Collins
Robert
French
Dictionary

HarperCollins Publishers
Westerhill Road
Bishopbriggs
Glasgow
G64 2QT
Great Britain

First published in this format by
HarperCollinsCanada 2008

www.collinslanguage.com

HarperCollins Publishers Ltd
2 Bloor Street East, 20th Floor
Toronto, Ontario
Canada M4W 1A8

ISBN 978-1-55468-175-4

www.collinsdictionaries.ca

Cataloguing in Publication Data is available
upon request

Dictionary text typeset by Thomas Callan

Supplement typeset by Davidson Pre-Press,
Glasgow

Printed in Canada

Pierre-Henri Cousin
Lorna Sinclair Knight
Jean-François Allain
Catherine E. Love
Lloyd Kelly

MANAGING EDITOR
Maree Airlie

EDITOR
Gaëlle Amiot-Cadey

Acknowledgements
We would like to thank those authors and
publishers who kindly gave permission for copyright material to be used in the Collins Word Web.
We would also like to thank Times Newspapers Ltd
for providing valuable data.

Table des matières

Contents

LES MARQUES DEPOSÉES

Les termes qui constituent à notre connaissance une marque déposée ont été désignés comme tels. La présence ou l'absence de cette désignation ne peut toutefois être considérée comme ayant valeur juridique.

NOTE ON TRADEMARKS

Words which we have reason to believe constitute trademarks have been designated as such. However, neither the presence nor the absence of such designation should be regarded as affecting the legal status of any trademark.

Introduction

You may be starting French for the first time, or you may wish to extend your knowledge of the language. Perhaps you want to read and study French books, newspapers and magazines, or perhaps simply have a conversation with French speakers. Whatever the reason, whether you're a student, a tourist or want to use French for business, this is the ideal book to help you understand and communicate. This modern, user-friendly dictionary gives priority to everyday vocabulary and the language of current affairs, business, computing and tourism, and, as in all Collins dictionaries, the emphasis is firmly placed on contemporary language and expressions.

How to use the dictionary
Below you will find an outline of how information is presented in your dictionary. Our aim is to give you the maximum amount of detail in the clearest and most helpful way.

Entries
A typical entry in your dictionary will be made up of the following elements:

Phonetic transcription
Phonetics appear in square brackets immediately after the headword. They are shown using the International Phonetic Alphabet (IPA), and a complete list of the symbols used in this system can be found on pages xii and xiii.

Grammatical information
All words belong to one of the following parts of speech: noun, verb, adjective, adverb, pronoun, article, conjunction, preposition.

Nouns can be singular or plural and, in French, masculine or feminine. Verbs can be transitive, intransitive, reflexive or impersonal. Parts of speech appear in *italics* immediately after the phonetic spelling of the headword. The gender of the translation appears in *italics* immediately following the key element of the translation.

Often a word can have more than one part of speech. Just as the English word **chemical** can be an adjective or a noun, the French word **rose** can be an adjective ("pink") or a feminine noun ("rose"). In the same way the verb **to walk** is sometimes transitive, ie it takes an object ("to walk the dog") and sometimes intransitive, ie it doesn't take an object ("to walk to school"). To help you find the meaning you are looking for quickly and for clarity of presentation, the different part of speech categories are separated by a right facing triangle ▷.

Meaning divisions

Most words have more than one meaning. Take, for example, **punch** which can be, amongst other things, a blow with the fist or an object used for making holes. Other words are translated differently depending on the context in which they are used. The transitive verb **to roll up**, for example, can be translated by "rouler" or "retrousser" depending on what it is you are rolling up. To help you select the most appropriate translation in every context, entries are divided according to meaning. Different meanings are introduced by an "indicator" in *italics* and in brackets. Thus, the examples given above will be shown as follows:

> **punch** n (*blow*) coup m de poing; (*tool*) poinçon m
> **roll up** vt (*carpet, cloth, map*) rouler; (*sleeves*) retrousser

Likewise, some words can have a different meaning when used to talk about a specific subject area or field. For example, **bishop**, which we generally use to mean a high-ranking clergyman, is also the name of a chess piece. To show English speakers which translation to use, we have added "subject field labels" in *italics*, starting with a capital letter, and in brackets, in this case (*Chess*):

> **bishop** n évêque m; (*Chess*) fou m

Field labels are often shortened to save space. You will find a complete list of abbreviations used in the dictionary on pages x and xi.

Translations

Most English words have a direct translation in French and vice versa, as shown in the examples given above. Sometimes, however, no exact equivalent exists in the target language. In such cases we have given an approximate equivalent, indicated by the sign ≈. An example is **National Insurance**, the French equivalent of which is "Sécurité Sociale". There is no exact equivalent since the systems of the two countries are quite different:

> **National Insurance** n (*Brit*) ≈ Sécurité Sociale

On occasion it is impossible to find even an approximate equivalent. This may be the case, for example, with the names of types of food:

> **mince pie** n *sorte de tarte aux fruits secs*

Here the translation (which doesn't exist) is replaced by an explanation. For increased clarity the explanation, or "gloss", is shown in *italics*.

It is often the case that a word, or a particular meaning of a word, cannot be translated in isolation. The translation of **Dutch**, for example, is "hollandais(e), neérlandais(e)". However, the phrase **to go Dutch** is rendered by "partager les frais".

Even an expression as simple as **washing powder** needs a separate translation since it translates as "lessive (en poudre)", not "poudre à laver". This is where your dictionary will prove to be particularly informative and useful since it contains an abundance of compounds, phrases and idiomatic expressions.

Levels of formality and familiarity

In English you instinctively know when to say "I don't have any money" and when to say "I'm broke" or "I'm a bit short of cash". When you are trying to understand someone who is speaking French, however, or when you yourself try to speak French, it is important to know what is polite and what is less so, and what you can say in a relaxed situation but not in a formal context. To help you with this, on the French–English side we have added the label (*inf*) to show that a French meaning or expression is colloquial, while those meanings or expressions which are vulgar are given an exclamation mark (*inf!*), warning you they can cause serious offence. Note also that on the English–French side, translations which are vulgar are followed by an exclamation mark in brackets.

Keywords

Words labelled in the text as KEYWORDS, such as **be** and **do** or their French equivalents **être** and **faire**, have been given special treatment because they form the basic elements of the language. This extra help will ensure that you know how to use these complex words with confidence.

Cultural information

Entries which appear distinguished in the text by a column of dots explain aspects of culture in French and English-speaking countries. Subject areas covered include politics, education, media and national festivals, for example **Assemblée nationale**, **baccalauréat**, **BBC** and **Hallowe'en**.

Abréviations

Abbreviations

Français	Abbr	English
abréviation	*ab(b)r*	abbreviation
adjectif, locution adjectivale	*adj*	adjective, adjectival phrase
administration	*Admin*	administration
adverbe, locution adverbiale	*adv*	adverb, adverbial phrase
agriculture	*Agr*	agriculture
anatomie	*Anat*	anatomy
architecture	*Archit*	architecture
article défini	*art déf*	definite article
article indéfini	*art indéf*	indefinite article
automobile	*Aut(o)*	the motor car and motoring
aviation, voyages aériens	*Aviat*	flying, air travel
biologie	*Bio(l)*	biology
botanique	*Bot*	botany
anglais britannique	*Brit*	British English
chimie	*Chem*	chemistry
cinéma	*Ciné, Cine*	cinema
commerce, finance, banque	*Comm*	commerce, finance, banking
informatique	*Comput*	computing
conjonction	*conj*	conjunction
construction	*Constr*	building
nom utilisé comme adjectif	*cpd*	compound element
cuisine	*Culin*	cookery
article défini	*def art*	definite article
déterminant: article; adjectif démonstratif *ou* indéfini etc	*dét*	determiner: article, demonstrative etc
économie	*Écon, Econ*	economics
électricité, électronique	*Élec, Elec*	electricity, electronics
en particulier	*esp*	especially
exclamation, interjection	*excl*	exclamation, interjection
féminin	*f*	feminine
langue familière (! emploi vulgaire)	*fam(!)*	colloquial usage (! particularly offensive)
emploi figuré	*fig*	figurative use
(verbe anglais) dont la particule est inséparable	*fus*	(phrasal verb) where the particle is inseparable
généralement	*gén, gen*	generally
géographie, géologie	*Géo, Geo*	geography, geology
géométrie	*Géom, Geom*	geometry
langue familière (! emploi vulgaire)	*inf(!)*	colloquial usage (! particularly offensive)
infinitif	*infin*	infinitive
informatique	*Inform*	computing
invariable	*inv*	invariable
irrégulier	*irrég, irreg*	irregular
domaine juridique	*Jur*	law

Abréviations

Abbreviations

grammaire, linguistique	*Ling*	grammar, linguistics
masculin	*m*	masculine
mathématiques, algèbre	*Math*	mathematics, calculus
médecine	*Méd, Med*	medical term, medicine
masculin *ou* féminin	*m/f*	masculine *or* feminine
domaine militaire, armée	*Mil*	military matters
musique	*Mus*	music
nom	*n*	noun
navigation, nautisme	*Navig, Naut*	sailing, navigation
nom *ou* adjectif numéral	*num*	numeral noun *or* adjective
	o.s.	oneself
péjoratif	*péj, pej*	derogatory, pejorative
photographie	*Phot(o)*	photography
physiologie	*Physiol*	physiology
pluriel	*pl*	plural
politique	*Pol*	politics
participe passé	*pp*	past participle
préposition	*prép, prep*	preposition
pronom	*pron*	pronoun
psychologie, psychiatrie	*Psych*	psychology, psychiatry
temps du passé	*pt*	past tense
quelque chose	*qch*	
quelqu'un	*qn*	
religion, domaine ecclésiastique	*Rel*	religion
	sb	somebody
enseignement, système scolaire et universitaire	*Scol*	schooling, schools and universities
singulier	*sg*	singular
	sth	something
subjonctif	*sub*	subjunctive
sujet (grammatical)	*su(b)j*	(grammatical) subject
superlatif	*superl*	superlative
techniques, technologie	*Tech*	technical term, technology
télécommunications	*Tél, Tel*	telecommunications
télévision	*TV*	television
typographie	*Typ(o)*	typography, printing
anglais des USA	*US*	American English
verbe (auxiliare)	*vb (aux)*	(auxiliary) verb
verbe intransitif	*vi*	intransitive verb
verbe transitif	*vt*	transitive verb
zoologie	*Zool*	zoology
marque déposée	®	registered trademark
indique une équivalence culturelle	≈	introduces a cultural equivalent

Transcription phonétique

Phonetic transcription

Consonnes

Consonants

poupée	p	*puppy*
bombe	b	*baby*
tente thermal	t	*tent*
dinde	d	*daddy*
coq qui képi	k	*cork kiss chord*
gag bague	g	*gag guess*
sale ce nation	s	*so rice kiss*
zéro rose	z	*cousin buzz*
tache chat	ʃ	*sheep sugar*
gilet juge	ʒ	*pleasure beige*
	tʃ	*church*
	dʒ	*judge general*
fer phare	f	*farm raffle*
valve	v	*very rev*
	θ	*thin maths*
	ð	*that other*
lent salle	l	*little ball*
rare rentrer	ʀ	
	r	*rat rare*
maman femme	m	*mummy comb*
non nonne	n	*no ran*
agneau vigne	ɲ	
	ŋ	*singing bank*
hop!	h	*hat reheat*
yeux paille pied	j	*yet*
nouer oui	w	*wall bewail*
huile lui	ɥ	
	x	*loch*

Divers

Miscellaneous

pour l'anglais: le "r" final se prononce en liaison devant une voyelle	ʳ	in English transcription: final "r" can be pronounced before a vowel
pour l'anglais: précède la syllabe accentuée	ˈ	in French wordlist: no liaison before aspirate "h"

NB: p, b, t, d, k, g sont suivis d'une aspiration en anglais.
p, b, t, d, k, g are not aspirated in French.

En règle générale, la prononciation est donnée entre crochets après chaque entrée. Toutefois, du côté anglais-français et dans le cas des expressions composées de deux ou plusieurs mots non réunis par un trait d'union et faisant l'objet d'une entrée séparée, la prononciation doit être cherchée sous chacun des mots constitutifs de l'expression en question.

Transcription phonétique

Phonetic transcription

Voyelles

Vowels

ici v*ie* l*y*rique	i iː	h*ee*l b*ea*d
	ɪ	h*i*t p*i*ty
jo*uer été*	e	
l*ai*t jou*e*t m*e*rci	ɛ	s*e*t t*e*nt
pl*a*t *a*mour	a æ	b*a*t *a*pple
b*a*s p*â*te	ɑ ɑː	*a*fter c*a*r c*a*lm
	ʌ	f*u*n c*ou*sin
l*e* pr*e*mier	ə	*o*ver *a*bove
b*eu*rre p*eu*r	œ	
p*eu* d*eu*x	ø əː	*u*rgent f*er*n w*or*k
*o*r h*o*mme	ɔ	w*a*sh p*o*t
m*o*t *eau* g*au*che	o ɔː	b*or*n c*or*k
gen*ou* r*ou*e	u	f*u*ll h*oo*k
	uː	b*oo*m sh*oe*
r*ue* *u*rne	y	

Diphtongues

Diphthongs

	ɪə	b*eer* t*ier*
	ɛə	t*ear* f*air* th*ere*
	eɪ	d*a*te pl*ai*ce d*ay*
	aɪ	l*i*fe b*uy* cr*y*
	au	*ow*l f*ou*l n*ow*
	əu	l*ow* n*o*
	ɔɪ	b*oi*l b*oy* *oi*ly
	uə	p*oor* t*our*

Nasales

Nasal vowels

mat*in* pl*ein*	ɛ̃	
br*un*	œ̃	
s*an*g *an* d*an*s	ɑ̃	
n*on* p*on*t	ɔ̃	

NB: La mise en équivalence de certains sons n'indique qu'une ressemblance approximative.
The pairing of some vowel sounds only indicates approximate equivalence.

In general, we give the pronunciation of each entry in square brackets after the word in question. However, on the English-French side, where the entry is composed of two or more unhyphenated words, each of which is given elsewhere in this dictionary, you will find the pronunciation of each word in its alphabetical position.

Le verbe anglais

present	pt	pp
arise	arose	arisen
awake	awoke	awoken
be (am, is, are; being)	was, were	been
bear	bore	born(e)
beat	beat	beaten
become	became	become
befall	befell	befallen
begin	began	begun
behold	beheld	beheld
bend	bent	bent
beset	beset	beset
bet	bet, betted	bet, betted
bid (at auction, cards)	bid	bid
bid (say)	bade	bidden
bind	bound	bound
bite	bit	bitten
bleed	bled	bled
blow	blew	blown
break	broke	broken
breed	bred	bred
bring	brought	brought
build	built	built
burn	burnt, burned	burnt, burned
burst	burst	burst
buy	bought	bought
can	could	(been able)
cast	cast	cast
catch	caught	caught
choose	chose	chosen
cling	clung	clung
come	came	come
cost	cost	cost
cost (work out price of)	costed	costed
creep	crept	crept
cut	cut	cut
deal	dealt	dealt
dig	dug	dug
do (3rd person: he/she/it does)	did	done
draw	drew	drawn
dream	dreamed, dreamt	dreamed, dreamt
drink	drank	drunk
drive	drove	driven

English verb forms

present	pt	pp
dwell	dwelt	dwelt
eat	ate	eaten
fall	fell	fallen
feed	fed	fed
feel	felt	felt
fight	fought	fought
find	found	found
flee	fled	fled
fling	flung	flung
fly	flew	flown
forbid	forbad(e)	forbidden
forecast	forecast	forecast
forget	forgot	forgotten
forgive	forgave	forgiven
forsake	forsook	forsaken
freeze	froze	frozen
get	got	got, (US) gotten
give	gave	given
go (goes)	went	gone
grind	ground	ground
grow	grew	grown
hang	hung	hung
hang (execute)	hanged	hanged
have	had	had
hear	heard	heard
hide	hid	hidden
hit	hit	hit
hold	held	held
hurt	hurt	hurt
keep	kept	kept
kneel	knelt, kneeled	knelt, kneeled
know	knew	known
lay	laid	laid
lead	led	led
lean	leant, leaned	leant, leaned
leap	leapt, leaped	leapt, leaped
learn	learnt, learned	learnt, learned
leave	left	left
lend	lent	lent
let	let	let
lie (lying)	lay	lain
light	lit, lighted	lit, lighted

present	pt	pp	present	pt	pp
lose	lost	lost	speak	spoke	spoken
make	made	made	speed	sped,	sped,
may	might	—		speeded	speeded
mean	meant	meant	spell	spelt,	spelt,
meet	met	met		spelled	spelled
mistake	mistook	mistaken	spend	spent	spent
mow	mowed	mown,	spill	spilt,	spilt,
		mowed		spilled	spilled
must	(had to)	(had to)	spin	spun	spun
pay	paid	paid	spit	spat	spat
put	put	put	spoil	spoiled,	spoiled,
quit	quit,	quit,		spoilt	spoilt
	quitted	quitted	spread	spread	spread
read	read	read	spring	sprang	sprung
rid	rid	rid	stand	stood	stood
ride	rode	ridden	steal	stole	stolen
ring	rang	rung	stick	stuck	stuck
rise	rose	risen	sting	stung	stung
run	ran	run	stink	stank	stunk
saw	sawed	sawed,	stride	strode	stridden
		sawn	strike	struck	struck
say	said	said	strive	strove	striven
see	saw	seen	swear	swore	sworn
seek	sought	sought	sweep	swept	swept
sell	sold	sold	swell	swelled	swollen,
send	sent	sent			swelled
set	set	set	swim	swam	swum
sew	sewed	sewn	swing	swung	swung
shake	shook	shaken	take	took	taken
shear	sheared	shorn,	teach	taught	taught
		sheared	tear	tore	torn
shed	shed	shed	tell	told	told
shine	shone	shone	think	thought	thought
shoot	shot	shot	throw	threw	thrown
show	showed	shown	thrust	thrust	thrust
shrink	shrank	shrunk	tread	trod	trodden
shut	shut	shut	wake	woke,	woken,
sing	sang	sung		waked	waked
sink	sank	sunk	wear	wore	worn
sit	sat	sat	weave	wove	woven
slay	slew	slain	weave	weaved	weaved
sleep	slept	slept	(wind)		
slide	slid	slid	wed	wedded,	wedded,
sling	slung	slung		wed	wed
slit	slit	slit	weep	wept	wept
smell	smelt,	smelt,	win	won	won
	smelled	smelled	wind	wound	wound
sow	sowed	sown,	wring	wrung	wrung
		sowed	write	wrote	written

Le verbe français

French verb forms

1 Present participle 2 Past participle 3 Present 4 Imperfect 5 Future 6 Conditional
7 Present subjunctive 8 Impératif

acquérir 1 acquérant 2 acquis 3 acquiers,
acquérons, acquièrent 4 acquérais
5 acquerrai 7 acquière

ALLER 1 allant 2 allé 3 vais, vas, va, allons,
allez, vont 4 allais 5 irai 6 irais 7 aille

asseoir 1 asseyant 2 assis 3 assieds,
asseyons, asseyez, asseyent 4 asseyais
5 assiérai 7 asseye

atteindre 1 atteignant 2 atteint 3 atteins,
atteignons 4 atteignais 7 atteigne

AVOIR 1 ayant 2 eu 3 ai, as, a, avons, avez,
ont 4 avais 5 aurai 6 aurais 7 aie, aies, ait,
ayons, ayez, aient

battre 1 battant 2 battu 3 bats, bat, battons
4 battais 7 batte

boire 1 buvant 2 bu 3 bois, buvons, boivent
4 buvais 7 boive

bouillir 1 bouillant 2 bouilli 3 bous,
bouillons 4 bouillais 7 bouille

conclure 1 concluant 2 conclu 3 conclus,
concluons 4 concluais 7 conclue

conduire 1 conduisant 2 conduit 3 conduis,
conduisons 4 conduisais 7 conduise

connaître 1 connaissant 2 connu 3 connais,
connaît, connaissons 4 connaissais
7 connaisse

coudre 1 cousant 2 cousu 3 couds, cousons,
cousez, cousent 4 cousais 7 couse

courir 1 courant 2 couru 3 cours, courons
4 courais 5 courrai 7 coure

couvrir 1 couvrant 2 couvert 3 couvre,
couvrons 4 couvrais 7 couvre

craindre 1 craignant 2 craint 3 crains,
craignons 4 craignais 7 craigne

croire 1 croyant 2 cru 3 crois, croyons,
croient 4 croyais 7 croie

croître 1 croissant 2 crû, crue, crus, crues
3 croîs, croissons 4 croissais 7 croisse

cueillir 1 cueillant 2 cueilli 3 cueille,
cueillons 4 cueillais 5 cueillerai 7 cueille

devoir 1 devant 2 dû, due, dus, dues 3 dois,
devons, doivent 4 devais 5 devrai 7 doive

dire 1 disant 2 dit 3 dis, disons, dites,
disent 4 disais 7 dise

dormir 1 dormant 2 dormi 3 dors, dormons
4 dormais 7 dorme

écrire 1 écrivant 2 écrit 3 écris, écrivons
4 écrivais 7 écrive

ÊTRE 1 étant 2 été 3 suis, es, est, sommes,
êtes, sont 4 étais 5 serai 6 serais 7 sois,
sois, soit, soyons, soyez, soient

FAIRE 1 faisant 2 fait 3 fais, fais, fait,
faisons, faites, font 4 faisais 5 ferai
6 ferais 7 fasse

falloir 2 fallu 3 faut 4 fallait 5 faudra
7 faille

FINIR 1 finissant 2 fini 3 finis, finis, finit,
finissons, finissez, finissent 4 finissais
5 finirai 6 finirais 7 finisse

fuir 1 fuyant 2 fui 3 fuis, fuyons, fuient
4 fuyais 7 fuie

joindre 1 joignant 2 joint 3 joins, joignons
4 joignais 7 joigne

lire 1 lisant 2 lu 3 lis, lisons 4 lisais 7 lise

luire 1 luisant 2 lui 3 luis, luisons 4 luisais
7 luise

maudire 1 maudissant 2 maudit
3 maudis, maudissons 4 maudissait
7 maudisse

mentir 1 mentant 2 menti 3 mens,
mentons 4 mentais 7 mente

mettre 1 mettant 2 mis 3 mets, mettons
4 mettais 7 mette

mourir 1 mourant 2 mort 3 meurs,
mourons, meurent 4 mourais 5 mourrai
7 meure

naître 1 naissant 2 né 3 nais, naît,
naissons 4 naissais 7 naisse

offrir 1 offrant 2 offert 3 offre, offrons
4 offrais 7 offre

PARLER 1 parlant 2 parlé 3 parle, parles,
parle, parlons, parlez, parlent 4 parlais,
parlais, parlait, parlions, parliez, parlaient
5 parlerai, parleras, parlera, parlerons,

parlerez, parleront **6** parlerais, parlerais, parlerait, parlerions, parleriez, parleraient **7** parle, parles, parle, parlions, parliez, parlent **8** parle! parlons! parlez!

partir **1** partant **2** parti **3** pars, partons **4** partais **7** parte

plaire **1** plaisant **2** plu **3** plais, plaît, plaisons **4** plaisais **7** plaise

pleuvoir **1** pleuvant **2** plu **3** pleut, pleuvent **4** pleuvait **5** pleuvra **7** pleuve

pourvoir **1** pourvoyant **2** pourvu **3** pourvois, pourvoyons, pourvoient **4** pourvoyais **7** pourvoie

pouvoir **1** pouvant **2** pu **3** peux, peut, pouvons, peuvent **4** pouvais **5** pourrai **7** puisse

prendre **1** prenant **2** pris **3** prends, prenons, prennent **4** prenais **7** prenne

prévoir *like* **voir** **5** prévoirai

RECEVOIR **1** recevant **2** reçu **3** reçois, reçois, reçoit, recevons, recevez, rerçoivent **4** recevais **5** recevrai **6** recevrais **7** reçoive

RENDRE **1** rendant **2** rendu **3** rends, rends, rend, rendons, rendez, rendent **4** rendais **5** rendrai **6** rendrais **7** rende

résoudre **1** résolvant **2** résolu **3** résous, résout, résolvons **4** résolvais **7** résolve

rire **1** riant **2** ri **3** ris, rions **4** riais **7** rie

savoir **1** sachant **2** su **3** sais, savons, savent **4** savais **5** saurai **7** sache **8** sache! sachons! sachez!

servir **1** servant **2** servi **3** sers, servons **4** servais **7** serve

sortir **1** sortant **2** sorti **3** sors, sortons **4** sortais **7** sorte

souffrir **1** souffrant **2** souffert **3** souffre, souffrons **4** souffrais **7** souffre

suffire **1** suffisant **2** suffi **3** suffis, suffisons **4** suffisais **7** suffise

suivre **1** suivant **2** suivi **3** suis, suivons **4** suivais **7** suive

taire **1** taisant **2** tu **3** tais, taisons **4** taisais **7** taise

tenir **1** tenant **2** tenu **3** tiens, tenons, tiennent **4** tenais **5** tiendrai **7** tienne

vaincre **1** vainquant **2** vaincu **3** vaincs, vainc, vainquons **4** vainquais **7** vainque

valoir **1** valant **2** valu **3** vaux, vaut, valons **4** valais **5** vaudrai **7** vaille

venir **1** venant **2** venu **3** viens, venons, viennent **4** venais **5** viendrai **7** vienne

vivre **1** vivant **2** vécu **3** vis, vivons **4** vivais **7** vive

voir **1** voyant **2** vu **3** vois, voyons, voient **4** voyais **5** verrai **7** voie

vouloir **1** voulant **2** voulu **3** veux, veut, voulons, veulent **4** voulais **5** voudrai **7** veuille **8** veuillez!

Les nombres

Numbers

un (une)	1	one
deux	2	two
trois	3	three
quatre	4	four
cinq	5	five
six	6	six
sept	7	seven
huit	8	eight
neuf	9	nine
dix	10	ten
onze	11	eleven
douze	12	twelve
treize	13	thirteen
quatorze	14	fourteen
quinze	15	fifteen
seize	16	sixteen
dix-sept	17	seventeen
dix-huit	18	eighteen
dix-neuf	19	nineteen
vingt	20	twenty
vingt et un (une)	21	twenty-one
vingt-deux	22	twenty-two
trente	30	thirty
quarante	40	forty
cinquante	50	fifty
soixante	60	sixty
soixante-dix	70	seventy
soixante-et-onze	71	seventy-one
soixante-douze	72	seventy
quatre-vingts	80	eighty
quatre-vingt-un (-une)	81	eighty-one
quatre-vingt-dix	90	ninety
cent	100	a hundred, one hundred
cent un (une)	101	a hundred and one
deux cents	200	two hundred
deux cent un (une)	201	two hundred and one
quatre cents	400	four hundred
mille	1 000	a thousand
cinq mille	5 000	five thousand
un million	1 000 000	a million

Les nombres

Numbers

premier (première), 1er (1ère)	first, 1st
deuxième, 2e *or* 2ème	second, 2nd
troisième, 3e *or* 3ème	third, 3rd
quatrième, 4e *or* 4ème	fourth, 4th
cinquième, 5e *or* 5ème	fifth, 5th
sixième, 6e *or* 6ème	sixth, 6th
septième	seventh
huitième	eighth
neuvième	ninth
dixième	tenth
onzième	eleventh
douzième	twelfth
treizième	thirteenth
quartorzième	fourteenth
quinzième	fifteenth
seizième	sixteenth
dix-septième	seventeenth
dix-huitième	eighteenth
dix-neuvième	nineteenth
vingtième	twentieth
vingt-et-unième	twenty-first
vingt-deuxième	twenty-second
trentième	thirtieth
centième	hundredth
cent-unième	hundred-and-first
millième	thousandth

L'heure

quelle heure est-il?
  il est …

minuit	midnight, twelve p.m.
une heure (du matin)	one o'clock (in the morning), one (a.m.)
une heure cinq	five past one
une heure dix	ten past one
une heure et quart	a quarter past one, one fifteen
une heure vingt-cinq	twenty-five past one, one twenty-five
une heure et demie,	half-past one,
une heure trente	one thirty
deux heures moins vingt-cinq,	twenty-five to two,
une heure trente-cinq	one thirty-five
deux heures moins vingt,	twenty to two,
une heure quarante	one forty
deux heures moins le quart,	a quarter to two,
une heure quarante-cinq	one forty-five
deux heures moins dix,	ten to two,
une heure cinquante	one fifty
midi	twelve o'clock, midday, noon
deux heures (de l'après-midi),	two o'clock (in the afternoon),
quatorze heures	two (p.m.)
sept heures (du soir),	seven o'clock (in the evening),
dix-sept heures	seven (p.m.)

à quelle heure?
à minuit
à sept heures

(at) what time?
at midnight
at seven o'clock

dans vingt minutes
il y a un quart d'heure

in twenty minutes
fifteen minutes ago

La date

The date

aujourd'hui	today
demain	tomorrow
après-demain	the day after tomorrow
hier	yesterday
avant-hier	the day before yesterday
la veille	the day before, the previous day
le lendemain	the next *or* following day
le matin	morning
le soir	evening
ce matin	this morning
ce soir	this evening
cet après-midi	this afternoon
hier matin	yesterday morning
hier soir	yesterday evening
demain matin	tomorrow morning
demain soir	tomorrow evening
dans la nuit du samedi au dimanche	during Saturday night, during the night of Saturday to Sunday
il viendra samedi	he's coming on Saturday
le samedi	on Saturdays
tous les samedis	every Saturday
samedi passé *ou* dernier	last Saturday
samedi prochain	next Saturday
samedi en huit	a week on Saturday
samedi en quinze	a fortnight *or* two weeks on Saturday
du lundi au samedi	from Monday to Saturday
tous les jours	every day
une fois par semaine	once a week
une fois par mois	once a month
deux fois par semaine	twice a week
il y a une semaine *ou* huit jours	a week ago
il y a quinze jours	a fortnight *or* two weeks ago
l'année passée *ou* dernière	last year
dans deux jours	in two days
dans huit jours *ou* une semaine	in a week
dans quinze jours	in a fortnight *or* two weeks
le mois prochain	next month
l'année prochaine	next year
quel jour sommes-nous?	*what day is it?*
le 1ᵉʳ/24 octobre 2007	the 1st/24th of October 2007, October 1st/24th 2007
en 2007	in 2007
mille neuf cent quatre-vingt seize	nineteen ninety-six
44 av. J.-C.	44 BC
14 apr. J.-C.	14 AD
au XIXᵉ (siècle)	in the nineteenth century
dans les années trente	in the thirties
il était une fois ...	once upon a time ...

Aa

A, a [ɑ] *nm inv* A, a ▷ *abr* = **anticyclone**; **are**; (*ampère*) amp; (*autoroute*) ≈ M (*Brit*); **A comme Anatole** A for Andrew (*Brit*) *ou* Able (*US*); **de a à z** from a to z; **prouver qch par a + b** to prove sth conclusively

a [a] *vb voir* **avoir**

○ MOT-CLÉ

à [a] (*à + le* = **au**, *à + les* = **aux**) *prép* **1** (*endroit, situation*) at, in; **être à Paris/au Portugal** to be in Paris/Portugal; **être à la maison/à l'école** to be at home/at school; **à la campagne** in the country; **c'est à 10 m/km/à 20 minutes (d'ici)** it's 10 m/km/20 minutes away
2 (*direction*) to; **aller à Paris/au Portugal** to go to Paris/Portugal; **aller à la maison/à l'école** to go home/to school; **à la campagne** to the country
3 (*temps*): **à 3 heures/minuit** at 3 o'clock/ midnight; **au printemps** in the spring; **au mois de juin** in June; **au départ** at the start, at the outset; **à demain/la semaine prochaine!** see you tomorrow/next week!; **visites de 5 heures à 6 heures** visiting from 5 to *ou* till 6 o'clock
4 (*attribution, appartenance*) to; **le livre est à Paul/à lui/à nous** this book is Paul's/his/ours; **donner qch à qn** to give sth to sb; **un ami à moi** a friend of mine; **c'est à moi de le faire** it's up to me to do it
5 (*moyen*) with; **se chauffer au gaz** to have gas heating; **à bicyclette** on a *ou* by bicycle; **à la main/machine** by hand/machine; **à la télévision/la radio** on television/the radio
6 (*provenance*) from; **boire à la bouteille** to drink from the bottle
7 (*caractérisation, manière*): **l'homme aux yeux bleus** the man with the blue eyes; **à la russe** the Russian way; **glace à la framboise** raspberry ice cream
8 (*but, destination*): **tasse à café** coffee cup; **maison à vendre** house for sale; **problème à régler** problem to sort out
9 (*rapport, évaluation, distribution*): **100 km/unités à l'heure** 100 km/units per *ou* an hour; **payé à**

l'heure paid by the hour; **cinq à six** five to six
10 (*conséquence, résultat*): **à ce qu'il prétend** according to him; **à leur grande surprise** much to their surprise; **à nous trois nous n'avons pas su le faire** we couldn't do it even between the three of us; **ils sont arrivés à quatre** four of them arrived (together)

Å *abr* (= *Ångstrom*) Å *ou* A
AB *abr* = **assez bien**
abaissement [abɛsmã] *nm* lowering; pulling down
abaisser [abese] *vt* to lower, bring down; (*manette*) to pull down; (*fig*) to debase; to humiliate; **s'abaisser** *vi* to go down; (*fig*) to demean o.s.; **s'~ à faire/à qch** to stoop *ou* descend to doing/to sth
abandon [abãdɔ̃] *nm* abandoning; deserting; giving up; withdrawal; surrender, relinquishing; (*fig*) lack of constraint; relaxed pose *ou* mood; **être à l'~** to be in a state of neglect; **laisser à l'~** to abandon
abandonné, e [abãdɔne] *adj* (*solitaire*) deserted; (*route, usine*) disused; (*jardin*) abandoned
abandonner [abãdɔne] *vt* to leave, abandon, desert; (*projet, activité*) to abandon, give up; (*Sport*) to retire *ou* withdraw from; (*Inform*) to abort; (*céder*) to surrender, relinquish; **s'abandonner** *vi* to let o.s. go; **s'~ à** (*paresse, plaisirs*) to give o.s. up to; **~ qch à qn** to give sth up to sb
abasourdir [abazuʀdiʀ] *vt* to stun, stagger
abat *etc* [aba] *vb voir* **abattre**
abat-jour [abaʒuʀ] *nm inv* lampshade
abats [aba] *vb voir* **abattre** ▷ *nmpl* (*de bœuf, porc*) offal *sg* (*Brit*), entrails (*US*); (*de volaille*) giblets
abattage [abataʒ] *nm* cutting down, felling
abattant [abatã] *vb voir* **abattre** ▷ *nm* leaf, flap
abattement [abatmã] *nm* (*physique*) enfeeblement; (*moral*) dejection, despondency; (*déduction*) reduction; **~ fiscal** ≈ tax allowance
abattis [abati] *vb voir* **abattre** ▷ *nmpl* giblets
abattoir [abatwaʀ] *nm* abattoir (*Brit*), slaughterhouse
abattre [abatʀ(ə)] *vt* (*arbre*) to cut down, fell; (*mur, maison*) to pull down; (*avion, personne*) to

shoot down; (*animal*) to shoot, kill; (*fig:
physiquement*) to wear out, tire out; (: *moralement*)
to demoralize; **s'abattre** *vi* to crash down; **s'~
sur** (*pluie*) to beat down on; (: *coups, injures*) to
rain down on; **~ ses cartes** (*aussi fig*) to lay one's
cards on the table; **~ du travail** *ou* **de la
besogne** to get through a lot of work

abattu, e [abaty] *pp de* **abattre** ▷ *adj* (*déprimé*)
downcast

abbatiale [abasjal] *nf* abbey (*church*)

abbaye [abei] *nf* abbey

abbé [abe] *nm* priest; (*d'une abbaye*) abbot; **M l'~**
Father

abbesse [abɛs] *nf* abbess

abc, ABC [abese] *nm* alphabet primer; (*fig*)
rudiments *pl*

abcès [apsɛ] *nm* abscess

abdication [abdikasjɔ̃] *nf* abdication

abdiquer [abdike] *vi* to abdicate ▷ *vt* to
renounce, give up

abdomen [abdɔmɛn] *nm* abdomen

abdominal, e, -aux [abdɔminal, -o] *adj*
abdominal ▷ *nmpl*: **faire des abdominaux** to
do exercises for the stomach muscles

abécédaire [abesedɛr] *nm* alphabet primer

abeille [abɛj] *nf* bee

aberrant, e [abɛrɑ̃, -ɑ̃t] *adj* absurd

aberration [abɛrasjɔ̃] *nf* aberration

abêtir [abetir] *vt* to make morons (*ou* a moron)
of

abêtissant, e [abetisɑ̃, -ɑ̃t] *adj* stultifying

abhorrer [abɔre] *vt* to abhor, loathe

abîme [abim] *nm* abyss, gulf

abîmer [abime] *vt* to spoil, damage; **s'abîmer** *vi*
to get spoilt *ou* damaged; (*fruits*) to spoil;
(*tomber*) to sink, founder; **s'~ les yeux** to ruin
one's eyes *ou* eyesight

abject, e [abʒɛkt] *adj* abject, despicable

abjurer [abʒyre] *vt* to abjure, renounce

ablatif [ablatif] *nm* ablative

ablation [ablasjɔ̃] *nf* removal

ablutions [ablysjɔ̃] *nfpl*: **faire ses ~** to perform
one's ablutions

abnégation [abnegasjɔ̃] *nf* (self-)abnegation

aboie *etc* [abwa] *vb voir* **aboyer**

aboiement [abwamɑ̃] *nm* bark, barking *no pl*

aboierai *etc* [abwajare] *vb voir* **aboyer**

abois [abwa] *nmpl*: **aux ~** at bay

abolir [abɔlir] *vt* to abolish

abolition [abɔlisjɔ̃] *nf* abolition

abolitionniste [abɔlisjɔnist(ə)] *adj, nm/f*
abolitionist

abominable [abɔminabl(ə)] *adj* abominable

abomination [abɔminasjɔ̃] *nf* abomination

abondamment [abɔ̃damɑ̃] *adv* abundantly

abondance [abɔ̃dɑ̃s] *nf* abundance; (*richesse*)
affluence; **en ~** in abundance

abondant, e [abɔ̃dɑ̃, -ɑ̃t] *adj* plentiful,
abundant, copious

abonder [abɔ̃de] *vi* to abound, be plentiful; **~ en**
to be full of, abound in; **~ dans le sens de qn** to
concur with sb

abonné, e [abɔne] *nm/f* subscriber; season
ticket holder ▷ *adj*: **être ~ à un journal** to
subscribe to *ou* have a subscription to a
periodical; **être ~ au téléphone** to be on the
(tele)phone

abonnement [abɔnmɑ̃] *nm* subscription; (*pour
transports en commun, concerts*) season ticket

abonner [abɔne] *vt*: **s'abonner à** to subscribe to,
take out a subscription to

abord [abɔr] *nm*: **être d'un ~ facile** to be
approachable; **être d'un ~ difficile** (*personne*) to
be unapproachable; (*lieu*) to be hard to reach *ou*
difficult to get to; **de prime ~, au premier ~** at
first sight; **d'~** *adv* first; **tout d'~** first of all

abordable [abɔrdabl(ə)] *adj* (*personne*)
approachable; (*marchandise*) reasonably priced;
(*prix*) affordable, reasonable

abordage [abɔrdaʒ] *nm* boarding

aborder [abɔrde] *vi* to land ▷ *vt* (*sujet, difficulté*)
to tackle; (*personne*) to approach; (*rivage etc*) to
reach; (*Navig: attaquer*) to board; (: *heurter*) to
collide with

abords [abɔr] *nmpl* surroundings

aborigène [abɔriʒɛn] *nm* aborigine, native

Abou Dhabî, Abu Dhabî [abudabi] *nm* Abu
Dhabi

aboulique [abulik] *adj* totally lacking in
willpower

aboutir [abutir] *vi* (*négociations etc*) to succeed;
(*abcès*) to come to a head; **~ à/dans/sur** to end
up at/in/on

aboutissants [abutisɑ̃] *nmpl voir* **tenants**

aboutissement [abutismɑ̃] *nm* success; (*de
concept, projet*) successful realization; (*d'années de
travail*) successful conclusion

aboyer [abwaje] *vi* to bark

abracadabrant, e [abrakadabrɑ̃, -ɑ̃t] *adj*
incredible, preposterous

abrasif, -ive [abrazif, -iv] *adj, nm* abrasive

abrégé [abreʒe] *nm* summary; **en ~** in a
shortened *ou* abbreviated form

abréger [abreʒe] *vt* (*texte*) to shorten, abridge;
(*mot*) to shorten, abbreviate; (*réunion, voyage*) to
cut short, shorten

abreuver [abrœve] *vt* to water; (*fig*): **~ qn de** to
shower ou swamp sb with; (*injures etc*) to shower
sb with; **s'abreuver** *vi* to drink

abreuvoir [abrœvwar] *nm* watering place

abréviation [abrevjasjɔ̃] *nf* abbreviation

abri [abri] *nm* shelter; **à l'~** under cover; **être/
se mettre à l'~** to be/get under cover *ou* shelter;
à l'~ de sheltered from; (*fig*) safe from

Abribus® [abribys] *nm* bus shelter

abricot [abriko] *nm* apricot

abricotier [abrikɔtje] *nm* apricot tree

abrité, e [abrite] *adj* sheltered

abriter [abrite] *vt* to shelter; (*loger*) to
accommodate; **s'abriter** *vi* to shelter, take
cover

abrogation [abrɔgasjɔ̃] *nf* (*Jur*) repeal,
abrogation

abroger [abrɔʒe] *vt* to repeal, abrogate

abrupt, e [abʀypt] *adj* sheer, steep; *(ton)* abrupt

abruti, e [abʀyti] *nm/f (fam)* idiot, moron

abrutir [abʀytiʀ] *vt* to daze; *(fatiguer)* to exhaust; *(abêtir)* to stupefy

abrutissant, e [abʀytisɑ̃, -ɑ̃t] *adj (bruit, travail)* stupefying

abscisse [apsis] *nf* X axis, abscissa

absence [apsɑ̃s] *nf* absence; *(Méd)* blackout; *(distraction)* mental blank; **en l'~ de** in the absence of

absent, e [apsɑ̃, -ɑ̃t] *adj* absent; *(chose)* missing, lacking; *(distrait: air)* vacant, faraway ▷ *nm/f* absentee

absentéisme [apsɑ̃teism(ə)] *nm* absenteeism

absenter [apsɑ̃te]: **s'absenter** *vi* to take time off work; *(sortir)* to leave, go out

abside [apsid] *nf (Archit)* apse

absinthe [apsɛ̃t] *nf (boisson)* absinth(e); *(Bot)* wormwood, absinth(e)

absolu, e [apsɔly] *adj* absolute; *(caractère)* rigid, uncompromising ▷ *nm (Philosophie)*: **l'~** the Absolute; **dans l'~** in the absolute, in a vacuum

absolument [apsɔlymɑ̃] *adv* absolutely

absolution [apsɔlysjɔ̃] *nf* absolution; *(Jur)* dismissal *(of case)*

absolutisme [apsɔlytism(ə)] *nm* absolutism

absolvais *etc* [apsɔlvɛ] *vb voir* **absoudre**

absorbant, e [apsɔʀbɑ̃, -ɑ̃t] *adj* absorbent; *(tâche)* absorbing, engrossing

absorbé, e [apsɔʀbe] *adj* absorbed, engrossed

absorber [apsɔʀbe] *vt* to absorb; *(gén Méd: manger, boire)* to take; *(Écon: firme)* to take over, absorb

absorption [apsɔʀpsjɔ̃] *nf* absorption

absoudre [apsudʀ(ə)] *vt* to absolve; *(Jur)* to dismiss

absous, -oute [apsu, -ut] *pp de* **absoudre**

abstenir [apstəniʀ]: **s'abstenir** *vi (Pol)* to abstain; **s'~ de qch/de faire** to refrain from sth/from doing

abstention [apstɑ̃sjɔ̃] *nf* abstention

abstentionnisme [apstɑ̃sjɔnism(ə)] *nm* abstaining

abstentionniste [apstɑ̃sjɔnist(ə)] *nm* abstentionist

abstenu, e [apstəny] *pp de* **abstenir**

abstiendrai [apstjɛ̃dʀe], **abstiens** *etc* [apstjɛ̃] *vb voir* **abstenir**

abstinence [apstinɑ̃s] *nf* abstinence; **faire ~** to abstain *(from meat on Fridays)*

abstint *etc* [apstɛ̃] *vb voir* **abstenir**

abstraction [apstʀaksjɔ̃] *nf* abstraction; **faire ~ de** to set *ou* leave aside; **~ faite de ...** leaving aside ...

abstraire [apstʀɛʀ] *vt* to abstract; **s'abstraire** *vi*: **s'~ (de)** *(s'isoler)* to cut o.s. off (from)

abstrait, e [apstʀɛ, -ɛt] *pp de* **abstraire** ▷ *adj* abstract ▷ *nm*: **dans l'~** in the abstract

abstraitement [apstʀɛtmɑ̃] *adv* abstractly

abstrayais *etc* [apstʀɛjɛ] *vb voir* **abstraire**

absurde [apsyʀd(ə)] *adj* absurd ▷ *nm* absurdity; *(Philosophie)*: **l'~** absurd; **par l'~** ad absurdio

absurdité [apsyʀdite] *nf* absurdity

abus [aby] *nm (excès)* abuse, misuse; *(injustice)* abuse; **~ de confiance** breach of trust; *(détournement de fonds)* embezzlement

abuser [abyze] *vi* to go too far, overstep the mark ▷ *vt* to deceive, mislead; **s'abuser** *vi (se méprendre)* to be mistaken; **~ de** *vt (force, droit)* to misuse; *(alcool)* to take to excess; *(violer, duper)* to take advantage of

abusif, -ive [abyzif, -iv] *adj* exorbitant; *(punition)* excessive; *(pratique)* improper

abusivement [abyzivmɑ̃] *adv* exorbitantly; excessively; improperly

AC *sigle f* = **appellation contrôlée**

acabit [akabi] *nm*: **du même ~** of the same type

acacia [akasja] *nm (Bot)* acacia

académicien, ne [akademisjɛ̃, -ɛn] *nm/f* academician

académie [akademi] *nf (société)* learned society; *(école: d'art, de danse)* academy; *(Art: nu)* nude; *(Scol: circonscription)* ≈ regional education authority; **l'A~ (française)** the French Academy; *see note*

● **ACADÉMIE FRANÇAISE**
●
● The Académie française was founded by
● Cardinal Richelieu in 1635, during the reign
● of Louis XIII. It is made up of forty elected
● scholars and writers who are known as "les
● Quarante" or "les Immortels". One of the
● Académie's functions is to keep an eye on the
● development of the French language, and
● its recommendations are frequently the
● subject of lively public debate. It has
● produced several editions of its famous
● dictionary and also awards various literary
● prizes.

académique [akademik] *adj* academic

Acadie [akadi] *nf*: **l'~** the Maritime Provinces

acadien, ne [akadjɛ̃, -ɛn] *adj* Acadian, of *ou* from the Maritime Provinces

acajou [akaʒu] *nm* mahogany

acariâtre [akaʀjɑtʀ(ə)] *adj* sour(-tempered) *(Brit)*, cantankerous

accablant, e [akablɑ̃, -ɑ̃t] *adj (témoignage, preuve)* overwhelming

accablement [akabləmɑ̃] *nm* deep despondency

accabler [akable] *vt* to overwhelm, overcome; *(témoignage)* to condemn, damn; **~ qn d'injures** to heap *ou* shower abuse on sb; **~ qn de travail** to overburden sb with work; **accablé de dettes/soucis** weighed down with debts/cares

accalmie [akalmi] *nf* lull

accaparant, e [akapaʀɑ̃, -ɑ̃t] *adj* that takes up all one's time *ou* attention

accaparer [akapaʀe] *vt* to monopolize; *(travail etc)* to take up (all) the time *ou* attention of

accéder [aksede]: **~ à** *vt (lieu)* to reach; *(fig: pouvoir)* to accede to; *(: poste)* to attain; *(accorder:*

requête) to grant, accede to

accélérateur [akseleRatœR] *nm* accelerator

accélération [akseleRasjɔ̃] *nf* speeding up; acceleration

accéléré [akseleRe] *nm*: **en ~** (*Ciné*) speeded up

accélérer [akseleRe] *vt* (*mouvement, travaux*) to speed up ▷ *vi* (*Auto*) to accelerate

accent [aksɑ̃] *nm* accent; (*inflexions expressives*) tone (of voice); (*Phonétique, fig*) stress; **aux ~s de** (*musique*) to the strains of; **mettre l'~ sur** (*fig*) to stress; **~ aigu/grave/circonflexe** acute/grave/circumflex accent

accentuation [aksɑ̃tɥasjɔ̃] *nf* accenting; stressing

accentué, e [aksɑ̃tɥe] *adj* marked, pronounced

accentuer [aksɑ̃tɥe] *vt* (*Ling: orthographe*) to accent; (*: phonétique*) to stress, accent; (*fig*) to accentuate, emphasize; (*effort, pression*) to increase; **s'accentuer** *vi* to become more marked *ou* pronounced

acceptable [aksɛptabl(ə)] *adj* satisfactory, acceptable

acceptation [aksɛptasjɔ̃] *nf* acceptance

accepter [aksɛpte] *vt* to accept; (*tolérer*): **~ que qn fasse** to agree to sb doing; **~ de faire** to agree to do

acception [aksɛpsjɔ̃] *nf* meaning, sense; **dans toute l'~ du terme** in the full sense *ou* meaning of the word

accès [aksɛ] *nm* (*à un lieu, Inform*) access; (*Méd*) attack; (*: de toux*) fit, bout ▷ *nmpl* (*routes etc*) means of access, approaches; **d'~ facile/ malaisé** easily/not easily accessible; **donner ~ à** (*lieu*) to give access to; (*carrière*) to open the door to; **avoir ~ auprès de qn** to have access to sb; **l'~ aux quais est interdit aux personnes non munies d'un billet** ticket-holders only on platforms, no access to platforms without a ticket; **~ de colère** fit of anger; **~ de joie** burst of joy

accessible [aksesibl(ə)] *adj* accessible; (*personne*) approachable; (*livre, sujet*): **~ à qn** within the reach of sb; (*sensible*): **~ à la pitié/l'amour** open to pity/love

accession [aksesjɔ̃] *nf*: **~ à** accession to; (*à un poste*) attainment of; **~ à la propriété** home-ownership

accessit [aksesit] *nm* (*Scol*) ≈ certificate of merit

accessoire [akseswaR] *adj* secondary, of secondary importance; (*frais*) incidental ▷ *nm* accessory; (*Théât*) prop

accessoirement [akseswaRmɑ̃] *adv* secondarily; incidentally

accessoiriste [akseswaRist(ə)] *nm/f* (*TV, Ciné*) property man/woman

accident [aksidɑ̃] *nm* accident; **par ~** by chance; **~ de parcours** mishap; **~ de la route** road accident; **~ du travail** accident at work; industrial injury *ou* accident; **~s de terrain** unevenness of the ground

accidenté, e [aksidɑ̃te] *adj* damaged *ou* injured (in an accident); (*relief, terrain*) uneven; hilly

accidentel, le [aksidɑ̃tɛl] *adj* accidental

accidentellement [aksidɑ̃tɛlmɑ̃] *adv* (*par hasard*) accidentally; (*mourir*) in an accident

accise [aksiz] *nf*: **droit d'~(s)** excise duty

acclamation [aklamasjɔ̃] *nf*: **par ~** (*vote*) by acclamation; **acclamations** *nfpl* cheers, cheering *sg*

acclamer [aklame] *vt* to cheer, acclaim

acclimatation [aklimatasjɔ̃] *nf* acclimatization

acclimater [aklimate] *vt* to acclimatize; **s'acclimater** *vi* to become acclimatized

accointances [akwɛ̃tɑ̃s] *nfpl*: **avoir des ~ avec** to have contacts with

accolade [akɔlad] *nf* (*amicale*) embrace; (*signe*) brace; **donner l'~ à qn** to embrace sb

accoler [akɔle] *vt* to place side by side

accommodant, e [akɔmɔdɑ̃, -ɑ̃t] *adj* accommodating, easy-going

accommodement [akɔmɔdmɑ̃] *nm* compromise

accommoder [akɔmɔde] *vt* (*Culin*) to prepare; (*points de vue*) to reconcile; **~ qch à** (*adapter*) to adapt sth to; **s'accommoder de** to put up with; (*se contenter de*) to make do with; **s'~ à** (*s'adapter*) to adapt to

accompagnateur, -trice [akɔ̃paɲatœR, -tRis] *nm/f* (*Mus*) accompanist; (*de voyage*) guide; (*de voyage organisé*) courier; (*d'enfants*) accompanying adult

accompagnement [akɔ̃paɲmɑ̃] *nm* (*Mus*) accompaniment; (*Mil*) support

accompagner [akɔ̃paɲe] *vt* to accompany, be *ou* go *ou* come with; (*Mus*) to accompany; **s'accompagner de** to bring, be accompanied by

accompli, e [akɔ̃pli] *adj* accomplished

accomplir [akɔ̃pliR] *vt* (*tâche, projet*) to carry out; (*souhait*) to fulfil; **s'accomplir** *vi* to be fulfilled

accomplissement [akɔ̃plismɑ̃] *nm* carrying out; fulfilment (*Brit*), fulfillment (*US*)

accord [akɔR] *nm* (*entente, convention, Ling*) agreement; (*entre des styles, tons etc*) harmony; (*consentement*) agreement, consent; (*Mus*) chord; **donner son ~** to give one's agreement; **mettre deux personnes d'~** to make two people come to an agreement, reconcile two people; **se mettre d'~** to come to an agreement (with each other); **être d'~** to agree; **être d'~ avec qn** to agree with sb; **d'~!** OK!, right!; **d'un commun ~** of one accord; **~ parfait** (*Mus*) tonic chord

accord-cadre [akɔRkadR(ə)] (*pl* **accords-cadres**) *nm* framework *ou* outline agreement

accordéon [akɔRdeɔ̃] *nm* (*Mus*) accordion

accordéoniste [akɔRdeɔnist(ə)] *nm/f* accordionist

accorder [akɔRde] *vt* (*faveur, délai*) to grant; (*attribuer*): **~ de l'importance/de la valeur à qch** to attach importance/value to sth; (*harmoniser*) to match; (*Mus*) to tune; **s'accorder** *vi* to get on together; (*être d'accord*) to agree; (*couleurs, caractères*) to go together, match; (*Ling*) to agree; **je vous accorde que ...** I grant you that ...

accordeur [akɔʀdœʀ] nm (Mus) tuner

accoster [akɔste] vt (Navig) to draw alongside; (personne) to accost ▷ vi (Navig) to berth

accotement [akɔtmā] nm (de route) verge (Brit), shoulder; ~ **stabilisé/non stabilisé** hard shoulder/soft verge ou shoulder

accoter [akɔte] vt: ~ **qch contre/à** to lean ou rest sth against/on; **s'~ contre/à** to lean against/on

accouchement [akuʃmā] nm delivery, (child)birth; (travail) labour (Brit), labor (US); ~ **à terme** delivery at (full) term; ~ **sans douleur** natural childbirth

accoucher [akuʃe] vi to give birth, have a baby; (être en travail) to be in labour (Brit) ou labor (US) ▷ vt to deliver; ~ **d'un garçon** to give birth to a boy

accoucheur [akuʃœʀ] nm: **(médecin)** ~ obstetrician

accoucheuse [akuʃøz] nf midwife

accouder [akude]: **s'accouder** vi: **s'~ à/contre/ sur** to rest one's elbows on/against/on; **accoudé à la fenêtre** leaning on the windowsill

accoudoir [akudwaʀ] nm armrest

accouplement [akupləmā] nm coupling; mating

accoupler [akuple] vt to couple; (pour la reproduction) to mate; **s'accoupler** vi to mate

accourir [akuʀiʀ] vi to rush ou run up

accoutrement [akutʀəmā] nm (péj) getup (Brit), outfit

accoutrer [akutʀe] (péj) vt to do ou get up; **s'accoutrer** to do ou get o.s. up

accoutumance [akutymās] nf (gén) adaptation; (Méd) addiction

accoutumé, e [akutyme] adj (habituel) customary, usual; **comme à l'~e** as is customary ou usual

accoutumer [akutyme] vt: ~ **qn à qch/faire** to accustom sb to sth/to doing; **s'accoutumer à** to get accustomed ou used to

accréditer [akʀedite] vt (nouvelle) to substantiate; ~ **qn (auprès de)** to accredit sb (to)

accro [akʀo] nm/f (fam: = accroché(e)) addict

accroc [akʀo] nm (déchirure) tear; (fig) hitch, snag; **sans** ~ without a hitch; **faire un** ~ **à** (vêtement) to make a tear in, tear; (fig: règle etc) to infringe

accrochage [akʀɔʃaʒ] nm hanging (up); hitching (up); (Auto) (minor) collision; (Mil) encounter, engagement; (dispute) clash, brush

accroche-cœur [akʀɔʃkœʀ] nm kiss-curl

accrocher [akʀɔʃe] vt (suspendre): ~ **qch à** to hang sth (up) on; (attacher: remorque) to hitch sth (up) to; (heurter) to catch; to hit; (déchirer): ~ **qch (à)** to catch sth (on); (Mil) to engage; (fig) to catch, attract ▷ vi to stick, get stuck; (fig: pourparlers etc) to hit a snag; (plaire: disque etc) to catch on; **s'accrocher** vi (se disputer) to have a clash ou brush; (ne pas céder) to hold one's own, hang on in (fam); **s'~ à** (rester pris à) to catch on;

(agripper, fig) to hang on ou cling to

accrocheur, -euse [akʀɔʃœʀ, -øz] adj (vendeur, concurrent) tenacious; (publicité) eye-catching; (titre) catchy, eye-catching

accroire [akʀwaʀ] vt: **faire** ou **laisser** ~ **à qn qch/que** to give sb to believe sth/that

accroîs [akʀwa], **accroissais** etc [akʀwasɛ] vb voir **accroître**

accroissement [akʀwasmā] nm increase

accroître [akʀwatʀ(ə)] vt, **s'accroître** vi to increase

accroupi, e [akʀupi] adj squatting, crouching (down)

accroupir [akʀupiʀ]: **s'accroupir** vi to squat, crouch (down)

accru, e [akʀy] pp de **accroître**

accu [aky] nm (fam: = accumulateur) accumulator, battery

accueil [akœj] nm welcome; (endroit) reception (desk); (: dans une gare) information kiosk; **comité/centre d'~** reception committee/ centre

accueillant, e [akœjā, -āt] adj welcoming, friendly

accueillir [akœjiʀ] vt to welcome; (loger) to accommodate

acculer [akyle] vt: ~ **qn à** ou **contre** to drive sb back against; ~ **qn dans** to corner sb in; ~ **qn à** (faillite) to drive sb to the brink of

accumulateur [akymylatœʀ] nm accumulator, battery

accumulation [akymylɑsjɔ̃] nf accumulation; **chauffage/radiateur à** ~ (night-)storage heating/heater

accumuler [akymyle] vt to accumulate, amass; **s'accumuler** vi to accumulate; to pile up

accusateur, -trice [akyzatœʀ, -tʀis] nm/f accuser ▷ adj accusing; (document, preuve) incriminating

accusatif [akyzatif] nm (Ling) accusative

accusation [akyzɑsjɔ̃] nf (gén) accusation; (Jur) charge; (partie): **l'~** the prosecution; **mettre en** ~ to indict; **acte d'~** bill of indictment

accusé, e [akyze] nm/f accused; (prévenu(e)) defendant ▷ nm: ~ **de réception** acknowledgement of receipt

accuser [akyze] vt to accuse; (fig) to emphasize, bring out; (: montrer) to show; **s'accuser** vi (s'accentuer) to become more marked; ~ **qn de** to accuse sb of; (Jur) to charge sb with; ~ **qn/qch de qch** (rendre responsable) to blame sb/sth for sth; **s'~ de qch/d'avoir fait qch** to admit sth/ having done sth; to blame o.s. for sth/for having done sth; ~ **réception de** to acknowledge receipt of; ~ **le coup** (aussi fig) to be visibly affected

acerbe [asɛʀb(ə)] adj caustic, acid

acéré, e [aseʀe] adj sharp

acétate [asetat] nm acetate

acétique [asetik] adj: **acide** ~ acetic acid

acétone [asetɔn] nf acetone

acétylène [asetilɛn] nm acetylene

ach. *abr* = **achète**

acharné, e [aʃaʀne] *adj (lutte, adversaire)* fierce, bitter; *(travail)* relentless, unremitting

acharnement [aʃaʀnəmã] *nm* fierceness; relentlessness

acharner [aʃaʀne]: **s'acharner** *vi*: **s'~ sur** to go at fiercely, hound; **s'~ contre** to set o.s. against; to dog, pursue; *(malchance)* to hound; **s'~ à faire** to try doggedly to do; to persist in doing

achat [aʃa] *nm* buying *no pl*; *(article acheté)* purchase; **faire l'~ de** to buy, purchase; **faire des ~s** to do some shopping, buy a few things

acheminement [aʃminmã] *nm* conveyance

acheminer [aʃmine] *vt (courrier)* to forward, dispatch; *(troupes)* to convey, transport; *(train)* to route; **s'acheminer vers** to head for

acheter [aʃte] *vt* to buy, purchase; *(soudoyer)* to buy, bribe; **~ qch à** *(marchand)* to buy *ou* purchase sth from; *(ami etc: offrir)* to buy sth for; **~ à crédit** to buy on credit

acheteur, -euse [aʃtœʀ, -øz] *nm/f* buyer; shopper; *(Comm)* buyer; *(Jur)* vendee, purchaser

achevé, e [aʃve] *adj*: **d'un ridicule ~** thoroughly *ou* absolutely ridiculous; **d'un comique ~** absolutely hilarious

achèvement [aʃevmã] *nm* completion, finishing

achever [aʃve] *vt* to complete, finish; *(blessé)* to finish off; **s'achever** *vi* to end

achoppement [aʃɔpmã] *nm*: **pierre d'~** stumbling block

acide [asid] *adj* sour, sharp; *(ton)* acid, biting; *(Chimie)* acid(ic) ▷ *nm* acid

acidifier [asidifje] *vt* to acidify

acidité [asidite] *nf* sharpness; acidity

acidulé, e [asidyle] *adj* slightly acid; **bonbons ~s** acid drops *(Brit)*, ≈ lemon drops *(US)*

acier [asje] *nm* steel; **~ inoxydable** stainless steel

aciérie [asjeʀi] *nf* steelworks *sg*

acné [akne] *nf* acne

acolyte [akɔlit] *nm (péj)* associate

acompte [akɔ̃t] *nm* deposit; *(versement régulier)* instalment; *(sur somme due)* payment on account; *(sur salaire)* advance; **un ~ de 10 euros** 10 euros on account

acoquiner [akɔkine]: **s'acoquiner avec** *vt (péj)* to team up with

Açores [asɔʀ] *nfpl*: **les ~** the Azores

à-côté [akote] *nm* side-issue; *(argent)* extra

à-coup [aku] *nm (du moteur)* (hic)cough; *(fig)* jolt; **sans ~s** smoothly; **par ~s** by fits and starts

acoustique [akustik] *nf (d'une salle)* acoustics *pl*; *(science)* acoustics *sg* ▷ *adj* acoustic

acquéreur [akeʀœʀ] *nm* buyer, purchaser; **se porter/se rendre ~ de qch** to announce one's intention to purchase/to purchase sth

acquérir [akeʀiʀ] *vt* to acquire; *(par achat)* to purchase, acquire; *(valeur)* to gain; *(résultats)* to achieve; **ce que ses efforts lui ont acquis** what his efforts have won *ou* gained (for) him

acquiers *etc* [akjɛʀ] *vb voir* **acquérir**

acquiescement [akjɛsmã] *nm* acquiescence, agreement

acquiescer [akjese] *vi (opiner)* to agree; *(consentir)*: **~ (à qch)** to acquiesce *ou* assent (to sth)

acquis, e [aki, -iz] *pp de* **acquérir** ▷ *nm* (accumulated) experience; *(avantage)* gain ▷ *adj (voir acquérir)* acquired; gained; achieved; **être ~ à** *(plan, idée)* to be in full agreement with; **son aide nous est ~e** we can count on *ou* be sure of his help; **tenir qch pour ~** to take sth for granted

acquisition [akizisjɔ̃] *nf* acquisition; *(achat)* purchase; **faire l'~ de** to acquire; to purchase

acquit [aki] *vb voir* **acquérir** ▷ *nm (quittance)* receipt; **pour ~** received; **par ~ de conscience** to set one's mind at rest

acquittement [akitmã] *nm* acquittal; payment, settlement

acquitter [akite] *vt (Jur)* to acquit; *(facture)* to pay, settle; **s'acquitter de** to discharge; *(promesse, tâche)* to fulfil *(Brit)*, fulfill *(US)*, carry out

âcre [ɑkʀ(ə)] *adj* acrid, pungent

âcreté [ɑkʀəte] *nf* acridness, pungency

acrimonie [akʀimɔni] *nf* acrimony

acrobate [akʀɔbat] *nm/f* acrobat

acrobatie [akʀɔbasi] *nf (art)* acrobatics *sg*; *(exercice)* acrobatic feat; **~ aérienne** aerobatics *sg*

acrobatique [akʀɔbatik] *adj* acrobatic

acronyme [akʀɔnim] *nm* acronym

Acropole [akʀɔpɔl] *nf*: **l'~** the Acropolis

acrylique [akʀilik] *adj, nm* acrylic

acte [akt(ə)] *nm* act, action; *(Théât)* act; **actes** *nmpl (compte-rendu)* proceedings; **prendre ~ de** to note, take note of; **faire ~ de présence** to put in an appearance; **faire ~ de candidature** to submit an application; **~ d'accusation** charge *(Brit)*, bill of indictment; **~ de baptême** baptismal certificate; **~ de mariage/naissance** marriage/birth certificate; **~ de vente** bill of sale

acteur [aktœʀ] *nm* actor

actif, -ive [aktif, -iv] *adj* active ▷ *nm (Comm)* assets *pl*; *(Ling)* active (voice); *(fig)*: **avoir à son ~** to have to one's credit; **actifs** *nmpl* people in employment; **mettre à son ~** to add to one's list of achievements; **l'~ et le passif** assets and liabilities; **prendre une part active à qch** to take an active part in sth; **population active** working population

action [aksjɔ̃] *nf (gén)* action; *(Comm)* share; **une bonne/mauvaise ~** a good/an unkind deed; **mettre en ~** to put into action; **passer à l'~** to take action; **sous l'~ de** under the effect of; **l'~ syndicale** (the) union action; **un film d'~** an action film *ou* movie; **~ en diffamation** libel action; **~ de grâce(s)** *(Rel)* thanksgiving

actionnaire [aksjɔnɛʀ] *nm/f* shareholder

actionner [aksjɔne] *vt* to work; to activate; to operate

active [aktiv] *adj f voir* **actif**

activement [aktivmɑ̃] *adv* actively

activer [aktive] *vt* to speed up; (*Chimie*) to activate; **s'activer** *vi* (*s'affairer*) to bustle about; (*se hâter*) to hurry up

activisme [aktivism(ə)] *nm* activism

activiste [aktivist(ə)] *nm/f* activist

activité [aktivite] *nf* activity; **en ~** (*volcan*) active; (*fonctionnaire*) in active life; (*militaire*) on active service

actrice [aktʀis] *nf* actress

actualiser [aktɥalize] *vt* to actualize; (*mettre à jour*) to bring up to date

actualité [aktɥalite] *nf* (*d'un problème*) topicality; (*événements*): **l'~** current events; **les ~s** (*Ciné, TV*) the news; **l'~ politique/sportive** the political/sports *ou* sporting news; **les ~s télévisées** the television news; **d'~** topical

actuel, le [aktɥɛl] *adj* (*présent*) present; (*d'actualité*) topical; (*non virtuel*) actual; **à l'heure ~le** at this moment in time, at the moment

actuellement [aktɥɛlmɑ̃] *adv* at present, at the present time

acuité [akɥite] *nf* acuteness

acuponcteur, acupuncteur [akypɔ̃ktœʀ] *nm* acupuncturist

acuponcture, acupuncture [akypɔ̃ktyʀ] *nf* acupuncture

adage [adaʒ] *nm* adage

adagio [ada(d)ʒjo] *adv, nm* adagio

adaptable [adaptabl(ə)] *adj* adaptable

adaptateur, -trice [adaptatœʀ, -tʀis] *nm/f* adapter

adaptation [adaptɑsjɔ̃] *nf* adaptation

adapter [adapte] *vt* to adapt; **s'adapter (à)** (*personne*) to adapt (to); (: *objet, prise etc*) to apply (to); **~ qch à** (*approprier*) to adapt sth to (fit); **~ qch sur/dans/à** (*fixer*) to fit sth on/into/to

addenda [adɛ̃da] *nm inv* addenda

Addis-Ababa [adisababa], **Addis-Abeba** [adisabəba] *n* Addis Ababa

additif [aditif] *nm* additional clause; (*substance*) additive; **~ alimentaire** food additive

addition [adisjɔ̃] *nf* addition; (*au café*) bill

additionnel, le [adisjɔnɛl] *adj* additional

additionner [adisjɔne] *vt* to add (up); **s'additionner** *vi* to add up; **~ un produit d'eau** to add water to a product

adduction [adyksjɔ̃] *nf* (*de gaz, d'eau*) conveyance

adepte [adɛpt(ə)] *nm/f* follower

adéquat, e [adekwa, -at] *adj* appropriate, suitable

adéquation [adekwɑsjɔ̃] *nf* appropriateness; (*Ling*) adequacy

adhérence [adeʀɑ̃s] *nf* adhesion

adhérent, e [adeʀɑ̃, -ɑ̃t] *nm/f* (*de club*) member

adhérer [adeʀe] *vi* (*coller*) to adhere, stick; **~ à** (*coller*) to adhere *ou* stick to; (*se rallier à: parti, club*) to join; to be a member of; (: *opinion, mouvement*) to support

adhésif, -ive [adezif, -iv] *adj* adhesive, sticky ▷ *nm* adhesive

adhésion [adezjɔ̃] *nf* (*à un club*) joining; membership; (*à une opinion*) support

ad hoc [adɔk] *adj* ad hoc

adieu, x [adjø] *excl* goodbye ▷ *nm* farewell; **dire ~ à qn** to say goodbye *ou* farewell to sb; **dire ~ à qch** (*renoncer*) to say *ou* wave goodbye to sth

adipeux, -euse [adipø, -øz] *adj* bloated, fat; (*Anat*) adipose

adjacent, e [adʒasɑ̃, -ɑ̃t] *adj*: **~ (à)** adjacent (to)

adjectif [adʒɛktif] *nm* adjective; **~ attribut** adjectival complement; **~ épithète** attributive adjective

adjectival, e, -aux [adʒɛktival, -o] *adj* adjectival

adjoignais *etc* [adʒwaɲɛ] *vb voir* **adjoindre**

adjoindre [adʒwɛ̃dʀ(ə)] *vt*: **~ qch à** to attach sth to; (*ajouter*) to add sth to; **~ qn à** (*personne*) to appoint sb as an assistant to; (*comité*) to appoint sb to, attach sb to; **s'adjoindre** *vt* (*collaborateur etc*) to take on, appoint

adjoint, e [adʒwɛ̃, -wɛ̃t] *pp de* **adjoindre** ▷ *nm/f* assistant; **directeur ~** assistant manager

adjonction [adʒɔ̃ksjɔ̃] *nf* (*voir adjoindre*) attaching; addition; appointment

adjudant [adʒydɑ̃] *nm* (*Mil*) warrant officer; **~-chef** ≈ warrant officer 1st class (*Brit*), ≈ chief warrant officer (*US*)

adjudicataire [adʒydikatɛʀ] *nm/f* successful bidder, purchaser; (*pour travaux*) successful tenderer (*Brit*) *ou* bidder (*US*)

adjudicateur, -trice [adʒydikatœʀ, -tʀis] *nm/f* (*aux enchères*) seller

adjudication [adʒydikɑsjɔ̃] *nf* sale by auction; (*pour travaux*) invitation to tender (*Brit*) *ou* bid (*US*)

adjuger [adʒyʒe] *vt* (*prix, récompense*) to award; (*lors d'une vente*) to auction (off); **s'adjuger** *vt* to take for o.s.; **adjugé!** (*vendu*) gone!, sold!

adjurer [adʒyʀe] *vt*: **~ qn de faire** to implore *ou* beg sb to do

adjuvant [adʒyvɑ̃] *nm* (*médicament*) adjuvant; (*additif*) additive; (*stimulant*) stimulant

admettre [admɛtʀ(ə)] *vt* (*visiteur, nouveau-venu*) to admit, let in; (*candidat: Scol*) to pass; (*Tech: gaz, eau, air*) to admit; (*tolérer*) to allow, accept; (*reconnaître*) to admit, acknowledge; (*supposer*) to suppose; **j'admets que ...** I admit that ...; **je n'admets pas que tu fasses cela** I won't allow you to do that; **admettons que ...** let's suppose that ...; **admettons** let's suppose so

administrateur, -trice [administʀatœʀ, -tʀis] *nm/f* (*Comm*) director; (*Admin*) administrator; **~ délégué** managing director; **~ judiciaire** receiver

administratif, -ive [administʀatif, -iv] *adj* administrative ▷ *nm* person in administration

administration [administʀɑsjɔ̃] *nf* administration; **l'A~** ≈ the Civil Service

administré, e [administʀe] *nm/f* ≈ citizen

administrer [administʀe] *vt* (*firme*) to manage, run; (*biens, remède, sacrement etc*) to administer

admirable [admiʀabl(ə)] *adj* admirable, wonderful

admirablement [admiʀabləmɑ̃] *adv* admirably

admirateur, -trice [admiʀatœʀ, -tʀis] *nm/f* admirer

admiratif, -ive [admiʀatif, -iv] *adj* admiring

admiration [admiʀɑsjɔ̃] *nf* admiration; **être en ~ devant** to be lost in admiration before

admirativement [admiʀativmɑ̃] *adv* admiringly

admirer [admiʀe] *vt* to admire

admis, e [admi, -iz] *pp de* **admettre**

admissibilité [admisibilite] *nf* eligibility; admissibility, acceptability

admissible [admisibl(ə)] *adj* (*candidat*) eligible; (*comportement*) admissible, acceptable; (*Jur*) receivable

admission [admisjɔ̃] *nf* admission; **tuyau d'~** intake pipe; **demande d'~** application for membership; **service des ~s** admissions

admonester [admɔnɛste] *vt* to admonish

ADN *sigle m* (= *acide désoxyribonucléique*) DNA

ado [ado] *nm/f* (*fam*: = *adolescent(e)*) adolescent, teenager

adolescence [adɔlesɑ̃s] *nf* adolescence

adolescent, e [adɔlesɑ̃, -ɑ̃t] *nm/f* adolescent, teenager

adonner [adɔne]: **s'adonner à** *vt* (*sport*) to devote o.s. to; (*boisson*) to give o.s. over to

adopter [adɔpte] *vt* to adopt; (*projet de loi etc*) to pass

adoptif, -ive [adɔptif, -iv] *adj* (*parents*) adoptive; (*fils, patrie*) adopted

adoption [adɔpsjɔ̃] *nf* adoption; **son pays/sa ville d'~** his adopted country/town

adorable [adɔʀabl(ə)] *adj* adorable

adoration [adɔʀɑsjɔ̃] *nf* adoration; (*Rel*) worship; **être en ~ devant** to be lost in adoration before

adorer [adɔʀe] *vt* to adore; (*Rel*) to worship

adosser [adose] *vt*: **~ qch à** *ou* **contre** to stand sth against; **s'~ à** *ou* **contre** to lean with one's back against; **être adossé à** *ou* **contre** to be leaning with one's back against

adoucir [adusiʀ] *vt* (*goût, température*) to make milder; (*avec du sucre*) to sweeten; (*peau, voix, eau*) to soften; (*caractère, personne*) to mellow; (*peine*) to soothe, allay; **s'adoucir** *vi* to become milder; to soften; to mellow

adoucissement [adusismɑ̃] *nm* becoming milder; sweetening; softening; mellowing; soothing

adoucisseur [adusisœʀ] *nm*: **~ (d'eau)** water softener

adr. *abr* = **adresse; adresser**

adrénaline [adʀenalin] *nf* adrenaline

adresse [adʀɛs] *nf* (*voir adroit*) skill, dexterity; (*domicile, Inform*) address; **à l'~ de** (*pour*) for the benefit of

adresser [adʀese] *vt* (*lettre: expédier*) to send; (: *écrire l'adresse sur*) to address; (*injure, compliments*) to address; **~ qn à un docteur/bureau** to refer *ou* send sb to a doctor/an office; **~ la parole à qn** to speak to *ou* address sb; **s'adresser à** (*parler à*)

to speak to, address; (*s'informer auprès de*) to go and see, go and speak to; (: *bureau*) to enquire at; (*livre, conseil*) to be aimed at

Adriatique [adʀijatik] *nf*: **l'~** the Adriatic

adroit, e [adʀwa, -wat] *adj* (*joueur, mécanicien*) skilful (*Brit*), skillful (*US*), dext(e)rous; (*politicien etc*) shrewd, skilled

adroitement [adʀwatmɑ̃] *adv* skilfully (*Brit*), skillfully (*US*), dext(e)rously; shrewdly

AdS *sigle f* = **Académie des Sciences**

ADSL *sigle m* (= *asymmetrical digital subscriber line*) ADSL; **avoir l'~** to have broadband

aduler [adyle] *vt* to adulate

adulte [adylt(ə)] *nm/f* adult, grown-up ▷ *adj* (*personne, attitude*) adult, grown-up; (*chien, arbre*) fully-grown, mature; **l'âge ~** adulthood; **formation/film pour ~s** adult training/film

adultère [adyltɛʀ] *adj* adulterous ▷ *nm/f* adulterer/adulteress ▷ *nm* (*acte*) adultery

adultérin, e [adylteʀɛ̃, -in] *adj* born of adultery

advenir [advəniʀ] *vi* to happen; **qu'est-il advenu de ...?** what has become of ...?; **quoi qu'il advienne** whatever befalls *ou* happens

adventiste [advɑ̃tist(ə)] *nm/f* (*Rel*) Adventist

adverbe [advɛʀb(ə)] *nm* adverb; **~ de manière** adverb of manner

adverbial, e, -aux [advɛʀbjal, -o] *adj* adverbial

adversaire [advɛʀsɛʀ] *nm/f* (*Sport, gén*) opponent, adversary; (*Mil*) adversary, enemy

adverse [advɛʀs(ə)] *adj* opposing

adversité [advɛʀsite] *nf* adversity

AELE *sigle f* (= *Association européenne de libre-échange*) EFTA (= *European Free Trade Association*)

AEN *sigle f* (= *Agence pour l'énergie nucléaire*) ≈ AEA = **Atomic Energy Authority**

aérateur [aeʀatœʀ] *nm* ventilator

aération [aeʀɑsjɔ̃] *nf* airing; (*circulation de l'air*) ventilation; **conduit d'~** ventilation shaft; **bouche d'~** air vent

aéré, e [aeʀe] *adj* (*pièce, local*) airy, well-ventilated; (*tissu*) loose-woven; **centre ~** outdoor centre

aérer [aeʀe] *vt* to air; (*fig*) to lighten; **s'aérer** *vi* to get some (fresh) air

aérien, ne [aeʀjɛ̃, -ɛn] *adj* (*Aviat*) air *cpd*, aerial; (*câble, métro*) overhead; (*fig*) light; **compagnie ~ne** airline (company); **ligne ~ne** airline

aérobic [aeʀɔbik] *nf* aerobics *sg*

aérobie [aeʀɔbi] *adj* aerobic

aéro-club [aeʀɔklœb] *nm* flying club

aérodrome [aeʀɔdʀɔm] *nm* airfield, aerodrome

aérodynamique [aeʀɔdinamik] *adj* aerodynamic, streamlined ▷ *nf* aerodynamics *sg*

aérofrein [aeʀɔfʀɛ̃] *nm* air brake

aérogare [aeʀɔgaʀ] *nf* airport (buildings); (*en ville*) air terminal

aéroglisseur [aeʀɔglisœʀ] *nm* hovercraft

aérogramme [aeʀɔgʀam] *nm* air letter, aerogram(me)

aéromodélisme [aeʀɔmɔdelism(ə)] *nm* model aircraft making

aéronaute [aeʀɔnot] *nm/f* aeronaut

aéronautique [aeʀɔnotik] *adj* aeronautical ▷ *nf* aeronautics *sg*

aéronaval, e [aeʀɔnaval] *adj* air and sea *cpd*

Aéronavale [aeʀɔnaval] *nf* ≈ Fleet Air Arm (*Brit*), ≈ Naval Air Force (*US*)

aéronef [aeʀɔnɛf] *nm* aircraft

aérophagie [aeʀɔfaʒi] *nf*: **il fait de l'~** he suffers from abdominal wind

aéroport [aeʀɔpɔʀ] *nm* airport; **~ d'embarquement** departure airport

aéroporté, e [aeʀɔpɔʀte] *adj* airborne, airlifted

aéroportuaire [aeʀɔpɔʀtɥɛʀ] *adj* of an *ou* the airport, airport *cpd*

aéropostal, e, -aux [aeʀɔpɔstal, -o] *adj* airmail *cpd*

aérosol [aeʀɔsɔl] *nm* aerosol

aérospatial, e, -aux [aeʀɔspasjal, -o] *adj* aerospace ▷ *nf* the aerospace industry

aérostat [aeʀɔsta] *nm* aerostat

aérotrain [aeʀɔtʀɛ̃] *nm* hovertrain

AF *sigle fpl* = **allocations familiales** ▷ *sigle f* (*Suisse*) = **Assemblée fédérale**

AFAT [afat] *sigle m* (= *Auxiliaire féminin de l'armée de terre*) *member of the women's army*

affabilité [afabilite] *nf* affability

affable [afabl(ə)] *adj* affable

affabulateur, -trice [afabylatœʀ, -tʀis] *nm/f* storyteller

affabulation [afabylɑsjɔ̃] *nf* invention, fantasy

affabuler [afabyle] *vi* to make up stories

affacturage [afaktyʀaʒ] *nm* factoring

affadir [afadiʀ] *vt* to make insipid *ou* tasteless

affaiblir [afebliʀ] *vt* to weaken; **s'affaiblir** *vi* to weaken, grow weaker; (*vue*) to grow dim

affaiblissement [afeblismɑ̃] *nm* weakening

affaire [afɛʀ] *nf* (*problème, question*) matter; (*criminelle, judiciaire*) case; (*scandaleuse etc*) affair; (*entreprise*) business; (*marché, transaction*) (business) deal, (piece of) business *no pl*; (*occasion intéressante*) good deal; **affaires** *nfpl* affairs; (*activité commerciale*) business *sg*; (*effets personnels*) things, belongings; **tirer qn/se tirer d'~** to get sb/o.s. out of trouble; **ceci fera l'~** this will do (nicely); **avoir ~ à** (*comme adversaire*) to be faced with; (*en contact*) to be dealing with; **tu auras ~ à moi!** (*menace*) you'll have me to contend with!; **c'est une ~ de goût/d'argent** it's a question *ou* matter of taste/money; **c'est l'~ d'une minute/heure** it'll only take a minute/an hour; **ce sont mes ~s** (*cela me concerne*) that's my business; **toutes ~s cessantes** forthwith; **les ~s étrangères** (*Pol*) foreign affairs

affairé, e [afeʀe] *adj* busy

affairer [afeʀe]: **s'affairer** *vi* to busy o.s., bustle about

affairisme [afeʀism(ə)] *nm* (political) racketeering

affaissement [afɛsmɑ̃] *nm* subsidence; collapse

affaisser [afese]: **s'affaisser** *vi* (*terrain, immeuble*) to subside, sink; (*personne*) to collapse

affaler [afale]: **s'affaler** *vi*: **s'~ dans/sur** to collapse *ou* slump into/onto

affamé, e [afame] *adj* starving, famished

affamer [afame] *vt* to starve

affectation [afɛktɑsjɔ̃] *nf* (*voir affecter*) allotment; appointment; posting; (*voir affecté*) affectedness

affecté, e [afɛkte] *adj* affected

affecter [afɛkte] *vt* (*émouvoir*) to affect, move; (*feindre*) to affect, feign; (*telle ou telle forme etc*) to take on, assume; **~ qch à** to allocate *ou* allot sth to; **~ qn à** to appoint sb to; (*diplomate*) to post sb to; **~ qch de** (*de coefficient*) to modify sth by

affectif, -ive [afɛktif, -iv] *adj* emotional, affective

affection [afɛksjɔ̃] *nf* affection; (*mal*) ailment; **avoir de l'~ pour** to feel affection for; **prendre en ~** to become fond of

affectionner [afɛksjɔne] *vt* to be fond of

affectueusement [afɛktɥøzmɑ̃] *adv* affectionately

affectueux, -euse [afɛktɥø, -øz] *adj* affectionate

afférent, e [afeʀɑ̃, -ɑ̃t] *adj*: **~ à** pertaining *ou* relating to

affermir [afɛʀmiʀ] *vt* to consolidate, strengthen

affichage [afiʃaʒ] *nm* billposting, billsticking; (*électronique*) display; **"~ interdit"** "stick no bills", "billsticking prohibited"; **~ à cristaux liquides** liquid crystal display, LCD; **~ numérique** *ou* **digital** digital display

affiche [afiʃ] *nf* poster; (*officielle*) (public) notice; (*Théât*) bill; **être à l'~** (*Théât*) to be on; **tenir l'~** to run

afficher [afiʃe] *vt* (*affiche*) to put up, post up; (*réunion*) to put up a notice about; (*électroniquement*) to display; (*fig*) to exhibit, display; **s'afficher** *vi* (*péj*) to flaunt o.s.; **"défense d'~"** "stick no bills"

affichette [afiʃɛt] *nf* small poster *ou* notice

affilé, e [afile] *adj* sharp

affilée [afile]: **d'~** *adv* at a stretch

affiler [afile] *vt* to sharpen

affiliation [afiljɑsjɔ̃] *nf* affiliation

affilié, e [afilje] *adj*: **être ~ à** to be affiliated to ▷ *nm/f* affiliated party *ou* member

affilier [afilje] *vt*: **s'affilier à** to become affiliated to

affiner [afine] *vt* to refine; **s'affiner** *vi* to become (more) refined

affinité [afinite] *nf* affinity

affirmatif, -ive [afiʀmatif, -iv] *adj* affirmative ▷ *nf*: **répondre par l'affirmative** to reply in the affirmative; **dans l'affirmative** (*si oui*) if (the answer is) yes ..., if he does (*ou* you do *etc*) ...

affirmation [afiʀmɑsjɔ̃] *nf* assertion

affirmativement [afiʀmativmɑ̃] *adv* affirmatively, in the affirmative

affirmer [afiʀme] *vt* (*prétendre*) to maintain, assert; (*autorité etc*) to assert; **s'affirmer** *vi* to assert o.s.; to assert itself

affleurer [aflœʀe] *vi* to show on the surface

affliction [afliksjɔ̃] *nf* affliction

affligé, e [afliʒe] *adj* distressed, grieved; ~ **de** (*maladie, tare*) afflicted with

affligeant, e [afliʒɑ̃, -ɑ̃t] *adj* distressing

affliger [afliʒe] *vt* (*peiner*) to distress, grieve

affluence [aflyɑ̃s] *nf* crowds *pl*; **heures d'~** rush hour *sg*; **jours d'~** busiest days

affluent [aflyɑ̃] *nm* tributary

affluer [aflye] *vi* (*secours, biens*) to flood in, pour in; (*sang*) to rush, flow

afflux [afly] *nm* flood, influx; rush

affolant, e [afɔlɑ̃, -ɑ̃t] *adj* terrifying

affolé, e [afɔle] *adj* panic-stricken, panicky

affolement [afɔlmɑ̃] *nm* panic

affoler [afɔle] *vt* to throw into a panic; **s'affoler** *vi* to panic

affranchir [afʀɑ̃ʃiʀ] *vt* to put a stamp *ou* stamps on; (*à la machine*) to frank (*Brit*), meter (*US*); (*esclave*) to enfranchise, emancipate; (*fig*) to free, liberate; **s'affranchir de** to free o.s. from; **machine à ~** franking machine, postage meter

affranchissement [afʀɑ̃ʃismɑ̃] *nm* franking (*Brit*), metering (*US*); freeing; (*Postes: prix payé*) postage; **tarifs d'~** postage rates

affres [afʀ(ə)] *nfpl*: **dans les ~ de** in the throes of

affréter [afʀete] *vt* to charter

affreusement [afʀøzmɑ̃] *adv* dreadfully, awfully

affreux, -euse [afʀø, -øz] *adj* dreadful, awful

affriolant, e [afʀijɔlɑ̃, -ɑ̃t] *adj* tempting, enticing

affront [afʀɔ̃] *nm* affront

affrontement [afʀɔ̃tmɑ̃] *nm* (*Mil, Pol*) clash, confrontation

affronter [afʀɔ̃te] *vt* to confront, face; **s'affronter** to confront each other

affubler [afyble] *vt* (*péj*): ~ **qn de** to rig *ou* deck sb out in; (*surnom*) to attach to sb

affût [afy] *nm* (*de canon*) gun carriage; **à l'~ (de)** (*gibier*) lying in wait (for); (*fig*) on the look-out (for)

affûter [afyte] *vt* to sharpen, grind

afghan, e [afgɑ̃, -an] *adj* Afghan

Afghanistan [afganistɑ̃] *nm*: **l'~** Afghanistan

afin [afɛ̃]: ~ **que** *conj* so that, in order that; ~ **de faire** in order to do, so as to do

AFNOR [afnɔʀ] *sigle f* (= *Association française de normalisation*) *industrial standards authority*

a fortiori [afɔʀsjɔʀi] *adv* all the more, a fortiori

AFP *sigle f* = **Agence France-Presse**

AFPA *sigle f* = **Association pour la formation professionnelle des adultes**

africain, e [afʀikɛ̃, -ɛn] *adj* African ▷ *nm/f*: **Africain, e** African

afrikaans [afʀikɑ̃] *nm, adj inv* Afrikaans

Afrique [afʀik] *nf*: **l'~** Africa; **l'~ australe/du Nord/du Sud** southern/North/South Africa

afro [afʀo] *adj inv*: **coupe ~** afro hairstyle ▷ *nm/f*: **Afro** Afro

afro-américain, e [afʀoameʀikɛ̃, -ɛn] *adj* Afro-American

AG *sigle f* = **assemblée générale**

ag. *abr* = **agence**

agaçant, e [agasɑ̃, -ɑ̃t] *adj* irritating, aggravating

agacement [agasmɑ̃] *nm* irritation, aggravation

agacer [agase] *vt* to pester, tease; (*involontairement*) to irritate, aggravate; (*aguicher*) to excite, lead on

agapes [agap] *nfpl* (*humoristique: festin*) feast

agate [agat] *nf* agate

AGE *sigle f* = **assemblée générale extraordinaire**

âge [ɑʒ] *nm* age; **quel ~ as-tu?** how old are you?; **une femme d'un certain ~** a middle-aged woman, a woman who is getting on (in years); **bien porter son ~** to wear well; **prendre de l'~** to be getting on (in years), grow older; **limite d'~** age limit; **dispense d'~** special exemption from age limit; **troisième ~** (*période*) retirement; (*personnes âgées*) senior citizens; **l'~ ingrat** the awkward *ou* difficult age; ~ **légal** legal age; ~ **mental** mental age; **l'~ mûr** maturity, middle age; ~ **de raison** age of reason

âgé, e [ɑʒe] *adj* old, elderly; ~ **de 10 ans** 10 years old

agence [aʒɑ̃s] *nf* agency, office; (*succursale*) branch; ~ **immobilière** estate agent's (office) (*Brit*), real estate office (*US*); ~ **matrimoniale** marriage bureau; ~ **de placement** employment agency; ~ **de publicité** advertising agency; ~ **de voyages** travel agency

agencé, e [aʒɑ̃se] *adj*: **bien/mal ~** well/badly put together; well/badly laid out *ou* arranged

agencement [aʒɑ̃smɑ̃] *nm* putting together; arrangement, laying out

agencer [aʒɑ̃se] *vt* to put together; (*local*) to arrange, lay out

agenda [aʒɛ̃da] *nm* diary

agenouiller [aʒnuje]: **s'agenouiller** *vi* to kneel (down)

agent [aʒɑ̃] *nm* (*aussi*: **agent de police**) policeman; (*Admin*) official, officer; (*fig: élément, facteur*) agent; ~ **d'assurances** insurance broker; ~ **de change** stockbroker; ~ **commercial** sales representative; ~ **immobilier** estate agent (*Brit*), realtor (*US*); ~ **(secret)** (secret) agent

agglo [aglo] *nm* (*fam*) = **aggloméré**

agglomérat [aglɔmeʀa] *nm* (*Géo*) agglomerate

agglomération [aglɔmeʀasjɔ̃] *nf* town; (*Auto*) built-up area; **l'~ parisienne** the urban area of Paris

aggloméré [aglɔmeʀe] *nm* (*bois*) chipboard; (*pierre*) conglomerate

agglomérer [aglɔmeʀe] *vt* to pile up; (*Tech: bois, pierre*) to compress; **s'agglomérer** *vi* to pile up

agglutiner [aglytine] *vt* to stick together; **s'agglutiner** *vi* to congregate

aggravant, e [agʀavɑ̃, -ɑ̃t] *adj*: **circonstances ~es** aggravating circumstances

aggravation [agravɑsjɔ̃] *nf* worsening, aggravation; increase

aggraver [agrave] *vt* to worsen, aggravate; (*Jur: peine*) to increase; **s'aggraver** *vi* to worsen; ~ **son cas** to make one's case worse

agile [aʒil] *adj* agile, nimble

agilement [aʒilmɑ̃] *adv* nimbly

agilité [aʒilite] *nf* agility, nimbleness

agio [aʒjo] *nm* (bank) charges *pl*

agir [aʒiʀ] *vi* (*se comporter*) to behave, act; (*faire quelque chose*) to act, take action; (*avoir de l'effet*) to act; **il s'agit de** it's a matter *ou* question of; it is about; (*il importe que*): **il s'agit de faire** we (*ou* you *etc*) must do; **de quoi s'agit-il?** what is it about?

agissements [aʒismɑ̃] *nmpl* (*gén péj*) schemes, intrigues

agitateur, -trice [aʒitatœʀ, -tʀis] *nm/f* agitator

agitation [aʒitɑsjɔ̃] *nf* (hustle and) bustle; (*trouble*) agitation, excitement; (*politique*) unrest, agitation

agité, e [aʒite] *adj* (*remuant*) fidgety, restless; (*trouble*) agitated, perturbed; (*journée*) hectic; (*mer*) rough; (*sommeil*) disturbed, broken

agiter [aʒite] *vt* (*bouteille, chiffon*) to shake; (*bras, mains*) to wave; (*préoccuper, exciter*) to trouble, perturb; **s'agiter** *vi* to bustle about; (*dormeur*) to toss and turn; (*enfant*) to fidget; (*Pol*) to grow restless; **"~ avant l'emploi"** "shake before use"

agneau, x [aɲo] *nm* lamb; (*toison*) lambswool

agnelet [aɲlɛ] *nm* little lamb

agnostique [agnɔstik] *adj, nm/f* agnostic

agonie [agɔni] *nf* mortal agony, death pangs *pl*; (*fig*) death throes *pl*

agonir [agɔniʀ] *vt*: ~ **qn d'injures** to hurl abuse at sb

agoniser [agɔnize] *vi* to be dying; (*fig*) to be in its death throes

agrafe [agʀaf] *nf* (*de vêtement*) hook, fastener; (*de bureau*) staple; (*Méd*) clip

agrafer [agʀafe] *vt* to fasten; to staple

agrafeuse [agʀaføz] *nf* stapler

agraire [agʀɛʀ] *adj* agrarian; (*mesure, surface*) land *cpd*

agrandir [agʀɑ̃diʀ] *vt* (*magasin, domaine*) to extend, enlarge; (*trou*) to enlarge, make bigger; (*Photo*) to enlarge, blow up; **s'agrandir** *vi* to be extended; to be enlarged

agrandissement [agʀɑ̃dismɑ̃] *nm* extension; enlargement; (*photographie*) enlargement

agrandisseur [agʀɑ̃disœʀ] *nm* (*Photo*) enlarger

agréable [agʀeabl(ə)] *adj* pleasant, nice

agréablement [agʀeabləmɑ̃] *adv* pleasantly

agréé, e [agʀee] *adj*: **concessionnaire ~** registered dealer; **magasin ~** registered dealer('s)

agréer [agʀee] *vt* (*requête*) to accept; **~ à** *vt* to please, suit; **veuillez ~ ...** (*formule épistolaire*) yours faithfully

agrég [agʀɛg] *nf* (*fam*) = **agrégation**

agrégat [agʀega] *nm* aggregate

agrégation [agʀegɑsjɔ̃] *nf* highest teaching diploma in France; *see note*

● AGRÉGATION

●
● The *agrégation*, informally known as the
● "*agrég*", is a prestigious competitive
● examination for the recruitment of
● secondary school teachers in France. The
● number of candidates always far exceeds
● the number of vacant posts. Most teachers
● of 'classes préparatoires' and most
● university lecturers have passed the
● *agrégation*.

agrégé, e [agʀeʒe] *nm/f* holder of the *agrégation*

agréger [agʀeʒe]: **s'agréger** *vi* to aggregate

agrément [agʀemɑ̃] *nm* (*accord*) consent, approval; (*attraits*) charm, attractiveness; (*plaisir*) pleasure; **voyage d'~** pleasure trip

agrémenter [agʀemɑ̃te] *vt*: ~ (**de**) to embellish (with), adorn (with)

agrès [agʀɛ] *nmpl* (gymnastics) apparatus *sg*

agresser [agʀese] *vt* to attack

agresseur [agʀesœʀ] *nm* aggressor

agressif, -ive [agʀesif, -iv] *adj* aggressive

agression [agʀesjɔ̃] *nf* attack; (*Pol, Mil, Psych*) aggression

agressivement [agʀesivmɑ̃] *adv* aggressively

agressivité [agʀesivite] *nf* aggressiveness

agreste [agʀɛst(ə)] *adj* rustic

agricole [agʀikɔl] *adj* agricultural, farm *cpd*

agriculteur, -trice [agʀikyltœʀ, -tʀis] *nm/f* farmer

agriculture [agʀikyltyʀ] *nf* agriculture; farming

agripper [agʀipe] *vt* to grab, clutch; (*pour arracher*) to snatch, grab; **s'agripper à** to cling (on) to, clutch, grip

agroalimentaire [agʀɔalimɑ̃tɛʀ] *adj* farming *cpd* ▷ *nm*: **l'~** agribusiness

agronome [agʀɔnɔm] *nm/f* agronomist

agronomie [agʀɔnɔmi] *nf* agronomy

agronomique [agʀɔnɔmik] *adj* agronomic(al)

agrumes [agʀym] *nmpl* citrus fruit(s)

aguerrir [ageʀiʀ] *vt* to harden; **s'aguerrir (contre)** to become hardened (to)

aguets [agɛ]: **aux ~** *adv*: **être aux ~** to be on the look-out

aguichant, e [agiʃɑ̃, -ɑ̃t] *adj* enticing

aguicher [agiʃe] *vt* to entice

aguicheur, -euse [agiʃœʀ, -øz] *adj* enticing

ah [ɑ] *excl* ah!; **ah bon?** really?, is that so?; **ah mais ...** yes, but ...; **ah non!** oh no!

ahuri, e [ayʀi] *adj* (*stupéfait*) flabbergasted; (*idiot*) dim-witted

ahurir [ayʀiʀ] *vt* to stupefy, stagger

ahurissant, e [ayʀisɑ̃, -ɑ̃t] *adj* stupefying, staggering, mind-boggling

ai [e] *vb voir* **avoir**

aide [ɛd] *nm/f* assistant ▷ *nf* assistance, help; (*secours financier*) aid; **à l'~ de** with the help *ou* aid of; **aller à l'~ de qn** to go to sb's aid, go to help sb; **venir en ~ à qn** to help sb, come to sb's assistance; **appeler (qn) à l'~** to call for help (from sb); **à l'~!** help!; **~ de camp** nm aide-de-camp; **~ comptable** nm accountant's assistant; **~ électricien** nm electrician's mate; **~ familiale** nf mother's help, ≈ home help; **~ judiciaire** nf legal aid; **~ de laboratoire** nm/f laboratory assistant; **~ ménagère** nf ≈ home help; **~ sociale** nf (assistance) state aid; **~ soignant, e** nm/f auxiliary nurse; **~ technique** nf ≈ VSO (Brit), ≈ Peace Corps (US)

aide-éducateur, -trice [ɛdmedykatœʀ, tʀis] nm/f classroom assistant

aide-mémoire [ɛdmemwaʀ] nm inv (key facts) handbook

aider [ede] vt to help; **~ à qch** to help (towards) sth; **~ qn à faire qch** to help sb to do sth; **s'aider de** (se servir de) to use, make use of

aide-soignant, e [ɛdswanjɑ̃, ɑ̃t] nm/f auxiliary nurse

aie etc [ɛ] vb voir **avoir**

aïe [aj] excl ouch!

AIEA sigle f (= Agence internationale de l'énergie atomique) IAEA (= International Atomic Energy Agency)

aïeul, e [ajœl] nm/f grandparent, grandfather/grandmother; (ancêtre) forebear

aïeux [ajø] nmpl grandparents; forebears, forefathers

aigle [ɛgl(ə)] nm eagle

aiglefin [ɛgləfɛ̃] nm = **églefin**

aigre [ɛgʀ(ə)] adj sour, sharp; (fig) sharp, cutting; **tourner à l'~** to turn sour

aigre-doux, -douce [ɛgʀədu, -dus] adj (fruit) bitter-sweet; (sauce) sweet and sour

aigrefin [ɛgʀəfɛ̃] nm swindler

aigrelet, te [ɛgʀəlɛ, -ɛt] adj (goût) sourish; (voix, son) sharpish

aigrette [ɛgʀɛt] nf (plume) feather

aigreur [ɛgʀœʀ] nf sourness; sharpness; **~s d'estomac** heartburn sg

aigri, e [egʀi] adj embittered

aigrir [egʀiʀ] vt (personne) to embitter; (caractère) to sour; **s'aigrir** vi to become embittered; to sour; (lait etc) to turn sour

aigu, ë [egy] adj (objet, arête) sharp, pointed; (son, voix) high-pitched, shrill; (note) high(-pitched); (douleur, intelligence) acute, sharp

aigue-marine [ɛgmaʀin] (pl **aigues-marines**) nf aquamarine

aiguillage [eguijaʒ] nm (Rail) points pl

aiguille [eguij] nf needle; (de montre) hand; **~ à tricoter** knitting needle

aiguiller [eguije] vt (orienter) to direct; (Rail) to shunt

aiguillette [eguijɛt] nf (Culin) aiguillette

aiguilleur [eguijœʀ] nm: **~ du ciel** air traffic controller

aiguillon [eguijɔ̃] nm (d'abeille) sting; (fig) spur, stimulus

aiguillonner [eguijɔne] vt to spur ou goad on

aiguiser [egize] vt to sharpen, grind; (fig) to stimulate; (: esprit) to sharpen; (: sens) to excite

aiguisoir [egizwaʀ] nm sharpener

aïkido [ajkido] nm aikido

ail [aj] nm garlic

aile [ɛl] nf wing; (de voiture) wing (Brit), fender (US); **battre de l'~** (fig) to be in a sorry state; **voler de ses propres ~s** to stand on one's own two feet; **~ libre** hang-glider

ailé, e [ele] adj winged

aileron [ɛlʀɔ̃] nm (de requin) fin; (d'avion) aileron

ailette [ɛlɛt] nf (Tech) fin; (: de turbine) blade

ailier [elje] nm (Sport) winger

aille etc [aj] vb voir **aller**

ailleurs [ajœʀ] adv elsewhere, somewhere else; **partout/nulle part ~** everywhere/nowhere else; **d'~** adv (du reste) moreover, besides; **par ~** adv (d'autre part) moreover, furthermore

ailloli [ajɔli] nm garlic mayonnaise

aimable [ɛmabl(ə)] adj kind, nice; **vous êtes bien ~** that's very nice ou kind of you, how kind (of you)!

aimablement [ɛmabləmɑ̃] adv kindly

aimant¹ [ɛmɑ̃] nm magnet

aimant², e [ɛmɑ̃, -ɑ̃t] adj loving, affectionate

aimanté, e [ɛmɑ̃te] adj magnetic

aimanter [ɛmɑ̃te] vt to magnetize

aimer [eme] vt to love; (d'amitié, affection, par goût) to like; (souhait): **j'aimerais ...** I would like ...; **s'aimer** to love each other; to like each other; **je n'aime pas beaucoup Paul** I don't like Paul much, I don't care much for Paul; **~ faire qch** to like doing sth, like to do sth; **aimeriez-vous que je vous accompagne?** would you like me to come with you?; **j'aimerais (bien) m'en aller** I should (really) like to go; **bien ~ qn/qch** to like sb/sth; **j'aime mieux Paul (que Pierre)** I prefer Paul (to Pierre); **j'aime mieux ou autant vous dire que** I may as well tell you that; **j'aimerais autant ou mieux y aller maintenant** I'd sooner ou rather go now; **j'aime assez aller au cinéma** I quite like going to the cinema

aine [ɛn] nf groin

aîné, e [ene] adj elder, older; (le plus âgé) eldest, oldest ▷ nm/f oldest child ou one, oldest boy ou son/girl ou daughter; **aînés** nmpl (fig: anciens) elders; **il est mon ~ (de 2 ans)** he's (2 years) older than me, he's (2 years) my senior

aînesse [ɛnɛs] nf: **droit d'~** birthright

ainsi [ɛ̃si] adv (de cette façon) like this, in this way, thus; (ce faisant) thus ou thus, so; **~ que** (comme) (just) as; (et aussi) as well as; **pour ~ dire** so to speak, as it were; **~ donc** and so; **~ soit-il** (Rel) so be it; **et ~ de suite** and so on (and so forth)

aïoli [ajɔli] nm = **ailloli**

air [ɛʀ] nm air; (mélodie) tune; (expression) look, air; (atmosphère, ambiance): **dans l'~** in the air (fig); **prendre de grands ~s (avec qn)** to give o.s. airs (with sb); **en l'~** (up) into the air; **tirer en l'~** to fire shots in the air; **paroles/menaces**

en l'~ idle words/threats; **prendre l'~** to get some (fresh) air; (avion) to take off; **avoir l'~ triste** to look ou seem sad; **avoir l'~ de qch** to look like sth; **avoir l'~ de faire** to look as though one is doing, appear to be doing; **courant d'~** draught (Brit), draft (US); **le grand ~** the open air; **mal de l'~** air-sickness; **tête en l'~** scatterbrain; **~ comprimé** compressed air; **~ conditionné** air-conditioning

airbag [ɛʀbag] nm airbag

aire [ɛʀ] nf (zone, fig, Math) area; (nid) eyrie (Brit), aerie (US); **~ d'atterrissage** landing strip; landing patch; **~ de jeu** play area; **~ de lancement** launching site; **~ de stationnement** parking area

airelle [ɛʀɛl] nf bilberry

aisance [ɛzɑ̃s] nf ease; (Couture) easing, freedom of movement; (richesse) affluence; **être dans l'~** to be well-off ou affluent

aise [ɛz] nf comfort ▷ adj: **être bien ~ de/que** to be delighted to/that; **aises** nfpl: **aimer ses ~s** to like one's (creature) comforts; **prendre ses ~s** to make o.s. comfortable; **frémir d'~** to shudder with pleasure; **être à l'~** ou **à son ~** to be comfortable; (pas embarrassé) to be at ease; (financièrement) to be comfortably off; **se mettre à l'~** to make o.s. comfortable; **être mal à l'~** ou **à son ~** to be uncomfortable; (gêné) to be ill at ease; **mettre qn à l'~** to put sb at his (ou her) ease; **mettre qn mal à l'~** to make sb feel ill at ease; **à votre ~** please yourself, just as you like; **en faire à son ~** to do as one likes; **en prendre à son ~ avec qch** to be free and easy with sth, do as one likes with sth

aisé, e [eze] adj easy; (assez riche) well-to-do, well-off

aisément [ezemɑ̃] adv easily

aisselle [ɛsɛl] nf armpit

ait [ɛ] vb voir **avoir**

ajonc [aʒɔ̃] nm gorse no pl

ajouré, e [aʒuʀe] adj openwork cpd

ajournement [aʒuʀnəmɑ̃] nm adjournment; deferment, postponement

ajourner [aʒuʀne] vt (réunion) to adjourn; (décision) to defer, postpone; (candidat) to refer; (conscrit) to defer

ajout [aʒu] nm addition

ajouter [aʒute] vt to add; **~ à** (accroître) to add to; **s'ajouter à** to add to; **~ que** to add that; **~ foi à** to lend ou give credence to

ajustage [aʒystaʒ] nm fitting

ajusté, e [aʒyste] adj: **bien ~** (robe etc) close-fitting

ajustement [aʒystəmɑ̃] nm adjustment

ajuster [aʒyste] vt (régler) to adjust; (vêtement) to alter; (arranger): **~ sa cravate** to adjust one's tie; (coup de fusil) to aim; (cible) to aim at; (adapter): **~ qch à** to fit sth to

ajusteur [aʒystœʀ] nm metal worker

alaise [alɛz] nf = **alèse**

alambic [alɑ̃bik] nm still

alambiqué, e [alɑ̃bike] adj convoluted,

overcomplicated

alangui, e [alɑ̃gi] adj languid

alanguir [alɑ̃giʀ]: **s'alanguir** vi to grow languid

alarmant, e [alaʀmɑ̃, -ɑ̃t] adj alarming

alarme [alaʀm(ə)] nf alarm; **donner l'~** to give ou raise the alarm; **jeter l'~** to cause alarm

alarmer [alaʀme] vt to alarm; **s'alarmer** vi to become alarmed

alarmiste [alaʀmist(ə)] adj alarmist

Alaska [alaska] nm: **l'~** Alaska

albanais, e [albanɛ, -ɛz] adj Albanian ▷ nm (Ling) Albanian ▷ nm/f: **Albanais, e** Albanian

Albanie [albani] nf: **l'~** Albania

albâtre [albɑtʀ(ə)] nm alabaster

albatros [albatʀos] nm albatross

albigeois, e [albiʒwa, -waz] adj of ou from Albi

albinos [albinos] nm/f albino

album [albɔm] nm album; **~ à colorier** colouring book; **~ de timbres** stamp album

albumen [albymɛn] nm albumen

albumine [albymin] nf albumin; **avoir** ou **faire de l'~** to suffer from albuminuria

alcalin, e [alkalɛ̃, -in] adj alkaline

alchimie [alʃimi] nf alchemy

alchimiste [alʃimist(ə)] nm alchemist

alcool [alkɔl] nm: **l'~** alcohol; **un ~** a spirit, a brandy; **~ à brûler** methylated spirits (Brit), wood alcohol (US); **~ à 90°** surgical spirit; **~ camphré** camphorated alcohol; **~ de prune** etc plum etc brandy

alcoolémie [alkɔlemi] nf blood alcohol level

alcoolique [alkɔlik] adj, nm/f alcoholic

alcoolisé, e [alkɔlize] adj alcoholic

alcoolisme [alkɔlism(ə)] nm alcoholism

alcootest®, alcotest® [alkɔtɛst] nm (objet) Breathalyser®; (test) breath-test; **faire subir l'alco(o)test à qn** to Breathalyse® sb

alcôve [alkov] nf alcove, recess

aléas [alea] nmpl hazards

aléatoire [aleatwaʀ] adj uncertain; (Inform, Statistique) random

alémanique [alemanik] adj: **la Suisse ~** German-speaking Switzerland

ALENA [alena] sigle m (= Accord de libre-échange nord-américain) NAFTA (= North American Free Trade Agreement)

alentour [alɑ̃tuʀ] adv around (about); **alentours** nmpl surroundings; **aux ~s de** in the vicinity ou neighbourhood of, around about; (temps) around about

alerte [alɛʀt(ə)] adj agile, nimble; (style) brisk, lively ▷ nf alert; warning; **donner l'~** to give the alert; **à la première ~** at the first sign of trouble ou danger; **~ à la bombe** bomb scare

alerter [alɛʀte] vt to alert

alèse [alɛz] nf (drap) undersheet, drawsheet

aléser [aleze] vt to ream

alevin [alvɛ̃] nm alevin, young fish

alevinage [alvinaʒ] nm fish farming

Alexandrie [alɛksɑ̃dʀi] n Alexandria

alexandrin [alɛksɑ̃dʀɛ̃] nm alexandrine

alezan, e [alzɑ̃, -an] adj chestnut

algarade [algaʀad] *nf* row, dispute
algèbre [alʒɛbʀ(ə)] *nf* algebra
algébrique [alʒebʀik] *adj* algebraic
Alger [alʒe] *n* Algiers
Algérie [alʒeʀi] *nf*: **l'~** Algeria
algérien, ne [alʒeʀjɛ̃, -ɛn] *adj* Algerian ▷ *nm/f*:
Algérien, ne Algerian
algérois, e [alʒeʀwa, -waz] *adj* of *ou* from
Algiers ▷ *nm*: **l'A~** (*région*) the Algiers region
algorithme [algɔʀitm(ə)] *nm* algorithm
algue [alg(ə)] *nf* seaweed *no pl*
alias [aljas] *adv* alias
alibi [alibi] *nm* alibi
aliénation [aljenɑsjɔ̃] *nf* alienation
aliéné, e [aljene] *nm/f* insane person, lunatic
(*péj*)
aliéner [aljene] *vt* to alienate; (*bien, liberté*) to
give up; **s'aliéner** *vt* to alienate
alignement [aliɲmɑ̃] *nm* alignment, lining up;
à l'~ in line
aligner [aliɲe] *vt* to align, line up; (*idées, chiffres*)
to string together; (*adapter*): **~ qch sur** to bring
sth into alignment with; **s'aligner** *vi* (*soldats*
etc) to line up; **s'~ sur** (*Pol*) to align o.s. with
aliment [alimɑ̃] *nm* food; **~ complet** whole food
alimentaire [alimɑ̃tɛʀ] *adj* food *cpd*; (*péj: besogne*)
done merely to earn a living; **produits ~s**
foodstuffs, foods
alimentation [alimɑ̃tɑsjɔ̃] *nf* feeding;
supplying, supply; (*commerce*) food trade;
(*produits*) groceries *pl*; (*régime*) diet; (*Inform*) feed;
~ (générale) (general) grocer's; **~ de base**
staple diet; **~ en feuilles/en continu/en**
papier form/stream/sheet feed
alimenter [alimɑ̃te] *vt* to feed; (*Tech*): **~ (en)** to
supply (with), feed (with); (*fig*) to sustain, keep
going
alinéa [alinea] *nm* paragraph; **"nouvel ~"** "new
line"
aliter [alite]: **s'aliter** *vi* to take to one's bed;
infirme alité bedridden person *ou* invalid
alizé [alize] *adj, nm*: **(vent) ~** trade wind
allaitement [alɛtmɑ̃] *nm* feeding; **~ maternel/**
au biberon breast-/bottle-feeding; **~ mixte**
mixed feeding
allaiter [alete] *vt* (*femme*) to (breast-)feed, nurse;
(*animal*) to suckle; **~ au biberon** to bottle-feed
allant [alɑ̃] *nm* drive, go
alléchant, e [aleʃɑ̃, -ɑ̃t] *adj* tempting, enticing
allécher [aleʃe] *vt*: **~ qn** to make sb's mouth
water; to tempt sb, entice sb
allée [ale] *nf* (*de jardin*) path; (*en ville*) avenue,
drive; **~s et venues** comings and goings
allégation [alegɑsjɔ̃] *nf* allegation
allégé, e [aleʒe] *adj* (*yaourt etc*) low-fat
alléger [aleʒe] *vt* (*voiture*) to make lighter;
(*chargement*) to lighten; (*souffrance*) to alleviate,
soothe
allégorie [alegɔʀi] *nf* allegory
allégorique [alegɔʀik] *adj* allegorical
allègre [alɛgʀ(ə)] *adj* lively, jaunty (*Brit*);
(*personne*) gay, cheerful

allégresse [alegʀɛs] *nf* elation, gaiety
allegretto [al(l)egʀɛt(t)o] *adv, nm* allegretto
allegro [al(l)egʀo] *adv, nm* allegro
alléguer [alege] *vt* to put forward (as proof *ou* an
excuse)
Allemagne [aləmaɲ] *nf*: **l'~** Germany; **l'~ de**
l'Est/Ouest East/West Germany; **l'~ fédérale**
(RFA) the Federal Republic of Germany (FRG)
allemand, e [almɑ̃, -ɑ̃d] *adj* German ▷ *nm* (*Ling*)
German ▷ *nm/f*: **Allemand, e** German; **A~ de**
l'Est/l'Ouest East/West German
aller [ale] *nm* (*trajet*) outward journey; (*billet*): **~**
(simple) single (*Brit*) *ou* one-way ticket; **~ (et)**
retour (AR) (*trajet*) return trip *ou* journey (*Brit*),
round trip (*US*); (*billet*) return (*Brit*) *ou* round-
trip (*US*) ticket ▷ *vi* (*gén*) to go; **~ à** (*convenir*) to
suit; (*forme, pointure etc*) to fit; **cela me va**
(*couleur*) that suits me; (*vêtement*) that suits me;
that fits me; (*projet, disposition*) that suits me,
that's fine *ou* OK by me; **~ à la chasse/pêche** to
go hunting/fishing; **~ avec** (*couleurs, style etc*) to
go (well) with; **je vais le faire/me fâcher** I'm
going to do it/to get angry; **~ voir/chercher qn**
to go and see/look for sb; **comment allez-**
vous? how are you?; **comment ça va?** how are
you?; (*affaires etc*) how are things?; **ça va? — oui**
(ça va)! how are things? — fine!; **pour ~ à** how
do I get to; **ça va (comme ça)** that's fine (as it
is); **il va bien/mal** he's well/ not well, he's fine/
ill; **ça va bien/mal** (*affaires etc*) it's going well/
not going well; **tout va bien** everything's fine;
ça ne va pas! (*mauvaise humeur etc*) that's not on!,
hey, come on!; **ça ne va pas sans difficultés**
it's not without difficulties; **~ mieux** to be
better; **il y va de leur vie** their lives are at
stake; **se laisser ~** to let o.s. go; **s'en aller** *vi*
(*partir*) to be off, go, leave; (*disparaître*) to go away;
~ jusqu'à to go as far as; **ça va de soi**, **ça va**
sans dire that goes without saying; **tu y vas**
un peu fort you're going a bit (too) far; **allez!**
go on!; come on!; **allons-y!** let's go!; **allez, au**
revoir! right *ou* OK then, bye-bye!
allergène [alɛʀʒɛn] *nm* allergen
allergie [alɛʀʒi] *nf* allergy
allergique [alɛʀʒik] *adj* allergic; **~ à** allergic to
allez [ale] *vb voir* **aller**
alliage [aljaʒ] *nm* alloy
alliance [aljɑ̃s] *nf* (*Mil, Pol*) alliance; (*mariage*)
marriage; (*bague*) wedding ring; **neveu par ~**
nephew by marriage
allié, e [alje] *nm/f* ally; **parents et ~s** relatives
and relatives by marriage
allier [alje] *vt* (*métaux*) to alloy; (*Pol, gén*) to ally;
(*fig*) to combine; **s'allier** *vi* to become allies;
(*éléments, caractéristiques*) to combine; **s'~ à** to
become allied to *ou* with
alligator [aligatɔʀ] *nm* alligator
allitération [aliteʀɑsjɔ̃] *nf* alliteration
allô [alo] *excl* hullo, hallo
allocataire [alɔkatɛʀ] *nm/f* beneficiary
allocation [alɔkɑsjɔ̃] *nf* allowance; **~ (de)**
chômage unemployment benefit; **~ (de)**

logement rent allowance; **~s familiales**
≈ child benefit *no pl*; **~s de maternité** maternity
allowance

allocution [alɔkysjɔ̃] *nf* short speech

allongé, e [alɔ̃ʒe] *adj* (*étendu*): **être ~** to be
stretched out *ou* lying down; (*long*) long; (*étiré*)
elongated; (*oblong*) oblong; **rester ~** to be lying
down; **mine ~e** long face

allonger [alɔ̃ʒe] *vt* to lengthen, make longer;
(*étendre: bras, jambe*) to stretch (out); (*sauce*) to
spin out, make go further; **s'allonger** *vi* to get
longer; (*se coucher*) to lie down, stretch out; **~ le
pas** to hasten one's step(s)

allouer [alwe] *vt*: **~ qch à** to allocate sth to, allot
sth to

allumage [alymaʒ] *nm* (*Auto*) ignition

allume-cigare [alymsigaR] *nm inv* cigar lighter

allume-gaz [alymgɑz] *nm inv* gas lighter

allumer [alyme] *vt* (*lampe, phare, radio*) to put *ou*
switch on; (*pièce*) to put *ou* switch the light(s)
on in; (*feu, bougie, cigare, pipe, gaz*) to light;
(*chauffage*) to put on; **s'allumer** *vi* (*lumière, lampe*)
to come *ou* go on; **~ (la lumière *ou* l'électricité)**
to put on the light

allumette [alymɛt] *nf* match; (*morceau de bois*)
matchstick; (*Culin*): **~ au fromage** cheese
straw; **~ de sûreté** safety match

allumeuse [alymøz] *nf* (*péj*) tease (*woman*)

allure [alyR] *nf* (*vitesse*) speed; (: *à pied*) pace;
(*démarche*) walk; (*maintien*) bearing; (*aspect, air*)
look; **avoir de l' ~** to have style *ou* a certain
elegance; **à toute ~** at top *ou* full speed

allusion [alyzjɔ̃] *nf* allusion; (*sous-entendu*) hint;
faire ~ à to allude *ou* refer to; to hint at

alluvions [alyvjɔ̃] *nfpl* alluvial deposits,
alluvium *sg*

almanach [almana] *nm* almanac

aloès [alɔɛs] *nm* (*Bot*) aloe

aloi [alwa] *nm*: **de bon/mauvais ~** of genuine/
doubtful worth *ou* quality

 MOT-CLÉ

alors [alɔR] *adv* **1** (*à ce moment-là*) then, at that
time; **il habitait alors à Paris** he lived in Paris
at that time; **jusqu'alors** up till *ou* until then
2 (*par conséquent*) then; **tu as fini? alors je m'en
vais** have you finished? I'm going then
3 (*expressions*): **alors? quoi de neuf?** well *ou* so?
what's new?; **et alors?** so (what)?; **ça alors!**
(well) really!
▷ *conj*: **alors que 1** (*au moment où*) when, as; **il
est arrivé alors que je partais** he arrived as I
was leaving
2 (*pendant que*) while, when; **alors qu'il était à
Paris, il a visité ...** while *ou* when he was in
Paris, he visited ...
3 (*tandis que*) whereas, while; **alors que son
frère travaillait dur, lui se reposait** while his
brother was working hard, HE would rest

alouette [alwɛt] *nf* (sky)lark

alourdir [aluRdiR] *vt* to weigh down, make
heavy; **s'alourdir** *vi* to grow heavy *ou* heavier

aloyau [alwajo] *nm* sirloin

alpaga [alpaga] *nm* (*tissu*) alpaca

alpage [alpaʒ] *nm* high mountain pasture

Alpes [alp(ə)] *nfpl*: **les ~** the Alps

alpestre [alpɛstR(ə)] *adj* alpine

alphabet [alfabɛ] *nm* alphabet; (*livre*) ABC
(book), primer

alphabétique [alfabetik] *adj* alphabetic(al);
par ordre ~ in alphabetical order

alphabétisation [alfabetizasjɔ̃] *nf* literacy
teaching

alphabétiser [alfabetize] *vt* to teach to read
and write; (*pays*) to eliminate illiteracy in

alphanumérique [alfanymeRik] *adj*
alphanumeric

alpin, e [alpɛ̃, -in] *adj* (*plante etc*) alpine; (*club*)
climbing

alpinisme [alpinism(ə)] *nm* mountaineering,
climbing

alpiniste [alpinist(ə)] *nm/f* mountaineer,
climber

Alsace [alzas] *nf*: **l' ~** Alsace

alsacien, ne [alzasjɛ̃, -ɛn] *adj* Alsatian

altercation [altɛRkasjɔ̃] *nf* altercation

alter ego [altɛRego] *nm* alter ego

altérer [alteRe] *vt* (*faits, vérité*) to falsify, distort;
(*qualité*) to debase, impair; (*données*) to corrupt;
(*donner soif à*) to make thirsty; **s'altérer** *vi* to
deteriorate; to spoil

altermondialisme [altɛRmɔ̃djalism] *nm* anti-
globalism

altermondialiste [altɛRmɔ̃djalist] *adj, nm/f*
anti-globalist

alternance [altɛRnɑ̃s] *nf* alternation; **en ~**
alternately; **formation en ~** sandwich course

alternateur [altɛRnatœR] *nm* alternator

alternatif, -ive [altɛRnatif, -iv] *adj* alternating
▷ *nf* alternative

alternativement [altɛRnativmɑ̃] *adv*
alternately

alterner [altɛRne] *vt* to alternate ▷ *vi*: **~ (avec)**
to alternate (with); (**faire**) **~ qch avec qch** to
alternate sth with sth

Altesse [altɛs] *nf* Highness

altier, -ière [altje, -jɛR] *adj* haughty

altimètre [altimetR(ə)] *nm* altimeter

altiport [altipɔR] *nm* mountain airfield

altiste [altist(ə)] *nm/f* viola player, violist

altitude [altityd] *nf* altitude, height; **à 1000 m
d'~** at a height *ou* an altitude of 1000 m; **en ~** at
high altitudes; **perdre/prendre de l'~** to lose/
gain height; **voler à haute/basse ~** to fly at a
high/low altitude

alto [alto] *nm* (*instrument*) viola ▷ *nf* (*contr*)alto

altruisme [altRɥism(ə)] *nm* altruism

altruiste [altRɥist(ə)] *adj* altruistic

aluminium [alyminjɔm] *nm* aluminium (*Brit*),
aluminum (*US*)

alun [alœ̃] *nm* alum

alunir [alyniR] *vi* to land on the moon

alunissage [alynisaʒ] *nm* (moon) landing
alvéole [alveɔl] *nm ou f* (*de ruche*) alveolus
alvéolé, e [alveɔle] *adj* honeycombed
AM *sigle f* = **assurance maladie**
amabilité [amabilite] *nf* kindness; **il a eu l'~ de**
he was kind *ou* good enough to
amadou [amadu] *nm* touchwood, amadou
amadouer [amadwe] *vt* to coax, cajole; (*adoucir*)
to mollify, soothe
amaigrir [amegʀiʀ] *vt* to make thin *ou* thinner
amaigrissant, e [amegʀisɑ̃, -ɑ̃t] *adj*: **régime ~**
slimming (*Brit*) *ou* weight-reduction (*US*) diet
amalgame [amalgam] *nm* amalgam; (*fig: de
gens, d'idées*) hotch-potch, mixture
amalgamer [amalgame] *vt* to amalgamate
amande [amɑ̃d] *nf* (*de l'amandier*) almond; (*de
noyau de fruit*) kernel; **en ~** (*yeux*) almond *cpd*,
almond-shaped
amandier [amɑ̃dje] *nm* almond (tree)
amanite [amanit] *nf* (*Bot*) mushroom of the genus
Amanita; **~ tue-mouches** fly agaric
amant [amɑ̃] *nm* lover
amarre [amaʀ] *nf* (*Navig*) (mooring) rope *ou* line;
amarres *nfpl* moorings
amarrer [amaʀe] *vt* (*Navig*) to moor; (*gén*) to
make fast
amaryllis [amaʀilis] *nf* amaryllis
amas [amɑ] *nm* heap, pile
amasser [amɑse] *vt* to amass; **s'amasser** *vi* to
pile up, accumulate; (*foule*) to gather
amateur [amatœʀ] *nm* amateur; **en ~** (*péj*)
amateurishly; **musicien/sportif ~** amateur
musician/sportsman; **~ de musique/sport** *etc*
music/sport *etc* lover
amateurisme [amatœʀism(ə)] *nm*
amateurism; (*péj*) amateurishness
Amazone [amazon] *nf*: **l'~** the Amazon
amazone [amazon] *nf* horsewoman; **en ~** sidesaddle
Amazonie [amazoni] *nf*: **l'~** Amazonia
ambages [ɑ̃baʒ]: **sans ~** *adv* without beating
about the bush, plainly
ambassade [ɑ̃basad] *nf* embassy; (*mission*): **en ~**
on a mission
ambassadeur, -drice [ɑ̃basadœʀ, -dʀis] *nm/f*
ambassador/ambassadress
ambiance [ɑ̃bjɑ̃s] *nf* atmosphere; **il y a de l'~**
everyone's having a good time
ambiant, e [ɑ̃bjɑ̃, -ɑ̃t] *adj* (*air, milieu*)
surrounding; (*température*) ambient
ambidextre [ɑ̃bidɛkstʀ(ə)] *adj* ambidextrous
ambigu, ë [ɑ̃bigy] *adj* ambiguous
ambiguïté [ɑ̃bigɥite] *nf* ambiguousness *no pl*,
ambiguity
ambitieux, -euse [ɑ̃bisjø, -øz] *adj* ambitious
ambition [ɑ̃bisjɔ̃] *nf* ambition
ambitionner [ɑ̃bisjone] *vt* to have as one's aim
ou ambition
ambivalent, e [ɑ̃bivalɑ̃, -ɑ̃t] *adj* ambivalent
amble [ɑ̃bl(ə)] *nm*: **aller l'~** to amble
ambre [ɑ̃bʀ(ə)] *nm*: **~ (jaune)** amber; **~ gris**
ambergris

ambré, e [ɑ̃bʀe] *adj* (*couleur*) amber; (*parfum*)
ambergris-scented
ambulance [ɑ̃bylɑ̃s] *nf* ambulance
ambulancier, -ière [ɑ̃bylɑ̃sje, -jɛʀ] *nm/f*
ambulanceman/woman (*Brit*), paramedic (*US*)
ambulant, e [ɑ̃bylɑ̃, -ɑ̃t] *adj* travelling,
itinerant
âme [ɑm] *nf* soul; **rendre l'~** to give up the
ghost; **bonne ~** (*aussi ironique*) kind soul; **un
joueur/tricheur dans l'~** a gambler/cheat
through and through; **~ sœur** kindred spirit
amélioration [ameljɔʀasjɔ̃] *nf* improvement
améliorer [ameljɔʀe] *vt* to improve;
s'améliorer *vi* to improve, get better
aménagement [amenaʒmɑ̃] *nm* fitting out;
laying out; development; **aménagements** *nmpl*
developments; **l'~ du territoire** town and
country planning; **~s fiscaux** tax adjustments
aménager [amenaʒe] *vt* (*agencer: espace, local*) to
fit out; (: *terrain*) to lay out; (: *quartier, territoire*) to
develop; (*installer*) to fix up, put in; **ferme
aménagée** converted farmhouse
amende [amɑ̃d] *nf* fine; **mettre à l'~** to
penalize; **faire ~ honorable** to make amends
amendement [amɑ̃dmɑ̃] *nm* (*Jur*) amendment
amender [amɑ̃de] *vt* (*loi*) to amend; (*terre*) to
enrich; **s'amender** *vi* to mend one's ways
amène [amɛn] *adj* affable; **peu ~** unkind
amener [amne] *vt* to bring; (*causer*) to bring
about; (*baisser: drapeau, voiles*) to strike; **s'amener**
vi (*fam*) to show up, turn up; **~ qn à qch/à faire**
to lead sb to sth/to do
amenuiser [amənɥize]: **s'amenuiser** *vi* to
dwindle; (*chances*) to grow slimmer, lessen
amer, amère [amɛʀ] *adj* bitter
amèrement [amɛʀmɑ̃] *adv* bitterly
américain, e [ameʀikɛ̃, -ɛn] *adj* American ▷ *nm*
(*Ling*) American (English) ▷ *nm/f*: **Américain, e**
American; **en vedette ~e** as a special guest
(star)
américaniser [ameʀikanize] *vt* to Americanize
américanisme [ameʀikanism(ə)] *nm*
Americanism
amérindien, ne [ameʀɛ̃djɛ̃, -ɛn] *adj*
Amerindian, American Indian
Amérique [ameʀik] *nf* America; **l'~ centrale**
Central America; **l'~ latine** Latin America; **l'~
du Nord** North America; **l'~ du Sud** South
America
Amerloque [amɛʀlɔk] *nm/f* (*fam*) Yank, Yankee
amerrir [ameʀiʀ] *vi* to land (on the sea); (*capsule
spatiale*) to splash down
amerrissage [ameʀisaʒ] *nm* landing (on the
sea); splash-down
amertume [amɛʀtym] *nf* bitterness
améthyste [ametist(ə)] *nf* amethyst
ameublement [amœbləmɑ̃] *nm* furnishing;
(*meubles*) furniture; **articles d'~** furnishings;
tissus d'~ soft furnishings, furnishing fabrics
ameuter [amøte] *vt* (*badauds*) to draw a crowd
of; (*peuple*) to rouse, stir up
ami, e [ami] *nm/f* friend; (*amant/maîtresse*)

boyfriend/girlfriend ▷ *adj*: **pays/groupe ~** friendly country/group; **être (très) ~ avec qn** to be (very) friendly with sb; **être ~ de l'ordre** to be a lover of order; **un ~ des arts** a patron of the arts; **un ~ des chiens** a dog lover; **petit ~/ petite ~e** (*fam*) boyfriend/girlfriend

amiable [amjabl(ə)]: **à l'~** *adv* (*Jur*) out of court; (*gén*) amicably

amiante [amjɑ̃t] *nm* asbestos

amibe [amib] *nf* amoeba

amical, e, -aux [amikal, -o] *adj* friendly ▷ *nf* (*club*) association

amicalement [amikalmɑ̃] *adv* in a friendly way; (*formule épistolaire*) regards

amidon [amidɔ̃] *nm* starch

amidonner [amidɔne] *vt* to starch

amincir [amɛ̃siʁ] *vt* (*objet*) to thin (down); **s'amincir** *vi* to get thinner *ou* slimmer; **~ qn** to make sb thinner *ou* slimmer

amincissant, e [amɛ̃sisɑ̃, -ɑ̃t] *adj* slimming

aminé, e [amine] *adj*: **acide ~** amino acid

amiral, -aux [amiʁal, -o] *nm* admiral

amirauté [amiʁote] *nf* admiralty

amitié [amitje] *nf* friendship; **prendre en ~ to** take a liking to; **faire** *ou* **présenter ses ~s à qn** to send sb one's best wishes; **~s** (*formule épistolaire*) (with) best wishes

ammoniac [amɔnjak] *nm*: **(gaz) ~** ammonia

ammoniaque [amɔnjak] *nf* ammonia (water)

amnésie [amnezi] *nf* amnesia

amnésique [amnezik] *adj* amnesic

Amnesty International [amnɛsti-] *n* Amnesty International

amniocentèse [amnjosɛ̃tez] *nf* amniocentesis

amnistie [amnisti] *nf* amnesty

amnistier [amnistje] *vt* to amnesty

amocher [amɔʃe] *vt* (*fam*) to mess up

amoindrir [amwɛ̃dʁiʁ] *vt* to reduce

amollir [amɔliʁ] *vt* to soften

amonceler [amɔ̃sle] *vt*: **s'amonceler** to pile *ou* heap up; (*fig*) to accumulate

amoncellement [amɔ̃sɛlmɑ̃] *nm* piling *ou* heaping up; accumulation; (*tas*) pile, heap, accumulation

amont [amɔ̃]: **en ~** *adv* upstream; (*sur une pente*) uphill; **en ~ de** *prép* upstream from; uphill from, above

amoral, e, -aux [amɔʁal, -o] *adj* amoral

amorce [amɔʁs(ə)] *nf* (*sur un hameçon*) bait; (*explosif*) cap; (*tube*) primer; (: *contenu*) priming; (*fig: début*) beginning(s), start

amorcer [amɔʁse] *vt* to bait; to prime; (*commencer*) to begin, start

amorphe [amɔʁf(ə)] *adj* passive, lifeless

amortir [amɔʁtiʁ] *vt* (*atténuer: choc*) to absorb, cushion; (*bruit, douleur*) to deaden; (*Comm: dette*) to pay off, amortize; (: *mise de fonds, matériel*) to write off; **~ un abonnement** to make a season ticket pay (for itself)

amortissable [amɔʁtisabl(ə)] *adj* (*Comm*) that can be paid off

amortissement [amɔʁtismɑ̃] *nm* (*de matériel*)

writing off; (*d'une dette*) paying off

amortisseur [amɔʁtisœʁ] *nm* shock absorber

amour [amuʁ] *nm* love; (*liaison*) love affair, love; (*statuette etc*) cupid; **un ~ de** a lovely little; **faire l'~** to make love

amouracher [amuʁaʃe]: **s'amouracher de** *vt* (*péj*) to become infatuated with

amourette [amuʁɛt] *nf* passing fancy

amoureusement [amuʁøzmɑ̃] *adv* lovingly

amoureux, -euse [amuʁø, -øz] *adj* (*regard, tempérament*) amorous; (*vie, problèmes*) love *cpd*; (*personne*): **~ (de qn)** in love (with sb) ▷ *nm/f* lover ▷ *nmpl* courting couple(s); **tomber ~ de qn** to fall in love with sb; **être ~ de qch** to be passionately fond of sth; **un ~ de la nature** a nature lover

amour-propre [amuʁpʁɔpʁ(ə)] (*pl* **amours-propres**) *nm* self-esteem

amovible [amɔvibl(ə)] *adj* removable, detachable

ampère [ɑ̃pɛʁ] *nm* amp(ere)

ampèremètre [ɑ̃pɛʁmɛtʁ(ə)] *nm* ammeter

amphétamine [ɑ̃fetamin] *nf* amphetamine

amphi [ɑ̃fi] *nm* (*Scol fam: = amphithéâtre*) lecture hall *ou* theatre

amphibie [ɑ̃fibi] *adj* amphibious

amphibien [ɑ̃fibjɛ̃] *nm* (*Zool*) amphibian

amphithéâtre [ɑ̃fiteɑtʁ(ə)] *nm* amphitheatre; (*d'université*) lecture hall *ou* theatre

amphore [ɑ̃fɔʁ] *nf* amphora

ample [ɑ̃pl(ə)] *adj* (*vêtement*) roomy, ample; (*gestes, mouvement*) broad; (*ressources*) ample; **jusqu'à plus ~ informé** (*Admin*) until further details are available

amplement [ɑ̃pləmɑ̃] *adv* amply; **~ suffisant** ample, more than enough

ampleur [ɑ̃plœʁ] *nf* scale, size; extent, magnitude

ampli [ɑ̃pli] *nm* (*fam: = amplificateur*) amplifier, amp

amplificateur [ɑ̃plifikatœʁ] *nm* amplifier

amplification [ɑ̃plifikasjɔ̃] *nf* amplification; expansion, increase

amplifier [ɑ̃plifje] *vt* (*son, oscillation*) to amplify; (*fig*) to expand, increase

amplitude [ɑ̃plityd] *nf* amplitude; (*des températures*) range

ampoule [ɑ̃pul] *nf* (*électrique*) bulb; (*de médicament*) phial; (*aux mains, pieds*) blister

ampoulé, e [ɑ̃pule] *adj* (*péj*) pompous, bombastic

amputation [ɑ̃pytɑsjɔ̃] *nf* amputation

amputer [ɑ̃pyte] *vt* (*Méd*) to amputate; (*fig*) to cut *ou* reduce drastically; **~ qn d'un bras/pied** to amputate sb's arm/foot

Amsterdam [amstɛʁdam] *n* Amsterdam

amulette [amylɛt] *nf* amulet

amusant, e [amyzɑ̃, -ɑ̃t] *adj* (*divertissant, spirituel*) entertaining, amusing; (*comique*) funny, amusing

amusé, e [amyze] *adj* amused

amuse-gueule [amyzgœl] *nm inv* appetizer,

snack

amusement [amyzmɑ̃] *nm* (*voir amusé*) amusement; (*voir amuser*) entertaining, amusing; (*jeu etc*) pastime, diversion

amuser [amyze] *vt* (*divertir*) to entertain, amuse; (*égayer, faire rire*) to amuse; (*détourner l'attention de*) to distract; **s'amuser** *vi* (*jouer*) to amuse o.s., play; (*se divertir*) to enjoy o.s., have fun; (*fig*) to mess around; **s'~ de qch** (*trouver comique*) to find sth amusing; **s'~ avec** *ou* **de qn** (*duper*) to make a fool of sb

amusette [amyzɛt] *nf* idle pleasure, trivial pastime

amuseur [amyzœʀ] *nm* entertainer; (*péj*) clown

amygdale [amidal] *nf* tonsil; **opérer qn des ~s** to take sb's tonsils out

amygdalite [amidalit] *nf* tonsillitis

AN *sigle f* = **Assemblée nationale**

an [ɑ̃] *nm* year; **être âgé de** *ou* **avoir 3 ans** to be 3 (years old); **en l'an 1980** in the year 1980; **le jour de l'an, le premier de l'an, le nouvel an** New Year's Day

anabolisant [anabɔlizɑ̃] *nm* anabolic steroid

anachronique [anakʀɔnik] *adj* anachronistic

anachronisme [anakʀɔnism(ə)] *nm* anachronism

anaconda [anakɔ̃da] *nm* (*Zool*) anaconda

anaérobie [anaeʀɔbi] *adj* anaerobic

anagramme [anagʀam] *nf* anagram

ANAH *sigle f* = **Agence nationale pour l'amélioration de l'habitat**

anal, e, -aux [anal, -o] *adj* anal

analgésique [analʒezik] *nm* analgesic

anallergique [analɛʀʒik] *adj* hypoallergenic

analogie [analɔʒi] *nf* analogy

analogique [analɔʒik] *adj* (*Logique: raisonnement*) analogical; (*calculateur, montre etc*) analogue; (*Inform*) analog

analogue [analɔg] *adj*: **~ (à)** analogous (to), similar (to)

analphabète [analfabɛt] *nm/f* illiterate

analphabétisme [analfabetism(ə)] *nm* illiteracy

analyse [analiz] *nf* analysis; (*Méd*) test; **faire l'~ de** to analyse; **une ~ approfondie** an in-depth analysis; **en dernière ~** in the last analysis; **avoir l'esprit d'~** to have an analytical turn of mind; **~ grammaticale** grammatical analysis, parsing (*Scol*)

analyser [analize] *vt* to analyse; (*Méd*) to test

analyste [analist(ə)] *nm/f* analyst; (*psychanalyste*) (psycho) analyst

analyste-programmeur, -euse [analist-] (*pl* **analystes-programmeurs, -euses**) *nm/f* systems analyst

analytique [analitik] *adj* analytical

analytiquement [analitikmɑ̃] *adv* analytically

ananas [anana] *nm* pineapple

anarchie [anaʀʃi] *nf* anarchy

anarchique [anaʀʃik] *adj* anarchic

anarchisme [anaʀʃism(ə)] *nm* anarchism

anarchiste [anaʀʃist(ə)] *adj* anarchistic ▷ *nm/f* anarchist

anathème [anatɛm] *nm*: **jeter l'~ sur, lancer l'~ contre** to anathematize, curse

anatomie [anatɔmi] *nf* anatomy

anatomique [anatɔmik] *adj* anatomical

ancestral, e, -aux [ɑ̃sɛstʀal, -o] *adj* ancestral

ancêtre [ɑ̃sɛtʀ(ə)] *nm/f* ancestor; (*fig*): **l'~ de** the forerunner of

anche [ɑ̃ʃ] *nf* reed

anchois [ɑ̃ʃwa] *nm* anchovy

ancien, ne [ɑ̃sjɛ̃, -ɛn] *adj* old; (*de jadis, de l'antiquité*) ancient; (*précédent, ex-*) former, old ▷ *nm* (*mobilier ancien*): **l'~** antiques *pl* ▷ *nm/f* (*dans une tribu etc*) elder; **un ~ ministre** a former minister; **mon ~ne voiture** my previous car; **être plus ~ que qn dans une maison** to have been in a firm longer than sb; (*dans la hiérarchie*) to be senior to sb in a firm; **~ combattant** ex-serviceman; **~ (élève)** (*Scol*) ex-pupil (*Brit*), alumnus (*US*)

anciennement [ɑ̃sjɛnmɑ̃] *adv* formerly

ancienneté [ɑ̃sjɛnte] *nf* oldness; antiquity; (*Admin*) (length of) service; seniority

ancrage [ɑ̃kʀaʒ] *nm* anchoring; (*Navig*) anchorage; (*Constr*) anchor

ancre [ɑ̃kʀ(ə)] *nf* anchor; **jeter/lever l'~** to cast/weigh anchor; **à l'~** at anchor

ancrer [ɑ̃kʀe] *vt* (*Constr*) to anchor; (*fig*) to fix firmly; **s'ancrer** *vi* (*Navig*) to (cast) anchor

andalou, -ouse [ɑ̃dalu, -uz] *adj* Andalusian

Andalousie [ɑ̃daluzi] *nf*: **l'~** Andalusia

andante [ɑ̃dɑ̃t] *adv, nm* andante

Andes [ɑ̃d] *nfpl*: **les ~** the Andes

Andorre [ɑ̃dɔʀ] *nf* Andorra

andouille [ɑ̃duj] *nf* (*Culin*) sausage made of chitterlings; (*fam*) clot, nit

andouillette [ɑ̃dujɛt] *nf* small andouille

âne [ɑn] *nm* donkey, ass; (*péj*) dunce, fool

anéantir [aneɑ̃tiʀ] *vt* to annihilate, wipe out; (*fig*) to obliterate, destroy; (*déprimer*) to overwhelm

anecdote [anɛkdɔt] *nf* anecdote

anecdotique [anɛkdɔtik] *adj* anecdotal

anémie [anemi] *nf* anaemia

anémié, e [anemje] *adj* anaemic; (*fig*) enfeebled

anémique [anemik] *adj* anaemic

anémone [anemɔn] *nf* anemone; **~ de mer** sea anemone

ânerie [ɑnʀi] *nf* stupidity; (*parole etc*) stupid *ou* idiotic comment *etc*

anéroïde [aneʀɔid] *adj voir* **baromètre**

ânesse [ɑnɛs] *nf* she-ass

anesthésie [anɛstezi] *nf* anaesthesia; **sous ~** under anaesthetic; **~ générale/locale** general/local anaesthetic; **faire une ~ locale à qn** to give sb a local anaesthetic

anesthésier [anɛstezje] *vt* to anaesthetize

anesthésique [anɛstezik] *adj* anaesthetic

anesthésiste [anɛstezist(ə)] *nm/f* anaesthetist

anfractuosité [ɑ̃fʀaktɥozite] *nf* crevice

ange [ɑ̃ʒ] *nm* angel; **être aux ~s** to be over the moon; **~ gardien** guardian angel

angélique [ãʒelik] *adj* angelic(al) ▷ *nf* angelica
angelot [ãʒlo] *nm* cherub
angélus [ãʒelys] *nm* angelus; *(cloches)* evening bells *pl*
angevin, e [ãʒvɛ̃, -in] *adj* of *ou* from Anjou; of *ou* from Angers
angine [ãʒin] *nf* sore throat, throat infection; ~ **de poitrine** angina (pectoris)
angiome [ãʒjom] *nm* angioma
anglais, e [ãglɛ, -ɛz] *adj* English ▷ *nm* *(Ling)* English ▷ *nm/f*: **Anglais, e** Englishman/woman; **les A~** the English; **filer à l'~e** to take French leave; **à l'~e** *(Culin)* boiled
anglaises [ãglɛz] *nfpl* *(cheveux)* ringlets
angle [ãgl(ə)] *nm* angle; *(coin)* corner; ~ **droit/obtus/aigu/mort** right/obtuse/acute/dead angle
Angleterre [ãglətɛʀ] *nf*: **l'~** England
anglican, e [ãglikã, -an] *adj, nm/f* Anglican
anglicanisme [ãglikanism(ə)] *nm* Anglicanism
anglicisme [ãglisism(ə)] *nm* anglicism
angliciste [ãglisist(ə)] *nm/f* English scholar; *(étudiant)* student of English
anglo... [ãglɔ] *préfixe* Anglo-, anglo(-)
anglo-américain, e [ãglɔameʀikɛ̃, -ɛn] *adj* Anglo-American ▷ *nm* *(Ling)* American English
anglo-arabe [ãglɔaʀab] *adj* Anglo-Arab
anglo-canadien, ne [ãglɔkanadjɛ̃, -ɛn] *adj* Anglo-Canadian ▷ *nm* *(Ling)* Canadian English
anglo-normand, e [ãglɔnɔʀmã, -ãd] *adj* Anglo-Norman; **les îles ~es** the Channel Islands
anglophile [ãglɔfil] *adj* anglophilic
anglophobe [ãglɔfɔb] *adj* anglophobic
anglophone [ãglɔfɔn] *adj* English-speaking
anglo-saxon, ne [ãglɔsaksɔ̃, -ɔn] *adj* Anglo-Saxon
angoissant, e [ãgwasã, -ãt] *adj* harrowing
angoisse [ãgwas] *nf*: **l'~** anguish *no pl*
angoissé, e [ãgwase] *adj* anguished; *(personne)* full of anxieties *ou* hang-ups *(fam)*
angoisser [ãgwase] *vt* to harrow, cause anguish to ▷ *vi* to worry, fret
Angola [ãgɔla] *nm*: **l'~** Angola
angolais, e [ãgɔlɛ, -ɛz] *adj* Angolan
angora [ãgɔʀa] *adj, nm* angora
anguille [ãgij] *nf* eel; ~ **de mer** conger (eel); **il y a ~ sous roche** *(fig)* there's something going on, there's something beneath all this
angulaire [ãgylɛʀ] *adj* angular
anguleux, -euse [ãgylø, -øz] *adj* angular
anhydride [anidʀid] *nm* anhydride
anicroche [anikʀɔʃ] *nf* hitch, snag
animal, e, -aux [animal, -o] *adj, nm* animal; ~ **domestique/sauvage** domestic/wild animal
animalier [animalje] *adj*: **peintre ~** animal painter
animateur, -trice [animatœʀ, -tʀis] *nm/f* *(de télévision)* host; *(de music-hall)* compère; *(de groupe)* leader, organizer; *(Ciné: technicien)* animator
animation [animasjɔ̃] *nf* *(voir animé)* busyness; liveliness; *(Ciné: technique)* animation; **animations** *nfpl* *(activité)* activities; **centre d'~**

≈ community centre
animé, e [anime] *adj* *(rue, lieu)* busy, lively; *(conversation, réunion)* lively, animated; *(opposé à inanimé, aussi Ling)* animate
animer [anime] *vt* *(ville, soirée)* to liven up, enliven; *(mettre en mouvement)* to drive; *(stimuler)* to drive, impel; **s'animer** *vi* to liven up, come to life
animosité [animozite] *nf* animosity
anis [ani] *nm* *(Culin)* aniseed; *(Bot)* anise
anisette [anizɛt] *nf* anisette
Ankara [ãkaʀa] *n* Ankara
ankyloser [ãkiloze]: **s'ankyloser** *vi* to get stiff
annales [anal] *nfpl* annals
anneau, x [ano] *nm* ring; *(de chaîne)* link; *(Sport)*: **exercices aux ~x** ring exercises
année [ane] *nf* year; **souhaiter la bonne ~ à qn** to wish sb a Happy New Year; **tout au long de l'~** all year long; **d'une ~ à l'autre** from one year to the next; **d'~ en ~** from year to year; **l'~ scolaire/fiscale** the school/tax year
année-lumière [anelymjɛʀ] *(pl* **années-lumières)** *nf* light year
annexe [anɛks(ə)] *adj* *(problème)* related; *(document)* appended; *(salle)* adjoining ▷ *nf* *(bâtiment)* annex(e); *(de document, ouvrage)* annex, appendix; *(jointe à une lettre, un dossier)* enclosure
annexer [anɛkse] *vt* to annex; **s'annexer** *(pays)* to annex; ~ **qch à** *(joindre)* to append sth to
annexion [anɛksjɔ̃] *nf* annexation
annihiler [aniile] *vt* to annihilate
anniversaire [anivɛʀsɛʀ] *nm* birthday; *(d'un événement, bâtiment)* anniversary ▷ *adj*: **jour ~** anniversary
annonce [anɔ̃s] *nf* announcement; *(signe, indice)* sign; *(aussi:* **annonce publicitaire)** advertisement; *(Cartes)* declaration; ~ **personnelle** personal message; **les petites ~s** the small *ou* classified ads
annoncer [anɔ̃se] *vt* to announce; *(être le signe de)* to herald; *(Cartes)* to declare; **je vous annonce que ...** I wish to tell you that ...; **s'annoncer bien/difficile** *vi* to look promising/difficult; ~ **la couleur** *(fig)* to lay one's cards on the table
annonceur, -euse [anɔ̃sœʀ, -øz] *nm/f* *(TV, Radio: speaker)* announcer; *(publicitaire)* advertiser
annonciateur, -trice [anɔ̃sjatœʀ, -tʀis] *adj*: ~ **d'un événement** presaging an event
Annonciation [anɔ̃sjasjɔ̃] *nf*: **l'~** *(Rel)* the Annunciation; *(jour)* Annunciation Day
annotation [anɔtasjɔ̃] *nf* annotation
annoter [anɔte] *vt* to annotate
annuaire [anɥɛʀ] *nm* yearbook, annual; ~ **téléphonique** (telephone) directory, phone book
annuel, le [anɥɛl] *adj* annual, yearly
annuellement [anɥɛlmã] *adv* annually, yearly
annuité [anɥite] *nf* annual instalment
annulaire [anylɛʀ] *nm* ring *ou* third finger
annulation [anylasjɔ̃] *nf* cancellation; annulment; quashing, repeal

annuler [anyle] vt (rendez-vous, voyage) to cancel, call off; (mariage) to annul; (jugement) to quash (Brit), repeal (US); (résultats) to declare void; (Math, Physique) to cancel out; **s'annuler** to cancel each other out

anoblir [anɔbliʀ] vt to ennoble

anode [anɔd] nf anode

anodin, e [anɔdɛ̃, -in] adj harmless; (sans importance) insignificant, trivial

anomalie [anɔmali] nf anomaly

ânon [anɔ̃] nm baby donkey; (petit âne) little donkey

ânonner [anɔne] vi, vt to read in a drone; (hésiter) to read in a fumbling manner

anonymat [anɔnima] nm anonymity; **garder l'~** to remain anonymous

anonyme [anɔnim] adj anonymous; (fig) impersonal

anonymement [anɔnimmɑ̃] adv anonymously

anorak [anɔrak] nm anorak

anorexie [anɔrɛksi] nf anorexia

anorexique [anɔrɛksik] adj, nm/f anorexic

anormal, e, -aux [anɔrmal, -o] adj abnormal; (insolite) unusual, abnormal

anormalement [anɔrmalmɑ̃] adv abnormally; unusually

ANPE sigle f (= Agence nationale pour l'emploi) national employment agency (functions include job creation)

anse [ɑ̃s] nf handle; (Géo) cove

antagonisme [ɑ̃tagɔnism(ə)] nm antagonism

antagoniste [ɑ̃tagɔnist(ə)] adj antagonistic ⊳ nm antagonist

antan [ɑ̃tɑ̃]: **d'~** adj of yesteryear, of long ago

antarctique [ɑ̃taʀktik] adj Antarctic ⊳ nm: **l'A~** the Antarctic; **le cercle A~** the Antarctic Circle; **l'océan A~** the Antarctic Ocean

antécédent [ɑ̃tesedɑ̃] nm (Ling) antecedent; **antécédents** nmpl (Méd etc) past history sg; **~s professionnels** record, career to date

antédiluvien, ne [ɑ̃tedilyvjɛ̃, -ɛn] adj (fig) ancient, antediluvian

antenne [ɑ̃tɛn] nf (de radio, télévision) aerial; (d'insecte) antenna (pl -ae), feeler; (poste avancé) outpost; (petite succursale) sub-branch; **sur l'~** on the air; **passer à/avoir l'~** to go/be on the air; **deux heures d'~** two hours' broadcasting time; **hors ~** off the air; **~ chirurgicale** (Mil) advance surgical unit

antépénultième [ɑ̃tepenyltjɛm] adj antepenultimate

antérieur, e [ɑ̃teʀjœʀ] adj (d'avant) previous, earlier; (de devant) front; **~ à** prior ou previous to; **passé/futur ~** (Ling) past/future anterior

antérieurement [ɑ̃teʀjœʀmɑ̃] adv earlier; (précédemment) previously; **~ à** prior ou previous to

antériorité [ɑ̃teʀjɔʀite] nf precedence (in time)

anthologie [ɑ̃tɔlɔʒi] nf anthology

anthracite [ɑ̃tʀasit] nm anthracite ⊳ adj: **(gris) ~** charcoal (grey)

anthropologie [ɑ̃tʀɔpɔlɔʒi] nf anthropology

anthropologue [ɑ̃tʀɔpɔlɔg] nm/f anthropologist

anthropomorphisme [ɑ̃tʀɔpɔmɔʀfism(ə)] nm anthropomorphism

anthropophage [ɑ̃tʀɔpɔfaʒ] adj cannibalistic

anthropophagie [ɑ̃tʀɔpɔfaʒi] nf cannibalism, anthropophagy

anti... [ɑ̃ti] préfixe anti...

antiaérien, ne [ɑ̃tiaeʀjɛ̃, -ɛn] adj anti-aircraft; **abri ~** air-raid shelter

antialcoolique [ɑ̃tialkɔlik] adj anti-alcohol; **ligue ~** temperance league

antiatomique [ɑ̃tiatɔmik] adj: **abri ~** fallout shelter

antibiotique [ɑ̃tibjɔtik] nm antibiotic

antibrouillard [ɑ̃tibʀujaʀ] adj: **phare ~** fog lamp

antibruit [ɑ̃tibʀɥi] adj inv: **mur ~** (sur autoroute) sound-muffling wall

antibuée [ɑ̃tibɥe] adj inv: **dispositif ~** demister; **bombe ~** demister spray

anticancéreux, -euse [ɑ̃tikɑ̃seʀø, -øz] adj cancer cpd

anticasseur, anticasseurs [ɑ̃tikɑsœʀ] adj: **loi/mesure ~(s)** law/measure against damage done by demonstrators

antichambre [ɑ̃tiʃɑ̃bʀ(ə)] nf antechamber, anteroom; **faire ~** to wait (for an audience)

antichar [ɑ̃tiʃaʀ] adj antitank

antichoc [ɑ̃tiʃɔk] adj shockproof

anticipation [ɑ̃tisipɑsjɔ̃] nf anticipation; (Comm) payment in advance; **par ~** in anticipation, in advance; **livre/film d'~** science fiction book/film

anticipé, e [ɑ̃tisipe] adj (règlement, paiement) early, in advance; (joie etc) anticipated, early; **avec mes remerciements ~s** thanking you in advance ou anticipation

anticiper [ɑ̃tisipe] vt to anticipate, foresee; (paiement) to pay ou make in advance ⊳ vi to look ou think ahead; (en racontant) to jump ahead; (prévoir) to anticipate; **~ sur** to anticipate

anticlérical, e, -aux [ɑ̃tikleʀikal, -o] adj anticlerical

anticoagulant, e [ɑ̃tikɔagylɑ̃, -ɑ̃t] adj, nm anticoagulant

anticolonialisme [ɑ̃tikɔlɔnjalism(ə)] nm anticolonialism

anticonceptionnel, le [ɑ̃tikɔ̃sɛpsjɔnɛl] adj contraceptive

anticonformisme [ɑ̃tikɔ̃fɔʀmism(ə)] nm nonconformism

anticonstitutionnel, le [ɑ̃tikɔ̃stitysjɔnɛl] adj unconstitutional

anticorps [ɑ̃tikɔʀ] nm antibody

anticyclone [ɑ̃tisiklon] nm anticyclone

antidater [ɑ̃tidate] vt to backdate, predate

antidémocratique [ɑ̃tidemɔkʀatik] adj antidemocratic; (peu démocratique) undemocratic

antidépresseur [ɑ̃tidepʀesœʀ] nm antidepressant

antidérapant, e [ɑ̃tideʀapɑ̃, -ɑ̃t] adj nonskid

antidopage [ɑ̃tidɔpaʒ], **antidoping** [ɑ̃tidɔpiŋ] *adj* (*lutte*) antidoping; (*contrôle*) dope *cpd*
antidote [ɑ̃tidɔt] *nm* antidote
antienne [ɑ̃tjɛn] *nf* (*fig*) chant, refrain
antigang [ɑ̃tigɑ̃g] *adj inv*: **brigade ~** commando unit
antigel [ɑ̃tiʒɛl] *nm* antifreeze
antigène [ɑ̃tiʒɛn] *nm* antigen
antigouvernemental, e, -aux [ɑ̃tiguvɛʀnəmɑ̃tal, -o] *adj* antigovernment
Antigua et Barbude [ɑ̃tigaebaʀbyd] *nf* Antigua and Barbuda
antihistaminique [ɑ̃tiistaminik] *nm* antihistamine
anti-inflammatoire [ɑ̃tiɛ̃flamatwaʀ] *adj* anti-inflammatory
anti-inflationniste [ɑ̃tiɛ̃flasjɔnist(ə)] *adj* anti-inflationary
antillais, e [ɑ̃tijɛ, -ɛz] *adj* West Indian
Antilles [ɑ̃tij] *nfpl*: **les ~** the West Indies; **les Grandes/Petites ~** the Greater/Lesser Antilles
antilope [ɑ̃tilɔp] *nf* antelope
antimilitarisme [ɑ̃timilitaʀism(ə)] *nm* antimilitarism
antimilitariste [ɑ̃timilitaʀist(ə)] *adj* antimilitarist
antimissile [ɑ̃timisil] *adj* antimissile
antimite, antimites [ɑ̃timit] *adj,nm*: (**produit**) **~(s)** mothproofer, moth repellent
antimondialisation [ɑ̃timɔ̃djalizasjɔ̃] *nf* anti-globalization
antinucléaire [ɑ̃tinykleeʀ] *adj* antinuclear
antioxydant [ɑ̃tiɔksidɑ̃] *nm* antioxidant
antiparasite [ɑ̃tipaʀazit] *adj* (*Radio, TV*) anti-interference; **dispositif ~** suppressor
antipathie [ɑ̃tipati] *nf* antipathy
antipathique [ɑ̃tipatik] *adj* unpleasant, disagreeable
antipelliculaire [ɑ̃tipelikylɛʀ] *adj* anti-dandruff
antiphrase [ɑ̃tifʀaz] *nf*: **par ~** ironically
antipodes [ɑ̃tipɔd] *nmpl* (*Géo*): **les ~** the antipodes; (*fig*): **être aux ~ de** to be the opposite extreme of
antipoison [ɑ̃tipwazɔ̃] *adj inv*: **centre ~** poison centre
antipoliomyélitique [ɑ̃tipɔljɔmjelitik] *adj* polio *cpd*
antiquaire [ɑ̃tikɛʀ] *nm/f* antique dealer
antique [ɑ̃tik] *adj* antique; (*très vieux*) ancient, antiquated
antiquité [ɑ̃tikite] *nf* (*objet*) antique; **l'A~** Antiquity; **magasin/marchand d'~s** antique shop/dealer
antirabique [ɑ̃tiʀabik] *adj* rabies *cpd*
antiraciste [ɑ̃tiʀasist(ə)] *adj* antiracist, antiracialist
antireflet [ɑ̃tiʀəflɛ] *adj inv* (*verres*) antireflective
antirépublicain, e [ɑ̃tiʀepyblikɛ̃, -ɛn] *adj* antirepublican
antirides [ɑ̃tiʀid] *adj* (*crème*) antiwrinkle
antirouille [ɑ̃tiʀuj] *adj inv*: **peinture ~** antirust

paint; **traitement ~** rustproofing
antisémite [ɑ̃tisemit] *adj* anti-Semitic
antisémitisme [ɑ̃tisemitism(ə)] *nm* anti-Semitism
antiseptique [ɑ̃tisɛptik] *adj,nm* antiseptic
antisocial, e, -aux [ɑ̃tisɔsjal, -o] *adj* antisocial
antispasmodique [ɑ̃tispasmɔdik] *adj,nm* antispasmodic
antisportif, -ive [ɑ̃tispɔʀtif, -iv] *adj* unsporting; (*hostile au sport*) antisport
antitétanique [ɑ̃titetanik] *adj* tetanus *cpd*
antithèse [ɑ̃titɛz] *nf* antithesis
antitrust [ɑ̃titʀœst] *adj inv* (*loi, mesures*) antimonopoly
antituberculeux, -euse [ɑ̃titybɛʀkylø, -øz] *adj* tuberculosis *cpd*
antitussif, -ive [ɑ̃titysif, -iv] *adj* antitussive, cough *cpd*
antivariolique [ɑ̃tivaʀɔlik] *adj* smallpox *cpd*
antivirus [ɑ̃tiviʀys] *nm* (*Inform*) antivirus (program)
antivol [ɑ̃tivɔl] *adj,nm*: (**dispositif**) **~** antitheft device; (*pour vélo*) padlock
antonyme [ɑ̃tɔnim] *nm* antonym
antre [ɑ̃tʀ(ə)] *nm* den, lair
anus [anys] *nm* anus
Anvers [ɑ̃vɛʀ] *n* Antwerp
anxiété [ɑ̃ksjete] *nf* anxiety
anxieusement [ɑ̃ksjøzmɑ̃] *adv* anxiously
anxieux, -euse [ɑ̃ksjø, -øz] *adj* anxious, worried; **être ~ de faire** to be anxious to do
AOC *sigle f* (= *Appellation d'origine contrôlée*) *guarantee of quality of wine*; *see note*

● AOC

● AOC ("appellation d'origine contrôlée") is
● the highest French wine classification. It
● indicates that the wine meets strict
● requirements concerning vineyard of
● origin, type of grape, method of production
● and alcoholic strength.

aorte [aɔʀt(ə)] *nf* aorta
août [u] *nm* August; *voir aussi* **juillet; Assomption**
aoûtien, ne [ausjɛ̃, -ɛn] *nm/f* August holiday-maker
AP *sigle f* = **Assistance publique**
apaisant, e [apɛzɑ̃, -ɑ̃t] *adj* soothing
apaisement [apɛzmɑ̃] *nm* calming; soothing; (*aussi Pol*) appeasement; **apaisements** *nmpl* soothing reassurances; (*pour calmer*) pacifying words
apaiser [apeze] *vt* (*colère*) to calm, quell, soothe; (*faim*) to appease, assuage; (*douleur*) to soothe; (*personne*) to calm (down), pacify; **s'apaiser** *vi* (*tempête, bruit*) to die down, subside
apanage [apanaʒ] *nm*: **être l'~ de** to be the privilege ou prerogative of
aparté [apaʀte] *nm* (*Théât*) aside; (*entretien*) private conversation; **en ~** *adv* in an aside (*Brit*);

(entretien) in private

apartheid [apaʀtɛd] *nm* apartheid

apathie [apati] *nf* apathy

apathique [apatik] *adj* apathetic

apatride [apatʀid] *nm/f* stateless person

APCE *sigle f* (= *Agence pour la création d'entreprises*) business start-up agency

apercevoir [apɛʀsəvwaʀ] *vt* to see; **s'apercevoir de** *vt* to notice; **s'~ que** to notice that; **sans s'en ~** without realizing *ou* noticing

aperçu, e [apɛʀsy] *pp de* **apercevoir** ▷ *nm* (*vue d'ensemble*) general survey; (*intuition*) insight

apéritif, -ive [apeʀitif, -iv] *adj* which stimulates the appetite ▷ *nm* (*boisson*) aperitif; (*réunion*) (pre-lunch *ou* -dinner) drinks *pl*; **prendre l'~** to have drinks (before lunch *ou* dinner) *ou* an aperitif

apesanteur [apəzɑ̃tœʀ] *nf* weightlessness

à-peu-près [apøpʀɛ] *nm inv* (*péj*) vague approximation

apeuré, e [apœʀe] *adj* frightened, scared

aphasie [afazi] *nm* aphasia

aphone [afɔn] *adj* voiceless

aphorisme [afɔʀism(ə)] *nm* aphorism

aphrodisiaque [afʀɔdizjak] *adj, nm* aphrodisiac

aphte [aft(ə)] *nm* mouth ulcer

aphteuse [aftøz] *adj f*: **fièvre ~** foot-and-mouth disease

à-pic [apik] *nm* cliff, drop

apicole [apikɔl] *adj* beekeeping *cpd*

apiculteur, -trice [apikyltœʀ, -tʀis] *nm/f* beekeeper

apiculture [apikyltyʀ] *nf* beekeeping, apiculture

apitoiement [apitwamɑ̃] *nm* pity, compassion

apitoyer [apitwaje] *vt* to move to pity; **~ qn sur qn/qch** to move sb to pity for sb/over sth; **s'~ (sur qn/qch)** to feel pity *ou* compassion (for sb/ over sth)

ap. J.-C. *abr* (= *après Jésus-Christ*) AD

APL *sigle f* (= *aide personnalisée au logement*) housing benefit

aplanir [aplaniʀ] *vt* to level; (*fig*) to smooth away, iron out

aplati, e [aplati] *adj* flat, flattened

aplatir [aplatiʀ] *vt* to flatten; **s'aplatir** *vi* to become flatter; (*écrasé*) to be flattened; (*fig*) to lie flat on the ground; (: *fam*) to fall flat on one's face; (: *péj*) to grovel

aplomb [aplɔ̃] *nm* (*équilibre*) balance, equilibrium; (*fig*) self-assurance; (: *péj*) nerve; **d'~** *adv* steady; (*Constr*) plumb

apocalypse [apɔkalips(ə)] *nf* apocalypse

apocalyptique [apɔkaliptik] *adj* (*fig*) apocalyptic

apocryphe [apɔkʀif] *adj* apocryphal

apogée [apɔʒe] *nm* (*fig*) peak, apogee

apolitique [apɔlitik] *adj* (*indifférent*) apolitical; (*indépendant*) unpolitical, non-political

apologie [apɔlɔʒi] *nf* praise; (*Jur*) vindication

apoplexie [apɔplɛksi] *nf* apoplexy

a posteriori [apɔsteʀjɔʀi] *adv* after the event, with hindsight, a posteriori

apostolat [apɔstɔla] *nm* (*Rel*) apostolate, discipleship; (*gén*) evangelism

apostolique [apɔstɔlik] *adj* apostolic

apostrophe [apɔstʀɔf] *nf* (*signe*) apostrophe; (*appel*) interpellation

apostropher [apɔstʀɔfe] *vt* (*interpeller*) to shout at, address sharply

apothéose [apɔteoz] *nf* pinnacle (of achievement); (*Mus etc*) grand finale

apothicaire [apɔtikɛʀ] *nm* apothecary

apôtre [apotʀ(ə)] *nm* apostle, disciple

apparaître [apaʀɛtʀ(ə)] *vi* to appear ▷ *vb copule* to appear, seem

apparat [apaʀa] *nm*: **tenue/dîner d'~** ceremonial dress/dinner

appareil [apaʀɛj] *nm* (*outil, machine*) piece of apparatus, device; (*électrique etc*) appliance; (*politique, syndical*) machinery; (*avion*) (aero)plane (Brit), (air)plane (US), aircraft *inv*; (*téléphonique*) telephone; (*dentier*) brace (Brit), braces (US); **~ digestif/reproducteur** digestive/reproductive system *ou* apparatus; **l'~ productif** the means of production; **qui est à l'~?** who's speaking?; **dans le plus simple ~** in one's birthday suit; **~ (photographique)** camera; **~ 24 x 36** *ou* **petit format** 35 mm camera

appareillage [apaʀejaʒ] *nm* (*appareils*) equipment; (*Navig*) casting off, getting under way

appareiller [apaʀeje] *vi* (*Navig*) to cast off, get under way ▷ *vt* (*assortir*) to match up

appareil-photo [apaʀejfoto] (*pl* **appareils-photos**) *nm* camera

apparemment [apaʀamɑ̃] *adv* apparently

apparence [apaʀɑ̃s] *nf* appearance; **malgré les ~s** despite appearances; **en ~** apparently, seemingly

apparent, e [apaʀɑ̃, -ɑ̃t] *adj* visible; (*évident*) obvious; (*superficiel*) apparent; **coutures ~es** topstitched seams; **poutres ~es** exposed beams

apparenté, e [apaʀɑ̃te] *adj*: **~ à** related to; (*fig*) similar to

apparenter [apaʀɑ̃te]: **s'apparenter à** *vt* to be similar to

apparier [apaʀje] *vt* (*gants*) to pair, match

appariteur [apaʀitœʀ] *nm* attendant, porter (in French universities)

apparition [apaʀisjɔ̃] *nf* appearance; (*surnaturelle*) apparition; **faire son ~** to appear

appartement [apaʀtəmɑ̃] *nm* flat (Brit), apartment (US)

appartenance [apaʀtənɑ̃s] *nf*: **~ à** belonging to, membership of

appartenir [apaʀtəniʀ]: **~ à** *vt* to belong to; (*faire partie de*) to belong to, be a member of; **il lui appartient de** it is up to him to

appartiendrai [apaʀtjɛ̃dʀe], **appartiens** *etc* [apaʀtjɛ̃] *vb voir* **appartenir**

apparu, e [apaʀy] *pp de* **apparaître**

appas [apɑ] *nmpl* (*d'une femme*) charms

appât [apɑ] *nm* (*Pêche*) bait; (*fig*) lure, bait
appâter [apɑte] *vt* (*hameçon*) to bait; (*poisson, fig*) to lure, entice
appauvrir [apovʀiʀ] *vt* to impoverish; **s'appauvrir** *vi* to grow poorer, become impoverished
appauvrissement [apovʀismɑ̃] *nm* impoverishment
appel [apɛl] *nm* call; (*nominal*) roll call; (: *Scol*) register; (*Mil: recrutement*) call-up; (*Jur*) appeal; **faire ~ à** (*invoquer*) to appeal to; (*avoir recours à*) to call on; (*nécessiter*) to call for, require; **faire** *ou* **interjeter ~** (*Jur*) to appeal, lodge an appeal; **faire l'~** to call the roll; to call the register; **indicatif d'~** call sign; **numéro d'~** (*Tél*) number; **produit d'~** (*Comm*) loss leader; **sans ~** (*fig*) final, irrevocable; **~ d'air** in-draught; **~ d'offres** (*Comm*) invitation to tender; **faire un ~ de phares** to flash one's headlights; **~ (téléphonique)** (tele)phone call
appelé [aple] *nm* (*Mil*) conscript
appeler [aple] *vt* to call; (*Tél*) to call, ring; (*faire venir: médecin etc*) to call, send for; (*fig: nécessiter*) to call for, demand; **~ au secours** to call for help; **~ qn à l'aide** *ou* **au secours** to call to sb for help; **~ qn à un poste/des fonctions** to appoint sb to a post/assign duties to sb; **être appelé à** (*fig*) to be destined to; **~ qn à comparaître** (*Jur*) to summon sb to appear; **en ~ à** to appeal to; **s'appeler: elle s'appelle Gabrielle** her name is Gabrielle, she's called Gabrielle; **comment ça s'appelle?** what is it *ou* that called?
appellation [apelɑsjɔ̃] *nf* designation, appellation; **vin d'~ contrôlée** "appellation contrôlée" wine, *wine guaranteed of a certain quality*
appelle *etc* [apɛl] *vb voir* **appeler**
appendice [apɛ̃dis] *nm* appendix
appendicite [apɑ̃disit] *nf* appendicitis
appentis [apɑti] *nm* lean-to
appert [apɛʀ] *vb*: **il ~ que** it appears that, it is evident that
appesantir [apzɑtiʀ]: **s'appesantir** *vi* to grow heavier; **s'~ sur** (*fig*) to dwell at length on
appétissant, e [apetisɑ̃, -ɑ̃t] *adj* appetizing, mouth-watering
appétit [apeti] *nm* appetite; **couper l'~ à qn** to take away sb's appetite; **bon ~!** enjoy your meal!
applaudimètre [aplodimɛtʀ(ə)] *nm* applause meter
applaudir [aplodiʀ] *vt* to applaud ▷ *vi* to applaud, clap; **~ à** *vt* (*décision*) to applaud, commend
applaudissements [aplodismɑ̃] *nmpl* applause *sg*, clapping *sg*
applicable [aplikabl(ə)] *adj* applicable
applicateur [aplikatœʀ] *nm* applicator
application [aplikɑsjɔ̃] *nf* application; (*d'une loi*) enforcement; **mettre en ~** to implement
applique [aplik] *nf* wall lamp
appliqué, e [aplike] *adj* (*élève etc*) industrious,

assiduous; (*science*) applied
appliquer [aplike] *vt* to apply; (*loi*) to enforce; (*donner: gifle, châtiment*) to give; **s'appliquer** *vi* (*élève etc*) to apply o.s.; **s'~ à** (*loi, remarque*) to apply to; **s'~ à faire qch** to apply o.s. to doing sth, take pains to do sth; **s'~ sur** (*coïncider avec*) to fit over
appoint [apwɛ̃] *nm* (extra) contribution *ou* help; **avoir/faire l'~** (*en payant*) to have/give the right change *ou* money; **chauffage d'~** extra heating
appointements [apwɛ̃tmɑ̃] *nmpl* salary *sg*, stipend
appointer [apwɛ̃te] *vt*: **être appointé à l'année/au mois** to be paid yearly/monthly
appontage [apɔ̃taʒ] *nm* landing (*on an aircraft carrier*)
appontement [apɔ̃tmɑ̃] *nm* landing stage, wharf
apponter [apɔ̃te] *vi* (*avion, hélicoptère*) to land
apport [apɔʀ] *nm* supply; (*argent, biens etc*) contribution
apporter [apɔʀte] *vt* to bring; (*preuve*) to give, provide; (*modification*) to make; (*remarque*) to contribute, add
apposer [apoze] *vt* to append; (*sceau etc*) to affix
apposition [apozisjɔ̃] *nf* appending; affixing; (*Ling*): **en ~** in apposition
appréciable [apʀesjabl(ə)] *adj* (*important*) appreciable, significant
appréciation [apʀesjɑsjɔ̃] *nf* appreciation; estimation, assessment; **appréciations** *nfpl* (*avis*) assessment *sg*, appraisal *sg*
apprécier [apʀesje] *vt* to appreciate; (*évaluer*) to estimate, assess; **j'~ais que tu ...** I should appreciate (it) if you ...
appréhender [apʀeɑ̃de] *vt* (*craindre*) to dread; (*arrêter*) to apprehend; **~ que** to fear that; **~ de faire** to dread doing
appréhensif, -ive [apʀeɑ̃sif, -iv] *adj* apprehensive
appréhension [apʀeɑ̃sjɔ̃] *nf* apprehension
apprendre [apʀɑ̃dʀ(ə)] *vt* to learn; (*événement, résultats*) to learn of, hear of; **~ qch à qn** (*informer*) to tell sb (of) sth; (*enseigner*) to teach sb sth; **tu me l'apprends!** that's news to me!; **~ à faire qch** to learn to do sth; **~ à qn à faire qch** to teach sb to do sth
apprenti, e [apʀɑti] *nm/f* apprentice; (*fig*) novice, beginner
apprentissage [apʀɑtisaʒ] *nm* learning; (*Comm, Scol: période*) apprenticeship; **école** *ou* **centre d'~** training school *ou* centre; **faire l'~ de qch** (*fig*) to be initiated into sth
apprêt [apʀɛ] *nm* (*sur un cuir, une étoffe*) dressing; (*sur un mur*) size; (*sur un papier*) finish; **sans ~** (*fig*) without artifice, unaffectedly
apprêté, e [apʀete] *adj* (*fig*) affected
apprêter [apʀete] *vt* to dress, finish; **s'apprêter** *vi*: **s'~ à qch/à faire qch** to prepare for sth/for doing sth
appris, e [apʀi, -iz] *pp de* **apprendre**
apprivoisé, e [apʀivwaze] *adj* tame, tamed

apprivoiser [apʀivwaze] *vt* to tame

approbateur, -trice [apʀɔbatœʀ, -tʀis] *adj* approving

approbatif, -ive [apʀɔbatif, -iv] *adj* approving

approbation [apʀɔbasjɔ̃] *nf* approval; **digne d'~** (*conduite, travail*) praiseworthy, commendable

approchant, e [apʀɔʃɑ̃, -ɑ̃t] *adj* similar, close; **quelque chose d'~** something similar

approche [apʀɔʃ] *nf* approaching; (*arrivée, attitude*) approach; **approches** *nfpl* (*abords*) surroundings; **à l'~ du bateau/de l'ennemi** as the ship/enemy approached *ou* drew near; **l'~ d'un problème** the approach to a problem; **travaux d'~** (*fig*) manoeuvrings

approché, e [apʀɔʃe] *adj* approximate

approcher [apʀɔʃe] *vi* to approach, come near ▷ *vt* (*vedette, artiste*) to come close to, approach; (*rapprocher*): **~ qch (de qch)** to bring *ou* put *ou* move sth near (to sth); **~ de** *vt* to draw near to; (*quantité, moment*) to approach; **s'approcher de** *vt* to approach, go *ou* come *ou* move near to; **approchez-vous** come *ou* go nearer

approfondi, e [apʀɔfɔ̃di] *adj* thorough, detailed

approfondir [apʀɔfɔ̃diʀ] *vt* to deepen; (*question*) to go further into; **sans ~** without going too deeply into it

appropriation [apʀɔpʀijɑsjɔ̃] *nf* appropriation

approprié, e [apʀɔpʀije] *adj*: **~ (à)** appropriate (to), suited (to)

approprier [apʀɔpʀije] *vt* (*adapter*) adapt; **s'approprier** *vt* to appropriate, take over

approuver [apʀuve] *vt* to agree with; (*autoriser: loi, projet*) to approve, pass; (*trouver louable*) to approve of; **je vous approuve entièrement/ne vous approuve pas** I agree with you entirely/don't agree with you; **lu et approuvé** (read and) approved

approvisionnement [apʀɔvizjɔnmɑ̃] *nm* supplying; (*provisions*) supply, stock

approvisionner [apʀɔvizjɔne] *vt* to supply; (*compte bancaire*) to pay funds into; **~ qn en** to supply sb with; **s'approvisionner** *vi*: **s'~ dans un certain magasin/au marché** to shop in a certain shop/at the market; **s'~ en** to stock up with

approximatif, -ive [apʀɔksimatif, -iv] *adj* approximate, rough; (*imprécis*) vague

approximation [apʀɔksimɑsjɔ̃] *nf* approximation

approximativement [apʀɔksimativmɑ̃] *adv* approximately, roughly; vaguely

appt *abr* = **appartement**

appui [apɥi] *nm* support; **prendre ~ sur** to lean on; (*objet*) to rest on; **point d'~** fulcrum; (*fig*) something to lean on; **à l'~ de** (*pour prouver*) in support of; **à l'~** *adv* to support one's argument; **l'~ de la fenêtre** the windowsill, the window ledge

appuie *etc* [apɥi] *vb voir* **appuyer**

appui-tête, appuie-tête [apɥitɛt] *nm inv* headrest

appuyé, e [apɥije] *adj* (*regard*) meaningful; (: *insistant*) intent, insistent; (*excessif: politesse, compliment*) exaggerated, overdone

appuyer [apɥije] *vt* (*poser*): **~ qch sur/contre/à** to lean *ou* rest sth on/against/on; (*soutenir: personne, demande*) to support, back (up) ▷ *vi*: **~ sur** (*bouton, frein*) to press, push; (*mot, détail*) to stress, emphasize; (*chose: peser sur*) to rest (heavily) on, press against; **s'appuyer sur** *vt* to lean on; (*compter sur*) to rely on; **s'~ sur qn** to lean on sb; **~ contre** (*toucher: mur, porte*) to lean *ou* rest against; **~ à droite** *ou* **sur sa droite** to bear (to the) right; **~ sur le champignon** to put one's foot down

apr. *abr* = **après**

âpre [ɑpʀ(ə)] *adj* acrid, pungent; (*fig*) harsh; (*lutte*) bitter; **~ au gain** grasping, greedy

après [apʀɛ] *prép* after ▷ *adv* afterwards; **deux heures ~** two hours later; **~ qu'il est parti/avoir fait** after he left/having done; **courir ~ qn** to run after sb; **crier ~ qn** to shout at sb; **être toujours ~ qn** (*critiquer etc*) to be always on at sb; **~ quoi** after which; **d'~** *prép* (*selon*) according to; **d'~ lui** according to him; **d'~ moi** in my opinion; **~ coup** *adv* after the event, afterwards; **~ tout** *adv* (*au fond*) after all; **et (puis) ~?** so what?

après-demain [apʀɛdmɛ̃] *adv* the day after tomorrow

après-guerre [apʀɛgɛʀ] *nm* post-war years *pl*; **d'~** *adj* post-war

après-midi [apʀɛmidi] *nm ou f inv* afternoon

après-rasage [apʀɛʀazaʒ] *nm inv*: **(lotion) ~** after-shave (lotion)

après-shampooing [apʀɛʃɑ̃pwɛ̃] *nm inv* conditioner

après-ski [apʀɛski] *nm inv* (*chaussure*) snow boot; (*moment*) après-ski

après-soleil [apʀɛsɔlɛj] *adj inv* after-sun *cpd* ▷ *nm* after-sun cream *ou* lotion

après-vente [apʀɛvɑ̃t] *adj inv* after-sales *cpd*

âpreté [ɑpʀəte] *nf* (*voir âpre*) pungency; harshness; bitterness

à-propos [apʀopo] *nm* (*d'une remarque*) aptness; **faire preuve d'~** to show presence of mind, do the right thing; **avec ~** suitably, aptly

apte [apt(ə)] *adj*: **~ à qch/faire qch** capable of sth/doing sth; **~ (au service)** (*Mil*) fit (for service)

aptitude [aptityd] *nf* ability, aptitude

apurer [apyʀe] *vt* (*Comm*) to clear

aquaculture [akwakyltyʀ] *nf* fish farming

aquaplanage [akwaplanaʒ] *nm* (*Auto*) aquaplaning

aquaplane [akwaplan] *nm* (*planche*) aquaplane; (*sport*) aquaplaning

aquaplaning [akwaplaniŋ] *nm* aquaplaning

aquarelle [akwaʀɛl] *nf* (*tableau*) watercolour (*Brit*), watercolor (*US*); (*genre*) watercolo(u)rs *pl*, aquarelle

aquarelliste [akwaʀelist(ə)] *nm/f* painter in watercolo(u)rs

aquarium [akwaʀjɔm] *nm* aquarium
aquatique [akwatik] *adj* aquatic, water *cpd*
aqueduc [akdyk] *nm* aqueduct
aqueux, -euse [akø, -øz] *adj* aqueous
aquilin [akilɛ̃] *adj m*: **nez ~** aquiline nose
AR *sigle m* = **accusé de réception; lettre/paquet
avec AR** = recorded delivery letter/parcel; (*Aviat,
Rail etc*) = **aller (et) retour** ▷ *abr* (*Auto*) = **arrière**
arabe [aʀab] *adj* Arabic; (*désert, cheval*) Arabian;
(*nation, peuple*) Arab ▷ *nm* (*Ling*) Arabic ▷ *nm/f*:
Arabe Arab
arabesque [aʀabɛsk(ə)] *nf* arabesque
Arabie [aʀabi] *nf*: **l'~** Arabia; **l'~ Saoudite** *ou*
Séoudite Saudi Arabia
arable [aʀabl(ə)] *adj* arable
arachide [aʀaʃid] *nf* groundnut (plant); (*graine*)
peanut, groundnut
araignée [aʀeɲe] *nf* spider; **~ de mer** spider
crab
araser [aʀɑze] *vt* to level; (*en rabotant*) to plane
(down)
aratoire [aʀatwaʀ] *adj*: **instrument ~**
ploughing implement
arbalète [aʀbalɛt] *nf* crossbow
arbitrage [aʀbitʀaʒ] *nm* refereeing; umpiring;
arbitration
arbitraire [aʀbitʀɛʀ] *adj* arbitrary
arbitre [aʀbitʀ(ə)] *nm* (*Sport*) referee; (: *Tennis,
Cricket*) umpire; (*fig*) arbiter, judge; (*Jur*)
arbitrator
arbitrer [aʀbitʀe] *vt* to referee; to umpire; to
arbitrate
arborer [aʀbɔʀe] *vt* to bear, display; (*avec
ostentation*) to sport
arborescence [aʀbɔʀesɑ̃s] *nf* tree structure
arboricole [aʀbɔʀikɔl] *adj* (*animal*) arboreal;
(*technique*) arboricultural
arboriculture [aʀbɔʀikyltyʀ] *nf* arboriculture;
~ fruitière fruit (tree) growing
arbre [aʀbʀ(ə)] *nm* tree; (*Tech*) shaft; **~ à cames**
(*Auto*) camshaft; **~ fruitier** fruit tree; **~
généalogique** family tree; **~ de Noël**
Christmas tree; **~ de transmission** (*Auto*)
driveshaft
arbrisseau, x [aʀbʀiso] *nm* shrub
arbuste [aʀbyst(ə)] *nm* small shrub, bush
arc [aʀk] *nm* (*arme*) bow; (*Géom*) arc; (*Archit*) arch;
~ de cercle arc of a circle; **en ~ de cercle** *adj*
semi-circular
arcade [aʀkad] *nf* arch(way); **~s** arcade *sg*,
arches; **~ sourcilière** arch of the eyebrows
arcanes [aʀkan] *nmpl* mysteries
arc-boutant [aʀkbutɑ̃] (*pl* **arcs-boutants**) *nm*
flying buttress
arc-bouter [aʀkbute]: **s'arc-bouter** *vi*: **s'~
contre** to lean *ou* press against
arceau, x [aʀso] *nm* (*métallique etc*) hoop
arc-en-ciel [aʀkɑ̃sjɛl] (*pl* **arcs-en-ciel**) *nm*
rainbow
archaïque [aʀkaik] *adj* archaic
archaïsme [aʀkaism(ə)] *nm* archaism
archange [aʀkɑ̃ʒ] *nm* archangel

arche [aʀʃ(ə)] *nf* arch; **~ de Noé** Noah's Ark
archéologie [aʀkeɔlɔʒi] *nf* arch(a)eology
archéologique [aʀkeɔlɔʒik] *adj*
arch(a)eological
archéologue [aʀkeɔlɔg] *nm/f* arch(a)eologist
archer [aʀʃe] *nm* archer
archet [aʀʃɛ] *nm* bow
archevêché [aʀʃəveʃe] *nm* archbishopric;
(*palais*) archbishop's palace
archevêque [aʀʃəvɛk] *nm* archbishop
archi... [aʀʃi] *préfixe* (*très*) dead, extra
archibondé, e [aʀʃibɔ̃de] *adj* chock-a-block
(*Brit*), packed solid
archiduc [aʀʃidyk] *nm* archduke
archiduchesse [aʀʃidyʃɛs] *nf* archduchess
archipel [aʀʃipɛl] *nm* archipelago
archisimple [aʀʃisɛ̃pl(ə)] *adj* dead easy *ou*
simple
architecte [aʀʃitɛkt(ə)] *nm* architect
architectural, e, -aux [aʀʃitɛktyʀal, -o] *adj*
architectural
architecture [aʀʃitɛktyʀ] *nf* architecture
archive [aʀʃiv] *nf* file; **archives** *nfpl* archives
archiver [aʀʃive] *vt* to file
archiviste [aʀʃivist(ə)] *nm/f* archivist
arçon [aʀsɔ̃] *nm voir* **cheval**
arctique [aʀktik] *adj* Arctic ▷ *nm*: **l'A~** the
Arctic; **le cercle A~** the Arctic Circle; **l'océan
A~** the Arctic Ocean
ardemment [aʀdamɑ̃] *adv* ardently, fervently
ardent, e [aʀdɑ̃, -ɑ̃t] *adj* (*soleil*) blazing; (*fièvre*)
raging; (*amour*) ardent, passionate; (*prière*)
fervent
ardeur [aʀdœʀ] *nf* blazing heat; (*fig*) fervour,
ardour
ardoise [aʀdwaz] *nf* slate
ardu, e [aʀdy] *adj* arduous, difficult; (*pente*)
steep, abrupt
are [aʀ] *nm* are, 100 square metres
arène [aʀɛn] *nf* arena; (*fig*): **l'~ politique** the
political arena; **arènes** *nfpl* bull-ring *sg*
arête [aʀɛt] *nf* (*de poisson*) bone; (*d'une montagne*)
ridge; (*Géom etc*) edge (*where two faces meet*)
arg. *abr* = **argus**
argent [aʀʒɑ̃] *nm* (*métal*) silver; (*monnaie*)
money; (*couleur*) silver; **en avoir pour son ~** to
get value for money; **gagner beaucoup d'~** to
earn a lot of money; **~ comptant** (hard) cash; **~
liquide** ready money, (ready) cash; **~ de poche**
pocket money
argenté, e [aʀʒɑ̃te] *adj* silver(y); (*métal*) silver-
plated
argenter [aʀʒɑ̃te] *vt* to silver(-plate)
argenterie [aʀʒɑ̃tʀi] *nf* silverware; (*en métal
argenté*) silver plate
argentin, e [aʀʒɑ̃tɛ̃, -in] *adj* Argentinian,
Argentine ▷ *nm/f*: **Argentin, e** Argentinian,
Argentine
Argentine [aʀʒɑ̃tin] *nf*: **l'~** Argentina, the
Argentine
argentique [aʀʒɑ̃tik] *adj* (*appareil-photo*) film *cpd*
argile [aʀʒil] *nf* clay

argileux, -euse [aʀʒilø, -øz] *adj* clayey
argot [aʀgo] *nm* slang; *see note*

● **ARGOT**
●
● *Argot* was the term originally used to
● describe the jargon of the criminal
● underworld, characterized by colourful
● images and distinctive intonation and
● designed to confuse the outsider. Some
● French authors write in *argot* and so have
● helped it spread and grow. More generally,
● the special vocabulary used by any social or
● professional group is also known as *argot*.

argotique [aʀgotik] *adj* slang *cpd*; *(très familier)* slangy
arguer [aʀgɥe]: **~ de** *vt* to put forward as a pretext *ou* reason; **~ que** to argue that
argument [aʀgymɑ̃] *nm* argument
argumentaire [aʀgymɑ̃tɛʀ] *nm* list of sales points; *(brochure)* sales leaflet
argumentation [aʀgymɑ̃tasjɔ̃] *nf (fait d'argumenter)* arguing; *(ensemble des arguments)* argument
argumenter [aʀgymɑ̃te] *vi* to argue
argus [aʀgys] *nm* guide to second-hand car etc prices
arguties [aʀgysi] *nfpl* pettifoggery *sg (Brit)*, quibbles
aride [aʀid] *adj* arid
aridité [aʀidite] *nf* aridity
arien, ne [aʀjɛ̃, -ɛn] *adj* Arian
aristocrate [aʀistokʀat] *nm/f* aristocrat
aristocratie [aʀistokʀasi] *nf* aristocracy
aristocratique [aʀistokʀatik] *adj* aristocratic
arithmétique [aʀitmetik] *adj* arithmetic(al)
▷ *nf* arithmetic
armada [aʀmada] *nf (fig)* army
armagnac [aʀmaɲak] *nm* armagnac
armateur [aʀmatœʀ] *nm* shipowner
armature [aʀmatyʀ] *nf* framework; *(de tente etc)* frame; *(de corset)* bone; *(de soutien-gorge)* wiring
arme [aʀm(ə)] *nf* weapon; *(section de l'armée)* arm; **armes** *nfpl* weapons, arms; *(blason)* (coat of) arms; **les ~s** *(profession)* soldiering *sg*; **à ~s égales** on equal terms; **en ~s** up in arms; **passer par les ~s** to execute (by firing squad); **prendre/présenter les ~s** to take up/present arms; **se battre à l'~ blanche** to fight with blades; **~ à feu** firearm; **~s de destruction massive** weapons of mass destruction
armé, e [aʀme] *adj* armed; **~ de** armed with
armée [aʀme] *nf* army; **~ de l'air** Air Force; **l'~ du Salut** the Salvation Army; **~ de terre** Army
armement [aʀməmɑ̃] *nm (matériel)* arms *pl*, weapons *pl*; *(: d'un pays)* arms *pl*, armament; *(action d'équiper: d'un navire)* fitting out; **~s nucléaires** nuclear armaments; **course aux ~s** arms race
Arménie [aʀmeni] *nf*: **l'~** Armenia
arménien, ne [aʀmenjɛ̃, -ɛn] *adj* Armenian
▷ *nm (Ling)* Armenian ▷ *nm/f*: **Arménien, ne** Armenian

armer [aʀme] *vt* to arm; *(arme à feu)* to cock; *(appareil-photo)* to wind on; **~ qch de** to fit sth with; *(renforcer)* to reinforce sth with; **~ qn de** to arm *ou* equip sb with; **s'armer de** to arm o.s. with
armistice [aʀmistis] *nm* armistice; **l'A~** ≈ Remembrance *(Brit) ou* Veterans *(US)* Day
armoire [aʀmwaʀ] *nf* (tall) cupboard; *(penderie)* wardrobe *(Brit)*, closet *(US)*; **~ à pharmacie** medicine chest
armoiries [aʀmwaʀi] *nfpl* coat of arms *sg*
armure [aʀmyʀ] *nf* armour *no pl*, suit of armour
armurerie [aʀmyʀʀi] *nf* arms factory; *(magasin)* gunsmith's (shop)
armurier [aʀmyʀje] *nm* gunsmith; *(Mil, d'armes blanches)* armourer
ARN *sigle m* (= *acide ribonucléique*) RNA
arnaque [aʀnak] *nf*: **de l'~** daylight robbery
arnaquer [aʀnake] *vt* to do *(fam)*, swindle; **se faire ~** to be had *(fam) ou* done
arnaqueur [aʀnakœʀ] *nm* swindler
arnica [aʀnika] *nm*: **(teinture d')~** arnica
arobase [aʀobaz] *nf (Inform)* "at" symbol, @; **"paul ~ société point fr"** "paul at société dot fr"
aromates [aʀomat] *nmpl* seasoning *sg*, herbs (and spices)
aromathérapie [aʀomateʀapi] *nf* aromatherapy
aromatique [aʀomatik] *adj* aromatic
aromatisé, e [aʀomatize] *adj* flavoured
arôme [aʀom] *nm* aroma; *(d'une fleur etc)* fragrance
arpège [aʀpɛʒ] *nm* arpeggio
arpentage [aʀpɑ̃taʒ] *nm* (land) surveying
arpenter [aʀpɑ̃te] *vt* to pace up and down
arpenteur [aʀpɑ̃tœʀ] *nm* land surveyor
arqué, e [aʀke] *adj* arched; *(jambes)* bow *cpd*, bandy
arr. *abr* = **arrondissement**
arrachage [aʀaʃaʒ] *nm*: **~ des mauvaises herbes** weeding
arraché [aʀaʃe] *nm (Sport)* snatch; **obtenir à l'~** *(fig)* to snatch
arrache-pied [aʀaʃpje]: **d'~** *adv* relentlessly
arracher [aʀaʃe] *vt* to pull out; *(page etc)* to tear off, tear out; *(déplanter: légume)* to lift; *(: herbe, souche)* to pull up; *(bras etc: par explosion)* to blow off; *(: par accident)* to tear off; **s'arracher** *vt* *(article très recherché)* to fight over; **~ qch à qn** to snatch sth from sb; *(fig)* to wring sth out of sb, wrest sth from sb; **~ qn à** *(solitude, rêverie)* to drag sb out of; *(famille etc)* to tear *ou* wrench sb away from; **se faire ~ une dent** to have a tooth out *ou* pulled *(US)*; **s'~ de** *(lieu)* to tear o.s. away from; *(habitude)* to force o.s. out of
arraisonner [aʀɛzone] *vt* to board and search
arrangeant, e [aʀɑ̃ʒɑ̃, -ɑ̃t] *adj* accommodating, obliging
arrangement [aʀɑ̃ʒmɑ̃] *nm* arrangement
arranger [aʀɑ̃ʒe] *vt* to arrange; *(réparer)* to fix, put right; *(régler)* to settle, sort out; *(convenir à)* to suit, be convenient for; **s'arranger** *vi (se mettre*

d'accord) to come to an agreement *ou* arrangement; (*s'améliorer: querelle, situation*) to be sorted out; (*se débrouiller*): **s'~ pour que ...** to arrange things so that ...; **je vais m'~** I'll manage; **ça va s'~** it'll sort itself out; **s'~ pour faire** to make sure that *ou* see to it that one can do

arrangeur [aʀɑ̃ʒœʀ] *nm* (*Mus*) arranger

arrestation [aʀɛstasjɔ̃] *nf* arrest

arrêt [aʀɛ] *nm* stopping; (*de bus etc*) stop; (*Jur*) judgment, decision; (*Football*) save; **arrêts** *nmpl* (*Mil*) arrest *sg*; **être à l'~** to be stopped, have come to a halt; **rester** *ou* **tomber en ~ devant** to stop short in front of; **sans ~** without stopping, non-stop; (*fréquemment*) continually; **~ d'autobus** bus stop; **~ facultatif** request stop; **~ de mort** capital sentence; **~ de travail** stoppage (of work)

arrêté, e [aʀete] *adj* (*idées*) firm, fixed ▷ *nm* order, decree; **~ municipal** ≈ bylaw, byelaw

arrêter [aʀete] *vt* to stop; (*chauffage etc*) to turn off, switch off; (*Comm: compte*) to settle; (*Couture: point*) to fasten off; (*fixer: date etc*) to appoint, decide on; (*criminel, suspect*) to arrest; **s'arrêter** *vi* to stop; (*s'interrompre*) to stop o.s.; **~ de faire** to stop doing; **arrête de te plaindre** stop complaining; **ne pas ~ de faire** to keep on doing; **s'~ de faire** to stop doing; **s'~ sur** (*choix, regard*) to fall on

arrhes [aʀ] *nfpl* deposit *sg*

arrière [aʀjɛʀ] *nm* back; (*Sport*) fullback ▷ *adj inv*: **siège/roue ~** back *ou* rear seat/wheel; **arrières** *nmpl* (*fig*) **protéger ses ~s** to protect the rear; **à l'~** *adv* behind, at the back; **en ~** *adv* behind; (*regarder*) back, behind; (*tomber, aller*) backwards; **en ~ de** *prép* behind

arriéré, e [aʀjeʀe] *adj* (*péj*) backward ▷ *nm* (*d'argent*) arrears *pl*

arrière-boutique [aʀjɛʀbutik] *nf* back shop

arrière-cour [aʀjɛʀkuʀ] *nf* backyard

arrière-cuisine [aʀjɛʀkɥizin] *nf* scullery

arrière-garde [aʀjɛʀɡaʀd(ə)] *nf* rearguard

arrière-goût [aʀjɛʀɡu] *nm* aftertaste

arrière-grand-mère [aʀjɛʀɡʀɑ̃mɛʀ] (*pl* **-s**) *nf* great-grandmother

arrière-grand-père [aʀjɛʀɡʀɑ̃pɛʀ] (*pl* **arrière-grands-pères**) *nm* great-grandfather

arrière-grands-parents [aʀjɛʀɡʀɑ̃paʀɑ̃] *nmpl* great-grandparents

arrière-pays [aʀjɛʀpei] *nm inv* hinterland

arrière-pensée [aʀjɛʀpɑ̃se] *nf* ulterior motive; (*doute*) mental reservation

arrière-petite-fille [aʀjɛʀpətitfij] (*pl* **arrière-petites-filles**) *nf* great-granddaughter

arrière-petit-fils [aʀjɛʀpətifis] (*pl* **arrière-petits-fils**) *nm* great-grandson

arrière-petits-enfants [aʀjɛʀpətizɑ̃fɑ̃] *nmpl* great-grandchildren

arrière-plan [aʀjɛʀplɑ̃] *nm* background; **d'~** *adj* (*Inform*) background *cpd*

arriérer [aʀjeʀe]: **s'arriérer** *vi* (*Comm*) to fall into arrears

arrière-saison [aʀjɛʀsezɔ̃] *nf* late autumn

arrière-salle [aʀjɛʀsal] *nf* back room

arrière-train [aʀjɛʀtʀɛ̃] *nm* hindquarters *pl*

arrimer [aʀime] *vt* to stow; (*fixer*) to secure, fasten securely

arrivage [aʀivaʒ] *nm* arrival

arrivant, e [aʀivɑ̃, -ɑ̃t] *nm/f* newcomer

arrivée [aʀive] *nf* arrival; (*ligne d'arrivée*) finish; **~ d'air/de gaz** air/gas inlet; **courrier à l'~** incoming mail; **à mon ~** when I arrived

arriver [aʀive] *vi* to arrive; (*survenir*) to happen, occur; **j'arrive!** (I'm) just coming!; **il arrive à Paris à 8 h** he gets to *ou* arrives in Paris at 8; **~ à destination** to arrive at one's destination; **~ à** (*atteindre*) to reach; **~ à (faire) qch** (*réussir*) to manage (to do) sth; **~ à échéance** to fall due; **en ~ à faire ...** to end up doing ..., get to the point of doing ...; **il arrive que ...** it happens that ...; **il lui arrive de faire ...** he sometimes does ...

arrivisme [aʀivism(ə)] *nm* ambition, ambitiousness

arriviste [aʀivist(ə)] *nm/f* go-getter

arrogance [aʀɔɡɑ̃s] *nf* arrogance

arrogant, e [aʀɔɡɑ̃, -ɑ̃t] *adj* arrogant

arroger [aʀɔʒe]: **s'arroger** *vt* to assume (without right); **s'~ le droit de ...** to assume the right to ...

arrondi, e [aʀɔ̃di] *adj* round ▷ *nm* roundness

arrondir [aʀɔ̃diʀ] *vt* (*forme, objet*) to round; (*somme*) to round off; **s'arrondir** *vi* to become round(ed); **~ ses fins de mois** to supplement one's pay

arrondissement [aʀɔ̃dismɑ̃] *nm* (*Admin*) ≈ district

arrosage [aʀozaʒ] *nm* watering; **tuyau d'~** hose(pipe)

arroser [aʀoze] *vt* to water; (*victoire etc*) to celebrate (over a drink); (*Culin*) to baste

arroseur [aʀozœʀ] *nm* (*tourniquet*) sprinkler

arroseuse [aʀozøz] *nf* water cart

arrosoir [aʀozwaʀ] *nm* watering can

arrt *abr* = **arrondissement**

arsenal, -aux [aʀsənal, -o] *nm* (*Navig*) naval dockyard; (*Mil*) arsenal; (*fig*) gear, paraphernalia

art [aʀ] *nm* art; **avoir l'~ de faire** (*fig: personne*) to have a talent for doing; **les ~s** the arts; **livre/ critique d'~** art book/ critic; **objet d'~** objet d'art; **~ dramatique** dramatic art; **~s martiaux** martial arts; **~s et métiers** applied arts and crafts; **~s ménagers** home economics *sg*; **~s plastiques** plastic arts

art. *abr* = **article**

artère [aʀtɛʀ] *nf* (*Anat*) artery; (*rue*) main road

artériel, le [aʀteʀjɛl] *adj* arterial

artériosclérose [aʀteʀjɔskleʀoz] *nf* arteriosclerosis

arthrite [aʀtʀit] *nf* arthritis

arthrose [aʀtʀoz] *nf* (degenerative) osteoarthritis

artichaut [aʀtiʃo] *nm* artichoke

article [aʀtikl(ə)] *nm* article; (*Comm*) item, article; **faire l'~** (*Comm*) to do one's sales spiel; **faire l'~ de** (*fig*) to sing the praises of; **à l'~ de la mort** at the point of death; **~ défini/indéfini** definite/indefinite article; **~ de fond** (*Presse*) feature article; **~s de bureau** office equipment; **~s de voyage** travel goods *ou* items

articulaire [aʀtikylɛʀ] *adj* of the joints, articular

articulation [aʀtikylɑsjɔ̃] *nf* articulation; (*Anat*) joint

articulé, e [aʀtikyle] *adj* (*membre*) jointed; (*poupée*) with moving joints

articuler [aʀtikyle] *vt* to articulate; **s'articuler (sur)** *vi* (*Anat, Tech*) to articulate (with); **s'~ autour de** (*fig*) to centre around *ou* on, turn on

artifice [aʀtifis] *nm* device, trick

artificiel, le [aʀtifisjɛl] *adj* artificial

artificiellement [aʀtifisjɛlmɑ̃] *adv* artificially

artificier [aʀtifisje] *nm* pyrotechnist

artificieux, -euse [aʀtifisjø, -øz] *adj* guileful, deceitful

artillerie [aʀtijʀi] *nf* artillery, ordnance

artilleur [aʀtijœʀ] *nm* artilleryman, gunner

artisan [aʀtizɑ̃] *nm* artisan, (self-employed) craftsman; **l'~ de la victoire/du malheur** the architect of victory/of the disaster

artisanal, e, -aux [aʀtizanal, -o] *adj* of *ou* made by craftsmen; (*péj*) cottage industry *cpd*, unsophisticated

artisanalement [aʀtizanalmɑ̃] *adv* by craftsmen

artisanat [aʀtizana] *nm* arts and crafts *pl*

artiste [aʀtist(ə)] *nm/f* artist; (*Théât, Mus*) artist, performer; (: *de variétés*) entertainer

artistique [aʀtistik] *adj* artistic

artistiquement [aʀtistikmɑ̃] *adv* artistically

aryen, ne [aʀjɛ̃, -ɛn] *adj* Aryan

AS *sigle fpl* (*Admin*) = **assurances sociales** ▷ *sigle f* (*Sport*: = *Association sportive*) ≈ FC (= Football Club)

as *vb* [a] *voir* **avoir** ▷ *nm* [ɑs] ace

a/s *abr* (= *aux soins de*) c/o

ASBL *sigle f* (= *association sans but lucratif*) non-profit-making organization

asc. *abr* = **ascenseur**

ascendance [asɑ̃dɑ̃s] *nf* (*origine*) ancestry; (*Astrologie*) ascendant

ascendant, e [asɑ̃dɑ̃, -ɑ̃t] *adj* upward ▷ *nm* influence; **ascendants** *nmpl* ascendants

ascenseur [asɑ̃sœʀ] *nm* lift (*Brit*), elevator (*US*)

ascension [asɑ̃sjɔ̃] *nf* ascent; climb; **l'A~** (*Rel*) the Ascension; (: *jour férié*) Ascension (Day); *see note*; **(île de) l'A~** Ascension Island

● **L'ASCENSION**
●
● The *fête de l'Ascension* is a public holiday in
● France. It always falls on a Thursday, usually
● in May. Many French people take the
● following Friday off work and enjoy a
● long weekend.

ascète [asɛt] *nm/f* ascetic

ascétique [asetik] *adj* ascetic

ascétisme [asetism(ə)] *nm* asceticism

ascorbique [askɔʀbik] *adj*: **acide ~** ascorbic acid

ASE *sigle f* (= *Agence spatiale européenne*) ESA (= *European Space Agency*)

asepsie [asɛpsi] *nf* asepsis

aseptique [asɛptik] *adj* aseptic

aseptisé, e [asɛptize] (*péj*) *adj* sanitized

asexué, e [asɛksɥe] *adj* asexual

asiatique [azjatik] *adj* Asian, Asiatic ▷ *nm/f*: **Asiatique** Asian

Asie [azi] *nf*: **l'~** Asia

asile [azil] *nm* (*refuge*) refuge, sanctuary; (*Pol*): **droit d'~** (political) asylum; (*pour malades, vieillards etc*) home; **accorder l'~ politique à qn** to grant *ou* give sb political asylum; **chercher/trouver ~ quelque part** to seek/find refuge somewhere

asocial, e, -aux [asɔsjal, -o] *adj* antisocial

aspect [aspɛ] *nm* appearance, look; (*fig*) aspect, side; (*Ling*) aspect; **à l'~ de** at the sight of

asperge [aspɛʀʒ(ə)] *nf* asparagus *no pl*

asperger [aspɛʀʒe] *vt* to spray, sprinkle

aspérité [asperite] *nf* excrescence, protruding bit (of rock *etc*)

aspersion [aspɛʀsjɔ̃] *nf* spraying, sprinkling

asphalte [asfalt(ə)] *nm* asphalt

asphyxiant, e [asfiksjɑ̃, -ɑ̃t] *adj* suffocating; **gaz ~** poison gas

asphyxie [asfiksi] *nf* suffocation, asphyxia, asphyxiation

asphyxier [asfiksje] *vt* to suffocate, asphyxiate; (*fig*) to stifle; **mourir asphyxié** to die of suffocation *ou* asphyxiation

aspic [aspik] *nm* (*Zool*) asp; (*Culin*) aspic

aspirant, e [aspirɑ̃, -ɑ̃t] *adj*: **pompe ~e** suction pump ▷ *nm* (*Navig*) midshipman

aspirateur [aspiʀatœʀ] *nm* vacuum cleaner, hoover®

aspiration [aspiʀɑsjɔ̃] *nf* inhalation, sucking (up); drawing up; **aspirations** *nfpl* (*ambitions*) aspirations

aspirer [aspiʀe] *vt* (*air*) to inhale; (*liquide*) to suck (up); (*appareil*) to suck *ou* draw up; **~ à** *vt* to aspire to

aspirine [aspiʀin] *nf* aspirin

assagir [asaʒiʀ] *vt*, **s'assagir** *vi* to quieten down, sober down

assaillant, e [asajɑ̃, -ɑ̃t] *nm/f* assailant, attacker

assaillir [asajiʀ] *vt* to assail, attack; **~ qn de** (*questions*) to assail *ou* bombard sb with

assainir [aseniʀ] *vt* to clean up; (*eau, air*) to purify

assainissement [asenismɑ̃] *nm* cleaning up; purifying

assaisonnement [asɛzɔnmɑ̃] *nm* seasoning

assaisonner [asɛzɔne] *vt* to season; **bien assaisonné** highly seasoned

assassin [asasɛ̃] *nm* murderer; assassin

assassinat [asasina] *nm* murder; assassination

assassiner [asasine] *vt* to murder; (*surtout Pol*) to assassinate

assaut [aso] *nm* assault, attack; **prendre d'**~ to (take by) storm, assault; **donner l'**~ **(à)** to attack; **faire** ~ **de** (*rivaliser*) to vie with *ou* rival each other in

assèchement [aseʃmã] *nm* draining, drainage

assécher [aseʃe] *vt* to drain

ASSEDIC [asedik] *sigle f* (= *Association pour l'emploi dans l'industrie et le commerce*) unemployment insurance scheme

assemblage [asãblaʒ] *nm* assembling; (*Menuiserie*) joint; **un** ~ **de** (*fig*) a collection of; **langage d'**~ (*Inform*) assembly language

assemblée [asãble] *nf* (*réunion*) meeting; (*public, assistance*) gathering; assembled people; (*Pol*) assembly; (*Rel*): **l'**~ **des fidèles** the congregation; **l'A**~ **nationale (AN)** the (French) National Assembly; *see note*

● **ASSEMBLÉE NATIONALE**

The *Assemblée nationale* is the lower house of the French Parliament, the upper house being the "Sénat". It is housed in the Palais Bourbon in Paris. Its members, or "députés" are elected every five years.

assembler [asãble] *vt* (*joindre, monter*) to assemble, put together; (*amasser*) to gather (together), collect (together); **s'assembler** *vi* to gather, collect

assembleur [asãblœʀ] *nm* assembler, fitter; (*Inform*) assembler

assener, asséner [asene] *vt*: ~ **un coup à qn** to deal sb a blow

assentiment [asãtimã] *nm* assent, consent; (*approbation*) approval

asseoir [aswaʀ] *vt* (*malade, bébé*) to sit up; (*personne debout*) to sit down; (*autorité, réputation*) to establish; **s'asseoir** *vi* to sit (o.s.) up; to sit (o.s.) down; **faire** ~ **qn** to ask sb to sit down; **asseyez-vous!, assieds-toi!** sit down!; ~ **qch sur** to build sth on; (*appuyer*) to base sth on

assermenté, e [asɛʀmãte] *adj* sworn, on oath

assertion [asɛʀsjõ] *nf* assertion

asservir [asɛʀviʀ] *vt* to subjugate, enslave

asservissement [asɛʀvismã] *nm* (*action*) enslavement; (*état*) slavery

assesseur [asesœʀ] *nm* (*Jur*) assessor

asseyais *etc* [asejɛ] *vb voir* **asseoir**

assez [ase] *adv* (*suffisamment*) enough, sufficiently; (*passablement*) rather, quite, fairly; ~! enough!, that'll do!; ~/**pas** ~ **cuit** well enough done/underdone; **est-il** ~ **fort/rapide?** is he strong/fast enough?; **il est passé** ~ **vite** he went past rather *ou* quite *ou* fairly fast; ~ **de pain/livres** enough *ou* sufficient bread/books; **vous en avez** ~? have you got enough?; **en avoir** ~ **de qch** (*en être fatigué*) to have had enough of sth; **travailler** ~ to work (hard) enough

assidu, e [asidy] *adj* assiduous, painstaking; (*régulier*) regular; ~ **auprès de qn** attentive

towards sb

assiduité [asidɥite] *nf* assiduousness, painstaking regularity; attentiveness; **assiduités** *nfpl* assiduous attentions

assidûment [asidymã] *adv* assiduously, painstakingly; attentively

assied *etc* [asje] *vb voir* **asseoir**

assiégé, e [asjeʒe] *adj* under siege, besieged

assiéger [asjeʒe] *vt* to besiege, lay siege to; (*foule, touristes*) to mob, besiege

assiérai *etc* [asjeʀe] *vb voir* **asseoir**

assiette [asjɛt] *nf* plate; (*contenu*) plate(ful); (*équilibre*) seat; (*de colonne*) seating; (*de navire*) trim; ~ **anglaise** assorted cold meats; ~ **creuse** (soup) dish, soup plate; ~ **à dessert** dessert *ou* side plate; ~ **de l'impôt** basis of (tax) assessment; ~ **plate** (dinner) plate

assiettée [asjete] *nf* plateful

assignation [asiɲasjõ] *nf* assignation; (*Jur*) summons; (: *de témoin*) subpoena; ~ **à résidence** compulsory order of residence

assigner [asiɲe] *vt*: ~ **qch à** to assign *ou* allot sth to; (*valeur, importance*) to attach sth to; (*somme*) to allocate sth to; (*limites*) to set *ou* fix sth to; (*cause, effet*) to ascribe *ou* attribute sth to; ~ **qn à** (*affecter*) to assign sb to; ~ **qn à résidence** (*Jur*) to give sb a compulsory order of residence

assimilable [asimilabl(ə)] *adj* easily assimilated *ou* absorbed

assimilation [asimilasjõ] *nf* assimilation, absorption

assimiler [asimile] *vt* to assimilate, absorb; (*comparer*): ~ **qch/qn à** to liken *ou* compare sth/sb to; **s'assimiler** *vi* (*s'intégrer*) to be assimilated *ou* absorbed; **ils sont assimilés aux infirmières** (*Admin*) they are classed as nurses

assis, e [asi, -iz] *pp de* **asseoir** ▷ *adj* sitting (down), seated ▷ *nf* (*Constr*) course; (*Géo*) stratum (*pl* -a); (*fig*) basis (*pl* bases), foundation; ~ **en tailleur** sitting cross-legged

assises [asiz] *nfpl* (*Jur*) assizes; (*congrès*) (annual) conference

assistanat [asistana] *nm* assistantship; (*à l'université*) probationary lectureship

assistance [asistãs] *nf* (*public*) audience; (*aide*) assistance; **porter** *ou* **prêter** ~ **à qn** to give sb assistance; **A**~ **publique (AP)** *public health service*; **enfant de l'A**~ **(publique)** child in care; ~ **technique** technical aid

assistant, e [asistã, -ãt] *nm/f* assistant; (*d'université*) probationary lecturer; **les assistants** *nmpl* (*auditeurs etc*) those present; ~**e sociale** social worker

assisté, e [asiste] *adj* (*Auto*) power assisted ▷ *nm/f* person receiving aid from the State

assister [asiste] *vt* to assist; ~ **à** *vt* (*scène, événement*) to witness; (*conférence*) to attend, be (present) at; (*spectacle, match*) to be at, see

association [asɔsjasjõ] *nf* association; (*Comm*) partnership; ~ **d'idées/images** association of ideas/images

associé, e [asɔsje] *nm/f* associate; (*Comm*)

partner

associer [asɔsje] vt to associate; ~ qn à (profits) to give sb a share of; (affaire) to make sb a partner in; (joie, triomphe) to include sb in; ~ **qch à** (joindre, allier) to combine sth with; **s'associer** vi to join together; (Comm) to form a partnership ▷ vt (collaborateur) to take on (as a partner); **s'~ à** to be combined with; (opinions, joie de qn) to share in; **s'~ à** ou **avec qn pour faire** to join (forces) ou join together with sb to do

assoie etc [aswa] vb voir **asseoir**

assoiffé, e [aswafe] adj thirsty; (fig): ~ **de** (sang) thirsting for; (gloire) thirsting after

assoirai [aswaʀe], **assois** etc [aswa] vb voir **asseoir**

assolement [asɔlmã] nm (systematic) rotation of crops

assombrir [asɔ̃bʀiʀ] vt to darken; (fig) to fill with gloom; **s'assombrir** vi to darken; (devenir nuageux, fig: visage) to cloud over; (fig) to become gloomy

assommer [asɔme] vt (étourdir, abrutir) to knock out, stun; (fam: ennuyer) to bore stiff

Assomption [asɔ̃psjɔ̃] nf: **l'~** the Assumption; see note

assorti, e [asɔʀti] adj matched, matching; **fromages/légumes ~s** assorted cheeses/vegetables; ~ **à** matching; ~ **de** accompanied with; (conditions, conseils) coupled with; **bien/mal ~** well/ill-matched

assortiment [asɔʀtimã] nm (choix) assortment, selection; (harmonie de couleurs, formes) arrangement; (Comm: lot, stock) selection

assortir [asɔʀtiʀ] vt to match; **s'assortir** vi to go well together, match; ~ **qch à** to match sth with; ~ **qch de** to accompany sth with; **s'~ de** to be accompanied by

assoupi, e [asupi] adj dozing, sleeping; (fig) (be)numbed; (sens) dulled

assoupir [asupiʀ]: **s'assoupir** vi (personne) to doze off; (sens) to go numb

assoupissement [asupismã] nm (sommeil) dozing; (fig: somnolence) drowsiness

assouplir [asupliʀ] vt to make supple, soften; (membres, corps) to limber up, make supple; (fig) to relax; (: caractère) to soften, make more flexible; **s'assouplir** vi to soften; to limber up; to relax; to become more flexible

assouplissant [asuplisã] nm (fabric) softener

assouplissement [asuplismã] nm softening; limbering up; relaxation; **exercices d'~** limbering up exercises

assourdir [asuʀdiʀ] vt (bruit) to deaden, muffle; (bruit) to deafen

assourdissant, e [asuʀdisã, -ãt] adj (bruit) deafening

assouvir [asuviʀ] vt to satisfy, appease

assoyais etc [aswajɛ] vb voir **asseoir**

assujetti, e [asyʒeti] adj: ~ (**à**) subject (to); (Admin): ~ **à l'impôt** subject to tax(ation)

assujettir [asyʒetiʀ] vt to subject, subjugate; (fixer: planches, tableau) to fix securely; ~ **qn à** (règle, impôt) to subject sb to

assujettissement [asyʒetismã] nm subjection, subjugation

assumer [asyme] vt (fonction, emploi) to assume, take on; (accepter: conséquence, situation) to accept

assurance [asyʀãs] nf (certitude) assurance; (confiance en soi) (self-)confidence; (contrat) insurance (policy); (secteur commercial) insurance; **prendre une ~ contre** to take out insurance ou an insurance policy against; ~ **contre l'incendie** fire insurance; ~ **contre le vol** insurance against theft; **société d'~**, **compagnie d'~s** insurance company; ~ **maladie (AM)** health insurance; ~ **au tiers** third party insurance; ~ **tous risques** (Auto) comprehensive insurance; ~**s sociales (AS)** ≈ National Insurance (Brit), ≈ Social Security (US)

assurance-vie [asyʀãsvi] (pl **assurances-vie**) nf life assurance ou insurance

assurance-vol [asyʀãsvɔl] (pl **assurances-vol**) nf insurance against theft

assuré, e [asyʀe] adj (victoire etc) certain, sure; (démarche, voix) assured, (self-)confident; (certain): ~ **de** confident of; (Assurances) insured ▷ nm/f insured (person); ~ **social** ≈ member of the National Insurance (Brit) ou Social Security (US) scheme

assurément [asyʀemã] adv assuredly, most certainly

assurer [asyʀe] vt (Comm) to insure; (stabiliser) to steady, stabilize; (victoire etc) to ensure, make certain; (frontières, pouvoir) to make secure; (service, garde) to provide, operate; ~ **qch à qn** (garantir) to secure ou guarantee sth for sb; (certifier) to assure sb of sth; ~ **à qn que** to assure sb that; **je vous assure que non/si** I assure you that that is not the case/is the case; ~ **qn de** to assure sb of; ~ **ses arrières** (fig) to be sure one has something to fall back on; **s'assurer (contre)** vi (Comm) to insure o.s. (against); **s'~ de/que** (vérifier) to make sure of/that; **s'~ (de)** (aide de qn) to secure; **s'~ sur la vie** to take out life insurance; **s'~ le concours/la collaboration de qn** to secure sb's aid/collaboration

assureur [asyʀœʀ] nm insurance agent; (société) insurers pl

Assyrie [asiʀi] nf: **l'~** Assyria

astérisque [asteʀisk(ə)] nm asterisk

astéroïde [asteʀɔid] nm asteroid

asthmatique [asmatik] adj asthmatic

asthme [asm(ə)] nm asthma

asticot [astiko] *nm* maggot
asticoter [astikɔte] *vt (fam)* to needle, get at
astigmate [astigmat] *adj (Méd: personne)*
astigmatic, having an astigmatism
astiquer [astike] *vt* to polish, shine
astrakan [astʀakɑ̃] *nm* astrakhan
astral, e, -aux [astʀal, -o] *adj* astral
astre [astʀ(ə)] *nm* star
astreignant, e [astʀɛɲɑ̃, -ɑ̃t] *adj* demanding
astreindre [astʀɛ̃dʀ(ə)] *vt*: ~ **qn à qch** to force
sth upon sb; ~ **qn à faire** to compel *ou* force sb
to do; **s'astreindre à** to compel *ou* force o.s. to
astringent, e [astʀɛ̃ʒɑ̃, -ɑ̃t] *adj* astringent
astrologie [astʀɔlɔʒi] *nf* astrology
astrologique [astʀɔlɔʒik] *adj* astrological
astrologue [astʀɔlɔg] *nm/f* astrologer
astronaute [astʀɔnot] *nm/f* astronaut
astronautique [astʀɔnotik] *nf* astronautics *sg*
astronome [astʀɔnɔm] *nm/f* astronomer
astronomie [astʀɔnɔmi] *nf* astronomy
astronomique [astʀɔnɔmik] *adj* astronomic(al)
astrophysicien, ne [astʀɔfizisjɛ̃, -ɛn] *nm/f*
astrophysicist
astrophysique [astʀɔfizik] *nf* astrophysics *sg*
astuce [astys] *nf* shrewdness, astuteness; *(truc)*
trick, clever way; *(plaisanterie)* wisecrack
astucieusement [astysjøzmɑ̃] *adv* shrewdly,
cleverly, astutely
astucieux, -euse [astysjø, -øz] *adj* shrewd,
clever, astute
asymétrique [asimetʀik] *adj* asymmetric(al)
AT *sigle m (= Ancien Testament)* OT
atavisme [atavism(ə)] *nm* atavism, heredity
atelier [atəlje] *nm* workshop; *(de peintre)* studio
atermoiements [atɛʀmwamɑ̃] *nmpl*
procrastination *sg*
atermoyer [atɛʀmwaje] *vi* to temporize,
procrastinate
athée [ate] *adj* atheistic ▷ *nm/f* atheist
athéisme [ateism(ə)] *nm* atheism
Athènes [atɛn] *n* Athens
athénien, ne [atenjɛ̃, -ɛn] *adj* Athenian
athlète [atlɛt] *nm/f (Sport)* athlete; *(costaud)*
muscleman
athlétique [atletik] *adj* athletic
athlétisme [atletism(ə)] *nm* athletics *sg*; **faire
de l'**~ to do athletics; **tournoi d'**~ athletics
meeting
Atlantide [atlɑ̃tid] *nf*: **l'**~ Atlantis
atlantique [atlɑ̃tik] *adj* Atlantic ▷ *nm*: **l'(océan)
A**~ the Atlantic (Ocean)
atlantiste [atlɑ̃tist(ə)] *adj, nm/f* Atlanticist
Atlas [atlɑs] *nm*: **l'**~ the Atlas Mountains
atlas [atlɑs] *nm* atlas
atmosphère [atmɔsfɛʀ] *nf* atmosphere
atmosphérique [atmɔsfeʀik] *adj* atmospheric
atoll [atɔl] *nm* atoll
atome [atom] *nm* atom
atomique [atɔmik] *adj* atomic, nuclear; *(usine)*
nuclear; *(nombre, masse)* atomic
atomiseur [atɔmizœʀ] *nm* atomizer
atomiste [atɔmist(ə)] *nm/f (aussi:* **savant,**

ingénieur *etc* **atomiste)** atomic scientist
atone [atɔn] *adj* lifeless; *(Ling)* unstressed,
unaccented
atours [atuʀ] *nmpl* attire *sg*, finery *sg*
atout [atu] *nm* trump; *(fig)* asset; (: *plus fort)*
trump card; **"~ pique/trèfle"** "spades/clubs
are trumps"
ATP *sigle f (= Association des tennismen professionnels)*
ATP (= *Association of Tennis Professionals*) ▷ *sigle mpl*
= **arts et traditions populaires**; **musée des** ~
≈ folk museum
âtre [ɑtʀ(ə)] *nm* hearth
atroce [atʀɔs] *adj* atrocious, horrible
atrocement [atʀɔsmɑ̃] *adv* atrociously, horribly
atrocité [atʀɔsite] *nf* atrocity
atrophie [atʀɔfi] *nf* atrophy
atrophier [atʀɔfje]: **s'atrophier** *vi* to atrophy
attabler [atable]: **s'attabler** *vi* to sit down at
(the) table; **s'~ à la terrasse** to sit down (at a
table) on the terrace
ATTAC *sigle f (= Association pour la Taxation des
Transactions pour l'Aide aux Citoyens)* ATTAC,
*organization critical of globalization originally set up to
demand a tax on foreign currency speculation*
attachant, e [ataʃɑ̃, -ɑ̃t] *adj* engaging, likeable
attache [ataʃ] *nf* clip, fastener; *(fig)* tie;
attaches *nfpl (relations)* connections; **à l'**~ *(chien)*
tied up
attaché, e [ataʃe] *adj*: **être** ~ **à** *(aimer)* to be
attached to ▷ *nm (Admin)* attaché; ~ **de presse/
d'ambassade** press/embassy attaché; ~
commercial commercial attaché
attaché-case [ataʃekɛz] *nm inv* attaché case
(Brit), briefcase
attachement [ataʃmɑ̃] *nm* attachment
attacher [ataʃe] *vt* to tie up; *(étiquette)* to attach,
tie on; *(souliers)* to do up ▷ *vi (poêle, riz)* to stick;
s'attacher *vi (robe etc)* to do up; **s'~ à** *(par
affection)* to become attached to; **s'~ à faire qch**
to endeavour to do sth; ~ **qch à** to tie *ou* fasten
ou attach sth to; ~ **qn à** *(fig: lier)* to attach sb to; ~
du prix/de l'importance à to attach great
value/attach importance to
attaquant [atakɑ̃] *nm (Mil)* attacker; *(Sport)*
striker, forward
attaque [atak] *nf* attack; *(cérébrale)* stroke;
(d'épilepsie) fit; **être/se sentir d'**~ to be/feel on
form; ~ **à main armée** armed attack
attaquer [atake] *vt* to attack; *(en justice)* to bring
an action against, sue; *(travail)* to tackle, set
about ▷ *vi* to attack; **s'attaquer à** *vt* to attack;
(épidémie, misère) to tackle, attack
attardé, e [ataʀde] *adj (passants)* late; *(enfant)*
backward; *(conceptions)* old-fashioned
attarder [ataʀde]: **s'attarder** *vi (sur qch, en
chemin)* to linger; *(chez qn)* to stay on
atteignais *etc* [atɛɲɛ] *vb voir* **atteindre**
atteindre [atɛ̃dʀ(ə)] *vt* to reach; *(blesser)* to hit;
(contacter) to reach, contact, get in touch with;
(émouvoir) to affect
atteint, e [atɛ̃, -ɛ̃t] *pp de* **atteindre** ▷ *adj (Méd)*:
être ~ **de** to be suffering from ▷ *nf* attack; **hors**

d'~e out of reach; **porter ~e à** to strike a blow at, undermine

attelage [atlaʒ] nm (de remorque etc) coupling (Brit), (trailer) hitch (US); (animaux) team; (harnachement) harness; (: de bœufs) yoke

atteler [atle] vt (cheval, bœufs) to hitch up; (wagons) to couple; **s'atteler à** (travail) to buckle down to

attelle [atɛl] nf splint

attenant, e [atnɑ̃, -ɑ̃t] adj: **~ (à)** adjoining

attendant [atɑ̃dɑ̃]: **en ~** adv (dans l'intervalle) meanwhile, in the meantime

attendre [atɑ̃dʀ(ə)] vt to wait for; (être destiné ou réservé à) to await, be in store for ▷ vi to wait; **je n'attends plus rien (de la vie)** I expect nothing more (from life); **attendez que je réfléchisse** wait while I think; **s'~ à (ce que)** (escompter) to expect (that); **je ne m'y attendais pas** I didn't expect that; **ce n'est pas ce à quoi je m'attendais** that's not what I expected; **~ un enfant** to be expecting a baby; **~ de pied ferme** to wait determinedly; **~ de faire/d'être** to wait until one does/is; **~ que** to wait until; **~ qch de** to expect sth of; **faire ~ qn** to keep sb waiting; **se faire ~** to keep people (ou us etc) waiting; **en attendant** adv voir **attendant**

attendri, e [atɑ̃dʀi] adj tender

attendrir [atɑ̃dʀiʀ] vt to move (to pity); (viande) to tenderize; **s'attendrir (sur)** to be moved ou touched (by)

attendrissant, e [atɑ̃dʀisɑ̃, -ɑ̃t] adj moving, touching

attendrissement [atɑ̃dʀismɑ̃] nm (tendre) emotion; (apitoyé) pity

attendrisseur [atɑ̃dʀisœʀ] nm tenderizer

attendu, e [atɑ̃dy] pp de **attendre** ▷ adj long-awaited; (prévu) expected ▷ nm: **~s** reasons adduced for a judgment; **~ que** conj considering that, since

attentat [atɑ̃ta] nm (contre une personne) assassination attempt; (contre un bâtiment) attack; **~ à la bombe** bomb attack; **~ à la pudeur** (exhibitionnisme) indecent exposure no pl; (agression) indecent assault no pl; **~ suicide** suicide bombing

attente [atɑ̃t] nf wait; (espérance) expectation; **contre toute ~** contrary to (all) expectations

attenter [atɑ̃te]: **~ à** vt (liberté) to violate; **~ à la vie de qn** to make an attempt on sb's life; **~ à ses jours** to make an attempt on one's life

attentif, -ive [atɑ̃tif, -iv] adj (auditeur) attentive; (soin) scrupulous; (travail) careful; **~ à** paying attention to; (devoir) mindful of; **~ à faire** careful to do

attention [atɑ̃sjɔ̃] nf attention; (prévenance) attention, thoughtfulness no pl; **mériter ~** to be worthy of attention; **à l'~ de** for the attention of; **porter qch à l'~ de qn** to bring sth to sb's attention; **attirer l'~ de qn sur qch** to draw sb's attention to sth; **faire ~ (à)** to be careful (of); **faire ~ (à ce) que** to be ou make sure that; **~!** careful!, watch!, watch ou mind (Brit) out!; **~,**

si vous ouvrez cette lettre (sanction) just watch out, if you open that letter; **~, respectez les consignes de sécurité** be sure to observe the safety instructions

attentionné, e [atɑ̃sjɔne] adj thoughtful, considerate

attentisme [atɑ̃tism(ə)] nm wait-and-see policy

attentiste [atɑ̃tist(ə)] adj (politique) wait-and-see ▷ nm/f believer in a wait-and-see policy

attentivement [atɑ̃tivmɑ̃] adv attentively

atténuant, e [atenɥɑ̃, -ɑ̃t] adj: **circonstances ~es** extenuating circumstances

atténuer [atenɥe] vt to alleviate, ease; (diminuer) to lessen; (amoindrir) to mitigate the effects of; **s'atténuer** vi to ease; (violence etc) to abate

atterrer [ateʀe] vt to dismay, appal

atterrir [ateʀiʀ] vi to land

atterrissage [ateʀisaʒ] nm landing; **~ sur le ventre/sans visibilité/forcé** belly/blind/forced landing

attestation [atɛstasjɔ̃] nf certificate, testimonial; **~ médicale** doctor's certificate

attester [atɛste] vt to testify to, vouch for; (démontrer) to attest, testify to; **~ que** to testify that

attiédir [atjediʀ]: **s'attiédir** vi to become lukewarm; (fig) to cool down

attifé, e [atife] adj (fam) got up (Brit), decked out

attifer [atife] vt to get (Brit) ou do up, deck out

attique [atik] nm: **appartement en ~** penthouse (flat (Brit) ou apartment (US))

attirail [atiʀaj] nm gear; (péj) paraphernalia

attirance [atiʀɑ̃s] nf attraction; (séduction) lure

attirant, e [atiʀɑ̃, -ɑ̃t] adj attractive, appealing

attirer [atiʀe] vt to attract; (appâter) to lure, entice; **~ qn dans un coin/vers soi** to draw sb into a corner/towards one; **~ l'attention de qn** to attract sb's attention; **~ l'attention de qn sur qch** to draw sb's attention to sth; **~ des ennuis à qn** to make trouble for sb; **s'~ des ennuis** to bring trouble upon o.s., get into trouble

attiser [atize] vt (feu) to poke (up), stir up; (fig) to fan the flame of, stir up

attitré, e [atitʀe] adj qualified; (agréé) accredited, appointed

attitude [atityd] nf attitude; (position du corps) bearing

attouchements [atuʃmɑ̃] nmpl touching sg; (sexuels) fondling sg, stroking sg

attractif, -ive [atʀaktif, -iv] adj attractive

attraction [atʀaksjɔ̃] nf attraction; (de cabaret, cirque) number

attrait [atʀɛ] nm appeal, attraction; (plus fort) lure; **attraits** nmpl attractions; **éprouver de l'~ pour** to be attracted to

attrape [atʀap] nf voir **farce**

attrape-nigaud [atʀapnigo] nm con

attraper [atʀape] vt to catch; (habitude, amende) to get, pick up; (fam: duper) to take in (Brit), con

attrayant, e [atʀɛjɑ̃, -ɑ̃t] *adj* attractive
attribuer [atʀibɥe] *vt* (*prix*) to award; (*rôle, tâche*) to allocate, assign; (*imputer*): **~ qch à** to attribute sth to, ascribe sth to, put sth down to; **s'attribuer** *vt* (*s'approprier*) to claim for o.s.
attribut [atʀiby] *nm* attribute; (*Ling*) complement
attribution [atʀibysjɔ̃] *nf* (*voir attribuer*) awarding; allocation, assignment; attribution; **attributions** *nfpl* (*compétence*) attributions; **complément d'~** (*Ling*) indirect object
attristant, e [atʀistɑ̃, -ɑ̃t] *adj* saddening
attrister [atʀiste] *vt* to sadden; **s'~ de qch** to be saddened by sth
attroupement [atʀupmɑ̃] *nm* crowd, mob
attrouper [atʀupe]: **s'attrouper** *vi* to gather
au [o] *prép voir* **à**
aubade [obad] *nf* dawn serenade
aubaine [obɛn] *nf* godsend; (*financière*) windfall; (*Comm*) bonanza
aube [ob] *nf* dawn, daybreak; (*Rel*) alb; **à l'~** at dawn *ou* daybreak; **à l'~ de** (*fig*) at the dawn of
aubépine [obepin] *nf* hawthorn
auberge [obɛʀ3(ə)] *nf* inn; **~ de jeunesse** youth hostel
aubergine [obɛʀ3in] *nf* aubergine (*Brit*), eggplant (*US*)
aubergiste [obɛʀ3ist(ə)] *nm/f* inn-keeper, hotel-keeper
auburn [obœʀn] *adj inv* auburn
aucun, e [okœ̃, -yn] *adj, pron* no; (*positif*) any ▷ *pron* none; (*positif*) any(one); **il n'y a ~ livre** there isn't any book, there is no book; **je n'en vois ~ qui** … I can't see any which …, I (can) see none which …; **~ homme** no man; **sans ~ doute** without any doubt; **sans ~e hésitation** without hesitation; **plus qu'~ autre** more than any other; **plus qu'~ de ceux qui** … more than any of those who …; **en ~e façon** in no way at all; **~ des deux** neither of the two; **~ d'entre eux** none of them; **d'~s** (*certains*) some
aucunement [okynmɑ̃] *adv* in no way, not in the least
audace [odas] *nf* daring, boldness; (*péj*) audacity; **il a eu l'~ de** … he had the audacity to …; **vous ne manquez pas d'~!** you're not lacking in nerve *ou* cheek!
audacieux, -euse [odasjø, -øz] *adj* daring, bold
au-dedans [odədɑ̃] *adv, prép* inside
au-dehors [odəɔʀ] *adv, prép* outside
au-delà [odla] *adv* beyond ▷ *nm*: **l'~** the hereafter; **~ de** *prép* beyond
au-dessous [odsu] *adv* underneath; below; **~ de** *prép* under(neath), below; (*limite, somme etc*) below, under; (*dignité, condition*) below
au-dessus [odsy] *adv* above; **~ de** *prép* above
au-devant [odvɑ̃] *adv*: **aller ~ de** to go (out) and meet; (*souhaits de qn*) to anticipate
audible [odibl(ə)] *adj* audible
audience [odjɑ̃s] *nf* audience; (*Jur: séance*) hearing; **trouver ~ auprès de** to arouse much interest among, get the (interested) attention of

audimat® [odimat] *nm* (*taux d'écoute*) ratings *pl*
audio-visuel, le [odjovizɥɛl] *adj* audio-visual ▷ *nm* (*équipement*) audio-visual aids *pl*; (*méthodes*) audio-visual methods *pl*; **l'~** radio and television
auditeur, -trice [oditœʀ, -tʀis] *nm/f* (*à la radio*) listener; (*à une conférence*) member of the audience, listener; **~ libre** unregistered student (*attending lectures*), auditor (*US*)
auditif, -ive [oditif, -iv] *adj* (*mémoire*) auditory; **appareil ~** hearing aid
audition [odisjɔ̃] *nf* (*ouïe, écoute*) hearing; (*Jur: de témoins*) examination; (*Mus, Théât: épreuve*) audition
auditionner [odisjɔne] *vt, vi* to audition
auditoire [oditwaʀ] *nm* audience
auditorium [oditɔʀjɔm] *nm* (*public*) studio
auge [o3] *nf* trough
augmentation [ɔgmɑ̃tasjɔ̃] *nf* (*action*) increasing; raising; (*résultat*) increase; **~ (de salaire)** rise (in salary) (*Brit*), (pay) raise (*US*)
augmenter [ɔgmɑ̃te] *vt* to increase; (*salaire, prix*) to increase, raise, put up; (*employé*) to increase the salary of, give a (salary) rise (*Brit*) *ou* (pay) raise (*US*) to ▷ *vi* to increase; **~ de poids/volume** to gain (in) weight/volume
augure [ɔgyʀ] *nm* soothsayer, oracle; **de bon/mauvais ~** of good/ill omen
augurer [ɔgyʀe] *vt*: **~ qch de** to foresee sth (coming) from *ou* out of; **~ bien de** to augur well for
auguste [ɔgyst(ə)] *adj* august, noble, majestic
aujourd'hui [oʒuʀdɥi] *adv* today; **aujourd'hui en huit/quinze** a week/two weeks today, a week/two weeks from now; **à dater** *ou* **partir d'aujourd'hui** from today('s date)
aumône [omon] *nf* alms *sg* (*pl inv*); **faire l'~ (à qn)** to give alms (to sb); **faire l'~ de qch à qn** (*fig*) to favour sb with sth
aumônerie [omonʀi] *nf* chaplaincy
aumônier [omonje] *nm* chaplain
auparavant [opaʀavɑ̃] *adv* before(hand)
auprès [opʀɛ]: **~ de** *prép* next to, close to; (*recourir, s'adresser*) to; (*en comparaison de*) compared with, next to; (*dans l'opinion de*) in the opinion of
auquel [okɛl] *pron voir* **lequel**
aura *etc* [ɔʀa] *vb voir* **avoir**
aurai *etc* [ɔʀe] *vb voir* **avoir**
auréole [ɔʀeɔl] *nf* halo; (*tache*) ring
auréolé, e [ɔʀeɔle] *adj* (*fig*): **~ de gloire** crowned with *ou* in glory
auriculaire [ɔʀikylɛʀ] *nm* little finger
aurons *etc* [ɔʀɔ̃] *vb voir* **avoir**
aurore [ɔʀɔʀ] *nf* dawn, daybreak; **~ boréale** northern lights *pl*
ausculter [ɔskylte] *vt* to sound
auspices [ɔspis] *nmpl*: **sous les ~ de** under the patronage *ou* auspices of; **sous de bons/mauvais ~** under favourable/unfavourable auspices
aussi [osi] *adv* (*également*) also, too; (*de*

comparaison) as ▷ *conj* therefore, consequently; ~
fort que as strong as; **lui** ~ (*sujet*) he too; (*objet*)
him too; ~ **bien que** (*de même que*) as well as
aussitôt [osito] *adv* straight away,
immediately; ~ **que** as soon as; ~ **envoyé** as
soon as it is (*ou* was) sent; ~ **fait** no sooner done
austère [ostɛʀ] *adj* austere; (*sévère*) stern
austérité [osteʀite] *nf* austerity; **plan/budget**
d'~ austerity plan/budget
austral, e [ostʀal] *adj* southern; **l'océan A~** the
Antarctic Ocean; **les Terres A~es** Antarctica
Australie [ostʀali] *nf*: **l'**~ Australia
australien, ne [ostʀaljɛ̃, -ɛn] *adj* Australian
▷ *nm/f*: **Australien, ne** Australian
autant [otɑ̃] *adv* so much; (*comparatif*): ~ **(que)**
as much (as); (*nombre*) as many (as); ~ **(de)** so
much (*ou* many); as much (*ou* many);
n'importe qui aurait pu en faire ~ anyone
could have done the same *ou* as much; ~ **partir**
we (*ou* you *etc*) may as well leave; ~ **ne rien dire**
best not say anything; ~ **dire que** ... one might
as well say that ...; **fort** ~ **que courageux** as
strong as he is brave; **il n'est pas découragé**
pour ~ he isn't discouraged for all that; **pour** ~
que *conj* assuming, as long as; **d'**~ *adv*
accordingly, in proportion; **d'**~ **plus/mieux**
(que) all the more/the better (since)
autarcie [otaʀsi] *nf* autarky, self-sufficiency
autel [otɛl] *nm* altar
auteur [otœʀ] *nm* author; **l'**~ **de cette**
remarque the person who said that; **droit d'**~
copyright
auteur-compositeur [otœʀkɔ̃pozitœʀ] *nm/f*
composer-songwriter
authenticité [otɑ̃tisite] *nf* authenticity
authentifier [otɑ̃tifje] *vt* to authenticate
authentique [otɑ̃tik] *adj* authentic, genuine
autiste [otist] *adj* autistic
auto [oto] *nf* car; ~**s tamponneuses** bumper
cars, dodgems
auto... [oto] *préfixe* auto..., self-
autobiographie [otobjɔgʀafi] *nf* autobiography
autobiographique [otobjɔgʀafik] *adj*
autobiographical
autobronzant [otobʀɔ̃zɑ̃] *nm* self-tanning
cream (*or* lotion *etc*)
autobus [otobys] *nm* bus
autocar [otokaʀ] *nm* coach
autochtone [otokton] *nm/f* native
autocollant, e [otokɔlɑ̃, -ɑ̃t] *adj* self-adhesive;
(*enveloppe*) self-seal ▷ *nm* sticker
auto-couchettes [otokuʃɛt] *adj inv*: **train** ~ car
sleeper train, motorail® train (*Brit*)
autocratique [otokʀatik] *adj* autocratic
autocritique [otokʀitik] *nf* self-criticism
autocuiseur [otokwizœʀ] *nm* (*Culin*) pressure
cooker
autodéfense [otodefɑ̃s] *nf* self-defence;
groupe d'~ vigilante committee
autodétermination [otodetɛʀminasjɔ̃] *nf* self-
determination
autodidacte [otodidakt(ə)] *nm/f* self-taught

person
autodiscipline [otodisiplin] *nf* self-discipline
autodrome [otodʀom] *nm* motor-racing
stadium
auto-école [otoekɔl] *nf* driving school
autofinancement [otofinɑ̃smɑ̃] *nm* self-
financing
autogéré, e [otoʒeʀe] *adj* self-managed,
managed internally
autogestion [otoʒɛstjɔ̃] *nf* joint worker-
management control
autographe [otogʀaf] *nm* autograph
autoguidé, e [otogide] *adj* self-guided
automate [otomat] *nm* (*robot*) automaton;
(*machine*) (automatic) machine
automatique [otomatik] *adj, nm* automatic; **l'**~
(*Tél*) ≈ direct dialling
automatiquement [otomatikmɑ̃] *adv*
automatically
automatisation [otomatizasjɔ̃] *nf* automation
automatiser [otomatize] *vt* to automate
automédication [otomedikasjɔ̃] *nf* self-
medication
automitrailleuse [otomitʀajøz] *nf* armoured
car
automnal, e, -aux [otonal, -o] *adj* autumnal
automne [oton] *nm* autumn (*Brit*), fall (*US*)
automobile [otomɔbil] *adj* motor *cpd* ▷ *nf*
(motor) car; **l'**~ motoring; (*industrie*) the car *ou*
automobile (*US*) industry
automobiliste [otomɔbilist(ə)] *nm/f* motorist
autonettoyant, e [otonɛtwajɑ̃, -ɑ̃t] *adj*: **four** ~
self-cleaning oven
autonome [otonom] *adj* autonomous
autonomie [otonomi] *nf* autonomy; (*Pol*) self-
government, autonomy; ~ **de vol** range
autonomiste [otonomist(ə)] *nm/f* separatist
autoportrait [otopɔʀtʀɛ] *nm* self-portrait
autopsie [otopsi] *nf* post-mortem
(examination), autopsy
autopsier [otopsje] *vt* to carry out a post-
mortem *ou* an autopsy on
autoradio [otoʀadjo] *nf* car radio
autorail [otoʀaj] *nm* railcar
autorisation [otoʀizasjɔ̃] *nf* permission,
authorization; (*papiers*) permit; **donner à qn l'**~
de to give sb permission to, authorize sb to;
avoir l'~ **de faire** to be allowed *ou* have
permission to do, be authorized to do
autorisé, e [otoʀize] *adj* (*opinion, sources*)
authoritative; (*permis*): ~ **à faire** authorized *ou*
permitted to do; **dans les milieux** ~**s** in official
circles
autoriser [otoʀize] *vt* to give permission for,
authorize; (*fig*) to allow (of), sanction; ~ **qn à**
faire to give permission to sb to do, authorize
sb to do
autoritaire [otoʀitɛʀ] *adj* authoritarian
autoritarisme [otoʀitaʀism(ə)] *nm*
authoritarianism
autorité [otoʀite] *nf* authority; **faire** ~ to be
authoritative; ~**s constituées** constitutional

authorities

autoroute [otoʀut] *nf* motorway (*Brit*), expressway (*US*); **~ de l'information** (*Tél*) information highway

autoroutier, -ière [otoʀutje, -jɛʀ] *adj* motorway *cpd* (*Brit*), expressway *cpd* (*US*)

autosatisfaction [otosatisfaksjɔ̃] *nf* self-satisfaction

auto-stop [otostop] *nm*: **l'~** hitch-hiking; **faire de l'~** to hitch-hike; **prendre qn en ~** to give sb a lift

auto-stoppeur, -euse [otostopœʀ, -øz] *nm/f* hitch-hiker, hitcher (*Brit*)

autosuffisant, e [otosyfizɑ̃, -ɑ̃t] *adj* self-sufficient

autosuggestion [otosygʒɛstjɔ̃] *nf* autosuggestion

autour [otuʀ] *adv* around; **~ de** *prép* around; (*environ*) around, about; **tout ~** *adv* all around

 MOT-CLÉ

autre [otʀ(ə)] *adj* **1** (*différent*) other, different; **je préférerais un autre verre** I'd prefer another *ou* a different glass; **d'autres verres** different glasses; **se sentir autre** to feel different; **la difficulté est autre** the difficulty is *ou* lies elsewhere
2 (*supplémentaire*) other; **je voudrais un autre verre d'eau** I'd like another glass of water
3: **autre chose** something else; **autre part** somewhere else; **d'autre part** on the other hand
▷ *pron* **1**: **un autre** another (one); **nous/vous autres** us/you; **d'autres** others; **l'autre** the other (one); **les autres** the others; (*autrui*) others; **l'un et l'autre** both of them; **ni l'un ni l'autre** neither of them; **se détester l'un l'autre/les uns les autres** to hate each other *ou* one another; **d'une semaine/minute à l'autre** from one week/minute *ou* moment to the next; (*incessamment*) any week/minute *ou* moment now; **de temps à autre** from time to time; **entre autres** among other things
2 (*expressions*): **j'en ai vu d'autres** I've seen worse; **à d'autres!** pull the other one!

autrefois [otʀəfwa] *adv* in the past

autrement [otʀəmɑ̃] *adv* differently; (*d'une manière différente*) in another way; (*sinon*) otherwise; **je n'ai pas pu faire ~** I couldn't do anything else, I couldn't do otherwise; **~ dit** in other words; (*c'est-à-dire*) that is to say

Autriche [otʀiʃ] *nf*: **l'~** Austria

autrichien, ne [otʀiʃjɛ̃, -ɛn] *adj* Austrian ▷ *nm/f*: **Autrichien, ne** Austrian

autruche [otʀyʃ] *nf* ostrich; **faire l'~** (*fig*) to bury one's head in the sand

autrui [otʀɥi] *pron* others

auvent [ovɑ̃] *nm* canopy

auvergnat, e [ovɛʀɲa, -at] *adj* of *ou* from the Auvergne

Auvergne [ovɛʀɲ(ə)] *nf*: **l'~** the Auvergne

aux [o] *prép voir* **à**

auxiliaire [oksiljɛʀ] *adj, nm/f* auxiliary

auxquels, auxquelles [okɛl] *pron voir* **lequel**

AV *sigle m* (*Banque*: = *avis de virement*) advice of bank transfer ▷ *abr* (*Auto*) = **avant**

av. *abr* (= *avenue*) Av(e)

avachi, e [avaʃi] *adj* limp, flabby; (*chaussure, vêtement*) out-of-shape; (*personne*): **~ sur qch** slumped on *ou* across sth

avais *etc* [avɛ] *vb voir* **avoir**

aval [aval] *nm* (*accord*) endorsement, backing; (*Géo*): **en ~** downstream, downriver; (*sur une pente*) downhill; **en ~ de** downstream *ou* downriver from; downhill from

avalanche [avalɑ̃ʃ] *nf* avalanche; **~ poudreuse** powder snow avalanche

avaler [avale] *vt* to swallow

avaliser [avalize] *vt* (*plan, entreprise*) to back, support; (*Comm, Jur*) to guarantee

avance [avɑ̃s] *nf* (*de troupes etc*) advance; (*progrès*) progress; (*d'argent*) advance; (*opposé à retard*) lead; being ahead of schedule; **avances** *nfpl* overtures; (*amoureuses*) advances; **une ~ de 300 m/4 h** (*Sport*) a 300 m/4 hour lead; **(être) en ~** (to be) early; (*sur un programme*) (to be) ahead of schedule; **on n'est pas en ~!** we're kind of late!; **être en ~ sur qn** to be ahead of sb; **d'~, à l'~, par ~** in advance; **~ (du) papier** (*Inform*) paper advance

avancé, e [avɑ̃se] *adj* advanced; (*travail etc*) well on, well under way; (*fruit, fromage*) overripe ▷ *nf* projection; overhang; **il est ~ pour son âge** he is advanced for his age

avancement [avɑ̃smɑ̃] *nm* (*professionnel*) promotion; (*de travaux*) progress

avancer [avɑ̃se] *vi* to move forward, advance; (*projet, travail*) to make progress; (*être en saillie*) to overhang; to project; (*montre, réveil*) to be fast; (: *d'habitude*) to gain ▷ *vt* to move forward, advance; (*argent*) to advance; (*montre, pendule*) to put forward; (*faire progresser: travail etc*) to advance, move on; **s'avancer** *vi* to move forward, advance; (*fig*) to commit o.s.; (*faire saillie*) to overhang; to project; **j'avance (d'une heure)** fast

avanies [avani] *nfpl* snubs (*Brit*), insults

avant [avɑ̃] *prép* before ▷ *adv*: **trop/plus ~** too far/further forward ▷ *adj inv*: **siège/roue ~** front seat/wheel ▷ *nm* front; (*Sport: joueur*) forward; **~ qu'il parte/de partir** before he leaves/leaving; **~ qu'il (ne) pleuve** before it rains (*ou* rained); **~ tout** (*surtout*) above all; **à l'~** (*dans un véhicule*) in (the) front; **en ~** *adv* forward(s); **en ~ de** *prép* in front of; **aller de l'~** to steam ahead (*fig*), make good progress

avantage [avɑ̃taʒ] *nm* advantage; (*Tennis*): **~ service/dehors** advantage *ou* van (*Brit*) *ou* ad (*US*) in/out; **tirer ~ de** to take advantage of; **vous auriez ~ à faire** you would be well-advised to do, it would be to your advantage to do; **à l'~ de qn** to sb's advantage; **être à son ~**

to be at one's best; **~s en nature** benefits in kind; **~s sociaux** fringe benefits

avantager [avɑ̃taʒe] *vt* (*favoriser*) to favour; (*embellir*) to flatter

avantageux, -euse [avɑ̃taʒø, -øz] *adj* attractive; (*intéressant*) attractively priced; (*portrait, coiffure*) flattering; **conditions avantageuses** favourable terms

avant-bras [avɑ̃bʀa] *nm inv* forearm

avant-centre [avɑ̃sɑ̃tʀ(ə)] *nm* centre-forward

avant-coureur [avɑ̃kuʀœʀ] *adj inv* (*bruit etc*) precursory; **signe ~** advance indication *ou* sign

avant-dernier, -ière [avɑ̃dɛʀnje, -jɛʀ] *adj, nm/f* next to last, last but one

avant-garde [avɑ̃gaʀd(ə)] *nf* (*Mil*) vanguard; (*fig*) avant-garde; **d'~** avant-garde

avant-goût [avɑ̃gu] *nm* foretaste

avant-hier [avɑ̃tjɛʀ] *adv* the day before yesterday

avant-poste [avɑ̃pɔst(ə)] *nm* outpost

avant-première [avɑ̃pʀəmjɛʀ] *nf* (*de film*) preview; **en ~** as a preview, in a preview showing

avant-projet [avɑ̃pʀɔʒɛ] *nm* preliminary draft

avant-propos [avɑ̃pʀɔpo] *nm* foreword

avant-veille [avɑ̃vɛj] *nf*: **l'~** two days before

avare [avaʀ] *adj* miserly, avaricious ▷ *nm/f* miser; **~ de compliments** stingy *ou* sparing with one's compliments

avarice [avaʀis] *nf* avarice, miserliness

avarié, e [avaʀje] *adj* (*viande, fruits*) rotting, going off (*Brit*); (*Navig: navire*) damaged

avaries [avaʀi] *nfpl* (*Navig*) damage *sg*

avatar [avataʀ] *nm* misadventure; (*transformation*) metamorphosis

avec [avɛk] *prép* with; (*à l'égard de*) to(wards), with ▷ *adv* (*fam*) with it (*ou* him *etc*); **~ habileté/ lenteur** skilfully/slowly; **~ eux/ces maladies** with them/these diseases; **~ ça** (*malgré ça*) for all that; **et ~ ça?** (*dans un magasin*) anything *ou* something else?

avenant, e [avnɑ̃, -ɑ̃t] *adj* pleasant ▷ *nm* (*Assurances*) additional clause; **à l'~** *adv* in keeping

avènement [avɛnmɑ̃] *nm* (*d'un roi*) accession, succession; (*d'un changement*) advent; (*d'une politique, idée*) coming

avenir [avniʀ] *nm*: **l'~** the future; **à l'~** in future; **sans ~** with no future, without a future; **carrière/politicien d'~** career/politician with prospects *ou* a future

Avent [avɑ̃] *nm*: **l'~** Advent

aventure [avɑ̃tyʀ] *nf*: **l'~** adventure; **une ~** an adventure; (*amoureuse*) an affair; **partir à l'~** to go off in search of adventure; (*au hasard*) to go where one's fancy takes one; **roman/film d'~** adventure story/film

aventurer [avɑ̃tyʀe] *vt* (*somme, réputation, vie*) to stake; (*remarque, opinion*) to venture; **s'aventurer** *vi* to venture; **s'~ à faire qch** to venture into sth

aventureux, -euse [avɑ̃tyʀø, -øz] *adj* adventurous, venturesome; (*projet*) risky,

chancy

aventurier, -ière [avɑ̃tyʀje, -jɛʀ] *nm/f* adventurer ▷ *nf* (*péj*) adventuress

avenu, e [avny] *adj*: **nul et non ~** null and void

avenue [avny] *nf* avenue

avéré, e [aveʀe] *adj* recognized, acknowledged

avérer [aveʀe]: **s'avérer** *vr*: **s'~ faux/coûteux** to prove (to be) wrong/expensive

averse [avɛʀs(ə)] *nf* shower

aversion [avɛʀsjɔ̃] *nf* aversion, loathing

averti, e [avɛʀti] *adj* (well-)informed

avertir [avɛʀtiʀ] *vt*: **~ qn (de qch/que)** to warn sb (of sth/that); (*renseigner*) to inform sb (of sth/ that); **~ qn de ne pas faire qch** to warn sb not to do sth

avertissement [avɛʀtismɑ̃] *nm* warning

avertisseur [avɛʀtisœʀ] *nm* horn, siren; **~ (d'incendie)** (fire) alarm

aveu, x [avø] *nm* confession; **passer aux ~x** to make a confession; **de l'~ de** according to

aveuglant, e [avœglɑ̃, -ɑ̃t] *adj* blinding

aveugle [avœgl(ə)] *adj* blind ▷ *nm/f* blind person; **les ~s** the blind; **test en (double) ~** (double) blind test

aveuglement [avœgləmɑ̃] *nm* blindness

aveuglément [avœglemɑ̃] *adv* blindly

aveugler [avœgle] *vt* to blind

aveuglette [avœglɛt]: **à l'~** *adv* groping one's way along; (*fig*) in the dark, blindly

avez [ave] *vb voir* **avoir**

aviateur, -trice [avjatœʀ, -tʀis] *nm/f* aviator, pilot

aviation [avjɑsjɔ̃] *nf* (*secteur commercial*) aviation; (*sport, métier de pilote*) flying; (*Mil*) air force; **terrain d'~** airfield; **~ de chasse** fighter force

aviculteur, -trice [avikyltœʀ, -tʀis] *nm/f* poultry farmer; bird breeder

aviculture [avikyltyʀ] *nf* (*de volailles*) poultry farming

avide [avid] *adj* eager; (*péj*) greedy, grasping; **~ de** (*sang etc*) thirsting for; **~ d'honneurs/ d'argent** greedy for honours/money; **~ de connaître/d'apprendre** eager to know/learn

avidité [avidite] *nf* eagerness; greed

avilir [aviliʀ] *vt* to debase

avilissant, e [avilisɑ̃, -ɑ̃t] *adj* degrading

aviné, e [avine] *adj* drunken

avion [avjɔ̃] *nm* (aero)plane (*Brit*), (air)plane (*US*); **aller (quelque part) en ~** to go (somewhere) by plane, fly (somewhere); **par ~** by airmail; **~ de chasse** fighter; **~ de ligne** airliner; **~ à réaction** jet (plane)

avion-cargo [avjɔ̃kaʀgo] *nm* air freighter

avion-citerne [avjɔ̃sitɛʀn(ə)] *nm* air tanker

aviron [aviʀɔ̃] *nm* oar; (*sport*): **l'~** rowing

avis [avi] *nm* opinion; (*notification*) notice; (*Comm*): **~ de crédit/débit** credit/debit advice; **à mon ~** in my opinion; **je suis de votre ~** I share your opinion, I am of your opinion; **être d'~ que** to be of the opinion that; **changer d'~** to change one's mind; **sauf ~ contraire** unless you hear to the contrary; **sans ~ préalable**

without notice; **jusqu'à nouvel ~** until further notice; **~ de décès** death announcement

avisé, e [avize] *adj* sensible, wise; **être bien/mal ~ de faire** to be well-/ill-advised to do

aviser [avize] *vt* (*voir*) to notice, catch sight of; (*informer*): **~ qn de/que** to advise *ou* inform *ou* notify sb of/that ▷ *vi* to think about things, assess the situation; **s'~ de qch/que** to become suddenly aware of sth/that; **s'~ de faire** to take it into one's head to do

aviver [avive] *vt* (*douleur, chagrin*) to intensify; (*intérêt, désir*) to sharpen; (*colère, querelle*) to stir up; (*couleur*) to brighten up

av. J.-C. *abr* (= *avant Jésus-Christ*) BC

avocat, e [avɔka, -at] *nm/f* (*Jur*) ≈ barrister (*Brit*), lawyer; (*fig*) advocate, champion ▷ *nm* (*Culin*) avocado (pear); **se faire l'~ du diable** to be the devil's advocate; **l'~ de la défense/partie civile** the counsel for the defence/plaintiff; **~ d'affaires** business lawyer; **~ général** assistant public prosecutor

avocat-conseil [avɔkakɔ̃sɛj] (*pl* **avocats-conseils**) *nm* ≈ barrister (*Brit*)

avocat-stagiaire [avɔkastaʒjɛR] (*pl* **avocats-stagiaires**) *nm* ≈ barrister doing his articles (*Brit*)

avoine [avwan] *nf* oats *pl*

 MOT-CLÉ

avoir [avwaʀ] *nm* assets *pl*, resources *pl*; (*Comm*) credit; **avoir fiscal** tax credit
▷ *vt* **1** (*posséder*) to have; **elle a deux enfants/une belle maison** she has (got) two children/a lovely house; **il a les yeux bleus** he has (got) blue eyes
2 (*éprouver*): **qu'est-ce que tu as?, qu'as-tu?** what's wrong?, what's the matter?; *voir aussi* **faim, peur** *etc*
3 (*âge, dimensions*) to be; **il a 3 ans** he is 3 (years old); **le mur a 3 mètres de haut** the wall is 3 metres high
4 (*fam: duper*) to do, have; **on vous a eu!** you've been done *ou* had!
5: **en avoir contre qn** to have a grudge against sb; **en avoir assez** to be fed up; **j'en ai pour une demi-heure** it'll take me half an hour; **n'avoir que faire de qch** to have no use for sth
▷ *vb aux* **1** to have; **avoir mangé/dormi** to have eaten/slept; **hier je n'ai pas mangé** I didn't eat yesterday
2 (*avoir +à +infinitif*): **avoir à faire qch** to have to do sth; **vous n'avez qu'à lui demander** you only have to ask him; **tu n'as pas à me poser**

des questions it's not for you to ask me questions
▷ *vb impers* **1**: **il y a** (+ *singulier*) there is; (+ *pluriel*) there are; **qu'y-a-t-il?, qu'est-ce qu'il y a?** what's the matter?, what is it?; **il doit y avoir une explication** there must be an explanation; **il n'y a qu'à ...** we (*ou* you *etc*) will just have to ...; **il ne peut y en avoir qu'un** there can only be one
2 (*temporel*): **il y a 10 ans** 10 years ago; **il y a 10 ans/longtemps que je le connais** I've known him for 10 years/a long time; **il y a 10 ans qu'il est arrivé** it's 10 years since he arrived

avoisinant, e [avwazinã, -ãt] *adj* neighbouring

avoisiner [avwazine] *vt* to be near *ou* close to; (*fig*) to border *ou* verge on

avons [avɔ̃] *vb voir* **avoir**

avortement [avɔRtəmã] *nm* abortion

avorter [avɔRte] *vi* (*Méd*) to have an abortion; (*fig*) to fail; **faire ~** to abort; **se faire ~** to have an abortion

avorton [avɔRtɔ̃] *nm* (*péj*) little runt

avouable [avwabl(ə)] *adj* respectable; **des pensées non ~s** unrepeatable thoughts

avoué, e [avwe] *adj* avowed ▷ *nm* (*Jur*) ≈ solicitor (*Brit*), lawyer

avouer [avwe] *vt* (*crime, défaut*) to confess (to) ▷ *vi* (*se confesser*) to confess; (*admettre*) to admit; **~ avoir fait/que** to admit *ou* confess to having done/that; **~ que oui/non** to admit that that is so/not so

avril [avril] *nm* April; *voir aussi* **juillet**

axe [aks(ə)] *nm* axis (*pl* axes); (*de roue etc*) axle; **dans l'~ de** directly in line with; (*fig*) main line; **~ routier** trunk road, main road

axer [akse] *vt*: **~ qch sur** to centre sth on

axial, e, -aux [aksjal, -o] *adj* axial

axiome [aksjom] *nm* axiom

ayant [ɛjã] *vb voir* **avoir** ▷ *nm*: **~ droit** assignee; **~ droit à** (*pension etc*) person eligible for *ou* entitled to

ayons *etc* [ɛjɔ̃] *vb voir* **avoir**

azalée [azale] *nf* azalea

Azerbaïdjan [azɛRbaidʒã] *nm* Azerbaijan

azimut [azimyt] *nm* azimuth; **tous ~s** *adj* (*fig*) omnidirectional

azote [azɔt] *nm* nitrogen

azoté, e [azɔte] *adj* nitrogenous

AZT *sigle m* (= *azidothymidine*) AZT

aztèque [aztɛk] *adj* Aztec

azur [azyR] *nm* (*couleur*) azure, sky blue; (*ciel*) sky, skies *pl*

azyme [azim] *adj*: **pain ~** unleavened bread

Bb

B, b [be] *nm inv* B, b ▷ *abr* = **bien; B comme Bertha** B for Benjamin (*Brit*) *ou* Baker (*US*)

BA *sigle f* (= *bonne action*) good deed

baba [baba] *adj inv*: **en être ~** (*fam*) to be flabbergasted ▷ *nm*: **~ au rhum** rum baba

babil [babi] *nm* prattle

babillage [babijaʒ] *nm* chatter

babiller [babije] *vi* to prattle, chatter; (*bébé*) to babble

babines [babin] *nfpl* chops

babiole [babjɔl] *nf* (*bibelot*) trinket; (*vétille*) trifle

bâbord [babɔʀ] *nm*: **à** *ou* **par ~** to port, on the port side

babouin [babwɛ̃] *nm* baboon

baby-foot [babifut] *nm inv* table football

Babylone [babilɔn] *n* Babylon

babylonien, ne [babilɔnjɛ̃, -ɛn] *adj* Babylonian

baby-sitter [babisitœʀ] *nm/f* baby-sitter

baby-sitting [babisitiŋ] *nm* baby-sitting; **faire du ~** to baby-sit

bac [bak] *nm* (*Scol*) = **baccalauréat**; (*bateau*) ferry; (*récipient*) tub; (: *Photo etc*) tray; (: *Industrie*) tank; **~ à glace** ice-tray; **~ à légumes** vegetable compartment *ou* rack

baccalauréat [bakalɔʀea] *nm* ≈ A-levels *pl* (*Brit*), ≈ high school diploma (*US*); *see note*

● BACCALAURÉAT

The *baccalauréat* or "bac" is the school-leaving examination taken at a French "lycée" at the age of 18; it marks the end of seven years' secondary education. Several subject combinations are available, although in all cases a broad range is studied. Successful candidates can go on to university, if they so wish.

bâche [baʃ] *nf* tarpaulin, canvas sheet

bachelier, -ière [baʃəlje, -jɛʀ] *nm/f* holder of the *baccalauréat*

bâcher [baʃe] *vt* to cover (with a canvas sheet *ou* a tarpaulin)

bachot [baʃo] *nm* = **baccalauréat**

bachotage [baʃotaʒ] *nm* (*Scol*) cramming

bachoter [baʃote] *vi* (*Scol*) to cram (for an exam)

bacille [basil] *nm* bacillus

bâcler [bakle] *vt* to botch (up)

bacon [bekɔn] *nm* bacon

bactéricide [bakteʀisid] *nm* (*Méd*) bactericide

bactérie [bakteʀi] *nf* bacterium

bactérien, ne [bakteʀjɛ̃, -ɛn] *adj* bacterial

bactériologie [bakteʀjɔlɔʒi] *nf* bacteriology

bactériologique [bakteʀjɔlɔʒik] *adj* bacteriological

bactériologiste [bakteʀjɔlɔʒist(ə)] *nm/f* bacteriologist

badaud, e [bado, -od] *nm/f* idle onlooker

baderne [badɛʀn(ə)] *nf* (*péj*): **(vieille) ~** old fossil

badge [badʒ(ə)] *nm* badge

badigeon [badiʒɔ̃] *nm* distemper; colourwash

badigeonner [badiʒɔne] *vt* to distemper; to colourwash; (*péj: barbouiller*) to daub; (*Méd*) to paint

badin, e [badɛ̃, -in] *adj* light-hearted, playful

badinage [badinaʒ] *nm* banter

badine [badin] *nf* switch (*stick*)

badiner [badine] *vi*: **~ avec qch** to treat sth lightly; **ne pas ~ avec qch** not to trifle with sth

badminton [badmintɔn] *nm* badminton

BAFA [bafa] *sigle m* (= *Brevet d'aptitude aux fonctions d'animation*) diploma for youth leaders and workers

baffe [baf] *nf* (*fam*) slap, clout

Baffin [bafin] *nf*: **terre de ~** Baffin Island

baffle [bafl(ə)] *nm* baffle (board)

bafouer [bafwe] *vt* to deride, ridicule

bafouillage [bafujaʒ] *nm* (*fam: propos incohérents*) jumble of words

bafouiller [bafuje] *vi, vt* to stammer

bâfrer [bafʀe] *vi, vt* (*fam*) to guzzle, gobble

bagage [bagaʒ] *nm*: **~s** luggage *sg*, baggage *sg*; **faire ses ~s** to pack (one's bags); **~ littéraire** (stock of) literary knowledge; **~s à main** hand-luggage

bagarre [bagaʀ] *nf* fight, brawl; **il aime la ~** he loves a fight, he likes fighting

bagarrer [bagaʀe]: **se bagarrer** *vi* to (have a) fight

bagarreur, -euse [bagaʀœʀ, -øz] *adj* pugnacious ▷ *nm/f*: **il est ~** he loves a fight

bagatelle [bagatɛl] *nf* trifle, trifling sum (*ou* matter)

Bagdad, Baghdâd [bagdad] *n* Baghdad

bagnard [baɲaʀ] *nm* convict

bagne [baɲ] *nm* penal colony; **c'est le ~** (*fig*) it's forced labour

bagnole [baɲɔl] *nf* (*fam*) car, wheels *pl* (*Brit*)

bagout [bagu] *nm* glibness; **avoir du ~** to have the gift of the gab

bague [bag] *nf* ring; **~ de fiançailles** engagement ring; **~ de serrage** clip

baguenauder [bagnode]: **se baguenauder** *vi* to trail around, loaf around

baguer [bage] *vt* to ring

baguette [bagɛt] *nf* stick; (*cuisine chinoise*) chopstick; (*de chef d'orchestre*) baton; (*pain*) stick of (French) bread; (*Constr: moulure*) beading; **mener qn à la ~** to rule sb with a rod of iron; **~ magique** magic wand; **~ de sourcier** divining rod; **~ de tambour** drumstick

Bahamas [baamas] *nfpl*: **les (îles) ~** the Bahamas

Bahrein [baʀɛn] *nm* Bahrain *ou* Bahrein

bahut [bay] *nm* chest

bai, e [bɛ] *adj* (*cheval*) bay

baie [bɛ] *nf* (*Géo*) bay; (*fruit*) berry; **~ (vitrée)** picture window

baignade [bɛɲad] *nf* (*action*) bathing; (*bain*) bathe; (*endroit*) bathing place

baigné, e [beɲe] *adj*: **~ de** bathed in; (*trempé*) soaked with; (*inondé*) flooded with

baigner [beɲe] *vt* (*bébé*) to bath ▷ *vi*: **~ dans son sang** to lie in a pool of blood; **~ dans la brume** to be shrouded in mist; **se baigner** *vi* to go swimming *ou* bathing; (*dans une baignoire*) to have a bath; **ça baigne!** (*fam*) everything's great!

baigneur, -euse [beɲœʀ, -øz] *nm/f* bather ▷ *nm* (*poupée*) baby doll

baignoire [beɲwaʀ] *nf* bath(tub); (*Théât*) ground-floor box

bail, baux [baj, bo] *nm* lease; **donner** *ou* **prendre qch à ~** to lease sth

bâillement [bɑjmɑ̃] *nm* yawn

bâiller [bɑje] *vi* to yawn; (*être ouvert*) to gape

bailleur [bajœʀ] *nm*: **~ de fonds** sponsor, backer; (*Comm*) sleeping *ou* silent partner

bâillon [bɑjɔ̃] *nm* gag

bâillonner [bɑjɔne] *vt* to gag

bain [bɛ̃] *nm* (*dans une baignoire, Photo, Tech*) bath; (*dans la mer, une piscine*) swim; **costume de ~** bathing costume (*Brit*), swimsuit; **prendre un ~** to have a bath; **se mettre dans le ~** (*fig*) to get into (the way of) it *ou* things; **~ de bouche** mouthwash; **~ de foule** walkabout; **~ de pieds** footbath; (*au bord de la mer*) paddle; **~ de siège** hip bath; **~ de soleil** sunbathing *no pl*; **prendre un ~ de soleil** to sunbathe; **~s de mer** sea bathing *sg*; **~s(-douches) municipaux** public baths

bain-marie [bɛ̃maʀi] (*pl* **bains-marie**) *nm* double boiler; **faire chauffer au ~** (*boîte etc*) to immerse in boiling water

baïonnette [bajɔnɛt] *nf* bayonet; (*Élec*): **douille à ~** bayonet socket; **ampoule à ~** bulb with a bayonet fitting

baisemain [bɛzmɛ̃] *nm* kissing a lady's hand

baiser [beze] *nm* kiss ▷ *vt* (*main, front*) to kiss; (*fam!*) to screw (!)

baisse [bɛs] *nf* fall, drop; (*Comm*): **"~ sur la viande"** "meat prices down"; **en ~** (*cours, action*) falling; **à la ~** downwards

baisser [bese] *vt* to lower; (*radio, chauffage*) to turn down; (*Auto: phares*) to dip (*Brit*), lower (*US*) ▷ *vi* to fall, drop, go down; **se baisser** *vi* to bend down

bajoues [baʒu] *nfpl* chaps, chops

bal [bal] *nm* dance; (*grande soirée*) ball; **~ costumé/masqué** fancy-dress/masked ball; **~ musette** dance (*with accordion accompaniment*)

balade [balad] *nf* walk, stroll; (*en voiture*) drive; **faire une ~** to go for a walk *ou* stroll; to go for a drive

balader [balade] *vt* (*traîner*) to trail around; **se balader** *vi* to go for a walk *ou* stroll; to go for a drive

baladeur [baladœʀ] *nm* personal stereo; **~ numérique** MP3 player

baladeuse [baladøz] *nf* inspection lamp

baladin [baladɛ̃] *nm* wandering entertainer

balafre [balafʀ(ə)] *nf* gash, slash; (*cicatrice*) scar

balafrer [balafʀe] *vt* to gash, slash

balai [balɛ] *nm* broom, brush; (*Auto: d'essuie-glace*) blade; (*Mus: de batterie etc*) brush; **donner un coup de ~** to give the floor a sweep; **~ mécanique** carpet sweeper

balai-brosse [balɛbʀɔs] (*pl* **balais-brosses**) *nm* (long-handled) scrubbing brush

balance [balɑ̃s] *nf* (*à plateaux*) scales *pl*; (*de précision*) balance; (*Comm, Pol*): **~ des comptes** *ou* **paiements** balance of payments; (*signe*): **la B~** Libra, the Scales; **être de la B~** to be Libra; **~ commerciale** balance of trade; **~ des forces** balance of power; **~ romaine** steelyard

balancelle [balɑ̃sɛl] *nf* garden hammock-seat

balancer [balɑ̃se] *vt* to swing; (*lancer*) to fling, chuck; (*renvoyer, jeter*) to chuck out ▷ *vi* to swing; **se balancer** *vi* to swing; (*bateau*) to rock; (*branche*) to sway; **se ~ de qch** (*fam*) not to give a toss about sth

balancier [balɑ̃sje] *nm* (*de pendule*) pendulum; (*de montre*) balance wheel; (*perche*) (balancing) pole

balançoire [balɑ̃swaʀ] *nf* swing; (*sur pivot*) seesaw

balayage [balɛjaʒ] *nm* sweeping; scanning

balayer [baleje] *vt* (*feuilles etc*) to sweep up, brush up; (*pièce, cour*) to sweep; (*chasser*) to sweep away *ou* aside; (*radar*) to scan; (: *phares*) to sweep across

balayette [balɛjɛt] *nf* small brush

balayeur, -euse [balɛjœʀ, -øz] *nm/f* road sweeper ▷ *nf* (*engin*) road sweeper

balayures [balɛjyʀ] *nfpl* sweepings

balbutiement [balbysimɑ̃] *nm* (*paroles*) stammering *no pl*; **balbutiements** *nmpl* (*fig*:

débuts) first faltering steps

balbutier [balbysje] *vi, vt* to stammer

balcon [balkɔ̃] *nm* balcony; (*Théât*) dress circle

baldaquin [baldakɛ̃] *nm* canopy

Bâle [bɑl] *n* Basle *ou* Basel

Baléares [baleaʀ] *nfpl*: **les ~** the Balearic Islands

baleine [balɛn] *nf* whale; (*de parapluie*) rib; (*de corset*) bone

baleinier [balenje] *nm* (*Navig*) whaler

baleinière [balenjɛʀ] *nf* whaleboat

balisage [balizaʒ] *nm* (*signaux*) beacons *pl*; buoys *pl*; runway lights *pl*; signs *pl*, markers *pl*

balise [baliz] *nf* (*Navig*) beacon, (marker) buoy; (*Aviat*) runway light, beacon; (*Auto, Ski*) sign

baliser [balize] *vt* to mark out (with beacons *ou* lights *etc*)

balistique [balistik] *adj* (*engin*) ballistic ▷ *nf* ballistics

balivernes [balivɛʀn(ə)] *nfpl* twaddle *sg* (*Brit*), nonsense *sg*

balkanique [balkanik] *adj* Balkan

Balkans [balkɑ̃] *nmpl*: **les ~** the Balkans

ballade [balad] *nf* ballad

ballant, e [balɑ̃, -ɑ̃t] *adj* dangling

ballast [balast] *nm* ballast

balle [bal] *nf* (*de fusil*) bullet; (*de sport*) ball; (*du blé*) chaff; (*paquet*) bale; (*fam: franc*) franc; **~ perdue** stray bullet

ballerine [balʀin] *nf* ballet dancer; (*chaussure*) pump, ballerina

ballet [balɛ] *nm* ballet; (*fig*): **~ diplomatique** diplomatic to-ings and fro-ings

ballon [balɔ̃] *nm* (*de sport*) ball; (*jouet, Aviat, de bande dessinée*) balloon; (*de vin*) glass; **~ d'essai** (*météorologique*) pilot balloon; (*fig*) feeler(s); **~ de football** football; **~ d'oxygène** oxygen bottle

ballonner [balɔne] *vt*: **j'ai le ventre ballonné** I feel bloated

ballon-sonde [balɔ̃sɔ̃d] (*pl* **ballons-sondes**) *nm* sounding balloon

ballot [balo] *nm* bundle; (*péj*) nitwit

ballottage [balɔtaʒ] *nm* (*Pol*) second ballot

ballotter [balɔte] *vi* to roll around; (*bateau etc*) to toss ▷ *vt* to shake *ou* throw about; to toss; **être ballotté entre** (*fig*) to be shunted between; (: *indécis*) to be torn between

ballottine [balɔtin] *nf* (*Culin*): **~ de volaille** meat loaf made with poultry

ball-trap [baltʀap] *nm* (*appareil*) trap; (*tir*) clay pigeon shooting

balluchon [balyʃɔ̃] *nm* bundle (of clothes)

balnéaire [balneɛʀ] *adj* seaside *cpd*

balnéothérapie [balneɔteʀapi] *nf* spa bath therapy

BALO *sigle m* (= *Bulletin des annonces légales obligatoires*) ≈ Public Notices (*in newspapers etc*)

balourd, e [baluʀ, -uʀd(ə)] *adj* clumsy ▷ *nm/f* clodhopper

balourdise [baluʀdiz] *nf* clumsiness; (*gaffe*) blunder

balte [balt] *adj* Baltic ▷ *nm/f*: **Balte** native of the Baltic States

baltique [baltik] *adj* Baltic ▷ *nf*: **la (mer) B~** the Baltic (Sea)

baluchon [balyʃɔ̃] *nm* = **balluchon**

balustrade [balystʀad] *nf* railings *pl*, handrail

bambin [bɑ̃bɛ̃] *nm* little child

bambou [bɑ̃bu] *nm* bamboo

ban [bɑ̃] *nm* round of applause, cheer; **être/ mettre au ~ de** to be outlawed/to outlaw from; **le ~ et l'arrière-~ de sa famille** every last one of his relatives; **~s (de mariage)** banns, bans

banal, e [banal] *adj* banal, commonplace; (*péj*) trite; **four/moulin ~** village oven/mill

banalisé, e [banalize] *adj* (*voiture de police*) unmarked

banalité [banalite] *nf* banality; (*remarque*) truism, trite remark

banane [banan] *nf* banana

bananeraie [bananʀɛ] *nf* banana plantation

bananier [bananje] *nm* banana tree; (*bateau*) banana boat

banc [bɑ̃] *nm* seat, bench; (*de poissons*) shoal; **~ des accusés** dock; **~ d'essai** (*fig*) testing ground; **~ de sable** sandbank; **~ des témoins** witness box; **~ de touche** dugout

bancaire [bɑ̃kɛʀ] *adj* banking, bank *cpd*

bancal, e [bɑ̃kal] *adj* wobbly; (*personne*) bow-legged; (*fig: projet*) shaky

bandage [bɑ̃daʒ] *nm* bandaging; (*pansement*) bandage; **~ herniaire** truss

bande [bɑ̃d] *nf* (*de tissu etc*) strip; (*Méd*) bandage; (*motif, dessin*) stripe; (*Ciné*) film; (*Radio, groupe*) band; (*péj*): **une ~ de** a bunch *ou* crowd of; **par la ~** in a roundabout way; **donner de la ~** to list; **faire ~ à part** to keep to o.s.; **~ dessinée (BD)** strip cartoon (*Brit*), comic strip; **~ magnétique** magnetic tape; **~ passante** (*Inform*) bandwidth; **~ perforée** punched tape; **~ de roulement** (*de pneu*) tread; **~ sonore** sound track; **~ de terre** strip of land; **~ Velpeau**® (*Méd*) crêpe bandage

bandé, e [bɑ̃de] *adj* bandaged; **les yeux ~s** blindfold

bande-annonce [bɑ̃danɔ̃s] (*pl* **bandes-annonces**) *nf* (*Ciné*) trailer

bandeau, x [bɑ̃do] *nm* headband; (*sur les yeux*) blindfold; (*Méd*) head bandage

bandelette [bɑ̃dlɛt] *nf* strip of cloth, bandage

bander [bɑ̃de] *vt* to bandage; (*muscle*) to tense; (*arc*) to bend ▷ *vi* (*fam!*) to have a hard on (!); **~ les yeux à qn** to blindfold sb

banderole [bɑ̃dʀɔl] *nf* banderole; (*dans un défilé etc*) streamer

bande-son [bɑ̃dsɔ̃] (*pl* **bandes-son**) *nf* (*Ciné*) soundtrack

bandit [bɑ̃di] *nm* bandit

banditisme [bɑ̃ditism(ə)] *nm* violent crime, armed robberies *pl*

bandoulière [bɑ̃duljɛʀ] *nf*: **en ~** (slung *ou* worn) across the shoulder

Bangkok [bɑ̃ŋkɔk] *n* Bangkok

Bangladesh [bɑ̃ɡladɛʃ] *nm*: **le ~** Bangladesh

banjo [bɑ̃(d)ʒo] *nm* banjo

banlieue [bãljø] *nf* suburbs *pl*; **quartiers de ~** suburban areas; **trains de ~** commuter trains

banlieusard, e [bãljøzaʀ, -aʀd(ə)] *nm/f* suburbanite

bannière [banjɛʀ] *nf* banner

bannir [baniʀ] *vt* to banish

banque [bãk] *nf* bank; (*activités*) banking; **~ des yeux/du sang** eye/blood bank; **~ d'affaires** merchant bank; **~ de dépôt** deposit bank; **~ de données** (*Inform*) data bank; **~ d'émission** bank of issue

banqueroute [bãkʀut] *nf* bankruptcy

banquet [bãkɛ] *nm* (*de club*) dinner; (*de noces*) reception; (*d'apparat*) banquet

banquette [bãkɛt] *nf* seat

banquier [bãkje] *nm* banker

banquise [bãkiz] *nf* ice field

bantou, e [bãtu] *adj* Bantu

baptême [batɛm] *nm* (*sacrement*) baptism; (*cérémonie*) christening, baptism; (*d'un navire*) launching; (*d'une cloche*) consecration, dedication; **~ de l'air** first flight

baptiser [batize] *vt* to christen; to baptize; to launch; to consecrate, dedicate

baptiste [batist(ə)] *adj*, *nm/f* Baptist

baquet [bakɛ] *nm* tub, bucket

bar [baʀ] *nm* bar; (*poisson*) bass

baragouin [baʀagwɛ̃] *nm* gibberish

baragouiner [baʀagwine] *vi* to gibber, jabber

baraque [baʀak] *nf* shed; (*fam*) house; **~ foraine** fairground stand

baraqué, e [baʀake] *adj* well-built, hefty

baraquements [baʀakmã] *nmpl* huts (*for refugees, workers etc*)

baratin [baʀatɛ̃] *nm* (*fam*) smooth talk, patter

baratiner [baʀatine] *vt* to chat up

baratte [baʀat] *nf* churn

Barbade [baʀbad] *nf*: **la ~** Barbados

barbant, e [baʀbã, -ãt] *adj* (*fam*) deadly (boring)

barbare [baʀbaʀ] *adj* barbaric ▷ *nm/f* barbarian

Barbarie [baʀbaʀi] *nf*: **la ~** the Barbary Coast

barbarie [baʀbaʀi] *nf* barbarism; (*cruauté*) barbarity

barbarisme [baʀbaʀism(ə)] *nm* (*Ling*) barbarism

barbe [baʀb(ə)] *nf* beard; (*fam*) **à la ~ de qn** (*fig*) under sb's very nose; **quelle ~!** (*fam*) what a drag *ou* bore!; **~ à papa** candy-floss (*Brit*), cotton candy (*US*)

barbecue [baʀbəkju] *nm* barbecue

barbelé [baʀbəle] *nm* barbed wire *no pl*

barber [baʀbe] *vt* (*fam*) to bore stiff

barbiche [baʀbiʃ] *nf* goatee

barbichette [baʀbiʃɛt] *nf* small goatee

barbiturique [baʀbityʀik] *nm* barbiturate

barboter [baʀbɔte] *vi* to paddle, dabble ▷ *vt* (*fam*) to filch

barboteuse [baʀbɔtøz] *nf* rompers *pl*

barbouiller [baʀbuje] *vt* to daub; (*péj: écrire, dessiner*) to scribble; **avoir l'estomac barbouillé** to feel queasy *ou* sick

barbu, e [baʀby] *adj* bearded

barbue [baʀby] *nf* (*poisson*) brill

Barcelone [baʀsələn] *n* Barcelona

barda [baʀda] *nm* (*fam*) kit, gear

barde [baʀd(ə)] *nf* (*Culin*) piece of fat bacon ▷ *nm* (*poète*) bard

bardé, e [baʀde] *adj*: **~ de médailles** *etc* bedecked with medals *etc*

bardeaux [baʀdo] *nmpl* shingle *no pl*

barder [baʀde] *vt* (*Culin: rôti, volaille*) to bard ▷ *vi* (*fam*): **ça va ~** sparks will fly

barème [baʀɛm] *nm* scale; (*liste*) table; **~ des salaires** salary scale

barge [baʀʒ] *nf* barge

baril [baʀil] *nm* (*tonneau*) barrel; (*de poudre*) keg

barillet [baʀijɛ] *nm* (*de revolver*) cylinder

bariolé, e [baʀjɔle] *adj* many-coloured, rainbow-coloured

barman [baʀman] *nm* barman

baromètre [baʀɔmɛtʀ(ə)] *nm* barometer; **~ anéroïde** aneroid barometer

baron [baʀɔ̃] *nm* baron

baronne [baʀɔn] *nf* baroness

baroque [baʀɔk] *adj* (*Art*) baroque; (*fig*) weird

baroud [baʀud] *nm*: **~ d'honneur** gallant last stand

baroudeur [baʀudœʀ] *nm* (*fam*) fighter

barque [baʀk(ə)] *nf* small boat

barquette [baʀkɛt] *nf* small boat-shaped tart; (*récipient: en aluminium*) tub; (: *en bois*) basket

barracuda [baʀakyda] *nm* barracuda

barrage [baʀaʒ] *nm* dam; (*sur route*) roadblock, barricade; **~ de police** police roadblock

barre [baʀ] *nf* (*de fer etc*) rod; (*Navig*) helm; (*écrite*) line, stroke; (*Danse*) barre; (*niveau*): **la livre a franchi la ~ des 1,70 euros** the pound has broken the 1.70 euros barrier; (*Jur*): **comparaître à la ~** to appear as a witness; **être à** *ou* **tenir la ~** (*Navig*) to be at the helm; **coup de ~** (*fig*): **c'est le coup de ~!** it's daylight robbery!; **j'ai le coup de ~!** I'm all in!; **~ fixe** (*Gym*) horizontal bar; **~ de mesure** (*Mus*) bar line; **~ à mine** crowbar; **~s parallèles/asymétriques** (*Gym*) parallel/asymmetric bars

barreau, x [baʀo] *nm* bar; (*Jur*): **le ~** the Bar

barrer [baʀe] *vt* (*route etc*) to block; (*mot*) to cross out; (*chèque*) to cross (*Brit*); (*Navig*) to steer; **se barrer** *vi* (*fam*) to clear off

barrette [baʀɛt] *nf* (*pour cheveux*) (hair) slide (*Brit*) *ou* clip (*US*); (*broche*) brooch

barreur [baʀœʀ] *nm* helmsman; (*aviron*) coxswain

barricade [baʀikad] *nf* barricade

barricader [baʀikade] *vt* to barricade; **se ~ chez soi** (*fig*) to lock o.s. in

barrière [baʀjɛʀ] *nf* fence; (*obstacle*) barrier; (*porte*) gate; **la Grande B~** the Great Barrier Reef; **~ de dégel** (*Admin: on roadsigns*) no heavy vehicles -- road liable to subsidence due to thaw; **~s douanières** trade barriers

barrique [baʀik] *nf* barrel, cask

barrir [baʀiʀ] *vi* to trumpet

bar-tabac [baʀtaba] *nm* bar (*which sells tobacco and stamps*)

baryton [baʀitɔ̃] *nm* baritone
bas, basse [bɑ, bɑs] *adj* low; (*action*) low, ignoble
▷ *nm* (*vêtement*) stocking; (*partie inférieure*): **le ~
de** the lower part *ou* foot *ou* bottom of ▷ *nf* (*Mus*)
bass ▷ *adv* low; (*parler*) softly; **plus ~** lower
down; more softly; (*dans un texte*) further on,
below; **la tête ~se** with lowered head; (*fig*)
with head hung low; **avoir la vue ~se** to be
short-sighted; **au ~ mot** at the lowest estimate;
enfant en ~ âge infant, young child; **en ~**
down below; at (*ou* to) the bottom; (*dans une
maison*) downstairs; **en ~ de** at the bottom of;
de ~ en haut upwards; from the bottom to the
top; **des hauts et des ~** ups and downs; **un ~
de laine** (*fam: économies*) money under the
mattress (*fig*); **mettre ~** *vi* (*animal*) to give birth;
à ~ la dictature! down with dictatorship!; **~
morceaux** (*viande*) cheap cuts
basalte [bazalt(ə)] *nm* basalt
basané, e [bazane] *adj* (*teint*) tanned, bronzed;
(*foncé; péj*) swarthy
bas-côté [bakote] *nm* (*de route*) verge (*Brit*),
shoulder (*US*); (*d'église*) (side) aisle
bascule [baskyl] *nf*: (**jeu de**) ~ seesaw; (**balance
à**) ~ scales *pl*; **fauteuil à ~** rocking chair;
système à ~ tip-over device; rocker device
basculer [baskyle] *vi* to fall over, topple (over);
(*benne*) to tip up ▷ *vt* (*aussi*: **faire basculer**) to
topple over; to tip out, tip up
base [baz] *nf* base; (*Pol*): **la ~** the rank and file,
the grass roots; (*fondement, principe*) basis (*pl
bases*); **jeter les ~s de** to lay the foundations of;
à la ~ de (*fig*) at the root of; **sur la ~ de** (*fig*) on
the basis of; **de ~** basic; **à ~ de café** *etc* coffee *etc*
-based; **~ de données** (*Inform*) database; **~ de
lancement** launching site
base-ball [bɛzbol] *nm* baseball
baser [baze] *vt*: **~ qch sur** to base sth on; **se ~
sur** (*données, preuves*) to base one's argument on;
être basé à/dans (*Mil*) to be based at/in
bas-fond [bafɔ̃] *nm* (*Navig*) shallow; **bas-fonds**
nmpl (*fig*) dregs
basilic [bazilik] *nm* (*Culin*) basil
basilique [bazilik] *nf* basilica
basket [baskɛt], **basket-ball** [baskɛtbol] *nm*
basketball
baskets [baskɛt] *nfpl* (*chaussures*) trainers (*Brit*),
sneakers (*US*)
basketteur, -euse [baskɛtœʀ, -øz] *nm/f*
basketball player
basquaise [baskɛz] *adj f* Basque ▷ *nf*: **B~** Basque
basque [bask(ə)] *adj, nm* (*Ling*) Basque ▷ *nm/f*:
Basque Basque; **le Pays ~** the Basque country
basques [bask(ə)] *nfpl* skirts; **pendu aux ~ de
qn** constantly pestering sb; (*mère etc*) hanging
on sb's apron strings
bas-relief [baʀəljɛf] *nm* bas-relief
basse [bɑs] *adj f, nf voir* **bas**
basse-cour [baskuʀ] (*pl* **basses-cours**) *nf*
farmyard; (*animaux*) farmyard animals
bassement [bɑsmɑ̃] *adv* basely
bassesse [bɑsɛs] *nf* baseness; (*acte*) base act

basset [bɑsɛ] *nm* (*Zool*) basset (hound)
bassin [bɑsɛ̃] *nm* (*cuvette*) bowl; (*pièce d'eau*) pond,
pool; (*de fontaine, Géo*) basin; (*Anat*) pelvis;
(*portuaire*) dock; **~ houiller** coalfield
bassine [basin] *nf* basin; (*contenu*) bowl, bowlful
bassiner [basine] *vt* (*plaie*) to bathe; (*lit*) to
warm with a warming pan; (*fam: ennuyer*) to
bore; (: *importuner*) to bug, pester
bassiste [basist(ə)] *nm/f* (double) bass player
basson [basɔ̃] *nm* bassoon
bastide [bastid] *nf* (*maison*) country house (*in
Provence*); (*ville*) walled town (*in SW France*)
bastion [bastjɔ̃] *nm* (*aussi fig, Pol*) bastion
bas-ventre [bavɑ̃tʀ(ə)] *nm* (lower part of the)
stomach
bât [bɑ] *nm* packsaddle
bataille [bataj] *nf* battle; **en ~** (*en travers*) at an
angle; (*en désordre*) awry; **~ rangée** pitched
battle
bataillon [batajɔ̃] *nm* battalion
bâtard, e [bɑtaʀ, -aʀd(ə)] *adj* (*enfant*)
illegitimate; (*fig*) hybrid ▷ *nm/f* illegitimate
child, bastard (*péj*) ▷ *nm* (*Boulangerie*) ≈ Vienna
loaf; **chien ~** mongrel
batavia [batavja] *nf* ≈ Webb lettuce
bateau, x [bato] *nm* boat; (*grand*) ship ▷ *adj inv*
(*banal, rebattu*) hackneyed; **~ de pêche/à
moteur/à voiles** fishing/motor/sailing boat
bateau-citerne [batositɛʀn(ə)] *nm* tanker
bateau-mouche [batomuʃ] *nm* (passenger)
pleasure boat (*on the Seine*)
bateau-pilote [batopilɔt] *nm* pilot ship
bateleur, -euse [batlœʀ, -øz] *nm/f* street
performer
batelier, -ière [batəlje, -jɛʀ] *nm/f* ferryman/-
woman
bâti, e [bati] *adj* (*terrain*) developed ▷ *nm*
(*armature*) frame; (*Couture*) tacking; **bien ~**
(*personne*) well-built
batifoler [batifɔle] *vi* to frolic *ou* lark about
batik [batik] *nm* batik
bâtiment [batimɑ̃] *nm* building; (*Navig*) ship,
vessel; (*industrie*): **le ~** the building trade
bâtir [batiʀ] *vt* to build; (*Couture: jupe, ourlet*) to
tack; **fil à ~** (*Couture*) tacking thread
bâtisse [batis] *nf* building
bâtisseur, -euse [batisœʀ, -øz] *nm/f* builder
batiste [batist(ə)] *nf* (*Couture*) batiste, cambric
bâton [batɔ̃] *nm* stick; **mettre des ~s dans les
roues à qn** to put a spoke in sb's wheel; **à ~s
rompus** informally; **~ de rouge (à lèvres)**
lipstick; **~ de ski** ski stick
bâtonnet [batɔnɛ] *nm* short stick *ou* rod
bâtonnier [batɔnje] *nm* (*Jur*) ≈ President of the
Bar
batraciens [batʀasjɛ̃] *nmpl* amphibians
bats [ba] *vb voir* **battre**
battage [bataʒ] *nm* (*publicité*) (hard) plugging
battant, e [batɑ̃, -ɑ̃t] *vb voir* **battre** ▷ *adj*: **pluie
~e** lashing rain ▷ *nm* (*de cloche*) clapper; (*de
volets*) shutter, flap; (*de porte*) side; (*fig: personne*)
fighter; **porte à double ~** double door;

tambour ~ briskly

batte [bat] *nf* (*Sport*) bat

battement [batmã] *nm* (*de cœur*) beat; (*intervalle*) interval (*between classes, trains etc*); ~ **de paupières** blinking *no pl* (of eyelids); **un** ~ **de 10 minutes, 10 minutes de** ~ 10 minutes to spare

batterie [batʀi] *nf* (*Mil, Élec*) battery; (*Mus*) drums *pl*, drum kit; ~ **de cuisine** kitchen utensils *pl*; (*casseroles etc*) pots and pans *pl*; **une** ~ **de tests** a string of tests

batteur [batœʀ] *nm* (*Mus*) drummer; (*appareil*) whisk

batteuse [batøz] *nf* (*Agr*) threshing machine

battoir [batwaʀ] *nm* (*à linge*) beetle (*for laundry*); (*à tapis*) (carpet) beater

battre [batʀ(ə)] *vt* to beat; (*pluie, vagues*) to beat *ou* lash against; (*œufs etc*) to beat up, whisk; (*blé*) to thresh; (*cartes*) to shuffle; (*passer au peigne fin*) to scour ▷ *vi* (*cœur*) to beat; (*volets etc*) to bang, rattle; **se battre** *vi* to fight; ~ **la mesure** to beat time; ~ **en brèche** (*Mil: mur*) to batter; (*fig: théorie*) to demolish; (*: institution etc*) to attack; ~ **son plein** to be at its height, be going full swing; ~ **pavillon britannique** to fly the British flag; ~ **des mains** to clap one's hands; ~ **des ailes** to flap its wings; ~ **de l'aile** (*fig*) to be in a bad way *ou* in bad shape; ~ **la semelle** to stamp one's feet; ~ **en retraite** to beat a retreat

battu, e [baty] *pp de* **battre** ▷ *nf* (*chasse*) beat; (*policière etc*) search, hunt

baud [bo(d)] *nm* baud

baudruche [bodʀyʃ] *nf*: **ballon en** ~ (toy) balloon; (*fig*) windbag

baume [bom] *nm* balm

bauxite [boksit] *nf* bauxite

bavard, e [bavaʀ, -aʀd(ə)] *adj* (very) talkative; gossipy

bavardage [bavaʀdaʒ] *nm* chatter *no pl*; gossip *no pl*

bavarder [bavaʀde] *vi* to chatter; (*indiscrètement*) to gossip; (*: révéler un secret*) to blab

bavarois, e [bavaʀwa, -waz] *adj* Bavarian ▷ *nm ou f* (*Culin*) bavarois

bave [bav] *nf* dribble; (*de chien etc*) slobber, slaver (*Brit*), drool (*US*); (*d'escargot*) slime

baver [bave] *vi* to dribble; to slobber, slaver (*Brit*), drool (*US*); (*encre, couleur*) to run; **en** ~ (*fam*) to have a hard time (of it)

bavette [bavɛt] *nf* bib

baveux, -euse [bavø, -øz] *adj* dribbling; (*omelette*) runny

Bavière [bavjɛʀ] *nf*: **la** ~ Bavaria

bavoir [bavwaʀ] *nm* (*de bébé*) bib

bavure [bavyʀ] *nf* smudge; (*fig*) hitch; blunder

bayer [baje] *vi*: ~ **aux corneilles** to stand gaping

bazar [bazaʀ] *nm* general store; (*fam*) jumble

bazarder [bazaʀde] *vt* (*fam*) to chuck out

BCBG *sigle adj* (= *bon chic bon genre*) ≈ preppy

BCG *sigle m* (= *bacille Calmette-Guérin*) BCG

bcp *abr* = **beaucoup**

BD *sigle f* = **bande dessinée**; (= *base de données*) DB

bd *abr* = **boulevard**

b.d.c. *abr* (*Typo*: = *bas de casse*) l.c.

béant, e [beã, -ãt] *adj* gaping

béarnais, e [beaʀnɛ, -ɛz] *adj* of *ou* from the Béarn

béat, e [bea, -at] *adj* showing open-eyed wonder; (*sourire etc*) blissful

béatitude [beatityd] *nf* bliss

beau, bel, belle, beaux [bo, bɛl] *adj* beautiful, lovely; (*homme*) handsome ▷ *nf* (*Sport*) decider ▷ *adv*: **il fait** ~ the weather's fine ▷ *nm*: **avoir le sens du** ~ to have an aesthetic sense; **le temps est au** ~ the weather is set fair; **un** ~ **geste** (*fig*) a fine gesture; **un** ~ **salaire** a good salary; **un** ~ **gâchis/rhume** a fine mess/nasty cold; **en faire/dire de belles** to do/say (some) stupid things; **le** ~ **monde** high society; ~ **parleur** smooth talker; **un** ~ **jour** one (fine) day; **de plus belle** more than ever, even more; **bel et bien** well and truly; (*vraiment*) really (and truly); **le plus** ~ **c'est que** ... the best of it is that ...; **c'est du** ~! that's great, that is!; **on a** ~ **essayer** however hard *ou* no matter how hard we try; **il a** ~ **jeu de protester** *etc* it's easy for him to protest *etc*; **faire le** ~ (*chien*) to sit up and beg

 MOT-CLÉ

beaucoup [boku] *adv* **1** a lot; **il boit beaucoup** he drinks a lot; **il ne boit pas beaucoup** he doesn't drink much *ou* a lot

2 (*suivi de plus, trop etc*) much, a lot, far; **il est beaucoup plus grand** he is much *ou* a lot *ou* far taller

3: **beaucoup de** (*nombre*) many, a lot of; (*quantité*) a lot of; **pas beaucoup de** (*nombre*) not many, not a lot of; (*quantité*) not much, not a lot of; **beaucoup d'étudiants/de touristes** a lot of *ou* many students/tourists; **beaucoup de courage** a lot of courage; **il n'a pas beaucoup d'argent** he hasn't got much *ou* a lot of money; **il n'y a pas beaucoup de touristes** there aren't many *ou* a lot of tourists

4: **de beaucoup** by far

▷ *pron*: **beaucoup le savent** lots of people know that

beau-fils [bofis] (*pl* **beaux-fils**) *nm* son-in-law; (*remariage*) stepson

beau-frère [bofʀɛʀ] (*pl* **beaux-frères**) *nm* brother-in-law

beau-père [bopɛʀ] (*pl* **beaux-pères**) *nm* father-in-law; (*remariage*) stepfather

beauté [bote] *nf* beauty; **de toute** ~ beautiful; **en** ~ *adv* with a flourish, brilliantly

beaux-arts [bozaʀ] *nmpl* fine arts

beaux-parents [bopaʀã] *nmpl* wife's/husband's family, in-laws

bébé [bebe] *nm* baby

bébé-éprouvette [bebeepʀuvɛt] (*pl* **bébés-éprouvette**) *nm* test-tube baby

bec [bɛk] *nm* beak, bill; (*de plume*) nib; (*de cafetière etc*) spout; (*de casserole etc*) lip; (*d'une clarinette etc*) mouthpiece; (*fam*) mouth; **clouer le ~ à qn** (*fam*) to shut sb up; **ouvrir le ~** (*fam*) to open one's mouth; **~ de gaz** (street) gaslamp; **~ verseur** pouring lip

bécane [bekan] *nf* (*fam*) bike

bécarre [bekaʀ] *nm* (*Mus*) natural

bécasse [bekas] *nf* (*Zool*) woodcock; (*fam*) silly goose

bec-de-cane [bɛkdəkan] (*pl* **becs-de-cane**) *nm* (*poignée*) door handle

bec-de-lièvre [bɛkdəljɛvʀ(ə)] (*pl* **becs-de-lièvre**) *nm* harelip

béchamel [beʃamɛl] *nf*: (**sauce**) ~ white sauce, bechamel sauce

bêche [bɛʃ] *nf* spade

bêcher [beʃe] *vt* (*terre*) to dig; (*personne: critiquer*) to slate; (: *snober*) to look down on

bêcheur, -euse [beʃœʀ, -øz] *adj* (*fam*) stuck-up ▷ *nm/f* fault-finder; (*snob*) stuck-up person

bécoter [bekɔte]: **se bécoter** *vi* to smooch

becquée [beke] *nf*: **donner la ~ à** to feed

becqueter [bɛkte] *vt* (*fam*) to eat

bedaine [bədɛn] *nf* paunch

bédé [bede] *nf* (*fam*) = **bande dessinée**

bedeau, x [bədo] *nm* beadle

bedonnant, e [bədɔnã, -ãt] *adj* paunchy, potbellied

bée [be] *adj*: **bouche ~** gaping

beffroi [befʀwa] *nm* belfry

bégaiement [begɛmã] *nm* stammering, stuttering

bégayer [begeje] *vt, vi* to stammer

bégonia [begɔnja] *nm* (*Bot*) begonia

bègue [bɛg] *nm/f*: **être ~** to have a stammer

bégueule [begœl] *adj* prudish

beige [bɛʒ] *adj* beige

beignet [beɲɛ] *nm* fritter

bel [bɛl] *adj m voir* **beau**

bêler [bele] *vi* to bleat

belette [bəlɛt] *nf* weasel

belge [bɛlʒ(ə)] *adj* Belgian ▷ *nm/f*: **Belge** Belgian; *see note*

⬤ **FÊTE NATIONALE BELGE**
⬤
⬤ The *fête nationale belge*, on 21 July, marks the
⬤ day in 1831 when Leopold of Saxe-Coburg
⬤ Gotha was crowned King Leopold I.

Belgique [bɛlʒik] *nf*: **la ~** Belgium

Belgrade [bɛlgʀad] *n* Belgrade

bélier [belje] *nm* ram; (*engin*) (battering) ram; (*signe*): **le B~** Aries, the Ram; **être du B~** to be Aries

Bélize [beliz] *nm*: **le ~** Belize

bellâtre [bɛlɑtʀ(ə)] *nm* dandy

belle [bɛl] *adj f, nf voir* **beau**

belle-famille [bɛlfamij] (*pl* **belles-familles**) *nf* (*fam*) in-laws *pl*

belle-fille [bɛlfij] (*pl* **belles-filles**) *nf* daughter-in-law; (*remariage*) stepdaughter

belle-mère [bɛlmɛʀ] (*pl* **belles-mères**) *nf*

mother-in-law; (*remariage*) stepmother

belle-sœur [bɛlsœʀ] (*pl* **belles-sœurs**) *nf* sister-in-law

belliciste [belisist(ə)] *adj* warmongering

belligérance [beliʒeʀãs] *nf* belligerence

belligérant, e [beliʒeʀã, -ãt] *adj* belligerent

belliqueux, -euse [belikø, -øz] *adj* aggressive, warlike

belote [bəlɔt] *nf* belote (*card game*)

belvédère [bɛlvedɛʀ] *nm* panoramic viewpoint (*or small building there*)

bémol [bemɔl] *nm* (*Mus*) flat

ben [bɛ̃] *excl* (*fam*) well

bénédiction [benediksjɔ̃] *nf* blessing

bénéfice [benefis] *nm* (*Comm*) profit; (*avantage*) benefit; **au ~ de** in aid of

bénéficiaire [benefisjɛʀ] *nm/f* beneficiary

bénéficier [benefisje] *vi*: **~ de** to enjoy; (*profiter*) to benefit by *ou* from; (*obtenir*) to get, be given

bénéfique [benefik] *adj* beneficial

Bénélux [benelyks] *nm*: **le ~** Benelux, the Benelux countries

benêt [bənɛ] *nm* simpleton

bénévolat [benevɔla] *nm* voluntary service *ou* work

bénévole [benevɔl] *adj* voluntary, unpaid

bénévolement [benevɔlmã] *adv* voluntarily

Bengale [bɛ̃gal] *nm*: **le ~** Bengal; **le golfe du ~** the Bay of Bengal

bengali [bɛ̃gali] *adj* Bengali, Bengalese ▷ *nm* (*Ling*) Bengali

Bénin [benɛ̃] *nm*: **le ~** Benin

bénin, -igne [benɛ̃, -iɲ] *adj* minor, mild; (*tumeur*) benign

bénir [beniʀ] *vt* to bless

bénit, e [beni, -it] *adj* consecrated; **eau ~e** holy water

bénitier [benitje] *nm* stoup, font (*for holy water*)

benjamin, e [bɛ̃ʒamɛ̃, -in] *nm/f* youngest child; (*Sport*) under-13

benne [bɛn] *nf* skip; (*de téléphérique*) (cable) car; **~ basculante** tipper (*Brit*), dump *ou* dumper truck

benzine [bɛ̃zin] *nf* benzine

béotien, ne [beɔsjɛ̃, -ɛn] *nm/f* philistine

BEP *sigle m* (= *Brevet d'études professionnelles*) school-leaving diploma, taken at approx. 18 years

BEPC *sigle m* (= *Brevet d'études du premier cycle*) former school certificate (taken at approx. 16 years)

béquille [bekij] *nf* crutch; (*de bicyclette*) stand

berbère [bɛʀbɛʀ] *adj* Berber ▷ *nm* (*Ling*) Berber ▷ *nm/f*: **Berbère** Berber

bercail [bɛʀkaj] *nm* fold

berceau, x [bɛʀso] *nm* cradle, crib

bercer [bɛʀse] *vt* to rock, cradle; (*musique etc*) to lull; **~ qn de** (*promesses etc*) to delude sb with

berceur, -euse [bɛʀsœʀ, -øz] *adj* soothing ▷ *nf* (*chanson*) lullaby

BERD [bɛʀd] *sigle f* (= *Banque européenne pour la reconstruction et le développement*) EBRD

béret [beʀɛ], **béret basque** [beʀɛbask(ə)] *nm* beret

bergamote [bɛʀgamɔt] *nf* (*Bot*) bergamot

berge [bɛʀʒ(ə)] *nf* bank

berger, -ère [bɛʀʒe, -ɛʀ] *nm/f* shepherd/ shepherdess; **~ allemand** (*chien*) alsatian (dog) (*Brit*), German shepherd (dog) (*US*)

bergerie [bɛʀʒəʀi] *nf* sheep pen

bergeronnette [bɛʀʒəʀɔnɛt] *nf* wagtail

béribéri [beʀibeʀi] *nm* beriberi

Berlin [bɛʀlɛ̃] *n* Berlin; **~-Est/-Ouest** East/West Berlin

berline [bɛʀlin] *nf* (*Auto*) saloon (car) (*Brit*), sedan (*US*)

berlingot [bɛʀlɛ̃go] *nm* (*emballage*) carton (*pyramid shaped*); (*bonbon*) lozenge

berlinois, e [bɛʀlinwa, -waz] *adj* of *ou* from Berlin ▷ *nm/f*: **Berlinois, e** Berliner

berlue [bɛʀly] *nf*: **j'ai la ~** I must be seeing things

bermuda [bɛʀmyda] *nm* (*short*) Bermuda shorts

Bermudes [bɛʀmyd] *nfpl*: **les (îles) ~** Bermuda

Berne [bɛʀn(ə)] *n* Bern

berne [bɛʀn(ə)] *nf*: **en ~** at half-mast; **mettre en ~** to fly at half-mast

berner [bɛʀne] *vt* to fool

bernois, e [bɛʀnwa, -waz] *adj* Bernese

berrichon, ne [bɛʀiʃɔ̃, -ɔn] *adj* of *ou* from the Berry

besace [bəzas] *nf* beggar's bag

besogne [bəzɔɲ] *nf* work *no pl*, job

besogneux, -euse [bəzɔɲø, -øz] *adj* hard-working

besoin [bəzwɛ̃] *nm* need; (*pauvreté*): **le ~** need, want; **le ~ d'argent/de gloire** the need for money/glory; **~s (naturels)** nature's needs; **faire ses ~s** to relieve o.s.; **avoir ~ de qch/faire qch** to need sth/to do sth; **il n'y a pas ~ de (faire)** there is no need to (do); **au ~, si ~ est** if need be; **pour les ~s de la cause** for the purpose in hand

bestial, e, -aux [bɛstjal, -o] *adj* bestial, brutish ▷ *nmpl* cattle

bestiole [bɛstjɔl] *nf* (tiny) creature

bétail [betaj] *nm* livestock, cattle *pl*

bétaillère [betajɛʀ] *nf* livestock truck

bête [bɛt] *nf* animal; (*bestiole*) insect, creature ▷ *adj* stupid, silly; **les ~s** (the) animals; **chercher la petite ~** to nit-pick; **~ noire** pet hate, bugbear (*Brit*); **~ sauvage** wild beast; **~ de somme** beast of burden

bêtement [bɛtmɑ̃] *adv* stupidly; **tout ~** quite simply

Bethléem [bɛtleɛm] *n* Bethlehem

bêtifier [betifje] *vi* to talk nonsense

bêtise [betiz] *nf* stupidity; (*action, remarque*) stupid thing (to say *ou* do); (*bonbon*) type of mint sweet (*Brit*) *ou* candy (*US*); **faire/dire une ~** to do/say something stupid

béton [betɔ̃] *nm* concrete; **(en) ~** (*fig*: *alibi, argument*) cast iron; **~ armé** reinforced concrete; **~ précontraint** prestressed concrete

bétonner [betɔne] *vt* to concrete (over)

bétonnière [betɔnjɛʀ] *nf* cement mixer

bette [bɛt] *nf* (*Bot*) (Swiss) chard

betterave [bɛtʀav] *nf* (*rouge*) beetroot (*Brit*), beet (*US*); **~ fourragère** mangel-wurzel; **~ sucrière** sugar beet

beugler [bøgle] *vi* to low; (*péj*: *radio etc*) to blare ▷ *vt* (*péj*: *chanson etc*) to bawl out

Beur [bœʀ] *adj, nm/f see note*

● **Beur**

● *Beur* is a term used to refer to a person born
● in France of North African immigrant
● parents. It is not racist and is often used by
● the media, anti-racist groups and second-
● generation North Africans themselves. The
● word itself comes from back slang or
● "verlan".

beurre [bœʀ] *nm* butter; **mettre du ~ dans les épinards** (*fig*) to add a little to the kitty; **~ de cacao** cocoa butter; **~ noir** brown butter (sauce)

beurrer [bœʀe] *vt* to butter

beurrier [bœʀje] *nm* butter dish

beuverie [bœvʀi] *nf* drinking session

bévue [bevy] *nf* blunder

Beyrouth [beʀut] *n* Beirut

Bhoutan [butɑ̃] *nm*: **le ~** Bhutan

bi... [bi] *préfixe* bi..., two-

Biafra [bjafʀa] *nm*: **le ~** Biafra

biafrais, e [bjafʀɛ, -ɛz] *adj* Biafran

biais [bjɛ] *nm* (*moyen*) device, expedient; (*aspect*) angle; (*bande de tissu*) piece of cloth cut on the bias; **en ~, de ~** (*obliquement*) at an angle; (*fig*) indirectly

biaiser [bjeze] *vi* (*fig*) to sidestep the issue

biathlon [biatlɔ̃] *nm* biathlon

bibelot [biblo] *nm* trinket, curio

biberon [bibʀɔ̃] *nm* (feeding) bottle; **nourrir au ~** to bottle-feed

bible [bibl(ə)] *nf* bible

bibliobus [biblijɔbys] *nm* mobile library van

bibliographie [biblijɔgʀafi] *nf* bibliography

bibliophile [biblijɔfil] *nm/f* book-lover

bibliothécaire [biblijɔtekɛʀ] *nm/f* librarian

bibliothèque [biblijɔtɛk] *nf* library; (*meuble*) bookcase; **~ municipale** public library

biblique [biblik] *adj* biblical

bic® [bik] *nm* Biro®

bicarbonate [bikaʀbɔnat] *nm*: **~ (de soude)** bicarbonate of soda

bicentenaire [bisɑ̃tnɛʀ] *nm* bicentenary

biceps [bisɛps] *nm* biceps

biche [biʃ] *nf* doe

bichonner [biʃɔne] *vt* to groom

bicolore [bikɔlɔʀ] *adj* two-coloured (*Brit*), two-colored (*US*)

bicoque [bikɔk] *nf* (*péj*) shack, dump

bicorne [bikɔʀn(ə)] *nm* cocked hat

bicyclette [bisiklɛt] *nf* bicycle

bidasse [bidas] *nm* (*fam*) squaddie (*Brit*)

bide [bid] *nm* (*fam*: *ventre*) belly; (*Théât*) flop

bidet [bidɛ] *nm* bidet

bidoche [bidɔʃ] *nf* (*fam*) meat

bidon [bidɔ̃] *nm* can ▷ *adj inv* (*fam*) phoney
bidonnant, e [bidɔnɑ̃, -ɑ̃t] *adj* (*fam*) hilarious
bidonville [bidɔ̃vil] *nm* shanty town
bidule [bidyl] *nm* (*fam*) thingamajig
bielle [bjɛl] *nf* connecting rod; (*Auto*) track rod
biélorusse [bjelɔRys] *adj* Belarussian ▷ *nm/f*:
  Biélorusse Belarussian
Biélorussie [bjelɔRysi] *nf* Belorussia

 MOT-CLÉ

bien [bjɛ̃] *nm* **1** (*avantage, profit*): **faire le bien** to
do good; **faire du bien à qn** to do sb good; **ça
fait du bien de faire** it does you good to do;
dire du bien de to speak well of; **c'est pour
son bien** it's for his own good; **changer en
bien** to change for the better; **le bien public**
the public good; **vouloir du bien à qn** (*vouloir
aider*) to have sb's (best) interests at heart; **je te
veux du bien** (*pour mettre en confiance*) I don't
wish you any harm
2 (*possession, patrimoine*) possession, property;
son bien le plus précieux his most treasured
possession; **avoir du bien** to have property;
biens (de consommation *etc*) (consumer *etc*)
goods; **biens durables** (consumer) durables
3 (*moral*): **le bien** good; **distinguer le bien du
mal** to tell good from evil
▷ *adv* **1** (*de façon satisfaisante*) well; **elle travaille/
mange bien** she works/eats well; **aller** *or* **se
porter bien** to be well; **croyant bien faire, je/
il ...** thinking I/he was doing the right thing, I/
he ...
2 (*valeur intensive*) quite; **bien jeune** quite
young; **bien assez** quite enough; **bien mieux**
(very) much better; **bien du temps/des gens**
quite a time/a number of people; **j'espère bien
y aller** I do hope to go; **je veux bien le faire**
(*concession*) I'm quite willing to do it; **il faut
bien le faire** it has to be done; **il y a bien deux
ans** at least two years ago; **il semble bien que**
it really seems that; **peut-être bien** it could
well be; **aimer bien** to like; **Paul est bien
venu, n'est-ce pas?** Paul HAS come, hasn't
he?; **où peut-il bien être passé?** where on
earth can he have got to?
3 (*conséquence, résultat*): **si bien que** with the
result that; **on verra bien** we'll see; **faire bien
de ...** to be right to ...
▷ *excl* right!, OK!, fine!; **eh bien!** well!; **(c'est)
bien fait!** it serves you (*ou* him *etc*) right!; **bien
sûr!, bien entendu!** certainly!, of course!
▷ *adj inv* **1** (*en bonne forme, à l'aise*): **je me sens
bien, je suis bien** I feel fine; **je ne me sens pas
bien, je ne suis pas bien** I don't feel well; **on
est bien dans ce fauteuil** this chair is very
comfortable
2 (*joli, beau*) good-looking; **tu es bien dans
cette robe** you look good in that dress
3 (*satisfaisant*) good; **elle est bien, cette
maison/secrétaire** it's a good house/she's a
good secretary; **c'est très bien (comme ça)** it's

fine (like that); **ce n'est pas si bien que ça** it's
not as good *ou* great as all that; **c'est bien?** is
that all right?
4 (*moralement*) right; (: *personne*) good, nice;
(*respectable*) respectable; **ce n'est pas bien de ...**
it's not right to ...; **elle est bien, cette femme**
she's a nice woman, she's a good sort; **des gens
bien** respectable people
5 (*en bons termes*): **être bien avec qn** to be on
good terms with sb

bien-aimé, e [bjɛ̃neme] *adj, nm/f* beloved
bien-être [bjɛ̃nɛtR(ə)] *nm* well-being
bienfaisance [bjɛ̃fəzɑ̃s] *nf* charity
bienfaisant, e [bjɛ̃fəzɑ̃, -ɑ̃t] *adj* (*chose*) beneficial
bienfait [bjɛ̃fɛ] *nm* act of generosity,
  benefaction; (*de la science etc*) benefit
bienfaiteur, -trice [bjɛ̃fɛtœR, -tRis] *nm/f*
  benefactor/benefactress
bien-fondé [bjɛ̃fɔ̃de] *nm* soundness
bien-fonds [bjɛ̃fɔ̃] *nm* property
bienheureux, -euse [bjɛ̃nœRø, -øz] *adj* happy;
  (*Rel*) blessed, blest
biennal, e, -aux [bjenal, -o] *adj* biennial
bien-pensant, e [bjɛ̃pɑ̃sɑ̃, -ɑ̃t] *adj* right-
  thinking ▷ *nm/f*: **les ~s** right-minded people
bien que [bjɛ̃k(ə)] *conj* although
bienséance [bjɛ̃seɑ̃s] *nf* propriety, decorum *no
  pl*; **les ~s** (*convenances*) the proprieties
bienséant, e [bjɛ̃seɑ̃, -ɑ̃t] *adj* proper, seemly
bientôt [bjɛ̃to] *adv* soon; **à ~** see you soon
bienveillance [bjɛ̃vɛjɑ̃s] *nf* kindness
bienveillant, e [bjɛ̃vɛjɑ̃, -ɑ̃t] *adj* kindly
bienvenu, e [bjɛ̃vny] *adj* welcome ▷ *nm/f*: **être
  le ~/la ~e** to be welcome ▷ *nf*: **souhaiter la ~e**
  to welcome; **~e à** welcome to
bière [bjɛR] *nf* (*boisson*) beer; (*cercueil*) bier; **~
  blonde** lager; **~ brune** brown ale; **~ (à la)
  pression** draught beer
biffer [bife] *vt* to cross out
bifteck [biftɛk] *nm* steak
bifurcation [bifyRkasjɔ̃] *nf* fork (*in road*); (*fig*)
  new direction
bifurquer [bifyRke] *vi* (*route*) to fork; (*véhicule*) to
  turn off
bigame [bigam] *adj* bigamous
bigamie [bigami] *nf* bigamy
bigarré, e [bigaRe] *adj* multicoloured (*Brit*),
  multicolored (*US*); (*disparate*) motley
bigarreau, x [bigaRo] *nm* type of cherry
bigleux, -euse [biglø, -øz] *adj* (*fam: qui louche*)
  cross-eyed; (: *qui voit mal*) short-sighted; **il est
  complètement ~** he's as blind as a bat
bigorneau, x [bigɔRno] *nm* winkle
bigot, e [bigo, -ɔt] (*péj*) *adj* bigoted ▷ *nm/f* bigot
bigoterie [bigɔtRi] *nf* bigotry
bigoudi [bigudi] *nm* curler
bigrement [bigRəmɑ̃] *adv* (*fam*) fantastically
bijou, x [biʒu] *nm* jewel
bijouterie [biʒutRi] *nf* (*magasin*) jeweller's
  (shop) (*Brit*), jewelry store (*US*); (*bijoux*)
  jewellery, jewelry

bijoutier, -ière [biʒutje, -jɛʀ] *nm/f* jeweller (*Brit*), jeweler (*US*)

bikini [bikini] *nm* bikini

bilan [bilɑ̃] *nm* (*Comm*) balance sheet(s); (*annuel*) end of year statement; (*fig*) (net) outcome; (: *de victimes*) toll; **faire le ~ de** to assess; to review; **déposer son ~** to file a bankruptcy statement; **~ de santé** (*Méd*) check-up; **~ social** *statement of a firm's policies towards its employees*

bilatéral, e, -aux [bilateʀal, -o] *adj* bilateral

bilboquet [bilbɔkɛ] *nm* (*jouet*) cup-and-ball game

bile [bil] *nf* bile; **se faire de la ~** (*fam*) to worry o.s. sick

biliaire [biljɛʀ] *adj* biliary

bilieux, -euse [biljø, -øz] *adj* bilious; (*fig: colérique*) testy

bilingue [bilɛ̃g] *adj* bilingual

bilinguisme [bilɛ̃gɥism(ə)] *nm* bilingualism

billard [bijaʀ] *nm* billiards *sg*; (*table*) billiard table; **c'est du ~** (*fam*) it's a cinch; **passer sur le ~** (*fam*) to have an (*ou* one's) operation; **~ électrique** pinball

bille [bij] *nf* ball; (*du jeu de billes*) marble; (*de bois*) log; **jouer aux ~s** to play marbles

billet [bijɛ] *nm* (*aussi*: **billet de banque**) (bank)note; (*de cinéma, de bus etc*) ticket; (*courte lettre*) note; **~ à ordre** *ou* **de commerce** (*Comm*) promissory note, IOU; **~ d'avion/de train** plane/train ticket; **~ circulaire** round-trip ticket; **~ doux** love letter; **~ de faveur** complimentary ticket; **~ de loterie** lottery ticket; **~ de quai** platform ticket; **~ électronique** e-ticket

billetterie [bijɛtʀi] *nf* ticket office; (*distributeur*) ticket dispenser; (*Banque*) cash dispenser

billion [biljɔ̃] *nm* billion (*Brit*), trillion (*US*)

billot [bijo] *nm* block

bimbeloterie [bɛ̃blɔtʀi] *nf* (*objets*) fancy goods

bimensuel, le [bimɑ̃sɥɛl] *adj* bimonthly, twice-monthly

bimestriel, le [bimɛstʀijɛl] *adj* bimonthly, two-monthly

bimoteur [bimɔtœʀ] *adj* twin-engined

binaire [binɛʀ] *adj* binary

biner [bine] *vt* to hoe

binette [binɛt] *nf* (*outil*) hoe

binoclard, e [binɔklaʀ, -aʀd(ə)] (*fam*) *adj* specky ▷ *nm/f* four-eyes

binocle [binɔkl(ə)] *nm* pince-nez

binoculaire [binɔkylɛʀ] *adj* binocular

binôme [binom] *nm* binomial

bio [bjo] *adj* (*fam*) = **biologique**; (*produits, aliments*) organic

bio... [bjɔ] *préfixe* bio...

biocarburant [bjokaʀbyʀɑ̃] *nm* biofuel

biochimie [bjɔʃimi] *nf* biochemistry

biochimique [bjɔʃimik] *adj* biochemical

biochimiste [bjɔʃimist(ə)] *nm/f* biochemist

biodégradable [bjɔdegʀadabl(ə)] *adj* biodegradable

biodiversité [bjodivɛʀsite] *nf* biodiversity

bioéthique [bjoetik] *nf* bioethics *sg*

biographe [bjɔgʀaf] *nm/f* biographer

biographie [bjɔgʀafi] *nf* biography

biographique [bjɔgʀafik] *adj* biographical

biologie [bjɔlɔʒi] *nf* biology

biologique [bjɔlɔʒik] *adj* biological

biologiste [bjɔlɔʒist(ə)] *nm/f* biologist

biomasse [bjomas] *nf* biomass

biopsie [bjɔpsi] *nf* (*Méd*) biopsy

biosphère [bjɔsfɛʀ] *nf* biosphere

biotechnologie [bjotɛknɔlɔʒi] *nf* biotechnology

bioterrorisme [bjotɛʀɔʀism] *nm* bioterrorism

bioterroriste [bjotɛʀɔʀist] *nm/f* bioterrorist

biotope [bjɔtɔp] *nm* biotope

bipartisme [bipaʀtism(ə)] *nm* two-party system

bipartite [bipaʀtit] *adj* (*Pol*) two-party, bipartisan

bipède [bipɛd] *nm* biped, two-footed creature

biphasé, e [bifaze] *adj* (*Élec*) two-phase

biplace [biplas] *adj, nm* (*avion*) two-seater

biplan [biplɑ̃] *nm* biplane

bique [bik] *nf* nanny goat; (*péj*) old hag

biquet, te [bikɛ, -ɛt] *nm/f*: **mon ~** (*fam*) my lamb

BIRD [biʀd] *sigle f* (= *Banque internationale pour la reconstruction et le développement*) IBRD

biréacteur [biʀeaktœʀ] *nm* twin-engined jet

birman, e [biʀmɑ̃, -an] *adj* Burmese

Birmanie [biʀmani] *nf*: **la ~** Burma

bis, e [bi, biz] *adj* (*couleur*) greyish brown ▷ *adv* [bis]: **12 ~** 12a *ou* A ▷ *excl, nm* [bis] encore ▷ *nf* (*baiser*) kiss; (*vent*) North wind; **faire une** *ou* **la ~ à qn** to kiss sb

bisaïeul, e [bizajœl] *nm/f* great-grandfather/great-grandmother

bisannuel, le [bizanɥɛl] *adj* biennial

bisbille [bisbij] *nf*: **être en ~ avec qn** to be at loggerheads with sb

Biscaye [biske] *nf*: **le golfe de ~** the Bay of Biscay

biscornu, e [biskɔʀny] *adj* crooked; (*bizarre*) weird(-looking)

biscotte [biskɔt] *nf* (breakfast) rusk

biscuit [biskɥi] *nm* biscuit (*Brit*), cookie (*US*); (*gateau*) sponge cake; **~ à la cuiller** sponge finger

biscuiterie [biskɥitʀi] *nf* biscuit manufacturing

bise [biz] *adj f, nf voir* **bis**

biseau, x [bizo] *nm* bevelled edge; **en ~** bevelled

biseauter [bizote] *vt* to bevel

bisexué, e [bisɛksɥe] *adj* bisexual

bisexuel, le [bisɛksɥɛl] *adj, nm/f* bisexual

bismuth [bismyt] *nm* bismuth

bison [bizɔ̃] *nm* bison

bisou [bizu] *nm* (*fam*) kiss

bisque [bisk(ə)] *nf*: **~ d'écrevisses** shrimp bisque

bissectrice [bisɛktʀis] *nf* bisector

bisser [bise] *vt* (*faire rejouer: artiste, chanson*) to encore; (*rejouer: morceau*) to give an encore of

bissextile [bisɛkstil] *adj*: **année ~** leap year

47

bistouri [bisturi] *nm* lancet
bistre [bistʀ(ə)] *adj* (*couleur*) bistre; (*peau, teint*) tanned
bistro, bistrot [bistʀo] *nm* bistro, café
BIT *sigle m* (= *Bureau international du travail*) ILO
bit [bit] *nm* (*Inform*) bit
biterrois, e [biterwa, -waz] *adj* of *ou* from Béziers
bitte [bit] *nf*: ~ **d'amarrage** bollard (*Naut*)
bitume [bitym] *nm* asphalt
bitumer [bityme] *vt* to asphalt
bivalent, e [bivalã, -ãt] *adj* bivalent
bivouac [bivwak] *nm* bivouac
bizarre [bizaʀ] *adj* strange, odd
bizarrement [bizaʀmã] *adv* strangely, oddly
bizarrerie [bizaʀʀi] *nf* strangeness, oddness
blackbouler [blakbule] *vt* (*à une élection*) to blackball
blafard, e [blafaʀ, -aʀd(ə)] *adj* wan
blague [blag] *nf* (*propos*) joke; (*farce*) trick; **sans** ~! no kidding!; ~ **à tabac** tobacco pouch
blaguer [blage] *vi* to joke ▷ *vt* to tease
blagueur, -euse [blagœʀ, -øz] *adj* teasing ▷ *nm/f* joker
blair [blɛʀ] *nm* (*fam*) conk
blaireau, x [blɛʀo] *nm* (*Zool*) badger; (*brosse*) shaving brush
blairer [blɛʀe] *vt*: **je ne peux pas le ~** I can't bear *ou* stand him
blâmable [blɑmabl(ə)] *adj* blameworthy
blâme [blɑm] *nm* blame; (*sanction*) reprimand
blâmer [blɑme] *vt* (*réprouver*) to blame; (*réprimander*) to reprimand
blanc, blanche [blã, blãʃ] *adj* white; (*non imprimé*) blank; (*innocent*) pure ▷ *nm/f* white, white man/woman ▷ *nm* (*couleur*) white; (*linge*): **le ~** whites *pl*; (*espace non écrit*) blank; (*aussi:* **blanc d'œuf**) (egg-)white; (*aussi:* **blanc de poulet**) breast, white meat; (*aussi:* **vin blanc**) white wine ▷ *nf* (*Mus*) minim (*Brit*), half-note (*US*); (*fam: drogue*) smack; **d'une voix blanche** in a toneless voice; **aux cheveux ~s** white-haired; **le ~ de l'œil** the white of the eye; **laisser en ~** to leave blank; **chèque en ~** blank cheque; **à ~** *adv* (*chauffer*) white-hot; (*tirer, charger*) with blanks; **saigner à ~** to bleed white; ~ **cassé** off-white
blanc-bec [blãbɛk] (*pl* **blancs-becs**) *nm* greenhorn
blanchâtre [blãʃatʀ(ə)] *adj* (*teint, lumière*) whitish
blancheur [blãʃœʀ] *nf* whiteness
blanchir [blãʃiʀ] *vt* (*gén*) to whiten; (*linge, fig: argent*) to launder; (*Culin*) to blanch; (*fig: disculper*) to clear ▷ *vi* to grow white; (*cheveux*) to go white; **blanchi à la chaux** whitewashed
blanchissage [blãʃisaʒ] *nm* (*du linge*) laundering
blanchisserie [blãʃisʀi] *nf* laundry
blanchisseur, -euse [blãʃisœʀ, -øz] *nm/f* launderer
blanc-seing [blãsɛ̃] (*pl* **blancs-seings**) *nm* signed blank paper

blanquette [blãkɛt] *nf* (*Culin*): ~ **de veau** veal in a white sauce, blanquette de veau
blasé, e [blaze] *adj* blasé
blaser [blaze] *vt* to make blasé
blason [blazɔ̃] *nm* coat of arms
blasphémateur, -trice [blasfematœʀ, -tʀis] *nm/f* blasphemer
blasphématoire [blasfematwaʀ] *adj* blasphemous
blasphème [blasfɛm] *nm* blasphemy
blasphémer [blasfeme] *vi* to blaspheme ▷ *vt* to blaspheme against
blatte [blat] *nf* cockroach
blazer [blazɛʀ] *nm* blazer
blé [ble] *nm* wheat; ~ **en herbe** wheat on the ear; ~ **noir** buckwheat
bled [blɛd] *nm* (*péj*) hole; (*en Afrique du Nord*): **le ~** the interior
blême [blɛm] *adj* pale
blêmir [blemiʀ] *vi* (*personne*) to (turn) pale; (*lueur*) to grow pale
blennorragie [blenɔʀaʒi] *nf* blennorrhoea
blessant, e [blɛsã, -ãt] *adj* hurtful
blessé, e [blese] *adj* injured ▷ *nm/f* injured person, casualty; **un ~ grave, un grand ~** a seriously injured *ou* wounded person
blesser [blese] *vt* to injure; (*délibérément: Mil etc*) to wound; (*souliers etc, offenser*) to hurt; **se blesser** to injure o.s.; **se ~ au pied** *etc* to injure one's foot *etc*
blessure [blesyʀ] *nf* injury; wound
blet, te [blɛ, blɛt] *adj* overripe
blette [blɛt] *nf* = **bette**
bleu, e [blø] *adj* blue; (*bifteck*) very rare ▷ *nm* (*couleur*) blue; (*novice*) greenhorn; (*contusion*) bruise; (*vêtement: aussi:* **bleus**) overalls *pl* (*Brit*), coveralls *pl* (*US*); **avoir une peur ~e** to be scared stiff; **zone ~e** ≈ restricted parking area; **fromage ~** blue cheese; **au ~** (*Culin*) au bleu; ~ (**de lessive**) ≈ blue bag; ~ **de méthylène** (*Méd*) methylene blue; ~ **marine/nuit/roi** navy/midnight/royal blue
bleuâtre [bløɑtʀ(ə)] *adj* (*fumée etc*) bluish, blueish
bleuet [bløɛ] *nm* cornflower
bleuir [bløiʀ] *vt, vi* to turn blue
bleuté, e [bløte] *adj* blue-shaded
blindage [blɛ̃daʒ] *nm* armo(u)r-plating
blindé, e [blɛ̃de] *adj* armoured (*Brit*), armored (*US*); (*fig*) hardened ▷ *nm* armoured *ou* armored car; (*char*) tank
blinder [blɛ̃de] *vt* to armour (*Brit*), armor (*US*); (*fig*) to harden
blizzard [blizaʀ] *nm* blizzard
bloc [blɔk] *nm* (*de pierre etc, Inform*) block; (*de papier à lettres*) pad; (*ensemble*) group, block; **serré à ~** tightened right down; **en ~** as a whole; wholesale; **faire ~** to unite; ~ **opératoire** operating *ou* theatre block; ~ **sanitaire** toilet block; ~ **sténo** shorthand notebook
blocage [blɔkaʒ] *nm* (*voir bloquer*) blocking; jamming; freezing; (*Psych*) hang-up

bloc-cuisine [blɔkkɥizin] (pl **blocs-cuisines**) nm kitchen unit

bloc-cylindres [blɔksilɛ̃dʀ(ə)] (pl **blocs-cylindres**) nm cylinder block

bloc-évier [blɔkevje] (pl **blocs-éviers**) nm sink unit

bloc-moteur [blɔkmɔtœʀ] (pl **blocs-moteurs**) nm engine block

bloc-notes [blɔknɔt] (pl **blocs-notes**) nm note pad

blocus [blɔkys] nm blockade

blog, blogue [blɔg] nm blog

bloguer [blɔge] vi to blog

blond, e [blɔ̃, -ɔ̃d] adj fair; (plus clair) blond; (sable, blés) golden ▷ nm/f fair-haired ou blond man/woman; ~ **cendré** ash blond

blondeur [blɔ̃dœʀ] nf fairness; blondness

blondin, e [blɔ̃dɛ̃, -in] nm/f fair-haired ou blond child ou young person

blondinet, te [blɔ̃dinɛ, -ɛt] nm/f blondy

blondir [blɔ̃diʀ] vi (personne, cheveux) to go fair ou blond

bloquer [blɔke] vt (passage) to block; (pièce mobile) to jam; (crédits, compte) to freeze; (personne, négociations etc) to hold up; (regrouper) to group; ~ **les freins** to jam on the brakes

blottir [blɔtiʀ]: **se blottir** vi to huddle up

blousant, e [bluzɑ̃, ɑ̃t] adj blousing out

blouse [bluz] nf overall

blouser [bluze] vi to blouse out

blouson [bluzɔ̃] nm blouson (jacket); ~ **noir** (fig) ≈ rocker

blue-jean [bludʒin], **blue-jeans** [bludʒins] nm jeans

blues [bluz] nm blues pl

bluet [blyɛ] nm = **bleuet**

bluff [blœf] nm bluff

bluffer [blœfe] vi, vt to bluff

BNF sigle f = **Bibliothèque nationale de France**

boa [bɔa] nm (Zool): ~ (**constricteur**) boa (constrictor); (tour de cou) (feather ou fur) boa

bob [bɔb] nm = **bobsleigh**

bobard [bɔbaʀ] nm (fam) tall story

bobèche [bɔbɛʃ] nf candle-ring

bobine [bɔbin] nf (de fil) reel; (de machine à coudre) spool; (de machine à écrire) ribbon; (Élec) coil; ~ (**d'allumage**) (Auto) coil; ~ **de pellicule** (Photo) roll of film

bobo [bobo] nm sore spot

bobsleigh [bɔbslɛg] nm bob(sleigh)

bocage [bɔkaʒ] nm (Géo) bocage, farmland criss-crossed by hedges and trees; (bois) grove, copse (Brit)

bocal, -aux [bɔkal, -o] nm jar

bock [bɔk] nm (beer) glass; (contenu) glass of beer

body [bɔdi] nm body(suit); (Sport) leotard

bœuf [bœf, pl bø] nm ox, steer; (Culin) beef; (Mus: fam) jam session

bof [bɔf] excl (fam: indifférence) don't care!; (: pas terrible) nothing special

Bogota [bɔgɔta] n Bogotá

bogue [bɔg] nf (Bot) husk ▷ nm (Inform) bug

Bohème [bɔɛm] nf: **la ~** Bohemia

bohème [bɔɛm] adj happy-go-lucky, unconventional

bohémien, ne [bɔemjɛ̃, -ɛn] adj Bohemian ▷ nm/f gipsy

boire [bwaʀ] vt to drink; (s'imprégner de) to soak up; ~ **un coup** to have a drink

bois [bwa] vb voir **boire** ▷ nm wood; (Zool) antler; (Mus): **les ~** the woodwind; **de ~, en ~** wooden; ~ **vert** green wood; ~ **mort** deadwood; ~ **de lit** bedstead

boisé, e [bwaze] adj woody, wooded

boiser [bwaze] vt (galerie de mine) to timber; (chambre) to panel; (terrain) to plant with trees

boiseries [bwazʀi] nfpl panelling sg

boisson [bwasɔ̃] nf drink; **pris de ~** drunk, intoxicated; **~s alcoolisées** alcoholic beverages ou drinks; **~s non alcoolisées** soft drinks

boit [bwa] vb voir **boire**

boîte [bwat] nf box; (fam: entreprise) firm, company; **aliments en ~** canned ou tinned (Brit) foods; ~ **de sardines/petits pois** can ou tin (Brit) of sardines/peas; **mettre qn en ~** (fam) to have a laugh at sb's expense; ~ **d'allumettes** box of matches; (vide) matchbox; ~ **de conserves** can ou tin (Brit) (of food); ~ **crânienne** cranium; ~ **à gants** glove compartment; ~ **aux lettres** letter box, mailbox (US); (Inform) mailbox; ~ **à musique** musical box; ~ **noire** (Aviat) black box; ~ **de nuit** night club; ~ **à ordures** dustbin (Brit), trash can (US); ~ **postale (BP)** PO box; ~ **de vitesses** gear box; ~ **vocale** voice mail

boiter [bwate] vi to limp; (fig) to wobble; (raisonnement) to be shaky

boiteux, -euse [bwatø, -øz] adj lame; wobbly; shaky

boîtier [bwatje] nm case; (d'appareil-photo) body; ~ **de montre** watch case

boitiller [bwatije] vi to limp slightly, have a slight limp

boive etc [bwav] vb voir **boire**

bol [bɔl] nm bowl; (contenu): **un ~ de café** etc a bowl of coffee etc; **un ~ d'air** a breath of fresh air; **en avoir ras le ~** (fam) to have had a bellyful

bolée [bɔle] nf bowlful

boléro [bɔleʀo] nm bolero

bolet [bɔlɛ] nm boletus (mushroom)

bolide [bɔlid] nm racing car; **comme un ~** like a rocket

Bolivie [bɔlivi] nf: **la ~** Bolivia

bolivien, ne [bɔlivjɛ̃, -ɛn] adj Bolivian ▷ nm/f: **Bolivien, ne** Bolivian

bolognais, e [bɔlɔɲɛ, -ɛz] adj Bolognese

Bologne [bɔlɔɲ] n Bologna

bombance [bɔ̃bɑ̃s] nf: **faire ~** to have a feast, revel

bombardement [bɔ̃baʀdəmɑ̃] nm bombing

bombarder [bɔ̃baʀde] vt to bomb; ~ **qn de** (cailloux, lettres) to bombard sb with; ~ **qn directeur** to thrust sb into the director's seat

bombardier [bɔ̃baʀdje] nm (avion) bomber; (aviateur) bombardier

49

bombe [bɔ̃b] *nf* bomb; (*atomiseur*) (aerosol) spray; (*Équitation*) riding cap; **faire la ~** (*fam*) to go on a binge; **~ atomique** atomic bomb; **~ à retardement** time bomb

bombé, e [bɔ̃be] *adj* rounded; (*mur*) bulging; (*front*) domed; (*route*) steeply cambered

bomber [bɔ̃be] *vi* to bulge; (*route*) to camber ▷ *vt*: **~ le torse** to swell out one's chest

 MOT-CLÉ

bon, bonne [bɔ̃, bɔn] *adj* **1** (*agréable, satisfaisant*) good; **un bon repas/restaurant** a good meal/restaurant; **être bon en maths** to be good at maths

2 (*charitable*): **être bon (envers)** to be good (to), to be kind (to); **vous êtes trop bon** you're too kind

3 (*correct*) right; **le bon numéro/moment** the right number/moment

4 (*souhaits*): **bon anniversaire** happy birthday; **bon courage** good luck; **bon séjour** enjoy your stay; **bon voyage** have a good trip; **bon week-end** have a good weekend; **bonne année** happy New Year; **bonne chance** good luck; **bonne fête** happy holiday; **bonne nuit** good night

5 (*approprié*): **bon à/pour** fit to/for; **bon à jeter** fit for the bin; **c'est bon à savoir** that's useful to know; **à quoi bon (...)?** what's the point *ou* use (of ...)?

6 (*intensif*): **ça m'a pris deux bonnes heures** it took me a good two hours; **un bon nombre de** a good number of

7: **bon enfant** *adj inv* accommodating, easy-going; **bonne femme** (*péj*) woman; **de bonne heure** early; **bon marché** cheap; **bon mot** witticism; **pour faire bon poids ...** to make up for it ...; **bon sens** common sense; **bon vivant** jovial chap; **bonnes œuvres** charitable works, charities; **bonne sœur** nun

▷ *nm* **1** (*billet*) voucher; (*aussi*: **bon cadeau**) gift voucher; **bon de caisse** cash voucher; **bon d'essence** petrol coupon; **bon à tirer** pass for press; **bon du Trésor** Treasury bond

2: **avoir du bon** to have its good points; **il y a du bon dans ce qu'il dit** there's some sense in what he says; **pour de bon** for good

▷ *nm/f*: **un bon à rien** a good-for-nothing

▷ *adv*: **il fait bon** it's *ou* the weather is fine; **sentir bon** to smell good; **tenir bon** to stand firm; **juger bon de faire ...** to think fit to do ...

▷ *excl* right!, good!; **ah bon?** really?; **bon, je reste** right, I'll stay; *voir aussi* **bonne**

bonasse [bɔnas] *adj* soft, meek

bonbon [bɔ̃bɔ̃] *nm* (boiled) sweet

bonbonne [bɔ̃bɔn] *nf* demijohn; carboy

bonbonnière [bɔ̃bɔnjɛʀ] *nf* sweet (*Brit*) *ou* candy (*US*) box

bond [bɔ̃] *nm* leap; (*d'une balle*) rebound, ricochet; **faire un ~** to leap in the air; **d'un seul ~** in one bound, with one leap; **~ en avant** (*fig: progrès*) leap forward

bonde [bɔ̃d] *nf* (*d'évier etc*) plug; (: *trou*) plughole; (*de tonneau*) bung; bunghole

bondé, e [bɔ̃de] *adj* packed (full)

bondieuserie [bɔ̃djøzʀi] *nf* (*péj: objet*) religious knick-knack

bondir [bɔ̃diʀ] *vi* to leap; **~ de joie** (*fig*) to jump for joy; **~ de colère** (*fig*) to be hopping mad

bonheur [bɔnœʀ] *nm* happiness; **avoir le ~ de** to have the good fortune to; **porter ~ (à qn)** to bring (sb) luck; **au petit ~** haphazardly; **par ~** fortunately

bonhomie [bɔnɔmi] *nf* good-naturedness

bonhomme [bɔnɔm] (*pl* **bonshommes** [bɔ̃zɔm]) *nm* fellow ▷ *adj* good-natured; **un vieux ~** an old chap; **aller son ~ de chemin** to carry on in one's own sweet way; **~ de neige** snowman

boni [bɔni] *nm* profit

bonification [bɔnifikasjɔ̃] *nf* bonus

bonifier [bɔnifje]: **se bonifier** *vi* to improve

boniment [bɔnimɑ̃] *nm* patter *no pl*

bonjour [bɔ̃ʒuʀ] *excl, nm* hello; (*selon l'heure*) good morning (*ou* afternoon); **donner** *ou* **souhaiter le ~ à qn** to bid sb good morning *ou* afternoon

Bonn [bɔn] *n* Bonn

bonne [bɔn] *adj f voir* **bon** ▷ *nf* (*domestique*) maid; **~ à toute faire** general help; **~ d'enfant** nanny

bonne-maman [bɔnmamɑ̃] (*pl* **bonnes-mamans**) *nf* granny, grandma, gran

bonnement [bɔnmɑ̃] *adv*: **tout ~** quite simply

bonnet [bɔnɛ] *nm* bonnet, hat; (*de soutien-gorge*) cup; **~ d'âne** dunce's cap; **~ de bain** bathing cap; **~ de nuit** nightcap

bonneterie [bɔnɛtʀi] *nf* hosiery

bon-papa [bɔ̃papa] (*pl* **bons-papas**) *nm* grandpa, grandad

bonsoir [bɔ̃swaʀ] *excl* good evening

bonté [bɔ̃te] *nf* kindness *no pl*; **avoir la ~ de** to be kind *ou* good enough to

bonus [bɔnys] *nm* (*Assurances*) no-claims bonus

bonze [bɔ̃z] *nm* (*Rel*) bonze

boomerang [bumʀɑ̃g] *nm* boomerang

boots [buts] *nfpl* boots

borborygme [bɔʀbɔʀigm(ə)] *nm* rumbling noise

bord [bɔʀ] *nm* (*de table, verre, falaise*) edge; (*de rivière, lac*) bank; (*de route*) side; (*de vêtement*) edge, border; (*de chapeau*) brim; (**monter) à ~** (to go) on board; **jeter par-dessus ~** to throw overboard; **le commandant de ~/les hommes du ~** the ship's master/crew; **du même ~** (*fig*) of the same opinion; **au ~ de la mer/route** at the seaside/roadside; **être au ~ des larmes** to be on the verge of tears; **virer de ~** (*Navig*) to tack; **sur les ~s** (*fig*) slightly; **de tous ~s** on all sides; **~ du trottoir** kerb (*Brit*), curb (*US*)

bordeaux [bɔʀdo] *nm* Bordeaux ▷ *adj inv* maroon

bordée [bɔʀde] *nf* broadside; **une ~ d'injures** a volley of abuse; **tirer une ~** to go on the town

bordel [bɔʀdɛl] *nm* brothel; (*fam!*) bloody (*Brit*)

ou goddamn (*US*) mess (*!*) ▷ *excl* hell!

bordelais, e [bɔʀdəlɛ, -ɛz] *adj* of *ou* from Bordeaux

border [bɔʀde] *vt* (*être le long de*) to border, line; (*garnir*): **~ qch de** to line sth with; to trim sth with; (*qn dans son lit*) to tuck up

bordereau, x [bɔʀdəʀo] *nm* docket, slip

bordure [bɔʀdyʀ] *nf* border; (*sur un vêtement*) trim(ming), border; **en ~ de** on the edge of

boréal, e, aux [bɔʀeal, -o] *adj* boreal, northern

borgne [bɔʀɲ(ə)] *adj* one-eyed; **hôtel ~** shady hotel; **fenêtre ~** obstructed window

bornage [bɔʀnaʒ] *nm* (*d'un terrain*) demarcation

borne [bɔʀn(ə)] *nf* boundary stone; (*aussi:* **borne kilométrique**) kilometre-marker, ≈ milestone; **bornes** *nfpl* (*fig*) limits; **dépasser les ~s** to go too far; **sans ~(s)** boundless

borné, e [bɔʀne] *adj* narrow; (*obtus*) narrow-minded

Bornéo [bɔʀneo] *nm:* **le ~** Borneo

borner [bɔʀne] *vt* (*délimiter*) to limit; (*limiter*) to confine; **se ~ à faire** to content o.s. with doing; to limit o.s. to doing

bosniaque [bɔznjak] *adj* Bosnian ▷ *nm/f:* **Bosniaque** Bosnian

Bosnie [bɔzni] *nf* Bosnia

Bosnie-Herzégovine [bɔzniɛʀzegɔvin] *nf* Bosnia-Herzegovina

bosnien, ne [bɔznjɛ̃, -ɛn] *adj* Bosnian ▷ *nm/f:* **Bosnien, ne** Bosnian

Bosphore [bɔsfɔʀ] *nm:* **le ~** the Bosphorus

bosquet [bɔskɛ] *nm* copse (*Brit*), grove

bosse [bɔs] *nf* (*de terrain etc*) bump; (*enflure*) lump; (*du bossu, du chameau*) hump; **avoir la ~ des maths** *etc* to have a gift for maths *etc*; **il a roulé sa ~** he's been around

bosseler [bɔsle] *vt* (*ouvrer*) to emboss; (*abîmer*) to dent

bosser [bɔse] *vi* (*fam*) to work; (: *dur*) to slog (hard) (*Brit*), slave (away)

bosseur, -euse [bɔsœʀ, -øz] *nm/f* (hard) worker, slogger (*Brit*)

bossu, e [bɔsy] *nm/f* hunchback

bot [bo] *adj m:* **pied ~** club foot

botanique [bɔtanik] *nf* botany ▷ *adj* botanic(al)

botaniste [bɔtanist(ə)] *nm/f* botanist

Botswana [bɔtswana] *nm:* **le ~** Botswana

botte [bɔt] *nf* (*soulier*) (high) boot; (*Escrime*) thrust; (*gerbe*): **~ de paille** bundle of straw; **~ de radis/d'asperges** bunch of radishes/asparagus; **~s de caoutchouc** wellington boots

botter [bɔte] *vt* to put boots on; (*donner un coup de pied à*) to kick; (*fam*): **ça me botte** I fancy that

bottier [bɔtje] *nm* bootmaker

bottillon [bɔtijɔ̃] *nm* bootee

bottin® [bɔtɛ̃] *nm* directory

bottine [bɔtin] *nf* ankle boot

botulisme [bɔtylism(ə)] *nm* botulism

bouc [buk] *nm* goat; (*barbe*) goatee; **~ émissaire** scapegoat

boucan [bukɑ̃] *nm* din, racket

bouche [buʃ] *nf* mouth; **une ~ à nourrir** a mouth to feed; **les ~s inutiles** the non-productive members of the population; **faire du ~ à ~ à qn** to give sb the kiss of life (*Brit*), give sb mouth-to-mouth resuscitation; **de ~ à oreille** confidentially; **pour la bonne ~** (*pour la fin*) till last; **faire venir l'eau à la ~** to make one's mouth water; **~ cousue!** mum's the word!; **~ d'aération** air vent; **~ de chaleur** hot air vent; **~ d'égout** manhole; **~ d'incendie** fire hydrant; **~ de métro** métro entrance

bouché, e [buʃe] *adj* (*flacon etc*) stoppered; (*temps, ciel*) overcast; (*carrière*) blocked; (*péj: personne*) thick; (*trompette*) muted; **avoir le nez ~** to have a blocked(-up) nose

bouchée [buʃe] *nf* mouthful; **ne faire qu'une ~ de** (*fig*) to make short work of; **pour une ~ de pain** (*fig*) for next to nothing; **~s à la reine** chicken vol-au-vents

boucher [buʃe] *nm* butcher ▷ *vt* (*pour colmater*) to stop up; to fill up; (*obstruer*) to block (up); **se boucher** (*tuyau etc*) to block up, get blocked up; **se ~ le nez** to hold one's nose

bouchère [buʃɛʀ] *nf* butcher; (*femme du boucher*) butcher's wife

boucherie [buʃʀi] *nf* butcher's (shop); (*métier*) butchery; (*fig*) slaughter, butchery

bouche-trou [buʃtʀu] *nm* (*fig*) stop-gap

bouchon [buʃɔ̃] *nm* (*en liège*) cork; (*autre matière*) stopper; (*fig: embouteillage*) holdup; (*Pêche*) float; **~ doseur** measuring cap

bouchonner [buʃɔne] *vt* to rub down ▷ *vi* to form a traffic jam

bouchot [buʃo] *nm* mussel bed

bouclage [buklaʒ] *nm* sealing off

boucle [bukl(ə)] *nf* (*forme, figure, aussi Inform*) loop; (*objet*) buckle; **~ (de cheveux)** curl; **~ d'oreilles** earring

bouclé, e [bukle] *adj* curly; (*tapis*) uncut

boucler [bukle] *vt* (*fermer: ceinture etc*) to fasten; (: *magasin*) to shut; (*terminer*) to finish off; (: *circuit*) to complete; (*budget*) to balance; (*enfermer*) to shut away; (: *condamné*) to lock up; (: *quartier*) to seal off ▷ *vi* to curl; **faire ~** (*cheveux*) to curl; **~ la boucle** (*Aviat*) to loop the loop

bouclette [buklɛt] *nf* small curl

bouclier [buklije] *nm* shield

bouddha [buda] *nm* Buddha

bouddhisme [budism(ə)] *nm* Buddhism

bouddhiste [budist(ə)] *nm/f* Buddhist

bouder [bude] *vi* to sulk ▷ *vt* (*chose*) to turn one's nose up at; (*personne*) to refuse to have anything to do with

bouderie [budʀi] *nf* sulking *no pl*

boudeur, -euse [budœʀ, -øz] *adj* sullen, sulky

boudin [budɛ̃] *nm* (*Culin*) black pudding; (*Tech*) roll; **~ blanc** white pudding

boudiné, e [budine] *adj* (*doigt*) podgy; (*serré*): **~ dans** (*vêtement*) bulging out of

boudoir [budwaʀ] *nm* boudoir; (*biscuit*) sponge finger

boue [bu] *nf* mud

bouée [bwe] *nf* buoy; (*de baigneur*) rubber ring; **~**

(de sauvetage) lifebuoy; *(fig)* lifeline

boueux, -euse [bwø, -øz] *adj* muddy ▷ *nm (fam)* refuse *(Brit) ou* garbage *(US)* collector

bouffant, e [bufã, -ãt] *adj* puffed out

bouffe [buf] *nf (fam)* grub, food

bouffée [bufe] *nf* puff; **~ de chaleur** *(gén)* blast of hot air; *(Méd)* hot flush *(Brit) ou* flash *(US)*; **~ de fièvre/de honte** flush of fever/shame; **~ d'orgueil** fit of pride

bouffer [bufe] *vi (fam)* to eat; *(Couture)* to puff out ▷ *vt (fam)* to eat

bouffi, e [bufi] *adj* swollen

bouffon, ne [bufõ, -ɔn] *adj* farcical, comical ▷ *nm* jester

bouge [buʒ] *nm (bar louche)* (low) dive; *(taudis)* hovel

bougeoir [buʒwaʀ] *nm* candlestick

bougeotte [buʒɔt] *nf*: **avoir la ~** to have the fidgets

bouger [buʒe] *vi* to move; *(dent etc)* to be loose; *(changer)* to alter; *(agir)* to stir ▷ *vt* to move; **se bouger** *(fam)* to move (oneself)

bougie [buʒi] *nf* candle; *(Auto)* spark(ing) plug

bougon, ne [bugõ, -ɔn] *adj* grumpy

bougonner [bugɔne] *vi, vt* to grumble

bougre [bugʀ(ə)] *nm* chap; *(fam)*: **ce ~ de ...** that confounded ...

boui-boui [bwibwi] *nm (fam)* greasy spoon

bouillabaisse [bujabɛs] *nf type of fish soup*

bouillant, e [bujã, -ãt] *adj (qui bout)* boiling; *(très chaud)* boiling (hot); *(fig: ardent)* hot-headed; **~ de colère** *etc* seething with anger *etc*

bouille [buj] *nf (fam)* mug

bouilleur [bujœʀ] *nm*: **~ de cru** (home) distiller

bouillie [buji] *nf* gruel; *(de bébé)* cereal; **en ~** *(fig)* crushed

bouillir [bujiʀ] *vi* to boil ▷ *vt (aussi*: **faire bouillir**: *Culin)* to boil; **~ de colère** *etc* to seethe with anger *etc*

bouilloire [bujwaʀ] *nf* kettle

bouillon [bujõ] *nm (Culin)* stock *no pl*; *(bulles, écume)* bubble; **~ de culture** culture medium

bouillonnement [bujɔnmã] *nm (d'un liquide)* bubbling; *(des idées)* ferment

bouillonner [bujɔne] *vi* to bubble; *(fig)* to bubble up; *(torrent)* to foam

bouillotte [bujɔt] *nf* hot-water bottle

boulanger, -ère [bulãʒe, -ɛʀ] *nm/f* baker ▷ *nf (femme du boulanger)* baker's wife

boulangerie [bulãʒʀi] *nf* bakery, baker's (shop); *(commerce)* bakery; **~ industrielle** bakery

boulangerie-pâtisserie [bulãʒʀipatisʀi] *(pl* **boulangeries-pâtisseries)** *nf* baker's and confectioner's (shop)

boule [bul] *nf (gén)* ball; *(pour jouer)* bowl; *(de machine à écrire)* golf ball; **roulé en ~** curled up in a ball; **se mettre en ~** *(fig)* to fly off the handle, blow one's top; **perdre la ~** *(fig: fam)* to go off one's rocker; **~ de gomme** *(bonbon)* gum(drop), pastille; **~ de neige** snowball; **faire ~ de neige** *(fig)* to snowball

bouleau, x [bulo] *nm* (silver) birch

bouledogue [buldɔg] *nm* bulldog

bouler [bule] *vi (fam)*: **envoyer ~ qn** to send sb packing; **je me suis fait ~** *(à un examen)* they flunked me

boulet [bulɛ] *nm (aussi*: **boulet de canon**) cannonball; *(de bagnard)* ball and chain; *(charbon)* (coal) nut

boulette [bulɛt] *nf* ball

boulevard [bulvaʀ] *nm* boulevard

bouleversant, e [bulvɛʀsã, -ãt] *adj (récit)* deeply distressing; *(nouvelle)* shattering

bouleversé, e [bulvɛʀse] *adj (ému)* deeply distressed; shattered

bouleversement [bulvɛʀsəmã] *nm (politique, social)* upheaval

bouleverser [bulvɛʀse] *vt (émouvoir)* to overwhelm; *(causer du chagrin à)* to distress; *(pays, vie)* to disrupt; *(papiers, objets)* to turn upside down, upset

boulier [bulje] *nm* abacus; *(de jeu)* scoring board

boulimie [bulimi] *nf* bulimia; compulsive eating

boulimique [bulimik] *adj* bulimic

boulingrin [bulɛ̃gʀɛ̃] *nm* lawn

bouliste [bulist(ə)] *nm/f* bowler

boulocher [bulɔʃe] *vi (laine etc)* to develop little snarls

boulodrome [bulɔdʀɔm] *nm* bowling pitch

boulon [bulõ] *nm* bolt

boulonner [bulɔne] *vt* to bolt

boulot [bulo] *nm (fam: travail)* work

boulot, te [bulo, -ɔt] *adj* plump, tubby

boum [bum] *nm* bang ▷ *nf* party

bouquet [bukɛ] *nm (de fleurs)* bunch (of flowers), bouquet; *(de persil etc)* bunch; *(parfum)* bouquet; *(fig)* crowning piece; **c'est le ~!** that's the last straw!; **~ garni** *(Culin)* bouquet garni

bouquetin [buktɛ̃] *nm* ibex

bouquin [bukɛ̃] *nm (fam)* book

bouquiner [bukine] *vi (fam)* to read

bouquiniste [bukinist(ə)] *nm/f* bookseller

bourbeux, -euse [buʀbø, -øz] *adj* muddy

bourbier [buʀbje] *nm* (quag)mire

bourde [buʀd(ə)] *nf (erreur)* howler; *(gaffe)* blunder

bourdon [buʀdõ] *nm* bumblebee

bourdonnement [buʀdɔnmã] *nm* buzzing *no pl*, buzz; **avoir des ~s d'oreilles** to have a buzzing (noise) in one's ears

bourdonner [buʀdɔne] *vi* to buzz; *(moteur)* to hum

bourg [buʀ] *nm* small market town *(ou* village)

bourgade [buʀgad] *nf* township

bourgeois, e [buʀʒwa, -waz] *adj (péj)* ≈ (upper) middle class; bourgeois; *(maison etc)* very comfortable ▷ *nm/f (autrefois)* burgher

bourgeoisie [buʀʒwazi] *nf* ≈ upper middle classes *pl*; bourgeoisie; **petite ~** middle classes

bourgeon [buʀʒõ] *nm* bud

bourgeonner [buʀʒɔne] *vi* to bud

Bourgogne [buʀgɔɲ] *nf*: **la ~** Burgundy ▷ *nm*: **bourgogne** Burgundy (wine)

bourguignon, ne [buʀɡiɲɔ̃, -ɔn] *adj* of *ou* from Burgundy, Burgundian; **bœuf ~** bœuf bourguignon

bourlinguer [buʀlɛ̃ɡe] *vi* to knock about a lot, get around a lot

bourrade [buʀad] *nf* shove, thump

bourrage [buʀaʒ] *nm* (*papier*) jamming; **~ de crâne** brainwashing; (*Scol*) cramming

bourrasque [buʀask(ə)] *nf* squall

bourratif, -ive [buʀatif, -iv] *adj* filling, stodgy

bourre [buʀ] *nf* (*de coussin, matelas etc*) stuffing

bourré, e [buʀe] *adj* (*rempli*): **~ de** crammed full of; (*fam: ivre*) pickled, plastered

bourreau, x [buʀo] *nm* executioner; (*fig*) torturer; **~ de travail** workaholic, glutton for work

bourrelé, e [buʀle] *adj*: **être ~ de remords** to be racked by remorse

bourrelet [buʀlɛ] *nm* draught (*Brit*) *ou* draft (*US*) excluder; (*de peau*) fold *ou* roll (of flesh)

bourrer [buʀe] *vt* (*pipe*) to fill; (*poêle*) to pack; (*valise*) to cram (full); **~ de** to cram (full) with, stuff with; **~ de coups** to hammer blows on, pummel; **~ le crâne à qn** to pull the wool over sb's eyes; (*endoctriner*) to brainwash sb

bourricot [buʀiko] *nm* small donkey

bourrique [buʀik] *nf* (*âne*) ass

bourru, e [buʀy] *adj* surly, gruff

bourse [buʀs(ə)] *nf* (*subvention*) grant; (*porte-monnaie*) purse; **sans ~ délier** without spending a penny; **la B~** the Stock Exchange; **~ du travail** ≈ trades union council (regional headquarters)

boursicoter [buʀsikɔte] *vi* (*Comm*) to dabble on the Stock Market

boursier, -ière [buʀsje, -jɛʀ] *adj* (*Comm*) Stock Market *cpd* ▷ *nm/f* (*Scol*) grant-holder

boursouflé, e [buʀsufle] *adj* swollen, puffy; (*fig*) bombastic, turgid

boursoufler [buʀsufle] *vt* to puff up, bloat; **se boursoufler** *vi* (*visage*) to swell *ou* puff up; (*peinture*) to blister

boursouflure [buʀsuflyʀ] *nf* (*du visage*) swelling, puffiness; (*de la peinture*) blister; (*fig: du style*) pomposity

bous [bu] *vb voir* **bouillir**

bousculade [buskylad] *nf* (*hâte*) rush; (*poussée*) crush

bousculer [buskyle] *vt* to knock over; to knock into; (*fig*) to push, rush

bouse [buz] *nf*: **~ (de vache)** (cow) dung *no pl* (*Brit*), manure *no pl*

bousiller [buzije] *vt* (*fam*) to wreck

boussole [busɔl] *nf* compass

bout [bu] *vb voir* **bouillir** ▷ *nm* bit; (*extrémité: d'un bâton etc*) tip; (: *d'une ficelle, table, rue, période*) end; **au ~ de** at the end of, after; **au ~ du compte** at the end of the day; **pousser qn à ~** to push sb to the limit (of his patience); **venir à ~ de** to manage to finish (off) *ou* overcome; **~ à ~** end to end; **à tout ~ de champ** at every turn; **d'un ~ à l'autre, de ~ en ~** from one end to the other; **à ~**

portant at point-blank range; **un ~ de chou** (*enfant*) a little tot; **~ d'essai** (*Ciné etc*) screen test; **~ filtre** filter tip

boutade [butad] *nf* quip, sally

boute-en-train [butɑ̃tʀɛ̃] *nm inv* live wire (*fig*)

bouteille [butɛj] *nf* bottle; (*de gaz butane*) cylinder

boutiquaire [butikɛʀ] *adj*: **niveau ~** shopping level

boutique [butik] *nf* shop (*Brit*), store (*US*); (*de grand couturier, de mode*) boutique

boutiquier, -ière [butikje, -jɛʀ] *nm/f* shopkeeper (*Brit*), storekeeper (*US*)

boutoir [butwaʀ] *nm*: **coup de ~** (*choc*) thrust; (*fig: propos*) barb

bouton [butɔ̃] *nm* (*de vêtement, électrique etc*) button; (*Bot*) bud; (*sur la peau*) spot; (*de porte*) knob; **~ de manchette** cuff-link; **~ d'or** buttercup

boutonnage [butɔnaʒ] *nm* (*action*) buttoning(-up); **un manteau à double ~** a coat with two rows of buttons

boutonner [butɔne] *vt* to button up, do up; **se boutonner** to button one's clothes up

boutonneux, -euse [butɔnø, -øz] *adj* spotty

boutonnière [butɔnjɛʀ] *nf* buttonhole

bouton-poussoir [butɔ̃puswaʀ] (*pl* **boutons-poussoirs**) *nm* pushbutton

bouton-pression [butɔ̃pʀesjɔ̃] (*pl* **boutons-pression**) *nm* press stud, snap fastener

bouture [butyʀ] *nf* cutting; **faire des ~s** to take cuttings

bouvreuil [buvʀœj] *nm* bullfinch

bovidé [bɔvide] *nm* bovine

bovin, e [bɔvɛ̃, -in] *adj* bovine ▷ *nm*: **~s** cattle

bowling [bɔliŋ] *nm* (tenpin) bowling; (*salle*) bowling alley

box [bɔks] *nm* lock-up (garage); (*de salle, dortoir*) cubicle; (*d'écurie*) loose-box; (*aussi*: **box-calf**) box calf; **le ~ des accusés** the dock

boxe [bɔks(ə)] *nf* boxing

boxer [bɔkse] *vi* to box ▷ *nm* [bɔksɛʀ] (*chien*) boxer

boxeur [bɔksœʀ] *nm* boxer

boyau, x [bwajo] *nm* (*corde de raquette etc*) (cat) gut; (*galerie*) passage(way); (narrow) gallery; (*pneu de bicyclette*) tubeless tyre ▷ *nmpl* (*viscères*) entrails, guts

boyaux [bwajo] *nmpl* (*viscères*) entrails, guts

boycottage [bɔjkɔtaʒ] *nm* (*d'un produit*) boycotting

boycotter [bɔjkɔte] *vt* to boycott

BP *sigle f* = **boîte postale**

brabançon, ne [bʀabɑ̃sɔ̃, -ɔn] *adj* of *ou* from Brabant

Brabant [bʀabɑ̃] *nm*: **le ~** Brabant

bracelet [bʀaslɛ] *nm* bracelet

bracelet-montre [bʀaslɛmɔ̃tʀ(ə)] *nm* wristwatch

braconnage [bʀakɔnaʒ] *nm* poaching

braconner [bʀakɔne] *vi* to poach

braconnier [bʀakɔnje] *nm* poacher

brader [bʀade] *vt* to sell off, sell cheaply

braderie [bʀadʀi] *nf* clearance sale; *(par des particuliers)* ≈ car boot sale (Brit), ≈ garage sale (US); *(magasin)* discount store; *(sur marché)* cut-price (Brit) *ou* cut-rate (US) stall

braguette [bʀagɛt] *nf* fly, flies *pl* (Brit), zipper (US)

braillard, e [bʀajaʀ, -aʀd] *adj (fam)* bawling, yelling

braille [bʀaj] *nm* Braille

braillement [bʀajmɑ̃] *nm (cri)* bawling *no pl*, yelling *no pl*

brailler [bʀaje] *vi* to bawl, yell ▷ *vt* to bawl out, yell out

braire [bʀɛʀ] *vi* to bray

braise [bʀɛz] *nf* embers *pl*

braiser [bʀeze] *vt* to braise; **bœuf braisé** braised steak

bramer [bʀame] *vi* to bell; *(fig)* to wail

brancard [bʀɑ̃kaʀ] *nm (civière)* stretcher; *(bras, perche)* shaft

brancardier [bʀɑ̃kaʀdje] *nm* stretcher-bearer

branchages [bʀɑ̃ʃaʒ] *nmpl* branches, boughs

branche [bʀɑ̃ʃ] *nf* branch; *(de lunettes)* side(-piece)

branché, e [bʀɑ̃ʃe] *adj (fam)* switched-on, trendy ▷ *nm/f (fam)* trendy

branchement [bʀɑ̃ʃmɑ̃] *nm* connection

brancher [bʀɑ̃ʃe] *vt* to connect (up); *(en mettant la prise)* to plug in; **~ qn/qch sur** *(fig)* to get sb/sth launched onto

branchies [bʀɑ̃ʃi] *nfpl* gills

brandade [bʀɑ̃dad] *nf* brandade (cod dish)

brandebourgeois, e [bʀɑ̃dəbuʀʒwa, -waz] *adj* of *ou* from Brandenburg

brandir [bʀɑ̃diʀ] *vt (arme)* to brandish, wield; *(document)* to flourish, wave

brandon [bʀɑ̃dɔ̃] *nm* firebrand

branlant, e [bʀɑ̃lɑ̃, -ɑ̃t] *adj (mur, meuble)* shaky

branle [bʀɑ̃l] *nm*: **mettre en ~** to set swinging; **donner le ~ à** to set in motion

branle-bas [bʀɑ̃lba] *nm inv* commotion

branler [bʀɑ̃le] *vi* to be shaky, be loose ▷ *vt*: **~ la tête** to shake one's head

braquage [bʀakaʒ] *nm (fam)* stick-up, hold-up; *(Auto)*: **rayon de ~** turning circle

braque [bʀak] *nm (Zool)* pointer

braquer [bʀake] *vi (Auto)* to turn (the wheel) ▷ *vt (revolver etc)*: **~ qch sur** to aim sth at, point sth at; *(mettre en colère)*: **~ qn** to antagonize sb, put sb's back up; **~ son regard sur** to fix one's gaze on; **se braquer** *vi*: **se ~ (contre)** to take a stand (against)

bras [bʀa] *nm* arm; *(de fleuve)* branch ▷ *nmpl (fig: travailleurs)* labour *sg* (Brit), labor *sg* (US), hands; **~ dessus ~ dessous** arm in arm; **à ~ raccourcis** with fists flying; **à tour de ~** with all one's might; **baisser les ~** to give up; **~ droit** *(fig)* right hand man; **~ de fer** arm-wrestling; **une partie de ~ de fer** *(fig)* a trial of strength; **~ de levier** lever arm; **~ de mer** arm of the sea, sound

brasero [bʀazeʀo] *nm* brazier

brasier [bʀazje] *nm* blaze, (blazing) inferno; *(fig)* inferno

Brasilia [bʀazilja] *n* Brasilia

bras-le-corps [bʀalkɔʀ]: **à ~** *adv* (a)round the waist

brassage [bʀasaʒ] *nm (de la bière)* brewing; *(fig)* mixing

brassard [bʀasaʀ] *nm* armband

brasse [bʀas] *nf (nage)* breast-stroke; *(mesure)* fathom; **~ papillon** butterfly(-stroke)

brassée [bʀase] *nf* armful; **une ~ de** *(fig)* a number of

brasser [bʀase] *vt (bière)* to brew; *(remuer: salade)* to toss; *(: cartes)* to shuffle; *(fig)* to mix; **~ l'argent/les affaires** to handle a lot of money/business

brasserie [bʀasʀi] *nf (restaurant)* bar (selling food), brasserie; *(usine)* brewery

brasseur [bʀasœʀ] *nm (de bière)* brewer; **~ d'affaires** big businessman

brassière [bʀasjɛʀ] *nf* (baby's) vest (Brit) *ou* undershirt (US); *(de sauvetage)* life jacket

bravache [bʀavaʃ] *nm* blusterer, braggart

bravade [bʀavad] *nf*: **par ~** out of bravado

brave [bʀav] *adj (courageux)* brave; *(bon, gentil)* good, kind

bravement [bʀavmɑ̃] *adv* bravely; *(résolument)* boldly

braver [bʀave] *vt* to defy

bravo [bʀavo] *excl* bravo! ▷ *nm* cheer

bravoure [bʀavuʀ] *nf* bravery

BRB *sigle f (Police)*: = *Brigade de répression du banditisme)* ≈ serious crime squad

break [bʀɛk] *nm (Auto)* estate car (Brit), station wagon (US)

brebis [bʀəbi] *nf* ewe; **~ galeuse** black sheep

brèche [bʀɛʃ] *nf* breach, gap; **être sur la ~** *(fig)* to be on the go

bredouille [bʀəduj] *adj* empty-handed

bredouiller [bʀəduje] *vi, vt* to mumble, stammer

bref, brève [bʀɛf, bʀɛv] *adj* short, brief ▷ *adv* in short ▷ *nf (voyelle)* short vowel; *(information)* brief news item; **d'un ton ~** sharply, curtly; **en ~** in short, in brief; **à ~ délai** shortly

brelan [bʀəlɑ̃] *nm*: **un ~** three of a kind; **un ~ d'as** three aces

breloque [bʀəlɔk] *nf* charm

brème [bʀɛm] *nf* bream

Brésil [bʀezil] *nm*: **le ~** Brazil

brésilien, ne [bʀeziljɛ̃, -ɛn] *adj* Brazilian ▷ *nm/f*: **Brésilien, ne** Brazilian

bressan, e [bʀesɑ̃, -an] *adj* of *ou* from Bresse

Bretagne [bʀətaɲ] *nf*: **la ~** Brittany

bretelle [bʀətɛl] *nf (de fusil etc)* sling; *(de vêtement)* strap; *(d'autoroute)* slip road (Brit), entrance *ou* exit ramp (US); **bretelles** *nfpl (pour pantalon)* braces (Brit), suspenders (US); **~ de contournement** *(Auto)* bypass; **~ de raccordement** *(Auto)* access road

breton, ne [bʀətɔ̃, -ɔn] *adj* Breton ▷ *nm (Ling)* Breton ▷ *nm/f*: **Breton, ne** Breton

breuvage [bʀœvaʒ] *nm* beverage, drink
brève [bʀɛv] *adj f, nf voir* **bref**
brevet [bʀəvɛ] *nm* diploma, certificate; ~
  (**d'invention**) patent; ~ **d'apprentissage**
  certificate of apprenticeship; ~ (**des collèges**)
  school certificate, taken at approx. 16 years
breveté, e [bʀəvte] *adj* patented; (*diplômé*)
  qualified
breveter [bʀəvte] *vt* to patent
bréviaire [bʀevjɛʀ] *nm* breviary
BRGM *sigle m* = **Bureau de recherches**
  géologiques et minières
briard, e [bʀijaʀ, -aʀd(ə)] *adj* of *ou* from Brie
  ▷ *nm* (*chien*) briard
bribes [bʀib] *nfpl* bits, scraps; (*d'une conversation*)
  snatches; **par ~** piecemeal
bric [bʀik]: **de ~ et de broc** *adv* with any old
  thing
bric-à-brac [bʀikabʀak] *nm inv* bric-a-brac,
  jumble
bricolage [bʀikɔlaʒ] *nm*: **le ~** do-it-yourself
  (jobs); (*péj*) patched-up job
bricole [bʀikɔl] *nf* (*babiole, chose insignifiante*)
  trifle; (*petit travail*) small job
bricoler [bʀikɔle] *vi* to do odd jobs; (*en amateur*)
  to do DIY jobs; (*passe-temps*) to potter about ▷ *vt*
  (*réparer*) to fix up; (*mal réparer*) to tinker with;
  (*trafiquer: voiture etc*) to doctor, fix
bricoleur, -euse [bʀikɔlœʀ, -øz] *nm/f*
  handyman/woman, DIY enthusiast
bride [bʀid] *nf* bridle; (*d'un bonnet*) string, tie; **à ~**
  abattue flat out, hell for leather; **tenir en ~** to
  keep in check; **lâcher la ~ à, laisser la ~ sur le**
  cou à to give free rein to
bridé, e [bʀide] *adj*: **yeux ~s** slit eyes
brider [bʀide] *vt* (*réprimer*) to keep in check;
  (*cheval*) to bridle; (*Culin: volaille*) to truss
bridge [bʀidʒ(ə)] *nm* bridge
brie [bʀi] *nm* Brie (cheese)
brièvement [bʀijɛvmɑ̃] *adv* briefly
brièveté [bʀijɛvte] *nf* brevity
brigade [bʀigad] *nf* squad; (*Mil*) brigade
brigadier [bʀigadje] *nm* (*Police*) ≈ sergeant; (*Mil*)
  bombardier; corporal
brigadier-chef [bʀigadjeʃɛf] (*pl* **brigadiers-**
  chefs) *nm* ≈ lance-sergeant
brigand [bʀigɑ̃] *nm* brigand
brigandage [bʀigɑ̃daʒ] *nm* robbery
briguer [bʀige] *vt* to aspire to; (*suffrages*) to
  canvass
brillamment [bʀijamɑ̃] *adv* brilliantly
brillant, e [bʀijɑ̃, -ɑ̃t] *adj* brilliant; bright;
  (*luisant*) shiny, shining ▷ *nm* (*diamant*) brilliant
briller [bʀije] *vi* to shine
brimade [bʀimad] *nf* vexation, harassment *no*
  pl; bullying *no pl*
brimbaler [bʀɛ̃bale] *vb* = **bringuebaler**
brimer [bʀime] *vt* to harass; to bully
brin [bʀɛ̃] *nm* (*de laine, ficelle etc*) strand; (*fig*): **un ~**
  de a bit of; **un ~ mystérieux** *etc* (*fam*) a weeny
  bit mysterious *etc*; ~ **d'herbe** blade of grass; ~
  de muguet sprig of lily of the valley; ~ **de**

paille wisp of straw
brindille [bʀɛ̃dij] *nf* twig
bringue [bʀɛ̃g] *nf* (*fam*): **faire la ~** to go on a
  binge
bringuebaler [bʀɛ̃gbale] *vi* to shake (about) ▷ *vt*
  to cart about
brio [bʀijo] *nm* brilliance; (*Mus*) brio; **avec ~**
  brilliantly, with panache
brioche [bʀijɔʃ] *nf* brioche (bun); (*fam: ventre*)
  paunch
brioché, e [bʀijɔʃe] *adj* brioche-style
brique [bʀik] *nf* brick; (*fam*) 10 000 francs ▷ *adj*
  inv brick red
briquer [bʀike] *vt* (*fam*) to polish up
briquet [bʀikɛ] *nm* (cigarette) lighter
briqueterie [bʀiktʀi] *nf* brickyard
bris [bʀi] *nm*: ~ **de clôture** (*Jur*) breaking in; ~ **de**
  glaces (*Auto*) breaking of windows
brisant [bʀizɑ̃] *nm* reef; (*vague*) breaker
brise [bʀiz] *nf* breeze
brisé, e [bʀize] *adj* broken; ~ (**de fatigue**)
  exhausted; **d'une voix ~e** in a voice broken
  with emotion; **pâte ~e** shortcrust pastry
brisées [bʀize] *nfpl*: **aller** *ou* **marcher sur les ~**
  de qn to compete with sb in his own province
brise-glace, brise-glaces [bʀizglas] *nm inv*
  (*navire*) icebreaker
brise-jet [bʀizʒɛ] *nm inv* tap swirl
brise-lames [bʀizlam] *nm inv* breakwater
briser [bʀize] *vt* to break; **se briser** *vi* to break
brise-tout [bʀiztu] *nm inv* wrecker
briseur, -euse [bʀizœʀ, -øz] *nm/f*: ~ **de grève**
  strike-breaker
brise-vent [bʀizvɑ̃] *nm inv* windbreak
bristol [bʀistɔl] *nm* (*carte de visite*) visiting card
britannique [bʀitanik] *adj* British ▷ *nm/f*:
  Britannique Briton, British person; **les B~s** the
  British
broc [bʀo] *nm* pitcher
brocante [bʀɔkɑ̃t] *nf* (*objets*) secondhand goods
  pl, junk; (*commerce*) secondhand trade; junk
  dealing
brocanteur, -euse [bʀɔkɑ̃tœʀ, -øz] *nm/f* junk
  shop owner; junk dealer
brocart [bʀɔkaʀ] *nm* brocade
broche [bʀɔʃ] *nf* brooch; (*Culin*) spit; (*fiche*)
  spike, peg; (*Méd*) pin; **à la ~** spit-roasted,
  roasted on a spit
broché, e [bʀɔʃe] *adj* (*livre*) paper-backed; (*tissu*)
  brocaded
brochet [bʀɔʃɛ] *nm* pike *inv*
brochette [bʀɔʃɛt] *nf* skewer; ~ **de décorations**
  row of medals
brochure [bʀɔʃyʀ] *nf* pamphlet, brochure,
  booklet
brocoli [bʀɔkɔli] *nm* broccoli
brodequins [bʀɔdkɛ̃] *nmpl* (*de marche*) (lace-up)
  boots
broder [bʀɔde] *vt* to embroider ▷ *vi*: ~ (**sur des**
  faits *ou* **une histoire**) to embroider the facts
broderie [bʀɔdʀi] *nf* embroidery
bromure [bʀɔmyʀ] *nm* bromide

55

broncher [bʀɔ̃ʃe] vi: **sans ~** without flinching, without turning a hair

bronches [bʀɔ̃ʃ] nfpl bronchial tubes

bronchite [bʀɔ̃ʃit] nf bronchitis

broncho-pneumonie [bʀɔ̃kɔpnømɔni] nf broncho-pneumonia no pl

bronzage [bʀɔ̃zaʒ] nm (hâle) (sun)tan

bronze [bʀɔ̃z] nm bronze

bronzé, e [bʀɔ̃ze] adj tanned

bronzer [bʀɔ̃ze] vt to tan ▷ vi to get a tan; **se bronzer** to sunbathe

brosse [bʀɔs] nf brush; **donner un coup de ~ à qch** to give sth a brush; **coiffé en ~** with a crewcut; **~ à cheveux** hairbrush; **~ à dents** toothbrush; **~ à habits** clothesbrush

brosser [bʀɔse] vt (nettoyer) to brush; (fig: tableau etc) to paint; to draw; **se brosser** vt, vi to brush one's clothes; **se ~ les dents** to brush one's teeth; **tu peux te ~!** (fam) you can sing for it!

brou [bʀu] nm: **~ de noix** (pour bois) walnut stain; (liqueur) walnut liqueur

brouette [bʀuɛt] nf wheelbarrow

brouhaha [bʀuaa] nm hubbub

brouillage [bʀujaʒ] nm (d'une émission) jamming

brouillard [bʀujaʀ] nm fog; **être dans le ~** (fig) to be all at sea

brouille [bʀuj] nf quarrel

brouillé, e [bʀuje] adj (fâché): **il est ~ avec ses parents** he has fallen out with his parents; (teint) muddy

brouiller [bʀuje] vt to mix up; to confuse; (Radio) to cause interference to; (: délibérément) to jam; (rendre trouble) to cloud; (désunir: amis) to set at odds; **se brouiller** vi (ciel, vue) to cloud over; (détails) to become confused; **se ~ (avec)** to fall out (with); **~ les pistes** to cover one's tracks; (fig) to confuse the issue

brouillon, ne [bʀujɔ̃, -ɔn] adj disorganized, unmethodical ▷ nm (first) draft; **cahier de ~** rough (work) book

broussailles [bʀusaj] nfpl undergrowth sg

broussailleux, -euse [bʀusajø, -øz] adj bushy

brousse [bʀus] nf: **la ~** the bush

brouter [bʀute] vt to graze on ▷ vi to graze; (Auto) to judder

broutille [bʀutij] nf trifle

broyer [bʀwaje] vt to crush; **~ du noir** to be down in the dumps

bru [bʀy] nf daughter-in-law

brucelles [bʀysɛl] nfpl: **(pinces) ~** tweezers

brugnon [bʀyɲɔ̃] nm nectarine

bruine [bʀɥin] nf drizzle

bruiner [bʀɥine] vb impers: **il bruine** it's drizzling, there's a drizzle

bruire [bʀɥiʀ] vi (eau) to murmur; (feuilles, étoffe) to rustle

bruissement [bʀɥismã] nm murmuring; rustling

bruit [bʀɥi] nm: **un ~** a noise, a sound; (fig: rumeur) a rumour (Brit), a rumor (US); **le ~** noise; **pas/trop de ~** no/too much noise; **sans ~** without a sound, noiselessly; **faire du ~** to make a noise; **~ de fond** background noise

bruitage [bʀɥitaʒ] nm sound effects pl

bruiteur, -euse [bʀɥitœʀ, -øz] nm/f sound-effects engineer

brûlant, e [bʀylã, -ãt] adj burning (hot); (liquide) boiling (hot); (regard) fiery; (sujet) red-hot

brûlé, e [bʀyle] adj (fig: démasqué) blown; (: homme politique etc) discredited ▷ nm: **odeur de ~** smell of burning

brûle-pourpoint [bʀylpuʀpwɛ̃]: **à ~** adv point-blank

brûler [bʀyle] vt to burn; (eau bouillante) to scald; (consommer: électricité, essence) to use; (feu rouge, signal) to go through (without stopping) ▷ vi to burn; (jeu): **tu brûles** you're getting warm ou hot; **se brûler** to burn o.s.; to scald o.s.; **se ~ la cervelle** to blow one's brains out; **~ les étapes** to make rapid progress; (aller trop vite) to cut corners; **~ (d'impatience) de faire qch** to burn with impatience to do sth, be dying to do sth

brûleur [bʀylœʀ] nm burner

brûlot [bʀylo] nm (Culin) flaming brandy; **un ~ de contestation** (fig) a hotbed of dissent

brûlure [bʀylyʀ] nf (lésion) burn; (sensation) burning no pl, burning sensation; **~s d'estomac** heartburn sg

brume [bʀym] nf mist

brumeux, -euse [bʀymø, -øz] adj misty; (fig) hazy

brumisateur [bʀymizatœʀ] nm atomizer

brun, e [bʀœ̃, -yn] adj brown; (cheveux, personne) dark ▷ nm (couleur) brown ▷ nf (cigarette) cigarette made of dark tobacco; (bière) ≈ brown ale, ≈ stout

brunâtre [bʀynɑtʀ(ə)] adj brownish

brunch [bʀœntʃ] nm brunch

Brunei [bʀynei] nm: **le ~** Brunei

brunir [bʀyniʀ] vi: **se brunir** to get a tan ▷ vt to tan

brushing [bʀœʃiŋ] nm blow-dry

brusque [bʀysk(ə)] adj (soudain) abrupt, sudden; (rude) abrupt, brusque

brusquement [bʀyskəmã] adv (soudainement) abruptly, suddenly

brusquer [bʀyske] vt to rush

brusquerie [bʀyskəʀi] nf abruptness, brusqueness

brut, e [bʀyt] adj raw, crude, rough; (diamant) uncut; (soie, minéral, Inform: données) raw; (Comm) gross ▷ nf brute; **(champagne) ~** brut champagne; **(pétrole) ~** crude (oil)

brutal, e, -aux [bʀytal, -o] adj brutal

brutalement [bʀytalmã] adv brutally

brutaliser [bʀytalize] vt to handle roughly, manhandle

brutalité [bʀytalite] nf brutality no pl

brute [bʀyt] adj f, nf voir **brut**

Bruxelles [bʀysɛl] n Brussels

bruxellois, e [bʀysɛlwa, -waz] adj of ou from Brussels ▷ nm/f: **Bruxellois, e** inhabitant ou native of Brussels

bruyamment [bʀɥijamã] adv noisily

bruyant, e [bʀɥijã, -ãt] adj noisy

bruyère [bʀyjɛʀ] *nf* heather

BT *sigle m* (= *Brevet de technicien*) *vocational training certificate, taken at approx. 18 years*

BTA *sigle m* (= *Brevet de technicien agricole*) *agricultural training certificate, taken at approx. 18 years*

BTP *sigle mpl* (= *Bâtiments et travaux publics*) *public buildings and works sector*

BTS *sigle m* (= *Brevet de technicien supérieur*) *vocational training certificate taken at end of two-year higher education course*

BU *sigle f* = **Bibliothèque universitaire**

bu, e [by] *pp de* **boire**

buanderie [bɥɑ̃dʀi] *nf* laundry

Bucarest [bykaʀɛst] *n* Bucharest

buccal, e, -aux [bykal, -o] *adj*: **par voie ~e** orally

bûche [byʃ] *nf* log; **prendre une ~** (*fig*) to come a cropper (*Brit*), fall flat on one's face; **~ de Noël** Yule log

bûcher [byʃe] *nm* pyre; bonfire ▷ *vi* (*fam: étudier*) to swot (*Brit*), grind (*US*) ▷ *vt* to swot up (*Brit*), cram

bûcheron [byʃʀɔ̃] *nm* woodcutter

bûchette [byʃɛt] *nf* (*de bois*) stick, twig; (*pour compter*) rod

bûcheur, -euse [byʃœʀ, -øz] *nm/f* (*fam: étudiant*) swot (*Brit*), grind (*US*)

bucolique [bykɔlik] *adj* bucolic, pastoral

Budapest [bydapɛst] *n* Budapest

budget [bydʒɛ] *nm* budget

budgétaire [bydʒetɛʀ] *adj* budgetary, budget *cpd*

budgétiser [bydʒetize] *vt* to budget (for)

buée [bɥe] *nf* (*sur une vitre*) mist; (*de l'haleine*) steam

Buenos Aires [bwenɔzɛʀ] *n* Buenos Aires

buffet [byfɛ] *nm* (*meuble*) sideboard; (*de réception*) buffet; **~ (de gare)** (station) buffet, snack bar

buffle [byfl(ə)] *nm* buffalo

buis [bɥi] *nm* box tree; (*bois*) box(wood)

buisson [bɥisɔ̃] *nm* bush

buissonnière [bɥisɔnjɛʀ] *adj f*: **faire l'école ~** to play truant (*Brit*), skip school

bulbe [bylb(ə)] *nm* (*Bot, Anat*) bulb; (*coupole*) onion-shaped dome

bulgare [bylgaʀ] *adj* Bulgarian ▷ *nm* (*Ling*) Bulgarian ▷ *nm/f*: **Bulgare** Bulgarian, Bulgar

Bulgarie [bylgaʀi] *nf*: **la ~** Bulgaria

bulldozer [buldozœʀ] *nm* bulldozer

bulle [byl] *adj, nm*: **(papier) ~** manil(l)a paper ▷ *nf* bubble; (*de bande dessinée*) balloon; (*papale*) bull; **~ de savon** soap bubble

bulletin [byltɛ̃] *nm* (*communiqué, journal*) bulletin; (*papier*) form; (: *de bagages*) ticket; (*Scol*) report; **~ d'informations** news bulletin; **~ météorologique** weather report; **~ de naissance** birth certificate; **~ de salaire** pay slip; **~ de santé** medical bulletin; **~ (de vote)** ballot paper

buraliste [byʀalist(ə)] *nm/f* (*de bureau de tabac*) tobacconist; (*de poste*) clerk

bure [byʀ] *nf* homespun; (*de moine*) frock

bureau, x [byʀo] *nm* (*meuble*) desk; (*pièce, service*) office; **~ de change** (foreign) exchange office *ou* bureau; **~ d'embauche** ≈ job centre; **~ d'études** design office; **~ de location** box office; **~ des objets trouvés** lost property office (*Brit*), lost and found (*US*); **~ de placement** employment agency; **~ de poste** post office; **~ de tabac** tobacconist's (shop), smoke shop (*US*); **~ de vote** polling station

bureaucrate [byʀokʀat] *nm* bureaucrat

bureaucratie [byʀokʀasi] *nf* bureaucracy

bureaucratique [byʀokʀatik] *adj* bureaucratic

bureautique [byʀotik] *nf* office automation

burette [byʀɛt] *nf* (*de mécanicien*) oilcan; (*de chimiste*) burette

burin [byʀɛ̃] *nm* cold chisel; (*Art*) burin

buriné, e [byʀine] *adj* (*fig: visage*) craggy, seamed

Burkina [byʀkina], **Burkina-Faso** [byʀkinafaso] *nm*: **le ~(-Faso)** Burkina Faso

burlesque [byʀlɛsk(ə)] *adj* ridiculous; (*Littérature*) burlesque

burnous [byʀnu(s)] *nm* burnous

Burundi [buʀundi] *nm*: **le ~** Burundi

bus *vb* [by] *voir* **boire** ▷ *nm* [bys] (*véhicule, aussi Inform*) bus

busard [byzaʀ] *nm* harrier

buse [byz] *nf* buzzard

busqué, e [byske] *adj*: **nez ~** hook(ed) nose

buste [byst(ə)] *nm* (*Anat*) chest; (: *de femme*) bust; (*sculpture*) bust

bustier [bystje] *nm* (*soutien-gorge*) long-line bra

but [by] *vb voir* **boire** ▷ *nm* (*cible*) target; (*fig*) goal, aim; (*Football etc*) goal; **de ~ en blanc** point-blank; **avoir pour ~ de faire** to aim to do; **dans le ~ de** with the intention of

butane [bytan] *nm* butane; (*domestique*) calor gas® (*Brit*), butane

buté, e [byte] *adj* stubborn, obstinate ▷ *nf* (*Archit*) abutment; (*Tech*) stop

buter [byte] *vi*: **~ contre** *ou* **sur** to bump into; (*trébucher*) to stumble against ▷ *vt* to antagonize; **se buter** *vi* to get obstinate, dig in one's heels

buteur [bytœʀ] *nm* striker

butin [bytɛ̃] *nm* booty, spoils *pl*; (*d'un vol*) loot

butiner [bytine] *vi* to gather nectar

butor [bytɔʀ] *nm* (*fig*) lout

butte [byt] *nf* mound, hillock; **être en ~ à** to be exposed to

buvable [byvabl(ə)] *adj* (*eau, vin*) drinkable; (*Méd: ampoule etc*) to be taken orally; (*fig: roman etc*) reasonable

buvais *etc* [byvɛ] *vb voir* **boire**

buvard [byvaʀ] *nm* blotter

buvette [byvɛt] *nf* refreshment room *ou* stall; (*comptoir*) bar

buveur, -euse [byvœʀ, -øz] *nm/f* drinker

buvons *etc* [byvɔ̃] *vb voir* **boire**

BVP *sigle m* (= *Bureau de vérification de la publicité*) *advertising standards authority*

Byzance [bizɑ̃s] *n* Byzantium

byzantin, e [bizɑ̃tɛ̃, -in] *adj* Byzantine

BZH *abr* (= *Breizh*) Brittany

Cc

C, c [se] *nm inv* C, c ▷ *abr* (= *centime*) c; (= *Celsius*) C;
C comme Célestin C for Charlie

c' [s] *pron voir* **ce**

CA *sigle m* = **chiffre d'affaires; conseil
d'administration; corps d'armée** ▷ *sigle f* =
chambre d'agriculture

ça [sa] *pron* (*pour désigner*) this; (: *plus loin*) that;
(*comme sujet indéfini*) it; **ça m'étonne que** it
surprises me that; **ça va?** how are you?; how
are things?; (*d'accord?*) OK?, all right?; **ça alors!**
(*désapprobation*) well!, really!; (*étonnement*)
heavens!; **c'est ça** that's right

çà [sa] *adv*: **çà et là** here and there

cabale [kabal] *nf* (*Théât, Pol*) cabal, clique

caban [kabã] *nm* reefer jacket, donkey jacket

cabane [kaban] *nf* hut, cabin

cabanon [kabanɔ̃] *nm* chalet, (country) cottage

cabaret [kabaʀɛ] *nm* night club

cabas [kaba] *nm* shopping bag

cabestan [kabɛstã] *nm* capstan

cabillaud [kabijo] *nm* cod *inv*

cabine [kabin] *nf* (*de bateau*) cabin; (*de plage*)
(beach) hut; (*de piscine etc*) cubicle; (*de camion,
train*) cab; (*d'avion*) cockpit; **~ (d'ascenseur)** lift
cage; **~ d'essayage** fitting room; **~ de
projection** projection room; **~ spatiale** space
capsule; **~ (téléphonique)** call *ou* (tele)phone
box, (tele)phone booth

cabinet [kabinɛ] *nm* (*petite pièce*) closet; (*de
médecin*) surgery (Brit), office (US); (*de notaire etc*)
office; (: *clientèle*) practice; (*Pol*) cabinet; (*d'un
ministre*) advisers *pl*; **cabinets** *nmpl* (*w.-c.*) toilet
sg; **~ d'affaires** business consultants' (bureau),
business partnership; **~ de toilette** toilet; **~ de
travail** study

câble [kɑbl(ə)] *nm* cable; **le ~** (TV) cable
television, cablevision (US)

câblé, e [kɑble] *adj* (*fam*) switched on; (*Tech*)
linked to cable television

câbler [kɑble] *vt* to cable; **~ un quartier** (TV) to
put cable television into an area

cabosser [kabɔse] *vt* to dent

cabot [kabo] *nm* (*péj: chien*) mutt

cabotage [kabɔtaʒ] *nm* coastal navigation

caboteur [kabɔtœʀ] *nm* coaster

cabotin, e [kabɔtɛ̃, -in] *nm/f* (*péj: personne*

maniérée) poseur; (: *acteur*) ham ▷ *adj* dramatic,
theatrical

cabotinage [kabɔtinaʒ] *nm* playacting; third-
rate acting, ham acting

cabrer [kabʀe]: **se cabrer** *vi* (*cheval*) to rear up;
(*avion*) to nose up; (*fig*) to revolt, rebel; to jib

cabri [kabʀi] *nm* kid

cabriole [kabʀijɔl] *nf* caper; (*gymnastique etc*)
somersault

cabriolet [kabʀijɔlɛ] *nm* convertible

CAC [kak] *sigle f* = **Compagnie des agents de
change; indice ~** ≈ FT index (Brit), ≈ Dow Jones
average (US)

caca [kaka] *nm* (*langage enfantin*) pooh; (*couleur*):
~ d'oie greeny-yellow; **faire ~** (*fam*) to do a pooh

cacahuète [kakayɛt] *nf* peanut

cacao [kakao] *nm* cocoa (powder); (*boisson*) cocoa

cachalot [kaʃalo] *nm* sperm whale

cache [kaʃ] *nm* mask, card (*for masking*) ▷ *nf*
hiding place

cache-cache [kaʃkaʃ] *nm*: **jouer à ~** to play
hide-and-seek

cache-col [kaʃkɔl] *nm* scarf

cachemire [kaʃmiʀ] *nm* cashmere ▷ *adj*: **dessin
~** paisley pattern; **le C~** Kashmir

cache-nez [kaʃne] *nm inv* scarf, muffler

cache-pot [kaʃpo] *nm inv* flower-pot holder

cache-prise [kaʃpʀiz] *nm inv* socket cover

cacher [kaʃe] *vt* to hide, conceal; **~ qch à qn** to
hide *ou* conceal sth from sb; **se cacher** to hide;
to be hidden *ou* concealed; **il ne s'en cache pas**
he makes no secret of it

cache-sexe [kaʃsɛks] *nm inv* G-string

cachet [kaʃɛ] *nm* (*comprimé*) tablet; (*sceau: du roi*)
seal; (: *de la poste*) postmark; (*rétribution*) fee; (*fig*)
style, character

cacheter [kaʃte] *vt* to seal; **vin cacheté** vintage
wine

cachette [kaʃɛt] *nf* hiding place; **en ~** on the sly,
secretly

cachot [kaʃo] *nm* dungeon

cachotterie [kaʃɔtʀi] *nf* mystery; **faire des ~s**
to be secretive

cachottier, -ière [kaʃɔtje, -jɛʀ] *adj* secretive

cachou [kaʃu] *nm*: **pastille de ~** cachou (*sweet*)

cacophonie [kakɔfɔni] *nf* cacophony, din

cacophonique [kakɔfɔnik] *adj* cacophonous

cactus [kaktys] *nm* cactus

c.-à-d. *abr* (= *c'est-à-dire*) i.e.

cadastre [kadastʀ(ə)] *nm* land register

cadavéreux, -euse [kadaveʀø, -øz] *adj* (*teint, visage*) deathly pale

cadavérique [kadaveʀik] *adj* deathly (pale), deadly pale

cadavre [kadɑvʀ(ə)] *nm* corpse, (dead) body

Caddie® [kadi] *nm* (supermarket) trolley

cadeau, x [kado] *nm* present, gift; **faire un ~ à qn** to give sb a present *ou* gift; **faire ~ de qch à qn** to make a present of sth to sb, give sb sth as a present

cadenas [kadnɑ] *nm* padlock

cadenasser [kadnase] *vt* to padlock

cadence [kadɑ̃s] *nf* (*Mus*) cadence; (: *rythme*) rhythm; (*de travail etc*) rate; **cadences** *nfpl* (*en usine*) production rate *sg*; **en ~** rhythmically; in time

cadencé, e [kadɑ̃se] *adj* rhythmic(al); **au pas ~** (*Mil*) in quick time

cadet, te [kadɛ, -ɛt] *adj* younger; (*le plus jeune*) youngest ▷ *nm/f* youngest child *ou* one, youngest boy *ou* son/girl *ou* daughter; **il est mon ~ de deux ans** he's two years younger than me, he's two years my junior; **les ~s** (*Sport*) the minors (*15–17 years*); **le ~ de mes soucis** the least of my worries

cadrage [kadʀaʒ] *nm* framing (*of shot*)

cadran [kadʀɑ̃] *nm* dial; **~ solaire** sundial

cadre [kadʀ(ə)] *nm* frame; (*environnement*) surroundings *pl*; (*limites*) scope ▷ *nm/f* (*Admin*) managerial employee, executive ▷ *adj*: **loi ~** outline *ou* blueprint law; **~ moyen/supérieur** (*Admin*) middle/senior management employee, junior/senior executive; **rayer qn des ~s** to discharge sb; to dismiss sb; **dans le ~ de** (*fig*) within the framework *ou* context of

cadrer [kadʀe] *vi*: **~ avec** to tally *ou* correspond with ▷ *vt* (*Ciné, Photo*) to frame

cadreur, -euse [kadʀœʀ, -øz] *nm/f* (*Ciné*) cameraman/woman

caduc, -uque [kadyk] *adj* obsolete; (*Bot*) deciduous

CAF *sigle f* (= *Caisse d'allocations familiales*) family allowance office

caf *abr* (*coût, assurance, fret*) cif

cafard [kafaʀ] *nm* cockroach; **avoir le ~** to be down in the dumps, be feeling low

cafardeux, -euse [kafaʀdø, -øz] *adj* (*personne, ambiance*) depressing, melancholy

café [kafe] *nm* coffee; (*bistro*) café ▷ *adj inv* coffee *cpd*; **~ crème** coffee with cream; **~ au lait** white coffee; **~ noir** black coffee; **~ en grains** coffee beans; **~ en poudre** instant coffee; **~ tabac** *tobacconist's or newsagent's also serving coffee and spirits*; **~ liégeois** *coffee ice cream with whipped cream*

café-concert [kafekɔ̃sɛʀ] (*pl* **cafés-concerts**) *nm* (*aussi*: **caf'conc'**) *café with a cabaret*

caféine [kafein] *nf* caffeine

cafétéria [kafeteʀja] *nf* cafeteria

café-théâtre [kafeteɑtʀ(ə)] (*pl* **cafés-théâtres**) *nm café used as a venue by (experimental) theatre groups*

cafetière [kaftjɛʀ] *nf* (*pot*) coffee-pot

cafouillage [kafujaʒ] *nm* shambles *sg*

cafouiller [kafuje] *vi* to get in a shambles; (*machine etc*) to work in fits and starts

cage [kaʒ] *nf* cage; **~ (des buts)** goal; **en ~** in a cage, caged up *ou* in; **~ d'ascenseur** lift shaft; **~ d'escalier** (stair)well; **~ thoracique** rib cage

cageot [kaʒo] *nm* crate

cagibi [kaʒibi] *nm* shed

cagneux, -euse [kaɲø, -øz] *adj* knock-kneed

cagnotte [kaɲɔt] *nf* kitty

cagoule [kagul] *nf* cowl; hood; (*Ski etc*) cagoule

cahier [kaje] *nm* notebook; (*Typo*) signature; (*revue*): **~s** journal; **~ de revendications/doléances** list of claims/grievances; **~ de brouillons** rough book, jotter; **~ des charges** specification; **~ d'exercices** exercise book

cahin-caha [kaɛ̃kaa] *adv*: **aller ~** to jog along; (*fig*) to be so-so

cahot [kao] *nm* jolt, bump

cahoter [kaɔte] *vi* to bump along, jog along

cahoteux, -euse [kaɔtø, -øz] *adj* bumpy

cahute [kayt] *nf* shack, hut

caïd [kaid] *nm* big chief, boss

caillasse [kajas] *nf* (*pierraille*) loose stones *pl*

caille [kaj] *nf* quail

caillé, e [kaje] *adj*: **lait ~** curdled milk, curds *pl*

caillebotis [kajbɔti] *nm* duckboard

cailler [kaje] *vi* (*lait*) to curdle; (*sang*) to clot; (*fam*) to be cold

caillot [kajo] *nm* (*blood*) clot

caillou, x [kaju] *nm* (little) stone

caillouter [kajute] *vt* (*chemin*) to metal

caillouteux, -euse [kajutø, -øz] *adj* stony; pebbly

cailloutis [kajuti] *nm* (*petits graviers*) gravel

caïman [kaimɑ̃] *nm* cayman

Caïmans [kaimɑ̃] *nfpl*: **les ~** the Cayman Islands

Caire [kɛʀ] *nm*: **le ~** Cairo

caisse [kɛs] *nf* box; (*où l'on met la recette*) cashbox; (: *machine*) till; (*où l'on paye*) cash desk (*Brit*), checkout counter; (: *au supermarché*) checkout; (*de banque*) cashier's desk; (*Tech*) case, casing; **faire sa ~** (*Comm*) to count the takings; **~ claire** (*Mus*) side *ou* snare drum; **~ éclair** express checkout; **~ enregistreuse** cash register; **~ d'épargne (CE)** savings bank; **~ noire** slush fund; **~ de retraite** pension fund; **~ de sortie** checkout; *voir* **grosse**

caissier, -ière [kesje, -jɛʀ] *nm/f* cashier

caisson [kɛsɔ̃] *nm* box, case

cajoler [kaʒole] *vt* to wheedle, coax; to surround with love and care, make a fuss of

cajoleries [kaʒɔlʀi] *nfpl* coaxing *sg*, flattery *sg*

cajou [kaʒu] *nm* cashew nut

cake [kɛk] *nm* fruit cake

CAL *sigle m* (= *Comité d'action lycéen*) pupils' action group seeking to reform school system

cal [kal] *nm* callus

cal. *abr* = **calorie**

calamar [kalamaʀ] nm = **calmar**

calaminé, e [kalamine] adj (Auto) coked up

calamité [kalamite] nf calamity, disaster

calandre [kalɑ̃dʀ(ə)] nf radiator grill; (machine) calender, mangle

calanque [kalɑ̃k] nf rocky inlet

calcaire [kalkɛʀ] nm limestone ▷ adj (eau) hard; (Géo) limestone cpd

calciné, e [kalsine] adj burnt to ashes

calcium [kalsjɔm] nm calcium

calcul [kalkyl] nm calculation; **le ~** (Scol) arithmetic; **~ différentiel/intégral** differential/integral calculus; **~ mental** mental arithmetic; **~ (biliaire)** (gall)stone; **~ (rénal)** (kidney) stone; **d'après mes ~s** by my reckoning

calculateur [kalkylatœʀ] nm, **calculatrice** [kalkylatʀis] nf calculator

calculé, e [kalkyle] adj: **risque ~** calculated risk

calculer [kalkyle] vt to calculate, work out, reckon; (combiner) to calculate; **~ qch de tête** to work sth out in one's head

calculette [kalkylɛt] nf (pocket) calculator

cale [kal] nf (de bateau) hold; (en bois) wedge, chock; **~ sèche** ou **de radoub** dry dock

calé, e [kale] adj (fam) clever, bright

calebasse [kalbɑs] nf calabash, gourd

calèche [kalɛʃ] nf horse-drawn carriage

caleçon [kalsɔ̃] nm pair of underpants, trunks pl; **~ de bain** bathing trunks pl

calembour [kalɑ̃buʀ] nm pun

calendes [kalɑ̃d] nfpl: **renvoyer aux ~ grecques** to postpone indefinitely

calendrier [kalɑ̃dʀije] nm calendar; (fig) timetable

cale-pied [kalpje] nm inv toe clip

calepin [kalpɛ̃] nm notebook

caler [kale] vt to wedge, chock up; **~ (son moteur/véhicule)** to stall (one's engine/vehicle); **se ~ dans un fauteuil** to make o.s. comfortable in an armchair

calfater [kalfate] vt to caulk

calfeutrage [kalføtʀaʒ] nm draughtproofing (Brit), draftproofing (US)

calfeutrer [kalføtʀe] vt to (make) draughtproof (Brit) ou draftproof (US); **se calfeutrer** vi to make o.s. snug and comfortable

calibre [kalibʀ(ə)] nm (d'un fruit) grade; (d'une arme) bore, calibre (Brit), caliber (US); (fig) calibre, caliber

calibrer [kalibʀe] vt to grade

calice [kalis] nm (Rel) chalice; (Bot) calyx

calicot [kaliko] nm (tissu) calico

calife [kalif] nm caliph

Californie [kalifɔʀni] nf: **la ~** California

californien, ne [kalifɔʀnjɛ̃, -ɛn] adj Californian

califourchon [kalifuʀʃɔ̃]: **à ~** adv astride; **à ~ sur** astride, straddling

câlin, e [kɑlɛ̃, -in] adj cuddly, cuddlesome; tender

câliner [kɑline] vt to fondle, cuddle

câlineries [kɑlinʀi] nfpl cuddles

calisson [kalisɔ̃] nm diamond-shaped sweet or candy made with ground almonds

calleux, -euse [kalø, -øz] adj horny, callous

calligraphie [kaligʀafi] nf calligraphy

callosité [kalozite] nf callus

calmant [kalmɑ̃] nm tranquillizer, sedative; (contre la douleur) painkiller

calmar [kalmaʀ] nm squid

calme [kalm(ə)] adj calm, quiet ▷ nm calm(ness), quietness; **sans perdre son ~** without losing one's cool ou calmness; **~ plat** (Navig) dead calm

calmement [kalməmɑ̃] adv calmly, quietly

calmer [kalme] vt to calm (down); (douleur, inquiétude) to ease, soothe; **se calmer** vi to calm down

calomniateur, -trice [kalɔmnjatœʀ, -tʀis] nm/f slanderer; libeller

calomnie [kalɔmni] nf slander; (écrite) libel

calomnier [kalɔmnje] vt to slander; to libel

calomnieux, -euse [kalɔmnjø, -øz] adj slanderous; libellous

calorie [kalɔʀi] nf calorie

calorifère [kalɔʀifɛʀ] nm stove

calorifique [kalɔʀifik] adj calorific

calorifuge [kalɔʀifyʒ] adj (heat-)insulating, heat-retaining

calot [kalo] nm forage cap

calotte [kalɔt] nf (coiffure) skullcap; (gifle) slap; **la ~** (péj: clergé) the cloth, the clergy; **~ glaciaire** icecap

calque [kalk(ə)] nm (aussi: **papier calque**) tracing paper; (dessin) tracing; (fig) carbon copy

calquer [kalke] vt to trace; (fig) to copy exactly

calvados [kalvados] nm Calvados (apple brandy)

calvaire [kalvɛʀ] nm (croix) wayside cross, calvary; (souffrances) suffering, martyrdom

calvitie [kalvisi] nf baldness

camaïeu [kamajø] nm: **(motif en) ~** monochrome motif

camarade [kamaʀad] nm/f friend, pal; (Pol) comrade

camaraderie [kamaʀadʀi] nf friendship

camarguais, e [kamaʀgɛ, -ɛz] adj of ou from the Camargue

Camargue [kamaʀg] nf: **la ~** the Camargue

cambiste [kɑ̃bist(ə)] nm (Comm) foreign exchange dealer, exchange agent

Cambodge [kɑ̃bɔdʒ] nm: **le ~** Cambodia

cambodgien, ne [kɑ̃bɔdʒjɛ̃, -ɛn] adj Cambodian ▷ nm/f: **Cambodgien, ne** Cambodian

cambouis [kɑ̃bwi] nm dirty oil ou grease

cambré, e [kɑ̃bʀe] adj: **avoir les reins ~s** to have an arched back; **avoir le pied très ~** to have very high arches ou insteps

cambrer [kɑ̃bʀe] vt to arch; **se cambrer** vi to arch one's back; **~ la taille** ou **les reins** to arch one's back

cambriolage [kɑ̃bʀijɔlaʒ] nm burglary

cambrioler [kɑ̃bʀijɔle] vt to burgle (Brit), burglarize (US)

cambrioleur, -euse [kɑ̃bʀijɔlœʀ, -øz] nm/f

burglar

cambrure [kɑ̃bʀyʀ] nf (du pied) arch; (de la route) camber; **~ des reins** small of the back

cambuse [kɑ̃byz] nf storeroom

came [kam] nf: **arbre à ~s** camshaft; **arbre à ~s en tête** overhead camshaft

camée [kame] nm cameo

caméléon [kameleɔ̃] nm chameleon

camélia [kamelja] nm camellia

camelot [kamlo] nm street pedlar

camelote [kamlɔt] nf rubbish, trash, junk

camembert [kamɑ̃bɛʀ] nm Camembert (cheese)

caméra [kameʀa] nf (Ciné, TV) camera; (d'amateur) cine-camera

caméraman [kameʀaman] nm cameraman/- woman

Cameroun [kamʀun] nm: **le ~** Cameroon

camerounais, e [kamʀunɛ, -ɛz] adj Cameroonian

caméscope® [kameskɔp] nm camcorder

camion [kamjɔ̃] nm lorry (Brit), truck; (plus petit, fermé) van; (charge): **~ de sable/cailloux** lorry- load (Brit) ou truck-load of sand/stones; **~ de dépannage** breakdown (Brit) ou tow (US) truck

camion-citerne [kamjɔ̃sitɛʀn(ə)] (pl **camions- citernes**) nm tanker

camionnage [kamjɔnaʒ] nm haulage (Brit), trucking (US); **frais/entreprise de ~** haulage costs/business

camionnette [kamjɔnɛt] nf (small) van

camionneur [kamjɔnœʀ] nm (entrepreneur) haulage contractor (Brit), trucker (US); (chauffeur) lorry (Brit) ou truck driver; van driver

camisole [kamizɔl] nf: **~ (de force)** straitjacket

camomille [kamɔmij] nf camomile; (boisson) camomile tea

camouflage [kamuflaʒ] nm camouflage

camoufler [kamufle] vt to camouflage; (fig) to conceal, cover up

camouflet [kamuflɛ] nm (fam) snub

camp [kɑ̃] nm camp; (fig) side; **~ de nudistes/ vacances** nudist/holiday camp; **~ de concentration** concentration camp

campagnard, e [kɑ̃paɲaʀ, -aʀd(ə)] adj country cpd ▷ nm/f countryman/woman

campagne [kɑ̃paɲ] nf country, countryside; (Mil, Pol, Comm) campaign; **en ~** (Mil) in the field; **à la ~** in/to the country; **faire ~ pour** to campaign for; **~ électorale** election campaign; **~ de publicité** advertising campaign

campanile [kɑ̃panil] nm (tour) bell tower

campé, e [kɑ̃pe] adj: **bien ~** (personnage, tableau) well-drawn

campement [kɑ̃pmɑ̃] nm camp, encampment

camper [kɑ̃pe] vi to camp ▷ vt (chapeau etc) to pull ou put on firmly; (dessin) to sketch; **se ~ devant** to plant o.s. in front of

campeur, -euse [kɑ̃pœʀ, -øz] nm/f camper

camphre [kɑ̃fʀ(ə)] nm camphor

camphré, e [kɑ̃fʀe] adj camphorated

camping [kɑ̃piŋ] nm camping; **(terrain de) ~** campsite, camping site; **faire du ~** to go

camping; **faire du ~ sauvage** to camp rough

camping-car [kɑ̃piŋkaʀ] nm caravanette, camper (US)

camping-gaz® [kɑ̃piŋgaz] nm inv camp(ing) stove

campus [kɑ̃pys] nm campus

camus, e [kamy, -yz] adj: **nez ~** pug nose

Canada [kanada] nm: **le ~** Canada

canadair® [kanadɛʀ] nm fire-fighting plane

canadien, ne [kanadjɛ̃, -ɛn] adj Canadian ▷ nm/f: **Canadien, ne** Canadian ▷ nf (veste) fur-lined jacket

canaille [kanɑj] nf (péj) scoundrel; (populace) riff-raff ▷ adj raffish, rakish

canal, -aux [kanal, -o] nm canal; (naturel) channel; (Admin): **par le ~ de** through (the medium of), via; **~ de distribution/télévision** distribution/television channel; **~ de Panama/ Suez** Panama/Suez Canal

canalisation [kanalizasjɔ̃] nf (tuyau) pipe

canaliser [kanalize] vt to canalize; (fig) to channel

canapé [kanape] nm settee, sofa; (Culin) canapé, open sandwich

canapé-lit [kanapeli] (pl **canapés-lits**) nm sofa bed

canaque [kanak] adj of ou from New Caledonia ▷ nm/f: **Canaque** native of New Caledonia

canard [kanaʀ] nm duck

canari [kanaʀi] nm canary

Canaries [kanaʀi] nfpl: **les (îles) ~** the Canary Islands, the Canaries

cancaner [kɑ̃kane] vi to gossip (maliciously); (canard) to quack

cancanier, -ière [kɑ̃kanje, -jɛʀ] adj gossiping

cancans [kɑ̃kɑ̃] nmpl (malicious) gossip sg

cancer [kɑ̃sɛʀ] nm cancer; (signe): **le C~** Cancer, the Crab; **être du C~** to be Cancer; **il a un ~** he has cancer

cancéreux, -euse [kɑ̃seʀø, -øz] adj cancerous; (personne) suffering from cancer

cancérigène [kɑ̃seʀiʒɛn] adj carcinogenic

cancérologue [kɑ̃seʀɔlɔg] nm/f cancer specialist

cancre [kɑ̃kʀ(ə)] nm dunce

cancrelat [kɑ̃kʀəla] nm cockroach

candélabre [kɑ̃delabʀ(ə)] nm candelabrum; (lampadaire) street lamp, lamppost

candeur [kɑ̃dœʀ] nf ingenuousness

candi [kɑ̃di] adj inv: **sucre ~** (sugar-)candy

candidat, e [kɑ̃dida, -at] nm/f candidate; (à un poste) applicant, candidate

candidature [kɑ̃didatyʀ] nf candidacy; application; **poser sa ~** to submit an application, apply; **~ spontanée** unsolicited job application

candide [kɑ̃did] adj ingenuous, guileless, naïve

cane [kan] nf (female) duck

caneton [kantɔ̃] nm duckling

canette [kanɛt] nf (de bière) (flip-top) bottle; (de machine à coudre) spool

canevas [kanva] nm (Couture) canvas (for tapestry work); (fig) framework, structure

caniche [kaniʃ] nm poodle
caniculaire [kanikylɛʀ] adj (chaleur, jour) scorching
canicule [kanikyl] nf scorching heat; midsummer heat, dog days pl
canif [kanif] nm penknife, pocket knife
canin, e [kanɛ̃, -in] adj canine ▷ nf canine (tooth), eye tooth; **exposition ~e** dog show
caniveau, x [kanivo] nm gutter
cannabis [kanabis] nm cannabis
canne [kan] nf (walking) stick; **~ à pêche** fishing rod; **~ à sucre** sugar cane; **les ~s blanches** (les aveugles) the blind
canné, e [kane] adj (chaise) cane cpd
cannelé, e [kanle] adj fluted
cannelle [kanɛl] nf cinnamon
cannelure [kanlyʀ] nf fluting no pl
canner [kane] vt (chaise) to make ou repair with cane
cannibale [kanibal] nm/f cannibal
cannibalisme [kanibalism(ə)] nm cannibalism
canoë [kanɔe] nm canoe; (sport) canoeing; **~ (kayak)** kayak
canon [kanɔ̃] nm (arme) gun; (Hist) cannon; (d'une arme: tube) barrel; (fig) model; (Mus) canon ▷ adj: **droit ~** canon law; **~ rayé** rifled barrel
cañon [kanɔ̃] nm canyon
canonique [kanɔnik] adj: **âge ~** respectable age
canoniser [kanɔnize] vt to canonize
canonnade [kanɔnad] nf cannonade
canonnier [kanɔnje] nm gunner
canonnière [kanɔnjɛʀ] nf gunboat
canot [kano] nm boat, ding(h)y; **~ pneumatique** rubber ou inflatable ding(h)y; **~ de sauvetage** lifeboat
canotage [kanɔtaʒ] nm rowing
canoter [kanɔte] vi to go rowing
canoteur, -euse [kanɔtœʀ, -øz] nm/f rower
canotier [kanɔtje] nm boater
Cantal [kɑ̃tal] nm: **le ~** Cantal
cantate [kɑ̃tat] nf cantata
cantatrice [kɑ̃tatʀis] nf (opera) singer
cantilène [kɑ̃tilɛn] nf (Mus) cantilena
cantine [kɑ̃tin] nf canteen; (réfectoire d'école) dining hall
cantique [kɑ̃tik] nm hymn
canton [kɑ̃tɔ̃] nm district (consisting of several communes); see note; (en Suisse) canton

● CANTON
●
● A French canton is the administrative
● division represented by a councillor in the
● "Conseil général". It comprises a number of
● "communes" and is, in turn, a subdivision
● of an "arrondissement". In Switzerland the
● cantons are the 23 autonomous political
● divisions which make up the Swiss
● confederation.

cantonade [kɑ̃tɔnad]: **à la ~** adv to everyone in general; (crier) from the rooftops

cantonais, e [kɑ̃tɔnɛ, -ɛz] adj Cantonese ▷ nm (Ling) Cantonese
cantonal, e, -aux [kɑ̃tɔnal, -o] adj cantonal, ≈ district
cantonnement [kɑ̃tɔnmɑ̃] nm (lieu) billet; (action) billeting
cantonner [kɑ̃tɔne] vt (Mil) to billet (Brit), quarter; to station; **se ~ dans** to confine o.s. to
cantonnier [kɑ̃tɔnje] nm roadmender
canular [kanylaʀ] nm hoax
CAO sigle f (= conception assistée par ordinateur) CAD
caoutchouc [kautʃu] nm rubber; **~ mousse** foam rubber; **en ~** rubber cpd
caoutchouté, e [kautʃute] adj rubberized
caoutchouteux, -euse [kautʃutø, -øz] adj rubbery
CAP sigle m (= Certificat d'aptitude professionnelle) vocational training certificate taken at secondary school
cap [kap] nm (Géo) cape; headland; (fig) hurdle; watershed; (Navig): **changer de ~** to change course; **mettre le ~ sur** to head ou steer for; **doubler** ou **passer le ~** (fig) to get over the worst; **Le C~** Cape Town; **le ~ de Bonne Espérance** the Cape of Good Hope; **le ~ Horn** Cape Horn; **les îles du C~ Vert** (aussi: **le Cap-Vert**) the Cape Verde Islands
capable [kapabl(ə)] adj able, capable; **~ de qch/faire** capable of sth/doing; **il est ~ d'oublier** he could easily forget; **spectacle ~ d'intéresser** show likely to be of interest
capacité [kapasite] nf (compétence) ability; (Jur, Inform, d'un récipient) capacity; **~ (en droit)** basic legal qualification
caparaçonner [kapaʀasɔne] vt (fig) to clad
cape [kap] nf cape, cloak; **rire sous ~** to laugh up one's sleeve
capeline [kaplin] nf wide-brimmed hat
CAPES [kapɛs] sigle m (= Certificat d'aptitude au professorat de l'enseignement du second degré) secondary teaching diploma; see note

● CAPES
●
● The French CAPES ("certificat d'aptitude au
● professorat de l'enseignement du second
● degré") is a competitive examination sat by
● prospective secondary school teachers after
● the 'licence'. Successful candidates become
● fully qualified teachers ("professeurs
● certifiés").

capésien, ne [kapesjɛ̃, -ɛn] nm/f person who holds the CAPES
CAPET [kapɛt] sigle m (= Certificat d'aptitude au professorat de l'enseignement technique) technical teaching diploma
capharnaüm [kafaʀnaɔm] nm shambles sg
capillaire [kapilɛʀ] adj (soins, lotion) hair cpd; (vaisseau etc) capillary; **artiste ~** hair artist ou designer
capillarité [kapilaʀite] nf capillary action
capilotade [kapilɔtad]: **en ~** adv crushed to a

pulp; smashed to pieces

capitaine [kapitɛn] *nm* captain; **~ des pompiers** fire chief (*Brit*), fire marshal (*US*); **~ au long cours** master mariner

capitainerie [kapitɛnʀi] *nf* (*du port*) harbour (*Brit*) *ou* harbor (*US*) master's (office)

capital, e, -aux [kapital, -o] *adj* major; fundamental; (*Jur*) capital ▷ *nm* capital; (*fig*) stock; asset ▷ *nf* (*ville*) capital; (*lettre*) capital (letter) ▷ *nmpl* (*fonds*) capital *sg*, money *sg*; **les sept péchés capitaux** the seven deadly sins; **peine ~e** capital punishment; **~ (social)** authorized capital; **~ d'exploitation** working capital

capitaliser [kapitalize] *vt* to amass, build up; (*Comm*) to capitalize ▷ *vi* to save

capitalisme [kapitalism(ə)] *nm* capitalism

capitaliste [kapitalist(ə)] *adj, nm/f* capitalist

capiteux, -euse [kapitø, -øz] *adj* (*vin, parfum*) heady; (*sensuel*) sensuous, alluring

capitonnage [kapitɔnaʒ] *nm* padding

capitonné, e [kapitɔne] *adj* padded

capitonner [kapitɔne] *vt* to pad

capitulation [kapitylasjɔ̃] *nf* capitulation

capituler [kapityle] *vi* to capitulate

caporal, -aux [kapɔʀal, -o] *nm* lance corporal

caporal-chef [kapɔʀalʃɛf, kapɔʀo-] (*pl* **caporaux-chefs**) *nm* corporal

capot [kapo] *nm* (*Auto*) bonnet (*Brit*), hood (*US*)

capote [kapɔt] *nf* (*de voiture*) hood (*Brit*), top (*US*); (*de soldat*) greatcoat; **~ (anglaise)** (*fam*) rubber, condom

capoter [kapɔte] *vi* to overturn; (*négociations*) to founder

câpre [kɑpʀ(ə)] *nf* caper

caprice [kapʀis] *nm* whim, caprice; passing fancy; **caprices** *nmpl* (*de la mode etc*) vagaries; **faire un ~** to throw a tantrum; **faire des ~s** to be temperamental

capricieux, -euse [kapʀisjø, -øz] *adj* capricious; whimsical; temperamental

Capricorne [kapʀikɔʀn] *nm*: **le ~** Capricorn, the Goat; **être du ~** to be Capricorn

capsule [kapsyl] *nf* (*de bouteille*) cap; (*amorce*) primer; cap; (*Bot etc, spatiale*) capsule

captage [kaptaʒ] *nm* (*d'une émission de radio*) picking-up; (*d'énergie, d'eau*) harnessing

capter [kapte] *vt* (*ondes radio*) to pick up; (*eau*) to harness; (*fig*) to win, capture

capteur [kaptœʀ] *nm*: **~ solaire** solar collector

captieux, -euse [kapsjø, -øz] *adj* specious

captif, -ive [kaptif, -iv] *adj, nm/f* captive

captivant, e [kaptivɑ̃, -ɑ̃t] *adj* captivating

captiver [kaptive] *vt* to captivate

captivité [kaptivite] *nf* captivity; **en ~** in captivity

capture [kaptyʀ] *nf* capture, catching *no pl*; catch

capturer [kaptyʀe] *vt* to capture, catch

capuche [kapyʃ] *nf* hood

capuchon [kapyʃɔ̃] *nm* hood; (*de stylo*) cap, top

capucin [kapysɛ̃] *nm* Capuchin monk

capucine [kapysin] *nf* (*Bot*) nasturtium

Cap-Vert [kabvɛʀ] *nm*: **le ~** Cape Verde

caquelon [kaklɔ̃] *nm* (*ustensile de cuisson*) fondue pot

caquet [kakɛ] *nm*: **rabattre le ~ à qn** to bring sb down a peg or two

caqueter [kakte] *vi* (*poule*) to cackle; (*fig*) to prattle

car [kaʀ] *nm* coach (*Brit*), bus ▷ *conj* because, for; **~ de police** police van; **~ de reportage** broadcasting *ou* radio van

carabine [kaʀabin] *nf* carbine, rifle; **~ à air comprimé** airgun

carabiné, e [kaʀabine] *adj* violent; (*cocktail, amende*) stiff

Caracas [kaʀakas] *n* Caracas

caracoler [kaʀakɔle] *vi* to caracole, prance

caractère [kaʀaktɛʀ] *nm* (*gén*) character; **en ~s gras** in bold type; **en petits ~s** in small print; **en ~s d'imprimerie** in block capitals; **avoir du ~** to have character; **avoir bon/mauvais ~** to be good-/ill-natured *ou* tempered; **~ de remplacement** wild card (*Inform*); **~s/seconde (cps)** characters per second (cps)

caractériel, le [kaʀakteʀjɛl] *adj* (*enfant*) (emotionally) disturbed ▷ *nm/f* problem child; **troubles ~s** emotional problems

caractérisé, e [kaʀakteʀize] *adj*: **c'est une grippe/de l'insubordination ~e** it is a clear(-cut) case of flu/insubordination

caractériser [kaʀakteʀize] *vt* to characterize; **se ~ par** to be characterized *ou* distinguished by

caractéristique [kaʀakteʀistik] *adj, nf* characteristic

carafe [kaʀaf] *nf* decanter; carafe

carafon [kaʀafɔ̃] *nm* small carafe

caraïbe [kaʀaib] *adj* Caribbean; **les Caraïbes** *nfpl* the Caribbean (Islands); **la mer des C~s** the Caribbean Sea

carambolage [kaʀɑ̃bɔlaʒ] *nm* multiple crash, pileup

caramel [kaʀamɛl] *nm* (*bonbon*) caramel, toffee; (*substance*) caramel

caraméliser [kaʀamelize] *vt* to caramelize

carapace [kaʀapas] *nf* shell

carapater [kaʀapate]: **se carapater** *vi* to take to one's heels, scram ·

carat [kaʀa] *nm* carat; **or à 18 ~s** 18-carat gold

caravane [kaʀavan] *nf* caravan

caravanier [kaʀavanje] *nm* caravanner

caravaning [kaʀavaniŋ] *nm* caravanning; (*emplacement*) caravan site

caravelle [kaʀavɛl] *nf* caravel

carbonate [kaʀbɔnat] *nm* (*Chimie*): **~ de soude** sodium carbonate

carbone [kaʀbɔn] *nm* carbon; (*feuille*) carbon, sheet of carbon paper; (*double*) carbon (copy)

carbonique [kaʀbɔnik] *adj*: **gaz ~** carbon dioxide; **neige ~** dry ice

carbonisé, e [kaʀbɔnize] *adj* charred; **mourir ~** to be burned to death

carboniser [kaʀbɔnize] *vt* to carbonize; (*brûler*

complètement) to burn down, reduce to ashes

carburant [kaʀbyʀɑ̃] *nm* (motor) fuel

carburateur [kaʀbyʀatœʀ] *nm* carburettor

carburation [kaʀbyʀasjɔ̃] *nf* carburation

carburer [kaʀbyʀe] *vi* (*moteur*): **bien/mal ~** to be well/badly tuned

carcan [kaʀkɑ̃] *nm* (*fig*) yoke, shackles *pl*

carcasse [kaʀkas] *nf* carcass; (*de véhicule etc*) shell

carcéral, e, -aux [kaʀseʀal, -o] *adj* prison *cpd*

carcinogène [kaʀsinɔʒɛn] *adj* carcinogenic

cardan [kaʀdɑ̃] *nm* universal joint

carder [kaʀde] *vt* to card

cardiaque [kaʀdjak] *adj* cardiac, heart *cpd* ▷ *nm/f* heart patient; **être ~** to have a heart condition

cardigan [kaʀdigɑ̃] *nm* cardigan

cardinal, e, -aux [kaʀdinal, -o] *adj* cardinal ▷ *nm* (*Rel*) cardinal

cardiologie [kaʀdjɔlɔʒi] *nf* cardiology

cardiologue [kaʀdjɔlɔg] *nm/f* cardiologist, heart specialist

cardio-vasculaire [kaʀdjovaskylɛʀ] *adj* cardiovascular

cardon [kaʀdɔ̃] *nm* cardoon

carême [kaʀɛm] *nm*: **le C~** Lent

carence [kaʀɑ̃s] *nf* incompetence, inadequacy; (*manque*) deficiency; **~ vitaminique** vitamin deficiency

carène [kaʀɛn] *nf* hull

caréner [kaʀene] *vt* (*Navig*) to careen; (*carrosserie*) to streamline

caressant, e [kaʀɛsɑ̃, -ɑ̃t] *adj* affectionate; caressing, tender

caresse [kaʀɛs] *nf* caress

caresser [kaʀese] *vt* to caress, stroke, fondle; (*fig: projet, espoir*) to toy with

cargaison [kaʀgɛzɔ̃] *nf* cargo, freight

cargo [kaʀgo] *nm* cargo boat, freighter; **~ mixte** cargo and passenger ship

cari [kaʀi] *nm* = **curry**

caricatural, e, -aux [kaʀikatyʀal, -o] *adj* caricatural, caricature-like

caricature [kaʀikatyʀ] *nf* caricature; (*politique etc*) (satirical) cartoon

caricaturer [kaʀikatyʀe] *vt* (*personne*) to caricature; (*politique etc*) to satirize

caricaturiste [kaʀikatyʀist(ə)] *nm/f* caricaturist, (satirical) cartoonist

carie [kaʀi] *nf*: **la ~ (dentaire)** tooth decay; **une ~** a bad tooth

carié, e [kaʀje] *adj*: **dent ~e** bad *ou* decayed tooth

carillon [kaʀijɔ̃] *nm* (*d'église*) bells *pl*; (*de pendule*) chimes *pl*; (*de porte*): **~ (électrique)** (electric) door chime *ou* bell

carillonner [kaʀijɔne] *vi* to ring, chime, peal

caritatif, -ive [kaʀitatif, -iv] *adj* charitable

carlingue [kaʀlɛ̃g] *nf* cabin

carmélite [kaʀmelit] *nf* Carmelite nun

carmin [kaʀmɛ̃] *adj inv* crimson

carnage [kaʀnaʒ] *nm* carnage, slaughter

carnassier, -ière [kaʀnasje, -jɛʀ] *adj*

carnivorous ▷ *nm* carnivore

carnation [kaʀnɑsjɔ̃] *nf* complexion; **carnations** *nfpl* (*Peinture*) flesh tones

carnaval [kaʀnaval] *nm* carnival

carné, e [kaʀne] *adj* meat *cpd*, meat-based

carnet [kaʀnɛ] *nm* (*calepin*) notebook; (*de tickets, timbres etc*) book; (*d'école*) school report; (*journal intime*) diary; **~ d'adresses** address book; **~ de chèques** cheque book (*Brit*), checkbook (*US*); **~ de commandes** order book; **~ de notes** (*Scol*) (school) report; **~ à souches** counterfoil book

carnier [kaʀnje] *nm* gamebag

carnivore [kaʀnivɔʀ] *adj* carnivorous ▷ *nm* carnivore

Carolines [kaʀɔlin] *nfpl*: **les ~** the Caroline Islands

carotide [kaʀɔtid] *nf* carotid (artery)

carotte [kaʀɔt] *nf* (*aussi fig*) carrot

Carpates [kaʀpat] *nfpl*: **les ~** the Carpathians, the Carpathian Mountains

carpe [kaʀp(ə)] *nf* carp

carpette [kaʀpɛt] *nf* rug

carquois [kaʀkwa] *nm* quiver

carre [kaʀ] *nf* (*de ski*) edge

carré, e [kaʀe] *adj* square; (*fig: franc*) straightforward ▷ *nm* (*de terrain, jardin*) patch, plot; (*Navig: salle*) wardroom; (*Math*) square; **~ blanc** (*TV*) "adults only" symbol; (*Cartes*): **~ d'as/de rois** four aces/kings; **élever un nombre au ~** to square a number; **mètre/ kilomètre ~** square metre/kilometre; **~ de soie** silk headsquare *ou* headscarf; **~ d'agneau** loin of lamb

carreau, x [kaʀo] *nm* (*en faïence etc*) (floor) tile, (wall) tile; (*window*) pane; (*motif*) check, square; (*Cartes: couleur*) diamonds *pl*; (: *carte*) diamond; **tissu à ~x** checked fabric; **papier à ~x** squared paper

carrefour [kaʀfuʀ] *nm* crossroads *sg*

carrelage [kaʀlaʒ] *nm* tiling; (tiled) floor

carreler [kaʀle] *vt* to tile

carrelet [kaʀlɛ] *nm* (*poisson*) plaice

carreleur [kaʀlœʀ] *nm* (floor) tiler

carrément [kaʀemɑ̃] *adv* (*franchement*) straight out, bluntly; (*sans détours, sans hésiter*) straight; (*nettement*) definitely; **il l'a ~ mis à la porte** he threw him straight out

carrer [kaʀe]: **se carrer** *vi*: **se ~ dans un fauteuil** to settle o.s. comfortably *ou* ensconce o.s. in an armchair

carrier [kaʀje] *nm*: **(ouvrier) ~** quarryman, quarrier

carrière [kaʀjɛʀ] *nf* (*de roches*) quarry; (*métier*) career; **militaire de ~** professional soldier; **faire ~ dans** to make one's career in

carriériste [kaʀjeʀist(ə)] *nm/f* careerist

carriole [kaʀjɔl] *nf* (*péj*) old cart

carrossable [kaʀɔsabl(ə)] *adj* suitable for (motor) vehicles

carrosse [kaʀɔs] *nm* (horse-drawn) coach

carrosserie [kaʀɔsʀi] *nf* body, bodywork *no pl* (*Brit*); (*activité, commerce*) coachwork (*Brit*), (car) body manufacturing; **atelier de ~** (*pour réparations*) body shop, panel beaters' (yard) (*Brit*)

carrossier [kaʀɔsje] *nm* coachbuilder (*Brit*), (car) body repairer; (*dessinateur*) car designer

carrousel [kaʀuzɛl] *nm* (*Équitation*) carousel; (*fig*) merry-go-round

carrure [kaʀyʀ] *nf* build; (*fig*) stature

cartable [kaʀtabl(ə)] *nm* (*d'écolier*) satchel, (school)bag

carte [kaʀt(ə)] *nf* (*de géographie*) map; (*marine, du ciel*) chart; (*de fichier, d'abonnement etc, à jouer*) card; (*au restaurant*) menu; (*aussi:* **carte postale**) (post)card; (*aussi:* **carte de visite**) (visiting) card; **avoir/donner ~ blanche** to have/give carte blanche *ou* a free hand; **tirer les ~s à qn** to read sb's cards; **jouer aux ~s** to play cards; **jouer ~s sur table** (*fig*) to put one's cards on the table; **à la ~** (*au restaurant*) à la carte; **~ à circuit imprimé** printed circuit; **~ à puce** smartcard; **~ bancaire** cash card; **C~ Bleue**® debit card; **~ de crédit** credit card; **~ d'état-major** ≈ Ordnance (*Brit*) *ou* Geological (*US*) Survey map; **la ~ grise** (*Auto*) ≈ the (car) registration document; **~ d'identité** identity card; **~ jeune** young person's railcard; **~ perforée** punch(ed) card; **~ routière** road map; **~ de séjour** residence permit; **~ SIM** SIM card; **~ téléphonique** phonecard; **la ~ verte** (*Auto*) the green card; **la ~ des vins** the wine list

cartel [kaʀtɛl] *nm* cartel

carte-lettre [kaʀtəlɛtʀ(ə)] (*pl* **cartes-lettres**) *nf* letter-card

carte-mère [kaʀtəmɛʀ] (*pl* **cartes-mères**) *nf* (*Inform*) mother board

carter [kaʀtɛʀ] *nm* (*Auto: d'huile*) sump (*Brit*), oil pan (*US*); (: *de la boîte de vitesses*) casing; (*de bicyclette*) chain guard

carte-réponse [kaʀt(ə)ʀepɔ̃s] (*pl* **cartes-réponses**) *nf* reply card

cartésien, ne [kaʀtezjɛ̃, -ɛn] *adj* Cartesian

Carthage [kaʀtaʒ] *n* Carthage

carthaginois, e [kaʀtaʒinwa, -waz] *adj* Carthaginian

cartilage [kaʀtilaʒ] *nm* (*Anat*) cartilage

cartilagineux, -euse [kaʀtilaʒinø, -øz] *adj* (*viande*) gristly

cartographe [kaʀtɔgʀaf] *nm/f* cartographer

cartographie [kaʀtɔgʀafi] *nf* cartography, map-making

cartomancie [kaʀtɔmɑ̃si] *nf* fortune-telling, card-reading

cartomancien, ne [kaʀtɔmɑ̃sjɛ̃, -ɛn] *nm/f* fortune-teller (*with cards*)

carton [kaʀtɔ̃] *nm* (*matériau*) cardboard; (*boîte*) (cardboard) box; (*d'invitation*) invitation card; (*Art*) sketch; cartoon; **en ~** cardboard *cpd*; **faire un ~** (*au tir*) to have a go at the rifle range; to score a hit; **~ (à dessin)** portfolio

cartonnage [kaʀtɔnaʒ] *nm* cardboard (packing)

cartonné, e [kaʀtɔne] *adj* (*livre*) hardback, cased

carton-pâte [kaʀtɔ̃pat] *nm* pasteboard; **de ~** (*fig*) cardboard *cpd*

cartouche [kaʀtuʃ] *nf* cartridge; (*de cigarettes*) carton

cartouchière [kaʀtuʃjɛʀ] *nf* cartridge belt

cas [ka] *nm* case; **faire peu de ~/grand ~ de** to attach little/great importance to; **le ~ échéant** if need be; **en aucun ~** on no account, under no circumstances (whatsoever); **au ~ où** in case; **dans ce ~** in that case; **en ~ de** in case of, in the event of; **en ~ de besoin** if need be; **en ~ d'urgence** in an emergency; **en ce ~** in that case; **en tout ~** in any case, at any rate; **~ de conscience** matter of conscience; **~ de force majeure** case of absolute necessity; (*Assurances*) act of God; **~ limite** borderline case; **~ social** social problem

Casablanca [kazablɑ̃ka] *n* Casablanca

casanier, -ière [kazanje, -jɛʀ] *adj* stay-at-home

casaque [kazak] *nf* (*de jockey*) blouse

cascade [kaskad] *nf* waterfall, cascade; (*fig*) stream, torrent

cascadeur, -euse [kaskadœʀ, -øz] *nm/f* stuntman/girl

case [kaz] *nf* (*hutte*) hut; (*compartiment*) compartment; (*pour le courrier*) pigeonhole; (*de mots croisés, d'échiquier*) square; (*sur un formulaire*) box

casemate [kazmat] *nf* blockhouse

caser [kaze] *vt* (*mettre*) to put; (*loger*) to put up; (*péj*) to find a job for; to marry off; **se caser** *vi* (*personne*) to settle down

caserne [kazɛʀn(ə)] *nf* barracks

casernement [kazɛʀnəmɑ̃] *nm* barrack buildings *pl*

cash [kaʃ] *adv*: **payer ~** to pay cash down

casier [kazje] *nm* (*à journaux etc*) rack; (*de bureau*) filing cabinet; (: *à cases*) set of pigeonholes; (*case*) compartment; pigeonhole; (: *à clef*) locker; (*Pêche*) lobster pot; **~ à bouteilles** bottle rack; **~ judiciaire** police record

casino [kazino] *nm* casino

casque [kask(ə)] *nm* helmet; (*chez le coiffeur*) (hair-)dryer; (*pour audition*) (head-)phones *pl*, headset; **les C~s bleus** the UN peacekeeping force

casquer [kaske] *vi* (*fam*) to cough up, stump up (*Brit*)

casquette [kaskɛt] *nf* cap

cassable [kasabl(ə)] *adj* (*fragile*) breakable

cassant, e [kasɑ̃, -ɑ̃t] *adj* brittle; (*fig*) brusque, abrupt

cassate [kasat] *nf*: **(glace) ~** cassata

cassation [kasasjɔ̃] *nf*: **se pourvoir en ~** to lodge an appeal; **recours en ~** appeal to the Supreme Court

casse [kas] *nf* (*pour voitures*): **mettre à la ~** to scrap, send to the breakers (*Brit*); (*dégâts*): **il y a eu de la ~** there were a lot of breakages; (*Typo*): **haut/bas de ~** upper/lower case

cassé, e [kase] *adj* (*voix*) cracked; (*vieillard*) bent

casse-cou [kasku] *adj inv* daredevil, reckless; **crier ~ à qn** to warn sb (*against a risky undertaking*)

casse-croûte [kaskʀut] *nm inv* snack

casse-noisettes [kɑsnwazɛt], **casse-noix** [kɑsnwa] *nm inv* nutcrackers *pl*

casse-pieds [kɑspje] *adj, nm/f inv (fam)*: **il est ~, c'est un ~** he's a pain (in the neck)

casser [kɑse] *vt* to break; (*Admin: gradé*) to demote; (*Jur*) to quash; (*Comm*): ~ **les prix** to slash prices; **se casser** *vi* to break; (*fam*) to go, leave ▷ *vt*: **se ~ la jambe/une jambe** to break one's leg/a leg; **à tout ~** fantastic, brilliant; **se ~ net** to break clean off

casserole [kɑsʀɔl] *nf* saucepan; **à la ~** (*Culin*) braised

casse-tête [kɑstɛt] *nm inv* (*fig*) brain teaser; (*difficultés*) headache (*fig*)

cassette [kɑsɛt] *nf* (*bande magnétique*) cassette; (*coffret*) casket; ~ **numérique** digital compact cassette; ~ **vidéo** video

casseur [kɑsœʀ] *nm* hooligan; rioter

cassis [kasis] *nm* blackcurrant; (*de la route*) dip, bump

cassonade [kasɔnad] *nf* brown sugar

cassoulet [kasulɛ] *nm* sausage and bean hotpot

cassure [kɑsyʀ] *nf* break, crack

castagnettes [kastaɲɛt] *nfpl* castanets

caste [kast(ə)] *nf* caste

castillan, e [kastijɑ̃, -an] *adj* Castilian ▷ *nm* (*Ling*) Castilian

Castille [kastij] *nf*: **la ~** Castile

castor [kastɔʀ] *nm* beaver

castrer [kastʀe] *vt* (*mâle*) to castrate; (*femelle*) to spay; (*cheval*) to geld; (*chat, chien*) to doctor (*Brit*), fix (*US*)

cataclysme [kataklism(ə)] *nm* cataclysm

catacombes [katakɔ̃b] *nfpl* catacombs

catadioptre [katadjɔptʀ(ə)] *nm* = **cataphote**

catafalque [katafalk(ə)] *nm* catafalque

catalan, e [katalɑ̃, -an] *adj* Catalan, Catalonian ▷ *nm* (*Ling*) Catalan

Catalogne [katalɔɲ] *nf*: **la ~** Catalonia

catalogue [katalɔg] *nm* catalogue

cataloguer [katalɔge] *vt* to catalogue, list; (*péj*) to put a label on

catalyse [kataliz] *nf* catalysis

catalyser [katalize] *vt* to catalyze

catalyseur [katalizœʀ] *nm* catalyst

catalytique [katalitik] *adj* catalytic

catamaran [katamaʀɑ̃] *nm* (*voilier*) catamaran

cataphote [katafɔt] *nm* reflector

cataplasme [kataplasm(ə)] *nm* poultice

catapulte [katapylt(ə)] *nf* catapult

catapulter [katapylte] *vt* to catapult

cataracte [kataʀakt(ə)] *nf* cataract; **opérer qn de la ~** to operate on sb for a cataract

catarrhe [kataʀ] *nm* catarrh

catarrheux, -euse [kataʀø, -øz] *adj* catarrhal

catastrophe [katastʀɔf] *nf* catastrophe, disaster; **atterrir en ~** to make an emergency landing; **partir en ~** to rush away

catastropher [katastʀɔfe] *vt* (*personne*) to shatter

catastrophique [katastʀɔfik] *adj* catastrophic, disastrous

catch [katʃ] *nm* (all-in) wrestling

catcheur, -euse [katʃœʀ, -øz] *nm/f* (all-in) wrestler

catéchiser [kateʃize] *vt* to indoctrinate; to lecture

catéchisme [kateʃism(ə)] *nm* catechism

catéchumène [katekymɛn] *nm/f* catechumen, *person attending religious instruction prior to baptism*

catégorie [kategɔʀi] *nf* category; (*Boucherie*): **morceaux de première/deuxième ~** prime/second cuts

catégorique [kategɔʀik] *adj* categorical

catégoriquement [kategɔʀikmɑ̃] *adv* categorically

catégoriser [kategɔʀize] *vt* to categorize

caténaire [katenɛʀ] *nf* (*Rail*) catenary

cathédrale [katedʀal] *nf* cathedral

cathéter [katetɛʀ] *nm* (*Méd*) catheter

cathode [katɔd] *nf* cathode

cathodique [katɔdik] *adj*: **rayons ~s** cathode rays; **tube/écran ~** cathode-ray tube/screen

catholicisme [katɔlisism(ə)] *nm* (Roman) Catholicism

catholique [katɔlik] *adj, nm/f* (Roman) Catholic; **pas très ~** a bit shady *ou* fishy

catimini [katimini]: **en ~** *adv* on the sly, on the quiet

catogan [katɔgɑ̃] *nm* bow (*tying hair on neck*)

Caucase [kɔkaz] *nm*: **le ~** the Caucasus (Mountains)

caucasien, ne [kɔkazjɛ̃, -ɛn] *adj* Caucasian

cauchemar [kɔʃmaʀ] *nm* nightmare

cauchemardesque [kɔʃmaʀdɛsk(ə)] *adj* nightmarish

causal, e [kozal] *adj* causal

causalité [kozalite] *nf* causality

causant, e [kozɑ̃, -ɑ̃t] *adj* chatty, talkative

cause [koz] *nf* cause; (*Jur*) lawsuit, case; brief; **faire ~ commune avec qn** to take sides with sb; **être ~ de** to be the cause of; **à ~ de** because of, owing to; **pour ~ de** on account of; owing to; **(et) pour ~** and for (a very) good reason; **être en ~** (*intérêts*) to be at stake; (*personne*) to be involved; (*qualité*) to be in question; **mettre en ~** to implicate; to call into question; **remettre en ~** to challenge, call into question; **c'est hors de ~** it's out of the question; **en tout état de ~** in any case

causer [koze] *vt* to cause ▷ *vi* to chat, talk

causerie [kozʀi] *nf* talk

causette [kozɛt] *nf*: **faire la** *ou* **un brin de ~** to have a chat

caustique [kostik] *adj* caustic

cauteleux, -euse [kotlø, -øz] *adj* wily

cautériser [koteʀize] *vt* to cauterize

caution [kosjɔ̃] *nf* guarantee, security; deposit; (*Jur*) bail (bond); (*fig*) backing, support; **payer la ~ de qn** to stand bail for sb; **se porter ~ pour qn** to stand security for sb; **libéré sous ~** released on bail; **sujet à ~** unconfirmed

cautionnement [kosjɔnmɑ̃] *nm* (*somme*) guarantee, security

cautionner [kosjɔne] vt to guarantee; (soutenir) to support

cavalcade [kavalkad] nf (fig) stampede

cavale [kaval] nf: **en ~** on the run

cavalerie [kavalʀi] nf cavalry

cavalier, -ière [kavalje, -jɛʀ] adj (désinvolte) offhand ▷ nm/f rider; (au bal) partner ▷ nm (Échecs) knight; **faire ~ seul** to go it alone; **allée** ou **piste cavalière** riding path

cavalièrement [kavaljɛʀmɑ̃] adv offhandedly

cave [kav] nf cellar; (cabaret) (cellar) nightclub ▷ adj: **yeux ~s** sunken eyes; **joues ~s** hollow cheeks

caveau, x [kavo] nm vault

caverne [kavɛʀn(ə)] nf cave

caverneux, -euse [kavɛʀnø, -øz] adj cavernous

caviar [kavjaʀ] nm caviar(e)

cavité [kavite] nf cavity

Cayenne [kajɛn] n Cayenne

CB [sibi] sigle f (= citizens' band, canaux banalisés) CB = **carte bancaire**

CC sigle m = **corps consulaire**; **compte courant**

CCI sigle f = **Chambre de commerce et d'industrie**

CCP sigle m = **compte chèque postal**

CD sigle m (= chemin départemental) secondary road, ≈ B road (Brit); (= compact disc) CD; (= comité directeur) steering committee; (Pol) = **corps diplomatique**

CDD sigle m (= contrat à durée déterminée) fixed-term contract

CDI sigle m (= Centre de documentation et d'information) school library; (= contrat à durée indéterminée) permanent ou open-ended contract

CD-ROM [sederɔm] nm inv (= Compact Disc Read Only Memory) CD-Rom

CDS sigle m (= Centre des démocrates sociaux) political party

CE sigle f (= Communauté européenne) EC; (Comm) = **caisse d'épargne** ▷ sigle m (Industrie) = **comité d'entreprise**; (Scol) = **cours élémentaire**

 MOT-CLÉ

ce, cette [sə, sɛt] (devant nm **cet** + voyelle ou h aspiré; pl **ces**) adj dém (proximité) this; these pl; (non-proximité) that; those pl; **cette maison(-ci/là)** this/that house; **cette nuit** (qui vient) tonight; (passée) last night

▷ pron **1**: **c'est** it's, it is; **c'est petit/grand/un livre** it's ou it is small/big/a book; **c'est un peintre** he's ou he is a painter; **ce sont des peintres** they're ou they are painters; **c'est le facteur** etc (à la porte) it's the postman etc; **qui est-ce?** who is it?; (en désignant) who is he/she?; **qu'est-ce?** what is it?; **c'est toi qui lui as parlé** it was you who spoke to him

2: **c'est que**: **c'est qu'il est lent/qu'il n'a pas faim** the fact is, he's slow/he's not hungry

3 (expressions): **c'est ça** (correct) that's it, that's right; **c'est toi qui le dis!** that's what YOU say!; voir aussi **c'est-à-dire**; voir **-ci**; **est-ce que**; **n'est-ce pas**

4: **ce qui, ce que** what; (chose qui): **il est bête, ce qui me chagrine** he's stupid, which saddens me; **tout ce qui bouge** everything that ou which moves; **tout ce que je sais** all I know; **ce dont j'ai parlé** what I talked about; **ce que c'est grand!** it's so big!

CEA sigle m (= Commissariat à l'énergie atomique) ≈ AEA (= Atomic Energy Authority) (Brit) ≈ AEC = **Atomic Energy Commission** (US)

CECA [seka] sigle f (= Communauté européenne du charbon et de l'acier) ECSC (= European Coal and Steel Community)

ceci [səsi] pron this

cécité [sesite] nf blindness

céder [sede] vt to give up ▷ vi (pont, barrage) to give way; (personne) to give in; **~ à** to yield to, give in to

cédérom [sederɔm] nm CD-ROM

CEDEX [sedɛks] sigle m (= courrier d'entreprise à distribution exceptionnelle) accelerated postal service for bulk users

cédille [sedij] nf cedilla

cèdre [sɛdʀ(ə)] nm cedar

CEE sigle f (= Communauté économique européenne) EEC

CEI sigle f (= Communauté des États indépendants) CIS

ceindre [sɛ̃dʀ(ə)] vt (mettre) to put on; (entourer): **~ qch de qch** to put sth round sth

ceinture [sɛ̃tyʀ] nf belt; (taille) waist; (fig) ring; belt; circle; **~ de sauvetage** lifebelt (Brit), life preserver (US); **~ de sécurité** safety ou seat belt; **~ (de sécurité) à enrouleur** inertia reel seat belt; **~ verte** green belt

ceinturer [sɛ̃tyʀe] vt (saisir) to grasp (round the waist); (entourer) to surround

ceinturon [sɛ̃tyʀɔ̃] nm belt

cela [səla] pron that; (comme sujet indéfini) it; **~ m'étonne que** it surprises me that; **quand/où ~?** when/where (was that)?

célébrant [selebʀɑ̃] nm (Rel) celebrant

célébration [selebʀasjɔ̃] nf celebration

célèbre [selɛbʀ(ə)] adj famous

célébrer [selebʀe] vt to celebrate; (louer) to extol

célébrité [selebʀite] nf fame; (star) celebrity

céleri [sɛlʀi] nm: **~(-rave)** celeriac; **~ (en branche)** celery

célérité [selerite] nf speed, swiftness

céleste [selɛst(ə)] adj celestial; heavenly

célibat [seliba] nm celibacy, bachelor/spinsterhood

célibataire [selibatɛʀ] adj single, unmarried ▷ nm/f bachelor/unmarried ou single woman; **mère ~** single ou unmarried mother

celle, celles [sɛl] pron voir **celui**

cellier [selje] nm storeroom

cellophane® [selɔfan] nf cellophane

cellulaire [selylɛʀ] adj (Bio) cell cpd, cellular; **voiture** ou **fourgon ~** prison ou police van; **régime ~** confinement

cellule [selyl] nf (gén) cell; **~ (photo-électrique)**

electronic eye

cellulite [selylit] *nf* cellulite

celluloïd® [selylɔid] *nm* Celluloid

cellulose [selyloz] *nf* cellulose

celte [sɛlt(ə)], **celtique** [sɛltik] *adj* Celt, Celtic

 MOT-CLÉ

celui, celle [səlɥi, sɛl] (*mpl* **ceux**, *fpl* **celles**) *pron*
1: **celui-ci/là, celle-ci/là** this one/that one;
ceux-ci, celles-ci these (ones); **ceux-là, celles-là** those (ones); **celui de mon frère** my brother's; **celui du salon/du dessous** the one in (*ou* from) the lounge/below
2: **celui qui bouge** the one which *ou* that moves; (*personne*) the one who moves; **celui que je vois** the one (which *ou* that) I see; (*personne*) the one (whom) I see; **celui dont je parle** the one I'm talking about
3 (*valeur indéfinie*): **celui qui veut** whoever wants

cénacle [senakl(ə)] *nm* (literary) coterie *ou* set

cendre [sɑ̃dR(ə)] *nf* ash; **~s** (*d'un foyer*) ash(es), cinders; (*volcaniques*) ash *sg*; (*d'un défunt*) ashes; **sous la ~** (*Culin*) in (the) embers

cendré, e [sɑ̃dRe] *adj* (*couleur*) ashen; (**piste**) **~e** cinder track

cendreux, -euse [sɑ̃dRø, -øz] *adj* (*terrain, substance*) cindery; (*teint*) ashen

cendrier [sɑ̃dRije] *nm* ashtray

cène [sɛn] *nf*: **la ~** (Holy) Communion; (*Art*) the Last Supper

censé, e [sɑ̃se] *adj*: **être ~ faire** to be supposed to do

censément [sɑ̃semɑ̃] *adv* supposedly

censeur [sɑ̃sœR] *nm* (*Scol*) deputy head (*Brit*), vice-principal (*US*); (*Ciné, Pol*) censor

censure [sɑ̃syR] *nf* censorship

censurer [sɑ̃syRe] *vt* (*Ciné, Presse*) to censor; (*Pol*) to censure

cent [sɑ̃] *num* a hundred, one hundred; **pour ~** (%) per cent (%); **faire les ~ pas** to pace up and down ▷ *nm* (*US, Canada, partie de l'euro etc*) cent

centaine [sɑ̃tɛn] *nf*: **une ~ (de)** about a hundred, a hundred or so; (*Comm*) a hundred; **plusieurs ~s (de)** several hundred; **des ~s (de)** hundreds (of)

centenaire [sɑ̃tnɛR] *adj* hundred-year-old ▷ *nm/f* centenarian ▷ *nm* (*anniversaire*) centenary

centième [sɑ̃tjɛm] *num* hundredth

centigrade [sɑ̃tigRad] *nm* centigrade

centigramme [sɑ̃tigRam] *nm* centigramme

centilitre [sɑ̃tilitR(ə)] *nm* centilitre (*Brit*), centiliter (*US*)

centime [sɑ̃tim] *nm* centime; **~ d'euro** euro cent

centimètre [sɑ̃timɛtR(ə)] *nm* centimetre (*Brit*), centimeter (*US*); (*ruban*) tape measure, measuring tape

centrafricain, e [sɑ̃tRafRikɛ̃, -ɛn] *adj* of *ou* from the Central African Republic

central, e, -aux [sɑ̃tRal, -o] *adj* central ▷ *nm*: **~ (téléphonique)** (telephone) exchange ▷ *nf*: **~e d'achat** (*Comm*) central buying service; **~e électrique/nucléaire** electric/nuclear power station; **~e syndicale** group of affiliated trade unions

centralisation [sɑ̃tRalizasjɔ̃] *nf* centralization

centraliser [sɑ̃tRalize] *vt* to centralize

centralisme [sɑ̃tRalism(ə)] *nm* centralism

centraméricain, e [sɑ̃tRameRikɛ̃, -ɛn] *adj* Central American

centre [sɑ̃tR(ə)] *nm* centre (*Brit*), center (*US*); **~ commercial/sportif/culturel** shopping/sports/arts centre; **~ aéré** outdoor centre; **~ d'appels** call centre; **~ d'apprentissage** training college; **~ d'attraction** centre of attraction; **~ de gravité** centre of gravity; **~ de loisirs** leisure centre; **~ d'enfouissement des déchets** landfill site; **~ hospitalier** hospital complex; **~ de tri** (*Postes*) sorting office; **~s nerveux** (*Anat*) nerve centres

centrer [sɑ̃tRe] *vt* to centre (*Brit*), center (*US*) ▷ *vi* (*Football*) to centre the ball

centre-ville [sɑ̃tRəvil] (*pl* **centres-villes**) *nm* town centre (*Brit*) *ou* center (*US*), downtown (area) (*US*)

centrifuge [sɑ̃tRify3] *adj*: **force ~** centrifugal force

centrifuger [sɑ̃tRify3e] *vt* to centrifuge

centrifugeuse [sɑ̃tRify3øz] *nf* (*pour fruits*) juice extractor

centripète [sɑ̃tRipɛt] *adj*: **force ~** centripetal force

centrisme [sɑ̃tRism(ə)] *nm* centrism

centriste [sɑ̃tRist(ə)] *adj, nm/f* centrist

centuple [sɑ̃typl(ə)] *nm*: **le ~ de qch** a hundred times sth; **au ~** a hundredfold

centupler [sɑ̃typle] *vi, vt* to increase a hundredfold

CEP *sigle m* = **Certificat d'études (primaires)**

cep [sɛp] *nm* (vine) stock

cépage [sepa3] *nm* (type of) vine

cèpe [sɛp] *nm* (edible) boletus

cependant [səpɑ̃dɑ̃] *adv* however, nevertheless

céramique [seRamik] *adj* ceramic ▷ *nf* ceramic; (*art*) ceramics *sg*

céramiste [seRamist(ə)] *nm/f* ceramist

cerbère [sɛRbɛR] *nm* (*fig: péj*) bad-tempered doorkeeper

cerceau, x [sɛRso] *nm* (*d'enfant, de tonnelle*) hoop

cercle [sɛRkl(ə)] *nm* circle; (*objet*) band, hoop; **décrire un ~** (*avion*) to circle; (*projectile*) to describe a circle; **~ d'amis** circle of friends; **~ de famille** family circle; **~ vicieux** vicious circle

cercler [sɛRkle] *vt*: **lunettes cerclées d'or** gold-rimmed glasses

cercueil [sɛRkœj] *nm* coffin

céréale [seReal] *nf* cereal

céréalier, -ière [seRealje, -jɛR] *adj* (*production, cultures*) cereal *cpd*

cérébral, e, -aux [seRebRal, -o] *adj* (*Anat*) cerebral, brain *cpd*; (*fig*) mental, cerebral

cérémonial [seʀemɔnjal] *nm* ceremonial
cérémonie [seʀemɔni] *nf* ceremony;
cérémonies *nfpl* (*péj*) fuss *sg*, to-do *sg*
cérémonieux, -euse [seʀemɔnjø, -øz] *adj*
ceremonious, formal
cerf [sɛʀ] *nm* stag
cerfeuil [sɛʀfœj] *nm* chervil
cerf-volant [sɛʀvɔlã] *nm* kite; **jouer au ~** to fly
a kite
cerisaie [səʀize] *nf* cherry orchard
cerise [səʀiz] *nf* cherry
cerisier [səʀizje] *nm* cherry (tree)
CERN [sɛʀn] *sigle m* (= *Centre européen de recherche
nucléaire*) CERN
cerné, e [sɛʀne] *adj*: **les yeux ~s** with dark rings
ou shadows under the eyes
cerner [sɛʀne] *vt* (*Mil etc*) to surround; (*fig:
problème*) to delimit, define
cernes [sɛʀn(ə)] *nfpl* (dark) rings, shadows
(under the eyes)
certain, e [sɛʀtɛ̃, -ɛn] *adj* certain; (*sûr*): **~ (de/
que)** certain *ou* sure (of/ that); **d'un ~ âge** past
one's prime, not so young; **un ~ temps** (quite)
some time; **sûr et ~** absolutely certain; **~s** *pron*
some
certainement [sɛʀtɛnmã] *adv* (*probablement*)
most probably *ou* likely; (*bien sûr*) certainly, of
course
certes [sɛʀt(ə)] *adv* admittedly; of course;
indeed (yes)
certificat [sɛʀtifika] *nm* certificate; **C~
d'études (primaires)** *former school leaving
certificate* (*taken at the end of primary education*); **C~
de fin d'études secondaires** school leaving
certificate
certifié, e [sɛʀtifje] *adj*: **professeur ~** qualified
teacher; (*Admin*): **copie ~e conforme (à
l'original)** certified copy (of the original)
certifier [sɛʀtifje] *vt* to certify, guarantee; **~ à
qn que** to assure sb that, guarantee to sb that; **~
qch à qn** to guarantee sth to sb
certitude [sɛʀtityd] *nf* certainty
cérumen [seʀymɛn] *nm* (ear)wax
cerveau, x [sɛʀvo] *nm* brain; **~ électronique**
electronic brain
cervelas [sɛʀvəla] *nm* saveloy
cervelle [sɛʀvɛl] *nf* (*Anat*) brain; (*Culin*) brain(s);
se creuser la ~ to rack one's brains
cervical, e, -aux [sɛʀvikal, -o] *adj* cervical
cervidés [sɛʀvide] *nmpl* cervidae
CES *sigle m* (= *Collège d'enseignement secondaire*)
≈ (junior) secondary school (*Brit*), ≈ junior high
school (*US*)
ces [se] *adj dém voir* **ce**
césarienne [sezaʀjɛn] *nf* caesarean (*Brit*) *ou*
cesarean (*US*) (section)
cessantes [sɛsãt] *adj fpl*: **toutes affaires ~**
forthwith
cessation [sɛsasjõ] *nf*: **~ des hostilités**
cessation of hostilities; **~ de paiements/
commerce** suspension of payments/trading
cesse [sɛs]: **sans ~** *adv* continually, constantly;

continuously; **il n'avait de ~ que** he would not
rest until
cesser [sese] *vt* to stop ▷ *vi* to stop, cease; **~ de
faire** to stop doing; **faire ~** (*bruit, scandale*) to put
a stop to
cessez-le-feu [seselfø] *nm inv* ceasefire
cession [sɛsjõ] *nf* transfer
c'est [sɛ] *voir* **ce**
c'est-à-dire [sɛtadiʀ] *adv* that is (to say);
(*demander de préciser*): **c'est-à-dire?** what does
that mean?; **c'est-à-dire que ...** (*en conséquence*)
which means that ...; (*manière d'excuse*) well, in
fact ...
CET *sigle m* (= *Collège d'enseignement technique*)
(*formerly*) technical school
cet [sɛt] *adj dém voir* **ce**
cétacé [setase] *nm* cetacean
cette [sɛt] *adj dém voir* **ce**
ceux [sø] *pron voir* **celui**
cévenol, e [sevnɔl] *adj* of *ou* from the Cévennes
region
cf. *abr* (= *confer*) cf, cp
CFAO *sigle f* (= *conception de fabrication assistée par
ordinateur*) CAM
CFC *sigle mpl* (= *chlorofluorocarbures*) CFC
CFDT *sigle f* (= *Confédération française démocratique du
travail*) trade union
CFF *sigle m* (= *Chemins de fer fédéraux*) Swiss railways
CFL *sigle m* (= *Chemins de fer luxembourgeois*)
Luxembourg railways
CFP *sigle m* = **Centre de formation
professionnelle** ▷ *sigle f* = **Compagnie française
des pétroles**
CFTC *sigle f* (= *Confédération française des travailleurs
chrétiens*) trade union
CGC *sigle f* (= *Confédération générale des cadres*)
management union
CGPME *sigle f* = **Confédération générale des
petites et moyennes entreprises**
CGT *sigle f* (= *Confédération générale du travail*) trade
union
CH *abr* (= *Confédération helvétique*) CH
ch. *abr* = **charges; chauffage; cherche**
chacal [ʃakal] *nm* jackal
chacun, e [ʃakœ̃, -yn] *pron* each; (*indéfini*)
everyone, everybody
chagrin, e [ʃagʀɛ̃, -in] *adj* morose ▷ *nm* grief,
sorrow; **avoir du ~** to be grieved *ou* sorrowful
chagriner [ʃagʀine] *vt* to grieve, distress;
(*contrarier*) to bother, worry
chahut [ʃay] *nm* uproar
chahuter [ʃayte] *vt* to rag, bait ▷ *vi* to make an
uproar
chahuteur, -euse [ʃaytœʀ, -øz] *nm/f* rowdy
chai [ʃɛ] *nm* wine and spirit store(house)
chaîne [ʃɛn] *nf* chain; (*Radio, TV*) channel;
(*Inform*) string; **chaînes** *nfpl* (*liens, asservissement*)
fetters, bonds; **travail à la ~** production line
work; **réactions en ~** chain reactions; **faire la
~** to form a (human) chain; **~ alimentaire** food
chain; **~ compacte** music centre; **~ d'entraide**
mutual aid association; **~ (haute-fidélité** *ou*

hi-fi) hi-fi system; **~ (de montage** ou **de fabrication)** production ou assembly line; **~ (de montagnes)** (mountain) range; **~ de solidarité** solidarity network; **~ (stéréo** ou **audio)** stereo (system)

chaînette [ʃɛnɛt] nf (small) chain

chaînon [ʃɛnɔ̃] nm link

chair [ʃɛʀ] nf flesh ▷ adj: **(couleur) ~** flesh-coloured; **avoir la ~ de poule** to have goose pimples ou goose flesh; **bien en ~** plump, well-padded; **en ~ et en os** in the flesh; **~ à saucisses** sausage meat

chaire [ʃɛʀ] nf (d'église) pulpit; (d'université) chair

chaise [ʃɛz] nf chair; **~ de bébé** high chair; **~ électrique** electric chair; **~ longue** deckchair

chaland [ʃalɑ̃] nm (bateau) barge

châle [ʃɑl] nm shawl

chalet [ʃalɛ] nm chalet

chaleur [ʃalœʀ] nf heat; (fig) warmth; fire, fervour (Brit), fervor (US); heat; **en ~** (Zool) on heat

chaleureusement [ʃalœʀøzmɑ̃] adv warmly

chaleureux, -euse [ʃalœʀø, -øz] adj warm

challenge [ʃalɑ̃ʒ] nm contest, tournament

challenger [ʃalɑ̃ʒɛʀ] nm (Sport) challenger

chaloupe [ʃalup] nf launch; (de sauvetage) lifeboat

chalumeau, x [ʃalymo] nm blowlamp (Brit), blowtorch

chalut [ʃaly] nm trawl (net); **pêcher au ~** to trawl

chalutier [ʃalytje] nm trawler; (pêcheur) trawlerman

chamade [ʃamad] nf: **battre la ~** to beat wildly

chamailler [ʃamaje]: **se chamailler** vi to squabble, bicker

chamarré, e [ʃamaʀe] adj richly brocaded

chambard [ʃɑ̃baʀ] nm rumpus

chambardement [ʃɑ̃baʀdəmɑ̃] nm: **c'est le grand ~** everything has been (ou is being) turned upside down

chambarder [ʃɑ̃baʀde] vt to turn upside down

chamboulement [ʃɑ̃bulmɑ̃] nm disruption

chambouler [ʃɑ̃bule] vt to disrupt, turn upside down

chambranle [ʃɑ̃bʀɑ̃l] nm (door) frame

chambre [ʃɑ̃bʀ(ə)] nf bedroom; (Tech) chamber; (Pol) chamber, house; (Jur) court; (Comm) chamber; federation; **faire ~ à part** to sleep in separate rooms; **stratège/alpiniste en ~** armchair strategist/mountaineer; **~ à un lit/deux lits** single/twin-bedded room; **~ pour une/deux personne(s)** single/double room; **~ d'accusation** court of criminal appeal; **~ d'agriculture (CA)** body responsible for the agricultural interests of a département; **~ à air** (de pneu) (inner) tube; **~ d'amis** spare ou guest room; **~ de combustion** combustion chamber; **~ de commerce et d'industrie (CCI)** chamber of commerce and industry; **~ à coucher** bedroom; **la C~ des députés** the Chamber of Deputies, ≈ the House (of Commons) (Brit), ≈ the House of Representatives (US); **~ forte** strongroom; **~ froide** ou **frigorifique** cold room; **~ à gaz** gas chamber; **~ d'hôte** ≈ bed and breakfast (in private home); **~ des machines** engine-room; **~ des métiers (CM)** chamber of commerce for trades; **~ meublée** bedsit(ter) (Brit), furnished room; **~ noire** (Photo) dark room

chambrée [ʃɑ̃bʀe] nf room

chambrer [ʃɑ̃bʀe] vt (vin) to bring to room temperature

chameau, x [ʃamo] nm camel

chamois [ʃamwa] nm chamois ▷ adj: **(couleur) ~** fawn, buff

champ [ʃɑ̃] nm (aussi Inform) field; (Photo: aussi: **dans le champ)** in the picture; **prendre du ~** to draw back; **laisser le ~ libre à qn** to leave sb a clear field; **~ d'action** sphere of operation(s); **~ de bataille** battlefield; **~ de courses** racecourse; **~ d'honneur** field of honour; **~ de manœuvre** (Mil) parade ground; **~ de mines** minefield; **~ de tir** shooting ou rifle range; **~ visuel** field of vision

Champagne [ʃɑ̃paɲ] nf: **la ~** Champagne, the Champagne region

champagne [ʃɑ̃paɲ] nm champagne

champenois, e [ʃɑ̃pənwa, -waz] adj of ou from Champagne; (vin): **méthode ~e** champagne-type

champêtre [ʃɑ̃pɛtʀ(ə)] adj country cpd, rural

champignon [ʃɑ̃piɲɔ̃] nm mushroom; (terme générique) fungus; (fam: accélérateur) accelerator, gas pedal (US); **~ de couche** ou **de Paris** button mushroom; **~ vénéneux** toadstool, poisonous mushroom

champion, ne [ʃɑ̃pjɔ̃, -ɔn] adj, nm/f champion

championnat [ʃɑ̃pjɔna] nm championship

chance [ʃɑ̃s] nf: **la ~** luck; **une ~** a stroke ou piece of luck ou good fortune; (occasion) a lucky break; **chances** nfpl (probabilités) chances; **avoir de la ~** to be lucky; **il a des ~s de gagner** he has a chance of winning; **il y a de fortes ~s pour que Paul soit malade** it's highly probable that Paul is ill; **bonne ~!** good luck!; **encore une ~ que tu viennes!** it's lucky you're coming!; **je n'ai pas de ~** I'm out of luck; (toujours) I never have any luck; **donner sa ~ à qn** to give sb a chance

chancelant, e [ʃɑ̃slɑ̃, -ɑ̃t] adj (personne) tottering; (santé) failing

chanceler [ʃɑ̃sle] vi to totter

chancelier [ʃɑ̃səlje] nm (allemand) chancellor; (d'ambassade) secretary

chancellerie [ʃɑ̃sɛlʀi] nf (en France) ministry of justice; (en Allemagne) chancellery; (d'ambassade) chancery

chanceux, -euse [ʃɑ̃sø, -øz] adj lucky, fortunate

chancre [ʃɑ̃kʀ(ə)] nm canker

chandail [ʃɑ̃daj] nm (thick) jumper ou sweater

Chandeleur [ʃɑ̃dlœʀ] nf: **la ~** Candlemas

chandelier [ʃɑ̃dəlje] nm candlestick; (à plusieurs branches) candelabra

chandelle [ʃɑ̃dɛl] nf (tallow) candle; (Tennis):

faire une ~ to lob; (*Aviat*): **monter en ~** to climb vertically; **tenir la ~** to play gooseberry; **dîner aux ~s** candlelight dinner

change [ʃɑ̃ʒ] *nm* (*Comm*) exchange; **opérations de ~** (foreign) exchange transactions; **contrôle des ~s** exchange control; **gagner/perdre au ~** to be better/worse off (for it); **donner le ~ à qn** (*fig*) to lead sb up the garden path

changeant, e [ʃɑ̃ʒɑ̃, -ɑ̃t] *adj* changeable, fickle

changement [ʃɑ̃ʒmɑ̃] *nm* change; **~ de vitesse** (*dispositif*) gears *pl*; (*action*) gear change

changer [ʃɑ̃ʒe] *vt* (*modifier*) to change, alter; (*remplacer, Comm, rhabiller*) to change ▷ *vi* to change, alter; **se changer** *vi* to change (o.s.); **~ de** (*remplacer: adresse, nom, voiture etc*) to change one's; **~ de train** to change trains; **~ d'air** to get a change of air; **~ de couleur/direction** to change colour/direction; **~ d'idée** to change one's mind; **~ de place avec qn** to change places with sb; **~ de vitesse** (*Auto*) to change gear; **~ qn/qch de place** to move sb/sth to another place; **~ (de bus** *etc***)** to change (buses *etc*); **~ qch en** to change sth into

changeur [ʃɑ̃ʒœʀ] *nm* (*personne*) moneychanger; **~ automatique** change machine; **~ de disques** record changer, autochange

chanoine [ʃanwan] *nm* canon

chanson [ʃɑ̃sɔ̃] *nf* song

chansonnette [ʃɑ̃sɔnɛt] *nf* ditty

chansonnier [ʃɑ̃sɔnje] *nm* cabaret artist (*specializing in political satire*); (*recueil*) song book

chant [ʃɑ̃] *nm* song; (*art vocal*) singing; (*d'église*) hymn; (*de poème*) canto; (*Tech*): **posé de** *ou* **sur ~** placed edgeways; **~ de Noël** Christmas carol

chantage [ʃɑ̃taʒ] *nm* blackmail; **faire du ~** to use blackmail; **soumettre qn à un ~** to blackmail sb

chantant, e [ʃɑ̃tɑ̃, -ɑ̃t] *adj* (*accent, voix*) sing-song

chanter [ʃɑ̃te] *vt, vi* to sing; **~ juste/faux** to sing in tune/out of tune; **si cela lui chante** (*fam*) if he feels like it *ou* fancies it

chanterelle [ʃɑ̃tʀɛl] *nf* chanterelle (*edible mushroom*)

chanteur, -euse [ʃɑ̃tœʀ, -øz] *nm/f* singer; **~ de charme** crooner

chantier [ʃɑ̃tje] *nm* (building) site; (*sur une route*) roadworks *pl*; **mettre en ~** to start work on; **~ naval** shipyard

chantilly [ʃɑ̃tiji] *nf voir* **crème**

chantonner [ʃɑ̃tɔne] *vi, vt* to sing to oneself, hum

chantre [ʃɑ̃tʀ(ə)] *nm* (*fig*) eulogist

chanvre [ʃɑ̃vʀ(ə)] *nm* hemp

chaos [kao] *nm* chaos

chaotique [kaɔtik] *adj* chaotic

chap. *abr* (= *chapitre*) ch

chapardage [ʃapaʀdaʒ] *nm* pilfering

chaparder [ʃapaʀde] *vt* to pinch

chapeau, x [ʃapo] *nm* hat; (*Presse*) introductory paragraph; **~!** well done!; **~ melon** bowler hat; **~ mou** trilby; **~x de roues** hub caps

chapeauter [ʃapote] *vt* (*Admin*) to head, oversee

chapelain [ʃaplɛ̃] *nm* (*Rel*) chaplain

chapelet [ʃaplɛ] *nm* (*Rel*) rosary; (*fig*): **un ~ de** a string of; **dire son ~** to tell one's beads

chapelier, -ière [ʃapəlje, -jɛʀ] *nm/f* hatter; milliner

chapelle [ʃapɛl] *nf* chapel; **~ ardente** chapel of rest

chapellerie [ʃapɛlʀi] *nf* (*magasin*) hat shop; (*commerce*) hat trade

chapelure [ʃaplyʀ] *nf* (dried) breadcrumbs *pl*

chaperon [ʃapʀɔ̃] *nm* chaperon

chaperonner [ʃapʀɔne] *vt* to chaperon

chapiteau, x [ʃapito] *nm* (*Archit*) capital; (*de cirque*) marquee, big top

chapitre [ʃapitʀ(ə)] *nm* chapter; (*fig*) subject, matter; **avoir voix au ~** to have a say in the matter

chapitrer [ʃapitʀe] *vt* to lecture, reprimand

chapon [ʃapɔ̃] *nm* capon

chaque [ʃak] *adj* each, every; (*indéfini*) every

char [ʃaʀ] *nm* (*à foin etc*) cart, waggon; (*de carnaval*) float; **~ (d'assaut)** tank

charabia [ʃaʀabja] *nm* (*péj*) gibberish, gobbledygook (*Brit*)

charade [ʃaʀad] *nf* riddle; (*mimée*) charade

charbon [ʃaʀbɔ̃] *nm* coal; **~ de bois** charcoal

charbonnage [ʃaʀbɔnaʒ] *nm*: **les ~s de France** the (French) Coal Board *sg*

charbonnier [ʃaʀbɔnje] *nm* coalman

charcuterie [ʃaʀkytʀi] *nf* (*magasin*) pork butcher's shop and delicatessen; (*produits*) cooked pork meats *pl*

charcutier, -ière [ʃaʀkytje, -jɛʀ] *nm/f* pork butcher

chardon [ʃaʀdɔ̃] *nm* thistle

chardonneret [ʃaʀdɔnʀɛ] *nm* goldfinch

charentais, e [ʃaʀɑ̃tɛ, -ɛz] *adj* *ou* from Charente ▷ *nf* (*pantoufle*) slipper

charge [ʃaʀʒ(ə)] *nf* (*fardeau*) load; (*explosif, Élec, Mil, Jur*) charge; (*rôle, mission*) responsibility; **charges** *nfpl* (*du loyer*) service charges; **à la ~ de** (*dépendant de*) dependent upon, supported by; (*aux frais de*) chargeable to, payable by; **j'accepte, à ~ de revanche** I accept, provided I can do the same for you (in return) one day; **prendre en ~** to take charge of; (*véhicule*) to take on; (*dépenses*) to take care of; **~ utile** (*Auto*) live load; (*Comm*) payload; **~s sociales** social security contributions

chargé [ʃaʀʒe] *adj* (*voiture, animal, personne*) laden; (*fusil, batterie, caméra*) loaded; (*occupé: emploi du temps, journée*) busy, full; (*estomac*) heavy, full; (*langue*) furred; (*décoration, style*) heavy, ornate ▷ *nm*: **~ d'affaires** chargé d'affaires; **~ de cours** ≈ lecturer; **~ de** (*responsable de*) responsible for

chargement [ʃaʀʒəmɑ̃] *nm* (*action*) loading; charging; (*objets*) load

charger [ʃaʀʒe] *vt* (*voiture, fusil, caméra*) to load; (*batterie*) to charge ▷ *vi* (*Mil etc*) to charge; **se ~ de** *vt* to see to, take care of; **~ qn de qch/faire qch** to give sb the responsibility for sth/of doing sth; to put sb in charge of sth/doing sth;

se ~ **de faire qch** to take it upon o.s. to do sth

chargeur [ʃaʀʒœʀ] *nm* (*dispositif: d'arme à feu*) magazine; (: *Photo*) cartridge; ~ **de batterie** (*Élec*) battery charger

chariot [ʃaʀjo] *nm* trolley; (*charrette*) waggon; (*de machine à écrire*) carriage; ~ **élévateur** fork-lift truck

charisme [kaʀism(ə)] *nm* charisma

charitable [ʃaʀitabl(ə)] *adj* charitable; kind

charité [ʃaʀite] *nf* charity; **faire la** ~ to give to charity; to do charitable works; **faire la** ~ **à** to give (something) to; **fête/vente de** ~ fête/sale in aid of charity

charivari [ʃaʀivaʀi] *nm* hullabaloo

charlatan [ʃaʀlatã] *nm* charlatan

charlotte [ʃaʀlɔt] *nf* (*Culin*) charlotte

charmant, e [ʃaʀmã, -ãt] *adj* charming

charme [ʃaʀm(ə)] *nm* charm; **charmes** *nmpl* (*appas*) charms; **c'est ce qui en fait le** ~ that is its attraction; **faire du** ~ to be charming, turn on the charm; **aller** *ou* **se porter comme un** ~ to be in the pink

charmer [ʃaʀme] *vt* to charm; **je suis charmé de** … I'm delighted to …

charmeur, -euse [ʃaʀmœʀ, -øz] *nm/f* charmer; ~ **de serpents** snake charmer

charnel, le [ʃaʀnɛl] *adj* carnal

charnier [ʃaʀnje] *nm* mass grave

charnière [ʃaʀnjɛʀ] *nf* hinge; (*fig*) turning-point

charnu, e [ʃaʀny] *adj* fleshy

charogne [ʃaʀɔɲ] *nf* carrion *no pl*; (*fam!*) bastard (!)

charolais, e [ʃaʀɔlɛ, -ɛz] *adj* of *ou* from the Charolais

charpente [ʃaʀpãt] *nf* frame(work); (*fig*) structure, framework; (*carrure*) build, frame

charpenté, e [ʃaʀpãte] *adj*: **bien** *ou* **solidement** ~ (*personne*) well-built; (*texte*) well-constructed

charpenterie [ʃaʀpãtʀi] *nf* carpentry

charpentier [ʃaʀpãtje] *nm* carpenter

charpie [ʃaʀpi] *nf*: **en** ~ (*fig*) in shreds *ou* ribbons

charretier [ʃaʀtje] *nm* carter; **de** ~ (*péj: langage, manières*) uncouth

charrette [ʃaʀɛt] *nf* cart

charrier [ʃaʀje] *vt* to carry (along); to cart, carry ▷ *vi* (*fam*) to exaggerate

charrue [ʃaʀy] *nf* plough (*Brit*), plow (*US*)

charte [ʃaʀt(ə)] *nf* charter

charter [tʃaʀtœʀ] *nm* (*vol*) charter flight; (*avion*) charter plane

chasse [ʃas] *nf* hunting; (*au fusil*) shooting; (*poursuite*) chase; (*aussi:* **chasse d'eau**) flush; **la** ~ **est ouverte** the hunting season is open; **la** ~ **est fermée** it is the close (*Brit*) *ou* closed (*US*) season; **aller à la** ~ to go hunting; **prendre en** ~, **donner la** ~ **à** to give chase to; **tirer la** ~ **(d'eau)** to flush the toilet, pull the chain; ~ **aérienne** aerial pursuit; ~ **à courre** hunting; ~ **à l'homme** manhunt; ~ **gardée** private hunting grounds *pl*; ~ **sous-marine** underwater fishing

châsse [ʃas] *nf* reliquary, shrine

chassé-croisé [ʃasekʀwaze] (*pl* **chassés-croisés**) *nm* (*Danse*) chassé-croisé; (*fig*) mix-up (*where people miss each other in turn*)

chasse-neige [ʃasnɛʒ] *nm inv* snowplough (*Brit*), snowplow (*US*)

chasser [ʃase] *vt* to hunt; (*expulser*) to chase away *ou* out, drive away *ou* out; (*dissiper*) to chase *ou* sweep away; to dispel, drive away

chasseur, -euse [ʃasœʀ, -øz] *nm/f* hunter ▷ *nm* (*avion*) fighter; (*domestique*) page (boy), messenger (boy); ~ **d'images** roving photographer; ~ **de têtes** (*fig*) headhunter; ~**s alpins** mountain infantry

chassieux, -euse [ʃasjø, -øz] *adj* sticky, gummy

châssis [ʃasi] *nm* (*Auto*) chassis; (*cadre*) frame; (*de jardin*) cold frame

chaste [ʃast(ə)] *adj* chaste

chasteté [ʃastəte] *nf* chastity

chasuble [ʃazybl(ə)] *nf* chasuble; **robe** ~ pinafore dress (*Brit*), jumper (*US*)

chat¹ [ʃa] *nm* cat; ~ **sauvage** wildcat

chat² [tʃat] *nm* (*Internet*) chat

châtaigne [ʃatɛɲ] *nf* chestnut

châtaignier [ʃatɛɲe] *nm* chestnut (tree)

châtain [ʃatɛ̃] *adj inv* chestnut (brown); (*personne*) chestnut-haired

château, x [ʃato] *nm* castle; ~ **d'eau** water tower; ~ **fort** stronghold, fortified castle; ~ **de sable** sand castle

châtelain, e [ʃatlɛ̃, -ɛn] *nm/f* lord/lady of the manor ▷ *nf* (*ceinture*) chatelaine

châtier [ʃatje] *vt* to punish, castigate; (*fig: style*) to polish, refine

chatière [ʃatjɛʀ] *nf* (*porte*) cat flap

châtiment [ʃatimã] *nm* punishment, castigation; ~ **corporel** corporal punishment

chatoiement [ʃatwamã] *nm* shimmer(ing)

chaton [ʃatɔ̃] *nm* (*Zool*) kitten; (*Bot*) catkin; (*de bague*) bezel; stone

chatouillement [ʃatujmã] *nm* (*gén*) tickling; (*dans le nez, la gorge*) tickle

chatouiller [ʃatuje] *vt* to tickle; (*l'odorat, le palais*) to titillate

chatouilleux, -euse [ʃatujø, -øz] *adj* ticklish; (*fig*) touchy, over-sensitive

chatoyant, e [ʃatwajã, -ãt] *adj* (*reflet, étoffe*) shimmering; (*couleurs*) sparkling

chatoyer [ʃatwaje] *vi* to shimmer

châtrer [ʃatʀe] *vt* (*mâle*) to castrate; (*femelle*) to spay; (*cheval*) to geld; (*chat, chien*) to doctor (*Brit*), fix (*US*); (*fig*) to mutilate

chatte [ʃat] *nf* (she-)cat

chatter [tʃate] *vi* (*Internet*) to chat

chatterton [ʃatɛʀtɔn] *nm* (*ruban isolant: Élec*) (adhesive) insulating tape

chaud, e [ʃo, -od] *adj* (*gén*) warm; (*très chaud*) hot; (*fig: félicitations*) hearty; (*discussion*) heated; **il fait** ~ it's warm; it's hot; **manger** ~ to have something hot to eat; **avoir** ~ to be warm; to be hot; **tenir** ~ to keep hot; **ça me tient** ~ it keeps me warm; **tenir au** ~ to keep in a warm place;

rester au ~ to stay in the warm

chaudement [ʃodmɑ̃] *adv* warmly; (*fig*) hotly

chaudière [ʃodjɛʀ] *nf* boiler

chaudron [ʃodʀɔ̃] *nm* cauldron

chaudronnerie [ʃodʀɔnʀi] *nf* (*usine*) boilerworks; (*activité*) boilermaking; (*boutique*) coppersmith's workshop

chauffage [ʃofaʒ] *nm* heating; ~ **au gaz/à l'électricité/au charbon** gas/electric/solid fuel heating; ~ **central** central heating; ~ **par le sol** underfloor heating

chauffagiste [ʃofaʒist(ə)] *nm* (*installateur*) heating engineer

chauffant, e [ʃofɑ̃, -ɑ̃t] *adj*: **couverture ~e** electric blanket; **plaque ~e** hotplate

chauffard [ʃofaʀ] *nm* (*péj*) reckless driver; road hog; (*après un accident*) hit-and-run driver

chauffe-bain [ʃofbɛ̃] *nm* = **chauffe-eau**

chauffe-biberon [ʃofbibʀɔ̃] *nm* (baby's) bottle warmer

chauffe-eau [ʃofo] *nm inv* water heater

chauffe-plats [ʃofpla] *nm inv* dish warmer

chauffer [ʃofe] *vt* to heat ▷ *vi* to heat up, warm up; (*trop chauffer: moteur*) to overheat; **se chauffer** *vi* (*se mettre en train*) to warm up; (*au soleil*) to warm o.s.

chaufferie [ʃofʀi] *nf* boiler room

chauffeur [ʃofœʀ] *nm* driver; (*privé*) chauffeur; **voiture avec/sans ~** chauffeur-driven/self-drive car; ~ **de taxi** taxi driver

chauffeuse [ʃoføz] *nf* fireside chair

chauler [ʃole] *vt* (*mur*) to whitewash

chaume [ʃom] *nm* (*du toit*) thatch; (*tiges*) stubble

chaumière [ʃomjɛʀ] *nf* (thatched) cottage

chaussée [ʃose] *nf* road(way); (*digue*) causeway

chausse-pied [ʃospje] *nm* shoe-horn

chausser [ʃose] *vt* (*bottes, skis*) to put on; (*enfant*) to put shoes on; (*soulier*) to fit; ~ **du 38/42** to take size 38/42; ~ **grand/bien** to be big-/well-fitting; **se chausser** to put one's shoes on

chausse-trappe [ʃostʀap] *nf* trap

chaussette [ʃosɛt] *nf* sock

chausseur [ʃosœʀ] *nm* (*marchand*) footwear specialist, shoemaker

chausson [ʃosɔ̃] *nm* slipper; (*de bébé*) bootee; ~ **(aux pommes)** (apple) turnover

chaussure [ʃosyʀ] *nf* shoe; (*commerce*): **la ~** the shoe industry *ou* trade; **~s basses** flat shoes; **~s montantes** ankle boots; **~s de ski** ski boots

chaut [ʃo] *vb*: **peu me ~** it matters little to me

chauve [ʃov] *adj* bald

chauve-souris [ʃovsuʀi] (*pl* **chauves-souris**) *nf* bat

chauvin, e [ʃovɛ̃, -in] *adj* chauvinistic; jingoistic

chauvinisme [ʃovinism(ə)] *nm* chauvinism; jingoism

chaux [ʃo] *nf* lime; **blanchi à la ~** whitewashed

chavirer [ʃaviʀe] *vi* to capsize, overturn

chef [ʃɛf] *nm* head, leader; (*patron*) boss; (*de cuisine*) chef; **au premier ~** extremely, to the nth degree; **de son propre ~** on his *ou* her own initiative; **général/commandant en ~**

general-/commander-in-chief; ~ **d'accusation** (*Jur*) charge, count (of indictment); ~ **d'atelier** (shop) foreman; ~ **de bureau** head clerk; ~ **de clinique** senior hospital lecturer; ~ **d'entreprise** company head; ~ **d'équipe** team leader; ~ **d'état** head of state; ~ **de famille** head of the family; ~ **de file** (*de parti etc*) leader; ~ **de gare** station master; ~ **d'orchestre** conductor (*Brit*), leader (*US*); ~ **de rayon** department(al) supervisor; ~ **de service** departmental head

chef-d'œuvre [ʃɛdœvʀ(ə)] (*pl* **chefs-d'œuvre**) *nm* masterpiece

chef-lieu [ʃɛfljø] (*pl* **chefs-lieux**) *nm* county town

cheftaine [ʃɛftɛn] *nf* (guide) captain

cheik, cheikh [ʃɛk] *nm* sheik

chemin [ʃəmɛ̃] *nm* path; (*itinéraire, direction, trajet*) way; **en ~, ~ faisant** on the way; ~ **de fer** railway (*Brit*), railroad (*US*); **par ~ de fer** by rail; **les ~s de fer** the railways (*Brit*), the railroad (*US*); ~ **de terre** dirt track

cheminée [ʃəmine] *nf* chimney; (*à l'intérieur*) chimney piece, fireplace; (*de bateau*) funnel

cheminement [ʃəminmɑ̃] *nm* progress; course

cheminer [ʃəmine] *vi* to walk (along)

cheminot [ʃəmino] *nm* railwayman (*Brit*), railroad worker (*US*)

chemise [ʃəmiz] *nf* shirt; (*dossier*) folder; ~ **de nuit** nightdress

chemiserie [ʃəmizʀi] *nf* (gentlemen's) outfitters'

chemisette [ʃəmizɛt] *nf* short-sleeved shirt

chemisier [ʃəmizje] *nm* blouse

chenal, -aux [ʃənal, -o] *nm* channel

chenapan [ʃənapɑ̃] *nm* (*garnement*) rascal; (*péj: vaurien*) rogue

chêne [ʃɛn] *nm* oak (tree); (*bois*) oak

chenet [ʃənɛ] *nm* fire-dog, andiron

chenil [ʃənil] *nm* kennels *pl*

chenille [ʃənij] *nf* (*Zool*) caterpillar; (*Auto*) caterpillar track; **véhicule à ~s** tracked vehicle, caterpillar

chenillette [ʃənijɛt] *nf* tracked vehicle

cheptel [ʃɛptɛl] *nm* livestock

chèque [ʃɛk] *nm* cheque (*Brit*), check (*US*); **faire/toucher un ~** to write/cash a cheque; **par ~** by cheque; ~ **barré/sans provision** crossed (*Brit*) / bad cheque; ~ **en blanc** blank cheque; ~ **au porteur** cheque to bearer; ~ **postal** post office cheque, ≈ giro cheque (*Brit*); ~ **de voyage** traveller's cheque

chèque-cadeau [ʃɛkkado] (*pl* **chèques-cadeaux**) *nm* gift token

chèque-repas (*pl* **chèques-repas**) [ʃɛkʀəpa], **chèque-restaurant** (*pl* **chèques-restaurant**) [ʃɛkʀɛstɔʀɑ̃] *nm* ≈ luncheon voucher

chéquier [ʃekje] *nm* cheque book (*Brit*), checkbook (*US*)

cher, -ère [ʃɛʀ] *adj* (*aimé*) dear; (*coûteux*) expensive, dear ▷ *adv*: **coûter/payer ~** to cost/pay a lot ▷ *nf*: **la bonne chère** good food; **cela**

coûte ~ it's expensive, it costs a lot of money; **mon** ~, **ma chère** my dear

chercher [ʃɛRʃe] vt to look for; (gloire etc) to seek; ~ **des ennuis/la bagarre** to be looking for trouble/a fight; **aller** ~ to go for, go and fetch; ~ **à faire** to try to do

chercheur, -euse [ʃɛRʃœR, -øz] nm/f researcher, research worker; ~ **de** seeker of; hunter of; ~ **d'or** gold digger

chère [ʃɛR] adj f, nf voir **cher**

chèrement [ʃɛRmã] adv dearly

chéri, e [ʃeRi] adj beloved, dear; (**mon**) ~ darling

chérir [ʃeRiR] vt to cherish

cherté [ʃɛRte] nf: **la ~ de la vie** the high cost of living

chérubin [ʃeRybɛ̃] nm cherub

chétif, -ive [ʃetif, -iv] adj puny, stunted

cheval, -aux [ʃəval, -o] nm horse; (Auto): ~ (**vapeur**) (**CV**) horsepower no pl; **50 chevaux** (**au frein**) 50 brake horsepower, 50 b.h.p.; **10 chevaux (fiscaux)** 10 horsepower (for tax purposes); **faire du** ~ to ride; **à** ~ on horseback; **à** ~ **sur** astride, straddling; (fig) overlapping; ~ **d'arçons** vaulting horse; ~ **à bascule** rocking horse; ~ **de bataille** charger; (fig) hobby-horse; ~ **de course** race horse; **chevaux de bois** (des manèges) wooden (fairground) horses; (manège) merry-go-round

chevaleresque [ʃəvalRɛsk(ə)] adj chivalrous

chevalerie [ʃəvalRi] nf chivalry; knighthood

chevalet [ʃəvalɛ] nm easel

chevalier [ʃəvalje] nm knight; ~ **servant** escort

chevalière [ʃəvaljɛR] nf signet ring

chevalin, e [ʃəvalɛ̃, -in] adj of horses, equine; (péj) horsy; **boucherie ~e** horse-meat butcher's

cheval-vapeur [ʃəvalvapœR, ʃəvo-] (pl **chevaux-vapeur**) nm voir **cheval**

chevauchée [ʃəvoʃe] nf ride; cavalcade

chevauchement [ʃəvoʃmã] nm overlap

chevaucher [ʃəvoʃe] vi (aussi: **se chevaucher**) to overlap (each other) ▷ vt to be astride, straddle

chevaux [ʃəvo] nmpl voir **cheval**

chevelu, e [ʃəvly] adj with a good head of hair, hairy (péj)

chevelure [ʃəvlyR] nf hair no pl

chevet [ʃəvɛ] nm: **au ~ de qn** at sb's bedside; **lampe de ~** bedside lamp

cheveu, x [ʃəvø] nm hair ▷ nmpl (chevelure) hair sg; **avoir les ~x courts/en brosse** to have short hair/a crew cut; **se faire couper les ~x** to get ou have one's hair cut; **tiré par les ~x** (histoire) far-fetched

cheville [ʃəvij] nf (Anat) ankle; (de bois) peg; (pour enfoncer une vis) plug; **être en ~ avec qn** to be in cahoots with sb; ~ **ouvrière** (fig) kingpin

chèvre [ʃɛvR(ə)] nf (she-)goat; **ménager la ~ et le chou** to try to please everyone

chevreau, x [ʃəvRo] nm kid

chèvrefeuille [ʃɛvRəfœj] nm honeysuckle

chevreuil [ʃəvRœj] nm roe deer inv; (Culin) venison

chevron [ʃəvRɔ̃] nm (poutre) rafter; (motif) chevron, v(-shape); **à ~s** chevron-patterned; (petits) herringbone

chevronné, e [ʃəvRɔne] adj seasoned, experienced

chevrotant, e [ʃəvRɔtã, -ãt] adj quavering

chevroter [ʃəvRɔte] vi (personne, voix) to quaver

chevrotine [ʃəvRɔtin] nf buckshot no pl

chewing-gum [ʃwiŋɡɔm] nm chewing gum

 MOT-CLÉ

chez [ʃe] prép **1** (à la demeure de) at; (: direction) to; **chez qn** at/to sb's house ou place; **chez moi** at home; (direction) home
2 (à l'entreprise de): **il travaille chez Renault** he works for Renault, he works at Renault('s)
3 (+profession) at; (: direction) to; **chez le boulanger/dentiste** at ou to the baker's/dentist's
4 (dans le caractère, l'œuvre de) in; **chez les renards/Racine** in foxes/Racine; **chez les Français** among the French; **chez lui, c'est un devoir** for him, it's a duty
▷ nm inv: **mon chez moi/ton chez toi** etc my/your etc home ou place

chez-soi [ʃeswa] nm inv home

Chf. cent. abr (= chauffage central) c.h

chiadé, e [ʃjade] adj (fam: fignolé, soigné) wicked

chialer [ʃjale] vi (fam) to blubber; **arrête de ~!** stop blubbering!

chiant, e [ʃjã, -ãt] adj (fam!) bloody annoying (vulgar: Brit) damn annoying; **qu'est-ce qu'il est ~!** he's such a bloody pain! (!)

chic [ʃik] adj inv chic, smart; (généreux) nice, decent ▷ nm stylishness; **avoir le ~ de ou pour** to have the knack of ou for; **de ~** adv off the cuff; **~!** great!, terrific!

chicane [ʃikan] nf (obstacle) zigzag; (querelle) squabble

chicaner [ʃikane] vi (ergoter): ~ **sur** to quibble about

chiche [ʃiʃ] adj (mesquin) niggardly, mean; (pauvre) meagre (Brit), meager (US) ▷ excl (en réponse à un défi) you're on!; **tu n'es pas ~ de lui parler!** you wouldn't (dare) speak to her!

chichement [ʃiʃmã] adv (pauvrement) meagrely (Brit); (mesquinement) meanly

chichi [ʃiʃi] nm (fam) fuss; **faire des ~s** to make a fuss

chichis [ʃiʃi] (fam) nmpl fuss sg

chicorée [ʃikɔRe] nf (café) chicory; (salade) endive; ~ **frisée** curly endive

chicot [ʃiko] nm stump

chien [ʃjɛ̃] nm dog; (de pistolet) hammer; **temps de ~** rotten weather; **vie de ~** dog's life; **couché en ~ de fusil** curled up; ~ **d'aveugle** guide dog; ~ **de chasse** gun dog; ~ **de garde** guard dog; ~ **policier** police dog; ~ **de race** pedigree dog; ~ **de traîneau** husky

chiendent [ʃjɛ̃dã] nm couch grass

chien-loup [ʃjɛ̃lu] (pl **chiens-loups**) nm

wolfhound

chienne [ʃjɛn] nf (she-)dog, bitch

chier [ʃje] vi (fam!) to crap (!), shit (!); **faire ~ qn** (importuner) to bug sb; (causer des ennuis à) to piss sb around (!); **se faire ~** (s'ennuyer) to be bored rigid

chiffe [ʃif] nf: **il est mou comme une ~, c'est une ~ molle** he's spineless ou wet

chiffon [ʃifɔ̃] nm (piece of) rag

chiffonné, e [ʃifɔne] adj (fatigué: visage) worn-looking

chiffonner [ʃifɔne] vt to crumple, crease; (tracasser) to concern

chiffonnier [ʃifɔnje] nm ragman, rag-and-bone man; (meuble) chiffonier

chiffrable [ʃifʀabl(ə)] adj numerable

chiffre [ʃifʀ(ə)] nm (représentant un nombre) figure; numeral; (montant, total) total, sum; (d'un code) code, cipher; **~s romains/arabes** roman/arabic figures ou numerals; **en ~s ronds** in round figures; **écrire un nombre en ~s** to write a number in figures; **~ d'affaires (CA)** turnover; **~ de ventes** sales figures

chiffrer [ʃifʀe] vt (dépense) to put a figure to, assess; (message) to (en)code, cipher ▷ vi: **~ à, se ~ à** to add up to

chignole [ʃiɲɔl] nf drill

chignon [ʃiɲɔ̃] nm chignon, bun

chiite [ʃiit] adj Shiite ▷ nm/f: **Chiite** Shiite

Chili [ʃili] nm: **le ~** Chile

chilien, ne [ʃiljɛ̃, -ɛn] adj Chilean ▷ nm/f: **Chilien, ne** Chilean

chimère [ʃimɛʀ] nf (wild) dream, pipe dream, idle fancy

chimérique [ʃimeʀik] adj (utopique) fanciful

chimie [ʃimi] nf chemistry

chimio [ʃimjɔ], **chimiothérapie** [ʃimjɔteʀapi] nf chemotherapy

chimique [ʃimik] adj chemical; **produits ~s** chemicals

chimiste [ʃimist(ə)] nm/f chemist

chimpanzé [ʃɛ̃pɑ̃ze] nm chimpanzee

chinchilla [ʃɛ̃ʃila] nm chinchilla

Chine [ʃin] nf: **la ~** China; **la ~ libre, la république de ~** the Republic of China, Nationalist China (Taiwan)

chine [ʃin] nm rice paper; (porcelaine) china (vase)

chiné, e [ʃine] adj flecked

chinois, e [ʃinwa, -waz] adj Chinese; (fig: péj) pernickety, fussy ▷ nm (Ling) Chinese ▷ nm/f: **Chinois, e** Chinese

chinoiserie [ʃinwazʀi], **chinoiseries** nf(pl) (péj) red tape, fuss

chiot [ʃjo] nm pup(py)

chiper [ʃipe] vt (fam) to pinch

chipie [ʃipi] nf shrew

chipolata [ʃipɔlata] nf chipolata

chipoter [ʃipɔte] vi (manger) to nibble; (ergoter) to quibble, haggle

chips [ʃips] nfpl (aussi: **pommes chips**) crisps (Brit), (potato) chips (US)

chique [ʃik] nf quid, chew

chiquenaude [ʃiknod] nf flick, flip

chiquer [ʃike] vi to chew tobacco

chiromancie [kiʀɔmɑ̃si] nf palmistry

chiromancien, ne [kiʀɔmɑ̃sjɛ̃, -ɛn] nm/f palmist

chiropracteur [kiʀɔpʀaktœʀ] nm, **chiropraticien, ne** [kiʀɔpʀatisjɛ̃, -ɛn] nm/f chiropractor

chirurgical, e, -aux [ʃiʀyʀʒikal, -o] adj surgical

chirurgie [ʃiʀyʀʒi] nf surgery; **~ esthétique** cosmetic ou plastic surgery

chirurgien [ʃiʀyʀʒjɛ̃] nm surgeon; **~ dentiste** dental surgeon

chiure [ʃjyʀ] nf: **~s de mouche** fly specks

ch.-l. abr = **chef-lieu**

chlore [klɔʀ] nm chlorine

chloroforme [klɔʀɔfɔʀm(ə)] nm chloroform

chlorophylle [klɔʀɔfil] nf chlorophyll

chlorure [klɔʀyʀ] nm chloride

choc [ʃɔk] nm impact; shock; crash; (moral) shock; (affrontement) clash ▷ adj: **prix ~** amazing ou incredible price/prices; **de ~** (troupe, traitement) shock cpd; (patron etc) high-powered; **~ opératoire/nerveux** post-operative/nervous shock; **~ en retour** return shock; (fig) backlash

chocolat [ʃɔkɔla] nm chocolate; (boisson) (hot) chocolate; **~ chaud** hot chocolate; **~ à cuire** cooking chocolate; **~ au lait** milk chocolate; **~ en poudre** drinking chocolate

chocolaté, e [ʃɔkɔlate] adj chocolate cpd, chocolate-flavoured

chocolaterie [ʃɔkɔlatʀi] nf (fabrique) chocolate factory

chocolatier, -ière [ʃɔkɔlatje, -jɛʀ] nm/f chocolate maker

chœur [kœʀ] nm (chorale) choir; (Opéra, Théât) chorus; (Archit) choir, chancel; **en ~** in chorus

choir [ʃwaʀ] vi to fall

choisi, e [ʃwazi] adj (de premier choix) carefully chosen; select; **textes ~s** selected writings

choisir [ʃwaziʀ] vt to choose; (entre plusieurs) to choose, select; **~ de faire qch** to choose ou opt to do sth

choix [ʃwa] nm choice; selection; **avoir le ~** to have the choice; **je n'avais pas le ~** I had no choice; **de premier ~** (Comm) class ou grade one; **de ~** choice cpd, selected; **au ~** as you wish ou prefer; **de mon/son ~** of my/his ou her choosing

choléra [kɔleʀa] nm cholera

cholestérol [kɔlesteʀɔl] nm cholesterol

chômage [ʃomaʒ] nm unemployment; **mettre au ~** to make redundant, put out of work; **être au ~** to be unemployed ou out of work; **~ partiel** short-time working; **~ structurel** structural unemployment; **~ technique** lay-offs pl

chômer [ʃome] vi to be unemployed, be idle; **jour chômé** public holiday

chômeur, -euse [ʃomœʀ, -øz] nm/f unemployed person, person out of work

chope [ʃɔp] nf tankard

choper [ʃɔpe] (fam) vt (objet, maladie) to catch

choquant, e [ʃɔkɑ̃, -ɑ̃t] adj shocking

choquer [ʃɔke] *vt* (*offenser*) to shock;
(*commotionner*) to shake (up)
choral, e [kɔʀal] *adj* choral ▷ *nf* choral society,
choir
chorégraphe [kɔʀegʀaf] *nm/f* choreographer
chorégraphie [kɔʀegʀafi] *nf* choreography
choriste [kɔʀist(ə)] *nm/f* choir member; (*Opéra*)
chorus member
chorus [kɔʀys] *nm*: **faire ~ (avec)** to voice one's
agreement (with)
chose [ʃoz] *nf* thing ▷ *nm* (*fam: machin*)
thingamajig ▷ *adj inv*: **être/se sentir tout ~**
(*bizarre*) to be/feel a bit odd; (*malade*) to be/feel
out of sorts; **dire bien des ~s à qn** to give sb's
regards to sb; **parler de ~(s) et d'autre(s)** to
talk about one thing and another; **c'est peu de
~** it's nothing much
chou, x [ʃu] *nm* cabbage ▷ *adj inv* cute; **mon
petit ~** (my) sweetheart; **faire ~ blanc** to draw
a blank; **feuille de ~** (*fig: journal*) rag; **~ à la
crème** cream bun (*made of choux pastry*); **~ de
Bruxelles** Brussels sprout
choucas [ʃuka] *nm* jackdaw
chouchou, te [ʃuʃu, -ut] *nm/f* (*Scol*) teacher's pet
chouchouter [ʃuʃute] *vt* to pet
choucroute [ʃukʀut] *nf* sauerkraut; **~ garnie**
sauerkraut with cooked meats and potatoes
chouette [ʃwɛt] *nf* owl ▷ *adj* (*fam*) great,
smashing
chou-fleur [ʃuflœʀ] (*pl* **choux-fleurs**) *nm*
cauliflower
chou-rave [ʃuʀav] (*pl* **choux-raves**) *nm* kohlrabi
choyer [ʃwaje] *vt* to cherish; to pamper
CHR *sigle m* = **Centre hospitalier régional**
chrétien, ne [kʀetjɛ̃, -ɛn] *adj, nm/f* Christian
chrétiennement [kʀetjɛnmɑ̃] *adv* in a
Christian way *ou* spirit
chrétienté [kʀetjɛ̃te] *nf* Christendom
Christ [kʀist] *nm*: **le ~** Christ; **christ** (*crucifix etc*)
figure of Christ; **Jésus ~** Jesus Christ
christianiser [kʀistjanize] *vt* to convert to
Christianity
christianisme [kʀistjanism(ə)] *nm* Christianity
chromatique [kʀɔmatik] *adj* chromatic
chrome [kʀom] *nm* chromium; (*revêtement*)
chrome, chromium
chromé, e [kʀome] *adj* chrome-plated,
chromium-plated
chromosome [kʀomozom] *nm* chromosome
chronique [kʀɔnik] *adj* chronic ▷ *nf* (*de journal*)
column, page; (*historique*) chronicle; (*Radio, TV*):
la ~ sportive/théâtrale the sports/theatre
review; **la ~ locale** local news and gossip
chroniqueur [kʀɔnikœʀ] *nm* columnist;
chronicler
chrono [kʀɔno] *nm* (*fam*) = **chronomètre**
chronologie [kʀɔnɔlɔʒi] *nf* chronology
chronologique [kʀɔnɔlɔʒik] *adj* chronological
chronologiquement [kʀɔnɔlɔʒikmɑ̃] *adv*
chronologically
chronomètre [kʀɔnɔmɛtʀ(ə)] *nm* stopwatch
chronométrer [kʀɔnɔmetʀe] *vt* to time

chronométreur [kʀɔnɔmetʀœʀ] *nm*
timekeeper
chrysalide [kʀizalid] *nf* chrysalis
chrysanthème [kʀizɑ̃tɛm] *nm*
chrysanthemum
CHU *sigle m* (= *Centre hospitalo-universitaire*)
≈ (teaching) hospital
chu, e [ʃy] *pp de* **choir**
chuchotement [ʃyʃɔtmɑ̃] *nm* whisper
chuchoter [ʃyʃɔte] *vt, vi* to whisper
chuintement [ʃɥɛ̃tmɑ̃] *nm* hiss
chuinter [ʃɥɛ̃te] *vi* to hiss
chut *excl* [ʃyt] sh! ▷ *vb* [ʃy] *voir* **choir**
chute [ʃyt] *nf* fall; (*de bois, papier: déchet*) scrap; **la
~ des cheveux** hair loss; **faire une ~ (de 10 m)**
to fall (10 m); **~s de pluie/neige** rain/snowfalls;
~ (d'eau) waterfall; **~ du jour** nightfall; **~ libre**
free fall; **~ des reins** small of the back
Chypre [ʃipʀ] *nm* Cyprus
chypriote [ʃipʀiɔt] *adj, nm/f* = **cypriote**
-ci, ci- [si] *adv voir* **par**; **ci-contre**; **ci-joint** *etc* ▷ *adj
dém*: **ce garçon~/-là** this/that boy; **ces
femmes~/-là** these/those women
CIA *sigle f* CIA
cial *abr* = **commercial**
ciao [tʃao] *excl* (*fam*) (bye-)bye
ci-après [siapʀɛ] *adv* hereafter
cibiste [sibist(ə)] *nm* CB enthusiast
cible [sibl(ə)] *nf* target
cibler [sible] *vt* to target
ciboire [sibwaʀ] *nm* ciborium (*vessel*)
ciboule [sibul] *nf* (large) chive
ciboulette [sibulet] *nf* (small) chive
ciboulot [sibulo] *nm* (*fam*) head, nut; **il n'a rien
dans le ~** he's got nothing between his ears
cicatrice [sikatʀis] *nf* scar
cicatriser [sikatʀize] *vt* to heal; **se cicatriser** to
heal (up), form a scar
ci-contre [sikɔ̃tʀ(ə)] *adv* opposite
CICR *sigle m* (= *Comité international de la Croix-Rouge*)
ICRC
ci-dessous [sidəsu] *adv* below
ci-dessus [sidəsy] *adv* above
ci-devant [sidəvɑ̃] *nm/f inv* aristocrat who lost his/
her title in the French Revolution
CIDJ *sigle m* (= *Centre d'information et de
documentation de la jeunesse*) careers advisory service
cidre [sidʀ(ə)] *nm* cider
cidrerie [sidʀəʀi] *nf* cider factory
Cie *abr* (= *compagnie*) Co
ciel [sjɛl] *nm* sky; (*Rel*) heaven; **ciels** *nmpl*
(*Peinture etc*) skies; **cieux** *nmpl* sky *sg*, skies; (*Rel*)
heaven *sg*; **à ~ ouvert** open-air; (*mine*) opencast;
tomber du ~ (*arriver à l'improviste*) to appear out
of the blue; (*être stupéfait*) to be unable to believe
one's eyes; **C~!** good heavens!; **~ de lit** canopy
cierge [sjɛʀʒ(ə)] *nm* candle; **~ pascal** Easter
candle
cieux [sjø] *nmpl voir* **ciel**
cigale [sigal] *nf* cicada
cigare [sigaʀ] *nm* cigar
cigarette [sigaʀɛt] *nf* cigarette; **~ (à) bout**

filtre filter cigarette

ci-gît [siʒi] *adv* here lies

cigogne [sigɔɲ] *nf* stork

ciguë [sigy] *nf* hemlock

ci-inclus, e [siɛ̃kly, -yz] *adj, adv* enclosed

ci-joint, e [siʒwɛ̃, -ɛ̃t] *adj, adv* enclosed; **veuillez trouver** ~ please find enclosed

cil [sil] *nm* (eye)lash

ciller [sije] *vi* to blink

cimaise [simɛz] *nf* picture rail

cime [sim] *nf* top; (*montagne*) peak

ciment [simɑ̃] *nm* cement; ~ **armé** reinforced concrete

cimenter [simɑ̃te] *vt* to cement

cimenterie [simɑ̃tʀi] *nf* cement works *sg*

cimetière [simtjɛʀ] *nm* cemetery; (*d'église*) churchyard; ~ **de voitures** scrapyard

cinéaste [sineast(ə)] *nm/f* film-maker

ciné-club [sineklœb] *nm* film club; film society

cinéma [sinema] *nm* cinema; **aller au** ~ to go to the cinema *ou* pictures *ou* movies; ~ **d'animation** cartoon (film)

cinémascope® [sinemaskɔp] *nm* Cinemascope®

cinémathèque [sinematɛk] *nf* film archives *pl ou* library

cinématographie [sinematɔgʀafi] *nf* cinematography

cinématographique [sinematɔgʀafik] *adj* film *cpd*, cinema *cpd*

cinéphile [sinefil] *nm/f* film buff

cinérama® [sinerama] *nm*: **en** ~ in Cinerama®

cinétique [sinetik] *adj* kinetic

cingalais, cinghalais, e [sɛ̃galɛ, -ɛz] *adj* Sin(g)halese

cinglant, e [sɛ̃glɑ̃, -ɑ̃t] *adj* (*propos, ironie*) scathing, biting; (*échec*) crushing

cinglé, e [sɛ̃gle] *adj* (*fam*) crazy

cingler [sɛ̃gle] *vt* to lash; (*fig*) to sting ▷ *vi* (*Navig*): ~ **vers** to make *ou* head for

cinq [sɛ̃k] *num* five

cinquantaine [sɛ̃kɑ̃tɛn] *nf*: **une** ~ (**de**) about fifty; **avoir la** ~ (*âge*) to be around fifty

cinquante [sɛ̃kɑ̃t] *num* fifty

cinquantenaire [sɛ̃kɑ̃tnɛʀ] *adj, nm/f* fifty-year-old

cinquantième [sɛ̃kɑ̃tjɛm] *num* fiftieth

cinquième [sɛ̃kjɛm] *num* fifth

cinquièmement [sɛ̃kjɛmmɑ̃] *adv* fifthly

cintre [sɛ̃tʀ(ə)] *nm* coat-hanger; (*Archit*) arch; **plein** ~ semicircular arch

cintré, e [sɛ̃tʀe] *adj* curved; (*chemise*) fitted, slim-fitting

CIO *sigle m* (= *Comité international olympique*) IOC (= *International Olympic Committee*); (= *centre d'information et d'orientation*) careers advisory centre

cirage [siʀaʒ] *nm* (shoe) polish

circoncis, e [siʀkɔ̃si, -iz] *adj* circumcized

circoncision [siʀkɔ̃sizjɔ̃] *nf* circumcision

circonférence [siʀkɔ̃feʀɑ̃s] *nf* circumference

circonflexe [siʀkɔ̃flɛks(ə)] *adj*: **accent** ~ circumflex accent

circonlocution [siʀkɔ̃lɔkysjɔ̃] *nf* circumlocution

circonscription [siʀkɔ̃skʀipsjɔ̃] *nf* district; ~ **électorale** (*d'un député*) constituency; ~ **militaire** military area

circonscrire [siʀkɔ̃skʀiʀ] *vt* to define, delimit; (*incendie*) to contain; (*propriété*) to mark out; (*sujet*) to define

circonspect, e [siʀkɔ̃spɛkt] *adj* circumspect, cautious

circonspection [siʀkɔ̃spɛksjɔ̃] *nf* circumspection, caution

circonstance [siʀkɔ̃stɑ̃s] *nf* circumstance; (*occasion*) occasion; **œuvre de** ~ occasional work; **air de** ~ fitting air; **tête de** ~ appropriate demeanour (*Brit*) *ou* demeanor (*US*); ~**s atténuantes** mitigating circumstances

circonstancié, e [siʀkɔ̃stɑ̃sje] *adj* detailed

circonstanciel, le [siʀkɔ̃stɑ̃sjɛl] *adj*: **complément/proposition** ~(**le**) adverbial phrase/clause

circonvenir [siʀkɔ̃vniʀ] *vt* to circumvent

circonvolutions [siʀkɔ̃vɔlysjɔ̃] *nfpl* twists, convolutions

circuit [siʀkчi] *nm* (*trajet*) tour, (round) trip; (*Élec, Tech*) circuit; ~ **automobile** motor circuit; ~ **de distribution** distribution network; ~ **fermé** closed circuit; ~ **intégré** integrated circuit

circulaire [siʀkylɛʀ] *adj, nf* circular

circulation [siʀkylɑsjɔ̃] *nf* circulation; (*Auto*): **la** ~ (the) traffic; **bonne/mauvaise** ~ good/bad circulation; **mettre en** ~ to put into circulation

circulatoire [siʀkylatwaʀ] *adj*: **avoir des troubles** ~**s** to have problems with one's circulation

circuler [siʀkyle] *vi* to drive (along); to walk along; (*train etc*) to run; (*sang, devises*) to circulate; **faire** ~ (*nouvelle*) to spread (about), circulate; (*badauds*) to move on

cire [siʀ] *nf* wax; ~ **à cacheter** sealing wax

ciré [siʀe] *nm* oilskin

cirer [siʀe] *vt* to wax, polish

cireur [siʀœʀ] *nm* shoeshine boy

cireuse [siʀøz] *nf* floor polisher

cireux, -euse [siʀø, -øz] *adj* (*fig: teint*) sallow, waxen

cirque [siʀk(ə)] *nm* circus; (*arène*) amphitheatre (*Brit*), amphitheater (*US*); (*Géo*) cirque; (*fig: désordre*) chaos, bedlam; (: *chichis*) carry-on

cirrhose [siʀoz] *nf*: ~ **du foie** cirrhosis of the liver

cisaille [sizaj], **cisailles** *nf(pl)* (gardening) shears *pl*

cisailler [sizaje] *vt* to clip

ciseau, x [sizo] *nm*: ~ (**à bois**) chisel ▷ *nmpl* (pair of) scissors; **sauter en** ~**x** to do a scissors jump; ~ **à froid** cold chisel

ciseler [sizle] *vt* to chisel, carve

ciselure [sizlyʀ] *nf* engraving; (*bois*) carving

Cisjordanie [sisʒɔʀdani] *nf*: **la ~** the West Bank (of Jordan)

citadelle [sitadɛl] *nf* citadel

citadin, e [sitadɛ̃, -in] *nm/f* city dweller ▷ *adj* town *cpd*, city *cpd*, urban

citation [sitasjɔ̃] *nf* (*d'auteur*) quotation; (*Jur*) summons *sg*; (*Mil*: *récompense*) mention

cité [site] *nf* town; (*plus grande*) city; **~ ouvrière** (workers') housing estate; **~ universitaire** students' residences *pl*

cité-dortoir [sitedɔʀtwaʀ] (*pl* **cités-dortoirs**) *nf* dormitory town

cité-jardin [siteʒaʀdɛ̃] (*pl* **cités-jardins**) *nf* garden city

citer [site] *vt* (*un auteur*) to quote (from); (*nommer*) to name; (*Jur*) to summon; **~ (en exemple)** (*personne*) to hold up (as an example); **je ne veux ~ personne** I don't want to name names

citerne [sitɛʀn(ə)] *nf* tank

cithare [sitaʀ] *nf* zither

citoyen, ne [sitwajɛ̃, -ɛn] *nm/f* citizen

citoyenneté [sitwajɛnte] *nf* citizenship

citrique [sitʀik] *adj*: **acide ~** citric acid

citron [sitʀɔ̃] *nm* lemon; **~ pressé** (fresh) lemon juice; **~ vert** lime

citronnade [sitʀɔnad] *nf* lemonade

citronné, e [sitʀɔne] *adj* (*boisson*) lemon-flavoured (*Brit*) *ou* -flavored (*US*); (*eau de toilette*) lemon-scented

citronnelle [sitʀɔnɛl] *nf* citronella

citronnier [sitʀɔnje] *nm* lemon tree

citrouille [sitʀuj] *nf* pumpkin

cive [siv] *nf* chive

civet [sivɛ] *nm* stew; **~ de lièvre** jugged hare

civette [sivɛt] *nf* (*Bot*) chives *pl*; (*Zool*) civet (cat)

civière [sivjɛʀ] *nf* stretcher

civil, e [sivil] *adj* (*Jur, Admin, poli*) civil; (*non militaire*) civilian ▷ *nm* civilian; **en ~** in civilian clothes; **dans le ~** in civilian life

civilement [sivilmɑ̃] *adv* (*poliment*) civilly; **se marier ~** to have a civil wedding

civilisation [sivilizasjɔ̃] *nf* civilization

civilisé, e [sivilize] *adj* civilized

civiliser [sivilize] *vt* to civilize

civilité [sivilite] *nf* civility; **présenter ses ~s** to present one's compliments

civique [sivik] *adj* civic; **instruction ~** (*Scol*) civics *sg*

civisme [sivism(ə)] *nm* public-spiritedness

cl. *abr* (= *centilitre*) cl

clafoutis [klafuti] *nm* batter pudding (*containing fruit*)

claie [klɛ] *nf* grid, riddle

clair, e [klɛʀ] *adj* light; (*chambre*) light, bright; (*eau, son, fig*) clear ▷ *adv*: **voir ~** to see clearly ▷ *nm*: **mettre au ~** (*notes etc*) to tidy up; **tirer qch au ~** to clear sth up, clarify sth; **bleu ~** light blue; **pour être ~** so as to make it plain; **y voir ~** (*comprendre*) to understand, see; **le plus ~ de son temps/argent** the better part of his time/money; **en ~** (*non codé*) in clear; **~ de lune** moonlight

claire [klɛʀ] *nf*: **(huître de) ~** fattened oyster

clairement [klɛʀmɑ̃] *adv* clearly

claire-voie [klɛʀvwa]: **à ~** *adj* letting the light through; openwork *cpd*

clairière [klɛʀjɛʀ] *nf* clearing

clair-obscur [klɛʀɔpskyʀ] (*pl* **clairs-obscurs**) *nm* half-light; (*fig*) uncertainty

clairon [klɛʀɔ̃] *nm* bugle

claironner [klɛʀɔne] *vt* (*fig*) to trumpet, shout from the rooftops

clairsemé, e [klɛʀsəme] *adj* sparse

clairvoyance [klɛʀvwajɑ̃s] *nf* clear-sightedness

clairvoyant, e [klɛʀvwajɑ̃, -ɑ̃t] *adj* perceptive, clear-sighted

clam [klam] *nm* (*Zool*) clam

clamer [klame] *vt* to proclaim

clameur [klamœʀ] *nf* clamour (*Brit*), clamor (*US*)

clan [klɑ̃] *nm* clan

clandestin, e [klɑ̃dɛstɛ̃, -in] *adj* clandestine, covert; (*Pol*) underground, clandestine; **passager ~** stowaway

clandestinement [klɑ̃dɛstinmɑ̃] *adv* secretly; **s'embarquer ~** to stow away

clandestinité [klɑ̃dɛstinite] *nf*: **dans la ~** (*en secret*) under cover; (*en se cachant*: *vivre*) underground; **entrer dans la ~** to go underground

clapet [klapɛ] *nm* (*Tech*) valve

clapier [klapje] *nm* (rabbit) hutch

clapotement [klapɔtmɑ̃] *nm* lap(ping)

clapoter [klapɔte] *vi* to lap

clapotis [klapɔti] *nm* lap(ping)

claquage [klakaʒ] *nm* pulled *ou* strained muscle

claque [klak] *nf* (*gifle*) slap; (*Théât*) claque ▷ *nm* (*chapeau*) opera hat

claquement [klakmɑ̃] *nm* (*de porte*: *bruit répété*) banging; (: *bruit isolé*) slam

claquemurer [klakmyʀe]: **se claquemurer** *vi* to shut o.s. away, closet o.s

claquer [klake] *vi* (*drapeau*) to flap; (*porte*) to bang, slam; (*coup de feu*) to ring out ▷ *vt* (*porte*) to slam, bang; (*doigts*) to snap; **elle claquait des dents** her teeth were chattering; **se ~ un muscle** to pull *ou* strain a muscle

claquettes [klakɛt] *nfpl* tap-dancing *sg*

clarification [klaʀifikasjɔ̃] *nf* (*fig*) clarification

clarifier [klaʀifje] *vt* (*fig*) to clarify

clarinette [klaʀinɛt] *nf* clarinet

clarinettiste [klaʀinetist(ə)] *nm/f* clarinettist

clarté [klaʀte] *nf* lightness; brightness; (*d'un son, de l'eau*) clearness; (*d'une explication*) clarity

classe [klɑs] *nf* class; (*Scol*: *local*) class(room); (: *leçon*) class; (: *élèves*) class, form; **1ère/2ème ~** 1st/2nd class; **un (soldat de) deuxième ~** (*Mil*: *armée de terre*) ≈ private (soldier); (: *armée de l'air*) ≈ aircraftman (*Brit*), ≈ airman basic (*US*); **de ~** luxury *cpd*; **faire ses ~s** (*Mil*) to do one's (recruit's) training; **faire la ~** (*Scol*) to be a *ou* the teacher; to teach; **aller en ~** to go to school; **aller en ~ verte/de neige/de mer** to go to the countryside/skiing/to the seaside with the school; ~ **préparatoire** *class which prepares students for the Grandes Écoles entry exams; see note;* ~ **sociale** social class; ~ **touriste** economy class

● **CLASSES PRÉPARATOIRES**
●
● *Classes préparatoires* are the two years of
● intensive study which coach students for
● the competitive entry examinations to the
● "grandes écoles". These extremely
● demanding courses follow the
● "baccalauréat" and are usually done at a
● "lycée". Schools which provide such classes
● are more highly regarded than those which
● do not.

classement [klɑsmɑ̃] *nm* classifying; filing; grading; closing; (*rang: Scol*) place; (: *Sport*) placing; (*liste: Scol*) class list (in order of merit); (: *Sport*) placings *pl*; **premier au ~ général** (*Sport*) first overall

classer [klɑse] *vt* (*idées, livres*) to classify; (*papiers*) to file; (*candidat, concurrent*) to grade; (*personne: juger: péj*) to rate; (*Jur: affaire*) to close; **se ~ premier/dernier** to come first/last; (*Sport*) to finish first/last

classeur [klɑsœʀ] *nm* file; (*meuble*) filing cabinet; ~ **à feuillets mobiles** ring binder

classification [klasifikɑsjɔ̃] *nf* classification

classifier [klasifje] *vt* to classify

classique [klasik] *adj* classical; (*habituel*) standard, classic ▷ *nm* classic; classical author; **études ~s** classical studies, classics

claudication [klodikɑsjɔ̃] *nf* limp

clause [kloz] *nf* clause

claustrer [klostʀe] *vt* to confine

claustrophobie [klostʀofɔbi] *nf* claustrophobia

clavecin [klavsɛ̃] *nm* harpsichord

claveciniste [klavsinist(ə)] *nm/f* harpsichordist

clavicule [klavikyl] *nf* clavicle, collarbone

clavier [klavje] *nm* keyboard

clé, clef [kle] *nf* key; (*Mus*) clef; (*de mécanicien*) spanner (*Brit*), wrench (*US*) ▷ *adj*: **problème/position ~** key problem/position; **mettre sous ~** to place under lock and key; **prendre la ~ des champs** to run away, make off; **prix ~s en main** (*d'une voiture*) on-the-road price; (*d'un appartement*) price with immediate entry; ~ **de sol/de fa/d'ut** treble/bass/alto clef; **livre/film** *etc* **à ~** *book/film etc in which real people are depicted under fictitious names;* **à la ~** (*à la fin*) at the end of it all; ~ **anglaise** = **clé à molette**; ~ **de contact** ignition key; ~ **à molette** adjustable spanner (*Brit*) *ou* wrench, monkey wrench; ~ **USB** USB key; ~ **de voûte** keystone

clématite [klematit] *nf* clematis

clémence [klemɑ̃s] *nf* mildness; leniency

clément, e [klemɑ̃, -ɑ̃t] *adj* (*temps*) mild; (*indulgent*) lenient

clémentine [klemɑ̃tin] *nf* (*Bot*) clementine

clenche [klɑ̃ʃ] *nf* latch

cleptomane [klɛptɔman] *nm/f* = **kleptomane**

clerc [klɛʀ] *nm*: ~ **de notaire** *ou* **d'avoué** lawyer's clerk

clergé [klɛʀʒe] *nm* clergy

clérical, e, -aux [kleʀikal, -o] *adj* clerical

cliché [kliʃe] *nm* (*Photo*) negative; print; (*Typo*) (printing) plate; (*Ling*) cliché

client, e [klijɑ̃, -ɑ̃t] *nm/f* (*acheteur*) customer, client; (*d'hôtel*) guest, patron; (*du docteur*) patient; (*de l'avocat*) client

clientèle [klijɑ̃tɛl] *nf* (*du magasin*) customers *pl*, clientèle; (*du docteur, de l'avocat*) practice; **accorder sa ~ à** to give one's custom to; **retirer sa ~ à** to take one's business away from

cligner [kliɲe] *vi*: ~ **des yeux** to blink (one's eyes); ~ **de l'œil** to wink

clignotant [kliɲɔtɑ̃] *nm* (*Auto*) indicator

clignoter [kliɲɔte] *vi* (*étoiles etc*) to twinkle; (*lumière: à intervalles réguliers*) to flash; (: *vaciller*) to flicker; (*yeux*) to blink

climat [klima] *nm* climate

climatique [klimatik] *adj* climatic

climatisation [klimatizɑsjɔ̃] *nf* air conditioning

climatisé, e [klimatize] *adj* air-conditioned

climatiseur [klimatizœʀ] *nm* air conditioner

clin d'œil [klɛ̃dœj] *nm* wink; **en un clin d'œil** in a flash

clinique [klinik] *adj* clinical ▷ *nf* nursing home, (*private*) clinic

clinquant, e [klɛ̃kɑ̃, -ɑ̃t] *adj* flashy

clip [klip] *nm* (*pince*) clip; (*vidéo*) pop (*ou* promotional) video

clique [klik] *nf* (*péj: bande*) clique, set; **prendre ses ~s et ses claques** to pack one's bags

cliquer [klike] *vi* (*Inform*) to click; ~ **deux fois** to double-click

cliqueter [klikte] *vi* to clash; (*ferraille, clefs, monnaie*) to jangle, jingle; (*verres*) to chink

cliquetis [klikti] *nm* jangle; jingle; chink

clitoris [klitɔʀis] *nm* clitoris

clivage [klivaʒ] *nm* cleavage; (*fig*) rift, split

cloaque [klɔak] *nm* (*fig*) cesspit

clochard, e [klɔʃaʀ, -aʀd(ə)] *nm/f* tramp

cloche [klɔʃ] *nf* (*d'église*) bell; (*fam*) clot; (*chapeau*) cloche (hat); ~ **à fromage** cheese-cover

cloche-pied [klɔʃpje]: **à ~** *adv* on one leg, hopping (along)

clocher [klɔʃe] *nm* church tower; (*en pointe*) steeple ▷ *vi* (*fam*) to be *ou* go wrong; **de ~** (*péj*) parochial

clocheton [klɔʃtɔ̃] *nm* pinnacle

clochette [klɔʃɛt] *nf* bell

clodo [klɔdo] *nm* (*fam*: = *clochard*) tramp

cloison [klwazɔ̃] *nf* partition (wall); ~ **étanche** (*fig*) impenetrable barrier, brick wall (*fig*)

cloisonner [klwazɔne] *vt* to partition (off), to divide up; (*fig*) to compartmentalize

cloître [klwatʀ(ə)] *nm* cloister

cloîtrer [klwatʀe] *vt*: **se cloîtrer** to shut o.s. away; (*Rel*) to enter a convent *ou* monastery

clonage [klonaʒ] *nm* cloning

clone [klon] *nm* clone

cloner [klone] vt to clone
clope [klɔp] (fam) nm ou f fag (Brit), cigarette
clopin-clopant [klɔpɛ̃klɔpɑ̃] adv hobbling along; (fig) so-so
clopiner [klɔpine] vi to hobble along
cloporte [klɔpɔʀt(ə)] nm woodlouse
cloque [klɔk] nf blister
cloqué, e [klɔke] adj: **étoffe ~e** seersucker
cloquer [klɔke] vi (peau, peinture) to blister
clore [klɔʀ] vt to close; **~ une session** (Inform) to log out
clos, e [klo, -oz] pp de **clore** ▷ adj voir **maison; huis; vase** ▷ nm (enclosed) field
clôt [klo] vb voir **clore**
clôture [klotyʀ] nf closure, closing; (barrière) enclosure, fence
clôturer [klotyʀe] vt (terrain) to enclose, close off; (festival, débats) to close
clou [klu] nm nail; (Méd) boil; **clous** nmpl = **passage clouté; pneus à ~s** studded tyres; **le ~ du spectacle** the highlight of the show; **~ de girofle** clove
clouer [klue] vt to nail down (ou up); (fig): **~ sur/contre** to pin to/against
clouté, e [klute] adj studded
clown [klun] nm clown; **faire le ~** (fig) to clown (about), play the fool
clownerie [klunʀi] nf clowning no pl; **faire des ~s** to clown around
club [klœb] nm club
CM sigle f = **chambre des métiers** ▷ sigle m = **conseil municipal;** (Scol) = **cours moyen**
cm. abr (= centimètre) cm
CMU sigle f (= couverture maladie universelle) system of free health care for those on low incomes
CNAT sigle f (= Commission nationale d'aménagement du territoire) national development agency
CNC sigle m (= Conseil national de la consommation) national consumers' council
CNDP sigle m = **Centre national de documentation pédagogique**
CNE sigle m (= Contrat nouvelles embauches) less stringent type of employment contract for use by small companies
CNED sigle m (= Centre national d'enseignement à distance) ≈ Open University
CNIL sigle f (= Commission nationale de l'informatique et des libertés) board which enforces law on data protection
CNIT sigle m (= Centre national des industries et des techniques) exhibition centre in Paris
CNJA sigle m (= Centre national des jeunes agriculteurs) farmers' union
CNL sigle f (= Confédération nationale du logement) consumer group for housing
CNRS sigle m = **Centre national de la recherche scientifique**
c/o abr (= care of) c/o
coagulant [kɔagylɑ̃] nm (Méd) coagulant
coaguler [kɔagyle]: **se coaguler** vi to coagulate
coaliser [kɔalize]: **se coaliser** vi to unite, join forces

coalition [kɔalisjɔ̃] nf coalition
coasser [kɔase] vi to croak
coauteur [kɔotœʀ] nm co-author
coaxial, e, -aux [kɔaksjal, -o] adj coaxial
cobaye [kɔbaj] nm guinea-pig
cobra [kɔbʀa] nm cobra
coca® [kɔka] nm Coke®
cocagne [kɔkaɲ] nf: **pays de ~** land of plenty; **mât de ~** greasy pole (fig)
cocaïne [kɔkain] nf cocaine
cocarde [kɔkaʀd(ə)] nf rosette
cocardier, -ière [kɔkaʀdje, -jɛʀ] adj jingoistic, chauvinistic; militaristic
cocasse [kɔkas] adj comical, funny
coccinelle [kɔksinɛl] nf ladybird (Brit), ladybug (US)
coccyx [kɔksis] nm coccyx
cocher [kɔʃe] nm coachman ▷ vt to tick off; (entailler) to notch
cochère [kɔʃɛʀ] adj f voir **porte**
cochon, ne [kɔʃɔ̃, -ɔn] nm pig ▷ nm/f (péj: sale) (filthy) pig; (: méchant) swine ▷ adj (fam) dirty, smutty; **~ d'Inde** guinea-pig; **~ de lait** (Culin) sucking pig
cochonnaille [kɔʃɔnaj] nf (péj: charcuterie) (cold) pork
cochonnerie [kɔʃɔnʀi] nf (fam: saleté) filth; (: marchandises) rubbish, trash
cochonnet [kɔʃɔnɛ] nm (Boules) jack
cocker [kɔkɛʀ] nm cocker spaniel
cocktail [kɔktɛl] nm cocktail; (réception) cocktail party
coco [kɔko] nm voir **noix;** (fam) bloke (Brit), dude (US)
cocon [kɔkɔ̃] nm cocoon
cocorico [kɔkɔʀiko] excl, nm cock-a-doodle-do
cocotier [kɔkɔtje] nm coconut palm
cocotte [kɔkɔt] nf (en fonte) casserole; **ma ~** (fam) sweetie (pie); **~ (minute)®** pressure cooker; **~ en papier** paper shape
cocu [kɔky] nm cuckold
code [kɔd] nm code; **se mettre en ~(s)** to dip (Brit) ou dim (US) one's (head)lights; **~ à barres** bar code; **~ de caractère** (Inform) character code; **~ civil** Common Law; **~ machine** machine code; **~ pénal** penal code; **~ postal** (numéro) postcode (Brit), zip code (US); **~ de la route** highway code; **~ secret** cipher
codéine [kɔdein] nf codeine
coder [kɔde] vt to (en)code
codétenu, e [kɔdetny] nm/f fellow prisoner ou inmate
codicille [kɔdisil] nm codicil
codifier [kɔdifje] vt to codify
codirecteur, -trice [kɔdiʀɛktœʀ, -tʀis] nm/f co-director
coéditeur, -trice [kɔeditœʀ, -tʀis] nm/f co-publisher; (rédacteur) co-editor
coefficient [kɔefisjɑ̃] nm coefficient; **~ d'erreur** margin of error
coéquipier, -ière [kɔekipje, -jɛʀ] nm/f team-mate, partner

coercition [kɔɛRsisjɔ̃] nf coercion
cœur [kœR] nm heart; (Cartes: couleur) hearts pl; (: carte) heart; (Culin): ~ **de laitue/d'artichaut** lettuce/artichoke heart; (fig): ~ **du débat** heart of the debate; ~ **de l'été** height of summer; ~ **de la forêt** depths pl of the forest; **affaire de** ~ love affair; **avoir bon** ~ to be kind-hearted; **avoir mal au** ~ to feel sick; **contre** ou **sur son** ~ to one's breast; **opérer qn à** ~ **ouvert** to perform open-heart surgery on sb; **recevoir qn à** ~ **ouvert** to welcome sb with open arms; **parler à** ~ **ouvert** to open one's heart; **de tout son** ~ with all one's heart; **avoir le** ~ **gros** ou **serré** to have a heavy heart; **en avoir le** ~ **net** to be clear in one's own mind (about it); **par** ~ by heart; **de bon** ~ willingly; **avoir à** ~ **de faire** to be very keen to do; **cela lui tient à** ~ that's (very) close to his heart; **prendre les choses à** ~ to take things to heart; **à** ~ **joie** to one's heart's content; **être de tout** ~ **avec qn** to be (completely) in accord with sb
coexistence [kɔɛgzistɑ̃s] nf coexistence
coexister [kɔɛgziste] vi to coexist
coffrage [kɔfRaʒ] nm (Constr: dispositif) form(work)
coffre [kɔfR(ə)] nm (meuble) chest; (coffre-fort) safe; (d'auto) boot (Brit), trunk (US); **avoir du** ~ (fam) to have a lot of puff
coffre-fort [kɔfRəfɔR] (pl **coffres-forts**) nm safe
coffrer [kɔfRe] vt (fam) to put inside, lock up
coffret [kɔfRɛ] nm casket; ~ **à bijoux** jewel box
cogérant, e [kɔʒeRɑ̃, -ɑ̃t] nm/f joint manager/ manageress
cogestion [kɔʒestjɔ̃] nf joint management
cogiter [kɔʒite] vi to cogitate
cognac [kɔɲak] nm brandy, cognac
cognement [kɔɲmɑ̃] nm knocking
cogner [kɔɲe] vi to knock, bang; **se cogner** vi to bump o.s.
cohabitation [kɔabitasjɔ̃] nf living together; (Pol, Jur) cohabitation
cohabiter [kɔabite] vi to live together
cohérence [kɔeRɑ̃s] nf coherence
cohérent, e [kɔeRɑ̃, -ɑ̃t] adj coherent
cohésion [kɔezjɔ̃] nf cohesion
cohorte [kɔɔRt(ə)] nf troop
cohue [kɔy] nf crowd
coi, coite [kwa, kwat] adj: **rester** ~ to remain silent
coiffe [kwaf] nf headdress
coiffé, e [kwafe] adj: **bien/mal** ~ with tidy/ untidy hair; ~ **d'un béret** wearing a beret; ~ **en arrière** with one's hair brushed ou combed back; ~ **en brosse** with a crew cut
coiffer [kwafe] vt (fig) to cover, top; ~ **qn** to do sb's hair; ~ **qn d'un béret** to put a beret on sb; **se coiffer** vi to do one's hair; to put on a ou one's hat
coiffeur, -euse [kwafœR, -øz] nm/f hairdresser ▷ nf (table) dressing table
coiffure [kwafyR] nf (cheveux) hairstyle, hairdo; (chapeau) hat, headgear no pl; (art): **la** ~ hairdressing

coin [kwɛ̃] nm corner; (pour graver) die; (pour coincer) wedge; (poinçon) hallmark; **l'épicerie du** ~ the local grocer; **dans le** ~ (aux alentours) in the area, around about; locally; **au** ~ **du feu** by the fireside; **du** ~ **de l'œil** out of the corner of one's eye; **regard en** ~ side(ways) glance; **sourire en** ~ half-smile
coincé, e [kwɛ̃se] adj stuck, jammed; (fig: inhibé) inhibited, with hang-ups
coincer [kwɛ̃se] vt to jam; (fam) to catch (out); to nab; **se coincer** vi to get stuck ou jammed
coïncidence [kɔɛ̃sidɑ̃s] nf coincidence
coïncider [kɔɛ̃side] vi: ~ **(avec)** to coincide (with); (correspondre: témoignage etc) to correspond ou tally (with)
coin-coin [kwɛ̃kwɛ̃] nm inv quack
coing [kwɛ̃] nm quince
coït [kɔit] nm coitus
coite [kwat] adj f voir coi
coke [kɔk] nm coke
col [kɔl] nm (de chemise) collar; (encolure, cou) neck; (de montagne) pass; ~ **roulé** polo-neck; ~ **de l'utérus** cervix
coléoptère [kɔleɔptɛR] nm beetle
colère [kɔlɛR] nf anger; **une** ~ a fit of anger; **être en** ~ **(contre qn)** to be angry (with sb); **mettre qn en** ~ to make sb angry; **se mettre en** ~ to get angry
coléreux, -euse [kɔleRø, -øz] adj, **colérique** [kɔleRik] ▷ adj quick-tempered, irascible
colibacille [kɔlibasil] nm colon bacillus
colibacillose [kɔlibasiloz] nf colibacillosis
colifichet [kɔlifiʃɛ] nm trinket
colimaçon [kɔlimasɔ̃] nm: **escalier en** ~ spiral staircase
colin [kɔlɛ̃] nm hake
colin-maillard [kɔlɛ̃majaR] nm (jeu) blind man's buff
colique [kɔlik] nf diarrhoea (Brit), diarrhea (US); (douleurs) colic (pains pl); (fam: personne ou chose ennuyeuse) pain
colis [kɔli] nm parcel; **par** ~ **postal** by parcel post
colistier, -ière [kɔlistje, -jɛR] nm/f fellow candidate
colite [kɔlit] nf colitis
coll. abr = **collection**; (= collaborateurs): **et** ~ et al
collaborateur, -trice [kɔlabɔRatœR, -tRis] nm/f (aussi Pol) collaborator; (d'une revue) contributor
collaboration [kɔlabɔRasjɔ̃] nf collaboration
collaborer [kɔlabɔRe] vi to collaborate; (aussi: **collaborer à**) to collaborate on; (revue) to contribute to
collage [kɔlaʒ] nm (Art) collage
collagène [kɔlaʒɛn] nm collagen
collant, e [kɔlɑ̃, -ɑ̃t] adj sticky; (robe etc) clinging, skintight; (péj) clinging ▷ nm (bas) tights pl
collatéral, e, -aux [kɔlateRal, -o] nm/f collateral
collation [kɔlasjɔ̃] nf light meal
colle [kɔl] nf glue; (à papiers peints) (wallpaper)

paste; *(devinette)* teaser, riddle; *(Scol fam)* detention; **~ forte** superglue®

collecte [kɔlɛkt(ə)] *nf* collection; **faire une ~** to take up a collection

collecter [kɔlɛkte] *vt* to collect

collecteur [kɔlɛktœʀ] *nm* (*égout*) main sewer

collectif, -ive [kɔlɛktif, -iv] *adj* collective; *(visite, billet etc)* group *cpd* ▷ *nm:* **~ budgétaire** mini-budget *(Brit)*, mid-term budget; **immeuble ~** block of flats

collection [kɔlɛksjɔ̃] *nf* collection; *(Édition)* series; **pièce de ~** collector's item; **faire (la) ~ de** to collect; **(toute) une ~ de ...** *(fig)* a (complete) set of ...

collectionner [kɔlɛksjɔne] *vt* (*tableaux, timbres*) to collect

collectionneur, -euse [kɔlɛksjɔnœʀ, -øz] *nm/f* collector

collectivement [kɔlɛktivmɑ̃] *adv* collectively

collectiviser [kɔlɛktivize] *vt* to collectivize

collectivisme [kɔlɛktivism(ə)] *nm* collectivism

collectiviste [kɔlɛktivist(ə)] *adj* collectivist

collectivité [kɔlɛktivite] *nf* group; **la ~** the community, the collectivity; **les ~s locales** local authorities

collège [kɔlɛʒ] *nm* (*école*) (secondary) school; *see note*; *(assemblée)* body; **~ électoral** electoral college

● **COLLÈGE**
●
● A *collège* is a state secondary school for
● children between 11 and 15 years of age.
● Pupils follow a national curriculum which
● prescribes a common core along with
● several options. Schools are free to arrange
● their own timetable and choose their own
● teaching methods. Before leaving this
● phase of their education, students are
● assessed by examination and course work
● for their "brevet des collèges".

collégial, e, -aux [kɔleʒjal, -o] *adj* collegiate

collégien, ne [kɔleʒjɛ̃, -ɛn] *nm/f* secondary school pupil *(Brit)*, high school student *(US)*

collègue [kɔlɛg] *nm/f* colleague

coller [kɔle] *vt* (*papier, timbre*) to stick (on); *(affiche)* to stick up; *(appuyer, placer contre)*: **~ son front à la vitre** to press one's face to the window; *(enveloppe)* to stick down; *(morceaux)* to stick *ou* glue together; *(fam: mettre, fourrer)* to stick, shove; *(Scol fam)* to keep in, give detention to ▷ *vi* (*être collant*) to be sticky; *(adhérer)* to stick; **~ qch sur** to stick (*ou* paste *ou* glue) sth on(to); **~ à** to stick to; *(fig)* to cling to

collerette [kɔlʀɛt] *nf* ruff; *(Tech)* flange

collet [kɔlɛ] *nm* (*piège*) snare, noose; *(cou):* **prendre qn au ~** to grab sb by the throat; **~ monté** *adj inv* straight-laced

colleter [kɔlte] *vt* (*adversaire*) to collar, grab by the throat; **se ~ avec** to wrestle with

colleur [kɔlœʀ] *nm:* **~ d'affiches** bill-poster

collier [kɔlje] *nm* (*bijou*) necklace; *(de chien, Tech)* collar; **~ (de barbe), barbe en ~** narrow beard along the line of the jaw; **~ de serrage** choke collar

collimateur [kɔlimatœʀ] *nm:* **être dans le ~** *(fig)* to be in the firing line; **avoir qn/qch dans le ~** *(fig)* to have sb/sth in one's sights

colline [kɔlin] *nf* hill

collision [kɔlizjɔ̃] *nf* collision, crash; **entrer en ~ (avec)** to collide (with)

colloque [kɔlɔk] *nm* colloquium, symposium

collusion [kɔlyzjɔ̃] *nf* collusion

collutoire [kɔlytwaʀ] *nm* (*Méd*) oral medication; *(en bombe)* throat spray

collyre [kɔliʀ] *nm* (*Méd*) eye lotion

colmater [kɔlmate] *vt* (*fuite*) to seal off; *(brèche)* to plug, fill in

Cologne [kɔlɔɲ] *n* Cologne

colombage [kɔlɔ̃baʒ] *nm* half-timbering; **une maison à ~s** a half-timbered house

colombe [kɔlɔ̃b] *nf* dove

Colombie [kɔlɔ̃bi] *nf:* **la ~** Colombia

colombien, ne [kɔlɔ̃bjɛ̃, -ɛn] *adj* Colombian ▷ *nm/f:* **Colombien, ne** Colombian

colon [kɔlɔ̃] *nm* settler; *(enfant)* boarder (*in children's holiday camp*)

côlon [kolɔ̃] *nm* colon (*Méd*)

colonel [kɔlɔnɛl] *nm* colonel; *(de l'armée de l'air)* group captain

colonial, e, -aux [kɔlɔnjal, -o] *adj* colonial

colonialisme [kɔlɔnjalism(ə)] *nm* colonialism

colonialiste [kɔlɔnjalist(ə)] *adj, nm/f* colonialist

colonie [kɔlɔni] *nf* colony; **~ (de vacances)** holiday camp (*for children*)

colonisation [kɔlɔnizɑsjɔ̃] *nf* colonization

coloniser [kɔlɔnize] *vt* to colonize

colonnade [kɔlɔnad] *nf* colonnade

colonne [kɔlɔn] *nf* column; **se mettre en ~ par deux/quatre** to get into twos/fours; **en ~ par deux** in double file; **~ de secours** rescue party; **~ (vertébrale)** spine, spinal column

colonnette [kɔlɔnɛt] *nf* small column

colophane [kɔlɔfan] *nf* rosin

colorant [kɔlɔʀɑ̃] *nm* colo(u)ring

coloration [kɔlɔʀɑsjɔ̃] *nf* colour(ing) (*Brit*), color(ing) (*US*); **se faire faire une ~** (*chez le coiffeur*) to have one's hair dyed

coloré, e [kɔlɔʀe] *adj* (*fig*) colo(u)rful

colorer [kɔlɔʀe] *vt* to colour (*Brit*), color (*US*); **se colorer** *vi* to turn red; to blush

coloriage [kɔlɔʀjaʒ] *nm* colo(u)ring

colorier [kɔlɔʀje] *vt* to colo(u)r (in); **album à ~** colouring book

coloris [kɔlɔʀi] *nm* colo(u)r, shade

coloriste [kɔlɔʀist(ə)] *nm/f* colo(u)rist

colossal, e, -aux [kɔlɔsal, -o] *adj* colossal, huge

colosse [kɔlɔs] *nm* giant

colostrum [kɔlɔstʀɔm] *nm* colostrum

colporter [kɔlpɔʀte] *vt* to peddle

colporteur, -euse [kɔlpɔʀtœʀ, -øz] *nm/f*

hawker, pedlar

colt [kɔlt] *nm* revolver, Colt®

coltiner [kɔltine] *vt* to lug about

colza [kɔlza] *nm* rape(seed)

coma [kɔma] *nm* coma; **être dans le ~** to be in a coma

comateux, -euse [kɔmatø, -øz] *adj* comatose

combat [kɔ̃ba] *vb voir* **combattre** ▷ *nm* fight; fighting *no pl*; **~ de boxe** boxing match; **~ de rues** street fighting *no pl*; **~ singulier** single combat

combatif, -ive [kɔ̃batif, -iv] *adj* with a lot of fight

combativité [kɔ̃bativite] *nf* fighting spirit

combattant [kɔ̃batɑ̃] *vb voir* **combattre** ▷ *nm* combatant; (*d'une rixe*) brawler; **ancien ~** war veteran

combattre [kɔ̃batʀ(ə)] *vi* to fight ▷ *vt* to fight; (*épidémie, ignorance*) to combat

combien [kɔ̃bjɛ̃] *adv* (*quantité*) how much; (*nombre*) how many; (*exclamatif*) how; **~ de** how much; how many; **~ de temps** how long, how much time; **c'est ~?, ça fait ~?** how much is it?; **~ coûte/pèse ceci?** how much does this cost/weigh?; **vous mesurez ~?** what size are you?; **ça fait ~ en largeur?** how wide is that?

combinaison [kɔ̃binɛzɔ̃] *nf* combination; (*astuce*) device, scheme; (*de femme*) slip; (*d'aviateur*) flying suit; (*d'homme-grenouille*) wetsuit; (*bleu de travail*) boilersuit (*Brit*), coveralls *pl* (*US*)

combine [kɔ̃bin] *nf* trick; (*péj*) scheme, fiddle (*Brit*)

combiné [kɔ̃bine] *nm* (*aussi:* **combiné téléphonique**) receiver; (*Ski*) combination (event); (*vêtement de femme*) corselet

combiner [kɔ̃bine] *vt* to combine; (*plan, horaire*) to work out, devise

comble [kɔ̃bl(ə)] *adj* (*salle*) packed (full) ▷ *nm* (*du bonheur, plaisir*) height; **combles** *nmpl* (*Constr*) attic *sg*, loft *sg*; **de fond en ~** from top to bottom; **pour ~ de malchance** to cap it all; **c'est le ~!** that beats everything!, that takes the biscuit! (*Brit*); **sous les ~s** in the attic

combler [kɔ̃ble] *vt* (*trou*) to fill in; (*besoin, lacune*) to fill; (*déficit*) to make good; (*satisfaire*) to gratify, fulfil (*Brit*), fulfill (*US*); **~ qn de joie** to fill sb with joy; **~ qn d'honneurs** to shower sb with honours

combustible [kɔ̃bystibl(ə)] *adj* combustible ▷ *nm* fuel

combustion [kɔ̃bystjɔ̃] *nf* combustion

COMECON [kɔmekɔn] *sigle m* Comecon

comédie [kɔmedi] *nf* comedy; (*fig*) playacting *no pl*; **jouer la ~** (*fig*) to put on an act; **la C~ française**; *see note*; **~ musicale** musical

comédien, ne [kɔmedjɛ̃, -ɛn] *nm/f* actor/actress; (*comique*) comedy actor/actress, comedian/comedienne; (*fig*) sham

comestible [kɔmɛstibl(ə)] *adj* edible; **comestibles** *nmpl* foods

comète [kɔmɛt] *nf* comet

comice [kɔmis] *nm:* **~ agricole** agricultural show

comique [kɔmik] *adj* (*drôle*) comical; (*Théât*) comic ▷ *nm* (*artiste*) comic, comedian; **le ~ de qch** the funny *ou* comical side of sth

comité [kɔmite] *nm* committee; **petit ~** select group; **~ directeur** management committee; **~ d'entreprise (CE)** works council; **~ des fêtes** festival committee

commandant [kɔmɑ̃dɑ̃] *nm* (*gén*) commander, commandant; (*Mil: grade*) major; (: *armée de l'air*) squadron leader; (*Navig*) captain; **~ (de bord)** (*Aviat*) captain

commande [kɔmɑ̃d] *nf* (*Comm*) order; (*Inform*) command; **commandes** *nfpl* (*Aviat etc*) controls; **passer une ~ (de)** to put in an order (for); **sur ~** to order; **~ à distance** remote control; **véhicule à double ~** vehicle with dual controls

commandement [kɔmɑ̃dmɑ̃] *nm* command; (*ordre*) command, order; (*Rel*) commandment

commander [kɔmɑ̃de] *vt* (*Comm*) to order; (*diriger, ordonner*) to command; **~ à** (*Mil*) to command; (*contrôler, maîtriser*) to have control over; **~ à qn de faire** to command *ou* order sb to do

commanditaire [kɔmɑ̃ditɛʀ] *nm* sleeping (*Brit*) *ou* silent (*US*) partner

commandite [kɔmɑ̃dit] *nf:* **(société en) ~** limited partnership

commanditer [kɔmɑ̃dite] *vt* (*Comm*) to finance, back; to commission

commando [kɔmɑ̃do] *nm* commando (squad)

 MOT-CLÉ

comme [kɔm] *prép* **1** (*comparaison*) like; **tout comme son père** just like his father; **fort comme un bœuf** as strong as an ox; **joli comme tout** ever so pretty

2 (*manière*) like; **faites-le comme ça** do it like this, do it this way; **comme ça ou cela on n'aura pas d'ennuis** that way we won't have any problems; **comme ci, comme ça** so-so, middling; **comment ça va? — comme ça** how are things? — OK; **comme on dit** as they say

3 (*en tant que*) as a; **donner comme prix** to give as a prize; **travailler comme secrétaire** to work as a secretary

4: **comme quoi** (*d'où il s'ensuit que*) which shows that; **il a écrit une lettre comme quoi il ...** he's written a letter saying that ...

5: **comme il faut** *adv* properly

▷ *adj* (*correct*) proper, correct

▷ *conj* **1** (*ainsi que*) as; **elle écrit comme elle parle** she writes as she talks; **comme si** as if **2** (*au moment où, alors que*) as; **il est parti comme j'arrivais** he left as I arrived **3** (*parce que, puisque*) as, since; **comme il était en retard, il … ** as he was late, he …

▷ *adv*: **comme il est fort/c'est bon!** he's so strong/it's so good!; **il est malin comme c'est pas permis** he's as smart as anything

commémoratif, -ive [kɔmɛmɔratif, -iv] *adj* commemorative; **un monument ~** a memorial
commémoration [kɔmemɔʀasjɔ̃] *nf* commemoration
commémorer [kɔmemɔʀe] *vt* to commemorate
commencement [kɔmɑ̃smɑ̃] *nm* beginning, start, commencement; **commencements** *nmpl* (*débuts*) beginnings
commencer [kɔmɑ̃se] *vt* to begin, start, commence ▷ *vi* to begin, start, commence; **~ à** *ou* **de faire** to begin *ou* start doing; **~ par qch** to begin with sth; **~ par faire qch** to begin by doing sth
commensal, e, -aux [kɔmɑ̃sal, -o] *nm/f* companion at table
comment [kɔmɑ̃] *adv* how; **~?** (*que dites-vous*) (I beg your) pardon?; **~!** what! ▷ *nm*: **le ~ et le pourquoi** the whys and wherefores; **et ~!** and how!; **~ donc!** of course!; **~ faire?** how will we do it?; **~ se fait-il que …?** how is it that …?
commentaire [kɔmɑ̃tɛʀ] *nm* comment; remark; **~ (de texte)** (*Scol*) commentary; **~ sur image** voice-over
commentateur, -trice [kɔmɑ̃tatœʀ, -tʀis] *nm/f* commentator
commenter [kɔmɑ̃te] *vt* (*jugement, événement*) to comment (up)on; (*Radio, TV*: *match, manifestation*) to cover, give a commentary on
commérages [kɔmeʀaʒ] *nmpl* gossip *sg*
commerçant, e [kɔmɛʀsɑ̃, -ɑ̃t] *adj* commercial; trading; (*rue*) shopping *cpd*; (*personne*) commercially shrewd ▷ *nm/f* shopkeeper, trader
commerce [kɔmɛʀs(ə)] *nm* (*activité*) trade, commerce; (*boutique*) business; **le petit ~** small shop owners *pl*, small traders *pl*; **faire ~ de** to trade in; (*fig: péj*) to trade on; **chambre de ~** Chamber of Commerce; **livres de ~** (account) books; **vendu dans le ~** sold in the shops; **vendu hors-~** sold directly to the public; **~ en** *ou* **de gros/détail** wholesale/retail trade; **~ électronique** e-commerce; **~ équitable** fair trade; **~ intérieur/extérieur** home/foreign trade
commercer [kɔmɛʀse] *vi*: **~ avec** to trade with
commercial, e, -aux [kɔmɛʀsjal, -o] *adj* commercial, trading; (*péj*) commercial ▷ *nm*: **les commerciaux** the commercial people
commercialisable [kɔmɛʀsjalizabl(ə)] *adj* marketable
commercialisation [kɔmɛʀsjalizasjɔ̃] *nf* marketing
commercialiser [kɔmɛʀsjalize] *vt* to market
commère [kɔmɛʀ] *nf* gossip
commettant [kɔmetɑ̃] *vb voir* **commettre** ▷ *nm* (*Jur*) principal
commettre [kɔmɛtʀ(ə)] *vt* to commit; **se commettre** *vi* to compromise one's good name
commis¹ [kɔmi] *nm* (*de magasin*) (shop) assistant (*Brit*), sales clerk (*US*); (*de banque*) clerk; **~ voyageur** commercial traveller (*Brit*) *ou* traveler (*US*)
commis², e [kɔmi, -iz] *pp de* **commettre**
commisération [kɔmizeʀasjɔ̃] *nf* commiseration
commissaire [kɔmisɛʀ] *nm* (*de police*) ≈ (police) superintendent (*Brit*), ≈ (police) captain (*US*); (*de rencontre sportive etc*) steward; **~ du bord** (*Navig*) purser; **~ aux comptes** (*Admin*) auditor
commissaire-priseur [kɔmisɛʀpʀizœʀ] (*pl* **commissaires-priseurs**) *nm* (official) auctioneer
commissariat [kɔmisaʀja] *nm*: **~ (de police)** police station; (*Admin*) commissionership
commission [kɔmisjɔ̃] *nf* (*comité, pourcentage*) commission; (*message*) message; (*course*) errand; **commissions** *nfpl* (*achats*) shopping *sg*; **~ d'examen** examining board
commissionnaire [kɔmisjɔnɛʀ] *nm* delivery boy (*ou* man); messenger; (*Transports*) (forwarding) agent
commissure [kɔmisyʀ] *nf*: **les ~s des lèvres** the corners of the mouth
commode [kɔmɔd] *adj* (*pratique*) convenient, handy; (*facile*) easy; (*air, personne*) easy-going; (*personne*): **pas ~** awkward (to deal with) ▷ *nf* chest of drawers
commodité [kɔmɔdite] *nf* convenience
commotion [kɔmosjɔ̃] *nf*: **~ (cérébrale)** concussion
commotionné, e [kɔmosjɔne] *adj* shocked, shaken
commuer [kɔmɥe] *vt* to commute
commun, e [kɔmœ̃, -yn] *adj* common; (*pièce*) communal, shared; (*réunion, effort*) joint ▷ *nf* (*Admin*) commune, ≈ district; (*: urbaine*) ≈ borough; **communs** *nmpl* (*bâtiments*) outbuildings; **cela sort du ~** it's out of the ordinary; **le ~ des mortels** the common run of people; **sans ~e mesure** incomparable; **être ~ à** (*chose*) to be shared by; **en ~** (*faire*) jointly; **mettre en ~** to pool, share; **peu ~** unusual; **d'un ~ accord** of one accord; with one accord
communal, e, -aux [kɔmynal, -o] *adj* (*Admin*) of the commune, ≈ (district *ou* borough) council *cpd*
communard, e [kɔmynaʀ, -aʀd(ə)] *nm/f* (*Hist*) Communard; (*péj: communiste*) commie
communautaire [kɔmynotɛʀ] *adj* community *cpd*
communauté [kɔmynote] *nf* community; (*Jur*): **régime de la ~** communal estate settlement
commune [kɔmyn] *adj f, nf voir* **commun**

communément [kɔmynemɑ̃] *adv* commonly

Communes [kɔmyn] *nfpl* (*en Grande-Bretagne: parlement*) Commons

communiant, e [kɔmynjɑ̃, -ɑ̃t] *nm/f* communicant; **premier ~** child taking his first communion

communicant, e [kɔmynikɑ̃, -ɑ̃t] *adj* communicating

communicatif, -ive [kɔmynikatif, -iv] *adj* (*personne*) communicative; (*rire*) infectious

communication [kɔmynikasjɔ̃] *nf* communication; **~ (téléphonique)** (telephone) call; **avoir la ~ (avec)** to get *ou* be through (to); **vous avez la ~** you're through; **donnez-moi la ~ avec** put me through to; **mettre qn en ~ avec qn** (*en contact*) to put sb in touch with sb; (*au téléphone*) to connect sb with sb; **~ interurbaine** long-distance call; **~ en PCV** reverse charge (*Brit*) *ou* collect (*US*) call; **~ avec préavis** personal call

communier [kɔmynje] *vi* (*Rel*) to receive communion; (*fig*) to be united

communion [kɔmynjɔ̃] *nf* communion

communiqué [kɔmynike] *nm* communiqué; **~ de presse** press release

communiquer [kɔmynike] *vt* (*nouvelle, dossier*) to pass on, convey; (*maladie*) to pass on; (*peur etc*) to communicate; (*chaleur, mouvement*) to transmit ▷ *vi* to communicate; **~ avec** (*salle*) to communicate with; **se ~ à** (*se propager*) to spread to

communisme [kɔmynism(ə)] *nm* communism

communiste [kɔmynist(ə)] *adj, nm/f* communist

commutateur [kɔmytatœʀ] *nm* (*Élec*) (change-over) switch, commutator

commutation [kɔmytasjɔ̃] *nf* (*Inform*): **~ de messages** message switching; **~ de paquets** packet switching

Comores [kɔmɔʀ] *nfpl*: **les (îles) ~** the Comoros (Islands)

comorien, ne [kɔmɔʀjɛ̃, -ɛn] *adj* of *ou* from the Comoros

compact, e [kɔ̃pakt] *adj* dense; compact

compagne [kɔ̃paɲ] *nf* companion

compagnie [kɔ̃paɲi] *nf* (*firme, Mil*) company; (*groupe*) gathering; (*présence*): **la ~ de qn** sb's company; **homme/femme de ~** escort; **tenir ~ à qn** to keep sb company; **fausser ~ à qn** to give sb the slip, slip *ou* sneak away from sb; **en ~ de** in the company of; **Dupont et ~**, **Dupont et Cie** Dupont and Company, Dupont and Co; **~ aérienne** airline (company)

compagnon [kɔ̃paɲɔ̃] *nm* companion; (*autrefois: ouvrier*) craftsman; journeyman

comparable [kɔ̃paʀabl(ə)] *adj*: **~ (à)** comparable (to)

comparaison [kɔ̃paʀɛzɔ̃] *nf* comparison; (*métaphore*) simile; **en ~ (de)** in comparison (with); **par ~ (à)** by comparison (with)

comparaître [kɔ̃paʀɛtʀ(ə)] *vi*: **~ (devant)** to appear (before)

comparatif, -ive [kɔ̃paʀatif, -iv] *adj, nm* comparative

comparativement [kɔ̃paʀativmɑ̃] *adv* comparatively; **~ à** by comparison with

comparé, e [kɔ̃paʀe] *adj*: **littérature** *etc* **~e** comparative literature *etc*

comparer [kɔ̃paʀe] *vt* to compare; **~ qch/qn à** *ou* **et** (*pour choisir*) to compare sth/sb with *ou* and; (*pour établir une similitude*) to compare sth/sb to *ou* and

comparse [kɔ̃paʀs(ə)] *nm/f* (*péj*) associate, stooge

compartiment [kɔ̃paʀtimɑ̃] *nm* compartment

compartimenté, e [kɔ̃paʀtimɑ̃te] *adj* partitioned; (*fig*) compartmentalized

comparu, e [kɔ̃paʀy] *pp de* **comparaître**

comparution [kɔ̃paʀysjɔ̃] *nf* appearance

compas [kɔ̃pa] *nm* (*Géom*) (pair of) compasses *pl*; (*Navig*) compass

compassé, e [kɔ̃pase] *adj* starchy, formal

compassion [kɔ̃pasjɔ̃] *nf* compassion

compatibilité [kɔ̃patibilite] *nf* compatibility

compatible [kɔ̃patibl(ə)] *adj*: **~ (avec)** compatible (with)

compatir [kɔ̃patiʀ] *vi*: **~ (à)** to sympathize (with)

compatissant, e [kɔ̃patisɑ̃, -ɑ̃t] *adj* sympathetic

compatriote [kɔ̃patʀijɔt] *nm/f* compatriot, fellow countryman/woman

compensateur, -trice [kɔ̃pɑ̃satœʀ, -tʀis] *adj* compensatory

compensation [kɔ̃pɑ̃sasjɔ̃] *nf* compensation; (*Banque*) clearing; **en ~** *ou* as compensation

compensé, e [kɔ̃pɑ̃se] *adj*: **semelle ~e** platform sole

compenser [kɔ̃pɑ̃se] *vt* to compensate for, make up for

compère [kɔ̃pɛʀ] *nm* accomplice; fellow musician *ou* comedian *etc*

compétence [kɔ̃petɑ̃s] *nf* competence

compétent, e [kɔ̃petɑ̃, -ɑ̃t] *adj* (*apte*) competent, capable; (*Jur*) competent

compétitif, -ive [kɔ̃petitif, -iv] *adj* competitive

compétition [kɔ̃petisjɔ̃] *nf* (*gén*) competition; (*Sport: épreuve*) event; **la ~** competitive sport; **être en ~ avec** to be competing with; **la ~ automobile** motor racing

compétitivité [kɔ̃petitivite] *nf* competitiveness

compilateur [kɔ̃pilatœʀ] *nm* (*Inform*) compiler

compiler [kɔ̃pile] *vt* to compile

complainte [kɔ̃plɛ̃t] *nf* lament

complaire [kɔ̃plɛʀ]: **se complaire** *vi*: **se ~ dans/parmi** to take pleasure in/in being among

complaisais *etc* [kɔ̃plɛzɛ] *vb voir* **complaire**

complaisamment [kɔ̃plɛzamɑ̃] *adv* kindly; complacently

complaisance [kɔ̃plɛzɑ̃s] *nf* kindness; (*péj*) indulgence; (*: fatuité*) complacency; **attestation de ~** *certificate produced to oblige a patient etc*; **pavillon de ~** flag of convenience

complaisant, e [kɔ̃plɛzɑ̃, -ɑ̃t] *vb voir* **complaire**

▷ adj (aimable) kind; obliging; (péj) accommodating; (: fat) complacent

complaît [kɔ̃plɛ] vb voir **complaire**

complément [kɔ̃plemɑ̃] nm complement; (reste) remainder; (Ling) complement; ~ **d'information** (Admin) supplementary ou further information; ~ **d'agent** agent; ~ **(d'objet) direct/indirect** direct/indirect object; ~ **(circonstanciel) de lieu/temps** adverbial phrase of place/time; ~ **de nom** possessive phrase

complémentaire [kɔ̃plemɑ̃tɛʀ] adj complementary; (additionnel) supplementary

complet, -ète [kɔ̃plɛ, -ɛt] adj complete; (plein: hôtel etc) full ▷ nm (aussi: **complet-veston**) suit; **au (grand)** ~ all together

complètement [kɔ̃plɛtmɑ̃] adv (en entier) completely; (absolument: fou, faux etc) absolutely; (à fond: étudier etc) fully, in depth

compléter [kɔ̃plete] vt (porter à la quantité voulue) to complete; (augmenter) to complement, supplement; to add to; **se compléter** vi (personnes) to complement one another; (collection etc) to become complete

complexe [kɔ̃plɛks(ə)] adj complex ▷ nm (Psych) complex, hang-up; (bâtiments): ~ **hospitalier/industriel** hospital/industrial complex

complexé, e [kɔ̃plɛkse] adj mixed-up, hung-up

complexité [kɔ̃plɛksite] nf complexity

complication [kɔ̃plikɑsjɔ̃] nf complexity, intricacy; (difficulté, ennui) complication; **complications** nfpl (Méd) complications

complice [kɔ̃plis] nm accomplice

complicité [kɔ̃plisite] nf complicity

compliment [kɔ̃plimɑ̃] nm (louange) compliment; **compliments** nmpl (félicitations) congratulations

complimenter [kɔ̃plimɑ̃te] vt: ~ **qn (sur** ou **de)** to congratulate ou compliment sb (on)

compliqué, e [kɔ̃plike] adj complicated, complex, intricate; (personne) complicated

compliquer [kɔ̃plike] vt to complicate; **se compliquer** vi (situation) to become complicated; **se ~ la vie** to make life difficult ou complicated for o.s

complot [kɔ̃plo] nm plot

comploter [kɔ̃plɔte] vi, vt to plot

complu, e [kɔ̃ply] pp de **complaire**

comportement [kɔ̃pɔʀtəmɑ̃] nm behaviour (Brit), behavior (US); (Tech: d'une pièce, d'un véhicule) behavio(u)r, performance

comporter [kɔ̃pɔʀte] vt to be composed of, consist of, comprise; (être équipé de) to have; (impliquer) to entail, involve; **se comporter** vi to behave; (Tech) to behave, perform

composant [kɔ̃pozɑ̃] nm component, constituent

composante [kɔ̃pozɑ̃t] nf component

composé, e [kɔ̃poze] adj (visage, air) studied; (Bio, Chimie, Ling) compound ▷ nm (Chimie, Ling) compound; ~ **de** made up of

composer [kɔ̃poze] vt (musique, texte) to

compose; (mélange, équipe) to make up; (faire partie de) to make up, form; (Typo) to (type)set ▷ vi (Scol) to sit ou do a test; (transiger) to come to terms; **se ~ de** to be composed of, be made up of; ~ **un numéro** (au téléphone) to dial a number

composite [kɔ̃pozit] adj heterogeneous

compositeur, -trice [kɔ̃pozitœʀ, -tʀis] nm/f (Mus) composer; (Typo) compositor, typesetter

composition [kɔ̃pozisjɔ̃] nf composition; (Scol) test; (Typo) (type)setting, composition; **de bonne** ~ (accommodant) easy to deal with; **amener qn à** ~ to get sb to come to terms; ~ **française** (Scol) French essay

compost [kɔ̃pɔst] nm compost

composter [kɔ̃pɔste] vt to date-stamp; to punch

composteur [kɔ̃pɔstœʀ] nm date stamp; punch; (Typo) composing stick

compote [kɔ̃pɔt] nf stewed fruit no pl; ~ **de pommes** stewed apples

compotier [kɔ̃pɔtje] nm fruit dish ou bowl

compréhensible [kɔ̃pʀeɑ̃sibl(ə)] adj comprehensible; (attitude) understandable

compréhensif, -ive [kɔ̃pʀeɑ̃sif, -iv] adj understanding

compréhension [kɔ̃pʀeɑ̃sjɔ̃] nf understanding; comprehension

comprendre [kɔ̃pʀɑ̃dʀ(ə)] vt to understand; (se composer de) to comprise, consist of; (inclure) to include; **se faire** ~ to make o.s. understood; to get one's ideas across; **mal** ~ to misunderstand

compresse [kɔ̃pʀɛs] nf compress

compresser [kɔ̃pʀese] vt to squash in, crush together; (Inform) to zip

compresseur [kɔ̃pʀesœʀ] adj m voir **rouleau**

compressible [kɔ̃pʀesibl(ə)] adj (Physique) compressible; (dépenses) reducible

compression [kɔ̃pʀesjɔ̃] nf compression; (d'un crédit etc) reduction

comprimé, e [kɔ̃pʀime] adj: **air** ~ compressed air ▷ nm tablet

comprimer [kɔ̃pʀime] vt to compress; (fig: crédit etc) to reduce, cut down

compris, e [kɔ̃pʀi, -iz] pp de **comprendre** ▷ adj (inclus) included; ~? understood?, is that clear?; ~ **entre** (situé) contained between; **la maison** ~**e/non** ~**e, y/non** ~ **la maison** including/excluding the house; **service** ~ service (charge) included; **100 euros tout** ~ 100 euros all inclusive ou all-in

compromettant, e [kɔ̃pʀɔmetɑ̃, -ɑ̃t] adj compromising

compromettre [kɔ̃pʀɔmɛtʀ(ə)] vt to compromise

compromis [kɔ̃pʀɔmi] vb voir **compromettre** ▷ nm compromise

compromission [kɔ̃pʀɔmisjɔ̃] nf compromise, deal

comptabiliser [kɔ̃tabilize] vt (valeur) to post; (fig) to evaluate

comptabilité [kɔ̃tabilite] nf (activité, technique) accounting, accountancy; (d'une société: comptes) accounts *pl*, books *pl*; (: *service*) accounts office *ou* department; **~ à partie double** double-entry book-keeping

comptable [kɔ̃tabl(ə)] *nm/f* accountant ▷ *adj* accounts *cpd*, accounting

comptant [kɔ̃tɑ̃] *adv*: **payer ~** to pay cash; **acheter ~** to buy for cash

compte [kɔ̃t] *nm* count, counting; (*total, montant*) count, (right) number; (*bancaire, facture*) account; **comptes** *nmpl* accounts, books; (*fig*) explanation *sg*; **ouvrir un ~** to open an account; **rendre des ~s à qn** (*fig*) to be answerable to sb; **faire le ~ de** to count up, make a count of; **tout ~ fait** on the whole; **à ce ~-là** (*dans ce cas*) in that case; (*à ce train-là*) at that rate; **en fin de ~** (*fig*) all things considered, weighing it all up; **au bout du ~** in the final analysis; **à bon ~** at a favourable price; (*fig*) lightly; **avoir son ~** (*fig: fam*) to have had it; **pour le ~ de** on behalf of; **pour son propre ~** for one's own benefit; **sur le ~ de qn** (*à son sujet*) about sb; **travailler à son ~** to work for oneself; **mettre qch sur le ~ de qn** (*le rendre responsable*) to attribute sth to sb; **prendre qch à son ~** to take responsibility for sth; **trouver son ~ à qch** to do well out of sth; **régler un ~** (*s'acquitter de qch*) to settle an account; (*se venger*) to get one's own back; **rendre ~ (à qn) de qch** to give (sb) an account of sth; **tenir ~ de qch** to take sth into account; **~ tenu de** taking into account; **~ en banque** bank account; **~ chèque(s)** current account; **~ chèque postal (CCP)** Post Office account; **~ client** (*sur bilan*) accounts receivable; **~ courant (CC)** current account; **~ de dépôt** deposit account; **~ d'exploitation** operating account; **~ fournisseur** (*sur bilan*) accounts payable; **~ à rebours** countdown; **~ rendu** account, report; (*de film, livre*) review; *voir aussi* **rendre**

compte-gouttes [kɔ̃tgut] *nm inv* dropper

compter [kɔ̃te] *vt* to count; (*facturer*) to charge for; (*avoir à son actif, comporter*) to have; (*prévoir*) to allow, reckon; (*tenir compte de, inclure*) to include; (*penser, espérer*): **~ réussir/revenir** to expect to succeed/return ▷ *vi* to count; (*être économe*) to economize; (*être non négligeable*) to count, matter; (*valoir*): **~ pour** to count for; (*figurer*): **~ parmi** to be *ou* rank among; **~ sur** to count (up)on; **~ avec qch/qn** to reckon with *ou* take account of sth/sb; **~ sans qch/qn** to reckon without sth/sb; **sans ~ que** besides which; **à ~ du 10 janvier** (*Comm*) (as) from 10th January

compte-tours [kɔ̃ttuʀ] *nm inv* rev(olution) counter

compteur [kɔ̃tœʀ] *nm* meter; **~ de vitesse** speedometer

comptine [kɔ̃tin] *nf* nursery rhyme

comptoir [kɔ̃twaʀ] *nm* (*de magasin*) counter; (*de café*) counter, bar; (*colonial*) trading post

compulser [kɔ̃pylse] *vt* to consult

comte, comtesse [kɔ̃t, kɔ̃tɛs] *nm/f* count/countess

con, ne [kɔ̃, kɔn] *adj* (*fam!*) bloody (*Brit*) *ou* damned stupid (*!*)

concasser [kɔ̃kase] *vt* (*pierre, sucre*) to crush; (*poivre*) to grind

concave [kɔ̃kav] *adj* concave

concéder [kɔ̃sede] *vt* to grant; (*défaite, point*) to concede; **~ que** to concede that

concentration [kɔ̃sɑ̃tʀasjɔ̃] *nf* concentration

concentrationnaire [kɔ̃sɑ̃tʀasjɔnɛʀ] *adj* of *ou* in concentration camps

concentré [kɔ̃sɑ̃tʀe] *nm* concentrate; **~ de tomates** tomato purée

concentrer [kɔ̃sɑ̃tʀe] *vt* to concentrate; **se concentrer** to concentrate

concentrique [kɔ̃sɑ̃tʀik] *adj* concentric

concept [kɔ̃sɛpt] *nm* concept

concepteur, -trice [kɔ̃sɛptœʀ, -tʀis] *nm/f* designer

conception [kɔ̃sɛpsjɔ̃] *nf* conception; (*d'une machine etc*) design

concernant [kɔ̃sɛʀnɑ̃] *prép* (*se rapportant à*) concerning; (*en ce qui concerne*) as regards

concerner [kɔ̃sɛʀne] *vt* to concern; **en ce qui me concerne** as far as I am concerned; **en ce qui concerne ceci** as far as this is concerned, with regard to this

concert [kɔ̃sɛʀ] *nm* concert; **de ~** *adv* in unison; together

concertation [kɔ̃sɛʀtasjɔ̃] *nf* (*échange de vues*) dialogue; (*rencontre*) meeting

concerter [kɔ̃sɛʀte] *vt* to devise; **se concerter** *vi* (*collaborateurs etc*) to put our (*ou* their *etc*) heads together, consult (each other)

concertiste [kɔ̃sɛʀtist(ə)] *nm/f* concert artist

concerto [kɔ̃sɛʀto] *nm* concerto

concession [kɔ̃sesjɔ̃] *nf* concession

concessionnaire [kɔ̃sesjɔnɛʀ] *nm/f* agent, dealer

concevable [kɔ̃svabl(ə)] *adj* conceivable

concevoir [kɔ̃svwaʀ] *vt* (*idée, projet*) to conceive (of); (*méthode, plan d'appartement, décoration etc*) to plan, design; (*enfant*) to conceive; **maison bien/mal conçue** well-/badly-designed *ou* -planned house

concierge [kɔ̃sjɛʀʒ(ə)] *nm/f* caretaker; (*d'hôtel*) head porter

conciergerie [kɔ̃sjɛʀʒəʀi] *nf* caretaker's lodge

concile [kɔ̃sil] *nm* council, synod

conciliable [kɔ̃siljabl(ə)] *adj* (*opinions etc*) reconcilable

conciliabules [kɔ̃siljabyl] *nmpl* (private) discussions, confabulations (*Brit*)

conciliant, e [kɔ̃siljɑ̃, -ɑ̃t] *adj* conciliatory

conciliateur, -trice [kɔ̃siljatœʀ, -tʀis] *nm/f* mediator, go-between

conciliation [kɔ̃siljasjɔ̃] *nf* conciliation

concilier [kɔ̃silje] *vt* to reconcile; **se concilier qn/l'appui de qn** to win sb over/sb's support

concis, e [kɔ̃si, -iz] *adj* concise

concision [kɔ̃sizjɔ̃] *nf* concision, conciseness

concitoyen, ne [kɔ̃sitwajɛ̃, -ɛn] *nm/f* fellow citizen

conclave [kɔ̃klav] *nm* conclave
concluant, e [kɔ̃klyã, -ãt] *vb voir* **conclure** ▷ *adj* conclusive
conclure [kɔ̃klyʀ] *vt* to conclude; (*signer: accord, pacte*) to enter into; (*déduire*): ~ **qch de qch** to deduce sth from sth; ~ **à l'acquittement** to decide in favour of an acquittal; ~ **au suicide** to come to the conclusion (*ou* (*Jur*) to pronounce) that it is a case of suicide; ~ **un marché** to clinch a deal; **j'en conclus que** from that I conclude that
conclusion [kɔ̃klyzjɔ̃] *nf* conclusion; **conclusions** *nfpl* (*Jur*) submissions; findings; **en** ~ in conclusion
concocter [kɔ̃kɔkte] *vt* to concoct
conçois [kɔ̃swa], **conçoive** *etc* [kɔ̃swav] *vb voir* **concevoir**
concombre [kɔ̃kɔ̃bʀ(ə)] *nm* cucumber
concomitant, e [kɔ̃kɔmitã, -ãt] *adj* concomitant
concordance [kɔ̃kɔʀdãs] *nf* concordance; **la** ~ **des temps** (*Ling*) the sequence of tenses
concordant, e [kɔ̃kɔʀdã, -ãt] *adj* (*témoignages, versions*) corroborating
concorde [kɔ̃kɔʀd(ə)] *nf* concord
concorder [kɔ̃kɔʀde] *vi* to tally, agree
concourir [kɔ̃kuʀiʀ] *vi* (*Sport*) to compete; ~ **à** *vt* (*effet etc*) to work towards
concours [kɔ̃kuʀ] *vb voir* **concourir** ▷ *nm* competition; (*Scol*) competitive examination; (*assistance*) aid, help; **recrutement par voie de** ~ recruitment by (competitive) examination; **apporter son** ~ **à** to give one's support to; ~ **de circonstances** combination of circumstances; ~ **hippique** horse show; *voir* **hors-concours**
concret, -ète [kɔ̃kʀɛ, -ɛt] *adj* concrete
concrètement [kɔ̃kʀɛtmã] *adv* in concrete terms
concrétisation [kɔ̃kʀetizasjɔ̃] *nf* realization
concrétiser [kɔ̃kʀetize] *vt* to realize; **se concrétiser** *vi* to materialize
conçu, e [kɔ̃sy] *pp de* **concevoir**
concubin, e [kɔ̃kybɛ̃, -in] *nm/f* (*Jur*) cohabitant
concubinage [kɔ̃kybinaʒ] *nm* (*Jur*) cohabitation
concupiscence [kɔ̃kypisãs] *nf* concupiscence
concurremment [kɔ̃kyʀamã] *adv* concurrently; jointly
concurrence [kɔ̃kyʀãs] *nf* competition; **jusqu'à** ~ **de** up to; ~ **déloyale** unfair competition
concurrencer [kɔ̃kyʀãse] *vt* to compete with; **ils nous concurrencent dangereusement** they are a serious threat to us
concurrent, e [kɔ̃kyʀã, -ãt] *adj* competing ▷ *nm/f* (*Sport, Écon etc*) competitor; (*Scol*) candidate
concurrentiel, le [kɔ̃kyʀãsjɛl] *adj* competitive
conçus [kɔ̃sy] *vb voir* **concevoir**
condamnable [kɔ̃danabl(ə)] *adj* (*action, opinion*) reprehensible
condamnation [kɔ̃danasjɔ̃] *nf* (*action*) condemnation; sentencing; (*peine*) sentence;

conviction; ~ **à mort** death sentence
condamné, e [kɔ̃dane] *nm/f* (*Jur*) convict
condamner [kɔ̃dane] *vt* (*blâmer*) to condemn; (*Jur*) to sentence; (*porte, ouverture*) to fill in, block up; (*malade*) to give up (hope for); (*obliger*): ~ **qn à qch/à faire** to condemn sb to sth/to do; ~ **qn à deux ans de prison** to sentence sb to two years' imprisonment; ~ **qn à une amende** to impose a fine on sb
condensateur [kɔ̃dãsatœʀ] *nm* condenser
condensation [kɔ̃dãsasjɔ̃] *nf* condensation
condensé [kɔ̃dãse] *nm* digest
condenser [kɔ̃dãse]: **se condenser** *vi* to condense
condescendance [kɔ̃desãdãs] *nf* condescension
condescendant, e [kɔ̃desãdã, -ãt] *adj* (*personne, attitude*) condescending
condescendre [kɔ̃desãdʀ(ə)] *vi*: ~ **à** to condescend to
condiment [kɔ̃dimã] *nm* condiment
condisciple [kɔ̃disipl(ə)] *nm/f* school fellow, fellow student
condition [kɔ̃disjɔ̃] *nf* condition; **conditions** *nfpl* (*tarif, prix*) terms; (*circonstances*) conditions; **sans** ~ *adj* unconditional ▷ *adv* unconditionally; **sous** ~ **que** on condition that; **à** ~ **de** *ou* **que** provided that; **en bonne** ~ in good condition; **mettre en** ~ (*Sport etc*) to get fit; (*Psych*) to condition (mentally); ~**s de vie** living conditions
conditionnel, le [kɔ̃disjɔnɛl] *adj* conditional ▷ *nm* conditional (tense)
conditionnement [kɔ̃disjɔnmã] *nm* (*emballage*) packaging; (*fig*) conditioning
conditionner [kɔ̃disjɔne] *vt* (*déterminer*) to determine; (*Comm: produit*) to package; (*fig: personne*) to condition; **air conditionné** air conditioning; **réflexe conditionné** conditioned reflex
condoléances [kɔ̃dɔleãs] *nfpl* condolences
conducteur, -trice [kɔ̃dyktœʀ, -tʀis] *adj* (*Élec*) conducting ▷ *nm/f* (*Auto etc*) driver; (*d'une machine*) operator ▷ *nm* (*Élec etc*) conductor
conduire [kɔ̃dɥiʀ] *vt* (*véhicule, passager*) to drive; (*délégation, troupeau*) to lead; **se conduire** *vi* to behave; ~ **vers/à** to lead towards/to; ~ **qn quelque part** to take sb somewhere; to drive sb somewhere
conduit, e [kɔ̃dɥi, -it] *pp de* **conduire** ▷ *nm* (*Tech*) conduit, pipe; (*Anat*) duct, canal
conduite [kɔ̃dɥit] *nf* (*en auto*) driving; (*comportement*) behaviour (*Brit*), behavior (*US*); (*d'eau, de gaz*) pipe; **sous la** ~ **de** led by; ~ **forcée** pressure pipe; ~ **à gauche** left-hand drive; ~ **intérieure** saloon (car)
cône [kon] *nm* cone; **en forme de** ~ cone-shaped
conf. *abr* = **confort**; **tt** ~ all mod cons (*Brit*)
confection [kɔ̃fɛksjɔ̃] *nf* (*fabrication*) making; (*Couture*): **la** ~ the clothing industry, the rag trade (*fam*); **vêtement de** ~ ready-to-wear *ou*

off-the-peg garment

confectionner [kɔ̃fɛksjɔne] vt to make

confédération [kɔ̃fedeRɑsjɔ̃] nf confederation

conférence [kɔ̃feRɑ̃s] nf (exposé) lecture; (pourparlers) conference; ~ **de presse** press conference; ~ **au sommet** summit (conference)

conférencier, -ière [kɔ̃feRɑ̃sje, -jɛR] nm/f lecturer

conférer [kɔ̃feRe] vt: ~ **à qn** (titre, grade) to confer on sb; ~ **à qch/qn** (aspect etc) to endow sth/sb with, give (to) sth/sb

confesser [kɔ̃fese] vt to confess; **se confesser** vi (Rel) to go to confession

confesseur [kɔ̃fesœR] nm confessor

confession [kɔ̃fɛsjɔ̃] nf confession; (culte: catholique etc) denomination

confessionnal, -aux [kɔ̃fesjɔnal, -o] nm confessional

confessionnel, le [kɔ̃fesjɔnɛl] adj denominational

confetti [kɔ̃feti] nm confetti no pl

confiance [kɔ̃fjɑ̃s] nf confidence, trust; faith; **avoir ~ en** to have confidence ou faith in, trust; **faire ~ à** to trust; **en toute ~** with complete confidence; **de ~** trustworthy, reliable; **mettre qn en ~** to win sb's trust; **vote de ~** (Pol) vote of confidence; **inspirer ~ à** to inspire confidence in; ~ **en soi** self-confidence; voir **question**

confiant, e [kɔ̃fjɑ̃, -ɑ̃t] adj confident; trusting

confidence [kɔ̃fidɑ̃s] nf confidence

confident, e [kɔ̃fidɑ̃, -ɑ̃t] nm/f confidant/confidante

confidentiel, le [kɔ̃fidɑ̃sjɛl] adj confidential

confidentiellement [kɔfidɑ̃sjɛlmɑ̃] adv in confidence, confidentially

confier [kɔ̃fje] vt: ~ **à qn** (objet en dépôt, travail etc) to entrust to sb; (secret, pensée) to confide to sb; **se confier à qn** to confide in sb

configuration [kɔ̃figyRɑsjɔ̃] nf configuration, layout; (Inform) configuration

configurer [kɔ̃figyRe] vt to configure

confiné, e [kɔ̃fine] adj enclosed; (air) stale

confiner [kɔ̃fine] vt: ~ **à** to confine to; (toucher) to border on; **se ~ dans** ou **à** to confine o.s. to

confins [kɔ̃fɛ̃] nmpl: **aux ~ de** on the borders of

confirmation [kɔ̃fiRmɑsjɔ̃] nf confirmation

confirmer [kɔ̃fiRme] vt to confirm; ~ **qn dans une croyance/ses fonctions** to strengthen sb in a belief/his duties

confiscation [kɔ̃fiskɑsjɔ̃] nf confiscation

confiserie [kɔ̃fizRi] nf (magasin) confectioner's ou sweet shop (Brit), candy store (US); **confiseries** nfpl (bonbons) confectionery sg, sweets, candy no pl

confiseur, -euse [kɔ̃fizœR, -øz] nm/f confectioner

confisquer [kɔ̃fiske] vt to confiscate

confit, e [kɔ̃fi, -it] adj: **fruits ~s** crystallized fruits ▷ nm: ~ **d'oie** potted goose

confiture [kɔ̃fityR] nf jam; ~ **d'oranges** (orange) marmalade

conflagration [kɔ̃flagRɑsjɔ̃] nf cataclysm

conflictuel, le [kɔ̃fliktɥɛl] adj full of clashes ou conflicts

conflit [kɔ̃fli] nm conflict

confluent [kɔ̃flyɑ̃] nm confluence

confondre [kɔ̃fɔ̃dR(ə)] vt (jumeaux, faits) to confuse, mix up; (témoin, menteur) to confound; **se confondre** vi to merge; **se ~ en excuses** to offer profuse apologies, apologize profusely; ~ **qch/qn avec qch/qn d'autre** to mistake sth/sb for sth/sb else

confondu, e [kɔ̃fɔ̃dy] pp de **confondre** ▷ adj (stupéfait) speechless, overcome; **toutes catégories ~es** taking all categories together

conformation [kɔ̃fɔRmɑsjɔ̃] nf conformation

conforme [kɔ̃fɔRm(ə)] adj: ~ **à** (en accord avec) in accordance with, in keeping with; (identique à) true to; **copie certifiée ~** (Admin) certified copy; ~ **à la commande** as per order

conformé, e [kɔ̃fɔRme] adj: **bien ~** well-formed

conformément [kɔ̃fɔRmemɑ̃] adv: ~ **à** in accordance with

conformer [kɔ̃fɔRme] vt: ~ **qch à** to model sth on; **se ~ à** to conform to

conformisme [kɔ̃fɔRmism(ə)] nm conformity

conformiste [kɔ̃fɔRmist(ə)] adj, nm/f conformist

conformité [kɔ̃fɔRmite] nf conformity; agreement; **en ~ avec** in accordance with

confort [kɔ̃fɔR] nm comfort; **tout ~** (Comm) with all mod cons (Brit) ou modern conveniences

confortable [kɔ̃fɔRtabl(ə)] adj comfortable

confortablement [kɔ̃fɔRtabləmɑ̃] adv comfortably

conforter [kɔ̃fɔRte] vt to reinforce, strengthen

confrère [kɔ̃fRɛR] nm colleague; fellow member

confrérie [kɔ̃fReRi] nf brotherhood

confrontation [kɔ̃fRɔ̃tɑsjɔ̃] nf confrontation

confronté, e [kɔ̃fRɔ̃te] adj: ~ **à** confronted by, facing

confronter [kɔ̃fRɔ̃te] vt to confront; (textes) to compare, collate

confus, e [kɔ̃fy, -yz] adj (vague) confused; (embarrassé) embarrassed

confusément [kɔ̃fyzemɑ̃] adv (distinguer, ressentir) vaguely; (parler) confusedly

confusion [kɔ̃fyzjɔ̃] nf (voir confus) confusion; embarrassment; (voir confondre) confusion; mixing up; (erreur) confusion; ~ **des peines** (Jur) concurrency of sentences

congé [kɔ̃ʒe] nm (vacances) holiday; (arrêt de travail) time off no pl, leave no pl; (Mil) leave no pl; (avis de départ) notice; **en ~** on holiday; off (work); on leave; **semaine/jour de ~** week/day off; **prendre ~ de qn** to take one's leave of sb; **donner son ~ à** to hand ou give in one's notice to; ~ **de maladie** sick leave; ~ **de maternité** maternity leave; ~**s payés** paid holiday ou leave

congédier [kɔ̃ʒedje] vt to dismiss

congélateur [kɔ̃ʒelatœR] nm freezer, deep freeze

congélation [kɔ̃ʒelɑsjɔ̃] nf freezing; (de l'huile)

89

congealing

congeler [kɔ̃ʒle]: **se congeler** vi to freeze

congénère [kɔ̃ʒenɛʀ] nm/f fellow (bear ou lion etc), fellow creature

congénital, e, -aux [kɔ̃ʒenital, -o] adj congenital

congère [kɔ̃ʒɛʀ] nf snowdrift

congestion [kɔ̃ʒɛstjɔ̃] nf congestion; ~ **cérébrale** stroke; ~ **pulmonaire** congestion of the lungs

congestionner [kɔ̃ʒɛstjɔne] vt to congest; (Méd) to flush

conglomérat [kɔ̃glɔmeʀa] nm conglomerate

Congo [kɔ̃go] nm: **le** ~ (pays, fleuve) the Congo

congolais, e [kɔ̃gɔlɛ, -ɛz] adj Congolese ▷ nm/f: **Congolais, e** Congolese

congratuler [kɔ̃gʀatyle] vt to congratulate

congre [kɔ̃gʀ(ə)] nm conger (eel)

congrégation [kɔ̃gʀegasjɔ̃] nf (Rel) congregation; (gén) assembly; gathering

congrès [kɔ̃gʀɛ] nm congress

congressiste [kɔ̃gʀesist(ə)] nm/f delegate, participant (at a congress)

congru, e [kɔ̃gʀy] adj: **la portion ~e** the smallest ou meanest share

conifère [kɔnifɛʀ] nm conifer

conique [kɔnik] adj conical

conjecture [kɔ̃ʒɛktyʀ] nf conjecture, speculation no pl

conjecturer [kɔ̃ʒɛktyʀe] vt, vi to conjecture

conjoint, e [kɔ̃ʒwɛ̃, -wɛ̃t] adj joint ▷ nm/f spouse

conjointement [kɔ̃ʒwɛ̃tmã] adv jointly

conjonctif, -ive [kɔ̃ʒɔ̃ktif, -iv] adj: **tissu ~** connective tissue

conjonction [kɔ̃ʒɔ̃ksjɔ̃] nf (Ling) conjunction

conjonctivite [kɔ̃ʒɔ̃ktivit] nf conjunctivitis

conjoncture [kɔ̃ʒɔ̃ktyʀ] nf circumstances pl; **la** ~ **(économique)** the economic climate ou situation

conjoncturel, le [kɔ̃ʒɔ̃ktyʀɛl] adj: **variations/ tendances ~les** economic fluctuations/trends

conjugaison [kɔ̃ʒygɛzɔ̃] nf (Ling) conjugation

conjugal, e, -aux [kɔ̃ʒygal, -o] adj conjugal; married

conjugué, e [kɔ̃ʒyge] adj combined

conjuguer [kɔ̃ʒyge] vt (Ling) to conjugate; (efforts etc) to combine

conjuration [kɔ̃ʒyʀasjɔ̃] nf conspiracy

conjuré, e [kɔ̃ʒyʀe] nm/f conspirator

conjurer [kɔ̃ʒyʀe] vt (sort, maladie) to avert; (implorer): ~ **qn de faire qch** to beseech ou entreat sb to do sth

connais [kɔnɛ], **connaissais** etc [kɔnɛsɛ] vb voir **connaître**

connaissance [kɔnɛsãs] nf (savoir) knowledge no pl; (personne connue) acquaintance; (conscience) consciousness; **connaissances** nfpl knowledge no pl; **être sans** ~ to be unconscious; **perdre/ reprendre** ~ to lose/regain consciousness; **à ma/sa** ~ to (the best of) my/his knowledge; **faire** ~ **avec qn** ou **la** ~ **de qn** (rencontrer) to meet

sb; (apprendre à connaître) to get to know sb; **avoir** ~ **de** to be aware of; **prendre** ~ **de** (document etc) to peruse; **en** ~ **de cause** with full knowledge of the facts; **de** ~ (personne, visage) familiar

connaissant etc [kɔnɛsã] vb voir **connaître**

connaissement [kɔnɛsmã] nm bill of lading

connaisseur, -euse [kɔnɛsœʀ, -øz] nm/f connoisseur ▷ adj expert

connaître [kɔnɛtʀ(ə)] vt to know; (éprouver) to experience; (avoir) to have; to enjoy; ~ **de nom/ vue** to know by name/sight; **se connaître** vi to know each other; (soi-même) to know o.s.; **ils se sont connus à Genève** they (first) met in Geneva; **s'y** ~ **en qch** to know about sth

connasse [kɔnas] nf (fam!) stupid bitch (!) ou cow (!)

connecté, e [kɔnɛkte] adj (Inform) on line

connecter [kɔnɛkte] vt to connect; **se connecter à Internet** to log onto the internet

connerie [kɔnʀi] nf (fam) (bloody) stupid (Brit) ou damn-fool (US) thing to do ou say

connexe [kɔnɛks(ə)] adj closely related

connexion [kɔnɛksjɔ̃] nf connection

connivence [kɔnivãs] nf connivance

connotation [kɔnɔtasjɔ̃] nf connotation

connu, e [kɔny] pp de **connaître** ▷ adj (célèbre) well-known

conque [kɔ̃k] nf (coquille) conch (shell)

conquérant, e [kɔ̃keʀã, -ãt] nm/f conqueror

conquérir [kɔ̃keʀiʀ] vt to conquer, win

conquerrai etc [kɔ̃kɛʀʀe] vb voir **conquérir**

conquête [kɔ̃kɛt] nf conquest

conquière, conquiers etc [kɔ̃kjɛʀ] vb voir **conquérir**

conquis, e [kɔ̃ki, -iz] pp de **conquérir**

consacrer [kɔ̃sakʀe] vt (Rel) ~ **qch (à)** to consecrate sth (to); (fig: usage etc) to sanction, establish; (employer): ~ **qch à** to devote ou dedicate sth to; **se consacrer à qch/faire** to dedicate ou devote o.s. to sth/to doing

consanguin, e [kɔ̃sãgɛ̃, -in] adj between blood relations; **frère** ~ half-brother (on father's side); **mariage** ~ intermarriage

consciemment [kɔ̃sjamã] adv consciously

conscience [kɔ̃sjãs] nf conscience; (perception) consciousness; **avoir/prendre** ~ **de** to be/ become aware of; **perdre/reprendre** ~ to lose/ regain consciousness; **avoir bonne/mauvaise** ~ to have a clear/guilty conscience; **en (toute)** ~ in all conscience

consciencieux, -euse [kɔ̃sjãsjø, -øz] adj conscientious

conscient, e [kɔ̃sjã, -ãt] adj conscious; ~ **de** aware ou conscious of

conscription [kɔ̃skʀipsjɔ̃] nf conscription

conscrit [kɔ̃skʀi] nm conscript

consécration [kɔ̃sekʀasjɔ̃] nf consecration

consécutif, -ive [kɔ̃sekytif, -iv] adj consecutive; ~ **à** following upon

consécutivement [kɔ̃sekytivmã] adv consecutively; ~ **à** following on

conseil [kɔ̃sɛj] nm (avis) piece of advice, advice no

pl; (*assemblée*) council; (*expert*): **~ en
recrutement** recruitment consultant ▷ *adj*:
ingénieur-~ engineering consultant; **tenir ~**
to hold a meeting; to deliberate; **donner un ~**
ou **des ~s à qn** to give sb (a piece of) advice;
demander ~ à qn to ask sb's advice; **prendre ~
(auprès de qn)** to take advice (from sb); **~
d'administration (CA)** board (of directors); **~
de classe** (*Scol*) *meeting of teachers, parents and class
representatives to discuss pupils' progress*; **~ de
discipline** disciplinary committee; **~ général**
regional council; *see note*; **~ de guerre** court-
martial; **le ~ des ministres** ≈ the Cabinet; **~
municipal (CM)** town council; **~ régional**
regional board of elected representatives; **~ de
révision** recruitment *ou* draft (US) board

● **CONSEIL GÉNÉRAL**
●
● Each "département" of France is run by a
● *Conseil général*, whose remit covers personnel,
● transport infrastructure, housing, school
● grants and economic development. The
● council is made up of "conseillers
● généraux", each of whom represents a
● "canton" and is elected for a six-year term.
● Half of the council's membership are
● elected every three years.

conseiller[1] [kɔ̃seje] *vt* (*personne*) to advise;
(*méthode, action*) to recommend, advise; **~ qch à
qn** to recommend sth to sb; **~ à qn de faire qch**
to advise sb to do sth
conseiller[2]**, -ière** [kɔ̃seje, -ɛʀ] *nm/f* adviser; **~
général** regional councillor; **~ matrimonial**
marriage guidance counsellor; **~ municipal**
town councillor; **~ d'orientation** (*Scol*) careers
adviser (Brit), (school) counselor (US)
consensuel, le [kɔ̃sɑ̃sɥɛl] *adj* consensual
consensus [kɔ̃sɛ̃sys] *nm* consensus
consentement [kɔ̃sɑ̃tmɑ̃] *nm* consent
consentir [kɔ̃sɑ̃tiʀ] *vt*: **~ (à qch/faire)** to agree
ou consent (to sth/to doing); **~ qch à qn** to grant
sb sth
conséquence [kɔ̃sekɑ̃s] *nf* consequence,
outcome; **conséquences** *nfpl* consequences,
repercussions; **en ~** (*donc*) consequently; (*de
façon appropriée*) accordingly; **ne pas tirer à ~** to
be unlikely to have any repercussions; **sans ~**
unimportant; **de ~** important
conséquent, e [kɔ̃sekɑ̃, -ɑ̃t] *adj* logical,
rational; (*fam: important*) substantial; **par ~**
consequently
conservateur, -trice [kɔ̃sɛʀvatœʀ, -tʀis] *adj*
conservative ▷ *nm/f* (*Pol*) conservative; (*de
musée*) curator
conservation [kɔ̃sɛʀvasjɔ̃] *nf* retention;
keeping; preservation
conservatisme [kɔ̃sɛʀvatism(ə)] *nm*
conservatism
conservatoire [kɔ̃sɛʀvatwaʀ] *nm* academy;
(*Écologie*) conservation area

conserve [kɔ̃sɛʀv(ə)] *nf* (*gén pl*) canned *ou* tinned
(Brit) food; **~s de poisson** canned *ou* tinned (Brit)
fish; **en ~** canned, tinned (Brit); **de ~** (*ensemble*)
in concert; (*naviguer*) in convoy
conservé, e [kɔ̃sɛʀve] *adj*: **bien ~** (*personne*) well-
preserved
conserver [kɔ̃sɛʀve] *vt* (*faculté*) to retain, keep;
(*habitude*) to keep up; (*amis, livres*) to keep;
(*préserver, Culin*) to preserve; **se conserver** *vi*
(*aliments*) to keep; (*aussi:* **"conserver au frais"**)
"store in a cool place"
conserverie [kɔ̃sɛʀvəʀi] *nf* canning factory
considérable [kɔ̃sideʀabl(ə)] *adj* considerable,
significant, extensive
considération [kɔ̃sideʀasjɔ̃] *nf* consideration;
(*estime*) esteem, respect; **considérations** *nfpl*
(*remarques*) reflections; **prendre en ~** to take
into consideration *ou* account; **ceci mérite ~**
this is worth considering; **en ~ de** given,
because of
considéré, e [kɔ̃sideʀe] *adj* respected; **tout
bien ~** all things considered
considérer [kɔ̃sideʀe] *vt* to consider; (*regarder*)
to consider, study; **~ qch comme** to regard sth
as
consigne [kɔ̃siɲ] *nf* (*Comm*) deposit; (*de gare*) left
luggage (office) (Brit), checkroom (US); (*punition:
Scol*) detention; (*: Mil*) confinement to barracks;
(*ordre, instruction*) instructions *pl*; **~
automatique** left-luggage locker; **~s de
sécurité** safety instructions
consigné, e [kɔ̃siɲe] *adj* (*Comm: bouteille,
emballage*) returnable; **non ~** non-returnable
consigner [kɔ̃siɲe] *vt* (*note, pensée*) to record;
(*marchandises*) to deposit; (*punir: Mil*) to confine
to barracks; (*: élève*) to put in detention; (*Comm*)
to put a deposit on
consistance [kɔ̃sistɑ̃s] *nf* consistency
consistant, e [kɔ̃sistɑ̃, -ɑ̃t] *adj* thick; solid
consister [kɔ̃siste] *vi*: **~ en/dans/à faire** to
consist of/in/in doing
consœur [kɔ̃sœʀ] *nf* (lady) colleague; fellow
member
consolation [kɔ̃sɔlasjɔ̃] *nf* consolation *no pl*,
comfort *no pl*
console [kɔ̃sɔl] *nf* console; **~ graphique** *ou* **de
visualisation** (*Inform*) visual display unit, VDU;
~ de jeux games console
consoler [kɔ̃sɔle] *vt* to console; **se ~ (de qch)** to
console o.s. (for sth)
consolider [kɔ̃sɔlide] *vt* to strengthen,
reinforce; (*fig*) to consolidate; **bilan consolidé**
consolidated balance sheet
consommateur, -trice [kɔ̃sɔmatœʀ, -tʀis] *nm/f*
(*Écon*) consumer; (*dans un café*) customer
consommation [kɔ̃sɔmasjɔ̃] *nf* consumption;
(*Jur*) consummation; (*boisson*) drink; **~ aux 100
km** (*Auto*) (fuel) consumption per 100 km,
≈ miles per gallon (mpg), ≈ gas mileage (US); **de
~** (*biens, société*) consumer *cpd*
consommé, e [kɔ̃sɔme] *adj* consummate ▷ *nm*
consommé

consommer [kɔsɔme] *vt* (*personne*) to eat *ou*
drink, consume; (*voiture, usine, poêle*) to use,
consume; (*Jur*) to consummate ▷ *vi* (*dans un café*)
to (have a) drink
consonance [kɔsɔnɑ̃s] *nf* consonance; **nom à ~
étrangère** foreign-sounding name
consonne [kɔsɔn] *nf* consonant
consortium [kɔsɔRsjɔm] *nm* consortium
consorts [kɔsɔR] *nmpl*: **et ~** (*péj*) and company,
and his bunch *ou* like
conspirateur, -trice [kɔspiRatœR, -tRis] *nm/f*
conspirator, plotter
conspiration [kɔspiRasjɔ̃] *nf* conspiracy
conspirer [kɔspiRe] *vi* to conspire, plot; **~ à**
(*tendre à*) to conspire to
conspuer [kɔspɥe] *vt* to boo, shout down
constamment [kɔstamɑ̃] *adv* constantly
constance [kɔstɑ̃s] *nf* permanence, constancy;
(*d'une amitié*) steadfastness; **travailler avec ~** to
work steadily; **il faut de la ~ pour la
supporter** (*fam*) you need a lot of patience to
put up with her
constant, e [kɔstɑ̃, -ɑ̃t] *adj* constant; (*personne*)
steadfast ▷ *nf* constant
Constantinople [kɔstɑ̃tinɔpl(ə)] *n*
Constantinople
constat [kɔsta] *nm* (*d'huissier*) certified report (*by
bailiff*); (*de police*) report; (*observation*) (observed)
fact, observation; (*affirmation*) statement; **~ (à
l'amiable)** (*jointly agreed*) *statement for insurance
purposes*
constatation [kɔstatasjɔ̃] *nf* noticing;
certifying; (*remarque*) observation
constater [kɔstate] *vt* (*remarquer*) to note, notice;
(*Admin, Jur: attester*) to certify; (*dégâts*) to note; **~
que** (*dire*) to state that
constellation [kɔstelasjɔ̃] *nf* constellation
constellé, e [kɔstele] *adj*: **~ de** (*étoiles*) studded *ou*
spangled with; (*taches*) spotted with
consternant, e [kɔstɛRnɑ̃ -ɑ̃t] *adj* (*nouvelle*)
dismaying; (*attristant, étonnant: bêtise*) appalling
consternation [kɔstɛRnasjɔ̃] *nf* consternation,
dismay
consterner [kɔstɛRne] *vt* to dismay
constipation [kɔstipasjɔ̃] *nf* constipation
constipé, e [kɔstipe] *adj* constipated; (*fig*) stiff
constituant, e [kɔstitɥɑ̃, -ɑ̃t] *adj* (*élément*)
constituent; **assemblée ~e** (*Pol*) constituent
assembly
constitué, e [kɔstitɥe] *adj*: **~ de** made up *ou*
composed of; **bien ~** of sound constitution;
well-formed
constituer [kɔstitɥe] *vt* (*comité, équipe*) to set up,
form; (*dossier, collection*) to put together, build
up; (*éléments, parties: composer*) to make up,
constitute; (*représenter, être*) to constitute; **se ~
prisonnier** to give o.s. up; **se ~ partie civile** *to
bring an independent action for damages*
constitution [kɔstitysjɔ̃] *nf* setting up;
building up; (*composition*) composition, make-
up; (*santé, Pol*) constitution
constitutionnel, le [kɔstitysjɔnɛl] *adj*
constitutional
constructeur [kɔstRyktœR] *nm* manufacturer,
builder
constructif, -ive [kɔstRyktif, -iv] *adj* (*positif*)
constructive
construction [kɔstRyksjɔ̃] *nf* construction,
building
construire [kɔstRɥiR] *vt* to build, construct; **se
construire** *vi*: **l'immeuble s'est construit
très vite** the building went up *ou* was built very
quickly
consul [kɔsyl] *nm* consul
consulaire [kɔsylɛR] *adj* consular
consulat [kɔsyla] *nm* consulate
consultant, e [kɔsyltɑ̃, -ɑ̃t] *adj* consultant
consultatif, -ive [kɔsyltatif, -iv] *adj* advisory
consultation [kɔsyltasjɔ̃] *nf* consultation;
consultations *nfpl* (*Pol*) talks; **être en ~**
(*délibération*) to be in consultation; (*médecin*) to be
consulting; **aller à la ~** (*Méd*) to go to the
surgery (*Brit*) *ou* doctor's office (*US*); **heures de
~** (*Méd*) surgery (*Brit*) *ou* office (*US*) hours
consulter [kɔsylte] *vt* to consult ▷ *vi* (*médecin*) to
hold surgery (Brit), be in (the office) (*US*); **se
consulter** *vi* to confer
consumer [kɔsyme] *vt* to consume; **se
consumer** *vi* to burn; **se ~ de chagrin/douleur**
to be consumed with sorrow/grief
consumérisme [kɔsymeRism(ə)] *nm*
consumerism
contact [kɔtakt] *nm* contact; **au ~ de** (*air, peau*)
on contact with; (*gens*) through contact with;
mettre/couper le ~ (*Auto*) to switch on/off the
ignition; **entrer en ~** (*fils, objets*) to come into
contact, make contact; **se mettre en ~ avec**
(*Radio*) to make contact with; **prendre ~ avec**
(*relation d'affaires, connaissance*) to get in touch *ou*
contact with
contacter [kɔtakte] *vt* to contact, get in touch
with
contagieux, -euse [kɔtaʒjø, -øz] *adj*
contagious; infectious
contagion [kɔtaʒjɔ̃] *nf* contagion
container [kɔtenɛR] *nm* container
contamination [kɔtaminasjɔ̃] *nf* infection;
contamination
contaminer [kɔtamine] *vt* (*par un virus*) to infect;
(*par des radiations*) to contaminate
conte [kɔt] *nm* tale; **~ de fées** fairy tale
contemplatif, -ive [kɔtɑ̃platif, -iv] *adj*
contemplative
contemplation [kɔtɑ̃plasjɔ̃] *nf* contemplation;
(*Rel, Philosophie*) meditation
contempler [kɔtɑ̃ple] *vt* to contemplate, gaze at
contemporain, e [kɔtɑ̃pɔRɛ̃, -ɛn] *adj, nm/f*
contemporary
contenance [kɔtnɑ̃s] *nf* (*d'un récipient*) capacity;
(*attitude*) bearing, attitude; **perdre ~** to lose
one's composure; **se donner une ~** to give the
impression of composure; **faire bonne ~
(devant)** to put on a bold front (in the face of)
conteneur [kɔtnœR] *nm* container; **~ (de**

bouteilles) bottle bank

conteneurisation [kɔ̃tnœʀizasjɔ̃] *nf* containerization

contenir [kɔ̃tniʀ] *vt* to contain; *(avoir une capacité de)* to hold; **se contenir** *vi (se retenir)* to control o.s. *ou* one's emotions, contain o.s.

content, e [kɔ̃tɑ̃, -ɑ̃t] *adj* pleased, glad; **~ de** pleased with; **je serais ~ que tu ...** I would be pleased if you ...

contentement [kɔ̃tɑ̃tmɑ̃] *nm* contentment, satisfaction

contenter [kɔ̃tɑ̃te] *vt* to satisfy, please; *(envie)* to satisfy; **se ~ de** to content o.s. with

contentieux [kɔ̃tɑ̃sjø] *nm (Comm)* litigation; *(: service)* litigation department; *(Pol etc)* contentious issues *pl*

contenu, e [kɔ̃tny] *pp de* **contenir** ▷ *nm (d'un bol)* contents *pl*; *(d'un texte)* content

conter [kɔ̃te] *vt* to recount, relate; **en ~ de belles à qn** to tell tall stories to sb

contestable [kɔ̃tɛstabl(ə)] *adj* questionable

contestataire [kɔ̃tɛstatɛʀ] *adj (journal, étudiant)* anti-establishment ▷ *nm/f* (anti-establishment) protester

contestation [kɔ̃tɛstasjɔ̃] *nf* questioning, contesting; *(Pol)*: **la ~** anti-establishment activity, protest

conteste [kɔ̃tɛst(ə)]: **sans ~** *adv* unquestionably, indisputably

contesté, e [kɔ̃tɛste] *adj (roman, écrivain)* controversial

contester [kɔ̃tɛste] *vt* to question, contest ▷ *vi (Pol: gén)* to protest, rebel (against established authority)

conteur, -euse [kɔ̃tœʀ, -øz] *nm/f* story-teller

contexte [kɔ̃tɛkst(ə)] *nm* context

contiendrai [kɔ̃tjɛ̃dʀe], **contiens** *etc* [kɔ̃tjɛ̃] *vb voir* **contenir**

contigu, ë [kɔ̃tigy] *adj*: **~ (à)** adjacent (to)

continent [kɔ̃tinɑ̃] *nm* continent

continental, e, -aux [kɔ̃tinɑ̃tal, -o] *adj* continental

contingences [kɔ̃tɛ̃ʒɑ̃s] *nfpl* contingencies

contingent [kɔ̃tɛ̃ʒɑ̃] *nm (Mil)* contingent; *(Comm)* quota

contingenter [kɔ̃tɛ̃ʒɑ̃te] *vt (Comm)* to fix a quota on

contins *etc* [kɔ̃tɛ̃] *vb voir* **contenir**

continu, e [kɔ̃tiny] *adj* continuous; **(courant) ~** direct current, DC

continuation [kɔ̃tinɥasjɔ̃] *nf* continuation

continuel, le [kɔ̃tinɥɛl] *adj (qui se répète)* constant, continual; *(continu)* continuous

continuellement [kɔ̃tinɥɛlmɑ̃] *adv* continually; continuously

continuer [kɔ̃tinɥe] *vt (travail, voyage etc)* to continue (with), carry on (with), go on with; *(prolonger: alignement, rue)* to continue ▷ *vi (pluie, vie, bruit)* to continue, go on; *(voyageur)* to go on; **se continuer** *vi* to carry on; **~ à** *ou* **de faire** to go on *ou* continue doing

continuité [kɔ̃tinɥite] *nf* continuity;

continuation

contondant, e [kɔ̃tɔ̃dɑ̃, -ɑ̃t] *adj*: **arme ~e** blunt instrument

contorsion [kɔ̃tɔʀsjɔ̃] *nf* contortion

contorsionner [kɔ̃tɔʀsjɔne]: **se contorsionner** *vi* to contort o.s., writhe about

contorsionniste [kɔ̃tɔʀsjɔnist(ə)] *nm/f* contortionist

contour [kɔ̃tuʀ] *nm* outline, contour; **contours** *nmpl (d'une rivière etc)* windings

contourner [kɔ̃tuʀne] *vt* to bypass, walk *ou* drive) round

contraceptif, -ive [kɔ̃tʀasɛptif, -iv] *adj, nm* contraceptive

contraception [kɔ̃tʀasɛpsjɔ̃] *nf* contraception

contracté, e [kɔ̃tʀakte] *adj (muscle)* tense, contracted; *(personne: tendu)* tense, tensed up; **article ~** *(Ling)* contracted article

contracter [kɔ̃tʀakte] *vt (muscle etc)* to tense, contract; *(maladie, dette, obligation)* to contract; *(assurance)* to take out; **se contracter** *vi (métal, muscles)* to contract

contraction [kɔ̃tʀaksjɔ̃] *nf* contraction

contractuel, le [kɔ̃tʀaktɥɛl] *adj* contractual ▷ *nm/f (agent)* traffic warden; *(employé)* contract employee

contradiction [kɔ̃tʀadiksjɔ̃] *nf* contradiction

contradictoire [kɔ̃tʀadiktwaʀ] *adj* contradictory, conflicting; **débat ~** (open) debate

contraignant, e [kɔ̃tʀɛɲɑ̃, -ɑ̃t] *vb voir* **contraindre** ▷ *adj* restricting

contraindre [kɔ̃tʀɛ̃dʀ(ə)] *vt*: **~ qn à faire** to force *ou* compel sb to do

contraint, e [kɔ̃tʀɛ̃, -ɛ̃t] *pp de* **contraindre** ▷ *adj (mine, air)* constrained, forced ▷ *nf* constraint; **sans ~e** unrestrainedly, unconstrainedly

contraire [kɔ̃tʀɛʀ] *adj, nm* opposite; **~ à** contrary to; **au ~** *adv* on the contrary

contrairement [kɔ̃tʀɛʀmɑ̃] *adv*: **~ à** contrary to, unlike

contralto [kɔ̃tʀalto] *nm* contralto

contrariant, e [kɔ̃tʀaʀjɑ̃, -ɑ̃t] *adj (personne)* contrary, perverse; *(incident)* annoying

contrarier [kɔ̃tʀaʀje] *vt (personne)* to annoy, bother; *(fig)* to impede; to thwart, frustrate

contrariété [kɔ̃tʀaʀjete] *nf* annoyance

contraste [kɔ̃tʀast(ə)] *nm* contrast

contraster [kɔ̃tʀaste] *vt, vi* to contrast

contrat [kɔ̃tʀa] *nm* contract; *(fig: accord, pacte)* agreement; **~ de travail** employment contract

contravention [kɔ̃tʀavɑ̃sjɔ̃] *nf (infraction)*: **~ à** contravention of; *(amende)* fine; *(PV pour stationnement interdit)* parking ticket; **dresser ~ à** *(automobiliste)* to book; to write out a parking ticket for

contre [kɔ̃tʀ(ə)] *prép* against; *(en échange)* (in exchange) for; **par ~** on the other hand

contre-amiral, -aux [kɔ̃tʀamiʀal, -o] *nm* rear admiral

contre-attaque [kɔ̃tʀatak] *nf* counterattack

contre-attaquer [kɔ̃tʀatake] *vi* to

counterattack

contre-balancer [kɔ̃tRəbalɑ̃se] *vt* to counterbalance; (*fig*) to offset

contrebande [kɔ̃tRəbɑ̃d] *nf* (*trafic*) contraband, smuggling; (*marchandise*) contraband, smuggled goods *pl*; **faire la ~ de** to smuggle

contrebandier, -ière [kɔ̃tRəbɑ̃dje, -jɛR] *nm/f* smuggler

contrebas [kɔ̃tRəba]: **en ~** *adv* (down) below

contrebasse [kɔ̃tRəbas] *nf* (double) bass

contrebassiste [kɔ̃tRəbasist(ə)] *nm/f* (double) bass player

contre-braquer [kɔ̃tRəbRake] *vi* to steer into a skid

contrecarrer [kɔ̃tRəkaRe] *vt* to thwart

contrechamp [kɔ̃tRəʃɑ̃] *nm* (*Ciné*) reverse shot

contrecœur [kɔ̃tRəkœR]: **à ~** *adv* (be)grudgingly, reluctantly

contrecoup [kɔ̃tRəku] *nm* repercussions *pl*; **par ~** as an indirect consequence

contre-courant [kɔ̃tRəkuRɑ̃]: **à ~** *adv* against the current

contredire [kɔ̃tRədiR] *vt* (*personne*) to contradict; (*témoignage, assertion, faits*) to refute; **se contredire** *vi* to contradict o.s.

contredit, e [kɔ̃tRədi, -it] *pp de* **contredire** ▷ *nm*: **sans ~** without question

contrée [kɔ̃tRe] *nf* region; land

contre-écrou [kɔ̃tRekRu] *nm* lock nut

contre-enquête [kɔ̃tRɑ̃kɛt] *nf* counter-inquiry

contre-espionnage [kɔ̃tRɛspjɔnaʒ] *nm* counter-espionage

contre-exemple [kɔ̃tRɛgzɑ̃pl(ə)] *nf* counter-example

contre-expertise [kɔ̃tRɛkspɛRtiz] *nf* second (expert) assessment

contrefaçon [kɔ̃tRəfasɔ̃] *nf* forgery; **~ de brevet** patent infringement

contrefaire [kɔ̃tRəfɛR] *vt* (*document, signature*) to forge, counterfeit; (*personne, démarche*) to mimic; (*dénaturer: sa voix etc*) to disguise

contrefait, e [kɔ̃tRəfɛ, -ɛt] *pp de* **contrefaire** ▷ *adj* misshapen, deformed

contrefasse [kɔ̃tRəfas], **contreferai** *etc* [kɔ̃tRəfRe] *vb voir* **contrefaire**

contre-filet [kɔ̃tRəfilɛ] *nm* (*Culin*) sirloin

contreforts [kɔ̃tRəfɔR] *nmpl* foothills

contre-haut [kɔ̃tRəo]: **en ~** *adv* (up) above

contre-indication [kɔ̃tRɛ̃dikasjɔ̃] *nf* contraindication

contre-indiqué, e [kɔ̃tRɛ̃dike] *adj* (*Méd*) contraindicated

contre-interrogatoire [kɔ̃tRɛ̃teRɔgatwaR] *nm*: **faire subir un ~ à qn** to cross-examine sb

contre-jour [kɔ̃tRəʒuR]: **à ~** *adv* against the light

contremaître [kɔ̃tRəmɛtR(ə)] *nm* foreman

contre-manifestant, e [kɔ̃tRəmanifɛstɑ̃, -ɑ̃t] *nm/f* counter-demonstrator

contre-manifestation [kɔ̃tRəmanifɛstasjɔ̃] *nf* counter-demonstration

contremarque [kɔ̃tRəmaRk(ə)] *nf* (*ticket*) pass-out ticket

contre-offensive [kɔ̃tRɔfɑ̃siv] *nf* counteroffensive

contre-ordre [kɔ̃tRɔRdR(ə)] *nm* = **contrordre**

contrepartie [kɔ̃tRəpaRti] *nf* compensation; **en ~** in compensation; in return

contre-performance [kɔ̃tRəpɛRfɔRmɑ̃s] *nf* below-average performance

contrepèterie [kɔ̃tRəpetRi] *nf* spoonerism

contre-pied [kɔ̃tRəpje] *nm* (*inverse, opposé*): **le ~ de ...** the exact opposite of ...; **prendre le ~ de** to take the opposing view of; to take the opposite course to; **prendre qn à ~** (*Sport*) to wrong-foot sb

contre-plaqué [kɔ̃tRəplake] *nm* plywood

contre-plongée [kɔ̃tRəplɔ̃ʒe] *nf* low-angle shot

contrepoids [kɔ̃tRəpwa] *nm* counterweight, counterbalance; **faire ~** to act as a counterbalance

contrepoil [kɔ̃tRəpwal]: **à ~** *adv* the wrong way

contrepoint [kɔ̃tRəpwɛ̃] *nm* counterpoint

contrepoison [kɔ̃tRəpwazɔ̃] *nm* antidote

contrer [kɔ̃tRe] *vt* to counter

contre-révolution [kɔ̃tRəRevɔlysjɔ̃] *nf* counter-revolution

contre-révolutionnaire [kɔ̃tRəRevɔlysjɔnɛR] *nm/f* counter-revolutionary

contresens [kɔ̃tRəsɑ̃s] *nm* misinterpretation; (*mauvaise traduction*) mistranslation; (*absurdité*) nonsense *no pl*; **à ~** *adv* the wrong way

contresigner [kɔ̃tRəsiɲe] *vt* to countersign

contretemps [kɔ̃tRətɑ̃] *nm* hitch, contretemps; **à ~** *adv* (*Mus*) out of time; (*fig*) at an inopportune moment

contre-terrorisme [kɔ̃tRəteRɔRism(ə)] *nm* counter-terrorism

contre-terroriste [kɔ̃tRəteRɔRist(ə)] *nm/f* counter-terrorist

contre-torpilleur [kɔ̃tRətɔRpijœR] *nm* destroyer

contrevenant, e [kɔ̃tRəvnɑ̃, -ɑ̃t] *vb voir* **contrevenir** ▷ *nm/f* offender

contrevenir [kɔ̃tRəvniR]: **~ à** *vt* to contravene

contre-voie [kɔ̃tRəvwa]: **à ~** *adv* (*en sens inverse*) on the wrong track; (*du mauvais côté*) on the wrong side

contribuable [kɔ̃tRibɥabl(ə)] *nm/f* taxpayer

contribuer [kɔ̃tRibɥe]: **~ à** *vt* to contribute towards

contribution [kɔ̃tRibysjɔ̃] *nf* contribution; **les ~s** (*bureaux*) the tax office; **mettre à ~** to call upon; **~s directes/indirectes** direct/indirect taxation

contrit, e [kɔ̃tRi, -it] *adj* contrite

contrôlable [kɔ̃tRolabl(ə)] *adj* (*maîtrisable: situation, débit*) controllable; (*alibi, déclarations*) verifiable

contrôle [kɔ̃tRol] *nm* checking *no pl*, check; supervision; monitoring; (*test*) test, examination; **perdre le ~ de son véhicule** to lose control of one's vehicle; **~ des changes** (*Comm*) exchange controls; **~ continu** (*Scol*) continuous assessment; ~ **d'identité** identity check; ~ **des naissances** birth control; ~ **des prix** price control

contrôler [kɔ̃tʀole] vt (*vérifier*) to check; (*surveiller*) to supervise; to monitor, control; (*maîtriser*, Comm: *firme*) to control; **se contrôler** vi to control o.s.

contrôleur, -euse [kɔ̃tʀolœʀ, -øz] nm/f (*de train*) (ticket) inspector; (*de bus*) (bus) conductor/tress; ~ **de la navigation aérienne**, ~ **aérien** air traffic controller; ~ **financier** financial controller

contrordre [kɔ̃tʀɔʀdʀ(ə)] nm counter-order, countermand; **sauf** ~ unless otherwise directed

controverse [kɔ̃tʀɔvɛʀs(ə)] nf controversy

controversé, e [kɔ̃tʀɔvɛʀse] adj (*personnage, question*) controversial

contumace [kɔ̃tymas]: **par** ~ adv in absentia

contusion [kɔ̃tyzjɔ̃] nf bruise, contusion

contusionné, e [kɔ̃tyzjɔne] adj bruised

conurbation [kɔnyʀbasjɔ̃] nf conurbation

convaincant, e [kɔ̃vɛ̃kɑ̃, -ɑ̃t] vb voir **convaincre** ▷ adj convincing

convaincre [kɔ̃vɛ̃kʀ(ə)] vt: ~ **qn (de qch)** to convince sb (of sth); ~ **qn (de faire)** to persuade sb (to do); ~ **qn de** (Jur: *délit*) to convict sb of

convaincu, e [kɔ̃vɛ̃ky] pp de **convaincre** ▷ adj: **d'un ton** ~ with conviction

convainquais etc [kɔ̃vɛ̃kɛ] vb voir **convaincre**

convalescence [kɔ̃valesɑ̃s] nf convalescence; **maison de** ~ convalescent home

convalescent, e [kɔ̃valesɑ̃, -ɑ̃t] adj, nm/f convalescent

convenable [kɔ̃vnabl(ə)] adj suitable; (*décent*) acceptable, proper; (*assez bon*) decent, acceptable; adequate, passable

convenablement [kɔ̃vnabləmɑ̃] adv (*placé, choisi*) suitably; (*s'habiller, s'exprimer*) properly; (*payé, logé*) decently

convenance [kɔ̃vnɑ̃s] nf: **à ma/votre** ~ to my/your liking; **convenances** nfpl proprieties

convenir [kɔ̃vniʀ] vt to be suitable; ~ **à** to suit; **il convient de** it is advisable to; (*bienséant*) it is right ou proper to; ~ **de** (*bien-fondé de qch*) to admit (to), acknowledge; (*date, somme etc*) to agree upon; ~ **que** (*admettre*) to admit that, acknowledge the fact that; ~ **de faire qch** to agree to do sth; **il a été convenu que** it has been agreed that; **comme convenu** as agreed

convention [kɔ̃vɑ̃sjɔ̃] nf convention; **conventions** nfpl (*convenances*) convention sg, social conventions; **de** ~ conventional; ~ **collective** (Écon) collective agreement

conventionnalisme [kɔ̃vɑ̃sjɔnalism(ə)] nm (*des idées*) conventionality

conventionné, e [kɔ̃vɑ̃sjɔne] adj (Admin) applying charges laid down by the state

conventionnel, le [kɔ̃vɑ̃sjɔnɛl] adj conventional

conventionnellement [kɔ̃vɑ̃sjɔnɛlmɑ̃] adv conventionally

conventuel, le [kɔ̃vɑ̃tɥɛl] adj monastic; monastery cpd, conventual, convent cpd

convenu, e [kɔ̃vny] pp de **convenir** ▷ adj agreed

convergent, e [kɔ̃vɛʀʒɑ̃, -ɑ̃t] adj convergent

converger [kɔ̃vɛʀʒe] vi to converge; ~ **vers** ou **sur** to converge on

conversation [kɔ̃vɛʀsasjɔ̃] nf conversation; **avoir de la** ~ to be a good conversationalist

converser [kɔ̃vɛʀse] vi to converse

conversion [kɔ̃vɛʀsjɔ̃] nf conversion; (Ski) kick turn

convertible [kɔ̃vɛʀtibl(ə)] adj (Écon) convertible; (**canapé**) ~ sofa bed

convertir [kɔ̃vɛʀtiʀ] vt: ~ **qn (à)** to convert sb (to); ~ **qch en** to convert sth into; **se** ~ **(à)** to be converted (to)

convertisseur [kɔ̃vɛʀtisœʀ] nm (Élec) converter

convexe [kɔ̃vɛks(ə)] adj convex

conviction [kɔ̃viksjɔ̃] nf conviction

conviendrai [kɔ̃vjɛ̃dʀe], **conviens** etc [kɔ̃vjɛ̃] vb voir **convenir**

convier [kɔ̃vje] vt: ~ **qn à** (*dîner etc*) to (cordially) invite sb to; ~ **qn à faire** to urge sb to do

convint etc [kɔ̃vɛ̃] vb voir **convenir**

convive [kɔ̃viv] nm/f guest (*at table*)

convivial, e [kɔ̃vivjal] adj (Inform) user-friendly

convocation [kɔ̃vɔkasjɔ̃] nf (*voir convoquer*) convening, convoking; summoning; invitation; (*document*) notification to attend; summons sg

convoi [kɔ̃vwa] nm (*de voitures, prisonniers*) convoy; (*train*) train; ~ (**funèbre**) funeral procession

convoiter [kɔ̃vwate] vt to covet

convoitise [kɔ̃vwatiz] nf covetousness; (*sexuelle*) lust, desire

convoler [kɔ̃vɔle] vi: ~ (**en justes noces**) to be wed

convoquer [kɔ̃vɔke] vt (*assemblée*) to convene, convoke; (*subordonné, témoin*) to summon; (*candidat*) to ask to attend; ~ **qn (à)** (*réunion*) to invite sb (to attend)

convoyer [kɔ̃vwaje] vt to escort

convoyeur [kɔ̃vwajœʀ] nm (Navig) escort ship; ~ **de fonds** security guard

convulsé, e [kɔ̃vylse] adj (*visage*) distorted

convulsif, -ive [kɔ̃vylsif, -iv] adj convulsive

convulsions [kɔ̃vylsjɔ̃] nfpl convulsions

coopérant [kɔɔpeʀɑ̃] nm ≈ person doing Voluntary Service Overseas (Brit), ≈ member of the Peace Corps (US)

coopératif, -ive [kɔɔpeʀatif, -iv] adj, nf co-operative

coopération [kɔɔpeʀasjɔ̃] nf co-operation; (Admin): **la C~** ≈ Voluntary Service Overseas (Brit) ou the Peace Corps (US) (*done as alternative to military service*)

coopérer [kɔɔpeʀe] vi: ~ **(à)** to co-operate (in)

coordination [kɔɔʀdinasjɔ̃] nf coordination

coordonnateur, -trice [kɔɔʀdɔnatœʀ, -tʀis] adj coordinating ▷ nm/f coordinator

coordonné, e [kɔɔʀdɔne] adj coordinated ▷ nf (Ling) coordinate clause; **coordonnés** nmpl

(*vêtements*) coordinates; **coordonnées** *nfpl*
(*Math*) coordinates; (*détails personnels*) address,
phone number, schedule *etc*; whereabouts;
donnez-moi vos ~ (*fam*) can I have your details
please?

coordonner [kɔɔrdɔne] *vt* to coordinate

copain, copine [kɔpɛ̃, kɔpin] *nm/f* mate (*Brit*),
pal ▷ *adj*: **être ~ avec** to be pally with

copeau, x [kɔpo] *nm* shaving; (*de métal*) turning

Copenhague [kɔpənag] *n* Copenhagen

copie [kɔpi] *nf* copy; (*Scol*) script, paper;
exercise; **~ certifiée conforme** certified copy;
~ papier (*Inform*) hard copy

copier [kɔpje] *vt, vi* to copy; **~ sur** to copy from

copieur [kɔpjœr] *nm* (photo)copier

copieusement [kɔpjøzmã] *adv* copiously

copieux, -euse [kɔpjø, -øz] *adj* copious, hearty

copilote [kɔpilɔt] *nm* (*Aviat*) co-pilot; (*Auto*) co-
driver, navigator

copinage [kɔpinaʒ] *nm*: **obtenir qch par ~** to
get sth through contacts

copine [kɔpin] *nf voir* **copain**

copiste [kɔpist(ə)] *nm/f* copyist, transcriber

coproduction [kɔprɔdyksjɔ̃] *nf* coproduction,
joint production

copropriétaire [kɔprɔprijetɛr] *nm/f* co-owner

copropriété [kɔprɔprijete] *nf* co-ownership,
joint ownership; **acheter en ~** to buy on a co-
ownership basis

copulation [kɔpylasjɔ̃] *nf* copulation

copyright [kɔpirajt] *nm* copyright

coq [kɔk] *nm* cockerel, rooster ▷ *adj inv* (*Boxe*):
poids ~ bantamweight; **~ de bruyère** grouse; **~
du village** (*fig: péj*) ladykiller; **~ au vin** coq au
vin

coq-à-l'âne [kɔkalan] *nm inv* abrupt change of
subject

coque [kɔk] *nf* (*de noix, mollusque*) shell; (*de bateau*)
hull; **à la ~** (*Culin*) (soft-)boiled

coquelet [kɔklɛ] *nm* (*Culin*) cockerel

coquelicot [kɔkliko] *nm* poppy

coqueluche [kɔklyʃ] *nf* whooping-cough; (*fig*):
être la ~ de qn to be sb's flavour of the month

coquet, te [kɔkɛ, -ɛt] *adj* appearance-conscious;
(*joli*) pretty

coquetier [kɔktje] *nm* egg-cup

coquettement [kɔkɛtmã] *adv* (*s'habiller*)
attractively; (*meubler*) prettily

coquetterie [kɔkɛtri] *nf* appearance-
consciousness

coquillage [kɔkijaʒ] *nm* (*mollusque*) shellfish *inv*;
(*coquille*) shell

coquille [kɔkij] *nf* shell; (*Typo*) misprint; **~ de
beurre** shell of butter; **~ d'œuf** *adj* (*couleur*)
eggshell; **~ de noix** nutshell; **~ St Jacques**
scallop

coquillettes [kɔkijɛt] *nfpl* pasta shells

coquin, e [kɔkɛ̃, -in] *adj* mischievous, roguish;
(*polisson*) naughty ▷ *nm/f* (*péj*) rascal

cor [kɔr] *nm* (*Mus*) horn; (*Méd*): **~ (au pied)** corn;
réclamer à ~ et à cri to clamour for; **~ anglais**
cor anglais; **~ de chasse** hunting horn

corail, -aux [kɔraj, -o] *nm* coral *no pl*

Coran [kɔrã] *nm*: **le ~** the Koran

coraux [kɔro] *nmpl de* **corail**

corbeau, x [kɔrbo] *nm* crow

corbeille [kɔrbɛj] *nf* basket; (*Inform*) recycle bin;
(*Bourse*): **la ~** = the floor (of the Stock Exchange);
~ de mariage (*fig*) wedding presents *pl*; **~ à
ouvrage** work-basket; **~ à pain** breadbasket; **~
à papier** waste paper basket *ou* bin

corbillard [kɔrbijar] *nm* hearse

cordage [kɔrdaʒ] *nm* rope; **cordages** *nmpl* (*de
voilure*) rigging *sg*

corde [kɔrd(ə)] *nf* rope; (*de violon, raquette, d'arc*)
string; (*trame*): **la ~** the thread; (*Athlétisme,
Auto*): **la ~** the rails *pl*; **les ~s** (*Boxe*) the ropes; **les
(instruments à) ~s** (*Mus*) the strings, the
stringed instruments; **semelles de ~** rope
soles; **tenir la ~** (*Athlétisme, Auto*) to be in the
inside lane; **tomber des ~s** to rain cats and
dogs; **tirer sur la ~** to go too far; **la ~ sensible**
the right chord; **usé jusqu'à la ~** threadbare; **~
à linge** washing *ou* clothes line; **~ lisse**
(climbing) rope; **~ à nœuds** knotted climbing
rope; **~ raide** tightrope; **~ à sauter** skipping
rope; **~s vocales** vocal cords

cordeau, x [kɔrdo] *nm* string, line; **tracé au ~**
as straight as a die

cordée [kɔrde] *nf* (*d'alpinistes*) rope, roped party

cordelière [kɔrdəljɛr] *nf* cord (belt)

cordial, e, aux [kɔrdjal, -o] *adj* warm, cordial
▷ *nm* cordial, pick-me-up

cordialement [kɔrdjalmã] *adv* cordially,
heartily; (*formule épistolaire*) (kind) regards

cordialité [kɔrdjalite] *nf* warmth, cordiality

cordillère [kɔrdijɛr] *nf*: **la ~ des Andes** the
Andes cordillera *ou* range

cordon [kɔrdɔ̃] *nm* cord, string; **~ sanitaire/de
police** sanitary/police cordon; **~ littoral**
sandbank, sandbar; **~ ombilical** umbilical cord

cordon-bleu [kɔrdɔ̃blø] *adj, nm/f* cordon bleu

cordonnerie [kɔrdɔnri] *nf* shoe repairer's *ou*
mender's (shop)

cordonnier [kɔrdɔnje] *nm* shoe repairer *ou*
mender, cobbler

cordouan, e [kɔrduã, -an] *adj* Cordovan

Cordoue [kɔrdu] *n* Cordoba

Corée [kɔre] *nf*: **la ~** Korea; **la ~ du Sud/du
Nord** South/North Korea; **la République
(démocratique populaire) de ~** the
(Democratic People's) Republic of Korea

coréen, ne [kɔreɛ̃, -ɛn] *adj* Korean ▷ *nm* (*Ling*)
Korean ▷ *nm/f*: **Coréen, ne** Korean

coreligionnaire [kɔrəliʒjɔnɛr] *nm/f* fellow
Christian/Muslim/Jew *etc*

Corfou [kɔrfu] *n* Corfu

coriace [kɔrjas] *adj* tough

coriandre [kɔrjãdr(ə)] *nf* coriander

Corinthe [kɔrɛ̃t] *n* Corinth

cormoran [kɔrmɔrã] *nm* cormorant

cornac [kɔrnak] *nm* elephant driver

corne [kɔrn(ə)] *nf* horn; (*de cerf*) antler; (*de la
peau*) callus; **~ d'abondance** horn of plenty; **~**

de brume (Navig) foghorn
cornée [kɔʀne] nf cornea
corneille [kɔʀnɛj] nf crow
cornélien, ne [kɔʀneljɛ̃, -ɛn] adj (débat etc)
where love and duty conflict
cornemuse [kɔʀnəmyz] nf bagpipes pl; **joueur de ~** piper
corner[1] [kɔʀnɛʀ] nm (Football) corner (kick)
corner[2] [kɔʀne] vt (pages) to make dog-eared ▷ vi
(klaxonner) to blare out
cornet [kɔʀnɛ] nm (paper) cone; (de glace)
cornet, cone; **~ à pistons** cornet
cornette [kɔʀnɛt] nf cornet (headgear)
corniaud [kɔʀnjo] nm (chien) mongrel; (péj) twit,
clot
corniche [kɔʀniʃ] nf (de meuble, neigeuse) cornice;
(route) coast road
cornichon [kɔʀniʃɔ̃] nm gherkin
Cornouailles [kɔʀnwaj] nf(pl) Cornwall
cornue [kɔʀny] nf retort
corollaire [kɔʀɔlɛʀ] nm corollary
corolle [kɔʀɔl] nf corolla
coron [kɔʀɔ̃] nm mining cottage; mining village
coronaire [kɔʀɔnɛʀ] adj coronary
corporation [kɔʀpɔʀasjɔ̃] nf corporate body;
(au Moyen-Âge) guild
corporel, le [kɔʀpɔʀɛl] adj bodily; (punition)
corporal; **soins ~s** care sg of the body
corps [kɔʀ] nm (gén) body; (cadavre) (dead) body;
à son ~ défendant against one's will; **à ~
perdu** headlong; **perdre ~ et biens** lost with all
hands; **prendre ~** to take shape; **faire ~ avec** to
be joined to; to form one body with; **~ d'armée
(CA)** army corps; **~ de ballet** corps de ballet; **~
constitués** (Pol) constitutional bodies; **le ~
consulaire (CC)** the consular corps; **~ à ~** adv
hand-to-hand ▷ nm clinch; **le ~ du délit** (Jur)
corpus delicti; **le ~ diplomatique (CD)** the
diplomatic corps; **le ~ électoral** the electorate;
le ~ enseignant the teaching profession; **~
étranger** (Méd) foreign body; **~
expéditionnaire** task force; **~ de garde**
guardroom; **~ législatif** legislative body; **le ~
médical** the medical profession
corpulence [kɔʀpylɑ̃s] nf build; (embonpoint)
stoutness (Brit), corpulence; **de forte ~** of large
build
corpulent, e [kɔʀpylɑ̃, -ɑ̃t] adj stout (Brit),
corpulent
corpus [kɔʀpys] nm (Ling) corpus
correct, e [kɔʀɛkt] adj (exact) accurate, correct;
(bienséant, honnête) correct; (passable) adequate
correctement [kɔʀɛktəmɑ̃] adv accurately;
correctly; adequately
correcteur, -trice [kɔʀɛktœʀ, -tʀis] nm/f (Scol)
examiner, marker; (Typo) proofreader
correctif, -ive [kɔʀɛktif, -iv] adj corrective ▷ nm
(mise au point) rider, qualification
correction [kɔʀɛksjɔ̃] nf (voir corriger) correction;
marking; (voir correct) correctness; (rature,
surcharge) correction, emendation; (coups)
thrashing; **~ sur écran** (Inform) screen editing;

~ (des épreuves) proofreading
correctionnel, le [kɔʀɛksjɔnɛl] adj (Jur):
tribunal ~ ≈ criminal court
corrélation [kɔʀelasjɔ̃] nf correlation
correspondance [kɔʀɛspɔ̃dɑ̃s] nf
correspondence; (de train, d'avion) connection;
ce train assure la ~ avec l'avion de 10 heures
this train connects with the 10 o'clock plane;
cours par ~ correspondence course; **vente par
~** mail-order business
correspondancier, -ière [kɔʀɛspɔ̃dɑ̃sje, -jɛʀ]
nm/f correspondence clerk
correspondant, e [kɔʀɛspɔ̃dɑ̃, -ɑ̃t] nm/f
correspondent; (Tél) person phoning (ou being
phoned)
correspondre [kɔʀɛspɔ̃dʀ(ə)] vi (données,
témoignages) to correspond, tally; (chambres) to
communicate; **~ à** to correspond to; **~ avec qn**
to correspond with sb
Corrèze [kɔʀɛz] nf: **la ~** the Corrèze
corrézien, ne [kɔʀezjɛ̃, -ɛn] adj of ou from the
Corrèze
corrida [kɔʀida] nf bullfight
corridor [kɔʀidɔʀ] nm corridor, passage
corrigé [kɔʀiʒe] nm (Scol) correct version; fair
copy
corriger [kɔʀiʒe] vt (devoir) to correct, mark;
(texte) to correct, emend; (erreur, défaut) to
correct, put right; (punir) to thrash; **~ qn de**
(défaut) to cure sb of; **se ~ de** to cure o.s. of
corroborer [kɔʀɔbɔʀe] vt to corroborate
corroder [kɔʀɔde] vt to corrode
corrompre [kɔʀɔ̃pʀ(ə)] vt (dépraver) to corrupt;
(acheter: témoin etc) to bribe
corrompu, e [kɔʀɔ̃py] adj corrupt
corrosif, -ive [kɔʀozif, -iv] adj corrosive
corrosion [kɔʀozjɔ̃] nf corrosion
corruption [kɔʀypsjɔ̃] nf corruption; bribery
corsage [kɔʀsaʒ] nm (d'une robe) bodice;
(chemisier) blouse
corsaire [kɔʀsɛʀ] nm pirate, corsair; privateer
corse [kɔʀs(ə)] adj Corsican ▷ nm/f: **Corse**
Corsican ▷ nf: **la C~** Corsica
corsé, e [kɔʀse] adj vigorous; (café etc) full-
flavoured (Brit) ou flavored (US); (goût) full; (fig)
spicy; tricky
corselet [kɔʀsəlɛ] nm corselet
corser [kɔʀse] vt (difficulté) to aggravate;
(intrigue) to liven up; (sauce) to add spice to
corset [kɔʀsɛ] nm corset; (d'une robe) bodice; **~
orthopédique** surgical corset
corso [kɔʀso] nm: **~ fleuri** procession of floral
floats
cortège [kɔʀtɛʒ] nm procession
cortisone [kɔʀtizɔn] nf (Méd) cortisone
corvée [kɔʀve] nf chore, drudgery no pl; (Mil)
fatigue (duty)
cosaque [kɔzak] nm cossack
cosignataire [kɔsiɲatɛʀ] adj, nm/f co-signatory
cosinus [kɔsinys] nm (Math) cosine
cosmétique [kɔsmetik] nm (pour les cheveux)
hair-oil; (produit de beauté) beauty care product

cosmétologie [kɔsmetɔlɔʒi] *nf* beauty care
cosmique [kɔsmik] *adj* cosmic
cosmonaute [kɔsmɔnot] *nm/f* cosmonaut, astronaut
cosmopolite [kɔsmɔpɔlit] *adj* cosmopolitan
cosmos [kɔsmɔs] *nm* outer space; cosmos
cosse [kɔs] *nf* (*Bot*) pod, hull
cossu, e [kɔsy] *adj* opulent-looking, well-to-do
Costa Rica [kɔstaʀika] *nm*: **le ~** Costa Rica
costaricien, ne [kɔstaʀisjɛ̃, -ɛn] *adj* Costa Rican ▷ *nm/f*: **Costaricien, ne** Costa Rican
costaud, e [kɔsto, -od] *adj* strong, sturdy
costume [kɔstym] *nm* (*d'homme*) suit; (*de théâtre*) costume
costumé, e [kɔstyme] *adj* dressed up
costumier, -ière [kɔstymje, -jɛʀ] *nm/f* (*fabricant, loueur*) costumier; (*Théât*) wardrobe master/mistress
cotangente [kɔtɑ̃ʒɑ̃t] *nf* (*Math*) cotangent
cotation [kɔtasjɔ̃] *nf* quoted value
cote [kɔt] *nf* (*en Bourse etc*) quotation; quoted value; (*d'un cheval*): **la ~ de** the odds *pl* on; (*d'un candidat etc*) rating; (*mesure: sur une carte*) spot height; (: *sur un croquis*) dimension; (*de classement*) (classification) mark; reference number; **avoir la ~** to be very popular; **inscrit à la ~** quoted on the Stock Exchange; **~ d'alerte** danger *ou* flood level; **~ mal taillée** (*fig*) compromise; **~ de popularité** popularity rating
coté, e [kɔte] *adj*: **être ~** to be listed *ou* quoted; **être ~ en Bourse** to be quoted on the Stock Exchange; **être bien/mal ~** to be highly/poorly rated
côte [kot] *nf* (*rivage*) coast(line); (*pente*) slope; (: *sur une route*) hill; (*Anat*) rib; (*d'un tricot, tissu*) rib, ribbing *no pl*; **~ à ~** *adv* side by side; **la C~ (d'Azur)** the (French) Riviera; **la C~ d'Ivoire** the Ivory Coast; **~ de porc** pork chop
côté [kote] *nm* (*gén*) side; (*direction*) way, direction; **de chaque ~ (de)** on each side of; **de tous les ~s** from all directions; **de quel ~ est-il parti?** which way *ou* in which direction did he go?; **de ce/de l'autre ~** this/the other way; **d'un ~ ... de l'autre ~ ...** (*alternative*) on (the) one hand ... on the other (hand) ...; **du ~ de** (*provenance*) from; (*direction*) towards; **du ~ de Lyon** (*proximité*) near Lyons; **du ~ gauche** on the left-hand side; **de ~** *adv* sideways; on one side; to one side; aside; **laisser de ~** to leave on one side; **mettre de ~** to put on one side, put aside; **de mon ~** (*quant à moi*) for my part; **à ~** *adv* (*right*) nearby; beside next door; (*d'autre part*) besides; **à ~ de** beside; next to; (*fig*) in comparison to; **à ~ (de la cible)** off target, wide (of the mark); **être aux ~s de** to be by the side of
coteau, x [kɔto] *nm* hill
côtelé, e [kotle] *adj* ribbed; **pantalon en velours ~** corduroy trousers *pl*
côtelette [kotlɛt] *nf* chop
coter [kɔte] *vt* (*Bourse*) to quote

coterie [kɔtʀi] *nf* set
côtier, -ière [kotje, -jɛʀ] *adj* coastal
cotisation [kɔtizasjɔ̃] *nf* subscription, dues *pl*; (*pour une pension*) contributions *pl*
cotiser [kɔtize] *vi*: **~ (à)** to pay contributions (to); (*à une association*) to subscribe (to); **se cotiser** to club together
coton [kɔtɔ̃] *nm* cotton; **~ hydrophile** cotton wool (*Brit*), absorbent cotton (*US*)
cotonnade [kɔtɔnad] *nf* cotton (fabric)
Coton-Tige® [kɔtɔ̃tiʒ] *nm* cotton bud®
côtoyer [kotwaje] *vt* to be close to; (*rencontrer*) to rub shoulders with; (*longer*) to run alongside; (*fig: friser*) to be bordering *ou* verging on
cotte [kɔt] *nf*: **~ de mailles** coat of mail
cou [ku] *nm* neck
couac [kwak] *nm* (*fam*) bum note
couard, e [kwaʀ, -aʀd(ə)] *adj* cowardly
couchage [kuʃaʒ] *nm voir* **sac**
couchant [kuʃɑ̃] *adj*: **soleil ~** setting sun
couche [kuʃ] *nf* (*strate: gén, Géo*) layer, stratum (*pl* -a); (*de peinture, vernis*) coat; (*de poussière, crème*) layer; (*de bébé*) nappy (*Brit*), diaper (*US*); **~ d'ozone** ozone layer; **couches** *nfpl* (*Méd*) confinement *sg*; **~s sociales** social levels *ou* strata
couché, e [kuʃe] *adj* (*étendu*) lying down; (*au lit*) in bed
couche-culotte [kuʃkylɔt] (*pl* **couches-culottes**) *nf* (plastic-coated) disposable nappy (*Brit*) *ou* diaper (*US*)
coucher [kuʃe] *nm* (*du soleil*) setting ▷ *vt* (*personne*) to put to bed; (: *loger*) to put up; (*objet*) to lay on its side; (*écrire*) to inscribe, couch ▷ *vi* (*dormir*) to sleep, spend the night; **~ avec qn** to sleep with sb, go to bed with sb; **se coucher** *vi* (*pour dormir*) to go to bed; (*pour se reposer*) to lie down; (*soleil*) to set, go down; **à prendre avant le ~** (*Méd*) take at night *ou* before going to bed; **~ de soleil** sunset
couchette [kuʃɛt] *nf* couchette; (*de marin*) bunk
coucheur [kuʃœʀ] *nm*: **mauvais ~** awkward customer
couci-couça [kusikusa] *adv* (*fam*) so-so
coucou [kuku] *nm* cuckoo ▷ *excl* peek-a-boo
coude [kud] *nm* (*Anat*) elbow; (*de tuyau, de la route*) bend; **~ à ~** *adv* shoulder to shoulder, side by side
coudée [kude] *nf*: **avoir ses ~s franches** (*fig*) to have a free rein
cou-de-pied [kudpje] (*pl* **cous-de-pied**) *nm* instep
coudoyer [kudwaje] *vt* to brush past *ou* against; (*fig*) to rub shoulders with
coudre [kudʀ(ə)] *vt* (*bouton*) to sew on; (*robe*) to sew (up) ▷ *vi* to sew
couenne [kwan] *nf* (*de lard*) rind
couette [kwɛt] *nf* duvet, (continental) quilt; **couettes** *nfpl* (*cheveux*) bunches
couffin [kufɛ̃] *nm* Moses basket; (straw) basket
couilles [kuj] *nfpl* (*fam!*) balls (!)
couiner [kwine] *vi* to squeal

coulage [kulaʒ] *nm* (*Comm*) loss of stock (*due to theft or negligence*)

coulant, e [kulɑ̃, -ɑ̃t] *adj* (*indulgent*) easy-going; (*fromage etc*) runny

coulée [kule] *nf* (*de lave, métal en fusion*) flow; **~ de neige** snowslide

couler [kule] *vi* to flow, run; (*fuir: stylo, récipient*) to leak; (*sombrer: bateau*) to sink ▷ *vt* (*cloche, sculpture*) to cast; (*bateau*) to sink; (*fig*) to ruin, bring down; (: *passer*): **~ une vie heureuse** to enjoy a happy life; **se ~ dans** (*interstice etc*) to slip into; **faire ~** (*eau*) to run; **faire ~ un bain** to run a bath; **il a coulé une bielle** (*Auto*) his big end went; **~ de source** to follow on naturally; **~ à pic** to sink *ou* go straight to the bottom

couleur [kulœR] *nf* colour (*Brit*), color (*US*); (*Cartes*) suit; **couleurs** *nfpl* (*du teint*) colo(u)r *sg*; **les ~s** (*Mil*) the colo(u)rs; **en ~s** (*film*) in colo(u)r; **télévision en ~s** colo(u)r television; **de ~** (*homme, femme*) colo(u)red; **sous ~ de** on the pretext of; **de quelle ~** of what colo(u)r

couleuvre [kulœvR(ə)] *nf* grass snake

coulisse [kulis] *nf* (*Tech*) runner; **coulisses** *nfpl* (*Théât*) wings; (*fig*): **dans les ~s** behind the scenes; **porte à ~** sliding door

coulisser [kulise] *vi* to slide, run

couloir [kulwaR] *nm* corridor, passage; (*d'avion*) aisle; (*de bus*) gangway; (: *sur la route*) bus lane; (*Sport: de piste*) lane; (*Géo*) gully; **~ aérien** air corridor *ou* lane; **~ de navigation** shipping lane

coulpe [kulp(ə)] *nf*: **battre sa ~** to repent openly

coup [ku] *nm* (*heurt, choc*) knock; (*affectif*) blow, shock; (*agressif*) blow; (*avec arme à feu*) shot; (*de l'horloge*) chime; stroke; (*Sport*) stroke; shot; blow; (*fam: fois*) time; (*Échecs*) move; **~ de coude/genou** nudge (with the elbow)/ with the knee; **à ~s de hache/marteau** (hitting) with an axe/a hammer; **~ de tonnerre** clap of thunder; **~ de sonnette** ring of the bell; **~ de crayon/pinceau** stroke of the pencil/brush; **donner un ~ de balai** to sweep up, give the floor a sweep; **donner un ~ de chiffon** to go round with the duster; **avoir le ~** (*fig*) to have the knack; **être dans le/hors du ~** to be in/not to be in on it; **boire un ~** to have a drink; **d'un seul ~** (*subitement*) suddenly; (*à la fois*) at one go; in one blow; **du ~** so (you see); **du premier ~** first time *ou* go, at the first attempt; **du même ~** at the same time; **à ~ sûr** definitely, without fail; **après ~** afterwards; **~ sur ~** in quick succession; **être sur un ~** to be on to something; **sur le ~** outright; **sous le ~ de** (*surprise etc*) under the influence of; **tomber sous le ~ de la loi** to constitute a statutory offence; **à tous les ~s** every time; **il a raté son ~** he missed his turn; **pour le ~** for once; **~ bas** (*fig*): **donner un ~ bas à qn** to hit sb below the belt; **~ de chance** stroke of luck; **~ de chapeau** (*fig*) pat on the back; **~ de couteau** stab (of a knife); **~ dur** hard blow; **~ d'éclat** (great) feat; **~ d'envoi** kick-off; **~ d'essai** first attempt; **~ d'état** coup d'état; **~ de feu** shot; **~ de filet**

(*Police*) haul; **~ de foudre** (*fig*) love at first sight; **~ fourré** stab in the back; **~ franc** free kick; **~ de frein** (sharp) braking *no pl*; **~ de fusil** rifle shot; **~ de grâce** coup de grâce; **~ du lapin** (*Auto*) whiplash; **~ de main**: **donner un ~ de main à qn** to give sb a (helping) hand; **~ de maître** master stroke; **~ d'œil** glance; **~ de pied** kick; **~ de poing** punch; **~ de soleil** sunburn *no pl*; **~ de téléphone** phone call; **~ de tête** (*fig*) (sudden) impulse; **~ de théâtre** (*fig*) dramatic turn of events; **~ de vent** gust of wind; **en ~ de vent** (*rapidement*) in a tearing hurry

coupable [kupabl(ə)] *adj* guilty; (*pensée*) guilty, culpable ▷ *nm/f* (*gén*) culprit; (*Jur*) guilty party; **~ de** guilty of

coupant, e [kupɑ̃, -ɑ̃t] *adj* (*lame*) sharp; (*fig: voix, ton*) cutting

coupe [kup] *nf* (*verre*) goblet; (*à fruits*) dish; (*Sport*) cup; (*de cheveux, de vêtement*) cut; (*graphique, plan*) (cross) section; **être sous la ~ de** to be under the control of; **faire des ~s sombres dans** to make drastic cuts in

coupé, e [kupe] *adj* (*communications, route*) cut, blocked; (*vêtement*): **bien/mal ~** well/badly cut ▷ *nm* (*Auto*) coupé ▷ *nf* (*Navig*) gangway

coupe-circuit [kupsiRkɥi] *nm inv* cutout, circuit breaker

coupe-feu [kupfø] *nm inv* firebreak

coupe-gorge [kupgɔRʒ(ə)] *nm inv* cut-throats' den

coupe-ongles [kupɔ̃gl(ə)] *nm inv* (*pince*) nail clippers; (*ciseaux*) nail scissors

coupe-papier [kuppapje] *nm inv* paper knife

couper [kupe] *vt* to cut; (*retrancher*) to cut (out), take out; (*route, courant*) to cut off; (*appétit*) to take away; (*fièvre*) to take down, reduce; (*vin, cidre*) to blend; (: *à table*) to dilute (with water) ▷ *vi* to cut; (*prendre un raccourci*) to take a short-cut; (*Cartes: diviser le paquet*) to cut; (: *avec l'atout*) to trump; **se couper** *vi* (*se blesser*) to cut o.s.; (*en témoignant etc*) to give o.s. away; **~ l'appétit à qn** to spoil sb's appetite; **~ la parole à qn** to cut sb short; **~ les vivres à qn** to cut off sb's vital supplies; **~ le contact** *ou* **l'allumage** (*Auto*) to turn off the ignition; **~ les ponts avec qn** to break with sb; **se faire ~ les cheveux** to have *ou* get one's hair cut

couperet [kupRɛ] *nm* cleaver, chopper

couperosé, e [kupRoze] *adj* blotchy

couple [kupl(ə)] *nm* couple; **~ de torsion** torque

coupler [kuple] *vt* to couple (together)

couplet [kuplɛ] *nm* verse

coupleur [kuplœR] *nm*: **~ acoustique** acoustic coupler

coupole [kupɔl] *nf* dome; cupola

coupon [kupɔ̃] *nm* (*ticket*) coupon; (*de tissu*) remnant; roll

coupon-réponse [kupɔ̃Repɔ̃s] (*pl* **coupons-réponses**) *nm* reply coupon

coupure [kupyR] *nf* cut; (*billet de banque*) note; (*de journal*) cutting; **~ de courant** power cut

cour [kuʀ] *nf* (*de ferme, jardin*) (court)yard; (*d'immeuble*) back yard; (*Jur, royale*) court; **faire la ~ à qn** to court sb; **~ d'appel** appeal court (*Brit*), appellate court (*US*); **~ d'assises** court of assizes, ≈ Crown Court (*Brit*); **~ de cassation** final court of appeal; **~ des comptes** (*Admin*) revenue court; **~ martiale** court-martial; **~ de récréation** (*Scol*) schoolyard, playground

courage [kuʀaʒ] *nm* courage, bravery

courageusement [kuʀaʒøzmɑ̃] *adv* bravely, courageously

courageux, -euse [kuʀaʒø, -øz] *adj* brave, courageous

couramment [kuʀamɑ̃] *adv* commonly; (*parler*) fluently

courant, e [kuʀɑ̃, -ɑ̃t] *adj* (*fréquent*) common; (*Comm, gén: normal*) standard; (*en cours*) current ▷ *nm* current; (*fig*) movement; trend; **être au ~ (de)** (*fait, nouvelle*) to know (about); **mettre qn au ~ (de)** (*fait, nouvelle*) to tell sb (about); (*nouveau travail etc*) to teach sb the basics (of), brief sb (about); **se tenir au ~ (de)** (*techniques etc*) to keep o.s. up-to-date (on); **dans le ~ de** (*pendant*) in the course of; **~ octobre** *etc* in the course of October *etc*; **le 10 ~** (*Comm*) the 10th inst.; **~ d'air** draught (*Brit*), draft (*US*); **~ électrique** (electric) current, power

courbature [kuʀbatyʀ] *nf* ache

courbaturé, e [kuʀbatyʀe] *adj* aching

courbe [kuʀb(ə)] *adj* curved ▷ *nf* curve; **~ de niveau** contour line

courber [kuʀbe] *vt* to bend; **~ la tête** to bow one's head; **se courber** *vi* (*branche etc*) to bend, curve; (*personne*) to bend (down)

courbette [kuʀbɛt] *nf* low bow

coure *etc* [kuʀ] *vb voir* **courir**

coureur, -euse [kuʀœʀ, -øz] *nm/f* (*Sport*) runner (*ou* driver); (*péj*) womanizer/manhunter; **~ cycliste/automobile** racing cyclist/driver

courge [kuʀʒ(ə)] *nf* (*Bot*) gourd; (*Culin*) marrow

courgette [kuʀʒɛt] *nf* courgette (*Brit*), zucchini (*US*)

courir [kuʀiʀ] *vi* (*gén*) to run; (*se dépêcher*) to rush; (*fig: rumeurs*) to go round; (*Comm: intérêt*) to accrue ▷ *vt* (*Sport: épreuve*) to run; (*risque*) to run; (*danger*) to face; **~ les cafés/bals** to do the rounds of the cafés/ dances; **le bruit court que** the rumour is going round that; **par les temps qui courent** at the present time; **~ après qn** to run after sb, chase (after) sb; **laisser ~** to let things alone; **faire ~ qn** to make sb run around (all over the place); **tu peux (toujours) ~!** you've got a hope!

couronne [kuʀɔn] *nf* crown; (*de fleurs*) wreath, circlet; **~ (funéraire** *ou* **mortuaire)** (funeral) wreath

couronnement [kuʀɔnmɑ̃] *nm* coronation, crowning; (*fig*) crowning achievement

couronner [kuʀɔne] *vt* to crown

courons [kuʀɔ̃], **courrai** *etc* [kuʀe] *vb voir* **courir**

courre [kuʀ] *vb voir* **chasse**

courriel [kuʀjɛl] *nm* email; **envoyer qch par ~** to email sth

courrier [kuʀje] *nm* mail, post; (*lettres à écrire*) letters *pl*; (*rubrique*) column; **qualité ~** letter quality; **long/moyen ~** *adj* (*Aviat*) long-/medium-haul; **~ du cœur** problem page; **~ électronique** electronic mail, E-mail

courroie [kuʀwa] *nf* strap; (*Tech*) belt; **~ de transmission/de ventilateur** driving/fan belt

courrons *etc* [kuʀɔ̃] *vb voir* **courir**

courroucé, e [kuʀuse] *adj* wrathful

cours [kuʀ] *vb voir* **courir** ▷ *nm* (*leçon*) lesson; class; (*série de leçons*) course; (*cheminement*) course; (*écoulement*) flow; (*avenue*) walk; (*Comm*) rate; price; (*Bourse*) quotation; **donner libre ~ à** to give free expression to; **avoir ~** (*monnaie*) to be legal tender; (*fig*) to be current; (*Scol*) to have a class *ou* lecture; **en ~** (*année*) current; (*travaux*) in progress; **en ~ de route** on the way; **au ~ de** in the course of, during; **le ~ du change** the exchange rate; **~ d'eau** waterway; **~ élémentaire (CE)** *2nd and 3rd years of primary school*; **~ moyen (CM)** *4th and 5th years of primary school*; **~ préparatoire** ≈ infants' class (*Brit*), ≈ 1st grade (*US*); **~ du soir** night school

course [kuʀs(ə)] *nf* running; (*Sport: épreuve*) race; (*trajet: du soleil*) course; (: *d'un projectile*) flight; (: *d'une pièce mécanique*) travel; (*excursion*) outing; climb; (*d'un taxi, autocar*) journey, trip; (*petite mission*) errand; **courses** *nfpl* (*achats*) shopping *sg*; (*Hippisme*) races; **faire les** *ou* **ses ~s** to go shopping; **jouer aux ~s** to bet on the races; **à bout de ~** (*épuisé*) exhausted; **~ automobile** car race; **~ de côte** (*Auto*) hill climb; **~ par étapes** *ou* **d'étapes** race in stages; **~ d'obstacles** obstacle race; **~ à pied** walking race; **~ de vitesse** sprint; **~s de chevaux** horse racing

coursier, -ière [kuʀsje, -jɛʀ] *nm/f* courier

court, e [kuʀ, kuʀt(ə)] *adj* short ▷ *adv* short ▷ *nm*: **~ (de tennis)** (tennis) court; **tourner ~** to come to a sudden end; **couper ~ à** to cut short; **à ~ de** short of; **prendre qn de ~** to catch sb unawares; **pour faire ~** briefly, to cut a long story short; **ça fait ~** that's not very long; **tirer à la ~e paille** to draw lots; **faire la ~e échelle à qn** to give sb a leg up; **~ métrage** (*Ciné*) short (film)

court-bouillon [kuʀbujɔ̃] (*pl* **courts-bouillons**) *nm* court-bouillon

court-circuit [kuʀsiʀkɥi] (*pl* **courts-circuits**) *nm* short-circuit

court-circuiter [kuʀsiʀkɥite] *vt* (*fig*) to bypass

courtier, -ière [kuʀtje, -jɛʀ] *nm/f* broker

courtisan [kuʀtizɑ̃] *nm* courtier

courtisane [kuʀtizan] *nf* courtesan

courtiser [kuʀtize] *vt* to court, woo

courtois, e [kuʀtwa, -waz] *adj* courteous

courtoisement [kuʀtwazmɑ̃] *adv* courteously

courtoisie [kuʀtwazi] *nf* courtesy

couru, e [kuʀy] *pp de* **courir** ▷ *adj* (*spectacle etc*) popular; **c'est ~ (d'avance)!** (*fam*) it's a safe bet!

cousais *etc* [kuzɛ] *vb voir* **coudre**

couscous [kuskus] *nm* couscous

cousin, e [kuzɛ̃, -in] *nm/f* cousin ▷ *nm* (*Zool*) mosquito; **~ germain** first cousin

cousons *etc* [kuzɔ̃] *vb voir* **coudre**

coussin [kusɛ̃] *nm* cushion; **~ d'air** (*Tech*) air cushion

cousu, e [kuzy] *pp de* **coudre** ▷ *adj*: **~ d'or** rolling in riches

coût [ku] *nm* cost; **le ~ de la vie** the cost of living

coûtant [kutɑ̃] *adj m*: **au prix ~** at cost price

couteau, x [kuto] *nm* knife; **~ à cran d'arrêt** flick-knife; **~ de cuisine** kitchen knife; **~ à pain** bread knife; **~ de poche** pocket knife

couteau-scie [kutosi] (*pl* **couteaux-scies**) *nm* serrated(-edged) knife

coutelier, -ière [kutəlje, -jɛR] *adj*: **l'industrie coutelière** the cutlery industry ▷ *nm/f* cutler

coutellerie [kutɛlRi] *nf* cutlery shop; cutlery

coûter [kute] *vt* to cost ▷ *vi*: **~ à qn** to cost sb a lot; **~ cher** to be expensive; **~ cher à qn** (*fig*) to cost sb dear *ou* dearly; **combien ça coûte?** how much is it?, what does it cost?; **coûte que coûte** at all costs

coûteux, -euse [kutø, -øz] *adj* costly, expensive

coutume [kutym] *nf* custom; **de ~** usual, customary

coutumier, -ière [kutymje, -jɛR] *adj* customary; **elle est coutumière du fait** that's her usual trick

couture [kutyR] *nf* sewing; dress-making; (*points*) seam

couturier [kutyRje] *nm* fashion designer, couturier

couturière [kutyRjɛR] *nf* dressmaker

couvée [kuve] *nf* brood, clutch

couvent [kuvɑ̃] *nm* (*de sœurs*) convent; (*de frères*) monastery; (*établissement scolaire*) convent (school)

couver [kuve] *vt* to hatch; (*maladie*) to be sickening for ▷ *vi* (*feu*) to smoulder (*Brit*), smolder (*US*); (*révolte*) to be brewing; **~ qn/qch des yeux** to look lovingly at sb/sth; (*convoiter*) to look longingly at sb/sth

couvercle [kuvɛRkl(ə)] *nm* lid; (*de bombe aérosol etc, qui se visse*) cap, top

couvert, e [kuvɛR, -ɛRt(ə)] *pp de* **couvrir** ▷ *adj* (*ciel*) overcast; (*coiffé d'un chapeau*) wearing a hat ▷ *nm* place setting; (*place à table*) place; (*au restaurant*) cover charge; **couverts** *nmpl* place settings; cutlery *sg*; **~ de** covered with *ou* in; **bien ~** (*habillé*) well wrapped up; **mettre le ~** to lay the table; **à ~** under cover; **sous le ~ de** under the shelter of; (*fig*) under cover of

couverture [kuvɛRtyR] *nf* (*de lit*) blanket; (*de bâtiment*) roofing; (*de livre, fig: d'un espion etc, Assurances*) cover; (*Presse*) coverage; **de ~** (*lettre etc*) covering; **~ chauffante** electric blanket

couveuse [kuvøz] *nf* (*à poules*) sitter, brooder; (*de maternité*) incubator

couvre *etc* [kuvR(ə)] *vb voir* **couvrir**

couvre-chef [kuvRəʃɛf] *nm* hat

couvre-feu, x [kuvRəfø] *nm* curfew

couvre-lit [kuvRəli] *nm* bedspread

couvre-pieds [kuvRəpje] *nm inv* quilt

couvreur [kuvRœR] *nm* roofer

couvrir [kuvRiR] *vt* to cover; (*dominer, étouffer: voix, pas*) to drown out; (*erreur*) to cover up; (*Zool: s'accoupler à*) to cover; **se couvrir** *vi* (*ciel*) to cloud over; (*s'habiller*) to cover up, wrap up; (*se coiffer*) to put on one's hat; (*par une assurance*) to cover o.s.; **se ~ de** (*fleurs, boutons*) to become covered in

cover-girl [kɔvœRg[ʷœR]l] *nf* model

cow-boy [kɔbɔj] *nm* cowboy

coyote [kɔjɔt] *nm* coyote

CP *sigle m* = **cours préparatoire**

CPAM *sigle f* (= *Caisse primaire d'assurances maladie*) health insurance office

cps *abr* (= *caractères par seconde*) cps

cpt *abr* = **comptant**

CQFD *abr* (= *ce qu'il fallait démontrer*) QED = **quod erat demonstrandum**

CR *sigle m* = **compte rendu**

crabe [kRab] *nm* crab

crachat [kRaʃa] *nm* spittle *no pl*, spit *no pl*

craché, e [kRaʃe] *adj*: **son père tout ~** the spitting image of his (*ou* her) father

cracher [kRaʃe] *vi* to spit ▷ *vt* to spit out; (*fig: lave etc*) to belch (out); **~ du sang** to spit blood

crachin [kRaʃɛ̃] *nm* drizzle

crachiner [kRaʃine] *vi* to drizzle

crachoir [kRaʃwaR] *nm* spittoon; (*de dentiste*) bowl

crachotement [kRaʃɔtmɑ̃] *nm* crackling *no pl*

crachoter [kRaʃɔte] *vi* (*haut-parleur, radio*) to crackle

crack [kRak] *nm* (*intellectuel*) whiz kid; (*sportif*) ace; (*poulain*) hot favourite (*Brit*) *ou* favorite (*US*)

Cracovie [kRakɔvi] *n* Cracow

cradingue [kRadɛ̃g] *adj* (*fam*) disgustingly dirty, filthy-dirty

craie [kRɛ] *nf* chalk

craignais *etc* [kRɛɲɛ] *vb voir* **craindre**

craindre [kRɛ̃dR(ə)] *vt* to fear, be afraid of; (*être sensible à: chaleur, froid*) to be easily damaged by; **~ de/que** to be afraid of/that; **je crains qu'il (ne) vienne** I am afraid he may come

crainte [kRɛ̃t] *nf* fear; **de ~ de/que** for fear of/ that

craintif, -ive [kRɛ̃tif, -iv] *adj* timid

craintivement [kRɛ̃tivmɑ̃] *adv* timidly

cramer [kRame] *vi* (*fam*) to burn

cramoisi, e [kRamwazi] *adj* crimson

crampe [kRɑ̃p] *nf* cramp; **~ d'estomac** stomach cramp

crampon [kRɑ̃pɔ̃] *nm* (*de semelle*) stud; (*Alpinisme*) crampon

cramponner [kRɑ̃pɔne]: **se cramponner** *vi*: **se ~ (à)** to hang *ou* cling on (to)

cran [kRɑ̃] *nm* (*entaille*) notch; (*de courroie*) hole; (*courage*) guts *pl*; **~ d'arrêt/de sûreté** safety catch; **~ de mire** bead

crâne [kRɑn] *nm* skull

crâner [kRɑne] *vi* (*fam*) to swank, show off

crânien, ne [kRɑnjɛ̃, -ɛn] *adj* cranial, skull *cpd*,

brain *cpd*

crapaud [kʀapo] *nm* toad

crapule [kʀapyl] *nf* villain

crapuleux, -euse [kʀapylø, -øz] *adj*: **crime ~** villainous crime

craquelure [kʀaklyʀ] *nf* crack; crackle *no pl*

craquement [kʀakmɑ̃] *nm* crack, snap; (*du plancher*) creak, creaking *no pl*

craquer [kʀake] *vi* (*bois, plancher*) to creak; (*fil, branche*) to snap; (*couture*) to come apart, burst; (*fig*) to break down, fall apart; (: *être enthousiasmé*) to go wild ▷ *vt*: **~ une allumette** to strike a match

crasse [kʀas] *nf* grime, filth ▷ *adj* (*fig: ignorance*) crass

crasseux, -euse [kʀasø, øz] *adj* filthy

crassier [kʀasje] *nm* slag heap

cratère [kʀatɛʀ] *nm* crater

cravache [kʀavaʃ] *nf* (riding) crop

cravacher [kʀavaʃe] *vt* to use the crop on

cravate [kʀavat] *nf* tie

cravater [kʀavate] *vt* to put a tie on; (*fig*) to grab round the neck

crawl [kʀol] *nm* crawl

crawlé, e [kʀole] *adj*: **dos ~** backstroke

crayeux, -euse [kʀɛjø, -øz] *adj* chalky

crayon [kʀɛjɔ̃] *nm* pencil; (*de rouge à lèvres etc*) stick, pencil; **écrire au ~** to write in pencil; **~ à bille** ball-point pen; **~ de couleur** crayon; **~ optique** light pen

crayon-feutre [kʀɛjɔ̃føtʀ(ə)] (*pl* **crayons-feutres**) *nm* felt(-tip) pen

crayonner [kʀɛjone] *vt* to scribble, sketch

CRDP *sigle m* (= *Centre régional de documentation pédagogique*) teachers' resource centre

créance [kʀeɑ̃s] *nf* (*Comm*) (financial) claim, (recoverable) debt; **donner ~ à qch** to lend credence to sth

créancier, -ière [kʀeɑ̃sje, -jɛʀ] *nm/f* creditor

créateur, -trice [kʀeatœʀ, -tʀis] *adj* creative ▷ *nm/f* creator; **le C~** (*Rel*) the Creator

créatif, -ive [kʀeatif, -iv] *adj* creative

création [kʀeasjɔ̃] *nf* creation

créativité [kʀeativite] *nf* creativity

créature [kʀeatyʀ] *nf* creature

crécelle [kʀesɛl] *nf* rattle

crèche [kʀɛʃ] *nf* (*de Noël*) crib; *see note*; (*garderie*) crèche, day nursery

⬤ **CRÈCHE**
⬤
⬤ In France the Christmas crib (*crèche*) usually
⬤ contains figurines representing a miller, a
⬤ wood-cutter and other villagers as well as
⬤ the Holy Family and the traditional cow,
⬤ donkey and shepherds. The Three Wise Men
⬤ are added to the nativity scene at Epiphany
⬤ (6 January, Twelfth Night).

crédence [kʀedɑ̃s] *nf* (small) sideboard

crédibilité [kʀedibilite] *nf* credibility

crédible [kʀedibl(ə)] *adj* credible

crédit [kʀedi] *nm* (*gén*) credit; **crédits** *nmpl* funds; **acheter à ~** to buy on credit *ou* on easy terms; **faire ~ à qn** to give sb credit; **~ municipal** pawnshop; **~ relais** bridging loan

crédit-bail [kʀedibaj] (*pl* **crédits-bails**) *nm* (*Écon*) leasing

créditer [kʀedite] *vt*: **~ un compte (de)** to credit an account (with)

créditeur, -trice [kʀeditœʀ, -tʀis] *adj* in credit, credit *cpd* ▷ *nm/f* customer in credit

credo [kʀedo] *nm* credo, creed

crédule [kʀedyl] *adj* credulous, gullible

crédulité [kʀedylite] *nf* credulity, gullibility

créer [kʀee] *vt* to create; (*Théât: pièce*) to produce (for the first time); (: *rôle*) to create

crémaillère [kʀemajɛʀ] *nf* (*Rail*) rack; (*tige crantée*) trammel; **direction à ~** (*Auto*) rack and pinion steering; **pendre la ~** to have a house-warming party

crémation [kʀemasjɔ̃] *nf* cremation

crématoire [kʀematwaʀ] *adj*: **four ~** crematorium

crématorium [kʀematɔʀjɔm] *nm* crematorium

crème [kʀɛm] *nf* cream; (*entremets*) cream dessert ▷ *adj inv* cream; **un (café) ~** ≈ a white coffee; **~ chantilly** whipped cream, crème Chantilly; **~ fouettée** whipped cream; **~ glacée** ice cream; **~ à raser** shaving cream; **~ solaire** sun cream

crémerie [kʀɛmʀi] *nf* dairy; (*tearoom*) teashop

crémeux, -euse [kʀemø, -øz] *adj* creamy

crémier, -ière [kʀemje, -jɛʀ] *nm/f* dairyman/-woman

créneau, x [kʀeno] *nm* (*de fortification*) crenel(le); (*fig, aussi Comm*) gap, slot; (*Auto*): **faire un ~** to reverse into a parking space (*between cars alongside the kerb*)

créole [kʀeɔl] *adj, nm/f* Creole

crêpe [kʀɛp] *nf* (*galette*) pancake ▷ *nm* (*tissu*) crêpe; (*de deuil*) black mourning crêpe; (*ruban*) black armband (*ou* hatband *ou* ribbon); **semelle (de) ~** crêpe sole; **~ de Chine** crêpe de Chine

crêpé, e [kʀepe] *adj* (*cheveux*) backcombed

crêperie [kʀɛpʀi] *nf* pancake shop *ou* restaurant

crépi [kʀepi] *nm* roughcast

crépir [kʀepiʀ] *vt* to roughcast

crépitement [kʀepitmɑ̃] *nm* (*du feu*) crackling *no pl*; (*d'une arme automatique*) rattle *no pl*

crépiter [kʀepite] *vi* to sputter, splutter, crackle

crépon [kʀepɔ̃] *nm* seersucker

CREPS [kʀɛps] *sigle m* (= *Centre régional d'éducation physique et sportive*) ≈ sports *ou* leisure centre

crépu, e [kʀepy] *adj* frizzy, fuzzy

crépuscule [kʀepyskyl] *nm* twilight, dusk

crescendo [kʀeʃɛndo] *nm, adv* (*Mus*) crescendo; **aller ~** (*fig*) to rise higher and higher, grow ever greater

cresson [kʀesɔ̃] *nm* watercress

Crète [kʀɛt] *nf*: **la ~** Crete

crête [kʀɛt] *nf* (*de coq*) comb; (*de vague, montagne*) crest

crétin, e [kʀetɛ̃, -in] *nm/f* cretin

crétois, e [kʀetwa, -waz] *adj* Cretan

cretonne [kʀətɔn] *nf* cretonne

creuser [kʀøze] *vt* (*trou, tunnel*) to dig; (*sol*) to dig a hole in; (*bois*) to hollow out; (*fig*) to go (deeply) into; **ça creuse** that gives you a real appetite; **se ~ (la cervelle)** to rack one's brains

creuset [kʀøzɛ] *nm* crucible; (*fig*) melting pot, (*severe*) test

creux, -euse [kʀø, -øz] *adj* hollow ▷ *nm* hollow; (*fig: sur graphique etc*) trough; **heures creuses** slack periods; off-peak periods; **le ~ de l'estomac** the pit of the stomach

crevaison [kʀəvɛzɔ̃] *nf* puncture, flat

crevant, e [kʀəvɑ, -ɑ̃t] *adj* (*fam: fatigant*) knackering; (: *très drôle*) priceless

crevasse [kʀəvas] *nf* (*dans le sol*) crack, fissure; (*de glacier*) crevasse; (*de la peau*) crack

crevé, e [kʀəve] *adj* (*fam: fatigué*) worn out, dead beat

crève-cœur [kʀɛvkœʀ] *nm inv* heartbreak

crever [kʀəve] *vt* (*papier*) to tear, break; (*tambour, ballon*) to burst ▷ *vi* (*pneu*) to burst; (*automobiliste*) to have a puncture (*Brit*) *ou* a flat (tire) (*US*); (*abcès, outre, nuage*) to burst (open); (*fam*) to die; **cela lui a crevé un œil** it blinded him in one eye; **~ l'écran** to have real screen presence

crevette [kʀəvɛt] *nf*: **~ (rose)** prawn; **~ grise** shrimp

CRF *sigle f* (= *Croix-Rouge française*) French Red Cross

cri [kʀi] *nm* cry, shout; (*d'animal: spécifique*) cry, call; **à grands ~s** at the top of one's voice; **c'est le dernier ~** (*fig*) it's the latest fashion

criant, e [kʀijɑ̃, -ɑ̃t] *adj* (*injustice*) glaring

criard, e [kʀijaʀ, -aʀd(ə)] *adj* (*couleur*) garish, loud; (*voix*) yelling

crible [kʀibl(ə)] *nm* riddle; (*mécanique*) screen, jig; **passer qch au ~** to put sth through a riddle; (*fig*) to go over sth with a fine-tooth comb

criblé, e [kʀible] *adj*: **~ de** riddled with

cric [kʀik] *nm* (*Auto*) jack

cricket [kʀikɛt] *nm* cricket

criée [kʀije] *nf*: **(vente à la) ~** (sale by) auction

crier [kʀije] *vi* (*pour appeler*) to shout, cry (out); (*de peur, de douleur etc*) to scream, yell; (*fig: grincer*) to squeal, screech ▷ *vt* (*ordre, injure*) to shout (out), yell (out); **sans ~ gare** without warning; **~ grâce** to cry for mercy; **~ au secours** to shout for help

crieur, -euse [kʀijœʀ, -øz] *nm/f*: **~ de journaux** newspaper seller

crime [kʀim] *nm* crime; (*meurtre*) murder

Crimée [kʀime] *nf*: **la ~** the Crimea

criminalité [kʀiminalite] *nf* criminality, crime

criminel, le [kʀiminɛl] *adj* criminal ▷ *nm/f* criminal; murderer; **~ de guerre** war criminal

criminologie [kʀiminɔlɔʒi] *nf* criminology

criminologiste [kʀiminɔlɔʒist(ə)] *nm/f* criminologist

criminologue [kʀiminɔlɔg] *nm/f* criminologist

crin [kʀɛ̃] *nm* hair *no pl*; (*fibre*) horsehair; **à tous ~s, à tout ~** diehard, out-and-out

crinière [kʀinjɛʀ] *nf* mane

crique [kʀik] *nf* creek, inlet

criquet [kʀikɛ] *nm* grasshopper

crise [kʀiz] *nf* crisis (*pl* crises); (*Méd*) attack; fit; **~ cardiaque** heart attack; **~ de foi** crisis of belief; **~ de foie** bilious attack; **~ de nerfs** attack of nerves

crispant, e [kʀispɑ̃, -ɑ̃t] *adj* annoying, irritating

crispation [kʀispasjɔ̃] *nf* (*spasme*) twitch; (*contraction*) contraction; tenseness

crispé, e [kʀispe] *adj* tense, nervous

crisper [kʀispe] *vt* to tense; (*poings*) to clench; **se crisper** to tense; to clench; (*personne*) to get tense

crissement [kʀismɑ̃] *nm* crunch; rustle; screech

crisser [kʀise] *vi* (*neige*) to crunch; (*tissu*) to rustle; (*pneu*) to screech

cristal, -aux [kʀistal, -o] *nm* crystal; **crystaux** *nmpl* (*objets*) crystal(ware) *sg*; **~ de plomb** (lead) crystal; **~ de roche** rock-crystal; **cristaux de soude** washing soda *sg*

cristallin, e [kʀistalɛ̃, -in] *adj* crystal-clear ▷ *nm* (*Anat*) crystalline lens

cristalliser [kʀistalize] *vi, vt*, **se cristalliser** *vi* to crystallize

critère [kʀitɛʀ] *nm* criterion (*pl* -ia)

critiquable [kʀitikabl(ə)] *adj* open to criticism

critique [kʀitik] *adj* critical ▷ *nm/f* (*de théâtre, musique*) critic ▷ *nf* criticism; (*Théât etc: article*) review; **la ~** (*activité*) criticism; (*personnes*) the critics *pl*

critiquer [kʀitike] *vt* (*dénigrer*) to criticize; (*évaluer, juger*) to assess, examine (critically)

croasser [kʀɔase] *vi* to caw

croate [kʀɔat] *adj* Croatian ▷ *nm* (*Ling*) Croat, Croatian

Croatie [kʀɔasi] *nf*: **la ~** Croatia

croc [kʀo] *nm* (*dent*) fang; (*de boucher*) hook

croc-en-jambe [kʀɔkɑ̃ʒɑ̃b] (*pl* **crocs-en-jambe**) *nm*: **faire un ~ à qn** to trip sb up

croche [kʀɔʃ] *nf* (*Mus*) quaver (*Brit*), eighth note (*US*); **double ~** semiquaver (*Brit*), sixteenth note (*US*)

croche-pied [kʀɔʃpje] *nm* = **croc-en-jambe**

crochet [kʀɔʃɛ] *nm* hook; (*clef*) picklock; (*détour*) detour; (*Boxe*): **~ du gauche** left hook; (*Tricot: aiguille*) crochet hook; (: *technique*) crochet; **crochets** *nmpl* (*Typo*) square brackets; **vivre aux ~s de qn** to live *ou* sponge off sb

crocheter [kʀɔʃte] *vt* (*serrure*) to pick

crochu, e [kʀɔʃy] *adj* hooked; claw-like

crocodile [kʀɔkɔdil] *nm* crocodile

crocus [kʀɔkys] *nm* crocus

croire [kʀwaʀ] *vt* to believe; **~ qn honnête** to believe sb (to be) honest; **se ~ fort** to think one is strong; **~ que** to believe *ou* think that; **vous croyez?** do you think so?; **~ être/faire** to think one is/does; **~ à, ~ en** to believe in

croîs *etc* [kʀwa] *vb voir* **croître**

croisade [kʀwazad] *nf* crusade

croisé, e [kʀwaze] *adj* (*veston*) double-breasted ▷ *nm* (*guerrier*) crusader ▷ *nf* (*fenêtre*) window, casement; **~e d'ogives** intersecting ribs; **à la ~e des chemins** at the crossroads

croisement [kʀwazmã] *nm* (*carrefour*) crossroads *sg*; (*Bio*) crossing; crossbreed

croiser [kʀwaze] *vt* (*personne, voiture*) to pass; (*route*) to cross, cut across; (*Bio*) to cross ▷ *vi* (*Navig*) to cruise; **~ les jambes/bras** to cross one's legs/ fold one's arms; **se croiser** *vi* (*personnes, véhicules*) to pass each other; (*routes*) to cross, intersect; (*lettres*) to cross (in the post); (*regards*) to meet; **se ~ les bras** (*fig*) to twiddle one's thumbs

croiseur [kʀwazœʀ] *nm* cruiser (*warship*)

croisière [kʀwazjɛʀ] *nf* cruise; **vitesse de ~** (*Auto etc*) cruising speed

croisillon [kʀwazijõ] *nm*: **motif/fenêtre à ~s** lattice pattern/window

croissais *etc* [kʀwasɛ] *vb voir* **croître**

croissance [kʀwasãs] *nf* growing, growth; **troubles de la ~** growing pains; **maladie de ~** growth disease; **~ économique** economic growth

croissant, e [kʀwasã, -ãt] *vb voir* **croître** ▷ *adj* growing; rising ▷ *nm* (*à manger*) croissant; (*motif*) crescent; **~ de lune** crescent moon

croître [kʀwatʀ(ə)] *vi* to grow; (*lune*) to wax

croix [kʀwa] *nf* cross; **en ~** *adj, adv* in the form of a cross; **la C~ Rouge** the Red Cross

croquant, e [kʀɔkã, -ãt] *adj* crisp, crunchy ▷ *nm/f* (*péj*) yokel, (country) bumpkin

croque-madame [kʀɔkmadam] *nm inv* toasted *cheese sandwich with a fried egg on top*

croque-mitaine [kʀɔkmitɛn] *nm* bog(e)y-man (*pl* -men)

croque-monsieur [kʀɔkməsjø] *nm inv* toasted *ham and cheese sandwich*

croque-mort [kʀɔkmɔʀ] *nm* (*péj*) pallbearer

croquer [kʀɔke] *vt* (*manger*) to crunch; to munch; (*dessiner*) to sketch ▷ *vi* to be crisp *ou* crunchy; **chocolat à ~** plain dessert chocolate

croquet [kʀɔkɛ] *nm* croquet

croquette [kʀɔkɛt] *nf* croquette

croquis [kʀɔki] *nm* sketch

cross [kʀɔs], **cross-country** [kʀɔskuntʀi] (*pl* -(-countries)) *nm* cross-country race *ou* run; cross-country racing *ou* running

crosse [kʀɔs] *nf* (*de fusil*) butt; (*de revolver*) grip; (*d'évêque*) crook, crosier; (*de hockey*) hockey stick

crotale [kʀɔtal] *nm* rattlesnake

crotte [kʀɔt] *nf* droppings *pl*; **~!** (*fam*) damn!

crotté, e [kʀɔte] *adj* muddy, mucky

crottin [kʀɔtɛ̃] *nm*: **~ (de cheval)** (horse) dung *ou* manure

croulant, e [kʀulã, -ãt] *nm/f* (*fam*) old fogey

crouler [kʀule] *vi* (*s'effondrer*) to collapse; (*être délabré*) to be crumbling

croupe [kʀup] *nf* croup, rump; **en ~** pillion

croupier [kʀupje] *nm* croupier

croupion [kʀupjõ] *nm* (*d'un oiseau*) rump; (*Culin*) parson's nose

croupir [kʀupiʀ] *vi* to stagnate

CROUS [kʀus] *sigle m* (= *Centre régional des œuvres universitaires et scolaires*) students' representative body

croustade [kʀustad] *nf* (*Culin*) croustade

croustillant, e [kʀustijã, -ãt] *adj* crisp; (*fig*) spicy

croustiller [kʀustije] *vi* to be crisp *ou* crusty

croûte [kʀut] *nf* crust; (*du fromage*) rind; (*de vol-au-vent*) case; (*Méd*) scab; **en ~** (*Culin*) in pastry, in a pie; **~ aux champignons** mushrooms on toast; **~ au fromage** cheese on toast *no pl*; **~ de pain** (*morceau*) crust (of bread); **~ terrestre** earth's crust

croûton [kʀutõ] *nm* (*Culin*) crouton; (*bout du pain*) crust, heel

croyable [kʀwajabl(ə)] *adj* believable, credible

croyais *etc* [kʀwajɛ] *vb voir* **croire**

croyance [kʀwajãs] *nf* belief

croyant, e [kʀwajã, -ãt] *vb voir* **croire** ▷ *adj*: **être/ne pas être ~** to be/not to be a believer ▷ *nm/f* believer

Crozet [kʀɔzɛ] *n*: **les îles ~** the Crozet Islands

CRS *sigle fpl* (= *Compagnies républicaines de sécurité*) state security police force ▷ *sigle m* member of the CRS

cru, e [kʀy] *pp de* **croire** ▷ *adj* (*non cuit*) raw; (*lumière, couleur*) harsh; (*description*) crude; (*paroles, langage: franc*) blunt; (*: grossier*) crude ▷ *nm* (*vignoble*) vineyard; (*vin*) wine ▷ *nf* (*d'un cours d'eau*) swelling, rising; **de son (propre) ~** (*fig*) of his own devising; **monter à ~** to ride bareback; **du ~** local; **en ~e** in spate

crû [kʀy] *pp de* **croître**

cruauté [kʀyote] *nf* cruelty

cruche [kʀyʃ] *nf* pitcher, (earthenware) jug

crucial, e, -aux [kʀysjal, -o] *adj* crucial

crucifier [kʀysifje] *vt* to crucify

crucifix [kʀysifi] *nm* crucifix

crucifixion [kʀysifiksjõ] *nf* crucifixion

cruciforme [kʀysifɔʀm(ə)] *adj* cruciform, cross-shaped

cruciverbiste [kʀysivɛʀbist(ə)] *nm/f* crossword puzzle enthusiast

crudité [kʀydite] *nf* crudeness *no pl*; harshness *no pl*; **crudités** *nfpl* (*Culin*) mixed salads (*as hors-d'œuvre*)

crue [kʀy] *nf voir* **cru**

cruel, le [kʀyɛl] *adj* cruel

cruellement [kʀyɛlmã] *adv* cruelly

crûment [kʀymã] *adv* (*voir cru*) harshly; bluntly; crudely

crus, crûs *etc* [kʀy] *vb voir* **croire**; **croître**

crustacés [kʀystase] *nmpl* shellfish

crypte [kʀipt(ə)] *nf* crypt

CSA *sigle f* (= *Conseil supérieur de l'audiovisuel*) French broadcasting regulatory body, ≈ IBA (*Brit*), ≈ FCC (*US*)

cse *abr* = **cause**

CSEN *sigle f* (= *Confédération syndicale de l'éducation nationale*) group of teachers' unions

CSG *sigle f* (= *contribution sociale généralisée*) supplementary social security contribution in aid of the underprivileged

CSM *sigle m* (= *Conseil supérieur de la magistrature*)

French magistrates' council

Cte *abr* = **Comtesse**

CU *sigle f* = **communauté urbaine**

Cuba [kyba] *nm*: **le** ~ Cuba

cubage [kybaʒ] *nm* cubage, cubic content

cubain, e [kybɛ̃, -ɛn] *adj* Cuban ▷ *nm/f*: **Cubain, e** Cuban

cube [kyb] *nm* cube; (*jouet*) brick, building block; **gros** ~ powerful motorbike; **mètre** ~ cubic metre; **2 au** ~ **= 8** 2 cubed is 8; **élever au** ~ to cube

cubique [kybik] *adj* cubic

cubisme [kybism(ə)] *nm* cubism

cubiste [kybist(ə)] *adj, nm/f* cubist

cubitus [kybitys] *nm* ulna

cueillette [kœjɛt] *nf* picking, gathering; harvest *ou* crop (of fruit)

cueillir [kœjiʀ] *vt* (*fruits, fleurs*) to pick, gather; (*fig*) to catch

cuiller, cuillère [kɥijɛʀ] *nf* spoon; ~ **à café** coffee spoon; (*Culin*) ≈ teaspoonful; ~ **à soupe** soup spoon; (*Culin*) ≈ tablespoonful

cuillerée [kɥijʀe] *nf* spoonful; (*Culin*): ~ **à soupe/café** tablespoonful/teaspoonful

cuir [kɥiʀ] *nm* leather; (*avant tannage*) hide; ~ **chevelu** scalp

cuirasse [kɥiʀas] *nf* breastplate

cuirassé [kɥiʀase] *nm* (*Navig*) battleship

cuire [kɥiʀ] *vt*: (**faire**) ~ (*aliments*) to cook; (*au four*) to bake; (*poterie*) to fire ▷ *vi* to cook; (*picoter*) to smart, sting, burn; **bien cuit** (*viande*) well done; **trop cuit** overdone; **pas assez cuit** underdone; **cuit à point** medium done; done to a turn

cuisant, e [kɥizɑ̃, -ɑ̃t] *vb voir* **cuire** ▷ *adj* (*douleur*) smarting, burning; (*fig: souvenir, échec*) bitter

cuisine [kɥizin] *nf* (*pièce*) kitchen; (*art culinaire*) cookery, cooking; (*nourriture*) cooking, food; **faire la** ~ to cook

cuisiné, e [kɥizine] *adj*: **plat** ~ ready-made meal *ou* dish

cuisiner [kɥizine] *vt* to cook; (*fam*) to grill ▷ *vi* to cook

cuisinette [kɥizinɛt] *nf* kitchenette

cuisinier, -ière [kɥizinje, -jɛʀ] *nm/f* cook ▷ *nf* (*poêle*) cooker; **cuisinière électrique/à gaz** electric/gas cooker

cuisis *etc* [kɥizi] *vb voir* **cuire**

cuissardes [kɥisaʀd] *nfpl* (*de pêcheur*) waders; (*de femme*) thigh boots

cuisse [kɥis] *nf* (*Anat*) thigh; (*Culin*) leg

cuisson [kɥisɔ̃] *nf* cooking; (*de poterie*) firing

cuissot [kɥiso] *nm* haunch

cuistre [kɥistʀ(ə)] *nm* prig

cuit, e [kɥi, -it] *pp de* **cuire** ▷ *nf* (*fam*): **prendre une** ~ to get plastered *ou* smashed

cuivre [kɥivʀ(ə)] *nm* copper; **les ~s** (*Mus*) the brass; ~ **rouge** copper; ~ **jaune** brass

cuivré, e [kɥivʀe] *adj* coppery; (*peau*) bronzed

cul [ky] *nm* (*fam!*) arse (*Brit !*), ass (*US !*), bum (*Brit*); ~ **de bouteille** bottom of a bottle

culasse [kylas] *nf* (*Auto*) cylinder-head; (*de*

fusil) breech

culbute [kylbyt] *nf* somersault; (*accidentelle*) tumble, fall

culbuter [kylbyte] *vi* to (take a) tumble, fall (head over heels)

culbuteur [kylbytœʀ] *nm* (*Auto*) rocker arm

cul-de-jatte [kydʒat] (*pl* **culs-de-jatte**) *nm/f* legless cripple

cul-de-sac [kydsak] (*pl* **culs-de-sac**) *nm* cul-de-sac

culinaire [kylinɛʀ] *adj* culinary

culminant, e [kylminɑ̃, -ɑ̃t] *adj*: **point** ~ highest point; (*fig*) height, climax

culminer [kylmine] *vi* to reach its highest point; to tower

culot [kylo] *nm* (*d'ampoule*) cap; (*effronterie*) cheek, nerve

culotte [kylɔt] *nf* (*de femme*) panties *pl*, knickers *pl* (*Brit*); (*d'homme*) underpants *pl*; (*pantalon*) trousers *pl* (*Brit*), pants *pl* (*US*); ~ **de cheval** riding breeches *pl*

culotté, e [kylɔte] *adj* (*pipe*) seasoned; (*cuir*) mellowed; (*effronté*) cheeky

culpabiliser [kylpabilize] *vt*: ~ **qn** to make sb feel guilty

culpabilité [kylpabilite] *nf* guilt

culte [kylt(ə)] *adj*: **livre/film** ~ cult film/book ▷ *nm* (*religion*) religion; (*hommage, vénération*) worship; (*protestant*) service

cultivable [kyltivabl(ə)] *adj* cultivable

cultivateur, -trice [kyltivatœʀ, -tʀis] *nm/f* farmer

cultivé, e [kyltive] *adj* (*personne*) cultured, cultivated

cultiver [kyltive] *vt* to cultivate; (*légumes*) to grow, cultivate

culture [kyltyʀ] *nf* cultivation; growing; (*connaissances etc*) culture; (**champs de**) ~**s** land(s) under cultivation; ~ **physique** physical training

culturel, le [kyltyʀɛl] *adj* cultural

culturisme [kyltyʀism(ə)] *nm* body-building

culturiste [kyltyʀist(ə)] *nm/f* body-builder

cumin [kymɛ̃] *nm* (*Culin*) cumin

cumul [kymyl] *nm* (*voir* **cumuler**) holding (*ou* drawing) concurrently; ~ **de peines** sentences to run consecutively

cumulable [kymylabl(ə)] *adj* (*fonctions*) which may be held concurrently

cumuler [kymyle] *vt* (*emplois, honneurs*) to hold concurrently; (*salaires*) to draw concurrently; (*Jur: droits*) to accumulate

cupide [kypid] *adj* greedy, grasping

cupidité [kypidite] *nf* greed

curable [kyʀabl(ə)] *adj* curable

Curaçao [kyʀaso] *n* Curaçao ▷ *nm*: **curaçao** curaçao

curare [kyʀaʀ] *nm* curare

curatif, -ive [kyʀatif, -iv] *adj* curative

cure [kyʀ] *nf* (*Méd*) course of treatment; (*Rel*) cure, ≈ living; presbytery, ≈ vicarage; **faire une** ~ **de fruits** to go on a fruit cure *ou* diet; **faire**

une ~ **thermale** to take the waters; **n'avoir ~ de** to pay no attention to; **~ d'amaigrissement** slimming course; **~ de repos** rest cure; **~ de sommeil** sleep therapy *no pl*

curé [kyʀe] *nm* parish priest; **M le ~ ≈** Vicar

cure-dent [kyʀdɑ̃] *nm* toothpick

curée [kyʀe] *nf* (*fig*) scramble for the pickings

cure-ongles [kyʀɔ̃gl(ə)] *nm inv* nail cleaner

cure-pipe [kyʀpip] *nm* pipe cleaner

curer [kyʀe] *vt* to clean out; **se ~ les dents** to pick one's teeth

curetage [kyʀtaʒ] *nm* (*Méd*) curettage

curieusement [kyʀjøzmɑ̃] *adv* oddly

curieux, -euse [kyʀjø, -øz] *adj* (*étrange*) strange, curious; (*indiscret*) curious, inquisitive; (*intéressé*) inquiring, curious ▷ *nmpl* (*badauds*) onlookers, bystanders

curiosité [kyʀjozite] *nf* curiosity, inquisitiveness; (*objet*) curio(sity); (*site*) unusual feature *ou* sight

curiste [kyʀist(ə)] *nm/f person taking the waters at a spa*

curriculum vitae [kyʀikylɔmvite] *nm inv* curriculum vitae

curry [kyʀi] *nm* curry; **poulet au ~** curried chicken, chicken curry

curseur [kyʀsœʀ] *nm* (*Inform*) cursor; (*de règle*) slide; (*de fermeture-éclair*) slider

cursif, -ive [kyʀsif, -iv] *adj*: **écriture cursive** cursive script

cursus [kyʀsys] *nm* degree course

curviligne [kyʀviliɲ] *adj* curvilinear

cutané, e [kytane] *adj* cutaneous, skin *cpd*

cuti-réaction [kytiʀeaksjɔ̃] *nf* (*Méd*) skin-test

cuve [kyv] *nf* vat; (*à mazout etc*) tank

cuvée [kyve] *nf* vintage

cuvette [kyvɛt] *nf* (*récipient*) bowl, basin; (*du lavabo*) (wash)basin; (*des w.-c.*) pan; (*Géo*) basin

CV *sigle m* (*Auto*) = **cheval vapeur**; (*Admin*) = **curriculum vitae**

CVS *sigle adj* (= *corrigées des variations saisonnières*) seasonally adjusted

cx *abr* (= *coefficient de pénétration dans l'air*) drag coefficient

cyanure [sjanyʀ] *nm* cyanide

cybercafé [sibɛʀkafe] *nm* cybercafé

cyberculture [sibɛʀkyltyʀ] *nf* cyberculture

cyberespace [sibɛʀɛspas] *nm* cyberspace

cybernaute [sibɛʀnot] *nm/f* Internet user

cybernétique [sibɛʀnetik] *nf* cybernetics *sg*

cyclable [siklabl(ə)] *adj*: **piste ~** cycle track

cyclamen [siklamɛn] *nm* cyclamen

cycle [sikl(ə)] *nm* cycle; (*Scol*): **premier/second ~ ≈** middle/upper school (*Brit*), ≈ junior/senior high school (*US*)

cyclique [siklik] *adj* cyclic(al)

cyclisme [siklism(ə)] *nm* cycling

cycliste [siklist(ə)] *nm/f* cyclist ▷ *adj* cycle *cpd*; **coureur ~** racing cyclist

cyclo-cross [siklɔkʀɔs] *nm* (*Sport*) cyclo-cross; (*épreuve*) cyclo-cross race

cyclomoteur [siklɔmɔtœʀ] *nm* moped

cyclomotoriste [siklɔmɔtɔʀist(ə)] *nm/f* moped rider

cyclone [siklon] *nm* hurricane

cyclotourisme [siklɔtuʀism(ə)] *nm* (bi)cycle touring

cygne [siɲ] *nm* swan

cylindre [silɛ̃dʀ(ə)] *nm* cylinder; **moteur à 4 ~s en ligne** straight-4 engine

cylindrée [silɛ̃dʀe] *nf* (*Auto*) (cubic) capacity; **une (voiture de) grosse ~** a big-engined car

cylindrique [silɛ̃dʀik] *adj* cylindrical

cymbale [sɛ̃bal] *nf* cymbal

cynique [sinik] *adj* cynical

cyniquement [sinikmɑ̃] *adv* cynically

cynisme [sinism(ə)] *nm* cynicism

cyprès [sipʀɛ] *nm* cypress

cypriote [sipʀijɔt] *adj* Cypriot ▷ *nm/f*: **Cypriote** Cypriot

cyrillique [siʀilik] *adj* Cyrillic

cystite [sistit] *nf* cystitis

cytise [sitiz] *nm* laburnum

cytologie [sitɔlɔʒi] *nf* cytology

Dd

D, d [de] *nm inv* D, d ▷ *abr:* **D** (*Météorologie:*
= *dépression*) low, depression; **D comme Désiré**
D for David (*Brit*) *ou* Dog (*US*); *voir* **système**
d' *prép, art voir* **de**
Dacca [daka] *n* Dacca
dactylo [daktilo] *nf* (*aussi:* **dactylographe**)
typist; (*aussi:* **dactylographie**) typing,
typewriting
dactylographier [daktilɔgʀafje] *vt* to type (out)
dada [dada] *nm* hobby-horse
dadais [dadɛ] *nm* ninny, lump
dague [dag] *nf* dagger
dahlia [dalja] *nm* dahlia
dahoméen, ne [daɔmeɛ̃, -ɛn] *adj* Dahomean
Dahomey [daɔme] *nm:* **le ~** Dahomey
daigner [deɲe] *vt* to deign
daim [dɛ̃] *nm* (fallow) deer *inv*; (*peau*) buckskin;
(*imitation*) suede
dais [dɛ] *nm* (*tenture*) canopy
Dakar [dakaʀ] *n* Dakar
dal. *abr* (= *décalitre*) dal.
dallage [dalaʒ] *nm* paving
dalle [dal] *nf* slab; (*au sol*) paving stone,
flag(stone); **que ~** nothing at all, damn all (*Brit*)
daller [dale] *vt* to pave
dalmatien, ne [dalmasjɛ̃, -ɛn] *nm/f* (*chien*)
Dalmatian
daltonien, ne [daltɔnjɛ̃, -ɛn] *adj* colour-blind
(*Brit*), color-blind (*US*)
daltonisme [daltɔnism(ə)] *nm* colour (*Brit*) *ou*
color (*US*) blindness
dam [dam] *nm:* **au grand ~ de** much to the
detriment (*ou* annoyance) of
Damas [dama] *n* Damascus
damas [dama] *nm* (*étoffe*) damask
damassé, e [damase] *adj* damask *cpd*
dame [dam] *nf* lady; (*Cartes, Échecs*) queen;
dames *nfpl* (*jeu*) draughts *sg* (*Brit*), checkers *sg*
(*US*); **les** (**toilettes des**) **~s** the ladies' (toilets);
~ de charité benefactress; **~ de compagnie**
lady's companion
dame-jeanne [damʒɑn] (*pl* **dames-jeannes**) *nf*
demijohn
damer [dame] *vt* to ram *ou* pack down; **~ le pion
à** (*fig*) to get the better of
damier [damje] *nm* draughts board (*Brit*),

checkerboard (*US*); (*dessin*) check (pattern); **en ~**
check
damner [dane] *vt* to damn
dancing [dɑ̃siŋ] *nm* dance hall
dandiner [dɑ̃dine]: **se dandiner** *vi* to sway
about; (*en marchant*) to waddle along
Danemark [danmaʀk] *nm:* **le ~** Denmark
danger [dɑ̃ʒe] *nm* danger; **mettre en ~** to
endanger, put in danger; **être en ~ de mort** to
be in peril of one's life; **être hors de ~** to be out
of danger
dangereusement [dɑ̃ʒʀøzmɑ̃] *adv* dangerously
dangereux, -euse [dɑ̃ʒʀø, -øz] *adj* dangerous
danois, e [danwa, -waz] *adj* Danish ▷ *nm* (*Ling*)
Danish ▷ *nm/f:* **Danois, e** Dane

 MOT-CLÉ

dans [dɑ̃] *prép* **1** (*position*) in; (*à l'intérieur de*)
inside; **c'est dans le tiroir/le salon** it's in the
drawer/lounge; **dans la boîte** in *ou* inside the
box; **marcher dans la ville/la rue** to walk
about the town/along the street; **je l'ai lu dans
le journal** I read it in the newspaper; **être
dans les meilleurs** to be among *ou* one of the
best
2 (*direction*) into; **elle a couru dans le salon** she
ran into the lounge
3 (*provenance*) out of, from; **je l'ai pris dans le
tiroir/salon** I took it out of *ou* from the drawer/
lounge; **boire dans un verre** to drink out of *ou*
from a glass
4 (*temps*) in; **dans deux mois** in two months, in
two months' time
5 (*approximation*) about; **dans les 20 euros**
about 20 euros

dansant, e [dɑ̃sɑ̃, -ɑ̃t] *adj:* **soirée ~e** evening of
dancing; (*bal*) dinner dance
danse [dɑ̃s] *nf:* **la ~** dancing; (*classique*) (ballet)
dancing; **une ~** a dance; **~ du ventre** belly
dancing
danser [dɑ̃se] *vi, vt* to dance
danseur, -euse [dɑ̃sœʀ, -øz] *nm/f* ballet dancer;
(*au bal etc*) dancer; (: *cavalier*) partner; **~ de
claquettes** tap-dancer; **en danseuse** (*à vélo*)

standing on the pedals

Danube [danyb] *nm*: **le** ~ the Danube

DAO *sigle m* (= *dessin assisté par ordinateur*) CAD

dard [daʀ] *nm* sting (*organ*)

darder [daʀde] *vt* to shoot, send forth

dare-dare [daʀdaʀ] *adv* in double quick time

Dar-es-Salaam, Dar-es-Salam [daʀɛsalam] *n* Dar-es-Salaam

darne [daʀn] *nf* steak (*of fish*)

darse [daʀs(ə)] *nf* sheltered dock (*in a Mediterranean port*)

dartre [daʀtʀ(ə)] *nf* (*Méd*) sore

datation [datasjɔ̃] *nf* dating

date [dat] *nf* date; **faire** ~ to mark a milestone; **de longue** ~ *adj* longstanding; ~ **de naissance** date of birth; ~ **limite** deadline; (*d'un aliment: aussi:* **date limite de vente**) sell-by date

dater [date] *vt, vi* to date; ~ **de** to date from, go back to; **à** ~ **de** (as) from

dateur [datœʀ] *nm* (*de montre*) date indicator; **timbre** ~ date stamp

datif [datif] *nm* dative

datte [dat] *nf* date

dattier [datje] *nm* date palm

daube [dob] *nf*: **bœuf en** ~ beef casserole

dauphin [dofɛ̃] *nm* (*Zool*) dolphin; (*du roi*) dauphin; (*fig*) heir apparent

Dauphiné [dofine] *nm*: **le** ~ the Dauphiné

dauphinois, e [dofinwa, -waz] *adj* of *ou* from the Dauphiné

daurade [dɔʀad] *nf* sea bream

davantage [davɑ̃taʒ] *adv* more; (*plus longtemps*) longer; ~ **de** more; ~ **que** more than

DB *sigle f* (*Mil*) = **division blindée**

DCA *sigle f* (= *défense contre avions*) anti-aircraft defence

DCT *sigle m* (= *diphtérie coqueluche tétanos*) DPT

DDASS [das] *sigle f* (= *Direction départementale d'action sanitaire et sociale*) ≈ DWP (= *Department of Work and Pensions* (*Brit*)), ≈ SSA (= *Social Security Administration* (US))

DDT *sigle m* (= *dichloro-diphénol-trichloréthane*) DDT

 MOT-CLÉ

de, d' (*de + le* = **du**, *de + les* = **des**) *prép* **1** (*appartenance*) of; **le toit de la maison** the roof of the house; **la voiture d'Elisabeth/de mes parents** Elizabeth's/my parents' car

2 (*provenance*) from; **il vient de Londres** he comes from London; **de Londres à Paris** from London to Paris; **elle est sortie du cinéma** she came out of the cinema

3 (*moyen*) with; **je l'ai fait de mes propres mains** I did it with my own two hands

4 (*caractérisation, mesure*): **un mur de brique/ bureau d'acajou** a brick wall/mahogany desk; **un billet de 10 euros** a 10 euro note; **une pièce de 2 m de large** *ou* **large de 2 m** a room 2 m wide, a 2m-wide room; **un bébé de 10 mois** a 10-month-old baby; **12 mois de crédit/travail** 12 months' credit/work; **elle est payée 20**

euros de l'heure she's paid 20 euros an hour *ou* per hour; **augmenter de 10 euros** to increase by 10 euros; **trois jours de libres** three free days, three days free; **un verre d'eau** a glass of water; **il mange de tout** he'll eat anything

5 (*rapport*) from; **de quatre à six** from four to six

6 (*de la part de*): **estimé de ses collègues** respected by his colleagues

7 (*cause*): **mourir de faim** to die of hunger; **rouge de colère** red with fury

8 (*vb + de + infin*) to; **il m'a dit de rester** he told me to stay

9 (*en apposition*): **cet imbécile de Paul** that idiot Paul; **le terme de franglais** the term "franglais"

▷ *art* **1** (*phrases affirmatives*) some (*souvent omis*); **du vin, de l'eau, des pommes** (some) wine, (some) water, (some) apples; **des enfants sont venus** some children came; **pendant des mois** for months

2 (*phrases interrogatives et négatives*) any; **a-t-il du vin?** has he got any wine?; **il n'a pas de pommes/d'enfants** he hasn't (got) any apples/ children, he has no apples/children

dé [de] *nm* (*à jouer*) die *ou* dice; (*aussi:* **dé à coudre**) thimble; **dés** *nmpl* (*jeu*) (game of) dice; **un coup de dés** a throw of the dice; **couper en dés** (*Culin*) to dice

DEA *sigle m* (= *Diplôme d'études approfondies*) postgraduate diploma

dealer [dilœʀ] *nm* (*fam*) (drug) pusher

déambulateur [deɑ̃bylatœʀ] *nm* zimmer®

déambuler [deɑ̃byle] *vi* to stroll about

déb. *abr* = **débutant**; (*Comm*) = **à débattre**

débâcle [debɑkl(ə)] *nf* rout

déballage [debalaʒ] *nm* (*de marchandises*) display (*of loose goods*); (*fig: fam*) outpourings *pl*

déballer [debale] *vt* to unpack

débandade [debɑ̃dad] *nf* scattering; (*déroute*) rout

débander [debɑ̃de] *vt* to unbandage

débaptiser [debatize] *vt* (*rue*) to rename

débarbouiller [debaʀbuje] *vt* to wash; **se débarbouiller** *vi* to wash (one's face)

débarcadère [debaʀkadɛʀ] *nm* landing stage (*Brit*), wharf

débardeur [debaʀdœʀ] *nm* docker, stevedore; (*maillot*) slipover, tank top

débarquement [debaʀkəmɑ̃] *nm* unloading, landing; disembarcation; (*Mil*) landing; **le D~** the Normandy landings

débarquer [debaʀke] *vt* to unload, land ▷ *vi* to disembark; (*fig*) to turn up

débarras [debaʀa] *nm* lumber room; (*placard*) junk cupboard; (*remise*) outhouse; **bon ~!** good riddance!

débarrasser [debaʀase] *vt* to clear ▷ *vi* (*enlever le couvert*) to clear away; ~ **qn de** (*vêtements, paquets*) to relieve sb of; (*habitude, ennemi*) to rid sb of; ~ **qch de** (*fouillis etc*) to clear sth of; **se débarrasser**

de *vt* to get rid of; to rid o.s. of

débat [deba] *vb voir* **débattre** ▷ *nm* discussion, debate; **débats** *nmpl* (Pol) proceedings, debates

débattre [debatʀ(ə)] *vt* to discuss, debate; **se débattre** *vi* to struggle

débauchage [deboʃaʒ] *nm* (*licenciement*) laying off (of staff); (*par un concurrent*) poaching

débauche [deboʃ] *nf* debauchery; **une ~ de** (*fig*) a profusion of; (: *de couleurs*) a riot of

débauché, e [deboʃe] *adj* debauched ▷ *nm/f* profligate

débaucher [deboʃe] *vt* (*licencier*) to lay off, dismiss; (*salarié d'une autre entreprise*) to poach; (*entraîner*) to lead astray, debauch; (*inciter à la grève*) to incite

débile [debil] *adj* weak, feeble; (*fam: idiot*) dim-witted ▷ *nm/f*: **~ mental, e** mental defective

débilitant, e [debilitɑ̃, -ɑ̃t] *adj* debilitating

débilité [debilite] *nf* debility; (*fam: idiotie*) stupidity; **~ mentale** mental debility

débiner [debine]: **se débiner** *vi* to do a bunk (*Brit*), clear out

débit [debi] *nm* (*d'un liquide, fleuve*) (rate of) flow; (*d'un magasin*) turnover (of goods); (*élocution*) delivery; (*bancaire*) debit; **avoir un ~ de 10 euros** to be 10 euros in debit; **~ de boissons** drinking establishment; **~ de tabac** tobacconist's (shop) (*Brit*), tobacco *ou* smoke shop (*US*)

débiter [debite] *vt* (*compte*) to debit; (*liquide, gaz*) to yield, produce, give out; (*couper: bois, viande*) to cut up; (*vendre*) to retail; (*péj: paroles etc*) to come out with, churn out

débiteur, -trice [debitœʀ, -tʀis] *nm/f* debtor ▷ *adj* in debit; (*compte*) debit *cpd*

déblai [deblɛ] *nm* (*nettoyage*) clearing; **déblais** *nmpl* (*terre*) earth; (*décombres*) rubble

déblaiement [deblɛmɑ̃] *nm* clearing; **travaux de ~** earth moving *sg*

déblatérer [deblateʀe] *vi*: **~ contre** to go on about

déblayer [debleje] *vt* to clear; **~ le terrain** (*fig*) to clear the ground

déblocage [deblɔkaʒ] *nm* (*des prix, cours*) unfreezing

débloquer [deblɔke] *vt* (*frein, fonds*) to release; (*prix*) to unfreeze ▷ *vi* (*fam*) to talk rubbish

débobiner [debɔbine] *vt* to unwind

déboires [debwaʀ] *nmpl* setbacks

déboisement [debwazmɑ̃] *nm* deforestation

déboiser [debwaze] *vt* to clear of trees; (*région*) to deforest; **se déboiser** *vi* (*colline, montagne*) to become bare of trees

déboîter [debwate] *vt* (*Auto*) to pull out; **se ~ le genou** *etc* to dislocate one's knee *etc*

débonnaire [debɔnɛʀ] *adj* easy-going, good-natured

débordant, e [debɔʀdɑ̃, -ɑ̃t] *adj* (*joie*) unbounded; (*activité*) exuberant

débordé, e [debɔʀde] *adj*: **être ~ de** (*travail, demandes*) to be snowed under with

débordement [debɔʀdəmɑ̃] *nm* overflowing

déborder [debɔʀde] *vi* to overflow; (*lait etc*) to boil over ▷ *vt* (*Mil, Sport*) to outflank; **~ (de) qch** (*dépasser*) to extend beyond sth; **~ de** (*joie, zèle*) to be brimming over with *ou* bursting with

débouché [debuʃe] *nm* (*pour vendre*) outlet; (*perspective d'emploi*) opening; (*sortie*): **au ~ de la vallée** where the valley opens out (onto the plain)

déboucher [debuʃe] *vt* (*évier, tuyau etc*) to unblock; (*bouteille*) to uncork, open ▷ *vi*: **~ de** to emerge from, come out of; **~ sur** to come out onto; to open out onto; (*fig*) to arrive at, lead up to

débouler [debule] *vi* to go (*ou* come) tumbling down; (*sans tomber*) to come careering down ▷ *vt*: **~ l'escalier** to belt down the stairs

déboulonner [debulɔne] *vt* to dismantle; (*fig: renvoyer*) to dismiss; (: *détruire le prestige de*) to discredit

débours [debuʀ] *nmpl* outlay

débourser [debuʀse] *vt* to pay out, lay out

déboussoler [debusɔle] *vt* to disorientate, disorient

debout [dəbu] *adv*: **être ~** (*personne*) to be standing, stand; (: *levé, éveillé*) to be up (and about); (*chose*) to be upright; **être encore ~** (*fig: en état*) to be still going; to be still standing; to be still up; **mettre qn ~** to get sb to his feet; **mettre qch ~** to stand sth up; **se mettre ~** to get up (on one's feet); **se tenir ~** to stand; **~!** get up!; **cette histoire ne tient pas ~** this story doesn't hold water

débouter [debute] *vt* (*Jur*) to dismiss; **~ qn de sa demande** to dismiss sb's petition

déboutonner [debutɔne] *vt* to undo, unbutton; **se déboutonner** *vi* to come undone *ou* unbuttoned

débraillé, e [debʀaje] *adj* slovenly, untidy

débrancher [debʀɑ̃ʃe] *vt* (*appareil électrique*) to unplug; (*téléphone, courant électrique*) to disconnect, cut off

débrayage [debʀɛjaʒ] *nm* (*Auto*) clutch; (: *action*) disengaging the clutch; (*grève*) stoppage; **faire un double ~** to double-declutch

débrayer [debʀeje] *vi* (*Auto*) to declutch, disengage the clutch; (*cesser le travail*) to stop work

débridé, e [debʀide] *adj* unbridled, unrestrained

débrider [debʀide] *vt* (*cheval*) to unbridle; (*Culin: volaille*) to untruss

débris [debʀi] *nm* (*fragment*) fragment ▷ *nmpl* (*déchets*) pieces, debris *sg*; rubbish *sg* (*Brit*), garbage *sg* (*US*)

débrouillard, e [debʀujaʀ, -aʀd(ə)] *adj* smart, resourceful

débrouillardise [debʀujaʀdiz] *nf* smartness, resourcefulness

débrouiller [debʀuje] *vt* to disentangle, untangle; (*fig*) to sort out, unravel; **se débrouiller** *vi* to manage

débroussailler [debʀusaje] *vt* to clear (of

brushwood)

débusquer [debyske] *vt* to drive out (from cover)

début [deby] *nm* beginning, start; **débuts** *nmpl* beginnings; (*de carrière*) début *sg*; **faire ses ~s** to start out; **au ~** in *ou* at the beginning, at first; **au ~ de** at the beginning *ou* start of; **dès le ~** from the start

débutant, e [debytã, -ãt] *nm/f* beginner, novice

débuter [debyte] *vi* to begin, start; (*faire ses débuts*) to start out

deçà [dəsa]: **en ~ de** *prép* this side of; **en ~** *adv* on this side

décacheter [dekaʃte] *vt* to unseal, open

décade [dekad] *nf* (*10 jours*) (period of) ten days; (*10 ans*) decade

décadence [dekadãs] *nf* decadence; decline

décadent, e [dekadã, -ãt] *adj* decadent

décaféiné, e [dekafeine] *adj* decaffeinated, caffeine-free

décalage [dekalaʒ] *nm* move forward *ou* back; shift forward *ou* back; (*écart*) gap; (*désaccord*) discrepancy; **~ horaire** time difference (between time zones), time-lag

décalaminer [dekalamine] *vt* to decoke

décalcification [dekalsifikasjõ] *nf* decalcification

décalcifier [dekalsifje]: **se décalcifier** *vr* to decalcify

décalcomanie [dekalkɔmani] *nf* transfer

décaler [dekale] *vt* (*dans le temps: avancer*) to bring forward; (*: retarder*) to put back; (*changer de position*) to shift forward *ou* back; **~ de 10 cm** to move forward *ou* back by 10 cm; **~ de deux heures** to bring *ou* move forward two hours; to put back two hours

décalitre [dekalitʀ(ə)] *nm* decalitre (*Brit*), decaliter (*US*)

décalogue [dekalɔg] *nm* Decalogue

décalquer [dekalke] *vt* to trace; (*par pression*) to transfer

décamètre [dekamɛtʀ(ə)] *nm* decametre (*Brit*), decameter (*US*)

décamper [dekãpe] *vi* to clear out *ou* off

décan [dekã] *nm* (*Astrologie*) decan

décanter [dekãte] *vt* to (allow to) settle (and decant); **se décanter** *vi* to settle

décapage [dekapaʒ] *nm* stripping; scouring; sanding

décapant [dekapã] *nm* acid solution; scouring agent; paint stripper

décaper [dekape] *vt* to strip; (*avec abrasif*) to scour; (*avec papier de verre*) to sand

décapiter [dekapite] *vt* to behead; (*par accident*) to decapitate; (*fig*) to cut the top off; (*: organisation*) to remove the top people from

décapotable [dekapɔtabl(ə)] *adj* convertible

décapoter [dekapɔte] *vt* to put down the top of

décapsuler [dekapsyle] *vt* to take the cap *ou* top off

décapsuleur [dekapsylœʀ] *nm* bottle-opener

décarcasser [dekaʀkase] *vt*: **se ~ pour qn/pour**

faire qch (*fam*) to slog one's guts out for sb/to do sth

décathlon [dekatlõ] *nm* decathlon

décati, e [dekati] *adj* faded, aged

décédé, e [desede] *adj* deceased

décéder [desede] *vi* to die

décelable [des(ə)labl(ə)] *adj* discernible

déceler [desle] *vt* to discover, detect; (*révéler*) to indicate, reveal

décélération [deseleʀasjõ] *nf* deceleration

décélérer [deseleʀe] *vi* to decelerate, slow down

décembre [desãbʀ(ə)] *nm* December; *voir aussi* **juillet**

décemment [desamã] *adv* decently

décence [desãs] *nf* decency

décennal, e, -aux [desenal, -o] *adj* (*qui dure dix ans*) having a term of ten years, ten-year; (*qui revient tous les dix ans*) ten-yearly

décennie [deseni] *nf* decade

décent, e [desã, -ãt] *adj* decent

décentralisation [desãtʀalizasjõ] *nf* decentralization

décentraliser [desãtʀalize] *vt* to decentralize

décentrer [desãtʀe] *vt* to throw off centre; **se décentrer** *vi* to move off-centre

déception [desɛpsjõ] *nf* disappointment

décerner [desɛʀne] *vt* to award

décès [desɛ] *nm* death, decease; **acte de ~** death certificate

décevant, e [desvã, -ãt] *adj* disappointing

décevoir [desvwaʀ] *vt* to disappoint

déchaîné, e [deʃene] *adj* unbridled, raging

déchaînement [deʃenmã] *nm* (*de haine, violence*) outbreak, outburst

déchaîner [deʃene] *vt* (*passions, colère*) to unleash; (*rires etc*) to give rise to, arouse; **se déchaîner** *vi* to be unleashed; (*rires*) to burst out; (*se mettre en colère*) to fly into a rage; **se ~ contre qn** to unleash one's fury on sb

déchanter [deʃãte] *vi* to become disillusioned

décharge [deʃaʀʒ(ə)] *nf* (*dépôt d'ordures*) rubbish tip *ou* dump; (*électrique*) electrical discharge; (*salve*) volley of shots; **à la ~ de** in defence of

déchargement [deʃaʀʒəmã] *nm* unloading

décharger [deʃaʀʒe] *vt* (*marchandise, véhicule*) to unload; (*Élec*) to discharge; (*arme: neutraliser*) to unload; (*: faire feu*) to discharge, fire; **~ qn de** (*responsabilité*) to relieve sb of, release sb from; **~ sa colère (sur)** to vent one's anger (on); **~ sa conscience** to unburden one's conscience; **se ~ dans** (*se déverser*) to flow into; **se ~ d'une affaire sur qn** to hand a matter over to sb

décharné, e [deʃaʀne] *adj* bony, emaciated, fleshless

déchaussé, e [deʃose] *adj* (*dent*) loose

déchausser [deʃose] *vt* (*personne*) to take the shoes off; (*skis*) to take off; **se déchausser** *vi* to take off one's shoes; (*dent*) to come *ou* work loose

dèche [dɛʃ] *nf* (*fam*): **être dans la ~** to be flat broke

déchéance [deʃeãs] *nf* (*déclin*) degeneration,

decay, decline; (*chute*) fall

déchet [deʃɛ] *nm* (*de bois, tissu etc*) scrap; (*perte: gén Comm*) wastage, waste; **déchets** *nmpl* (*ordures*) refuse *sg*, rubbish *sg* (*Brit*), garbage *sg* (*US*); **~s radioactifs** radioactive waste

déchiffrage [deʃifʀaʒ] *nm* sight-reading

déchiffrer [deʃifʀe] *vt* to decipher

déchiqueté, e [deʃikte] *adj* jagged(-edged), ragged

déchiqueter [deʃikte] *vt* to tear *ou* pull to pieces

déchirant, e [deʃiʀɑ̃, -ɑ̃t] *adj* heart-breaking, heart-rending

déchiré, e [deʃiʀe] *adj* torn; (*fig*) heart-broken

déchirement [deʃiʀmɑ̃] *nm* (*chagrin*) wrench, heartbreak; (*gén pl: conflit*) rift, split

déchirer [deʃiʀe] *vt* to tear, rip; (*mettre en morceaux*) to tear up; (*pour ouvrir*) to tear off; (*arracher*) to tear out; (*fig*) to tear apart; **se déchirer** *vi* to tear, rip; **se ~ un muscle/tendon** to tear a muscle/ tendon

déchirure [deʃiʀyʀ] *nf* (*accroc*) tear, rip; **~ musculaire** torn muscle

déchoir [deʃwaʀ] *vi* (*personne*) to lower o.s., demean o.s.; **~ de** to fall from

déchu, e [deʃy] *pp de* **déchoir** ▷ *adj* fallen; (*roi*) deposed

décibel [desibɛl] *nm* decibel

décidé, e [deside] *adj* (*personne, air*) determined; **c'est ~** it's decided; **être ~ à faire** to be determined to do

décidément [desidemɑ̃] *adv* undoubtedly; really

décider [deside] *vt*: **~ qch** to decide on sth; **~ de faire/que** to decide to do/that; **~ qn (à faire qch)** to persuade *ou* induce sb (to do sth); **~ de qch** to decide upon sth; (*chose*) to determine sth; **se décider** *vi* (*personne*) to decide, make up one's mind; (*problème, affaire*) to be resolved; **se ~ à qch** to decide on sth; **se ~ à faire** to decide *ou* make up one's mind to do; **se ~ pour qch** to decide on *ou* in favour of sth

décideur [desidœʀ] *nm* decision-maker

décilitre [desilitʀ(ə)] *nm* decilitre (*Brit*), deciliter (*US*)

décimal, e, -aux [desimal, -o] *adj, nf* decimal

décimalisation [desimalizasjɔ̃] *nf* decimalization

décimaliser [desimalize] *vt* to decimalize

décimer [desime] *vt* to decimate

décimètre [desimɛtʀ(ə)] *nm* decimetre (*Brit*), decimeter (*US*); **double ~** (20 cm) ruler

décisif, -ive [desizif, -iv] *adj* decisive; (*qui l'emporte*): **le facteur/l'argument ~** the deciding factor/argument

décision [desizjɔ̃] *nf* decision; (*fermeté*) decisiveness, decision; **prendre une ~** to make a decision; **prendre la ~ de faire** to take the decision to do; **emporter** *ou* **faire la ~** to be decisive

déclamation [deklamasjɔ̃] *nf* declamation; (*péj*) ranting, spouting

déclamatoire [deklamatwaʀ] *adj* declamatory

déclamer [deklame] *vt* to declaim; (*péj*) to spout ▷ *vi*: **~ contre** to rail against

déclarable [deklaʀabl(ə)] *adj* (*marchandise*) dutiable; (*revenus*) declarable

déclaration [deklaʀasjɔ̃] *nf* declaration; registration; (*discours: Pol etc*) statement; (*compte rendu*) report; **fausse ~** misrepresentation; **~ (d'amour)** declaration; **~ de décès** registration of death; **~ de guerre** declaration of war; **~ (d'impôts)** statement of income, tax declaration, ≈ tax return; **~ (de sinistre)** (insurance) claim; **~ de revenus** statement of income

déclaré, e [deklaʀe] *adj* (*juré*) avowed

déclarer [deklaʀe] *vt* to declare, announce; (*revenus, employés, marchandises*) to declare; (*décès, naissance*) to register; (*vol etc: à la police*) to report; **rien à ~** nothing to declare; **se déclarer** *vi* (*feu, maladie*) to break out; **~ la guerre** to declare war

déclassé, e [deklɑse] *adj* relegated, downgraded; (*matériel*) (to be) sold off

déclassement [deklɑsmɑ̃] *nm* relegation, downgrading; (*Rail etc*) change of class

déclasser [deklɑse] *vt* to relegate, downgrade; (*déranger: fiches, livres*) to get out of order

déclenchement [deklɑ̃ʃmɑ̃] *nm* release; setting off

déclencher [deklɑ̃ʃe] *vt* (*mécanisme etc*) to release; (*sonnerie*) to set off, activate; (*attaque, grève*) to launch; (*provoquer*) to trigger off; **se déclencher** *vi* to release itself; to go off

déclencheur [deklɑ̃ʃœʀ] *nm* release mechanism

déclic [deklik] *nm* trigger mechanism; (*bruit*) click

déclin [deklɛ̃] *nm* decline

déclinaison [deklinɛzɔ̃] *nf* declension

décliner [dekline] *vi* to decline ▷ *vt* (*invitation*) to decline, refuse; (*responsabilité*) to refuse to accept; (*nom, adresse*) to state; (*Ling*) to decline; **se décliner** (*Ling*) to decline

déclivité [deklivite] *nf* slope, incline; **en ~** sloping, on the incline

décloisonner [deklwazɔne] *vt* to decompartmentalize

déclouer [deklue] *vt* to unnail

décocher [dekɔʃe] *vt* to hurl; (*flèche, regard*) to shoot

décoction [dekɔksjɔ̃] *nf* decoction

décodage [dekɔdaʒ] *nm* deciphering, decoding

décoder [dekɔde] *vt* to decipher, decode

décodeur [dekɔdœʀ] *nm* decoder

décoiffé, e [dekwafe] *adj*: **elle est toute ~e** her hair is in a mess

décoiffer [dekwafe] *vt*: **~ qn** to disarrange *ou* mess up sb's hair; to take sb's hat off; **se décoiffer** *vi* to take off one's hat

décoincer [dekwɛ̃se] *vt* to unjam, loosen

déçois *etc* [deswa], **déçoive** *etc* [deswav] *vb voir* **décevoir**

décolérer [dekɔleʀe] *vi*: **il ne décolère pas** he's still angry, he hasn't calmed down

décollage [dekɔlaʒ] nm (Aviat, Écon) takeoff
décollé, e [dekɔle] adj: **oreilles ~es** sticking-out ears
décollement [dekɔlmɑ̃] nm (Méd): **~ de la rétine** retinal detachment
décoller [dekɔle] vt to unstick ▷ vi to take off; (projet, entreprise) to take off, get off the ground; **se décoller** vi to come unstuck
décolleté, e [dekɔlte] adj low-necked, low-cut; (femme) wearing a low-cut dress ▷ nm low neck(line); (épaules) (bare) neck and shoulders; (plongeant) cleavage
décolleter [dekɔlte] vt (vêtement) to give a low neckline to; (Tech) to cut
décolonisation [dekɔlɔnizasjɔ̃] nf decolonization
décoloniser [dekɔlɔnize] vt to decolonize
décolorant [dekɔlɔRɑ̃] nm decolorant, bleaching agent
décoloration [dekɔlɔRasjɔ̃] nf: **se faire faire une ~** (chez le coiffeur) to have one's hair bleached ou lightened
décoloré, e [dekɔlɔRe] adj (vêtement) faded; (cheveux) bleached
décolorer [dekɔlɔRe] vt (tissu) to fade; (cheveux) to bleach, lighten; **se décolorer** vi to fade
décombres [dekɔ̃bR(ə)] nmpl rubble sg, debris sg
décommander [dekɔmɑ̃de] vt to cancel; (invités) to put off; **se décommander** vi to cancel, cry off
décomposé, e [dekɔ̃poze] adj (pourri) decomposed; (visage) haggard, distorted
décomposer [dekɔ̃poze] vt to break up; (Chimie) to decompose; (Math) to factorize; **se décomposer** vi to decompose
décomposition [dekɔ̃pozisjɔ̃] nf breaking up; decomposition; factorization; **en ~** (organisme) in a state of decay, decomposing
décompresser [dekɔ̃pRese] vi (fam: se détendre) to unwind
décompresseur [dekɔ̃pResœR] nm decompressor
décompression [dekɔ̃pResjɔ̃] nf decompression
décomprimer [dekɔ̃pRime] vt to decompress
décompte [dekɔ̃t] nm deduction; (facture) breakdown (of an account), detailed account
décompter [dekɔ̃te] vt to deduct
déconcentration [dekɔ̃sɑ̃tRasjɔ̃] nf (des industries etc) dispersal; **~ des pouvoirs** devolution
déconcentré, e [dekɔ̃sɑ̃tRe] adj (sportif etc) who has lost (his/her) concentration
déconcentrer [dekɔ̃sɑ̃tRe] vt (Admin) to disperse; **se déconcentrer** vi to lose (one's) concentration
déconcertant, e [dekɔ̃sɛRtɑ̃, -ɑ̃t] adj disconcerting
déconcerter [dekɔ̃sɛRte] vt to disconcert, confound
déconditionner [dekɔ̃disjɔne] vt: **~ l'opinion américaine** to change the way the Americans have been forced to think

déconfit, e [dekɔ̃fi, -it] adj crestfallen, downcast
déconfiture [dekɔ̃fityR] nf collapse, ruin; (morale) defeat
décongélation [dekɔ̃ʒelasjɔ̃] nf defrosting, thawing
décongeler [dekɔ̃ʒle] vt to thaw (out)
décongestionner [dekɔ̃ʒɛstjɔne] vt (Méd) to decongest; (rues) to relieve congestion in
déconnecter [dekɔnɛkte] vt to disconnect
déconner [dekɔne] vi (fam!: en parlant) to talk (a load of) rubbish (Brit) ou garbage (US); (: faire des bêtises) to muck about; **sans ~** no kidding
déconseiller [dekɔ̃seje] vt: **~ qch (à qn)** to advise (sb) against sth; **~ à qn de faire** to advise sb against doing; **c'est déconseillé** it's not advised ou advisable
déconsidérer [dekɔ̃sideRe] vt to discredit
décontamination [dekɔ̃taminasjɔ̃] nf decontamination
décontaminer [dekɔ̃tamine] vt to decontaminate
décontenancer [dekɔ̃tnɑ̃se] vt to disconcert, discountenance
décontracté, e [dekɔ̃tRakte] adj relaxed
décontracter [dekɔ̃tRakte] vt, **se décontracter** vi to relax
décontraction [dekɔ̃tRaksjɔ̃] nf relaxation
déconvenue [dekɔ̃vny] nf disappointment
décor [dekɔR] nm décor; (paysage) scenery; **décors** nmpl (Théât) scenery, decor sg; (Ciné) set sg; **changement de ~** (fig) change of scene; **entrer dans le ~** (fig) to run off the road; **en ~ naturel** (Ciné) on location
décorateur, -trice [dekɔRatœR, -tRis] nm/f (interior) decorator; (Ciné) set designer
décoratif, -ive [dekɔRatif, -iv] adj decorative
décoration [dekɔRasjɔ̃] nf decoration
décorer [dekɔRe] vt to decorate
décortiqué, e [dekɔRtike] adj shelled; hulled
décortiquer [dekɔRtike] vt to shell; (riz) to hull; (fig) to dissect
décorum [dekɔRɔm] nm decorum; etiquette
décote [dekɔt] nf tax relief
découcher [dekuʃe] vi to spend the night away
découdre [dekudR(ə)] vt (vêtement, couture) to unpick, take the stitching out of; (bouton) to take off; **se découdre** vi to come unstitched; (bouton) to come off; **en ~** (fig) to fight, do battle
découler [dekule] vi: **~ de** to ensue ou follow from
découpage [dekupaʒ] nm cutting up; carving; (image) cut-out (figure); **~ électoral** division into constituencies
découper [dekupe] vt (papier, tissu etc) to cut up; (volaille, viande) to carve; (détacher: manche, article) to cut out; **se ~ sur** (ciel, fond) to stand out against
découplé, e [dekuple] adj: **bien ~** well-built, well-proportioned
découpure [dekupyR] nf: **~s** (morceaux) cut-out bits; (d'une côte, arête) indentations, jagged

outline *sg*

décourageant, e [dekuʀaʒɑ̃, ɑ̃t] *adj*
discouraging; (*personne, attitude*) discouraging,
negative

découragement [dekuʀaʒmɑ̃] *nm*
discouragement, despondency

décourager [dekuʀaʒe] *vt* to discourage,
dishearten; (*dissuader*) to discourage, put off; **se
décourager** *vi* to lose heart, become
discouraged; **~ qn de faire/de qch** to
discourage sb from doing/from sth, put sb off
doing/sth

décousu, e [dekuzy] *pp de* **découdre** ▷ *adj*
unstitched; (*fig*) disjointed, disconnected

découvert, e [dekuvɛʀ, -ɛʀt(ə)] *pp de* **découvrir**
▷ *adj* (*tête*) bare, uncovered; (*lieu*) open, exposed
▷ *nm* (*bancaire*) overdraft ▷ *nf* discovery; **à ~** *adv*
(*Mil*) exposed, without cover; (*fig*) openly ▷ *adj*
(*Comm*) overdrawn; **à visage ~** openly; **aller à la
~e de** to go in search of

découvrir [dekuvʀiʀ] *vt* to discover; (*apercevoir*)
to see; (*enlever ce qui couvre ou protège*) to uncover;
(*montrer, dévoiler*) to reveal; **se découvrir** *vi* to
take off one's hat; (*se déshabiller*) to take
something off; (*au lit*) to uncover o.s.; (*ciel*) to
clear; **se ~ des talents** to find hidden talents
in o.s.

décrasser [dekʀase] *vt* to clean

décrêper [dekʀepe] *vt* (*cheveux*) to straighten

décrépi, e [dekʀepi] *adj* peeling; with roughcast
rendering removed

décrépit, e [dekʀepi, -it] *adj* decrepit

décrépitude [dekʀepityd] *nf* decrepitude; decay

decrescendo [dekʀeʃɛndo] *nm* (*Mus*)
decrescendo; **aller ~** (*fig*) to decline, be on the
wane

décret [dekʀɛ] *nm* decree

décréter [dekʀete] *vt* to decree; (*ordonner*) to order

décret-loi [dekʀɛlwa] *nm* statutory order

décrié, e [dekʀije] *adj* disparaged

décrire [dekʀiʀ] *vt* to describe; (*courbe, cercle*) to
follow, describe

décrisper [dekʀispe] *vt* to defuse

décrit, e [dekʀi, -it] *pp de* **décrire**

décrivais *etc* [dekʀivɛ] *vb voir* **décrire**

décrochage [dekʀɔʃaʒ] *nm*: **~ scolaire** (*Scol*)
≈ truancy

décrochement [dekʀɔʃmɑ̃] *nm* (*d'un mur etc*)
recess

décrocher [dekʀɔʃe] *vt* (*dépendre*) to take down;
(*téléphone*) to take off the hook; (: *pour répondre*): **~
(le téléphone)** to pick up *ou* lift the receiver;
(*fig: contrat etc*) to get, land ▷ *vi* to drop out; to
switch off; **se décrocher** *vi* (*tableau, rideau*) to
fall down

décroîs *etc* [dekʀwa] *vb voir* **décroître**

décroiser [dekʀwaze] *vt* (*bras*) to unfold; (*jambes*)
to uncross

décroissant, e [dekʀwasɑ̃, -ɑ̃t] *vb voir* **décroître**
▷ *adj* decreasing, declining, diminishing; **par
ordre ~** in descending order

décroître [dekʀwatʀ(ə)] *vi* to decrease,

decline diminish

décrotter [dekʀɔte] *vt* (*chaussures*) to clean the
mud from; **se ~ le nez** to pick one's nose

décru, e [dekʀy] *pp de* **décroître**

décrue [dekʀy] *nf* drop in level (of the waters)

décrypter [dekʀipte] *vt* to decipher

déçu, e [desy] *pp de* **décevoir** ▷ *adj* disappointed

déculotter [dekylɔte] *vt*: **~ qn** to take off *ou*
down sb's trousers; **se déculotter** *vi* to take off
ou down one's trousers

déculpabiliser [dekylpabilize] *vt* (*personne*) to
relieve of guilt; (*chose*) to decriminalize

décuple [dekypl(ə)] *nm*: **le ~ de** ten times; **au ~**
tenfold

décupler [dekyple] *vt, vi* to increase tenfold

déçut *etc* [desy] *vb voir* **décevoir**

dédaignable [dedɛɲabl(ə)] *adj*: **pas ~** not to be
despised

dédaigner [dedeɲe] *vt* to despise, scorn;
(*négliger*) to disregard, spurn; **~ de faire** to
consider it beneath one to do, not deign to do

dédaigneusement [dedɛɲøzmɑ̃] *adv*
scornfully, disdainfully

dédaigneux, -euse [dedɛɲø, -øz] *adj* scornful,
disdainful

dédain [dedɛ̃] *nm* scorn, disdain

dédale [dedal] *nm* maze

dedans [dədɑ̃] *adv* inside; (*pas en plein air*)
indoors, inside ▷ *nm* inside; **au ~** on the inside;
inside; **en ~** (*vers l'intérieur*) inwards; *voir aussi* **là**

dédicace [dedikas] *nf* (*imprimée*) dedication;
(*manuscrite, sur une photo etc*) inscription

dédicacer [dedikase] *vt*: **~ (à qn)** to sign (for sb),
autograph (for sb), inscribe (to sb)

dédié, e [dedje] *adj*: **ordinateur ~** dedicated
computer

dédier [dedje] *vt* to dedicate

dédire [dediʀ]: **se dédire** *vi* to go back on one's
word; (*se rétracter*) to retract, recant

dédit, e [dedi, -it] *pp de* **dédire** ▷ *nm* (*Comm*)
forfeit, penalty

dédommagement [dedɔmaʒmɑ̃] *nm*
compensation

dédommager [dedɔmaʒe] *vt*: **~ qn (de)** to
compensate sb (for); (*fig*) to repay sb (for)

dédouaner [dedwane] *vt* to clear through
customs

dédoublement [dedubləmɑ̃] *nm* splitting;
(*Psych*): **~ de la personnalité** split *ou* dual
personality

dédoubler [deduble] *vt* (*classe, effectifs*) to split
(into two); (*couverture etc*) to unfold; (*manteau*) to
remove the lining of; **~ un train/les trains** to
run a relief train/additional trains; **se
dédoubler** *vi* (*Psych*) to have a split personality

dédramatiser [dedʀamatize] *vt* (*situation*) to
defuse; (*événement*) to play down

déductible [dedyktibl(ə)] *adj* deductible

déduction [dedyksjɔ̃] *nf* (*d'argent*) deduction;
(*raisonnement*) deduction, inference

déduire [dedɥiʀ] *vt*: **~ qch (de)** (*ôter*) to deduct
sth (from); (*conclure*) to deduce *ou* infer sth (from)

déesse [deɛs] nf goddess

DEFA sigle m (= Diplôme d'État relatif aux fonctions d'animation) diploma for senior youth leaders

défaillance [defajãs] nf (syncope) blackout; (fatigue) (sudden) weakness no pl; (technique) fault, failure; (morale etc) weakness; ~ **cardiaque** heart failure

défaillant, e [defajã, -ãt] adj defective; (Jur: témoin) defaulting

défaillir [defajiʀ] vi to faint; to feel faint; (mémoire etc) to fail

défaire [defɛʀ] vt (installation, échafaudage) to take down, dismantle; (paquet etc, nœud, vêtement) to undo; (bagages) to unpack; (ouvrage) to undo, unpick; (cheveux) to take out; **se défaire** vi to come undone; **se ~ de** vt (se débarrasser de) to get rid of; (se séparer de) to part with; ~ **le lit** (pour changer les draps) to strip the bed; (pour se coucher) to turn back the bedclothes

défait, e [defɛ, -ɛt] pp de **défaire** ▷ adj (visage) haggard, ravaged ▷ nf defeat

défaites [defɛt] vb voir **défaire**

défaitisme [defetism(ə)] nm defeatism

défaitiste [defetist(ə)] adj, nm/f defeatist

défalcation [defalkɑsjɔ̃] nf deduction

défalquer [defalke] vt to deduct

défasse etc [defas] vb voir **défaire**

défausser [defose] vt to get rid of; **se défausser** vi (Cartes) to discard

défaut [defo] nm (moral) fault, failing, defect; (d'étoffe, métal) fault, flaw, defect; (manque, carence): ~ **de** lack of; shortage of; (Inform) bug; ~ **de la cuirasse** (fig) chink in the armour (Brit) ou armor (US); **en** ~ at fault; in the wrong; **faire** ~ (manquer) to be lacking; **à** ~ adv failing that; **à** ~ **de** for lack ou want of; **par** ~ (Jur) in his (ou her etc) absence

défaveur [defavœʀ] nf disfavour (Brit), disfavor (US)

défavorable [defavɔʀabl(ə)] adj unfavourable (Brit), unfavorable (US)

défavoriser [defavɔʀize] vt to put at a disadvantage

défectif, -ive [defɛktif, -iv] adj: **verbe** ~ defective verb

défection [defɛksjɔ̃] nf defection, failure to give support ou assistance; failure to appear; **faire** ~ (d'un parti etc) to withdraw one's support, leave

défectueux, -euse [defɛktɥø, -øz] adj faulty, defective

défectuosité [defɛktɥozite] nf defectiveness no pl; (défaut) defect, fault

défendable [defãdabl(ə)] adj defensible

défendeur, -eresse [defãdœʀ, -dʀɛs] nm/f (Jur) defendant

défendre [defãdʀ(ə)] vt to defend; (interdire) to forbid; ~ **à qn qch/de faire** to forbid sb sth/to do; **il est défendu de cracher** spitting (is) prohibited ou is not allowed; **c'est défendu** it is forbidden; **se défendre** vi to defend o.s.; **il se défend** (fig) he can hold his own; **ça se défend**

(fig) it holds together; **se ~ de/contre** (se protéger) to protect o.s. from/against; **se ~ de** (se garder de) to refrain from; (nier): **se ~ de vouloir** to deny wanting

défenestrer [defənɛstʀe] vt to throw out of the window

défense [defãs] nf defence (Brit), defense (US); (d'éléphant etc) tusk; **ministre de la** ~ Minister of Defence (Brit), Defence Secretary; **la** ~ **nationale** defence, the defence of the realm (Brit); **la** ~ **contre avions** anti-aircraft defence; **"~ de fumer/cracher"** "no smoking/spitting", "smoking/spitting prohibited"; **prendre la ~ de qn** to stand up for sb; ~ **des consommateurs** consumerism

défenseur [defãsœʀ] nm defender; (Jur) counsel for the defence

défensif, -ive [defãsif, -iv] adj, nf defensive; **être sur la défensive** to be on the defensive

déféquer [defeke] vi to defecate

déferai etc [defʀe] vb voir **défaire**

déférence [deferãs] nf deference

déférent, e [deferã, -ãt] adj (poli) deferential, deferent

déférer [defere] vt (Jur) to refer; ~ **à** vt (requête, décision) to defer to; ~ **qn à la justice** to hand sb over to justice

déferlant, e [defɛʀlã, -ãt] adj: **vague ~e** breaker

déferlement [defɛʀləmã] nm breaking; surge

déferler [defɛʀle] vi (vagues) to break; (fig) to surge

défi [defi] nm (provocation) challenge; (bravade) defiance; **mettre qn au ~ de faire qch** to challenge sb to do sth; **relever un ~** to take up ou accept a challenge

défiance [defjãs] nf mistrust, distrust

déficeler [defisle] vt (paquet) to undo, untie

déficience [defisjãs] nf deficiency

déficient, e [defisjã, -ãt] adj deficient

déficit [defisit] nm (Comm) deficit; (Psych etc: manque) defect; ~ **budgétaire** budget deficit; **être en** ~ to be in deficit

déficitaire [defisitɛʀ] adj (année, récolte) bad; **entreprise/budget** ~ business/budget in deficit

défier [defje] vt (provoquer) to challenge; (fig) to defy, brave; **se ~ de** (se méfier de) to distrust, mistrust; ~ **qn de faire** to challenge ou defy sb to do; ~ **qn à** to challenge sb to; ~ **toute comparaison/concurrence** to be incomparable/unbeatable

défigurer [defigyʀe] vt to disfigure; (boutons etc) to mar ou spoil (the looks of); (fig: œuvre) to mutilate, deface

défilé [defile] nm (Géo) (narrow) gorge ou pass; (soldats) parade; (manifestants) procession, march; **un ~ de** (voitures, visiteurs etc) a stream of

défiler [defile] vi (troupes) to march past; (sportifs) to parade; (manifestants) to march; (visiteurs) to pour, stream; **se défiler** vi (se dérober) to slip away, sneak off; **faire ~** (bande, film) to put on; (Inform) to scroll

défini, e [defini] *adj* definite
définir [definiʀ] *vt* to define
définissable [definisabl(ə)] *adj* definable
définitif, -ive [definitif, -iv] *adj* (*final*) final, definitive; (*pour longtemps*) permanent, definitive; (*sans appel*) final, definite ▷ *nf:* **en définitive** eventually; (*somme toute*) when all is said and done
définition [definisjɔ̃] *nf* definition; (*de mots croisés*) clue; (TV) (picture) resolution
définitivement [definitivmã] *adv* definitively; permanently; definitely
défit *etc* [defi] *vb voir* **défaire**
déflagration [deflagʀasjɔ̃] *nf* explosion
déflation [deflasjɔ̃] *nf* deflation
déflationniste [deflasjɔnist(ə)] *adj* deflationist, deflationary
déflecteur [deflɛktœʀ] *nm* (Auto) quarterlight (Brit), deflector (US)
déflorer [deflɔʀe] *vt* (*jeune fille*) to deflower; (*fig*) to spoil the charm of
défoncé, e [defɔ̃se] *adj* smashed in; broken down; (*route*) full of potholes ▷ *nm/f* addict
défoncer [defɔ̃se] *vt* (*caisse*) to stave in; (*porte*) to smash in *ou* down; (*lit, fauteuil*) to burst (the springs of); (*terrain, route*) to rip *ou* plough up; **se défoncer** *vi* (*se donner à fond*) to give it all one's got
défont [defɔ̃] *vb voir* **défaire**
déformant, e [defɔʀmã, -ãt] *adj:* **glace ~e** *ou* **miroir ~** distorting mirror
déformation [defɔʀmasjɔ̃] *nf* loss of shape; deformation; distortion; **~ professionnelle** conditioning by one's job
déformer [defɔʀme] *vt* to put out of shape; (*corps*) to deform; (*pensée, fait*) to distort; **se déformer** *vi* to lose its shape
défoulement [defulmã] *nm* release of tension; unwinding
défouler [defule]: **se défouler** *vi* (Psych) to work off one's tensions, release one's pent-up feelings; (*gén*) to unwind, let off steam
défraîchi, e [defʀeʃi] *adj* faded; (*article à vendre*) shop-soiled
défraîchir [defʀeʃiʀ]: **se défraîchir** *vi* to fade; to become shop-soiled
défrayer [defʀeje] *vt:* **~ qn** to pay sb's expenses; **~ la chronique** to be in the news; **~ la conversation** to be the main topic of conversation
défrichement [defʀiʃmã] *nm* clearance
défricher [defʀiʃe] *vt* to clear (for cultivation)
défriser [defʀize] *vt* (*cheveux*) to straighten; (*fig*) to annoy
défroisser [defʀwase] *vt* to smooth out
défroque [defʀɔk] *nf* cast-off
défroqué [defʀɔke] *nm* former monk (*ou* priest)
défroquer [defʀɔke] *vi* (*aussi:* **se défroquer**) to give up the cloth, renounce one's vows
défunt, e [defœ̃, -œ̃t] *adj:* **son ~ père** his late father ▷ *nm/f* deceased
dégagé, e [degaʒe] *adj* clear; (*ton, air*) casual,

jaunty
dégagement [degaʒmã] *nm* emission; freeing; clearing; (*espace libre*) clearing; passage; clearance; (Football) clearance; **voie de ~** slip road; **itinéraire de ~** alternative route (*to relieve traffic congestion*)
dégager [degaʒe] *vt* (*exhaler*) to give off, emit; (*délivrer*) to free, extricate; (Mil: *troupes*) to relieve; (*désencombrer*) to clear; (*isoler, mettre en valeur*) to bring out; (*crédits*) to release; **se dégager** *vi* (*odeur*) to emanate, be given off; (*passage, ciel*) to clear; **~ qn de** (*engagement, parole etc*) to release *ou* free sb from; **se ~ de** (*fig: engagement etc*) to get out of; (*: promesse*) to go back on
dégaine [degɛn] *nf* awkward way of walking
dégainer [degene] *vt* to draw
dégarni, e [degaʀni] *adj* bald
dégarnir [degaʀniʀ] *vt* (*vider*) to empty, clear; **se dégarnir** *vi* to empty; to be cleaned out *ou* cleared; (*tempes, crâne*) to go bald
dégâts [dega] *nmpl* damage *sg;* **faire des ~** to damage
dégauchir [degoʃiʀ] *vt* (Tech) to surface
dégazer [degaze] *vi* (*pétrolier*) to clean its tanks
dégel [deʒɛl] *nm* thaw; (*fig: des prix etc*) unfreezing
dégeler [deʒle] *vt* to thaw (out); (*fig*) to unfreeze ▷ *vi* to thaw (out); **se dégeler** *vi* (*fig*) to thaw out
dégénéré, e [deʒeneʀe] *adj, nm/f* degenerate
dégénérer [deʒeneʀe] *vi* to degenerate; (*empirer*) to go from bad to worse; (*devenir*) **~ en** to degenerate into
dégénérescence [deʒeneʀesãs] *nf* degeneration
dégingandé, e [deʒɛ̃gãde] *adj* gangling, lanky
dégivrage [deʒivʀaʒ] *nm* defrosting; de-icing
dégivrer [deʒivʀe] *vt* (*frigo*) to defrost; (*vitres*) to de-ice
dégivreur [deʒivʀœʀ] *nm* defroster; de-icer
déglinguer [deglɛ̃ge] *vt* to bust
déglutir [deglytiʀ] *vt, vi* to swallow
déglutition [deglytisjɔ̃] *nf* swallowing
dégonflé, e [degɔ̃fle] *adj* (*pneu*) flat; (*fam*) chicken ▷ *nm/f* (*fam*) chicken
dégonfler [degɔ̃fle] *vt* (*pneu, ballon*) to let down, deflate ▷ *vi* (*désenfler*) to go down; **se dégonfler** *vi* (*fam*) to chicken out
dégorger [degɔʀʒe] *vi* (Culin): **faire ~** to leave to sweat; (*aussi:* **se dégorger**: *rivière*): **~ dans** to flow into ▷ *vt* to disgorge
dégoter [degɔte] *vt* (*fam*) to dig up, find
dégouliner [deguline] *vi* to trickle, drip; **~ de** to be dripping with
dégoupiller [degupije] *vt* (*grenade*) to take the pin out of
dégourdi, e [deguʀdi] *adj* smart, resourceful
dégourdir [deguʀdiʀ] *vt* to warm (up); **se ~ (les jambes)** to stretch one's legs
dégoût [degu] *nm* disgust, distaste
dégoûtant, e [degutã, -ãt] *adj* disgusting
dégoûté, e [degute] *adj* disgusted; **~ de** sick of
dégoûter [degute] *vt* to disgust; **cela me**

dégoûte I find this disgusting *ou* revolting; ~ **qn de qch** to put sb off sth; **se ~ de** to get *ou* become sick of

dégoutter [degute] *vi* to drip; ~ **de** to be dripping with

dégradant, e [degradɑ̃, -ɑ̃t] *adj* degrading

dégradation [degradasjɔ̃] *nf* reduction in rank; defacement; degradation, debasement; deterioration; (*aussi:* **dégradations**: *dégâts*) damage *no pl*

dégradé, e [degrade] *adj* (*couleur*) shaded off; (*teintes*) faded; (*cheveux*) layered ▷ *nm* (*Peinture*) gradation

dégrader [degrade] *vt* (*Mil: officier*) to degrade; (*abîmer*) to damage, deface; (*avilir*) to degrade, debase; **se dégrader** *vi* (*relations, situation*) to deteriorate

dégrafer [degrafe] *vt* to unclip, unhook, unfasten

dégraissage [degrɛsaʒ] *nm* (*Écon*) cutbacks *pl*; ~ **et nettoyage à sec** dry cleaning

dégraissant [degrɛsɑ̃] *nm* spot remover

dégraisser [degrese] *vt* (*soupe*) to skim; (*vêtement*) to take the grease marks out of; (*Écon*) to cut back; (: *entreprise*) to slim down

degré [dəgre] *nm* degree; (*d'escalier*) step; **brûlure au 1er/2ème ~** 1st/2nd degree burn; **équation du 1er/2ème ~** linear/quadratic equation; **le premier ~** (*Scol*) primary level; **alcool à 90 ~s** surgical spirit; **vin de 10 ~s** 10° wine (*on Gay-Lussac scale*); **par ~(s)** *adv* by degrees, gradually

dégressif, -ive [degresif, -iv] *adj* on a decreasing scale, degressive; **tarif ~** decreasing rate of charge

dégrèvement [degrɛvmɑ̃] *nm* tax relief

dégrever [degrəve] *vt* to grant tax relief to; to reduce the tax burden on

dégriffé, e [degrife] *adj* (*vêtement*) sold without the designer's label; **voyage ~** discount holiday

dégringolade [degrɛ̃gɔlad] *nf* tumble; (*fig*) collapse

dégringoler [degrɛ̃gɔle] *vi* to tumble (down); (*fig: prix, monnaie etc*) to collapse

dégriser [degrize] *vt* to sober up

dégrossir [degrosir] *vt* (*bois*) to trim; (*fig*) to work out roughly; (: *personne*) to knock the rough edges off

déguenillé, e [degnije] *adj* ragged, tattered

déguerpir [degɛrpir] *vi* to clear off

dégueulasse [degœlas] *adj* (*fam*) disgusting

dégueuler [degœle] *vi* (*fam*) to puke, throw up

déguisé, e [degize] *adj* disguised; dressed up; ~ **en** disguised (*ou* dressed up) as

déguisement [degizmɑ̃] *nm* disguise; (*habits: pour s'amuser*) dressing-up clothes; (: *pour tromper*) disguise

déguiser [degize] *vt* to disguise; **se déguiser (en)** *vi* (*se costumer*) to dress up (as); (*pour tromper*) to disguise o.s. (as)

dégustation [degystasjɔ̃] *nf* tasting; sampling; savouring (*Brit*), savoring (*US*); (*séance*): ~ **de vin(s)** wine-tasting

déguster [degyste] *vt* (*vins*) to taste; (*fromages etc*) to sample; (*savourer*) to enjoy, savour (*Brit*), savor (*US*)

déhancher [deɑ̃ʃe]: **se déhancher** *vi* to sway one's hips; to lean (one's weight) on one hip

dehors [dəɔr] *adv* outside; (*en plein air*) outdoors, outside ▷ *nm* outside ▷ *nmpl* (*apparences*) appearances, exterior *sg*; **mettre** *ou* **jeter ~** to throw out; **au ~** outside; (*en apparence*) outwardly; **au ~ de** outside; **de ~** from outside; **en ~** outside; outwards; **en ~ de** apart from

déifier [deifje] *vt* to deify

déjà [deʒa] *adv* already; (*auparavant*) before, already; **as-tu ~ été en France?** have you been to France before?; **c'est ~ pas mal** that's not too bad (at all); **au ~** outside; (*en apparence*) **c'est ~ quelque chose** (at least) it's better than nothing; **quel nom, ~?** what was the name again?

déjanter [deʒɑ̃te]: **se déjanter** *vi* (*pneu*) to come off the rim

déjà-vu [deʒavy] *nm*: **c'est du ~** there's nothing new in that

déjeté, e [deʒte] *adj* lop-sided, crooked

déjeuner [deʒœne] *vi* to (have) lunch; (*le matin*) to have breakfast ▷ *nm* lunch; (*petit déjeuner*) breakfast; ~ **d'affaires** business lunch

déjouer [deʒwe] *vt* to elude, to foil, thwart

déjuger [deʒyʒe]: **se déjuger** *vi* to go back on one's opinion

delà [dəla] *adv*: **par ~, en ~ (de), au ~ (de)** beyond

délabré, e [delabre] *adj* dilapidated, broken-down

délabrement [delabrəmɑ̃] *nm* decay, dilapidation

délabrer [delabre]: **se délabrer** *vi* to fall into decay, become dilapidated

délacer [delase] *vt* to unlace, undo

délai [delɛ] *nm* (*attente*) waiting period; (*sursis*) extension (of time); (*temps accordé: aussi:* **délais**) time limit; **sans ~** without delay; **à bref ~** shortly, very soon; at short notice; **dans les ~s** within the time limit; **un ~ de 30 jours** a period of 30 days; **comptez un ~ de livraison de 10 jours** allow 10 days for delivery

délaissé, e [delese] *adj* abandoned, deserted; neglected

délaisser [delese] *vt* (*abandonner*) to abandon, desert; (*négliger*) to neglect

délassant, e [delasɑ̃, -ɑ̃t] *adj* relaxing

délassement [delasmɑ̃] *nm* relaxation

délasser [delase] *vt* (*reposer*) to relax; (*divertir*) to divert, entertain; **se délasser** *vi* to relax

délateur, -trice [delatœr, -tris] *nm/f* informer

délation [delasjɔ̃] *nf* denouncement, informing

délavé, e [delave] *adj* faded

délayage [delɛjaʒ] *nm* mixing; thinning down

délayer [deleje] *vt* (*Culin*) to mix (with water *etc*); (*peinture*) to thin down; (*fig*) to pad out, spin out

delco® [dɛlko] *nm* (*Auto*) distributor; **tête de delco** distributor cap

délectation [delɛktasjɔ̃] *nf* delight

délecter [delɛkte]: **se délecter** *vi*: **se ~ de** to revel *ou* delight in

délégation [delegɑsjɔ̃] *nf* delegation; **~ de pouvoir** delegation of power

délégué, e [delege] *adj* delegated ▷ *nm/f* delegate; representative; **ministre ~ à** minister with special responsibility for

déléguer [delege] *vt* to delegate

délestage [delɛstaʒ] *nm*: **itinéraire de ~** alternative route (*to relieve traffic congestion*)

délester [delɛste] *vt* (*navire*) to unballast; **~ une route** to relieve traffic congestion on a road by diverting traffic

Delhi [deli] *n* Delhi

délibérant, e [delibeʀɑ̃, -ɑ̃t] *adj*: **assemblée ~e** deliberative assembly

délibératif, -ive [delibeʀatif, -iv] *adj*: **avoir voix délibérative** to have voting rights

délibération [delibeʀɑsjɔ̃] *nf* deliberation

délibéré, e [delibeʀe] *adj* (*conscient*) deliberate; (*déterminé*) determined, resolute; **de propos ~** (*à dessein, exprès*) intentionally

délibérément [delibeʀemɑ̃] *adv* deliberately; (*résolument*) resolutely

délibérer [delibeʀe] *vi* to deliberate

délicat, e [delika, -at] *adj* delicate; (*plein de tact*) tactful; (*attentionné*) thoughtful; (*exigeant*) fussy, particular; **procédés peu ~s** unscrupulous methods

délicatement [delikatmɑ̃] *adv* delicately; (*avec douceur*) gently

délicatesse [delikatɛs] *nf* delicacy; tactfulness; thoughtfulness; **délicatesses** *nfpl* attentions, consideration *sg*

délice [delis] *nm* delight

délicieusement [delisjøzmɑ̃] *adv* deliciously; delightfully

délicieux, -euse [delisjø, -øz] *adj* (*au goût*) delicious; (*sensation, impression*) delightful

délictueux, -euse [deliktɥø, -øz] *adj* criminal

délié, e [delje] *adj* nimble, agile; (*mince*) slender, fine ▷ *nm*: **les ~s** the upstrokes (*in handwriting*)

délier [delje] *vt* to untie; **~ qn de** (*serment etc*) to free *ou* release sb from

délimitation [delimitɑsjɔ̃] *nf* delimitation

délimiter [delimite] *vt* to delimit

délinquance [delɛ̃kɑ̃s] *nf* criminality; **~ juvénile** juvenile delinquency

délinquant, e [delɛ̃kɑ̃, -ɑ̃t] *adj, nm/f* delinquent

déliquescence [delikesɑ̃s] *nf*: **en ~** in a state of decay

déliquescent, e [delikesɑ̃, -ɑ̃t] *adj* decaying

délirant, e [deliʀɑ̃, -ɑ̃t] *adj* (*Méd: fièvre*) delirious; (*imagination*) frenzied; (*fam: déraisonnable*) crazy

délire [deliʀ] *nm* (*fièvre*) delirium; (*fig*) frenzy; (: *folie*) lunacy

délirer [deliʀe] *vi* to be delirious; (*fig*) to be raving

délit [deli] *nm* (criminal) offence; **~ de droit commun** violation of common law; **~ de fuite** failure to stop after an accident; **~ d'initiés** insider dealing *ou* trading; **~ de presse**

violation of the press laws

délivrance [delivʀɑ̃s] *nf* freeing, release; (*sentiment*) relief

délivrer [delivʀe] *vt* (*prisonnier*) to (set) free, release; (*passeport, certificat*) to issue; **~ qn de** (*ennemis*) to set sb free from, deliver *ou* free sb from; (*fig*) to rid sb of

délocalisation [delɔkalizɑsjɔ̃] *nf* relocation

délocaliser [delɔkalize] *vt* (*entreprise, emplois*) relocate

déloger [delɔʒe] *vt* (*locataire*) to turn out; (*objet coincé, ennemi*) to dislodge

déloyal, e, -aux [delwajal, -o] *adj* (*personne, conduite*) disloyal; (*procédé*) unfair

Delphes [dɛlf] *n* Delphi

delta [dɛlta] *nm* (*Géo*) delta

deltaplane® [dɛltaplan] *nm* hang-glider

déluge [delyʒ] *nm* (*biblique*) Flood, Deluge; (*grosse pluie*) downpour, deluge; (*grand nombre*): **~ de** flood of

déluré, e [delyʀe] *adj* smart, resourceful; (*péj*) forward, pert

démagnétiser [demaɲetize] *vt* to demagnetize

démagogie [demagɔʒi] *nf* demagogy

démagogique [demagɔʒik] *adj* demagogic, popularity-seeking; (*Pol*) vote-catching

démagogue [demagɔg] *adj* demagogic ▷ *nm* demagogue

démaillé, e [demaje] *adj* (*bas*) laddered (*Brit*), with a run (*ou* runs)

demain [dəmɛ̃] *adv* tomorrow; **~ matin/soir** tomorrow morning/evening; **~ midi** tomorrow at midday; **à ~!** see you tomorrow!

demande [dəmɑ̃d] *nf* (*requête*) request; (*revendication*) demand; (*Admin, formulaire*) application; (*Écon*): **la ~** demand; **"~s d'emploi"** "situations wanted"; **à la ~ générale** by popular request; **~ en mariage** (marriage) proposal; **faire sa ~ (en mariage)** to propose (marriage); **~ de naturalisation** application for naturalization; **~ de poste** job application

demandé, e [dəmɑ̃de] *adj* (*article etc*): **très ~** (very) much in demand

demander [dəmɑ̃de] *vt* to ask for; (*question: date, heure, chemin*) to ask; (*requérir, nécessiter*) to require, demand; **~ qch à qn** to ask sb for sth, ask sb sth; **ils demandent deux secrétaires et un ingénieur** they're looking for two secretaries and an engineer; **~ la main de qn** to ask for sb's hand (in marriage); **~ pardon à qn** to apologize to sb; **~ à ou de voir/faire** to ask to see/ask if one can do; **~ à qn de faire** to ask sb to do; **~ que/ pourquoi** to ask that/why; **se ~ si/pourquoi** *etc* to wonder if/why *etc*; (*sens purement réfléchi*) to ask o.s. if/why *etc*; **on vous demande au téléphone** you're wanted on the phone, there's someone for you on the phone; **il ne demande que ça** that's all he wants; **je ne demande pas mieux** I'm asking nothing more; **il ne demande qu'à faire** all he wants is to do

demandeur, -euse [dəmɑ̃dœʀ, -øz] *nm/f*: **~**

d'emploi job-seeker

démangeaison [demɑ̃ʒɛzɔ̃] *nf* itching

démanger [demɑ̃ʒe] *vi* to itch; **la main me démange** my hand is itching; **l'envie** *ou* **ça me démange de faire** I'm itching to do

démantèlement [demɑ̃tɛlmɑ̃] *nm* breaking up

démanteler [demɑ̃tle] *vt* to break up; to demolish

démaquillant [demakijɑ̃] *nm* make-up remover

démaquiller [demakije] *vt*: **se démaquiller** to remove one's make-up

démarcage [demaʀkaʒ] *nm* = **démarquage**

démarcation [demaʀkasjɔ̃] *nf* demarcation

démarchage [demaʀʃaʒ] *nm* (*Comm*) door-to-door selling

démarche [demaʀʃ(ə)] *nf* (*allure*) gait, walk; (*intervention*) step; approach; (*fig: intellectuelle*) thought processes *pl*; approach; **faire** *ou* **entreprendre des ~s** to take action; **faire des ~s auprès de qn** to approach sb

démarcheur, -euse [demaʀʃœʀ, -øz] *nm/f* (*Comm*) door-to-door salesman/woman; (*Pol etc*) canvasser

démarquage [demaʀkaʒ] *nm* marking down

démarque [demaʀk(ə)] *nf* (*Comm: d'un article*) mark-down

démarqué, e [demaʀke] *adj* (*Football*) unmarked; (*Comm*) reduced; **prix ~s** marked-down prices

démarquer [demaʀke] *vt* (*prix*) to mark down; (*joueur*) to stop marking; **se démarquer** *vi* (*Sport*) to shake off one's marker

démarrage [demaʀaʒ] *nm* starting *no pl*, start; **~ en côte** hill start

démarrer [demaʀe] *vt* to start up ▷ *vi* (*conducteur*) to start (up); (*véhicule*) to move off; (*travaux, affaire*) to get moving; (*coureur: accélérer*) to pull away

démarreur [demaʀœʀ] *nm* (*Auto*) starter

démasquer [demaske] *vt* to unmask; **se démasquer** to unmask; (*fig*) to drop one's mask

démâter [demɑte] *vt* to dismast ▷ *vi* to be dismasted

démêlant, e [demelɑ̃, -ɑ̃t] *adj*: **baume ~, crème ~e** (hair) conditioner

démêler [demele] *vt* to untangle, disentangle

démêlés [demele] *nmpl* problems

démembrement [demɑ̃bʀəmɑ̃] *nm* dismemberment

démembrer [demɑ̃bʀe] *vt* to dismember

déménagement [demenaʒmɑ̃] *nm* (*du point de vue du locataire etc*) move; (*: du déménageur*) removal (*Brit*), moving (*US*); **entreprise/camion de ~** removal (*Brit*) *ou* moving (*US*) firm/van

déménager [demenaʒe] *vt* (*meubles*) to (re)move ▷ *vi* to move (house)

déménageur [demenaʒœʀ] *nm* removal man (*Brit*), (furniture) mover (*US*); (*entrepreneur*) furniture remover

démence [demɑ̃s] *nf* madness, insanity; (*Méd*) dementia

démener [demne]: **se démener** *vi* to thrash about; (*fig*) to exert o.s.

dément, e [demɑ̃, -ɑ̃t] *vb voir* **démentir** ▷ *adj* (*fou*) mad (*Brit*), crazy; (*fam*) brilliant, fantastic

démenti [demɑ̃ti] *nm* refutation

démentiel, le [demɑ̃sjɛl] *adj* insane

démentir [demɑ̃tiʀ] *vt* (*nouvelle, témoin*) to refute; (*faits etc*) to belie, refute; **~ que** to deny that; **ne pas se ~** not to fail, keep up

démerder [demɛʀde]: **se démerder** *vi* (*fam!*) to bloody well manage for o.s.

démériter [demeʀite] *vi*: **~ auprès de qn** to come down in sb's esteem

démesure [deməzyʀ] *nf* immoderation, immoderateness

démesuré, e [deməzyʀe] *adj* immoderate, disproportionate

démesurément [deməzyʀemɑ̃] *adv* disproportionately

démettre [demɛtʀ(ə)] *vt*: **~ qn de** (*fonction, poste*) to dismiss sb from; **se ~ (de ses fonctions)** to resign (from) one's duties; **se ~ l'épaule** *etc* to dislocate one's shoulder *etc*

demeurant [dəmœʀɑ̃]: **au ~** *adv* for all that

demeure [dəmœʀ] *nf* residence; **dernière ~** (*fig*) last resting place; **mettre qn en ~ de faire** to enjoin *ou* order sb to do; **à ~** *adv* permanently

demeuré, e [dəmœʀe] *adj* backward ▷ *nm/f* backward person

demeurer [dəmœʀe] *vi* (*habiter*) to live; (*séjourner*) to stay; (*rester*) to remain; **en ~ là** (*personne*) to leave it at that; (*: choses*) to be left at that

demi, e [dəmi] *adj*: **et ~, trois heures/bouteilles et ~es** three and a half hours/bottles, three hours/bottles and a half ▷ *nm* (*bière: = 0.25 litre*) ≈ half-pint; (*Football*) half-back; **il est 2 heures et ~e** it's half past 2; **il est midi et ~** it's half past 12; **~ de mêlée/d'ouverture** (*Rugby*) scrum/fly half; **à ~** *adv* half-; **ouvrir à ~** to half-open; **faire les choses à ~** to do things by halves; **à la ~e** (*heure*) on the half-hour

demi... [dəmi] *préfixe* half-, semi..., demi-

demi-bas [dəmiba] *nm inv* (*chaussette*) knee-sock

demi-bouteille [dəmibutɛj] *nf* half-bottle

demi-cercle [dəmisɛʀkl(ə)] *nm* semicircle; **en ~** *adj* semicircular ▷ *adv* in a semicircle

demi-douzaine [dəmiduzɛn] *nf* half-dozen, half a dozen

demi-finale [dəmifinal] *nf* semifinal

demi-finaliste [dəmifinalist(ə)] *nm/f* semifinalist

demi-fond [dəmifɔ̃] *nm* (*Sport*) medium-distance running

demi-frère [dəmifʀɛʀ] *nm* half-brother

demi-gros [dəmigʀo] *nm inv* wholesale trade

demi-heure [dəmijœʀ] *nf*: **une ~** a half-hour, half an hour

demi-jour [dəmiʒuʀ] *nm* half-light

demi-journée [dəmiʒuʀne] *nf* half-day, half a day

démilitariser [demilitaʀize] vt to demilitarize

demi-litre [dəmilitʀ(ə)] nm half-litre (Brit), half-liter (US), half a litre ou liter

demi-livre [dəmilivʀ(ə)] nf half-pound, half a pound

demi-longueur [dəmilɔ̃gœʀ] nf (Sport) half-length, half a length

demi-lune [dəmilyn]: **en ~** adj inv semicircular

demi-mal [dəmimal] nm: **il n'y a que ~** there's not much harm done

demi-mesure [dəmimzyʀ] nf half-measure

demi-mot [dəmimo]: **à ~** adv without having to spell things out

déminer [demine] vt to clear of mines

démineur [deminœʀ] nm bomb disposal expert

demi-pension [dəmipɑ̃sjɔ̃] nf half-board; **être en ~** (Scol) to take school meals

demi-pensionnaire [dəmipɑ̃sjɔnɛʀ] nm/f (Scol) half-boarder

demi-place [dəmiplas] nf half-price; (Transports) half-fare

démis, e [demi, -iz] pp de **démettre** ▷ adj (épaule etc) dislocated

demi-saison [dəmisɛzɔ̃] nf: **vêtements de ~** spring ou autumn clothing

demi-sel [dəmisɛl] adj inv slightly salted

demi-sœur [dəmisœʀ] nf half-sister

demi-sommeil [dəmisɔmɛj] nm doze

demi-soupir [dəmisupiʀ] nm (Mus) quaver (Brit) ou eighth note (US) rest

démission [demisjɔ̃] nf resignation; **donner sa ~** to give ou hand in one's notice, hand in one's resignation

démissionnaire [demisjɔnɛʀ] adj outgoing ▷ nm/f person resigning

démissionner [demisjɔne] vi (de son poste) to resign, give ou hand in one's notice

demi-tarif [dəmitaʀif] nm half-price; (Transports) half-fare

demi-ton [dəmitɔ̃] nm (Mus) semitone

demi-tour [dəmituʀ] nm about-turn; **faire un ~** (Mil etc) to make an about-turn; **faire ~** to turn (and go) back; (Auto) to do a U-turn

démobilisation [demɔbilizasjɔ̃] nf demobilization; (fig) demotivation, demoralization

démobiliser [demɔbilize] vt to demobilize; (fig) to demotivate, demoralize

démocrate [demɔkʀat] adj democratic ▷ nm/f democrat

démocrate-chrétien, ne [demɔkʀatkʀetjɛ̃, -ɛn] nm/f Christian Democrat

démocratie [demɔkʀasi] nf democracy; **~ populaire/libérale** people's/liberal democracy

démocratique [demɔkʀatik] adj democratic

démocratiquement [demɔkʀatikmɑ̃] adv democratically

démocratisation [demɔkʀatizasjɔ̃] nf democratization

démocratiser [demɔkʀatize] vt to democratize

démodé, e [demɔde] adj old-fashioned

démoder [demɔde]: **se démoder** vi to go out of fashion

démographe [demɔgʀaf] nm/f demographer

démographie [demɔgʀafi] nf demography

démographique [demɔgʀafik] adj demographic; **poussée ~** increase in population

demoiselle [dəmwazɛl] nf (jeune fille) young lady; (célibataire) single lady, maiden lady; **~ d'honneur** bridesmaid

démolir [demɔliʀ] vt to demolish; (fig: personne) to do for

démolisseur [demɔlisœʀ] nm demolition worker

démolition [demɔlisjɔ̃] nf demolition

démon [demɔ̃] nm demon, fiend; evil spirit; (enfant turbulent) devil, demon; **le ~ du jeu/des femmes** a mania for gambling/women; **le D~** the Devil

démonétiser [demɔnetize] vt to demonetize

démoniaque [demɔnjak] adj fiendish

démonstrateur, -trice [demɔ̃stʀatœʀ, -tʀis] nm/f demonstrator

démonstratif, -ive [demɔ̃stʀatif, -iv] adj, nm (aussi Ling) demonstrative

démonstration [demɔ̃stʀasjɔ̃] nf demonstration; (aérienne, navale) display

démontable [demɔ̃tabl(ə)] adj folding

démontage [demɔ̃taʒ] nm dismantling

démonté, e [demɔ̃te] adj (fig) raging, wild

démonte-pneu [demɔ̃təpnø] nm tyre lever (Brit), tire iron (US)

démonter [demɔ̃te] vt (machine etc) to take down, dismantle; (pneu, porte) to take off; (cavalier) to throw, unseat; (fig: personne) to disconcert; **se démonter** vi (personne) to lose countenance

démontrable [demɔ̃tʀabl(ə)] adj demonstrable

démontrer [demɔ̃tʀe] vt to demonstrate, show

démoralisant, e [demɔʀalizɑ̃, -ɑ̃t] adj demoralizing

démoralisateur, -trice [demɔʀalizatœʀ, -tʀis] adj demoralizing

démoraliser [demɔʀalize] vt to demoralize

démordre [demɔʀdʀ] vi (aussi: **ne pas démordre de**) to refuse to give up, stick to

démouler [demule] vt (gâteau) to turn out

démultiplication [demyltiplikasjɔ̃] nf reduction; reduction ratio

démuni, e [demyni] adj (sans argent) impoverished; **~ de** without, lacking in

démunir [demyniʀ] vt: **~ qn de** to deprive sb of; **se ~ de** to part with, give up

démuseler [demyzle] vt to unmuzzle

démystifier [demistifje] vt to demystify

démythifier [demitifje] vt to demythologize

dénatalité [denatalite] nf fall in the birth rate

dénationalisation [denasjɔnalizasjɔ̃] nf denationalization

dénationaliser [denasjɔnalize] vt to denationalize

dénaturé, e [denatyʀe] adj (alcool) denaturized; (goûts) unnatural

dénaturer [denatyʀe] vt (goût) to alter (completely); (pensée, fait) to distort, misrepresent

dénégations [denegɑsjɔ̃] nfpl denials

déneigement [denɛʒmɑ̃] nm snow clearance

déneiger [deneʒe] vt to clear snow from

déni [deni] nm: ~ (de justice) denial of justice

déniaiser [denjeze] vt: ~ qn to teach sb about life

dénicher [deniʃe] vt to unearth

dénicotinisé, e [denikɔtinize] adj nicotine-free

denier [dənje] nm (monnaie) formerly, a coin of small value; (de bas) denier; ~ du culte contribution to parish upkeep; ~s publics public money; de ses (propres) ~s out of one's own pocket

dénier [denje] vt to deny; ~ qch à qn to deny sb sth

dénigrement [denigʀəmɑ̃] nm denigration; **campagne de** ~ smear campaign

dénigrer [denigʀe] vt to denigrate, run down

dénivelé, e [denivle] adj (chaussée) on a lower level ▷ nm difference in height

déniveler [denivle] vt to make uneven; to put on a lower level

dénivellation [denivɛlɑsjɔ̃] nf, **dénivellement** [denivɛlmɑ̃] ▷ nm difference in level; (pente) ramp; (creux) dip

dénombrer [denɔ̃bʀe] vt (compter) to count; (énumérer) to enumerate, list

dénominateur [denɔminatœʀ] nm denominator; ~ **commun** common denominator

dénomination [denɔminɑsjɔ̃] nf designation, appellation

dénommé, e [denɔme] adj: **le** ~ **Dupont** the man by the name of Dupont

dénommer [denɔme] vt to name

dénoncer [denɔ̃se] vt to denounce; **se dénoncer** vi to give o.s. up, come forward

dénonciation [denɔ̃sjɑsjɔ̃] nf denunciation

dénoter [denɔte] vt to denote

dénouement [denumɑ̃] nm outcome, conclusion; (Théât) dénouement

dénouer [denwe] vt to unknot, undo

dénoyauter [denwajote] vt to stone; **appareil à** ~ stoner

dénoyauteur [denwajotœʀ] nm stoner

denrée [dɑ̃ʀe] nf commodity; (aussi: **denrée alimentaire**) food(stuff)

dense [dɑ̃s] adj dense

densité [dɑ̃site] nf denseness; (Physique) density

dent [dɑ̃] nf tooth; **avoir/garder une** ~ **contre qn** to have/hold a grudge against sb; **se mettre qch sous la** ~ to eat sth; **être sur les** ~**s** to be on one's last legs; **faire ses** ~**s** to teethe, cut (one's) teeth; **en** ~**s de scie** serrated; (irrégulier) jagged; **avoir les** ~**s longues** (fig) to be ruthlessly ambitious; ~ **de lait/sagesse** milk/wisdom tooth

dentaire [dɑ̃tɛʀ] adj dental; **cabinet** ~ dental surgery; **école** ~ dental school

denté, e [dɑ̃te] adj: **roue** ~**e** cog wheel

dentelé, e [dɑ̃tle] adj jagged, indented

dentelle [dɑ̃tɛl] nf lace no pl

dentelure [dɑ̃tlyʀ] nf (aussi: **dentelures**) jagged outline

dentier [dɑ̃tje] nm denture

dentifrice [dɑ̃tifʀis] adj, nm: (**pâte**) ~ toothpaste; **eau** ~ mouthwash

dentiste [dɑ̃tist(ə)] nm/f dentist

dentition [dɑ̃tisjɔ̃] nf teeth pl, dentition

dénucléariser [denykleaʀize] vt to make nuclear-free

dénudé, e [denyde] adj bare

dénuder [denyde] vt to bare; **se dénuder** (personne) to strip

dénué, e [denɥe] adj: ~ **de** lacking in; (intérêt) devoid of

dénuement [denymɑ̃] nm destitution

dénutrition [denytʀisjɔ̃] nf undernourishment

déodorant [deɔdɔʀɑ̃] nm deodorant

déodoriser [deɔdɔʀize] vt to deodorize

déontologie [deɔ̃tɔlɔʒi] nf code of ethics; (professionnelle) (professional) code of practice

dép. abr (= département) dept; (= départ) dep.

dépannage [depanaʒ] nm: **service/camion de** ~ (Auto) breakdown service/truck

dépanner [depane] vt (voiture, télévision) to fix, repair; (fig) to bail out, help out

dépanneur [depanœʀ] nm (Auto) breakdown mechanic; (TV) television engineer

dépanneuse [depanøz] nf breakdown lorry (Brit), tow truck (US)

dépareillé, e [depaʀeje] adj (collection, service) incomplete; (gant, volume, objet) odd

déparer [depaʀe] vt to spoil, mar

départ [depaʀ] nm leaving no pl, departure; (Sport) start; (sur un horaire) departure; **à son** ~ when he left; **au** ~ (au début) initially, at the start; **courrier au** ~ outgoing mail

départager [depaʀtaʒe] vt to decide between

département [depaʀtəmɑ̃] nm department; see note

● **DÉPARTEMENTS**
●
● France is divided into 96 administrative
● units called départements. These local
● government divisions are headed by a state-
● appointed 'préfet', and administered by an
● elected 'Conseil général'. Départements are
● usually named after prominent
● geographical features such as rivers or
● mountain ranges.

départemental, e, -aux [depaʀtəmɑ̃tal, -o] adj departmental

départementaliser [depaʀtəmɑ̃talize] vt to devolve authority to

départir [depaʀtiʀ]: **se** ~ **de** vt to abandon, depart from

dépassé, e [depɑse] adj superseded, outmoded; (fig) out of one's depth

dépassement [depɑsmɑ̃] nm (Auto)

overtaking *no pl*

dépasser [depɑse] *vt* (*véhicule, concurrent*) to overtake; (*endroit*) to pass, go past; (*somme, limite*) to exceed; (*fig: en beauté etc*) to surpass, outshine; (*être en saillie sur*) to jut out above (*ou* in front of); (*dérouter*): **cela me dépasse** it's beyond me ▷ *vi* (*Auto*) to overtake; (*jupon*) to show; **se dépasser** *vi* to excel o.s.

dépassionner [depɑsjɔne] *vt* (*débat etc*) to take the heat out of

dépaver [depave] *vt* to remove the cobblestones from

dépaysé, e [depeize] *adj* disorientated

dépaysement [depeizmɑ̃] *nm* disorientation; change of scenery

dépayser [depeize] *vt* (*désorienter*) to disorientate; (*changer agréablement*) to provide with a change of scenery.

dépecer [depəse] *vt* (*boucher*) to joint, cut up; (*animal*) to dismember

dépêche [depɛʃ] *nf* dispatch; ~ **(télégraphique)** telegram, wire

dépêcher [depeʃe] *vt* to dispatch; **se dépêcher** *vi* to hurry; **se ~ de faire qch** to hasten to do sth, hurry (in order) to do sth

dépeindre [depɛ̃dʀ(ə)] *vt* to depict

dépénalisation [depenalizɑsjɔ̃] *nf* decriminalization

dépendance [depɑ̃dɑ̃s] *nf* (*interdépendance*) dependence *no pl*, dependency; (*bâtiment*) outbuilding

dépendant, e [depɑ̃dɑ̃, -ɑ̃t] *vb voir* **dépendre** ▷ *adj* (*financièrement*) dependent

dépendre [depɑ̃dʀ(ə)] *vt* (*tableau*) to take down; **~ de** *vt* to depend on, to be dependent on; (*appartenir*) to belong to; **ça dépend** it depends

dépens [depɑ̃] *nmpl*: **aux ~ de** at the expense of

dépense [depɑ̃s] *nf* spending *no pl*, expense, expenditure *no pl*; (*fig*) consumption; (: *de temps, de forces*) expenditure; **pousser qn à la ~** to make sb incur an expense; **~ physique** (physical) exertion; **~s de fonctionnement** revenue expenditure; **~s d'investissement** capital expenditure; **~s publiques** public expenditure

dépenser [depɑ̃se] *vt* to spend; (*gaz, eau*) to use; (*fig*) to expend, use up; **se dépenser** *vi* (*se fatiguer*) to exert o.s.

dépensier, -ière [depɑ̃sje, -jɛʀ] *adj*: **il est ~** he's a spendthrift

déperdition [depɛʀdisjɔ̃] *nf* loss

dépérir [depeʀiʀ] *vi* (*personne*) to waste away; (*plante*) to wither

dépersonnaliser [depɛʀsɔnalize] *vt* to depersonalize

dépêtrer [depetʀe] *vt*: **se ~ de** (*situation*) to extricate o.s. from

dépeuplé, e [depœple] *adj* depopulated

dépeuplement [depœpləmɑ̃] *nm* depopulation

dépeupler [depœple] *vt* to depopulate; **se dépeupler** *vi* to be depopulated

déphasage [defɑzaʒ] *nm* (*fig*) being out of touch

déphasé, e [defɑze] *adj* (*Élec*) out of phase; (*fig*) out of touch

déphaser [defɑze] *vt* (*fig*) to put out of touch

dépilation [depilɑsjɔ̃] *nf* hair loss; hair removal

dépilatoire [depilatwaʀ] *adj* depilatory, hair-removing

dépiler [depile] *vt* (*épiler*) to depilate, remove hair from

dépistage [depistaʒ] *nm* (*Méd*) screening

dépister [depiste] *vt* to detect; (*Méd*) to screen; (*voleur*) to track down; (*poursuivants*) to throw off the scent

dépit [depi] *nm* vexation, frustration; **en ~ de** *prép* in spite of; **en ~ du bon sens** contrary to all good sense

dépité, e [depite] *adj* vexed, frustrated

dépiter [depite] *vt* to vex, frustrate

déplacé, e [deplase] *adj* (*propos*) out of place, uncalled-for; **personne ~e** displaced person

déplacement [deplasmɑ̃] *nm* moving; shifting; transfer; (*voyage*) trip, travelling *no pl* (Brit), traveling *no pl* (US); **en ~** away (on a trip); **~ d'air** displacement of air; **~ de vertèbre** slipped disc

déplacer [deplase] *vt* (*table, voiture*) to move, shift; (*employé*) to transfer, move; **se déplacer** *vi* (*objet*) to move; (*organe*) to become displaced; (*personne: bouger*) to move, walk; (: *voyager*) to travel ▷ *vt* (*vertèbre etc*) to displace

déplaire [deplɛʀ] *vi*: **ceci me déplaît** I don't like this, I dislike this; **il cherche à nous ~** he's trying to displease us *ou* be disagreeable to us; **se ~ quelque part** to dislike it *ou* be unhappy somewhere

déplaisant, e [deplɛzɑ̃, -ɑ̃t] *vb voir* **déplaire** ▷ *adj* disagreeable, unpleasant

déplaisir [depleziʀ] *nm* displeasure, annoyance

déplaît [deplɛ] *vb voir* **déplaire**

dépliant [deplijɑ̃] *nm* leaflet

déplier [deplije] *vt* to unfold; **se déplier** *vi* (*parachute*) to open

déplisser [deplise] *vt* to smooth out

déploiement [deplwamɑ̃] *nm* (*voir déployer*) deployment; display

déplomber [deplɔ̃be] *vt* (*caisse, compteur*) to break (open) the seal of; (*Inform*) to hack into

déplorable [deplɔʀabl(ə)] *adj* deplorable; lamentable

déplorer [deplɔʀe] *vt* (*regretter*) to deplore; (*pleurer sur*) to lament

déployer [deplwaje] *vt* to open out, spread; (*Mil*) to deploy; (*montrer*) to display, exhibit

déplu [deply] *pp de* **déplaire**

dépointer [depwɛ̃te] *vi* to clock out

dépoli, e [depɔli] *adj*: **verre ~** frosted glass

dépolitiser [depɔlitize] *vt* to depoliticize

dépopulation [depɔpylɑsjɔ̃] *nf* depopulation

déportation [depɔʀtɑsjɔ̃] *nf* deportation

déporté, e [depɔʀte] *nm/f* deportee; (1939–45) concentration camp prisoner

déporter [depɔʀte] *vt* (*Pol*) to deport; (*dévier*) to carry off course; **se déporter** *vi* (*voiture*) to swerve

déposant, e [depozɑ̃, -ɑ̃t] *nm/f* (*épargnant*) depositor

dépose [depoz] *nf* taking out; taking down

déposé, e [depoze] *adj* registered; *voir aussi* **marque**

déposer [depoze] *vt* (*gén: mettre, poser*) to lay down, put down, set down; (*à la banque, à la consigne*) to deposit; (*caution*) to put down; (*passager*) to drop (off), set down; (*démonter: serrure, moteur*) to take out; (*: rideau*) to take down; (*roi*) to depose; (*Admin: faire enregistrer*) to file; to register ▷ *vi* to form a sediment *ou* deposit; (*Jur*): ~ **(contre)** to testify *ou* give evidence (against); **se déposer** *vi* to settle; ~ **son bilan** (*Comm*) to go into (voluntary) liquidation

dépositaire [depoziteʀ] *nm/f* (*Jur*) depository; (*Comm*) agent; ~ **agréé** authorized agent

déposition [depozisjɔ̃] *nf* (*Jur*) deposition

déposséder [deposede] *vt* to dispossess

dépôt [depo] *nm* (*à la banque, sédiment*) deposit; (*entrepôt, réserve*) warehouse, store; (*gare*) depot; (*prison*) cells *pl*; ~ **d'ordures** rubbish (*Brit*) *ou* garbage (*US*) dump, tip (*Brit*); ~ **de bilan** (voluntary) liquidation; ~ **légal** registration of copyright

dépoter [depote] *vt* (*plante*) to take from the pot, transplant

dépotoir [depotwaʀ] *nm* dumping ground, rubbish (*Brit*) *ou* garbage (*US*) dump; ~ **nucléaire** nuclear (waste) dump

dépouille [depuj] *nf* (*d'animal*) skin, hide; (*humaine*): ~ **(mortelle)** mortal remains *pl*

dépouillé, e [depuje] *adj* (*fig*) bare, bald; ~ **de** stripped of; lacking in

dépouillement [depujmɑ̃] *nm* (*de scrutin*) count, counting *no pl*

dépouiller [depuje] *vt* (*animal*) to skin; (*spolier*) to deprive of one's possessions; (*documents*) to go through, peruse; ~ **qn/qch de** to strip sb/sth of; ~ **le scrutin** to count the votes

dépourvu, e [depuʀvy] *adj*: ~ **de** lacking in, without; **au** ~ *adv*: **prendre qn au** ~ to catch sb unawares

dépoussiérer [depusjeʀe] *vt* to remove dust from

dépravation [depʀavasjɔ̃] *nf* depravity

dépravé, e [depʀave] *adj* depraved

dépraver [depʀave] *vt* to deprave

dépréciation [depʀesjasjɔ̃] *nf* depreciation

déprécier [depʀesje] *vt* to reduce the value of; **se déprécier** *vi* to depreciate

déprédations [depʀedasjɔ̃] *nfpl* damage *sg*

dépressif, -ive [depʀesif, -iv] *adj* depressive

dépression [depʀesjɔ̃] *nf* depression; ~ **(nerveuse)** (nervous) breakdown

déprimant, e [depʀimɑ̃, -ɑ̃t] *adj* depressing

déprime [depʀim] *nf* (*fam*): **la** ~ depression

déprimé, e [depʀime] *adj* (*découragé*) depressed

déprimer [depʀime] *vt* to depress

déprogrammer [depʀɔgʀame] *vt* (*supprimer*) to cancel

DEPS *sigle* (= *dernier entré premier sorti*) LIFO (= *last in first out*)

dépt *abr* (= *département*) dept

dépuceler [depysle] *vt* (*fam*) to take the virginity of

 MOT-CLÉ

depuis [dəpɥi] *prép* **1** (*point de départ dans le temps*) since; **il habite Paris depuis 1983/l'an dernier** he has been living in Paris since 1983/ last year; **depuis quand?** since when?; **depuis quand le connaissez-vous?** how long have you known him?; **depuis lors** since then
2 (*temps écoulé*) for; **il habite Paris depuis cinq ans** he has been living in Paris for five years; **je le connais depuis trois ans** I've known him for three years; **depuis combien de temps êtes-vous ici?** how long have you been here?
3 (*lieu*): **il a plu depuis Metz** it's been raining since Metz; **elle a téléphoné depuis Valence** she rang from Valence
4 (*quantité, rang*) from; **depuis les plus petits jusqu'aux plus grands** from the youngest to the oldest
▷ *adv* (*temps*) since (then); **je ne lui ai pas parlé depuis** I haven't spoken to him since (then); **depuis que** *conj* (ever) since; **depuis qu'il m'a dit ça** (ever) since he said that to me

dépuratif, -ive [depyʀatif, -iv] *adj* depurative, purgative

députation [depytɑsjɔ̃] *nf* deputation; (*fonction*) position of deputy; ≈ parliamentary seat (*Brit*), ≈ seat in Congress (*US*)

député, e [depyte] *nm/f* (*Pol*) deputy, ≈ Member of Parliament (*Brit*), ≈ Congressman/woman (*US*)

députer [depyte] *vt* to delegate; ~ **qn auprès de** to send sb (as a representative) to

déracinement [deʀasinmɑ̃] *nm* (*gén*) uprooting; (*d'un préjugé*) eradication

déraciner [deʀasine] *vt* to uproot

déraillement [deʀajmɑ̃] *nm* derailment

dérailler [deʀaje] *vi* (*train*) to be derailed, go off *ou* jump the rails; (*fam*) to be completely off the track; **faire** ~ to derail

dérailleur [deʀajœʀ] *nm* (*de vélo*) dérailleur gears *pl*

déraison [deʀezɔ̃] *nf* unreasonableness

déraisonnable [deʀezɔnabl(ə)] *adj* unreasonable

déraisonner [deʀezɔne] *vi* to talk nonsense, rave

dérangement [deʀɑ̃ʒmɑ̃] *nm* (*gêne, déplacement*) trouble; (*gastrique etc*) disorder; (*mécanique*) breakdown; **en** ~ (*téléphone*) out of order

déranger [deʀɑ̃ʒe] *vt* (*personne*) to trouble, bother, disturb; (*projets*) to disrupt, upset; (*objets, vêtements*) to disarrange; **se déranger** to put o.s. out; (*se déplacer*) to (take the trouble to) come (*ou* go) out; **est-ce que cela vous dérange si ...?** do you mind if ...?; **ça te**

dérangerait de faire ...? would you mind doing ...?; **ne vous dérangez pas** don't go to any trouble; don't disturb yourself

dérapage [deʀapaʒ] *nm* skid, skidding *no pl*; going out of control

déraper [deʀape] *vi* (*voiture*) to skid; (*personne, semelles, couteau*) to slip; (*fig: économie etc*) to go out of control

dératé, e [deʀate] *nm/f*: **courir comme un ~** to run like the clappers

dératiser [deʀatize] *vt* to rid of rats

déréglé, e [deʀegle] *adj* (*mœurs*) dissolute

dérèglement [deʀɛɡləmɑ̃] *nm* upsetting *no pl*, upset

déréglementation [deʀɛɡləmɑ̃tasjɔ̃] *nf* deregulation

dérégler [deʀegle] *vt* (*mécanisme*) to put out of order, cause to break down; (*estomac*) to upset; **se dérégler** *vi* to break down, go wrong

dérider [deʀide] *vt*, **se dérider** *vi* to cheer up

dérision [deʀizjɔ̃] *nf* derision; **tourner en ~** to deride; **par ~** in mockery

dérisoire [deʀizwaʀ] *adj* derisory

dérivatif [deʀivatif] *nm* distraction

dérivation [deʀivasjɔ̃] *nf* derivation; diversion

dérive [deʀiv] *nf* (*de dériveur*) centre-board; **aller à la ~** (*Navig, fig*) to drift; **~ des continents** (*Géo*) continental drift

dérivé, e [deʀive] *adj* derived ▷ *nm* (*Ling*) derivative; (*Tech*) by-product ▷ *nf* (*Math*) derivative

dériver [deʀive] *vt* (*Math*) to derive; (*cours d'eau etc*) to divert ▷ *vi* (*bateau*) to drift; **~ de** to derive from

dériveur [deʀivœʀ] *nm* sailing dinghy

dermatite [dɛʀmatit] *nf* dermatitis

dermato [dɛʀmato] *nm/f* (*fam: = dermatologue*) dermatologist

dermatologie [dɛʀmatɔlɔʒi] *nf* dermatology

dermatologue [dɛʀmatɔlɔg] *nm/f* dermatologist

dermatose [dɛʀmatoz] *nf* dermatosis

dermite [dɛʀmit] *nf* = **dermatite**

dernier, -ière [dɛʀnje, -jɛʀ] *adj* (*dans le temps, l'espace*) last; (*le plus récent: gén avant n*) latest, last; (*final, ultime: effort*) final; (*échelon, grade*) top, highest ▷ *nm* (*étage*) top floor; **lundi/le mois ~** last Monday/month; **du ~ chic** extremely smart; **le ~ cri** the last word (in fashion); **les ~s honneurs** the last tribute; **le ~ soupir, rendre le ~ soupir** to breathe one's last; **en ~** *adv* last; **ce ~, cette dernière** the latter

dernièrement [dɛʀnjɛʀmɑ̃] *adv* recently

dernier-né, dernière-née [dɛʀnjene, dɛʀnjɛʀne] *nm/f* (*enfant*) last-born

dérobade [deʀɔbad] *nf* side-stepping *no pl*

dérobé, e [deʀɔbe] *adj* (*porte*) secret, hidden; **à la ~e** surreptitiously

dérober [deʀɔbe] *vt* to steal; (*cacher*): **~ qch à (la vue de) qn** to conceal *ou* hide sth from sb('s view); **se dérober** *vi* (*s'esquiver*) to slip away; (*fig*) to shy away; **se ~ sous** (*s'effondrer*) to give way

beneath; **se ~ à** (*justice, regards*) to hide from; (*obligation*) to shirk

dérogation [deʀɔɡasjɔ̃] *nf* (special) dispensation

déroger [deʀɔʒe]: **~ à** *vt* to go against, depart from

dérouiller [deʀuje] *vt*: **se ~ les jambes** to stretch one's legs

déroulement [deʀulmɑ̃] *nm* (*d'une opération etc*) progress

dérouler [deʀule] *vt* (*ficelle*) to unwind; (*papier*) to unroll; **se dérouler** *vi* to unwind; to unroll, come unrolled; (*avoir lieu*) to take place; (*se passer*) to go

déroutant, e [deʀutɑ̃, -ɑ̃t] *adj* disconcerting

déroute [deʀut] *nf* (*Mil*) rout; (*fig*) total collapse; **mettre en ~** to rout; **en ~** routed

dérouter [deʀute] *vt* (*avion, train*) to reroute, divert; (*étonner*) to disconcert, throw (out)

derrick [deʀik] *nm* derrick (*over oil well*)

derrière [deʀjɛʀ] *adv, prép* behind ▷ *nm* (*d'une maison*) back; (*postérieur*) behind, bottom; **les pattes de ~** the back legs, the hind legs; **par ~** from behind; (*fig*) in an underhand way, behind one's back

derviche [dɛʀviʃ] *nm* dervish

DES *sigle m* (= *diplôme d'études supérieures*) university post-graduate degree

des [de] *art voir* **de**

dès [dɛ] *prép* from; **~ que** *conj* as soon as; **~ à présent** here and now; **~ son retour** as soon as he was (*ou* is) back; **~ réception** upon receipt; **~ lors** *adv* from then on; **~ lors que** *conj* from the moment (that)

désabusé, e [dezabyze] *adj* disillusioned

désaccord [dezakɔʀ] *nm* disagreement

désaccordé, e [dezakɔʀde] *adj* (*Mus*) out of tune

désacraliser [desakʀalize] *vt* to deconsecrate; (*fig: profession, institution*) to take the mystique out of

désaffecté, e [dezafɛkte] *adj* disused

désaffection [dezafɛksjɔ̃] *nf*: **~ pour** estrangement from

désagréable [dezagʀeablə] *adj* unpleasant, disagreeable

désagréablement [dezagʀeabləmɑ̃] *adv* disagreeably, unpleasantly

désagrégation [dezagʀegasjɔ̃] *nf* disintegration

désagréger [dezagʀeʒe]: **se désagréger** *vi* to disintegrate, break up

désagrément [dezagʀemɑ̃] *nm* annoyance, trouble *no pl*

désaltérant, e [dezalteʀɑ̃, -ɑ̃t] *adj* thirst-quenching

désaltérer [dezalteʀe] *vt*: **se désaltérer** to quench one's thirst; **ça désaltère** it's thirst-quenching, it quenches your thirst

désamorcer [dezamɔʀse] *vt* to remove the primer from; (*fig*) to defuse; (: *prévenir*) to forestall

désappointé, e [dezapwɛ̃te] *adj* disappointed

désapprobateur, -trice [dezapʀɔbatœʀ, -tʀis] *adj* disapproving

désapprobation [dezapʀɔbasjɔ̃] *nf* disapproval

désapprouver [dezapʀuve] *vt* to disapprove of

désarçonner [dezaʀsɔne] *vt* to unseat, throw; *(fig)* to throw, nonplus *(Brit)*, disconcert

désargenté, e [dezaʀʒɑ̃te] *adj* impoverished

désarmant, e [dezaʀmɑ̃, -ɑ̃t] *adj* disarming

désarmé, e [dezaʀme] *adj (fig)* disarmed

désarmement [dezaʀməmɑ̃] *nm* disarmament

désarmer [dezaʀme] *vt (Mil, aussi fig)* to disarm; *(Navig)* to lay up; *(fusil)* to unload; *(: mettre le cran de sûreté)* to put the safety catch on ▷ *vi (pays)* to disarm; *(haine)* to wane; *(personne)* to give up

désarroi [dezaʀwa] *nm* helplessness, disarray

désarticulé, e [dezaʀtikyle] *adj (pantin, corps)* dislocated

désarticuler [dezaʀtikyle] *vt:* **se désarticuler** to contort (o.s.)

désassorti, e [dezasɔʀti] *adj* non-matching, unmatched; *(magasin, marchand)* sold out

désastre [dezastʀ(ə)] *nm* disaster

désastreux, -euse [dezastʀø, -øz] *adj* disastrous

désavantage [dezavɑ̃taʒ] *nm* disadvantage; *(inconvénient)* drawback, disadvantage

désavantager [dezavɑ̃taʒe] *vt* to put at a disadvantage

désavantageux, -euse [dezavɑ̃taʒø, -øz] *adj* unfavourable, disadvantageous

désaveu [dezavø] *nm* repudiation; *(déni)* disclaimer

désavouer [dezavwe] *vt* to disown, repudiate, disclaim

désaxé, e [dezakse] *adj (fig)* unbalanced

désaxer [dezakse] *vt (roue)* to put out of true; *(personne)* to throw off balance

desceller [desele] *vt (pierre)* to pull free

descendance [desɑ̃dɑ̃s] *nf (famille)* descendants *pl*, issue; *(origine)* descent

descendant, e [desɑ̃dɑ̃, -ɑ̃t] *vb voir* **descendre** ▷ *nm/f* descendant

descendeur, -euse [desɑ̃dœʀ, -øz] *nm/f (Sport)* downhiller

descendre [desɑ̃dʀ(ə)] *vt (escalier, montagne)* to go *(ou* come) down; *(valise, paquet)* to take *ou* get down; *(étagère etc)* to lower; *(fam: abattre)* to shoot down; *(: boire)* to knock back ▷ *vi* to go *(ou* come) down; *(passager: s'arrêter)* to get out, alight; *(niveau, température)* to go *ou* come down, fall, drop; *(marée)* to go out; **~ à pied/en voiture** to walk/drive down, go down on foot/by car; **~ de** *(famille)* to be descended from; **~ du train** to get out of *ou* off the train; **~ d'un arbre** to climb down from a tree; **~ de cheval** to dismount, get off one's horse; **~ à l'hôtel** to stay at a hotel; **~ dans la rue** *(manifester)* to take to the streets; **~ en ville** to go into town, go down town

descente [desɑ̃t] *nf* descent, going down; *(chemin)* way down; *(Ski)* downhill (race); **au milieu de la ~** halfway down; **freinez dans les ~s** use the brakes going downhill; **~ de lit**
bedside rug; **~ (de police)** (police) raid

descriptif, -ive [dɛskʀiptif, -iv] *adj* descriptive ▷ *nm* explanatory leaflet

description [dɛskʀipsjɔ̃] *nf* description

désembourber [dezɑ̃buʀbe] *vt* to pull out of the mud

désembourgeoiser [dezɑ̃buʀʒwaze] *vt:* **~ qn** to get sb out of his *(ou* her) middle-class attitudes

désembuer [dezɑ̃bɥe] *vt* to demist

désemparé, e [dezɑ̃paʀe] *adj* bewildered, distraught; *(bateau, avion)* crippled

désemparer [dezɑ̃paʀe] *vi:* **sans ~** without stopping

désemplir [dezɑ̃pliʀ] *vi:* **ne pas ~** to be always full

désenchanté, e [dezɑ̃ʃɑ̃te] *adj* disenchanted, disillusioned

désenchantement [dezɑ̃ʃɑ̃tmɑ̃] *nm* disenchantment, disillusion

désenclaver [dezɑ̃klave] *vt* to open up

désencombrer [dezɑ̃kɔ̃bʀe] *vt* to clear

désenfler [dezɑ̃fle] *vi* to become less swollen

désengagement [dezɑ̃gaʒmɑ̃] *nm (Pol)* disengagement

désensabler [dezɑ̃sable] *vt* to pull out of the sand

désensibiliser [desɑ̃sibilize] *vt (Méd)* to desensitize

désenvenimer [dezɑ̃vnime] *vt (plaie)* to remove the poison from; *(fig)* to take the sting out of

désépaissir [dezepesiʀ] *vt* to thin (out)

déséquilibre [dezekilibʀ(ə)] *nm (position):* **être en ~** to be unsteady; *(fig: des forces, du budget)* imbalance; *(Psych)* unbalance

déséquilibré, e [dezekilibʀe] *nm/f (Psych)* unbalanced person

déséquilibrer [dezekilibʀe] *vt* to throw off balance

désert, e [dezɛʀ, -ɛʀt(ə)] *adj* deserted ▷ *nm* desert

déserter [dezɛʀte] *vi, vt* to desert

déserteur [dezɛʀtœʀ] *nm* deserter

désertion [dezɛʀsjɔ̃] *nf* desertion

désertique [dezɛʀtik] *adj* desert *cpd*; *(inculte)* barren, empty

désescalade [dezeskalad] *nf (Mil)* de-escalation

désespérant, e [dezɛspeʀɑ̃, -ɑ̃t] *adj* hopeless, despairing

désespéré, e [dezɛspeʀe] *adj* desperate; *(regard)* despairing; **état ~** *(Méd)* hopeless condition

désespérément [dezɛspeʀemɑ̃] *adv* desperately

désespérer [dezɛspeʀe] *vt* to drive to despair ▷ *vi,* **se désespérer** *vi* to despair; **~ de** to despair of

désespoir [dezɛspwaʀ] *nm* despair; **être** *ou* **faire le ~ de qn** to be the despair of sb; **en ~ de cause** in desperation

déshabillé, e [dezabije] *adj* undressed ▷ *nm* négligée

déshabiller [dezabije] *vt* to undress; **se déshabiller** *vi* to undress (o.s.)

déshabituer [dezabitɥe] *vt:* **se ~ de** to get out of

the habit of

désherbant [dezɛrbã] *nm* weed-killer

désherber [dezɛrbe] *vt* to weed

déshérité, e [dezerite] *adj* disinherited ▷ *nm/f*: **les ~s** (*pauvres*) the underprivileged, the deprived

déshériter [dezerite] *vt* to disinherit

déshonneur [dezɔnœr] *nm* dishonour (*Brit*), dishonor (*US*), disgrace

déshonorer [dezɔnɔre] *vt* to dishonour (*Brit*), dishonor (*US*), bring disgrace upon; **se déshonorer** *vi* to bring dishono(u)r on o.s.

déshumaniser [dezymanize] *vt* to dehumanize

déshydratation [dezidratasjɔ̃] *nf* dehydration

déshydraté, e [dezidrate] *adj* dehydrated

déshydrater [dezidrate] *vt* to dehydrate

desiderata [deziderata] *nmpl* requirements

design [dizajn] *adj* (*mobilier*) designer *cpd* ▷ *nm* (industrial) design

désignation [dezinasjɔ̃] *nf* naming, appointment; (*signe, mot*) name, designation

designer [dizajnɛr] *nm* designer

désigner [dezine] *vt* (*montrer*) to point out, indicate; (*dénommer*) to denote, refer to; (*nommer: candidat etc*) to name, appoint

désillusion [dezilyzjɔ̃] *nf* disillusion(ment)

désillusionner [dezilyzjɔne] *vt* to disillusion

désincarné, e [dezɛ̃karne] *adj* disembodied

désinence [dezinãs] *nf* ending, inflexion

désinfectant, e [dezɛ̃fɛktã, -ãt] *adj, nm* disinfectant

désinfecter [dezɛ̃fɛkte] *vt* to disinfect

désinfection [dezɛ̃fɛksjɔ̃] *nf* disinfection

désinformation [dezɛ̃fɔrmasjɔ̃] *nf* disinformation

désintégration [dezɛ̃tegrasjɔ̃] *nf* disintegration

désintégrer [dezɛ̃tegre] *vt* to break up; **se désintégrer** *vi* to disintegrate

désintéressé, e [dezɛ̃terese] *adj* (*généreux, bénévole*) disinterested, unselfish

désintéressement [dezɛ̃terɛsmã] *nm* (*générosité*) disinterestedness

désintéresser [dezɛ̃terese] *vt*: **se désintéresser (de)** to lose interest (in)

désintérêt [dezɛ̃terɛ] *nm* (*indifférence*) disinterest

désintoxication [dezɛ̃tɔksikasjɔ̃] *nf* treatment for alcoholism (*ou* drug addiction); **faire une cure de ~** to have *ou* undergo treatment for alcoholism (*ou* drug addiction)

désintoxiquer [dezɛ̃tɔksike] *vt* to treat for alcoholism (*ou* drug addiction)

désinvolte [dezɛ̃vɔlt(ə)] *adj* casual, off-hand

désinvolture [dezɛ̃vɔltyr] *nf* casualness

désir [dezir] *nm* wish; (*fort, sensuel*) desire

désirable [dezirabl(ə)] *adj* desirable

désirer [dezire] *vt* to want, wish for; (*sexuellement*) to desire; **je désire ...** (*formule de politesse*) I would like ...; **il désire que tu l'aides** he would like *ou* he wants you to help him; **~ faire** to want *ou* wish to do; **ça laisse à ~** it

leaves something to be desired

désireux, -euse [dezirø, -øz] *adj*: **~ de faire** anxious to do

désistement [dezistəmã] *nm* withdrawal

désister [deziste]: **se désister** *vi* to stand down, withdraw

désobéir [dezɔbeir] *vi*: **~ (à qn/qch)** to disobey (sb/sth)

désobéissance [dezɔbeisãs] *nf* disobedience

désobéissant, e [dezɔbeisã, -ãt] *adj* disobedient

désobligeant, e [dezɔbliʒã, -ãt] *adj* disagreeable, unpleasant

désobliger [dezɔbliʒe] *vt* to offend

désodorisant [dezɔdɔrizã] *nm* air freshener, deodorizer

désodoriser [dezɔdɔrize] *vt* to deodorize

désœuvré, e [dezœvre] *adj* idle

désœuvrement [dezœvrəmã] *nm* idleness

désolant, e [dezɔlã, -ãt] *adj* distressing

désolation [dezɔlasjɔ̃] *nf* (*affliction*) distress, grief; (*d'un paysage etc*) desolation, devastation

désolé, e [dezɔle] *adj* (*paysage*) desolate; **je suis ~** I'm sorry

désoler [dezɔle] *vt* to distress, grieve; **se désoler** *vi* to be upset

désolidariser [desɔlidarize] *vt*: **se ~ de** *ou* **d'avec** to dissociate o.s. from

désopilant, e [dezɔpilã, -ãt] *adj* screamingly funny, hilarious

désordonné, e [dezɔrdɔne] *adj* untidy, disorderly

désordre [dezɔrdr(ə)] *nm* disorder(liness), untidiness; (*anarchie*) disorder; **désordres** *nmpl* (*Pol*) disturbances, disorder *sg*; **en ~** in a mess, untidy

désorganiser [dezɔrganize] *vt* to disorganize

désorienté, e [dezɔrjãte] *adj* disorientated; (*fig*) bewildered

désorienter [dezɔrjãte] *vt* (*fig*) to confuse

désormais [dezɔrmɛ] *adv* in future, from now on

désosser [dezɔse] *vt* to bone

despote [dɛspɔt] *nm* despot; (*fig*) tyrant

despotique [dɛspɔtik] *adj* despotic

despotisme [dɛspɔtism(ə)] *nm* despotism

desquamer [dɛskwame]: **se desquamer** *vi* to flake off

desquels, desquelles [dekɛl] *prép + pron voir* **lequel**

DESS *sigle m* (= *Diplôme d'études supérieures spécialisées*) post-graduate diploma

dessaisir [desezir] *vt*: **~ un tribunal d'une affaire** to remove a case from a court; **se ~ de** *vt* to give up, part with

dessaler [desale] *vt* (*eau de mer*) to desalinate; (*Culin: morue etc*) to soak; (*fig fam: délurer*): **~ qn** to teach sb a thing or two ▷ *vi* (*voilier*) to capsize

Desse *abr* = **duchesse**

desséché, e [deseʃe] *adj* dried up

dessèchement [desɛʃmã] *nm* drying out; dryness; hardness

dessécher [deseʃe] *vt* (*terre, plante*) to dry out,

parch; (*peau*) to dry out; (*volontairement: aliments etc*) to dry, dehydrate; (*fig: cœur*) to harden; **se dessécher** *vi* to dry out; (*peau, lèvres*) to go dry

dessein [desɛ̃] *nm* design; **dans le ~ de** with the intention of; **à ~** intentionally, deliberately

desseller [desele] *vt* to unsaddle

desserrer [deseRe] *vt* to loosen; (*frein*) to release; (*poing, dents*) to unclench; (*objets alignés*) to space out; **ne pas ~ les dents** not to open one's mouth

dessert [desɛR] *vb voir* **desservir** ▷ *nm* dessert, pudding

desserte [desɛRt(ə)] *nf* (*table*) side table; (*transport*): **la ~ du village est assurée par autocar** there is a coach service to the village; **chemin** *ou* **voie de ~** service road

desservir [desɛRviR] *vt* (*ville, quartier*) to serve; (: *voie de communication*) to lead into; (*vicaire: paroisse*) to serve; (*nuire à: personne*) to do a disservice to; (*débarrasser*): **~ (la table)** to clear the table

dessiller [desije] *vt* (*fig*): **~ les yeux à qn** to open sb's eyes

dessin [desɛ̃] *nm* (*œuvre, art*) drawing; (*motif*) pattern, design; (*contour*) (out)line; **le ~ industriel** draughtsmanship (*Brit*), draftsmanship (*US*); **~ animé** cartoon (film); **~ humoristique** cartoon

dessinateur, -trice [desinatœR, -tRis] *nm/f* drawer; (*de bandes dessinées*) cartoonist; (*industriel*) draughtsman (*Brit*), draftsman (*US*); **dessinatrice de mode** fashion designer

dessiner [desine] *vt* to draw; (*concevoir: carrosserie, maison*) to design; (*robe: taille*) to show off; **se dessiner** *vi* (*forme*) to be outlined; (*fig: solution*) to emerge

dessoûler [desule] *vt, vi* to sober up

dessous [dəsu] *adv* underneath, beneath ▷ *nm* underside; (*étage inférieur*): **les voisins du ~** the downstairs neighbours ▷ *nmpl* (*sous-vêtements*) underwear *sg*; (*fig*) hidden aspects; **en ~** underneath; below; (*fig: en catimini*) slyly, on the sly; **par ~** underneath; below; **de ~ le lit** from under the bed; **au-~** *adv* below; **au-~ de** *prép* below; (*peu digne de*) beneath; **au-~ de tout** the (absolute) limit; **avoir le ~** to get the worst of it

dessous-de-bouteille [dəsudbutɛj] *nm* bottle mat

dessous-de-plat [dəsudpla] *nm inv* tablemat

dessous-de-table [dəsudtabl(ə)] *nm* (*fig*) bribe, under-the-counter payment

dessus [dəsy] *adv* on top; (*collé, écrit*) on it ▷ *nm* top; (*étage supérieur*): **les voisins/ l'appartement du ~** the upstairs neighbours/ flat; **en ~** above; **par ~** *adv* over it ▷ *prép* over; **au-~** above; **au-~ de** above; **avoir/prendre le ~** to have/get the upper hand; **reprendre le ~** to get over it; **bras ~ bras dessous** arm in arm; **sens ~ dessous** upside down; *voir* **ci-**; **là-**

dessus-de-lit [dəsydli] *nm inv* bedspread

déstabiliser [destabilize] *vt* (*Pol*) to destabilize

destin [destɛ̃] *nm* fate; (*avenir*) destiny

destinataire [dɛstinatɛR] *nm/f* (*Postes*) addressee; (*d'un colis*) consignee; (*d'un mandat*) payee; **aux risques et périls du ~** at owner's risk

destination [dɛstinasjɔ̃] *nf* (*lieu*) destination; (*usage*) purpose; **à ~ de** (*avion etc*) bound for; (*voyageur*) bound for, travelling to

destinée [dɛstine] *nf* fate; (*existence, avenir*) destiny

destiner [dɛstine] *vt*: **~ qn à** (*poste, sort*) to destine sb for; **~ qn/qch à** (*prédestiner*) to mark sb/sth out for; **~ qch à** (*envisager d'affecter*) to intend to use sth for; **~ qch à qn** (*envisager de donner*) to intend to give sth to sb, intend sb to have sth; (*adresser*) to intend sth for sb; **se ~ à l'enseignement** to intend to become a teacher; **être destiné à** (*sort*) to be destined to + *verbe*; (*usage*) to be intended *ou* meant for; (*sort*) to be in store for

destituer [dɛstitɥe] *vt* to depose; **~ qn de ses fonctions** to relieve sb of his duties

destitution [dɛstitysjɔ̃] *nf* deposition

destructeur, -trice [dɛstRyktœR, -tRis] *adj* destructive

destructif, -ive [dɛstRyktif, -iv] *adj* destructive

destruction [dɛstRyksjɔ̃] *nf* destruction

déstructuré, e [destRyktyRe] *adj*: **vêtements ~s** casual clothes

déstructurer [destRyktyRe] *vt* to break down, take to pieces

désuet, -ète [desɥɛ, -ɛt] *adj* outdated, outmoded

désuétude [desɥetyd] *nf*: **tomber en ~** to fall into disuse, become obsolete

désuni, e [dezyni] *adj* divided, disunited

désunion [dezynjɔ̃] *nf* disunity

désunir [dezyniR] *vt* to disunite; **se désunir** *vi* (*athlète*) to get out of one's stride

détachable [detaʃabl(ə)] *adj* (*coupon etc*) tear-off *cpd*; (*capuche etc*) detachable

détachant [detaʃɑ̃] *nm* stain remover

détaché, e [detaʃe] *adj* (*fig*) detached ▷ *nm/f* (*représentant*) person on secondment (*Brit*) *ou* a posting

détachement [detaʃmɑ̃] *nm* detachment; (*fonctionnaire, employé*): **être en ~** to be on secondment (*Brit*) *ou* a posting

détacher [detaʃe] *vt* (*enlever*) to detach, remove; (*délier*) to untie; (*Admin*): **~ qn (auprès de** *ou* **à)** to send sb on secondment (to) (*Brit*), post sb (to); (*Mil*) to detail; (*vêtement: nettoyer*) to remove the stains from; **se détacher** *vi* (*tomber*) to come off; to come out; (*se défaire*) to come undone; (*Sport*) to pull *ou* break away; (*se délier: chien, prisonnier*) to break loose; **se ~ sur** to stand out against; **se ~ de** (*se désintéresser*) to grow away from

détail [detaj] *nm* detail; (*Comm*): **le ~** retail; **prix de ~** retail price; **au ~** *adv* (*Comm*) retail; (: *individuellement*) separately; **donner le ~ de** to give a detailed account of; (*compte*) to give a breakdown of; **en ~** in detail

détaillant, e [detajɑ̃, -ɑ̃t] *nm/f* retailer

détaillé, e [detaje] *adj* (*récit*) detailed
détailler [detaje] *vt* (*Comm*) to sell retail; to sell separately; (*expliquer*) to explain in detail; to detail; (*examiner*) to look over, examine
détaler [detale] *vi* (*lapin*) to scamper off; (*fam: personne*) to make off, scarper (*fam*)
détartrant [detartrã] *nm* descaling agent (*Brit*), scale remover
détartrer [detartre] *vt* to descale; (*dents*) to scale
détaxe [detaks(ə)] *nf* (*réduction*) reduction in tax; (*suppression*) removal of tax; (*remboursement*) tax refund
détaxer [detakse] *vt* (*réduire*) to reduce the tax on; (*ôter*) to remove the tax on
détecter [detɛkte] *vt* to detect
détecteur [detɛktœr] *nm* detector, sensor; **~ de mensonges** lie detector; **~ (de mines)** mine detector
détection [detɛksjɔ̃] *nf* detection
détective [detɛktiv] *nm* detective; **~ (privé)** private detective *ou* investigator
déteindre [detɛ̃dr(ə)] *vi* to fade; (*fig*): **~ sur** to rub off on
déteint, e [detɛ̃, -ɛ̃t] *pp de* **déteindre**
dételer [detle] *vt* to unharness; (*voiture, wagon*) to unhitch ▷ *vi* (*fig: s'arrêter*) to leave off (working)
détendeur [detãdœr] *nm* (*de bouteille à gaz*) regulator
détendre [detãdr(ə)] *vt* (*fil*) to slacken, loosen; (*personne, atmosphère*) to relax; (*: situation*) to relieve; **se détendre** *vi* to lose its tension; to relax
détendu, e [detãdy] *adj* relaxed
détenir [detnir] *vt* (*fortune, objet, secret*) to be in possession of; (*prisonnier*) to detain; (*record*) to hold; **~ le pouvoir** to be in power
détente [detãt] *nf* relaxation; (*Pol*) détente; (*d'une arme*) trigger; (*d'un athlète qui saute*) spring
détenteur, -trice [detãtœr, -tris] *nm/f* holder
détention [detãsjɔ̃] *nf* (*voir détenir*) possession; detention; holding; **~ préventive** (pre-trial) custody
détenu, e [detny] *pp de* **détenir** ▷ *nm/f* prisoner
détergent [detɛrʒã] *nm* detergent
détérioration [deterjɔrasjɔ̃] *nf* damaging; deterioration
détériorer [deterjɔre] *vt* to damage; **se détériorer** *vi* to deteriorate
déterminant, e [detɛrminã, -ãt] *adj*: **un facteur ~** a determining factor ▷ *nm* (*Ling*) determiner
détermination [detɛrminasjɔ̃] *nf* determining; (*résolution*) decision; (*fermeté*) determination
déterminé, e [detɛrmine] *adj* (*résolu*) determined; (*précis*) specific, definite
déterminer [detɛrmine] *vt* (*fixer*) to determine; (*décider*): **~ qn à faire** to decide sb to do; **se ~ à faire** to make up one's mind to do
déterminisme [detɛrminism(ə)] *nm* determinism

déterré, e [detere] *nm/f*: **avoir une mine de ~** to look like death warmed up (*Brit*) *ou* warmed over (*US*)
déterrer [detere] *vt* to dig up
détersif, -ive [detɛrsif, -iv] *adj, nm* detergent
détestable [detɛstabl(ə)] *adj* foul, detestable
détester [detɛste] *vt* to hate, detest
détiendrai [detjɛ̃dre], **détiens** *etc* [detjɛ̃] *vb voir* **détenir**
détonant, e [detɔnã, -ãt] *adj*: **mélange ~** explosive mixture
détonateur [detɔnatœr] *nm* detonator
détonation [detɔnasjɔ̃] *nf* detonation, bang, report (of a gun)
détoner [detɔne] *vi* to detonate, explode
détonner [detɔne] *vi* (*Mus*) to go out of tune; (*fig*) to clash
détordre [detɔrdr(ə)] *vt* to untwist, unwind
détour [detur] *nm* detour; (*tournant*) bend, curve; (*fig: subterfuge*) roundabout means; **sans ~** (*fig*) plainly
détourné, e [deturne] *adj* (*sentier, chemin, moyen*) roundabout
détournement [deturnəmã] *nm* diversion, rerouting; **~ d'avion** hijacking; **~ (de fonds)** embezzlement *ou* misappropriation (of funds); **~ de mineur** corruption of a minor
détourner [deturne] *vt* to divert; (*avion*) to divert, reroute; (*: par la force*) to hijack; (*yeux, tête*) to turn away; (*de l'argent*) to embezzle, misappropriate; **se détourner** to turn away; **~ la conversation** to change the subject; **~ qn de son devoir** to divert sb from his duty; **~ l'attention (de qn)** to distract *ou* divert (sb's) attention
détracteur, -trice [detraktœr, -tris] *nm/f* disparager, critic
détraqué, e [detrake] *adj* (*machine, santé*) broken-down ▷ *nm/f* (*fam*): **c'est un ~** he's unhinged
détraquer [detrake] *vt* to put out of order; (*estomac*) to upset; **se détraquer** *vi* to go wrong
détrempe [detrãp] *nf* (*Art*) tempera
détrempé, e [detrãpe] *adj* (*sol*) sodden, waterlogged
détremper [detrãpe] *vt* (*peinture*) to water down
détresse [detrɛs] *nf* distress; **en ~** (*avion etc*) in distress; **appel/signal de ~** distress call/signal
détriment [detrimã] *nm*: **au ~ de** to the detriment of
détritus [detritys] *nmpl* rubbish *sg*, refuse *sg*, garbage *sg* (*US*)
détroit [detrwa] *nm* strait; **le ~ de Bering** *ou* **Behring** the Bering Strait; **le ~ de Gibraltar** the Straits of Gibraltar; **le ~ du Bosphore** the Bosphorus; **le ~ de Magellan** the Strait of Magellan, the Magellan Strait
détromper [detrɔ̃pe] *vt* to disabuse; **se détromper** *vi*: **détrompez-vous** don't believe it
détrôner [detrone] *vt* to dethrone, depose; (*fig*) to oust, dethrone
détrousser [detruse] *vt* to rob

détruire [detʀɥiʀ] *vt* to destroy; *(fig: santé, réputation)* to ruin; *(documents)* to shred

détruit, e [detʀɥi, -it] *pp de* **détruire**

dette [dɛt] *nf* debt; ~ **publique** *ou* **de l'État** national debt

DEUG [døg] *sigle m* = **Diplôme d'études universitaires générales**; *see note*

● **DEUG**

French students sit their DEUG ('diplôme d'études universitaires générales') after two years at university. They can then choose to leave university altogether, or go on to study for their 'licence'. The certificate specifies the student's major subject and may be awarded with distinction.

deuil [dœj] *nm (perte)* bereavement; *(période)* mourning; *(chagrin)* grief; **porter le ~** to wear mourning; **prendre le/être en ~** to go into/be in mourning

DEUST [dœst] *sigle m* = **Diplôme d'études universitaires scientifiques et techniques**

deux [dø] *num* two; **les ~** both; **ses ~ mains** both his hands, his two hands; **à ~ pas** a short distance away; **tous les ~ mois** every two months, every other month; **~ points** colon *sg*

deuxième [døzjɛm] *num* second

deuxièmement [døzjɛmmã] *adv* secondly, in the second place

deux-pièces [døpjɛs] *nm inv (tailleur)* two-piece (suit); *(de bain)* two-piece (swimsuit); *(appartement)* two-roomed flat *(Brit) ou* apartment *(US)*

deux-roues [døʀu] *nm* two-wheeled vehicle

deux-temps [døtã] *adj* two-stroke

devais *etc* [dəvɛ] *vb voir* **devoir**

dévaler [devale] *vt* to hurtle down

dévaliser [devalize] *vt* to rob, burgle

dévalorisant, e [devalɔʀizã, -ãt] *adj* depreciatory

dévalorisation [devalɔʀizasjɔ̃] *nf* depreciation

dévaloriser [devalɔʀize] *vt* to reduce the value of; **se dévaloriser** *vi* to depreciate

dévaluation [devalɥasjɔ̃] *nf* depreciation; *(Écon: mesure)* devaluation

dévaluer [devalɥe] *vt*, **se dévaluer** *vi* to devalue

devancer [dəvãse] *vt* to be ahead of; *(distancer)* to get ahead of; *(arriver avant)* to arrive before; *(prévenir)* to anticipate; ~ **l'appel** *(Mil)* to enlist before call-up

devancier, -ière [dəvãsje, -jɛʀ] *nm/f* precursor

devant [dəvã] *vb voir* **devoir** ▷ *adv* in front; *(à distance: en avant)* ahead ▷ *prép* in front of; ahead of; *(avec mouvement: passer)* past; *(fig)* before, in front of; *(: face à)* faced with, in the face of; *(: vu)* in view of ▷ *nm* front; **prendre les ~s** to make the first move; **de ~** *(roue, porte)* front; **les pattes de ~** the front legs, the forelegs; **par ~** *(boutonner)* at the front; *(entrer)* the front way; **par-~ notaire** in the presence of a notary; **aller**

au-~ de qn to go out to meet sb; **aller au-~ de** *(désirs de qn)* to anticipate; **aller au-~ des ennuis** *ou* **difficultés** to be asking for trouble

devanture [dəvãtyʀ] *nf (façade)* (shop) front; *(étalage)* display; (shop) window

dévastateur, -trice [devastatœʀ, -tʀis] *adj* devastating

dévastation [devastasjɔ̃] *nf* devastation

dévaster [devaste] *vt* to devastate

déveine [devɛn] *nf* rotten luck *no pl*

développement [devlɔpmã] *nm* development

développer [devlɔpe] *vt*, **se développer** *vi* to develop

devenir [dəvniʀ] *vi* to become; ~ **instituteur** to become a teacher; **que sont-ils devenus?** what has become of them?

devenu, e [dəvny] *pp de* **devenir**

dévergondé, e [devɛʀgɔ̃de] *adj* wild, shameless

dévergonder [devɛʀgɔ̃de] *vt*, **se dévergonder** *vi* to get into bad ways

déverrouiller [devɛʀuje] *vt* to unbolt

devers [dəvɛʀ] *adv*: **par ~ soi** to oneself

déverser [devɛʀse] *vt (liquide)* to pour (out); *(ordures)* to tip (out); **se ~ dans** *(fleuve, mer)* to flow into

déversoir [devɛʀswaʀ] *nm* overflow

dévêtir [devetiʀ] *vt*, **se dévêtir** *vi* to undress

devez [dəve] *vb voir* **devoir**

déviation [devjasjɔ̃] *nf* deviation; *(Auto)* diversion *(Brit)*, detour *(US)*; ~ **de la colonne (vertébrale)** curvature of the spine

dévider [devide] *vt* to unwind

dévidoir [devidwaʀ] *nm* reel

deviendrai [dəvjɛ̃dʀe], **deviens** *etc* [dəvjɛ̃] *vb voir* **devenir**

dévier [devje] *vt (fleuve, circulation)* to divert; *(coup)* to deflect ▷ *vi* to veer (off course); **(faire) ~** *(projectile)* to deflect; *(véhicule)* to push off course

devin [dəvɛ̃] *nm* soothsayer, seer

deviner [dəvine] *vt* to guess; *(prévoir)* to foretell, foresee; *(apercevoir)* to distinguish

devinette [dəvinɛt] *nf* riddle

devint *etc* [dəvɛ̃] *vb voir* **devenir**

devis [dəvi] *nm* estimate, quotation; ~ **descriptif/estimatif** detailed/preliminary estimate

dévisager [devizaʒe] *vt* to stare at

devise [dəviz] *nf (formule)* motto, watchword; *(Écon: monnaie)* currency; **devises** *nfpl (argent)* currency *sg*

deviser [dəvize] *vi* to converse

dévisser [devise] *vt* to unscrew, undo; **se dévisser** *vi* to come unscrewed

de visu [devizy] *adv*: **se rendre compte de qch ~** to see sth for o.s.

dévitaliser [devitalize] *vt (dent)* to remove the nerve from

dévoiler [devwale] *vt* to unveil

devoir [dəvwaʀ] *nm* duty; *(Scol)* piece of homework, homework *no pl*; *(: en classe)* exercise ▷ *vt (argent, respect)*: ~ **qch (à qn)** to owe (sb) sth;

(*suivi de l'infinitif: obligation*): **il doit le faire** he has to do it, he must do it; (: *fatalité*): **cela devait arriver un jour** it was bound to happen; (: *intention*): **il doit partir demain** he is (due) to leave tomorrow; (: *probabilité*): **il doit être tard** it must be late; **se faire un ~ de faire qch** to make it one's duty to do sth; **~s de vacances** homework set for the holidays; **se ~ de faire qch** to be duty bound to do sth; **je devrais faire** I ought to *ou* should do; **tu n'aurais pas dû** you ought not to have *ou* shouldn't have; **comme il se doit** (*comme il faut*) as is right and proper

dévolu, e [devɔly] *adj*: **~ à** allotted to ▷ *nm*: **jeter son ~ sur** to fix one's choice on

devons [dəvɔ̃] *vb voir* **devoir**

dévorant, e [devɔrɑ̃, -ɑ̃t] *adj* (*faim, passion*) raging

dévorer [devɔre] *vt* to devour; (*feu, soucis*) to consume; **~ qn/qch des yeux** *ou* **du regard** (*fig*) to eye sb/sth intently; (: *convoitise*) to eye sb/sth greedily

dévot, e [devo, -ɔt] *adj* devout, pious ▷ *nm/f* devout person; **un faux ~** a falsely pious person

dévotion [devosjɔ̃] *nf* devoutness; **être à la ~ de qn** to be totally devoted to sb; **avoir une ~ pour qn** to worship sb

dévoué, e [devwe] *adj* devoted

dévouement [devumɑ̃] *nm* devotion, dedication

dévouer [devwe]: **se dévouer** *vi* (*se sacrifier*): **se ~ (pour)** to sacrifice o.s. (for); (*se consacrer*): **se ~ à** to devote *ou* dedicate o.s. to

dévoyé, e [devwaje] *adj* delinquent

dévoyer [devwaje] *vt* to lead astray; **se dévoyer** *vi* to go off the rails; **~ l'opinion publique** to influence public opinion

devrai *etc* [dəvre] *vb voir* **devoir**

dextérité [dɛksterite] *nf* skill, dexterity

dézipper [dezipe] *vt* (*Inform*) to unzip

dfc *abr* (= *désire faire connaissance*) in personal column of newspaper

DG *sigle m* = **directeur général**

dg. *abr* (= *décigramme*) dg.

DGE *sigle f* (= *Dotation globale d'équipement*) state contribution to local government budget

DGSE *sigle f* (= *Direction générale de la sécurité extérieure*) ≈ MI6 (*Brit*), ≈ CIA (*US*)

diabète [djabɛt] *nm* diabetes *sg*

diabétique [djabetik] *nm/f* diabetic

diable [djɑbl(ə)] *nm* devil; **une musique du ~** an unholy racket; **il fait une chaleur du ~** it's fiendishly hot; **avoir le ~ au corps** to be the very devil

diablement [djɑbləmɑ̃] *adv* fiendishly

diableries [djɑbləri] *nfpl* (*d'enfant*) devilment *sg*, mischief *sg*

diablesse [djɑblɛs] *nf* (*petite fille*) little devil

diablotin [djɑblɔtɛ̃] *nm* imp; (*pétard*) cracker

diabolique [djɑbɔlik] *adj* diabolical

diabolo [djɑbɔlo] *nm* (*jeu*) diabolo; (*boisson*) lemonade and fruit cordial; **~(-menthe)** lemonade and mint cordial

diacre [djakʀ(ə)] *nm* deacon

diadème [djadɛm] *nm* diadem

diagnostic [djagnɔstik] *nm* diagnosis *sg*

diagnostiquer [djagnɔstike] *vt* to diagnose

diagonal, e, -aux [djagɔnal, -o] *adj, nf* diagonal; **en ~e** diagonally; **lire en ~e** (*fig*) to skim through

diagramme [djagʀam] *nm* chart, graph

dialecte [djalɛkt(ə)] *nm* dialect

dialectique [djalɛktik] *adj* dialectic(al)

dialogue [djalɔg] *nm* dialogue; **~ de sourds** dialogue of the deaf

dialoguer [djalɔge] *vi* to converse; (*Pol*) to have a dialogue

dialoguiste [djalɔgist(ə)] *nm/f* dialogue writer

dialyse [djaliz] *nf* dialysis

diamant [djamɑ̃] *nm* diamond

diamantaire [djamɑ̃tɛʀ] *nm* diamond dealer

diamétralement [djametʀalmɑ̃] *adv* diametrically; **~ opposés** (*opinions*) diametrically opposed

diamètre [djamɛtʀ(ə)] *nm* diameter

diapason [djapazɔ̃] *nm* tuning fork; (*fig*): **être/ se mettre au ~ (de)** to be/get in tune (with)

diaphane [djafan] *adj* diaphanous

diaphragme [djafʀagm(ə)] *nm* (*Anat, Photo*) diaphragm; (*contraceptif*) diaphragm, cap; **ouverture du ~** (*Photo*) aperture

diapo [djapo], **diapositive** [djapozitiv] *nf* transparency, slide

diaporama [djapɔʀama] *nm* slide show

diapré, e [djapʀe] *adj* many-coloured (*Brit*), many-colored (*US*)

diarrhée [djaʀe] *nf* diarrhoea (*Brit*), diarrhea (*US*)

diatribe [djatʀib] *nf* diatribe

dichotomie [dikɔtɔmi] *nf* dichotomy

dictaphone [diktafɔn] *nm* Dictaphone®

dictateur [diktatœʀ] *nm* dictator

dictatorial, e, -aux [diktatɔʀjal, -o] *adj* dictatorial

dictature [diktatyʀ] *nf* dictatorship

dictée [dikte] *nf* dictation; **prendre sous ~** to take down (*sth dictated*)

dicter [dikte] *vt* to dictate

diction [diksjɔ̃] *nf* diction, delivery; **cours de ~** speech production lesson(s)

dictionnaire [diksjɔnɛʀ] *nm* dictionary; **~ géographique** gazetteer

dicton [diktɔ̃] *nm* saying, dictum

didacticiel [didaktisjɛl] *nm* educational software

didactique [didaktik] *adj* didactic

dièse [djɛz] *nm* (*Mus*) sharp

diesel [djezɛl] *nm, adj inv* diesel

diète [djɛt] *nf* diet; **être à la ~** to be on a diet

diététicien, ne [djetetisjɛ̃, -ɛn] *nm/f* dietician

diététique [djetetik] *nf* dietetics *sg* ▷ *adj*: **magasin ~** health food shop (*Brit*) *ou* store (*US*)

dieu, x [djø] *nm* god; **D~** God; **le bon D~** the good Lord; **mon D~!** good heavens!

diffamant, e [difamɑ̃, -ɑ̃t] *adj* slanderous, defamatory; libellous

diffamation [difamɑsjɔ̃] *nf* slander; (*écrite*) libel; **attaquer qn en ~** to sue sb for slander (*ou* libel)

diffamatoire [difamatwaʀ] *adj* slanderous, defamatory; libellous

diffamer [difame] *vt* to slander, defame; to libel

différé [difeʀe] *adj* (*Inform*): **traitement ~** batch processing; **crédit ~** deferred credit ▷ *nm* (TV): **en ~** (pre-)recorded

différemment [difeʀamɑ̃] *adv* differently

différence [difeʀɑ̃s] *nf* difference; **à la ~ de** unlike

différenciation [difeʀɑ̃sjɑsjɔ̃] *nf* differentiation

différencier [difeʀɑ̃sje] *vt* to differentiate; **se différencier** *vi* (*organisme*) to become differentiated; **se ~ de** to differentiate o.s. from; (*être différent*) to differ from

différend [difeʀɑ̃] *nm* difference (of opinion), disagreement

différent, e [difeʀɑ̃, -ɑ̃t] *adj*: **~ (de)** different (from); **~s objets** different *ou* various objects; **à ~es reprises** on various occasions

différentiel, le [difeʀɑ̃sjɛl] *adj*, *nm* differential

différer [difeʀe] *vt* to postpone, put off ▷ *vi*: **~ (de)** to differ (from); **~ de faire** (*tarder*) to delay doing

difficile [difisil] *adj* difficult; (*exigeant*) hard to please, difficult (to please); **faire le** *ou* **la ~** to be hard to please, be difficult

difficilement [difisilmɑ̃] *adv* (*marcher, s'expliquer etc*) with difficulty; **~ lisible/compréhensible** difficult *ou* hard to read/understand

difficulté [difikylte] *nf* difficulty; **en ~** (*bateau, alpiniste*) in trouble *ou* difficulties; **avoir de la ~ à faire** to have difficulty (in) doing

difforme [difɔʀm(ə)] *adj* deformed, misshapen

difformité [difɔʀmite] *nf* deformity

diffracter [difʀakte] *vt* to diffract

diffus, e [dify, -yz] *adj* diffuse

diffuser [difyze] *vt* (*chaleur, bruit, lumière*) to diffuse; (*émission, musique*) to broadcast; (*nouvelle, idée*) to circulate; (*Comm: livres, journaux*) to distribute

diffuseur [difyzœʀ] *nm* diffuser; distributor

diffusion [difyzjɔ̃] *nf* diffusion, broadcast(ing); circulation; distribution

digérer [diʒeʀe] *vt* (*personne*) to digest; (: *machine*) to process; (*fig: accepter*) to stomach, put up with

digeste [diʒɛst(ə)] *adj* easily digestible

digestible [diʒɛstibl(ə)] *adj* digestible

digestif, -ive [diʒɛstif, -iv] *adj* digestive ▷ *nm* (after-dinner) liqueur

digestion [diʒɛstjɔ̃] *nf* digestion

digit [didʒit] *nm*: **~ binaire** binary digit

digital, e, -aux [diʒital, -o] *adj* digital

digitale [diʒital] *nf* digitalis, foxglove

digne [diɲ] *adj* dignified; **~ de** worthy of; **~ de foi** trustworthy

dignitaire [diɲitɛʀ] *nm* dignitary

dignité [diɲite] *nf* dignity

digression [digʀesjɔ̃] *nf* digression

digue [dig] *nf* dike, dyke; (*pour protéger la côte*) sea wall

dijonnais, e [diʒɔnɛ, -ɛz] *adj* of *ou* from Dijon ▷ *nm/f*: **Dijonnais, e** inhabitant *ou* native of Dijon

diktat [diktat] *nm* diktat

dilapidation [dilapidɑsjɔ̃] *nf* (*voir vb*) squandering; embezzlement, misappropriation

dilapider [dilapide] *vt* to squander, waste; (*détourner: biens, fonds publics*) to embezzle, misappropriate

dilater [dilate] *vt* to dilate; (*gaz, métal*) to cause to expand; (*ballon*) to distend; **se dilater** *vi* to expand

dilemme [dilɛm] *nm* dilemma

dilettante [diletɑ̃t] *nm/f* dilettante; **en ~** in a dilettantish way

dilettantisme [diletɑ̃tism(ə)] *nm* dilettant(e)ism

diligence [diliʒɑ̃s] *nf* stagecoach, diligence; (*empressement*) despatch; **faire ~** to make haste

diligent, e [diliʒɑ̃, -ɑ̃t] *adj* prompt and efficient; diligent

diluant [dilɥɑ̃] *nm* thinner(s)

diluer [dilɥe] *vt* to dilute

dilution [dilysjɔ̃] *nf* dilution

diluvien, ne [dilyvjɛ̃, -ɛn] *adj*: **pluie ~ne** torrential rain

dimanche [dimɑ̃ʃ] *nm* Sunday; **le ~ des Rameaux/de Pâques** Palm/Easter Sunday; *voir aussi* **lundi**

dîme [dim] *nf* tithe

dimension [dimɑ̃sjɔ̃] *nf* (*grandeur*) size; (*gén pl: cotes, Math: de l'espace*) dimension

diminué, e [diminɥe] *adj* (*personne: physiquement*) run-down; (: *mentalement*) less alert

diminuer [diminɥe] *vt* to reduce, decrease; (*ardeur etc*) to lessen; (*personne: physiquement*) to undermine; (*dénigrer*) to belittle ▷ *vi* to decrease, diminish

diminutif [diminytif] *nm* (*Ling*) diminutive; (*surnom*) pet name

diminution [diminysjɔ̃] *nf* decreasing, diminishing

dînatoire [dinatwaʀ] *adj*: **goûter ~** ≈ high tea (*Brit*); **apéritif ~** ≈ evening buffet

dinde [dɛ̃d] *nf* turkey; (*femme stupide*) goose

dindon [dɛ̃dɔ̃] *nm* turkey

dindonneau, x [dɛ̃dɔno] *nm* turkey poult

dîner [dine] *nm* dinner ▷ *vi* to have dinner; **~ d'affaires/de famille** business/family dinner

dînette [dinɛt] *nf* (*jeu*): **jouer à la ~** to play at tea parties

dingue [dɛ̃g] *adj* (*fam*) crazy

dinosaure [dinozɔʀ] *nm* dinosaur

diocèse [djɔsɛz] *nm* diocese

diode [djɔd] *nf* diode

diphasé, e [difaze] *adj* (*Élec*) two-phase

diphtérie [difteʀi] *nf* diphtheria

diphtongue [diftɔ̃g] *nf* diphthong

diplomate [diplɔmat] *adj* diplomatic ▷ *nm* diplomat; (*fig: personne habile*) diplomatist; (*Culin: gâteau*) *dessert made of sponge cake, candied fruit and custard*, ≈ trifle (*Brit*)

diplomatie [diplɔmasi] *nf* diplomacy

diplomatique [diplɔmatik] *adj* diplomatic

diplôme [diplom] *nm* diploma certificate; (*examen*) (diploma) examination

diplômé, e [diplome] *adj* qualified

dire [diʀ] *nm*: **au ~ de** according to; **leurs ~s** what they say ▷ *vt* to say; (*secret, mensonge*) to tell; **~ l'heure/la vérité** to tell the time/the truth; **dis pardon/merci** say sorry/thank you; **~ qch à qn** to tell sb sth; **~ à qn qu'il fasse** *ou* **de faire** to tell sb to do; **~ que** to say that; **on dit que** they say that; **comme on dit** as they say; **on dirait que** it looks (*ou* sounds *etc*) as though; **on dirait du vin** you'd *ou* one would think it was wine; **que dites-vous de** (*penser*) what do you think of; **si cela lui dit** if he feels like it, if he fancies it; **cela ne me dit rien** that doesn't appeal to me; **à vrai ~** truth to tell; **pour ainsi ~** so to speak; **cela va sans ~** that goes without saying; **dis donc!, dites donc!** (*pour attirer l'attention*) hey!; (*au fait*) by the way; **et ~ que ...** and to think that ...; **ceci** *ou* **cela dit** that being said; (*à ces mots*) whereupon; **c'est dit, voilà qui est dit** so that's settled; **il n'y a pas à ~** there's no getting away from it; **c'est ~ si ...** that just shows that ...; **c'est beaucoup/peu ~** that's saying a lot/not saying much; **se dire** *vi* (*à soi-même*) to say to oneself; (*se prétendre*): **se ~ malade** *etc* to say (that) one is ill *etc*; **ça se dit ... en anglais** that is ... in English; **cela ne se dit pas comme ça** you don't say it like that; **se ~ au revoir** to say goodbye (to each other)

direct, e [diʀɛkt] *adj* direct ▷ *nm* (*train*) through train; **en ~** (*émission*) live; **train/bus ~** express train/bus

directement [diʀɛktəmã] *adv* directly

directeur, -trice [diʀɛktœʀ, -tʀis] *nm/f* (*d'entreprise*) director; (*de service*) manager/eress; (*d'école*) head(teacher) (*Brit*), principal (*US*); **comité ~** management *ou* steering committee; **~ général** general manager; **~ de thèse** ≈ PhD supervisor

direction [diʀɛksjõ] *nf* management; conducting; supervision; (*Auto*) steering; (*sens*) direction; **sous la ~ de** (*Mus*) conducted by; **en ~ de** (*avion, train, bateau*) for; **"toutes ~s"** (*Auto*) "all routes"

directive [diʀɛktiv] *nf* directive, instruction

directorial, e, -aux [diʀɛktɔʀjal, -o] *adj* (*bureau*) director's; manager's; head teacher's

directrice [diʀɛktʀis] *adj f, nf voir* **directeur**

dirent [diʀ] *vb voir* **dire**

dirigeable [diʀiʒabl(ə)] *adj, nm*: **(ballon) ~** dirigible

dirigeant, e [diʀiʒã, -ãt] *adj* managerial; (*classes*) ruling ▷ *nm/f* (*d'un parti etc*) leader; (*d'entreprise*) manager, member of the management

diriger [diʀiʒe] *vt* (*entreprise*) to manage, run; (*véhicule*) to steer; (*orchestre*) to conduct; (*recherches, travaux*) to supervise, be in charge of; (*braquer: regard, arme*): **~ sur** to point *ou* level *ou* aim at; (*fig: critiques*): **~ contre** to aim at; **se diriger** *vi* (*s'orienter*) to find one's way; **se ~ vers** *ou* **sur** to make *ou* head for

dirigisme [diʀiʒism(ə)] *nm* (*Écon*) state intervention, interventionism

dirigiste [diʀiʒist(ə)] *adj* interventionist

dis [di], **disais** *etc* [dizɛ] *vb voir* **dire**

discal, e, -aux [diskal, -o] *adj* (*Méd*): **hernie ~e** slipped disc

discernement [disɛʀnəmã] *nm* discernment, judgment

discerner [disɛʀne] *vt* to discern, make out

disciple [disipl(ə)] *nm/f* disciple

disciplinaire [disiplinɛʀ] *adj* disciplinary

discipline [disiplin] *nf* discipline

discipliné, e [disipline] *adj* (well-)disciplined

discipliner [disipline] *vt* to discipline; (*cheveux*) to control

discobole [diskɔbɔl] *nm/f* discus thrower

discographie [diskɔgʀafi] *nf* discography

discontinu, e [diskõtiny] *adj* intermittent; (*bande: sur la route*) broken

discontinuer [diskõtinɥe] *vi*: **sans ~** without stopping, without a break

disconvenir [diskõvniʀ] *vi*: **ne pas ~ de qch/que** not to deny sth/that

discophile [diskɔfil] *nm/f* record enthusiast

discordance [diskɔʀdãs] *nf* discordance; conflict

discordant, e [diskɔʀdã, -ãt] *adj* discordant; conflicting

discorde [diskɔʀd(ə)] *nf* discord, dissension

discothèque [diskɔtɛk] *nf* (*disques*) record collection; (*: dans une bibliothèque*): **~ (de prêt)** record library; (*boîte de nuit*) disco(thèque)

discourais *etc* [diskuʀɛ] *vb voir* **discourir**

discourir [diskuʀiʀ] *vi* to discourse, hold forth

discours [diskuʀ] *vb voir* **discourir** ▷ *nm* speech; **~ direct/indirect** (*Ling*) direct/indirect *ou* reported speech

discourtois, e [diskuʀtwa, waz] *adj* discourteous

discrédit [diskʀedi] *nm*: **jeter le ~ sur** to discredit

discréditer [diskʀedite] *vt* to discredit

discret, -ète [diskʀɛ, -ɛt] *adj* discreet; (*fig: musique, style*) unobtrusive; (*: endroit*) quiet

discrètement [diskʀɛtmã] *adv* discreetly

discrétion [diskʀesjõ] *nf* discretion; **à la ~ de qn** at sb's discretion; in sb's hands; **à ~** (*boisson etc*) unlimited, as much as one wants

discrétionnaire [diskʀesjɔnɛʀ] *adj* discretionary

discrimination [diskʀiminasjõ] *nf* discrimination; **sans ~** indiscriminately

discriminatoire [diskʀiminatwaʀ] *adj* discriminatory

disculper [diskylpe] *vt* to exonerate

discussion [diskysjɔ̃] *nf* discussion
discutable [diskytabl(ə)] *adj* (*contestable*)
doubtful; (*à débattre*) debatable
discuté, e [diskyte] *adj* controversial
discuter [diskyte] *vt* (*contester*) to question,
dispute; (*débattre: prix*) to discuss ▷ *vi* to talk;
(*ergoter*) to argue; **~ de** to discuss
dise *etc* [diz] *vb voir* **dire**
disert, e [dizɛʀ, -ɛʀt(ə)] *adj* loquacious
disette [dizɛt] *nf* food shortage
diseuse [dizøz] *nf*: **~ de bonne aventure**
fortune-teller
disgrâce [disgʀɑs] *nf* disgrace; **être en ~** to be
in disgrace
disgracié, e [disgʀasje] *adj* (*en disgrâce*) disgraced
disgracieux, -euse [disgʀasjø, -øz] *adj*
ungainly, awkward
disjoindre [disʒwɛ̃dʀ(ə)] *vt* to take apart; **se**
disjoindre *vi* to come apart
disjoint, e [disʒwɛ̃, -wɛ̃t] *pp de* **disjoindre** ▷ *adj*
loose
disjoncteur [disʒɔ̃ktœʀ] *nm* (*Élec*) circuit
breaker
dislocation [dislɔkasjɔ̃] *nf* dislocation
disloquer [dislɔke] *vt* (*membre*) to dislocate;
(*chaise*) to dismantle; (*troupe*) to disperse; **se**
disloquer *vi* (*parti, empire*) to break up; **se ~**
l'épaule to dislocate one's shoulder
disons *etc* [dizɔ̃] *vb voir* **dire**
disparaître [dispaʀɛtʀ(ə)] *vi* to disappear; (*à la*
vue) to vanish, disappear; to be hidden *ou*
concealed; (*être manquant*) to go missing,
disappear; (*se perdre: traditions etc*) to die out;
(*personne: mourir*) to die; **faire ~** (*objet, tache, trace*)
to remove; (*personne*) to get rid of
disparate [dispaʀat] *adj* disparate; (*couleurs*) ill-
assorted
disparité [dispaʀite] *nf* disparity
disparition [dispaʀisjɔ̃] *nf* disappearance
disparu, e [dispaʀy] *pp de* **disparaître** ▷ *nm/f*
missing person; (*défunt*) departed; **être porté ~**
to be reported missing
dispendieux, -euse [dispɑ̃djø, -øz] *adj*
extravagant, expensive
dispensaire [dispɑ̃sɛʀ] *nm* community clinic
dispense [dispɑ̃s] *nf* exemption; (*permission*)
special permission; **~ d'âge** special exemption
from age limit
dispenser [dispɑ̃se] *vt* (*donner*) to lavish, bestow;
(*exempter*): **~ qn de** to exempt sb from; **se ~ de** *vt*
to avoid, get out of
disperser [dispɛʀse] *vt* to scatter; (*fig: son*
attention) to dissipate; **se disperser** *vi* to scatter;
(*fig*) to dissipate one's efforts
dispersion [dispɛʀsjɔ̃] *nf* scattering; (*des efforts*)
dissipation
disponibilité [dispɔnibilite] *nf* availability;
(*Admin*): **être en ~** to be on leave of absence;
disponibilités *nfpl* (*Comm*) liquid assets
disponible [dispɔnibl(ə)] *adj* available
dispos [dispo] *adj m*: **(frais et) ~** fresh (as a
daisy)

disposé, e [dispoze] *adj* (*d'une certaine manière*)
arranged, laid-out; **bien/mal ~** (*humeur*) in a
good/bad mood; **bien/mal ~ pour** *ou* **envers qn**
well/badly disposed towards sb; **~ à** (*prêt à*)
willing *ou* prepared to
disposer [dispoze] *vt* (*arranger, placer*) to arrange;
(*inciter*): **~ qn à qch/faire qch** to dispose *ou*
incline sb towards sth/to do sth ▷ *vi*: **vous**
pouvez ~ you may leave; **~ de** *vt* to have (at
one's disposal); **se ~ à faire** to prepare to do, be
about to do
dispositif [dispozitif] *nm* device; (*fig*) system,
plan of action; set-up; (*d'un texte de loi*) operative
part; **~ de sûreté** safety device
disposition [dispozisjɔ̃] *nf* (*arrangement*)
arrangement, layout; (*humeur*) mood; (*tendance*)
tendency; **dispositions** *nfpl* (*mesures*) steps,
measures; (*préparatifs*) arrangements; (*de loi,*
testament) provisions; (*aptitudes*) bent *sg*,
aptitude *sg*; **à la ~ de qn** at sb's disposal
disproportion [dispʀɔpɔʀsjɔ̃] *nf* disproportion
disproportionné, e [dispʀɔpɔʀsjone] *adj*
disproportionate, out of all proportion
dispute [dispyt] *nf* quarrel, argument
disputer [dispyte] *vt* (*match*) to play; (*combat*) to
fight; (*course*) to run; **se disputer** *vi* to quarrel,
have a quarrel; (*match, combat, course*) to take
place; **~ qch à qn** to fight with sb for *ou* over sth
disquaire [diskɛʀ] *nm/f* record dealer
disqualification [diskalifikasjɔ̃] *nf*
disqualification
disqualifier [diskalifje] *vt* to disqualify; **se**
disqualifier *vi* to bring discredit on o.s.
disque [disk(ə)] *nm* (*Mus*) record; (*Inform*) disk,
disc; (*forme, pièce*) disc; (*Sport*) discus; **~ compact**
compact disc; **~ compact interactif** CD-I®; **~**
dur hard disk; **~ d'embrayage** (*Auto*) clutch
plate; **~ laser** compact disc; **~ de**
stationnement parking disc; **~ système**
system disk
disquette [diskɛt] *nf* diskette, floppy (disk)
dissection [disɛksjɔ̃] *nf* dissection
dissemblable [disɑ̃blabl(ə)] *adj* dissimilar
dissemblance [disɑ̃blɑ̃s] *nf* dissimilarity,
difference
dissémination [diseminasjɔ̃] *nf* (*voir vb*)
scattering; dispersal; (*des armes*) proliferation
disséminer [disemine] *vt* to scatter; (*troupes: sur*
un territoire) to disperse
dissension [disɑ̃sjɔ̃] *nf* dissension; **dissensions**
nfpl dissension
disséquer [diseke] *vt* to dissect
dissertation [disɛʀtasjɔ̃] *nf* (*Scol*) essay
disserter [disɛʀte] *vi*: **~ sur** to discourse upon
dissidence [disidɑ̃s] *nf* (*concept*) dissidence;
rejoindre la ~ to join the dissidents
dissident, e [disidɑ̃, -ɑ̃t] *adj, nm/f* dissident
dissimilitude [disimilityd] *nf* dissimilarity
dissimulateur, -trice [disimyltœʀ, -tʀis] *adj*
dissembling ▷ *nm/f* dissembler
dissimulation [disimylasjɔ̃] *nf* concealing;
(*duplicité*) dissimulation; **~ de bénéfices/de**

revenus concealment of profits/income

dissimulé, e [disimyle] *adj* (*personne: secret*) secretive; (: *fourbe, hypocrite*) deceitful

dissimuler [disimyle] *vt* to conceal; **se dissimuler** *vi* to conceal o.s.; to be concealed

dissipation [disipasjɔ̃] *nf* squandering; unruliness; (*débauche*) dissipation

dissipé, e [disipe] *adj* (*indiscipliné*) unruly

dissiper [disipe] *vt* to dissipate; (*fortune*) to squander, fritter away; **se dissiper** *vi* (*brouillard*) to clear, disperse; (*doutes*) to disappear, melt away; (*élève*) to become undisciplined *ou* unruly

dissociable [disɔsjabl(ə)] *adj* separable

dissocier [disɔsje] *vt* to dissociate; **se dissocier** *vi* (*éléments, groupe*) to break up, split up; **se ~ de** (*groupe, point de vue*) to dissociate o.s. from

dissolu, e [disɔly] *adj* dissolute

dissoluble [disɔlybl(ə)] *adj* (Pol: *assemblée*) dissolvable

dissolution [disɔlysjɔ̃] *nf* dissolving; (*Pol, Jur*) dissolution

dissolvant, e [disɔlvɑ̃, -ɑ̃t] *vb voir* **dissoudre** ▷ *nm* (*Chimie*) solvent; **~ (gras)** nail polish remover

dissonant, e [disɔnɑ̃, -ɑ̃t] *adj* discordant

dissoudre [disudʀ(ə)] *vt*, **se dissoudre** *vi* to dissolve

dissous, -oute [disu, -ut] *pp de* **dissoudre**

dissuader [disɥade] *vt*: **~ qn de faire/de qch** to dissuade sb from doing/from sth

dissuasif, -ive [disɥazif, iv] *adj* dissuasive

dissuasion [disɥazjɔ̃] *nf* dissuasion; **force de ~** deterrent power

distance [distɑ̃s] *nf* distance; (*fig: écart*) gap; **à ~** at *ou* from a distance; (*mettre en marche, commander*) by remote control; **(situé) à ~** (*Inform*) remote; **tenir qn à ~** to keep sb at a distance; **se tenir à ~** to keep one's distance; **à une ~ de 10 km, à 10 km de ~** 10 km away, at a distance of 10 km; **à deux ans de ~** with a gap of two years; **prendre ses ~s** to space out; **garder ses ~s** to keep one's distance; **tenir la ~** (*Sport*) to cover the distance, last the course; **~ focale** (*Photo*) focal length

distancer [distɑ̃se] *vt* to outdistance, leave behind

distancier [distɑ̃sje]: **se distancier** *vi* to distance o.s.

distant, e [distɑ̃, -ɑ̃t] *adj* (*réservé*) distant, aloof; (*éloigné*) distant, far away; **~ de** (*lieu*) far away *ou* a long way from; **~ de 5 km (d'un lieu)** 5 km away (from a place)

distendre [distɑ̃dʀ(ə)] *vt*, **se distendre** *vi* to distend

distillation [distilasjɔ̃] *nf* distillation, distilling

distillé, e [distile] *adj*: **eau ~e** distilled water

distiller [distile] *vt* to distil; (*fig*) to exude; to elaborate

distillerie [distilʀi] *nf* distillery

distinct, e [distɛ̃(kt), distɛ̃kt(ə)] *adj* distinct

distinctement [distɛ̃ktəmɑ̃] *adv* distinctly

distinctif, -ive [distɛ̃ktif, -iv] *adj* distinctive

distinction [distɛ̃ksjɔ̃] *nf* distinction

distingué, e [distɛ̃ge] *adj* distinguished

distinguer [distɛ̃ge] *vt* to distinguish; **se distinguer** *vi* (*s'illustrer*) to distinguish o.s.; (*différer*): **se ~ (de)** to distinguish o.s. *ou* be distinguished (from)

distinguo [distɛ̃go] *nm* distinction

distorsion [distɔʀsjɔ̃] *nf* (*gén*) distortion; (*fig: déséquilibre*) disparity, imbalance

distraction [distʀaksjɔ̃] *nf* (*manque d'attention*) absent-mindedness; (*oubli*) lapse (in concentration *ou* attention; (*détente*) diversion, recreation; (*passe-temps*) distraction, entertainment

distraire [distʀɛʀ] *vt* (*déranger*) to distract; (*divertir*) to entertain, divert; (*détourner: somme d'argent*) to divert, misappropriate; **se distraire** *vi* to amuse *ou* enjoy o.s.

distrait, e [distʀɛ, -ɛt] *pp de* **distraire** ▷ *adj* absent-minded

distraitement [distʀɛtmɑ̃] *adv* absent-mindedly

distrayant, e [distʀɛjɑ̃, -ɑ̃t] *vb voir* **distraire** ▷ *adj* entertaining

distribuer [distʀibɥe] *vt* to distribute; to hand out; (*Cartes*) to deal (out); (*courrier*) to deliver

distributeur [distʀibytœʀ] *nm* (*Auto, Comm*) distributor; (*automatique*) (vending) machine; **~ de billets** (*Rail*) ticket machine; (*Banque*) cash dispenser

distribution [distʀibysjɔ̃] *nf* distribution; (*postale*) delivery; (*choix d'acteurs*) casting; **circuits de ~** (*Comm*) distribution network; **~ des prix** (*Scol*) prize giving

district [distʀik(t)] *nm* district

dit, e [di, dit] *pp de* **dire** ▷ *adj* (*fixé*): **le jour ~** the arranged day; (*surnommé*): **X, ~ Pierrot** X, known as *ou* called Pierrot

dites [dit] *vb voir* **dire**

dithyrambique [ditiʀɑ̃bik] *adj* eulogistic

DIU *sigle m* (= *dispositif intra-utérin*) IUD

diurétique [djyʀetik] *adj, nm* diuretic

diurne [djyʀn(ə)] *adj* diurnal, daytime *cpd*

divagations [divagasjɔ̃] *nfpl* ramblings; ravings

divaguer [divage] *vi* to ramble; (*malade*) to rave

divan [divɑ̃] *nm* divan

divan-lit [divɑ̃li] *nm* divan (bed)

divergence [divɛʀʒɑ̃s] *nf* divergence; **des ~s d'opinion au sein de ...** differences of opinion within ...

divergent, e [divɛʀʒɑ̃, -ɑ̃t] *adj* divergent

diverger [divɛʀʒe] *vi* to diverge

divers, e [divɛʀ, -ɛʀs(ə)] *adj* (*varié*) diverse, varied; (*différent*) different, various; **(frais) ~** (*Comm*) sundries, miscellaneous (expenses); **"~"** (*rubrique*) "miscellaneous"

diversement [divɛʀsəmɑ̃] *adv* in various *ou* diverse ways

diversification [divɛʀsifikasjɔ̃] *nf* diversification

diversifier [divɛʀsifje] *vt*, **se diversifier** *vi* to diversify

diversion [divɛʀsjɔ̃] *nf* diversion; **faire** ~ to create a diversion

diversité [divɛʀsite] *nf* diversity, variety

divertir [divɛʀtiʀ] *vt* to amuse, entertain; **se divertir** *vi* to amuse *ou* enjoy o.s.

divertissant, e [divɛʀtisɑ̃, -ɑ̃t] *adj* entertaining

divertissement [divɛʀtismɑ̃] *nm* entertainment; (*Mus*) divertimento, divertissement

dividende [dividɑ̃d] *nm* (*Math, Comm*) dividend

divin, e [divɛ̃, -in] *adj* divine; (*fig: excellent*) heavenly, divine

divinateur, -trice [divinatœʀ, -tʀis] *adj* perspicacious

divinatoire [divinatwaʀ] *adj* (*art, science*) divinatory; **baguette** ~ divining rod

diviniser [divinize] *vt* to deify

divinité [divinite] *nf* divinity

divisé, e [divize] *adj* divided

diviser [divize] *vt* (*gén, Math*) to divide; (*morceler, subdiviser*) to divide (up), split (up); **se** ~ **en** to divide into; ~ **par** to divide by

diviseur [divizœʀ] *nm* (*Math*) divisor

divisible [divizibl(ə)] *adj* divisible

division [divizjɔ̃] *nf* (*gén*) division; ~ **du travail** (*Écon*) division of labour

divisionnaire [divizjɔnɛʀ] *adj*: **commissaire** ~ ≈ chief superintendent (*Brit*), ≈ police chief (*US*)

divorce [divɔʀs(ə)] *nm* divorce

divorcé, e [divɔʀse] *nm/f* divorcee

divorcer [divɔʀse] *vi* to get a divorce, get divorced; ~ **de** *ou* **d'avec qn** to divorce sb

divulgation [divylgasjɔ̃] *nf* disclosure

divulguer [divylge] *vt* to divulge, disclose

dix [di, dis, diz] *num* ten

dix-huit [dizɥit] *num* eighteen

dix-huitième [dizɥitjɛm] *num* eighteenth

dixième [dizjɛm] *num* tenth

dix-neuf [diznœf] *num* nineteen

dix-neuvième [diznœvjɛm] *num* nineteenth

dix-sept [disɛt] *num* seventeen

dix-septième [disɛtjɛm] *num* seventeenth

dizaine [dizɛn] *nf* (10) ten; (*environ 10*): **une** ~ **(de)** about ten, ten or so

Djakarta [dʒakaʀta] *n* Djakarta

Djibouti [dʒibuti] *n* Djibouti

dl *abr* (= *décilitre*) dl

DM *abr* (= *Deutschmark*) DM

dm. *abr* (= *décimètre*) dm.

do [do] *nm* (*note*) C; (*en chantant la gamme*) do(h)

docile [dɔsil] *adj* docile

docilement [dɔsilmɑ̃] *adv* docilely

docilité [dɔsilite] *nf* docility

dock [dɔk] *nm* dock; (*hangar, bâtiment*) warehouse

docker [dɔkɛʀ] *nm* docker

docte [dɔkt(ə)] *adj* (*péj*) learned

docteur, e [dɔktœʀ] *nm/f* doctor; ~ **en médecine** doctor of medicine

doctoral, e, -aux [dɔktɔʀal, -o] *adj* pompous, bombastic

doctorat [dɔktɔʀa] *nm*: ~ **(d'Université)** ≈ doctorate; ~ **d'État** ≈ PhD; ~ **de troisième cycle** ≈ doctorate

doctoresse [dɔktɔʀɛs] *nf* lady doctor

doctrinaire [dɔktʀinɛʀ] *adj* doctrinaire; (*sentencieux*) pompous, sententious

doctrinal, e, -aux [dɔktʀinal, o] *adj* doctrinal

doctrine [dɔktʀin] *nf* doctrine

document [dɔkymɑ̃] *nm* document

documentaire [dɔkymɑ̃tɛʀ] *adj, nm* documentary

documentaliste [dɔkymɑ̃talist(ə)] *nm/f* archivist; (*Presse, TV*) researcher

documentation [dɔkymɑ̃tasjɔ̃] *nf* documentation, literature; (*Presse, TV: service*) research

documenté, e [dɔkymɑ̃te] *adj* well-informed, well-documented; well-researched

documenter [dɔkymɑ̃te] *vt*: **se** ~ **(sur)** to gather information *ou* material (on *ou* about)

Dodécanèse [dɔdekanɛz] *nm* Dodecanese (Islands)

dodeliner [dɔdline] *vi*: ~ **de la tête** to nod one's head gently

dodo [dɔdo] *nm*: **aller faire** ~ to go to beddy-byes

dodu, e [dɔdy] *adj* plump

dogmatique [dɔgmatik] *adj* dogmatic

dogmatisme [dɔgmatism(ə)] *nm* dogmatism

dogme [dɔgm(ə)] *nm* dogma

dogue [dɔg] *nm* mastiff

doigt [dwa] *nm* finger; **à deux ~s de** within an ace (*Brit*) *ou* an inch of; **un** ~ **de lait/whisky** a drop of milk/whisky; **désigner** *ou* **montrer du** ~ to point at; **au** ~ **et à l'œil** to the letter; **connaître qch sur le bout du** ~ to know sth backwards; **mettre le** ~ **sur la plaie** (*fig*) to find the sensitive spot; ~ **de pied** toe

doigté [dwate] *nm* (*Mus*) fingering; (*fig: habileté*) diplomacy, tact

doigtier [dwatje] *nm* fingerstall

dois *etc* [dwa] *vb voir* **devoir**

doit *etc* [dwa] *vb voir* **devoir**

doive *etc* [dwav] *vb voir* **devoir**

doléances [dɔleɑ̃s] *nfpl* complaints; (*réclamations*) grievances

dolent, e [dɔlɑ̃, -ɑ̃t] *adj* doleful, mournful

dollar [dɔlaʀ] *nm* dollar

dolmen [dɔlmɛn] *nm* dolmen

DOM [dɔm] *sigle m ou mpl* = **Département(s) d'outre-mer**

domaine [dɔmɛn] *nm* estate, property; (*fig*) domain, field; **tomber dans le** ~ **public** (*livre etc*) to be out of copyright; **dans tous les ~s** in all areas

domanial, e, -aux [dɔmanjal, -o] *adj* national, state *cpd*

dôme [dom] *nm* dome

domestication [dɔmɛstikasjɔ̃] *nf* (*voir domestiquer*) domestication; harnessing

domesticité [dɔmɛstisite] *nf* (domestic) staff

domestique [dɔmɛstik] *adj* domestic ▷ *nm/f* servant, domestic

domestiquer [dɔmɛstike] *vt* to domesticate; (*vent, marées*) to harness

domicile [dɔmisil] *nm* home, place of residence; **à ~** at home; **élire ~ à** to take up residence in; **sans ~ fixe** of no fixed abode; **~ conjugal** marital home; **~ légal** domicile

domicilié, e [dɔmisilje] *adj*: **être ~ à** to have one's home in *ou* at

dominant, e [dɔminɑ̃, -ɑ̃t] *adj* dominant; (*plus important*) predominant ▷ *nf* (*caractéristique*) dominant characteristic; (*couleur*) dominant colour

dominateur, -trice [dɔminatœʀ, -tʀis] *adj* dominating; (*qui aime à dominer*) domineering

domination [dɔminasjɔ̃] *nf* domination

dominer [dɔmine] *vt* to dominate; (*passions etc*) to control, master; (*surpasser*) to outclass, surpass; (*surplomber*) to tower above, dominate ▷ *vi* to be in the dominant position; **se dominer** *vi* to control o.s.

dominicain, e [dɔminikɛ̃, -ɛn] *adj* Dominican

dominical, e, -aux [dɔminikal, -o] *adj* Sunday *cpd*, dominical

Dominique [dɔminik] *nf*: **la ~** Dominica

domino [dɔmino] *nm* domino; **dominos** *nmpl* (*jeu*) dominoes *sg*

dommage [dɔmaʒ] *nm* (*préjudice*) harm, injury; (*dégâts, pertes*) damage *no pl*; **c'est ~ de faire/que** it's a shame *ou* pity to do/that; **quel ~!** what a pity *ou* shame!; **~s corporels** physical injury

dommages-intérêts [dɔmaʒ(əz)ɛ̃teʀɛ] *nmpl* damages

dompter [dɔ̃te] *vt* to tame

dompteur, -euse [dɔ̃tœʀ, -øz] *nm/f* trainer; (*de lion*) lion tamer

DOM-ROM [dɔmʀɔm], **DOM-TOM** [dɔmtɔm] *sigle m ou mpl* (= *Département(s) et Régions/ Territoire(s) d'outre-mer*) French overseas departments and regions; *see note*

DOM-TOM, ROM ET COM

There are four "Départements d'outre-mer" or *DOMs*: Guadeloupe, Martinique, La Réunion and French Guyana. They are run in the same way as metropolitan "départements" and their inhabitants are French citizens. In administrative terms they are also "Régions", and in this regard are also referred to as "ROM" (Régions d'outre-mer"). The term "DOM-TOM" is still commonly used, but the term "Territoire d'outre-mer" has been superseded by that of "Collectivité d'outre-mer" (COM). The COMs include French Polynesia, Wallis-and-Futuna, New Caledonia and polar territories. They are independent, but each is supervised by a representative of the French government.

don [dɔ̃] *nm* (*cadeau*) gift; (*charité*) donation; (*aptitude*) gift, talent; **avoir des ~s pour** to have a gift *ou* talent for; **faire ~ de** to make a gift of; **~ en argent** cash donation

donateur, -trice [dɔnatœʀ, -tʀis] *nm/f* donor

donation [dɔnasjɔ̃] *nf* donation

donc [dɔ̃k] *conj* therefore, so; (*après une digression*) so, then; (*intensif*): **voilà ~ la solution** so there's the solution; **je disais ~ que ...** as I was saying, ...; **venez ~ dîner à la maison** do come for dinner; **allons ~!** come now!; **faites ~** go ahead

donjon [dɔ̃ʒɔ̃] *nm* keep

don Juan [dɔ̃ʒɥɑ̃] *nm* Don Juan

donnant, e [dɔnɑ̃, -ɑ̃t] *adj*: **~, ~** fair's fair

donne [dɔn] *nf* (*Cartes*): **il y a mauvaise** *ou* **fausse ~** there's been a misdeal

donné, e [dɔne] *adj* (*convenu*) given; (*pas cher*) very cheap ▷ *nf* (*Math, Inform, gén*) datum; **c'est ~** it's a gift; **étant ~ ...** given ...

données [dɔne] *nfpl* data

donner [dɔne] *vt* to give; (*vieux habits etc*) to give away; (*spectacle*) to put on; (*film*) to show; **~ qch à qn** to give sb sth, give sth to sb; **~ sur** (*fenêtre, chambre*) to look (out) onto; **~ dans** (*piège etc*) to fall into; **faire ~ l'infanterie** (*Mil*) to send in the infantry; **~ l'heure à qn** to tell sb the time; **~ le ton** (*fig*) to set the tone; **~ à penser/ entendre que ...** to make one think/give one to understand that ...; **se ~ à fond (à son travail)** to give one's all (to one's work); **se ~ du mal** *ou* **de la peine (pour faire qch)** to go to a lot of trouble (to do sth); **s'en ~ à cœur joie** (*fam*) to have a great time (of it)

donneur, -euse [dɔnœʀ, -øz] *nm/f* (*Méd*) donor; (*Cartes*) dealer; **~ de sang** blood donor

 MOT-CLÉ

dont [dɔ̃] *pron relatif* **1** (*appartenance: objets*) whose, of which; (: *êtres animés*) whose; **la maison dont le toit est rouge** the house the roof of which is red, the house whose roof is red; **l'homme dont je connais la sœur** the man whose sister I know

2 (*parmi lesquel(le)s*): **deux livres, dont l'un est ...** two books, one of which is ...; **il y avait plusieurs personnes, dont Gabrielle** there were several people, among them Gabrielle; **10 blessés, dont 2 grièvement** 10 injured, 2 of them seriously

3 (*complément d'adjectif, de verbe*): **le fils dont il est si fier** the son he's so proud of; **ce dont je parle** what I'm talking about; **la façon dont il l'a fait** the way (in which) he did it

donzelle [dɔ̃zɛl] *nf* (*péj*) young madam

dopage [dɔpaʒ] *nm* doping

dopant [dɔpɑ̃] *nm* dope

doper [dɔpe] *vt* to dope; **se doper** *vi* to take dope

doping [dɔpiŋ] *nm* doping; (*excitant*) dope

dorade [dɔʀad] *nf* = **daurade**

doré, e [dɔʀe] *adj* golden; (*avec dorure*) gilt, gilded

dorénavant [dɔʀenavɑ̃] *adv* from now on, henceforth

dorer [dɔʀe] vt (cadre) to gild; **(faire)** ~ (Culin) to brown; (: gâteau) to glaze; **se ~ au soleil** to sunbathe; **~ la pilule à qn** to sugar the pill for sb

dorloter [dɔʀlɔte] vt to pamper, cosset (Brit); **se faire ~** to be pampered ou cosseted

dormant, e [dɔʀmɑ̃, -ɑ̃t] adj: **eau ~e** still water

dorme etc [dɔʀm(ə)] vb voir **dormir**

dormeur, -euse [dɔʀmœʀ, -øz] nm/f sleeper

dormir [dɔʀmiʀ] vi to sleep; (être endormi) to be asleep; **à poings fermés** to sleep very soundly

dorsal, e, -aux [dɔʀsal, -o] adj dorsal; voir **rouleau**

dortoir [dɔʀtwaʀ] nm dormitory

dorure [dɔʀyʀ] nf gilding

doryphore [dɔʀifɔʀ] nm Colorado beetle

dos [do] nm back; (de livre) spine; **"voir au ~"** "see over"; **robe décolletée dans le ~** low-backed dress; **de ~** from the back, from behind; **~ à ~** back to back; **sur le ~** on one's back; **à ~ de chameau** riding on a camel; **avoir bon ~** to be a good excuse; **se mettre qn à ~** to turn sb against one

dosage [dozaʒ] nm mixture

dos-d'âne [dodɑn] nm humpback; **pont en dos-d'âne** humpbacked bridge

dose [doz] nf (Méd) dose; **forcer la ~** (fig) to overstep the mark

doser [doze] vt to measure out; (mélanger) to mix in the correct proportions; (fig) to expend in the right amounts ou proportions; to strike a balance between

doseur [dozœʀ] nm measure; **bouchon ~** measuring cap

dossard [dosaʀ] nm number (worn by competitor)

dossier [dosje] nm (renseignements, fichier) file; (enveloppe) folder, file; (de chaise) back; (Presse) feature; **le ~ social/monétaire** (fig) the social/financial question; **~ suspendu** suspension file

dot [dɔt] nf dowry

dotation [dɔtasjɔ̃] nf block grant; endowment

doté, e [dɔte] adj: **~ de** equipped with

doter [dɔte] vt: **~ qn/qch de** to equip sb/sth with

douairière [dwɛʀjɛʀ] nf dowager

douane [dwan] nf (poste, bureau) customs pl; (taxes) (customs) duty; **passer la ~** to go through customs; **en ~** (marchandises, entrepôt) bonded

douanier, -ière [dwanje, -jɛʀ] adj customs cpd ▷ nm customs officer

doublage [dublaʒ] nm (Ciné) dubbing

double [dubl(ə)] adj, adv double ▷ nm (2 fois plus): **le ~ (de)** twice as much (ou many) (as), double the amount (ou number) (of); (autre exemplaire) duplicate, copy; (sosie) double; (Tennis) doubles sg; **voir ~** to see double; **en ~ (exemplaire)** in duplicate; **faire ~ emploi** to be redundant; **à ~ sens** with a double meaning; **à ~ tranchant** two-edged; **~ carburateur** twin carburettor; **à ~s commandes** dual-control; **~ messieurs/ mixte** men's/mixed doubles sg; **~ toit** (de tente)

fly sheet; **~ vue** second sight

doublé, e [duble] adj (vêtement): **~ (de)** lined (with)

double-cliquer [dubl(ə)klike] vi (Inform) to double-click

doublement [dubləmɑ̃] nm doubling; twofold increase ▷ adv doubly; (pour deux raisons) in two ways, on two counts

doubler [duble] vt (multiplier par 2) to double; (vêtement) to line; (dépasser) to overtake, pass; (film) to dub; (acteur) to stand in for ▷ vi to double, increase twofold; **se ~ de** to be coupled with; **~ (la classe)** (Scol) to repeat a year; **~ un cap** (Navig) to round a cape; (fig) to get over a hurdle

doublure [dublyʀ] nf lining; (Ciné) stand-in

douce [dus] adj f voir **doux**

douceâtre [dusatʀ(ə)] adj sickly sweet

doucement [dusmɑ̃] adv gently; (à voix basse) softly; (lentement) slowly

doucereux, -euse [dusʀø, -øz] adj (péj) sugary

douceur [dusœʀ] nf softness; sweetness; mildness; gentleness; **douceurs** nfpl (friandises) sweets (Brit), candy sg (US); **en ~** gently

douche [duʃ] nf shower; **douches** nfpl shower room sg; **prendre une ~** to have ou take a shower; **~ écossaise** (fig): **~ froide** (fig) let-down

doucher [duʃe] vt: **~ qn** to give sb a shower; (mouiller) to drench sb; (fig) to give sb a telling-off; **se doucher** vi to have ou take a shower

doudoune [dudun] nf padded jacket; (fam) boob

doué, e [dwe] adj gifted, talented; **~ de** endowed with; **être ~ pour** to have a gift for

douille [duj] nf (Élec) socket; (de projectile) case

douillet, te [dujɛ, -ɛt] adj cosy; (péj) soft

douleur [dulœʀ] nf pain; (chagrin) grief, distress; **ressentir des ~s** to feel pain; **il a eu la ~ de perdre son père** he suffered the grief of losing his father

douloureux, -euse [duluʀø, -øz] adj painful

doute [dut] nm doubt; **sans ~** adv no doubt; (probablement) probably; **sans nul** ou **aucun ~** without (a) doubt; **hors de ~** beyond doubt; **nul ~ que** there's no doubt that; **mettre en ~** to call into question; **mettre en ~ que** to question whether

douter [dute] vt to doubt; **~ de** vt (allié) to doubt, have (one's) doubts about; (résultat) to be doubtful of; **~ que** to doubt whether ou if; **j'en doute** I have my doubts; **se ~ de qch/que** to suspect sth/that; **je m'en doutais** I suspected as much; **il ne se doutait de rien** he didn't suspect a thing

douteux, -euse [dutø, -øz] adj (incertain) doubtful; (discutable) dubious, questionable; (péj) dubious-looking

douve [duv] nf (de château) moat; (de tonneau) stave

Douvres [duvʀ(ə)] n Dover

doux, douce [du, dus] adj (lisse, moelleux, pas vif: couleur, non calcaire: eau) soft; (sucré, agréable) sweet; (peu fort: moutarde etc, clément: climat) mild;

(*pas brusque*) gentle; **en douce** (*partir etc*) on the quiet

douzaine [duzɛn] *nf* (12) dozen; (*environ 12*): **une ~ (de)** a dozen or so, twelve or so

douze [duz] *num* twelve; **les D~** (*membres de la CEE*) the Twelve

douzième [duzjɛm] *num* twelfth

doyen, ne [dwajɛ̃, -ɛn] *nm/f* (*en âge, ancienneté*) most senior member; (*de faculté*) dean

DPLG *sigle* (= *diplômé par le gouvernement*) extra certificate for architects, engineers etc

Dr *abr* (= *docteur*) Dr

dr. *abr* (= *droit(e)*) R, r

draconien, ne [dʀakɔnjɛ̃, -ɛn] *adj* draconian, stringent

dragage [dʀagaʒ] *nm* dredging

dragée [dʀaʒe] *nf* sugared almond; (*Méd*) (sugar-coated) pill

dragéifié, e [dʀaʒeifje] *adj* (*Méd*) sugar-coated

dragon [dʀagɔ̃] *nm* dragon

drague [dʀag] *nf* (*filet*) dragnet; (*bateau*) dredger

draguer [dʀage] *vt* (*rivière: pour nettoyer*) to dredge; (: *pour trouver qch*) to drag; (*fam*) to try and pick up, chat up (*Brit*) ▷ *vi* (*fam*) to try and pick sb up, chat sb up (*Brit*)

dragueur [dʀagœʀ] *nm* (*aussi*: **dragueur de mines**) minesweeper; (*fam*): **quel ~!** he's a great one for picking up girls!

drain [dʀɛ̃] *nm* (*Méd*) drain

drainage [dʀɛnaʒ] *nm* drainage

drainer [dʀene] *vt* to drain; (*fig: visiteurs, région*) to drain off

dramatique [dʀamatik] *adj* dramatic; (*tragique*) tragic ▷ *nf* (*TV*) (television) drama

dramatisation [dʀamatizasjɔ̃] *nf* dramatization

dramatiser [dʀamatize] *vt* to dramatize

dramaturge [dʀamatyʀʒ(ə)] *nm* dramatist, playwright

drame [dʀam] *nm* (*Théât*) drama; (*catastrophe*) drama, tragedy; **~ familial** family drama

drap [dʀa] *nm* (*de lit*) sheet; (*tissu*) woollen fabric; **~ de plage** beach towel

drapé [dʀape] *nm* (*d'un vêtement*) hang

drapeau, x [dʀapo] *nm* flag; **sous les ~x** with the colours (*Brit*) *ou* colors (*US*), in the army

draper [dʀape] *vt* to drape; (*robe, jupe*) to arrange

draperies [dʀapʀi] *nfpl* hangings

drap-housse [dʀaus] (*pl* **draps-housses**) *nm* fitted sheet

drapier [dʀapje] *nm* (*woollen*) cloth manufacturer; (*marchand*) clothier

drastique [dʀastik] *adj* drastic

dressage [dʀɛsaʒ] *nm* training

dresser [dʀese] *vt* (*mettre vertical, monter: tente*) to put up, erect; (*fig: liste, bilan, contrat*) to draw up; (*animal*) to train; **se dresser** *vi* (*falaise, obstacle*) to stand; (*avec grandeur, menace*) to tower (up); (*personne*) to draw o.s. up; **~ l'oreille** to prick up one's ears; **~ la table** to set *ou* lay the table; **~ qn contre qn d'autre** to set sb against sb else; **~ un procès-verbal** *ou* **une contravention à qn** to book sb

dresseur, -euse [dʀɛsœʀ, -øz] *nm/f* trainer

dressoir [dʀɛswaʀ] *nm* dresser

dribbler [dʀible] *vt, vi* (*Sport*) to dribble

drille [dʀij] *nm*: **joyeux ~** cheerful sort

drogue [dʀɔg] *nf* drug; **la ~** drugs *pl*; **~ dure/douce** hard/soft drugs *pl*

drogué, e [dʀɔge] *nm/f* drug addict

droguer [dʀɔge] *vt* (*victime*) to drug; (*malade*) to give drugs to; **se droguer** *vi* (*aux stupéfiants*) to take drugs; (*péj: de médicaments*) to dose o.s. up

droguerie [dʀɔgʀi] *nf* ≈ hardware shop (*Brit*) *ou* store (*US*)

droguiste [dʀɔgist(ə)] *nm* ≈ keeper (*ou* owner) of a hardware shop *ou* store

droit, e [dʀwa, dʀwat] *adj* (*non courbe*) straight; (*vertical*) upright, straight; (*fig: loyal, franc*) upright, straight(forward); (*opposé à gauche*) right, right-hand ▷ *adv* straight ▷ *nm* (*prérogative, Boxe*) right; (*taxe*) duty, tax; (: *d'inscription*) fee; (*lois, branche*): **le ~** law ▷ *nf* (*Pol*) right (wing); (*ligne*) straight line; **~ au but** *ou* **au fait/cœur** straight to the point/heart; **avoir le ~ de** to be allowed to; **avoir ~ à** to be entitled to; **être en ~ de** to have a *ou* the right to; **faire ~ à** to grant, accede to; **être dans son ~** to be within one's rights; **à bon ~** (*justement*) with good reason; **de quel ~?** by what right?; **à qui de ~** to whom it may concern; **à ~e** on the right; (*direction*) (to the) right; **à ~e de** to the right of; **de ~e, sur votre ~e** on your right; (*Pol*) right-wing; **~ d'auteur** copyright; **avoir ~ de cité (dans)** (*fig*) to belong (to); **~ coutumier** common law; **~ de regard** right of access *ou* inspection; **~ de réponse** right to reply; **~ de visite** (right of) access; **~ de vote** (right to) vote; **~s d'auteur** royalties; **~s de douane** customs duties; **~s de l'homme** human rights; **~s d'inscription** enrolment *ou* registration fees

droitement [dʀwatmɑ̃] *adv* (*agir*) uprightly

droitier, -ière [dʀwatje, -jɛʀ] *nm/f* right-handed person

droiture [dʀwatyʀ] *nf* uprightness, straightness

drôle [dʀol] *adj* (*amusant*) funny, amusing; (*bizarre*) funny, peculiar; **un ~ de ...** (*bizarre*) a strange *ou* funny ...; (*intensif*) an incredible ..., a terrific ...

drôlement [dʀolmɑ̃] *adv* funnily; peculiarly; (*très*) terribly, awfully; **il fait ~ froid** it's awfully cold

drôlerie [dʀolʀi] *nf* funniness; funny thing

dromadaire [dʀɔmadɛʀ] *nm* dromedary

dru, e [dʀy] *adj* (*cheveux*) thick, bushy; (*pluie*) heavy ▷ *adv* (*pousser*) thickly; (*tomber*) heavily

drugstore [dʀœgstɔʀ] *nm* drugstore

druide [dʀɥid] *nm* Druid

ds *abr* = **dans**

DST *sigle f* (= *Direction de la surveillance du territoire*) internal security service, ≈ MI5 (*Brit*)

DT *sigle m* (= *diphtérie tétanos*) vaccine

DTCP *sigle m* (= *diphtérie tétanos coqueluche polio*) *vaccine*

DTP *sigle m* (= *diphtérie tétanos polio*) *vaccine*

DTTAB *sigle m* (= *diphtérie tétanos typhoïde A et B*) *vaccine*

du [dy] *art voir* **de**

dû, due [dy] *pp de* **devoir** ▷ *adj* (*somme*) owing, owed; (: *venant à échéance*) due; (*causé par*): **dû à** due to ▷ *nm* due; (*somme*) dues *pl*

dualisme [dɥalism(ə)] *nm* dualism

Dubaï, Dubay [dybaj] *n* Dubai

dubitatif, -ive [dybitatif, -iv] *adj* doubtful, dubious

Dublin [dyblɛ̃] *n* Dublin

duc [dyk] *nm* duke

duché [dyʃe] *nm* dukedom, duchy

duchesse [dyʃɛs] *nf* duchess

duel [dɥɛl] *nm* duel

duettiste [dɥetist(ə)] *nm/f* duettist

duffel-coat [dœfœlkot] *nm* duffel coat

dûment [dymɑ̃] *adv* duly

dumping [dœmpiŋ] *nm* dumping

dune [dyn] *nf* dune

Dunkerque [dœ̃kɛrk] *n* Dunkirk

duo [dɥo] *nm* (*Mus*) duet; (*fig: couple*) duo, pair

dupe [dyp] *nf* dupe ▷ *adj*: (**ne pas**) **être ~ de** (not) to be taken in by

duper [dype] *vt* to dupe, deceive

duperie [dypri] *nf* deception, dupery

duplex [dyplɛks] *nm* (*appartement*) split-level apartment, duplex; (*TV*): **émission en ~** link-up

duplicata [dyplikata] *nm* duplicate

duplicateur [dyplikatœr] *nm* duplicator; **~ à alcool** spirit duplicator

duplicité [dyplisite] *nf* duplicity

duquel [dykɛl] *prép+pron voir* **lequel**

dur, e [dyr] *adj* (*pierre, siège, travail, problème*) hard; (*lumière, voix, climat*) harsh; (*sévère*) hard, harsh; (*cruel*) hard(-hearted); (*porte, col*) stiff; (*viande*) tough ▷ *adv* hard ▷ *nf*: **à la ~e** rough; **mener la vie ~e à qn** to give sb a hard time; **~ d'oreille** hard of hearing

durabilité [dyrabilite] *nf* durability

durable [dyrabl(ə)] *adj* lasting

durablement [dyrabləmɑ̃] *adv* for the long term

durant [dyrɑ̃] *prép* (*au cours de*) during; (*pendant*) for; **~ des mois, des mois ~** for months

durcir [dyrsir] *vt, vi*, **se durcir** *vi* to harden

durcissement [dyrsismɑ̃] *nm* hardening

durée [dyre] *nf* length; (*d'une pile etc*) life; (*déroulement: des opérations etc*) duration; **pour une ~ illimitée** for an unlimited length of time; **de courte ~** (*séjour, répit*) brief, short-term; **de longue ~** (*effet*) long-term; **pile de longue ~** long-life battery

durement [dyrmɑ̃] *adv* harshly

durent [dyr] *vb voir* **devoir**

durer [dyre] *vi* to last

dureté [dyrte] *nf* (*voir dur*) hardness; harshness; stiffness; toughness

durillon [dyrijɔ̃] *nm* callus

durit® [dyrit] *nf* (*car radiator*) hose

DUT *sigle m* = **Diplôme universitaire de technologie**

dut *etc* [dy] *vb voir* **devoir**

duvet [dyvɛ] *nm* down; (**sac de couchage en**) **~** down-filled sleeping bag

duveteux, -euse [dyvtø, -øz] *adj* downy

DVD *sigle m* (= *digital versatile disc*) DVD

dynamique [dinamik] *adj* dynamic

dynamiser [dinamize] *vt* to pep up, enliven; (*équipe, service*) to inject some dynamism into

dynamisme [dinamism(ə)] *nm* dynamism

dynamite [dinamit] *nf* dynamite

dynamiter [dinamite] *vt* to (blow up with) dynamite

dynamo [dinamo] *nf* dynamo

dynastie [dinasti] *nf* dynasty

dysenterie [disɑ̃tri] *nf* dysentery

dyslexie [dislɛksi] *nf* dyslexia, word blindness

dyslexique [dislɛksik] *adj* dyslexic

dyspepsie [dispɛpsi] *nf* dyspepsia

Ee

E, e [ə] *nm inv* E, e ▷ *abr* (= *Est*) E; **E comme Eugène** E for Edward (*Brit*) *ou* Easy (*US*)

EAO *sigle m* (= *enseignement assisté par ordinateur*) CAL (= *computer-aided learning*)

EAU *sigle mpl* (= *Émirats arabes unis*) UAE (= *United Arab Emirates*)

eau, x [o] *nf* water ▷ *nfpl* waters; **prendre l'~** (*chaussure etc*) to leak, let in water; **prendre les ~x** to take the waters; **faire ~** to leak; **tomber à l'~** (*fig*) to fall through; **à l'~ de rose** slushy, sentimental; **~ bénite** holy water; **~ de Cologne** eau de Cologne; **~ courante** running water; **~ distillée** distilled water; **~ douce** fresh water; **~ de Javel** bleach; **~ lourde** heavy water; **~ minérale** mineral water; **~ oxygénée** hydrogen peroxide; **~ plate** still water; **~ de pluie** rainwater; **~ salée** salt water; **~ de toilette** toilet water; **~x ménagères** dirty water (*from washing up etc*); **~x territoriales** territorial waters; **~x usées** liquid waste

eau-de-vie [odvi] (*pl* **eaux-de-vie**) *nf* brandy

eau-forte [ofɔʀt(ə)] (*pl* **eaux-fortes**) *nf* etching

ébahi, e [ebai] *adj* dumbfounded, flabbergasted

ébahir [ebaiʀ] *vt* to astonish, astound

ébats [eba] *vb voir* **ébattre** ▷ *nmpl* frolics, gambols

ébattre [ebatʀ(ə)]: **s'ébattre** *vi* to frolic

ébauche [eboʃ] *nf* (rough) outline, sketch

ébaucher [eboʃe] *vt* to sketch out, outline; (*fig*): **~ un sourire/geste** to give a hint of a smile/ make a slight gesture; **s'ébaucher** *vi* to take shape

ébène [ebɛn] *nf* ebony

ébéniste [ebenist(ə)] *nm* cabinetmaker

ébénisterie [ebenistʀi] *nf* cabinetmaking; (*bâti*) cabinetwork

éberlué, e [ebɛʀlɥe] *adj* astounded, flabbergasted

éblouir [ebluiʀ] *vt* to dazzle

éblouissant, e [ebluisɑ̃, -ɑ̃t] *adj* dazzling

éblouissement [ebluismɑ̃] *nm* dazzle; (*faiblesse*) dizzy turn

ébonite [ebɔnit] *nf* vulcanite

éborgner [ebɔʀɲe] *vt*: **~ qn** to blind sb in one eye

éboueur [ebwœʀ] *nm* dustman (*Brit*), garbage man (*US*)

ébouillanter [ebujɑ̃te] *vt* to scald; (*Culin*) to blanch; **s'ébouillanter** *vi* to scald o.s

éboulement [ebulmɑ̃] *nm* falling rocks *pl*, rock fall; (*amas*) heap of boulders *etc*

ébouler [ebule]: **s'ébouler** *vi* to crumble, collapse

éboulis [ebuli] *nmpl* fallen rocks

ébouriffé, e [ebuʀife] *adj* tousled, ruffled

ébouriffer [ebuʀife] *vt* to tousle, ruffle

ébranlement [ebʀɑ̃lmɑ̃] *nm* shaking

ébranler [ebʀɑ̃le] *vt* to shake; (*rendre instable: mur, santé*) to weaken; **s'ébranler** *vi* (*partir*) to move off

ébrécher [ebʀeʃe] *vt* to chip

ébriété [ebʀijete] *nf*: **en état d'~** in a state of intoxication

ébrouer [ebʀue]: **s'ébrouer** *vi* (*souffler*) to snort; (*s'agiter*) to shake o.s.

ébruiter [ebʀɥite] *vt*, **s'ébruiter** *vi* to spread

ébullition [ebylisjɔ̃] *nf* boiling point; **en ~** boiling; (*fig*) in an uproar

écaille [ekaj] *nf* (*de poisson*) scale; (*de coquillage*) shell; (*matière*) tortoiseshell; (*de roc etc*) flake

écaillé, e [ekaje] *adj* (*peinture*) flaking

écailler [ekaje] *vt* (*poisson*) to scale; (*huître*) to open; **s'écailler** *vi* to flake *ou* peel (off)

écarlate [ekaʀlat] *adj* scarlet

écarquiller [ekaʀkije] *vt*: **~ les yeux** to stare wide-eyed

écart [ekaʀ] *nm* gap; (*embardée*) swerve; (*saut*) sideways leap; (*fig*) departure, deviation; **à l'~** *adv* out of the way; **à l'~ de** *prép* away from; (*fig*) out of; **faire le grand ~** (*Danse, Gymnastique*) to do the splits; **~ de conduite** misdemeanour

écarté, e [ekaʀte] *adj* (*lieu*) out-of-the-way, remote; (*ouvert*): **les jambes ~es** legs apart; **les bras ~s** arms outstretched

écarteler [ekaʀtəle] *vt* to quarter; (*fig*) to tear

écartement [ekaʀtəmɑ̃] *nm* space, gap; (*Rail*) gauge

écarter [ekaʀte] *vt* (*séparer*) to move apart, separate; (*éloigner*) to push back, move away; (*ouvrir: bras, jambes*) to spread, open; (*: rideau*) to draw (back); (*éliminer: candidat, possibilité*) to dismiss; (*Cartes*) to discard; **s'écarter** *vi* to part; (*personne*) to move away; **s'~ de** to wander from

ecchymose [ekimoz] *nf* bruise
ecclésiastique [eklezjastik] *adj* ecclesiastical
▷ *nm* ecclesiastic
écervelé, e [esɛʀvəle] *adj* scatterbrained,
featherbrained
ECG *sigle m* (= *électrocardiogramme*) ECG
échafaud [eʃafo] *nm* scaffold
échafaudage [eʃafodaʒ] *nm* scaffolding; (*fig*)
heap, pile
échafauder [eʃafode] *vt* (*plan*) to construct
échalas [eʃala] *nm* stake, pole; (*personne*)
beanpole
échalote [eʃalɔt] *nf* shallot
échancré, e [eʃɑ̃kʀe] *adj* (*robe, corsage*) low-
necked; (*côte*) indented
échancrure [eʃɑ̃kʀyʀ] *nf* (*de robe*) scoop neckline;
(*de côte, arête rocheuse*) indentation
échange [eʃɑ̃ʒ] *nm* exchange; **en ~** in exchange;
en ~ de in exchange *ou* return for; **libre ~** free
trade; **~ de lettres/politesses/vues** exchange
of letters/civilities/views; **~s commerciaux**
trade; **~s culturels** cultural exchanges
échangeable [eʃɑ̃ʒabl(ə)] *adj* exchangeable
échanger [eʃɑ̃ʒe] *vt*: **~ qch (contre)** to exchange
sth (for)
échangeur [eʃɑ̃ʒœʀ] *nm* (*Auto*) interchange
échantillon [eʃɑ̃tijɔ̃] *nm* sample
échantillonnage [eʃɑ̃tijɔnaʒ] *nm* selection of
samples
échappatoire [eʃapatwaʀ] *nf* way out
échappée [eʃape] *nf* (*vue*) vista; (*Cyclisme*)
breakaway
échappement [eʃapmɑ̃] *nm* (*Auto*) exhaust; **~
libre** cutout
échapper [eʃape]: **~ à** *vt* (*gardien*) to escape
(from); (*punition, péril*) to escape; **~ à qn** (*détail,
sens*) to escape sb; (*objet qu'on tient: aussi:*
échapper des mains de qn) to slip out of sb's
hands; **laisser ~** to let fall; (*cri etc*) to let out;
s'échapper *vi* to escape; **l'~ belle** to have a
narrow escape
écharde [eʃaʀd(ə)] *nf* splinter (of wood)
écharpe [eʃaʀp(ə)] *nf* scarf; (*de maire*) sash; (*Méd*)
sling; **prendre en ~** (*dans une collision*) to hit
sideways on
écharper [eʃaʀpe] *vt* to tear to pieces
échasse [eʃas] *nf* stilt
échassier [eʃasje] *nm* wader
échauder [eʃode] *vt*: **se faire ~** (*fig*) to get one's
fingers burnt
échauffement [eʃofmɑ̃] *nm* overheating; (*Sport*)
warm-up
échauffer [eʃofe] *vt* (*métal, moteur*) to overheat;
(*fig: exciter*) to fire, excite; **s'échauffer** *vi* (*Sport*)
to warm up; (*discussion*) to become heated
échauffourée [eʃofuʀe] *nf* clash, brawl; (*Mil*)
skirmish
échéance [eʃeɑ̃s] *nf* (*d'un paiement: date*)
settlement date; (*: somme due*) financial
commitment(s); (*fig*) deadline; **à brève/longue
~** *adj* short-/long-term ▷ *adv* in the short/long
term

échéancier [eʃeɑ̃sje] *nm* schedule
échéant [eʃeɑ̃]: **le cas ~** *adv* if the case arises
échec [eʃɛk] *nm* failure; (*Échecs*): **~ et mat/au
roi** checkmate/check; **échecs** *nmpl* (*jeu*) chess
sg; **mettre en ~** to put in check; **tenir en ~** to
hold in check; **faire ~ à** to foil, thwart
échelle [eʃɛl] *nf* ladder; (*fig, d'une carte*) scale; **à
l'~ de** on the scale of; **sur une grande/petite ~**
on a large/small scale; **faire la courte ~ à qn** to
give sb a leg up; **~ de corde** rope ladder
échelon [eʃlɔ̃] *nm* (*d'échelle*) rung; (*Admin*) grade
échelonner [eʃlɔne] *vt* to space out, spread out;
(versement) échelonné (payment) by
instalments
écheveau, x [eʃvo] *nm* skein, hank
échevelé, e [eʃəvle] *adj* tousled, dishevelled;
(*fig*) wild, frenzied
échine [eʃin] *nf* backbone, spine
échiner [eʃine]: **s'échiner** *vi* (*se fatiguer*) to work
o.s. to the bone
échiquier [eʃikje] *nm* chessboard
écho [eko] *nm* echo; **échos** *nmpl* (*potins*) gossip
sg, rumours; (*Presse: rubrique*) "news in brief";
rester sans ~ (*suggestion etc*) to come to nothing;
se faire l'~ de to repeat, spread about
échographie [ekɔgʀafi] *nf* ultrasound (scan)
échoir [eʃwaʀ] *vi* (*dette*) to fall due; (*délais*) to
expire; **~ à** *vt* to fall to
échoppe [eʃɔp] *nf* stall, booth
échouer [eʃwe] *vi* to fail; (*débris etc: sur la plage*) to
be washed up; (*aboutir: personne dans un café etc*) to
arrive ▷ *vt* (*bateau*) to ground; **s'échouer** *vi* to
run aground
échu, e [eʃy] *pp de* **échoir** ▷ *adj* due, mature
échut *etc* [eʃy] *vb voir* **échoir**
éclabousser [eklabuse] *vt* to splash; (*fig*) to
tarnish
éclaboussure [eklabusyʀ] *nf* splash; (*fig*) stain
éclair [eklɛʀ] *nm* (*d'orage*) flash of lightning,
lightning *no pl*; (*Photo: de flash*) flash; (*fig*) flash,
spark; (*gâteau*) éclair
éclairage [eklɛʀaʒ] *nm* lighting
éclairagiste [eklɛʀaʒist(ə)] *nm/f* lighting
engineer
éclaircie [eklɛʀsi] *nf* bright *ou* sunny interval
éclaircir [eklɛʀsiʀ] *vt* to lighten; (*fig*) to clear up,
clarify; (*Culin*) to thin (down); **s'éclaircir** *vi* (*ciel*)
to brighten up, clear; (*cheveux*) to go thin;
(*situation etc*) to become clearer; **s'~ la voix** to
clear one's throat
éclaircissement [eklɛʀsismɑ̃] *nm* clearing up,
clarification
éclairer [eklɛʀe] *vt* (*lieu*) to light (up); (*personne:
avec une lampe de poche etc*) to light the way for;
(*fig: instruire*) to enlighten; (*: rendre comprehensible*)
to shed light on ▷ *vi*: **~ mal/bien** to give a poor/
good light; **s'éclairer** *vi* (*phare, rue*) to light up;
(*situation etc*) to become clearer; **s'~ à la bougie/
l'électricité** to use candlelight/have electric
lighting
éclaireur, -euse [eklɛʀœʀ, -øz] *nm/f* (*scout*) (boy)
scout/(girl) guide ▷ *nm* (*Mil*) scout; **partir en ~**

to go off to reconnoitre

éclat [ekla] *nm* (*de bombe, de verre*) fragment; (*du soleil, d'une couleur etc*) brightness, brilliance; (*d'une cérémonie*) splendour; (*scandale*): **faire un ~** to cause a commotion; **action d'~** outstanding action; **voler en ~s** to shatter; **des ~s de verre** broken glass; flying glass; **~ de rire** burst *ou* roar of laughter; **~ de voix** shout

éclatant, e [eklatã, -ãt] *adj* brilliant, bright; (*succès*) resounding; (*revanche*) devastating

éclater [eklate] *vi* (*pneu*) to burst; (*bombe*) to explode; (*guerre, épidémie*) to break out; (*groupe, parti*) to break up; **~ de rire/en sanglots** to burst out laughing/sobbing

éclectique [eklɛktik] *adj* eclectic

éclipse [eklips(ə)] *nf* eclipse

éclipser [eklipse] *vt* to eclipse; **s'éclipser** *vi* to slip away

éclopé, e [eklope] *adj* lame

éclore [eklɔʀ] *vi* (*œuf*) to hatch; (*fleur*) to open (out)

éclosion [eklozjɔ̃] *nf* blossoming

écluse [eklyz] *nf* lock

éclusier [eklyzje] *nm* lock keeper

éco- [eko] *préfixe* eco-

écœurant, e [ekœʀã, -ãt] *adj* sickening; (*gâteau etc*) sickly

écœurement [ekœʀmã] *nm* disgust

écœurer [ekœʀe] *vt*: **~ qn** to make sb feel sick; (*fig: démoraliser*) to disgust sb

école [ekɔl] *nf* school; **aller à l'~** to go to school; **faire ~** to collect a following; **les grandes ~s** *prestige university-level colleges with competitive entrance examinations*; **~ maternelle** nursery school; *see note*; **~ primaire** primary (*Brit*) *ou* grade (*US*) school; **~ secondaire** secondary (*Brit*) *ou* high (*US*) school; **~ privée/publique/élementaire** private/state/elementary school; **~ de dessin/danse/musique** art/dancing/music school; **~ hôtelière** catering college; **~ normale (d'instituteurs) (ENI)** *primary school teachers' training college*; **~ normale supérieure (ENS)** *grande école for training secondary school teachers*; **~ de secrétariat** secretarial college

○ **ÉCOLE MATERNELLE**
○
○
○ Nursery school (kindergarten) (*l'école*
○ *maternelle*) is publicly funded in France and,
○ though not compulsory, is attended by most
○ children between the ages of three and six.
○ Statutory education begins with primary
○ (grade) school (*l'école primaire*) and is attended
○ by children between the ages of six and 10 or
○ 11.

écolier, -ière [ekɔlje, -jɛʀ] *nm/f* schoolboy/girl

écolo [ekolo] *nm/f* (*fam*) ecologist ▷ *adj* ecological

écologie [ekɔlɔʒi] *nf* ecology; (*sujet scolaire*) environmental studies *pl*

écologique [ekɔlɔʒik] *adj* ecological; environmental

écologiste [ekɔlɔʒist(ə)] *nm/f* ecologist; environmentalist

éconduire [ekɔ̃dɥiʀ] *vt* to dismiss

économat [ekɔnɔma] *nm* (*fonction*) bursarship (*Brit*), treasurership (*US*); (*bureau*) bursar's office (*Brit*), treasury (*US*)

économe [ekɔnɔm] *adj* thrifty ▷ *nm/f* (*de lycée etc*) bursar (*Brit*), treasurer (*US*)

économétrie [ekɔnɔmetʀi] *nf* econometrics *sg*

économie [ekɔnɔmi] *nf* (*vertu*) economy, thrift; (*gain: d'argent, de temps etc*) saving; (*science*) economics *sg*; (*situation économique*) economy; **économies** *nfpl* (*pécule*) savings; **faire des ~s** to save up; **une ~ de temps/d'argent** a saving in time/of money; **~ dirigée** planned economy; **~ de marché** market economy

économique [ekɔnɔmik] *adj* (*avantageux*) economical; (*Écon*) economic

économiquement [ekɔnɔmikmã] *adv* economically; **les ~ faibles** (*Admin*) the low-paid, people on low incomes

économiser [ekɔnɔmize] *vt, vi* to save

économiseur [ekɔnɔmizœʀ] *nm*: **~ d'écran** (*Inform*) screen saver

économiste [ekɔnɔmist(ə)] *nm/f* economist

écoper [ekɔpe] *vi* to bale out; (*fig*) to cop it; **~ (de)** *vt* to get

écorce [ekɔʀs(ə)] *nf* bark; (*de fruit*) peel

écorcer [ekɔʀse] *vt* to bark

écorché, e [ekɔʀʃe] *adj*: **~ vif** flayed alive ▷ *nm* cut-away drawing

écorcher [ekɔʀʃe] *vt* (*animal*) to skin; (*égratigner*) to graze; **~ une langue** to speak a language brokenly; **s'~ le genou** *etc* to scrape *ou* graze one's knee *etc*

écorchure [ekɔʀʃyʀ] *nf* graze

écorner [ekɔʀne] *vt* (*taureau*) to dehorn; (*livre*) to make dog-eared

écossais, e [ekɔsɛ, -ɛz] *adj* Scottish, Scots; (*whisky, confiture*) Scotch; (*écharpe, tissu*) tartan ▷ *nm* (*Ling*) Scots; (: *gaélique*) Gaelic; (*tissu*) tartan (cloth) ▷ *nm/f*: **Écossais, e** Scot, Scotsman/woman; **les É~** the Scots

Écosse [ekɔs] *nf*: **l'~** Scotland

écosser [ekɔse] *vt* to shell

écosystème [ekɔsistɛm] *nm* ecosystem

écot [eko] *nm*: **payer son ~** to pay one's share

écoulement [ekulmã] *nm* (*de faux billets*) circulation; (*de stock*) selling

écouler [ekule] *vt* to dispose of; **s'écouler** *vi* (*eau*) to flow (out); (*foule*) to drift away; (*jours, temps*) to pass (by)

écourter [ekuʀte] *vt* to curtail, cut short

écoute [ekut] *nf* (*Navig: cordage*) sheet; (*Radio, TV*): **temps d'~** (listening *ou* viewing) time; **heure de grande ~** peak listening *ou* viewing time; **prendre l'~** to tune in; **rester à l'~ (de)** to stay tuned in (to); **~s téléphoniques** phone tapping *sg*

écouter [ekute] *vt* to listen to

écouteur [ekutœʀ] *nm* (*Tél*) (additional)

earpiece; **écouteurs** nmpl (Radio) headphones, headset sg

écoutille [ekutij] nf hatch

écr. abr = **écrire**

écrabouiller [ekʀabuje] vt to squash, crush

écran [ekʀɑ̃] nm screen; (Inform) screen, VDU; ~ **de fumée/d'eau** curtain of smoke/water; **porter à l'~** (Ciné) to adapt for the screen; **le petit ~** television, the small screen

écrasant, e [ekʀazɑ̃, -ɑ̃t] adj overwhelming

écraser [ekʀaze] vt to crush; (piéton) to run over; (Inform) to overwrite; **se faire ~** to be run over; **écrase(-toi)!** shut up!; **s'~ (au sol)** to crash; **s'~ contre** to crash into

écrémé, e [ekʀeme] adj (lait) skimmed

écrémer [ekʀeme] vt to skim

écrevisse [ekʀəvis] nf crayfish inv

écrier [ekʀije]: **s'écrier** vi to exclaim

écrin [ekʀɛ̃] nm case, box

écrire [ekʀiʀ] vt, vi to write ▷ vi: **ça s'écrit comment?** how is it spelt?; **~ à qn que** to write and tell sb that; **s'écrire** vi to write to one another

écrit, e [ekʀi, -it] pp de **écrire** ▷ adj: **bien/mal ~** well/badly written ▷ nm document; (examen) written paper; **par ~** in writing

écriteau, x [ekʀito] nm notice, sign

écritoire [ekʀitwaʀ] nf writing case

écriture [ekʀityʀ] nf writing; (Comm) entry; **écritures** nfpl (Comm) accounts, books; **l'É~ (sainte), les É~s** the Scriptures

écrivain [ekʀivɛ̃] nm writer

écrivais etc [ekʀivɛ] vb voir **écrire**

écrou [ekʀu] nm nut

écrouer [ekʀue] vt to imprison; (provisoirement) to remand in custody

écroulé, e [ekʀule] adj (de fatigue) exhausted; (par un malheur) overwhelmed; **~ (de rire)** in stitches

écroulement [ekʀulmɑ̃] nm collapse

écrouler [ekʀule]: **s'écrouler** vi to collapse

écru, e [ekʀy] adj (toile) raw, unbleached; (couleur) off-white, écru

écu [eky] nm (bouclier) shield; (monnaie: ancienne) crown; (: de la CEE) ecu

écueil [ekœj] nm reef; (fig) pitfall; stumbling block

écuelle [ekɥɛl] nf bowl

éculé, e [ekyle] adj (chaussure) down-at-heel; (fig: péj) hackneyed

écume [ekym] nf foam; (Culin) scum; **~ de mer** meerschaum

écumer [ekyme] vt (Culin) to skim; (fig) to plunder ▷ vi (mer) to foam; (fig) to boil with rage

écumoire [ekymwaʀ] nf skimmer

écureuil [ekyʀœj] nm squirrel

écurie [ekyʀi] nf stable

écusson [ekysɔ̃] nm badge

écuyer, -ère [ekɥije, -ɛʀ] nm/f rider

eczéma [ɛgzema] nm eczema

éd. abr = **édition**

édam [edam] nm (fromage) edam

edelweiss [edɛlvajs] nm inv edelweiss

éden [edɛn] nm Eden

édenté, e [edɑ̃te] adj toothless

EDF sigle f (= Électricité de France) national electricity company

édifiant, e [edifjɑ̃, -ɑ̃t] adj edifying

édification [edifikasjɔ̃] nf (d'un bâtiment) building, erection

édifice [edifis] nm building, edifice

édifier [edifje] vt to build, erect; (fig) to edify

édiles [edil] nmpl city fathers

Édimbourg [edɛ̃buʀ] n Edinburgh

édit [edi] nm edict

édit. abr = **éditeur**

éditer [edite] vt (publier) to publish; (: disque) to produce; (préparer: texte, Inform) to edit

éditeur, -trice [editœʀ, -tʀis] nm/f publisher; editor; **~ de textes** (Inform) text editor

édition [edisjɔ̃] nf editing no pl; (série d'exemplaires) edition; (industrie du livre): **l'~** publishing; **~ sur écran** (Inform) screen editing

édito [edito] nm (fam: éditorial) editorial, leader

éditorial, -aux [editɔʀjal, -o] nm editorial, leader

éditorialiste [editɔʀjalist(ə)] nm/f editorial ou leader writer

édredon [edʀədɔ̃] nm eiderdown, comforter (US)

éducateur, -trice [edykatœʀ, -tʀis] nm/f teacher; **~ spécialisé** specialist teacher

éducatif, -ive [edykatif, -iv] adj educational

éducation [edykasjɔ̃] nf education; (familiale) upbringing; (manières) (good) manners pl; **bonne/mauvaise ~** good/bad upbringing; **sans ~** bad-mannered, ill-bred; **l'É~ (nationale)** ≈ the Department for Education; **~ permanente** continuing education; **~ physique** physical education

édulcorant [edylkɔʀɑ̃] nm sweetener

édulcorer [edylkɔʀe] vt to sweeten; (fig) to tone down

éduquer [edyke] vt to educate; (élever) to bring up; (faculté) to train; **bien/mal éduqué** well/badly brought up

EEG sigle m (= électroencéphalogramme) EEG

effacé, e [efase] adj (fig) retiring, unassuming

effacer [efase] vt to erase, rub out; (bande magnétique) to erase; (Inform: fichier, fiche) to delete; **s'effacer** vi (inscription etc) to wear off; (pour laisser passer) to step aside; **~ le ventre** to pull one's stomach in

effarant, e [efaʀɑ̃, -ɑ̃t] adj alarming

effaré, e [efaʀe] adj alarmed

effarement [efaʀmɑ̃] nm alarm

effarer [efaʀe] vt to alarm

effarouchement [efaʀuʃmɑ̃] nm alarm

effaroucher [efaʀuʃe] vt to frighten ou scare away; (personne) to alarm

effectif, -ive [efɛktif, -iv] adj real; effective ▷ nm (Mil) strength; (Scol) total number of pupils, size; **~s** numbers, strength sg; (Comm) manpower sg; **réduire l'~ de** to downsize

effectivement [efɛktivmɑ̃] adv effectively;

(*réellement*) actually, really; (*en effet*) indeed
effectuer [efɛktɥe] *vt* (*opération, mission*) to carry out; (*déplacement, trajet*) to make, complete; (*mouvement*) to execute, make; **s'effectuer** *vi* to be carried out
efféminé, e [efemine] *adj* effeminate
effervescence [efɛʀvesɑ̃s] *nf* (*fig*): **en ~** in a turmoil
effervescent, e [efɛʀvesɑ̃, -ɑ̃t] *adj* (*cachet, boisson*) effervescent; (*fig*) agitated, in a turmoil
effet [efɛ] *nm* (*résultat, artifice*) effect; (*impression*) impression; (*Comm*) bill; (*Jur: d'une loi, d'un jugement*): **avec ~ rétroactif** applied retrospectively; **effets** *nmpl* (*vêtements etc*) things; **~ de style/couleur/lumière** stylistic/colour/lighting effect; **~s de voix** dramatic effects with one's voice; **faire de l'~** (*médicament, menace*) to have an effect, be effective; **sous l'~ de** under the effect of; **donner de l'~ à une balle** (*Tennis*) to put some spin on a ball; **à cet ~** to that end; **en ~** *adv* indeed; **~ (de commerce)** bill of exchange; **~ de serre** greenhouse effect; **~s spéciaux** (*Ciné*) special effects
effeuiller [efœje] *vt* to remove the leaves (*ou* petals) from
efficace [efikas] *adj* (*personne*) efficient; (*action, médicament*) effective
efficacité [efikasite] *nf* efficiency; effectiveness
effigie [efiʒi] *nf* effigy; **brûler qn en ~** to burn an effigy of sb
effilé, e [efile] *adj* slender; (*pointe*) sharp; (*carrosserie*) streamlined
effiler [efile] *vt* (*cheveux*) to thin (out); (*tissu*) to fray
effilocher [efiloʃe]: **s'effilocher** *vi* to fray
efflanqué, e [eflɑ̃ke] *adj* emaciated
effleurement [eflœʀmɑ̃] *nm*: **touche à ~** touch-sensitive control *ou* key
effleurer [eflœʀe] *vt* to brush (against); (*sujet*) to touch upon; (*idée, pensée*): **~ qn** to cross sb's mind
effluves [eflyv] *nmpl* exhalation(s)
effondré, e [efɔ̃dʀe] *adj* (*abattu: par un malheur, échec*) overwhelmed
effondrement [efɔ̃dʀəmɑ̃] *nm* collapse
effondrer [efɔ̃dʀe]: **s'effondrer** *vi* to collapse
efforcer [efɔʀse]: **s'efforcer de** *vt*: **s'~ de faire** to try hard to do
effort [efɔʀ] *nm* effort; **faire un ~** to make an effort; **faire tous ses ~s** to try one's hardest; **faire l'~ de ...** to make the effort to ...; **sans ~** *adj* effortless ▷ *adv* effortlessly; **~ de mémoire** attempt to remember; **~ de volonté** effort of will
effraction [efʀaksjɔ̃] *nf* breaking-in; **s'introduire par ~ dans** to break into
effrangé, e [efʀɑ̃ʒe] *adj* fringed; (*effiloché*) frayed
effrayant, e [efʀɛjɑ̃, -ɑ̃t] *adj* frightening, fearsome; (*sens affaibli*) dreadful
effrayer [efʀeje] *vt* to frighten, scare; (*rebuter*) to put off; **s'effrayer (de)** *vi* to be frightened *ou* scared (by)
effréné, e [efʀene] *adj* wild
effritement [efʀitmɑ̃] *nm* crumbling; erosion; slackening off
effriter [efʀite]: **s'effriter** *vi* to crumble; (*monnaie*) to be eroded; (*valeurs*) to slacken off
effroi [efʀwɑ] *nm* terror, dread *no pl*
effronté, e [efʀɔ̃te] *adj* insolent
effrontément [efʀɔ̃temɑ̃] *adv* insolently
effronterie [efʀɔ̃tʀi] *nf* insolence
effroyable [efʀwajabl(ə)] *adj* horrifying, appalling
effusion [efyzjɔ̃] *nf* effusion; **sans ~ de sang** without bloodshed
égailler [egaje]: **s'égailler** *vi* to scatter, disperse
égal, e, -aux [egal, -o] *adj* (*identique, ayant les mêmes droits*) equal; (*plan: surface*) even, level; (*constant: vitesse*) steady; (*équitable*) even ▷ *nm/f* equal; **être ~ à** (*prix, nombre*) to be equal to; **ça m'est ~** it's all the same to me, it doesn't matter to me, I don't mind; **c'est ~, ...** all the same, ...; **sans ~** matchless, unequalled; **à l'~ de** (*comme*) just like; **d'~ à ~** as equals
également [egalmɑ̃] *adv* equally; evenly; steadily; (*aussi*) too, as well
égaler [egale] *vt* to equal
égalisateur, -trice [egalizatœʀ, -tʀis] *adj* (*Sport*): **but ~** equalizing goal, equalizer
égalisation [egalizasjɔ̃] *nf* (*Sport*) equalization
égaliser [egalize] *vt* (*sol, salaires*) to level (out); (*chances*) to equalize ▷ *vi* (*Sport*) to equalize
égalitaire [egalitɛʀ] *adj* egalitarian
égalitarisme [egalitaʀism(ə)] *nm* egalitarianism
égalité [egalite] *nf* equality; evenness; steadiness; (*Math*) identity; **être à ~ (de points)** to be level; **~ de droits** equality of rights; **~ d'humeur** evenness of temper
égard [egaʀ] *nm*: **~s** *nmpl* consideration *sg*; **à cet ~** in this respect; **à certains ~s/tous ~s** in certain respects/all respects; **eu ~ à** in view of; **par ~ pour** out of consideration for; **sans ~ pour** without regard for; **à l'~ de** *prép* towards; (*en ce qui concerne*) concerning, as regards
égaré, e [egaʀe] *adj* lost
égarement [egaʀmɑ̃] *nm* distraction; aberration
égarer [egaʀe] *vt* (*objet*) to mislay; (*moralement*) to lead astray; **s'égarer** *vi* to get lost, lose one's way; (*objet*) to go astray; (*fig: dans une discussion*) to wander
égayer [egeje] *vt* (*personne*) to amuse; (: *remonter*) to cheer up; (*récit, endroit*) to brighten up, liven up
Égée [eʒe] *adj*: **la mer ~** the Aegean (Sea)
égéen, ne [eʒeɛ̃, -ɛn] *adj* Aegean
égérie [eʒeʀi] *nf*: **l'~ de qn/qch** the brains behind sb/sth
égide [eʒid] *nf*: **sous l'~ de** under the aegis of
églantier [eglɑ̃tje] *nm* wild *ou* dog rose(-bush)
églantine [eglɑ̃tin] *nf* wild *ou* dog rose
églefin [egləfɛ̃] *nm* haddock

église [egliz] *nf* church
égocentrique [egɔsãtʀik] *adj* egocentric, self-centred
égocentrisme [egɔsãtʀism(ə)] *nm* egocentricity
égoïne [egɔin] *nf* handsaw
égoïsme [egɔism(ə)] *nm* selfishness, egoism
égoïste [egɔist(ə)] *adj* selfish, egoistic ▷ *nm/f* egoist
égoïstement [egɔistəmã] *adv* selfishly
égorger [egɔʀʒe] *vt* to cut the throat of
égosiller [egozije]: **s'égosiller** *vi* to shout o.s. hoarse
égotisme [egɔtism(ə)] *nm* egotism, egoism
égout [egu] *nm* sewer; **eaux d'~** sewage
égoutier [egutje] *nm* sewer worker
égoutter [egute] *vt* (*linge*) to wring out; (*vaisselle, fromage*) to drain ▷ *vi*, **s'égoutter** *vi* to drip
égouttoir [egutwaʀ] *nm* draining board; (*mobile*) draining rack
égratigner [egʀatiɲe] *vt* to scratch; **s'égratigner** *vi* to scratch o.s.
égratignure [egʀatiɲyʀ] *nf* scratch
égrener [egʀəne] *vt*: **~ une grappe, ~ des raisins** to pick grapes off a bunch; **s'égrener** *vi* (*fig: heures etc*) to pass by; (: *notes*) to chime out
égrillard, e [egʀijaʀ, -aʀd(ə)] *adj* ribald, bawdy
Égypte [eʒipt] *nf*: **l'~** Egypt
égyptien, ne [eʒipsjɛ̃, -ɛn] *adj* Egyptian ▷ *nm/f*: **Égyptien, ne** Egyptian
égyptologue [eʒiptɔlɔg] *nm/f* Egyptologist
eh [e] *excl* hey!; **eh bien** well
éhonté, e [eõte] *adj* shameless, brazen (*Brit*)
éjaculation [eʒakylɑsjõ] *nf* ejaculation
éjaculer [eʒakyle] *vi* to ejaculate
éjectable [eʒɛktabl(ə)] *adj*: **siège ~** ejector seat
éjecter [eʒɛkte] *vt* (*Tech*) to eject; (*fam*) to kick *ou* chuck out
éjection [eʒɛksjõ] *nf* ejection
élaboration [elabɔʀɑsjõ] *nf* elaboration
élaboré, e [elabɔʀe] *adj* (*complexe*) elaborate
élaborer [elabɔʀe] *vt* to elaborate; (*projet, stratégie*) to work out; (*rapport*) to draft
élagage [elagaʒ] *nm* pruning
élaguer [elage] *vt* to prune
élan [elã] *nm* (*Zool*) elk, moose; (*Sport: avant le saut*) run up; (*de véhicule*) momentum; (*fig: de tendresse etc*) surge; **prendre son ~/de l'~** to take a run up/gather speed; **perdre son ~** to lose one's momentum
élancé, e [elãse] *adj* slender
élancement [elãsmã] *nm* shooting pain
élancer [elãse]: **s'élancer** *vi* to dash, hurl o.s.; (*fig: arbre, clocher*) to soar (upwards)
élargir [elaʀʒiʀ] *vt* to widen; (*vêtement*) to let out; (*Jur*) to release; **s'élargir** *vi* to widen; (*vêtement*) to stretch
élargissement [elaʀʒismã] *nm* widening; letting out
élasticité [elastisite] *nf* (*aussi Écon*) elasticity; **~ de l'offre/de la demande** flexibility of supply/demand

élastique [elastik] *adj* elastic ▷ *nm* (*de bureau*) rubber band; (*pour la couture*) elastic *no pl*
élastomère [elastɔmɛʀ] *nm* elastomer
Elbe [ɛlb] *nf*: **l'île d'~** (the Island of) Elba; (*fleuve*): **l'~** the Elbe
eldorado [ɛldɔʀado] *nm* Eldorado
électeur, -trice [elɛktœʀ, -tʀis] *nm/f* elector, voter
électif, -ive [elɛktif, -iv] *adj* elective
élection [elɛksjõ] *nf* election; **élections** *nfpl* (*Pol*) election(s); **sa terre/patrie d'~** the land/country of one's choice; **~ partielle** ≈ by-election; **~s législatives/présidentielles** general/presidential election *sg*; *see note*

électoral, e, -aux [elɛktɔʀal, -o] *adj* electoral, election *cpd*
électoralisme [elɛktɔʀalism(ə)] *nm* electioneering
électorat [elɛktɔʀa] *nm* electorate
électricien, ne [elɛktʀisjɛ̃, -ɛn] *nm/f* electrician
électricité [elɛktʀisite] *nf* electricity; **allumer/éteindre l'~** to put on/off the light; **~ statique** static electricity
électrification [elɛktʀifikɑsjõ] *nf* (*Rail*) electrification; (*d'un village etc*) laying on of electricity
électrifier [elɛktʀifje] *vt* (*Rail*) to electrify
électrique [elɛktʀik] *adj* electric(al)
électriser [elɛktʀize] *vt* to electrify
électro... [elɛktʀɔ] *préfixe* electro...
électro-aimant [elɛktʀɔemã] *nm* electromagnet
électrocardiogramme [elɛktʀɔkaʀdjɔgʀam] *nm* electrocardiogram
électrocardiographe [elɛktʀɔkaʀdjɔgʀaf] *nm* electrocardiograph
électrochoc [elɛktʀɔʃɔk] *nm* electric shock treatment
électrocuter [elɛktʀɔkyte] *vt* to electrocute
électrocution [elɛktʀɔkysjõ] *nf* electrocution
électrode [elɛktʀɔd] *nf* electrode
électro-encéphalogramme [elɛktʀɔãsefalɔgʀam] *nm* electroencephalogram
électrogène [elɛktʀɔʒɛn] *adj*: **groupe ~** generating set
électrolyse [elɛktʀɔliz] *nf* electrolysis *sg*
électromagnétique [elɛktʀɔmaɲetik] *adj* electromagnetic
électroménager [elɛktʀɔmenaʒe] *adj*:

appareils ~s domestic (electrical) appliances
▷ *nm*: **l'**~ household appliances
électron [elɛktrɔ̃] *nm* electron
électronicien, ne [elɛktrɔnisjɛ̃, -ɛn] *nm/f*
electronics (Brit) *ou* electrical (US) engineer
électronique [elɛktrɔnik] *adj* electronic ▷ *nf*
(*science*) electronics *sg*
électronucléaire [elɛktrɔnykleɛr] *adj* nuclear
power *cpd* ▷ *nm*: **l'**~ nuclear power
électrophone [elɛktrɔfɔn] *nm* record player
électrostatique [elɛktrɔstatik] *adj*
electrostatic ▷ *nf* electrostatics *sg*
élégamment [elegamɑ̃] *adv* elegantly
élégance [elegɑ̃s] *nf* elegance
élégant, e [elegɑ̃, -ɑ̃t] *adj* elegant; (*solution*)
neat, elegant; (*attitude, procédé*) courteous,
civilized
élément [elemɑ̃] *nm* element; (*pièce*)
component, part; **éléments** *nmpl* elements
élémentaire [elemɑ̃tɛr] *adj* elementary;
(*Chimie*) elemental
éléphant [elefɑ̃] *nm* elephant; ~ **de mer**
elephant seal
éléphanteau, x [elefɑ̃to] *nm* baby elephant
éléphantesque [elefɑ̃tɛsk(ə)] *adj* elephantine
élevage [ɛlvaʒ] *nm* breeding; (*de bovins*) cattle
breeding *ou* rearing; (*ferme*) cattle farm
élévateur [elevatœr] *nm* elevator
élévation [elevasjɔ̃] *nf* (*gén*) elevation; (*voir
élever*) raising; (*voir s'élever*) rise
élevé, e [ɛlve] *adj* (*prix, sommet*) high; (*fig: noble*)
elevated; **bien/mal** ~ well-/ill-mannered
élève [elɛv] *nm/f* pupil; ~ **infirmière** student
nurse
élever [ɛlve] *vt* (*enfant*) to bring up, raise; (*bétail,
volaille*) to breed; (*abeilles*) to keep; (*hausser: taux,
niveau*) to raise; (*fig: âme, esprit*) to elevate; (*édifier:
monument*) to put up, erect; **s'élever** *vi* (*avion,
alpiniste*) to go up; (*niveau, température, aussi: cri etc*)
to rise; (*survenir: difficultés*) to arise; **s'~ à** (*frais,
dégâts*) to amount to, add up to; **s'~ contre** to
rise up against; ~ **une protestation/critique**
to raise a protest/make a criticism; ~ **qn au
rang de** to raise *ou* elevate sb to the rank of; ~
un nombre au carré/au cube to square/cube a
number
éleveur, -euse [ɛlvœr, -øz] *nm/f* stock breeder
elfe [ɛlf(ə)] *nm* elf
élidé, e [elide] *adj* elided
élider [elide] *vt* to elide
éligibilité [eliʒibilite] *nf* eligibility
éligible [eliʒibl(ə)] *adj* eligible
élimé, e [elime] *adj* worn (thin), threadbare
élimination [eliminasjɔ̃] *nf* elimination
éliminatoire [eliminatwar] *adj* eliminatory;
(*Sport*) disqualifying ▷ *nf* (*Sport*) heat
éliminer [elimine] *vt* to eliminate
élire [elir] *vt* to elect; ~ **domicile à** to take up
residence in *ou* at
élision [elizjɔ̃] *nf* elision
élite [elit] *nf* elite; **tireur d'**~ crack rifleman;
chercheur d'~ top-notch researcher

élitisme [elitism(ə)] *nm* elitism
élitiste [elitist(ə)] *adj* elitist
élixir [eliksir] *nm* elixir
elle [ɛl] *pron* (*sujet*) she; (: *chose*) it; (*complément*)
her; it; ~**s** (*sujet*) they; (*complément*) them;
~**-même** herself; itself; ~**s-mêmes** themselves;
voir **il**
ellipse [elips(ə)] *nf* ellipse; (*Ling*) ellipsis *sg*
elliptique [eliptik] *adj* elliptical
élocution [elɔkysjɔ̃] *nf* delivery; **défaut d'**~
speech impediment
éloge [elɔʒ] *nm* praise *gen no pl*; **faire l'**~ **de** to
praise
élogieusement [elɔʒjøzmɑ̃] *adv* very
favourably
élogieux, -euse [elɔʒjø, -øz] *adj* laudatory, full
of praise
éloigné, e [elwaɲe] *adj* distant, far-off
éloignement [elwaɲmɑ̃] *nm* removal; putting
off; estrangement; (*fig: distance*) distance
éloigner [elwaɲe] *vt* (*objet*): ~ **qch (de)** to move
ou take sth away (from); (*personne*): ~ **qn (de)** to
take sb away *ou* remove sb (from); (*échéance*) to
put off, postpone; (*soupçons, danger*) to ward off;
s'éloigner (de) *vi* (*personne*) to go away (from);
(*véhicule*) to move away (from); (*affectivement*) to
become estranged (from)
élongation [elɔ̃gasjɔ̃] *nf* strained muscle
éloquence [elɔkɑ̃s] *nf* eloquence
éloquent, e [elɔkɑ̃, -ɑ̃t] *adj* eloquent
élu, e [ely] *pp de* **élire** ▷ *nm/f* (*Pol*) elected
representative
élucider [elyside] *vt* to elucidate
élucubrations [elykybrasjɔ̃] *nfpl* wild
imaginings
éluder [elyde] *vt* to evade
élus *etc* [ely] *vb voir* **élire**
élusif, -ive [elyzif, -iv] *adj* elusive
Élysée [elize] *nm*: (**le palais de**) **l'**~ the Élysée
palace; *see note*; **les Champs ~s** the Champs
Élysées

L'ÉLYSÉE

The *palais de l'Élysée*, situated in the heart of
Paris just off the Champs Élysées, is the
official residence of the French President.
Built in the eighteenth century, it has
performed its present function since 1876.
A shorter form of its name, "l'Élysée" is
frequently used to refer to the presidency
itself.

émacié, e [emasje] *adj* emaciated
émail, -aux [emaj, -o] *nm* enamel
e-mail [imɛl] *nm* email; **envoyer qch par** ~ to
email sth
émaillé, e [emaje] *adj* enamelled; (*fig*): ~ **de**
dotted with
émailler [emaje] *vt* to enamel
émanation [emanasjɔ̃] *nf* emanation
émancipation [emɑ̃sipasjɔ̃] *nf* emancipation

émancipé, e [emãsipe] *adj* emancipated

émanciper [emãsipe] *vt* to emancipate; **s'émanciper** *(fig)* to become emancipated *ou* liberated

émaner [emane]: **~ de** *vt* to emanate from; *(Admin)* to proceed from

émarger [emaʀʒe] *vt* to sign; **~ de 1000 euros à un budget** to receive 1000 euros out of a budget

émasculer [emaskyle] *vt* to emasculate

emballage [ãbalaʒ] *nm* wrapping; packing; *(papier)* wrapping; *(carton)* packaging

emballer [ãbale] *vt* to wrap (up); *(dans un carton)* to pack (up); *(fig: fam)* to thrill (to bits); **s'emballer** *vi (moteur)* to race; *(cheval)* to bolt; *(fig: personne)* to get carried away

emballeur, -euse [ãbalœʀ, -øz] *nm/f* packer

embarcadère [ãbaʀkadɛʀ] *nm* landing stage *(Brit)*, pier

embarcation [ãbaʀkasjɔ̃] *nf* (small) boat, (small) craft *inv*

embardée [ãbaʀde] *nf* swerve; **faire une ~** to swerve

embargo [ãbaʀgo] *nm* embargo; **mettre l'~ sur** to put an embargo on, embargo

embarquement [ãbaʀkəmã] *nm* embarkation; loading; boarding

embarquer [ãbaʀke] *vt (personne)* to embark; *(marchandise)* to load; *(fam)* to cart off; *(: arrêter)* to nick ▷ *vi (passager)* to board; *(Navig)* to ship water; **s'embarquer** *vi* to board; **s'~ dans** *(affaire, aventure)* to embark upon

embarras [ãbaʀa] *nm (obstacle)* hindrance; *(confusion)* embarrassment; *(ennuis)*: **être dans l'~** to be in a predicament *ou* an awkward position; *(gêne financière)* to be in difficulties; **~ gastrique** stomach upset

embarrassant, e [ãbaʀasã, -ãt] *adj* cumbersome; embarrassing; awkward

embarrassé, e [ãbaʀase] *adj (encombré)* encumbered; *(gêné)* embarrassed; *(explications etc)* awkward

embarrasser [ãbaʀase] *vt (encombrer)* to clutter (up); *(gêner)* to hinder, hamper; *(fig)* to cause embarrassment to; to put in an awkward position; **s'embarrasser de** *vi* to burden o.s. with

embauche [ãboʃ] *nf* hiring; **bureau d'~** labour office

embaucher [ãboʃe] *vt* to take on, hire; **s'embaucher comme** *vi* to get (o.s.) a job as

embauchoir [ãboʃwaʀ] *nm* shoetree

embaumer [ãbome] *vt* to embalm; *(parfumer)* to fill with its fragrance; **~ la lavande** to be fragrant with (the scent of) lavender

embellie [ãbeli] *nf* bright spell, brighter period

embellir [ãbeliʀ] *vt* to make more attractive; *(une histoire)* to embellish ▷ *vi* to grow lovelier *ou* more attractive

embellissement [ãbelismã] *nm* embellishment

embêtant, e [ãbɛtã, -ãt] *adj* annoying

embêtement [ãbɛtmã] *nm* problem, difficulty; **embêtements** *nmpl* trouble *sg*

embêter [ãbete] *vt* to bother; **s'embêter** *vi (s'ennuyer)* to be bored; **ça m'embête** it bothers me; **il ne s'embête pas!** *(ironique)* he does all right for himself!

emblée [ãble]: **d'~** *adv* straightaway

emblème [ãblɛm] *nm* emblem

embobiner [ãbɔbine] *vt (enjôler)*: **~ qn** to get round sb

emboîtable [ãbwatabl(ə)] *adj* interlocking

emboîter [ãbwate] *vt* to fit together; **s'emboîter dans** to fit into; **s'~ (l'un dans l'autre)** to fit together; **~ le pas à qn** to follow in sb's footsteps

embolie [ãbɔli] *nf* embolism

embonpoint [ãbɔ̃pwɛ̃] *nm* stoutness *(Brit)*, corpulence; **prendre de l'~** to grow stout *(Brit) ou* corpulent

embouché, e [ãbuʃe] *adj*: **mal ~** foul-mouthed

embouchure [ãbuʃyʀ] *nf (Géo)* mouth; *(Mus)* mouthpiece

embourber [ãbuʀbe]: **s'embourber** *vi* to get stuck in the mud; *(fig)*: **s'~ dans** to sink into

embourgeoiser [ãbuʀʒwaze]: **s'embourgeoiser** *vi* to adopt a middle-class outlook

embout [ãbu] *nm (de canne)* tip; *(de tuyau)* nozzle

embouteillage [ãbuteJaʒ] *nm* traffic jam, (traffic) holdup *(Brit)*

embouteiller [ãbuteje] *vt (véhicules etc)* to block

emboutir [ãbutiʀ] *vt (Tech)* to stamp; *(heurter)* to crash into, ram

embranchement [ãbʀãʃmã] *nm (routier)* junction; *(classification)* branch

embrancher [ãbʀãʃe] *vt (tuyaux)* to join; **~ qch sur** to join sth to

embraser [ãbʀaze]: **s'embraser** *vi* to flare up

embrassade [ãbʀasad] *nf (gén pl)* hugging and kissing *no pl*

embrasse [ãbʀas] *nf (de rideau)* tie-back, loop

embrasser [ãbʀase] *vt* to kiss; *(sujet, période)* to embrace, encompass; *(carrière)* to embark on; *(métier)* to go in for, take up; **~ du regard** to take in (with eyes); **s'embrasser** *vi* to kiss (each other)

embrasure [ãbʀazyʀ] *nf*: **dans l'~ de la porte** in the door(way)

embrayage [ãbʀɛjaʒ] *nm* clutch

embrayer [ãbʀeje] *vi (Auto)* to let in the clutch ▷ *vt (fig: affaire)* to set in motion; **~ sur qch** to begin on sth

embrigader [ãbʀigade] *vt* to recruit

embrocher [ãbʀɔʃe] *vt* to (put on a) spit *(ou* skewer)

embrouillamini [ãbʀujamini] *nm (fam)* muddle

embrouillé, e [ãbʀuje] *adj (affaire)* confused, muddled

embrouiller [ãbʀuje] *vt (fils)* to tangle (up); *(fiches, idées, personne)* to muddle up; **s'embrouiller** *vi* to get in a muddle

embroussaillé, e [ãbʀusaje] *adj* overgrown,

scrubby; (*cheveux*) bushy, shaggy

embruns [ɑ̃bʀœ̃] *nmpl* sea spray *sg*

embryologie [ɑ̃bʀijɔlɔʒi] *nf* embryology

embryon [ɑ̃bʀijɔ̃] *nm* embryo

embryonnaire [ɑ̃bʀijɔnɛʀ] *adj* embryonic

embûches [ɑ̃byʃ] *nfpl* pitfalls, traps

embué, e [ɑ̃bɥe] *adj* misted up; **yeux ~s de larmes** eyes misty with tears

embuscade [ɑ̃byskad] *nf* ambush; **tendre une ~ à** to lay an ambush for

embusqué, e [ɑ̃byske] *adj* in ambush ▷ *nm* (*péj*) shirker, skiver (*Brit*)

embusquer [ɑ̃byske]: **s'embusquer** *vi* to take up position (for an ambush)

éméché, e [emeʃe] *adj* tipsy, merry

émeraude [ɛmʀod] *nf* emerald ▷ *adj inv* emerald-green

émergence [emɛʀʒɑ̃s] *nf* (*fig*) emergence

émerger [emɛʀʒe] *vi* to emerge; (*faire saillie, aussi fig*) to stand out

émeri [ɛmʀi] *nm*: **toile** *ou* **papier ~** emery paper

émérite [emeʀit] *adj* highly skilled

émerveillement [emɛʀvɛjmɑ̃] *nm* wonderment

émerveiller [emɛʀveje] *vt* to fill with wonder; **s'émerveiller de** *vi* to marvel at

émet *etc* [emɛ] *vb voir* **émettre**

émétique [emetik] *nm* emetic

émetteur, -trice [emetœʀ, -tʀis] *adj* transmitting; (**poste**) ~ transmitter

émetteur-récepteur [emetœʀʀesɛptœʀ] (*pl* **émetteurs-récepteurs**) *nm* transceiver

émettre [emɛtʀ(ə)] *vt* (*son, lumière*) to give out, emit; (*message etc: Radio*) to transmit; (*billet, timbre, emprunt, chèque*) to issue; (*hypothèse, avis*) to voice, put forward; (*vœu*) to express ▷ *vi*: **~ sur ondes courtes** to broadcast on short wave

émeus *etc* [emø] *vb voir* **émouvoir**

émeute [emøt] *nf* riot

émeutier, -ière [emøtje, -jɛʀ] *nm/f* rioter

émeuve *etc* [emœv] *vb voir* **émouvoir**

émietter [emjete] *vt* (*pain, terre*) to crumble; (*fig*) to split up, disperse; **s'émietter** *vi* (*pain, terre*) to crumble

émigrant, e [emigʀɑ̃, -ɑ̃t] *nm/f* emigrant

émigration [emigʀasjɔ̃] *nf* emigration

émigré, e [emigʀe] *nm/f* expatriate

émigrer [emigʀe] *vi* to emigrate

émincer [emɛ̃se] *vt* (*Culin*) to slice thinly

éminemment [eminamɑ̃] *adv* eminently

éminence [eminɑ̃s] *nf* distinction; (*colline*) knoll, hill; **Son É~** His Eminence; **~ grise** éminence grise

éminent, e [eminɑ̃, -ɑ̃t] *adj* distinguished

émir [emiʀ] *nm* emir

émirat [emiʀa] *nm* emirate; **les É~s arabes unis (EAU)** the United Arab Emirates (UAE)

émis, e [emi, -iz] *pp de* **émettre**

émissaire [emisɛʀ] *nm* emissary

émission [emisjɔ̃] *nf* (*voir* émettre) emission; transmission; issue; (*Radio, TV*) programme,

broadcast

émit *etc* [emi] *vb voir* **émettre**

emmagasinage [ɑ̃magazinaʒ] *nm* storage; storing away

emmagasiner [ɑ̃magazine] *vt* to (put into) store; (*fig*) to store up

emmailloter [ɑ̃majɔte] *vt* to wrap up

emmanchure [ɑ̃mɑ̃ʃyʀ] *nf* armhole

emmêlement [ɑ̃mɛlmɑ̃] *nm* (*état*) tangle

emmêler [ɑ̃mele] *vt* to tangle (up); (*fig*) to muddle up; **s'emmêler** *vi* to get into a tangle

emménagement [ɑ̃menaʒmɑ̃] *nm* settling in

emménager [ɑ̃menaʒe] *vi* to move in; **~ dans** to move into

emmener [ɑ̃mne] *vt* to take (with one); (*comme otage, capture*) to take away; **~ qn au concert** to take sb to a concert

emmental, emmenthal [emɛ̃tal] *nm* (*fromage*) Emmenthal

emmerder [ɑ̃mɛʀde] (*fam!*) *vt* to bug, bother; **s'emmerder** *vi* (*s'ennuyer*) to be bored stiff; **je t'emmerde!** to hell with you!

emmitoufler [ɑ̃mitufle] *vt* to wrap up (warmly); **s'emmitoufler** to wrap (o.s.) up (warmly)

emmurer [ɑ̃myʀe] *vt* to wall up, immure

émoi [emwa] *nm* (*agitation, effervescence*) commotion; (*trouble*) agitation; **en ~** (*sens*) excited, stirred

émollient, e [emɔljɑ̃, -ɑ̃t] *adj* (*Méd*) emollient

émoluments [emɔlymɑ̃] *nmpl* remuneration *sg*, fee *sg*

émonder [emɔ̃de] *vt* (*arbre etc*) to prune; (*amande etc*) to blanch

émoticone [emɔticon] *nm* (*Inform*) smiley

émotif, -ive [emɔtif, -iv] *adj* emotional

émotion [emosjɔ̃] *nf* emotion; **avoir des ~s** (*fig*) to get a fright; **donner des ~s à** to give a fright to; **sans ~** without emotion, coldly

émotionnant, e [emosjɔnɑ̃, -ɑ̃t] *adj* upsetting

émotionnel, le [emosjɔnɛl] *adj* emotional

émotionner [emosjɔne] *vt* to upset

émoulu, e [emuly] *adj*: **frais ~ de** fresh from, just out of

émoussé, e [emuse] *adj* blunt

émousser [emuse] *vt* to blunt; (*fig*) to dull

émoustiller [emustije] *vt* to titillate, arouse

émouvant, e [emuvɑ̃, -ɑ̃t] *adj* moving

émouvoir [emuvwaʀ] *vt* (*troubler*) to stir, affect; (*toucher, attendrir*) to move; (*indigner*) to rouse; (*effrayer*) to disturb, worry; **s'émouvoir** *vi* to be affected; to be moved; to be roused; to be disturbed *ou* worried

empailler [ɑ̃paje] *vt* to stuff

empailleur, -euse [ɑ̃pajœʀ, -øz] *nm/f* (*d'animaux*) taxidermist

empaler [ɑ̃pale] *vt* to impale

empaquetage [ɑ̃paktaʒ] *nm* packing, packaging

empaqueter [ɑ̃pakte] *vt* to pack up

emparer [ɑ̃paʀe]: **s'emparer de** *vt* (*objet*) to seize, grab; (*comme otage, Mil*) to seize; (*peur etc*) to take hold of

empâter [ɑ̃pɑte]: **s'empâter** vi to thicken out

empattement [ɑ̃patmɑ̃] nm (Auto) wheelbase; (Typo) serif

empêché, e [ɑ̃peʃe] adj detained

empêchement [ɑ̃pɛʃmɑ̃] nm (unexpected) obstacle, hitch

empêcher [ɑ̃peʃe] vt to prevent; ~ **qn de faire** to prevent ou stop sb (from) doing; ~ **que qch (n')arrive/qn (ne) fasse** to prevent sth from happening/sb from doing; **il n'empêche que** nevertheless, be that as it may; **il n'a pas pu s'~ de rire** he couldn't help laughing

empêcheur [ɑ̃peʃœʀ] nm: ~ **de danser en rond** spoilsport, killjoy (Brit)

empeigne [ɑ̃pɛɲ] nf upper (of shoe)

empennage [ɑ̃pɛnaʒ] nm (Aviat) tailplane

empereur [ɑ̃pʀœʀ] nm emperor

empesé, e [ɑ̃pəze] adj (fig) stiff, starchy

empeser [ɑ̃pəze] vt to starch

empester [ɑ̃pɛste] vt (lieu) to stink out ▷ vi to stink, reek; ~ **le tabac/le vin** to stink ou reek of tobacco/wine

empêtrer [ɑ̃petʀe] vt: **s'empêtrer dans** (fils etc, aussi fig) to get tangled up in

emphase [ɑ̃faz] nf pomposity, bombast; **avec ~** pompously

emphatique [ɑ̃fatik] adj emphatic

empiècement [ɑ̃pjɛsmɑ̃] nm (Couture) yoke

empierrer [ɑ̃pjeʀe] vt (route) to metal

empiéter [ɑ̃pjete]: ~ **sur** vt to encroach upon

empiffrer [ɑ̃pifʀe]: **s'empiffrer** vi (péj) to stuff o.s.

empiler [ɑ̃pile] vt to pile (up), stack (up); **s'empiler** vi to pile up

empire [ɑ̃piʀ] nm empire; (fig) influence; **style E~** Empire style; **sous l'~ de** in the grip of

empirer [ɑ̃piʀe] vi to worsen, deteriorate

empirique [ɑ̃piʀik] adj empirical

empirisme [ɑ̃piʀism(ə)] nm empiricism

emplacement [ɑ̃plasmɑ̃] nm site; **sur l'~ de** on the site of

emplâtre [ɑ̃plɑtʀ(ə)] nm plaster; (fam) twit

emplette [ɑ̃plɛt] nf: **faire l'~ de** to purchase; **emplettes** shopping sg; **faire des ~s** to go shopping

emplir [ɑ̃pliʀ] vt to fill; **s'emplir (de)** vi to fill (with)

emploi [ɑ̃plwa] nm use; (Comm, Écon): **l'~** employment; (poste) job, situation; **d'~ facile** easy to use; **le plein ~** full employment; ~ **du temps** timetable, schedule

emploie etc [ɑ̃plwa] vb voir **employer**

employé, e [ɑ̃plwaje] nm/f employee; ~ **de bureau/banque** office/bank employee ou clerk; ~ **de maison** domestic (servant)

employer [ɑ̃plwaje] vt (outil, moyen, méthode, mot) to use; (ouvrier, main-d'œuvre) to employ; **s'~ à qch/à faire** to apply ou devote o.s. to sth/to doing

employeur, -euse [ɑ̃plwajœʀ, -øz] nm/f employer

empocher [ɑ̃pɔʃe] vt to pocket

empoignade [ɑ̃pwaɲad] nf row, set-to

empoigne [ɑ̃pwaɲ] nf: **foire d'~** free-for-all

empoigner [ɑ̃pwaɲe] vt to grab; **s'empoigner** vi (fig) to have a row ou set-to

empois [ɑ̃pwa] nm starch

empoisonnement [ɑ̃pwazɔnmɑ̃] nm poisoning; (fam: ennui) annoyance, irritation

empoisonner [ɑ̃pwazɔne] vt to poison; (empester: air, pièce) to stink out; (fam): ~ **qn** to drive sb mad; **s'empoisonner** vi to poison o.s.; ~ **l'atmosphère** (aussi fig) to poison the atmosphere; (aussi: **il nous empoisonne l'existence**) he's the bane of our life

empoissonner [ɑ̃pwasɔne] vt (étang, rivière) to stock with fish

emporté, e [ɑ̃pɔʀte] adj (personne, caractère) fiery

emportement [ɑ̃pɔʀtəmɑ̃] nm fit of rage, anger no pl

emporte-pièce [ɑ̃pɔʀtəpjɛs] nm inv (Tech) punch; **à l'~** adj (fig) incisive

emporter [ɑ̃pɔʀte] vt to take (with one); (en dérobant ou enlevant, emmener: blessés, voyageurs) to take away; (entraîner) to carry away ou along; (arracher) to tear off; (rivière, vent) to carry away; (Mil: position) to take; (avantage, approbation) to win; **s'emporter** vi (de colère) to fly into a rage, lose one's temper; **la maladie qui l'a emporté** the illness which caused his death; **l'~** to gain victory; **l'~ (sur)** to get the upper hand (of); (méthode etc) to prevail (over); **boissons à ~** take-away drinks

empoté, e [ɑ̃pɔte] adj (maladroit) clumsy

empourpré, e [ɑ̃puʀpʀe] adj crimson

empreint, e [ɑ̃pʀɛ̃, -ɛ̃t] adj: ~ **de** marked with; tinged with ▷ nf (de pied, main) print; (fig) stamp, mark; ~**e (digitale)** fingerprint; ~**e écologique** carbon footprint

empressé, e [ɑ̃pʀese] adj attentive; (péj) overanxious to please, overattentive

empressement [ɑ̃pʀɛsmɑ̃] nm eagerness

empresser [ɑ̃pʀese]: **s'empresser** vi: **s'~ auprès de qn** to surround sb with attentions; **s'~ de faire** to hasten to do

emprise [ɑ̃pʀiz] nf hold, ascendancy; **sous l'~ de** under the influence of

emprisonnement [ɑ̃pʀizɔnmɑ̃] nm imprisonment

emprisonner [ɑ̃pʀizɔne] vt to imprison, jail

emprunt [ɑ̃pʀœ̃] nm borrowing no pl, loan (from debtor's point of view); (Ling etc) borrowing; **nom d'~** assumed name; ~ **d'État** government ou state loan; ~ **public à 5%** 5% public loan

emprunté, e [ɑ̃pʀœ̃te] adj (fig) ill-at-ease, awkward

emprunter [ɑ̃pʀœ̃te] vt to borrow; (itinéraire) to take, follow; (style, manière) to adopt, assume

emprunteur, -euse [ɑ̃pʀœ̃tœʀ, -øz] nm/f borrower

empuantir [ɑ̃pɥɑ̃tiʀ] vt to stink out

EMT sigle f (= éducation manuelle et technique) handwork as a school subject

ému, e [emy] *pp de* **émouvoir** ▷ *adj* excited; touched; moved

émulation [emylɑsjɔ̃] *nf* emulation

émule [emyl] *nm/f* imitator

émulsion [emylsjɔ̃] *nf* emulsion; (*cosmétique*) (water-based) lotion

émut *etc* [emy] *vb voir* **émouvoir**

EN *sigle f* = **Éducation nationale**; *voir* **éducation**

 MOT-CLÉ

en [ɑ̃] *prép* **1** (*endroit, pays*) in; (*direction*) to; **habiter en France/ville** to live in France/town; **aller en France/ville** to go to France/town **2** (*moment, temps*) in; **en été/juin** in summer/ June; **en 3 jours/20 ans** in 3 days/20 years **3** (*moyen*) by; **en avion/taxi** by plane/taxi **4** (*composition*) made of; **c'est en verre/coton/ laine** it's (made of) glass/cotton/wool; **en metal/plastique** made of metal/plastic; **un collier en argent** a silver necklace; **en deux volumes/une pièce** in two volumes/one piece **5** (*description, état*): **une femme (habillée) en rouge** a woman (dressed) in red; **peindre qch en rouge** to paint sth red; **en T/étoile** T-/star-shaped; **en chemise/chaussettes** in one's shirt sleeves/socks; **en soldat** as a soldier; **en civil** in civilian clothes; **cassé en plusieurs morceaux** broken into several pieces; **en réparation** being repaired, under repair; **en vacances** on holiday; **en bonne santé** healthy, in good health; **en deuil** in mourning; **le même en plus grand** the same but *ou* only bigger **6** (*avec gérondif*) while; on; **en dormant** while sleeping, as one sleeps; **en sortant** on going out, as he *etc* went out; **sortir en courant** to run out; **en apprenant la nouvelle, il s'est évanoui** he fainted at the news *ou* when he heard the news **7** (*matière*): **fort en math** good at maths; **expert en** expert in **8** (*conformité*): **en tant que** as; **en bon politicien, il …** good politician that he is, he …, like a good politician. true politician, he …; **je te parle en ami** I'm talking to you as a friend ▷ *pron* **1** (*indéfini*): **j'en ai/veux** I have/want some; **en as-tu?** have you got any?; **il n'y en a pas** there isn't *ou* aren't any; **je n'en veux pas** I don't want any; **j'en ai deux** I've got two; **combien y en a-t-il?** how many (of them) are there?; **j'en ai assez** I've got enough (of it *ou* them); (*j'en ai marre*) I've had enough; **où en étais-je?** where was I? **2** (*provenance*) from there; **j'en viens** I've come from there **3** (*cause*): **il en est malade/perd le sommeil** he is ill/can't sleep because of it **4** (*de la part de*): **elle en est aimée** she is loved by him (*ou* them *etc*) **5** (*complément de nom, d'adjectif, de verbe*): **j'en connais les dangers** I know its *ou* the dangers;

j'en suis fier/ai besoin I am proud of it/need it; **il en est ainsi** *ou* **de même pour moi** it's the same for me, same here

ENA [ena] *sigle f* (= *École nationale d'administration*) *grande école for training civil servants*

énarque [enaʀk(ə)] *nm/f* former ENA student

encablure [ɑ̃kablyʀ] *nf* (*Navig*) cable's length

encadrement [ɑ̃kadʀəmɑ̃] *nm* framing; training; (*de porte*) frame; **~ du crédit** credit restrictions

encadrer [ɑ̃kadʀe] *vt* (*tableau, image*) to frame; (*fig: entourer*) to surround; (*personnel, soldats etc*) to train; (*Comm: crédit*) to restrict

encadreur [ɑ̃kadʀœʀ] *nm* (picture) framer

encaisse [ɑ̃kɛs] *nf* cash in hand; **~ or/ métallique** gold/gold and silver reserves

encaissé, e [ɑ̃kese] *adj* (*vallée*) steep-sided; (*rivière*) with steep banks

encaisser [ɑ̃kese] *vt* (*chèque*) to cash; (*argent*) to collect; (*fig: coup, défaite*) to take

encaisseur [ɑ̃kesœʀ] *nm* collector (*of debts etc*)

encan [ɑ̃kɑ̃]: **à l'~** *adv* by auction

encanailler [ɑ̃kanaje]: **s'encanailler** *vi* to become vulgar *ou* common; to mix with the riff-raff

encart [ɑ̃kaʀ] *nm* insert; **~ publicitaire** publicity insert

encarter [ɑ̃kaʀte] *vt* to insert

en-cas [ɑ̃ka] *nm inv* snack

encastrable [ɑ̃kastʀabl(ə)] *adj* (*four, élément*) that can be built in

encastré, e [ɑ̃kastʀe] *adj* (*four, baignoire*) built-in

encastrer [ɑ̃kastʀe] *vt*: **~ qch dans** (*mur*) to embed sth in(to); (*boîtier*) to fit sth into; **s'encastrer dans** *vi* to fit into; (*heurter*) to crash into

encaustique [ɑ̃kɔstik] *nf* polish, wax

encaustiquer [ɑ̃kɔstike] *vt* to polish, wax

enceinte [ɑ̃sɛ̃t] *adj f*: **~ (de six mois)** (six months) pregnant ▷ *nf* (*mur*) wall; (*espace*) enclosure; **~ (acoustique)** speaker

encens [ɑ̃sɑ̃] *nm* incense

encenser [ɑ̃sɑ̃se] *vt* to (in)cense; (*fig*) to praise to the skies

encensoir [ɑ̃sɑ̃swaʀ] *nm* thurible (*Brit*), censer

encéphalogramme [ɑ̃sefalɔgʀam] *nm* encephalogram

encercler [ɑ̃sɛʀkle] *vt* to surround

enchaîné [ɑ̃ʃene] *nm* (*Ciné*) link shot

enchaînement [ɑ̃ʃɛnmɑ̃] *nm* (*fig*) linking

enchaîner [ɑ̃ʃene] *vt* to chain up; (*mouvements, séquences*) to link (together) ▷ *vi* to carry on

enchanté, e [ɑ̃ʃɑ̃te] *adj* (*ravi*) delighted; (*ensorcelé*) enchanted; **~ (de faire votre connaissance)** pleased to meet you, how do you do?

enchantement [ɑ̃ʃɑ̃tmɑ̃] *nm* delight; (*magie*) enchantment; **comme par ~** as if by magic

enchanter [ɑ̃ʃɑ̃te] *vt* to delight

enchanteur, -teresse [ɑ̃ʃɑ̃tœʀ, -tʀɛs] *adj* enchanting

enchâsser [ɑ̃ʃase] *vt*: ~ **qch (dans)** to set sth (in)
enchère [ɑ̃ʃɛʀ] *nf* bid; **faire une** ~ to (make a)
bid; **mettre/vendre aux ~s** to put up for (sale
by)/sell by auction; **les ~s montent** the bids are
rising; **faire monter les ~s** (*fig*) to raise the
bidding
enchérir [ɑ̃ʃeʀiʀ] *vi*: ~ **sur qn** (*aux enchères, aussi
fig*) to outbid sb
enchérisseur, -euse [ɑ̃ʃeʀisœʀ, -øz] *nm/f* bidder
enchevêtrement [ɑ̃ʃvɛtʀəmɑ̃] *nm* tangle
enchevêtrer [ɑ̃ʃvetʀe] *vt* to tangle (up)
enclave [ɑ̃klav] *nf* enclave
enclaver [ɑ̃klave] *vt* to enclose, hem in
enclencher [ɑ̃klɑ̃ʃe] *vt* (*mécanisme*) to engage;
(*fig: affaire*) to set in motion; **s'enclencher** *vi* to
engage
enclin, e [ɑ̃klɛ̃, -in] *adj*: ~ **à qch/à faire** inclined
ou prone to sth/to do
enclore [ɑ̃klɔʀ] *vt* to enclose
enclos [ɑ̃klo] *nm* enclosure; (*clôture*) fence
enclume [ɑ̃klym] *nf* anvil
encoche [ɑ̃kɔʃ] *nf* notch
encoder [ɑ̃kɔde] *vt* to encode
encodeur [ɑ̃kɔdœʀ] *nm* encoder
encoignure [ɑ̃kɔɲyʀ] *nf* corner
encoller [ɑ̃kɔle] *vt* to paste
encolure [ɑ̃kɔlyʀ] *nf* (*tour de cou*) collar size; (*col,
cou*) neck
encombrant, e [ɑ̃kɔ̃bʀɑ̃, -ɑ̃t] *adj* cumbersome,
bulky
encombre [ɑ̃kɔ̃bʀ(ə)]: **sans** ~ *adv* without
mishap *ou* incident
encombré, e [ɑ̃kɔ̃bʀe] *adj* (*pièce, passage*)
cluttered; (*lignes téléphoniques*) engaged; (*marché*)
saturated
encombrement [ɑ̃kɔ̃bʀəmɑ̃] *nm* (*d'un lieu*)
cluttering (up); (*d'un objet: dimensions*) bulk
encombrer [ɑ̃kɔ̃bʀe] *vt* to clutter (up); (*gêner*) to
hamper; **s'encombrer de** *vi* (*bagages etc*) to load
ou burden o.s. with; ~ **le passage** to block *ou*
obstruct the way
encontre [ɑ̃kɔ̃tʀ(ə)]: **à l'~ de** *prép* against,
counter to
encorbellement [ɑ̃kɔʀbɛlmɑ̃] *nm*: **fenêtre en** ~
oriel window
encorder [ɑ̃kɔʀde] *vt*: **s'encorder** (*Alpinisme*) to
rope up

 MOT-CLÉ

encore [ɑ̃kɔʀ] *adv* **1** (*continuation*) still; **il y
travaille encore** he's still working on it; **pas
encore** not yet
2 (*de nouveau*) again; **j'irai encore demain** I'll
go again tomorrow; **encore une fois** (once)
again; **encore un effort** one last effort;
encore deux jours two more days
3 (*intensif*) even, still; **encore plus fort/mieux**
even louder/better, louder/better still; **hier
encore** even yesterday; **non seulement ...,
mais encore ...** not only ..., but also ...;
encore! (*insatisfaction*) not again!; **quoi encore?**

what now?
4 (*restriction*) even so *ou* then, only; **encore
pourrais-je le faire si ...** even so, I might be
able to do it if ...; **si encore** if only; **encore que**
conj although

encourageant, e [ɑ̃kuʀaʒɑ̃, -ɑ̃t] *adj*
encouraging
encouragement [ɑ̃kuʀaʒmɑ̃] *nm*
encouragement; (*récompense*) incentive
encourager [ɑ̃kuʀaʒe] *vt* to encourage; ~ **qn à
faire qch** to encourage sb to do sth
encourir [ɑ̃kuʀiʀ] *vt* to incur
encrasser [ɑ̃kʀase] *vt* to foul up; (*Auto etc*) to
soot up
encre [ɑ̃kʀ(ə)] *nf* ink; ~ **de Chine** Indian ink; ~
indélébile indelible ink; ~ **sympathique**
invisible ink
encrer [ɑ̃kʀe] *vt* to ink
encreur [ɑ̃kʀœʀ] *adj m*: **rouleau** ~ inking roller
encrier [ɑ̃kʀije] *nm* inkwell
encroûter [ɑ̃kʀute]: **s'encroûter** *vi* (*fig*) to get
into a rut, get set in one's ways
encyclique [ɑ̃siklik] *nf* encyclical
encyclopédie [ɑ̃siklɔpedi] *nf* encyclopaedia
(*Brit*), encyclopedia (*US*)
encyclopédique [ɑ̃siklɔpedik] *adj*
encyclopaedic (*Brit*), encyclopedic (*US*)
endémique [ɑ̃demik] *adj* endemic
endetté, e [ɑ̃dete] *adj* in debt; (*fig*): **très** ~
envers qn deeply indebted to sb
endettement [ɑ̃dɛtmɑ̃] *nm* debts *pl*
endetter [ɑ̃dete] *vt*, **s'endetter** *vi* to get into
debt
endeuiller [ɑ̃dœje] *vt* to plunge into mourning;
manifestation endeuillée par event over
which a tragic shadow was cast by
endiablé, e [ɑ̃djable] *adj* furious; (*enfant*)
boisterous
endiguer [ɑ̃dige] *vt* to dyke (up); (*fig*) to check,
hold back
endimanché, e [ɑ̃dimɑ̃ʃe] *adj* in one's Sunday
best
endimancher [ɑ̃dimɑ̃ʃe] *vt*: **s'endimancher** to
put on one's Sunday best; **avoir l'air
endimanché** to be all done up to the nines
(*fam*)
endive [ɑ̃div] *nf* chicory *no pl*
endocrine [ɑ̃dɔkʀin] *adj f*: **glande** ~ endocrine
(gland)
endoctrinement [ɑ̃dɔktʀinmɑ̃] *nm*
indoctrination
endoctriner [ɑ̃dɔktʀine] *vt* to indoctrinate
endolori, e [ɑ̃dɔlɔʀi] *adj* painful
endommager [ɑ̃dɔmaʒe] *vt* to damage
endormant, e [ɑ̃dɔʀmɑ̃, -ɑ̃t] *adj* dull, boring
endormi, e [ɑ̃dɔʀmi] *pp de* **endormir** ▷ *adj*
(*personne*) asleep; (*fig: indolent, lent*) sluggish;
(*engourdi: main, pied*) numb
endormir [ɑ̃dɔʀmiʀ] *vt* to put to sleep; (*chaleur
etc*) to send to sleep; (*Méd: dent, nerf*) to
anaesthetize; (*fig: soupçons*) to allay; **s'endormir**

vi to fall asleep, go to sleep

endoscope [ɑ̃dɔskɔp] *nm* (*Méd*) endoscope

endoscopie [ɑ̃dɔskɔpi] *nf* endoscopy

endosser [ɑ̃dose] *vt* (*responsabilité*) to take, shoulder; (*chèque*) to endorse; (*uniforme, tenue*) to put on, don

endroit [ɑ̃dRwa] *nm* place; (*localité*) **les gens de l'~** the local people; (*opposé à l'envers*) right side; **à cet ~** in this place; **à l'~** right side out; the right way up; (*vêtement*) the right way out; **à l'~ de** *prép* regarding, with regard to; **par ~s** in places

enduire [ɑ̃dɥiR] *vt* to coat; **~ qch de** to coat sth with

enduit, e [ɑ̃dɥi, -it] *pp de* **enduire** ▷ *nm* coating

endurance [ɑ̃dyRɑ̃s] *nf* endurance

endurant, e [ɑ̃dyRɑ̃, -ɑ̃t] *adj* tough, hardy

endurcir [ɑ̃dyRsiR] *vt* (*physiquement*) to toughen; (*moralement*) to harden; **s'endurcir** *vi* to become tougher; to become hardened

endurer [ɑ̃dyRe] *vt* to endure, bear

énergétique [enɛRʒetik] *adj* (*ressources etc*) energy *cpd*; (*aliment*) energizing

énergie [enɛRʒi] *nf* (*Physique*) energy; (*Tech*) power; (*fig: physique*) energy; (*: morale*) vigour, spirit; **~ éolienne/solaire** wind/solar power

énergique [enɛRʒik] *adj* energetic; vigorous; (*mesures*) drastic, stringent

énergiquement [enɛRʒikmɑ̃] *adv* energetically; drastically

énergisant, e [enɛRʒizɑ̃, -ɑ̃t] *adj* energizing

énergumène [enɛRgymɛn] *nm* rowdy character *ou* customer

énervant, e [enɛRvɑ̃, -ɑ̃t] *adj* irritating

énervé, e [enɛRve] *adj* nervy, on edge; (*agacé*) irritated

énervement [enɛRvəmɑ̃] *nm* nerviness; irritation

énerver [enɛRve] *vt* to irritate, annoy; **s'énerver** *vi* to get excited, get worked up

enfance [ɑ̃fɑ̃s] *nf* (*âge*) childhood; (*fig*) infancy; (*enfants*) children *pl*; **c'est l'~ de l'art** it's child's play; **petite ~** infancy; **souvenir/ami d'~** childhood memory/friend; **retomber en ~** to lapse into one's second childhood

enfant [ɑ̃fɑ̃] *nm/f* child; **~ adoptif/naturel** adopted/natural child; **bon ~** *adj* good-natured, easy-going; **~ de chœur** *nm* (*Rel*) altar boy; **~ prodige** child prodigy; **~ unique** only child

enfanter [ɑ̃fɑ̃te] *vi* to give birth ▷ *vt* to give birth to

enfantillage [ɑ̃fɑ̃tijaʒ] *nm* (*péj*) childish behaviour *no pl*

enfantin, e [ɑ̃fɑ̃tɛ̃, -in] *adj* childlike; (*péj*) childish; (*langage*) child *cpd*

enfer [ɑ̃fɛR] *nm* hell; **allure/bruit d'~** horrendous speed/noise

enfermer [ɑ̃fɛRme] *vt* to shut up; (*à clef, interner*) to lock up; **s'enfermer** to shut o.s. away; **s'~ à clé** to lock o.s. in; **s'~ dans la solitude/le mutisme** to retreat into solitude/silence

enferrer [ɑ̃feRe]: **s'enferrer** *vi*: **s'~ dans** to tangle o.s. up in

enfiévré, e [ɑ̃fjevRe] *adj* (*fig*) feverish

enfilade [ɑ̃filad] *nf*: **une ~ de** a series *ou* line of; **prendre des rues en ~** to cross directly from one street into the next

enfiler [ɑ̃file] *vt* (*vêtement*): **~ qch** to slip sth on, slip into sth; (*insérer*): **~ qch dans** to stick sth into; (*rue, couloir*) to take; (*perles*) to string; (*aiguille*) to thread; **s'enfiler dans** *vi* to disappear into

enfin [ɑ̃fɛ̃] *adv* at last; (*en énumérant*) lastly; (*de restriction, résignation*) still; (*eh bien*) well; (*pour conclure*) in a word

enflammé, e [ɑ̃flame] *adj* (*torche, allumette*) burning; (*Méd: plaie*) inflamed; (*fig: nature, discours, déclaration*) fiery

enflammer [ɑ̃flame] *vt* to set fire to; (*Méd*) to inflame; **s'enflammer** *vi* to catch fire; to become inflamed

enflé, e [ɑ̃fle] *adj* swollen; (*péj: style*) bombastic, turgid

enfler [ɑ̃fle] *vi* to swell (up); **s'enfler** *vi* to swell

enflure [ɑ̃flyR] *nf* swelling

enfoncé, e [ɑ̃fɔ̃se] *adj* staved-in, smashed-in; (*yeux*) deep-set

enfoncement [ɑ̃fɔ̃smɑ̃] *nm* (*recoin*) nook

enfoncer [ɑ̃fɔ̃se] *vt* (*clou*) to drive in; (*faire pénétrer*): **~ qch dans** to push (*ou* drive) sth into; (*forcer: porte*) to break open; (*: plancher*) to cause to cave in; (*défoncer: côtes etc*) to smash; (*fam: surpasser*) to lick, beat (hollow) ▷ *vi* (*dans la vase etc*) to sink in; (*sol, surface porteuse*) to give way; **s'enfoncer** *vi* to sink; **s'~ dans** to sink into; (*forêt, ville*) to disappear into; **~ un chapeau sur la tête** to cram *ou* jam a hat on one's head; **~ qn dans la dette** to drag sb into debt

enfouir [ɑ̃fwiR] *vt* (*dans le sol*) to bury; (*dans un tiroir etc*) to tuck away; **s'enfouir dans/sous** to bury o.s. in/under

enfourcher [ɑ̃fuRʃe] *vt* to mount; **~ son dada** (*fig*) to get on one's hobby-horse

enfourner [ɑ̃fuRne] *vt* to put in the oven; (*poterie*) to put in the kiln; **~ qch dans** to shove *ou* stuff sth into; **s'enfourner dans** (*personne*) to dive into

enfreignais *etc* [ɑ̃fRɛɲɛ] *vb voir* **enfreindre**

enfreindre [ɑ̃fRɛ̃dR(ə)] *vt* to infringe, break

enfuir [ɑ̃fɥiR]: **s'enfuir** *vi* to run away *ou* off

enfumer [ɑ̃fyme] *vt* to smoke out

enfuyais *etc* [ɑ̃fɥijɛ] *vb voir* **enfuir**

engagé, e [ɑ̃gaʒe] *adj* (*littérature etc*) engagé, committed

engageant, e [ɑ̃gaʒɑ̃, -ɑ̃t] *adj* attractive, appealing

engagement [ɑ̃gaʒmɑ̃] *nm* taking on, engaging; starting; investing; (*promesse*) commitment; (*Mil: combat*) engagement; (*: recrutement*) enlistment; (*Sport*) entry; **prendre l'~ de faire** to undertake to do; **sans ~** (*Comm*) without obligation

engager [ɑ̃gaʒe] *vt* (*embaucher*) to take on,

engage; (*commencer*) to start; (*lier*) to bind, commit; (*impliquer, entraîner*) to involve; (*investir*) to invest, lay out; (*faire intervenir*) to engage; (*Sport: concurrents, chevaux*) to enter; (*inciter*): **~ qn à faire** to urge sb to do; (*faire pénétrer*): **~ qch dans** to insert sth into; **~ qn à qch** to urge sth on sb; **s'engager** *vi* to get taken on; (*Mil*) to enlist; (*promettre, politiquement*) to commit o.s.; (*débuter*) to start (up); **s'~ à faire** to undertake to do; **s'~ dans** (*rue, passage*) to enter, turn into; (*s'emboîter*) to engage *ou* fit into; (*fig: affaire, discussion*) to enter into, embark on

engazonner [ɑ̃gazɔne] *vt* to turf
engeance [ɑ̃ʒɑ̃s] *nf* mob
engelures [ɑ̃ʒlyʀ] *nfpl* chilblains
engendrer [ɑ̃ʒɑ̃dʀe] *vt* to father; (*fig*) to create, breed
engin [ɑ̃ʒɛ̃] *nm* machine instrument; vehicle; (*péj*) gadget; (*Aviat: avion*) aircraft *inv*; (: *missile*) missile; **~ blindé** armoured vehicle; **~ (explosif)** (explosive) device; **~s (spéciaux)** missiles
englober [ɑ̃glɔbe] *vt* to include
engloutir [ɑ̃glutiʀ] *vt* to swallow up; (*fig: dépenses*) to devour; **s'engloutir** *vi* to be engulfed
englué, e [ɑ̃glye] *adj* sticky
engoncé, e [ɑ̃gɔ̃se] *adj*: **~ dans** cramped in
engorgement [ɑ̃gɔʀʒəmɑ̃] *nm* blocking; (*Méd*) engorgement
engorger [ɑ̃gɔʀʒe] *vt* to obstruct, block; **s'engorger** *vi* to become blocked
engouement [ɑ̃gumɑ̃] *nm* (sudden) passion
engouffrer [ɑ̃gufʀe] *vt* to swallow up, devour; **s'engouffrer dans** to rush into
engourdi, e [ɑ̃guʀdi] *adj* numb
engourdir [ɑ̃guʀdiʀ] *vt* to numb; (*fig*) to dull, blunt; **s'engourdir** *vi* to go numb
engrais [ɑ̃gʀɛ] *nm* manure; **~ (chimique)** (chemical) fertilizer; **~ organique/ inorganique** organic/inorganic fertilizer
engraisser [ɑ̃gʀese] *vt* to fatten (up); (*terre: fertiliser*) to fertilize ▷ *vi* (*péj*) to get fat(ter)
engranger [ɑ̃gʀɑ̃ʒe] *vt* (*foin*) to bring in; (*fig*) to store away
engrenage [ɑ̃gʀənaʒ] *nm* gears *pl*, gearing; (*fig*) chain
engueuler [ɑ̃gœle] *vt* (*fam*) to bawl at *ou* out
enguirlander [ɑ̃giʀlɑ̃de] *vt* (*fam*) to give sb a bawling out, bawl at
enhardir [ɑ̃aʀdiʀ]: **s'enhardir** *vi* to grow bolder
ENI [eni] *sigle f* = **école normale (d'instituteurs)**
énième [enjɛm] *adj* = **nième**
énigmatique [enigmatik] *adj* enigmatic
énigmatiquement [enigmatikmɑ̃] *adv* enigmatically
énigme [enigm(ə)] *nf* riddle
enivrant, e [ɑ̃nivʀɑ̃, -ɑ̃t] *adj* intoxicating
enivrer [ɑ̃nivʀe] *vt*: **s'enivrer** to get drunk; **s'~ de** (*fig*) to become intoxicated with
enjambée [ɑ̃ʒɑ̃be] *nf* stride; **d'une ~** with one stride
enjamber [ɑ̃ʒɑ̃be] *vt* to stride over; (*pont etc*) to

span, straddle
enjeu, x [ɑ̃ʒø] *nm* stakes *pl*
enjoindre [ɑ̃ʒwɛ̃dʀ(ə)] *vt*: **~ à qn de faire** to enjoin *ou* order sb to do
enjôler [ɑ̃ʒole] *vt* to coax, wheedle
enjôleur, -euse [ɑ̃ʒolœʀ, -øz] *adj* (*sourire, paroles*) winning
enjolivement [ɑ̃ʒɔlivmɑ̃] *nm* embellishment
enjoliver [ɑ̃ʒɔlive] *vt* to embellish
enjoliveur [ɑ̃ʒɔlivœʀ] *nm* (*Auto*) hub cap
enjoué, e [ɑ̃ʒwe] *adj* playful
enlacer [ɑ̃lase] *vt* (*étreindre*) to embrace, hug; (*lianes*) to wind round, entwine
enlaidir [ɑ̃lediʀ] *vt* to make ugly ▷ *vi* to become ugly
enlevé, e [ɑ̃lve] *adj* (*morceau de musique*) played brightly
enlèvement [ɑ̃lɛvmɑ̃] *nm* removal; (*rapt*) abduction, kidnapping; **l'~ des ordures ménagères** refuse collection
enlever [ɑ̃lve] *vt* (*ôter: gén*) to remove; (: *vêtement, lunettes*) to take off; (: *Méd: organe*) to remove; (*emporter: ordures etc*) to collect, take away; (*kidnapper*) to abduct, kidnap; (*obtenir: prix, contrat*) to win; (*Mil: position*) to take; (*morceau de piano etc*) to execute with spirit *ou* brio; (*prendre*): **~ qch à qn** to take sth (away) from sb; **s'enlever** *vi* (*tache*) to come out *ou* off; **la maladie qui nous l'a enlevé** (*euphémisme*) the illness which took him from us
enliser [ɑ̃lize]: **s'enliser** *vi* to sink, get stuck; (*dialogue etc*) to get bogged down
enluminure [ɑ̃lyminyʀ] *nf* illumination
ENM *sigle f* (= *École nationale de la magistrature*) grande école for law students
enneigé, e [ɑ̃neʒe] *adj* snowy; (*col*) snowed-up; (*maison*) snowed-in
enneigement [ɑ̃neʒmɑ̃] *nm* depth of snow, snowfall; **bulletin d'~** snow report
ennemi, e [ɛnmi] *adj* hostile; (*Mil*) enemy *cpd* ▷ *nm/f* enemy; **être ~ de** to be strongly averse *ou* opposed to
ennième [ɛnjɛm] *adj* = **nième**
ennoblir [ɑ̃nɔbliʀ] *vt* to ennoble
ennui [ɑ̃nɥi] *nm* (*lassitude*) boredom; (*difficulté*) trouble *no pl*; **avoir des ~s** to have problems; **s'attirer des ~s** to cause problems for o.s.
ennuie *etc* [ɑ̃nɥi] *vb voir* **ennuyer**
ennuyé, e [ɑ̃nɥije] *adj* (*air, personne*) preoccupied, worried
ennuyer [ɑ̃nɥije] *vt* to bother; (*lasser*) to bore; **s'ennuyer** *vi* to be bored; (*s'ennuyer de: regretter*) to miss; **si cela ne vous ennuie pas** if it's no trouble to you
ennuyeux, -euse [ɑ̃nɥijø, -øz] *adj* boring, tedious; (*agaçant*) annoying
énoncé [enɔ̃se] *nm* terms *pl*; wording; (*Ling*) utterance
énoncer [enɔ̃se] *vt* to say, express; (*conditions*) to set out, lay down, state
énonciation [enɔ̃sjasjɔ̃] *nf* statement
enorgueillir [ɑ̃nɔʀgœjiʀ]: **s'enorgueillir de** *vt* to

pride o.s. on; to boast

énorme [enɔʀm(ə)] *adj* enormous, huge

énormément [enɔʀmemɑ̃] *adv* enormously, tremendously; **~ de neige/gens** an enormous amount of snow/number of people

énormité [enɔʀmite] *nf* enormity, hugeness; (*propos*) outrageous remark

en part. *abr* (= *en particulier*) esp.

enquérir [ɑ̃keʀiʀ]: **s'enquérir de** *vt* to inquire about

enquête [ɑ̃kɛt] *nf* (*de journaliste, de police*) investigation; (*judiciaire, administrative*) inquiry; (*sondage d'opinion*) survey

enquêter [ɑ̃kete] *vi* to investigate; to hold an inquiry; (*faire un sondage*): **~ (sur)** to do a survey (on), carry out an opinion poll (on)

enquêteur, -euse *ou* **-trice** [ɑ̃kɛtœʀ, -øz, -tʀis] *nm/f* officer in charge of an investigation; person conducting a survey; pollster

enquiers, enquière *etc* [ɑ̃kjɛʀ] *vb voir* **enquérir**

enquiquiner [ɑ̃kikine] *vt* to rile, irritate

enquis, e [ɑ̃ki, -iz] *pp de* **enquérir**

enraciné, e [ɑ̃ʀasine] *adj* deep-rooted

enragé, e [ɑ̃ʀaʒe] *adj* (*Méd*) rabid, with rabies; (*furieux*) furiously angry; (*fig*) fanatical; **~ de** wild about

enrageant, e [ɑ̃ʀaʒɑ̃, -ɑ̃t] *adj* infuriating

enrager [ɑ̃ʀaʒe] *vi* to be furious, be in a rage; **faire ~ qn** to make sb wild with anger

enrayer [ɑ̃ʀeje] *vt* to check, stop; **s'enrayer** *vi* (*arme à feu*) to jam

enrégimenter [ɑ̃ʀeʒimɑ̃te] *vt* (*péj*) to enlist

enregistrement [ɑ̃ʀʒistʀəmɑ̃] *nm* recording; (*Admin*) registration; **~ des bagages** (*à l'aéroport*) baggage check-in; **~ magnétique** tape-recording

enregistrer [ɑ̃ʀʒistʀe] *vt* (*Mus*) to record; (*Inform*) to save; (*remarquer, noter*) to note, record; (*Comm: commande*) to note, enter; (*fig: mémoriser*) to make a mental note of; (*Admin*) to register; (*aussi:* **faire enregistrer**: *bagages: par train*) to register; (: *à l'aéroport*) to check in

enregistreur, -euse [ɑ̃ʀʒistʀœʀ, -øz] *adj* (*machine*) recording *cpd* ▷ *nm* (*appareil*): **~ de vol** (*Aviat*) flight recorder

enrhumé, e [ɑ̃ʀyme] *adj*: **il est ~** he has a cold

enrhumer [ɑ̃ʀyme]: **s'enrhumer** *vi* to catch a cold

enrichir [ɑ̃ʀiʃiʀ] *vt* to make rich(er); (*fig*) to enrich; **s'enrichir** *vi* to get rich(er)

enrichissant, e [ɑ̃ʀiʃisɑ̃, -ɑ̃t] *adj* instructive

enrichissement [ɑ̃ʀiʃismɑ̃] *nm* enrichment

enrober [ɑ̃ʀobe] *vt*: **~ qch de** to coat sth with; (*fig*) to wrap sth up in

enrôlement [ɑ̃ʀolmɑ̃] *nm* enlistment

enrôler [ɑ̃ʀole] *vt* to enlist; **s'enrôler (dans)** *vi* to enlist (in)

enroué, e [ɑ̃ʀwe] *adj* hoarse

enrouer [ɑ̃ʀwe]: **s'enrouer** *vi* to go hoarse

enrouler [ɑ̃ʀule] *vt* (*fil, corde*) to wind (up); **s'enrouler** to coil up; **~ qch autour de** to wind sth (a)round

enrouleur, -euse [ɑ̃ʀulœʀ, -øz] *adj* (*Tech*) winding ▷ *nm voir* **ceinture**

enrubanné, e [ɑ̃ʀybane] *adj* trimmed with ribbon

ENS *sigle f* = **école normale supérieure**

ensabler [ɑ̃sable] *vt* (*port, canal*) to silt up, sand up; (*embarcation*) to strand (on a sandbank); **s'ensabler** *vi* to silt up; to get stranded

ensacher [ɑ̃saʃe] *vt* to pack into bags

ENSAM *sigle f* (= *École nationale supérieure des arts et métiers*) *grande école for engineering students*

ensanglanté, e [ɑ̃sɑ̃glɑ̃te] *adj* covered with blood

enseignant, e [ɑ̃sɛɲɑ̃, -ɑ̃t] *adj* teaching ▷ *nm/f* teacher

enseigne [ɑ̃sɛɲ] *nf* sign ▷ *nm*: **~ de vaisseau** lieutenant; **à telle ~ que** so much so that; **être logés à la même ~** (*fig*) to be in the same boat; **~ lumineuse** neon sign

enseignement [ɑ̃sɛɲmɑ̃] *nm* teaching; **~ ménager** home economics; **~ primaire** primary (*Brit*) *ou* grade school (*US*) education; **~ secondaire** secondary (*Brit*) *ou* high school (*US*) education

enseigner [ɑ̃seɲe] *vt, vi* to teach; **~ qch à qn/à qn que** to teach sb sth/sb that

ensemble [ɑ̃sɑ̃bl(ə)] *adv* together ▷ *nm* (*assemblage, Math*) set; (*totalité*): **l'~ du/de la** the whole *ou* entire; (*vêtement féminin*) ensemble, suit; (*unité, harmonie*) unity; (*résidentiel*) housing development; **aller ~** to go together; **impression/idée d'~** overall *ou* general impression/idea; **dans l'~** (*en gros*) on the whole; **dans son ~** overall, in general; **~ vocal/musical** vocal/musical ensemble

ensemblier [ɑ̃sɑ̃blije] *nm* interior designer

ensemencer [ɑ̃smɑ̃se] *vt* to sow

enserrer [ɑ̃seʀe] *vt* to hug (tightly)

ENSET [ɛnsɛt] *sigle f* (= *École normale supérieure de l'enseignement technique*) *grande école for training technical teachers*

ensevelir [ɑ̃səvliʀ] *vt* to bury

ensilage [ɑ̃silaʒ] *nm* (*aliment*) silage

ensoleillé, e [ɑ̃sɔleje] *adj* sunny

ensoleillement [ɑ̃sɔlɛjmɑ̃] *nm* period *ou* hours *pl* of sunshine

ensommeillé, e [ɑ̃sɔmeje] *adj* sleepy, drowsy

ensorceler [ɑ̃sɔʀsəle] *vt* to enchant, bewitch

ensuite [ɑ̃sɥit] *adv* then, next; (*plus tard*) afterwards, later; **~ de quoi** after which

ensuivre [ɑ̃sɥivʀ(ə)]: **s'ensuivre** *vi* to follow, ensue; **il s'ensuit que ...** it follows that ...; **et tout ce qui s'ensuit** and all that goes with it

entaché, e [ɑ̃taʃe] *adj*: **~ de** marred by; **~ de nullité** null and void

entacher [ɑ̃taʃe] *vt* to soil

entaille [ɑ̃taj] *nf* (*encoche*) notch; (*blessure*) cut; **se faire une ~** to cut o.s.

entailler [ɑ̃taje] *vt* to notch; to cut; **s'~ le doigt** to cut one's finger

entamer [ɑ̃tame] *vt* to start; (*hostilités, pourparlers*) to open; (*fig: altérer*) to make a dent in; to damage

entartrer [ɑ̃taʀtʀe]: **s'entartrer** vi to fur up; (dents) to become covered with plaque

entassement [ɑ̃tɑsmɑ̃] nm (tas) pile, heap

entasser [ɑ̃tɑse] vt (empiler) to pile up, heap up; (tenir à l'étroit) to cram together; **s'entasser** vi to pile up; to cram; **s'~ dans** to cram into

entendement [ɑ̃tɑ̃dmɑ̃] nm understanding

entendre [ɑ̃tɑ̃dʀ(ə)] vt to hear; (comprendre) to understand; (vouloir dire) to mean; (vouloir): **~ être obéi/que** to intend ou mean to be obeyed/that; **j'ai entendu dire que** I've heard (it said) that; **je suis heureux de vous l'~ dire** I'm pleased to hear you say it; **~ parler de** to hear of; **laisser ~ que, donner à ~ que** to let it be understood that; **~ raison** to see sense, listen to reason; **qu'est-ce qu'il ne faut pas ~!** whatever next!; **j'ai mal entendu** I didn't catch what was said; **je vous entends très mal** I can hardly hear you; **s'entendre** vi (sympathiser) to get on; (se mettre d'accord) to agree; **s'~ à qch/à faire** (être compétent) to be good at sth/doing; **ça s'entend** (est audible) it's audible; **je m'entends** I mean; **entendons-nous!** let's be clear what we mean

entendu, e [ɑ̃tɑ̃dy] pp de **entendre** ▷ adj (réglé) agreed; (au courant: air) knowing; **étant ~ que** since (it's understood ou agreed that); **(c'est) ~** all right, agreed; **c'est ~** (concession) all right, granted; **bien ~** of course

entente [ɑ̃tɑ̃t] nf (entre amis, pays) understanding, harmony; (accord, traité) agreement, understanding; **à double ~** (sens) with a double meaning

entériner [ɑ̃teʀine] vt to ratify, confirm

entérite [ɑ̃teʀit] nf enteritis no pl

enterrement [ɑ̃tɛʀmɑ̃] nm burying; (cérémonie) funeral, burial; (cortège funèbre) funeral procession

enterrer [ɑ̃teʀe] vt to bury

entêtant, e [ɑ̃tɛtɑ̃, -ɑ̃t] adj heady

en-tête [ɑ̃tɛt] nm heading; (de papier à lettres) letterhead; **papier à ~** headed notepaper

entêté, e [ɑ̃tete] adj stubborn

entêtement [ɑ̃tɛtmɑ̃] nm stubbornness

entêter [ɑ̃tete]: **s'entêter** vi: **s'~ (à faire)** to persist (in doing)

enthousiasmant, e [ɑ̃tuzjasmɑ̃, -ɑ̃t] adj exciting

enthousiasme [ɑ̃tuzjasm(ə)] nm enthusiasm; **avec ~** enthusiastically

enthousiasmé, e [ɑ̃tuzjasme] adj filled with enthusiasm

enthousiasmer [ɑ̃tuzjasme] vt to fill with enthusiasm; **s'~ (pour qch)** to get enthusiastic (about sth)

enthousiaste [ɑ̃tuzjast(ə)] adj enthusiastic

enticher [ɑ̃tiʃe]: **s'enticher de** vt to become infatuated with

entier, -ière [ɑ̃tje, -jɛʀ] adj (non entamé, en totalité) whole; (total, complet) complete; (fig: caractère) unbending, averse to compromise ▷ nm (Math)

whole; **en ~** totally; in its entirety; **se donner tout ~ à qch** to devote o.s. completely to sth; **lait ~** full-cream milk; **pain ~** wholemeal bread; **nombre ~** whole number

entièrement [ɑ̃tjɛʀmɑ̃] adv entirely, completely, wholly

entité [ɑ̃tite] nf entity

entomologie [ɑ̃tɔmɔlɔʒi] nf entomology

entonner [ɑ̃tɔne] vt (chanson) to strike up

entonnoir [ɑ̃tɔnwaʀ] nm (ustensile) funnel; (trou) shell-hole, crater

entorse [ɑ̃tɔʀs(ə)] nf (Méd) sprain; (fig): **~ à la loi/au règlement** infringement of the law/rule; **se faire une ~ à la cheville/au poignet** to sprain one's ankle/wrist

entortiller [ɑ̃tɔʀtije] vt (envelopper): **~ qch dans/avec** to wrap sth in/with; (enrouler): **~ qch autour de** to twist ou wind sth (a)round; (fam): **~ qn** to get (a)round sb; (: duper) to hoodwink sb (Brit), trick sb; **s'entortiller dans** vi (draps) to roll o.s. up in; (fig: réponses) to get tangled up in

entourage [ɑ̃tuʀaʒ] nm circle; family (circle); (d'une vedette etc) entourage; (ce qui enclôt) surround

entouré, e [ɑ̃tuʀe] adj (recherché, admiré) popular; **~ de** surrounded by

entourer [ɑ̃tuʀe] vt to surround; (apporter son soutien à) to rally round; **~ de** to surround with; (trait) to encircle with; **s'entourer de** vi to surround o.s. with; **s'~ de précautions** to take all possible precautions

entourloupette [ɑ̃tuʀlupɛt] nf mean trick

entournures [ɑ̃tuʀnyʀ] nfpl: **gêné aux ~** in financial difficulties; (fig) a bit awkward

entracte [ɑ̃tʀakt(ə)] nm interval

entraide [ɑ̃tʀɛd] nf mutual aid ou assistance

entraider [ɑ̃tʀede]: **s'entraider** vi to help each other

entrailles [ɑ̃tʀaj] nfpl entrails; (humaines) bowels

entrain [ɑ̃tʀɛ̃] nm spirit; **avec ~** (répondre, travailler) energetically; **faire qch sans ~** to do sth half-heartedly ou without enthusiasm

entraînant, e [ɑ̃tʀɛnɑ̃, -ɑ̃t] adj (musique) stirring, rousing

entraînement [ɑ̃tʀɛnmɑ̃] nm training; (Tech): **~ à chaîne/galet** chain/wheel drive; **manquer d'~** to be unfit; **~ par ergots/friction** (Inform) tractor/friction feed

entraîner [ɑ̃tʀene] vt (tirer: wagons) to pull; (charrier) to carry ou drag along; (Tech) to drive; (emmener: personne) to take (off); (mener à l'assaut, influencer) to lead; (Sport) to train; (impliquer) to entail; (causer) to lead to, bring about; **~ qn à faire** (inciter) to lead sb to do; **s'entraîner** vi (Sport) to train; **s'~ à qch/à faire** to train o.s. for sth/to do

entraîneur [ɑ̃tʀɛnœʀ] nm (Sport) coach, trainer; (Hippisme) trainer

entraîneuse [ɑ̃tʀɛnøz] nf (de bar) hostess

entrapercevoir [ɑ̃tʀapɛʀsəvwaʀ] vt to catch a glimpse of

entrave [ãtʀav] *nf* hindrance
entraver [ãtʀave] *vt* (*circulation*) to hold up; (*action, progrès*) to hinder, hamper
entre [ãtʀ(ə)] *prép* between; (*parmi*) among(st); **l'un d'~ eux/nous** one of them/us; **le meilleur d'~ eux/nous** the best of them/us; **ils préfèrent rester ~ eux** they prefer to keep to themselves; **~ autres (choses)** among other things; **~ nous, ...** between ourselves ..., between you and me ...; **ils se battent ~ eux** they are fighting among(st) themselves
entrebâillé, e [ãtʀəbaje] *adj* half-open, ajar
entrebâillement [ãtʀəbajmã] *nm*: **dans l'~ (de la porte)** in the half-open door
entrebâiller [ãtʀəbaje] *vt* to half open
entrechat [ãtʀəʃa] *nm* leap
entrechoquer [ãtʀəʃɔke]: **s'entrechoquer** *vi* to knock *ou* bang together
entrecôte [ãtʀəkot] *nf* entrecôte *ou* rib steak
entrecoupé, e [ãtʀəkupe] *adj* (*paroles, voix*) broken
entrecouper [ãtʀəkupe] *vt*: **~ qch de** to intersperse sth with; **~ un récit/voyage de** to interrupt a story/journey with; **s'entrecouper** *vi* (*traits, lignes*) to cut across each other
entrecroiser [ãtʀəkʀwaze] *vt*, **s'entrecroiser** *vi* to intertwine
entrée [ãtʀe] *nf* entrance; (*accès: au cinéma etc*) admission; (*billet*) (admission) ticket; (*Culin*) first course; (*Comm: de marchandises*) entry; (*Inform*) entry, input; **entrées** *nfpl*: **avoir ses ~s chez** *ou* **auprès de** to be a welcome visitor to; **d'~** *adv* from the outset; **erreur d'~** input error; **"~ interdite"** "no admittance *ou* entry"; **~ des artistes** stage door; **~ en matière** introduction; **~ principale** main entrance; **~ en scène** entrance; **~ de service** service entrance
entrefaites [ãtʀəfɛt]: **sur ces ~** *adv* at this juncture
entrefilet [ãtʀəfilɛ] *nm* (*article*) paragraph, short report
entregent [ãtʀəʒã] *nm*: **avoir de l'~** to have an easy manner
entrejambes [ãtʀəʒãb] *nm inv* crotch
entrelacement [ãtʀəlasmã] *nm*: **un ~ de ...** a network of ...
entrelacer [ãtʀəlase] *vt*, **s'entrelacer** *vi* to intertwine
entrelarder [ãtʀəlaʀde] *vt* to lard; (*fig*): **entrelardé de** interspersed with
entremêler [ãtʀəmele] *vt*: **~ qch de** to (inter)mingle sth with
entremets [ãtʀəmɛ] *nm* (cream) dessert
entremetteur, -euse [ãtʀəmɛtœʀ, -øz] *nm/f* go-between
entremettre [ãtʀəmɛtʀ(ə)]: **s'entremettre** *vi* to intervene
entremise [ãtʀəmiz] *nf* intervention; **par l'~ de** through
entrepont [ãtʀəpõ] *nm* steerage; **dans l'~** in steerage

entreposer [ãtʀəpoze] *vt* to store, put into storage
entrepôt [ãtʀəpo] *nm* warehouse
entreprenant, e [ãtʀəpʀənã, -ãt] *vb voir* **entreprendre** ▷ *adj* (*actif*) enterprising; (*trop galant*) forward
entreprendre [ãtʀəpʀãdʀ(ə)] *vt* (*se lancer dans*) to undertake; (*commencer*) to begin *ou* start (upon); (*personne*) to buttonhole; **~ qn sur un sujet** to tackle sb on a subject; **~ de faire** to undertake to do
entrepreneur [ãtʀəpʀənœʀ] *nm*: **~ (en bâtiment)** (building) contractor; **~ de pompes funèbres** funeral director, undertaker
entreprenne *etc* [ãtʀəpʀɛn] *vb voir* **entreprendre**
entrepris, e [ãtʀəpʀi, -iz] *pp de* **entreprendre** ▷ *nf* (*société*) firm, business; (*action*) undertaking, venture
entrer [ãtʀe] *vi* to go (*ou* come) in, enter ▷ *vt* (*Inform*) to input, enter; **(faire) ~ qch dans** to get sth into; **~ dans** (*gén*) to enter; (*pièce*) to go (*ou* come) into, enter; (*club*) to join; (*heurter*) to run into; (*partager: vues, craintes de qn*) to share; (*être une composante de*) to go into; (*faire partie de*) to form part of; **~ au couvent** to enter a convent; **~ à l'hôpital** to go into hospital; **~ dans le système** (*Inform*) to log in; **~ en fureur** to become angry; **~ en ébullition** to start to boil; **~ en scène** to come on stage; **laisser ~ qn/qch** to let sb/sth in; **faire ~** (*visiteur*) to show in
entresol [ãtʀəsɔl] *nm* entresol, mezzanine
entre-temps [ãtʀətã] *adv* meanwhile, (in the) meantime
entretenir [ãtʀətniʀ] *vt* to maintain; (*amitié*) to keep alive; (*famille, maîtresse*) to support, keep; **~ qn (de)** to speak to sb (about); **s'entretenir (de)** to converse (about); **~ qn dans l'erreur** to let sb remain in ignorance
entretenu, e [ãtʀətny] *pp de* **entretenir** ▷ *adj* (*femme*) kept; **bien/mal ~** (*maison, jardin*) well/badly kept
entretien [ãtʀətjɛ̃] *nm* maintenance; (*discussion*) discussion, talk; (*audience*) interview; **frais d'~** maintenance charges
entretiendrai [ãtʀətjɛ̃dʀe], **entretiens** *etc* [ãtʀətjɛ̃] *vb voir* **entretenir**
entretuer [ãtʀətɥe]: **s'entretuer** *vi* to kill one another
entreverrai [ãtʀəveʀe], **entrevit** *etc* [ãtʀəvi] *vb voir* **entrevoir**
entrevoir [ãtʀəvwaʀ] *vt* (*à peine*) to make out; (*brièvement*) to catch a glimpse of
entrevu, e [ãtʀəvy] *pp de* **entrevoir** ▷ *nf* meeting; (*audience*) interview
entrouvert, e [ãtʀuveʀ, -ɛʀt(ə)] *pp de* **entrouvrir** ▷ *adj* half-open
entrouvrir [ãtʀuvʀiʀ] *vt*, **s'entrouvrir** *vi* to half open
énumération [enymeʀasjõ] *nf* enumeration
énumérer [enymeʀe] *vt* to list, enumerate
envahir [ãvaiʀ] *vt* to invade; (*inquiétude, peur*) to

come over

envahissant, e [ãvaisã, -ãt] *adj* (*péj: personne*) interfering, intrusive

envahissement [ãvaismã] *nm* invasion

envahisseur [ãvaisœʀ] *nm* (*Mil*) invader

envasement [ãnvazmã] *nm* silting up

envaser [ãvaze]: **s'envaser** *vi* to get bogged down (in the mud)

enveloppe [ãvlɔp] *nf* (*de lettre*) envelope; (*Tech*) casing; outer layer; **mettre sous ~** to put in an envelope; **~ autocollante** self-seal envelope; **~ budgétaire** budget; **~ à fenêtre** window envelope

envelopper [ãvlɔpe] *vt* to wrap; (*fig*) to envelop, shroud; **s'~ dans un châle/une couverture** to wrap o.s. in a shawl/blanket

envenimer [ãvnime] *vt* to aggravate; **s'envenimer** *vi* (*plaie*) to fester; (*situation, relations*) to worsen

envergure [ãvɛʀgyʀ] *nf* (*d'un oiseau, avion*) wingspan; (*fig: étendue*) scope; (: *valeur*) calibre

enverrai *etc* [ãvɛʀe] *vb voir* **envoyer**

envers [ãvɛʀ] *prép* towards, to ▷ *nm* other side; (*d'une étoffe*) wrong side; **à l'~** upside down; back to front; (*vêtement*) inside out; **~ et contre tous** *ou* **tout** against all opposition

enviable [ãvjabl(ə)] *adj* enviable; **peu ~** unenviable

envie [ãvi] *nf* (*sentiment*) envy; (*souhait*) desire, wish; (*tache sur la peau*) birthmark; (*filet de peau*) hangnail; **avoir ~ de** to feel like; (*désir plus fort*) to want; **avoir ~ de faire** to feel like doing; to want to do; **avoir ~ que** to wish that; **donner à qn l'~ de faire** to make sb want to do; **ça lui fait ~** he would like that

envier [ãvje] *vt* to envy; **~ qch à qn** to envy sb sth; **n'avoir rien à ~ à** to have no cause to be envious of

envieux, -euse [ãvjø, -øz] *adj* envious

environ [ãviʀɔ̃] *adv*: **~ 3 h/2 km, 3 h/2km ~** (around) about 3 o'clock/2 km, 3 o'clock/2 km or so

environnant, e [ãviʀɔnã, -ãt] *adj* surrounding

environnement [ãviʀɔnmã] *nm* environment

environnementaliste [ãviʀɔnmãtalist(ə)] *nm/f* environmentalist

environner [ãviʀɔne] *vt* to surround

environs [ãviʀɔ̃] *nmpl* surroundings; **aux ~ de** around

envisageable [ãvizaʒabl(ə)] *adj* conceivable

envisager [ãvizaʒe] *vt* (*examiner, considérer*) to view, contemplate; (*avoir en vue*) to envisage; **~ de faire** to consider doing

envoi [ãvwa] *nm* sending; (*paquet*) parcel, consignment; **~ contre remboursement** (*Comm*) cash on delivery

envoie *etc* [ãvwa] *vb voir* **envoyer**

envol [ãvɔl] *nm* takeoff

envolée [ãvɔle] *nf* (*fig*) flight

envoler [ãvɔle]: **s'envoler** *vi* (*oiseau*) to fly away *ou* off; (*avion*) to take off; (*papier, feuille*) to blow away; (*fig*) to vanish (into thin air)

envoûtant, e [ãvutã, -ãt] *adj* enchanting

envoûtement [ãvutmã] *nm* bewitchment

envoûter [ãvute] *vt* to bewitch

envoyé, e [ãvwaje] *nm/f* (*Pol*) envoy; (*Presse*) correspondent ▷ *adj*: **bien ~** (*remarque, réponse*) well-aimed

envoyer [ãvwaje] *vt* to send; (*lancer*) to hurl, throw; **~ une gifle/un sourire à qn** to aim a blow/flash a smile at sb; **~ les couleurs** to run up the colours; **~ chercher** to send for; **~ par le fond** (*bateau*) to send to the bottom

envoyeur, -euse [ãvwajœʀ, -øz] *nm/f* sender

enzyme [ãzim] *nf ou m* enzyme

éolien, ne [eɔljɛ̃, -ɛn] *adj* wind *cpd* ▷ *nf* wind turbine; **pompe ~ne** windpump

EOR *sigle m* (= *élève officier de réserve*) ≈ military cadet

éosine [eɔzin] *nf* eosin (*antiseptic used in France to treat skin ailments*)

épagneul, e [epaɲœl] *nm/f* spaniel

épais, se [epɛ, -ɛs] *adj* thick

épaisseur [epɛsœʀ] *nf* thickness

épaissir [epesiʀ] *vt*, **s'épaissir** *vi* to thicken

épaississement [epesismã] *nm* thickening

épanchement [epãʃmã] *nm*: **un ~ de sinovie** water on the knee; **épanchements** *nmpl* (*fig*) (sentimental) outpourings

épancher [epãʃe] *vt* to give vent to; **s'épancher** *vi* to open one's heart; (*liquide*) to pour out

épandage [epãdaʒ] *nm* manure spreading

épanoui, e [epanwi] *adj* (*éclos, ouvert, développé*) blooming; (*radieux*) radiant

épanouir [epanwiʀ]: **s'épanouir** *vi* (*fleur*) to bloom, open out; (*visage*) to light up; (*fig: se développer*) to blossom (out); (: *mentalement*) to open up

épanouissement [epanwismã] *nm* blossoming; opening up

épargnant, e [epaʀɲã, -ãt] *nm/f* saver, investor

épargne [epaʀɲ(ə)] *nf* saving; **l'~-logement** property investment

épargner [epaʀɲe] *vt* to save; (*ne pas tuer ou endommager*) to spare ▷ *vi* to save; **~ qch à qn** to spare sb sth

éparpillement [epaʀpijmã] *nm* (*de papier*) scattering; (*des efforts*) dissipation

éparpiller [epaʀpije] *vt* to scatter; (*pour répartir*) to disperse; (*fig: efforts*) to dissipate; **s'éparpiller** *vi* to scatter; (*fig*) to dissipate one's efforts

épars, e [epaʀ, -aʀs(ə)] *adj* (*maisons*) scattered; (*cheveux*) sparse

épatant, e [epatã, -ãt] *adj* (*fam*) super, splendid

épaté, e [epate] *adj*: **nez ~** flat nose (with wide nostrils)

épater [epate] *vt* to amaze; (*impressionner*) to impress

épaule [epol] *nf* shoulder

épaulé-jeté [epoleʒəte] (*pl* **épaulés-jetés**) *nm* (*Sport*) clean-and-jerk

épaulement [epolmã] *nm* escarpment; (*mur*) retaining wall

épauler [epole] *vt* (*aider*) to back up, support;

(*arme*) to raise (to one's shoulder) ▷ *vi* to (take) aim

épaulette [epolɛt] *nf* (*Mil, d'un veston*) epaulette; (*de combinaison*) shoulder strap

épave [epav] *nf* wreck

épée [epe] *nf* sword

épeler [eple] *vt* to spell

éperdu, e [epɛRdy] *adj* (*personne*) overcome; (*sentiment*) passionate; (*fuite*) frantic

éperdument [epɛRdymã] *adv* (*aimer*) wildly; (*espérer*) fervently

éperlan [epɛRlã] *nm* (*Zool*) smelt

éperon [epRɔ̃] *nm* spur

éperonner [epRɔne] *vt* to spur (on); (*navire*) to ram

épervier [epɛRvje] *nm* (*Zool*) sparrowhawk; (*Pêche*) casting net

éphèbe [efɛb] *nm* beautiful young man

éphémère [efemɛR] *adj* ephemeral, fleeting

éphéméride [efemeRid] *nf* block *ou* tear-off calendar

épi [epi] *nm* (*de blé, d'orge*) ear; **~ de cheveux** tuft of hair; **stationnement/se garer en ~** parking/to park at an angle to the kerb

épice [epis] *nf* spice

épicé, e [epise] *adj* highly spiced, spicy; (*fig*) spicy

épicéa [episea] *nm* spruce

épicentre [episãtR(ə)] *nm* epicentre

épicer [epise] *vt* to spice; (*fig*) to add spice to

épicerie [episRi] *nf* (*magasin*) grocer's shop; (*denrées*) groceries *pl*; **~ fine** delicatessen (shop)

épicier, -ière [episje, -jɛR] *nm/f* grocer

épicurien, ne [epikyRjɛ̃, -ɛn] *adj* epicurean

épidémie [epidemi] *nf* epidemic

épidémique [epidemik] *adj* epidemic

épiderme [epidɛRm(ə)] *nm* skin, epidermis

épidermique [epidɛRmik] *adj* skin *cpd*, epidermic

épier [epje] *vt* to spy on, watch closely; (*occasion*) to look out for

épieu, x [epjø] *nm* (hunting-)spear

épigramme [epigRam] *nf* epigram

épigraphe [epigRaf] *nf* epigraph

épilation [epilasjɔ̃] *nf* removal of unwanted hair

épilatoire [epilatwaR] *adj* depilatory, hair-removing

épilepsie [epilɛpsi] *nf* epilepsy

épileptique [epilɛptik] *adj, nm/f* epileptic

épiler [epile] *vt* (*jambes*) to remove the hair from; (*sourcils*) to pluck; **s'~ les jambes** to remove the hair from one's legs; **s'~ les sourcils** to pluck one's eyebrows; **se faire ~** to get unwanted hair removed; **crème à ~** hair-removing *ou* depilatory cream; **pince à ~** eyebrow tweezers

épilogue [epilog] *nm* (*fig*) conclusion, dénouement

épiloguer [epiloge] *vi*: **~ sur** to hold forth on

épinards [epinaR] *nmpl* spinach *sg*

épine [epin] *nf* thorn, prickle; (*d'oursin etc*) spine, prickle; **~ dorsale** backbone

épineux, -euse [epinø, -øz] *adj* thorny, prickly

épinglage [epɛ̃glaʒ] *nm* pinning

épingle [epɛ̃gl(ə)] *nf* pin; **tirer son ~ du jeu** to play one's game well; **tiré à quatre ~s** well turned-out; **monter qch en ~** to build sth up, make a thing of sth (*fam*); **~ à chapeau** hatpin; **~ à cheveux** hairpin; **virage en ~ à cheveux** hairpin bend; **~ de cravate** tie pin; **~ de nourrice** *ou* **de sûreté** *ou* **double** safety pin, nappy (*Brit*) *ou* diaper (*US*) pin

épingler [epɛ̃gle] *vt* (*badge, décoration*): **~ qch sur** to pin sth on(to); (*Couture: tissu, robe*) to pin together; (*fam*) to catch, nick

épinière [epinjɛR] *adj f voir* **moelle**

Épiphanie [epifani] *nf* Epiphany

épique [epik] *adj* epic

épiscopal, e, -aux [episkɔpal, -o] *adj* episcopal

épiscopat [episkɔpa] *nm* bishopric, episcopate

épisiotomie [epizjɔtomi] *nf* (*Méd*) episiotomy

épisode [epizɔd] *nm* episode; **film/roman à ~s** serialized film/novel, serial

épisodique [epizɔdik] *adj* occasional

épisodiquement [epizɔdikmã] *adv* occasionally

épissure [episyR] *nf* splice

épistémologie [epistemɔlɔʒi] *nf* epistemology

épistolaire [epistɔlɛR] *adj* epistolary; **être en relations ~s avec qn** to correspond with sb

épitaphe [epitaf] *nf* epitaph

épithète [epitɛt] *nf* (*nom, surnom*) epithet; **adjectif ~** attributive adjective

épître [epitR(ə)] *nf* epistle

éploré, e [eplɔRe] *adj* in tears, tearful

épluchage [eplyʃaʒ] *nm* peeling; (*de dossier etc*) careful reading *ou* analysis

épluche-légumes [eplyʃlegym] *nm inv* potato peeler

éplucher [eplyʃe] *vt* (*fruit, légumes*) to peel; (*comptes, dossier*) to go over with a fine-tooth comb

éplucheur [eplyʃœR] *nm* (automatic) peeler

épluchures [eplyʃyR] *nfpl* peelings

épointer [epwɛ̃te] *vt* to blunt

éponge [epɔ̃ʒ] *nf* sponge; **passer l'~ (sur)** (*fig*) to let bygones be bygones (with regard to); **jeter l'~** (*fig*) to throw in the towel; **~ métallique** scourer

éponger [epɔ̃ʒe] *vt* (*liquide*) to mop *ou* sponge up; (*surface*) to sponge; (*fig: déficit*) to soak up, absorb; **s'~ le front** to mop one's brow

épopée [epɔpe] *nf* epic

époque [epɔk] *nf* (*de l'histoire*) age, era; (*de l'année, la vie*) time; **d'~** *adj* (*meuble*) period *cpd*; **à cette ~** at this (*ou* that) time *ou* period; **faire ~** to make history

épouiller [epuje] *vt* to pick lice off; (*avec un produit*) to delouse

époumoner [epumɔne]: **s'époumoner** *vi* to shout (*ou* sing) o.s. hoarse

épouse [epuz] *nf* wife

épouser [epuze] *vt* to marry; (*fig: idées*) to espouse; (: *forme*) to fit

époussetage [epustaʒ] *nm* dusting
épousseter [epuste] *vt* to dust
époustouflant, e [epustuflɑ̃, -ɑ̃t] *adj*
staggering, mind-boggling
époustoufler [epustufle] *vt* to flabbergast,
astound
épouvantable [epuvɑ̃tabl(ə)] *adj* appalling,
dreadful
épouvantablement [epuvɑ̃tabləmɑ̃] *adj*
terribly, dreadfully
épouvantail [epuvɑ̃taj] *nm* (à moineaux)
scarecrow; (fig) bog(e)y; bugbear
épouvante [epuvɑ̃t] *nf* terror; **film d'~** horror
film
épouvanter [epuvɑ̃te] *vt* to terrify
époux [epu] *nm* husband ▷ *nmpl*: **les ~** the
(married) couple, the husband and wife
éprendre [epRɑ̃dR(ə)]: **s'éprendre de** *vt* to fall in
love with
épreuve [epRœv] *nf* (d'examen) test; (malheur,
difficulté) trial, ordeal; (Photo) print; (Typo) proof;
(Sport) event; **à l'~ des balles/du feu** (vêtement)
bulletproof/fireproof; **à toute ~** unfailing;
mettre à l'~ to put to the test; **~ de force** trial
of strength; (fig) showdown; **~ de résistance**
test of resistance; **~ de sélection** (Sport) heat
épris, e [epRi, -iz] *vb voir* **éprendre** ▷ *adj*: **~ de** in
love with
éprouvant, e [epRuvɑ̃, -ɑ̃t] *adj* trying
éprouvé, e [epRuve] *adj* tested, proven
éprouver [epRuve] *vt* (tester) to test; (mettre à
l'épreuve) to put to the test; (marquer, faire souffrir)
to afflict, distress; (ressentir) to experience
éprouvette [epRuvεt] *nf* test tube
EPS *sigle f* (= Éducation physique et sportive) ≈ PE
épuisant, e [epɥizɑ̃, -ɑ̃t] *adj* exhausting
épuisé, e [epɥize] *adj* exhausted; (livre) out of
print
épuisement [epɥizmɑ̃] *nm* exhaustion;
jusqu'à ~ des stocks while stocks last
épuiser [epɥize] *vt* (fatiguer) to exhaust, wear ou
tire out; (stock, sujet) to exhaust; **s'épuiser** *vi* to
wear ou tire o.s. out, exhaust o.s.; (stock) to run
out
épuisette [epɥizεt] *nf* landing net; shrimping
net
épuration [epyRɑsjɔ̃] *nf* purification; purging;
refinement
épure [epyR] *nf* working drawing
épurer [epyRe] *vt* (liquide) to purify; (parti,
administration) to purge; (langue, texte) to refine
équarrir [ekaRiR] *vt* (pierre, arbre) to square (off);
(animal) to quarter
équateur [ekwatœR] *nm* equator; **(la
république de) l'É~** Ecuador
équation [ekwasjɔ̃] *nf* equation; **mettre en ~**
to equate; **~ du premier/second degré** simple/
quadratic equation
équatorial, e, -aux [ekwatɔRjal, -o] *adj*
equatorial
équatorien, ne [ekwatɔRjɛ̃, -εn] *adj* Ecuadorian
▷ *nm/f*: **Équatorien, ne** Ecuadorian

équerre [ekεR] *nf* (à dessin) (set) square; (pour
fixer) brace; **en ~** at right angles; **à l'~, d'~**
straight; **double ~** T-square
équestre [ekεstR(ə)] *adj* equestrian
équeuter [ekøte] *vt* (Culin) to remove the stalk(s)
from
équidé [ekide] *nm* (Zool) member of the horse
family
équidistance [ekɥidistɑ̃s] *nf*: **à ~ (de)**
equidistant (from)
équidistant, e [ekɥidistɑ̃, -ɑ̃t] *adj*: **~ (de)**
equidistant (from)
équilatéral, e, -aux [ekɥilateRal, -o] *adj*
equilateral
équilibrage [ekilibRaʒ] *nm* (Auto): **~ des roues**
wheel balancing
équilibre [ekilibR(ə)] *nm* balance; (d'une balance)
equilibrium; **~ budgétaire** balanced budget;
garder/perdre l'~ to keep/lose one's balance;
être en ~ to be balanced; **mettre en ~** to make
steady; **avoir le sens de l'~** to be well-balanced
équilibré, e [ekilibRe] *adj* (fig) well-balanced,
stable
équilibrer [ekilibRe] *vt* to balance; **s'équilibrer**
vi (poids) to balance; (fig: défauts etc) to balance
each other out
équilibriste [ekilibRist(ə)] *nm/f* tightrope
walker
équinoxe [ekinɔks] *nm* equinox
équipage [ekipaʒ] *nm* crew; **en grand ~** in great
array
équipe [ekip] *nf* team; (bande: parfois péj) bunch;
travailler par ~s to work in shifts; **travailler
en ~** to work as a team; **faire ~ avec** to team up
with; **~ de chercheurs** research team; **~ de
secours** ou **de sauvetage** rescue team
équipé, e [ekipe] *adj* (cuisine etc) equipped,
fitted(-out) ▷ *nf* escapade
équipement [ekipmɑ̃] *nm* equipment;
équipements *nmpl* amenities, facilities;
installations; **biens/dépenses d'~** capital
goods/expenditure; **ministère de l'É~**
department of public works; **~s sportifs/
collectifs** sports/community facilities ou
resources
équiper [ekipe] *vt* to equip; (voiture, cuisine) to
equip, fit out; **~ qn/qch de** to equip sb/sth with;
s'équiper *vi* (sportif) to equip o.s., kit o.s. out
équipier, -ière [ekipje, -jεR] *nm/f* team member
équitable [ekitabl(ə)] *adj* fair
équitablement [ekitabləmɑ̃] *adv* fairly,
equitably
équitation [ekitɑsjɔ̃] *nf* (horse-)riding; **faire
de l'~** to go (horse-)riding
équité [ekite] *nf* equity
équivaille *etc* [ekivaj] *vb voir* **équivaloir**
équivalence [ekivalɑ̃s] *nf* equivalence
équivalent, e [ekivalɑ̃, -ɑ̃t] *adj, nm* equivalent
équivaloir [ekivalwaR]: **~ à** *vt* to be equivalent
to; (représenter) to amount to
équivaut *etc* [ekivo] *vb voir* **équivaloir**
équivoque [ekivɔk] *adj* equivocal, ambiguous;

(louche) dubious ▷ nf ambiguity

érable [eʀabl(ə)] nm maple

éradication [eʀadikasjɔ̃] nf eradication

éradiquer [eʀadike] vt to eradicate

érafler [eʀafle] vt to scratch; **s'~ la main/les jambes** to scrape ou scratch one's hand/legs

éraflure [eʀaflyʀ] nf scratch

éraillé, e [eʀaje] adj (voix) rasping, hoarse

ère [eʀ] nf era; **en l'an 1050 de notre ~** in the year 1050 A.D.

érection [eʀɛksjɔ̃] nf erection

éreintant, e [eʀɛ̃tɑ̃, -ɑ̃t] adj exhausting

éreinté, e [eʀɛ̃te] adj exhausted

éreintement [eʀɛ̃tmɑ̃] nm exhaustion

éreinter [eʀɛ̃te] vt to exhaust, wear out; (fig: critiquer) to slate; **s'~ (à faire qch/à qch)** to wear o.s. out (doing sth/with sth)

ergonomie [eʀgɔnɔmi] nf ergonomics sg

ergonomique [eʀgɔnɔmik] adj ergonomic

ergot [eʀgo] nm (de coq) spur; (Tech) lug

ergoter [eʀgɔte] vi to split hairs, argue over details

ergoteur, -euse [eʀgɔtœʀ, -øz] nm/f hairsplitter

ériger [eʀiʒe] vt (monument) to erect; **~ qch en principe/loi** to make sth a principle/law; **s'~ en critique (de)** to set o.s. up as a critic (of)

ermitage [eʀmitaʒ] nm retreat

ermite [eʀmit] nm hermit

éroder [eʀɔde] vt to erode

érogène [eʀɔʒɛn] adj erogenous

érosion [eʀozjɔ̃] nf erosion

érotique [eʀɔtik] adj erotic

érotiquement [eʀɔtikmɑ̃] adv erotically

érotisme [eʀɔtism(ə)] nm eroticism

errance [eʀɑ̃s] nf wandering

errant, e [eʀɑ̃, -ɑ̃t] adj: **un chien ~** a stray dog

erratum [eʀatɔm, -a] (pl **errata**) nm erratum

errements [eʀmɑ̃] nmpl misguided ways

errer [eʀe] vi to wander

erreur [eʀœʀ] nf mistake, error; (Inform) error; (morale): **~s** nfpl errors; **être dans l'~** to be wrong; **induire qn en ~** to mislead sb; **par ~** by mistake; **sauf ~** unless I'm mistaken; **faire ~** to be mistaken; **~ de date** mistake in the date; **~ de fait** error of fact; **~ d'impression** (Typo) misprint; **~ judiciaire** miscarriage of justice; **~ de jugement** error of judgment; **~ matérielle** ou **d'écriture** clerical error; **~ tactique** tactical error

erroné, e [eʀɔne] adj wrong, erroneous

ersatz [eʀzats] nm substitute, ersatz; **~ de café** coffee substitute

éructer [eʀykte] vi to belch

érudit, e [eʀydi, -it] adj erudite, learned ▷ nm/f scholar

érudition [eʀydisjɔ̃] nf erudition, scholarship

éruptif, -ive [eʀyptif, -iv] adj eruptive

éruption [eʀypsjɔ̃] nf eruption; (cutanée) outbreak; (: boutons) rash; (fig: de joie, colère, folie) outburst

E/S abr (= entrée/sortie) I/O (= in/out)

es [ɛ] vb voir **être**

ès [ɛs] prép: **licencié ès lettres/sciences** ≈ Bachelor of Arts/Science; **docteur ès lettres** ≈ doctor of philosophy, ≈ PhD

esbroufe [ɛsbʀuf] nf: **faire de l'~** to have people on

escabeau, x [ɛskabo] nm (tabouret) stool; (échelle) stepladder

escadre [ɛskadʀ(ə)] nf (Navig) squadron; (Aviat) wing

escadrille [ɛskadʀij] nf (Aviat) flight

escadron [ɛskadʀɔ̃] nm squadron

escalade [ɛskalad] nf climbing no pl; (Pol etc) escalation

escalader [ɛskalade] vt to climb, scale

escalator [ɛskalatɔʀ] nm escalator

escale [ɛskal] nf (Navig) call; (: port) port of call; (Aviat) stop(over); **faire ~ à** to put in at, call in at; to stop over at; **~ technique** (Aviat) refuelling stop

escalier [ɛskalje] nm stairs pl; **dans l'~** ou **les ~s** on the stairs; **descendre l'~** ou **les ~s** to go downstairs; **~ mécanique** ou **roulant** escalator; **~ de secours** fire escape; **~ de service** backstairs; **~ à vis** ou **en colimaçon** spiral staircase

escalope [ɛskalɔp] nf escalope

escamotable [ɛskamɔtabl(ə)] adj (train d'atterrissage, antenne) retractable; (table, lit) fold-away

escamoter [ɛskamɔte] vt (esquiver) to get round, evade; (faire disparaître) to conjure away; (dérober: portefeuille etc) to snatch; (train d'atterrissage) to retract; (mots) to miss out

escapade [ɛskapad] nf: **faire une ~** to go on a jaunt; (s'enfuir) to run away ou off

escarbille [ɛskaʀbij] nf bit of grit

escarcelle [ɛskaʀsɛl] nf: **faire tomber dans l'~** (argent) to bring in

escargot [ɛskaʀgo] nm snail

escarmouche [ɛskaʀmuʃ] nf (Mil) skirmish; (fig: propos hostiles) angry exchange

escarpé, e [ɛskaʀpe] adj steep

escarpement [ɛskaʀpəmɑ̃] nm steep slope

escarpin [ɛskaʀpɛ̃] nm flat(-heeled) shoe

escarre [ɛskaʀ] nf bedsore

Escaut [ɛsko] nm: **l'~** the Scheldt

escient [esjɑ̃] nm: **à bon ~** advisedly

esclaffer [ɛsklafe]: **s'esclaffer** vi to guffaw

esclandre [ɛsklɑ̃dʀ(ə)] nm scene, fracas

esclavage [ɛsklavaʒ] nm slavery

esclavagiste [ɛsklavaʒist(ə)] adj pro-slavery ▷ nm/f supporter of slavery

esclave [ɛsklav] nm/f slave; **être ~ de** (fig) to be a slave of

escogriffe [ɛskɔgʀif] nm (péj) beanpole

escompte [ɛskɔ̃t] nm discount

escompter [ɛskɔ̃te] vt (Comm) to discount; (espérer) to expect, reckon upon; **~ que** to reckon ou expect that

escorte [ɛskɔʀt(ə)] nf escort; **faire ~ à** to escort

escorter [ɛskɔʀte] vt to escort

escorteur [ɛskɔʀtœʀ] nm (Navig) escort (ship)

escouade [ɛskwad] *nf* squad; *(fig: groupe de personnes)* group

escrime [ɛskʀim] *nf* fencing; **faire de l'~** to fence

escrimer [ɛskʀime]: **s'escrimer** *vi*: **s'~ à faire** to wear o.s. out doing

escrimeur, -euse [ɛskʀimœʀ, -øz] *nm/f* fencer

escroc [ɛskʀo] *nm* swindler, con-man

escroquer [ɛskʀɔke] *vt*: **~ qn (de qch)/qch à qn** to swindle sb (out of sth)/sth out of sb

escroquerie [ɛskʀɔkʀi] *nf* swindle

ésotérique [ezɔteʀik] *adj* esoteric

espace [ɛspas] *nm* space; **~ publicitaire** advertising space; **~ vital** living space

espacé, e [ɛspase] *adj* spaced out

espacement [ɛspasmɑ̃] *nm*: **~ proportionnel** proportional spacing *(on printer)*

espacer [ɛspase] *vt* to space out; **s'espacer** *vi (visites etc)* to become less frequent

espadon [ɛspadɔ̃] *nm* swordfish *inv*

espadrille [ɛspadʀij] *nf* rope-soled sandal

Espagne [ɛspaɲ(ə)] *nf*: **l'~** Spain

espagnol, e [ɛspaɲɔl] *adj* Spanish ▷ *nm (Ling)* Spanish ▷ *nm/f*: **Espagnol, e** Spaniard

espagnolette [ɛspaɲɔlɛt] *nf (window)* catch; **fermé à l'~** resting on the catch

espalier [ɛspalje] *nm (arbre fruitier)* espalier

espèce [ɛspɛs] *nf (Bio, Bot, Zool)* species *inv*; *(gén: sorte)* sort, kind, type; *(péj)*: **~ de maladroit/de brute!** you clumsy oaf/you brute!; **espèces** *nfpl (Comm)* cash *sg*; *(Rel)* species; **de toute ~** of all kinds *ou* sorts; **en l'~** *adv* in the case in point; **payer en ~s** to pay (in) cash; **cas d'~** individual case; **l'~ humaine** humankind

espérance [ɛspeʀɑ̃s] *nf* hope; **~ de vie** life expectancy

espéranto [ɛspeʀɑ̃to] *nm* esperanto

espérer [ɛspeʀe] *vt* to hope for; **j'espère (bien)** I hope so; **~ que/faire** to hope that/to do; **~ en** to trust in

espiègle [ɛspjɛgl(ə)] *adj* mischievous

espièglerie [ɛspjɛgləʀi] *nf* mischievousness; *(tour, farce)* piece of mischief, prank

espion, ne [ɛspjɔ̃, -ɔn] *nm/f* spy; **avion ~** spy plane

espionnage [ɛspjɔnaʒ] *nm* espionage, spying; **film/roman d'~** spy film/novel

espionner [ɛspjɔne] *vt* to spy (up)on

esplanade [ɛsplanad] *nf* esplanade

espoir [ɛspwaʀ] *nm* hope; **l'~ de qch/de faire qch** the hope of sth/of doing sth; **avoir bon ~ que ...** to have high hopes that ...; **garder l'~ que ...** to remain hopeful that ...; **un ~ de la boxe/du ski** one of boxing's/skiing's hopefuls, one of the hopes of boxing/skiing; **sans ~** *adj* hopeless

esprit [ɛspʀi] *nm (pensée, intellect)* mind; *(humour, ironie)* wit; *(mentalité, d'une loi etc, fantôme etc)* spirit; **l'~ d'équipe/de compétition** team/competitive spirit; **faire de l'~** to try to be witty; **reprendre ses ~s** to come to; **perdre l'~** to lose one's mind; **avoir bon/mauvais ~** to be of a good/bad disposition; **avoir l'~ à faire qch** to have a mind to do sth; **avoir l'~ critique** to be critical; **~ de contradiction** contrariness; **~ de corps** esprit de corps; **~ de famille** family loyalty; **l'~ malin** *(le diable)* the Evil One; **~s chagrins** fault-finders

esquif [ɛskif] *nm* skiff

esquimau, de, -x [ɛskimo, -od] *adj* Eskimo ▷ *nm (Ling)* Eskimo; *(glace)*: **E-®** ice lolly *(Brit)*, popsicle *(US)* ▷ *nm/f*: **Esquimau, de** Eskimo; **chien ~** husky

esquinter [ɛskɛ̃te] *vt (fam)* to mess up; **s'esquinter** *vi*: **s'~ à faire qch** to knock o.s. out doing sth

esquisse [ɛskis] *nf* sketch; **l'~ d'un sourire/changement** a hint of a smile/of change

esquisser [ɛskise] *vt* to sketch; **s'esquisser** *vi (amélioration)* to begin to be detectable; **~ un sourire** to give a hint of a smile

esquive [ɛskiv] *nf (Boxe)* dodging; *(fig)* sidestepping

esquiver [ɛskive] *vt* to dodge; **s'esquiver** *vi* to slip away

essai [esɛ] *nm* trying; *(tentative)* attempt, try; *(Rugby)* try; *(Littérature)* essay; **essais** *nmpl (Auto)* trials; **à l'~** on a trial basis; **~ gratuit** *(Comm)* free trial

essaim [esɛ̃] *nm* swarm

essaimer [eseme] *vi* to swarm; *(fig)* to spread, expand

essayage [esɛjaʒ] *nm (d'un vêtement)* trying on, fitting; **salon d'~** fitting room; **cabine d'~** fitting room *(cubicle)*

essayer [eseje] *vt (gén)* to try; *(vêtement, chaussures)* to try (on); *(restaurant, méthode, voiture)* to try (out) ▷ *vi* to try; **~ de faire** to try *ou* attempt to do; **s'~ à faire** to try one's hand at doing; **essayez un peu!** *(menace)* just you try!

essayeur, -euse [esɛjœʀ, -øz] *nm/f (chez un tailleur etc)* fitter

essayiste [esejist(ə)] *nm/f* essayist

ESSEC [esɛk] *sigle f (= École supérieure des sciences économiques et sociales) grande école for management and business studies*

essence [esɑ̃s] *nf (de voiture)* petrol *(Brit)*, gas(oline) *(US)*; *(extrait de plante, Philosophie)* essence; *(espèce: d'arbre)* species *inv*; **prendre de l'~** to get (some) petrol *ou* gas; **par ~** *(essentiellement)* essentially; **~ de citron/rose** lemon/rose oil; **~ sans plomb** unleaded petrol; **~ de térébenthine** turpentine

essentiel, le [esɑ̃sjɛl] *adj* essential ▷ *nm*: **l'~ d'un discours/d'une œuvre** the essence of a speech/work of art; **emporter l'~** to take the essentials; **c'est l'~** *(ce qui importe)* that's the main thing; **l'~ de** *(la majeure partie)* the main part of

essentiellement [esɑ̃sjɛlmɑ̃] *adv* essentially

esseulé, e [esœle] *adj* forlorn

essieu, x [esjø] *nm* axle

essor [esɔʀ] *nm (de l'économie etc)* rapid expansion; **prendre son ~** *(oiseau)* to fly off

essorage [esɔʀaʒ] *nm* wringing out; spin-drying; spinning; shaking

essorer [esɔʀe] *vt* (*en tordant*) to wring (out); (*par la force centrifuge*) to spin-dry; (*salade*) to spin; (: *en secouant*) to shake dry

essoreuse [esɔʀøz] *nf* mangle, wringer; (*à tambour*) spin-dryer

essoufflé, e [esufle] *adj* out of breath, breathless

essouffler [esufle] *vt* to make breathless; **s'essouffler** *vi* to get out of breath; (*fig: économie*) to run out of steam

essuie *etc* [esɥi] *vb voir* **essuyer**

essuie-glace [esɥiglas] *nm* windscreen (*Brit*) *ou* windshield (*US*) wiper

essuie-mains [esɥimɛ̃] *nm inv* hand towel

essuierai *etc* [esɥiʀe] *vb voir* **essuyer**

essuie-tout [esɥitu] *nm inv* kitchen paper

essuyer [esɥije] *vt* to wipe; (*fig: subir*) to suffer; **s'essuyer** (*après le bain*) to dry o.s.; **~ la vaisselle** to dry up, dry the dishes

est [ɛ] *vb voir* **être** ▷ *nm* [ɛst]: **l'~** the east ▷ *adj inv* east; (*région*) east(ern); **à l'~** in the east; (*direction*) to the east, east(wards); **à l'~ de** (to the) east of; **les pays de l'E~** the eastern countries

estafette [ɛstafɛt] *nf* (*Mil*) dispatch rider

estafilade [ɛstafilad] *nf* gash, slash

est-allemand, e [ɛstalmɑ̃, -ɑ̃d] *adj* East German

estaminet [ɛstaminɛ] *nm* tavern

estampe [ɛstɑ̃p] *nf* print, engraving

estamper [ɛstɑ̃pe] *vt* (*monnaies etc*) to stamp; (*fam: escroquer*) to swindle

estampille [ɛstɑ̃pij] *nf* stamp

est-ce que [ɛskə] *adv*: **~ c'est cher/c'était bon?** is it expensive/was it good?; **quand est-ce qu'il part?** when does he leave?, when is he leaving?; **où est-ce qu'il va?** where's he going?; *voir aussi* **que**

este [ɛst(ə)] *adj* Estonian ▷ *nm/f*: **Este** Estonian

esthète [ɛstɛt] *nm/f* aesthete

esthéticienne [ɛstetisjɛn] *nf* beautician

esthétique [ɛstetik] *adj* (*sens, jugement*) aesthetic; (*beau*) attractive, aesthetically pleasing ▷ *nf* aesthetics *sg*; **l'~ industrielle** industrial design

esthétiquement [ɛstetikmɑ̃] *adv* aesthetically

estimable [ɛstimabl(ə)] *adj* respected

estimatif, -ive [ɛstimatif, -iv] *adj* estimated

estimation [ɛstimasjɔ̃] *nf* valuation; assessment; **d'après mes ~s** according to my calculations

estime [ɛstim] *nf* esteem, regard; **avoir de l'~ pour qn** to think highly of sb

estimer [ɛstime] *vt* (*respecter*) to esteem, hold in high regard; (*expertiser*) to value; (*évaluer*) to assess, estimate; (*penser*): **~ que/être** to consider that/o.s. to be; **s'estimer satisfait/heureux** *vi* to feel satisfied/happy; **j'estime la distance à 10 km** I reckon the distance to be 10 km

estival, e, -aux [ɛstival, -o] *adj* summer *cpd*;

station ~e (summer) holiday resort

estivant, e [ɛstivɑ̃, -ɑ̃t] *nm/f* (summer) holiday-maker

estoc [ɛstɔk] *nm*: **frapper d'~ et de taille** to cut and thrust

estocade [ɛstɔkad] *nf* death-blow

estomac [ɛstɔma] *nm* stomach; **avoir mal à l'~** to have stomach ache; **avoir l'~ creux** to have an empty stomach

estomaqué, e [ɛstɔmake] *adj* flabbergasted

estompe [ɛstɔ̃p] *nf* stump; (*dessin*) stump drawing

estompé, e [ɛstɔ̃pe] *adj* blurred

estomper [ɛstɔ̃pe] *vt* (*Art*) to shade off; (*fig*) to blur, dim; **s'estomper** *vi* (*sentiments*) to soften; (*contour*) to become blurred

Estonie [ɛstɔni] *nf*: **l'~** Estonia

estonien, ne [ɛstɔnjɛ̃, -ɛn] *adj* Estonian ▷ *nm* (*Ling*) Estonian ▷ *nm/f*: **Estonien, ne** Estonian

estrade [ɛstʀad] *nf* platform, rostrum

estragon [ɛstʀagɔ̃] *nm* tarragon

estropié, e [ɛstʀɔpje] *nm/f* cripple

estropier [ɛstʀɔpje] *vt* to cripple, maim; (*fig*) to twist, distort

estuaire [ɛstɥɛʀ] *nm* estuary

estudiantin, e [ɛstydjɑ̃tɛ̃, -in] *adj* student *cpd*

esturgeon [ɛstyʀʒɔ̃] *nm* sturgeon

et [e] *conj* and; **et lui?** what about him?; **et alors?, et (puis) après?** so what?; (*ensuite*) and then?

ét. *abr* = **étage**

ETA [eta] *sigle m* (*Pol*) ETA

étable [etabl(ə)] *nf* cowshed

établi, e [etabli] *adj* established ▷ *nm* (work)bench

établir [etabliʀ] *vt* (*papiers d'identité, facture*) to make out; (*liste, programme*) to draw up; (*gouvernement, artisan etc: aider à s'installer*) to set up, establish; (*entreprise, atelier, camp*) to set up; (*réputation, usage, fait, culpabilité, relations*) to establish; (*Sport: record*) to set; **s'établir** *vi* (*se faire: entente etc*) to be established; **s'~ (à son compte)** to set up in business; **s'~ à/près de** to settle in/near

établissement [etablismɑ̃] *nm* making out; drawing up; setting up, establishing; (*entreprise, institution*) establishment; **~ de crédit** credit institution; **~ hospitalier** hospital complex; **~ industriel** industrial plant, factory; **~ scolaire** school, educational establishment

étage [etaʒ] *nm* (*d'immeuble*) storey (*Brit*), story (*US*), floor; (*de fusée*) stage; (*Géo: de culture, végétation*) level; **au 2ème ~** on the 2nd (*Brit*) *ou* 3rd (*US*) floor; **à l'~** upstairs; **maison à deux ~s** two-storey *ou* -story house; **de bas ~** *adj* low-born; (*médiocre*) inferior

étager [etaʒe] *vt* (*cultures*) to lay out in tiers; **s'étager** *vi* (*prix*) to range; (*zones, cultures*) to lie on different levels

étagère [etaʒɛʀ] *nf* (*rayon*) shelf; (*meuble*) shelves *pl*, set of shelves

étai [etɛ] *nm* stay, prop

étain [etɛ̃] *nm* tin; (*Orfèvrerie*) pewter *no pl*

étais *etc* [etɛ] *vb voir* **être**

étal [etal] *nm* stall

étalage [etalaʒ] *nm* display; (*vitrine*) display window; **faire ~ de** to show off, parade

étalagiste [etalaʒist(ə)] *nm/f* window-dresser

étale [etal] *adj* (*mer*) slack

étalement [etalmɑ̃] *nm* spreading; (*échelonnement*) staggering

étaler [etale] *vt* (*carte, nappe*) to spread (out); (*peinture, liquide*) to spread; (*échelonner: paiements, dates, vacances*) to spread, stagger; (*exposer: marchandises*) to display; (*richesses, connaissances*) to parade; **s'étaler** *vi* (*liquide*) to spread out; (*fam*) to come a cropper (*Brit*), fall flat on one's face; **s'~ sur** (*paiements etc*) to be spread over

étalon [etalɔ̃] *nm* (*mesure*) standard; (*cheval*) stallion; **l'~-or** the gold standard

étalonner [etalone] *vt* to calibrate

étamer [etame] *vt* (*casserole*) to tin(plate); (*glace*) to silver

étamine [etamin] *nf* (*Bot*) stamen; (*tissu*) butter muslin

étanche [etɑ̃ʃ] *adj* (*récipient, aussi fig*) watertight; (*montre, vêtement*) waterproof; **~ à l'air** airtight

étanchéité [etɑ̃ʃeite] *nf* watertightness; airtightness

étancher [etɑ̃ʃe] *vt* (*liquide*) to stop (flowing); **~ sa soif** to quench *ou* slake one's thirst

étançon [etɑ̃sɔ̃] *nm* (*Tech*) prop

étançonner [etɑ̃sone] *vt* to prop up

étang [etɑ̃] *nm* pond

étant [etɑ̃] *vb voir* **être; donné**

étape [etap] *nf* stage; (*lieu d'arrivée*) stopping place; (*Cyclisme*) staging point; **faire ~ à** to stop off at; **brûler les ~s** (*fig*) to cut corners

état [eta] *nm* (*Pol, condition*) state; (*d'un article d'occasion etc*) condition, state; (*liste*) inventory, statement; (*condition: professionnelle*) profession, trade; (*: sociale*) status; **en bon/mauvais ~** in good/poor condition; **en ~ (de marche)** in (working) order; **remettre en ~** to repair; **hors d'~** out of order; **être en ~/hors d'~ de faire** to be in a state/in no fit state to do; **en tout ~ de cause** in any event; **être dans tous ses ~s** to be in a state; **faire ~ de** (*alléguer*) to put forward; **en ~ d'arrestation** under arrest; **~ de grâce** (*Rel*) state of grace; (*fig*) honeymoon period; **en ~ de grâce** (*fig*) inspired; **en ~ d'ivresse** under the influence of drink; **~ de choses** (*situation*) state of affairs; **~ civil** civil status; (*bureau*) registry office (*Brit*); **~ d'esprit** frame of mind; **~ des lieux** inventory of fixtures; **~ de santé** state of health; **~ de siège/d'urgence** state of siege/emergency; **~ de veille** (*Psych*) waking state; **~s d'âme** moods; **les É~s barbaresques** the Barbary States; **les É~s du Golfe** the Gulf States; **~s de service** service record *sg*

étatique [etatik] *adj* state *cpd*, State *cpd*

étatisation [etatizasjɔ̃] *nf* nationalization

étatiser [etatize] *vt* to bring under state control

étatisme [etatism(ə)] *nm* state control

étatiste [etatist(ə)] *adj* (*doctrine etc*) of state control ▷ *nm/f* partisan of state control

état-major [etamaʒɔR] (*pl* **états-majors**) *nm* (*Mil*) staff; (*d'un parti etc*) top advisers *pl*; (*d'une entreprise*) top management

État-providence [etapRɔvidɑ̃s] *nm* welfare state

États-Unis [etazyni] *nmpl*: **les ~ (d'Amérique)** the United States (of America)

étau, x [eto] *nm* vice (*Brit*), vise (*US*)

étayer [eteje] *vt* to prop *ou* shore up; (*fig*) to back up

et cætera, et cetera [ɛtseteRa], **etc.** *adv* et cetera, and so on, etc

été [ete] *pp de* **être** ▷ *nm* summer; **en ~** in summer

éteignais *etc* [etɛɲɛ] *vb voir* **éteindre**

éteignoir [etɛɲwaR] *nm* (*candle*) snuffer; (*péj*) killjoy, wet blanket

éteindre [etɛ̃dR(ə)] *vt* (*lampe, lumière, radio, chauffage*) to turn *ou* switch off; (*cigarette, incendie, bougie*) to put out, extinguish; (*Jur: dette*) to extinguish; **s'éteindre** *vi* to go off; to go out; (*mourir*) to pass away

éteint, e [etɛ̃, -ɛ̃t] *pp de* **éteindre** ▷ *adj* (*fig*) lacklustre, dull; (*volcan*) extinct; **tous feux ~s** (*Auto: rouler*) without lights

étendard [etɑ̃daR] *nm* standard

étendre [etɑ̃dR(ə)] *vt* (*appliquer: pâte, liquide*) to spread; (*déployer: carte etc*) to spread out; (*sur un fil: lessive, linge*) to hang up *ou* out; (*bras, jambes, par terre: blessé*) to stretch out; (*diluer*) to dilute, thin; (*fig: agrandir*) to extend; (*fam: adversaire*) to floor; **s'étendre** *vi* (*augmenter, se propager*) to spread; (*terrain, forêt etc*): **s'~ jusqu'à/de ... à** to stretch as far as/from ... to; **s'~ (sur)** (*s'allonger*) to stretch out (upon); (*se coucher*) to lie down (on); (*fig: expliquer*) to elaborate *ou* enlarge (upon)

étendu, e [etɑ̃dy] *adj* extensive ▷ *nf* (*d'eau, de sable*) stretch, expanse; (*importance*) extent

éternel, le [etɛRnɛl] *adj* eternal; **les neiges ~les** perpetual snow

éternellement [etɛRnɛlmɑ̃] *adv* eternally

éterniser [etɛRnize]: **s'éterniser** *vi* to last for ages; (*personne*) to stay for ages

éternité [etɛRnite] *nf* eternity; **il y a** *ou* **ça fait une ~ que** it's ages since; **de toute ~** from time immemorial

éternuement [etɛRnymɑ̃] *nm* sneeze

éternuer [etɛRnɥe] *vi* to sneeze

êtes [ɛt] *vb voir* **être**

étêter [etete] *vt* (*arbre*) to poll(ard); (*clou, poisson*) to cut the head off

éther [etɛR] *nm* ether

éthéré, e [etere] *adj* ethereal

Éthiopie [etjɔpi] *nf*: **l'~** Ethiopia

éthiopien, ne [etjɔpjɛ̃, -ɛn] *adj* Ethiopian

éthique [etik] *adj* ethical ▷ *nf* ethics *sg*

ethnie [ɛtni] *nf* ethnic group

ethnique [ɛtnik] *adj* ethnic

ethnographe [ɛtnɔgRaf] *nm/f* ethnographer

ethnographie [ɛtnɔgRafi] *nf* ethnography

ethnographique [ɛtnɔɡʀafik] *adj*
ethnographic(al)
ethnologie [ɛtnɔlɔʒi] *nf* ethnology
ethnologique [ɛtnɔlɔʒik] *adj* ethnological
ethnologue [ɛtnɔlɔɡ] *nm/f* ethnologist
éthylique [etilik] *adj* alcoholic
éthylisme [etilism(ə)] *nm* alcoholism
étiage [etjaʒ] *nm* low water
étiez [etje] *vb voir* **être**
étincelant, e [etɛ̃slɑ̃, -ɑ̃t] *adj* sparkling
étinceler [etɛ̃sle] *vi* to sparkle
étincelle [etɛ̃sɛl] *nf* spark
étioler [etjɔle]: **s'étioler** *vi* to wilt
étions [etjɔ̃] *vb voir* **être**
étique [etik] *adj* skinny, bony
étiquetage [etiktaʒ] *nm* labelling
étiqueter [etikte] *vt* to label
étiquette [etikɛt] *vb voir* **étiqueter** ▷ *nf* label;
(*protocole*): **l'~** etiquette
étirer [etiʀe] *vt* to stretch; (*ressort*) to stretch out;
s'étirer *vi* (*personne*) to stretch; (*convoi, route*): **s'~
sur** to stretch out over
étoffe [etɔf] *nf* material, fabric; **avoir l'~ d'un
chef** *etc* to be cut out to be a leader *etc*; **avoir de
l'~** to be a forceful personality
étoffer [etɔfe] *vt* to flesh out; **s'étoffer** *vi* to fill
out
étoile [etwal] *nf* star ▷ *adj*: **danseuse** *ou*
danseur ~ leading dancer; **la bonne/mauvaise
~ de qn** sb's lucky/unlucky star; **à la belle ~**
(out) in the open; **~ filante** shooting star; **~ de
mer** starfish; **~ polaire** pole star
étoilé, e [etwale] *adj* starry
étole [etɔl] *nf* stole
étonnamment [etɔnamɑ̃] *adv* amazingly
étonnant, e [etɔnɑ̃, -ɑ̃t] *adj* surprising
étonné, e [etɔne] *adj* surprised
étonnement [etɔnmɑ̃] *nm* surprise; **à mon
grand ~ ...** to my great surprise *ou*
amazement ...
étonner [etɔne] *vt* to surprise; **s'étonner que/
de** to be surprised that/at; **cela m'~ait (que)**
(*j'en doute*) I'd be (very) surprised (if)
étouffant, e [etufɑ̃, -ɑ̃t] *adj* stifling
étouffé, e [etufe] *adj* (*asphyxié*) suffocated;
(*assourdi: cris, rires*) smothered ▷ *nf* (*Culin:
poisson, légumes*) steamed; (: *viande*) braised
étouffement [etufmɑ̃] *nm* suffocation
étouffer [etufe] *vt* to suffocate; (*bruit*) to muffle;
(*scandale*) to hush up ▷ *vi* to suffocate; (*avoir trop
chaud; aussi fig*) to feel stifled; **s'étouffer** *vi* (*en
mangeant etc*) to choke
étouffoir [etufwaʀ] *nm* (*Mus*) damper
étourderie [etuʀdəʀi] *nf* heedlessness *no pl*;
thoughtless blunder; **faute d'~** careless
mistake
étourdi, e [etuʀdi] *adj* (*distrait*) scatterbrained,
heedless
étourdiment [etuʀdimɑ̃] *adv* rashly
étourdir [etuʀdiʀ] *vt* (*assommer*) to stun, daze;
(*griser*) to make dizzy *ou* giddy
étourdissant, e [etuʀdisɑ̃, -ɑ̃t] *adj* staggering

étourdissement [etuʀdismɑ̃] *nm* dizzy spell
étourneau, x [etuʀno] *nm* starling
étrange [etʀɑ̃ʒ] *adj* strange
étrangement [etʀɑ̃ʒmɑ̃] *adv* strangely
étranger, -ère [etʀɑ̃ʒe, -ɛʀ] *adj* foreign; (*pas de la
famille, non familier*) strange ▷ *nm/f* foreigner;
stranger ▷ *nm*: **l'~** foreign countries; **à l'~**
abroad; **de l'~** from abroad; **~ à** (*mal connu*)
unfamiliar to; (*sans rapport*) irrelevant to
étrangeté [etʀɑ̃ʒte] *nf* strangeness
étranglé, e [etʀɑ̃gle] *adj*: **d'une voix ~e** in a
strangled voice
étranglement [etʀɑ̃gləmɑ̃] *nm* (*d'une vallée etc*)
constriction, narrow passage
étrangler [etʀɑ̃gle] *vt* to strangle; (*fig: presse,
libertés*) to stifle; **s'étrangler** *vi* (*en mangeant etc*)
to choke; (*se resserrer*) to make a bottleneck
étrave [etʀav] *nf* stem

 MOT-CLÉ

être [ɛtʀ(ə)] *nm* being; **être humain** human
being
▷ *vb copule* **1** (*état, description*) to be; **il est
instituteur** he is *ou* he's a teacher; **vous êtes
grand/intelligent/fatigué** you are *ou* you're
tall/clever/tired
2 (+*à: appartenir*) to be; **le livre est à Paul** the
book is Paul's *ou* belongs to Paul; **c'est à moi/
eux** it is *ou* it's mine/theirs
3 (+*de: provenance*): **il est de Paris** he is from
Paris; (*appartenance*;): **il est des nôtres** he is
one of us
4 (*date*): **nous sommes le 10 janvier** it's the
10th of January (today)
▷ *vi* to be; **je ne serai pas ici demain** I won't be
here tomorrow
▷ *vb aux* **1** to have; to be; **être arrivé/allé** to
have arrived/gone; **il est parti** he has left, he
has gone
2 (*forme passive*) to be; **être fait par** to be made
by; **il a été promu** he has been promoted
3 (+*à* +*inf: obligation, but*): **c'est à réparer** it
needs repairing; **c'est à essayer** it should be
tried; **il est à espérer que ...** it is *ou* it's to be
hoped that ...
▷ *vb impers* **1**: **il est** (*avec adjectif*) it is; **il est
impossible de le faire** it's impossible to do it
2 (*heure, date*): **il est 10 heures** it is *ou* it's 10
o'clock
3 (*emphatique*): **c'est moi** it's me; **c'est à lui de
le faire** it's up to him to do it; *voir aussi* **est-ce
que**; **n'est-ce pas**; **c'est-à-dire**; **ce**

étreindre [etʀɛ̃dʀ(ə)] *vt* to clutch, grip;
(*amoureusement, amicalement*) to embrace;
s'étreindre to embrace
étreinte [etʀɛ̃t] *nf* clutch, grip; embrace;
resserrer son ~ autour de (*fig*) to tighten one's
grip on *ou* around
étrenner [etʀene] *vt* to use (*ou* wear) for the first
time

étrennes [etʀɛn] *nfpl* (*cadeaux*) New Year's present; (*gratifications*) ≈ Christmas box *sg*, ≈ Christmas bonus

étrier [etʀije] *nm* stirrup

étriller [etʀije] *vt* (*cheval*) to curry; (*fam: battre*) to slaughter (*fig*)

étriper [etʀipe] *vt* to gut; (*fam*): ~ **qn** to tear sb's guts out

étriqué, e [etʀike] *adj* skimpy

étroit, e [etʀwa, -wat] *adj* narrow; (*vêtement*) tight; (*fig: serré*) close, tight; **à l'~** cramped; ~ **d'esprit** narrow-minded

étroitement [etʀwatmã] *adv* closely

étroitesse [etʀwatɛs] *nf* narrowness; ~ **d'esprit** narrow-mindedness

étrusque [etʀysk(ə)] *adj* Etruscan

étude [etyd] *nf* studying; (*ouvrage, rapport, Mus*) study; (*de notaire: bureau*) office; (*: charge*) practice; (*Scol: salle de travail*) study room; **études** *nfpl* (*Scol*) studies; **être à l'~** (*projet etc*) to be under consideration; **faire des ~s (de droit/ médecine)** to study (law/medicine); **~s secondaires/supérieures** secondary/higher education; **~ de cas** case study; **~ de faisabilité** feasibility study; **~ de marché** (*Écon*) market research

étudiant, e [etydjã, -ãt] *adj, nm/f* student

étudié, e [etydje] *adj* (*démarche*) studied; (*système*) carefully designed; (*prix*) keen

étudier [etydje] *vt, vi* to study

étui [etɥi] *nm* case

étuve [etyv] *nf* steamroom; (*appareil*) sterilizer

étuvée [etyve]: **à l'~** *adv* braised

étymologie [etimɔlɔʒi] *nf* etymology

étymologique [etimɔlɔʒik] *adj* etymological

eu, eue [y] *pp de* **avoir**

EU *sigle mpl* (= *États-Unis*) US

EUA *sigle mpl* (= *États-Unis d'Amérique*) USA

eucalyptus [økaliptys] *nm* eucalyptus

Eucharistie [økaʀisti] *nf*: **l'~** the Eucharist, the Lord's Supper

eucharistique [økaʀistik] *adj* eucharistic

euclidien, ne [øklidjɛ̃, -ɛn] *adj* Euclidian

eugénique [øʒenik] *adj* eugenic ▷ *nf* eugenics *sg*

eugénisme [øʒenism(ə)] *nm* eugenics *sg*

euh [ø] *excl* er

eunuque [ønyk] *nm* eunuch

euphémique [øfemik] *adj* euphemistic

euphémisme [øfemism(ə)] *nm* euphemism

euphonie [øfɔni] *nf* euphony

euphorbe [øfɔʀb(ə)] *nf* (*Bot*) spurge

euphorie [øfɔʀi] *nf* euphoria

euphorique [øfɔʀik] *adj* euphoric

euphorisant, e [øfɔʀizã, -ãt] *adj* exhilarating

eurafricain, e [øʀafʀikɛ̃, -ɛn] *adj* Eurafrican

eurasiatique [øʀazjatik] *adj* Eurasiatic

Eurasie [øʀazi] *nf*: **l'~** Eurasia

eurasien, ne [øʀazjɛ̃, -ɛn] *adj* Eurasian

EURATOM [øʀatɔm] *sigle f* Euratom

eurent [yʀ(ə)] *vb voir* **avoir**

euro [øʀo] *nm* euro

euro- [øʀo] *préfixe* Euro-

eurocrate [øʀɔkʀat] *nm/f* (*péj*) Eurocrat

eurodevise [øʀɔdəviz] *nf* Eurocurrency

eurodollar [øʀɔdɔlaʀ] *nm* Eurodollar

Euroland [øʀɔlãd] *nm* Euroland

euromonnaie [øʀɔmɔnɛ] *nf* Eurocurrency

Europe [øʀɔp] *nf*: **l'~** Europe; **l'~ centrale** Central Europe; **l'~ verte** European agriculture

européanisation [øʀɔpeanizasjɔ̃] *nf* Europeanization

européaniser [øʀɔpeanize] *vt* to Europeanize

européen, ne [øʀɔpeɛ̃, -ɛn] *adj* European ▷ *nm/f*: **Européen, ne** European

eurosceptique [øʀɔsɛptik] *nm/f* Eurosceptic

Eurovision [øʀovizjɔ̃] *nf* Eurovision; **émission en ~** Eurovision broadcast

eus *etc* [y] *vb voir* **avoir**

euthanasie [øtanazi] *nf* euthanasia

eux [ø] *pron* (*sujet*) they; (*objet*) them; **~, ils ont fait ...** THEY did ...

évacuation [evakɥasjɔ̃] *nf* evacuation

évacué, e [evakɥe] *nm/f* evacuee

évacuer [evakɥe] *vt* (*salle, région*) to evacuate, clear; (*occupants, population*) to evacuate; (*toxine etc*) to evacuate, discharge

évadé, e [evade] *adj* escaped ▷ *nm/f* escapee

évader [evade]: **s'évader** *vi* to escape

évaluation [evalɥasjɔ̃] *nf* assessment, evaluation

évaluer [evalɥe] *vt* to assess, evaluate

évanescent, e [evanesã, -ãt] *adj* evanescent

évangélique [evãʒelik] *adj* evangelical

évangélisation [evãʒelizasjɔ̃] *nf* evangelization

évangéliser [evãʒelize] *vt* to evangelize

évangéliste [evãʒelist(ə)] *nm* evangelist

évangile [evãʒil] *nm* gospel; (*texte de la Bible*): **É~** Gospel; **ce n'est pas l'É~** (*fig*) it's not gospel

évanoui, e [evanwi] *adj* in a faint; **tomber ~** to faint

évanouir [evanwiʀ]: **s'évanouir** *vi* to faint, pass out; (*disparaître*) to vanish, disappear

évanouissement [evanwismã] *nm* (*syncope*) fainting fit; (*Méd*) loss of consciousness

évaporation [evapɔʀasjɔ̃] *nf* evaporation

évaporé, e [evapɔʀe] *adj* giddy, scatterbrained

évaporer [evapɔʀe]: **s'évaporer** *vi* to evaporate

évasé, e [evaze] *adj* (*jupe etc*) flared

évaser [evaze] *vt* (*tuyau*) to widen, open out; (*jupe, pantalon*) to flare; **s'évaser** *vi* to widen, open out

évasif, -ive [evazif, -iv] *adj* evasive

évasion [evazjɔ̃] *nf* escape; **littérature d'~** escapist literature; **~ des capitaux** (*Écon*) flight of capital; **~ fiscale** tax avoidance

évasivement [evazivmã] *adv* evasively

évêché [eveʃe] *nm* (*fonction*) bishopric; (*palais*) bishop's palace

éveil [evɛj] *nm* awakening; **être en ~** to be alert; **mettre qn en ~, donner l'~ à qn** to arouse sb's suspicions; **activités d'~** early-learning activities

éveillé, e [eveje] *adj* awake; (*vif*) alert, sharp
éveiller [eveje] *vt* to (a)waken; **s'éveiller** *vi* to (a)waken; (*fig*) to be aroused
événement [evɛnmɑ̃] *nm* event
éventail [evɑ̃taj] *nm* fan; (*choix*) range; **en ~** fanned out; fan-shaped
éventaire [evɑ̃tɛʀ] *nm* stall, stand
éventé, e [evɑ̃te] *adj* (*parfum, vin*) stale
éventer [evɑ̃te] *vt* (*secret, complot*) to uncover; (*avec un éventail*) to fan; **s'éventer** *vi* (*parfum, vin*) to go stale
éventrer [evɑ̃tʀe] *vt* to disembowel; (*fig*) to tear *ou* rip open
éventualité [evɑ̃tɥalite] *nf* eventuality; possibility; **dans l' ~ de** in the event of; **parer à toute ~** to guard against all eventualities
éventuel, le [evɑ̃tɥɛl] *adj* possible
éventuellement [evɑ̃tɥɛlmɑ̃] *adv* possibly
évêque [evɛk] *nm* bishop
Everest [ɛvʀɛst] *nm*: (**mont**) **~** (Mount) Everest
évertuer [evɛʀtɥe]: **s'évertuer** *vi*: **s' ~ à faire** to try very hard to do
éviction [eviksjɔ̃] *nf* ousting, supplanting; (*de locataire*) eviction
évidemment [evidamɑ̃] *adv* obviously
évidence [evidɑ̃s] *nf* obviousness; (*fait*) obvious fact; **se rendre à l' ~** to bow before the evidence; **nier l' ~** to deny the evidence; **à l' ~** evidently; **de toute ~** quite obviously *ou* evidently; **en ~** conspicuous; **mettre en ~** to bring to the fore
évident, e [evidɑ̃, -ɑ̃t] *adj* obvious, evident; **ce n'est pas ~** (*cela pose des problèmes*) it's not (all that) straightforward, it's not as simple as all that
évider [evide] *vt* to scoop out
évier [evje] *nm* (kitchen) sink
évincer [evɛ̃se] *vt* to oust, supplant
évitable [evitabl(ə)] *adj* avoidable
évitement [evitmɑ̃] *nm*: **place d' ~** (*Auto*) passing place
éviter [evite] *vt* to avoid; **~ de faire/que qch ne se passe** to avoid doing/sth happening; **~ qch à qn** to spare sb sth
évocateur, -trice [evɔkatœʀ, -tʀis] *adj* evocative, suggestive
évocation [evɔkasjɔ̃] *nf* evocation
évolué, e [evɔlɥe] *adj* advanced; (*personne*) broad-minded
évoluer [evɔlɥe] *vi* (*enfant, maladie*) to develop; (*situation, moralement*) to evolve, develop; (*aller et venir: danseur etc*) to move about, circle
évolutif, -ive [evɔlytif, -iv] *adj* evolving
évolution [evɔlysjɔ̃] *nf* development; evolution; **évolutions** *nfpl* movements
évolutionnisme [evɔlysjɔnism(ə)] *nm* evolutionism
évoquer [evɔke] *vt* to call to mind, evoke; (*mentionner*) to mention
ex. *abr* (= *exemple*) ex.
ex- [ɛks] *préfixe* ex-
exacerbé, e [ɛgzasɛʀbe] *adj* (*orgueil, sensibilité*) exaggerated

exacerber [ɛgzasɛʀbe] *vt* to exacerbate
exact, e [ɛgzakt] *adj* (*précis*) exact, accurate, precise; (*correct*) correct; (*ponctuel*) punctual; **l'heure ~e** the right *ou* exact time
exactement [ɛgzaktəmɑ̃] *adv* exactly, accurately, precisely; correctly; (*c'est cela même*) exactly
exaction [ɛgzaksjɔ̃] *nf* (*d'argent*) exaction; (*gén pl: actes de violence*) abuse(s)
exactitude [ɛgzaktityd] *nf* exactitude, accurateness, precision
ex aequo [ɛgzeko] *adj* equally placed; **classé 1er ~** placed equal first
exagération [ɛgzaʒeʀasjɔ̃] *nf* exaggeration
exagéré, e [ɛgzaʒeʀe] *adj* (*prix etc*) excessive
exagérément [ɛgzaʒeʀemɑ̃] *adv* excessively
exagérer [ɛgzaʒeʀe] *vt* to exaggerate ▷ *vi* (*abuser*) to go too far; (*dépasser les bornes*) to overstep the mark; (*déformer les faits*) to exaggerate; **s'exagérer qch** to exaggerate sth
exaltant, e [ɛgzaltɑ̃, -ɑ̃t] *adj* exhilarating
exaltation [ɛgzaltasjɔ̃] *nf* exaltation
exalté, e [ɛgzalte] *adj* (over)excited ▷ *nm/f* (*péj*) fanatic
exalter [ɛgzalte] *vt* (*enthousiasmer*) to excite, elate; (*glorifier*) to exalt
examen [ɛgzamɛ̃] *nm* examination; (*Scol*) exam, examination; **à l' ~** (*dossier, projet*) under consideration; (*Comm*) on approval; **~ blanc** mock exam(ination); **~ de la vue** sight test
examinateur, -trice [ɛgzaminatœʀ, -tʀis] *nm/f* examiner
examiner [ɛgzamine] *vt* to examine
exaspérant, e [ɛgzaspeʀɑ̃, -ɑ̃t] *adj* exasperating
exaspération [ɛgzaspeʀasjɔ̃] *nf* exasperation
exaspéré, e [ɛgzaspeʀe] *adj* exasperated
exaspérer [ɛgzaspeʀe] *vt* to exasperate; (*aggraver*) to exacerbate
exaucer [ɛgzose] *vt* (*vœu*) to grant, fulfil; **~ qn** to grant sb's wishes
ex cathedra [ɛkskatedʀa] *adj, adv* ex cathedra
excavateur [ɛkskavatœʀ] *nm* excavator, mechanical digger
excavation [ɛkskavasjɔ̃] *nf* excavation
excavatrice [ɛkskavatʀis] *nf* = **excavateur**
excédent [ɛksedɑ̃] *nm* surplus; **en ~** surplus; **payer 60 euros d' ~** (*de bagages*) to pay 60 euros excess baggage; **~ de bagages** excess baggage; **~ commercial** trade surplus
excédentaire [ɛksedɑ̃tɛʀ] *adj* surplus, excess
excéder [ɛksede] *vt* (*dépasser*) to exceed; (*agacer*) to exasperate; **excédé de fatigue** exhausted; **excédé de travail** worn out with work
excellence [ɛksɛlɑ̃s] *nf* excellence; (*titre*) Excellency; **par ~** par excellence
excellent, e [ɛksɛlɑ̃, -ɑ̃t] *adj* excellent
exceller [ɛksele] *vi*: **~ (dans)** to excel (in)
excentricité [ɛksɑ̃tʀisite] *nf* eccentricity
excentrique [ɛksɑ̃tʀik] *adj* eccentric; (*quartier*) outlying ▷ *nm/f* eccentric
excentriquement [ɛksɑ̃tʀikmɑ̃] *adv* eccentrically

excepté, e [ɛksɛpte] *adj, prép*: **les élèves ~s, ~ les élèves** except for *ou* apart from the pupils; **~ si/ quand** except if/when; **~ que** except that
excepter [ɛksɛpte] *vt* to except
exception [ɛksɛpsjɔ̃] *nf* exception; **faire ~** to be an exception; **faire une ~** to make an exception; **sans ~** without exception; **à l'~ de** except for, with the exception of; **d'~** (*mesure, loi*) special, exceptional
exceptionnel, le [ɛksɛpsjɔnɛl] *adj* exceptional; (*prix*) special
exceptionnellement [ɛksɛpsjɔnɛlmɑ̃] *adv* exceptionally; (*par exception*) by way of an exception, on this occasion
excès [ɛksɛ] *nm* surplus ▷ *nmpl* excesses; **à l'~** (*méticuleux, généreux*) to excess; **avec ~** to excess; **sans ~** in moderation; **tomber dans l'~ inverse** to go to the opposite extreme; **~ de langage** immoderate language; **~ de pouvoir** abuse of power; **~ de vitesse** speeding *no pl*, exceeding the speed limit; **~ de zèle** overzealousness *no pl*
excessif, -ive [ɛksesif, -iv] *adj* excessive
excessivement [ɛksesivmɑ̃] *adv* (*trop: cher*) excessively, inordinately; (*très: riche, laid*) extremely, incredibly; **manger/boire ~** to eat/drink to excess
exciper [ɛksipe]: **~ de** *vt* to plead
excipient [ɛksipjɑ̃] *nm* (*Méd*) inert base, excipient
exciser [ɛksize] *vt* (*Méd*) to excise
excision [ɛksizjɔ̃] *nf* (*Méd*) excision; (*rituelle*) circumcision
excitant, e [ɛksitɑ̃, -ɑ̃t] *adj* exciting ▷ *nm* stimulant
excitation [ɛksitasjɔ̃] *nf* (*état*) excitement
excité, e [ɛksite] *adj* excited
exciter [ɛksite] *vt* to excite; (*café etc*) to stimulate; **s'exciter** *vi* to get excited; **~ qn à** (*révolte etc*) to incite sb to
exclamation [ɛksklamasjɔ̃] *nf* exclamation
exclamer [ɛksklame]: **s'exclamer** *vi* to exclaim
exclu, e [ɛkskly] *pp de* **exclure** ▷ *adj*: **il est/n'est pas ~ que ...** it's out of the question/not impossible that ...; **ce n'est pas ~** it's not impossible, I don't rule that out
exclure [ɛksklyʀ] *vt* (*faire sortir*) to expel; (*ne pas compter*) to exclude, leave out; (*rendre impossible*) to exclude, rule out
exclusif, -ive [ɛksklyzif, -iv] *adj* exclusive; **avec la mission exclusive/dans le but ~ de ...** with the sole mission/aim of ...; **agent ~** sole agent
exclusion [ɛksklyzjɔ̃] *nf* expulsion; **à l'~ de** with the exclusion *ou* exception of
exclusivement [ɛksklyzivmɑ̃] *adv* exclusively
exclusivité [ɛksklyzivite] *nf* exclusiveness; (*Comm*) exclusive rights *pl*; **passer en ~** (*film*) to go on general release
excommunier [ɛkskɔmynje] *vt* to excommunicate
excréments [ɛkskʀemɑ̃] *nmpl* excrement *sg*, faeces

excréter [ɛkskʀete] *vt* to excrete
excroissance [ɛkskʀwasɑ̃s] *nf* excrescence, outgrowth
excursion [ɛkskyʀsjɔ̃] *nf* (*en autocar*) excursion, trip; (*à pied*) walk, hike; **faire une ~** to go on an excursion *ou* a trip; to go on a walk *ou* hike
excursionniste [ɛkskyʀsjɔnist(ə)] *nm/f* tripper; hiker
excusable [ɛkskyzabl(ə)] *adj* excusable
excuse [ɛkskyz] *nf* excuse; **excuses** *nfpl* apology *sg*, apologies; **faire des ~s** to apologize; **faire ses ~s** to offer one's apologies; **mot d'~** (*Scol*) note from one's parent(s) (*to explain absence etc*); **lettre d'~s** letter of apology
excuser [ɛkskyze] *vt* to excuse; **~ qn de qch** (*dispenser*) to excuse sb from sth; **s'excuser (de)** to apologize (for); **"excusez-moi"** "I'm sorry"; (*pour attirer l'attention*) "excuse me"; **se faire ~** to ask to be excused
exécrable [ɛgzekʀabl(ə)] *adj* atrocious
exécrer [ɛgzekʀe] *vt* to loathe, abhor
exécutant, e [ɛgzekytɑ̃, -ɑ̃t] *nm/f* performer
exécuter [ɛgzekyte] *vt* (*prisonnier*) to execute; (*tâche etc*) to execute, carry out; (*Mus: jouer*) to perform, execute; (*Inform*) to run; **s'exécuter** *vi* to comply
exécuteur, -trice [ɛgzekytœʀ, -tʀis] *nm/f* (*testamentaire*) executor ▷ *nm* (*bourreau*) executioner
exécutif, -ive [ɛgzekytif, -iv] *adj, nm* (*Pol*) executive
exécution [ɛgzekysjɔ̃] *nf* execution; carrying out; **mettre à ~** to carry out
exécutoire [ɛgzekytwaʀ] *adj* (*Jur*) (legally) binding
exégèse [ɛgzeʒɛz] *nf* exegesis
exégète [ɛgzeʒɛt] *nm* exegete
exemplaire [ɛgzɑ̃plɛʀ] *adj* exemplary ▷ *nm* copy
exemple [ɛgzɑ̃pl(ə)] *nm* example; **par ~** for instance, for example; (*valeur intensive*) really!; **sans ~** (*bêtise, gourmandise etc*) unparalleled; **donner l'~** to set an example; **prendre ~ sur** to take as a model; **à l'~ de** just like; **pour l'~** (*punir*) as an example
exempt, e [ɛgzɑ̃, -ɑ̃t] *adj*: **~ de** (*dispensé de*) exempt from; (*sans*) free from; **~ de taxes** tax-free
exempter [ɛgzɑ̃te] *vt*: **~ de** to exempt from
exercé, e [ɛgzɛʀse] *adj* trained
exercer [ɛgzɛʀse] *vt* (*pratiquer*) to exercise, practise; (*faire usage de: prérogative*) to exercise; (*effectuer: influence, contrôle, pression*) to exert; (*former*) to exercise, train ▷ *vi* (*médecin*) to be in practice; **s'exercer** (*sportif, musicien*) to practise; (*se faire sentir: pression etc*): **s'~** (**sur** *ou* **contre**) to be exerted (on); **s'~ à faire qch** to train o.s. to do sth
exercice [ɛgzɛʀsis] *nm* practice; exercising; (*tâche, travail*) exercise; (*Comm, Admin: période*) accounting period; **l'~** (*sportive etc*) exercise; (*Mil*) drill; **en ~** (*juge*) in office; (*médecin*)

practising; **dans l'~ de ses fonctions** in the discharge of his duties; **~s d'assouplissement** limbering-up (exercises)

exergue [ɛgzɛʀg(ə)] *nm*: **mettre en ~** (*inscription*) to inscribe; **porter en ~** to be inscribed with

exhalaison [ɛgzalɛzɔ̃] *nf* exhalation

exhaler [ɛgzale] *vt* (*parfum*) to exhale; (*souffle, son, soupir*) to utter, breathe; **s'exhaler** *vi* to rise (up)

exhausser [ɛgzose] *vt* to raise (up)

exhausteur [ɛgzostœʀ] *nm* extractor fan

exhaustif, -ive [ɛgzostif, -iv] *adj* exhaustive

exhiber [ɛgzibe] *vt* (*montrer: papiers, certificat*) to present, produce; (*péj*) to display, flaunt; **s'exhiber** (*personne*) to parade; (*exhibitionniste*) to expose o.s.

exhibitionnisme [ɛgzibisjɔnism(ə)] *nm* exhibitionism

exhibitionniste [ɛgzibisjɔnist(ə)] *nm/f* exhibitionist

exhortation [ɛgzɔʀtɑsjɔ̃] *nf* exhortation

exhorter [ɛgzɔʀte] *vt*: **~ qn à faire** to urge sb to do

exhumer [ɛgzyme] *vt* to exhume

exigeant, e [ɛgziʒɑ̃, -ɑ̃t] *adj* demanding; (*péj*) hard to please

exigence [ɛgziʒɑ̃s] *nf* demand, requirement

exiger [ɛgziʒe] *vt* to demand, require

exigible [ɛgziʒibl(ə)] *adj* (*Comm, Jur*) payable

exigu, ë [ɛgzigy] *adj* cramped, tiny

exiguïté [ɛgzigɥite] *nf* (*d'un lieu*) cramped nature

exil [ɛgzil] *nm* exile; **en ~** in exile

exilé, e [ɛgzile] *nm/f* exile

exiler [ɛgzile] *vt* to exile; **s'exiler** to go into exile

existant, e [ɛgzistɑ̃, -ɑ̃t] *adj* (*actuel, présent*) existing

existence [ɛgzistɑ̃s] *nf* existence; **dans l'~** in life

existentialisme [ɛgzistɑ̃sjalism(ə)] *nm* existentialism

existentiel, le [ɛgzistɑ̃sjɛl] *adj* existential

exister [ɛgziste] *vi* to exist; **il existe un/des** there is a/are (some)

exode [ɛgzɔd] *nm* exodus

exonération [ɛgzɔneʀɑsjɔ̃] *nf* exemption

exonéré, e [ɛgzɔneʀe] *adj*: **~ de TVA** zero-rated (for VAT)

exonérer [ɛgzɔneʀe] *vt*: **~ de** to exempt from

exorbitant, e [ɛgzɔʀbitɑ̃, -ɑ̃t] *adj* exorbitant

exorbité, e [ɛgzɔʀbite] *adj*: **yeux ~s** bulging eyes

exorciser [ɛgzɔʀsize] *vt* to exorcize

exorde [ɛgzɔʀd(ə)] *nm* introduction

exotique [ɛgzɔtik] *adj* exotic

exotisme [ɛgzɔtism(ə)] *nm* exoticism

expansif, -ive [ɛkspɑ̃sif, -iv] *adj* expansive, communicative

expansion [ɛkspɑ̃sjɔ̃] *nf* expansion

expansionniste [ɛkspɑ̃sjɔnist(ə)] *adj* expansionist

expansivité [ɛkspɑ̃sivite] *nf* expansiveness

expatrié, e [ɛkspatʀije] *nm/f* expatriate

expatrier [ɛkspatʀije] *vt* (*argent*) to take *ou* send

out of the country; **s'expatrier** to leave one's country

expectative [ɛkspɛktativ] *nf*: **être dans l'~** to be waiting to see

expectorant, e [ɛkspɛktɔʀɑ̃, -ɑ̃t] *adj*: **sirop ~** expectorant (syrup)

expectorer [ɛkspɛktɔʀe] *vi* to expectorate

expédient [ɛkspedjɑ̃] *nm* (*parfois péj*) expedient; **vivre d'~s** to live by one's wits

expédier [ɛkspedje] *vt* (*lettre, paquet*) to send; (*troupes, renfort*) to dispatch; (*péj: travail etc*) to dispose of, dispatch

expéditeur, -trice [ɛkspeditœʀ, -tʀis] *nm/f* (*Postes*) sender

expéditif, -ive [ɛkspeditif, -iv] *adj* quick, expeditious

expédition [ɛkspedisjɔ̃] *nf* sending; (*scientifique, sportive, Mil*) expedition; **~ punitive** punitive raid

expéditionnaire [ɛkspedisjɔnɛʀ] *adj*: **corps ~** (*Mil*) task force

expérience [ɛkspeʀjɑ̃s] *nf* (*de la vie, des choses*) experience; (*scientifique*) experiment; **avoir de l'~** to have experience, be experienced; **avoir l'~ de** to have experience of; **faire l'~ de qch** to experience sth; **~ de chimie/d'électricité** chemical/electrical experiment

expérimental, e, -aux [ɛkspeʀimɑtal, -o] *adj* experimental

expérimentalement [ɛkspeʀimɑtalmɑ̃] *adv* experimentally

expérimenté, e [ɛkspeʀimɑ̃te] *adj* experienced

expérimenter [ɛkspeʀimɑ̃te] *vt* (*machine, technique*) to test out, experiment with

expert, e [ɛkspɛʀ, -ɛʀt(ə)] *adj*: **~ en** expert in ▷ *nm* (*spécialiste*) expert; **~ en assurances** insurance valuer

expert-comptable [ɛkspɛʀkɔ̃tabl(ə)] (*pl* **experts-comptables**) *nm* ≈ chartered (*Brit*) *ou* certified public (*US*) accountant

expertise [ɛkspɛʀtiz] *nf* valuation; assessment; valuer's (*ou* assessor's) report; (*Jur*) (forensic) examination

expertiser [ɛkspɛʀtize] *vt* (*objet de valeur*) to value; (*voiture accidentée etc*) to assess damage to

expier [ɛkspje] *vt* to expiate, atone for

expiration [ɛkspiʀɑsjɔ̃] *nf* expiry (*Brit*), expiration; breathing out *no pl*

expirer [ɛkspiʀe] *vi* (*prendre fin, littéraire: mourir*) to expire; (*respirer*) to breathe out

explétif, -ive [ɛkspletif, -iv] *adj* (*Ling*) expletive

explicable [ɛksplikabl(ə)] *adj*: **pas ~** inexplicable

explicatif, -ive [ɛksplikatif, -iv] *adj* (*mot, texte, note*) explanatory

explication [ɛksplikɑsjɔ̃] *nf* explanation; (*discussion*) discussion; **~ de texte** (*Scol*) critical analysis (of a text)

explicite [ɛksplisit] *adj* explicit

explicitement [ɛksplisitmɑ̃] *adv* explicitly

expliciter [ɛksplisite] *vt* to make explicit

expliquer [ɛksplike] *vt* to explain; **~ (à qn)**

comment/que to point out *ou* explain (to sb) how/that; **s'expliquer** (*se faire comprendre: personne*) to explain o.s.; (*discuter*) to discuss things; (*se disputer*) to have it out; (*comprendre*): **je m'explique son retard/absence** I understand his lateness/absence; **son erreur s'explique** one can understand his mistake

exploit [ɛksplwa] *nm* exploit, feat

exploitable [ɛskplwatabl(ə)] *adj* (*gisement etc*) that can be exploited; **~ par une machine** machine-readable

exploitant [ɛksplwatɑ̃] *nm* farmer

exploitation [ɛksplwatasjɔ̃] *nf* exploitation; running; (*entreprise*): **~ agricole** farming concern

exploiter [ɛksplwate] *vt* to exploit; (*entreprise, ferme*) to run, operate

exploiteur, -euse [ɛksplwatœʀ, -øz] *nm/f* (*péj*) exploiter

explorateur, -trice [ɛksplɔʀatœʀ, -tʀis] *nm/f* explorer

exploration [ɛksplɔʀasjɔ̃] *nf* exploration

explorer [ɛksplɔʀe] *vt* to explore

exploser [ɛksploze] *vi* to explode, blow up; (*engin explosif*) to go off; (*fig: joie, colère*) to burst out, explode; (: *personne: de colère*) to explode, flare up; **faire ~** (*bombe*) to explode, detonate; (*bâtiment, véhicule*) to blow up

explosif, -ive [ɛksplozif, -iv] *adj, nm* explosive

explosion [ɛksplozjɔ̃] *nf* explosion; **~ de joie/colère** outburst of joy/rage; **~ démographique** population explosion

exponentiel, le [ɛksponɑ̃sjɛl] *adj* exponential

exportateur, -trice [ɛkspɔʀtatœʀ, -tʀis] *adj* exporting ▷ *nm* exporter

exportation [ɛkspɔʀtasjɔ̃] *nf* export

exporter [ɛkspɔʀte] *vt* to export

exposant [ɛkspozɑ̃] *nm* exhibitor; (*Math*) exponent

exposé, e [ɛkspoze] *nm* (*écrit*) exposé; (*oral*) talk ▷ *adj*: **~ au sud** facing south, with a southern aspect; **bien ~** well situated; **très ~** very exposed

exposer [ɛkspoze] *vt* (*montrer: marchandise*) to display; (: *peinture*) to exhibit, show; (*parler de: problème, situation*) to explain, expose, set out; (*mettre en danger, orienter: maison etc*) to expose; **~ qn/qch à** to expose sb/sth to; **~ sa vie** to risk one's life; **s'exposer à** (*soleil, danger*) to expose o.s. to; (*critiques, punition*) to lay o.s. open to

exposition [ɛkspozisjɔ̃] *nf* (*voir exposer*) displaying; exhibiting; explanation, exposition; exposure; (*voir exposé*) aspect, situation; (*manifestation*) exhibition; (*Photo*) exposure; (*introduction*) exposition

exprès¹ [ɛkspʀɛ] *adv* (*délibérément*) on purpose; (*spécialement*) specially; **faire ~ de faire qch** to do sth on purpose

exprès², -esse [ɛkspʀɛs] *adj* (*ordre, défense*) express, formal ▷ *adj inv, adv* (*Postes*) express; **envoyer qch en ~** to send sth express

express [ɛkspʀɛs] *adj, nm*: (**café**) **~** espresso;

(**train**) **~** fast train

expressément [ɛkspʀɛsemɑ̃] *adv* expressly, specifically

expressif, -ive [ɛkspʀɛsif, -iv] *adj* expressive

expression [ɛkspʀɛsjɔ̃] *nf* expression; **réduit à sa plus simple ~** reduced to its simplest terms; **liberté/moyens d'~** freedom/means of expression; **~ toute faite** set phrase

expressionnisme [ɛkspʀɛsjɔnism(ə)] *nm* expressionism

expressivité [ɛkspʀɛsivite] *nf* expressiveness

exprimer [ɛkspʀime] *vt* (*sentiment, idée*) to express; (*faire sortir: jus, liquide*) to press out; **s'exprimer** *vi* (*personne*) to express o.s.

expropriation [ɛkspʀɔpʀijasjɔ̃] *nf* expropriation; **frapper d'~** to put a compulsory purchase order on

exproprier [ɛkspʀɔpʀije] *vt* to buy up (*ou* buy the property of) by compulsory purchase, expropriate

expulser [ɛkspylse] *vt* (*d'une salle, d'un groupe*) to expel; (*locataire*) to evict; (*Football*) to send off

expulsion [ɛkspylsjɔ̃] *nf* expulsion; eviction; sending off

expurger [ɛkspyʀʒe] *vt* to expurgate, bowdlerize

exquis, e [ɛkski, -iz] *adj* (*gâteau, parfum, élégance*) exquisite; (*personne, temps*) delightful

exsangue [ɛksɑ̃g] *adj* bloodless, drained of blood

exsuder [ɛksyde] *vt* to exude

extase [ɛkstaz] *nf* ecstasy; **être en ~** to be in raptures

extasier [ɛkstazje]: **s'extasier** *vi*: **s'~ sur** to go into raptures over

extatique [ɛkstatik] *adj* ecstatic

extenseur [ɛkstɑ̃sœʀ] *nm* (*Sport*) chest expander

extensible [ɛkstɑ̃sibl(ə)] *adj* extensible

extensif, -ive [ɛkstɑ̃sif, -iv] *adj* extensive

extension [ɛkstɑ̃sjɔ̃] *nf* (*d'un muscle, ressort*) stretching; (*Méd*): **à l'~** in traction; (*fig*) extension; expansion

exténuant, e [ɛkstenɥɑ̃, -ɑ̃t] *adj* exhausting

exténuer [ɛkstenɥe] *vt* to exhaust

extérieur, e [ɛksteʀjœʀ] *adj* (*de dehors: porte, mur etc*) outer, outside; (: *commerce, politique*) foreign; (: *influences, pressions*) external; (*au dehors: escalier, w.-c.*) outside; (*apparent: calme, gaieté etc*) outer ▷ *nm* (*d'une maison, d'un récipient etc*) outside, exterior; (*d'une personne: apparence*) exterior; (*d'un pays, d'un groupe social*): **l'~** the outside world; **à l'~** (*dehors*) outside; (*fig: à l'étranger*) abroad

extérieurement [ɛksteʀjœʀmɑ̃] *adv* (*de dehors*) on the outside; (*en apparence*) on the surface

extérioriser [ɛksteʀjɔʀize] *vt* to exteriorize

extermination [ɛkstɛʀminasjɔ̃] *nf* extermination, wiping out

exterminer [ɛkstɛʀmine] *vt* to exterminate, wipe out

externat [ɛkstɛʀna] *nm* day school

externe [ɛkstɛʀn(ə)] *adj* external, outer ▷ *nm/f* (*Méd*) non-resident medical student, extern

(US); (Scol) day pupil

extincteur [ɛkstɛ̃ktœʀ] nm (fire) extinguisher

extinction [ɛkstɛ̃ksjɔ̃] nf extinction; (Jur: d'une dette) extinguishment; ~ **de voix** (Méd) loss of voice

extirper [ɛkstiʀpe] vt (tumeur) to extirpate; (plante) to root out, pull up; (préjugés) to eradicate

extorquer [ɛkstɔʀke] vt (de l'argent, un renseignement): ~ **qch à qn** to extort sth from sb

extorsion [ɛkstɔʀsjɔ̃] nf: ~ **de fonds** extortion of money

extra [ɛkstʀa] adj inv first-rate; (marchandises) top-quality ▷ nm inv extra help ▷ préfixe extra(-)

extraction [ɛkstʀaksjɔ̃] nf extraction

extrader [ɛkstʀade] vt to extradite

extradition [ɛkstʀadisjɔ̃] nf extradition

extra-fin, e [ɛkstʀafɛ̃, -in] adj extra-fine

extra-fort, e [ɛkstʀafɔʀ] adj extra strong

extraire [ɛkstʀɛʀ] vt to extract

extrait, e [ɛkstʀɛ, -ɛt] pp de **extraire** ▷ nm (de plante) extract; (de film, livre) extract, excerpt; ~ **de naissance** birth certificate

extra-lucide [ɛkstʀalysid] adj: **voyante** ~ clairvoyant

extraordinaire [ɛkstʀaɔʀdinɛʀ] adj extraordinary; (Pol, Admin) special; **ambassadeur** ~ ambassador extraordinary; **assemblée** ~ extraordinary meeting; **par** ~ by some unlikely chance

extraordinairement [ɛkstʀaɔʀdinɛʀmɑ̃] adv extraordinarily

extrapoler [ɛkstʀapɔle] vt, vi to extrapolate

extra-sensoriel, le [ɛkstʀasɑ̃sɔʀjɛl] adj extrasensory

extra-terrestre [ɛkstʀatɛʀɛstʀ(ə)] nm/f extraterrestrial

extra-utérin, e [ɛkstʀayteʀɛ̃, -in] adj extrauterine

extravagance [ɛkstʀavagɑ̃s] nf extravagance no pl; extravagant behaviour no pl

extravagant, e [ɛkstʀavagɑ̃, -ɑ̃t] adj (personne, attitude) extravagant; (idée) wild

extraverti, e [ɛkstʀavɛʀti] adj extrovert

extrayais etc [ɛkstʀɛjɛ] vb voir **extraire**

extrême [ɛkstʀɛm] adj, nm extreme; (intensif): **d'une ~ simplicité/brutalité** extremely simple/brutal; **d'un ~ à l'autre** from one extreme to another; **à l'~** in the extreme; **à l'~ rigueur** in the absolute extreme

extrêmement [ɛkstʀɛmmɑ̃] adv extremely

extrême-onction [ɛkstʀɛmɔ̃ksjɔ̃] (pl **extrêmes-onctions**) nf (Rel) last rites pl, Extreme Unction

Extrême-Orient [ɛkstʀɛmɔʀjɑ̃] nm: **l'~** the Far East

extrême-oriental, e, -aux [ɛkstʀɛmɔʀjɑ̃tal, -o] adj Far Eastern

extrémisme [ɛkstʀemism(ə)] nm extremism

extrémiste [ɛkstʀemist(ə)] adj, nm/f extremist

extrémité [ɛkstʀemite] nf (bout) end; (situation) straits pl, plight; (geste désespéré) extreme action; **extrémités** nfpl (pieds et mains) extremities; **à la dernière** ~ (à l'agonie) on the point of death

extroverti, e [ɛkstʀovɛʀti] adj = **extraverti**

exubérance [ɛgzybeʀɑ̃s] nf exuberance

exubérant, e [ɛgzybeʀɑ̃, -ɑ̃t] adj exuberant

exulter [ɛgzylte] vi to exult

exutoire [ɛgzytwaʀ] nm outlet, release

ex-voto [ɛksvoto] nm inv ex-voto

eye-liner [ajlajnœʀ] nm eyeliner

Ff

F, f [ɛf] *nm inv* F, f ▷ *abr* = **féminin**; (= *franc*) fr.; (= *Fahrenheit*) F; (= *frère*) Br(o).; (= *femme*) W; (*appartement*): **un F2/F3** a 2-/3-roomed flat (Brit) *ou* apartment (US); **F comme François** F for Frederick (Brit) *ou* Fox (US)

fa [fa] *nm inv* (Mus) F; (*en chantant la gamme*) fa

fable [fabl(ə)] *nf* fable; (*mensonge*) story, tale

fabricant [fabʀikɑ̃] *nm* manufacturer, maker

fabrication [fabʀikasjɔ̃] *nf* manufacture, making

fabrique [fabʀik] *nf* factory

fabriquer [fabʀike] *vt* to make; (*industriellement*) to manufacture, make; (*construire: voiture*) to manufacture, build; (: *maison*) to build; (*fig: inventer: histoire, alibi*) to make up; (*fam*): **qu'est-ce qu'il fabrique?** what is he up to?; **~ en série** to mass-produce

fabulateur, -trice [fabylatœʀ, -tʀis] *nm/f*: **c'est un ~** he fantasizes, he makes up stories

fabulation [fabylasjɔ̃] *nf* (Psych) fantasizing

fabuleusement [fabyløzmɑ̃] *adv* fabulously, fantastically

fabuleux, -euse [fabylø, -øz] *adj* fabulous, fantastic

fac [fak] *abr f* (*fam*: = *faculté*) Uni (Brit: *fam*) ≈ college (US)

façade [fasad] *nf* front, façade; (*fig*) façade

face [fas] *nf* face; (*fig: aspect*) side ▷ *adj*: **le côté ~** heads; **perdre/sauver la ~** to lose/save face; **regarder qn en ~** to look sb in the face; **la maison/le trottoir d'en ~** the house/pavement opposite; **en ~ de** *prép* opposite; (*fig*) in front of; **de ~** *adv* from the front; face on; **~ à** *prép* facing; (*fig*) faced with, in the face of; **faire ~ à** to face; **faire ~ à la demande** (Comm) to meet the demand; **~ à ~** *adv* facing each other ▷ *nm inv* encounter

face-à-main [fasamɛ̃] (*pl* **faces-à-main**) *nm* lorgnette

facéties [fasesi] *nfpl* jokes, pranks

facétieux, -euse [fasesjø, -øz] *adj* mischievous

facette [fasɛt] *nf* facet

fâché, e [faʃe] *adj* angry; (*désolé*) sorry

fâcher [faʃe] *vt* to anger; **se fâcher** *vi* to get angry; **se ~ avec** (*se brouiller*) to fall out with

fâcherie [faʃʀi] *nf* quarrel

fâcheusement [faʃøzmɑ̃] *adv* unpleasantly; (*impressionné etc*) badly; **avoir ~ tendance à** to have an irritating tendency to

fâcheux, -euse [faʃø, -øz] *adj* unfortunate, regrettable

facho [faʃo] *adj, nm/f* (*fam*: = *fasciste*) fascist

facial, e, -aux [fasjal, -o] *adj* facial

faciès [fasjɛs] *nm* (*visage*) features *pl*

facile [fasil] *adj* easy; (*accommodant*) easy-going

facilement [fasilmɑ̃] *adv* easily

facilité [fasilite] *nf* easiness; (*disposition, don*) aptitude; (*moyen, occasion, possibilité*): **il a la ~ de rencontrer les gens** he has every opportunity to meet people; **facilités** *nfpl* facilities; (Comm) terms; **~s de crédit** credit terms; **~s de paiement** easy terms

faciliter [fasilite] *vt* to make easier

façon [fasɔ̃] *nf* (*manière*) way; (*d'une robe etc*) making-up; cut; (: *main-d'œuvre*) labour (Brit), labor (US); (*imitation*): **châle ~ cachemire** cashmere-style shawl; **façons** *nfpl* (*péj*) fuss *sg*; **faire des ~s** (*péj: être affecté*) to be affected; (: *faire des histoires*) to make a fuss; **de quelle ~?** (in) what way?; **sans ~** *adv* without fuss ▷ *adj* unaffected; **d'une autre ~** in another way; **en aucune ~** in no way; **de ~ à** so as to; **de ~ à ce que, de (telle) ~ que** so that; **de toute ~** anyway, in any case; (**c'est une**) **~ de parler** it's a way of putting it; **travail à ~** tailoring

façonner [fasɔne] *vt* (*fabriquer*) to manufacture; (*travailler: matière*) to shape, fashion; (*fig*) to mould, shape

fac-similé [faksimile] *nm* facsimile

facteur, -trice [faktœʀ, -tʀis] *nm/f* postman/woman (Brit), mailman/woman (US) ▷ *nm* (Math, *gén*) factor; **~ d'orgues** organ builder; **~ de pianos** piano maker; **~ rhésus** rhesus factor

factice [faktis] *adj* artificial

faction [faksjɔ̃] *nf* (*groupe*) faction; (Mil) guard *ou* sentry (duty); watch; **en ~** on guard; standing watch

factionnaire [faksjɔnɛʀ] *nm* guard, sentry

factoriel, le [faktɔʀjɛl] *adj, nf* factorial

factotum [faktɔtɔm] *nm* odd-job man, dogsbody (Brit)

factuel, le [faktɥɛl] *adj* factual

facturation [faktyʁasjɔ̃] *nf* invoicing; (*bureau*) invoicing (office)

facture [faktyʁ] *nf* (*à payer: gén*) bill; (: *Comm*) invoice; (*d'un artisan, artiste*) technique, workmanship

facturer [faktyʁe] *vt* to invoice

facturier, -ière [faktyʁje, -jɛʁ] *nm/f* invoice clerk

facultatif, -ive [fakyltatif, -iv] *adj* optional; (*arrêt de bus*) request *cpd*

faculté [fakylte] *nf* (*intellectuelle, d'université*) faculty; (*pouvoir, possibilité*) power

fadaises [fadɛz] *nfpl* twaddle *sg*

fade [fad] *adj* insipid

fading [fadiŋ] *nm* (*Radio*) fading

fagot [fago] *nm* (*de bois*) bundle of sticks

fagoté, e [fagɔte] *adj* (*fam*): **drôlement ~** oddly dressed

faible [fɛbl(ə)] *adj* weak; (*voix, lumière, vent*) faint; (*élève, copie*) poor; (*rendement, intensité, revenu etc*) low ▷ *nm* weak point; (*pour quelqu'un*) weakness, soft spot; **~ d'esprit** feeble-minded

faiblement [fɛbləmɑ̃] *adv* weakly; (*peu: éclairer etc*) faintly

faiblesse [fɛblɛs] *nf* weakness

faiblir [febliʁ] *vi* to weaken; (*lumière*) to dim; (*vent*) to drop

faïence [fajɑ̃s] *nf* earthenware *no pl*; (*objet*) piece of earthenware

faignant, e [fɛɲɑ̃, -ɑ̃t] *nm/f* = **fainéant, e**

faille [faj] *vb voir* **falloir** ▷ *nf* (*Géo*) fault; (*fig*) flaw, weakness

failli, e [faji] *adj, nm/f* bankrupt

faillible [fajibl(ə)] *adj* fallible

faillir [fajiʁ] *vi*: **j'ai failli tomber/lui dire** I almost *ou* nearly fell/told him; **~ à une promesse/un engagement** to break a promise/an agreement

faillite [fajit] *nf* bankruptcy; (*échec: d'une politique etc*) collapse; **être en ~** to be bankrupt; **faire ~** to go bankrupt

faim [fɛ̃] *nf* hunger; (*fig*): **~ d'amour/de richesse** hunger *ou* yearning for love/wealth; **avoir ~** to be hungry; **rester sur sa ~** (*aussi fig*) to be left wanting more

fainéant, e [feneɑ̃, -ɑ̃t] *nm/f* idler, loafer

fainéantise [feneɑ̃tiz] *nf* idleness, laziness

 MOT-CLÉ

faire [fɛʁ] *vt* **1** (*fabriquer, être l'auteur de*) to make; (*produire*) to produce; (*construire: maison, bateau*) to build; **faire du vin/une offre/un film** to make wine/an offer/a film; **faire du bruit** to make a noise

2 (*effectuer: travail, opération*) to do; **que faites-vous?** (*quel métier etc*) what do you do?; (*quelle activité: au moment de la question*) what are you doing?; **que faire?** what are we going to do?, what can be done (about it)?; **faire la lessive/le ménage** to do the washing/the housework

3 (*études*) to do; (*sport, musique*) to play; **faire du droit/du français** to do law/French; **faire du rugby/piano** to play rugby/the piano; **faire du cheval/du ski** to go riding/skiing

4 (*visiter*): **faire les magasins** to go shopping; **faire l'Europe** to tour *ou* do Europe

5 (*simuler*): **faire le malade/l'ignorant** to act the invalid/the fool

6 (*transformer, avoir un effet sur*): **faire de qn un frustré/avocat** to make sb frustrated/a lawyer; **ça ne me fait rien** (*m'est égal*) I don't care *ou* mind; (*me laisse froid*) it has no effect on me; **ça ne fait rien** it doesn't matter; **faire que** (*impliquer*) to mean that

7 (*calculs, prix, mesures*): **deux et deux font quatre** two and two are *ou* make four; **ça fait 10 m/15 euros** it's 10 m/15 euros; **je vous le fais 10 euros** I'll let you have it for 10 euros

8 (*vb +de*): **qu'a-t-il fait de sa valise/de sa sœur?** what has he done with his case/his sister?

9: **ne faire que**: **il ne fait que critiquer** (*sans cesse*) all he (ever) does is criticize; (*seulement*) he's only criticizing

10 (*dire*) to say; **vraiment? fit-il** really? he said

11 (*maladie*) to have; **faire du diabète/de la tension** to have diabetes *sg*/high blood pressure

▷ *vi* **1** (*agir, s'y prendre*) to act, do; **il faut faire vite** we (*ou* you *etc*) must act quickly; **comment a-t-il fait pour?** how did he manage to?; **faites comme chez vous** make yourself at home; **je n'ai pas pu faire autrement** there was nothing else I could do

2 (*paraître*) to look; **faire vieux/démodé** to look old/old-fashioned; **ça fait bien** it looks good; **tu fais jeune dans cette robe** that dress makes you look young(er)

3 (*remplaçant un autre verbe*) to do; **ne le casse pas comme je l'ai fait** don't break it as I did; **je peux le voir? — faites!** can I see it? — please do!; **remets-le en place — je viens de le faire** put it back in its place — I just have (done)

▷ *vb impers* **1**: **il fait beau** *etc* the weather is fine *etc*; *voir aussi* **jour**; **froid** *etc*

2 (*temps écoulé, durée*): **ça fait deux ans qu'il est parti** it's two years since he left; **ça fait deux ans qu'il y est** he's been there for two years

▷ *vb aux* **1**: **faire** (*+infinitif: action directe*) to make; **faire tomber/bouger qch** to make sth fall/move; **faire démarrer un moteur/chauffer de l'eau** to start up an engine/heat some water; **cela fait dormir** it makes you sleep; **faire travailler les enfants** to make the children work *ou* get the children to work; **il m'a fait traverser la rue** he helped me to cross the road

2 (*indirectement, par un intermédiaire*): **faire réparer qch** to get *ou* have sth repaired; **faire punir les enfants** to have the children punished; **il m'a fait ouvrir la porte** he got me to open the door

se faire *vi* **1** (*vin, fromage*) to mature

2: **cela se fait beaucoup/ne se fait pas** it's

done a lot/not done

3 (+*nom ou pron*): **se faire une jupe** to make o.s. a
skirt; **se faire des amis** to make friends; **se
faire du souci** to worry; **se faire des illusions**
to delude o.s.; **se faire beaucoup d'argent** to
make a lot of money; **il ne s'en fait pas** he
doesn't worry

4 (+*adj*: *devenir*): **se faire vieux** to be getting old;
(*délibérément*): **se faire beau** to do o.s. up

5: **se faire à** (*s'habituer*) to get used to; **je
n'arrive pas à me faire à la nourriture/au
climat** I can't get used to the food/climate

6 (+*infinitif*): **se faire examiner la vue/opérer**
to have one's eyes tested/have an operation; **se
faire couper les cheveux** to get one's hair cut;
il va se faire tuer/punir he's going to get
himself killed/get (himself) punished; **il s'est
fait aider** he got somebody to help him; **il
s'est fait aider par Simon** he got Simon to
help him; **se faire faire un vêtement** to get a
garment made for o.s.

7 (*impersonnel*): **comment se fait-il/faisait-il
que?** how is it/was it that?; **il peut se faire que
nous utilisions ...** it's possible that we could
use ...

faire-part [fɛʀpaʀ] *nm inv* announcement (*of
birth, marriage etc*)
fair-play [fɛʀplɛ] *adj inv* fair play
fais [fɛ] *vb voir* **faire**
faisabilité [fəzabilite] *nf* feasibility
faisable [fəzabl(ə)] *adj* feasible
faisais *etc* [fəzɛ] *vb voir* **faire**
faisan, e [fəzɑ̃, -an] *nm/f* pheasant
faisandé, e [fəzɑ̃de] *adj* high (*bad*); (*fig péj*)
corrupt, decadent
faisceau, x [fɛso] *nm* (*de lumière etc*) beam; (*de
branches etc*) bundle
faiseur, -euse [fəzœʀ, -øz] *nm/f* (*gén: péj*): **~ de**
maker of ▷ *nm* (*bespoke*) tailor; **~ d'embarras**
fusspot; **~ de projets** schemer
faisons *etc* [fəzɔ̃] *vb voir* **faire**
faisselle [fɛsɛl] *nf* cheese strainer
fait¹ [fɛ] *vb voir* **faire** ▷ *nm* (*événement*) event,
occurrence; (*réalité, donnée*) fact; **le ~ que/de
manger** the fact that/of eating; **être le ~ de**
(*causé par*) to be the work of; **être au ~ (de)** to be
informed (of); **mettre qn au ~** to inform sb,
put sb in the picture; **au ~** (*à propos*) by the way;
en venir au ~ to get to the point; **de ~** *adj*
(*opposé à: de droit*) de facto ▷ *adv* in fact; **du ~ de
ceci/qu'il a menti** because of *ou* on account of
this/his having lied; **de ce ~** therefore, for this
reason; **en ~** in fact; **en ~ de repas** by way of a
meal; **prendre ~ et cause pour qn** to support
sb, side with sb; **prendre qn sur le ~** to catch sb
in the act; **dire à qn son ~** to give sb a piece of
one's mind; **hauts ~s** (*exploits*) exploits; **~
d'armes** feat of arms; **~ divers** (*short*) news
item; **les ~s et gestes de qn** sb's actions *ou*
doings
fait², e [fɛ, fɛt] *pp de* **faire** ▷ *adj* (*mûr: fromage,*

melon) ripe; (*maquillé: yeux*) made-up; (*vernis:
ongles*) painted, polished; **un homme ~** a grown
man; **tout(e) ~(e)** (*préparé à l'avance*) ready-made;
c'en est ~ de notre tranquillité that's the end
of our peace; **c'est bien ~ (pour lui** *ou* **eux** *etc***)** it
serves him (*ou* them *etc*) right
faîte [fɛt] *nm* top; (*fig*) pinnacle, height
faites [fɛt] *vb voir* **faire**
faîtière [fɛtjɛʀ] *nf* (*de tente*) ridge pole
faitout [fɛtu] *nm* stewpot
fakir [fakiʀ] *nm* (*Théât*) wizard
falaise [falɛz] *nf* cliff
falbalas [falbala] *nmpl* fripperies, frills
fallacieux, -euse [falasjø, -øz] *adj* (*raisonnement*)
fallacious; (*apparences*) deceptive; (*espoir*)
illusory
falloir [falwaʀ] *vb impers*: **il faut faire les lits** we
(*ou* you *etc*) have to *ou* must make the beds; **il
faut que je fasse les lits** I have to *ou* must
make the beds; **il a fallu qu'il parte** he had to
leave; **il faudrait qu'elle rentre** she ought to
go home; **il va ~ 10 euros** we'll (*ou* I'll *etc*) need
10 euros; **il doit ~ du temps** that must take
time; **il vous faut tourner à gauche après
l'église** you have to turn left past the church;
nous avons ce qu'il (nous) faut we have what
we need; **il faut qu'il ait oublié** he must have
forgotten; **il a fallu qu'il l'apprenne** he would
have to hear about it; **il ne fallait pas** (*pour
remercier*) you shouldn't have (done); **faut le
faire!** (it) takes some doing! ▷ *vi*: **s'en falloir: il
s'en est fallu de 10 euros/5 minutes** we (*ou*
they *etc*) were 10 euros short/5 minutes late (*ou*
early); **il s'en faut de beaucoup qu'il soit ...**
he is far from being ...; **il s'en est fallu de peu
que cela n'arrive** it very nearly happened; **ou
peu s'en faut** or just about, or as good as;
comme il faut *adj* proper ▷ *adv* properly
fallu [faly] *pp de* **falloir**
falot, -ote [falo, -ɔt] *adj* dreary, colourless (*Brit*),
colorless (*US*) ▷ *nm* lantern
falsification [falsifikasjɔ̃] *nf* falsification
falsifier [falsifje] *vt* to falsify
famé, e [fame] *adj*: **mal ~** disreputable, of ill
repute
famélique [famelik] *adj* half-starved
fameux, -euse [famø, -øz] *adj* (*illustre: parfois péj*)
famous; (*bon: repas, plat etc*) first-rate, first-class;
(*intensif*): **un ~ problème** *etc* a real problem *etc*;
pas ~ not great, not much good
familial, e, -aux [familjal, -o] *adj* family *cpd* ▷ *nf*
(*Auto*) family estate car (*Brit*), station wagon
(*US*)
familiariser [familjaʀize] *vt*: **~ qn avec** to
familiarize sb with; **se ~ avec** to familiarize o.s.
with
familiarité [familjaʀite] *nf* familiarity;
informality; **familiarités** *nfpl* familiarities; **~
avec** (*sujet, science*) familiarity with
familier, -ière [familje, -jɛʀ] *adj* (*connu,
impertinent*) familiar; (*dénotant une certaine
intimité*) informal, friendly; (*Ling*) informal,

colloquial ▷ nm regular (visitor)

familièrement [familjɛʀmɑ̃] adv (sans façon: s'entretenir) informally; (cavalièrement) familiarly

famille [famij] nf family; **il a de la ~ à Paris** he has relatives in Paris

famine [famin] nf famine

fan [fan] nm/f fan

fana [fana] adj, nm/f (fam) = **fanatique**

fanal, -aux [fanal, -o] nm beacon; lantern

fanatique [fanatik] adj: ~ **(de)** fanatical (about) ▷ nm/f fanatic

fanatisme [fanatism(ə)] nm fanaticism

fane [fan] nf top

fané, e [fane] adj faded

faner [fane]: **se faner** vi to fade

faneur, -euse [fanœʀ, -øz] nm/f haymaker ▷ nf (Tech) tedder

fanfare [fɑ̃faʀ] nf (orchestre) brass band; (musique) fanfare; **en ~** (avec bruit) noisily

fanfaron, ne [fɑ̃faʀɔ̃, -ɔn] nm/f braggart

fanfaronnades [fɑ̃faʀɔnad] nfpl bragging no pl

fanfreluches [fɑ̃fʀəlyʃ] nfpl trimming no pl

fange [fɑ̃ʒ] nf mire

fanion [fanjɔ̃] nm pennant

fanon [fanɔ̃] nm (de baleine) plate of baleen; (repli de peau) dewlap, wattle

fantaisie [fɑ̃tezi] nf (spontanéité) fancy, imagination; (caprice) whim; extravagance; (Mus) fantasia ▷ adj: **bijou (de) ~** (piece of) costume jewellery (Brit) ou jewelry (US); **pain (de) ~** fancy bread

fantaisiste [fɑ̃tezist(ə)] adj (péj) unorthodox, eccentric ▷ nm/f (de music-hall) variety artist ou entertainer

fantasmagorique [fɑ̃tasmagɔʀik] adj phantasmagorical

fantasme [fɑ̃tasm(ə)] nm fantasy

fantasmer [fɑ̃tasme] vi to fantasize

fantasque [fɑ̃task(ə)] adj whimsical, capricious; fantastic

fantassin [fɑ̃tasɛ̃] nm infantryman

fantastique [fɑ̃tastik] adj fantastic

fantoche [fɑ̃tɔʃ] nm (péj) puppet

fantomatique [fɑ̃tɔmatik] adj ghostly

fantôme [fɑ̃tom] nm ghost, phantom

FAO sigle f (= Food and Agricultural Organization) FAO

faon [fɑ̃] nm fawn (deer)

FAQ abr f (= foire aux questions) FAQ pl (= frequently asked questions)

faramineux, -euse [faʀaminø, -øz] adj (fam) fantastic

farandole [faʀɑ̃dɔl] nf farandole

farce [faʀs(ə)] nf (viande) stuffing; (blague) (practical) joke; (Théât) farce; **faire une ~ à qn** to play a (practical) joke on sb; **~s et attrapes** jokes and novelties

farceur, -euse [faʀsœʀ, -øz] nm/f practical joker; (fumiste) clown

farci, e [faʀsi] adj (Culin) stuffed

farcir [faʀsiʀ] vt (viande) to stuff; (fig): ~ **qch de** to stuff sth with; **se farcir** (fam): **je me suis farci la vaisselle** I've got stuck ou landed with

the washing-up

fard [faʀ] nm make-up; ~ **à joues** blusher

fardeau, x [faʀdo] nm burden

farder [faʀde] vt to make up; (vérité) to disguise; **se farder** to make o.s. up

farfelu, e [faʀfəly] adj wacky (fam), hare-brained

farfouiller [faʀfuje] vi (péj) to rummage around

fariboles [faʀibɔl] nfpl nonsense no pl

farine [faʀin] nf flour; ~ **de blé** wheatflour; ~ **de maïs** cornflour (Brit), cornstarch (US); ~ **lactée** (pour bouillie) baby cereal

fariner [faʀine] vt to flour

farineux, -euse [faʀinø, -øz] adj (sauce, pomme) floury ▷ nmpl (aliments) starchy foods

farniente [faʀnjɛnte] nm idleness

farouche [faʀuʃ] adj shy, timid; (sauvage) savage, wild; (violent) fierce

farouchement [faʀuʃmɑ̃] adv fiercely

fart [faʀ(t)] nm (ski) wax

farter [faʀte] vt to wax

fascicule [fasikyl] nm volume

fascinant, e [fasinɑ̃, -ɑ̃t] adj fascinating

fascination [fasinɑsjɔ̃] nf fascination

fasciner [fasine] vt to fascinate

fascisant, e [faʃizɑ̃, -ɑ̃t] adj fascistic

fascisme [faʃism(ə)] nm fascism

fasciste [faʃist(ə)] adj, nm/f fascist

fasse etc [fas] vb voir **faire**

faste [fast(ə)] nm splendour (Brit), splendor (US) ▷ adj: **c'est un jour ~** it's his (ou our etc) lucky day

fastidieux, -euse [fastidjø, -øz] adj tedious, tiresome

fastueux, -euse [fastɥø, -øz] adj sumptuous, luxurious

fat [fa] adj m conceited, smug

fatal, e [fatal] adj fatal; (inévitable) inevitable

fatalement [fatalmɑ̃] adv inevitably

fatalisme [fatalism(ə)] nm fatalism

fataliste [fatalist(ə)] adj fatalistic

fatalité [fatalite] nf (destin) fate; (coïncidence) fateful coincidence; (caractère inévitable) inevitability

fatidique [fatidik] adj fateful

fatigant, e [fatigɑ̃, -ɑ̃t] adj tiring; (agaçant) tiresome

fatigue [fatig] nf tiredness, fatigue; (détérioration) fatigue; **les ~s du voyage** the wear and tear of the journey

fatigué, e [fatige] adj tired

fatiguer [fatige] vt to tire, make tired; (Tech) to put a strain on, strain; (fig: importuner) to wear out ▷ vi (moteur) to labour (Brit), labor (US), strain; **se fatiguer** vi to get tired; to tire o.s. (out); **se ~ à faire qch** to tire o.s. out doing sth

fatras [fatʀa] nm jumble, hotchpotch

fatuité [fatɥite] nf conceitedness, smugness

faubourg [fobuʀ] nm suburb

faubourien, ne [fobuʀjɛ̃, -ɛn] adj (accent) working-class

fauché, e [foʃe] adj (fam) broke

faucher [foʃe] vt (herbe) to cut; (champs, blés) to reap; (fig) to cut down; to mow down; (fam: voler) to pinch, nick

faucheur, -euse [foʃœR, -øz] nm/f reaper, mower

faucille [fosij] nf sickle

faucon [fokɔ̃] nm falcon, hawk

faudra etc [fodRa] vb voir **falloir**

faufil [fofil] nm (Couture) tacking thread

faufilage [fofilaʒ] nm (Couture) tacking

faufiler [fofile] vt to tack, baste; **se faufiler** vi: **se ~ dans** to edge one's way into; **se ~ parmi/ entre** to thread one's way among/between

faune [fon] nf (Zool) wildlife, fauna; (fig péj) set, crowd ▷ nm faun; **~ marine** marine (animal) life

faussaire [fosɛR] nm/f forger

fausse [fos] adj f voir **faux**

faussement [fosmɑ̃] adv (accuser) wrongly, wrongfully; (croire) falsely, erroneously

fausser [fose] vt (objet) to bend, buckle; (fig) to distort; **~ compagnie à qn** to give sb the slip

fausset [fosɛ] nm: **voix de ~** falsetto voice

fausseté [foste] nf wrongness; falseness

faut [fo] vb voir **falloir**

faute [fot] nf (erreur) mistake, error; (péché, manquement) misdemeanour; (Football etc) offence; (Tennis) fault; (responsabilité): **par la ~ de** through the fault of, because of; **c'est de sa/ ma ~** it's his/my fault; **être en ~** to be in the wrong; **prendre qn en ~** to catch sb out; **~ de** (temps, argent) for ou through lack of; **~ de mieux** for want of anything ou something better; **sans ~** adv without fail; **~ de frappe** typing error; **~ d'inattention** careless mistake; **~ d'orthographe** spelling mistake; **~ professionnelle** professional misconduct no pl

fauteuil [fotœj] nm armchair; **~ à bascule** rocking chair; **~ club** (big) easy chair; **~ d'orchestre** seat in the front stalls (Brit) ou the orchestra (US); **~ roulant** wheelchair

fauteur [fotœR] nm: **~ de troubles** trouble-maker

fautif, -ive [fotif, -iv] adj (incorrect) incorrect, inaccurate; (responsable) at fault, in the wrong; (coupable) guilty ▷ nm/f culprit

fauve [fov] nm wildcat; (peintre) Fauve ▷ adj (couleur) fawn

fauvette [fovɛt] nf warbler

fauvisme [fovism(ə)] nm (Art) Fauvism

faux¹ [fo] nf scythe

faux², fausse [fo, fos] adj (inexact) wrong; (piano, voix) out of tune; (falsifié) fake, forged; (sournois, postiche) false ▷ adv (Mus) out of tune ▷ nm (copie) fake, forgery; (opposé au vrai): **le ~** falsehood; **le ~ numéro/la fausse clé** the wrong number/key; **faire fausse route** to go the wrong way; **faire ~ bond à qn** to let sb down; **~ ami** (Ling) faux ami; **~ col** detachable collar; **~ départ** (Sport, fig) false start; **~ frais** nmpl extras, incidental expenses; **~ frère** (fig péj) false friend; **~ mouvement** awkward movement; **~ nez** false nose; **~ nom** assumed name; **~ pas** tripping no pl; (fig) faux pas; **~ témoignage** (délit) perjury; **fausse alerte** false alarm; **fausse clé** skeleton key; **fausse couche** (Méd) miscarriage; **fausse joie** vain joy; **fausse note** wrong note

faux-filet [fofilɛ] nm sirloin

faux-fuyant [fofɥijɑ̃] nm equivocation

faux-monnayeur [fomɔnɛjœR] nm counterfeiter, forger

faux-semblant [fosɑ̃blɑ̃] nm pretence (Brit), pretense (US)

faux-sens [fosɑ̃s] nm mistranslation

faveur [favœR] nf favour (Brit), favor (US); **traitement de ~** preferential treatment; **à la ~ de** under cover of; (grâce à) thanks to; **en ~ de** in favo(u)r of

favorable [favɔRabl(ə)] adj favo(u)rable

favori, te [favɔRi, -it] adj, nm/f favo(u)rite

favoris [favɔRi] nmpl (barbe) sideboards (Brit), sideburns

favoriser [favɔRize] vt to favour (Brit), favor (US)

favoritisme [favɔRitism(ə)] nm (péj) favo(u)ritism

fax [faks] nm fax

faxer vt to fax

fayot [fajo] nm (fam) crawler

FB abr (= franc belge) BF, FB

FBI sigle m FBI

FC sigle m (= Football Club) FC

fébrile [febRil] adj feverish, febrile; **capitaux ~s** (Écon) hot money

fébrilement [febRilmɑ̃] adv feverishly

fécal, e, -aux [fekal, -o] adj voir **matière**

fécond, e [fekɔ̃, -ɔ̃d] adj fertile

fécondation [fekɔ̃dasjɔ̃] nf fertilization

féconder [fekɔ̃de] vt to fertilize

fécondité [fekɔ̃dite] nf fertility

fécule [fekyl] nf potato flour

féculent [fekylɑ̃] nm starchy food

fédéral, e, -aux [federal, -o] adj federal

fédéralisme [federalism(ə)] nm federalism

fédéraliste [federalist(ə)] adj federalist

fédération [federasjɔ̃] nf federation; **la F~ française de football** the French football association

fée [fe] nf fairy

féerie [feRi] nf enchantment

féerique [feRik] adj magical, fairytale cpd

feignant, e [fɛɲɑ̃, -ɑ̃t] nm/f = **fainéant, e**

feindre [fɛ̃dR(ə)] vt to feign ▷ vi to dissemble; **~ de faire** to pretend to do

feint, e [fɛ̃, fɛ̃t] pp de **feindre** ▷ adj feigned ▷ nf (Sport: escrime) feint; (: Football, Rugby) dummy (Brit), fake (US); (fam: ruse) sham

feinter [fɛ̃te] vi (Sport: escrime) to feint; (: Football, Rugby) to dummy (Brit), fake (US) ▷ vt (fam: tromper) to fool

fêlé, e [fele] adj (aussi fig) cracked

fêler [fele] vt to crack

félicitations [felisitasjɔ̃] nfpl congratulations

félicité [felisite] nf bliss

féliciter [felisite] *vt*: ~ **qn (de)** to congratulate sb (on)

félin, e [felɛ̃, -in] *adj* feline ▷ *nm* (big) cat

félon, ne [felɔ̃, -ɔn] *adj* perfidious, treacherous

félonie [felɔni] *nf* treachery

fêlure [felyR] *nf* crack

femelle [fəmɛl] *adj* (*aussi Élec, Tech*) female ▷ *nf* female

féminin, e [feminɛ̃, -in] *adj* feminine; (*sexe*) female; (*équipe, vêtements etc*) women's; (*parfois péj: homme*) effeminate ▷ *nm* (*Ling*) feminine

féminiser [feminize] *vt* to feminize; (*rendre efféminé*) to make effeminate; **se féminiser** *vi*: **cette profession se féminise** this profession is attracting more women

féminisme [feminism(ə)] *nm* feminism

féministe [feminist(ə)] *adj*, *nf* feminist

féminité [feminite] *nf* femininity

femme [fam] *nf* woman; (*épouse*) wife; **être très ~** to be very much a woman; **devenir ~** to attain womanhood; **~ d'affaires** businesswoman; **~ de chambre** chambermaid; **~ fatale** femme fatale; **~ au foyer** housewife; **~ d'intérieur** (*real*) homemaker; **~ de ménage** domestic help, cleaning lady; **~ du monde** society woman; **~-objet** sex object; **~ de tête** determined, intellectual woman

fémoral, e, -aux [femɔral, -o] *adj* femoral

fémur [femyR] *nm* femur, thighbone

FEN [fɛn] *sigle f* (= *Fédération de l'Éducation nationale*) teachers' trades union

fenaison [fənɛzɔ̃] *nf* haymaking

fendillé, e [fɑ̃dije] *adj* (*terre etc*) crazed

fendre [fɑ̃dR(ə)] *vt* (*couper en deux*) to split; (*fissurer*) to crack; (*fig: traverser*) to cut through; to push one's way through; **se fendre** *vi* to crack

fendu, e [fɑ̃dy] *adj* (*sol, mur*) cracked; (*jupe*) slit

fenêtre [fənɛtR(ə)] *nf* window; **~ à guillotine** sash window

fennec [fenɛk] *nm* fennec

fenouil [fənuj] *nm* fennel

fente [fɑ̃t] *nf* slit; (*fissure*) crack

féodal, e, -aux [feɔdal, -o] *adj* feudal

féodalisme [feɔdalism(ə)] *nm* feudalism

feodalité [feɔdalite] *nf* feudalism

fer [fɛR] *nm* iron; (*de cheval*) shoe; **fers** *nmpl* (*Méd*) forceps; **mettre aux ~s** (*enchaîner*) to put in chains; **au ~ rouge** with a red-hot iron; **santé/main de ~** iron constitution/hand; **~ à cheval** horseshoe; **en ~ à cheval** (*fig*) horseshoe-shaped; **~ forgé** wrought iron; **~ à friser** curling tongs; **~ de lance** spearhead; **~ à repasser** iron; **~ à souder** soldering iron

ferai *etc* [fəRe] *vb voir* **faire**

fer-blanc [fɛRblɑ̃] *nm* tin(plate)

ferblanterie [fɛRblɑ̃tRi] *nf* tinplate making; (*produit*) tinware

ferblantier [fɛRblɑ̃tje] *nm* tinsmith

férié, e [feRje] *adj*: **jour ~** public holiday

ferions *etc* [fəRjɔ̃] *vb voir* **faire**

férir [feRiR]: **sans coup ~** *adv* without meeting any opposition

fermage [fɛRmaʒ] *nm* tenant farming

ferme [fɛRm(ə)] *adj* firm ▷ *adv* (*travailler etc*) hard; (*discuter*) ardently ▷ *nf* (*exploitation*) farm; (*maison*) farmhouse; **tenir ~** to stand firm

fermé, e [fɛRme] *adj* closed, shut; (*gaz, eau etc*) off; (*fig: personne*) uncommunicative; (: *milieu*) exclusive

fermement [fɛRməmɑ̃] *adv* firmly

ferment [fɛRmɑ̃] *nm* ferment

fermentation [fɛRmɑ̃tasjɔ̃] *nf* fermentation

fermenter [fɛRmɑ̃te] *vi* to ferment

fermer [fɛRme] *vt* to close, shut; (*cesser l'exploitation de*) to close down, shut down; (*eau, lumière, électricité, robinet*) to put off, turn off; (*aéroport, route*) to close ▷ *vi* to close, shut; to close down, shut down; **se fermer** *vi* (*yeux*) to close, shut; (*fleur, blessure*) to close up; **~ à clef** to lock; **~ au verrou** to bolt; **~ les yeux (sur qch)** (*fig*) to close one's eyes (to sth); **se ~ à** (*pitié, amour*) to close one's heart *ou* mind to

fermeté [fɛRməte] *nf* firmness

fermette [fɛRmɛt] *nf* farmhouse

fermeture [fɛRmətyR] *nf* closing; shutting; closing *ou* shutting down; putting *ou* turning off; (*dispositif*) catch; fastening, fastener; **heure de ~** (*Comm*) closing time; **jour de ~** (*Comm*) day on which the shop (*etc*) is closed; **~ éclair**® *ou* **à glissière** zip (fastener) (*Brit*), zipper; *voir* **fermer**

fermier, -ière [fɛRmje, -jɛR] *nm/f* farmer ▷ *nf* (*femme de fermier*) farmer's wife ▷ *adj*: **beurre/cidre ~** farm butter/cider

fermoir [fɛRmwaR] *nm* clasp

féroce [feRɔs] *adj* ferocious, fierce

férocement [feRɔsmɑ̃] *adv* ferociously

férocité [feRɔsite] *nf* ferocity, ferociousness

ferons *etc* [fəRɔ̃] *vb voir* **faire**

ferraille [fɛRaj] *nf* scrap iron; **mettre à la ~** to scrap; **bruit de ~** clanking

ferrailler [fɛRaje] *vi* to clank

ferrailleur [fɛRajœR] *nm* scrap merchant

ferrant [fɛRɑ̃] *adj m voir* **maréchal-ferrant**

ferré, e [fɛRe] *adj* (*chaussure*) hobnailed; (*canne*) steel-tipped; **~ sur** (*fam: savant*) well up on

ferrer [fɛRe] *vt* (*cheval*) to shoe; (*chaussure*) to nail; (*canne*) to tip; (*poisson*) to strike

ferreux, -euse [fɛRø, -øz] *adj* ferrous

ferronnerie [fɛRɔnRi] *nf* ironwork; **~ d'art** wrought iron work

ferronnier [fɛRɔnje] *nm* craftsman in wrought iron; (*marchand*) ironware merchant

ferroviaire [fɛRɔvjɛR] *adj* rail *cpd*, railway *cpd* (*Brit*), railroad *cpd* (*US*)

ferrugineux, -euse [fɛRyʒinø, -øz] *adj* ferruginous

ferrure [fɛRyR] *nf* (*ornamental*) hinge

ferry [fɛRe], **ferry-boat** [fɛRebot] *nm* ferry

fertile [fɛRtil] *adj* fertile; **~ en incidents** eventful, packed with incidents

fertilisant [fɛRtilizɑ̃] *nm* fertilizer

fertilisation [fɛRtilizasjɔ̃] *nf* fertilization

fertiliser [fɛRtilize] *vt* to fertilize

fertilité [fɛRtilite] *nf* fertility

féru, e [feʀy] *adj*: **~ de** with a keen interest in

férule [feʀyl] *nf*: **être sous la ~ de qn** to be under sb's (iron) rule

fervent, e [fɛʀvɑ̃, -ɑ̃t] *adj* fervent

ferveur [fɛʀvœʀ] *nf* fervour (*Brit*), fervor (*US*)

fesse [fɛs] *nf* buttock; **les ~s** the bottom *sg*, the buttocks

fessée [fese] *nf* spanking

fessier [fesje] *nm* (*fam*) behind

festin [fɛstɛ̃] *nm* feast

festival [fɛstival] *nm* festival

festivalier [fɛstivalje] *nm* festival-goer

festivités [fɛstivite] *nfpl* festivities, merrymaking *sg*

feston [fɛstɔ̃] *nm* (*Archit*) festoon; (*Couture*) scallop

festoyer [fɛstwaje] *vi* to feast

fêtard [fɛtaʀ] *nm* (*péj*) high liver, merrymaker

fête [fɛt] *nf* (*religieuse*) feast; (*publique*) holiday; (*en famille etc*) celebration; (*kermesse*) fête, fair, festival; (*du nom*) feast day, name day; **faire la ~** to live it up; **faire ~ à qn** to give sb a warm welcome; **se faire une ~ de** to look forward to; to enjoy; **ça va être sa ~!** (*fam*) he's going to get it!; **jour de ~** holiday; **les ~s (de fin d'année)** the festive season; **la salle/le comité des ~s** the village hall/festival committee; **la ~ des Mères/Pères** Mother's/Father's Day; **~ de charité** charity fair *ou* fête; **~ foraine** (fun)fair; **la ~ de la musique**; *see note*; **~ mobile** movable feast (day); **la F~ Nationale** the national holiday

⬤ **FÊTE DE LA MUSIQUE**
⬤
⬤ The *fête de la musique* is a music festival which
⬤ has taken place every year since 1981. On 21
⬤ June throughout France local musicians
⬤ perform free of charge in parks, streets and
⬤ squares.

Fête-Dieu [fɛtdjø] *nf*: **la ~** Corpus Christi

fêter [fete] *vt* to celebrate; (*personne*) to have a celebration for

fétiche [fetiʃ] *nm* fetish; **animal ~**, **objet ~** mascot

fétichisme [fetiʃism(ə)] *nm* fetishism

fétichiste [fetiʃist(ə)] *adj* fetishist

fétide [fetid] *adj* fetid

fétu [fety] *nm*: **~ de paille** wisp of straw

feu¹ [fø] *adj inv*: **~ son père** his late father

feu², x [fø] *nm* (*gén*) fire; (*signal lumineux*) light; (*de cuisinière*) ring; (*sensation de brûlure*) burning (sensation); **feux** *nmpl* fire *sg*; (*Auto*) (traffic) lights; **tous ~x éteints** (*Navig, Auto*) without lights; **au ~!** (*incendie*) fire!; **à ~ doux/vif** over a slow/brisk heat; **à petit ~** (*Culin*) over a gentle heat; (*fig*) slowly; **faire ~** to fire; **ne pas faire long ~** (*fig*) not to last long; **commander le ~** (*Mil*) to give the order to (open) fire; **tué au ~** (*Mil*) killed in action; **mettre à ~** (*fusée*) to fire off; **pris entre deux ~x** caught in the crossfire;

en ~ on fire; **être tout ~ tout flamme (pour)** (*passion*) to be aflame with passion (for); (*enthousiasme*) to be fired with enthusiasm (for); **prendre ~** to catch fire; **mettre le ~ à** to set fire to, set on fire; **faire du ~** to make a fire; **avez-vous du ~?** (*pour cigarette*) have you (got) a light?; **~ rouge/vert/orange** (*Auto*) red/green/amber (*Brit*) *ou* yellow (*US*) light; **donner le ~ vert à qch/qn** (*fig*) to give sth/sb the go-ahead *ou* green light; **~ arrière** (*Auto*) rear light; **~ d'artifice** firework; (*spectacle*) fireworks *pl*; **~ de camp** campfire; **~ de cheminée** chimney fire; **~ de joie** bonfire; **~ de paille** (*fig*) flash in the pan; **~x de brouillard** (*Auto*) fog lights *ou* lamps; **~x de croisement** (*Auto*) dipped (*Brit*) *ou* dimmed (*US*) headlights; **~x de position** (*Auto*) sidelights; **~x de route** (*Auto*) headlights (on full (*Brit*) *ou* high (*US*) beam); **~x de stationnement** parking lights

feuillage [fœjaʒ] *nm* foliage, leaves *pl*

feuille [fœj] *nf* (*d'arbre*) leaf; **~ (de papier)** sheet (of paper); **rendre ~ blanche** (*Scol*) to give in a blank paper; **~ d'or/de métal** gold/metal leaf; **~ de chou** (*péj: journal*) rag; **~ d'impôts** tax form; **~ de maladie** medical expenses claim form; **~ morte** dead leaf; **~ de paye** pay slip; **~ de présence** attendance sheet; **~ de température** temperature chart; **~ de vigne** (*Bot*) vine leaf; (*sur statue*) fig leaf; **~ volante** loose sheet

feuillet [fœjɛ] *nm* leaf, page

feuilletage [fœjtaʒ] *nm* (*aspect feuilleté*) flakiness

feuilleté, e [fœjte] *adj* (*Culin*) flaky; (*verre*) laminated

feuilleter [fœjte] *vt* (*livre*) to leaf through

feuilleton [fœjtɔ̃] *nm* serial

feuillette *etc* [fœjɛt] *vb voir* **feuilleter**

feuillu, e [fœjy] *adj* leafy ▷ *nm* broad-leaved tree

feulement [følmɑ̃] *nm* growl

feutre [føtʀ(ə)] *nm* felt; (*chapeau*) felt hat; (*stylo*) felt-tip(ped pen)

feutré, e [føtʀe] *adj* feltlike; (*pas, voix*) muffled

feutrer [føtʀe] *vt* to felt; (*fig: bruits*) to muffle ▷ *vi*, **se feutrer** *vi* (*tissu*) to felt

feutrine [føtʀin] *nf* (lightweight) felt

fève [fɛv] *nf* broad bean; (*dans la galette des Rois*) charm (*hidden in cake eaten on Twelfth Night*)

février [fevʀije] *nm* February; *voir aussi* **juillet**

fez [fɛz] *nm* fez

FF *abr* (= franc français) FF

FFA *sigle fpl* (= Forces françaises en Allemagne) French forces in Germany

FFF *abr* = **Fédération française de football**

FFI *sigle fpl* = **Forces françaises de l'intérieur (1942–45)** ▷ *sigle m* member of the FFI

FFL *sigle fpl* (= Forces françaises libres) Free French Army

Fg *abr* = **faubourg**

FGA *sigle m* (= Fonds de garantie automobile) fund financed through insurance premiums, to compensate victims of uninsured losses

FGEN *sigle f* (= Fédération générale de l'éducation nationale) teachers' trade union

fi [fi] *excl*: **faire fi de** to snap one's fingers at

fiabilité [fjabilite] *nf* reliability

fiable [fjabl(ə)] *adj* reliable

fiacre [fjakʀ(ə)] *nm* (hackney) cab *ou* carriage

fiançailles [fjɑ̃saj] *nfpl* engagement *sg*

fiancé, e [fjɑ̃se] *nm/f* fiancé (fiancée) ▷ *adj*: **être ~ (à)** to be engaged (to)

fiancer [fjɑ̃se]: **se fiancer** *vi*: **se ~ (avec)** to become engaged (to)

fiasco [fjasko] *nm* fiasco

fibranne [fibʀan] *nf* bonded fibre *ou* fiber (*US*)

fibre [fibʀ(ə)] *nf* fibre, fiber (*US*); **avoir la ~ paternelle/militaire** to be a born father/ soldier; **~ optique** optical fibre *ou* fiber; **~ de verre** fibreglass (*Brit*), fiberglass (*US*), glass fibre *ou* fiber

fibreux, -euse [fibʀø, -øz] *adj* fibrous; (*viande*) stringy

fibrome [fibʀom] *nm* (*Méd*) fibroma

ficelage [fislaʒ] *nm* tying (up)

ficelé, e [fisle] *adj* (*fam*): **être mal ~** (*habillé*) to be badly got up; **bien/mal ~** (*conçu: roman, projet*) well/badly put together

ficeler [fisle] *vt* to tie up

ficelle [fisɛl] *nf* string *no pl*; (*morceau*) piece *ou* length of string; (*pain*) stick of French bread; **ficelles** *nfpl* (*fig*) strings; **tirer sur la ~** (*fig*) to go too far

fiche [fiʃ] *nf* (*carte*) (index) card; (*formulaire*) form; (*Élec*) plug; **~ de paye** pay slip; **~ signalétique** (*Police*) identification card; **~ technique** data sheet, specification *ou* spec sheet

ficher [fiʃe] *vt* (*dans un fichier*) to file; (: *Police*) to put on file; (*fam*) to do; (: *donner*) to give; (: *mettre*) to stick *ou* shove; (*planter*): **~ qch dans** to stick *ou* drive sth into; **~ qn à la porte** (*fam*) to chuck sb out; **fiche(-moi) le camp** (*fam*) clear off; **fiche-moi la paix** (*fam*) leave me alone; **se ~ dans** (*s'enfoncer*) to get stuck in, embed itself in; **se ~ de** (*fam*) to make fun of; not to care about

fichier [fiʃje] *nm* (*gén, Inform*) file; (*à cartes*) card index; **~ actif** *ou* **en cours d'utilisation** (*Inform*) active file; **~ d'adresses** mailing list; **~ d'archives** (*Inform*) archive file

fichu, e [fiʃy] *pp de* **ficher** (*fam*) ▷ *adj* (*fam: fini, inutilisable*) bust, done for; (: *intensif*) wretched, darned ▷ *nm* (*foulard*) (head)scarf; **être ~ de** to be capable of; **mal ~** feeling lousy; useless; **bien ~** great

fictif, -ive [fiktif, -iv] *adj* fictitious

fiction [fiksjɔ̃] *nf* fiction; (*fait imaginé*) invention

fictivement [fiktivmɑ̃] *adv* fictitiously

fidèle [fidɛl] *adj*: **~ (à)** faithful (to) ▷ *nm/f* (*Rel*): **les ~s** the faithful; (*à l'église*) the congregation

fidèlement [fidɛlmɑ̃] *adv* faithfully

fidélité [fidelite] *nf* faithfulness

Fidji [fidʒi] *nfpl*: **(les îles) ~** Fiji

fiduciaire [fidysjɛʀ] *adj* fiduciary; **héritier ~** heir, trustee; **monnaie ~** flat money

fief [fjɛf] *nm* fief; (*fig*) preserve; stronghold

fieffé, e [fjefe] *adj* (*ivrogne, menteur*) arrant, out-and-out

fiel [fjɛl] *nm* gall

fiente [fjɑ̃t] *nf* (*bird*) droppings *pl*

fier¹ [fje]: **se ~ à** *vt* to trust

fier², fière [fjɛʀ] *adj* proud; **~ de** proud of; **avoir fière allure** to cut a fine figure

fièrement [fjɛʀmɑ̃] *adv* proudly

fierté [fjɛʀte] *nf* pride

fièvre [fjɛvʀ(ə)] *nf* fever; **avoir de la ~/39 de ~** to have a high temperature/a temperature of 39° C; **~ typhoïde** typhoid fever

fiévreusement [fjevʀøzmɑ̃] *adv* (*fig*) feverishly

fiévreux, -euse [fjevʀø, -øz] *adj* feverish

FIFA [fifa] *sigle f* (= *Fédération internationale de Football association*) FIFA

fifre [fifʀ(ə)] *nm* fife; (*personne*) fife-player

fig *abr* (= *figure*) fig

figé, e [fiʒe] *adj* (*manières*) stiff; (*société*) rigid; (*sourire*) set

figer [fiʒe] *vt* to congeal; (*fig: personne*) to freeze, root to the spot; **se figer** *vi* to congeal; to freeze; (*institutions etc*) to become set, stop evolving

fignoler [fiɲɔle] *vt* to put the finishing touches to

figue [fig] *nf* fig

figuier [figje] *nm* fig tree

figurant, e [figyʀɑ̃, -ɑ̃t] *nm/f* (*Théât*) walk-on; (*Ciné*) extra

figuratif, -ive [figyʀatif, -iv] *adj* representational, figurative

figuration [figyʀasjɔ̃] *nf* walk-on parts *pl*; extras *pl*

figure [figyʀ] *nf* (*visage*) face; (*image, tracé, forme, personnage*) figure; (*illustration*) picture, diagram; **faire ~ de** to look like; **faire bonne ~** to put up a good show; **faire triste ~** to be a sorry sight; **~ de rhétorique** figure of speech

figuré, e [figyʀe] *adj* (*sens*) figurative

figurer [figyʀe] *vi* to appear ▷ *vt* to represent; **se ~ que** to imagine that; **figurez-vous que ...** would you believe that ...?

figurine [figyʀin] *nf* figurine

fil [fil] *nm* (*brin, fig: d'une histoire*) thread; (*du téléphone*) cable, wire; (*textile de lin*) linen; (*d'un couteau: tranchant*) edge; **au ~ des années** with the passing of the years; **au ~ de l'eau** with the stream *ou* current; **de ~ en aiguille** one thing leading to another; **ne tenir qu'à un ~** (*vie, réussite etc*) to hang by a thread; **donner du ~ à retordre à qn** to make life difficult for sb; **donner/recevoir un coup de ~** to make/get a phone call; **~ à coudre** (*sewing*) thread *ou* yarn; **~ dentaire** dental floss; **~ électrique** electric wire; **~ de fer** wire; **~ de fer barbelé** barbed wire; **~ à pêche** fishing line; **~ à plomb** plumb line; **~ à souder** soldering wire

filament [filamɑ̃] *nm* (*Élec*) filament; (*de liquide*) trickle, thread

filandreux, -euse [filɑ̃dʀø, -øz] *adj* stringy

filant, e [filɑ̃, -ɑ̃t] *adj*: **étoile ~e** shooting star

filasse [filas] *adj inv* white blond

filature [filatyʀ] *nf* (*fabrique*) mill; (*policière*) shadowing *no pl*, tailing *no pl*; **prendre qn en ~** to shadow *ou* tail sb

file [fil] *nf* line; **~ (d'attente)** queue (*Brit*), line (*US*); **prendre la ~** to join (the end of the) queue *ou* line; **prendre la ~ de droite** (*Auto*) to move into the right-hand lane; **se mettre en ~** to form a line; (*Auto*) to get into lane; **stationner en double ~** (*Auto*) to double-park; **à la ~** *adv* (*d'affilée*) in succession; (*à la suite*) one after another; **à la** *ou* **en ~ indienne** in single file

filer [file] *vt* (*tissu, toile, verre*) to spin; (*dérouler: câble etc*) to pay *ou* let out; (*prendre en filature*) to shadow, tail; (*fam: donner*): **~ qch à qn** to slip sb sth ▷ *vi* (*bas, maille, liquide, pâte*) to run; (*aller vite*) to fly past *ou* by; (*fam: partir*) to make off; **~ à l'anglaise** to take French leave; **~ doux** to behave o.s., toe the line; **~ un mauvais coton** to be in a bad way

filet [file] *nm* net; (*Culin*) fillet; (*d'eau, de sang*) trickle; **tendre un ~** (*police*) to set a trap; **~ (à bagages)** (*Rail*) luggage rack; **~ (à provisions)** string bag

filetage [filtaʒ] *nm* threading; thread

fileter [filte] *vt* to thread

filial, e, -aux [filjal, -o] *adj* filial ▷ *nf* (*Comm*) subsidiary; affiliate

filiation [filjasjɔ̃] *nf* filiation

filière [filjɛʀ] *nf*: **passer par la ~** to go through the (administrative) channels; **suivre la ~** to work one's way up (through the hierarchy)

filiforme [filifɔʀm(ə)] *adj* spindly; threadlike

filigrane [filigʀan] *nm* (*d'un billet, timbre*) watermark; **en ~** (*fig*) showing just beneath the surface

filin [filɛ̃] *nm* (*Navig*) rope

fille [fij] *nf* girl; (*opposé à fils*) daughter; **vieille ~** old maid; **~ de joie** prostitute; **~ de salle** waitress

fille-mère [fijmɛʀ] (*pl* **filles-mères**) *nf* unmarried mother

fillette [fijɛt] *nf* (little) girl

filleul, e [fijœl] *nm/f* godchild, godson (goddaughter)

film [film] *nm* (*pour photo*) (roll of) film; (*œuvre*) film, picture, movie; (*couche*) film; **~ muet/ parlant** silent/talking picture *ou* movie; **~ alimentaire** clingfilm; **~ d'amour/ d'animation/d'horreur** romantic/animated/ horror film; **~ comique** comedy; **~ policier** thriller

filmer [filme] *vt* to film

filon [filɔ̃] *nm* vein, lode; (*fig*) lucrative line, money-spinner

filou [filu] *nm* (*escroc*) swindler

fils [fis] *nm* son; **~ de famille** moneyed young man; **~ à papa** (*péj*) daddy's boy

filtrage [filtʀaʒ] *nm* filtering

filtrant, e [filtʀɑ̃, -ɑ̃t] *adj* (*huile solaire etc*) filtering

filtre [filtʀ(ə)] *nm* filter; **"~ ou sans ~?"** (*cigarettes*) "tipped or plain?"; **~ à air** air filter

filtrer [filtʀe] *vt* to filter; (*fig: candidats, visiteurs*)

to screen ▷ *vi* to filter (through)

fin¹ [fɛ̃] *nf* end; **fins** *nfpl* (*but*) ends; **à (la) ~ mai**, **~ mai** at the end of May; **en ~ de semaine** at the end of the week; **prendre ~** to come to an end; **toucher à sa ~** to be drawing to a close; **mettre ~ à** to put an end to; **mener à bonne ~** to bring to a successful conclusion; **à cette ~** to this end; **à toutes ~s utiles** for your information; **à la ~** in the end, eventually; **sans ~** *adj* endless ▷ *adv* endlessly; **~ de non-recevoir** (*Jur, Admin*) objection; **~ de section** (*de ligne d'autobus*) (fare) stage

fin², e [fɛ̃, fin] *adj* (*papier, couche, fil*) thin; (*cheveux, poudre, pointe, visage*) fine; (*taille*) neat, slim; (*esprit, remarque*) subtle; shrewd ▷ *adv* (*moudre, couper*) finely ▷ *nm*: **vouloir jouer au plus ~ (avec qn)** to try to outsmart sb ▷ *nf* (*alcool*) liqueur brandy; **c'est ~!** (*ironique*) how clever!; **~ prêt/soûl** quite ready/drunk; **un ~ gourmet** a gourmet; **un ~ tireur** a crack shot; **avoir la vue/l'ouïe ~e** to have sharp eyes/ears, have keen eyesight/hearing; **or/linge/vin ~** fine gold/linen/wine; **le ~ fond de** the very depths of; **le ~ mot de** the real story behind; **la ~e fleur de** the flower of; **une ~e mouche** (*fig*) a sly customer; **~es herbes** mixed herbs

final, e [final] *adj, nf* final ▷ *nm* (*Mus*) finale; **quarts de ~e** quarter finals; **8èmes/16èmes de ~e** 2nd/1st round (*in 5 round knock-out competition*)

finalement [finalmɑ̃] *adv* finally, in the end; (*après tout*) after all

finaliste [finalist(ə)] *nm/f* finalist

finalité [finalite] *nf* (*but*) aim, goal; (*fonction*) purpose

finance [finɑ̃s] *nf* finance; **finances** *nfpl* (*situation financière*) finances; (*activités financières*) finance *sg*; **moyennant ~** for a fee *ou* consideration

financement [finɑ̃smɑ̃] *nm* financing

financer [finɑ̃se] *vt* to finance

financier, -ière [finɑ̃sje, -jɛʀ] *adj* financial ▷ *nm* financier

financièrement [finɑ̃sjɛʀmɑ̃] *adv* financially

finasser [finase] *vi* (*péj*) to wheel and deal

finaud, e [fino, -od] *adj* wily

fine [fin] *adj f, nf voir* **fin, e**

finement [finmɑ̃] *adv* thinly; finely; neatly, slimly; subtly; shrewdly

finesse [finɛs] *nf* thinness; fineness; neatness, slimness; subtlety; shrewdness; **finesses** *nfpl* (*subtilités*) niceties; finer points

fini, e [fini] *adj* finished; (*Math*) finite; (*intensif*): **un menteur ~** a liar through and through ▷ *nm* (*d'un objet manufacturé*) finish

finir [finiʀ] *vt* to finish ▷ *vi* to finish, end; **~ quelque part** to end *ou* finish up somewhere; **~ de faire** to finish doing; (*cesser*) to stop doing; **~ par faire** to end *ou* finish up doing; **il finit par m'agacer** he's beginning to get on my nerves; **~ en pointe/tragédie** to end in a point/in tragedy; **en ~ avec** to be *ou* have done with; **à n'en plus ~** (*route, discussions*) never-ending; **il**

va mal ~ he will come to a bad end; **c'est bientôt fini?** (*reproche*) have you quite finished?

finish [finiʃ] *nm* (*Sport*) finish

finissage [finisaʒ] *nm* finishing

finisseur, -euse [finisœʀ, -øz] *nm/f* (*Sport*) strong finisher

finition [finisjɔ̃] *nf* finishing; finish

finlandais, e [fɛ̃lɑ̃dɛ, -ɛz] *adj* Finnish ▷ *nm/f*: **Finlandais, e** Finn

Finlande [fɛ̃lɑ̃d] *nf*: **la** ~ Finland

finnois, e [finwa, -waz] *adj* Finnish ▷ *nm* (*Ling*) Finnish

fiole [fjɔl] *nf* phial

fiord [fjɔʀ(d)] *nm* = **fjord**

fioriture [fjɔʀityʀ] *nf* embellishment, flourish

fioul [fjul] *nm* fuel oil

firent [fiʀ] *vb voir* **faire**

firmament [fiʀmamɑ̃] *nm* firmament, skies *pl*

firme [fiʀm(ə)] *nf* firm

fis [fi] *vb voir* **faire**

fisc [fisk] *nm* tax authorities *pl*, ≈ Inland Revenue (*Brit*), ≈ Internal Revenue Service (*US*)

fiscal, e, -aux [fiskal, -o] *adj* tax *cpd*, fiscal

fiscaliser [fiskalize] *vt* to subject to tax

fiscaliste [fiskalist(ə)] *nm/f* tax specialist

fiscalité [fiskalite] *nf* tax system; (*charges*) taxation

fissible [fisibl(ə)] *adj* fissile

fission [fisjɔ̃] *nf* fission

fissure [fisyʀ] *nf* crack

fissurer [fisyʀe] *vt*, **se fissurer** *vi* to crack

fiston [fistɔ̃] *nm* (*fam*) son, lad

fit [fi] *vb voir* **faire**

FIV *sigle f* (= *fécondation in vitro*) IVF

fixage [fiksaʒ] *nm* (*Photo*) fixing

fixateur [fiksatœʀ] *nm* (*Photo*) fixer; (*pour cheveux*) hair cream

fixatif [fiksatif] *nm* fixative

fixation [fiksasjɔ̃] *nf* fixing; fastening; setting; (*de ski*) binding; (*Psych*) fixation

fixe [fiks(ə)] *adj* fixed; (*emploi*) steady, regular ▷ *nm* (*salaire*) basic salary; **à heure** ~ at a set time; **menu à prix** ~ set menu

fixé, e [fikse] *adj* (*heure, jour*) appointed; **être** ~ **(sur)** to have made up one's mind (about); to know for certain (about)

fixement [fiksəmɑ̃] *adv* fixedly, steadily

fixer [fikse] *vt* (*attacher*): ~ **qch (à/sur)** to fix *ou* fasten sth (to/onto); (*déterminer*) to fix, set; (*Chimie, Photo*) to fix; (*poser son regard sur*) to look hard at, stare at; **se fixer** (*s'établir*) to settle down; ~ **son choix sur qch** to decide on sth; **se** ~ **sur** (*attention*) to focus on

fixité [fiksite] *nf* fixedness

fjord [fjɔʀ(d)] *nm* fjord, fiord

fl. *abr* (= *fleuve*) r, R; (= *florin*) fl

flacon [flakɔ̃] *nm* bottle

flagada [flagada] *adj inv* (*fam: fatigué*) shattered

flagellation [flaʒɛlɑsjɔ̃] *nf* flogging

flageller [flaʒele] *vt* to flog, scourge

flageoler [flaʒɔle] *vi* to have knees like jelly

flageolet [flaʒɔlɛ] *nm* (*Mus*) flageolet; (*Culin*) dwarf kidney bean

flagornerie [flagɔʀnəʀi] *nf* toadying, fawning

flagorneur, -euse [flagɔʀnœʀ, -øz] *nm/f* toady, fawner

flagrant, e [flagʀɑ̃, -ɑ̃t] *adj* flagrant, blatant; **en** ~ **délit** in the act, in flagrante delicto

flair [flɛʀ] *nm* sense of smell; (*fig*) intuition

flairer [fleʀe] *vt* (*humer*) to sniff (at); (*détecter*) to scent

flamand, e [flamɑ̃, -ɑ̃d] *adj* Flemish ▷ *nm* (*Ling*) Flemish ▷ *nm/f*: **Flamand, e** Fleming; **les F~s** the Flemish

flamant [flamɑ̃] *nm* flamingo

flambant [flɑ̃bɑ̃] *adv*: ~ **neuf** brand new

flambé, e [flɑ̃be] *adj* (*Culin*) flambé ▷ *nf* blaze; (*fig*) flaring-up, explosion

flambeau, x [flɑ̃bo] *nm* (*flaming*) torch; **se passer le** ~ (*fig*) to hand down the (*ou* a) tradition

flambée [flɑ̃be] *nf* (*feu*) blaze; (*Comm*): ~ **des prix** (*sudden*) shooting up of prices

flamber [flɑ̃be] *vi* to blaze (up) ▷ *vt* (*poulet*) to singe; (*aiguille*) to sterilize

flambeur, -euse [flɑ̃bœʀ, -øz] *nm/f* big-time gambler

flamboyant, e [flɑ̃bwajɑ̃, -ɑ̃t] *adj* blazing; flaming

flamboyer [flɑ̃bwaje] *vi* to blaze (up); (*fig*) to flame

flamenco [flamɛnko] *nm* flamenco

flamingant, e [flamɛ̃gɑ̃, -ɑ̃t] *adj* Flemish-speaking ▷ *nm/f*: **Flamingant, e** Flemish speaker; (*Pol*) Flemish nationalist

flamme [flam] *nf* flame; (*fig*) fire, fervour; **en** ~**s** on fire, ablaze

flammèche [flamɛʃ] *nf* (*flying*) spark

flammerole [flamʀɔl] *nf* will-o'-the-wisp

flan [flɑ̃] *nm* (*Culin*) custard tart *ou* pie

flanc [flɑ̃] *nm* side; (*Mil*) flank; **à ~ de colline** on the hillside; **prêter le** ~ **à** (*fig*) to lay o.s. open to

flancher [flɑ̃ʃe] *vi* (*cesser de fonctionner*) to fail, pack up; (*armée*) to quit

Flandre [flɑ̃dʀ(ə)] *nf*: **la** ~ (*aussi*: **les Flandres**) Flanders

flanelle [flanɛl] *nf* flannel

flâner [flɑne] *vi* to stroll

flânerie [flɑnʀi] *nf* stroll

flâneur, -euse [flɑnœʀ, -øz] *adj* idle ▷ *nm/f* stroller

flanquer [flɑ̃ke] *vt* to flank; (*fam: jeter*): ~ **par terre/à la porte** to fling to the ground/chuck out; (: *donner*): ~ **la frousse à qn** to put the wind up sb, give sb an awful fright

flapi, e [flapi] *adj* dog-tired

flaque [flak] *nf* (*d'eau*) puddle; (*d'huile, de sang etc*) pool

flash [flaʃ] (*pl* -**es**) *nm* (*Photo*) flash; ~ **(d'information)** newsflash

flasque [flask(ə)] *adj* flabby ▷ *nf* (*flacon*) flask

flatter [flate] *vt* to flatter; (*caresser*) to stroke; **se** ~ **de qch** to pride o.s. on sth

flatterie [flatʀi] *nf* flattery

flatteur, -euse [flatœʀ, -øz] *adj* flattering ▷ *nm/f* flatterer

flatulence [flatylɑ̃s], **flatuosité** [flatɥozite] *nf* (*Méd*) flatulence, wind

FLB *abr* (= *franco long du bord*) FAS ▷ *sigle m* (*Pol*) = **Front de libération de la Bretagne**

FLC *sigle m* = **Front de libération de la Corse**

fléau, x [fleo] *nm* scourge, curse; (*de balance*) beam; (*pour le blé*) flail

fléchage [fleʃaʒ] *nm* (*d'un itinéraire*) signposting

flèche [flɛʃ] *nf* arrow; (*de clocher*) spire; (*de grue*) jib; (*trait d'esprit, critique*) shaft; **monter en ~** (*fig*) to soar, rocket; **partir en ~** (*fig*) to be off like a shot; **à ~ variable** (*avion*) swing-wing *cpd*

flécher [fleʃe] *vt* to arrow, mark with arrows

fléchette [fleʃɛt] *nf* dart; **fléchettes** *nfpl* (*jeu*) darts *sg*

fléchir [fleʃiʀ] *vt* (*corps, genou*) to bend; (*fig*) to sway, weaken ▷ *vi* (*poutre*) to sag, bend; (*fig*) to weaken, flag; (: *baisser: prix*) to fall off

fléchissement [fleʃismɑ̃] *nm* bending; sagging; flagging; (*de l'économie*) dullness

flegmatique [flɛgmatik] *adj* phlegmatic

flegme [flɛgm(ə)] *nm* composure

flemmard, e [flemaʀ, -aʀd(ə)] *nm/f* lazybones *sg*, loafer

flemme [flɛm] *nf* (*fam*): **j'ai la ~ de le faire** I can't be bothered

flétan [fletɑ̃] *nm* (*Zool*) halibut

flétrir [fletʀiʀ] *vt* to wither; (*stigmatiser*) to condemn (in the most severe terms); **se flétrir** *vi* to wither

fleur [flœʀ] *nf* flower; (*d'un arbre*) blossom; **être en ~** (*arbre*) to be in blossom; **tissu à ~s** flowered *ou* flowery fabric; **la (fine) ~ de** (*fig*) the flower of; **être ~ bleue** to be soppy *ou* sentimental; **à ~ de terre** just above the ground; **faire une ~ à qn** to do sb a favour (*Brit*) *ou* favor (*US*); **~ de lis** fleur-de-lis

fleurer [flœʀe] *vt*: **~ la lavande** to have the scent of lavender

fleuret [flœʀɛ] *nm* (*arme*) foil; (*sport*) fencing

fleurette [flœʀɛt] *nf*: **conter ~ à qn** to whisper sweet nothings to sb

fleuri, e [flœʀi] *adj* in flower *ou* bloom; surrounded by flowers; (*fig: style*) flowery; (: *teint*) glowing

fleurir [flœʀiʀ] *vi* (*rose*) to flower; (*arbre*) to blossom; (*fig*) to flourish ▷ *vt* (*tombe*) to put flowers on; (*chambre*) to decorate with flowers

fleuriste [flœʀist(ə)] *nm/f* florist

fleuron [flœʀɔ̃] *nm* jewel (*fig*)

fleuve [flœv] *nm* river; **roman-~** saga; **discours-~** interminable speech

flexibilité [flɛksibilite] *nf* flexibility

flexible [flɛksibl(ə)] *adj* flexible

flexion [flɛksjɔ̃] *nf* flexing, bending; (*Ling*) inflection

flibustier [flibystje] *nm* buccaneer

flic [flik] *nm* (*fam: péj*) cop

flingue [flɛ̃g] *nm* (*fam*) shooter

flipper *nm* [flipœʀ] pinball (machine) ▷ *vi*

[flipe] (*fam: être déprimé*) to feel down, be on a downer; (: *être exalté*) to freak out

flirt [flœʀt] *nm* flirting; (*personne*) boyfriend, girlfriend

flirter [flœʀte] *vi* to flirt

FLN *sigle m* = **Front de libération nationale (during the Algerian war)**

FLNKS *sigle m* (= *Front de libération nationale kanak et socialiste*) *political movement in New Caledonia*

flocon [flɔkɔ̃] *nm* flake; (*de laine etc: boulette*) flock; **~s d'avoine** oat flakes, porridge oats

floconneux, -euse [flɔkɔnø, -øz] *adj* fluffy, fleecy

flonflons [flɔ̃flɔ̃] *nmpl* blare *sg*

flopée [flɔpe] *nf*: **une ~ de** loads of

floraison [flɔʀɛzɔ̃] *nf* flowering; blossoming; flourishing; *voir* **fleurir**

floral, e, -aux [flɔʀal, -o] *adj* floral, flower *cpd*

floralies [flɔʀali] *nfpl* flower show *sg*

flore [flɔʀ] *nf* flora

Florence [flɔʀɑ̃s] *n* (*ville*) Florence

florentin, e [flɔʀɑ̃tɛ̃, -in] *adj* Florentine

floriculture [flɔʀikyltyʀ] *nf* flower-growing

florissant, e [flɔʀisɑ̃, -ɑ̃t] *vb voir* **fleurir** ▷ *adj* flourishing; (*santé, teint, mine*) blooming

flot [flo] *nm* flood, stream; (*marée*) flood tide; **flots** *nmpl* (*de la mer*) waves; **être à ~** (*Navig*) to be afloat; (*fig*) to be on an even keel; **à ~s** (*couler*) in torrents; **entrer à ~s** to stream *ou* pour in

flottage [flɔtaʒ] *nm* (*du bois*) floating

flottaison [flɔtɛzɔ̃] *nf*: **ligne de ~** waterline

flottant, e [flɔtɑ̃, -ɑ̃t] *adj* (*vêtement*) loose(-fitting); (*cours, barème*) floating

flotte [flɔt] *nf* (*Navig*) fleet; (*fam*) water; rain

flottement [flɔtmɑ̃] *nm* (*fig*) wavering, hesitation; (*Écon*) floating

flotter [flɔte] *vi* to float; (*nuage, odeur*) to drift; (*drapeau*) to fly; (*vêtements*) to hang loose ▷ *vb impers* (*fam: pleuvoir*): **il flotte** it's raining ▷ *vt* to float; **faire ~** to float

flotteur [flɔtœʀ] *nm* float

flottille [flɔtij] *nf* flotilla

flou, e [flu] *adj* fuzzy, blurred; (*fig*) woolly (*Brit*), vague; (*non ajusté: robe*) loose(-fitting)

flouer [flue] *vt* to swindle

FLQ *abr* (= *franco long du quai*) FAQ

fluctuant, e [flyktɥɑ̃, -ɑ̃t] *adj* (*prix, cours*) fluctuating; (*opinions*) changing

fluctuation [flyktɥasjɔ̃] *nf* fluctuation

fluctuer [flyktɥe] *vi* to fluctuate

fluet, te [flyɛ, -ɛt] *adj* thin, slight; (*voix*) thin

fluide [flyid] *adj* fluid; (*circulation etc*) flowing freely ▷ *nm* fluid; (*force*) (mysterious) power

fluidifier [flyidifje] *vt* to make fluid

fluidité [flyidite] *nf* fluidity; free flow

fluor [flyɔʀ] *nm* fluorine

fluoré, e [flyɔʀe] *adj* fluoridated

fluorescent, e [flyɔʀesɑ̃, -ɑ̃t] *adj* fluorescent

flûte [flyt] *nf* (*aussi:* **flûte traversière**) flute; (*verre*) flute glass; (*pain*) long loaf; **petite ~** piccolo; **~! drat it!**; **~ (à bec)** recorder; **~ de Pan** panpipes *pl*

flûtiste [flytist(ə)] *nm/f* flautist, flute player

fluvial, e, -aux [flyvjal, -o] *adj* river *cpd*, fluvial

flux [fly] *nm* incoming tide; (*écoulement*) flow; **le ~ et le re~** the ebb and flow

fluxion [flyksjɔ̃] *nf*: **~ de poitrine** pneumonia

FM *sigle f* (= *frequency modulation*) FM

Fme *abr* (= *femme*) W

FMI *sigle m* (= *Fonds monétaire international*) IMF

FN *sigle m* (= *Front national*) ≈ NF (= *National Front*)

FNAC [fnak] *sigle f* (= *Fédération nationale des achats des cadres*) *chain of discount shops (hi-fi, photo etc)*

FNSEA *sigle f* (= *Fédération nationale des syndicats d'exploitants agricoles*) *farmers' union*

FO *sigle f* (= *Force ouvrière*) *trades union*

foc [fɔk] *nm* jib

focal, e, -aux [fɔkal, -o] *adj* focal ▷ *nf* focal length

focaliser [fɔkalize] *vt* to focus

foehn [føn] *nm* foehn, föhn

fœtal, e, -aux [fetal, -o] *adj* fetal, foetal (*Brit*)

fœtus [fetys] *nm* fetus, foetus (*Brit*)

foi [fwa] *nf* faith; **sous la ~ du serment** under *ou* on oath; **ajouter ~ à** to lend credence to; **faire ~** (*prouver*) to be evidence; **digne de ~** reliable; **sur la ~ de** on the word *ou* strength of; **être de bonne/mauvaise ~** to be in good faith/not to be in good faith; **ma ~!** well!

foie [fwa] *nm* liver; **~ gras** foie gras

foin [fwɛ̃] *nm* hay; **faire les ~s** to make hay; **faire du ~** (*fam*) to kick up a row

foire [fwaʀ] *nf* fair; (*fête foraine*) (fun) fair; (*fig: désordre, confusion*) bear garden; **~ aux questions** (*Internet*) frequently asked questions; **faire la ~** to whoop it up; **~ (exposition)** trade fair

fois [fwa] *nf* time; **une/deux ~** once/twice; **trois/vingt ~** three/twenty times; **deux ~ deux** twice two; **deux/quatre ~ plus grand (que)** twice/four times as big (as); **une ~** (*passé*) once; (*futur*) sometime; **une (bonne) ~ pour toutes** once and for all; **encore une ~** again, once more; **il était une ~** once upon a time; **une ~ que c'est fait** once it's done; **une ~ parti** once he (*ou* I *etc*) had left; **des ~** (*parfois*) sometimes; **si des ~ ...** (*fam*) if ever ...; **non mais des ~!** (*fam*) (now) look here!; **à la ~** (*ensemble*) (all) at once; **à la ~ grand et beau** both tall and handsome

foison [fwazɔ̃] *nf*: **une ~ de** an abundance of; **à ~** *adv* in plenty

foisonnant, e [fwazɔnɑ̃, -ɑ̃t] *adj* teeming

foisonnement [fwazɔnmɑ̃] *nm* profusion, abundance

foisonner [fwazɔne] *vi* to abound; **~ en** *ou* **de** to abound in

fol [fɔl] *adj m voir* **fou**

folâtre [fɔlɑtʀ(ə)] *adj* playful

folâtrer [fɔlɑtʀe] *vi* to frolic (about)

folichon, ne [fɔliʃɔ̃, -ɔn] *adj*: **ça n'a rien de ~** it's not a lot of fun

folie [fɔli] *nf* (*d'une décision, d'un acte*) madness, folly; (*état*) madness, insanity; (*acte*) folly; **la ~ des grandeurs** delusions of grandeur; **faire des ~s** (*en dépenses*) to be extravagant

folklore [fɔlklɔʀ] *nm* folklore

folklorique [fɔlklɔʀik] *adj* folk *cpd*; (*fam*) weird

folle [fɔl] *adj f, nf voir* **fou**

follement [fɔlmɑ̃] *adv* (*très*) madly, wildly

follet [fɔlɛ] *adj m*: **feu ~** will-o'-the-wisp

fomentateur, -trice [fɔmɑ̃tatœʀ, -tʀis] *nm/f* agitator

fomenter [fɔmɑ̃te] *vt* to stir up, foment

foncé, e [fɔ̃se] *adj* dark; **bleu ~** dark blue

foncer [fɔ̃se] *vt* to make darker; (*Culin: moule etc*) to line ▷ *vi* to go darker; (*fam: aller vite*) to tear *ou* belt along; **~ sur** to charge at

fonceur, -euse [fɔ̃sœʀ, -øz] *nm/f* whizz kid

foncier, -ière [fɔ̃sje, -jɛʀ] *adj* (*honnêteté etc*) basic, fundamental; (*malhonnêteté*) deep-rooted; (*Comm*) real estate *cpd*

foncièrement [fɔ̃sjɛʀmɑ̃] *adv* basically; (*absolument*) thoroughly

fonction [fɔ̃ksjɔ̃] *nf* (*rôle, Math, Ling*) function; (*emploi, poste*) post, position; **fonctions** *nfpl* (*professionnelles*) duties; **entrer en ~s** to take up one's post *ou* duties; to take up office; **voiture de ~** company car; **être ~ de** (*dépendre de*) to depend on; **en ~ de** (*par rapport à*) according to; **faire ~ de** to serve as; **la ~ publique** the state *ou* civil (*Brit*) service

fonctionnaire [fɔ̃ksjɔnɛʀ] *nm/f* state employee *ou* official; (*dans l'administration*) ≈ civil servant (*Brit*)

fonctionnariser [fɔ̃ksjɔnaʀize] *vt* (*Admin: personne*) to give the status of a state employee to

fonctionnel, le [fɔ̃ksjɔnɛl] *adj* functional

fonctionnellement [fɔ̃ksjɔnɛlmɑ̃] *adv* functionally

fonctionnement [fɔ̃ksjɔnmɑ̃] *nm* working; functioning; operation

fonctionner [fɔ̃ksjɔne] *vi* to work, function; (*entreprise*) to operate, function; **faire ~** to work, operate

fond [fɔ̃] *nm voir aussi* **fonds**; (*d'un récipient, trou*) bottom; (*d'une salle, scène*) back; (*d'un tableau, décor*) background; (*opposé à la forme*) content; (*petite quantité*): **un ~ de verre** a drop; (*Sport*): **le ~** long distance (running); **course/épreuve de ~** long-distance race/trial; **au ~ de** at the bottom of; at the back of; **aller au ~ des choses** to get to the root of things; **le ~ de sa pensée** his (*ou* her) true thoughts *ou* feelings; **sans ~** *adj* bottomless; **envoyer par le ~** (*Navig: couler*) to sink, scuttle; **à ~** *adv* (*connaître, soutenir*) thoroughly; (*appuyer, visser*) right down *ou* home; **à ~ (de train)** *adv* (*fam*) full tilt; **dans le ~, au ~** *adv* (*en somme*) basically, really; **de ~ en comble** *adv* from top to bottom; **~ sonore** background noise; background music; **~ de teint** foundation

fondamental, e, -aux [fɔ̃damɑ̃tal, -o] *adj* fundamental

fondamentalement [fɔ̃damɑ̃talmɑ̃] *adv* fundamentally

fondamentalisme [fɔ̃damɑ̃talism(ə)] *nm* fundamentalism

fondamentaliste [fɔ̃damɑ̃talist(ə)] *adj, nm/f* fundamentalist

fondant, e [fɔ̃dɑ̃, -ɑ̃t] *adj* (*neige*) melting; (*poire*) that melts in the mouth; (*chocolat*) fondant

fondateur, -trice [fɔ̃datœʀ, -tʀis] *nm/f* founder; **membre ~** founder (*Brit*) *ou* founding (*US*) member

fondation [fɔ̃dɑsjɔ̃] *nf* founding; (*établissement*) foundation; **fondations** *nfpl* (*d'une maison*) foundations; **travail de ~** foundation works *pl*

fondé, e [fɔ̃de] *adj* (*accusation etc*) well-founded ▷ *nm:* **~ de pouvoir** authorized representative; **mal ~** unfounded; **être ~ à croire** to have grounds for believing *ou* good reason to believe

fondement [fɔ̃dmɑ̃] *nm* (*derrière*) behind; **fondements** *nmpl* foundations; **sans ~** *adj* (*rumeur etc*) groundless, unfounded

fonder [fɔ̃de] *vt* to found; (*fig*): **~ qch sur** to base sth on; **se ~ sur** (*personne*) to base o.s. on; **~ un foyer** (*se marier*) to set up home

fonderie [fɔ̃dʀi] *nf* smelting works *sg*

fondeur, -euse [fɔ̃dœʀ, -øz] *nm/f* (*skieur*) long-distance skier ▷ *nm:* (**ouvrier**) **~** caster

fondre [fɔ̃dʀ(ə)] *vt* to melt; (*dans l'eau: sucre, sel*) to dissolve; (*fig: mélanger*) to merge, blend ▷ *vi* to melt; to dissolve; (*fig*) to melt away; (*se précipiter*): **~ sur** to swoop down on; **se fondre** *vi* (*se combiner, se confondre*) to merge into each other; to dissolve; **~ en larmes** to dissolve into tears

fondrière [fɔ̃dʀijeʀ] *nf* rut

fonds [fɔ̃] *nm* (*de bibliothèque*) collection; (*Comm*): **~ (de commerce)** business; (*fig*): **~ de probité** *etc* fund of integrity *etc* ▷ *nmpl* (*argent*) funds; **à ~ perdus** *adv* with little or no hope of getting the money back; **être en ~** to be in funds; **mise de ~** investment, (capital) outlay; **F~ monétaire international (FMI)** International Monetary Fund (IMF); **~ de roulement** *nm* float

fondu, e [fɔ̃dy] *adj* (*beurre, neige*) melted; (*métal*) molten ▷ *nm* (*Ciné*): **~ (enchaîné)** dissolve ▷ *nf* (*Culin*) fondue

fongicide [fɔ̃ʒisid] *nm* fungicide

font [fɔ̃] *vb voir* **faire**

fontaine [fɔ̃tɛn] *nf* fountain; (*source*) spring

fontanelle [fɔ̃tanɛl] *nf* fontanelle

fonte [fɔ̃t] *nf* melting; (*métal*) cast iron; **la ~ des neiges** the (spring) thaw

fonts baptismaux [fɔ̃batismo] *nmpl* (baptismal) font *sg*

foot [fut], **football** [futbol] *nm* football, soccer

footballeur, -euse [futbolœʀ, -øz] *nm/f* footballer (*Brit*), football *ou* soccer player

footing [futiŋ] *nm* jogging; **faire du ~** to go jogging

for [fɔʀ] *nm:* **dans** *ou* **en son ~ intérieur** in one's heart of hearts

forage [foʀaʒ] *nm* drilling, boring

forain, e [foʀɛ̃, -ɛn] *adj* fairground *cpd* ▷ *nm* (*marchand*) stallholder; (*acteur etc*) fairground entertainer

forban [fɔʀbɑ̃] *nm* (*pirate*) pirate; (*escroc*) crook

forçat [fɔʀsa] *nm* convict

force [fɔʀs(ə)] *nf* strength; (*puissance: surnaturelle etc*) power; (*Physique, Mécanique*) force; **forces** *nfpl* (*physiques*) strength *sg*; (*Mil*) forces; (*effectifs*): **d'importantes ~s de police** large contingents of police; **avoir de la ~** to be strong; **être à bout de ~** to have no strength left; **à la ~ du poignet** (*fig*) by the sweat of one's brow; **à ~ de faire** by dint of doing; **arriver en ~** (*nombreux*) to arrive in force; **cas de ~ majeure** case of absolute necessity; (*Assurances*) act of God; **~ de la nature** natural force; **de ~** *adv* forcibly, by force; **de toutes mes/ses ~s** with all my/his strength; **par la ~** using force; **par la ~ des choses/ d'habitude** by force of circumstances/habit; **à toute ~** (*absolument*) at all costs; **faire ~ de rames/voiles** to ply the oars/cram on sail; **être de ~ à faire** to be up to doing; **de première ~** first class; **la ~ armée** (*les troupes*) the army; **~ d'âme** fortitude; **~ de frappe** strike force; **~ d'inertie** force of inertia; **la ~ publique** the authorities responsible for public order; **~s d'intervention** (*Mil, Police*) peace-keeping force *sg*; **les ~s de l'ordre** the police

forcé, e [fɔʀse] *adj* forced; (*bain*) unintended; (*inévitable*): **c'est ~!** it's inevitable!, it HAS to be!

forcément [fɔʀsemɑ̃] *adv* necessarily; inevitably; (*bien sûr*) of course

forcené, e [fɔʀsəne] *adj* frenzied ▷ *nm/f* maniac

forceps [fɔʀsɛps] *nm* forceps *pl*

forcer [fɔʀse] *vt* (*contraindre*): **~ qn à faire** to force sb to do; (*porte, serrure, plante*) to force; (*moteur, voix*) to strain ▷ *vi* (*Sport*) to overtax o.s.; **se ~ à faire qch** to force o.s. to do sth; **~ la dose/ l'allure** to overdo it/increase the pace; **~ l'attention/le respect** to command attention/ respect; **~ la consigne** to bypass orders

forcing [fɔʀsiŋ] *nm* (*Sport*): **faire le ~** to pile on the pressure

forcir [fɔʀsiʀ] *vi* (*grossir*) to broaden out; (*vent*) to freshen

forclore [fɔʀklɔʀ] *vt* (*Jur: personne*) to debar

forclusion [fɔʀklyzjɔ̃] *nf* (*Jur*) debarment

forer [fɔʀe] *vt* to drill, bore

forestier, -ière [fɔʀɛstje, -jɛʀ] *adj* forest *cpd*

foret [fɔʀɛ] *nm* drill

forêt [fɔʀɛ] *nf* forest; **Office National des F~s** (*Admin*) ≈ Forestry Commission (*Brit*), ≈ National Forest Service (*US*); **la F~ Noire** the Black Forest

foreuse [fɔʀøz] *nf* (electric) drill

forfait [fɔʀfɛ] *nm* (*Comm*) fixed *ou* set price; all-in deal *ou* price; (*crime*) infamy; **déclarer ~** to withdraw; **gagner par ~** to win by a walkover; **travailler à ~** to work for a lump sum

forfaitaire [fɔʀfɛtɛʀ] *adj* set; inclusive

forfait-vacances [fɔʀfɛvakɑ̃s] (*pl* **forfaits-vacances**) *nm* package holiday

forfanterie [fɔʀfɑ̃tʀi] *nf* boastfulness *no pl*

forge [fɔʀʒ(ə)] *nf* forge, smithy

forgé, e [fɔʀʒe] *adj:* **~ de toutes pièces** (*histoire*) completely fabricated

forger [fɔʀʒe] vt to forge; (fig: personnalité) to form; (: prétexte) to contrive, make up

forgeron [fɔʀʒəʀɔ̃] nm (black)smith

formaliser [fɔʀmalize]: **se formaliser** vi: **se ~ (de)** to take offence (at)

formalisme [fɔʀmalism(ə)] nm formality

formalité [fɔʀmalite] nf formality

format [fɔʀma] nm size; **petit ~** small size; (Photo) 35 mm (film)

formater [fɔʀmate] vt (disque) to format; **non formaté** unformatted

formateur, -trice [fɔʀmatœʀ, -tʀis] adj formative

formation [fɔʀmasjɔ̃] nf forming; (éducation) training; (Mus) group; (Mil, Aviat, Géo) formation; **la ~ permanente** ou **continue** continuing education; **la ~ professionnelle** vocational training

forme [fɔʀm(ə)] nf (gén) form; (d'un objet) shape, form; **formes** nfpl (bonnes manières) proprieties; (d'une femme) figure sg; **en ~ de poire** pear-shaped, in the shape of a pear; **sous ~ de** in the form of; in the guise of; **sous ~ de cachets** in the form of tablets; **être en (bonne** ou **pleine) ~**, **avoir la ~** (Sport etc) to be on form; **en bonne et due ~** in due form; **pour la ~** for the sake of form; **sans autre ~ de procès** (fig) without further ado; **prendre ~** to take shape

formel, le [fɔʀmɛl] adj (preuve, décision) definite, positive; (logique) formal

formellement [fɔʀmɛlmɑ̃] adv (interdit) strictly

former [fɔʀme] vt (gén) to form; (éduquer: soldat, ingénieur etc) to train; **se former** to form; to train

formidable [fɔʀmidabl(ə)] adj tremendous

formidablement [fɔʀmidabləmɑ̃] adv tremendously

formol [fɔʀmɔl] nm formalin, formol

formosan, e [fɔʀmozɑ̃, -an] adj Formosan

Formose [fɔʀmoz] nf Formosa

formulaire [fɔʀmylɛʀ] nm form

formulation [fɔʀmylasjɔ̃] nf formulation; expression; voir **formuler**

formule [fɔʀmyl] nf (gén) formula; (formulaire) form; **selon la ~ consacrée** as one says; **~ de politesse** polite phrase; (en fin de lettre) letter ending

formuler [fɔʀmyle] vt (émettre: réponse, vœux) to formulate; (expliciter: sa pensée) to express

forniquer [fɔʀnike] vi to fornicate

fort, e [fɔʀ, fɔʀt(ə)] adj strong; (intensité, rendement) high, great; (corpulent) large; (doué): **être ~ (en)** to be good (at) ▷ adv (serrer, frapper) hard; (sonner) loud(ly); (beaucoup) greatly, very much; (très) very ▷ nm (édifice) fort; (point fort) strong point, forte; (gén pl: personne, pays): **le ~**, **les ~s** the strong; **c'est un peu ~!** it's a bit much!; **à plus ~e raison** even more so, all the more reason; **avoir ~ à faire avec qn** to have a hard job with sb; **se faire ~ de faire** to claim one can do; **~ bien/peu** very well/few; **au plus ~ de** (au milieu de) in the thick of, at the height of; **~e tête** rebel

fortement [fɔʀtəmɑ̃] adv strongly; (s'intéresser) deeply

forteresse [fɔʀtəʀɛs] nf fortress

fortifiant [fɔʀtifjɑ̃] nm tonic

fortifications [fɔʀtifikasjɔ̃] nfpl fortifications

fortifier [fɔʀtifje] vt to strengthen, fortify; (Mil) to fortify; **se fortifier** vi (personne, santé) to grow stronger

fortin [fɔʀtɛ̃] nm (small) fort

fortiori [fɔʀtjɔʀi]: **à ~** adv all the more so

FORTRAN [fɔʀtʀɑ̃] nm FORTRAN

fortuit, e [fɔʀtɥi, -it] adj fortuitous, chance cpd

fortuitement [fɔʀtɥitmɑ̃] adv fortuitously

fortune [fɔʀtyn] nf fortune; **faire ~** to make one's fortune; **de ~** adj makeshift; (compagnon) chance cpd

fortuné, e [fɔʀtyne] adj wealthy, well-off

forum [fɔʀɔm] nm forum

fosse [fos] nf (grand trou) pit; (tombe) grave; **la ~ aux lions/ours** the lions' den/bear pit; **~ commune** common ou communal grave; **~ (d'orchestre)** (orchestra) pit; **~ à purin** cesspit; **~ septique** septic tank; **~s nasales** nasal fossae

fossé [fose] nm ditch; (fig) gulf, gap

fossette [fosɛt] nf dimple

fossile [fosil] nm fossil ▷ adj fossilized, fossil cpd

fossilisé, e [fosilize] adj fossilized

fossoyeur [foswajœʀ] nm gravedigger

fou, fol, folle [fu, fɔl] adj mad, crazy; (déréglé etc) wild, erratic; (mèche) stray; (herbe) wild; (fam: extrême, très grand) terrific, tremendous ▷ nm/f madman/woman ▷ nm (du roi) jester, fool; (Échecs) bishop; **~ à lier**, **~ furieux (folle furieuse)** raving mad; **être ~ de** to be mad ou crazy about; (chagrin, joie, colère) to be wild with; **faire le ~** to play ou act the fool; **avoir le ~ rire** to have the giggles

foucade [fukad] nf caprice

foudre [fudʀ(ə)] nf lightning; **foudres** nfpl (fig: colère) wrath sg

foudroyant, e [fudʀwajɑ̃, -ɑ̃t] adj devastating; (maladie, poison) violent

foudroyer [fudʀwaje] vt to strike down; **~ qn du regard** to look daggers at sb; **il a été foudroyé** he was struck by lightning

fouet [fwɛ] nm whip; (Culin) whisk; **de plein ~** adv head on

fouettement [fwɛtmɑ̃] nm lashing no pl

fouetter [fwete] vt to whip; to whisk

fougasse [fugas] nf type of flat pastry

fougère [fuʒɛʀ] nf fern

fougue [fug] nf ardour (Brit), ardor (US), spirit

fougueusement [fugøzmɑ̃] adv ardently

fougueux, -euse [fugø, -øz] adj fiery, ardent

fouille [fuj] nf search; **fouilles** nfpl (archéologiques) excavations; **passer à la ~** to be searched

fouillé, e [fuje] adj detailed

fouiller [fuje] vt to search; (creuser) to dig; (: archéologie) to excavate; (approfondir: étude etc) to go into ▷ vi (archéologue) to excavate; **~ dans/ parmi** to rummage in/among

fouillis [fuji] *nm* jumble, muddle
fouine [fwin] *nf* stone marten
fouiner [fwine] *vi* (*péj*): ~ **dans** to nose around *ou* about in
fouineur, -euse [fwinœR, -øz] *adj* nosey ▷ *nm/f* nosey parker, snooper
fouir [fwiR] *vt* to dig
fouisseur, -euse [fwisœR, -øz] *adj* burrowing
foulage [fulaʒ] *nm* pressing
foulante [fulɑ̃t] *adjf*: **pompe** ~ force pump
foulard [fulaR] *nm* scarf
foule [ful] *nf* crowd; **une** ~ **de** masses of; **venir en** ~ to come in droves
foulée [fule] *nf* stride; **dans la** ~ **de** on the heels of
fouler [fule] *vt* to press; (*sol*) to tread upon; **se fouler** *vi* (*fam*) to overexert o.s.; **se** ~ **la cheville** to sprain one's ankle; ~ **aux pieds** to trample underfoot
foulure [fulyR] *nf* sprain
four [fuR] *nm* oven; (*de potier*) kiln; (*Théât: échec*) flop; **allant au** ~ ovenproof
fourbe [fuRb(ə)] *adj* deceitful
fourberie [fuRbəRi] *nf* deceit
fourbi [fuRbi] *nm* (*fam*) gear, junk
fourbir [fuRbiR] *vt*: ~ **ses armes** (*fig*) to get ready for the fray
fourbu, e [fuRby] *adj* exhausted
fourche [fuRʃ(ə)] *nf* pitchfork; (*de bicyclette*) fork
fourcher [fuRʃe] *vi*: **ma langue a fourché** it was a slip of the tongue
fourchette [fuRʃɛt] *nf* fork; (*Statistique*) bracket, margin
fourchu, e [fuRʃy] *adj* split; (*arbre etc*) forked
fourgon [fuRgɔ̃] *nm* van; (*Rail*) wag(g)on; ~ **mortuaire** hearse
fourgonnette [fuRgɔnɛt] *nf* (delivery) van
fourmi [fuRmi] *nf* ant; **avoir des** ~**s** (*fig*) to have pins and needles
fourmilière [fuRmiljeR] *nf* ant-hill; (*fig*) hive of activity
fourmillement [fuRmijmɑ̃] *nm* (*démangeaison*) pins and needles *pl*; (*grouillement*) swarming *no pl*
fourmiller [fuRmije] *vi* to swarm; ~ **de** to be teeming with, be swarming with
fournaise [fuRnɛz] *nf* blaze; (*fig*) furnace, oven
fourneau, x [fuRno] *nm* stove
fournée [fuRne] *nf* batch
fourni, e [fuRni] *adj* (*barbe, cheveux*) thick; (*magasin*): **bien** ~ **(en)** well stocked (with)
fournil [fuRni] *nm* bakehouse
fournir [fuRniR] *vt* to supply; (*preuve, exemple*) to provide, supply; (*effort*) to put in; ~ **qch à qn** to supply sth to sb, supply *ou* provide sb with sth; ~ **qn en** (*Comm*) to supply sb with; **se** ~ **chez** to shop at
fournisseur, -euse [fuRnisœR, -øz] *nm/f* supplier; (*Internet*): ~ **d'accès à Internet** (Internet) service provider
fourniture [fuRnityR] *nf* supply(ing); **fournitures** *nfpl* supplies; ~**s de bureau** office

supplies, stationery; ~**s scolaires** school stationery
fourrage [fuRaʒ] *nm* fodder
fourrager¹ [fuRaʒe] *vi*: ~ **dans/parmi** to rummage through/among
fourrager², -ère [fuRaʒe, -ɛR] *adj* fodder *cpd* ▷ *nf* (*Mil*) fourragère
fourré, e [fuRe] *adj* (*bonbon, chocolat*) filled; (*manteau, botte*) fur-lined ▷ *nm* thicket
fourreau, x [fuRo] *nm* sheath; (*de parapluie*) cover; **robe** ~ figure-hugging dress
fourrer [fuRe] *vt* (*fam*): ~ **qch dans** to stick *ou* shove sth into; **se** ~ **dans/sous** to get into/under; **se** ~ **dans** (*une mauvaise situation*) to land o.s. in
fourre-tout [fuRtu] *nm inv* (*sac*) holdall; (*péj*) junk room (*ou* cupboard); (*fig*) rag-bag
fourreur [fuRœR] *nm* furrier
fourrière [fuRjeR] *nf* pound
fourrure [fuRyR] *nf* fur; (*sur l'animal*) coat; **manteau/col de** ~ fur coat/collar
fourvoyer [fuRvwaje]: **se fourvoyer** *vi* to go astray, stray; **se** ~ **dans** to stray into
foutre [futR(ə)] *vt* (*fam!*) = **ficher♯**; (*fam*)
foutu, e [futy] *adj* (*fam!*) = **fichu**
foyer [fwaje] *nm* (*de cheminée*) hearth; (*fig*) seat, centre; (*famille*) family; (*domicile*) home; (*local de réunion*) (social) club; (*résidence*) hostel; (*salon*) foyer; (*Optique, Photo*) focus; **lunettes à double** ~ bi-focal glasses
FP *sigle f* (= *franchise postale*) exemption from postage
FPA *sigle f* (= *Formation professionnelle pour adultes*) adult education
FPLP *sigle m* (= *Front populaire de la libération de la Palestine*) PFLP (= *Popular Front for the Liberation of Palestine*)
fracas [fRaka] *nm* din; crash
fracassant, e [fRakasɑ̃, -ɑ̃t] *adj* sensational, staggering
fracasser [fRakase] *vt* to smash; **se fracasser contre** *ou* **sur** to crash against
fraction [fRaksjɔ̃] *nf* fraction
fractionnement [fRaksjɔnmɑ̃] *nm* division
fractionner [fRaksjɔne] *vt* to divide (up), split (up)
fracture [fRaktyR] *nf* fracture; ~ **du crâne** fractured skull; ~ **de la jambe** broken leg
fracturer [fRaktyRe] *vt* (*coffre, serrure*) to break open; (*os, membre*) to fracture
fragile [fRaʒil] *adj* fragile, delicate; (*fig*) frail
fragiliser [fRaʒilize] *vt* to weaken, make fragile
fragilité [fRaʒilite] *nf* fragility
fragment [fRagmɑ̃] *nm* (*d'un objet*) fragment, piece; (*d'un texte*) passage, extract
fragmentaire [fRagmɑ̃tɛR] *adj* sketchy
fragmenter [fRagmɑ̃te] *vt* to split up
frai [fRɛ] *nm* spawn; (*ponte*) spawning
fraîche [fRɛʃ] *adjf voir* **frais**
fraîchement [fRɛʃmɑ̃] *adv* (*sans enthousiasme*) coolly; (*récemment*) freshly, newly
fraîcheur [fRɛʃœR] *nf* coolness; freshness; *voir* **frais**

fraîchir [fʀeʃiʀ] *vi* to get cooler; (*vent*) to freshen

frais, fraîche [fʀɛ, fʀɛʃ] *adj* (*air, eau, accueil*) cool; (*petit pois, œufs, nouvelles, couleur, troupes*) fresh; **le voilà ~!** he's in a (right) mess! ▷ *adv* (*récemment*) newly, fresh(ly); **il fait ~** it's cool; **servir ~** chill before serving, serve chilled ▷ *nm*: **mettre au ~** to put in a cool place; **prendre le ~** to take a breath of cool air ▷ *nmpl* (*débours*) expenses; (*Comm*) costs; charges; **faire des ~** to spend; to go to a lot of expense; **faire les ~ de** to bear the brunt of; **faire les ~ de la conversation** (*parler*) to do most of the talking; (*en être le sujet*) to be the topic of conversation; **il en a été pour ses ~** he could have spared himself the trouble; **rentrer dans ses ~** to recover one's expenses; **~ de déplacement** travel(ling) expenses; **~ d'entretien** upkeep; **~ généraux** overheads; **~ de scolarité** school fees, tuition (*US*)

fraise [fʀɛz] *nf* strawberry; (*Tech*) countersink (bit); (*de dentiste*) drill; **~ des bois** wild strawberry

fraiser [fʀeze] *vt* to countersink; (*Culin: pâte*) to knead

fraiseuse [fʀɛzøz] *nf* (*Tech*) milling machine

fraisier [fʀɛzje] *nm* strawberry plant

framboise [fʀɑ̃bwaz] *nf* raspberry

framboisier [fʀɑ̃bwazje] *nm* raspberry bush

franc, franche [fʀɑ̃, fʀɑ̃ʃ] *adj* (*personne*) frank, straightforward; (*visage*) open; (*net: refus, couleur*) clear; (*: coupure*) clean; (*intensif*) downright; (*exempt*): **~ de port** post free, postage paid; (*zone, port*) free; (*boutique*) duty-free ▷ *adv*: **parler ~** to be frank *ou* candid ▷ *nm* franc

français, e [fʀɑ̃sɛ, -ɛz] *adj* French ▷ *nm* (*Ling*) French ▷ *nm/f*: **Français, e** Frenchman/woman; **les F~** the French

franc-comtois, e (*mpl* **francs-comtois**) [fʀɑ̃kɔ̃twa, -waz] *adj* of *ou* from (the) Franche-Comté

France [fʀɑ̃s] *nf*: **la ~** France; **en ~** in France; **~ 2, ~ 3** public-sector television channels; *see note*

◉ FRANCE TÉLÉVISION

◉
◉ *France 2* and *France 3* are public-sector
◉ television channels. France 2 is a national
◉ general interest and entertainment
◉ channel; France 3 provides regional news
◉ and information as well as programmes for
◉ the national network.

Francfort [fʀɑ̃kfɔʀ] *n* Frankfurt

franche [fʀɑ̃ʃ] *adj f voir* **franc**

Franche-Comté [fʀɑ̃ʃkõte] *nf* Franche-Comté

franchement [fʀɑ̃ʃmɑ̃] *adv* frankly; clearly; (*tout à fait*) downright ▷ *excl* well, really!; *voir* **franc**

franchir [fʀɑ̃ʃiʀ] *vt* (*obstacle*) to clear, get over; (*seuil, ligne, rivière*) to cross; (*distance*) to cover

franchisage [fʀɑ̃ʃizaʒ] *nm* (*Comm*) franchising

franchise [fʀɑ̃ʃiz] *nf* frankness; (*douanière, d'impôt*) exemption; (*Assurances*) excess; (*Comm*)

franchise; **~ de bagages** baggage allowance

franchissable [fʀɑ̃ʃisabl(ə)] *adj* (*obstacle*) surmountable

francilien, ne [fʀɑ̃siljɛ̃, -ɛn] *adj* of *ou* from the Île-de-France region ▷ *nm/f*: **Francilien, ne** person from the Île-de-France region

franciscain, e [fʀɑ̃siskɛ̃, -ɛn] *adj* Franciscan

franciser [fʀɑ̃size] *vt* to gallicize, Frenchify

franc-jeu [fʀɑ̃ʒø] *nm*: **jouer ~** to play fair

franc-maçon [fʀɑ̃masɔ̃] (*pl* **francs-maçons**) *nm* Freemason

franc-maçonnerie [fʀɑ̃masɔnʀi] *nf* Freemasonry

franco [fʀɑ̃ko] *adv* (*Comm*): **~ (de port)** postage paid

franco... [fʀɑ̃ko] *préfixe* franco-

franco-canadien [fʀɑ̃kɔkanadjɛ̃] *nm* (*Ling*) Canadian French

francophile [fʀɑ̃kɔfil] *adj* Francophile

francophobe [fʀɑ̃kɔfɔb] *adj* Francophobe

francophone [fʀɑ̃kɔfɔn] *adj* French-speaking ▷ *nm/f* French speaker

francophonie [fʀɑ̃kɔfɔni] *nf* French-speaking communities *pl*

franco-québécois [fʀɑ̃kɔkebekwa] *nm* (*Ling*) Quebec French

franc-parler [fʀɑ̃paʀle] *nm inv* outspokenness

franc-tireur [fʀɑ̃tiʀœʀ] *nm* (*Mil*) irregular; (*fig*) freelance

frange [fʀɑ̃ʒ] *nf* fringe; (*cheveux*) fringe (*Brit*), bangs (*US*)

frangé, e [fʀɑ̃ʒe] *adj* (*tapis, nappe*): **~ de** trimmed with

frangin [fʀɑ̃ʒɛ̃] *nm* (*fam*) brother

frangine [fʀɑ̃ʒin] *nf* (*fam*) sis, sister

frangipane [fʀɑ̃ʒipan] *nf* almond paste

franglais [fʀɑ̃glɛ] *nm* Franglais

franquette [fʀɑ̃kɛt]: **à la bonne ~** *adv* without any fuss

frappant, e [fʀapɑ̃, -ɑ̃t] *adj* striking

frappe [fʀap] *nf* (*d'une dactylo, pianiste, machine à écrire*) touch; (*Boxe*) punch; (*péj*) hood, thug

frappé, e [fʀape] *adj* (*Culin*) iced; **~ de panique** panic-stricken; **~ de stupeur** thunderstruck, dumbfounded

frapper [fʀape] *vt* to hit, strike; (*étonner*) to strike; (*monnaie*) to strike, stamp; **se frapper** *vi* (*s'inquiéter*) to get worked up; **~ à la porte** to knock at the door; **~ dans ses mains** to clap one's hands; **~ du poing sur** to bang one's fist on; **~ un grand coup** (*fig*) to strike a blow

frasques [fʀask(ə)] *nfpl* escapades; **faire des ~** to get up to mischief

fraternel, le [fʀatɛʀnɛl] *adj* brotherly, fraternal

fraternellement [fʀatɛʀnɛlmɑ̃] *adv* in a brotherly way

fraterniser [fʀatɛʀnize] *vi* to fraternize

fraternité [fʀatɛʀnite] *nf* brotherhood

fratricide [fʀatʀisid] *adj* fratricidal

fraude [fʀod] *nf* fraud; (*Scol*) cheating; **passer qch en ~** to smuggle sth in (*ou* out); **~ fiscale** tax evasion

frauder [fʀode] *vi, vt* to cheat; ~ **le fisc** to evade paying tax(es)

fraudeur, -euse [fʀodœʀ, -øz] *nm/f* person guilty of fraud; *(candidat)* candidate who cheats; *(au fisc)* tax evader

frauduleusement [fʀodyløzmɑ̃] *adv* fraudulently

frauduleux, -euse [fʀodylø, -øz] *adj* fraudulent

frayer [fʀeje] *vt* to open up, clear ▷ *vi* to spawn; *(fréquenter)*: ~ **avec** to mix *ou* associate with; **se ~ un passage dans** to clear o.s. a path through, force one's way through

frayeur [fʀejœʀ] *nf* fright

fredaines [fʀədɛn] *nfpl* mischief *sg*, escapades

fredonner [fʀədɔne] *vt* to hum

freezer [fʀizœʀ] *nm* freezing compartment

frégate [fʀegat] *nf* frigate

frein [fʀɛ̃] *nm* brake; **mettre un ~ à** *(fig)* to put a brake on, check; **sans ~** *(sans limites)* unchecked; ~ **à main** handbrake; ~ **moteur** engine braking; ~**s à disques** disc brakes; ~**s à tambour** drum brakes

freinage [fʀɛnaʒ] *nm* braking; **distance de ~** braking distance; **traces de ~** tyre *(Brit)* ou tire *(US)* marks

freiner [fʀene] *vi* to brake ▷ *vt* *(progrès etc)* to check

frelaté, e [fʀəlate] *adj* adulterated; *(fig)* tainted

frêle [fʀɛl] *adj* frail, fragile

frelon [fʀəlɔ̃] *nm* hornet

freluquet [fʀəlykɛ] *nm* *(péj)* whippersnapper

frémir [fʀemiʀ] *vi* *(de froid, de peur)* to tremble, shiver; *(de joie)* to quiver; *(eau)* to (begin to) bubble

frémissement [fʀemismɑ̃] *nm* shiver; quiver; bubbling *no pl*

frêne [fʀɛn] *nm* ash (tree)

frénésie [fʀenezi] *nf* frenzy

frénétique [fʀenetik] *adj* frenzied, frenetic

frénétiquement [fʀenetikmɑ̃] *adv* frenetically

fréon® [fʀeɔ̃] *nm* Freon®

fréquemment [fʀekamɑ̃] *adv* frequently

fréquence [fʀekɑ̃s] *nf* frequency

fréquent, e [fʀekɑ̃, -ɑ̃t] *adj* frequent

fréquentable [fʀekɑ̃tabl(ə)] *adj*: **il est peu ~** he's not the type one can associate oneself with

fréquentation [fʀekɑ̃tasjɔ̃] *nf* frequenting; seeing; **fréquentations** *nfpl* company *sg*

fréquenté, e [fʀekɑ̃te] *adj*: **très ~** (very) busy; **mal ~** patronized by disreputable elements

fréquenter [fʀekɑ̃te] *vt* *(lieu)* to frequent; *(personne)* to see; **se fréquenter** to see a lot of each other

frère [fʀɛʀ] *nm* brother ▷ *adj*: **partis/pays ~s** sister parties/countries

fresque [fʀɛsk(ə)] *nf* *(Art)* fresco

fret [fʀɛ] *nm* freight

fréter [fʀete] *vt* to charter

frétiller [fʀetije] *vi* to wriggle; to quiver; ~ **de la queue** to wag its tail

fretin [fʀətɛ̃] *nm*: **le menu ~** the small fry

freudien, ne [fʀødjɛ̃, -ɛn] *adj* Freudian

freux [fʀø] *nm* *(Zool)* rook

friable [fʀijabl(ə)] *adj* crumbly

friand, e [fʀijɑ̃, -ɑ̃d] *adj*: ~ **de** very fond of ▷ *nm* *(Culin)* small minced-meat *(Brit)* ou ground-meat *(US)* pie; *(: sucré)* small almond cake

friandise [fʀijɑ̃diz] *nf* sweet

fric [fʀik] *nm* *(fam)* cash, bread

fricassée [fʀikase] *nf* fricassee

fric-frac [fʀikfʀak] *nm* break-in

friche [fʀiʃ] *nf*: **en ~** *adj, adv* (lying) fallow

friction [fʀiksjɔ̃] *nf* *(massage)* rub, rub-down; *(chez le coiffeur)* scalp massage; *(Tech, fig)* friction

frictionner [fʀiksjɔne] *vt* to rub (down); to massage

frigidaire® [fʀiʒidɛʀ] *nm* refrigerator

frigide [fʀiʒid] *adj* frigid

frigidité [fʀiʒidite] *nf* frigidity

frigo [fʀigo] *nm* *(= frigidaire)* fridge

frigorifier [fʀigɔʀifje] *vt* to refrigerate; *(fig: personne)* to freeze

frigorifique [fʀigɔʀifik] *adj* refrigerating

frileusement [fʀiløzmɑ̃] *adv* with a shiver

frileux, -euse [fʀilø, -øz] *adj* sensitive to (the) cold; *(fig)* overcautious

frimas [fʀimɑ] *nmpl* wintry weather *sg*

frime [fʀim] *nf* *(fam)*: **c'est de la ~** it's all put on; **pour la ~** just for show

frimer [fʀime] *vi* to put on an act

frimeur, -euse [fʀimœʀ, -øz] *nm/f* poser

frimousse [fʀimus] *nf* *(sweet)* little face

fringale [fʀɛ̃gal] *nf*: **avoir la ~** to be ravenous

fringant, e [fʀɛ̃gɑ̃, -ɑ̃t] *adj* dashing

fringues [fʀɛ̃g] *nfpl* *(fam)* clothes, gear *no pl*

fripé, e [fʀipe] *adj* crumpled

friperie [fʀipʀi] *nf* *(commerce)* secondhand clothes shop; *(vêtements)* secondhand clothes

fripes [fʀip] *nfpl* secondhand clothes

fripier, -ière [fʀipje, -jɛʀ] *nm/f* secondhand clothes dealer

fripon, ne [fʀipɔ̃, -ɔn] *adj* roguish, mischievous ▷ *nm/f* rascal, rogue

fripouille [fʀipuj] *nf* scoundrel

frire [fʀiʀ] *vt* *(aussi:* **faire frire***)* ▷ *vi* to fry

Frisbee® [fʀizbi] *nm* Frisbee®

frise [fʀiz] *nf* frieze

frisé, e [fʀize] *adj* curly, curly-haired ▷ *nf*: **(chicorée) ~e** curly endive

friser [fʀize] *vt* to curl; *(fig: surface)* to skim, graze; *(: mort)* to come within a hair's breadth of; *(: hérésie)* to verge on ▷ *vi* *(cheveux)* to curl; *(personne)* to have curly hair; **se faire ~** to have one's hair curled

frisette [fʀizɛt] *nf* little curl

frisotter [fʀizɔte] *vi* *(cheveux)* to curl tightly

frisquet [fʀiskɛ] *adj m* chilly

frisson [fʀisɔ̃], **frissonnement** [fʀisɔnmɑ̃] *nm* shudder, shiver; quiver

frissonner [fʀisɔne] *vi* *(personne)* to shudder, shiver; *(feuilles)* to quiver

frit, e [fʀi, fʀit] *pp de* **frire** ▷ *adj* fried ▷ *nf*: **(pommes) ~es** chips *(Brit)*, French fries

friterie [fʀitʀi] *nf* ≈ chip shop *(Brit)*,

≈ hamburger stand (US)

friteuse [fʀitøz] nf chip pan (Brit), deep (fat) fryer

friture [fʀityʀ] nf (huile) (deep) fat; (plat): **~ (de poissons)** fried fish; (Radio) crackle, crackling no pl; **fritures** nfpl (aliments frits) fried food sg

frivole [fʀivɔl] adj frivolous

frivolité [fʀivɔlite] nf frivolity

froc [fʀɔk] nm (Rel) habit; (fam: pantalon) trousers pl, pants pl

froid, e [fʀwa, fʀwad] adj cold ▷ nm cold; (absence de sympathie) coolness no pl; **il fait ~** it's cold; **avoir ~** to be cold; **prendre ~** to catch a chill ou cold; **à ~** adv (démarrer) (from) cold; **(pendant) les grands ~s** (in) the depths of winter, (during) the cold season; **jeter un ~** (fig) to cast a chill; **être en ~ avec** to be on bad terms with; **battre ~ à qn** to give sb the cold shoulder

froidement [fʀwadmɑ̃] adv (accueillir) coldly; (décider) coolly

froideur [fʀwadœʀ] nf coolness no pl

froisser [fʀwase] vt to crumple (up), crease; (fig) to hurt, offend; **se froisser** vi to crumple, crease; to take offence (Brit) ou offense (US); **se ~ un muscle** to strain a muscle

frôlement [fʀolmɑ̃] nm (contact) light touch

frôler [fʀole] vt to brush against; (projectile) to skim past; (fig) to come within a hair's breadth of, come very close to

fromage [fʀɔmaʒ] nm cheese; **~ blanc** soft white cheese; **~ de tête** pork brawn

fromager, -ère [fʀɔmaʒe, -ɛʀ] nm/f cheese merchant ▷ adj (industrie) cheese cpd

fromagerie [fʀɔmaʒʀi] nf cheese dairy

froment [fʀɔmɑ̃] nm wheat

fronce [fʀɔ̃s] nf (de tissu) gather

froncement [fʀɔ̃smɑ̃] nm: **~ de sourcils** frown

froncer [fʀɔ̃se] vt to gather; **~ les sourcils** to frown

frondaisons [fʀɔ̃dɛzɔ̃] nfpl foliage sg

fronde [fʀɔ̃d] nf sling; (fig) rebellion, rebelliousness

frondeur, -euse [fʀɔ̃dœʀ, -øz] adj rebellious

front [fʀɔ̃] nm forehead, brow; (Mil, Météorologie, Pol) front; **avoir le ~ de faire** to have the effrontery to do; **de ~** adv (se heurter) head-on; (rouler) together (2 or 3 abreast); (simultanément) at once; **faire ~ à** to face up to; **~ de mer** (sea) front

frontal, e, -aux [fʀɔ̃tal, -o] adj frontal

frontalier, -ière [fʀɔ̃talje, -jɛʀ] adj border cpd, frontier cpd ▷ nm/f: **(travailleurs) ~s** workers who cross the border to go to work, commuters from across the border

frontière [fʀɔ̃tjɛʀ] nf (Géo, Pol) frontier, border; (fig) frontier, boundary

frontispice [fʀɔ̃tispis] nm frontispiece

fronton [fʀɔ̃tɔ̃] nm pediment; (de pelote basque) (front) wall

frottement [fʀɔtmɑ̃] nm rubbing, scraping; **frottements** nmpl (fig: difficultés) friction sg

frotter [fʀɔte] vi to rub, scrape ▷ vt to rub; (pour nettoyer) to rub (up); (: avec une brosse) to scrub; **~ une allumette** to strike a match; **se ~ à qn** to cross swords with sb; **se ~ à qch** to come up against sth; **se ~ les mains** (fig) to rub one's hands (gleefully)

frottis [fʀɔti] nm (Méd) smear

frottoir [fʀɔtwaʀ] nm (d'allumettes) friction strip; (pour encaustiquer) (long-handled) brush

frou-frou [fʀufʀu] (pl **frous-frous**) nm rustle

frousse [fʀus] nf (fam: peur): **avoir la ~** to be in a blue funk

fructifier [fʀyktifje] vi to yield a profit; **faire ~** to turn to good account

fructueux, -euse [fʀyktɥø, -øz] adj fruitful; profitable

frugal, e, -aux [fʀygal, -o] adj frugal

frugalement [fʀygalmɑ̃] adv frugally

frugalité [fʀygalite] nf frugality

fruit [fʀɥi] nm fruit gen no pl; **~s de mer** (Culin) seafood(s); **~s secs** dried fruit sg

fruité, e [fʀɥite] adj (vin) fruity

fruiterie [fʀɥitʀi] nf (boutique) greengrocer's (Brit), fruit (and vegetable) store (US)

fruitier, -ière [fʀɥitje, -jɛʀ] adj: **arbre ~** fruit tree ▷ nm/f fruiterer (Brit), fruit merchant (US)

fruste [fʀyst(ə)] adj unpolished, uncultivated

frustrant, e [fʀystʀɑ̃, -ɑ̃t] adj frustrating

frustration [fʀystʀasjɔ̃] nf frustration

frustré, e [fʀystʀe] adj frustrated

frustrer [fʀystʀe] vt to frustrate; (priver): **~ qn de qch** to deprive sb of sth

FS abr (= franc suisse) FS, SF

FSE sigle m (= foyer socio-éducatif) community home

FTP sigle mpl (= Francs-tireurs et partisans) Communist Resistance in 1940–45

fuchsia [fyʃja] nm fuchsia

fuel [fjul], **fuel-oil** [fjulɔjl] nm fuel oil; (pour chauffer) heating oil

fugace [fygas] adj fleeting

fugitif, -ive [fyʒitif, -iv] adj (lueur, amour) fleeting; (prisonnier etc) runaway ▷ nm/f fugitive, runaway

fugue [fyg] nf (d'un enfant) running away no pl; (Mus) fugue; **faire une ~** to run away, abscond

fuir [fɥiʀ] vt to flee from; (éviter) to shun ▷ vi to run away; (gaz, robinet) to leak

fuite [fɥit] nf flight; (écoulement) leak, leakage; (divulgation) leak; **être en ~** to be on the run; **mettre en ~** to put to flight; **prendre la ~** to take flight

fulgurant, e [fylgyʀɑ̃, -ɑ̃t] adj lightning cpd, dazzling

fulminant, e [fylminɑ̃, -ɑ̃t] adj (lettre, regard) furious; **~ de colère** raging with anger

fulminer [fylmine] vi: **~ (contre)** to thunder forth (against)

fumant, e [fymɑ̃, -ɑ̃t] adj smoking; (liquide) steaming; **un coup ~** (fam) a master stroke

fumé, e [fyme] adj (Culin) smoked; (verre) tinted ▷ nf smoke; **partir en ~e** to go up in smoke

fume-cigarette [fymsigaʀɛt] nm inv cigarette

holder

fumer [fyme] *vi* to smoke; *(liquide)* to steam ▷ *vt* to smoke; *(terre, champ)* to manure

fumerie [fymʀi] *nf*: ~ **d'opium** opium den

fumerolles [fymʀɔl] *nfpl* gas and smoke *(from volcano)*

fûmes [fym] *vb voir* **être**

fumet [fymɛ] *nm* aroma

fumeur, -euse [fymœʀ, -øz] *nm/f* smoker; **(compartiment)** ~**s** smoking compartment

fumeux, -euse [fymø, -øz] *adj (péj)* woolly *(Brit)*, hazy

fumier [fymje] *nm* manure

fumigation [fymigɑsjɔ̃] *nf* fumigation

fumigène [fymiʒɛn] *adj* smoke *cpd*

fumiste [fymist(ə)] *nm (ramoneur)* chimney sweep ▷ *nm/f (péj: paresseux)* shirker; *(charlatan)* phoney

fumisterie [fymistəʀi] *nf (péj)* fraud, con

fumoir [fymwaʀ] *nm* smoking room

funambule [fynɑ̃byl] *nm* tightrope walker

funèbre [fynɛbʀ(ə)] *adj* funeral *cpd*; *(fig)* doleful; funereal

funérailles [fyneʀaj] *nfpl* funeral *sg*

funéraire [fyneʀɛʀ] *adj* funeral *cpd*, funerary

funeste [fynɛst(ə)] *adj* disastrous; deathly

funiculaire [fynikylɛʀ] *nm* funicular (railway)

FUNU [fyny] *sigle f* (= Force d'urgence des Nations unies) UNEF (= United Nations Emergency Forces)

fur [fyʀ]: **au ~ et à mesure** *adv* as one goes along; **au ~ et à mesure que** as; **au ~ et à mesure de leur progression** as they advance *(ou* advanced)

furax [fyʀaks] *adj inv (fam)* livid

furent [fyʀ] *vb voir* **être**

furet [fyʀɛ] *nm* ferret

fureter [fyʀte] *vi (péj)* to nose about

fureur [fyʀœʀ] *nf* fury; *(passion)*: ~ **de** passion for; **faire** ~ to be all the rage

furibard, e [fyʀibaʀ, -aʀd(ə)] *adj (fam)* livid, absolutely furious

furibond, e [fyʀibɔ̃, -ɔ̃d] *adj* livid, absolutely furious

furie [fyʀi] *nf* fury; *(femme)* shrew, vixen; **en ~** *(mer)* raging

furieusement [fyʀjøzmɑ̃] *adv* furiously

furieux, -euse [fyʀjø, -øz] *adj* furious

furoncle [fyʀɔ̃kl(ə)] *nm* boil

furtif, -ive [fyʀtif, -iv] *adj* furtive

furtivement [fyʀtivmɑ̃] *adv* furtively

fus [fy] *vb voir* **être**

fusain [fyzɛ̃] *nm (Bot)* spindle-tree; *(Art)* charcoal

fuseau, x [fyzo] *nm (pantalon)* (ski-)pants *pl*; *(pour filer)* spindle; **en ~** *(jambes)* tapering; *(colonne)* bulging; ~ **horaire** time zone

fusée [fyze] *nf* rocket; ~ **éclairante** flare

fuselage [fyzlaʒ] *nm* fuselage

fuselé, e [fyzle] *adj* slender; *(galbé)* tapering

fuser [fyze] *vi (rires etc)* to burst forth

fusible [fyzibl(ə)] *nm (Élec: fil)* fuse wire; *(: fiche)* fuse

fusil [fyzi] *nm (de guerre, à canon rayé)* rifle, gun; *(de chasse, à canon lisse)* shotgun, gun; ~ **à deux coups** double-barrelled rifle *ou* shotgun; ~ **sous-marin** spear-gun

fusilier [fyzilje] *nm (Mil)* rifleman

fusillade [fyzijad] *nf* gunfire *no pl*, shooting *no pl*; *(combat)* gun battle

fusiller [fyzije] *vt* to shoot; ~ **qn du regard** to look daggers at sb

fusil-mitrailleur [fyzimitʀajœʀ] *(pl* **fusils-mitrailleurs)** *nm* machine gun

fusion [fyzjɔ̃] *nf* fusion, melting; *(fig)* merging; *(Comm)* merger; **en ~** *(métal, roches)* molten

fusionnement [fyzjɔnmɑ̃] *nm* merger

fusionner [fyzjɔne] *vi* to merge

fustiger [fystiʒe] *vt* to denounce

fut [fy] *vb voir* **être**

fût [fy] *vb voir* **être** ▷ *nm (tonneau)* barrel, cask; *(de canon)* stock; *(d'arbre)* bole, trunk; *(de colonne)* shaft

futaie [fytɛ] *nf* forest, plantation

futé, e [fyte] *adj* crafty

fûtes [fyt] *vb voir* **être**

futile [fytil] *adj (inutile)* futile; *(frivole)* frivolous

futilement [fytilmɑ̃] *adv* frivolously

futilité [fytilite] *nf* futility; frivolousness; *(chose futile)* futile pursuit *(ou* thing *etc)*

futon [fytɔ̃] *nm* futon

futur, e [fytyʀ] *adj, nm* future; **son ~ époux** her husband-to-be; **au ~** *(Ling)* in the future

futuriste [fytyʀist(ə)] *adj* futuristic

futurologie [fytyʀɔlɔʒi] *nf* futurology

fuyant, e [fɥijɑ̃, -ɑ̃t] *vb voir* **fuir** ▷ *adj (regard etc)* evasive; *(lignes etc)* receding; *(perspective)* vanishing

fuyard, e [fɥijaʀ, -aʀd(ə)] *nm/f* runaway

fuyons *etc* [fɥijɔ̃] *vb voir* **fuir**

Gg

G, g [ʒe] *nm inv* G, g ▷ *abr* (= *gramme*) g; (= *gauche*) L, l; **G comme Gaston** G for George; **le G8** (*Pol*) the G8 nations, the Group of Eight

gabardine [gabaʀdin] *nf* gabardine

gabarit [gabaʀi] *nm* (*fig: dimension, taille*) size; (: *valeur*) calibre; (*Tech*) template; **du même ~** (*fig*) of the same type, of that ilk

gabegie [gabʒi] *nf* (*péj*) chaos

Gabon [gabɔ̃] *nm*: **le ~** Gabon

gabonais, e [gabɔnɛ, -ɛz] *adj* Gabonese

gâcher [gaʃe] *vt* (*gâter*) to spoil, ruin; (*gaspiller*) to waste; (*plâtre*) to temper; (*mortier*) to mix

gâchette [gaʃɛt] *nf* trigger

gâchis [gaʃi] *nm* (*désordre*) mess; (*gaspillage*) waste *no pl*

gadget [gadʒɛt] *nm* thingumajig; (*nouveauté*) gimmick

gadin [gadɛ̃] *nm* (*fam*): **prendre un ~** to come a cropper (*Brit*)

gadoue [gadu] *nf* sludge

gaélique [gaelik] *adj* Gaelic ▷ *nm* (*Ling*) Gaelic

gaffe [gaf] *nf* (*instrument*) boat hook; (*fam: erreur*) blunder; **faire ~** (*fam*) to watch out

gaffer [gafe] *vi* to blunder

gaffeur, -euse [gafœʀ, -øz] *nm/f* blunderer

gag [gag] *nm* gag

gaga [gaga] *adj* (*fam*) gaga

gage [gaʒ] *nm* (*dans un jeu*) forfeit; (*fig: de fidélité*) token; **gages** *nmpl* (*salaire*) wages; (*garantie*) guarantee *sg*; **mettre en ~** to pawn; **laisser en ~** to leave as security

gager [gaʒe] *vt*: **~ que** to bet *ou* wager that

gageure [gaʒyʀ] *nf*: **c'est une ~** it's attempting the impossible

gagnant, e [gaɲɑ̃, -ɑ̃t] *adj*: **billet/numéro ~** winning ticket/number ▷ *adv*: **jouer ~** (*aux courses*) to be bound to win ▷ *nm/f* winner

gagne-pain [gaɲpɛ̃] *nm inv* job

gagne-petit [gaɲpəti] *nm inv* low wage earner

gagner [gaɲe] *vt* (*concours, procès, pari*) to win; (*somme d'argent, revenu*) to earn; (*aller vers, atteindre*) to reach; (*s'emparer de*) to overcome; (*envahir*) to spread to; (*se concilier*): **~ qn** to win sb over ▷ *vi* to win; (*fig*) to gain; **~ du temps/de la place** to gain time/save space; **~ sa vie** to earn one's living; **~ du terrain** (*aussi fig*) to gain ground; **~**

qn de vitesse to outstrip sb; (*aussi fig*): **~ à faire** (*s'en trouver bien*) to be better off doing; **il y gagne** it's in his interest, it's to his advantage

gagneur [gaɲœʀ] *nm* winner

gai, e [ge] *adj* cheerful; (*livre, pièce de théâtre*) light-hearted; (*un peu ivre*) merry

gaiement [gemɑ̃] *adv* cheerfully

gaieté [gete] *nf* cheerfulness; **gaietés** *nfpl* (*souvent ironique*) delights; **de ~ de cœur** with a light heart

gaillard, e [gajaʀ, -aʀd(ə)] *adj* (*robuste*) sprightly; (*grivois*) bawdy, ribald ▷ *nm/f* (*strapping*) fellow/wench

gaillardement [gajaʀdəmɑ̃] *adv* cheerfully

gain [gɛ̃] *nm* (*revenu*) earnings *pl*; (*bénéfice: gén pl*) profits *pl*; (*au jeu: gén pl*) winnings *pl*; (*fig: de temps, place*) saving; (: *avantage*) benefit; (: *lucre*) gain; **avoir ~ de cause** to win the case; (*fig*) to be proved right; **obtenir ~ de cause** (*fig*) to win out

gaine [gɛn] *nf* (*corset*) girdle; (*fourreau*) sheath; (*de fil électrique etc*) outer covering

gaine-culotte [gɛnkylɔt] (*pl* **gaines-culottes**) *nf* pantie girdle

gainer [gene] *vt* to cover

gala [gala] *nm* official reception; **soirée de ~** gala evening

galamment [galamɑ̃] *adv* courteously

galant, e [galɑ̃, -ɑ̃t] *adj* (*courtois*) courteous, gentlemanly; (*entreprenant*) flirtatious, gallant; (*aventure, poésie*) amorous; **en ~e compagnie** (*homme*) with a lady friend; (*femme*) with a gentleman friend

galanterie [galɑ̃tʀi] *nf* gallantry

galantine [galɑ̃tin] *nf* galantine

Galapagos [galapagɔs] *nfpl*: **les (îles) ~** the Galapagos Islands

galaxie [galaksi] *nf* galaxy

galbe [galb(ə)] *nm* curve(s); shapeliness

galbé, e [galbe] *adj* (*jambes*) (well-)rounded; **bien ~** shapely

gale [gal] *nf* (*Méd*) scabies *sg*; (*de chien*) mange

galéjade [galeʒad] *nf* tall story

galère [galɛʀ] *nf* galley

galérer [galeʀe] *vi* (*fam*) to work hard, slave (away)

galerie [galʀi] *nf* gallery; (*Théât*) circle; (*de voiture*) roof rack; (*fig: spectateurs*) audience; ~ **marchande** shopping mall; ~ **de peinture** (private) art gallery

galérien [galeʀjɛ̃] *nm* galley slave

galet [galɛ] *nm* pebble; (*Tech*) wheel; **galets** *nmpl* pebbles, shingle *sg*

galette [galɛt] *nf* (*gâteau*) flat pastry cake; (*crêpe*) savoury pancake; **la ~ des Rois** *cake traditionally eaten on Twelfth Night*

galeux, -euse [galø, -øz] *adj*: **un chien ~** a mangy dog

Galice [galis] *nf*: **la ~** Galicia (*in Spain*)

Galicie [galisi] *nf*: **la ~** Galicia; (*in Central Europe*)

galiléen, ne [galileɛ̃, -ɛn] *adj* Galilean

galimatias [galimatja] *nm* (*péj*) gibberish

galipette [galipɛt] *nf*: **faire des ~s** to turn somersaults

Galles [gal] *nfpl*: **le pays de ~** Wales

gallicisme [galisism(ə)] *nm* French idiom; (*tournure fautive*) gallicism

gallois, e [galwa, -waz] *adj* Welsh ▷ *nm* (*Ling*) Welsh ▷ *nm/f*: **Gallois, e** Welshman(-woman)

gallo-romain, e [galoʀɔmɛ̃, -ɛn] *adj* Gallo-Roman

galoche [galɔʃ] *nf* clog

galon [galɔ̃] *nm* (*Mil*) stripe; (*décoratif*) piece of braid; **prendre du ~** to be promoted

galop [galo] *nm* gallop; **au ~** at a gallop; ~ **d'essai** (*fig*) trial run

galopade [galɔpad] *nf* stampede

galopant, e [galɔpɑ̃, -ɑ̃t] *adj*: **inflation ~e** galloping inflation; **démographie ~e** exploding population

galoper [galɔpe] *vi* to gallop

galopin [galɔpɛ̃] *nm* urchin, ragamuffin

galvaniser [galvanize] *vt* to galvanize

galvaudé, e [galvode] *adj* (*expression*) hackneyed; (*mot*) clichéd

galvauder [galvode] *vt* to debase

gambade [gɑ̃bad] *nf*: **faire des ~s** to skip *ou* frisk about

gambader [gɑ̃bade] *vi* to skip *ou* frisk about

gamberger [gɑ̃bɛʀʒe] (*fam*) *vi* to (have a) think ▷ *vt* to dream up

Gambie [gɑ̃bi] *nf*: **la ~** (*pays*) Gambia; (*fleuve*) the Gambia

gamelle [gamɛl] *nf* mess tin; billy can; (*fam*): **ramasser une ~** to fall flat on one's face

gamin, e [gamɛ̃, -in] *nm/f* kid ▷ *adj* mischievous, playful

gaminerie [gaminʀi] *nf* mischievousness, playfulness

gamme [gam] *nf* (*Mus*) scale; (*fig*) range

gammé, e [game] *adj*: **croix ~e** swastika

Gand [gɑ̃] *n* Ghent

gang [gɑ̃g] *nm* gang

Gange [gɑ̃ʒ] *nm*: **le ~** the Ganges

ganglion [gɑ̃glijɔ̃] *nm* ganglion; (*lymphatique*) gland; **avoir des ~s** to have swollen glands

gangrène [gɑ̃gʀɛn] *nf* gangrene; (*fig*) corruption; corrupting influence

gangster [gɑ̃gstɛʀ] *nm* gangster

gangstérisme [gɑ̃gsteʀism(ə)] *nm* gangsterism

gangue [gɑ̃g] *nf* coating

ganse [gɑ̃s] *nf* braid

gant [gɑ̃] *nm* glove; **prendre des ~s** (*fig*) to handle the situation with kid gloves; **relever le ~** (*fig*) to take up the gauntlet; ~ **de crin** massage glove; ~ **de toilette** (face) flannel (*Brit*), face cloth; ~**s de boxe** boxing gloves; ~**s de caoutchouc** rubber gloves

ganté, e [gɑ̃te] *adj*: ~ **de blanc** wearing white gloves

ganterie [gɑ̃tʀi] *nf* glove trade; (*magasin*) glove shop

garage [gaʀaʒ] *nm* garage; ~ **à vélos** bicycle shed

garagiste [gaʀaʒist(ə)] *nm/f* (*propriétaire*) garage owner; (*mécanicien*) garage mechanic

garant, e [gaʀɑ̃, -ɑ̃t] *nm/f* guarantor ▷ *nm* guarantee; **se porter ~ de** to vouch for; to be answerable for

garantie [gaʀɑ̃ti] *nf* guarantee, warranty; (*gage*) security, surety; (**bon de**) ~ guarantee *ou* warranty slip; ~ **de bonne exécution** performance bond

garantir [gaʀɑ̃tiʀ] *vt* to guarantee; (*protéger*): ~ **de** to protect from; **je vous garantis que** I can assure you that; **garanti pure laine/2 ans** guaranteed pure wool/for 2 years

garce [gaʀs(ə)] *nf* (*péj*) bitch

garçon [gaʀsɔ̃] *nm* boy; (*célibataire*) bachelor; (*jeune homme*) boy, lad; (*aussi*: **garçon de café**) waiter; ~ **boucher/coiffeur** butcher's/hairdresser's assistant; ~ **de courses** messenger; ~ **d'écurie** stable lad; ~ **manqué** tomboy

garçonnet [gaʀsɔnɛ] *nm* small boy

garçonnière [gaʀsɔnjɛʀ] *nf* bachelor flat

garde [gaʀd(ə)] *nm* (*de prisonnier*) guard; (*de domaine etc*) warden; (*soldat, sentinelle*) guardsman ▷ *nf* guarding; looking after; (*soldats, Boxe, Escrime*) guard; (*faction*) watch; (*d'une arme*) hilt; (*Typo: aussi*: **page** *ou* **feuille de garde**) flyleaf; (: **collée**) endpaper; **de ~** *adj, adv* on duty; **monter la ~** to stand guard; **être sur ses ~s** to be on one's guard; **mettre en ~** to warn; **mise en ~** warning; **prendre ~ (à)** to be careful (of); **avoir la ~ des enfants** (*après divorce*) to have custody of the children; ~ **champêtre** *nm* rural policeman; ~ **du corps** *nm* bodyguard; ~ **d'enfants** *nf* child minder; ~ **forestier** *nm* forest warden; ~ **mobile** *nm, nf* mobile guard; ~ **des Sceaux** *nm* ≈ Lord Chancellor (*Brit*), ≈ Attorney General (*US*); ~ **à vue** *nf* (*Jur*) ≈ police custody

garde-à-vous [gaʀdavu] *nm inv*: **être/se mettre au ~** to be at/stand to attention; ~ **(fixe)!** (*Mil*) attention!

garde-barrière [gaʀdəbaʀjɛʀ] (*pl* **gardes-barrière(s)**) *nm/f* level-crossing keeper

garde-boue [gaʀdəbu] *nm inv* mudguard

garde-chasse [gaʀdəʃas] (*pl* **gardes-chasse(s)**)

nm gamekeeper

garde-côte [gaʀdəkot] *nm* (*vaisseau*) coastguard boat

garde-feu [gaʀdəfø] *nm inv* fender

garde-fou [gaʀdəfu] *nm* railing, parapet

garde-malade [gaʀdəmalad] (*pl* **gardes-malade(s)**) *nf* home nurse

garde-manger [gaʀdmãʒe] *nm inv* (*boîte*) meat safe; (*placard*) pantry, larder

garde-meuble [gaʀdəmœbl(ə)] *nm* furniture depository

garde-pêche [gaʀdəpɛʃ] *nm inv* (*personne*) water bailiff; (*navire*) fisheries protection ship

garder [gaʀde] *vt* (*conserver*) to keep; (: *sur soi: vêtement, chapeau*) to keep on; (*surveiller: enfants*) to look after; (: *immeuble, lieu, prisonnier*) to guard; **se garder** *vi* (*aliment: se conserver*) to keep; **se ~ de faire** to be careful not to do; **~ le lit/la chambre** to stay in bed/indoors; **~ le silence** to keep silent *ou* quiet; **~ la ligne** to keep one's figure; **~ à vue** to keep in custody; **pêche/chasse gardée** private fishing/hunting (ground)

garderie [gaʀdəʀi] *nf* day nursery, crèche

garde-robe [gaʀdəʀɔb] *nf* wardrobe

gardeur, -euse [gaʀdœʀ, -øz] *nm/f* (*de vaches*) cowherd; (*de chèvres*) goatherd

gardian [gaʀdjã] *nm* cowboy (*in the Camargue*)

gardien, ne [gaʀdjɛ̃, -ɛn] *nm/f* (*garde*) guard; (*de prison*) warder; (*de domaine, réserve*) warden; (*de musée etc*) attendant; (*de phare, cimetière*) keeper; (*d'immeuble*) caretaker; (*fig*) guardian; **~ de but** goalkeeper; **~ de nuit** night watchman; **~ de la paix** policeman

gardiennage [gaʀdjɛnaʒ] *nm* (*emploi*) caretaking; **société de ~** security firm

gardon [gaʀdɔ̃] *nm* roach

gare [gaʀ] *nf* (*railway*) station, train station (US) ▷ *excl*: **~ à ...** mind ...!, watch out for ...!; **~ à ne pas ...** mind you don't ...; **~ à toi!** watch out!; **sans crier ~** without warning; **~ maritime** harbour station; **~ routière** coach (*Brit*) *ou* bus station; (*de camions*) haulage (*Brit*) *ou* trucking (US) depot; **~ de triage** marshalling yard

garenne [gaʀɛn] *nf voir* **lapin**

garer [gaʀe] *vt* to park; **se garer** to park; (*pour laisser passer*) to draw into the side

gargantuesque [gaʀgãtɥɛsk(ə)] *adj* gargantuan

gargariser [gaʀgaʀize]: **se gargariser** *vi* to gargle; **se ~ de** (*fig*) to revel in

gargarisme [gaʀgaʀism(ə)] *nm* gargling *no pl*; (*produit*) gargle

gargote [gaʀgɔt] *nf* cheap restaurant, greasy spoon (*fam*)

gargouille [gaʀguj] *nf* gargoyle

gargouillement [gaʀgujmã] *nm* = **gargouillis**

gargouiller [gaʀguje] *vi* (*estomac*) to rumble; (*eau*) to gurgle

gargouillis [gaʀguji] *nm* (*gén pl: voir vb*) rumbling; gurgling

garnement [gaʀnəmã] *nm* rascal, scallywag

garni, e [gaʀni] *adj* (*plat*) served with vegetables (*and chips, pasta or rice*) ▷ *nm* (*appartement*) furnished accommodation *no pl* (*Brit*) *ou* accommodations *pl* (US)

garnir [gaʀniʀ] *vt* to decorate; (*remplir*) to fill; (*recouvrir*) to cover; **se garnir** *vi* (*pièce, salle*) to fill up; **~ qch de** (*orner*) to decorate sth with; to trim sth with; (*approvisionner*) to fill *ou* stock sth with; (*protéger*) to fit sth with; (*Culin*) to garnish sth with

garnison [gaʀnizɔ̃] *nf* garrison

garniture [gaʀnityʀ] *nf* (*Culin: légumes*) vegetables *pl*; (: *persil etc*) garnish; (: *farce*) filling; (*décoration*) trimming; (*protection*) fittings *pl*; **~ de cheminée** mantelpiece ornaments *pl*; **~ de frein** (*Auto*) brake lining; **~ intérieure** (*Auto*) interior trim; **~ périodique** sanitary towel (*Brit*) *ou* napkin (US)

garrigue [gaʀig] *nf* scrubland

garrot [gaʀo] *nm* (*Méd*) tourniquet; (*torture*) garrotte

garrotter [gaʀote] *vt* to tie up; (*fig*) to muzzle

gars [ga] *nm* lad; (*type*) guy

Gascogne [gaskɔɲ] *nf*: **la ~** Gascony

gascon, ne [gaskɔ̃, -ɔn] *adj* Gascon ▷ *nm*: **G~** (*hâbleur*) braggart

gas-oil [gazɔjl] *nm* diesel oil

gaspillage [gaspijaʒ] *nm* waste

gaspiller [gaspije] *vt* to waste

gaspilleur, -euse [gaspijœʀ, -øz] *adj* wasteful

gastrique [gastʀik] *adj* gastric, stomach *cpd*

gastro-entérite [gastʀoãteʀit] *nf* (*Méd*) gastro-enteritis

gastro-intestinal, e, -aux [gastʀoɛ̃tɛstinal, -o] *adj* gastrointestinal

gastronome [gastʀonɔm] *nm/f* gourmet

gastronomie [gastʀonɔmi] *nf* gastronomy

gastronomique [gastʀonɔmik] *adj*: **menu ~** gourmet menu

gâteau, x [gato] *nm* cake ▷ *adj inv* (*fam: trop indulgent*): **papa-/maman-~** doting father/mother; **~ d'anniversaire** birthday cake; **~ de riz** ≈ rice pudding; **~ sec** biscuit

gâter [gate] *vt* to spoil; **se gâter** *vi* (*dent, fruit*) to go bad; (*temps, situation*) to change for the worse

gâterie [gatʀi] *nf* little treat

gâteux, -euse [gatø, -øz] *adj* senile

gâtisme [gatism(ə)] *nm* senility

GATT [gat] *sigle m* (= *General Agreement on Tariffs and Trade*) GATT

gauche [goʃ] *adj* left, left-hand; (*maladroit*) awkward, clumsy ▷ *nf* (*Pol*) left (wing); (*Boxe*) left; **à ~** on the left; (*direction*) (to the) left; **à ~ de** (on *ou* to the) left of; **à la ~ de** to the left of; **sur votre ~** on your left; **de ~** (*Pol*) left-wing

gauchement [goʃmã] *adv* awkwardly, clumsily

gaucher, -ère [goʃe, -ɛʀ] *adj* left-handed

gaucherie [goʃʀi] *nf* awkwardness, clumsiness

gauchir [goʃiʀ] *vt* (*planche, objet*) to warp; (*fig: fait, idée*) to distort

gauchisant, e [goʃizã, -ãt] *adj* with left-wing tendencies

gauchisme [goʃism(ə)] *nm* leftism

gauchiste [goʃist(ə)] *adj, nm/f* leftist

gaufre [gofʀ(ə)] *nf* (*pâtisserie*) waffle; (*de cire*) honeycomb

gaufrer [gofʀe] *vt* (*papier*) to emboss; (*tissu*) to goffer

gaufrette [gofʀɛt] *nf* wafer

gaufrier [gofʀije] *nm* (*moule*) waffle iron

Gaule [gol] *nf*: **la ~** Gaul

gaule [gol] *nf* (*perche*) (long) pole; (*canne à pêche*) fishing rod

gauler [gole] *vt* (*arbre*) to beat (*using a long pole to bring down fruit*); (*fruits*) to beat down (*with a pole*)

gaullisme [golism(ə)] *nm* Gaullism

gaulliste [golist(ə)] *adj, nm/f* Gaullist

gaulois, e [golwa, -waz] *adj* Gallic; (*grivois*) bawdy ▷ *nm/f*: **Gaulois, e** Gaul

gauloiserie [golwazʀi] *nf* bawdiness

gausser [gose]: **se ~ de** *vt* to deride

gaver [gave] *vt* to force-feed; (*fig*): **~ de** to cram with, fill up with; (*personne*): **se ~ de** to stuff o.s. with

gay [gɛ] *adj, nm* (*fam*) gay

gaz [gaz] *nm inv* gas; **mettre les ~** (*Auto*) to put one's foot down; **chambre/masque à ~** gas chamber/mask; **~ en bouteille** bottled gas; **~ butane** Calor gas® (*Brit*), butane gas; **~ carbonique** carbon dioxide; **~ hilarant** laughing gas; **~ lacrymogène** tear gas; **~ naturel** natural gas; **~ de ville** town gas (*Brit*), manufactured domestic gas

gaze [gaz] *nf* gauze

gazéifié, e [gazeifje] *adj* carbonated, aerated

gazelle [gazɛl] *nf* gazelle

gazer [gaze] *vt* to gas ▷ *vi* (*fam*) to be going *ou* working well

gazette [gazɛt] *nf* news sheet

gazeux, -euse [gazø, -øz] *adj* gaseous; (*eau*) sparkling; (*boisson*) fizzy

gazoduc [gazɔdyk] *nm* gas pipeline

gazole [gazɔl] *nm* = **gas-oil**

gazomètre [gazɔmɛtʀ(ə)] *nm* gasometer

gazon [gazɔ̃] *nm* (*herbe*) turf, grass; (*pelouse*) lawn

gazonner [gazɔne] *vt* (*terrain*) to grass over

gazouillement [gazujmɑ̃] *nm* (*voir vb*) chirping; babbling

gazouiller [gazuje] *vi* (*oiseau*) to chirp; (*enfant*) to babble

gazouillis [gazuji] *nmpl* chirp *sg*

GB *sigle f* (= *Grande Bretagne*) GB

gd *abr* (= *grand*) L

GDF *sigle m* (= *Gaz de France*) national gas company

geai [ʒɛ] *nm* jay

géant, e [ʒeɑ̃, -ɑ̃t] *adj* gigantic, giant; (*Comm*) giant-size ▷ *nm/f* giant

geignement [ʒɛɲmɑ̃] *nm* groaning, moaning

geindre [ʒɛ̃dʀ(ə)] *vi* to groan, moan

gel [ʒɛl] *nm* frost; (*de l'eau*) freezing; (*fig: des salaires, prix*) freeze; freezing; (*produit de beauté*) gel; **~ douche** shower gel

gélatine [ʒelatin] *nf* gelatine

gélatineux, -euse [ʒelatinø, -øz] *adj* jelly-like, gelatinous

gelé, e [ʒəle] *adj* frozen ▷ *nf* jelly; (*gel*) frost; **~ blanche** hoarfrost, white frost

geler [ʒəle] *vt, vi* to freeze; **il gèle** it's freezing

gélule [ʒelyl] *nf* capsule

gelures [ʒəlyʀ] *nfpl* frostbite *sg*

Gémeaux [ʒemo] *nmpl*: **les ~** Gemini, the Twins; **être des ~** to be Gemini

gémir [ʒemiʀ] *vi* to groan, moan

gémissement [ʒemismɑ̃] *nm* groan, moan

gemme [ʒɛm] *nf* gem(stone)

gémonies [ʒemɔni] *nfpl*: **vouer qn aux ~** to subject sb to public scorn

gén. *abr* (= *généralement*) gen.

gênant, e [ʒɛnɑ̃, -ɑ̃t] *adj* (*objet*) awkward, in the way; (*histoire, personne*) embarrassing

gencive [ʒɑ̃siv] *nf* gum

gendarme [ʒɑ̃daʀm(ə)] *nm* gendarme

gendarmer [ʒɑ̃daʀme]: **se gendarmer** *vi* to kick up a fuss

gendarmerie [ʒɑ̃daʀməʀi] *nf* military police force in countryside and small towns; their police station or barracks

gendre [ʒɑ̃dʀ(ə)] *nm* son-in-law

gène [ʒɛn] *nm* (*Bio*) gene

gêne [ʒɛn] *nf* (*à respirer, bouger*) discomfort, difficulty; (*dérangement*) bother, trouble; (*manque d'argent*) financial difficulties *pl ou* straits *pl*; (*confusion*) embarrassment; **sans ~** *adj* inconsiderate

gêné, e [ʒene] *adj* embarrassed; (*dépourvu d'argent*) short (of money)

généalogie [ʒenealɔʒi] *nf* genealogy

généalogique [ʒenealɔʒik] *adj* genealogical

gêner [ʒene] *vt* (*incommoder*) to bother; (*encombrer*) to hamper; (*bloquer le passage*) to be in the way of; (*déranger*) to bother; (*embarrasser*): **~ qn** to make sb feel ill-at-ease; **se gêner** to put o.s. out; **ne vous gênez pas!** (*ironique*) go right ahead!, don't mind me!; **je vais me ~!** (*ironique*) why should I care?

général, e, -aux [ʒeneʀal, -o] *adj, nm* general ▷ *nf*: (**répétition**) **~e** final dress rehearsal; **en ~** usually, in general; **à la satisfaction ~e** to everyone's satisfaction

généralement [ʒeneʀalmɑ̃] *adv* generally

généralisable [ʒeneʀalizabl(ə)] *adj* generally applicable

généralisation [ʒeneʀalizasjɔ̃] *nf* generalization

généraliser [ʒeneʀalize] *vt, vi* to generalize; **se généraliser** *vi* to become widespread

généraliste [ʒeneʀalist(ə)] *nm/f* (*Méd*) general practitioner, GP

généralité [ʒeneʀalite] *nf*: **la ~ des ...** the majority of ...; **généralités** *nfpl* generalities; (*introduction*) general points

générateur, -trice [ʒeneʀatœʀ, -tʀis] *adj*: **~ de** which causes *ou* brings about ▷ *nf* (*Élec*) generator

génération [ʒeneʀasjɔ̃] *nf* generation

généreusement [ʒenerøzmɑ̃] *adv* generously
généreux, -euse [ʒenerø, -øz] *adj* generous
générique [ʒenerik] *adj* generic ▷ *nm* (*Ciné, TV*) credits *pl*, credit titles *pl*
générosité [ʒenerozite] *nf* generosity
Gênes [ʒɛn] *n* Genoa
genèse [ʒənɛz] *nf* genesis
genêt [ʒənɛ] *nm* (*Bot*) broom *no pl*
généticien, ne [ʒenetisjɛ̃, -ɛn] *nm/f* geneticist
génétique [ʒenetik] *adj* genetic ▷ *nf* genetics *sg*
génétiquement [ʒenetikmɑ̃] *adv* genetically
gêneur, -euse [ʒɛnœr, -øz] *nm/f* (*personne qui gêne*) obstacle; (*importun*) intruder
Genève [ʒənɛv] *n* Geneva
genevois, e [ʒənəvwa, -waz] *adj* Genevan
genévrier [ʒənevrije] *nm* juniper
génial, e, -aux [ʒenjal, -o] *adj* of genius; (*fam*) fantastic, brilliant
génie [ʒeni] *nm* genius; (*Mil*): **le ~** ≈ the Engineers *pl*; **avoir du ~** to have genius; **~ civil** civil engineering; **~ génétique** genetic engineering
genièvre [ʒənjɛvr(ə)] *nm* (*Bot*) juniper (tree); (*boisson*) Dutch gin; **grain de ~** juniper berry
génisse [ʒenis] *nf* heifer; **foie de ~** ox liver
génital, e, -aux [ʒenital, -o] *adj* genital
génitif [ʒenitif] *nm* genitive
génocide [ʒenɔsid] *nm* genocide
génois, e [ʒenwa, -waz] *adj* Genoese ▷ *nf* (*gâteau*) ≈ sponge cake
genou, x [ʒnu] *nm* knee; **à ~x** on one's knees; **se mettre à ~x** to kneel down
genouillère [ʒənujɛr] *nf* (*Sport*) kneepad
genre [ʒɑ̃r] *nm* (*espèce, sorte*) kind, type, sort; (*allure*) manner; (*Ling*) gender; (*Art*) genre; (*Zool etc*) genus; **se donner du ~** to give o.s. airs; **avoir du ~** to have style; **avoir mauvais ~** to be ill-mannered
gens [ʒɑ̃] *nmpl* (*f in some phrases*) people *pl*; **les ~ d'Église** the clergy; **les ~ du monde** society people; **~ de maison** domestics
gentiane [ʒɑ̃sjan] *nf* gentian
gentil, le [ʒɑ̃ti, -ij] *adj* kind; (*enfant: sage*) good; (*sympa: endroit etc*) nice; **c'est très ~ à vous** it's very kind *ou* good *ou* nice of you
gentilhommière [ʒɑ̃tijɔmjɛr] *nf* (small) manor house *ou* country seat
gentillesse [ʒɑ̃tijɛs] *nf* kindness
gentillet, te [ʒɑ̃tijɛ, -ɛt] *adj* nice little
gentiment [ʒɑ̃timɑ̃] *adv* kindly
génuflexion [ʒenyflɛksjɔ̃] *nf* genuflexion
géo *abr* (= *géographie*) geography
géodésique [ʒeɔdezik] *adj* geodesic
géographe [ʒeɔgraf] *nm/f* geographer
géographie [ʒeɔgrafi] *nf* geography
géographique [ʒeɔgrafik] *adj* geographical
geôlier [ʒolje] *nm* jailer
géologie [ʒeɔlɔʒi] *nf* geology
géologique [ʒeɔlɔʒik] *adj* geological
géologiquement [ʒeɔlɔʒikmɑ̃] *adv* geologically
géologue [ʒeɔlɔg] *nm/f* geologist
géomètre [ʒeɔmɛtr(ə)] *nm*: **(arpenteur-)~**

(land) surveyor
géométrie [ʒeɔmetri] *nf* geometry; **à ~ variable** (*Aviat*) swing-wing
géométrique [ʒeɔmetrik] *adj* geometric
géophysique [ʒeɔfizik] *nf* geophysics *sg*
géopolitique [ʒeɔpɔlitik] *nf* geopolitics *sg*
Géorgie [georʒi] *nf*: **la ~** (*URSS, USA*) Georgia; **la ~ du Sud** South Georgia
géorgien, ne [georʒjɛ̃, -ɛn] *adj* Georgian
géostationnaire [ʒeɔstasjɔnɛr] *adj* geostationary
géothermique [ʒeɔtɛrmik] *adj*: **énergie ~** geothermal energy
gérance [ʒerɑ̃s] *nf* management; **mettre en ~** to appoint a manager for; **prendre en ~** to take over (the management of)
géranium [ʒeranjɔm] *nm* geranium
gérant, e [ʒerɑ̃, -ɑ̃t] *nm/f* manager/manageress; **~ d'immeuble** managing agent
gerbe [ʒɛrb(ə)] *nf* (*de fleurs, d'eau*) spray; (*de blé*) sheaf; (*fig*) shower, burst
gercé, e [ʒɛrse] *adj* chapped
gercer [ʒɛrse] *vi*, **se gercer** *vi* to chap
gerçure [ʒɛrsyr] *nf* crack
gérer [ʒere] *vt* to manage
gériatrie [ʒerjatri] *nf* geriatrics *sg*
gériatrique [ʒerjatrik] *adj* geriatric
germain, e [ʒɛrmɛ̃, -ɛn] *adj*: **cousin ~** first cousin
germanique [ʒɛrmanik] *adj* Germanic
germaniste [ʒɛrmanist(ə)] *nm/f* German scholar
germe [ʒɛrm(ə)] *nm* germ
germer [ʒɛrme] *vi* to sprout; (*semence, aussi fig*) to germinate
gérondif [ʒerɔ̃dif] *nm* gerund; (*en latin*) gerundive
gérontologie [ʒerɔ̃tɔlɔʒi] *nf* gerontology
gérontologue [ʒerɔ̃tɔlɔg] *nm/f* gerontologist
gésier [ʒezje] *nm* gizzard
gésir [ʒezir] *vi* to be lying (down); *voir aussi* **ci-gît**
gestation [ʒɛstasjɔ̃] *nf* gestation
geste [ʒɛst(ə)] *nm* gesture; move; motion; **il fit un ~ de la main pour m'appeler** he signed to me to come over, he waved me over; **ne faites pas un ~** (*ne bougez pas*) don't move
gesticuler [ʒɛstikyle] *vi* to gesticulate
gestion [ʒɛstjɔ̃] *nf* management; **~ des disques** (*Inform*) housekeeping; **~ de fichier(s)** (*Inform*) file management
gestionnaire [ʒɛstjɔnɛr] *nm/f* administrator; **~ de fichiers** (*Inform*) file manager
geyser [ʒɛzɛr] *nm* geyser
Ghana [gana] *nm*: **le ~** Ghana
ghetto [gɛto] *nm* ghetto
gibecière [ʒibsjɛr] *nf* (*de chasseur*) gamebag; (*sac en bandoulière*) shoulder bag
gibelotte [ʒiblɔt] *nf* rabbit fricassee in white wine
gibet [ʒibɛ] *nm* gallows *pl*
gibier [ʒibje] *nm* (*animaux*) game; (*fig*) prey
giboulée [ʒibule] *nf* sudden shower
giboyeux, -euse [ʒibwajø, -øz] *adj* well-stocked

with game
Gibraltar [ʒibʀaltaʀ] nm Gibraltar
gibus [ʒibys] nm opera hat
giclée [ʒikle] nf spurt, squirt
gicler [ʒikle] vi to spurt, squirt
gicleur [ʒiklœʀ] nm (Auto) jet
GIE sigle m = **groupement d'intérêt économique**
gifle [ʒifl(ə)] nf slap (in the face)
gifler [ʒifle] vt to slap (in the face)
gigantesque [ʒigɑ̃tɛsk(ə)] adj gigantic
gigantisme [ʒigɑ̃tism(ə)] nm (Méd) gigantism; (des mégalopoles) vastness
gigaoctet [ʒigaɔktɛ] nm gigabyte
GIGN sigle m (= Groupe d'intervention de la gendarmerie nationale) special crack force of the gendarmerie, ≈ SAS (Brit)
gigogne [ʒigɔɲ] adj: **lits ~s** truckle (Brit) ou trundle (US) beds; **tables/poupées ~s** nest of tables/dolls
gigolo [ʒigɔlo] nm gigolo
gigot [ʒigo] nm leg (of mutton ou lamb)
gigoter [ʒigɔte] vi to wriggle (about)
gilet [ʒilɛ] nm waistcoat; (pull) cardigan; (de corps) vest; ~ **pare-balles** bulletproof jacket; ~ **de sauvetage** life jacket
gin [dʒin] nm gin
gingembre [ʒɛ̃ʒɑ̃bʀ(ə)] nm ginger
gingivite [ʒɛ̃ʒivit] nf inflammation of the gums, gingivitis
ginseng [ʒinsɛŋ] nm ginseng
girafe [ʒiʀaf] nf giraffe
giratoire [ʒiʀatwaʀ] adj: **sens ~** roundabout
girofle [ʒiʀɔfl(ə)] nm: **clou de ~** clove
giroflée [ʒiʀɔfle] nf wallflower
girolle [ʒiʀɔl] nf chanterelle
giron [ʒiʀɔ̃] nm (genoux) lap; (fig: sein) bosom
Gironde [ʒiʀɔ̃d] nf: **la ~** the Gironde
girophare [ʒiʀɔfaʀ] nm revolving (flashing) light
girouette [ʒiʀwɛt] nf weather vane ou cock
gis [ʒi], **gisais** etc [ʒizɛ] vb voir **gésir**
gisement [ʒizmɑ̃] nm deposit
gît [ʒi] vb voir **gésir**
gitan, e [ʒitɑ̃, -an] nm/f gipsy
gîte [ʒit] nm home; shelter; (du lièvre) form; ~ **(rural)** (country) holiday cottage ou apartment
gîter [ʒite] vi (Navig) to list
givrage [ʒivʀaʒ] nm icing
givrant, e [ʒivʀɑ̃, -ɑ̃t] adj: **brouillard ~** freezing fog
givre [ʒivʀ(ə)] nm (hoar)frost
givré, e [ʒivʀe] adj: **citron ~/orange ~e** lemon/orange sorbet (served in fruit skin)
glabre [ɡlɑbʀ(ə)] adj hairless; (menton) clean-shaven
glaçage [ɡlasaʒ] nm (au sucre) icing; (au blanc d'œuf, de la viande) glazing
glace [ɡlas] nf glace ice; (crème glacée) ice cream; (verre) sheet of glass; (miroir) mirror; (de voiture) window; **glaces** nfpl (Géo) ice sheets, ice sg; **de ~** (fig: accueil, visage) frosty, icy; **rester de ~** to remain unmoved

glacé, e [ɡlase] adj icy; (boisson) iced
glacer [ɡlase] vt to freeze; (boisson) to chill, ice; (gâteau) to ice (Brit), frost (US); (papier, tissu) to glaze; (fig): ~ **qn** to chill sb; (fig) to make sb's blood run cold
glaciaire [ɡlasjɛʀ] adj (période) ice cpd; (relief) glacial
glacial, e [ɡlasjal] adj icy
glacier [ɡlasje] nm (Géo) glacier; (marchand) ice-cream maker
glacière [ɡlasjɛʀ] nf icebox
glaçon [ɡlasɔ̃] nm icicle; (pour boisson) ice cube
gladiateur [ɡladjatœʀ] nm gladiator
glaïeul [ɡlajœl] nm gladiola
glaire [ɡlɛʀ] nf (Méd) phlegm no pl
glaise [ɡlɛz] nf clay
glaive [ɡlɛv] nm two-edged sword
gland [ɡlɑ̃] nm (de chêne) acorn; (décoration) tassel; (Anat) glans
glande [ɡlɑ̃d] nf gland
glander [ɡlɑ̃de] vi (fam) to fart around (Brit) (!), screw around (US) (!)
glaner [ɡlane] vt, vi to glean
glapir [ɡlapiʀ] vi to yelp
glapissement [ɡlapismɑ̃] nm yelping
glas [ɡlɑ] nm knell, toll
glauque [ɡlok] adj dull blue-green
glissade [ɡlisad] nf (par jeu) slide; (chute) slip; (dérapage) skid; **faire des ~s** to slide
glissant, e [ɡlisɑ̃, -ɑ̃t] adj slippery
glisse [ɡlis] nf: **sports de ~** sports involving sliding or gliding (eg skiing, surfing, windsurfing)
glissement [ɡlismɑ̃] nm sliding; (fig) shift; ~ **de terrain** landslide
glisser [ɡlise] vi (avancer) to glide ou slide along; (coulisser, tomber) to slide; (déraper) to slip; (être glissant) to be slippery ▷ vt: ~ **qch sous/dans/à** to slip sth under/into/to; ~ **sur** (fig: détail etc) to skate over; **se ~ dans/entre** to slip into/between
glissière [ɡlisjɛʀ] nf slide channel; **à ~** (porte, fenêtre) sliding; ~ **de sécurité** (Auto) crash barrier
glissoire [ɡliswaʀ] nf slide
global, e, -aux [ɡlɔbal, -o] adj overall
globalement [ɡlɔbalmɑ̃] adv taken as a whole
globe [ɡlɔb] nm globe; **sous ~** under glass; ~ **oculaire** eyeball; **le ~ terrestre** the globe
globe-trotter [ɡlɔbtʀɔtœʀ] nm globe-trotter
globule [ɡlɔbyl] nm (du sang): ~ **blanc/rouge** white/red corpuscle
globuleux, -euse [ɡlɔbylø, -øz] adj: **yeux ~** protruding eyes
gloire [ɡlwaʀ] nf glory; (mérite) distinction, credit; (personne) celebrity
glorieux, -euse [ɡlɔʀjø, -øz] adj glorious
glorifier [ɡlɔʀifje] vt to glorify, extol; **se ~ de** to glory in
gloriole [ɡlɔʀjɔl] nf vainglory
glose [ɡloz] nf gloss
glossaire [ɡlɔsɛʀ] nm glossary
glotte [ɡlɔt] nf (Anat) glottis
glouglouter [ɡluɡlute] vi to gurgle

gloussement [glusmɑ̃] nm (de poule) cluck; (rire) chuckle

glousser [gluse] vi to cluck; (rire) to chuckle

glouton, ne [glutɔ̃, -ɔn] adj gluttonous, greedy

gloutonnerie [glutɔnʀi] nf gluttony

glu [gly] nf birdlime

gluant, e [glyɑ̃, -ɑ̃t] adj sticky, gummy

glucide [glysid] nm carbohydrate

glucose [glykoz] nm glucose

gluten [glytɛn] nm gluten

glycérine [gliseʀin] nf glycerine

glycine [glisin] nf wisteria

GMT sigle adj (= Greenwich Mean Time) GMT

gnangnan [ɲɑ̃ɲɑ̃] adj inv (fam: livre, film) soppy

GNL sigle m (= gaz naturel liquéfié) LNG (= liquefied natural gas)

gnôle [njol] nf (fam) booze no pl; **un petit verre de ~** a drop of the hard stuff

gnome [gnom] nm gnome

gnon [ɲɔ̃] nm (fam: coup de poing) bash; (: marque) dent

GO sigle fpl (= grandes ondes) LW ▷ sigle m (= gentil organisateur) title given to leaders on Club Méditerranée holidays; extended to refer to easy-going leader of any group

Go abr (= gigaoctet) GB

go [go]: **tout de go** adv straight out

goal [gol] nm goalkeeper

gobelet [gɔblɛ] nm (en métal) tumbler; (en plastique) beaker; (à dés) cup

gober [gɔbe] vt to swallow

goberger [gɔbɛʀʒe]: **se goberger** vi to cosset o.s.

Gobi [gɔbi] n: **désert de ~** Gobi Desert

godasse [gɔdas] nf (fam) shoe

godet [gɔdɛ] nm pot; (Couture) unpressed pleat

godiller [gɔdije] vi (Navig) to scull; (Ski) to wedeln

goéland [gɔelɑ̃] nm (sea)gull

goélette [gɔelɛt] nf schooner

goémon [gɔemɔ̃] nm wrack

gogo [gɔgo] nm (péj) mug, sucker; **à ~** adv galore

goguenard, e [gɔgnaʀ, -aʀd(ə)] adj mocking

goguette [gɔgɛt] nf: **en ~** on the binge

goinfre [gwɛ̃fʀ(ə)] nm glutton

goinfrer [gwɛ̃fʀe]: **se goinfrer** vi to make a pig of o.s.; **se ~ de** to guzzle

goitre [gwatʀ(ə)] nm goitre

golf [gɔlf] nm (jeu) golf; (terrain) golf course; **~ miniature** crazy ou miniature golf

golfe [gɔlf(ə)] nm gulf; bay; **le ~ d'Aden** the Gulf of Aden; **le ~ de Gascogne** the Bay of Biscay; **le ~ du Lion** the Gulf of Lions; **le ~ Persique** the Persian Gulf

golfeur, -euse [gɔlfœʀ, -øz] nm/f golfer

gominé, e [gɔmine] adj slicked down

gomme [gɔm] nf (à effacer) rubber (Brit), eraser; (résine) gum; **boule** ou **pastille de ~** throat pastille

gommé, e [gɔme] adj: **papier ~** gummed paper

gommer [gɔme] vt (effacer) to rub out (Brit), erase; (enduire de gomme) to gum

gond [gɔ̃] nm hinge; **sortir de ses ~s** (fig) to fly off the handle

gondole [gɔ̃dɔl] nf gondola; (pour l'étalage) shelves pl, gondola

gondoler [gɔ̃dɔle]: **se gondoler** vi to warp, buckle; (fam: rire) to hoot with laughter; to be in stitches

gondolier [gɔ̃dɔlje] nm gondolier

gonflable [gɔ̃flabl(ə)] adj inflatable

gonflage [gɔ̃flaʒ] nm inflating, blowing up

gonflé, e [gɔ̃fle] adj swollen; (ventre) bloated; (fam: culotté): **être ~** to have a nerve

gonflement [gɔ̃fləmɑ̃] nm inflation; (Méd) swelling

gonfler [gɔ̃fle] vt (pneu, ballon) to inflate, blow up; (nombre, importance) to inflate ▷ vi (pied etc) to swell (up); (Culin: pâte) to rise

gonfleur [gɔ̃flœʀ] nm air pump

gong [gɔ̃g] nm gong

gonzesse [gɔ̃zɛs] nf (fam) chick, bird (Brit)

goret [gɔʀɛ] nm piglet

gorge [gɔʀʒ(ə)] nf (Anat) throat; (poitrine) breast; (Géo) gorge; (rainure) groove; **avoir mal à la ~** to have a sore throat; **avoir la ~ serrée** to have a lump in one's throat

gorgé, e [gɔʀʒe] adj: **~ de** filled with; (eau) saturated with ▷ nf mouthful; sip; gulp; **boire à petites/grandes ~es** to take little sips/big gulps

gorille [gɔʀij] nm gorilla; (fam) bodyguard

gosier [gozje] nm throat

gosse [gɔs] nm/f kid

gothique [gɔtik] adj gothic

gouache [gwaʃ] nf gouache

gouaille [gwaj] nf street wit, cocky humour (Brit) ou humor (US)

goudron [gudʀɔ̃] nm (asphalte) tar(mac) (Brit), asphalt; (du tabac) tar

goudronner [gudʀone] vt to tar(mac) (Brit), asphalt

gouffre [gufʀ(ə)] nm abyss, gulf

goujat [guʒa] nm boor

goujon [guʒɔ̃] nm gudgeon

goulée [gule] nf gulp

goulet [gulɛ] nm bottleneck

goulot [gulo] nm neck; **boire au ~** to drink from the bottle

goulu, e [guly] adj greedy

goulûment [gulymɑ̃] adv greedily

goupille [gupij] nf (metal) pin

goupiller [gupije] vt to pin (together)

goupillon [gupijɔ̃] nm (Rel) sprinkler; (brosse) bottle brush; **le ~** (fig) the cloth, the clergy

gourd, e [guʀ, guʀd(ə)] adj numb (with cold); (fam) oafish

gourde [guʀd(ə)] nf (récipient) flask; (fam) (clumsy) clot ou oaf

gourdin [guʀdɛ̃] nm club, bludgeon

gourer [guʀe] (fam): **se gourer** vi to boob

gourmand, e [guʀmɑ̃, -ɑ̃d] adj greedy

gourmandise [guʀmɑ̃diz] nf greed; (bonbon) sweet (Brit), piece of candy (US)

gourmet [guʀmɛ] nm epicure

gourmette [guʀmɛt] nf chain bracelet

gourou [guʀu] nm guru

gousse [gus] *nf* (*de vanille etc*) pod; ~ **d'ail** clove of garlic

gousset [gusɛ] *nm* (*de gilet*) fob

goût [gu] *nm* taste; (*fig: appréciation*) taste, liking; **le (bon)** ~ good taste; **de bon** ~ in good taste, tasteful; **de mauvais** ~ in bad taste, tasteless; **avoir bon/mauvais** ~ (*aliment*) to taste nice/ nasty; (*personne*) to have good/bad taste; **avoir du/manquer de** ~ to have/lack taste; **avoir du** ~ **pour** to have a liking for; **prendre** ~ **à** to develop a taste *ou* a liking for

goûter [gute] *vt* (*essayer*) to taste; (*apprécier*) to enjoy ▷ *vi* to have (afternoon) tea ▷ *nm* (afternoon) tea; ~ **à** to taste, sample; ~ **de** to have a taste of; ~ **d'enfants/d'anniversaire** children's tea/birthday party

goutte [gut] *nf* drop; (*Méd*) gout; (*alcool*) nip (Brit), tot (Brit), drop (US); **gouttes** *nfpl* (*Méd*) drops; ~ **à** ~ *adv* a drop at a time; **tomber** ~ **à** ~ to drip

goutte-à-goutte [gutagut] *nm inv* (*Méd*) drip; **alimenter au** ~ to drip-feed

gouttelette [gutlɛt] *nf* droplet

goutter [gute] *vi* to drip

gouttière [gutjɛR] *nf* gutter

gouvernail [guvɛRnaj] *nm* rudder; (*barre*) helm, tiller

gouvernant, e [guvɛRnã, -ãt] *adj* ruling *cpd* ▷ *nf* housekeeper; (*d'un enfant*) governess

gouverne [guvɛRn(ə)] *nf*: **pour sa** ~ for his guidance

gouvernement [guvɛRnəmã] *nm* government

gouvernemental, e, -aux [guvɛRnəmãtal, -o] *adj* (*politique*) government *cpd*; (*journal, parti*) pro-government

gouverner [guvɛRne] *vt* to govern; (*diriger*) to steer; (*fig*) to control

gouverneur [guvɛRnœR] *nm* governor; (*Mil*) commanding officer

goyave [gɔjav] *nf* guava

GPL *sigle m* (= *gaz de pétrole liquéfié*) LPG (= *liquefied petroleum gas*)

GQG *sigle m* (= *grand quartier général*) GHQ

grabataire [gRabatɛR] *adj* bedridden ▷ *nm/f* bedridden invalid

grâce [gRas] *nf* grace; (*faveur*) favour; (*Jur*) pardon; **grâces** *nfpl* (*Rel*) grace *sg*; **de bonne/ mauvaise** ~ with (a) good/bad grace; **dans les bonnes** ~**s de qn** in favour with sb; **faire** ~ **à qn de qch** to spare sb sth; **rendre** ~**(s) à** to give thanks to; **demander** ~ to beg for mercy; **droit de** ~ right of reprieve; **recours en** ~ plea for pardon; ~ **à** *prép* thanks to

gracier [gRasje] *vt* to pardon

gracieusement [gRasjøzmã] *adv* graciously, kindly; (*gratuitement*) freely; (*avec grâce*) gracefully

gracieux, -euse [gRasjø, -øz] *adj* (*charmant, élégant*) graceful; (*aimable*) gracious, kind; **à titre** ~ free of charge

gracile [gRasil] *adj* slender

gradation [gRadasjɔ̃] *nf* gradation

grade [gRad] *nm* (*Mil*) rank; (*Scol*) degree; **monter en** ~ to be promoted

gradé [gRade] *nm* (*Mil*) officer

gradin [gRadɛ̃] *nm* (*dans un théâtre*) tier; (*de stade*) step; **gradins** *nmpl* (*de stade*) terracing *no pl* (Brit), standing area; **en** ~**s** terraced

graduation [gRadɥasjɔ̃] *nf* graduation

gradué, e [gRadɥe] *adj* (*exercices*) graded (for difficulty); (*thermomètre, verre*) graduated

graduel, le [gRadɥɛl] *adj* gradual; progressive

graduer [gRadɥe] *vt* (*effort etc*) to increase gradually; (*règle, verre*) to graduate

graffiti [gRafiti] *nmpl* graffiti

grain [gRɛ̃] *nm* (*gén*) grain; (*de chapelet*) bead; (*Navig*) squall; (*averse*) heavy shower; (*fig: petite quantité*): **un** ~ **de** a touch of; ~ **de beauté** beauty spot; ~ **de café** coffee bean; ~ **de poivre** peppercorn; ~ **de poussière** speck of dust; ~ **de raisin** grape

graine [gRɛn] *nf* seed; **mauvaise** ~ (*mauvais sujet*) bad lot; **une** ~ **de voyou** a hooligan in the making

graineterie [gRɛntRi] *nf* seed merchant's (shop)

grainetier, -ière [gRɛntje, -jɛR] *nm/f* seed merchant

graissage [gRɛsaʒ] *nm* lubrication, greasing

graisse [gRɛs] *nf* fat; (*lubrifiant*) grease; ~ **saturée** saturated fat

graisser [gRese] *vt* to lubricate, grease; (*tacher*) to make greasy

graisseux, -euse [gRɛsø, -øz] *adj* greasy; (*Anat*) fatty

grammaire [gRamɛR] *nf* grammar

grammatical, e, -aux [gRamatikal, -o] *adj* grammatical

gramme [gRam] *nm* gramme

grand, e [gRã, gRãd] *adj* (*haut*) tall; (*gros, vaste, large*) big, large; (*long*) long; (*sens abstraits*) great ▷ *adv*: ~ **ouvert** wide open; **un** ~ **buveur** a heavy drinker; **un** ~ **homme** a great man; **son** ~ **frère** his big *ou* older brother; **avoir** ~ **besoin de** to be in dire *ou* desperate need of; **il est** ~ **temps de** it's high time to; **il est assez** ~ **pour** he's big *ou* old enough to; **voir** ~ to think big; **en** ~ on a large scale; **au** ~ **air** in the open (air); **les** ~**s blessés/brûlés** the severely injured/burned; **de** ~ **matin** at the crack of dawn; ~ **écart** splits *pl*; ~ **ensemble** housing scheme; ~ **jour** broad daylight; ~ **livre** (*Comm*) ledger; ~ **magasin** department store; ~ **malade** very sick person; ~ **public** general public; ~**e personne** grown-up; ~**e surface** hypermarket, superstore; ~**es écoles** prestige university-level colleges with competitive entrance examinations; *see note*; ~**es lignes** (*Rail*) main lines; ~**es vacances** summer holidays

● **GRANDES ÉCOLES**
●
● The *grandes écoles* are highly-respected
● institutes of higher education which train
● students for specific careers. Students who

- have spent two years after the
- "baccalauréat" in the "classes
- préparatoires" are recruited by competitive
- entry examination. The prestigious *grandes*
- *écoles* have a strong corporate identity and
- tend to furnish France with its intellectual,
- administrative and political élite.

grand-angle [gʀɑ̃tɑ̃gl(ə)] (*pl* **grands-angles**) *nm* (*Photo*) wide-angle lens
grand-angulaire [gʀɑ̃tɑ̃gylɛʀ] (*pl* **grands-angulaires**) *nm* (*Photo*) wide-angle lens
grand-chose [gʀɑ̃ʃoz] *nm/f inv*: **pas** ~ not much
Grande-Bretagne [gʀɑ̃dbʀətaɲ] *nf*: **la** ~ (Great) Britain; **en** ~ in (Great) Britain
grandement [gʀɑ̃dmɑ̃] *adv* (*tout à fait*) greatly; (*largement*) easily; (*généreusement*) lavishly
grandeur [gʀɑ̃dœʀ] *nf* (*dimension*) size; (*fig: ampleur, importance*) magnitude; (: *gloire, puissance*) greatness; ~ **nature** *adj* life-size
grand-guignolesque [gʀɑ̃giɲolɛsk(ə)] *adj* gruesome
grandiloquent, e [gʀɑ̃dilokɑ̃, -ɑ̃t] *adj* bombastic, grandiloquent
grandiose [gʀɑ̃djoz] *adj* (*paysage, spectacle*) imposing
grandir [gʀɑ̃diʀ] *vi* (*enfant, arbre*) to grow; (*bruit, hostilité*) to increase, grow ▷ *vt*: ~ **qn** (*vêtement, chaussure*) to make sb look taller; (*fig*) to make sb grow in stature
grandissant, e [gʀɑ̃disɑ̃, -ɑ̃t] *adj* growing
grand-mère [gʀɑ̃mɛʀ] (*pl* **grand(s)-mères**) *nf* grandmother
grand-messe [gʀɑ̃mɛs] *nf* high mass
grand-oncle [gʀɑ̃tɔ̃kl(ə), gʀɑ̃zɔ̃kl(ə)] (*pl* **grands-oncles**) *nm* great-uncle
grand-peine [gʀɑ̃pɛn]: **à** ~ *adv* with (great) difficulty
grand-père [gʀɑ̃pɛʀ] (*pl* **grands-pères**) *nm* grandfather
grand-route [gʀɑ̃ʀut] *nf* main road
grand-rue [gʀɑ̃ʀy] *nf* high street
grands-parents [gʀɑ̃paʀɑ̃] *nmpl* grandparents
grand-tante [gʀɑ̃tɑ̃t] (*pl* **grand(s)-tantes**) *nf* great-aunt
grand-voile [gʀɑ̃vwal] *nf* mainsail
grange [gʀɑ̃ʒ] *nf* barn
granit, granite [gʀanit] *nm* granite
granitique [gʀanitik] *adj* granite; (*terrain*) granitic
granule [gʀanyl] *nm* small pill
granulé [gʀanyle] *nm* granule
granuleux, -euse [gʀanylø, -øz] *adj* granular
graphe [gʀaf] *nm* graph
graphie [gʀafi] *nf* written form
graphique [gʀafik] *adj* graphic ▷ *nm* graph
graphisme [gʀafism(ə)] *nm* graphic arts *pl*; graphics *sg*; (*écriture*) handwriting
graphiste [gʀafist(ə)] *nm/f* graphic designer
graphologie [gʀafoloʒi] *nf* graphology
graphologue [gʀafolog] *nm/f* graphologist
grappe [gʀap] *nf* cluster; ~ **de raisin** bunch of grapes

grappiller [gʀapije] *vt* to glean
grappin [gʀapɛ̃] *nm* grapnel; **mettre le** ~ **sur** (*fig*) to get one's claws on
gras, se [gʀɑ, gʀɑs] *adj* (*viande, soupe*) fatty; (*personne*) fat; (*surface, main, cheveux*) greasy; (*terre*) sticky; (*toux*) loose, phlegmy; (*rire*) throaty; (*plaisanterie*) coarse; (*crayon*) soft-lead; (*Typo*) bold ▷ *nm* (*Culin*) fat; **faire la** ~**se matinée** to have a lie-in (*Brit*), sleep late; **matière** ~**se** fat (content)
gras-double [gʀɑdubl(ə)] *nm* (*Culin*) tripe
grassement [gʀɑsmɑ̃] *adv* (*généreusement*): ~ **payé** handsomely paid; (*grossièrement: rire*) coarsely
grassouillet, te [gʀɑsujɛ, -ɛt] *adj* podgy, plump
gratifiant, e [gʀatifjɑ̃, -ɑ̃t] *adj* gratifying, rewarding
gratification [gʀatifikasjɔ̃] *nf* bonus
gratifier [gʀatifje] *vt*: ~ **qn de** to favour (*Brit*) *ou* favor (*US*) sb with; to reward sb with; (*sourire etc*) to favo(u)r sb with
gratin [gʀatɛ̃] *nm* (*Culin*) cheese- (*ou* crumb-)topped dish; (: *croûte*) topping; **au** ~ au gratin; **tout le** ~ **parisien** all the best people of Paris
gratiné [gʀatine] *adj* (*Culin*) au gratin; (*fam*) hellish ▷ *nf* (*soupe*) onion soup au gratin
gratis [gʀatis] *adv, adj* free
gratitude [gʀatityd] *nf* gratitude
gratte-ciel [gʀatsjɛl] *nm inv* skyscraper
grattement [gʀatmɑ̃] *nm* (*bruit*) scratching (noise)
gratte-papier [gʀatpapje] *nm inv* (*péj*) penpusher
gratter [gʀate] *vt* (*frotter*) to scrape; (*enlever*) to scrape off; (*bras, bouton*) to scratch; **se gratter** to scratch o.s.
grattoir [gʀatwaʀ] *nm* scraper
gratuit, e [gʀatɥi, -ɥit] *adj* (*entrée*) free; (*billet*) free, complimentary; (*fig*) gratuitous
gratuité [gʀatɥite] *nf* being free (of charge); gratuitousness
gratuitement [gʀatɥitmɑ̃] *adv* (*sans payer*) free; (*sans preuve, motif*) gratuitously
gravats [gʀava] *nmpl* rubble *sg*
grave [gʀav] *adj* (*dangereux: maladie, accident*) serious, bad; (*sérieux: sujet, problème*) serious, grave; (*personne, air*) grave, solemn; (*voix, son*) deep, low-pitched ▷ *nm* (*Mus*) low register; **ce n'est pas** ~! it's all right, don't worry; **blessé** ~ seriously injured person
graveleux, -euse [gʀavlø, -øz] *adj* (*terre*) gravelly; (*fruit*) gritty; (*contes, propos*) smutty
gravement [gʀavmɑ̃] *adv* seriously; badly; gravely
graver [gʀave] *vt* (*plaque, nom*) to engrave; (*CD, DVD*) to burn; (*fig*): ~ **qch dans son esprit/sa mémoire** to etch sth in one's mind/memory
graveur [gʀavœʀ] *nm* engraver; ~ **de CD/DVD** CD/DVD burner *or* writer
gravier [gʀavje] *nm* (loose) gravel *no pl*
gravillons [gʀavijɔ̃] *nmpl* gravel *sg*, loose

chippings *ou* gravel

gravir [gʀaviʀ] *vt* to climb (up)

gravitation [gʀavitasjɔ̃] *nf* gravitation

gravité [gʀavite] *nf* (*voir* grave) seriousness; gravity; (*Physique*) gravity

graviter [gʀavite] *vi*: ~ **autour de** to revolve around

gravure [gʀavyʀ] *nf* engraving; (*reproduction*) print; plate

gré [gʀe] *nm*: **à son** ~ *adj* to his liking ▷ *adv* as he pleases; **au** ~ **de** according to, following; **contre le** ~ **de qn** against sb's will; **de son (plein)** ~ of one's own free will; **de** ~ **ou de force** whether one likes it or not; **de bon** ~ willingly; **bon** ~ **mal** ~ like it or not; willy-nilly; **de** ~ **à** ~ (*Comm*) by mutual agreement; **savoir (bien)** ~ **à qn de qch** to be (most) grateful to sb for sth

grec, grecque [gʀɛk] *adj* Greek; (*classique: vase etc*) Grecian ▷ *nm* (*Ling*) Greek ▷ *nm/f*: **Grec, Grecque** Greek

Grèce [gʀɛs] *nf*: **la** ~ Greece

gredin, e [gʀədɛ̃, -in] *nm/f* rogue, rascal

gréement [gʀemɑ̃] *nm* rigging

greffe [gʀɛf] *nf* graft; transplant ▷ *nm* (*Jur*) office

greffer [gʀefe] *vt* (*Bot, Méd: tissu*) to graft; (*Méd: organe*) to transplant

greffier [gʀefje] *nm* clerk of the court

grégaire [gʀegɛʀ] *adj* gregarious

grège [gʀɛʒ] *adj*: **soie** ~ raw silk

grêle [gʀɛl] *adj* (very) thin ▷ *nf* hail

grêlé, e [gʀele] *adj* pockmarked

grêler [gʀele] *vb impers*: **il grêle** it's hailing ▷ *vt*: **la région a été grêlée** the region was damaged by hail

grêlon [gʀelɔ̃] *nm* hailstone

grelot [gʀəlo] *nm* little bell

grelottant, e [gʀələtɑ̃, -ɑ̃t] *adj* shivering, shivery

grelotter [gʀələte] *vi* (*trembler*) to shiver

Grenade [gʀənad] *n* Granada ▷ *nf* (*île*) Grenada

grenade [gʀənad] *nf* (*explosive*) grenade; (*Bot*) pomegranate; ~ **lacrymogène** teargas grenade

grenadier [gʀənadje] *nm* (*Mil*) grenadier; (*Bot*) pomegranate tree

grenadine [gʀənadin] *nf* grenadine

grenat [gʀəna] *adj inv* dark red

grenier [gʀənje] *nm* (*de maison*) attic; (*de ferme*) loft

grenouille [gʀənuj] *nf* frog

grenouillère [gʀənujɛʀ] *nf* (*de bébé*) leggings; (*: combinaison*) sleepsuit

grenu, e [gʀəny] *adj* grainy, grained

grès [gʀɛ] *nm* (*roche*) sandstone; (*poterie*) stoneware

grésil [gʀezi] *nm* (fine) hail

grésillement [gʀezijmɑ̃] *nm* sizzling; crackling

grésiller [gʀezije] *vi* to sizzle; (*Radio*) to crackle

grève [gʀɛv] *nf* (*d'ouvriers*) strike; (*plage*) shore; **se mettre en/faire** ~ to go on/be on strike; ~ **bouchon** partial strike (*in key areas of a company*);

~ **de la faim** hunger strike; ~ **perlée** go-slow (*Brit*), slowdown (*US*); ~ **sauvage** wildcat strike; ~ **de solidarité** sympathy strike; ~ **surprise** lightning strike; ~ **sur le tas** sit down strike; ~ **tournante** strike by rota; ~ **du zèle** work-to-rule (*Brit*), slowdown (*US*)

grever [gʀəve] *vt* (*budget, économie*) to put a strain on; **grevé d'impôts** crippled by taxes; **grevé d'hypothèques** heavily mortgaged

gréviste [gʀevist(ə)] *nm/f* striker

gribouillage [gʀibujaʒ] *nm* scribble, scrawl

gribouiller [gʀibuje] *vt* to scribble, scrawl ▷ *vi* to doodle

gribouillis [gʀibuji] *nm* (*dessin*) doodle; (*action*) doodling *no pl*; (*écriture*) scribble

grief [gʀijɛf] *nm* grievance; **faire** ~ **à qn de** to reproach sb for

grièvement [gʀijɛvmɑ̃] *adv* seriously

griffe [gʀif] *nf* claw; (*fig*) signature; (: *d'un couturier, parfumeur*) label, signature

griffé, e [gʀife] *adj* designer(-label) *cpd*

griffer [gʀife] *vt* to scratch

griffon [gʀifɔ̃] *nm* (*chien*) griffon

griffonnage [gʀifɔnaʒ] *nm* scribble

griffonner [gʀifɔne] *vt* to scribble

griffure [gʀifyʀ] *nf* scratch

grignoter [gʀiɲɔte] *vt, vi* to nibble

gril [gʀil] *nm* steak *ou* grill pan

grillade [gʀijad] *nf* grill

grillage [gʀijaʒ] *nm* (*treillis*) wire netting; (*clôture*) wire fencing

grillager [gʀijaʒe] *vt* (*objet*) to put wire netting on; (*périmètre, jardin*) to put wire fencing around

grille [gʀij] *nf* (*portail*) (metal) gate; (*clôture*) railings *pl*; (*d'égout*) (metal) grate; (*fig*) grid

grille-pain [gʀijpɛ̃] *nm inv* toaster

griller [gʀije] *vt* (*aussi*: **faire griller**: *pain*) to toast; (: *viande*) to grill (*Brit*), broil (*US*); (: *café*) to roast; (*fig: ampoule etc*) to burn out, blow; ~ **un feu rouge** to jump the lights (*Brit*), run a stoplight (*US*) ▷ *vi* (*brûler*) to be roasting

grillon [gʀijɔ̃] *nm* (*Zool*) cricket

grimace [gʀimas] *nf* grimace; (*pour faire rire*): **faire des** ~**s** to pull *ou* make faces

grimacer [gʀimase] *vi* to grimace

grimacier, -ière [gʀimasje, -jɛʀ] *adj*: **c'est un enfant** ~ that child is always pulling faces

grimer [gʀime] *vt* to make up

grimoire [gʀimwaʀ] *nm* (*illisible*) unreadable scribble; (*livre de magie*) book of magic spells

grimpant, e [gʀɛ̃pɑ̃, -ɑ̃t] *adj*: **plante** ~**e** climbing plant, climber

grimper [gʀɛ̃pe] *vi, vt* to climb ▷ *nm*: **le** ~ (*Sport*) rope-climbing; ~ **à/sur** to climb (up)/climb onto

grimpeur, -euse [gʀɛ̃pœʀ, -øz] *nm/f* climber

grinçant, e [gʀɛ̃sɑ̃, -ɑ̃t] *adj* grating

grincement [gʀɛ̃smɑ̃] *nm* grating (noise); creaking (noise)

grincer [gʀɛ̃se] *vi* (*porte, roue*) to grate; (*plancher*) to creak; ~ **des dents** to grind one's teeth

grincheux, -euse [gʀɛ̃ʃø, -øz] *adj* grumpy

gringalet [gʀɛ̃galɛ] *adj m* puny ▷ *nm* weakling
griotte [gʀijɔt] *nf* Morello cherry
grippal, e, -aux [gʀipal, -o] *adj* (*état*) flu-like
grippe [gʀip] *nf* flu, influenza; **avoir la ~** to have (the) flu; **prendre qn/qch en ~** (*fig*) to take a sudden dislike to sb/sth; **~ aviaire** bird flu
grippé, e [gʀipe] *adj*: **être ~** to have (the) flu; (*moteur*) to have seized up (*Brit*) *ou* jammed
gripper [gʀipe] *vt, vi* to jam
grippe-sou [gʀipsu] *nm/f* penny pincher
gris, e [gʀi, gʀiz] *adj* grey (*Brit*), gray (*US*); (*ivre*) tipsy ▷ *nm* (*couleur*) grey (*Brit*), gray (*US*); **il fait ~** it's a dull *ou* grey day; **faire ~e mine** to look miserable *ou* morose; **faire ~e mine à qn** to give sb a cool reception
grisaille [gʀizaj] *nf* greyness (*Brit*), grayness (*US*), dullness
grisant, e [gʀizɑ̃, -ɑ̃t] *adj* intoxicating, exhilarating
grisâtre [gʀizɑtʀ(ə)] *adj* greyish (*Brit*), grayish (*US*)
griser [gʀize] *vt* to intoxicate; **se ~ de** (*fig*) to become intoxicated with
griserie [gʀizʀi] *nf* intoxication
grisonnant, e [gʀizɔnɑ̃, -ɑ̃t] *adj* greying (*Brit*), graying (*US*)
grisonner [gʀizɔne] *vi* to be going grey (*Brit*) *ou* gray (*US*)
Grisons [gʀizɔ̃] *nmpl*: **les ~** Graubünden
grisou [gʀizu] *nm* firedamp
gris-vert [gʀivɛʀ] *adj* grey-green
grive [gʀiv] *nf* (*Zool*) thrush
grivois, e [gʀivwa, -waz] *adj* saucy
grivoiserie [gʀivwazʀi] *nf* sauciness
Groenland [gʀɔɛnlɑ̃d] *nm*: **le ~** Greenland
grog [gʀɔg] *nm* grog
groggy [gʀɔgi] *adj inv* dazed
grogne [gʀɔɲ] *nf* grumble
grognement [gʀɔɲmɑ̃] *nm* grunt; growl
grogner [gʀɔɲe] *vi* to growl; (*fig*) to grumble
grognon, ne [gʀɔɲɔ̃, -ɔn] *adj* grumpy, grouchy
groin [gʀwɛ̃] *nm* snout
grommeler [gʀɔmle] *vi* to mutter to o.s.
grondement [gʀɔ̃dmɑ̃] *nm* rumble; growl
gronder [gʀɔ̃de] *vi* (*canon, moteur, tonnerre*) to rumble; (*animal*) to growl; (*fig: révolte*) to be brewing ▷ *vt* to scold
groom [gʀum] *nm* page, bellhop (*US*)
gros, se [gʀo, gʀos] *adj* big, large; (*obèse*) fat; (*problème, quantité*) great; (*travaux, dégâts*) extensive; (*large: trait, fil*) thick, heavy ▷ *adv*: **risquer/gagner ~** to risk/win a lot ▷ *nm* (*Comm*): **le ~** the wholesale business; **écrire ~** to write in big letters; **prix de ~** wholesale price; **par ~ temps/~se mer** in rough weather/heavy seas; **le ~ de** the main body of; (*du travail etc*) the bulk of; **en avoir ~ sur le cœur** to be upset; **en ~** roughly; (*Comm*) wholesale; **~ intestin** large intestine; **~ lot** jackpot; **~ mot** coarse word, vulgarity; **~ œuvre** shell (of building); **~ plan** (*Photo*) close-up; **~ porteur** wide-bodied aircraft, jumbo (jet); **~ sel** cooking salt; **~ titre**

headline; **~se caisse** big drum
groseille [gʀozɛj] *nf*: **~ (rouge)/(blanche)** red/white currant; **~ à maquereau** gooseberry
groseillier [gʀozeje] *nm* red *ou* white currant bush; gooseberry bush
grosse [gʀos] *adj f voir* **gros** ▷ *nf* (*Comm*) gross
grossesse [gʀosɛs] *nf* pregnancy; **~ nerveuse** phantom pregnancy
grosseur [gʀosœʀ] *nf* size; fatness; (*tumeur*) lump
grossier, -ière [gʀosje, -jɛʀ] *adj* coarse; (*travail*) rough; crude; (*évident: erreur*) gross
grossièrement [gʀosjɛʀmɑ̃] *adv* coarsely; roughly; crudely; (*en gros*) roughly
grossièreté [gʀosjɛʀte] *nf* coarseness; rudeness
grossir [gʀosiʀ] *vi* (*personne*) to put on weight; (*fig*) to grow, get bigger; (*rivière*) to swell ▷ *vt* to increase; (*exagérer*) to exaggerate; (*au microscope*) to magnify, enlarge; (*vêtement*): **~ qn** to make sb look fatter
grossissant, e [gʀosisɑ̃, -ɑ̃t] *adj* magnifying, enlarging
grossissement [gʀosismɑ̃] *nm* (*optique*) magnification
grossiste [gʀosist(ə)] *nm/f* wholesaler
grosso modo [gʀosomɔdo] *adv* roughly
grotesque [gʀɔtɛsk(ə)] *adj* grotesque
grotte [gʀɔt] *nf* cave
grouiller [gʀuje] *vi* (*foule*) to mill about; (*fourmis*) to swarm about; **~ de** to be swarming with
groupe [gʀup] *nm* group; **cabinet de ~** group practice; **médecine de ~** group practice; **~ électrogène** generator; **~ de parole** support group; **~ de pression** pressure group; **~ sanguin** blood group; **~ scolaire** school complex
groupement [gʀupmɑ̃] *nm* grouping; (*groupe*) group; **~ d'intérêt économique (GIE)** ≈ trade association
grouper [gʀupe] *vt* to group; (*ressources, moyens*) to pool; **se grouper** to get together
groupuscule [gʀupyskyl] *nm* clique
gruau [gʀyo] *nm*: **pain de ~** wheaten bread
grue [gʀy] *nf* crane; **faire le pied de ~** (*fam*) to hang around (waiting), kick one's heels (*Brit*)
gruger [gʀyʒe] *vt* to cheat, dupe
grumeaux [gʀymo] *nmpl* (*Culin*) lumps
grumeleux, -euse [gʀymlø, -øz] *adj* (*sauce etc*) lumpy; (*peau etc*) bumpy
grutier [gʀytje] *nm* crane driver
gruyère [gʀyjɛʀ] *nm* gruyère (*Brit*) *ou* Swiss cheese
Guadeloupe [gwadlup] *nf*: **la ~** Guadeloupe
guadeloupéen, ne [gwadlupeɛ̃, -ɛn] *adj* Guadelupian
Guatémala [gwatemala] *nm*: **le ~** Guatemala
guatémalien, ne [gwatemaljɛ̃, -ɛn] *adj* Guatemalan
guatémaltèque [gwatemaltɛk] *adj* Guatemalan
gué [ge] *nm* ford; **passer à ~** to ford
guenilles [gənij] *nfpl* rags

guenon [gənɔ̃] nf female monkey
guépard [gepaʀ] nm cheetah
guêpe [gɛp] nf wasp
guêpier [gepje] nm (fig) trap
guère [gɛʀ] adv (avec adjectif, adverbe): **ne ... ~** hardly; (avec verbe): **ne ... ~** (tournure négative) much; hardly ever; (very) long; **il n'y a ~ que/ de** there's hardly anybody (ou anything) but/ hardly any
guéridon [geʀidɔ̃] nm pedestal table
guérilla [geʀija] nf guerrilla warfare
guérillero [geʀijeʀo] nm guerrilla
guérir [geʀiʀ] vt (personne, maladie) to cure; (membre, plaie) to heal ▷ vi (personne) to recover, be cured; (plaie, chagrin) to heal; **~ de** to be cured of, recover from; **~ qn de** to cure sb of
guérison [geʀizɔ̃] nf curing; healing; recovery
guérissable [geʀisabl(ə)] adj curable
guérisseur, -euse [geʀisœʀ, -øz] nm/f healer
guérite [geʀit] nf (Mil) sentry box; (sur un chantier) (workman's) hut
Guernesey [gɛʀnəzɛ] nf Guernsey
guernesiais, e [gɛʀnəzjɛ, -ɛz] adj of ou from Guernsey
guerre [gɛʀ] nf war; (méthode): **~ atomique/de tranchées** atomic/trench warfare no pl; **en ~** at war; **faire la ~ à** to wage war against; **de ~ lasse** (fig) tired of fighting ou resisting; **de bonne ~** fair and square; **~ civile/mondiale** civil/world war; **~ froide/sainte** cold/holy war; **~ d'usure** war of attrition
guerrier, -ière [gɛʀje, -jɛʀ] adj warlike ▷ nm/f warrior
guerroyer [gɛʀwaje] vi to wage war
guet [gɛ] nm: **faire le ~** to be on the watch ou look-out
guet-apens [gɛtapɑ̃] (pl **guets-apens**) nm ambush
guêtre [gɛtʀ(ə)] nf gaiter
guetter [gete] vt (épier) to watch (intently); (attendre) to watch (out) for; (: pour surprendre) to be lying in wait for
guetteur [gɛtœʀ] nm look-out
gueule [gœl] nf mouth; (fam: visage) mug; (: bouche) gob (!), mouth; **ta ~!** (fam) shut up!; **~ de bois** (fam) hangover
gueule-de-loup [gœldəlu] (pl **gueules-de-loup**) nf snapdragon
gueuler [gœle] vi (fam) to bawl
gueuleton [gœltɔ̃] nm (fam) blowout (Brit), big meal
gueux [gø] nm beggar; (coquin) rogue
gui [gi] nm mistletoe
guibole [gibɔl] nf (fam) leg
guichet [giʃɛ] nm (de bureau, banque) counter, window; (d'une porte) wicket, hatch; **les ~s** (à la gare, au théâtre) the ticket office; **jouer à ~s fermés** to play to a full house
guichetier, -ière [giʃtje, -jɛʀ] nm/f counter clerk
guide [gid] nm guide; (livre) guide(book) ▷ nf (fille scout) (girl) guide (Brit), girl scout (US); **guides** nfpl (d'un cheval) reins
guider [gide] vt to guide
guidon [gidɔ̃] nm handlebars pl
guigne [giɲ] nf (fam): **avoir la ~** to be jinxed
guignol [giɲɔl] nm ≈ Punch and Judy show; (fig) clown
guillemets [gijmɛ] nmpl: **entre ~** in inverted commas ou quotation marks; **~ de répétition** ditto marks
guilleret, te [gijʀɛ, -ɛt] adj perky, bright
guillotine [gijɔtin] nf guillotine
guillotiner [gijɔtine] vt to guillotine
guimauve [gimov] nf (Bot) marshmallow; (fig) sentimentality, sloppiness
guimbarde [gɛ̃baʀd(ə)] nf old banger (Brit), jalopy
guindé, e [gɛ̃de] adj stiff, starchy
Guinée [gine] nf: **la (République de) ~** (the Republic of) Guinea; **la ~ équatoriale** Equatorial Guinea
Guinée-Bissau [ginebiso] nf: **la ~** Guinea-Bissau
guinéen, ne [gineɛ̃, -ɛn] adj Guinean
guingois [gɛ̃gwa]: **de ~** adv askew
guinguette [gɛ̃gɛt] nf open-air café or dance hall
guirlande [giʀlɑ̃d] nf garland; (de papier) paper chain; **~ lumineuse** lights pl, fairy lights pl (Brit); **~ de Noël** tinsel no pl
guise [giz] nf: **à votre ~** as you wish ou please; **en ~ de** by way of
guitare [gitaʀ] nf guitar
guitariste [gitaʀist(ə)] nm/f guitarist, guitar player
gustatif, -ive [gystatif, -iv] adj gustatory; voir **papille**
guttural, e, -aux [gytyʀal, -o] adj guttural
guyanais, e [gɥijanɛ, -ɛz] adj Guyanese, Guyanan; (français) Guianese, Guianan
Guyane [gɥijan] nf: **la ~** Guyana; **la ~ (française)** (French) Guiana
gvt abr (= gouvernement) govt
gym [ʒim] nf (exercices) gym
gymkhana [ʒimkana] nm rally; **~ motocycliste** (motorbike) scramble (Brit), motocross
gymnase [ʒimnɑz] nm gym(nasium)
gymnaste [ʒimnast(ə)] nm/f gymnast
gymnastique [ʒimnastik] nf gymnastics sg; (au réveil etc) keep-fit exercises pl; **~ corrective** remedial gymnastics
gynécologie [ʒinekɔlɔʒi] nf gynaecology (Brit), gynecology (US)
gynécologique [ʒinekɔlɔʒik] adj gynaecological (Brit), gynecological (US)
gynécologue [ʒinekɔlɔg] nm/f gynaecologist (Brit), gynecologist (US)
gypse [ʒips(ə)] nm gypsum
gyrophare [ʒiʀɔfaʀ] nm (sur une voiture) revolving (flashing) light

Hh

H, h [aʃ] *nm inv* H, h ▷ *abr* (= *homme*) M;
(= *hydrogène*) H = **heure**; **à l'heure H** at zero
hour; **bombe H** H bomb; **H comme Henri** H
for Harry (*Brit*) *ou* How (*US*)

ha. *abr* (= *hectare*) ha.

hab. *abr* = **habitant**

habile [abil] *adj* skilful; (*malin*) clever

habilement [abilmɑ̃] *adv* skilfully; cleverly

habileté [abilte] *nf* skill, skilfulness; cleverness

habilité, e [abilite] *adj*: ~ **à faire** entitled to do,
empowered to do

habiliter [abilite] *vt* to empower, entitle

habillage [abijaʒ] *nm* dressing

habillé, e [abije] *adj* dressed; (*chic*) dressy;
(*Tech*): ~ **de** covered with; encased in

habillement [abijmɑ̃] *nm* clothes *pl*; (*profession*)
clothing industry

habiller [abije] *vt* to dress; (*fournir en vêtements*) to
clothe; **s'habiller** to dress (o.s.); (*se déguiser,
mettre des vêtements chic*) to dress up; **s'~ de/en** to
dress in/dress up as; **s'~ chez/à** to buy one's
clothes from/at

habilleuse [abijøz] *nf* (*Ciné, Théât*) dresser

habit [abi] *nm* outfit; **habits** *nmpl* (*vêtements*)
clothes; ~ **(de soirée)** tails *pl*; evening dress;
prendre l'~ (*Rel: entrer en religion*) to enter (holy)
orders

habitable [abitabl(ə)] *adj* (in)habitable

habitacle [abitakl(ə)] *nm* cockpit; (*Auto*)
passenger cell

habitant, e [abitɑ̃, -ɑ̃t] *nm/f* inhabitant; (*d'une
maison*) occupant, occupier; **loger chez l'~** to
stay with the locals

habitat [abita] *nm* housing conditions *pl*; (*Bot,
Zool*) habitat

habitation [abitasjɔ̃] *nf* living; (*demeure*)
residence, home; (*maison*) house; **~s à loyer
modéré (HLM)** low-rent, state-owned housing,
≈ council housing *sg* (*Brit*), ≈ public housing
units (*US*)

habité, e [abite] *adj* inhabited; lived in

habiter [abite] *vt* to live in; (*sentiment*) to dwell
in ▷ *vi*: ~ **à/dans** to live in *ou* at/in; ~ **chez** *ou*
avec qn to live with sb; **~ 16 rue Montmartre**
to live at number 16 rue Montmartre; **~ rue
Montmartre** to live in rue Montmartre

habitude [abityd] *nf* habit; **avoir l'~ de faire** to
be in the habit of doing; **avoir l'~ des enfants**
to be used to children; **prendre l'~ de faire qch**
to get into the habit of doing sth; **perdre une ~**
to get out of a habit; **d'~** usually; **comme d'~** as
usual; **par ~** out of habit

habitué, e [abitɥe] *adj*: **être ~ à** to be used *ou*
accustomed to ▷ *nm/f* regular visitor; (*client*)
regular (customer)

habituel, le [abitɥel] *adj* usual

habituellement [abitɥɛlmɑ̃] *adv* usually

habituer [abitɥe] *vt*: ~ **qn à** to get sb used to;
s'habituer à to get used to

'hâbleur, -euse [ˈɑblœʀ, -øz] *adj* boastful

'hache [ˈaʃ] *nf* axe

'haché, e [ˈaʃe] *adj* minced (*Brit*), ground (*US*);
(*persil*) chopped; (*fig*) jerky

'hache-légumes [ˈaʃlegym] *nm inv* vegetable
chopper

'hacher [ˈaʃe] *vt* (*viande*) to mince (*Brit*), grind
(*US*); (*persil*) to chop; **~ menu** to mince *ou* grind
finely; to chop finely

'hachette [ˈaʃɛt] *nf* hatchet

'hache-viande [ˈaʃvjɑ̃d] *nm inv* (meat) mincer
(*Brit*) *ou* grinder (*US*); (*couteau*) (meat) cleaver

'hachis [ˈaʃi] *nm* mince *no pl* (*Brit*), hamburger
meat (*US*); **~ de viande** minced (*Brit*) *ou* ground
(*US*) meat

'hachisch [ˈaʃiʃ] *nm* hashish

'hachoir [ˈaʃwaʀ] *nm* chopper; (meat) mincer
(*Brit*) *ou* grinder (*US*); (*planche*) chopping board

'hachurer [ˈaʃyʀe] *vt* to hatch

'hachures [ˈaʃyʀ] *nfpl* hatching *sg*

'hagard, e [ˈagaʀ, -aʀd(ə)] *adj* wild, distraught

'haie [ˈɛ] *nf* hedge; (*Sport*) hurdle; (*fig: rang*) line,
row; **200 m ~s** 200 m hurdles; **~ d'honneur**
guard of honour

'haillons [ˈajɔ̃] *nmpl* rags

'haine [ˈɛn] *nf* hatred

'haineux, -euse [ˈɛnø, -øz] *adj* full of hatred

'haïr [ˈaiʀ] *vt* to detest, hate; **se 'haïr** to hate
each other

'hais [ˈɛ], **'haïs** *etc* [ˈai] *vb voir* **'haïr**

'haïssable [ˈaisabl(ə)] *adj* detestable

Haïti [aiti] *n* Haiti

haïtien, ne [aisjɛ̃, -ɛn] *adj* Haitian

'halage ['alaʒ] *nm*: **chemin de ~** towpath
'hâle ['ɑl] *nm* (sun)tan
'hâlé, e ['ɑle] *adj* (sun)tanned, sunburnt
haleine [alɛn] *nf* breath; **perdre ~** to get out of breath; **à perdre ~** until one is gasping for breath; **avoir mauvaise ~** to have bad breath; **reprendre ~** to get one's breath back; **hors d'~** out of breath; **tenir en ~** to hold spellbound; (*en attente*) to keep in suspense; **de longue ~** *adj* long-term
'haler ['ale] *vt* to haul in; (*remorquer*) to tow
'haleter ['alte] *vi* to pant
'hall ['ol] *nm* hall
hallali [alali] *nm* kill
'halle ['al] *nf* (covered) market; **'halles** *nfpl* central food market *sg*
'hallebarde ['albaʀd] *nf* halberd; **il pleut des ~s** (*fam*) it's bucketing down
hallucinant, e [alysinɑ̃, -ɑ̃t] *adj* staggering
hallucination [alysinasjɔ̃] *nf* hallucination
hallucinatoire [alysinatwaʀ] *adj* hallucinatory
halluciné, e [alysine] *nm/f* person suffering from hallucinations; (*fou*) (raving) lunatic
hallucinogène [a(l)lysinɔʒɛn] *adj* hallucinogenic ▷ *nm* hallucinogen
'halo ['alo] *nm* halo
halogène [alɔʒɛn] *nm*: **lampe (à) ~** halogen lamp
'halte ['alt(ə)] *nf* stop, break; (*escale*) stopping place; (*Rail*) halt ▷ *excl* stop!; **faire ~** to stop
'halte-garderie ['altgaʀdəʀi] (*pl* **'haltes-garderies**) *nf* crèche
haltère [altɛʀ] *nm* (*à boules, disques*) dumbbell, barbell; **(poids et) ~s** weightlifting
haltérophile [alteʀɔfil] *nm/f* weightlifter
haltérophilie [alteʀɔfili] *nf* weightlifting
'hamac ['amak] *nm* hammock
'Hambourg ['ɑ̃buʀ] *n* Hamburg
'hamburger ['ɑ̃buʀɡœʀ] *nm* hamburger
'hameau, x ['amo] *nm* hamlet
hameçon [amsɔ̃] *nm* (fish) hook
'hampe ['ɑ̃p] *nf* (*de drapeau etc*) pole; (*de lance*) shaft
'hamster ['amstɛʀ] *nm* hamster
'hanche ['ɑ̃ʃ] *nf* hip
'hand-ball ['ɑ̃dbal] *nm* handball
'handballeur, -euse ['ɑ̃dbalœʀ, -øz] *nm/f* handball player
'handicap ['ɑ̃dikap] *nm* handicap
'handicapé, e ['ɑ̃dikape] *adj* handicapped ▷ *nm/f* physically (*ou* mentally) handicapped person; **~ moteur** spastic
'handicaper ['ɑ̃dikape] *vt* to handicap
'hangar ['ɑ̃ɡaʀ] *nm* shed; (*Aviat*) hangar
'hanneton ['antɔ̃] *nm* cockchafer
'Hanovre ['anɔvʀ(ə)] *n* Hanover
'hanter ['ɑ̃te] *vt* to haunt
'hantise ['ɑ̃tiz] *nf* obsessive fear
'happer ['ape] *vt* to snatch; (*train etc*) to hit
'harangue ['aʀɑ̃ɡ] *nf* harangue
'haranguer ['aʀɑ̃ɡe] *vt* to harangue
'haras ['aʀɑ] *nm* stud farm

'harassant, e ['aʀasɑ̃, -ɑ̃t] *adj* exhausting
'harcèlement ['aʀsɛlmɑ̃] *nm* harassment; **~ sexuel** sexual harassment
'harceler ['aʀsəle] *vt* (*Mil, Chasse*) to harass, harry; (*importuner*) to plague
'hardes ['aʀd(ə)] *nfpl* rags
'hardi, e ['aʀdi] *adj* bold, daring
'hardiesse ['aʀdjɛs] *nf* audacity; **avoir la ~ de** to have the audacity *ou* effrontery to
'harem ['aʀɛm] *nm* harem
'hareng ['aʀɑ̃] *nm* herring
'hargne ['aʀɲ(ə)] *nf* aggressivity, aggressiveness
'hargneusement ['aʀɲøzmɑ̃] *adv* belligerently, aggressively
'hargneux, -euse ['aʀɲø, -øz] *adj* (*propos, personne*) belligerent, aggressive; (*chien*) fierce
'haricot ['aʀiko] *nm* bean; **~ blanc/rouge** haricot/kidney bean; **~ vert** French (*Brit*) *ou* green bean
harmonica [aʀmɔnika] *nm* mouth organ
harmonie [aʀmɔni] *nf* harmony
harmonieux, -euse [aʀmɔnjø, -øz] *adj* harmonious
harmonique [aʀmɔnik] *adj, nm ou f* harmonic
harmoniser [aʀmɔnize] *vt* to harmonize; **s'harmoniser** (*couleurs, teintes*) to go well together
harmonium [aʀmɔnjɔm] *nm* harmonium
'harnaché, e ['aʀnaʃe] *adj* (*fig*) rigged out
'harnachement ['aʀnaʃmɑ̃] *nm* (*habillement*) rig-out; (*équipement*) harness, equipment
'harnacher ['aʀnaʃe] *vt* to harness
'harnais ['aʀnɛ] *nm* harness
'haro ['aʀo] *nm*: **crier ~ sur qn/qch** to inveigh against sb/sth
'harpe ['aʀp(ə)] *nf* harp
'harpie ['aʀpi] *nf* harpy
'harpiste ['aʀpist(ə)] *nm/f* harpist
'harpon ['aʀpɔ̃] *nm* harpoon
'harponner ['aʀpɔne] *vt* to harpoon; (*fam*) to collar
'hasard ['azaʀ] *nm*: **le ~** chance, fate; **un ~** a coincidence; (*aubaine, chance*) a stroke of luck; **au ~** (*sans but*) aimlessly; (*à l'aveuglette*) at random, haphazardly; **par ~** by chance; **comme par ~** as if by chance; **à tout ~** on the off chance; (*en cas de besoin*) just in case
'hasarder ['azaʀde] *vt* (*mot*) to venture; (*fortune*) to risk; **se ~ à faire** to risk doing, venture to do
'hasardeux, -euse ['azaʀdø, -øz] *adj* hazardous, risky; (*hypothèse*) rash
'haschisch ['aʃiʃ] *nm* hashish
'hâte ['ɑt] *nf* haste; **à la ~** hurriedly, hastily; **en ~** posthaste, with all possible speed; **avoir ~ de** to be eager *ou* anxious to
'hâter ['ɑte] *vt* to hasten; **se 'hâter** to hurry; **se ~ de** to hurry *ou* hasten to
'hâtif, -ive ['ɑtif, -iv] *adj* (*travail*) hurried; (*décision*) hasty; (*légume*) early
'hâtivement ['ɑtivmɑ̃] *adv* hurriedly; hastily
'hauban ['obɑ̃] *nm* (*Navig*) shroud
'hausse ['os] *nf* rise, increase; (*de fusil*) backsight

adjuster; **à la** ~ upwards; **en** ~ rising

'hausser ['ose] *vt* to raise; ~ **les épaules** to shrug (one's shoulders); **se** ~ **sur la pointe des pieds** to stand (up) on tiptoe *ou* tippy-toe (US)

'haut, e ['o, 'ot] *adj* high; (*grand*) tall; (*son, voix*) high(-pitched) ▷ *adv* high ▷ *nm* top (part); **de 3 m de** ~, ~ **de 3 m** 3 m high, 3 m in height; **en** ~e **montagne** high up in the mountains; **en** ~ **lieu** in high places; **à** ~e **voix**, (**tout**) ~ aloud, out loud; **des** ~s **et des bas** ups and downs; **du** ~ **de** from the top of; **tomber de** ~ to fall from a height; (*fig*) to have one's hopes dashed; **dire qch bien** ~ to say sth plainly; **prendre qch de** (**très**) ~ to react haughtily to sth; **traiter qn de** ~ to treat sb with disdain; **de** ~ **en bas** from top to bottom; downwards; ~ **en couleur** (*chose*) highly coloured; (*personne*): **un personnage** ~ **en couleur** a colourful character; **plus** ~ higher up, further up; (*dans un texte*) above; (*parler*) louder; **en** ~ up above; at (*ou* to) the top; (*dans une maison*) upstairs; **en** ~ **de** at the top of; ~ **les mains!** hands up!, stick 'em up!; **la** ~e **couture/coiffure** haute couture/coiffure; ~ **débit** (*Inform*) broadband; ~e **fidélité** hi-fi, high fidelity; **la** ~e **finance** high finance; ~e **trahison** high treason

'hautain, e ['otɛ̃, -ɛn] *adj* (*personne, regard*) haughty

'hautbois ['obwa] *nm* oboe

'hautboïste ['oboist(ə)] *nm/f* oboist

'haut-de-forme ['odfɔrm(ə)] (*pl* **'hauts-de-forme**) *nm* top hat

'haute-contre ['otkɔ̃tr(ə)] (*pl* **'hautes-contre**) *nf* counter-tenor

'hautement ['otmã] *adv* (*ouvertement*) openly; (*supérieurement*): ~ **qualifié** highly qualified

'hauteur ['otœr] *nf* height; (*Géo*) height, hill; (*fig*) loftiness; haughtiness; **à** ~ **de** up to (the level of); **à** ~ **des yeux** at eye level; **à la** ~ **de** (*sur la même ligne*) level with; by; (*fig*) equal to; **à la** ~ (*fig*) up to it, equal to the task

'Haute-Volta ['otvolta] *nf*: **la** ~ Upper Volta

'haut-fond ['ofɔ̃] (*pl* **'hauts-fonds**) *nm* shallow

'haut-fourneau ['ofurno] (*pl* **'hauts-fourneaux**) *nm* blast *ou* smelting furnace

'haut-le-cœur ['olkœr] *nm inv* retch, heave

'haut-le-corps ['olkɔr] *nm inv* start, jump

'haut-parleur ['oparlœr] (*pl* **-s**) *nm* (loud)speaker

'hauturier, -ière ['otyrje, -jɛr] *adj* (*Navig*) deep-sea

'havanais, e ['avanɛ, -ɛz] *adj* of *ou* from Havana

'Havane ['avan] *nf*: **la** ~ Havana ▷ *nm*: **'havane** (*cigare*) Havana

'hâve ['av] *adj* gaunt

'havrais, e ['avrɛ, -ɛz] *adj* of *ou* from Le Havre

'havre ['avr(ə)] *nm* haven

'havresac ['avrəsak] *nm* haversack

Hawaï [awai] *n* Hawaii; **les îles** ~ the Hawaiian Islands

hawaïen, ne [awajɛ̃, -ɛn] *adj* Hawaiian ▷ *nm* (*Ling*) Hawaiian

'Haye ['ɛ] *n*: **la** ~ the Hague

'hayon ['ɛjɔ̃] *nm* tailgate

HCR *sigle m* (= *Haut-Commissariat des Nations unies pour les réfugiés*) UNHCR

hdb. *abr* (= *heures de bureau*) o.h. = **office hours**

'hé ['e] *excl* hey!

hebdo [ɛbdo] *nm* (*fam*) weekly

hebdomadaire [ɛbdɔmadɛr] *adj, nm* weekly

hébergement [ebɛrʒəmã] *nm* accommodation, lodging; taking in

héberger [ebɛrʒe] *vt* to accommodate, lodge; (*réfugiés*) to take in

hébergeur [ebɛrʒœr] *nm* (*Internet*) host

hébété, e [ebete] *adj* dazed

hébétude [ebetyd] *nf* stupor

hébraïque [ebraik] *adj* Hebrew, Hebraic

hébreu, x [ebrø] *adj m, nm* Hebrew

Hébrides [ebrid] *nf*: **les** ~ the Hebrides

HEC *sigle fpl* (= *École des hautes études commerciales*) *grande école for management and business studies*

hécatombe [ekatɔ̃b] *nf* slaughter

hectare [ɛktar] *nm* hectare, 10,000 square metres

hecto... [ɛkto] *préfixe* hecto...

hectolitre [ɛktɔlitr(ə)] *nm* hectolitre

hédoniste [edɔnist(ə)] *adj* hedonistic

hégémonie [eʒemɔni] *nf* hegemony

'hein ['ɛ̃] *excl* eh?; (*sollicitant l'approbation*): **tu m'approuves, ~?** so I did the right thing then?; **Paul est venu, ~?** Paul came, did he?; **que fais-tu, ~?** hey! what are you doing?

'hélas ['elas] *excl* alas! ▷ *adv* unfortunately

'héler ['ele] *vt* to hail

hélice [elis] *nf* propeller

hélicoïdal, e, -aux [elikɔidal, -o] *adj* helical; helicoid

hélicoptère [elikɔptɛr] *nm* helicopter

héliogravure [eljɔgravyr] *nf* heliogravure

héliomarin, e [eljɔmarɛ̃, -in] *adj*: **centre** ~ *centre offering sea and sun therapy*

héliotrope [eljɔtrɔp] *nm* (*Bot*) heliotrope

héliport [elipɔr] *nm* heliport

héliporté, e [elipɔrte] *adj* transported by helicopter

hélium [eljɔm] *nm* helium

hellénique [elenik] *adj* Hellenic

hellénisant, e [elenizã, -ãt], **helléniste** [elenist(ə)] *nm/f* hellenist

Helsinki [ɛlzinki] *n* Helsinki

helvète [ɛlvɛt] *adj* Helvetian ▷ *nm/f*: **Helvète** Helvetian

Helvétie [elvesi] *nf*: **la** ~ Helvetia

helvétique [ɛlvetik] *adj* Swiss

hématologie [ematɔlɔʒi] *nf* (*Méd*) haematology.

hématome [ematom] *nm* haematoma

hémicycle [emisikl(ə)] *nm* semicircle; (*Pol*): **l'**~ the benches (in French parliament)

hémiplégie [emipleʒi] *nf* paralysis of one side, hemiplegia

hémisphère [emisfɛr] *nf*: ~ **nord/sud** northern/southern hemisphere

hémisphérique [emisferik] *adj* hemispherical

hémoglobine [emɔglɔbin] *nf* haemoglobin (*Brit*), hemoglobin (*US*)

hémophile [emɔfil] *adj* haemophiliac (*Brit*), hemophiliac (*US*)

hémophilie [emɔfili] *nf* haemophilia (*Brit*), hemophilia (*US*)

hémorragie [emɔraʒi] *nf* bleeding *no pl*, haemorrhage (*Brit*), hemorrhage (*US*); ~ **cérébrale** cerebral haemorrhage; ~ **interne** internal bleeding *ou* haemorrhage

hémorroïdes [emɔrɔid] *nfpl* piles, haemorrhoids (*Brit*), hemorrhoids (*US*)

hémostatique [emɔstatik] *adj* haemostatic (*Brit*), hemostatic (*US*)

'henné ['ene] *nm* henna

'hennir ['enir] *vi* to neigh, whinny

'hennissement ['enismã] *nm* neighing, whinnying

'hep ['ɛp] *excl* hey!

hépatite [epatit] *nf* hepatitis, liver infection

héraldique [eraldik] *adj* heraldry

herbacé, e [ɛrbase] *adj* herbaceous

herbage [ɛrbaʒ] *nm* pasture

herbe [ɛrb(ə)] *nf* grass; (*Culin, Méd*) herb; **en ~** unripe; (*fig*) budding; **touffe/brin d'~** clump/blade of grass

herbeux, -euse [ɛrbø, -øz] *adj* grassy

herbicide [ɛrbisid] *nm* weed-killer

herbier [ɛrbje] *nm* herbarium

herbivore [ɛrbivɔr] *nm* herbivore

herboriser [ɛrbɔrize] *vi* to collect plants

herboriste [ɛrbɔrist(ə)] *nm/f* herbalist

herboristerie [ɛrbɔristri] *nf* (*magasin*) herbalist's shop; (*commerce*) herb trade

herculéen, ne [ɛrkyleɛ̃, -ɛn] *adj* (*fig*) herculean

'hère ['ɛr] *nm:* **pauvre ~** poor wretch

héréditaire [erediter] *adj* hereditary

hérédité [eredite] *nf* heredity

hérésie [erezi] *nf* heresy

hérétique [eretik] *nm/f* heretic

'hérissé, e ['erise] *adj* bristling; ~ **de** spiked with; (*fig*) bristling with

'hérisser ['erise] *vt:* ~ **qn** (*fig*) to ruffle sb; **se 'hérisser** *vi* to bristle, bristle up

'hérisson ['erisɔ̃] *nm* hedgehog

héritage [eritaʒ] *nm* inheritance; (*fig*) heritage; (*: legs*) legacy; **faire un (petit) ~** to come into (a little) money

hériter [erite] *vi:* ~ **de qch (de qn)** to inherit sth (from sb); ~ **de qn** to inherit sb's property

héritier, -ière [eritje, -jɛr] *nm/f* heir/heiress

hermaphrodite [ɛrmafrɔdit] *adj* (*Bot, Zool*) hermaphrodite

hermétique [ɛrmetik] *adj* (*à l'air*) airtight; (*à l'eau*) watertight; (*fig: écrivain, style*) abstruse; (*: visage*) impenetrable

hermétiquement [ɛrmetikmã] *adv* hermetically

hermine [ɛrmin] *nf* ermine

'hernie ['ɛrni] *nf* hernia

héroïne [erɔin] *nf* heroine; (*drogue*) heroin

héroïnomane [erɔinɔman] *nm/f* heroin addict

héroïque [erɔik] *adj* heroic

héroïquement [erɔikmã] *adv* heroically

héroïsme [erɔism(ə)] *nm* heroism

'héron ['erɔ̃] *nm* heron

'héros ['ero] *nm* hero

herpès [ɛrpɛs] *nm* herpes

'herse ['ɛrs(ə)] *nf* harrow; (*de château*) portcullis

hertz [ɛrts] *nm* (*Élec*) hertz

hertzien, ne [ɛrtsjɛ̃, -ɛn] *adj* (*Élec*) Hertzian

hésitant, e [ezitã, -ãt] *adj* hesitant

hésitation [ezitasjɔ̃] *nf* hesitation

hésiter [ezite] *vi:* ~ **(à faire)** to hesitate (to do); ~ **sur qch** to hesitate over sth

hétéro [etero] *adj inv* (*hétérosexuel(le)*) hetero

hétéroclite [eterɔklit] *adj* heterogeneous; (*objets*) sundry

hétérogène [eterɔʒɛn] *adj* heterogeneous

hétérosexuel, le [eterɔsɛkɥɛl] *adj* heterosexual

'hêtre ['ɛtr(ə)] *nm* beech

heure [œr] *nf* hour; (*Scol*) period; (*moment, moment fixé*) time; **c'est l'~** it's time; **pourriez-vous me donner l'~, s'il vous plaît?** could you tell me the time, please?; **quelle ~ est-il?** what time is it?; **2 ~s (du matin)** 2 o'clock (in the morning); **à la bonne ~!** (*parfois ironique*) splendid!; **être à l'~** to be on time; (*montre*) to be right; **le bus passe à l'~** the bus runs on the hour; **mettre à l'~** to set right; **100 km à l'~** ≈ 60 miles an *ou* per hour; **à toute ~** at any time; **24 ~s sur 24** round the clock, 24 hours a day; **à l'~ qu'il est** at this time (of day); (*fig*) now; **à l'~ actuelle** at the present time; **sur l'~** at once; **pour l'~** for the time being; **d'~ en ~** from one hour to the next; (*régulièrement*) hourly; **d'une ~ à l'autre** from hour to hour; **de bonne ~** early; **deux ~s de marche/travail** two hours' walking/work; **une ~ d'arrêt** an hour's break *ou* stop; ~ **d'été** summer time (*Brit*), daylight saving time (*US*); ~ **de pointe** rush hour; ~**s de bureau** office hours; ~**s supplémentaires** overtime *sg*

heureusement [œrøzmã] *adv* (*par bonheur*) fortunately, luckily; ~ **que ...** it's a good job that ..., fortunately ...

heureux, -euse [œrø, -øz] *adj* happy; (*chanceux*) lucky, fortunate; (*judicieux*) felicitous, fortunate; **être ~ de qch** to be pleased *ou* happy about sth; **être ~ de faire/que** to be pleased *ou* happy to do/that; **s'estimer ~ de qch/que** to consider o.s. fortunate with sth/that; **encore ~ que ...** just as well that ...

'heurt ['œr] *nm* (*choc*) collision; **'heurts** *nmpl* (*fig*) clashes

'heurté, e ['œrte] *adj* (*fig*) jerky, uneven; (*: couleurs*) clashing

'heurter ['œrte] *vt* (*mur*) to strike, hit; (*personne*) to collide with; (*fig*) to go against, upset; **se 'heurter** (*couleurs, tons*) to clash; **se ~ à** to collide with; (*fig*) to come up against; ~ **qn de front** to clash head-on with sb

'heurtoir ['œrtwar] *nm* door knocker

hévéa [evea] *nm* rubber tree

hexagonal, e, -aux [ɛgzagɔnal, -o] *adj*
hexagonal; (*français*) French (*see note at hexagone*)
hexagone [ɛgzagɔn] *nm* hexagon; (*la France*)
France (*because of its roughly hexagonal shape*)
HF *sigle f* (= *haute fréquence*) HF
hiatus [jatys] *nm* hiatus
hibernation [ibɛʀnɑsjɔ̃] *nf* hibernation
hiberner [ibɛʀne] *vi* to hibernate
hibiscus [ibiskys] *nm* hibiscus
'hibou, x ['ibu] *nm* owl
'hic ['ik] *nm* (*fam*) snag
'hideusement ['idøzmɑ̃] *adv* hideously
'hideux, -euse ['idø, -øz] *adj* hideous
hier [jɛʀ] *adv* yesterday; **~ matin/soir/midi**
yesterday morning/evening/at midday; **toute
la journée d'~** all day yesterday; **toute la
matinée d'~** all yesterday morning
'hiérarchie ['jeʀaʀʃi] *nf* hierarchy
'hiérarchique ['jeʀaʀʃik] *adj* hierarchic
'hiérarchiquement ['jeʀaʀʃikmɑ̃] *adv*
hierarchically
'hiérarchiser ['jeʀaʀʃize] *vt* to organize into a
hierarchy
'hiéroglyphe ['jeʀɔglif] *nm* hieroglyphic
'hiéroglyphique ['jeʀɔglifik] *adj* hieroglyphic
'hi-fi ['ifi] *nf inv* hi-fi
hilarant, e [ilaʀɑ̃, -ɑ̃t] *adj* hilarious
hilare [ilaʀ] *adj* mirthful
hilarité [ilaʀite] *nf* hilarity, mirth
Himalaya [imalaja] *nm*: **l'~** the Himalayas *pl*
himalayen, ne [imalajɛ̃, -ɛn] *adj* Himalayan
hindou, e [ɛ̃du] *adj, nm/f* Hindu; (*Indien*) Indian
hindouisme [ɛ̃duism(ə)] *nm* Hinduism
Hindoustan [ɛ̃dustɑ̃] *nm*: **l'~** Hindustan
'hippie ['ipi] *nm/f* hippy
hippique [ipik] *adj* equestrian, horse *cpd*
hippisme [ipism(ə)] *nm* (horse-)riding
hippocampe [ipɔkɑ̃p] *nm* sea horse
hippodrome [ipɔdʀom] *nm* racecourse
hippophagique [ipɔfaʒik] *adj*: **boucherie ~**
horse butcher's
hippopotame [ipɔpɔtam] *nm* hippopotamus
hirondelle [iʀɔ̃dɛl] *nf* swallow
hirsute [iʀsyt] *adj* (*personne*) hairy; (*barbe*)
shaggy; (*tête*) tousled
hispanique [ispanik] *adj* Hispanic
hispanisant, e [ispanizɑ̃, -ɑ̃t], **hispaniste**
[ispanist(ə)] *nm/f* Hispanist
hispano-américain, e [ispanɔameʀikɛ̃, -ɛn] *adj*
Spanish-American
hispano-arabe [ispanɔaʀab] *adj* Hispano-
Moresque
'hisser ['ise] *vt* to hoist, haul up; **se 'hisser sur**
to haul o.s. up onto
histoire [istwaʀ] *nf* (*science, événements*) history;
(*anecdote, récit, mensonge*) story; (*affaire*) business
no pl; (*chichis: gén pl*) fuss *no pl*; **histoires** *nfpl*
(*ennuis*) trouble *sg*; **l'~ de France** French history,
the history of France; **l'~ sainte** biblical
history; **une ~ de** (*fig*) a question of
histologie [istɔlɔʒi] *nf* histology
historien, ne [istɔʀjɛ̃, -ɛn] *nm/f* historian

historique [istɔʀik] *adj* historical; (*important*)
historic ▷ *nm* (*exposé, récit*): **faire l'~ de** to give
the background to
historiquement [istɔʀikmɑ̃] *adv* historically
'hit-parade ['itpaʀad] *nm*: **le ~** the charts
HIV *sigle m* (= *human immunodeficiency virus*) HIV
hiver [ivɛʀ] *nm* winter; **en ~** in winter
hivernal, e, -aux [ivɛʀnal, -o] *adj* (*de l'hiver*)
winter *cpd*; (*comme en hiver*) wintry
hivernant, e [ivɛʀnɑ̃, -ɑ̃t] *nm/f* winter holiday-
maker
hiverner [ivɛʀne] *vi* to winter
HLM *sigle m ou f* (= *habitations à loyer modéré*) low-
rent, state-owned housing; **un(e) ~** ≈ a council flat
(*ou* house) (*Brit*), ≈ a public housing unit (*US*)
Hme *abr* (= *homme*) M
HO *abr* (= *hors œuvre*) labour not included (*on
invoices*)
'hobby ['ɔbi] *nm* hobby
'hochement ['ɔʃmɑ̃] *nm*: **~ de tête** nod; shake of
the head
'hocher ['ɔʃe] *vt*: **~ la tête** to nod; (*signe négatif ou
dubitatif*) to shake one's head
'hochet ['ɔʃɛ] *nm* rattle
'hockey ['ɔkɛ] *nm*: **~ (sur glace/gazon)** (ice/
field) hockey
'hockeyeur, -euse ['ɔkɛjœʀ, -øz] *nm/f* hockey
player
'holà ['ɔla] *nm*: **mettre le ~ à qch** to put a stop to
sth
'holding ['ɔldiŋ] *nm* holding company
'hold-up ['ɔldœp] *nm inv* hold-up
'hollandais, e ['ɔlɑ̃dɛ, -ɛz] *adj* Dutch ▷ *nm* (*Ling*)
Dutch ▷ *nm/f*: **'Hollandais, e** Dutchman/
woman; **les 'Hollandais** the Dutch
'Hollande ['ɔlɑ̃d] *nf*: **la ~** Holland ▷ *nm*:
'hollande (*fromage*) Dutch cheese
holocauste [ɔlɔkost(ə)] *nm* holocaust
hologramme [ɔlɔgʀam] *nm* hologram
'homard ['ɔmaʀ] *nm* lobster
homéopathe [ɔmeɔpat] *n* homoeopath
homéopathie [ɔmeɔpati] *nf* homoeopathy
homéopathique [ɔmeɔpatik] *adj*
homoeopathic
homérique [ɔmeʀik] *adj* Homeric
homicide [ɔmisid] *nm* murder ▷ *nm/f*
murderer/eress; **~ involontaire** manslaughter
hommage [ɔmaʒ] *nm* tribute; **hommages** *nmpl*:
présenter ses ~s to pay one's respects; **rendre
~ à** to pay tribute *ou* homage to; **en ~ de** as a
token of; **faire ~ de qch à qn** to present sb with
sth
homme [ɔm] *nm* man; (*espèce humaine*): **l'~** man,
mankind; **~ d'affaires** businessman; **~ des
cavernes** caveman; **~ d'Église** churchman,
clergyman; **~ d'État** statesman; **~ de loi**
lawyer; **~ de main** hired man; **~ de paille**
stooge; **~ politique** politician; **l'~ de la rue** the
man in the street; **~ à tout faire** odd-job man
homme-grenouille [ɔmgʀənuj] (*pl* **hommes-
grenouilles**) *nm* frogman
homme-orchestre [ɔmɔʀkɛstʀ(ə)] (*pl* **hommes-**

orchestres) *nm* one-man band

homme-sandwich [ɔmsɑ̃dwitʃ] (*pl* **hommes-sandwichs**) *nm* sandwich (board) man

homo [ɔmo] *adj, nm/f* = **homosexuel**

homogène [ɔmɔʒɛn] *adj* homogeneous

homogénéisé, e [ɔmɔʒeneize] *adj*: **lait ~** homogenized milk

homogénéité [ɔmɔʒeneite] *nf* homogeneity

homologation [ɔmɔlɔgɑsjɔ̃] *nf* ratification; official recognition

homologue [ɔmɔlɔg] *nm/f* counterpart, opposite number

homologué, e [ɔmɔlɔge] *adj* (*Sport*) officially recognized, ratified; (*tarif*) authorized

homologuer [ɔmɔlɔge] *vt* (*Jur*) to ratify; (*Sport*) to recognize officially, ratify

homonyme [ɔmɔnim] *nm* (*Ling*) homonym; (*d'une personne*) namesake

homosexualité [ɔmɔsɛksɥalite] *nf* homosexuality

homosexuel, le [ɔmɔsɛksɥɛl] *adj* homosexual

'Honduras ['ɔ̃dyRɑs] *nm*: **le ~** Honduras

'hondurien, ne ['ɔ̃dyRjɛ̃, -ɛn] *adj* Honduran

'Hong-Kong ['ɔ̃gkɔ̃g] *n* Hong Kong

'hongre ['ɔ̃gR(ə)] *adj* (*cheval*) gelded ▷ *nm* gelding

'Hongrie ['ɔ̃gRi] *nf*: **la ~** Hungary

'hongrois, e ['ɔ̃gRwa, -waz] *adj* Hungarian ▷ *nm* (*Ling*) Hungarian ▷ *nm/f*: **'Hongrois, e** Hungarian

honnête [ɔnɛt] *adj* (*intègre*) honest; (*juste, satisfaisant*) fair

honnêtement [ɔnɛtmɑ̃] *adv* honestly

honnêteté [ɔnɛtte] *nf* honesty

honneur [ɔnœR] *nm* honour; (*mérite*): **l'~ lui revient** the credit is his; **à qui ai-je l'~?** to whom have I the pleasure of speaking?; **"j'ai l'~ de ..."** "I have the honour of ..."; **en l'~ de** (*personne*) in honour of; (*événement*) on the occasion of; **faire ~ à** (*engagements*) to honour; (*famille, professeur*) to be a credit to; (*fig: repas etc*) to do justice to; **être à l'~** to be in the place of honour; **être en ~** to be in favour; **membre d'~** honorary member; **table d'~** top table

Honolulu [ɔnɔlyly] *n* Honolulu

honorable [ɔnɔRabl(ə)] *adj* worthy, honourable; (*suffisant*) decent

honorablement [ɔnɔRabləmɑ̃] *adv* honourably; decently

honoraire [ɔnɔRɛR] *adj* honorary; **honoraires** *nmpl* fees; **professeur ~** professor emeritus

honorer [ɔnɔRe] *vt* to honour; (*estimer*) to hold in high regard; (*faire honneur à*) to do credit to; **~ qn de** to honour sb with; **s'honorer de** to pride o.s. upon

honorifique [ɔnɔRifik] *adj* honorary

'honte ['ɔ̃t] *nf* shame; **avoir ~ de** to be ashamed of; **faire ~ à qn** to make sb (feel) ashamed

'honteusement ['ɔ̃tøzmɑ̃] *adv* ashamedly; shamefully

'honteux, -euse ['ɔ̃tø, -øz] *adj* ashamed; (*conduite, acte*) shameful, disgraceful

hôpital, -aux [ɔpital, -o] *nm* hospital

'hoquet ['ɔkɛ] *nm* hiccough; **avoir le ~** to have (the) hiccoughs

'hoqueter ['ɔkte] *vi* to hiccough

horaire [ɔRɛR] *adj* hourly ▷ *nm* timetable, schedule; **horaires** *nmpl* (*heures de travail*) hours; **~ flexible** *ou* **mobile** *ou* **à la carte** *ou* **souple** flex(i)time

'horde ['ɔRd(ə)] *nf* horde

'horions ['ɔRjɔ̃] *nmpl* blows

horizon [ɔRizɔ̃] *nm* horizon; (*paysage*) landscape, view; **sur l'~** on the skyline *ou* horizon

horizontal, e, -aux [ɔRizɔ̃tal, -o] *adj* horizontal ▷ *nf*: **à l'~e** on the horizontal

horizontalement [ɔRizɔ̃talmɑ̃] *adv* horizontally

horloge [ɔRlɔʒ] *nf* clock; **l'~ parlante** the speaking clock; **~ normande** grandfather clock; **~ physiologique** biological clock

horloger, -ère [ɔRlɔʒe, -ɛR] *nm/f* watchmaker; clockmaker

horlogerie [ɔRlɔʒRi] *nf* watchmaking; watchmaker's (shop); clockmaker's (shop); **pièces d'~** watch parts *ou* components

'hormis ['ɔRmi] *prép* save

hormonal, e, -aux [ɔRmɔnal, -o] *adj* hormonal

hormone [ɔRmɔn] *nf* hormone

horodaté, e [ɔRɔdate] *adj* (*ticket*) time- and date-stamped; (*stationnement*) pay and display

horodateur, -trice [ɔRɔdatœR, -tRis] *adj* (*appareil*) for stamping the time and date ▷ *nm/f* (*parking*) ticket machine

horoscope [ɔRɔskɔp] *nm* horoscope

horreur [ɔRœR] *nf* horror; **avoir ~ de** to loathe, detest; **quelle ~!** how awful!; **cela me fait ~** I find that awful

horrible [ɔRibl(ə)] *adj* horrible

horriblement [ɔRibləmɑ̃] *adv* horribly

horrifiant, e [ɔRifjɑ̃, -ɑ̃t] *adj* horrifying

horrifier [ɔRifje] *vt* to horrify

horrifique [ɔRifik] *adj* horrific

horripilant, e [ɔRipilɑ̃, -ɑ̃t] *adj* exasperating

horripiler [ɔRipile] *vt* to exasperate

'hors ['ɔR] *prép* except (for); **~ de** out of; **~ ligne** (*Inform*) off line; **~ pair** outstanding; **~ de propos** inopportune; **~ série** (*sur mesure*) made-to-order; (*exceptionnel*) exceptional; **~ service (HS), ~ d'usage** out of service; **être ~ de soi** to be beside o.s.

'hors-bord ['ɔRbɔR] *nm inv* outboard motor; (*canot*) speedboat (with outboard motor)

'hors-concours ['ɔRkɔ̃kuR] *adj inv* ineligible to compete; (*fig*) in a class of one's own

'hors-d'œuvre ['ɔRdœvR(ə)] *nm inv* hors d'œuvre

'hors-jeu ['ɔRʒø] *nm inv* being offside *no pl*

'hors-la-loi ['ɔRlalwa] *nm inv* outlaw

'hors-piste, 'hors-pistes ['ɔRpist] *nm inv* (*Ski*) cross-country

hors-taxe [ɔRtaks] *adj* (*sur une facture, prix*) excluding VAT; (*boutique, marchandises*) duty-free

'hors-texte ['ɔRtɛkst(ə)] *nm inv* plate

hortensia [ɔʀtɑ̃sja] nm hydrangea
horticole [ɔʀtikɔl] adj horticultural
horticulteur, -trice [ɔʀtikyltœʀ, -tʀis] nm/f horticulturalist (Brit), horticulturist (US)
horticulture [ɔʀtikyltyʀ] nf horticulture
hospice [ɔspis] nm (de vieillards) home; (asile) hospice
hospitalier, -ière [ɔspitalje, -jɛʀ] adj (accueillant) hospitable; (Méd: service, centre) hospital cpd
hospitalisation [ɔspitalizɑsjɔ̃] nf hospitalization
hospitaliser [ɔspitalize] vt to take (ou send) to hospital, hospitalize
hospitalité [ɔspitalite] nf hospitality
hospitalo-universitaire [ɔspitalɔyniveʀsitɛʀ] adj: **centre ~ (CHU)** ≈ (teaching) hospital
hostie [ɔsti] nf host (Rel)
hostile [ɔstil] adj hostile
hostilité [ɔstilite] nf hostility; **hostilités** nfpl hostilities
hôte [ot] nm (maître de maison) host; (client) patron; (fig) inhabitant, occupant ▷ nm/f (invité) guest; ~ **payant** paying guest
hôtel [otɛl] nm hotel; **aller à l'~** to stay in a hotel; ~ **(particulier)** (private) mansion; ~ **de ville** town hall
hôtelier, -ière [otəlje, -jɛʀ] adj hotel cpd ▷ nm/f hotelier, hotel-keeper
hôtellerie [otɛlʀi] nf (profession) hotel business; (auberge) inn
hôtesse [otɛs] nf hostess; ~ **de l'air** flight attendant; ~ **(d'accueil)** receptionist
'hotte ['ɔt] nf (panier) basket (carried on the back); (de cheminée) hood; ~ **aspirante** cooker hood
'houblon ['ublɔ̃] nm (Bot) hop; (pour la bière) hops pl
'houe ['u] nf hoe
'houille ['uj] nf coal; ~ **blanche** hydroelectric power
'houiller, -ère ['uje, -ɛʀ] adj coal cpd; (terrain) coal-bearing ▷ nf coal mine
'houle ['ul] nf swell
'houlette ['ulɛt] nf: **sous la ~ de** under the guidance of
'houleux, -euse ['ulø, -øz] adj heavy, swelling; (fig) stormy, turbulent
'houppe ['up], **'houppette** ['upɛt] nf powder puff; (cheveux) tuft
'hourra ['uʀa] nm cheer ▷ excl hurrah!
'houspiller ['uspije] vt to scold
'housse ['us] nf cover; (pour protéger provisoirement) dust cover; (pour recouvrir à neuf) loose ou stretch cover; ~ **(penderie)** hanging wardrobe
'houx ['u] nm holly
hovercraft [ovœʀkʀaft] nm hovercraft
HS abr = **hors service**
HT abr = **hors taxe**
'hublot ['yblo] nm porthole
'huche ['yʃ] nf: ~ **à pain** bread bin
'huées ['ɥe] nfpl boos
'huer ['ɥe] vt to boo; (hibou, chouette) to hoot
huile [ɥil] nf oil; (Art) oil painting; (fam) bigwig;

mer d'~ (très calme) glassy sea, sea of glass; **faire tache d'~** (fig) to spread; ~ **d'arachide** groundnut oil; ~ **essentielle** essential oil; ~ **de foie de morue** cod-liver oil; ~ **de ricin** castor oil; ~ **solaire** suntan oil; ~ **de table** salad oil
huiler [ɥile] vt to oil
huilerie [ɥilʀi] nf (usine) oil-works
huileux, -euse [ɥilø, -øz] adj oily
huilier [ɥilje] nm (oil and vinegar) cruet
huis [ɥi] nm: **à - clos** in camera
huissier [ɥisje] nm usher; (Jur) ≈ bailiff
'huit ['ɥi(t)] num eight; **samedi en ~** a week on Saturday; **dans ~ jours** in a week('s time)
'huitaine ['ɥitɛn] nf: **une ~ de** about eight, eight or so; **une ~ de jours** a week or so
'huitante ['ɥitɑ̃t] num (Suisse) eighty
'huitième ['ɥitjɛm] num eighth
huître [ɥitʀ(ə)] nf oyster
'hululement ['ylylmɑ̃] nm hooting
'hululer ['ylyle] vi to hoot
humain, e [ymɛ̃, -ɛn] adj human; (compatissant) humane ▷ nm human (being)
humainement [ymɛnmɑ̃] adv humanly; humanely
humanisation [ymanizɑsjɑ̃] nf humanization
humaniser [ymanize] vt to humanize
humaniste [ymanist(ə)] nm/f (Ling) classicist; humanist
humanitaire [ymanitɛʀ] adj humanitarian
humanitarisme [ymanitaʀism(ə)] nm humanitarianism
humanité [ymanite] nf humanity
humanoïde [ymanɔid] nm/f humanoid
humble [œ̃bl(ə)] adj humble
humblement [œ̃bləmɑ̃] adv humbly
humecter [ymɛkte] vt to dampen; **s'~ les lèvres** to moisten one's lips
'humer ['yme] vt to inhale; (pour sentir) to smell
humérus [ymeʀys] nm (Anat) humerus
humeur [ymœʀ] nf mood; (tempérament) temper; (irritation) bad temper; **de bonne/mauvaise ~** in a good/bad mood; **être d'~ à faire qch** to be in the mood for doing sth
humide [ymid] adj (linge) damp; (main, yeux) moist; (climat, chaleur) humid; (saison, route) wet
humidificateur [ymidifikatœʀ] nm humidifier
humidifier [ymidifje] vt to humidify
humidité [ymidite] nf humidity; dampness; **traces d'~** traces of moisture ou damp
humiliant, e [ymiljɑ̃, -ɑ̃t] adj humiliating
humiliation [ymiljɑsjɔ̃] nf humiliation
humilier [ymilje] vt to humiliate; **s'~ devant qn** to humble o.s. before sb
humilité [ymilite] nf humility
humoriste [ymɔʀist(ə)] nm/f humorist
humoristique [ymɔʀistik] adj humorous; humoristic
humour [ymuʀ] nm humour; **avoir de l'~** to have a sense of humour; ~ **noir** sick humour
humus [ymys] nm humus
'huppé, e ['ype] adj crested; (fam) posh
'hurlement ['yʀləmɑ̃] nm howling no pl, howl;

yelling *no pl*, yell

'**hurler** ['yʀle] *vi* to howl, yell; (*fig*: *vent*) to howl; (: *couleurs etc*) to clash; ~ **à la mort** (*chien*) to bay at the moon

hurluberlu [yʀlybɛʀly] *nm* (*péj*) crank ▷ *adj* cranky

'**hutte** ['yt] *nf* hut

hybride [ibʀid] *adj* hybrid

hydratant, e [idʀatã, -ãt] *adj* (*crème*) moisturizing

hydrate [idʀat] *nm*: ~**s de carbone** carbohydrates

hydrater [idʀate] *vt* to hydrate

hydraulique [idʀolik] *adj* hydraulic

hydravion [idʀavjõ] *nm* seaplane, hydroplane

hydro... [idʀo] *préfixe* hydro...

hydrocarbure [idʀokaʀbyʀ] *nm* hydrocarbon

hydrocution [idʀokysjõ] *nf* immersion syncope

hydro-électrique [idʀoelɛktʀik] *adj* hydroelectric

hydrogène [idʀoʒɛn] *nm* hydrogen

hydroglisseur [idʀoglisœʀ] *nm* hydroplane

hydrographie [idʀogʀafi] *nf* (*fleuves*) hydrography

hydrophile [idʀofil] *adj voir* **coton**

hyène [jɛn] *nf* hyena

hygiène [iʒjɛn] *nf* hygiene; ~ **intime** personal hygiene

hygiénique [iʒenik] *adj* hygienic

hymne [imn(ə)] *nm* hymn; ~ **national** national anthem

hyper... [ipɛʀ] *préfixe* hyper...

hyperlien [ipɛʀljẽ] *nm* (*Inform*) hyperlink

hypermarché [ipɛʀmaʀʃe] *nm* hypermarket

hypermétrope [ipɛʀmetʀop] *adj* long-sighted

hypernerveux, -euse [ipɛʀnɛʀvø, -øz] *adj* highly-strung

hypersensible [ipɛʀsãsibl(ə)] *adj*

hypersensitive

hypertendu, e [ipɛʀtãdy] *adj* having high blood pressure, hypertensive

hypertension [ipɛʀtãsjõ] *nf* high blood pressure, hypertension

hypertexte [ipɛʀtɛkst] *nm* (*Inform*) hypertext

hypertrophié, e [ipɛʀtʀofje] *adj* hypertrophic

hypnose [ipnoz] *nf* hypnosis

hypnotique [ipnotik] *adj* hypnotic

hypnotiser [ipnotize] *vt* to hypnotize

hypnotiseur [ipnotizœʀ] *nm* hypnotist

hypnotisme [ipnotism(ə)] *nm* hypnotism

hypocondriaque [ipokõdʀijak] *adj* hypochondriac

hypocrisie [ipokʀizi] *nf* hypocrisy

hypocrite [ipokʀit] *adj* hypocritical ▷ *nm/f* hypocrite

hypocritement [ipokʀitmã] *adv* hypocritically

hypotendu, e [ipotãdy] *adj* having low blood pressure, hypotensive

hypotension [ipotãsjõ] *nf* low blood pressure, hypotension

hypoténuse [ipotenyz] *nf* hypotenuse

hypothécaire [ipotekɛʀ] *adj* mortgage; **garantie/prêt** ~ mortgage security/loan

hypothèque [ipotɛk] *nf* mortgage

hypothéquer [ipoteke] *vt* to mortgage

hypothermie [ipotɛʀmi] *nf* hypothermia

hypothèse [ipotɛz] *nf* hypothesis; **dans l'**~ **où** assuming that

hypothétique [ipotetik] *adj* hypothetical

hypothétiquement [ipotetikmã] *adv* hypothetically

hystérectomie [isteʀɛktomi] *nf* hysterectomy

hystérie [isteʀi] *nf* hysteria; ~ **collective** mass hysteria

hystérique [isteʀik] *adj* hysterical

Hz *abr* (= *Hertz*) Hz

I i

I, i [i] *nm inv* I, i; **I comme Irma** I for Isaac (*Brit*)
ou Item (*US*)

IAC *sigle f* (= *insémination artificielle entre conjoints*)
AIH

IAD *sigle f* (= *insémination artificielle par donneur
extérieur*) AID

ibère [ibɛʀ] *adj* Iberian ▷ *nm/f*: **Ibère** Iberian

ibérique [ibeʀik] *adj*: **la péninsule ~** the Iberian
peninsula

ibid. [ibid] *abr* (= *ibidem*) ibid., ib.

iceberg [isbɛʀg] *nm* iceberg

ici [isi] *adv* here; **jusqu'~** as far as this; (*temporel*)
until now; **d'~ là** by then; (*en attendant*) in the
meantime; **d'~ peu** before long

icône [ikon] *nf* (*aussi Inform*) icon

iconoclaste [ikɔnɔklast(ə)] *nm/f* iconoclast

iconographie [ikɔnɔgʀafi] *nf* iconography;
(*illustrations*) (collection of) illustrations

id. [id] *abr* (= *idem*) id.

idéal, e, -aux [ideal, -o] *adj* ideal ▷ *nm* ideal;
(*système de valeurs*) ideals *pl*

idéalement [idealmɑ̃] *adv* ideally

idéalisation [idealizasjɔ̃] *nf* idealization

idéaliser [idealize] *vt* to idealize

idéalisme [idealism(ə)] *nm* idealism

idéaliste [idealist(ə)] *adj* idealistic ▷ *nm/f*
idealist

idée [ide] *nf* idea; (*illusion*): **se faire des ~s** to
imagine things, get ideas into one's head;
avoir dans l'~ que to have an idea that; **mon ~,
c'est que ...** I suggest that ..., I think that ...; **à
l'~ de/que** at the idea of/that, at the thought of/
that; **je n'ai pas la moindre ~** I haven't the
faintest idea; **avoir ~ que** to have an idea that;
avoir des ~s larges/étroites to be broad-/
narrow-minded; **venir à l'~ de qn** to occur to
sb; **en voilà des ~s!** the very idea!; **~ fixe** idée
fixe, obsession; **~s noires** black *ou* dark
thoughts; **~s reçues** accepted ideas *ou* wisdom

identifiable [idɑ̃tifjabl(ə)] *adj* identifiable

identifiant [idɑ̃tifjɑ̃] *nm* (*Inform*) login

identification [idɑ̃tifikasjɔ̃] *nf* identification

identifier [idɑ̃tifje] *vt* to identify; **~ qch/qn à** to
identify sth/sb with; **s'~ avec** *ou* **à qn/qch** (*héros
etc*) to identify with sb/sth

identique [idɑ̃tik] *adj*: **~ (à)** identical (to)

identité [idɑ̃tite] *nf* identity; **~ judiciaire**
(*Police*) ≈ Criminal Records Office

idéogramme [ideɔgʀam] *nm* ideogram

idéologie [ideɔlɔʒi] *nf* ideology

idéologique [ideɔlɔʒik] *adj* ideological

idiomatique [idjɔmatik] *adj*: **expression ~**
idiom, idiomatic expression

idiome [idjom] *nm* (*Ling*) idiom

idiot, e [idjo, idjɔt] *adj* idiotic ▷ *nm/f* idiot

idiotie [idjɔsi] *nf* idiocy; (*propos*) idiotic remark

idiotisme [idjɔtism(ə)] *nm* idiom, idiomatic
phrase

idoine [idwan] *adj* fitting

idolâtrer [idolɑtʀe] *vt* to idolize

idolâtrie [idolɑtʀi] *nf* idolatry

idole [idɔl] *nf* idol

idylle [idil] *nf* idyll

idyllique [idilik] *adj* idyllic

if [if] *nm* yew

IFOP [ifɔp] *sigle m* (= *Institut français d'opinion
publique*) French market research institute

IGH *sigle m* = **immeuble de grande hauteur**

igloo [iglu] *nm* igloo

IGN *sigle m* = **Institut géographique national**

ignare [iɲaʀ] *adj* ignorant

ignifuge [iɲifyʒ] *adj* fireproofing ▷ *nm*
fireproofing (substance)

ignifuger [iɲifyʒe] *vt* to fireproof

ignoble [iɲɔbl(ə)] *adj* vile

ignominie [iɲɔmini] *nf* ignominy; (*acte*)
ignominious *ou* base act

ignominieux, -euse [iɲɔminjø, øz] *adj*
ignominious

ignorance [iɲɔʀɑ̃s] *nf* ignorance; **dans l'~ de** in
ignorance of, ignorant of

ignorant, e [iɲɔʀɑ̃, -ɑ̃t] *adj* ignorant ▷ *nm/f*:
faire l'~ to pretend one doesn't know; **~ de**
ignorant of, not aware of; **~ en** ignorant of,
knowing nothing of

ignoré, e [iɲɔʀe] *adj* unknown

ignorer [iɲɔʀe] *vt* (*ne pas connaître*) not to know,
be unaware *ou* ignorant of; (*être sans expérience de*:
plaisir, guerre etc) not to know about, have no
experience of; (*bouder: personne*) to ignore;
j'ignore comment/si I do not know how/if; **~
que** to be unaware that, not to know that; **je**

n'ignore pas que ... I'm not forgetting that ..., I'm not unaware that ...; **je l'ignore** I don't know

IGPN sigle f (= Inspection générale de la police nationale) police disciplinary body

IGS sigle f (= Inspection générale des services) police disciplinary body for Paris

iguane [igwan] nm iguana

il [il] pron he; (animal, chose, en tournure impersonnelle) it; NB: en anglais les navires et les pays sont en général assimilés aux femelles, et les bébés aux choses, si le sexe n'est pas spécifié; **ils** they; **il neige** it's snowing; voir aussi **avoir**

île [il] nf island; **les Î~s** the West Indies; **l'~ de Beauté** Corsica; **l'~ Maurice** Mauritius; **les ~s anglo-normandes** the Channel Islands; **les ~s Britanniques** the British Isles; **les ~s Cocos** ou **Keeling** the Cocos ou Keeling Islands; **les ~s Cook** the Cook Islands; **les ~s Scilly** the Scilly Isles, the Scillies; **les ~s Shetland** the Shetland Islands, Shetland; **les ~s Sorlingues**; = **les îles Scilly**; **les ~s Vierges** the Virgin Islands

iliaque [iljak] adj (Anat): **os/artère ~** iliac bone/ artery

illégal, e, -aux [ilegal, -o] adj illegal, unlawful (Admin)

illégalement [ilegalmā] adv illegally

illégalité [ilegalite] nf illegality; unlawfulness; **être dans l'~** to be outside the law

illégitime [ileʒitim] adj illegitimate; (optimisme, sévérité) unjustified, unwarranted

illégitimement [ileʒitimmā] adv illegitimately

illégitimité [ileʒitimite] nf illegitimacy; **gouverner dans l'~** to rule illegally

illettré, e [iletRe] adj, nm/f illiterate

illicite [ilisit] adj illicit

illicitement [ilisitmā] adv illicitly

illico [iliko] adv (fam) pronto

illimité, e [ilimite] adj (immense) boundless, unlimited; (congé, durée) indefinite, unlimited

illisible [ilizibl(ə)] adj illegible; (roman) unreadable

illisiblement [iliziblǝmā] adv illegibly

illogique [ilɔʒik] adj illogical

illogisme [ilɔʒism(ə)] nm illogicality

illumination [ilyminɑsjɔ̃] nf illumination, floodlighting; (inspiration) flash of inspiration; **illuminations** nfpl illuminations, lights

illuminé, e [ilymine] adj lit up; illuminated, floodlit ▷ nm/f (fig: péj) crank

illuminer [ilymine] vt to light up; (monument, rue: pour une fête) to illuminate, floodlight; **s'illuminer** vi to light up

illusion [ilyzjɔ̃] nf illusion; **se faire des ~s** to delude o.s.; **faire ~** to delude ou fool people; **~ d'optique** optical illusion

illusionner [ilyzjɔne] vt to delude; **s'~** (sur qn/ qch) to delude o.s. (about sb/sth)

illusionnisme [ilyzjɔnism(ə)] nm conjuring

illusionniste [ilyzjɔnist(ə)] nm/f conjuror

illusoire [ilyzwaR] adj illusory, illusive

illustrateur [ilystRatœR] nm illustrator

illustratif, -ive [ilystRatif, -iv] adj illustrative

illustration [ilystRɑsjɔ̃] nf illustration; (d'un ouvrage: photos) illustrations pl

illustre [ilystR(ə)] adj illustrious, renowned

illustré, e [ilystRe] adj illustrated ▷ nm illustrated magazine; (pour enfants) comic

illustrer [ilystRe] vt to illustrate; **s'illustrer** to become famous, win fame

îlot [ilo] nm small island, islet; (de maisons) block; (petite zone): **un ~ de verdure** an island of greenery, a patch of green

ils [il] pron voir **il**

image [imaʒ] nf (gén) picture; (comparaison, ressemblance, Optique) image; **~ de** picture ou image of; **~ d'Épinal** (social) stereotype; **~ de marque** brand image; (d'une personne) (public) image; (d'une entreprise) corporate image; **~ pieuse** holy picture

imagé, e [imaʒe] adj full of imagery

imaginable [imaʒinabl(ə)] adj imaginable; **difficilement ~** hard to imagine

imaginaire [imaʒinɛR] adj imaginary

imaginatif, -ive [imaʒinatif, -iv] adj imaginative

imagination [imaʒinɑsjɔ̃] nf imagination; (chimère) fancy, imagining; **avoir de l'~** to be imaginative, have a good imagination

imaginer [imaʒine] vt to imagine; (croire): **qu'allez-vous ~ là?** what on earth are you thinking of?; (inventer: expédient, mesure) to devise, think up; **s'imaginer** vt (se figurer: scène etc) to imagine, picture; **s'~ à 60 ans** to picture ou imagine o.s. at 60; **s'~ que** to imagine that; **s'~ pouvoir faire qch** to think one can do sth; **j'imagine qu'il a voulu plaisanter** I suppose he was joking; **~ de faire** (se mettre dans l'idée de) to dream up the idea of doing

imbattable [ɛ̃batabl(ə)] adj unbeatable

imbécile [ɛ̃besil] adj idiotic ▷ nm/f idiot; (Méd) imbecile

imbécillité [ɛ̃besilite] nf idiocy; imbecility; idiotic action (ou remark etc)

imberbe [ɛ̃bɛRb(ə)] adj beardless

imbiber [ɛ̃bibe] vt: **~ qch de** to moisten ou wet sth with; **s'imbiber de** to become saturated with; **imbibé(e) d'eau** (chaussures, étoffe) saturated; (terre) waterlogged

imbriqué, e [ɛ̃bRike] adj overlapping

imbriquer [ɛ̃bRike]: **s'imbriquer** vi to overlap (each other); (fig) to become interlinked ou interwoven

imbroglio [ɛ̃bRɔljo] nm imbroglio

imbu, e [ɛ̃by] adj: **~ de** full of; **~ de soi-même/sa supériorité** full of oneself/one's superiority

imbuvable [ɛ̃byvabl(ə)] adj undrinkable

imitable [imitabl(ə)] adj imitable; **facilement ~** easily imitated

imitateur, -trice [imitatœR, -tRis] nm/f (gén) imitator; (Music-Hall: d'une personnalité) impersonator

imitation [imitɑsjɔ̃] nf imitation; impersonation; **sac ~ cuir** bag in imitation ou simulated leather; **à l'~ de** in imitation of

imiter [imite] *vt* to imitate; (*personne*) to imitate, impersonate; (*contrefaire: signature, document*) to forge, copy; (*ressembler à*) to look like; **il se leva et je l'imitai** he got up and I did likewise

imm. *abr* = **immeuble**

immaculé, e [imakyle] *adj* spotless, immaculate; **l'I~e Conception** (*Rel*) the Immaculate Conception

immanent, e [imanã, -ãt] *adj* immanent

immangeable [ɛ̃mãʒabl(ə)] *adj* inedible, uneatable

immanquable [ɛ̃mãkabl(ə)] *adj* (*cible*) impossible to miss; (*fatal, inévitable*) bound to happen, inevitable

immanquablement [ɛ̃mãkabləmã] *adv* inevitably

immatériel, le [imateʀjɛl] *adj* ethereal; (*Philosophie*) immaterial

immatriculation [imatʀikylasjɔ̃] *nf* registration

immatriculer [imatʀikyle] *vt* to register; **faire/se faire ~** to register; **voiture immatriculée dans la Seine** car with a Seine registration (number)

immature [imatyʀ] *adj* immature

immaturité [imatyʀite] *nf* immaturity

immédiat, e [imedja, -at] *adj* immediate ▷ *nm*: **dans l'~** for the time being; **dans le voisinage ~ de** in the immediate vicinity of

immédiatement [imedjatmã] *adv* immediately

immémorial, e, -aux [imemɔʀjal, -o] *adj* ancient, age-old

immense [imãs] *adj* immense

immensément [imãsemã] *adv* immensely

immensité [imãsite] *nf* immensity

immerger [imɛʀʒe] *vt* to immerse, submerge; (*câble etc*) to lay under water; (*déchets*) to dump at sea; **s'immerger** *vi* (*sous-marin*) to dive, submerge

immérité, e [imeʀite] *adj* undeserved

immersion [imɛʀsjɔ̃] *nf* immersion

immettable [ɛ̃mɛtabl(ə)] *adj* unwearable

immeuble [imœbl(ə)] *nm* building ▷ *adj* (*Jur*) immovable, real; **~ locatif** block of rented flats (*Brit*), rental building (*US*); **~ de rapport** investment property

immigrant, e [imigʀã, -ãt] *nm/f* immigrant

immigration [imigʀasjɔ̃] *nf* immigration

immigré, e [imigʀe] *nm/f* immigrant

immigrer [imigʀe] *vi* to immigrate

imminence [iminãs] *nf* imminence

imminent, e [iminã, -ãt] *adj* imminent, impending

immiscer [imise]: **s'immiscer** *vi*: **s'~ dans** to interfere in *ou* with

immixtion [imiksjɔ̃] *nf* interference

immobile [imɔbil] *adj* still, motionless; (*pièce de machine*) fixed; (*fig*) unchanging; **rester/se tenir ~** to stay/keep still

immobilier, -ière [imɔbilje, -jɛʀ] *adj* property

cpd, in real property ▷ *nm*: **l'~** the property *ou* the real estate business

immobilisation [imɔbilizasjɔ̃] *nf* immobilization; **immobilisations** *nfpl* (*Jur*) fixed assets

immobiliser [imɔbilize] *vt* (*gén*) to immobilize; (*circulation, véhicule, affaires*) to bring to a standstill; **s'immobiliser** (*personne*) to stand still; (*machine, véhicule*) to come to a halt *ou* a standstill

immobilisme [imɔbilism(ə)] *nm* strong resistance *ou* opposition to change

immobilité [imɔbilite] *nf* immobility

immodéré, e [imɔdeʀe] *adj* immoderate, inordinate

immodérément [imɔdeʀemã] *adv* immoderately

immoler [imɔle] *vt* to sacrifice

immonde [imɔ̃d] *adj* foul; (*sale: ruelle, taudis*) squalid

immondices [imɔ̃dis] *nfpl* (*ordures*) refuse *sg*; (*saletés*) filth *sg*

immoral, e, -aux [imɔʀal, -o] *adj* immoral

immoralisme [imɔʀalism(ə)] *nm* immoralism

immoralité [imɔʀalite] *nf* immorality

immortaliser [imɔʀtalize] *vt* to immortalize

immortel, le [imɔʀtɛl] *adj* immortal ▷ *nf* (*Bot*) everlasting (flower)

immuable [imɥabl(ə)] *adj* (*inébranlable*) immutable; (*qui ne change pas*) unchanging; (*personne*): **~ dans ses convictions** immoveable (in one's convictions)

immunisation [imynizasjɔ̃] *nf* immunization

immunisé, e [im(m)ynize] *adj*: **~ contre** immune to

immuniser [imynize] *vt* (*Méd*) to immunize; **~ qn contre** to immunize sb against; (*fig*) to make sb immune to

immunitaire [imynitɛʀ] *adj* immune

immunité [imynite] *nf* immunity; **~ diplomatique** diplomatic immunity; **~ parlementaire** parliamentary privilege

immunologie [imynɔlɔʒi] *nf* immunology

immutabilité [imytabilite] *nf* immutability

impact [ɛ̃pakt] *nm* impact; **point d'~** point of impact

impair, e [ɛ̃pɛʀ] *adj* odd ▷ *nm* faux pas, blunder; **numéros ~s** odd numbers

impalpable [ɛ̃palpabl(ə)] *adj* impalpable

impaludation [ɛ̃palydasjɔ̃] *nf* inoculation against malaria

imparable [ɛ̃paʀabl(ə)] *adj* unstoppable

impardonnable [ɛ̃paʀdɔnabl(ə)] *adj* unpardonable, unforgivable; **vous êtes ~ d'avoir fait cela** it's unforgivable of you to have done that

imparfait, e [ɛ̃paʀfɛ, -ɛt] *adj* imperfect ▷ *nm* (*Ling*) imperfect (tense)

imparfaitement [ɛ̃paʀfɛtmã] *adv* imperfectly

impartial, e, -aux [ɛ̃paʀsjal, -o] *adj* impartial, unbiased

impartialité [ɛ̃paʀsjalite] *nf* impartiality

impartir [ɛ̃paʀtiʀ] *vt*: ~ **qch à qn** to assign sth to sb; *(dons)* to bestow sth upon sb; **dans les délais impartis** in the time allowed
impasse [ɛ̃pɑs] *nf* dead-end, cul-de-sac; *(fig)* deadlock; **être dans l'**~ *(négociations)* to have reached deadlock; ~ **budgétaire** budget deficit
impassibilité [ɛ̃pasibilite] *nf* impassiveness
impassible [ɛ̃pasibl(ə)] *adj* impassive
impassiblement [ɛ̃pasibləmɑ̃] *adv* impassively
impatiemment [ɛ̃pasjamɑ̃] *adv* impatiently
impatience [ɛ̃pasjɑ̃s] *nf* impatience
impatient, e [ɛ̃pasjɑ̃, -ɑ̃t] *adj* impatient; ~ **de faire qch** keen *ou* impatient to do sth
impatienter [ɛ̃pasjɑ̃te] *vt* to irritate, annoy; **s'impatienter** *vi* to get impatient; **s'**~ **de/ contre** to lose patience at/with, grow impatient at/with
impayable [ɛ̃pɛjabl(ə)] *adj* *(drôle)* priceless
impayé, e [ɛ̃peje] *adj* unpaid, outstanding
impeccable [ɛ̃pekabl(ə)] *adj* faultless, impeccable; *(propre)* spotlessly clean; *(chic)* impeccably dressed; *(fam)* smashing
impeccablement [ɛ̃pekabləmɑ̃] *adv* impeccably
impénétrable [ɛ̃penetʀabl(ə)] *adj* impenetrable
impénitent, e [ɛ̃penitɑ̃, -ɑ̃t] *adj* unrepentant
impensable [ɛ̃pɑ̃sabl(ə)] *adj* unthinkable, unbelievable
imper [ɛ̃pɛʀ] *nm (imperméable)* mac
impératif, -ive [ɛ̃peʀatif, -iv] *adj* imperative; *(Jur)* mandatory ▷ *nm (Ling)* imperative; **impératifs** *nmpl* requirements; demands
impérativement [ɛ̃peʀativmɑ̃] *adv* imperatively
impératrice [ɛ̃peʀatʀis] *nf* empress
imperceptible [ɛ̃pɛʀsɛptibl(ə)] *adj* imperceptible
imperceptiblement [ɛ̃pɛʀsɛptibləmɑ̃] *adv* imperceptibly
imperdable [ɛ̃pɛʀdabl(ə)] *adj* that cannot be lost
imperfectible [ɛ̃pɛʀfɛktibl(ə)] *adj* which cannot be perfected
imperfection [ɛ̃pɛʀfɛksjɔ̃] *nf* imperfection
impérial, e, -aux [ɛ̃peʀjal, -o] *adj* imperial ▷ *nf* upper deck; **autobus à** ~**e** double-decker bus
impérialisme [ɛ̃peʀjalism(ə)] *nm* imperialism
impérialiste [ɛ̃peʀjalist(ə)] *adj* imperialist
impérieusement [ɛ̃peʀjøzmɑ̃] *adv*: **avoir** ~ **besoin de qch** to have urgent need of sth
impérieux, -euse [ɛ̃peʀjø, -øz] *adj (caractère, ton)* imperious; *(obligation, besoin)* pressing, urgent
impérissable [ɛ̃peʀisabl(ə)] *adj* undying, imperishable
imperméabilisation [ɛ̃pɛʀmeabilizasjɔ̃] *nf* waterproofing
imperméabiliser [ɛ̃pɛʀmeabilize] *vt* to waterproof
imperméable [ɛ̃pɛʀmeabl(ə)] *adj* waterproof; *(Géo)* impermeable; *(fig)*: ~ **à** impervious to ▷ *nm* raincoat; ~ **à l'air** airtight
impersonnel, le [ɛ̃pɛʀsɔnɛl] *adj* impersonal

impertinemment [ɛ̃pɛʀtinamɑ̃] *adv* impertinently
impertinence [ɛ̃pɛʀtinɑ̃s] *nf* impertinence
impertinent, e [ɛ̃pɛʀtinɑ̃, -ɑ̃t] *adj* impertinent
imperturbable [ɛ̃pɛʀtyʀbabl(ə)] *adj (personne)* imperturbable; *(sang-froid)* unshakeable; **rester** ~ to remain unruffled
imperturbablement [ɛ̃pɛʀtyʀbabləmɑ̃] *adv* imperturbably; unshakeably
impétrant, e [ɛ̃petʀɑ̃, -ɑ̃t] *nm/f (Jur)* applicant
impétueux, -euse [ɛ̃petɥø, -øz] *adj* fiery
impétuosité [ɛ̃petɥozite] *nf* fieriness
impie [ɛ̃pi] *adj* impious, ungodly
impiété [ɛ̃pjete] *nf* impiety
impitoyable [ɛ̃pitwajabl(ə)] *adj* pitiless, merciless
impitoyablement [ɛ̃pitwajabləmɑ̃] *adv* mercilessly
implacable [ɛ̃plakabl(ə)] *adj* implacable
implacablement [ɛ̃plakabləmɑ̃] *adv* implacably
implant [ɛ̃plɑ̃] *nm (Méd)* implant
implantation [ɛ̃plɑ̃tasjɔ̃] *nf* establishment; settling; implantation
implanter [ɛ̃plɑ̃te] *vt (usine, industrie, usage)* to establish; *(colons etc)* to settle; *(idée, préjugé)* to implant; **s'implanter dans** *vi* to be established in; to settle in; to become implanted in
implémenter [ɛ̃plemɑ̃te] *vt (aussi Inform)* to implement
implication [ɛ̃plikasjɔ̃] *nf* implication
implicite [ɛ̃plisit] *adj* implicit
implicitement [ɛ̃plisitmɑ̃] *adv* implicitly
impliquer [ɛ̃plike] *vt* to imply; ~ **qn (dans)** to implicate sb (in)
implorant, e [ɛ̃plɔʀɑ̃, -ɑ̃t] *adj* imploring
implorer [ɛ̃plɔʀe] *vt* to implore
imploser [ɛ̃plɔze] *vi* to implode
implosion [ɛ̃plozjɔ̃] *nf* implosion
impoli, e [ɛ̃pɔli] *adj* impolite, rude
impoliment [ɛ̃pɔlimɑ̃] *adv* impolitely
impolitesse [ɛ̃pɔlitɛs] *nf* impoliteness, rudeness; *(propos)* impolite *ou* rude remark
impondérable [ɛ̃pɔ̃deʀabl(ə)] *nm* imponderable
impopulaire [ɛ̃pɔpylɛʀ] *adj* unpopular
impopularité [ɛ̃pɔpylaʀite] *nf* unpopularity
importable [ɛ̃pɔʀtabl(ə)] *adj (Comm: marchandise)* importable; *(vêtement: immettable)* unwearable
importance [ɛ̃pɔʀtɑ̃s] *nf* importance; **avoir de l'**~ to be important; **sans** ~ unimportant; **d'**~ important, considerable; **quelle** ~**?** what does it matter?
important, e [ɛ̃pɔʀtɑ̃, -ɑ̃t] *adj* important; *(en quantité)* considerable, sizeable; *(: gamme, dégâts)* extensive; *(péj: airs, ton)* self-important ▷ *nm*: **l'**~ the important thing
importateur, -trice [ɛ̃pɔʀtatœʀ, -tʀis] *adj* importing ▷ *nm/f* importer; **pays** ~ **de blé** wheat-importing country
importation [ɛ̃pɔʀtasjɔ̃] *nf* import; introduction; *(produit)* import
importer [ɛ̃pɔʀte] *vt (Comm)* to import;

(*maladies, plantes*) to introduce ▷ *vi* (*être important*) to matter; **~ à qn** to matter to sb; **il importe de** it is important to; **il importe qu'il fasse** he must do, it is important that he should do; **peu m'importe** I don't mind, I don't care; **peu importe** it doesn't matter; **peu importe (que)** it doesn't matter (if); **peu importe le prix** never mind the price; *voir aussi* **n'importe**

import-export [ɛ̃pɔʀɛkspɔʀ] *nm* import-export business

importun, e [ɛ̃pɔʀtœ̃, -yn] *adj* irksome, importunate; (*arrivée, visite*) inopportune, ill-timed ▷ *nm* intruder

importuner [ɛ̃pɔʀtyne] *vt* to bother

imposable [ɛ̃pozabl(ə)] *adj* taxable

imposant, e [ɛ̃pozɑ̃, -ɑ̃t] *adj* imposing

imposé, e [ɛ̃poze] *adj* (*soumis à l'impôt*) taxed; (*Gym etc*: *figures*) set

imposer [ɛ̃poze] *vt* (*taxer*) to tax; (*Rel*): **~ les mains** to lay on hands; **~ qch à qn** to impose sth on sb; **s'imposer** *vi* (*être nécessaire*) to be imperative; (*montrer sa proéminence*) to stand out, emerge; (*artiste*: *se faire connaître*) to win recognition, come to the fore; **en ~** to be imposing; **en ~ à** to impress; **ça s'impose** it's essential, it's vital

imposition [ɛ̃pozisjɔ̃] *nf* (*Admin*) taxation

impossibilité [ɛ̃pɔsibilite] *nf* impossibility; **être dans l'~ de faire** to be unable to do, find it impossible to do

impossible [ɛ̃pɔsibl(ə)] *adj* impossible ▷ *nm*: **l'~** the impossible; **~ à faire** impossible to do; **il m'est ~ de le faire** it is impossible for me to do it, I can't possibly do it; **faire l'~ (pour que)** to do one's utmost (so that); **si, par ~ ...** if, by some miracle ...

imposteur [ɛ̃pɔstœʀ] *nm* impostor

imposture [ɛ̃pɔstyʀ] *nf* imposture, deception

impôt [ɛ̃po] *nm* tax; (*taxes*) taxation, taxes *pl*; **impôts** *nmpl* (*contributions*) (income) tax *sg*; **payer 1000 euros d'~s** to pay 1,000 euros in tax; **~ direct/indirect** direct/indirect tax; **~ sur le chiffre d'affaires** tax on turnover; **~ foncier** land tax; **~ sur la fortune** wealth tax; **~ sur les plus-values** capital gains tax; **~ sur le revenu** income tax; **~ sur le RPP** personal income tax; **~ sur les sociétés** tax on companies; **~s locaux** rates, local taxes (*US*), ≈ council tax (*Brit*)

impotence [ɛ̃pɔtɑ̃s] *nf* disability

impotent, e [ɛ̃pɔtɑ̃, -ɑ̃t] *adj* disabled

impraticable [ɛ̃pʀatikabl(ə)] *adj* (*projet*) impracticable, unworkable; (*piste*) impassable

imprécation [ɛ̃pʀekasjɔ̃] *nf* imprecation

imprécis, e [ɛ̃pʀesi, -iz] *adj* (*contours, souvenir*) imprecise, vague; (*tir*) inaccurate, imprecise

imprécision [ɛ̃pʀesizjɔ̃] *nf* imprecision

imprégner [ɛ̃pʀeɲe] *vt* (*tissu, tampon*): **~ (de)** to soak *ou* impregnate (with); (*lieu, air*): **~ (de)** to fill (with); (*amertume, ironie*) to pervade; **s'imprégner de** *vi* to become impregnated with; to be filled with; (*fig*) to absorb

imprenable [ɛ̃pʀənabl(ə)] *adj* (*forteresse*) impregnable; **vue ~** unimpeded outlook

impresario [ɛ̃pʀesaʀjo] *nm* manager, impresario

impression [ɛ̃pʀesjɔ̃] *nf* impression; (*d'un ouvrage, tissu*) printing; (*Photo*) exposure; **faire bonne ~** to make a good impression; **donner une ~ de/l'~ que** to give the impression of/that; **avoir l'~ de/que** to have the impression of/that; **faire ~** to make an impression; **~s de voyage** impressions of one's journey

impressionnable [ɛ̃pʀesjɔnabl(ə)] *adj* impressionable

impressionnant, e [ɛ̃pʀesjɔnɑ̃, -ɑ̃t] *adj* impressive; upsetting

impressionner [ɛ̃pʀesjɔne] *vt* (*frapper*) to impress; (*troubler*) to upset; (*Photo*) to expose

impressionnisme [ɛ̃pʀesjɔnism(ə)] *nm* impressionism

impressionniste [ɛ̃pʀesjɔnist(ə)] *adj, nm/f* impressionist

imprévisible [ɛ̃pʀevizibl(ə)] *adj* unforeseeable; (*réaction, personne*) unpredictable

imprévoyance [ɛ̃pʀevwajɑ̃s] *nf* lack of foresight

imprévoyant, e [ɛ̃pʀevwajɑ̃, -ɑ̃t] *adj* lacking in foresight; (*en matière d'argent*) improvident

imprévu, e [ɛ̃pʀevy] *adj* unforeseen, unexpected ▷ *nm* unexpected incident; **l'~** the unexpected; **en cas d'~** if anything unexpected happens; **sauf ~** barring anything unexpected

imprimante [ɛ̃pʀimɑ̃t] *nf* (*Inform*) printer; **~ à bulle d'encre** bubblejet printer; **~ à jet d'encre** ink-jet printer; **~ à laser** laser printer; **~ (ligne par) ligne** line printer; **~ à marguerite** daisy-wheel printer

imprimé [ɛ̃pʀime] *nm* (*formulaire*) printed form; (*Postes*) printed matter *no pl*; (*tissu*) printed fabric; **un ~ à fleurs/pois** (*tissu*) a floral/polka-dot print

imprimer [ɛ̃pʀime] *vt* to print; (*Inform*) to print (out); (*apposer*: *visa, cachet*) to stamp; (*empreinte etc*) to imprint; (*publier*) to publish; (*communiquer*: *mouvement, impulsion*) to impart, transmit

imprimerie [ɛ̃pʀimʀi] *nf* printing; (*établissement*) printing works *sg*; (*atelier*) printing house, printery

imprimeur [ɛ̃pʀimœʀ] *nm* printer; **~-éditeur/-libraire** printer and publisher/bookseller

improbable [ɛ̃pʀɔbabl(ə)] *adj* unlikely, improbable

improductif, -ive [ɛ̃pʀɔdyktif, -iv] *adj* unproductive

impromptu, e [ɛ̃pʀɔ̃pty] *adj* impromptu; (*départ*) sudden

imprononçable [ɛ̃pʀɔnɔ̃sabl(ə)] *adj* unpronounceable

impropre [ɛ̃pʀɔpʀ(ə)] *adj* inappropriate; **~ à** unsuitable for

improprement [ɛ̃pʀɔpʀəmɑ̃] *adv* improperly

impropriété [ɛ̃pʀɔpʀijete] *nf*: **~ (de langage)** incorrect usage *no pl*

improvisation [ɛ̃pʀɔvizasjɔ̃] *nf* improvization

improvisé, e [ɛ̃pʀɔvize] *adj* makeshift, improvized; *(jeu etc)* scratch, improvized; **avec des moyens ~s** using whatever comes to hand

improviser [ɛ̃pʀɔvize] *vt, vi* to improvize; **s'improviser** *(secours, réunion)* to be improvized; **s'~ cuisinier** to (decide to) act as cook; **~ qn cuisinier** to get sb to act as cook

improviste [ɛ̃pʀɔvist(ə)]: **à l'~** *adv* unexpectedly, without warning

imprudemment [ɛ̃pʀydamɑ̃] *adv* carelessly; unwisely, imprudently

imprudence [ɛ̃pʀydɑ̃s] *nf* carelessness *no pl*; imprudence *no pl*; act of carelessness; (:) foolish *ou* unwise action

imprudent, e [ɛ̃pʀydɑ̃, -ɑ̃t] *adj* (*conducteur, geste, action*) careless; (*remarque*) unwise, imprudent; (*projet*) foolhardy

impubère [ɛ̃pybɛʀ] *adj* below the age of puberty

impubliable [ɛ̃pyblijabl(ə)] *adj* unpublishable

impudemment [ɛ̃pydamɑ̃] *adv* impudently

impudence [ɛ̃pydɑ̃s] *nf* impudence

impudent, e [ɛ̃pydɑ̃, -ɑ̃t] *adj* impudent

impudeur [ɛ̃pydœʀ] *nf* shamelessness

impudique [ɛ̃pydik] *adj* shameless

impuissance [ɛ̃pɥisɑ̃s] *nf* helplessness; ineffectualness; impotence

impuissant, e [ɛ̃pɥisɑ̃, -ɑ̃t] *adj* helpless; (*sans effet*) ineffectual; (*sexuellement*) impotent ▷ *nm* impotent man; **~ à faire qch** powerless to do sth

impulsif, -ive [ɛ̃pylsif, -iv] *adj* impulsive

impulsion [ɛ̃pylsjɔ̃] *nf* (*Élec, instinct*) impulse; (*élan, influence*) impetus

impulsivement [ɛ̃pylsivmɑ̃] *adv* impulsively

impulsivité [ɛ̃pylsivite] *nf* impulsiveness

impunément [ɛ̃pynemɑ̃] *adv* with impunity

impuni, e [ɛ̃pyni] *adj* unpunished

impunité [ɛ̃pynite] *nf* impunity

impur, e [ɛ̃pyʀ] *adj* impure

impureté [ɛ̃pyʀte] *nf* impurity

imputable [ɛ̃pytabl(ə)] *adj* (*attribuable*): **~ à** imputable to, ascribable to; (*Comm: somme*): **~ sur** chargeable to

imputation [ɛ̃pytasjɔ̃] *nf* imputation, charge

imputer [ɛ̃pyte] *vt* (*attribuer*): **~ qch à** to ascribe *ou* impute sth to; (*Comm*): **~ qch à** *ou* **sur** to charge sth to

imputrescible [ɛ̃pytʀesibl(ə)] *adj* rotproof

in [in] *adj inv* in, trendy

INA [ina] *sigle m* (= *Institut national de l'audio-visuel*) library of television archives

inabordable [inabɔʀdabl(ə)] *adj* (*lieu*) inaccessible; (*cher*) prohibitive

inaccentué, e [inaksɑ̃tɥe] *adj* (*Ling*) unstressed

inacceptable [inaksɛptabl(ə)] *adj* unacceptable

inaccessible [inaksesibl(ə)] *adj* inaccessible; (*objectif*) unattainable; (*insensible*): **~ à** impervious to

inaccoutumé, e [inakutyme] *adj* unaccustomed

inachevé, e [inaʃve] *adj* unfinished

inactif, -ive [inaktif, -iv] *adj* inactive, idle

inaction [inaksjɔ̃] *nf* inactivity

inactivité [inaktivite] *nf* (*Admin*): **en ~** out of active service

inadaptation [inadaptasjɔ̃] *nf* (*Psych*) maladjustment

inadapté, e [inadapte] *adj* (*Psych: adulte, enfant*) maladjusted ▷ *nm/f* (*péj: adulte: asocial*) misfit; **~ à** not adapted to, unsuited to

inadéquat, e [inadekwa, wat] *adj* inadequate

inadéquation [inadekwasjɔ̃] *nf* inadequacy

inadmissible [inadmisibl(ə)] *adj* inadmissible

inadvertance [inadvɛʀtɑ̃s]: **par ~** *adv* inadvertently

inaliénable [inaljenabl(ə)] *adj* inalienable

inaltérable [inalteʀabl(ə)] *adj* (*matière*) stable; (*fig*) unchanging; **~ à** unaffected by; **couleur ~ (au lavage/à la lumière)** fast colour/fade-resistant colour

inamovible [inamɔvibl(ə)] *adj* fixed; (*Jur*) irremovable

inanimé, e [inanime] *adj* (*matière*) inanimate; (*évanoui*) unconscious; (*sans vie*) lifeless

inanité [inanite] *nf* futility

inanition [inanisjɔ̃] *nf*: **tomber d'~** to faint with hunger (and exhaustion)

inaperçu, e [inapɛʀsy] *adj*: **passer ~** to go unnoticed

inappétence [inapetɑ̃s] *nf* lack of appetite

inapplicable [inaplikabl(ə)] *adj* inapplicable

inapplication [inaplikasjɔ̃] *nf* lack of application

inappliqué, e [inaplike] *adj* lacking in application

inappréciable [inapʀesjabl(ə)] *adj* (*service*) invaluable; (*différence, nuance*) inappreciable

inapte [inapt(ə)] *adj*: **~ à** incapable of; (*Mil*) unfit for

inaptitude [inaptityd] *nf* inaptitude; unfitness

inarticulé, e [inaʀtikyle] *adj* inarticulate

inassimilable [inasimilabl(ə)] *adj* that cannot be assimilated

inassouvi, e [inasuvi] *adj* unsatisfied, unfulfilled

inattaquable [inatakabl(ə)] *adj* (*Mil*) unassailable; (*texte, preuve*) irrefutable

inattendu, e [inatɑ̃dy] *adj* unexpected ▷ *nm*: **l'~** the unexpected

inattentif, -ive [inatɑ̃tif, -iv] *adj* inattentive; **~ à** (*dangers, détails*) heedless of

inattention [inatɑ̃sjɔ̃] *nf* inattention; (*inadvertance*): **une minute d'~** a minute of inattention, a minute's carelessness; **par ~** inadvertently; **faute d'~** careless mistake

inaudible [inodibl(ə)] *adj* inaudible

inaugural, e, -aux [inoɡyʀal, -o] *adj* (*cérémonie*) inaugural, opening; (*vol, voyage*) maiden

inauguration [inoɡyʀasjɔ̃] *nf* unveiling; opening; **discours/cérémonie d'~** inaugural speech/ceremony

inaugurer [inoɡyʀe] *vt* (*monument*) to unveil; (*exposition, usine*) to open; (*fig*) to inaugurate

inauthenticité [inotɑ̃tisite] *nf* inauthenticity

inavouable [inavwabl(ə)] *adj* undisclosable; (*honteux*) shameful

inavoué, e [inavwe] *adj* unavowed

INC *sigle m* (= *Institut national de la consommation*) consumer research organization

inca [ɛ̃ka] *adj inv* Inca ▷ *nm/f*: **Inca** Inca

incalculable [ɛ̃kalkylabl(ə)] *adj* incalculable; **un nombre ~ de** countless numbers of

incandescence [ɛ̃kɑ̃desɑ̃s] *nf* incandescence; **en ~** incandescent, white-hot; **porter à ~** to heat white-hot; **lampe/manchon à ~** incandescent lamp/(gas) mantle

incandescent, e [ɛ̃kɑ̃desɑ̃, -ɑ̃t] *adj* incandescent, white-hot

incantation [ɛ̃kɑ̃tasjɔ̃] *nf* incantation

incantatoire [ɛ̃kɑ̃tatwaʀ] *adj*: **formule ~** incantation

incapable [ɛ̃kapabl(ə)] *adj* incapable; **~ de faire** incapable of doing; (*empêché*) unable to do

incapacitant, e [ɛ̃kapasitɑ̃, -ɑ̃t] *adj* (*Mil*) incapacitating

incapacité [ɛ̃kapasite] *nf* incapability; (*Jur*) incapacity; **être dans l'~ de faire** to be unable to do; **~ permanente/de travail** permanent/ industrial disablement; **~ électorale** ineligibility to vote

incarcération [ɛ̃kaʀseʀasjɔ̃] *nf* incarceration

incarcérer [ɛ̃kaʀseʀe] *vt* to incarcerate

incarnat, e [ɛ̃kaʀna, -at] *adj* (rosy) pink

incarnation [ɛ̃kaʀnasjɔ̃] *nf* incarnation

incarné, e [ɛ̃kaʀne] *adj* incarnate; (*ongle*) ingrown

incarner [ɛ̃kaʀne] *vt* to embody, personify; (*Théât*) to play; (*Rel*) to incarnate; **s'incarner dans** *vi* (*Rel*) to be incarnate in

incartade [ɛ̃kaʀtad] *nf* prank, escapade

incassable [ɛ̃kɑsabl(ə)] *adj* unbreakable

incendiaire [ɛ̃sɑ̃djɛʀ] *adj* incendiary; (*fig*: *discours*) inflammatory ▷ *nm/f* fire-raiser, arsonist

incendie [ɛ̃sɑ̃di] *nm* fire; **~ criminel** arson *no pl*; **~ de forêt** forest fire

incendier [ɛ̃sɑ̃dje] *vt* (*mettre le feu à*) to set fire to, set alight; (*brûler complètement*) to burn down

incertain, e [ɛ̃sɛʀtɛ̃, -ɛn] *adj* uncertain; (*temps*) uncertain, unsettled; (*imprécis*: *contours*) indistinct, blurred

incertitude [ɛ̃sɛʀtityd] *nf* uncertainty

incessamment [ɛ̃sɛsamɑ̃] *adv* very shortly

incessant, e [ɛ̃sɛsɑ̃, -ɑ̃t] *adj* incessant, unceasing

incessible [ɛ̃sesibl(ə)] *adj* (*Jur*) non-transferable

inceste [ɛ̃sɛst(ə)] *nm* incest

incestueux, -euse [ɛ̃sɛstɥø, -øz] *adj* incestuous

inchangé, e [ɛ̃ʃɑ̃ʒe] *adj* unchanged, unaltered

inchantable [ɛ̃ʃɑ̃tabl(ə)] *adj* unsingable

inchauffable [ɛ̃ʃofabl(ə)] *adj* impossible to heat

incidemment [ɛ̃sidamɑ̃] *adv* in passing

incidence [ɛ̃sidɑ̃s] *nf* (*effet, influence*) effect; (*Physique*) incidence

incident [ɛ̃sidɑ̃] *nm* incident; **~ de frontière** border incident; **~ de parcours** minor hitch *ou*

setback; **~ technique** technical difficulties *pl*, technical hitch

incinérateur [ɛ̃sineʀatœʀ] *nm* incinerator

incinération [ɛ̃sineʀasjɔ̃] *nf* (*d'ordures*) incineration; (*crémation*) cremation

incinérer [ɛ̃sineʀe] *vt* (*ordures*) to incinerate; (*mort*) to cremate

incise [ɛ̃siz] *nf* (*Ling*) interpolated clause

inciser [ɛ̃size] *vt* to make an incision in; (*abcès*) to lance

incisif, -ive [ɛ̃sizif, -iv] *adj* incisive, cutting ▷ *nf* incisor

incision [ɛ̃sizjɔ̃] *nf* incision; (*d'un abcès*) lancing

incitation [ɛ̃sitasjɔ̃] *nf* (*encouragement*) incentive; (*provocation*) incitement

inciter [ɛ̃site] *vt*: **~ qn à (faire) qch** to prompt *ou* encourage sb to do sth; (*à la révolte etc*) to incite sb to do sth

incivil, e [ɛ̃sivil] *adj* uncivil

incivilité [ɛ̃sivilite] *nf* (*grossièreté*) incivility; **incivilités** *nfpl* antisocial behaviour *sg*

inclinable [ɛ̃klinabl(ə)] *adj* (*dossier etc*) tilting; **siège à dossier ~** reclining seat

inclinaison [ɛ̃klinezɔ̃] *nf* (*déclivité: d'une route etc*) incline; (: *d'un toit*) slope; (*état penché: d'un mur*) lean; (: *de la tête*) tilt; (: *d'un navire*) list

inclination [ɛ̃klinasjɔ̃] *nf* (*penchant*) inclination, tendency; **montrer de l'~ pour les sciences** *etc* to show an inclination for the sciences *etc*; **~s égoïstes/altruistes** egoistic/altruistic tendencies; **~ de (la) tête** nod (of the head); **~ (de buste)** bow

incliner [ɛ̃kline] *vt* (*bouteille*) to tilt; (*tête*) to incline; (*inciter*): **~ qn à qch/à faire** to encourage sb towards sth/to do ▷ *vi*: **à qch/à faire** (*tendre à, pencher pour*) to incline towards sth/doing, tend towards sth/to do; **s'incliner** *vi* (*route*) to slope; (*toit*) to be sloping; **s'~ (devant)** to bow (before)

inclure [ɛ̃klyʀ] *vt* to include; (*joindre à un envoi*) to enclose; **jusqu'au 10 mars inclus** until 10th March inclusive

inclus, e [ɛ̃kly, -yz] *pp de* **inclure** ▷ *adj* (*joint à un envoi*) enclosed; (*compris: frais, dépense*) included; (*Math: ensemble*): **~ dans** included in; **jusqu'au troisième chapitre ~** up to and including the third chapter

inclusion [ɛ̃klyzjɔ̃] *nf* (*voir inclure*) inclusion; enclosing

inclusivement [ɛ̃klyzivmɑ̃] *adv* inclusively

inclut [ɛ̃kly] *vb voir* **inclure**

incoercible [ɛ̃kɔɛʀsibl(ə)] *adj* uncontrollable

incognito [ɛ̃kɔɲito] *adv* incognito ▷ *nm*: **garder l'~** to remain incognito

incohérence [ɛ̃kɔeʀɑ̃s] *nf* inconsistency; incoherence

incohérent, e [ɛ̃kɔeʀɑ̃, -ɑ̃t] *adj* inconsistent; incoherent

incollable [ɛ̃kɔlabl(ə)] *adj* (*riz*) that does not stick; (*fam: personne*): **il est ~** he's got all the answers

incolore [ɛ̃kɔlɔʀ] *adj* colourless

215

incomber [ɛ̃kɔ̃be]: ~ **à** vt (devoirs, responsabilité) to rest ou be incumbent upon; (: frais, travail) to be the responsibility of

incombustible [ɛ̃kɔ̃bystibl(ə)] adj incombustible

incommensurable [ɛ̃kɔmɑ̃syRabl(ə)] adj immeasurable

incommodant, e [ɛ̃kɔmɔdɑ̃, -ɑ̃t] adj (bruit) annoying; (chaleur) uncomfortable

incommode [ɛ̃kɔmɔd] adj inconvenient; (posture, siège) uncomfortable

incommodément [ɛ̃kɔmɔdemɑ̃] adv (installé, assis) uncomfortably; (logé, situé) inconveniently

incommoder [ɛ̃kɔmɔde] vt: ~ **qn** to bother ou inconvenience sb; (embarrasser) to make sb feel uncomfortable ou ill at ease

incommodité [ɛ̃kɔmɔdite] nf inconvenience

incommunicable [ɛ̃kɔmynikabl(ə)] adj (Jur: droits, privilèges) non-transferable; (pensée) incommunicable

incomparable [ɛ̃kɔ̃paRabl(ə)] adj not comparable; (inégalable) incomparable, matchless

incomparablement [ɛ̃kɔ̃paRabləmɑ̃] adv incomparably

incompatibilité [ɛ̃kɔ̃patibilite] nf incompatibility; ~ **d'humeur** (mutual) incompatibility

incompatible [ɛ̃kɔ̃patibl(ə)] adj incompatible

incompétence [ɛ̃kɔ̃petɑ̃s] nf lack of expertise; incompetence

incompétent, e [ɛ̃kɔ̃petɑ̃, -ɑ̃t] adj (ignorant) inexpert; (incapable) incompetent, not competent

incomplet, -ète [ɛ̃kɔ̃plɛ, -ɛt] adj incomplete

incomplètement [ɛ̃kɔ̃plɛtmɑ̃] adv not completely, incompletely

incompréhensible [ɛ̃kɔ̃pReɑ̃sibl(ə)] adj incomprehensible

incompréhensif, -ive [ɛ̃kɔ̃pReɑ̃sif, -iv] adj lacking in understanding, unsympathetic

incompréhension [ɛ̃kɔ̃pReɑ̃sjɔ̃] nf lack of understanding

incompressible [ɛ̃kɔ̃pResibl(ə)] adj (Physique) incompressible; (fig: dépenses) that cannot be reduced; (Jur: peine) irreducible

incompris, e [ɛ̃kɔ̃pRi, -iz] adj misunderstood

inconcevable [ɛ̃kɔ̃svabl(ə)] adj (conduite etc) inconceivable; (mystère) incredible

inconciliable [ɛ̃kɔ̃siljabl(ə)] adj irreconcilable

inconditionnel, le [ɛ̃kɔ̃disjɔnɛl] adj unconditional; (partisan) unquestioning ▷ nm/f (partisan) unquestioning supporter

inconditionnellement [ɛ̃kɔ̃disjɔnɛlmɑ̃] adv unconditionally

inconduite [ɛ̃kɔ̃dɥit] nf bad ou unsuitable behaviour no pl

inconfort [ɛ̃kɔ̃fɔR] nm lack of comfort, discomfort

inconfortable [ɛ̃kɔ̃fɔRtabl(ə)] adj uncomfortable

inconfortablement [ɛ̃kɔ̃fɔRtabləmɑ̃] adv uncomfortably

incongru, e [ɛ̃kɔ̃gRy] adj unseemly; (remarque) ill-chosen, incongruous

incongruité [ɛ̃kɔ̃gRyite] nf unseemliness; incongruity; (parole incongrue) ill-chosen remark

inconnu, e [ɛ̃kɔny] adj unknown; (sentiment, plaisir) new, strange ▷ nm/f stranger; unknown person (ou artist etc) ▷ nm: l'~ the unknown ▷ nf (Math) unknown; (fig) unknown factor

inconsciemment [ɛ̃kɔ̃sjamɑ̃] adv unconsciously

inconscience [ɛ̃kɔ̃sjɑ̃s] nf unconsciousness; recklessness

inconscient, e [ɛ̃kɔ̃sjɑ̃, -ɑ̃t] adj unconscious; (irréfléchi) reckless ▷ nm (Psych): l'~ the subconscious, the unconscious; ~ **de** unaware of

inconséquence [ɛ̃kɔ̃sekɑ̃s] nf inconsistency; thoughtlessness; (action, parole) thoughtless thing to do (ou say)

inconséquent, e [ɛ̃kɔ̃sekɑ̃, -ɑ̃t] adj (illogique) inconsistent; (irréfléchi) thoughtless

inconsidéré, e [ɛ̃kɔ̃sideRe] adj ill-considered

inconsidérément [ɛ̃kɔ̃sideRemɑ̃] adv thoughtlessly

inconsistant, e [ɛ̃kɔ̃sistɑ̃, -ɑ̃t] adj flimsy, weak; (crème etc) runny

inconsolable [ɛ̃kɔ̃sɔlabl(ə)] adj inconsolable

inconstance [ɛ̃kɔ̃stɑ̃s] nf inconstancy, fickleness

inconstant, e [ɛ̃kɔ̃stɑ̃, -ɑ̃t] adj inconstant, fickle

inconstitutionnel, le [ɛ̃kɔ̃stitysjɔnɛl] adj unconstitutional

incontestable [ɛ̃kɔ̃tɛstabl(ə)] adj unquestionable, indisputable

incontestablement [ɛ̃kɔ̃tɛstabləmɑ̃] adv unquestionably, indisputably

incontesté, e [ɛ̃kɔ̃tɛste] adj undisputed

incontinence [ɛ̃kɔ̃tinɑ̃s] nf (Méd) incontinence

incontinent, e [ɛ̃kɔ̃tinɑ̃, -ɑ̃t] adj (Méd) incontinent ▷ adv (tout de suite) forthwith

incontournable [ɛ̃kɔ̃tuRnabl(ə)] adj unavoidable

incontrôlable [ɛ̃kɔ̃tRolabl(ə)] adj unverifiable

incontrôlé, e [ɛ̃kɔ̃tRole] adj uncontrolled

inconvenance [ɛ̃kɔ̃vnɑ̃s] nf (parole, action) impropriety

inconvenant, e [ɛ̃kɔ̃vnɑ̃, -ɑ̃t] adj unseemly, improper

inconvénient [ɛ̃kɔ̃venjɑ̃] nm (d'une situation, d'un projet) disadvantage, drawback; (d'un remède, changement etc) risk, inconvenience; **si vous n'y voyez pas d'~** if you have no objections; **y a-t-il un ~ à ...?** (risque) isn't there a risk in ...?; (objection) is there any objection to ...?

inconvertible [ɛ̃kɔ̃vɛRtibl(ə)] adj inconvertible

incorporation [ɛ̃kɔRpɔRasjɔ̃] nf (Mil) call-up

incorporé, e [ɛ̃kɔRpɔRe] adj (micro etc) built-in

incorporel, le [ɛ̃kɔRpɔRɛl] adj (Jur): **biens ~s** intangible property

incorporer [ɛ̃kɔRpɔRe] vt: ~ **(à)** to mix in (with); (paragraphe etc): ~ **(dans)** to incorporate (in);

(*territoire, immigrants*): ~ **(dans)** to incorporate (into); (*Mil: appeler*) to recruit, call up; (: *affecter*): ~ **qn dans** to enlist sb into

incorrect, e [ɛ̃kɔʀɛkt] *adj* (*impropre, inconvenant*) improper; (*défectueux*) faulty; (*inexact*) incorrect; (*impoli*) impolite; (*déloyal*) underhand

incorrectement [ɛ̃kɔʀɛktəmɑ̃] *adv* improperly; faultily; incorrectly; impolitely; in an underhand way

incorrection [ɛ̃kɔʀɛksjɔ̃] *nf* impropriety; incorrectness; underhand nature; (*terme impropre*) impropriety; (*action, remarque*) improper behaviour (*ou* remark)

incorrigible [ɛ̃kɔʀiʒibl(ə)] *adj* incorrigible

incorruptible [ɛ̃kɔʀyptibl(ə)] *adj* incorruptible

incrédibilité [ɛ̃kʀedibilite] *nf* incredibility

incrédule [ɛ̃kʀedyl] *adj* incredulous; (*Rel*) unbelieving

incrédulité [ɛ̃kʀedylite] *nf* incredulity; **avec ~** incredulously

increvable [ɛ̃kʀəvabl(ə)] *adj* (*pneu*) puncture-proof; (*fam*) tireless

incriminer [ɛ̃kʀimine] *vt* (*personne*) to incriminate; (*action, conduite*) to bring under attack; (*bonne foi, honnêteté*) to call into question; **livre/article incriminé** offending book/article

incrochetable [ɛ̃kʀɔʃtabl(ə)] *adj* (*serrure*) that can't be picked, burglarproof

incroyable [ɛ̃kʀwajabl(ə)] *adj* incredible, unbelievable

incroyablement [ɛ̃kʀwajabləmɑ̃] *adv* incredibly, unbelievably

incroyant, e [ɛ̃kʀwajɑ̃, -ɑ̃t] *nm/f* non-believer

incrustation [ɛ̃kʀystasjɔ̃] *nf* inlaying *no pl*; inlay; (*dans une chaudière etc*) fur *no pl*, scale *no pl*

incruster [ɛ̃kʀyste] *vt* (*Art*) ~ **qch dans/qch de** to inlay sth into/sth with; (*radiateur etc*) to coat with scale *ou* fur; **s'incruster** *vi* (*invité*) to take root; (*radiateur etc*) to become coated with scale *ou* fur; **s'~ dans** (*corps étranger, caillou*) to become embedded in

incubateur [ɛ̃kybatœʀ] *nm* incubator

incubation [ɛ̃kybasjɔ̃] *nf* incubation

inculpation [ɛ̃kylpasjɔ̃] *nf* charging *no pl*; charge; **sous l'~ de** on a charge of

inculpé, e [ɛ̃kylpe] *nm/f* accused

inculper [ɛ̃kylpe] *vt*: ~ **(de)** to charge (with)

inculquer [ɛ̃kylke] *vt*: ~ **qch à** to inculcate sth in, instil sth into

inculte [ɛ̃kylt(ə)] *adj* uncultivated; (*esprit, peuple*) uncultured; (*barbe*) unkempt

incultivable [ɛ̃kyltivabl(ə)] *adj* (*terrain*) unworkable

inculture [ɛ̃kyltyʀ] *nf* lack of education

incurable [ɛ̃kyʀabl(ə)] *adj* incurable

incurie [ɛ̃kyʀi] *nf* carelessness

incursion [ɛ̃kyʀsjɔ̃] *nf* incursion, foray

incurvé, e [ɛ̃kyʀve] *adj* curved

incurver [ɛ̃kyʀve] *vt* (*barre de fer*) to bend into a curve; **s'incurver** *vi* (*planche, route*) to bend

Inde [ɛ̃d] *nf*: **l'~** India

indécemment [ɛ̃desamɑ̃] *adv* indecently

indécence [ɛ̃desɑ̃s] *nf* indecency; (*propos, acte*) indecent remark (*ou* act *etc*)

indécent, e [ɛ̃desɑ̃, -ɑ̃t] *adj* indecent

indéchiffrable [ɛ̃deʃifʀabl(ə)] *adj* indecipherable

indéchirable [ɛ̃deʃiʀabl(ə)] *adj* tear-proof

indécis, e [ɛ̃desi, -iz] *adj* indecisive; (*perplexe*) undecided

indécision [ɛ̃desizjɔ̃] *nf* indecision, indecisiveness

indéclinable [ɛ̃deklinabl(ə)] *adj* (*Ling: mot*) indeclinable

indécomposable [ɛ̃dekɔ̃pozabl(ə)] *adj* that cannot be broken down

indécrottable [ɛ̃dekʀɔtabl(ə)] *adj* (*fam*) hopeless

indéfectible [ɛ̃defɛktibl(ə)] *adj* (*attachement*) indestructible

indéfendable [ɛ̃defɑ̃dabl(ə)] *adj* indefensible

indéfini, e [ɛ̃defini] *adj* (*imprécis, incertain*) undefined; (*illimité, Ling*) indefinite

indéfiniment [ɛ̃definimɑ̃] *adv* indefinitely

indéfinissable [ɛ̃definisabl(ə)] *adj* indefinable

indéformable [ɛ̃defɔʀmabl(ə)] *adj* that keeps its shape

indélébile [ɛ̃delebil] *adj* indelible

indélicat, e [ɛ̃delika, -at] *adj* tactless; (*malhonnête*) dishonest

indélicatesse [ɛ̃delikatɛs] *nf* tactlessness; dishonesty

indémaillable [ɛ̃demajabl(ə)] *adj* run-resist

indemne [ɛ̃dɛmn(ə)] *adj* unharmed

indemnisable [ɛ̃dɛmnizabl(ə)] *adj* entitled to compensation

indemnisation [ɛ̃dɛmnizasjɔ̃] *nf* (*somme*) indemnity, compensation

indemniser [ɛ̃dɛmnize] *vt*: ~ **qn (de)** to compensate sb (for); **se faire ~** to get compensation

indemnité [ɛ̃dɛmnite] *nf* (*dédommagement*) compensation *no pl*; (*allocation*) allowance; ~ **de licenciement** redundancy payment; ~ **de logement** housing allowance; ~ **parlementaire** ≈ MP's (*Brit*) *ou* Congressman's (US) salary

indémontable [ɛ̃demɔ̃tabl(ə)] *adj* (*meuble etc*) that cannot be dismantled, in one piece

indéniable [ɛ̃denjabl(ə)] *adj* undeniable, indisputable

indéniablement [ɛ̃denjabləmɑ̃] *adv* undeniably

indépendamment [ɛ̃depɑ̃damɑ̃] *adv* independently; ~ **de** independently of; (*abstraction faite de*) irrespective of; (*en plus de*) over and above

indépendance [ɛ̃depɑ̃dɑ̃s] *nf* independence; ~ **matérielle** financial independence

indépendant, e [ɛ̃depɑ̃dɑ̃, -ɑ̃t] *adj* independent; ~ **de** independent of; **chambre ~e** room with private entrance; **travailleur ~** self-employed worker

indépendantiste [ɛ̃depɑ̃dɑ̃tist(ə)] *adj, nm/f* separatist

indéracinable [ɛ̃deʀasinabl(ə)] *adj (fig: croyance etc)* ineradicable

indéréglable [ɛ̃deʀeglabl(ə)] *adj* which will not break down

indescriptible [ɛ̃dɛskʀiptibl(ə)] *adj* indescribable

indésirable [ɛ̃deziʀabl(ə)] *adj* undesirable

indestructible [ɛ̃dɛstʀyktibl(ə)] *adj* indestructible; *(marque, impression)* indelible

indéterminable [ɛ̃detɛʀminabl(ə)] *adj* indeterminable

indétermination [ɛ̃detɛʀminasjɔ̃] *nf* indecision, indecisiveness

indéterminé, e [ɛ̃detɛʀmine] *adj* unspecified; indeterminate; indeterminable

index [ɛ̃dɛks] *nm (doigt)* index finger; *(d'un livre etc)* index; **mettre à l'~** to blacklist

indexation [ɛ̃dɛksasjɔ̃] *nf* indexing

indexé, e [ɛ̃dɛkse] *adj (Écon):* ~ **(sur)** index-linked (to)

indexer [ɛ̃dɛkse] *vt (salaire, emprunt):* ~ **(sur)** to index (on)

indicateur [ɛ̃dikatœʀ] *nm (Police)* informer; *(livre)* guide; (*: liste*) directory; *(Tech)* gauge; indicator; *(Écon)* indicator ▷ *adj:* **poteau ~** signpost; **tableau ~** indicator (board); ~ **des chemins de fer** railway timetable; ~ **de direction** *(Auto)* indicator; ~ **immobilier** property gazette; ~ **de niveau** level, gauge; ~ **de pression** pressure gauge; ~ **de rues** street directory; ~ **de vitesse** speedometer

indicatif, -ive [ɛ̃dikatif, -iv] *adj:* **à titre ~** for (your) information ▷ *nm (Ling)* indicative; *(d'une émission)* theme *ou* signature tune; *(Tél)* dialling code; ~ **d'appel** *(Radio)* call sign

indication [ɛ̃dikasjɔ̃] *nf* indication; *(renseignement)* information *no pl;* **indications** *nfpl (directives)* instructions; ~ **d'origine** *(Comm)* place of origin

indice [ɛ̃dis] *nm (marque, signe)* indication, sign; *(Police: lors d'une enquête)* clue; *(Jur: présomption)* piece of evidence; *(Science, Écon, Tech)* index; *(Admin)* grading; rating; ~ **du coût de la vie** cost-of-living index; ~ **inférieur** subscript; ~ **d'octane** octane rating; ~ **des prix** price index; ~ **de traitement** salary grading

indicible [ɛ̃disibl(ə)] *adj* inexpressible

indien, ne [ɛ̃djɛ̃, -ɛn] *adj* Indian ▷ *nm/f:* **Indien, ne** *(d'Amérique)* Native American; *(d'Inde)* Indian

indifféremment [ɛ̃difeʀamɑ̃] *adv (sans distinction)* equally; indiscriminately

indifférence [ɛ̃difeʀɑ̃s] *nf* indifference

indifférencié, e [ɛ̃difeʀɑ̃sje] *adj* undifferentiated

indifférent, e [ɛ̃difeʀɑ̃, -ɑ̃t] *adj (peu intéressé)* indifferent; ~ **à** *(insensible à)* indifferent to, unconcerned about; *(peu intéressant pour)* indifferent to; immaterial to; **ça m'est ~ (que ...)** it doesn't matter to me (whether ...)

indifférer [ɛ̃difeʀe] *vt:* **cela m'indiffère** I'm indifferent about it

indigence [ɛ̃diʒɑ̃s] *nf* poverty; **être dans l'~** to be destitute

indigène [ɛ̃diʒɛn] *adj* native, indigenous; *(de la région)* local ▷ *nm/f* native

indigent, e [ɛ̃diʒɑ̃, -ɑ̃t] *adj* destitute, poverty-stricken; *(fig)* poor

indigeste [ɛ̃diʒɛst(ə)] *adj* indigestible

indigestion [ɛ̃diʒɛstjɔ̃] *nf* indigestion *no pl;* **avoir une ~** to have indigestion

indignation [ɛ̃diɲasjɔ̃] *nf* indignation; **avec ~** indignantly

indigne [ɛ̃diɲ] *adj:* ~ **(de)** unworthy (of)

indigné, e [ɛ̃diɲe] *adj* indignant

indignement [ɛ̃diɲmɑ̃] *adv* shamefully

indigner [ɛ̃diɲe] *vt* to make indignant; **s'indigner (de/contre)** *vi* to be (*ou* become) indignant (at)

indignité [ɛ̃diɲite] *nf* unworthiness *no pl; (acte)* shameful act

indigo [ɛ̃digo] *nm* indigo

indiqué, e [ɛ̃dike] *adj (date, lieu)* given, appointed; *(adéquat)* appropriate, suitable; *(conseillé)* advisable; *(remède, traitement)* appropriate

indiquer [ɛ̃dike] *vt (désigner):* ~ **qch/qn à qn** to point sth/sb out to sb; *(pendule, aiguille)* to show; *(étiquette, plan)* to show, indicate; *(faire connaître: médecin, lieu):* ~ **qch/qn à qn** to tell sb of sth/sb; *(renseigner sur)* to point out, tell; *(déterminer: date, lieu)* to give, state; *(dénoter)* to indicate, point to; ~ **du doigt** to point out; ~ **de la main** to indicate with one's hand; ~ **du regard** to glance towards *ou* in the direction of; **pourriez-vous m'~ les toilettes/l'heure?** could you direct me to the toilets/tell me the time?

indirect, e [ɛ̃diʀɛkt] *adj* indirect

indirectement [ɛ̃diʀɛktəmɑ̃] *adv* indirectly; *(apprendre)* in a roundabout way

indiscernable [ɛ̃disɛʀnabl(ə)] *adj* undiscernable

indiscipline [ɛ̃disiplin] *nf* lack of discipline

indiscipliné, e [ɛ̃disipline] *adj* undisciplined; *(fig)* unmanageable

indiscret, -ète [ɛ̃diskʀɛ, -ɛt] *adj* indiscreet

indiscrétion [ɛ̃diskʀesjɔ̃] *nf* indiscretion; **sans ~, ...** without wishing to be indiscreet, ...

indiscutable [ɛ̃diskytabl(ə)] *adj* indisputable

indiscutablement [ɛ̃diskytabləmɑ̃] *adv* indisputably

indiscuté, e [ɛ̃dispyte] *adj (incontesté: droit, chef)* undisputed

indispensable [ɛ̃dispɑ̃sabl(ə)] *adj* indispensable, essential; ~ **à qn/pour faire qch** essential for sb/to do sth

indisponibilité [ɛ̃dispɔnibilite] *nf* unavailability

indisponible [ɛ̃dispɔnibl(ə)] *adj* unavailable

indisposé, e [ɛ̃dispoze] *adj* indisposed, unwell

indisposer [ɛ̃dispoze] *vt (incommoder)* to upset; *(déplaire à)* to antagonize

indisposition [ɛ̃dispozisjɔ̃] *nf* (slight) illness, indisposition

indissociable [ɛ̃disɔsjabl(ə)] *adj* indissociable

indissoluble [ɛ̃disɔlybl(ə)] *adj* indissoluble

indissolublement [ɛ̃disɔlybləmɑ̃] *adv* indissolubly

indistinct, e [ɛ̃distɛ̃, -ɛ̃kt(ə)] *adj* indistinct

indistinctement [ɛ̃distɛ̃ktəmɑ̃] *adv* (*voir, prononcer*) indistinctly; (*sans distinction*) without distinction, indiscriminately

individu [ɛ̃dividy] *nm* individual

individualiser [ɛ̃dividɥalize] *vt* to individualize; (*personnaliser*) to tailor to individual requirements; **s'individualiser** *vi* to develop one's own identity

individualisme [ɛ̃dividɥalism(ə)] *nm* individualism

individualiste [ɛ̃dividɥalist(ə)] *nm/f* individualist

individualité [ɛ̃dividɥalite] *nf* individuality

individuel, le [ɛ̃dividɥɛl] *adj* (*gén*) individual; (*opinion, livret, contrôle, avantages*) personal; **chambre ~le** single room; **maison ~le** detached house; **propriété ~le** personal *ou* private property

individuellement [ɛ̃dividɥɛlmɑ̃] *adv* individually

indivis, e [ɛ̃divi, -iz] *adj* (*Jur: bien, succession*) indivisible; (: *cohéritiers, propriétaires*) joint

indivisible [ɛ̃divizibl(ə)] *adj* indivisible

Indochine [ɛ̃dɔʃin] *nf*: **l'~** Indochina

indochinois, e [ɛ̃dɔʃinwa, -waz] *adj* Indochinese

indocile [ɛ̃dɔsil] *adj* unruly

indo-européen, ne [ɛ̃dɔøRɔpeɛ̃, -ɛn] *adj* Indo-European ▷ *nm* (*Ling*) Indo-European

indolence [ɛ̃dɔlɑ̃s] *nf* indolence

indolent, e [ɛ̃dɔlɑ̃, -ɑ̃t] *adj* indolent

indolore [ɛ̃dɔlɔR] *adj* painless

indomptable [ɛ̃dɔ̃tabl(ə)] *adj* untameable; (*fig*) invincible, indomitable

indompté, e [ɛ̃dɔ̃te] *adj* (*cheval*) unbroken

Indonésie [ɛ̃donezi] *nf*: **l'~** Indonesia

indonésien, ne [ɛ̃donezjɛ̃, -ɛn] *adj* Indonesian ▷ *nm/f*: **Indonésien, ne** Indonesian

indu, e [ɛ̃dy] *adj*: **à des heures ~es** at an ungodly hour

indubitable [ɛ̃dybitabl(ə)] *adj* indubitable

indubitablement [ɛ̃dybitabləmɑ̃] *adv* indubitably

induction [ɛ̃dyksjɔ̃] *nf* induction

induire [ɛ̃dɥiR] *vt*: **~ qch de** to induce sth from; **~ qn en erreur** to lead sb astray, mislead sb

indulgence [ɛ̃dylʒɑ̃s] *nf* indulgence; leniency; **avec ~** indulgently; leniently

indulgent, e [ɛ̃dylʒɑ̃, -ɑ̃t] *adj* (*parent, regard*) indulgent; (*juge, examinateur*) lenient

indûment [ɛ̃dymɑ̃] *adv* without due cause; (*illégitimement*) wrongfully

industrialisation [ɛ̃dystRijalizɑsjɔ̃] *nf* industrialization

industrialisé, e [ɛ̃dystRijalize] *adj* industrialized

industrialiser [ɛ̃dystRijalize] *vt* to industrialize; **s'industrialiser** *vi* to become industrialized

industrie [ɛ̃dystRi] *nf* industry; **~ automobile/ textile** car/textile industry; **~ du spectacle** entertainment business

industriel, le [ɛ̃dystRijɛl] *adj* industrial; (*produit industriellement: pain etc*) mass-produced, factory-produced ▷ *nm* industrialist; (*fabricant*) manufacturer

industriellement [ɛ̃dystRijɛlmɑ̃] *adv* industrially

industrieux, -euse [ɛ̃dystRijø, -øz] *adj* industrious

inébranlable [inebRɑlabl(ə)] *adj* (*masse, colonne*) solid; (*personne, certitude, foi*) steadfast, unwavering

inédit, e [inedi, -it] *adj* (*correspondance etc*) (hitherto) unpublished; (*spectacle, moyen*) novel, original

ineffable [inefabl(ə)] *adj* inexpressible, ineffable

ineffaçable [inefasabl(ə)] *adj* indelible

inefficace [inefikas] *adj* (*remède, moyen*) ineffective; (*machine, employé*) inefficient

inefficacité [inefikasite] *nf* ineffectiveness; inefficiency

inégal, e, -aux [inegal, -o] *adj* unequal; (*irrégulier*) uneven

inégalable [inegalabl(e)] *adj* matchless

inégalé, e [inegale] *adj* unmatched, unequalled

inégalement [inegalmɑ̃] *adv* unequally

inégalité [inegalite] *nf* inequality; unevenness *no pl*; **~ de deux hauteurs** difference *ou* disparity between two heights; **~s de terrain** uneven ground

inélégance [inelegɑ̃s] *nf* inelegance

inélégant, e [inelegɑ̃, -ɑ̃t] *adj* inelegant; (*indélicat*) discourteous

inéligible [ineliʒibl(ə)] *adj* ineligible

inéluctable [inelyktabl(ə)] *adj* inescapable

inéluctablement [inelyktabləmɑ̃] *adv* inescapably

inemployable [inɑ̃plwajabl(ə)] *adj* unusable

inemployé, e [inɑ̃plwaje] *adj* unused

inénarrable [inenaRabl(ə)] *adj* hilarious

inepte [inɛpt(ə)] *adj* inept

ineptie [inɛpsi] *nf* ineptitude; (*propos*) nonsense *no pl*

inépuisable [inepɥizabl(ə)] *adj* inexhaustible

inéquitable [inekitabl(ə)] *adj* inequitable

inerte [inɛRt(ə)] *adj* lifeless; (*apathique*) passive, inert; (*Physique, Chimie*) inert

inertie [inɛRsi] *nf* inertia

inescompté, e [inɛskɔ̃te] *adj* unexpected, unhoped-for

inespéré, e [inɛspeRe] *adj* unhoped-for, unexpected

inesthétique [inɛstetik] *adj* unsightly

inestimable [inɛstimabl(e)] *adj* priceless; (*fig: bienfait*) invaluable

inévitable [inevitabl(ə)] *adj* unavoidable; (*fatal, habituel*) inevitable

inévitablement [inevitabləmɑ̃] *adv* inevitably

inexact, e [inɛgzakt] *adj* inaccurate, inexact; *(non ponctuel)* unpunctual

inexactement [inɛgzaktəmɑ̃] *adv* inaccurately

inexactitude [inɛgzaktityd] *nf* inaccuracy

inexcusable [inɛkskyzabl(ə)] *adj* inexcusable, unforgivable

inexécutable [inɛgzekytabl(ə)] *adj* impracticable, unworkable; *(Mus)* unplayable

inexistant, e [inɛgzistɑ̃, -ɑ̃t] *adj* non-existent

inexorable [inɛgzɔRabl(ə)] *adj* inexorable; *(personne: dur)*: ~ **(à)** unmoved (by)

inexorablement [inɛgzɔRabləmɑ̃] *adv* inexorably

inexpérience [inɛkspeRjɑ̃s] *nf* inexperience, lack of experience

inexpérimenté, e [inɛkspeRimɑ̃te] *adj* inexperienced; *(arme, procédé)* untested

inexplicable [inɛksplikabl(ə)] *adj* inexplicable

inexplicablement [inɛksplikabləmɑ̃] *adv* inexplicably

inexpliqué, e [inɛksplike] *adj* unexplained

inexploitable [inɛksplwatabl(ə)] *adj (gisement, richesse)* unexploitable; *(données, renseignements)* unusable

inexploité, e [inɛksplwate] *adj* unexploited, untapped

inexploré, e [inɛksplɔRe] *adj* unexplored

inexpressif, -ive [inɛkspResif, -iv] *adj* inexpressive; *(regard etc)* expressionless

inexpressivité [inɛkspResivite] *nf* expressionlessness

inexprimable [inɛkspRimabl(ə)] *adj* inexpressible

inexprimé, e [inɛkspRime] *adj* unspoken, unexpressed

inexpugnable [inɛkspygnabl(ə)] *adj* impregnable

inextensible [inɛkstɑ̃sibl(ə)] *adj (tissu)* non-stretch

in extenso [inɛkstɛ̃so] *adv* in full

inextinguible [inɛkstɛ̃gibl(ə)] *adj (soif)* unquenchable; *(rire)* uncontrollable

in extremis [inɛkstRemis] *adv* at the last minute ▷ *adj* last-minute; *(testament)* death bed *cpd*

inextricable [inɛkstRikabl(ə)] *adj* inextricable

inextricablement [inɛkstRikabləmɑ̃] *adv* inextricably

infaillibilité [ɛ̃fajibilite] *nf* infallibility

infaillible [ɛ̃fajibl(ə)] *adj* infallible; *(instinct)* infallible, unerring

infailliblement [ɛ̃fajibləmɑ̃] *adv (certainement)* without fail

infaisable [ɛ̃fəzabl(ə)] *adj (travail etc)* impossible, impractical

infamant, e [ɛ̃famɑ̃, -ɑ̃t] *adj* libellous, defamatory

infâme [ɛ̃fam] *adj* vile

infamie [ɛ̃fami] *nf* infamy

infanterie [ɛ̃fɑ̃tRi] *nf* infantry

infanticide [ɛ̃fɑ̃tisid] *nm/f* child-murderer, murderess ▷ *nm (meurtre)* infanticide

infantile [ɛ̃fɑ̃til] *adj (Méd)* infantile, child *cpd*; *(péj: ton, réaction)* infantile, childish

infantilisme [ɛ̃fɑ̃tilism(ə)] *nm* infantilism

infarctus [ɛ̃faRktys] *nm*: ~ **(du myocarde)** coronary (thrombosis)

infatigable [ɛ̃fatigabl(ə)] *adj* tireless, indefatigable

infatigablement [ɛ̃fatigabləmɑ̃] *adv* tirelessly, indefatigably

infatué, e [ɛ̃fatɥe] *adj* conceited; ~ **de** full of

infécond, e [ɛ̃fekɔ̃, -ɔ̃d] *adj* infertile, barren

infect, e [ɛ̃fɛkt] *adj* vile, foul; *(repas, vin)* revolting, foul

infecter [ɛ̃fɛkte] *vt (atmosphère, eau)* to contaminate; *(Méd)* to infect; **s'infecter** *vi* to become infected *ou* septic

infectieux, -euse [ɛ̃fɛksjø, -øz] *adj* infectious

infection [ɛ̃fɛksjɔ̃] *nf* infection

inféoder [ɛ̃feɔde] *vt*: **s'inféoder à** to pledge allegiance to

inférer [ɛ̃feRe] *vt*: ~ **qch de** to infer sth from

inférieur, e [ɛ̃feRjœR] *adj* lower; *(en qualité, intelligence)* inferior ▷ *nm/f* inferior; ~ **à** *(somme, quantité)* less *ou* smaller than; *(moins bon que)* inferior to; *(tâche: pas à la hauteur de)* unequal to

infériorité [ɛ̃feRjɔRite] *nf* inferiority; ~ **en nombre** inferiority in numbers

infernal, e, -aux [ɛ̃fɛRnal, -o] *adj (chaleur, rythme)* infernal; *(méchanceté, complot)* diabolical

infester [ɛ̃fɛste] *vt* to infest; **infesté de moustiques** infested with mosquitoes, mosquito-ridden

infidèle [ɛ̃fidɛl] *adj* unfaithful; *(Rel)* infidel

infidélité [ɛ̃fidelite] *nf* unfaithfulness *no pl*

infiltration [ɛ̃filtRɑsjɔ̃] *nf* infiltration

infiltrer [ɛ̃filtRe] : **s'infiltrer** *vi*: **s'~ dans** to penetrate into; *(liquide)* to seep into; *(fig: noyauter)* to infiltrate

infime [ɛ̃fim] *adj* minute, tiny; *(inférieur)* lowly

infini, e [ɛ̃fini] *adj* infinite ▷ *nm* infinity; **à l'~** *(Math)* to infinity; *(discourir)* ad infinitum, endlessly; *(agrandir, varier)* infinitely; *(à perte de vue)* endlessly (into the distance)

infiniment [ɛ̃finimɑ̃] *adv* infinitely; ~ **grand/ petit** *(Math)* infinitely great/infinitessimal

infinité [ɛ̃finite] *nf*: **une ~ de** an infinite number of

infinitésimal, e, -aux [ɛ̃finitezimal, -o] *adj* infinitesimal

infinitif, -ive [ɛ̃finitif, -iv] *adj, nm* infinitive

infirme [ɛ̃fiRm(ə)] *adj* disabled ▷ *nm/f* disabled person; ~ **de guerre** war cripple; ~ **du travail** industrially disabled person

infirmer [ɛ̃fiRme] *vt* to invalidate

infirmerie [ɛ̃fiRməRi] *nf* sick bay

infirmier, -ière [ɛ̃fiRmje, -jɛR] *nm/f* nurse ▷ *adj*: **élève ~** student nurse; **infirmière chef** sister; **infirmière diplômée** registered nurse; **infirmière visiteuse** visiting nurse, ≈ district nurse *(Brit)*

infirmité [ɛ̃fiRmite] *nf* disability

inflammable [ɛ̃flamabl(ə)] *adj* (in)flammable
inflammation [ɛ̃flamasjɔ̃] *nf* inflammation
inflammatoire [ɛ̃flamatwaʀ] *adj* (*Méd*) inflammatory
inflation [ɛ̃flɑsjɔ̃] *nf* inflation; **~ rampante/galopante** creeping/galloping inflation
inflationniste [ɛ̃flɑsjɔnist(ə)] *adj* inflationist
infléchir [ɛ̃fleʃiʀ] *vt* (*fig: politique*) to reorientate, redirect; **s'infléchir** *vi* (*poutre, tringle*) to bend, sag
inflexibilité [ɛ̃flɛksibilite] *nf* inflexibility
inflexible [ɛ̃flɛksibl(ə)] *adj* inflexible
inflexion [ɛ̃flɛksjɔ̃] *nf* inflexion; **~ de la tête** slight nod (of the head)
infliger [ɛ̃fliʒe] *vt:* **~ qch (à qn)** to inflict sth (on sb); (*amende, sanction*) to impose sth (on sb)
influençable [ɛ̃flyɑ̃sabl(ə)] *adj* easily influenced
influence [ɛ̃flyɑ̃s] *nf* influence; (*d'un médicament*) effect
influencer [ɛ̃flyɑ̃se] *vt* to influence
influent, e [ɛ̃flyɑ̃, -ɑ̃t] *adj* influential
influer [ɛ̃flye]: **~ sur** *vt* to have an influence upon
influx [ɛ̃fly] *nm:* **~ nerveux** (nervous) impulse
infobulle [ɛ̃fobyl] *nf* (*Inform*) help bubble
infographie [ɛ̃fɔgʀafi] *nf* computer graphics *sg*
informateur, -trice [ɛ̃fɔʀmatœʀ, -tʀis] *nm/f* informant
informaticien, ne [ɛ̃fɔʀmatisjɛ̃, -ɛn] *nm/f* computer scientist
informatif, -ive [ɛ̃fɔʀmatif, -iv] *adj* informative
information [ɛ̃fɔʀmɑsjɔ̃] *nf* (*renseignement*) piece of information; (*Presse, TV: nouvelle*) item of news; (*diffusion de renseignements, Inform*) information; (*Jur*) inquiry, investigation; **informations** *nfpl* (*TV*) news *sg*; **voyage d'~** fact-finding trip; **agence d'~** news agency; **journal d'~** quality (*Brit*) *ou* serious newspaper
informatique [ɛ̃fɔʀmatik] *nf* (*technique*) data processing; (*science*) computer science ▷ *adj* computer *cpd*
informatisation [ɛ̃fɔʀmatizɑsjɔ̃] *nf* computerization
informatiser [ɛ̃fɔʀmatize] *vt* to computerize
informe [ɛ̃fɔʀm(ə)] *adj* shapeless
informé, e [ɛ̃fɔʀme] *adj:* **jusqu'à plus ample ~** until further information is available
informel, le [ɛ̃fɔʀmɛl] *adj* informal
informer [ɛ̃fɔʀme] *vt:* **~ qn (de)** to inform sb (of) ▷ *vi* (*Jur*): **~ contre qn/sur qch** to initiate inquiries about sb/sth; **s'informer (sur)** to inform o.s. (about); **s'~ (de qch/si)** to inquire *ou* find out (about sth/whether *ou* if)
informulé, e [ɛ̃fɔʀmyle] *adj* unformulated
infortune [ɛ̃fɔʀtyn] *nf* misfortune
infos [ɛ̃fo] *nfpl* (= **informations**) news
infraction [ɛ̃fʀaksjɔ̃] *nf* offence; **~ à** violation *ou* breach of; **être en ~** to be in breach of the law
infranchissable [ɛ̃fʀɑ̃ʃisabl(ə)] *adj* impassable; (*fig*) insuperable
infrarouge [ɛ̃fʀaʀuʒ] *adj, nm* infrared
infrason [ɛ̃fʀasɔ̃] *nm* infrasonic vibration

infrastructure [ɛ̃fʀastʀyktyʀ] *nf* (*d'une route etc*) substructure; (*Aviat, Mil*) ground installations *pl*; (*touristique etc*) facilities *pl*
infréquentable [ɛ̃fʀekɑ̃tabl(ə)] *adj* not to be associated with
infroissable [ɛ̃fʀwasabl(ə)] *adj* crease-resistant
infructueux, -euse [ɛ̃fʀyktɥø, -øz] *adj* fruitless, unfruitful
infus, e [ɛ̃fy, -yz] *adj:* **avoir la science ~e** to have innate knowledge
infuser [ɛ̃fyze] *vt* (*aussi:* **faire infuser**: *thé*) to brew; (: *tisane*) to infuse ▷ *vi* to brew; to infuse; **laisser ~** (to leave) to brew
infusion [ɛ̃fyzjɔ̃] *nf* (*tisane*) infusion, herb tea
ingambe [ɛ̃gɑ̃b] *adj* spry, nimble
ingénier [ɛ̃ʒenje]: **s'ingénier** *vi:* **s'~ à faire** to strive to do
ingénierie [ɛ̃ʒeniʀi] *nf* engineering
ingénieur [ɛ̃ʒenjœʀ] *nm* engineer; **~ agronome/chimiste** agricultural/chemical engineer; **~ conseil** consulting engineer; **~ du son** sound engineer
ingénieusement [ɛ̃ʒenjøzmɑ̃] *adv* ingeniously
ingénieux, -euse [ɛ̃ʒenjø, -øz] *adj* ingenious, clever
ingéniosité [ɛ̃ʒenjozite] *nf* ingenuity
ingénu, e [ɛ̃ʒeny] *adj* ingenuous, artless ▷ *nf* (*Théât*) ingénue
ingénuité [ɛ̃ʒenɥite] *nf* ingenuousness
ingénument [ɛ̃ʒenymɑ̃] *adv* ingenuously
ingérence [ɛ̃ʒeʀɑ̃s] *nf* interference
ingérer [ɛ̃ʒeʀe]: **s'ingérer** *vi:* **s'~ dans** to interfere in
ingouvernable [ɛ̃guvɛʀnabl(ə)] *adj* ungovernable
ingrat, e [ɛ̃gʀa, -at] *adj* (*personne*) ungrateful; (*sol*) poor; (*travail, sujet*) arid, thankless; (*visage*) unprepossessing
ingratitude [ɛ̃gʀatityd] *nf* ingratitude
ingrédient [ɛ̃gʀedjɑ̃] *nm* ingredient
inguérissable [ɛ̃geʀisabl(ə)] *adj* incurable
ingurgiter [ɛ̃gyʀʒite] *vt* to swallow; **faire ~ qch à qn** to make sb swallow sth; (*fig: connaissances*) to force sth into sb
inhabile [inabil] *adj* clumsy; (*fig*) inept
inhabitable [inabitabl(ə)] *adj* uninhabitable
inhabité, e [inabite] *adj* (*régions*) uninhabited; (*maison*) unoccupied
inhabituel, le [inabitɥɛl] *adj* unusual
inhalateur [inalatœʀ] *nm* inhaler; **~ d'oxygène** oxygen mask
inhalation [inalɑsjɔ̃] *nf* (*Méd*) inhalation; **faire des ~s** to use an inhalation bath
inhaler [inale] *vt* to inhale
inhérent, e [ineʀɑ̃, -ɑ̃t] *adj:* **~ à** inherent in
inhiber [inibe] *vt* to inhibit
inhibition [inibisjɔ̃] *nf* inhibition
inhospitalier, -ière [inɔspitalje, -jɛʀ] *adj* inhospitable
inhumain, e [inymɛ̃, -ɛn] *adj* inhuman
inhumation [inymɑsjɔ̃] *nf* interment, burial
inhumer [inyme] *vt* to inter, bury

inimaginable [inimaʒinabl(ə)] *adj*
unimaginable

inimitable [inimitabl(ə)] *adj* inimitable

inimitié [inimitje] *nf* enmity

ininflammable [inɛ̃flamabl(ə)] *adj* non-
flammable

inintelligent, e [inɛ̃teliʒɑ̃, -ɑ̃t] *adj* unintelligent

inintelligible [inɛ̃teliʒibl(ə)] *adj* unintelligible

inintelligiblement [inɛ̃teliʒibləmɑ̃] *adv*
unintelligibly

inintéressant, e [inɛ̃teʀesɑ̃, -ɑ̃t] *adj*
uninteresting

ininterrompu, e [inɛ̃tɛʀɔ̃py] *adj* (*file, série*)
unbroken; (*flot, vacarme*) uninterrupted, non-
stop; (*effort*) unremitting, continuous

iniquité [inikite] *nf* iniquity

initial, e, -aux [inisjal, -o] *adj, nf* initial;
initiales *nfpl* initials

initialement [inisjalmɑ̃] *adv* initially

initialiser [inisjalize] *vt* to initialize

initiateur, -trice [inisjatœʀ, -tʀis] *nm/f*
initiator; (*d'une mode, technique*) innovator,
pioneer

initiation [inisjɑsjɔ̃] *nf* initiation

initiatique [inisjatik] *adj* (*rites, épreuves*)
initiatory

initiative [inisjativ] *nf* initiative; **prendre l'~
de qch/de faire** to take the initiative for sth/of
doing; **avoir de l'~** to have initiative, show
enterprise; **esprit/qualités d'~** spirit/qualities
of initiative; **à** *ou* **sur l'~ de qn** on sb's
initiative; **de sa propre ~** on one's own
initiative

initié, e [inisje] *adj* initiated ▷ *nm/f* initiate

initier [inisje] *vt* to initiate; **~ qn à** to initiate sb
into; (*faire découvrir: art, jeu*) to introduce sb to;
s'initier à *vi* (*métier, profession, technique*) to
become initiated into

injectable [ɛ̃ʒɛktabl(ə)] *adj* injectable

injecté, e [ɛ̃ʒɛkte] *adj*: **yeux ~s de sang**
bloodshot eyes

injecter [ɛ̃ʒɛkte] *vt* to inject

injection [ɛ̃ʒɛksjɔ̃] *nf* injection; **à ~** (*Auto*) fuel
injection *cpd*

injonction [ɛ̃ʒɔ̃ksjɔ̃] *nf* injunction, order; **~ de
payer** (*Jur*) order to pay

injouable [ɛ̃ʒwabl(ə)] *adj* unplayable

injure [ɛ̃ʒyʀ] *nf* insult, abuse *no pl*

injurier [ɛ̃ʒyʀje] *vt* to insult, abuse

injurieux, -euse [ɛ̃ʒyʀjø, -øz] *adj* abusive,
insulting

injuste [ɛ̃ʒyst(ə)] *adj* unjust, unfair

injustement [ɛ̃ʒystəmɑ̃] *adv* unjustly, unfairly

injustice [ɛ̃ʒystis] *nf* injustice

injustifiable [ɛ̃ʒystifjabl(ə)] *adj* unjustifiable

injustifié, e [ɛ̃ʒystifje] *adj* unjustified,
unwarranted

inlassable [ɛ̃lasabl(ə)] *adj* tireless,
indefatigable

inlassablement [ɛ̃lasabləmɑ̃] *adv* tirelessly

inné, e [ine] *adj* innate, inborn

innocemment [inɔsamɑ̃] *adv* innocently

innocence [inɔsɑ̃s] *nf* innocence

innocent, e [inɔsɑ̃, -ɑ̃t] *adj* innocent ▷ *nm/f*
innocent person; **faire l'~** to play *ou* come the
innocent

innocenter [inɔsɑ̃te] *vt* to clear, prove innocent

innocuité [inɔkɥite] *nf* innocuousness

innombrable [inɔ̃bʀabl(ə)] *adj* innumerable

innommable [inɔmabl(ə)] *adj* unspeakable

innovateur, -trice [inɔvatœʀ, -tʀis] *adj*
innovatory

innovation [inɔvasjɔ̃] *nf* innovation

innover [inɔve] *vi*: **~ en matière d'art** to break
new ground in the field of art

inobservance [inɔpsɛʀvɑ̃s] *nf* non-observance

inobservation [inɔpsɛʀvasjɔ̃] *nf* non-
observation, inobservance

inoccupé, e [inɔkype] *adj* unoccupied

inoculer [inɔkyle] *vt*: **~ qch à qn** (*volontairement*)
to inoculate sb with sth; (*accidentellement*) to
infect sb with sth; **~ qn contre** to inoculate sb
against

inodore [inɔdɔʀ] *adj* (*gaz*) odourless; (*fleur*)
scentless

inoffensif, -ive [inɔfɑ̃sif, -iv] *adj* harmless,
innocuous

inondable [inɔ̃dabl(ə)] *adj* (*zone etc*) liable to
flooding

inondation [inɔ̃dasjɔ̃] *nf* flooding *no pl*; (*torrent,
eau*) flood

inonder [inɔ̃de] *vt* to flood; (*fig*) to inundate,
overrun; **~ de** (*fig*) to flood *ou* swamp with

inopérable [inɔpeʀabl(ə)] *adj* inoperable

inopérant, e [inɔpeʀɑ̃, -ɑ̃t] *adj* inoperative,
ineffective

inopiné, e [inɔpine] *adj* unexpected, sudden

inopinément [inɔpinemɑ̃] *adv* unexpectedly

inopportun, e [inɔpɔʀtœ̃, -yn] *adj* ill-timed,
untimely; inappropriate; (*moment*) inopportune

inorganisation [inɔʀganizasjɔ̃] *nf* lack of
organization

inorganisé, e [inɔʀganize] *adj* (*travailleurs*) non-
organized

inoubliable [inublijabl(ə)] *adj* unforgettable

inouï, e [inwi] *adj* unheard-of, extraordinary

inox [inɔks] *adj, nm* (= *inoxydable*) stainless (steel)

inoxydable [inɔksidabl(ə)] *adj* stainless;
(*couverts*) stainless steel *cpd*

inqualifiable [ɛ̃kalifjabl(ə)] *adj* unspeakable

inquiet, -ète [ɛ̃kjɛ, -ɛt] *adj* (*par nature*) anxious;
(*momentanément*) worried; **~ de qch/au sujet de
qn** worried about sth/sb

inquiétant, e [ɛ̃kjetɑ̃, -ɑ̃t] *adj* worrying,
disturbing

inquiéter [ɛ̃kjete] *vt* to worry, disturb; (*harceler*)
to harass; **s'inquiéter** to worry, become
anxious; **s'~ de** to worry about; (*s'enquérir de*) to
inquire about

inquiétude [ɛ̃kjetyd] *nf* anxiety; **donner de l'~**
ou **des ~s à** to worry; **avoir de l'~** *ou* **des ~s au
sujet de** to feel anxious *ou* worried about

inquisiteur, -trice [ɛ̃kizitœʀ, -tʀis] *adj* (*regards,
questions*) inquisitive, prying

inquisition [ɛ̃kizisjɔ̃] *nf* inquisition

INRA [inʀa] *sigle m* = **Institut national de la recherche agronomique**

inracontable [ɛ̃ʀakɔ̃tabl(ə)] *adj* (*trop osé*) unrepeatable; (*trop compliqué*): **l'histoire est ~** the story is too complicated to relate

insaisissable [ɛ̃sezisabl(ə)] *adj* elusive

insalubre [ɛ̃salybʀ(ə)] *adj* unhealthy, insalubrious

insalubrité [ɛ̃salybʀite] *nf* unhealthiness, insalubrity

insanité [ɛ̃sanite] *nf* madness *no pl*, insanity *no pl*

insatiable [ɛ̃sasjabl(ə)] *adj* insatiable

insatisfaction [ɛ̃satisfaksjɔ̃] *nf* dissatisfaction

insatisfait, e [ɛ̃satisfɛ, -ɛt] *adj* (*non comblé*) unsatisfied; (: *passion, envie*) unfulfilled; (*mécontent*) dissatisfied

inscription [ɛ̃skʀipsjɔ̃] *nf* (*sur un mur, écriteau etc*) inscription; (*à une institution*: *voir s'inscrire*) enrolment; registration

inscrire [ɛ̃skʀiʀ] *vt* (*marquer*: *sur son calepin etc*) to note *ou* write down; (: *sur un mur, une affiche etc*) to write; (: *dans la pierre, le métal*) to inscribe; (*mettre*: *sur une liste, un budget etc*) to put down; (*enrôler*: *soldat*) to enlist; **~ qn à** (*club, école etc*) to enrol sb at; **s'inscrire** *vi* (*pour une excursion etc*) to put one's name down; **s'~ (à)** (*club, parti*) to join; (*université*) to register *ou* enrol (at); (*examen, concours*) to register *ou* enter (for); **s'~ dans** (*se situer*: *négociations etc*) to come within the scope of; **s'~ en faux contre** to deny (strongly); (*Jur*) to challenge

inscrit, e [ɛ̃skʀi, it] *pp de* **inscrire** ▷ *adj* (*étudiant, électeur etc*) registered

insécable [ɛ̃sekabl(ə)] *adj* (*Inform*) indivisible; **espace ~** hard space

insecte [ɛ̃sɛkt(ə)] *nm* insect

insecticide [ɛ̃sɛktisid] *nm* insecticide

insécurité [ɛ̃sekyʀite] *nf* insecurity, lack of security

INSEE [inse] *sigle m* (= *Institut national de la statistique et des études économiques*) *national institute of statistical and economic information*

insémination [ɛ̃seminasjɔ̃] *nf* insemination

insensé, e [ɛ̃sɑ̃se] *adj* insane, mad

insensibiliser [ɛ̃sɑ̃sibilize] *vt* to anaesthetize; (*à une allergie*) to desensitize; **à qch** (*fig*) to cause to become insensitive to sth

insensibilité [ɛ̃sɑ̃sibilite] *nf* insensitivity

insensible [ɛ̃sɑ̃sibl(ə)] *adj* (*nerf, membre*) numb; (*dur, indifférent*) insensitive; (*imperceptible*) imperceptible

insensiblement [ɛ̃sɑ̃sibləmɑ̃] *adv* (*doucement, peu à peu*) imperceptibly

inséparable [ɛ̃sepaʀabl(ə)] *adj*: **~ (de)** inseparable (from) ▷ *nmpl*: **~s** (*oiseaux*) lovebirds

insérer [ɛ̃seʀe] *vt* to insert; **s'~ dans** to fit into; (*fig*) to come within

INSERM [ɛ̃sɛʀm] *sigle m* (= *Institut national de la santé et de la recherche médicale*) *national institute for medical research*

insert [ɛ̃sɛʀ] *nm* *enclosed fireplace burning solid fuel*

insertion [ɛ̃sɛʀsjɔ̃] *nf* (*d'une personne*) integration

insidieusement [ɛ̃sidjøzmɑ̃] *adv* insidiously

insidieux, -euse [ɛ̃sidjø, -øz] *adj* insidious

insigne [ɛ̃siɲ] *nm* (*d'un parti, club*) badge ▷ *adj* distinguished; **insignes** *nmpl* (*d'une fonction*) insignia *pl*

insignifiant, e [ɛ̃siɲifjɑ̃, -ɑ̃t] *adj* insignificant; (*somme, affaire, détail*) trivial, insignificant

insinuant, e [ɛ̃sinɥɑ̃, -ɑ̃t] *adj* ingratiating

insinuation [ɛ̃sinɥasjɔ̃] *nf* innuendo, insinuation

insinuer [ɛ̃sinɥe] *vt* to insinuate, imply; **s'insinuer dans** *vi* to seep into; (*fig*) to worm one's way into, creep into

insipide [ɛ̃sipid] *adj* insipid

insistance [ɛ̃sistɑ̃s] *nf* insistence; **avec ~** insistently

insistant, e [ɛ̃sistɑ̃, -ɑ̃t] *adj* insistent

insister [ɛ̃siste] *vi* to insist; (*s'obstiner*) to keep on; **~ sur** (*détail, note*) to stress; **~ pour qch/ pour faire qch** to be insistent about sth/about doing sth

insociable [ɛ̃sɔsjabl(ə)] *adj* unsociable

insolation [ɛ̃sɔlasjɔ̃] *nf* (*Méd*) sunstroke *no pl*; (*ensoleillement*) period of sunshine

insolence [ɛ̃sɔlɑ̃s] *nf* insolence *no pl*; **avec ~** insolently

insolent, e [ɛ̃sɔlɑ̃, -ɑ̃t] *adj* insolent

insolite [ɛ̃sɔlit] *adj* strange, unusual

insoluble [ɛ̃sɔlybl(ə)] *adj* insoluble

insolvable [ɛ̃sɔlvabl(ə)] *adj* insolvent

insomniaque [ɛ̃sɔmnjak] *adj, nm/f* insomniac

insomnie [ɛ̃sɔmni] *nf* insomnia *no pl*, sleeplessness *no pl*; **avoir des ~s** to suffer from insomnia

insondable [ɛ̃sɔ̃dabl(ə)] *adj* unfathomable

insonore [ɛ̃sɔnɔʀ] *adj* soundproof

insonorisation [ɛ̃sɔnɔʀizasjɔ̃] *nf* soundproofing

insonoriser [ɛ̃sɔnɔʀize] *vt* to soundproof

insouciance [ɛ̃susjɑ̃s] *nf* carefree attitude; heedless attitude

insouciant, e [ɛ̃susjɑ̃, -ɑ̃t] *adj* carefree; (*imprévoyant*) heedless

insoumis, e [ɛ̃sumi, -iz] *adj* (*caractère, enfant*) rebellious, refractory; (*contrée, tribu*) unsubdued; (*Mil*: *soldat*) absent without leave ▷ *nm* (*Mil*: *soldat*) absentee

insoumission [ɛ̃sumisjɔ̃] *nf* rebelliousness; (*Mil*) absence without leave

insoupçonnable [ɛ̃supsɔnabl(ə)] *adj* above suspicion

insoupçonné, e [ɛ̃supsɔne] *adj* unsuspected

insoutenable [ɛ̃sutnabl(ə)] *adj* (*argument*) untenable; (*chaleur*) unbearable

inspecter [ɛ̃spɛkte] *vt* to inspect

inspecteur, -trice [ɛ̃spɛktœʀ, -tʀis] *nm/f* inspector; (*des assurances*) assessor; **~ d'Académie** (regional) director of education; **~ (de l'enseignement) primaire** primary school inspector; **~ des finances** ≈ tax inspector (*Brit*),

≈ Internal Revenue Service agent (US); ~ **(de police)** (police) inspector

inspection [ɛ̃spɛksjɔ̃] *nf* inspection

inspirateur, -trice [ɛ̃spiRatœR, -tRis] *nm/f* (*instigateur*) instigator; (*animateur*) inspirer

inspiration [ɛ̃spiRasjɔ̃] *nf* inspiration; breathing in *no pl*; (*idée*) flash of inspiration, brainwave; **sous l'~ de** prompted by

inspiré, e [ɛ̃spiRe] *adj*: **être bien/mal ~ de faire qch** to be well-advised/ill-advised to do sth

inspirer [ɛ̃spiRe] *vt* (*gén*) to inspire ▷ *vi* (*aspirer*) to breathe in; **s'inspirer de** (*artiste*) to draw one's inspiration from; (*tableau*) to be inspired by; **~ qch à qn** (*œuvre, project, action*) to inspire sb with sth; (*dégoût, crainte, horreur*) to fill sb with sth; **ça ne m'inspire pas** I'm not keen on the idea

instabilité [ɛ̃stabilite] *nf* instability

instable [ɛ̃stabl(ə)] *adj* (*meuble, équilibre*) unsteady; (*population, temps*) unsettled; (*paix, régime, caractère*) unstable

installateur [ɛ̃stalatœR] *nm* fitter

installation [ɛ̃stalasjɔ̃] *nf* installation; putting in *ou* up; fitting out; settling in; (*appareils etc*) fittings *pl*, installations *pl*; **installations** *nfpl* installations; (*industrielles*) plant *sg*; (*de loisirs*) facilities

installé, e [ɛ̃stale] *adj*: **bien/mal ~** well/poorly equipped; (*personne*) well/not very well set up *ou* organized

installer [ɛ̃stale] *vt* (*loger*): **~ qn** to get sb settled, install sb; (*asseoir, coucher*) to settle (down); (*placer*) to put, place; (*meuble*) to put in; (*rideau, étagère, tente*) to put up; (*gaz, électricité etc*) to put in, install; (*appartement*) to fit out; (*aménager*): **~ une salle de bains dans une pièce** to fit out a room with a bathroom suite; **s'installer** *vi* (*s'établir: artisan, dentiste etc*) to set o.s. up; (*se loger*): **s'~ à l'hôtel/chez qn** to move into a hotel/in with sb; (*emménager*) to settle in; (*sur un siège, à un emplacement*) to settle (down); (*fig: maladie, grève*) to take a firm hold *ou* grip

instamment [ɛ̃stamɑ̃] *adv* urgently

instance [ɛ̃stɑ̃s] *nf* (*Jur: procédure*) (legal) proceedings *pl*; (*Admin: autorité*) authority; **instances** *nfpl* (*prières*) entreaties; **affaire en ~** matter pending; **courrier en ~** mail ready for posting; **être en ~ de divorce** to be awaiting a divorce; **train en ~ de départ** train on the point of departure; **tribunal de première ~** court of first instance; **en seconde ~** on appeal

instant [ɛ̃stɑ̃] *nm* moment, instant; **dans un ~** in a moment; **à l'~** this instant; **je l'ai vu à l'~** I've just this minute seen him, I saw him a moment ago; **à l'~ (même) où** at the (very) moment that *ou* when, (just) as; **à chaque ~, à tout ~** at any moment; constantly; **pour l'~** for the moment, for the time being; **par ~s** at times; **de tous les ~s** perpetual; **dès l'~ où** *ou* **que ...** from the moment when ..., since that moment when ...

instantané, e [ɛ̃stɑ̃tane] *adj* (*lait, café*) instant;

(*explosion, mort*) instantaneous ▷ *nm* snapshot

instantanément [ɛ̃stɑ̃tanemɑ̃] *adv* instantaneously

instar [ɛ̃staR]: **à l'~ de** *prép* following the example of, like

instaurer [ɛ̃stoRe] *vt* to institute; **s'instaurer** *vi* to set o.s. up; (*collaboration etc*) to be established

instigateur, -trice [ɛ̃stigatœR, -tRis] *nm/f* instigator

instigation [ɛ̃stigasjɔ̃] *nf*: **à l'~ de qn** at sb's instigation

instiller [ɛ̃stile] *vt* to instil, apply

instinct [ɛ̃stɛ̃] *nm* instinct; **d'~** (*spontanément*) instinctively; **~ grégaire** herd instinct; **~ de conservation** instinct of self-preservation

instinctif, -ive [ɛ̃stɛ̃ktif, -iv] *adj* instinctive

instinctivement [ɛ̃stɛ̃ktivmɑ̃] *adv* instinctively

instit [ɛ̃stit] (*fam*) *nm/f* (primary school) teacher

instituer [ɛ̃stitɥe] *vt* to institute, set up; **s'~ défenseur d'une cause** to set o.s up as defender of a cause

institut [ɛ̃stity] *nm* institute; **~ de beauté** beauty salon; **~ médico-légal** mortuary; **I-universitaire de technologie (IUT)** technical college

instituteur, -trice [ɛ̃stitytœR, -tRis] *nm/f* (primary (*Brit*) *ou* grade (*US*) school) teacher

institution [ɛ̃stitysjɔ̃] *nf* institution; (*collège*) private school

institutionnaliser [ɛ̃stitysjɔnalize] *vt* to institutionalize

instructeur, -trice [ɛ̃stRyktœR, -tRis] *adj* (*Mil*): **sergent ~** drill sergeant; (*Jur*): **juge ~** examining (*Brit*) *ou* committing (*US*) magistrate ▷ *nm/f* instructor

instructif, -ive [ɛ̃stRyktif, -iv] *adj* instructive

instruction [ɛ̃stRyksjɔ̃] *nf* (*enseignement, savoir*) education; (*Jur*: preliminary) investigation and hearing; (*directive*) instruction; (*Admin: document*) directive; **instructions** *nfpl* instructions; (*mode d'emploi*) directions, instructions; **~ civique** civics *sg*; **~ primaire/publique** primary/public education; **~ religieuse** religious instruction; **~ professionnelle** vocational training

instruire [ɛ̃stRɥiR] *vt* (*élèves*) to teach; (*recrues*) to train; (*Jur: affaire*) to conduct the investigation for; **s'instruire** to educate o.s.; **s'~ auprès de qn de qch** (*s'informer*) to find sth out from sb; **~ qn de qch** (*informer*) to inform *ou* advise sb of sth; **~ contre qn** (*Jur*) to investigate sb

instruit, e [ɛ̃stRɥi, -it] *pp de* **instruire** ▷ *adj* educated

instrument [ɛ̃stRymɑ̃] *nm* instrument; **~ à cordes/vent** stringed/wind instrument; **~ de mesure** measuring instrument; **~ de musique** musical instrument; **~ de travail** (working) tool

instrumental, e, -aux [ɛ̃stRymɑ̃tal, -o] *adj* instrumental

instrumentation [ɛ̃stRymɑ̃tasjɔ̃] *nf* instrumentation

instrumentiste [ɛ̃stʀymɑ̃tist(ə)] *nm/f*
instrumentalist
insu [ɛ̃sy] *nm*: **à l'~ de qn** without sb knowing
insubmersible [ɛ̃sybmɛʀsibl(ə)] *adj* unsinkable
insubordination [ɛ̃sybɔʀdinasjɔ̃] *nf*
rebelliousness; (*Mil*) insubordination
insubordonné, e [ɛ̃sybɔʀdɔne] *adj*
insubordinate
insuccès [ɛ̃syksɛ] *nm* failure
insuffisamment [ɛ̃syfizamɑ̃] *adv* insufficiently
insuffisance [ɛ̃syfizɑ̃s] *nf* insufficiency;
inadequacy; **insuffisances** *nfpl* (*lacunes*)
inadequacies; **~ cardiaque** cardiac
insufficiency *no pl*; **~ hépatique** liver deficiency
insuffisant, e [ɛ̃syfizɑ̃, -ɑ̃t] *adj* insufficient;
(*élève, travail*) inadequate
insuffler [ɛ̃syfle] *vt*: **~ qch dans** to blow sth into;
~ qch à qn to inspire sb with sth
insulaire [ɛ̃sylɛʀ] *adj* island *cpd*; (*attitude*)
insular
insularité [ɛ̃sylaʀite] *nf* insularity
insuline [ɛ̃sylin] *nf* insulin
insultant, e [ɛ̃syltɑ̃, -ɑ̃t] *adj* insulting
insulte [ɛ̃sylt(ə)] *nf* insult
insulter [ɛ̃sylte] *vt* to insult
insupportable [ɛ̃sypɔʀtabl(ə)] *adj* unbearable
insurgé, e [ɛ̃syʀʒe] *adj, nm/f* insurgent, rebel
insurger [ɛ̃syʀʒe]: **s'insurger** *vi*: **s'~ (contre)** to
rise up *ou* rebel (against)
insurmontable [ɛ̃syʀmɔ̃tabl(ə)] *adj* (*difficulté*)
insuperable; (*aversion*) unconquerable
insurpassable [ɛ̃syʀpɑsabl(ə)] *adj*
unsurpassable, unsurpassed
insurrection [ɛ̃syʀɛksjɔ̃] *nf* insurrection, revolt
insurrectionnel, le [ɛ̃syʀɛksjɔnɛl] *adj*
insurrectionary
intact, e [ɛ̃takt] *adj* intact
intangible [ɛ̃tɑ̃ʒibl(ə)] *adj* intangible; (*principe*)
inviolable
intarissable [ɛ̃taʀisabl(ə)] *adj* inexhaustible
intégral, e, -aux [ɛ̃tegʀal, -o] *adj* complete ▷ *nf*
(*Math*) integral; (*œuvres complètes*) complete
works
intégralement [ɛ̃tegʀalmɑ̃] *adv* in full, fully
intégralité [ɛ̃tegʀalite] *nf* (*d'une somme, d'un
revenu*) whole (*ou* full) amount; **dans son ~** in its
entirety
intégrant, e [ɛ̃tegʀɑ̃, -ɑ̃t] *adj*: **faire partie ~e de**
to be an integral part of, be part and parcel of
intégration [ɛ̃tegʀasjɔ̃] *nf* integration
intégrationniste [ɛ̃tegʀasjɔnist(ə)] *adj, nm/f*
integrationist
intégré, e [ɛ̃tegʀe] *adj*: **circuit ~** integrated
circuit
intègre [ɛ̃tɛgʀ(ə)] *adj* perfectly honest, upright
intégrer [ɛ̃tegʀe] *vt*: **~ qch à** *ou* **dans** to
integrate sth into; **s'~ à** *ou* **dans** to become
integrated into
intégrisme [ɛ̃tegʀism(ə)] *nm* fundamentalism
intégriste [ɛ̃tegʀist(ə)] *adj, nm/f*
fundamentalist
intégrité [ɛ̃tegʀite] *nf* integrity

intellect [ɛ̃telɛkt] *nm* intellect
intellectuel, le [ɛ̃telɛktɥɛl] *adj, nm/f*
intellectual; (*péj*) highbrow
intellectuellement [ɛ̃telɛktɥɛlmɑ̃] *adv*
intellectually
intelligemment [ɛ̃teliʒamɑ̃] *adv* intelligently
intelligence [ɛ̃teliʒɑ̃s] *nf* intelligence;
(*compréhension*): **l'~ de** the understanding of;
(*complicité*): **regard d'~** glance of complicity,
meaningful *ou* knowing look; (*accord*): **vivre en
bonne ~ avec qn** to be on good terms with sb;
intelligences *nfpl* (*Mil, fig*) secret contacts; **être
d'~** to have an understanding; **~ artificielle**
artificial intelligence (A.I.)
intelligent, e [ɛ̃teliʒɑ̃, -ɑ̃t] *adj* intelligent;
(*capable*): **~ en affaires** competent in business
intelligentsia [ɛ̃telidʒɛnsja] *nf* intelligentsia
intelligible [ɛ̃teliʒibl(ə)] *adj* intelligible
intello [ɛ̃telo] *adj, nm/f* (*fam*) highbrow
intempérance [ɛ̃tɑ̃peʀɑ̃s] *nf* overindulgence *no
pl*; intemperance *no pl*
intempérant, e [ɛ̃tɑ̃peʀɑ̃, -ɑ̃t] *adj*
overindulgent; (*moralement*) intemperate
intempéries [ɛ̃tɑ̃peʀi] *nfpl* bad weather *sg*
intempestif, -ive [ɛ̃tɑ̃pɛstif, -iv] *adj* untimely
intenable [ɛ̃tnabl(ə)] *adj* unbearable
intendance [ɛ̃tɑ̃dɑ̃s] *nf* (*Mil*) supply corps;
(: *bureau*) supplies office; (*Scol*) bursar's office
intendant, e [ɛ̃tɑ̃dɑ̃, -ɑ̃t] *nm/f* (*Mil*)
quartermaster; (*Scol*) bursar; (*d'une propriété*)
steward
intense [ɛ̃tɑ̃s] *adj* intense
intensément [ɛ̃tɑ̃semɑ̃] *adv* intensely
intensif, -ive [ɛ̃tɑ̃sif, -iv] *adj* intensive; **cours ~**
crash course; **~ en main-d'œuvre** labour-
intensive; **~ en capital** capital-intensive
intensification [ɛ̃tɑ̃sifikasjɔ̃] *nf* intensification
intensifier [ɛ̃tɑ̃sifje] *vt*, **s'intensifier** *vi* to
intensify
intensité [ɛ̃tɑ̃site] *nf* intensity
intensivement [ɛ̃tɑ̃sivmɑ̃] *adv* intensively
intenter [ɛ̃tɑ̃te] *vt*: **~ un procès contre** *ou* **à qn**
to start proceedings against sb
intention [ɛ̃tɑ̃sjɔ̃] *nf* intention; (*Jur*) intent;
avoir l'~ de faire to intend to do, have the
intention of doing; **dans l'~ de faire qch** with
a view to doing sth; **à l'~ de** *prép* for;
(*renseignement*) for the benefit *ou* information of;
(*film, ouvrage*) aimed at; **à cette ~** with this aim
in view; **sans ~** unintentionally; **faire qch
sans mauvaise ~** to do sth without ill intent;
agir dans une bonne ~ to act with good
intentions
intentionné, e [ɛ̃tɑ̃sjɔne] *adj*: **bien ~** well-
meaning *ou* -intentioned; **mal ~** ill-
intentioned
intentionnel, le [ɛ̃tɑ̃sjɔnɛl] *adj* intentional,
deliberate
intentionnellement [ɛ̃tɑ̃sjɔnɛlmɑ̃] *adv*
intentionally, deliberately
inter [ɛ̃tɛʀ] *nm* (*Tél*: *interurbain*) long-distance
call service; (*Sport*): **~ gauche/droit** inside-

left/-right

interactif, -ive [ɛ̃tɛʀaktif, -iv] *adj* (*aussi Inform*) interactive

interaction [ɛ̃tɛʀaksjɔ̃] *nf* interaction

interbancaire [ɛ̃tɛʀbɑ̃kɛʀ] *adj* interbank

intercalaire [ɛ̃tɛʀkalɛʀ] *adj, nm*: (**feuillet**) ~ insert; (**fiche**) ~ divider

intercaler [ɛ̃tɛʀkale] *vt* to insert; **s'intercaler entre** *vi* to come in between; to slip in between

intercéder [ɛ̃tɛʀsede] *vi*: ~ (**pour qn**) to intercede (on behalf of sb)

intercepter [ɛ̃tɛʀsɛpte] *vt* to intercept; (*lumière, chaleur*) to cut off

intercepteur [ɛ̃tɛʀsɛptœʀ] *nm* (*Aviat*) interceptor

interception [ɛ̃tɛʀsɛpsjɔ̃] *nf* interception; **avion d'**~ interceptor

intercession [ɛ̃tɛʀsesjɔ̃] *nf* intercession

interchangeable [ɛ̃tɛʀʃɑ̃ʒabl(ə)] *adj* interchangeable

interclasse [ɛ̃tɛʀklas] *nm* (*Scol*) break (between classes)

interclubs [ɛ̃tɛʀklœb] *adj inv* interclub

intercommunal, e, -aux [ɛ̃tɛʀkɔmynal, -o] *adj* intervillage, intercommunity

intercommunautaire [ɛ̃tɛʀkɔmynotɛʀ] *adj* intercommunity

intercontinental, e, -aux [ɛ̃tɛʀkɔ̃tinɑ̃tal, -o] *adj* intercontinental

intercostal, e, -aux [ɛ̃tɛʀkɔstal, -o] *adj* intercostal, between the ribs

interdépartemental, e, -aux [ɛ̃tɛʀdepaʀtəmɑ̃tal, -o] *adj* interdepartmental

interdépendance [ɛ̃tɛʀdepɑ̃dɑ̃s] *nf* interdependence

interdépendant, e [ɛ̃tɛʀdepɑ̃dɑ̃, -ɑ̃t] *adj* interdependent

interdiction [ɛ̃tɛʀdiksjɔ̃] *nf* ban; ~ **de faire qch** ban on doing sth; ~ **de séjour** (*Jur*) *order banning ex-prisoner from frequenting specified places*

interdire [ɛ̃tɛʀdiʀ] *vt* to forbid; (*Admin: stationnement, meeting, passage*) to ban, prohibit; (: *journal, livre*) to ban; ~ **qch à qn** to forbid sb sth; ~ **à qn de faire** to forbid sb to do, prohibit sb from doing; (*empêchement*) to prevent *ou* preclude sb from doing; **s'interdire qch** *vi* (*éviter*) to refrain *ou* abstain from sth; (*se refuser*): **il s'interdit d'y penser** he doesn't allow himself to think about it

interdisciplinaire [ɛ̃tɛʀdisiplinɛʀ] *adj* interdisciplinary

interdit, e [ɛ̃tɛʀdi, -it] *pp de* **interdire** ▷ *adj* (*stupéfait*) taken aback; (*défendu*) forbidden, prohibited ▷ *nm* interdict, prohibition; **film** ~ **aux moins de 18/13 ans** ≈ 18-/PG-rated film; **sens** ~ one way; **stationnement** ~ no parking; ~ **de chéquier** having cheque book facilities suspended; ~ **de séjour** subject to an "interdiction de séjour"

intéressant, e [ɛ̃teʀesɑ̃, -ɑ̃t] *adj* interesting; **faire l'**~ to draw attention to o.s.

intéressé, e [ɛ̃teʀese] *adj* (*parties*) involved, concerned; (*amitié, motifs*) self-interested ▷ *nm*: **l'**~ the interested party; **les ~s** those concerned *ou* involved

intéressement [ɛ̃teʀesmɑ̃] *nm* (*Comm*) profit-sharing

intéresser [ɛ̃teʀese] *vt* to interest; (*toucher*) to be of interest *ou* concern to; (*Admin: concerner*) to affect, concern; (*Comm: travailleur*) to give a share in the profits to; (: *partenaire*) to interest (in the business); **s'intéresser à** *vi* to take an interest in, be interested in; ~ **qn à qch** to get sb interested in sth

intérêt [ɛ̃teʀɛ] *nm* (*aussi Comm*) interest; (*égoïsme*) self-interest; **porter de l'**~ **à qn** to take an interest in sb; **agir par** ~ to act out of self-interest; **avoir des ~s dans** (*Comm*) to have a financial interest *ou* a stake in; **avoir ~ à faire** to do well to do; **il y a ~ à ...** it would be a good thing to ...; ~ **composé** compound interest

interface [ɛ̃tɛʀfas] *nf* (*Inform*) interface

interférence [ɛ̃tɛʀfeʀɑ̃s] *nf* interference

interférer [ɛ̃tɛʀfeʀe] *vi*: ~ (**avec**) to interfere (with)

intergouvernemental, e, -aux [ɛ̃tɛʀguvɛʀnəmɑ̃tal, -o] *adj* intergovernmental

intérieur, e [ɛ̃teʀjœʀ] *adj* (*mur, escalier, poche*) inside; (*commerce, politique*) domestic; (*cour, calme, vie*) inner; (*navigation*) inland ▷ *nm* (*d'une maison, d'un récipient etc*) inside; (*d'un pays, aussi: décor, mobilier*) interior; (*Pol*): **l'I** (the Department of) the Interior, ≈ the Home Office (*Brit*); **à l'**~ (**de**) inside; (*fig*) within; **de l'**~ (*fig*) from the inside; **en** ~ (*Ciné*) in the studio; **vêtement d'**~ indoor garment

intérieurement [ɛ̃teʀjœʀmɑ̃] *adv* inwardly

intérim [ɛ̃teʀim] *nm* (*période*) interim period; (*travail*) temping; **agence d'**~ temping agency; **assurer l'**~ (**de**) to deputize (for); **président par** ~ interim president; **travailler en** ~ to temp

intérimaire [ɛ̃teʀimɛʀ] *adj* temporary, interim ▷ *nm/f* (*secrétaire etc*) temporary, temp (*Brit*); (*suppléant*) deputy

intérioriser [ɛ̃teʀjɔʀize] *vt* to internalize

interjection [ɛ̃tɛʀʒɛksjɔ̃] *nf* interjection

interjeter [ɛ̃tɛʀʒəte] *vt* (*Jur*): ~ **appel** to lodge an appeal

interligne [ɛ̃tɛʀliɲ] *nm* inter-line space ▷ *nf* (*Typo*) lead, leading; **simple/double** ~ single/double spacing

interlocuteur, -trice [ɛ̃tɛʀlɔkytœʀ, -tʀis] *nm/f* speaker; (*Pol*): ~ **valable** valid representative; **son** ~ the person he *ou* she was speaking to

interlope [ɛ̃tɛʀlɔp] *adj* illicit; (*milieu, bar*) shady

interloquer [ɛ̃tɛʀlɔke] *vt* to take aback

interlude [ɛ̃tɛʀlyd] *nm* interlude

intermède [ɛ̃tɛʀmɛd] *nm* interlude

intermédiaire [ɛ̃tɛʀmedjɛʀ] *adj* intermediate; middle; half-way ▷ *nm/f* intermediary; (*Comm*) middleman; **sans** ~ directly; **par l'**~ **de** through

interminable [ɛ̃tɛʀminabl(ə)] *adj* never-ending

interminablement [ɛ̃tɛʀminabləmɑ̃] *adv* interminably

interministériel, le [ɛ̃tɛʀministeʀjɛl] *adj*: **comité** ~ interdepartmental committee

intermittence [ɛ̃tɛʀmitɑ̃s] *nf*: **par** ~ intermittently, sporadically

intermittent, e [ɛ̃tɛʀmitɑ̃, -ɑ̃t] *adj* intermittent, sporadic

internat [ɛ̃tɛʀna] *nm* (*Scol*) boarding school

international, e, -aux [ɛ̃tɛʀnasjɔnal, -o] *adj*, *nm/f* international

internationalisation [ɛ̃tɛʀnasjɔnalizasjɔ̃] *nf* internationalization

internationaliser [ɛ̃tɛʀnasjɔnalize] *vt* to internationalize

internationalisme [ɛ̃tɛʀnasjɔnalism(ə)] *nm* internationalism

internaute [ɛ̃tɛʀnot] *nm/f* Internet user

interne [ɛ̃tɛʀn(ə)] *adj* internal ▷ *nm/f* (*Scol*) boarder; (*Méd*) houseman (*Brit*), intern (*US*)

internement [ɛ̃tɛʀnəmɑ̃] *nm* (*Pol*) internment; (*Méd*) confinement

interner [ɛ̃tɛʀne] *vt* (*Pol*) to intern; (*Méd*) to confine to a mental institution

Internet [ɛ̃tɛʀnɛt] *nm*: **l'**~ the Internet

interparlementaire [ɛ̃tɛʀpaʀləmɑ̃tɛʀ] *adj* interparliamentary

interpellation [ɛ̃tɛʀpelasjɔ̃] *nf* interpellation; (*Pol*) question

interpeller [ɛ̃tɛʀpele] *vt* (*appeler*) to call out to; (*apostropher*) to shout at; (*Police*) to take in for questioning; (*Pol*) to question; **s'interpeller** *vi* to exchange insults

interphone [ɛ̃tɛʀfɔn] *nm* intercom

interplanétaire [ɛ̃tɛʀplanetɛʀ] *adj* interplanetary

Interpol [ɛ̃tɛʀpɔl] *sigle m* Interpol

interpoler [ɛ̃tɛʀpole] *vt* to interpolate

interposer [ɛ̃tɛʀpoze] *vt* to interpose; **s'interposer** *vi* to intervene; **par personnes interposées** through a third party

interprétariat [ɛ̃tɛʀpʀetaʀja] *nm* interpreting

interprétation [ɛ̃tɛʀpʀetasjɔ̃] *nf* interpretation

interprète [ɛ̃tɛʀpʀɛt] *nm/f* interpreter; (*porte-parole*) spokesman

interpréter [ɛ̃tɛʀpʀete] *vt* to interpret

interprofessionnel, le [ɛ̃tɛʀpʀɔfesjɔnɛl] *adj* interprofessional

interrogateur, -trice [ɛ̃teʀɔgatœʀ, -tʀis] *adj* questioning, inquiring ▷ *nm/f* (*Scol*) (oral) examiner

interrogatif, -ive [ɛ̃teʀɔgatif, -iv] *adj* (*Ling*) interrogative

interrogation [ɛ̃teʀɔgasjɔ̃] *nf* question; (*Scol*) (written *ou* oral) test

interrogatoire [ɛ̃teʀɔgatwaʀ] *nm* (*Police*) questioning *no pl*; (*Jur*) cross-examination, interrogation

interroger [ɛ̃teʀɔʒe] *vt* to question; (*Inform*) to search; (*Scol: candidat*) to test; ~ **qn (sur qch)** to question sb (about sth); ~ **qn du regard** to look questioningly at sb, give sb a questioning look;

s'~ **sur qch** to ask o.s. about sth, ponder (about) sth

interrompre [ɛ̃teʀɔ̃pʀ(ə)] *vt* (*gén*) to interrupt; (*travail, voyage*) to break off, interrupt; **s'interrompre** *vi* to break off

interrupteur [ɛ̃teʀyptœʀ] *nm* switch

interruption [ɛ̃teʀypsjɔ̃] *nf* interruption; **sans** ~ without a break; ~ **de grossesse** termination of pregnancy; ~ **volontaire de grossesse** voluntary termination of pregnancy, abortion

interscolaire [ɛ̃tɛʀskɔlɛʀ] *adj* interschool(s)

intersection [ɛ̃tɛʀsɛksjɔ̃] *nf* intersection

intersidéral, e, -aux [ɛ̃tɛʀsideʀal, -o] *adj* interstellar

interstice [ɛ̃tɛʀstis] *nm* crack, slit

intersyndical, e, -aux [ɛ̃tɛʀsɛ̃dikal, -o] *adj* interunion

interurbain [ɛ̃tɛʀyʀbɛ̃] (*Tél*) *nm* long-distance call service ▷ *adj* long-distance

intervalle [ɛ̃tɛʀval] *nm* (*espace*) space; (*de temps*) interval; **dans l'**~ in the meantime; **à deux mois d'**~ after a space of two months; **à ~s rapprochés** at close intervals; **par ~s** at intervals

intervenant, e [ɛ̃tɛʀvənɑ̃, -ɑ̃t] *vb voir* **intervenir** ▷ *nm/f* speaker (*at conference*)

intervenir [ɛ̃tɛʀvəniʀ] *vi* (*gén*) to intervene; (*survenir*) to take place; (*faire une conférence*) to give a talk *ou* lecture; ~ **auprès de/en faveur de qn** to intervene with/on behalf of sb; **la police a dû** ~ police had to step in *ou* intervene; **les médecins ont dû** ~ the doctors had to operate

intervention [ɛ̃tɛʀvɑ̃sjɔ̃] *nf* intervention; (*conférence*) talk, paper; ~ **(chirurgicale)** operation

interventionnisme [ɛ̃tɛʀvɑ̃sjɔnism(ə)] *nm* interventionism

interventionniste [ɛ̃tɛʀvɑ̃sjɔnist(ə)] *adj* interventionist

intervenu, e [ɛ̃tɛʀv(ə)ny] *pp de* **intervenir**

intervertible [ɛ̃tɛʀvɛʀtibl(ə)] *adj* interchangeable

intervertir [ɛ̃tɛʀvɛʀtiʀ] *vt* to invert (the order of), reverse

interviendrai [ɛ̃tɛʀvjɛ̃dʀe], **interviens** *etc* [ɛ̃tɛʀvjɛ̃] *vb voir* **intervenir**

interview [ɛ̃tɛʀvju] *nf* interview

interviewer [ɛ̃tɛʀvjuve] *vt* to interview ▷ *nm* [ɛ̃tɛʀvjuvœʀ] (*journaliste*) interviewer

intervins *etc* [ɛ̃tɛʀvɛ̃] *vb voir* **intervenir**

intestat [ɛ̃tɛsta] *adj* (*Jur*): **décéder** ~ to die intestate

intestin, e [ɛ̃tɛstɛ̃, -in] *adj* internal ▷ *nm* intestine; ~ **grêle** small intestine

intestinal, e, -aux [ɛ̃tɛstinal, -o] *adj* intestinal

intime [ɛ̃tim] *adj* intimate; (*vie, journal*) private; (*convictions*) inmost; (*dîner, cérémonie*) held among friends, quiet ▷ *nm/f* close friend

intimement [ɛ̃timmɑ̃] *adv* (*profondément*) deeply, firmly; (*étroitement*) intimately

intimer [ɛ̃time] *vt* (*Jur*) to notify; ~ **à qn l'ordre de faire** to order sb to do

intimidant, e [ɛ̃timidɑ̃, -ɑ̃t] *adj* intimidating
intimidation [ɛ̃timidasjɔ̃] *nf* intimidation;
manœuvres d'~ (*action*) acts of intimidation;
(*stratégie*) intimidatory tactics
intimider [ɛ̃timide] *vt* to intimidate
intimité [ɛ̃timite] *nf* intimacy; (*vie privée*)
privacy; private life; **dans l'~** in private; (*sans
formalités*) with only a few friends, quietly
intitulé [ɛ̃tityle] *nm* title
intituler [ɛ̃tityle] *vt*: **comment a-t-il intitulé
son livre?** what title did he give his book?;
s'intituler *vi* to be entitled; (*personne*) to call o.s.
intolérable [ɛ̃tɔlerabl(ə)] *adj* intolerable
intolérance [ɛ̃tɔlerɑ̃s] *nf* intolerance; **~ aux
antibiotiques** intolerance to antibiotics
intolérant, e [ɛ̃tɔlerɑ̃, -ɑ̃t] *adj* intolerant
intonation [ɛ̃tɔnasjɔ̃] *nf* intonation
intouchable [ɛ̃tuʃabl(ə)] *adj* (*fig*) above the law,
sacrosanct; (*Rel*) untouchable
intox [ɛ̃tɔks] (*fam*) *nf* brainwashing
intoxication [ɛ̃tɔksikasjɔ̃] *nf* poisoning *no pl*;
(*toxicomanie*) drug addiction; (*fig*) brainwashing;
~ alimentaire food poisoning
intoxiqué, e [ɛ̃tɔksike] *nm/f* addict
intoxiquer [ɛ̃tɔksike] *vt* to poison; (*fig*) to
brainwash; **s'intoxiquer** to poison o.s.
intradermique [ɛ̃tradɛrmik] *adj, nf*:
(**injection**) **~** intradermal *ou* intracutaneous
injection
intraduisible [ɛ̃traduizibl(ə)] *adj*
untranslatable; (*fig*) inexpressible
intraitable [ɛ̃trɛtabl(ə)] *adj* inflexible,
uncompromising
intramusculaire [ɛ̃tramyskylɛr] *adj, nf*:
(**injection**) **~** intramuscular injection
intranet [ɛ̃tranɛt] *nm* intranet
intransigeance [ɛ̃trɑ̃ziʒɑ̃s] *nf* intransigence
intransigeant, e [ɛ̃trɑ̃ziʒɑ̃, -ɑ̃t] *adj*
intransigent; (*morale, passion*) uncompromising
intransitif, -ive [ɛ̃trɑ̃zitif, -iv] *adj* (*Ling*)
intransitive
intransportable [ɛ̃trɑ̃spɔrtabl(ə)] *adj* (*blessé*)
unable to travel
intraveineux, -euse [ɛ̃travɛnø, -øz] *adj*
intravenous
intrépide [ɛ̃trepid] *adj* dauntless, intrepid
intrépidité [ɛ̃trepidite] *nf* dauntlessness
intrigant, e [ɛ̃trigɑ̃, -ɑ̃t] *nm/f* schemer
intrigue [ɛ̃trig] *nf* intrigue; (*scénario*) plot
intriguer [ɛ̃trige] *vi* to scheme ▷ *vt* to puzzle,
intrigue
intrinsèque [ɛ̃trɛ̃sɛk] *adj* intrinsic
introductif, -ive [ɛ̃trɔdyktif, -iv] *adj*
introductory
introduction [ɛ̃trɔdyksjɔ̃] *nf* introduction;
paroles/chapitre d'~ introductory words/
chapter; **lettre/mot d'~** letter/note of
introduction
introduire [ɛ̃trɔduir] *vt* to introduce; (*visiteur*)
to show in; (*aiguille, clef*): **~ qch dans** to insert *ou*
introduce sth into; (*personne*): **à qch** to
introduce to sth; (: *présenter*): **~ qn à qn/dans un**

club to introduce sb to sb/to a club; **s'introduire**
vi (*techniques, usages*) to be introduced; **s'~ dans**
to gain entry into; to get o.s. accepted into; (*eau,
fumée*) to get into; **~ au clavier** to key in
introduit, e [ɛ̃trɔdui, -it] *pp de* **introduire** ▷ *adj*:
bien ~ (*personne*) well-received
introniser [ɛ̃trɔnize] *vt* to enthrone
introspection [ɛ̃trɔspɛksjɔ̃] *nf* introspection
introuvable [ɛ̃truvabl(ə)] *adj* which cannot be
found; (*Comm*) unobtainable
introverti, e [ɛ̃trɔvɛrti] *nm/f* introvert
intrus, e [ɛ̃try, -yz] *nm/f* intruder
intrusion [ɛ̃tryzjɔ̃] *nf* intrusion; (*ingérence*)
interference
intuitif, -ive [ɛ̃tuitif, -iv] *adj* intuitive
intuition [ɛ̃tuisjɔ̃] *nf* intuition; **avoir une ~** to
have a feeling; **avoir l'~ de qch** to have an
intuition of sth; **avoir de l'~** to have intuition
intuitivement [ɛ̃tuitivmɑ̃] *adv* intuitively
inusable [inyzabl(ə)] *adj* hard-wearing
inusité, e [inyzite] *adj* rarely used
inutile [inytil] *adj* useless; (*superflu*)
unnecessary
inutilement [inytilmɑ̃] *adv* needlessly
inutilisable [inytilizabl(ə)] *adj* unusable
inutilisé, e [inytilize] *adj* unused
inutilité [inytilite] *nf* uselessness
invaincu, e [ɛ̃vɛ̃ky] *adj* unbeaten; (*armée, peuple*)
unconquered
invalide [ɛ̃valid] *adj* disabled ▷ *nm/f*: **~ de
guerre** disabled ex-serviceman; **~ du travail**
industrially disabled person
invalider [ɛ̃valide] *vt* to invalidate
invalidité [ɛ̃validite] *nf* disability
invariable [ɛ̃varjabl(ə)] *adj* invariable
invariablement [ɛ̃varjabləmɑ̃] *adv* invariably
invasion [ɛ̃vazjɔ̃] *nf* invasion
invective [ɛ̃vɛktiv] *nf* invective
invectiver [ɛ̃vɛktive] *vt* to hurl abuse at ▷ *vi*: **~
contre** to rail against
invendable [ɛ̃vɑ̃dabl(ə)] *adj* unsaleable,
unmarketable
invendu, e [ɛ̃vɑ̃dy] *adj* unsold ▷ *nm* return;
invendus *nmpl* unsold goods
inventaire [ɛ̃vɑ̃tɛr] *nm* inventory; (*Comm: liste*)
stocklist; (: *opération*) stocktaking *no pl*; (*fig*)
survey; **faire un ~** to make an inventory;
(*Comm*) to take stock; **faire** *ou* **procéder à l'~** to
take stock
inventer [ɛ̃vɑ̃te] *vt* to invent; (*subterfuge*) to
devise, invent; (*histoire, excuse*) to make up,
invent; **~ de faire** to hit on the idea of doing
inventeur, -trice [ɛ̃vɑ̃tœr, -tris] *nm/f* inventor
inventif, -ive [ɛ̃vɑ̃tif, -iv] *adj* inventive
invention [ɛ̃vɑ̃sjɔ̃] *nf* invention; (*imagination,
inspiration*) inventiveness
inventivité [ɛ̃vɑ̃tivite] *nf* inventiveness
inventorier [ɛ̃vɑ̃tɔrje] *vt* to make an inventory
of
invérifiable [ɛ̃verifjabl(ə)] *adj* unverifiable
inverse [ɛ̃vɛrs(ə)] *adj* (*ordre*) reverse; (*sens*)
opposite; (*rapport*) inverse ▷ *nm* reverse; inverse;

en proportion ~ in inverse proportion; **dans le sens ~ des aiguilles d'une montre** anticlockwise; **en sens ~** in (ou from) the opposite direction; **à l'~** conversely

inversement [ɛ̃vɛʀsəmɑ̃] adv conversely

inverser [ɛ̃vɛʀse] vt to reverse, invert; (Élec) to reverse

inversion [ɛ̃vɛʀsjɔ̃] nf reversal; inversion

invertébré, e [ɛ̃vɛʀtebʀe] adj, nm invertebrate

inverti, e [ɛ̃vɛʀti] nm/f homosexual

investigation [ɛ̃vɛstigasjɔ̃] nf investigation, inquiry

investir [ɛ̃vɛstiʀ] vt to invest; **s'investir** vi (Psych) to involve o.s.; **~ qn de** to vest ou invest sb with

investissement [ɛ̃vɛstismɑ̃] nm investment; (Psych) involvement

investisseur [ɛ̃vɛstisœʀ] nm investor

investiture [ɛ̃vɛstityʀ] nf investiture; (à une élection) nomination

invétéré, e [ɛ̃vetere] adj (habitude) ingrained; (bavard, buveur) inveterate

invincible [ɛ̃vɛ̃sibl(ə)] adj invincible, unconquerable

invinciblement [ɛ̃vɛ̃sibləmɑ̃] adv (fig) invincibly

inviolabilité [ɛ̃vjɔlabilite] nf: **~ parlementaire** parliamentary immunity

inviolable [ɛ̃vjɔlabl(ə)] adj inviolable

invisible [ɛ̃vizibl(ə)] adj invisible; (fig: personne) not available

invitation [ɛ̃vitasjɔ̃] nf invitation; **à/sur l'~ de qn** at/on sb's invitation; **carte/lettre d'~** invitation card/letter

invite [ɛ̃vit] nf invitation

invité, e [ɛ̃vite] nm/f guest

inviter [ɛ̃vite] vt to invite; **~ qn à faire qch** to invite sb to do sth; (chose) to induce ou tempt sb to do sth

invivable [ɛ̃vivabl(ə)] adj unbearable, impossible

involontaire [ɛ̃vɔlɔ̃tɛʀ] adj (mouvement) involuntary; (insulte) unintentional; (complice) unwitting

involontairement [ɛ̃vɔlɔ̃tɛʀmɑ̃] adv involuntarily

invoquer [ɛ̃vɔke] vt (Dieu, muse) to call upon, invoke; (prétexte) to put forward (as an excuse); (témoignage) to call upon; (loi, texte) to refer to; **~ la clémence de qn** to beg sb ou appeal to sb for clemency

invraisemblable [ɛ̃vʀɛsɑ̃blabl(ə)] adj unlikely, improbable; (bizarre) incredible

invraisemblance [ɛ̃vʀɛsɑ̃blɑ̃s] nf unlikelihood no pl, improbability

invulnérable [ɛ̃vylneʀabl(ə)] adj invulnerable

iode [jɔd] nm iodine

iodé, e [jɔde] adj iodized

ion [jɔ̃] nm ion

ionique [jɔnik] adj (Archit) Ionic; (Science) ionic

ioniseur [jɔnizœʀ] nm ionizer

iota [jɔta] nm: **sans changer un ~** without

changing one iota ou the tiniest bit

IPC sigle m (= Indice des prix à la consommation) CPI

IR. abr = **infrarouge**

IRA sigle f (= Irish Republican Army) IRA

irai etc [iʀe] vb voir **aller**

Irak [iʀak] nm: **l'~** Iraq ou Irak

irakien, ne [iʀakjɛ̃, -ɛn] adj Iraqi ▷ nm/f: **Irakien, ne** Iraqi

Iran [iʀɑ̃] nm: **l'~** Iran

iranien, ne [iʀanjɛ̃, -ɛn] adj Iranian ▷ nm (Ling) Iranian ▷ nm/f: **Iranien, ne** Iranian

Iraq [iʀak] nm = **Irak**

iraquien, ne [iʀakjɛ̃, -ɛn] adj, nm/f = **irakien, ne**

irascible [iʀasibl(ə)] adj short-tempered, irascible

irions etc [iʀjɔ̃] vb voir **aller**

iris [iʀis] nm iris

irisé, e [iʀize] adj iridescent

irlandais, e [iʀlɑ̃dɛ, -ɛz] adj, nm (Ling) Irish ▷ nm/f: **Irlandais, e** Irishman/woman; **les I-** the Irish

Irlande [iʀlɑ̃d] nf: **l'~** (pays) Ireland; (état) the Irish Republic, the Republic of Ireland, Eire; **~ du Nord** Northern Ireland, Ulster; **~ du Sud** Southern Ireland, Irish Republic, Eire; **la mer d'~** the Irish Sea

ironie [iʀɔni] nf irony

ironique [iʀɔnik] adj ironical

ironiquement [iʀɔnikmɑ̃] adv ironically

ironiser [iʀɔnize] vi to be ironical

irons etc [iʀɔ̃] vb voir **aller**

IRPP sigle m (= impôt sur le revenu des personnes physiques) income tax

irradiation [iʀadjasjɔ̃] nf irradiation

irradier [iʀadje] vi to radiate ▷ vt to irradiate

irraisonné, e [iʀezone] adj irrational, unreasoned

irrationnel, le [iʀasjɔnɛl] adj irrational

irrattrapable [iʀatʀapabl(ə)] adj (retard) that cannot be made up; (bévue) that cannot be made good

irréalisable [iʀealizabl(ə)] adj unrealizable; (projet) impracticable

irréalisme [iʀealism(ə)] nm lack of realism

irréaliste [iʀealist(ə)] adj unrealistic

irréalité [iʀealite] nf unreality

irrecevable [iʀsəvabl(ə)] adj unacceptable

irréconciliable [iʀekɔ̃siljabl(ə)] adj irreconcilable

irrécouvrable [iʀekuvʀabl(ə)] adj irrecoverable

irrécupérable [iʀekypeʀabl(ə)] adj unreclaimable, beyond repair; (personne) beyond redemption ou recall

irrécusable [iʀekyzabl(ə)] adj (témoignage) unimpeachable; (preuve) incontestable, indisputable

irréductible [iʀedyktibl(ə)] adj indomitable, implacable; (Math: fraction, équation) irreducible

irréductiblement [iʀedyktibləmɑ̃] adv implacably

irréel, le [iʀeɛl] adj unreal

irréfléchi, e [iʀefleʃi] adj thoughtless

irréfutable [iʀefytabl(ə)] adj irrefutable

irréfutablement [iʀefytabləmɑ̃] *adv* irrefutably

irrégularité [iʀegylaʀite] *nf* irregularity; unevenness *no pl*

irrégulier, -ière [iʀegylje, -jɛʀ] *adj* irregular; *(surface, rythme, écriture)* uneven, irregular; *(élève, athlète)* erratic

irrégulièrement [iʀegyljɛʀmɑ̃] *adv* irregularly

irrémédiable [iʀemedjabl(ə)] *adj* irreparable

irrémédiablement [iʀemedjabləmɑ̃] *adv* irreparably

irremplaçable [iʀɑ̃plasabl(ə)] *adj* irreplaceable

irréparable [iʀepaʀabl(ə)] *adj* beyond repair, irreparable; *(fig)* irreparable

irrépréhensible [iʀepʀeɑ̃sibl(ə)] *adj* irreproachable

irrépressible [iʀepʀesibl(ə)] *adj* irrepressible

irréprochable [iʀepʀɔʃabl(ə)] *adj* irreproachable, beyond reproach; *(tenue, toilette)* impeccable

irrésistible [iʀezistibl(ə)] *adj* irresistible; *(preuve, logique)* compelling

irrésistiblement [iʀezistibləmɑ̃] *adv* irresistibly

irrésolu, e [iʀezɔly] *adj* irresolute

irrésolution [iʀezɔlysjɔ̃] *nf* irresoluteness

irrespectueux, -euse [iʀɛspɛktɥø, -øz] *adj* disrespectful

irrespirable [iʀɛspiʀabl(ə)] *adj* unbreathable; *(fig)* oppressive, stifling

irresponsabilité [iʀɛspɔ̃sabilite] *nf* irresponsibility

irresponsable [iʀɛspɔ̃sabl(ə)] *adj* irresponsible

irrévérencieux, -euse [iʀeveʀɑ̃sjø, -øz] *adj* irreverent

irréversible [iʀeveʀsibl(ə)] *adj* irreversible

irréversiblement [iʀeveʀsibləmɑ̃] *adv* irreversibly

irrévocable [iʀevɔkabl(ə)] *adj* irrevocable

irrévocablement [iʀevɔkabləmɑ̃] *adv* irrevocably

irrigation [iʀigasjɔ̃] *nf* irrigation

irriguer [iʀige] *vt* to irrigate

irritabilité [iʀitabilite] *nf* irritability

irritable [iʀitabl(ə)] *adj* irritable

irritant, e [iʀitɑ̃, -ɑ̃t] *adj* irritating; *(Méd)* irritant

irritation [iʀitasjɔ̃] *nf* irritation

irrité, e [iʀite] *adj* irritated

irriter [iʀite] *vt (agacer)* to irritate, annoy; *(Méd: enflammer)* to irritate; **s'~ contre qn/de qch** to get annoyed *ou* irritated with sb/at sth

irruption [iʀypsjɔ̃] *nf* irruption *no pl*; **faire ~ dans** to burst into

ISBN *sigle m* (= *International Standard Book Number*) ISBN

ISF *sigle m* (= *impôt de solidarité sur la fortune*) wealth tax

Islam [islam] *nm* Islam

islamique [islamik] *adj* Islamic

islamiste [islamist(ə)] *adj, nm/f* Islamic

islandais, e [islɑ̃dɛ, -ez] *adj* Icelandic ▷ *nm* *(Ling)* Icelandic ▷ *nm/f*: **I~, e** Icelander

Islande [islɑ̃d] *nf*: **l'~** Iceland

ISMH *sigle m* = **Inventaire supplémentaire des monuments historiques**; **monument inscrit à l'~** ≈ listed building

isocèle [izɔsɛl] *adj* isoceles

isolant, e [izɔlɑ̃, -ɑ̃t] *adj* insulating; *(insonorisant)* soundproofing ▷ *nm* insulator

isolateur [izɔlatœʀ] *nm (Élec)* insulator

isolation [izɔlasjɔ̃] *nf* insulation; **~ acoustique/thermique** sound/thermal insulation

isolationnisme [izɔlasjɔnism(ə)] *nm* isolationism

isolé, e [izɔle] *adj* isolated; *(Élec)* insulated

isolement [izɔlmɑ̃] *nm* isolation; solitary confinement

isolément [izɔlemɑ̃] *adv* in isolation

isoler [izɔle] *vt* to isolate; *(prisonnier)* to put in solitary confinement; *(ville)* to cut off, isolate; *(Élec)* to insulate

isoloir [izɔlwaʀ] *nm* polling booth

isorel® [izɔʀɛl] *nm* hardboard

isotherme [izɔtɛʀm(ə)] *adj (camion)* refrigerated

Israël [isʀaɛl] *nm*: **l'~** Israel

israélien, ne [isʀaeljɛ̃, -ɛn] *adj* Israeli ▷ *nm/f*: **Israélien, ne** Israeli

israélite [isʀaelit] *adj* Jewish; *(dans l'Ancien Testament)* Israelite ▷ *nm/f*: **Israélite** Jew/Jewess; Israelite

issu, e [isy] *adj*: **~ de** descended from; *(fig)* stemming from ▷ *nf (ouverture, sortie)* exit; *(solution)* way out, solution; *(dénouement)* outcome; **à l'~e de** at the conclusion *ou* close of; **rue sans ~e** dead end, no through road *(Brit)*, no outlet *(US)*; **~e de secours** emergency exit

Istamboul, Istanbul [istɑ̃bul] *n* Istanbul

isthme [ism(ə)] *nm* isthmus

Italie [itali] *nf*: **l'~** Italy

italien, ne [italjɛ̃, -ɛn] *adj* Italian ▷ *nm (Ling)* Italian ▷ *nm/f*: **Italien, ne** Italian

italique [italik] *nm*: **en ~(s)** in italics

item [itɛm] *nm* item; *(question)* question, test

itinéraire [itineʀɛʀ] *nm* itinerary, route

itinérant, e [itineʀɑ̃, -ɑ̃t] *adj* itinerant, travelling

ITP *sigle m* (= *ingénieur des travaux publics*) civil engineer

IUT *sigle m* = **Institut universitaire de technologie**

IVG *sigle f* (= *interruption volontaire de grossesse*) abortion

ivoire [ivwaʀ] *nm* ivory

ivoirien, ne [ivwaʀjɛ̃, -ɛn] *adj* of *ou* from the Ivory Coast

ivraie [ivʀɛ] *nf*: **séparer le bon grain de l'~** *(fig)* to separate the wheat from the chaff

ivre [ivʀ(ə)] *adj* drunk; **~ de** *(colère)* wild with; *(bonheur)* drunk *ou* intoxicated with; **~ mort** dead drunk

ivresse [ivʀɛs] *nf* drunkenness; *(euphorie)* intoxication

ivrogne [ivʀɔɲ] *nm/f* drunkard

Jj

J, j [ʒi] *nm inv* J, j ▷ *abr* = **jour**; **jour** J D-day;
(= *Joule*) J; **J comme Joseph** J for Jack (*Brit*) *ou* Jig
(*US*)

j' [ʒ] *pron voir* **je**

jabot [ʒabo] *nm* (*Zool*) crop; (*de vêtement*) jabot

jacasser [ʒakase] *vi* to chatter

jachère [ʒaʃɛʀ] *nf*: **(être) en ~** (to lie) fallow

jacinthe [ʒasɛ̃t] *nf* hyacinth; **~ des bois**
bluebell

jack [dʒak] *nm* jack plug

jacquard [ʒakaʀ] *adj inv* Fair Isle

jacquerie [ʒakʀi] *nf* riot

jade [ʒad] *nm* jade

jadis [ʒadis] *adv* in times past, formerly

jaguar [ʒagwaʀ] *nm* (*Zool*) jaguar

jaillir [ʒajiʀ] *vi* (*liquide*) to spurt out, gush out;
(*lumière*) to flood out; (*fig*) to rear up; to burst out

jaillissement [ʒajismɑ̃] *nm* spurt, gush

jais [ʒɛ] *nm* jet; **(d'un noir) de ~** jet-black

jalon [ʒalɔ̃] *nm* range pole; (*fig*) milestone;
poser des ~s (*fig*) to pave the way

jalonner [ʒalɔne] *vt* to mark out; (*fig*) to mark,
punctuate

jalousement [ʒaluzmɑ̃] *adv* jealously

jalouser [ʒaluze] *vt* to be jealous of

jalousie [ʒaluzi] *nf* jealousy; (*store*) (venetian)
blind

jaloux, -ouse [ʒalu, -uz] *adj* jealous; **être ~ de
qn/qch** to be jealous of sb/sth

jamaïquain, e [ʒamaikɛ̃, -ɛn] *adj* Jamaican

Jamaïque [ʒamaik] *nf*: **la ~** Jamaica

jamais [ʒamɛ] *adv* never; (*sans négation*) ever;
ne ... ~ never; **~ de la vie!** never!; **si ... ~** if ever ...;
à (tout) ~, **pour ~** for ever, for ever and ever

jambage [ʒɑ̃baʒ] *nm* (*de lettre*) downstroke; (*de
porte*) jamb

jambe [ʒɑ̃b] *nf* leg; **à toutes ~s** as fast as one's
legs can carry one

jambières [ʒɑ̃bjɛʀ] *nfpl* legwarmers; (*Sport*) shin
pads

jambon [ʒɑ̃bɔ̃] *nm* ham

jambonneau, x [ʒɑ̃bɔno] *nm* knuckle of ham

jante [ʒɑ̃t] *nf* (wheel) rim

janvier [ʒɑ̃vje] *nm* January; *voir aussi* **juillet**

Japon [ʒapɔ̃] *nm*: **le ~** Japan

japonais, e [ʒapɔnɛ, -ɛz] *adj* Japanese ▷ *nm*
(*Ling*) Japanese ▷ *nm/f*: **Japonais, e** Japanese

japonaiserie [ʒapɔnɛzʀi] *nf* (*bibelot*) Japanese
curio

jappement [ʒapmɑ̃] *nm* yap, yelp

japper [ʒape] *vi* to yap, yelp

jaquette [ʒakɛt] *nf* (*de cérémonie*) morning coat;
(*de femme*) jacket; (*de livre*) dust cover, (dust)
jacket

jardin [ʒaʀdɛ̃] *nm* garden; **~ d'acclimatation**
zoological gardens *pl*; **~ botanique** botanical
gardens *pl*; **~ d'enfants** nursery school; **~
potager** vegetable garden; **~ public** (public)
park, public gardens *pl*; **~s suspendus** hanging
gardens; **~ zoologique** zoological gardens

jardinage [ʒaʀdinaʒ] *nm* gardening

jardiner [ʒaʀdine] *vi* to garden, do some
gardening

jardinet [ʒaʀdinɛ] *nm* little garden

jardinier, -ière [ʒaʀdinje, -jɛʀ] *nm/f* gardener
▷ *nf* (*de fenêtre*) window box; **jardinière
d'enfants** nursery school teacher; **jardinière
(de légumes)** (*Culin*) mixed vegetables

jargon [ʒaʀgɔ̃] *nm* (*charabia*) gibberish;
(*publicitaire, scientifique etc*) jargon

jarre [ʒaʀ] *nf* (earthenware) jar

jarret [ʒaʀɛ] *nm* back of knee; (*Culin*) knuckle,
shin

jarretelle [ʒaʀtɛl] *nf* suspender (*Brit*), garter (*US*)

jarretière [ʒaʀtjɛʀ] *nf* garter

jars [ʒaʀ] *nm* (*Zool*) gander

jaser [ʒaze] *vi* to chatter, prattle; (*indiscrètement*)
to gossip

jasmin [ʒasmɛ̃] *nm* jasmine

jaspe [ʒasp(ə)] *nm* jasper

jaspé, e [ʒaspe] *adj* marbled, mottled

jatte [ʒat] *nf* basin, bowl

jauge [ʒoʒ] *nf* (*capacité*) capacity, tonnage;
(*instrument*) gauge; **~ (de niveau) d'huile**
dipstick

jauger [ʒoʒe] *vt* to gauge the capacity of; (*fig*) to
size up; **~ 3 000 tonneaux** to measure 3,000
tons

jaunâtre [ʒonɑtʀ(ə)] *adj* (*couleur, teint*) yellowish

jaune [ʒon] *adj, nm* yellow ▷ *nm/f* Asiatic; (*briseur
de grève*) blackleg ▷ *adv* (*fam*): **rire ~** to laugh on
the other side of one's face; **~ d'œuf** (egg) yolk

jaunir [ʒoniʀ] *vi, vt* to turn yellow
jaunisse [ʒonis] *nf* jaundice
Java [ʒava] *nf* Java
java [ʒava] *nf (fam)*: **faire la ~** to live it up, have a real party
javanais, e [ʒavanɛ, -ɛz] *adj* Javanese
Javel [ʒavɛl] *nf voir* **eau**
javelliser [ʒavelize] *vt (eau)* to chlorinate
javelot [ʒavlo] *nm* javelin; *(Sport)*: **faire du ~** to throw the javelin
jazz [dʒaz] *nm* jazz
J.-C. *abr* = **Jésus-Christ**
je, j' [ʒ(ə)] *pron* I
jean [dʒin] *nm* jeans *pl*
jeannette [ʒanɛt] *nf (planchette)* sleeve board; *(petite fille scout)* Brownie
jeep® [(d)ʒip] *nf (Auto)* Jeep®
jérémiades [ʒeʀemjad] *nfpl* moaning *sg*
jerrycan [ʒeʀikan] *nm* jerry can
Jersey [ʒɛʀzɛ] *nf* Jersey
jersey [ʒɛʀzɛ] *nm* jersey; *(Tricot)*: **pointe de ~** stocking stitch
jersiais, e [ʒɛʀzjɛ, -ɛz] *adj* Jersey *cpd*, of *ou* from Jersey
Jérusalem [ʒeʀyzalɛm] *n* Jerusalem
jésuite [ʒezɥit] *nm* Jesuit
Jésus-Christ [ʒezykri(st)] *n* Jesus Christ; **600 avant/après ~ *ou* J.-C.** 600 B.C./A.D.
jet¹ [ʒɛ] *nm (lancer)* throwing *no pl*, throw; *(jaillissement)* jet; spurt; *(de tuyau)* nozzle; *(fig)*: **premier ~** *(ébauche)* rough outline; **arroser au ~** to hose; **d'un (seul) ~** *(d'un seul coup)* at *(ou* in) one go; **du premier ~** at the first attempt *ou* shot; **~ d'eau** spray; *(fontaine)* fountain
jet² [dʒɛt] *nm (avion)* jet
jetable [ʒətabl(ə)] *adj* disposable
jeté [ʒəte] *nm (Tricot)*: **un ~** make one; **~ de table** (table) runner; **~ de lit** bedspread
jetée [ʒəte] *nf* jetty; pier
jeter [ʒəte] *vt (gén)* to throw; *(se défaire de)* to throw away *ou* out; *(son, lueur etc)* to give out; **~ qch à qn** to throw sth to sb; *(de façon agressive)* to throw sth at sb; *(Navig)*: **~ l'ancre** to cast anchor; **~ un coup d'œil (à)** to take a look (at); **~ les bras en avant/la tête en arrière** to throw one's arms forward/one's head back(ward); **~ l'effroi parmi** to spread fear among; **~ un sort à qn** to cast a spell on sb; **~ qn dans la misère** to reduce sb to poverty; **~ qn dehors/en prison** to throw sb out/into prison; **~ l'éponge** *(fig)* to throw in the towel; **~ des fleurs à qn** *(fig)* to say lovely things to sb; **~ la pierre à qn** *(accuser, blâmer)* to accuse sb; **se ~ sur** to throw o.s. onto; **se ~ dans** *(fleuve)* to flow into; **se ~ par la fenêtre** to throw o.s. out of the window; **se ~ à l'eau** *(fig)* to take the plunge
jeton [ʒətɔ̃] *nm (au jeu)* counter; *(de téléphone)* token; **~s de présence** (director's) fees
jette *etc* [ʒɛt] *vb voir* **jeter**
jeu, x [ʒø] *nm (divertissement, Tech: d'une pièce)* play; *(défini par des règles, Tennis: partie, Football etc: façon de jouer)* game; *(Théât etc)* acting; *(fonctionnement)*

working, interplay; *(série d'objets, jouet)* set; *(Cartes)* hand; *(au casino)*: **le ~** gambling; **cacher son ~** *(fig)* to keep one's cards hidden, conceal one's hand; **c'est un ~ d'enfant!** *(fig)* it's child's play!; **en ~** at stake; at work; *(Football)* in play; **remettre en ~** to throw in; **entrer/mettre en ~** to come/bring into play; **par ~** *(pour s'amuser)* for fun; **d'entrée de ~** *(tout de suite, dès le début)* from the outset; **entrer dans le ~/le ~ de qn** *(fig)* to play the game/sb's game; **jouer gros ~** to play for high stakes; **se piquer/se prendre au ~** to get excited over/get caught up in the game; **~ d'arcade** video game; **~ de boules** game of bowls; *(endroit)* bowling pitch; *(boules)* set of bowls; **~ de cartes** card game; *(paquet)* pack of cards; **~ de construction** building set; **~ d'échecs** chess set; **~ d'écritures** *(Comm)* paper transaction; **~ électronique** electronic game; **~ de hasard** game of chance; **~ de mots** pun; **le ~ de l'oie** snakes and ladders *sg*; **~ d'orgue(s)** organ stop; **~ de patience** puzzle; **~ de physionomie** facial expressions *pl*; **~ de société** parlour game; **~ télévisé** television game; **~ vidéo** computer game; **~x de lumière** lighting effects; **J~x olympiques (JO)** Olympic Games
jeu-concours [ʒøkɔ̃kuʀ] *(pl* **jeux-concours**) *nm* competition
jeudi [ʒødi] *nm* Thursday; **~ saint** Maundy Thursday; *voir aussi* **lundi**
jeun [ʒœ̃]: **à ~** *adv* on an empty stomach
jeune [ʒœn] *adj* young ▷ *adv*: **faire/s'habiller ~** to look/dress young; **les ~s** young people, the young; **~ fille** *nf* girl; **~ homme** *nm* young man; **~ loup** *nm (Pol, Écon)* young go-getter; **~ premier** leading man; **~s gens** *nmpl* young people; **~s mariés** *nmpl* newly weds
jeûne [ʒøn] *nm* fast
jeûner [ʒøne] *vt* to fast, go without food
jeunesse [ʒœnɛs] *nf* youth; *(aspect)* youthfulness; *(jeunes)* young people *pl*, youth
jf *sigle f* = **jeune fille**
jh *sigle m* = **jeune homme**
JI *sigle m* = **juge d'instruction**
jiu-jitsu [ʒyʒitsy] *nm inv (Sport)* jujitsu
JMF *sigle f (= Jeunesses musicales de France)* association to promote music among the young
JO *sigle m* = **Journal officiel** ▷ *sigle mpl* = **Jeux olympiques**
joaillerie [ʒɔajʀi] *nf* jewel trade; jewellery *(Brit)*, jewelry *(US)*
joaillier, -ière [ʒɔaje, -jɛʀ] *nm/f* jeweller *(Brit)*, jeweler *(US)*
job [dʒɔb] *nm* job
jobard [ʒɔbaʀ] *nm (péj)* sucker, mug
jockey [ʒɔkɛ] *nm* jockey
jodler [ʒɔdle] *vi* to yodel
jogging [dʒɔgiŋ] *nm* tracksuit *(Brit)*, sweatsuit *(US)*; **faire du ~** to jog, go jogging
joie [ʒwa] *nf* joy
joignais *etc* [ʒwaɲɛ] *vb voir* **joindre**
joindre [ʒwɛ̃dʀ(ə)] *vt* to join; **~ qch à** *(à une lettre)*

to enclose sth with; *(à un mail)* to attach sth to; *(contacter)* to contact, get in touch with; **~ les mains/talons** to put one's hands/heels together; **les deux bouts** *(fig: du mois)* to make ends meet; **se joindre** *(mains etc)* to come together; **se ~ à qn** to join sb; **se ~ à qch** to join in sth

joint, e [ʒwɛ̃, -ɛ̃t] *pp de* **joindre** ▷ *adj*: **~ (à)** *(lettre, paquet)* attached (to), enclosed (with); **pièce ~e** *(de lettre)* enclosure; *(de mail)* attachment ▷ *nm* joint; *(ligne)* join; *(de ciment etc)* pointing *no pl*; **chercher/trouver le ~** *(fig)* to look for/come up with the answer; **~ de cardan** cardan joint; **~ de culasse** cylinder head gasket; **~ de robinet** washer; **~ universel** universal joint

jointure [ʒwɛ̃tyʀ] *nf (Anat: articulation)* joint; *(Tech: assemblage)* joint; *(: ligne)* join

joker [ʒɔkɛʀ] *nm (Cartes)* joker; *(Inform)*: **(caractère) ~** wild card

joli, e [ʒɔli] *adj* pretty, attractive; **une ~e somme/situation** a nice little sum/situation; **un ~ gâchis** *etc* a nice mess *etc*; **c'est du ~!** that's very nice!; **tout ça, c'est bien ~ mais ...** that's all very well but ...

joliment [ʒɔlimɑ̃] *adv* prettily, attractively; *(fam: très)* pretty

jonc [ʒɔ̃] *nm (bul)*rush; *(bague, bracelet)* band

joncher [ʒɔ̃ʃe] *vt (choses)* to be strewed on; **jonché de** strewn with

jonction [ʒɔ̃ksjɔ̃] *nf* joining; **(point de) ~** *(de routes)* junction; *(de fleuves)* confluence; **opérer une ~** *(Mil etc)* to rendez-vous

jongler [ʒɔ̃gle] *vi* to juggle; *(fig)*: **~ avec** to juggle with, play with

jongleur, -euse [ʒɔ̃glœʀ, -øz] *nm/f* juggler

jonquille [ʒɔ̃kij] *nf* daffodil

Jordanie [ʒɔʀdani] *nf*: **la ~** Jordan

jordanien, ne [ʒɔʀdanjɛ̃, -ɛn] *adj* Jordanian ▷ *nm/f*: **Jordanien, ne** Jordanian

jouable [ʒwabl(ə)] *adj* playable

joue [ʒu] *nf* cheek; **mettre en ~** to take aim at

jouer [ʒwe] *vt (partie, carte, coup, Mus: morceau)* to play; *(somme d'argent, réputation)* to stake, wager; *(pièce, rôle)* to perform; *(film)* to show; *(simuler: sentiment)* to affect, feign ▷ *vi* to play; *(Théât, Ciné)* to act, perform; *(bois, porte: se voiler)* to warp; *(clef, pièce: avoir du jeu)* to be loose; *(entrer ou être en jeu)* to come into play, come into it; **~ sur** *(miser)* to gamble on; **~ de** *(Mus)* to play; **~ du couteau/des coudes** to use knives/one's elbows; **~ à** *(jeu, sport, roulette)* to play; **~ au héros** to act *ou* play the hero; **~ avec** *(risquer)* to gamble with; **se ~ de** *(difficultés)* to make light of; **se ~ de qn** to deceive ou dupe sb; **~ un tour à qn** to play a trick on sb; **~ la comédie** *(fig)* to put on an act, put it on; **~ aux courses** to back horses, bet on horses; **~ à la baisse/hausse** *(Bourse)* to play for a fall/rise; **~ serré** to play a close game; **~ de malchance** to be dogged with ill-luck; **~ sur les mots** to play with words; **à toi/nous de ~** it's your/our go *ou* turn

jouet [ʒwɛ] *nm* toy; **être le ~ de** *(illusion etc)* to be the victim of

joueur, -euse [ʒwœʀ, -øz] *nm/f* player ▷ *adj (enfant, chat)* playful; **être beau/mauvais ~** to be a good/bad loser

joufflu, e [ʒufly] *adj* chubby(-cheeked)

joug [ʒu] *nm* yoke

jouir [ʒwiʀ]: **~ de** *vt* to enjoy

jouissance [ʒwisɑ̃s] *nf* pleasure; *(Jur)* use

jouisseur, -euse [ʒwisœʀ, -øz] *nm/f* sensualist

joujou [ʒuʒu] *nm (fam)* toy

jour [ʒuʀ] *nm* day; *(opposé à la nuit)* day, daytime; *(clarté)* daylight; *(fig: aspect)*: **sous un ~ favourable/nouveau** in a favourable/new light; *(ouverture)* opening; *(Couture)* openwork *no pl*; **au ~ le ~** from day to day; **de nos ~s** these days, nowadays; **tous les ~s** every day; **de ~ en ~** day by day; **d'un ~ à l'autre** from one day to the next; **du ~ au lendemain** overnight; **il fait ~** it's daylight; **en plein ~** in broad daylight; **au ~** in daylight; **au petit ~** at daybreak; **au grand ~** *(fig)* in the open; **mettre au ~** to uncover, disclose; **être à ~** to be up to date; **mettre à ~** to bring up to date, update; **mise à ~** updating; **donner le ~ à** to give birth to; **voir le ~** to be born; **se faire ~** *(fig)* to become clear; **~ férié** public holiday; **le ~ J** D-day; **~ ouvrable** working day

Jourdain [ʒuʀdɛ̃] *nm*: **le ~** the (River) Jordan

journal, -aux [ʒuʀnal, -o] *nm* (news)paper; *(personnel)* journal, diary; **~ de bord** log; **~ de mode** fashion magazine; **le J~ officiel (de la République française) (JO)** *bulletin giving details of laws and official announcements*; **~ parlé/télévisé** radio/television news *sg*

journalier, -ière [ʒuʀnalje, -jɛʀ] *adj* daily; *(banal)* everyday ▷ *nm* day labourer

journalisme [ʒuʀnalism(ə)] *nm* journalism

journaliste [ʒuʀnalist(ə)] *nm/f* journalist

journalistique [ʒuʀnalistik] *adj* journalistic

journée [ʒuʀne] *nf* day; **la ~ continue** the 9 to 5 working day *(with short lunch break)*

journellement [ʒuʀnɛlmɑ̃] *adv (tous les jours)* daily; *(souvent)* every day

joute [ʒut] *nf (tournoi)* duel; *(verbale)* duel, battle of words

jouvence [ʒuvɑ̃s] *nf*: **bain de ~** rejuvenating experience

jouxter [ʒukste] *vt* to adjoin

jovial [ʒɔvjal] *adj* jovial, jolly

jovialité [ʒɔvjalite] *nf* joviality

joyau, x [ʒwajo] *nm* gem, jewel

joyeusement [ʒwajøzmɑ̃] *adv* joyfully, gladly

joyeux, -euse [ʒwajø, -øz] *adj* joyful, merry; **~ Noël!** Merry *ou* Happy Christmas!; **joyeuses Pâques!** Happy Easter!; **~ anniversaire!** many happy returns!

JT *sigle m* = **journal télévisé**

jubilation [ʒybilasjɔ̃] *nf* jubilation

jubilé [ʒybile] *nm* jubilee

jubiler [ʒybile] *vi* to be jubilant, exult

jucher [ʒyʃe] *vt*: **~ qch sur** to perch sth (up)on ▷ *vi (oiseau)*: **~ sur** to perch (up)on; **se ~ sur** to

233

perch o.s. (up)on

judaïque [ʒydaik] *adj (loi)* Judaic; *(religion)* Jewish

judaïsme [ʒydaism(ə)] *nm* Judaism

judas [ʒyda] *nm (trou)* spy-hole

Judée [ʒyde] *nf:* **la ~** Jud(a)ea

judéo- [ʒydeɔ] *préfixe* Judeo-

judéo-allemand, e [ʒydeɔalmã, -ãd] *adj, nm* Yiddish

judéo-chrétien, ne [ʒydeɔkʀetjɛ̃, -ɛn] *adj* Judeo-Christian

judiciaire [ʒydisjɛʀ] *adj* judicial

judicieusement [ʒydisjøzmã] *adv* judiciously

judicieux, -euse [ʒydisjø, -øz] *adj* judicious

judo [ʒydo] *nm* judo

judoka [ʒydɔka] *nm/f* judoka

juge [ʒyʒ] *nm* judge; **~ d'instruction** examining *(Brit) ou* committing *(US)* magistrate; **~ de paix** justice of the peace; **~ de touche** linesman

jugé [ʒyʒe]: **au ~** *adv* by guesswork

jugement [ʒyʒmã] *nm* judgment; *(Jur: au pénal)* sentence; (: *au civil)* decision; **~ de valeur** value judgment

jugeote [ʒyʒɔt] *nf (fam)* gumption

juger [ʒyʒe] *vt* to judge ▷ *nm:* **au ~** by guesswork; **~ qn/qch satisfaisant** to consider sb/sth (to be) satisfactory; **~ que** to think *ou* consider that; **~ bon de faire** to consider it a good idea to do, see fit to do; **~ de** *vt* to judge; **jugez de ma surprise** imagine my surprise

jugulaire [ʒygylɛʀ] *adj* jugular ▷ *nf (Mil)* chinstrap

juguler [ʒygyle] *vt (maladie)* to halt; *(révolte)* to suppress; *(inflation etc)* to control, curb

juif, -ive [ʒɥif, -iv] *adj* Jewish ▷ *nm/f:* **Juif, ive** Jew/Jewess *ou* Jewish woman

juillet [ʒɥijɛ] *nm* July; **le premier ~** the first of July *(Brit),* July first *(US);* **le deux/onze ~** the second/eleventh of July, July second/eleventh; **il est venu le 5 ~** he came on 5th July *ou* July 5th; **en ~** in July; **début/fin ~** at the beginning/ end of July; *see note*

● LE 14 JUILLET

- ●
- ● *Le 14 juillet* is a national holiday in France and
- ● commemorates the storming of the Bastille
- ● during the French Revolution. Throughout
- ● the country there are celebrations, which
- ● feature parades, music, dancing and
- ● firework displays. In Paris a military parade
- ● along the Champs-Élysées is attended by
- ● the President.

juin [ʒɥɛ̃] *nm* June; *voir aussi* **juillet**

juive [ʒɥiv] *adj, nf voir* **juif**

jumeau, -elle, -x [ʒymo, -ɛl] *adj, nm/f* twin; **maisons jumelles** semidetached houses

jumelage [ʒymlaʒ] *nm* twinning

jumeler [ʒymle] *vt* to twin; **roues jumelées** double wheels; **billets de loterie jumelés**

double series lottery tickets; **pari jumelé** double bet

jumelle [ʒymɛl] *adj f, nf voir* **jumeau** ▷ *vb voir* **jumeler**

jumelles [ʒymɛl] *nfpl* binoculars

jument [ʒymã] *nf* mare

jungle [ʒɔ̃gl(ə)] *nf* jungle

junior [ʒynjɔʀ] *adj* junior

junte [ʒɔ̃t] *nf* junta

jupe [ʒyp] *nf* skirt

jupe-culotte [ʒypkylɔt] *(pl* **jupes-culottes)** *nf* divided skirt, culotte(s)

jupette [ʒypɛt] *nf* short skirt

jupon [ʒypɔ̃] *nm* waist slip *ou* petticoat

Jura [ʒyʀa] *nm:* **le ~** the Jura (Mountains)

jurassien, ne [ʒyʀasjɛ̃, -ɛn] *adj* of *ou* from the Jura Mountains

juré, e [ʒyʀe] *nm/f* juror ▷ *adj:* **ennemi ~** sworn *ou* avowed enemy

jurer [ʒyʀe] *vt (obéissance etc)* to swear, vow ▷ *vi (dire des jurons)* to swear, curse; *(dissoner):* **~ (avec)** to clash (with); *(s'engager):* **~ de faire/que** to swear *ou* vow to do/that; *(affirmer):* **~ que** to swear *ou* vouch that; **~ de qch** *(s'en porter garant)* to swear to sth; **ils ne jurent que par lui** they swear by him; **je vous jure!** honestly!

juridiction [ʒyʀidiksjɔ̃] *nf* jurisdiction; *(tribunal, tribunaux)* court(s) of law

juridique [ʒyʀidik] *adj* legal

juridiquement [ʒyʀidikmã] *adv (devant la justice)* juridically; *(du point de vue du droit)* legally

jurisconsulte [ʒyʀikɔ̃sylt(ə)] *nm* jurisconsult

jurisprudence [ʒyʀispʀydãs] *nf (Jur: décisions)* (legal) precedents; *(principes juridiques)* jurisprudence; **faire ~** *(faire autorité)* to set a precedent

juriste [ʒyʀist(ə)] *nm/f* jurist; lawyer

juron [ʒyʀɔ̃] *nm* curse, swearword

jury [ʒyʀi] *nm (Jur)* jury; *(Scol)* board (of examiners), jury

jus [ʒy] *nm* juice; *(de viande)* gravy, (meat) juice; **~ de fruits** fruit juice; **~ de raisin/tomates** grape/tomato juice

jusant [ʒyzã] *nm* ebb (tide)

jusqu'au-boutiste [ʒyskobutist(ə)] *nm/f* extremist, hardliner

jusque [ʒysk(ə)]: **jusqu'à** *prép (endroit)* as far as, (up) to; *(moment)* until, till; *(limite)* up to; **~ sur/ dans** up to, as far as; *(y compris)* even on/in; **~ vers** until about; **jusqu'à ce que** *conj* until; **~- là** *(temps)* until then; *(espace)* up to there; **jusqu'ici** *(temps)* until now; *(espace)* up to here; **jusqu'à présent** until now, so far

justaucorps [ʒystokɔʀ] *nm inv (Danse, Sport)* leotard

juste [ʒyst(ə)] *adj (équitable)* just, fair; *(légitime)* just, justified; *(exact, vrai)* right; *(étroit, insuffisant)* tight ▷ *adv* right; tight; *(chanter)* in tune; *(seulement)* just; **~ assez/au-dessus** just enough/above; **pouvoir tout ~ faire** to be only just able to do; **au ~** exactly, actually; **comme de ~** of course, naturally; **le ~ milieu** the happy medium; **à ~ titre** rightfully

justement [ʒystəmã] *adv* rightly; justly; (*précisément*): **c'est ~ ce qu'il fallait faire** that's just *ou* precisely what needed doing

justesse [ʒystɛs] *nf* (*précision*) accuracy; (*d'une remarque*) aptness; (*d'une opinion*) soundness; **de ~** just, by a narrow margin

justice [ʒystis] *nf* (*équité*) fairness, justice; (*Admin*) justice; **rendre la ~** to dispense justice; **traduire en ~** to bring before the courts; **obtenir ~** to obtain justice; **rendre ~ à qn** to do sb justice; **se faire ~** to take the law into one's own hands; (*se suicider*) to take one's life

justiciable [ʒystisjabl(ə)] *adj*: **~ de** (*Jur*) answerable to

justicier, -ière [ʒystisje, -jɛR] *nm/f* judge, righter of wrongs

justifiable [ʒystifjabl(ə)] *adj* justifiable

justificatif, -ive [ʒystifikatif, -iv] *adj* (*document etc*) supporting ▷ *nm* supporting proof

justification [ʒystifikɑsjɔ̃] *nf* justification

justifier [ʒystifje] *vt* to justify; **~ de** *vt* to prove; **non justifié** unjustified; **justifié à droite/ gauche** ranged right/left

jute [ʒyt] *nm* jute

juteux, -euse [ʒytø, -øz] *adj* juicy

juvénile [ʒyvenil] *adj* young, youthful

juxtaposer [ʒykstapoze] *vt* to juxtapose

juxtaposition [ʒykstapozisjɔ̃] *nf* juxtaposition

Kk

K, k [kɑ] *nm inv* K, k ▷ *abr* (= *kilo*) kg; **K comme Kléber** K for King
K 7 [kasɛt] *nf* cassette
Kaboul, Kabul [kabul] *n* Kabul
kabyle [kabil] *adj* Kabyle ▷ *nm* (*Ling*) Kabyle ▷ *nm/f*: **Kabyle** Kabyle
Kabylie [kabili] *nf*: **la ~** Kabylia
kafkaïen, ne [kafkajɛ̃, -ɛn] *adj* Kafkaesque
kaki [kaki] *adj inv* khaki
Kalahari [kalaaʀi] *n*: **désert de ~** Kalahari Desert
kaléidoscope [kaleidɔskɔp] *nm* kaleidoscope
Kampala [kɑ̃pala] *n* Kampala
Kampuchéa [kɑ̃putʃea] *nm*: **le ~ (démocratique)** (the People's Republic of) Kampuchea
kangourou [kɑ̃guʀu] *nm* kangaroo
kaolin [kaɔlɛ̃] *nm* kaolin
kapok [kapɔk] *nm* kapok
karaoke [kaʀaoke] *nm* karaoke
karaté [kaʀate] *nm* karate
kart [kaʀt] *nm* go-cart
karting [kaʀtiŋ] *nm* go-carting, karting
kascher [kaʃɛʀ] *adj inv* kosher
kayak [kajak] *nm* kayak
Kazakhstan [kaʒakstɑ̃] *nm* Kazakhstan
Kenya [kenja] *nm*: **le ~** Kenya
kenyan, e [kenjɑ̃, -an] *adj* Kenyan ▷ *nm/f*: **Kenyan, e** Kenyan
képi [kepi] *nm* kepi
Kerguelen [kɛʀgelɛn] *nfpl*: **les (îles) ~** Kerguelen
kermesse [kɛʀmɛs] *nf* bazaar, (charity) fête; village fair
kérosène [keʀozɛn] *nm* jet fuel; rocket fuel
kg *abr* (= *kilogramme*) kg
KGB *sigle m* KGB
khmer, -ère [kmɛʀ] *adj* Khmer ▷ *nm* (*Ling*) Khmer
khôl [kol] *nm* khol
kibboutz [kibuts] *nm* kibbutz
kidnapper [kidnape] *vt* to kidnap
kidnappeur, -euse [kidnapœʀ, -øz] *nm/f* kidnapper
kidnapping [kidnapiŋ] *nm* kidnapping
Kilimandjaro [kilimɑ̃dʒaʀo] *nm*: **le ~** Mount Kilimanjaro
kilo [kilo] *nm* kilo
kilogramme [kilɔgʀam] *nm* kilogramme (*Brit*), kilogram (*US*)
kilométrage [kilɔmetʀaʒ] *nm* number of kilometres travelled, ≈ mileage
kilomètre [kilɔmetʀ(ə)] *nm* kilometre (*Brit*), kilometer (*US*); **~s-heure** kilometres per hour
kilométrique [kilɔmetʀik] *adj* (*distance*) in kilometres; **compteur ~** ≈ mileage indicator
kilooctet [kilɔɔktɛ] *nm* kilobyte
kilowatt [kilɔwat] *nm* kilowatt
kinésithérapeute [kineziteʀapøt] *nm/f* physiotherapist
kinésithérapie [kineziteʀapi] *nf* physiotherapy
kiosque [kjɔsk(ə)] *nm* kiosk, stall; (*Tél etc*) *telephone and/or videotext information service*; **~ à journaux** newspaper kiosk
kir [kiʀ] *nm* kir (*white wine with blackcurrant liqueur*)
Kirghizistan [kiʀgizistɑ̃] *nm* Kirghizia
kirsch [kiʀʃ] *nm* kirsch
kit [kit] *nm* kit; **~ piéton** *ou* **mains libres** hands-free kit; **en ~** in kit form
kitchenette [kitʃ(ə)nɛt] *nf* kitchenette
kiwi [kiwi] *nm* (*Zool*) kiwi; (*Bot*) kiwi (fruit)
klaxon [klaksɔn] *nm* horn
klaxonner [klaksɔne] *vi, vt* to hoot (*Brit*), honk (one's horn) (*US*)
kleptomane [klɛptɔman] *nm/f* kleptomaniac
km *abr* (= *kilomètre*) km
km/h *abr* = **kilomètres/heure**
knock-out [nɔkawt] *nm* knock-out
Ko *abr* (*Inform*: = *kilooctet*) kB
K.-O. [kao] *adj inv* (knocked) out, out for the count
koala [kɔala] *nm* koala (bear)
kolkhoze [kɔlkoz] *nm* kolkhoz
Kosovo [kɔsɔvo] *nm*: **le ~** Kosovo
Koweit [kɔwɛt] *nm*: **le ~** Kuwait, Koweit
koweitien, ne [kɔwɛtjɛ̃, -ɛn] *adj* Kuwaiti ▷ *nm/f*: **Koweitien, ne** Kuwaiti
krach [kʀak] *nm* (*Écon*) crash
kraft [kʀaft] *nm* brown *ou* kraft paper
Kremlin [kʀɛmlɛ̃] *nm*: **le ~** the Kremlin
Kuala Lumpur [kwalalympuʀ] *n* Kuala

Lumpur

kurde [kyʀd(ə)] *adj* Kurdish ▷ *nm* (*Ling*) Kurdish
▷ *nm/f*: **Kurde** Kurd

Kurdistan [kyʀdistɑ̃] *nm*: **le ~** Kurdistan

Kuweit [kɔwɛt] *nm* = **Koweit**

kW *abr* (= *kilowatt*) kW

k-way® [kawɛ] *nm* (lightweight nylon) cagoule

kW/h *abr* (= *kilowatt/heure*) kW/h

kyrielle [kiʀjɛl] *nf*: **une ~ de** a stream of

kyste [kist(ə)] *nm* cyst

Ll

L, l [εl] *nm inv* L, l ▷ *abr* (= *litre*) l; (*Scol*): **L ès L**
= **Licence ès Lettres**; **L en D** = **Licence en Droit**;
L comme Louis L for Lucy (*Brit*) *ou* Love (*US*)
l' [l] *art déf voir* **le**
la [la] *art déf, pron voir* **le** ▷ *nm* (*Mus*) A; (*en chantant
la gamme*) la
là [la] *adv voir aussi* **-ci**; **celui** there; (*ici*) here; (*dans
le temps*) then; **est-ce que Catherine est là?** is
Catherine there (*ou* here)?; **c'est là que** this is
where; **là où** where; **de là** (*fig*) hence; **par là**
(*fig*) by that; **tout est là** (*fig*) that's what it's all
about
là-bas [laba] *adv* there
label [label] *nm* stamp, seal
labeur [labœʀ] *nm* toil *no pl*, toiling *no pl*
labo [labo] *nm* (= *laboratoire*) lab
laborantin, e [labɔʀɑ̃tɛ̃, -in] *nm/f* laboratory
assistant
laboratoire [labɔʀatwaʀ] *nm* laboratory; **~ de
langues/d'analyses** language-/(medical)
analysis laboratory
laborieusement [labɔʀjøzmɑ̃] *adv* laboriously
laborieux, -euse [labɔʀjø, -øz] *adj* (*tâche*)
laborious; **classes laborieuses** working
classes
labour [labuʀ] *nm* ploughing *no pl* (*Brit*),
plowing *no pl* (*US*); **labours** *nmpl* (*champs*)
ploughed fields; **cheval de ~** plough- *ou* cart-
horse; **bœuf de ~** ox
labourage [labuʀaʒ] *nm* ploughing (*Brit*),
plowing (*US*)
labourer [labuʀe] *vt* to plough (*Brit*), plow (*US*);
(*fig*) to make deep gashes *ou* furrows in
laboureur [labuʀœʀ] *nm* ploughman (*Brit*),
plowman (*US*)
labrador [labʀadɔʀ] *nm* (*chien*) labrador; (*Géo*):
le L~ Labrador
labyrinthe [labiʀɛ̃t] *nm* labyrinth, maze
lac [lak] *nm* lake; **le ~ Léman** Lake Geneva; **les
Grands L~s** the Great Lakes; *voir aussi* **lacs**
lacer [lase] *vt* to lace *ou* do up
lacérer [laseʀe] *vt* to tear to shreds
lacet [lasɛ] *nm* (*de chaussure*) lace; (*de route*) sharp
bend; (*piège*) snare; **chaussures à ~s** lace-up *ou*
lacing shoes
lâche [lɑʃ] *adj* (*poltron*) cowardly; (*desserré*) loose,

slack; (*morale, mœurs*) lax ▷ *nm/f* coward
lâchement [lɑʃmɑ̃] *adv* (*par peur*) like a coward;
(*par bassesse*) despicably
lâcher [lɑʃe] *nm* (*de ballons, oiseaux*) release ▷ *vt* to
let go of; (*ce qui tombe, abandonner*) to drop; (*oiseau,
animal: libérer*) to release, set free; (*fig: mot,
remarque*) to let slip, come out with; (*Sport:
distancer*) to leave behind ▷ *vi* (*fil, amarres*) to
break, give way; (*freins*) to fail; **~ les amarres**
(*Navig*) to cast off (the moorings); **~ prise** to let
go
lâcheté [lɑʃte] *nf* cowardice; (*bassesse*) lowness
lacis [lasi] *nm* (*de ruelles*) maze
laconique [lakɔnik] *adj* laconic
laconiquement [lakɔnikmɑ̃] *adv* laconically
lacrymal, e, aux [lakʀimal, -o] *adj* (*canal, glande*)
tear *cpd*
lacrymogène [lakʀimɔʒɛn] *adj*: **grenade/gaz ~**
tear gas grenade/tear gas
lacs [lɑ] *nm* (*piège*) snare
lactation [laktasjɔ̃] *nf* lactation
lacté, e [lakte] *adj* milk *cpd*
lactique [laktik] *adj*: **acide/ferment ~** lactic
acid/ferment
lactose [laktoz] *nm* lactose, milk sugar
lacune [lakyn] *nf* gap
lacustre [lakystʀ(ə)] *adj* lake *cpd*, lakeside *cpd*
lad [lad] *nm* stable-lad
là-dedans [laddɑ̃] *adv* inside (there), in it; (*fig*)
in that
là-dehors [ladəɔʀ] *adv* out there
là-derrière [ladɛʀjɛʀ] *adv* behind there; (*fig*)
behind that
là-dessous [ladsu] *adv* underneath, under
there; (*fig*) behind that
là-dessus [ladsy] *adv* on there; (*fig*) at that
point; (: *à ce sujet*) about that
là-devant [ladvɑ̃] *adv* there (in front)
ladite [ladit] *adj voir* **ledit**
ladre [lɑdʀ(ə)] *adj* miserly
lagon [lagɔ̃] *nm* lagoon
Lagos [lagɔs] *n* Lagos
lagune [lagyn] *nf* lagoon
là-haut [lao] *adv* up there
laïc [laik] *adj, nm/f* = **laïque**
laïciser [laisize] *vt* to secularize

laïcité [laisite] *nf* secularity, secularism
laid, e [lɛ, lɛd] *adj* ugly; (*fig: acte*) mean, cheap
laideron [lɛdRɔ̃] *nm* ugly girl
laideur [lɛdœR] *nf* ugliness *no pl*; meanness *no pl*
laie [lɛ] *nf* wild sow
lainage [lɛnaʒ] *nm* woollen garment; (*étoffe*) woollen material
laine [lɛn] *nf* wool; ~ **peignée** worsted (wool); ~ **à tricoter** knitting wool; ~ **de verre** glass wool; ~ **vierge** new wool
laineux, -euse [lɛnø, -øz] *adj* woolly
lainier, -ière [lenje, -jɛR] *adj* (*industrie etc*) woollen
laïque [laik] *adj* lay, civil; (*Scol*) state *cpd* (*as opposed to private and Roman Catholic*) ▷ *nm/f* layman(-woman)
laisse [lɛs] *nf* (*de chien*) lead, leash; **tenir en** ~ to keep on a lead *ou* leash
laissé-pour-compte, laissée-, laissés- [lesepuRkɔ̃t] *adj* (*Comm*) unsold; (: *refusé*) returned ▷ *nm/f* (*fig*) reject; **les laissés-pour-compte de la reprise économique** those who are left out of the economic upturn
laisser [lese] *vt* to leave ▷ *vb aux*: ~ **qn faire** to let sb do; **se** ~ **exploiter** to let o.s. be exploited; **se** ~ **aller** to let o.s. go; ~ **qn tranquille** to let *ou* leave sb alone; **laisse-toi faire** let me (*ou* him) do it; **rien ne laisse penser que ...** there is no reason to think that ...; **cela ne laisse pas de surprendre** nonetheless it is surprising
laisser-aller [leseale] *nm* carelessness, slovenliness
laisser-faire [lesefɛR] *nm* laissez-faire
laissez-passer [lesepase] *nm inv* pass
lait [lɛ] *nm* milk; **frère/sœur de** ~ foster brother/sister; ~ **écrémé/concentré/condensé** skimmed/condensed/evaporated milk; ~ **en poudre** powdered milk, milk powder; ~ **de chèvre/vache** goat's/cow's milk; ~ **maternel** mother's milk; ~ **démaquillant/de beauté** cleansing/beauty lotion
laitage [lɛtaʒ] *nm* milk product
laiterie [lɛtRi] *nf* dairy
laiteux, -euse [lɛtø, -øz] *adj* milky
laitier, -ière [letje, -jɛR] *adj* dairy ▷ *nm/f* milkman (dairywoman)
laiton [lɛtɔ̃] *nm* brass
laitue [lety] *nf* lettuce
laïus [lajys] *nm* (*péj*) spiel
lama [lama] *nm* llama
lambeau, x [lɑ̃bo] *nm* scrap; **en ~x** in tatters, tattered
lambin, e [lɑ̃bɛ̃, -in] *adj* (*péj*) slow
lambiner [lɑ̃bine] *vi* (*péj*) to dawdle
lambris [lɑ̃bRi] *nm* panelling *no pl*
lambrissé, e [lɑ̃bRise] *adj* panelled
lame [lam] *nf* blade; (*vague*) wave; (*lamelle*) strip; ~ **de fond** ground swell *no pl*; ~ **de rasoir** razor blade
lamé [lame] *nm* lamé
lamelle [lamɛl] *nf* (*lame*) small blade; (*morceau*) sliver; (*de champignon*) gill; **couper en ~s** to slice

thinly
lamentable [lamɑ̃tabl(ə)] *adj* (*déplorable*) appalling; (*pitoyable*) pitiful
lamentablement [lamɑ̃tabləmɑ̃] *adv* (*échouer*) miserably; (*se conduire*) appallingly
lamentation [lamɑ̃tasjɔ̃] *nf* wailing *no pl*, lamentation; moaning *no pl*
lamenter [lamɑ̃te]: **se lamenter** *vi*: **se** ~ **(sur)** to moan (over)
laminage [laminaʒ] *nm* lamination
laminer [lamine] *vt* to laminate; (*fig: écraser*) to wipe out
laminoir [laminwaR] *nm* rolling mill; **passer au** ~ (*fig*) to go (*ou* put) through the mill
lampadaire [lɑ̃padɛR] *nm* (*de salon*) standard lamp; (*dans la rue*) street lamp
lampe [lɑ̃p(ə)] *nf* lamp; (*Tech*) valve; ~ **à alcool** spirit lamp; ~ **à bronzer** sunlamp; ~ **de poche** torch (*Brit*), flashlight (*US*); ~ **à souder** blowlamp; ~ **témoin** warning light
lampée [lɑ̃pe] *nf* gulp, swig
lampe-tempête [lɑ̃ptɑ̃pɛt] (*pl* **lampes-tempête**) *nf* storm lantern
lampion [lɑ̃pjɔ̃] *nm* Chinese lantern
lampiste [lɑ̃pist(ə)] *nm* light (maintenance) man; (*fig*) underling
lamproie [lɑ̃pRwa] *nf* lamprey
lance [lɑ̃s] *nf* spear; ~ **d'arrosage** garden hose; ~ **à eau** water hose; ~ **d'incendie** fire hose
lancée [lɑ̃se] *nf*: **être/continuer sur sa** ~ to be under way/keep going
lance-flammes [lɑ̃sflam] *nm inv* flamethrower
lance-fusées [lɑ̃sfyze] *nm inv* rocket launcher
lance-grenades [lɑ̃sgRənad] *nm inv* grenade launcher
lancement [lɑ̃smɑ̃] *nm* launching *no pl*, launch; **offre de** ~ introductory offer
lance-missiles [lɑ̃smisil] *nm inv* missile launcher
lance-pierres [lɑ̃spjɛR] *nm inv* catapult
lancer [lɑ̃se] *nm* (*Sport*) throwing *no pl*, throw; (*Pêche*) rod and reel fishing ▷ *vt* to throw; (*émettre, projeter*) to throw out, send out; (*produit, fusée, bateau, artiste*) to launch; (*injure*) to hurl, fling; (*proclamation, mandat d'arrêt*) to issue; (*emprunt*) to float; (*moteur*) to send roaring away; ~ **qch à qn** to throw sth to sb; (*de façon agressive*) to throw sth at sb; ~ **un cri** *ou* **un appel** to shout *ou* call out; **se lancer** *vi* (*prendre de l'élan*) to build up speed; (*se précipiter*): **se** ~ **sur** *ou* **contre** to rush at; **se** ~ **dans** (*discussion*) to launch into; (*aventure*) to embark on; (*les affaires, la politique*) to go into; ~ **du poids** *nm* putting the shot
lance-roquettes [lɑ̃sRɔkɛt] *nm inv* rocket launcher
lance-torpilles [lɑ̃stɔRpij] *nm inv* torpedo tube
lanceur, -euse [lɑ̃sœR, -øz] *nm/f* bowler; (*Baseball*) pitcher ▷ *nm* (*Espace*) launcher
lancinant, e [lɑ̃sinɑ̃, -ɑ̃t] *adj* (*regrets etc*) haunting; (*douleur*) shooting
lanciner [lɑ̃sine] *vi* to throb; (*fig*) to nag

landais, e [lɑ̃dɛ, -ɛz] adj of ou from the Landes
landau [lɑ̃do] nm pram (Brit), baby carriage (US)
lande [lɑ̃d] nf moor
Landes [lɑ̃d] nfpl: **les ~** the Landes
langage [lɑ̃gaʒ] nm language; **~ d'assemblage**
(Inform) assembly language; **~ du corps** body
language; **~ évolué/machine** (Inform) high-
level/machine language; **~ de**
programmation (Inform) programming
language
lange [lɑ̃ʒ] nm flannel blanket; **langes** nmpl
swaddling clothes
langer [lɑ̃ʒe] vt to change (the nappy (Brit) ou
diaper (US) of); **table à ~** changing table
langoureusement [lɑ̃guʀøzmɑ̃] adv
languorously
langoureux, -euse [lɑ̃guʀø, -øz] adj
languorous
langouste [lɑ̃gust(ə)] nf crayfish inv
langoustine [lɑ̃gustin] nf Dublin Bay prawn
langue [lɑ̃g] nf (Anat, Culin) tongue; (Ling)
language; (bande): **~ de terre** spit of land;
tirer la ~ (à) to stick out one's tongue (at);
donner sa ~ au chat to give up, give in; **de ~**
française French-speaking; **~ de bois**
officialese; **~ maternelle** native language,
mother tongue; **~ verte** slang; **~ vivante**
modern language
langue-de-chat [lɑ̃gdəʃa] nf finger biscuit
languedocien, ne [lɑ̃gdɔsjɛ̃, -ɛn] adj of ou from
the Languedoc
languette [lɑ̃gɛt] nf tongue
langueur [lɑ̃gœʀ] nf languidness
languir [lɑ̃giʀ] vi to languish; (conversation) to
flag; **se languir** vi to be languishing; **faire ~ qn**
to keep sb waiting
languissant, e [lɑ̃gisɑ̃, -ɑ̃t] adj languid
lanière [lanjɛʀ] nf (de fouet) lash; (de valise,
bretelle) strap
lanoline [lanɔlin] nf lanolin
lanterne [lɑ̃tɛʀn(ə)] nf (portable) lantern;
(électrique) light, lamp; (de voiture) (side)light; **~**
rouge (fig) tail-ender; **~ vénitienne** Chinese
lantern
lanterneau, x [lɑ̃tɛʀno] nm skylight
lanterner [lɑ̃tɛʀne] vi: **faire ~ qn** to keep sb
hanging around
Laos [laɔs] nm: **le ~** Laos
laotien, ne [laɔsjɛ̃, -ɛn] adj Laotian
lapalissade [lapalisad] nf statement of the
obvious
La Paz [lapaz] n La Paz
laper [lape] vt to lap up
lapereau, x [lapʀo] nm young rabbit
lapidaire [lapidɛʀ] adj stone cpd; (fig) terse
lapider [lapide] vt to stone
lapin [lapɛ̃] nm rabbit; (fourrure) cony; **coup du ~**
rabbit punch; **poser un ~ à qn** to stand sb up; **~**
de garenne wild rabbit
lapis [lapis], **lapis-lazuli** [lapislazyli] nm inv
lapis lazuli
lapon, e [lapɔ̃, -ɔn] adj Lapp, Lappish ▷ nm (Ling)

Lapp, Lappish ▷ nm/f: **Lapon, e** Lapp, Laplander
Laponie [lapɔni] nf: **la ~** Lapland
laps [laps] nm: **~ de temps** space of time, time
no pl
lapsus [lapsys] nm slip
laquais [lakɛ] nm lackey
laque [lak] nf lacquer; (brute) shellac; (pour
cheveux) hair spray ▷ nm lacquer; piece of
lacquer ware
laqué, e [lake] adj lacquered
laquelle [lakɛl] pron voir **lequel**
larbin [laʀbɛ̃] nm (péj) flunkey
larcin [laʀsɛ̃] nm theft
lard [laʀ] nm (graisse) fat; (bacon) (streaky)
bacon
larder [laʀde] vt (Culin) to lard
lardon [laʀdɔ̃] nm (Culin) piece of chopped
bacon; (fam: enfant) kid
large [laʀʒ(ə)] adj wide; broad; (fig) generous
▷ adv: **calculer/voir ~** to allow extra/think big
▷ nm (largeur): **5 m de ~** 5 m wide ou in width;
(mer): **le ~** the open sea; **en ~** adv sideways; **au ~**
de off; **~ d'esprit** broad-minded; **ne pas en**
mener ~ to have one's heart in one's boots
largement [laʀʒəmɑ̃] adv widely; (de loin)
greatly; (amplement, au minimum) easily; (sans
compter: donner etc) generously
largesse [laʀʒɛs] nf generosity; **largesses** nfpl
liberalities
largeur [laʀʒœʀ] nf (qu'on mesure) width;
(impression visuelle) wideness, width; breadth;
broadness
larguer [laʀge] vt to drop; (fam: se débarrasser de)
to get rid of; **~ les amarres** to cast off (the
moorings)
larme [laʀm(ə)] nf tear; (fig): **une ~ de** a drop of;
en ~s in tears; **pleurer à chaudes ~s** to cry
one's eyes out, cry bitterly
larmoyant, e [laʀmwajɑ̃, -ɑ̃t] adj tearful
larmoyer [laʀmwaje] vi (yeux) to water; (se
plaindre) to whimper
larron [laʀɔ̃] nm thief
larve [laʀv(ə)] nf (Zool) larva; (fig) worm
larvé, e [laʀve] adj (fig) latent
laryngite [laʀɛ̃ʒit] nf laryngitis
laryngologiste [laʀɛ̃gɔlɔʒist(ə)] nm/f throat
specialist
larynx [laʀɛ̃ks] nm larynx
las, lasse [lɑ, lɑs] adj weary
lasagne [lazaɲ] nf lasagne
lascar [laskaʀ] nm character; (malin) rogue
lascif, -ive [lasif, -iv] adj lascivious
laser [lazɛʀ] nm: **(rayon) ~** laser (beam); **chaîne**
ou platine ~ compact disc (player); **disque ~**
compact disc
lassant, e [lɑsɑ̃, -ɑ̃t] adj tiresome, wearisome
lasse [lɑs] adj f voir **las**
lasser [lɑse] vt to weary, tire; **se ~ de** to grow
weary ou tired of
lassitude [lɑsityd] nf lassitude, weariness
lasso [laso] nm lasso; **prendre au ~** to lasso
latent, e [latɑ̃, -ɑ̃t] adj latent

latéral, e, aux [lateʀal, -o] *adj* side *cpd*, lateral
latéralement [lateʀalmɑ̃] *adv* edgeways; (*arriver, souffler*) from the side
latex [latɛks] *nm inv* latex
latin, e [latɛ̃, -in] *adj* Latin ▷ *nm* (*Ling*) Latin ▷ *nm/f*: **Latin, e** Latin; **j'y perds mon ~** it's all Greek to me
latiniste [latinist(ə)] *nm/f* Latin scholar (*ou* student)
latino-américain, e [latinɔameʀikɛ̃, -ɛn] *adj* Latin-American
latitude [latityd] *nf* latitude; (*fig*): **avoir la ~ de faire** to be left free *ou* be at liberty to do; **à 48° de ~ Nord** at latitude 48° North; **sous toutes les ~s** (*fig*) world-wide, throughout the world
latrines [latʀin] *nfpl* latrines
latte [lat] *nf* lath, slat; (*de plancher*) board
lattis [lati] *nm* lathwork
laudanum [lodanɔm] *nm* laudanum
laudatif, -ive [lodatif, -iv] *adj* laudatory
lauréat, e [lɔʀea, -at] *nm/f* winner
laurier [lɔʀje] *nm* (*Bot*) laurel; (*Culin*) bay leaves *pl*; **lauriers** *nmpl* (*fig*) laurels
laurier-rose [lɔʀjeʀoz] (*pl* **lauriers-roses**) *nm* oleander
laurier-tin [lɔʀjetɛ̃] (*pl* **lauriers-tins**) *nm* laurustinus
lavable [lavabl(ə)] *adj* washable
lavabo [lavabo] *nm* washbasin; **lavabos** *nmpl* toilet *sg*
lavage [lavaʒ] *nm* washing *no pl*, wash; **~ d'estomac/d'intestin** stomach/intestinal wash; **~ de cerveau** brainwashing *no pl*
lavande [lavɑ̃d] *nf* lavender
lavandière [lavɑ̃djɛʀ] *nf* washerwoman
lave [lav] *nf* lava *no pl*
lave-glace [lavglas] *nm* (*Auto*) windscreen (*Brit*) *ou* windshield (*US*) washer
lave-linge [lavlɛʒ] *nm inv* washing machine
lavement [lavmɑ̃] *nm* (*Méd*) enema
laver [lave] *vt* to wash; (*tache*) to wash off; (*fig: affront*) to avenge; **se laver** to have a wash, wash; **se ~ les mains/dents** to wash one's hands/clean one's teeth; **~ la vaisselle/le linge** to wash the dishes/clothes; **~ qn de** (*accusation*) to clear sb of
laverie [lavʀi] *nf*: **~ (automatique)** launderette
lavette [lavɛt] *nf* (*chiffon*) dish cloth; (*brosse*) dish mop; (*fam: homme*) wimp, drip
laveur, -euse [lavœʀ, -øz] *nm/f* cleaner
lave-vaisselle [lavvɛsɛl] *nm inv* dishwasher
lavis [lavi] *nm* (*technique*) washing; (*dessin*) wash drawing
lavoir [lavwaʀ] *nm* wash house; (*bac*) washtub
laxatif, -ive [laksatif, -iv] *adj, nm* laxative
laxisme [laksism(ə)] *nm* laxity
laxiste [laksist(ə)] *adj* lax
layette [lɛjɛt] *nf* layette
layon [lɛjɔ̃] *nm* trail
lazaret [lazaʀɛ] *nm* quarantine area
lazzi [ladzi] *nm* gibe

LCR *sigle f* (= *Ligue communiste révolutionnaire*) political party

 MOT-CLÉ

le, l', la [l(ə)] (*pl* **les**) *art déf* **1** the; **le livre/la pomme/l'arbre** the book/the apple/the tree; **les étudiants** the students
2 (*noms abstraits*): **le courage/l'amour/la jeunesse** courage/love/youth
3 (*indiquant la possession*): **se casser la jambe** *etc* to break one's leg *etc*; **levez la main** put your hand up; **avoir les yeux gris/le nez rouge** to have grey eyes/a red nose
4 (*temps*): **le matin/soir** in the morning/evening; mornings/evenings; **le jeudi** *etc* (*d'habitude*) on Thursdays *etc*; (*ce jeudi-là etc*) on (the) Thursday; **nous venons le 3 décembre** (*parlé*) we're coming on the 3rd of December *ou* on December the 3rd; (*écrit*) we're coming (on) 3rd *ou* 3 December
5 (*distribution, évaluation*) a, an; **trois euros le mètre/kilo** three euros a *ou* per metre/kilo; **le tiers/quart de** a third/quarter of
▷ *pron* **1** (*personne: mâle*) him; (: *femelle*) her; (: *pluriel*) them; **je le/la/les vois** I can see him/her/them
2 (*animal, chose: singulier*) it; (: *pluriel*) them; **je le** (*ou* **la**) **vois** I can see it; **je les vois** I can see them
3 (*remplaçant une phrase*): **je ne le savais pas** I didn't know (about it); **il était riche et ne l'est plus** he was once rich but no longer is

lé [le] *nm* (*de tissu*) width; (*de papier peint*) strip, length
leader [lidœʀ] *nm* leader
leadership [lidœʀʃip] *nm* (*Pol*) leadership
leasing [liziŋ] *nm* leasing
lèche-bottes [lɛʃbɔt] *nm inv* bootlicker
lèchefrite [lɛʃfʀit] *nf* dripping pan *ou* tray
lécher [leʃe] *vt* to lick; (*laper: lait, eau*) to lick *ou* lap up; (*finir, polir*) to over-refine; **~ les vitrines** to go window-shopping; **se ~ les doigts/lèvres** to lick one's fingers/lips
lèche-vitrines [lɛʃvitʀin] *nm inv*: **faire du ~** to go window-shopping
leçon [ləsɔ̃] *nf* lesson; **faire la ~** to teach; **faire la ~ à** (*fig*) to give a lecture to; **~s de conduite** driving lessons; **~s particulières** private lessons *ou* tuition *sg* (*Brit*)
lecteur, -trice [lɛktœʀ, -tʀis] *nm/f* reader; (*d'université*) (foreign language) assistant (*Brit*), (foreign) teaching assistant (*US*) ▷ *nm* (*Tech*): **~ de cassettes** cassette player; **~ de CD/DVD** (*Inform: d'ordinateur*) CD/DVD drive; (*de salon*) CD/DVD player; **~ MP3** MP3 player
lectorat [lɛktɔʀa] *nm* (foreign language *ou* teaching) assistantship
lecture [lɛktyʀ] *nf* reading
LED [lɛd] *sigle f* (= *light emitting diode*) LED
ledit [lədi], **ladite** [ladit] (*mpl* **lesdits** [ledi]) (*fpl*

lesdites [ledit]) *adj* the aforesaid
légal, e, -aux [legal, -o] *adj* legal
légalement [legalmã] *adv* legally
légalisation [legalizasjɔ̃] *nf* legalization
légaliser [legalize] *vt* to legalize
légalité [legalite] *nf* legality, lawfulness; **être dans/sortir de la ~** to be within/step outside the law
légat [lega] *nm* (*Rel*) legate
légataire [legatɛR] *nm* legatee
légendaire [leʒɑ̃dɛR] *adj* legendary
légende [leʒɑ̃d] *nf* (*mythe*) legend; (*de carte, plan*) key, legend; (*de dessin*) caption
léger, -ère [leʒe, -ɛR] *adj* light; (*bruit, retard*) slight; (*boisson, parfum*) weak; (*couche, étoffe*) thin; (*superficiel*) thoughtless; (*volage*) free and easy; flighty; (*peu sérieux*) lightweight; **blessé ~** slightly injured person; **à la légère** *adv* (*parler, agir*) rashly, thoughtlessly
légèrement [leʒɛRmɑ̃] *adv* lightly; thoughtlessly, rashly; **~ plus grand** slightly bigger
légèreté [leʒɛRte] *nf* lightness; thoughtlessness
légiférer [leʒifere] *vi* to legislate
légion [leʒjɔ̃] *nf* legion; **la L~ étrangère** the Foreign Legion; **la L~ d'honneur** the Legion of Honour; *see note*

légionnaire [leʒjɔnɛR] *nm* (*Mil*) legionnaire; (*de la Légion d'honneur*) holder of the Legion of Honour
législateur [leʒislatœR] *nm* legislator, lawmaker
législatif, -ive [leʒislatif, -iv] *adj* legislative; **législatives** *nfpl* general election *sg*
législation [leʒislasjɔ̃] *nf* legislation
législature [leʒislatyR] *nf* legislature; (*période*) term (of office)
légiste [leʒist(ə)] *nm* jurist ▷ *adj*: **médecin ~** forensic scientist (*Brit*), medical examiner (*US*)
légitime [leʒitim] *adj* (*Jur*) lawful, legitimate; (*enfant*) legitimate; (*fig*) rightful, legitimate; **en état de ~ défense** in self-defence
légitimement [leʒitimmɑ̃] *adv* lawfully; legitimately; rightfully
légitimer [leʒitime] *vt* (*enfant*) to legitimize; (*justifier: conduite etc*) to justify
légitimité [leʒitimite] *nf* (*Jur*) legitimacy
legs [lɛg] *nm* legacy
léguer [lege] *vt*: **~ qch à qn** (*Jur*) to bequeath sth to sb; (*fig*) to hand sth down *ou* pass sth on to sb
légume [legym] *nm* vegetable; **~s verts** green

vegetables; **~s secs** pulses
légumier [legymje] *nm* vegetable dish
leitmotiv [lejtmɔtiv] *nm* leitmotiv, leitmotif
Léman [lemɑ̃] *nm voir* **lac**
lendemain [lɑ̃dmɛ̃] *nm*: **le ~** the next *ou* following day; **le ~ matin/soir** the next *ou* following morning/evening; **le ~ de** the day after; **au ~ de** in the days following; in the wake of; **penser au ~** to think of the future; **sans ~** short-lived; **de beaux ~s** bright prospects; **des ~s qui chantent** a rosy future
lénifiant, e [lenifjɑ̃, -ɑ̃t] *adj* soothing
léniniste [leninist(ə)] *adj, nm/f* Leninist
lent, e [lɑ̃, lɑ̃t] *adj* slow
lente [lɑ̃t] *nf* nit
lentement [lɑ̃tmɑ̃] *adv* slowly
lenteur [lɑ̃tœR] *nf* slowness *no pl*; **lenteurs** *nfpl* (*actions, décisions lentes*) slowness *sg*
lentille [lɑ̃tij] *nf* (*Optique*) lens *sg*; (*Bot*) lentil; **~ d'eau** duckweed; **~s de contact** contact lenses
léonin, e [leɔnɛ̃, -in] *adj* (*fig: contrat etc*) one-sided
léopard [leɔpaR] *nm* leopard
LEP [lɛp] *sigle m* (= *lycée d'enseignement professionnel*) *secondary school for vocational training, pre-1986*
lèpre [lɛpR(ə)] *nf* leprosy
lépreux, -euse [lepRø, -øz] *nm/f* leper ▷ *adj* (*fig*) flaking, peeling

MOT-CLÉ

lequel, laquelle [ləkɛl, lakɛl] (*mpl* **lesquels**, *fpl* **lesquelles**) (*à + lequel = **auquel**, de + lequel = **duquel***) *pron* **1** (*interrogatif*) which, which one **2** (*relatif: personne: sujet*) who; (*: objet, après préposition*) whom; (*sujet: possessif*) whose; (*: chose*) which; **je l'ai proposé au directeur, lequel est d'accord** I suggested it to the director, who agrees; **la femme à laquelle j'ai acheté mon chien** the woman from whom I bought my dog; **le pont sur lequel nous sommes passés** the bridge (over) which we crossed; **un homme sur la compétence duquel on peut compter** a man whose competence one can count on ▷ *adj*: **auquel cas** in which case

les [le] *art déf, pron voir* **le**
lesbienne [lɛsbjɛn] *nf* lesbian
lesdits [ledi], **lesdites** [ledit] *adj voir* **ledit**
lèse-majesté [lɛzmaʒeste] *nf inv*: **crime de ~** crime of lese-majesty
léser [leze] *vt* to wrong; (*Méd*) to injure
lésiner [lezine] *vt*: **~ (sur)** to skimp (on)
lésion [lezjɔ̃] *nf* lesion, damage *no pl*; **~s cérébrales** brain damage
Lesotho [lezɔto] *nm*: **le ~** Lesotho
lesquels, lesquelles [lekɛl] *pron voir* **lequel**
lessivable [lesivabl(ə)] *adj* washable
lessive [lesiv] *nf* (*poudre*) washing powder; (*linge*) washing *no pl*, wash; (*opération*) washing *no pl*; **faire la ~** to do the washing
lessivé, e [lesive] *adj* (*fam*) washed out
lessiver [lesive] *vt* to wash

lessiveuse [lesivøz] *nf* (*récipient*) washtub

lessiviel [lesivjɛl] *adj* detergent

lest [lɛst] *nm* ballast; **jeter** *ou* **lâcher du ~** (*fig*) to make concessions

leste [lɛst(ə)] *adj* (*personne, mouvement*) sprightly, nimble; (*désinvolte: manières*) offhand; (*osé: plaisanterie*) risqué

lestement [lɛstəmã] *adv* nimbly

lester [lɛste] *vt* to ballast

letchi [lɛtʃi] *nm* = **litchi**

léthargie [letaʀʒi] *nf* lethargy

léthargique [letaʀʒik] *adj* lethargic

letton, ne [lɛtɔ̃, -ɔn] *adj* Latvian, Lett

Lettonie [lɛtɔni] *nf*: **la ~** Latvia

lettre [lɛtʀ(ə)] *nf* letter; **lettres** *nfpl* (*étude, culture*) literature *sg*; (*Scol*) arts (subjects); **à la ~** (*au sens propre*) literally; (*ponctuellement*) to the letter; **en ~s majuscules** *ou* **capitales** in capital letters, in capitals; **en toutes ~s** in words, in full; **~ de change** bill of exchange; **~ piégée** letter bomb; **~ de voiture (aérienne)** (air) waybill, (air) bill of lading; **~s de noblesse** pedigree

lettré, e [letʀe] *adj* well-read, scholarly

lettre-transfert [lɛtʀətʀɑ̃sfɛʀ] (*pl* **lettres-transferts**) *nf* (pressure) transfer

leu [lø] *nm voir* **queue**

leucémie [løsemi] *nf* leukaemia

⬤ MOT-CLÉ

leur [lœʀ] *adj poss* their; **leur maison** their house; **leurs amis** their friends; **à leur approche** as they came near; **à leur vue** at the sight of them
▷ *pron* **1** (*objet indirect*) (to) them; **je leur ai dit la vérité** I told them the truth; **je le leur ai donné** I gave it to them, I gave them it
2 (*possessif*): **le (la) leur, les leurs** theirs

leurre [lœʀ] *nm* (*appât*) lure; (*fig*) delusion; (*: piège*) snare

leurrer [lœʀe] *vt* to delude, deceive

leurs [lœʀ] *adj voir* **leur**

levain [ləvɛ̃] *nm* leaven; **sans ~** unleavened

levant, e [ləvã, -ãt] *adj*: **soleil ~** rising sun ▷ *nm*: **le L~** the Levant; **au soleil ~** at sunrise

levantin, e [ləvãtɛ̃, -in] *adj* Levantine ▷ *nm/f*: **Levantin, e** Levantine

levé, e [ləve] *adj*: **être ~** to be up ▷ *nm*: **~ de terrain** land survey; **à mains ~es** (*vote*) by a show of hands; **au pied ~** at a moment's notice

levée [ləve] *nf* (*Postes*) collection; (*Cartes*) trick; **~ de boucliers** general outcry; **~ du corps** collection of the body from house of the deceased, before funeral; **~ d'écrou** release from custody; **~ de terre** levee; **~ de troupes** levy

lever [ləve] *vt* (*vitre, bras etc*) to raise; (*soulever de terre, supprimer: interdiction, siège*) to lift; (*: difficulté*) to remove; (*séance*) to close; (*impôts, armée*) to levy; (*Chasse: lièvre*) to start; (*: perdrix*) to flush;

(*fam: fille*) to pick up ▷ *vi* (*Culin*) to rise ▷ *nm*: **au ~** on getting up; **se lever** *vi* to get up; (*soleil*) to rise; (*jour*) to break; (*brouillard*) to lift; **levez-vous!, lève-toi!** stand up!, get up!; **ça va se ~** the weather will clear; **~ du jour** daybreak; **~ du rideau** (*Théât*) curtain; **~ de rideau** (*pièce*) curtain raiser; **~ de soleil** sunrise

lève-tard [lɛvtaʀ] *nm/f inv* late riser

lève-tôt [lɛvto] *nm/f inv* early riser, early bird

levier [ləvje] *nm* lever; **faire ~ sur** to lever up (*ou* off); **~ de changement de vitesse** gear lever

lévitation [levitasjɔ̃] *nf* levitation

levraut [ləvʀo] *nm* (*Zool*) leveret

lèvre [lɛvʀ(ə)] *nf* lip; **lèvres** *nfpl* (*d'une plaie*) edges; **petites/grandes ~s** labia minora/majora; **du bout des ~s** half-heartedly

lévrier [levʀije] *nm* greyhound

levure [ləvyʀ] *nf* yeast; **~ chimique** baking powder

lexical, e, -aux [lɛksikal, -o] *adj* lexical

lexicographe [lɛksikɔgʀaf] *nm/f* lexicographer

lexicographie [lɛksikɔgʀafi] *nf* lexicography, dictionary writing

lexicologie [lɛksikɔlɔʒi] *nf* lexicology

lexique [lɛksik] *nm* vocabulary, lexicon; (*glossaire*) vocabulary

lézard [lezaʀ] *nm* lizard; (*peau*) lizard skin

lézarde [lezaʀd(ə)] *nf* crack

lézarder [lezaʀde]: **se lézarder** *vi* to crack

liaison [ljɛzɔ̃] *nf* (*rapport*) connection, link; (*Rail, Aviat etc*) link; (*relation: d'amitié*) friendship; (*: d'affaires*) relationship; (*: amoureuse*) affair; (*Culin, Phonétique*) liaison; **entrer/être en ~ avec** to get/be in contact with; **~ radio** radio contact; **~ (de transmission de données)** (*Inform*) data link

liane [ljan] *nf* creeper

liant, e [ljã, -ãt] *adj* sociable

liasse [ljas] *nf* wad, bundle

Liban [libã] *nm*: **le ~** (the) Lebanon

libanais [libanɛ, -ɛz] *adj* Lebanese ▷ *nm/f*: **Libanais, e** Lebanese

libations [libasjɔ̃] *nfpl* libations

libelle [libɛl] *nm* lampoon

libellé [libele] *nm* wording

libeller [libele] *vt* (*chèque, mandat*): **~ (au nom de)** to make out (to); (*lettre*) to word

libellule [libelyl] *nf* dragonfly

libéral, e, -aux [libeʀal, -o] *adj, nm/f* liberal; **les professions ~es** the professions

libéralement [libeʀalmã] *adv* liberally

libéralisation [libeʀalizasjɔ̃] *nf* liberalization; **~ du commerce** easing of trade restrictions

libéraliser [libeʀalize] *vt* to liberalize

libéralisme [libeʀalism(ə)] *nm* liberalism

libéralité [libeʀalite] *nf* liberality *no pl*, generosity *no pl*

libérateur, -trice [libeʀatœʀ, -tʀis] *adj* liberating ▷ *nm/f* liberator

libération [libeʀasjɔ̃] *nf* liberation, freeing; release; discharge; **~ conditionnelle** release on parole

libéré, e [libeʀe] *adj* liberated; ~ **de** freed from; **être ~ sous caution/sur parole** to be released on bail/on parole

libérer [libeʀe] *vt* (*délivrer*) to free, liberate; (: *moralement, Psych*) to liberate; (*relâcher: prisonnier*) to release; (: *soldat*) to discharge; (*dégager: gaz, cran d'arrêt*) to release; (*Écon: échanges commerciaux*) to ease restrictions on; **se libérer** (*de rendez-vous*) to try and be free, get out of previous engagements; ~ **qn de** (*liens, dette*) to free sb from; (*promesse*) to release sb from

Libéria [libeʀja] *nm*: **le ~** Liberia

libérien, ne [libeʀjɛ̃, -ɛn] *adj* Liberian ▷ *nm/f*: **Libérien, ne** Liberian

libéro [libeʀo] *nm* (*Football*) sweeper

libertaire [libɛʀtɛʀ] *adj* libertarian

liberté [libɛʀte] *nf* freedom; (*loisir*) free time; **libertés** *nfpl* (*privautés*) liberties; **mettre/être en ~** to set/be free; **en ~ provisoire/surveillée/conditionnelle** on bail/probation/parole; **~ d'association** right of association; **~ de conscience** freedom of conscience; **~ du culte** freedom of worship; **~ d'esprit** independence of mind; **~ d'opinion** freedom of thought; **~ de la presse** freedom of the press; **~ de réunion** right to hold meetings; **~ syndicale** union rights *pl*; **~s individuelles** personal freedom *sg*; **~s publiques** civil rights

libertin, e [libɛʀtɛ̃, -in] *adj* libertine, licentious

libertinage [libɛʀtinaʒ] *nm* licentiousness

libidineux, -euse [libidinø, -øz] *adj* lustful

libido [libido] *nf* libido

libraire [libʀɛʀ] *nm/f* bookseller

libraire-éditeur [libʀɛʀeditœʀ] (*pl* **libraires-éditeurs**) *nm* publisher and bookseller

librairie [libʀeʀi] *nf* bookshop

librairie-papeterie [libʀeʀipapetʀi] (*pl* **librairies-papeteries**) *nf* bookseller's and stationer's

libre [libʀ(ə)] *adj* free; (*route*) clear; (*place etc*) vacant, free; (*fig: propos, manières*) open; (*Scol*) private and Roman Catholic (*as opposed to "laïque"*); **de ~** (*place*) free; **~ de qch/de faire** free from sth/to do; **vente ~** (*Comm*) unrestricted sale; **~ arbitre** free will; **~ concurrence** free-market economy; **~ entreprise** free enterprise

libre-échange [libʀeʃɑ̃ʒ] *nm* free trade

librement [libʀəmɑ̃] *adv* freely

libre-penseur, -euse [libʀəpɑ̃sœʀ, -øz] *nm/f* free thinker

libre-service [libʀəsɛʀvis] *nm inv* (*magasin*) self-service store; (*restaurant*) self-service restaurant

librettiste [libʀetist(ə)] *nm/f* librettist

Libye [libi] *nf*: **la ~** Libya

libyen, ne [libjɛ̃, -ɛn] *adj* Libyan ▷ *nm/f*: **Libyen, ne** Libyan

lice [lis] *nf*: **entrer en ~** (*fig*) to enter the lists

licence [lisɑ̃s] *nf* (*permis*) permit; (*diplôme*) (first) degree; *see note*; (*liberté*) liberty; (*poétique, orthographique*) licence (Brit), license (US); (*des mœurs*) licentiousness; **~ ès lettres/en droit** arts/law degree

● **LICENCE**
●
● After the "DEUG", French university
● students undertake a third year of study to
● complete their licence. This is roughly
● equivalent to a bachelor's degree in Britain.

licencié, e [lisɑ̃sje] *nm/f* (*Scol*): **~ ès lettres/en droit** ≈ Bachelor of Arts/Law, arts/law graduate; (*Sport*) permit-holder

licenciement [lisɑ̃simɑ̃] *nm* dismissal; redundancy; laying off *no pl*

licencier [lisɑ̃sje] *vt* (*renvoyer*) to dismiss; (*débaucher*) to make redundant; to lay off

licencieux, -euse [lisɑ̃sjø, -øz] *adj* licentious

lichen [likɛn] *nm* lichen

licite [lisit] *adj* lawful

licorne [likɔʀn(ə)] *nf* unicorn

licou [liku] *nm* halter

lie [li] *nf* dregs *pl*, sediment

lié, e [lje] *adj*: **très ~ avec** (*fig*) very friendly with *ou* close to; **~ par** (*serment, promesse*) bound by; **avoir partie ~e (avec qn)** to be involved (with sb)

Liechtenstein [liʃtɛnʃtajn] *nm*: **le ~** Liechtenstein

lie-de-vin [lidvɛ̃] *adj inv* wine(-coloured)

liège [ljɛʒ] *nm* cork

liégeois, e [ljeʒwa, -waz] *adj* of *ou* from Liège ▷ *nm/f*: **Liégeois, e** inhabitant *ou* native of Liège; **café/chocolat ~** *coffee/chocolate ice cream topped with whipped cream*

lien [ljɛ̃] *nm* (*corde, fig: affectif, culturel*) bond; (*rapport*) link, connection; (*analogie*) link; **~ de parenté** family tie

lier [lje] *vt* (*attacher*) to tie up; (*joindre*) to link up; (*fig: unir, engager*) to bind; (*Culin*) to thicken; **~ qch à** (*attacher*) to tie sth to; (*associer*) to link sth to; **~ conversation (avec)** to strike up a conversation (with); **se lier avec** to make friends with

lierre [ljɛʀ] *nm* ivy

liesse [ljɛs] *nf*: **être en ~** to be jubilant

lieu, x [ljø] *nm* place; **lieux** *nmpl* (*locaux*) premises; (*endroit: d'un accident etc*) scene *sg*; **en ~ sûr** in a safe place; **en haut ~** in high places; **vider** *ou* **quitter les ~x** to leave the premises; **arriver/être sur les ~x** to arrive/be on the scene; **en premier ~** in the first place; **en dernier ~** lastly; **avoir ~** to take place; **avoir ~ de faire** to have grounds *ou* good reason for doing; **tenir ~ de** to take the place of; (*servir de*) to serve as; **donner ~ à** to give rise to, give cause for; **au ~ de** instead of; **au ~ qu'il y aille** instead of him going; **~ commun** commonplace; **~ géométrique** locus; **~ de naissance** place of birth

lieu-dit [ljødi] (*pl* **lieux-dits**) *nm* locality

lieue [ljø] *nf* league

lieutenant [ljøtnɑ̃] *nm* lieutenant; **~ de vaisseau** (*Navig*) lieutenant

lieutenant-colonel [ljøtnɑ̃kɔlɔnɛl] (*pl* **lieutenants-colonels**) *nm* (*armée de terre*) lieutenant colonel; (*armée de l'air*) wing commander (*Brit*), lieutenant colonel (*US*)

lièvre [ljɛvʀ(ə)] *nm* hare; (*coureur*) pacemaker; **lever un ~** (*fig*) to bring up a prickly subject

liftier, -ière [liftje, -jɛʀ] *nm,f* lift (*Brit*) *ou* elevator (*US*) attendant

lifting [liftiŋ] *nm* face lift

ligament [ligamɑ̃] *nm* ligament

ligature [ligatyʀ] *nf* ligature

lige [liʒ] *adj*: **homme ~** (*péj*) henchman

ligne [liɲ] *nf* (*gén*) line; (*Transports: liaison*) service; (: *trajet*) route; (*silhouette*): **garder la ~** to keep one's figure; **en ~** (*Inform*) on line; **en ~ droite** as the crow flies; **"à la ~"** "new paragraph"; **entrer en ~ de compte** to be taken into account; to come into it; **~ de but/médiane** goal/halfway line; **~ d'arrivée/de départ** finishing/starting line; **~ de conduite** course of action; **~ directrice** guiding line; **~ fixe** (*Tél*) fixed line (phone); **~ d'horizon** skyline; **~ de mire** line of sight; **~ de touche** touchline

ligné, e [liɲe] *adj*: **papier ~** ruled paper ▷ *nf* (*race, famille*) line, lineage; (*postérité*) descendants *pl*

ligneux, -euse [liɲø, -øz] *adj* ligneous, woody

lignite [liɲit] *nm* lignite

ligoter [ligɔte] *vt* to tie up

ligue [lig] *nf* league

liguer [lige]: **se liguer** *vi* to form a league; **se ~ contre** (*fig*) to combine against

lilas [lila] *nm* lilac

lillois, e [lilwa, -waz] *adj* of *ou* from Lille

Lima [lima] *n* Lima

limace [limas] *nf* slug

limaille [limaj] *nf*: **~ de fer** iron filings *pl*

limande [limɑ̃d] *nf* dab

limande-sole [limɑ̃dsɔl] *nf* lemon sole

limbes [lɛ̃b] *nmpl* limbo *sg*; **être dans les ~** (*fig: projet etc*) to be up in the air

lime [lim] *nf* (*Tech*) file; (*Bot*) lime; **~ à ongles** nail file

limer [lime] *vt* (*bois, métal*) to file (down); (*ongles*) to file; (*fig: prix*) to pare down

limier [limje] *nm* (*Zool*) bloodhound; (*détective*) sleuth

liminaire [liminɛʀ] *adj* (*propos*) introductory

limitatif, -ive [limitatif, -iv] *adj* restrictive

limitation [limitasjɔ̃] *nf* limitation, restriction; **sans ~ de temps** with no time limit; **~ des naissances** birth control; **~ de vitesse** speed limit

limite [limit] *nf* (*de terrain*) boundary; (*partie ou point extrême*) limit; **dans la ~ de** within the limits of; **à la ~** (*au pire*) if the worst comes (*ou* came) to the worst; **sans ~s** (*bêtise, richesse, pouvoir*) limitless, boundless; **vitesse/charge ~** maximum speed/load; **cas ~** borderline case; **date ~** deadline; **date ~ de vente/**

consommation sell-by/best-before date; **prix ~** upper price limit; **~ d'âge** maximum age, age limit

limiter [limite] *vt* (*restreindre*) to limit, restrict; (*délimiter*) to border, form the boundary of; **se ~ (à qch/à faire)** (*personne*) to limit *ou* confine o.s. (to sth/to doing sth); **se ~ à** (*chose*) to be limited to

limitrophe [limitʀɔf] *adj* border *cpd*; **~ de** bordering on

limogeage [limɔʒaʒ] *nm* dismissal

limoger [limɔʒe] *vt* to dismiss

limon [limɔ̃] *nm* silt

limonade [limɔnad] *nf* lemonade (*Brit*), (lemon) soda (*US*)

limonadier, -ière [limɔnadje, -jɛʀ] *nm/f* (*commerçant*) café owner; (*fabricant de limonade*) soft drinks manufacturer

limoneux, -euse [limɔnø, -øz] *adj* muddy

limousin, e [limuzɛ̃, -in] *adj* of *ou* from Limousin ▷ *nm* (*région*): **le L~** the Limousin ▷ *nf* limousine

limpide [lɛ̃pid] *adj* limpid

lin [lɛ̃] *nm* (*Bot*) flax; (*tissu, toile*) linen

linceul [lɛ̃sœl] *nm* shroud

linéaire [lineɛʀ] *adj* linear ▷ *nm*: **~ (de vente)** shelves *pl*

linéament [lineamɑ̃] *nm* outline

linge [lɛ̃ʒ] *nm* (*serviettes etc*) linen; (*pièce de tissu*) cloth; (*aussi*: **linge de corps**) underwear; (*aussi*: **linge de toilette**) towel; (*lessive*) washing; **~ sale** dirty linen

lingère [lɛ̃ʒɛʀ] *nf* linen maid

lingerie [lɛ̃ʒʀi] *nf* lingerie, underwear

lingot [lɛ̃go] *nm* ingot

linguiste [lɛ̃gɥist(ə)] *nm/f* linguist

linguistique [lɛ̃gɥistik] *adj* linguistic ▷ *nf* linguistics *sg*

lino [lino], **linoléum** [linɔleɔm] *nm* lino(leum)

linotte [linɔt] *nf*: **tête de ~** bird brain

linteau, x [lɛ̃to] *nm* lintel

lion, ne [ljɔ̃, ljɔn] *nm/f* lion (lioness); (*signe*): **le L~** Leo, the Lion; **être du L~** to be Leo; **~ de mer** sea lion

lionceau, x [ljɔ̃so] *nm* lion cub

liposuccion [liposyksjɔ̃] *nf* liposuction

lippu, e [lipy] *adj* thick-lipped

liquéfier [likefje] *vt* to liquefy; **se liquéfier** *vi* (*gaz etc*) to liquefy; (*fig: personne*) to succumb

liqueur [likœʀ] *nf* liqueur

liquidateur, -trice [likidatœʀ, -tʀis] *nm/f* (*Jur*) receiver; **~ judiciaire** official liquidator

liquidation [likidasjɔ̃] *nf* liquidation; (*Comm*) clearance (sale); **~ judiciaire** compulsory liquidation

liquide [likid] *adj* liquid ▷ *nm* liquid; (*Comm*): **en ~** in ready money *ou* cash

liquider [likide] *vt* (*société, biens, témoin gênant*) to liquidate; (*compte, problème*) to settle; (*Comm: articles*) to clear, sell off

liquidités [likidite] *nfpl* (*Comm*) liquid assets

liquoreux, -euse [likɔʀø, -øz] *adj* syrupy

lire [liʀ] nf (monnaie) lira ▷ vt, vi to read; **~ qch à qn** to read sth (out) to sb

lis vb [li] voir **lire** ▷ nm [lis] = **lys**

lisais etc [lizɛ] vb voir **lire**

Lisbonne [lizbɔn] n Lisbon

lise etc [liz] vb voir **lire**

liseré [lizʀe] nm border, edging

liseron [lizʀɔ̃] nm bindweed

liseuse [lizøz] nf book-cover; (veste) bed jacket

lisible [lizibl(ə)] adj legible; (digne d'être lu) readable

lisiblement [lizibləmɑ̃] adv legibly

lisière [lizjɛʀ] nf (de forêt) edge; (de tissu) selvage

lisons [lizɔ̃] vb voir **lire**

lisse [lis] adj smooth

lisser [lise] vt to smooth

listage [listaʒ] nm (Inform) listing

liste [list(ə)] nf list; (Inform) listing; **faire la ~ de** to list, make out a list of; **~ d'attente** waiting list; **~ civile** civil list; **~ électorale** electoral roll; **~ de mariage** wedding (present) list; **~ noire** hit list

lister [liste] vt to list

listéria [listeʀja] nf listeria

listing [listiŋ] nm (Inform) listing; **qualité ~** draft quality

lit [li] nm (gén) bed; **faire son ~** to make one's bed; **aller/se mettre au ~** to go to/get into bed; **chambre avec un grand ~** room with a double bed; **prendre le ~** to take to one's bed; **d'un premier ~** (Jur) of a first marriage; **~ de camp** camp bed (Brit), cot (US); **~ d'enfant** cot (Brit), crib (US)

litanie [litani] nf litany

lit-cage [likaʒ] (pl **lits-cages**) nm folding bed

litchi [litʃi] nm lychee

literie [litʀi] nf bedding; (linge) bedding, bedclothes pl

litho [lito], **lithographie** [litɔgʀafi] nf litho(graphy); (épreuve) litho(graph)

litière [litjɛʀ] nf litter

litige [litiʒ] nm dispute; **en ~** in contention

litigieux, -euse [litiʒjø, -øz] adj litigious, contentious

litote [litɔt] nf understatement

litre [litʀ(ə)] nm litre; (récipient) litre measure

littéraire [liteʀɛʀ] adj literary

littéral, e, -aux [liteʀal, -o] adj literal

littéralement [liteʀalmɑ̃] adv literally

littérature [liteʀatyʀ] nf literature

littoral, e, -aux [litɔʀal, -o] adj coastal ▷ nm coast

Lituanie [litɥani] nf: **la ~** Lithuania

lituanien, ne [litɥanjɛ̃, -ɛn] adj Lithuanian ▷ nm (Ling) Lithuanian ▷ nm/f: **Lituanien, ne** Lithuanian

liturgie [lityʀʒi] nf liturgy

liturgique [lityʀʒik] adj liturgical

livide [livid] adj livid, pallid

living [liviŋ], **living-room** [liviŋʀum] nm living room

livrable [livʀabl(ə)] adj (Comm) that can be delivered

livraison [livʀɛzɔ̃] nf delivery; **~ à domicile** home delivery (service)

livre [livʀ(ə)] nm book; (imprimerie etc): **le ~** the book industry ▷ nf (poids, monnaie) pound; **traduire qch à ~ ouvert** to translate sth off the cuff ou at sight; **~ blanc** official report (on war, natural disaster etc, prepared by independent body); **~ de bord** (Navig) logbook; **~ de comptes** account(s) book; **~ de cuisine** cookery book (Brit), cookbook; **~ de messe** mass ou prayer book; **~ d'or** visitors' book; **~ de poche** paperback (small and cheap); **~ sterling** pound sterling; **~ verte** green pound

livré, e [livʀe] nf livery ▷ adj: **~ à** (l'anarchie etc) given over to; **~ à soi-même** left to oneself ou one's own devices

livrer [livʀe] vt (Comm) to deliver; (otage, coupable) to hand over; (secret, information) to give away; **se ~ à** (se confier) to confide in; (se rendre) to give o.s. up to; (s'abandonner à: débauche etc) to give o.s. up ou over to; (faire: pratiques, actes) to indulge in; (travail) to be engaged in, engage in; (: sport) to practise; (: enquête) to carry out; **~ bataille** to give battle

livresque [livʀɛsk(ə)] adj (péj) bookish

livret [livʀɛ] nm booklet; (d'opéra) libretto; **~ de caisse d'épargne** (savings) bank-book; **~ de famille** (official) family record book; **~ scolaire** (school) report book

livreur, -euse [livʀœʀ, -øz] nm/f delivery boy ou man/girl ou woman

LO sigle f (= Lutte ouvrière) political party

lob [lɔb] nm lob

lobe [lɔb] nm: **~ de l'oreille** ear lobe

lobé, e [lɔbe] adj (Archit) foiled

lober [lɔbe] vt to lob

local, e, -aux [lɔkal, -o] adj local ▷ nm (salle) premises pl ▷ nmpl premises

localement [lɔkalmɑ̃] adv locally

localisé, e [lɔkalize] adj localized

localiser [lɔkalize] vt (repérer) to locate, place; (limiter) to localize, confine

localité [lɔkalite] nf locality

locataire [lɔkatɛʀ] nm/f tenant; (de chambre) lodger

locatif, -ive [lɔkatif, -iv] adj (charges, réparations) incumbent upon the tenant; (valeur) rental; (immeuble) with rented flats, used as a letting ou rental (US) concern

location [lɔkasjɔ̃] nf (par le locataire) renting; (par l'usager: de voiture etc) hiring (Brit), renting (US); (par le propriétaire) renting out, letting; hiring out (Brit); (de billets, places) booking; (bureau) booking office; **"~ de voitures"** "car hire (Brit) ou rental (US)"

location-vente [lɔkasjɔ̃vɑ̃t] nf form of hire purchase (Brit) ou installment plan (US)

lock-out [lɔkawt] nm inv lockout

locomoteur, -trice [lɔkɔmɔtœʀ, -tʀis] adj, nf locomotive

locomotion [lɔkɔmosjɔ̃] nf locomotion

locomotive [lɔkɔmɔtiv] *nf* locomotive, engine; (*fig*) pacesetter, pacemaker

locuteur, -trice [lɔkytœʀ, -tʀis] *nm/f* (*Ling*) speaker

locution [lɔkysjɔ̃] *nf* phrase

loden [lɔdɛn] *nm* loden

lofer [lɔfe] *vi* (*Navig*) to luff

logarithme [lɔgaʀitm(ə)] *nm* logarithm

loge [lɔʒ] *nf* (*Théât: d'artiste*) dressing room; (: *de spectateurs*) box; (*de concierge, franc-maçon*) lodge

logeable [lɔʒabl(ə)] *adj* habitable; (*spacieux*) roomy

logement [lɔʒmɑ̃] *nm* flat (*Brit*), apartment (*US*); accommodation *no pl* (*Brit*), accommodations *pl* (*US*); **le ~** housing; **chercher un ~** to look for a flat *ou* apartment, look for accommodation(s); **construire des ~s bon marché** to build cheap housing *sg*; **crise du ~** housing shortage; **~ de fonction** (*Admin*) company flat *ou* apartment, accommodation(s) provided with one's job

loger [lɔʒe] *vt* to accommodate ▷ *vi* to live; **se loger: trouver à se ~** to find accommodation; **se ~ dans** (*balle, flèche*) to lodge itself in

logeur, -euse [lɔʒœʀ, -øz] *nm/f* landlord (landlady)

loggia [lɔdʒja] *nf* loggia

logiciel [lɔʒisjɛl] *nm* (*Inform*) piece of software

logicien, ne [lɔʒisjɛ̃, -ɛn] *nm/f* logician

logique [lɔʒik] *adj* logical ▷ *nf* logic; **c'est ~** it stands to reason

logiquement [lɔʒikmɑ̃] *adv* logically

logis [lɔʒi] *nm* home; abode, dwelling

logisticien, ne [lɔʒistisjɛ̃, -ɛn] *nm/f* logistician

logistique [lɔʒistik] *nf* logistics *sg* ▷ *adj* logistic

logo [lɔgo], **logotype** [lɔgɔtip] *nm* logo

loi [lwa] *nf* law; **faire la ~** to lay down the law; **les ~s de la mode** (*fig*) the dictates of fashion; **proposition de ~** (private member's) bill; **projet de ~** (government) bill

loi-cadre [lwakadʀ(ə)] (*pl* **lois-cadres**) *nf* (*Pol*) blueprint law

loin [lwɛ̃] *adv* far; (*dans le temps: futur*) a long way off; (: *passé*) a long time ago; **plus ~** further; **moins ~ (que)** not as far (as); **~ de** far from; **~ d'ici** a long way from here; **pas ~ de 100 euros** not far off 100 euros; **au ~** far off; **de ~** *adv* from a distance; (*fig: de beaucoup*) by far; **il vient de ~** he's come a long way; he comes from a long way away; **de ~ en ~** here and there; (*de temps en temps*) (every) now and then; **~ de là** (*au contraire*) far from it

lointain, e [lwɛ̃tɛ̃, -ɛn] *adj* faraway, distant; (*dans le futur, passé*) distant, far-off; (*cause, parent*) remote, distant ▷ *nm*: **dans le ~** in the distance

loi-programme [lwapʀɔgʀam] (*pl* **lois-programmes**) *nf* (*Pol*) act providing framework for government programme

loir [lwaʀ] *nm* dormouse

Loire [lwaʀ] *nf*: **la ~** the Loire

loisible [lwazibl(ə)] *adj*: **il vous est ~ de ...** you are free to ...

loisir [lwaziʀ] *nm*: **heures de ~** spare time;

loisirs *nmpl* leisure *sg*; (*activités*) leisure activities; **avoir le ~ de faire** to have the time *ou* opportunity to do; **(tout) à ~** (*en prenant son temps*) at leisure; (*autant qu'on le désire*) at one's pleasure

lombaire [lɔ̃bɛʀ] *adj* lumbar

lombalgie [lɔ̃balʒi] *nf* back pain

londonien, ne [lɔ̃dɔnjɛ̃, -ɛn] *adj* London *cpd*, of London ▷ *nm/f*: **Londonien, ne** Londoner

Londres [lɔ̃dʀ(ə)] *n* London

long, longue [lɔ̃, lɔ̃g] *adj* long ▷ *adv*: **en savoir ~** to know a great deal ▷ *nm*: **de 3 m de ~** 3 m long, 3 m in length ▷ *nf*: **à la longue** in the end; **faire ~ feu** to fizzle out; **ne pas faire ~ feu** not to last long; **au ~ cours** (*Navig*) ocean *cpd*, ocean-going; **de longue date** *adj* long-standing; **longue durée** *adj* long-term; **de longue haleine** *adj* long-term; **être ~ à faire** to take a long time to do; **en ~** *adv* lengthwise, lengthways; **(tout) le ~ de** (all) along; **tout au ~ de** (*année, vie*) throughout; **de ~ en large** (*marcher*) to and fro, up and down; **en ~ et en large** (*fig*) in every detail

longanimité [lɔ̃ganimite] *nf* forbearance

long-courrier [lɔ̃kuʀje] *nm* (*Aviat*) long-haul aircraft

longe [lɔ̃ʒ] *nf* (*corde: pour attacher*) tether; (*pour mener*) lead; (*Culin*) loin

longer [lɔ̃ʒe] *vt* to go (*ou* walk *ou* drive) along(side); (*mur, route*) to border

longévité [lɔ̃ʒevite] *nf* longevity

longiligne [lɔ̃ʒiliɲ] *adj* long-limbed

longitude [lɔ̃ʒityd] *nf* longitude; **à 45° de ~ ouest** at 45° longitude west

longitudinal, e, -aux [lɔ̃ʒitydinal, -o] *adj* longitudinal, lengthways; (*entaille, vallée*) running lengthways

longtemps [lɔ̃tɑ̃] *adv* (for) a long time, (for) long; **ça ne va pas durer ~** it won't last long; **avant ~** before long; **pour/pendant ~** for a long time; **je n'en ai pas pour ~** I shan't be long; **mettre ~ à faire** to take a long time to do; **il en a pour ~** he'll be a long time; **il y a ~ que je travaille** I have been working (for) a long time; **il n'y a pas ~ que je l'ai rencontré** it's not long since I met him

longue [lɔ̃g] *adj f voir* **long**

longuement [lɔ̃gmɑ̃] *adv* (*longtemps: parler, regarder*) for a long time; (*en détail: expliquer, raconter*) at length

longueur [lɔ̃gœʀ] *nf* length; **longueurs** *nfpl* (*fig: d'un film etc*) tedious parts; **sur une ~ de 10 km** for *ou* over 10 km; **en ~** *adv* lengthwise, lengthways; **tirer en ~** to drag on; **à ~ de journée** all day long; **d'une ~** (*gagner*) by a length; **~ d'onde** wavelength

longue-vue [lɔ̃gvy] *nf* telescope

look [luk] (*fam*) *nm* look, image

looping [lupiŋ] *nm* (*Aviat*): **faire des ~s** to loop the loop

lopin [lɔpɛ̃] *nm*: **~ de terre** patch of land

loquace [lɔkas] *adj* talkative, loquacious

loque [lɔk] *nf* (*personne*) wreck; **loques** *nfpl*
(*habits*) rags; **être** *ou* **tomber en ~s** to be in rags
loquet [lɔkɛ] *nm* latch
lorgner [lɔʀɲe] *vt* to eye; (*convoiter*) to have one's
eye on
lorgnette [lɔʀɲɛt] *nf* opera glasses *pl*
lorgnon [lɔʀɲɔ̃] *nm* (*face-à-main*) lorgnette;
(*pince-nez*) pince-nez
loriot [lɔʀjo] *nm* (golden) oriole
lorrain, e [lɔʀɛ̃, -ɛn] *adj* of *ou* from Lorraine;
quiche ~e quiche
lors [lɔʀ]: **~ de** *prép* (*au moment de*) at the time of;
(*pendant*) during; **~ même que** even though
lorsque [lɔʀsk(ə)] *conj* when, as
losange [lɔzɑ̃ʒ] *nm* diamond; (*Géom*) lozenge;
en ~ diamond-shaped
lot [lo] *nm* (*part*) share; (*de loterie*) prize; (*fig:
destin*) fate, lot; (*Comm, Inform*) batch; **~ de
consolation** consolation prize
loterie [lɔtʀi] *nf* lottery; (*tombola*) raffle; **L~
nationale** French national lottery
loti, e [lɔti] *adj*: **bien/mal ~** well-/badly off,
lucky/unlucky
lotion [losjɔ̃] *nf* lotion; **~ après rasage** after-
shave (lotion); **~ capillaire** hair lotion
lotir [lɔtiʀ] *vt* (*terrain: diviser*) to divide into plots;
(: *vendre*) to sell by lots
lotissement [lɔtismɑ̃] *nm* (*groupe de maisons,
d'immeubles*) housing development; (*parcelle*)
(building) plot, lot
loto [lɔto] *nm* lotto
lotte [lɔt] *nf* (*Zool: de rivière*) burbot; (: *de mer*)
monkfish
louable [lwabl(ə)] *adj* (*appartement, garage*)
rentable; (*action, personne*) praiseworthy,
commendable
louage [lwaʒ] *nm*: **voiture de ~** hired (*Brit*) *ou*
rented (*US*) car; (*à louer*) hire (*Brit*) *ou* rental (*US*)
car
louange [lwɑ̃ʒ] *nf*: **à la ~ de** in praise of;
louanges *nfpl* praise *sg*
loubar, loubard [lubaʀ] *nm* (*fam*) lout
louche [luʃ] *adj* shady, dubious ▷ *nf* ladle
loucher [luʃe] *vi* to squint; (*fig*): **~ sur** to have
one's (beady) eye on
louer [lwe] *vt* (*maison: propriétaire*) to let, rent
(out); (: *locataire*) to rent; (*voiture etc*) to hire out
(*Brit*), rent (out); to hire (*Brit*), rent; (*réserver*) to
book; (*faire l'éloge de*) to praise; **"à ~"** "to let"
(*Brit*), "for rent" (*US*); **~ qn de** to praise sb for; **se
~ de** to congratulate o.s. on
loufoque [lufɔk] *adj* (*fam*) crazy, zany
loukoum [lukum] *nm* Turkish delight
loulou [lulu] *nm* (*chien*) spitz; **~ de Poméranie**
Pomeranian (dog)
loup [lu] *nm* wolf; (*poisson*) bass; (*masque*) (eye)
mask; **jeune ~** young go-getter; **~ de mer**
(*marin*) old seadog
loupe [lup] *nf* magnifying glass; **~ de noyer**
burr walnut; **à la ~** (*fig*) in minute detail
louper [lupe] *vt* (*fam: manquer*) to miss; (: *gâcher*)
to mess up, bungle

lourd, e [luʀ, luʀd(ə)] *adj* heavy; (*chaleur, temps*)
sultry; (*fig: personne, style*) heavy-handed ▷ *adv*:
peser ~ to be heavy; **~ de** (*menaces*) charged
with; (*conséquences*) fraught with; **artillerie/
industrie ~e** heavy artillery/industry
lourdaud, e [luʀdo, -od] *adj* oafish
lourdement [luʀdəmɑ̃] *adv* heavily; **se
tromper ~** to make a big mistake
lourdeur [luʀdœʀ] *nf* heaviness; **~ d'estomac**
indigestion *no pl*
loustic [lustik] *nm* (*fam péj*) joker
loutre [lutʀ(ə)] *nf* otter; (*fourrure*) otter skin
louve [luv] *nf* she-wolf
louveteau, x [luvto] *nm* (*Zool*) wolf-cub; (*scout*)
cub (scout)
louvoyer [luvwaje] *vi* (*Navig*) to tack; (*fig*) to
hedge, evade the issue
lover [lɔve]: **se lover** *vi* to coil up
loyal, e, -aux [lwajal, -o] *adj* (*fidèle*) loyal,
faithful; (*fair-play*) fair
loyalement [lwajalmɑ̃] *adv* loyally, faithfully;
fairly
loyalisme [lwajalism(ə)] *nm* loyalty
loyauté [lwajote] *nf* loyalty, faithfulness;
fairness
loyer [lwaje] *nm* rent; **~ de l'argent** interest
rate
LP *sigle m* (= *lycée professionnel*) *secondary school for
vocational training*
LPO *sigle f* (= *Ligue pour la protection des oiseaux*) *bird
protection society*
LSD *sigle m* (= *Lyserg Säure Diäthylamid*) LSD
lu, e [ly] *pp de* **lire**
lubie [lybi] *nf* whim, craze
lubricité [lybʀisite] *nf* lust
lubrifiant [lybʀifjɑ̃] *nm* lubricant
lubrifier [lybʀifje] *vt* to lubricate
lubrique [lybʀik] *adj* lecherous
lucarne [lykaʀn(ə)] *nf* skylight
lucide [lysid] *adj* (*conscient*) lucid, conscious;
(*perspicace*) clear-headed
lucidité [lysidite] *nf* lucidity
luciole [lysjɔl] *nf* firefly
lucratif, -ive [lykʀatif, -iv] *adj* lucrative;
profitable; **à but non ~** non profit-making
ludique [lydik] *adj* play *cpd*, playing
ludothèque [lydɔtɛk] *nf* toy library
luette [lɥɛt] *nf* uvula
lueur [lɥœʀ] *nf* (*chatoyante*) glimmer *no pl*;
(*métallique, mouillée*) gleam *no pl*; (*rougeoyante*)
glow *no pl*; (*pâle*) (faint) light; (*fig*) spark;
(: *d'espérance*) glimmer, gleam
luge [lyʒ] *nf* sledge (*Brit*), sled (*US*); **faire de la ~**
to sledge (*Brit*), sled (*US*), toboggan
lugubre [lygybʀ(ə)] *adj* gloomy; dismal

 MOT-CLÉ

lui [lɥi] *pp de* **luire**
▷ *pron* **1** (*objet indirect: mâle*) (to) him; (: *femelle*)
(to) her; (: *chose, animal*) (to) it; **je lui ai parlé** I
have spoken to him (*ou* to her); **il lui a offert**

un cadeau he gave him (*ou* her) a present; **je le lui ai donné** I gave it to him (*ou* her)

2 (*après préposition, comparatif: personne*) him; (*: chose, animal*) it; **elle est contente de lui** she is pleased with him; **je la connais mieux que lui** I know her better than he does; **cette voiture est à lui** this car belongs to him, this is HIS car

3 (*sujet, forme emphatique*) he; **lui, il est à Paris** HE is in Paris; **c'est lui qui l'a fait** HE did it

lui-même [lɥimɛm] *pron* (*personne*) himself; (*chose*) itself

luire [lɥir] *vi* (*gén*) to shine, gleam; (*surface mouillée*) to glisten; (*reflets chauds, cuivrés*) to glow

luisant, e [lɥizɑ̃, -ɑ̃t] *vb voir* **luire** ▷ *adj* shining, gleaming

lumbago [lɔ̃bago] *nm* lumbago

lumière [lymjɛr] *nf* light; **lumières** *nfpl* (*d'une personne*) knowledge *sg*, wisdom *sg*; **à la ~ de** by the light of; (*fig: événements*) in the light of; **fais de la ~** let's have some light, give us some light; **faire (toute) la ~ sur** (*fig*) to clarify (completely); **mettre en ~** (*fig*) to highlight; **~ du jour/soleil** day/sunlight

luminaire [lyminɛr] *nm* lamp, light

lumineux, -euse [lyminø, -øz] *adj* (*émettant de la lumière*) luminous; (*éclairé*) illuminated; (*ciel, journée, couleur*) bright; (*relatif à la lumière: rayon etc*) of light, light *cpd*; (*fig: regard*) radiant

luminosité [lyminɔzite] *nf* (*Tech*) luminosity

lump [lœp] *nm*: **œufs de ~** lump-fish roe

lunaire [lynɛr] *adj* lunar, moon *cpd*

lunatique [lynatik] *adj* whimsical, temperamental

lunch [lœntʃ] *nm* (*réception*) buffet lunch

lundi [lœdi] *nm* Monday; **on est ~** it's Monday; **le ~ 20 août** Monday 20th August; **il est venu ~** he came on Monday; **le(s) ~(s)** on Mondays; **à ~!** see you (on) Monday!; **~ de Pâques** Easter Monday; **~ de Pentecôte** Whit Monday (*Brit*)

lune [lyn] *nf* moon; **pleine/nouvelle ~** full/new moon; **être dans la ~** (*distrait*) to have one's head in the clouds; **~ de miel** honeymoon

luné, e [lyne] *adj*: **bien/mal ~** in a good/bad mood

lunette [lynɛt] *nf*: **~s** *nfpl* glasses, spectacles; (*protectrices*) goggles; **~ d'approche** telescope; **~ arrière** (*Auto*) rear window; **~s noires** dark glasses; **~s de soleil** sunglasses

lurent [lyr] *vb voir* **lire**

lurette [lyrɛt] *nf*: **il y a belle ~** ages ago

luron, ne [lyrɔ̃, -ɔn] *nm/f* lad/lass; **joyeux** *ou* **gai ~** gay dog

lus *etc* [ly] *vb voir* **lire**

lustre [lystr(ə)] *nm* (*de plafond*) chandelier; (*fig: éclat*) lustre

lustrer [lystre] *vt*: **~ qch** (*faire briller*) to make sth shine; (*user*) to make sth shiny

lut [ly] *vb voir* **lire**

luth [lyt] *nm* lute

luthier [lytje] *nm* (stringed-)instrument maker

lutin [lytɛ̃] *nm* imp, goblin

lutrin [lytrɛ̃] *nm* lectern

lutte [lyt] *nf* (*conflit*) struggle; (*Sport*): **la ~** wrestling; **de haute ~** after a hard-fought struggle; **~ des classes** class struggle; **~ libre** (*Sport*) all-in wrestling

lutter [lyte] *vi* to fight, struggle; (*Sport*) to wrestle

lutteur, -euse [lytœr, -øz] *nm/f* (*Sport*) wrestler; (*fig*) battler, fighter

luxation [lyksasjɔ̃] *nf* dislocation

luxe [lyks(ə)] *nm* luxury; **un ~ de** (*détails, précautions*) a wealth of; **de ~** *adj* luxury *cpd*

Luxembourg [lyksɑ̃bur] *nm*: **le ~** Luxembourg

luxembourgeois, e [lyksɑ̃burʒwa, -waz] *adj* of *ou* from Luxembourg ▷ *nm/f*: **Luxembourgeois, e** inhabitant *ou* native of Luxembourg

luxer [lykse] *vt*: **se ~ l'épaule** to dislocate one's shoulder

luxueusement [lyksɥøzmɑ̃] *adv* luxuriously

luxueux, -euse [lyksɥø, -øz] *adj* luxurious

luxure [lyksyr] *nf* lust

luxuriant, e [lyksyrjɑ̃, -ɑ̃t] *adj* luxuriant, lush

luzerne [lyzɛrn(ə)] *nf* lucerne, alfalfa

lycée [lise] *nm* (state) secondary (*Brit*) *ou* high (*US*) school; **~ technique** technical secondary *ou* high school; *see note*

lycéen, ne [liseɛ̃, -ɛn] *nm/f* secondary school pupil

Lycra® [likra] *nm* Lycra®

lymphatique [lɛ̃fatik] *adj* (*fig*) lethargic, sluggish

lymphe [lɛ̃f] *nf* lymph

lyncher [lɛ̃ʃe] *vt* to lynch

lynx [lɛ̃ks] *nm* lynx

Lyon [ljɔ̃] *n* Lyons

lyonnais, e [ljɔnɛ, -ɛz] *adj* of *ou* from Lyons; (*Culin*) Lyonnaise

lyophilisé, e [ljɔfilize] *adj* freeze-dried

lyre [lir] *nf* lyre

lyrique [lirik] *adj* lyrical; (*Opéra*) lyric; **artiste ~** opera singer; **comédie ~** comic opera; **théâtre ~** opera house (*for light opera*)

lyrisme [lirism(ə)] *nm* lyricism

lys [lis] *nm* lily

Mm

M, m [ɛm] *nm inv* M, m ▷ *abr* = **majeur;**
masculin; mètre; Monsieur; (= *million*) M; **M**
comme Marcel M for Mike
m' [m] *pron voir* **me**
MA *sigle m* = **maître auxiliaire**
ma [ma] *adj poss voir* **mon**
maboul, e [mabul] *adj* (*fam*) loony
macabre [makɑbʀ(ə)] *adj* macabre, gruesome
macadam [makadam] *nm* tarmac (*Brit*), asphalt
macaron [makaʀɔ̃] *nm* (*gâteau*) macaroon;
(*insigne*) (round) badge
macaroni [makaʀɔni] *nm*, **macaronis** *nmpl*
macaroni *sg*; **~(s) au gratin** macaroni cheese
(*Brit*), macaroni and cheese (*US*)
Macédoine [masedwan] *nf* Macedonia
macédoine [masedwan] *nf*: **~ de fruits** fruit
salad; **~ de légumes** mixed vegetables *pl*
macérer [maseʀe] *vi, vt* to macerate
mâchefer [mɑʃfɛʀ] *nm* clinker, cinders *pl*
mâcher [mɑʃe] *vt* to chew; **ne pas ~ ses mots**
not to mince one's words; **~ le travail à qn** (*fig*)
to spoon-feed sb, do half sb's work for him
machiavélique [makjavelik] *adj* Machiavellian
machin [maʃɛ̃] *nm* (*fam*) thingamajig, thing;
(*personne*): **M~** what's-his-name
machinal, e, -aux [maʃinal, -o] *adj* mechanical,
automatic
machinalement [maʃinalmmɑ̃] *adv*
mechanically, automatically
machination [maʃinasjɔ̃] *nf* scheming, frame-
up
machine [maʃin] *nf* machine; (*locomotive; de*
navire etc) engine; (*fig: rouages*) machinery; (*fam:*
personne): **M~** what's-her-name; **faire ~ arrière**
(*Navig*) to go astern; (*fig*) to back-pedal; **~ à**
laver/coudre/tricoter washing/sewing/
knitting machine; **~ à écrire** typewriter; **~ à**
sous fruit machine; **~ à vapeur** steam engine
machine-outil [maʃinuti] (*pl* **machines-outils**)
nf machine tool
machinerie [maʃinʀi] *nf* machinery, plant;
(*d'un navire*) engine room
machinisme [maʃinism(ə)] *nm* mechanization
machiniste [maʃinist(ə)] *nm* (*Théât*) scene
shifter; (*de bus, métro*) driver
macho [matʃo] (*fam*) *nm* male chauvinist

mâchoire [mɑʃwaʀ] *nf* jaw; **~ de frein** brake
shoe
mâchonner [mɑʃone] *vt* to chew (at)
maçon [masɔ̃] *nm* bricklayer; (*constructeur*)
builder
mâcon [mɑkɔ̃] *nm* Mâcon wine
maçonner [masɔne] *vt* (*revêtir*) to face, render
(with cement); (*boucher*) to brick up
maçonnerie [masɔnʀi] *nf* (*murs: de brique*)
brickwork; (: *de pierre*) masonry, stonework;
(*activité*) bricklaying; building; **~ de béton**
concrete
maçonnique [masɔnik] *adj* masonic
macramé [makʀame] *nm* macramé
macrobiotique [makʀɔbjɔtik] *adj* macrobiotic
macrocosme [makʀɔkɔsm(ə)] *nm* macrocosm
macro-économie [makʀɔekɔnɔmi] *nf*
macroeconomics *sg*
maculer [makyle] *vt* to stain; (*Typo*) to mackle
Madagascar [madagaskaʀ] *nf* Madagascar
Madame [madam] (*pl* **Mesdames** [medam]) *nf*:
~ X Mrs X; **occupez-vous de ~/Monsieur/**
Mademoiselle please serve this lady/
gentleman/(young) lady; **bonjour ~/**
Monsieur/Mademoiselle good morning; (*ton*
déférent) good morning Madam/Sir/Madam; (*le*
nom est connu) good morning Mrs X/Mr X/Miss X;
~/Monsieur/Mademoiselle! (*pour appeler*)
excuse me!; (*ton déférent*) Madam/Sir/Miss!; **~/**
Monsieur/Mademoiselle (*sur lettre*) Dear
Madam/Sir/Madam; **chère ~/cher Monsieur/**
chère Mademoiselle Dear Mrs X/Mr X/Miss X;
~ la Directrice the director; the manageress;
the head teacher; **Mesdames** Ladies
Madeleine [madlɛn]: **îles de la ~** *nfpl* Magdalen
Islands
madeleine [madlɛn] *nf* madeleine, ≈ sponge
finger cake
Mademoiselle [madmwazɛl] (*pl*
Mesdemoiselles [medmwazɛl]) *nf* Miss; *voir*
aussi **Madame**
Madère [madɛʀ] *nf* Madeira ▷ *nm*: **madère**
Madeira (wine)
madone [madɔn] *nf* Madonna
madré, e [madʀe] *adj* crafty, wily
Madrid [madʀid] *n* Madrid

madrier [madʀije] *nm* beam
madrigal, -aux [madʀigal, -o] *nm* madrigal
madrilène [madʀilɛn] *adj* of *ou* from Madrid
maestria [maɛstʀija] *nf* (masterly) skill
maestro [maɛstʀo] *nm* maestro
mafia, maffia [mafja] *nf* Maf(f)ia
magasin [magazɛ̃] *nm* (*boutique*) shop; (*entrepôt*)
warehouse; (*d'arme, appareil-photo*) magazine; **en**
~ (*Comm*) in stock; **faire les ~s** to go (a)round
the shops, do the shops; ~ **d'alimentation**
grocer's (shop) (*Brit*), grocery store (*US*)
magasinier [magazinje] *nm* warehouseman
magazine [magazin] *nm* magazine
mage [maʒ] *nm*: **les Rois M~s** the Magi, the
(Three) Wise Men
Maghreb [magʀɛb] *nm*: **le ~** the Maghreb,
North(-West) Africa
maghrébin, e [magʀebɛ̃, -in] *adj* of *ou* from the
Maghreb ▷ *nm/f*: **Maghrébin, e** North African,
Maghrebi
magicien, ne [maʒisjɛ̃, -ɛn] *nm/f* magician
magie [maʒi] *nf* magic; ~ **noire** black magic
magique [maʒik] *adj* (*occulte*) magic; (*fig*)
magical
magistral, e, -aux [maʒistʀal, -o] *adj* (*œuvre,*
adresse) masterly; (*ton*) authoritative; (*gifle etc*)
sound, resounding; (*ex cathedra*):
enseignement ~ lecturing, lectures *pl*; **cours ~**
lecture
magistrat [maʒistʀa] *nm* magistrate
magistrature [maʒistʀatyʀ] *nf* magistracy,
magistrature; ~ **assise** judges *pl*, bench; ~
debout state prosecutors *pl*
magma [magma] *nm* (*Géo*) magma; (*fig*) jumble
magnanime [maɲanim] *adj* magnanimous
magnanimité [maɲanimite] *nf* magnanimity
magnat [magna] *nm* tycoon, magnate
magner [maɲe]: **se magner** *vi* (*fam*) to get a
move on
magnésie [maɲezi] *nf* magnesia
magnésium [maɲezjɔm] *nm* magnesium
magnétique [maɲetik] *adj* magnetic
magnétiser [maɲetize] *vt* to magnetize; (*fig*) to
mesmerize, hypnotize
magnétiseur, -euse [maɲetizœʀ, -øz] *nm/f*
hypnotist
magnétisme [maɲetism(ə)] *nm* magnetism
magnéto [maɲeto] *nm* (*à cassette*) cassette deck;
(*magnétophone*) tape recorder
magnétophone [maɲetɔfɔn] *nm* tape recorder;
~ **à cassettes** cassette recorder
magnétoscope [maɲetɔskɔp] *nm*: ~ **(à**
cassette) video (recorder)
magnificence [maɲifisɑ̃s] *nf* (*faste*)
magnificence, splendour (*Brit*), splendor (*US*);
(*générosité*) munificence, lavishness
magnifier [maɲifje] *vt* (*glorifier*) to glorify;
(*idéaliser*) to idealize
magnifique [maɲifik] *adj* magnificent
magnifiquement [maɲifikmɑ̃] *adv*
magnificently
magnolia [maɲɔlja] *nm* magnolia

magnum [magnɔm] *nm* magnum
magot [mago] *nm* (*argent*) pile (of money);
(*économies*) nest egg
magouille [maguj] *nf* (*fam*) scheming
magret [magʀɛ] *nm*: ~ **de canard** duck breast
mahométan, e [maɔmetɑ̃, -an] *adj*
Mohammedan, Mahometan
mai [mɛ] *nm* May; *see note*; *voir aussi* **juillet**

● LE PREMIER MAI

Le premier mai is a public holiday in France
and commemorates the trades union
demonstrations in the United States in 1886
when workers demanded the right to an
eight-hour working day. Sprigs of lily of the
valley are traditionally exchanged. *Le 8 mai* is
also a public holiday and commemorates
the surrender of the German army to
Eisenhower on 7 May, 1945. It is marked by
parades of ex-servicemen and ex-
servicewomen in most towns. The social
upheavals of May and June 1968, with their
student demonstrations, workers' strikes
and general rioting, are usually referred to
as "les événements de mai 68". De Gaulle's
Government survived, but reforms in
education and a move towards
decentralization ensued.

maigre [mɛgʀ(ə)] *adj* (very) thin, skinny;
(*viande*) lean; (*fromage*) low-fat; (*végétation*) thin,
sparse; (*fig*) poor, meagre, skimpy ▷ *adv*: **faire ~**
not to eat meat; **jours ~s** days of abstinence,
fish days
maigrelet, te [mɛgʀəlɛ, -ɛt] *adj* skinny, scrawny
maigreur [mɛgʀœʀ] *nf* thinness
maigrichon, ne [megʀiʃɔ̃, -ɔn] *adj* = **maigrelet,**
te
maigrir [megʀiʀ] *vi* to get thinner, lose weight
▷ *vt*: ~ **qn** (*vêtement*) to make sb look slim(mer)
mail [mɛl] *nm* email
mailing [mɛliŋ] *nm* direct mail *no pl*; **un ~** a
mailshot
maille [mɑj] *nf* (*boucle*) stitch; (*ouverture*) hole (in
the mesh); **avoir ~ à partir avec qn** to have a
brush with sb; ~ **à l'endroit/à l'envers** knit
one/purl one; (*boucle*) plain/purl stitch
maillechort [majʃɔʀ] *nm* nickel silver
maillet [majɛ] *nm* mallet
maillon [majɔ̃] *nm* link
maillot [majo] *nm* (*aussi*: **maillot de corps**) vest;
(*de danseur*) leotard; (*de sportif*) jersey; ~ **de bain**
bathing costume (*Brit*), swimsuit; (*d'homme*)
bathing trunks *pl*; ~ **deux pièces** two-piece
swimsuit, bikini; ~ **jaune** yellow jersey
main [mɛ̃] *nf* hand; **la ~ dans la ~** hand in hand;
à deux ~s with both hands; **à une ~** with one
hand; **à la ~** (*tenir, avoir*) in one's hand; (*faire,*
tricoter etc) by hand; **se donner la ~** to hold
hands; **donner** *ou* **tendre la ~ à qn** to hold out
one's hand to sb; **se serrer la ~** to shake hands;

serrer la ~ à qn to shake hands with sb; **sous la ~** to *ou* at hand; **haut les ~s!** hands up!; **à ~ levée** (*Art*) freehand; **à ~s levées** (*voter*) with a show of hands; **attaque à ~ armée** armed attack; **à ~ droite/gauche** to the right/left; **à remettre en ~s propres** to be delivered personally; **de première ~** (*renseignement*) first-hand; (*Comm: voiture etc*) with only one previous owner; **faire ~ basse sur** to help o.s. to; **mettre la dernière ~ à** to put the finishing touches to; **mettre la ~ à la pâte** (*fig*) to lend a hand; **avoir/passer la ~** (*Cartes*) to lead/hand over the lead; **s'en laver les ~s** (*fig*) to wash one's hands of it; **se faire/perdre la ~** to get one's hand in/lose one's touch; **avoir qch bien en ~** to have got the hang of sth; **en un tour de ~** (*fig*) in the twinkling of an eye; **~ courante** handrail

mainate [mɛnat] *nm* myna(h) bird

main-d'œuvre [mɛ̃dœvʀ(ə)] *nf* manpower, labour (*Brit*), labor (*US*)

main-forte [mɛ̃fɔʀt(ə)] *nf*: **prêter ~ à qn** to come to sb's assistance

mainmise [mɛ̃miz] *nf* seizure; (*fig*): **avoir la ~ sur** to have a grip *ou* stranglehold on

mains-libres [mɛ̃libʀ] *adj inv* (*téléphone, kit*) hands-free

maint, e [mɛ̃, mɛ̃t] *adj* many a; **~s** many; **à ~es reprises** time and (time) again

maintenance [mɛ̃tnɑ̃s] *nf* maintenance, servicing

maintenant [mɛ̃tnɑ̃] *adv* now; (*actuellement*) nowadays

maintenir [mɛ̃tniʀ] *vt* (*retenir, soutenir*) to support; (*contenir: foule etc*) to keep in check, hold back; (*conserver*) to maintain, uphold; (*affirmer*) to maintain; **se maintenir** *vi* (*paix, temps*) to hold; (*préjugé*) to persist; (*malade*) to remain stable

maintien [mɛ̃tjɛ̃] *nm* maintaining, upholding; (*attitude*) bearing; **~ de l'ordre** maintenance of law and order

maintiendrai [mɛ̃tjɛ̃dʀe], **maintiens** *etc* [mɛ̃tjɛ̃] *vb voir* **maintenir**

maire [mɛʀ] *nm* mayor

mairie [meʀi] *nf* (*endroit*) town hall; (*administration*) town council

mais [mɛ] *conj* but; **~ non!** of course not!; **~ enfin** but after all; (*indignation*) look here!; **~ encore?** is that all?

maïs [mais] *nm* maize (*Brit*), corn (*US*)

maison [mɛzɔ̃] *nf* (*bâtiment*) house; (*chez-soi*) home; (*Comm*) firm; (*famille*): **ami de la ~** friend of the family ▷ *adj inv* (*Culin*) home-made; (: *au restaurant*) made by the chef; (*Comm*) in-house, own; (*fam*) first-rate; **à la ~** at home; (*direction*) home; **~ d'arrêt** (short-stay) prison; **~ centrale** prison; **~ close** brothel; **~ de correction** ≈ remand home (*Brit*), ≈ reformatory (*US*); **~ de la culture** ≈ arts centre; **~ des jeunes** ≈ youth club; **~ mère** parent company; **~ de passe**; = **maison close**; **~ de repos** convalescent home; **~ de retraite** old people's home; **~ de santé** mental home

Maison-Blanche [mɛzɔ̃blɑ̃ʃ] *nf*: **la ~** the White House

maisonnée [mɛzɔne] *nf* household, family

maisonnette [mɛzɔnɛt] *nf* small house

maître, -esse [mɛtʀ(ə), mɛtʀɛs] *nm/f* master (mistress); (*Scol*) teacher, schoolmaster(-mistress) ▷ *nm* (*peintre etc*) master; (*titre*): **M~** (**Mᵉ**) Maître, *term of address for lawyers etc* ▷ *nf* (*amante*) mistress ▷ *adj* (*principal, essentiel*) main; **maison de ~** family seat; **être ~ de** (*soi-même, situation*) to be in control of; **se rendre ~ de** (*pays, ville*) to gain control of; (*situation, incendie*) to bring under control; **être passé ~ dans l'art de** to be a (past) master in the art of; **une maîtresse femme** a forceful woman; **~ d'armes** fencing master; **~ auxiliaire (MA)** (*Scol*) temporary teacher; **~ chanteur** blackmailer; **~ de chapelle** choirmaster; **~ de conférences** ≈ senior lecturer (*Brit*), ≈ assistant professor (*US*); **~/ maîtresse d'école** teacher, schoolmaster/-mistress; **~ d'hôtel** (*domestique*) butler; (*d'hôtel*) head waiter; **~ de maison** host; **~ nageur** lifeguard; **~ d'œuvre** (*Constr*) project manager; **~ d'ouvrage** (*Constr*) client; **~ queux** chef; **maîtresse de maison** hostess; (*ménagère*) housewife

maître-assistant, e [mɛtʀasistɑ̃, -ɑ̃t] (*pl* **maîtres-assistants, es**) *nm/f* ≈ lecturer

maîtrise [metʀiz] *nf* (*aussi*: **maîtrise de soi**) self-control; (*habileté*) skill, mastery; (*suprématie*) mastery, command; (*diplôme*) ≈ master's degree; *see note*; (*chefs d'équipe*) supervisory staff

● MAÎTRISE

The *maîtrise* is a French degree which is awarded to university students if they successfully complete two more years' study after the "DEUG". Students wishing to go on to do research or to take the "agrégation" must hold a *maîtrise*.

maîtriser [metʀize] *vt* (*cheval, incendie*) to (bring under) control; (*sujet*) to master; (*émotion*) to control; **se maîtriser** to control o.s.

majesté [maʒɛste] *nf* majesty

majestueux, -euse [maʒɛstɥø, -øz] *adj* majestic

majeur, e [maʒœʀ] *adj* (*important*) major; (*Jur*) of age; (*fig*) adult ▷ *nm/f* (*Jur*) person who has come of age *ou* attained his (*ou* her) majority ▷ *nm* (*doigt*) middle finger; **en ~e partie** for the most part; **la ~e partie de** the major part of

major [maʒɔʀ] *nm* adjutant; (*Scol*): **~ de la promotion** first in one's year

majoration [maʒɔʀasjɔ̃] *nf* increase

majordome [maʒɔʀdɔm] *nm* major-domo

majorer [maʒɔʀe] *vt* to increase

majorette [maʒɔʀɛt] *nf* majorette

majoritaire [maʒɔʀitɛʀ] *adj* majority *cpd*;

système/scrutin ~ majority system/ballot

majorité [maʒɔrite] *nf* (*gén*) majority; (*parti*) party in power; **en ~** (*composé etc*) mainly

Majorque [maʒɔrk(ə)] *nf* Majorca

majuscule [maʒyskyl] *adj*, *nf*: (**lettre**) **~** capital (letter)

mal, maux [mal, mo] *nm* (*opposé au bien*) evil; (*tort, dommage*) harm; (*douleur physique*) pain, ache; (*maladie*) illness, sickness *no pl*; (*difficulté, peine*) trouble; (*souffrance morale*) pain ▷ *adv* badly ▷ *adj*: **c'est ~ (de faire)** it's bad *ou* wrong (to do); **être ~** to be uncomfortable; **être ~ avec qn** to be on bad terms with sb; **être au plus ~** (*malade*) to be very bad; (*brouillé*) to be at daggers drawn; **il comprend ~** he has difficulty in understanding; **il a ~ compris** he misunderstood; **~ tourner** to go wrong; **dire/penser du ~ de** to speak/think ill of; **ne vouloir de ~ à personne** to wish nobody any ill; **il n'a rien fait de ~** he has done nothing wrong; **avoir du ~ à faire qch** to have trouble doing sth; **se donner du ~ pour faire qch** to go to a lot of trouble to do sth; **ne voir aucun ~ à** to see no harm in, see nothing wrong in; **craignant ~ faire** fearing he *etc* was doing the wrong thing; **sans penser** *ou* **songer à ~** without meaning any harm; **faire du ~ à qn** to hurt sb; to harm sb; **se faire ~** to hurt o.s.; **se faire ~ au pied** to hurt one's foot; **ça fait ~** it hurts; **j'ai ~ (ici)** it hurts (here); **j'ai ~ au dos** my back aches, I've got a pain in my back; **avoir ~ à la tête/à la gorge** to have a headache/a sore throat; **avoir ~ aux dents/à l'oreille** to have toothache/earache; **avoir le ~ de l'air** to be airsick; **avoir le ~ du pays** to be homesick; **~ de mer** seasickness; **~ de la route** carsickness; **~ en point** *adj inv* in a bad state; **maux de ventre** stomach ache *sg*; *voir aussi* **cœur**

malabar [malabar] *nm* (*fam*) muscle man

malade [malad] *adj* ill, sick; (*poitrine, jambe*) bad; (*plante*) diseased; (*fig: entreprise, monde*) ailing ▷ *nm/f* invalid, sick person; (*à l'hôpital etc*) patient; **tomber ~** to fall ill; **être ~ du cœur** to have heart trouble *ou* a bad heart; **grand ~** seriously ill person; **~ mental** mentally sick *ou* ill person

maladie [maladi] *nf* (*spécifique*) disease, illness; (*mauvaise santé*) illness, sickness; (*fig: manie*) mania; **être rongé par la ~** to be wasting away (through illness); **~ d'Alzheimer** Alzheimer's disease; **~ de peau** skin disease

maladif, -ive [maladif, -iv] *adj* sickly; (*curiosité, besoin*) pathological

maladresse [maladrɛs] *nf* clumsiness *no pl*; (*gaffe*) blunder

maladroit, e [maladrwa, -wat] *adj* clumsy

maladroitement [maladrwatmã] *adv* clumsily

mal-aimé, e [maleme] *nm/f* unpopular person; (*de la scène politique, de la société*) persona non grata

malais, e [malɛ, -ɛz] *adj* Malay, Malayan ▷ *nm* (*Ling*) Malay ▷ *nm/f*: **Malais, e** Malay, Malayan

malaise [malɛz] *nm* (*Méd*) feeling of faintness; feeling of discomfort; (*fig*) uneasiness, malaise; **avoir un ~** to feel faint *ou* dizzy

malaisé, e [maleze] *adj* difficult

Malaisie [malɛzi] *nf*: **la ~** Malaya, West Malaysia; **la péninsule de ~** the Malay Peninsula

malappris, e [malapri, -iz] *nm/f* ill-mannered *ou* boorish person

malaria [malarja] *nf* malaria

malavisé, e [malavize] *adj* ill-advised, unwise

Malawi [malawi] *nm*: **le ~** Malawi

malaxer [malakse] *vt* (*pétrir*) to knead; (*mêler*) to mix

Malaysia [malɛzja] *nf*: **la ~** Malaysia

malbouffe [malbuf] *nf* (*fam*): **la ~** junk food

malchance [malʃãs] *nf* misfortune, ill luck *no pl*; **par ~** unfortunately; **quelle ~!** what bad luck!

malchanceux, -euse [malʃãsø, -øz] *adj* unlucky

malcommode [malkɔmɔd] *adj* impractical, inconvenient

Maldives [maldiv] *nfpl*: **les ~** the Maldive Islands

maldonne [maldɔn] *nf* (*Cartes*) misdeal; **il y a ~** (*fig*) there's been a misunderstanding

mâle [mɑl] *adj* (*Élec, Tech*) male; (*viril: voix, traits*) manly ▷ *nm* male

malédiction [malediksjɔ̃] *nf* curse

maléfice [malefis] *nm* evil spell

maléfique [malefik] *adj* evil, baleful

malencontreusement [malãkɔ̃trøzmã] *adv* (*arriver*) at the wrong moment; (*rappeler, mentionner*) inopportunely

malencontreux, -euse [malãkɔ̃trø, -øz] *adj* unfortunate, untoward

malentendant, e [malãtãdã, -ãt] *nm/f*: **les ~s** the hard of hearing

malentendu [malãtãdy] *nm* misunderstanding

malfaçon [malfasɔ̃] *nf* fault

malfaisant, e [malfəzã, -ãt] *adj* evil, harmful

malfaiteur [malfɛtœr] *nm* lawbreaker, criminal; (*voleur*) thief

malfamé, e [malfame] *adj* disreputable, of ill repute

malfrat [malfra] *nm* villain, crook

malgache [malgaʃ] *adj* Malagasy, Madagascan ▷ *nm* (*Ling*) Malagasy ▷ *nm/f*: **Malgache** Malagasy, Madagascan

malgré [malgre] *prép* in spite of, despite; **~ tout** *adv* in spite of everything

malhabile [malabil] *adj* clumsy

malheur [malœr] *nm* (*situation*) adversity, misfortune; (*événement*) misfortune; (*: plus fort*) disaster, tragedy; **par ~** unfortunately; **quel ~!** what a shame *ou* pity!; **faire un ~** (*fam: un éclat*) to do something desperate; (*: avoir du succès*) to be a smash hit

malheureusement [malœrøzmã] *adv* unfortunately

malheureux, -euse [malœrø, -øz] *adj* (*triste*) unhappy, miserable; (*infortuné, regrettable*) unfortunate; (*malchanceux*) unlucky; (*insignifiant*) wretched ▷ *nm/f* (*infortuné, misérable*) poor soul; (*indigent, miséreux*) unfortunate

creature; **les ~** the destitute; **avoir la main
malheureuse** (au jeu) to be unlucky; (tout casser)
to be ham-fisted

malhonnête [malɔnɛt] adj dishonest

malhonnêtement [malɔnɛtmɑ̃] adv
dishonestly

malhonnêteté [malɔnɛtte] nf dishonesty;
rudeness no pl

Mali [mali] nm: **le ~** Mali

malice [malis] nf mischievousness;
(méchanceté): **par ~** out of malice ou spite; **sans ~**
guileless

malicieusement [malisjøzmɑ̃] adv
mischievously

malicieux, -euse [malisjø, -øz] adj mischievous

malien, ne [maljɛ̃, -ɛn] adj Malian

malignité [maliɲite] nf (d'une tumeur, d'un mal)
malignancy

malin, -igne [malɛ̃, -iɲ] adj (futé: f gén: **maline**)
smart, shrewd; (: sourire) knowing; (Méd,
influence) malignant; **faire le ~** to show off;
éprouver un ~ plaisir à to take malicious
pleasure in

malingre [malɛ̃gʀ(ə)] adj puny

malintentionné, e [malɛ̃tɑ̃sjɔne] adj ill-
intentioned, malicious

malle [mal] nf trunk; (Auto): **~ (arrière)** boot
(Brit), trunk (US)

malléable [maleabl(ə)] adj malleable

malle-poste [malpɔst(ə)] (pl **malles-poste**) nf
mail coach

mallette [malɛt] nf (valise) (small) suitcase;
(aussi: **mallette de voyage**) overnight case; (pour
documents) attaché case

malmener [malməne] vt to manhandle; (fig) to
give a rough ride to

malnutrition [malnytʀisjɔ̃] nf malnutrition

malodorant, e [malɔdɔʀɑ̃, -ɑ̃t] adj foul-
smelling

malotru [malɔtʀy] nm lout, boor

Malouines [malwin] nfpl: **les ~** the Falklands,
the Falkland Islands

malpoli, e [malpɔli] nm/f rude individual

malpropre [malpʀɔpʀ(ə)] adj (personne, vêtement)
dirty; (travail) slovenly; (histoire, plaisanterie)
unsavoury (Brit), unsavory (US), smutty;
(malhonnête) dishonest

malpropreté [malpʀɔpʀəte] nf dirtiness

malsain, e [malsɛ̃, -ɛn] adj unhealthy

malséant, e [malseɑ̃, -ɑ̃t] adj unseemly,
unbecoming

malsonnant, e [malsɔnɑ̃, -ɑ̃t] adj offensive

malt [malt] nm malt; **pur ~** (whisky) malt
(whisky)

maltais, e [maltɛ, -ɛz] adj Maltese

Malte [malt(ə)] nf Malta

malté, e [malte] adj (lait etc) malted

maltraiter [maltʀete] vt (brutaliser) to
manhandle, ill-treat; (critiquer, éreinter) to slate
(Brit), roast

malus [malys] nm (Assurances) car insurance
weighting, penalty

malveillance [malvɛjɑ̃s] nf (animosité) ill will;
(intention de nuire) malevolence; (Jur) malicious
intent no pl

malveillant, e [malvɛjɑ̃, -ɑ̃t] adj malevolent,
malicious

malvenu, e [malvəny] adj: **être ~ de** ou **à faire
qch** not to be in a position to do sth

malversation [malvɛʀsasjɔ̃] nf embezzlement,
misappropriation (of funds)

mal-vivre [malvivʀ] nm inv malaise

maman [mamɑ̃] nf mum(my) (Brit), mom (US)

mamelle [mamɛl] nf teat

mamelon [mamlɔ̃] nm (Anat) nipple; (colline)
knoll, hillock

mamie [mami] nf (fam) granny

mammifère [mamifɛʀ] nm mammal

mammouth [mamut] nm mammoth

manager [manadʒɛʀ] nm (Sport) manager;
(Comm): **~ commercial** commercial director

manche [mɑ̃ʃ] nf (de vêtement) sleeve; (d'un jeu,
tournoi) round; (Géo): **la M~** the (English)
Channel ▷ nm (d'outil, casserole) handle; (de pelle,
pioche etc) shaft; (de violon, guitare) neck; (fam)
clumsy oaf; **faire la ~** to pass the hat; **~ à air** nf
(Aviat) wind-sock; **~ à balai** nm broomstick;
(Aviat, Inform) joystick

manchette [mɑ̃ʃɛt] nf (de chemise) cuff; (coup)
forearm blow; (titre) headline

manchon [mɑ̃ʃɔ̃] nm (de fourrure) muff; **~ à
incandescence** incandescent (gas) mantle

manchot [mɑ̃ʃo] nm one-armed man; armless
man; (Zool) penguin

mandarine [mɑ̃daʀin] nf mandarin (orange),
tangerine

mandat [mɑ̃da] nm (postal) postal ou money
order; (d'un député etc) mandate; (procuration)
power of attorney, proxy; (Police) warrant; **~
d'amener** summons sg; **~ d'arrêt** warrant for
arrest; **~ de dépôt** committal order; **~ de
perquisition** (Police) search warrant

mandataire [mɑ̃datɛʀ] nm/f (représentant,
délégué) representative; (Jur) proxy

mandat-carte [mɑ̃dakaʀt(ə)] (pl **mandats-
cartes**) nm money order (in postcard form)

mandater [mɑ̃date] vt (personne) to appoint;
(Pol: député) to elect

mandat-lettre [mɑ̃dalɛtʀ(ə)] (pl **mandats-
lettres**) nm money order (with space for
correspondence)

mandchou, e [mɑ̃tʃu] adj Manchu,
Manchurian ▷ nm (Ling) Manchu ▷ nm/f:
Mandchou, e Manchu

Mandchourie [mɑ̃tʃuʀi] nf: **la ~** Manchuria

mander [mɑ̃de] vt to summon

mandibule [mɑ̃dibyl] nf mandible

mandoline [mɑ̃dɔlin] nf mandolin(e)

manège [manɛʒ] nm riding school; (à la foire)
roundabout (Brit), merry-go-round; (fig) game,
ploy; **faire un tour de ~** to go for a ride on a ou
the roundabout etc; **~ (de chevaux de bois)**
roundabout (Brit), merry-go-round

manette [manɛt] nf lever, tap; **~ de jeu** (Inform)

joystick

manganèse [mɑ̃ganɛz] *nm* manganese

mangeable [mɑ̃ʒabl(ə)] *adj* edible, eatable

mangeaille [mɑ̃ʒaj] *nf* (*péj*) grub

mangeoire [mɑ̃ʒwaʀ] *nf* trough, manger

manger [mɑ̃ʒe] *vt* to eat; (*ronger: rouille etc*) to eat into *ou* away; (*utiliser, consommer*) to eat up ▷ *vi* to eat

mange-tout [mɑ̃ʒtu] *nm inv* mange-tout

mangeur, -euse [mɑ̃ʒœʀ, -øz] *nm/f* eater

mangouste [mɑ̃gust(ə)] *nf* mongoose

mangue [mɑ̃g] *nf* mango

maniabilité [manjabilite] *nf* (*d'un outil*) handiness; (*d'un véhicule, voilier*) manoeuvrability

maniable [manjabl(ə)] *adj* (*outil*) handy; (*voiture, voilier*) easy to handle; manoeuvrable (*Brit*), maneuverable (*US*); (*fig: personne*) easily influenced, manipulable

maniaque [manjak] *adj* (*pointilleux, méticuleux*) finicky, fussy; (*atteint de manie*) suffering from a mania ▷ *nm/f* maniac

manie [mani] *nf* mania; (*tic*) odd habit

maniement [manimɑ̃] *nm* handling; **~ d'armes** arms drill

manier [manje] *vt* to handle; **se manier** *vi* (*fam*) to get a move on

maniéré, e [manjeʀe] *adj* affected

manière [manjɛʀ] *nf* (*façon*) way, manner; (*genre, style*) style; **manières** *nfpl* (*attitude*) manners; (*chichis*) fuss *sg*; **de ~ à** so as to; **de telle ~ que** in such a way that; **de cette ~** in this way *ou* manner; **d'une ~ générale** generally speaking, as a general rule; **de toute ~** in any case; **d'une certaine ~** in a (certain) way; **faire des ~s** to put on airs; **employer la ~ forte** to use strong-arm tactics

manif [manif] *nf* (*manifestation*) demo

manifestant, e [manifɛstɑ̃, -ɑ̃t] *nm/f* demonstrator

manifestation [manifɛstasjɔ̃] *nf* (*de joie, mécontentement*) expression, demonstration; (*symptôme*) outward sign; (*fête etc*) event; (*Pol*) demonstration

manifeste [manifɛst(ə)] *adj* obvious, evident ▷ *nm* manifesto

manifestement [manifɛstəmɑ̃] *adv* obviously

manifester [manifɛste] *vt* (*volonté, intentions*) to show, indicate; (*joie, peur*) to express, show ▷ *vi* (*Pol*) to demonstrate; **se manifester** *vi* (*émotion*) to show *ou* express itself; (*difficultés*) to arise; (*symptômes*) to appear; (*témoin etc*) to come forward

manigance [manigɑ̃s] *nf* scheme

manigancer [manigɑ̃se] *vt* to plot, devise

Manille [manij] *n* Manila

manioc [manjɔk] *nm* cassava, manioc

manipulateur, -trice [manipylatœʀ, -tʀis] *nm/f* (*technicien*) technician, operator; (*prestidigitateur*) conjurer; (*péj*) manipulator

manipulation [manipylasjɔ̃] *nf* handling; manipulation

manipuler [manipyle] *vt* to handle; (*fig*) to manipulate

manivelle [manivɛl] *nf* crank

manne [man] *nf* (*Rel*) manna; (*fig*) godsend

mannequin [mankɛ̃] *nm* (*Couture*) dummy; (*Mode*) model

manœuvrable [manœvʀabl(ə)] *adj* (*bateau, véhicule*) manoeuvrable (*Brit*), maneuverable (*US*)

manœuvre [manœvʀ(ə)] *nf* (*gén*) manoeuvre (*Brit*), maneuver (*US*) ▷ *nm* (*ouvrier*) labourer (*Brit*), laborer (*US*)

manœuvrer [manœvʀe] *vt* to manoeuvre (*Brit*), maneuver (*US*); (*levier, machine*) to operate; (*personne*) to manipulate ▷ *vi* to manoeuvre *ou* maneuver

manoir [manwaʀ] *nm* manor *ou* country house

manomètre [manɔmɛtʀ(ə)] *nm* gauge, manometer

manquant, e [mɑ̃kɑ̃, -ɑ̃t] *adj* missing

manque [mɑ̃k] *nm* (*insuffisance*): **~ de** lack of; (*vide*) emptiness, gap; (*Méd*) withdrawal; **manques** *nmpl* (*lacunes*) faults, defects; **par ~ de** for want of; **~ à gagner** loss of profit *ou* earnings

manqué [mɑ̃ke] *adj* failed; **garçon ~** tomboy

manquement [mɑ̃kmɑ̃] *nm*: **~ à** (*discipline, règle*) breach of

manquer [mɑ̃ke] *vi* (*faire défaut*) to be lacking; (*être absent*) to be missing; (*échouer*) to fail ▷ *vt* to miss ▷ *vb impers*: **il (nous) manque encore 10 euros** we are still 10 euros short; **il manque des pages (au livre)** there are some pages missing *ou* some pages are missing (from the book); **l'argent qui leur manque** the money they need *ou* are short of; **le pied/la voix lui manqua** he missed his footing/his voice failed him; **~ à qn** (*absent etc*): **il/cela me manque** I miss him/that; **~ à** *vt* (*règles etc*) to be in breach of, fail to observe; **~ de** *vt* to lack; (*Comm*) to be out of (stock of); **ne pas ~ de faire: il n'a pas manqué de le dire** he certainly said it; **~ (de) faire: il a manqué (de) se tuer** he very nearly got killed; **il ne manquerait plus qu'il fasse** all we need now is for him to do; **je n'y manquerai pas** leave it to me, I'll definitely do it

mansarde [mɑ̃saʀd(ə)] *nf* attic

mansardé, e [mɑ̃saʀde] *adj* attic *cpd*

mansuétude [mɑ̃sɥetyd] *nf* leniency

mante [mɑ̃t] *nf*: **~ religieuse** praying mantis

manteau, x [mɑ̃to] *nm* coat; **~ de cheminée** mantelpiece; **sous le ~** (*fig*) under cover

mantille [mɑ̃tij] *nf* mantilla

manucure [manykyʀ] *nf* manicurist

manuel, le [manɥɛl] *adj* manual ▷ *nm/f* manually gifted pupil (*as opposed to intellectually gifted*) ▷ *nm* (*ouvrage*) manual, handbook

manuellement [manɥɛlmɑ̃] *adv* manually

manufacture [manyfaktyʀ] *nf* (*établissement*) factory; (*fabrication*) manufacture

manufacturé, e [manyfaktyʀe] *adj* manufactured

manufacturier, -ière [manyfaktyʀje, -jɛʀ] *nm/f* factory owner

manuscrit, e [manyskʀi, -it] *adj* handwritten ▷ *nm* manuscript

manutention [manytɑ̃sjɔ̃] *nf* (*Comm*) handling; (*local*) storehouse

manutentionnaire [manytɑ̃sjɔnɛʀ] *nm/f* warehouseman(-woman), packer

manutentionner [manytɑ̃sjɔne] *vt* to handle

mappemonde [mapmɔ̃d] *nf* (*plane*) map of the world; (*sphère*) globe

maquereau, x [makʀo] *nm* mackerel *inv*; (*fam: proxénète*) pimp

maquerelle [makʀɛl] *nf* (*fam*) madam

maquette [makɛt] *nf* (*d'un décor, bâtiment, véhicule*) (scale) model; (*Typo*) mockup; (: *d'une page illustrée, affiche*) paste-up; (: *prêt à la réproduction*) artwork

maquignon [makiɲɔ̃] *nm* horse-dealer

maquillage [makijaʒ] *nm* making up; faking; (*produits*) make-up

maquiller [makije] *vt* (*personne, visage*) to make up; (*truquer: passeport, statistique*) to fake; (: *voiture volée*) to do over (*respray etc*); **se maquiller** to make o.s. up

maquilleur, -euse [makijœʀ, -øz] *nm/f* make-up artist

maquis [maki] *nm* (*Géo*) scrub; (*fig*) tangle; (*Mil*) maquis, underground fighting *no pl*

maquisard, e [makizaʀ, -aʀd(ə)] *nm/f* maquis, member of the Resistance

marabout [maʀabu] *nm* (*Zool*) marabou(t)

maraîcher, -ère [maʀeʃe, maʀeʃɛʀ] *adj*: **cultures maraîchères** market gardening *sg* ▷ *nm/f* market gardener

marais [maʀɛ] *nm* marsh, swamp; **~ salant** saltworks

marasme [maʀasm(ə)] *nm* (*Pol, Écon*) stagnation, sluggishness; (*accablement*) dejection, depression

marathon [maʀatɔ̃] *nm* marathon

marâtre [maʀɑtʀ(ə)] *nf* cruel mother

maraude [maʀod] *nf* pilfering, thieving (*of poultry, crops*); (*dans un verger*) scrumping; (*vagabondage*) prowling; **en ~** on the prowl; (*taxi*) cruising

maraudeur, -euse [maʀodœʀ, -øz] *nm/f* marauder; prowler

marbre [maʀbʀ(ə)] *nm* (*pierre, statue*) marble; (*d'une table, commode*) marble top; (*Typo*) stone, bed; **rester de ~** to remain stonily indifferent

marbrer [maʀbʀe] *vt* to mottle, blotch; (*Tech: papier*) to marble

marbrerie [maʀbʀəʀi] *nf* (*atelier*) marble mason's workshop; (*industrie*) marble industry

marbrures [maʀbʀyʀ] *nfpl* blotches *pl*; (*Tech*) marbling *sg*

marc [maʀ] *nm* (*de raisin, pommes*) marc; **~ de café** coffee grounds *pl ou* dregs *pl*

marcassin [maʀkasɛ̃] *nm* young wild boar

marchand, e [maʀʃɑ̃, -ɑ̃d] *nm/f* shopkeeper, tradesman(-woman); (*au marché*) stallholder; (*spécifique*): **~ de cycles/tapis** bicycle/carpet dealer; **~ de charbon/vins** coal/wine merchant ▷ *adj*: **prix/valeur ~(e)** market price/value; **qualité ~e** standard quality; **~ en gros/au détail** wholesaler/retailer; **~ de biens** real estate agent; **~ de canons** (*péj*) arms dealer; **~ de couleurs** ironmonger (*Brit*), hardware dealer (*US*); **~/e de fruits** fruiterer (*Brit*), fruit seller (*US*); **~/e de journaux** newsagent; **~/e de légumes** greengrocer (*Brit*), produce dealer (*US*); **~/e de poisson** fishmonger (*Brit*), fish seller (*US*); **~/e de(s) quatre-saisons** costermonger (*Brit*), street vendor (selling fresh fruit and vegetables); **~ de sable** (*fig*) sandman; **~ de tableaux** art dealer

marchandage [maʀʃɑ̃daʒ] *nm* bargaining; (*péj: électoral*) bargaining, manoeuvring

marchander [maʀʃɑ̃de] *vt* (*article*) to bargain *ou* haggle over; (*éloges*) to be sparing with ▷ *vi* to bargain, haggle

marchandisage [maʀʃɑ̃dizaʒ] *nm* merchandizing

marchandise [maʀʃɑ̃diz] *nf* goods *pl*, merchandise *no pl*

marche [maʀʃ(ə)] *nf* (*d'escalier*) step; (*activité*) walking; (*promenade, trajet, allure*) walk; (*démarche*) walk, gait; (*Mil etc, Mus*) march; (*fonctionnement*) running; (*progression*) progress; course; **à une heure de ~** an hour's walk (away); **ouvrir/fermer la ~** to lead the way/bring up the rear; **dans le sens de la ~** (*Rail*) facing the engine; **en ~** (*monter etc*) while the vehicle is moving *ou* in motion; **mettre en ~** to start; **remettre qch en ~** to set *ou* start sth going again; **se mettre en ~** (*personne*) to get moving; (*machine*) to start; **~ arrière** (*Auto*) reverse (gear); **faire ~ arrière** (*Auto*) to reverse; (*fig*) to backtrack, back-pedal; **~ à suivre** (correct) procedure; (*sur notice*) (step by step) instructions *pl*

marché [maʀʃe] *nm* (*lieu, Comm, Écon*) market; (*ville*) trading centre; (*transaction*) bargain, deal; **par-dessus le ~** into the bargain; **faire son ~** to do one's shopping; **mettre le ~ en main à qn** to tell sb to take it or leave it; **~ au comptant** (*Bourse*) spot market; **~ aux fleurs** flower market; **~ noir** black market; **faire du ~ noir** to buy and sell on the black market; **~ aux puces** flea market; **~ à terme** (*Bourse*) forward market; **~ du travail** labour market

marchepied [maʀʃəpje] *nm* (*Rail*) step; (*Auto*) running board; (*fig*) stepping stone

marcher [maʀʃe] *vi* to walk; (*Mil*) to march; (*aller: voiture, train, affaires*) to go; (*prospérer*) to go well; (*fonctionner*) to work, run; (*fam*) to go along, agree; (: *croire naïvement*) to be taken in; **~ sur** to walk on; (*mettre le pied sur*) to step on *ou* in; (*Mil*) to march upon; **~ dans** (*herbe etc*) to walk in *ou* on; (*flaque*) to step in; **faire ~ qn** (*pour rire*) to pull sb's leg; (*pour tromper*) to lead sb up the garden path

marcheur, -euse [maʀʃœʀ, -øz] *nm/f* walker

mardi [maʀdi] *nm* Tuesday; **M~ gras** Shrove Tuesday; *voir aussi* **lundi**

mare [maʀ] *nf* pond; **~ de sang** pool of blood

marécage [maʀekaʒ] *nm* marsh, swamp

marécageux, -euse [maʀekaʒø, -øz] *adj* marshy, swampy

maréchal, -aux [maʀeʃal, -o] *nm* marshal; **~ des logis** (*Mil*) sergeant

maréchal-ferrant [maʀeʃalfɛʀɑ̃, maʀeʃo-] (*pl* **maréchaux-ferrants**) *nm* blacksmith

maréchaussée [maʀeʃose] *nf* (*humoristique*: *gendarmes*) constabulary (*Brit*), police

marée [maʀe] *nf* tide; (*poissons*) fresh (sea) fish; **~ haute/basse** high/low tide; **~ montante/descendante** rising/ebb tide; **~ noire** oil slick

marelle [maʀɛl] *nf*: (**jouer à**) **la ~** (to play) hopscotch

marémotrice [maʀemɔtʀis] *adj f* tidal

mareyeur, -euse [maʀɛjœʀ, -øz] *nm/f* wholesale (sea) fish merchant

margarine [maʀgaʀin] *nf* margarine

marge [maʀʒ(ə)] *nf* margin; **en ~** in the margin; **en ~ de** (*fig*) on the fringe of; (*en dehors de*) cut off from; (*qui se rapporte à*) connected with; **~ bénéficiaire** profit margin, mark-up; **~ de sécurité** safety margin

margelle [maʀʒɛl] *nf* coping

margeur [maʀʒœʀ] *nm* margin stop

marginal, e, -aux [maʀʒinal, -o] *adj* marginal ▷ *nm/f* dropout

marguerite [maʀgəʀit] *nf* marguerite, (oxeye) daisy

marguillier [maʀgije] *nm* churchwarden

mari [maʀi] *nm* husband

mariage [maʀjaʒ] *nm* (*union, état, fig*) marriage; (*noce*) wedding; **~ civil/religieux** registry office (*Brit*) *ou* civil/church wedding; **un ~ de raison/d'amour** a marriage of convenience/a love match; **~ blanc** unconsummated marriage; **~ en blanc** white wedding

marié, e [maʀje] *adj* married ▷ *nm/f* (bride)groom/bride; **les ~s** the bride and groom; **les (jeunes) ~s** the newly-weds

marier [maʀje] *vt* to marry; (*fig*) to blend; **se ~ (avec)** to marry, get married (to); (*fig*) to blend (with)

marijuana [maʀiʒwana] *nf* marijuana

marin, e [maʀɛ̃, -in] *adj* sea *cpd*, marine ▷ *nm* sailor ▷ *nf* navy; (*Art*) seascape; (*couleur*) navy (blue); **avoir le pied ~** to be a good sailor; (*garder son équilibre*) to have one's sea legs; **~e de guerre** navy; **~e marchande** merchant navy; **~e à voiles** sailing ships *pl*

marina [maʀina] *nf* marina

marinade [maʀinad] *nf* marinade

marine [maʀin] *adj f, nf voir* **marin** ▷ *adj inv* navy (blue) ▷ *nm* (*Mil*) marine

mariner [maʀine] *vi, vt* to marinate, marinade

marinier [maʀinje] *nm* bargee

marinière [maʀinjɛʀ] *nf* (*blouse*) smock ▷ *adj inv*: **moules ~** (*Culin*) mussels in white wine

marionnette [maʀjɔnɛt] *nf* puppet

marital, e, -aux [maʀital, -o] *adj*: **autorisation ~e** husband's permission

maritalement [maʀitalmɑ̃] *adv*: **vivre ~** to live together (as husband and wife)

maritime [maʀitim] *adj* sea *cpd*, maritime; (*ville*) coastal, seaside; (*droit*) shipping, maritime

marjolaine [maʀʒɔlɛn] *nf* marjoram

marketing [maʀkətiŋ] *nm* (*Comm*) marketing

marmaille [maʀmɑj] *nf* (*péj*) (gang of) brats *pl*

marmelade [maʀməlad] *nf* (*compote*) stewed fruit, compote; **~ d'oranges** (orange) marmalade; **en ~** (*fig*) crushed (to a pulp)

marmite [maʀmit] *nf* (cooking-)pot

marmiton [maʀmitɔ̃] *nm* kitchen boy

marmonner [maʀmɔne] *vt, vi* to mumble, mutter

marmot [maʀmo] *nm* (*fam*) brat

marmotte [maʀmɔt] *nf* marmot

marmotter [maʀmɔte] *vt* (*prière*) to mumble, mutter

marne [maʀn(ə)] *nf* (*Géo*) marl

Maroc [maʀɔk] *nm*: **le ~** Morocco

marocain, e [maʀɔkɛ̃, -ɛn] *adj* Moroccan ▷ *nm/f*: **Marocain, e** Moroccan

maroquin [maʀɔkɛ̃] *nm* (*peau*) morocco (leather); (*fig*) (minister's) portfolio

maroquinerie [maʀɔkinʀi] *nf* (*industrie*) leather craft; (*commerce*) leather shop; (*articles*) fine leather goods *pl*

maroquinier [maʀɔkinje] *nm* (*fabricant*) leather craftsman; (*marchand*) leather dealer

marotte [maʀɔt] *nf* fad

marquant, e [maʀkɑ̃, -ɑ̃t] *adj* outstanding

marque [maʀk(ə)] *nf* mark; (*Sport, Jeu*) score; (*Comm*: *de produits*) brand, make; (: *de disques*) label; (*insigne*: *d'une fonction*) badge; (*fig*): **~ d'affection** token of affection; **~ de joie** sign of joy; **à vos ~s!** (*Sport*) on your marks!; **de ~** *adj* (*Comm*) brand-name *cpd*; proprietary; (*fig*) high-class; (: *personnage, hôte*) distinguished; **produit de ~** quality product; **~ déposée** registered trademark; **~ de fabrique** trademark

marqué, e [maʀke] *adj* marked

marquer [maʀke] *vt* to mark; (*inscrire*) to write down; (*bétail*) to brand; (*Sport*: *but etc*) to score; (: *joueur*) to mark; (*accentuer*: *taille etc*) to emphasize; (*manifester*: *refus, intérêt*) to show ▷ *vi* (*événement, personnalité*) to stand out, be outstanding; (*Sport*) to score; **~ qn de son influence/empreinte** to have an influence/leave its impression on sb; **~ un temps d'arrêt** to pause momentarily; **~ le pas** (*fig*) to mark time; **il a marqué ce jour-là d'une pierre blanche** that was a red-letter day for him; **~ les points** (*tenir la marque*) to keep the score

marqueté, e [maʀkəte] *adj* inlaid

marqueterie [maʀkətʀi] *nf* inlaid work, marquetry

marqueur, -euse [maʀkœʀ, -øz] *nm/f* (*Sport*: *de but*) scorer ▷ *nm* (*crayon feutre*) marker pen

marquis, e [maʀki, -iz] *nm/f* marquis *ou* marquess (marchioness) ▷ *nf* (*auvent*) glass canopy *ou* awning

Marquises [maʀkiz] *nfpl*: **les (îles)** ~ the Marquesas Islands

marraine [maʀɛn] *nf* godmother; *(d'un navire, d'une rose etc)* namer

Marrakech [maʀakɛʃ] *n* Marrakech *ou* Marrakesh

marrant, e [maʀɑ̃, -ɑ̃t] *adj (fam)* funny

marre [maʀ] *adv (fam)*: **en avoir** ~ **de** to be fed up with

marrer [maʀe]: **se marrer** *vi (fam)* to have a (good) laugh

marron, ne [maʀɔ̃, -ɔn] *nm (fruit)* chestnut ▷ *adj inv* brown ▷ *adj (péj)* crooked; *(: faux)* bogus; ~**s glacés** marrons glacés

marronnier [maʀɔnje] *nm* chestnut (tree)

Mars [maʀs] *nm ou f* Mars

mars [maʀs] *nm* March; *voir aussi* **juillet**

marseillais, e [maʀsɛjɛ, -ɛz] *adj* of *ou* from Marseilles ▷ *nf*: **la M~e** *the French national anthem; see note*

◉ **LA MARSEILLAISE**
◉
◉
◉ The *Marseillaise* has been France's national
◉ anthem since 1879. The words of the "Chant
◉ de guerre de l'armée du Rhin", as the song
◉ was originally called, were written to an
◉ anonymous tune by an army captain called
◉ Rouget de Lisle in 1792. Adopted as a
◉ marching song by the Marseille battalion, it
◉ was finally popularized as the *Marseillaise*.

Marseille [maʀsɛj] *n* Marseilles

marsouin [maʀswɛ̃] *nm* porpoise

marsupiaux [maʀsypjo] *nmpl* marsupials

marteau, x [maʀto] *nm* hammer; *(de porte)* knocker; ~ **pneumatique** pneumatic drill

marteau-pilon [maʀtopilɔ̃] *(pl* **marteaux-pilons**) *nm* power hammer

marteau-piqueur [maʀtopikœʀ] *(pl* **marteaux-piqueurs**) *nm* pneumatic drill

martel [maʀtɛl] *nm*: **se mettre** ~ **en tête** to worry o.s.

martèlement [maʀtɛlmɑ̃] *nm* hammering

marteler [maʀtəle] *vt* to hammer; *(mots, phrases)* to rap out

martial, e, -aux [maʀsjal, -o] *adj* martial; **cour** ~**e** court-martial

martien, ne [maʀsjɛ̃, -ɛn] *adj* Martian, of *ou* from Mars

martinet [maʀtinɛ] *nm (fouet)* small whip; *(Zool)* swift

martingale [maʀtɛ̃gal] *nf (Couture)* half-belt; *(Jeu)* winning formula

martiniquais, e [maʀtinikɛ, -ɛz] *adj* of *ou* from Martinique

Martinique [maʀtinik] *nf*: **la** ~ Martinique

martin-pêcheur *(pl* **martins-pêcheurs**) [maʀtɛ̃pɛʃœʀ] *nm* kingfisher

martre [maʀtʀ(ə)] *nf* marten; ~ **zibeline** sable

martyr, e [maʀtiʀ] *nm/f* martyr ▷ *adj* martyred; **enfants** ~**s** battered children

martyre [maʀtiʀ] *nm* martyrdom; *(fig: sens affaibli)* agony, torture; **souffrir le** ~ to suffer agonies

martyriser [maʀtiʀize] *vt (Rel)* to martyr; *(fig)* to bully; *(: enfant)* to batter

mas [mɑ(s)] *nm* traditional house or farm in Provence

mascara [maskaʀa] *nm* mascara

mascarade [maskaʀad] *nf* masquerade

mascotte [maskɔt] *nf* mascot

masculin, e [maskylɛ̃, -in] *adj* masculine; *(sexe, population)* male; *(équipe, vêtements)* men's; *(viril)* manly ▷ *nm* masculine

masochisme [mazɔʃism(ə)] *nm* masochism

masochiste [mazɔʃist(ə)] *adj* masochistic ▷ *nm/f* masochist

masque [mask(ə)] *nm* mask; ~ **de beauté** face pack; ~ **à gaz** gas mask; ~ **de plongée** diving mask

masqué, e [maske] *adj* masked

masquer [maske] *vt (cacher: porte, goût)* to hide, conceal; *(dissimuler: vérité, projet)* to mask, obscure

massacrant, e [masakʀɑ̃, -ɑ̃t] *adj*: **humeur** ~**e** foul temper

massacre [masakʀ(ə)] *nm* massacre, slaughter; **jeu de** ~ *(fig)* wholesale slaughter

massacrer [masakʀe] *vt* to massacre, slaughter; *(fig: adversaire)* to slaughter; *(: texte etc)* to murder

massage [masaʒ] *nm* massage

masse [mas] *nf* mass; *(péj)*: **la** ~ the masses *pl*; *(Élec)* earth; *(maillet)* sledgehammer; **masses** *nfpl* masses; **une** ~ **de, des** ~**s de** *(fam)* masses *ou* loads of; **en** ~ *adv (en bloc)* in bulk; *(en foule)* en masse ▷ *adj (exécutions, production)* mass *cpd*; ~ **monétaire** *(Écon)* money supply; ~ **salariale** *(Comm)* wage(s) bill

massepain [maspɛ̃] *nm* marzipan

masser [mase] *vt (assembler)* to gather; *(pétrir)* to massage; **se masser** *vi* to gather

masseur, -euse [masœʀ, -øz] *nm/f (personne)* masseur(-euse) ▷ *nm (appareil)* massager

massicot [masiko] *nm (Typo)* guillotine

massif, -ive [masif, -iv] *adj (porte)* solid, massive; *(visage)* heavy, large; *(bois, or)* solid; *(dose)* massive; *(déportations etc)* mass *cpd* ▷ *nm (montagneux)* massif; *(de fleurs)* clump, bank

massivement [masivmɑ̃] *adv (répondre)* en masse; *(administrer, injecter)* in massive doses

massue [masy] *nf* club, bludgeon ▷ *adj inv*: **argument** ~ sledgehammer argument

mastectomie [mastɛktɔmi] *nf* mastectomy

mastic [mastik] *nm (pour vitres)* putty; *(pour fentes)* filler

masticage [mastikaʒ] *nm (d'une fente)* filling; *(d'une vitre)* puttying

mastication [mastikasjɔ̃] *nf* chewing, mastication

mastiquer [mastike] *vt (aliment)* to chew, masticate; *(fente)* to fill; *(vitre)* to putty

mastoc [mastɔk] *adj inv* hefty

mastodonte [mastɔdɔ̃t] *nm* monster *(fig)*

masturbation [mastyʀbasjɔ̃] *nf* masturbation

masturber [mastyʀbe] *vt*: **se masturber** to masturbate

m'as-tu-vu [matyvy] *nm/f inv* show-off

masure [mazyʀ] *nf* tumbledown cottage

mat, e [mat] *adj (couleur, métal)* mat(t); *(bruit, son)* dull ▷ *adj inv (Échecs)*: **être ~** to be checkmate

mât [mɑ] *nm (Navig)* mast; *(poteau)* pole, post

matamore [matamɔʀ] *nm* braggart, blusterer

match [matʃ] *nm* match; **~ nul** draw, tie (US); **faire ~ nul** to draw (Brit), tie (US); **~ aller** first leg; **~ retour** second leg, return match

matelas [matla] *nm* mattress; **~ pneumatique** air bed *ou* mattress; **~ à ressorts** spring *ou* interior-sprung mattress

matelassé, e [matlase] *adj* padded; *(tissu)* quilted

matelasser [matlase] *vt* to pad

matelot [matlo] *nm* sailor, seaman

mater [mate] *vt (personne)* to bring to heel, subdue; *(révolte)* to put down; *(fam)* to watch, look at

matérialisation [mateʀjalizasjɔ̃] *nf* materialization

matérialiser [mateʀjalize]: **se matérialiser** *vi* to materialize

matérialisme [mateʀjalism(ə)] *nm* materialism

matérialiste [mateʀjalist(ə)] *adj* materialistic ▷ *nm/f* materialist

matériau, x [mateʀjo] *nm* material; **matériaux** *nmpl* material(s); **~x de construction** building materials

matériel, le [mateʀjɛl] *adj* material; *(organisation, aide, obstacle)* practical; *(fig: péj: personne)* materialistic ▷ *nm* equipment *no pl*; *(de camping etc)* gear *no pl*; *(Inform)* hardware; **il n'a pas le temps ~ de le faire** he doesn't have the time (needed) to do it; **~ d'exploitation** (Comm) plant; **~ roulant** rolling stock

matériellement [mateʀjɛlmɑ̃] *adv (financièrement)* materially; **~ à l'aise** comfortably off; **je n'en ai ~ pas le temps** I simply do not have the time

maternel, le [matɛʀnɛl] *adj (amour, geste)* motherly, maternal; *(grand-père, oncle)* maternal ▷ *nf (aussi:* **école maternelle)** (state) nursery school

materner [matɛʀne] *vt (personne)* to mother

maternisé, e [matɛʀnize] *adj*: **lait ~** (infant) formula

maternité [matɛʀnite] *nf (établissement)* maternity hospital; *(état de mère)* motherhood, maternity; *(grossesse)* pregnancy

math [mat] *nfpl* maths (Brit), math (US)

mathématicien, ne [matematisjɛ̃, -ɛn] *nm/f* mathematician

mathématique [matematik] *adj* mathematical

mathématiques [matematik] *nfpl* mathematics *sg*

matheux, -euse [matø, -øz] *nm/f (fam)* maths (Brit) *ou* math (US) student; *(fort en math)* mathematical genius

maths [mat] *nfpl* maths (Brit), math (US)

matière [matjɛʀ] *nf (Physique)* matter; *(Comm, Tech)* material; matter *no pl*; *(fig: d'un livre etc)* subject matter; *(Scol)* subject; **en ~ de** as regards; **donner ~ à** to give cause to; **~ plastique** plastic; **~s fécales** faeces; **~s grasses** fat (content) *sg*; **~s premières** raw materials

MATIF [matif] *sigle m (= Marché à terme des instruments financiers)* body which regulates the activities of the French Stock Exchange

Matignon [matiɲɔ̃] *nm*: **(l'hôtel) ~** the French Prime Minister's residence; *see note*

⬤ **HÔTEL MATIGNON**

⬤
⬤ The *hôtel Matignon* is the Paris office and
⬤ residence of the French Prime Minister. By
⬤ extension, the term "Matignon" is often
⬤ used to refer to the Prime Minister and his
⬤ or her staff.

matin [matɛ̃] *nm, adv* morning; **le ~** *(pendant le matin)* in the morning; **demain ~** tomorrow morning; **le lendemain ~** (the) next morning; **du ~ au soir** from morning till night; **une heure du ~** one o'clock in the morning; **de grand** *ou* **bon ~** early in the morning

matinal, e, -aux [matinal, -o] *adj (toilette, gymnastique)* morning *cpd*; *(de bonne heure)* early; **être ~** *(personne)* to be up early; *(: habituellement)* to be an early riser

matinée [matine] *nf* morning; *(spectacle)* matinée, afternoon performance

matois, e [matwa, -waz] *adj* wily

matou [matu] *nm* tom(cat)

matraquage [matʀakaʒ] *nm* beating up; **~ publicitaire** plug, plugging

matraque [matʀak] *nf (de malfaiteur)* cosh (Brit), club; *(de policier)* truncheon (Brit), billy (US)

matraquer [matʀake] *vt* to beat up (with a truncheon *ou* billy); to cosh (Brit), club; *(fig: touristes etc)* to rip off; *(: disque)* to plug

matriarcal, e, -aux [matʀijaʀkal, -o] *adj* matriarchal

matrice [matʀis] *nf (Anat)* womb; *(Tech)* mould; *(Math etc)* matrix

matricule [matʀikyl] *nf (aussi:* **registre matricule)** roll, register ▷ *nm (aussi:* **numéro matricule**: Mil) regimental number; *(: Admin)* reference number

matrimonial, e, -aux [matʀimɔnjal, -o] *adj* marital, marriage *cpd*

matrone [matʀon] *nf* matron

mâture [mɑtyʀ] *nf* masts *pl*

maturité [matyʀite] *nf* maturity; *(d'un fruit)* ripeness, maturity

maudire [modiʀ] *vt* to curse

maudit, e [modi, -it] *adj (fam: satané)* blasted, confounded

maugréer [mogʀee] *vi* to grumble

mauresque [moʀɛsk(ə)] *adj* Moorish

Maurice [moʀis] *nf*: **(l'île) ~** Mauritius

mauricien, ne [mɔʀisjɛ̃, -ɛn] *adj* Mauritian
Mauritanie [mɔʀitani] *nf*: **la ~** Mauritania
mauritanien, ne [mɔʀitanjɛ̃, -ɛn] *adj*
Mauritanian
mausolée [mozɔle] *nm* mausoleum
maussade [mosad] *adj* (*air, personne*) sullen; (*ciel, temps*) dismal
mauvais, e [mɔvɛ, -ɛz] *adj* bad; (*méchant, malveillant*) malicious, spiteful; (*faux*): **le ~ numéro** the wrong number ▷ *nm*: **le ~** the bad side ▷ *adv*: **il fait ~** the weather is bad; **sentir ~** to have a nasty smell, smell bad *ou* nasty; **la mer est ~e** the sea is rough; **~ coucheur** awkward customer; **~ coup** (*fig*) criminal venture; **~ garçon** tough; **~ pas** tight spot; **~ plaisant** hoaxer; **~ traitements** ill treatment *sg*; **~e herbe** weed; **~e langue** gossip, scandalmonger (*Brit*); **~e passe** difficult situation; (*période*) bad patch; **~e tête** rebellious *ou* headstrong customer
mauve [mov] *adj* (*couleur*) mauve ▷ *nf* (*Bot*) mallow
mauviette [movjɛt] *nf* (*péj*) weakling
maux [mo] *nmpl voir* **mal**
max. *abr* (= *maximum*) max
maximal, e, -aux [maksimal, -o] *adj* maximal
maxime [maksim] *nf* maxim
maximum [maksimɔm] *adj, nm* maximum; **atteindre un/son ~** to reach a/his peak; **au ~** *adv* (*le plus possible*) to the full; as much as one can; (*tout au plus*) at the (very) most *ou* maximum
Mayence [majɑ̃s] *n* Mainz
mayonnaise [majɔnɛz] *nf* mayonnaise
Mayotte [majɔt] *nf* Mayotte
mazout [mazut] *nm* (fuel) oil; **chaudière/ poêle à ~** oil-fired boiler/stove
mazouté, e [mazute] *adj* oil-polluted
MDM *sigle mpl* (= *Médecins du Monde*) *medical association for aid to Third World countries*
Me *abr* = **Maître**
me, m' [m(ə)] *pron* me; (*réfléchi*) myself
méandres [meɑ̃dʀ(ə)] *nmpl* meanderings
mec [mɛk] *nm* (*fam*) guy, bloke (*Brit*)
mécanicien, ne [mekanisjɛ̃, -ɛn] *nm/f* mechanic; (*Rail*) (train *ou* engine) driver; **~ navigant** *ou* **de bord** (*Aviat*) flight engineer
mécanique [mekanik] *adj* mechanical ▷ *nf* (*science*) mechanics *sg*; (*technologie*) mechanical engineering; (*mécanisme*) mechanism; engineering; works *pl*; **ennui ~** engine trouble *no pl*; **s'y connaître en ~** to be mechanically minded; **~ hydraulique** hydraulics *sg*; **~ ondulatoire** wave mechanics *sg*
mécaniquement [mekanikmɑ̃] *adv* mechanically
mécanisation [mekanizasjɔ̃] *nf* mechanization
mécaniser [mekanize] *vt* to mechanize
mécanisme [mekanism(ə)] *nm* mechanism; **~ des taux de change** exchange rate mechanism
mécano [mekano] *nm* (*fam*) mechanic
mécène [mesɛn] *nm* patron
méchamment [meʃamɑ̃] *adv* nastily, maliciously; spitefully; viciously
méchanceté [meʃɑ̃ste] *nf* (*d'une personne, d'une parole*) nastiness, maliciousness, spitefulness; (*parole, action*) nasty *ou* spiteful *ou* malicious remark (*ou* action)
méchant, e [meʃɑ̃, -ɑ̃t] *adj* nasty, malicious, spiteful; (*enfant: pas sage*) naughty; (*animal*) vicious; (*avant le nom: péjorative*) nasty
mèche [mɛʃ] *nf* (*de lampe, bougie*) wick; (*d'un explosif*) fuse; (*Méd*) pack, dressing; (*de vilebrequin, perceuse*) bit; (*de dentiste*) drill; (*de fouet*) lash; (*de cheveux*) lock; **se faire faire des ~s** (*chez le coiffeur*) to have one's hair streaked, have highlights put in one's hair; **vendre la ~** to give the game away; **de ~ avec** in league with
méchoui [meʃwi] *nm* whole sheep barbecue
mécompte [mekɔ̃t] *nm* (*erreur*) miscalculation; (*déception*) disappointment
méconnais etc [mekɔnɛ] *vb voir* **méconnaître**
méconnaissable [mekɔnɛsabl(ə)] *adj* unrecognizable
méconnaissais etc [mekɔnɛsɛ] *vb voir* **méconnaître**
méconnaissance [mekɔnɛsɑ̃s] *nf* ignorance
méconnaître [mekɔnɛtʀ(ə)] *vt* (*ignorer*) to be unaware of; (*mésestimer*) to misjudge
méconnu, e [mekɔny] *pp de* **méconnaître** ▷ *adj* (*génie etc*) unrecognized
mécontent, e [mekɔ̃tɑ̃, -ɑ̃t] *adj*: **~ (de)** (*insatisfait*) discontented *ou* dissatisfied *ou* displeased (with); (*contrarié*) annoyed (at) ▷ *nm/f* malcontent, dissatisfied person
mécontentement [mekɔ̃tɑ̃tmɑ̃] *nm* dissatisfaction, discontent, displeasure; annoyance
mécontenter [mekɔ̃tɑ̃te] *vt* to displease
Mecque [mɛk] *nf*: **la ~** Mecca
mécréant, e [mekʀeɑ̃, -ɑ̃t] *adj* (*peuple*) infidel; (*personne*) atheistic
méd. *abr* = **médecin**
médaille [medaj] *nf* medal
médaillé, e [medaje] *nm/f* (*Sport*) medal-holder
médaillon [medajɔ̃] *nm* (*portrait*) medallion; (*bijou*) locket; (*Culin*) médaillon; **en ~** *adj* (*carte etc*) inset
médecin [medsɛ̃] *nm* doctor; **~ du bord** (*Navig*) ship's doctor; **~ généraliste** general practitioner, GP; **~ légiste** forensic scientist (*Brit*), medical examiner (*US*); **~ traitant** family doctor, GP
médecine [medsin] *nf* medicine; **~ générale** general medicine; **~ infantile** paediatrics *sg* (*Brit*), pediatrics *sg* (*US*); **~ légale** forensic medicine; **~ préventive** preventive medicine; **~ du travail** occupational *ou* industrial medicine; **~s parallèles** *ou* **douces** alternative medicine
MEDEF [medɛf] *sigle m* (= *Mouvement des entreprises de France*) *French employers' confederation*
médian, e [medjɑ̃, -an] *adj* median
médias [medja] *nmpl*: **les ~** the media
médiateur, -trice [medjatœʀ, -tʀis] *nm/f voir*

médiation mediator; arbitrator
médiathèque [medjatɛk] *nf* media library
médiation [medjasjɔ̃] *nf* mediation; *(dans conflit social etc)* arbitration
médiatique [medjatik] *adj* media *cpd*
médiatisé, e [medjatize] *adj* reported in the media; **ce procès a été très ~** *(péj)* this trial was turned into a media event
médiator [medjatɔʀ] *nm* plectrum
médical, e, -aux [medikal, -o] *adj* medical; **visiteur** *ou* **délégué ~** medical rep *ou* representative
médicalement [medikalmɑ̃] *adv* medically
médicament [medikamɑ̃] *nm* medicine, drug
médicamenteux, -euse [medikamɑ̃tø, -øz] *adj* medicinal
médication [medikasjɔ̃] *nf* medication
médicinal, e, -aux [medisinal, -o] *adj* medicinal
médico-légal, e, -aux [medikɔlegal, -o] *adj* forensic
médico-social, e, -aux [medikɔsɔsjal, -o] *adj*: **assistance ~e** medical and social assistance
médiéval, e, -aux [medjeval, -o] *adj* medieval
médiocre [medjɔkʀ(ə)] *adj* mediocre, poor
médiocrité [medjɔkʀite] *nf* mediocrity
médire [mediʀ] *vi*: **~ de** to speak ill of
médisance [medizɑ̃s] *nf* scandalmongering *no pl (Brit)*, mud-slinging *no pl*; *(propos)* piece of scandal *ou* malicious gossip
médisant, e [medizɑ̃, -ɑ̃t] *vb voir* **médire** ▷ *adj* slanderous, malicious
médit, e [medi, -it] *pp de* **médire**
méditatif, -ive [meditatif, -iv] *adj* thoughtful
méditation [meditasjɔ̃] *nf* meditation
méditer [medite] *vt (approfondir)* to meditate on, ponder (over); *(combiner)* to meditate ▷ *vi* to meditate; **~ de faire** to contemplate doing, plan to do
Méditerranée [mediteʀane] *nf*: **la (mer) ~** the Mediterranean (Sea)
méditerranéen, ne [mediteʀaneɛ̃, -ɛn] *adj* Mediterranean ▷ *nm/f*: **Méditerranéen, ne** Mediterranean
médium [medjɔm] *nm* medium *(spiritualist)*
médius [medjys] *nm* middle finger
méduse [medyz] *nf* jellyfish
méduser [medyze] *vt* to dumbfound
meeting [mitiŋ] *nm (Pol, Sport)* rally, meeting; **~ d'aviation** air show
méfait [mefɛ] *nm (faute)* misdemeanour, wrongdoing; **méfaits** *nmpl (ravages)* ravages
méfiance [mefjɑ̃s] *nf* mistrust, distrust
méfiant, e [mefjɑ̃, -ɑ̃t] *adj* mistrustful, distrustful
méfier [mefje]: **se méfier** *vi* to be wary; *(faire attention)* to be careful; **se ~ de** *vt* to mistrust, distrust, be wary of; to be careful about
mégalomane [megalɔman] *adj* megalomaniac
mégalomanie [megalɔmani] *nf* megalomania
mégalopole [megalɔpɔl] *nf* megalopolis
méga-octet [megaɔktɛ] *nm* megabyte
mégarde [megaʀd(ə)] *nf*: **par ~** accidentally;

(par erreur) by mistake
mégatonne [megatɔn] *nf* megaton
mégère [meʒɛʀ] *nf (péj: femme)* shrew
mégot [mego] *nm* cigarette end *ou* butt
mégoter [megɔte] *vi* to nitpick
meilleur, e [mɛjœʀ] *adj, adv* better; *(valeur superlative)* best ▷ *nm*: **le ~** *(celui qui ...)* the best (one); *(ce qui ...)* the best ▷ *nf*: **la ~e** the best (one); **le ~ des deux** the better of the two; **de ~e heure** earlier; **~ marché** cheaper
méjuger [meʒyʒe] *vt* to misjudge
mél [mɛl] *nm* e-mail
mélancolie [melɑ̃kɔli] *nf* melancholy, gloom
mélancolique [melɑ̃kɔlik] *adj* melancholy, gloomy
mélange [melɑ̃ʒ] *nm (opération)* mixing; blending; *(résultat)* mixture; blend; **sans ~** unadulterated
mélanger [melɑ̃ʒe] *vt (substances)* to mix; *(vins, couleurs)* to blend; *(mettre en désordre, confondre)* to mix up, muddle (up); **se mélanger** *(liquides, couleurs)* to blend, mix
mélanine [melanin] *nf* melanin
mélasse [melas] *nf* treacle, molasses *sg*
mêlée [mele] *nf (bataille, cohue)* mêlée, scramble; *(lutte, conflit)* tussle, scuffle; *(Rugby)* scrum(mage)
mêler [mele] *vt (substances, odeurs, races)* to mix; *(embrouiller)* to muddle (up), mix up; **se mêler** to mix; *(se joindre, s'allier)* to mingle; **se ~ à** *(personne)* to join; to mix with; *(: odeurs etc)* to mingle with; **se ~ de** *(personne)* to meddle with, interfere in; **mêle-toi de tes affaires!** mind your own business!; **~ à** *ou* **avec** *ou* **de** to mix with; to mingle with; **~ qn à** *(affaire)* to get sb mixed up *ou* involved in
mélo [melo] *nm adj* = **mélodrame**; **mélodramatique**
mélodie [melɔdi] *nf* melody
mélodieux, -euse [melɔdjø, -øz] *adj* melodious, tuneful
mélodique [melɔdik] *adj* melodic
mélodramatique [melɔdʀamatik] *adj* melodramatic
mélodrame [melɔdʀam] *nm* melodrama
mélomane [melɔman] *nm/f* music lover
melon [məlɔ̃] *nm (Bot)* (honeydew) melon; *(aussi:* **chapeau melon)** bowler (hat); **~ d'eau** watermelon
mélopée [melɔpe] *nf* monotonous chant
membrane [mɑ̃bʀan] *nf* membrane
membre [mɑ̃bʀ(ə)] *nm (Anat)* limb; *(personne, pays, élément)* member ▷ *adj* member; **être ~ de** to be a member of; **~ (viril)** (male) organ
mémé [meme] *nf (fam)* granny; *(: vieille femme)* old dear

 MOT-CLÉ

même [mɛm] *adj* **1** *(avant le nom)* same; **en même temps** at the same time; **ils ont les mêmes goûts** they have the same *ou* similar tastes

2 (*après le nom: renforcement*): **il est la loyauté même** he is loyalty itself; **ce sont ses paroles/celles-là même** they are his very words/the very ones

▷ *pron:* **le (la) même** the same one

▷ *adv* **1** (*renforcement*): **il n'a même pas pleuré** he didn't even cry; **même lui l'a dit** even HE said it; **ici même** at this very place; **même si** even if

2: **à même: à même la bouteille** straight from the bottle; **à même la peau** next to the skin; **être à même de faire** to be in a position to do, be able to do; **mettre qn à même de faire** to enable sb to do

3: **de même** likewise; **faire de même** to do likewise *ou* the same; **lui de même** so does (*ou* did *ou* is) he; **de même que** just as; **il en va de même pour** the same goes for

mémento [memɛ̃to] *nm* (*agenda*) appointments diary; (*ouvrage*) summary

mémo [memo] (*fam*) *nm* memo

mémoire [memwaʀ] *nf* memory ▷ *nm* (*Admin, Jur*) memorandum; (*Scol*) dissertation, paper; **avoir la ~ des visages/chiffres** to have a (good) memory for faces/figures; **n'avoir aucune ~** to have a terrible memory; **avoir de la ~** to have a good memory; **à la ~ de** to the *ou* in memory of; **pour ~** *adv* for the record; **de ~** *adv* from memory; **de ~ d'homme** in living memory; **mettre en ~** (*Inform*) to store; **~ morte** ROM; **~ vive** RAM

mémoires [memwaʀ] *nmpl* memoirs

mémorable [memɔʀabl(ə)] *adj* memorable

mémorandum [memɔʀɑ̃dɔm] *nm* memorandum; (*carnet*) notebook

mémorial, -aux [memɔʀjal, -o] *nm* memorial

mémoriser [memɔʀize] *vt* to memorize; (*Inform*) to store

menaçant, e [mənasɑ̃, -ɑ̃t] *adj* threatening, menacing

menace [mənas] *nf* threat; **~ en l'air** empty threat

menacer [mənase] *vt* to threaten; **~ qn de qch/de faire qch** to threaten sb with sth/to do sth

ménage [menaʒ] *nm* (*travail*) housekeeping, housework; (*couple*) (married) couple; (*famille, Admin*) household; **faire le ~** to do the housework; **faire des ~s** to work as a cleaner (*in private homes*); **monter son ~** to set up house; **se mettre en ~** (*avec*) to set up house (with); **heureux en ~** happily married; **faire bon ~ avec** to get on well with; **~ de poupée** doll's kitchen set; **~ à trois** love triangle

ménagement [menaʒmɑ̃] *nm* care and attention; **ménagements** *nmpl* (*égards*) consideration *sg*, attention *sg*

ménager[1] [menaʒe] *vt* (*traiter avec mesure*) to handle with tact; to treat considerately; (*utiliser*) to use with care; (: *avec économie*) to use sparingly; (*prendre soin de*) to take (great) care of,

look after; (*organiser*) to arrange; (*installer*) to put in; to make; **se ménager** to look after o.s.; **~ qch à qn** (*réserver*) to have sth in store for sb

ménager[2]**, -ère** [menaʒe, -ɛʀ] *adj* household *cpd*, domestic ▷ *nf* (*femme*) housewife; (*couverts*) canteen (of cutlery)

ménagerie [menaʒʀi] *nf* menagerie

mendiant, e [mɑ̃djɑ̃, -ɑ̃t] *nm/f* beggar

mendicité [mɑ̃disite] *nf* begging

mendier [mɑ̃dje] *vi* to beg ▷ *vt* to beg (for); (*fig: éloges, compliments*) to fish for

menées [məne] *nfpl* intrigues, manœuvres (*Brit*), maneuvers (*US*); (*Comm*) activities

mener [məne] *vt* to lead; (*enquête*) to conduct; (*affaires*) to manage, conduct, run ▷ *vi*: **~ (à la marque)** to lead, be in the lead; **~ à/dans** (*emmener*) to take to/into; **~ qch à bonne fin** *ou* **à terme** *ou* **à bien** to see sth through (to a successful conclusion), complete sth successfully

meneur, -euse [mənœʀ, -øz] *nm/f* leader; (*péj: agitateur*) ringleader; **~ d'hommes** born leader; **~ de jeu** host, quizmaster (*Brit*)

menhir [meniʀ] *nm* standing stone

méningite [menɛ̃ʒit] *nf* meningitis *no pl*

ménisque [menisk] *nm* (*Anat*) meniscus

ménopause [menɔpoz] *nf* menopause

menotte [mənɔt] *nf* (*langage enfantin*) handie; **menottes** *nfpl* handcuffs; **passer les ~s à** to handcuff

mens [mɑ̃] *vb voir* **mentir**

mensonge [mɑ̃sɔ̃ʒ] *nm*: **le ~** lying *no pl*; **un ~** a lie

mensonger, -ère [mɑ̃sɔ̃ʒe, -ɛʀ] *adj* false

menstruation [mɑ̃stʀyasjɔ̃] *nf* menstruation

menstruel, le [mɑ̃stʀyɛl] *adj* menstrual

mensualiser [mɑ̃syalize] *vt* to pay monthly

mensualité [mɑ̃syalite] *nf* (*somme payée*) monthly payment; (*somme perçue*) monthly salary

mensuel, le [mɑ̃syɛl] *adj* monthly ▷ *nm/f* (*employé*) employee paid monthly ▷ *nm* (*Presse*) monthly

mensuellement [mɑ̃syɛlmɑ̃] *adv* monthly

mensurations [mɑ̃syʀasjɔ̃] *nfpl* measurements

mentais *etc* [mɑ̃tɛ] *vb voir* **mentir**

mental, e, -aux [mɑ̃tal, -o] *adj* mental

mentalement [mɑ̃talmɑ̃] *adv* in one's head, mentally

mentalité [mɑ̃talite] *nf* mentality

menteur, -euse [mɑ̃tœʀ, -øz] *nm/f* liar

menthe [mɑ̃t] *nf* mint; **~ (à l'eau)** peppermint cordial

mentholé, e [mɑ̃tɔle] *adj* menthol *cpd*, mentholated

mention [mɑ̃sjɔ̃] *nf* (*note*) note, comment; (*Scol*): **~ (très) bien/passable** (very) good/satisfactory pass; **faire ~ de** to mention; **"rayer la ~ inutile"** "delete as appropriate"

mentionner [mɑ̃sjɔne] *vt* to mention

mentir [mɑ̃tiʀ] *vi* to lie

menton [mɑ̃tɔ̃] *nm* chin

mentonnière [mãtɔnjɛʀ] *nf* chin strap
menu, e [məny] *adj* (*mince*) thin; (*petit*) tiny; (*frais, difficulté*) minor ▷ *adv* (*couper, hacher*) very fine ▷ *nm* menu; **par le ~** (*raconter*) in minute detail; **~ touristique** popular *ou* tourist menu; **~e monnaie** small change
menuet [mənɥɛ] *nm* minuet
menuiserie [mənɥizʀi] *nf* (*travail*) joinery, carpentry; (*d'amateur*) woodwork; (*local*) joiner's workshop; (*ouvrages*) woodwork *no pl*
menuisier [mənɥizje] *nm* joiner, carpenter
méprendre [mepʀãdʀ(ə)]: **se méprendre** *vi*: **se méprendre sur** to be mistaken about
mépris, e [mepʀi, -iz] *pp de* **méprendre** ▷ *nm* (*dédain*) contempt, scorn; (*indifférence*): **le ~ de** contempt *ou* disregard for; **au ~ de** regardless of, in defiance of
méprisable [mepʀizabl(ə)] *adj* contemptible, despicable
méprisant, e [mepʀizã, -ãt] *adj* contemptuous, scornful
méprise [mepʀiz] *nf* mistake, error; (*malentendu*) misunderstanding
mépriser [mepʀize] *vt* to scorn, despise; (*gloire, danger*) to scorn, spurn
mer [mɛʀ] *nf* sea; (*marée*) tide; **~ fermée** inland sea; **en ~** at sea; **prendre la ~** to put out to sea; **en haute** *ou* **pleine ~** off shore, on the open sea; **la ~ Adriatique** the Adriatic (Sea); **la ~ des Antilles** *ou* **des Caraïbes** the Caribbean (Sea); **la ~ Baltique** the Baltic (Sea); **la ~ Caspienne** the Caspian Sea; **la ~ de Corail** the Coral Sea; **la ~ Égée** the Aegean (Sea); **la ~ Ionienne** the Ionian Sea; **la ~ Morte** the Dead Sea; **la ~ Noire** the Black Sea; **la ~ du Nord** the North Sea; **la ~ Rouge** the Red Sea; **la ~ des Sargasses** the Sargasso Sea; **les ~s du Sud** the South Seas; **la ~ Tyrrhénienne** the Tyrrhenian Sea
mercantile [mɛʀkãtil] *adj* (*péj*) mercenary
mercantilisme [mɛʀkãtilism(ə)] *nm* (*esprit mercantile*) mercenary attitude
mercenaire [mɛʀsənɛʀ] *nm* mercenary
mercerie [mɛʀsəʀi] *nf* (*Couture*) haberdashery (*Brit*), notions *pl* (*US*); (*boutique*) haberdasher's (shop) (*Brit*), notions store (*US*)
merci [mɛʀsi] *excl* thank you ▷ *nf*: **à la ~ de qn/qch** at sb's mercy/the mercy of sth; **~ beaucoup** thank you very much; **~ de** *ou* **pour** thank you for; **sans ~** *adj* merciless ▷ *adv* mercilessly
mercier, -ière [mɛʀsje, -jɛʀ] *nm/f* haberdasher
mercredi [mɛʀkʀədi] *nm* Wednesday; **~ des Cendres** Ash Wednesday; *voir aussi* **lundi**
mercure [mɛʀkyʀ] *nm* mercury
merde [mɛʀd(ə)] (*fam!*) *nf* shit (!) ▷ *excl* (bloody) hell (!)
merdeux, -euse [mɛʀdø, -øz] *nm/f* (*fam!*) little bugger (*Brit*) (!), little devil
mère [mɛʀ] *nf* mother ▷ *adj inv* mother *cpd*; **~ célibataire** single parent, unmarried mother
merguez [mɛʀgɛz] *nf* spicy North African sausage
méridien [meʀidjɛ̃] *nm* meridian
méridional, e, -aux [meʀidjɔnal, -o] *adj*

southern; (*du midi de la France*) Southern (French) ▷ *nm/f* Southerner
meringue [məʀɛ̃g] *nf* meringue
mérinos [meʀinos] *nm* merino
merisier [məʀizje] *nm* wild cherry (tree)
méritant, e [meʀitã, -ãt] *adj* deserving
mérite [meʀit] *nm* merit; **le ~ (de ceci) lui revient** the credit (for this) is his
mériter [meʀite] *vt* to deserve; **~ de réussir** to deserve to succeed; **il mérite qu'on fasse ...** he deserves people to do ...
méritocratie [meʀitɔkʀasi] *nf* meritocracy
méritoire [meʀitwaʀ] *adj* praiseworthy, commendable
merlan [mɛʀlã] *nm* whiting
merle [mɛʀl(ə)] *nm* blackbird
mérou [meʀu] *nm* grouper (*fish*)
merveille [mɛʀvɛj] *nf* marvel, wonder; **faire ~** *ou* **des ~s** to work wonders; **à ~** perfectly, wonderfully
merveilleux, -euse [mɛʀvɛjø, -øz] *adj* marvellous, wonderful
mes [me] *adj poss voir* **mon**
mésalliance [mezaljãs] *nf* misalliance, mismatch
mésallier [mezalje]: **se mésallier** *vi* to marry beneath (*ou* above) o.s.
mésange [mezãʒ] *nf* tit(mouse); **~ bleue** bluetit
mésaventure [mezavãtyʀ] *nf* misadventure, misfortune
Mesdames [medam] *nfpl voir* **Madame**
Mesdemoiselles [medmwazɛl] *nfpl voir* **Mademoiselle**
mésentente [mezãtãt] *nf* dissension, disagreement
mésestimer [mezɛstime] *vt* to underestimate, underrate
Mésopotamie [mezɔpɔtami] *nf*: **la ~** Mesopotamia
mesquin, e [mɛskɛ̃, -in] *adj* mean, petty
mesquinerie [mɛskinʀi] *nf* meanness *no pl*, pettiness *no pl*
mess [mɛs] *nm* mess
message [mesaʒ] *nm* message; **~ d'erreur** (*Inform*) error message; **~ électronique** (*Inform*) email; **~ publicitaire** ad, advertisement; **~ téléphoné** telegram dictated by telephone
messager, -ère [mesaʒe, -ɛʀ] *nm/f* messenger
messagerie [mesaʒʀi] *nf*: **~ électronique** electronic mail, email; **~ rose** *lonely hearts and contact service on videotext*; **~s aériennes/ maritimes** air freight/shipping service *sg*; **~s de presse** press distribution service; **~ vocale** voice mail
messe [mɛs] *nf* mass; **aller à la ~** to go to mass; **~ de minuit** midnight mass; **faire des ~s basses** (*fig, péj*) to mutter
messie [mesi] *nm*: **le M~** the Messiah
Messieurs [mesjø] *nmpl voir* **Monsieur**
mesure [məzyʀ] *nf* (*évaluation, dimension*) measurement; (*étalon, récipient, contenu*) measure; (*Mus: cadence*) time, tempo; (: *division*)

bar; (*retenue*) moderation; (*disposition*) measure, step; **unité/système de ~** unit/system of measurement; **sur ~** (*costume*) made-to-measure; (*fig*) personally adapted; **à la ~ de** (*fig: personne*) worthy of; (*chambre etc*) on the same scale as; **dans la ~ où** insofar as, inasmuch as; **dans une certaine ~** to some *ou* a certain extent; **à ~ que** as; **en ~** (*Mus*) in time *ou* tempo; **être en ~ de** to be in a position to; **dépasser la ~** (*fig*) to overstep the mark

mesuré, e [məzyʀe] *adj* (*ton, effort*) measured; (*personne*) restrained

mesurer [məzyʀe] *vt* to measure; (*juger*) to weigh up, assess; (*limiter*) to limit, ration; (*modérer*) to moderate; (*proportionner*): **~ qch à** to match sth to, gear sth to; **se ~ avec** to have a confrontation with; to tackle; **il mesure 1 m 80** he's 1 m 80 tall

met [mɛ] *vb voir* **mettre**

métabolisme [metabɔlism(ə)] *nm* metabolism

métairie [meteʀi] *nf* smallholding

métal, -aux [metal, -o] *nm* metal

métalangage [metalɑ̃gaʒ] *nm* metalanguage

métallique [metalik] *adj* metallic

métallisé, e [metalize] *adj* metallic

métallurgie [metalyʀʒi] *nf* metallurgy

métallurgique [metalyʀʒik] *adj* steel *cpd*, metal *cpd*

métallurgiste [metalyʀʒist(ə)] *nm/f* (*ouvrier*) steel *ou* metal worker; (*industriel*) metallurgist

métamorphose [metamɔʀfoz] *nf* metamorphosis

métamorphoser [metamɔʀfoze] *vt* to transform

métaphore [metafɔʀ] *nf* metaphor

métaphorique [metafɔʀik] *adj* metaphorical, figurative

métaphoriquement [metafɔʀikmɑ̃] *adv* metaphorically

métaphysique [metafizik] *nf* metaphysics *sg* ▷ *adj* metaphysical

métapsychique [metapsiʃik] *adj* psychic, parapsychological

métayer, -ère [meteje, metejɛʀ] *nm/f* (*tenant*) farmer

météo [meteo] *nf* (*bulletin*) (weather) forecast; (*service*) ≈ Met Office (*Brit*), ≈ National Weather Service (*US*)

météore [meteɔʀ] *nm* meteor

météorite [meteɔʀit] *nm ou f* meteorite

météorologie [meteɔʀɔlɔʒi] *nf* (*étude*) meteorology; (*service*) ≈ Meteorological Office (*Brit*), ≈ National Weather Service (*US*)

météorologique [meteɔʀɔlɔʒik] *adj* meteorological, weather *cpd*

météorologue [meteɔʀɔlɔg], **météorologiste** [meteɔʀɔlɔʒist(ə)] *nm/f* meteorologist, weather forecaster

métèque [metɛk] *nm* (*péj*) wop (!)

méthane [metan] *nm* methane

méthanier [metanje] *nm* (*bateau*) (liquefied) gas carrier *ou* tanker

méthode [metɔd] *nf* method; (*livre, ouvrage*) manual, tutor

méthodique [metɔdik] *adj* methodical

méthodiquement [metɔdikmɑ̃] *adv* methodically

méthodiste [metɔdist(ə)] *adj, nm/f* (*Rel*) Methodist

méthylène [metilɛn] *nm*: **bleu de ~** *nm* methylene blue

méticuleux, -euse [metikylø, -øz] *adj* meticulous

métier [metje] *nm* (*profession: gén*) job; (: *manuel*) trade; (: *artisanal*) craft; (*technique, expérience*) (acquired) skill *ou* technique; (*aussi*: **métier à tisser**) (weaving) loom; **être du ~** to be in the trade *ou* profession

métis, se [metis] *adj, nm/f* half-caste, half-breed

métisser [metise] *vt* to cross(breed)

métrage [metʀaʒ] *nm* (*de tissu*) length; (*Ciné*) footage, length; **long/moyen/court ~** feature *ou* full-length/medium-length/short film

mètre [mɛtʀ(ə)] *nm* metre (*Brit*), meter (*US*); (*règle*) (metre *ou* meter) rule; (*ruban*) tape measure; **~ carré/cube** square/cubic metre *ou* meter

métrer [metʀe] *vt* (*Tech*) to measure (in metres *ou* meters); (*Constr*) to survey

métreur, -euse [metʀœʀ, -øz] *nm/f*: **~ (vérificateur), métreuse (vérificatrice)** (quantity) surveyor

métrique [metʀik] *adj* metric ▷ *nf* metrics *sg*

métro [metʀo] *nm* underground (*Brit*), subway (*US*)

métronome [metʀɔnɔm] *nm* metronome

métropole [metʀɔpɔl] *nf* (*capitale*) metropolis; (*pays*) home country

métropolitain, e [metʀɔpɔlitɛ̃, -ɛn] *adj* metropolitan

mets [mɛ] *nm* dish ▷ *vb voir* **mettre**

mettable [mɛtabl(ə)] *adj* fit to be worn, decent

metteur [mɛtœʀ] *nm*: **~ en scène** (*Théât*) producer; (*Ciné*) director; **~ en ondes** (*Radio*) producer

 MOT-CLÉ

mettre [mɛtʀ(ə)] *vt* **1** (*placer*) to put; **mettre en bouteille/en sac** to bottle/put in bags *ou* sacks; **mettre qch à la poste** to post sth (*Brit*), mail sth (*US*); **mettre en examen (pour)** to charge (with) (*Brit*), indict (for) (*US*); **mettre une note gaie/amusante** to inject a cheerful/an amusing note; **mettre qn debout/assis** to help sb up *ou* to their feet/help sb to sit down

2 (*vêtements: revêtir*) to put on; (: *porter*) to wear; **mets ton gilet** put your cardigan on; **je ne mets plus mon manteau** I no longer wear my coat

3 (*faire fonctionner: chauffage, électricité*) to put on; (: *réveil, minuteur*) to set; (*installer: gaz, eau*) to put in, lay on; **mettre en marche** to start up

4 (*consacrer*): **mettre du temps/deux heures à**

faire qch to take time/two hours to do sth; **y mettre du sien** to pull one's weight

5 (*noter, écrire*) to say, put (down); **qu'est-ce qu'il a mis sur la carte?** what did he say *ou* write on the card?; **mettez au pluriel ...** put ... into the plural

6 (*supposer*): **mettons que ...** let's suppose *ou* say that ...

7 (*faire* + *vb*): **faire mettre le gaz/l'électricité** to have gas/electricity put in *ou* installed

se mettre *vi* **1** (*se placer*): **vous pouvez vous mettre là** you can sit (*ou* stand) there; **où ça se met?** where does it go?; **se mettre au lit** to get into bed; **se mettre au piano** to sit down at the piano; **se mettre à l'eau** to get into the water; **se mettre de l'encre sur les doigts** to get ink on one's fingers

2 (*s'habiller*): **se mettre en maillot de bain** to get into *ou* put on a swimsuit; **n'avoir rien à se mettre** to have nothing to wear

3 (*dans rapports*): **se mettre bien/mal avec qn** to get on the right/wrong side of sb; **se mettre qn à dos** to get on sb's bad side; **se mettre avec qn** (*prendre parti*) to side with sb; (*faire équipe*) to team up with sb; (*en ménage*) to move in with sb

4: **se mettre à** to begin, start; **se mettre à faire** to begin *ou* start doing *ou* to do; **se mettre au piano** to start learning the piano; **se mettre au régime** to go on a diet; **se mettre au travail/à l'étude** to get down to work/one's studies; **il est temps de s'y mettre** it's time we got down to it *ou* got on with it

meublant, e [mœblɑ̃, -ɑ̃t] *adj* (*tissus etc*) effective (in the room)

meuble [mœbl(ə)] *nm* (*objet*) piece of furniture; (*ameublement*) furniture *no pl* ▷ *adj* (*terre*) loose, friable; (*Jur*): **biens ~s** movables

meublé [mœble] *nm* (*pièce*) furnished room; (*appartement*) furnished flat (*Brit*) *ou* apartment (*US*)

meubler [mœble] *vt* to furnish; (*fig*): **~ qch (de)** to fill sth (with); **se meubler** to furnish one's house

meuf [mœf] *nf* (*fam*) woman

meugler [møgle] *vi* to low, moo

meule [møl] *nf* (*à broyer*) millstone; (*à aiguiser*) grindstone; (*à polir*) buff wheel; (*de foin, blé*) stack; (*de fromage*) round

meunerie [mønʀi] *nf* (*industrie*) flour trade; (*métier*) milling

meunier, -ière [mønje, -jɛʀ] *nm* miller ▷ *nf* miller's wife ▷ *adj f* (*Culin*) meunière

meurs *etc* [mœʀ] *vb voir* **mourir**

meurtre [mœʀtʀ(ə)] *nm* murder

meurtrier, -ière [mœʀtʀije, -jɛʀ] *adj* (*arme, épidémie, combat*) deadly; (*accident*) fatal; (*carrefour, route*) lethal; (*fureur, instincts*) murderous ▷ *nm/f* murderer(-ess) ▷ *nf* (*ouverture*) loophole

meurtrir [mœʀtʀiʀ] *vt* to bruise; (*fig*) to wound

meurtrissure [mœʀtʀisyʀ] *nf* bruise; (*fig*) scar

meus *etc* [mœ] *vb voir* **mouvoir**

Meuse [mœz] *nf*: **la ~** the Meuse

meute [møt] *nf* pack

meuve *etc* [mœv] *vb voir* **mouvoir**

mévente [mevɑ̃t] *nf* slump (in sales)

mexicain, e [mɛksikɛ̃, -ɛn] *adj* Mexican ▷ *nm/f*: **Mexicain, e** Mexican

Mexico [mɛksiko] *n* Mexico City

Mexique [mɛksik] *nm*: **le ~** Mexico

mezzanine [mɛdzanin] *nf* mezzanine (floor)

MF *sigle mpl* = **millions de francs** ▷ *sigle f* (*Radio*: = *modulation de fréquence*) FM

Mgr *abr* = **Monseigneur**

mi [mi] *nm* (*Mus*) E; (*en chantant la gamme*) mi

mi... [mi] *préfixe* half(-), mid-; **à la mi-janvier** in mid-January; **mi-bureau, mi-chambre** half office, half bedroom; **à mi-jambes/-corps** (up *ou* down) to the knees/waist; **à mi-hauteur/-pente** halfway up (*ou* down)/up (*ou* down) the hill

miaou [mjau] *nm* miaow

miaulement [mjolmɑ̃] *nm* (*cri*) miaow; (*continu*) miaowing *no pl*

miauler [mjole] *vi* to miaow

mi-bas [miba] *nm inv* knee-length sock

mica [mika] *nm* mica

mi-carême [mikaʀɛm] *nf*: **la ~** the third Thursday in Lent

miche [miʃ] *nf* round *ou* cob loaf

mi-chemin [miʃmɛ̃]: **à ~** *adv* halfway, midway

mi-clos, e [miklo, -kloz] *adj* half-closed

micmac [mikmak] *nm* (*péj*) carry-on

mi-côte [mikot]: **à ~** *adv* halfway up (*ou* down) the hill

mi-course [mikuʀs]: **à ~** *adv* halfway through the race

micro [mikʀo] *nm* mike, microphone; **~ cravate** lapel mike

microbe [mikʀob] *nm* germ, microbe

microbiologie [mikʀobjɔlɔʒi] *nf* microbiology

microchirurgie [mikʀoʃiʀyʀʒi] *nf* microsurgery

microclimat [mikʀoklima] *nm* microclimate

microcosme [mikʀokosm(ə)] *nm* microcosm

micro-édition [mikʀoedisjɔ̃] *nf* desk-top publishing

micro-électronique [mikʀoelɛktʀonik] *nf* microelectronics *sg*

microfiche [mikʀofiʃ] *nf* microfiche

microfilm [mikʀofilm] *nm* microfilm

micro-onde [mikʀoɔ̃d] *nf*: **four à ~s** microwave oven

micro-ordinateur [mikʀoɔʀdinatœʀ] *nm* microcomputer

micro-organisme [mikʀooʀganism(ə)] *nm* micro-organism

microphone [mikʀofɔn] *nm* microphone

microplaquette [mikʀoplakɛt] *nf* microchip

microprocesseur [mikʀopʀosɛsœʀ] *nm* microprocessor

microscope [mikʀoskop] *nm* microscope; **au ~** under *ou* through the microscope

microscopique [mikʀoskopik] *adj* microscopic

microsillon [mikʀosijɔ̃] *nm* long-playing record

MIDEM [midɛm] *sigle m* (= *Marché international du disque et de l'édition musicale*) music industry trade fair
midi [midi] *nm* (*milieu du jour*) midday, noon; (*moment du déjeuner*) lunchtime; (*sud*) south; (*: de la France*): **le M~** the South (of France), the Midi; **à ~** at 12 (o'clock) *ou* midday *ou* noon; **tous les ~s** every lunchtime; **le repas de ~** lunch; **en plein ~** (right) in the middle of the day; (*sud*) facing south
midinette [midinɛt] *nf* silly young townie
mie [mi] *nf* inside (of the loaf)
miel [mjɛl] *nm* honey; **être tout ~** (*fig*) to be all sweetness and light
mielleux, -euse [mjɛlø, -øz] *adj* (*péj*) sugary, honeyed
mien, ne [mjɛ̃, mjɛn] *adj, pron*: **le (la) ~(ne), les ~s** mine; **les ~s** (*ma famille*) my family
miette [mjɛt] *nf* (*de pain, gâteau*) crumb; (*fig: de la conversation etc*) scrap; **en ~s** (*fig*) in pieces *ou* bits

 MOT-CLÉ

mieux [mjø] *adv* **1** (*d'une meilleure façon*): **mieux (que)** better (than); **elle travaille/mange mieux** she works/eats better; **aimer mieux** to prefer; **j'attendais mieux de vous** I expected better of you; **elle va mieux** she is better; **de mieux en mieux** better and better
2 (*de la meilleure façon*) best; **ce que je sais le mieux** what I know best; **les livres les mieux faits** the best made books
3 (*intensif*): **vous feriez mieux de faire ...** you would be better to do ...; **crier à qui mieux mieux** to try to shout each other down
▷ *adj* **1** (*plus à l'aise, en meilleure forme*) better; **se sentir mieux** to feel better
2 (*plus satisfaisant*) better; **c'est mieux ainsi** it's better like this; **c'est le mieux des deux** it's the better of the two; **le/la mieux, les mieux** the best; **demandez-lui, c'est le mieux** ask him, it's the best thing
3 (*plus joli*) better-looking; (*plus gentil*) nicer; **il est mieux que son frère** (*plus beau*) he's better-looking than his brother; (*plus gentil*) he's nicer than his brother; **il est mieux sans moustache** he looks better without a moustache
4: **au mieux** at best; **au mieux avec** on the best of terms with; **pour le mieux** for the best; **qui mieux est** even better, better still
▷ *nm* **1** (*progrès*) improvement
2: **de mon/ton mieux** as best I/you can (*ou* could); **faire de son mieux** to do one's best; **du mieux qu'il peut** the best he can; **faute de mieux** for lack *ou* want of anything better, failing anything better

mieux-être [mjøzɛtʀ(ə)] *nm* greater well-being; (*financier*) improved standard of living
mièvre [mjɛvʀ(ə)] *adj* sickly sentimental
mignon, ne [miɲɔ̃, -ɔn] *adj* sweet, cute
migraine [migʀɛn] *nf* headache; migraine

migrant, e [migʀɑ̃, -ɑ̃t] *adj, nm/f* migrant
migrateur, -trice [migʀatœʀ, -tʀis] *adj* migratory
migration [migʀasjɔ̃] *nf* migration
mijaurée [miʒɔʀe] *nf* pretentious (young) madam
mijoter [miʒɔte] *vt* to simmer; (*préparer avec soin*) to cook lovingly; (*affaire, projet*) to plot, cook up ▷ *vi* to simmer
mil [mil] *num* = **mille**
Milan [milɑ̃] *n* Milan
milanais, e [milanɛ, -ɛz] *adj* Milanese
mildiou [mildju] *nm* mildew
milice [milis] *nf* militia
milicien, ne [milisjɛ̃, -ɛn] *nm/f* militiaman(-woman)
milieu, x [miljø] *nm* (*centre*) middle; (*fig*) middle course *ou* way; (*aussi*: **juste milieu**) happy medium; (*Bio, Géo*) environment; (*entourage social*) milieu; (*familial*) background; circle; (*pègre*): **le ~** the underworld; **au ~ de** in the middle of; **au beau** *ou* **en plein ~ (de)** right in the middle (of); **~ de terrain** (*Football: joueur*) midfield player; (*: joueurs*) midfield
militaire [militɛʀ] *adj* military ▷ *nm* serviceman; **service ~** military service
militant, e [militɑ̃, -ɑ̃t] *adj, nm/f* militant
militantisme [militɑ̃tism(ə)] *nm* militancy
militariser [militaʀize] *vt* to militarize
militarisme [militaʀism(ə)] *nm* (*péj*) militarism
militer [milite] *vi* to be a militant; **~ pour/contre** to militate in favour of/against
milk-shake [milkʃɛk] *nm* milk shake
mille [mil] *num* a *ou* one thousand ▷ *nm* (*mesure*): **~ (marin)** nautical mile; **mettre dans le ~** to hit the bull's-eye; (*fig*) to be bang on (target)
millefeuille [milfœj] *nm* cream *ou* vanilla slice
millénaire [milenɛʀ] *nm* millennium ▷ *adj* thousand-year-old; (*fig*) ancient
mille-pattes [milpat] *nm inv* centipede
millésime [milezim] *nm* year
millésimé, e [milezime] *adj* vintage *cpd*
millet [mijɛ] *nm* millet
milliard [miljaʀ] *nm* milliard, thousand million (*Brit*), billion (*US*)
milliardaire [miljaʀdɛʀ] *nm/f* multimillionaire (*Brit*), billionaire (*US*)
millième [miljɛm] *num* thousandth
millier [milje] *nm* thousand; **un ~ (de)** a thousand or so, about a thousand; **par ~s** in (their) thousands, by the thousand
milligramme [miligʀam] *nm* milligramme (*Brit*), milligram (*US*)
millimétré, e [milimetʀe] *adj*: **papier ~** graph paper
millimètre [milimɛtʀ(ə)] *nm* millimetre (*Brit*), millimeter (*US*)
million [miljɔ̃] *nm* million; **deux ~s de** two million; **riche à ~s** worth millions
millionième [miljɔnjɛm] *num* millionth
millionnaire [miljɔnɛʀ] *nm/f* millionaire
mi-lourd [miluʀ] *adj m, nm* light heavyweight

mime [mim] *nm/f* (*acteur*) mime(r); (*imitateur*) mimic ⊳ *nm* (*art*) mime, miming

mimer [mime] *vt* to mime; (*singer*) to mimic, take off

mimétisme [mimetism(ə)] *nm* (*Bio*) mimicry

mimique [mimik] *nf* (*funny*) face; (*signes*) gesticulations *pl*, sign language *no pl*

mimosa [mimoza] *nm* mimosa

mi-moyen [mimwajɛ̃] *adj m, nm* welterweight

MIN *sigle m* (= *Marché d'intérêt national*) *wholesale market for fruit, vegetables and agricultural produce*

min. *abr* (= *minimum*) min

minable [minabl(ə)] *adj* (*personne*) shabby (-looking); (*travail*) pathetic

minaret [minaʀɛ] *nm* minaret

minauder [minode] *vi* to mince, simper

minauderies [minodʀi] *nfpl* simpering *sg*

mince [mɛ̃s] *adj* thin; (*personne, taille*) slim; (*fig: profit, connaissances*) slight, small; (: *prétexte*) weak ⊳ *excl*: ~ **(alors)!** darn it!

minceur [mɛ̃sœʀ] *nf* thinness slimness, slenderness

mincir [mɛ̃siʀ] *vi* to get slimmer *ou* thinner

mine [min] *nf* (*physionomie*) expression, look; (*extérieur*) exterior, appearance; (*de crayon*) lead; (*gisement, exploitation, explosif*) mine; **mines** *nfpl* (*péj*) simpering airs; **les M~s** (*Admin*) *the national mining and geological service, the government vehicle testing department*; **avoir bonne ~** (*personne*) to look well; (*ironique*) to look an utter idiot; **avoir mauvaise ~** to look unwell; **faire ~ de faire** to make a pretence of doing; **ne pas payer de ~** to be not much to look at; **~ de rien** *adv* with a casual air; although you wouldn't think so; **~ de charbon** coal mine; **~ à ciel ouvert** opencast (*Brit*) *ou* open-air (*US*) mine

miner [mine] *vt* (*saper*) to undermine, erode; (*Mil*) to mine

minerai [minʀɛ] *nm* ore

minéral, e, -aux [mineʀal, -o] *adj* mineral; (*Chimie*) inorganic ⊳ *nm* mineral

minéralier [mineʀalje] *nm* (*bateau*) ore tanker

minéralisé, e [mineʀalize] *adj* mineralized

minéralogie [mineʀalɔʒi] *nf* mineralogy

minéralogique [mineʀalɔʒik] *adj* mineralogical; **plaque ~** number (*Brit*) *ou* license (*US*) plate; **numéro ~** registration (*Brit*) *ou* license (*US*) number

minet, te [minɛ, -ɛt] *nm/f* (*chat*) pussy-cat; (*péj*) young trendy

mineur, e [minœʀ] *adj* minor ⊳ *nm/f* (*Jur*) minor ⊳ *nm* (*travailleur*) miner; (*Mil*) sapper; **~ de fond** face worker

miniature [minjatyʀ] *adj, nf* miniature

miniaturisation [minjatyʀizɑsjɔ̃] *nf* miniaturization

miniaturiser [minjatyʀize] *vt* to miniaturize

minibus [minibys] *nm* minibus

mini-cassette [minikasɛt] *nf* cassette (recorder)

minichaîne [miniʃɛn] *nf* mini system

minier, -ière [minje, -jɛʀ] *adj* mining

mini-jupe [miniʒyp] *nf* mini-skirt

minimal, e, -aux [minimal, -o] *adj* minimum

minimaliste [minimalist(ə)] *adj* (*Art*) minimalist

minime [minim] *adj* minor, minimal ⊳ *nm/f* (*Sport*) junior

minimessage [minimesaʒ] *nm* text message

minimiser [minimize] *vt* to minimize; (*fig*) to play down

minimum [minimɔm] *adj, nm* minimum; **au ~** at the very least; **~ vital** (*salaire*) living wage; (*niveau de vie*) subsistence level

mini-ordinateur [miniɔʀdinatœʀ] *nm* minicomputer

ministère [ministɛʀ] *nm* (*cabinet*) government; (*département*) ministry (*Brit*), department; (*Rel*) ministry; **~ public** (*Jur*) Prosecution, State Prosecutor

ministériel, le [ministeʀjɛl] *adj* government *cpd*; ministerial, departmental; (*partisan*) pro-government

ministrable [ministʀabl(ə)] *adj* (*Pol*): **il est ~** he's a potential minister

ministre [ministʀ(ə)] *nm* minister (*Brit*), secretary; (*Rel*) minister; **~ d'État** senior minister *ou* secretary

Minitel® [minitɛl] *nm* *videotext terminal and service*

minium [minjɔm] *nm* red lead paint

minois [minwa] *nm* little face

minorer [minɔʀe] *vt* to cut, reduce

minoritaire [minɔʀitɛʀ] *adj* minority *cpd*

minorité [minɔʀite] *nf* minority; **être en ~** to be in the *ou* a minority; **mettre en ~** (*Pol*) to defeat

Minorque [minɔʀk] *nf* Minorca

minorquin, e [minɔʀkɛ̃, -in] *adj* Minorcan

minoterie [minɔtʀi] *nf* flour-mill

minuit [minɥi] *nm* midnight

minuscule [minyskyl] *adj* minute, tiny ⊳ *nf*: **(lettre) ~** small letter

minutage [minytaʒ] *nm* timing

minute [minyt] *nf* minute; (*Jur: original*) minute, draft ⊳ *excl* just a minute!, hang on!; **à la ~** (*présent*) (just) this instant; (*passé*) there and then; **entrecôte** *ou* **steak ~** minute steak

minuter [minyte] *vt* to time

minuterie [minytʀi] *nf* time switch

minuteur [minytœʀ] *nm* timer

minutie [minysi] *nf* meticulousness; minute detail; **avec ~** meticulously; in minute detail

minutieusement [minysjøzmɑ̃] *adv* (*organiser, travailler*) meticulously; (*examiner*) minutely

minutieux, -euse [minysjø, -øz] *adj* (*personne*) meticulous; (*inspection*) minutely detailed; (*travail*) requiring painstaking attention to detail

mioche [mjɔʃ] *nm* (*fam*) nipper, brat

mirabelle [miʀabɛl] *nf* (*fruit*) (cherry) plum; (*eau-de-vie*) plum brandy

miracle [miʀakl(ə)] *nm* miracle

miraculé, e [miʀakyle] *adj* who has been miraculously cured (*ou* rescued)

miraculeux, -euse [miʀakylø, -øz] *adj*
miraculous
mirador [miʀadɔʀ] *nm* (*Mil*) watchtower
mirage [miʀaʒ] *nm* mirage
mire [miʀ] *nf* (*d'un fusil*) sight; (*TV*) test card;
point de ~ target; (*fig*) focal point; **ligne de ~**
line of sight
mirent [miʀ] *vb voir* **mettre**
mirer [miʀe] *vt* (*œufs*) to candle; **se mirer** *vi*: **se ~**
dans (*personne*) to gaze at one's reflection in;
(: *chose*) to be mirrored in
mirifique [miʀifik] *adj* wonderful
mirobolant, e [miʀɔbɔlɑ̃, -ɑ̃t] *adj* fantastic
miroir [miʀwaʀ] *nm* mirror
miroiter [miʀwate] *vi* to sparkle, shimmer;
faire ~ qch à qn to paint sth in glowing colours
for sb, dangle sth in front of sb's eyes
miroiterie [miʀwatʀi] *nf* (*usine*) mirror factory;
(*magasin*) mirror dealer's (shop)
Mis *abr* = **marquis**
mis, e [mi, miz] *pp de* **mettre** ▷ *adj* (*couvert, table*)
set, laid; (*personne*): **bien ~** well dressed ▷ *nf*
(*argent: au jeu*) stake; (*tenue*) clothing; attire;
être de ~e to be acceptable *ou* in season; **~e en**
bouteilles bottling; **~e à examen** charging,
indictment; **~e à feu** blast-off; **~e de fonds**
capital outlay; **~e à jour** (*Inform*) update; **~e à**
mort kill; **~e à pied** (*d'un employé*) suspension;
lay-off; **~e sur pied** (*d'une affaire, entreprise*)
setting up; **~e en plis** set; **~e au point** (*Photo*)
focusing; (*fig*) clarification; **~e à prix** reserve
(*Brit*) *ou* upset price; **~e en scène** production
misaine [mizɛn] *nf*: **mât de ~** foremast
misanthrope [mizɑ̃tʀɔp] *nm/f* misanthropist
Mise *abr* = **marquise**
mise [miz] *adj f, nf voir* **mis**
miser [mize] *vt* (*enjeu*) to stake, bet; **~ sur** *vt*
(*cheval, numéro*) to bet on; (*fig*) to bank *ou* count
on
misérable [mizeʀabl(ə)] *adj* (*lamentable,*
malheureux) pitiful, wretched; (*pauvre*) poverty-
stricken; (*insignifiant, mesquin*) miserable ▷ *nm/f*
wretch; (*miséreux*) poor wretch
misère [mizɛʀ] *nf* (*pauvreté*) (extreme) poverty,
destitution; **misères** *nfpl* (*malheurs*) woes,
miseries; (*ennuis*) little troubles; **être dans la ~**
to be destitute *ou* poverty-stricken; **salaire de ~**
starvation wage; **faire des ~s à qn** to torment
sb; **~ noire** utter destitution, abject poverty
miséreux, -euse [mizeʀø, -øz] *adj* poverty-
stricken ▷ *nm/f* down-and-out
miséricorde [mizeʀikɔʀd(ə)] *nf* mercy,
forgiveness
miséricordieux, -euse [mizeʀikɔʀdjø, -øz] *adj*
merciful, forgiving
misogyne [mizɔʒin] *adj* misogynous ▷ *nm/f*
misogynist
missel [misɛl] *nm* missal
missile [misil] *nm* missile
mission [misjɔ̃] *nf* mission; **partir en ~** (*Admin,*
Pol) to go on an assignment
missionnaire [misjɔnɛʀ] *nm/f* missionary

missive [misiv] *nf* missive
mistral [mistʀal] *nm* mistral (wind)
mit [mi] *vb voir* **mettre**
mitaine [mitɛn] *nf* mitt(en)
mite [mit] *nf* clothes moth
mité, e [mite] *adj* moth-eaten
mi-temps [mitɑ̃] *nf inv* (*Sport: période*) half;
(: *pause*) half-time; **à ~** *adj, adv* part-time
miteux, -euse [mitø, -øz] *adj* seedy, shabby
mitigé, e [mitiʒe] *adj* (*conviction, ardeur*)
lukewarm; (*sentiments*) mixed
mitonner [mitɔne] *vt* (*préparer*) to cook with
loving care; (*fig*) to cook up quietly
mitoyen, ne [mitwajɛ̃, -ɛn] *adj* common, party
cpd; **maisons ~nes** semi-detached houses; (*plus*
de deux) terraced (*Brit*) *ou* row (*US*) houses
mitraille [mitʀaj] *nf* (*balles de fonte*) grapeshot;
(*décharge d'obus*) shellfire
mitrailler [mitʀaje] *vt* to machine-gun; (*fig:*
photographier) to snap away at; **~ qn de** to pelt *ou*
bombard sb with
mitraillette [mitʀajɛt] *nf* submachine gun
mitrailleur [mitʀajœʀ] *nm* machine gunner
▷ *adj m*: **fusil ~** machine gun
mitrailleuse [mitʀajøz] *nf* machine gun
mitre [mitʀ(ə)] *nf* mitre
mitron [mitʀɔ̃] *nm* baker's boy
mi-voix [mivwa]: **à ~** *adv* in a low *ou* hushed
voice
mixage [miksaʒ] *nm* (*Ciné*) (sound) mixing
mixer, mixeur [miksœʀ] *nm* (*Culin*) (food)
mixer
mixité [miksite] *nf* (*Scol*) coeducation
mixte [mikst(ə)] *adj* (*gén*) mixed; (*Scol*) mixed,
coeducational; **à usage ~** dual-purpose;
cuisinière ~ combined gas and electric cooker;
équipe ~ combined team
mixture [mikstyʀ] *nf* mixture; (*fig*) concoction
MJC *sigle f* (= *maison des jeunes et de la culture*)
community arts centre and youth club
ml *abr* (= *millilitre*) ml
MLF *sigle m* (= *Mouvement de libération de la femme*)
Women's Movement
Mlle (*pl* **-s**) *abr* = **Mademoiselle**
MM *abr* = **Messieurs**; *voir* **Monsieur**
Mme (*pl* **-s**) *abr* = **Madame**
MMS *sigle m* (= *Multimedia messaging service*) MMS
mn. *abr* (= *minute*) min
mnémotechnique [mnemɔtɛknik] *adj*
mnemonic
MNS *sigle m* (= *maître nageur sauveteur*) ≈ lifeguard
MO *sigle f* (= *main-d'œuvre*) labour costs (on invoices)
Mo *abr* = **méga-octet; métro**
mobile [mɔbil] *adj* mobile; (*amovible*) loose,
removable; (*pièce de machine*) moving; (*élément de*
meuble etc) movable ▷ *nm* (*motif*) motive; (*œuvre*
d'art) mobile; (*Physique*) moving object *ou* body;
(téléphone) ~ mobile (phone) (*Brit*), cell
(phone) (*US*)
mobilier, -ière [mɔbilje, -jɛʀ] *adj* (*Jur*) personal
▷ *nm* (*meubles*) furniture; **valeurs mobilières**
transferable securities; **vente mobilière** sale

of personal property *ou* chattels

mobilisation [mɔbilizasjɔ̃] *nf* mobilization

mobiliser [mɔbilize] *vt* (*Mil, gén*) to mobilize

mobilité [mɔbilite] *nf* mobility

mobylette® [mɔbilɛt] *nf* moped

mocassin [mɔkasɛ̃] *nm* moccasin

moche [mɔʃ] *adj* (*fam: laid*) ugly; (: *mauvais, méprisable*) rotten

modalité [mɔdalite] *nf* form, mode; **modalités** *nfpl* (*d'un accord etc*) clauses, terms; **~s de paiement** methods of payment

mode [mɔd] *nf* fashion; (*commerce*) fashion trade *ou* industry ▷ *nm* (*manière*) form, mode, method; (*Ling*) mood; (*Inform, Mus*) mode; **travailler dans la ~** to be in the fashion business; **à la ~** fashionable, in fashion; **~ dialogué** (*Inform*) interactive *ou* conversational mode; **~ d'emploi** directions *pl* (for use); **~ de vie** way of life

modelage [mɔdlaʒ] *nm* modelling

modelé [mɔdle] *nm* (*Géo*) relief; (*du corps etc*) contours *pl*

modèle [mɔdɛl] *adj* model ▷ *nm* model; (*qui pose: de peintre*) sitter; (*type*) type; (*gabarit, patron*) pattern; **~ courant** *ou* **de série** (*Comm*) production model; **~ déposé** registered design; **~ réduit** small-scale model

modeler [mɔdle] *vt* (*Art*) to model, mould; (*vêtement, érosion*) to mould, shape; **~ qch sur/ d'après** to model sth on

modélisation [mɔdelizasjɔ̃] *nf* (*Math*) modelling

modéliste [mɔdelist(ə)] *nm/f* (*Couture*) designer; (*de modèles réduits*) model maker

modem [mɔdɛm] *nm* (*Inform*) modem

modérateur, -trice [mɔdeʀatœʀ, -tʀis] *adj* moderating ▷ *nm/f* moderator

modération [mɔdeʀasjɔ̃] *nf* moderation; **~ de peine** reduction of sentence

modéré, e [mɔdeʀe] *adj, nm/f* moderate

modérément [mɔdeʀemɑ̃] *adv* moderately, in moderation

modérer [mɔdeʀe] *vt* to moderate; **se modérer** *vi* to restrain o.s

moderne [mɔdɛʀn(ə)] *adj* modern ▷ *nm* (*Art*) modern style; (*ameublement*) modern furniture

modernisation [mɔdɛʀnizasjɔ̃] *nf* modernization

moderniser [mɔdɛʀnize] *vt* to modernize

modernisme [mɔdɛʀnism(ə)] *nm* modernism

modernité [mɔdɛʀnite] *nf* modernity

modeste [mɔdɛst(ə)] *adj* modest; (*origine*) humble, lowly

modestement [mɔdɛstəmɑ̃] *adv* modestly

modestie [mɔdɛsti] *nf* modesty; **fausse ~** false modesty

modicité [mɔdisite] *nf*: **la ~ des prix** *etc* the low prices *etc*

modificatif, -ive [mɔdifikatif, -iv] *adj* modifying

modification [mɔdifikasjɔ̃] *nf* modification

modifier [mɔdifje] *vt* to modify, alter; (*Ling*) to

modify; **se modifier** *vi* to alter

modique [mɔdik] *adj* (*salaire, somme*) modest

modiste [mɔdist(ə)] *nf* milliner

modulaire [mɔdylɛʀ] *adj* modular

modulation [mɔdylasjɔ̃] *nf* modulation; **~ de fréquence (FM** *ou* **MF)** frequency modulation (FM)

module [mɔdyl] *nm* module

moduler [mɔdyle] *vt* to modulate; (*air*) to warble

moelle [mwal] *nf* marrow; (*fig*) pith, core; **~ épinière** spinal chord

moelleux, -euse [mwalø, -øz] *adj* soft; (*au goût, à l'ouïe*) mellow; (*gracieux, souple*) smooth

moellon [mwalɔ̃] *nm* rubble stone

mœurs [mœʀ] *nfpl* (*conduite*) morals; (*manières*) manners; (*pratiques sociales*) habits; (*mode de vie*) life style *sg*; (*d'une espèce animale*) behaviour *sg* (*Brit*), behavior *sg* (*US*); **femme de mauvaises ~** loose woman; **passer dans les ~** to become the custom; **contraire aux bonnes ~** contrary to proprieties

mohair [mɔɛʀ] *nm* mohair

moi [mwa] *pron* me; (*emphatique*): **~, je ...** for my part, I ..., I myself ... ▷ *nm inv* (*Psych*) ego, self; **à ~!** (*à l'aide*) help (me)!

moignon [mwaɲɔ̃] *nm* stump

moi-même [mwamɛm] *pron* myself; (*emphatique*) I myself

moindre [mwɛ̃dʀ(ə)] *adj* lesser; lower; **le (la) ~, les ~s** the least; the slightest; **le (la) ~ de** the least of; **c'est la ~ des choses** it's nothing at all

moindrement [mwɛ̃dʀəmɑ̃] *adv*: **pas le ~** not in the least

moine [mwan] *nm* monk, friar

moineau, x [mwano] *nm* sparrow

 MOT-CLÉ

moins [mwɛ̃] *adv* **1** (*comparatif*): **moins (que)** less (than); **moins grand que** less tall than, not as tall as; **il a trois ans de moins que moi** he's three years younger than me; **il est moins intelligent que moi** he's not as clever as me, he's less clever than me; **moins je travaille, mieux je me porte** the less I work, the better I feel

2 (*superlatif*): **le moins** (the) least; **c'est ce que j'aime le moins** it's what I like (the) least; **le(la) moins doué(e)** the least gifted; **au moins, du moins** at least; **pour le moins** at the very least

3: **moins de** (*quantité*) less (than); (*nombre*) fewer (than); **moins de sable/d'eau** less sand/water; **moins de livres/gens** fewer books/people; **moins de deux ans** less than two years; **moins de midi** not yet midday

4: **de moins, en moins: 100 euros/3 jours de moins** 100 euros/3 days less; **trois livres en moins** three books fewer; three books too few; **de l'argent en moins** less money; **le soleil en moins** but for the sun, minus the sun; **de**

moins en moins less and less; **en moins de deux** in a flash *ou* a trice
5: **à moins de, à moins que** unless; **à moins de faire** unless we do (*ou* he does *etc*); **à moins que tu ne fasses** unless you do; **à moins d'un accident** barring any accident
▷ *prép*: **quatre moins deux** four minus two; **dix heures moins cinq** five to ten; **il fait moins cinq** it's five (degrees) below (freezing), it's minus five; **il est moins cinq** it's five to
▷ *nm* (*signe*) minus sign

moins-value [mwɛ̃valy] *nf* (Écon, Comm) depreciation
moire [mwaʀ] *nf* moiré
moiré, e [mwaʀe] *adj* (*tissu, papier*) moiré, watered; (*reflets*) shimmering
mois [mwa] *nm* month; (*salaire, somme dû*) (monthly) pay *ou* salary; **treizième ~, double ~** extra month's salary
moïse [mɔiz] *nm* Moses basket
moisi, e [mwazi] *adj* mouldy (Brit), moldy (US), mildewed ▷ *nm* mould, mold, mildew; **odeur de ~** musty smell
moisir [mwaziʀ] *vi* to go mouldy (Brit) *ou* moldy (US); (*fig*) to rot; (*personne*) to hang about ▷ *vt* to make mouldy *ou* moldy
moisissure [mwazisyʀ] *nf* mould *no pl* (Brit), mold *no pl* (US)
moisson [mwasɔ̃] *nf* harvest; (*époque*) harvest (time); (*fig*): **faire une ~ de** to gather a wealth of
moissonner [mwasɔne] *vt* to harvest, reap; (*fig*) to collect
moissonneur, -euse [mwasɔnœʀ, -øz] *nm/f* harvester, reaper ▷ *nf* (*machine*) harvester
moissonneuse-batteuse [mwasɔnøzbatøz] (*pl* **moissonneuses-batteuses**) *nf* combine harvester
moite [mwat] *adj* (*peau, mains*) sweaty, sticky; (*atmosphère*) muggy
moitié [mwatje] *nf* half; (*épouse*): **sa ~** his better half; **la ~** half; **la ~ de** half (of), half the amount (*ou* number) of; **la ~ du temps/des gens** half the time/the people; **à la ~ de** halfway through; **~ moins grand** half as tall; **~ plus long** half as long again, longer by half; **à ~** half (*avant le verbe*), half- (*avant l'adjectif*); **à ~ prix** (at) half price, half-price; **de ~** by half; **~ ~** half-and-half
moka [mɔka] *nm* (*café*) mocha coffee; (*gâteau*) mocha cake
mol [mɔl] *adj m voir* **mou**
molaire [mɔlɛʀ] *nf* molar
moldave [mɔldav] *adj* Moldavian
Moldavie [mɔldavi] *nf*: **la ~** Moldavia
môle [mol] *nm* jetty
moléculaire [mɔlekylɛʀ] *adj* molecular
molécule [mɔlekyl] *nf* molecule
moleskine [mɔlɛskin] *nf* imitation leather
molester [mɔlɛste] *vt* to manhandle, maul (about)
molette [mɔlɛt] *nf* toothed *ou* cutting wheel

mollasse [mɔlas] *adj* (*péj: sans énergie*) sluggish; (: *flasque*) flabby
molle [mɔl] *adj f voir* **mou**
mollement [mɔlmɑ̃] *adv* softly; (*péj*) sluggishly; (*protester*) feebly
mollesse [mɔlɛs] *nf* (*voir mou*) softness; flabbiness; limpness; sluggishness; feebleness
mollet [mɔlɛ] *nm* calf ▷ *adj m*: **œuf ~** soft-boiled egg
molletière [mɔltjɛʀ] *adj f*: **bande ~** puttee
molleton [mɔltɔ̃] *nm* (Textiles) felt
molletonné, e [mɔltɔne] *adj* (*gants etc*) fleece-lined
mollir [mɔliʀ] *vi* (*jambes*) to give way; (Navig: *vent*) to drop, die down; (*fig: personne*) to relent; (: *courage*) to fail, flag
mollusque [mɔlysk(ə)] *nm* (Zool) mollusc; (*fig: personne*) lazy lump
molosse [mɔlɔs] *nm* big ferocious dog
môme [mom] *nm/f* (*fam: enfant*) brat; (: *fille*) bird (Brit), chick
moment [mɔmɑ̃] *nm* moment; (*occasion*): **profiter du ~** to take (advantage of) the opportunity; **ce n'est pas le ~** this is not the right time; **à un certain ~** at some point; **à un ~ donné** at a certain point; **à quel ~?** when exactly?; **au même ~** at the same time; (*instant*) at the same moment; **pour un bon ~** for a good while; **pour le ~** for the moment, for the time being; **au ~ de** at the time of; **au ~ où** as; at a time when; **à tout ~** at any time *ou* moment; (*continuellement*) constantly, continually; **en ce ~** at the moment; (*aujourd'hui*) at present; **sur le ~** at the time; **par ~s** now and then, at times; **d'un ~ à l'autre** any time (now); **du ~ où** *ou* **que** seeing that, since; **n'avoir pas un ~ à soi** not to have a minute to oneself
momentané, e [mɔmɑ̃tane] *adj* temporary, momentary
momentanément [mɔmɑ̃tanemɑ̃] *adv* for a moment, for a while
momie [mɔmi] *nf* mummy
mon [mɔ̃], **ma** [ma] (*pl* **mes** [me]) *adj poss* my
monacal, e, -aux [mɔnakal, -o] *adj* monastic
Monaco [mɔnako] *nm*: **le ~** Monaco
monarchie [mɔnaʀʃi] *nf* monarchy
monarchiste [mɔnaʀʃist(ə)] *adj, nm/f* monarchist
monarque [mɔnaʀk(ə)] *nm* monarch
monastère [mɔnastɛʀ] *nm* monastery
monastique [mɔnastik] *adj* monastic
monceau, x [mɔ̃so] *nm* heap
mondain, e [mɔ̃dɛ̃, -ɛn] *adj* (*soirée, vie*) society *cpd*; (*obligations*) social; (*peintre, écrivain*) fashionable; (*personne*) society *cpd* ▷ *nm/f* society man/woman, socialite ▷ *nf*: **la Mondaine, la police ~** ≈ the vice squad
mondanités [mɔ̃danite] *nfpl* (*vie mondaine*) society life *sg*; (*paroles*) (society) small talk *sg*; (*Presse*) (society) gossip column *sg*
monde [mɔ̃d] *nm* world; (*personnes mondaines*): **le ~** (high) society; (*milieu*): **être du même ~** to

move in the same circles; (*gens*): **il y a du ~**
(*beaucoup de gens*) there are a lot of people;
(*quelques personnes*) there are some people; **y a-t-
il du ~ dans le salon?** is there anybody in the
lounge?; **beaucoup/peu de ~** many/few people;
le meilleur *etc* **du ~** the best *etc* in the world;
mettre au ~ to bring into the world; **pas le
moins du ~** not in the least; **se faire un ~ de
qch** to make a great deal of fuss about sth; **tour
du ~** round-the-world trip; **homme/femme
du ~** society man/woman

mondial, e, -aux [mɔ̃djal, -o] *adj* (*population*)
world *cpd*; (*influence*) world-wide

mondialement [mɔ̃djalmɑ̃] *adv* throughout
the world

mondialisation [mɔ̃djalizɑsjɔ̃] *nf* (*d'une
technique*) global application; (*d'un conflit*) global
spread

mondovision [mɔ̃dovizjɔ̃] *nf* (world coverage
by) satellite television

monégasque [mɔnegask(ə)] *adj* Monegasque,
of *ou* from Monaco ▷ *nm/f*: **Monégasque**
Monegasque

monétaire [mɔnetɛR] *adj* monetary

monétarisme [mɔnetaRism(ə)] *nm*
monetarism

monétique [mɔnetik] *nf* electronic money

mongol, e [mɔ̃gɔl] *adj* Mongol, Mongolian ▷ *nm*
(*Ling*) Mongolian ▷ *nm/f*: **Mongol, e** (*Méd*)
Mongol, Mongoloid; (*de la Mongolie*) Mongolian

Mongolie [mɔ̃gɔli] *nf*: **la ~** Mongolia

mongolien, ne [mɔ̃gɔljɛ̃, -ɛn] *adj, nm/f* mongol

mongolisme [mɔ̃gɔlism(ə)] *nm* mongolism,
Down's syndrome

moniteur, -trice [mɔnitœR, -tRis] *nm/f* (*Sport*)
instructor (instructress); (*de colonie de vacances*)
supervisor ▷ *nm* (*écran*) monitor; **~ cardiaque**
cardiac monitor; **~ d'auto-école** driving
instructor

monitorage [mɔnitoRaʒ] *nm* monitoring

monitorat [mɔnitoRa] *nm* (*formation*)
instructor's training (course); (*fonction*)
instructorship

monnaie [mɔnɛ] *nf* (*pièce*) coin; (*Écon: gén: moyen
d'échange*) currency; (*petites pièces*): **avoir de la ~**
to have (some) change; **faire de la ~** to get
(some) change; **avoir/faire la ~ de 20 euros** to
have change of/get change for 20 euros; **faire
ou donner à qn la ~ de 20 euros** to give sb
change for 20 euros, change 20 euros for sb;
rendre à qn la ~ (sur 20 euros) to give sb the
change (from *ou* out of 20 euros); **servir de ~
d'échange** (*fig*) to be used as a bargaining
counter *ou* as bargaining counters; **payer en ~
de singe** to fob (sb) off with empty promises;
c'est ~ courante it's a common occurrence; **~
légale** legal tender

monnayable [mɔnɛjabl(ə)] *adj* (*vendable*)
convertible into cash; **mes services sont ~s**
my services are worth money

monnayer [mɔneje] *vt* to convert into cash;
(*talent*) to capitalize on

monnayeur [mɔnɛjœR] *nm voir* **faux**

mono [mɔno] *nf* (*monophonie*) mono ▷ *nm*
(*monoski*) monoski

monochrome [mɔnɔkRom] *adj* monochrome

monocle [mɔnɔkl(ə)] *nm* monocle, eyeglass

monocoque [mɔnɔkɔk] *adj* (*voiture*) monocoque
▷ *nm* (*voilier*) monohull

monocorde [mɔnɔkɔRd(ə)] *adj* monotonous

monoculture [mɔnɔkyltyR] *nf* single-crop
farming, monoculture

monogamie [mɔnɔgami] *nf* monogamy

monogramme [mɔnɔgRam] *nm* monogram

monokini [mɔnɔkini] *nm* one-piece bikini,
bikini pants *pl*

monolingue [mɔnɔlɛ̃g] *adj* monolingual

monolithique [mɔnɔlitik] *adj* (*lit, fig*)
monolithic

monologue [mɔnɔlɔg] *nm* monologue,
soliloquy; **~ intérieur** stream of consciousness

monologuer [mɔnɔlɔge] *vi* to soliloquize

monôme [mɔnom] *nm* (*Math*) monomial;
(*d'étudiants*) students' rag procession

monoparental, e, -aux [mɔnɔpaRɑ̃tal, -o] *adj*:
famille ~e single-parent *ou* one-parent family

monophasé, e [mɔnɔfaze] *adj* single-phase *cpd*

monophonie [mɔnɔfɔni] *nf* monophony

monoplace [mɔnɔplas] *adj, nm, nf* single-seater,
one-seater

monoplan [mɔnɔplɑ̃] *nm* monoplane

monopole [mɔnɔpɔl] *nm* monopoly

monopolisation [mɔnɔpolizɑsjɔ̃] *nf*
monopolization

monopoliser [mɔnɔpolize] *vt* to monopolize

monorail [mɔnɔRaj] *nm* monorail; monorail
train

monoski [mɔnɔski] *nm* monoski

monosyllabe [mɔnɔsilab] *nm* monosyllable,
word of one syllable

monosyllabique [mɔnɔsilabik] *adj*
monosyllabic

monotone [mɔnɔtɔn] *adj* monotonous

monotonie [mɔnɔtɔni] *nf* monotony

monseigneur [mɔ̃sɛɲœR] *nm* (*archevêque, évêque*)
Your (*ou* His) Grace; (*cardinal*) Your (*ou* His)
Eminence; **M~ Thomas** Bishop Thomas;
Cardinal Thomas

Monsieur [məsjø] (*pl* **Messieurs** [mesjø]) *nm*
(*titre*) Mr; (*homme quelconque*): **un/le monsieur**
a/the gentleman; *voir aussi* **Madame**

monstre [mɔ̃stR(ə)] *nm* monster ▷ *adj* (*fam: effet,
publicité*) massive; **un travail ~** a fantastic
amount of work; an enormous job; **~ sacré**
superstar

monstrueux, -euse [mɔ̃stRyø, -øz] *adj*
monstrous

monstruosité [mɔ̃stRyozite] *nf* monstrosity

mont [mɔ̃] *nm*: **par ~s et par vaux** up hill and
down dale; **le M~ Blanc** Mont Blanc; **~ de
Vénus** mons veneris

montage [mɔ̃taʒ] *nm* putting up; (*d'un bijou*)
mounting, setting; (*d'une machine etc*) assembly;
(*Photo*) photomontage; (*Ciné*) editing; **~ sonore**

sound editing

montagnard, e [mɔ̃taɲaʀ, -aʀd(ə)] *adj* mountain *cpd* ▷ *nm/f* mountain-dweller

montagne [mɔ̃taɲ] *nf* (*cime*) mountain; (*région*): **la ~** the mountains *pl*; **la haute ~** the high mountains; **les ~s Rocheuses** the Rocky Mountains, the Rockies; **~s russes** big dipper *sg*, switchback *sg*

montagneux, -euse [mɔ̃taɲø, -øz] *adj* mountainous; hilly

montant, e [mɔ̃tɑ̃, -ɑ̃t] *adj* (*mouvement, marée*) rising; (*chemin*) uphill; (*robe, corsage*) high-necked ▷ *nm* (*somme, total*) (sum) total, (total) amount; (*de fenêtre*) upright; (*de lit*) post

mont-de-piété [mɔ̃dpjete] (*pl* **monts-de-piété**) *nm* pawnshop

monte [mɔ̃t] *nf* (*accouplement*): **la ~** stud; (*d'un jockey*) seat

monté, e [mɔ̃te] *adj*: **être ~ contre qn** to be angry with sb; (*fourni, équipé*): **~ en** equipped with

monte-charge [mɔ̃tʃaʀʒ(ə)] *nm inv* goods lift, hoist

montée [mɔ̃te] *nf* rising, rise; (*escalade*) ascent, climb; (*chemin*) way up; **au milieu de la ~** halfway up; **le moteur chauffe dans les ~s** the engine overheats going uphill

Monténégro [mɔ̃tenegʀo] *nm*: **le ~** Montenegro

monte-plats [mɔ̃tpla] *nm inv* service lift

monter [mɔ̃te] *vt* (*escalier, côte*) to go (*ou* come) up; (*valise, paquet*) to take (*ou* bring) up; (*cheval*) to mount; (*femelle*) to cover, serve; (*tente, échafaudage*) to put up; (*machine*) to assemble; (*bijou*) to mount, set; (*Couture*) to sew on; (: *manche*) to set in; (*Ciné*) to edit; (*Théât*) to put on, stage; (*société, coup etc*) to set up; (*fournir, équiper*) to equip ▷ *vi* to go (*ou* come) up; (*avion, voiture*) to climb, go up; (*chemin, niveau, température, voix, prix*) to go up, rise; (*brouillard, bruit*) to rise, come up; (*passager*) to get on; (*à cheval*): **~ bien/mal** to ride well/badly; **~ à cheval/bicyclette** to get on *ou* mount a horse/bicycle; (*faire du cheval etc*) to ride (a horse), to (ride a) bicycle; **~ à pied/en voiture** to walk/drive up, go up on foot/by car; **~ dans le train/l'avion** to get into the train/plane, board the train/plane; **~ sur** to climb up onto; **~ sur** *ou* **à un arbre/une échelle** to climb (up) a tree/ladder; **~ à bord** to (get on) board; **~ à la tête de qn** to go to sb's head; **~ sur les planches** to go on the stage; **~ en grade** to be promoted; **se monter** (*s'équiper*) to equip o.s., get kitted out (*Brit*); **se ~ à** (*frais etc*) to add up to, come to; **~ qn contre qn** to set sb against sb; **~ la tête à qn** to give sb ideas

monteur, -euse [mɔ̃tœʀ, -øz] *nm/f* (*Tech*) fitter; (*Ciné*) (film) editor

montgolfière [mɔ̃ɡɔlfjɛʀ] *nf* hot-air balloon

monticule [mɔ̃tikyl] *nm* mound

montmartrois, e [mɔ̃maʀtʀwa, -waz] *adj* of *ou* from Montmartre

montre [mɔ̃tʀ(ə)] *nf* watch; (*ostentation*): **pour la ~** for show; **~ en main** exactly, to the minute; **faire ~ de** to show, display; **contre la ~** (*Sport*) against the clock; **~ de plongée** diver's watch

montréalais, e [mɔ̃ʀealɛ, -ɛz] *adj* of *ou* from Montreal ▷ *nm/f*: **Montréalais, e** Montrealer

montre-bracelet [mɔ̃tʀəbʀaslɛ] (*pl* **montres-bracelets**) *nf* wrist watch

montrer [mɔ̃tʀe] *vt* to show; **se montrer** to appear; **~ qch à qn** to show sb sth; **~ qch du doigt** to point to sth, point one's finger at sth; **se ~ intelligent** to prove (to be) intelligent

montreur, -euse [mɔ̃tʀœʀ, -øz] *nm/f*: **~ de marionnettes** puppeteer

monture [mɔ̃tyʀ] *nf* (*bête*) mount; (*d'une bague*) setting; (*de lunettes*) frame

monument [mɔnymɑ̃] *nm* monument; **~ aux morts** war memorial

monumental, e, -aux [mɔnymɑ̃tal, -o] *adj* monumental

moquer [mɔke]: **se ~ de** *vt* to make fun of, laugh at; (*fam: se désintéresser de*) not to care about; (*tromper*): **se ~ de qn** to take sb for a ride

moquerie [mɔkʀi] *nf* mockery *no pl*

moquette [mɔkɛt] *nf* fitted carpet, wall-to-wall carpeting *no pl*

moquetter [mɔkete] *vt* to carpet

moqueur, -euse [mɔkœʀ, -øz] *adj* mocking

moral, e, -aux [mɔʀal, -o] *adj* moral ▷ *nm* morale ▷ *nf* (*conduite*) morals *pl* (*règles*), moral code, ethic; (*valeurs*) moral standards *pl*, morality; (*science*) ethics *sg*, moral philosophy; (*conclusion: d'une fable etc*) moral; **au ~, sur le plan ~** morally; **avoir le ~ à zéro** to be really down; **faire la ~e à** to lecture, preach at

moralement [mɔʀalmɑ̃] *adv* morally

moralisateur, -trice [mɔʀalizatœʀ, -tʀis] *adj* moralizing, sanctimonious ▷ *nm/f* moralizer

moraliser [mɔʀalize] *vt* (*sermonner*) to lecture, preach at

moraliste [mɔʀalist(ə)] *nm/f* moralist ▷ *adj* moralistic

moralité [mɔʀalite] *nf* (*d'une action, attitude*) morality; (*conduite*) morals *pl*; (*conclusion, enseignement*) moral

moratoire [mɔʀatwaʀ] *adj m*: **intérêts ~s** (*Écon*) interest on arrears

morbide [mɔʀbid] *adj* morbid

morceau, x [mɔʀso] *nm* piece, bit; (*d'une œuvre*) passage, extract; (*Mus*) piece; (*Culin: de viande*) cut; **mettre en ~x** to pull to pieces *ou* bits

morceler [mɔʀsəle] *vt* to break up, divide up

morcellement [mɔʀsɛlmɑ̃] *nm* breaking up

mordant, e [mɔʀdɑ̃, -ɑ̃t] *adj* scathing, cutting; (*froid*) biting ▷ *nm* (*dynamisme, énergie*) spirit; (*fougue*) bite, punch

mordicus [mɔʀdikys] *adv* (*fam*) obstinately, stubbornly

mordiller [mɔʀdije] *vt* to nibble at, chew at

mordoré, e [mɔʀdɔʀe] *adj* lustrous bronze

mordre [mɔʀdʀ(ə)] *vt* to bite; (*lime, vis*) to bite into ▷ *vi* (*poisson*) to bite; **~ dans** to bite into; **~ sur** (*fig*) to go over into, overlap into; **~ à qch**

(*comprendre, aimer*) to take to; **~ à l'hameçon** to bite, rise to the bait

mordu, e [mɔʀdy] *pp de* **mordre** ▷ *adj* (*amoureux*) smitten ▷ *nm/f*: **un ~ du jazz/de la voile** a jazz/ sailing fanatic *ou* buff

morfondre [mɔʀfɔ̃dʀ(ə)]: **se morfondre** *vi* to mope

morgue [mɔʀg(ə)] *nf* (*arrogance*) haughtiness; (*lieu: de la police*) morgue; (: *à l'hôpital*) mortuary

moribond, e [mɔʀibɔ̃, -ɔ̃d] *adj* dying, moribund

morille [mɔʀij] *nf* morel (*mushroom*)

mormon, e [mɔʀmɔ̃, -ɔn] *adj, nm/f* Mormon

morne [mɔʀn(ə)] *adj* (*personne, visage*) glum, gloomy; (*temps, vie*) dismal, dreary

morose [mɔʀoz] *adj* sullen, morose; (*marché*) sluggish

morphine [mɔʀfin] *nf* morphine

morphinomane [mɔʀfinɔman] *nm/f* morphine addict

morphologie [mɔʀfɔlɔʒi] *nf* morphology

morphologique [mɔʀfɔlɔʒik] *adj* morphological

mors [mɔʀ] *nm* bit

morse [mɔʀs(ə)] *nm* (*Zool*) walrus; (*Tél*) Morse (code)

morsure [mɔʀsyʀ] *nf* bite

mort¹ [mɔʀ] *nf* death; **se donner la ~** to take one's own life; **de ~** (*silence, pâleur*) deathly; **blessé à ~** fatally wounded *ou* injured; **à la vie, à la ~** for better, for worse; **~ clinique** brain death; **~ subite du nourrisson, ~ au berceau** cot death

mort² [mɔʀ, mɔʀt(ə)] *pp de* **mourir** ▷ *adj* dead ▷ *nm/f* (*défunt*) dead man/woman; (*victime*): **il y a eu plusieurs ~s** several people were killed, there were several killed ▷ *nm* (*Cartes*) dummy; **~ ou vif** dead or alive; **~ de peur/fatigue** frightened to death/dead tired; **~s et blessés** casualties; **faire le ~** (*fig*) to play dead; to lie low

mortadelle [mɔʀtadɛl] *nf* mortadella

mortalité [mɔʀtalite] *nf* mortality, death rate

mort-aux-rats [mɔʀtoʀa] *nf inv* rat poison

mortel, le [mɔʀtɛl] *adj* (*poison etc*) deadly, lethal; (*accident, blessure*) fatal; (*Rel: danger, frayeur*) mortal; (*fig: froid*) deathly; (: *ennui, soirée*) deadly (boring) ▷ *nm/f* mortal

mortellement [mɔʀtɛlmɑ̃] *adv* (*blessé etc*) fatally, mortally; (*pâle etc*) deathly; (*fig: ennuyeux etc*) deadly

morte-saison [mɔʀtəsɛzɔ̃] (*pl* **mortes-saisons**) *nf* slack *ou* off season

mortier [mɔʀtje] *nm* (*gén*) mortar

mortifier [mɔʀtifje] *vt* to mortify

mort-né, e [mɔʀne] *adj* (*enfant*) stillborn; (*fig*) abortive

mortuaire [mɔʀtɥɛʀ] *adj* funeral *cpd*; **avis ~s** death announcements, intimations; **chapelle ~** mortuary chapel; **couronne ~** (funeral) wreath; **domicile ~** house of the deceased; **drap ~** pall

morue [mɔʀy] *nf* (*Zool*) cod *inv*; (*Culin: salée*) salt-cod

morvandeau, -elle, x [mɔʀvɑ̃do, -ɛl] *adj* of *ou* from the Morvan region

morveux, -euse [mɔʀvø, -øz] *adj* (*fam*) snotty-nosed

mosaïque [mɔzaik] *nf* (*Art*) mosaic; (*fig*) patchwork

Moscou [mɔsku] *n* Moscow

moscovite [mɔskɔvit] *adj* of *ou* from Moscow, Moscow *cpd* ▷ *nm/f*: **Moscovite** Muscovite

mosquée [mɔske] *nf* mosque

mot [mo] *nm* word; (*message*) line, note; (*bon mot etc*) saying; **le ~ de la fin** the last word; **~ à ~** *adj, adv* word for word; **~ pour ~** word for word, verbatim; **sur** *ou* **à ces ~s** with these words; **en un ~** in a word; **à ~s couverts** in veiled terms; **prendre qn au ~** to take sb at his word; **se donner le ~** to send the word round; **avoir son ~ à dire** to have a say; **~ d'ordre** watchword; **~ de passe** password; **~s croisés** crossword (puzzle) *sg*

motard [mɔtaʀ] *nm* biker; (*policier*) motorcycle cop

motel [mɔtɛl] *nm* motel

moteur, -trice [mɔtœʀ, -tʀis] *adj* (*Anat, Physiol*) motor; (*Tech*) driving; (*Auto*): **à 4 roues motrices** 4-wheel drive ▷ *nm* engine, motor; (*fig*) mover, mainspring; **à ~** power-driven, motor *cpd*; **~ à deux temps** two-stroke engine; **~ à explosion** internal combustion engine; **~ à réaction** jet engine; **~ de recherche** search engine; **~ thermique** heat engine

motif [mɔtif] *nm* (*cause*) motive; (*décoratif*) design, pattern, motif; (*d'un tableau*) subject, motif; (*Mus*) figure, motif; **motifs** *nmpl* (*Jur*) grounds *pl*; **sans ~** *adj* groundless

motion [mosjɔ̃] *nf* motion; **~ de censure** motion of censure, vote of no confidence

motivation [mɔtivasjɔ̃] *nf* motivation

motivé, e [mɔtive] *adj* (*acte*) justified; (*personne*) motivated

motiver [mɔtive] *vt* (*justifier*) to justify, account for; (*Admin, Jur, Psych*) to motivate

moto [mɔto] *nf* (motor)bike; **~ verte** *ou* **de trial** trail (*Brit*) *ou* dirt (*US*) bike

moto-cross [mɔtokʀɔs] *nm* motocross

motoculteur [mɔtokyltœʀ] *nm* (motorized) cultivator

motocyclette [mɔtosiklɛt] *nf* motorbike, motorcycle

motocyclisme [mɔtosiklism(ə)] *nm* motorcycle racing

motocycliste [mɔtosiklist(ə)] *nm/f* motorcyclist

motoneige [mɔtonɛʒ] *nf* snow bike

motorisé, e [mɔtoʀize] *adj* (*troupe*) motorized; (*personne*) having one's own transport

motrice [mɔtʀis] *adj f voir* **moteur**

motte [mɔt] *nf*: **~ de terre** lump of earth, clod (of earth); **~ de gazon** turf, sod; **~ de beurre** lump of butter

motus [mɔtys] *excl*: **~ (et bouche cousue)!** mum's the word!

mou, mol, molle [mu, mɔl] *adj* soft; (*péj: visage, traits*) flabby; (: *geste*) limp; (: *personne*) sluggish; (: *résistance, protestations*) feeble ▷ *nm* (*homme mou*) wimp; (*abats*) lights *pl*, lungs *pl*; (*de la corde*): **avoir du ~** to be slack; **donner du ~** to slacken, loosen; **avoir les jambes molles** to be weak at the knees

mouchard, e [muʃaʀ, -aʀd(ə)] *nm/f* (*péj: Scol*) sneak; (: *Police*) stool pigeon, grass (*Brit*) ▷ *nm* (*appareil*) control device; (: *de camion*) tachograph

mouche [muʃ] *nf* fly; (*Escrime*) button; (*de taffetas*) patch; **prendre la ~** to go into a huff; **faire ~** to score a bull's-eye

moucher [muʃe] *vt* (*enfant*) to blow the nose of; (*chandelle*) to snuff (out); **se moucher** to blow one's nose

moucheron [muʃʀɔ̃] *nm* midge

moucheté, e [muʃte] *adj* (*cheval*) dappled; (*laine*) flecked; (*Escrime*) buttoned

mouchoir [muʃwaʀ] *nm* handkerchief, hanky; **~ en papier** tissue, paper hanky

moudre [mudʀ(ə)] *vt* to grind

moue [mu] *nf* pout; **faire la ~** to pout; (*fig*) to pull a face

mouette [mwɛt] *nf* (sea)gull

moufette, mouffette [mufɛt] *nf* skunk

moufle [mufl(ə)] *nf* (*gant*) mitt(en); (*Tech*) pulley block

mouflon [muflɔ̃] *nm* mouf(f)lon

mouillage [muja3] *nm* (*Navig: lieu*) anchorage, moorings *pl*

mouillé, e [muje] *adj* wet

mouiller [muje] *vt* (*humecter*) to wet, moisten; (*tremper*): **~ qn/qch** to make sb/sth wet; (*Culin: ragoût*) to add stock *ou* wine to; (*couper, diluer*) to water down; (*mine etc*) to lay ▷ *vi* (*Navig*) to lie *ou* be at anchor; **se mouiller** to get wet; (*fam*) to commit o.s; to get (o.s.) involved; **~ l'ancre** to drop *ou* cast anchor

mouillette [mujɛt] *nf* (bread) finger

mouillure [mujyʀ] *nf* wet *no pl*; (*tache*) wet patch

moulage [mula3] *nm* moulding (*Brit*), molding (*US*); casting; (*objet*) cast

moulais *etc* [mulɛ] *vb voir* **moudre**

moulant, e [mulɑ̃, -ɑ̃t] *adj* figure-hugging

moule [mul] *vb voir* **moudre** ▷ *nf* (*mollusque*) mussel ▷ *nm* (*creux, Culin*) mould (*Brit*), mold (*US*); (*modèle plein*) cast; **~ à gâteau** *nm* cake tin (*Brit*) *ou* pan (*US*); **~ à gaufre** *nm* waffle iron; **~ à tarte** *nm* pie *ou* flan dish

moulent [mul] *vb voir* **moudre; mouler**

mouler [mule] *vt* (*brique*) to mould (*Brit*), mold (*US*); (*statue*) to cast; (*visage, bas-relief*) to make a cast of; (*lettre*) to shape with care; (*vêtement*) to hug, fit closely round; **~ qch sur** (*fig*) to model sth on

moulin [mulɛ̃] *nm* mill; (*fam*) engine; **~ à café** coffee mill; **~ à eau** watermill; **~ à légumes** (vegetable) shredder; **~ à paroles** (*fig*) chatterbox; **~ à poivre** pepper mill; **~ à prières** prayer wheel; **~ à vent** windmill

mouliner [muline] *vt* to shred

moulinet [mulinɛ] *nm* (*de treuil*) winch; (*de canne à pêche*) reel; (*mouvement*): **faire des ~s avec qch** to whirl sth around

moulinette® [mulinɛt] *nf* (vegetable) shredder

moulons *etc* [mulɔ̃] *vb voir* **moudre**

moulu, e [muly] *pp de* **moudre** ▷ *adj* (*café*) ground

moulure [mulyʀ] *nf* (*ornement*) moulding (*Brit*), molding (*US*)

mourant, e [muʀɑ̃, -ɑ̃t] *vb voir* **mourir** ▷ *adj* dying ▷ *nm/f* dying man/woman

mourir [muʀiʀ] *vi* to die; (*civilisation*) to die out; **~ assassiné** to be murdered; **~ de froid/faim/vieillesse** to die of exposure/hunger/old age; **~ de faim/d'ennui** (*fig*) to be starving/be bored to death; **~ d'envie de faire** to be dying to do; **s'ennuyer à ~** to be bored to death

mousquetaire [muskətɛʀ] *nm* musketeer

mousqueton [muskətɔ̃] *nm* (*fusil*) carbine; (*anneau*) snap-link, karabiner

moussant, e [musɑ̃, -ɑ̃t] *adj* foaming; **bain ~** foam *ou* bubble bath, bath foam

mousse [mus] *nf* (*Bot*) moss; (*écume: sur eau, bière*) froth, foam; (: *shampooing*) lather; (*de champagne*) bubbles *pl*; (*Culin*) mousse; (*en caoutchouc etc*) foam ▷ *nm* (*Navig*) ship's boy; **bain de ~** bubble bath; **bas ~** stretch stockings; **balle ~** rubber ball; **~ carbonique** (fire-fighting) foam; **~ de nylon** nylon foam; (*tissu*) stretch nylon; **~ à raser** shaving foam

mousseline [muslin] *nf* (*Textiles*) muslin; chiffon; **pommes ~** (*Culin*) creamed potatoes

mousser [muse] *vi* to foam; to lather

mousseux, -euse [musø, -øz] *adj* (*chocolat*) frothy; (*eau*) foamy, frothy; (*vin*) sparkling ▷ *nm*: **(vin) ~** sparkling wine

mousson [musɔ̃] *nf* monsoon

moussu, e [musy] *adj* mossy

moustache [mustaʃ] *nf* moustache; **moustaches** *nfpl* (*d'animal*) whiskers *pl*

moustachu, e [mustaʃy] *adj* wearing a moustache

moustiquaire [mustikɛʀ] *nf* (*rideau*) mosquito net; (*chassis*) mosquito screen

moustique [mustik] *nm* mosquito

moutarde [mutaʀd(ə)] *nf* mustard ▷ *adj inv* mustard(-coloured)

moutardier [mutaʀdje] *nm* mustard jar

mouton [mutɔ̃] *nm* (*Zool, péj*) sheep *inv*; (*peau*) sheepskin; (*Culin*) mutton

mouture [mutyʀ] *nf* grinding; (*péj*) rehash

mouvant, e [muvɑ̃, -ɑ̃t] *adj* unsettled; changing; shifting

mouvement [muvmɑ̃] *nm* (*gen, aussi: mécanisme*) movement; (*ligne courbe*) contours *pl*; (*fig: tumulte, agitation*) activity, bustle; (: *impulsion*) impulse; reaction; (*geste*) gesture; (*Mus: rythme*) tempo; **en ~** in motion; on the move; **mettre qch en ~** to set sth in motion, set sth going; **~ d'humeur** fit *ou* burst of temper; **~ d'opinion** trend of (public) opinion; **le ~ perpétuel** perpetual motion

mouvementé, e [muvmɑ̃te] *adj* (*vie, poursuite*)
eventful; (*réunion*) turbulent
mouvoir [muvwaʀ] *vt* (*levier, membre*) to move;
(*machine*) to drive; **se mouvoir** to move
moyen, ne [mwajɛ̃, -ɛn] *adj* average; (*tailles, prix*)
medium; (*de grandeur moyenne*) medium-sized
▷ *nm* (*façon*) means *sg*, way ▷ *nf* average;
(*Statistique*) mean; (*Scol: à l'examen*) pass mark;
(*Auto*) average speed; **moyens** *nmpl* (*capacités*)
means; **au ~ de** by means of; **y a-t-il ~ de ...?** is
it possible to ...?; can one ...?; **par quel ~?** how?,
which way?, by which means?; **par tous les ~s**
by every possible means, every possible way;
avec les ~s du bord (*fig*) with what's available
ou what comes to hand; **employer les grands
~s** to resort to drastic measures; **par ses
propres ~s** all by oneself; **en ~ne** on (an)
average; **faire la ~ne** to work out the average; **~
de locomotion/d'expression** means of
transport/expression; **~ âge** Middle Ages; **~ de
transport** means of transport; **~ne d'âge**
average age; **~ne entreprise** (*Comm*) medium-
sized firm
moyenâgeux, -euse [mwajɛnaʒø, -øz] *adj*
medieval
moyen-courrier [mwajɛ̃kuʀje] *nm* (*Aviat*)
medium-haul aircraft
moyennant [mwajɛnɑ̃] *prép* (*somme*) for; (*service,
conditions*) in return for; (*travail, effort*) with
moyennement [mwajɛnmɑ̃] *adv* fairly,
moderately; (*faire*) fairly *ou* moderately well
Moyen-Orient [mwajɛ̃nɔʀjɑ̃] *nm*: **le ~** the
Middle East
moyeu, x [mwajø] *nm* hub
mozambicain, e [mɔzɑ̃bikɛ̃, -ɛn] *adj*
Mozambican
Mozambique [mɔzɑ̃bik] *nm*: **le ~** Mozambique
MRAP *sigle m* = **Mouvement contre le racisme et
pour l'amitié entre les peuples**
MRG *sigle m* (= *Mouvement des radicaux de gauche*)
political party
ms *abr* (= *manuscrit*) MS., ms
MSF *sigle mpl* = **Médecins sans frontières**
MST *sigle f* (= *maladie sexuellement transmissible*) STD
(= *sexually transmitted disease*)
mû, mue [my] *pp de* **mouvoir**
mucosité [mykozite] *nf* mucus *no pl*
mucus [mykys] *nm* mucus *no pl*
mue [my] *pp de* **mouvoir** ▷ *nf* moulting (*Brit*),
molting (*US*); sloughing; breaking of the voice
muer [mɥe] *vi* (*oiseau, mammifère*) to moult (*Brit*),
molt (*US*); (*serpent*) to slough (its skin); (*jeune
garçon*): **il mue** his voice is breaking; **se ~ en** to
transform into
muet, te [mɥɛ, -ɛt] *adj* dumb; (*fig*): **~
d'admiration** *etc* speechless with admiration
etc; (*joie, douleur, Ciné*) silent; (*Ling: lettre*) silent,
mute; (*carte*) blank ▷ *nm/f* mute ▷ *nm*: **le ~** (*Ciné*)
the silent cinema *ou* (*esp US*) movies
mufle [myfl(ə)] *nm* muzzle; (*goujat*) boor ▷ *adj*
boorish
mugir [myʒiʀ] *vi* (*bœuf*) to bellow; (*vache*) to low,

moo; (*fig*) to howl
mugissement [myʒismɑ̃] *nm* (*voir mugir*)
bellowing; lowing, mooing; howling
muguet [mygɛ] *nm* (*Bot*) lily of the valley; (*Méd*)
thrush
mulâtre, tresse [mylɑtʀ(ə), -tʀɛs] *nm/f*
mulatto
mule [myl] *nf* (*Zool*) (she-)mule
mules [myl] *nfpl* (*pantoufles*) mules
mulet [mylɛ] *nm* (*Zool*) (he-)mule; (*poisson*)
mullet
muletier, -ière [myltje, -jɛʀ] *adj*: **sentier** *ou*
chemin ~ mule track
mulot [mylo] *nm* fieldmouse
multicolore [myltikɔlɔʀ] *adj* multicoloured
(*Brit*), multicolored (*US*)
multicoque [myltikɔk] *nm* multihull
multidisciplinaire [myltidisiplinɛʀ] *adj*
multidisciplinary
multiforme [myltifɔʀm(ə)] *adj* many-sided
multilatéral, e, -aux [myltilateʀal, -o] *adj*
multilateral
multimilliardaire [myltimiljaʀdɛʀ],
multimillionnaire [myltimiljɔnɛʀ] *adj, nm/f*
multimillionaire
multinational, e, -aux [myltinasjɔnal, -o] *adj,
nf* multinational
multiple [myltipl(ə)] *adj* multiple, numerous;
(*varié*) many, manifold ▷ *nm* (*Math*) multiple
multiplex [myltiplɛks] *nm* (*Radio*) live link-up
multiplicateur [myltiplikatœʀ] *nm* multiplier
multiplication [myltiplikasjɔ̃] *nf*
multiplication
multiplicité [myltiplisite] *nf* multiplicity
multiplier [myltiplije] *vt* to multiply; **se
multiplier** *vi* to multiply; (*fig: personne*) to be
everywhere at once
multiprogrammation [myltipʀɔgʀamasjɔ̃] *nf*
(*Inform*) multiprogramming
multipropriété [myltipʀɔpʀijete] *nf*
timesharing *no pl*
multirisque [myltiʀisk] *adj*: **assurance ~**
multiple-risk insurance
multisalles [myltisal] *adj*: (**cinéma**) **~**
multiplex (cinema)
multitraitement [myltitʀɛtmɑ̃] *nm* (*Inform*)
multiprocessing
multitude [myltityd] *nf* multitude; mass; **une
~ de** a vast number of, a multitude of
Munich [mynik] *n* Munich
munichois, e [mynikwa, -waz] *adj* of *ou* from
Munich
municipal, e, -aux [mynisipal, -o] *adj*
municipal; town *cpd*
municipalité [mynisipalite] *nf* (*corps municipal*)
town council, corporation; (*commune*) town,
municipality
munificence [mynifisɑ̃s] *nf* munificence
munir [myniʀ] *vt*: **~ qn/qch de** to equip sb/sth
with; **se ~ de** to provide o.s. with
munitions [mynisjɔ̃] *nfpl* ammunition *sg*
muqueuse [mykøz] *nf* mucous membrane

mur [myʀ] *nm* wall; *(fig)* stone *ou* brick wall;
faire le ~ *(interne, soldat)* to jump the wall; **~ du
son** sound barrier
mûr, e [myʀ] *adj* ripe; *(personne)* mature ▷ *nf (de
la ronce)* blackberry; *(du mûrier)* mulberry
muraille [myʀaj] *nf* (high) wall
mural, e, -aux [myʀal, -o] *adj* wall *cpd* ▷ *nm* (Art)
mural
mûre [myʀ] *nf voir* **mûr**
mûrement [myʀmɑ̃] *adv:* **ayant ~ réfléchi**
having given the matter much thought
murène [myʀɛn] *nf* moray (eel)
murer [myʀe] *vt (enclos)* to wall (in); *(porte, issue)*
to wall up; *(personne)* to wall up *ou* in
muret [myʀɛ] *nm* low wall
mûrier [myʀje] *nm* mulberry tree; *(ronce)*
blackberry bush
mûrir [myʀiʀ] *vi (fruit, blé)* to ripen; *(abcès,
furoncle)* to come to a head; *(fig: idée, personne)* to
mature; *(projet)* to develop ▷ *vt (fruit, blé)* to
ripen; *(personne)* to (make) mature; *(pensée,
projet)* to nurture
murmure [myʀmyʀ] *nm* murmur; **murmures**
nmpl (plaintes) murmurings, mutterings
murmurer [myʀmyʀe] *vi* to murmur; *(se
plaindre)* to mutter, grumble
mus *etc* [my] *vb voir* **mouvoir**
musaraigne [myzaʀɛɲ] *nf* shrew
musarder [myzaʀde] *vi* to idle (about); *(en
marchant)* to dawdle (along)
musc [mysk] *nm* musk
muscade [myskad] *nf (aussi:* **noix muscade)**
nutmeg
muscat [myska] *nm (raisin)* muscat grape; *(vin)*
muscatel (wine)
muscle [myskl(ə)] *nm* muscle
musclé, e [myskle] *adj (personne, corps)* muscular;
(fig: politique, régime etc) strong-arm *cpd*
muscler [myskle] *vt* to develop the muscles of
musculaire [myskylɛʀ] *adj* muscular
musculation [myskylasjɔ̃] *nf:* **exercices de ~**
muscle-developing exercises
musculature [myskylatyʀ] *nf* muscle
structure, muscles *pl*, musculature
muse [myz] *nf* muse
museau, x [myzo] *nm* muzzle
musée [myze] *nm* museum; *(de peinture)* art
gallery
museler [myzle] *vt* to muzzle
muselière [myzəljɛʀ] *nf* muzzle
musette [myzɛt] *nf (sac)* lunch bag ▷ *adj inv
(orchestre etc)* accordion *cpd*
muséum [myzeɔm] *nm* museum
musical, e, -aux [myzikal, -o] *adj* musical
music-hall [myzikol] *nm* variety theatre; *(genre)*
variety
musicien, ne [myzisjɛ̃, -ɛn] *adj* musical ▷ *nm/f*
musician
musique [myzik] *nf* music; *(fanfare)* band; **faire
de la ~** to make music; *(jouer d'un instrument)* to

play an instrument; **~ de chambre** chamber
music; **~ de fond** background music
musqué, e [myske] *adj* musky
must [mœst] *nm* must
musulman, e [myzylmɑ̃, -an] *adj, nm/f* Moslem,
Muslim
mutant, e [mytɑ̃, -ɑ̃t] *nm/f* mutant
mutation [mytasjɔ̃] *nf (Admin)* transfer; *(Bio)*
mutation
muter [myte] *vt (Admin)* to transfer
mutilation [mytilasjɔ̃] *nf* mutilation
mutilé, e [mytile] *nm/f* disabled person *(through
loss of limbs)*; **~ de guerre** disabled ex-
serviceman; **grand ~** severely disabled person
mutiler [mytile] *vt* to mutilate, maim; *(fig)* to
mutilate, deface
mutin, e [mytɛ̃, -in] *adj (enfant, air, ton)*
mischievous, impish ▷ *nm/f (Mil, Navig)*
mutineer
mutiner [mytine]: **se mutiner** *vi* to mutiny
mutinerie [mytinʀi] *nf* mutiny
mutisme [mytism(ə)] *nm* silence
mutualiste [mytɥalist(ə)] *adj:* **société ~**
mutual benefit society, ≈ Friendly Society
mutualité [mytɥalite] *nf (assurance)* mutual
(benefit) insurance scheme
mutuel, le [mytɥɛl] *adj* mutual ▷ *nf* mutual
benefit society
mutuellement [mytɥɛlmɑ̃] *adv* each other, one
another
Myanmar [mjanmaʀ] *nm* Myanmar
myocarde [mjɔkaʀd(ə)] *nm voir* **infarctus**
myope [mjɔp] *adj* short-sighted
myopie [mjɔpi] *nf* short-sightedness, myopia
myosotis [mjɔzɔtis] *nm* forget-me-not
myriade [miʀjad] *nf* myriad
myrtille [miʀtij] *nf* bilberry (Brit), blueberry
(US), whortleberry
mystère [mistɛʀ] *nm* mystery
mystérieusement [misteʀjøzmɑ̃] *adv*
mysteriously
mystérieux, -euse [misteʀjø, -øz] *adj*
mysterious
mysticisme [mistisism(ə)] *nm* mysticism
mystificateur, -trice [mistifikatœʀ, -tʀis] *nm/f*
hoaxer, practical joker
mystification [mistifikasjɔ̃] *nf (tromperie,
mensonge)* hoax; *(mythe)* mystification
mystifier [mistifje] *vt* to fool, take in; *(tromper)*
to mystify
mystique [mistik] *adj* mystic, mystical ▷ *nm/f*
mystic
mythe [mit] *nm* myth
mythifier [mitifje] *vt* to turn into a myth,
mythologize
mythique [mitik] *adj* mythical
mythologie [mitɔlɔʒi] *nf* mythology
mythologique [mitɔlɔʒik] *adj* mythological
mythomane [mitɔman] *adj, nm/f*
mythomaniac

Nn

N, n [ɛn] *nm inv* N, n ▷ *abr* (= *nord*) N; **N comme Nicolas** N for Nelly (*Brit*) *ou* Nan (*US*)

n' [n] *adv voir* **ne**

nabot [nabo] *nm* dwarf

nacelle [nasɛl] *nf* (*de ballon*) basket

nacre [nakʀ(ə)] *nf* mother-of-pearl

nacré, e [nakʀe] *adj* pearly

nage [naʒ] *nf* swimming; (*manière*) style of swimming, stroke; **traverser/s'éloigner à la ~** to swim across/away; **en ~** bathed in perspiration; **~ indienne** sidestroke; **~ libre** freestyle; **~ papillon** butterfly

nageoire [naʒwaʀ] *nf* fin

nager [naʒe] *vi* to swim; (*fig: ne rien comprendre*) to be all at sea; **~ dans** to be swimming in; (*vêtements*) to be lost in; **~ dans le bonheur** to be overjoyed

nageur, -euse [naʒœʀ, -øz] *nm/f* swimmer

naguère [nagɛʀ] *adv* (*il y a peu de temps*) not long ago; (*autrefois*) formerly

naïf, -ïve [naif, naiv] *adj* naïve

nain, e [nɛ̃, nɛn] *adj, nm/f* dwarf

Nairobi [naiʀɔbi] *n* Nairobi

nais [nɛ], **naissais** *etc* [nɛsɛ] *vb voir* **naître**

naissance [nɛsɑ̃s] *nf* birth; **donner ~ à** to give birth to; (*fig*) to give rise to; **prendre ~** to originate; **aveugle de ~** born blind; **Français de ~** French by birth; **à la ~ des cheveux** at the roots of the hair; **lieu de ~** place of birth

naissant, e [nɛsɑ̃, -ɑ̃t] *vb voir* **naître** ▷ *adj* budding, incipient; (*jour*) dawning

naît [nɛ] *vb voir* **naître**

naître [nɛtʀ(ə)] *vi* to be born; (*conflit, complications*): **~ de** to arise from, be born out of; **~ à** (*amour, poésie*) to awaken to; **je suis né en 1960** I was born in 1960; **il naît plus de filles que de garçons** there are more girls born than boys; **faire ~** (*fig*) to give rise to, arouse

naïvement [naivmɑ̃] *adv* naïvely

naïveté [naivte] *nf* naivety

nana [nana] *nf* (*fam: fille*) bird (*Brit*), chick

nantais, e [nɑ̃tɛ, -ɛz] *adj* of *ou* from Nantes

nantir [nɑ̃tiʀ] *vt*: **~ qn de** to provide sb with; **les nantis** (*péj*) the well-to-do

napalm [napalm] *nm* napalm

naphtaline [naftalin] *nf*: **boules de ~** mothballs

Naples [napl(ə)] *n* Naples

napolitain, e [napɔlitɛ̃, -ɛn] *adj* Neapolitan; **tranche ~e** Neapolitan ice cream

nappe [nap] *nf* tablecloth; (*fig*) sheet; layer; **~ de mazout** oil slick; **~ (phréatique)** water table

napper [nape] *vt*: **~ qch de** to coat sth with

napperon [napʀɔ̃] *nm* table-mat; **~ individuel** place mat

naquis *etc* [naki] *vb voir* **naître**

narcisse [naʀsis] *nm* narcissus

narcissique [naʀsisik] *adj* narcissistic

narcissisme [naʀsisism(ə)] *nm* narcissism

narcodollars [naʀkodɔlaʀ] *nmpl* drug money *no pl*

narcotique [naʀkɔtik] *adj, nm* narcotic

narguer [naʀge] *vt* to taunt

narine [naʀin] *nf* nostril

narquois, e [naʀkwa, -waz] *adj* derisive, mocking

narrateur, -trice [naʀatœʀ, -tʀis] *nm/f* narrator

narration [naʀasjɔ̃] *nf* narration, narrative; (*Scol*) essay

narrer [naʀe] *vt* to tell the story of, recount

NASA [nasa] *sigle f* (= *National Aeronautics and Space Administration*) NASA

nasal, e, -aux [nazal, -o] *adj* nasal

naseau, x [nazo] *nm* nostril

nasillard, e [nazijaʀ, -aʀd(ə)] *adj* nasal

nasiller [nazije] *vi* to speak with a (nasal) twang

nasse [nas] *nf* fish-trap

natal, e [natal] *adj* native

nataliste [natalist(ə)] *adj* supporting a rising birth rate

natalité [natalite] *nf* birth rate

natation [natasjɔ̃] *nf* swimming; **faire de la ~** to go swimming (*regularly*)

natif, -ive [natif, -iv] *adj* native

nation [nɑsjɔ̃] *nf* nation; **les N~s unies (NU)** the United Nations (UN)

national, e, -aux [nasjɔnal, -o] *adj* national ▷ *nf*: **(route) ~e** ≈ A road (*Brit*), ≈ state highway (*US*); **obsèques ~es** state funeral

nationalisation [nasjɔnalizasjɔ̃] *nf* nationalization

nationaliser [nasjɔnalize] *vt* to nationalize

nationalisme [nasjɔnalism(ə)] *nm* nationalism

nationaliste [nasjɔnalist(ə)] *adj, nm/f* nationalist

nationalité [nasjɔnalite] *nf* nationality; **de ~ française** of French nationality

natte [nat] *nf* (*tapis*) mat; (*cheveux*) plait

natter [nate] *vt* (*cheveux*) to plait

naturalisation [natyʀalizɑsjɔ̃] *nf* naturalization

naturaliser [natyʀalize] *vt* to naturalize; (*empailler*) to stuff

naturaliste [natyʀalist(ə)] *nm/f* naturalist; (*empailleur*) taxidermist

nature [natyʀ] *nf* nature ▷ *adj, adv* (*Culin*) plain, without seasoning or sweetening; (*café, thé: sans lait*) black; (: *sans sucre*) without sugar; **payer en ~** to pay in kind; **peint d'après ~** painted from life; **être de ~ à faire qch** (*propre à*) to be the sort of thing (*ou* person) to do sth; **~ morte** still-life

naturel, le [natyʀɛl] *adj* natural ▷ *nm* naturalness; (*caractère*) disposition, nature; (*autochtone*) native; (*aussi*: **au naturel**: *Culin*) in water; in its own juices

naturellement [natyʀɛlmɑ̃] *adv* naturally; (*bien sûr*) of course

naturisme [natyʀism(ə)] *nm* naturism

naturiste [natyʀist(ə)] *nm/f* naturist

naufrage [nofʀaʒ] *nm* (ship)wreck; (*fig*) wreck; **faire ~** to be shipwrecked

naufragé, e [nofʀaʒe] *nm/f* shipwreck victim, castaway

nauséabond, e [nozeabɔ̃, -ɔ̃d] *adj* foul, nauseous

nausée [noze] *nf* nausea; **avoir la ~** to feel sick; **avoir des ~s** to have waves of nausea, feel nauseous *ou* sick

nautique [notik] *adj* nautical, water *cpd*; **sports ~s** water sports

nautisme [notism(ə)] *nm* water sports *pl*

naval, e [naval] *adj* naval

navarrais, e [navaʀɛ, -ɛz] *adj* Navarrian

navet [navɛ] *nm* turnip; (*péj*) third-rate film

navette [navɛt] *nf* shuttle; (*en car etc*) shuttle (service); **faire la ~ (entre)** to go to and fro (between), shuttle (between); **~ spatiale** space shuttle

navigabilité [navigabilite] *nf* (*d'un navire*) seaworthiness; (*d'un avion*) airworthiness

navigable [navigabl(ə)] *adj* navigable

navigant, e [navigɑ̃, -ɑ̃t] *adj* (*Aviat: personnel*) flying ▷ *nm/f*: **les ~s** the flying staff *ou* personnel

navigateur [navigatœʀ] *nm* (*Navig*) seafarer, sailor; (*Aviat*) navigator; (*Inform*) browser

navigation [navigasjɔ̃] *nf* navigation, sailing; (*Comm*) shipping; **compagnie de ~** shipping company; **~ spatiale** space navigation

naviguer [navige] *vi* to navigate, sail

navire [naviʀ] *nm* ship; **~ de guerre** warship; **~ marchand** merchantman

navire-citerne [naviʀsitɛʀn(ə)] (*pl* **navires-citernes**) *nm* tanker

navire-hôpital [naviʀɔpital, -to] (*pl* **navires-hôpitaux**) *nm* hospital ship

navrant, e [navʀɑ̃, -ɑ̃t] *adj* (*affligeant*) upsetting; (*consternant*) annoying

navrer [navʀe] *vt* to upset, distress; **je suis navré (de/de faire/que)** I'm so sorry (for/for doing/that)

NB *abr* (= *nota bene*) NB

nbr. *abr* = **nombreux**

nbses *abr* = **nombreuses**

ND *sigle f* = **Notre Dame**

NDA *sigle f* = **note de l'auteur**

NDE *sigle f* = **note de l'éditeur**

NDLR *sigle f* = **note de la rédaction**

NDT *sigle f* = **note du traducteur**

ne, n' [n(ə)] *adv voir* **pas; plus; jamais** *etc*; (*explétif*) *non traduit*

né, e [ne] *pp de* **naître; né en 1960** born in 1960; **née Scott** née Scott; **né(e) de ... et de ...** son/daughter of ... and of ...; **né d'une mère française** having a French mother; **né pour commander** born to lead ▷ *adj*: **un comédien né** a born comedian

néanmoins [neɑ̃mwɛ̃] *adv* nevertheless, yet

néant [neɑ̃] *nm* nothingness; **réduire à ~** to bring to nought; (*espoir*) to dash

nébuleux, -euse [nebylø, -øz] *adj* (*ciel*) cloudy; (*fig*) nebulous ▷ *nf* (*Astronomie*) nebula

nébuliser [nebylize] *vt* (*liquide*) to spray

nébulosité [nebylozite] *nf* cloud cover; **~ variable** cloudy in places

nécessaire [neseseʀ] *adj* necessary ▷ *nm* necessary; (*sac*) kit; **faire le ~** to do the necessary; **n'emporter que le strict ~** to take only what is strictly necessary; **~ de couture** sewing kit; **~ de toilette** toilet bag; **~ de voyage** overnight bag

nécessairement [neseseʀmɑ̃] *adv* necessarily

nécessité [nesesite] *nf* necessity; **se trouver dans la ~ de faire qch** to find it necessary to do sth; **par ~** out of necessity

nécessiter [nesesite] *vt* to require

nécessiteux, -euse [nesesitø, -øz] *adj* needy

nec plus ultra [nekplysyltʀa] *nm*: **le ~ de** the last word in

nécrologie [nekʀɔlɔʒi] *nf* obituary

nécrologique [nekʀɔlɔʒik] *adj*: **article ~** obituary; **rubrique ~** obituary column

nécromancie [nekʀɔmɑ̃si] *nf* necromancy

nécrose [nekʀoz] *nf* necrosis

nectar [nɛktaʀ] *nm* nectar

nectarine [nɛktaʀin] *nf* nectarine

néerlandais, e [neɛʀlɑ̃dɛ, -ɛz] *adj* Dutch, of the Netherlands ▷ *nm* (*Ling*) Dutch ▷ *nm/f*: **Néerlandais, e** Dutchman/woman; **les N~** the Dutch

nef [nɛf] *nf* (*d'église*) nave

néfaste [nefast(ə)] *adj* baneful; ill-fated

négatif, -ive [negatif, iv] *adj* negative ▷ *nm* (*Photo*) negative

négation [negasjɔ̃] *nf* denial; (*Ling*) negation

négativement [negativmɑ̃] *adv*: **répondre ~** to give a negative response

négligé, e [negliʒe] *adj* (*en désordre*) slovenly ▷ *nm* (*tenue*) negligee

négligeable [negliʒabl(ə)] *adj* insignificant,

negligible

négligemment [negliʒamɑ̃] *adv* carelessly

négligence [negliʒɑ̃s] *nf* carelessness *no pl*;
(*faute*) careless omission

négligent, e [negliʒɑ̃, -ɑ̃t] *adj* careless; (*Jur etc*)
negligent

négliger [negliʒe] *vt* (*épouse, jardin*) to neglect;
(*tenue*) to be careless about; (*avis, précautions*) to
disregard, overlook; **~ de faire** to fail to do, not
bother to do; **se négliger** to neglect o.s

négoce [negɔs] *nm* trade

négociable [negɔsjabl(ə)] *adj* negotiable

négociant [negɔsjɑ̃] *nm* merchant

négociateur [negɔsjatœr] *nm* negotiator

négociation [negɔsjasjɔ̃] *nf* negotiation; **~s
collectives** collective bargaining *sg*

négocier [negɔsje] *vi, vt* to negotiate

nègre [nɛgr(ə)] *nm* (*péj*) Negro; (*péj: écrivain*)
ghost writer ▷ *adj* (*péj*) Negro

négresse [negres] *nf* (*péj*) Negress

négrier [negrije] *nm* (*fig*) slave driver

neige [nɛʒ] *nf* snow; **battre les œufs en ~**
(*Culin*) to whip *ou* beat the egg whites until stiff;
~ carbonique dry ice; **~ fondue** (*par terre*) slush;
(*qui tombe*) sleet; **~ poudreuse** powdery snow

neiger [neʒe] *vi* to snow

neigeux, -euse [nɛʒø, -øz] *adj* snowy, snow-
covered

nénuphar [nenyfar] *nm* water-lily

néo-calédonien, ne [neɔkaledɔnjɛ̃, -ɛn] *adj*
New Caledonian ▷ *nm/f*: **Néo-calédonien, ne**
native of New Caledonia

néocapitalisme [neokapitalism(ə)] *nm*
neocapitalism

néo-colonialisme [neokɔlɔnjalism(ə)] *nm*
neocolonialism

néologisme [neɔlɔʒism(ə)] *nm* neologism

néon [neɔ̃] *nm* neon

néo-natal, e [neonatal] *adj* neonatal

néophyte [neɔfit] *nm/f* novice

néo-zélandais, e [neozelɑ̃dɛ, -ɛz] *adj* New
Zealand *cpd* ▷ *nm/f*: **Néo-zélandais, e** New
Zealander

Népal [nepal] *nm*: **le ~** Nepal

népalais, e [nepalɛ, -ɛz] *adj* Nepalese, Nepali
▷ *nm* (*Ling*) Nepalese, Nepali ▷ *nm/f*: **Népalais, e**
Nepalese, Nepali

néphrétique [nefretik] *adj* (*Méd: colique*)
nephritic

néphrite [nefrit] *nf* (*Méd*) nephritis

népotisme [nepɔtism(ə)] *nm* nepotism

nerf [nɛr] *nm* nerve; (*fig*) spirit; (: *forces*)
stamina; **nerfs** *nmpl* nerves; **être** *ou* **vivre sur
les ~s** to live on one's nerves; **être à bout de ~s**
to be at the end of one's tether; **passer ses ~s
sur qn** to take it out on sb

nerveusement [nɛrvøzmɑ̃] *adv* nervously

nerveux, -euse [nɛrvø, -øz] *adj* nervous;
(*cheval*) highly-strung; (*voiture*) nippy,
responsive; (*tendineux*) sinewy

nervosité [nɛrvozite] *nf* nervousness;
(*émotivité*) excitability

nervure [nɛrvyr] *nf* (*de feuille*) vein; (*Archit, Tech*)
rib

n'est-ce pas [nɛspɑ] *adv* isn't it?, won't you? *etc*
(*selon le verbe qui précède*); **c'est bon, n'est-ce pas?**
it's good, isn't it?; **il a peur, n'est-ce pas?** he's
afraid, isn't he?; **n'est-ce pas que c'est bon?**
don't you think it's good?; **lui, n'est-ce pas, il
peut se le permettre** he, of course, can afford
to do that, can't he?

net, nette [nɛt] *adj* (*sans équivoque, distinct*) clear;
(*photo*) sharp; (*évident*) definite; (*propre*) neat,
clean; (*Comm: prix, salaire, poids*) net ▷ *adv* (*refuser*)
flatly ▷ *nm*: **mettre au ~** to copy out; **s'arrêter
~** to stop dead; **la lame a cassé ~** the blade
snapped clean through; **faire place nette** to
make a clean sweep; **~ d'impôt** tax free

Net [nɛt] *nm* (*Internet*): **le ~** the Net

nettement [nɛtmɑ̃] *adv* (*distinctement*) clearly;
(*évidemment*) definitely; (*avec comparatif,
superlatif*): **~ mieux** definitely *ou* clearly better

netteté [nɛtte] *nf* clearness

nettoie *etc* [nɛtwa] *vb voir* **nettoyer**

nettoiement [netwamɑ̃] *nm* (*Admin*) cleaning;
service du ~ refuse collection

nettoierai *etc* [nɛtware] *vb voir* **nettoyer**

nettoyage [nɛtwajaʒ] *nm* cleaning; **~ à sec** dry
cleaning

nettoyant [netwajɑ̃] *nm* (*produit*) cleaning agent

nettoyer [nɛtwaje] *vt* to clean; (*fig*) to clean out

neuf¹ [nœf] *num* nine

neuf², neuve [nœf, nœv] *adj* new ▷ *nm*:
repeindre à ~ to redecorate; **remettre à ~** to do
up (as good as new), refurbish; **n'acheter que du
~** to buy everything new; **quoi de ~?** what's new?

neurasthénique [nørastenik] *adj* neurasthenic

neurochirurgie [nøroʃiryrʒi] *nf* neurosurgery

neurochirurgien [nøroʃiryrʒjɛ̃] *nm*
neurosurgeon

neuroleptique [nørɔlɛptik] *adj* neuroleptic

neurologie [nørɔlɔʒi] *nf* neurology

neurologique [nørɔlɔʒik] *adj* neurological

neurologue [nørɔlɔg] *nm/f* neurologist

neurone [nørɔn] *nm* neuron(e)

neuropsychiatre [nøropsikjatr(ə)] *nm/f*
neuropsychiatrist

neutralisation [nøtralizasjɔ̃] *nf* neutralization

neutraliser [nøtralize] *vt* to neutralize

neutralisme [nøtralism(ə)] *nm* neutralism

neutraliste [nøtralist(ə)] *adj* neutralist

neutralité [nøtralite] *nf* neutrality

neutre [nøtr(ə)] *adj, nm* (*Ling*) neutral

neutron [nøtrɔ̃] *nm* neutron

neuve [nœv] *adj f voir* **neuf**

neuvième [nœvjɛm] *num* ninth

neveu, x [nəvø] *nm* nephew

névralgie [nevralʒi] *nf* neuralgia

névralgique [nevralʒik] *adj* (*fig: sensible*)
sensitive; **centre ~** nerve centre

névrite [nevrit] *nf* neuritis

névrose [nevroz] *nf* neurosis

névrosé, e [nevroze] *adj, nm/f* neurotic

névrotique [nevrɔtik] *adj* neurotic

New York [njujɔʀk] *n* New York
new-yorkais, e [njujɔʀkɛ, -ɛz] *adj* of *ou* from New York, New York *cpd* ▷ *nm/f*: **New-Yorkais, e** New Yorker
nez [ne] *nm* nose; **rire au ~ de qn** to laugh in sb's face; **avoir du ~** to have flair; **avoir le ~ fin** to have foresight; **~ à ~ avec** face to face with; **à vue de ~** roughly
NF *sigle mpl* = **nouveaux francs** ▷ *sigle f* (*Industrie*: = *norme française*) industrial standard
ni [ni] *conj*: **ni l'un ni l'autre ne sont** *ou* **n'est** neither one nor the other is; **il n'a rien dit ni fait** he hasn't said or done anything
Niagara [njagaʀa] *nm*: **les chutes du ~** the Niagara Falls
niais, e [njɛ, -ɛz] *adj* silly, thick
niaiserie [njɛzʀi] *nf* gullibility; (*action, propos, futilité*) silliness
Nicaragua [nikaʀagwa] *nm*: **le ~** Nicaragua
nicaraguayen, ne [nikaʀagwajɛ̃, -ɛn] *adj* Nicaraguan ▷ *nm/f*: **Nicaraguayen, ne** Nicaraguan
Nice [nis] *n* Nice
niche [niʃ] *nf* (*du chien*) kennel; (*de mur*) recess, niche; (*farce*) trick
nichée [niʃe] *nf* brood, nest
nicher [niʃe] *vi* to nest; **se ~ dans** (*personne: se blottir*) to snuggle into; (: *se cacher*) to hide in; (*objet*) to lodge itself in
nichon [niʃɔ̃] *nm* (*fam*) boob, tit
nickel [nikɛl] *nm* nickel
niçois, e [niswa, -waz] *adj* of *ou* from Nice; (*Culin*) Nicoise
nicotine [nikɔtin] *nf* nicotine
nid [ni] *nm* nest; (*fig: repaire etc*) den, lair; **~ d'abeilles** (*Couture, Textile*) honeycomb stitch; **~ de poule** pothole
nièce [njɛs] *nf* niece
nième [ɛnjɛm] *adj*: **la ~ fois** the nth *ou* umpteenth time
nier [nje] *vt* to deny
nigaud, e [nigo, -od] *nm/f* booby, fool
Niger [niʒɛʀ] *nm*: **le ~** Niger; (*fleuve*) the Niger
Nigéria [niʒeʀja] *nm ou f* Nigeria
nigérian, e [niʒeʀjɑ̃, -an] *adj* Nigerian ▷ *nm/f*: **Nigérian, e** Nigerian
nigérien, ne [niʒeʀjɛ̃, -ɛn] *adj* of *ou* from Niger
night-club [najtklœb] *nm* nightclub
nihilisme [niilism(ə)] *nm* nihilism
nihiliste [niilist(ə)] *adj* nihilist, nihilistic
Nil [nil] *nm*: **le ~** the Nile
n'importe [nɛ̃pɔʀt(ə)] *adv*: **n'importe!** no matter!; **n'importe qui/quoi/où** anybody/anything/anywhere; **n'importe quoi!** (*fam: désapprobation*) what rubbish!; **n'importe quand** any time; **n'importe quel/quelle** any; **n'importe lequel/laquelle** any (one); **n'importe comment** (*sans soin*) carelessly; **n'importe comment, il part ce soir** he's leaving tonight in any case
nippes [nip] *nfpl* (*fam*) togs
nippon, e *ou* **ne** [nipɔ̃, -ɔn] *adj* Japanese

nique [nik] *nf*: **faire la ~ à** to thumb one's nose at (*fig*)
nitouche [nituʃ] *nf* (*péj*): **c'est une sainte ~** she looks as if butter wouldn't melt in her mouth
nitrate [nitʀat] *nm* nitrate
nitrique [nitʀik] *adj*: **acide ~** nitric acid
nitroglycérine [nitʀɔgliseʀin] *nf* nitroglycerin(e)
niveau, x [nivo] *nm* level; (*des élèves, études*) standard; **au ~ de** at the level of; (*personne*) on a level with; **de ~ (avec)** level (with); **le ~ de la mer** sea level; **~ (à bulle)** spirit level; **~ (d'eau)** water level; **~ de vie** standard of living
niveler [nivle] *vt* to level
niveleuse [nivløz] *nf* (*Tech*) grader
nivellement [nivɛlmɑ̃] *nm* levelling
nivernais, e [nivɛʀnɛ, -ɛz] *adj* of *ou* from Nevers (and region) ▷ *nm/f*: **Nivernais, e** inhabitant *ou* native of Nevers (and region)
NL *sigle f* = **nouvelle lune**
NN *abr* (= *nouvelle norme*) revised standard of hotel classification
n° *abr* (*numéro*) no
nobiliaire [nɔbiljɛʀ] *adj f* *voir* **particule**
noble [nɔbl(ə)] *adj* noble; (*de qualité: métal etc*) precious ▷ *nm/f* noble(man/-woman)
noblesse [nɔblɛs] *nf* (*classe sociale*) nobility; (*d'une action etc*) nobleness
noce [nɔs] *nf* wedding; (*gens*) wedding party (*ou* guests *pl*); **il l'a épousée en secondes ~s** she was his second wife; **faire la ~** (*fam*) to go on a binge; **~s d'or/d'argent/de diamant** golden/silver/diamond wedding
noceur [nɔsœʀ] *nm* (*fam*): **c'est un sacré ~** he's a real party animal
nocif, -ive [nɔsif, -iv] *adj* harmful, noxious
noctambule [nɔktɑ̃byl] *nm* night-bird
nocturne [nɔktyʀn(ə)] *adj* nocturnal ▷ *nf* (*Sport*) floodlit fixture; (*d'un magasin*) late opening
Noël [nɔɛl] *nm* Christmas; **la (fête de) ~** Christmas time
nœud [nø] *nm* (*de corde, du bois, Navig*) knot; (*ruban*) bow; (*fig: liens*) bond, tie; (: *d'une question*) crux; (*Théât etc*): **le ~ de l'action** the web of events; **~ coulant** noose; **~ gordien** Gordian knot; **~ papillon** bow tie
noie *etc* [nwa] *vb voir* **noyer**
noir, e [nwaʀ] *adj* black; (*obscur, sombre*) dark ▷ *nm/f* black man/woman ▷ *nm*: **dans le ~** in the dark ▷ *nf* (*Mus*) crotchet (*Brit*), quarter note (*US*); **il fait ~** it is dark; **au ~** *adv* (*acheter, vendre*) on the black market; **travail au ~** moonlighting
noirâtre [nwaʀɑtʀ(ə)] *adj* (*teinte*) blackish
noirceur [nwaʀsœʀ] *nf* blackness; darkness
noircir [nwaʀsiʀ] *vt, vi* to blacken
noise [nwaz] *nf*: **chercher ~ à** to try and pick a quarrel with
noisetier [nwaztje] *nm* hazel (tree)
noisette [nwazɛt] *nf* hazelnut; (*morceau: de beurre etc*) small knob ▷ *adj* (*yeux*) hazel
noix [nwa] *nf* walnut; (*fam*) twit; (*Culin*): **une ~**

de beurre a knob of butter; **à la ~** (*fam*) worthless; **~ de cajou** cashew nut; **~ de coco** coconut; **~ muscade** nutmeg; **~ de veau** (*Culin*) round fillet of veal

nom [nɔ̃] *nm* name; (*Ling*) noun; **connaître qn de ~** to know sb by name; **au ~ de** in the name of; **~ d'une pipe** *ou* **d'un chien!** (*fam*) for goodness' sake!; **~ de Dieu!** (*fam!*) bloody hell! (*Brit*), my God!; **~ commun/propre** common/ proper noun; **~ composé** (*Ling*) compound noun; **~ déposé** trade name; **~ d'emprunt** assumed name; **~ de famille** surname; **~ de fichier** file name; **~ de jeune fille** maiden name

nomade [nɔmad] *adj* nomadic ▷ *nm/f* nomad

nombre [nɔ̃bʀ(ə)] *nm* number; **venir en ~** to come in large numbers; **depuis ~ d'années** for many years; **ils sont au ~ de trois** there are three of them; **au ~ de mes amis** among my friends; **sans ~** countless; **(bon) ~ de** (*beaucoup, plusieurs*) a (large) number of; **~ premier/entier** prime/whole number

nombreux, -euse [nɔ̃bʀø, -øz] *adj* many, numerous; (*avec nom sg*: *foule etc*) large; **peu ~** few; small; **de ~ cas** many cases

nombril [nɔ̃bʀi] *nm* navel

nomenclature [nɔmɑ̃klatyʀ] *nf* wordlist; list of items

nominal, e, -aux [nɔminal, -o] *adj* nominal; (*appel, liste*) of names

nominatif, -ive [nɔminatif, -iv] *nm* (*Ling*) nominative ▷ *adj*: **liste nominative** list of names; **carte nominative** calling card; **titre ~** registered name

nomination [nɔminasjɔ̃] *nf* nomination

nommément [nɔmemɑ̃] *adv* (*désigner*) by name

nommer [nɔme] *vt* (*baptiser*) to name, give a name to; (*qualifier*) to call; (*mentionner*) to name, give the name of; (*élire*) to appoint, nominate; **se nommer**: **il se nomme Pascal** his name's Pascal, he's called Pascal

non [nɔ̃] *adv* (*réponse*) no; (*suivi d'un adjectif, adverbe*) not; **Paul est venu, ~?** Paul came, didn't he?; **répondre** *ou* **dire que ~** to say no; **~ pas que** not that; **~ plus**: **moi ~ plus** neither do I, I don't either; **je préférerais que ~** I would prefer not; **il se trouve que ~** perhaps not; **je pense que ~** I don't think so; **~ mais!** well really!; **~ mais des fois!** you must be joking!; **~ alcoolisé** non-alcoholic; **~ loin/seulement** not far/only

nonagénaire [nɔnaʒenɛʀ] *nm/f* nonagenarian

non-agression [nɔnagʀesjɔ̃] *nf*: **pacte de ~** non-aggression pact

nonante [nɔnɑ̃t] *num* (*Belgique, Suisse*) ninety

non-assistance [nɔnasistɑ̃s] *nf* (*Jur*): **~ à personne en danger** failure to render assistance to a person in danger

nonce [nɔ̃s] *nm* (*Rel*) nuncio

nonchalamment [nɔ̃ʃalamɑ̃] *adv* nonchalantly

nonchalance [nɔ̃ʃalɑ̃s] *nf* nonchalance, casualness

nonchalant, e [nɔ̃ʃalɑ̃, -ɑ̃t] *adj* nonchalant, casual

non-conformisme [nɔ̃kɔ̃fɔʀmism(ə)] *nm* nonconformism

non-conformiste [nɔ̃kɔ̃fɔʀmist(ə)] *adj, nm/f* non-conformist

non-conformité [nɔ̃kɔ̃fɔʀmite] *nf* nonconformity

non-croyant, e [nɔ̃kʀwajɑ̃, -ɑ̃t] *nm/f* (*Rel*) non-believer

non-engagé, e [nɔnɑ̃gaʒe] *adj* non-aligned

non-fumeur [nɔ̃fymœʀ] *nm* non-smoker

non-ingérence [nɔnɛ̃ʒeʀɑ̃s] *nf* non-interference

non-initié, e [nɔninisje] *nm/f* lay person; **les ~s** the uninitiated

non-inscrit, e [nɔnɛ̃skʀi, -it] *nm/f* (*Pol*: *député*) independent

non-intervention [nɔnɛ̃tɛʀvɑ̃sjɔ̃] *nf* non-intervention

non-lieu [nɔ̃ljø] *nm*: **il y a eu ~** the case was dismissed

nonne [nɔn] *nf* nun

nonobstant [nɔnɔpstɑ̃] *prép* notwithstanding

non-paiement [nɔ̃pɛmɑ̃] *nm* non-payment

non-prolifération [nɔ̃pʀɔlifeʀasjɔ̃] *nf* non-proliferation

non-résident [nɔ̃ʀezidɑ̃] *nm* (*Écon*) non-resident

non-retour [nɔ̃ʀətuʀ] *nm*: **point de ~** point of no return

non-sens [nɔ̃sɑ̃s] *nm* absurdity

non-spécialiste [nɔ̃spesjalist(ə)] *nm/f* non-specialist

non-stop [nɔnstɔp] *adj inv* nonstop

non-syndiqué, e [nɔ̃sɛ̃dike] *nm/f* non-union member

non-violence [nɔ̃vjɔlɑ̃s] *nf* nonviolence

non-violent, e [nɔ̃vjɔlɑ̃, -ɑ̃t] *adj* non-violent

nord [nɔʀ] *nm* North ▷ *adj* northern; north; **au ~** (*situation*) in the north; (*direction*) to the north; **au ~ de** north of, to the north of; **perdre le ~** to lose one's way (*fig*)

nord-africain, e [nɔʀafʀikɛ̃, -ɛn] *adj* North-African ▷ *nm/f*: **Nord-Africain, e** North African

nord-américain, e [nɔʀameʀikɛ̃, -ɛn] *adj* North American ▷ *nm/f*: **Nord-Américain, e** North American

nord-coréen, ne [nɔʀkɔʀeɛ̃, -ɛn] *adj* North Korean ▷ *nm/f*: **Nord-Coréen, ne** North Korean

nord-est [nɔʀɛst] *nm* North-East

nordique [nɔʀdik] *adj* (*pays, race*) Nordic; (*langues*) Scandinavian, Nordic ▷ *nm/f*: **Nordique** Scandinavian

nord-ouest [nɔʀwɛst] *nm* North-West

nord-vietnamien, ne [nɔʀvjɛtnamjɛ̃, -ɛn] *adj* North Vietnamese ▷ *nm/f*: **Nord-Vietnamien, ne** North Vietnamese

normal, e, -aux [nɔʀmal, -o] *adj* normal ▷ *nf*: **la ~e** the norm, the average

normalement [nɔʀmalmɑ̃] *adv* (*en général*) normally; (*comme prévu*) **~, il le fera demain** he should be doing it tomorrow, he's supposed to do it tomorrow

normalien, ne [nɔʀmaljɛ̃, -ɛn] *nm/f student of*
École normale supérieure

normalisation [nɔʀmalizasjɔ̃] *nf*
standardization; normalization

normaliser [nɔʀmalize] *vt* (*Comm, Tech*) to
standardize; (*Pol*) to normalize

normand, e [nɔʀmɑ̃, -ɑ̃d] *adj* (*de Normandie*)
Norman ▷ *nm/f:* **Normand, e** (*de Normandie*)
Norman

Normandie [nɔʀmɑ̃di] *nf:* **la ~** Normandy

norme [nɔʀm(ə)] *nf* norm; (*Tech*) standard

Norvège [nɔʀvɛʒ] *nf:* **la ~** Norway

norvégien, ne [nɔʀveʒjɛ̃, -ɛn] *adj* Norwegian
▷ *nm* (*Ling*) Norwegian ▷ *nm/f:* **Norvégien, ne**
Norwegian

nos [no] *adj poss voir* **notre**

nostalgie [nɔstalʒi] *nf* nostalgia

nostalgique [nɔstalʒik] *adj* nostalgic

notable [nɔtabl(ə)] *adj* notable, noteworthy;
(*marqué*) noticeable, marked ▷ *nm* prominent
citizen

notablement [nɔtabləmɑ̃] *adv* notably;
(*sensiblement*) noticeably

notaire [nɔtɛʀ] *nm* notary; solicitor

notamment [nɔtamɑ̃] *adv* in particular, among
others

notariat [nɔtaʀja] *nm* profession of notary (*ou*
solicitor)

notarié, e [nɔtaʀje] *adj:* **acte ~** deed drawn up
by a notary (*ou* solicitor)

notation [nɔtasjɔ̃] *nf* notation

note [nɔt] *nf* (*écrite, Mus*) note; (*Scol*) mark (*Brit*),
grade; (*facture*) bill; **prendre des ~s** to take
notes; **prendre ~ de** to note; (*par écrit*) to note,
write down; **dans la ~** exactly right; **forcer la ~**
to exaggerate; **une ~ de tristesse/de gaieté** a
sad/happy note; **~ de service** memorandum

noté, e [nɔte] *adj:* **être bien/mal ~** (*employé etc*)
to have a good/bad record

noter [nɔte] *vt* (*écrire*) to write down, note;
(*remarquer*) to note, notice; (*Scol, Admin: donner une*
appréciation) to mark, give a grade to; **notez bien**
que ... (please) note that ...

notice [nɔtis] *nf* summary, short article;
(*brochure*): **~ explicative** explanatory leaflet,
instruction booklet

notification [nɔtifikasjɔ̃] *nf* notification

notifier [nɔtifje] *vt:* **~ qch à qn** to notify sb of
sth, notify sth to sb

notion [nosjɔ̃] *nf* notion, idea; **notions** *nfpl*
(*rudiments*) rudiments

notoire [nɔtwaʀ] *adj* widely known; (*en mal*)
notorious; **le fait est ~** the fact is common
knowledge

notoriété [nɔtɔʀjete] *nf:* **c'est de ~ publique**
it's common knowledge

notre, nos [nɔtʀ(ə), no] *adj poss* our

nôtre [notʀ(ə)] *adj* ours ▷ *pron:* **le/la ~** ours; **les**
~s ours; (*alliés etc*) our own people; **soyez des ~s**
join us

nouba [nuba] *nf* (*fam*): **faire la ~** to live it up

nouer [nwe] *vt* to tie, knot; (*fig: alliance etc*) to
strike up; **~ la conversation** to start a
conversation; **se nouer** *vi:* **c'est là où**
l'intrigue se noue it's at that point that the
strands of the plot come together; **ma gorge se**
noua a lump came to my throat

noueux, -euse [nwø, -øz] *adj* gnarled

nougat [nuga] *nm* nougat

nougatine [nugatin] *nf* kind of nougat

nouille [nuj] *nf* (*fam*) noodle (*Brit*), fathead;
nouilles *nfpl* (*pâtes*) noodles; pasta *sg*

nounou [nunu] *nf* nanny

nounours [nunuʀs] *nm* teddy (bear)

nourri, e [nuʀi] *adj* (*feu etc*) sustained

nourrice [nuʀis] *nf* ≈ baby-minder; (*autrefois*)
wet-nurse

nourrir [nuʀiʀ] *vt* to feed; (*fig: espoir*) to harbour,
nurse; **logé nourri** with board and lodging; **~**
au sein to breast-feed; **se ~ de légumes** to live
on vegetables

nourrissant, e [nuʀisɑ̃, -ɑ̃t] *adj* nourishing,
nutritious

nourrisson [nuʀisɔ̃] *nm* (unweaned) infant

nourriture [nuʀityʀ] *nf* food

nous [nu] *pron* (*sujet*) we; (*objet*) us

nous-mêmes [numɛm] *pron* ourselves

nouveau, nouvel, -elle, x [nuvo, -ɛl] *adj* new;
(*original*) novel ▷ *nm/f* new pupil (*ou* employee)
▷ *nm:* **il y a du ~** there's something new ▷ *nf*
(piece of) news *sg*; (*Littérature*) short story;
nouvelles *nfpl* (*Presse, TV*) news; **de ~ à ~** again;
je suis sans nouvelles de lui I haven't heard
from him; **Nouvel An** New Year; **~ venu,**
nouvelle venue newcomer; **~x mariés** newly-
weds; **nouvelle vague** new wave

nouveau-né, e [nuvone] *nm/f* newborn (baby)

nouveauté [nuvote] *nf* novelty; (*chose nouvelle*)
innovation, something new; (*Comm*) new film
(*ou* book *ou* creation *etc*)

nouvel *adj m*, **nouvelle** *adj f, nf* [nuvɛl] *voir*
nouveau

Nouvelle-Angleterre [nuvɛlɑ̃glətɛʀ] *nf:* **la ~**
New England

Nouvelle-Calédonie [nuvɛlkaledɔni] *nf:* **la ~**
New Caledonia

Nouvelle-Écosse [nuvɛlekɔs] *nf:* **la ~** Nova
Scotia

Nouvelle-Galles du Sud [nuvɛlgaldysyd] *nf:* **la**
~ New South Wales

Nouvelle-Guinée [nuvɛlgine] *nf:* **la ~** New
Guinea

nouvellement [nuvɛlmɑ̃] *adv* (*arrivé etc*)
recently, newly

Nouvelle-Orléans [nuvɛlɔʀleɑ̃] *nf:* **la ~** New
Orleans

Nouvelles-Hébrides [nuvɛlsebʀid] *nfpl:* **les ~**
the New Hebrides

Nouvelle-Zélande [nuvɛlzelɑ̃d] *nf:* **la ~** New
Zealand

nouvelliste [nuvelist(ə)] *nm/f* editor *ou* writer of
short stories

novateur, -trice [nɔvatœʀ, -tʀis] *adj* innovative
▷ *nm/f* innovator

novembre [nɔvɑ̃bʀ(ə)] *nm* November; *see note; voir aussi* **juillet**

see note; voir aussi **juillet**

⬤ **LE 11 NOVEMBRE**

⬤
⬤ *Le 11 novembre* is a public holiday in France
⬤ and commemorates the signing of the
⬤ armistice, near Compiègne, at the end of the
⬤ First World War.

novice [nɔvis] *adj* inexperienced ▷ *nm/f* novice
noviciat [nɔvisja] *nm* (*Rel*) noviciate
noyade [nwajad] *nf* drowning *no pl*
noyau, x [nwajo] *nm* (*de fruit*) stone; (*Bio, Physique*) nucleus; (*Élec, Géo, fig: centre*) core; (*fig: d'artistes etc*) group; (*: de résistants etc*) cell
noyautage [nwajotaʒ] *nm* (*Pol*) infiltration
noyauter [nwajote] *vt* (*Pol*) to infiltrate
noyé, e [nwaje] *nm/f* drowning (*ou* drowned) man/woman ▷ *adj* (*fig: dépassé*) out of one's depth
noyer [nwaje] *nm* walnut (tree); (*bois*) walnut ▷ *vt* to drown; (*fig*) to flood; to submerge; (*Auto: moteur*) to flood; **se noyer** to be drowned, drown; (*suicide*) to drown o.s.; **~ son chagrin** to drown one's sorrows; **~ le poisson** to duck the issue
NSP *sigle m* (*Rel*) = **Notre Saint Père**; (*dans les sondages*: = *ne sais pas*) don't know
NT *sigle m* (= *Nouveau Testament*) NT
NU *sigle fpl* (= *Nations unies*) UN
nu, e [ny] *adj* naked; (*membres*) naked, bare; (*chambre, fil, plaine*) bare ▷ *nm* (*Art*) nude; **le nu intégral** total nudity; **se mettre nu** to strip; **mettre à nu** to bare
nuage [nɥaʒ] *nm* cloud; **être dans les ~s** (*distrait*) to have one's head in the clouds; **~ de lait** drop of milk
nuageux, -euse [nɥaʒø, -øz] *adj* cloudy
nuance [nɥɑ̃s] *nf* (*de couleur, sens*) shade; **il y a une ~ (entre)** there's a slight difference (between); **une ~ de tristesse** a tinge of sadness
nuancé, e [nɥɑ̃se] *adj* (*opinion*) finely-shaded, subtly differing; **être ~ dans ses opinions** to have finely-shaded opinions
nuancer [nɥɑ̃se] *vt* (*pensée, opinion*) to qualify
nubile [nybil] *adj* nubile
nucléaire [nykleɛʀ] *adj* nuclear ▷ *nm* nuclear power
nudisme [nydism(ə)] *nm* nudism
nudiste [nydist(ə)] *adj, nm/f* nudist
nudité [nydite] *nf voir* **nu** nudity, nakedness; bareness
nuée [nɥe] *nf*: **une ~ de** a cloud *ou* host *ou* swarm of
nues [ny] *nfpl*: **tomber des ~** to be taken aback; **porter qn aux ~** to praise sb to the skies
nui [nɥi] *pp de* **nuire**
nuire [nɥiʀ] *vi* to be harmful; **~ à** to harm, do damage to
nuisance [nɥizɑ̃s] *nf* nuisance; **nuisances** *nfpl*

pollution *sg*
nuisible [nɥizibl(ə)] *adj* harmful; (**animal**) **~** pest
nuisis *etc* [nɥizi] *vb voir* **nuire**
nuit [nɥi] *nf* night; **payer sa ~** to pay for one's overnight accommodation; **il fait ~** it's dark; **cette ~** (*hier*) last night; (*aujourd'hui*) tonight; **de ~** (*vol, service*) night *cpd*; **~ blanche** sleepless night; **~ de noces** wedding night; **~ de Noël** Christmas Eve
nuitamment [nɥitamɑ̃] *adv* by night
nuitées [nɥite] *nfpl* overnight stays, beds occupied (*in statistics*)
nul, nulle [nyl] *adj* (*aucun*) no; (*minime*) nil, non-existent; (*non valable*) null; (*péj*) useless, hopeless ▷ *pron* none, no one; **résultat ~**, **match ~** draw; **nulle part** *adv* nowhere
nullement [nylmɑ̃] *adv* by no means
nullité [nylite] *nf* nullity; (*péj*) hopelessness; (*: personne*) hopeless individual, nonentity
numéraire [nymeʀɛʀ] *nm* cash; metal currency
numéral, e, -aux [nymeʀal, -o] *adj* numeral
numérateur [nymeʀatœʀ] *nm* numerator
numération [nymeʀɑsjɔ̃] *nf*: **~ décimale/binaire** decimal/binary notation; **~ globulaire** blood count
numérique [nymeʀik] *adj* numerical; (*Inform*) digital
numériquement [nymeʀikmɑ̃] *adv* numerically; (*Inform*) digitally
numériser [nymeʀize] *vt* (*Inform*) to digitize
numéro [nymeʀo] *nm* number; (*spectacle*) act, turn; **faire** *ou* **composer un ~** to dial a number; **~ d'identification personnel** personal identification number (PIN); **~ d'immatriculation** *ou* **minéralogique** *ou* **de police** registration (*Brit*) *ou* license (*US*) number; **~ de téléphone** (tele)phone number; **~ vert** ≈ Freefone® number (*Brit*); ≈ toll-free number (*US*)
numérotage [nymeʀotaʒ] *nm* numbering
numérotation [nymeʀotasjɔ̃] *nf* numeration
numéroter [nymeʀote] *vt* to number
numerus clausus [nymeʀysklozys] *nm inv* restriction *ou* limitation of numbers
numismate [nymismat] *nm/f* numismatist, coin collector
nu-pieds [nypje] *nm inv* sandal ▷ *adj inv* barefoot
nuptial, e, -aux [nypsjal, -o] *adj* nuptial; wedding *cpd*
nuptialité [nypsjalite] *nf*: **taux de ~** marriage rate
nuque [nyk] *nf* nape of the neck
nu-tête [nytɛt] *adj inv* bareheaded
nutritif, -ive [nytʀitif, -iv] *adj* nutritional; (*aliment*) nutritious, nourishing
nutrition [nytʀisjɔ̃] *nf* nutrition
nutritionnel, le [nytʀisjɔnɛl] *adj* nutritional
nutritionniste [nytʀisjɔnist(ə)] *nm/f* nutritionist
nylon [nilɔ̃] *nm* nylon
nymphomane [nɛ̃fɔman] *adj, nf* nymphomaniac

Oo

O, o [o] *nm inv* O, o ▷ *abr* (= *ouest*) W; **O comme Oscar** O for Oliver (*Brit*) *ou* Oboe (*US*)

OAS *sigle f* (= *Organisation de l'armée secrète*) *organization opposed to Algerian independence* (1961–63)

oasis [ɔazis] *nf ou m* oasis

obédience [ɔbedjɑ̃s] *nf* allegiance

obéir [ɔbeiʀ] *vi* to obey; ~ **à** to obey; (*moteur, véhicule*) to respond to

obéissance [ɔbeisɑ̃s] *nf* obedience

obéissant, e [ɔbeisɑ̃, -ɑ̃t] *adj* obedient

obélisque [ɔbelisk(ə)] *nm* obelisk

obèse [ɔbɛz] *adj* obese

obésité [ɔbezite] *nf* obesity

objecter [ɔbʒɛkte] *vt* (*prétexter*) to plead, put forward as an excuse; ~ **qch à** (*argument*) to put forward sth against; ~ **(à qn) que** to object (to sb) that

objecteur [ɔbʒɛktœʀ] *nm*: ~ **de conscience** conscientious objector

objectif, -ive [ɔbʒɛktif, -iv] *adj* objective ▷ *nm* (*Optique, Photo*) lens *sg*; (*Mil: fig*) objective; ~ **grand angulaire/à focale variable** wide-angle/zoom lens

objection [ɔbʒɛksjɔ̃] *nf* objection; ~ **de conscience** conscientious objection

objectivement [ɔbʒɛktivmɑ̃] *adv* objectively

objectivité [ɔbʒɛktivite] *nf* objectivity

objet [ɔbʒɛ] *nm* (*chose*) object; (*d'une discussion, recherche*) subject; **être** *ou* **faire l'~ de** (*discussion*) to be the subject of; (*soins*) to be given *ou* shown; **sans ~** *adj* purposeless; (*sans fondement*) groundless; ~ **d'art** objet d'art; ~**s personnels** personal items; ~**s de toilette** toiletries; ~**s trouvés** lost property *sg* (*Brit*), lost-and-found *sg* (*US*); ~**s de valeur** valuables

obligataire [ɔbligatɛʀ] *adj* bond *cpd* ▷ *nm/f* bondholder, debenture holder

obligation [ɔbligasjɔ̃] *nf* obligation; (*gén pl: devoir*) duty; (*Comm*) bond, debenture; **sans ~ d'achat** with no obligation (to buy); **être dans l'~ de faire** to be obliged to do; **avoir l'~ de faire** to be under an obligation to do; ~**s familiales** family obligations *ou* responsibilities; ~**s militaires** military obligations *ou* duties

obligatoire [ɔbligatwaʀ] *adj* compulsory, obligatory

obligatoirement [ɔbligatwaʀmɑ̃] *adv* compulsorily; (*fatalement*) necessarily

obligé, e [ɔbliʒe] *adj* (*redevable*): **être très ~ à qn** to be most obliged to sb; (*contraint*): **je suis (bien) ~ (de le faire)** I have to (do it); (*nécessaire: conséquence*) necessary; **c'est ~!** it's inevitable!

obligeamment [ɔbliʒamɑ̃] *adv* obligingly

obligeance [ɔbliʒɑ̃s] *nf*: **avoir l'~ de** to be kind *ou* good enough to

obligeant, e [ɔbliʒɑ̃, -ɑ̃t] *adj* obliging; kind

obliger [ɔbliʒe] *vt* (*contraindre*): ~ **qn à faire** to force *ou* oblige sb to do; (*Jur: engager*) to bind; (*rendre service à*) to oblige

oblique [ɔblik] *adj* oblique; **regard ~** sidelong glance; **en ~** *adv* diagonally

obliquer [ɔblike] *vi*: ~ **vers** to turn off towards

oblitération [ɔbliteʀasjɔ̃] *nf* cancelling *no pl*, cancellation; obstruction

oblitérer [ɔblitere] *vt* (*timbre-poste*) to cancel; (*Méd: canal, vaisseau*) to obstruct

oblong, oblongue [ɔblɔ̃, ɔblɔ̃g] *adj* oblong

obnubiler [ɔbnybile] *vt* to obsess

obole [ɔbɔl] *nf* offering

obscène [ɔpsɛn] *adj* obscene

obscénité [ɔpsenite] *nf* obscenity

obscur, e [ɔpskyʀ] *adj* (*sombre*) dark; (*fig: raisons*) obscure; (: *sentiment, malaise*) vague; (: *personne, vie*) humble, lowly

obscurcir [ɔpskyʀsiʀ] *vt* to darken; (*fig*) to obscure; **s'obscurcir** *vi* to grow dark

obscurité [ɔpskyʀite] *nf* darkness; **dans l'~** in the dark, in darkness; (*anonymat, médiocrité*) in obscurity

obsédant, e [ɔpsedɑ̃, -ɑ̃t] *adj* obsessive

obsédé, e [ɔpsede] *nm/f* fanatic; ~**(e) sexuel(le)** sex maniac

obséder [ɔpsede] *vt* to obsess, haunt

obsèques [ɔpsɛk] *nfpl* funeral *sg*

obséquieux, -euse [ɔpsekjø, -øz] *adj* obsequious

observance [ɔpsɛʀvɑ̃s] *nf* observance

observateur, -trice [ɔpsɛʀvatœʀ, -tʀis] *adj* observant, perceptive ▷ *nm/f* observer

observation [ɔpsɛʀvasjɔ̃] *nf* observation; (*d'un règlement etc*) observance; (*commentaire*) observation, remark; (*reproche*) reproof; **en ~** (*Méd*) under observation

observatoire [ɔpsɛʀvatwaʀ] *nm* observatory; (*lieu élevé*) observation post, vantage point

observer [ɔpsɛʀve] *vt* (*regarder*) to observe, watch; (*examiner*) to examine; (*scientifiquement, aussi: règlement, jeûne etc*) to observe; (*surveiller*) to watch; (*remarquer*) to observe, notice; **faire ~ qch à qn** (*dire*) to point out sth to sb; **s'observer** *vi* (*se surveiller*) to keep a check on o.s.

obsession [ɔpsesjɔ̃] *nf* obsession; **avoir l'~ de** to have an obsession with

obsessionnel, le [ɔpsesjɔnɛl] *adj* obsessive

obsolescent, e [ɔpsɔlesɑ̃, -ɑ̃t] *adj* obsolescent

obstacle [ɔpstakl(ə)] *nm* obstacle; (*Équitation*) jump, hurdle; **faire ~ à** (*lumière*) to block out; (*projet*) to hinder, put obstacles in the path of; **~s antichars** tank defences

obstétricien, ne [ɔpstetʀisjɛ̃, -ɛn] *nm/f* obstetrician

obstétrique [ɔpstetʀik] *nf* obstetrics *sg*

obstination [ɔpstinasjɔ̃] *nf* obstinacy

obstiné, e [ɔpstine] *adj* obstinate

obstinément [ɔpstinemɑ̃] *adv* obstinately

obstiner [ɔpstine]: **s'obstiner** *vi* to insist, dig one's heels in; **s'~ à faire** to persist (obstinately) in doing; **s'~ sur qch** to keep working at sth, labour away at sth

obstruction [ɔpstʀyksjɔ̃] *nf* obstruction, blockage; (*Sport*) obstruction; **faire de l'~** (*fig*) to be obstructive

obstruer [ɔpstʀye] *vt* to block, obstruct; **s'obstruer** *vi* to become blocked

obtempérer [ɔptɑ̃peʀe] *vi* to obey; **~ à** to obey, comply with

obtenir [ɔptəniʀ] *vt* to obtain, get; (*total*) to arrive at, reach; (*résultat*) to achieve, obtain; **~ de pouvoir faire** to obtain permission to do; **~ qch à qn** to obtain sth for sb; **~ de qn qu'il fasse** to get sb to agree to do(ing)

obtention [ɔptɑ̃sjɔ̃] *nf* obtaining

obtenu, e [ɔpt(ə)ny] *pp de* **obtenir**

obtiendrai [ɔptjɛ̃dʀe], **obtiens** [ɔptjɛ̃], **obtint** *etc* [ɔptɛ̃] *vb voir* **obtenir**

obturateur [ɔptyʀatœʀ] *nm* (*Photo*) shutter; **~ à rideau** focal plane shutter

obturation [ɔptyʀasjɔ̃] *nf* closing (up); **~ (dentaire)** filling; **vitesse d'~** (*Photo*) shutter speed

obturer [ɔptyʀe] *vt* to close (up); (*dent*) to fill

obtus, e [ɔpty, -yz] *adj* obtuse

obus [ɔby] *nm* shell; **~ explosif** high-explosive shell; **~ incendiaire** incendiary device, fire bomb

obvier [ɔbvje]: **~ à** *vt* to obviate

OC *sigle fpl* (= *ondes courtes*) SW

occasion [ɔkazjɔ̃] *nf* (*aubaine, possibilité*) opportunity; (*circonstance*) occasion; (*Comm: article non neuf*) secondhand buy; (: *acquisition avantageuse*) bargain; **à plusieurs ~s** on several occasions; **à la première ~** at the first *ou* earliest opportunity; **avoir l'~ de faire** to have

the opportunity to do; **être l'~ de** to occasion, give rise to; **à l'~** *adv* sometimes, on occasions; (*un jour*) some time; **à l'~ de** on the occasion of; **d'~** *adj, adv* secondhand

occasionnel, le [ɔkazjɔnɛl] *adj* (*fortuit*) chance *cpd*; (*non régulier*) occasional; (: *travail*) casual

occasionnellement [ɔkazjɔnɛlmɑ̃] *adv* occasionally, from time to time

occasionner [ɔkazjɔne] *vt* to cause, bring about; **~ qch à qn** to cause sb sth

occident [ɔksidɑ̃] *nm*: **l'O~** the West

occidental, e, -aux [ɔksidɑ̃tal, -o] *adj* western; (*Pol*) Western ▷ *nm/f* Westerner

occidentaliser [ɔksidɑ̃talize] *vt* (*coutumes, mœurs*) to westernize

occiput [ɔksipyt] *nm* back of the head, occiput

occire [ɔksiʀ] *vt* to slay

occitan, e [ɔksitɑ̃, -an] *adj* of the langue d'oc, of Provençal French

occlusion [ɔklyzjɔ̃] *nf*: **~ intestinale** obstruction of the bowel

occulte [ɔkylt(ə)] *adj* occult, supernatural

occulter [ɔkylte] *vt* (*fig*) to overshadow

occupant, e [ɔkypɑ̃, -ɑ̃t] *adj* occupying ▷ *nm/f* (*d'un appartement*) occupier, occupant; (*d'un véhicule*) occupant ▷ *nm* (*Mil*) occupying forces *pl*; (*Pol: d'usine etc*) occupier

occupation [ɔkypasjɔ̃] *nf* occupation; **l'O~** the Occupation (of France)

occupationnel, le [ɔkypasjɔnɛl] *adj*: **thérapie ~le** occupational therapy

occupé, e [ɔkype] *adj* (*Mil, Pol*) occupied; (*personne: affairé, pris*) busy; (*esprit: absorbé*) occupied; (*place, sièges*) taken; (*toilettes, ligne*) engaged

occuper [ɔkype] *vt* to occupy; (*poste, fonction*) to hold; (*main-d'œuvre*) to employ; **s'~ (à qch)** to occupy o.s ou keep o.s. busy (with sth); **s'~ de** (*être responsable de*) to be in charge of; (*se charger de: affaire*) to take charge of, deal with; (: *clients etc*) to attend to; (*s'intéresser à, pratiquer: politique etc*) to be involved in; **ça occupe trop de place** it takes up too much room

occurrence [ɔkyʀɑ̃s] *nf*: **en l'~** in this case

OCDE *sigle f* (= *Organisation de coopération et de développement économique*) OECD

océan [ɔseɑ̃] *nm* ocean; **l'~ Indien** the Indian Ocean

Océanie [ɔseani] *nf*: **l'~** Oceania, South Sea Islands

océanique [ɔseanik] *adj* oceanic

océanographe [ɔseanɔgʀaf] *nm/f* oceanographer

océanographie [ɔseanɔgʀafi] *nf* oceanography

océanologie [ɔseanɔlɔʒi] *nf* oceanology

ocelot [ɔslo] *nm* (*Zool*) ocelot; (*fourrure*) ocelot fur

ocre [ɔkʀ(ə)] *adj inv* ochre

octane [ɔktan] *nm* octane

octante [ɔktɑ̃t] *num* (*Belgique, Suisse*) eighty

octave [ɔktav] *nf* octave

octet [ɔktɛ] *nm* byte

octobre [ɔktɔbʀ(ə)] *nm* October; *voir aussi* **juillet**

octogénaire [ɔktɔʒenɛʀ] *adj, nm/f* octogenarian
octogonal, e, -aux [ɔktɔgɔnal, -o] *adj* octagonal
octogone [ɔktɔgɔn] *nm* octagon
octroi [ɔktʀwa] *nm* granting
octroyer [ɔktʀwaje] *vt*: ~ **qch à qn** to grant sth to sb, grant sb sth
oculaire [ɔkylɛʀ] *adj* ocular, eye *cpd* ▷ *nm* (*de microscope*) eyepiece
oculiste [ɔkylist(ə)] *nm/f* eye specialist, oculist
ode [ɔd] *nf* ode
odeur [ɔdœʀ] *nf* smell
odieusement [ɔdjøzmɑ̃] *adv* odiously
odieux, -euse [ɔdjø, -øz] *adj* odious, hateful
odontologie [ɔdɔ̃tɔlɔʒi] *nf* odontology
odorant, e [ɔdɔʀɑ̃, -ɑ̃t] *adj* sweet-smelling, fragrant
odorat [ɔdɔʀa] *nm* (sense of) smell; **avoir l'~ fin** to have a keen sense of smell
odoriférant, e [ɔdɔʀiferɑ̃, -ɑ̃t] *adj* sweet-smelling, fragrant
odyssée [ɔdise] *nf* odyssey
OEA *sigle f* (= *Organisation des États américains*) OAS
œcuménique [ekymenik] *adj* ecumenical
œdème [edɛm] *nm* oedema (*Brit*), edema (*US*)
œil [œj] (*pl* **yeux** [jø]) *nm* eye; **avoir un ~ poché** *ou* **au beurre noir** to have a black eye; **à l'~** (*fam*) for free; **à l'~ nu** with the naked eye; **tenir qn à l'~** to keep an eye *ou* a watch on sb; **avoir l'~ à** to keep an eye on; **faire de l'~ à qn** to make eyes at sb; **voir qch d'un bon/mauvais ~** to view sth in a favourable/an unfavourable light; **à l'~ vif** with a lively expression; **à mes/ses yeux** in my/his eyes; **de ses propres yeux** with his own eyes; **fermer les yeux (sur)** (*fig*) to turn a blind eye (to); **les yeux fermés** (*aussi fig*) with one's eyes shut; **fermer l'~** to get a moment's sleep; **~ pour ~, dent pour dent** an eye for an eye, a tooth for a tooth; **pour les beaux yeux de qn** (*fig*) for love of sb; **~ de verre** glass eye
œil-de-bœuf [œjdəbœf] (*pl* **œils-de-bœuf**) *nm* bull's-eye (window)
œillade [œjad] *nf*: **lancer une ~ à qn** to wink at sb, give sb a wink; **faire des ~s à** to make eyes at
œillères [œjɛʀ] *nfpl* blinkers (*Brit*), blinders (*US*); **avoir des ~** (*fig*) to be blinkered, wear blinders
œillet [œjɛ] *nm* (*Bot*) carnation; (*trou*) eyelet
œnologue [enɔlɔg] *nm/f* wine expert
œsophage [ezɔfaʒ] *nm* oesophagus (*Brit*), esophagus (*US*)
œstrogène [ɛstʀɔʒɛn] *adj* oestrogen (*Brit*), estrogen (*US*)
œuf [œf] *nm* egg; **étouffer dans l'~** to nip in the bud; **~ à la coque/dur/mollet** boiled/hard-boiled/soft-boiled egg; **~ au plat/poché** fried/poached egg; **~s brouillés** scrambled eggs; **~ de Pâques** Easter egg; **~ à repriser** darning egg
œuvre [œvʀ(ə)] *nf* (*tâche*) task, undertaking; (*ouvrage achevé, livre, tableau etc*) work; (*ensemble de la production artistique*) works *pl*; (*organisation charitable*) charity ▷ *nm* (*d'un artiste*) works *pl*; (*Constr*): **le gros ~** the shell; **œuvres** *nfpl* (*actes*)

deeds, works; **être/se mettre à l'~** to be at/get (down) to work; **mettre en ~** (*moyens*) to make use of; (*plan, loi, projet etc*) to implement; **~ d'art** work of art; **bonnes ~s** good works *ou* deeds; **~s de bienfaisance** charitable works
OFCE *sigle m* (= *Observatoire français des conjonctures économiques*) economic research institute
offensant, e [ɔfɑ̃sɑ̃, -ɑ̃t] *adj* offensive, insulting
offense [ɔfɑ̃s] *nf* (*affront*) insult; (*Rel*): **péché**) transgression, trespass
offenser [ɔfɑ̃se] *vt* to offend, hurt; (*principes, Dieu*) to offend against; **s'offenser de** *vi* to take offence (*Brit*) *ou* offense (*US*) at
offensif, -ive [ɔfɑ̃sif, -iv] *adj* (*armes, guerre*) offensive ▷ *nf* offensive; (*fig: du froid, de l'hiver*) onslaught; **passer à l'offensive** to go into the attack *ou* offensive
offert, e [ɔfɛʀ, -ɛʀt(ə)] *pp de* **offrir**
offertoire [ɔfɛʀtwaʀ] *nm* offertory
office [ɔfis] *nm* (*charge*) office; (*agence*) bureau, agency; (*Rel*) service ▷ *nm ou f* (*pièce*) pantry; **faire ~ de** to act as; to do duty as; **d'~** *adv* automatically; **bons ~s** (*Pol*) good offices; **~ du tourisme** tourist bureau
officialiser [ɔfisjalize] *vt* to make official
officiel, le [ɔfisjɛl] *adj, nm/f* official
officiellement [ɔfisjɛlmɑ̃] *adv* officially
officier [ɔfisje] *nm* officer ▷ *vi* (*Rel*) to officiate; **~ de l'état-civil** registrar; **~ ministériel** member of the legal profession; **~ de police** = police officer
officieusement [ɔfisjøzmɑ̃] *adv* unofficially
officieux, -euse [ɔfisjø, -øz] *adj* unofficial
officinal, e, -aux [ɔfisinal, -o] *adj*: **plantes ~es** medicinal plants
officine [ɔfisin] *nf* (*de pharmacie*) dispensary; (*Admin: pharmacie*) pharmacy; (*gén péj: bureau*) agency, office
offrais *etc* [ɔfʀɛ] *vb voir* **offrir**
offrande [ɔfʀɑ̃d] *nf* offering
offrant [ɔfʀɑ̃] *nm*: **au plus ~** to the highest bidder
offre [ɔfʀ(ə)] *vb voir* **offrir** ▷ *nf* offer; (*aux enchères*) bid; (*Admin: soumission*) tender; (*Écon*): **l'~** supply; **~ d'emploi** job advertised; **"~s d'emploi"** "situations vacant"; **~ publique d'achat (OPA)** takeover bid; **~s de service** offer of service
offrir [ɔfʀiʀ] *vt*: **~ (à qn)** to offer (to sb); (*faire cadeau*) to give to (sb); **s'offrir** *vi* (*se présenter: occasion, paysage*) to present itself ▷ *vt* (*se payer: vacances, voiture*) to treat o.s. to; **~ (à qn) de faire qch** to offer to do sth (for sb); **~ à boire à qn** to offer sb a drink; **s'~ à faire qch** to offer *ou* volunteer to do sth; **s'~ comme guide/en otage** to offer one's services as (a) guide/offer o.s. as (a) hostage; **s'~ aux regards** (*personne*) to expose o.s. to the public gaze
offset [ɔfsɛt] *nm* offset (printing)
offusquer [ɔfyske] *vt* to offend; **s'offusquer de** to take offence (*Brit*) *ou* offense (*US*) at, be offended by

ogive [ɔʒiv] *nf* (*Archit*) diagonal rib; (*d'obus, de missile*) nose cone; **voûte en ~** rib vault; **arc en ~** lancet arch; **~ nucléaire** nuclear warhead

OGM *sigle m* GMO

ogre [ɔgʀ(ə)] *nm* ogre

oh [o] *excl* oh!; **oh la la!** oh (dear)!; **pousser des oh! et des ah!** to gasp with admiration

oie [wa] *nf* (*Zool*) goose; **~ blanche** (*fig*) young innocent

oignon [ɔɲɔ̃] *nm* (*Culin*) onion; (*de tulipe etc: bulbe*) bulb; (*Méd*) bunion; **ce ne sont pas tes ~s** (*fam*) that's none of your business

oindre [wɛ̃dʀ(ə)] *vt* to anoint

oiseau, x [wazo] *nm* bird; **~ de proie** bird of prey

oiseau-mouche [wazomuʃ] (*pl* **oiseaux-mouches**) *nm* hummingbird

oiseleur [wazlœʀ] *nm* bird-catcher

oiselier, -ière [wazəlje, -jɛʀ] *nm/f* bird-seller

oisellerie [wazɛlʀi] *nf* bird shop

oiseux, -euse [wazø, -øz] *adj* pointless, idle; (*sans valeur, importance*) trivial

oisif, -ive [wazif, -iv] *adj* idle ▷ *nm/f* (*péj*) man/lady of leisure

oisillon [wazijɔ̃] *nm* little *ou* baby bird

oisiveté [wazivte] *nf* idleness

OIT *sigle f* (= *Organisation internationale du travail*) ILO

OK [okɛ] *excl* OK!, all right!

OL *sigle fpl* (= *ondes longues*) LW

oléagineux, -euse [ɔleaʒinø, -øz] *adj* oleaginous, oil-producing

oléiculture [ɔleikyltyʀ] *nm* olive growing

oléoduc [ɔleɔdyk] *nm* (oil) pipeline

olfactif, -ive [ɔlfaktif, -iv] *adj* olfactory

olibrius [ɔlibʀijys] *nm* oddball

oligarchie [ɔligaʀʃi] *nf* oligarchy

oligo-élément [ɔligɔelemɑ̃] *nm* trace element

oligopole [ɔligɔpɔl] *nm* oligopoly

olivâtre [ɔlivɑtʀ(ə)] *adj* olive-greenish; (*teint*) sallow

olive [ɔliv] *nf* (*Bot*) olive ▷ *adj inv* olive-green

oliveraie [ɔlivʀɛ] *nf* olive grove

olivier [ɔlivje] *nm* olive (tree); (*bois*) olive (wood)

olographe [ɔlɔgʀaf] *adj*: **testament ~** *will* written, dated and signed by the testator

OLP *sigle f* (= *Organisation de libération de la Palestine*) PLO

olympiade [ɔlɛ̃pjad] *nf* (*période*) Olympiad; **les ~s** (*jeux*) the Olympiad *sg*

olympien, ne [ɔlɛ̃pjɛ̃, -ɛn] *adj* Olympian, of Olympian aloofness

olympique [ɔlɛ̃pik] *adj* Olympic

OM *sigle fpl* (= *ondes moyennes*) MW

Oman [ɔman] *nm*: **l'~, le sultanat d'~** (the Sultanate of) Oman

ombilical, e, -aux [ɔ̃bilikal, -o] *adj* umbilical

ombrage [ɔ̃bʀaʒ] *nm* (*ombre*) (leafy) shade; (*fig*): **prendre ~ de** to take umbrage at; **faire** *ou* **porter ~ à qn** to offend sb

ombragé, e [ɔ̃bʀaʒe] *adj* shaded, shady

ombrageux, -euse [ɔ̃bʀaʒø, -øz] *adj* (*cheval*) skittish, nervous; (*personne*) touchy, easily offended

ombre [ɔ̃bʀ(ə)] *nf* (*espace non ensoleillé*) shade; (*ombre portée, tache*) shadow; **à l'~** in the shade; (*fam: en prison*) behind bars; **à l'~ de** in the shade of; (*tout près de, fig*) in the shadow of; **tu me fais de l'~** you're in my light; **ça nous donne de l'~** it gives us (some) shade; **il n'y a pas l'~ d'un doute** there's not the shadow of a doubt; **dans l'~** in the shade; **vivre dans l'~** (*fig*) to live in obscurity; **laisser dans l'~** (*fig*) to leave in the dark; **~ à paupières** eye shadow; **~ portée** shadow; **~s chinoises** (*spectacle*) shadow show *sg*

ombrelle [ɔ̃bʀɛl] *nf* parasol, sunshade

ombrer [ɔ̃bʀe] *vt* to shade

OMC *sigle f* (= *organisation mondiale du commerce*) WTO

omelette [ɔmlɛt] *nf* omelette; **~ baveuse** runny omelette; **~ au fromage/au jambon** cheese/ham omelette; **~ aux herbes** omelette with herbs; **~ norvégienne** baked Alaska

omettre [ɔmɛtʀ(ə)] *vt* to omit, leave out; **~ de faire** to fail *ou* omit to do

omis, e [ɔmi, -iz] *pp* de **omettre**

omission [ɔmisjɔ̃] *nf* omission

omnibus [ɔmnibys] *nm* slow *ou* stopping train

omnipotent, e [ɔmnipɔtɑ̃, -ɑ̃t] *adj* omnipotent

omnipraticien, ne [ɔmnipʀatisjɛ̃, -ɛn] *nm/f* (*Méd*) general practitioner

omniprésent, e [ɔmnipʀezɑ̃, -ɑ̃t] *adj* omnipresent

omniscient, e [ɔmnisjɑ̃, -ɑ̃t] *adj* omniscient

omnisports [ɔmnispɔʀ] *adj inv* (*club*) general sports *cpd*; (*salle*) multi-purpose *cpd*; (*terrain*) all-purpose *cpd*

omnium [ɔmnjɔm] *nm* (*Comm*) corporation; (*Cyclisme*) omnium; (*Courses*) open handicap

omnivore [ɔmnivɔʀ] *adj* omnivorous

omoplate [ɔmɔplat] *nf* shoulder blade

OMS *sigle f* (= *Organisation mondiale de la santé*) WHO

 MOT-CLÉ

on [ɔ̃] *pron* **1** (*indéterminé*) you, one; **on peut le faire ainsi** you *ou* one can do it like this, it can be done like this; **on dit que ...** they say that ..., it is said that ..

2 (*quelqu'un*): **on les a attaqués** they were attacked; **on vous demande au téléphone** there's a phone call for you, you're wanted on the phone; **on frappe à la porte** someone's knocking at the door

3 (*nous*) we; **on va y aller demain** we're going tomorrow

4 (*les gens*) they; **autrefois, on croyait ...** they used to believe ..

5: **on ne peut plus** *adv*: **on ne peut plus stupide** as stupid as can be

once [ɔ̃s] *nf*: **une ~ de** an ounce of

oncle [ɔ̃kl(ə)] nm uncle
onction [ɔ̃ksjɔ̃] nf voir **extrême-onction**
onctueux, -euse [ɔ̃ktɥø, -øz] adj creamy, smooth; (fig) smooth, unctuous
onde [ɔ̃d] nf (Physique) wave; **sur l'~** on the waters; **sur les ~s** on the radio; **mettre en ~s** to produce for the radio; **~ de choc** shock wave; **~s courtes (OC)** short wave sg; **petites ~s (PO)**, **~s moyennes (OM)** medium wave sg; **grandes ~s (GO)**, **~s longues (OL)** long wave sg; **~s sonores** sound waves
ondée [ɔ̃de] nf shower
on-dit [ɔ̃di] nm inv rumour
ondoyer [ɔ̃dwaje] vi to ripple, wave ▷ vt (Rel) to baptize (in an emergency)
ondulant, e [ɔ̃dylɑ̃, -ɑ̃t] adj (démarche) swaying; (ligne) undulating
ondulation [ɔ̃dylasjɔ̃] nf undulation; wave
ondulé, e [ɔ̃dyle] adj undulating; wavy
onduler [ɔ̃dyle] vi to undulate; (cheveux) to wave
onéreux, -euse [ɔnerø, -øz] adj costly; **à titre ~** in return for payment
ONF sigle m (= Office national des forêts) ≈ Forestry Commission (Brit), ≈ National Forest Service (US)
ONG sigle f (= organisation non-gouvernementale) NGO
ongle [ɔ̃gl(ə)] nm (Anat) nail; **manger** ou **ronger ses ~s** to bite one's nails; **se faire les ~s** to do one's nails
onglet [ɔ̃glɛ] nm (rainure) (thumbnail) groove; (bande de papier) tab
onguent [ɔ̃gɑ̃] nm ointment
onirique [ɔnirik] adj dreamlike, dream cpd
onirisme [ɔnirism(ə)] nm dreams pl
onomatopée [ɔnɔmatɔpe] nf onomatopoeia
ont [ɔ̃] vb voir **avoir**
ontarien, ne [ɔ̃tarjɛ̃, -ɛn] adj Ontarian
ONU [ɔny] sigle f (= Organisation des Nations unies) UN(O)
onusien, ne [ɔnyzjɛ̃, -ɛn] adj of the UN(O), of the United Nations (Organization)
onyx [ɔniks] nm onyx
onze [ɔ̃z] num eleven
onzième [ɔ̃zjɛm] num eleventh
op [ɔp] nf (opération): **salle d'op** (operating) theatre
OPA sigle f = **offre publique d'achat**
opacité [ɔpasite] nf opaqueness
opale [ɔpal] nf opal
opalescent, e [ɔpalesɑ̃, -ɑ̃t] adj opalescent
opalin, e [ɔpalɛ̃, -in] adj, nf opaline
opaque [ɔpak] adj (vitre, verre) opaque; (brouillard, nuit) impenetrable
OPE sigle f (= offre publique d'échange) take-over bid where bidder offers shares in his company in exchange for shares in target company
OPEP [ɔpɛp] sigle f (= Organisation des pays exportateurs de pétrole) OPEC
opéra [ɔpera] nm opera; (édifice) opera house
opérable [ɔperabl(ə)] adj operable
opéra-comique [ɔperakɔmik] (pl **opéras-comiques**) nm light opera, opéra comique

opérant, e [ɔperɑ̃, -ɑ̃t] adj (mesure) effective
opérateur, -trice [ɔperatœr, -tris] nm/f operator; **~ (de prise de vues)** cameraman
opération [ɔperasjɔ̃] nf operation; (Comm) dealing; **salle/table d'~** operating theatre/ table; **~ de sauvetage** rescue operation; **~ à cœur ouvert** open-heart surgery no pl
opérationnel, le [ɔperasjɔnel] adj operational
opératoire [ɔperatwar] adj (manœuvre, méthode) operating; (choc etc) post-operative
opéré, e [ɔpere] nm/f post-operative patient
opérer [ɔpere] vt (Méd) to operate on; (faire, exécuter) to carry out, make ▷ vi (remède: faire effet) to act, work; (procéder) to proceed; (Méd) to operate; **s'opérer** vi (avoir lieu) to occur, take place; **se faire ~** to have an operation; **se faire ~ des amygdales/du cœur** to have one's tonsils out/have a heart operation
opérette [ɔperɛt] nf operetta, light opera
ophtalmique [ɔftalmik] adj ophthalmic
ophtalmologie [ɔftalmɔlɔʒi] nf ophthalmology
ophtalmologue [ɔftalmɔlɔg] nm/f ophthalmologist
opiacé, e [ɔpjase] adj opiate
opiner [ɔpine] vi: **~ de la tête** to nod assent ▷ vt: **~ à** to consent to
opiniâtre [ɔpinjatr(ə)] adj stubborn
opiniâtreté [ɔpinjatrəte] nf stubbornness
opinion [ɔpinjɔ̃] nf opinion; **l'~ (publique)** public opinion; **avoir bonne/mauvaise ~ de** to have a high/low opinion of
opiomane [ɔpjɔman] nm/f opium addict
opium [ɔpjɔm] nm opium
OPJ sigle m (= officier de police judiciaire) ≈ DC (= Detective Constable)
opportun, e [ɔpɔrtœ̃, -yn] adj timely, opportune; **en temps ~** at the appropriate time
opportunément [ɔpɔrtynemɑ̃] adv opportunely
opportunisme [ɔpɔrtynism(ə)] nm opportunism
opportuniste [ɔpɔrtynist(ə)] adj, nm/f opportunist
opportunité [ɔpɔrtynite] nf timeliness, opportuneness
opposant, e [ɔpozɑ̃, -ɑ̃t] adj opposing ▷ nm/f opponent
opposé, e [ɔpoze] adj (direction, rive) opposite; (faction) opposing; (couleurs) contrasting; (opinions, intérêts) conflicting; (contre): **~ à** opposed to, against ▷ nm: **l'~** the other ou opposite side (ou direction); (contraire) the opposite; **être ~ à** to be opposed to; **à l'~** (fig) on the other hand; **à l'~ de** on the other ou opposite side from; (fig) contrary to, unlike
opposer [ɔpoze] vt (meubles, objets) to place opposite each other; (personnes, armées, équipes) to oppose; (couleurs, termes, tons) to contrast; (comparer: livres, avantages) to contrast; **~ qch à** (comme obstacle, défense) to set sth against; (comme objection) to put sth forward against; (en contraste) to set sth opposite; to match sth with;

s'opposer vi (sens réciproque) to conflict; to clash; to face each other; to contrast; **s'~ à** (interdire, empêcher) to oppose; (tenir tête à) to rebel against; **sa religion s'y oppose** it's against his religion; **s'~ à ce que qn fasse** to be opposed to sb's doing

opposition [ɔpozisjɔ̃] nf opposition; **par ~** in contrast; **par ~ à** as opposed to, in contrast with; **entrer en ~ avec** to come into conflict with; **être en ~ avec** (idées, conduite) to be at variance with; **faire ~ à un chèque** to stop a cheque

oppressant, e [ɔpʀesɑ̃, -ɑ̃t] adj oppressive

oppresser [ɔpʀese] vt to oppress; **se sentir oppressé** to feel breathless

oppresseur [ɔpʀesœʀ] nm oppressor

oppressif, -ive [ɔpʀesif, -iv] adj oppressive

oppression [ɔpʀesjɔ̃] nf oppression; (malaise) feeling of suffocation

opprimer [ɔpʀime] vt (asservir: peuple, faibles) to oppress; (étouffer: liberté, opinion) to suppress, stifle; (chaleur etc) to suffocate, oppress

opprobre [ɔpʀɔbʀ(ə)] nm disgrace

opter [ɔpte] vi: **~ pour** to opt for; **~ entre** to choose between

opticien, ne [ɔptisjɛ̃, -ɛn] nm/f optician

optimal, e, -aux [ɔptimal, -o] adj optimal

optimisation [ɔptimizasjɔ̃] nf optimization

optimiser [ɔptimize] vt to optimize

optimisme [ɔptimism(ə)] nm optimism

optimiste [ɔptimist(ə)] adj optimistic ▷ nm/f optimist

optimum [ɔptimɔm] adj, nm optimum

option [ɔpsjɔ̃] nf option; (Auto: supplément) optional extra; **matière à ~** (Scol) optional subject (Brit), elective (US); **prendre une ~ sur** to take (out) an option on; **~ par défaut** (Inform) default (option)

optionnel, le [ɔpsjɔnɛl] adj optional

optique [ɔptik] adj (nerf) optic; (verres) optical ▷ nf (Photo: lentilles etc) optics pl; (science, industrie) optics sg; (fig: manière de voir) perspective

opulence [ɔpylɑ̃s] nf wealth, opulence

opulent, e [ɔpylɑ̃, -ɑ̃t] adj wealthy, opulent; (formes, poitrine) ample, generous

OPV sigle f (= offre publique de vente) public offer of sale

or [ɔʀ] nm gold ▷ conj now, but; **d'or** (fig) golden; **en or** gold cpd; (occasion) golden; **un mari/ enfant en or** a treasure; **une affaire en or** (achat) a real bargain; (commerce) a gold mine; **plaqué or** gold-plated; **or noir** black gold

oracle [ɔʀakl(ə)] nm oracle

orage [ɔʀaʒ] nm (thunder)storm

orageux, -euse [ɔʀaʒø, -øz] adj stormy

oraison [ɔʀɛzɔ̃] nf orison, prayer; **~ funèbre** funeral oration

oral, e, -aux [ɔʀal, -o] adj (déposition, promesse) oral, verbal; (Méd): **par voie ~e** by mouth, orally ▷ nm (Scol) oral

oralement [ɔʀalmɑ̃] adv orally

orange [ɔʀɑ̃ʒ] adj inv, nf orange; **~ sanguine** blood orange; **~ pressée** freshly-squeezed orange juice

orangé, e [ɔʀɑ̃ʒe] adj orangey, orange-coloured

orangeade [ɔʀɑ̃ʒad] nf orangeade

oranger [ɔʀɑ̃ʒe] nm orange tree

orangeraie [ɔʀɑ̃ʒʀɛ] nf orange grove

orangerie [ɔʀɑ̃ʒʀi] nf orangery

orang-outan, orang-outang [ɔʀɑ̃utɑ̃] nm orang-utan

orateur [ɔʀatœʀ] nm speaker; orator

oratoire [ɔʀatwaʀ] nm (lieu, chapelle) oratory; (au bord du chemin) wayside shrine ▷ adj oratorical

oratorio [ɔʀatɔʀjo] nm oratorio

orbital, e, -aux [ɔʀbital, -o] adj orbital; **station ~e** space station

orbite [ɔʀbit] nf (Anat) (eye-)socket; (Physique) orbit; **mettre sur ~** to put into orbit; (fig) to launch; **dans l'~ de** (fig) within the sphere of influence of

Orcades [ɔʀkad] nfpl: **les ~** the Orkneys, the Orkney Islands

orchestral, e, -aux [ɔʀkɛstʀal, -o] adj orchestral

orchestrateur, -trice [ɔʀkɛstʀatœʀ, -tʀis] nm/f orchestrator

orchestration [ɔʀkɛstʀasjɔ̃] nf orchestration

orchestre [ɔʀkɛstʀ(ə)] nm orchestra; (de jazz, danse) band; (places) stalls pl (Brit), orchestra (US)

orchestrer [ɔʀkɛstʀe] vt (Mus) to orchestrate; (fig) to mount, stage-manage

orchidée [ɔʀkide] nf orchid

ordinaire [ɔʀdinɛʀ] adj ordinary; (coutumier: maladresse etc) usual; (de tous les jours) everyday; (modèle, qualité) standard ▷ nm ordinary; (menus) everyday fare ▷ nf (essence) ≈ two-star (petrol) (Brit), ≈ regular (gas) (US); **d'~** usually, normally; **à l'~** usually, ordinarily

ordinairement [ɔʀdinɛʀmɑ̃] adv ordinarily, usually

ordinal, e, -aux [ɔʀdinal, -o] adj ordinal

ordinateur [ɔʀdinatœʀ] nm computer; **mettre sur ~** to computerize, put on computer; **~ de bureau** desktop computer; **~ individuel** ou **personnel** personal computer; **~ portable** laptop (computer)

ordination [ɔʀdinasjɔ̃] nf ordination

ordonnance [ɔʀdɔnɑ̃s] nf organization; (groupement, disposition) layout; (Méd) prescription; (Jur) order; (Mil) orderly, batman (Brit); **d'~** (Mil) regulation cpd; **officier d'~** aide-de-camp

ordonnateur, -trice [ɔʀdɔnatœʀ, -tʀis] nm/f (d'une cérémonie, fête) organizer; **~ des pompes funèbres** funeral director

ordonné, e [ɔʀdɔne] adj tidy, orderly; (Math) ordered ▷ nf (Math) Y-axis, ordinate

ordonner [ɔʀdɔne] vt (agencer) to organize, arrange; (: meubles, appartement) to lay out, arrange; (donner un ordre): **~ à qn de faire** to order sb to do; (Math) to (arrange in) order; (Rel) to ordain; (Méd) to prescribe; (Jur) to order; **s'ordonner** vi (faits) to organize themselves

ordre [ɔRdR(ə)] *nm* (*gén*) order; (*propreté et soin*) orderliness, tidiness; (*association professionnelle, honorifique*) association; (*Comm*): **à l'~ de** payable to; (*nature*): **d'~ pratique** of a practical nature; **ordres** *nmpl* (*Rel*) holy orders; **avoir de l'~** to be tidy *ou* orderly; **mettre en ~** to tidy (up), put in order; **mettre bon ~ à** to put to rights, sort out; **procéder par ~** to take things one at a time; **être aux ~s de qn/sous les ~s de qn** to be at sb's disposal/under sb's command; **rappeler qn à l'~** to call sb to order; **jusqu'à nouvel ~** until further notice; **dans le même ~ d'idées** in this connection; **par ~ d'entrée en scène** in order of appearance; **un ~ de grandeur** some idea of the size (*ou* amount); **de premier ~** first-rate; **~ de grève** strike call; **~ du jour** (*d'une réunion*) agenda; (*Mil*) order of the day; **à l'~ du jour** on the agenda; (*fig*) topical; (*Mil: citer*) in dispatches; **~ de mission** (*Mil*) orders *pl*; **~ public** law and order; **~ de route** marching orders *pl*

ordure [ɔRdyR] *nf* filth *no pl*; (*propos, écrit*) obscenity, (piece of) filth; **ordures** *nfpl* (*balayures, déchets*) rubbish *sg*, refuse *sg*; **~s ménagères** household refuse

ordurier, -ière [ɔRdyRje, -jɛR] *adj* lewd, filthy

oreille [ɔRɛj] *nf* (*Anat*) ear; (*de marmite, tasse*) handle; (*Tech: d'un écrou*) wing; **avoir de l'~** to have a good ear (for music); **avoir l'~ fine** to have good *ou* sharp ears; **l'~ basse** crestfallen, dejected; **se faire tirer l'~** to take a lot of persuading; **dire qch à l'~ de qn** to have a word in sb's ear (about sth)

oreiller [ɔReje] *nm* pillow

oreillette [ɔRɛjɛt] *nf* (*Anat*) auricle

oreillons [ɔRɛjɔ̃] *nmpl* mumps *sg*

ores [ɔR]: **d'~ et déjà** *adv* already

orfèvre [ɔRfɛvR(ə)] *nm* goldsmith; silversmith

orfèvrerie [ɔRfɛvRəRi] *nf* (*art, métier*) goldsmith's (*ou* silversmith's) trade; (*ouvrage*) (silver *ou* gold) plate

orfraie [ɔRfRɛ] *nm* white-tailed eagle; **pousser des cris d'~** to yell at the top of one's voice

organe [ɔRgan] *nm* organ; (*véhicule, instrument*) instrument; (*voix*) voice; (*porte-parole*) representative, mouthpiece; **~s de commande** (*Tech*) controls; **~s de transmission** (*Tech*) transmission system *sg*

organigramme [ɔRganigRam] *nm* (*hiérarchique, structure*) organization chart; (*des opérations*) flow chart

organique [ɔRganik] *adj* organic

organisateur, -trice [ɔRganizatœR, -tRis] *nm/f* organizer

organisation [ɔRganizasjɔ̃] *nf* organization; **O~ des Nations unies (ONU)** United Nations (Organization) (UN, UNO); **O~ mondiale de la santé (OMS)** World Health Organization (WHO); **O~ du traité de l'Atlantique Nord (OTAN)** North Atlantic Treaty Organization (NATO)

organisationnel, le [ɔRganizasjɔnɛl] *adj* organizational

organiser [ɔRganize] *vt* to organize; (*mettre sur pied: service etc*) to set up; **s'organiser** *vi* to get organized

organisme [ɔRganism(ə)] *nm* (*Bio*) organism; (*corps humain*) body; (*Admin, Pol etc*) body, organism

organiste [ɔRganist(ə)] *nm/f* organist

orgasme [ɔRgasm(ə)] *nm* orgasm, climax

orge [ɔR3(ə)] *nf* barley

orgeat [ɔR3a] *nm*: **sirop d'~** barley water

orgelet [ɔR3əlɛ] *nm* sty(e)

orgie [ɔR3i] *nf* orgy

orgue [ɔRg(ə)] *nm* organ; **orgues** *nfpl* organ *sg*; **~ de Barbarie** barrel *ou* street organ

orgueil [ɔRgœj] *nm* pride

orgueilleux, -euse [ɔRgœjø, -øz] *adj* proud

Orient [ɔRjɑ̃] *nm*: **l'~** the East, the Orient

orientable [ɔRjɑ̃tabl(ə)] *adj* (*phare, lampe etc*) adjustable

oriental, e, -aux [ɔRjɑ̃tal, -o] *adj* oriental, eastern; (*frontière*) eastern ▷ *nm/f*: **Oriental, e** Oriental

orientation [ɔRjɑ̃tasjɔ̃] *nf* positioning; adjustment; orientation; direction; (*d'une maison etc*) aspect; (*d'un journal*) leanings *pl*; **avoir le sens de l'~** to have a (good) sense of direction; **course d'~** orienteering exercise; **~ professionnelle** careers advice *ou* guidance; (*service*) careers advisory service

orienté, e [ɔRjɑ̃te] *adj* (*fig: article, journal*) slanted; **bien/mal ~** (*appartement*) well/badly positioned; **~ au sud** facing south, with a southern aspect

orienter [ɔRjɑ̃te] *vt* (*situer*) to position; (*placer, disposer: pièce mobile*) to adjust, position; (*tourner*) to direct, turn; (*voyageur, touriste, recherches*) to direct; (*fig: élève*) to orientate; **s'orienter** *vi* (*se repérer*) to find one's bearings; **s'~ vers** (*fig*) to turn towards

orienteur, -euse [ɔRjɑ̃tœR, -øz] *nm/f* (*Scol*) careers adviser

orifice [ɔRifis] *nm* opening, orifice

oriflamme [ɔRiflam] *nf* banner, standard

origan [ɔRigɑ̃] *nm* oregano

originaire [ɔRiʒinɛR] *adj* original; **être ~ de** (*pays, lieu*) to be a native of; (*provenir de*) to originate from; to be native to

original, e, -aux [ɔRiʒinal, -o] *adj* original; (*bizarre*) eccentric ▷ *nm/f* (*fam: excentrique*) eccentric; (: *fantaisiste*) joker ▷ *nm* (*document etc, Art*) original; (*dactylographie*) top copy

originalité [ɔRiʒinalite] *nf* (*d'un nouveau modèle*) originality *no pl*; (*excentricité, bizarrerie*) eccentricity

origine [ɔRiʒin] *nf* origin; (*d'un message, appel téléphonique*) source; (*d'une révolution, réussite*) root; **origines** *nfpl* (*d'une personne*) origins; **d'~** of origin; (*pneus etc*) original; (*bureau postal*) dispatching; **d'~ française** of French origin; **dès l'~** at *ou* from the outset; **à l'~** originally; **avoir son ~ dans** to have its origins in, originate in

originel, le [ɔʀiʒinɛl] *adj* original
originellement [ɔʀiʒinɛlmɑ̃] *adv* (*à l'origine*)
originally; (*dès l'origine*) from the beginning
oripeaux [ɔʀipo] *nmpl* rags
ORL *sigle f* (= *oto-rhino-laryngologie*) ENT ▷ *sigle m/f*
(= *oto-rhino-laryngologiste*) ENT specialist; **être en**
~ (*malade*) to be in the ENT hospital *ou*
department
orme [ɔʀm(ə)] *nm* elm
orné, e [ɔʀne] *adj* ornate; ~ **de** adorned *ou*
decorated with
ornement [ɔʀnəmɑ̃] *nm* ornament; (*fig*)
embellishment, adornment; ~**s sacerdotaux**
vestments
ornemental, e, -aux [ɔʀnəmɑ̃tal, -o] *adj*
ornamental
ornementer [ɔʀnəmɑ̃te] *vt* to ornament
orner [ɔʀne] *vt* to decorate, adorn; ~ **qch de** to
decorate sth with
ornière [ɔʀnjɛʀ] *nf* rut; (*fig*): **sortir de l'~**
(*routine*) to get out of the rut; (*impasse*) to get out
of a spot
ornithologie [ɔʀnitɔlɔʒi] *nf* ornithology
ornithologue [ɔʀnitɔlɔg] *nm/f* ornithologist; ~
amateur birdwatcher
orphelin, e [ɔʀfəlɛ̃, -in] *adj* orphan(ed) ▷ *nm/f*
orphan; ~ **de père/mère** fatherless/motherless
orphelinat [ɔʀfəlina] *nm* orphanage
ORSEC [ɔʀsɛk] *sigle f* = **Organisation des**
secours; **le plan** ~ *disaster contingency plan*
ORSECRAD [ɔʀsɛkʀad] *sigle m* = **ORSEC en cas**
d'accident nucléaire
orteil [ɔʀtɛj] *nm* toe; **gros** ~ big toe
ORTF *sigle m* (= *Office de radio-diffusion télévision*
française) (*former*) French broadcasting corporation
orthodontiste [ɔʀtɔdɔ̃tist(ə)] *nm/f*
orthodontist
orthodoxe [ɔʀtɔdɔks(ə)] *adj* orthodox
orthodoxie [ɔʀtɔdɔksi] *nf* orthodoxy
orthogénie [ɔʀtɔʒeni] *nf* family planning
orthographe [ɔʀtɔgʀaf] *nf* spelling
orthographier [ɔʀtɔgʀafje] *vt* to spell; **mal**
orthographié misspelt
orthopédie [ɔʀtɔpedi] *nf* orthopaedics *sg* (*Brit*),
orthopedics *sg* (*US*)
orthopédique [ɔʀtɔpedik] *adj* orthopaedic
(*Brit*), orthopedic (*US*)
orthopédiste [ɔʀtɔpedist(ə)] *nm/f* orthopaedic
(*Brit*) *ou* orthopedic (*US*) specialist
orthophonie [ɔʀtɔfɔni] *nf* (*Méd*) speech
therapy; (*Ling*) correct pronunciation
orthophoniste [ɔʀtɔfɔnist(ə)] *nm/f* speech
therapist
ortie [ɔʀti] *nf* (stinging) nettle; ~ **blanche**
white dead-nettle
OS *sigle m* = **ouvrier spécialisé**
os [ɔs] *nm* bone; **sans os** (*Boucherie*) off the bone,
boned; **os à moelle** marrowbone
oscillation [ɔsilasjɔ̃] *nf* oscillation; **oscillations**
nfpl (*fig*) fluctuations
osciller [ɔsile] *vi* (*pendule*) to swing; (*au vent etc*)
to rock; (*Tech*) to oscillate; (*fig*): ~ **entre** to

waver *ou* fluctuate between
osé, e [oze] *adj* daring, bold
oseille [ozɛj] *nf* sorrel
oser [oze] *vi, vt* to dare; ~ **faire** to dare (to) do
osier [ozje] *nm* (*Bot*) willow; **d'**~, **en** ~
wicker(work) *cpd*
Oslo [ɔslo] *n* Oslo
osmose [ɔsmoz] *nf* osmosis
ossature [ɔsatyʀ] *nf* (*Anat*: *squelette*) frame,
skeletal structure; (: *du visage*) bone structure;
(*fig*) framework
osselet [ɔslɛ] *nm* (*Anat*) ossicle; **jouer aux** ~**s** to
play jacks
ossements [ɔsmɑ̃] *nmpl* bones
osseux, -euse [ɔsø, -øz] *adj* bony; (*tissu, maladie,*
greffe) bone *cpd*
ossifier [ɔsifje]: **s'ossifier** *vi* to ossify
ossuaire [ɔsɥɛʀ] *nm* ossuary
Ostende [ɔstɑ̃d] *n* Ostend
ostensible [ɔstɑ̃sibl(ə)] *adj* conspicuous
ostensiblement [ɔstɑ̃sibləmɑ̃] *adv*
conspicuously
ostensoir [ɔstɑ̃swaʀ] *nm* monstrance
ostentation [ɔstɑ̃tasjɔ̃] *nf* ostentation; **faire** ~
de to parade, make a display of
ostentatoire [ɔstɑ̃tatwaʀ] *adj* ostentatious
ostracisme [ɔstʀasism(ə)] *nm* ostracism;
frapper d'~ to ostracize
ostréicole [ɔstʀeikɔl] *adj* oyster *cpd*
ostréiculture [ɔstʀeikyltyʀ] *nf* oyster-farming
otage [ɔtaʒ] *nm* hostage; **prendre qn comme** ~
to take sb hostage
OTAN [ɔtɑ̃] *sigle f* (= *Organisation du traité de*
l'Atlantique Nord) NATO
otarie [ɔtaʀi] *nf* sea-lion
ôter [ote] *vt* to remove; (*soustraire*) to take away;
~ **qch à qn** to take sth (away) from sb; ~ **qch de**
to remove sth from; **six ôté de dix égale**
quatre six from ten equals *ou* is four
otite [ɔtit] *nf* ear infection
oto-rhino [ɔtɔʀinɔ(-)], **oto-rhino-**
laryngologiste *nm/f* ear, nose and throat
specialist.
ottomane [ɔtɔman] *nf* ottoman
ou [u] *conj* or; **ou ... ou** either ... or; **ou bien** or
(else)

 MOT-CLÉ

où [u] *pron relatif* **1** (*position, situation*) where, that
(*souvent omis*); **la chambre où il était** the room
(that) he was in, the room where he was; **la**
ville où je l'ai rencontré the town where I met
him; **la pièce d'où il est sorti** the room he
came out of; **le village d'où je viens** the village
I come from; **les villes par où il est passé** the
towns he went through
2 (*temps, état*) that (*souvent omis*); **le jour où il est**
parti the day (that) he left; **au prix où c'est** at
the price it is
▷ *adv* **1** (*interrogation*) where; **où est-il/va-t-il?**
where is he/is he going?; **par où?** which way?;

d'où vient que ...? how come ...?
2 (*position*) where; **je sais où il est** I know where he is; **où que l'on aille** wherever you go

OUA *sigle f* (= *Organisation de l'unité africaine*) OAU (= *Organization of African Unity*)
ouais [wɛ] *excl* yeah
ouate [wat] *nf* cotton wool (*Brit*), cotton (*US*); (*bourre*) padding, wadding; **~ (hydrophile)** cotton wool (*Brit*), (absorbent) cotton (*US*)
ouaté, e [wate] *adj* cotton-wool; (*doublé*) padded; (*fig: atmosphère*) cocoon-like; (*: pas, bruit*) muffled
oubli [ubli] *nm* (*acte*): **l'~ de** forgetting; (*étourderie*) forgetfulness *no pl*; (*négligence*) omission, oversight; (*absence de souvenirs*) oblivion; **~ de soi** self-effacement, self-negation
oublier [ublije] *vt* (*gén*) to forget; (*ne pas voir: erreurs etc*) to miss; (*ne pas mettre: virgule, nom*) to leave out, forget; (*laisser quelque part: chapeau etc*) to leave behind; **s'oublier** *vi* to forget o.s.; (*enfant, animal*) to have an accident (*euphemism*); **~ l'heure** to forget (about) the time
oubliettes [ublijɛt] *nfpl* dungeon *sg*; **(jeter) aux ~** (*fig*) (to put) completely out of mind
oublieux, -euse [ublijø, -øz] *adj* forgetful
oued [wed] *nm* wadi
ouest [wɛst] *nm* west ▷ *adj inv* west; (*région*) western; **à l'~** in the west, (to the) west, westwards; **à l'~ de** (to the) west of; **vent d'~** westerly wind
ouest-allemand, e [wɛstalmɑ̃, -ɑ̃d] *adj* West German
ouf [uf] *excl* phew!
Ouganda [ugɑ̃da] *nm:* **l'~** Uganda
ougandais, e [ugɑ̃dɛ, -ɛz] *adj* Ugandan
oui [wi] *adv* yes; **répondre (par) ~** to answer yes; **mais ~, bien sûr** yes, of course; **je pense que ~** I think so; **pour un ~ ou pour un non** for no apparent reason
ouï-dire [widiʀ]: **par ~** *adv* by hearsay
ouïe [wi] *nf* hearing; **ouïes** *nfpl* (*de poisson*) gills; (*de violon*) sound-hole *sg*
ouïr [wiʀ] *vt* to hear; **avoir ouï dire que** to have heard it said that
ouistiti [wistiti] *nm* marmoset
ouragan [uʀagɑ̃] *nm* hurricane; (*fig*) storm
Oural [uʀal] *nm:* **l'~** (*fleuve*) the Ural; (*aussi:* **les monts Oural**) the Urals, the Ural Mountains
ourdir [uʀdiʀ] *vt* (*complot*) to hatch
ourdou [uʀdu] *adj inv* Urdu ▷ *nm* (*Ling*) Urdu
ourlé, e [uʀle] *adj* hemmed; (*fig*) rimmed
ourler [uʀle] *vt* to hem
ourlet [uʀlɛ] *nm* hem; (*de l'oreille*) rim; **faire un ~ à** to hem
ours [uʀs] *nm* bear; **~ brun/blanc** brown/polar bear; **~ marin** fur seal; **~ mal léché** uncouth fellow; **~ (en peluche)** teddy (bear)
ourse [uʀs(ə)] *nf* (*Zool*) she-bear; **la Grande/ Petite O~** the Great/Little Bear, Ursa Major/ Minor

oursin [uʀsɛ̃] *nm* sea urchin
ourson [uʀsɔ̃] *nm* (bear-)cub
ouste [ust(ə)] *excl* hop it!
outil [uti] *nm* tool
outillage [utijaʒ] *nm* set of tools; (*d'atelier*) equipment *no pl*
outiller [utije] *vt* (*ouvrier, usine*) to equip
outrage [utʀaʒ] *nm* insult; **faire subir les derniers ~s à** (*femme*) to ravish; **~ aux bonnes mœurs** (*Jur*) outrage to public decency; **~ à magistrat** (*Jur*) contempt of court; **~ à la pudeur** (*Jur*) indecent behaviour *no pl*
outragé, e [utʀaʒe] *adj* offended; outraged
outrageant, e [utʀaʒɑ̃, -ɑ̃t] *adj* offensive
outrager [utʀaʒe] *vt* to offend gravely; (*fig: contrevenir à*) to outrage, insult
outrageusement [utʀaʒøzmɑ̃] *adv* outrageously
outrance [utʀɑ̃s] *nf* excessiveness *no pl*, excess; **à ~** *adv* excessively, to excess
outrancier, -ière [utʀɑ̃sje, -jɛʀ] *adj* extreme
outre [utʀ(ə)] *nf* goatskin, water skin ▷ *prép* besides ▷ *adv:* **passer ~** to carry on regardless; **passer ~ à** to disregard, take no notice of; **en ~** besides, moreover; **~ que** apart from the fact that; **~ mesure** immoderately; unduly
outré, e [utʀe] *adj* (*flatterie, éloge*) excessive, exaggerated; (*indigné, scandalisé*) outraged
outre-Atlantique [utʀatlɑ̃tik] *adv* across the Atlantic
outrecuidance [utʀəkɥidɑ̃s] *nf* presumptuousness *no pl*
outre-Manche [utʀəmɑ̃ʃ] *adv* across the Channel
outremer [utʀəmɛʀ] *adj inv* ultramarine
outre-mer [utʀəmɛʀ] *adv* overseas; **d'~** overseas
outrepasser [utʀəpase] *vt* to go beyond, exceed
outrer [utʀe] *vt* (*pensée, attitude*) to exaggerate; (*indigner: personne*) to outrage
outre-Rhin [utʀəʀɛ̃] *adv* across the Rhine, in Germany
outsider [awtsajdœʀ] *nm* outsider
ouvert, e [uvɛʀ, -ɛʀt(ə)] *pp de* **ouvrir** ▷ *adj* open; (*robinet, gaz etc*) on; **à bras ~s** with open arms
ouvertement [uvɛʀtəmɑ̃] *adv* openly
ouverture [uvɛʀtyʀ] *nf* opening; (*Mus*) overture; (*Pol*): **l'~** the widening of the political spectrum; (*Photo*): **~ (du diaphragme)** aperture; **ouvertures** *nfpl* (*propositions*) overtures; **~ d'esprit** open-mindedness; **heures d'~** (*Comm*) opening hours; **jours d'~** (*Comm*) days of opening
ouvrable [uvʀabl(ə)] *adj:* **jour ~** working day, weekday; **heures ~s** business hours
ouvrage [uvʀaʒ] *nm* (*tâche, de tricot etc, Mil*) work *no pl*; (*objet: Couture, Art*) (piece of) work; (*texte, livre*) work; **panier ou corbeille à ~** work basket; **~ d'art** (*Génie Civil*) bridge or tunnel etc
ouvragé, e [uvʀaʒe] *adj* finely embroidered (*ou* worked *ou* carved)
ouvrant, e [uvʀɑ̃, -ɑ̃t] *vb voir* **ouvrir** ▷ *adj:* **toit ~**

sunroof

ouvré, e [uvʀe] *adj* finely-worked; **jour ~** working day

ouvre-boîte, ouvre-boîtes [uvʀəbwat] *nm inv* tin (*Brit*) *ou* can opener

ouvre-bouteille, ouvre-bouteilles [uvʀəbutɛj] *nm inv* bottle-opener

ouvreuse [uvʀøz] *nf* usherette

ouvrier, -ière [uvʀije, -jɛʀ] *nm/f* worker ▷ *nf* (*Zool*) worker (bee) ▷ *adj* working-class; (*problèmes, conflit*) industrial, labour *cpd* (*Brit*), labor *cpd* (*US*); (*revendications*) workers'; **classe ouvrière** working class; **~ agricole** farmworker; **~ qualifié** skilled worker; **~ spécialisé (OS)** semiskilled worker; **~ d'usine** factory worker

ouvrir [uvʀiʀ] *vt* (*gén*) to open; (*brèche, passage*) to open up; (*commencer l'exploitation de, créer*) to open (up); (*eau, électricité, chauffage, robinet*) to turn on; (*Méd: abcès*) to open up, cut open ▷ *vi* to open; to open up; (*Cartes*): **~ à trèfle** to open in clubs; **s'ouvrir** *vi* to open; **s'~ à** (*art etc*) to open one's mind to; **s'~ à qn (de qch)** to open one's heart to sb (about sth); **s'~ les veines** to slash *ou* cut one's wrists; **~ sur** to open onto; **~ l'appétit à qn** to whet sb's appetite; **~ des horizons** to open up new horizons; **~ l'esprit** to broaden one's horizons; **~ une session** (*Inform*) to log in

ouvroir [uvʀwaʀ] *nm* workroom, sewing room

ovaire [ɔvɛʀ] *nm* ovary

ovale [ɔval] *adj* oval

ovation [ɔvɑsjɔ̃] *nf* ovation

ovationner [ɔvɑsjɔne] *vt*: **~ qn** to give sb an ovation

ovin, e [ɔvɛ̃, -in] *adj* ovine

OVNI [ɔvni] *sigle m* (= *objet volant non identifié*) UFO

ovoïde [ɔvɔid] *adj* egg-shaped

ovulation [ɔvylɑsjɔ̃] *nf* (*Physiol*) ovulation

ovule [ɔvyl] *nm* (*Physiol*) ovum; (*Méd*) pessary

oxfordien, ne [ɔksfɔʀdjɛ̃, -ɛn] *adj* Oxonian ▷ *nm/f*: **Oxfordien, ne** Oxonian

oxydable [ɔksidabl(ə)] *adj* liable to rust

oxyde [ɔksid] *nm* oxide; **~ de carbone** carbon monoxide

oxyder [ɔkside]: **s'oxyder** *vi* to become oxidized

oxygéné, e [ɔksiʒene] *adj*: **eau ~e** hydrogen peroxide; **cheveux ~s** bleached hair

oxygène [ɔksiʒɛn] *nm* oxygen; (*fig*): **cure d'~** fresh air cure

ozone [ozɔn] *nm* ozone; **trou dans la couche d'~** hole in the ozone layer

Pp

P, p [pe] *nm inv* P, p ▷ *abr* (= *Père*) Fr; (= *page*) p; **P comme Pierre** P for Peter

PA *sigle fpl* = **petites annonces**

PAC *sigle f* (= *Politique agricole commune*) CAP

pacage [pakaʒ] *nm* grazing, pasture

pacemaker [pɛsmɛkœʀ] *nm* pacemaker

pachyderme [paʃidɛʀm(ə)] *nm* pachyderm; elephant

pacificateur, -trice [pasifikatœʀ, -tʀis] *adj* pacificatory

pacification [pasifikasjɔ̃] *nf* pacification

pacifier [pasifje] *vt* to pacify

pacifique [pasifik] *adj* (*personne*) peaceable; (*intentions, coexistence*) peaceful ▷ *nm*: **le P~, l'océan P~** the Pacific (Ocean)

pacifiquement [pasifikmɑ̃] *adv* peaceably; peacefully

pacifisme [pasifism(ə)] *nm* pacifism

pacifiste [pasifist(ə)] *nm/f* pacifist

pack [pak] *nm* pack

pacotille [pakɔtij] *nf* (*péj*) cheap goods *pl*; **de ~** cheap

PACS [paks] *sigle m* (= *pacte civil de solidarité*) ≈ civil partnership

pacser [pakse]: **se pacser** *vi* ≈ to form a civil partnership

pacte [pakt(ə)] *nm* pact, treaty

pactiser [paktize] *vi*: **~ avec** to come to terms with

pactole [paktɔl] *nm* gold mine (*fig*)

paddock [padɔk] *nm* paddock

Padoue [padu] *n* Padua

PAF *sigle f* (= *Police de l'air et des frontières*) *police authority responsible for civil aviation, border control etc* ▷ *sigle m* (= *paysage audiovisuel français*) *French broadcasting scene*

pagaie [pagɛ] *nf* paddle

pagaille [pagaj] *nf* mess, shambles *sg*; **il y en a en ~** there are loads *ou* heaps of them

paganisme [paganism(ə)] *nm* paganism

pagayer [pageje] *vi* to paddle

page [paʒ] *nf* page; (*passage: d'un roman*) passage ▷ *nm* page (boy); **mettre en ~s** to make up (into pages); **mise en ~** layout; **à la ~** (*fig*) up-to-date; **~ d'accueil** (*Inform*) home page; **~ blanche** blank page; **~ de garde** endpaper; **~ Web**

(*Inform*) web page

page-écran [paʒekʀɑ̃] (*pl* **pages-écrans**) *nf* (*Inform*) screen page

pagination [paʒinasjɔ̃] *nf* pagination

paginer [paʒine] *vt* to paginate

pagne [paɲ] *nm* loincloth

pagode [pagɔd] *nf* pagoda

paie [pɛ] *nf* = **paye**

paiement [pɛmɑ̃] *nm* = **payement**

païen, ne [pajɛ̃, -ɛn] *adj, nm/f* pagan, heathen

paillard, e [pajaʀ, -aʀd(ə)] *adj* bawdy

paillasse [pajas] *nf* (*matelas*) straw mattress; (*d'un évier*) draining board

paillasson [pajasɔ̃] *nm* doormat

paille [paj] *nf* straw; (*défaut*) flaw; **être sur la ~** to be ruined; **~ de fer** steel wool

paillé, e [paje] *adj* with a straw seat

pailleté, e [pajte] *adj* sequined

paillette [pajɛt] *nf* speck, flake; **paillettes** *nfpl* (*décoratives*) sequins, spangles; **lessive en ~s** soapflakes *pl*

pain [pɛ̃] *nm* (*substance*) bread; (*unité*) loaf (of bread); (*morceau*): **~ de cire** *etc* bar of wax *etc*; (*Culin*): **~ de poisson/légumes** fish/vegetable loaf; **petit ~** (bread) roll, **~ bis/complet** brown/wholemeal (*Brit*) *ou* wholewheat (*US*) bread; **~ de campagne** farmhouse bread; **~ d'épice** ≈ gingerbread; **~ grillé** toast; **~ de mie** sandwich loaf; **~ perdu** French toast; **~ de seigle** rye bread; **~ de sucre** sugar loaf

pair, e [pɛʀ] *adj* (*nombre*) even ▷ *nm* peer; **aller de ~ (avec)** to go hand in hand *ou* together (with); **au ~** (*Finance*) at par; **valeur au ~** par value; **jeune fille au ~** au pair

paire [pɛʀ] *nf* pair; **une ~ de lunettes/tenailles** a pair of glasses/pincers; **faire la ~: les deux font la ~** they are two of a kind

pais [pɛ] *vb voir* **paître**

paisible [pezibl(ə)] *adj* peaceful, quiet

paisiblement [peziblǝmɑ̃] *adv* peacefully, quietly

paître [pɛtʀ(ə)] *vi* to graze

paix [pɛ] *nf* peace; (*fig*) peacefulness, peace; **faire la ~ avec** to make peace with; **avoir la ~** to have peace (and quiet)

Pakistan [pakistɑ̃] *nm*: **le ~** Pakistan

pakistanais, e [pakistanɛ, -ɛz] *adj* Pakistani
PAL *sigle m* (= *Phase Alternation Line*) PAL
palabrer [palabʀe] *vi* to argue endlessly
palabres [palabʀ(ə)] *nfpl ou mpl* endless
  discussions
palace [palas] *nm* luxury hotel
palais [palɛ] *nm* palace; (*Anat*) palate; **le P~**
  Bourbon *the seat of the French National Assembly*; **le**
  P~ de l'Élysée the Élysée Palace; **~ des**
  expositions exhibition centre; **le P~ de**
  Justice the Law Courts *pl*
palan [palɑ̃] *nm* hoist
pale [pal] *nf* (*d'hélice, de rame*) blade; (*de roue*)
  paddle
pâle [pɑl] *adj* pale; (*fig*): **une ~ imitation** a pale
  imitation; **bleu ~** pale blue; **~ de colère** white
  ou pale with anger
palefrenier [palfʀənje] *nm* groom (*for horses*)
paléontologie [paleɔ̃tɔlɔʒi] *nf* paleontology
paléontologiste [paleɔ̃tɔlɔʒist(ə)],
  paléontologue [paleɔ̃tɔlɔg] *nm/f*
  paleontologist
Palerme [palɛʀm(ə)] *n* Palermo
Palestine [palɛstin] *nf*: **la ~** Palestine
palestinien, ne [palɛstinjɛ̃, -ɛn] *adj* Palestinian
  ▷ *nm/f*: **Palestinien, ne** Palestinian
palet [palɛ] *nm* disc; (*Hockey*) puck
paletot [palto] *nm* (short) coat
palette [palɛt] *nf* palette; (*de produits*) range
palétuvier [paletyvje] *nm* mangrove
pâleur [pɑlœʀ] *nf* paleness
palier [palje] *nm* (*d'escalier*) landing; (*fig*) level,
  plateau; (*: phase stable*) levelling (*Brit*) *ou* leveling
  (*US*) off, new level; (*Tech*) bearing; **nos voisins**
  de ~ our neighbo(u)rs across the landing (*Brit*)
  ou the hall (*US*); **en ~** *adv* level; **par ~s** in stages
palière [paljɛʀ] *adj f* landing *cpd*
pâlir [paliʀ] *vi* to turn *ou* go pale; (*couleur*) to
  fade; **faire ~ qn** (*de jalousie*) to make sb green
  (with envy)
palissade [palisad] *nf* fence
palissandre [palisɑ̃dʀ(ə)] *nm* rosewood
palliatif [paljatif] *nm* palliative; (*expédient*)
  stopgap measure
pallier [palje] *vt*: **~ à** *vt* to offset, make up for
palmarès [palmaʀɛs] *nm* record (of
  achievements); (*Scol*) prize list; (*Sport*) list of
  winners
palme [palm(ə)] *nf* (*Bot*) palm leaf; (*symbole*)
  palm; (*de plongeur*) flipper; **~s (académiques)**
  decoration for services to education
palmé, e [palme] *adj* (*pattes*) webbed
palmeraie [palməʀɛ] *nf* palm grove
palmier [palmje] *nm* palm tree
palmipède [palmipɛd] *nm* palmiped,
  webfooted bird
palois, e [palwa, -waz] *adj* of *ou* from Pau ▷ *nm/f*:
  Palois, e inhabitant *ou* native of Pau
palombe [palɔ̃b] *nf* woodpigeon, ringdove
pâlot, te [pɑlo, -ɔt] *adj* pale, peaky
palourde [paluʀd(ə)] *nf* clam
palpable [palpabl(ə)] *adj* tangible, palpable

palper [palpe] *vt* to feel, finger
palpitant, e [palpitɑ̃, -ɑ̃t] *adj* thrilling, gripping
palpitation [palpitasjɔ̃] *nf* palpitation
palpiter [palpite] *vi* (*cœur, pouls*) to beat; (*: plus*
  fort) to pound, throb; (*narines, chair*) to quiver
paludisme [palydism(ə)] *nm* malaria
palustre [palystʀ(ə)] *adj* (*coquillage etc*) marsh
  cpd; (*fièvre*) malarial
pâmer [pɑme]: **se pâmer** *vi* to swoon; (*fig*): **se ~**
  devant to go into raptures over
pâmoison [pɑmwazɔ̃] *nf*: **tomber en ~** to
  swoon
pampa [pɑ̃pa] *nf* pampas *pl*
pamphlet [pɑ̃flɛ] *nm* lampoon, satirical tract
pamphlétaire [pɑ̃fletɛʀ] *nm/f* lampoonist
pamplemousse [pɑ̃pləmus] *nm* grapefruit
pan [pɑ̃] *nm* section, piece; (*côté: d'un prisme, d'une*
  tour) side, face ▷ *excl* bang!; **~ de chemise** shirt
  tail; **~ de mur** section of wall
panacée [panase] *nf* panacea
panachage [panaʃaʒ] *nm* blend, mix; (*Pol*) voting
  for candidates from different parties instead of for the set
  list of one party
panache [panaʃ] *nm* plume; (*fig*) spirit, panache
panaché, e [panaʃe] *adj*: **œillet ~** variegated
  carnation; **glace ~e** mixed ice cream; **salade ~e**
  mixed salad; **bière ~e** shandy
panais [panɛ] *nm* parsnip
Panama [panama] *nm*: **le ~** Panama
panaméen, ne [panameɛ̃, -ɛn] *adj* Panamanian
  ▷ *nm/f*: **Panaméen, ne** Panamanian
panaris [panaʀi] *nm* whitlow
pancarte [pɑ̃kaʀt(ə)] *nf* sign, notice; (*dans un*
  défilé) placard
pancréas [pɑ̃kʀeas] *nm* pancreas
panda [pɑ̃da] *nm* panda
pané, e [pane] *adj* fried in breadcrumbs
panégyrique [paneʒiʀik] *nm*: **faire le ~ de qn**
  to extol sb's merits *ou* virtues
panier [panje] *nm* basket; (*à diapositives*)
  magazine; **mettre au ~** to chuck away; **~ de**
  crabes: **c'est un ~ de crabes** (*fig*) they're
  constantly at one another's throats; **~ percé**
  (*fig*) spendthrift; **~ à provisions** shopping
  basket; **~ à salade** (*Culin*) salad shaker; (*Police*)
  paddy wagon, police van
panier-repas [panjeʀ(ə)pa] (*pl* **paniers-repas**)
  nm packed lunch
panification [panifikasjɔ̃] *nf* bread-making
panique [panik] *adj* panicky ▷ *nf* panic
paniquer [panike] *vi* to panic
panne [pan] *nf* (*d'un mécanisme, moteur*)
  breakdown; **être/tomber en ~** to have broken
  down/break down; **être en ~ d'essence** *ou* **en ~**
  sèche to have run out of petrol (*Brit*) *ou* gas (*US*);
  mettre en ~ (*Navig*) to bring to; **~ d'électricité**
  ou **de courant** power *ou* electrical failure
panneau, x [pano] *nm* (*écriteau*) sign, notice; (*de*
  boiserie, de tapisserie etc) panel; **tomber dans le ~**
  (*fig*) to walk into the trap; **~ d'affichage** notice
  (*Brit*) *ou* bulletin (*US*) board; **~ électoral** board
  for election poster; **~ indicateur** signpost; **~**

publicitaire hoarding (*Brit*), billboard (*US*); ~ **de signalisation** roadsign; ~ **solaire** solar panel

panonceau, x [panɔso] *nm* (*de magasin etc*) sign; (*de médecin etc*) plaque

panoplie [panɔpli] *nf* (*jouet*) outfit; (*d'armes*) display; (*fig*) array

panorama [panɔrama] *nm* (*vue*) all-round view, panorama; (*peinture*) panorama; (*fig: étude complète*) complete overview

panoramique [panɔramik] *adj* panoramic; (*carrosserie*) with panoramic windows ▷ *nm* (*Ciné, TV*) panoramic shot

panse [pɑ̃s] *nf* paunch

pansement [pɑ̃smɑ̃] *nm* dressing, bandage; ~ **adhésif** sticking plaster (*Brit*), bandaid® (*US*)

panser [pɑ̃se] *vt* (*plaie*) to dress, bandage; (*bras*) to put a dressing on, bandage; (*cheval*) to groom

pantacourt [pɑ̃takur] *nm* cropped trousers *pl*

pantalon [pɑ̃talɔ̃] *nm* trousers *pl* (*Brit*), pants *pl* (*US*), pair of trousers *ou* pants; ~ **de ski** ski pants *pl*

pantalonnade [pɑ̃talɔnad] *nf* slapstick (comedy)

pantelant, e [pɑ̃tlɑ̃, -ɑ̃t] *adj* gasping for breath, panting

panthère [pɑ̃tɛr] *nf* panther

pantin [pɑ̃tɛ̃] *nm* (*jouet*) jumping jack; (*péj: personne*) puppet

pantois [pɑ̃twa] *adj m*: **rester** ~ to be flabbergasted

pantomime [pɑ̃tɔmim] *nf* mime; (*pièce*) mime show; (*péj*) fuss, carry-on

pantouflard, e [pɑ̃tuflar, -ard(ə)] *adj* (*péj*) stay-at-home

pantoufle [pɑ̃tufl(ə)] *nf* slipper

panure [panyr] *nf* breadcrumbs *pl*

PAO *sigle f* (= *publication assistée par ordinateur*) DTP

paon [pɑ̃] *nm* peacock

papa [papa] *nm* dad(dy)

papauté [papote] *nf* papacy

papaye [papaj] *nf* pawpaw

pape [pap] *nm* pope

paperasse [papras] *nf* (*péj*) bumf *no pl*, papers *pl*; forms *pl*

paperasserie [paprasri] *nf* (*péj*) red tape *no pl*; paperwork *no pl*

papeterie [papetri] *nf* (*fabrication du papier*) paper-making (industry); (*usine*) paper mill; (*magasin*) stationer's (shop (*Brit*)); (*articles*) stationery

papetier, -ière [paptje, -jɛr] *nm/f* paper-maker; stationer

papetier-libraire [paptjɛlibrɛr] (*pl* **papetiers-libraires**) *nm* bookseller and stationer

papi [papi] *nm* (*fam*) granddad

papier [papje] *nm* paper; (*feuille*) sheet *ou* piece of paper; (*article*) article; (*écrit officiel*) document; **papiers** *nmpl* (*aussi*: **papiers d'identité**) (identity) papers; **sur le** ~ (*théoriquement*) on paper; **noircir du** ~ to write page after page; ~ **couché/glacé** art/glazed paper; ~

(d')aluminium aluminium (*Brit*) *ou* aluminum (*US*) foil, tinfoil; ~ **d'Arménie** incense paper; ~ **bible** India *ou* bible paper; ~ **de brouillon** rough *ou* scrap paper; ~ **bulle** manil(l)a paper; ~ **buvard** blotting paper; ~ **calque** tracing paper; ~ **carbone** carbon paper; ~ **collant** Sellotape® (*Brit*), Scotch tape® (*US*), sticky tape; ~ **en continu** continuous stationery; ~ **à dessin** drawing paper; ~ **d'emballage** wrapping paper; ~ **gommé** gummed paper; ~ **hygiénique** toilet paper; ~ **journal** newsprint; (*pour emballer*) newspaper; ~ **à lettres** writing paper, notepaper; ~ **mâché** papier-mâché; ~ **machine** typing paper; ~ **peint** wallpaper; ~ **pelure** India paper; ~ **à pliage accordéon** fanfold paper; ~ **de soie** tissue paper; ~ **thermique** thermal paper; ~ **de tournesol** litmus paper; ~ **de verre** sandpaper

papier-filtre [papjefiltr(ə)] (*pl* **papiers-filtres**) *nm* filter paper

papier-monnaie [papjemɔnɛ] (*pl* **papiers-monnaies**) *nm* paper money

papille [papij] *nf*: ~**s gustatives** taste buds

papillon [papijɔ̃] *nm* butterfly; (*fam: contravention*) (parking) ticket; (*Tech: écrou*) wing *ou* butterfly nut; ~ **de nuit** moth

papillonner [papijɔne] *vi* to flit from one thing (*ou* person) to another

papillote [papijɔt] *nf* (*pour cheveux*) curlpaper; (*de gigot*) (paper) frill

papilloter [papijɔte] *vi* (*yeux*) to blink; (*paupières*) to flutter; (*lumière*) to flicker

papotage [papɔtaʒ] *nm* chitchat

papoter [papɔte] *vi* to chatter

papou, e [papu] *adj* Papuan

Papouasie-Nouvelle-Guinée [papwazinuvɛlgine] *nf*: **la** ~ Papua-New-Guinea

paprika [paprika] *nm* paprika

papyrus [papirys] *nm* papyrus

pâque [pɑk] *nf*: **la** ~ Passover; *voir aussi* **Pâques**

paquebot [pakbo] *nm* liner

pâquerette [pɑkrɛt] *nf* daisy

Pâques [pɑk] *nm, nfpl*: **faire ses** ~ to do one's Easter duties; **l'île de** ~ Easter Island

paquet [pakɛ] *nm* packet; (*colis*) parcel; (*ballot*) bundle; (*dans négociations*) package (deal); (*fig: tas*): ~ **de** pile *ou* heap of; **paquets** *nmpl* (*bagages*) bags; **mettre le** ~ (*fam*) to give one's all; ~ **de mer** big wave

paquetage [paktaʒ] *nm* (*Mil*) kit, pack

paquet-cadeau [pakkado] (*pl* **paquets-cadeaux**) *nm* gift-wrapped parcel

par [par] *prép* by; **finir** *etc* ~ to end *etc* with; ~ **amour** out of love; **passer** ~ **Lyon/la côte** to go via *ou* through Lyons/along by the coast; ~ **la fenêtre** (*jeter, regarder*) out of the window; **trois** ~ **jour/personne** three a *ou* per day/head; **deux** ~ **deux** two at a time; (*marcher etc*) in twos; ~ **où?** which way?; ~ **ici** this way; (*dans le coin*) round here; ~**-ci**, ~**-là** here and there

para [para] *nm* (*parachutiste*) para

parabole [parabɔl] *nf* (*Rel*) parable; (*Géom*)

parabola

parabolique [paʀabɔlik] *adj* parabolic;
antenne ~ satellite dish

parachever [paʀaʃve] *vt* to perfect

parachutage [paʀaʃytaʒ] *nm* (*de soldats, vivres*)
parachuting-in; **nous sommes contre le ~
d'un candidat parisien dans notre
circonscription** (*Pol, fig*) we are against a
Parisian candidate being landed on us

parachute [paʀaʃyt] *nm* parachute

parachuter [paʀaʃyte] *vt* (*soldat etc*) to
parachute; (*fig*) to pitchfork; **il a été
parachuté à la tête de l'entreprise** he was
brought in from outside as head of the
company

parachutisme [paʀaʃytism(ə)] *nm* parachuting

parachutiste [paʀaʃytist(ə)] *nm/f* parachutist;
(*Mil*) paratrooper

parade [paʀad] *nf* (*spectacle, défilé*) parade;
(*Escrime, Boxe*) parry; (*ostentation*): **faire ~ de** to
display, show off; (*défense, riposte*): **trouver la ~
à une attaque** to find the answer to an attack;
de ~ *adj* ceremonial; (*superficiel*) superficial,
outward

parader [paʀade] *vi* to swagger (around), show
off

paradis [paʀadi] *nm* heaven, paradise; **P~
terrestre** (*Rel*) Garden of Eden; (*fig*) heaven on
earth

paradisiaque [paʀadizjak] *adj* heavenly, divine

paradoxal, e, -aux [paʀadɔksal, -o] *adj*
paradoxical

paradoxalement [paʀadɔksalmɑ̃] *adv*
paradoxically

paradoxe [paʀadɔks(ə)] *nm* paradox

parafe [paʀaf] *nm*, **parafer** [paʀafe] ▷ *vt* =
paraphe; parapher

paraffine [paʀafin] *nf* paraffin; paraffin wax

paraffiné, e [paʀafine] *adj*: **papier ~** wax(ed)
paper

parafoudre [paʀafudʀ(ə)] *nm* (*Élec*) lightning
conductor

parages [paʀaʒ] *nmpl* (*Navig*) waters; **dans les ~
(de)** in the area *ou* vicinity (of)

paragraphe [paʀagʀaf] *nm* paragraph

Paraguay [paʀagwɛ] *nm*: **le ~** Paraguay

paraguayen, ne [paʀagwajɛ̃, -ɛn] *adj*
Paraguayan ▷ *nm/f*: **Paraguayen, ne**
Paraguayan

paraître [paʀɛtʀ(ə)] *vb copule* to seem, look,
appear ▷ *vi* to appear; (*être visible*) to show;
(*Presse, Édition*) to be published, come out,
appear; (*briller*) to show off; **laisser ~ qch** to let
(sth) show ▷ *vb impers*: **il paraît que** it seems *ou*
appears that; **il me paraît que** it seems to me
that; **il paraît absurde de** it seems absurd to;
il ne paraît pas son âge he doesn't look his
age; **~ en justice** to appear before the court(s);
~ en scène/en public/à l'écran to appear on
stage/in public/on the screen

parallèle [paʀalɛl] *adj* parallel; (*police, marché*)
unofficial; (*société, énergie*) alternative ▷ *nm*

(*comparaison*): **faire un ~ entre** to draw a
parallel between; (*Géo*) parallel ▷ *nf* parallel
(line); **en ~** in parallel; **mettre en ~** (*choses
opposées*) to compare; (*choses semblables*) to
parallel

parallèlement [paʀalɛlmɑ̃] *adv* in parallel; (*fig:
en même temps*) at the same time

parallélépipède [paʀalelepipɛd] *nm*
parallelepiped

parallélisme [paʀalelism(ə)] *nm* parallelism;
(*Auto*) wheel alignment

parallélogramme [paʀalelɔgʀam] *nm*
parallelogram

paralyser [paʀalize] *vt* to paralyze

paralysie [paʀalizi] *nf* paralysis

paralytique [paʀalitik] *adj, nm/f* paralytic

paramédical, e, -aux [paʀamedikal, -o] *adj*
paramedical

paramètre [paʀamɛtʀ(ə)] *nm* parameter

paramilitaire [paʀamilitɛʀ] *adj* paramilitary

paranoïa [paʀanɔja] *nf* paranoia

paranoïaque [paʀanɔjak] *nm/f* paranoiac

paranormal, e, -aux [paʀanɔʀmal, -o] *adj*
paranormal

parapet [paʀapɛ] *nm* parapet

paraphe [paʀaf] *nm* (*trait*) flourish; (*signature*)
initials *pl*; signature

parapher [paʀafe] *vt* to initial; to sign

paraphrase [paʀafʀɑz] *nf* paraphrase

paraphraser [paʀafʀɑze] *vt* to paraphrase

paraplégie [paʀapleʒi] *nf* paraplegia

paraplégique [paʀapleʒik] *adj, nm/f* paraplegic

parapluie [paʀaplɥi] *nm* umbrella; **~ atomique
ou nucléaire** nuclear umbrella; **~ pliant**
telescopic umbrella

parapsychique [paʀapsiʃik] *adj*
parapsychological

parapsychologie [paʀapsikɔlɔʒi] *nf*
parapsychology

parapublic, -ique [paʀapyblik] *adj* partly state-
controlled

parascolaire [paʀaskɔlɛʀ] *adj* extracurricular

parasitaire [paʀazitɛʀ] *adj* parasitic(al)

parasite [paʀazit] *nm* parasite ▷ *adj* (*Bot, Bio*)
parasitic(al); **parasites** *nmpl* (*Tél*)
interference *sg*

parasitisme [paʀazitism(ə)] *nm* parasitism

parasol [paʀasɔl] *nm* parasol, sunshade

paratonnerre [paʀatɔnɛʀ] *nm* lightning
conductor

paravent [paʀavɑ̃] *nm* folding screen; (*fig*)
screen

parc [paʀk] *nm* (public) park, gardens *pl*; (*de
château etc*) grounds *pl*; (*pour le bétail*) pen,
enclosure; (*d'enfant*) playpen; (*Mil: entrepôt*)
depot; (*ensemble d'unités*) stock; (*de voitures etc*)
fleet; **~ d'attractions** amusement park; **~
automobile** (*d'un pays*) number of cars on the
roads; **~ à huîtres** oyster bed; **~ à thème** theme
park; **~ national** national park; **~ naturel**
nature reserve; **~ de stationnement** car park;
~ zoologique zoological gardens *pl*

parcelle [paʀsɛl] *nf* fragment, scrap; *(de terrain)* plot, parcel

parcelliser [paʀselize] *vt* to divide *ou* split up

parce que [paʀsk(ə)] *conj* because

parchemin [paʀʃəmɛ̃] *nm* parchment

parcheminé, e [paʀʃəmine] *adj* wrinkled; *(papier)* with a parchment finish

parcimonie [paʀsimɔni] *nf* parsimony, parsimoniousness

parcimonieux, -euse [paʀsimɔnjø, -øz] *adj* parsimonious, miserly

parcmètre [paʀkmɛtʀ(ə)], **parcomètre** [paʀkɔmɛtʀ(ə)] *nm* parking meter

parcotrain [paʀkɔtʀɛ̃] *nm* station car park (Brit) *ou* parking lot (US), park-and-ride car park (Brit)

parcourir [paʀkuʀiʀ] *vt* (trajet, distance) to cover; *(article, livre)* to skim *ou* glance through; *(lieu)* to go all over, travel up and down; *(frisson, vibration)* to run through; **~ des yeux** to run one's eye over

parcours [paʀkuʀ] *vb voir* **parcourir** ▷ *nm* (trajet) journey; *(itinéraire)* route; *(Sport: terrain)* course; *(: tour)* round; run; lap; **~ du combattant** assault course

parcouru, e [paʀkuʀy] *pp de* **parcourir**

par-delà [paʀdəla] *prép* beyond

par-dessous [paʀdəsu] *prép, adv* under(neath)

pardessus [paʀdəsy] *nm* overcoat

par-dessus [paʀdəsy] *prép* over (the top of) ▷ *adv* over (the top); **~ le marché** on top of it all

par-devant [paʀdəvɑ̃] *prép* in the presence of, before ▷ *adv* at the front; round the front

pardon [paʀdɔ̃] *nm* forgiveness *no pl* ▷ *excl* *(excuses)* (I'm) sorry; *(pour interpeller etc)* excuse me; *(demander de répéter)* (I beg your) pardon? (Brit), pardon me? (US)

pardonnable [paʀdɔnabl(ə)] *adj* forgivable, excusable

pardonner [paʀdɔne] *vt* to forgive; **~ qch à qn** to forgive sb for sth; **qui ne pardonne pas** *(maladie, erreur)* fatal

paré, e [paʀe] *adj* ready, prepared

pare-balles [paʀbal] *adj inv* bulletproof

pare-boue [paʀbu] *nm inv* mudflap

pare-brise [paʀbʀiz] *nm inv* windscreen (Brit), windshield (US)

pare-chocs [paʀʃɔk] *nm inv* bumper (Brit), fender (US)

pare-étincelles [paʀetɛ̃sɛl] *nm inv* fireguard

pare-feu [paʀfø] *nm inv* firebreak ▷ *adj inv*: **portes ~** fire (resistant) doors

pareil, le [paʀɛj] *adj* (identique) the same, alike; *(similaire)* similar; *(tel)*: **un courage/livre ~** such courage/a book, courage/a book like this; **de ~s livres** such books ▷ *adv*: **habillés ~** dressed the same (way), dressed alike; **faire ~** to do the same (thing); **j'en veux un ~** I'd like one just like it; **rien de ~** no (ou any) such thing, nothing (ou anything) like it; **ses ~s** one's fellow men; one's peers; **ne pas avoir son (sa) ~(le)** to be second to none; **~ à** the same as; similar to; **sans ~** unparalleled, unequalled;

c'est du ~ au même it comes to the same thing, it's six (of one) and half-a-dozen (of the other); **en ~ cas** in such a case; **rendre la ~le à qn** to pay sb back in his own coin

pareillement [paʀɛjmɑ̃] *adv* the same, alike; in such a way; *(également)* likewise

parement [paʀmɑ̃] *nm* (Constr: revers d'un col, d'une manche) facing; *(Rel)*: **~ d'autel** antependium

parent, e [paʀɑ̃, -ɑ̃t] *nm/f*: **un/une ~/e** a relative *ou* relation ▷ *adj*: **être ~ de** to be related to; **parents** *nmpl* (père et mère) parents; *(famille, proches)* relatives, relations; **~ unique** lone parent; **~s par alliance** relatives *ou* relations by marriage; **~s en ligne directe** blood relations

parental, e, -aux [paʀɑ̃tal, -o] *adj* parental

parenté [paʀɑ̃te] *nf* (lien) relationship; *(personnes)* relatives pl, relations pl

parenthèse [paʀɑ̃tɛz] *nf* (ponctuation) bracket, parenthesis; *(Math)* bracket; *(digression)* parenthesis, digression; **ouvrir/fermer la ~** to open/close brackets; **entre ~s** in brackets; *(fig)* incidentally

parer [paʀe] *vt* to adorn; *(Culin)* to dress, trim; *(éviter)* to ward off; **~ à** *(danger)* to ward off; *(inconvénient)* to deal with; **se ~ de** (fig: qualité, titre) to assume; **~ à toute éventualité** to be ready for every eventuality; **~ au plus pressé** to attend to what's most urgent

pare-soleil [paʀsɔlɛj] *nm inv* sun visor

paresse [paʀɛs] *nf* laziness

paresser [paʀese] *vi* to laze around

paresseusement [paʀɛsøzmɑ̃] *adv* lazily; sluggishly

paresseux, -euse [paʀɛsø, -øz] *adj* lazy; *(fig)* slow, sluggish ▷ *nm* (Zool) sloth

parfaire [paʀfɛʀ] *vt* to perfect, complete

parfait, e [paʀfɛ, -ɛt] *pp de* **parfaire** ▷ *adj* perfect ▷ *nm* (Ling) perfect (tense); *(Culin)* parfait ▷ *excl* fine, excellent

parfaitement [paʀfɛtmɑ̃] *adv* perfectly ▷ *excl* (most) certainly

parfaites [paʀfɛt], **parfasse** [paʀfas], **parferai** *etc* [paʀfʀe] *vb voir* **parfaire**

parfois [paʀfwa] *adv* sometimes

parfum [paʀfœ̃] *nm* (produit) perfume, scent; *(odeur: de fleur)* scent, fragrance; *(: de tabac, vin)* aroma; *(goût: de glace, milk-shake)* flavour (Brit), flavor (US)

parfumé, e [paʀfyme] *adj* (fleur, fruit) fragrant; *(papier à lettres etc)* scented; *(femme)* wearing perfume *ou* scent, perfumed; *(aromatisé)*: **~ au café** coffee-flavoured (Brit) *ou* -flavored (US)

parfumer [paʀfyme] *vt* (odeur, bouquet) to perfume; *(mouchoir)* to put scent *ou* perfume on; *(crème, gâteau)* to flavour (Brit), flavor (US); **se parfumer** to put on (some) perfume *ou* scent; *(d'habitude)* to use perfume *ou* scent

parfumerie [paʀfymʀi] *nf* (commerce) perfumery; *(produits)* perfumes; *(boutique)* perfume shop (Brit) *ou* store (US)

pari [paʀi] *nm* bet, wager; *(Sport)* bet; **~ mutuel urbain (PMU)** *system of betting on horses*

paria [paʀja] *nm* outcast

parier [paʀje] *vt* to bet; **j'aurais parié que si/non** I'd have said he (*ou* you *etc*) would/wouldn't

parieur [paʀjœʀ] *nm* (*turfiste etc*) punter

Paris [paʀi] *n* Paris

parisien, ne [paʀizjɛ̃, -ɛn] *adj* Parisian; (*Géo, Admin*) Paris *cpd* ▷ *nm/f*: **Parisien, ne** Parisian

paritaire [paʀitɛʀ] *adj*: **commission** ~ joint commission

parité [paʀite] *nf* parity; ~ **de change** (*Écon*) exchange parity

parjure [paʀʒyʀ] *nm* (*faux serment*) false oath, perjury; (*violation de serment*) breach of oath, perjury ▷ *nm/f* perjurer

parjurer [paʀʒyʀe]: **se parjurer** *vi* to perjure o.s

parka [paʀka] *nf* parka

parking [paʀkiŋ] *nm* (*lieu*) car park (*Brit*), parking lot (*US*)

parlant, e [paʀlɑ̃, -ɑ̃t] *adj* (*fig*) graphic, vivid; (: *comparaison, preuve*) eloquent; (*Ciné*) talking ▷ *adv*: **généralement** ~ generally speaking

parlé, e [paʀle] *adj*: **langue** ~**e** spoken language

parlement [paʀləmɑ̃] *nm* parliament; **le P~ européen** the European Parliament

parlementaire [paʀləmɑ̃tɛʀ] *adj* parliamentary ▷ *nm/f* (*député*) ≈ Member of Parliament (*Brit*) *ou* Congress (*US*); parliamentarian; (*négociateur*) negotiator, mediator

parlementarisme [paʀləmɑ̃taʀism(ə)] *nm* parliamentary government

parlementer [paʀləmɑ̃te] *vi* (*ennemis*) to negotiate, parley; (*s'entretenir, discuter*) to argue at length, have lengthy talks

parler [paʀle] *nm* speech; dialect ▷ *vi* to speak, talk; (*avouer*) to talk; ~ **(à qn) de** to talk *ou* speak (to sb) about; ~ **pour qn** (*intercéder*) to speak for sb; ~ **en l'air** to say the first thing that comes into one's head; ~ **le/en français** to speak French/in French; ~ **affaires** to talk business; ~ **en dormant/du nez** to talk in one's sleep/through one's nose; **sans** ~ **de** (*fig*) not to mention, to say nothing of; **tu parles!** you must be joking!; **n'en parlons plus!** let's forget it!

parleur [paʀlœʀ] *nm*: **beau** ~ fine talker

parloir [paʀlwaʀ] *nm* (*d'une prison, d'un hôpital*) visiting room; (*Rel*) parlour (*Brit*), parlor (*US*)

parlote [paʀlɔt] *nf* chitchat

Parme [paʀm(ə)] *n* Parma

parme [paʀm(ə)] *adj* violet (blue)

parmesan [paʀməzɑ̃] *nm* Parmesan (cheese)

parmi [paʀmi] *prép* among(st)

parodie [paʀɔdi] *nf* parody

parodier [paʀɔdje] *vt* (*œuvre, auteur*) to parody

paroi [paʀwa] *nf* wall; (*cloison*) partition; ~ **rocheuse** rock face

paroisse [paʀwas] *nf* parish

paroissial, e, -aux [paʀwasjal, -o] *adj* parish *cpd*

paroissien, ne [paʀwasjɛ̃, -ɛn] *nm/f* parishioner ▷ *nm* prayer book

parole [paʀɔl] *nf* (*faculté*): **la** ~ speech; (*mot, promesse*) word; (*Rel*): **la bonne** ~ the word of God; **paroles** *nfpl* (*Mus*) words, lyrics; **tenir** ~ to keep one's word; **avoir la** ~ to have the floor; **n'avoir qu'une** ~ to be true to one's word; **donner la** ~ **à qn** to hand over to sb; **prendre la** ~ to speak; **demander la** ~ to ask for permission to speak; **perdre la** ~ to lose the power of speech; (*fig*) to lose one's tongue; **je le crois sur** ~ I'll take his word for it, I'll take him at his word; **temps de** ~ (*TV, Radio etc*) discussion time; **ma** ~! my word!, good heavens!; ~ **d'honneur** word of honour (*Brit*) *ou* honor (*US*)

parolier, -ière [paʀɔlje, -jɛʀ] *nm/f* lyricist; (*Opéra*) librettist

paroxysme [paʀɔksism(ə)] *nm* height, paroxysm

parpaing [paʀpɛ̃] *nm* bond-stone, parpen

parquer [paʀke] *vt* (*voiture, matériel*) to park; (*bestiaux*) to pen (in *ou* up); (*prisonniers*) to pack in

parquet [paʀkɛ] *nm* (*parquet*) floor; (*Jur: bureau*) public prosecutor's office; **le** ~ **(général)** (*magistrats*) ≈ the Bench

parqueter [paʀkəte] *vt* to lay a parquet floor in

parrain [paʀɛ̃] *nm* godfather; (*d'un navire*) namer; (*d'un nouvel adhérent*) sponsor, proposer

parrainage [paʀɛnaʒ] *nm* sponsorship

parrainer [paʀene] *vt* (*nouvel adhérent*) to sponsor, propose; (*entreprise*) to promote, sponsor

parricide [paʀisid] *nm, nf* parricide

pars [paʀ] *vb voir* **partir**

parsemer [paʀsəme] *vt* (*feuilles, papiers*) to be scattered over; ~ **qch de** to scatter sth with

parsi, e [paʀsi] *adj* Parsee

part [paʀ] *vb voir* **partir** ▷ *nf* (*qui revient à qn*) share; (*fraction, partie*) part; (*de gâteau, fromage*) portion; (*Finance*) (non-voting) share; **prendre** ~ **à** (*débat etc*) to take part in; (*soucis, douleur de qn*) to share in; **faire** ~ **de qch à qn** to announce sth to sb, inform sb of sth; **pour ma** ~ as for me, as far as I'm concerned; **à** ~ **entière** *adj* full; **de la** ~ **de** (*au nom de*) on behalf of; (*donné par*) from; **c'est de la** ~ **de qui?** (*au téléphone*) who's calling *ou* speaking (please)?; **de toute(s)** ~**(s)** from all sides *ou* quarters; **de** ~ **et d'autre** on both sides, on either side; **de** ~ **en** ~ right through; **d'une** ~ **... d'autre** ~ on the one hand ... on the other hand; **nulle/autre/quelque** ~ nowhere/elsewhere/somewhere; **à** ~ *adv* separately; (*de côté*) aside ▷ *prép* apart from, except for ▷ *adj* exceptional, special; **pour une large** *ou* **bonne** ~ to a great extent; **prendre qch en bonne/mauvaise** ~ to take sth well/badly; **faire la** ~ **des choses** to make allowances; **faire la** ~ **du feu** (*fig*) to cut one's losses; **faire la** ~ **(trop) belle à qn** to give sb more than his (*ou* her) share

part. *abr* = **particulier**

partage [paʀtaʒ] *nm voir* **partager** sharing (out) *no pl*, share-out; sharing; dividing up; (*Pol: de suffrages*) share; **recevoir qch en** ~ to receive sth as one's share (*ou* lot); **sans** ~ undivided

partagé, e [paʁtaʒe] *adj* (*opinions etc*) divided; (*amour*) shared; **être ~ entre** to be shared between; **être ~ sur** to be divided about

partager [paʁtaʒe] *vt* to share; (*distribuer, répartir*) to share (out); (*morceler, diviser*) to divide (up); **se partager** *vt* (*héritage etc*) to share between themselves (*ou* ourselves *etc*)

partance [paʁtɑ̃s]: **en ~** *adv* outbound, due to leave; **en ~ pour** (bound) for

partant, e [paʁtɑ̃, -ɑ̃t] *vb voir* **partir** ▷ *adj*: **être ~ pour qch** (*d'accord pour*) to be quite ready for sth ▷ *nm* (*Sport*) starter; (*Hippisme*) runner

partenaire [paʁtənɛʁ] *nm/f* partner; **~s sociaux** management and workforce

parterre [paʁtɛʁ] *nm* (*de fleurs*) (flower) bed, border; (*Théât*) stalls *pl*

parti [paʁti] *nm* (*Pol*) party; (*décision*) course of action; (*personne à marier*) match; **tirer ~ de** to take advantage of, turn to good account; **prendre le ~ de faire** to make up one's mind to do, resolve to do; **prendre le ~ de qn** to stand up for sb, side with sb; **prendre ~ (pour/contre)** to take sides *ou* a stand (for/against); **prendre son ~ de** to come to terms with; **~ pris** bias

partial, e, -aux [paʁsjal, -o] *adj* biased, partial

partialement [paʁsjalmɑ̃] *adv* in a biased way

partialité [paʁsjalite] *nf* bias, partiality

participant, e [paʁtisipɑ̃, -ɑ̃t] *nm/f* participant; (*à un concours*) entrant; (*d'une société*) member

participation [paʁtisipasjɔ̃] *nf* participation; sharing; (*Comm*) interest; **la ~ aux bénéfices** profit-sharing; **la ~ ouvrière** worker participation; **"avec la ~ de ..."** "featuring ..."

participe [paʁtisip] *nm* participle; **~ passé/présent** past/present participle

participer [paʁtisipe]: **~ à** *vt* (*course, réunion*) to take part in; (*profits etc*) to share in; (*frais etc*) to contribute to; (*entreprise: financièrement*) to cooperate in; (*chagrin, succès de qn*) to share (in); **~ de** *vt* to partake of.

particulariser [paʁtikylaʁize] *vt*: **se particulariser** to mark o.s. (*ou* itself) out

particularisme [paʁtikylaʁism(ə)] *nm* sense of identity

particularité [paʁtikylaʁite] *nf* particularity; (*distinctive*) characteristic, feature

particule [paʁtikyl] *nf* particle; **~ (nobiliaire)** nobiliary particle

particulier, -ière [paʁtikylje, -jɛʁ] *adj* (*personnel, privé*) private; (*spécial*) special, particular; (*caractéristique*) characteristic, distinctive; (*spécifique*) particular ▷ *nm* (*individu: Admin*) private individual; **"~ vend ..."** (*Comm*) "for sale privately ...", "for sale by owner ..." (*US*); **~ à** peculiar to; **en ~** *adv* (*surtout*) in particular, particularly; (*à part*) separately; (*en privé*) in private

particulièrement [paʁtikyljɛʁmɑ̃] *adv* particularly

partie [paʁti] *nf* (*gén*) part; (*profession, spécialité*) field, subject; (*Jur etc: protagonistes*) party; (*de cartes, tennis etc*) game; (*fig: lutte, combat*) struggle, fight; **une ~ de campagne/de pêche** an outing in the country/a fishing party *ou* trip; **en ~** *adv* partly, in part; **faire ~ de** to belong to; (*chose*) to be part of; **prendre qn à ~** to take sb to task; (*malmener*) to set on sb; **en grande ~** largely, in the main; **ce n'est que ~ remise** it will be for another time *ou* the next time; **avoir ~ liée avec qn** to be in league with sb; **~ civile** (*Jur*) party claiming damages in a criminal case

partiel, le [paʁsjɛl] *adj* partial ▷ *nm* (*Scol*) class exam

partiellement [paʁsjɛlmɑ̃] *adv* partially, partly

partir [paʁtiʁ] *vi* (*gén*) to go; (*quitter*) to go, leave; (*s'éloigner*) to go (*ou* drive *etc*) away *ou* off; (*moteur*) to start; (*pétard*) to go off; (*bouchon*) to come out; (*bouton*) to come off; **~ de** (*lieu: quitter*) to leave; (: *commencer à*) to start from; (*date*) to run *ou* start from; **~ pour/à** (*lieu, pays etc*) to leave for/go off to; **à ~ de** from

partisan, e [paʁtizɑ̃, -an] *nm/f* partisan; (*d'un parti, régime etc*) supporter ▷ *adj* (*lutte, querelle*) partisan, one-sided; **être ~ de qch/faire** to be in favour (*Brit*) *ou* favor (*US*) of sth/doing

partitif, -ive [paʁtitif, -iv] *adj*: **article ~** partitive article

partition [paʁtisjɔ̃] *nf* (*Mus*) score

partout [paʁtu] *adv* everywhere; **~ où il allait** everywhere *ou* wherever he went; **trente ~** (*Tennis*) thirty all

paru [paʁy] *pp de* **paraître**

parure [paʁyʁ] *nf* (*bijoux etc*) finery *no pl*; jewellery *no pl* (*Brit*), jewelry *no pl* (*US*); (*assortiment*) set

parus *etc* [paʁy] *vb voir* **paraître**

parution [paʁysjɔ̃] *nf* publication, appearance

parvenir [paʁvəniʁ]: **~ à** *vt* (*atteindre*) to reach; (*obtenir, arriver à*) to attain; (*réussir*): **~ à faire** to manage to do, succeed in doing; **faire ~ qch à qn** to have sth sent to sb

parvenu, e [paʁvəny] *pp de* **parvenir** ▷ *nm/f* (*péj*) parvenu, upstart

parviendrai [paʁvjɛ̃dʁe], **parviens** *etc* [paʁvjɛ̃] *vb voir* **parvenir**

parvis [paʁvi] *nm* square (*in front of a church*)

 MOT-CLÉ

pas¹ [pɑ] *adv* **1** (*en corrélation avec ne, non etc*) not; **il ne pleure pas** (*habituellement*) he does not *ou* doesn't cry; (*maintenant*) he's not *ou* isn't crying; **je ne mange pas de viande** I don't *ou* do not eat meat; **il n'a pas pleuré/ne pleurera pas** he did not *ou* didn't/will not *ou* won't cry; **ils n'ont pas de voiture/d'enfants** they haven't got a car/any children, they have no car/children; **il m'a dit de ne pas le faire** he told me not to do it; **non pas que ...** not that ..

2 (*employé sans ne etc*): **pas moi** not me, not I, I don't (*ou* can't *etc*); **elle travaille, (mais) lui pas** *ou* **pas lui** she works but he doesn't *ou* does not; **une pomme pas mûre** an apple which isn't ripe; **pas plus tard qu'hier** only yesterday; **pas du tout** not at all; **pas de sucre, merci** no sugar, thanks; **ceci est à vous ou pas?** is this yours or not?, is this yours or isn't it?

3: **pas mal** (*joli: personne, maison*) not bad; **pas mal fait** not badly done *ou* made; **comment ça va? — pas mal** how are things? — not bad; **pas mal de** quite a lot of

pas² [pɑ] *nm* (*allure, mesure*) pace; (*démarche*) tread; (*enjambée, Danse, fig: étape*) step; (*bruit*) (foot)step; (*trace*) footprint; (*allure*) pace; (*d'un cheval*) walk; (*mesure*) pace; (*Tech: de vis, d'écrou*) thread; **~ à ~** step by step; **au ~** at a walking pace; **de ce ~** (*à l'instant même*) straightaway, at once; **marcher à grands ~** to stride along; **mettre qn au ~** to bring sb to heel; **au ~ de gymnastique/de course** at a jog trot/at a run; **à ~ de loup** stealthily; **faire les cent ~** to pace up and down; **faire les premiers ~** to make the first move; **retourner** *ou* **revenir sur ses ~** to retrace one's steps; **se tirer d'un mauvais ~** to get o.s. out of a tight spot; **sur le ~ de la porte** on the doorstep; **le ~ de Calais** (*détroit*) the Straits *pl* of Dover; **~ de porte** (*fig*) key money

pascal, e, -aux [paskal, -o] *adj* Easter *cpd*
passable [pɑsabl(ə)] *adj* passable, tolerable
passablement [pɑsabləmɑ̃] *adv* (*pas trop mal*) reasonably well; (*beaucoup*) quite a lot
passade [pɑsad] *nf* passing fancy, whim
passage [pɑsaʒ] *nm* (*fait de passer*) *voir* **passer**; (*lieu, prix de la traversée, extrait de livre etc*) passage; (*chemin*) way; (*itinéraire*) **sur le ~ du cortège** along the route of the procession; **"laissez/ n'obstruez pas le ~"** "keep clear/do not obstruct"; **de ~** (*en passant*) as I (*ou* he *etc*) went by; **de ~** (*touristes*) passing through; (*amants etc*) casual; **~ clouté** pedestrian crossing; **"~ interdit"** "no entry"; **~ à niveau** level (*Brit*) *ou* grade (*US*) crossing; **"~ protégé"** right of way over secondary road(s) on your right; **~ souterrain** subway (*Brit*), underpass; **~ à tabac** beating-up; **~ à vide** (*fig*) bad patch
passager, -ère [pɑsaʒe, -ɛʀ] *adj* passing; (*hôte*) short-stay *cpd*; (*oiseau*) migratory ▷ *nm/f* passenger; **~ clandestin** stowaway
passagèrement [pɑsaʒɛʀmɑ̃] *adv* temporarily, for a short time
passant, e [pɑsɑ̃, -ɑ̃t] *adj* (*rue, endroit*) busy ▷ *nm/f* passer-by ▷ *nm* (*pour ceinture etc*) loop; **en ~: remarquer qch en ~** to notice sth in passing
passation [pɑsɑsjɔ̃] *nf* (*Jur: d'un acte*) signing; **~ des pouvoirs** transfer *ou* handover of power
passe [pɑs] *nf* (*Sport, magnétique*) pass; (*Navig*) channel ▷ *nm* (*passe-partout*) master *ou* skeleton key; **être en ~ de faire** to be on the way to doing; **être dans une mauvaise ~** (*fig*) to be going through a bad patch; **être dans une bonne ~** (*fig*) to be in a healthy situation; **~ d'armes** (*fig*) heated exchange
passé, e [pɑse] *adj* (*événement, temps*) past;

(*couleur, tapisserie*) faded; (*précédent*): **dimanche ~** last Sunday ▷ *prép* after ▷ *nm* past; (*Ling*) past (tense); **il est ~ midi** *ou* **midi ~** it's gone (*Brit*) *ou* past twelve; **~ de mode** out of fashion; **~ composé** perfect (tense); **~ simple** past historic
passe-droit [pɑsdʀwa] *nm* special privilege
passéiste [pɑseist(ə)] *adj* backward-looking
passementerie [pɑsmɑ̃tʀi] *nf* trimmings *pl*
passe-montagne [pɑsmɔ̃taɲ] *nm* balaclava
passe-partout [pɑspaʀtu] *nm inv* master *ou* skeleton key ▷ *adj inv* all-purpose
passe-passe [pɑspas] *nm*: **tour de ~** trick, sleight of hand *no pl*
passe-plat [pɑspla] *nm* serving hatch
passeport [pɑspɔʀ] *nm* passport
passer [pɑse] *vi* (*se rendre, aller*) to go; (*voiture, piétons: défiler*) to pass (by), go by; (*faire une halte rapide: facteur, laitier etc*) to come, call; (: *pour rendre visite*) to call *ou* drop in; (*courant, air, lumière, franchir un obstacle etc*) to get through; (*accusé, projet de loi*): **~ devant** to come before; (*film, émission*) to be on; (*temps, jours*) to pass, go by; (*liquide, café*) to go through; (*être digéré, avalé*) to go down; (*couleur, papier*) to fade; (*mode*) to die out; (*douleur*) to pass, go away; (*Cartes*) to pass; (*Scol*) to go up (to the next class); (*devenir*): **~ président** to be appointed *ou* become president ▷ *vt* (*frontière, rivière etc*) to cross; (*douane*) to go through; (*examen*) to sit, take; (*visite médicale etc*) to have; (*journée, temps*) to spend; (*donner*): **~ qch à qn** to pass sth to sb; to give sb sth; (*transmettre*): **~ qch à qn** to pass sth on to sb; (*enfiler: vêtement*) to slip on; (*faire entrer, mettre*): **(faire) ~ qch dans/par** to get sth into/through; (*café*) to pour the water on; (*thé, soupe*) to strain; (*film, pièce*) to show, put on; (*disque*) to play, put on; (*marché, accord*) to agree on; (*tolérer*): **~ qch à qn** to let sb get away with sth; **se passer** *vi* (*avoir lieu: scène, action*) to take place; (*se dérouler: entretien etc*) to go; (*arriver*): **que s'est-il passé?** what happened?; (*s'écouler: semaine etc*) to pass, go by; **se ~ de** *vt* to go *ou* do without; **se ~ les mains sous l'eau/de l'eau sur le visage** to put one's hands under the tap/run water over one's face; **en passant** in passing; **~ par** to go through; **passez devant/par ici** go front/ this way; **~ sur** *vt* (*faute, détail inutile*) to pass over; **~ dans les mœurs/l'usage** to become the custom/normal usage; **~ avant qch/qn** (*fig*) to come before sth/sb; **laisser ~** (*air, lumière, personne*) to let through; (*occasion*) to let slip, miss; (*erreur*) to overlook; **faire ~** (*message*) to get over *ou* across; **faire ~ à qn le goût de qch** to cure sb of his (*ou* her) taste for sth; **~ à la radio/ fouille** to be X-rayed/searched; **~ à la radio/ télévision** to be on the radio/on television; **~ à table** to sit down to eat; **~ au salon** to go through to *ou* into the sitting room; **~ à l'opposition** to go over to the opposition; **~ aux aveux** to confess, make a confession; **~ à l'action** to go into action; **~ pour riche** to be

taken for a rich man; **il passait pour avoir** he was said to have; **faire ~ qn/qch pour** to make sb/sth out to be; **passe encore de le penser, mais de le dire!** it's one thing to think it, but to say it!; **passons!** let's say no more (about it); **et j'en passe!** and that's not all!; **~ en seconde, ~ la seconde** (*Auto*) to change into second; **~ qch en fraude** to smuggle sth in (*ou* out); **~ la main par la portière** to stick one's hand out of the door; **~ le balai/l'aspirateur** to sweep up/ hoover; **~ commande/la parole à qn** to hand over to sb; **je vous passe M. X** (*je vous mets en communication avec lui*) I'm putting you through to Mr X; (*je lui passe l'appareil*) here is Mr X, I'll hand you over to Mr X; **~ prendre** to (come and) collect

passereau, x [pɑsʀo] *nm* sparrow
passerelle [pɑsʀɛl] *nf* footbridge; (*de navire, avion*) gangway; (*Navig*): **~ (de commandement)** bridge
passe-temps [pɑstɑ̃] *nm inv* pastime
passette [pɑsɛt] *nf* (tea-)strainer
passeur, -euse [pɑsœʀ, -øz] *nm/f* smuggler
passible [pɑsibl(ə)] *adj*: **~ de** liable to
passif, -ive [pasif, -iv] *adj* passive ▷ *nm* (*Ling*) passive; (*Comm*) liabilities *pl*
passion [pɑsjɔ̃] *nf* passion; **avoir la ~ de** to have a passion for; **fruit de la ~** passion fruit
passionnant, e [pɑsjɔnɑ̃, -ɑ̃t] *adj* fascinating
passionné, e [pɑsjɔne] *adj* (*personne, tempérament*) passionate; (*description*) impassioned ▷ *nm/f*: **c'est un ~ d'échecs** he's a chess fanatic; **être ~ de** *ou* **pour qch** to have a passion for sth
passionnel, le [pɑsjɔnɛl] *adj* of passion
passionnément [pɑsjɔnemɑ̃] *adv* passionately
passionner [pɑsjɔne] *vt* (*personne*) to fascinate, grip; (*débat, discussion*) to inflame; **se ~ pour** to take an avid interest in; to have a passion for
passivement [pasivmɑ̃] *adv* passively
passivité [pasivite] *nf* passivity, passiveness
passoire [pɑswaʀ] *nf* sieve; (*à légumes*) colander; (*à thé*) strainer
pastel [pastɛl] *nm, adj inv* (*Art*) pastel
pastèque [pastɛk] *nf* watermelon
pasteur [pastœʀ] *nm* (*protestant*) minister, pastor
pasteurisation [pastœʀizasjɔ̃] *nf* pasteurization
pasteurisé, e [pastœʀize] *adj* pasteurized
pasteuriser [pastœʀize] *vt* to pasteurize
pastiche [pastiʃ] *nm* pastiche
pastille [pastij] *nf* (*à sucer*) lozenge, pastille; (*de papier etc*) (small) disc; **~s pour la toux** cough drops *ou* lozenges
pastis [pastis] *nm anise-flavoured alcoholic drink*
pastoral, e, -aux [pastɔʀal, -o] *adj* pastoral
patagon, ne [patagɔ̃, -ɔn] *adj* Patagonian
Patagonie [patagɔni] *nf*: **la ~** Patagonia
patate [patat] *nf* spud; **~ douce** sweet potato
pataud, e [pato, -od] *adj* lumbering
patauger [patoʒe] *vi* (*pour s'amuser*) to splash

about; (*avec effort*) to wade about; (*fig*) to flounder; **~ dans** (*en marchant*) to wade through
patch [patʃ] *nm* nicotine patch
patchouli [patʃuli] *nm* patchouli
patchwork [patʃwœʀk] *nm* patchwork
pâte [pɑt] *nf* (*à tarte*) pastry; (*à pain*) dough; (*à frire*) batter; (*substance molle*) paste; cream; **pâtes** *nfpl* (*macaroni etc*) pasta *sg*; **fromage à ~ dure/ molle** hard/soft cheese; **~ d'amandes** almond paste; **~ brisée** shortcrust (*Brit*) *ou* pie crust (*US*) pastry; **~ à choux/feuilletée** choux/puff *ou* flaky (*Brit*) pastry; **~ de fruits** crystallized fruit *no pl*; **~ à modeler** modelling clay, Plasticine® (*Brit*); **~ à papier** paper pulp
pâté [pɑte] *nm* (*charcuterie: terrine*) pâté; (*tache*) ink blot; (*de sable*) sandpie; **~ (en croûte)** ≈ meat pie; **~ de foie** liver pâté; **~ de maisons** block (of houses)
pâtée [pɑte] *nf* mash, feed
patelin [patlɛ̃] *nm* little place
patente [patɑ̃t] *nf* (*Comm*) trading licence (*Brit*) *ou* license (*US*)
patenté, e [patɑ̃te] *adj* (*Comm*) licensed; (*fig: attitré*) registered, (officially) recognized
patère [patɛʀ] *nf* (coat-)peg
paternalisme [patɛʀnalism(ə)] *nm* paternalism
paternaliste [patɛʀnalist(ə)] *adj* paternalistic
paternel, le [patɛʀnɛl] *adj* (*amour, soins*) fatherly; (*ligne, autorité*) paternal
paternité [patɛʀnite] *nf* paternity, fatherhood
pâteux, -euse [pɑtø, -øz] *adj* thick; pasty; **avoir la bouche** *ou* **langue pâteuse** to have a furred (*Brit*) *ou* coated tongue
pathétique [patetik] *adj* pathetic, moving
pathologie [patɔlɔʒi] *nf* pathology
pathologique [patɔlɔʒik] *adj* pathological
patibulaire [patibylɛʀ] *adj* sinister
patiemment [pasjamɑ̃] *adv* patiently
patience [pasjɑ̃s] *nf* patience; **être à bout de ~** to have run out of patience; **perdre/prendre ~** to lose (one's)/have patience
patient, e [pasjɑ̃, -ɑ̃t] *adj, nm/f* patient
patienter [pasjɑ̃te] *vi* to wait
patin [patɛ̃] *nm* skate; (*sport*) skating; (*de traîneau, luge*) runner; (*pièce de tissu*) cloth pad (*used as slippers to protect polished floor*); **~ (de frein)** brake block; **~s (à glace)** (ice) skates; **~s à roulettes** roller skates
patinage [patinaʒ] *nm* skating; **~ artistique/ de vitesse** figure/speed skating
patine [patin] *nf* sheen
patiner [patine] *vi* to skate; (*embrayage*) to slip; (*roue, voiture*) to spin; **se patiner** *vi* (*meuble, cuir*) to acquire a sheen, become polished
patineur, -euse [patinœʀ, -øz] *nm/f* skater
patinoire [patinwaʀ] *nf* skating rink, (ice) rink
patio [patjo] *nm* patio
pâtir [pɑtiʀ]: **~ de** *vt* to suffer because of
pâtisserie [pɑtisʀi] *nf* (*boutique*) cake shop; (*métier*) confectionery; (*à la maison*) pastry- *ou* cake-making, baking; **pâtisseries** *nfpl* (*gâteaux*)

pastries, cakes

pâtissier, -ière [pɑtisje, -jɛʀ] *nm/f* pastrycook; confectioner

patois [patwa] *nm* dialect, patois

patraque [patʀak] *(fam) adj* peaky, off-colour

patriarche [patʀijaʀʃ(ə)] *nm* patriarch

patrie [patʀi] *nf* homeland

patrimoine [patʀimwan] *nm* inheritance, patrimony; *(culture)* heritage; ~ **génétique** *ou* **héréditaire** genetic inheritance

patriote [patʀijɔt] *adj* patriotic ▷ *nm/f* patriot

patriotique [patʀijɔtik] *adj* patriotic

patriotisme [patʀijɔtism(ə)] *nm* patriotism

patron, ne [patʀɔ̃, -ɔn] *nm/f (chef)* boss, manager(-ess); *(propriétaire)* owner, proprietor(-tress); *(employeur)* employer; *(Méd)* ≈ senior consultant; *(Rel)* patron saint ▷ *nm (Couture)* pattern; ~ **de thèse** supervisor (of postgraduate thesis)

patronage [patʀɔnaʒ] *nm* patronage; *(organisation, club)* (parish) youth club; (parish) children's club

patronal, e, -aux [patʀɔnal, -o] *adj (syndicat, intérêts)* employers'

patronat [patʀɔna] *nm* employers *pl*

patronner [patʀɔne] *vt* to sponsor, support

patronnesse [patʀɔnɛs] *adj f:* **dame** ~ patroness

patronyme [patʀɔnim] *nm* name

patronymique [patʀɔnimik] *adj:* **nom** ~ patronymic (name)

patrouille [patʀuj] *nf* patrol

patrouiller [patʀuje] *vi* to patrol, be on patrol

patrouilleur [patʀujœʀ] *nm (Aviat)* scout (plane); *(Navig)* patrol boat

patte [pat] *nf (jambe)* leg; *(pied: de chien, chat)* paw; *(: d'oiseau)* foot; *(languette)* strap; *(: de poche)* flap; *(favoris)*: ~**s (de lapin)** (short) sideburns; **à ~s d'éléphant** *adj (pantalon)* flared; ~**s de mouche** *(fig)* spidery scrawl *sg*; ~**s d'oie** *(fig)* crow's feet

pattemouille [patmuj] *nf* damp cloth *(for ironing)*

pâturage [pɑtyʀaʒ] *nm* pasture

pâture [pɑtyʀ] *nf* food

paume [pom] *nf* palm

paumé, e [pome] *nm/f (fam)* drop-out

paumer [pome] *vt (fam)* to lose

paupérisation [popeʀizasjɔ̃] *nf* pauperization

paupérisme [popeʀism(ə)] *nm* pauperism

paupière [popjɛʀ] *nf* eyelid

paupiette [popjɛt] *nf:* ~**s de veau** veal olives

pause [poz] *nf (arrêt)* break; *(en parlant, Mus)* pause; ~ **de midi** lunch break

pause-café [pozkafe] *(pl* **pauses-café***) nf* coffee-break

pauvre [povʀ(ə)] *adj* poor ▷ *nm/f* poor man/ woman; **les ~s** the poor; ~ **en calcium** low in calcium

pauvrement [povʀəmɑ̃] *adv* poorly

pauvreté [povʀəte] *nf (état)* poverty

pavage [pavaʒ] *nm* paving; cobbles *pl*

pavaner [pavane]: **se pavaner** *vi* to strut about

pavé, e [pave] *adj (cour)* paved; *(rue)* cobbled

▷ *nm (bloc)* paving stone; cobblestone; *(pavage)* paving; *(bifteck)* slab of steak; *(fam: livre)* hefty tome; **être sur le** ~ *(sans domicile)* to be on the streets; *(sans emploi)* to be out of a job; ~ **numérique** *(Inform)* keypad

pavillon [pavijɔ̃] *nm (de banlieue)* small (detached) house; *(kiosque)* lodge; pavilion; *(d'hôpital)* ward; *(Mus: de cor etc)* bell; *(Anat: de l'oreille)* pavilion, pinna; *(Navig)* flag; ~ **de complaisance** flag of convenience

pavoiser [pavwaze] *vt* to deck with flags ▷ *vi* to put out flags; *(fig)* to rejoice, exult

pavot [pavo] *nm* poppy

payable [pɛjabl(ə)] *adj* payable

payant, e [pɛjɑ̃, -ɑ̃t] *adj (spectateurs etc)* paying; *(billet)* that you pay for, to be paid for; *(fig: entreprise)* profitable; **c'est** ~ you have to pay, there is a charge

paye [pɛj] *nf* pay, wages *pl*

payement [pɛjmɑ̃] *nm* payment

payer [peje] *vt (créancier, employé, loyer)* to pay; *(achat, réparations, fig: faute)* to pay for ▷ *vi* to pay; *(métier)* to pay, be well-paid; *(effort, tactique etc)* to pay off; **être bien/mal payé** to be well/badly paid; **il me l'a fait** ~ **10 euros** he charged me 10 euros for it; ~ **qn de** *(ses efforts, peines)* to reward sb for; ~ **qch à qn** to buy sth for sb, buy sb sth; **ils nous ont payé le voyage** they paid for our trip; ~ **de sa personne** to give of oneself; ~ **d'audace** to act with great daring; ~ **cher qch** to pay dear(ly) for sth; **cela ne paie pas de mine** it doesn't look much; **se** ~ **qch** to buy o.s. sth; **se** ~ **de mots** to shoot one's mouth off; **se** ~ **la tête de qn** to take the mickey out of sb *(Brit)*, make a fool of sb; *(duper)* to take sb for a ride

payeur, -euse [pɛjœʀ, -øz] *adj (organisme, bureau)* payments *cpd* ▷ *nm/f* payer

pays [pei] *nm (territoire, habitants)* country, land; *(région)* region; *(village)* village; **du** ~ *adj* local; **le** ~ **de Galles** Wales

paysage [peizaʒ] *nm* landscape

paysager, -ère [peizaʒe, -ɛʀ] *adj (jardin, parc)* landscaped

paysagiste [peizaʒist(ə)] *nm/f (de jardin)* landscape gardener; *(Art)* landscapist, landscape painter

paysan, ne [peizɑ̃, -an] *nm/f* countryman/- woman; farmer; *(péj)* peasant ▷ *adj* country *cpd*, farming, farmers'

paysannat [peizana] *nm* peasantry

Pays-Bas [peiba] *nmpl:* **les** ~ the Netherlands

PC *sigle m (Pol)* = **parti communiste**; *(Inform: = personal computer)* PC; *(= prêt conventionné) type of loan for house purchase*; *(Constr)* = **permis de construire**; *(Mil)* = **poste de commandement**

pcc *abr (= pour copie conforme)* c.c

Pce *abr* = **prince**

Pcesse *abr* = **princesse**

PCV *abr* = **percevoir**; *voir* **communication**

PDA *sigle m (= personal digital assistant)* PDA

p de p *abr* = **pas de porte**

PDG *sigle m* = **président directeur général**
p.-ê. *abr* = **peut-être**
PEA *sigle m* (= *plan d'épargne en actions*) building society savings plan
péage [peaʒ] *nm* toll; (*endroit*) tollgate; **pont à ~** toll bridge
peau, x [po] *nf* skin; (*cuir*): **gants de ~** leather gloves; **être bien/mal dans sa ~** to be at ease/odds with oneself; **se mettre dans la ~ de qn** to put o.s. in sb's place *ou* shoes; **faire ~ neuve** (*se renouveler*) to change one's image; **~ de chamois** (*chiffon*) chamois leather, shammy; **~ d'orange** orange peel
peaufiner [pofine] *vt* to polish (up)
Peau-Rouge [poruʒ] *nm/f* Red Indian, red skin
peccadille [pekadij] *nf* trifle, peccadillo
péché [peʃe] *nm* sin; **~ mignon** weakness
pêche [pɛʃ] *nf* (*sport, activité*) fishing; (*poissons pêchés*) catch; (*fruit*) peach; **aller à la ~** to go fishing; **avoir la ~** (*fam*) to be on (top) form; **~ à la ligne** (*en rivière*) angling; **~ sous-marine** deep-sea fishing
pêche-abricot [pɛʃabriko] (*pl* **pêches-abricots**) *nf* yellow peach
pécher [peʃe] *vi* (*Rel*) to sin; (*fig: personne*) to err; (: *chose*) to be flawed; **~ contre la bienséance** to break the rules of good behaviour
pêcher [peʃe] *nm* peach tree ▷ *vi* to go fishing; (*en rivière*) to go angling ▷ *vt* (*attraper*) to catch, land; (*chercher*) to fish for; **~ au chalut** to trawl
pécheur, -eresse [peʃœr, peʃrɛs] *nm/f* sinner
pêcheur [peʃœr] *nm* voir **pêche** fisherman; angler; **~ de perles** pearl diver
pectine [pɛktin] *nf* pectin
pectoral, e, -aux [pɛktɔral, -o] *adj* (*Anat*) pectoral; (*sirop*) throat *cpd*, cough *cpd* ▷ *nmpl* pectoral muscles
pécule [pekyl] *nm* savings *pl*, nest egg; (*d'un détenu*) earnings *pl* (*paid on release*)
pécuniaire [pekynjɛr] *adj* financial
pédagogie [pedagɔʒi] *nf* educational methods *pl*, pedagogy
pédagogique [pedagɔʒik] *adj* educational; **formation ~** teacher training
pédagogue [pedagɔg] *nm/f* teacher, education(al)ist
pédale [pedal] *nf* pedal; **mettre la ~ douce** to soft-pedal
pédaler [pedale] *vi* to pedal
pédalier [pedalje] *nm* pedal and gear mechanism
pédalo [pedalo] *nm* pedalo, pedal-boat
pédant, e [pedɑ̃, -ɑ̃t] *adj* (*péj*) pedantic ▷ *nm/f* pedant
pédantisme [pedɑ̃tism(ə)] *nm* pedantry
pédéraste [pederast(ə)] *nm* homosexual, pederast
pédérastie [pederasti] *nf* homosexuality, pederasty
pédestre [pedɛstr(ə)] *adj*: **tourisme ~** hiking; **randonnée ~** (*activité*) rambling; (*excursion*) ramble

pédiatre [pedjatr(ə)] *nm/f* paediatrician (*Brit*), pediatrician *ou* pediatrist (*US*), child specialist
pédiatrie [pedjatri] *nf* paediatrics *sg* (*Brit*), pediatrics *sg* (*US*)
pédicure [pedikyr] *nm/f* chiropodist
pedigree [pedigre] *nm* pedigree
peeling [piliŋ] *nm* exfoliation treatment
PEEP *sigle f* = **Fédération des parents d'élèves de l'enseignement public**
pègre [pɛgr(ə)] *nf* underworld
peignais *etc* [peɲɛ] *vb* voir **peindre**
peigne [pɛɲ] *vb* voir **peindre**; **peigner** ▷ *nm* comb
peigné, e [peɲe] *adj*: **laine ~e** wool worsted; combed wool
peigner [peɲe] *vt* to comb (the hair of); **se peigner** to comb one's hair
peignez *etc* [peɲe] *vb* voir **peindre**
peignoir [peɲwar] *nm* dressing gown; **~ de bain** bathrobe; **~ de plage** beach robe
peignons [peɲɔ̃] *vb* voir **peindre**
peinard, e [penar, -ard(ə)] *adj* (*emploi*) cushy (*Brit*), easy; (*personne*): **on est ~ ici** we're left in peace here
peindre [pɛ̃dr(ə)] *vt* to paint; (*fig*) to portray, depict
peine [pɛn] *nf* (*affliction*) sorrow, sadness *no pl*; (*mal, effort*) trouble *no pl*, effort; (*difficulté*) difficulty; (*punition, châtiment*) punishment; (*Jur*) sentence; **faire de la ~ à qn** to distress *ou* upset sb; **prendre la ~ de faire** to go to the trouble of doing; **se donner de la ~** to make an effort; **ce n'est pas la ~ de faire** there's no point in doing, it's not worth doing; **ce n'est pas la ~ que vous fassiez** there's no point (in) you doing; **avoir de la ~ à faire** to have difficulty doing; **donnez-vous** *ou* **veuillez-vous donner la ~ d'entrer** please do come in; **c'est ~ perdue** it's a waste of time (and effort); **à ~** *adv* scarcely, hardly, barely; **à ~ ... que** hardly ... than; **c'est à ~ si ...** it's (*ou* it was) a job to ...; **sous ~:** **sous ~ d'être puni** for fear of being punished; **défense d'afficher sous ~ d'amende** billposters will be fined; **~ capitale** capital punishment; **~ de mort** death sentence *ou* penalty
peiner [pene] *vi* to work hard; to struggle; (*moteur, voiture*) to labour (*Brit*), labor (*US*) ▷ *vt* to grieve, sadden
peint, e [pɛ̃, pɛ̃t] *pp de* **peindre**
peintre [pɛ̃tr(ə)] *nm* painter; **~ en bâtiment** house painter, painter and decorator; **~ d'enseignes** signwriter
peinture [pɛ̃tyr] *nf* painting; (*couche de couleur, couleur*) paint; (*surfaces peintes: aussi:* **peintures**) paintwork; **je ne peux pas le voir en ~** I can't stand the sight of him; **~ mate/brillante** matt/gloss paint; **"~ fraîche"** "wet paint"
péjoratif, -ive [peʒɔratif, -iv] *adj* pejorative, derogatory
Pékin [pekɛ̃] *n* Peking
pékinois, e [pekinwa, -waz] *adj* Peking(g)ese ▷ *nm* (*chien*) peke, pekin(g)ese; (*Ling*) Mandarin,

Pekin(g)ese ▷ nm/f: **Pékinois, e** Pekin(g)ese

PEL sigle m (= plan d'épargne logement) savings scheme providing lower-interest mortgages

pelade [pəlad] nf alopecia

pelage [pəlaʒ] nm coat, fur

pelé, e [pəle] adj (chien) hairless; (vêtement) threadbare; (terrain) bare

pêle-mêle [pɛlmɛl] adv higgledy-piggledy

peler [pəle] vt, vi to peel

pèlerin [pɛlʀɛ̃] nm pilgrim

pèlerinage [pɛlʀinaʒ] nm (voyage) pilgrimage; (lieu) place of pilgrimage, shrine

pèlerine [pɛlʀin] nf cape

pélican [pelikɑ̃] nm pelican

pelisse [pəlis] nf fur-lined cloak

pelle [pɛl] nf shovel; (d'enfant, de terrassier) spade; **~ à gâteau** cake slice; **~ mécanique** mechanical digger

pelletée [pɛlte] nf shovelful; spadeful

pelleter [pɛlte] vt to shovel (up)

pelleteuse [pɛltøz] nf mechanical digger, excavator

pelletier [pɛltje] nm furrier

pellicule [pelikyl] nf film; **pellicules** nfpl (Méd) dandruff sg

Péloponnèse [peloponɛz] nm: **le ~** the Peloponnese

pelote [pəlɔt] nf (de fil, laine) ball; (d'épingles) pin cushion; **~ basque** pelota

peloter [pəlɔte] vt (fam) to feel (up); **se peloter** vi to pet

peloton [pəlɔtɔ̃] nm (groupe: de personnes) group; (: de pompiers, gendarmes) squad; (: Sport) pack; (de laine) ball; **~ d'exécution** firing squad

pelotonner [pəlɔtɔne]: **se pelotonner** vi to curl (o.s.) up

pelouse [pəluz] nf lawn; (Hippisme) spectating area inside racetrack

peluche [pəlyʃ] nf (bit of) fluff; **animal en ~** soft toy, fluffy animal

pelucher [p(ə)lyʃe] vi to become fluffy, fluff up

pelucheux, -euse [p(ə)lyʃø, -øz] adj fluffy

pelure [pəlyʀ] nf peeling, peel no pl; **~ d'oignon** onion skin

pénal, e, -aux [penal, -o] adj penal

pénalisation [penalizasjɔ̃] nf (Sport) sanction, penalty

pénaliser [penalize] vt to penalize

pénalité [penalite] nf penalty

penalty, ies [penalti, -z] nm (Sport) penalty (kick)

pénard, e [penaʀ, -aʀd(ə)] adj = peinard

pénates [penat] nmpl: **regagner ses ~** to return to the bosom of one's family

penaud, e [pəno, -od] adj sheepish, contrite

penchant [pɑ̃ʃɑ̃] nm: **un ~ à faire/à qch** a tendency to do/to sth; **un ~ pour qch** a liking ou fondness for sth

penché, e [pɑ̃ʃe] adj slanting

pencher [pɑ̃ʃe] vi to tilt, lean over ▷ vt to tilt; **se pencher** vi to lean over; (se baisser) to bend down; **se ~ sur** to bend over; (fig: problème) to

look into; **se ~ au dehors** to lean out; **~ pour** to be inclined to favour (Brit) ou favor (US)

pendable [pɑ̃dabl(ə)] adj: **tour ~** rotten trick; **c'est un cas ~!** he (ou she) deserves to be shot!

pendaison [pɑ̃dɛzɔ̃] nf hanging

pendant, e [pɑ̃dɑ̃, -ɑ̃t] adj hanging (out); (Admin, Jur) pending ▷ nm counterpart; matching piece ▷ prép during; **faire ~ à** to match; to be the counterpart of; **~ que** while; **~s d'oreilles** drop ou pendant earrings

pendeloque [pɑ̃dlɔk] nf pendant

pendentif [pɑ̃dɑ̃tif] nm pendant

penderie [pɑ̃dʀi] nf wardrobe; (placard) walk-in cupboard

pendiller [pɑ̃dije] vi to flap (about)

pendre [pɑ̃dʀ(ə)] vt, vi to hang; **se ~ (à)** (se suicider) to hang o.s. (on); **~ à** to hang (down) from; **~ qch à** (mur) to hang sth (up) on; (plafond) to hang sth (up) from; **se ~ à** (se suspendre) to hang from

pendu, e [pɑ̃dy] pp de **pendre** ▷ nm/f hanged man (ou woman)

pendulaire [pɑ̃dylɛʀ] adj pendular, of a pendulum

pendule [pɑ̃dyl] nf clock ▷ nm pendulum

pendulette [pɑ̃dylɛt] nf small clock

pêne [pɛn] nm bolt

pénétrant, e [penetʀɑ̃, -ɑ̃t] adj (air, froid) biting; (pluie) that soaks right through you; (fig: odeur) noticeable; (œil, regard) piercing; (clairvoyant, perspicace) perceptive ▷ nf (route) expressway

pénétration [penetʀasjɔ̃] nf (fig: d'idées etc) penetration; (perspicacité) perception

pénétré, e [penetʀe] adj (air, ton) earnest; **être ~ de soi-même/son importance** to be full of oneself/one's own importance

pénétrer [penetʀe] vi to come ou get in ▷ vt to penetrate; **~ dans** to enter; (froid, projectile) to penetrate; (: air, eau) to come into, get into; (mystère, secret) to fathom; **se ~ de qch** to get sth firmly set in one's mind

pénible [penibl(ə)] adj (astreignant) hard; (affligeant) painful; (personne, caractère) tiresome; **il m'est ~ de ...** I'm sorry to ...

péniblement [peniblǝmɑ̃] adv with difficulty

péniche [peniʃ] nf barge; **~ de débarquement** landing craft inv

pénicilline [penisilin] nf penicillin

péninsulaire [penɛ̃sylɛʀ] adj peninsular

péninsule [penɛ̃syl] nf peninsula

pénis [penis] nm penis

pénitence [penitɑ̃s] nf (repentir) penitence; (peine) penance; (punition, châtiment) punishment; **mettre un enfant en ~** ≈ to make a child stand in the corner; **faire ~** to do a penance

pénitencier [penitɑ̃sje] nm prison, penitentiary (US)

pénitent, e [penitɑ̃, -ɑ̃t] adj penitent

pénitentiaire [penitɑ̃sjɛʀ] adj prison cpd, penitentiary (US)

pénombre [penɔ̃bʀ(ə)] nf half-light

pensable [pɑ̃sabl(ə)] *adj*: **ce n'est pas** ~ it's unthinkable

pensant, e [pɑ̃sɑ̃, -ɑ̃t] *adj*: **bien** ~ right-thinking

pense-bête [pɑ̃sbɛt] *nm* aide-mémoire, mnemonic device

pensée [pɑ̃se] *nf* thought; (*démarche, doctrine*) thinking *no pl*; (*Bot*) pansy; **se représenter qch par la** ~ to conjure up a mental picture of sth; **en** ~ in one's mind

penser [pɑ̃se] *vi* to think ▷ *vt* to think; (*concevoir: problème, machine*) to think out; ~ **à** to think of; (*songer à: ami, vacances*) to think of *ou* about; (*réfléchir à: problème, offre*) ~ **à qch** to think about sth, think sth over; ~ **à faire qch** to think of doing sth; ~ **faire qch** to be thinking of doing sth, intend to do sth; **faire** ~ **à** to remind one of; **n'y pensons plus** let's forget it; **vous n'y pensez pas!** don't let it bother you!; **sans** ~ **à mal** without meaning any harm; **je le pense aussi** I think so too; **je pense que oui/non** I think so/don't think so

penseur [pɑ̃sœʀ] *nm* thinker; **libre** ~ free-thinker

pensif, -ive [pɑ̃sif, -iv] *adj* pensive, thoughtful

pension [pɑ̃sjɔ̃] *nf* (*allocation*) pension; (*prix du logement*) board and lodging, bed and board; (*maison particulière*) boarding house; (*hôtel*) guesthouse, hotel; (*école*) boarding school; **prendre** ~ **chez** to take board and lodging at; **prendre qn en** ~ to take sb (in) as a lodger; **mettre en** ~ to send to boarding school; ~ **alimentaire** (*d'étudiant*) living allowance; (*de divorcée*) maintenance allowance; alimony; ~ **complète** full board; ~ **de famille** boarding house, guesthouse; ~ **de guerre/d'invalidité** war/disablement pension

pensionnaire [pɑ̃sjɔnɛʀ] *nm/f* boarder; guest

pensionnat [pɑ̃sjɔna] *nm* boarding school

pensionné, e [pɑ̃sjɔne] *nm/f* pensioner

pensivement [pɑ̃sivmɑ̃] *adv* pensively, thoughtfully

pensum [pɛ̃sɔm] *nm* (*Scol*) punishment exercise; (*fig*) chore

pentagone [pɛ̃tagɔn] *nm* pentagon; **le P~** the Pentagon

pentathlon [pɛ̃tatlɔ̃] *nm* pentathlon

pente [pɑ̃t] *nf* slope; **en** ~ *adj* sloping

Pentecôte [pɑ̃tkot] *nf*: **la** ~ Whitsun (*Brit*), Pentecost; (*dimanche*) Whitsunday (*Brit*); **lundi de** ~ Whit Monday (*Brit*)

pénurie [penyʀi] *nf* shortage; ~ **de main-d'œuvre** undermanning

PEP [pɛp] *sigle m* (= *plan d'épargne populaire*) *individual savings plan*

pépé [pepe] *nm* (*fam*) grandad

pépère [pepɛʀ] *adj* (*fam*) cushy; (*fam*) quiet ▷ *nm* (*fam*) grandad

pépier [pepje] *vi* to chirp, tweet

pépin [pepɛ̃] *nm* (*Bot: graine*) pip; (*fam: ennui*) snag, hitch; (: *parapluie*) brolly (*Brit*), umbrella

pépinière [pepinjɛʀ] *nf* nursery; (*fig*) nest, breeding-ground

pépiniériste [pepinjeʀist(ə)] *nm* nurseryman

pépite [pepit] *nf* nugget

PEPS *abr* (= *premier entré premier sorti*) first in first out

PER [pɛʀ] *sigle m* (= *plan d'épargne retraite*) *type of personal pension plan*

perçant, e [pɛʀsɑ̃, -ɑ̃t] *adj* (*vue, regard, yeux*) sharp, keen; (*cri, voix*) piercing, shrill

percée [pɛʀse] *nf* (*trouée*) opening; (*Mil, Comm: fig*) breakthrough; (*Sport*) break

perce-neige [pɛʀsənɛʒ] *nm ou f inv* snowdrop

perce-oreille [pɛʀsɔʀɛj] *nm* earwig

percepteur [pɛʀsɛptœʀ] *nm* tax collector

perceptible [pɛʀsɛptibl(ə)] *adj* (*son, différence*) perceptible; (*impôt*) payable, collectable

perception [pɛʀsɛpsjɔ̃] *nf* perception; (*d'impôts etc*) collection; (*bureau*) tax (collector's) office

percer [pɛʀse] *vt* to pierce; (*ouverture etc*) to make; (*mystère, énigme*) to penetrate ▷ *vi* to come through; (*réussir*) to break through; ~ **une dent** to cut a tooth

perceuse [pɛʀsøz] *nf* drill; ~ **à percussion** hammer drill

percevable [pɛʀsəvabl(ə)] *adj* collectable, payable

percevoir [pɛʀsəvwaʀ] *vt* (*distinguer*) to perceive, detect; (*taxe, impôt*) to collect; (*revenu, indemnité*) to receive

perche [pɛʀʃ(ə)] *nf* (*Zool*) perch; (*bâton*) pole; ~ **à son** (sound) boom

percher [pɛʀʃe] *vt*: ~ **qch sur** to perch sth on ▷ *vi*, **se percher** *vi* (*oiseau*) to perch

perchiste [pɛʀʃist(ə)] *nm/f* (*Sport*) pole vaulter; (*TV etc*) boom operator

perchoir [pɛʀʃwaʀ] *nm* perch; (*fig*) presidency of the French National Assembly

perclus, e [pɛʀkly, -yz] *adj*: ~ **de** (*rhumatismes*) crippled with

perçois *etc* [pɛʀswa] *vb voir* **percevoir**

percolateur [pɛʀkɔlatœʀ] *nm* percolator

perçu, e [pɛʀsy] *pp de* **percevoir**

percussion [pɛʀkysjɔ̃] *nf* percussion

percussionniste [pɛʀkysjɔnist(ə)] *nm/f* percussionist

percutant, e [pɛʀkytɑ̃, -ɑ̃t] *adj* (*article etc*) resounding, forceful

percuter [pɛʀkyte] *vt* to strike; (*véhicule*) to crash into ▷ *vi*: ~ **contre** to crash into

percuteur [pɛʀkytœʀ] *nm* firing pin, hammer

perdant, e [pɛʀdɑ̃, -ɑ̃t] *nm/f* loser ▷ *adj* losing

perdition [pɛʀdisjɔ̃] *nf* (*morale*) ruin; **en** ~ (*Navig*) in distress; **lieu de** ~ den of vice

perdre [pɛʀdʀ(ə)] *vt* to lose; (*gaspiller: temps, argent*) to waste; (: *occasion*) to waste, miss; (*personne: moralement etc*) to ruin ▷ *vi* to lose; (*sur une vente etc*) to lose out; (*récipient*) to leak; **se perdre** *vi* (*s'égarer*) to get lost, lose one's way; (*fig: se gâter*) to go to waste; (*disparaître*) to disappear, vanish; **il ne perd rien pour attendre** it can wait, it'll keep

perdreau, x [pɛʀdʀo] *nm* (young) partridge

perdrix [pɛʀdʀi] *nf* partridge

perdu, e [pɛʀdy] *pp de* **perdre** ▷ *adj* (*enfant, cause, objet*) lost; (*isolé*) out-of-the-way; (*Comm: emballage*) non-returnable; (*récolte etc*) ruined; (*malade*): **il est ~** there's no hope left for him; **à vos moments ~s** in your spare time

père [pɛʀ] *nm* father; **pères** *nmpl* (*ancêtres*) forefathers; **de ~ en fils** from father to son; **~ de famille** father; family man; **mon ~** (*Rel*) Father; **le ~ Noël** Father Christmas

pérégrinations [peʀegʀinasjɔ̃] *nfpl* travels

péremption [peʀɑ̃psjɔ̃] *nf*: **date de ~** expiry date

péremptoire [peʀɑ̃ptwaʀ] *adj* peremptory

pérennité [peʀenite] *nf* durability, lasting quality

péréquation [peʀekwasjɔ̃] *nf* (*des salaires*) realignment; (*des prix, impôts*) equalization

perfectible [pɛʀfɛktibl(ə)] *adj* perfectible

perfection [pɛʀfɛksjɔ̃] *nf* perfection; **à la ~** *adv* to perfection

perfectionné, e [pɛʀfɛksjɔne] *adj* sophisticated

perfectionnement [pɛʀfɛksjɔnmɑ̃] *nm* improvement

perfectionner [pɛʀfɛksjɔne] *vt* to improve, perfect; **se ~ en anglais** to improve one's English

perfectionniste [pɛʀfɛksjɔnist(ə)] *nm/f* perfectionist

perfide [pɛʀfid] *adj* perfidious, treacherous

perfidie [pɛʀfidi] *nf* treachery

perforant, e [pɛʀfɔʀɑ̃, -ɑ̃t] *adj* (*balle*) armour-piercing (*Brit*), armor-piercing (*US*)

perforateur, -trice [pɛʀfɔʀatœʀ, -tʀis] *nm/f* punch-card operator ▷ *nm* (*perceuse*) borer; drill ▷ *nf* (*perceuse*) borer; drill; (*pour cartes*) card-punch; (*de bureau*) punch

perforation [pɛʀfɔʀasjɔ̃] *nf* perforation; punching; (*trou*) hole

perforatrice [pɛʀfɔʀatʀis] *nf voir* **perforateur**

perforé, e [pɛʀfɔʀe] *adj*: **bande ~** punched tape; **carte ~** punch card

perforer [pɛʀfɔʀe] *vt* to perforate, punch a hole *ou* holes in; (*ticket, bande, carte*) to punch

perforeuse [pɛʀfɔʀøz] *nf* (*machine*) (card) punch; (*personne*) card punch operator

performance [pɛʀfɔʀmɑ̃s] *nf* performance

performant, e [pɛʀfɔʀmɑ̃, -ɑ̃t] *adj* (*Écon: produit, entreprise*) high-return *cpd*; (*Tech: appareil, machine*) high-performance *cpd*

perfusion [pɛʀfyzjɔ̃] *nf* perfusion; **faire une ~ à qn** to put sb on a drip

péricliter [peʀiklite] *vi* to go downhill

péridurale [peʀidyʀal] *nf* epidural

périgourdin, e [peʀiguʀdɛ̃, -in] *adj* of *ou* from the Périgord

péril [peʀil] *nm* peril; **au ~ de sa vie** at the risk of his life; **à ses risques et ~s** at his (*ou* her) own risk

périlleux, -euse [peʀijø, -øz] *adj* perilous

périmé, e [peʀime] *adj* (out)dated; (*Admin*) out-of-date, expired

périmètre [peʀimɛtʀ(ə)] *nm* perimeter

périnatal, e [peʀinatal] *adj* perinatal

période [peʀjɔd] *nf* period

périodique [peʀjɔdik] *adj* (*phases*) periodic; (*publication*) periodical; (*Math: fraction*) recurring ▷ *nm* periodical; **garniture** *ou* **serviette ~** sanitary towel (*Brit*) *ou* napkin (*US*)

périodiquement [peʀjɔdikmɑ̃] *adv* periodically

péripéties [peʀipesi] *nfpl* events, episodes

périphérie [peʀifeʀi] *nf* periphery; (*d'une ville*) outskirts *pl*

périphérique [peʀifeʀik] *adj* (*quartiers*) outlying; (*Anat, Tech*) peripheral; (*station de radio*) operating from a neighbouring country ▷ *nm* (*Inform*) peripheral; (*Auto*): (**boulevard**) **~** ring road (*Brit*), beltway (*US*)

périphrase [peʀifʀaz] *nf* circumlocution

périple [peʀipl(ə)] *nm* journey

périr [peʀiʀ] *vi* to die, perish

périscolaire [peʀiskɔlɛʀ] *adj* extracurricular

périscope [peʀiskɔp] *nm* periscope

périssable [peʀisabl(ə)] *adj* perishable

péristyle [peʀistil] *nm* peristyle

péritonite [peʀitɔnit] *nf* peritonitis

perle [pɛʀl(ə)] *nf* pearl; (*de plastique, métal, sueur*) bead; (*personne, chose*) gem, treasure; (*erreur*) gem, howler

perlé, e [pɛʀle] *adj* (*rire*) rippling, tinkling; (*travail*) exquisite; (*orge*) pearl *cpd*; **grève ~e** go-slow, selective strike (action)

perler [pɛʀle] *vi* to form in droplets

perlier, -ière [pɛʀlje, -jɛʀ] *adj* pearl *cpd*

permanence [pɛʀmanɑ̃s] *nf* permanence; (*local*) (duty) office, strike headquarters; (*service des urgences*) emergency service; (*Scol*) study room; **assurer une ~** (*service public, bureaux*) to operate *ou* maintain a basic service; **être de ~** to be on call *ou* duty; **en ~** *adv* (*toujours*) permanently; (*continûment*) continuously

permanent, e [pɛʀmanɑ̃, -ɑ̃t] *adj* permanent; (*spectacle*) continuous; (*armée, comité*) standing ▷ *nf* perm ▷ *nm/f* (*d'un syndicat, parti*) paid official

perméable [pɛʀmeabl(ə)] *adj* (*terrain*) permeable; **~ à** (*fig*) receptive *ou* open to

permettre [pɛʀmɛtʀ(ə)] *vt* to allow, permit; **~ à qn de faire/qch** to allow sb to do/sth; **se ~ de faire qch** to take the liberty of doing sth; **permettez!** excuse me!

permis, e [pɛʀmi, -iz] *pp de* **permettre** ▷ *nm* permit, licence (*Brit*), license (*US*); **~ de chasse** hunting permit; **~ (de conduire)** (driving) licence (*Brit*), (driver's) license (*US*); **~ de construire** planning permission (*Brit*), building permit (*US*); **~ d'inhumer** burial certificate; **~ poids lourds** ≈ HGV (driving) licence (*Brit*), ≈ class E (driver's) license (*US*); **~ de séjour** residence permit; **~ de travail** work permit

permissif, -ive [pɛʀmisif, -iv] *adj* permissive

permission [pɛʀmisjɔ̃] *nf* permission; (*Mil*) leave; (*: papier*) pass; **en ~** on leave; **avoir la ~ de faire** to have permission to do, be allowed to do

permissionnaire [pɛʀmisjɔnɛʀ] *nm* soldier on leave

permutable [pɛʀmytabl(ə)] *adj* which can be changed *ou* switched around

permuter [pɛʀmyte] *vt* to change around, permutate ▷ *vi* to change, swap

pernicieux, -euse [pɛʀnisjø, -øz] *adj* pernicious

péroné [peʀɔne] *nm* fibula

pérorer [peʀɔʀe] *vi* to hold forth

Pérou [peʀu] *nm*: **le ~** Peru

perpendiculaire [pɛʀpɑ̃dikylɛʀ] *adj, nf* perpendicular

perpendiculairement [pɛʀpɑ̃dikylɛʀmɑ̃] *adv* perpendicularly

perpète [pɛʀpɛt] *nf*: **à ~** (*fam: loin*) miles away; (*: longtemps*) forever

perpétrer [pɛʀpetʀe] *vt* to perpetrate

perpétuel, le [pɛʀpetɥɛl] *adj* perpetual; (*Admin etc*) permanent; for life

perpétuellement [pɛʀpetɥɛlmɑ̃] *adv* perpetually, constantly

perpétuer [pɛʀpetɥe] *vt* to perpetuate; **se perpétuer** (*usage, injustice*) to be perpetuated; (*espèces*) to survive

perpétuité [pɛʀpetɥite] *nf*: **à ~** *adj, adv* for life; **être condamné à ~** to be sentenced to life imprisonment, receive a life sentence

perplexe [pɛʀplɛks(ə)] *adj* perplexed, puzzled

perplexité [pɛʀplɛksite] *nf* perplexity

perquisition [pɛʀkizisjɔ̃] *nf* (police) search

perquisitionner [pɛʀkizisjɔne] *vi* to carry out a search

perron [peʀɔ̃] *nm* steps *pl* (*in front of mansion etc*)

perroquet [peʀɔkɛ] *nm* parrot

perruche [peʀyʃ] *nf* budgerigar (*Brit*), budgie (*Brit*), parakeet (*US*)

perruque [peʀyk] *nf* wig

persan, e [pɛʀsɑ̃, -an] *adj* Persian ▷ *nm* (*Ling*) Persian

perse [pɛʀs(ə)] *adj* Persian ▷ *nm* (*Ling*) Persian ▷ *nm/f*: **Perse** Persian ▷ *nf*: **la P~** Persia

persécuter [pɛʀsekyte] *vt* to persecute

persécution [pɛʀsekysjɔ̃] *nf* persecution

persévérance [pɛʀseveʀɑ̃s] *nf* perseverance

persévérant, e [pɛʀseveʀɑ̃, -ɑ̃t] *adj* persevering

persévérer [pɛʀseveʀe] *vi* to persevere; **~ à croire que** to continue to believe that

persiennes [pɛʀsjɛn] *nfpl* (slatted) shutters

persiflage [pɛʀsiflaʒ] *nm* mockery *no pl*

persifleur, -euse [pɛʀsiflœʀ, -øz] *adj* mocking

persil [pɛʀsi] *nm* parsley

persillé, e [pɛʀsije] *adj* (sprinkled) with parsley; (*fromage*) veined; (*viande*) marbled, with fat running through

Persique [pɛʀsik] *adj*: **le golfe ~** the (Persian) Gulf

persistance [pɛʀsistɑ̃s] *nf* persistence

persistant, e [pɛʀsistɑ̃, -ɑ̃t] *adj* persistent; (*feuilles*) evergreen; **à feuillage ~** evergreen

persister [pɛʀsiste] *vi* to persist; **~ à faire qch** to persist in doing sth

personnage [pɛʀsɔnaʒ] *nm* (*notable*) personality; figure; (*individu*) character, individual; (*Théât*) character; (*Peinture*) figure

personnaliser [pɛʀsɔnalize] *vt* to personalize; (*appartement*) to give a personal touch to

personnalité [pɛʀsɔnalite] *nf* personality; (*personnage*) prominent figure

personne [pɛʀsɔn] *nf* person ▷ *pron* nobody, no one; (*quelqu'un*) anybody, anyone; **personnes** *nfpl* people *pl*; **il n'y a ~** there's nobody in *ou* there, there isn't anybody in *ou* there; **10 euros par ~** 10 euros per person *ou* a head; **en ~** personally, in person; **~ âgée** elderly person; **~ à charge** (*Jur*) dependent; **~ morale** *ou* **civile** (*Jur*) legal entity

personnel, le [pɛʀsɔnɛl] *adj* personal; (*égoïste: personne*) selfish, self-centred; (*idée, opinion*): **j'ai des idées ~les à ce sujet** I have my own ideas about that ▷ *nm* personnel, staff; **service du ~** personnel department

personnellement [pɛʀsɔnɛlmɑ̃] *adv* personally

personnification [pɛʀsɔnifikasjɔ̃] *nf* personification; **c'est la ~ de la cruauté** he's cruelty personified

personnifier [pɛʀsɔnifje] *vt* to personify; to typify; **c'est l'honnêteté personnifiée** he (*ou* she *etc*) is honesty personified

perspective [pɛʀspɛktiv] *nf* (*Art*) perspective; (*vue, coup d'œil*) view; (*point de vue*) viewpoint, angle; (*chose escomptée, envisagée*) prospect; **en ~** in prospect

perspicace [pɛʀspikas] *adj* clear-sighted, gifted with *ou* showing) insight

perspicacité [pɛʀspikasite] *nf* insight, perspicacity

persuader [pɛʀsɥade] *vt*: **~ qn (de/de faire)** to persuade sb (of/to do); **j'en suis persuadé** I'm quite sure *ou* convinced (of it)

persuasif, -ive [pɛʀsɥazif, -iv] *adj* persuasive

persuasion [pɛʀsɥazjɔ̃] *nf* persuasion

perte [pɛʀt(ə)] *nf* loss; (*de temps*) waste; (*fig: morale*) ruin; **pertes** *nfpl* losses; **à ~** (*Comm*) at a loss; **à ~ de vue** as far as the eye can (*ou* could) see; (*fig*) interminably; **en pure ~** for absolutely nothing; **courir à sa ~** to be on the road to ruin; **être en ~ de vitesse** (*fig*) to be losing momentum; **avec ~ et fracas** forcibly; **~ de chaleur** heat loss; **~ sèche** dead loss; **~s blanches** (vaginal) discharge *sg*

pertinemment [pɛʀtinamɑ̃] *adv* to the point; (*savoir*) perfectly well, full well

pertinence [pɛʀtinɑ̃s] *nf* pertinence, relevance; discernment

pertinent, e [pɛʀtinɑ̃, -ɑ̃t] *adj* (*remarque*) apt, pertinent, relevant; (*analyse*) discerning, judicious

perturbateur, -trice [pɛʀtyʀbatœʀ, -tʀis] *adj* disruptive

perturbation [pɛʀtyʀbasjɔ̃] *nf* (*dans un service public*) disruption; (*agitation, trouble*) perturbation; **~ (atmosphérique)** atmospheric disturbance

perturber [pɛʀtyʀbe] *vt* to disrupt; (*Psych*) to perturb, disturb

péruvien, ne [peʀyvjɛ̃, -ɛn] *adj* Peruvian ▷ *nm/f*:

Péruvien, ne Peruvian

pervenche [pɛʀvɑ̃ʃ] *nf* periwinkle; (*fam*) traffic warden (*Brit*), meter maid (*US*)

pervers, e [pɛʀvɛʀ, -ɛʀs(ə)] *adj* perverted, depraved; (*malfaisant*) perverse

perversion [pɛʀvɛʀsjɔ̃] *nf* perversion

perversité [pɛʀvɛʀsite] *nf* depravity; perversity

perverti, e [pɛʀvɛʀti] *nm/f* pervert

pervertir [pɛʀvɛʀtiʀ] *vt* to pervert

pesage [pəzaʒ] *nm* weighing; (*Hippisme: action*) weigh-in; (*: salle*) weighing room; (*: enceinte*) enclosure

pesamment [pəzamɑ̃] *adv* heavily

pesant, e [pəzɑ̃, -ɑ̃t] *adj* heavy; (*fig*) burdensome ▷ *nm*: **valoir son ~ de** to be worth one's weight in

pesanteur [pəzɑ̃tœʀ] *nf* gravity

pèse-bébé [pɛzbebe] *nm* (baby) scales *pl*

pesée [pəze] *nf* weighing; (*Boxe*) weigh-in; (*pression*) pressure

pèse-lettre [pɛzlɛtʀ(ə)] *nm* letter scales *pl*

pèse-personne [pɛzpɛʀsɔn] *nm* (bathroom) scales *pl*

peser [pəze] *vt* to weigh; (*considérer, comparer*) to weigh up ▷ *vi* to be heavy; (*fig*) to carry weight; **~ sur** (*levier, bouton*) to press, push; (*fig: accabler*) to lie heavy on; (*: influencer*) to influence; **~ à qn** to weigh heavy on sb

pessaire [pɛsɛʀ] *nm* pessary

pessimisme [pesimism(ə)] *nm* pessimism

pessimiste [pesimist(ə)] *adj* pessimistic ▷ *nm/f* pessimist

peste [pɛst(ə)] *nf* plague; (*fig*) pest, nuisance

pester [pɛste] *vi*: **~ contre** to curse

pesticide [pɛstisid] *nm* pesticide

pestiféré, e [pɛstifeʀe] *nm/f* plague victim

pestilentiel, le [pɛstilɑ̃sjɛl] *adj* foul

pet [pɛ] *nm* (*fam!*) fart (!)

pétale [petal] *nm* petal

pétanque [petɑ̃k] *nf* *type of bowls*; *see note*

⬤ **PÉTANQUE**
⬤
⬤ *Pétanque* is a version of the game of "boules",
⬤ played on a variety of hard surfaces.
⬤ Standing with their feet together, players
⬤ throw steel bowls at a wooden jack. *Pétanque*
⬤ originated in the South of France and is still
⬤ very much associated with that area.

pétarade [petaʀad] *nf* backfiring *no pl*

pétarader [petaʀade] *vi* to backfire

pétard [petaʀ] *nm* (*feu d'artifice*) banger (*Brit*), firecracker; (*de cotillon*) cracker; (*Rail*) detonator

pet-de-nonne [pɛdnɔn] (*pl* **pets-de-nonne**) *nm* ≈ choux bun

péter [pete] *vi* (*fam: casser, sauter*) to burst; to bust; (*fam!*) to fart (!)

pète-sec [pɛtsɛk] *adj inv* abrupt, sharp (-tongued)

pétillant, e [petijɑ̃, -ɑ̃t] *adj* sparkling

pétiller [petije] *vi* (*flamme, bois*) to crackle;

(*mousse, champagne*) to bubble; (*pierre, métal*) to glisten; (*yeux*) to sparkle; (*fig*) **~ d'esprit** to sparkle with wit

petit, e [pəti, -it] *adj* (*gén*) small; (*main, objet, colline, en âge: enfant*) small, little; (*mince, fin: personne, taille, pluie*) slight; (*voyage*) short, little; (*bruit etc*) faint, slight; (*mesquin*) mean; (*peu important*) minor ▷ *nm/f* (*petit enfant*) little one, child; **petits** *nmpl* (*d'un animal*) young *pl*; **faire des ~s** to have kittens (*ou* puppies *etc*); **en ~** in miniature; **mon ~** son; little one; **ma ~e** dear; little one; **pauvre ~** poor little thing; **la classe des ~s** the infant class; **pour ~s et grands** for children and adults; **les tout-~s** the little ones, the tiny tots; **~ à ~** bit by bit, gradually; **~(e) ami/e** boyfriend/girlfriend; **les ~es annonces** the small ads; **~ déjeuner** breakfast; **~ doigt** little finger; **le ~ écran** the small screen; **~ four** petit four; **~ pain** (bread) roll; **~e monnaie** small change; **~e vérole** smallpox; **~s pois** petit pois *pl*, garden peas; **~es gens** people of modest means

petit-beurre [pətibœʀ] (*pl* **petits-beurre**) *nm* sweet butter biscuit (*Brit*) ou cookie (*US*)

petit-bourgeois, petite-bourgeoise [pətibuʀʒwa, pətitbuʀʒwaz] (*pl* **petit(e)s-bourgeois(es)**) *adj* (*péj*) petit-bourgeois, middle-class

petite-fille [pətitfij] (*pl* **petites-filles**) *nf* granddaughter

petitement [pətitmɑ̃] *adv* poorly; meanly; **être logé ~** to be in cramped accommodation

petitesse [pətitɛs] *nf* smallness; (*d'un salaire, de revenus*) modestness; (*mesquinerie*) meanness

petit-fils [pətifis] (*pl* **petits-fils**) *nm* grandson

pétition [petisjɔ̃] *nf* petition; **faire signer une ~** to get up a petition

pétitionnaire [petisjɔnɛʀ] *nm/f* petitioner

pétitionner [petisjɔne] *vi* to petition

petit-lait [pətilɛ] (*pl* **petits-laits**) *nm* whey *no pl*

petit-nègre [pətinɛgʀ(ə)] *nm* (*péj*) pidgin French

petits-enfants [pətizɑ̃fɑ̃] *nmpl* grandchildren

petit-suisse [pətisɥis] (*pl* **petits-suisses**) *nm* *small individual pot of cream cheese*

pétoche [petɔʃ] *nf* (*fam*): **avoir la ~** to be scared out of one's wits

pétri, e [petʀi] *adj*: **~ d'orgueil** filled with pride

pétrifier [petʀifje] *vt* to petrify; (*fig*) to paralyze, transfix

pétrin [petʀɛ̃] *nm* kneading-trough; (*fig*): **dans le ~** in a jam *ou* fix

pétrir [petʀiʀ] *vt* to knead

pétrochimie [petʀɔʃimi] *nf* petrochemistry

pétrochimique [petʀɔʃimik] *adj* petrochemical

pétrodollar [petʀɔdɔlaʀ] *nm* petrodollar

pétrole [petʀɔl] *nm* oil; (*aussi*: **pétrole lampant**) paraffin (*Brit*), kerosene (*US*)

pétrolier, -ière [petʀɔlje, -jɛʀ] *adj* oil *cpd*; (*pays*) oil-producing ▷ *nm* (*navire*) oil tanker; (*financier*) oilman; (*technicien*) petroleum engineer

pétrolifère [petʀɔlifɛʀ] *adj* oil(-bearing)

P et T *sigle fpl* = **postes et télécommunications**

pétulant, e [petylɑ̃, -ɑ̃t] *adj* exuberant

○ MOT-CLÉ

peu [pø] *adv* **1** (*modifiant verbe, adjectif, adverbe*): **il boit peu** he doesn't drink (very) much; **il est peu bavard** he's not very talkative; **peu avant/après** shortly before/afterwards; **pour peu qu'il fasse** if he should do, if by any chance he does
2 (*modifiant nom*): **peu de: peu de gens/d'arbres** few *ou* not (very) many people/trees; **il a peu d'espoir** he hasn't (got) much hope, he has little hope; **pour peu de temps** for (only) a short while; **à peu de frais** for very little cost
3: **peu à peu** little by little; **à peu près** just about, more or less; **à peu près 10 kg/10 euros** approximately 10 kg/10 euros
▷ *nm* **1**: **le peu de gens qui** the few people who; **le peu de sable qui** what little sand, the little sand which
2: **un peu** a little; **un petit peu** a little bit; **un peu d'espoir** a little hope; **elle est un peu bavarde** she's rather talkative; **un peu plus/moins de** slightly more/less (*ou* fewer) than; **pour un peu il ..., un peu plus et il ...** he very nearly *ou* all but ...; **essayez un peu!** have a go!, just try it!
▷ *pron*: **peu le savent** few know (it); **avant** *ou* **sous peu** shortly, before long; **depuis peu** for a short *ou* little while; (*au passé*) a short *ou* little while ago; **de peu** (only) just; **c'est peu de chose** it's nothing; **il est de peu mon cadet** he's just a little *ou* bit younger than me

peuplade [pœplad] *nf* (*horde, tribu*) tribe, people
peuple [pœpl(ə)] *nm* people; (*masse*): **un ~ de vacanciers** a crowd of holiday-makers; **il y a du ~** there are a lot of people
peuplé, e [pœple] *adj*: **très/peu ~** densely/sparsely populated
peupler [pœple] *vt* (*pays, région*) to populate; (*étang*) to stock; (*hommes, poissons*) to inhabit; (*fig: imagination, rêves*) to fill; **se peupler** *vi* (*ville, région*) to become populated; (*fig: s'animer*) to fill (up), be filled
peuplier [pøplije] *nm* poplar (tree)
peur [pœʀ] *nf* fear; **avoir ~ (de/de faire/que)** to be frightened *ou* afraid (of/of doing/that); **prendre ~** to take fright; **faire ~ à** to frighten; **de ~ de/que** for fear of/that; **j'ai ~ qu'il ne soit trop tard** I'm afraid it might be too late; **j'ai ~ qu'il (ne) vienne (pas)** I'm afraid he may (not) come
peureux, -euse [pœʀø, -øz] *adj* fearful, timorous
peut [pø] *vb voir* **pouvoir**
peut-être [pøtɛtʀ(ə)] *adv* perhaps, maybe; **~ que** perhaps, maybe; **~ bien qu'il fera/est** he may well do/be
peuvent [pœv], **peux** *etc* [pø] *vb voir* **pouvoir**
p. ex. *abr* (= *par exemple*) e.g

phalange [falɑ̃ʒ] *nf* (*Anat*) phalanx; (*Mil: fig*) phalanx
phallique [falik] *adj* phallic
phallocrate [falɔkʀat] *nm* male chauvinist
phallocratie [falɔkʀasi] *nf* male chauvinism
phallus [falys] *nm* phallus
pharaon [faʀaɔ̃] *nm* Pharaoh
phare [faʀ] *nm* (*en mer*) lighthouse; (*d'aéroport*) beacon; (*de véhicule*) headlight, headlamp (*Brit*)
▷ *adj*: **produit ~** leading product; **se mettre en ~s, mettre ses ~s** to put on one's headlights; **~s de recul** reversing (*Brit*) *ou* back-up (*US*) lights
pharmaceutique [faʀmasøtik] *adj* pharmaceutic(al)
pharmacie [faʀmasi] *nf* (*science*) pharmacology; (*magasin*) chemist's (*Brit*), pharmacy; (*officine*) dispensary; (*produits*) pharmaceuticals *pl*; (*armoire*) medicine chest *ou* cupboard, first-aid cupboard
pharmacien, ne [faʀmasjɛ̃, -ɛn] *nm/f* pharmacist, chemist (*Brit*)
pharmacologie [faʀmakɔlɔʒi] *nf* pharmacology
pharyngite [faʀɛ̃ʒit] *nf* pharyngitis *no pl*
pharynx [faʀɛ̃ks] *nm* pharynx
phase [fɑz] *nf* phase
phénoménal, e, -aux [fenɔmenal, -o] *adj* phenomenal
phénomène [fenɔmɛn] *nm* phenomenon; (*monstre*) freak
philanthrope [filɑ̃tʀɔp] *nm/f* philanthropist
philanthropie [filɑ̃tʀɔpi] *nf* philanthropy
philanthropique [filɑ̃tʀɔpik] *adj* philanthropic
philatélie [filateli] *nf* philately, stamp collecting
philatélique [filatelik] *adj* philatelic
philatéliste [filatelist(ə)] *nm/f* philatelist, stamp collector
philharmonique [filaʀmɔnik] *adj* philharmonic
philippin, e [filipɛ̃, -in] *adj* Filipino
Philippines [filipin] *nfpl*: **les ~** the Philippines
philistin [filistɛ̃] *nm* philistine
philo [filo] *nf* (*fam*: = *philosophie*) philosophy
philosophe [filozɔf] *nm/f* philosopher ▷ *adj* philosophical
philosopher [filozofe] *vi* to philosophize
philosophie [filozofi] *nf* philosophy
philosophique [filozofik] *adj* philosophical
philosophiquement [filozofikmɑ̃] *adv* philosophically
philtre [filtʀ(ə)] *nm* philtre, love potion
phlébite [flebit] *nf* phlebitis
phlébologue [flebolog] *nm/f* vein specialist
phobie [fɔbi] *nf* phobia
phonétique [fɔnetik] *adj* phonetic ▷ *nf* phonetics *sg*
phonétiquement [fɔnetikmɑ̃] *adv* phonetically
phonographe [fɔnɔgʀaf] *nm* (wind-up) gramophone
phoque [fɔk] *nm* seal; (*fourrure*) sealskin

phosphate [fɔsfat] *nm* phosphate
phosphaté, e [fɔsfate] *adj* phosphate-enriched
phosphore [fɔsfɔʀ] *nm* phosphorus
phosphoré, e [fɔsfɔʀe] *adj* phosphorous
phosphorescent, e [fɔsfɔʀesɑ̃, -ɑ̃t] *adj* luminous
phosphorique [fɔsfɔʀik] *adj*: **acide ~** phosphoric acid
photo [fɔto] *nf* (*photographie*) photo ▷ *adj*: **appareil/pellicule ~** camera/film; **en ~** in *ou* on a photo; **prendre en ~** to take a photo of; **aimer la/faire de la ~** to like taking/take photos; **~ en couleurs** colour photo; **~ d'identité** passport photo
photo... [fɔtɔ] *préfixe* photo...
photocopie [fɔtɔkɔpi] *nf* (*procédé*) photocopying; (*document*) photocopy
photocopier [fɔtɔkɔpje] *vt* to photocopy
photocopieur [fɔtɔkɔpjœʀ] *nm*, **photocopieuse** [fɔtɔkɔpjøz] *nf* (photo)copier
photo-électrique [fɔtɔelɛktʀik] *adj* photo-electric
photo-finish [fɔtofiniʃ] (*pl* **photos-finish**) *nf* (*appareil*) photo finish camera; (*photo*) photo finish picture; **il y a eu ~ pour la troisième place** there was a photo finish for third place
photogénique [fɔtɔʒenik] *adj* photogenic
photographe [fɔtɔgʀaf] *nm/f* photographer
photographie [fɔtɔgʀafi] *nf* (*procédé, technique*) photography; (*cliché*) photograph; **faire de la ~** to do photography as a hobby; (*comme métier*) to be a photographer
photographier [fɔtɔgʀafje] *vt* to photograph, take
photographique [fɔtɔgʀafik] *adj* photographic
photogravure [fɔtɔgʀavyʀ] *nf* photoengraving
photomaton® [fɔtɔmatɔ̃] *nm* photo-booth, photomat
photomontage [fɔtɔmɔ̃taʒ] *nm* photomontage
photophone [fɔtɔfɔn] *nm* camera phone
photo-robot [fɔtɔʀɔbo] *nf* Identikit® (picture)
photosensible [fɔtɔsɑ̃sibl(ə)] *adj* photosensitive
photostat [fɔtɔsta] *nm* photostat
phrase [fʀɑz] *nf* (*Ling*) sentence; (*propos, Mus*) phrase; **phrases** *nfpl* (*péj*) flowery language *sg*
phraséologie [fʀazeɔlɔʒi] *nf* phraseology; (*rhétorique*) flowery language
phraseur, -euse [fʀazœʀ, -øz] *nm/f*: **c'est un ~** he uses such flowery language
phrygien, ne [fʀiʒjɛ̃, -ɛn] *adj*: **bonnet ~** Phrygian cap
phtisie [ftizi] *nf* consumption
phylloxéra [filɔkseʀa] *nm* phylloxera
physicien, ne [fizisjɛ̃, -ɛn] *nm/f* physicist
physiologie [fizjɔlɔʒi] *nf* physiology
physiologique [fizjɔlɔʒik] *adj* physiological
physiologiquement [fizjɔlɔʒikmɑ̃] *adv* physiologically
physionomie [fizjɔnɔmi] *nf* face; (*d'un paysage etc*) physiognomy

physionomiste [fizjɔnɔmist(ə)] *nm/f* good judge of faces; person who has a good memory for faces
physiothérapie [fizjɔteʀapi] *nf* natural medicine, alternative medicine
physique [fizik] *adj* physical ▷ *nm* physique ▷ *nf* physics *sg*; **au ~** physically
physiquement [fizikmɑ̃] *adv* physically
phytothérapie [fitɔteʀapi] *nf* herbal medicine
p.i. *abr* = **par intérim**; *voir* **intérim**
piaffer [pjafe] *vi* to stamp
piaillement [pjɑjmɑ̃] *nm* squawking *no pl*
piailler [pjɑje] *vi* to squawk
pianiste [pjanist(ə)] *nm/f* pianist
piano [pjano] *nm* piano; **~ à queue** grand piano
pianoter [pjanɔte] *vi* to tinkle away (at the piano); (*tapoter*): **~ sur** to drum one's fingers on
piaule [pjol] *nf* (*fam*) pad
piauler [pjole] *vi* (*enfant*) to whimper; (*oiseau*) to cheep
PIB *sigle m* (= *produit intérieur brut*) GDP
pic [pik] *nm* (*instrument*) pick(axe); (*montagne*) peak; (*Zool*) woodpecker; **à ~** *adv* vertically; (*fig*) just at the right time; **couler à ~** (*bateau*) to go straight down; **~ à glace** ice pick
picard, e [pikaʀ, -aʀd(ə)] *adj* of *ou* from Picardy
Picardie [pikaʀdi] *nf*: **la ~** Picardy
picaresque [pikaʀɛsk(ə)] *adj* picaresque
piccolo [pikɔlo] *nm* piccolo
pichenette [piʃnɛt] *nf* flick
pichet [piʃɛ] *nm* jug
pickpocket [pikpɔkɛt] *nm* pickpocket
pick-up [pikœp] *nm inv* record player
picorer [pikɔʀe] *vt* to peck
picot [piko] *nm* sprocket; **entraînement par roue à ~s** sprocket feed
picotement [pikɔtmɑ̃] *nm* smarting *no pl*, prickling *no pl*
picoter [pikɔte] *vt* (*oiseau*) to peck ▷ *vi* (*irriter*) to smart, prickle
pictural, e, -aux [piktyʀal, -o] *adj* pictorial
pie [pi] *nf* magpie; (*fig*) chatterbox ▷ *adj inv*: **cheval ~** piebald; **vache ~** black and white cow
pièce [pjɛs] *nf* (*d'un logement*) room; (*Théât*) play; (*de mécanisme, machine*) part; (*de monnaie*) coin; (*Couture*) patch; (*document*) document; (*de drap, fragment, d'une collection*) piece; (*de bétail*) head; **mettre en ~s** to smash to pieces; **deux euros ~** two euros each; **vendre à la ~** to sell separately *ou* individually; **travailler/payer à la ~** to do piecework/pay piece rate; **de toutes ~s: c'est inventé de toutes ~s** it's a complete fabrication; **un maillot une ~** a one-piece swimsuit; **un deux-~s cuisine** a two-room(ed) flat (*Brit*) *ou* apartment (*US*) with kitchen; **tout d'une ~** (*personne: franc*) blunt; (: *sans souplesse*) inflexible; **~ à conviction** exhibit; **~ d'eau** ornamental lake *ou* pond; **~ d'identité: avez-vous une ~ d'identité?** have you got any (means of) identification?; **~ jointe** (*Inform*) attachment; **~ montée** tiered cake; **~ de rechange** spare (part); **~ de résistance** pièce de

résistance; (*plat*) main dish; **~s détachées** spares, (spare) parts; **en ~s détachées** (*à monter*) in kit form; **~s justificatives** supporting documents

pied [pje] *nm* foot; (*de verre*) stem; (*de table*) leg; (*de lampe*) base; (*plante*) plant; **~s nus** barefoot; **à ~** on foot; **à ~ sec** without getting one's feet wet; **à ~ d'œuvre** ready to start (work); **au ~ de la lettre** literally; **au ~ levé** at a moment's notice; **de ~ en cap** from head to foot; **en ~** (*portrait*) full-length; **avoir ~** to be able to touch the bottom, not to be out of one's depth; **avoir le ~ marin** to be a good sailor; **perdre ~** to lose one's footing; (*fig*) to get out of one's depth; **sur ~** (*Agr*) on the stalk, uncut; (*debout, rétabli*) up and about; **mettre sur ~** (*entreprise*) to set up; **mettre à ~** to suspend; to lay off; **mettre qn au ~ du mur** to get sb with his (*ou* her) back to the wall; **sur le ~ de guerre** ready for action; **sur un ~ d'égalité** on an equal footing; **sur ~ d'intervention** on stand-by; **faire du ~ à qn** (*prévenir*) to give sb a (warning) kick; (*galamment*) to play footsie with sb; **mettre les ~s quelque part** to set foot somewhere; **faire des ~s et des mains** (*fig*) to move heaven and earth, pull out all the stops; **c'est le ~!** (*fam*) it's terrific!; **se lever du bon ~/du ~ gauche** to get out of bed on the right/wrong side; **~ de lit** footboard; **~ de nez: faire un ~ de nez à** to thumb one's nose at; **~ de vigne** vine

pied-à-terre [pjetatεR] *nm inv* pied-à-terre

pied-bot [pjebo] (*pl* **pieds-bots**) *nm* person with a club foot

pied-de-biche [pjedbiʃ] (*pl* **pieds-de-biche**) *nm* claw; (*Couture*) presser foot

pied-de-poule [pjedpul] *adj inv* hound's-tooth

piédestal, -aux [pjedεstal, -o] *nm* pedestal

pied-noir [pjenwaR] (*pl* **pieds-noirs**) *nm* Algerian-born Frenchman

piège [pjεʒ] *nm* trap; **prendre au ~** to trap

piéger [pjeʒe] *vt* (*animal, fig*) to trap; (*avec une bombe*) to booby-trap; **lettre/voiture piégée** letter-/car-bomb

piercing [pjεRsiŋ] *nm* piercing

pierraille [pjεRaj] *nf* loose stones *pl*

pierre [pjεR] *nf* stone; **première ~** (*d'un édifice*) foundation stone; **mur de ~s sèches** drystone wall; **faire d'une ~ deux coups** to kill two birds with one stone; **~ à briquet** flint; **~ fine** semiprecious stone; **~ ponce** pumice stone; **~ de taille** freestone *no pl*; **~ tombale** tombstone, gravestone; **~ de touche** touchstone

pierreries [pjεRRi] *nfpl* gems, precious stones

pierreux, -euse [pjεRø, -øz] *adj* stony

piété [pjete] *nf* piety

piétinement [pjetinmɑ̃] *nm* stamping *no pl*

piétiner [pjetine] *vi* (*trépigner*) to stamp (one's foot); (*marquer le pas*) to stand about; (*fig*) to be at a standstill ▷ *vt* to trample on

piéton, ne [pjetɔ̃, -ɔn] *nm/f* pedestrian ▷ *adj* pedestrian *cpd*

piétonnier, -ière [pjetɔnje, -jεR] *adj* pedestrian *cpd*

piètre [pjεtR(ə)] *adj* poor, mediocre

pieu, x [pjø] *nm* (*piquet*) post; (*pointu*) stake; (*fam: lit*) bed

pieusement [pjøzmɑ̃] *adv* piously

pieuvre [pjœvR(ə)] *nf* octopus

pieux, -euse [pjø, -øz] *adj* pious

pif [pif] *nm* (*fam*) conk (*Brit*), beak; **au ~** = **au pifomètre**

piffer [pife] *vt* (*fam*): **je ne peux pas le ~** I can't stand him

pifomètre [pifɔmεtR(ə)] *nm* (*fam*): **choisir** *etc* **au ~** to follow one's nose when choosing *etc*

pige [piʒ] *nf* piecework rate

pigeon [piʒɔ̃] *nm* pigeon; **~ voyageur** homing pigeon

pigeonnant, e [piʒɔnɑ̃, -ɑ̃t] *adj* full, well-developed

pigeonneau, x [piʒɔno] *nm* young pigeon

pigeonnier [piʒɔnje] *nm* pigeon loft, dovecot(e)

piger [piʒe] *vi* (*fam*) to get it ▷ *vt* (*fam*) to get, understand

pigiste [piʒist(ə)] *nm/f* (*typographe*) typesetter on piecework; (*journaliste*) freelance journalist (*paid by the line*)

pigment [pigmɑ̃] *nm* pigment

pignon [piɲɔ̃] *nm* (*de mur*) gable; (*d'engrenage*) cog(wheel), gearwheel; (*graine*) pine kernel; **avoir ~ sur rue** (*fig*) to have a prosperous business

pile [pil] *nf* (*tas, pilier*) pile; (*Élec*) battery ▷ *adj*: **le côté ~** tails ▷ *adv* (*net, brusquement*) dead; (*à temps, à point nommé*) just at the right time; **à deux heures ~** at two on the dot; **jouer à ~ ou face** to toss up (for it); **~ ou face?** heads or tails?

piler [pile] *vt* to crush, pound

pileux, -euse [pilø, -øz] *adj*: **système ~** (body) hair

pilier [pilje] *nm* (*colonne, support*) pillar; (*personne*) mainstay; (*Rugby*) prop (forward)

pillage [pijaʒ] *nm* pillaging, plundering, looting

pillard, e [pijaR, -aRd(ə)] *nm/f* looter; plunderer

piller [pije] *vt* to pillage, plunder, loot

pilleur, -euse [pijœR, -øz] *nm/f* looter

pilon [pilɔ̃] *nm* (*instrument*) pestle; (*de volaille*) drumstick; **mettre un livre au ~** to pulp a book

pilonner [pilɔne] *vt* to pound

pilori [pilɔRi] *nm*: **mettre** *ou* **clouer au ~** to pillory

pilotage [pilɔtaʒ] *nm* piloting; flying; **~ automatique** automatic piloting; **~ sans visibilité** blind flying

pilote [pilɔt] *nm* pilot; (*de char, voiture*) driver ▷ *adj* pilot *cpd*; **usine/ferme ~** experimental factory/farm; **~ de chasse/d'essai/de ligne** fighter/test/airline pilot; **~ de course** racing driver

piloter [pilɔte] *vt* (*navire*) to pilot; (*avion*) to fly; (*automobile*) to drive; (*fig*): **~ qn** to guide sb round

pilotis [pilɔti] *nm* pile; stilt

pilule [pilyl] *nf* pill; **prendre la ~** to be on the

pill; **~ du lendemain** morning-after pill

pimbêche [pɛ̃bɛʃ] *nf* (*péj*) stuck-up girl

piment [pimɑ̃] *nm* (*Bot*) pepper, capsicum; (*fig*) spice, piquancy; **~ rouge** (*Culin*) chilli

pimenté, e [pimɑ̃te] *adj* hot and spicy

pimenter [pimɑ̃te] *vt* (*plat*) to season (with peppers *ou* chillis); (*fig*) to add *ou* give spice to

pimpant, e [pɛ̃pɑ̃, -ɑ̃t] *adj* spruce

pin [pɛ̃] *nm* pine (tree); (*bois*) pine(wood)

pinacle [pinakl(ə)] *nm*: **porter qn au ~** (*fig*) to praise sb to the skies

pinard [pinaʀ] *nm* (*fam*) (cheap) wine, plonk (*Brit*)

pince [pɛ̃s] *nf* (*outil*) pliers *pl*; (*de homard, crabe*) pincer, claw; (*Couture: pli*) dart; **~ à sucre/glace** sugar/ice tongs *pl*; **~ à épiler** tweezers *pl*; **~ à linge** clothes peg (*Brit*) *ou* pin (*US*); **~ universelle** (universal) pliers *pl*; **~s de cycliste** bicycle clips

pincé, e [pɛ̃se] *adj* (*air*) stiff; (*mince: bouche*) pinched ▷ *nf*: **une ~e de** a pinch of

pinceau, x [pɛ̃so] *nm* (paint)brush

pincement [pɛ̃smɑ̃] *nm*: **~ au cœur** twinge of regret

pince-monseigneur [pɛ̃smɔ̃sɛɲœʀ] (*pl* **pinces-monseigneur**) *nf* crowbar

pince-nez [pɛ̃sne] *nm inv* pince-nez

pincer [pɛ̃se] *vt* to pinch; (*Mus: cordes*) to pluck; (*Couture*) to dart, put darts in; (*fam*) to nab; **se ~ le doigt** to squeeze *ou* nip one's finger; **se ~ le nez** to hold one's nose

pince-sans-rire [pɛ̃ssɑ̃ʀiʀ] *adj inv* deadpan

pincettes [pɛ̃sɛt] *nfpl* tweezers; (*pour le feu*) (fire) tongs

pinçon [pɛ̃sɔ̃] *nm* pinch mark

pinède [pinɛd] *nf* pinewood, pine forest

pingouin [pɛ̃gwɛ̃] *nm* penguin

ping-pong [piŋpɔ̃g] *nm* table tennis

pingre [pɛ̃gʀ(ə)] *adj* niggardly

pinson [pɛ̃sɔ̃] *nm* chaffinch

pintade [pɛ̃tad] *nf* guinea-fowl

pin up [pinœp] *nf inv* pin-up (girl)

pioche [pjɔʃ] *nf* pickaxe

piocher [pjɔʃe] *vt* to dig up (with a pickaxe); (*fam*) to swot (*Brit*) *ou* grind (*US*) at; **~ dans** to dig into

piolet [pjɔlɛ] *nm* ice axe

pion, ne [pjɔ̃, pjɔn] *nm/f* (*Scol: péj*) student paid to supervise schoolchildren ▷ *nm* (*Échecs*) pawn; (*Dames*) piece, draught (*Brit*), checker (*US*)

pionnier [pjɔnje] *nm* pioneer

pipe [pip] *nf* pipe; **fumer la** *ou* **une ~** to smoke a pipe; **~ de bruyère** briar pipe

pipeau, x [pipo] *nm* (reed-)pipe

pipe-line [piplin] *nm* pipeline

piper [pipe] *vt* (*dé*) to load; (*carte*) to mark; **sans ~ mot** (*fam*) without a squeak; **les dés sont pipés** (*fig*) the dice are loaded

pipette [pipɛt] *nf* pipette

pipi [pipi] *nm* (*fam*): **faire ~** to have a wee

piquant, e [pikɑ̃, -ɑ̃t] *adj* (*barbe, rosier etc*) prickly; (*saveur, sauce*) hot, pungent; (*fig: description, style*) racy; (: *mordant, caustique*) biting ▷ *nm* (*épine*) thorn, prickle; (*de hérisson*) quill, spine; (*fig*) spiciness, spice

pique [pik] *nf* (*arme*) pike; (*fig*): **envoyer** *ou* **lancer des ~s à qn** to make cutting remarks to sb ▷ *nm* (*Cartes: couleur*) spades *pl*; (: *carte*) spade

piqué, e [pike] *adj* (*Couture*) (machine-)stitched; quilted; (*livre, glace*) mildewed; (*vin*) sour; (*Mus: note*) staccato; (*fam: personne*) nuts ▷ *nm* (*Aviat*) dive; (*Textiles*) piqué

pique-assiette [pikasjɛt] *nm/f inv* (*péj*) scrounger, sponger

pique-fleurs [pikflœʀ] *nm inv* flower holder

pique-nique [piknik] *nm* picnic

pique-niquer [piknike] *vi* to (have a) picnic

pique-niqueur, -euse [piknikœʀ, -øz] *nm/f* picnicker

piquer [pike] *vt* (*percer*) to prick; (*Méd*) to give an injection to; (: *animal blessé etc*) to put to sleep; (*insecte, fumée, ortie*) to sting; (: *poivre*) to burn; (: *froid*) to bite; (*Couture*) to machine (stitch); (*intérêt etc*) to arouse; (*fam: prendre*) to pick up; (: *voler*) to pinch; (: *arrêter*) to nab; (*planter*): **~ qch dans** to stick sth into; (*fixer*): **~ qch à** *ou* **sur** to pin sth onto ▷ *vi* (*oiseau, avion*) to go into a dive; (*saveur*) to be pungent; to be sour; **se piquer** (*avec une aiguille*) to prick o.s.; (*se faire une piqûre*) to inject o.s.; (*se vexer*) to get annoyed; **se ~ de faire** to pride o.s. on doing; **~ sur** to swoop down on; to head straight for; **~ du nez** (*avion*) to go into a nose-dive; **~ une tête** (*plonger*) to dive headfirst; **~ un galop/un cent mètres** to break into a gallop/put on a sprint; **~ une crise** to throw a fit; **~ au vif** (*fig*) to sting

piquet [pikɛ] *nm* (*pieu*) post, stake; (*de tente*) peg; **mettre un élève au ~** to make a pupil stand in the corner; **~ de grève** (strike) picket; **~ d'incendie** fire-fighting squad

piqueté, e [pikte] *adj*: **~ de** dotted with

piquette [pikɛt] *nf* (*fam*) cheap wine, plonk (*Brit*)

piqûre [pikyʀ] *nf* (*d'épingle*) prick; (*d'ortie*) sting; (*de moustique*) bite; (*Méd*) injection, shot (*US*); (*Couture*) (straight) stitch; straight stitching; (*de ver*) hole; (*tache*) (spot of) mildew; **faire une ~ à qn** to give sb an injection

piranha [piʀana] *nm* piranha

piratage [piʀataʒ] *nm* (*Inform*) piracy

pirate [piʀat] *adj* pirate *cpd* ▷ *nm* pirate; (*fig: escroc*) crook, shark; (*Inform*) hacker; **~ de l'air** hijacker

pirater [piʀate] *vi* (*Inform*) to hack ▷ *vt* (*Inform*) to hack into

piraterie [piʀatʀi] *nf* (act of) piracy; **~ aérienne** hijacking

pire [piʀ] *adj* (*comparatif*) worse; (*superlatif*): **le (la) ~ ...** the worst ... ▷ *nm*: **le ~ (de)** the worst (of)

Pirée [piʀe] *n* Piraeus

pirogue [piʀɔg] *nf* dugout (canoe)

pirouette [piʀwɛt] *nf* pirouette; (*fig: volte-face*) about-turn

pis [pi] *nm* (*de vache*) udder; (*pire*): **le ~** the worst

▷ *adj, adv* worse; **qui ~ est** what is worse; **au ~ aller** if the worst comes to the worst, at worst

pis-aller [pizale] *nm inv* stopgap

pisciculture [pisikyltyʀ] *nf* fish farming

piscine [pisin] *nf* (swimming) pool; **~ couverte** indoor (swimming) pool

Pise [piz] *n* Pisa

pissenlit [pisɑ̃li] *nm* dandelion

pisser [pise] *vi* (*fam!*) to pee

pissotière [pisɔtjɛʀ] *nf* (*fam*) public urinal

pistache [pistaʃ] *nf* pistachio (nut)

pistard [pistaʀ] *nm* (*Cyclisme*) track cyclist

piste [pist(ə)] *nf* (*d'un animal, sentier*) track, trail; (*indice*) lead; (*de stade, de magnétophone: de cirque*) ring; (*de danse*) floor; (*de patinage*) rink; (*de ski*) run; (*Aviat*) runway; **~ cavalière** bridle path; **~ cyclable** cycle track, bikeway (*US*); **~ sonore** sound track

pister [piste] *vt* to track, trail

pisteur [pistœʀ] *nm* (*Ski*) member of the ski patrol

pistil [pistil] *nm* pistil

pistolet [pistɔlɛ] *nm* (*arme*) pistol, gun; (*à peinture*) spray gun; **~ à bouchon/air comprimé** popgun/airgun; **~ à eau** water pistol

pistolet-mitrailleur [pistɔlɛmitʀajœʀ] (*pl* **pistolets-mitrailleurs**) *nm* submachine gun

piston [pistɔ̃] *nm* (*Tech*) piston; (*Mus*) valve; (*fig: appui*) string-pulling

pistonner [pistɔne] *vt* (*candidat*) to pull strings for

pitance [pitɑ̃s] *nf* (*péj*) (means of) sustenance

piteusement [pitøzmɑ̃] *adv* (*échouer*) miserably

piteux, -euse [pitø, -øz] *adj* pitiful, sorry (*avant le nom*); **en ~ état** in a sorry state

pitié [pitje] *nf* pity; **sans ~** *adj* pitiless, merciless; **faire ~** to inspire pity; **il me fait ~** I pity him, I feel sorry for him; **avoir ~ de** (*compassion*) to pity, feel sorry for; (*merci*) to have pity *ou* mercy on; **par ~!** for pity's sake!

piton [pitɔ̃] *nm* (*clou*) peg, bolt; **~ rocheux** rocky outcrop

pitoyable [pitwajabl(ə)] *adj* pitiful

pitre [pitʀ(ə)] *nm* clown

pitrerie [pitʀəʀi] *nf* tomfoolery *no pl*

pittoresque [pitɔʀɛsk(ə)] *adj* picturesque; (*expression, détail*) colourful (*Brit*), colorful (*US*)

pivert [pivɛʀ] *nm* green woodpecker

pivoine [pivwan] *nf* peony

pivot [pivo] *nm* pivot; (*d'une dent*) post

pivoter [pivɔte] *vi* (*fauteuil*) to swivel; (*porte*) to revolve; **~ sur ses talons** to swing round

pixel [piksɛl] *nm* pixel

pizza [pidza] *nf* pizza

PJ *sigle f* = **police judiciaire** ▷ *sigle fpl* (= **pièces jointes**) encl

PL *sigle m* (*Auto*) = **poids lourd**

Pl. *abr* = **place**

placage [plakaʒ] *nm* (*bois*) veneer

placard [plakaʀ] *nm* (*armoire*) cupboard; (*affiche*) poster, notice; (*Typo*) galley; **~ publicitaire** display advertisement

placarder [plakaʀde] *vt* (*affiche*) to put up; (*mur*) to stick posters on

place [plas] *nf* (*emplacement, situation, classement*) place; (*de ville, village*) square; (*Écon*): **~ financière/boursière** money/stock market; (*espace libre*) room, space; (*de parking*) space; (*siège: de train, cinéma, voiture*) seat; (*prix: au cinéma etc*) price; (: *dans un bus, taxi*) fare; (*emploi*) job; **en ~** (*mettre*) in its place; **de ~ en ~**, **par ~s** here and there, in places; **sur ~** on the spot; **faire ~ à** to give way to; **faire de la ~ à** to make room for; **ça prend de la ~** it takes up a lot of room *ou* space; **prendre ~** to take one's place; **remettre qn à sa ~** to put sb in his (*ou* her) place; **ne pas rester** *ou* **tenir en ~** to be always on the go; **à la ~ de** in place of, instead of; **une quatre ~s** (*Auto*) a four-seater; **il y a 20 ~s assises/debout** there are 20 seats/there is standing room for 20; **~ forte** fortified town; **~ d'honneur** place (*ou* seat) of honour (*Brit*) *ou* honor (*US*)

placé, e [plase] *adj* (*Hippisme*) placed; **haut ~** (*fig*) high-ranking; **être bien/mal ~** to be well/badly placed; (*spectateur*) to have a good/bad seat; **être bien/mal ~ pour faire** to be in/not to be in a position to do

placebo [plasebo] *nm* placebo

placement [plasmɑ̃] *nm* placing; (*Finance*) investment; **agence** *ou* **bureau de ~** employment agency

placenta [plasɑ̃ta] *nm* placenta

placer [plase] *vt* to place, put; (*convive, spectateur*) to seat; (*capital, argent*) to place, invest; (*dans la conversation*) to put *ou* get in; **~ qn chez** to get sb a job at (*ou* with); **se ~ au premier rang** to go and stand (*ou* sit) in the first row

placide [plasid] *adj* placid

placidité [plasidite] *nf* placidity

placier, -ière [plasje, -jɛʀ] *nm/f* commercial rep(resentative), salesman/woman

Placoplâtre® [plakoplatʀ] *nm* plasterboard

plafond [plafɔ̃] *nm* ceiling

plafonner [plafɔne] *vt* (*pièce*) to put a ceiling (up) in ▷ *vi* to reach one's (*ou* a) ceiling

plafonnier [plafɔnje] *nm* ceiling light; (*Auto*) interior light

plage [plaʒ] *nf* beach; (*station*) (seaside) resort; (*fig*) band, bracket; (*de disque*) track, band; **~ arrière** (*Auto*) parcel *ou* back shelf

plagiaire [plaʒjɛʀ] *nm/f* plagiarist

plagiat [plaʒja] *nm* plagiarism

plagier [plaʒje] *vt* to plagiarize

plagiste [plaʒist(ə)] *nm/f* beach attendant

plaid [plɛd] *nm* (*tartan*) car rug, lap robe (*US*)

plaidant, e [plɛdɑ̃, -ɑ̃t] *adj* litigant

plaider [plede] *vi* (*avocat*) to plead; (*plaignant*) to go to court, litigate ▷ *vt* to plead; **~ pour** (*fig*) to speak for

plaideur, -euse [plɛdœʀ, -øz] *nm/f* litigant

plaidoirie [plɛdwaʀi] *nf* (*Jur*) speech for the defence (*Brit*) *ou* defense (*US*)

plaidoyer [plɛdwaje] *nm* (*Jur*) speech for the defence (*Brit*) *ou* defense (*US*); (*fig*) plea

plaie [plɛ] *nf* wound

plaignant, e [plɛɲɑ̃, -ɑ̃t] *vb voir* **plaindre** ▷ *nm/f* plaintiff

plaindre [plɛ̃dʀ(ə)] *vt* to pity, feel sorry for; **se plaindre** *vi* (*gémir*) to moan; (*protester, rouspéter*): **se ~ (à qn) (de)** to complain (to sb) (about); (*souffrir*): **se ~ de** to complain of

plaine [plɛn] *nf* plain

plain-pied [plɛ̃pje]: **de ~** *adv* at street-level; (*fig*) straight; **de ~ (avec)** on the same level (as)

plaint, e [plɛ̃, -ɛ̃t] *pp de* **plaindre** ▷ *nf* (*gémissement*) moan, groan; (*doléance*) complaint; **porter ~e** to lodge a complaint

plaintif, -ive [plɛ̃tif, -iv] *adj* plaintive

plaire [plɛʀ] *vi* to be a success, be successful; to please; **~ à: cela me plaît** I like it; **essayer de ~ à qn** (*en étant serviable etc*) to try and please sb; **elle plaît aux hommes** she's a success with men, men like her; **se ~ quelque part** to like being somewhere, like it somewhere; **se ~ à faire** to take pleasure in doing; **ce qu'il vous plaira** what(ever) you like *ou* wish; **s'il vous plaît** please

plaisamment [plɛzamɑ̃] *adv* pleasantly

plaisance [plɛzɑ̃s] *nf* (*aussi*: **navigation de plaisance**) (pleasure) sailing, yachting

plaisancier [plɛzɑ̃sje] *nm* amateur sailor, yachting enthusiast

plaisant, e [plɛzɑ̃, -ɑ̃t] *adj* pleasant; (*histoire, anecdote*) amusing

plaisanter [plɛzɑ̃te] *vi* to joke ▷ *vt* (*personne*) to tease, make fun of; **pour ~** for a joke; **on ne plaisante pas avec cela** that's no joking matter; **tu plaisantes!** you're joking *ou* kidding!

plaisanterie [plɛzɑ̃tʀi] *nf* joke; joking *no pl*

plaisantin [plɛzɑ̃tɛ̃] *nm* joker; (*fumiste*) fly-by-night

plaise *etc* [plɛz] *vb voir* **plaire**

plaisir [pleziʀ] *nm* pleasure; **faire ~ à qn** (*délibérément*) to be nice to sb, please sb; (*cadeau, nouvelle etc*): **ceci me fait ~** I'm delighted *ou* very pleased with this; **prendre ~ à/à faire** to take pleasure in/in doing; **j'ai le ~ de ...** it is with great pleasure that I ...; **M. et Mme X ont le ~ de vous faire part de ...** M. and Mme X are pleased to announce ...; **se faire un ~ de faire qch** to be (only too) pleased to do sth; **faites-moi le ~ de ...** would you mind ..., would you be kind enough to ...; **à ~** freely; for the sake of it; **au ~ (de vous revoir)** (I hope to) see you again; **pour le** *ou* **pour son** *ou* **par ~** for pleasure

plaît [plɛ] *vb voir* **plaire**

plan, e [plɑ̃, -an] *adj* flat ▷ *nm* plan; (*Géom*) plane; (*fig*) level, plane; (*Ciné*) shot; **au premier/second ~** in the foreground/middle distance; **à l'arrière ~** in the background; **mettre qch au premier ~** (*fig*) to consider sth to be of primary importance; **sur le ~ sexuel** sexually, as far as sex is concerned; **laisser/rester en ~** to abandon/be abandoned; **~ d'action** plan of action; **~ directeur** (*Écon*)

master plan; **~ d'eau** lake; pond; **~ de travail** work-top, work surface; **~ de vol** (*Aviat*) flight plan

planche [plɑ̃ʃ] *nf* (*pièce de bois*) plank, (wooden) board; (*illustration*) plate; (*de salades, radis, poireaux*) bed; (*d'un plongeoir*) (diving) board; **les ~s** (*Théât*) the boards; **en ~s** *adj* wooden; **faire la ~** (*dans l'eau*) to float on one's back; **avoir du pain sur la ~** to have one's work cut out; **~ à découper** chopping board; **~ à dessin** drawing board; **~ à pain** breadboard; **~ à repasser** ironing board; **~ (à roulettes)** (*planche*) skateboard; (*sport*) skateboarding; **~ de salut** (*fig*) sheet anchor; **~ à voile** (*planche*) windsurfer, sailboard; (*sport*) windsurfing

plancher [plɑ̃ʃe] *nm* floor; (*planches*) floorboards *pl*; (*fig*) minimum level ▷ *vi* to work hard

planchiste [plɑ̃ʃist(ə)] *nm/f* windsurfer

plancton [plɑ̃ktɔ̃] *nm* plankton

planer [plane] *vi* (*oiseau, avion*) to glide; (*fumée, vapeur*) to float, hover; (*drogué*) to be (on a) high; **~ sur** (*fig*) to hang over; to hover above

planétaire [planetɛʀ] *adj* planetary

planétarium [planetaʀjɔm] *nm* planetarium

planète [planɛt] *nf* planet

planeur [planœʀ] *nm* glider

planification [planifikasjɔ̃] *nf* (economic) planning

planifier [planifje] *vt* to plan

planisphère [planisfɛʀ] *nm* planisphere

planning [planiŋ] *nm* programme (*Brit*), program (*US*), schedule; **~ familial** family planning

planque [plɑ̃k] *nf* (*fam: combine, filon*) cushy (*Brit*) *ou* easy number; (: *cachette*) hideout

planquer [plɑ̃ke] *vt* (*fam*) to hide (away), stash away; **se planquer** to hide

plant [plɑ̃] *nm* seedling, young plant

plantage [plɑ̃taʒ] *nm* (*d'ordinateur*) crash

plantaire [plɑ̃tɛʀ] *adj voir* **voûte**

plantation [plɑ̃tasjɔ̃] *nf* planting; (*de fleurs, légumes*) bed; (*exploitation*) plantation

plante [plɑ̃t] *nf* plant; **~ d'appartement** house *ou* pot plant; **~ du pied** sole (of the foot); **~ verte** house plant

planter [plɑ̃te] *vt* (*plante*) to plant; (*enfoncer*) to hammer *ou* drive in; (*tente*) to put up, pitch; (*drapeau, échelle, décors*) to put up; (*fam: mettre*) to dump; (: *abandonner*): **~ là** to ditch; **se planter** *vi* (*fam: se tromper*) to get it wrong; (*ordinateur*) to crash; **~ qch dans** to hammer *ou* drive sth into; to stick sth into; **se ~ dans** to sink into; to get stuck in; **se ~ devant** to plant o.s. in front of

planteur [plɑ̃tœʀ] *nm* planter

planton [plɑ̃tɔ̃] *nm* orderly

plantureux, -euse [plɑ̃tyʀø, -øz] *adj* (*repas*) copious, lavish; (*femme*) buxom

plaquage [plakaʒ] *nm* (*Rugby*) tackle

plaque [plak] *nf* plate; (*de verre*) sheet; (*de verglas, d'eczéma*) patch; (*dentaire*) plaque; (*avec inscription*) plaque; **~ (minéralogique** *ou* **de police** *ou* **d'immatriculation)** number (*Brit*) *ou* license

(US) plate; ~ **de beurre** slab of butter; ~ **chauffante** hotplate; ~ **de chocolat** bar of chocolate; ~ **de cuisson** hob; ~ **d'identité** identity disc; ~ **tournante** (fig) centre (Brit), center (US)

plaqué, e [plake] adj: ~ **or/argent** gold-/silver-plated ▷ nm: ~ **or/argent** gold/silver plate; ~ **acajou** with a mahogany veneer

plaquer [plake] vt (bijou) to plate; (bois) to veneer; (aplatir): ~ **qch sur/contre** to make sth stick ou cling to; (Rugby) to bring down; (fam: laisser tomber) to drop, ditch; **se ~ contre** to flatten o.s. against; ~ **qn contre** to pin sb to

plaquette [plakɛt] nf tablet; (de chocolat) bar; (de beurre) slab, packet; (livre) small volume; (Méd: de pilules, gélules) pack, packet; ~ **de frein** (Auto) brake pad

plasma [plasma] nm plasma

plastic [plastik] nm plastic explosive

plastifié, e [plastifje] adj plastic-coated

plastifier [plastifje] vt (document, photo) to laminate

plastiquage [plastikaʒ] nm bombing, bomb attack

plastique [plastik] adj plastic ▷ nm plastic ▷ nf plastic arts pl; (d'une statue) modelling

plastiquer [plastike] vt to blow up

plastiqueur [plastikœʀ] nm terrorist (planting a plastic bomb)

plastron [plastʀɔ̃] nm shirt front

plastronner [plastʀɔne] vi to swagger

plat, e [pla, -at] adj flat; (fade: vin) flat-tasting, insipid; (personne, livre) dull ▷ nm (récipient, Culin) dish; (d'un repas): **le premier ~** the first course; (partie plate): **le ~ de la main** the flat of the hand; (: d'une route) flat (part); **à ~ ventre** adv face down; (tomber) flat on one's face; **à ~** adj (pneu, batterie) flat; (fam: fatigué) dead beat, tired out; ~ **cuisiné** pre-cooked meal (ou dish); ~ **du jour** dish of the day; ~ **principal** ou **de résistance** main course; ~s **préparés** convenience food(s)

platane [platan] nm plane tree

plateau, x [plato] nm (support) tray; (d'une table) top; (d'une balance) pan; (Géo) plateau; (de tourne-disques) turntable; (Ciné) set; (TV): **nous avons deux journalistes sur le ~ ce soir** we have two journalists with us tonight; ~ **à fromages** cheeseboard

plateau-repas [platoʀəpɑ] (pl **plateaux-repas**) nm tray meal, TV dinner (US)

plate-bande [platbɑ̃d] (pl **plates-bandes**) nf flower bed

platée [plate] nf dish(ful)

plate-forme [platfɔʀm(ə)] (pl **plates-formes**) nf platform; ~ **de forage/pétrolière** drilling/oil rig

platine [platin] nm platinum ▷ nf (d'un tourne-disque) turntable; ~ **disque/cassette** record/cassette deck; ~ **laser** ou **compact-disc** compact disc (player)

platitude [platityd] nf platitude

platonique [platɔnik] adj platonic

plâtras [platʀa] nm rubble no pl

plâtre [platʀ(ə)] nm (matériau) plaster; (statue) plaster statue; (Méd) (plaster) cast; **plâtres** nmpl plasterwork sg; **avoir un bras dans le ~** to have an arm in plaster

plâtrer [platʀe] vt to plaster; (Méd) to set ou put in a (plaster) cast

plâtrier [platʀije] nm plasterer

plausible [plozibl(ə)] adj plausible

play-back [plɛbak] nm miming

play-boy [plɛbɔj] nm playboy

plébiscite [plebisit] nm plebiscite

plébisciter [plebisite] vt (approuver) to give overwhelming support to; (élire) to elect by an overwhelming majority

plectre [plɛktʀ(ə)] nm plectrum

plein, e [plɛ̃, -ɛn] adj full; (porte, roue) solid; (chienne, jument) big (with young) ▷ nm: **faire le ~ (d'essence)** to fill up (with petrol (Brit) ou gas (US)) ▷ prép: **avoir de l'argent ~ les poches** to have loads of money; ~ **de** full of; **avoir les mains ~es** to have one's hands full; **à ~es mains** (ramasser) in handfuls; (empoigner) firmly; **à ~ régime** at maximum revs; (fig) at full speed; **à ~ temps** full-time; **en ~ air** in the open air; **jeux en ~ air** outdoor games; **en ~e mer** on the open sea; **en ~ soleil** in direct sunlight; **en ~e nuit/rue** in the middle of the night/street; **en ~ milieu** right in the middle; **en ~ jour** in broad daylight; **les ~s** the downstrokes (in handwriting); **faire le ~ des voix** to get the maximum number of votes possible; **en ~ sur** right on; **en avoir ~ le dos** (fam) to have had it up to here

pleinement [plɛnmã] adv fully; to the full

plein-emploi [plɛnãplwa] nm full employment

plénière [plenjɛʀ] adj f: **assemblée ~** plenary assembly

plénipotentiaire [plenipɔtãsjɛʀ] nm plenipotentiary

plénitude [plenityd] nf fullness

pléthore [pletɔʀ] nf: ~ **de** overabundance ou plethora of

pléthorique [pletɔʀik] adj (classes) overcrowded; (documentation) excessive

pleurer [plœʀe] vi to cry; (yeux) to water ▷ vt to mourn (for); ~ **sur** vt to lament (over), bemoan; ~ **de rire** to laugh till one cries

pleurésie [plœʀezi] nf pleurisy

pleureuse [plœʀøz] nf professional mourner

pleurnicher [plœʀniʃe] vi to snivel, whine

pleurs [plœʀ] nmpl: **en ~** in tears

pleut [plø] vb voir **pleuvoir**

pleutre [pløtʀ(ə)] adj cowardly

pleuvait etc [pløvɛ] vb voir **pleuvoir**

pleuviner [pløvine] vb impers to drizzle

pleuvoir [pløvwaʀ] vb impers to rain ▷ vi (fig): ~ **(sur)** to shower down (upon), be showered upon; **il pleut** it's raining; **il pleut des cordes** ou **à verse** ou **à torrents** it's pouring (down), it's raining cats and dogs

pleuvra etc [pløvʀa] vb voir **pleuvoir**
plexiglas® [plɛksiglas] nm Plexiglas® (US)
pli [pli] nm fold; (dejupe) pleat; (de pantalon)
crease; (aussi: **faux pli**) crease; (enveloppe)
envelope; (lettre) letter; (Cartes) trick; **prendre
le ~ de faire** to get into the habit of doing; **ça
ne fait pas un ~!** don't you worry!; **~ d'aisance**
inverted pleat
pliable [plijabl(ə)] adj pliable, flexible
pliage [plijaʒ] nm folding; (Art) origami
pliant, e [plijɑ̃, -ɑ̃t] adj folding ▷ nm folding
stool, campstool
plier [plije] vt to fold; (pour ranger) to fold up;
(table pliante) to fold down; (genou, bras) to bend
▷ vi to bend; (fig) to yield; **se ~ à** to submit to; **~
bagages** (fig) to pack up (and go)
plinthe [plɛ̃t] nf skirting board
plissé, e [plise] adj (jupe, robe) pleated; (peau)
wrinkled; (Géo) folded ▷ nm (Couture) pleats pl
plissement [plismɑ̃] nm (Géo) fold
plisser [plise] vt (chiffonner: papier, étoffe) to crease;
(rider: front) to furrow, wrinkle; (: bouche) to
pucker; (jupe) to put pleats in; **se plisser** vi
(vêtement, étoffe) to crease
pliure [plijyʀ] nf (du bras, genou) bend; (d'un ourlet)
fold
plomb [plɔ̃] nm (métal) lead; (d'une cartouche)
(lead) shot; (Pêche) sinker; (sceau) (lead) seal;
(Élec) fuse; **de ~** (soleil) blazing; **sans ~** (essence)
unleaded; **sommeil de ~** heavy ou very deep
sleep; **mettre à ~** to plumb
plombage [plɔ̃baʒ] nm (de dent) filling
plomber [plɔ̃be] vt (canne, ligne) to weight (with
lead); (colis, wagon) to put a lead seal on; (Tech:
mur) to plumb; (dent) to fill (Brit), stop (US);
(Inform) to protect
plomberie [plɔ̃bʀi] nf plumbing
plombier [plɔ̃bje] nm plumber
plonge [plɔ̃ʒ] nf: **faire la ~** to be a washer-up
(Brit) ou dishwasher (person)
plongeant, e [plɔ̃ʒɑ̃, -ɑ̃t] adj (vue) from above;
(tir, décolleté) plunging
plongée [plɔ̃ʒe] nf (Sport) diving no pl; (: sans
scaphandre) skin diving; (de sous-marin)
submersion, dive; **en ~** (sous-marin) submerged;
(prise de vue) high angle
plongeoir [plɔ̃ʒwaʀ] nm diving board
plongeon [plɔ̃ʒɔ̃] nm dive
plonger [plɔ̃ʒe] vi to dive ▷ vt: **~ qch dans** to
plunge sth into; **~ dans un sommeil profond**
to sink straight into a deep sleep; **~ qn dans
l'embarras** to throw sb into a state of
confusion
plongeur, -euse [plɔ̃ʒœʀ, -øz] nm/f diver; (de
café) washer-up (Brit), dishwasher (person)
plot [plo] nm (Élec) contact
ploutocratie [plutɔkʀasi] nf plutocracy
ploutocratique [plutɔkʀatik] adj plutocratic
ployer [plwaje] vt to bend ▷ vi to bend;
(plancher) to sag
plu [ply] pp de **plaire**; **pleuvoir**
pluie [plɥi] nf rain; (averse, ondée): **une ~ brève** a

shower; (fig): **~ de** shower of; **une ~ fine** fine
rain; **retomber en ~** to shower down; **sous la ~**
in the rain
plumage [plymaʒ] nm plumage no pl, feathers pl
plume [plym] nf feather; (pour écrire) (pen) nib;
(fig) pen; **dessin à la ~** pen and ink drawing
plumeau, x [plymo] nm feather duster
plumer [plyme] vt to pluck
plumet [plymɛ] nm plume
plumier [plymje] nm pencil box
plupart [plypaʀ]: **la ~** pron the majority, most
(of them); **la ~ des** most, the majority of; **la ~
du temps/d'entre nous** most of the time/of
us; **pour la ~** adv for the most part, mostly
pluralisme [plyʀalism(ə)] nm pluralism
pluralité [plyʀalite] nf plurality
pluridisciplinaire [plyʀidisiplinɛʀ] adj
multidisciplinary
pluriel [plyʀjɛl] nm plural; **au ~** in the plural
plus[1] [ply] vb voir **plaire**

 MOT-CLÉ

plus[2] [ply] adv **1** (forme négative): **ne ... plus** no
more, no longer; **je n'ai plus d'argent** I've got
no more money ou no money left; **il ne
travaille plus** he's no longer working, he
doesn't work any more
2 [ply, plyz] (+voyelle: comparatif) more, ...+er;
(superlatif): **le plus** the most, the ...+est; **plus
grand/intelligent (que)** bigger/more
intelligent (than); **le plus grand/intelligent**
the biggest/most intelligent; **tout au plus** at
the very most
3 [plys] (davantage) more; **il travaille plus (que)**
he works more (than); **plus il travaille, plus il
est heureux** the more he works, the happier he
is; **plus de pain** more bread; **plus de 10
personnes/trois heures/quatre kilos** more
than ou over 10 people/three hours/four kilos;
trois heures de plus que three hours more
than; **plus de minuit** after ou past midnight;
de plus what's more, moreover; **il a trois ans
de plus que moi** he's three years older than
me; **trois kilos en plus** three kilos more; **en
plus de** in addition to; **de plus en plus** more
and more; **en plus de cela ...** what is more ...;
plus ou moins more or less; **ni plus ni moins**
no more, no less; **sans plus** (but) no more than
that, (but) that's all; **qui plus est** what is more
▷ prép [plys]: **quatre plus deux** four plus two

plusieurs [plyzjœʀ] adj, pron several; **ils sont ~**
there are several of them
plus-que-parfait [plyskəpaʀfɛ] nm pluperfect,
past perfect
plus-value [plyvaly] nf (d'un bien) appreciation;
(bénéfice) capital gain; (budgétaire) surplus
plut [ply] vb voir **plaire**; **pleuvoir**
plutonium [plytɔnjɔm] nm plutonium
plutôt [plyto] adv rather; **je ferais ~ ceci** I'd
rather ou sooner do this; **fais ~ comme ça** try

this way instead; **~ que (de) faire** rather than *ou* instead of doing

pluvial, e, -aux [plyvjal, -o] *adj (eaux)* rain *cpd*

pluvieux, -euse [plyvjø, -øz] *adj* rainy, wet

pluviosité [plyvjozite] *nf* rainfall

PM *sigle f* = **Police militaire**

p.m. *abr* (= *pour mémoire*) for the record

PME *sigle fpl* = **petites et moyennes entreprises**

PMI *sigle fpl* = **petites et moyennes industries** ▷ *sigle f* = **protection maternelle et infantile**

PMU *sigle m* = **pari mutuel urbain**; (*café*) betting agency; *see note*

● PMU
●
●
● The *PMU* ("pari mutuel urbain") is a
● Government-regulated network of betting
● counters run from bars displaying the PMU
● sign. Punters buy fixed-price tickets
● predicting winners or finishing positions in
● horse races. The traditional bet is the
● "tiercé", a triple bet, although other
● multiple bets ("quarté" and so on) are
● becoming increasingly popular.

PNB *sigle m* (= *produit national brut*) GNP

pneu [pnø] *nm* (*de roue*) tyre (*Brit*), tire (*US*); (*message*) letter sent by pneumatic tube

pneumatique [pnømatik] *adj* pneumatic; (*gonflable*) inflatable ▷ *nm* tyre (*Brit*), tire (*US*)

pneumonie [pnømɔni] *nf* pneumonia

PO *sigle fpl* (= *petites ondes*) MW

po [po] *abr voir* **science**

p.o. *abr* (= *par ordre*) p.p. (*on letters etc*)

Pô [po] *nm*: **le Pô** the Po

poche [pɔʃ] *nf* pocket; (*déformation*): **faire une/ des ~(s)** to bag; (*sous les yeux*) bag, pouch; (*Zool*) pouch ▷ *nm* (*livre de poche*) (pocket-size) paperback; **de ~** pocket *cpd*; **en être de sa ~** to be out of pocket; **c'est dans la ~** it's in the bag

poché, e [pɔʃe] *adj*: **œuf ~** poached egg; **œil ~** black eye

pocher [pɔʃe] *vt* (*Culin*) to poach; (*Art*) to sketch ▷ *vi* (*vêtement*) to bag

poche-revolver [pɔʃʀəvɔlvɛʀ] (*pl* **poches-revolver**) *nf* hip pocket

pochette [pɔʃɛt] *nf* (*de timbres*) wallet, envelope; (*d'aiguilles etc*) case; (*sac: de femme*) clutch bag, purse; (: *d'homme*) bag; (*sur veston*) breast pocket; (*mouchoir*) breast pocket handkerchief; **~ d'allumettes** book of matches; **~ de disque** record sleeve; **~ surprise** lucky bag

pochoir [pɔʃwaʀ] *nm* (*Art: cache*) stencil; (: *tampon*) transfer

podcast [pɔdkast] *nm* (*Inform*) podcast

podcaster [pɔdkaste] *vi* (*Inform*) to podcast

podium [pɔdjɔm] *nm* podium

poêle [pwal] *nm* stove ▷ *nf*: **~ (à frire)** frying pan

poêlon [pwalɔ̃] *nm* casserole

poème [pɔɛm] *nm* poem

poésie [pɔezi] *nf* (*poème*) poem; (*art*): **la ~** poetry

poète [pɔɛt] *nm* poet; (*fig*) dreamer ▷ *adj* poetic

poétique [pɔetik] *adj* poetic

pognon [pɔɲɔ̃] *nm* (*fam: argent*) dough

poids [pwa] *nm* weight; (*Sport*) shot; **vendre au ~** to sell by weight; **de ~** *adj* (*argument etc*) weighty; **prendre du ~** to put on weight; **faire le ~** (*fig*) to measure up; **~ plume/mouche/coq/ moyen** (*Boxe*) feather/fly/bantam/ middleweight; **~ et haltères** weight lifting *sg*; **~ lourd** (*Boxe*) heavyweight; (*camion: aussi*: **PL**) (big) lorry (*Brit*), truck (*US*); (: *Admin*) large goods vehicle (*Brit*), truck (*US*); **~ mort** dead weight; **~ utile** net weight

poignant, e [pwaɲɑ̃, -ɑ̃t] *adj* poignant, harrowing

poignard [pwaɲaʀ] *nm* dagger

poignarder [pwaɲaʀde] *vt* to stab, knife

poigne [pwaɲ] *nf* grip; (*fig*) firm-handedness; **à ~** firm-handed

poignée [pwaɲe] *nf* (*de sel etc, fig*) handful; (*de couvercle, porte*) handle; **~ de main** handshake

poignet [pwaɲɛ] *nm* (*Anat*) wrist; (*de chemise*) cuff

poil [pwal] *nm* (*Anat*) hair; (*de pinceau, brosse*) bristle; (*de tapis, tissu*) strand; (*pelage*) coat; (*ensemble des poils*): **avoir du ~ sur la poitrine** to have hair(s) on one's chest, have a hairy chest; **à ~** *adj* (*fam*) starkers; **au ~** *adj* (*fam*) hunky-dory; **de tout ~** of all kinds; **être de bon/ mauvais ~** to be in a good/bad mood; **~ à gratter** itching powder

poilu, e [pwaly] *adj* hairy

poinçon [pwɛ̃sɔ̃] *nm* awl; bodkin; (*marque*) hallmark

poinçonner [pwɛ̃sɔne] *vt* (*marchandise*) to stamp; (*bijou etc*) to hallmark; (*billet, ticket*) to clip, punch

poinçonneuse [pwɛ̃sɔnøz] *nf* (*outil*) punch

poindre [pwɛ̃dʀ(ə)] *vi* (*fleur*) to come up; (*aube*) to break; (*jour*) to dawn

poing [pwɛ̃] *nm* fist; **dormir à ~s fermés** to sleep soundly

point [pwɛ̃] *vb voir* **poindre** ▷ *nm* (*marque, signe*) dot; (: *de ponctuation*) full stop, period (*US*); (*moment, de score etc, fig: question*) point; (*endroit*) spot; (*Couture, Tricot*) stitch ▷ *adv* = **pas**; **ne ... ~** not (at all); **faire le ~** (*Navig*) to take a bearing; (*fig*) to take stock (of the situation); **faire le ~ sur** to review; **en tout ~** in every respect; **sur le ~ de faire** (just) about to do; **au ~ que, à tel ~ que** so much so that; **mettre au ~** (*mécanisme, procédé*) to develop; (*appareil-photo*) to focus; (*affaire*) to settle; **à ~** (*Culin*) just right; (: *viande*) medium; **à ~ (nommé)** just at the right time; **~ de croix/tige/chaînette** (*Couture*) cross/stem/ chain stitch; **~ mousse/jersey** (*Tricot*) garter/ stocking stitch; **~ de départ/d'arrivée/d'arrêt** departure/arrival/stopping point; **~ chaud** (*Mil, Pol*) hot spot; **~ de chute** landing place; (*fig*) stopping-off point; **~ (de côté)** stitch (*pain*); **~ culminant** summit; (*fig*) height, climax; **~ d'eau** spring, water point; **~ d'exclamation**

exclamation mark; ~ **faible** weak spot; ~ **final** full stop, period (US); ~ **d'interrogation** question mark; ~ **mort** (Finance) break-even point; **au ~ mort** (Auto) in neutral; (affaire, entreprise) at a standstill; ~ **noir** (sur le visage) blackhead; (Auto) accident black spot; ~ **de non-retour** point of no return; ~ **de repère** landmark; (dans le temps) point of reference; ~ **de vente** retail outlet; ~ **de vue** viewpoint; (fig: opinion) point of view; **du ~ de vue de** from the point of view of; ~**s cardinaux** points of the compass, cardinal points; ~**s de suspension** suspension points

pointage [pwɛtaʒ] nm ticking off; checking in
pointe [pwɛt] nf point; (de la côte) headland; (allusion) dig; sally; (fig): **une ~ d'ail/d'accent** a touch ou hint of garlic/of an accent; **pointes** nfpl (Danse) points, point shoes; **être à la ~ de** (fig) to be in the forefront of; **faire** ou **pousser une ~ jusqu'à ...** to press on as far as ...; **sur la ~ des pieds** on tiptoe; **en ~** adv (tailler) into a point ▷ adj pointed, tapered; **de ~** adj (technique etc) leading; (vitesse) maximum, top; **heures/ jours de ~** peak hours/days; **faire du 180 en ~** (Auto) to have a top ou maximum speed of 180; **faire des ~s** (Danse) to dance on points; ~ **d'asperge** asparagus tip; ~ **de courant** surge (of current); ~ **de vitesse** burst of speed
pointer [pwɛte] vt (cocher) to tick off; (employés etc) to check in; (diriger: canon, longue-vue, doigt): ~ **vers qch** to point at sth; (Mus: note) to dot ▷ vi (employé) to clock in ou on; (pousses) to come through; (jour) to break; ~ **les oreilles** (chien) to prick up its ears
pointeur, -euse [pwɛtœʀ, -øz] nm/f time-keeper ▷ nf timeclock ▷ nm (Inform) cursor
pointillé [pwɛtije] nm (trait) dotted line; (Art) stippling no pl
pointilleux, -euse [pwɛtijø, -øz] adj particular, pernickety
pointu, e [pwɛty] adj pointed; (clou) sharp; (voix) shrill; (analyse) precise
pointure [pwɛtyʀ] nf size
point-virgule [pwɛviʀgyl] (pl **points-virgules**) nm semi-colon
poire [pwaʀ] nf pear; (fam: péj) mug; ~ **électrique** (pear-shaped) switch; ~ **à injections** syringe
poireau, x [pwaʀo] nm leek
poireauter [pwaʀote] vi (fam) to hang about (waiting)
poirier [pwaʀje] nm pear tree; (Sport): **faire le ~** to do a headstand
pois [pwa] nm (Bot) pea; (sur une étoffe) dot, spot; **à ~** (cravate etc) spotted, polka-dot cpd; ~ **chiche** chickpea; ~ **de senteur** sweet pea; ~ **cassés** split peas
poison [pwazɔ̃] nm poison
poisse [pwas] nf rotten luck
poisser [pwase] vt to make sticky
poisseux, -euse [pwasø, -øz] adj sticky
poisson [pwasɔ̃] nm fish gen inv; **les P~s** (signe)

Pisces, the Fish; **être des P~s** to be Pisces; **pêcher** ou **prendre du ~** ou **des ~s** to fish; ~ **d'avril** April fool; (blague) April fool's day trick; see note; ~ **rouge** goldfish

poisson-chat [pwasɔ̃ʃa] (pl **poissons-chats**) nm catfish
poissonnerie [pwasɔnʀi] nf fishmonger's (Brit), fish store (US)
poissonneux, -euse [pwasɔnø, -øz] adj abounding in fish
poissonnier, -ière [pwasɔnje, -jɛʀ] nm/f fishmonger (Brit), fish merchant (US) ▷ nf (ustensile) fish kettle
poisson-scie [pwasɔ̃si] (pl **poissons-scies**) nm sawfish
poitevin, e [pwatvɛ̃, -in] adj (région) of ou from Poitou; (ville) of ou from Poitiers
poitrail [pwatʀaj] nm (d'un cheval etc) breast
poitrine [pwatʀin] nf (Anat) chest; (seins) bust, bosom; (Culin) breast; ~ **de bœuf** brisket
poivre [pwavʀ(ə)] nm pepper; ~ **en grains/ moulu** whole/ground pepper; ~ **de cayenne** cayenne (pepper); ~ **et sel** adj (cheveux) pepper-and-salt
poivré, e [pwavʀe] adj peppery
poivrer [pwavʀe] vt to pepper
poivrier [pwavʀije] nm (Bot) pepper plant
poivrière [pwavʀijɛʀ] nf pepperpot, pepper shaker (US)
poivron [pwavʀɔ̃] nm pepper, capsicum; ~ **vert/ rouge** green/red pepper
poix [pwa] nf pitch (tar)
poker [pɔkɛʀ] nm: **le ~** poker; **partie de ~** (fig) gamble; ~ **d'as** four aces
polaire [pɔlɛʀ] adj polar
polar [pɔlaʀ] (fam) nm detective novel
polarisation [pɔlaʀizasjɔ̃] nf (Physique, Élec) polarization; (fig) focusing
polariser [pɔlaʀize] vt to polarize; (fig: attirer) to attract; (: réunir, concentrer) to focus; **être polarisé sur** (personne) to be completely bound up with ou absorbed by
pôle [pol] nm (Géo, Élec) pole; **le ~ Nord/Sud** the North/South Pole; ~ **d'attraction** (fig) centre of attraction
polémique [pɔlemik] adj controversial, polemic(al) ▷ nf controversy
polémiquer [pɔlemike] vi to be involved in controversy
polémiste [pɔlemist(ə)] nm/f polemist, polemicist
poli, e [pɔli] adj polite; (lisse) smooth; polished
police [pɔlis] nf police; (discipline): **assurer la ~ de** ou **dans** to keep order in; **peine de simple ~**

sentence given by a magistrates' or police court; ~ **(d'assurance)** (insurance) policy; ~ **(de caractères)** (Typo, Inform) font, typeface; ~ **judiciaire (PJ)** ≈ Criminal Investigation Department (CID) (Brit), ≈ Federal Bureau of Investigation (FBI) (US); ~ **des mœurs** ≈ vice squad; ~ **secours** ≈ emergency services pl

polichinelle [pɔliʃinɛl] nm Punch; (péj) buffoon; **secret de** ~ open secret

policier, -ière [pɔlisje, -jɛʀ] adj police cpd ▷ nm policeman; (aussi: **roman policier**) detective novel

policlinique [pɔliklinik] nf ≈ outpatients sg (clinic)

poliment [pɔlimɑ̃] adv politely

polio [pɔljo] nf (aussi: **poliomyélite**) polio ▷ nm/f (aussi: **poliomyélitique**) polio patient ou case

poliomyélite [pɔljɔmjelit] nf poliomyelitis

poliomyélitique [pɔljɔmjelitik] nm/f polio patient ou case

polir [pɔliʀ] vt to polish

polisson, ne [pɔlisɔ̃, -ɔn] adj naughty

politesse [pɔlitɛs] nf politeness; **politesses** nfpl (exchange of) courtesies; **rendre une ~ à qn** to return sb's favour (Brit) ou favor (US)

politicard [pɔlitikaʀ] nm (péj) politico, political schemer

politicien, ne [pɔlitisjɛ̃, -ɛn] adj political ▷ nm/f politician

politique [pɔlitik] adj political ▷ nf (science, activité) politics sg; (principes, tactique) policy, policies pl ▷ nm (politicien) politician; ~ **étrangère/intérieure** foreign/domestic policy

politique-fiction [pɔlitikfiksjɔ̃] nf political fiction

politiquement [pɔlitikmɑ̃] adv politically

politisation [pɔlitizasjɔ̃] nf politicization

politiser [pɔlitize] vt to politicize; ~ **qn** to make sb politically aware

pollen [pɔlɛn] nm pollen

polluant, e [pɔlɥɑ̃, -ɑ̃t] adj polluting ▷ nm polluting agent, pollutant

polluer [pɔlɥe] vt to pollute

pollueur, -euse [pɔlɥœʀ, -øz] nm/f polluter

pollution [pɔlysjɔ̃] nf pollution

polo [pɔlo] nm (sport) polo; (tricot) polo shirt

Pologne [pɔlɔɲ] nf: **la** ~ Poland

polonais, e [pɔlɔnɛ, -ɛz] adj Polish ▷ nm (Ling) Polish ▷ nm/f: **Polonais, e** Pole

poltron, ne [pɔltʀɔ̃, -ɔn] adj cowardly

poly... [pɔli] préfixe poly...

polyamide [pɔliamid] nf polyamide

polychrome [pɔlikʀom] adj polychrome, polychromatic

polyclinique [pɔliklinik] nf (private) clinic (treating different illnesses)

polycopie [pɔlikɔpi] nf (procédé) duplicating; (reproduction) duplicated copy

polycopié, e [pɔlikɔpje] adj duplicated ▷ nm handout, duplicated notes pl

polycopier [pɔlikɔpje] vt to duplicate

polyculture [pɔlikyltyʀ] nf mixed farming

polyester [pɔliɛstɛʀ] nm polyester

polyéthylène [pɔlietilɛn] nm polyethylene

polygame [pɔligam] adj polygamous

polygamie [pɔligami] nf polygamy

polyglotte [pɔliglɔt] adj polyglot

polygone [pɔligɔn] nm polygon

Polynésie [pɔlinezi] nf: **la** ~ Polynesia; **la** ~ **française** French Polynesia

polynésien, ne [pɔlinezjɛ̃, -ɛn] adj Polynesian

polynôme [pɔlinom] nm polynomial

polype [pɔlip] nm polyp

polystyrène [pɔlistiʀɛn] nm polystyrene

polytechnicien, ne [pɔliteknisjɛ̃, -ɛn] nm/f student or former student of the École polytechnique

Polytechnique [pɔliteknik] nf: **(École)** ~ prestigious military academy producing high-ranking officers and engineers

polyvalent, e [pɔlivalɑ̃, -ɑ̃t] adj (vaccin) polyvalent; (personne) versatile; (salle) multi-purpose ▷ nm ≈ tax inspector

pomélo [pɔmelo] nm pomelo, grapefruit

pommade [pɔmad] nf ointment, cream

pomme [pɔm] nf (Bot) apple; (boule décorative) knob; (pomme de terre): **steak ~s (frites)** steak and chips (Brit) ou (French) fries (US); **tomber dans les ~s** (fam) to pass out; ~ **d'Adam** Adam's apple; ~**s allumettes** French fries (thin-cut); ~ **d'arrosoir** (sprinkler) rose; ~ **de pin** pine ou fir cone; ~ **de terre** potato; ~**s vapeur** boiled potatoes

pommé, e [pɔme] adj (chou etc) firm

pommeau, x [pɔmo] nm (boule) knob; (de selle) pommel

pommelé, e [pɔmle] adj: **gris** ~ dapple grey

pommette [pɔmɛt] nf cheekbone

pommier [pɔmje] nm apple tree

pompe [pɔ̃p] nf pump; (faste) pomp (and ceremony); ~ **à eau/essence** water/petrol pump; ~ **à huile** oil pump; ~ **à incendie** fire engine (apparatus); ~**s funèbres** undertaker's sg, funeral parlour (Brit), mortician's sg (US)

Pompéi [pɔ̃pei] n Pompeii

pompéien, ne [pɔ̃pejɛ̃, -ɛn] adj Pompeiian

pomper [pɔ̃pe] vt to pump; (évacuer) to pump out; (aspirer) to pump up; (absorber) to soak up ▷ vi to pump

pompeusement [pɔ̃pøzmɑ̃] adv pompously

pompeux, -euse [pɔ̃pø, -øz] adj pompous

pompier [pɔ̃pje] nm fireman ▷ adj m (style) pretentious, pompous

pompiste [pɔ̃pist(ə)] nm/f petrol (Brit) ou gas (US) pump attendant

pompon [pɔ̃pɔ̃] nm pompom, bobble

pomponner [pɔ̃pɔne] vt to titivate (Brit), dress up

ponce [pɔ̃s] nf: **pierre** ~ pumice stone

poncer [pɔ̃se] vt to sand (down)

ponceuse [pɔ̃søz] nf sander

poncif [pɔ̃sif] nm cliché

ponction [pɔ̃ksjɔ̃] nf (d'argent etc) withdrawal; ~ **lombaire** lumbar puncture

ponctualité [pɔ̃ktɥalite] nf punctuality

ponctuation [pɔ̃ktɥasjɔ̃] *nf* punctuation

ponctuel, le [pɔ̃ktɥɛl] *adj* (*à l'heure*, *Tech*) punctual; (*fig: opération etc*) one-off, single; (*scrupuleux*) punctilious, meticulous

ponctuellement [pɔ̃ktɥɛlmɑ̃] *adv* punctually; punctiliously, meticulously

ponctuer [pɔ̃ktɥe] *vt* to punctuate; (*Mus*) to phrase

pondéré, e [pɔ̃deʀe] *adj* level-headed, composed

pondérer [pɔ̃deʀe] *vt* to balance

pondeuse [pɔ̃døz] *nf* layer, laying hen

pondre [pɔ̃dʀ(ə)] *vt* to lay; (*fig*) to produce ▷ *vi* to lay

poney [pɔnɛ] *nm* pony

pongiste [pɔ̃ʒist(ə)] *nm/f* table tennis player

pont [pɔ̃] *nm* bridge; (*Auto*) ~ **arrière/avant** rear/front axle; (*Navig*) deck; **faire le** ~ to take the extra day off; *see note*; **faire un ~ d'or à qn** to offer sb a fortune to take a job; ~ **aérien** airlift; ~ **basculant** bascule bridge; ~ **d'envol** flight deck; ~ **élévateur** hydraulic ramp; ~ **de graissage** ramp (*in garage*); ~ **à péage** tollbridge; ~ **roulant** travelling crane; ~ **suspendu** suspension bridge; ~ **tournant** swing bridge; **P~s et Chaussées** highways department

⬤ **FAIRE LE PONT**
⬤
⬤ The expression "faire le pont" refers to the
⬤ practice of taking a Monday or Friday off to
⬤ make a long weekend if a public holiday
⬤ falls on a Tuesday or Thursday. The French
⬤ commonly take an extra day off work to give
⬤ four consecutive days' holiday at
⬤ "l'Ascension", "le 14 juillet" and le "15 août".

ponte [pɔ̃t] *nf* laying; (*œufs pondus*) clutch ▷ *nm* (*fam*) big shot

pontife [pɔ̃tif] *nm* pontiff

pontifier [pɔ̃tifje] *vi* to pontificate

pont-levis [pɔ̃lvi] (*pl* **ponts-levis**) *nm* drawbridge

ponton [pɔ̃tɔ̃] *nm* pontoon (*on water*)

pop [pɔp] *adj inv* pop ▷ *nm:* **le** ~ pop (music)

pop-corn [pɔpkɔʀn] *nm* popcorn

popeline [pɔplin] *nf* poplin

populace [pɔpylas] *nf* (*péj*) rabble

populaire [pɔpylɛʀ] *adj* popular; (*manifestation*) mass *cpd*, of the people; (*milieux, clientèle*) working-class; (*Ling: mot etc*) used by the lower classes (of society)

populariser [pɔpylaʀize] *vt* to popularize

popularité [pɔpylaʀite] *nf* popularity

population [pɔpylasjɔ̃] *nf* population; ~ **active/ agricole** working/farming population

populeux, -euse [pɔpylø, -øz] *adj* densely populated

porc [pɔʀ] *nm* (*Zool*) pig; (*Culin*) pork; (*peau*) pigskin

porcelaine [pɔʀsəlɛn] *nf* (*substance*) porcelain, china; (*objet*) piece of china(ware)

porcelet [pɔʀsəlɛ] *nm* piglet

porc-épic [pɔʀkepik] (*pl* **porcs-épics**) *nm* porcupine

porche [pɔʀʃ(ə)] *nm* porch

porcher, -ère [pɔʀʃe, -ɛʀ] *nm/f* pig-keeper

porcherie [pɔʀʃəʀi] *nf* pigsty

porcin, e [pɔʀsɛ̃, -in] *adj* (*race*) porcine; (*élevage*) pig *cpd*; (*fig*) piglike

pore [pɔʀ] *nm* pore

poreux, -euse [pɔʀø, -øz] *adj* porous

porno [pɔʀno] *adj* porno ▷ *nm* porn

pornographie [pɔʀnɔgʀafi] *nf* pornography

pornographique [pɔʀnɔgʀafik] *adj* pornographic

port [pɔʀ] *nm* (*Navig*) harbour (*Brit*), harbor (*US*), port; (*ville, Inform*) port; (*de l'uniforme etc*) wearing; (*pour lettre*) postage; (*pour colis, aussi: posture*) carriage; ~ **de commerce/de pêche** commercial/fishing port; **arriver à bon** ~ to arrive safe and sound; ~ **d'arme** (*Jur*) carrying of a firearm; ~ **d'attache** (*Navig*) port of registry; (*fig*) home base; ~ **d'escale** port of call; ~ **franc** free port

portable [pɔʀtabl(ə)] *adj* (*vêtement*) wearable; (*portatif*) portable; (*téléphone*) mobile (*Brit*), cell (*US*) ▷ *nm* (*Inform*) laptop (computer); (*téléphone*) mobile (phone) (*Brit*), cell (phone) (*US*)

portail [pɔʀtaj] *nm* gate; (*de cathédrale*) portal

portant, e [pɔʀtɑ̃, -ɑ̃t] *adj* (*murs*) structural, supporting; (*roues*) running; **bien/mal** ~ in good/poor health

portatif, -ive [pɔʀtatif, -iv] *adj* portable

porte [pɔʀt(ə)] *nf* door; (*de ville, forteresse, Ski*) gate; **mettre à la** ~ to throw out; **prendre la** ~ to leave, go away; **à ma/sa** ~ (*tout près*) on my/his (*ou* her) doorstep; ~ **(d'embarquement)** (*Aviat*) (departure) gate; ~ **d'entrée** front door; ~ **à** ~ *nm* door-to-door selling; ~ **de secours** emergency exit; ~ **de service** service entrance

porté, e [pɔʀte] *adj:* **être** ~ **à faire qch** to be apt to do sth, tend to do sth; **être** ~ **sur qch** to be partial to sth

porte-à-faux [pɔʀtafo] *nm:* **en** ~ cantilevered; (*fig*) in an awkward position

porte-aiguilles [pɔʀtegɥij] *nm inv* needle case

porte-avions [pɔʀtavjɔ̃] *nm inv* aircraft carrier

porte-bagages [pɔʀtbagaʒ] *nm inv* luggage rack (*ou* basket *etc*)

porte-bébé [pɔʀtbebe] *nm* baby sling *ou* carrier

porte-bonheur [pɔʀtbɔnœʀ] *nm inv* lucky charm

porte-bouteilles [pɔʀtbutɛj] *nm inv* bottle carrier; (*à casiers*) wine rack

porte-cartes [pɔʀtəkaʀt(ə)] *nm inv* (*de cartes d'identité*) card holder; (*de cartes géographiques*) map wallet

porte-cigarettes [pɔʀtsigaʀɛt] *nm inv* cigarette case

porte-clefs [pɔʀtəkle] *nm inv* key ring

porte-conteneurs [pɔʀtəkɔ̃tnœʀ] *nm inv* container ship

porte-couteau, x [pɔʀtkuto] *nm* knife rest

porte-crayon [pɔʀtkʀɛjɔ̃] *nm* pencil holder
porte-documents [pɔʀtdɔkymɑ̃] *nm inv*
attaché *ou* document case
porte-drapeau, x [pɔʀtdʀapo] *nm* standard
bearer
portée [pɔʀte] *nf* (*d'une arme*) range; (*fig:
importance*) impact, import; (: *capacités*) scope,
capability; (*de chatte etc*) litter; (*Mus*) stave, staff;
à/hors de ~ (de) within/out of reach (of); **à ~ de
(la) main** within (arm's) reach; **à ~ de voix**
within earshot; **à la ~ de qn** (*fig*) at sb's level,
within sb's capabilities; **à la ~ de toutes les
bourses** to suit every pocket, within everyone's
means
portefaix [pɔʀtəfɛ] *nm inv* porter
porte-fenêtre [pɔʀtfənɛtʀ(ə)] (*pl* **portes-
fenêtres**) *nf* French window
portefeuille [pɔʀtəfœj] *nm* wallet; (*Pol, Bourse*)
portfolio; **faire un lit en ~** to make an apple-
pie bed
porte-jarretelles [pɔʀtʒaʀtɛl] *nm inv* suspender
belt (*Brit*), garter belt (*US*)
porte-jupe [pɔʀtəʒyp] *nm* skirt hanger
portemanteau, x [pɔʀtmɑ̃to] *nm* coat rack
porte-mine [pɔʀtəmin] *nm* propelling (*Brit*) *ou*
mechanical (*US*) pencil
porte-monnaie [pɔʀtmɔnɛ] *nm inv* purse
porte-parapluies [pɔʀtpaʀaplɥi] *nm inv*
umbrella stand
porte-parole [pɔʀtpaʀɔl] *nm inv* spokesperson
porte-plume [pɔʀtəplym] *nm inv* penholder
porter [pɔʀte] *vt* (*charge ou sac etc, aussi: fœtus*) to
carry; (*sur soi: vêtement, barbe, bague*) to wear; (*fig:
responsabilité etc*) to bear, carry; (*inscription, marque,
titre, patronyme: arbre: fruits, fleurs*) to bear;
(*jugement*) to pass; (*apporter*): **~ qch quelque
part/à qn** to take sth somewhere/to sb;
(*inscrire*): **~ qch sur** to put sth down on; to enter
sth in ▷ *vi* (*voix, regard, canon*) to carry; (*coup,
argument*) to hit home; **se porter** *vi* (*se sentir*): **se
~ bien/mal** to be well/unwell; (*aller*): **se ~ vers**
to go towards; **~ sur** (*peser*) to rest on; (*accent*) to
fall on; (*conférence etc*) to concern; (*heurter*) to
strike; **être porté à faire** to be apt *ou* inclined
to do; **elle portait le nom de Rosalie** she was
called Rosalie; **~ qn au pouvoir** to bring sb to
power; **~ bonheur à qn** to bring sb luck; **~ qn à
croire** to lead sb to believe; **~ son âge** to look
one's age; **~ un toast** to drink a toast; **~ de
l'argent au crédit d'un compte** to credit an
account with some money; **se ~ partie civile** *to
associate in a court action with the public prosecutor*; **se
~ garant de qch** to guarantee sth, vouch for
sth; **se ~ candidat à la députation** ≈ to stand
for Parliament (*Brit*), ≈ run for Congress (*US*); **se
faire ~ malade** to report sick; **~ la main à son
chapeau** to raise one's hand to one's hat; **~ son
effort sur** to direct one's efforts towards; **~ un
fait à la connaissance de qn** to bring a fact to
sb's attention *ou* notice
porte-savon [pɔʀtsavɔ̃] *nm* soap dish
porte-serviettes [pɔʀtsɛʀvjɛt] *nm inv* towel rail

portes-ouvertes [pɔʀtuvɛʀt(ə)] *adj inv:*
journée ~ open day
porteur, -euse [pɔʀtœʀ, -øz] *adj* (*Comm*) strong,
promising; (*nouvelle, chèque etc*): **être ~ de** to be
the bearer of ▷ *nm/f* (*de messages*) bearer ▷ *nm* (*de
bagages*) porter; (*Comm: de chèque*) bearer;
(: *d'actions*) holder; (**avion**) **gros ~** wide-bodied
aircraft, jumbo (jet)
porte-voix [pɔʀtəvwa] *nm inv* megaphone,
loudhailer (*Brit*)
portier [pɔʀtje] *nm* doorman,
commissionnaire (*Brit*)
portière [pɔʀtjɛʀ] *nf* door
portillon [pɔʀtijɔ̃] *nm* gate
portion [pɔʀsjɔ̃] *nf* (*part*) portion, share; (*partie*)
portion, section
portique [pɔʀtik] *nm* (*Sport*) crossbar; (*Archit*)
portico; (*Rail*) gantry
porto [pɔʀto] *nm* port (wine)
portoricain, e [pɔʀtɔʀikɛ̃, -ɛn] *adj* Puerto Rican
Porto Rico [pɔʀtɔʀiko] *nf* Puerto Rico
portrait [pɔʀtʀɛ] *nm* portrait; (*photographie*)
photograph; (*fig*): **elle est le ~ de sa mère** she's
the image of her mother
portraitiste [pɔʀtʀetist(ə)] *nm/f* portrait
painter
portrait-robot [pɔʀtʀeʀɔbo] *nm* Identikit® *ou*
Photo-fit ® (*Brit*) picture
portuaire [pɔʀtɥɛʀ] *adj* port *cpd*, harbour *cpd*
(*Brit*), harbor *cpd* (*US*)
portugais, e [pɔʀtygɛ, -ɛz] *adj* Portuguese ▷ *nm*
(*Ling*) Portuguese ▷ *nm/f:* **Portugais, e**
Portuguese
Portugal [pɔʀtygal] *nm:* **le ~** Portugal
POS *sigle m* (= *plan d'occupation des sols*) zoning
ordinances *ou* regulations
pose [poz] *nf* (*de moquette*) laying; (*de rideaux,
papier peint*) hanging; (*attitude, d'un modèle*) pose;
(*Photo*) exposure
posé, e [poze] *adj* calm, unruffled
posément [pozemɑ̃] *adv* calmly
posemètre [pozmɛtʀ(ə)] *nm* exposure meter
poser [poze] *vt* (*déposer*): **~ qch (sur)/qn à** to put
sth down (on)/drop sb at; (*placer*): **~ qch sur/
quelque part** to put sth on/somewhere;
(*installer: moquette, carrelage*) to lay; (*rideaux, papier
peint*) to hang; (*Math: chiffre*) to put (down);
(*question*) to ask; (*principe, conditions*) to lay *ou* set
down; (*problème*) to formulate; (*difficulté*) to
pose; (*personne: mettre en valeur*) to give standing
to ▷ *vi* (*modèle*) to pose; to sit; **se poser** (*oiseau,
avion*) to land; (*question*) to arise; **se ~ en** to pass
o.s off as, pose as; **~ son ou un regard sur qn/
qch** to turn one's gaze on sb/sth; **~ sa
candidature** to apply; (*Pol*) to put o.s. up for
election
poseur, -euse [pozœʀ, -øz] *nm/f* (*péj*) show-off,
poseur; **~ de parquets/carrelages** floor/tile
layer
positif, -ive [pozitif, -iv] *adj* positive
position [pozisjɔ̃] *nf* position; **prendre ~** (*fig*) to
take a stand

positionner [pozisjɔne] *vt* to position; *(compte en banque)* to calculate the balance of

positivement [pozitivmɑ̃] *adv* positively

posologie [pozɔlɔʒi] *nf* directions *pl* for use, dosage

possédant, e [posedɑ̃, -ɑ̃t] *adj (classe)* wealthy ▷ *nm/f:* **les ~s** the haves, the wealthy

possédé, e [posede] *nm/f* person possessed

posséder [posede] *vt* to own, possess; *(qualité, talent)* to have, possess; *(bien connaître: métier, langue)* to have mastered, have a thorough knowledge of; *(sexuellement, aussi: suj: colère)* to possess; *(fam: duper)* to take in

possesseur [posesœʀ] *nm* owner

possessif, -ive [posesif, -iv] *adj, nm (Ling)* possessive

possession [posesjɔ̃] *nf* ownership *no pl*; possession; *(aussi:* **être/entrer en possession de qch)** to be in/take possession of sth

possibilité [posibilite] *nf* possibility; **possibilités** *nfpl (moyens)* means; *(potentiel)* potential *sg*; **avoir la ~ de faire** to be in a position to do; to have the opportunity to do

possible [posibl(ə)] *adj* possible; *(projet, entreprise)* feasible ▷ *nm:* **faire son ~** to do all one can, do one's utmost; **(ce n'est) pas ~!** impossible!; **le plus/moins de livres ~** as many/few books as possible; **dès que ~** as soon as possible; **gentil** *etc* **au ~** as nice *etc* as it is possible to be

postal, e, -aux [postal, -o] *adj* postal, post office *cpd;* **sac ~** mailbag, postbag

postdater [postdate] *vt* to postdate

poste [post(ə)] *nf (service)* post, postal service; *(administration, bureau)* post office ▷ *nm (fonction, Mil)* post; *(Tél)* extension; *(de radio etc)* set; *(de budget)* item; **postes** *nfpl* post office *sg*; **P~s télécommunications et télédiffusion (PTT)** *postal and telecommunications service;* **agent** *ou* **employé des ~s** post office worker; **mettre à la ~** to post; **~ de commandement (PC)** *nm (Mil etc)* headquarters; **~ de contrôle** *nm* checkpoint; **~ de douane** *nm* customs post; **~ émetteur** *nm* transmitting set; **~ d'essence** *nm* filling station; **~ d'incendie** *nm* fire point; **~ de péage** *nm* tollgate; **~ de pilotage** *nm* cockpit; **~ (de police)** *nm* police station; **~ de radio** *nm* radio set; **~ restante (PR)** *nf* poste restante *(Brit)*, general delivery *(US)*; **~ de secours** *nm* first-aid post; **~ de télévision** *nm* television set; **~ de travail** *nm* work station

poster *vt* [poste] to post ▷ *nm* [postɛʀ] poster; **se poster** to position o.s

postérieur, e [posteʀjœʀ] *adj (date)* later; *(partie)* back ▷ *nm (fam)* behind

postérieurement [posteʀjœʀmɑ̃] *adv* later, subsequently; **~ à** after

posteriori [posteʀjɔʀi]: **a ~** *adv* with hindsight, a posteriori

postérité [posteʀite] *nf* posterity

postface [postfas] *nf* appendix

posthume [postym] *adj* posthumous

postiche [postiʃ] *adj* false ▷ *nm* hairpiece

postier, -ière [postje, -jɛʀ] *nm/f* post office worker

postillon [postijɔ̃] *nm:* **envoyer des ~s** to splutter

postillonner [postijɔne] *vi* to splutter

post-natal, e [postnatal] *adj* postnatal

postopératoire [postopeʀatwaʀ] *adj* post-operative

postscolaire [postskɔlɛʀ] *adj* further, continuing

post-scriptum [postskʀiptɔm] *nm inv* postscript

postsynchronisation [postsɛ̃kʀɔnizasjɔ̃] *nf* dubbing

postsynchroniser [postsɛ̃kʀɔnize] *vt* to dub

postulant, e [postylɑ̃, -ɑ̃t] *nm/f (candidat)* applicant; *(Rel)* postulant

postulat [postyla] *nm* postulate

postuler [postyle] *vt (emploi)* to apply for, put in for

posture [postyʀ] *nf* posture, position; *(fig)* position

pot [po] *nm* jar, pot; *(en plastique, carton)* carton; *(en métal)* tin; *(fam):* **avoir du ~** to be lucky; **boire** *ou* **prendre un ~** *(fam)* to have a drink; **découvrir le ~ aux roses** to find out what's been going on; **~ catalytique** catalytic converter; **~ (de chambre)** (chamber)pot; **~ d'échappement** exhaust pipe; **~ de fleurs** plant pot, flowerpot; *(plante)* pot plant; **~ à tabac** tobacco jar

potable [potabl(ə)] *adj (fig: boisson)* drinkable; *(: travail, devoir)* decent; **eau (non) ~** (not) drinking water

potache [potaʃ] *nm* schoolboy

potage [potaʒ] *nm* soup

potager, -ère [potaʒe, -ɛʀ] *adj (plante)* edible, vegetable *cpd;* **(jardin) ~** kitchen *ou* vegetable garden

potasse [potas] *nf* potassium hydroxide; *(engrais)* potash

potasser [potase] *vt (fam)* to swot up *(Brit)*, cram

potassium [potasjɔm] *nm* potassium

pot-au-feu [potofø] *nm inv (beef)* stew; *(viande)* stewing beef ▷ *adj (fam: personne)* stay-at-home

pot-de-vin [podvɛ̃] *(pl* **pots-de-vin)** *nm* bribe

pote [pot] *nm (fam)* mate *(Brit)*, pal

poteau, x [poto] *nm* post; **~ de départ/arrivée** starting/finishing post; **~ (d'exécution)** execution post, stake; **~ indicateur** signpost; **~ télégraphique** telegraph pole; **~x (de but)** goal-posts

potée [pote] *nf* hotpot *(of pork and cabbage)*

potelé, e [potle] *adj* plump, chubby

potence [potɑ̃s] *nf* gallows *sg;* **en ~** T-shaped

potentat [potɑ̃ta] *nm* potentate; *(fig: péj)* despot

potentiel, le [potɑ̃sjɛl] *adj, nm* potential

potentiellement [potɑ̃sjɛlmɑ̃] *adv* potentially

poterie [potʀi] *nf (fabrication)* pottery; *(objet)* piece of pottery

potiche [potiʃ] *nf* large vase

potier [potje] *nm* potter

potins [potɛ̃] *nmpl* gossip *sg*

potion [posjɔ̃] *nf* potion
potiron [pɔtiRɔ̃] *nm* pumpkin
pot-pourri [popuRi] (*pl* **pots-pourris**) *nm* (*Mus*) medley
pou, x [pu] *nm* louse
pouah [pwa] *excl* ugh!, yuk!
poubelle [pubɛl] *nf* (dust)bin
pouce [pus] *nm* thumb; **se tourner** *ou* **se rouler les ~s** (*fig*) to twiddle one's thumbs; **manger sur le ~** to eat on the run, snatch something to eat
poudre [pudR(ə)] *nf* powder; (*fard*) (face) powder; (*explosif*) gunpowder; **en ~: café en ~** instant coffee; **savon en ~** soap powder; **lait en ~** dried *ou* powdered milk; **~ à canon** gunpowder; **~ à éternuer** sneezing powder; **~ à récurer** scouring powder; **~ de riz** face powder
poudrer [pudRe] *vt* to powder
poudreux, -euse [pudRø, -øz] *adj* dusty; (*neige*) powdery, powder *cpd*
poudrier [pudRije] *nm* (powder) compact
poudrière [pudRijɛR] *nf* powder magazine; (*fig*) powder keg
pouf [puf] *nm* pouffe
pouffer [pufe] *vi*: **~ (de rire)** to snigger; to giggle
pouffiasse [pufjas] *nf* (*fam*) fat cow; (*prostituée*) tart
pouilleux, -euse [pujø, -øz] *adj* flea-ridden; (*fig*) seedy
poulailler [pulaje] *nm* henhouse; (*Théât*): **le ~** the gods *sg*
poulain [pulɛ̃] *nm* foal; (*fig*) protégé
poularde [pulaRd(ə)] *nf* fatted chicken
poule [pul] *nf* (*Zool*) hen; (*Culin*) (boiling) fowl; (*Sport*) (round-robin) tournament; (*Rugby*) group; (*fam*) bird (*Brit*), chick, broad (*US*); (*prostituée*) tart; **~ d'eau** moorhen; **~ mouillée** coward; **~ pondeuse** laying hen, layer; **~ au riz** chicken and rice
poulet [pulɛ] *nm* chicken; (*fam*) cop
poulette [pulɛt] *nf* (*jeune poule*) pullet
pouliche [puliʃ] *nf* filly
poulie [puli] *nf* pulley
poulpe [pulp(ə)] *nm* octopus
pouls [pu] *nm* pulse; (*Anat*): **prendre le ~ de qn** to take sb's pulse
poumon [pumɔ̃] *nm* lung; **~ d'acier** *ou* **artificiel** iron *ou* artificial lung
poupe [pup] *nf* stern; **en ~** astern
poupée [pupe] *nf* doll; **jouer à la ~** to play with one's doll (*ou* dolls); **de ~** (*très petit*): **jardin de ~** doll's garden, pocket-handkerchief-sized garden
poupin, e [pupɛ̃, -in] *adj* chubby
poupon [pupɔ̃] *nm* babe-in-arms
pouponner [pupɔne] *vi* to fuss (around)
pouponnière [pupɔnjɛR] *nf* crèche, day nursery
pour [puR] *prép* for ▷ *nm*: **le ~ et le contre** the pros and cons; **~ faire** (so as) to do, in order to do; **~ avoir fait** for having done; **~ que** so that, in order that; **~ moi** (*à mon avis, pour ma part*) for my part, personally; **~ riche qu'il soit** rich

though he may be; **~ 20 euros d'essence** 20 euros' worth of petrol; **~ cent** per cent; **~ ce qui est de** as for; **y être ~ quelque chose** to have something to do with it
pourboire [puRbwaR] *nm* tip
pourcentage [puRsɑ̃taʒ] *nm* percentage; **travailler au ~** to work on commission
pourchasser [puRʃase] *vt* to pursue
pourfendeur [puRfɑ̃dœR] *nm* sworn opponent
pourfendre [puRfɑ̃dR(ə)] *vt* to assail
pourlécher [puRleʃe]: **se pourlécher** *vi* to lick one's lips
pourparlers [puRpaRle] *nmpl* talks, negotiations; **être en ~ avec** to be having talks with
pourpre [puRpR(ə)] *adj* crimson
pourquoi [puRkwa] *adv, conj* why ▷ *nm inv*: **le ~ (de)** the reason (for)
pourrai *etc* [puRe] *vb voir* **pouvoir**
pourri, e [puRi] *adj* rotten; (*roche, pierre*) crumbling; (*temps, climat*) filthy, foul ▷ *nm*: **sentir le ~** to smell rotten
pourriel [puRjɛl] *nm* (*Inform*) spam
pourrir [puRiR] *vi* to rot; (*fruit*) to go rotten *ou* bad; (*fig: situation*) to deteriorate ▷ *vt* to rot; (*fig: corrompre: personne*) to corrupt; (: *gâter: enfant*) to spoil thoroughly
pourrissement [puRismɑ̃] *nm* deterioration
pourriture [puRityR] *nf* rot
pourrons *etc* [puRɔ̃] *vb voir* **pouvoir**
poursuis *etc* [puRsɥi] *vb voir* **poursuivre**
poursuite [puRsɥit] *nf* pursuit, chase; **poursuites** *nfpl* (*Jur*) legal proceedings; **(course) ~** track race; (*fig*) chase
poursuivant, e [puRsɥivɑ̃, -ɑ̃t] *vb voir* **poursuivre** ▷ *nm/f* pursuer; (*Jur*) plaintiff
poursuivre [puRsɥivR(ə)] *vt* to pursue, chase (after); (*relancer*) to hound, harry; (*obséder*) to haunt; (*Jur*) to bring proceedings against, prosecute; (: *au civil*) to sue; (*but*) to strive towards; (*voyage, études*) to carry on with, continue ▷ *vi* to carry on, go on; **se poursuivre** *vi* to go on, continue
pourtant [puRtɑ̃] *adv* yet; **mais ~** but nevertheless, but even so; **c'est ~ facile** (and) yet it's easy
pourtour [puRtuR] *nm* perimeter
pourvoi [puRvwa] *nm* appeal
pourvoir [puRvwaR] *nm* (*Comm*) supply ▷ *vt*: **~ qch/qn de** to equip sth/sb with ▷ *vi*: **~ à** to provide for; (*emploi*) to fill; **se pourvoir** *vi* (*Jur*): **se ~ en cassation** to take one's case to the Court of Appeal
pourvoyeur, -euse [puRvwajœR, -øz] *nm/f* supplier
pourvu, e [puRvy] *pp de* **pourvoir** ▷ *adj*: **~ de** equipped with; **~ que** *conj* (*si*) provided that, so long as; (*espérons que*) let's hope (that)
pousse [pus] *nf* growth; (*bourgeon*) shoot
poussé, e [puse] *adj* sophisticated, advanced; (*moteur*) souped-up
pousse-café [puskafe] *nm inv* (after-dinner)

liqueur

poussée [puse] *nf* thrust; (*coup*) push; (*Méd*) eruption; (*fig*) upsurge

pousse-pousse [puspus] *nm inv* rickshaw

pousser [puse] *vt* to push; (*acculer*) to drive sb to do sth; (*moteur, voiture*) to drive hard; (*émettre: cri etc*) to give; (*stimuler*) to urge on; to drive hard; (*poursuivre*) to carry on; (*inciter*): ~ **qn à faire qch** to urge *ou* press sb to do sth ▷ *vi* to push; (*croître*) to grow; (*aller*): ~ **plus loin** to push on a bit further; **se pousser** *vi* to move over; **faire ~** (*plante*) to grow; ~ **le dévouement** *etc* **jusqu'à …** to take devotion *etc* as far as …

poussette [puset] *nf* (*voiture d'enfant*) pushchair (*Brit*), stroller (*US*)

poussette-canne [pusɛtkan] (*pl* **poussettes-cannes**) *nf* baby buggy (*Brit*), (folding) stroller (*US*)

poussier [pusje] *nm* coaldust

poussière [pusjɛʀ] *nf* dust; (*grain*) speck of dust; **et des ~s** (*fig*) and a bit; ~ **de charbon** coaldust

poussiéreux, -euse [pusjeʀø, -øz] *adj* dusty

poussif, -ive [pusif, -iv] *adj* wheezy, wheezing

poussin [pusɛ̃] *nm* chick

poussoir [puswaʀ] *nm* button

poutre [putʀ(ə)] *nf* beam; (*en fer, ciment armé*) girder; ~**s apparentes** exposed beams

poutrelle [putʀɛl] *nf* (*petite poutre*) small beam; (*barre d'acier*) girder

 MOT-CLÉ

pouvoir [puvwaʀ] *nm* power; (*Pol: dirigeants*): **le pouvoir** those in power; **les pouvoirs publics** the authorities; **avoir pouvoir de faire** (*autorisation*) to have (the) authority to do; (*droit*) to have the right to do; **pouvoir absolu** absolute power; **pouvoir absorbant** absorbency; **pouvoir d'achat** purchasing power; **pouvoir calorifique** calorific value ▷ *vb semi-aux* **1** (*être en état de*) can, be able to; **je ne peux pas le réparer** I can't *ou* I am not able to repair it; **déçu de ne pas pouvoir le faire** disappointed not to be able to do it
2 (*avoir la permission*) can, may, be allowed to; **vous pouvez aller au cinéma** you can *ou* may go to the pictures
3 (*probabilité, hypothèse*) may, might, could; **il a pu avoir un accident** he may *ou* might *ou* could have had an accident; **il aurait pu le dire!** he might *ou* could have said (so)!
4 (*expressions*): **tu ne peux pas savoir!** you have no idea!; **tu peux le dire!** you can say that again!
▷ *vb impers* may, might, could; **il peut arriver que** it may *ou* might *ou* could happen that; **il pourrait pleuvoir** it might rain
▷ *vt* **1** can, be able to; **j'ai fait tout ce que j'ai pu** I did all I could; **je n'en peux plus** (*épuisé*) I'm exhausted; (*à bout*) I can't take any more
2 (*vb +adj ou adv comparatif*): **je me porte on ne peut mieux** I'm absolutely fine, I couldn't be

better; **elle est on ne peut plus gentille** she couldn't be nicer, she's as nice as can be
se pouvoir *vi*: **il se peut que** it may *ou* might be that; **cela se pourrait** that's quite possible

PP *sigle f* (= *préventive de la pellagre: vitamine*) niacin ▷ *abr* (= *pages*) pp

p.p. *abr* (= *par procuration*) p.p.

p.p.c.m. *sigle m* (*Math: = plus petit commun multiple*) LCM (= *lowest common multiple*)

PQ *sigle f* (*Canada: = province de Québec*) PQ

PR *sigle m* = **parti républicain** ▷ *sigle f* = **poste restante**

pr *abr* = **pour**

pragmatique [pʀagmatik] *adj* pragmatic

pragmatisme [pʀagmatism(ə)] *nm* pragmatism

Prague [pʀag] *n* Prague

prairie [pʀeʀi] *nf* meadow

praline [pʀalin] *nf* (*bonbon*) sugared almond; (*au chocolat*) praline

praliné, e [pʀaline] *adj* (*amande*) sugared; (*chocolat, glace*) praline *cpd*

praticable [pʀatikabl(ə)] *adj* (*route etc*) passable, practicable; (*projet*) practicable

praticien, ne [pʀatisjɛ̃, -ɛn] *nm/f* practitioner

pratiquant, e [pʀatikɑ̃, -ɑ̃t] *adj* practising (*Brit*), practicing (*US*)

pratique [pʀatik] *nf* practice ▷ *adj* practical; (*commode: horaire etc*) convenient; (: *outil*) handy, useful; **dans la ~** in (actual) practice; **mettre en ~** to put into practice

pratiquement [pʀatikmɑ̃] *adv* (*dans la pratique*) in practice; (*pour ainsi dire*) practically, virtually

pratiquer [pʀatike] *vt* to practise (*Brit*), practice (*US*); (*Sport etc*) to go in for, play; (*appliquer: méthode, théorie*) to apply; (*intervention, opération*) to carry out; (*ouverture, abri*) to make ▷ *vi* (*Rel*) to be a churchgoer

pré [pʀe] *nm* meadow

préados [pʀeado] *nmpl* pre-teens

préalable [pʀealabl(ə)] *adj* preliminary; **condition ~ (de)** precondition (for), prerequisite (for); **sans avis ~** without prior *ou* previous notice; **au ~** first, beforehand

préalablement [pʀealabləmɑ̃] *adv* first, beforehand

Préalpes [pʀealp(ə)] *nfpl*: **les ~** the Pre-Alps

préalpin, e [pʀealpɛ̃, -in] *adj* of the Pre-Alps

préambule [pʀeɑ̃byl] *nm* preamble; (*fig*) prelude; **sans ~** straight away

préau, x [pʀeo] *nm* (*d'une cour d'école*) covered playground; (*d'un monastère, d'une prison*) inner courtyard

préavis [pʀeavi] *nm* notice; ~ **de congé** notice; **communication avec ~** (*Tél*) personal *ou* person-to-person call

prébende [pʀebɑ̃d] *nf* (*péj*) remuneration

précaire [pʀekɛʀ] *adj* precarious

précaution [pʀekosjɔ̃] *nf* precaution; **avec ~** cautiously; **prendre des** *ou* **ses ~s** to take precautions; **par ~** as a precaution; **pour plus**

de ~ to be on the safe side; **~s oratoires** carefully phrased remarks

précautionneux, -euse [pʀekosjɔnø, -øz] *adj* cautious, careful

précédemment [pʀesedamɑ̃] *adv* before, previously

précédent, e [pʀesedɑ̃, -ɑ̃t] *adj* previous ▷ *nm* precedent; **sans ~** unprecedented; **le jour ~** the day before, the previous day

précéder [pʀesede] *vt* to precede; (*marcher ou rouler devant*) to be in front of; (*arriver avant*) to get ahead of

précepte [pʀesɛpt(ə)] *nm* precept

précepteur, -trice [pʀesɛptœʀ, -tʀis] *nm/f* (private) tutor

préchauffer [pʀeʃofe] *vt* to preheat

prêcher [pʀeʃe] *vt, vi* to preach

prêcheur, -euse [pʀeʃœʀ, -øz] *adj* moralizing ▷ *nm/f* (*Rel*) preacher; (*fig*) moralizer

précieusement [pʀesjøzmɑ̃] *adv* (*avec soin*) carefully; (*avec préciosité*) preciously

précieux, -euse [pʀesjø, -øz] *adj* precious; (*collaborateur, conseils*) invaluable; (*style, écrivain*) précieux, precious

préciosité [pʀesjozite] *nf* preciosity, preciousness

précipice [pʀesipis] *nm* drop, chasm; (*fig*) abyss; **au bord du ~** at the edge of the precipice

précipitamment [pʀesipitamɑ̃] *adv* hurriedly, hastily

précipitation [pʀesipitasjɔ̃] *nf* (*hâte*) haste; **~s (atmosphériques)** precipitation *sg*

précipité, e [pʀesipite] *adj* (*respiration*) fast; (*pas*) hurried; (*départ*) hasty

précipiter [pʀesipite] *vt* (*faire tomber*): **~ qn/qch du haut de** to throw *ou* hurl sb/sth off *ou* from; (*hâter: marche*) to quicken; (: *départ*) to hasten; **se précipiter** *vi* (*événements*) to move faster; (*respiration*) to speed up; **se ~ sur/vers** to rush at/towards; **se ~ au-devant de qn** to throw o.s. before sb

précis, e [pʀesi, -iz] *adj* precise; (*tir, mesures*) accurate, precise ▷ *nm* handbook

précisément [pʀesizemɑ̃] *adv* precisely; **ma vie n'est pas ~ distrayante** my life is not exactly entertaining

préciser [pʀesize] *vt* (*expliquer*) to be more specific about, clarify; (*spécifier*) to state, specify; **se préciser** *vi* to become clear(er)

précision [pʀesizjɔ̃] *nf* precision; accuracy; (*détail*) point *ou* detail (*made clear or to be clarified*); **précisions** *nfpl* further details

précoce [pʀekɔs] *adj* early; (*enfant*) precocious; (*calvitie*) premature

précocité [pʀekɔsite] *nf* earliness; precociousness

préconçu, e [pʀekɔ̃sy] *adj* preconceived

préconiser [pʀekɔnize] *vt* to advocate

précuit, e [pʀekɥi, -it] *adj* precooked

précurseur [pʀekyʀsœʀ] *adj m* precursory ▷ *nm* forerunner, precursor

prédateur [pʀedatœʀ] *nm* predator

prédécesseur [pʀedesesœʀ] *nm* predecessor

prédécoupé, e [pʀedekupe] *adj* pre-cut

prédestiner [pʀedɛstine] *vt*: **~ qn à qch/à faire** to predestine sb for sth/to do

prédicateur [pʀedikatœʀ] *nm* preacher

prédiction [pʀediksjɔ̃] *nf* prediction

prédilection [pʀedilɛksjɔ̃] *nf*: **avoir une ~ pour** to be partial to; **de ~** favourite (*Brit*), favorite (*US*)

prédire [pʀediʀ] *vt* to predict

prédisposer [pʀedispoze] *vt*: **~ qn à qch/à faire** to predispose sb to sth/to do

prédisposition [pʀedispozisjɔ̃] *nf* predisposition

prédit, e [pʀedi, -it] *pp de* **prédire**

prédominance [pʀedɔminɑ̃s] *nf* predominance

prédominant, e [pʀedɔminɑ̃, -ɑ̃t] *adj* predominant; prevailing

prédominer [pʀedɔmine] *vi* to predominate; (*avis*) to prevail

pré-électoral, e, -aux [pʀeelɛktɔʀal, -o] *adj* pre-election *cpd*

pré-emballé, e [pʀeɑ̃bale] *adj* pre-packed

prééminent, e [pʀeeminɑ̃, -ɑ̃t] *adj* pre-eminent

préemption [pʀeɑ̃psjɔ̃] *nf*: **droit de ~** (*Jur*) pre-emptive right

pré-encollé, e [pʀeɑ̃kɔle] *adj* pre-pasted

préétabli, e [pʀeetabli] *adj* pre-established

préexistant, e [pʀeɛgzistɑ̃, -ɑ̃t] *adj* pre-existing

préfabriqué, e [pʀefabʀike] *adj* prefabricated; (*péj: sourire*) artificial ▷ *nm* prefabricated material

préface [pʀefas] *nf* preface

préfacer [pʀefase] *vt* to write a preface for

préfectoral, e, -aux [pʀefɛktɔʀal, -o] *adj* prefectorial

préfecture [pʀefɛktyʀ] *nf* prefecture; *see note*; **~ de police** police headquarters

PRÉFECTURE

The *préfecture* is the administrative headquarters of the "département". The "préfet", a senior civil servant appointed by the government, is responsible for putting government policy into practice. France's 22 regions, each comprising a number of "départements", also have a "préfet de région".

préférable [pʀefeʀabl(ə)] *adj* preferable

préféré, e [pʀefeʀe] *adj, nm/f* favourite (*Brit*), favorite (*US*)

préférence [pʀefeʀɑ̃s] *nf* preference; **de ~** preferably; **de *ou* par ~ à** in preference to, rather than; **donner la ~ à qn** to give preference to sb; **par ordre de ~** in order of preference; **obtenir la ~ sur** to have preference over

préférentiel, le [pʀefeʀɑ̃sjɛl] *adj* preferential

préférer [pʀefeʀe] *vt*: **~ qn/qch (à)** to prefer sb/sth (to), like sb/sth better (than); **~ faire** to prefer to do; **je préférerais du thé** I would rather have tea, I'd prefer tea

préfet [pʀefɛ] *nm* prefect; **~ de police** ≈ Chief Constable (*Brit*), ≈ Police Commissioner (*US*)

préfigurer [pʀefigyʀe] *vt* to prefigure

préfixe [pʀefiks(ə)] *nm* prefix

préhistoire [pʀeistwaʀ] *nf* prehistory

préhistorique [pʀeistɔʀik] *adj* prehistoric

préjudice [pʀeʒydis] *nm* (*matériel*) loss; (*moral*) harm *no pl*; **porter ~ à** to harm, be detrimental to; **au ~ de** at the expense of

préjudiciable [pʀeʒydisjabl(ə)] *adj*: **~ à** prejudicial *ou* harmful to

préjugé [pʀeʒyʒe] *nm* prejudice; **avoir un ~ contre** to be prejudiced against; **bénéficier d'un ~ favorable** to be viewed favourably

préjuger [pʀeʒyʒe]: **~ de** *vt* to prejudge

prélasser [pʀelase]: **se prélasser** *vi* to lounge

prélat [pʀela] *nm* prelate

prélavage [pʀelavaʒ] *nm* pre-wash

prélèvement [pʀelɛvmɑ̃] *nm* deduction; withdrawal; **faire un ~ de sang** to take a blood sample

prélever [pʀelve] *vt* (*échantillon*) to take; **~ (sur)** (*argent*) to deduct (from); (: *sur son compte*) to withdraw (from)

préliminaire [pʀeliminɛʀ] *adj* preliminary; **préliminaires** *nmpl* preliminaries; (*négociations*) preliminary talks

prélude [pʀelyd] *nm* prelude; (*avant le concert*) warm-up

prématuré, e [pʀematyʀe] *adj* premature; (*retraite*) early ▷ *nm* premature baby

prématurément [pʀematyʀemɑ̃] *adv* prematurely

préméditation [pʀemeditasjɔ̃] *nf*: **avec ~** *adj* premeditated ▷ *adv* with intent

préméditer [pʀemedite] *vt* to premeditate, plan

prémices [pʀemis] *nfpl* beginnings

premier, -ière [pʀəmje, -jɛʀ] *adj* first; (*branche, marche, grade*) bottom; (*fig: fondamental*) basic; prime; (*en importance*) first, foremost ▷ *nm* (*premier étage*) first (*Brit*) *ou* second (*US*) floor ▷ *nf* (*Auto*) first (gear); (*Rail, Aviat etc*) first class; (*Scol: classe*) penultimate school year (*age 16–17*); (*Théât*) first night; (*Ciné*) première; (*exploit*) first; **au ~ abord** at first sight; **au** *ou* **du ~ coup** at the first attempt *ou* go; **de ~ ordre** first-class, first-rate; **de première qualité**, **de ~ choix** best *ou* top quality; **de première importance** of the highest importance; **de première nécessité** absolutely essential; **le ~ venu** the first person to come along; **jeune ~** leading man; **le ~ de l'an** New Year's Day; **enfant du ~ lit** child of a first marriage; **en ~ lieu** in the first place; **~ âge** (*d'un enfant*) the first three months (of life); **P~ Ministre** Prime Minister

premièrement [pʀəmjɛʀmɑ̃] *adv* firstly

première-née [pʀəmjɛʀne] (*pl* **premières-nées**) *nf* first-born

premier-né [pʀəmjene] (*pl* **premiers-nés**) *nm* first-born

prémisse [pʀemis] *nf* premise

prémolaire [pʀemɔlɛʀ] *nf* premolar

prémonition [pʀemɔnisjɔ̃] *nf* premonition

prémonitoire [pʀemɔnitwaʀ] *adj* premonitory

prémunir [pʀemyniʀ]: **se prémunir** *vi*: **se ~ contre** to protect o.s. from, guard against

prenant, e [pʀənɑ̃, -ɑ̃t] *vb voir* **prendre** ▷ *adj* absorbing, engrossing

prénatal, e [pʀenatal] *adj* (*Méd*) antenatal; (*allocation*) maternity *cpd*

prendre [pʀɑ̃dʀ(ə)] *vt* to take; (*aller chercher*) to get, fetch; (*se procurer*) to get; (*réserver: place*) to book; (*acquérir: du poids, de la valeur*) to put on, gain; (*malfaiteur, poisson*) to catch; (*passager*) to pick up; (*personnel, aussi: couleur, goût*) to take on; (*locataire*) to take in; (*traiter: enfant, problème*) to handle; (*voix, ton*) to put on; (*prélever: pourcentage, argent*) to take off; (*ôter*): **~ qch à** to take sth from; (*coincer*): **se ~ les doigts dans** to get one's fingers caught in ▷ *vi* (*liquide, ciment*) to set; (*greffe, vaccin*) to take; (*mensonge*) to be successful; (*feu: foyer*) to go; (: *incendie*) to start; (*allumette*) to light; (*se diriger*): **~ à gauche** to turn (to the) left; **~ son origine** *ou* **sa source** (*mot, rivière*) to have its source; **~ qn pour** to take sb for; **se ~ pour** to think one is; **~ sur soi de faire qch** to take it upon o.s. to do sth; **~ qn en sympathie/horreur** to get to like/loathe sb; **à tout ~** all things considered; **s'en ~ à** (*agresser*) to set about; (*passer sa colère sur*) to take it out on; (*critiquer*) to attack; (*remettre en question*) to challenge; **se ~ d'amitié/d'affection pour** to befriend/become fond of; **s'y ~** (*procéder*) to set about it; **s'y ~ à l'avance** to see to it in advance; **s'y ~ à deux fois** to try twice, make two attempts

preneur [pʀənœʀ] *nm*: **être ~** to be willing to buy; **trouver ~** to find a buyer

preniez [pʀənje] *vb voir* **prendre**

prenne *etc* [pʀɛn] *vb voir* **prendre**

prénom [pʀenɔ̃] *nm* first name

prénommer [pʀenɔme] *vt*: **elle se prénomme Claude** her (first) name is Claude

prénuptial, e, -aux [pʀenypsjal, -o] *adj* premarital

préoccupant, e [pʀeɔkypɑ̃, -ɑ̃t] *adj* worrying

préoccupation [pʀeɔkypasjɔ̃] *nf* (*souci*) concern; (*idée fixe*) preoccupation

préoccupé, e [pʀeɔkype] *adj* concerned; preoccupied

préoccuper [pʀeɔkype] *vt* (*tourmenter, tracasser*) to concern; (*absorber, obséder*) to preoccupy; **se ~ de qch** to be concerned about sth; to show concern about sth

préparateur, -trice [pʀepaʀatœʀ, -tʀis] *nm/f* assistant

préparatifs [pʀepaʀatif] *nmpl* preparations

préparation [pʀepaʀasjɔ̃] *nf* preparation; (*Scol*) piece of homework

préparatoire [pʀepaʀatwaʀ] *adj* preparatory

préparer [pʀepaʀe] *vt* to prepare; (*café, repas*) to

first-born

make; (examen) to prepare for; (voyage, entreprise) to plan; **se préparer** vi (orage, tragédie) to brew, be in the air; **se ~ (à qch/à faire)** to prepare (o.s.) ou get ready (for sth/to do); **~ qch à qn** (surprise etc) to have sth in store for sb; **~ qn à qch** (nouvelle etc) to prepare sb for sth

prépondérance [pʀepɔ̃deʀɑ̃s] nf: **~ (sur)** predominance (over)

prépondérant, e [pʀepɔ̃deʀɑ̃, -ɑ̃t] adj major, dominating; **voix ~e** casting vote

préposé, e [pʀepoze] adj: **~ à** in charge of ▷ nm/f (gén: employé) employee; (Admin: facteur) postman/woman (Brit), mailman/woman (US); (de la douane etc) official; (de vestiaire) attendant

préposer [pʀepoze] vt: **~ qn à qch** to appoint sb to sth

préposition [pʀepozisjɔ̃] nf preposition

prérentrée [pʀeʀɑ̃tʀe] nf in-service training period before start of school term

préretraite [pʀeʀətʀɛt] nf early retirement

prérogative [pʀeʀɔgativ] nf prerogative

près [pʀɛ] adv near, close; **~ de** prép near (to), close to; (environ) nearly, almost; **~ d'ici** near here; **de ~** adv closely; **à cinq kg ~** to within about five kg; **à cela ~ que** apart from the fact that; **je ne suis pas ~ de lui pardonner** I'm nowhere near ready to forgive him; **on n'est pas à un jour ~** one day (either way) won't make any difference, we're not going to quibble over the odd day

présage [pʀezaʒ] nm omen

présager [pʀezaʒe] vt (prévoir) to foresee; (annoncer) to portend

pré-salé [pʀesale] (pl **prés-salés**) nm (Culin) salt-meadow lamb

presbyte [pʀɛsbit] adj long-sighted (Brit), far-sighted (US)

presbytère [pʀɛsbitɛʀ] nm presbytery

presbytérien, ne [pʀɛsbiteʀjɛ̃, -ɛn] adj, nm/f Presbyterian

presbytie [pʀɛsbisi] nf long-sightedness (Brit), far-sightedness (US)

prescience [pʀesjɑ̃s] nf prescience, foresight

préscolaire [pʀeskɔlɛʀ] adj preschool cpd

prescription [pʀɛskʀipsjɔ̃] nf (instruction) order, instruction; (Méd, Jur) prescription

prescrire [pʀɛskʀiʀ] vt to prescribe; **se prescrire** vi (Jur) to lapse

prescrit, e [pʀɛskʀi, -it] pp de **prescrire** ▷ adj (date etc) stipulated

préséance [pʀeseɑ̃s] nf precedence no pl

présélection [pʀeselɛksjɔ̃] nf (de candidats) short-listing; **effectuer une ~** to draw up a shortlist

présélectionner [pʀeselɛksjɔne] vt to preselect; (dispositif) to preset; (candidats) to make an initial selection from among, short-list (Brit)

présence [pʀezɑ̃s] nf presence; (au bureau etc) attendance; **en ~** face to face; **en ~ de** in (the) presence of; (fig) in the face of; **faire acte de ~** to put in a token appearance; **~ d'esprit** presence of mind

présent, e [pʀezɑ̃, -ɑ̃t] adj, nm present; (Admin, Comm): **la ~e lettre/loi** this letter/law ▷ nm/f: **les ~s** (personnes) those present ▷ nf (Comm: lettre): **la ~e** this letter; **à ~** now, at present; **dès à ~** here and now; **jusqu'à ~** up till now, until now; **à ~ que** now that

présentable [pʀezɑ̃tabl(ə)] adj presentable

présentateur, -trice [pʀezɑ̃tatœʀ, -tʀis] nm/f presenter

présentation [pʀezɑ̃tasjɔ̃] nf presentation; introduction; (allure) appearance

présenter [pʀezɑ̃te] vt to present; (invité, candidat) to introduce; (félicitations, condoléances) to offer; (montrer: billet, pièce d'identité) to show, produce; (faire inscrire: candidat) to put forward; (soumettre) to submit ▷ vi: **~ mal/bien** to have an unattractive/a pleasing appearance; **se présenter** vi (sur convocation) to report, come; (se faire connaître) to come forward; (à une élection) to stand; (occasion) to arise; **se ~ à un examen** to sit an exam; **se ~ bien/mal** to look good/not too good

présentoir [pʀezɑ̃twaʀ] nm (étagère) display shelf; (vitrine) showcase; (étal) display stand

préservatif [pʀezɛʀvatif] nm condom, sheath

préservation [pʀezɛʀvasjɔ̃] nf protection, preservation

préserver [pʀezɛʀve] vt: **~ de** (protéger) to protect from; (sauver) to save from

présidence [pʀezidɑ̃s] nf presidency; chairmanship

président [pʀezidɑ̃] nm (Pol) president; (d'une assemblée, Comm) chairman; **~ directeur général (PDG)** chairman and managing director (Brit), chairman and president (US); **~ du jury** (Jur) foreman of the jury; (d'examen) chief examiner

présidente [pʀezidɑ̃t] nf president; (femme du président) president's wife; (d'une réunion) chairwoman

présidentiable [pʀezidɑ̃sjabl(ə)] adj, nm/f potential president

présidentiel, le [pʀezidɑ̃sjɛl] adj presidential; **présidentielles** nfpl presidential election(s)

présider [pʀezide] vt to preside over; (dîner) to be the guest of honour (Brit) ou honor (US) at; **~ à** vt to direct; to govern

présomption [pʀezɔ̃psjɔ̃] nf presumption

présomptueux, -euse [pʀezɔ̃ptɥø, -øz] adj presumptuous

presque [pʀɛsk(ə)] adv almost, nearly; **~ rien** hardly anything; **~ pas** hardly (at all); **~ pas de** hardly any; **personne, ou ~** next to nobody, hardly anyone; **la ~ totalité (de)** almost ou nearly all

presqu'île [pʀɛskil] nf peninsula

pressant, e [pʀesɑ̃, -ɑ̃t] adj urgent; (personne) insistent; **se faire ~** to become insistent

presse [pʀɛs] nf press; (affluence): **heures de ~** busy times; **sous ~** gone to press; **mettre sous ~** to send to press; **avoir une bonne/mauvaise ~** to have a good/bad press; **~ féminine**

women's magazines *pl*; ~ **d'information** quality newspapers *pl*

pressé, e [pRese] *adj* in a hurry; *(air)* hurried; *(besogne)* urgent ▷ *nm*: **aller au plus** ~ to see to first things first; **être ~ de faire qch** to be in a hurry to do sth; **orange ~e** freshly squeezed orange juice

presse-citron [pREssitRɔ̃] *nm inv* lemon squeezer

presse-fruits [pREsfRɥi] *nm inv* lemon squeezer

pressentiment [pResɑ̃timɑ̃] *nm* foreboding, premonition

pressentir [pResɑ̃tiR] *vt* to sense; *(prendre contact avec)* to approach

presse-papiers [pREspapje] *nm inv* paperweight

presse-purée [pREspyRe] *nm inv* potato masher

presser [pRese] *vt* (fruit, éponge) to squeeze; *(interrupteur, bouton)* to press, push; *(allure, affaire)* to speed up; *(débiteur etc)* to press; *(inciter)*: ~ **qn de faire** to urge *ou* press sb to do ▷ *vi* to be urgent; **se presser** *(se hâter)* to hurry (up); *(se grouper)* to crowd; **rien ne presse** there's no hurry; **se ~ contre qn** to squeeze up against sb; ~ **le pas** to quicken one's step; ~ **qn entre ses bras** to squeeze sb tight

pressing [pResiŋ] *nm* (repassage) steam-pressing; *(magasin)* dry-cleaner's

pression [pResjɔ̃] *nf* pressure; *(bouton)* press stud (Brit), snap fastener; **faire ~ sur** to put pressure on; **sous ~** pressurized, under pressure; *(fig)* keyed up; ~ **artérielle** blood pressure

pressoir [pReswaR] *nm* (wine *ou* oil *etc*) press

pressurer [pResyRe] *vt* (fig) to squeeze

pressurisé, e [pResyRize] *adj* pressurized

prestance [pREstɑ̃s] *nf* presence, imposing bearing

prestataire [pREstatER] *nm/f* person receiving benefits; *(Comm)*: ~ **de services** provider of services

prestation [pREstasjɔ̃] *nf* (allocation) benefit; *(d'une assurance)* cover *no pl*; *(d'une entreprise)* service provided; *(d'un joueur, artiste)* performance; ~ **de serment** taking the oath; ~ **de service** provision of a service; ~**s familiales** ≈ child benefit

preste [pREst(ə)] *adj* nimble

prestement [pREstəmɑ̃] *adv* nimbly

prestidigitateur, -trice [pREstidiʒitatœR, -tRis] *nm/f* conjurer

prestidigitation [pREstidiʒitasjɔ̃] *nf* conjuring

prestige [pREstiʒ] *nm* prestige

prestigieux, -euse [pREstiʒjø, -øz] *adj* prestigious

présumer [pRezyme] *vt*: ~ **que** to presume *ou* assume that; ~ **de** to overrate; ~ **qn coupable** to presume sb guilty

présupposé [pResypoze] *nm* presupposition

présupposer [pResypoze] *vt* to presuppose

présupposition [pResypozisjɔ̃] *nf* presupposition

présure [pRezyR] *nf* rennet

prêt, e [pRe, pREt] *adj* ready ▷ *nm* lending *no pl*; *(somme prêtée)* loan; ~ **à faire** ready to do; ~ **à tout** ready for anything; ~ **sur gages** pawnbroking *no pl*

prêt-à-porter [pREtapɔRte] (*pl* **prêts-à-porter**) *nm* ready-to-wear *ou* off-the-peg (Brit) clothes *pl*

prétendant [pRetɑ̃dɑ̃] *nm* pretender; *(d'une femme)* suitor

prétendre [pRetɑ̃dR(ə)] *vt* (affirmer): ~ **que** to claim that; *(avoir l'intention de)*: ~ **faire qch** to mean *ou* intend to do sth; ~ **à** *vt* (droit, titre) to lay claim to

prétendu, e [pRetɑ̃dy] *adj* (supposé) so-called

prétendument [pRetɑ̃dymɑ̃] *adv* allegedly

prête-nom [pREtnɔ̃] *nm* (péj) figurehead; *(Comm etc)* dummy

prétentieux, -euse [pRetɑ̃sjø, -øz] *adj* pretentious

prétention [pRetɑ̃sjɔ̃] *nf* pretentiousness; *(exigence, ambition)* claim; **sans ~** unpretentious

prêter [pRete] *vt* (livres, argent): ~ **qch (à)** to lend sth (to); *(supposer)*: ~ **à qn** (caractère, propos) to attribute to sb ▷ *vi*: **se prêter** *(tissu, cuir)* to give; ~ **à** *(commentaires etc)* to be open to, give rise to; **se ~ à** to lend o.s. to; *(manigances etc)* to go along with; ~ **assistance à** to give help to; ~ **attention** to pay attention; ~ **serment** to take the oath; ~ **l'oreille** to listen

prêteur, -euse [pRetœR, -øz] *nm/f* moneylender; ~ **sur gages** pawnbroker

prétexte [pRetEkst(ə)] *nm* pretext, excuse; **sous aucun ~** on no account; **sous (le) ~ que/de** on the pretext that/of

prétexter [pRetEkste] *vt* to give as a pretext *ou* an excuse

prêtre [pRetR(ə)] *nm* priest

prêtre-ouvrier [pREtRuvRije] (*pl* **prêtres-ouvriers**) *nm* worker-priest

prêtrise [pREtRiz] *nf* priesthood

preuve [pRœv] *nf* proof; *(indice)* proof, evidence *no pl*; **jusqu'à ~ du contraire** until proved otherwise; **faire ~ de** to show; **faire ses ~s** to prove o.s. *(ou* itself); ~ **matérielle** material evidence

prévaloir [pRevalwaR] *vi* to prevail; **se ~ de** *vt* to take advantage of; *(tirer vanité de)* to pride o.s. on

prévarication [pRevaRikasjɔ̃] *nf* maladministration

prévaut *etc* [pRevo] *vb voir* **prévaloir**

prévenances [pRevnɑ̃s] *nfpl* thoughtfulness *sg*, kindness *sg*

prévenant, e [pRevnɑ̃, -ɑ̃t] *adj* thoughtful, kind

prévenir [pRevniR] *vt* (éviter) to avoid, prevent; *(anticiper)* to anticipate; ~ **qn (de)** (avertir) to warn sb (about); *(informer)* to tell *ou* inform sb (about); ~ **qn contre** (influencer) to prejudice sb against

préventif, -ive [pRevɑ̃tif, -iv] *adj* preventive

prévention [pRevɑ̃sjɔ̃] *nf* prevention; *(préjugé)* prejudice; *(Jur)* custody, detention; ~ **routière** road safety

prévenu, e [pʀevny] nm/f (Jur) defendant, accused

prévisible [pʀevizibl(ə)] adj foreseeable

prévision [pʀevizjɔ̃] nf: **~s** predictions; (météorologiques, économiques) forecast sg; **en ~ de** in anticipation of; **~s météorologiques** ou **du temps** weather forecast sg

prévisionnel, le [pʀevizjɔnɛl] adj concerned with future requirements

prévit etc [pʀevi] vb voir **prévoir**

prévoir [pʀevwaʀ] vt (deviner) to foresee; (s'attendre à) to expect, reckon on; (prévenir) to anticipate; (organiser) to plan; (préparer, réserver) to allow; **prévu pour quatre personnes** designed for four people; **prévu pour 10 h** scheduled for 10 o'clock

prévoyance [pʀevwajɑ̃s] nf foresight; **société/ caisse de ~** provident society/contingency fund

prévoyant, e [pʀevwajɑ̃, -ɑ̃t] vb voir **prévoir** ▷ adj gifted with (ou showing) foresight, far-sighted

prévu, e [pʀevy] pp de **prévoir**

prier [pʀije] vi to pray ▷ vt (Dieu) to pray to; (implorer) to beg; (demander): **~ qn de faire** to ask sb to do; (inviter): **~ qn à dîner** to invite sb to dinner; **se faire ~** to need coaxing ou persuading; **je vous en prie** (allez-y) please do; (de rien) don't mention it; **je vous prie de faire** please (would you) do

prière [pʀijɛʀ] nf prayer; (demande instante) plea, entreaty; **"~ de faire ..."** "please do ..."

primaire [pʀimɛʀ] adj primary; (péj: personne) simple-minded; (: idées) simplistic ▷ nm (Scol) primary education

primauté [pʀimote] nf (fig) primacy

prime [pʀim] nf (bonification) bonus; (subside) allowance; (Comm: cadeau) free gift; (Assurances, Bourse) premium ▷ adj: **de ~ abord** at first glance; **~ de risque** danger money no pl; **~ de transport** travel allowance

primer [pʀime] vt (l'emporter sur) to prevail over; (récompenser) to award a prize to ▷ vi to dominate, prevail

primesautier, -ière [pʀimsotje, -jɛʀ] adj impulsive

primeur [pʀimœʀ] nf: **avoir la ~ de** to be the first to hear (ou see etc); **primeurs** nfpl (fruits, légumes) early fruits and vegetables; **marchand de ~** greengrocer (Brit), produce dealer (US)

primevère [pʀimvɛʀ] nf primrose

primitif, -ive [pʀimitif, -iv] adj primitive; (originel) original ▷ nm/f primitive

primo [pʀimo] adv first (of all), firstly

primordial, e, -aux [pʀimɔʀdjal, -o] adj essential, primordial

prince [pʀɛ̃s] nm prince; **~ charmant** Prince Charming; **~ de Galles** nm inv (tissu) check cloth; **~ héritier** crown prince

princesse [pʀɛ̃sɛs] nf princess

princier, -ière [pʀɛ̃sje, -jɛʀ] adj princely

principal, e, -aux [pʀɛ̃sipal, -o] adj principal, main ▷ nm (Scol) head (teacher) (Brit), principal

(US); (essentiel) main thing ▷ nf (Ling): **(proposition) ~e** main clause

principalement [pʀɛ̃sipalmɑ̃] adv principally, mainly

principauté [pʀɛ̃sipote] nf principality

principe [pʀɛ̃sip] nm principle; **partir du ~ que** to work on the principle ou assumption that; **pour le ~** on principle, for the sake of it; **de ~** adj (hostilité) automatic; (accord) in principle; **par ~** on principle; **en ~** (habituellement) as a rule; (théoriquement) in principle

printanier, -ière [pʀɛ̃tanje, -jɛʀ] adj spring, spring-like

printemps [pʀɛ̃tɑ̃] nm spring; **au ~** in spring

priori [pʀijɔʀi]: **a ~** adv at first glance, initially; a priori

prioritaire [pʀijɔʀitɛʀ] adj having priority; (Auto) having right of way; (Inform) foreground

priorité [pʀijɔʀite] nf (Auto): **avoir la ~ (sur)** to have right of way (over); **~ à droite** right of way to vehicles coming from the right; **en ~** as a (matter of) priority

pris, e [pʀi, pʀiz] pp de **prendre** ▷ adj (place) taken; (billets) sold; (journée, mains) full; (personne) busy; (crème, ciment) set; (Méd: enflammé): **avoir le nez/la gorge ~(e)** to have a stuffy nose/a bad throat; (saisi): **être ~ de peur/ de fatigue** to be stricken with fear/overcome with fatigue

prise [pʀiz] nf (d'une ville) capture; (Pêche, Chasse) catch; (de judo ou catch, point d'appui ou pour empoigner) hold; (Élec: fiche) plug; (: femelle) socket; (: au mur) point; **en ~** (Auto) in gear; **être aux ~s avec** to be grappling with; to be battling with; **lâcher ~** to let go; **donner ~ à** (fig) to give rise to; **avoir ~ sur qn** to have a hold over sb; **~ en charge** (taxe) pick-up charge; (par la sécurité sociale) undertaking to reimburse costs; **~ de contact** initial meeting, first contact; **~ de courant** power point; **~ d'eau** water (supply) point; tap; **~ multiple** adaptor; **~ d'otages** hostage-taking; **~ à partie** (Jur) action against a judge; **~ de sang** blood test; **~ de son** sound recording; **~ de tabac** pinch of snuff; **~ de terre** earth; **~ de vue** (photo) shot; (action): **~ de vue(s)** filming, shooting

priser [pʀize] vt (tabac, héroïne) to take; (estimer) to prize, value ▷ vi to take snuff

prisme [pʀism(ə)] nm prism

prison [pʀizɔ̃] nf prison; **aller/être en ~** to go to/be in prison ou jail; **faire de la ~** to serve time; **être condamné à cinq ans de ~** to be sentenced to five years' imprisonment ou five years in prison

prisonnier, -ière [pʀizɔnje, -jɛʀ] nm/f prisoner ▷ adj captive; **faire qn ~** to take sb prisoner

prit [pʀi] vb voir **prendre**

privatif, -ive [pʀivatif, -iv] adj (jardin etc) private; (peine) which deprives one of one's liberties

privations [pʀivasjɔ̃] nfpl privations, hardships

privatisation [pʀivatizasjɔ̃] nf privatization

privatiser [pʀivatize] vt to privatize

privautés [pʀivote] *nfpl* liberties

privé, e [pʀive] *adj* private; (*dépourvu*): ~ **de** without, lacking; **en** ~, **dans le** ~ in private

priver [pʀive] *vt*: ~ **qn de** to deprive sb of; **se** ~ **de** to go *ou* do without; **ne pas se** ~ **de faire** not to refrain from doing

privilège [pʀivilɛʒ] *nm* privilege

privilégié, e [pʀivileʒje] *adj* privileged

privilégier [pʀivileʒje] *vt* to favour (*Brit*), favor (*US*)

prix [pʀi] *nm* (*valeur*) price; (*récompense, Scol*) prize; **mettre à** ~ to set a reserve (*Brit*) *ou* an upset (*US*) price on; **au** ~ **fort** at a very high price; **acheter qch à** ~ **d'or** to pay a (small) fortune for sth; **hors de** ~ exorbitantly priced; **à aucun** ~ not at any price; **à tout** ~ at all costs; **grand** ~ (*Sport*) Grand Prix; ~ **d'achat/de vente/ de revient** purchasing/selling/cost price; ~ **conseillé** manufacturer's recommended price (MRP)

pro [pʀo] *nm* (= *professionnel*) pro

probabilité [pʀobabilite] *nf* probability; **selon toute** ~ in all probability

probable [pʀobabl(ə)] *adj* likely, probable

probablement [pʀobabləmã] *adv* probably

probant, e [pʀobã, -ãt] *adj* convincing

probatoire [pʀobatwaʀ] *adj* (*examen, test*) preliminary; (*stage*) probationary, trial *cpd*

probité [pʀobite] *nf* integrity, probity

problématique [pʀoblematik] *adj* problematic(al) ▷ *nf* problematics *sg*; (*problème*) problem

problème [pʀoblɛm] *nm* problem

procédé [pʀosede] *nm* (*méthode*) process; (*comportement*) behaviour *no pl* (*Brit*), behavior *no pl* (*US*)

procéder [pʀosede] *vi* to proceed; to behave; ~ **à** *vt* to carry out

procédure [pʀosedyʀ] *nf* (*Admin, Jur*) procedure

procès [pʀosɛ] *nm* (*Jur*) trial; (: *poursuites*) proceedings *pl*; **être en** ~ **avec** to be involved in a lawsuit with; **faire le** ~ **de qn/qch** (*fig*) to put sb/sth on trial; **sans autre forme de** ~ without further ado

processeur [pʀosesœʀ] *nm* processor

procession [pʀosesjõ] *nf* procession

processus [pʀosesys] *nm* process

procès-verbal, -aux [pʀosɛvɛʀbal, -o] *nm* (*constat*) statement; (*aussi*: **PV**): **avoir un** ~ to get a parking ticket; to be booked; (*de réunion*) minutes *pl*

prochain, e [pʀoʃɛ̃, -ɛn] *adj* next; (*proche*) impending; near ▷ *nm* fellow man; **la** ~**e fois/ semaine** ~**e** next time/week; **à la** ~**e!** (*fam*): **à la** ~**e fois** see you!, till the next time!; **un** ~ **jour** (some day) soon

prochainement [pʀoʃɛnmã] *adv* soon, shortly

proche [pʀoʃ] *adj* nearby; (*dans le temps*) imminent; close at hand; (*parent, ami*) close; **proches** *nmpl* (*parents*) close relatives, next of kin; (*amis*): **l'un de ses** ~**s** one of those close to him (*ou* her); **être** ~ **(de)** to be near, be close (to);

de ~ **en** ~ gradually

Proche-Orient [pʀoʃoʀjã] *nm*: **le** ~ the Near East

proclamation [pʀoklamasjõ] *nf* proclamation

proclamer [pʀoklame] *vt* to proclaim; (*résultat d'un examen*) to announce

procréer [pʀokʀee] *vt* to procreate

procuration [pʀokyʀasjõ] *nf* proxy; power of attorney; **voter par** ~ to vote by proxy

procurer [pʀokyʀe] *vt* (*fournir*): ~ **qch à qn** to get *ou* obtain sth for sb; (*causer: plaisir etc*): ~ **qch à qn** to bring *ou* give sb sth; **se procurer** *vt* to get

procureur [pʀokyʀœʀ] *nm* public prosecutor; ~ **général** public prosecutor (*in appeal court*)

prodigalité [pʀodigalite] *nf* (*générosité*) generosity; (*extravagance*) extravagance, wastefulness

prodige [pʀodiʒ] *nm* (*miracle, merveille*) marvel, wonder; (*personne*) prodigy

prodigieusement [pʀodiʒjøzmã] *adv* tremendously

prodigieux, -euse [pʀodiʒjø, -øz] *adj* prodigious; phenomenal

prodigue [pʀodig] *adj* (*généreux*) generous; (*dépensier*) extravagant, wasteful; **fils** ~ prodigal son

prodiguer [pʀodige] *vt* (*argent, biens*) to be lavish with; (*soins, attentions*): ~ **qch à qn** to lavish sth on sb

producteur, -trice [pʀodyktœʀ, -tʀis] *adj*: ~ **de blé** wheat-producing; (*Ciné*): **société productrice** film *ou* movie company ▷ *nm/f* producer

productif, -ive [pʀodyktif, -iv] *adj* productive

production [pʀodyksjõ] *nf* (*gén*) production; (*rendement*) output; (*produits*) products *pl*, goods *pl*; (*œuvres*): **la** ~ **dramatique du XVIIe siècle** the plays of the 17th century

productivité [pʀodyktivite] *nf* productivity

produire [pʀodɥiʀ] *vt, vi* to produce; **se produire** *vi* (*acteur*) to perform, appear; (*événement*) to happen, occur

produit, e [pʀodɥi, -it] *pp de* **produire** ▷ *nm* (*gén*) product; ~ **d'entretien** cleaning product; ~ **national brut (PNB)** gross national product (GNP); ~ **net** net profit; ~ **pour la vaisselle** washing-up (*Brit*) *ou* dish-washing (*US*) liquid; ~ **des ventes** income from sales; ~**s agricoles** farm produce *sg*; ~**s alimentaires** foodstuffs; ~**s de beauté** beauty products, cosmetics

proéminent, e [pʀoeminã, -ãt] *adj* prominent

prof [pʀof] *nm* (*fam*: = *professeur*) teacher; professor; lecturer

prof. [pʀof] *abr* = **professeur; professionnel**

profane [pʀofan] *adj* (*Rel*) secular; (*ignorant, non initié*) uninitiated ▷ *nm/f* layman

profaner [pʀofane] *vt* to desecrate; (*fig: sentiment*) to defile; (: *talent*) to debase

proférer [pʀofeʀe] *vt* to utter

professer [pʀofese] *vt* to profess

professeur, e [pʀofesœʀ] *nm/f* teacher; (*titulaire d'une chaire*) professor; ~ **(de faculté)** (university) lecturer

profession [pʀɔfɛsjɔ̃] nf (libérale) profession; (gén) occupation; **faire ~ de** (opinion, religion) to profess; **de ~** by profession; **"sans ~"** "unemployed"; (femme mariée) "housewife"

professionnel, le [pʀɔfɛsjɔnɛl] adj professional ▷ nm/f professional; (ouvrier qualifié) skilled worker

professoral, e, -aux [pʀɔfɛsɔʀal, -o] adj professorial; **le corps ~** the teaching profession

professorat [pʀɔfɛsɔʀa] nm: **le ~** the teaching profession

profil [pʀɔfil] nm profile; (d'une voiture) line, contour; **de ~** in profile

profilé, e [pʀɔfile] adj shaped; (aile etc) streamlined

profiler [pʀɔfile] vt to streamline; **se profiler** vi (arbre, tour) to stand out, be silhouetted

profit [pʀɔfi] nm (avantage) benefit, advantage; (Comm, Finance) profit; **au ~ de** in aid of; **tirer** ou **retirer ~ de** to profit from; **mettre à ~** to take advantage of; to turn to good account; **~s et pertes** (Comm) profit and loss(es)

profitable [pʀɔfitabl(ə)] adj beneficial; profitable

profiter [pʀɔfite] vi: **~ de** to take advantage of; to make the most of; **~ de ce que ...** to take advantage of the fact that ...; **~ à** to be of benefit to, benefit; to be profitable to

profiteur, -euse [pʀɔfitœʀ, -øz] nm/f (péj) profiteer

profond, e [pʀɔfɔ̃, -ɔ̃d] adj deep; (méditation, mépris) profound; **peu ~** (eau, vallée, puits) shallow; (coupure) superficial; **au plus ~ de** in the depths of, at the (very) bottom of; **la France ~e** the heartlands of France

profondément [pʀɔfɔ̃demã] adv deeply; profoundly

profondeur [pʀɔfɔ̃dœʀ] nf depth

profusément [pʀɔfyzemã] adv profusely

profusion [pʀɔfyzjɔ̃] nf profusion; **à ~** in plenty

progéniture [pʀɔʒenityʀ] nf offspring inv

progiciel [pʀɔʒisjɛl] nm (Inform) (software) package; **~ d'application** applications package, applications software no pl

progouvernemental, e, -aux [pʀɔguvɛʀnəmãtal, -o] adj pro-government cpd

programmable [pʀɔgʀamabl(ə)] adj programmable

programmateur, -trice [pʀɔgʀamatœʀ, -tʀis] nm/f (Ciné, TV) programme (Brit) ou program (US) planner ▷ nm (de machine à laver etc) timer

programmation [pʀɔgʀamasjɔ̃] nf programming

programme [pʀɔgʀam] nm programme (Brit), program (US); (TV, Radio) program(me)s pl; (Scol) syllabus, curriculum; (Inform) program; **au ~ de ce soir** (TV) among tonight's program(me)s

programmé, e [pʀɔgʀame] adj: **enseignement ~** programmed learning

programmer [pʀɔgʀame] vt (TV, Radio) to put on, show; (organiser, prévoir) to schedule; (Inform) to program

programmeur, -euse [pʀɔgʀamœʀ, -øz] nm/f (computer) programmer

progrès [pʀɔgʀɛ] nm progress no pl; **faire des/être en ~** to make/be making progress

progresser [pʀɔgʀese] vi to progress; (troupes etc) to make headway ou progress

progressif, -ive [pʀɔgʀesif, -iv] adj progressive

progression [pʀɔgʀesjɔ̃] nf progression; (d'une troupe etc) advance, progress

progressiste [pʀɔgʀesist(ə)] adj progressive

progressivement [pʀɔgʀesivmã] adv progressively

prohiber [pʀɔibe] vt to prohibit, ban

prohibitif, -ive [pʀɔibitif, -iv] adj prohibitive

prohibition [pʀɔibisjɔ̃] nf ban, prohibition; (Hist) Prohibition

proie [pʀwa] nf prey no pl; **être la ~ de** to fall prey to; **être en ~ à** (doutes, sentiment) to be prey to; (douleur, mal) to be suffering

projecteur [pʀɔʒɛktœʀ] nm projector; (de théâtre, cirque) spotlight

projectile [pʀɔʒɛktil] nm missile; (d'arme) projectile, bullet (ou shell etc)

projection [pʀɔʒɛksjɔ̃] nf projection; showing; **conférence avec ~s** lecture with slides (ou a film)

projectionniste [pʀɔʒɛksjɔnist(ə)] nm/f (Ciné) projectionist

projet [pʀɔʒɛ] nm plan; (ébauche) draft; **faire des ~s** to make plans; **~ de loi** bill

projeter [pʀɔʒte] vt (envisager) to plan; (film, photos) to project; (passer) to show; (ombre, lueur) to throw, cast, project; (jeter) to throw up (ou off ou out); **~ de faire qch** to plan to do sth

prolétaire [pʀɔletɛʀ] adj, nm/f proletarian

prolétariat [pʀɔletaʀja] nm proletariat

prolétarien, -ne [pʀɔletaʀjɛ̃, -ɛn] adj proletarian

prolifération [pʀɔlifeʀasjɔ̃] nf proliferation

proliférer [pʀɔlifeʀe] vi to proliferate

prolifique [pʀɔlifik] adj prolific

prolixe [pʀɔliks(ə)] adj verbose

prolo [pʀɔlo] nm/f (fam: = prolétaire) prole (péj)

prologue [pʀɔlɔg] nm prologue

prolongateur [pʀɔlɔ̃gatœʀ] nm (Élec) extension cable

prolongation [pʀɔlɔ̃gasjɔ̃] nf prolongation; extension; **prolongations** nfpl (Football) extra time sg

prolongement [pʀɔlɔ̃ʒmã] nm extension; **prolongements** nmpl (fig) repercussions, effects; **dans le ~ de** running on from

prolonger [pʀɔlɔ̃ʒe] vt (débat, séjour) to prolong; (délai, billet, rue) to extend; (chose) to be a continuation ou an extension of; **se prolonger** vi to go on

promenade [pʀɔmnad] nf walk (ou drive ou ride); **faire une ~** to go for a walk; **une ~ (à pied)/en voiture/à vélo** a walk/drive/(bicycle) ride

promener [pʀɔmne] vt (personne, chien) to take out for a walk; (fig) to carry around; to trail

round; *(doigts, regard)*: **~ qch sur** to run sth over;
se promener *vi (à pied)* to go for *(ou* be out for) a
walk; *(en voiture)* to go for *(ou* be out for) a drive;
(fig): **se ~ sur** to wander over

promeneur, -euse [pʀɔmnœʀ, -øz] *nm/f*
walker, stroller

promenoir [pʀɔmənwaʀ] *nm* gallery, (covered)
walkway

promesse [pʀɔmɛs] *nf* promise; **~ d'achat**
commitment to buy

prometteur, -euse [pʀɔmɛtœʀ, -øz] *adj*
promising

promettre [pʀɔmɛtʀ(ə)] *vt* to promise ▷ *vi*
(récolte, arbre) to look promising; *(enfant, musicien)*
to be promising; **se ~ de faire** to resolve *ou*
mean to do; **~ à qn de faire** to promise sb that
one will do

promeus *etc* [pʀɔmø] *vb voir* **promouvoir**

promis, e [pʀɔmi, -iz] *pp de* **promettre** ▷ *adj*:
être ~ à qch *(destiné)* to be destined for sth

promiscuité [pʀɔmiskɥite] *nf* crowding; lack of
privacy

promit [pʀɔmi] *vb voir* **promettre**

promontoire [pʀɔmɔ̃twaʀ] *nm* headland

promoteur, -trice [pʀɔmɔtœʀ, -tʀis] *nm/f*
(instigateur) instigator, promoter; **~
(immobilier)** property developer *(Brit)*, real
estate promoter *(US)*

promotion [pʀɔmɔsjɔ̃] *nf (avancement)*
promotion; *(Scol)* year *(Brit)*, class; **en ~** *(Comm)*
on promotion, on (special) offer

promotionnel, le [pʀɔmɔsjɔnɛl] *adj (article)* on
promotion, on (special) offer; *(vente)*
promotional

promouvoir [pʀɔmuvwaʀ] *vt* to promote

prompt, e [pʀɔ̃, pʀɔ̃t] *adj* swift, rapid;
(intervention, changement) sudden; **~ à faire qch**
quick to do sth

promptement [pʀɔ̃ptəmɑ̃] *adv* swiftly

prompteur® [pʀɔ̃tœʀ] *nm* Autocue® *(Brit)*,
Teleprompter® *(US)*

promptitude [pʀɔ̃tityd] *nf* swiftness, rapidity

promu, e [pʀɔmy] *pp de* **promouvoir**

promulguer [pʀɔmylge] *vt* to promulgate

prôner [pʀone] *vt (louer)* to laud, extol;
(préconiser) to advocate, commend

pronom [pʀɔnɔ̃] *nm* pronoun

pronominal, e, -aux [pʀɔnɔminal, -o] *adj*
pronominal; *(verbe)* reflexive, pronominal

prononcé, e [pʀɔnɔ̃se] *adj* pronounced, marked

prononcer [pʀɔnɔ̃se] *vt (son, mot, jugement)* to
pronounce; *(dire)* to utter; *(allocution)* to deliver
▷ *vi (Jur)* to deliver *ou* give a verdict; **~ bien/mal**
to have good/poor pronunciation; **se
prononcer** *vi* to reach a decision, give a verdict;
se ~ sur to give an opinion on; **se ~ contre** to
come down against; **ça se prononce
comment?** how do you pronounce this?

prononciation [pʀɔnɔ̃sjasjɔ̃] *nf* pronunciation

pronostic [pʀɔnɔstik] *nm (Méd)* prognosis; *(fig:
aussi: **pronostics**)* forecast

pronostiquer [pʀɔnɔstike] *vt (Méd)* to

prognosticate; *(annoncer, prévoir)* to forecast,
foretell

pronostiqueur, -euse [pʀɔnɔstikœʀ, -øz] *nm/f*
forecaster

propagande [pʀɔpagɑ̃d] *nf* propaganda; **faire
de la ~ pour qch** to plug *ou* push sth

propagandiste [pʀɔpagɑ̃dist(ə)] *nm/f*
propagandist

propagation [pʀɔpagasjɔ̃] *nf* propagation

propager [pʀɔpaʒe] *vt* to spread; **se propager** *vi*
to spread; *(Physique)* to be propagated

propane [pʀɔpan] *nm* propane

propension [pʀɔpɑ̃sjɔ̃] *nf*: **~ à (faire) qch**
propensity to (do) sth

prophète [pʀɔfɛt], **prophétesse** [pʀɔfetɛs]
nm/f prophet(ess)

prophétie [pʀɔfesi] *nf* prophecy

prophétique [pʀɔfetik] *adj* prophetic

prophétiser [pʀɔfetize] *vt* to prophesy

prophylactique [pʀɔfilaktik] *adj* prophylactic

propice [pʀɔpis] *adj* favourable *(Brit)*,
favorable *(US)*

proportion [pʀɔpɔʀsjɔ̃] *nf* proportion; **il n'y a
aucune ~ entre le prix demandé et le prix
réel** the asking price bears no relation to the
real price; **à ~ de** proportionally to, in
proportion to; **en ~ (de)** in proportion (to); **hors
de ~** out of proportion; **toute(s) ~(s) gardée(s)**
making due allowance(s)

proportionné, e [pʀɔpɔʀsjɔne] *adj*: **bien ~** well-
proportioned; **~ à** proportionate to

proportionnel, le [pʀɔpɔʀsjɔnɛl] *adj*
proportional; **~ à** proportional to ▷ *nf*
proportional representation

proportionnellement [pʀɔpɔʀsjɔnɛlmɑ̃] *adv*
proportionally, proportionately

proportionner [pʀɔpɔʀsjɔne] *vt*: **~ qch à** to
proportion *ou* adjust sth to

propos [pʀɔpo] *nm (paroles)* talk *no pl*, remark;
(intention, but) intention, aim; *(sujet)*: **à quel ~?**
what about?; **à ~ de** about, regarding; **à tout ~**
for no reason at all; **à ce ~** on that subject, in
this connection; **à ~** *adv* by the way;
(opportunément) (just) at the right moment; **hors
de ~, mal à ~** *adv* at the wrong moment

proposer [pʀɔpoze] *vt (suggérer)*: **~ qch (à qn)/de
faire** to suggest sth (to sb)/doing, propose sth
(to sb)/(to) do; *(offrir)*: **~ qch à qn/de faire** to
offer sb sth/to do; *(candidat)* to nominate, put
forward; *(loi, motion)* to propose; **se ~ (pour
faire)** to offer one's services (to do); **se ~ de
faire** to intend *ou* propose to do

proposition [pʀɔpozisjɔ̃] *nf* suggestion;
proposal; offer; *(Ling)* clause; **sur la ~ de** at the
suggestion of; **~ de loi** private bill

propre [pʀɔpʀ(ə)] *adj* clean; *(net)* neat, tidy; *(qui
ne salit pas: chien, chat)* house-trained; *(: enfant)*
toilet-trained; *(fig: honnête)* honest; *(possessif)*
own; *(sens)* literal; *(particulier)*: **~ à** peculiar to,
characteristic of; *(approprié)*: **~ à** suitable *ou*
appropriate for; *(de nature à)*: **~ à faire** likely to
do, that will do ▷ *nm*: **recopier au ~** to make a

fair copy of; (*particularité*): **le ~ de** the peculiarity of, the distinctive feature of; **au ~** (*Ling*) literally; **appartenir à qn en ~** to belong to sb (exclusively); **~ à rien** *nm/f* (*péj*) good-for-nothing

proprement [pʀɔpʀəmɑ̃] *adv* cleanly; neatly, tidily; **à ~ parler** strictly speaking; **le village ~ dit** the actual village, the village itself

propret, te [pʀɔpʀɛ, -ɛt] *adj* neat and tidy, spick-and-span

propreté [pʀɔpʀəte] *nf* cleanliness, cleanness; neatness, tidiness

propriétaire [pʀɔpʀijetɛʀ] *nm/f* owner; (*d'hôtel etc*) proprietor(-tress), owner; (*pour le locataire*) landlord(-lady); **~ (immobilier)** house-owner; householder; **~ récoltant** grower; **~ (terrien)** landowner

propriété [pʀɔpʀijete] *nf* (*droit*) ownership; (*objet, immeuble etc*) property *gen no pl*; (*villa*) residence, property; (*terres*) property *gen no pl*, land *gen no pl*; (*qualité, Chimie, Math*) property; (*correction*) appropriateness, suitability; **~ artistique et littéraire** artistic and literary copyright; **~ industrielle** patent rights *pl*

propulser [pʀɔpylse] *vt* (*missile*) to propel; (*projeter*) to hurl, fling

propulsion [pʀɔpylsjɔ̃] *nf* propulsion

prorata [pʀɔʀata] *nm inv*: **au ~ de** in proportion to, on the basis of

prorogation [pʀɔʀɔgasjɔ̃] *nf* deferment; extension; adjournment

proroger [pʀɔʀɔʒe] *vt* to put back, defer; (*prolonger*) to extend; (*assemblée*) to adjourn, prorogue

prosaïque [pʀɔzaik] *adj* mundane, prosaic

proscription [pʀɔskʀipsjɔ̃] *nf* banishment; (*interdiction*) banning; prohibition

proscrire [pʀɔskʀiʀ] *vt* (*bannir*) to banish; (*interdire*) to ban, prohibit

prose [pʀoz] *nf* prose (*style*)

prosélyte [pʀɔzelit] *nm/f* proselyte, convert

prospecter [pʀɔspɛkte] *vt* to prospect; (*Comm*) to canvass

prospecteur-placier [pʀɔspɛktœʀplasje] (*pl* **prospecteurs-placiers**) *nm* placement officer

prospectif, -ive [pʀɔspɛktif, -iv] *adj* prospective

prospectus [pʀɔspɛktys] *nm* (*feuille*) leaflet; (*dépliant*) brochure, leaflet

prospère [pʀɔspɛʀ] *adj* prosperous; (*santé, entreprise*) thriving, flourishing

prospérer [pʀɔspeʀe] *vi* to thrive

prospérité [pʀɔspeʀite] *nf* prosperity

prostate [pʀɔstat] *nf* prostate (gland)

prosterner [pʀɔstɛʀne]: **se prosterner** *vi* to bow low, prostrate o.s

prostituée [pʀɔstitɥe] *nf* prostitute

prostitution [pʀɔstitysjɔ̃] *nf* prostitution

prostré, e [pʀɔstʀe] *adj* prostrate

protagoniste [pʀɔtagɔnist(ə)] *nm* protagonist

protecteur, -trice [pʀɔtɛktœʀ, -tʀis] *adj* protective; (*air, ton*: *péj*) patronizing ▷ *nm/f* (*défenseur*) protector; (*des arts*) patron

protection [pʀɔtɛksjɔ̃] *nf* protection; (*d'un personnage influent: aide*) patronage; **écran de ~** protective screen; **~ civile** state-financed civilian rescue service; **~ maternelle et infantile (PMI)** social service concerned with child welfare

protectionnisme [pʀɔtɛksjɔnism(ə)] *nm* protectionism

protectionniste [pʀɔtɛksjɔnist(ə)] *adj* protectionist

protégé, e [pʀɔteʒe] *nm/f* protégé(e)

protège-cahier [pʀɔtɛʒkaje] *nm* exercise book cover

protéger [pʀɔteʒe] *vt* to protect; (*aider, patronner*: *personne, arts*) to be a patron of; (: *carrière*) to further; **se ~ de/contre** to protect o.s from

protège-slip [pʀɔtɛʒslip] *nm* panty liner

protéine [pʀɔtein] *nf* protein

protestant, e [pʀɔtɛstɑ̃, -ɑ̃t] *adj, nm/f* Protestant

protestantisme [pʀɔtɛstɑ̃tism(ə)] *nm* Protestantism

protestataire [pʀɔtɛstatɛʀ] *nm/f* protestor

protestation [pʀɔtɛstasjɔ̃] *nf* (*plainte*) protest; (*déclaration*) protestation, profession

protester [pʀɔtɛste] *vi*: **~ (contre)** to protest (against *ou* about); **~ de** (*son innocence, sa loyauté*) to protest

prothèse [pʀɔtɛz] *nf* artificial limb, prosthesis; **~ dentaire** (*appareil*) denture; (*science*) dental engineering

protocolaire [pʀɔtɔkɔlɛʀ] *adj* formal; (*questions, règles*) of protocol

protocole [pʀɔtɔkɔl] *nm* protocol; (*fig*) etiquette; **~ d'accord** draft treaty; **~ opératoire** (*Méd*) operating procedure

prototype [pʀɔtɔtip] *nm* prototype

protubérance [pʀɔtybeʀɑ̃s] *nf* bulge, protuberance

protubérant, e [pʀɔtybeʀɑ̃, -ɑ̃t] *adj* protruding, bulging, protuberant

proue [pʀu] *nf* bow(s *pl*), prow

prouesse [pʀuɛs] *nf* feat

prouver [pʀuve] *vt* to prove

provenance [pʀɔvnɑ̃s] *nf* origin; (*de mot, coutume*) source; **avion en ~ de** plane (arriving) from

provençal, e, -aux [pʀɔvɑ̃sal, -o] *adj* Provençal ▷ *nm* (*Ling*) Provençal

Provence [pʀɔvɑ̃s] *nf*: **la ~** Provence

provenir [pʀɔvniʀ]: **~ de** *vt* to come from; (*résulter de*) to be due to, be the result of

proverbe [pʀɔvɛʀb(ə)] *nm* proverb

proverbial, e, -aux [pʀɔvɛʀbjal, -o] *adj* proverbial

providence [pʀɔvidɑ̃s] *nf*: **la ~** providence

providentiel, le [pʀɔvidɑ̃sjɛl] *adj* providential

province [pʀɔvɛ̃s] *nf* province

provincial, e, -aux [pʀɔvɛ̃sjal, -o] *adj, nm/f* provincial

proviseur [pʀɔvizœʀ] *nm* ≈ head (teacher) (*Brit*), ≈ principal (*US*)

provision [pʀɔvizjɔ̃] *nf* (*réserve*) stock, supply; (*avance*: *à un avocat, avoué*) retainer, retaining fee;

(*Comm*) funds *pl* (in account); reserve; **provisions** *nfpl* (*vivres*) provisions, food *no pl*; **faire ~ de** to stock up with; **placard** *ou* **armoire à ~s** food cupboard

provisoire [pʀɔvizwaʀ] *adj* temporary; (*Jur*) provisional; **mise en liberté ~** release on bail

provisoirement [pʀɔvizwaʀmã] *adv* temporarily, for the time being

provocant, e [pʀɔvɔkã, -ãt] *adj* provocative

provocateur, -trice [pʀɔvɔkatœʀ, -tʀis] *adj* provocative ▷ *nm* (*meneur*) agitator

provocation [pʀɔvɔkasjɔ̃] *nf* provocation

provoquer [pʀɔvɔke] *vt* (*défier*) to provoke; (*causer*) to cause, bring about; (: *curiosité*) to arouse, give rise to; (: *aveux*) to prompt, elicit; (*inciter*): **~ qn à** to incite sb to

prox. *abr* = **proximité**

proxénète [pʀɔksenɛt] *nm* procurer

proxénétisme [pʀɔksenetism(ə)] *nm* procuring

proximité [pʀɔksimite] *nf* nearness, closeness, proximity; (*dans le temps*) imminence, closeness; **à ~** near *ou* close by; **à ~ de** near (to), close to

prude [pʀyd] *adj* prudish

prudemment [pʀydamã] *adv* (*voir prudent*) carefully; cautiously; prudently; wisely, sensibly

prudence [pʀydãs] *nf* carefulness; caution; prudence; **avec ~** carefully; cautiously; wisely; **par (mesure de) ~** as a precaution

prudent, e [pʀydã, -ãt] *adj* (*pas téméraire*) careful, cautious, prudent; (: *en général*) safety-conscious; (*sage, conseillé*) wise, sensible; (*réservé*) cautious; **ce n'est pas ~** it's risky; it's not sensible; **soyez ~** take care, be careful

prune [pʀyn] *nf* plum

pruneau, x [pʀyno] *nm* prune

prunelle [pʀynɛl] *nf* pupil; (*œil*) eye; (*Bot*) sloe; (*eau de vie*) sloe gin

prunier [pʀynje] *nm* plum tree

Prusse [pʀys] *nf*: **la ~** Prussia

PS *sigle m* = **parti socialiste**; (= *post-scriptum*) PS

psalmodier [psalmɔdje] *vt* to chant; (*fig*) to drone out

psaume [psom] *nm* psalm

pseudonyme [psødɔnim] *nm* (*gén*) fictitious name; (*d'écrivain*) pseudonym, pen name; (*de comédien*) stage name

PSIG *sigle m* (= *Peloton de surveillance et d'intervention de gendarmerie*) type of police commando squad

PSU *sigle m* = **parti socialiste unifié**

psy [psi] *nm/f* (*fam*: = *psychiatre, psychologue*) shrink

psychanalyse [psikanaliz] *nf* psychoanalysis

psychanalyser [psikanalize] *vt* to psychoanalyze; **se faire ~** to undergo (psycho)analysis

psychanalyste [psikanalist(ə)] *nm/f* psychoanalyst

psychanalytique [psikanalitik] *adj* psychoanalytical

psychédélique [psikedelik] *adj* psychedelic

psychiatre [psikjatʀ(ə)] *nm/f* psychiatrist

psychiatrie [psikjatʀi] *nf* psychiatry

psychiatrique [psikjatʀik] *adj* psychiatric;

(*hôpital*) mental, psychiatric

psychique [psiʃik] *adj* psychological

psychisme [psiʃism(ə)] *nm* psyche

psychologie [psikɔlɔʒi] *nf* psychology

psychologique [psikɔlɔʒik] *adj* psychological

psychologiquement [psikɔlɔʒikmã] *adv* psychologically

psychologue [psikɔlɔg] *nm/f* psychologist; **être ~** (*fig*) to be a good psychologist

psychomoteur, -trice [psikɔmɔtœʀ, -tʀis] *adj* psychomotor

psychopathe [psikɔpat] *nm/f* psychopath

psychopédagogie [psikɔpedagɔʒi] *nf* educational psychology

psychose [psikoz] *nf* (*Méd*) psychosis; (*obsession, idée fixe*) obsessive fear

psychosomatique [psikɔsɔmatik] *adj* psychosomatic

psychothérapie [psikɔteʀapi] *nf* psychotherapy

psychotique [psikɔtik] *adj* psychotic

PTCA *sigle m* = **poids total en charge autorisé**

Pte *abr* = **Porte**

pte *abr* (= *pointe*) pt

PTMA *sigle m* (= *poids total maximum autorisé*) maximum loaded weight

PTT *sigle fpl* = **poste**

pu [py] *pp de* **pouvoir**

puanteur [pɥãtœʀ] *nf* stink, stench

pub [pyb] *nf* (*fam*) = **publicité**; **la ~** advertising

pubère [pybɛʀ] *adj* pubescent

puberté [pybɛʀte] *nf* puberty

pubis [pybis] *nm* (*bas-ventre*) pubes *pl*; (*os*) pubis

public, -ique [pyblik] *adj* public; (*école, instruction*) state *cpd*; (*scrutin*) open ▷ *nm* public; (*assistance*) audience; **en ~** in public; **le grand ~** the general public

publication [pyblikasjɔ̃] *nf* publication

publiciste [pyblisist(ə)] *nm/f* adman

publicitaire [pyblisitɛʀ] *adj* advertising *cpd*; (*film, voiture*) publicity *cpd*; (*vente*) promotional ▷ *nm* adman; **rédacteur ~** copywriter

publicité [pyblisite] *nf* (*méthode, profession*) advertising; (*annonce*) advertisement; (*révélations*) publicity

publier [pyblije] *vt* to publish; (*nouvelle*) to publicize, make public

publipostage [pyblipɔstaʒ] *nm* mailshot, (mass) mailing

publique [pyblik] *adj f voir* **public**

publiquement [pyblikmã] *adv* publicly

puce [pys] *nf* flea; (*Inform*) chip; **(marché aux) ~s** flea market *sg*; **mettre la ~ à l'oreille de qn** to give sb something to think about

puceau, x [pyso] *adj m*: **être ~** to be a virgin

pucelle [pysɛl] *adj f*: **être ~** to be a virgin

puceron [pysʀɔ̃] *nm* aphid

pudeur [pydœʀ] *nf* modesty

pudibond, e [pydibɔ̃, -ɔ̃d] *adj* prudish

pudique [pydik] *adj* (*chaste*) modest; (*discret*) discreet

pudiquement [pydikmã] *adv* modestly

puer [pɥe] (péj) vi to stink ▷ vt to stink of, reek of
puéricultrice [pɥerikyltris] nf ≈ nursery nurse
puériculture [pɥerikyltyr] nf infant care
puéril, e [pɥeril] adj childish
puérilement [pɥerilmɑ̃] adv childishly
puérilité [pɥerilite] nf childishness; (acte, idée) childish thing
pugilat [pyʒila] nm (fist) fight
puis [pɥi] vb voir **pouvoir** ▷ adv (ensuite) then; (dans une énumération) next; (en outre): **et ~** and (then); **et ~ (après** ou **quoi)?** so (what)?
puisard [pɥizar] nm (égout) cesspool
puiser [pɥize] vt: **~ (dans)** to draw (from); **~ dans qch** to dip into sth
puisque [pɥisk(ə)] conj since; (valeur intensive): **~ je te le dis!** I'm telling you!
puissamment [pɥisamɑ̃] adv powerfully
puissance [pɥisɑ̃s] nf power; **en ~** adj potential; **deux (à la) ~ cinq** two to the power (of) five
puissant, e [pɥisɑ̃, -ɑ̃t] adj powerful
puisse etc [pɥis] vb voir **pouvoir**
puits [pɥi] nm well; **~ artésien** artesian well; **~ de mine** mine shaft; **~ de science** fount of knowledge
pull [pyl], **pull-over** [pylɔvœr] nm sweater, jumper (Brit)
pulluler [pylyle] vi to swarm; (fig: erreurs) to abound, proliferate
pulmonaire [pylmɔner] adj lung cpd; (artère) pulmonary
pulpe [pylp(ə)] nf pulp
pulsation [pylsasjɔ̃] nf (Méd) beat
pulsé [pylse] adj m: **chauffage à air ~** warm air heating
pulsion [pylsjɔ̃] nf (Psych) drive, urge
pulvérisateur [pylverizatœr] nm spray
pulvérisation [pylverizasjɔ̃] nf spraying
pulvériser [pylverize] vt (solide) to pulverize; (liquide) to spray; (fig: anéantir: adversaire) to pulverize; (: record) to smash, shatter; (: argument) to demolish
puma [pyma] nm puma, cougar
punaise [pynɛz] nf (Zool) bug; (clou) drawing pin (Brit), thumb tack (US)
punch [pɔ̃ʃ] nm (boisson) punch [pœnʃ] (Boxe) punching ability; (fig) punch
punching-ball [pœnʃiŋbol] nm punchball
punir [pynir] vt to punish; **~ qn de qch** to punish sb for sth
punitif, -ive [pynitif, -iv] adj punitive
punition [pynisjɔ̃] nf punishment
pupille [pypij] nf (Anat) pupil ▷ nm/f (enfant) ward; **~ de l'État** child in care; **~ de la Nation** war orphan
pupitre [pypitr(ə)] nm (Scol) desk; (Rel) lectern; (de chef d'orchestre) rostrum; **~ de commande** control panel

pur, e [pyr] adj pure; (vin) undiluted; (whisky) neat; (intentions) honourable (Brit), honorable (US) ▷ nm (personne) hard-liner; **en ~e perte** fruitlessly, to no avail
purée [pyre] nf: **~ (de pommes de terre)** ≈ mashed potatoes pl; **~ de marrons** chestnut purée; **~ de pois** (fig) peasoup(er)
purement [pyrmɑ̃] adv purely
pureté [pyrte] nf purity
purgatif [pyrgatif] nm purgative, purge
purgatoire [pyrgatwar] nm purgatory
purge [pyrʒ(ə)] nf (Pol) purge; (Méd) purging no pl; purge
purger [pyrʒe] vt (radiateur) to flush (out), drain; (circuit hydraulique) to bleed; (Méd, Pol) to purge; (Jur: peine) to serve
purification [pyrifikasjɔ̃] nf (de l'eau) purification; **~ ethnique** ethnic cleansing
purifier [pyrifje] vt to purify; (Tech: métal) to refine
purin [pyrɛ̃] nm liquid manure
puriste [pyrist(ə)] nm/f purist
puritain, e [pyritɛ̃, -ɛn] adj, nm/f Puritan
puritanisme [pyritanism(ə)] nm Puritanism
pur-sang [pyrsɑ̃] nm inv thoroughbred, purebred
purulent, e [pyrylɑ̃, -ɑ̃t] adj purulent
pus [py] vb voir **pouvoir** ▷ nm pus
pusillanime [pyzilanim] adj fainthearted
pustule [pystyl] nf pustule
putain [pytɛ̃] nf (fam!) whore (!); **ce/cette ~ de** ... this bloody (Brit) ou goddamn (US) ... (!)
putois [pytwa] nm polecat; **crier comme un ~** to yell one's head off
putréfaction [pytrefaksjɔ̃] nf putrefaction
putréfier [pytrefje] vt, **se putréfier** vi to putrefy, rot
putride [pytrid] adj putrid
putsch [putʃ] nm (Pol) putsch
puzzle [pœzl(ə)] nm jigsaw (puzzle)
PV sigle m = **procès-verbal**
PVC sigle f (= polychlorure de vinyle) PVC
PVD sigle mpl (= pays en voie de développement) developing countries
Px abr = **prix**
pygmée [pigme] nm pygmy
pyjama [piʒama] nm pyjamas pl, pair of pyjamas
pylône [pilon] nm pylon
pyramide [piramid] nf pyramid
pyrénéen, ne [pireneɛ̃, -ɛn] adj Pyrenean
Pyrénées [pirene] nfpl: **les ~** the Pyrenees
pyrex® [pirɛks] nm Pyrex®
pyrogravure [pirɔgravyr] nf poker-work
pyromane [pirɔman] nm/f arsonist
python [pitɔ̃] nm python

Qq

Q, q [ky] *nm inv* Q, q ▷ *abr* (= *quintal*) q; **Q comme Quintal** Q for Queen

Qatar [katar] *nm*: **le ~** Qatar

QCM *sigle m* (= *questionnaire à choix multiples*) multiple-choice test

QG *sigle m* (= *quartier général*) HQ

QHS *sigle m* (= *quartier de haute sécurité*) high-security wing *ou* prison

QI *sigle m* (= *quotient intellectuel*) IQ

qqch. *abr* (= *quelque chose*) sth

qqe *abr* = **quelque**

qqes *abr* = **quelques**

qqn *abr* (= *quelqu'un*) sb, s.o.

quadra [k(w)adra] (*fam*) *nm/f* (= *quadragénaire*) person in his (*ou* her) forties; **les ~s** forty somethings (*fam*)

quadragénaire [kadraʒenɛʀ] *nm/f* (*de quarante ans*) forty-year-old; (*de quarante à cinquante ans*) man/woman in his/her forties

quadrangulaire [kwadrãgylɛʀ] *adj* quadrangular

quadrature [kwadratyʀ] *nf*: **c'est la ~ du cercle** it's like trying to square the circle

quadrichromie [kwadrikʀɔmi] *nf* four-colour (*Brit*) *ou* -color (*US*) printing

quadrilatère [k(w)adrilatɛʀ] *nm* (*Géom, Mil*) quadrilateral; (*terrain*) four-sided area

quadrillage [kadrijaʒ] *nm* (*lignes etc*) square pattern, criss-cross pattern

quadrillé, e [kadrije] *adj* (*papier*) squared

quadriller [kadrije] *vt* (*papier*) to mark out in squares; (*Police: ville, région etc*) to keep under tight control, be positioned throughout

quadrimoteur [k(w)adrimɔtœʀ] *nm* four-engined plane

quadripartite [kwadripartit] *adj* (*entre pays*) four-power; (*entre partis*) four-party

quadriphonie [kadrifɔni] *nf* quadraphony

quadriréacteur [k(w)adrireaktœʀ] *nm* four-engined jet

quadrupède [k(w)adrypɛd] *nm* quadruped

quadruple [k(w)adrypl(ə)] *nm*: **le ~ de** four times as much as

quadrupler [k(w)adryple] *vt, vi* to quadruple, increase fourfold

quadruplés, -ées [k(w)adryple] *nm/fpl* quadruplets, quads

quai [ke] *nm* (*de port*) quay; (*de gare*) platform; (*de cours d'eau, canal*) embankment; **être à ~** (*navire*) to be alongside; (*train*) to be in the station; **le Q~ d'Orsay** offices of the French Ministry for Foreign Affairs; **le Q~ des Orfèvres** central police headquarters

qualifiable [kalifjabl(ə)] *adj*: **ce n'est pas ~** it defies description

qualificatif, -ive [kalifikatif, -iv] *adj* (*Ling*) qualifying ▷ *nm* (*terme*) term; (*Ling*) qualifier

qualification [kalifikɑsjɔ̃] *nf* qualification

qualifié, e [kalifje] *adj* qualified; (*main d'œuvre*) skilled

qualifier [kalifje] *vt* to qualify; (*appeler*): **~ qch/qn de** to describe sth/sb as; **se qualifier** *vi* (*Sport*) to qualify; **être qualifié pour** to be qualified for

qualitatif, -ive [kalitatif, -iv] *adj* qualitative

qualité [kalite] *nf* quality; (*titre, fonction*) position; **en ~ de** in one's capacity as; **ès ~s** in an official capacity; **avoir ~ pour** to have authority to; **de ~** *adj* quality *cpd*; **rapport ~- prix** value (for money)

quand [kã] *conj, adv* when; **~ je serai riche** when I'm rich; **~ même** (*cependant, pourtant*) nevertheless; (*tout de même*) all the same; really; **~ bien même** even though

quant [kã]: **~ à** *prép* (*pour ce qui est de*) as for, as to; (*au sujet de*) regarding

quant-à-soi [kãtaswa] *nm*: **rester sur son ~** to remain aloof

quantième [kãtjɛm] *nm* date, day (of the month)

quantifiable [kãtifjabl(ə)] *adj* quantifiable

quantifier [kãtifje] *vt* to quantify

quantitatif, -ive [kãtitatif, -iv] *adj* quantitative

quantitativement [kãtitativmã] *adv* quantitatively

quantité [kãtite] *nf* quantity, amount; (*Science*) quantity; (*grand nombre*): **une** *ou* **des ~(s) de** a great deal of; a lot of; **en grande ~** in large quantities; **en ~s industrielles** in vast amounts; **du travail en ~** a great deal of work; **~ de** many

quarantaine [kaʀãtɛn] *nf* (*isolement*)

quarantine; (*âge*): **avoir la ~** to be around forty; (*nombre*): **une ~ (de)** forty or so, about forty; **mettre en ~** to put into quarantine; (*fig*) to send to Coventry (*Brit*), ostracize

quarante [kaʀɑ̃t] *num* forty

quarantième [kaʀɑ̃tjɛm] *num* fortieth

quark [kwaʀk] *nm* quark

quart [kaʀ] *nm* (*fraction*) quarter; (*surveillance*) watch; (*partie*): **un ~ de poulet/fromage** a chicken quarter/a quarter of a cheese; **un ~ de beurre** a quarter kilo of butter, ≈ a half pound of butter; **un ~ de vin** a quarter litre of wine; **une livre un ~ ou et ~** one and a quarter pounds; **le ~ de** a quarter of; **~ d'heure** quarter of an hour; **deux heures et ou un ~** (a) quarter past two, (a) quarter after two (*US*); **il est le ~** it's (a) quarter past *ou* after (*US*); **une heure moins le ~** (a) quarter to one, (a) quarter of one (*US*); **il est moins le ~** it's (a) quarter to; **être de/prendre le ~** to keep/take the watch; **~ de tour** quarter turn; **au ~ de tour** (*fig*) straight off; **~s de finale** (*Sport*) quarter finals

quarté [kaʀte] *nm* (*Courses*) system of forecast betting giving first four horses

quarteron [kaʀtəʀɔ̃] *nm* (*péj*) small bunch, handful

quartette [kwaʀtɛt] *nm* quartet(te)

quartier [kaʀtje] *nm* (*de ville*) district, area; (*de bœuf, de la lune*) quarter; (*de fruit, fromage*) piece; **quartiers** *nmpl* (*Mil, Blason*) quarters; **cinéma/salle de ~** local cinema/hall; **avoir ~ libre** to be free; (*Mil*) to have leave from barracks; **ne pas faire de ~** to spare no one, give no quarter; **~ commerçant/résidentiel** shopping/residential area; **~ général (QG)** headquarters (HQ)

quartier-maître [kaʀtjemɛtʀ(ə)] *nm* ≈ leading seaman

quartz [kwaʀts] *nm* quartz

quasi [kazi] *adv* almost, nearly ▷ *préfixe*: **~-certitude** near certainty

quasiment [kazimɑ̃] *adv* almost, very nearly

quaternaire [kwatɛʀnɛʀ] *adj* (*Géo*) Quaternary

quatorze [katɔʀz(ə)] *num* fourteen

quatorzième [katɔʀzjɛm] *num* fourteenth

quatrain [katʀɛ̃] *nm* quatrain

quatre [katʀ(ə)] *num* four; **à ~ pattes** on all fours; **tiré à ~ épingles** dressed up to the nines; **faire les ~ cent coups** to be a bit wild; **se mettre en ~ pour qn** to go out of one's way for sb; **à ~** (*monter, descendre*) four at a time; **à ~ mains** (*jouer*) four-handed

quatre-vingt-dix [katʀəvɛ̃dis] *num* ninety

quatre-vingts [katʀəvɛ̃] *num* eighty

quatre-vingt-un *num* eighty-one

quatrième [katʀijɛm] *num* fourth

quatuor [kwatɥɔʀ] *nm* quartet(te)

 MOT-CLÉ

que [kə] *conj* **1** (*introduisant complétive*) that; **il sait que tu es là** he knows (that) you're here; **je**
veux que tu acceptes I want you to accept; **il a dit que oui** he said he would (*ou* it was *etc*)

2 (*reprise d'autres conjonctions*): **quand il rentrera et qu'il aura mangé** when he gets back and (when) he has eaten; **si vous y allez ou que vous …** if you go there or if you …

3 (*en tête de phrase: hypothèse, souhait etc*): **qu'il le veuille ou non** whether he likes it or not; **qu'il fasse ce qu'il voudra!** let him do as he pleases!

4 (*but*): **tenez-le qu'il ne tombe pas** hold it so (that) it doesn't fall

5 (*après comparatif*) than; as; *voir aussi* **plus; aussi; autant** *etc*

6 (*seulement*): **ne … que** only; **il ne boit que de l'eau** he only drinks water

7 (*temps*): **elle venait à peine de sortir qu'il se mit à pleuvoir** she had just gone out when it started to rain, no sooner had she gone out than it started to rain; **il y a quatre ans qu'il est parti** it is four years since he left, he left four years ago

▷ *adv* (*exclamation*): **qu'il** *ou* **qu'est-ce qu'il est bête/court vite!** he's so silly!/he runs so fast!; **que de livres!** what a lot of books!

▷ *pron* **1** (*relatif: personne*) whom; (: *chose*) that, which; **l'homme que je vois** the man (whom) I see; **le livre que tu vois** the book (that *ou* which) you see; **un jour que j'étais …** a day when I was ..

2 (*interrogatif*) what; **que fais-tu?, qu'est-ce que tu fais?** what are you doing?; **qu'est-ce que c'est?** what is it?, what's that?; **que faire?** what can one do?; **que préfères-tu, celui-ci ou celui-là?** which (one) do you prefer, this one or that one?

Québec [kebɛk] *n* (*ville*) Quebec ▷ *nm*: **le ~** Quebec (Province)

québécois, e [kebekwa, -waz] *adj* Quebec *cpd* ▷ *nm* (*Ling*) Quebec French ▷ *nm/f*: **Québécois, e** Quebecois, Quebec(k)er

 MOT-CLÉ

quel, quelle [kɛl] *adj* **1** (*interrogatif: personne*) who; (: *chose*) what; which; **quel est cet homme?** who is this man?; **quel est ce livre?** what is this book?; **quel livre/homme?** what book/man?; (*parmi un certain choix*) which book/man?; **quels acteurs préférez-vous?** which actors do you prefer?; **dans quels pays êtes-vous allé?** which *ou* what countries did you go to?

2 (*exclamatif*): **quelle surprise/coïncidence!** what a surprise/coincidence!

3: **quel(le) que soit le coupable** whoever is guilty; **quel que soit votre avis** whatever your opinion (may be)

quelconque [kɛlkɔ̃k] *adj* (*médiocre*) indifferent, poor; (*sans attrait*) ordinary, plain; (*indéfini*): **un ami/prétexte ~** some friend/pretext or other;

un livre ~ suffira any book will do; **pour une raison ~** for some reason (or other)

 MOT-CLÉ

quelque [kɛlkə] *adj* **1** some; a few; *(tournure interrogative)* any; **quelque espoir** some hope; **il a quelques amis** he has a few *ou* some friends; **a-t-il quelques amis?** has he any friends?; **les quelques livres qui** the few books which; **20 kg et quelque(s)** a bit over 20 kg; **il habite à quelque distance d'ici** he lives some distance *ou* way (away) from here
2: **quelque ... que** whatever, whichever; **quelque livre qu'il choisisse** whatever *(ou* whichever) book he chooses; **par quelque temps qu'il fasse** whatever the weather
3: **quelque chose** something; *(tournure interrogative)* anything; **quelque chose d'autre** something else; anything else; **y être pour quelque chose** to have something to do with it; **faire quelque chose à qn** to have an effect on sb, do something to sb; **quelque part** somewhere; anywhere; **en quelque sorte** as it were
▷ *adv* **1** *(environ)*: **quelque 100 mètres** some 100 metres
2: **quelque peu** rather, somewhat

quelquefois [kɛlkəfwa] *adv* sometimes
quelques-uns, --unes [kɛlkəzœ̃, -yn] *pron* some, a few; **~ des lecteurs** some of the readers
quelqu'un [kɛlkœ̃] *pron* someone, somebody; *(tournure interrogative ou négative +)* anyone *ou* anybody; **quelqu'un d'autre** someone *ou* somebody else; anybody else
quémander [kemɑ̃de] *vt* to beg for
qu'en dira-t-on [kɑ̃diratɔ̃] *nm inv*: **le qu'en dira-t-on** gossip, what people say
quenelle [kənɛl] *nf* quenelle
quenouille [kənuj] *nf* distaff
querelle [kərɛl] *nf* quarrel; **chercher ~ à qn** to pick a quarrel with sb
quereller [kərele]: **se quereller** *vi* to quarrel
querelleur, -euse [kərɛlœʀ, -øz] *adj* quarrelsome
qu'est-ce que [kɛskə] *voir* **que**
qu'est-ce qui [kɛski] *voir* **qui**
question [kɛstjɔ̃] *nf* *(gén)* question; *(fig)* matter; issue; **il a été ~ de** we *(ou* they) spoke about; **il est ~ de les emprisonner** there's talk of them being jailed; **c'est une ~ de temps** it's a matter *ou* question of time; **de quoi est-il ~?** what is it about?; **il n'en est pas ~** there's no question of it; **en ~** in question; **hors de ~** out of the question; **je ne me suis jamais posé la ~** I've never thought about it; **(re)mettre en ~** *(autorité, science)* to question; **poser la ~ de confiance** *(Pol)* to ask for a vote of confidence; **~ piège** *(d'apparence facile)* trick question; *(pour nuire)* loaded question; **~ subsidiaire** tiebreaker
questionnaire [kɛstjɔnɛʀ] *nm* questionnaire

questionner [kɛstjɔne] *vt* to question
quête [kɛt] *nf* *(collecte)* collection; *(recherche)* quest, search; **faire la ~** *(à l'église)* to take the collection; *(artiste)* to pass the hat round; **se mettre en ~ de qch** to go in search of sth
quêter [kete] *vi* *(à l'église)* to take the collection; *(dans la rue)* to collect money (for charity) ▷ *vt* to seek
quetsche [kwɛtʃ(ə)] *nf* damson
queue [kø] *nf* tail; *(fig: du classement)* bottom; (: *de poêle)* handle; (: *de fruit, feuille)* stalk; (: *de train, colonne, file)* rear; *(file: de personnes)* queue (Brit), line (US); **en ~ (de train)** at the rear (of the train); **faire la ~** to queue (up) (Brit), line up (US); **se mettre à la ~** to join the queue *ou* line; **histoire sans ~ ni tête** cock and bull story; **à la ~ leu leu** in single file; *(fig)* one after the other; **~ de cheval** ponytail; **~ de poisson**: **faire une ~ de poisson à qn** *(Auto)* to cut in front of sb; **finir en ~ de poisson** *(film)* to come to an abrupt end
queue-de-pie [kødpi] *(pl* **queues-de-pie**) *nf* *(habit)* tails *pl*, tail coat
queux [kø] *adj m* *voir* **maître**
qui [ki] *pron* *(personne)* who; *(avec préposition)* whom; *(chose, animal)* which, that; *(interrogatif indirect: sujet)*: **je me demande ~ est là?** I wonder who is there?; (: *objet)*: **elle ne sait à ~ se plaindre** she doesn't know who to complain to *ou* to whom to complain; **qu'est-ce ~ est sur la table?** what is on the table?; **à ~ est ce sac?** whose bag is this?; **à ~ parlais-tu?** who were you talking to?, to whom were you talking?; **chez ~ allez-vous?** whose house are you going to?; **amenez ~ vous voulez** bring who(ever) you like; **~ est-ce ~ ...?** who?; **~ est-ce que ...?** who?; whom?; **~ que ce soit** whoever it may be
quiche [kiʃ] *nf* quiche; **~ lorraine** quiche Lorraine
quiconque [kikɔ̃k] *pron* *(celui qui)* whoever, anyone who; *(n'importe qui, personne)* anyone, anybody
quidam [kɥidam] *nm* *(hum)* fellow
quiétude [kjetyd] *nf* *(d'un lieu)* quiet, tranquillity; *(d'une personne)* peace (of mind), serenity; **en toute ~** in complete peace; *(mentale)* with complete peace of mind
quignon [kiɲɔ̃] *nm*: **~ de pain** *(croûton)* crust of bread; *(morceau)* hunk of bread
quille [kij] *nf* ninepin, skittle (Brit); *(Navig: d'un bateau)* keel; **(jeu de) ~s** ninepins *sg*, skittles *sg* (Brit)
quincaillerie [kɛ̃kajʀi] *nf* *(ustensiles, métier)* hardware, ironmongery (Brit); *(magasin)* hardware shop *ou* store (US), ironmonger's (Brit)
quincaillier, -ière [kɛ̃kaje, -jɛʀ] *nm/f* hardware dealer, ironmonger (Brit)
quinconce [kɛ̃kɔ̃s] *nm*: **en ~** in staggered rows
quinine [kinin] *nf* quinine
quinqua [kɛ̃ka] *(fam)* *nm/f* (= *quinquagénaire)* person in his *(ou* her) fifties; **les ~s** fifty somethings *(fam)*

quinquagénaire [kɛ̃kaʒenɛʀ] *nm/f* (*de cinquante ans*) fifty-year old; (*de cinquante à soixante ans*) man/woman in his/her fifties

quinquennal, e, -aux [kɛ̃kenal, -o] *adj* five-year, quinquennial

quinquennat [kɛ̃kena] *nm* five year term of office (*of French President*)

quintal, -aux [kɛ̃tal, -o] *nm* quintal (*100 kg*)

quinte [kɛ̃t] *nf*: **~ (de toux)** coughing fit

quintessence [kɛ̃tesɑ̃s] *nf* quintessence, very essence

quintette [kɛ̃tɛt] *nm* quintet(te)

quintuple [kɛ̃typl(ə)] *nm*: **le ~ de** five times as much as

quintupler [kɛ̃typle] *vt, vi* to increase fivefold

quintuplés, -ées [kɛ̃typle] *nm/fpl* quintuplets, quins

quinzaine [kɛ̃zɛn] *nf*: **une ~ (de)** about fifteen, fifteen or so; **une ~ (de jours)** (*deux semaines*) a fortnight (*Brit*), two weeks; **~ publicitaire** *ou* **commerciale** (two-week) sale

quinze [kɛ̃z] *num* fifteen; **demain en ~ a** fortnight (*Brit*) *ou* two weeks tomorrow; **dans ~ jours** in a fortnight('s time) (*Brit*), in two weeks(' time)

quinzième [kɛ̃zjɛm] *num* fifteenth

quiproquo [kipʀɔko] *nm* (*méprise sur une personne*) mistake; (*malentendu sur un sujet*) misunderstanding; (*Théât*) (case of) mistaken identity

Quito [kito] *n* Quito

quittance [kitɑ̃s] *nf* (*reçu*) receipt; (*facture*) bill

quitte [kit] *adj*: **être ~ envers qn** to be no longer in sb's debt; (*fig*) to be quits with sb; **être ~ de** (*obligation*) to be clear of; **en être ~ à bon compte** to have got off lightly; **~ à faire** even if it means doing; **~ ou double** (*jeu*) double or quits; (*fig*): **c'est du ~ ou double** it's a big risk

quitter [kite] *vt* to leave; (*espoir, illusion*) to give up; (*vêtement*) to take off; **se quitter** (*couples, interlocuteurs*) to part; **ne quittez pas** (*au téléphone*) hold the line; **ne pas ~ qn d'une semelle** to stick to sb like glue

quitus [kitys] *nm* final discharge; **donner ~ à** to discharge

qui-vive [kiviv] *nm inv*: **être sur le ~** to be on the alert

quoi [kwa] *pron* (*interrogatif*) what; **~ de neuf** *ou* **de nouveau?** what's new *ou* the news?; **as-tu de ~ écrire?** have you anything to write with?; **il n'a pas de ~ se l'acheter** he can't afford it, he hasn't got the money to buy it; **il y a de ~ être fier** that's something to be proud of; **"il n'y a pas de ~"** "(please) don't mention it", "not at all"; **~ qu'il arrive** whatever happens; **~ qu'il en soit** be that as it may; **~ que ce soit** anything at all; **en ~ puis-je vous aider?** how can I help you?; **à ~ bon?** what's the use *ou* point?; **et puis ~ encore!** what(ever) next!; **~ faire?** what's to be done?; **sans ~** (*ou sinon*) otherwise

quoique [kwak(ə)] *conj* (al)though

quolibet [kɔlibɛ] *nm* gibe, jeer

quorum [kɔʀɔm] *nm* quorum

quota [kwɔta] *nm* quota

quote-part [kɔtpaʀ] *nf* share

quotidien, ne [kɔtidjɛ̃, -ɛn] *adj* (*journalier*) daily; (*banal*) ordinary, everyday ▷ *nm* (*journal*) daily (paper); (*vie quotidienne*) daily life, day-to-day existence; **les grands ~s** the big (national) dailies

quotidiennement [kɔtidjɛnmɑ̃] *adv* daily, every day

quotient [kɔsjɑ̃] *nm* (*Math*) quotient; **~ intellectuel (QI)** intelligence quotient (IQ)

quotité [kɔtite] *nf* (*Finance*) quota

Rr

R, r [ɛʀ] *nm inv* R, r ▷ *abr* = **route**; **rue**; **R comme Raoul** R for Robert (*Brit*) *ou* Roger (*US*)

rab [ʀab] (*fam*), **rabiot** [ʀabjo] *nm* extra, more

rabâcher [ʀabɑʃe] *vi* to harp on ▷ *vt* keep on repeating

rabais [ʀabɛ] *nm* reduction, discount; **au ~** at a reduction *ou* discount

rabaisser [ʀabese] *vt* (*rabattre*) to reduce; (*dénigrer*) to belittle

rabane [ʀaban] *nf* raffia (matting)

Rabat [ʀaba(t)] *n* Rabat

rabat [ʀaba] *vb voir* **rabattre** ▷ *nm* flap

rabat-joie [ʀabaʒwa] *nm/f inv* killjoy (*Brit*), spoilsport

rabatteur, -euse [ʀabatœʀ, -øz] *nm/f* (*de gibier*) beater; (*péj*) tout

rabattre [ʀabatʀ(ə)] *vt* (*couvercle, siège*) to pull down; (*col*) to turn down; (*couture*) to stitch down; (*gibier*) to drive; (*somme d'un prix*) to deduct, take off; (*orgueil, prétentions*) to humble; (*Tricot*) to decrease; **se rabattre** *vi* (*bords, couvercle*) to fall shut; (*véhicule, coureur*) to cut in; **se ~ sur** (*accepter*) to fall back on

rabattu, e [ʀabaty] *pp de* **rabattre** ▷ *adj* turned down

rabbin [ʀabɛ̃] *nm* rabbi

rabique [ʀabik] *adj* rabies *cpd*

râble [ʀɑbl(ə)] *nm* back; (*Culin*) saddle

râblé, e [ʀɑble] *adj* broad-backed, stocky

rabot [ʀabo] *nm* plane

raboter [ʀabɔte] *vt* to plane (down)

raboteux, -euse [ʀabɔtø, -øz] *adj* uneven, rough

rabougri, e [ʀabugʀi] *adj* stunted

rabrouer [ʀabʀue] *vt* to snub, rebuff

racaille [ʀakɑj] *nf* (*péj*) rabble, riffraff

raccommodage [ʀakɔmɔdaʒ] *nm* mending *no pl*, repairing *no pl*; darning *no pl*

raccommoder [ʀakɔmɔde] *vt* to mend, repair; (*chaussette etc*) to darn; (*fam: réconcilier: amis, ménage*) to bring together again; **se ~ (avec)** (*fam*) to patch it up (with)

raccompagner [ʀakɔ̃paɲe] *vt* to take *ou* see back

raccord [ʀakɔʀ] *nm* link; **~ de maçonnerie** pointing *no pl*; **~ de peinture** join; touch-up

raccordement [ʀakɔʀdəmɑ̃] *nm* joining up; connection

raccorder [ʀakɔʀde] *vt* to join (up), link up; (*pont etc*) to connect, link; **se ~ à** to join up with; (*fig: se rattacher à*) to tie in with; **~ au réseau du téléphone** to connect to the telephone service

raccourci [ʀakuʀsi] *nm* short cut; **en ~** in brief

raccourcir [ʀakuʀsiʀ] *vt* to shorten ▷ *vi* (*vêtement*) to shrink

raccroc [ʀakʀo]: **par ~** *adv* by chance

raccrocher [ʀakʀoʃe] *vt* (*tableau, vêtement*) to hang back up; (*récepteur*) to put down; (*fig: affaire*) to save ▷ *vi* (*Tél*) to hang up, ring off; **se ~ à** *vt* to cling to, hang on to; **ne raccrochez pas** (*Tél*) hold on, don't hang up

race [ʀas] *nf* race; (*d'animaux, fig: espèce*) breed; (*ascendance, origine*) stock, race; **de ~** *adj* purebred, pedigree

racé, e [ʀase] *adj* thoroughbred

rachat [ʀaʃa] *nm* buying; buying back; redemption; atonement

racheter [ʀaʃte] *vt* (*article perdu*) to buy another; (*davantage*): **~ du lait/trois œufs** to buy more milk/another three eggs *ou* three more eggs; (*après avoir vendu*) to buy back; (*d'occasion*) to buy; (*Comm: part, firme*) to buy up; (*: pension, rente*) to redeem; (*Rel: pécheur*) to redeem; (*: péché*) to atone for, expiate; (*mauvaise conduite, oubli, défaut*) to make up for; **se racheter** (*Rel*) to redeem o.s.; (*gén*) to make amends, make up for it

rachitique [ʀaʃitik] *adj* suffering from rickets; (*fig*) scraggy, scrawny

rachitisme [ʀaʃitism(ə)] *nm* rickets *sg*

racial, e, -aux [ʀasjal, -o] *adj* racial

racine [ʀasin] *nf* root; (*fig: attache*) roots *pl*; **~ carrée/cubique** square/cube root; **prendre ~** (*fig*) to take root; to put down roots

racisme [ʀasism(ə)] *nm* racism, racialism

raciste [ʀasist(ə)] *adj, nm/f* racist, racialist

racket [ʀakɛt] *nm* racketeering *no pl*

racketteur [ʀakɛtœʀ] *nm* racketeer

raclée [ʀɑkle] *nf* (*fam*) hiding, thrashing

raclement [ʀɑkləmɑ̃] *nm* (*bruit*) scraping (noise)

racler [ʀɑkle] *vt* (*os, plat*) to scrape; (*tache, boue*) to scrape off; (*fig: instrument*) to scrape on; (*chose: frotter contre*) to scrape (against)

raclette [ʀɑklɛt] *nf* (*Culin*) raclette (*Swiss cheese dish*)

racloir [ʀɑklwaʀ] *nm* (*outil*) scraper

racolage [ʀakɔlaʒ] *nm* soliciting; touting

racoler [ʀakɔle] *vt* (*attirer: prostituée*) to solicit; (: *parti, marchand*) to tout for; (*attraper*) to pick up

racoleur, -euse [ʀakɔlœʀ, -øz] *adj* (*péj*) cheap and alluring ▷ *nm* (*péj: de clients etc*) tout ▷ *nf* streetwalker

racontars [ʀakɔ̃taʀ] *nmpl* stories, gossip *sg*

raconter [ʀakɔ̃te] *vt*: ~ (**à qn**) (*décrire*) to relate (to sb), tell (sb) about; (*dire*) to tell (sb)

racorni, e [ʀakɔʀni] *adj* hard(ened)

racornir [ʀakɔʀniʀ] *vt* to harden

radar [ʀadaʀ] *nm* radar; **système** ~ radar system; **écran** ~ radar screen

rade [ʀad] *nf* (natural) harbour; **en** ~ **de Toulon** in Toulon harbour; **rester en** ~ (*fig*) to be left stranded

radeau, x [ʀado] *nm* raft; ~ **de sauvetage** life raft

radial, e, -aux [ʀadjal, -o] *adj* radial

radiant, e [ʀadjɑ̃, -ɑ̃t] *adj* radiant

radiateur [ʀadjatœʀ] *nm* radiator, heater; (*Auto*) radiator; ~ **électrique/à gaz** electric/gas heater *ou* fire

radiation [ʀadjɑsjɔ̃] *nf* (*d'un nom etc*) striking off *no pl*; (*Physique*) radiation

radical, e, -aux [ʀadikal, -o] *adj* radical ▷ *nm* (*Ling*) stem; (*Math*) root sign; (*Pol*) radical

radicalement [ʀadikalmɑ̃] *adv* radically, completely

radicaliser [ʀadikalize] *vt* (*durcir: opinions etc*) to harden; **se radicaliser** *vi* (*mouvement etc*) to become more radical

radicalisme [ʀadikalism(ə)] *nm* (*Pol*) radicalism

radier [ʀadje] *vt* to strike off

radiesthésie [ʀadjɛstezi] *nf* divination (by radiation)

radiesthésiste [ʀadjɛstezist(ə)] *nm/f* diviner

radieux, -euse [ʀadjø, -øz] *adj* (*visage, personne*) radiant; (*journée, soleil*) brilliant, glorious

radin, e [ʀadɛ̃, -in] *adj* (*fam*) stingy

radio [ʀadjo] *nf* radio; (*Méd*) X-ray ▷ *nm* (*personne*) radio operator; **à la** ~ on the radio; **avoir la** ~ to have a radio; **passer à la** ~ to be on the radio; **se faire faire une ~/une ~ des poumons** to have an X-ray/a chest X-ray

radio... [ʀadjo] *préfixe* radio...

radioactif, -ive [ʀadjoaktif, -iv] *adj* radioactive

radioactivité [ʀadjoaktivite] *nf* radioactivity

radioamateur [ʀadjoamatœʀ] *nm* (radio) ham

radiobalise [ʀadjobaliz] *nf* radio beacon

radiocassette [ʀadjokasɛt] *nf* cassette radio

radiodiffuser [ʀadjodifyze] *vt* to broadcast

radiodiffusion [ʀadjodifyzjɔ̃] *nf* (radio) broadcasting

radioélectrique [ʀadjoelɛktʀik] *adj* radio *cpd*

radiographie [ʀadjogʀafi] *nf* radiography; (*photo*) X-ray photograph, radiograph

radiographier [ʀadjogʀafje] *vt* to X-ray; **se faire** ~ to have an X-ray

radioguidage [ʀadjogidaʒ] *nm* (*Navig, Aviat*) radio control; (*Auto*) (broadcast of) traffic information

radioguider [ʀadjogide] *vt* (*Navig, Aviat*) to guide by radio, control by radio

radiologie [ʀadjolɔʒi] *nf* radiology

radiologique [ʀadjolɔʒik] *adj* radiological

radiologue [ʀadjolɔg] *nm/f* radiologist

radiophonique [ʀadjofɔnik] *adj*: **programme/ émission/jeu** ~ radio programme/broadcast/ game

radio-réveil [ʀadjoʀevɛj] *nm* clock radio

radioscopie [ʀadjoskɔpi] *nf* radioscopy

radio-taxi [ʀadjotaksi] *nm* radiotaxi

radiotélescope [ʀadjoteleskɔp] *nm* radiotelescope

radiotélévisé, e [ʀadjotelevize] *adj* broadcast on radio and television

radiothérapie [ʀadjoteʀapi] *nf* radiotherapy

radis [ʀadi] *nm* radish; ~ **noir** horseradish *no pl*

radium [ʀadjɔm] *nm* radium

radoter [ʀadote] *vi* to ramble on

radoub [ʀadu] *nm*: **bassin** *ou* **cale de** ~ dry dock

radouber [ʀadube] *vt* to repair, refit

radoucir [ʀadusiʀ]: **se radoucir** *vi* (*se réchauffer*) to become milder; (*se calmer*) to calm down; to soften

radoucissement [ʀadusismɑ̃] *nm* milder period, better weather

rafale [ʀafal] *nf* (*vent*) gust (of wind); (*de balles, d'applaudissements*) burst; ~ **de mitrailleuse** burst of machine-gun fire

raffermir [ʀafɛʀmiʀ] *vt*, **se raffermir** *vi* (*tissus, muscle*) to firm up; (*fig*) to strengthen

raffermissement [ʀafɛʀmismɑ̃] *nm* (*fig*) strengthening

raffinage [ʀafinaʒ] *nm* refining

raffiné, e [ʀafine] *adj* refined

raffinement [ʀafinmɑ̃] *nm* refinement

raffiner [ʀafine] *vt* to refine

raffinerie [ʀafinʀi] *nf* refinery

raffoler [ʀafole]: ~ **de** *vt* to be very keen on

raffut [ʀafy] *nm* (*fam*) row, racket

rafiot [ʀafjo] *nm* tub

rafistoler [ʀafistole] *vt* (*fam*) to patch up

rafle [ʀafl(ə)] *nf* (*de police*) roundup, raid

rafler [ʀafle] *vt* (*fam*) to swipe, nick

rafraîchir [ʀafʀeʃiʀ] *vt* (*atmosphère, température*) to cool (down); (*aussi*: **mettre à rafraîchir**) to chill; (*air, eau*) to freshen up; (: *boisson*) to refresh; (*fig: rénover*) to brighten up ▷ *vi*: **mettre du vin/une boisson à** ~ to chill wine/a drink; **se rafraîchir** to grow cooler; to freshen up; (*personne: en buvant etc*) to refresh o.s.; ~ **la mémoire à qn** to refresh sb's memory

rafraîchissant, e [ʀafʀeʃisɑ̃, -ɑ̃t] *adj* refreshing

rafraîchissement [ʀafʀeʃismɑ̃] *nm* cooling; (*boisson*) cool drink; **rafraîchissements** *nmpl* (*boissons, fruits etc*) refreshments

ragaillardir [ʀagajaʀdiʀ] *vt* (*fam*) to perk *ou* buck up

rage [ʀaʒ] *nf* (*Méd*): **la** ~ rabies; (*fureur*) rage, fury; **faire ~** to rage; **~ de dents** (raging) toothache

rager [ʀaʒe] *vi* to fume (with rage); **faire ~ qn** to enrage sb, get sb mad

rageur, -euse [ʀaʒœʀ, -øz] *adj* snarling; ill-tempered

raglan [ʀaglɑ̃] *adj inv* raglan

ragot [ʀago] *nm* (*fam*) malicious gossip *no pl*

ragoût [ʀagu] *nm* (*plat*) stew

ragoûtant, e [ʀagutɑ̃, -ɑ̃t] *adj*: **peu ~** unpalatable

rai [ʀɛ] *nm*: **un ~ de soleil/lumière** a shaft of sunlight/light

raid [ʀɛd] *nm* (*Mil*) raid; (*attaque aérienne*) air raid; (*Sport*) long-distance trek

raide [ʀɛd] *adj* (*tendu*) taut, tight; (*escarpé*) steep; (*droit: cheveux*) straight; (*ankylosé, dur, guindé*) stiff; (*fam: cher*) steep, stiff; (: *sans argent*) flat broke; (*osé, licencieux*) daring ▷ *adv* (*en pente*) steeply; **~ mort** stone dead

raideur [ʀɛdœʀ] *nf* steepness; stiffness

raidir [ʀediʀ] *vt* (*muscles*) to stiffen; (*câble*) to pull taut, tighten; **se raidir** *vi* to stiffen; to become taut; (*personne: se crisper*) to tense up; (: *devenir intransigeant*) to harden

raidissement [ʀedismɑ̃] *nm* stiffening; tightening; hardening

raie [ʀɛ] *nf* (*Zool*) skate, ray; (*rayure*) stripe; (*des cheveux*) parting

raifort [ʀɛfɔʀ] *nm* horseradish

rail [ʀaj] *nm* (*barre d'acier*) rail; (*chemins de fer*) railways *pl* (Brit), railroads *pl* (US); **les ~s** (*la voie ferrée*) the rails, the track *sg*; **par ~** by rail; **~ conducteur** live *ou* conductor rail

railler [ʀaje] *vt* to scoff at, jeer at

raillerie [ʀajʀi] *nf* mockery

railleur, -euse [ʀajœʀ, -øz] *adj* mocking

rainurage [ʀenyʀaʒ] *nm* (*Auto*) uneven road surface

rainure [ʀenyʀ] *nf* groove; slot

rais [ʀɛ] *nm inv* = **rai**

raisin [ʀɛzɛ̃] *nm* (*aussi*: **raisins**) grapes *pl*; (*variété*): **~ blanc/noir** white (*ou* green)/black grape; **~ muscat** muscat grape; **~s secs** raisins

raison [ʀɛzɔ̃] *nf* reason; **avoir ~** to be right; **donner ~ à qn** (*personne*) to agree with sb; (*fait*) to prove sb right; **avoir ~ de qn/qch** to get the better of sb/sth; **se faire une ~** to learn to live with it; **perdre la ~** to become insane; (*fig*) to take leave of one's senses; **recouvrer la ~** to come to one's senses; **ramener qn à la ~** to make sb see sense; **demander ~ à qn de** (*affront etc*) to demand satisfaction from sb for; **entendre ~** to listen to reason, see reason; **plus que de ~** too much, more than is reasonable; **~ de plus** all the more reason; **à plus forte ~** all the more so; **en ~ de** (*à cause de*) because of; (*à proportion de*) in proportion to; **à ~ de** at the rate of; **~ d'État** reason of state; **~ d'être** raison d'être; **~ sociale** corporate name

raisonnable [ʀɛzɔnabl(ə)] *adj* reasonable, sensible

raisonnablement [ʀɛzɔnabləmɑ̃] *adv* reasonably

raisonné, e [ʀɛzɔne] *adj* reasoned

raisonnement [ʀɛzɔnmɑ̃] *nm* reasoning; arguing; argument

raisonner [ʀɛzɔne] *vi* (*penser*) to reason; (*argumenter, discuter*) to argue ▷ *vt* (*personne*) to reason with; (*attitude: justifier*) to reason out; **se raisonner** to reason with oneself

raisonneur, -euse [ʀɛzɔnœʀ, -øz] *adj* (*péj*) quibbling

rajeunir [ʀaʒœniʀ] *vt* (*coiffure, robe*): **~ qn** to make sb look younger; (*cure etc*) to rejuvenate; (*fig: rafraîchir*) to brighten up; (: *moderniser*) to give a new look to; (: *en recrutant*) to inject new blood into ▷ *vi* (*personne*) to become (*ou* look) younger; (*entreprise, quartier*) to be modernized

rajout [ʀaʒu] *nm* addition

rajouter [ʀaʒute] *vt* (*commentaire*) to add; **~ du sel/un œuf** to add some more salt/another egg; **~ que** to add that; **en ~** to lay it on thick

rajustement [ʀaʒystəmɑ̃] *nm* adjustment

rajuster [ʀaʒyste] *vt* (*vêtement*) to straighten, tidy; (*salaires*) to adjust; (*machine*) to readjust; **se rajuster** to tidy *ou* straighten o.s. up

râle [ʀɑl] *nm* groan; **~ d'agonie** death rattle

ralenti [ʀalɑ̃ti] *nm*: **au ~** (*Ciné*) in slow motion; (*fig*) at a slower pace; **tourner au ~** (*Auto*) to tick over, idle

ralentir [ʀalɑ̃tiʀ] *vt, vi*, **se ralentir** *vi* to slow down

ralentissement [ʀalɑ̃tismɑ̃] *nm* slowing down

râler [ʀɑle] *vi* to groan; (*fam*) to grouse, moan (and groan)

ralliement [ʀalimɑ̃] *nm* (*rassemblement*) rallying; (*adhésion: à une cause, une opinion*) winning over; **point/signe de ~** rallying point/sign

rallier [ʀalje] *vt* (*rassembler*) to rally; (*rejoindre*) to rejoin; (*gagner à sa cause*) to win over; **se ~ à** (*avis*) to come over *ou* round to

rallonge [ʀalɔ̃ʒ] *nf* (*de table*) (extra) leaf; (*argent etc*) extra *no pl*; (*Élec*) extension (cable *ou* flex); (*fig: de crédit etc*) extension

rallonger [ʀalɔ̃ʒe] *vt* to lengthen

rallumer [ʀalyme] *vt* to light up again, relight; (*fig*) to revive; **se rallumer** *vi* (*lumière*) to come on again

rallye [ʀali] *nm* rally; (*Pol*) march

ramages [ʀamaʒ] *nmpl* (*dessin*) leaf pattern *sg*; (*chants*) songs

ramassage [ʀamasaʒ] *nm*: **~ scolaire** school bus service

ramassé, e [ʀamase] *adj* (*trapu*) squat, stocky; (*concis: expression etc*) compact

ramasse-miettes [ʀamasmjɛt] *nm inv* table-tidy

ramasser [ʀamase] *vt* (*objet tombé ou par terre: fam*) to pick up; (*recueillir*) to collect; (*récolter*) to gather; (: *pommes de terre*) to lift; **se ramasser** *vi* (*sur soi-même*) to huddle up; to crouch

ramasseur, -euse [ʀamasœʀ, -øz] *nm/f*: **~ de balles** ballboy/girl

ramassis [ʀamasi] nm (péj: de gens) bunch; (: de choses) jumble

rambarde [ʀɑ̃baʀd(ə)] nf guardrail

rame [ʀam] nf (aviron) oar; (de métro) train; (de papier) ream; ~ **de haricots** bean support; **faire force de ~s** to row hard

rameau, x [ʀamo] nm (small) branch; (fig) branch; **les R~x** (Rel) Palm Sunday sg

ramener [ʀamne] vt to bring back; (reconduire) to take back; (rabattre: couverture, visière): ~ **qch sur** to pull sth back over; ~ **qch à** (réduire à, Math) to reduce sth to; ~ **qn à la vie/raison** to bring sb back to life/bring sb to his (ou her) senses; **se ramener** vi (fam) to roll ou turn up; **se ~ à** (se réduire à) to come ou boil down to

ramequin [ʀamkɛ̃] nm ramekin

ramer [ʀame] vi to row

rameur, -euse [ʀamœʀ, -øz] nm/f rower

rameuter [ʀamøte] vt to gather together

ramier [ʀamje] nm: **(pigeon)** ~ woodpigeon

ramification [ʀamifikasjɔ̃] nf ramification

ramifier [ʀamifje]: **se ramifier** vi (tige, secte, réseau): **se ~ (en)** to branch out (into); (veines, nerfs) to ramify

ramolli, e [ʀamɔli] adj soft

ramollir [ʀamɔliʀ] vt to soften; **se ramollir** vi (os, tissus) to get (ou go) soft; (beurre, asphalte) to soften

ramonage [ʀamɔnaʒ] nm (chimney-)sweeping

ramoner [ʀamɔne] vt (cheminée) to sweep; (pipe) to clean

ramoneur [ʀamɔnœʀ] nm (chimney) sweep

rampe [ʀɑ̃p] nf (d'escalier) banister(s pl); (dans un garage, d'un terrain) ramp; (Théât): **la ~** the footlights pl; (lampes: lumineuse, de balisage) floodlights pl; **passer la ~** (toucher le public) to get across to the audience; ~ **de lancement** launching pad

ramper [ʀɑ̃pe] vi (reptile, animal) to crawl; (plante) to creep

rancard [ʀɑ̃kaʀ] nm (fam) date; tip

rancart [ʀɑ̃kaʀ] nm: **mettre au ~** (article, projet) to scrap; (personne) to put on the scrapheap

rance [ʀɑ̃s] adj rancid

rancir [ʀɑ̃siʀ] vi to go off, go rancid

rancœur [ʀɑ̃kœʀ] nf rancour (Brit), rancor (US), resentment

rançon [ʀɑ̃sɔ̃] nf ransom; (fig): **la ~ du succès** etc the price of success etc

rançonner [ʀɑ̃sɔne] vt to hold to ransom

rancune [ʀɑ̃kyn] nf grudge, rancour (Brit), rancor (US); **garder ~ à qn (de qch)** to bear sb a grudge (for sth); **sans ~!** no hard feelings!

rancunier, -ière [ʀɑ̃kynje, -jɛʀ] adj vindictive, spiteful

randonnée [ʀɑ̃dɔne] nf ride; (à pied) walk, ramble; hike, hiking no pl

randonneur, -euse [ʀɑ̃dɔnœʀ, -øz] nm/f hiker

rang [ʀɑ̃] nm (rangée) row; (de perles) row, string, rope; (grade, condition sociale, classement) rank; **rangs** nmpl (Mil) ranks; **se mettre en ~s/sur un ~** to get into ou form rows/a line; **sur trois ~s** (lined up) three deep; **se mettre en ~s par quatre** to form fours ou rows of four; **se mettre sur les ~s** (fig) to get into the running; **au premier ~** in the first row; (fig) ranking first; **rentrer dans le ~** to get into line; **au ~ de** (au nombre de) among (the ranks of); **avoir ~ de** to hold the rank of

rangé, e [ʀɑ̃ʒe] adj (sérieux) orderly, steady

rangée [ʀɑ̃ʒe] nf row

rangement [ʀɑ̃ʒmɑ̃] nm tidying-up, putting-away; **faire des ~s** to tidy up

ranger [ʀɑ̃ʒe] vt (classer, grouper) to order, arrange; (mettre à sa place) to put away; (voiture dans la rue) to park; (mettre de l'ordre dans) to tidy up; (arranger, disposer: en cercle etc) to arrange; (fig: classer): ~ **qn/qch parmi** to rank sb/sth among; **se ranger** vi (se placer, se disposer: autour d'une table etc) to take one's place, sit round; (véhicule, conducteur: s'écarter) to pull over; (: s'arrêter) to pull in; (piéton) to step aside; (s'assagir) to settle down; **se ~ à** (avis) to come round to, fall in with

ranimer [ʀanime] vt (personne évanouie) to bring round; (revigorer: forces, courage) to restore; (réconforter: troupes etc) to kindle new life in; (douleur, souvenir) to revive; (feu) to rekindle

rap [ʀap] nm rap (music)

rapace [ʀapas] nm bird of prey ▷ adj (péj) rapacious, grasping; ~ **diurne/nocturne** diurnal/nocturnal bird of prey

rapatrié, e [ʀapatʀije] nm/f repatriate (esp French North African settler)

rapatriement [ʀapatʀimɑ̃] nm repatriation

rapatrier [ʀapatʀije] vt to repatriate; (capitaux) to bring (back) into the country

râpe [ʀɑp] nf (Culin) grater; (à bois) rasp

râpé, e [ʀɑpe] adj (tissu) threadbare; (Culin) grated

râper [ʀɑpe] vt (Culin) to grate; (gratter, râcler) to rasp

rapetasser [ʀaptase] vt (fam) to patch up

rapetisser [ʀaptise] vt: ~ **qch** to shorten sth; to make sth look smaller ▷ vi, **se rapetisser** vi to shrink

râpeux, -euse [ʀɑpø, -øz] adj rough

raphia [ʀafja] nm raffia

rapide [ʀapid] adj fast; (prompt) quick; (intelligence) quick ▷ nm express (train); (de cours d'eau) rapid

rapidement [ʀapidmɑ̃] adv fast; quickly

rapidité [ʀapidite] nf speed; quickness

rapiécer [ʀapjese] vt to patch

rappel [ʀapɛl] nm (d'un ambassadeur, Mil) recall; (Théât) curtain call; (Méd: vaccination) booster; (Admin: de salaire) back pay no pl; (d'une aventure, d'un nom) reminder; (de limitation de vitesse: sur écriteau) speed limit sign (reminder); (Tech) return; (Navig) sitting out; (Alpinisme: aussi: **rappel de corde**) abseiling no pl, roping down no pl; abseil; ~ **à l'ordre** call to order

rappeler [ʀaple] vt (pour faire revenir, retéléphoner) to call back; (ambassadeur, Mil) to recall; (acteur) to call back (onto the stage); (faire se souvenir): ~

qch à qn to remind sb of sth; **se rappeler** *vt* (*se souvenir de*) to remember, recall; **~ qn à la vie** to bring sb back to life; **~ qn à la décence** to recall sb to a sense of decency; **ça rappelle la Provence** it's reminiscent of Provence, it reminds you of Provence; **se ~ que...** to remember that...

rappelle *etc* [Rapɛl] *vb voir* **rappeler**

rappliquer [Raplike] *vi* (*fam*) to turn up

rapport [RapɔR] *nm* (*compte rendu*) report; (*profit*) yield, return; revenue; (*lien, analogie*) relationship; (*corrélation*) connection; (*proportion*: *Math, Tech*) ratio; **rapports** *nmpl* (*entre personnes, pays*) relations; **avoir ~ à** to have something to do with, concern; **être en ~ avec** (*idée de corrélation*) to be related to; **être/se mettre en ~ avec qn** to be/get in touch with sb; **par ~ à** (*comparé à*) in relation to; (*à propos de*) with regard to; **sous le ~ de** from the point of view of; **sous tous (les) ~s** in all respects; **~s (sexuels)** (sexual) intercourse *sg*; **~ qualité-prix** value (for money)

rapporté, e [RapɔRte] *adj*: **pièce ~e** (*Couture*) patch

rapporter [RapɔRte] *vt* (*rendre, ramener*) to bring back; (*apporter davantage*) to bring more; (*Couture*) to sew on; (*investissement*) to yield; (: *activité*) to bring in; (*relater*) to report; (*Jur*: *annuler*) to revoke ▷ *vi* (*investissement*) to give a good return *ou* yield; (*activité*) to be very profitable; (*péj*: *moucharder*) to tell; **~ qch à** (*fig*: *rattacher*) to relate sth to; **se ~ à** (*correspondre à*) to relate to; **s'en ~ à** to rely on

rapporteur, -euse [RapɔRtœR, -øz] *nm/f* (*de procès, commission*) reporter; (*péj*) telltale ▷ *nm* (*Géom*) protractor

rapproché, e [RapRɔʃe] *adj* (*proche*) near, close at hand; **~s** (*l'un de l'autre*) at close intervals

rapprochement [RapRɔʃmɑ̃] *nm* (*réconciliation*: *de nations, familles*) reconciliation; (*analogie, rapport*) parallel

rapprocher [RapRɔʃe] *vt* (*chaise d'une table*): **~ qch (de)** to bring sth closer (to); (*deux objets*) to bring closer together; (*réunir*) to bring together; (*comparer*) to establish a parallel between; **se rapprocher** *vi* to draw closer *ou* nearer; (*fig*: *familles, pays*) to come together; to come closer together; **se ~ de** to come closer to; (*présenter une analogie avec*) to be close to

rapt [Rapt] *nm* abduction

raquette [Rakɛt] *nf* (*de tennis*) racket; (*de ping-pong*) bat; (*à neige*) snowshoe

rare [RaR] *adj* rare; (*main-d'œuvre, denrées*) scarce; (*cheveux, herbe*) sparse; **il est ~ que** it's rare that, it's unusual that; **se faire ~** to become scarce; (*fig*: *personne*) to make oneself scarce

raréfaction [RaRefaksjɔ̃] *nf* scarcity; (*de l'air*) rarefaction

raréfier [RaRefje]: **se raréfier** *vi* to grow scarce; (*air*) to rarefy

rarement [RaRmɑ̃] *adv* rarely, seldom

rareté [RaRte] *nf voir* **rare** rarity; scarcity

rarissime [RaRisim] *adj* extremely rare

RAS *abr* = **rien à signaler**

ras, e [Rɑ, Rɑz] *adj* (*tête, cheveux*) close-cropped; (*poil, herbe*) short; (*mesure, cuillère*) level ▷ *adv* short; **faire table ~e** to make a clean sweep; **en ~e campagne** in open country; **à ~ bords** to the brim; **au ~ de** level with; **en avoir ~ le bol** (*fam*) to be fed up; **~ du cou** *adj* (*pull, robe*) crew-neck

rasade [Razad] *nf* glassful

rasant, e [Razɑ̃, ɑ̃t] *adj* (*Mil*: *balle, tir*) grazing; (*fam*) boring

rascasse [Raskas] *nf* (*Zool*) scorpion fish

rasé, e [Raze] *adj*: **~ de frais** freshly shaven; **~ de près** close-shaven

rase-mottes [Razmɔt] *nm inv*: **faire du ~** to hedgehop; **vol en ~** hedgehopping

raser [Raze] *vt* (*barbe, cheveux*) to shave off; (*menton, personne*) to shave; (*fam*: *ennuyer*) to bore; (*démolir*) to raze (to the ground); (*frôler*) to graze, skim; **se raser** to shave; (*fam*) to be bored (to tears)

rasoir [RazwaR] *nm* razor; **~ électrique** electric shaver *ou* razor; **~ mécanique** *ou* **de sûreté** safety razor

rassasier [Rasazje] *vt* to satisfy; **être rassasié** (*dégoûté*) to be sated; to have had more than enough

rassemblement [Rasɑ̃bləmɑ̃] *nm* (*groupe*) gathering; (*Pol*) union; association; (*Mil*): **le ~** parade

rassembler [Rasɑ̃ble] *vt* (*réunir*) to assemble, gather; (*regrouper, amasser*) to gather together, collect; **se rassembler** *vi* to gather; **~ ses idées/ses esprits/son courage** to collect one's thoughts/gather one's wits/screw up one's courage

rasseoir [RaswaR]: **se rasseoir** *vi* to sit down again

rassir [RasiR] *vi* to go stale

rassis, e [Rasi, -iz] *adj* (*pain*) stale

rassurant, e [RasyRɑ̃, -ɑ̃t] *adj* (*nouvelles etc*) reassuring

rassuré, e [RasyRe] *adj*: **ne pas être très ~** to be rather ill at ease

rassurer [RasyRe] *vt* to reassure; **se rassurer** to be reassured; **rassure-toi** don't worry

rat [Ra] *nm* rat; **~ d'hôtel** hotel thief; **~ musqué** muskrat

ratatiné, e [Ratatine] *adj* shrivelled (up), wrinkled

ratatiner [Ratatine] *vt* to shrivel; (*peau*) to wrinkle; **se ratatiner** *vi* to shrivel; to become wrinkled

ratatouille [Ratatuj] *nf* (*Culin*) ratatouille

rate [Rat] *nf* female rat; (*Anat*) spleen

raté, e [Rate] *adj* (*tentative*) unsuccessful, failed ▷ *nm/f* failure ▷ *nm* misfiring *no pl*

râteau, x [Rɑto] *nm* rake

râtelier [Rɑtəlje] *nm* rack; (*fam*) false teeth *pl*

rater [Rate] *vi* (*ne pas partir*: *coup de feu*) to fail to go off; (*affaire, projet etc*) to go wrong, fail ▷ *vt* (*cible, train, occasion*) to miss; (*démonstration, plat*) to spoil; (*examen*) to fail; ~ **son coup** to fail, not to bring it off

raticide [Ratisid] *nm* rat poison

ratification [Ratifikasjɔ̃] *nf* ratification

ratifier [Ratifje] *vt* to ratify

ratio [Rasjo] *nm* ratio

ration [Rɑsjɔ̃] *nf* ration; (*fig*) share; ~ **alimentaire** food intake

rationalisation [Rasjɔnalizasjɔ̃] *nf* rationalization

rationaliser [Rasjɔnalize] *vt* to rationalize

rationnel, le [Rasjɔnɛl] *adj* rational

rationnellement [Rasjɔnɛlmɑ̃] *adv* rationally

rationnement [Rasjɔnmɑ̃] *nm* rationing; **ticket de** ~ ration coupon

rationner [Rasjɔne] *vt* to ration; (*personne*) to put on rations; **se rationner** to ration o.s.

ratisser [Ratise] *vt* (*allée*) to rake; (*feuilles*) to rake up; (*armée, police*) to comb; ~ **large** to cast one's net wide

raton [Ratɔ̃] *nm*: ~ **laveur** raccoon

RATP *sigle f* (= *Régie autonome des transports parisiens*) Paris transport authority

rattacher [Rataʃe] *vt* (*animal, cheveux*) to tie up again; (*incorporer: Admin etc*): ~ **qch à** to join sth to, unite sth with; (*fig: relier*): ~ **qch à** to link sth with, relate sth to; (: *lier*): ~ **qn à** to bind *ou* tie sb to; **se** ~ **à** (*fig: avoir un lien avec*) to be linked (*ou* connected) with

rattrapage [RatRapaʒ] *nm* (*Scol*) remedial classes *pl*; (*Écon*) catching up

rattraper [RatRape] *vt* (*fugitif*) to recapture; (*retenir, empêcher de tomber*) to catch (hold of); (*atteindre, rejoindre*) to catch up with; (*réparer: erreur*) to make up for; **se rattraper** *vi* (*regagner: du temps*) to make up for lost time; (: *de l'argent etc*) to make good one's losses; (*réparer une gaffe etc*) to make up for it; **se** ~ **(à)** (*se raccrocher*) to stop o.s. falling (by catching hold of); ~ **son retard/le temps perdu** to make up (for) lost time

rature [RatyR] *nf* deletion, erasure

raturer [RatyRe] *vt* to cross out, delete, erase

rauque [Rok] *adj* raucous; hoarse

ravagé, e [Ravaʒe] *adj* (*visage*) harrowed

ravager [Ravaʒe] *vt* to devastate, ravage

ravages [Ravaʒ] *nmpl* ravages; **faire des** ~ to wreak havoc; (*fig: séducteur*) to break hearts

ravalement [Ravalmɑ̃] *nm* restoration

ravaler [Ravale] *vt* (*mur, façade*) to restore; (*déprécier*) to lower; (*avaler de nouveau*) to swallow again; ~ **sa colère/son dégoût** to stifle one's anger/swallow one's distaste

ravauder [Ravode] *vt* to repair, mend

rave [Rav] *nf* (*Bot*) rape

ravi, e [Ravi] *adj* delighted; **être** ~ **de/que** to be delighted with/that

ravier [Ravje] *nm* hors d'œuvre dish

ravigote [Ravigɔt] *adj*: **sauce** ~ oil and vinegar dressing with shallots

ravigoter [Ravigɔte] *vt* (*fam*) to buck up

ravin [Ravɛ̃] *nm* gully, ravine

raviner [Ravine] *vt* to furrow, gully

ravioli [Ravjɔli] *nmpl* ravioli *sg*

ravir [RaviR] *vt* (*enchanter*) to delight; (*enlever*): ~ **qch à qn** to rob sb of sth; **à** ~ *adv* delightfully, beautifully; **être beau à** ~ to be ravishingly beautiful

raviser [Ravize]: **se raviser** *vi* to change one's mind

ravissant, e [Ravisɑ̃, -ɑ̃t] *adj* delightful

ravissement [Ravismɑ̃] *nm* (*enchantement, délice*) rapture

ravisseur, -euse [RavisœR, -øz] *nm/f* abductor, kidnapper

ravitaillement [Ravitajmɑ̃] *nm* resupplying; refuelling; (*provisions*) supplies *pl*; **aller au** ~ to go for fresh supplies; ~ **en vol** (*Aviat*) in-flight refuelling

ravitailler [Ravitaje] *vt* to resupply; (*véhicule*) to refuel; **se ravitailler** *vi* to get fresh supplies

raviver [Ravive] *vt* (*feu*) to rekindle, revive; (*douleur*) to revive; (*couleurs*) to brighten up

ravoir [RavwaR] *vt* to get back

rayé, e [Reje] *adj* (*à rayures*) striped; (*éraflé*) scratched

rayer [Reje] *vt* (*érafler*) to scratch; (*barrer*) to cross *ou* score out; (*d'une liste: radier*) to cross *ou* strike off

rayon [Rɛjɔ̃] *nm* (*de soleil etc*) ray; (*Géom*) radius; (*de roue*) spoke; (*étagère*) shelf; (*de grand magasin*) department; (*fig: domaine*) responsibility, concern; (*de ruche*) (honey)comb; **dans un** ~ **de** within a radius of; **rayons** *nmpl* (*radiothérapie*) radiation; ~ **d'action** range; ~ **de braquage** (*Auto*) turning circle; ~ **laser** laser beam; ~ **de soleil** sunbeam, ray of sunlight *ou* sunshine; ~**s X** X-rays

rayonnage [Rɛjɔnaʒ] *nm* set of shelves

rayonnant, e [Rɛjɔnɑ̃, -ɑ̃t] *adj* radiant

rayonne [Rɛjɔn] *nf* rayon

rayonnement [Rɛjɔnmɑ̃] *nm* radiation; (*fig: éclat*) radiance; (: *influence*) influence

rayonner [Rɛjɔne] *vi* (*chaleur, énergie*) to radiate; (*fig: émotion*) to shine forth; (: *visage*) to be radiant; (*avenues, axes*) to radiate; (*touriste*) to go touring (*from one base*)

rayure [RejyR] *nf* (*motif*) stripe; (*éraflure*) scratch; (*rainure, d'un fusil*) groove; **à** ~**s** striped

raz-de-marée [Radmare] *nm inv* tidal wave

razzia [Razja] *nf* raid, foray

RBE *sigle m* (= *revenu brut d'exploitation*) gross profit (*of a farm*)

R-D *sigle f* (= *Recherche-Développement*) R & D

RDA *sigle f* (= *République démocratique allemande*) GDR

rdc *abr* = **rez-de-chaussée**

ré [Re] *nm* (*Mus*) D; (*en chantant la gamme*) re

réabonnement [Reabɔnmɑ̃] *nm* renewal of subscription

réabonner [Reabɔne] *vt*: ~ **qn à** to renew sb's subscription to; **se** ~ **(à)** to renew one's subscription (to)

réac [Reak] *adj, nm/f* (*fam*: = *réactionnaire*)

reactionary

réacteur [ʀeaktœʀ] *nm* jet engine; **~ nucléaire** nuclear reactor

réactif [ʀeaktif] *nm* reagent

réaction [ʀeaksjɔ̃] *nf* reaction; **par ~** jet-propelled; **avion/moteur à ~** jet (plane)/jet engine; **~ en chaîne** chain reaction

réactionnaire [ʀeaksjɔnɛʀ] *adj, nm/f* reactionary

réactualiser [ʀeaktɥalize] *vt* to update, bring up to date

réadaptation [ʀeadaptɑsjɔ̃] *nf* readjustment; rehabilitation

réadapter [ʀeadapte] *vt* to readjust; (*Méd*) to rehabilitate; **se ~ (à)** to readjust (to)

réaffirmer [ʀeafiʀme] *vt* to reaffirm, reassert

réagir [ʀeaʒiʀ] *vi* to react

réajuster [ʀeaʒyste] *vt* = **rajuster**

réalisable [ʀealizabl(ə)] *adj* (*projet, plan*) feasible; (*Comm: valeur*) realizable

réalisateur, -trice [ʀealizatœʀ, -tʀis] *nm/f* (*TV, Ciné*) director

réalisation [ʀealizɑsjɔ̃] *nf* carrying out; realization; fulfilment; achievement; production; (*œuvre*) production, work; (*création*) creation

réaliser [ʀealize] *vt* (*projet, opération*) to carry out, realize; (*rêve, souhait*) to realize, fulfil; (*exploit*) to achieve; (*achat, vente*) to make; (*film*) to produce; (*se rendre compte de, Comm: bien, capital*) to realize; **se réaliser** *vi* to be realized

réalisme [ʀealism(ə)] *nm* realism

réaliste [ʀealist(ə)] *adj* realistic; (*peintre, roman*) realist ▷ *nm/f* realist

réalité [ʀealite] *nf* reality; **en ~** in (actual) fact; **dans la ~** in reality; **~ virtuelle** virtual reality

réanimation [ʀeanimɑsjɔ̃] *nf* resuscitation; **service de ~** intensive care unit

réanimer [ʀeanime] *vt* (*Méd*) to resuscitate

réapparaître [ʀeapaʀɛtʀ(ə)] *vi* to reappear

réapparition [ʀeapaʀisjɔ̃] *nf* reappearance

réapprovisionner [ʀeapʀɔvizjɔne] *vt* (*magasin*) to restock; **se ~ (en)** to restock (with)

réarmement [ʀeaʀməmɑ̃] *nm* rearmament

réarmer [ʀeaʀme] *vt* (*arme*) to reload ▷ *vi* (*état*) to rearm

réassortiment [ʀeasɔʀtimɑ̃] *nm* (*Comm*) restocking

réassortir [ʀeasɔʀtiʀ] *vt* to match up

réassurance [ʀeasyʀɑ̃s] *nf* reinsurance

réassurer [ʀeasyʀe] *vt* to reinsure

rebaptiser [ʀəbatize] *vt* (*rue*) to rename

rébarbatif, -ive [ʀebaʀbatif, -iv] *adj* forbidding; (*style*) off-putting (*Brit*), crabbed

rebattre [ʀəbatʀ(ə)] *vt*: **~ les oreilles à qn de qch** to keep harping on to sb about sth

rebattu, e [ʀəbaty] *pp de* **rebattre** ▷ *adj* hackneyed

rebelle [ʀəbɛl] *nm/f* rebel ▷ *adj* (*troupes*) rebel; (*enfant*) rebellious; (*mèche etc*) unruly; **~ à qch** unamenable to sth; **~ à faire** unwilling to do

rebeller [ʀəbele]: **se rebeller** *vi* to rebel

rébellion [ʀebeljɔ̃] *nf* rebellion; (*rebelles*) rebel forces *pl*

rebiffer [ʀəbife]: **se rebiffer** *vr* to fight back

reboisement [ʀəbwazmɑ̃] *nm* reafforestation

reboiser [ʀəbwaze] *vt* to replant with trees, reafforest

rebond [ʀəbɔ̃] *nm* (*voir rebondir*) bounce; rebound

rebondi, e [ʀəbɔ̃di] *adj* (*ventre*) rounded; (*joues*) chubby, well-rounded

rebondir [ʀəbɔ̃diʀ] *vi* (*ballon: au sol*) to bounce; (*: contre un mur*) to rebound; (*fig: procès, action, conversation*) to get moving again, be suddenly revived

rebondissement [ʀəbɔ̃dismɑ̃] *nm* new development

rebord [ʀəbɔʀ] *nm* edge

reboucher [ʀəbuʃe] *vt* (*flacon*) to put the stopper (*ou* top) back on, recork; (*trou*) to stop up

rebours [ʀəbuʀ]: **à ~** *adv* the wrong way

rebouteux, -euse [ʀəbutø, -øz] *nm/f* (*péj*) bonesetter

reboutonner [ʀəbutɔne] *vt* (*vêtement*) to button up (again)

rebrousse-poil [ʀəbʀuspwal]: **à ~** *adv* the wrong way

rebrousser [ʀəbʀuse] *vt* (*cheveux, poils*) to brush back, brush up; **~ chemin** to turn back

rebuffade [ʀəbyfad] *nf* rebuff

rébus [ʀebys] *nm inv* (*jeu d'esprit*) rebus; (*fig*) puzzle

rebut [ʀəby] *nm*: **mettre au ~** to scrap, discard

rebutant, e [ʀəbytɑ̃, -ɑ̃t] *adj* (*travail, démarche*) off-putting, disagreeable

rebuter [ʀəbyte] *vt* to put off

récalcitrant, e [ʀekalsitʀɑ̃, -ɑ̃t] *adj* refractory, recalcitrant

recaler [ʀəkale] *vt* (*Scol*) to fail

récapitulatif, -ive [ʀekapitylatif, -iv] *adj* (*liste, tableau*) summary *cpd*, that sums up

récapituler [ʀekapityle] *vt* to recapitulate; (*résumer*) to sum up

recel [ʀəsɛl] *nm* receiving (stolen goods)

receler [ʀəsəle] *vt* (*produit d'un vol*) to receive; (*malfaiteur*) to harbour; (*fig*) to conceal

receleur, -euse [ʀəsəlœʀ, -øz] *nm/f* receiver

récemment [ʀesamɑ̃] *adv* recently

recensement [ʀəsɑ̃smɑ̃] *nm* census; inventory

recenser [ʀəsɑ̃se] *vt* (*population*) to take a census of; (*inventorier*) to make an inventory of; (*dénombrer*) to list

récent, e [ʀesɑ̃, -ɑ̃t] *adj* recent

récépissé [ʀesepise] *nm* receipt

réceptacle [ʀesɛptakl(ə)] *nm* (*où les choses aboutissent*) recipient; (*où les choses sont stockées*) repository; (*Bot*) receptacle

récepteur, -trice [ʀesɛptœʀ, -tʀis] *adj* receiving ▷ *nm* receiver; **~ (de radio)** radio set *ou* receiver

réceptif, -ive [ʀesɛptif, -iv] *adj*: **~ (à)** receptive (to)

réception [ʀesɛpsjɔ̃] *nf* receiving *no pl*; (*d'une marchandise, commande*) receipt; (*accueil*) reception, welcome; (*bureau*) reception (desk);

(*réunion mondaine*) reception, party; (*pièces*) reception rooms *pl*; (*Sport: après un saut*) landing; (*du ballon*) catching *no pl*; **jour/heures de ~** day/hours for receiving visitors (*ou* students *etc*)

réceptionner [ʀesɛpsjɔne] *vt* (*Comm*) to take delivery of; (*Sport: ballon*) to catch (and control)

réceptionniste [ʀesɛpsjɔnist(ə)] *nm/f* receptionist

réceptivité [ʀesɛptivite] *nf* (*à une influence*) receptiveness; (*à une maladie*) susceptibility

récessif, -ive [ʀesesif, -iv] *adj* (*Biol*) recessive

récession [ʀesesjɔ̃] *nf* recession

recette [ʀəsɛt] *nf* (*Culin*) recipe; (*fig*) formula, recipe; (*Comm*) takings *pl*; (*Admin: bureau*) tax *ou* revenue office; **recettes** *nfpl* (*Comm: rentrées*) receipts; **faire ~** (*spectacle, exposition*) to be a winner

receveur, -euse [ʀəsvœʀ, -øz] *nm/f* (*des contributions*) tax collector; (*des postes*) postmaster/mistress; (*d'autobus*) conductor/conductress; (*Méd: de sang, organe*) recipient

recevoir [ʀəsvwaʀ] *vt* to receive; (*lettre, prime*) to receive, get; (*client, patient, représentant*) to see; (*jour, soleil: pièce*) to get; (*Scol: candidat*) to pass ▷ *vi* to receive visitors; to give parties; to see patients *etc*; **se recevoir** *vi* (*athlète*) to land; **~ qn à dîner** to invite sb to dinner; **il reçoit de huit à 10** he's at home from eight to 10, he will see visitors from eight to 10; (*docteur, dentiste etc*) he sees patients from eight to 10; **être reçu** (*à un examen*) to pass; **être bien/mal reçu** to be well/badly received

rechange [ʀəʃɑ̃ʒ]: **de ~** *adj* (*pièces, roue*) spare; (*fig: solution*) alternative; **des vêtements de ~** a change of clothes

rechaper [ʀəʃape] *vt* to remould (Brit), remold (US), retread

réchapper [ʀeʃape] *vt*: **~ de** *ou* **à** (*accident, maladie*) to come through; **va-t-il en ~?** is he going to get over it?, is he going to come through (it)?

recharge [ʀəʃaʀʒ(ə)] *nf* refill

rechargeable [ʀəʃaʀʒabl(ə)] *adj* refillable; rechargeable

recharger [ʀəʃaʀʒe] *vt* (*camion, fusil, appareil-photo*) to reload; (*briquet, stylo*) to refill; (*batterie*) to recharge

réchaud [ʀeʃo] *nm* (*portable*) stove, plate-warmer

réchauffé [ʀeʃofe] *nm* (*nourriture*) reheated food; (*fig*) stale news (*ou* joke *etc*)

réchauffement [ʀeʃofmɑ̃] *nm* warming (up); **le ~ de la planète** global warming

réchauffer [ʀeʃofe] *vt* (*plat*) to reheat; (*mains, personne*) to warm; **se réchauffer** *vi* to get warmer; **se ~ les doigts** to warm (up) one's fingers

rêche [ʀɛʃ] *adj* rough

recherche [ʀəʃɛʀʃ(ə)] *nf* (*action*): **la ~ de** the search for; (*raffinement*) affectedness, studied elegance; (*scientifique etc*): **la ~** research; **recherches** *nfpl* (*de la police*) investigations; (*scientifiques*) research *sg*; **être/se mettre à la ~ de** to be/go in search of

recherché, e [ʀəʃɛʀʃe] *adj* (*rare, demandé*) much sought-after; (*entouré: acteur, femme*) in demand; (*raffiné*) studied, affected

rechercher [ʀəʃɛʀʃe] *vt* (*objet égaré, personne*) to look for, search for; (*témoins, coupable, main-d'œuvre*) to look for; (*causes d'un phénomène, nouveau procédé*) to try to find; (*bonheur etc, l'amitié de qn*) to seek; **"~ et remplacer"** (*Inform*) "find and replace"

rechigner [ʀəʃiɲe] *vi*: **~ (à)** to balk (at)

rechute [ʀəʃyt] *nf* (*Méd*) relapse; (*dans le péché, le vice*) lapse; **faire une ~** to have a relapse

rechuter [ʀəʃyte] *vi* (*Méd*) to relapse

récidive [ʀesidiv] *nf* (*Jur*) second (*ou* subsequent) offence; (*fig*) repetition; (*Méd*) recurrence

récidiver [ʀesidive] *vi* to commit a second (*ou* subsequent) offence; (*fig*) to do it again

récidiviste [ʀesidivist(ə)] *nm/f* second (*ou* habitual) offender, recidivist

récif [ʀesif] *nm* reef

récipiendaire [ʀesipjɑ̃dɛʀ] *nm* recipient (*of diploma etc*); (*d'une société*) newly elected member

récipient [ʀesipjɑ̃] *nm* container

réciproque [ʀesipʀɔk] *adj* reciprocal ▷ *nf*: **la ~** (*l'inverse*) the converse

réciproquement [ʀesipʀɔkmɑ̃] *adv* reciprocally; **et ~** and vice versa

récit [ʀesi] *nm* (*action de narrer*) telling; (*conte, histoire*) story

récital [ʀesital] *nm* recital

récitant, e [ʀesitɑ̃, -ɑ̃t] *nm/f* narrator

récitation [ʀesitasjɔ̃] *nf* recitation

réciter [ʀesite] *vt* to recite

réclamation [ʀeklamasjɔ̃] *nf* complaint; **réclamations** *nfpl* (*bureau*) complaints department *sg*

réclame [ʀeklam] *nf*: **la ~** advertising; **une ~** an ad(vertisement), an advert (Brit); **faire de la ~ (pour qch/qn)** to advertise (sth/sb); **article en ~** special offer

réclamer [ʀeklame] *vt* (*aide, nourriture etc*) to ask for; (*revendiquer: dû, part, indemnité*) to claim, demand; (*nécessiter*) to demand, require ▷ *vi* to complain; **se ~ de** to give as one's authority; to claim filiation with

reclassement [ʀəklasmɑ̃] *nm* reclassifying; regrading; rehabilitation

reclasser [ʀəklase] *vt* (*fiches, dossiers*) to reclassify; (*fig: fonctionnaire etc*) to regrade; (: *ouvrier licencié*) to place, rehabilitate

reclus, e [ʀəkly, -yz] *nm/f* recluse

réclusion [ʀeklyzjɔ̃] *nf* imprisonment; **~ à perpétuité** life imprisonment

recoiffer [ʀəkwafe] *vt*: **~ un enfant** to do a child's hair again; **se recoiffer** to do one's hair again

recoin [ʀəkwɛ̃] *nm* nook, corner; (*fig*) hidden recess

reçois *etc* [ʀəswa] *vb voir* **recevoir**

reçoive *etc* [ʀəswav] *vb voir* **recevoir**

recoller [ʀəkɔle] vt (enveloppe) to stick back down

récolte [ʀekɔlt(ə)] nf harvesting, gathering; (produits) harvest, crop; (fig) crop, collection; (: d'observations) findings

récolter [ʀekɔlte] vt to harvest, gather (in); (fig) to get

recommandable [ʀəkɔmɑ̃dabl(ə)] adj commendable; **peu** ~ not very commendable

recommandation [ʀəkɔmɑ̃dɑsjɔ̃] nf recommendation

recommandé [ʀəkɔmɑ̃de] nm (méthode etc) recommended; (Postes): **en** ~ by registered mail

recommander [ʀəkɔmɑ̃de] vt to recommend; (qualités etc) to commend; (Postes) to register; ~ **qch à qn** to recommend sth to sb; ~ **à qn de faire** to recommend sb to do; ~ **qn auprès de qn** ou **à qn** to recommend sb to sb; **il est recommandé de faire ...** it is recommended that one does ...; **se ~ à qn** to commend o.s. to sb; **se ~ de qn** to give sb's name as a reference

recommencer [ʀəkɔmɑ̃se] vt (reprendre: lutte, séance) to resume, start again; (refaire: travail, explications) to start afresh, start (over) again; (récidiver: erreur) to make again ▷ vi to start again; (récidiver) to do it again; ~ **à faire** to start doing again; **ne recommence pas!** don't do that again!

récompense [ʀekɔ̃pɑ̃s] nf reward; (prix) award; **recevoir qch en** ~ to get sth as a reward, be rewarded with sth

récompenser [ʀekɔ̃pɑ̃se] vt: ~ **qn (de** ou **pour)** to reward sb (for)

réconciliation [ʀekɔ̃siljɑsjɔ̃] nf reconciliation

réconcilier [ʀekɔ̃silje] vt to reconcile; ~ **qn avec qn** to reconcile sb with sb; ~ **qn avec qch** to reconcile sb to sth; **se réconcilier (avec)** to be reconciled (with)

reconductible [ʀəkɔ̃dyktibl(ə)] adj (Jur: contrat, bail) renewable

reconduction [ʀəkɔ̃dyksjɔ̃] nf renewal; (Pol: d'une politique) continuation

reconduire [ʀəkɔ̃dɥiʀ] vt (raccompagner) to take ou see back; (: à la porte) to show out; (: à son domicile) to see home, take home; (Jur, Pol: renouveler) to renew

réconfort [ʀekɔ̃fɔʀ] nm comfort

réconfortant, e [ʀekɔ̃fɔʀtɑ̃, -ɑ̃t] adj (idée, paroles) comforting; (boisson) fortifying

réconforter [ʀekɔ̃fɔʀte] vt (consoler) to comfort; (revigorer) to fortify

reconnais etc [ʀ(ə)kɔnɛ] vb voir **reconnaître**

reconnaissable [ʀəkɔnɛsabl(ə)] adj recognizable

reconnaissance [ʀəkɔnɛsɑ̃s] nf recognition; acknowledgement; (gratitude) gratitude, gratefulness; (Mil) reconnaissance, recce; **en** ~ (Mil) on reconnaissance; ~ **de dette** acknowledgement of a debt, IOU

reconnaissant, e [ʀəkɔnɛsɑ̃, -ɑ̃t] vb voir **reconnaître** ▷ adj grateful; **je vous serais** ~ **de bien vouloir** I should be most grateful if you would (kindly)

reconnaître [ʀəkɔnɛtʀ(ə)] vt to recognize; (Mil: lieu) to reconnoitre; (Jur: enfant, dette, droit) to acknowledge; ~ **que** to admit ou acknowledge that; ~ **qn/qch à** (l'identifier grâce à) to recognize sb/sth by; ~ **à qn: je lui reconnais certaines qualités** I recognize certain qualities in him; **se ~ quelque part** (s'y retrouver) to find one's way around (a place)

reconnu, e [ʀ(ə)kɔny] pp de **reconnaître** ▷ adj (indiscuté, connu) recognized

reconquérir [ʀəkɔ̃keʀiʀ] vt to reconquer, recapture; (sa dignité etc) to recover

reconquête [ʀəkɔ̃kɛt] nf recapture; recovery

reconsidérer [ʀəkɔ̃sideʀe] vt to reconsider

reconstituant, e [ʀəkɔ̃stitɥɑ̃, -ɑ̃t] adj (régime) strength-building ▷ nm tonic, pick-me-up

reconstituer [ʀəkɔ̃stitɥe] vt (monument ancien) to recreate, build a replica of; (fresque, vase brisé) to piece together, reconstitute; (événement, accident) to reconstruct; (fortune, patrimoine) to rebuild; (Bio: tissus etc) to regenerate

reconstitution [ʀəkɔ̃stitysjɔ̃] nf (d'un accident etc) reconstruction

reconstruction [ʀəkɔ̃stʀyksjɔ̃] nf rebuilding, reconstruction

reconstruire [ʀəkɔ̃stʀɥiʀ] vt to rebuild, reconstruct

reconversion [ʀəkɔ̃vɛʀsjɔ̃] nf (du personnel) redeployment

reconvertir [ʀəkɔ̃vɛʀtiʀ] vt (usine) to reconvert; (personnel, troupes etc) to redeploy; **se ~ dans** (un métier, une branche) to move into, be redeployed into

recopier [ʀəkɔpje] vt (transcrire) to copy out again, write out again; (mettre au propre: devoir) to make a clean ou fair copy of

record [ʀəkɔʀ] nm, adj record; ~ **du monde** world record

recoucher [ʀəkuʃe] vt (enfant) to put back to bed

recoudre [ʀəkudʀ(ə)] vt (bouton) to sew back on; (plaie, incision) to sew (back) up, stitch up

recoupement [ʀəkupmɑ̃] nm: **faire un** ~ ou **des ~s** to cross-check; **par** ~ by cross-checking

recouper [ʀəkupe] vt (tranche) to cut again; (vêtement) to recut ▷ vi (Cartes) to cut again; **se recouper** vi (témoignages) to tie ou match up

recourais etc [ʀəkuʀɛ] vb voir **recourir**

recourbé, e [ʀəkuʀbe] adj curved; hooked; bent

recourber [ʀəkuʀbe] vt (branche, tige de métal) to bend

recourir [ʀəkuʀiʀ] vi (courir de nouveau) to run again; (refaire une course) to race again; ~ **à** vt (ami, agence) to turn ou appeal to; (force, ruse, emprunt) to resort to, have recourse to

recours [ʀəkuʀ] vb voir **recourir** ▷ nm (Jur) appeal; **avoir** ~ **à**; = **recourir à**; **dernier** ~ as a last resort; **sans** ~ final; with no way out; ~ **en grâce** plea for clemency (ou pardon)

recouru, e [ʀəkuʀy] pp de **recourir**

recousu, e [ʀəkuzy] pp de **recoudre**

recouvert, e [ʀəkuvɛʀ, -ɛʀt(ə)] pp de **recouvrir**

recouvrable [ʀəkuvʀabl(ə)] adj (somme)

recoverable

recouvrais *etc* [RəkuvRɛ] *vb voir* **recouvrer**; **recouvrir**

recouvrement [RəkuvRəmɑ̃] *nm* recovery

recouvrer [RəkuvRe] *vt* (*vue, santé etc*) to recover, regain; (*impôts*) to collect; (*créance*) to recover

recouvrir [RəkuvRiR] *vt* (*couvrir à nouveau*) to recover; (*couvrir entièrement: aussi fig*) to cover; (*cacher, masquer*) to conceal, hide; **se recouvrir** (*se superposer*) to overlap

recracher [RəkRaʃe] *vt* to spit out

récréatif, -ive [RekReatif, -iv] *adj* of entertainment; recreational

récréation [RekReasjɔ̃] *nf* recreation, entertainment; (*Scol*) break

recréer [RəkRee] *vt* to recreate

récrier [RekRije]: **se récrier** *vi* to exclaim

récriminations [RekRiminasjɔ̃] *nfpl* remonstrations, complaints

récriminer [RekRimine] *vi*: ~ **contre qn/qch** to remonstrate against sb/sth

recroqueviller [RəkRɔkvije]: **se recroqueviller** *vi* (*feuilles*) to curl *ou* shrivel up; (*personne*) to huddle up

recru, e [RəkRy] *adj*: ~ **de fatigue** exhausted ▷ *nf* recruit

recrudescence [RəkRydesɑ̃s] *nf* fresh outbreak

recrutement [RəkRytmɑ̃] *nm* recruiting, recruitment

recruter [RəkRyte] *vt* to recruit

rectal, e, -aux [Rɛktal, -o] *adj*: **par voie ~e** rectally

rectangle [Rɛktɑ̃gl(ə)] *nm* rectangle

rectangulaire [Rɛktɑ̃gylɛR] *adj* rectangular

recteur [RɛktœR] *nm* ≈ (regional) director of education (*Brit*), ≈ state superintendent of education (*US*)

rectificatif, -ive [Rɛktifikatif, -iv] *adj* corrected ▷ *nm* correction

rectification [Rɛktifikasjɔ̃] *nf* correction

rectifier [Rɛktifje] *vt* (*tracé, virage*) to straighten; (*calcul, adresse*) to correct; (*erreur, faute*) to rectify, put right

rectiligne [Rɛktiliɲ] *adj* straight; (*Géom*) rectilinear

rectitude [Rɛktityd] *nf* rectitude, uprightness

recto [Rɛkto] *nm* front (*of a sheet of paper*)

rectorat [RɛktɔRa] *nm* (*fonction*) position of recteur; (*bureau*) recteur's office; *voir aussi* **recteur**

rectum [Rɛktɔm] *nm* rectum

reçu, e [Rəsy] *pp de* **recevoir** ▷ *adj* (*admis, consacré*) accepted ▷ *nm* (*Comm*) receipt

recueil [Rəkœj] *nm* collection

recueillement [Rəkœjmɑ̃] *nm* meditation, contemplation

recueilli, e [Rəkœji] *adj* contemplative

recueillir [RəkœjiR] *vt* to collect; (*voix, suffrages*) to win; (*accueillir: réfugiés, chat*) to take in; **se recueillir** *vi* to gather one's thoughts; to meditate

recuire [RəkɥiR] *vi*: **faire ~** to recook

recul [Rəkyl] *nm* retreat; recession; decline;

(*d'arme à feu*) recoil, kick; **avoir un mouvement de ~** to recoil, start back; **prendre du ~** to stand back; **avec le ~** with the passing of time, in retrospect

reculade [Rəkylad] *nf* (*péj*) climb-down

reculé, e [Rəkyle] *adj* remote

reculer [Rəkyle] *vi* to move back, back away; (*Auto*) to reverse, back (up); (*fig: civilisation, épidémie*) to (be on the) decline; (: *se dérober*) to shrink back ▷ *vt* to move back; to reverse, back (up); (*fig: possibilités, limites*) to extend; (: *date, décision*) to postpone; ~ **devant** (*danger, difficulté*) to shrink from; ~ **pour mieux sauter** (*fig*) to postpone the evil day

reculons [Rəkylɔ̃]: **à ~** *adv* backwards

récupérable [RekypeRabl(ə)] *adj* (*créance*) recoverable; (*heures*) which can be made up; (*ferraille*) salvageable

récupération [RekypeRasjɔ̃] *nf* (*de métaux etc*) salvage, reprocessing; (*Pol*) bringing into line

récupérer [RekypeRe] *vt* (*rentrer en possession de*) to recover, get back; (: *forces*) to recover; (*déchets etc*) to salvage (for reprocessing); (*remplacer: journée, heures de travail*) to make up; (*délinquant etc*) to rehabilitate; (*Pol*) to bring into line ▷ *vi* to recover

récurer [RekyRe] *vt* to scour; **poudre à ~** scouring powder

reçus *etc* [Rəsy] *vb voir* **recevoir**

récusable [Rekyzabl(ə)] *adj* (*témoin*) challengeable; (*témoignage*) impugnable

récuser [Rekyze] *vt* to challenge; **se récuser** to decline to give an opinion

recyclage [Rəsiklaʒ] *nm* reorientation; retraining; recycling; **cours de ~** retraining course

recycler [Rəsikle] *vt* (*Scol*) to reorientate; (*employés*) to retrain; (*matériau*) to recycle; **se recycler** to retrain; to go on a retraining course

rédacteur, -trice [RedaktœR, -tRis] *nm/f* (*journaliste*) writer; subeditor; (*d'ouvrage de référence*) editor, compiler; ~ **en chef** chief editor; ~ **publicitaire** copywriter

rédaction [Redaksjɔ̃] *nf* writing; (*rédacteurs*) editorial staff; (*bureau*) editorial office(s); (*Scol: devoir*) essay, composition

reddition [Redisjɔ̃] *nf* surrender

redéfinir [RedefiniR] *vt* to redefine

redemander [Rədmɑ̃de] *vt* (*renseignement*) to ask again for; (*nourriture*): ~ **de** to ask for more (*ou* another); (*objet prêté*): ~ **qch** to ask for sth back

redémarrer [RedemaRe] *vi* (*véhicule*) to start again, get going again; (*fig: industrie etc*) to get going again

rédemption [Redɑ̃psjɔ̃] *nf* redemption

redéploiement [Redeplwamɑ̃] *nm* redeployment

redescendre [Rədesɑ̃dR(ə)] *vi* (*à nouveau*) to go back down; (*après la montée*) to go down (again) ▷ *vt* (*pente etc*) to go down

redevable [Rədvabl(ə)] *adj*: **être ~ de qch à qn** (*somme*) to owe sb sth; (*fig*) to be indebted to sb for sth

redevance [ʀədvɑ̃s] *nf* (*Tél*) rental charge; (*TV*) licence (*Brit*) *ou* license (*US*) fee

redevenir [ʀədvəniʀ] *vi* to become again

rédhibitoire [ʀedibitwaʀ] *adj*: **vice ~** (*Jur*) *latent defect in merchandise that renders the sales contract void*; (*fig*: *défaut*) crippling

rediffuser [ʀədifyze] *vt* (*Radio, TV*) to repeat, broadcast again

rediffusion [ʀədifyzjɔ̃] *nf* repeat (programme)

rédiger [ʀediʒe] *vt* to write; (*contrat*) to draw up

redire [ʀədiʀ] *vt* to repeat; **trouver à ~ à** to find fault with

redistribuer [ʀədistʀibɥe] *vt* (*cartes etc*) to deal again; (*richesses, tâches, revenus*) to redistribute

redite [ʀədit] *nf* (needless) repetition

redondance [ʀədɔ̃dɑ̃s] *nf* redundancy

redonner [ʀədɔne] *vt* (*restituer*) to give back, return; (*du courage, des forces*) to restore

redoublé, e [ʀəduble] *adj*: **à coups ~s** even harder, twice as hard

redoubler [ʀəduble] *vi* (*tempête, violence*) to intensify, get even stronger *ou* fiercer *etc*; (*Scol*) to repeat a year ▷ *vt* (*Scol: classe*) to repeat; (*Ling: lettre*) to double; **le vent redouble de violence** the wind is blowing twice as hard

redoutable [ʀədutabl(ə)] *adj* formidable, fearsome

redouter [ʀədute] *vt* to fear; (*appréhender*) to dread; **~ de faire** to dread doing

redoux [ʀədu] *nm* milder spell

redressement [ʀədʀɛsmɑ̃] *nm* (*de l'économie etc*) putting right; **maison de ~** reformatory; **~ fiscal** repayment of back taxes

redresser [ʀədʀese] *vt* (*arbre, mât*) to set upright, right; (*pièce tordue*) to straighten out; (*Aviat, Auto*) to straighten up; (*situation, économie*) to put right; **se redresser** *vi* (*objet penché*) to right itself; to straighten up; (*personne*) to sit (*ou* stand) up; to sit (*ou* stand) up straight; (*fig: pays, situation*) to recover; **~ (les roues)** (*Auto*) to straighten up

redresseur [ʀədʀɛsœʀ] *nm*: **~ de torts** righter of wrongs

réducteur, -trice [ʀedyktœʀ, -tʀis] *adj* simplistic

réduction [ʀedyksjɔ̃] *nf* reduction; **en ~** *adv* in miniature, scaled-down

réduire [ʀedɥiʀ] *vt* (*gén, Culin, Math*) to reduce; (*prix, dépenses*) to cut, reduce; (*carte*) to scale down, reduce; (*Méd: fracture*) to set; **~ qn/qch à** to reduce sb/sth to; **se ~ à** (*revenir à*) to boil down to; **se ~ en** (*se transformer en*) to be reduced to; **en être réduit à** to be reduced to

réduit, e [ʀedɥi, -it] *pp de* **réduire** ▷ *adj* (*prix, tarif, échelle*) reduced; (*mécanisme*) scaled-down; (*vitesse*) reduced ▷ *nm* tiny room; recess

rééditer [ʀeedite] *vt* to republish

réédition [ʀeedisjɔ̃] *nf* new edition

rééducation [ʀeedykɑsjɔ̃] *nf* (*d'un membre*) re-education; (*de délinquants, d'un blessé*) rehabilitation; **~ de la parole** speech therapy;

centre de ~ physiotherapy *ou* physical therapy (*US*) centre

rééduquer [ʀeedyke] *vt* to reeducate; to rehabilitate

réel, le [ʀeɛl] *adj* real ▷ *nm*: **le ~** reality

réélection [ʀeelɛksjɔ̃] *nf* re-election

rééligible [ʀeeliʒibl(ə)] *adj* re-eligible

réélire [ʀeeliʀ] *vt* to re-elect

réellement [ʀeɛlmɑ̃] *adv* really

réembaucher [ʀeɑ̃boʃe] *vt* to take on again

réemploi [ʀeɑ̃plwa] *nm* = **remploi**

réemployer [ʀeɑ̃plwaje] *vt* (*méthode, produit*) to re-use; (*argent*) to reinvest; (*personnel, employé*) to re-employ

rééquilibrer [ʀeekilibʀe] *vt* (*budget*) to balance (again)

réescompte [ʀeɛskɔ̃t] *nm* rediscount

réessayer [ʀeeseje] *vt* to try on again

réévaluation [ʀeevalɥasjɔ̃] *nf* revaluation

réévaluer [ʀeevalɥe] *vt* to revalue

réexaminer [ʀeɛgzamine] *vt* to re-examine

réexpédier [ʀeɛkspedje] *vt* (*à l'envoyeur*) to return, send back; (*au destinataire*) to send on, forward

réexporter [ʀeɛkspɔʀte] *vt* to re-export

réf. *abr* = **référence(s)**; **V/~.** Your ref

refaire [ʀəfɛʀ] *vt* (*faire de nouveau, recommencer*) to do again; (*réparer, restaurer*) to do up; **se refaire** *vi* (*en argent*) to make up one's losses; **se ~ une santé** to recuperate; **se ~ à qch** (*se réhabituer à*) to get used to sth again

refasse *etc* [ʀəfas] *vb voir* **refaire**

réfection [ʀefɛksjɔ̃] *nf* repair; **en ~** under repair

réfectoire [ʀefɛktwaʀ] *nm* refectory

referai *etc* [ʀ(ə)fʀe] *vb voir* **refaire**

référé [ʀefeʀe] *nm* (*Jur*) *emergency interim proceedings ou ruling*

référence [ʀefeʀɑ̃s] *nf* reference; **références** *nfpl* (*recommandations*) reference *sg*; **faire ~ à** to refer to; **ouvrage de ~** reference work; **ce n'est pas une ~** (*fig*) that's no recommendation

référendum [ʀefeʀɑ̃dɔm] *nm* referendum

référer [ʀefeʀe]: **se ~ à** *vt* to refer to; **en ~ à qn** to refer the matter to sb

refermer [ʀəfɛʀme] *vt* to close again, shut again

refiler [ʀəfile] *vt* (*fam*): **~ qch à qn** to palm (*Brit*) *ou* fob sth off on sb; to pass sth on to sb

refit *etc* [ʀəfi] *vb voir* **refaire**

réfléchi, e [ʀefleʃi] *adj* (*caractère*) thoughtful; (*action*) well-thought-out; (*Ling*) reflexive

réfléchir [ʀefleʃiʀ] *vt* to reflect ▷ *vi* to think; **~ à** *ou* **sur** to think about; **c'est tout réfléchi** my mind's made up

réflecteur [ʀeflɛktœʀ] *nm* (*Auto*) reflector

reflet [ʀəflɛ] *nm* reflection; (*sur l'eau etc*) sheen *no pl*, glint; **reflets** *nmpl* gleam *sg*

refléter [ʀəflete] *vt* to reflect; **se refléter** *vi* to be reflected

réflex [ʀeflɛks] *adj inv* (*Photo*) reflex

réflexe [ʀeflɛks(ə)] *adj, nm* reflex; **~ conditionné** conditioned reflex

réflexion [ʀeflɛksjɔ̃] *nf* (*de la lumière etc, pensée*) reflection; (*fait de penser*) thought; (*remarque*) remark; **réflexions** *nfpl* (*méditations*) thought *sg*, reflection *sg*; **sans ~** without thinking; **~ faite, à la ~** après réflexion, on reflection; **délai de ~** cooling-off period; **groupe de ~** think tank

réflexologie [ʀeflɛksɔlɔʒi] *nf* reflexology

refluer [ʀəflye] *vi* to flow back; (*foule*) to surge back

reflux [ʀəfly] *nm* (*de la mer*) ebb; (*fig*) backward surge

refondre [ʀəfɔ̃dʀ(ə)] *vt* (*texte*) to recast

refont [ʀ(ə)fɔ̃] *vb voir* **refaire**

reformater [ʀəfɔʀmate] *vt* to reformat

réformateur, -trice [ʀefɔʀmatœʀ, -tʀis] *nm/f* reformer ▷ *adj* (*mesures*) reforming

Réformation [ʀefɔʀmasjɔ̃] *nf*: **la ~** the Reformation

réforme [ʀefɔʀm(ə)] *nf* reform; (*Mil*) declaration of unfitness for service; discharge (*on health grounds*); (*Rel*): **la R~** the Reformation

réformé, e [ʀefɔʀme] *adj, nm/f* (*Rel*) Protestant

reformer [ʀəfɔʀme] *vt*, **se reformer** *vi* to reform; **~ les rangs** (*Mil*) to fall in again

réformer [ʀefɔʀme] *vt* to reform; (*Mil: recrue*) to declare unfit for service; (*: soldat*) to discharge, invalid out; (*matériel*) to scrap

réformisme [ʀefɔʀmism(ə)] *nm* reformism, policy of reform

réformiste [ʀefɔʀmist(ə)] *adj, nm/f* (*Pol*) reformist

refoulé, e [ʀəfule] *adj* (*Psych*) repressed

refoulement [ʀəfulmɑ̃] *nm* (*d'une armée*) driving back; (*Psych*) repression

refouler [ʀəfule] *vt* (*envahisseurs*) to drive back, repulse; (*liquide*) to force back; (*fig*) to suppress; (*Psych*) to repress

réfractaire [ʀefʀaktɛʀ] *adj* (*minerai*) refractory; (*brique*) fire *cpd*; (*maladie*) which is resistant to treatment; (*prêtre*) non-juring; **soldat ~** draft evader; **être ~ à** to resist

réfracter [ʀefʀakte] *vt* to refract

réfraction [ʀefʀaksjɔ̃] *nf* refraction

refrain [ʀəfʀɛ̃] *nm* (*Mus*) refrain, chorus; (*air, fig*) tune

refréner, réfréner [ʀəfʀene, ʀefʀene] *vt* to curb, check

réfrigérant, e [ʀefʀiʒeʀɑ̃, -ɑ̃t] *adj* refrigerant, cooling

réfrigérateur [ʀefʀiʒeʀatœʀ] *nm* refrigerator; **~-congélateur** fridge-freezer

réfrigération [ʀefʀiʒeʀasjɔ̃] *nf* refrigeration

réfrigéré, e [ʀefʀiʒeʀe] *adj* (*camion, wagon*) refrigerated

réfrigérer [ʀefʀiʒeʀe] *vt* to refrigerate; (*fam: glacer: aussi fig*) to cool

refroidir [ʀəfʀwadiʀ] *vt* to cool; (*fig*) to have a cooling effect on ▷ *vi* to cool (down); **se refroidir** *vi* (*prendre froid*) to catch a chill; (*temps*) to get cooler *ou* colder; (*fig*) to cool (off)

refroidissement [ʀəfʀwadismɑ̃] *nm* cooling; (*grippe etc*) chill

refuge [ʀəfyʒ] *nm* refuge; (*pour piétons*) (traffic) island; **demander ~ à qn** to ask sb for refuge

réfugié, e [ʀefyʒje] *adj, nm/f* refugee

réfugier [ʀefyʒje]: **se réfugier** *vi* to take refuge

refus [ʀəfy] *nm* refusal; **ce n'est pas de ~** I won't say no, it's very welcome

refuser [ʀəfyze] *vt* to refuse; (*Scol: candidat*) to fail ▷ *vi* to refuse; **~ qch à qn/de faire** to refuse sb sth/to do; **~ du monde** to have to turn people away; **se ~ à qch** *ou* **à faire qch** to refuse to do sth; **il ne se refuse rien** he doesn't stint himself; **se ~ à qn** to refuse sb

réfutable [ʀefytabl(ə)] *adj* refutable

réfuter [ʀefyte] *vt* to refute

regagner [ʀəgaɲe] *vt* (*argent, faveur*) to win back; (*lieu*) to get back to; **~ le temps perdu** to make up for lost time; **~ du terrain** to regain ground

regain [ʀəgɛ̃] *nm* (*herbe*) second crop of hay; (*renouveau*): **~ de qch** renewed sth

régal [ʀegal] *nm* treat; **un ~ pour les yeux** a pleasure *ou* delight to look at

régalade [ʀegalad] *adv*: **à la ~** from the bottle (held away from the lips)

régaler [ʀegale] *vt*: **~ qn** to treat sb to a delicious meal; **~ qn de** to treat sb to; **se régaler** *vi* to have a delicious meal; (*fig*) to enjoy o.s

regard [ʀəgaʀ] *nm* (*coup d'œil*) look, glance; (*expression*) look (in one's eye); **parcourir/menacer du ~** to cast an eye over/look threateningly at; **au ~ de** (*loi, morale*) from the point of view of; **en ~** (*vis à vis*) opposite; **en ~ de** in comparison with

regardant, e [ʀəgaʀdɑ̃, -ɑ̃t] *adj*: **très/peu ~ (sur)** quite fussy/very free (about); (*économe*) very tight-fisted/quite generous (with)

regarder [ʀəgaʀde] *vt* (*examiner, observer, lire*) to look at; (*film, télévision, match*) to watch; (*envisager: situation, avenir*) to view; (*considérer: son intérêt etc*) to be concerned with; (*être orienté vers*): **~ (vers)** to face; (*concerner*) to concern ▷ *vi* to look; **~ à** *vt* (*dépense, qualité, détails*) to be fussy with *ou* over; **~ à faire** to hesitate to do; **dépenser sans ~** to spend freely; **~ qn/qch comme** to regard sb/sth as; **~ (qch) dans le dictionnaire** to look (sth up) in the dictionary; **~ par la fenêtre** to look out of the window; **cela me regarde** it concerns me, it's my business

régate [ʀegat], **régates** *nf(pl)* regatta

régénérer [ʀeʒeneʀe] *vt* to regenerate; (*fig*) to revive

régent [ʀeʒɑ̃] *nm* regent

régenter [ʀeʒɑ̃te] *vt* to rule over; to dictate to

régie [ʀeʒi] *nf* (*Comm, Industrie*) state-owned company; (*Théât, Ciné*) production; (*Radio, TV*) control room; **la ~ de l'État** state control

regimber [ʀəʒɛ̃be] *vi* to balk, jib

régime [ʀeʒim] *nm* (*Pol Géo*) régime; (*Admin: carcéral, fiscal etc*) system; (*Méd*) diet; (*Tech*) (engine) speed; (*fig*) rate, pace; (*de bananes, dattes*) bunch; **se mettre au/suivre un ~** to go on/be on a diet; **~ sans sel** salt-free diet; **à bas/**

haut ~ (*Auto*) at low/high revs; **à plein ~** flat out, at full speed; **~ matrimonial** marriage settlement

régiment [ʀeʒimɑ̃] *nm* (*Mil: unité*) regiment; (*fig: fam*): **un ~ de** an army of; **un copain de ~** a pal from military service *ou* (one's) army days

région [ʀeʒjɔ̃] *nf* region; **la ~ parisienne** the Paris area

régional, e, -aux [ʀeʒjɔnal, -o] *adj* regional

régionalisation [ʀeʒjɔnalizɑsjɔ̃] *nf* regionalization

régionalisme [ʀeʒjɔnalism(ə)] *nm* regionalism

régir [ʀeʒiʀ] *vt* to govern

régisseur [ʀeʒisœʀ] *nm* (*d'un domaine*) steward; (*Ciné, TV*) assistant director; (*Théât*) stage manager

registre [ʀəʒistʀ(ə)] *nm* (*livre*) register; logbook; ledger; (*Mus, Ling*) register; (*d'orgue*) stop; **~ de comptabilité** ledger; **~ de l'état civil** register of births, marriages and deaths

réglable [ʀeglabl(ə)] *adj* (*siège, flamme etc*) adjustable; (*achat*) payable

réglage [ʀeglaʒ] *nm* (*d'une machine*) adjustment; (*d'un moteur*) tuning

réglé, e [ʀegle] *adj* well-ordered; stable, steady; (*papier*) ruled; (*arrangé*) settled

règle [ʀegl(ə)] *nf* (*instrument*) ruler; (*loi, prescription*) rule; **règles** *nfpl* (*Physiol*) period *sg*; **avoir pour ~ de** to make it a rule that *ou* to; **en ~** (*papiers d'identité*) in order; **être/se mettre en ~** to be/put o.s. straight with the authorities; **en ~ générale** as a (general) rule; **être la ~** to be the rule; **être de ~** to be usual; **~ à calcul** slide rule; **~ de trois** (*Math*) rule of three

règlement [ʀeglǝmɑ̃] *nm* settling; (*paiement*) settlement; (*arrêté*) regulation; (*règles, statuts*) regulations *pl*, rules *pl*; **~ à la commande** cash with order; **~ de compte(s)** settling of scores; **~ en espèces/par chèque** payment in cash/by cheque; **~ intérieur** (*Scol*) school rules *pl*; (*Admin*) by-laws *pl*; **~ judiciaire** compulsory liquidation

réglementaire [ʀeglǝmɑ̃tɛʀ] *adj* conforming to the regulations; (*tenue, uniforme*) regulation *cpd*

réglementation [ʀeglǝmɑ̃tɑsjɔ̃] *nf* regulation, control; (*règlements*) regulations *pl*

réglementer [ʀeglǝmɑ̃te] *vt* to regulate, control

régler [ʀegle] *vt* (*mécanisme, machine*) to regulate, adjust; (*moteur*) to tune; (*thermostat etc*) to set, adjust; (*emploi du temps etc*) to organize, plan; (*question, conflit, facture, dette*) to settle; (*fournisseur*) to settle up with, pay; (*papier*) to rule; **~ qch sur** to model sth on; **~ son compte** to sort sb out, settle sb; **~ un compte** to settle a score with sb

réglisse [ʀeglis] *nf ou m* liquorice; **bâton de ~** liquorice stick

règne [ʀɛɲ] *nm* (*d'un roi etc, fig*) reign; (*Bio*): **le ~ végétal/animal** the vegetable/animal kingdom

régner [ʀeɲe] *vi* (*roi*) to rule, reign; (*fig*) to reign

regonfler [ʀ(ə)gɔ̃fle] *vt* (*ballon, pneu*) to reinflate, blow up again

regorger [ʀəgɔʀʒe] *vi* to overflow; **~ de** to overflow with, be bursting with

régresser [ʀegʀese] *vi* (*phénomène*) to decline; (*enfant, malade*) to regress

régressif, -ive [ʀegʀesif, -iv] *adj* regressive

régression [ʀegʀesjɔ̃] *nf* decline; regression; **être en ~** to be on the decline

regret [ʀəgʀɛ] *nm* regret; **à ~** with regret; **avec ~** regretfully; **être au ~ de devoir/ne pas pouvoir faire** to regret to have to/that one is unable to do; **j'ai le ~ de vous informer que ...** I regret to inform you that ...

regrettable [ʀəgʀɛtabl(ə)] *adj* regrettable

regretter [ʀəgʀete] *vt* to regret; (*personne*) to miss; **~ d'avoir fait** to regret doing; **~ que** to regret that, be sorry that; **non, je regrette** no, I'm sorry

regroupement [ʀ(ə)gʀupmɑ̃] *nm* grouping together; (*groupe*) group

regrouper [ʀəgʀupe] *vt* (*grouper*) to group together; (*contenir*) to include, comprise; **se regrouper** *vi* to gather (together)

régularisation [ʀegylaʀizɑsjɔ̃] *nf* (*de papiers, passeport*) putting in order; (*de sa situation: par le mariage*) regularization; (*d'un mécanisme*) regulation

régulariser [ʀegylaʀize] *vt* (*fonctionnement, trafic*) to regulate; (*passeport, papiers*) to put in order; (*sa situation*) to straighten out, regularize

régularité [ʀegylaʀite] *nf* regularity

régulateur, -trice [ʀegylatœʀ, -tʀis] *adj* regulating ▷ *nm* (*Tech*): **~ de vitesse/de température** speed/temperature regulator

régulation [ʀegylɑsjɔ̃] *nf* (*du trafic*) regulation; **~ des naissances** birth control

régulier, -ière [ʀegylje, -jɛʀ] *adj* (*gén*) regular; (*vitesse, qualité*) steady; (*répartition, pression*) even; (*Transports: ligne, service*) scheduled, regular; (*légal, réglementaire*) lawful, in order; (*fam: correct*) straight, on the level

régulièrement [ʀegyljɛʀmɑ̃] *adv* regularly; steadily; evenly; normally

régurgiter [ʀegyʀʒite] *vt* to regurgitate

réhabiliter [ʀeabilite] *vt* to rehabilitate; (*fig*) to restore to favour (*Brit*) *ou* favor (*US*)

réhabituer [ʀeabitɥe] *vt*: **se ~ à qch/à faire qch** to get used to sth again/to doing sth again

rehausser [ʀəose] *vt* to heighten, raise; (*fig*) to set off, enhance

réimporter [ʀeɛ̃pɔʀte] *vt* to reimport

réimposer [ʀeɛ̃poze] *vt* (*Finance*) to reimpose; to tax again

réimpression [ʀeɛ̃pʀesjɔ̃] *nf* reprinting; (*ouvrage*) reprint

réimprimer [ʀeɛ̃pʀime] *vt* to reprint

Reims [ʀɛ̃s] *n* Rheims

rein [ʀɛ̃] *nm* kidney; **reins** *nmpl* (*dos*) back *sg*; **avoir mal aux ~s** to have backache; **~ artificiel** kidney machine

réincarnation [ʀeɛ̃kaʀnɑsjɔ̃] *nf* reincarnation

réincarner [ʀeɛ̃kaʀne]: **se réincarner** *vr* to be reincarnated

reine [ʀɛn] *nf* queen
reine-claude [ʀɛnklod] *nf* greengage
reinette [ʀɛnɛt] *nf* rennet, pippin
réinitialisation [ʀeinisjalizasjɔ̃] *nf* (*Inform*)
reset
réinscriptible [ʀeɛ̃skʀiptibl] *adj* (*CD, DVD*)
rewritable
réinsérer [ʀeɛ̃seʀe] *vt* (*délinquant, handicapé etc*) to
rehabilitate
réinsertion [ʀeɛ̃sɛʀsjɔ̃] *nf* rehabilitation
réintégrer [ʀeɛ̃tegʀe] *vt* (*lieu*) to return to;
(*fonctionnaire*) to reinstate
réitérer [ʀeiteʀe] *vt* to repeat, reiterate
rejaillir [ʀəʒajiʀ] *vi* to splash up; ~ **sur** to splash
up onto; (*fig*) to rebound on; to fall upon
rejet [ʀəʒɛ] *nm* (*action, aussi Méd*) rejection;
(*Poésie*) enjambement, rejet; (*Bot*) shoot
rejeter [ʀəʒte] *vt* (*relancer*) to throw back; (*vomir*)
to bring *ou* throw up; (*écarter*) to reject; (*déverser*)
to throw out, discharge; (*reporter*): ~ **un mot à
la fin d'une phrase** to transpose a word to the
end of a sentence; **se** ~ **sur qch** (*accepter faute de
mieux*) to fall back on sth; ~ **la tête/les épaules
en arrière** to throw one's head/pull one's
shoulders back; ~ **la responsabilité de qch
sur qn** to lay the responsibility for sth at sb's
door
rejeton [ʀəʒtɔ̃] *nm* offspring
rejette *etc* [ʀ(ə)ʒɛt] *vb voir* **rejeter**
rejoignais *etc* [ʀ(ə)ʒwaɲɛ] *vb voir* **rejoindre**
rejoindre [ʀəʒwɛ̃dʀ(ə)] *vt* (*famille, régiment*) to
rejoin, return to; (*lieu*) to get (back) to; (*route etc*)
to meet, join; (*rattraper*) to catch up (with); **se
rejoindre** *vi* to meet; **je te rejoins au café** I'll
see *ou* meet you at the café
réjoui, e [ʀeʒwi] *adj* joyous
réjouir [ʀeʒwiʀ] *vt* to delight; **se réjouir** *vi* to be
delighted; **se** ~ **de qch/de faire** to be delighted
about sth/to do; **se** ~ **que** to be delighted that
réjouissances [ʀeʒwisɑ̃s] *nfpl* (*joie*) rejoicing *sg*;
(*fête*) festivities, merry-making *sg*
réjouissant, e [ʀeʒwisɑ̃, -ɑ̃t] *adj* heartening,
delightful
relâche [ʀəlɑʃ]: **faire** ~ *vi* (*navire*) to put into
port; (*Ciné*) to be closed; **c'est le jour de** ~ (*Ciné*)
it's closed today; **sans** ~ *adv* without respite *ou*
a break
relâché, e [ʀəlɑʃe] *adj* loose, lax
relâchement [ʀəlɑʃmɑ̃] *nm* (*d'un prisonnier*)
release; (*de la discipline, musculaire*) relaxation
relâcher [ʀəlɑʃe] *vt* (*ressort, prisonnier*) to release;
(*étreinte, cordes*) to loosen; (*discipline*) to relax ▷ *vi*
(*Navig*) to put into port; **se relâcher** *vi* to loosen;
(*discipline*) to become slack *ou* lax; (*élève etc*) to
slacken off
relais [ʀəlɛ] *nm* (*Sport*): (**course de**) ~ relay
(race); (*Radio, TV*) relay; (*intermédiaire*) go-
between; **équipe de** ~ shift team; (*Sport*) relay
team; **prendre le** ~ (**de**) to take over (from); ~
de poste post house, coaching inn; ~ **routier**
≈ transport café (*Brit*), ≈ truck stop (*US*)
relance [ʀəlɑ̃s] *nf* boosting, revival; (*Écon*)

reflation
relancer [ʀəlɑ̃se] *vt* (*balle*) to throw back (again);
(*moteur*) to restart; (*fig*) to boost, revive;
(*personne*): ~ **qn** to pester sb; to get on to sb again
relater [ʀəlate] *vt* to relate, recount
relatif, -ive [ʀəlatif, -iv] *adj* relative
relation [ʀəlasjɔ̃] *nf* (*récit*) account, report;
(*rapport*) relation(ship); **relations** *nfpl* (*rapports*)
relations; relationship; (*connaissances*)
connections; **être/entrer en** ~(**s**) **avec** to be in
contact *ou* be dealing/get in contact with;
mettre qn en ~(**s**) **avec** to put sb in touch with;
~**s internationales** international relations; ~**s
publiques** public relations; ~**s** (**sexuelles**)
sexual relations, (sexual) intercourse *sg*
relativement [ʀəlativmɑ̃] *adv* relatively; ~ **à** in
relation to
relativiser [ʀəlativize] *vt* to see in relation to; to
put into context
relativité [ʀəlativite] *nf* relativity
relax [ʀəlaks] *adj inv*, **relaxe** [ʀəlaks(ə)] ▷ *adj*
relaxed, informal, casual; easy-going;
(**fauteuil-**)~ *nm* reclining chair
relaxant, e [ʀəlaksɑ̃, -ɑ̃t] *adj* (*cure, médicament*)
relaxant; (*ambiance*) relaxing
relaxation [ʀ(ə)laksasjɔ̃] *nf* relaxation
relaxer [ʀəlakse] *vt* to relax; (*Jur*) to discharge;
se relaxer *vi* to relax
relayer [ʀəleje] *vt* (*collaborateur, coureur etc*) to
relieve, take over from; (*Radio, TV*) to relay; **se
relayer** (*dans une activité*) to take it in turns
relecture [ʀ(ə)lɛktyʀ] *nf* rereading
relégation [ʀəlegasjɔ̃] *nf* (*Sport*) relegation
reléguer [ʀəlege] *vt* to relegate; ~ **au second
plan** to push into the background
relent [ʀəlɑ̃], **relents** *nm(pl)* stench *sg*
relevé, e [ʀəlve] *adj* (*bord de chapeau*) turned-up;
(*manches*) rolled-up; (*fig: style*) elevated; (*: sauce*)
highly-seasoned ▷ *nm* (*lecture*) reading; (*de
cotes*) plotting; (*liste*) statement; list; (*facture*)
account; ~ **de compte** bank statement; ~
d'identité bancaire (**RIB**) (bank) account
number
relève [ʀəlɛv] *nf* relief; (*équipe*) relief team (*ou*
troops *pl*); **prendre la** ~ to take over
relèvement [ʀəlɛvmɑ̃] *nm* (*d'un taux, niveau*)
raising
relever [ʀəlve] *vt* (*statue, meuble*) to stand up
again; (*personne tombée*) to help up; (*vitre, plafond,
niveau de vie*) to raise; (*pays, économie, entreprise*) to
put back on its feet; (*col*) to turn up; (*style,
conversation*) to elevate; (*plat, sauce*) to season;
(*sentinelle, équipe*) to relieve; (*souligner: fautes,
points*) to pick out; (*constater: traces etc*) to find,
pick up; (*répliquer à: remarque*) to react to, reply to;
(*: défi*) to accept, take up; (*noter: adresse etc*) to
take down, note; (*: plan*) to sketch; (*: cotes etc*) to
plot; (*compteur*) to read; (*ramasser: cahiers, copies*)
to collect, take in ▷ *vi* (*jupe, bord*) to ride up; ~ **de**
vt (*maladie*) to be recovering from; (*être du ressort
de*) to be a matter for; (*Admin: dépendre de*) to come
under; (*fig*) to pertain to; **se relever** *vi* (*se*

remettre debout) to get up; (*fig*): **se ~ (de)** to recover (from); **~ qn de** (*vœux*) to release sb from; (*fonctions*) to relieve sb of; **~ la tête** to look up; to hold up one's head

relief [Rəljɛf] *nm* relief; (*de pneu*) tread pattern; **reliefs** *nmpl* (*restes*) remains; **en ~** in relief; (*photographie*) three-dimensional; **mettre en ~** (*fig*) to bring out, highlight

relier [Rəlje] *vt* to link up; (*livre*) to bind; **~ qch à** to link sth to; **livre relié cuir** leather-bound book

relieur, -euse [Rəljœr, -øz] *nm/f* (book)binder

religieusement [R(ə)liჳjøzmã] *adv* religiously; (*enterré, mariés*) in church; **vivre ~** to lead a religious life

religieux, -euse [Rəliჳjø, -øz] *adj* religious ▷ *nm* monk ▷ *nf* nun; (*gâteau*) cream bun

religion [Rəliჳjõ] *nf* religion; (*piété, dévotion*) faith; **entrer en ~** to take one's vows

reliquaire [Rəlikɛr] *nm* reliquary

reliquat [Rəlika] *nm* (*d'une somme*) balance; (*Jur: de succession*) residue

relique [Rəlik] *nf* relic

relire [Rəlir] *vt* (*à nouveau*) to reread, read again; (*vérifier*) to read over; **se relire** to read through what one has written

reliure [Rəljyr] *nf* binding; (*art, métier*): **la ~** book-binding

reloger [R(ə)lɔჳe] *vt* (*locataires, sinistrés*) to rehouse

relu, e [Rəly] *pp de* **relire**

reluire [Rəlɥir] *vi* to gleam

reluisant, e [Rəlɥizã, -ãt] *vb voir* **reluire** ▷ *adj* gleaming; **peu ~** (*fig*) unattractive; unsavoury (*Brit*), unsavory (*US*)

reluquer [R(ə)lyke] *vt* (*fam*) to eye (up), ogle

remâcher [Rəmɑʃe] *vt* to chew *ou* ruminate over

remailler [Rəmɑje] *vt* (*tricot*) to darn; (*filet*) to mend

remaniement [Rəmanimã] *nm*: **~ ministériel** Cabinet reshuffle

remanier [Rəmanje] *vt* to reshape, recast; (*Pol*) to reshuffle

remarquable [Rəmarkabl(ə)] *adj* remarkable

remarquablement [R(ə)markabləmã] *adv* remarkably

remarque [Rəmark(ə)] *nf* remark; (*écrite*) note

remarquer [Rəmarke] *vt* (*voir*) to notice; (*dire*): **~ que** to remark that; **se ~** to be noticeable; **se faire ~** to draw attention to o.s.; **faire ~ (à qn) que** to point out (to sb) that; **faire ~ qch (à qn)** to point sth out (to sb); **remarquez, ...** mark you, ..., mind you, ...

remballer [Rãbale] *vt* to wrap up (again); (*dans un carton*) to pack up (again)

rembarrer [Rãbare] *vt*: **~ qn** (*repousser*) to rebuff sb; (*remettre à sa place*) to put sb in his (*ou* her) place

remblai [Rãblɛ] *nm* embankment

remblayer [Rãbleje] *vt* to bank up; (*fossé*) to fill

in

rembobiner [Rãbɔbine] *vt* to rewind

rembourrage [Rãbura3] *nm* stuffing; padding

rembourré, e [Rãbure] *adj* padded

rembourrer [Rãbure] *vt* to stuff; (*dossier, vêtement, souliers*) to pad

remboursable [Rãbursabl(ə)] *adj* repayable

remboursement [Rãbursəmã] *nm* repayment; **envoi contre ~** cash on delivery

rembourser [Rãburse] *vt* to pay back, repay

rembrunir [Rãbrynir]: **se rembrunir** *vi* to grow sombre (*Brit*) *ou* somber (*US*)

remède [Rəmɛd] *nm* (*médicament*) medicine; (*traitement, fig*) remedy, cure; **trouver un ~ à** (*Méd, fig*) to find a cure for

remédier [Rəmedje]: **~ à** *vt* to remedy

remembrement [Rəmãbrəmã] *nm* (*Agr*) regrouping of lands

remémorer [Rəmemɔre]: **se remémorer** *vt* to recall, recollect

remerciements [Rəmɛrsimã] *nmpl* thanks; **(avec) tous mes ~** (with) grateful *ou* many thanks

remercier [Rəmɛrsje] *vt* to thank; (*congédier*) to dismiss; **~ qn de/d'avoir fait** to thank sb for/ for having done; **non, je vous remercie** no thank you

remettre [Rəmɛtr(ə)] *vt* (*vêtement*): **~ qch** to put sth back on, put sth on again; (*replacer*): **~ qch quelque part** to put sth back somewhere; (*ajouter*): **~ du sel/un sucre** to add more salt/ another lump of sugar; (*rétablir: personne*): **~ qn** to set sb back on his (*ou* her) feet; (*rendre, restituer*): **~ qch à qn** to give sth back to sb, return sth to sb; (*donner, confier: paquet, argent*): **~ qch à qn** to hand sth over to sb, deliver sth to sb; (*prix, décoration*): **~ qch à qn** to present sb with sth; (*ajourner*): **~ qch (à)** to postpone sth *ou* put sth off (until); **se remettre** *vi* to get better, recover; **se ~ de** to recover from, get over; **s'en ~ à** to leave it (up) to; **se ~ à faire/qch** to start doing/sth again; **~ une pendule à l'heure** to put a clock right; **~ un moteur/une machine en marche** to get an engine/a machine going again; **~ en état/en ordre** to repair/sort out; **~ en cause/question** to challenge/question again; **~ sa démission** to hand in one's notice; **~ qch à neuf** to make sth as good as new; **~ qn à sa place** (*fig*) to put sb in his (*ou* her) place

réminiscence [Reminisãs] *nf* reminiscence

remis, e [Rəmi, -iz] *pp de* **remettre** ▷ *nf* delivery; presentation; (*rabais*) discount; (*local*) shed; **~ en marche/en ordre** starting up again/sorting out; **~ en cause/question** calling into question/challenging; **~ de fonds** remittance; **~ en jeu** (*Football*) throw-in; **~ à neuf** restoration; **~ de peine** remission of sentence

remiser [Rəmize] *vt* to put away

rémission [Remisjõ]: **sans ~** *adj* irremediable *adv* unremittingly

remodeler [Rəmɔdle] *vt* to remodel; (*fig: restructurer*) to restructure

rémois, e [ʀemwa, -waz] *adj* of *ou* from Rheims
▷ *nm/f*: **Rémois, e** inhabitant *ou* native of Rheims
remontant [ʀəmɔ̃tɑ̃] *nm* tonic, pick-me-up
remontée [ʀəmɔ̃te] *nf* rising; ascent; **~s
mécaniques** (Ski) ski lifts, ski tows
remonte-pente [ʀəmɔ̃tpɑ̃t] *nm* ski lift, (ski)
tow
remonter [ʀəmɔ̃te] *vi* (à nouveau) to go back up;
(à cheval) to remount; (après une descente) to go up
(again); (en voiture) to get back in; (jupe) to ride
up ▷ *vt* (pente) to go up; (fleuve) to sail (ou swim
etc) up; up; (manches, pantalon) to roll up; (col) to
turn up; (niveau, limite) to raise; (fig: personne) to
buck up; (moteur, meuble) to put back together,
reassemble; (garde-robe etc) to renew, replenish;
(montre, mécanisme) to wind up; **~ le moral à qn**
to raise sb's spirits; **~ à** (dater de) to date *ou* go
back to; **~ en voiture** to get back into the car
remontoir [ʀəmɔ̃twaʀ] *nm* winding
mechanism, winder
remontrance [ʀəmɔ̃tʀɑ̃s] *nf* reproof,
reprimand
remontrer [ʀəmɔ̃tʀe] *vt* (montrer de nouveau): **~
qch (à qn)** to show sth again (to sb); (fig): **en ~ à**
to prove one's superiority over
remords [ʀəmɔʀ] *nm* remorse *no pl*; **avoir des ~**
to feel remorse, be conscience-stricken
remorque [ʀəmɔʀk(ə)] *nf* trailer; **prendre/être
en ~** to tow/be on tow; **être à la ~** (fig) to tag
along (behind)
remorquer [ʀəmɔʀke] *vt* to tow
remorqueur [ʀəmɔʀkœʀ] *nm* tug(boat)
rémoulade [ʀemulad] *nf* dressing with mustard and
herbs
rémouleur [ʀemulœʀ] *nm* (knife- *ou* scissor-)
grinder
remous [ʀəmu] *nm* (d'un navire) (back)wash *no pl*;
(de rivière) swirl, eddy *pl*; (fig) stir *sg*
rempailler [ʀɑ̃paje] *vt* to reseat (with straw)
rempart [ʀɑ̃paʀ] *nm* rampart; **faire à qn un ~
de son corps** to shield sb with one's (own) body
remparts [ʀɑ̃paʀ] *nmpl* walls, ramparts
rempiler [ʀɑ̃pile] *vt* (dossiers, livres etc) to pile up
again ▷ *vi* (Mil: fam) to join up again
remplaçant, e [ʀɑ̃plasɑ̃, -ɑ̃t] *nm/f* replacement,
substitute, stand-in; (Théât) understudy; (Scol)
supply (Brit) *ou* substitute (US) teacher
remplacement [ʀɑ̃plasmɑ̃] *nm* replacement;
(job) replacement work *no pl*; (suppléance: Scol)
supply (Brit) *ou* substitute (US) teacher; **assurer
le ~ de qn** (remplaçant) to stand in *ou* substitute
for sb; **faire des ~s** (professeur) to do supply *ou*
substitute teaching; (médecin) to do locum work
remplacer [ʀɑ̃plase] *vt* to replace; (prendre
temporairement la place de) to stand in for; (tenir lieu
de) to take the place of, act as a substitute for; **~
qch/qn par** to replace sth/sb with
rempli, e [ʀɑ̃pli] *adj* (emploi du temps) full, busy; **~
de** full of, filled with
remplir [ʀɑ̃pliʀ] *vt* to fill (up); (questionnaire) to
fill out *ou* up; (obligations, fonction, condition) to
fulfil; **se remplir** *vi* to fill up; **~ qch de** to fill

sth with
remplissage [ʀɑ̃plisaʒ] *nm* (fig: péj) padding
remploi [ʀɑ̃plwa] *nm* re-use
rempocher [ʀɑ̃pɔʃe] *vt* to put back into one's
pocket
remporter [ʀɑ̃pɔʀte] *vt* (marchandise) to take
away; (fig) to win, achieve
rempoter [ʀɑ̃pɔte] *vt* to repot
remuant, e [ʀəmɥɑ̃, -ɑ̃t] *adj* restless
remue-ménage [ʀəmymenaʒ] *nm inv*
commotion
remuer [ʀəmɥe] *vt* to move; (café, sauce) to stir
▷ *vi* to move; (fig: opposants) to show signs of
unrest; **se remuer** *vi* to move; (se démener) to stir
o.s.; (fam) to get a move on
rémunérateur, -trice [ʀemyneʀatœʀ, -tʀis] *adj*
remunerative, lucrative
rémunération [ʀemyneʀasjɔ̃] *nf* remuneration
rémunérer [ʀemyneʀe] *vt* to remunerate, pay
renâcler [ʀənɑkle] *vi* to snort; (fig) to grumble,
balk
renaissance [ʀənɛsɑ̃s] *nf* rebirth, revival; **la R~**
the Renaissance
renaître [ʀənɛtʀ(ə)] *vi* to be revived; **~ à la vie** to
take on a new lease of life; **~ à l'espoir** to find
fresh hope
rénal, e, -aux [ʀenal, -o] *adj* renal, kidney *cpd*
renard [ʀənaʀ] *nm* fox
renardeau [ʀənaʀdo] *nm* fox cub
rencard [ʀɑ̃kaʀ] *nm* = **rancard**
rencart [ʀɑ̃kaʀ] *nm* = **rancart**
renchérir [ʀɑ̃ʃeʀiʀ] *vi* to become more
expensive; (fig): **~ (sur)** to add something (to)
renchérissement [ʀɑ̃ʃeʀismɑ̃] *nm* increase (in
the cost *ou* price of)
rencontre [ʀɑ̃kɔ̃tʀ(ə)] *nf* (de cours d'eau)
confluence; (de véhicules) collision; (entrevue,
congrès, match etc) meeting; (imprévue) encounter;
faire la ~ de qn to meet sb; **aller à la ~ de qn** to
go and meet sb; **amours de ~** casual love affairs
rencontrer [ʀɑ̃kɔ̃tʀe] *vt* to meet; (mot, expression)
to come across; (difficultés) to meet with; **se
rencontrer** to meet; (véhicules) to collide
rendement [ʀɑ̃dmɑ̃] *nm* (d'un travailleur, d'une
machine) output; (d'une culture) yield; (d'un
investissement) return; **à plein ~** at full capacity
rendez-vous [ʀɑ̃devu] *nm* (rencontre)
appointment; (: d'amoureux) date; (lieu) meeting
place; **donner ~ à qn** to arrange to meet sb;
recevoir sur ~ to have an appointment system;
fixer un ~ à qn to give sb an appointment;
avoir/prendre ~ (avec) to have/make an
appointment (with); **prendre ~ chez le
médecin** to make an appointment with the
doctor; **~ spatial** *ou* **orbital** docking (in space)
rendormir [ʀɑ̃dɔʀmiʀ]: **se rendormir** *vr* to go
back to sleep
rendre [ʀɑ̃dʀ(ə)] *vt* (livre, argent etc) to give back,
return; (otages, visite, politesse, d'un verdict) to
return; (honneurs) to pay; (sang, aliments) to bring
up; (sons: instrument) to produce, make; (exprimer,
traduire) to render; (jugement) to pronounce,

render; (faire devenir): ~ **qn célèbre/qch possible** to make sb famous/sth possible; **se rendre** vi (capituler) to surrender, give o.s. up; (aller): **se ~ quelque part** to go somewhere; **se ~ à** (arguments etc) to bow to; (ordres) to comply with; **se ~ compte de qch** to realize sth; **~ la vue/la santé à qn** to restore sb's sight/health; **~ la liberté à qn** to set sb free; **~ la monnaie** to give change; **se ~ insupportable/malade** to become unbearable/make o.s. ill

rendu, e [Rɑ̃dy] pp de **rendre** ▷ adj (fatigué) exhausted

renégat, e [Rǝnega, -at] nm/f renegade

renégocier [Rǝnegɔsje] vt to renegociate

rênes [Rɛn] nfpl reins

renfermé, e [Rɑ̃fɛRme] adj (fig) withdrawn ▷ nm: **sentir le ~** to smell stuffy

renfermer [Rɑ̃fɛRme] vt to contain; **se renfermer (sur soi-même)** to withdraw into o.s

renfiler [Rɑ̃file] vt (collier) to rethread; (pull) to slip on

renflé, e [Rɑ̃fle] adj bulging, bulbous

renflement [Rɑ̃flǝmɑ̃] nm bulge

renflouer [Rɑ̃flue] vt to refloat; (fig) to set back on its (ou his/her etc) feet (again)

renfoncement [Rɑ̃fɔ̃smɑ̃] nm recess

renforcer [Rɑ̃fɔRse] vt to reinforce; **~ qn dans ses opinions** to confirm sb's opinion

renfort [Rɑ̃fɔR] : **~s** nmpl reinforcements; **en ~** as a back-up; **à grand ~ de** with a great deal of

renfrogné, e [Rɑ̃fRɔɲe] adj sullen, scowling

renfrogner [Rɑ̃fRɔɲe]: **se renfrogner** vi to scowl

rengager [Rɑ̃gaʒe] vt (personnel) to take on again; **se rengager** (Mil) to re-enlist

rengaine [Rɑ̃gɛn] nf (péj) old tune

rengainer [Rɑ̃gene] vt (revolver) to put back in its holster; (épée) to sheathe; (fam: compliment, discours) to save, withhold

rengorger [Rɑ̃gɔRʒe]: **se rengorger** vi (fig) to puff o.s. up

renier [Rǝnje] vt (parents) to disown, repudiate; (engagements) to go back on; (foi) to renounce

renifler [Rǝnifle] vi to sniff ▷ vt (tabac) to sniff up; (odeur) to sniff

rennais, e [Rɛnɛ, -ɛz] adj of ou from Rennes ▷ nm/f: **Rennais, e** inhabitant ou native of Rennes

renne [Rɛn] nm reindeer inv

renom [Rǝnɔ̃] nm reputation; (célébrité) renown; **vin de grand ~** celebrated ou highly renowned wine

renommé, e [R(ǝ)nɔme] adj celebrated, renowned ▷ nf fame

renoncement [Rǝnɔ̃smɑ̃] nm abnegation, renunciation

renoncer [Rǝnɔ̃se] vi: **~ à** vt to give up; **~ à faire** to give up the idea of doing; **j'y renonce!** I give up!

renouer [Rǝnwe] vt (cravate etc) to retie; (fig: conversation, liaison) to renew, resume; **~ avec** (tradition) to revive; (habitude) to take up again; **~ avec qn** to take up with sb again

renouveau, x [Rǝnuvo] nm revival; **~ de succès**

renewed success

renouvelable [R(ǝ)nuvlabl(ǝ)] adj (contrat, bail, énergie) renewable; (expérience) which can be renewed

renouveler [Rǝnuvle] vt to renew; (exploit, méfait) to repeat; **se renouveler** vi (incident) to recur, happen again, be repeated; (cellules etc) to be renewed ou replaced; (artiste, écrivain) to try something new

renouvellement [R(ǝ)nuvɛlmɑ̃] nm renewal; recurrence

rénovation [Renɔvasjɔ̃] nf renovation; restoration; reform(ing); redevelopment

rénover [Renɔve] vt (immeuble) to renovate, do up; (meuble) to restore; (enseignement) to reform; (quartier) to redevelop

renseignement [Rɑ̃sɛɲmɑ̃] nm information no pl, piece of information; (Mil) intelligence no pl; **prendre des ~s sur** to make inquiries about, ask for information about; **(guichet des) ~s** information desk; **(service des) ~s** (Tél) directory inquiries (Brit), information (US); **service de ~s** (Mil) intelligence service; **les ~s généraux** ≈ the secret police

renseigner [Rɑ̃seɲe] vt: **~ qn (sur)** to give information to sb (about); **se renseigner** vi to ask for information, make inquiries

rentabiliser [Rɑ̃tabilize] vt (capitaux, production) to make profitable

rentabilité [Rɑ̃tabilite] nf profitability; cost-effectiveness; (d'un investissement) return; **seuil de ~** break-even point

rentable [Rɑ̃tabl(ǝ)] adj profitable; cost-effective

rente [Rɑ̃t] nf income; (pension) pension; (titre) government stock ou bond; **~ viagère** life annuity

rentier, -ière [Rɑ̃tje, -jɛR] nm/f person of private ou independent means

rentrée [Rɑ̃tRe] nf: **~ (d'argent)** cash no pl coming in; **la ~ (des classes)** the start of the new school year; **la ~ (parlementaire)** the reopening ou reassembly of parliament; **faire sa ~** (artiste, acteur) to make a comeback

rentrer [Rɑ̃tRe] vi (entrer de nouveau) to go (ou come) back in; (entrer) to go (ou come) in; (revenir chez soi) to go (ou come) (back) home; (air, clou: pénétrer) to go in; (revenu, argent) to come in ▷ vt (foins) to bring in; (véhicule) to put away; (chemise dans pantalon etc) to tuck in; (griffes) to draw in; (train d'atterrissage) to raise; (fig: larmes, colère etc) to hold back; **~ le ventre** to pull in one's stomach; **~ dans** to go (ou come) back into; to go (ou come) into; (famille, patrie) to go back ou return to; (heurter) to crash into; (appartenir à) to be included in; (: catégorie etc) to fall into; **~ dans l'ordre** to get back to normal; **~ dans ses frais** to recover one's expenses (ou initial outlay)

renverrai etc [Rɑ̃vere] vb voir **renvoyer**

renversant, e [Rɑ̃vɛRsɑ̃, -ɑ̃t] adj amazing, astounding

renverse [Rɑ̃vɛRs(ǝ)]: **à la ~** adv backwards

renversé, e [ʀɑ̃vɛʀse] *adj* (*écriture*) backhand; (*image*) reversed; (*stupéfait*) staggered

renversement [ʀɑ̃vɛʀsəmɑ̃] *nm* (*d'un régime, des traditions*) overthrow; **~ de la situation** reversal of the situation

renverser [ʀɑ̃vɛʀse] *vt* (*faire tomber: chaise, verre*) to knock over, overturn; (*piéton*) to knock down; (*liquide, contenu*) to spill, upset; (*retourner: verre, image*) to turn upside down, invert; (: *ordre des mots etc*) to reverse; (*fig: gouvernement etc*) to overthrow; (*stupéfier*) to bowl over, stagger; **se renverser** *vi* to fall over; to overturn; to spill; **se ~ (en arrière)** to lean back; **~ la tête/le corps (en arrière)** to tip one's head back/throw oneself back; **~ la vapeur** (*fig*) to change course

renvoi [ʀɑ̃vwa] *nm* dismissal; return; reflection; postponement; (*référence*) cross-reference; (*éructation*) belch

renvoyer [ʀɑ̃vwaje] *vt* to send back; (*congédier*) to dismiss; (*Tennis*) to return; (*lumière*) to reflect; (*son*) to echo; (*ajourner*): **~ qch (à)** to postpone sth (until); **~ qch à qn** (*rendre*) to return sth to sb; **~ qn à** (*fig*) to refer sb to

réorganisation [ʀeɔʀganizasjɔ̃] *nf* reorganization

réorganiser [ʀeɔʀganize] *vt* to reorganize

réorienter [ʀeɔʀjɑ̃te] *vt* to reorient(ate), redirect

réouverture [ʀeuvɛʀtyʀ] *nf* reopening

repaire [ʀəpɛʀ] *nm* den

repaître [ʀəpɛtʀ(ə)] *vt* to feast; to feed; **se ~ de** *vt* (*animal*) to feed on; (*fig*) to wallow *ou* revel in

répandre [ʀepɑ̃dʀ(ə)] *vt* (*renverser*) to spill; (*étaler, diffuser*) to spread; (*lumière*) to shed; (*chaleur, odeur*) to give off; **se répandre** *vi* to spill; to spread; **se ~ en** (*injures etc*) to pour out

répandu, e [ʀepɑ̃dy] *pp de* **répandre** ▷ *adj* (*opinion, usage*) widespread

réparable [ʀepaʀabl(ə)] *adj* (*montre etc*) repairable; (*perte etc*) which can be made up for

reparaître [ʀəpaʀɛtʀ(ə)] *vi* to reappear

réparateur, -trice [ʀepaʀatœʀ, -tʀis] *nm/f* repairer

réparation [ʀepaʀasjɔ̃] *nf* repairing *no pl*, repair; **en ~** (*machine etc*) under repair; **demander à qn ~ de** (*offense etc*) to ask sb to make amends for

réparer [ʀepaʀe] *vt* to repair; (*fig: offense*) to make up for, atone for; (: *oubli, erreur*) to put right

reparler [ʀəpaʀle] *vi*: **~ de qn/qch** to talk about sb/sth again; **~ à qn** to speak to sb again

repars *etc* [ʀəpaʀ] *vb voir* **repartir**

repartie [ʀəpaʀti] *nf* retort; **avoir de la ~** to be quick at repartee

repartir [ʀəpaʀtiʀ] *vi* to set off again; to leave again; (*fig*) to get going again, pick up again; **~ à zéro** to start from scratch (again)

répartir [ʀepaʀtiʀ] *vt* (*pour attribuer*) to share out; (*pour disperser, disposer*) to divide up; (*poids, chaleur*) to distribute; (*étaler: dans le temps*): **~ sur** to spread over; (*classer, diviser*): **~ en** to divide into,

split up into; **se répartir** *vt* (*travail, rôles*) to share out between themselves

répartition [ʀepaʀtisjɔ̃] *nf* sharing out; dividing up; distribution

repas [ʀəpa] *nm* meal; **à l'heure des ~** at mealtimes

repassage [ʀəpasaʒ] *nm* ironing

repasser [ʀəpase] *vi* to come (*ou* go) back ▷ *vt* (*vêtement, tissu*) to iron; (*examen*) to retake, resit; (*film*) to show again; (*lame*) to sharpen; (*leçon, rôle: revoir*) to go over (again); (*plat, pain*): **~ qch à qn** to pass sth back to sb

repasseuse [ʀəpasøz] *nf* (*machine*) ironing machine

repayer [ʀəpeje] *vt* to pay again

repêchage [ʀəpɛʃaʒ] *nm* (*Scol*): **question de ~** question to give candidates a second chance

repêcher [ʀəpeʃe] *vt* (*noyé*) to recover the body of, fish out; (*fam: candidat*) to pass (*by inflating marks*); to give a second chance to

repeindre [ʀəpɛ̃dʀ(ə)] *vt* to repaint

repentir [ʀəpɑ̃tiʀ] *nm* repentance; **se repentir** *vi*: **se ~ (de)** to repent (of)

répercussions [ʀepɛʀkysjɔ̃] *nfpl* repercussions

répercuter [ʀepɛʀkyte] *vt* (*réfléchir, renvoyer: son, voix*) to reflect; (*faire transmettre: consignes, charges etc*) to pass on; **se répercuter** *vi* (*bruit*) to reverberate; (*fig*): **se ~ sur** to have repercussions on

repère [ʀəpɛʀ] *nm* mark; (*monument etc*) landmark; **(point de) ~** point of reference

repérer [ʀəpeʀe] *vt* (*erreur, connaisance*) to spot; (*abri, ennemi*) to locate; **se repérer** *vi* to get one's bearings; **se faire ~** to be spotted

répertoire [ʀepɛʀtwaʀ] *nm* (*liste*) (alphabetical) list; (*carnet*) index notebook; (*Inform*) directory; (*de carnet*) thumb index; (*indicateur*) directory, index; (*d'un théâtre, artiste*) repertoire

répertorier [ʀepɛʀtɔʀje] *vt* to itemize, list

répéter [ʀepete] *vt* to repeat; (*préparer: leçon*) ▷ *aussi vi* to learn, go over; (*Théât*) to rehearse; **se répéter** (*redire*) to repeat o.s.; (*se reproduire*) to be repeated, recur

répéteur [ʀepetœʀ] *nm* (*Tél*) repeater

répétitif, -ive [ʀepetitif, -iv] *adj* repetitive

répétition [ʀepetisjɔ̃] *nf* repetition; (*Théât*) rehearsal; **répétitions** *nfpl* (*leçons*) private coaching *sg*; **armes à ~** repeater weapons; **~ générale** final dress rehearsal

repeupler [ʀəpœple] *vt* to repopulate; (*forêt, rivière*) to restock

repiquage [ʀəpikaʒ] *nm* pricking out, planting out; re-recording

repiquer [ʀəpike] *vt* (*plants*) to prick out, plant out; (*enregistrement*) to re-record

répit [ʀepi] *nm* respite; **sans ~** without letting up

replacer [ʀəplase] *vt* to replace, put back

replanter [ʀəplɑ̃te] *vt* to replant

replat [ʀəpla] *nm* ledge

replâtrer [ʀəplɑtʀe] *vt* (*mur*) to replaster

replet, -ète [ʀəplɛ, -ɛt] *adj* chubby, fat

repli [Rǝpli] *nm* (*d'une étoffe*) fold; (*Mil, fig*) withdrawal

replier [Rǝplije] *vt* (*rabattre*) to fold down *ou* over; **se replier** *vi* (*armée*) to withdraw, fall back; **se ~ sur soi-même** to withdraw into oneself

réplique [Replik] *nf* (*repartie, fig*) reply; (*objection*) retort; (*Théât*) line; (*copie*) replica; **donner la ~ à** to play opposite; **sans ~** *adj* no-nonsense; irrefutable

répliquer [Replike] *vi* to reply; (*avec impertinence*) to answer back; (*riposter*) to retaliate

replonger [Rǝplɔ̃ʒe] *vt*: **~ qch dans** to plunge sth back into; **se ~ dans** (*journal etc*) to immerse o.s. in again

répondant, e [Repɔ̃dã, -ãt] *nm/f* (*garant*) guarantor, surety

répondeur [Repɔ̃dœR] *nm* answering machine

répondre [Repɔ̃dR(ǝ)] *vi* to answer, reply; (*freins, mécanisme*) to respond; **~ à** *vt* to reply to, answer; (*avec impertinence*): **~ à qn** to answer sb back; (*invitation, convocation*) to reply to; (*affection, salut*) to return; (*provocation: mécanisme etc*) to respond to; (*correspondre à: besoin*) to answer; (*: conditions*) to meet; (*: description*) to match; **~ que** to answer *ou* reply that; **~ de** to answer for

réponse [Repɔ̃s] *nf* answer, reply; **avec ~ payée** (*Postes*) reply-paid, post-paid (US); **avoir ~ à tout** to have an answer for everything; **en ~ à** in reply to; **carte-/bulletin-~** reply card/slip

report [RǝpɔR] *nm* postponement; transfer; **~ d'incorporation** (*Mil*) deferment

reportage [RǝpɔRtaʒ] *nm* (*bref*) report; (*écrit: documentaire*) story; article; (*en direct*) commentary; (*genre, activité*): **le ~** reporting

reporter *nm* [RǝpɔRtER] reporter ▷ *vt* [RǝpɔRte] (*total*): **~ qch sur** to carry sth forward *ou* over to; (*ajourner*): **~ qch (à)** to postpone sth (until); (*transférer*): **~ qch sur** to transfer sth to; **se ~ à** (*époque*) to think back to; (*document*) to refer to

repos [Rǝpo] *nm* rest; (*fig*) peace (and quiet); (*mental*) peace of mind; (*Mil*): **~!** (stand) at ease!; **en ~** at rest; **au ~** at rest; (*soldat*) at ease; **de tout ~** safe

reposant, e [R(ǝ)pozã, -ãt] *adj* restful; (*sommeil*) refreshing

repose [Rǝpoz] *nf* refitting

reposé, e [Rǝpoze] *adj* fresh, rested; **à tête ~e** in a leisurely way, taking time to think

repose-pied [Rǝpozpje] *nm inv* footrest

reposer [Rǝpoze] *vt* (*verre, livre*) to put down; (*rideaux, carreaux*) to put back; (*délasser*) to rest; (*problème*) to reformulate ▷ *vi* (*liquide, pâte*) to settle, rest; (*personne*): **ici repose ...** here lies ...; **~ sur** to be built on; (*fig*) to rest on; **se reposer** *vi* to rest; **se ~ sur qn** to rely on sb

repoussant, e [Rǝpusã, -ãt] *adj* repulsive

repoussé, e [Rǝpuse] *adj* (*cuir*) embossed (by hand)

repousser [Rǝpuse] *vi* to grow again ▷ *vt* to repel, repulse; (*offre*) to turn down, reject; (*tiroir, personne*) to push back; (*différer*) to put back

répréhensible [RepReãsibl(ǝ)] *adj* reprehensible

reprendre [RǝpRãdR(ǝ)] *vt* (*prisonnier, ville*) to recapture; (*objet prêté, donné*) to take back; (*chercher*): **je viendrai te ~ à 4 h** I'll come and fetch you *ou* I'll come back for you at 4; (*se resservir de*): **~ du pain/un œuf** to take (*ou* eat) more bread/another egg; (*Comm: article usagé*) to take back; to take in part exchange; (*firme, entreprise*) to take over; (*travail, promenade*) to resume; (*emprunter: argument, idée*) to take up, use; (*refaire: article etc*) to go over again; (*jupe etc*) to alter; (*émission, pièce*) to put on again; (*réprimander*) to tell off; (*corriger*) to correct ▷ *vi* (*classes, pluie*) to start (up) again; (*activités, travaux, combats*) to resume, start (up) again; (*affaires, industrie*) to pick up; (*dire*): **reprit-il** he went on; **se reprendre** (*se ressaisir*) to recover, pull o.s. together; **s'y ~** to make another attempt; **~ des forces** to recover one's strength; **~ courage** to take new heart; **~ ses habitudes/ sa liberté** to get back into one's old habits/ regain one's freedom; **~ la route** to resume one's journey, set off again; **~ connaissance** to come to, regain consciousness; **~ haleine** *ou* **son souffle** to get one's breath back; **~ la parole** to speak again

repreneur [RǝpRǝnœR] *nm* company fixer *ou* doctor

reprenne *etc* [RǝpRɛn] *vb voir* **reprendre**

représailles [RǝpRezaj] *nfpl* reprisals, retaliation *sg*

représentant, e [RǝpRezãtã, -ãt] *nm/f* representative

représentatif, -ive [RǝpRezãtatif, -iv] *adj* representative

représentation [RǝpRezãtasjɔ̃] *nf* representation; performing; (*symbole, image*) representation; (*spectacle*) performance; (*Comm*): **la ~** commercial travelling; sales representation; **frais de ~** (*d'un diplomate*) entertainment allowance

représenter [RǝpRezãte] *vt* to represent; (*donner: pièce, opéra*) to perform; **se représenter** *vt* (*se figurer*) to imagine; to visualize ▷ *vi*: **se ~ à** (*Pol*) to stand *ou* run again at; (*Scol*) to resit

répressif, -ive [RepResif, -iv] *adj* repressive

répression [RepResjɔ̃] *nf voir* **réprimer** suppression; repression; (*Pol*): **la ~** repression; **mesures de ~** repressive measures

réprimande [Reprimãd] *nf* reprimand, rebuke

réprimander [Reprimãde] *vt* to reprimand, rebuke

réprimer [Reprime] *vt* (*émotions*) to suppress; (*peuple etc*) repress

repris, e [RǝpRi, -iz] *pp de* **reprendre** ▷ *nm*: **~ de justice** ex-prisoner, ex-convict

reprise [RǝpRiz] *nf* (*recommencement*) resumption; (*économique*) recovery; (*TV*) repeat; (*Ciné*) rerun; (*Boxe etc*) round; (*Auto*) acceleration *no pl*; (*Comm*) trade-in, part exchange; (*de location*) sum asked for any extras or improvements made to the property; (*raccommodage*) darn; mend; **la ~ des hostilités** the resumption of hostilities; **à**

plusieurs ~s on several occasions, several times

repriser [ʀəpʀize] *vt* to darn; to mend; **aiguille/coton à ~** darning needle/thread

réprobateur, -trice [ʀepʀɔbatœʀ, -tʀis] *adj* reproving

réprobation [ʀepʀɔbasjɔ̃] *nf* reprobation

reproche [ʀəpʀɔʃ] *nm* (*remontrance*) reproach; **ton/air de ~** reproachful tone/look; **faire des ~s à qn** to reproach sb; **faire ~ à qn de qch** to reproach sb for sth; **sans ~(s)** beyond *ou* above reproach

reprocher [ʀəpʀɔʃe] *vt*: **~ qch à qn** to reproach *ou* blame sb for sth; **~ qch à** (*machine, théorie*) to have sth against; **se ~ qch/d'avoir fait qch** to blame o.s for sth/for doing sth

reproducteur, -trice [ʀəpʀɔdyktœʀ, -tʀis] *adj* reproductive

reproduction [ʀəpʀɔdyksjɔ̃] *nf* reproduction; **~ interdite** all rights (of reproduction) reserved

reproduire [ʀəpʀɔdɥiʀ] *vt* to reproduce; **se reproduire** *vi* (*Bio*) to reproduce; (*recommencer*) to recur, re-occur

reprographie [ʀəpʀɔgʀafi] *nf* (photo)copying

réprouvé, e [ʀepʀuve] *nm/f* reprobate

réprouver [ʀepʀuve] *vt* to reprove

reptation [ʀɛptasjɔ̃] *nf* crawling

reptile [ʀɛptil] *nm* reptile

repu, e [ʀəpy] *pp de* **repaître** ▷ *adj* satisfied, sated

républicain, e [ʀepyblikɛ̃, -ɛn] *adj, nm/f* republican

république [ʀepyblik] *nf* republic; **R~ arabe du Yémen** Yemen Arab Republic; **R~ Centrafricaine** Central African Republic; **R~ de Corée** South Korea; **R~ dominicaine** Dominican Republic; **R~ d'Irlande** Irish Republic, Eire; **R~ populaire de Chine** People's Republic of China; **R~ populaire démocratique de Corée** Democratic People's Republic of Korea; **R~ populaire du Yémen** People's Democratic Republic of Yemen

répudier [ʀepydje] *vt* (*femme*) to repudiate; (*doctrine*) to renounce

répugnance [ʀepyɲɑ̃s] *nf* repugnance, loathing; **avoir** *ou* **éprouver de la ~ pour** (*médicament, comportement, travail etc*) to have an aversion to; **avoir** *ou* **éprouver de la ~ à faire qch** to be reluctant to do sth

répugnant, e [ʀepyɲɑ̃, -ɑ̃t] *adj* repulsive, loathsome

répugner [ʀepyɲe]: **~ à** *vt*: **~ à qn** to repel *ou* disgust sb; **~ à faire** to be loath *ou* reluctant to do

répulsion [ʀepylsjɔ̃] *nf* repulsion

réputation [ʀepytasjɔ̃] *nf* reputation; **avoir la ~ d'être …** to have a reputation for being …; **connaître qn/qch de ~** to know sb/sth by repute; **de ~ mondiale** world-renowned

réputé, e [ʀepyte] *adj* renowned; **être ~ pour** to have a reputation for, be renowned for

requérir [ʀəkeʀiʀ] *vt* (*nécessiter*) to require, call for; (*au nom de la loi*) to call upon; (*Jur: peine*) to call for, demand

requête [ʀəkɛt] *nf* request, petition; (*Jur*) petition

requiem [ʀekɥijɛm] *nm* requiem

requiers *etc* [ʀəkjɛʀ] *vb voir* **requérir**

requin [ʀəkɛ̃] *nm* shark

requinquer [ʀəkɛ̃ke] *vt* to set up, pep up

requis, e [ʀəki, -iz] *pp de* **requérir** ▷ *adj* required

réquisition [ʀekizisjɔ̃] *nf* requisition

réquisitionner [ʀekizisjɔne] *vt* to requisition

réquisitoire [ʀekizitwaʀ] *nm* (*Jur*) closing speech for the prosecution; (*fig*): **~ contre** indictment of

RER *sigle m* (= *Réseau express régional*) *Greater Paris high speed train service*

rescapé, e [ʀɛskape] *nm/f* survivor

rescousse [ʀɛskus] *nf*: **aller à la ~ de qn** to go to sb's aid *ou* rescue; **appeler qn à la ~** to call on sb for help

réseau, x [ʀezo] *nm* network

réséda [ʀezeda] *nm* (*Bot*) reseda, mignonette

réservation [ʀezɛʀvasjɔ̃] *nf* reservation; booking

réserve [ʀezɛʀv(ə)] *nf* (*retenue*) reserve; (*entrepôt*) storeroom; (*restriction, aussi: d'Indiens*) reservation; (*de pêche, chasse*) preserve; (*restrictions*): **faire des ~s** to have reservations; **officier de ~** reserve officer; **sous toutes ~s** with all reserve; (*dire*) with reservations; **sous ~ de** subject to; **sans ~** *adv* unreservedly; **en ~** in reserve; **de ~** (*provisions etc*) in reserve

réservé, e [ʀezɛʀve] *adj* (*discret*) reserved; (*chasse, pêche*) private; **~ à** *ou* **pour** reserved for

réserver [ʀezɛʀve] *vt* (*gén*) to reserve; (*chambre, billet etc*) to book, reserve; (*mettre de côté, garder*): **~ qch pour** *ou* **à** to keep *ou* save sth for; **~ qch à qn** to reserve (*ou* book) sth for sb; (*fig: destiner*) to have sth in store for sb; **se ~ le droit de faire** to reserve the right to do

réserviste [ʀezɛʀvist(ə)] *nm* reservist

réservoir [ʀezɛʀvwaʀ] *nm* tank

résidence [ʀezidɑ̃s] *nf* residence; **~ principale/secondaire** main/second home; **~ universitaire** hall of residence; **(en) ~ surveillée** (under) house arrest

résident, e [ʀezidɑ̃, -ɑ̃t] *nm/f* (*ressortissant*) foreign resident; (*d'un immeuble*) resident ▷ *adj* (*Inform*) resident

résidentiel, le [ʀezidɑ̃sjɛl] *adj* residential

résider [ʀezide] *vi*: **~ à** *ou* **dans** *ou* **en** to reside in; **~ dans** (*fig*) to lie in

résidu [ʀezidy] *nm* residue *no pl*

résiduel, le [ʀeziduɛl] *adj* residual

résignation [ʀeziɲasjɔ̃] *nf* resignation

résigné, e [ʀeziɲe] *adj* resigned

résigner [ʀeziɲe] *vt* to relinquish, resign; **se résigner** *vi*: **se ~ (à qch/à faire)** to resign o.s. (to sth/to doing)

résiliable [ʀeziljabl(ə)] *adj* which can be terminated

résilier [ʀezilje] *vt* to terminate

résille [ʀezij] *nf* (hair)net

résine [ʀezin] *nf* resin

résiné, e [ʀezine] *adj*: **vin ~** retsina

résineux, -euse [ʀezinø, -øz] *adj* resinous ▷ *nm* coniferous tree

résistance [ʀezistɑ̃s] *nf* resistance; (*de réchaud, bouilloire: fil*) element

résistant, e [ʀezistɑ̃, -ɑ̃t] *adj* (*personne*) robust, tough; (*matériau*) strong, hard-wearing ▷ *nm/f* (*patriote*) Resistance worker *ou* fighter

résister [ʀeziste] *vi* to resist; **~ à** *vt* (*assaut, tentation*) to resist; (*effort, souffrance*) to withstand; (*matériau, plante*) to stand up to, withstand; (*personne: désobéir à*) to stand up to, oppose

résolu, e [ʀezɔly] *pp de* **résoudre** ▷ *adj* (*ferme*) resolute; **être ~ à qch/faire** to be set upon sth/doing

résolument [ʀezɔlymɑ̃] *adv* resolutely, steadfastly; **~ contre qch** firmly against sth

résolution [ʀezɔlysjɔ̃] *nf* solving; (*fermeté, décision, Inform*) resolution; **prendre la ~ de** to make a resolution to

résolvais *etc* [ʀezɔlvɛ] *vb voir* **résoudre**

résonance [ʀezɔnɑ̃s] *nf* resonance

résonner [ʀezɔne] *vi* (*cloche, pas*) to reverberate, resound; (*salle*) to be resonant; **~ de** to resound with

résorber [ʀezɔʀbe]: **se résorber** *vi* (*Méd*) to be resorbed; (*fig*) to be absorbed

résoudre [ʀezudʀ(ə)] *vt* to solve; **~ qn à faire qch** to get sb to make up his (*ou* her) mind to do sth; **~ de faire** to resolve to do; **se ~ à faire** to bring o.s. to do

respect [ʀɛspɛ] *nm* respect; **tenir en ~** to keep at bay

respectabilité [ʀɛspɛktabilite] *nf* respectability

respectable [ʀɛspɛktabl(ə)] *adj* respectable

respecter [ʀɛspɛkte] *vt* to respect; **faire ~** to enforce; **le lexicographe qui se respecte** (*fig*) any self-respecting lexicographer

respectif, -ive [ʀɛspɛktif, -iv] *adj* respective

respectivement [ʀɛspɛktivmɑ̃] *adv* respectively

respectueusement [ʀɛspɛktɥøzmɑ̃] *adv* respectfully

respectueux, -euse [ʀɛspɛktɥø, -øz] *adj* respectful; **~ de** respectful of

respirable [ʀɛspiʀabl(ə)] *adj*: **peu ~** unbreathable

respiration [ʀɛspiʀasjɔ̃] *nf* breathing *no pl*; **faire une ~ complète** to breathe in and out; **retenir sa ~** to hold one's breath; **~ artificielle** artificial respiration

respiratoire [ʀɛspiʀatwaʀ] *adj* respiratory

respirer [ʀɛspiʀe] *vi* to breathe; (*fig: se reposer*) to get one's breath, have a break; (: *être soulagé*) to breathe again ▷ *vt* to breathe (in), inhale; (*manifester: santé, calme etc*) to exude

resplendir [ʀɛsplɑ̃diʀ] *vi* to shine; (*fig*): **~ (de)** to be radiant (with)

resplendissant, e [ʀɛsplɑ̃disɑ̃, -ɑ̃t] *adj* radiant

responsabilité [ʀɛspɔ̃sabilite] *nf* responsibility; (*légale*) liability; **refuser la ~ de** to deny responsibility (*ou* liability) for; **prendre ses ~s** to assume responsibility for one's actions; **~ civile** civil liability; **~ pénale/morale/collective** criminal/moral/collective responsibility

responsable [ʀɛspɔ̃sabl(ə)] *adj* responsible ▷ *nm/f* (*du ravitaillement etc*) person in charge; (*de parti, syndicat*) official; **~ de** responsible for; (*légalement: de dégâts etc*) liable for; (*chargé de*) in charge of, responsible for

resquiller [ʀɛskije] *vi* (*au cinéma, au stade*) to get in on the sly; (*dans le train*) to fiddle a free ride

resquilleur, -euse [ʀɛskijœʀ, -øz] *nm/f* (*qui n'est pas invité*) gatecrasher; (*qui ne paie pas*) fare dodger

ressac [ʀəsak] *nm* backwash

ressaisir [ʀəseziʀ]: **se ressaisir** *vi* to regain one's self-control; (*équipe sportive*) to rally

ressasser [ʀəsase] *vt* (*remâcher*) to keep turning over; (*redire*) to keep trotting out

ressemblance [ʀəsɑ̃blɑ̃s] *nf* (*visuelle*) resemblance, similarity, likeness; (: *Art*) likeness; (*analogie, trait commun*) similarity

ressemblant, e [ʀəsɑ̃blɑ̃, -ɑ̃t] *adj* (*portrait*) lifelike, true to life

ressembler [ʀəsɑ̃ble]: **~ à** *vt* to be like, resemble; (*visuellement*) to look like; **se ressembler** *vi* to be (*ou* look) alike

ressemeler [ʀəsəmle] *vt* to (re)sole

ressens *etc* [ʀ(ə)sɑ̃] *vb voir* **ressentir**

ressentiment [ʀəsɑ̃timɑ̃] *nm* resentment

ressentir [ʀəsɑ̃tiʀ] *vt* to feel; **se ~ de** to feel (*ou* show) the effects of

resserre [ʀəsɛʀ] *nf* shed

resserrement [ʀ(ə)sɛʀmɑ̃] *nm* narrowing; strengthening; (*goulet*) narrow part

resserrer [ʀəseʀe] *vt* (*pores*) to close; (*nœud, boulon*) to tighten (up); (*fig: liens*) to strengthen; **se resserrer** *vi* (*route, vallée*) to narrow; (*liens*) to strengthen; **se ~ (autour de)** to draw closer (around), to close in (on)

ressers *etc* [ʀ(ə)sɛʀ] *vb voir* **resservir**

resservir [ʀəsɛʀviʀ] *vi* to do *ou* serve again ▷ *vt*: **~ qch (à qn)** to serve sth up again (to sb); **~ de qch (à qn)** to give (sb) a second helping of sth; **~ qn (d'un plat)** to give sb a second helping (of a dish); **se ~ de** (*plat*) to take a second helping of; (*outil etc*) to use again

ressort [ʀəsɔʀ] *vb voir* **ressortir** ▷ *nm* (*pièce*) spring; (*force morale*) spirit; (*recours*): **en dernier ~** as a last resort; (*compétence*): **être du ~ de** to fall within the competence of

ressortir [ʀəsɔʀtiʀ] *vi* to go (*ou* come) out (again); (*contraster*) to stand out; **~ de** (*résulter de*): **il ressort de ceci que** it emerges from this that; **~ à** (*Jur*) to come under the jurisdiction of; (*Admin*) to be the concern of; **faire ~** (*fig: souligner*) to bring out

ressortissant, e [ʀəsɔʀtisɑ̃, -ɑ̃t] *nm/f* national

ressouder [ʀəsude] *vt* to solder together again

ressource, e [ʀəsuʀs(ə)] *nf*: **avoir la ~ de** to have the possibility of; **ressources** *nfpl* resources; (*fig*) possibilities; **leur seule ~ était de** the only course open to them was to; **~s d'énergie** energy resources

ressusciter [ʀesysite] *vt* to resuscitate, restore to life; (*fig*) to revive, bring back ▷ *vi* to rise (from the dead); (*fig: pays*) to come back to life

restant, e [ʀɛstɑ̃, -ɑ̃t] *adj* remaining ▷ *nm*: **le ~ (de)** the remainder (of); **un ~ de** (*de trop*) some leftover; (*fig: vestige*) a remnant *ou* last trace of

restaurant [ʀɛstɔʀɑ̃] *nm* restaurant; **manger au ~** to eat out; **~ d'entreprise** staff canteen *ou* cafeteria (US); **~ universitaire (RU)** university refectory *ou* cafeteria (US)

restaurateur, -trice [ʀɛstɔʀatœʀ, -tʀis] *nm/f* restaurant owner, restaurateur; (*de tableaux*) restorer

restauration [ʀɛstɔʀasjɔ̃] *nf* restoration; (*hôtellerie*) catering; **~ rapide** fast food

restaurer [ʀɛstɔʀe] *vt* to restore; **se restaurer** *vi* to have something to eat

restauroute [ʀɛstɔʀut] *nm* = **restoroute**

reste [ʀɛst(ə)] *nm* (*restant*): **le ~ (de)** the rest (of); (*de trop*): **un ~ (de)** some leftover; (*vestige*): **un ~ de** a remnant *ou* last trace of; (*Math*) remainder; **restes** *nmpl* leftovers; (*d'une cité etc, dépouille mortelle*) remains; **avoir du temps de ~** to have time to spare; **ne voulant pas être en ~** not wishing to be outdone; **partir sans attendre** *ou* **demander son ~** (*fig*) to leave without waiting to hear more; **du ~, au ~** *adv* besides, moreover; **pour le ~, quant au ~** *adv* as for the rest

rester [ʀɛste] *vi* (*dans un lieu, un état, une position*) to stay, remain; (*subsister*) to remain, be left; (*durer*) to last, live on ▷ *vb impers*: **il reste du pain/deux œufs** there's some bread/there are two eggs left (over); **il reste du temps/10 minutes** there's some time/there are 10 minutes left; **il me reste assez de temps** I have enough time left; **voilà tout ce qui (me) reste** that's all I've got left; **ce qui reste à faire** what remains to be done; **ce qui me reste à faire** what remains for me to do; **(il) reste à savoir/établir si ...** it remains to be seen/established if *ou* whether ...; **il n'en reste pas moins que ...** the fact remains that ..., it's nevertheless a fact that ...; **en ~ à** (*stade, menaces*) to go no further than, only go as far as; **restons-en là** let's leave it at that; **~ sur une impression** to retain an impression; **y ~**: **il a failli y ~** he nearly met his end

restituer [ʀɛstitɥe] *vt* (*objet, somme*): **~ qch (à qn)** to return *ou* restore sth (to sb); (*énergie*) to release; (*son*) to reproduce

restitution [ʀɛstitysjɔ̃] *nf* restoration

restoroute [ʀɛstɔʀut] *nm* motorway (Brit) *ou* highway (US) restaurant

restreindre [ʀɛstʀɛ̃dʀ(ə)] *vt* to restrict, limit; **se restreindre** (*dans ses dépenses etc*) to cut down; (*champ de recherches*) to narrow

restreint, e [ʀɛstʀɛ̃, -ɛ̃t] *pp de* **restreindre** ▷ *adj* restricted, limited

restrictif, -ive [ʀɛstʀiktif, -iv] *adj* restrictive, limiting

restriction [ʀɛstʀiksjɔ̃] *nf* restriction; (*condition*) qualification; **restrictions** *nfpl* (*mentales*) reservations; **sans ~** *adv* unreservedly

restructuration [ʀəstʀyktyʀasjɔ̃] *nf* restructuring

restructurer [ʀəstʀyktyʀe] *vt* to restructure

résultante [ʀezyltɑ̃t] *nf* (*conséquence*) result, consequence

résultat [ʀezylta] *nm* result; (*conséquence*) outcome *no pl*, result; (*d'élection etc*) results *pl*; **résultats** *nmpl* (*d'une enquête*) findings; **~s sportifs** sports results

résulter [ʀezylte]: **~ de** *vt* to result from, be the result of; **il résulte de ceci que ...** the result of this is that ...

résumé [ʀezyme] *nm* summary, résumé; **faire le ~ de** to summarize; **en ~** *adv* in brief; (*pour conclure*) to sum up

résumer [ʀezyme] *vt* (*texte*) to summarize; (*récapituler*) to sum up; (*fig*) to epitomize, typify; **se résumer** *vi* (*personne*) to sum up (one's ideas); **se ~ à** to come down to

resurgir [ʀəsyʀʒiʀ] *vi* to reappear, re-emerge

résurrection [ʀezyʀɛksjɔ̃] *nf* resurrection; (*fig*) revival

rétablir [ʀetabliʀ] *vt* to restore, re-establish; (*personne: traitement*): **~ qn** to restore sb to health, help sb recover; (*Admin*): **~ qn dans son emploi/ses droits** to reinstate sb in his post/restore sb's rights; **se rétablir** *vi* (*guérir*) to recover; (*silence, calme*) to return, be restored; (*Gym etc*): **se ~ (sur)** to pull o.s. up (onto)

rétablissement [ʀetablismɑ̃] *nm* restoring; recovery; pull-up

rétamer [ʀetame] *vt* to re-coat, re-tin

rétameur [ʀetamœʀ] *nm* tinker

retaper [ʀətape] *vt* (*maison, voiture etc*) to do up; (*fam: revigorer*) to buck up; (*redactylographier*) to retype

retard [ʀətaʀ] *nm* (*d'une personne attendue*) lateness *no pl*; (*sur l'horaire, un programme, une échéance*) delay; (*fig: scolaire, mental etc*) backwardness; **être en ~** (*pays*) to be backward; (*dans paiement, travail*) to be behind; **en ~ (de deux heures)** (two hours) late; **avoir un ~ de deux km** (*Sport*) to be two km behind; **rattraper son ~** to catch up; **avoir du ~** to be late; (*sur un programme*) to be behind (schedule); **prendre du ~** (*train, avion*) to be delayed; (*montre*) to lose (time); **sans ~** *adv* without delay; **~ à l'allumage** (*Auto*) retarded spark; **~ scolaire** backwardness at school

retardataire [ʀətaʀdatɛʀ] *adj* late; (*enfant, idées*) backward ▷ *nm/f* latecomer; backward child

retardé, e [ʀətaʀde] *adj* backward

retardement [ʀətaʀdəmɑ̃]: **à ~** *adj* delayed action *cpd*; **bombe à ~** time bomb

retarder [ʀətaʀde] *vt* (*sur un horaire*): **~ qn (d'une heure)** to delay sb (an hour); (*sur un programme*): **~ qn (de trois mois)** to set sb back *ou* delay sb

(three months); (*départ, date*): ~ **qch (de deux jours)** to put sth back (two days), delay sth (for *ou* by two days); (*horloge*) to put back ▷ *vi* (*montre*) to be slow; (: *habituellement*) to lose (time); **je retarde (d'une heure)** I'm (an hour) slow
retendre [RətɑdR(ə)] *vt* (*câble etc*) to stretch again; (*Mus*: *cordes*) to retighten
retenir [Rətnir] *vt* (*garder, retarder*) to keep, detain; (*maintenir*: *objet qui glisse, fig*: *colère, larmes, rire*) to hold back; (: *objet suspendu*) to hold; (: *chaleur, odeur*) to retain; (*fig*: *empêcher d'agir*): ~ **qn** to hold sb back (from doing); (*se rappeler*) to retain; (*réserver*) to reserve; (*accepter*) to accept; (*prélever*): ~ **qch (sur)** to deduct sth (from); **se retenir** (*euphémisme*) to hold on; (*se raccrocher*): **se ~ à** to hold onto; (*se contenir*): **se ~ de faire** to restrain o.s. from doing; ~ **son souffle** *ou* **haleine** to hold one's breath; ~ **qn à dîner** to ask sb to stay for dinner; **je pose trois et je retiens deux** put down three and carry two
rétention [Retɑsjɔ] *nf*: ~ **d'urine** urine retention
retentir [RətɑtiR] *vi* to ring out; (*salle*): ~ **de** to ring *ou* resound with; ~ **sur** *vt* (*fig*) to have an effect upon
retentissant, e [Rətɑtisɑ, -ɑt] *adj* resounding; (*fig*) impact-making
retentissement [Rətɑtismɑ] *nm* (*retombées*) repercussions *pl*; effect, impact
retenu, e [Rətny] *pp de* **retenir** ▷ *adj* (*place*) reserved; (*personne*: *empêché*) held up; (*propos*: *contenu, discret*) restrained ▷ *nf* (*prélèvement*) deduction; (*Math*) number to carry over; (*Scol*) detention; (*modération*) (self-)restraint; (*réserve*) reserve, reticence; (*Auto*) tailback
réticence [Retisɑs] *nf* reticence *no pl*, reluctance *no pl*; **sans ~** without hesitation
réticent, e [Retisɑ, -ɑt] *adj* reticent, reluctant
retiendrai [RətjēdRe], **retiens** etc [Rətjē] *vb voir* **retenir**
rétif, -ive [Retif, -iv] *adj* restive
rétine [Retin] *nf* retina
retint etc [Rətē] *vb voir* **retenir**
retiré, e [RətiRe] *adj* (*solitaire*) secluded; (*éloigné*) remote
retirer [RətiRe] *vt* to withdraw; (*vêtement, lunettes*) to take off, remove; (*enlever*) ~ **qch à qn** to take sth from sb; (*extraire*): ~ **qn/qch de** to take sb away from/sth out of, remove sb/sth from; (*reprendre*: *bagages, billets*) to collect, pick up; ~ **des avantages de** to derive advantages from; **se retirer** *vi* (*partir, reculer*) to withdraw; (*prendre sa retraite*) to retire; **se ~ de** to withdraw from; to retire from
retombées [Rətɔbe] *nfpl* (*radioactives*) fallout *sg*; (*fig*) fallout; spin-offs
retomber [Rətɔbe] *vi* (*à nouveau*) to fall again; (*rechuter*): ~ **malade/dans l'erreur** to fall ill again/fall back into error; (*atterrir*: *après un saut etc*) to land; (*tomber, redescendre*) to fall back; (*pendre*) to fall, hang (down); (*échoir*): ~ **sur qn** to fall on sb

retordre [RətɔRdR(ə)] *vt*: **donner du fil à ~ à qn** to make life difficult for sb
rétorquer [RetɔRke] *vt*: ~ **(à qn) que** to retort (to sb) that
retors, e [RətɔR, -ɔRs(ə)] *adj* wily
rétorsion [RetɔRsjɔ] *nf*: **mesures de ~** reprisals
retouche [Rətuʃ] *nf* touching up *no pl*; alteration; **faire une ~** *ou* **des ~s à** to touch up
retoucher [Rətuʃe] *vt* (*photographie, tableau*) to touch up; (*texte, vêtement*) to alter
retour [RətuR] *nm* return; **au ~** (*en arrivant*) when we (*ou* they *etc*) get (*ou* got) back; (*en route*) on the way back; **pendant le ~** on the way *ou* journey back; **à mon/ton ~** on my/your return; **au ~ de** on the return of; **être de ~ (de)** to be back (from); **de ~ à .../chez moi** back at .../back home; **en ~** *adv* in return; **par ~ du courrier** by return of post; **par un juste ~ des choses** by a favourable twist of fate; **match ~** return match; ~ **en arrière** (*Ciné*) flashback; (*mesure*) backward step; ~ **de bâton** kickback; ~ **de chariot** carriage return; ~ **à l'envoyeur** (*Postes*) return to sender; ~ **de flamme** backfire; ~ **(automatique) à la ligne** (*Inform*) wordwrap; ~ **de manivelle** (*fig*) backfire; ~ **offensif** renewed attack; ~ **aux sources** (*fig*) return to basics
retournement [RətuRnəmɑ] *nm* (*d'une personne*: *revirement*) turning (round); ~ **de la situation** reversal of the situation
retourner [RətuRne] *vt* (*dans l'autre sens*: *matelas, crêpe*) to turn (over); (: *caisse*) to turn upside down; (: *sac, vêtement*) to turn inside out; (*fig*: *argument*) to turn back; (*en remuant*: *terre, sol, foin*) to turn over; (*émouvoir*: *personne*) to shake; (*renvoyer, restituer*): ~ **qch à qn** to return sth to sb ▷ *vi* (*aller, revenir*): ~ **quelque part/à** to go back *ou* return somewhere/to; ~ **à** (*état, activité*) to return to, go back to; **se retourner** *vi* to turn over; (*tourner la tête*) to turn round; **s'en ~** to go back; **se retourner contre** (*fig*) to turn against; **savoir de quoi il retourne** to know what it is all about; ~ **sa veste** (*fig*) to turn one's coat; ~ **en arrière** *ou* **sur ses pas** to turn back, retrace one's steps; ~ **aux sources** to go back to basics
retracer [RətRase] *vt* to relate, recount
rétracter [RetRakte] *vt*, **se rétracter** *vi* to retract
retraduire [RətRaduiR] *vt* to translate again; (*dans la langue de départ*) to translate back
retrait [RətRE] *nm voir* **retirer** withdrawal; collection; *voir* **se retirer** withdrawal; (*rétrécissement*) shrinkage; **en ~** *adj* set back; **écrire en ~** to indent; ~ **du permis (de conduire)** disqualification from driving (*Brit*), revocation of driver's license (*US*)
retraite [RətRE] *nf* (*d'une armée, Rel, refuge*) retreat; (*d'un employé*) retirement; (*revenu*) (retirement) pension; **être/mettre à la ~** to be retired/pension off *ou* retire; **prendre sa ~** to retire; ~ **anticipée** early retirement; ~ **aux flambeaux** torchlight tattoo

retraité | révéler

retraité, e [RətRete] *adj* retired ▷ *nm/f* (old age) pensioner
retraitement [RətRɛtmã] *nm* reprocessing
retraiter [RətRete] *vt* to reprocess
retranchement [RətRãʃmã] *nm* entrenchment; **poursuivre qn dans ses derniers ~s** to drive sb into a corner
retrancher [RətRãʃe] *vt* (*passage, détails*) to take out, remove; (*nombre, somme*): **~ qch de** to take *ou* deduct sth from; (*couper*) to cut off; **se ~ derrière/dans** to entrench o.s. behind/in; (*fig*) to take refuge behind/in
retranscrire [RətRãskRiR] *vt* to retranscribe
retransmettre [RətRãsmɛtR(ə)] *vt* (*Radio*) to broadcast, relay; (*TV*) to show
retransmission [RətRãsmisjõ] *nf* broadcast; showing
retravailler [RətRavaje] *vi* to start work again ▷ *vt* to work on again
retraverser [RətRavɛRse] *vt* (*dans l'autre sens*) to cross back over
rétréci, e [Retresi] *adj* (*idées, esprit*) narrow
rétrécir [RetResiR] *vt* (*vêtement*) to take in ▷ *vi* to shrink; **se rétrécir** *vi* to narrow
rétrécissement [Retresismã] *nm* narrowing
retremper [RətRãpe] *vt*: **se ~ dans** (*fig*) to reimmerse o.s. in
rétribuer [RetRibɥe] *vt* (*travail*) to pay for; (*personne*) to pay
rétribution [RetRibysjõ] *nf* payment
rétro [RetRo] *adj inv* old-style ▷ *nm* (*rétroviseur*) (rear-view) mirror; **la mode ~** the nostalgia vogue
rétroactif, -ive [RetRoaktif, -iv] *adj* retroactive
rétrocéder [RetRosede] *vt* to retrocede
rétrocession [RetRosesjõ] *nf* retrocession
rétrofusée [RetRofyze] *nf* retrorocket
rétrograde [RetRogRad] *adj* reactionary, backward-looking
rétrograder [RetRogRade] *vi* (*élève*) to fall back; (*économie*) to regress; (*Auto*) to change down
rétroprojecteur [RetRopRoʒɛktœR] *nm* overhead projector
rétrospectif, -ive [RetRospɛktif, -iv] *adj, nf* retrospective
rétrospectivement [RetRospɛktivmã] *adv* in retrospect
retroussé, e [RətRuse] *adj*: **nez ~** turned-up nose
retrousser [RətRuse] *vt* to roll up; (*fig: nez*) to wrinkle; (: *lèvres*) to curl
retrouvailles [RətRuvaj] *nfpl* reunion *sg*
retrouver [RətRuve] *vt* (*fugitif, objet perdu*) to find; (*occasion*) to find again; (*calme, santé*) to regain; (*reconnaître: expression, style*) to recognize; (*revoir*) to see again; (*rejoindre*) to meet (again), join; **se retrouver** *vi* to meet; (*s'orienter*) to find one's way; **se ~ quelque part** to find o.s. somewhere; to end up somewhere; **se ~ seul/sans argent** to find o.s. alone/with no money; **se ~ dans** (*calculs, dossiers, désordre*) to make sense of; **s'y ~** (*rentrer dans ses frais*) to break even

rétroviseur [RetRovizœR] *nm* (rear-view) mirror
réunifier [Reynifje] *vt* to reunify
Réunion [Reynjõ] *nf*: **la ~, l'île de la ~** Réunion
réunion [Reynjõ] *nf* bringing together; joining; (*séance*) meeting
réunionnais, e [Reynjonɛ, -ɛz] *adj* of *ou* from Réunion
réunir [ReyniR] *vt* (*convoquer*) to call together; (*rassembler*) to gather together; (*cumuler*) to combine; (*rapprocher*) to bring together (again), reunite; (*rattacher*) to join (together); **se réunir** *vi* (*se rencontrer*) to meet; (*s'allier*) to unite
réussi, e [Reysi] *adj* successful
réussir [ReysiR] *vi* to succeed, be successful; (*à un examen*) to pass; (*plante, culture*) to thrive, do well ▷ *vt* to make a success of; to bring off; **~ à faire** to succeed in doing; **~ à qn** to go right for sb; (*aliment*) to agree with sb; **le travail/le mariage lui réussit** work/married life agrees with him
réussite [Reysit] *nf* success; (*Cartes*) patience
réutiliser [Reytilize] *vt* to re-use
revaloir [RəvalwaR] *vt*: **je vous revaudrai cela** I'll repay you some day; (*en mal*) I'll pay you back for this
revalorisation [RəvaloRizasjõ] *nf* revaluation; raising
revaloriser [RəvaloRize] *vt* (*monnaie*) to revalue; (*salaires, pensions*) to raise the level of; (*institution, tradition*) to reassert the value of
revanche [Rəvãʃ] *nf* revenge; **prendre sa ~ (sur)** to take one's revenge (on); **en ~** (*par contre*) on the other hand; (*en compensation*) in return
rêvasser [Rɛvase] *vi* to daydream
rêve [Rɛv] *nm* dream; (*activité psychique*): **le ~** dreaming; **paysage/silence de ~** dreamlike landscape/silence; **~ éveillé** daydreaming *no pl*, daydream
rêvé, e [Reve] *adj* (*endroit, mari etc*) ideal
revêche [Rəvɛʃ] *adj* surly, sour-tempered
réveil [Revɛj] *nm* (*d'un dormeur*) waking up *no pl*; (*fig*) awakening; (*pendule*) alarm (clock); **au ~** when I (*ou* you *etc*) wake (*ou* woke) up, on waking (up); **sonner le ~** (*Mil*) to sound the reveille
réveille-matin [Revɛjmatɛ̃] *nm inv* alarm clock
réveiller [Reveje] *vt* (*personne*) to wake up; (*fig*) to awaken, revive; **se réveiller** *vi* to wake up; (*fig*) to be revived, reawaken
réveillon [Revɛjõ] *nm* Christmas Eve; (*de la Saint-Sylvestre*) New Year's Eve; Christmas Eve (*ou* New Year's Eve) party *ou* dinner
réveillonner [Revɛjone] *vi* to celebrate Christmas Eve (*ou* New Year's Eve)
révélateur, -trice [RevelatœR, -tRis] *adj*: **~ (de qch)** revealing (sth) ▷ *nm* (*Photo*) developer
révélation [Revelasjõ] *nf* revelation
révéler [Revele] *vt* (*gén*) to reveal; (*divulguer*) to disclose, reveal; (*dénoter*) to reveal, show; (*faire connaître au public*): **~ qn/qch** to make sb/sth widely known, bring sb/sth to the public's notice; **se révéler** *vi* to be revealed, reveal

itself; **se ~ facile/faux** to prove (to be) easy/false; **se ~ cruel/un allié sûr** to show o.s. to be cruel/a trustworthy ally

revenant, e [Rəvnā, -āt] *nm/f* ghost

revendeur, -euse [Rəvādœʀ, -øz] *nm/f* (*détaillant*) retailer; (*d'occasions*) secondhand dealer

revendicatif, -ive [Rəvādikatif, -iv] *adj* (*mouvement*) protest *cpd*

revendication [Rəvādikasjɔ̃] *nf* claim, demand; **journée de ~** day of action (in support of one's claims)

revendiquer [Rəvādike] *vt* to claim, demand; (*responsabilité*) to claim ▷ *vi* to agitate in favour of one's claims

revendre [Rəvādʀ(ə)] *vt* (*d'occasion*) to resell; (*détailler*) to sell; (*vendre davantage de*): **~ du sucre/un foulard/deux bagues** to sell more sugar/another scarf/another two rings; **à ~** *adv* (*en abondance*) to spare

revenir [Rəvniʀ] *vi* to come back; (*Culin*): **faire ~** to brown; (*coûter*): **~ cher/à 100 euros (à qn)** to cost (sb) a lot/100 euros; **~ à** (*études, projet*) to return to, go back to; (*équivaloir à*) to amount to; **~ à qn** (*rumeur, nouvelle*) to get back to sb, reach sb's ears; (*part, honneur*) to go to sb, be sb's; (*souvenir, nom*) to come back to sb; **~ de** (*fig: maladie, étonnement*) to recover from; **~ sur** (*question, sujet*) to go back over; (*engagement*) to go back on; **~ à la charge** to return to the attack; **~ à soi** to come round; **n'en pas ~: je n'en reviens** I can't get over it; **~ sur ses pas** to retrace one's steps; **cela revient à dire que/au même** it amounts to saying that/to the same thing; **~ de loin** (*fig*) to have been at death's door

revente [Rəvāt] *nf* resale

revenu, e [Rəvny] *pp de* **revenir** ▷ *nm* income; (*de l'État*) revenue; (*d'un capital*) yield; **revenus** *nmpl* income *sg*; **~ national brut** gross national income

rêver [Reve] *vi, vt* to dream; (*rêvasser*) to (day)dream; **~ de** (*voir en rêve*) to dream of ou about; **~ de qch/de faire** to dream of sth/of doing; **~ à** to dream of

réverbération [RevɛRbeRasjɔ̃] *nf* reflection

réverbère [RevɛRbɛR] *nm* street lamp *ou* light

réverbérer [RevɛRbeRe] *vt* to reflect

reverdir [RəvɛRdiR] *vi* (*arbre etc*) to turn green again

révérence [ReveRās] *nf* (*vénération*) reverence; (*salut: d'homme*) bow; (: *de femme*) curtsey

révérencieux, -euse [ReveRāsjø, -øz] *adj* reverent

révérend, e [ReveRā, -ād] *adj*: **le ~ père Pascal** the Reverend Father Pascal

révérer [ReveRe] *vt* to revere

rêverie [Rɛvʀi] *nf* daydreaming *no pl*, daydream

reverrai *etc* [RəvɛRe] *vb voir* **revoir**

revers [RəvɛR] *nm* (*de feuille, main*) back; (*d'étoffe*) wrong side; (*de pièce, médaille*) back, reverse; (*Tennis, Ping-Pong*) backhand; (*de veston*) lapel; (*de*

pantalon) turn-up; (*fig: échec*) setback; **~ de fortune** reverse of fortune; **d'un ~ de main** with the back of one's hand; **le ~ de la médaille** (*fig*) the other side of the coin; **prendre à ~** (*Mil*) to take from the rear

reverser [RəvɛRse] *vt* (*reporter: somme etc*): **~ sur** to put back into; (*liquide*): **~ (dans)** to pour some more (into)

réversible [RevɛRsibl(ə)] *adj* reversible

revêtement [Rəvɛtmā] *nm* (*de paroi*) facing; (*des sols*) flooring; (*de chaussée*) surface; (*de tuyau etc: enduit*) coating

revêtir [Rəvetir] *vt* (*habit*) to don, put on; (*fig*) to take on; **~ qn de** to dress sb in; (*fig*) to endow ou invest sb with; **~ qch de** to cover sth with; (*fig*) to cloak sth in; **~ d'un visa** to append a visa to

rêveur, -euse [RɛvœR, -øz] *adj* dreamy ▷ *nm/f* dreamer

reviendrai *etc* [Rəvjɛ̃dRe] *vb voir* **revenir**

revienne *etc* [Rəvjɛn] *vb voir* **revenir**

revient [Rəvjɛ̃] *vb voir* **revenir** ▷ *nm*: **prix de ~** cost price

revigorer [RəvigɔRe] *vt* to invigorate, revive, buck up

revint *etc* [Rəvɛ̃] *vb voir* **revenir**

revirement [RəviRmā] *nm* change of mind; (*d'une situation*) reversal

revis *etc* [Rəvi] *vb voir* **revoir**

révisable [Revizabl(ə)] *adj* (*procès, taux etc*) reviewable, subject to review

réviser [Revize] *vt* (*texte, Scol: matière*) to revise; (*comptes*) to audit; (*machine, installation, moteur*) to overhaul, service; (*Jur: procès*) to review

révision [Revizjɔ̃] *nf* revision; auditing *no pl*; overhaul, servicing *no pl*; review; **conseil de ~** (*Mil*) recruiting board; **faire ses ~s** (*Scol*) to do one's revision (*Brit*), revise (*Brit*), review (*US*); **la ~ des 10 000 km** (*Auto*) the 10,000 km service

révisionnisme [Revizjɔnism(ə)] *nm* revisionism

revisser [Rəvise] *vt* to screw back again

revit [Rəvi] *vb voir* **revoir**

revitaliser [Rəvitalize] *vt* to revitalize

revivifier [Rəvivifje] *vt* to revitalize

revivre [RəvivR(ə)] *vi* (*reprendre des forces*) to come alive again; (*traditions*) to be revived ▷ *vt* (*épreuve, moment*) to relive; **faire ~** (*mode, institution, usage*) to bring back to life

révocable [Revɔkabl(ə)] *adj* (*délégué*) dismissible; (*contrat*) revocable

révocation [Revɔkasjɔ̃] *nf* dismissal; revocation

revoir [Rəvwaʀ] *vt* to see again; (*réviser*) to revise (*Brit*), review (*US*) ▷ *nm*: **au ~** goodbye; **dire au ~ à qn** to say goodbye to sb; **se revoir** (*amis*) to meet (again), see each other again

révoltant, e [Revɔltā, -āt] *adj* revolting

révolte [Revɔlt(ə)] *nf* rebellion, revolt

révolter [Revɔlte] *vt* to revolt, outrage; **se révolter** *vi*: **se ~ (contre)** to rebel (against); **se ~ (à)** to be outraged (by)

révolu, e [Revɔly] *adj* past; (*Admin*): **âgé de 18 ans ~s** over 18 years of age; **après trois ans ~s**

when three full years have passed

révolution [ʀevɔlysjɔ̃] *nf* revolution; **être en ~** (*pays etc*) to be in revolt; **la ~ industrielle** the industrial revolution

révolutionnaire [ʀevɔlysjɔnɛʀ] *adj, nm/f* revolutionary

révolutionner [ʀevɔlysjɔne] *vt* to revolutionize; (*fig*) to stir up

revolver [ʀevɔlvɛʀ] *nm* gun; (*à barillet*) revolver

révoquer [ʀevɔke] *vt* (*fonctionnaire*) to dismiss, remove from office; (*arrêt, contrat*) to revoke

revoyais *etc* [ʀəvwajɛ] *vb voir* **revoir**

revu, e [ʀəvy] *pp de* **revoir** ▷ *nf* (*inventaire, examen*) review; (*Mil: défilé*) review, march past; (*: inspection*) inspection, review; (*périodique*) review, magazine; (*pièce satirique*) revue; (*de music-hall*) variety show; **passer en ~** to review, inspect; (*fig*) to review; **~ de (la) presse** press review

révulsé, e [ʀevylse] *adj* (*yeux*) rolled upwards; (*visage*) contorted

Reykjavik [ʀekjavik] *n* Reykjavik

rez-de-chaussée [ʀedʃose] *nm inv* ground floor

rez-de-jardin [ʀedʒaʀdɛ̃] *nm inv* garden level

RF *sigle f* = **République française**

RFA *sigle f* (= *République fédérale d'Allemagne*) FRG

RFO *sigle f* (= *Radio-Télévision Française d'Outre-mer*) French overseas broadcasting service

RG *sigle mpl* (= *renseignements généraux*) security section of the police force

rhabiller [ʀabije] *vt*: **se rhabiller** to get dressed again, put one's clothes on again

rhapsodie [ʀapsɔdi] *nf* rhapsody

rhéostat [ʀeɔsta] *nm* rheostat

rhésus [ʀezys] *adj, nm* rhesus; **~ positif/négatif** rhesus positive/negative

rhétorique [ʀetɔʀik] *nf* rhetoric ▷ *adj* rhetorical

Rhin [ʀɛ̃] *nm*: **le ~** the Rhine

rhinite [ʀinit] *nf* rhinitis

rhinocéros [ʀinɔseʀɔs] *nm* rhinoceros

rhinopharyngite [ʀinɔfaʀɛ̃ʒit] *nf* throat infection

rhodanien, ne [ʀɔdanjɛ̃, -ɛn] *adj* Rhône *cpd*, of the Rhône

Rhodes [ʀɔd] *n*: (**l'île de**) **~** (the island of) Rhodes

Rhodésie [ʀɔdezi] *nf*: **la ~** Rhodesia

rhodésien, ne [ʀɔdezjɛ̃, -ɛn] *adj* Rhodesian

rhododendron [ʀɔdɔdɛ̃dʀɔ̃] *nm* rhododendron

Rhône [ʀon] *nm*: **le ~** the Rhone

rhubarbe [ʀybaʀb(ə)] *nf* rhubarb

rhum [ʀɔm] *nm* rum

rhumatisant, e [ʀymatizɑ̃, -ɑ̃t] *adj, nm/f* rheumatic

rhumatismal, e, -aux [ʀymatismal, -o] *adj* rheumatic

rhumatisme [ʀymatism(ə)] *nm* rheumatism *no pl*

rhumatologie [ʀymatɔlɔʒi] *nf* rheumatology

rhumatologue [ʀymatɔlɔg] *nm/f* rheumatologist

rhume [ʀym] *nm* cold; **~ de cerveau** head cold;

le ~ des foins hay fever

rhumerie [ʀɔmʀi] *nf* (*distillerie*) rum distillery

RI *sigle m* (*Mil*) = **régiment d'infanterie**

ri [ʀi] *pp de* **rire**

riant, e [ʀjɑ̃, -ɑ̃t] *vb voir* **rire** ▷ *adj* smiling, cheerful; (*campagne, paysage*) pleasant

RIB *sigle m* = **relevé d'identité bancaire**

ribambelle [ʀibɑ̃bɛl] *nf*: **une ~ de** a herd *ou* swarm of

ricain, e [ʀikɛ̃, -ɛn] *adj* (*fam*) Yank, Yankee

ricanement [ʀikanmɑ̃] *nm* snigger; giggle

ricaner [ʀikane] *vi* (*avec méchanceté*) to snigger; (*bêtement, avec gêne*) to giggle

riche [ʀiʃ] *adj* (*gén*) rich; (*personne, pays*) rich, wealthy; **~ en** rich in; **~ de** full of; rich in

richement [ʀiʃmɑ̃] *adv* richly

richesse [ʀiʃɛs] *nf* wealth; (*fig*) richness; **richesses** *nfpl* wealth *sg*; treasures; **~ en vitamines** high vitamin content

richissime [ʀiʃisim] *adj* extremely rich *ou* wealthy

ricin [ʀisɛ̃] *nm*: **huile de ~** castor oil

ricocher [ʀikɔʃe] *vi*: **~ (sur)** to rebound (off); (*sur l'eau*) to bounce (on *ou* off); **faire ~** (*galet*) to skim

ricochet [ʀikɔʃɛ] *nm* rebound; bounce; **faire ~** to rebound, bounce; (*fig*) to rebound; **faire des ~s** to skip stones; **par ~** *adv* on the rebound; (*fig*) as an indirect result

rictus [ʀiktys] *nm* grin, (snarling) grimace

ride [ʀid] *nf* wrinkle; (*fig*) ripple

ridé, e [ʀide] *adj* wrinkled

rideau, x [ʀido] *nm* curtain; **tirer/ouvrir les ~x** to draw/open the curtains; **~ de fer** metal shutter; (*Pol*): **le ~ de fer** the Iron Curtain

ridelle [ʀidɛl] *nf* slatted side (*of truck*)

rider [ʀide] *vt* to wrinkle; (*fig*) to ripple, ruffle the surface of; **se rider** *vi* to become wrinkled

ridicule [ʀidikyl] *adj* ridiculous ▷ *nm* ridiculousness *no pl*; **le ~** ridicule; (*travers: gén pl*) absurdities *pl*; **tourner en ~** to ridicule

ridiculement [ʀidikylmɑ̃] *adv* ridiculously

ridiculiser [ʀidikylize] *vt* to ridicule; **se ridiculiser** to make a fool of o.s

ridule [ʀidyl] *nf* (*euph: ride*) little wrinkle

rie *etc* [ʀi] *vb voir* **rire**

 MOT-CLÉ

rien [ʀjɛ̃] *pron* **1**: **(ne)... rien** nothing; (*tournure negative*) anything; **qu'est-ce que vous avez? — rien** what have you got? — nothing; **il n'a rien dit/fait** he said/did nothing, he hasn't said/done anything; **il n'a rien** (*n'est pas blessé*) he's all right; **ça ne fait rien** it doesn't matter; **il n'y est pour rien** he's got nothing to do with it

2 (*quelque chose*): **a-t-il jamais rien fait pour nous?** has he ever done anything for us?

3: **rien de**: **rien d'intéressant** nothing interesting; **rien d'autre** nothing else; **rien du tout** nothing at all; **il n'a rien d'un champion** he's no champion, there's nothing of the champion about him

4: **rien que** just, only; nothing but; **rien que pour lui faire plaisir** only *ou* just to please him; **rien que la vérité** nothing but the truth; **rien que cela** that alone
▷ *excl*: **de rien!** not at all!, don't mention it!; **il n'en est rien!** nothing of the sort!; **rien à faire!** it's no good!, it's no use!
▷ *nm*: **un petit rien** (*cadeau*) a little something; **des riens** trivia *pl*; **un rien de** a hint of; **en un rien de temps** in no time at all; **avoir peur d'un rien** to be frightened of the slightest thing

rieur, -euse [ʀjœʀ, -øz] *adj* cheerful
rigide [ʀiʒid] *adj* stiff; (*fig*) rigid; (*moralement*) strict
rigidité [ʀiʒidite] *nf* stiffness; **la ~ cadavérique** rigor mortis
rigolade [ʀigɔlad] *nf*: **la ~** fun; (*fig*): **c'est de la ~** it's a big farce; (*c'est facile*) it's a cinch
rigole [ʀigɔl] *nf* (*conduit*) channel; (*filet d'eau*) rivulet
rigoler [ʀigɔle] *vi* (*rire*) to laugh; (*s'amuser*) to have (some) fun; (*plaisanter*) to be joking *ou* kidding
rigolo, ote [ʀigɔlo, -ɔt] *adj* (*fam*) funny ▷ *nm/f* comic; (*péj*) fraud, phoney
rigorisme [ʀigɔʀism(ə)] *nm* (moral) rigorism
rigoriste [ʀigɔʀist(ə)] *adj* rigorist
rigoureusement [ʀiguʀøzmɑ̃] *adv* rigorously; **~ vrai/interdit** strictly true/forbidden
rigoureux, -euse [ʀiguʀø, -øz] *adj* (*morale*) rigorous, strict; (*personne*) stern, strict; (*climat, châtiment*) rigorous, harsh, severe; (*interdiction, neutralité*) strict; (*preuves, analyse, méthode*) rigorous
rigueur [ʀigœʀ] *nf* rigour (*Brit*), rigor (*US*); strictness; harshness; **"tenue de soirée de ~"** "evening dress (to be worn)"; **être de ~** to be the usual thing, be the rule; **à la ~** at a pinch; possibly; **tenir ~ à qn de qch** to hold sth against sb
riions *etc* [ʀijɔ̃] *vb voir* **rire**
rillettes [ʀijɛt] *nfpl* ≈ potted meat *sg*
rime [ʀim] *nf* rhyme; **n'avoir ni ~ ni raison** to have neither rhyme nor reason
rimer [ʀime] *vi*: **~ (avec)** to rhyme (with); **ne ~ à rien** not to make sense
Rimmel® [ʀimɛl] *nm* mascara
rinçage [ʀɛ̃saʒ] *nm* rinsing (out); (*opération*) rinse
rince-doigts [ʀɛ̃sdwa] *nm inv* finger-bowl
rincer [ʀɛ̃se] *vt* to rinse; (*récipient*) to rinse out; **se ~ la bouche** to rinse one's mouth out
ring [ʀiŋ] *nm* (boxing) ring; **monter sur le ~** (*aussi fig*) to enter the ring; (: *faire carrière de boxeur*) to take up boxing
ringard, e [ʀɛ̃gaʀ, -aʀd(ə)] *adj* (*péj*) old-fashioned
Rio de Janeiro [ʀiodʒaneʀ(o)] *n* Rio de Janeiro
rions [ʀiɔ̃] *vb voir* **rire**
ripaille [ʀipaj] *nf*: **faire ~** to feast
riper [ʀipe] *vi* to slip, slide

ripoliné, e [ʀipɔline] *adj* enamel-painted
riposte [ʀipɔst(ə)] *nf* retort, riposte; (*fig*) counter-attack, reprisal
riposter [ʀipɔste] *vi* to retaliate ▷ *vt*: **~ que** to retort that; **~ à** *vt* to counter; to reply to
ripper [ʀipe] *vt* (*Inform*) to rip
rire [ʀiʀ] *vi* to laugh; (*se divertir*) to have fun; (*plaisanter*) to joke ▷ *nm* laugh; **le ~** laughter; **~ de** *vt* to laugh at; **se ~ de** to make light of; **tu veux ~!** you must be joking!; **~ aux éclats/aux larmes** to roar with laughter/laugh until one cries; **~ jaune** to force oneself to laugh; **~ sous cape** to laugh up one's sleeve; **~ au nez de qn** to laugh in sb's face; **pour ~** (*pas sérieusement*) for a joke *ou* a laugh
ris [ʀi] *vb voir* **rire** ▷ *nm*: **~ de veau** (calf) sweetbread
risée [ʀize] *nf*: **être la ~ de** to be the laughing stock of
risette [ʀizɛt] *nf*: **faire ~ (à)** to give a nice little smile (to)
risible [ʀizibl(ə)] *adj* laughable, ridiculous
risque [ʀisk(ə)] *nm* risk; **l'attrait du ~** the lure of danger; **prendre des ~s** to take risks; **à ses ~s et périls** at his own risk; **au ~ de** at the risk of; **~ d'incendie** fire risk; **~ calculé** calculated risk
risqué, e [ʀiske] *adj* risky; (*plaisanterie*) risqué, daring
risquer [ʀiske] *vt* to risk; (*allusion, question*) to venture, hazard; **tu risques qu'on te renvoie** you risk being dismissed; **ça ne risque rien** it's quite safe; **~ de: il risque de se tuer** he could get *ou* risks getting himself killed; **il a risqué de se tuer** he almost got himself killed; **ce qui risque de se produire** what might *ou* could well happen; **il ne risque pas de recommencer** there's no chance of him doing that again; **se risquer dans** (*s'aventurer*) to venture into; **se risquer à faire** (*tenter*) to dare to do; **~ le tout pour le tout** to risk the lot
risque-tout [ʀiskətu] *nm/f inv* daredevil
rissoler [ʀisɔle] *vi, vt*: **(faire) ~** to brown
ristourne [ʀistuʀn(ə)] *nf* rebate; discount
rit *etc* [ʀi] *vb voir* **rire**
rite [ʀit] *nm* rite; (*fig*) ritual
ritournelle [ʀituʀnɛl] *nf* (*fig*) tune; **c'est toujours la même ~** (*fam*) it's always the same old story
rituel, le [ʀitɥɛl] *adj, nm* ritual
rituellement [ʀitɥɛlmɑ̃] *adv* religiously
riv. *abr* (= *rivière*) R
rivage [ʀivaʒ] *nm* shore
rival, e, -aux [ʀival, -o] *adj, nm/f* rival; **sans ~** *adj* unrivalled
rivaliser [ʀivalize] *vi*: **~ avec** to rival, vie with; (*être comparable*) to hold its own against, compare with; **~ avec qn de** (*élégance etc*) to vie with *ou* rival sb in
rivalité [ʀivalite] *nf* rivalry
rive [ʀiv] *nf* shore; (*de fleuve*) bank
river [ʀive] *vt* (*clou, pointe*) to clinch; (*plaques*) to

rivet together; **être rivé sur/à** to be riveted on/to

riverain, e [ʀivʀɛ̃, -ɛn] *adj* riverside *cpd*; lakeside *cpd*; roadside *cpd* ▷ *nm/f* riverside (*ou* lakeside) resident; local *ou* roadside resident

rivet [ʀivɛ] *nm* rivet

riveter [ʀivte] *vt* to rivet (together)

Riviera [ʀivjeʀa] *nf*: **la ~ (italienne)** the Italian Riviera

rivière [ʀivjɛʀ] *nf* river; **~ de diamants** diamond rivière

rixe [ʀiks(ə)] *nf* brawl, scuffle

Riyad [ʀijad] *n* Riyadh

riz [ʀi] *nm* rice; **~ au lait** ≈ rice pudding

rizière [ʀizjɛʀ] *nf* paddy field

RMC *sigle f* = **Radio Monte Carlo**

RMI *sigle m* (= *revenu minimum d'insertion*) ≈ income support (*Brit*), ≈ welfare (*US*)

RN *sigle f* = **route nationale**

robe [ʀɔb] *nf* dress; (*de juge, d'ecclésiastique*) robe; (*de professeur*) gown; (*pelage*) coat; **~ de soirée/de mariée** evening/wedding dress; **~ de baptême** christening robe; **~ de chambre** dressing gown; **~ de grossesse** maternity dress

robinet [ʀɔbinɛ] *nm* tap, faucet (*US*); **~ du gaz** gas tap; **~ mélangeur** mixer tap

robinetterie [ʀɔbinɛtʀi] *nf* taps *pl*, plumbing

roboratif, -ive [ʀɔbɔʀatif, -iv] *adj* bracing, invigorating

robot [ʀɔbo] *nm* robot; **~ de cuisine** food processor

robotique [ʀɔbɔtik] *nf* robotics *sg*

robotiser [ʀɔbɔtize] *vt* (*personne, travailleur*) to turn into a robot; (*monde, vie*) to automate

robuste [ʀɔbyst(ə)] *adj* robust, sturdy

robustesse [ʀɔbystɛs] *nf* robustness, sturdiness

roc [ʀɔk] *nm* rock

rocade [ʀɔkad] *nf* (*Auto*) bypass

rocaille [ʀɔkaj] *nf* (*pierres*) loose stones *pl*; (*terrain*) rocky *ou* stony ground; (*jardin*) rockery, rock garden ▷ *adj* (*style*) rocaille

rocailleux, -euse [ʀɔkajø, -øz] *adj* rocky, stony; (*voix*) harsh

rocambolesque [ʀɔkãbɔlɛsk(ə)] *adj* fantastic, incredible

roche [ʀɔʃ] *nf* rock

rocher [ʀɔʃe] *nm* rock; (*Anat*) petrosal bone

rochet [ʀɔʃɛ] *nm*: **roue à ~** ratchet wheel

rocheux, -euse [ʀɔʃø, -øz] *adj* rocky; **les (montagnes) Rocheuses** the Rockies, the Rocky Mountains

rock [ʀɔk], **rock and roll** [ʀɔkɛnʀɔl] *nm* (*musique*) rock(-'n'-roll); (*danse*) rock

rocker [ʀɔkœʀ] *nm* (*chanteur*) rock musician; (*adepte*) rock fan

rocking-chair [ʀɔkiŋ(t)ʃɛʀ] *nm* rocking chair

rococo [ʀɔkoko] *nm* rococo ▷ *adj* rococo

rodage [ʀɔdaʒ] *nm* running in (*Brit*), breaking in (*US*); **en ~** (*Auto*) running *ou* breaking in

rodé, e [ʀɔde] *adj* run in (*Brit*), broken in (*US*); (*personne*): **~ à qch** having got the hang of sth

rodéo [ʀɔdeo] *nm* rodeo

roder [ʀɔde] *vt* (*moteur, voiture*) to run in (*Brit*), break in (*US*); **~ un spectacle** to iron out the initial problems of a show

rôder [ʀɔde] *vi* to roam *ou* wander about; (*de façon suspecte*) to lurk (about *ou* around)

rôdeur, -euse [ʀɔdœʀ, -øz] *nm/f* prowler

rodomontades [ʀɔdɔmɔ̃tad] *nfpl* bragging *sg*; sabre rattling *sg*

rogatoire [ʀɔgatwaʀ] *adj*: **commission ~** letters rogatory

rogne [ʀɔɲ] *nf*: **être en ~** to be mad *ou* in a temper; **se mettre en ~** to get mad *ou* in a temper

rogner [ʀɔɲe] *vt* to trim; (*fig*) to whittle down; **~ sur** (*fig*) to cut down *ou* back on

rognons [ʀɔɲɔ̃] *nmpl* kidneys

rognures [ʀɔɲyʀ] *nfpl* trimmings

rogue [ʀɔg] *adj* arrogant

roi [ʀwa] *nm* king; **les R~s mages** the Three Wise Men, the Magi; **le jour** *ou* **la fête des R~s**, **les R~s** Twelfth Night; *see note*

● FÊTE DES ROIS

● The *'fête des Rois'* is celebrated on 6 January.
● Figurines representing the Three Wise Men
● are traditionally added to the Christmas
● crib ('crèche') and people eat 'galette des
● Rois', a flat cake in which a porcelain charm
● ('la fève') is hidden. Whoever finds the
● charm is king or queen for the day and can
● choose a partner.

roitelet [ʀwatlɛ] *nm* wren; (*péj*) kinglet

rôle [ʀol] *nm* role; (*contribution*) part

rollers [ʀɔlœʀ] *nmpl* Rollerblades®

rollmops [ʀɔlmɔps] *nm* rollmop

romain, e [ʀɔmɛ̃, -ɛn] *adj* Roman ▷ *nm/f*: **Romain, e** Roman ▷ *nf* (*Culin*) cos (lettuce)

roman, e [ʀɔmã, -an] *adj* (*Archit*) Romanesque; (*Ling*) Romance *cpd*, Romanic ▷ *nm* novel; **~ d'amour** love story; **~ d'espionnage** spy novel *ou* story; **~ noir** thriller; **~ policier** detective novel

romance [ʀɔmãs] *nf* ballad

romancer [ʀɔmãse] *vt* to romanticize

romanche [ʀɔmãʃ] *adj, nm* Romansh

romancier, -ière [ʀɔmãsje, -jɛʀ] *nm/f* novelist

romand, e [ʀɔmã, -ãd] *adj* of *ou* from French-speaking Switzerland ▷ *nm/f*: **Romand, e** French-speaking Swiss

romanesque [ʀɔmanɛsk(ə)] *adj* (*fantastique*) fantastic; storybook *cpd*; (*sentimental*) romantic; (*Littérature*) novelistic

roman-feuilleton [ʀɔmãfœjtɔ̃] (*pl* **romans-feuilletons**) *nm* serialized novel

roman-fleuve [ʀɔmãflœv] (*pl* **romans-fleuves**) *nm* saga, roman-fleuve

romanichel, le [ʀɔmaniʃɛl] *nm/f* gipsy

roman-photo [ʀɔmãfoto] (*pl* **romans-photos**) *nm* (*romantic*) picture story

romantique [ʀɔmãtik] *adj* romantic

romantisme [ʀɔmãtism(ə)] *nm* romanticism

romarin [ʀɔmaʀɛ̃] *nm* rosemary
rombière [ʀɔ̃bjɛʀ] *nf* (*péj*) old bag
Rome [ʀɔm] *n* Rome
rompre [ʀɔ̃pʀ(ə)] *vt* to break; (*entretien, fiançailles*) to break off ▷ *vi* (*fiancés*) to break it off; **se rompre** *vi* to break; (*Méd*) to burst, rupture; **se ~ les os** *ou* **le cou** to break one's neck; **~ avec** to break with; **à tout ~** *adv* wildly; **applaudir à tout ~** to bring down the house, applaud wildly; **~ la glace** (*fig*) to break the ice; **rompez (les rangs)!** (*Mil*) dismiss!, fall out!
rompu, e [ʀɔ̃py] *pp de* **rompre** ▷ *adj* (*fourbu*) exhausted, worn out; **~ à** with wide experience of; inured to
romsteck [ʀɔ̃mstɛk] *nm* rump steak *no pl*
ronce [ʀɔ̃s] *nf* (*Bot*) bramble branch; (*Menuiserie*): **~ de noyer** burr walnut; **ronces** *nfpl* brambles, thorns
ronchonner [ʀɔ̃ʃɔne] *vi* (*fam*) to grouse, grouch
rond, e [ʀɔ̃, ʀɔ̃d] *adj* round; (*joues, mollets*) well-rounded; (*fam: ivre*) tight; (*sincère, décidé*): **être ~ en affaires** to be on the level in business, do an honest deal ▷ *nm* (*cercle*) ring; (*fam: sou*): **je n'ai plus un ~** I haven't a penny left ▷ *nf* (*gén: de surveillance*) rounds *pl*, patrol; (*danse*) round (dance); (*Mus*) semibreve (*Brit*), whole note (*US*) ▷ *adv*: **tourner ~** (*moteur*) to run smoothly; **ça ne tourne pas ~** (*fig*) there's something not quite right about it; **pour faire un compte ~** to make (it) a round figure, to round (it) off; **avoir le dos ~** to be round-shouldered; **en ~** (*s'asseoir, danser*) in a ring; **à la ~e** (*alentour*): **à 10 km à la ~e** for 10 km round; (*à chacun son tour*): **passer qch à la ~e** to pass sth (a)round; **faire des ~s de jambe** to bow and scrape; **~ de serviette** napkin ring
rond-de-cuir [ʀɔ̃dkɥiʀ] (*pl* **ronds-de-cuir**) *nm* (*péj*) penpusher
rondelet, te [ʀɔ̃dlɛ, -ɛt] *adj* plump; (*fig: somme*) tidy; (*: bourse*) well-lined, fat
rondelle [ʀɔ̃dɛl] *nf* (*Tech*) washer; (*tranche*) slice, round
rondement [ʀɔ̃dmɑ̃] *adv* (*avec décision*) briskly; (*loyalement*) frankly
rondeur [ʀɔ̃dœʀ] *nf* (*d'un bras, des formes*) plumpness; (*bonhomie*) friendly straightforwardness; **rondeurs** *nfpl* (*d'une femme*) curves
rondin [ʀɔ̃dɛ̃] *nm* log
rond-point [ʀɔ̃pwɛ̃] (*pl* **ronds-points**) *nm* roundabout (*Brit*), traffic circle (*US*)
ronflant, e [ʀɔ̃flɑ̃, -ɑ̃t] *adj* (*péj*) high-flown, grand
ronflement [ʀɔ̃fləmɑ̃] *nm* snore, snoring *no pl*
ronfler [ʀɔ̃fle] *vi* to snore; (*moteur, poêle*) to hum; (*: plus fort*) to roar
ronger [ʀɔ̃ʒe] *vt* to gnaw (at); (*vers, rouille*) to eat into; **~ son frein** to champ (at) the bit; (*fig*): **se ~ de souci, se ~ les sangs** to worry o.s. sick, fret; **se ~ les ongles** to bite one's nails
rongeur, -euse [ʀɔ̃ʒœʀ, -øz] *nm/f* rodent
ronronnement [ʀɔ̃ʀɔnmɑ̃] *nm* purring; (*bruit*) purr
ronronner [ʀɔ̃ʀɔne] *vi* to purr
roque [ʀɔk] *nm* (*Échecs*) castling
roquefort [ʀɔkfɔʀ] *nm* Roquefort
roquer [ʀɔke] *vi* to castle
roquet [ʀɔkɛ] *nm* nasty little lap-dog
roquette [ʀɔkɛt] *nf* rocket; **~ antichar** antitank rocket
rosace [ʀozas] *nf* (*vitrail*) rose window, rosace; (*motif: de plafond etc*) rose
rosaire [ʀozɛʀ] *nm* rosary
rosbif [ʀɔsbif] *nm*: **du ~** roasting beef; (*cuit*) roast beef; **un ~** a joint of (roasting) beef
rose [ʀoz] *nf* rose; (*vitrail*) rose window ▷ *adj* pink; **~ bonbon** *adj inv* candy pink; **~ des vents** compass card
rosé, e [ʀoze] *adj* pinkish; **(vin) ~** rosé (wine)
roseau, x [ʀozo] *nm* reed
rosée [ʀoze] *adj f voir* **rosé** ▷ *nf*: **goutte de ~** dewdrop
roseraie [ʀozʀɛ] *nf* rose garden; (*plantation*) rose nursery
rosette [ʀozɛt] *nf* rosette (*gen of the Légion d'honneur*)
rosier [ʀozje] *nm* rosebush, rose tree
rosir [ʀoziʀ] *vi* to go pink
rosse [ʀɔs] *nf* (*péj: cheval*) nag ▷ *adj* nasty, vicious
rosser [ʀɔse] *vt* (*fam*) to thrash
rossignol [ʀɔsiɲɔl] *nm* (*Zool*) nightingale; (*crochet*) picklock
rot [ʀo] *nm* belch; (*de bébé*) burp
rotatif, -ive [ʀɔtatif, -iv] *adj* rotary ▷ *nf* rotary press
rotation [ʀɔtasjɔ̃] *nf* rotation; (*fig*) rotation, swap-around; (*renouvellement*) turnover; **par ~** on a rota (*Brit*) *ou* rotation (*US*) basis; **~ des cultures** crop rotation; **~ des stocks** stock turnover
rotatoire [ʀɔtatwaʀ] *adj*: **mouvement ~** rotary movement
roter [ʀɔte] *vi* (*fam*) to burp, belch
rôti [ʀoti] *nm*: **du ~** roasting meat; (*cuit*) roast meat; **un ~ de bœuf/porc** a joint of (roasting) beef/pork
rotin [ʀɔtɛ̃] *nm* rattan (cane); **fauteuil en ~** cane (arm)chair
rôtir [ʀotiʀ] *vt* (*aussi*: **faire rôtir**) to roast ▷ *vi* to roast; **se ~ au soleil** to bask in the sun
rôtisserie [ʀotisʀi] *nf* (*restaurant*) steakhouse; (*comptoir, magasin*) roast meat counter (*ou* shop)
rôtissoire [ʀotiswaʀ] *nf* (roasting) spit
rotonde [ʀɔtɔ̃d] *nf* (*Archit*) rotunda; (*Rail*) engine shed
rotondité [ʀɔtɔ̃dite] *nf* roundness
rotor [ʀɔtɔʀ] *nm* rotor
Rotterdam [ʀɔtɛʀdam] *n* Rotterdam
rotule [ʀɔtyl] *nf* kneecap, patella
roturier, -ière [ʀɔtyʀje, -jɛʀ] *nm/f* commoner
rouage [ʀwaʒ] *nm* cog(wheel), gearwheel; (*de montre*) part; (*fig*) cog; **rouages** *nmpl* (*fig*) internal structure *sg*
Rouanda [ʀwɑ̃da] *nm*: **le ~** Rwanda

roubaisien, ne [ʀubezjɛ̃, -ɛn] *adj* of *ou* from Roubaix

roublard, e [ʀublaʀ, -aʀd(ə)] *adj* (*péj*) crafty, wily

rouble [ʀubl(ə)] *nm* rouble

roucoulement [ʀukulmã] *nm* (*de pigeons, fig*) coo, cooing

roucouler [ʀukule] *vi* to coo; (*fig: péj*) to warble; (: *amoureux*) to bill and coo

roue [ʀu] *nf* wheel; **faire la ~** (*paon*) to spread *ou* fan its tail; (*Gym*) to do a cartwheel; **descendre en ~ libre** to freewheel *ou* coast down; **pousser à la ~** to put one's shoulder to the wheel; **grande ~** (*à la foire*) big wheel; **~ à aubes** paddle wheel; **~ dentée** cogwheel; **~ de secours** spare wheel

roué, e [ʀwe] *adj* wily

rouennais, e [ʀwanɛ, -ɛz] *adj* of *ou* from Rouen

rouer [ʀwe] *vt*: **~ qn de coups** to give sb a thrashing

rouet [ʀwɛ] *nm* spinning wheel

rouge [ʀuʒ] *adj, nm/f* red ▷ *nm* red; (*fard*) rouge; **(vin) ~** red wine; **passer au ~** (*signal*) to go red; (*automobiliste*) to go through a red light; **porter au ~** (*métal*) to bring to red heat; **sur la liste ~** (*Tél*) ex-directory (*Brit*), unlisted (*US*); **~ de honte/colère** red with shame/anger; **se fâcher tout/voir ~** to blow one's top/see red; **~ (à lèvres)** lipstick

rougeâtre [ʀuʒatʀ(ə)] *adj* reddish

rougeaud, e [ʀuʒo, -od] *adj* (*teint*) red; (*personne*) red-faced

rouge-gorge [ʀuʒgɔʀʒ(ə)] *nm* robin (redbreast)

rougeoiement [ʀuʒwamã] *nm* reddish glow

rougeole [ʀuʒɔl] *nf* measles *sg*

rougeoyant, e [ʀuʒwajã, -ãt] *adj* (*ciel, braises*) glowing; (*aube, reflets*) glowing red

rougeoyer [ʀuʒwaje] *vi* to glow red

rouget [ʀuʒɛ] *nm* mullet

rougeur [ʀuʒœʀ] *nf* redness; (*du visage*) red face; **rougeurs** *nfpl* (*Méd*) red blotches

rougir [ʀuʒiʀ] *vi* (*de honte, timidité*) to blush, flush; (*de plaisir, colère*) to flush; (*fraise, tomate*) to go *ou* turn red; (*ciel*) to redden

rouille [ʀuj] *adj inv* rust-coloured, rusty ▷ *nf* rust; (*Culin*) spicy (*Provençal*) *sauce served with fish dishes*

rouillé, e [ʀuje] *adj* rusty

rouiller [ʀuje] *vt* to rust ▷ *vi* to rust, go rusty; **se rouiller** *vi* to rust; (*fig: mentalement*) to become rusty; (: *physiquement*) to grow stiff

roulade [ʀulad] *nf* (*Gym*) roll; (*Culin*) rolled meat *no pl*; (*Mus*) roulade, run

roulage [ʀulaʒ] *nm* (*transport*) haulage

roulant, e [ʀulã, -ãt] *adj* (*meuble*) on wheels; (*surface, trottoir*) moving; **matériel ~** (*Rail*) rolling stock; **personnel ~** (*Rail*) train crews *pl*

roulé, e [ʀule] *adj*: **bien ~e** (*fam: femme*) shapely, curvy

rouleau, x [ʀulo] *nm* (*de papier, tissu, pièces de monnaie, Sport*) roll; (*de machine à écrire*) roller, platen; (*à mise en plis, à peinture, vague*) roller; **être au bout du ~** (*fig*) to be at the end of the line; **~**

compresseur steamroller; **~ à pâtisserie** rolling pin; **~ de pellicule** roll of film

roulé-boulé [ʀulebule] (*pl* **roulés-boulés**) (*Sport*) roll

roulement [ʀulmã] *nm* (*bruit*) rumbling *no pl*, rumble; (*rotation*) rotation; turnover; (: *de capitaux*) circulation; **par ~** on a rota (*Brit*) *ou* rotation (*US*) basis; **~ (à billes)** ball bearings *pl*; **~ de tambour** drum roll; **~ d'yeux** roll(ing) of the eyes

rouler [ʀule] *vt* to roll; (*papier, tapis*) to roll up; (*Culin: pâte*) to roll out; (*fam*) to do, con ▷ *vi* (*bille, boule*) to roll; (*voiture, train*) to go, run; (*automobiliste*) to drive; (*cycliste*) to ride; (*bateau*) to roll; (*tonnerre*) to rumble, roll; (*dégringoler*): **~ en bas de** to roll down; **~ sur** (*conversation*) to turn on; **se ~ dans** (*boue*) to roll in; (*couverture*) to roll o.s. (up) in; **~ dans la farine** (*fam*) to con; **~ les épaules/hanches** to sway one's shoulders/ wiggle one's hips; **~ les "r"** to roll one's r's; **~ sur l'or** to be rolling in money, be rolling in it; **~ (sa bosse)** to go places

roulette [ʀulɛt] *nf* (*de table, fauteuil*) castor; (*de pâtissier*) pastry wheel; (*jeu*): **la ~** roulette; **à ~s** on castors; **la ~ russe** Russian roulette

roulis [ʀuli] *nm* roll(ing)

roulotte [ʀulɔt] *nf* caravan

roumain, e [ʀumɛ̃, -ɛn] *adj* Rumanian, Romanian ▷ *nm* (*Ling*) Rumanian, Romanian ▷ *nm/f*: **Roumain, e** Rumanian, Romanian

Roumanie [ʀumani] *nf*: **la ~** Rumania, Romania

roupiller [ʀupije] *vi* (*fam*) to sleep

rouquin, e [ʀukɛ̃, -in] *nm/f* (*péj*) redhead

rouspéter [ʀuspete] *vi* (*fam*) to moan, grouse

rousse [ʀus] *adj f voir* **roux**

rousseur [ʀusœʀ] *nf*: **tache de ~** freckle

roussi [ʀusi] *nm*: **ça sent le ~** there's a smell of burning; (*fig*) I can smell trouble

roussir [ʀusiʀ] *vt* to scorch ▷ *vi* (*feuilles*) to go *ou* turn brown; (*Culin*): **faire ~** to brown

routage [ʀutaʒ] *nm* (*collective*) mailing

routard, e [ʀutaʀ, -aʀd(ə)] *nm/f* traveller

route [ʀut] *nf* road; (*fig: chemin*) way; (*itinéraire, parcours*) route; (*fig: voie*) road, path; **par (la) ~** by road; **il y a trois heures de ~** it's a three-hour ride *ou* journey; **en ~** *adv* on the way; **en ~!** let's go!; **en cours de ~** en route; **mettre en ~** to start up; **se mettre en ~** to set off; **faire ~ vers** to head towards; **faire fausse ~** (*fig*) to be on the wrong track; **~ nationale (RN)** ≈ A-road (*Brit*), ≈ state highway (*US*)

routier, -ière [ʀutje, -jɛʀ] *adj* road *cpd* ▷ *nm* (*camionneur*) (long-distance) lorry (*Brit*) *ou* truck driver; (*restaurant*) ≈ transport café (*Brit*), ≈ truck stop (*US*); (*scout*) ≈ rover; (*cycliste*) road racer ▷ *nf* (*voiture*) touring car; **vieux ~** old stager; **carte routière** road map

routine [ʀutin] *nf* routine; **visite/contrôle de ~** routine visit/check

routinier, -ière [ʀutinje, -jɛʀ] *adj* (*péj: travail*) humdrum, routine; (: *personne*) addicted to routine

rouvert, e [ʀuvɛʀ, -ɛʀt(ə)] *pp de* **rouvrir**

rouvrir [ʀuvʀiʀ] *vt, vi* to reopen, open again; **se rouvrir** *vi* (*blessure*) to open up again

roux, rousse [ʀu, ʀus] *adj* red; (*personne*) red-haired ▷ *nm/f* redhead ▷ *nm* (*Culin*) roux

royal, e, -aux [ʀwajal, -o] *adj* royal; (*fig*) fit for a king, princely; blissful; thorough

royalement [ʀwajalmɑ̃] *adv* royally

royaliste [ʀwajalist(ə)] *adj, nm/f* royalist

royaume [ʀwajom] *nm* kingdom; (*fig*) realm; **le ~ des cieux** the kingdom of heaven

Royaume-Uni [ʀwajomyni] *nm*: **le ~** the United Kingdom

royauté [ʀwajote] *nf* (*dignité*) kingship; (*régime*) monarchy

RP *sigle f* (= *recette principale*) ≈ main post office = **région parisienne** ▷ *sigle fpl* (= *relations publiques*) PR

RPR *sigle m* (= *Rassemblement pour la République*) political party

R.S.V.P. *abr* (= *répondez s'il vous plaît*) R.S.V.P

RTB *sigle f* = **Radio-Télévision belge**

Rte *abr* = **route**

RTL *sigle f* = **Radio-Télévision Luxembourg**

RU [ʀy] *sigle m* = **restaurant universitaire**

ruade [ʀyad] *nf* kick

Ruanda [ʀwɑ̃da] *nm*: **le ~** Rwanda

ruban [ʀybɑ̃] *nm* (*gén*) ribbon; (*pour ourlet, couture*) binding; (*de télescripteur etc*) tape; (*d'acier*) strip; **~ adhésif** adhesive tape; **~ carbone** carbon ribbon

rubéole [ʀybeɔl] *nf* German measles *sg*, rubella

rubicond, e [ʀybikɔ̃, -ɔ̃d] *adj* rubicund, ruddy

rubis [ʀybi] *nm* ruby; (*Horlogerie*) jewel; **payer ~ sur l'ongle** to pay cash on the nail

rubrique [ʀybʀik] *nf* (*titre, catégorie*) heading, rubric; (*Presse: article*) column

ruche [ʀyʃ] *nf* hive

rucher [ʀyʃe] *nm* apiary

rude [ʀyd] *adj* (*barbe, toile*) rough; (*métier, tâche*) hard, tough; (*climat*) severe, harsh; (*bourru*) harsh, rough; (*fruste*) rugged, tough; (*fam*) jolly good; **être mis à ~ épreuve** to be put through the mill

rudement [ʀydmɑ̃] *adv* (*tomber, frapper*) hard; (*traiter, reprocher*) harshly; (*fam: très*) terribly; (: *beaucoup*) terribly hard

rudesse [ʀydɛs] *nf* roughness; toughness; severity; harshness

rudimentaire [ʀydimɑ̃tɛʀ] *adj* rudimentary, basic

rudiments [ʀydimɑ̃] *nmpl* rudiments; basic knowledge *sg*; basic principles

rudoyer [ʀydwaje] *vt* to treat harshly

rue [ʀy] *nf* street; **être/jeter qn à la ~** to be on the streets/throw sb out onto the street

ruée [ʀye] *nf* rush; **la ~ vers l'or** the gold rush

ruelle [ʀyɛl] *nf* alley(way)

ruer [ʀye] *vi* (*cheval*) to kick out; **se ruer** *vi*: **se ~ sur** to pounce on; **se ~ vers/dans/hors de** to rush *ou* dash towards/into/out of; **~ dans les brancards** to become rebellious

rugby [ʀygbi] *nm* rugby (football); **~ à treize/quinze** rugby league/union

rugir [ʀyʒiʀ] *vi* to roar

rugissement [ʀyʒismɑ̃] *nm* roar, roaring *no pl*

rugosité [ʀygozite] *nf* roughness; (*aspérité*) rough patch

rugueux, -euse [ʀygø, -øz] *adj* rough

ruine [ʀɥin] *nf* ruin; **ruines** *nfpl* ruins; **tomber en ~** to fall into ruin(s)

ruiner [ʀɥine] *vt* to ruin

ruineux, -euse [ʀɥinø, -øz] *adj* terribly expensive to buy (*ou* run), ruinous; extravagant

ruisseau, x [ʀɥiso] *nm* stream, brook; (*caniveau*) gutter; (*fig*): **~x de larmes/sang** floods of tears/streams of blood

ruisselant, e [ʀɥislɑ̃, -ɑ̃t] *adj* streaming

ruisseler [ʀɥisle] *vi* to stream; **~ (d'eau)** to be streaming (with water); **~ de lumière** to stream with light

ruissellement [ʀɥisɛlmɑ̃] *nm* streaming; **~ de lumière** stream of light

rumeur [ʀymœʀ] *nf* (*bruit confus*) rumbling; hubbub *no pl*; (*protestation*) murmur(ing); (*nouvelle*) rumour (*Brit*), rumor (*US*)

ruminer [ʀymine] *vt* (*herbe*) to ruminate; (*fig*) to ruminate on *ou* over, chew over ▷ *vi* (*vache*) to chew the cud, ruminate

rumsteck [ʀɔ̃mstɛk] *nm* = **romsteck**

rupestre [ʀypɛstʀ(ə)] *adj* (*plante*) rock *cpd*; (*art*) wall *cpd*

rupture [ʀyptyʀ] *nf* (*de câble, digue*) breaking; (*de tendon*) rupture, tearing; (*de négociations etc*) breakdown; (*de contrat*) breach; (*séparation, désunion*) break-up, split; **en ~ de ban** at odds with authority; **en ~ de stock** (*Comm*) out of stock

rural, e, -aux [ʀyʀal, -o] *adj* rural, country *cpd* ▷ *nmpl*: **les ruraux** country people

ruse [ʀyz] *nf*: **la ~** cunning, craftiness; trickery; **une ~** a trick, a ruse; **par ~** by trickery

rusé, e [ʀyze] *adj* cunning, crafty

russe [ʀys] *adj* Russian ▷ *nm* (*Ling*) Russian ▷ *nm/f*: **Russe** Russian

Russie [ʀysi] *nf*: **la ~** Russia; **la ~ blanche** White Russia; **la ~ soviétique** Soviet Russia

rustine [ʀystin] *nf* repair patch (*for bicycle inner tube*)

rustique [ʀystik] *adj* rustic; (*plante*) hardy

rustre [ʀystʀ(ə)] *nm* boor

rut [ʀyt] *nm*: **être en ~** (*animal domestique*) to be in *ou* on heat; (*animal sauvage*) to be rutting

rutabaga [ʀytabaga] *nm* swede

rutilant, e [ʀytilɑ̃, -ɑ̃t] *adj* gleaming

RV *sigle m* = **rendez-vous**

Rwanda [ʀwɑ̃da] *nm*: **le ~** Rwanda

rythme [ʀitm(ə)] *nm* rhythm; (*vitesse*) rate; (: *de la vie*) pace, tempo; **au ~ de 10 par jour** at the rate of 10 a day

rythmé, e [ʀitme] *adj* rhythmic(al)

rythmer [ʀitme] *vt* to give rhythm to

rythmique [ʀitmik] *adj* rhythmic(al) ▷ *nf* rhythmics *sg*

Ss

S, s [ɛs] *nm inv* S, s ▷ *abr* (= *sud*) S; (= *seconde*) sec; (= *siècle*) c., century; **S comme Suzanne** S for Sugar

s' [s] *pron voir* **se**

s/ *abr* = **sur**

SA *sigle f* = **société anonyme**; (= *Son Altesse*) HH

sa [sa] *adj possessif voir* **son**

sabbatique [sabatik] *adj*: **année ~** sabbatical year

sable [sabl(ə)] *nm* sand; **~s mouvants** quicksand(s)

sablé [sable] *adj* (*allée*) sandy ▷ *nm* shortbread biscuit; **pâte ~e** (*Culin*) shortbread dough

sabler [sable] *vt* to sand; (*contre le verglas*) to grit; **~ le champagne** to drink champagne

sableux, -euse [sablø, -øz] *adj* sandy

sablier [sablije] *nm* hourglass; (*de cuisine*) egg timer

sablière [sablijɛʀ] *nf* sand quarry

sablonneux, -euse [sablɔnø, -øz] *adj* sandy

saborder [sabɔʀde] *vt* (*navire*) to scuttle; (*fig*) to wind up, shut down

sabot [sabo] *nm* clog; (*de cheval, bœuf*) hoof; **~ (de Denver)** (wheel) clamp; **~ de frein** brake shoe

sabotage [sabɔtaʒ] *nm* sabotage

saboter [sabɔte] *vt* (*travail, morceau de musique*) to botch, make a mess of; (*machine, installation, négociation etc*) to sabotage

saboteur, -euse [sabɔtœʀ, -øz] *nm/f* saboteur

sabre [sabʀ(ə)] *nm* sabre; **le ~** (*fig*) the sword, the army

sabrer [sabʀe] *vt* to cut down

sac [sak] *nm* bag; (*à charbon etc*) sack; (*pillage*) sack(ing); **mettre à ~** to sack; **~ à provisions/de voyage** shopping/travelling bag; **~ de couchage** sleeping bag; **~ à dos** rucksack; **~ à main** handbag; **~ de plage** beach bag

saccade [sakad] *nf* jerk; **par ~s** jerkily; haltingly

saccadé, e [sakade] *adj* jerky

saccage [sakaʒ] *nm* havoc

saccager [sakaʒe] *vt* (*piller*) to sack, lay waste; (*dévaster*) to create havoc in, wreck

saccharine [sakaʀin] *nf* saccharin(e)

saccharose [sakaʀoz] *nm* sucrose

SACEM [sasɛm] *sigle f* (= *Société des auteurs, compositeurs et éditeurs de musique*) body responsible for collecting and distributing royalties

sacerdoce [sasɛʀdɔs] *nm* priesthood; (*fig*) calling, vocation

sacerdotal, e, -aux [sasɛʀdɔtal, -o] *adj* priestly, sacerdotal

sachant *etc* [saʃɑ̃] *vb voir* **savoir**

sache *etc* [saʃ] *vb voir* **savoir**

sachet [saʃɛ] *nm* (small) bag; (*de lavande, poudre, shampooing*) sachet; **thé en ~s** tea bags; **~ de thé** tea bag

sacoche [sakɔʃ] *nf* (*gén*) bag; (*de bicyclette*) saddlebag; (*du facteur*) (post)bag; (*d'outils*) toolbag

sacquer [sake] *vt* (*fam: candidat, employé*) to sack; (: *réprimander, mal noter*) to plough

sacraliser [sakʀalize] *vt* to make sacred

sacre [sakʀ(ə)] *nm* coronation; consecration

sacré, e [sakʀe] *adj* sacred; (*fam: satané*) blasted; (: *fameux*): **un ~ ...** a heck of a ...; (*Anat*) sacral

sacrement [sakʀəmɑ̃] *nm* sacrament; **les derniers ~s** the last rites

sacrer [sakʀe] *vt* (*roi*) to crown; (*évêque*) to consecrate ▷ *vi* to curse, swear

sacrifice [sakʀifis] *nm* sacrifice; **faire le ~ de** to sacrifice

sacrificiel, le [sakʀifisjɛl] *adj* sacrificial

sacrifier [sakʀifje] *vt* to sacrifice; **~ à** *vt* to conform to; **se sacrifier** to sacrifice o.s; **articles sacrifiés** (*Comm*) items sold at rock-bottom *ou* give-away prices

sacrilège [sakʀilɛʒ] *nm* sacrilege ▷ *adj* sacrilegious

sacristain [sakʀistɛ̃] *nm* sexton; sacristan

sacristie [sakʀisti] *nf* sacristy; (*culte protestant*) vestry

sacro-saint, e [sakʀosɛ̃, -ɛ̃t] *adj* sacrosanct

sadique [sadik] *adj* sadistic ▷ *nm/f* sadist

sadisme [sadism(ə)] *nm* sadism

sadomasochisme [sadɔmazoʃism(ə)] *nm* sadomasochism

sadomasochiste [sadɔmazoʃist(ə)] *nm/f* sadomasochist

safari [safaʀi] *nm* safari; **faire un ~** to go on safari

safari-photo [safaʀifoto] *nm* photographic

safari

SAFER [safɛʀ] *sigle f* (= *Société d'aménagement foncier et d'établissement rural*) organization with the right to buy land in order to retain it for agricultural use

safran [safʀɑ̃] *nm* saffron

saga [saga] *nf* saga

sagace [sagas] *adj* sagacious, shrewd

sagacité [sagasite] *nf* sagacity, shrewdness

sagaie [sagɛ] *nf* assegai

sage [saʒ] *adj* wise; (*enfant*) good ▷ *nm* wise man; sage

sage-femme [saʒfam] *nf* midwife

sagement [saʒmɑ̃] *adv* (*raisonnablement*) wisely, sensibly; (*tranquillement*) quietly

sagesse [saʒɛs] *nf* wisdom

Sagittaire [saʒitɛʀ] *nm*: **le ~** Sagittarius, the Archer; **être du ~** to be Sagittarius

Sahara [saaʀa] *nm*: **le ~** the Sahara (Desert); **le ~ occidental** (*pays*) Western Sahara

saharien, ne [saaʀjɛ̃, -ɛn] *adj* Saharan ▷ *nf* safari jacket

Sahel [saɛl] *nm*: **le ~** the Sahel

sahélien, ne [saeljɛ̃, -ɛn] *adj* Sahelian

saignant, e [sɛɲɑ̃, -ɑ̃t] *adj* (*viande*) rare; (*blessure, plaie*) bleeding

saignée [seɲe] *nf* (*Méd*) bleeding *no pl*, bloodletting *no pl*; (*Anat*): **la ~ du bras** the bend of the arm; (*fig: Mil*) heavy losses *pl*; (: *prélèvement*) savage cut

saignement [sɛɲmɑ̃] *nm* bleeding; **~ de nez** nosebleed

saigner [seɲe] *vi* to bleed ▷ *vt* to bleed; (*animal*) to bleed to death; **~ qn à blanc** (*fig*) to bleed sb white; **~ du nez** to have a nosebleed

Saigon [sajgɔ̃] *n* Saigon

saillant, e [sajɑ̃, -ɑ̃t] *adj* (*pommettes, menton*) prominent; (*corniche etc*) projecting; (*fig*) salient, outstanding

saillie [saji] *nf* (*sur un mur etc*) projection; (*trait d'esprit*) witticism; (*accouplement*) covering, serving; **faire ~** to project, stick out; **en ~, formant ~** projecting, overhanging

saillir [sajiʀ] *vi* to project, stick out; (*veine, muscle*) to bulge ▷ *vt* (*Élevage*) to cover, serve

sain, e [sɛ̃, sɛn] *adj* healthy; (*dents, constitution*) healthy, sound; (*lectures*) wholesome; **~ et sauf** safe and sound, unharmed; **~ d'esprit** sound in mind, sane

saindoux [sɛ̃du] *nm* lard

sainement [sɛnmɑ̃] *adv* (*vivre*) healthily; (*raisonner*) soundly

saint, e [sɛ̃, sɛ̃t] *adj* holy; (*fig*) saintly ▷ *nm/f* saint; **la S~e Vierge** the Blessed Virgin

saint-bernard [sɛ̃bɛʀnaʀ] *nm inv* (*chien*) St Bernard

Sainte-Hélène [sɛ̃telɛn] *nf* St Helena

Sainte-Lucie [sɛ̃tlysi] *nf* Saint Lucia

Saint-Esprit [sɛ̃tɛspʀi] *nm*: **le ~** the Holy Spirit *ou* Ghost

sainteté [sɛ̃te] *nf* holiness; saintliness

Saint-Laurent [sɛ̃lɔʀɑ̃] *nm*: **le ~** the St Lawrence

Saint-Marin [sɛ̃maʀɛ̃] *nm*: **le ~** San Marino

Saint-Père [sɛ̃pɛʀ] *nm*: **le ~** the Holy Father, the Pontiff

Saint-Pierre [sɛ̃pjɛʀ] *nm* Saint Peter; (*église*) Saint Peter's

Saint-Pierre-et-Miquelon [sɛ̃pjɛʀemiklɔ̃] *nm* Saint Pierre and Miquelon

Saint-Siège [sɛ̃sjɛʒ] *nm*: **le ~** the Holy See

Saint-Sylvestre [sɛ̃silvɛstʀ(ə)] *nf*: **la ~** New Year's Eve

Saint-Thomas [sɛ̃tɔma] *nf* Saint Thomas

Saint-Vincent et les Grenadines [sɛ̃vɛ̃sɑ̃elegʀənadin] *nm* St Vincent and the Grenadines

sais *etc* [sɛ] *vb voir* **savoir**

saisie [sezi] *nf* seizure; **à la ~** (*texte*) being keyed; **~ (de données)** (data) capture

saisine [sezin] *nf* (*Jur*) *submission of a case to the court*

saisir [seziʀ] *vt* to take hold of, grab; (*fig: occasion*) to seize; (*comprendre*) to grasp; (*entendre*) to get, catch; (*émotions*) to take hold of, come over; (*Inform*) to capture, keyboard; (*Culin*) to fry quickly; (*Jur: biens, publication*) to seize; (: *juridiction*): **~ un tribunal d'une affaire** to submit *ou* refer a case to a court; **se ~ de** *vt* to seize; **être saisi** (*frappé de*) to be overcome

saisissant, e [sezisɑ̃, -ɑ̃t] *adj* startling, striking; (*froid*) biting

saisissement [sezismɑ̃] *nm*: **muet/figé de ~** speechless/frozen with emotion

saison [sɛzɔ̃] *nf* season; **la belle/mauvaise ~** the summer/winter months; **être de ~** to be in season; **en/hors ~** in/out of season; **haute/basse/morte ~** high/low/slack season; **la ~ des pluies/des amours** the rainy/mating season

saisonnier, -ière [sɛzɔnje, -jɛʀ] *adj* seasonal ▷ *nm* (*travailleur*) seasonal worker; (*vacancier*) seasonal holidaymaker

sait [sɛ] *vb voir* **savoir**

salace [salas] *adj* salacious

salade [salad] *nf* (*Bot*) lettuce *etc* (*generic term*); (*Culin*) (green) salad; (*fam*) tangle, muddle; **salades** *nfpl* (*fam*): **raconter des ~s** to tell tales (*fam*); **haricots en ~** bean salad; **~ de concombres** cucumber salad; **~ de fruits** fruit salad; **~ niçoise** salade niçoise; **~ russe** Russian salad; **~ de tomates** tomato salad; **~ verte** green salad

saladier [saladje] *nm* (salad) bowl

salaire [salɛʀ] *nm* (*annuel, mensuel*) salary; (*hebdomadaire, journalier*) pay, wages *pl*; (*fig*) reward; **~ de base** basic salary (*ou* wage); **~ de misère** starvation wage; **~ minimum interprofessionnel de croissance (SMIC)** index-linked guaranteed minimum wage

salaison [salɛzɔ̃] *nf* salting; **salaisons** *nfpl* salt meat *sg*

salamandre [salamɑ̃dʀ(ə)] *nf* salamander

salami [salami] *nm* salami *no pl*, salami sausage

salant [salɑ̃] *adj m*: **marais ~** salt pan

salarial, e, -aux [salaʀjal, -o] *adj* salary *cpd*, wage(s) *cpd*

salariat [salaʀja] *nm* salaried staff
salarié, e [salaʀje] *adj* salaried; wage-earning
▷ *nm/f* salaried employee; wage-earner
salaud [salo] *nm* (*fam!*) sod (!), bastard (!)
sale [sal] *adj* dirty; (*fig: avant le nom*) nasty
salé, e [sale] *adj* (*liquide, saveur*) salty; (*Culin*)
salted, salt *cpd*; (*fig*) spicy, juicy; (: *note, facture*)
steep, stiff ▷ *nm* (*porc salé*) salt pork; **petit ~**
≈ boiling bacon
salement [salmã] *adv* (*manger etc*) dirtily,
messily
saler [sale] *vt* to salt
saleté [salte] *nf* (*état*) dirtiness; (*crasse*) dirt,
filth; (*tache etc*) dirt *no pl*, something dirty, dirty
mark; (*fig: tour*) filthy trick; (: *chose sans valeur*)
rubbish *no pl*; (: *obscénité*) filth *no pl*; (: *microbe etc*)
bug; **vivre dans la ~** to live in squalor
salière [saljɛʀ] *nf* saltcellar
saligaud [saligo] *nm* (*fam!*) bastard (!), sod (!)
salin, e [salɛ̃, -in] *adj* saline ▷ *nf* saltworks *sg*
salinité [salinite] *nf* salinity, salt-content
salir [saliʀ] *vt* to (make) dirty; (*fig*) to soil the
reputation of; **se salir** to get dirty
salissant, e [salisã, -ãt] *adj* (*tissu*) which shows
the dirt; (*métier*) dirty, messy
salissure [salisyʀ] *nf* dirt *no pl*; (*tache*) dirty
mark
salive [saliv] *nf* saliva
saliver [salive] *vi* to salivate
salle [sal] *nf* room; (*d'hôpital*) ward; (*de restaurant*)
dining room; (*d'un cinéma*) auditorium; (: *public*)
audience; **faire ~ comble** to have a full house;
~ d'armes (*pour l'escrime*) arms room; **~
d'attente** waiting room; **~ de bain(s)**
bathroom; **~ de bal** ballroom; **~ de cinéma**
cinema; **~ de classe** classroom; **~ commune**
(*d'hôpital*) ward; **~ de concert** concert hall; **~ de
consultation** consulting room (*Brit*), office
(*US*); **~ de danse** dance hall; **~ de douches**
shower-room; **~ d'eau** shower-room; **~
d'embarquement** (*à l'aéroport*) departure
lounge; **~ d'exposition** showroom; **~ de jeux**
games room; playroom; **~ des machines**
engine room; **~ à manger** dining room;
(*mobilier*) dining room suite; **~ obscure** cinema
(*Brit*), movie theater (*US*); **~ d'opération**
(*d'hôpital*) operating theatre; **~ des professeurs**
staffroom; **~ de projection** film theatre; **~ de
séjour** living room; **~ de spectacle** theatre;
cinema; **~ des ventes** saleroom
salmonellose [salmɔneloz] *nf* (*Méd*) salmonella
poisoning
Salomon [salɔmɔ̃]: **les îles ~** the Solomon
Islands
salon [salɔ̃] *nm* lounge, sitting room; (*mobilier*)
lounge suite; (*exposition*) exhibition, show;
(*mondain, littéraire*) salon; **~ de coiffure**
hairdressing salon; **~ de discussion** (*Inform*)
chatroom; **~ de thé** tearoom
salopard [salɔpaʀ] *nm* (*fam!*) bastard (!)
salope [salɔp] *nf* (*fam!*) bitch (!)
saloper [salɔpe] *vt* (*fam!*) to muck up, mess up

saloperie [salɔpʀi] *nf* (*fam!*) filth *no pl*; dirty
trick, rubbish *no pl*
salopette [salɔpɛt] *nf* dungarees *pl*; (*d'ouvrier*)
overall(s)
salpêtre [salpɛtʀ(ə)] *nm* saltpetre
salsifis [salsifi] *nm* salsify, oyster plant
SALT [salt] *sigle* (= *Strategic Arms Limitation Talks ou
Treaty*) SALT
saltimbanque [saltɛ̃bãk] *nm/f* (travelling)
acrobat
salubre [salybʀ(ə)] *adj* healthy, salubrious
salubrité [salybʀite] *nf* healthiness, salubrity;
~ publique public health
saluer [salɥe] *vt* (*pour dire bonjour, fig*) to greet;
(*pour dire au revoir*) to take one's leave; (*Mil*) to
salute
salut [saly] *nm* (*sauvegarde*) safety; (*Rel*)
salvation; (*geste*) wave; (*parole*) greeting; (*Mil*)
salute ▷ *excl* (*fam: pour dire bonjour*) hi (there);
(: *pour dire au revoir*) see you!, bye!
salutaire [salytɛʀ] *adj* (*remède*) beneficial;
(*conseils*) salutary
salutations [salytɑsjɔ̃] *nfpl* greetings; **recevez
mes ~ distinguées** *ou* **respectueuses** yours
faithfully
salutiste [salytist(ə)] *nm/f* Salvationist
Salvador [salvadɔʀ] *nm*: **le ~** El Salvador
salve [salv(ə)] *nf* salvo; volley of shots; **~
d'applaudissements** burst of applause
Samarie [samaʀi] *nf*: **la ~** Samaria
samaritain [samaʀitɛ̃] *nm*: **le bon S~** the Good
Samaritan
samedi [samdi] *nm* Saturday; *voir aussi* **lundi**
Samoa [samɔa] *nfpl*: **les (îles) ~** Samoa, the
Samoa Islands
SAMU [samy] *sigle m* (= *service d'assistance médicale
d'urgence*) ≈ ambulance (service) (*Brit*),
≈ paramedics (*US*)
sanatorium [sanatɔʀjɔm] *nm* sanatorium
sanctifier [sãktifje] *vt* to sanctify
sanction [sãksjɔ̃] *nf* sanction; (*fig*) penalty;
prendre des ~s contre to impose sanctions on
sanctionner [sãksjɔne] *vt* (*loi, usage*) to
sanction; (*punir*) to punish
sanctuaire [sãktɥɛʀ] *nm* sanctuary
sandale [sãdal] *nf* sandal; **~s à lanières** strappy
sandals
sandalette [sãdalɛt] *nf* sandal
sandwich [sãdwitʃ] *nm* sandwich; **pris en ~**
sandwiched
sang [sã] *nm* blood; **en ~** covered in blood;
jusqu'au ~ (*mordre, pincer*) till the blood comes;
se faire du mauvais ~ to fret, get in a state
sang-froid [sãfʀwa] *nm* calm, sangfroid;
garder/perdre/reprendre son ~ to keep/lose/
regain one's cool; **de ~** in cold blood
sanglant, e [sãglã, -ãt] *adj* bloody, covered in
blood; (*combat*) bloody; (*fig: reproche, affront*) cruel
sangle [sãgl(ə)] *nf* strap; **sangles** *nfpl* (*pour lit etc*)
webbing *sg*
sangler [sãgle] *vt* to strap up; (*animal*) to girth
sanglier [sãglije] *nm* (wild) boar

sanglot | satisfait

sanglot [sãglo] *nm* sob
sangloter [sãglɔte] *vi* to sob
sangsue [sãsy] *nf* leech
sanguin, e [sãgɛ̃, -in] *adj* blood *cpd*; (*fig*) fiery ▷ *nf* blood orange; (*Art*) red pencil drawing
sanguinaire [sãginɛʀ] *adj* (*animal, personne*) bloodthirsty; (*lutte*) bloody
sanguinolent, e [sãginɔlã, -ãt] *adj* streaked with blood
Sanisette® [sanizɛt] *nf* coin-operated public lavatory
sanitaire [sanitɛʀ] *adj* health *cpd*; **sanitaires** *nmpl* (*salle de bain et w.-c.*) bathroom *sg*; **installation/appareil** ~ bathroom plumbing/appliance
sans [sã] *prép* without; ~ **qu'il s'en aperçoive** without him *ou* his noticing; ~ **scrupules** unscrupulous; ~ **manches** sleeveless
sans-abri [sãzabʀi] *nmpl* homeless
sans-emploi [sãzãplwa] *nmpl* jobless
sans-façon [sãfasɔ̃] *adj inv* fuss-free; free and easy
sans-gêne [sãʒɛn] *adj inv* inconsiderate ▷ *nm inv* (*attitude*) lack of consideration
sans-logis [sãlɔʒi] *nmpl* homeless
sans-souci [sãsusi] *adj inv* carefree
sans-travail [sãtʀavaj] *nmpl* unemployed, jobless
santal [sãtal] *nm* sandal(wood)
santé [sãte] *nf* health; **avoir une** ~ **de fer** to be bursting with health; **être en bonne** ~ to be in good health, be healthy; **boire à la** ~ **de qn** to drink (to) sb's health; **"à la** ~ **de"** "here's to"; **à ta** *ou* **votre** ~! cheers!; **service de** ~ (*dans un port etc*) quarantine service; **la** ~ **publique** public health
Santiago [sãtjago], **Santiago du Chili** [sãtjagodyfili] *n* Santiago (de Chile)
santon [sãtɔ̃] *nm ornamental figure at a Christmas crib*
saoudien, ne [saudjɛ̃, -ɛn] *adj* Saudi (Arabian) ▷ *nm/f*: **Saoudien, ne** Saudi (Arabian)
saoul, e [su, sul] *adj* = **soûl, e**
sape [sap] *nf*: **travail de** ~ (*Mil*) sap; (*fig*) insidious undermining process *ou* work; **sapes** *nfpl* (*fam*) gear *sg*, togs
saper [sape] *vt* to undermine, sap; **se saper** *vi* (*fam*) to dress
sapeur [sapœʀ] *nm* sapper
sapeur-pompier [sapœʀpɔ̃pje] *nm* fireman
saphir [safiʀ] *nm* sapphire; (*d'électrophone*) needle, sapphire
sapin [sapɛ̃] *nm* fir (tree); (*bois*) fir; ~ **de Noël** Christmas tree
sapinière [sapinjɛʀ] *nf* fir plantation *ou* forest
SAR *sigle f* (= *Son Altesse Royale*) HRH
sarabande [saʀabãd] *nf* saraband; (*fig*) hullabaloo; whirl
sarbacane [saʀbakan] *nf* blowpipe, blowgun; (*jouet*) peashooter
sarcasme [saʀkasm(ə)] *nm* sarcasm *no pl*; (*propos*) piece of sarcasm

sarcastique [saʀkastik] *adj* sarcastic
sarcastiquement [saʀkastikmã] *adv* sarcastically
sarclage [saʀklaʒ] *nm* weeding
sarcler [saʀkle] *vt* to weed
sarcloir [saʀklwaʀ] *nm* (weeding) hoe, spud
sarcophage [saʀkɔfaʒ] *nm* sarcophagus
Sardaigne [saʀdɛɲ] *nf*: **la** ~ Sardinia
sarde [saʀd(ə)] *adj* Sardinian
sardine [saʀdin] *nf* sardine; ~**s à l'huile** sardines in oil
sardinerie [saʀdinʀi] *nf* sardine cannery
sardinier, -ière [saʀdinje, -jɛʀ] *adj* (*pêche, industrie*) sardine *cpd* ▷ *nm* (*bateau*) sardine boat
sardonique [saʀdɔnik] *adj* sardonic
sari [saʀi] *nm* sari
SARL [saʀl] *sigle f* = **société à responsabilité limitée**
sarment [saʀmã] *nm*: ~ **(de vigne)** vine shoot
sarrasin [saʀazɛ̃] *nm* buckwheat
sarrau [saʀo] *nm* smock
Sarre [saʀ] *nf*: **la** ~ the Saar
sarriette [saʀjɛt] *nf* savory
sarrois, e [saʀwa, -waz] *adj* Saar *cpd* ▷ *nm/f*: **Sarrois, e** inhabitant *ou* native of the Saar
sas [sas] *nm* (*de sous-marin, d'engin spatial*) airlock; (*d'écluse*) lock
satané, e [satane] *adj* (*fam*) confounded
satanique [satanik] *adj* satanic, fiendish
satelliser [satelize] *vt* (*fusée*) to put into orbit; (*fig: pays*) to make into a satellite
satellite [satelit] *nm* satellite; **pays** ~ satellite country
satellite-espion [satelitɛspjɔ̃] (*pl* **satellites-espions**) *nm* spy satellite
satellite-observatoire [satelitɔpsɛʀvatwaʀ] (*pl* **satellites-observatoires**) *nm* observation satellite
satellite-relais [satelitʀəlɛ] (*pl* **satellites-relais**) *nm* (TV) relay satellite
satiété [sasjete] **à** ~ *adv* to satiety *ou* satiation; (*répéter*) ad nauseam
satin [satɛ̃] *nm* satin
satiné, e [satine] *adj* satiny; (*peau*) satin-smooth
satinette [satinɛt] *nf* satinet, sateen
satire [satiʀ] *nf* satire; **faire la** ~ to satirize
satirique [satiʀik] *adj* satirical
satiriser [satiʀize] *vt* to satirize
satiriste [satiʀist(ə)] *nm/f* satirist
satisfaction [satisfaksjɔ̃] *nf* satisfaction; **à ma grande** ~ to my great satisfaction; **obtenir** ~ to obtain *ou* get satisfaction; **donner** ~ **(à)** to give satisfaction (to)
satisfaire [satisfɛʀ] *vt* to satisfy; **se satisfaire de** to be satisfied *ou* content with; ~ **à** *vt* (*engagement*) to fulfil; (*revendications, conditions*) to satisfy, meet
satisfaisant, e [satisfəzã, -ãt] *vb voir* **satisfaire** ▷ *adj* satisfactory; (*qui fait plaisir*) satisfying
satisfait, e [satisfɛ, -ɛt] *pp de* **satisfaire** ▷ *adj* satisfied; ~ **de** happy *ou* satisfied with

375

satisfasse [satisfas], **satisferai** etc [satisfрRe] vb voir **satisfaire**

saturation [satyRasjɔ̃] nf saturation; **arriver à ~** to reach saturation point

saturer [satyRe] vt to saturate; **~ qn/qch de** to saturate sb/sth with

saturnisme [satyRnism(ə)] nm (Méd) lead poisoning

satyre [satiR] nm satyr; (péj) lecher

sauce [sos] nf sauce; (avec un rôti) gravy; **en ~** in a sauce; **~ blanche** white sauce; **~ chasseur** sauce chasseur; **~ tomate** tomato sauce

saucer [sose] vt (assiette) to soak up the sauce from

saucière [sosjɛR] nf sauceboat; gravy boat

saucisse [sosis] nf sausage

saucisson [sosisɔ̃] nm (slicing) sausage; **~ à l'ail** garlic sausage

saucissonner [sosisɔne] vt to cut up, slice ▷ vi to picnic

sauf¹ [sof] prép except; **~ si** (à moins que) unless; **~ avis contraire** unless you hear to the contrary; **~ empêchement** barring (any) problems; **~ erreur** if I'm not mistaken; **~ imprévu** unless anything unforeseen arises, barring accidents

sauf², sauve [sof, sov] adj unharmed, unhurt; (fig: honneur) intact, saved; **laisser la vie sauve à qn** to spare sb's life

sauf-conduit [sofkɔ̃dɥi] nm safe-conduct

sauge [soʒ] nf sage

saugrenu, e [sogRəny] adj preposterous, ludicrous

saule [sol] nm willow (tree); **~ pleureur** weeping willow

saumâtre [somatR(ə)] adj briny; (désagréable: plaisanterie) unsavoury (Brit), unsavory (US)

saumon [somɔ̃] nm salmon inv ▷ adj inv salmon (pink)

saumoné, e [somɔne] adj: **truite ~e** salmon trout

saumure [somyR] nf brine

sauna [sona] nm sauna

saupoudrer [sopudRe] vt: **~ qch de** to sprinkle sth with

saupoudreuse [sopudRøz] nf dredger

saur [sɔR] adj m: **hareng ~** smoked ou red herring, kipper

saurai etc [sɔRe] vb voir **savoir**

saut [so] nm jump; (discipline sportive) jumping; **faire un ~** to (make a) jump ou leap; **faire un ~ chez qn** to pop over to sb's (place); **au ~ du lit** on getting out of bed; **~ en hauteur/longueur** high/long jump; **~ à la corde** skipping; **~ de page/ligne** (Inform) page/line break; **~ en parachute** parachuting no pl; **~ à la perche** pole vaulting; **~ à l'élastique** bungee jumping; **~ périlleux** somersault

saute [sot] nf: **~ de vent/température** sudden change of wind direction/in the temperature; **avoir des ~s d'humeur** to have sudden changes of mood

sauté, e [sote] adj (Culin) sauté ▷ nm: **~ de veau** sauté of veal

saute-mouton [sotmutɔ̃] nm: **jouer à ~** to play leapfrog

sauter [sote] vi to jump, leap; (exploser) to blow up, explode; (: fusibles) to blow; (se rompre) to snap, burst; (se détacher) to pop out (ou off) ▷ vt to jump (over), leap (over); (fig: omettre) to skip, miss (out); **faire ~** to blow up; to burst open; (Culin) to sauté; **~ à pieds joints/à cloche-pied** to make a standing jump/to hop; **~ en parachute** to make a parachute jump; **~ à la corde** to skip; **~ de joie** to jump for joy; **~ de colère** to be hopping with rage ou hopping mad; **~ au cou de qn** to fly into sb's arms; **~ aux yeux** to be quite obvious; **~ au plafond** (fig) to hit the roof

sauterelle [sotRɛl] nf grasshopper

sauterie [sotRi] nf party, hop

sauteur, -euse [sotœR, -øz] nm/f (athlète) jumper ▷ nf (casserole) shallow pan, frying pan; **~ à la perche** pole vaulter; **~ à skis** skijumper

sautillement [sotijmɑ̃] nm hopping; skipping

sautiller [sotije] vi to hop; to skip

sautoir [sotwaR] nm chain; (Sport: emplacement) jumping pit; **~ (de perles)** string of pearls

sauvage [sovaʒ] adj (gén) wild; (peuplade) savage; (farouche) unsociable; (barbare) wild, savage; (non officiel) unauthorized, unofficial ▷ nm/f savage; (timide) unsociable type, recluse

sauvagement [sovaʒmɑ̃] adv savagely

sauvageon, ne [sovaʒɔ̃, -ɔn] nm/f little savage

sauvagerie [sovaʒRi] nf wildness; savagery; unsociability

sauve [sov] adj f voir **sauf**

sauvegarde [sovgaRd(ə)] nf safeguard; **sous la ~ de** under the protection of; **disquette/fichier de ~** (Inform) backup disk/file

sauvegarder [sovgaRde] vt to safeguard; (Inform: enregistrer) to save; (: copier) to back up

sauve-qui-peut [sovkipø] nm inv stampede, mad rush ▷ excl run for your life!

sauver [sove] vt to save; (porter secours à) to rescue; (récupérer) to salvage, rescue; **se sauver** vi (s'enfuir) to run away; (fam: partir) to be off; **~ qn de** to save sb from; **~ la vie à qn** to save sb's life; **~ les apparences** to keep up appearances

sauvetage [sovtaʒ] nm rescue; **~ en montagne** mountain rescue; **ceinture de ~** lifebelt (Brit), life preserver (US); **brassière ou gilet de ~** lifejacket (Brit), life preserver (US)

sauveteur [sovtœR] nm rescuer

sauvette [sovɛt]: **à la ~** adv (vendre) without authorization; (se marier etc) hastily, hurriedly; **vente à la ~** (unauthorized) street trading, (street) peddling

sauveur [sovœR] nm saviour (Brit), savior (US)

SAV sigle m = **service après-vente**

savais etc [save] vb voir **savoir**

savamment [savamɑ̃] adv (avec érudition) learnedly; (habilement) skilfully, cleverly

savane [savan] nf savannah

savant, e [savɑ̃, -ɑ̃t] adj scholarly, learned; (calé)

clever ▷ *nm* scientist; **animal** ~ performing animal

savate [savat] *nf* worn-out shoe; (*Sport*) French boxing

saveur [savœʀ] *nf* flavour (*Brit*), flavor (*US*); (*fig*) savour (*Brit*), savor (*US*)

Savoie [savwa] *nf*: **la** ~ Savoy

savoir [savwaʀ] *vt* to know; (*être capable de*): **il sait nager** he knows how to swim, he can swim ▷ *nm* knowledge; **se savoir** (*être connu*) to be known; **se savoir malade/incurable** to know that one is ill/incurably ill; **il est petit: tu ne peux pas ~!** you won't believe how small he is!; **vous n'êtes pas sans ~ que** you are not *ou* will not be unaware of the fact that; **je crois ~ que ...** I believe that ..., I think I know that ...; **je n'en sais rien** I (really) don't know; **à ~ (que)** that is, namely; **faire ~ qch à qn** to inform sb about sth, let sb know sth; **pas que je sache** not as far as I know; **sans le ~** *adv* unknowingly, unwittingly; **en ~ long** to know a lot

savoir-faire [savwaʀfɛʀ] *nm inv* savoir-faire, know-how

savoir-vivre [savwaʀvivʀ(ə)] *nm inv*: **le** ~ savoir-faire, good manners *pl*

savon [savɔ̃] *nm* (*produit*) soap; (*morceau*) bar *ou* tablet of soap; (*fam*): **passer un ~ à qn** to give sb a good dressing-down

savonner [savɔne] *vt* to soap

savonnerie [savɔnʀi] *nf* soap factory

savonnette [savɔnɛt] *nf* bar *ou* tablet of soap

savonneux, -euse [savɔnø, -øz] *adj* soapy

savons [savɔ̃] *vb voir* **savoir**

savourer [savuʀe] *vt* to savour (*Brit*), savor (*US*)

savoureux, -euse [savuʀø, -øz] *adj* tasty; (*fig*) spicy, juicy

savoyard, e [savwajaʀ, -aʀd(ə)] *adj* Savoyard

Saxe [saks(ə)] *nf*: **la** ~ Saxony

saxo [saksɔ], **saxophone** [saksɔfɔn] *nm* sax(ophone)

saxophoniste [saksɔfɔnist(ə)] *nm/f* saxophonist, sax(ophone) player

saynète [sɛnɛt] *nf* playlet

SBB *sigle f* (= *Schweizerische Bundesbahn*) *Swiss federal railways*

sbire [sbiʀ] *nm* (*péj*) henchman

sc. *abr* = **scène**

s/c *abr* (= *sous couvert de*) ≈ c/o

scabreux, -euse [skabʀø, -øz] *adj* risky; (*indécent*) improper, shocking

scalpel [skalpɛl] *nm* scalpel

scalper [skalpe] *vt* to scalp

scampi [skãpi] *nmpl* scampi

scandale [skãdal] *nm* scandal; (*tapage*): **faire du** ~ to make a scene, create a disturbance; **faire** ~ to scandalize people; **au grand** ~ **de ...** to the great indignation of ...

scandaleusement [skãdaløzmã] *adv* scandalously, outrageously

scandaleux, -euse [skãdalø, -øz] *adj* scandalous, outrageous

scandaliser [skãdalize] *vt* to scandalize; **se** ~ **(de)** to be scandalized (by)

scander [skãde] *vt* (*vers*) to scan; (*mots, syllabes*) to stress separately; (*slogans*) to chant

scandinave [skãdinav] *adj* Scandinavian ▷ *nm/f*: **Scandinave** Scandinavian

Scandinavie [skãdinavi] *nf*: **la** ~ Scandinavia

scanner [skanɛʀ] *nm* (*Méd*) scanner

scanographie [skanɔgʀafi] *nf* (*Méd*) scanning; (*image*) scan

scaphandre [skafãdʀ(ə)] *nm* (*de plongeur*) diving suit; (*de cosmonaute*) spacesuit; ~ **autonome** aqualung

scaphandrier [skafãdʀije] *nm* diver

scarabée [skaʀabe] *nm* beetle

scarlatine [skaʀlatin] *nf* scarlet fever

scarole [skaʀɔl] *nf* endive

scatologique [skatɔlɔʒik] *adj* scatological, lavatorial

sceau, x [so] *nm* seal; (*fig*) stamp, mark; **sous le** ~ **du secret** under the seal of secrecy

scélérat, e [seleʀa, -at] *nm/f* villain, blackguard ▷ *adj* villainous, blackguardly

sceller [sele] *vt* to seal

scellés [sele] *nmpl* seals

scénario [senaʀjo] *nm* (*Ciné*) screenplay, script; (: *idée, plan*) scenario; (*fig*) pattern; scenario

scénariste [senaʀist(ə)] *nm/f* scriptwriter

scène [sɛn] *nf* (*gén*) scene; (*estrade, fig: théâtre*) stage; **entrer en** ~ to come on stage; **mettre en** ~ (*Théât*) to stage; (*Ciné*) to direct; (*fig*) to present, introduce; **sur le devant de la** ~ (*en pleine actualité*) in the forefront; **porter à la** ~ to adapt for the stage; **faire une** ~ **(à qn)** to make a scene (with sb); ~ **de ménage** domestic fight *ou* scene

scénique [senik] *adj* (*effets*) theatrical; (*art*) scenic

scepticisme [sɛptisism(ə)] *nm* scepticism

sceptique [sɛptik] *adj* sceptical ▷ *nm/f* sceptic

sceptre [sɛptʀ(ə)] *nm* sceptre

schéma [ʃema] *nm* (*diagramme*) diagram, sketch; (*fig*) outline

schématique [ʃematik] *adj* diagrammatic(al), schematic; (*fig*) oversimplified

schématiquement [ʃematikmã] *adv* schematically, diagrammatically

schématisation [ʃematizasjɔ̃] *nf* schematization; oversimplification

schématiser [ʃematize] *vt* to schematize; to (over)simplify

schismatique [ʃismatik] *adj* schismatic

schisme [ʃism(ə)] *nm* schism; rift, split

schiste [ʃist(ə)] *nm* schist

schizophrène [skizɔfʀɛn] *nm/f* schizophrenic

schizophrénie [skizɔfʀeni] *nf* schizophrenia

sciatique [sjatik] *adj*: **nerf** ~ sciatic nerve ▷ *nf* sciatica

scie [si] *nf* saw; (*fam: rengaine*) catch-tune; (: *personne*) bore; ~ **à bois** wood saw; ~ **circulaire** circular saw; ~ **à découper** fretsaw; ~ **à métaux** hacksaw; ~ **sauteuse** jigsaw

sciemment [sjamã] *adv* knowingly, wittingly
science [sjãs] *nf* science; (*savoir*) knowledge; (*savoir-faire*) art, skill; **~s économiques** economics; **~s humaines/sociales** social sciences; **~s naturelles** natural science *sg*, biology *sg*; **~s po** political studies
science-fiction [sjãsfiksjɔ̃] *nf* science fiction
scientifique [sjãtifik] *adj* scientific ▷ *nm/f* (*savant*) scientist; (*étudiant*) science student
scientifiquement [sjãtifikmã] *adv* scientifically
scier [sje] *vt* to saw; (*retrancher*) to saw off
scierie [siRi] *nf* sawmill
scieur [sjœR] *nm*: **~ de long** pit sawyer
Scilly [sili]: **les îles ~** the Scilly Isles, the Scillies, the Isles of Scilly
scinder [sɛ̃de] *vt*, **se scinder** *vi* to split (up)
scintillant, e [sɛ̃tijã, -ãt] *adj* sparkling
scintillement [sɛ̃tijmã] *nm* sparkling *no pl*
scintiller [sɛ̃tije] *vi* to sparkle
scission [sisjɔ̃] *nf* split
sciure [sjyR] *nf*: **~ (de bois)** sawdust
sclérose [skleRoz] *nf* sclerosis; (*fig*) ossification; **~ en plaques (SEP)** multiple sclerosis (MS)
sclérosé, e [skleRoze] *adj* sclerosed, sclerotic; ossified
scléroser [skleRoze]: **se scléroser** *vi* to become sclerosed; (*fig*) to become ossified
scolaire [skɔlER] *adj* school *cpd*; (*péj*) schoolish; **l'année ~** the school year; (*à l'université*) the academic year; **en âge ~** of school age
scolarisation [skɔlaRizasjɔ̃] *nf* (*d'un enfant*) schooling; **la ~ d'une région** the provision of schooling in a region; **le taux de ~** the proportion of children in full-time education
scolariser [skɔlaRize] *vt* to provide with schooling (*ou* schools)
scolarité [skɔlaRite] *nf* schooling; **frais de ~** school fees (*Brit*), tuition (*US*)
scolastique [skɔlastik] *adj* (*péj*) scholastic
scoliose [skɔljoz] *nf* curvature of the spine, scoliosis
scoop [skup] *nm* (*Presse*) scoop, exclusive
scooter [skutœR] *nm* (motor) scooter
scorbut [skɔRbyt] *nm* scurvy
score [skɔR] *nm* score; (*électoral etc*) result
scories [skɔRi] *nfpl* scoria *pl*
scorpion [skɔRpjɔ̃] *nm* (*signe*): **le S~** Scorpio, the Scorpion; **être du S~** to be Scorpio
scotch [skɔtʃ] *nm* (*whisky*) scotch, whisky; (*adhésif*) Sellotape® (*Brit*), Scotch tape® (*US*)
scotcher [skɔtʃe] *vt* to sellotape® (*Brit*), scotchtape® (*US*)
scout, e [skut] *adj*, *nm* scout
scoutisme [skutism(ə)] *nm* (boy) scout movement; (*activités*) scouting
scribe [skRib] *nm* scribe; (*péj*) penpusher
scribouillard [skRibujaR] *nm* penpusher
script [skRipt(ə)] *nm* printing; (*Ciné*) (shooting) script
scripte [skRipt(ə)] *nf* continuity girl
script-girl [skRiptgœRl] *nf* continuity girl

scriptural, e, -aux [skRiptyRal, -o] *adj*: **monnaie ~e** bank money
scrupule [skRypyl] *nm* scruple; **être sans ~s** to be unscrupulous; **se faire un ~ de qch** to have scruples *ou* qualms about doing sth
scrupuleusement [skRypyløzmã] *adv* scrupulously
scrupuleux, -euse [skRypylø, -øz] *adj* scrupulous
scrutateur, -trice [skRytatœR, -tRis] *adj* searching ▷ *nm/f* scrutineer
scruter [skRyte] *vt* to search, scrutinize; (*l'obscurité*) to peer into; (*motifs, comportement*) to examine, scrutinize
scrutin [skRytɛ̃] *nm* (*vote*) ballot; (*ensemble des opérations*) poll; **~ proportionnel/majoritaire** election on a proportional/majority basis; **~ à deux tours** poll with two ballots *ou* rounds; **~ de liste** list system
sculpter [skylte] *vt* to sculpt; (*érosion*) to carve
sculpteur [skyltœR] *nm* sculptor
sculptural, e, -aux [skyltyRal, -o] *adj* sculptural; (*fig*) statuesque
sculpture [skyltyR] *nf* sculpture; **~ sur bois** wood carving
sdb. *abr* = **salle de bain**
SDF *sigle m* (= *sans domicile fixe*) homeless person; **les ~** the homeless
SDN *sigle f* (= *Société des Nations*) League of Nations
SE *sigle f* (= *Son Excellence*) HE

 MOT-CLÉ

se, s' [s(ə)] *pron* **1** (*emploi réfléchi*) oneself; (: *masc*) himself; (: *fém*) herself; (: *sujet non humain*) itself; (: *pl*) themselves; **se voir comme l'on est** to see o.s. as one is
2 (*réciproque*) one another, each other; **ils s'aiment** they love one another *ou* each other
3 (*passif*): **cela se répare facilement** it is easily repaired
4 (*possessif*): **se casser la jambe/laver les mains** to break one's leg/wash one's hands

séance [seãs] *nf* (*d'assemblée, récréative*) meeting, session; (*de tribunal*) sitting, session; (*musicale, Ciné, Théât*) performance; **ouvrir/lever la ~** to open/close the meeting; **~ tenante** forthwith
séant, e [seã, -ãt] *adj* seemly, fitting ▷ *nm* posterior
seau, x [so] *nm* bucket, pail; **~ à glace** ice bucket
sébum [sebɔm] *nm* sebum
sec, sèche [sɛk, sɛʃ] *adj* dry; (*raisins, figues*) dried; (*cœur, personne: insensible*) hard, cold; (*maigre, décharné*) spare, lean; (*réponse, ton*) sharp, curt; (*démarrage*) sharp, sudden ▷ *nm*: **tenir au ~** to keep in a dry place ▷ *adv* hard; (*démarrer*) sharply; **boire ~** to be a heavy drinker; **je le bois ~** I drink it straight *ou* neat; **à pied ~** without getting one's feet wet; **à ~** *adj* dried up; (*à court d'argent*) broke
SECAM [sekam] *sigle m* (= *procédé séquentiel à*

mémoire) SECAM

sécante [sekɑ̃t] *nf* secant

sécateur [sekatœʀ] *nm* secateurs *pl* (*Brit*), shears *pl*, pair of secateurs *ou* shears

sécession [sesesjɔ̃] *nf*: **faire ~** to secede; **la guerre de S~** the American Civil War

séchage [seʃaʒ] *nm* drying; (*de bois*) seasoning

sèche [sɛʃ] *adj f voir* **sec** ▷ *nf* (*fam*) cigarette, fag (*Brit*)

sèche-cheveux [sɛʃʃəvø] *nm inv* hair-drier

sèche-linge [sɛʃlɛ̃ʒ] *nm inv* drying cabinet

sèche-mains [sɛʃmɛ̃] *nm inv* hand drier

sèchement [sɛʃmɑ̃] *adv* (*frapper etc*) sharply; (*répliquer etc*) drily, sharply

sécher [seʃe] *vt* to dry; (*dessécher: peau, blé*) to dry (out); (*: étang*) to dry up; (*bois*) to season; (*fam: classe, cours*) to skip, miss ▷ *vi* to dry; to dry out; to dry up; (*fam: candidat*) to be stumped; **se sécher** (*après le bain*) to dry o.s.

sécheresse [seʃʀɛs] *nf* dryness; (*absence de pluie*) drought

séchoir [seʃwaʀ] *nm* drier

second, e [səɡɔ̃, -ɔ̃d] *adj* second ▷ *nm* (*assistant*) second in command; (*étage*) second floor (*Brit*), third floor (*US*); (*Navig*) first mate ▷ *nf* second; (*Scol*) ≈ fifth form (*Brit*), ≈ tenth grade (*US*); **en ~** (*en second rang*) in second place; **voyager en ~e** to travel second-class; **doué de ~e vue** having (the gift of) second sight; **trouver son ~ souffle** (*Sport, fig*) to get one's second wind; **être dans un état ~** to be in a daze (*ou* trance); **de ~e main** second-hand

secondaire [səɡɔ̃dɛʀ] *adj* secondary

seconder [səɡɔ̃de] *vt* to assist; (*favoriser*) to back

secouer [səkwe] *vt* to shake; (*passagers*) to rock; (*traumatiser*) to shake (up); **se secouer** (*chien*) to shake itself; (*fam: se démener*) to shake o.s. up; **~ la poussière d'un tapis** to shake the dust off a carpet; **~ la tête** to shake one's head

secourable [səkuʀabl(ə)] *adj* helpful

secourir [səkuʀiʀ] *vt* (*aller sauver*) to (go and) rescue; (*prodiguer des soins à*) to help, assist; (*venir en aide à*) to assist, aid

secourisme [səkuʀism(ə)] *nm* (*premiers soins*) first aid; (*sauvetage*) life saving

secouriste [səkuʀist(ə)] *nm/f* first-aid worker

secourons *etc* [səkuʀɔ̃] *vb voir* **secourir**

secours [səkuʀ] *vb voir* **secourir** ▷ *nm* help, aid, assistance ▷ *nmpl* aid *sg*; **cela lui a été d'un grand ~** this was a great help to him; **au ~!** help!; **appeler au ~** to shout *ou* call for help; **appeler qn à son ~** to call sb to one's assistance; **porter ~ à qn** to give sb assistance, help sb; **les premiers ~** first aid *sg*; **le ~ en montagne** mountain rescue

secouru, e [səkuʀy] *pp de* **secourir**

secousse [səkus] *nf* jolt, bump; (*électrique*) shock; (*fig: psychologique*) jolt, shock; **~ sismique** *ou* **tellurique** earth tremor

secret, -ète [səkʀɛ, -ɛt] *adj* secret; (*fig: renfermé*) reticent, reserved ▷ *nm* secret; (*discrétion absolue*): **le ~** secrecy; **en ~** in secret, secretly; **au**

~ in solitary confinement; **~ de fabrication** trade secret; **~ professionnel** professional secrecy

secrétaire [səkʀetɛʀ] *nm/f* secretary ▷ *nm* (*meuble*) writing desk, secretaire; **~ d'ambassade** embassy secretary; **~ de direction** private *ou* personal secretary; **~ d'État** ≈ junior minister; **~ général (SG)** Secretary-General; (*Comm*) company secretary; **~ de mairie** town clerk; **~ médicale** medical secretary; **~ de rédaction** sub-editor

secrétariat [s(ə)kʀetaʀja] *nm* (*profession*) secretarial work; (*bureau: d'entreprise, d'école*) (secretary's) office; (*: d'organisation internationale*) secretariat; (*Pol etc: fonction*) secretaryship, office of Secretary

secrètement [səkʀɛtmɑ̃] *adv* secretly

sécréter [sekʀete] *vt* to secrete

sécrétion [sekʀesjɔ̃] *nf* secretion

sectaire [sɛktɛʀ] *adj* sectarian, bigoted

sectarisme [sɛktaʀism(ə)] *nm* sectarianism

secte [sɛkt(ə)] *nf* sect

secteur [sɛktœʀ] *nm* sector; (*Admin*) district; (*Élec*): **branché sur le ~** plugged into the mains (supply); **fonctionne sur pile et ~** battery or mains operated; **le ~ privé/public** (*Écon*) the private/public sector; **le ~ primaire/tertiaire** the primary/tertiary sector

section [sɛksjɔ̃] *nf* section; (*de parcours d'autobus*) fare stage; (*Mil: unité*) platoon; **~ rythmique** rhythm section

sectionner [sɛksjɔne] *vt* to sever; **se sectionner** *vi* to be severed

sectionneur [sɛksjɔnœʀ] *nm* (*Élec*) isolation switch

sectoriel, le [sɛktɔʀjɛl] *adj* sector-based

sectorisation [sɛktɔʀizasjɔ̃] *nf* division into sectors

sectoriser [sɛktɔʀize] *vt* to divide into sectors

sécu [seky] *nf* (*fam: = sécurité sociale*) ≈ dole (*Brit*), ≈ Welfare (*US*)

séculaire [sekylɛʀ] *adj* secular; (*très vieux*) age-old

séculariser [sekylaʀize] *vt* to secularize

séculier, -ière [sekylje, -jɛʀ] *adj* secular

sécurisant, e [sekyʀizɑ̃, -ɑ̃t] *adj* secure, giving a sense of security

sécuriser [sekyʀize] *vt* to give a sense of security to

sécurité [sekyʀite] *nf* security; (*absence de danger*) safety; **impression de ~** sense of security; **la ~ internationale** international security; **système de ~** security (*ou* safety) system; **être en ~** to be safe; **la ~ de l'emploi** job security; **la ~ routière** road safety; **la ~ sociale** ≈ (the) Social Security (*Brit*), ≈ (the) Welfare (*US*)

sédatif, -ive [sedatif, -iv] *adj, nm* sedative

sédentaire [sedɑ̃tɛʀ] *adj* sedentary

sédiment [sedimɑ̃] *nm* sediment; **sédiments** *nmpl* (*alluvions*) sediment *sg*

sédimentaire [sedimɑ̃tɛʀ] *adj* sedimentary

sédimentation [sedimɑ̃tasjɔ̃] *nf*

sedimentation

séditieux, -euse [sedisjø, -øz] *adj* insurgent; seditious

sédition [sedisjɔ̃] *nf* insurrection; sedition

séducteur, -trice [sedyktœʀ, -tʀis] *adj* seductive ▷ *nm/f* seducer (seductress)

séduction [sedyksjɔ̃] *nf* seduction; *(charme, attrait)* appeal, charm

séduire [sedɥiʀ] *vt* to charm; *(femme: abuser de)* to seduce; *(chose)* to appeal to

séduisant, e [sedɥizɑ̃, -ɑ̃t] *vb voir* **séduire** ▷ *adj* *(femme)* seductive; *(homme, offre)* very attractive

séduit, e [sedɥi, -it] *pp de* **séduire**

segment [sɛgmɑ̃] *nm* segment; *(Auto):* ~ **(de piston)** piston ring; ~ **de frein** brake shoe

segmenter [sɛgmɑ̃te] *vt*, **se segmenter** *vi* to segment

ségrégation [segʀegasjɔ̃] *nf* segregation

ségrégationnisme [segʀegasjɔnism(ə)] *nm* segregationism

ségrégationniste [segʀegasjɔnist(ə)] *adj* segregationist

seiche [sɛʃ] *nf* cuttlefish

séide [seid] *nm* *(péj)* henchman

seigle [sɛgl(ə)] *nm* rye

seigneur [sɛɲœʀ] *nm* lord; **le S~** the Lord

seigneurial, e, -aux [sɛɲœʀjal, -o] *adj* lordly, stately

sein [sɛ̃] *nm* breast; *(entrailles)* womb; **au ~ de** *prép (équipe, institution)* within; *(flots, bonheur)* in the midst of; **donner le ~ à** *(bébé)* to feed (at the breast); to breast-feed; **nourrir au ~** to breast-feed

Seine [sɛn] *nf*: **la ~** the Seine

séisme [seism(ə)] *nm* earthquake

séismique *etc* [seismik] *voir* **sismique** *etc*

SEITA [seita] *sigle f* = **Société d'exploitation industrielle des tabacs et allumettes**

seize [sɛz] *num* sixteen

seizième [sɛzjɛm] *num* sixteenth

séjour [seʒuʀ] *nm* stay; *(pièce)* living room

séjourner [seʒuʀne] *vi* to stay

sel [sɛl] *nm* salt; *(fig)* wit; spice; ~ **de cuisine/de table** cooking/table salt; ~ **gemme** rock salt; ~**s de bain** bathsalts

sélect, e [selɛkt] *adj* select

sélectif, -ive [selɛktif, -iv] *adj* selective

sélection [selɛksjɔ̃] *nf* selection; **faire/opérer une ~ parmi** to make a selection from among; **épreuve de ~** *(Sport)* trial (for selection); ~ **naturelle** natural selection; ~ **professionnelle** professional recruitment

sélectionné, e [selɛksjɔne] *adj (joueur)* selected; *(produit)* specially selected

sélectionner [selɛksjɔne] *vt* to select

sélectionneur, -euse [selɛksjɔnœʀ, -øz] *nm/f* selector

sélectivement [selɛktivmɑ̃] *adv* selectively

sélectivité [selɛktivite] *nf* selectivity

self [sɛlf] *nm (fam)* self-service

self-service [sɛlfsɛʀvis] *adj* self-service ▷ *nm* self-service (restaurant); *(magasin)* self-service

shop

selle [sɛl] *nf* saddle; **selles** *nfpl (Méd)* stools; **aller à la ~** *(Méd)* to have a bowel movement; **se mettre en ~** to mount, get into the saddle

seller [sele] *vt* to saddle

sellette [sɛlɛt] *nf*: **être sur la ~** to be on the carpet *(fig)*

sellier [selje] *nm* saddler

selon [səlɔ̃] *prép* according to; *(en se conformant à)* in accordance with; ~ **moi** as I see it; ~ **que** according to, depending on whether

SEm *sigle f* (= *Son Éminence*) HE

semailles [səmɑj] *nfpl* sowing *sg*

semaine [səmɛn] *nf* week; *(salaire)* week's wages *ou* pay, weekly wages *ou* pay; **en ~** during the week, on weekdays; **à la petite ~** from day to day; **la ~ sainte** Holy Week

semainier [səmenje] *nm (bracelet)* bracelet made up of seven bands; *(calendrier)* desk diary; *(meuble)* chest of (seven) drawers

sémantique [semɑ̃tik] *adj* semantic ▷ *nf* semantics *sg*

sémaphore [semafɔʀ] *nm (Rail)* semaphore signal

semblable [sɑ̃blabl(ə)] *adj* similar; *(de ce genre):* **de ~s mésaventures** such mishaps ▷ *nm* fellow creature *ou* man; ~ **à** similar to, like

semblant [sɑ̃blɑ̃] *nm*: **un ~ de vérité** a semblance of truth; **faire ~ (de faire)** to pretend (to do)

sembler [sɑ̃ble] *vb copule* to seem ▷ *vb impers*: **il semble (bien) que/inutile de** it (really) seems *ou* appears that/useless to; **il me semble (bien) que** it (really) seems to me that, I (really) think that; **il me semble le connaître** I think *ou* I've a feeling I know him; ~ **être** to seem to be; **comme bon lui semble** as he sees fit; **me semble-t-il, à ce qu'il me semble** it seems to me, to my mind

semelle [səmɛl] *nf* sole; *(intérieure)* insole, inner sole; **battre la ~** to stamp one's feet (to keep them warm); *(fig)* to hang around (waiting); ~**s compensées** platform soles

semence [səmɑ̃s] *nf (graine)* seed; *(clou)* tack

semer [səme] *vt* to sow; *(fig: éparpiller)* to scatter; *(confusion)* to spread; *(: poursuivants)* to lose, shake off; ~ **la discorde parmi** to sow discord among; **semé de** *(difficultés)* riddled with

semestre [səmɛstʀ(ə)] *nm* half-year; *(Scol)* semester

semestriel, le [səmɛstʀijɛl] *adj* half-yearly; semestral

semeur, -euse [səmœʀ, -øz] *nm/f* sower

semi-automatique [səmiɔtɔmatik] *adj* semiautomatic

semiconducteur [səmikɔ̃dyktœʀ] *nm (Inform)* semiconductor

semi-conserve [səmikɔ̃sɛʀv(ə)] *nf* semi-perishable foodstuff

semi-fini [səmifini] *adj m (produit)* semi-finished

semi-liberté [səmilibɛʀte] *nf (Jur)* partial release from prison *(in order to follow a profession or* undergo medical treatment)

sémillant, e [semijã, -ãt] *adj* vivacious; dashing

séminaire [seminɛR] *nm* seminar; (*Rel*) seminary

séminariste [seminaRist(ə)] *nm* seminarist

sémiologie [semjɔlɔʒi] *nf* semiology

semi-public, -ique [səmipyblik] *adj* (*Jur*) semipublic

semi-remorque [səmiRəmɔRk(ə)] *nf* trailer
▷ *nm* articulated lorry (*Brit*), semi(trailer) (*US*)

semis [səmi] *nm* (*terrain*) seedbed, seed plot; (*plante*) seedling

sémite [semit] *adj* Semitic

sémitique [semitik] *adj* Semitic

semoir [səmwaR] *nm* seed-bag; seeder

semonce [səmɔ̃s] *nf*: **un coup de ~** a shot across the bows

semoule [səmul] *nf* semolina; **~ de riz** ground rice

sempiternel, le [sɛ̃pitɛRnɛl] *adj* eternal, never-ending

sénat [sena] *nm* senate; *see note*

SÉNAT

The *Sénat* is the upper house of the French parliament and is housed in the Palais du Luxembourg in Paris. One-third of its members, "sénateurs" are elected for a nine-year term every three years by an electoral college consisting of the "députés" and other elected representatives. The *Sénat* has a wide range of powers but can be overridden by the lower house, the "Assemblée nationale" in case of dispute.

sénateur [senatœR] *nm* senator

sénatorial, e, -aux [senatɔRjal, -o] *adj* senatorial, Senate *cpd*

Sénégal [senegal] *nm*: **le ~** Senegal

sénégalais, e [senegalɛ, -ɛz] *adj* Senegalese

sénevé [sɛnve] *nm* (*Bot*) mustard; (*graine*) mustard seed

sénile [senil] *adj* senile

sénilité [senilite] *nf* senility

senior [senjɔR] *nm/f* (*Sport*) senior

sens [sã] *vb voir* **sentir** ▷ *nm* [sãs] (*Physiol, instinct*) sense; (*signification*) meaning, sense; (*direction*) direction, way ▷ *nmpl* (*sensualité*) senses; **reprendre ses ~** to regain consciousness; **avoir le ~ des affaires/de la mesure** to have business sense/a sense of moderation; **ça n'a pas de ~** that doesn't make (any) sense; **en dépit du bon ~** contrary to all good sense; **tomber sous le ~** to stand to reason, be perfectly obvious; **en un ~, dans un ~** in a way; **en ce ~ que** in the sense that; **à mon ~** to my mind; **dans le ~ des aiguilles d'une montre** clockwise; **dans le ~ de la longueur/largeur** lengthways/widthways; **dans le mauvais ~** the wrong way; in the wrong direction; **bon ~** good sense; **~ commun** common sense; **~**

dessus dessous upside down; **~ interdit, ~ unique** one-way street

sensass [sãsas] *adj* (*fam*) fantastic

sensation [sãsasjɔ̃] *nf* sensation; **faire ~** to cause a sensation, create a stir; **à ~** (*péj*) sensational

sensationnel, le [sãsasjɔnɛl] *adj* sensational

sensé, e [sãse] *adj* sensible

sensibilisation [sãsibilizasjɔ̃] *nf* consciousness-raising; **une campagne de ~ de l'opinion** a campaign to raise public awareness

sensibiliser [sãsibilize] *vt* to sensitize; **~ qn (à)** to make sb sensitive (to)

sensibilité [sãsibilite] *nf* sensitivity; (*affectivité, émotivité*) sensibility

sensible [sãsibl(ə)] *adj* sensitive; (*aux sens*) perceptible; (*appréciable: différence, progrès*) appreciable, noticeable; (*quartier*) problem *cpd*; **~ à** sensitive to

sensiblement [sãsibləmã] *adv* (*notablement*) appreciably, noticeably; (*à peu près*): **ils ont ~ le même poids** they weigh approximately the same

sensiblerie [sãsibləRi] *nf* sentimentality; squeamishness

sensitif, -ive [sãsitif, -iv] *adj* (*nerf*) sensory; (*personne*) oversensitive

sensoriel, le [sãsɔRjɛl] *adj* sensory, sensorial

sensualité [sãsɥalite] *nf* sensuality, sensuousness

sensuel, le [sãsɥɛl] *adj* sensual; sensuous

sent [sã] *vb voir* **sentir**

sente [sãt] *nf* path

sentence [sãtãs] *nf* (*jugement*) sentence; (*adage*) maxim

sentencieusement [sãtãsjøzmã] *adv* sententiously

sentencieux, -euse [sãtãsjø, -øz] *adj* sententious

senteur [sãtœR] *nf* scent, perfume

senti, e [sãti] *adj*: **bien ~** (*mots etc*) well-chosen

sentier [sãtje] *nm* path

sentiment [sãtimã] *nm* feeling; (*conscience, impression*): **avoir le ~ de/que** to be aware of/ have the feeling that; **recevez mes ~s respectueux** yours faithfully; **faire du ~** (*péj*) to be sentimental; **si vous me prenez par les ~s** if you appeal to my feelings

sentimental, e, -aux [sãtimãtal, -o] *adj* sentimental; (*vie, aventure*) love *cpd*

sentimentalisme [sãtimãtalism(ə)] *nm* sentimentalism

sentimentalité [sãtimãtalite] *nf* sentimentality

sentinelle [sãtinɛl] *nf* sentry; **en ~** standing guard; (*soldat: en faction*) on sentry duty

sentir [sãtiR] *vt* (*par l'odorat*) to smell; (*par le goût*) to taste; (*au toucher, fig*) to feel; (*répandre une odeur de*) to smell of; (: *ressemblance*) to smell like; (*avoir la saveur de*) to taste of; to taste like; (*fig: dénoter, annoncer*) to be indicative of; to smack of; to foreshadow ▷ *vi* to smell; ~ **mauvais** to smell bad; **se ~ bien** to feel good; **se ~ mal** (*être indisposé*) to feel unwell *ou* ill; **se ~ le courage/la force de faire** to feel brave/strong enough to do; **ne plus se ~ de joie** to be beside o.s. with joy; **il ne peut pas le ~** (*fam*) he can't stand him

seoir [swaʀ]: **~ à** *vt* to become, befit; **comme il (leur) sied** as it is fitting (to them)

Seoul [seul] *n* Seoul

SEP *sigle f* (= *sclérose en plaques*) MS

séparation [separɑsjɔ̃] *nf* separation; (*cloison*) division, partition; **~ de biens** division of property (*in marriage settlement*); **~ de corps** legal separation

séparatisme [separatism(ə)] *nm* separatism

séparatiste [separatist(ə)] *adj, nm/f* (*Pol*) separatist

séparé, e [separe] *adj* (*appartements, pouvoirs*) separate; (*époux*) separated; **~ de** separate from; separated from

séparément [separemɑ̃] *adv* separately

séparer [separe] *vt* (*gén*) to separate; (*divergences etc*) to divide; to drive apart; (: *différences, obstacles*) to stand between; (*détacher*): **~ qch de** to pull sth (off) from; (*dissocier*) to distinguish between; (*diviser*): **~ qch par** to divide sth (up) with; **~ une pièce en deux** to divide a room into two; **se séparer** (*époux*) to separate, part; (*prendre congé: amis etc*) to part, leave each other; (*adversaires*) to separate; (*se diviser: route, tige etc*) to divide; (*se détacher*): **se ~ (de)** to split off (from); to come off; **se ~ de** (*époux*) to separate *ou* part from; (*employé, objet personnel*) to part with

sépia [sepja] *nf* sepia

sept [sɛt] *num* seven

septante [sɛptɑ̃t] *num* (*Belgique, Suisse*) seventy

septembre [sɛptɑ̃bʀ(ə)] *nm* September; *voir aussi* **juillet**

septennal, e, -aux [sɛptenal, -o] *adj* seven-year; (*festival*) seven-year, septennial

septennat [sɛptena] *nm* seven-year term (of office)

septentrional, e, -aux [sɛptɑ̃tʀijɔnal, -o] *adj* northern

septicémie [sɛptisemi] *nf* blood poisoning, septicaemia

septième [sɛtjɛm] *num* seventh; **être au ~ ciel** to be on cloud nine

septique [sɛptik] *adj*: **fosse ~** septic tank

septuagénaire [sɛptɥaʒenɛʀ] *adj, nm/f* septuagenarian

sépulcral, e, -aux [sepylkʀal, -o] *adj* (*voix*) sepulchral

sépulcre [sepylkʀ(ə)] *nm* sepulchre

sépulture [sepyltyʀ] *nf* burial; (*tombeau*) burial place, grave

séquelles [sekɛl] *nfpl* after-effects; (*fig*) aftermath *sg*; consequences

séquence [sekɑ̃s] *nf* sequence

séquentiel, le [sekɑ̃sjɛl] *adj* sequential

séquestration [sekɛstʀɑsjɔ̃] *nf* illegal confinement; impounding

séquestre [sekɛstʀ(ə)] *nm* impoundment; **mettre sous ~** to impound

séquestrer [sekɛstʀe] *vt* (*personne*) to confine illegally; (*biens*) to impound

serai *etc* [səʀe] *vb voir* **être**

sérail [seʀaj] *nm* seraglio; harem; **rentrer au ~** to return to the fold

serbe [sɛʀb(ə)] *adj* Serbian ▷ *nm* (*Ling*) Serbian ▷ *nm/f*: **Serbe** Serb

Serbie [sɛʀbi] *nf*: **la ~** Serbia

serbo-croate [sɛʀbɔkʀɔat] *adj* Serbo-Croat, Serbo-Croatian ▷ *nm* (*Ling*) Serbo-Croat

serein, e [səʀɛ̃, -ɛn] *adj* serene; (*jugement*) dispassionate

sereinement [səʀɛnmɑ̃] *adv* serenely

sérénade [seʀenad] *nf* serenade; (*fam*) hullabaloo

sérénité [seʀenite] *nf* serenity

serez [səʀe] *vb voir* **être**

serf, serve [sɛʀ, sɛʀv(ə)] *nm/f* serf

serfouette [sɛʀfwɛt] *nf* weeding hoe

serge [sɛʀʒ(ə)] *nf* serge

sergent [sɛʀʒɑ̃] *nm* sergeant

sergent-chef [sɛʀʒɑ̃ʃɛf] *nm* staff sergeant

sergent-major [sɛʀʒɑ̃maʒɔʀ] *nm* ≈ quartermaster sergeant

sériciculture [seʀisikyltyʀ] *nf* silkworm breeding, sericulture

série [seʀi] *nf* (*de questions, d'accidents, TV*) series *inv*; (*de clés, casseroles, outils*) set; (*catégorie: Sport*) rank; class; **en ~** in quick succession; (*Comm*) mass *cpd*; **de ~** *adj* standard; **hors ~** (*Comm*) custom-built; (*fig*) outstanding; **imprimante ~** (*Inform*) serial printer; **soldes de fin de ~s** end of line special offers; **~ noire** *nm* (crime) thriller ▷ *nf* (*suite de malheurs*) run of bad luck

sérier [seʀje] *vt* to classify, sort out

sérieusement [seʀjøzmɑ̃] *adv* seriously; reliably; responsibly; **il parle ~** he's serious, he means it; **~?** are you serious?, do you mean it?

sérieux, -euse [seʀjø, -øz] *adj* serious; (*élève, employé*) reliable, responsible; (*client, maison*) reliable, dependable; (*offre, proposition*) genuine, serious; (*grave, sévère*) serious, solemn; (*maladie, situation*) serious, grave; (*important*) considerable ▷ *nm* seriousness; reliability; **ce n'est pas ~** (*raisonnable*) that's not on; **garder son ~** to keep a straight face; **manquer de ~** not to be very responsible (*ou* reliable); **prendre qch/qn au ~** to take sth/sb seriously

sérigraphie [seʀigʀafi] *nf* silk screen printing

serin [səʀɛ̃] *nm* canary

seriner [səʀine] *vt*: **~ qch à qn** to drum sth into sb

seringue [səʀɛ̃g] *nf* syringe

serions *etc* [səʀjɔ̃] *vb voir* **être**

serment [sɛʀmɑ̃] *nm* (*juré*) oath; (*promesse*) pledge, vow; **prêter ~** to take the *ou* an oath; **faire le ~ de** to take a vow to, swear to; **sous ~** on *ou* under oath

sermon [sɛʀmɔ̃] *nm* sermon; (*péj*) sermon, lecture

sermonner [sɛʀmɔne] *vt* to lecture

SERNAM [sɛʀnam] *sigle m* (= *Service national de messageries*) rail delivery service

sérologie [seʀɔlɔʒi] *nf* serology

séronégatif, -ive [seʀonegatif, -iv] *adj* HIV negative

séropositif, -ive [seʀopozitif, -iv] *adj* HIV positive

serpe [sɛʀp(ə)] *nf* billhook

serpent [sɛʀpā] *nm* snake; **~ à sonnettes** rattlesnake; **~ monétaire (européen)** (European) monetary snake

serpenter [sɛʀpāte] *vi* to wind

serpentin [sɛʀpātē] *nm* (*tube*) coil; (*ruban*) streamer

serpillière [sɛʀpijɛʀ] *nf* floorcloth

serrage [sɛʀaʒ] *nm* tightening; **collier de ~** clamp

serre [sɛʀ] *nf* (*Agr*) greenhouse; **~ chaude** hothouse; **~ froide** unheated greenhouse

serré, e [seʀe] *adj* (*tissu*) closely woven; (*réseau*) dense; (*écriture*) close; (*habits*) tight; (*fig: lutte, match*) tight, close-fought; (*passagers etc*) (tightly) packed; (*café*) strong ▷ *adv*: **jouer ~** to play it close, play a close game; **écrire ~** to write a cramped hand; **avoir la gorge ~e** to have a lump in one's throat

serre-livres [sɛʀlivʀ(ə)] *nm inv* book ends *pl*

serrement [sɛʀmā] *nm*: **~ de main** handshake; **~ de cœur** pang of anguish

serrer [seʀe] *vt* (*tenir*) to grip *ou* hold tight; (*comprimer, coincer*) to squeeze; (*poings, mâchoires*) to clench; (*vêtement*) to be too tight for; to fit tightly; (*rapprocher*) to close up, move closer together; (*ceinture, nœud, frein, vis*) to tighten ▷ *vi*: **~ à droite** to keep to the right; to move into the right-hand lane; **se serrer** (*se rapprocher*) to squeeze up; **se ~ contre qn** to huddle up to sb; **se ~ les coudes** to stick together, back one another up; **se ~ la ceinture** to tighten one's belt; **~ la main à qn** to shake sb's hand; **~ qn dans ses bras** to hug sb, clasp sb in one's arms; **~ la gorge à qn** (*chagrin*) to bring a lump to sb's throat; **~ les dents** to clench *ou* grit one's teeth; **~ qn de près** to follow close behind sb; **~ le trottoir** to hug the kerb; **~ sa droite** to keep well to the right; **~ la vis à qn** to crack down harder on sb; **~ les rangs** to close ranks

serres [sɛʀ] *nfpl* (*griffes*) claws, talons

serre-tête [sɛʀtɛt] *nm inv* (*bandeau*) headband; (*bonnet*) skullcap

serrure [seʀyʀ] *nf* lock

serrurerie [seʀyʀʀi] *nf* (*métier*) locksmith's trade; (*ferronnerie*) ironwork; **~ d'art** ornamental ironwork

serrurier [seʀyʀje] *nm* locksmith

sers, sert [sɛʀ] *vb voir* **servir**

sertir [sɛʀtiʀ] *vt* (*pierre*) to set; (*pièces métalliques*) to crimp

sérum [seʀɔm] *nm* serum; **~ antivenimeux** snakebite serum; **~ sanguin** (blood) serum

servage [sɛʀvaʒ] *nm* serfdom

servant [sɛʀvā] *nm* server

servante [sɛʀvāt] *nf* (maid)servant

serve [sɛʀv] *nf voir* **serf** ▷ *vb voir* **servir**

serveur, -euse [sɛʀvœʀ, -øz] *nm/f* waiter (waitress) ▷ *nm* (*Inform*) server ▷ *adj*: **centre ~** (*Inform*) service centre

servi, e [sɛʀvi] *adj*: **être bien ~** to get a large helping (*ou* helpings); **vous êtes ~?** are you being served?

serviable [sɛʀvjabl(ə)] *adj* obliging, willing to help

service [sɛʀvis] *nm* (*gén*) service; (*série de repas*): **premier ~** first sitting; (*pourboire*) service (charge); (*assortiment de vaisselle*) set, service; (*linge de table*) set; (*bureau: de la vente etc*) department, section; (*travail*): **pendant le ~** on duty; **services** *nmpl* (*travail, Écon*) services, inclusive/exclusive of service; **faire le ~** to serve; **être en ~ chez qn** (*domestique*) to be in sb's service; **être au ~ de** (*patron, patrie*) to be in the service of; **être au ~ de qn** (*collaborateur, voiture*) to be at sb's service; **porte de ~** tradesman's entrance; **rendre ~ à** to help; **il aime rendre ~** he likes to help; **rendre un ~ à qn** to do sb a favour; **heures de ~** hours of duty; **être de ~** to be on duty; **reprendre du ~** to get back into action; **avoir 25 ans de ~** to have completed 25 years' service; **être/mettre en ~** to be in/put into service *ou* operation; **hors ~** not in use; out of order; **~ à thé/café** tea/coffee set *ou* service; **~ après-vente (SAV)** after-sales service; **en ~ commandé** on an official assignment; **~ funèbre** funeral service; **~ militaire** military service; *see note*; **~ d'ordre** police (*ou* stewards) in charge of maintaining order; **~s publics** public services, (public) utilities; **~s secrets** secret service *sg*; **~s sociaux** social services

● **SERVICE MILITAIRE**

Until 1997, French men over the age of 18 who were passed as fit, and who were not in full-time higher education, were required to do ten months' "service militaire". Conscientious objectors were required to do two years' community service. Since 1997, military service has been suspended in France. However, all sixteen-year-olds, both male and female, are required to register for a compulsory one-day training course, the "JAPD" ("journée d'appel de préparation à la défense"), which covers basic information on the principles and organization of defence in France, and also advises on career opportunities in the military and in the voluntary sector. Young people must attend the training day before their eighteenth birthday.

serviette [sɛʀvjɛt] *nf* (*de table*) (table) napkin, serviette; (*de toilette*) towel; (*porte-documents*) briefcase; **~ éponge** terry towel; **~ hygiénique** sanitary towel

servile [sɛʀvil] *adj* servile

servir [sɛʀviʀ] *vt* (*gén*) to serve; (*dîneur: au restaurant*) to wait on; (*client: au magasin*) to serve, attend to; (*fig: aider*): **~ qn** to aid sb; to serve sb's interests; to stand sb in good stead; (*Comm: rente*) to pay ▷ *vi* (*Tennis*) to serve; (*Cartes*) to deal; (*être militaire*) to serve; **~ qch à qn** to serve sb with sth, help sb to sth; **qu'est-ce que je vous sers?** what can I get you?; **se servir** (*prendre d'un plat*) to help o.s.; (*s'approvisionner*): **se ~ chez** to shop at; **se ~ de** (*plat*) to help o.s. to; (*voiture, outil, relations*) to use; **~ à qn** (*diplôme, livre*) to be of use to sb; **ça m'a servi pour faire** it was useful to me when I did; I used it to do; **~ à qch/à faire** (*outil etc*) to be used for sth/for doing; **ça peut ~** it may come in handy; **à quoi cela sert-il (de faire)?** what's the use (of doing)?; **cela ne sert à rien** it's no use; **~ (à qn) de ...** to serve as ... (for sb); **~ à dîner (à qn)** to serve dinner (to sb)

serviteur [sɛʀvitœʀ] *nm* servant

servitude [sɛʀvityd] *nf* servitude; (*fig*) constraint; (*Jur*) easement

servofrein [sɛʀvɔfʀɛ̃] *nm* servo(-assisted) brake

servomécanisme [sɛʀvɔmekanism(ə)] *nm* servo system

ses [se] *adj possessif voir* **son**

sésame [sezam] *nm* (*Bot*) sesame; (*graine*) sesame seed

session [sesjɔ̃] *nf* session

set [sɛt] *nm* set; (*napperon*) placemat; **~ de table** set of placemats

seuil [sœj] *nm* doorstep; (*fig*) threshold; **sur le ~ de la maison** in the doorway of his house, on his doorstep; **au ~ de** (*fig*) on the threshold *ou* brink *ou* edge of; **~ de rentabilité** (*Comm*) breakeven point

seul, e [sœl] *adj* (*sans compagnie*) alone; (*avec nuance affective: isolé*) lonely; (*unique*): **un ~ livre** only one book, a single book; **le ~ livre** the only book; **~ ce livre, ce livre ~** this book alone, only this book; **d'un ~ coup** (*soudainement*) all at once; (*à la fois*) at one blow ▷ *adv* (*vivre*) alone, on one's own; **parler tout ~** to talk to oneself; **faire qch (tout) ~** to do sth (all) on one's own *ou* (all) by oneself ▷ *nm, nf*: **il en reste un(e) ~(e)** there's only one left; **pas un(e) ~(e)** not a single; **à lui (tout) ~** single-handed, on his own; **~ à ~** in private

seulement [sœlmɑ̃] *adv* (*pas davantage*): **~ cinq, cinq ~** only five; (*exclusivement*): **~ eux** only them, them alone; (*pas avant*): **~ hier/à 10h** only yesterday/at 10 o'clock; (*mais, toutefois*): **il consent, ~ il demande des garanties** he agrees, only he wants guarantees; **non ~ ... mais aussi** *ou* **encore** not only ... but also

sève [sɛv] *nf* sap

sévère [sevɛʀ] *adj* severe

sévèrement [sevɛʀmɑ̃] *adv* severely

sévérité [severite] *nf* severity

sévices [sevis] *nmpl* (physical) cruelty *sg*, ill treatment *sg*

Séville [sevil] *n* Seville

sévir [seviʀ] *vi* (*punir*) to use harsh measures, crack down; (*fléau*) to rage, be rampant; **~ contre** (*abus*) to deal ruthlessly with, crack down on

sevrage [səvʀaʒ] *nm* weaning; deprivation; (*d'un toxicomane*) withdrawal

sevrer [səvʀe] *vt* to wean; (*fig*): **~ qn de** to deprive sb of

sexagénaire [sɛgzaʒenɛʀ] *adj, nm/f* sexagenarian

SExc *sigle f* (= *Son Excellence*) HE

sexe [sɛks(ə)] *nm* sex; (*organe mâle*) member

sexisme [sɛksism(ə)] *nm* sexism

sexiste [sɛksist(ə)] *adj, nm* sexist

sexologie [sɛksɔlɔʒi] *nf* sexology

sexologue [sɛksɔlɔg] *nm/f* sexologist, sex specialist

sextant [sɛkstɑ̃] *nm* sextant

sexualité [sɛksɥalite] *nf* sexuality

sexué, e [sɛksɥe] *adj* sexual

sexuel, le [sɛksɥɛl] *adj* sexual; **acte ~** sex act

sexuellement [sɛksɥɛlmɑ̃] *adv* sexually

seyait [sejɛ] *vb voir* **seoir**

seyant, e [sejɑ̃, -ɑ̃t] *vb voir* **seoir** ▷ *adj* becoming

Seychelles [seʃɛl] *nfpl*: **les ~** the Seychelles

SG *sigle m* = **secrétaire général**

SGEN *sigle m* (= *Syndicat général de l'éducation nationale*) trades union

shaker [ʃɛkœʀ] *nm* (cocktail) shaker

shampooiner [ʃɑ̃pwine] *vt* to shampoo

shampooineur, -euse [ʃɑ̃pwinœʀ, -øz] *nm/f* (*personne*) junior (*who does the shampooing*)

shampooing [ʃɑ̃pwɛ̃] *nm* shampoo; **se faire un ~** to shampoo one's hair; **~ colorant** (colour) rinse; **~ traitant** medicated shampoo

Shetland [ʃɛtlɑ̃d] *n*: **les îles ~** the Shetland Islands, Shetland

shoot [ʃut] *nm* (*Football*) shot

shooter [ʃute] *vi* (*Football*) to shoot; **se shooter** (*drogué*) to mainline

shopping [ʃɔpiŋ] *nm*: **faire du ~** to go shopping

short [ʃɔʀt] *nm* (pair of) shorts *pl*

SI *sigle m* = **syndicat d'initiative**

 MOT-CLÉ

si [si] *nm* (*Mus*) B; (*en chantant la gamme*) ti ▷ *adv* **1** (*oui*) yes; **"Paul n'est pas venu" — "si!"** "Paul hasn't come" — "Yes he has!"; **je vous assure que si** I assure you he did/she is *etc*
2 (*tellement*) so; **si gentil/rapidement** so kind/fast; (**tant et**) **si bien que** so much so that; **si rapide qu'il soit** however fast he may be
▷ *conj* if; **si tu veux** if you want; **je me demande si** I wonder if *ou* whether; **si j'étais toi** if I were you; **si seulement** if only; **si ce n'est que** apart from; **une des plus belles, si**

ce n'est la plus belle one of the most beautiful, if not THE most beautiful; **s'il est aimable, eux par contre ...** while ou whereas he's nice, they (on the other hand) ...

siamois, e [sjamwa, -waz] adj Siamese; **frères/ sœurs ~(es)** Siamese twins
Sibérie [sibeʀi] nf: **la ~** Siberia
sibérien, ne [sibeʀjɛ̃, -ɛn] adj Siberian ▷ nm/f: **Sibérien, ne** Siberian
sibyllin, e [sibilɛ̃, -in] adj sibylline
SICAV [sikav] sigle f (= société d'investissement à capital variable) open-ended investment trust, share in such a trust
Sicile [sisil] nf: **la ~** Sicily
sicilien, ne [sisiljɛ̃, -ɛn] adj Sicilian
sida [sida] nm (= syndrome immuno-déficitaire acquis) AIDS sg
sidéral, e, -aux [sideʀal, -o] adj sideral
sidérant, e [sideʀɑ̃, -ɑ̃t] adj staggering
sidéré, e [sideʀe] adj staggered
sidérurgie [sideʀyʀʒi] nf steel industry
sidérurgique [sideʀyʀʒik] adj steel cpd
sidérurgiste [sideʀyʀʒist(ə)] nm/f steel worker
siècle [sjɛkl(ə)] nm century; (époque): **le ~ des lumières/de l'atome** the age of enlightenment/atomic age; (Rel): **le ~** the world
sied [sje] vb voir **seoir**
siège [sjɛʒ] nm seat; (d'entreprise) head office; (d'organisation) headquarters pl; (Mil) siege; **lever le ~** to raise the siege; **mettre le ~ devant** to besiege; **présentation par le ~** (Méd) breech presentation; **~ avant/arrière** (Auto) front/back seat; **~ baquet** bucket seat; **~ social** registered office
siéger [sjeʒe] vi (assemblée, tribunal) to sit; (résider, se trouver) to lie, be located
sien, ne [sjɛ̃, sjɛn] pron: **le(la) ~(ne), les ~s(~nes)**; his; hers; (d'une chose) its; **y mettre du ~** to pull one's weight; **faire des ~nes** (fam) to be up to one's (usual) tricks; **les ~s** (sa famille) one's family
siérait etc [sjeʀɛ] vb voir **seoir**
Sierra Leone [sjɛʀaleɔne] nf: **la ~** Sierra Leone
sieste [sjɛst(ə)] nf (afternoon) snooze ou nap, siesta; **faire la ~** to have a snooze ou nap
sieur [sjœʀ] nm: **le ~ Thomas** Mr Thomas; (en plaisantant) Master Thomas
sifflant, e [siflɑ̃, -ɑ̃t] adj (bruit) whistling; (toux) wheezing; **(consonne) ~e** sibilant
sifflement [sifləmɑ̃] nm whistle, whistling no pl; wheezing no pl; hissing no pl
siffler [sifle] vi (gén) to whistle; (avec un sifflet) to blow (on) one's whistle; (en respirant) to wheeze; (serpent, vapeur) to hiss ▷ vt (chanson) to whistle; (chien etc) to whistle for; (fille) to whistle at; (pièce, orateur) to hiss, boo; (faute) to blow one's whistle at; (fin du match, départ) to blow one's whistle for; (fam: verre, bouteille) to guzzle, knock back (Brit)

sifflet [siflɛ] nm whistle; **sifflets** nmpl (de mécontentement) whistles, boos; **coup de ~** whistle
siffloter [siflɔte] vi, vt to whistle
sigle [sigl(ə)] nm acronym, (set of) initials pl
signal, -aux [siɲal, -o] nm (signe convenu, appareil) signal; (indice, écriteau) sign; **donner le ~ de** to give the signal for; **~ d'alarme** alarm signal; **~ d'alerte/de détresse** warning/distress signal; **~ horaire** time signal; **~ optique/sonore** warning light/sound; visual/acoustic signal; **signaux (lumineux)** (Auto) traffic signals; **signaux routiers** road signs; (lumineux) traffic lights
signalement [siɲalmɑ̃] nm description, particulars pl
signaler [siɲale] vt to indicate; to announce; to report; (être l'indice de) to indicate; (faire remarquer): **~ qch à qn/à qn que** to point out sth to sb/to sb that; (appeler l'attention sur): **~ qn à la police** to bring sb to the notice of the police; **se ~ par** to distinguish o.s. by; **se ~ à l'attention de qn** to attract sb's attention
signalétique [siɲaletik] adj: **fiche ~** identification sheet
signalisation [siɲalizɑsjɔ̃] nf signalling, signposting; signals pl; roadsigns pl; **panneau de ~** roadsign
signaliser [siɲalize] vt to put up roadsigns on; to put signals on
signataire [siɲatɛʀ] nm/f signatory
signature [siɲatyʀ] nf signature; (action) signing
signe [siɲ] nm sign; (Typo) mark; **ne pas donner ~ de vie** to give no sign of life; **c'est bon ~** it's a good sign; **c'est ~ que** it's a sign that; **faire un ~ de la main/tête** to give a sign with one's hand/shake one's head; **faire ~ à qn** (fig) to get in touch with sb; **faire ~ à qn d'entrer** to motion (to) sb to come in; **en ~ de** as a sign ou mark of; **le ~ de la croix** the sign of the Cross; **~ de ponctuation** punctuation mark; **~ du zodiaque** sign of the zodiac; **~s particuliers** distinguishing marks
signer [siɲe] vt to sign; **se signer** vi to cross o.s
signet [siɲɛ] nm bookmark
significatif, -ive [siɲifikatif, -iv] adj significant
signification [siɲifikɑsjɔ̃] nf meaning
signifier [siɲifje] vt (vouloir dire) to mean, signify; (faire connaître): **~ qch (à qn)** to make sth known (to sb); (Jur): **~ qch à qn** to serve notice of sth on sb
silence [silɑ̃s] nm silence; (Mus) rest; **garder le ~ (sur qch)** to keep silent (about sth), say nothing (about sth); **passer sous ~** to pass over (in silence); **réduire au ~** to silence
silencieusement [silɑ̃sjøzmɑ̃] adv silently
silencieux, -euse [silɑ̃sjø, -øz] adj quiet, silent ▷ nm silencer (Brit), muffler (US)
silex [silɛks] nm flint
silhouette [silwɛt] nf outline, silhouette;

(*lignes, contour*) outline; (*figure*) figure
silice [silis] *nf* silica
siliceux, -euse [silisø, -øz] *adj* (*terrain*) chalky
silicium [silisjɔm] *nm* silicon; **plaquette de ~** silicon chip
silicone [silikon] *nf* silicone
silicose [silikoz] *nf* silicosis, dust disease
sillage [sijaʒ] *nm* wake; (*fig*) trail; **dans le ~ de** (*fig*) in the wake of
sillon [sijɔ̃] *nm* (*d'un champ*) furrow; (*de disque*) groove
sillonner [sijɔne] *vt* (*creuser*) to furrow; (*traverser*) to cross, criss-cross
silo [silo] *nm* silo
simagrées [simagʀe] *nfpl* fuss *sg*; airs and graces
simiesque [simjɛsk(ə)] *adj* monkey-like, ape-like
similaire [similɛʀ] *adj* similar
similarité [similaʀite] *nf* similarity
simili [simili] *nm* imitation; (*Typo*) half-tone ▷ *nf* half-tone engraving
simili... [simili] *préfixe* imitation *cpd*, artificial
similicuir [similikɥiʀ] *nm* imitation leather
similigravure [similigʀavyʀ] *nf* half-tone engraving
similitude [similityd] *nf* similarity
simple [sɛ̃pl(ə)] *adj* (*gén*) simple; (*non multiple*) single; **simples** *nmpl* (*Méd*) medicinal plants; **~ messieurs** *nm* (*Tennis*) men's singles *sg*; **un ~ particulier** an ordinary citizen; **une ~ formalité** a mere formality; **cela varie du ~ au double** it can double, it can double the price *etc*; **dans le plus ~ appareil** in one's birthday suit; **~ course** *adj* single; **~ d'esprit** *nm/f* simpleton; **~ soldat** private
simplement [sɛ̃pləmɑ̃] *adv* simply
simplet, te [sɛ̃plɛ, -ɛt] *adj* (*personne*) simple-minded
simplicité [sɛ̃plisite] *nf* simplicity; **en toute ~** quite simply
simplification [sɛ̃plifikɑsjɔ̃] *nf* simplification
simplifier [sɛ̃plifje] *vt* to simplify
simpliste [sɛ̃plist(ə)] *adj* simplistic
simulacre [simylakʀ(ə)] *nm* enactment; (*péj*): **un ~ de** a pretence of, a sham
simulateur, -trice [simylatœʀ, -tʀis] *nm/f* shammer, pretender; (*qui prétend malade*) malingerer ▷ *nm*: **~ de vol** flight simulator
simulation [simylɑsjɔ̃] *nf* shamming, simulation; malingering
simuler [simyle] *vt* to sham, simulate
simultané, e [simyltane] *adj* simultaneous
simultanéité [simyltaneite] *nf* simultaneity
simultanément [simyltanemɑ̃] *adv* simultaneously
Sinaï [sinai] *nm*: **le ~** Sinai
sinapisme [sinapism(ə)] *nm* (*Méd*) mustard poultice
sincère [sɛ̃sɛʀ] *adj* sincere; genuine; heartfelt; **mes ~s condoléances** my deepest sympathy
sincèrement [sɛ̃sɛʀmɑ̃] *adv* sincerely;

genuinely
sincérité [sɛ̃seʀite] *nf* sincerity; **en toute ~** in all sincerity
sinécure [sinekyʀ] *nf* sinecure
sine die [sinedje] *adv* sine die, indefinitely
sine qua non [sinekwanɔn] *adj*: **condition ~** indispensable condition
Singapour [sɛ̃gapuʀ] *nm*: **le ~** Singapore
singe [sɛ̃ʒ] *nm* monkey; (*de grande taille*) ape
singer [sɛ̃ʒe] *vt* to ape, mimic
singeries [sɛ̃ʒʀi] *nfpl* antics; (*simagrées*) airs and graces
singulariser [sɛ̃gylaʀize] *vt* to mark out; **se singulariser** to call attention to o.s.
singularité [sɛ̃gylaʀite] *nf* peculiarity
singulier, -ière [sɛ̃gylje, -jɛʀ] *adj* remarkable, singular; (*Ling*) singular ▷ *nm* singular
singulièrement [sɛ̃gyljɛʀmɑ̃] *adv* singularly, remarkably
sinistre [sinistʀ(ə)] *adj* sinister; (*intensif*): **un ~ imbécile** an incredible idiot ▷ *nm* (*incendie*) blaze; (*catastrophe*) disaster; (*Assurances*) damage (*giving rise to a claim*)
sinistré, e [sinistʀe] *adj* disaster-stricken ▷ *nm/f* disaster victim
sinistrose [sinistʀoz] *nf* pessimism
sino... [sino] *préfixe*: **sino-indien** Sino-Indian, Chinese-Indian
sinon [sinɔ̃] *conj* (*autrement, sans quoi*) otherwise, or else; (*sauf*) except, other than; (*si ce n'est*) if not
sinueux, -euse [sinɥø, -øz] *adj* winding; (*fig*) tortuous
sinuosités [sinɥozite] *nfpl* winding *sg*, curves
sinus [sinys] *nm* (*Anat*) sinus; (*Géom*) sine
sinusite [sinyzit] *nf* sinusitis, sinus infection
sinusoïdal, e, -aux [sinyzɔidal, -o] *adj* sinusoidal
sinusoïde [sinyzɔid] *nf* sinusoid
sionisme [sjɔnism(ə)] *nm* Zionism
sioniste [sjɔnist(ə)] *adj*, *nm/f* Zionist
siphon [sifɔ̃] *nm* (*tube, d'eau gazeuse*) siphon; (*d'évier etc*) U-bend
siphonner [sifɔne] *vt* to siphon
sire [siʀ] *nm* (*titre*): **S~** Sire; **un triste ~** an unsavoury individual
sirène [siʀɛn] *nf* siren; **~ d'alarme** fire alarm; (*pendant la guerre*) air-raid siren
sirop [siʀo] *nm* (*à diluer: de fruit etc*) syrup, cordial (*Brit*); (*boisson*) fruit drink; (*pharmaceutique*) syrup, mixture; **~ de menthe** mint syrup *ou* cordial; **~ contre la toux** cough syrup *ou* mixture
siroter [siʀɔte] *vt* to sip
sirupeux, -euse [siʀypø, -øz] *adj* syrupy
sis, e [si, siz] *adj*: **~ rue de la Paix** located in the rue de la Paix
sisal [sizal] *nm* (*Bot*) sisal
sismique [sismik] *adj* seismic
sismographe [sismɔgʀaf] *nm* seismograph
sismologie [sismɔlɔʒi] *nf* seismology
site [sit] *nm* (*paysage, environnement*) setting;

(*d'une ville etc: emplacement*) site; **~ (pittoresque)** beauty spot; **~s touristiques** places of interest; **~s naturels/historiques** natural/historic sites; **~ web** (*Inform*) website

sitôt [sito] *adv*: **~ parti** as soon as he *etc* had left; **~ après** straight after; **pas de ~** not for a long time; **~ (après) que** as soon as

situation [sityasjɔ̃] *nf* (*gén*) situation; (*d'un édifice, d'une ville*) situation, position; (*emplacement*) location; **être en ~ de faire qch** to be in a position to do sth; **~ de famille** marital status

situé, e [sitye] *adj*: **bien ~** well situated, in a good location; **~ à/près de** situated at/near

situer [sitye] *vt* to site, situate; (*en pensée*) to set, place; **se situer** *vi*: **se ~ à/près de** to be situated at/near

SIVOM [sivɔm] *sigle m* (= *Syndicat intercommunal à vocation multiple*) association of "communes"

six [sis] *num* six

sixième [sizjɛm] *num* sixth; **en ~** (*Scol: classe*) first form (*Brit*), sixth grade (*US*)

skaï® [skaj] *nm* ≈ Leatherette®

skate [sket], **skate-board** [sketbɔʀd] *nm* (*sport*) skateboarding; (*planche*) skateboard

sketch [skɛtʃ] *nm* (variety) sketch

ski [ski] *nm* (*objet*) ski; (*sport*) skiing; **faire du ~** to ski; **~ alpin** Alpine skiing; **~ court** short ski; **~ évolutif** short ski method; **~ de fond** cross-country skiing; **~ nautique** water-skiing; **~ de piste** downhill skiing; **~ de randonnée** cross-country skiing

ski-bob [skibɔb] *nm* skibob

skier [skje] *vi* to ski

skieur, -euse [skjœʀ, -øz] *nm/f* skier

skif, skiff [skif] *nm* skiff

slalom [slalɔm] *nm* slalom; **faire du ~ entre** to slalom between

slalomer [slalɔme] *vi* (*entre des obstacles*) to weave in and out; (*Ski*) to slalom

slalomeur, -euse [slalɔmœʀ, -øz] *nm/f* (*Ski*) slalom skier

slave [slav] *adj* Slav(onic), Slavic ▷ *nm* (*Ling*) Slavonic ▷ *nm/f*: **Slave** Slav

slip [slip] *nm* (*sous-vêtement*) underpants *pl*, pants *pl* (*Brit*), briefs *pl*; (*de bain: d'homme*) (bathing *ou* swimming) trunks *pl*; (: *du bikini*) (bikini) briefs *pl ou* bottoms *pl*

slogan [slɔgɑ̃] *nm* slogan

slovaque [slɔvak] *adj* Slovak ▷ *nm* (*Ling*) Slovak ▷ *nm/f*: **Slovaque** Slovak

Slovaquie [slɔvaki] *nf*: **la ~** Slovakia

slovène [slɔvɛn] *adj* Slovene ▷ *nm* (*Ling*) Slovene ▷ *nm/f*: **Slovène** Slovene

Slovénie [slɔveni] *nf*: **la ~** Slovenia

slow [slo] *nm* (*danse*) slow number

SM *sigle f* (= *Sa Majesté*) HM

SMAG [smag] *sigle m* = **salaire minimum agricole garanti**

smasher [smaʃe] *vi* to smash the ball ▷ *vt* (*balle*) to smash

SMIC [smik] *sigle m* = **salaire minimum**

interprofessionnel de croissance; *see note*

⬤ **S M I C**

⬤ In France, the *SMIC* ("salaire minimum
⬤ interprofessionnel de croissance") is the
⬤ minimum hourly rate which workers over
⬤ the age of 18 must legally be paid. It is index-
⬤ linked and is raised each time the cost of
⬤ living rises by 2 per cent.

smicard, e [smikaʀ, -aʀd(ə)] *nm/f* minimum wage earner

smocks [smɔk] *nmpl* (*Couture*) smocking *no pl*

smoking [smɔkiŋ] *nm* dinner *ou* evening suit

SMS *sigle m* = **short message service**; (*message*) text (message)

SMUR [smyʀ] *sigle m* (= *service médical d'urgence et de réanimation*) specialist mobile emergency unit

snack [snak] *nm* snack bar

SNC *abr* = **service non compris**

SNCB *sigle f* (= *Société nationale des chemins de fer belges*) Belgian railways

SNCF *sigle f* (= *Société nationale des chemins de fer français*) French railways

SNES [snɛs] *sigle m* (= *Syndicat national de l'enseignement secondaire*) secondary teachers' union

SNE-sup [ɛsənəsyp] *sigle m* (= *Syndicat national de l'enseignement supérieur*) university teachers' union

SNJ *sigle m* (= *Syndicat national des journalistes*) journalists' union

snob [snɔb] *adj* snobbish ▷ *nm/f* snob

snober [snɔbe] *vt*: **~ qn** to give sb the cold shoulder, treat sb with disdain

snobinard, e [snɔbinaʀ, -aʀd(ə)] *nm/f* snooty *ou* stuck-up person

snobisme [snɔbism(ə)] *nm* snobbery

SNSM *sigle f* (= *Société nationale de sauvetage en mer*) national sea-rescue association

s.o. *abr* (= *sans objet*) no longer applicable

sobre [sɔbʀ(ə)] *adj* temperate, abstemious; (*élégance, style*) restrained, sober; **~ de** (*gestes, compliments*) sparing of

sobrement [sɔbʀəmɑ̃] *adv* in moderation, abstemiously; soberly

sobriété [sɔbʀijete] *nf* temperance, abstemiousness; sobriety

sobriquet [sɔbʀikɛ] *nm* nickname

soc [sɔk] *nm* ploughshare

sociabilité [sɔsjabilite] *nf* sociability

sociable [sɔsjabl(ə)] *adj* sociable

social, e, -aux [sɔsjal, -o] *adj* social

socialisant, e [sɔsjalizɑ̃, -ɑ̃t] *adj* with socialist tendencies

socialisation [sɔsjalizasjɔ̃] *nf* socialisation

socialiser [sɔsjalize] *vt* to socialize

socialisme [sɔsjalism(ə)] *nm* socialism

socialiste [sɔsjalist(ə)] *adj, nm/f* socialist

sociétaire [sɔsjetɛʀ] *nm/f* member

société [sɔsjete] *nf* society; (*d'abeilles, de fourmis*) colony; (*sportive*) club; (*Comm*) company; **la bonne ~** polite society; **se plaire dans la ~ de**

to enjoy the society of; **l'archipel de la S~** the Society Islands; **la ~ d'abondance/de consommation** the affluent/consumer society; **~ par actions** joint stock company; **~ anonyme (SA)** ≈ limited company (Ltd) (Brit), ≈ incorporated company (Inc.) (US); **~ d'investissement à capital variable (SICAV)** ≈ investment trust (Brit), ≈ mutual fund (US); **~ à responsabilité limitée (SARL)** type of limited liability company (with non-negotiable shares); **~ savante** learned society; **~ de services** service company

socioculturel, le [sɔsjokyltyʀɛl] adj sociocultural

socio-économique [sɔsjoekɔnɔmik] adj socioeconomic

socio-éducatif, --ive [sɔsjoedykatif, -iv] adj socioeducational

sociolinguistique [sɔsjolɛ̃gɥistik] adj sociolinguistic

sociologie [sɔsjɔlɔʒi] nf sociology

sociologique [sɔsjɔlɔʒik] adj sociological

sociologue [sɔsjɔlɔg] nm/f sociologist

socio-professionnel, le [sɔsjopʀɔfɛsjɔnɛl] adj socioprofessional

socle [sɔkl(ə)] nm (de colonne, statue) plinth, pedestal; (de lampe) base

socquette [sɔkɛt] nf ankle sock

soda [sɔda] nm (boisson) fizzy drink, soda (US)

sodium [sɔdjɔm] nm sodium

sodomie [sɔdɔmi] nf sodomy; buggery

sodomiser [sɔdɔmize] vt to sodomize; to bugger

sœur [sœʀ] nf sister; (religieuse) nun, sister; **~ Élisabeth** (Rel) Sister Elizabeth; **~ de lait** foster sister

sofa [sɔfa] nm sofa

Sofia [sɔfja] n Sofia

SOFRES [sɔfʀɛs] sigle f (= Société française d'enquête par sondage) company which conducts opinion polls

soi [swa] pron oneself; **cela va de ~** that ou it goes without saying, it stands to reason

soi-disant [swadizɑ̃] adj inv so-called ▷ adv supposedly

soie [swa] nf silk; (de porc, sanglier: poil) bristle

soient [swa] vb voir **être**

soierie [swaʀi] nf (industrie) silk trade; (tissu) silk

soif [swaf] nf thirst; (fig): **~ de** thirst ou craving for; **avoir ~** to be thirsty; **donner ~ à qn** to make sb thirsty

soigné, e [swaɲe] adj (tenue) well-groomed, neat; (travail) careful, meticulous; (fam) whopping; stiff

soigner [swaɲe] vt (malade, maladie: docteur) to treat; (: infirmière, mère) to nurse, look after; (blessé) to tend; (travail, détails) to take care over; (jardin, chevelure, invités) to look after

soigneur [swaɲœʀ] nm (Cyclisme, Football) trainer; (Boxe) second

soigneusement [swaɲøzmɑ̃] adv carefully

soigneux, -euse [swaɲø, -øz] adj (propre) tidy, neat; (méticuleux) painstaking, careful; **~ de** careful with

soi-même [swamɛm] pron oneself

soin [swɛ̃] nm (application) care; (propreté, ordre) tidiness, neatness; (responsabilité): **le ~ de qch** the care of sth; **soins** nmpl (à un malade, blessé) treatment sg, medical attention sg; (attentions, prévenance) care and attention sg; (hygiène) care sg; **~s de la chevelure/de beauté** hair/beauty care; **~s du corps/ménage** care of one's body/the home; **avoir** ou **prendre ~ de** to take care of, look after; **avoir** ou **prendre ~ de faire** to take care to do; **faire qch avec (grand) ~** to do sth (very) carefully; **sans ~** adj careless; untidy; **les premiers ~s** first aid sg; **aux bons ~s de** c/o, care of; **être aux petits ~s pour qn** to wait on sb hand and foot, see to sb's every need; **confier qn aux ~s de qn** to hand sb over to sb's care

soir [swaʀ] nm, adv evening; **le ~** in the evening(s); **ce ~** this evening, tonight; **à ce ~!** see you this evening (ou tonight)!; **la veille au ~** the previous evening; **sept/dix heures du ~** seven in the evening/ten at night; **le repas/journal du ~** the evening meal/newspaper; **dimanche ~** Sunday evening; **hier ~** yesterday evening; **demain ~** tomorrow evening, tomorrow night

soirée [swaʀe] nf evening; (réception) party; **donner en ~** (film, pièce) to give an evening performance of

soit [swa] vb voir **être** ▷ conj (à savoir) namely, to wit; (ou): **~ ... ~** either ... or ▷ adv so be it, very well; **~ un triangle ABC** let ABC be a triangle; **~ que ... ~ que** ou **ou que** whether ... or whether

soixantaine [swasɑ̃tɛn] nf: **une ~ (de)** sixty or so, about sixty; **avoir la ~** to be around sixty

soixante [swasɑ̃t] num sixty

soixante-dix [swasɑ̃tdis] num seventy

soixante-dixième [swasɑ̃tdizjɛm] num seventieth

soixante-huitard, e [swazɑ̃tɥitaʀ, -aʀd(ə)] adj relating to the demonstrations of May 1968 ▷ nm/f participant in the demonstrations of May 1968

soixantième [swasɑ̃tjɛm] num sixtieth

soja [sɔʒa] nm soya; (graines) soya beans pl; **germes de ~** beansprouts

sol [sɔl] nm ground; (de logement) floor; (revêtement) flooring no pl; (territoire, Agr, Géo) soil; (Mus) G; (: en chantant la gamme) so(h)

solaire [sɔlɛʀ] adj solar, sun cpd

solarium [sɔlaʀjɔm] nm solarium

soldat [sɔlda] nm soldier; **S~ inconnu** Unknown Warrior ou Soldier; **~ de plomb** tin ou toy soldier

solde [sɔld(ə)] nf pay ▷ nm (Comm) balance; **soldes** nmpl ou nfpl (Comm) sales; (articles) sale goods; **à la ~ de qn** (péj) in sb's pay; **~ créditeur/débiteur** credit/debit balance; **~ à payer** balance outstanding; **en ~** at sale price; **aux ~s** at the sales

solder [sɔlde] vt (compte) to settle; (marchandise) to sell at sale price, sell off; **se ~ par** (fig) to end in; **article soldé (à) 10 euros** item reduced to 10 euros

soldeur, -euse [sɔldœʀ, -øz] *nm/f* (*Comm*) discounter

sole [sɔl] *nf* sole *inv* (*fish*)

soleil [sɔlɛj] *nm* sun; (*lumière*) sun(light); (*temps ensoleillé*) sun(shine); (*feu d'artifice*) Catherine wheel; (*d'acrobate*) grand circle; (*Bot*) sunflower; **il y a** *ou* **il fait du ~** it's sunny; **au ~** in the sun; **en plein ~** in full sun; **le ~ levant/couchant** the rising/setting sun; **le ~ de minuit** the midnight sun

solennel, le [sɔlanɛl] *adj* solemn; ceremonial

solennellement [sɔlanɛlmɑ̃] *adv* solemnly

solennité [sɔlanite] *nf* (*d'une fête*) solemnity; **solennités** *nfpl* (*formalités*) formalities

solénoïde [sɔlenɔid] *nm* (*Élec*) solenoid

solfège [sɔlfɛʒ] *nm* rudiments *pl* of music; (*exercices*) ear training *no pl*

solfier [sɔlfje] *vt*: **~ un morceau** to sing a piece using the sol-fa

soli [sɔli] *nmpl de* **solo**

solidaire [sɔlidɛʀ] *adj* (*personnes*) who stand together, who show solidarity; (*pièces mécaniques*) interdependent; (*Jur: engagement*) binding on all parties; (: *débiteurs*) jointly liable; **être ~ de** (*collègues*) to stand by; (*mécanisme*) to be bound up with, be dependent on

solidairement [sɔlidɛʀmɑ̃] *adv* jointly

solidariser [sɔlidaʀize]: **se ~ avec** *vt* to show solidarity with

solidarité [sɔlidaʀite] *nf* (*entre personnes*) solidarity; (*de mécanisme, phénomènes*) interdependence; **par ~ (avec)** (*cesser le travail etc*) in sympathy (with)

solide [sɔlid] *adj* solid; (*mur, maison, meuble*) solid, sturdy; (*connaissances, argument*) sound; (*personne*) robust, sturdy; (*estomac*) strong ▷ *nm* solid; **avoir les reins ~s** (*fig*) to be in a good financial position; to have sound financial backing

solidement [sɔlidmɑ̃] *adv* solidly; (*fermement*) firmly

solidifier [sɔlidifje] *vt*, **se solidifier** *vi* to solidify

solidité [sɔlidite] *nf* solidity; sturdiness

soliloque [sɔlilɔk] *nm* soliloquy

soliste [sɔlist(ə)] *nm/f* soloist

solitaire [sɔlitɛʀ] *adj* (*sans compagnie*) solitary, lonely; (*isolé*) solitary, isolated, lone; (*lieu*) lonely ▷ *nm/f* recluse; loner ▷ *nm* (*diamant, jeu*) solitaire

solitude [sɔlityd] *nf* loneliness; (*paix*) solitude

solive [sɔliv] *nf* joist

sollicitations [sɔlisitasjɔ̃] *nfpl* (*requêtes*) entreaties, appeals; (*attractions*) enticements; (*Tech*) stress *sg*

solliciter [sɔlisite] *vt* (*personne*) to appeal to; (*emploi, faveur*) to seek; (*moteur*) to prompt; (*occupations, attractions etc*): **~ qn** to appeal to sb's curiosity *etc*; to entice sb; to make demands on sb's time; **~ qn de faire** to appeal to sb *ou* request sb to do

sollicitude [sɔlisityd] *nf* concern

solo [sɔlo] *nm* (*pl* **soli** [sɔli]) (*Mus*) solo

sol-sol [sɔlsɔl] *adj inv* surface-to-surface

solstice [sɔlstis] *nm* solstice; **~ d'hiver/d'été** winter/summer solstice

solubilisé, e [sɔlybilize] *adj* soluble

solubilité [sɔlybilite] *nf* solubility

soluble [sɔlybl(ə)] *adj* (*sucre, cachet*) soluble; (*problème etc*) soluble, solvable

soluté [sɔlyte] *nm* solution

solution [sɔlysjɔ̃] *nf* solution; **~ de continuité** gap, break; **~ de facilité** easy way out

solutionner [sɔlysjɔne] *vt* to solve, find a solution for

solvabilité [sɔlvabilite] *nf* solvency

solvable [sɔlvabl(ə)] *adj* solvent

solvant [sɔlvɑ̃] *nm* solvent

Somalie [sɔmali] *nf*: **la ~** Somalia

somalien, ne [sɔmaljɛ̃, -ɛn] *adj* Somalian

somatique [sɔmatik] *adj* somatic

sombre [sɔ̃bʀ(ə)] *adj* dark; (*fig*) sombre, gloomy; (*sinistre*) awful, dreadful

sombrer [sɔ̃bʀe] *vi* (*bateau*) to sink, go down; **~ corps et biens** to go down with all hands; **~ dans** (*misère, désespoir*) to sink into

sommaire [sɔmɛʀ] *adj* (*simple*) basic; (*expéditif*) summary ▷ *nm* summary; **faire le ~ de** to make a summary of, summarize; **exécution ~** summary execution

sommairement [sɔmɛʀmɑ̃] *adv* basically; summarily

sommation [sɔmɑsjɔ̃] *nf* (*Jur*) summons *sg*; (*avant de faire feu*) warning

somme [sɔm] *nf* (*Math*) sum; (*fig*) amount; (*argent*) sum, amount ▷ *nm*: **faire un ~** to have a (short) nap; **faire la ~ de** to add up; **en ~, ~ toute** *adv* all in all

sommeil [sɔmɛj] *nm* sleep; **avoir ~** to be sleepy; **avoir le ~ léger** to be a light sleeper; **en ~** (*fig*) dormant

sommeiller [sɔmeje] *vi* to doze; (*fig*) to lie dormant

sommelier [sɔməlje] *nm* wine waiter

sommer [sɔme] *vt*: **~ qn de faire** to command *ou* order sb to do; (*Jur*) to summon sb to do

sommes [sɔm] *vb voir* **être**; *voir aussi* **somme**

sommet [sɔmɛ] *nm* top; (*d'une montagne*) summit, top; (*fig: de la perfection, gloire*) height; (*Géom: d'angle*) vertex; (*conférence*) summit (conference)

sommier [sɔmje] *nm* bed base, bedspring (*US*); (*Admin: registre*) register; **~ à ressorts** (interior sprung) divan base (*Brit*), box spring (*US*); **~ à lattes** slatted bed base

sommité [sɔmite] *nf* prominent person, leading light

somnambule [sɔmnɑ̃byl] *nm/f* sleepwalker

somnambulisme [sɔmnɑ̃bylism(ə)] *nm* sleepwalking

somnifère [sɔmnifɛʀ] *nm* sleeping drug; (*comprimé*) sleeping pill *ou* tablet

somnolence [sɔmnɔlɑ̃s] *nf* drowsiness

somnolent, e [sɔmnɔlɑ̃, -ɑ̃t] *adj* sleepy, drowsy

somnoler [sɔmnɔle] *vi* to doze
somptuaire [sɔ̃ptɥɛʀ] *adj*: **lois ~s** sumptuary laws; **dépenses ~s** extravagant expenditure *sg*
somptueusement [sɔ̃ptɥøzmɑ̃] *adv* sumptuously
somptueux, -euse [sɔ̃ptɥø, -øz] *adj* sumptuous; (*cadeau*) lavish
somptuosité [sɔ̃ptɥozite] *nf* sumptuousness; (*d'un cadeau*) lavishness
son[1] [sɔ̃], **sa** [sa] (*pl* **ses** [se]) *adj possessif* (*antécédent humain mâle*) his; (: *femelle*) her; (: *valeur indéfinie*) one's, his (her); (: *non humain*) its; *voir* **il**
son[2] [sɔ̃] *nm* sound; (*de blé etc*) bran; ~ **et lumière** *adj inv* son et lumière
sonar [sɔnaʀ] *nm* (*Navig*) sonar
sonate [sɔnat] *nf* sonata
sondage [sɔ̃daʒ] *nm* (*de terrain*) boring, drilling; (*de mer, atmosphère*) sounding; probe; (*enquête*) survey, sounding out of opinion; ~ **(d'opinion)** (opinion) poll
sonde [sɔ̃d] *nf* (*Navig*) lead *ou* sounding line; (*Météorologie*) sonde; (*Méd*) probe; catheter; (*d'alimentation*) feeding tube; (*Tech*) borer, driller; (*de forage, sondage*) drill; (*pour fouiller etc*) probe; ~ **à avalanche** pole (*for probing snow and locating victims*); ~ **spatiale** probe
sonder [sɔ̃de] *vt* (*Navig*) to sound; (*atmosphère, plaie, bagages etc*) to probe; (*Tech*) to bore, drill; (*fig: personne*) to sound out; (: *opinion*) to probe; ~ **le terrain** (*fig*) to see how the land lies
songe [sɔ̃ʒ] *nm* dream
songer [sɔ̃ʒe] *vi* to dream; ~ **à** (*rêver à*) to muse over, think over; (*penser à*) to think of; (*envisager*) to contemplate, think of, consider; ~ **que** to consider that; to think that
songerie [sɔ̃ʒʀi] *nf* reverie
songeur, -euse [sɔ̃ʒœʀ, -øz] *adj* pensive; **ça me laisse ~** that makes me wonder
sonnailles [sɔnaj] *nfpl* jingle of bells
sonnant, e [sɔnɑ̃, -ɑ̃t] *adj*: **en espèces ~es et trébuchantes** in coin of the realm; **à huit heures ~es** on the stroke of eight
sonné, e [sɔne] *adj* (*fam*) cracked; (*passé*): **il est midi ~** it's gone twelve; **il a quarante ans bien ~s** he's well into his forties
sonner [sɔne] *vi* (*retentir*) to ring; (*donner une impression*) to sound ▷ *vt* (*cloche*) to ring; (*glas, tocsin*) to sound; (*portier, infirmière*) to ring for; (*messe*) to ring the bell for; (*fam: choc, coup*) to knock out; ~ **du clairon** to sound the bugle; ~ **bien/mal/creux** to sound good/bad/hollow; ~ **faux** (*instrument*) to sound out of tune; (*rire*) to ring false; ~ **les heures** to strike the hours; **minuit vient de ~** midnight has just struck; ~ **chez qn** to ring sb's doorbell, ring at sb's door
sonnerie [sɔnʀi] *nf* (*son*) ringing; (*sonnette*) bell; (*mécanisme d'horloge*) striking mechanism; (*de téléphone portable*) ringtone; ~ **d'alarme** alarm bell; ~ **de clairon** bugle call
sonnet [sɔnɛ] *nm* sonnet
sonnette [sɔnɛt] *nf* bell; ~ **d'alarme** alarm bell;

~ **de nuit** night-bell
sono [sɔno] *nf* (= *sonorisation*) PA (system); (*d'une discothèque*) sound system
sonore [sɔnɔʀ] *adj* (*voix*) sonorous, ringing; (*salle, métal*) resonant; (*ondes, film, signal*) sound *cpd*; (*Ling*) voiced; **effets ~s** sound effects
sonorisation [sɔnɔʀizasjɔ̃] *nf* (*installations*) public address system; (*d'une discothèque*) sound system
sonoriser [sɔnɔʀize] *vt* (*film, spectacle*) to add the sound track to; (*salle*) to fit with a public address system
sonorité [sɔnɔʀite] *nf* (*de piano, violon*) tone; (*de voix, mot*) sonority; (*d'une salle*) resonance; acoustics *pl*
sonothèque [sɔnɔtɛk] *nf* sound library
sont [sɔ̃] *vb voir* **être**
sophisme [sɔfism(ə)] *nm* sophism
sophiste [sɔfist(ə)] *nm/f* sophist
sophistication [sɔfistikasjɔ̃] *nf* sophistication
sophistiqué, e [sɔfistike] *adj* sophisticated
soporifique [sɔpɔʀifik] *adj* soporific
soprano [sɔpʀano] *nm/f* soprano
sorbet [sɔʀbɛ] *nm* water ice, sorbet
sorbetière [sɔʀbətjɛʀ] *nf* ice-cream maker
sorbier [sɔʀbje] *nm* service tree
sorcellerie [sɔʀsɛlʀi] *nf* witchcraft *no pl*, sorcery *no pl*
sorcier, -ière [sɔʀsje, -jɛʀ] *nm/f* sorcerer (witch *ou* sorceress) ▷ *adj*: **ce n'est pas ~** (*fam*) it's as easy as pie
sordide [sɔʀdid] *adj* sordid; squalid
Sorlingues [sɔʀlɛ̃g] *nfpl*: **les (îles) ~** the Scilly Isles, the Isles of Scilly, the Scillies
sornettes [sɔʀnɛt] *nfpl* twaddle *sg*
sort [sɔʀ] *vb voir* **sortir** ▷ *nm* (*fortune, destinée*) fate; (*condition, situation*) lot; (*magique*): **jeter un ~** to cast a spell; **un coup du ~** a blow dealt by fate; **le ~ en est jeté** the die is cast; **tirer au ~** to draw lots; **tirer qch au ~** to draw lots for sth
sortable [sɔʀtabl(ə)] *adj*: **il n'est pas ~** you can't take him anywhere
sortant, e [sɔʀtɑ̃, -ɑ̃t] *vb voir* **sortir** ▷ *adj* (*numéro*) which comes up (*in a draw etc*); (*député, président*) outgoing
sorte [sɔʀt(ə)] *vb voir* **sortir** ▷ *nf* sort, kind; **une ~ de** a sort of; **de la ~** *adv* in that way; **en quelque ~** in a way; **de ~ à** so as to, in order to; **de (telle) ~ que, en ~ que** (*de manière que*) so that; (*si bien que*) so much so that; **faire en ~ que** to see to it that
sortie [sɔʀti] *nf* (*issue*) way out, exit; (*Mil*) sortie; (*fig: verbale*) outburst; sally; (: *parole incongrue*) odd remark; (*d'un gaz, de l'eau*) outlet; (*promenade*) outing; (*le soir: au restaurant etc*) night out; (*de produits*) export; (*de capitaux*) outflow; (*Comm: somme*): **~s** items of expenditure; outgoings; (*Inform*) output; (*d'imprimante*) printout; **à sa ~** as he went out *ou* left; **à la ~ de l'école/l'usine** (*moment*) after school/work; when school/the factory comes out; (*lieu*) at the school/factory gates; **à la ~ de ce nouveau modèle** when this

new model comes (ou came) out, when they bring (ou brought) out this new model; **~ de bain** (vêtement) bathrobe; **"~ de camions"** "vehicle exit"; **~ papier** hard copy; **~ de secours** emergency exit

sortilège [sɔʀtileʒ] nm (magic) spell

sortir [sɔʀtiʀ] vi (gén) to come out; (partir, se promener, aller au spectacle etc) to go out; (bourgeon, plante, numéro gagnant) to come up ▷ vt (gén) to take out; (produit, ouvrage, modèle) to bring out; (boniments, incongruités) to come out with; (Inform) to output; (: sur papier) to print out; (fam: expulser) to throw out ▷ nm: **au ~ de l'hiver/l'enfance** as winter/childhood nears its end; **~ qch de** to take sth out of; **~ qn d'embarras** to get sb out of trouble; **~ de** (gén) to leave; (endroit) to go (ou come) out of, leave; (rainure etc) to come out of; (maladie) to get over; (époque) to get through; (cadre, compétence) to be outside; (provenir de: famille etc) to come from; **~ de table** to leave the table; **~ du système** (Inform) to log out; **~ de ses gonds** (fig) to fly off the handle; **se ~ de** (affaire, situation) to get out of; **s'en ~** (malade) to pull through; (d'une difficulté etc) to come through all right; to get through, be able to manage

SOS sigle m mayday, SOS

sosie [sɔzi] nm double

sot, sotte [so, sɔt] adj silly, foolish ▷ nm/f fool

sottement [sɔtmɑ̃] adv foolishly

sottise [sɔtiz] nf silliness no pl, foolishness no pl; (propos, acte) silly ou foolish thing (to do ou say)

sou [su] nm: **près de ses ~s** tight-fisted; **sans le ~** penniless; **~ à ~** penny by penny; **pas un ~ de bon sens** not a scrap ou an ounce of good sense; **de quatre ~s** worthless

souahéli, e [swaeli] adj Swahili ▷ nm (Ling) Swahili

soubassement [subasmɑ̃] nm base

soubresaut [subʀəso] nm (de peur etc) start; (cahot: d'un véhicule) jolt

soubrette [subʀɛt] nf soubrette, maidservant

souche [suʃ] nf (d'arbre) stump; (de carnet) counterfoil (Brit), stub; **dormir comme une ~** to sleep like a log; **de vieille ~** of old stock

souci [susi] nm (inquiétude) worry; (préoccupation) concern; (Bot) marigold; **se faire du ~** to worry; **avoir (le) ~ de** to have concern for; **par ~ de** for the sake of, out of concern for

soucier [susje]: **se ~ de** vt to care about

soucieux, -euse [susjø, -øz] adj concerned, worried; **~ de** concerned about; **peu ~ de/que** caring little about/whether

soucoupe [sukup] nf saucer; **~ volante** flying saucer

soudain, e [sudɛ̃, -ɛn] adj (douleur, mort) sudden ▷ adv suddenly, all of a sudden

soudainement [sudɛnmɑ̃] adv suddenly

soudaineté [sudɛnte] nf suddenness

Soudan [sudɑ̃] nm: **le ~** the Sudan

soudanais, e [sudanɛ, -ɛz] adj Sudanese

soude [sud] nf soda

soudé, e [sude] adj (fig: pétales, organes) joined

(together)

souder [sude] vt (avec fil à souder) to solder; (par soudure autogène) to weld; (fig) to bind ou knit together; to fuse (together); **se souder** vi (os) to knit (together)

soudeur, -euse [sudœʀ, -øz] nm/f (ouvrier) welder

soudoyer [sudwaje] vt (péj) to bribe, buy over

soudure [sudyʀ] nf soldering; welding; (joint) soldered joint; weld; **faire la ~** (Comm) to fill a gap; (fig: assurer une transition) to bridge the gap

souffert, e [sufɛʀ, -ɛʀt(ə)] pp de **souffrir**

soufflage [suflaʒ] nm (du verre) glass-blowing

souffle [sufl(ə)] nm (en expirant) breath; (en soufflant) puff, blow; (respiration) breathing; (d'explosion, de ventilateur) blast; (du vent) blowing; (fig) inspiration; **retenir son ~** to hold one's breath; **avoir du/manquer de ~** to have a lot of puff/be short of breath; **être à bout de ~** to be out of breath; **avoir le ~ court** to be short-winded; **un ~ d'air** ou **de vent** a breath of air, a puff of wind; **~ au cœur** (Méd) heart murmur

soufflé, e [sufle] adj (Culin) soufflé; (fam: ahuri, stupéfié) staggered ▷ nm (Culin) soufflé

souffler [sufle] vi (gén) to blow; (haleter) to puff (and blow) ▷ vt (feu, bougie) to blow out; (chasser: poussière etc) to blow away; (Tech: verre) to blow; (explosion) to destroy (with its blast); (dire): **~ qch à qn** to whisper sth to sb; (fam: voler): **~ qch à qn** to pinch sth from sb; **~ son rôle à qn** to prompt sb; **ne pas ~ mot** not to breathe a word; **laisser ~ qn** (fig) to give sb a breather

soufflet [suflɛ] nm (instrument) bellows pl; (entre wagons) vestibule; (Couture) gusset; (gifle) slap (in the face)

souffleur, -euse [suflœʀ, -øz] nm/f (Théât) prompter; (Tech) glass-blower

souffrance [sufʀɑ̃s] nf suffering; **en ~** (marchandise) awaiting delivery; (affaire) pending

souffrant, e [sufʀɑ̃, -ɑ̃t] adj unwell

souffre-douleur [sufʀədulœʀ] nm inv whipping boy (Brit), butt, underdog

souffreteux, -euse [sufʀətø, -øz] adj sickly

souffrir [sufʀiʀ] vi to suffer; (éprouver des douleurs) to be in pain ▷ vt to suffer, endure; (supporter) to bear, stand; (admettre: exception etc) to allow ou admit of; **~ de** (maladie, froid) to suffer from; **~ des dents** to have trouble with one's teeth; **ne pas pouvoir ~ qch/que ...** not to be able to endure ou bear sth/that ...; **faire ~ qn** (personne) to make sb suffer; (: dents, blessure etc) to hurt sb

soufre [sufʀ(ə)] nm sulphur (Brit), sulfur (US)

soufrer [sufʀe] vt (vignes) to treat with sulphur ou sulfur

souhait [swɛ] nm wish; **tous nos ~s de** good wishes ou our best wishes for; **riche** etc **à ~** as rich etc as one could wish; **à vos ~s!** bless you!

souhaitable [swɛtabl(ə)] adj desirable

souhaiter [swɛte] vt to wish for; **~ le bonjour à qn** to bid sb good day; **~ la bonne année à qn** to wish sb a happy New Year; **il est à ~ que** it is to be hoped that

souiller [suje] *vt* to dirty, soil; *(fig)* to sully, tarnish

souillure [sujyʀ] *nf* stain

soûl, e [su, sul] *adj* drunk; *(fig)*: **~ de musique/plaisirs** drunk with music/pleasure ▷ *nm*: **tout son ~** to one's heart's content

soulagement [sulaʒmɑ̃] *nm* relief

soulager [sulaʒe] *vt* to relieve; **~ qn de** to relieve sb of

soûler [sule] *vt*: **~ qn** to get sb drunk; *(boisson)* to make sb drunk; *(fig)* to make sb's head spin *ou* reel; **se soûler** to get drunk; **se ~ de** *(fig)* to intoxicate o.s with

soûlerie [sulʀi] *nf (péj)* drunken binge

soulèvement [sulɛvmɑ̃] *nm* uprising; *(Géo)* upthrust

soulever [sulve] *vt* to lift; *(vagues, poussière)* to send up; *(peuple)* to stir up (to revolt); *(enthousiasme)* to arouse; *(question, débat, protestations, difficultés)* to raise; **se soulever** *vi* *(peuple)* to rise up; *(personne couchée)* to lift o.s. up; *(couvercle etc)* to lift; **cela me soulève le cœur** it makes me feel sick

soulier [sulje] *nm* shoe; **~s bas** low-heeled shoes; **~s plats/à talons** flat/heeled shoes

souligner [suliɲe] *vt* to underline; *(fig)* to emphasize, stress

soumettre [sumɛtʀ(ə)] *vt (pays)* to subject, subjugate; *(rebelles)* to put down, subdue; **~ qn/qch à** to subject sb/sth to; **~ qch à qn** *(projet etc)* to submit sth to sb; **se ~ (à)** *(se rendre, obéir)* to submit (to); **se ~ à** *(formalités etc)* to submit to; *(régime etc)* to submit o.s. to

soumis, e [sumi, -iz] *pp de* **soumettre** ▷ *adj* submissive; **revenus ~ à l'impôt** taxable income

soumission [sumisjɔ̃] *nf (voir se soumettre)* submission; *(docilité)* submissiveness; *(Comm)* tender

soumissionner [sumisjɔne] *vt (Comm: travaux)* to bid for, tender for

soupape [supap] *nf* valve; **~ de sûreté** safety valve

soupçon [supsɔ̃] *nm* suspicion; *(petite quantité)*: **un ~ de** a hint *ou* touch of; **avoir ~ de** to suspect; **au dessus de tout ~** above (all) suspicion

soupçonner [supsɔne] *vt* to suspect; **~ qn de qch/d'être** to suspect sb of sth/of being

soupçonneux, -euse [supsɔnø, -øz] *adj* suspicious

soupe [sup] *nf* soup; **~ au lait** *adj inv* quick-tempered; **~ à l'oignon/de poisson** onion/fish soup; **~ populaire** soup kitchen

soupente [supɑ̃t] *nf (mansarde)* attic; *(placard)* cupboard *(Brit) ou* closet *(US)* under the stairs

souper [supe] *vi* to have supper ▷ *nm* supper; **avoir soupé de** *(fam)* to be sick and tired of

soupeser [supəze] *vt* to weigh in one's hand(s), feel the weight of; *(fig)* to weigh up

soupière [supjɛʀ] *nf* (soup) tureen

soupir [supiʀ] *nm* sigh; *(Mus)* crotchet rest *(Brit)*, quarter note rest *(US)*; **rendre le dernier ~** to breathe one's last

soupirail, -aux [supiʀaj, -o] *nm* (small) basement window

soupirant [supiʀɑ̃] *nm (péj)* suitor, wooer

soupirer [supiʀe] *vi* to sigh; **~ après qch** to yearn for sth

souple [supl(ə)] *adj* supple; *(col)* soft; *(fig: règlement, caractère)* flexible; *(: démarche, taille)* lithe, supple

souplesse [suplɛs] *nf* suppleness; flexibility

source [suʀs(ə)] *nf (point d'eau)* spring; *(d'un cours d'eau, fig)* source; **prendre sa ~ à/dans** *(cours d'eau)* to have its source at/in; **tenir qch de bonne ~/de ~ sûre** to have sth on good authority/from a reliable source; **~ thermale/d'eau minérale** hot *ou* thermal/mineral spring

sourcier, -ière [suʀsje, -jɛʀ] *nm* water diviner

sourcil [suʀsij] *nm* (eye)brow

sourcilière [suʀsiljɛʀ] *adj f voir* **arcade**

sourciller [suʀsije] *vi*: **sans ~** without turning a hair *ou* batting an eyelid

sourcilleux, -euse [suʀsijø, -øz] *adj (hautain, sévère)* haughty, supercilious; *(pointilleux)* finicky, pernickety

sourd, e [suʀ, suʀd(ə)] *adj* deaf; *(bruit, voix)* muffled; *(couleur)* muted; *(douleur)* dull; *(lutte)* silent, hidden; *(Ling)* voiceless ▷ *nm/f* deaf person; **être ~ à** to be deaf to

sourdement [suʀdəmɑ̃] *adv (avec un bruit sourd)* dully; *(secrètement)* silently

sourdine [suʀdin] *nf (Mus)* mute; **en ~** *adv* softly, quietly; **mettre une ~ à** *(fig)* to tone down

sourd-muet, sourde-muette [suʀmyɛ, suʀdmyɛt] *adj* deaf-and-dumb ▷ *nm/f* deaf-mute

sourdre [suʀdʀ(ə)] *vi (eau)* to spring up; *(fig)* to rise

souriant, e [suʀjɑ̃, -ɑ̃t] *vb voir* **sourire** ▷ *adj* cheerful

souricière [suʀisjɛʀ] *nf* mousetrap; *(fig)* trap

sourie *etc* [suʀi] *vb voir* **sourire**

sourire [suʀiʀ] *nm* smile ▷ *vi* to smile; **~ à qn** to smile at sb; *(fig)* to appeal to sb; *(: chance)* to smile on sb; **faire un ~ à qn** to give sb a smile; **garder le ~** to keep smiling

souris [suʀi] *nf (aussi Inform)* mouse

sournois, e [suʀnwa, -waz] *adj* deceitful, underhand

sournoisement [suʀnwazmɑ̃] *adv* deceitfully

sournoiserie [suʀnwazʀi] *nf* deceitfulness, underhandedness

sous [su] *prép (gén)* under; **~ la pluie/le soleil** in the rain/sunshine; **~ mes yeux** before my eyes; **~ terre** *adj, adv* underground; **~ vide** *adj, adv* vacuum-packed; **~ l'influence/l'action de** under the influence of/by the action of; **~ antibiotiques/perfusion** on antibiotics/a drip; **~ cet angle/ce rapport** from this angle/in this respect; **~ peu** *adv* shortly, before long

sous... [su, suz + *vowel*] *préfixe* sub-; under...

sous-alimentation [suzalimɑ̃tasjɔ̃] *nf* undernourishment

sous-alimenté, e [suzalimɑ̃te] *adj* undernourished

sous-bois [subwa] *nm inv* undergrowth

sous-catégorie [sukategɔʀi] *nf* subcategory

sous-chef [suʃɛf] *nm* deputy chief, second in command; **~ de bureau** deputy head clerk

sous-comité [sukɔmite] *nm* subcommittee

sous-commission [sukɔmisjɔ̃] *nf* subcommittee

sous-continent [sukɔ̃tinɑ̃] *nm* subcontinent

sous-couche [sukuʃ] *nf* (*de peinture*) undercoat

souscripteur, -trice [suskʀiptœʀ, -tʀis] *nm/f* subscriber

souscription [suskʀipsjɔ̃] *nf* subscription; **offert en ~** available on subscription

souscrire [suskʀiʀ]: **~ à** *vt* to subscribe to

sous-cutané, e [sukytane] *adj* subcutaneous

sous-développé, e [sudevlɔpe] *adj* underdeveloped

sous-développement [sudevlɔpmɑ̃] *nm* underdevelopment

sous-directeur, -trice [sudiʀɛktœʀ, -tʀis] *nm/f* assistant manager/manageress, submanager/ manageress

sous-emploi [suzɑ̃plwa] *nm* underemployment

sous-employé, e [suzɑ̃plwaje] *adj* underemployed

sous-ensemble [suzɑ̃sɑ̃bl(ə)] *nm* subset

sous-entendre [suzɑ̃tɑ̃dʀ(ə)] *vt* to imply, infer

sous-entendu, e [suzɑ̃tɑ̃dy] *adj* implied; (*Ling*) understood ▷ *nm* innuendo, insinuation

sous-équipé, e [suzekipe] *adj* under-equipped; **~ en infrastructures industrielles** (*Écon: pays, région*) with an insufficient industrial infrastructure

sous-estimer [suzɛstime] *vt* to underestimate

sous-exploiter [suzɛksplwate] *vt* to underexploit

sous-exposer [suzɛkspoze] *vt* to underexpose

sous-fifre [sufifʀ(ə)] *nm* (*péj*) underling

sous-groupe [sugʀup] *nm* subgroup

sous-homme [suzɔm] *nm* sub-human

sous-jacent, e [suʒasɑ̃, -ɑ̃t] *adj* underlying

sous-lieutenant [suljøtnɑ̃] *nm* sub-lieutenant

sous-locataire [sulɔkatɛʀ] *nm/f* subtenant

sous-location [sulɔkasjɔ̃] *nf* subletting

sous-louer [sulwe] *vt* to sublet

sous-main [sumɛ̃] *nm inv* desk blotter; **en ~** *adv* secretly

sous-marin, e [sumaʀɛ̃, -in] *adj* (*flore, volcan*) submarine; (*navigation, pêche, explosif*) underwater ▷ *nm* submarine

sous-médicalisé, e [sumedikalize] *adj* lacking adequate medical care

sous-nappe [sunap] *nf* undercloth

sous-officier [suzɔfisje] *nm* ≈ non-commissioned officer (NCO)

sous-ordre [suzɔʀdʀ(ə)] *nm* subordinate; **créancier en ~** creditor's creditor

sous-payé, e [supeje] *adj* underpaid

sous-préfecture [supʀefɛktyʀ] *nf* subprefecture

sous-préfet [supʀefɛ] *nm* sub-prefect

sous-production [supʀɔdyksjɔ̃] *nf* underproduction

sous-produit [supʀɔdɥi] *nm* by-product; (*fig: péj*) pale imitation

sous-programme [supʀɔgʀam] *nm* (*Inform*) subroutine

sous-pull [supul] *nm* thin poloneck sweater

sous-secrétaire [susəkʀetɛʀ] *nm*: **~ d'État** Under-Secretary of State

soussigné, e [susiɲe] *adj*: **je ~** I the undersigned

sous-sol [susɔl] *nm* basement; (*Géo*) subsoil

sous-tasse [sutas] *nf* saucer

sous-tendre [sutɑ̃dʀ(ə)] *vt* to underlie

sous-titre [sutitʀ(ə)] *nm* subtitle

sous-titré, e [sutitʀe] *adj* with subtitles

soustraction [sustʀaksjɔ̃] *nf* subtraction

soustraire [sustʀɛʀ] *vt* to subtract, take away; (*dérober*): **~ qch à qn** to remove sth from sb; **~ qn à** (*danger*) to shield sb from; **se ~ à** (*autorité, obligation, devoir*) to elude, escape from

sous-traitance [sutʀɛtɑ̃s(ə)] *nf* subcontracting

sous-traitant [sutʀɛtɑ̃] *nm* subcontractor

sous-traiter [sutʀete] *vt, vi* to subcontract

soustrayais *etc* [sustʀɛjɛ] *vb voir* **soustraire**

sous-verre [suvɛʀ] *nm inv* glass mount

sous-vêtement [suvɛtmɑ̃] *nm* undergarment, item of underwear; **sous-vêtements** *nmpl* underwear *sg*

soutane [sutan] *nf* cassock, soutane

soute [sut] *nf* hold; **~ à bagages** baggage hold

soutenable [sutnabl(ə)] *adj* (*opinion*) tenable, defensible

soutenance [sutnɑ̃s] *nf*: **~ de thèse** ≈ viva (voce)

soutènement [sutɛnmɑ̃] *nm*: **mur de ~** retaining wall

souteneur [sutnœʀ] *nm* procurer

soutenir [sutniʀ] *vt* to support; (*assaut, choc, regard*) to stand up to, withstand; (*intérêt, effort*) to keep up; (*assurer*): **~ que** to maintain that; **se soutenir** (*dans l'eau etc*) to hold o.s. up; (*être soutenable: point de vue*) to be tenable; (*s'aider mutuellement*) to stand by each other; **~ la comparaison avec** to bear *ou* stand comparison with; **~ le regard de qn** to be able to look sb in the face

soutenu, e [sutny] *pp de* **soutenir** ▷ *adj* (*efforts*) sustained, unflagging; (*style*) elevated; (*couleur*) strong

souterrain, e [sutɛʀɛ̃, -ɛn] *adj* underground; (*fig*) subterranean ▷ *nm* underground passage

soutien [sutjɛ̃] *nm* support; **apporter son ~ à** to lend one's support to; **~ de famille** breadwinner

soutiendrai *etc* [sutjɛ̃dʀe] *vb voir* **soutenir**

soutien-gorge [sutjɛ̃gɔʀʒ(ə)] (*pl* **soutiens-gorge**) *nm* bra; (*de maillot de bain*) top

soutiens [sutjɛ̃], **soutint** *etc* [sutɛ̃] *vb voir* **soutenir**

soutirer [sutiʀe] *vt*: **~ qch à qn** to squeeze *ou* get sth out of sb

souvenance [suvnɑ̃s] *nf:* **avoir ~ de** to recollect

souvenir [suvniʀ] *nm* (*réminiscence*) memory; (*cadeau*) souvenir, keepsake; (*de voyage*) souvenir ▷ *vb:* **se ~ de** *vt* to remember; **se ~ que** to remember that; **garder le ~ de** to retain the memory of; **en ~ de** in memory *ou* remembrance of; **avec mes affectueux/ meilleurs ~s, ...** with love from, .../regards, ...

souvent [suvɑ̃] *adv* often; **peu ~** seldom, infrequently; **le plus ~** more often than not, most often

souvenu, e [suvǝny] *pp de* **se souvenir**

souverain, e [suvʀɛ̃, -ɛn] *adj* sovereign; (*fig: mépris*) supreme ▷ *nm/f* sovereign, monarch

souverainement [suvʀɛnmɑ̃] *adv* (*sans appel*) with sovereign power; (*extrêmement*) supremely, intensely

souveraineté [suvʀɛnte] *nf* sovereignty

souviendrai [suvjɛ̃dʀe], **souviens** [suvjɛ̃], **souvint** *etc* [suvɛ̃] *vb voir* **se souvenir**

soviétique [sɔvjetik] *adj* Soviet ▷ *nm/f:* **Soviétique** Soviet citizen

soviétologue [sɔvjetɔlɔg] *nm/f* Kremlinologist

soyeux, -euse [swajø, -øz] *adj* silky

soyez *etc* [swaje] *vb voir* **être**

soyons *etc* [swajɔ̃] *vb voir* **être**

SPA *sigle f* (= *Société protectrice des animaux*) ≈ RSPCA (*Brit*), ≈ SPCA (*US*)

spacieux, -euse [spasjø, -øz] *adj* spacious; roomy

spaciosité [spasjɔzite] *nf* spaciousness

spaghettis [spageti] *nmpl* spaghetti *sg*

sparadrap [spaʀadʀa] *nm* adhesive *ou* sticking (*Brit*) plaster, bandaid® (*US*)

Sparte [spaʀt(ǝ)] *nf* Sparta

spartiate [spaʀsjat] *adj* Spartan; **spartiates** *nfpl* (*sandales*) Roman sandals

spasme [spazm(ǝ)] *nm* spasm

spasmodique [spazmɔdik] *adj* spasmodic

spatial, e, -aux [spasjal, -o] *adj* (*Aviat*) space *cpd*; (*Psych*) spatial

spatule [spatyl] *nf* (*ustensile*) slice; spatula; (*bout*) tip

speaker, ine [spikœʀ, -kʀin] *nm/f* announcer

spécial, e, -aux [spesjal, -o] *adj* special; (*bizarre*) peculiar

spécialement [spesjalmɑ̃] *adv* especially, particularly; (*tout exprès*) specially; **pas ~** not particularly

spécialisation [spesjalizasjɔ̃] *nf* specialization

spécialisé, e [spesjalize] *adj* specialised; **ordinateur ~** dedicated computer

spécialiser [spesjalize]: **se spécialiser** *vi* to specialize

spécialiste [spesjalist(ǝ)] *nm/f* specialist

spécialité [spesjalite] *nf* speciality; (*Scol*) special field; **~ pharmaceutique** patent medicine

spécieux, -euse [spesjø, -øz] *adj* specious

spécification [spesifikasjɔ̃] *nf* specification

spécificité [spesifisite] *nf* specificity

spécifier [spesifje] *vt* to specify, state

spécifique [spesifik] *adj* specific

spécifiquement [spesifikmɑ̃] *adv* (*typiquement*) typically; (*tout exprès*) specifically

spécimen [spesimɛn] *nm* specimen; (*revue etc*) specimen *ou* sample copy

spectacle [spɛktakl(ǝ)] *nm* (*tableau, scène*) sight; (*représentation*) show; (*industrie*) show business, entertainment; **se donner en ~** (*péj*) to make a spectacle *ou* an exhibition of o.s; **pièce/revue à grand ~** spectacular (play/revue); **au ~ de ...** at the sight of ...

spectaculaire [spɛktakylɛʀ] *adj* spectacular

spectateur, -trice [spɛktatœʀ, -tʀis] *nm/f* (*Ciné etc*) member of the audience; (*Sport*) spectator; (*d'un événement*) onlooker, witness

spectre [spɛktʀ(ǝ)] *nm* (*fantôme, fig*) spectre; (*Physique*) spectrum; **~ solaire** solar spectrum

spéculateur, -trice [spekylatœʀ, -tʀis] *nm/f* speculator

spéculatif, -ive [spekylatif, -iv] *adj* speculative

spéculation [spekylasjɔ̃] *nf* speculation

spéculer [spekyle] *vi* to speculate; **~ sur** (*Comm*) to speculate in; (*réfléchir*) to speculate on; (*tabler sur*) to bank *ou* rely on

spéléologie [speleɔlɔʒi] *nf* (*étude*) speleology; (*activité*) potholing

spéléologue [speleɔlɔg] *nm/f* speleologist; potholer

spermatozoïde [spɛʀmatozɔid] *nm* sperm, spermatozoon

sperme [spɛʀm(ǝ)] *nm* semen, sperm

spermicide [spɛʀmisid] *adj, nm* spermicide

sphère [sfɛʀ] *nf* sphere

sphérique [sferik] *adj* spherical

sphincter [sfɛ̃ktɛʀ] *nm* sphincter

sphinx [sfɛ̃ks] *nm inv* sphinx; (*Zool*) hawkmoth

spiral, -aux [spiʀal, -o] *nm* hairspring

spirale [spiʀal] *nf* spiral; **en ~** in a spiral

spire [spiʀ] *nf* (*d'une spirale*) turn; (*d'une coquille*) whorl

spiritisme [spiʀitism(ǝ)] *nm* spiritualism, spiritism

spirituel, le [spiʀitɥɛl] *adj* spiritual; (*fin, piquant*) witty; **musique ~le** sacred music; **concert ~** concert of sacred music

spirituellement [spiʀitɥɛlmɑ̃] *adv* spiritually; wittily

spiritueux [spiʀitɥø] *nm* spirit

splendeur [splɑ̃dœʀ] *nf* splendour (*Brit*), splendor (*US*)

splendide [splɑ̃did] *adj* splendid, magnificent

spolier [spɔlje] *vt:* **~ qn (de)** to despoil sb (of)

spongieux, -euse [spɔ̃ʒjø, -øz] *adj* spongy

sponsor [spɔ̃sɔʀ] *nm* sponsor

sponsoriser [spɔ̃sɔʀize] *vt* to sponsor

spontané, e [spɔ̃tane] *adj* spontaneous

spontanéité [spɔ̃taneite] *nf* spontaneity

spontanément [spɔ̃tanemɑ̃] *adv* spontaneously

sporadique [spɔʀadik] *adj* sporadic

sporadiquement [spɔʀadikmɑ̃] *adv*

sporadically

sport [spɔʀ] *nm* sport ▷ *adj inv* (*vêtement*) casual; (*fair-play*) sporting; **faire du ~** to do sport; **~ individuel/d'équipe** individual/team sport; **~ de combat** combative sport; **~s d'hiver** winter sports

sportif, -ive [spɔʀtif, -iv] *adj* (*journal, association, épreuve*) sports *cpd*; (*allure, démarche*) athletic; (*attitude, esprit*) sporting; **les résultats ~s** the sports results

sportivement [spɔʀtivmɑ̃] *adv* sportingly

sportivité [spɔʀtivite] *nf* sportsmanship

spot [spɔt] *nm* (*lampe*) spot(light); (*annonce*): **~ (publicitaire)** commercial (break)

spray [spʀɛ] *nm* spray, aerosol

sprint [spʀint] *nm* sprint; **piquer un ~** to put on a (final) spurt

sprinter *nm* [spʀintœʀ] sprinter ▷ *vi* [spʀinte] to sprint

squale [skwal] *nm* (*type of*) shark

square [skwaʀ] *nm* public garden(s)

squash [skwaʃ] *nm* squash

squat [skwat] *nm* (*lieu*) squat

squatter *nm* [skwatœʀ] squatter ▷ *vt* [skwate] to squat

squelette [skəlɛt] *nm* skeleton

squelettique [skəletik] *adj* scrawny; (*fig*) skimpy

SRAS *sigle m* (= *syndrome respiratoire aigu sévère*) SARS

Sri Lanka [sʀilɑ̃ka] *nm* Sri Lanka

sri-lankais, e [sʀilɑ̃kɛ, -ɛz] *adj* Sri-Lankan

SS *sigle f* = **sécurité sociale**; (= *Sa Sainteté*) HH

ss *abr* = **sous**

SSR *sigle f* (= *Société suisse romande*) the Swiss French-language broadcasting company

St, Ste *abr* (= *Saint(e)*) St

stabilisateur, -trice [stabilizatœʀ, -tʀis] *adj* stabilizing ▷ *nm* stabilizer; (*d'un véhicule*) anti-roll device; (*d'un avion*) tailplane

stabiliser [stabilize] *vt* to stabilize; (*terrain*) to consolidate

stabilité [stabilite] *nf* stability

stable [stabl(ə)] *adj* stable, steady

stade [stad] *nm* (*Sport*) stadium; (*phase, niveau*) stage

stadier [stadje] *nm* steward (*working in a stadium*), stage

stage [staʒ] *nm* training period; training course; (*d'avocat stagiaire*) articles *pl*; **~ en entreprise** work experience placement

stagiaire [staʒjɛʀ] *nm/f, adj* trainee (*cpd*)

stagnant, e [stagnɑ̃, -ɑ̃t] *adj* stagnant

stagnation [stagnasjɔ̃] *nf* stagnation

stagner [stagne] *vi* to stagnate

stalactite [stalaktit] *nf* stalactite

stalagmite [stalagmit] *nf* stalagmite

stalle [stal] *nf* stall, box

stand [stɑ̃d] *nm* (*d'exposition*) stand; (*de foire*) stall; **~ de tir** (*à la foire, Sport*) shooting range; **~ de ravitaillement** pit

standard [stɑ̃daʀ] *adj inv* standard ▷ *nm* (*type,*

norme) standard; (*téléphonique*) switchboard

standardisation [stɑ̃daʀdizasjɔ̃] *nf* standardization

standardiser [stɑ̃daʀdize] *vt* to standardize

standardiste [stɑ̃daʀdist(ə)] *nm/f* switchboard operator

standing [stɑ̃diŋ] *nm* standing; **immeuble de grand ~** block of luxury flats (*Brit*), condo(minium) (*US*)

star [staʀ] *nf* star

starlette [staʀlɛt] *nf* starlet

starter [staʀtœʀ] *nm* (*Auto*) choke; (*Sport: personne*) starter; **mettre le ~** to pull out the choke

station [stasjɔ̃] *nf* station; (*de bus*) stop; (*de villégiature*) resort; (*posture*): **la ~ debout** standing, an upright posture; **~ balnéaire** seaside resort; **~ de graissage** lubrication bay; **~ de lavage** carwash; **~ de ski** ski resort; **~ de sports d'hiver** winter sports resort; **~ de taxis** taxi rank (*Brit*) *ou* stand (*US*); **~ thermale** thermal spa; **~ de travail** workstation

stationnaire [stasjɔnɛʀ] *adj* stationary

stationnement [stasjɔnmɑ̃] *nm* parking; **zone de ~ interdit** no parking area; **~ alterné** parking on alternate sides

stationner [stasjɔne] *vi* to park

station-service [stasjɔ̃sɛʀvis] *nf* service station

statique [statik] *adj* static

statisticien, ne [statistisjɛ̃, -ɛn] *nm/f* statistician

statistique [statistik] *nf* (*science*) statistics *sg*; (*rapport, étude*) statistic ▷ *adj* statistical; **statistiques** *nfpl* (*données*) statistics *pl*

statistiquement [statistikmɑ̃] *adv* statistically

statue [staty] *nf* statue

statuer [statɥe] *vi*: **~ sur** to rule on, give a ruling on

statuette [statɥet] *nf* statuette

statu quo [statykwo] *nm* status quo

stature [statyʀ] *nf* stature; **de haute ~** of great stature

statut [staty] *nm* status; **statuts** *nmpl* (*Jur, Admin*) statutes

statutaire [statytɛʀ] *adj* statutory

Sté *abr* (= *société*) soc

steak [stɛk] *nm* steak

stèle [stɛl] *nf* stela, stele

stellaire [stelɛʀ] *adj* stellar

stencil [stɛnsil] *nm* stencil

sténo [stenɔ] *nm/f* (*aussi*: **sténographe**) shorthand typist (*Brit*), stenographer (*US*) ▷ *nf* (*aussi*: **sténographie**) shorthand; **prendre en ~** to take down in shorthand

sténodactylo [stenɔdaktilo] *nm/f* shorthand typist (*Brit*), stenographer (*US*)

sténodactylographie [stenɔdaktilɔgʀafi] *nf* shorthand typing (*Brit*), stenography (*US*)

sténographe [stenɔgʀaf] *nm/f* shorthand typist (*Brit*), stenographer (*US*)

sténographie [stenɔgʀafi] *nf* shorthand; **prendre en ~** to take down in shorthand

sténographier [stenɔgʀafje] vt to take down in shorthand

sténographique [stenɔgʀafik] adj shorthand cpd

stentor [stɑ̃tɔʀ] nm: **voix de ~** stentorian voice

step® [stɛp] nm step aerobics sg®, step Reebok®

stéphanois, e [stefanwa, -waz] adj of ou from Saint-Étienne

steppe [stɛp] nf steppe

stère [stɛʀ] nm stere

stéréo nf (aussi: **stéréophonie**) stereo; **émission en ~** stereo broadcast ▷ adj (aussi: **stéréophonique**) stereo

stéréophonie [steʀeɔfɔni] nf stereo(phony); **émission en ~** stereo broadcast

stéréophonique [steʀeɔfɔnik] adj stereo(phonic)

stéréoscope [steʀeɔskɔp] nm stereoscope

stéréoscopique [steʀeɔskɔpik] adj stereoscopic

stéréotype [steʀeɔtip] nm stereotype

stéréotypé, e [steʀeɔtipe] adj stereotyped

stérile [steʀil] adj sterile; (terre) barren; (fig) fruitless, futile

stérilement [steʀilmɑ̃] adv fruitlessly

stérilet [steʀilɛ] nm coil, loop

stérilisateur [steʀilizatœʀ] nm sterilizer

stérilisation [steʀilizasjɔ̃] nf sterilization

stériliser [steʀilize] vt to sterilize

stérilité [steʀilite] nf sterility

sternum [stɛʀnɔm] nm breastbone, sternum

stéthoscope [stetɔskɔp] nm stethoscope

stick [stik] nm stick

stigmates [stigmat] nmpl scars, marks; (Rel) stigmata pl

stigmatiser [stigmatize] vt to denounce, stigmatize

stimulant, e [stimylɑ̃, -ɑ̃t] adj stimulating ▷ nm (Méd) stimulant; (fig) stimulus, incentive

stimulateur [stimylatœʀ] nm: **~ cardiaque** pacemaker

stimulation [stimylasjɔ̃] nf stimulation

stimuler [stimyle] vt to stimulate

stimulus [stimylys] nm (pl **stimuli** [stimyli]) stimulus

stipulation [stipylasjɔ̃] nf stipulation

stipuler [stipyle] vt to stipulate, specify

stock [stɔk] nm stock; **en ~** in stock

stockage [stɔkaʒ] nm stocking; storage

stocker [stɔke] vt to stock; (déchets) to store

Stockholm [stɔkɔlm] n Stockholm

stockiste [stɔkist(ə)] nm stockist

stoïcisme [stɔisism(ə)] nm stoicism

stoïque [stɔik] adj stoic, stoical

stoïquement [stɔikmɑ̃] adv stoically

stomacal, e, -aux [stɔmakal, -o] adj gastric, stomach cpd

stomatologie [stɔmatɔlɔʒi] nf stomatology

stomatologue [stɔmatɔlɔg] nm/f stomatologist

stop [stɔp] nm (Auto: écriteau) stop sign; (: signal) brake-light; (dans un télégramme) stop ▷ excl stop!

stoppage [stɔpaʒ] nm invisible mending

stopper [stɔpe] vt to stop, halt; (Couture) to mend ▷ vi to stop, halt

store [stɔʀ] nm blind; (de magasin) shade, awning

strabisme [stʀabism(ə)] nm squint(ing)

strangulation [stʀɑ̃gylasjɔ̃] nf strangulation

strapontin [stʀapɔ̃tɛ̃] nm jump ou foldaway seat

Strasbourg [stʀazbuʀ] n Strasbourg

strass [stʀas] nm paste, strass

stratagème [stʀataʒɛm] nm stratagem

strate [stʀat] nf (Géo) stratum, layer

stratège [stʀatɛʒ] nm strategist

stratégie [stʀateʒi] nf strategy

stratégique [stʀateʒik] adj strategic

stratégiquement [stʀateʒikmɑ̃] adv strategically

stratifié, e [stʀatifje] adj (Géo) stratified; (Tech) laminated

stratosphère [stʀatɔsfɛʀ] nf stratosphere

stress [stʀɛs] nm inv stress

stressant, e [stʀɛsɑ̃, -ɑ̃t] adj stressful

stresser [stʀɛse] vt to stress, cause stress in

strict, e [stʀikt(ə)] adj strict; (tenue, décor) severe, plain; **son droit le plus ~** his most basic right; **dans la plus ~e intimité** strictly in private; **le ~ nécessaire/minimum** the bare essentials/minimum

strictement [stʀiktəmɑ̃] adv strictly; plainly

strident, e [stʀidɑ̃, -ɑ̃t] adj shrill, strident

stridulations [stʀidylasjɔ̃] nfpl stridulations, chirrings

strie [stʀi] nf streak; (Anat, Géo) stria

strier [stʀije] vt to streak; to striate

strip-tease [stʀiptiz] nm striptease

strip-teaseuse [stʀiptizøz] nf stripper, striptease artist

striures [stʀijyʀ] nfpl streaking sg

strophe [stʀɔf] nf verse, stanza

structure [stʀyktyʀ] nf structure; **~s d'accueil/touristiques** reception/tourist facilities

structurer [stʀyktyʀe] vt to structure

strychnine [stʀiknin] nf strychnine

stuc [styk] nm stucco

studieusement [stydjøzmɑ̃] adv studiously

studieux, -euse [stydjø, -øz] adj (élève) studious; (vacances) study cpd

studio [stydjo] nm (logement) studio flat (Brit) ou apartment (US); (d'artiste, TV etc) studio

stupéfaction [stypefaksjɔ̃] nf stupefaction, astonishment

stupéfait, e [stypefɛ, -ɛt] adj astonished

stupéfiant, e [stypefjɑ̃, -ɑ̃t] adj stunning, astonishing ▷ nm (Méd) drug, narcotic

stupéfier [stypefje] vt to stupefy; (étonner) to stun, astonish

stupeur [stypœʀ] nf (inertie, insensibilité) stupor; (étonnement) astonishment, amazement

stupide [stypid] adj stupid; (hébété) stunned

stupidement [stypidmɑ̃] adv stupidly

stupidité [stypidite] nf stupidity no pl; (propos, action) stupid thing (to say ou do)

stups [styp] *nmpl* = **stupéfiants**; **brigade des ~** narcotics bureau *ou* squad

style [stil] *nm* style; **meuble/robe de ~** piece of period furniture/period dress; **~ de vie** lifestyle

stylé, e [stile] *adj* well-trained

stylet [stilɛ] *nm* (*poignard*) stiletto; (*Chirurgie*) stylet

stylisé, e [stilize] *adj* stylized

styliste [stilist(ə)] *nm/f* designer; stylist

stylistique [stilistik] *nf* stylistics *sg* ▷ *adj* stylistic

stylo [stilo] *nm*: **~ (à encre)** (fountain) pen; **~ (à) bille** ballpoint pen

stylo-feutre [stilɔføtR(ə)] *nm* felt-tip pen

su, e [sy] *pp de* **savoir** ▷ *nm*: **au su de** with the knowledge of

suaire [sɥɛR] *nm* shroud

suant, e [sɥɑ̃, -ɑ̃t] *adj* sweaty

suave [sɥav] *adj* (*odeur*) sweet; (*voix*) suave, smooth; (*coloris*) soft, mellow

subalterne [sybaltɛRn(ə)] *adj* (*employé, officier*) junior; (*rôle*) subordinate, subsidiary ▷ *nm/f* subordinate, inferior

subconscient [sypkɔ̃sjɑ̃] *nm* subconscious

subdiviser [sybdivize] *vt* to subdivide

subdivision [sybdivizjɔ̃] *nf* subdivision

subir [sybiR] *vt* (*affront, dégâts, mauvais traitements*) to suffer; (*influence, charme*) to be under, be subjected to; (*traitement, opération, châtiment*) to undergo; (*personne*) to suffer, be subjected to

subit, e [sybi, -it] *adj* sudden

subitement [sybitmɑ̃] *adv* suddenly, all of a sudden

subjectif, -ive [sybʒɛktif, -iv] *adj* subjective

subjectivement [sybʒɛktivmɑ̃] *adv* subjectively

subjectivité [sybʒɛktivite] *nf* subjectivity

subjonctif [sybʒɔ̃ktif] *nm* subjunctive

subjuguer [sybʒyge] *vt* to subjugate

sublime [syblim] *adj* sublime

sublimer [syblime] *vt* to sublimate

submergé, e [sybmɛRʒe] *adj* submerged; (*fig*): **~ de** snowed under with; overwhelmed with

submerger [sybmɛRʒe] *vt* to submerge; (*foule*) to engulf; (*fig*) to overwhelm

submersible [sybmɛRsibl(ə)] *nm* submarine

subordination [sybɔRdinasjɔ̃] *nf* subordination

subordonné, e [sybɔRdɔne] *adj, nm/f* subordinate; **~ à** (*personne*) subordinate to; (*résultats etc*) subject to, depending on

subordonner [sybɔRdɔne] *vt*: **~ qn/qch à** to subordinate sb/sth to

subornation [sybɔRnasjɔ̃] *nf* bribing

suborner [sybɔRne] *vt* to bribe

subrepticement [sybRɛptismɑ̃] *adv* surreptitiously

subroger [sybRɔʒe] *vt* (*Jur*) to subrogate

subside [sypsid] *nm* grant

subsidiaire [sypsidjɛR] *adj* subsidiary; **question ~** deciding question

subsistance [sybzistɑ̃s] *nf* subsistence; **pourvoir à la ~ de qn** to keep sb, provide for sb's subsistence *ou* keep

subsister [sybziste] *vi* (*rester*) to remain, subsist; (*vivre*) to live; (*survivre*) to live on

subsonique [sybsɔnik] *adj* subsonic

substance [sypstɑ̃s] *nf* substance; **en ~** in substance

substantiel, le [sypstɑ̃sjɛl] *adj* substantial

substantif [sypstɑ̃tif] *nm* noun, substantive

substantiver [sypstɑ̃tive] *vt* to nominalize

substituer [sypstitɥe] *vt*: **~ qn/qch à** to substitute sb/sth for; **se ~ à qn** (*représenter*) to substitute for sb; (*évincer*) to substitute o.s. for sb

substitut [sypstity] *nm* (*Jur*) deputy public prosecutor; (*succédané*) substitute

substitution [sypstitysjɔ̃] *nf* substitution

subterfuge [syptɛRfyʒ] *nm* subterfuge

subtil, e [syptil] *adj* subtle

subtilement [syptilmɑ̃] *adv* subtly

subtiliser [syptilize] *vt*: **~ qch (à qn)** to spirit sth away (from sb)

subtilité [syptilite] *nf* subtlety

subtropical, e, -aux [sybtRɔpikal, -o] *adj* subtropical

suburbain, e [sybyRbɛ̃, -ɛn] *adj* suburban

subvenir [sybvəniR]: **~ à** *vt* to meet

subvention [sybvɑ̃sjɔ̃] *nf* subsidy, grant

subventionner [sybvɑ̃sjɔne] *vt* to subsidize

subversif, -ive [sybvɛRsif, -iv] *adj* subversive

subversion [sybvɛRsjɔ̃] *nf* subversion

suc [syk] *nm* (*Bot*) sap; (*de viande, fruit*) juice; **~s gastriques** gastric juices

succédané [syksedane] *nm* substitute

succéder [syksede]: **~ à** *vt* (*directeur, roi etc*) to succeed; (*venir après: dans une série*) to follow, succeed; **se succéder** *vi* (*accidents, années*) to follow one another

succès [syksɛ] *nm* success; **avec ~** successfully; **sans ~** unsuccessfully; **avoir du ~** to be a success, be successful; **à ~** successful; **livre à ~** bestseller; **~ de librairie** bestseller; **~ (féminins)** conquests

successeur [syksesœR] *nm* successor

successif, -ive [syksesif, -iv] *adj* successive

succession [syksesjɔ̃] *nf* (*série, Pol*) succession; (*Jur: patrimoine*) estate, inheritance; **prendre la ~ de** (*directeur*) to succeed, take over from; (*entreprise*) to take over

successivement [syksesivmɑ̃] *adv* successively

succinct, e [syksɛ̃, -ɛ̃t] *adj* succinct

succinctement [syksɛ̃tmɑ̃] *adv* succinctly

succion [syksjɔ̃] *nf*: **bruit de ~** sucking noise

succomber [sykɔ̃be] *vi* to die, succumb; (*fig*): **~ à** to give way to, succumb to

succulent, e [sykylɑ̃, -ɑ̃t] *adj* succulent

succursale [sykyRsal] *nf* branch; **magasin à ~s multiples** chain *ou* multiple store

sucer [syse] *vt* to suck

sucette [sysɛt] *nf* (*bonbon*) lollipop; (*de bébé*) dummy (*Brit*), comforter, pacifier (*US*)

suçoter [sysɔte] *vt* to suck

sucre [sykR(ə)] *nm* (*substance*) sugar; (*morceau*) lump of sugar, sugar lump *ou* cube; **~ de canne/**

betterave cane/beet sugar; ~ **en morceaux/
cristallisé/en poudre** lump ou cube/
granulated/caster sugar; ~ **glace** icing sugar; ~
d'orge barley sugar
sucré, e [sykʀe] adj (produit alimentaire)
sweetened; (au goût) sweet; (péj) sugary,
honeyed
sucrer [sykʀe] vt (thé, café) to sweeten, put sugar
in; ~ **qn** to put sugar in sb's tea (ou coffee etc); **se
sucrer** to help o.s. to sugar, have some sugar;
(fam) to line one's pocket(s)
sucrerie [sykʀəʀi] nf (usine) sugar refinery;
sucreries nfpl (bonbons) sweets, sweet things
sucrier, -ière [sykʀije, -jɛʀ] adj (industrie) sugar
cpd; (région) sugar-producing ▷ nm (fabricant)
sugar producer; (récipient) sugar bowl ou basin
sud [syd] nm: **le ~** the south ▷ adj inv south;
(côte) south, southern; **au ~** (situation) in the
south; (direction) to the south; **au ~ de** (to the)
south of
sud-africain, e [sydafʀikɛ̃, -ɛn] adj South
African ▷ nm/f: **Sud-Africain, e** South African
sud-américain, e [sydameʀikɛ̃, -ɛn] adj South
American ▷ nm/f: **Sud-Américain, e** South
American
sudation [sydasjɔ̃] nf sweating, sudation
sud-coréen, ne [sydkɔʀeɛ̃, -ɛn] adj South
Korean ▷ nm/f: **Sud-Coréen, ne** South Korean
sud-est [sydɛst] nm, adj inv south-east
sud-ouest [sydwɛst] nm, adj inv south-west
sud-vietnamien, ne [sydvjɛtnamjɛ̃, -ɛn] adj
South Vietnamese ▷ nm/f: **Sud-Vietnamien, ne**
South Vietnamese
Suède [sɥɛd] nf: **la ~** Sweden
suédois, e [sɥedwa, -waz] adj Swedish ▷ nm
(Ling) Swedish ▷ nm/f: **Suédois, e** Swede
suer [sɥe] vi to sweat; (suinter) to ooze ▷ vt (fig) to
exude; ~ **à grosses gouttes** to sweat profusely
sueur [sɥœʀ] nf sweat; **en ~** sweating, in a
sweat; **avoir des ~s froides** to be in a cold
sweat
suffire [syfiʀ] vi (être assez): ~ **(à qn/pour qch/
pour faire)** to be enough ou sufficient (for sb/
for sth/to do); (satisfaire): **cela lui suffit** he's
content with this, this is enough for him; **se
suffire** vi to be self-sufficient; **cela suffit pour
les irriter/qu'ils se fâchent** it's enough to
annoy them/for them to get angry; **il suffit
d'une négligence/qu'on oublie pour que** ... it
only takes one act of carelessness/one only
needs to forget for ...; **ça suffit!** that's enough!,
that'll do!
suffisamment [syfizamɑ̃] adv sufficiently,
enough; ~ **de** sufficient, enough
suffisance [syfizɑ̃s] nf (vanité) self-importance,
bumptiousness; (quantité): **en ~** in plenty
suffisant, e [syfizɑ̃, -ɑ̃t] adj (temps, ressources)
sufficient; (résultats) satisfactory; (vaniteux) self-
important, bumptious
suffisons etc [syfizɔ̃] vb voir **suffire**
suffixe [syfiks(ə)] nm suffix
suffocant, e [syfɔkɑ̃, -ɑ̃t] adj (étouffant)

suffocating; (stupéfiant) staggering
suffocation [syfɔkasjɔ̃] nf suffocation
suffoquer [syfɔke] vt to choke, suffocate;
(stupéfier) to stagger, astound ▷ vi to choke,
suffocate; ~ **de colère/d'indignation** to choke
with anger/indignation
suffrage [syfʀaʒ] nm (Pol: voix) vote; (: méthode): ~
universel/direct/indirect universal/direct/
indirect suffrage; (du public etc) approval no pl; ~**s
exprimés** valid votes
suggérer [sygʒeʀe] vt to suggest; ~ **que/de
faire** to suggest that/doing
suggestif, -ive [sygʒɛstif, -iv] adj suggestive
suggestion [sygʒɛstjɔ̃] nf suggestion
suggestivité [sygʒɛstivite] nf suggestiveness,
suggestive nature
suicidaire [sɥisidɛʀ] adj suicidal
suicide [sɥisid] nm suicide ▷ adj: **opération ~**
suicide mission
suicidé, e [sɥiside] nm/f suicide
suicider [sɥiside]: **se suicider** vi to commit
suicide
suie [sɥi] nf soot
suif [sɥif] nm tallow
suinter [sɥɛ̃te] vi to ooze
suis [sɥi] vb voir **être**; **suivre**
suisse [sɥis] adj Swiss ▷ nm (bedeau) ≈ verger
▷ nm/f: **Suisse** Swiss pl inv ▷ nf: **la S~**
Switzerland; **la S~ romande/allemande**
French-speaking/German-speaking
Switzerland; ~ **romand** Swiss French
suisse-allemand, e [sɥisalmɑ̃, -ɑ̃d] adj, nm/f
Swiss German
Suissesse [sɥisɛs] nf Swiss (woman ou girl)
suit [sɥi] vb voir **suivre**
suite [sɥit] nf (continuation: d'énumération etc) rest,
remainder; (: de feuilleton) continuation; (: second
film etc sur le même thème) sequel; (série: de maisons,
succès): **une ~ de** a series ou succession of;
(Math) series sg; (conséquence) result; (ordre, liaison
logique) coherence; (appartement, Mus) suite;
(escorte) retinue, suite; **suites** nfpl (d'une maladie
etc) effects; **prendre la ~ de** (directeur etc) to
succeed, take over from; **donner ~ à** (requête,
projet) to follow up; **faire ~ à** to follow; (faisant)
~ **à votre lettre du** further to your letter of the;
sans ~ adj incoherent, disjointed ▷ adv
incoherently, disjointedly; **de ~** adv (d'affilée) in
succession; (immédiatement) at once; **par la ~**
afterwards, subsequently; **à la ~** adv one after
the other; **à la ~ de** (derrière) behind; (en
conséquence de) following; **par ~ de** owing to, as a
result of; **avoir de la ~ dans les idées** to show
great singleness of purpose; **attendre la ~ des
événements** to (wait and see) what happens
suivant, e [sɥivɑ̃, -ɑ̃t] vb voir **suivre** ▷ adj next,
following; (ci-après): **l'exercice ~** the following
exercise ▷ prép (selon) according to; ~ **que**
according to whether; **au ~!** next!
suive etc [sɥiv] vb voir **suivre**
suiveur [sɥivœʀ] nm (Cyclisme) (official)
follower; (péj) (camp) follower

suivi, e [sɥivi] *pp de* **suivre** ▷ *adj* (*régulier*)
regular; (*Comm: article*) in general production;
(*cohérent*) consistent; coherent ▷ *nm* follow-up;
très/peu ~ (*cours*) well-/poorly-attended; (*mode*)
widely/not widely adopted; (*feuilleton etc*)
widely/not widely followed
suivre [sɥivʀ(ə)] *vt* (*gén*) to follow; (*Scol: cours*) to
attend; (: *leçon*) to follow, attend to; (: *programme*)
to keep up with; (*Comm: article*) to continue to
stock ▷ *vi* to follow; (*élève: écouter*) to attend, pay
attention; (: *assimiler le programme*) to keep up,
follow; **se suivre** (*accidents, personnes, voitures etc*)
to follow one after the other; (*raisonnement*) to be
coherent; **~ des yeux** to follow with one's eyes;
faire ~ (*lettre*) to forward; **~ son cours** (*enquête
etc*) to run *ou* take its course; **"à ~"** "to be
continued"
sujet, te [syʒɛ, -ɛt] *adj*: **être ~ à** (*accidents*) to be
prone to; (*vertige etc*) to be liable *ou* subject to
▷ *nm/f* (*d'un souverain*) subject ▷ *nm* subject; **un ~
de dispute/discorde/mécontentement** a
cause for argument/dissension/dissatisfaction;
c'est à quel ~? what is it about?; **avoir ~ de se
plaindre** to have cause for complaint; **au ~ de**
prép about; **~ à caution** *adj* questionable; **~ de
conversation** topic *ou* subject of conversation;
~ d'examen (*Scol*) examination question;
examination paper; **~ d'expérience** (*Bio etc*)
experimental subject
sujétion [syʒesjɔ̃] *nf* subjection; (*fig*)
constraint
sulfater [sylfate] *vt* to spray with copper
sulphate
sulfureux, -euse [sylfyʀø, -øz] *adj* sulphurous
(*Brit*), sulfurous (*US*)
sulfurique [sylfyʀik] *adj*: **acide ~** sulphuric (*Brit*)
ou sulfuric (*US*) acid
sulfurisé, e [sylfyʀize] *adj*: **papier ~** greaseproof
(*Brit*) *ou* wax (*US*) paper
Sumatra [symatʀa] *nf* Sumatra
summum [sɔmɔm] *nm*: **le ~ de** the height of
super [sypɛʀ] *adj inv* great, fantastic ▷ *nm*
(= *supercarburant*) ≈ 4-star (*Brit*), ≈ premium (*US*)
superbe [sypɛʀb(ə)] *adj* magnificent, superb
▷ *nf* arrogance
superbement [sypɛʀbəmɑ̃] *adv* superbly
supercarburant [sypɛʀkaʀbyʀɑ̃] *nm* ≈ 4-star
petrol (*Brit*), ≈ premium gas (*US*)
supercherie [sypɛʀʃəʀi] *nf* trick, trickery *no pl*;
(*fraude*) fraud
supérette [sypeʀɛt] *nf* minimarket
superfétatoire [sypɛʀfetatwaʀ] *adj*
superfluous
superficie [sypɛʀfisi] *nf* (surface) area; (*fig*)
surface
superficiel, le [sypɛʀfisjɛl] *adj* superficial
superficiellement [sypɛʀfisjɛlmɑ̃] *adv*
superficially
superflu, e [sypɛʀfly] *adj* superfluous ▷ *nm*: **le ~**
the superfluous
superforme [sypɛʀfɔʀm(ə)] *nf* (*fam*) top form,
excellent shape

super-grand [sypɛʀgʀɑ̃] *nm* superpower
super-huit [sypɛʀɥit] *adj*: **camera/film ~**
super-eight camera/film
supérieur, e [sypeʀjœʀ] *adj* (*lèvre, étages, classes*)
upper; (*plus élevé: température, niveau*): **~ (à)** higher
(than); (*meilleur: qualité, produit*): **~ (à)** superior
(to); (*excellent, hautain*) superior ▷ *nm/f* superior;
Mère ~e Mother Superior; **à l'étage ~** on the
next floor up; **~ en nombre** superior in number
supérieurement [sypeʀjœʀmɑ̃] *adv*
exceptionally well; (*avec adjectif*) exceptionally
supériorité [sypeʀjɔʀite] *nf* superiority
superlatif [sypɛʀlatif] *nm* superlative
supermarché [sypɛʀmaʀʃe] *nm* supermarket
supernova [sypɛʀnɔva] *nf* supernova
superposable [sypɛʀpozabl(ə)] *adj* (*figures*) that
may be superimposed; (*lits*) stackable
superposer [sypɛʀpoze] *vt* to superpose;
(*meubles, caisses*) to stack; (*faire chevaucher*) to
superimpose; **se superposer** (*images, souvenirs*)
to be superimposed; **lits superposés** bunk
beds
superposition [sypɛʀpozisjɔ̃] *nf* superposition;
superimposition
superpréfet [sypɛʀpʀefɛ] *nm* prefect in charge of a
region
superproduction [sypɛʀpʀɔdyksjɔ̃] *nf* (*film*)
spectacular
superpuissance [sypɛʀpɥisɑ̃s] *nf* superpower
supersonique [sypɛʀsɔnik] *adj* supersonic
superstitieux, -euse [sypɛʀstisjø, -øz] *adj*
superstitious
superstition [sypɛʀstisjɔ̃] *nf* superstition
superstructure [sypɛʀstʀyktyʀ] *nf*
superstructure
supertanker [sypɛʀtɑ̃kœʀ] *nm* supertanker
superviser [sypɛʀvize] *vt* to supervise
supervision [sypɛʀvizjɔ̃] *nf* supervision
suppl. *abr* = **supplément**
supplanter [syplɑ̃te] *vt* to supplant
suppléance [sypleɑ̃s] *nf* (*poste*) supply post (*Brit*),
substitute teacher's post (*US*)
suppléant, e [sypleɑ̃, -ɑ̃t] *adj* (*juge, fonctionnaire*)
deputy *cpd*; (*professeur*) supply *cpd* (*Brit*),
substitute *cpd* (*US*) ▷ *nm/f* deputy; supply *ou*
substitute teacher; **médecin ~** locum
suppléer [syplee] *vt* (*ajouter: mot manquant etc*) to
supply, provide; (*compenser: lacune*) to fill in;
(: *défaut*) to make up for; (*remplacer: professeur*) to
stand in for; (: *juge*) to deputize for; **~ à** *vt* to
make up for; to substitute for
supplément [syplemɑ̃] *nm* supplement; **un ~
de travail** extra *ou* additional work; **un ~ de
frites** *etc* an extra portion of chips *etc*; **un ~ de
10 euros** a supplement of 10 euros, an extra *ou*
additional 10 euros; **ceci est en ~** (*au menu etc*)
this is extra, there is an extra charge for this; **~
d'information** additional information
supplémentaire [syplemɑ̃tɛʀ] *adj* additional,
further; (*train, bus*) relief *cpd*, extra
supplétif, -ive [sypletif, -iv] *adj* (*Mil*) auxiliary
suppliant, e [syplijɑ̃, -ɑ̃t] *adj* imploring

supplication [syplikɑsjɔ̃] *nf* (*Rel*) supplication; **supplications** *nfpl* (*adjurations*) pleas, entreaties

supplice [syplis] *nm* (*peine corporelle*) torture *no pl*; form of torture; (*douleur physique, morale*) torture, agony; **être au ~** to be in agony

supplier [syplije] *vt* to implore, beseech

supplique [syplik] *nf* petition

support [sypɔʀ] *nm* support; (*pour livre, outils*) stand; **~ audio-visuel** audio-visual aid; **~ publicitaire** advertising medium

supportable [sypɔʀtabl(ə)] *adj* (*douleur, température*) bearable; (*procédé, conduite*) tolerable

supporter *nm* [sypɔʀtɛʀ] supporter, fan ▷ *vt* [sypɔʀte] (*poids, poussée, Sport: concurrent, équipe*) to support; (*conséquences, épreuve*) to bear, endure; (*défauts, personne*) to tolerate, put up with; (*chose: chaleur etc*) to withstand; (*personne: chaleur, vin*) to take

supposé, e [sypoze] *adj* (*nombre*) estimated; (*auteur*) supposed

supposer [sypoze] *vt* to suppose; (*impliquer*) to presuppose; **en supposant** *ou* **à ~ que** supposing (that)

supposition [sypozisjɔ̃] *nf* supposition

suppositoire [sypozitwaʀ] *nm* suppository

suppôt [sypo] *nm* (*péj*) henchman

suppression [sypʀesjɔ̃] *nf* (*voir supprimer*) removal; deletion; cancellation; suppression

supprimer [sypʀime] *vt* (*cloison, cause, anxiété*) to remove; (*clause, mot*) to delete; (*congés, service d'autobus etc*) to cancel; (*publication, article*) to suppress; (*emplois, privilèges, témoin gênant*) to do away with; **~ qch à qn** to deprive sb of sth

suppurer [sypyʀe] *vi* to suppurate

supputations [sypytɑsjɔ̃] *nfpl* calculations, reckonings

supputer [sypyte] *vt* to calculate, reckon

supranational, e, -aux [sypʀanasjɔnal, -o] *adj* supranational

suprématie [sypʀemasi] *nf* supremacy

suprême [sypʀɛm] *adj* supreme

suprêmement [sypʀɛmmɑ̃] *adv* supremely

 MOT-CLÉ

sur¹ [syʀ] *prép* **1** (*position*) on; (*par-dessus*) over; (*au-dessus*) above; **pose-le sur la table** put it on the table; **je n'ai pas d'argent sur moi** I haven't any money on me
2 (*direction*) towards; **en allant sur Paris** going towards Paris; **sur votre droite** on *ou* to your right
3 (*à propos de*) on, about; **un livre/une conférence sur Balzac** a book/lecture on *ou* about Balzac
4 (*proportion, mesures*) out of; by; **un sur 10** one in 10; (*Scol*) one out of 10; **sur 20, deux sont venus** out of 20, two came; **4 m sur 2** 4 m by 2; **avoir accident sur accident** to have one accident after another
5 (*cause*): **sur sa recommandation** on *ou* at his recommendation; **sur son invitation** at his invitation
6: **sur ce** *adv* whereupon; **sur ce, il faut que je vous quitte** and now I must leave you

sur², e [syʀ] *adj* sour

sûr, e [syʀ] *adj* sure, certain; (*digne de confiance*) reliable; (*sans danger*) safe; **peu ~** unreliable; **~ de qch** sure *ou* certain of sth; **être ~ de qn** to be sure of sb; **~ et certain** absolutely certain; **~ de soi** self-assured, self-confident; **le plus ~ est de** the safest thing is to

surabondance [syʀabɔ̃dɑ̃s] *nf* overabundance

surabondant, e [syʀabɔ̃dɑ̃, -ɑ̃t] *adj* overabundant

surabonder [syʀabɔ̃de] *vi* to be overabundant; **~ de** to abound with, have an overabundance of

suractivité [syʀaktivite] *nf* hyperactivity

suraigu, ë [syʀegy] *adj* very shrill

surajouter [syʀaʒute] *vt*: **~ qch à** to add sth to

suralimentation [syʀalimɑ̃tɑsjɔ̃] *nf* overfeeding; (*Tech: d'un moteur*) supercharging

suralimenté, e [syʀalimɑ̃te] *adj* (*personne*) overfed; (*moteur*) supercharged

suranné, e [syʀane] *adj* outdated, outmoded

surarmement [syʀaʀməmɑ̃] *nm* (*excess*) stockpiling of arms (*ou* weapons)

surbaissé, e [syʀbese] *adj* lowered, low

surcapacité [syʀkapasite] *nf* overcapacity

surcharge [syʀʃaʀʒ(ə)] *nf* (*de passagers, marchandises*) excess load; (*de détails, d'ornements*) overabundance, excess; (*correction*) alteration; (*Postes*) surcharge; **prendre des passagers en ~** to take on excess *ou* extra passengers; **~ de bagages** excess luggage; **~ de travail** extra work

surchargé, e [syʀʃaʀʒe] *adj* (*décoration, style*) over-elaborate, overfussy; (*voiture, emploi du temps*) overloaded

surcharger [syʀʃaʀʒe] *vt* to overload; (*timbre-poste*) to surcharge; (*décoration*) to overdo

surchauffe [syʀʃof] *nf* overheating

surchauffé, e [syʀʃofe] *adj* overheated; (*fig: imagination*) overactive

surchoix [syʀʃwa] *adj inv* top-quality

surclasser [syʀklase] *vt* to outclass

surconsommation [syʀkɔ̃sɔmɑsjɔ̃] *nf* (*Écon*) overconsumption

surcoté, e [syʀkɔte] *adj* overpriced

surcouper [syʀkupe] *vt* to overtrump

surcroît [syʀkʀwa] *nm*: **~ de qch** additional sth; **par** *ou* **de ~** moreover; **en ~** in addition

surdi-mutité [syʀdimytite] *nf*: **atteint de ~** deaf and dumb

surdité [syʀdite] *nf* deafness; **atteint de ~ totale** profoundly deaf

surdoué, e [syʀdwe] *adj* gifted

sureau, x [syʀo] *nm* elder (tree)

sureffectif [syʀefɛktif] *nm* overmanning

surélever [syʀelve] *vt* to raise, heighten

sûrement [syʀmɑ̃] *adv* reliably; safely, securely; (*certainement*) certainly; **~ pas** certainly not

suremploi [syʀɑ̃plwa] *nm* (*Écon*) overemployment

surenchère [syʀɑ̃ʃɛʀ] *nf* (*aux enchères*) higher bid; (*sur prix fixe*) overbid; (*fig*) overstatement; outbidding tactics *pl*; ~ **de violence** build-up of violence; ~ **électorale** political (*ou* electoral) one-upmanship

surenchérir [syʀɑ̃ʃeʀiʀ] *vi* to bid higher; to raise one's bid; (*fig*) to try and outbid each other

surendettement [syʀɑ̃dɛtmɑ̃] *nm* excessive debt

surent [syʀ] *vb voir* **savoir**

surentraîné, e [syʀɑ̃tʀene] *adj* overtrained

suréquipé, e [syʀekipe] *adj* overequipped

surestimer [syʀɛstime] *vt* (*tableau*) to overvalue; (*possibilité, personne*) to overestimate

sûreté [syʀte] *nf* (*voir sûr*) reliability; safety; (*Jur*) guaranty; surety; **mettre en** ~ to put in a safe place; **pour plus de** ~ as an extra precaution; to be on the safe side; **la** ~ **de l'État** State security; **la S~ (nationale)** *division of the Ministère de l'Intérieur heading all police forces except the gendarmerie and the Paris préfecture de police*

surexcité, e [syʀɛksite] *adj* overexcited

surexciter [syʀɛksite] *vt* (*personne*) to overexcite; **cela surexcite ma curiosité** it really rouses my curiosity

surexploiter [syʀɛksplwate] *vt* to overexploit

surexposer [syʀɛkspoze] *vt* to overexpose

surf [sœʀf] *nm* surfing; **faire du** ~ to go surfing

surface [syʀfas] *nf* surface; (*superficie*) surface area; **faire** ~ to surface; **en** ~ *adv* near the surface; (*fig*) superficially; **la pièce fait 100 m²** **de** ~ the room has a surface area of 100m²; ~ **de** **réparation** (*Sport*) penalty area; ~ **porteuse** *ou* **de sustentation** (*Aviat*) aerofoil

surfait, e [syʀfɛ, -ɛt] *adj* overrated

surfer [sœʀfe] *vi* to surf; ~ **sur Internet** to surf the Internet

surfeur, -euse [sœʀfʀ, -øz] *nm/f* surfer

surfiler [syʀfile] *vt* (*Couture*) to oversew

surfin, e [syʀfɛ̃, -in] *adj* superfine

surgélateur [syʀʒelatœʀ] *nm* deep freeze

surgélation [syʀʒelasjɔ̃] *nf* deep-freezing

surgelé, e [syʀʒəle] *adj* (deep-)frozen

surgeler [syʀʒəle] *vt* to (deep-)freeze

surgir [syʀʒiʀ] *vi* (*personne, véhicule*) to appear suddenly; (*jaillir*) to shoot up; (*montagne etc*) to rise up, loom up; (*fig: problème, conflit*) to arise

surhomme [syʀɔm] *nm* superman

surhumain, e [syʀymɛ̃, -ɛn] *adj* superhuman

surimposer [syʀɛ̃poze] *vt* to overtax

surimpression [syʀɛ̃pʀesjɔ̃] *nf* (*Photo*) double exposure; **en** ~ superimposed

surimprimer [syʀɛ̃pʀime] *vt* to overstrike, overprint

Surinam [syʀinam] *nm*: **le** ~ Surinam

surinfection [syʀɛ̃fɛksjɔ̃] *nf* (*Méd*) secondary infection

surjet [syʀʒɛ] *nm* (*Couture*) overcast seam

sur-le-champ [syʀləʃɑ̃] *adv* immediately

surlendemain [syʀlɑ̃dmɛ̃] *nm*: **le** ~ (**soir**) two days later (in the evening); **le** ~ **de** two days after

surligneur [syʀliɲœʀ] *nm* (*feutre*) highlighter (pen)

surmenage [syʀmənaʒ] *nm* overwork; **le** ~ **intellectuel** mental fatigue

surmené, e [syʀmene] *adj* overworked

surmener [syʀmene] *vt*, **se surmener** *vi* to overwork

surmonter [syʀmɔ̃te] *vt* (*coupole etc*) to surmount, top; (*vaincre*) to overcome, surmount

surmultiplié, e [syʀmyltiplije] *adj, nf*: (**vitesse**) ~**e** overdrive

surnager [syʀnaʒe] *vi* to float

surnaturel, le [syʀnatyʀɛl] *adj, nm* supernatural

surnom [syʀnɔ̃] *nm* nickname

surnombre [syʀnɔ̃bʀ(ə)] *nm*: **être en** ~ to be too many (*ou* one too many)

surnommer [syʀnɔme] *vt* to nickname

surnuméraire [syʀnymeʀɛʀ] *nm/f* supernumerary

suroît [syʀwa] *nm* sou'wester

surpasser [syʀpase] *vt* to surpass; **se surpasser** *vi* to surpass o.s., excel o.s.

surpayer [syʀpeje] *vt* (*personne*) to overpay; (*article etc*) to pay too much for

surpeuplé, e [syʀpœple] *adj* overpopulated

surpeuplement [syʀpœpləmɑ̃] *nm* overpopulation

surpiquer [syʀpike] *vt* (*Couture*) to overstitch

surpiqûre [syʀpikyʀ] *nf* (*Couture*) overstitching

surplace [syʀplas] *nm*: **faire du** ~ to mark time

surplis [syʀpli] *nm* surplice

surplomb [syʀplɔ̃] *nm* overhang; **en** ~ overhanging

surplomber [syʀplɔ̃be] *vi* to be overhanging ▷ *vt* to overhang; (*dominer*) to tower above

surplus [syʀply] *nm* (*Comm*) surplus; (*reste*): ~ **de** **bois** wood left over; **au** ~ moreover; ~ **américains** American army surplus *sg*

surpopulation [syʀpɔpylasjɔ̃] *nf* overpopulation

surprenant, e [syʀpʀənɑ̃, -ɑ̃t] *vb voir* **surprendre** ▷ *adj* amazing

surprendre [syʀpʀɑ̃dʀ(ə)] *vt* (*étonner, prendre à l'improviste*) to amaze, surprise; (*secret*) to discover; (*tomber sur: intrus etc*) to catch; (*fig*) to detect; to chance *ou* happen upon; (*clin d'œil*) to intercept; (*conversation*) to overhear; (*orage, nuit etc*) to catch out, take by surprise; ~ **la** **vigilance/bonne foi de qn** to catch sb out/ betray sb's good faith; **se** ~ **à faire** to catch *ou* find o.s. doing

surprime [syʀpʀim] *nf* additional premium

surpris, e [syʀpʀi, -iz] *pp de* **surprendre** ▷ *adj*: ~ **(de/que)** amazed *ou* surprised (at/that)

surprise [syʀpʀiz] *nf* surprise; **faire une** ~ **à qn** to give sb a surprise; **voyage sans** ~**s** uneventful journey; **par** ~ *adv* by surprise

surprise-partie [syʀpʀizpaʀti] *nf* party

surprit [syʀpʀi] *vb voir* **surprendre**

surproduction [syʀpʀɔdyksjɔ̃] *nf* overproduction

surréaliste [syʀʀealist(ə)] *adj, nm/f* surrealist

sursaut [syʀso] *nm* start, jump; ~ **de** (*énergie, indignation*) sudden fit *ou* burst of; **en ~** *adv* with a start

sursauter [syʀsote] *vi* to (give a) start, jump

surseoir [syʀswaʀ]: ~ **à** *vt* to defer; (*Jur*) to stay

sursis [syʀsi] *nm* (*Jur: gén*) suspended sentence; (*à l'exécution capitale, aussi fig*) reprieve; (*Mil*): ~ **(d'appel** *ou* **d'incorporation)** deferment; **condamné à cinq mois (de prison) avec ~** given a five-month suspended (prison) sentence

sursitaire [syʀsitɛʀ] *nm* (*Mil*) deferred conscript

sursois [syʀswa], **sursoyais** *etc* [syʀswaje] *vb voir* **surseoir**

surtaxe [syʀtaks(ə)] *nf* surcharge

surtension [syʀtɑ̃sjɔ̃] *nf* (*Élec*) overvoltage

surtout [syʀtu] *adv* (*avant tout, d'abord*) above all; (*spécialement, particulièrement*) especially; **il aime le sport, ~ le football** he likes sport, especially football; **cet été, il a ~ fait de la pêche** this summer he went fishing more than anything (else); ~ **pas d'histoires!** no fuss now!; ~, **ne dites rien!** whatever you do – don't say anything!; ~ **pas!** certainly *ou* definitely not!; ~ **que ...** especially as ...

survécu, e [syʀveky] *pp de* **survivre**

surveillance [syʀvɛjɑ̃s] *nf* watch; (*Police, Mil*) surveillance; **sous ~ médicale** under medical supervision; **la ~ du territoire** internal security; *voir aussi* **DST**

surveillant, e [syʀvɛjɑ̃, -ɑ̃t] *nm/f* (*de prison*) warder; (*Scol*) monitor; (*de travaux*) supervisor, overseer

surveiller [syʀveje] *vt* (*enfant, élèves, bagages*) to watch, keep an eye on; (*malade*) to watch over; (*prisonnier, suspect*) to keep (a) watch on; (*territoire, bâtiment*) to (keep) watch over; (*travaux, cuisson*) to supervise; (*Scol: examen*) to invigilate; **se surveiller** to keep a check *ou* watch on o.s.; ~ **son langage/sa ligne** to watch one's language/figure

survenir [syʀvəniʀ] *vi* (*incident, retards*) to occur, arise; (*événement*) to take place; (*personne*) to appear, arrive

survenu, e [syʀv(ə)ny] *pp de* **survenir**

survêt [syʀvɛt], **survêtement** [syʀvɛtmɑ̃] *nm* tracksuit (*Brit*), sweat suit (*US*)

survie [syʀvi] *nf* survival; (*Rel*) afterlife; **équipement de ~** survival equipment; **une ~ de quelques mois** a few more months of life

surviens [syʀvjɛ̃], **survint** *etc* [syʀvɛ̃] *vb voir* **survenir**

survit *etc* [syʀvi] *vb voir* **survivre**

survitrage [syʀvitʀaʒ] *nm* double-glazing

survivance [syʀvivɑ̃s] *nf* relic

survivant, e [syʀvivɑ̃, -ɑ̃t] *vb voir* **survivre** ▷ *nm/f* survivor

survivre [syʀvivʀ(ə)] *vi* to survive; ~ **à** *vt* (*accident etc*) to survive; (*personne*) to outlive; **la**

victime a peu de chance de ~ the victim has little hope of survival

survol [syʀvɔl] *nm* flying over

survoler [syʀvɔle] *vt* to fly over; (*fig: livre*) to skim through; (: *question, problèmes*) to skim over

survolté, e [syʀvɔlte] *adj* (*Élec*) stepped up, boosted; (*fig*) worked up

sus [sy(s)]: **en ~ de** *prép* in addition to, over and above; **en ~** *adv* in addition; ~ **à** *excl*: ~ **au tyran!** at the tyrant! ▷ *vb voir* **savoir**

susceptibilité [sysɛptibilite] *nf* sensitivity *no pl*

susceptible [sysɛptibl(ə)] *adj* touchy, sensitive; ~ **d'amélioration** *ou* **d'être amélioré** that can be improved, open to improvement; ~ **de faire** (*capacité*) able to do; (*probabilité*) liable to do

susciter [sysite] *vt* (*admiration*) to arouse; (*obstacles, ennuis*): ~ **(à qn)** to create (for sb)

susdit, e [sysdi, -dit] *adj* foresaid

susmentionné, e [sysmɑ̃sjɔne] *adj* above-mentioned

susnommé, e [sysnɔme] *adj* above-named

suspect, e [syspɛ(kt), -ɛkt(ə)] *adj* suspicious; (*témoignage, opinions, vin etc*) suspect ▷ *nm/f* suspect; **peu ~ de** most unlikely to be suspected of

suspecter [syspɛkte] *vt* to suspect; (*honnêteté de qn*) to question, have one's suspicions about; ~ **qn d'être/d'avoir fait qch** to suspect sb of being/having done sth

suspendre [syspɑ̃dʀ(ə)] *vt* (*accrocher: vêtement*): ~ **qch (à)** to hang sth up (on); (*fixer: lustre etc*): ~ **qch à** to hang sth from; (*interrompre, démettre*) to suspend; (*remettre*) to defer; **se ~ à** to hang from

suspendu, e [syspɑ̃dy] *pp de* **suspendre** ▷ *adj* (*accroché*): ~ **à** hanging on (*ou* from); (*perché*): ~ **au-dessus de** suspended over; (*Auto*): **bien/mal ~** with good/poor suspension; **être ~ aux lèvres de qn** to hang upon sb's every word

suspens [syspɑ̃]: **en ~** *adv* (*affaire*) in abeyance; **tenir en ~** to keep in suspense

suspense [syspɑ̃s] *nm* suspense

suspension [syspɑ̃sjɔ̃] *nf* suspension; deferment; (*Auto*) suspension; (*lustre*) pendant light fitting; **en ~** in suspension, suspended; ~ **d'audience** adjournment

suspicieux, -euse [syspisjø, -øz] *adj* suspicious

suspicion [syspisjɔ̃] *nf* suspicion

sustentation [systɑ̃tasjɔ̃] *nf* (*Aviat*) lift; **base** *ou* **polygone de ~** support polygon

sustenter [systɑ̃te]: **se sustenter** *vi* to take sustenance

susurrer [sysyʀe] *vt* to whisper

sut [sy] *vb voir* **savoir**

suture [sytyʀ] *nf*: **point de ~** stitch

suturer [sytyʀe] *vt* to stitch up, suture

suzeraineté [syzʀɛnte] *nf* suzerainty

svelte [svɛlt(ə)] *adj* slender, svelte

SVP *sigle* (= *s'il vous plaît*) please

Swaziland [swazilɑ̃d] *nm*: **le ~** Swaziland

sweat [swit] *nm* (*fam*) sweatshirt

sweat-shirt [switʃœʀt] (*pl* **-s**) *nm* sweatshirt

syllabe [silab] *nf* syllable

sylphide [silfid] *nf* (*fig*): **sa taille de ~** her sylph-like figure

sylvestre [silvɛstʀ(ə)] *adj*: **pin ~** Scots pine, Scotch fir

sylvicole [silvikɔl] *adj* forestry *cpd*

sylviculteur [silvikyltœʀ] *nm* forester

sylviculture [silvikyltyʀ] *nf* forestry, sylviculture

symbole [sɛ̃bɔl] *nm* symbol

symbolique [sɛ̃bɔlik] *adj* symbolic; (*geste, offrande*) token *cpd*; (*salaire, dommages-intérêts*) nominal

symboliquement [sɛ̃bɔlikmɑ̃] *adv* symbolically

symboliser [sɛ̃bɔlize] *vt* to symbolize

symétrie [simetʀi] *nf* symmetry

symétrique [simetʀik] *adj* symmetrical

symétriquement [simetʀikmɑ̃] *adv* symmetrically

sympa [sɛ̃pa] *adj inv* (= *sympathique*) nice; friendly; good

sympathie [sɛ̃pati] *nf* (*inclination*) liking; (*affinité*) fellow feeling; (*condoléances*) sympathy; **accueillir avec ~** (*projet*) to receive favourably; **avoir de la ~ pour qn** to like sb, have a liking for sb; **témoignages de ~** expressions of sympathy; **croyez à toute ma ~** you have my deepest sympathy

sympathique [sɛ̃patik] *adj* (*personne, figure*) nice, friendly, likeable; (*geste*) friendly; (*livre*) good; (*déjeuner*) nice; (*réunion, endroit*) pleasant, nice

sympathisant, e [sɛ̃patizɑ̃, -ɑ̃t] *nm/f* sympathizer

sympathiser [sɛ̃patize] *vi* (*voisins etc: s'entendre*) to get on (*Brit*) *ou* along (*US*) (well); (*: se fréquenter*) to socialize, see each other; **~ avec** to get on *ou* along (well) with, to see, socialize with

symphonie [sɛ̃fɔni] *nf* symphony

symphonique [sɛ̃fɔnik] *adj* (*orchestre, concert*) symphony *cpd*; (*musique*) symphonic

symposium [sɛ̃pozjɔm] *nm* symposium

symptomatique [sɛ̃ptɔmatik] *adj* symptomatic

symptôme [sɛ̃ptom] *nm* symptom

synagogue [sinagɔg] *nf* synagogue

synchrone [sɛ̃kʀɔn] *adj* synchronous

synchronique [sɛ̃kʀɔnik] *adj*: **tableau ~** synchronic table of events

synchronisation [sɛ̃kʀɔnizasjɔ̃] *nf* synchronization; (*Auto*): **~ des vitesses** synchromesh

synchronisé, e [sɛ̃kʀɔnize] *adj* synchronized

synchroniser [sɛ̃kʀɔnize] *vt* to synchronize

syncope [sɛ̃kɔp] *nf* (*Méd*) blackout; (*Mus*) syncopation; **tomber en ~** to faint, pass out

syncopé, e [sɛ̃kɔpe] *adj* syncopated

syndic [sɛ̃dik] *nm* managing agent

syndical, e, -aux [sɛ̃dikal, -o] *adj* (trade-)union *cpd*; **centrale ~e** group of affiliated trade unions

syndicalisme [sɛ̃dikalism(ə)] *nm* (*mouvement*) trade unionism; (*activités*) union(ist) activities *pl*

syndicaliste [sɛ̃dikalist(ə)] *nm/f* trade unionist

syndicat [sɛ̃dika] *nm* (*d'ouvriers, employés*) (trade(s)) union; (*autre association d'intérêts*) union, association; **~ d'initiative (SI)** tourist office *ou* bureau; **~ patronal** employers' syndicate, federation of employers; **~ de propriétaires** association of property owners

syndiqué, e [sɛ̃dike] *adj* belonging to a (trade) union; **non ~** non-union

syndiquer [sɛ̃dike]: **se syndiquer** *vi* to form a trade union; (*adhérer*) to join a trade union

syndrome [sɛ̃dʀom] *nm* syndrome; **~ prémenstruel** premenstrual syndrome (PMS)

synergie [sinɛʀʒi] *nf* synergy

synode [sinɔd] *nm* synod

synonyme [sinɔnim] *adj* synonymous ▷ *nm* synonym; **~ de** synonymous with

synopsis [sinɔpsis] *nm ou nf* synopsis

synoptique [sinɔptik] *adj*: **tableau ~** synoptic table

synovie [sinɔvi] *nf* synovia; **épanchement de ~** water on the knee

syntaxe [sɛ̃taks(ə)] *nf* syntax

synthèse [sɛ̃tɛz] *nf* synthesis; **faire la ~ de** to synthesize

synthétique [sɛ̃tetik] *adj* synthetic

synthétiser [sɛ̃tetize] *vt* to synthesize

synthétiseur [sɛ̃tetizœʀ] *nm* (*Mus*) synthesizer

syphilis [sifilis] *nf* syphilis

Syrie [siʀi] *nf*: **la ~** Syria

syrien, ne [siʀjɛ̃, -ɛn] *adj* Syrian ▷ *nm/f*: **Syrien, ne** Syrian

systématique [sistematik] *adj* systematic

systématiquement [sistematikmɑ̃] *adv* systematically

systématiser [sistematize] *vt* to systematize

système [sistɛm] *nm* system; **le ~ D** resourcefulness; **~ décimal** decimal system; **~ expert** expert system; **~ d'exploitation** (*Inform*) operating system; **~ immunitaire** immune system; **~ métrique** metric system; **~ solaire** solar system

Tt

T, t [te] *nm inv* T, t ▷ *abr* (= *tonne*) t; **T comme Thérèse** T for Tommy

t' [t(ə)] *pron voir* **te**

ta [ta] *adj poss voir* **ton**

tabac [taba] *nm* tobacco; (*aussi*: **débit** *ou* **bureau de tabac**) tobacconist's (shop) ▷ *adj inv*: (**couleur**) ~ buff, tobacco *cpd*; **passer qn à** ~ to beat sb up; **faire un** ~ (*fam*) to be a big hit; ~ **blond/brun** light/dark tobacco; ~ **gris** shag; ~ **à priser** snuff

tabagie [tabaʒi] *nf* smoke den

tabagisme [tabaʒism(ə)] *nm* nicotine addiction; ~ **passif** passive smoking

tabasser [tabase] *vt* to beat up

tabatière [tabatjɛʀ] *nf* snuffbox

tabernacle [tabɛʀnakl(ə)] *nm* tabernacle

table [tabl(ə)] *nf* table; **avoir une bonne** ~ to keep a good table; **à** ~! dinner *etc* is ready!; **se mettre à** ~ to sit down to eat; (*fig*: *fam*) to come clean; **mettre** *ou* **dresser/desservir la** ~ to lay *ou* set/clear the table; **faire** ~ **rase de** to make a clean sweep of; ~ **basse** coffee table; ~ **de cuisson** (*à l'électricité*) hotplate; (*au gas*) gas ring; ~ **d'écoute** wire-tapping set; ~ **d'harmonie** sounding board; ~ **d'hôte** set menu; ~ **de lecture** turntable; ~ **des matières** (table of) contents *pl*; ~ **de multiplication** multiplication table; ~ **des négociations** negotiating table; ~ **de nuit** *ou* **de chevet** bedside table; ~ **ronde** (*débat*) round table; ~ **roulante** (tea) trolley; ~ **de toilette** washstand; ~ **traçante** (*Inform*) plotter

tableau, x [tablo] *nm* (*Art*) painting; (*reproduction, fig*) picture; (*panneau*) board; (*schéma*) table, chart; ~ **d'affichage** notice board; ~ **de bord** dashboard; (*Aviat*) instrument panel; ~ **de chasse** tally; ~ **de contrôle** console, control panel; ~ **de maître** masterpiece; ~ **noir** blackboard

tablée [table] *nf* (*personnes*) table

tabler [table] *vi*: ~ **sur** to count *ou* bank on

tablette [tablɛt] *nf* (*planche*) shelf; ~ **de chocolat** bar of chocolate

tableur [tablœʀ] *nm* (*Inform*) spreadsheet

tablier [tablije] *nm* apron; (*de pont*) roadway; (*de cheminée*) (flue-)shutter

tabou, e [tabu] *adj, nm* taboo

tabouret [tabuʀɛ] *nm* stool

tabulateur [tabylatœʀ] *nm* (*Tech*) tabulator

tac [tak] *nm*: **du** ~ **au** ~ tit for tat

tache [taʃ] *nf* (*saleté*) stain, mark; (*Art*: *de couleur, lumière*) spot; splash, patch; **faire** ~ **d'huile** to spread, gain ground; ~ **de rousseur** *ou* **de son** freckle; ~ **de vin** (*sur la peau*) strawberry mark

tâche [tɑʃ] *nf* task; **travailler à la** ~ to do piecework

tacher [taʃe] *vt* to stain, mark; (*fig*) to sully, stain; **se tacher** *vi* (*fruits*) to become marked

tâcher [taʃe] *vi*: ~ **de faire** to try to do, endeavour (*Brit*) *ou* endeavor (*US*) to do

tâcheron [tɑʃʀɔ̃] *nm* (*fig*) drudge

tacheté, e [taʃte] *adj*: ~ **de** speckled *ou* spotted with

tachisme [taʃism(ə)] *nm* (*Peinture*) tachisme

tachygraphe [takigʀaf] *nm* tachograph

tachymètre [takimɛtʀ(ə)] *nm* tachometer

tacite [tasit] *adj* tacit

tacitement [tasitmɑ̃] *adv* tacitly

taciturne [tasityʀn(ə)] *adj* taciturn

tacot [tako] *nm* (*péj*: *voiture*) banger (*Brit*), clunker (*US*)

tact [takt] *nm* tact; **avoir du** ~ to be tactful, have tact

tacticien, ne [taktisjɛ̃, -ɛn] *nm/f* tactician

tactile [taktil] *adj* tactile

tactique [taktik] *adj* tactical ▷ *nf* (*technique*) tactics *nsg*; (*plan*) tactic

Tadjikistan [tadʒikistɑ̃] *nm* Tajikistan

taffetas [tafta] *nm* taffeta

Tage [taʒ] *nm*: **le** ~ the (river) Tagus

Tahiti [taiti] *nf* Tahiti

tahitien, ne [taisjɛ̃, -ɛn] *adj* Tahitian

taie [tɛ] *nf*: ~ (**d'oreiller**) pillowslip, pillowcase

taillader [tɑjade] *vt* to gash

taille [tɑj] *nf* cutting; pruning; (*milieu du corps*) waist; (*hauteur*) height; (*grandeur*) size; **de** ~ **à faire** capable of doing; **de** ~ *adj* sizeable; **quelle** ~ **faites- vous?** what size are you?

taillé, e [tɑje] *adj* (*moustache, ongles, arbre*) trimmed; ~ **pour** (*fait pour, apte à*) cut out for; tailor-made for; ~ **en pointe** sharpened to a point

taille-crayon, taille-crayons [tɑjkʀɛjɔ̃] *nm inv* pencil sharpener

tailler [tɑje] *vt* (*pierre, diamant*) to cut; (*arbre, plante*) to prune; (*vêtement*) to cut out; (*crayon*) to sharpen; **se tailler** *vt* (*ongles, barbe*) to trim, cut; (*fig: réputation*) to gain, win ▷ *vi* (*fam: s'enfuir*) to beat it; **~ dans** (*chair, bois*) to cut into; **~ grand/petit** to be on the large/small side

tailleur [tɑjœʀ] *nm* (*couturier*) tailor; (*vêtement*) suit, costume; **en ~** (*assis*) cross-legged; **~ de diamants** diamond-cutter

taillis [tɑji] *nm* copse

tain [tɛ̃] *nm* silvering; **glace sans ~** two-way mirror

taire [tɛʀ] *vt* to keep to o.s., conceal ▷ *vi*: **faire ~ qn** to make sb be quiet; (*fig*) to silence sb; **se taire** *vi* (*s'arrêter de parler*) to fall silent, stop talking; (*ne pas parler*) to be silent *ou* quiet; (*s'abstenir de s'exprimer*) to keep quiet; (*bruit, voix*) to disappear; **tais-toi!, taisez-vous!** be quiet!

Taiwan [tajwan] *nf* Taiwan

talc [talk] *nm* talc, talcum powder

talé, e [tale] *adj* (*fruit*) bruised

talent [talɑ̃] *nm* talent; **avoir du ~** to be talented, have talent

talentueux, -euse [talɑ̃tɥø, -øz] *adj* talented

talion [taljɔ̃] *nm*: **la loi du ~** an eye for an eye

talisman [talismɑ̃] *nm* talisman

talkie-walkie [tɔkiwɔki] *nm* walkie-talkie

taloche [talɔʃ] *nf* (*fam: claque*) slap; (*Tech*) plaster float

talon [talɔ̃] *nm* heel; (*de chèque, billet*) stub, counterfoil (*Brit*); **~s plats/aiguilles** flat/stiletto heels; **être sur les ~s de qn** to be on sb's heels; **tourner les ~s** to turn on one's heel; **montrer les ~s** (*fig*) to show a clean pair of heels

talonner [talɔne] *vt* to follow hard behind; (*fig*) to hound; (*Rugby*) to heel

talonnette [talɔnɛt] *nf* (*de chaussure*) heelpiece; (*de pantalon*) stirrup

talquer [talke] *vt* to put talc(um powder) on

talus [taly] *nm* embankment; **~ de remblai/déblai** embankment/excavation slope

tamarin [tamaʀɛ̃] *nm* (*Bot*) tamarind

tambour [tɑ̃buʀ] *nm* (*Mus, also Tech*) drum; (*musicien*) drummer; (*porte*) revolving door(s *pl*); **sans ~ ni trompette** unobtrusively

tambourin [tɑ̃buʀɛ̃] *nm* tambourine

tambouriner [tɑ̃buʀine] *vi*: **~ contre** to drum against *ou* on

tambour-major [tɑ̃buʀmaʒɔʀ] (*pl* **tambours-majors**) *nm* drum major

tamis [tami] *nm* sieve

Tamise [tamiz] *nf*: **la ~** the Thames

tamisé, e [tamize] *adj* (*fig*) subdued, soft

tamiser [tamize] *vt* to sieve, sift

tampon [tɑ̃pɔ̃] *nm* (*de coton, d'ouate*) pad; (*aussi*: **tampon hygiénique** *ou* **périodique**) tampon; (*amortisseur, Inform: aussi*: **mémoire tampon**) buffer; (*bouchon*) plug, stopper; (*cachet, timbre*) stamp; (*Chimie*) buffer; **~ buvard** blotter; **~ encreur** inking pad; **~ (à récurer)** scouring pad

tamponné, e [tɑ̃pɔne] *adj*: **solution ~e** buffer solution

tamponner [tɑ̃pɔne] *vt* (*timbres*) to stamp; (*heurter*) to crash *ou* ram into; (*essuyer*) to mop up; **se tamponner** (*voitures*) to crash (into each other)

tamponneuse [tɑ̃pɔnøz] *adj f*: **autos ~s** dodgems, bumper cars

tam-tam [tamtam] *nm* tomtom

tancer [tɑ̃se] *vt* to scold

tanche [tɑ̃ʃ] *nf* tench

tandem [tɑ̃dɛm] *nm* tandem; (*fig*) duo, pair

tandis [tɑ̃di]: **~ que** *conj* while

tangage [tɑ̃gaʒ] *nm* pitching (and tossing)

tangent, e [tɑ̃ʒɑ̃, -ɑ̃t] *adj* (*Math*): **~ à** tangential to; (*fam: de justesse*) close ▷ *nf* (*Math*) tangent

Tanger [tɑ̃ʒe] *n* Tangier

tango [tɑ̃go] *nm* (*Mus*) tango ▷ *adj inv* (*couleur*) dark orange

tanguer [tɑ̃ge] *vi* to pitch (and toss)

tanière [tanjɛʀ] *nf* lair, den

tanin [tanɛ̃] *nm* tannin

tank [tɑ̃k] *nm* tank

tanker [tɑ̃kɛʀ] *nm* tanker

tanné, e [tane] *adj* weather-beaten

tanner [tane] *vt* to tan

tannerie [tanʀi] *nf* tannery

tanneur [tanœʀ] *nm* tanner

tant [tɑ̃] *adv* so much; **~ de** (*sable, eau*) so much; (*gens, livres*) so many; **~ que** *conj* as long as; **~ que** (*comparatif*) as much as; **~ mieux** that's great; so much the better; **~ mieux pour lui** good for him; **~ pis** too bad; **un ~ soit peu** (*un peu*) a little bit; (*même un peu*) (even) remotely; **~ bien que mal** as well as can be expected; **~ s'en faut** far from it, not by a long way

tante [tɑ̃t] *nf* aunt

tantinet [tɑ̃tinɛ]: **un ~** *adv* a tiny bit

tantôt [tɑ̃to] *adv* (*parfois*): **~ ... ~** now ... now; (*cet après-midi*) this afternoon

Tanzanie [tɑ̃zani] *nf*: **la ~** Tanzania

tanzanien, ne [tɑ̃zanjɛ̃, -ɛn] *adj* Tanzanian

TAO *sigle f* (= *traduction assistée par ordinateur*) MAT (= *machine-aided translation*)

taon [tɑ̃] *nm* horsefly, gadfly

tapage [tapaʒ] *nm* uproar, din; (*fig*) fuss, row; **~ nocturne** (*Jur*) disturbance of the peace (*at night*)

tapageur, -euse [tapaʒœʀ, -øz] *adj* (*bruyant: enfants etc*) noisy; (*toilette*) loud, flashy; (*publicité*) obtrusive

tape [tap] *nf* slap

tape-à-l'œil [tapalœj] *adj inv* flashy, showy

taper [tape] *vt* (*personne*) to clout; (*porte*) to bang, slam; (*dactylographier*) to type (out); (*Inform*) to key(board); (*fam: emprunter*): **~ qn de 10 euros** to touch sb for 10 euros, cadge 10 euros off sb ▷ *vi* (*soleil*) to beat down; **se taper** *vt* (*fam: travail*) to get landed with; (: *boire, manger*) to down; **~ sur qn** to thump sb; (*fig*) to run sb down; **~ sur qch**

405

(*clou etc*) to hit sth; (*table etc*) to bang on sth; **~ à** (*porte etc*) to knock on; **~ dans** (*se servir*) to dig into; **~ des mains/pieds** to clap one's hands/ stamp one's feet; **~ (à la machine)** to type

tapi, e [tapi] *adj*: **~ dans/derrière** (*blotti*) crouching *ou* cowering in/behind; (*caché*) hidden away in/behind

tapinois [tapinwa]: **en ~** *adv* stealthily

tapioca [tapjɔka] *nm* tapioca

tapir [tapiʀ]: **se tapir** *vi* to hide away

tapis [tapi] *nm* carpet; (*de table*) cloth; **mettre sur le ~** (*fig*) to bring up for discussion; **aller au ~** (*Boxe*) to go down; **envoyer au ~** (*Boxe*) to floor; **~ roulant** conveyor belt; **~ de sol** (*de tente*) groundsheet; **~ de souris** (*Inform*) mouse mat

tapis-brosse [tapibʀɔs] *nm* doormat

tapisser [tapise] *vt* (*avec du papier peint*) to paper; (*recouvrir*): **~ qch (de)** to cover sth (with)

tapisserie [tapisʀi] *nf* (*tenture, broderie*) tapestry; (: *travail*) tapestry-making; (: *ouvrage*) tapestry work; (*papier peint*) wallpaper; (*fig*): **faire ~** to sit out, be a wallflower

tapissier, -ière [tapisje, -jɛʀ] *nm/f*: **~- décorateur** upholsterer and decorator

tapoter [tapɔte] *vt* to pat, tap

taquet [takɛ] *nm* (*cale*) wedge; (*cheville*) peg

taquin, e [takɛ̃, -in] *adj* teasing

taquiner [takine] *vt* to tease

taquinerie [takinʀi] *nf* teasing *no pl*

tarabiscoté, e [taʀabiskɔte] *adj* over-ornate, fussy

tarabuster [taʀabyste] *vt* to bother, worry

tarama [taʀama] *nm* (*Culin*) taramasalata

tarauder [taʀode] *vt* (*Tech*) to tap; to thread; (*fig*) to pierce

tard [taʀ] *adv* late; **au plus ~** at the latest; **plus ~** later (on) ▷ *nm*: **sur le ~** (*à une heure avancée*) late in the day; (*vers la fin de la vie*) late in life

tarder [taʀde] *vi* (*chose*) to be a long time coming; (*personne*): **~ à faire** to delay doing; **il me tarde d'être** I am longing to be; **sans (plus) ~** without (further) delay

tardif, -ive [taʀdif, -iv] *adj* (*heure, repas, fruit*) late; (*talent, goût*) late in developing

tardivement [taʀdivmɑ̃] *adv* late

tare [taʀ] *nf* (*Comm*) tare; (*fig*) defect; blemish

taré, e [taʀe] *nm/f* cretin

targette [taʀʒɛt] *nf* (*verrou*) bolt

targuer [taʀge]: **se ~ de** *vt* to boast about

tarif [taʀif] *nm* (*liste*) price list, tariff (*Brit*); (*barème*) rate, rates *pl*, tariff (*Brit*); (: *de taxis etc*) fares *pl*; **voyager à plein ~/à ~ réduit** to travel at full/reduced fare

tarifaire [taʀifɛʀ] *adj* (*voir tarif*) relating to price lists *etc*

tarifé, e [taʀife] *adj*: **~ 10 euros** priced at 10 euros

tarifer [taʀife] *vt* to fix the price *ou* rate for

tarification [taʀifikasjɔ̃] *nf* fixing of a price scale

tarir [taʀiʀ] *vi* to dry up, run dry ▷ *vt* to dry up

tarot [taʀo], **tarots** *nm(pl)* tarot cards

tartare [taʀtaʀ] *adj* (*Culin*) tartar(e)

tarte [taʀt(ə)] *nf* tart; **~ aux pommes/à la crème** apple/custard tart

tartelette [taʀtəlɛt] *nf* tartlet

tartine [taʀtin] *nf* slice of bread (and butter (*ou* jam)); **~ de miel** slice of bread and honey; **~ beurrée** slice of bread and butter

tartiner [taʀtine] *vt* to spread; **fromage à ~** cheese spread

tartre [taʀtʀ(ə)] *nm* (*des dents*) tartar; (*de chaudière*) fur, scale

tas [ta] *nm* heap, pile; (*fig*): **un ~ de** heaps of, lots of; **en ~** in a heap *ou* pile; **dans le ~** (*fig*) in the crowd; among them; **formé sur le ~** trained on the job

Tasmanie [tasmani] *nf*: **la ~** Tasmania

tasmanien, ne [tasmanjɛ̃, -ɛn] *adj* Tasmanian

tasse [tas] *nf* cup; **boire la ~** (*en se baignant*) to swallow a mouthful; **~ à café/thé** coffee/ teacup

tassé, e [tase] *adj*: **bien ~** (*café etc*) strong

tasseau, x [taso] *nm* length of wood

tassement [tasmɑ̃] *nm* (*de vertèbres*) compression; (*Écon, Pol*: *ralentissement*) fall-off, slowdown; (*Bourse*) dullness

tasser [tase] *vt* (*terre, neige*) to pack down; (*entasser*): **~ qch dans** to cram sth into; **se tasser** *vi* (*terrain*) to settle; (*personne*: *avec l'âge*) to shrink; (*fig*) to sort itself out, settle down

tâter [tate] *vt* to feel; (*fig*) to sound out; **~ de** (*prison etc*) to have a taste of; **se tâter** (*hésiter*) to be in two minds; **~ le terrain** (*fig*) to test the ground

tatillon, ne [tatijɔ̃, -ɔn] *adj* pernickety

tâtonnement [tatɔnmɑ̃] *nm*: **par ~s** (*fig*) by trial and error

tâtonner [tatɔne] *vi* to grope one's way along; (*fig*) to grope around (in the dark)

tâtons [tatɔ̃]: **à ~** *adv*: **chercher/avancer à ~** to grope around for/grope one's way forward

tatouage [tatwaʒ] *nm* tattooing; (*dessin*) tattoo

tatouer [tatwe] *vt* to tattoo

taudis [todi] *nm* hovel, slum

taule [tol] *nf* (*fam*) nick (*Brit*), jail

taupe [top] *nf* mole; (*peau*) moleskin

taupinière [topinjɛʀ] *nf* molehill

taureau, x [tɔro] *nm* bull; (*signe*): **le T~** Taurus, the Bull; **être du T~** to be Taurus

taurillon [tɔʀijɔ̃] *nm* bull-calf

tauromachie [tɔʀɔmaʃi] *nf* bullfighting

taux [to] *nm* rate; (*d'alcool*) level; **~ d'escompte** discount rate; **~ d'intérêt** interest rate; **~ de mortalité** mortality rate

tavelé, e [tavle] *adj* marked

taverne [tavɛʀn(ə)] *nf* inn, tavern

taxable [taksabl(ə)] *adj* taxable

taxation [taksasjɔ̃] *nf* taxation; (*Tél*) charges *pl*

taxe [taks(ə)] *nf* tax; (*douanière*) duty; **toutes ~s comprises (TTC)** inclusive of tax; **~ de base** (*Tél*) unit charge; **~ de séjour** tourist tax; **~ à *ou* sur la valeur ajoutée (TVA)** value added tax (VAT)

taxer [takse] *vt* (*personne*) to tax; (*produit*) to put a tax on, tax; ~ **qn de qch** (qualifier) to call sb sth; (accuser) to accuse sb of sth, tax sb with sth

taxi [taksi] nm taxi

taxidermie [taksidɛʀmi] nf taxidermy

taxidermiste [taksidɛʀmist(ə)] nm/f taxidermist

taximètre [taksimɛtʀ(ə)] nm (taxi)meter

taxiphone [taksifɔn] nm pay phone

TB abr = **très bien, très bon**

tbe abr (= très bon état) VGC, vgc

TCF sigle m (= Touring Club de France) ≈ AA ou RAC (Brit), ≈ AAA (US)

Tchad [tʃad] nm: **le ~** Chad

tchadien, ne [tʃadjɛ̃, -ɛn] adj Chad(ian), of ou from Chad

tchao [tʃao] excl (fam) bye(-bye)!

tchécoslovaque [tʃekɔslɔvak] adj Czechoslovak(ian) ▷ nm/f: **Tchécoslovaque** Czechoslovak(ian)

Tchécoslovaquie [tʃekɔslɔvaki] nf: **la ~** Czechoslovakia

tchèque [tʃɛk] adj Czech ▷ nm (Ling) Czech ▷ nm/f: **Tchèque** Czech; **la République ~** the Czech Republic

Tchétchénie [tʃetʃeni] nf: **la ~** Chechnya

TCS sigle m (= Touring Club de Suisse) ≈ AA ou RAC (Brit), ≈ AAA (US)

TD sigle mpl = **travaux dirigés**

te, t' [t(ə)] pron you; (réfléchi) yourself

té [te] nm T-square

technicien, ne [tɛknisjɛ̃, -ɛn] nm/f technician

technicité [tɛknisite] nf technical nature

technico-commercial, e, -aux [tɛknikokɔmɛʀsjal, -o] adj: **agent ~** sales technician

technique [tɛknik] adj technical ▷ nf technique

techniquement [tɛknikmɑ̃] adv technically

techno [tɛkno] nf (fam: Mus): **la (musique) ~** techno (music); (fam) = **technologie**

technocrate [tɛknɔkʀat] nm/f technocrat

technocratie [tɛknɔkʀasi] nf technocracy

technologie [tɛknɔlɔʒi] nf technology

technologique [tɛknɔlɔʒik] adj technological

technologue [tɛknɔlɔg] nm/f technologist

teck [tɛk] nm teak

teckel [tekɛl] nm dachshund

tee-shirt [tiʃœʀt] nm T-shirt, tee-shirt

Téhéran [teeʀɑ̃] n Teheran

teigne [tɛɲ] vb voir **teindre** ▷ nf (Zool) moth; (Méd) ringworm

teigneux, -euse [tɛɲø, -øz] adj (péj) nasty, scabby

teindre [tɛ̃dʀ(ə)] vt to dye; **se ~ (les cheveux)** to dye one's hair

teint, e [tɛ̃, tɛ̃t] pp de **teindre** ▷ adj dyed ▷ nm (du visage: permanent) complexion, colouring (Brit), coloring (US); (momentané) colour (Brit), color (US) ▷ nf shade, colour, color; (fig: petite dose): **une ~e de** a hint of; **grand ~** adj inv colourfast; **bon ~** adj inv (couleur) fast; (tissu) colourfast; (personne) staunch, firm

teinté, e [tɛ̃te] adj (verres) tinted; (bois) stained; **~ acajou** mahogany-stained; **~ de** (fig) tinged with

teinter [tɛ̃te] vt to tint; (bois) to stain; (fig: d'ironie etc) to tinge

teinture [tɛ̃tyʀ] nf dyeing; (substance) dye; (Méd): **~ d'iode** tincture of iodine

teinturerie [tɛ̃tyʀʀi] nf dry cleaner's

teinturier, -ière [tɛ̃tyʀje, -jɛʀ] nm/f dry cleaner

tel, telle [tɛl] adj (pareil) such; (indéfini) such-and-such a, a given; (comme): **~ un/des ...** like a/ like ...; (intensif): **un ~/de ~s ...** such (a)/such ...; **rien de ~** nothing like it, no such thing; **~ que** conj like, such as; **~ quel** as it is ou stands (ou was etc)

tél. abr = **téléphone**

Tel Aviv [tɛlaviv] n Tel Aviv

télé [tele] nf (télévision) TV, telly (Brit); **à la ~** on TV ou telly

télébenne [telebɛn] nm, nf telecabine, gondola

télécabine [telekabin] nm, nf telecabine, gondola

télécarte [telekaʀt(ə)] nf phonecard

téléchargeable [teleʃaʀʒabl] adj downloadable

téléchargement [teleʃaʀʒemɑ̃] nm (action) downloading; (fichier) download

télécharger [teleʃaʀʒe] vt (Inform) to download

TELECOM [telekɔm] abr (= Télécommunications) ≈ Telecom.

télécommande [telekɔmɑ̃d] nf remote control

télécommander [telekɔmɑ̃de] vt to operate by remote control, radio-control

télécommunications [telekɔmynikasjɔ̃] nfpl telecommunications

télécopie [telekɔpi] nf fax, telefax

télécopieur [telekɔpjœʀ] nm fax (machine)

télédétection [teledetɛksjɔ̃] nf remote sensing

télédiffuser [teledifyze] vt to broadcast (on television)

télédiffusion [teledifyzjɔ̃] nf television broadcasting

télédistribution [teledistʀibysjɔ̃] nf cable TV

téléenseignement [teleɑ̃sɛɲmɑ̃] nm distance teaching (ou learning)

téléférique [telefeʀik] nm = **téléphérique**

téléfilm [telefilm] nm film made for TV, TV film

télégramme [telegʀam] nm telegram

télégraphe [telegʀaf] nm telegraph

télégraphie [telegʀafi] nf telegraphy

télégraphier [telegʀafje] vt to telegraph, cable

télégraphique [telegʀafik] adj telegraph cpd, telegraphic; (fig) telegraphic

télégraphiste [telegʀafist(ə)] nm/f telegraphist

téléguider [telegide] vt to operate by remote control, radio-control

téléinformatique [teleɛ̃fɔʀmatik] nf remote access computing

téléjournal, -aux [teleʒuʀnal, -o] nm television news magazine programme

télématique [telematik] nf telematics nsg ▷ adj telematic

téléobjectif [teleɔbʒɛktif] nm telephoto lens nsg

407

téléopérateur, trice [teleɔpeʀatœʀ, tʀis] *nm/f* call-centre operator

télépathie [telepati] *nf* telepathy

téléphérique [telefeʀik] *nm* cable-car

téléphone [telefɔn] *nm* telephone; **avoir le ~** to be on the (tele)phone; **au ~** on the phone; **~ arabe** bush telegraph; **~ à carte** cardphone; **~ avec appareil photo** cameraphone; **~ mobile** *ou* **portable** mobile (phone) (*Brit*), cell (phone) (*US*); **~ rouge** hotline; **~ sans fil** cordless (tele)phone

téléphoner [telefɔne] *vt* to telephone ▷ *vi* to telephone; to make a phone call; **~ à** to phone up, ring up, call up

téléphonie [telefɔni] *nf* telephony

téléphonique [telefɔnik] *adj* telephone *cpd*, phone *cpd*; **cabine ~** call box (*Brit*), (tele)phone box (*Brit*) *ou* booth; **conversation/appel ~** (tele)phone conversation/call

téléphoniste [telefɔnist(ə)] *nm/f* telephonist, telephone operator; (*d'entreprise*) switchboard operator

téléport [telepɔʀ] *nm* teleport

téléprospection [telepʀɔspɛksjɔ̃] *nf* telesales

téléréalité [teleʀealite] *nf* reality TV

télescopage [telɛskɔpaʒ] *nm* crash

télescope [telɛskɔp] *nm* telescope

télescoper [telɛskɔpe] *vt* to smash up; **se télescoper** (*véhicules*) to collide, crash into each other

télescopique [telɛskɔpik] *adj* telescopic

téléscripteur [teleskʀiptœʀ] *nm* teleprinter

télésiège [telesjɛʒ] *nm* chairlift

téléski [teleski] *nm* ski-tow; **~ à archets** T-bar tow; **~ à perche** button lift

téléspectateur, -trice [telespɛktatœʀ, -tʀis] *nm/f* (television) viewer

télétexte® [teletɛkst] *nm* Teletext®

téléthon [teletɔ̃] *nm* telethon

télétransmission [teletʀɑ̃smisjɔ̃] *nf* remote transmission

télétype [teletip] *nm* teleprinter

télévente [televɑ̃t] *nf* telesales

téléviser [televize] *vt* to televise

téléviseur [televizœʀ] *nm* television set

télévision [televizjɔ̃] *nf* television; **(poste de) ~** television (set); **avoir la ~** to have a television; **à la ~** on television; **~ par câble/satellite** cable/satellite television

télex [telɛks] *nm* telex

télexer [telɛkse] *vt* to telex

télexiste [telɛksist(ə)] *nm/f* telex operator

telle [tɛl] *adj f voir* **tel**

tellement [tɛlmɑ̃] *adv* (*tant*) so much; (*si*) so; **~ plus grand (que)** so much bigger (than); **~ de** (*sable, eau*) so much; (*gens, livres*) so many; **il s'est endormi ~ il était fatigué** he was so tired (that) he fell asleep; **pas ~** not really; **pas ~ fort/lentement** not (all) that strong/slowly; **il ne mange pas ~** he doesn't eat (all that) much

tellurique [telyʀik] *adj*: **secousse ~** earth tremor

téméraire [temeʀɛʀ] *adj* reckless, rash

témérité [temeʀite] *nf* recklessness, rashness

témoignage [temwaɲaʒ] *nm* (*Jur: déclaration*) testimony *no pl*, evidence *no pl*; (: *faits*) evidence *no pl*; (*gén: rapport, récit*) account; (*fig: d'affection etc*) token, mark; expression

témoigner [temwaɲe] *vt* (*manifester: intérêt, gratitude*) to show ▷ *vi* (*Jur*) to testify, give evidence; **~ que** to testify that; (*fig: démontrer*) to reveal that, testify to the fact that; **~ de** *vt* (*confirmer*) to bear witness to, testify to

témoin [temwɛ̃] *nm* witness; (*fig*) testimony; (*Sport*) baton; (*Constr*) telltale ▷ *adj* control *cpd*, test *cpd*; **~ le fait que ...** (as) witness the fact that ...; **appartement-~** show flat (*Brit*), model apartment (*US*); **être ~ de** (*voir*) to witness; **prendre à ~** to call to witness; **~ à charge** witness for the prosecution; **T~ de Jehovah** Jehovah's Witness; **~ de moralité** character reference; **~ oculaire** eyewitness

tempe [tɑ̃p] *nf* (*Anat*) temple

tempérament [tɑ̃peʀamɑ̃] *nm* temperament, disposition; (*santé*) constitution; **à ~ (vente)** on deferred (payment) terms; (*achat*) by instalments, hire purchase *cpd*; **avoir du ~** to be hot-blooded

tempérance [tɑ̃peʀɑ̃s] *nf* temperance; **société de ~** temperance society

tempérant, e [tɑ̃peʀɑ̃, -ɑ̃t] *adj* temperate

température [tɑ̃peʀatyʀ] *nf* temperature; **prendre la ~ de** to take the temperature of; (*fig*) to gauge the feeling of; **avoir** *ou* **faire de la ~** to be running *ou* have a temperature

tempéré, e [tɑ̃peʀe] *adj* temperate

tempérer [tɑ̃peʀe] *vt* to temper

tempête [tɑ̃pɛt] *nf* storm; **~ de sable/neige** sand/snowstorm; **vent de ~** gale

tempêter [tɑ̃pete] *vi* to rant and rave

temple [tɑ̃pl(ə)] *nm* temple; (*protestant*) church

tempo [tɛmpo] *nm* tempo

temporaire [tɑ̃pɔʀɛʀ] *adj* temporary

temporairement [tɑ̃pɔʀɛʀmɑ̃] *adv* temporarily

temporel, le [tɑ̃pɔʀɛl] *adj* temporal

temporisateur, -trice [tɑ̃pɔʀizatœʀ, -tʀis] *adj* temporizing, delaying

temporisation [tɑ̃pɔʀizasjɔ̃] *nf* temporizing, playing for time

temporiser [tɑ̃pɔʀize] *vi* to temporize, play for time

temps [tɑ̃] *nm* (*atmosphérique*) weather; (*durée*) time; (*époque*) time, times *pl*; (*Ling*) tense; (*Mus*) beat; (*Tech*) stroke; **les ~ changent/sont durs** times are changing/hard; **il fait beau/mauvais ~** the weather is fine/bad; **avoir le ~/tout le ~/juste le ~** to have time/plenty of time/just enough time; **avoir fait son ~** (*fig*) to have had its (*ou* his *etc*) day; **en ~ de paix/guerre** in peacetime/wartime; **en ~ utile** *ou* **voulu** in due time *ou* course; **de ~ en ~, de ~ à autre** from time to time, now and again; **en même ~** at the same time; **à ~ (partir, arriver)** in time; **à plein/mi-~** *adv, adj* full-/part-time; **à ~ partiel** *adv, adj*

part-time; **dans le ~** at one time; **de tout ~**
always; **du ~ que** at the time when, in the days
when; **dans le** *ou* **du** *ou* **au ~ où** at the time
when; **pendant ce ~** in the meantime; **~
d'accès** (*Inform*) access time; **~ d'arrêt** pause,
halt; **~ mort** (*Sport*) stoppage (time); (*Comm*)
slack period; **~ partagé** (*Inform*) time-sharing; **~
réel** (*Inform*) real time
tenable [tənabl(ə)] *adj* bearable
tenace [tənas] *adj* tenacious, persistent
ténacité [tenasite] *nf* tenacity, persistence
tenailler [tənɑje] *vt* (*fig*) to torment, torture
tenailles [tənɑj] *nfpl* pincers
tenais *etc* [t(ə)nɛ] *vb voir* **tenir**
tenancier, -ière [tənɑsje, -jɛʀ] *nm/f* (*d'hôtel, de
bistro*) manager (manageress)
tenant, e [tənɑ̃, -ɑ̃t] *adj f voir* **séance** ▷ *nm/f*
(*Sport*): **~ du titre** title-holder ▷ *nm*: **d'un seul ~**
in one piece; **les ~s et les aboutissants** (*fig*) the
ins and outs
tendance [tɑ̃dɑ̃s] *nf* (*opinions*) leanings *pl*,
sympathies *pl*; (*inclination*) tendency; (*évolution*)
trend; **~ à la hausse/baisse** upward/downward
trend; **avoir ~ à** to have a tendency to, tend to
tendancieux, -euse [tɑ̃dɑ̃sjø, -øz] *adj*
tendentious
tendeur [tɑ̃dœʀ] *nm* (*de vélo*) chain-adjuster; (*de
câble*) wire-strainer; (*de tente*) runner; (*attache*)
elastic strap
tendinite [tɑ̃dinit] *nf* tendinitis, tendonitis
tendon [tɑ̃dɔ̃] *nm* tendon, sinew; **~ d'Achille**
Achilles' tendon
tendre [tɑ̃dʀ(ə)] *adj* (*viande, légumes*) tender; (*bois,
roche, couleur*) soft; (*affectueux*) tender, loving ▷ *vt*
(*élastique, peau*) to stretch, draw tight; (*muscle*) to
tense; (*donner*): **~ qch à qn** to hold sth out to sb;
to offer sb sth; (*fig: piège*) to set, lay; (*tapisserie*):
tendu de soie hung with silk, with silk
hangings; **se tendre** *vi* (*corde*) to tighten;
(*relations*) to become strained; **~ à qch/à faire** to
tend towards sth/to do; **~ l'oreille** to prick up
one's ears; **~ la main/le bras** to hold out one's
hand/stretch out one's arm; **~ la perche à qn**
(*fig*) to throw sb a line
tendrement [tɑ̃dʀəmɑ̃] *adv* tenderly, lovingly
tendresse [tɑ̃dʀɛs] *nf* tenderness; **tendresses**
nfpl (*caresses etc*) tenderness *no pl*, caresses
tendu, e [tɑ̃dy] *pp de* **tendre** ▷ *adj* tight; tensed;
strained
ténèbres [tenɛbʀ(ə)] *nfpl* darkness *nsg*
ténébreux, -euse [tenebʀø, -øz] *adj* obscure,
mysterious; (*personne*) saturnine
Ténérife [teneʀif] *nf* Tenerife
teneur [tənœʀ] *nf* content, substance; (*d'une
lettre*) terms *pl*, content; **~ en cuivre** copper
content
ténia [tenja] *nm* tapeworm
tenir [təniʀ] *vt* to hold; (*magasin, hôtel*) to run;
(*promesse*) to keep ▷ *vi* to hold; (*neige, gel*) to last;
(*survivre*) to survive; **se tenir** *vi* (*avoir lieu*) to be
held, take place; (*être: personne*) to stand; **se ~
droit** to stand up (*ou* sit up) straight; **bien se ~**

to behave well; **se ~ à qch** to hold on to sth;
s'en ~ à qch to confine o.s. to sth; to stick to sth;
~ à *vt* to be attached to, care about (*ou* for); (*avoir
pour cause*) to be due to, stem from; **~ à faire** to
want to do, be keen to do; **~ à ce que qn fasse
qch** to be anxious that sb should do sth; **~ de** *vt*
to partake of; (*ressembler à*) to take after; **ça ne
tient qu'à lui** it is entirely up to him; **~ qn
pour** to take sb for; **~ qch de qn** (*histoire*) to have
heard *ou* learnt sth from sb; (*qualité, défaut*) to
have inherited *ou* got sth from sb; **~ les
comptes** to keep the books; **~ un rôle** to play a
part; **~ de la place** to take up space *ou* room; **~
l'alcool** to be able to hold a drink; **~ le coup** to
hold out; **~ bon** to stand *ou* hold fast; **~ trois
jours/deux mois** (*résister*) to hold out *ou* last
three days/two months; **~ au chaud/à l'abri** to
keep hot/under shelter *ou* cover; **~ prêt** to have
ready; **~ sa langue** (*fig*) to hold one's tongue;
tiens (*ou* **tenez**), **voilà le stylo** there's the pen!;
tiens, Alain! look, here's Alain!; **tiens?**
(*surprise*) really?; **tiens-toi bien!** (*pour informer*)
brace yourself!, take a deep breath!
tennis [tenis] *nm* tennis; (*aussi*: **court de tennis**)
tennis court ▷ *nmpl ou fpl* (*aussi*: **chaussures de
tennis**) tennis *ou* gym shoes; **~ de table** table
tennis
tennisman [tenisman] *nm* tennis player
ténor [tenɔʀ] *nm* tenor
tension [tɑ̃sjɔ̃] *nf* tension; (*fig: des relations, de la
situation*) tension; (: *concentration, effort*) strain;
(*Méd*) blood pressure; **faire** *ou* **avoir de la ~** to
have high blood pressure; **~ nerveuse/raciale**
nervous/racial tension
tentaculaire [tɑ̃takylɛʀ] *adj* (*fig*) sprawling
tentacule [tɑ̃takyl] *nm* tentacle
tentant, e [tɑ̃tɑ̃, -ɑ̃t] *adj* tempting
tentateur, -trice [tɑ̃tatœʀ, -tʀis] *adj* tempting
▷ *nm* (*Rel*) tempter
tentation [tɑ̃tasjɔ̃] *nf* temptation
tentative [tɑ̃tativ] *nf* attempt, bid; **~ d'évasion**
escape bid; **~ de suicide** suicide attempt
tente [tɑ̃t] *nf* tent; **~ à oxygène** oxygen tent
tenter [tɑ̃te] *vt* (*éprouver, attirer*) to tempt;
(*essayer*): **~ qch/de faire** to attempt *ou* try sth/to
do; **être tenté de** to be tempted to; **~ sa chance**
to try one's luck
tenture [tɑ̃tyʀ] *nf* hanging
tenu, e [təny] *pp de* **tenir** ▷ *adj* (*maison, comptes*):
bien ~ well-kept; (*obligé*): **~ de faire** under an
obligation to do ▷ *nf* (*action de tenir*) running;
keeping; holding; (*vêtements*) clothes *pl*, gear;
(*allure*) dress *no pl*, appearance; (*comportement*)
manners *pl*, behaviour (*Brit*), behavior (*US*);
être en ~e to be dressed (up); **se mettre en ~e**
to dress (up); **en grande ~e** in full dress; **en
petite ~e** scantily dressed *ou* clad; **avoir de la
~e** to have good manners; (*journal*) to have a
high standard; **~e de combat** combat gear *ou*
dress; **~e de pompier** fireman's uniform; **~e
de route** (*Auto*) road-holding; **~e de soirée**
evening dress; **~e de sport/voyage** sports/

travelling clothes *pl ou* gear *no pl*

ténu, e [teny] *adj (indice, nuance)* tenuous, subtle; *(fil, objet)* fine; *(voix)* thin

TER *abr m* (= *Train Régional Express*) local train

ter [tɛʁ] *adj*: **16 ~ 16b** *ou* **B**

térébenthine [teʁebɑ̃tin] *nf*: **(essence de) ~** (oil of) turpentine

tergal® [tɛʁɡal] *nm* Terylene®

tergiversations [tɛʁʒivɛʁsasjɔ̃] *nfpl* shilly-shallying *no pl*

tergiverser [tɛʁʒivɛʁse] *vi* to shilly-shally

terme [tɛʁm(ə)] *nm* term; *(fin)* end; **être en bons/mauvais ~s avec qn** to be on good/bad terms with sb; **vente/achat à ~** *(Comm)* forward sale/purchase; **au ~ de** at the end of; **en d'autres ~s** in other words; **moyen ~** *(solution intermédiaire)* middle course; **à court/long ~** *adj* short-/long-term *ou* -range ▷ *adv* in the short/long term; **à ~** *adj (Méd)* full-term ▷ *adv* sooner or later, eventually; *(Méd)* at term; **avant ~** *(Méd)* ▷ *adj* premature ▷ *adv* prematurely; **mettre un ~ à** to put an end *ou* a stop to; **toucher à son ~** to be nearing its end

terminaison [tɛʁminɛzɔ̃] *nf (Ling)* ending

terminal, e, -aux [tɛʁminal, -o] *adj (partie, phase)* final; *(Méd)* terminal ▷ *nm* terminal ▷ *nf (Scol)* ≈ sixth form *ou* year *(Brit)*, ≈ twelfth grade *(US)*

terminer [tɛʁmine] *vt* to end; *(travail, repas)* to finish; **se terminer** *vi* to end; **se ~ par** to end with

terminologie [tɛʁminɔlɔʒi] *nf* terminology

terminus [tɛʁminys] *nm* terminus; **~!** all change!

termite [tɛʁmit] *nm* termite, white ant

termitière [tɛʁmitjɛʁ] *nf* ant-hill

ternaire [tɛʁnɛʁ] *adj* compound

terne [tɛʁn(ə)] *adj* dull

ternir [tɛʁniʁ] *vt* to dull; *(fig)* to sully, tarnish; **se ternir** *vi* to become dull

terrain [tɛʁɛ̃] *nm (sol, fig)* ground; *(Comm)* land *no pl*, plot (of land); (: *à bâtir*) site; **sur le ~** *(fig)* on the field; **~ de football/rugby** football/rugby pitch *(Brit) ou* field *(US)*; **~ d'atterrissage** landing strip; **~ d'aviation** airfield; **~ de camping** campsite; **un ~ d'entente** an area of agreement; **~ de golf** golf course; **~ de jeu** playground; *(Sport)* games field; **~ de sport** sports ground; **~ vague** waste ground *no pl*

terrasse [tɛʁas] *nf* terrace; *(de café)* pavement area, terrasse; **à la ~** *(café)* outside

terrassement [tɛʁasmɑ̃] *nm* earth-moving, earthworks *pl*; embankment

terrasser [tɛʁase] *vt (adversaire)* to floor, bring down; *(maladie etc)* to lay low

terrassier [tɛʁasje] *nm* navvy, roadworker

terre [tɛʁ] *nf (gén, aussi Élec)* earth; *(substance)* soil, earth; *(opposé à mer)* land *no pl*; *(contrée)* land; **terres** *nfpl (terrains)* lands, land *nsg*; **travail de la ~** work on the land; **en ~** *(pipe, poterie)* clay *cpd*; **mettre en ~** *(plante etc)* to plant; *(personne: enterrer)* to bury; **à** *ou* **par ~** *(mettre, être)* on the ground *(ou* floor); *(jeter, tomber)* to the ground,

down; **~ à ~** *adj inv* down-to-earth, matter-of-fact; **la T~ Adélie** Adélie Coast *ou* Land; **~ de bruyère** (heath-)peat; **~ cuite** earthenware; terracotta; **la ~ ferme** dry land, terra firma; **la T~ de Feu** Tierra del Fuego; **~ glaise** clay; **la T~ promise** the Promised Land; **la T~ Sainte** the Holy Land

terreau [tɛʁo] *nm* compost

Terre-Neuve [tɛʁnœv] *nf*: **la ~** *(aussi*: **l'île de Terre-Neuve)** Newfoundland

terre-plein [tɛʁplɛ̃] *nm* platform

terrer [tɛʁe]: **se terrer** *vi* to hide away; to go to ground

terrestre [tɛʁɛstʁ(ə)] *adj (surface)* earth's, of the earth; *(Bot, Zool, Mil)* land *cpd*; *(Rel)* earthly, worldly

terreur [tɛʁœʁ] *nf* terror *no pl*, fear

terreux, -euse [tɛʁø, -øz] *adj* muddy; *(goût)* earthy

terrible [tɛʁibl(ə)] *adj* terrible, dreadful; *(fam: fantastique)* terrific

terriblement [tɛʁibləmɑ̃] *adv (très)* terribly, awfully

terrien, ne [tɛʁjɛ̃, -ɛn] *adj*: **propriétaire ~** landowner ▷ *nm/f* countryman/woman, man/woman of the soil; *(non martien etc)* earthling; *(non marin)* landsman

terrier [tɛʁje] *nm* burrow, hole; *(chien)* terrier

terrifiant, e [tɛʁifjɑ̃, -ɑ̃t] *adj (effrayant)* terrifying; *(extraordinaire)* terrible, awful

terrifier [tɛʁifje] *vt* to terrify

terril [tɛʁil] *nm* slag heap

terrine [tɛʁin] *nf (récipient)* terrine; *(Culin)* pâté

territoire [tɛʁitwaʁ] *nm* territory; **T~ des Afars et des Issas** French Territory of Afars and Issas

territorial, e, -aux [tɛʁitɔʁjal, -o] *adj* territorial; **eaux ~es** territorial waters; **armée ~e** regional defence force, ≈ Territorial Army *(Brit)*; **collectivités ~es** local and regional authorities

terroir [tɛʁwaʁ] *nm (Agr)* soil; *(région)* region; **accent du ~** country *ou* rural accent

terroriser [tɛʁɔʁize] *vt* to terrorize

terrorisme [tɛʁɔʁism(ə)] *nm* terrorism

terroriste [tɛʁɔʁist(ə)] *nm/f* terrorist

tertiaire [tɛʁsjɛʁ] *adj* tertiary ▷ *nm (Écon)* tertiary sector, service industries *pl*

tertiarisation [tɛʁsjaʁizasjɔ̃] *nf* expansion or development of the service sector

tertre [tɛʁtʁ(ə)] *nm* hillock, mound

tes [te] *adj poss voir* **ton**

tesson [tesɔ̃] *nm*: **~ de bouteille** piece of broken bottle

test [tɛst] *nm* test; **~ de grossesse** pregnancy test

testament [tɛstamɑ̃] *nm (Jur)* will; *(fig)* legacy; *(Rel)*: **T~** Testament; **faire son ~** to make one's will

testamentaire [tɛstamɑ̃tɛʁ] *adj* of a will

tester [tɛste] *vt* to test

testicule [tɛstikyl] *nm* testicle

tétanie [tetani] *nf* tetany

tétanos [tetanos] *nm* tetanus

têtard [tɛtaʀ] *nm* tadpole

tête [tɛt] *nf* head; (*cheveux*) hair *no pl*; (*visage*) face; (*longueur*): **gagner d'une (courte)** ~ to win by a (short) head; (*Football*) header; **de** ~ *adj* (*wagon etc*) front *cpd*; (*concurrent*) leading ▷ *adv* (*calculer*) in one's head, mentally; **par** ~ (*par personne*) per head; **se mettre en** ~ **que** to get it into one's head that; **se mettre en** ~ **de faire** to take it into one's head to do; **prendre la** ~ **de qch** to take the lead in sth; **perdre la** ~ (*fig: s'affoler*) to lose one's head; (: *devenir fou*) to go off one's head; **ça ne va pas, la** ~**?** (*fam*) are you crazy?; **tenir** ~ **à qn** to stand up to *ou* defy sb; **la** ~ **en bas** with one's head down; **la** ~ **la première** (*tomber*) head-first; **la** ~ **basse** hanging one's head; **avoir la** ~ **dure** (*fig*) to be thickheaded; **faire une** ~ (*Football*) to head the ball; **faire la** ~ (*fig*) to sulk; **en** ~ (*Sport*) in the lead; at the front *ou* head; **de la** ~ **aux pieds** from head to toe; ~ **d'affiche** (*Théât etc*) top of the bill; ~ **de bétail** head *inv* of cattle; ~ **brûlée** desperado; ~ **chercheuse** homing device; ~ **d'enregistrement** recording head; ~ **d'impression** printhead; ~ **de lecture** (playback) head; ~ **de ligne** (*Transports*) start of the line; ~ **de liste** (*Pol*) chief candidate; ~ **de mort** skull and crossbones; ~ **de pont** (*Mil*) bridge- *ou* beachhead; ~ **de série** (*Tennis*) seeded player, seed; ~ **de Turc** (*fig*) whipping boy (*Brit*), butt; ~ **de veau** (*Culin*) calf's head

tête-à-queue [tɛtakø] *nm inv*: **faire un** ~ to spin round

tête-à-tête [tɛtatɛt] *nm inv* tête- à-tête; (*service*) breakfast set for two; **en** ~ in private, alone together

tête-bêche [tɛtbɛʃ] *adv* head to tail

tétée [tete] *nf* (*action*) sucking; (*repas*) feed

téter [tete] *vt*: ~ (**sa mère**) to suck at one's mother's breast, feed

tétine [tetin] *nf* teat; (*sucette*) dummy (*Brit*), pacifier (*US*)

téton [tetɔ̃] *nm* breast

têtu, e [tety] *adj* stubborn, pigheaded

texte [tɛkst(ə)] *nm* text; (*Scol: d'un devoir*) subject, topic; **apprendre son** ~ (*Théât*) to learn one's lines; **un** ~ **de loi** the wording of a law

textile [tɛkstil] *adj* textile *cpd* ▷ *nm* textile; (*industrie*) textile industry

Texto® [tɛksto] *nm* text (message)

texto [tɛksto] (*fam*) *adj* word for word

textuel, le [tɛkstɥɛl] *adj* literal, word for word

textuellement [tɛkstɥɛlmã] *adv* literally

texture [tɛkstyʀ] *nf* texture; (*fig: d'un texte, livre*) feel

TF1 *sigle f* (= Télévision française 1) TV channel

TG *sigle f* = **Trésorerie générale**

TGI *sigle m* = **tribunal de grande instance**

TGV *sigle m* = **train à grande vitesse**

thaï, e [taj] *adj* Thai ▷ *nm* (*Ling*) Thai

thaïlandais, e [tailãdɛ, -ez] *adj* Thai

Thaïlande [tailãd] *nf*: **la** ~ Thailand

thalassothérapie [talasɔteʀapi] *nf* sea-water therapy

thé [te] *nm* tea; (*réunion*) tea party; **prendre le** ~ to have tea; ~ **au lait/citron** tea with milk/lemon

théâtral, e, -aux [teɑtʀal, -o] *adj* theatrical

théâtre [teɑtʀ(ə)] *nm* theatre; (*techniques, genre*) drama, theatre; (*activité*) stage, theatre; (*œuvres*) plays *pl*, dramatic works *pl*; (*fig: lieu*): **le** ~ **de** the scene of; (*péj*) histrionics *pl*, playacting; **faire du** ~ (*en professionnel*) to be on the stage; (*en amateur*) to do some acting; ~ **filmé** filmed stage productions *pl*

thébain, e [tebɛ̃, -ɛn] *adj* Theban

Thèbes [tɛb] *n* Thebes

théière [tejɛʀ] *nf* teapot

théine [tein] *nf* theine

théisme [teism(ə)] *nm* theism

thématique [tematik] *adj* thematic

thème [tɛm] *nm* theme; (*Scol: traduction*) prose (composition); ~ **astral** birth chart

théocratie [teɔkʀasi] *nf* theocracy

théologie [teɔlɔʒi] *nf* theology

théologien, ne [teɔlɔʒjɛ̃, -ɛn] *nm* theologian

théologique [teɔlɔʒik] *adj* theological

théorème [teɔʀɛm] *nm* theorem

théoricien, ne [teɔʀisjɛ̃, -ɛn] *nm/f* theoretician, theorist

théorie [teɔʀi] *nf* theory; **en** ~ in theory

théorique [teɔʀik] *adj* theoretical

théoriquement [teɔʀikmã] *adv* theoretically

théoriser [teɔʀize] *vi* to theorize

thérapeutique [teʀapøtik] *adj* therapeutic ▷ *nf* (*Méd: branche*) therapeutics *nsg*; (: *traitement*) therapy

thérapie [teʀapi] *nf* therapy; ~ **de groupe** group therapy

thermal, e, -aux [tɛʀmal, -o] *adj* thermal; **station** ~**e** spa; **cure** ~**e** water cure

thermes [tɛʀm(ə)] *nmpl* thermal baths; (*romains*) thermae *pl*

thermique [tɛʀmik] *adj* (*énergie*) thermic; (*unité*) thermal

thermodynamique [tɛʀmɔdinamik] *nf* thermodynamics *nsg*

thermoélectrique [tɛʀmoelɛktʀik] *adj* thermoelectric

thermomètre [tɛʀmɔmɛtʀ(ə)] *nm* thermometer

thermonucléaire [tɛʀmɔnykleɛʀ] *adj* thermonuclear

thermos® [tɛʀmos] *nm ou nf*: (**bouteille**) **thermos** vacuum *ou* Thermos® flask (*Brit*) *ou* bottle (*US*)

thermostat [tɛʀmɔsta] *nm* thermostat

thésauriser [tezɔʀize] *vi* to hoard money

thèse [tɛz] *nf* thesis

Thessalie [tesali] *nf*: **la** ~ Thessaly

thibaude [tibod] *nf* carpet underlay

thon [tɔ̃] *nm* tuna (fish)

thonier [tɔnje] *nm* tuna boat

thoracique [tɔʀasik] *adj* thoracic

thorax [tɔʀaks] nm thorax
thrombose [tʀɔ̃boz] nf thrombosis
thym [tɛ̃] nm thyme
thyroïde [tiʀɔid] nf thyroid (gland)
TI sigle m = **tribunal d'instance**
tiare [tjaʀ] nf tiara
Tibet [tibɛ] nm: **le ~** Tibet
tibétain, e [tibetɛ̃, -ɛn] adj Tibetan
tibia [tibja] nm shin; (os) shinbone, tibia
Tibre [tibʀ(ə)] nm: **le ~** the Tiber
TIC sigle fpl (= technologies de l'information et de la communication) ICT sg
tic [tik] nm tic, (nervous) twitch; (de langage etc) mannerism
ticket [tikɛ] nm ticket; **~ de caisse** till receipt; **~ modérateur** patient's contribution towards medical costs; **~ de quai** platform ticket; **~ repas** luncheon voucher
tic-tac [tiktak] nm inv tick-tock
tictaquer [tiktake] vi to tick (away)
tiède [tjed] adj (bière etc) lukewarm; (thé, café etc) tepid; (bain, accueil, sentiment) lukewarm; (vent, air) mild, warm ▷ adv: **boire ~** to drink things lukewarm
tièdement [tjɛdmɑ̃] adv coolly, half-heartedly
tiédeur [tjedœʀ] nf lukewarmness; (du vent, de l'air) mildness
tiédir [tjediʀ] vi (se réchauffer) to grow warmer; (refroidir) to cool
tien, tienne [tjɛ̃, tjɛn] pron: **le ~ (la ~ne), les ~s (~nes)** yours; **à la ~ne!** cheers!
tiendrai etc [tjɛ̃dʀe] vb voir **tenir**
tienne [tjɛn] vb voir **tenir** ▷ pron voir **tien**
tiens [tjɛ̃] vb, excl voir **tenir**
tierce [tjɛʀs(ə)] adj f, nf voir **tiers**
tiercé [tjɛʀse] nm system of forecast betting giving first three horses
tiers, tierce [tjɛʀ, tjɛʀs(ə)] adj third ▷ nm (Jur) third party; (fraction) third ▷ nf (Mus) third; (Cartes) tierce; **une tierce personne** a third party; **assurance au ~** third-party insurance; **le ~ monde** the third world; **~ payant** direct payment by insurers of medical expenses; **~ provisionnel** interim payment of tax
tifs [tif] (fam) nmpl hair
TIG sigle m = **travail d'intérêt général**
tige [tiʒ] nf stem; (baguette) rod
tignasse [tiɲas] nf (péj) shock ou mop of hair
Tigre [tigʀ(ə)] nm: **le ~** the Tigris
tigre [tigʀ(ə)] nm tiger
tigré, e [tigʀe] adj (rayé) striped; (tacheté) spotted
tigresse [tigʀɛs] nf tigress
tilleul [tijœl] nm lime (tree), linden (tree); (boisson) lime(-blossom) tea
tilt [tilt(ə)] nm: **faire ~** (fig: échouer) to miss the target; (: inspirer) to ring a bell
timbale [tɛ̃bal] nf (metal) tumbler; **timbales** nfpl (Mus) timpani, kettledrums
timbrage [tɛ̃bʀaʒ] nm: **dispensé de ~** post(age) paid
timbre [tɛ̃bʀ(ə)] nm (tampon) stamp; (aussi: **timbre-poste**) (postage) stamp; (cachet de la

poste) postmark; (sonnette) bell; (Mus: de voix, instrument) timbre, tone; **~ anti-tabac** nicotine patch; **~ dateur** date stamp
timbré, e [tɛ̃bʀe] adj (enveloppe) stamped; (voix) resonant; (fam: fou) cracked, nuts
timbrer [tɛ̃bʀe] vt to stamp
timide [timid] adj (emprunté) shy, timid; (timoré) timid, timorous
timidement [timidmɑ̃] adv shyly; timidly
timidité [timidite] nf shyness; timidity
timonerie [timɔnʀi] nf wheelhouse
timonier [timɔnje] nm helmsman
timoré, e [timɔʀe] adj timorous
tint etc [tɛ̃] vb voir **tenir**
tintamarre [tɛ̃tamaʀ] nm din, uproar
tintement [tɛ̃tmɑ̃] nm ringing, chiming; **~s d'oreilles** ringing in the ears
tinter [tɛ̃te] vi to ring, chime; (argent, clés) to jingle
Tipp-Ex® [tipɛks] nm Tipp-Ex®
tique [tik] nf tick (insect)
tiquer [tike] vi (personne) to make a face
TIR sigle mpl (= Transports internationaux routiers) TIR
tir [tiʀ] nm (sport) shooting; (fait ou manière de tirer) firing no pl; (Football) shot; (stand) shooting gallery; **~ d'obus/de mitraillette** shell/ machine gun fire; **~ à l'arc** archery; **~ de barrage** barrage fire; **~ au fusil** (rifle) shooting; **~ au pigeon** (d'argile) clay pigeon shooting
tirade [tiʀad] nf tirade
tirage [tiʀaʒ] nm (action) printing; (Photo) print; (Inform) printout; (de journal) circulation; (de livre) (print-)run; edition; (de cheminée) draught (Brit), draft (US); (de loterie) draw; (fig: désaccord) friction; **~ au sort** drawing lots
tiraillement [tiʀajmɑ̃] nm (douleur) sharp pain; (fig: doutes) agony no pl of indecision; (conflits) friction no pl
tirailler [tiʀaje] vt to pull at, tug at; (fig) to gnaw at ▷ vi to fire at random
tirailleur [tiʀajœʀ] nm skirmisher
tirant [tiʀɑ̃] nm: **~ d'eau** draught (Brit), draft (US)
tire [tiʀ] nf: **vol à la ~** pickpocketing
tiré [tiʀe] adj (visage, traits) drawn ▷ nm (Comm) drawee; **~ par les cheveux** far-fetched; **~ à part** off-print
tire-au-flanc [tiʀoflɑ̃] nm inv (péj) skiver
tire-bouchon [tiʀbuʃɔ̃] nm corkscrew
tire-bouchonner [tiʀbuʃɔne] vt to twirl
tire-d'aile [tiʀdɛl]: **à tire-d'aile** adv swiftly
tire-fesses [tiʀfɛs] nm inv ski-tow
tire-lait [tiʀlɛ] nm inv breast-pump
tire-larigot [tiʀlaʀigo]: **à ~** adv as much as one likes, to one's heart's content
tirelire [tiʀliʀ] nf moneybox
tirer [tiʀe] vt (gén) to pull; (extraire): **~ qch de** to take ou pull sth out of; to get sth out of; to extract sth from; (tracer: ligne, trait) to draw, trace; (fermer: volet, porte, trappe) to pull to, close; (: rideau) to draw; (choisir: carte, conclusion, aussi:

Comm: *chèque*) to draw; (*en faisant feu: balle, coup*) to fire; (: *animal*) to shoot; (*journal, livre, photo*) to print; (*Football: corner etc*) to take ▷ *vi* (*faire feu*) to fire; (*faire du tir, Football*) to shoot; (*cheminée*) to draw; **se tirer** *vi* (*fam*) to push off; (*aussi:* **s'en tirer**) to pull through; **~ sur** (*corde, poignée*) to pull on *ou* at; (*faire feu sur*) to shoot *ou* fire at; (*pipe*) to draw on; (*fig: avoisiner*) to verge *ou* border on; **~ six mètres** (*Navig*) to draw six metres of water; **~ son nom de** to take *ou* get its name from; **~ la langue** to stick out one's tongue; **~ qn de** (*embarras etc*) to help *ou* get sb out of; **~ à l'arc/la carabine** to shoot with a bow and arrow/with a rifle; **~ en longueur** to drag on; **~ à sa fin** to be drawing to an end; **~ les cartes** to read *ou* tell the cards

tiret [tiʀɛ] *nm* dash; (*en fin de ligne*) hyphen

tireur [tiʀœʀ] *nm* gunman; (*Comm*) drawer; **bon ~** good shot; **~ d'élite** marksman; **~ de cartes** fortuneteller

tiroir [tiʀwaʀ] *nm* drawer

tiroir-caisse [tiʀwaʀkɛs] *nm* till

tisane [tizan] *nf* herb tea

tison [tizɔ̃] *nm* brand

tisonner [tizɔne] *vt* to poke

tisonnier [tizɔnje] *nm* poker

tissage [tisaʒ] *nm* weaving *no pl*

tisser [tise] *vt* to weave

tisserand, e [tisʀɑ̃, -ɑ̃d] *nm/f* weaver

tissu¹ [tisy] *nm* fabric, material, cloth *no pl*; (*fig*) fabric; (*Anat, Bio*) tissue; **~ de mensonges** web of lies

tissu², e [tisy] *adj*: **~ de** woven through with

tissu-éponge [tisyepɔ̃ʒ] *nm* (terry) towelling *no pl*

titane [titan] *nm* titanium

titanesque [titanɛsk(ə)] *adj* titanic

titiller [titile] *vt* to titillate

titrage [titʀaʒ] *nm* (*d'un film*) titling; (*d'un alcool*) determination of alcohol content

titre [titʀ(ə)] *nm* (*gén*) title; (*de journal*) headline; (*diplôme*) qualification; (*Comm*) security; (*Chimie*) titre; **en ~** (*champion, responsable*) official, recognized; **à juste ~** with just cause, rightly; **à quel ~?** on what grounds?; **à aucun ~** on no account; **au même ~ (que)** in the same way (as); **au ~ de la coopération** *etc* in the name of cooperation *etc*; **à ~ d'exemple** as an *ou* by way of an example; **à ~ exceptionnel** exceptionally; **à ~ d'information** for (your) information; **à ~ gracieux** free of charge; **à ~ d'essai** on a trial basis; **à ~ privé** in a private capacity; **~ courant** running head; **~ de propriété** title deed; **~ de transport** ticket

titré, e [titʀe] *adj* (*livre, film*) entitled; (*personne*) titled

titrer [titʀe] *vt* (*Chimie*) to titrate; to assay; (*Presse*) to run as a headline; (*vin*): **~ 10°** to be 10° proof

titubant, e [titybɑ̃, -ɑ̃t] *adj* staggering, reeling

tituber [titybe] *vi* to stagger *ou* reel (along)

titulaire [titylɛʀ] *adj* (*Admin*) appointed, with

tenure ▷ *nm* (*Admin*) incumbent; **être ~ de** to hold

titularisation [titylaʀizɑsjɔ̃] *nf* granting of tenure

titulariser [titylaʀize] *vt* to give tenure to

TNP *sigle m* = **Théâtre national populaire**

TNT *sigle m* (= *Trinitrotoluène*) TNT ▷ *sigle f* (= *Télévision numérique terrestre*) digital television

toast [tost] *nm* slice *ou* piece of toast; (*de bienvenue*) (welcoming) toast; **porter un ~ à qn** to propose *ou* drink a toast to sb

toboggan [tɔbɔgɑ̃] *nm* toboggan; (*jeu*) slide; (*Auto*) flyover (*Brit*), overpass (*US*); **~ de secours** (*Aviat*) escape chute

toc [tɔk] *nm*: **en ~** imitation *cpd*

tocsin [tɔksɛ̃] *nm* alarm (bell)

toge [tɔʒ] *nf* toga; (*de juge*) gown

Togo [tɔgo] *nm*: **le ~** Togo

togolais, e [tɔgolɛ, -ɛz] *adj* Togolese

tohu-bohu [tɔybɔy] *nm* (*désordre*) confusion; (*tumulte*) commotion

toi [twa] *pron* you; **~, tu l'as fait?** did YOU do it?

toile [twal] *nf* (*matériau*) cloth *no pl*; (*bâche*) piece of canvas; (*tableau*) canvas; **grosse ~** canvas; **tisser sa ~** (*araignée*) to spin its web; **~ d'araignée** spider's web; (*au plafond etc: à enlever*) cobweb; **~ cirée** oilcloth; **~ émeri** emery cloth; **~ de fond** (*fig*) backdrop; **~ de jute** hessian; **~ de lin** linen; **~ de tente** canvas

toilettage [twalɛtaʒ] *nm* grooming *no pl*; (*d'un texte*) tidying up

toilette [twalɛt] *nf* wash; (*s'habiller et se préparer*) getting ready, washing and dressing; (*habits*) outfit; dress *no pl*; **toilettes** *nfpl* toilet *nsg*; **les ~s des dames/messieurs** the ladies'/gents' (toilets) (*Brit*), the ladies'/men's (rest)room (*US*); **faire sa ~** to have a wash, get washed; **faire la ~ de** (*animal*) to groom; (*voiture etc*) to clean, wash; (*texte*) to tidy up; **articles de ~** toiletries; **~ intime** personal hygiene

toi-même [twamɛm] *pron* yourself

toise [twaz] *nf*: **passer à la ~** to have one's height measured

toiser [twaze] *vt* to eye up and down

toison [twazɔ̃] *nf* (*de mouton*) fleece; (*cheveux*) mane

toit [twa] *nm* roof; **~ ouvrant** sun roof

toiture [twatyʀ] *nf* roof

Tokyo [tɔkjo] *n* Tokyo

tôle [tol] *nf* sheet metal *no pl*; (*plaque*) steel (*ou* iron) sheet; **tôles** *nfpl* (*carosserie*) bodywork *nsg* (*Brit*), body *nsg*; panels; **~ d'acier** sheet steel *no pl*; **~ ondulée** corrugated iron

Tolède [tɔlɛd] *n* Toledo

tolérable [tɔleʀabl(ə)] *adj* tolerable, bearable

tolérance [tɔleʀɑ̃s] *nf* tolerance; (*hors taxe*) allowance

tolérant, e [tɔleʀɑ̃, -ɑ̃t] *adj* tolerant

tolérer [tɔleʀe] *vt* to tolerate; (*Admin: hors taxe etc*) to allow

tôlerie [tolʀi] *nf* sheet metal manufacture; (*atelier*) sheet metal workshop; (*ensemble des tôles*) panels *pl*

tollé [tɔle] *nm*: **un ~ (de protestations)** a general outcry

TOM [tɔm] *sigle nm(pl)* = **territoire(s) d'outre-mer**

tomate [tɔmat] *nf* tomato

tombal, e [tɔ̃bal] *adj*: **pierre ~e** tombstone, gravestone

tombant, e [tɔ̃bã, -ãt] *adj* (*fig*) drooping, sloping

tombe [tɔ̃b] *nf* (*sépulture*) grave; (*avec monument*) tomb

tombeau, x [tɔ̃bo] *nm* tomb; **à ~ ouvert** at breakneck speed

tombée [tɔ̃be] *nf*: **à la ~ du jour** *ou* **de la nuit** at the close of day, at nightfall

tomber [tɔ̃be] *vi* to fall ▷ *vt*: **~ la veste** to slip off one's jacket; **laisser ~** to drop; **~ sur** *vt* (*rencontrer*) to come across; (*attaquer*) to set about; **~ de fatigue/sommeil** to drop from exhaustion/be falling asleep on one's feet; **~ à l'eau** (*fig: projet etc*) to fall through; **~ en panne** to break down; **~ juste** (*opération, calcul*) to come out right; **~ en ruine** to fall into ruins; **ça tombe bien/mal** (*fig*) that's come at the right/wrong time; **il est bien/mal tombé** (*fig*) he's been lucky/unlucky

tombereau, x [tɔ̃bʀo] *nm* tipcart

tombeur [tɔ̃bœʀ] *nm* (*péj*) Casanova

tombola [tɔ̃bɔla] *nf* tombola

Tombouctou [tɔ̃buktu] *n* Timbuktu

tome [tɔm] *nm* volume

tommette [tɔmɛt] *nf* hexagonal floor tile

ton¹, ta (*pl* **tes**) [tɔ̃, ta, te] *adj poss* your

ton² [tɔ̃] *nm* (*gén*) tone; (*Mus*) key; (*couleur*) shade, tone; (*de la voix: hauteur*) pitch; **donner le ~** to set the tone; **élever** *ou* **hausser le ~** to raise one's voice; **de bon ~** in good taste; **si vous le prenez sur ce ~** if you're going to take it like that; **~ sur ~** in matching shades

tonal, e [tɔnal] *adj* tonal

tonalité [tɔnalite] *nf* (*au téléphone*) dialling tone; (*Mus*) tonality; (: *ton*) key; (*fig*) tone

tondeuse [tɔ̃døz] *nf* (*à gazon*) (lawn)mower; (*du coiffeur*) clippers *pl*; (*pour la tonte*) shears *pl*

tondre [tɔ̃dʀ(ə)] *vt* (*pelouse, herbe*) to mow; (*haie*) to cut, clip; (*mouton, toison*) to shear; (*cheveux*) to crop

tondu, e [tɔ̃dy] *pp de* **tondre** ▷ *adj* (*cheveux*) cropped; (*mouton, crâne*) shorn

Tonga [tɔ̃ga]: **les îles ~** Tonga

tongs [tɔ̃g] *nfpl* flip-flops (*Brit*), thongs (*US*)

tonicité [tɔnisite] *nf* (*Méd: des tissus*) tone; (*fig: de l'air, la mer*) bracing effect

tonifiant, e [tɔnifjã, -ãt] *adj* invigorating, revivifying

tonifier [tɔnifje] *vt* (*air, eau*) to invigorate; (*peau, organisme*) to tone up

tonique [tɔnik] *adj* fortifying; (*personne*) dynamic ▷ *nm, nf* tonic

tonitruant, e [tɔnitʀyã, -ãt] *adj*: **voix ~e** thundering voice

Tonkin [tɔ̃kɛ̃] *nm*: **le ~** Tonkin, Tongking

tonkinois, e [tɔ̃kinwa, -waz] *adj* Tonkinese

tonnage [tɔnaʒ] *nm* tonnage

tonnant, e [tɔnã, -ãt] *adj* thunderous

tonne [tɔn] *nf* metric ton, tonne

tonneau, x [tɔno] *nm* (*à vin, cidre*) barrel; (*Navig*) ton; **faire des ~x** (*voiture, avion*) to roll over

tonnelet [tɔnlɛ] *nm* keg

tonnelier [tɔnəlje] *nm* cooper

tonnelle [tɔnɛl] *nf* bower, arbour (*Brit*), arbor (*US*)

tonner [tɔne] *vi* to thunder; (*parler avec véhémence*): **~ contre qn/qch** to inveigh against sb/sth; **il tonne** it is thundering, there's some thunder

tonnerre [tɔnɛʀ] *nm* thunder; **coup de ~** (*fig*) thunderbolt, bolt from the blue; **un ~ d'applaudissements** thunderous applause; **du ~** *adj* (*fam*) terrific

tonsure [tɔ̃syʀ] *nf* bald patch; (*de moine*) tonsure

tonte [tɔ̃t] *nf* shearing

tonton [tɔ̃tɔ̃] *nm* uncle

tonus [tɔnys] *nm* (*des muscles*) tone; (*d'une personne*) dynamism

top [tɔp] *nm*: **au troisième ~** at the third stroke ▷ *adj*: **~ secret** top secret ▷ *excl* go!

topaze [tɔpaz] *nf* topaz

toper [tɔpe] *vi*: **tope-/topez-là** it's a deal!, you're on!

topinambour [tɔpinãbuʀ] *nm* Jerusalem artichoke

topo [tɔpo] *nm* (*discours, exposé*) talk; (*fam*) spiel

topographie [tɔpɔgʀafi] *nf* topography

topographique [tɔpɔgʀafik] *adj* topographical

toponymie [tɔpɔnimi] *nf* study of place names, toponymy

toquade [tɔkad] *nf* fad, craze

toque [tɔk] *nf* (*de fourrure*) fur hat; **~ de jockey/juge** jockey's/judge's cap; **~ de cuisinier** chef's hat

toqué, e [tɔke] *adj* (*fam*) touched, cracked

torche [tɔʀʃ(ə)] *nf* torch; **se mettre en ~** (*parachute*) to candle

torcher [tɔʀʃe] *vt* (*fam*) to wipe

torchère [tɔʀʃɛʀ] *nf* flare

torchon [tɔʀʃɔ̃] *nm* cloth, duster; (*à vaisselle*) tea towel *ou* cloth

tordre [tɔʀdʀ(ə)] *vt* (*chiffon*) to wring; (*barre, fig: visage*) to twist; **se tordre** *vi* (*barre*) to bend; (*roue*) to twist, buckle; (*ver, serpent*) to writhe; **se ~ le pied/bras** to twist one's foot/arm; **se ~ de douleur/rire** to writhe in pain/be doubled up with laughter

tordu, e [tɔʀdy] *pp de* **tordre** ▷ *adj* (*fig*) warped, twisted

torero [tɔʀeʀo] *nm* bullfighter

tornade [tɔʀnad] *nf* tornado

toron [tɔʀɔ̃] *nm* strand (of rope)

Toronto [tɔʀɔ̃to] *n* Toronto

torontois, e [tɔʀɔ̃twa, -waz] *adj* Torontonian ▷ *nm/f*: **Torontois, e** Torontonian

torpeur [tɔʀpœʀ] *nf* torpor, drowsiness

torpille [tɔʀpij] *nf* torpedo

torpiller [tɔʀpije] *vt* to torpedo
torpilleur [tɔʀpijœʀ] *nm* torpedo boat
torréfaction [tɔʀefaksjɔ̃] *nf* roasting
torréfier [tɔʀefje] *vt* to roast
torrent [tɔʀɑ̃] *nm* torrent, mountain stream;
(*fig*): **un ~ de** a torrent *ou* flood of; **il pleut à ~s**
the rain is lashing down
torrentiel, le [tɔʀɑ̃sjɛl] *adj* torrential
torride [tɔʀid] *adj* torrid
tors, torse *ou* **torte** [tɔʀ, tɔʀs(ə) ᵉᵒᵘʰtɔʀt(ə)] *adj*
twisted
torsade [tɔʀsad] *nf* twist; (*Archit*) cable
moulding (*Brit*) *ou* molding (*US*)
torsader [tɔʀsade] *vt* to twist
torse [tɔʀs(ə)] *nm* torso; (*poitrine*) chest
torsion [tɔʀsjɔ̃] *nf* (*action*) twisting; (*Tech,
Physique*) torsion
tort [tɔʀ] *nm* (*défaut*) fault; (*préjudice*) wrong *no pl*;
torts *nmpl* (*Jur*) fault *nsg*; **avoir ~** to be wrong;
être dans son ~ to be in the wrong; **donner ~ à**
qn to lay the blame on sb; (*fig*) to prove sb
wrong; **causer du ~ à** to harm; to be harmful *ou*
detrimental to; **en ~** in the wrong, at fault; **à ~**
wrongly; **à ~ ou à raison** rightly or wrongly; **à
~ et à travers** wildly
torte [tɔʀt(ə)] *adj f voir* **tors**
torticolis [tɔʀtikɔli] *nm* stiff neck
tortiller [tɔʀtije] *vt* (*corde, mouchoir*) to twist;
(*doigts*) to twiddle; **se tortiller** *vi* to wriggle,
squirm
tortionnaire [tɔʀsjɔnɛʀ] *nm* torturer
tortue [tɔʀty] *nf* tortoise; (*fig*) slowcoach (*Brit*),
slowpoke (*US*)
tortueux, -euse [tɔʀtɥø, -øz] *adj* (*rue*) twisting;
(*fig*) tortuous
torture [tɔʀtyʀ] *nf* torture
torturer [tɔʀtyʀe] *vt* to torture; (*fig*) to torment
torve [tɔʀv(ə)] *adj*: **regard ~** menacing *ou* grim
look
toscan, e [tɔskɑ̃, -an] *adj* Tuscan
Toscane [tɔskan] *nf*: **la ~** Tuscany
tôt [to] *adv* early; **~ ou tard** sooner or later; **si ~**
so early; (*déjà*) so soon; **au plus ~** at the earliest,
as soon as possible; **plus ~** earlier; **il eut ~ fait
de faire ...** he soon did ...
total, e, -aux [tɔtal, -o] *adj, nm* total; **au ~** in
total *ou* all; (*fig*) all in all; **faire le ~** to work out
the total
totalement [tɔtalmɑ̃] *adv* totally, completely
totalisateur [tɔtalizatœʀ] *nm* adding machine
totaliser [tɔtalize] *vt* to total (up)
totalitaire [tɔtalitɛʀ] *adj* totalitarian
totalitarisme [tɔtalitaʀism(ə)] *nm*
totalitarianism
totalité [tɔtalite] *nf*: **la ~ de**: **la ~ des élèves** all
(of) the pupils; **la ~ de la population/classe**
the whole population/class; **en ~** entirely
totem [tɔtɛm] *nm* totem
toubib [tubib] *nm* (*fam*) doctor
touchant, e [tuʃɑ̃, -ɑ̃t] *adj* touching
touche [tuʃ] *nf* (*de piano, de machine à écrire*) key;
(*de violon*) fingerboard; (*de télécommande etc*) key,

button; (*Peinture etc*) stroke, touch; (*fig: de couleur,
nostalgie*) touch, hint; (*Rugby*) line-out; (*Football:
aussi*: **remise en touche**) throw-in; (*aussi*: **ligne
de touche**) touch-line; (*Escrime*) hit; **en ~** in (*ou*
into*) touch; **avoir une drôle de ~** to look a
sight; **~ de commande/de fonction/de retour**
(*Inform*) control/function/return key; **~ à
effleurement** *ou* **sensitive** touch-sensitive
control *ou* key
touche-à-tout [tuʃatu] *nm inv* (*péj: gén: enfant*)
meddler; (: *fig: inventeur etc*) dabbler
toucher [tuʃe] *nm* touch ▷ *vt* to touch; (*palper*) to
feel; (*atteindre: d'un coup de feu etc*) to hit; (*affecter*)
to touch, affect; (*concerner*) to concern, affect;
(*contacter*) to reach, contact; (*recevoir: récompense*)
to receive, get; (: *salaire*) to draw, get; (*chèque*) to
cash; (*aborder: problème, sujet*) to touch on; **au ~** to
the touch; by the feel; **se toucher** (*être en contact*)
to touch; **~ à** to touch; (*modifier*) to touch,
tamper *ou* meddle with; (*traiter de, concerner*) to
have to do with, concern; **je vais lui en ~ un
mot** I'll have a word with him about it; **~ au
but** (*fig*) to near one's goal; **~ à sa fin** to be
drawing to a close
touffe [tuf] *nf* tuft
touffu, e [tufy] *adj* thick, dense; (*fig*) complex,
involved
toujours [tuʒuʀ] *adv* always; (*encore*) still;
(*constamment*) forever; **depuis ~** always; **essaie
~** (you can) try anyway; **pour ~** forever; **~ est-il
que** the fact remains that; **~ plus** more and
more
toulonnais, e [tulɔnɛ, -ɛz] *adj* of *ou* from Toulon
toulousain, e [tuluzɛ̃, -ɛn] *adj* of *ou* from
Toulouse
toupet [tupɛ] *nm* quiff (*Brit*), tuft; (*fam*) nerve,
cheek (*Brit*)
toupie [tupi] *nf* (spinning) top
tour [tuʀ] *nf* tower; (*immeuble*) high-rise block
(*Brit*) *ou* building (*US*), tower block (*Brit*); (*Échecs*)
castle, rook ▷ *nm* (*excursion: à pied*) stroll, walk;
(: *en voiture etc*) run, ride; (: *plus long*) trip; (*Sport:
aussi*: **tour de piste**) lap; (*d'être servi ou de jouer etc,
tournure, de vis ou clef*) turn; (*de roue etc*) revolution;
(*circonférence*): **de 3 m de ~** 3 m round, with a
circumference *ou* girth of 3 m; (*Pol: aussi*: **tour de
scrutin**) ballot; (*ruse, de prestidigitation, de cartes*)
trick; (*de potier*) wheel; (*à bois, métaux*) lathe;
faire le ~ de to go (a)round; (*à pied*) to walk
(a)round; (*fig*) to review; **faire le ~ de l'Europe**
to tour Europe; **faire un ~** to go for a walk; (*en
voiture etc*) to go for a ride; **faire 2 ~s** to go
(a)round twice; (*hélice etc*) to turn *ou* revolve
twice; **fermer à double ~** *vi* to double-lock the
door; **c'est au ~ de Renée** it's Renée's turn; **à ~
de rôle, ~ à ~** in turn; **à ~ de bras** with all one's
strength; (*fig*) non-stop, relentlessly; **~ de
taille/tête** waist/head measurement; **~ de
chant** song recital; **~ de contrôle** *nf* control
tower; **le T~ de France** the Tour de France; *see
note*; **~ de garde** spell of duty; **~ d'horizon** (*fig*)
general survey; **~ de lit** valance; **~ de main**

dexterity, knack; **en un ~ de main** (as) quick as a flash; **~ de passe-passe** trick, sleight of hand; **~ de reins** sprained back

● **TOUR DE FRANCE**

● The *Tour de France* is an annual road race for professional cyclists. It takes about three weeks to complete and is divided into daily stages, or "étapes" of approximately 175km (110 miles) over terrain of varying levels of difficulty. The leading cyclist wears a yellow jersey, the "maillot jaune". The route varies; it is not usually confined to France but always ends in Paris. In addition, there are a number of time trials.

tourangeau, elle, x [tuʀɑ̃ʒo, -ɛl] *adj* (*de la région*) of *ou* from Touraine; (*de la ville*) of *ou* from Tours
tourbe [tuʀb(ə)] *nf* peat
tourbière [tuʀbjɛʀ] *nf* peat-bog
tourbillon [tuʀbijɔ̃] *nm* whirlwind; (*d'eau*) whirlpool; (*fig*) whirl, swirl
tourbillonner [tuʀbijɔne] *vi* to whirl, swirl; (*objet, personne*) to whirl *ou* twirl round
tourelle [tuʀɛl] *nf* turret
tourisme [tuʀism(ə)] *nm* tourism; **agence de ~** tourist agency; **avion/voiture de ~** private plane/car; **faire du ~** to do some sightseeing, go touring
touriste [tuʀist(ə)] *nm/f* tourist
touristique [tuʀistik] *adj* tourist *cpd*; (*région*) touristic (*péj*), with tourist appeal
tourment [tuʀmɑ̃] *nm* torment
tourmente [tuʀmɑ̃t] *nf* storm
tourmenté, e [tuʀmɑ̃te] *adj* tormented, tortured; (*mer, période*) turbulent
tourmenter [tuʀmɑ̃te] *vt* to torment; **se tourmenter** *vi* to fret, worry o.s.
tournage [tuʀnaʒ] *nm* (*d'un film*) shooting
tournant, e [tuʀnɑ̃, -ɑ̃t] *adj* (*feu, scène*) revolving; (*chemin*) winding; (*escalier*) spiral *cpd*; (*mouvement*) circling ▷ *nm* (*de route*) bend (*Brit*), curve (*US*); (*fig*) turning point; *voir* **plaque**; **grève**
tourné, e [tuʀne] *adj* (*lait, vin*) sour, off; (*Menuiserie: bois*) turned; (*fig: compliment*) well-phrased; **bien ~** (*femme*) shapely; **mal ~** (*lettre*) badly expressed; **avoir l'esprit mal ~** to have a dirty mind
tournebroche [tuʀnəbʀɔʃ] *nm* roasting spit
tourne-disque [tuʀnədisk(ə)] *nm* record player
tournedos [tuʀnədo] *nm* tournedos
tournée [tuʀne] *nf* (*du facteur etc*) round; (*d'artiste, politicien*) tour; (*au café*) round (of drinks); **faire la ~ de** to go (a)round
tournemain [tuʀnəmɛ̃]: **en un ~** *adv* in a flash
tourner [tuʀne] *vt* to turn; (*sauce, mélange*) to stir; (*contourner*) to get (a)round; (*Ciné*) to shoot; to make ▷ *vi* to turn; (*moteur*) to run; (*compteur*) to tick away; (*lait etc*) to turn (sour); (*fig: chance, vie*) to turn out; **se tourner** *vi* to turn (a)round;

se ~ vers to turn to; to turn towards; **bien ~** to turn out well; **~ autour de** to go (a)round; (*planète*) to revolve (a)round; (*péj*) to hang (a)round); **~ autour du pot** (*fig*) to go (a)round in circles; **~ à/en** to turn into; **~ à la pluie/au rouge** to turn rainy/red; **~ en ridicule** to ridicule; **~ le dos à** (*mouvement*) to turn one's back on; (*position*) to have one's back to; **~ court** to come to a sudden end; **se ~ les pouces** to twiddle one's thumbs; **~ la tête** to look away; **~ la tête à qn** (*fig*) to go to sb's head; **~ de l'œil** to pass out; **~ la page** (*fig*) to turn the page
tournesol [tuʀnəsɔl] *nm* sunflower
tourneur [tuʀnœʀ] *nm* turner; lathe-operator
tournevis [tuʀnəvis] *nm* screwdriver
tourniquer [tuʀnike] *vi* to go (a)round in circles
tourniquet [tuʀnike] *nm* (*pour arroser*) sprinkler; (*portillon*) turnstile; (*présentoir*) revolving stand, spinner; (*Chirurgie*) tourniquet
tournis [tuʀni] *nm*: **avoir/donner le ~** to feel/make dizzy
tournoi [tuʀnwa] *nm* tournament
tournoyer [tuʀnwaje] *vi* (*oiseau*) to wheel (a)round; (*fumée*) to swirl (a)round
tournure [tuʀnyʀ] *nf* (*Ling: syntaxe*) turn of phrase; form; (*: d'une phrase*) phrasing; (*évolution*): **la ~ de qch** the way sth is developing; (*aspect*): **la ~ de** the look of; **la ~ des événements** the turn of events; **prendre ~** to take shape
tour-opérateur [tuʀɔpeʀatœʀ] *nm* tour operator
tourte [tuʀt(ə)] *nf* pie
tourteau, x [tuʀto] *nm* (*Agr*) oilcake, cattle-cake; (*Zool*) edible crab
tourtereaux [tuʀtəʀo] *nmpl* lovebirds
tourterelle [tuʀtəʀɛl] *nf* turtledove
tourtière [tuʀtjɛʀ] *nf* pie dish *ou* plate
tous [tu] *adj* [tus] ▷ *pron voir* **tout**
Toussaint [tusɛ̃] *nf*: **la ~** All Saints' Day
tousser [tuse] *vi* to cough
toussoter [tusɔte] *vi* to have a slight cough; (*pour avertir*) to give a slight cough

 MOT-CLÉ

tout, e [tu, tut] (*mpl* **tous**, *fpl* **toutes**) *adj* **1** (*avec article singulier*) all; **tout le lait** all the milk; **toute la nuit** all night, the whole night; **tout le livre** the whole book; **tout un pain** a whole loaf; **tout le temps** all the time, the whole time; **c'est tout le contraire** it's quite the opposite; **c'est toute une affaire** *ou* **histoire** it's quite a business, it's a whole rigmarole
2 (*avec article pluriel*) every; all; **tous les livres** all the books; **toutes les nuits** every night; **toutes les fois** every time; **toutes les trois/deux semaines** every third/other *ou* second week, every three/two weeks; **tous les deux** both *ou* each of us (*ou* them *ou* you); **toutes les trois** all three of us (*ou* them *ou* you)

3 (*sans article*): **à tout âge** at any age; **pour toute nourriture, il avait** ... his only food was ...; **de tous côtés, de toutes parts** from everywhere, from every side
▷ *pron* everything, all; **il a tout fait** he's done everything; **je les vois tous** I can see them all *ou* all of them; **nous y sommes tous allés** all of us went, we all went; **c'est tout** that's all; **en tout** in all; **en tout et pour tout** all in all; **tout ce qu'il sait** all he knows; **c'était tout ce qu'il y a de chic** it was the last word *ou* the ultimate in chic
▷ *nm* whole; **le tout** all of it (*ou* them); **le tout est de** ... the main thing is to ...; **pas du tout** not at all; **elle a tout d'une mère/d'une intrigante** she's a real *ou* true mother/schemer; **du tout au tout** utterly
▷ *adv* **1** (*très, complètement*) very; **tout près** *ou* **à côté** very near; **le tout premier** the very first; **tout seul** all alone; **il était tout rouge** he was really *ou* all red; **parler tout bas** to speak very quietly; **le livre tout entier** the whole book; **tout en haut** right at the top; **tout droit** straight ahead
2: **tout en** while; **tout en travaillant** while working, as he *etc* works
3: **tout d'abord** first of all; **tout à coup** suddenly; **tout à fait** absolutely; **tout à fait!** exactly!; **tout à l'heure** a short while ago; (*futur*) in a short while, shortly; **à tout à l'heure!** see you later!; **il répondit tout court que non** he just answered no (and that was all); **tout de même** all the same; **tout le monde** everybody; **tout ou rien** all or nothing; **tout simplement** quite simply; **tout de suite** immediately, straight away

tout-à-l'égout [tutalegu] *nm inv* mains drainage
toutefois [tutfwa] *adv* however
toutou [tutu] *nm* (*fam*) doggie
tout-petit [tup(ə)ti] *nm* toddler
tout-puissant, toute-puissante [tupɥisɑ̃, tutpɥisɑ̃t] *adj* all-powerful, omnipotent
tout-venant [tuvnɑ̃] *nm*: **le ~** everyday stuff
toux [tu] *nf* cough
toxémie [tɔksemi] *nf* toxaemia (*Brit*), toxemia (*US*)
toxicité [tɔksisite] *nf* toxicity
toxicologie [tɔksikɔlɔʒi] *nf* toxicology
toxicomane [tɔksikɔman] *nm/f* drug addict
toxicomanie [tɔksikɔmani] *nf* drug addiction
toxine [tɔksin] *nf* toxin
toxique [tɔksik] *adj* toxic, poisonous
toxoplasmose [tɔksoplasmoz] *nf* toxoplasmosis
TP *sigle mpl* = **travaux pratiques**; **travaux publics** ▷ *sigle m* = **trésor public**
TPG *sigle m* = **Trésorier-payeur général**
tps *abr* = **temps**
trac [tʀak] *nm* nerves *pl*; (*Théât*) stage fright; **avoir le ~** to get an attack of nerves; to have

stage fright; **tout à ~** all of a sudden
traçant, e [tʀasɑ̃, -ɑ̃t] *adj*: **table ~e** (*Inform*) (graph) plotter
tracas [tʀaka] *nm* bother *no pl*, worry *no pl*
tracasser [tʀakase] *vt* to worry, bother; (*harceler*) to harass; **se tracasser** *vi* to worry o.s., fret
tracasserie [tʀakasʀi] *nf* annoyance *no pl*; harassment *no pl*
tracassier, -ière [tʀakasje, -jɛʀ] *adj* irksome
trace [tʀas] *nf* (*empreintes*) tracks *pl*; (*marques, aussi fig*) mark; (*restes, vestige*) trace; (*indice*) sign; (*aussi*: **suivre à la trace**) to track; **~s de pas** footprints
tracé [tʀase] *nm* (*contour*) line; (*plan*) layout
tracer [tʀase] *vt* to draw; (*mot*) to trace; (*piste*) to open up; (*fig: chemin*) to show
traceur [tʀasœʀ] *nm* (*Inform*) plotter
trachée [tʀaʃe], **trachée-artère** [tʀaʃeaʀtɛʀ] *nf* windpipe, trachea
trachéite [tʀakeit] *nf* tracheitis
tract [tʀakt] *nm* tract, pamphlet; (*publicitaire*) handout
tractations [tʀaktɑsjɔ̃] *nfpl* dealings, bargaining *nsg*
tracter [tʀakte] *vt* to tow
tracteur [tʀaktœʀ] *nm* tractor
traction [tʀaksjɔ̃] *nf* traction; (*Gym*) pull-up; **~ avant/arrière** front-wheel/rear-wheel drive; **~ électrique** electric(al) traction *ou* haulage
trad. *abr* (= *traduit*) translated; (= *traduction*) translation; (= *traducteur*) translator
tradition [tʀadisjɔ̃] *nf* tradition
traditionalisme [tʀadisjɔnalism(ə)] *nm* traditionalism
traditionaliste [tʀadisjɔnalist(ə)] *adj, nm/f* traditionalist
traditionnel, le [tʀadisjɔnɛl] *adj* traditional
traditionnellement [tʀadisjɔnɛlmɑ̃] *adv* traditionally
traducteur, -trice [tʀadyktœʀ, -tʀis] *nm/f* translator
traduction [tʀadyksjɔ̃] *nf* translation
traduire [tʀadɥiʀ] *vt* to translate; (*exprimer*) to render, convey; **se ~ par** to find expression in; **~ en français** to translate into French; **~ en justice** to bring before the courts
traduis *etc* [tʀadɥi] *vb voir* **traduire**
traduisible [tʀadɥizibl(ə)] *adj* translatable
traduit, e [tʀadɥi, -it] *pp de* **traduire**
trafic [tʀafik] *nm* traffic; **~ d'armes** arms dealing; **~ de drogue** drug peddling
trafiquant, e [tʀafikɑ̃, -ɑ̃t] *nm/f* trafficker; dealer
trafiquer [tʀafike] *vt* (*péj*) to doctor, tamper with ▷ *vi* to traffic, be engaged in trafficking
tragédie [tʀaʒedi] *nf* tragedy
tragédien, ne [tʀaʒedjɛ̃, -ɛn] *nm/f* tragedian/tragedienne
tragi-comique [tʀaʒikɔmik] *adj* tragi-comic
tragique [tʀaʒik] *adj* tragic ▷ *nm*: **prendre qch au ~** to make a tragedy out of sth

tragiquement [tʀaʒikmɑ̃] *adv* tragically
trahir [tʀaiʀ] *vt* to betray; *(fig)* to give away, reveal; **se trahir** to betray o.s., give o.s. away
trahison [tʀaizɔ̃] *nf* betrayal; *(Jur)* treason
traie *etc* [tʀɛ] *vb voir* **traire**
train [tʀɛ̃] *nm* (*Rail*) train; *(allure)* pace; *(fig: ensemble)* set; **être en ~ de faire qch** to be doing sth; **mettre qch en ~** to get sth under way; **mettre qn en ~** to put sb in good spirits; **se mettre en ~** *(commencer)* to get started; *(faire de la gymnastique)* to warm up; **se sentir en ~** to feel in good form; **aller bon ~** to make good progress; **~ avant/arrière** front-wheel/rear-wheel axle unit; **~ à grande vitesse (TGV)** high-speed train; **~ d'atterrissage** undercarriage; **~ autos-couchettes** car-sleeper train; **~ électrique** *(jouet)* (electric) train set; **~ de pneus** set of tyres *ou* tires; **~ de vie** style of living
traînailler [tʀɛnaje] *vi* = **traînasser**
traînant, e [tʀɛnɑ̃, -ɑ̃t] *adj (voix, ton)* drawling
traînard, e [tʀɛnaʀ, -aʀd(ə)] *nm/f (péj)* slowcoach *(Brit)*, slowpoke *(US)*
traînasser [tʀɛnase] *vi* to dawdle
traîne [tʀɛn] *nf (de robe)* train; **être à la ~** to be in tow; *(en arrière)* to lag behind; *(en désordre)* to be lying around
traîneau, x [tʀɛno] *nm* sleigh, sledge
traînée [tʀɛne] *nf* streak, trail; *(péj)* slut
traîner [tʀɛne] *vt (remorque)* to pull; *(enfant, chien)* to drag *ou* trail along; *(maladie)*: **il traîne un rhume depuis l'hiver** he has a cold which has been dragging on since winter ▷ *vi (être en désordre)* to lie around; *(marcher lentement)* to dawdle (along); *(vagabonder)* to hang about; *(agir lentement)* to idle about; *(durer)* to drag on; **se traîner** *vi (ramper)* to crawl along; *(marcher avec difficulté)* to drag o.s. along; *(durer)* to drag on; **se ~ par terre** to crawl (on the ground); **~ qn au cinéma** to drag sb to the cinema; **~ les pieds** to drag one's feet; **~ par terre** to trail on the ground; **~ en longueur** to drag out
training [tʀɛniŋ] *nm (pull)* tracksuit top; *(chaussure)* trainer *(Brit)*, sneaker *(US)*
train-train [tʀɛ̃tʀɛ̃] *nm* humdrum routine
traire [tʀɛʀ] *vt* to milk
trait, e [tʀɛ, -ɛt] *pp de* **traire** ▷ *nm (ligne)* line; *(de dessin)* stroke; *(caractéristique)* feature, trait; *(flèche)* dart, arrow; shaft; **traits** *nmpl (du visage)* features; **d'un ~** *(boire)* in one gulp; **de ~** *adj (animal)* draught *(Brit)*, draft *(US)*; **avoir ~ à** to concern; **~ pour ~** line for line; **~ de caractère** characteristic, trait; **~ d'esprit** flash of wit; **~ de génie** brainwave; **~ d'union** hyphen; *(fig)* link
traitable [tʀɛtabl(ə)] *adj (personne)* accommodating; *(sujet)* manageable
traitant, e [tʀɛtɑ̃, -ɑ̃t] *adj:* **votre médecin ~** your usual *ou* family doctor; **shampooing ~** medicated shampoo; **crème ~e** conditioning cream, conditioner
traite [tʀɛt] *nf (Comm)* draft; *(Agr)* milking;

(trajet) stretch; **d'une (seule) ~** without stopping (once); **la ~ des noirs** the slave trade; **la ~ des blanches** the white slave trade
traité [tʀɛte] *nm* treaty
traitement [tʀɛtmɑ̃] *nm* treatment; processing; *(salaire)* salary; **suivre un ~** to undergo treatment; **mauvais ~** ill-treatment; **~ de données** *ou* **de l'information** *(Inform)* data processing; **~ hormono-supplétif** hormone replacement therapy; **~ par lots** *(Inform)* batch processing; **~ de texte** *(Inform)* word processing
traiter [tʀɛte] *vt (gén)* to treat; *(Tech: matériaux)* to process, treat; *(Inform)* to process; *(affaire)* to deal with, handle; *(qualifier):* **~ qn d'idiot** to call sb a fool ▷ *vi* to deal; **~ de** *vt* to deal with; **bien/mal ~** to treat well/ill-treat
traiteur [tʀɛtœʀ] *nm* caterer
traître, -esse [tʀɛtʀ(ə), -tʀɛs] *adj (dangereux)* treacherous ▷ *nm* traitor; **prendre qn en ~** to make an insidious attack on sb
traîtrise [tʀɛtʀiz] *nf* treachery
trajectoire [tʀaʒɛktwaʀ] *nf* trajectory, path
trajet [tʀaʒɛ] *nm* journey; *(itinéraire)* route; *(fig)* path, course
tralala [tʀalala] *nm (péj)* fuss
tram [tʀam] *nm* tram *(Brit)*, streetcar *(US)*
trame [tʀam] *nf (de tissu)* weft; *(fig)* framework; texture; *(Typo)* screen
tramer [tʀame] *vt* to plot, hatch
trampoline [tʀɑ̃pɔlin], **trampolino** [tʀɑ̃pɔlino] *nm* trampoline; *(Sport)* trampolining
tramway [tʀamwɛ] *nm* tram(way); *(voiture)* tram(car) *(Brit)*, streetcar *(US)*
tranchant, e [tʀɑ̃ʃɑ̃, -ɑ̃t] *adj* sharp; *(fig: personne)* peremptory; *(: couleurs)* striking ▷ *nm (d'un couteau)* cutting edge; *(de la main)* edge; **à double ~** *(argument, procédé)* double-edged
tranche [tʀɑ̃ʃ] *nf (morceau)* slice; *(arête)* edge; *(partie)* section; *(série)* block; *(d'impôts, revenus etc)* bracket; *(loterie)* issue; **~ d'âge** age bracket; **~ (de silicium)** wafer
tranché, e [tʀɑ̃ʃe] *adj (couleurs)* distinct, sharply contrasted; *(opinions)* clear-cut, definite ▷ *nf* trench
trancher [tʀɑ̃ʃe] *vt* to cut, sever; *(fig: résoudre)* to settle ▷ *vi* to be decisive; *(entre deux choses)* to settle the argument; **~ avec** to contrast sharply with
tranchet [tʀɑ̃ʃɛ] *nm* knife
tranchoir [tʀɑ̃ʃwaʀ] *nm* chopper
tranquille [tʀɑ̃kil] *adj* calm, quiet; *(enfant, élève)* quiet; *(rassuré)* easy in one's mind, with one's mind at rest; **se tenir ~** *(enfant)* to be quiet; **avoir la conscience ~** to have an easy conscience; **laisse-moi/laisse-ça ~** leave me/it alone
tranquillement [tʀɑ̃kilmɑ̃] *adv* calmly
tranquillisant, e [tʀɑ̃kilizɑ̃, -ɑ̃t] *adj (nouvelle)* reassuring ▷ *nm* tranquillizer
tranquilliser [tʀɑ̃kilize] *vt* to reassure; **se tranquilliser** to calm (o.s.) down
tranquillité [tʀɑ̃kilite] *nf* quietness, peace (and

quiet); **en toute** ~ with complete peace of mind; ~ **d'esprit** peace of mind

transaction [trɑ̃zaksjɔ̃] *nf* (*Comm*) transaction, deal

transafricain, e [trɑ̃safrikɛ̃, -ɛn] *adj* transafrican

transalpin, e [trɑ̃zalpɛ̃, -in] *adj* transalpine

transaméricain, e [trɑ̃zamerikɛ̃, -ɛn] *adj* transamerican

transat [trɑ̃zat] *nm* deckchair ▷ *nf* = **course transatlantique**

transatlantique [trɑ̃zatlɑ̃tik] *adj* transatlantic ▷ *nm* transatlantic liner

transborder [trɑ̃sbɔrde] *vt* to tran(s)ship

transcendant, e [trɑ̃sɑ̃dɑ̃, -ɑ̃t] *adj* (*Philosophie, Math*) transcendental; (*supérieur*) transcendent

transcodeur [trɑ̃skɔdœr] *nm* compiler

transcontinental, e, -aux [trɑ̃skɔ̃tinɑ̃tal, -o] *adj* transcontinental

transcription [trɑ̃skripsjɔ̃] *nf* transcription

transcrire [trɑ̃skrir] *vt* to transcribe

transe [trɑ̃s] *nf*: **entrer en** ~ to go into a trance; **transes** *nfpl* agony *nsg*

transférable [trɑ̃sferabl(ə)] *adj* transferable

transfèrement [trɑ̃sfermɑ̃] *nm* transfer

transférer [trɑ̃sfere] *vt* to transfer

transfert [trɑ̃sfer] *nm* transfer

transfiguration [trɑ̃sfigyrasjɔ̃] *nf* transformation, transfiguration

transfigurer [trɑ̃sfigyre] *vt* to transform

transfo [trɑ̃sfo] *nm* (= *transformateur*) transformer

transformable [trɑ̃sfɔrmabl(ə)] *adj* convertible

transformateur [trɑ̃sfɔrmatœr] *nm* transformer

transformation [trɑ̃sfɔrmasjɔ̃] *nf* transformation; (*Rugby*) conversion; **industries de** ~ processing industries

transformer [trɑ̃sfɔrme] *vt* to transform, alter (*"alter" implique un changement moins radical*); (*matière première, appartement, Rugby*) to convert; ~ **en** to transform into; to turn into; to convert into; **se transformer** *vi* to be transformed; to alter

transfuge [trɑ̃sfyʒ] *nm* renegade

transfuser [trɑ̃sfyze] *vt* to transfuse

transfusion [trɑ̃sfyzjɔ̃] *nf*: ~ **sanguine** blood transfusion

transgénique [trɑ̃sʒenik] *adj* transgenic

transgresser [trɑ̃sgrese] *vt* to contravene, disobey

transhumance [trɑ̃zymɑ̃s] *nf* transhumance, seasonal move to new pastures

transi, e [trɑ̃zi] *adj* numb (with cold), chilled to the bone

transiger [trɑ̃ziʒe] *vi* to compromise, come to an agreement; ~ **sur** *ou* **avec qch** to compromise on sth

transistor [trɑ̃zistɔr] *nm* transistor

transistorisé, e [trɑ̃zistɔrize] *adj* transistorized

transit [trɑ̃zit] *nm* transit; **de** ~ transit *cpd*; **en** ~ in transit

transitaire [trɑ̃zitɛr] *nm/f* forwarding agent

transiter [trɑ̃zite] *vi* to pass in transit

transitif, -ive [trɑ̃zitif, -iv] *adj* transitive

transition [trɑ̃zisjɔ̃] *nf* transition; **de** ~ transitional

transitoire [trɑ̃zitwar] *adj* (*mesure, gouvernement*) transitional, provisional; (*fugitif*) transient

translucide [trɑ̃slysid] *adj* translucent

transmet *etc* [trɑ̃smɛ] *vb voir* **transmettre**

transmettais *etc* [trɑ̃smɛtɛ] *vb voir* **transmettre**

transmetteur [trɑ̃smɛtœr] *nm* transmitter

transmettre [trɑ̃smɛtr(ə)] *vt* (*passer*): ~ **qch à qn** to pass sth on to sb; (*Tech, Tél, Méd*) to transmit; (*TV, Radio: retransmettre*) to broadcast

transmis, e [trɑ̃smi, -iz] *pp de* **transmettre**

transmissible [trɑ̃smisibl(ə)] *adj* transmissible

transmission [trɑ̃smisjɔ̃] *nf* transmission, passing on; (*Auto*) transmission; **transmissions** *nfpl* (*Mil*) ≈ signals corps *nsg*; ~ **de données** (*Inform*) data transmission; ~ **de pensée** thought transmission

transocéanien, ne [trɑ̃zɔseanjɛ̃, -ɛn] *adj*, **transocéanique** [trɑ̃zɔseanik] ▷ *adj* transoceanic

transparaître [trɑ̃sparɛtr(ə)] *vi* to show (through)

transparence [trɑ̃sparɑ̃s] *nf* transparence; **par** ~ (*regarder*) against the light; (*voir*) showing through

transparent, e [trɑ̃sparɑ̃, -ɑ̃t] *adj* transparent

transpercer [trɑ̃sperse] *vt* to go through, pierce

transpiration [trɑ̃spirasjɔ̃] *nf* perspiration

transpirer [trɑ̃spire] *vi* to perspire; (*information, nouvelle*) to come to light

transplant [trɑ̃splɑ̃] *nm* transplant

transplantation [trɑ̃splɑ̃tasjɔ̃] *nf* transplant

transplanter [trɑ̃splɑ̃te] *vt* (*Méd, Bot*) to transplant; (*personne*) to uproot, move

transport [trɑ̃spɔr] *nm* transport; (*émotions*): ~ **de colère** fit of rage; ~ **de joie** transport of delight; ~ **de voyageurs/marchandises** passenger/goods transportation; ~s **en commun** public transport *nsg*; ~s **routiers** haulage (*Brit*), trucking (*US*)

transportable [trɑ̃spɔrtabl(ə)] *adj* (*marchandises*) transportable; (*malade*) fit (enough) to be moved

transporter [trɑ̃spɔrte] *vt* to carry, move; (*Comm*) to transport, convey; (*fig*): ~ **qn (de joie)** to send sb into raptures; **se** ~ **quelque part** (*fig*) to let one's imagination carry one away (somewhere)

transporteur [trɑ̃spɔrtœr] *nm* haulage contractor (*Brit*), trucker (*US*)

transposer [trɑ̃spoze] *vt* to transpose

transposition [trɑ̃spozisjɔ̃] *nf* transposition

transrhénan, e [trɑ̃srenɑ̃, -an] *adj* transrhenane

transsaharien, ne [trɑ̃ssaarjɛ̃, -ɛn] *adj* trans-Saharan

transsexuel, le [tʀɑ̃ssɛksɥɛl] *adj, nm/f* transsexual

transsibérien, ne [tʀɑ̃ssibeʀjɛ̃, -ɛn] *adj* trans-Siberian

transvaser [tʀɑ̃svaze] *vt* to decant

transversal, e, -aux [tʀɑ̃svɛʀsal, -o] *adj* transverse, cross(-); (*route etc*) cross-country; (*mur, chemin, rue*) running at right angles; (*Auto*): **axe ~** main cross-country road (*Brit*) *ou* highway (*US*)

transversalement [tʀɑ̃svɛʀsalmɑ̃] *adv* crosswise

trapèze [tʀapɛz] *nm* (*Géom*) trapezium; (*au cirque*) trapeze

trapéziste [tʀapezist(ə)] *nm/f* trapeze artist

trappe [tʀap] *nf* (*de cave, grenier*) trap door; (*piège*) trap

trappeur [tʀapœʀ] *nm* trapper, fur trader

trapu, e [tʀapy] *adj* squat, stocky

traquenard [tʀaknaʀ] *nm* trap

traquer [tʀake] *vt* to track down; (*harceler*) to hound

traumatisant, e [tʀomatizɑ̃, -ɑ̃t] *adj* traumatic

traumatiser [tʀomatize] *vt* to traumatize

traumatisme [tʀomatism(ə)] *nm* traumatism

traumatologie [tʀomatɔlɔʒi] *nf* branch of *medicine concerned with accidents*

travail, -aux [tʀavaj, -o] *nm* (*gén*) work; (*tâche, métier*) work *no pl*, job; (*Écon, Méd*) labour (*Brit*), labor (*US*); (*Inform*) job ▷ *nmpl* (*de réparation, agricoles etc*) work *nsg*; (*sur route*) roadworks; (*de construction*) building (work) *nsg*; **être/entrer en ~** (*Méd*) to be in/go into labour; **être sans ~** (*employé*) to be out of work, be unemployed; **~ d'intérêt général (TIG)** ≈ community service; **~ (au) noir** moonlighting; **~ posté** shiftwork; **travaux des champs** farmwork *nsg*; **travaux dirigés (TD)** (*Scol*) supervised practical work *nsg*; **travaux forcés** hard labour *nsg*; **travaux manuels** (*Scol*) handicrafts; **travaux ménagers** housework *nsg*; **travaux pratiques (TP)** (*gén*) practical work; (*en laboratoire*) lab work (*Brit*), lab (*US*); **travaux publics (TP)** ≈ public works *nsg*

travaillé, e [tʀavaje] *adj* (*style*) polished

travailler [tʀavaje] *vi* to work; (*bois*) to warp ▷ *vt* (*bois, métal*) to work; (*pâte*) to knead; (*objet d'art, discipline, fig: influencer*) to work on; **cela le travaille** it is on his mind; **~ la terre** to work the land; **~ son piano** to do one's piano practice; **~ à** to work on; (*fig: contribuer à*) to work towards; **~ à faire** to endeavour (*Brit*) *ou* endeavor (*US*) to do

travailleur, -euse [tʀavajœʀ, -øz] *adj* hardworking ▷ *nm/f* worker; **~ de force** labourer (*Brit*), laborer (*US*); **~ intellectuel** non-manual worker; **~ social** social worker; **travailleuse familiale** home help

travailliste [tʀavajist(ə)] *adj* ≈ Labour *cpd* ▷ *nm/f* member of the Labour party

travée [tʀave] *nf* row; (*Archit*) bay; span

traveller's [tʀavlœʀs], **traveller's chèque**
[tʀavlœʀsʃɛk] *nm* traveller's cheque

travelling [tʀavliŋ] *nm* (*chariot*) dolly; (*technique*) tracking; **~ optique** zoom shots *pl*

travelo [tʀavlo] *nm* (*fam*) (drag) queen

travers [tʀavɛʀ] *nm* fault, failing; **en ~ (de)** across; **au ~ (de)** through; **de ~** *adj* askew ▷ *adv* sideways; (*fig*) the wrong way; **à ~** through; **regarder de ~** (*fig*) to look askance at

traverse [tʀavɛʀs(ə)] *nf* (*de voie ferrée*) sleeper; **chemin de ~** shortcut

traversée [tʀavɛʀse] *nf* crossing

traverser [tʀavɛʀse] *vt* (*gén*) to cross; (*ville, tunnel, aussi: percer, fig*) to go through; (*ligne, trait*) to run across

traversin [tʀavɛʀsɛ̃] *nm* bolster

travesti [tʀavɛsti] *nm* (*costume*) fancy dress; (*artiste de cabaret*) female impersonator, drag artist; (*pervers*) transvestite

travestir [tʀavɛstiʀ] *vt* (*vérité*) to misrepresent; **se travestir** (*se costumer*) to dress up; (*artiste*) to put on drag; (*Psych*) to dress as a woman

trayais *etc* [tʀɛjɛ] *vb voir* **traire**

trayeuse [tʀɛjøz] *nf* milking machine

trébucher [tʀebyʃe] *vi* **~ (sur)** to stumble (over), trip (over)

trèfle [tʀɛfl(ə)] *nm* (*Bot*) clover; (*Cartes: couleur*) clubs *pl*; (: *carte*) club; **~ à quatre feuilles** four-leaf clover

treillage [tʀejaʒ] *nm* lattice work

treille [tʀɛj] *nf* (*tonnelle*) vine arbour (*Brit*) *ou* arbor (*US*); (*vigne*) climbing vine

treillis [tʀeji] *nm* (*métallique*) wire-mesh; (*toile*) canvas; (*Mil: tenue*) combat uniform; (*pantalon*) combat trousers *pl*

treize [tʀɛz] *num* thirteen

treizième [tʀɛzjɛm] *num* thirteenth; *see note*

● TREIZIÈME MOIS

● The *treizième mois* is an end-of-year bonus
● roughly corresponding to one month's
● salary. For many employees it is a standard
● part of their salary package.

tréma [tʀema] *nm* diaeresis

tremblant, e [tʀɑ̃blɑ̃, -ɑ̃t] *adj* trembling, shaking

tremble [tʀɑ̃bl(ə)] *nm* (*Bot*) aspen

tremblé, e [tʀɑ̃ble] *adj* shaky

tremblement [tʀɑ̃bləmɑ̃] *nm* trembling *no pl*, shaking *no pl*, shivering *no pl*; **~ de terre** earthquake

trembler [tʀɑ̃ble] *vi* to tremble, shake; **~ de** (*froid, fièvre*) to shiver *ou* tremble with; (*peur*) to shake *ou* tremble with; **~ pour qn** to fear for sb

tremblotant, e [tʀɑ̃blɔtɑ̃, -ɑ̃t] *adj* trembling

trembloter [tʀɑ̃blɔte] *vi* to tremble *ou* shake slightly

trémolo [tʀemolo] *nm* (*d'un instrument*) tremolo; (*de la voix*) quaver

trémousser [tʀemuse]: **se trémousser** *vi* to jig about, wriggle about

trempe [tʀɑ̃p] *nf* (*fig*): **de cette/sa ~** of this/his calibre (*Brit*) *ou* caliber (*US*)

trempé, e [tʀɑ̃pe] *adj* soaking (wet), drenched; (*Tech*): **acier ~** tempered steel

tremper [tʀɑ̃pe] *vt* to soak, drench; (*aussi*: **faire tremper, mettre à tremper**) to soak; (*plonger*): **~ qch dans** to dip sth in(to) ▷ *vi* to soak; (*fig*): **~ dans** to be involved *ou* have a hand in; **se tremper** *vi* to have a quick dip; **se faire ~** to get soaked *ou* drenched

trempette [tʀɑ̃pɛt] *nf*: **faire ~** to go paddling

tremplin [tʀɑ̃plɛ̃] *nm* springboard; (*Ski*) ski jump

trentaine [tʀɑ̃tɛn] *nf* (*âge*): **avoir la ~** to be around thirty; **une ~ (de)** thirty or so, about thirty

trente [tʀɑ̃t] *num* thirty; **voir ~-six chandelles** (*fig*) to see stars; **être/se mettre sur son ~ et un** to be/get dressed to kill; **~-trois tours** *nm* long-playing record, LP

trentième [tʀɑ̃tjɛm] *num* thirtieth

trépanation [tʀepanasjɔ̃] *nf* trepan

trépaner [tʀepane] *vt* to trepan, trephine

trépasser [tʀepase] *vi* to pass away

trépidant, e [tʀepidɑ̃, -ɑ̃t] *adj* (*fig*: *rythme*) pulsating; (: *vie*) hectic

trépidation [tʀepidasjɔ̃] *nf* (*d'une machine, d'un moteur*) vibration; (*fig*: *de la vie*) whirl

trépider [tʀepide] *vi* to vibrate

trépied [tʀepje] *nm* (*d'appareil*) tripod; (*meuble*) trivet

trépignement [tʀepiɲmɑ̃] *nm* stamping (of feet)

trépigner [tʀepiɲe] *vi* to stamp (one's feet)

très [tʀɛ] *adv* very; **~ beau/bien** very beautiful/well; **~ critiqué** much criticized; **~ industrialisé** highly industrialized; **j'ai ~ faim** I'm very hungry

trésor [tʀezɔʀ] *nm* treasure; (*Admin*) finances *pl*; (*d'une organisation*) funds *pl*; **~ (public) (TP)** public revenue; (*service*) public revenue office

trésorerie [tʀezɔʀʀi] *nf* (*fonds*) funds *pl*; (*gestion*) accounts *pl*; (*bureaux*) accounts department; (*poste*) treasurership; **difficultés de ~** cash problems, shortage of cash *ou* funds; **~ générale (TG)** local government finance office

trésorier, -ière [tʀezɔʀje, -jɛʀ] *nm/f* treasurer

Trésorier-payeur [tʀezɔʀjepɛjœʀ] *nm*: **~ général (TPG)** paymaster

tressaillement [tʀesajmɑ̃] *nm* shiver, shudder; quiver

tressaillir [tʀesajiʀ] *vi* (*de peur etc*) to shiver, shudder; (*de joie*) to quiver

tressauter [tʀesote] *vi* to start, jump

tresse [tʀɛs] *nf* (*de cheveux*) braid, plait; (*cordon, galon*) braid

tresser [tʀese] *vt* (*cheveux*) to braid, plait; (*fil, jonc*) to plait; (*corbeille*) to weave; (*corde*) to twist

tréteau, x [tʀeto] *nm* trestle; **les ~x** (*fig*: *Théât*) the boards

treuil [tʀœj] *nm* winch

trêve [tʀɛv] *nf* (*Mil, Pol*) truce; (*fig*) respite; **sans ~** unremittingly; **~ de ... enough of this ...; les États de la T~** the Trucial States

tri [tʀi] *nm* (*voir trier*) sorting (out) *no pl*; selection; screening; (*Inform*) sort; (*Postes*: *action*) sorting; (: *bureau*) sorting office

triage [tʀijaʒ] *nm* (*Rail*) shunting; (*gare*) marshalling yard

trial [tʀijal] *nm* (*Sport*) scrambling

triangle [tʀijɑ̃gl(ə)] *nm* triangle; **~ isocèle/équilatéral** isosceles/equilateral triangle; **~ rectangle** right-angled triangle

triangulaire [tʀijɑ̃gylɛʀ] *adj* triangular

triathlon [tʀi(j)atlɔ̃] *nm* triathlon

tribal, e, -aux [tʀibal, -o] *adj* tribal

tribord [tʀibɔʀ] *nm*: **à ~** to starboard, on the starboard side

tribu [tʀiby] *nf* tribe

tribulations [tʀibylɑsjɔ̃] *nfpl* tribulations, trials

tribunal, -aux [tʀibynal, -o] *nm* (*Jur*) court; (*Mil*) tribunal; **~ de police/pour enfants** police/juvenile court; **~ d'instance (TI)** ≈ magistrates' court (*Brit*), ≈ district court (*US*); **~ de grande instance (TGI)** ≈ High Court (*Brit*), ≈ Supreme Court (*US*)

tribune [tʀibyn] *nf* (*estrade*) platform, rostrum; (*débat*) forum; (*d'église, de tribunal*) gallery; (*de stade*) stand; **~ libre** (*Presse*) opinion column

tribut [tʀiby] *nm* tribute

tributaire [tʀibytɛʀ] *adj*: **être ~ de** to be dependent on; (*Géo*) to be a tributary of

tricentenaire [tʀisɑ̃tnɛʀ] *nm* tercentenary, tricentennial

tricher [tʀiʃe] *vi* to cheat

tricherie [tʀiʃʀi] *nf* cheating *no pl*

tricheur, -euse [tʀiʃœʀ, -øz] *nm/f* cheat

trichromie [tʀikʀɔmi] *nf* three-colour (*Brit*) *ou* -color (*US*) printing

tricolore [tʀikɔlɔʀ] *adj* three-coloured (*Brit*), three-colored (*US*); (*français*: *drapeau*) red, white and blue; (: *équipe etc*) French

tricot [tʀiko] *nm* (*technique, ouvrage*) knitting *no pl*; (*tissu*) knitted fabric; (*vêtement*) jersey, sweater; **~ de corps** vest (*Brit*), undershirt (*US*)

tricoter [tʀikɔte] *vt* to knit; **machine/aiguille à ~** knitting machine/needle (*Brit*) *ou* pin (*US*)

trictrac [tʀiktʀak] *nm* backgammon

tricycle [tʀisikl(ə)] *nm* tricycle

tridimensionnel, le [tʀidimɑ̃sjɔnɛl] *adj* three-dimensional

triennal, e, -aux [tʀiɛnal, -o] *adj* (*prix, foire, élection*) three-yearly; (*charge, mandat, plan*) three-year

trier [tʀije] *vt* (*classer*) to sort (out); (*choisir*) to select; (*visiteurs*) to screen; (*Postes, Inform*) to sort

trieur, -euse [tʀijœʀ, -øz] *nm/f* sorter

trigonométrie [tʀigɔnɔmetʀi] *nf* trigonometry

trigonométrique [tʀigɔnɔmetʀik] *adj* trigonometric

trilingue [tʀilɛ̃g] *adj* trilingual

trilogie [tʀilɔʒi] *nf* trilogy

trimaran [tʀimaʀɑ̃] *nm* trimaran

trimbaler [tʀɛ̃bale] *vt* to cart around, trail

along

trimer [tʀime] *vi* to slave away

trimestre [tʀimɛstʀ(ə)] *nm* (*Scol*) term; (*Comm*) quarter

trimestriel, le [tʀimɛstʀijɛl] *adj* quarterly; (*Scol*) end-of-term

trimoteur [tʀimɔtœʀ] *nm* three-engined aircraft

tringle [tʀɛ̃gl(ə)] *nf* rod

Trinité [tʀinite] *nf* Trinity

Trinité et Tobago [tʀiniteetɔbago] *nf* Trinidad and Tobago

trinquer [tʀɛ̃ke] *vi* to clink glasses; (*fam*) to cop it; **~ à qch/la santé de qn** to drink to sth/sb

trio [tʀijo] *nm* trio

triolet [tʀijɔlɛ] *nm* (*Mus*) triplet

triomphal, e, -aux [tʀijɔ̃fal, -o] *adj* triumphant, triumphal

triomphalement [tʀijɔ̃falmɑ̃] *adv* triumphantly

triomphant, e [tʀijɔ̃fɑ̃, -ɑ̃t] *adj* triumphant

triomphateur, -trice [tʀijɔ̃fatœʀ, -tʀis] *nm/f* (triumphant) victor

triomphe [tʀijɔ̃f] *nm* triumph; **être reçu/ porté en ~** to be given a triumphant welcome/ be carried shoulder-high in triumph

triompher [tʀijɔ̃fe] *vi* to triumph; **~ de** to triumph over, overcome

triparti, e [tʀipaʀti] *adj* (*aussi:* **tripartite**: *réunion, assemblée*) tripartite, three-party

triperie [tʀipʀi] *nf* tripe shop

tripes [tʀip] *nfpl* (*Culin*) tripe *nsg*; (*fam*) guts

triplace [tʀiplas] *adj* three-seater *cpd*

triple [tʀipl(ə)] *adj* (*à trois éléments*) triple; (*trois fois plus grand*) treble ▷ *nm*: **le ~ (de)** (*comparaison*) three times as much (as); **en ~ exemplaire** in triplicate; **~ saut** (*Sport*) triple jump

triplé [tʀiple] *nm* hat-trick (*Brit*), triple success

triplement [tʀipləmɑ̃] *adv* (*à un degré triple*) three times over; (*de trois façons*) in three ways; (*pour trois raisons*) on three counts ▷ *nm* trebling, threefold increase

tripler [tʀiple] *vi, vt* to triple, treble, increase threefold

triplés, -ées [tʀiple] *nm/fpl* triplets

Tripoli [tʀipoli] *n* Tripoli

triporteur [tʀipɔʀtœʀ] *nm* delivery tricycle

tripot [tʀipo] *nm* (*péj*) dive

tripotage [tʀipɔtaʒ] *nm* (*péj*) jiggery-pokery

tripoter [tʀipɔte] *vt* to fiddle with, finger ▷ *vi* (*fam*) to rummage about

trique [tʀik] *nf* cudgel

trisannuel, le [tʀizanɥɛl] *adj* triennial

trisomie [tʀizɔmi] *nf* Down's syndrome

triste [tʀist(ə)] *adj* sad; (*péj*): **~ personnage/ affaire** sorry individual/affair; **c'est pas ~!** (*fam*) it's something else!

tristement [tʀistəmɑ̃] *adv* sadly

tristesse [tʀistɛs] *nf* sadness

triton [tʀitɔ̃] *nm* triton

triturer [tʀityʀe] *vt* (*pâte*) to knead; (*objets*) to manipulate

trivial, e, -aux [tʀivjal, -o] *adj* coarse, crude; (*commun*) mundane

trivialité [tʀivjalite] *nf* coarseness, crudeness; mundaneness

troc [tʀɔk] *nm* (*Écon*) barter; (*transaction*) exchange, swap

troène [tʀɔɛn] *nm* privet

troglodyte [tʀɔglɔdit] *nm/f* cave dweller, troglodyte

trognon [tʀɔɲɔ̃] *nm* (*de fruit*) core; (*de légume*) stalk

trois [tʀwa] *num* three

trois-huit [tʀwaɥit] *nmpl*: **faire les ~** to work eight-hour shifts (round the clock)

troisième [tʀwazjɛm] *num* third; **le ~ âge** the years of retirement

troisièmement [tʀwazjɛmmɑ̃] *adv* thirdly

trois quarts [tʀwakaʀ] *nmpl*: **les ~ de** three-quarters of

trolleybus [tʀɔlɛbys] *nm* trolley bus

trombe [tʀɔ̃b] *nf* waterspout; **des ~s d'eau** a downpour; **en ~** (*arriver, passer*) like a whirlwind

trombone [tʀɔ̃bɔn] *nm* (*Mus*) trombone; (*de bureau*) paper clip; **~ à coulisse** slide trombone

tromboniste [tʀɔ̃bɔnist(ə)] *nm/f* trombonist

trompe [tʀɔ̃p] *nf* (*d'éléphant*) trunk; (*Mus*) trumpet, horn; **~ d'Eustache** Eustachian tube; **~s utérines** Fallopian tubes

trompe-l'œil [tʀɔ̃plœj] *nm*: **en trompe-l'œil** in trompe-l'œil style

tromper [tʀɔ̃pe] *vt* to deceive; (*fig: espoir, attente*) to disappoint; (*vigilance, poursuivants*) to elude; **se tromper** *vi* to make a mistake, be mistaken; **se tromper de voiture/jour** to take the wrong car/ get the day wrong; **se ~ de 3 cm/20 euros** to be out by 3 cm/20 euros

tromperie [tʀɔ̃pʀi] *nf* deception, trickery *no pl*

trompette [tʀɔ̃pɛt] *nf* trumpet; **en ~** (*nez*) turned-up

trompettiste [tʀɔ̃petist(ə)] *nm/f* trumpet player

trompeur, -euse [tʀɔ̃pœʀ, -øz] *adj* deceptive, misleading

tronc [tʀɔ̃] *nm* (*Bot, Anat*) trunk; (*d'église*) collection box; **~ d'arbre** tree trunk; **~ commun** (*Scol*) common-core syllabus; **~ de cône** truncated cone

tronche [tʀɔ̃ʃ] *nf* (*fam*) mug, face

tronçon [tʀɔ̃sɔ̃] *nm* section

tronçonner [tʀɔ̃sɔne] *vt* (*arbre*) to saw up; (*pierre*) to cut up

tronçonneuse [tʀɔ̃sɔnøz] *nf* chain saw

trône [tʀon] *nm* throne; **monter sur le ~** to ascend the throne

trôner [tʀone] *vi* (*fig*) to have (*ou* take) pride of place (*Brit*), have the place of honour (*Brit*) *ou* honor (*US*)

tronquer [tʀɔ̃ke] *vt* to truncate; (*fig*) to curtail

trop [tʀo] *adv* (*avec verbe*) too much; (*aussi:* **trop nombreux**) too many; (*aussi:* **trop souvent**) too often; **~ peu (nombreux)** too few; **~ longtemps** (for) too long; **~ de** (*nombre*) too many; (*quantité*) too much; **de ~, en ~: des livres en ~** a few books too many, a few extra books; **du lait en ~** too much milk; **trois livres/cinq euros de ~** three books too many/ five euros too much

trophée [tʀɔfe] *nm* trophy

tropical, e, -aux [tʀɔpikal, -o] *adj* tropical

tropique [tʀɔpik] *nm* tropic; **tropiques** *nmpl* tropics; **~ du Cancer/Capricorne** Tropic of Cancer/Capricorn

trop-plein [tʀɔplɛ̃] *nm* (*tuyau*) overflow *ou* outlet (pipe); (*liquide*) overflow

troquer [tʀɔke] *vt*: **~ qch contre** to barter *ou* trade sth for; (*fig*) to swap sth for

trot [tʀo] *nm* trot; **aller au ~** to trot along; **partir au ~** to set off at a trot

trotter [tʀɔte] *vi* to trot; (*fig*) to scamper along (*ou* about)

trotteuse [tʀɔtøz] *nf* (*de montre*) second hand

trottiner [tʀɔtine] *vi* (*fig*) to scamper along (*ou* about)

trottinette [tʀɔtinɛt] *nf* (child's) scooter

trottoir [tʀɔtwaʀ] *nm* pavement (*Brit*), sidewalk (*US*); **faire le ~** (*péj*) to walk the streets; **~ roulant** moving pavement (*Brit*) *ou* walkway

trou [tʀu] *nm* hole; (*fig*) gap; (*Comm*) deficit; **~ d'aération** (air) vent; **~ d'air** air pocket; **~ de mémoire** blank, lapse of memory; **~ noir** black hole; **~ de la serrure** keyhole

troublant, e [tʀublɑ̃, -ɑ̃t] *adj* disturbing

trouble [tʀubl(ə)] *adj* (*liquide*) cloudy; (*image, mémoire*) indistinct, hazy; (*affaire*) shady, murky ▷ *adv* indistinctly ▷ *nm* (*désarroi*) distress, agitation; (*émoi sensuel*) turmoil, agitation; (*embarras*) confusion; (*zizanie*) unrest, discord; **troubles** *nmpl* (*Pol*) disturbances, troubles, unrest *nsg*; (*Méd*) trouble *nsg*, disorders; **~s de la personnalité** personality problems; **~s de la vision** eye trouble

trouble-fête [tʀubləfɛt] *nm/f inv* spoilsport

troubler [tʀuble] *vt* (*embarrasser*) to confuse, disconcert; (*émouvoir*) to agitate; to disturb; to perturb; (*perturber: ordre etc*) to disrupt, disturb; (*liquide*) to make cloudy; **se troubler** *vi* (*personne*) to become flustered *ou* confused; **~ l'ordre public** to cause a breach of the peace

troué, e [tʀue] *adj* with a hole (*ou* holes) in it ▷ *nf* gap; (*Mil*) breach

trouer [tʀue] *vt* to make a hole (*ou* holes) in; (*fig*) to pierce

trouille [tʀuj] *nf* (*fam*): **avoir la ~** to be scared stiff, be scared out of one's wits

troupe [tʀup] *nf* (*Mil*) troop; (*groupe*) troop, group; **la ~** (*Mil: l'armée*) the army; (: *les simples soldats*) the troops *pl*; **~ (de théâtre)** (theatrical) company; **~s de choc** shock troops

troupeau, x [tʀupo] *nm* (*de moutons*) flock; (*de vaches*) herd

trousse [tʀus] *nf* case, kit; (*d'écolier*) pencil case; (*de docteur*) instrument case; **aux ~s de** (*fig*) on the heels *ou* tail of; **~ à outils** toolkit; **~ de toilette** toilet *ou* sponge (*Brit*) bag

trousseau, x [tʀuso] *nm* (*de mariée*) trousseau; **~ de clefs** bunch of keys

trouvaille [tʀuvaj] *nf* find; (*fig: idée, expression etc*) brainwave

trouvé, e [tʀuve] *adj*: **tout ~** ready-made

trouver [tʀuve] *vt* to find; (*rendre visite*): **aller/ venir ~ qn** to go/come and see sb; **je trouve que** I find *ou* think that; **~ à boire/critiquer** to find something to drink/criticize; **~ asile/ refuge** to find refuge/shelter; **se trouver** *vi* (*être*) to be; (*être soudain*) to find o.s.; **se ~ être/ avoir** to happen to be/have; **il se trouve que** it happens that, it turns out that; **se ~ bien** to feel well; **se ~ mal** to pass out

truand [tʀyɑ̃] *nm* villain, crook

truander [tʀyɑ̃de] *vi* (*fam*) to cheat, do

trublion [tʀyblijɔ̃] *nm* troublemaker

truc [tʀyk] *nm* (*astuce*) way, device; (*de cinéma, prestidigitateur*) trick effect; (*chose*) thing; (*machin*) thingumajig, whatsit (*Brit*); **avoir le ~** to have the knack; **c'est pas son** (*ou* **mon** *etc*) **~** (*fam*) it's not really his (*ou* my *etc*) thing

truchement [tʀyʃmɑ̃] *nm*: **par le ~ de qn** through (the intervention of) sb

trucider [tʀyside] *vt* (*fam*) to do in, bump off

truculence [tʀykylɑ̃s] *nf* colourfulness (*Brit*), colorfulness (*US*)

truculent, e [tʀykylɑ̃, -ɑ̃t] *adj* colourful (*Brit*), colorful (*US*)

truelle [tʀyɛl] *nf* trowel

truffe [tʀyf] *nf* truffle; (*nez*) nose

truffé, e [tʀyfe] *adj*: **~ de** (*fig*) peppered with; (*fautes*) riddled with; (*pièges*) bristling with

truffer [tʀyfe] *vt* (*Culin*) to garnish with truffles; **truffé de** (*fig: citations*) peppered with; (: *pièges*) bristling with

truie [tʀɥi] *nf* sow

truite [tʀɥit] *nf* trout *inv*

truquage [tʀykaʒ] *nm* fixing; (*Ciné*) special effects *pl*

truquer [tʀyke] *vt* (*élections, serrure, dés*) to fix; (*Ciné*) to use special effects in

trust [tʀœst] *nm* (*Comm*) trust

truster [tʀœste] *vt* (*Comm*) to monopolize

ts *abr* = **tous**

tsar [dzaʀ] *nm* tsar

tsé-tsé [tsetse] *nf*: **mouche ~** tsetse fly

TSF *sigle f* (= *télégraphie sans fil*) wireless

tsigane [tsigan] *adj, nm/f* = **tzigane**

TSVP *abr* (= *tournez s'il vous plaît*) PTO

tt *abr* = **tout**

TT, TTA *sigle m* (= *transit temporaire (autorisé)*) vehicle registration for cars etc bought in France for export tax-free by non-residents

TTC *abr* = **toutes taxes comprises**

ttes *abr* = **toutes**

TU *sigle m* = **temps universel**

tu¹ [ty] *pron* you ▷ *nm*: **employer le tu** to use the "tu" form

tu², e [ty] *pp de* **taire**

tuant, e [tɥɑ̃, -ɑ̃t] *adj* (*épuisant*) killing; (*énervant*) infuriating

tuba [tyba] *nm* (*Mus*) tuba; (*Sport*) snorkel
tubage [tybaʒ] *nm* (*Méd*) intubation
tube [tyb] *nm* tube; (*de canalisation, métallique etc*)
pipe; (*chanson, disque*) hit song *ou* record; ~
digestif alimentary canal, digestive tract; ~ **à
essai** test tube
tuberculeux, -euse [tybɛʀkylø, -øz] *adj*
tubercular ▷ *nm/f* tuberculosis *ou* TB patient
tuberculose [tybɛʀkyloz] *nf* tuberculosis, TB
tubulaire [tybylɛʀ] *adj* tubular
tubulure [tybylyʀ] *nf* pipe; piping *no pl*; (*Auto*): ~
d'échappement/d'admission exhaust/inlet
manifold
TUC [tyk] *sigle m* (= *travail d'utilité collective*)
community work scheme for the young unemployed
tuciste [tysist(ə)] *nm/f* young person on a community
work scheme
tué, e [tɥe] *nm/f*: **cinq ~s** five killed *ou* dead
tue-mouche [tymuʃ] *adj*: **papier ~(s)** flypaper
tuer [tɥe] *vt* to kill; **se tuer** (*se suicider*) to kill o.s.;
(*dans un accident*) to be killed; **se ~ au travail** (*fig*)
to work o.s. to death
tuerie [tyʀi] *nf* slaughter *no pl*, massacre
tue-tête [tytɛt]: **à ~** *adv* at the top of one's voice
tueur [tɥœʀ] *nm* killer; **~ à gages** hired killer
tuile [tɥil] *nf* tile; (*fam*) spot of bad luck, blow
tulipe [tylip] *nf* tulip
tulle [tyl] *nm* tulle
tuméfié, e [tymefje] *adj* puffy, swollen
tumeur [tymœʀ] *nf* growth, tumour (*Brit*),
tumor (*US*)
tumulte [tymylt(ə)] *nm* commotion, hubbub
tumultueux, -euse [tymyltɥø, -øz] *adj* stormy,
turbulent
tuner [tynɛʀ] *nm* tuner
tungstène [tœ̃kstɛn] *nm* tungsten
tunique [tynik] *nf* tunic; (*de femme*) smock,
tunic
Tunis [tynis] *n* Tunis
Tunisie [tynizi] *nf*: **la ~** Tunisia
tunisien, ne [tynizjɛ̃, -ɛn] *adj* Tunisian ▷ *nm/f*:
Tunisien, ne Tunisian
tunisois, e [tynizwa, -waz] *adj* of *ou* from Tunis
tunnel [tynɛl] *nm* tunnel; **le ~ sous la Manche**
the Channel Tunnel, the Chunnel
TUP *sigle m* (= *titre universel de paiement*) ≈ payment
slip
turban [tyʀbɑ̃] *nm* turban
turbin [tyʀbɛ̃] *nm* (*fam*) work *no pl*
turbine [tyʀbin] *nf* turbine
turbo [tyʀbo] *nm* turbo; **un moteur ~** a
turbo(-charged) engine
turbomoteur [tyʀbomɔtœʀ] *nm*
turbo(-boosted) engine
turbopropulseur [tyʀbopʀɔpylsœʀ] *nm*
turboprop
turboréacteur [tyʀboʀeaktœʀ] *nm* turbojet
turbot [tyʀbo] *nm* turbot
turbotrain [tyʀbotʀɛ̃] *nm* turbotrain
turbulences [tyʀbylɑ̃s] *nfpl* (*Aviat*) turbulence *sg*
turbulent, e [tyʀbylɑ̃, -ɑ̃t] *adj* boisterous,
unruly

turc, turque [tyʀk(ə)] *adj* Turkish; (*w.-c.*)
seatless ▷ *nm* (*Ling*) Turkish ▷ *nm/f*: **Turc,
Turque** Turk/Turkish woman; **à la turque** *adv*
(*assis*) cross-legged
turf [tyʀf] *nm* racing
turfiste [tyʀfist(ə)] *nm/f* racegoer
Turks et Caïques [tyʀkekaik], **Turks et
Caicos** [tyʀkekaikɔs] *nfpl* Turks and Caicos
Islands
turpitude [tyʀpityd] *nf* base act, baseness *no pl*
turque [tyʀk(ə)] *adj f, nf voir* **turc**
Turquie [tyʀki] *nf*: **la ~** Turkey
turquoise [tyʀkwaz] *nf, adj inv* turquoise
tus *etc* [ty] *vb voir* **taire**
tut *etc* [ty] *vb voir* **taire**
tutelle [tytɛl] *nf* (*Jur*) guardianship; (*Pol*)
trusteeship; **sous la ~ de** (*fig*) under the
supervision of
tuteur, -trice [tytœʀ, -tʀis] *nm/f* (*Jur*) guardian;
(*de plante*) stake, support
tutoiement [tytwamɑ̃] *nm* use of familiar "tu"
form
tutoyer [tytwaje] *vt*: **~ qn** to address sb as "tu"
tutti quanti [tutikwɑ̃ti] *nmpl*: **et ~** and all the
rest (of them)
tutu [tyty] *nm* (*Danse*) tutu
tuyau, x [tɥijo] *nm* pipe; (*flexible*) tube; (*fam:
conseil*) tip; (: *mise au courant*) gen *no pl*; ~
d'arrosage hosepipe; **~ d'échappement**
exhaust pipe; **~ d'incendie** fire hose
tuyauté, e [tɥijote] *adj* fluted
tuyauterie [tɥijotʀi] *nf* piping *no pl*
tuyère [tɥijɛʀ] *nf* nozzle
TV [teve] *nf* TV, telly (*Brit*)
TVA *sigle f* = **taxe à** *ou sur la valeur ajoutée*
tweed [twid] *nm* tweed
tympan [tɛ̃pɑ̃] *nm* (*Anat*) eardrum
type [tip] *nm* type; (*personne, chose: représentant*)
classic example, epitome; (*fam*) chap, guy ▷ *adj*
typical, standard; **avoir le ~ nordique** to be
Nordic-looking
typé, e [tipe] *adj* ethnic (*euph*)
typhoïde [tifɔid] *nf* typhoid (fever)
typhon [tifɔ̃] *nm* typhoon
typhus [tifys] *nm* typhus (fever)
typique [tipik] *adj* typical
typiquement [tipikmɑ̃] *adv* typically
typographe [tipɔgʀaf] *nm/f* typographer
typographie [tipɔgʀafi] *nf* typography;
(*procédé*) letterpress (printing)
typographique [tipɔgʀafik] *adj* typographical;
letterpress *cpd*
typologie [tipɔlɔʒi] *nf* typology
tyran [tiʀɑ̃] *nm* tyrant
tyrannie [tiʀani] *nf* tyranny
tyrannique [tiʀanik] *adj* tyrannical
tyranniser [tiʀanize] *vt* to tyrannize
Tyrol [tiʀɔl] *nm*: **le ~** the Tyrol
tyrolien, ne [tiʀɔljɛ̃, -ɛn] *adj* Tyrolean
tzar [dzaʀ] *nm* = **tsar**
tzigane [dzigan] *adj* gipsy, tzigane ▷ *nm/f*
(Hungarian) gipsy, Tzigane

Uu

U, u [y] *nm inv* U, u; **U comme Ursule** U for Uncle
ubiquité [ybikɥite] *nf*: **avoir le don d'~** to be
everywhere at once, be ubiquitous
UDF *sigle f* (= *Union pour la démocratie française*)
political party
UE *sigle f* (= *Union européenne*) EU
UEFA [yefa] *sigle f* (= *Union of European Football
Associations*) UEFA
UEM *sigle f* (= *Union économique et monétaire*) EMU
UER *sigle f* (= *unité d'enseignement et de recherche*) old
title of UFR; (= *Union européenne de radiodiffusion*)
EBU (= *European Broadcasting Union*)
UFC *sigle f* (= *Union fédérale des consommateurs*)
national consumer group
UFR *sigle f* (= *unité de formation et de recherche*)
≈ university department
UHF *sigle f* (= *ultra-haute fréquence*) UHF
UHT *sigle* (= *ultra-haute température*) UHT
UIT *sigle f* (= *Union internationale des
télécommunications*) ITU (= *International
Telecommunications Union*)
Ukraine [ykrɛn] *nf*: **l'~** the Ukraine
ukrainien, ne [ykrɛnjɛ̃, -ɛn] *adj* Ukrainian ▷ *nm*
(*Ling*) Ukrainian ▷ *nm/f*: **Ukrainien, ne**
Ukrainian
ulcère [ylsɛʀ] *nm* ulcer; **~ à l'estomac** stomach
ulcer
ulcérer [ylseʀe] *vt* (*Méd*) to ulcerate; (*fig*) to
sicken, appal
ulcéreux, -euse [ylseʀø, -øz] *adj* (*plaie, lésion*)
ulcerous; (*membre*) ulcerated
ULM *sigle m* (= *ultra léger motorisé*) microlight
ultérieur, e [ylteʀjœʀ] *adj* later, subsequent;
remis à une date ~e postponed to a later date
ultérieurement [ylteʀjœʀmɑ̃] *adv* later
ultimatum [yltimatɔm] *nm* ultimatum
ultime [yltim] *adj* final
ultra... [yltʀa] *préfixe* ultra...
ultramoderne [yltʀamɔdɛʀn(ə)] *adj* ultra-
modern
ultra-rapide [yltʀaʀapid] *adj* ultra-fast
ultra-sensible [yltʀasɑ̃sibl(ə)] *adj* (*Photo*) high-
speed
ultrason, ultra-son [yltʀasɔ̃] *nm* ultrasound *no
pl*; **ultra(-)sons** *nmpl* ultrasonics
ultraviolet, ultra-violet, te [yltʀavjɔlɛ, -ɛt] *adj*

ultraviolet ▷ *nm*: **les ultra(-)violets** ultraviolet
rays
ululer [ylyle] *vi* = **hululer**
UME *sigle f* (= *Union monétaire européenne*) EMU
UMP *sigle f* (= *Union pour un mouvement populaire*)
political party

 MOT-CLÉ

un, une [œ̃, yn] *art indéf* a; (*devant voyelle*) an; **un
garçon/vieillard** a boy/an old man; **une fille** a
girl
▷ *pron* one; **l'un des meilleurs** one of the best;
l'un ..., l'autre (the) one ..., the other; **les
uns ..., les autres** some ..., others; **l'un et
l'autre** both (of them); **l'un ou l'autre** either
(of them); **l'un l'autre, les uns les autres**
each other, one another; **pas un seul** not a
single one; **un par un** one by one
▷ *num* one; **une pomme seulement** one apple
only
▷ *nf*: **la une** (*Presse*) the front page

unanime [ynanim] *adj* unanimous; **ils sont ~s
(à penser que)** they are unanimous (in
thinking that)
unanimement [ynanimmɑ̃] *adv* (*par tous*)
unanimously; (*d'un commun accord*) with one
accord
unanimité [ynanimite] *nf* unanimity; **à l'~**
unanimously; **faire l'~** to be approved
unanimously
UNEF [ynɛf] *sigle f* = **Union nationale des
étudiants de France**
UNESCO [ynɛsko] *sigle f* (= *United Nations
Educational, Scientific and Cultural Organization*)
UNESCO
Unetelle [yntɛl] *nf voir* **Untel**
UNI *sigle f* = **Union nationale interuniversitaire**
uni, e [yni] *adj* (*ton, tissu*) plain; (*surface*) smooth,
even; (*famille*) close(-knit); (*pays*) united
UNICEF [ynisɛf] *sigle m ou f* (= *United Nations
International Children's Emergency Fund*) UNICEF
unidirectionnel, le [ynidiʀɛksjɔnɛl] *adj*
unidirectional, one-way
unième [ynjɛm] *num*: **vingt/trente et ~**

twenty-/thirty-first; **cent ~** (one) hundred and first

unificateur, -trice [ynifikatœʀ, -tʀis] *adj* unifying

unification [ynifikɑsjɔ̃] *nf* uniting; unification; standardization

unifier [ynifje] *vt* to unite, unify; (*systèmes*) to standardize, unify; **s'unifier** *vi* to become united

uniforme [ynifɔʀm(ə)] *adj* (*mouvement*) regular, uniform; (*surface, ton*) even; (*objets, maisons*) uniform; (*fig: vie, conduite*) unchanging ▷ *nm* uniform; **être sous l'~** (*Mil*) to be serving

uniformément [ynifɔʀmemɑ̃] *adv* uniformly

uniformisation [ynifɔʀmizɑsjɔ̃] *nf* standardization

uniformiser [ynifɔʀmize] *vt* to make uniform; (*systèmes*) to standardize

uniformité [ynifɔʀmite] *nf* regularity; uniformity; evenness

unijambiste [yniʒɑ̃bist(ə)] *nm/f* one-legged man/woman

unilatéral, e, -aux [ynilateʀal, -o] *adj* unilateral; **stationnement ~** parking on one side only

unilatéralement [ynilateʀalmɑ̃] *adv* unilaterally

uninominal, e, -aux [yninɔminal, -o] *adj* uncontested

union [ynjɔ̃] *nf* union; **~ conjugale** union of marriage; **~ de consommateurs** consumers' association; **~ libre** free love; **l'U~ des Républiques socialistes soviétiques (URSS)** the Union of Soviet Socialist Republics (USSR); **l'U~ soviétique** the Soviet Union

unique [ynik] *adj* (*seul*) only; (*le même*): **un prix/ système ~** a single price/system; (*exceptionnel*) unique; **ménage à salaire ~** one-salary family; **route à voie ~** single-lane road; **fils/fille ~** only son/daughter, only child; **~ en France** the only one of its kind in France

uniquement [ynikmɑ̃] *adv* only, solely; (*juste*) only, merely

unir [yniʀ] *vt* (*nations*) to unite; (*éléments, couleurs*) to combine; (*en mariage*) to unite, join together; **~ qch à** to unite sth with; to combine sth with; **s'unir** *vi* to unite; (*en mariage*) to be joined together; **s'~ à** *ou* **avec** to unite with

unisexe [ynisɛks] *adj* unisex

unisson [ynisɔ̃] : **à l'~** *adv* in unison

unitaire [ynitɛʀ] *adj* unitary; (*Pol*) unitarian; **prix ~** unit price

unité [ynite] *nf* (*harmonie, cohésion*) unity; (*Comm, Mil, de mesure, Math*) unit; **~ centrale** central processing unit; **~ de valeur** (university) course, credit

univers [ynivɛʀ] *nm* universe

universalisation [ynivɛʀsalizɑsjɔ̃] *nf* universalization

universaliser [ynivɛʀsalize] *vt* to universalize

universalité [ynivɛʀsalite] *nf* universality

universel, le [ynivɛʀsɛl] *adj* universal; (*esprit*) all-embracing

universellement [ynivɛʀsɛlmɑ̃] *adv* universally

universitaire [ynivɛʀsitɛʀ] *adj* university *cpd*; (*diplôme, études*) academic, university *cpd* ▷ *nm/f* academic

université [ynivɛʀsite] *nf* university

univoque [ynivɔk] *adj* unambiguous; (*Math*) one-to-one

UNR *sigle f* (= *Union pour la nouvelle république*) former political party

UNSS *sigle f* = **Union nationale du sport scolaire**

Untel, Unetelle [œ̃tɛl, yntɛl] *nm/f*: **Monsieur ~** Mr so-and-so

uranium [yʀanjɔm] *nm* uranium

urbain, e [yʀbɛ̃, -ɛn] *adj* urban, city *cpd*, town *cpd*; (*poli*) urbane

urbanisation [yʀbanizɑsjɔ̃] *nf* urbanization

urbaniser [yʀbanize] *vt* to urbanize

urbanisme [yʀbanism(ə)] *nm* town planning

urbaniste [yʀbanist(ə)] *nm/f* town planner

urbanité [yʀbanite] *nf* urbanity

urée [yʀe] *nf* urea

urémie [yʀemi] *nf* uraemia (*Brit*), uremia (*US*)

urgence [yʀʒɑ̃s] *nf* urgency; (*Méd etc*) emergency; **d'~** *adj* emergency *cpd* ▷ *adv* as a matter of urgency; **en cas d'~** in case of emergency; **service des ~s** emergency service

urgent, e [yʀʒɑ̃, -ɑ̃t] *adj* urgent

urinaire [yʀinɛʀ] *adj* urinary

urinal, -aux [yʀinal, -o] *nm* (bed) urinal

urine [yʀin] *nf* urine

uriner [yʀine] *vi* to urinate

urinoir [yʀinwaʀ] *nm* (public) urinal

urne [yʀn(ə)] *nf* (*électorale*) ballot box; (*vase*) urn; **aller aux ~s** (*voter*) to go to the polls

urologie [yʀɔlɔʒi] *nf* urology

URSS [parfois : yʀs] *sigle f* (= *Union des Républiques Socialistes Soviétiques*) USSR

URSSAF [yʀsaf] *sigle f* (= *Union pour le recouvrement de la sécurité sociale et des allocations familiales*) administrative body responsible for social security funds and payments

urticaire [yʀtikɛʀ] *nf* nettle rash, urticaria

Uruguay [yʀygwɛ] *nm*: **l'~** Uruguay

uruguayen, ne [yʀygwajɛ̃, -ɛn] *adj* Uruguayan ▷ *nm/f*: **Uruguayen, ne** Uruguayan

us [ys] *nmpl*: **us et coutumes** (habits and) customs

USA *sigle mpl* (= *United States of America*) USA

usage [yzaʒ] *nm* (*emploi, utilisation*) use; (*coutume*) custom; (*éducation*) (good) manners *pl*, (good) breeding; (*Ling*): **l'~** usage; **faire ~ de** (*pouvoir, droit*) to exercise; **avoir l'~ de** to have the use of; **à l'~** *adv* with use; **à l'~ de** (*pour*) for (use of); **en ~** in use; **hors d'~** out of service; **à ~ interne** to be taken; **à ~ externe** for external use only

usagé, e [yzaʒe] *adj* (*usé*) worn; (*d'occasion*) used

usager, -ère [yzaʒe, -ɛʀ] *nm/f* user

usé, e [yze] *adj* worn (down *ou* out *ou* away); ruined; (*banal*) hackneyed

user [yze] *vt* (*outil*) to wear down; (*vêtement*) to

wear out; (*matière*) to wear away; (*consommer*: *charbon etc*) to use; (*fig: santé*) to ruin; (: *personne*) to wear out; **s'user** *vi* to wear; to wear out; (*fig*) to decline; **s'~ à la tâche** to wear o.s. out with work; **~ de** *vt* (*moyen, procédé*) to use, employ; (*droit*) to exercise

usine [yzin] *nf* factory; **~ atomique** nuclear power plant; **~ à gaz** gasworks *sg*; **~ marémotrice** tidal power station

usiner [yzine] *vt* (*Tech*) to machine; (*fabriquer*) to manufacture

usité, e [yzite] *adj* in common use, common; **peu ~** rarely used

ustensile [ystɑ̃sil] *nm* implement; **~ de cuisine** kitchen utensil

usuel, le [yzɥɛl] *adj* everyday, common

usufruit [yzyfʀɥi] *nm* usufruct

usuraire [yzyʀɛʀ] *adj* usurious

usure [yzyʀ] *nf* wear; worn state; (*de l'usurier*) usury; **avoir qn à l'~** to wear sb down; **~ normale** fair wear and tear

usurier, -ière [yzyʀje, -jɛʀ] *nm/f* usurer

usurpateur, -trice [yzyʀpatœʀ, -tʀis] *nm/f* usurper

usurpation [yzyʀpasjɔ̃] *nf* usurpation

usurper [yzyʀpe] *vt* to usurp

ut [yt] *nm* (*Mus*) C

UTA *sigle f* = **Union des transporteurs aériens**

utérin, e [yteʀɛ̃, -in] *adj* uterine

utérus [yteʀys] *nm* uterus, womb

utile [ytil] *adj* useful; **~ à qn/qch** of use to sb/sth

utilement [ytilmɑ̃] *adv* usefully

utilisable [ytilizabl(ə)] *adj* usable

utilisateur, -trice [ytilizatœʀ, -tʀis] *nm/f* user

utilisation [ytilizasjɔ̃] *nf* use

utiliser [ytilize] *vt* to use

utilitaire [ytilitɛʀ] *adj* utilitarian; (*objets*) practical ▷ *nm* (*Inform*) utility

utilité [ytilite] *nf* usefulness *no pl*; use; **jouer les ~s** (*Théât*) to play bit parts; **reconnu d'~ publique** state-approved; **c'est d'une grande ~** it's extremely useful; **il n'y a aucune ~ à ...** there's no use in ...

utopie [ytɔpi] *nf* (*idée, conception*) utopian idea *ou* view; (*société etc idéale*) utopia

utopique [ytɔpik] *adj* utopian

utopiste [ytɔpist(ə)] *nm/f* utopian

UV *sigle f* (*Scol*) = **unité de valeur** ▷ *sigle mpl* (= *ultra-violets*) UV

uvule [yvyl] *nf* uvula

Vv

V, v [ve] *nm inv* V, v ▷ *abr* (= *voir, verset*) v = **vers**;
(*de poésie*) l.; (: *en direction de*) toward(s); **V
comme Victor** V for Victor; **en V** V-shaped;
encolure en V V-neck; **décolleté en V**
plunging neckline

va [va] *vb voir* **aller**

vacance [vakɑ̃s] *nf* (*Admin*) vacancy; **vacances**
nfpl holiday(s) *pl* (*Brit*), vacation *sg* (*US*); **les
grandes ~s** the summer holidays *ou* vacation;
prendre des/ses ~s to take a holiday *ou*
vacation/one's holiday(s) *ou* vacation; **aller en
~s** to go on holiday *ou* vacation

vacancier, -ière [vakɑ̃sje, -jɛʀ] *nm/f*
holidaymaker (*Brit*), vacationer (*US*)

vacant, e [vakɑ̃, -ɑ̃t] *adj* vacant

vacarme [vakaʀm(ə)] *nm* row, din

vacataire [vakatɛʀ] *nm/f* temporary
(employee); (*enseignement*) supply (*Brit*) *ou*
substitute (*US*) teacher; (*Université*) part-time
temporary lecturer

vaccin [vaksɛ̃] *nm* vaccine; (*opération*)
vaccination

vaccination [vaksinɑsjɔ̃] *nf* vaccination

vacciner [vaksine] *vt* to vaccinate; (*fig*) to make
immune; **être vacciné** (*fig*) to be immune

vache [vaʃ] *nf* (*Zool*) cow; (*cuir*) cowhide ▷ *adj*
(*fam*) rotten, mean; **~ à eau** (*canvas*) water bag;
(**manger de la**) **~ enragée** (to go through) hard
times; **~ à lait** (*péj*) mug, sucker; **~ laitière**
dairy cow; **période des ~s maigres** lean times
pl, lean period

vachement [vaʃmɑ̃] *adv* (*fam*) damned, really

vacher, -ère [vaʃe, -ɛʀ] *nm/f* cowherd

vacherie [vaʃʀi] *nf* (*fam*) meanness *no pl*; (*action*)
dirty trick; (*propos*) nasty remark

vacherin [vaʃʀɛ̃] *nm* (*fromage*) vacherin cheese;
(*gâteau*): **~ glacé** vacherin (*type of cream gâteau*)

vachette [vaʃɛt] *nf* calfskin

vacillant, e [vasijɑ̃, -ɑ̃t] *adj* wobbly; flickering;
failing, faltering

vaciller [vasije] *vi* to sway, wobble; (*bougie,
lumière*) to flicker; (*fig*) to be failing, falter; **~
dans ses réponses** to falter in one's replies; **~
dans ses résolutions** to waver in one's
resolutions

vacuité [vakɥite] *nf* emptiness, vacuity

vade-mecum [vademekɔm] *nm inv* pocketbook

vadrouille [vadʀuj] *nf*: **être/partir en ~** to be
on/go for a wander

vadrouiller [vadʀuje] *vi* to wander around *ou*
about

va-et-vient [vaevjɛ̃] *nm inv* (*de pièce mobile*) to and
fro (*ou* up and down) movement; (*de personnes,
véhicules*) comings and goings *pl*, to-ings and
fro-ings *pl*; (*Élec*) two-way switch

vagabond, e [vagabɔ̃, -ɔ̃d] *adj* wandering;
(*imagination*) roaming, roving ▷ *nm* (*rôdeur*)
tramp, vagrant; (*voyageur*) wanderer

vagabondage [vagabɔ̃daʒ] *nm* roaming,
wandering; (*Jur*) vagrancy

vagabonder [vagabɔ̃de] *vi* to roam, wander

vagin [vaʒɛ̃] *nm* vagina

vaginal, e, -aux [vaʒinal, -o] *adj* vaginal

vagissement [vaʒismɑ̃] *nm* cry (*of newborn baby*)

vague [vag] *nf* wave ▷ *adj* vague; (*regard*)
faraway; (*manteau, robe*) loose(-fitting);
(*quelconque*): **un ~ bureau/cousin** some office/
cousin or other ▷ *nm*: **être dans le ~** to be
rather in the dark; **rester dans le ~** to keep
things rather vague; **regarder dans le ~** to
gaze into space; **~ à l'âme** *nm* vague
melancholy; **~ d'assaut** *nf* (*Mil*) wave of
assault; **~ de chaleur** *nf* heatwave; **~ de fond**
nf ground swell; **~ de froid** *nf* cold spell

vaguelette [vaglɛt] *nf* ripple

vaguement [vagmɑ̃] *adv* vaguely

vaillamment [vajamɑ̃] *adv* bravely, gallantly

vaillant, e [vajɑ̃, -ɑ̃t] *adj* (*courageux*) brave,
gallant; (*robuste*) vigorous, hale and hearty;
n'avoir plus un sou ~ to be penniless

vaille [vaj] *vb voir* **valoir**

vain, e [vɛ̃, vɛn] *adj* vain; **en ~** *adv* in vain

vaincre [vɛ̃kʀ(ə)] *vt* to defeat; (*fig*) to conquer,
overcome

vaincu, e [vɛ̃ky] *pp de* **vaincre** ▷ *nm/f* defeated
party

vainement [vɛnmɑ̃] *adv* vainly

vainquais *etc* [vɛ̃kɛ] *vb voir* **vaincre**

vainqueur [vɛ̃kœʀ] *nm* victor; (*Sport*) winner
▷ *adj m* victorious

vais [vɛ] *vb voir* **aller**

vaisseau, x [veso] *nm* (*Anat*) vessel; (*Navig*) ship, vessel; **~ spatial** spaceship

vaisselier [vɛsəlje] *nm* dresser

vaisselle [vɛsɛl] *nf* (*service*) crockery; (*plats etc à laver*) (dirty) dishes *pl*; **faire la ~** to do the washing-up (*Brit*) *ou* the dishes

val, vaux *ou* **vals** [val, vo] *nmpl* valley

valable [valabl(ə)] *adj* valid; (*acceptable*) decent, worthwhile

valablement [valabləmã] *adv* legitimately; (*de façon satisfaisante*) satisfactorily

Valence [valãs] *n* (*en Espagne*) Valencia; (*en France*) Valence

valent *etc* [val] *vb voir* **valoir**

valet [valɛ] *nm* valet; (*péj*) lackey; (*Cartes*) jack, knave (*Brit*); **~ de chambre** manservant, valet; **~ de pied** footman

valeur [valœR] *nf* (*gén*) value; (*mérite*) worth, merit; (*Comm: titre*) security; **mettre en ~** (*bien*) to exploit; (*terrain, région*) to develop; (*fig*) to highlight; to show off to advantage; **avoir de la ~** to be valuable; **prendre de la ~** to go up *ou* gain in value; **sans ~** worthless; **~ absolue** absolute value; **~ d'échange** exchange value; **~ nominale** face value; **~s mobilières** transferable securities

valeureux, -euse [valœRø, -øz] *adj* valorous

validation [validɑsjõ] *nf* validation

valide [valid] *adj* (*en bonne santé*) fit, well; (*indemne*) able-bodied, fit; (*valable*) valid

valider [valide] *vt* to validate

validité [validite] *nf* validity

valions *etc* [valjõ] *vb voir* **valoir**

valise [valiz] *nf* (suit)case; **faire sa ~** to pack one's (suit)case; **la ~ (diplomatique)** the diplomatic bag

vallée [vale] *nf* valley

vallon [valõ] *nm* small valley

vallonné, e [valɔne] *adj* undulating

vallonnement [valɔnmã] *nm* undulation

valoir [valwaR] *vi* (*être valable*) to hold, apply ▷ *vt* (*prix, valeur, effort*) to be worth; (*causer*): **~ qch à qn** to earn sb sth; **se valoir** to be of equal merit; (*péj*) to be two of a kind; **faire ~** (*droits, prérogatives*) to assert; (*domaine, capitaux*) to exploit; **faire ~ que** to point out that; **se faire ~** to make the most of o.s.; **à ~** on account; **à ~ sur** to be deducted from; **vaille que vaille** somehow or other; **cela ne me dit rien qui vaille** I don't like the look of it at all; **ce climat ne me vaut rien** this climate doesn't suit me; **~ la peine** to be worth the trouble, be worth it; **~ mieux: il vaut mieux se taire** it's better to say nothing; **il vaut mieux que je fasse/comme ceci** it's better if I do/like this; **ça ne vaut rien** it's worthless; **que vaut ce candidat?** how good is this applicant?

valorisation [valɔRizɑsjõ] *nf* (economic) development; increased standing

valoriser [valɔRize] *vt* (*Écon*) to develop (the economy of); (*produit*) to increase the value of; (*Psych*) to increase the standing of; (*fig*) to highlight, bring out

valse [vals(ə)] *nf* waltz; **c'est la ~ des étiquettes** the prices don't stay the same from one moment to the next

valser [valse] *vi* to waltz; (*fig*): **aller ~** to go flying

valu, e [valy] *pp de* **valoir**

valve [valv(ə)] *nf* valve

vamp [vɑ̃p] *nf* vamp

vampire [vɑ̃piR] *nm* vampire

van [vɑ̃] *nm* horse box (*Brit*) *ou* trailer (*US*)

vandale [vɑ̃dal] *nm/f* vandal

vandalisme [vɑ̃dalism(ə)] *nm* vandalism

vanille [vanij] *nf* vanilla; **glace à la ~** vanilla ice cream

vanillé, e [vanije] *adj* vanilla *cpd*

vanité [vanite] *nf* vanity

vaniteux, -euse [vanitø, -øz] *adj* vain, conceited

vanity-case [vaniti(e)kɛz] *nm* vanity case

vanne [van] *nf* gate; (*fam: remarque*) dig, (nasty) crack; **lancer une ~ à qn** to have a go at sb (*Brit*), knock sb

vanneau, x [vano] *nm* lapwing

vanner [vane] *vt* to winnow

vannerie [vanRi] *nf* basketwork

vantail, -aux [vɑ̃taj, -o] *nm* door, leaf

vantard, e [vɑ̃taR, -aRd(ə)] *adj* boastful

vantardise [vɑ̃taRdiz] *nf* boastfulness *no pl*; boast

vanter [vɑ̃te] *vt* to speak highly of, vaunt; **se vanter** *vi* to boast, brag; **se ~ de** to pride o.s. on; (*péj*) to boast of

va-nu-pieds [vanypje] *nm/f inv* tramp, beggar

vapeur [vapœR] *nf* steam; (*émanation*) vapour (*Brit*), vapor (*US*), fumes *pl*; (*brouillard, buée*) haze; **vapeurs** *nfpl* (*bouffées*) vapours, vapors; **à ~** steam-powered, steam *cpd*; **à toute ~** full steam ahead; (*fig*) at full tilt; **renverser la ~** to reverse engines; (*fig*) to backtrack, backpedal; **cuit à la ~** steamed

vapocuiseur [vapokyizœR] *nm* pressure cooker

vaporeux, -euse [vapoRø, -øz] *adj* (*flou*) hazy, misty; (*léger*) filmy, gossamer *cpd*

vaporisateur [vapoRizatœR] *nm* spray

vaporiser [vapoRize] *vt* (*Chimie*) to vaporize; (*parfum etc*) to spray

vaquer [vake] *vi* (*Admin*) to be on vacation; **~ à ses occupations** to attend to one's affairs, go about one's business

varappe [vaRap] *nf* rock climbing

varappeur, -euse [vaRapœR, -øz] *nm/f* (rock) climber

varech [vaRɛk] *nm* wrack, varec

vareuse [vaRøz] *nf* (*blouson*) pea jacket; (*d'uniforme*) tunic

variable [vaRjabl(ə)] *adj* variable; (*temps, humeur*) changeable; (*Tech: à plusieurs positions etc*) adaptable; (*Ling*) inflectional; (*divers: résultats*) varied, various ▷ *nf* (*Inform, Math*) variable

variante [vaRjãt] *nf* variant

variation [vaRjɑsjõ] *nf* variation; changing *no pl*, change; (*Mus*) variation

varice [vaʀis] *nf* varicose vein

varicelle [vaʀisɛl] *nf* chickenpox

varié, e [vaʀje] *adj* varied; (*divers*) various; **hors-d'œuvre ~s** selection of hors d'œuvres

varier [vaʀje] *vi* to vary; (*temps, humeur*) to change ▷ *vt* to vary

variété [vaʀjete] *nf* variety; **spectacle de ~s** variety show

variole [vaʀjɔl] *nf* smallpox

variqueux, -euse [vaʀikø, -øz] *adj* varicose

Varsovie [vaʀsɔvi] *n* Warsaw

vas [va] *vb voir* **aller**; **~-y!** [vazi] go on!

vasculaire [vaskylɛʀ] *adj* vascular

vase [vaz] *nm* vase ▷ *nf* silt, mud; **en ~ clos** in isolation; **~ de nuit** chamberpot; **~s communicants** communicating vessels

vasectomie [vazɛktɔmi] *nf* vasectomy

vaseline [vazlin] *nf* Vaseline®

vaseux, -euse [vazø, -øz] *adj* silty, muddy; (*fig: confus*) woolly, hazy; (: *fatigué*) peaky; (: *étourdi*) woozy

vasistas [vazistas] *nm* fanlight

vasque [vask(ə)] *nf* (*bassin*) basin; (*coupe*) bowl

vassal, e, -aux [vasal, -o] *nm/f* vassal

vaste [vast(ə)] *adj* vast, immense

Vatican [vatikɑ̃] *nm*: **le ~** the Vatican

vaticiner [vatisine] *vi* (*péj*) to make pompous predictions

va-tout [vatu] *nm*: **jouer son ~** to stake one's all

vaudeville [vodvil] *nm* vaudeville, light comedy

vaudrai *etc* [vodʀe] *vb voir* **valoir**

vau-l'eau [volo]: **à vau-l'eau** *adv* with the current; **s'en aller à vau-l'eau** (*fig: projets*) to be adrift

vaurien, ne [voʀjɛ̃, -ɛn] *nm/f* good-for-nothing, guttersnipe

vaut [vo] *vb voir* **valoir**

vautour [votuʀ] *nm* vulture

vautrer [votʀe]: **se vautrer** *vi*: **se ~ dans** to wallow in; **se ~ sur** to sprawl on

vaux [vo] *pl de* **val** ▷ *vb voir* **valoir**

va-vite [vavit]: **à la ~** *adv* in a rush

vd *abr* = **vend**

VDQS *sigle m* (= *vin délimité de qualité supérieure*) label guaranteeing quality of wine

vds *abr* = **vends**

veau, x [vo] *nm* (*Zool*) calf; (*Culin*) veal; (*peau*) calfskin; **tuer le ~ gras** to kill the fatted calf

vecteur [vɛktœʀ] *nm* vector; (*Mil, Bio*) carrier

vécu, e [veky] *pp de* **vivre** ▷ *adj* real(-life)

vedettariat [vədɛtaʀja] *nm* stardom; (*attitude*) acting like a star

vedette [vədɛt] *nf* (*artiste etc*) star; (*canot*) patrol boat; launch; **avoir la ~** to top the bill, get star billing; **mettre qn en ~** (*Ciné etc*) to give sb the starring role; (*fig*) to push sb into the limelight; **voler la ~ à qn** to steal the show from sb

végétal, e, -aux [veʒetal, -o] *adj* vegetable ▷ *nm* vegetable, plant

végétalien, ne [veʒetaljɛ̃, -ɛn] *adj, nm/f* vegan

végétalisme [veʒetalism(ə)] *nm* veganism

végétarien, ne [veʒetaʀjɛ̃, -ɛn] *adj, nm/f* vegetarian

végétarisme [veʒetaʀism(ə)] *nm* vegetarianism

végétatif, -ive [veʒetatif, -iv] *adj*: **une vie ~ive** a vegetable existence

végétation [veʒetasjɔ̃] *nf* vegetation; **végétations** *nfpl* (*Méd*) adenoids

végéter [veʒete] *vi* (*fig*) to vegetate

véhémence [veemɑ̃s] *nf* vehemence

véhément, e [veemɑ̃, -ɑ̃t] *adj* vehement

véhicule [veikyl] *nm* vehicle; **~ utilitaire** commercial vehicle

véhiculer [veikyle] *vt* (*personnes, marchandises*) to transport, convey; (*fig: idées, substances*) to convey, serve as a vehicle for

veille [vɛj] *nf* (*garde*) watch; (*Psych*) wakefulness; (*jour*) **la ~** the day before, the previous day; **la ~ au soir** the previous evening; **la ~ de** the day before; **à la ~ de** on the eve of; **l'état de ~** the waking state

veillée [veje] *nf* (*soirée*) evening; (*réunion*) evening gathering; **~ d'armes** night before combat; (*fig*) vigil; **~ (mortuaire)** watch

veiller [veje] *vi* (*rester debout*) to stay ou sit up; (*ne pas dormir*) to be awake; (*être de garde*) to be on watch; (*être vigilant*) to be watchful ▷ *vt* (*malade, mort*) to watch over, sit up with; **~ à** *vt* to attend to, see to; **~ à ce que** to make sure that, see to it that; **~ sur** *vt* to keep a watch ou an eye on

veilleur [vɛjœʀ] *nm*: **~ de nuit** night watchman

veilleuse [vɛjøz] *nf* (*lampe*) night light; (*Auto*) sidelight; (*flamme*) pilot light; **en ~** *adj* (*lampe*) dimmed; (*fig: affaire*) shelved, set aside

veinard, e [vɛnaʀ, -aʀd(ə)] *nm/f* (*fam*) lucky devil

veine [vɛn] *nf* (*Anat, du bois etc*) vein; (*filon*) vein, seam; (*fam: chance*): **avoir de la ~** to be lucky; (*inspiration*) inspiration

veiné, e [vene] *adj* veined; (*bois*) grained

veineux, -euse [venø, -øz] *adj* venous

Velcro® [vɛlkʀo] *nm* Velcro®

vêler [vele] *vi* to calve

vélin [velɛ̃] *nm*: **(papier) ~** vellum (paper)

véliplanchiste [veliplɑ̃ʃist(ə)] *nm/f* windsurfer

velléitaire [veleitɛʀ] *adj* irresolute, indecisive

velléités [veleite] *nfpl* vague impulses

vélo [velo] *nm* bike, cycle; **faire du ~** to go cycling

véloce [velɔs] *adj* swift

vélocité [velɔsite] *nf* (*Mus*) nimbleness, swiftness; (*vitesse*) velocity

vélodrome [velɔdʀom] *nm* velodrome

vélomoteur [velɔmotœʀ] *nm* moped

véloski [veloski] *nm* skibob

velours [vəluʀ] *nm* velvet; **~ côtelé** corduroy

velouté, e [vəlute] *adj* (*au toucher*) velvety; (*à la vue*) soft, mellow; (*au goût*) smooth, mellow ▷ *nm*: **~ d'asperges/de tomates** cream of asparagus/tomato soup

velouteux, -euse [vəlutø, -øz] *adj* velvety

velu, e [vəly] *adj* hairy

venais *etc* [vəne] *vb voir* **venir**

venaison [vənɛzɔ̃] *nf* venison

vénal, e, -aux [venal, -o] *adj* venal
vénalité [venalite] *nf* venality
venant [vənɑ̃]: **à tout ~** *adv* to all and sundry
vendable [vɑ̃dabl(ə)] *adj* saleable, marketable
vendange [vɑ̃dɑ̃ʒ] *nf* (*opération, période: aussi:* **vendanges**) grape harvest; (*raisins*) grape crop, grapes *pl*
vendanger [vɑ̃dɑ̃ʒe] *vi* to harvest the grapes
vendangeur, -euse [vɑ̃dɑ̃ʒœʀ, -øz] *nm/f* grape-picker
vendéen, ne [vɑ̃deɛ̃, -ɛn] *adj* of ou from the Vendée
vendeur, -euse [vɑ̃dœʀ, -øz] *nm/f* (*de magasin*) shop ou sales assistant (*Brit*), sales clerk (*US*); (*Comm*) salesman/woman ▷ *nm* (*Jur*) vendor, seller; **~ de journaux** newspaper seller
vendre [vɑ̃dʀ(ə)] *vt* to sell; **~ qch à qn** to sell sb sth; **cela se vend à la douzaine** these are sold by the dozen; **"à ~"** "for sale"
vendredi [vɑ̃dʀədi] *nm* Friday; **V~ saint** Good Friday; *voir aussi* **lundi**
vendu, e [vɑ̃dy] *pp de* **vendre** ▷ *adj* (*péj*) corrupt
venelle [vənɛl] *nf* alley
vénéneux, -euse [venenø, -øz] *adj* poisonous
vénérable [veneʀabl(ə)] *adj* venerable
vénération [veneʀasjɔ̃] *nf* veneration
vénérer [veneʀe] *vt* to venerate
vénerie [vɛnʀi] *nf* hunting
vénérien, ne [veneʀjɛ̃, -ɛn] *adj* venereal
Venezuela [venezɥela] *nm*: **le ~** Venezuela
vénézuélien, ne [venezɥeljɛ̃, -ɛn] *adj* Venezuelan ▷ *nm/f*: **Vénézuélien, ne** Venezuelan
vengeance [vɑ̃ʒɑ̃s] *nf* vengeance *no pl*, revenge *no pl*; (*acte*) act of vengeance *ou* revenge
venger [vɑ̃ʒe] *vt* to avenge; **se venger** *vi* to avenge o.s.; (*par rancune*) to take revenge; **se ~ de qch** to avenge o.s. for sth; to take one's revenge for sth; **se ~ de qn** to take revenge on sb; **se ~ sur** to wreak vengeance upon; to take revenge on ou through; to take it out on
vengeur, -eresse [vɑ̃ʒœʀ, -ʒʀɛs] *adj* vengeful ▷ *nm/f* avenger
véniel, le [venjɛl] *adj* venial
venimeux, -euse [vənimø, -øz] *adj* poisonous, venomous; (*fig: haineux*) venomous, vicious
venin [vənɛ̃] *nm* venom, poison; (*fig*) venom
venir [vəniʀ] *vi* to come; **~ de** to come from; **~ de faire**: **je viens d'y aller/de le voir** I've just been there/seen him; **s'il vient à pleuvoir** if it should rain, if it happens to rain; **en ~ à faire**: **j'en viens à croire que** I am coming to believe that; **où veux-tu en ~?** what are you getting at?; **il en est venu à mendier** he has been reduced to begging; **en ~ aux mains** to come to blows; **les années/générations à ~** the years/generations to come; **il me vient une idée** an idea has just occurred to me; **il me vient des soupçons** I'm beginning to be suspicious; **je te vois ~** I know what you're after; **faire ~** (*docteur, plombier*) to call (out); **d'où vient que ...?** how is it that ...?; **~ au monde** to come into the world
Venise [vəniz] *n* Venice

vénitien, ne [venisjɛ̃, -ɛn] *adj* Venetian
vent [vɑ̃] *nm* wind; **il y a du ~** it's windy; **c'est du ~** it's all hot air; **au ~** to windward; **sous le ~** to leeward; **avoir le ~ debout/arrière** to head into the wind/have the wind astern; **dans le ~** (*fam*) trendy; **prendre le ~** (*fig*) to see which way the wind blows; **avoir ~ de** to get wind of; **contre ~s et marées** come hell or high water
vente [vɑ̃t] *nf* sale; **la ~** (*activité*) selling; (*secteur*) sales *pl*; **mettre en ~** to put on sale; (*objets personnels*) to put up for sale; **~ de charité** jumble (*Brit*) ou rummage (*US*) sale; **~ par correspondance (VPC)** mail-order selling; **~ aux enchères** auction sale
venté, e [vɑ̃te] *adj* windswept, windy
venter [vɑ̃te] *vb impers*: **il vente** the wind is blowing
venteux, -euse [vɑ̃tø, -øz] *adj* windswept, windy
ventilateur [vɑ̃tilatœʀ] *nm* fan
ventilation [vɑ̃tilɑsjɔ̃] *nf* ventilation
ventiler [vɑ̃tile] *vt* to ventilate; (*total, statistiques*) to break down
ventouse [vɑ̃tuz] *nf* (*ampoule*) cupping glass; (*de caoutchouc*) suction pad; (*Zool*) sucker
ventre [vɑ̃tʀ(ə)] *nm* (*Anat*) stomach; (*fig*) belly; **prendre du ~** to be getting a paunch; **avoir mal au ~** to have (a) stomach ache
ventricule [vɑ̃tʀikyl] *nm* ventricle
ventriloque [vɑ̃tʀilɔk] *nm/f* ventriloquist
ventripotent, e [vɑ̃tʀipɔtɑ̃, -ɑ̃t] *adj* potbellied
ventru, e [vɑ̃tʀy] *adj* potbellied
venu, e [vəny] *pp de* **venir** ▷ *adj*: **être mal ~ à** ou **de faire** to have no grounds for doing, be in no position to do; **mal ~** ill-timed, unwelcome; **bien ~** timely, welcome ▷ *nf* coming
vêpres [vɛpʀ(ə)] *nfpl* vespers
ver [vɛʀ] *nm* worm; (*des fruits etc*) maggot; (*du bois*) woodworm *no pl*; **~ blanc** May beetle grub; **~ luisant** glow-worm; **~ à soie** silkworm; **~ solitaire** tapeworm; **~ de terre** earthworm
véracité [veʀasite] *nf* veracity
véranda [veʀɑ̃da] *nf* veranda(h)
verbal, e, -aux [vɛʀbal, -o] *adj* verbal
verbalement [vɛʀbalmɑ̃] *adv* verbally
verbaliser [vɛʀbalize] *vi* (*Police*) to book ou report an offender; (*Psych*) to verbalize
verbe [vɛʀb(ə)] *nm* (*Ling*) verb; (*voix*): **avoir le ~ sonore** to have a sonorous tone (of voice); (*expression*): **la magie du ~** the magic of language ou the word; (*Rel*): **le V~** the Word
verbeux, -euse [vɛʀbø, -øz] *adj* verbose, wordy
verbiage [vɛʀbjaʒ] *nm* verbiage
verbosité [vɛʀbozite] *nf* verbosity
verdâtre [vɛʀdɑtʀ(ə)] *adj* greenish
verdeur [vɛʀdœʀ] *nf* (*vigueur*) vigour (*Brit*), vigor (*US*), vitality; (*crudité*) forthrightness; (*défaut de maturité*) tartness, sharpness
verdict [vɛʀdik(t)] *nm* verdict
verdir [vɛʀdiʀ] *vi, vt* to turn green
verdoyant, e [vɛʀdwajɑ̃, -ɑ̃t] *adj* green, verdant
verdure [vɛʀdyʀ] *nf* (*arbres, feuillages*) greenery;

(*légumes verts*) green vegetables *pl*, greens *pl*

véreux, -euse [verø, -øz] *adj* worm-eaten; (*malhonnête*) shady, corrupt

verge [vɛrʒ(ə)] *nf* (*Anat*) penis; (*baguette*) stick, cane

verger [vɛrʒe] *nm* orchard

vergeture [vɛrʒətyr] *nf gén pl* stretch mark

verglacé, e [vɛrglase] *adj* icy, iced-over

verglas [vɛrgla] *nm* (black) ice

vergogne [vɛrgɔɲ]: **sans ~** *adv* shamelessly

véridique [veridik] *adj* truthful

vérificateur, -trice [verifikatœr, -tris] *nm/f* controller, checker ▷ *nf* (*machine*) verifier; **~ des comptes** (*Finance*) auditor

vérification [verifikasjɔ̃] *nf* checking *no pl*, check; **~ d'identité** identity check

vérifier [verifje] *vt* to check; (*corroborer*) to confirm, bear out; **se vérifier** *vi* to be confirmed *ou* verified

vérin [verɛ̃] *nm* jack

véritable [veritabl(ə)] *adj* real; (*ami, amour*) true; **un ~ désastre** an absolute disaster

véritablement [veritabləmã] *adv* (*effectivement*) really; (*absolument*) absolutely

vérité [verite] *nf* truth; (*d'un portrait*) lifelikeness; (*sincérité*) truthfulness, sincerity; **en ~, à la ~** to tell the truth

verlan [vɛrlã] *nm* (back) slang; *see note*

⬤ **VERLAN**

Verlan is a form of slang popularized in the 1950's. It consists of inverting a word's syllables, the term *verlan* itself coming from "l'envers" ("à l'envers" = back to front). Typical examples are "féca" ("café"), "ripou" ("pourri"), "meuf" ("femme"), and "beur" ("Arabe").

vermeil, le [vɛrmɛj] *adj* bright red, ruby red ▷ *nm* (*substance*) vermeil

vermicelles [vɛrmisɛl] *nmpl* vermicelli *sg*

vermifuge [vɛrmifyʒ] *nm*: **poudre ~** worm powder

vermillon [vɛrmijɔ̃] *adj inv* vermilion, scarlet

vermine [vɛrmin] *nf* vermin *pl*

vermoulu, e [vɛrmuly] *adj* worm-eaten, with woodworm

vermout, vermouth [vɛrmut] *nm* vermouth

verni, e [vɛrni] *adj* varnished; glazed; (*fam*) lucky; **cuir ~** patent leather; **souliers ~s** patent (leather) shoes

vernir [vɛrnir] *vt* (*bois, tableau, ongles*) to varnish; (*poterie*) to glaze

vernis [vɛrni] *nm* (*enduit*) varnish; glaze; (*fig*) veneer; **~ à ongles** nail varnish (*Brit*) *ou* polish

vernissage [vɛrnisaʒ] *nm* varnishing; glazing; (*d'une exposition*) preview

vernisser [vɛrnise] *vt* to glaze

vérole [verɔl] *nf* (*variole*) smallpox; (*fam: syphilis*) pox

Vérone [verɔn] *n* Verona

verrai *etc* [vɛre] *vb voir* **voir**

verre [vɛr] *nm* glass; (*de lunettes*) lens *sg*; **verres** *nmpl* (*lunettes*) glasses; **boire** *ou* **prendre un ~** to have a drink; **~ à vin/à liqueur** wine/liqueur glass; **~ à dents** tooth mug; **~ dépoli** frosted glass; **~ de lampe** lamp glass *ou* chimney; **~ de montre** watch glass; **~ à pied** stemmed glass; **~s de contact** contact lenses; **~s fumés** tinted lenses

verrerie [vɛrri] *nf* (*fabrique*) glassworks *sg*; (*activité*) glass-making, glass-working; (*objets*) glassware

verrier [vɛrje] *nm* glass-blower

verrière [vɛrjɛr] *nf* (*grand vitrage*) window; (*toit vitré*) glass roof

verrons *etc* [vɛrɔ̃] *vb voir* **voir**

verroterie [vɛrɔtri] *nf* glass beads *pl*, glass jewellery (*Brit*) *ou* jewelry (*US*)

verrou [vɛru] *nm* (*targette*) bolt; (*fig*) constriction; **mettre le ~** to bolt the door; **mettre qn sous les ~s** to put sb behind bars

verrouillage [vɛrujaʒ] *nm* (*dispositif*) locking mechanism; (*Auto*): **~ central** *ou* **centralisé** central locking

verrouiller [vɛruje] *vt* to bolt; to lock; (*Mil: brèche*) to close

verrue [vɛry] *nf* wart; (*plantaire*) verruca; (*fig*) eyesore

vers [vɛr] *nm* line ▷ *nmpl* (*poésie*) verse *sg* ▷ *prép* (*en direction de*) toward(s); (*près de*) around (about); (*temporel*) about, around

versant [vɛrsã] *nm* slopes *pl*, side

versatile [vɛrsatil] *adj* fickle, changeable

verse [vɛrs(ə)]: **à ~** *adv*: **il pleut à ~** it's pouring (with rain)

versé, e [vɛrse] *adj*: **être ~ dans** (*science*) to be (well-)versed in

Verseau [vɛrso] *nm*: **le ~** Aquarius, the water-carrier; **être du ~** to be Aquarius

versement [vɛrsəmã] *nm* payment; (*sur un compte*) deposit, remittance; **en trois ~s** in three instalments

verser [vɛrse] *vt* (*liquide, grains*) to pour; (*larmes, sang*) to shed; (*argent*) to pay; (*soldat: affecter*): **~ qn dans** to assign sb to ▷ *vi* (*véhicule*) to overturn; (*fig*): **~ dans** to lapse into; **~ à un compte** to pay into an account

verset [vɛrsɛ] *nm* verse; versicle

verseur [vɛrsœr] *adj m voir* **bec**; **bouchon**

versification [vɛrsifikasjɔ̃] *nf* versification

versifier [vɛrsifje] *vt* to put into verse ▷ *vi* to versify, write verse

version [vɛrsjɔ̃] *nf* version; (*Scol*) translation (*into the mother tongue*); **film en ~ originale** film in the original language

verso [vɛrso] *nm* back; **voir au ~** see over(leaf)

vert, e [vɛr, vɛrt(ə)] *adj* green; (*vin*) young; (*vigoureux*) sprightly; (*cru*) forthright ▷ *nm* green; **dire des ~es (et des pas mûres)** to say some pretty spicy things; **il en a vu des ~es** he's seen a thing or two; **~ bouteille** *adj inv* bottle-green; **~ d'eau** *adj inv* sea-green; **~**

pomme *adj inv* apple-green

vert-de-gris [vɛʀdəgʀi] *nm* verdigris ▷ *adj inv* grey(ish)-green

vertébral, e, aux [vɛʀtebʀal, -o] *adj* back *cpd*; *voir* **colonne**

vertébré, e [vɛʀtebʀe] *adj, nm* vertebrate

vertèbre [vɛʀtɛbʀ(ə)] *nf* vertebra

vertement [vɛʀtəmɑ̃] *adv* (*réprimander*) sharply

vertical, e, -aux [vɛʀtikal, -o] *adj, nf* vertical; **à la ~e** *adv* vertically

verticalement [vɛʀtikalmɑ̃] *adv* vertically

verticalité [vɛʀtikalite] *nf* verticalness, verticality

vertige [vɛʀtiʒ] *nm* (*peur du vide*) vertigo; (*étourdissement*) dizzy spell; (*fig*) fever; **ça me donne le ~** it makes me dizzy; (*fig*) it makes my head spin *ou* reel

vertigineux, -euse [vɛʀtiʒinø, -øz] *adj* (*hausse, vitesse*) breathtaking; (*altitude, gorge*) breathtakingly high (*ou* deep)

vertu [vɛʀty] *nf* virtue; **une ~** a saint, a paragon of virtue; **avoir la ~ de faire** to have the virtue of doing; **en ~ de** *prép* in accordance with

vertueusement [vɛʀtɥøzmɑ̃] *adv* virtuously

vertueux, -euse [vɛʀtɥø, -øz] *adj* virtuous

verve [vɛʀv(ə)] *nf* witty eloquence; **être en ~** to be in brilliant form

verveine [vɛʀvɛn] *nf* (*Bot*) verbena, vervain; (*infusion*) verbena tea

vésicule [vezikyl] *nf* vesicle; **~ biliaire** gall-bladder

vespasienne [vɛspazjɛn] *nf* urinal

vespéral, e, -aux [vɛspeʀal, -o] *adj* vespertine, evening *cpd*

vessie [vesi] *nf* bladder

veste [vɛst(ə)] *nf* jacket; **~ droite/croisée** single-/double-breasted jacket; **retourner sa ~** (*fig*) to change one's colours

vestiaire [vɛstjɛʀ] *nm* (*au théâtre etc*) cloakroom; (*de stade etc*) changing-room (*Brit*), locker-room (*US*); (*métallique*): (**armoire**) **~** locker

vestibule [vɛstibyl] *nm* hall

vestige [vɛstiʒ] *nm* (*objet*) relic; (*fragment*) trace; (*fig*) remnant, vestige; **vestiges** *nmpl* (*d'une ville*) remains; (*d'une civilisation, du passé*) remnants, relics

vestimentaire [vɛstimɑ̃tɛʀ] *adj* (*dépenses*) clothing; (*détail*) of dress; (*élégance*) sartorial

veston [vɛstɔ̃] *nm* jacket

Vésuve [vezyv] *nm*: **le ~** Vesuvius

vêtais *etc* [vɛtɛ] *vb voir* **vêtir**

vêtement [vɛtmɑ̃] *nm* garment, item of clothing; (*Comm*): **le ~** the clothing industry; **vêtements** *nmpl* clothes; **~s de sport** sportswear *sg*, sports clothes

vétéran [veteʀɑ̃] *nm* veteran

vétérinaire [veteʀinɛʀ] *adj* veterinary ▷ *nm/f* vet, veterinary surgeon (*Brit*), veterinarian (*US*)

vétille [vetij] *nf* trifle, triviality

vétilleux, -euse [vetijø, -øz] *adj* punctilious

vêtir [vetiʀ] *vt* to clothe, dress; **se vêtir** to dress (o.s.)

vêtit *etc* [veti] *vb voir* **vêtir**

vétiver [vetiveʀ] *nm* (*Bot*) vetiver

veto [veto] *nm* veto; **droit de ~** right of veto; **mettre** *ou* **opposer un ~ à** to veto

vêtu, e [vety] *pp de* **vêtir** ▷ *adj*: **~ de** dressed in, wearing; **chaudement ~** warmly dressed

vétuste [vetyst(ə)] *adj* ancient, timeworn

vétusté [vetyste] *nf* age, delapidation

veuf, veuve [vœf, v v] *adj* widowed ▷ *nm* widower ▷ *nf* widow

veuille [vœj], **veuillez** *etc* [vœje] *vb voir* **vouloir**

veule [vøl] *adj* spineless

veulent *etc* [vœl] *vb voir* **vouloir**

veulerie [vølʀi] *nf* spinelessness

veut [vø] *vb voir* **vouloir**

veuvage [vœvaʒ] *nm* widowhood

veuve [vœv] *adj f, nf voir* **veuf**

veux [vø] *vb voir* **vouloir**

vexant, e [vɛksɑ̃, -ɑ̃t] *adj* (*contrariant*) annoying; (*blessant*) upsetting

vexations [vɛksasjɔ̃] *nfpl* humiliations

vexatoire [vɛksatwaʀ] *adj*: **mesures ~s** harassment *sg*

vexer [vɛkse] *vt* to hurt, upset; **se vexer** *vi* to be hurt, get upset

VF *sigle f* (*Ciné*) = **version française**

VHF *sigle f* (= *Very High Frequency*) VHF

via [vja] *prép* via

viabiliser [vjabilize] *vt* to provide with services (*water etc*)

viabilité [vjabilite] *nf* viability; (*d'un chemin*) practicability

viable [vjabl(ə)] *adj* viable

viaduc [vjadyk] *nm* viaduct

viager, -ère [vjaʒe, -ɛʀ] *adj*: **rente viagère** life annuity ▷ *nm*: **mettre en ~** to sell in return for a life annuity

viande [vjɑ̃d] *nf* meat

viatique [vjatik] *nm* (*Rel*) viaticum; (*fig*) provisions *pl ou* money for the journey

vibrant, e [vibʀɑ̃, -ɑ̃t] *adj* vibrating; (*voix*) vibrant; (*émouvant*) emotive

vibraphone [vibʀafɔn] *nm* vibraphone, vibes *pl*

vibraphoniste [vibʀafɔnist(ə)] *nm/f* vibraphone player

vibration [vibʀasjɔ̃] *nf* vibration

vibratoire [vibʀatwaʀ] *adj* vibratory

vibrer [vibʀe] *vi* to vibrate; (*son, voix*) to be vibrant; (*fig*) to be stirred; **faire ~** to (cause to) vibrate; to stir, thrill

vibromasseur [vibʀomasœʀ] *nm* vibrator

vicaire [vikɛʀ] *nm* curate

vice... [vis] *préfixe* vice-

vice [vis] *nm* vice; (*défaut*) fault; **~ caché** (*Comm*) latent *ou* inherent defect; **~ de forme** legal flaw *ou* irregularity

vice-consul [viskɔ̃syl] *nm* vice-consul

vice-présidence [vispʀezidɑ̃s] *nf* (*d'un pays*) vice-presidency; (*d'une société*) vice-presidency, vice-chairmanship (*Brit*)

vice-président, e [vispʀezidɑ̃, -ɑ̃t] *nm/f* vice-president; vice-chairman

vice-roi [visrwa] *nm* viceroy

vice-versa [viseversa] *adv* vice versa

vichy [viʃi] *nm (toile)* gingham; *(eau)* Vichy water; **carottes V~** boiled carrots

vichyssois, e [viʃiswa, -waz] *adj* of *ou* from Vichy, Vichy *cpd* ▷ *nf (soupe)* vichyssoise (soup), cream of leek and potato soup ▷ *nm/f*: **Vichyssois, e** native *ou* inhabitant of Vichy

vicié, e [visje] *adj (air)* polluted, tainted; *(Jur)* invalidated

vicier [visje] *vt (Jur)* to invalidate

vicieux, -euse [visjø, -øz] *adj (pervers)* dirty(-minded); *(méchant)* nasty; *(fautif)* incorrect, wrong

vicinal, e, -aux [visinal, -o] *adj*: **chemin ~** byroad, byway

vicissitudes [visisityd] *nfpl* (trials and) tribulations

vicomte [vikɔ̃t] *nm* viscount

vicomtesse [vikɔ̃tɛs] *nf* viscountess

victime [viktim] *nf* victim; *(d'accident)* casualty; **être (la) ~ de** to be the victim of; **être ~ d'une attaque/d'un accident** to suffer a stroke/be involved in an accident

victoire [viktwar] *nf* victory

victorieusement [viktɔrjøzmɑ̃] *adv* triumphantly, victoriously

victorieux, -euse [viktɔrjø, -øz] *adj* victorious; *(sourire, attitude)* triumphant

victuailles [viktɥaj] *nfpl* provisions

vidange [vidɑ̃ʒ] *nf (d'un fossé, réservoir)* emptying; *(Auto)* oil change; *(de lavabo: bonde)* waste outlet; **vidanges** *nfpl (matières)* sewage *sg*; **faire la ~** *(Auto)* to change the oil, do an oil change; **tuyau de ~** drainage pipe

vidanger [vidɑ̃ʒe] *vt* to empty; **faire ~ la voiture** to have the oil changed in one's car

vide [vid] *adj* empty ▷ *nm (Physique)* vacuum; *(espace)* (empty) space, gap; *(sous soi: dans une falaise etc)* drop; *(futilité, néant)* void; **~ de** empty of; *(de sens etc)* devoid of; **sous ~** *adv* in a vacuum; **emballé sous ~** vacuum-packed; **regarder dans le ~** to stare into space; **avoir peur du ~** to be afraid of heights; **parler dans le ~** to waste one's breath; **faire le ~** *(dans son esprit)* to make one's mind go blank; **faire le ~ autour de qn** to isolate sb; **à ~** *adv (sans occupants)* empty; *(sans charge)* unladen; *(Tech)* without gripping *ou* being in gear

vidé, e [vide] *adj (épuisé)* done in, all in

vidéo [video] *nf, adj inv* video; **~ inverse** reverse video

vidéocassette [videokasɛt] *nf* video cassette

vidéoclip [videoklip] *nm* music video

vidéoclub [videoklœb] *nm* video club

vidéoconférence [videokɔ̃fe(ʀɑ̃s)] *nf* videoconference

vidéodisque [videodisk] *nm* videodisc

vide-ordures [vidɔʀdyʀ] *nm inv* (rubbish) chute

vidéotex® [videotɛks] *nm* teletext

vidéothèque [videotɛk] *nf* video library

vide-poches [vidpɔʃ] *nm inv* tidy; *(Auto)* glove compartment

vide-pomme [vidpɔm] *nm inv* apple-corer

vider [vide] *vt* to empty; *(Culin: volaille, poisson)* to gut, clean out; *(régler: querelle)* to settle; *(fatiguer)* to wear out; *(fam: expulser)* to throw out, chuck out; **se vider** *vi* to empty; **~ les lieux** to quit *ou* vacate the premises

videur [vidœʀ] *nm (de boîte de nuit)* bouncer

vie [vi] *nf* life; **être en ~** to be alive; **sans ~** lifeless; **à ~** for life; **membre à ~** life member; **dans la ~ courante** in everyday life; **avoir la ~ dure** to have nine lives; to die hard; **mener la ~ dure à qn** to make life a misery for sb

vieil [vjɛj] *adj m voir* **vieux**

vieillard [vjɛjaʀ] *nm* old man; **les ~s** old people, the elderly

vieille [vjɛj] *adj f, nf voir* **vieux**

vieilleries [vjɛjʀi] *nfpl* old things *ou* stuff *sg*

vieillesse [vjɛjɛs] *nf* old age; *(vieillards)*: **la ~** the old *pl*, the elderly *pl*

vieilli, e [vjeji] *adj (marqué par l'âge)* aged; *(suranné)* dated

vieillir [vjejiʀ] *vi (prendre de l'âge)* to grow old; *(population, vin)* to age; *(doctrine, auteur)* to become dated ▷ *vt* to age; **il a beaucoup vieilli** he has aged a lot; **se vieillir** to make o.s. older

vieillissement [vjejismɑ̃] *nm* growing old; ageing

vieillot, te [vjɛjo, -ɔt] *adj* antiquated, quaint

vielle [vjɛl] *nf* hurdy-gurdy

viendrai *etc* [vjɛ̃dʀe] *vb voir* **venir**

Vienne [vjɛn] *n (en Autriche)* Vienna

vienne [vjɛn], **viens** *etc* [vjɛ̃] *vb voir* **venir**

viennois, e [vjɛnwa, -waz] *adj* Viennese

viens [vjɛ̃] *vb voir* **venir**

vierge [vjɛʀʒ(ə)] *adj* virgin; *(film)* blank; *(page)* clean, blank; *(jeune fille)*: **être ~** to be a virgin ▷ *nf* virgin; *(signe)*: **la V~** Virgo, the Virgin; **être de la V~** to be Virgo; **~ de** *(sans)* free from, unsullied by

Viêtnam, Vietnam [vjɛtnam] *nm*: **le ~** Vietnam; **le ~ du Nord/du Sud** North/South Vietnam

vietnamien, ne [vjɛtnamjɛ̃, -ɛn] *adj* Vietnamese ▷ *nm (Ling)* Vietnamese ▷ *nm/f*: **Vietnamien, ne** Vietnamese; **V~, ne du Nord/Sud** North/South Vietnamese

vieux, vieil, vieille [vjø, vjɛj] *adj* old ▷ *nm/f* old man/woman ▷ *nmpl*: **les ~** the old, old people; *(fam: parents)* the old folk *ou* ones; **un petit ~** a little old man; **mon ~/ma vieille** *(fam)* old man/girl; **pauvre ~** poor old soul; **prendre un coup de ~** to put years on; **se faire ~** to make o.s. look older; **un ~ de la vieille** one of the old brigade; **~ garçon** *nm* bachelor; **~ jeu** *adj inv* old-fashioned; **~ rose** *adj inv* old rose; **vieil or** *adj inv* old gold; **vieille fille** *nf* spinster

vif, vive [vif, viv] *adj (animé)* lively; *(alerte)* sharp, quick; *(brusque)* sharp, brusque; *(aigu)* sharp; *(lumière, couleur)* brilliant; *(air)* crisp; *(vent, émotion)* keen; *(froid)* bitter; *(fort: regret, déception)* great, deep; *(vivant)*: **brûlé ~** burnt alive; **eau vive** running water; **de vive voix** personally;

piquer qn au ~ to cut sb to the quick; **tailler dans la** ~ to cut into the living flesh; **à** ~ *(plaie)* open; **avoir les nerfs à** ~ to be on edge; **sur le** ~ *(Art)* from life; **entrer dans le** ~ **du sujet** to get to the very heart of the matter

vif-argent [vifaʀʒɑ̃] *nm inv* quicksilver

vigie [viʒi] *nf (matelot)* look-out; *(poste)* look-out post, crow's nest

vigilance [viʒilɑ̃s] *nf* vigilance

vigilant, e [viʒilɑ̃, -ɑ̃t] *adj* vigilant

vigile [viʒil] *nm (veilleur de nuit)* (night) watchman; *(police privée)* vigilante

vigne [viɲ] *nf (plante)* vine; *(plantation)* vineyard; ~ **vierge** Virginia creeper

vigneron [viɲʀɔ̃] *nm* wine grower

vignette [viɲɛt] *nf (motif)* vignette; *(de marque)* manufacturer's label *ou* seal; *(petite illustration)* (small) illustration; *(Admin)* ≈ (road) tax disc *(Brit)*, ≈ license plate sticker *(US)*; *(: sur médicament)* price label *(on medicines for reimbursement by Social Security)*

vignoble [viɲɔbl(ə)] *nm (plantation)* vineyard; *(vignes d'une région)* vineyards *pl*

vigoureusement [viguʀøzmɑ̃] *adv* vigorously

vigoureux, -euse [viguʀø, -øz] *adj* vigorous, robust

vigueur [vigœʀ] *nf* vigour *(Brit)*, vigor *(US)*; **être/entrer en** ~ to be in/come into force; **en** ~ current

vil, e [vil] *adj* vile, base; **à** ~ **prix** at a very low price

vilain, e [vilɛ̃, -ɛn] *adj (laid)* ugly; *(affaire, blessure)* nasty; *(passage: enfant)* naughty ▷ *nm (paysan)* villein, villain; **ça va tourner au** ~ things are going to turn nasty; ~ **mot** bad word

vilainement [vilɛnmɑ̃] *adv* badly

vilebrequin [vilbʀəkɛ̃] *nm (outil)* (bit-)brace; *(Auto)* crankshaft

vilenie [vilni] *nf* vileness *no pl*, baseness *no pl*

vilipender [vilipɑ̃de] *vt* to revile, vilify

villa [vila] *nf* (detached) house

village [vilaʒ] *nm* village; ~ **de toile** tent village; ~ **de vacances** holiday village

villageois, e [vilaʒwa, -waz] *adj* village *cpd* ▷ *nm/f* villager

ville [vil] *nf* town; *(importante)* city; *(administration)*: **la** ~ ≈ the Corporation, ≈ the (town) council; **aller en** ~ to go to town; **habiter en** ~ to live in town; ~ **jumelée** twin town; ~ **nouvelle** new town

ville-champignon [vilʃɑ̃piɲɔ̃] *(pl* **villes-champignons**) *nf* boom town

ville-dortoir [vildɔʀtwaʀ] *(pl* **villes-dortoirs**) *nf* dormitory town

villégiature [vileʒjatyʀ] *nf (séjour)* holiday; *(lieu)* (holiday) resort

vin [vɛ̃] *nm* wine; **avoir le** ~ **gai/triste** to get happy/miserable after a few drinks; ~ **blanc/rosé/rouge** white/rosé/red wine; ~ **d'honneur** reception; *(with wine and snacks)*: ~ **de messe** altar wine; ~ **ordinaire** *ou* **de table** table wine; ~ **de pays** local wine; *voir aussi* **AOC**; **VDQS**

vinaigre [vinɛgʀ(ə)] *nm* vinegar; **tourner au** ~ *(fig)* to turn sour; ~ **de vin/d'alcool** wine/spirit vinegar

vinaigrette [vinɛgʀɛt] *nf* vinaigrette, French dressing

vinaigrier [vinɛgʀije] *nm (fabricant)* vinegar-maker; *(flacon)* vinegar cruet *ou* bottle

vinasse [vinas] *nf (péj)* cheap wine, plonk *(Brit)*

vindicatif, -ive [vɛ̃dikatif, -iv] *adj* vindictive

vindicte [vɛ̃dikt(ə)] *nf*: **désigner qn à la** ~ **publique** to expose sb to public condemnation

vineux, -euse [vinø, -øz] *adj* win(e)y

vingt [vɛ̃, vɛ̃t] *(+ voyelle following 2nd pron) num* twenty; ~-**quatre heures sur** ~-**quatre** twenty-four hours a day, round the clock

vingtaine [vɛ̃tɛn] *nf*: **une** ~ **(de)** around twenty, twenty or so

vingtième [vɛ̃tjɛm] *num* twentieth

vinicole [vinikɔl] *adj (production)* wine *cpd*; *(région)* wine-growing

vinification [vinifikasjɔ̃] *nf* wine-making, wine production; *(des sucres)* vinification

vins *etc* [vɛ̃] *vb voir* **venir**

vinyle [vinil] *nm* vinyl

viol [vjɔl] *nm (d'une femme)* rape; *(d'un lieu sacré)* violation

violacé, e [vjɔlase] *adj* purplish, mauvish

violation [vjɔlasjɔ̃] *nf* desecration; violation; *(d'un droit)* breach

violemment [vjɔlamɑ̃] *adv* violently

violence [vjɔlɑ̃s] *nf* violence; **violences** *nfpl* acts of violence; **faire** ~ **à qn** to do violence to sb; **se faire** ~ to force o.s

violent, e [vjɔlɑ̃, -ɑ̃t] *adj* violent; *(remède)* drastic; *(besoin, désir)* intense, urgent

violenter [vjɔlɑ̃te] *vt* to assault (sexually)

violer [vjɔle] *vt (femme)* to rape; *(sépulture)* to desecrate, violate; *(loi, traité)* to violate

violet, te [vjɔlɛ, -ɛt] *adj, nm* purple, mauve ▷ *nf (fleur)* violet

violeur [vjɔlœʀ] *nm* rapist

violine [vjɔlin] *nf* deep purple

violon [vjɔlɔ̃] *nm* violin; *(dans la musique folklorique etc)* fiddle; *(fam: prison)* lock-up; **premier** ~ first violin; ~ **d'Ingres** (artistic) hobby

violoncelle [vjɔlɔ̃sɛl] *nm* cello

violoncelliste [vjɔlɔ̃selist(ə)] *nm/f* cellist

violoniste [vjɔlɔnist(ə)] *nm/f* violinist, violin-player; *(folklorique etc)* fiddler

VIP *sigle m* (= *Very Important Person*) VIP

vipère [vipɛʀ] *nf* viper, adder

virage [viʀaʒ] *nm (d'un véhicule)* turn; *(d'une route, piste)* bend; *(Chimie)* change in colour *(Brit) ou* color *(US)*; *(de cuti-réaction)* positive reaction; *(Photo)* toning; *(fig: Pol)* about-turn; **prendre un** ~ to go into a bend, take a bend; ~ **sans visibilité** blind bend

viral, e, -aux [viʀal, -o] *adj* viral

virée [viʀe] *nf (courte)* run; *(: à pied)* walk; *(longue)* trip; hike, walking tour

virement [viʀmɑ̃] *nm (Comm)* transfer; ~ **bancaire** (bank) credit transfer, ≈ (bank) giro transfer (*Brit*); **~ postal** Post office credit transfer, ≈ Girobank® transfer (*Brit*)

virent [viʀ] *vb voir* **voir**

virer [viʀe] *vt* (*Comm*): **~ qch (sur)** to transfer sth (into); (*Photo*) to tone; (*fam: renvoyer*) to sack, boot out ▷ *vi* to turn; (*Chimie*) to change colour (*Brit*) *ou* color (*US*); (*cuti-réaction*) to come up positive; (*Photo*) to tone; **~ au bleu** to turn blue; **~ de bord** to tack; (*fig*) to change tack; **~ sur l'aile** to bank

virevolte [viʀvɔlt(ə)] *nf* twirl; (*d'avis, d'opinion*) about-turn

virevolter [viʀvɔlte] *vi* to twirl around

virginal, e, -aux [viʀʒinal, -o] *adj* virginal

virginité [viʀʒinite] *nf* virginity; (*fig*) purity

virgule [viʀgyl] *nf* comma; (*Math*) point; **quatre ~ deux** four point two; **~ flottante** floating decimal

viril, e [viʀil] *adj* (*propre à l'homme*) masculine; (*énergique, courageux*) manly, virile

viriliser [viʀilize] *vt* to make (more) manly *ou* masculine

virilité [viʀilite] *nf* (*attributs masculins*) masculinity; (*fermeté, courage*) manliness; (*sexuelle*) virility

virologie [viʀɔlɔʒi] *nf* virology

virtualité [viʀtɥalite] *nf* virtuality; potentiality

virtuel, le [viʀtɥɛl] *adj* potential; (*théorique*) virtual

virtuellement [viʀtɥɛlmɑ̃] *adj* potentially; (*presque*) virtually

virtuose [viʀtɥoz] *nm/f* (*Mus*) virtuoso; (*gén*) master

virtuosité [viʀtɥozite] *nf* virtuosity; masterliness, masterful skills *pl*

virulence [viʀylɑ̃s] *nf* virulence

virulent, e [viʀylɑ̃, -ɑ̃t] *adj* virulent

virus [viʀys] *nm* virus

vis *vb* [vi] *voir* **voir**; **vivre** ▷ *nf* [vis] screw; **~ à tête plate/ronde** flat-headed/round-headed screw; **~ platinées** (*Auto*) (contact) points; **~ sans fin** worm, endless screw

visa [viza] *nm* (*sceau*) stamp; (*validation de passeport*) visa; **~ de censure** (censor's) certificate

visage [vizaʒ] *nm* face; **à ~ découvert** (*franchement*) openly

visagiste [vizaʒist(ə)] *nm/f* beautician

vis-à-vis [vizavi] *adv* face to face ▷ *nm* person opposite; house *etc* opposite; **~ de** *prép* opposite; (*fig*) towards, vis-à-vis; **en ~** facing *ou* opposite each other; **sans ~** (*immeuble*) with an open outlook

viscéral, e, -aux [viseʀal, -o] *adj* (*fig*) deep-seated, deep-rooted

viscères [viseʀ] *nmpl* intestines, entrails

viscose [viskoz] *nf* viscose

viscosité [viskozite] *nf* viscosity

visée [vize] *nf* (*avec une arme*) aiming; (*Arpentage*) sighting; **visées** *nfpl* (*intentions*) designs; **avoir des ~s sur qn/qch** to have designs on sb/sth

viser [vize] *vi* to aim ▷ *vt* to aim at; (*concerner*) to

be aimed *ou* directed at; (*apposer un visa sur*) to stamp, visa; **~ à qch/faire** to aim at sth/at doing *ou* to do

viseur [vizœʀ] *nm* (*d'arme*) sights *pl*; (*Photo*) viewfinder

visibilité [vizibilite] *nf* visibility; **sans ~** (*pilotage, virage*) blind *cpd*

visible [vizibl(ə)] *adj* visible; (*disponible*): **est-il ~?** can he see me?, will he see visitors?

visiblement [vizibləmɑ̃] *adv* visibly, obviously

visière [vizjɛʀ] *nf* (*de casquette*) peak; (*qui s'attache*) eyeshade

vision [vizjɔ̃] *nf* vision; (*sens*) (eye)sight, vision; (*fait de voir*): **la ~ de** the sight of; **première ~** (*Ciné*) first showing

visionnaire [vizjɔnɛʀ] *adj, nm/f* visionary

visionner [vizjɔne] *vt* to view

visionneuse [vizjɔnøz] *nf* viewer

visiophone [vizjɔfɔn] *nm* videophone

visite [vizit] *nf* visit; (*visiteur*) visitor; (*touristique*: *d'un musée etc*) tour; (*Comm*: *de représentant*) call; (*expertise, d'inspection*) inspection; (*médicale, à domicile*) visit, call; **la ~** (*Méd*) medical examination; (*Mil*: *d'entrée*) medicals *pl*; (*: quotidienne*) sick parade; **faire une ~ à qn** to call on sb, pay sb a visit; **rendre ~ à qn** to visit sb, pay sb a visit; **être en ~ (chez qn)** to be visiting (sb); **heures de ~** (*hôpital, prison*) visiting hours; **le droit de ~** (*Jur*: *aux enfants*) right of access, access; **~ de douane** customs inspection *ou* examination; **~ guidée** guided tour

visiter [vizite] *vt* to visit; (*musée, ville*) to visit, go round

visiteur, -euse [vizitœʀ, -øz] *nm/f* visitor; **~ des douanes** customs inspector; **~ médical** medical rep(resentative); **~ de prison** prison visitor

vison [vizɔ̃] *nm* mink

visqueux, -euse [viskø, -øz] *adj* viscous; (*péj*) gooey; (*: manières*) slimy

visser [vise] *vt*: **~ qch** (*fixer, serrer*) to screw sth on

visu [vizy]: **de ~** *adv* with one's own eyes

visualisation [vizɥalizasjɔ̃] *nf* (*Inform*) display; **écran de ~** visual display unit (VDU)

visualiser [vizɥalize] *vt* to visualize; (*Inform*) to display, bring up on screen

visuel, le [vizɥɛl] *adj* visual

visuellement [vizɥɛlmɑ̃] *adv* visually

vit [vi] *vb voir* **vivre**; **voir**

vital, e, -aux [vital, -o] *adj* vital

vitalité [vitalite] *nf* vitality

vitamine [vitamin] *nf* vitamin

vitaminé, e [vitamine] *adj* with (added) vitamins

vitaminique [vitaminik] *adj* vitamin *cpd*

vite [vit] *adv* (*rapidement*) quickly, fast; (*sans délai*) quickly; soon; **faire ~** (*agir rapidement*) to act fast; (*se dépêcher*) to be quick; **ce sera ~ fini** this will soon be finished; **viens ~** come quick(ly)

vitesse [vites] *nf* speed; (*Auto*: *dispositif*) gear; **faire de la ~** to drive fast *ou* at speed; **prendre qn de ~** to outstrip sb, get ahead of sb; **prendre**

de la ~ to pick up *ou* gather speed; **à toute** ~ at full *ou* top speed; **en perte de** ~ (*avion*) losing lift; (*fig*) losing momentum; **changer de** ~ (*Auto*) to change gear; ~ **acquise** momentum; ~ **de croisière** cruising speed; ~ **de pointe** top speed; ~ **du son** speed of sound

viticole [vitikɔl] *adj* (*industrie*) wine *cpd*; (*région*) wine-growing

viticulteur [vitikyltœʀ] *nm* wine grower

viticulture [vitikyltyʀ] *nf* wine growing

vitrage [vitʀaʒ] *nm* (*cloison*) glass partition; (*toit*) glass roof; (*rideau*) net curtain

vitrail, -aux [vitʀaj, -o] *nm* stained-glass window

vitre [vitʀ(ə)] *nf* (window) pane; (*de portière, voiture*) window

vitré, e [vitʀe] *adj* glass *cpd*

vitrer [vitʀe] *vt* to glaze

vitreux, -euse [vitʀø, -øz] *adj* vitreous; (*terne*) glassy

vitrier [vitʀije] *nm* glazier

vitrifier [vitʀifje] *vt* to vitrify; (*parquet*) to glaze

vitrine [vitʀin] *nf* (*devanture*) (shop) window; (*étalage*) display; (*petite armoire*) display cabinet; **en** ~ in the window, on display; ~ **publicitaire** display case, showcase

vitriol [vitʀijɔl] *nm* vitriol; **au** ~ (*fig*) vitriolic

vitupérations [vitypeʀasjɔ̃] *nfpl* invective *sg*

vitupérer [vitypeʀe] *vi* to rant and rave; ~ **contre** to rail against

vivable [vivabl(ə)] *adj* (*personne*) livable-with; (*endroit*) fit to live in

vivace *adj* [vivas] (*arbre, plante*) hardy; (*fig*) enduring ▷ *adv* [vivatʃe] (*Mus*) vivace

vivacité [vivasite] *nf* (*voir vif*) liveliness, vivacity; sharpness; brilliance

vivant, e [vivã, -ãt] *vb voir* **vivre** ▷ *adj* (*qui vit*) living, alive; (*animé*) lively; (*preuve, exemple*) living; (*langue*) modern ▷ *nm*: **du** ~ **de qn** in sb's lifetime; **les ~s et les morts** the living and the dead

vivarium [vivaʀjɔm] *nm* vivarium

vivats [viva] *nmpl* cheers

vive [viv] *adj f voir* **vif** ▷ *vb voir* **vivre** ▷ *excl*: ~ **le roi!** long live the king!; ~ **les vacances!** hurrah for the holidays!

vivement [vivmã] *adv* vivaciously; sharply ▷ *excl*: ~ **les vacances!** I can't wait for the holidays!, roll on the holidays!

viveur [vivœʀ] *nm* (*péj*) high liver, pleasure-seeker

vivier [vivje] *nm* (*au restaurant etc*) fish tank; (*étang*) fishpond

vivifiant, e [vivifjã, -ãt] *adj* invigorating

vivifier [vivifje] *vt* to invigorate; (*fig: souvenirs, sentiments*) to liven up, enliven

vivions [vivjɔ̃] *vb voir* **vivre**

vivipare [vivipaʀ] *adj* viviparous

vivisection [vivisɛksjɔ̃] *nf* vivisection

vivoter [vivɔte] *vi* (*personne*) to scrape a living, get by; (*fig: affaire etc*) to struggle along

vivre [vivʀ(ə)] *vi, vt* to live ▷ *nm*: **le** ~ **et le**

logement board and lodging; **vivres** *nmpl* provisions, food supplies; **il vit encore** he is still alive; **se laisser** ~ to take life as it comes; **ne plus** ~ (*être anxieux*) to live on one's nerves; **il a vécu** (*eu une vie aventureuse*) he has seen life; **ce régime a vécu** this regime has had its day; **être facile à** ~ to be easy to get on with; **faire** ~ **qn** (*pourvoir à sa subsistance*) to provide (a living) for sb; ~ **mal** (*chichement*) to have a meagre existence; ~ **de** (*salaire etc*) to live on

vivrier, -ière [vivʀije, -jɛʀ] *adj* food-producing *cpd*

vlan [vlã] *excl* wham!, bang!

VO *sigle f* (*Ciné*) = **version originale**; **voir un film en VO** to see a film in its original language

v° *abr* = **verso**

vocable [vɔkabl(ə)] *nm* term

vocabulaire [vɔkabylɛʀ] *nm* vocabulary

vocal, e, -aux [vɔkal, -o] *adj* vocal

vocalique [vɔkalik] *adj* vocalic, vowel *cpd*

vocalise [vɔkaliz] *nf* singing exercise

vocaliser [vɔkalize] *vi* (*Ling*) to vocalize; (*Mus*) to do one's singing exercises

vocation [vɔkasjɔ̃] *nf* vocation, calling; **avoir la** ~ to have a vocation

vociférations [vɔsifeʀasjɔ̃] *nfpl* cries of rage, screams

vociférer [vɔsifeʀe] *vi, vt* to scream

vodka [vɔdka] *nf* vodka

vœu, x [vø] *nm* wish; (*à Dieu*) vow; **faire** ~ **de** to take a vow of; **avec tous nos ~x** with every good wish *ou* our best wishes; **meilleurs ~x** best wishes; (*sur une carte*) "Season's Greetings"; **~x de bonheur** best wishes for your future happiness; **~x de bonne année** best wishes for the New Year

vogue [vɔg] *nf* fashion, vogue; **en** ~ in fashion, in vogue

voguer [vɔge] *vi* to sail

voici [vwasi] *prép* (*pour introduire, désigner*) here is; (*+ sg*) here are; (*+ pl*): **et** ~ **que ...** and now it (*ou* he) ...; **il est parti** ~ **trois ans** he left three years ago; ~ **une semaine que je l'ai vue** it's a week since I've seen her; **me** ~ here I am; *voir aussi* **voilà**

voie [vwa] *vb voir* **voir** ▷ *nf* way; (*Rail*) track, line; (*Auto*) lane; **par** ~ **buccale** *ou* **orale** orally; **par** ~ **rectale** rectally; **suivre la** ~ **hiérarchique** to go through official channels; **ouvrir/montrer la** ~ to open up/show the way; **être en bonne** ~ to be shaping *ou* going well; **mettre qn sur la** ~ to put sb on the right track; **être en** ~ **d'achèvement/de rénovation** to be nearing completion/in the process of renovation; **à** ~ **étroite** narrow-gauge; **à** ~ **unique** single-track; **route à deux/trois ~s** two-/three-lane road; **par la** ~ **aérienne/maritime** by air/sea; ~ **d'eau** (*Navig*) leak; ~ **express** expressway; ~ **de fait** (*Jur*) assault (and battery); ~ **ferrée** track; railway line (*Brit*), railroad (*US*); **par** ~ **ferrée** by rail, by railroad; ~ **de garage** (*Rail*) siding; **la** ~ **lactée** the Milky Way; ~ **navigable** waterway;

~ **prioritaire** (*Auto*) road with right of way; ~ **privée** private road; **la ~ publique** the public highway

voilà [vwala] *prép* (*en désignant*) there is; (+*sg*) there are; (+*pl*): **les ~** *ou* **voici** here *ou* there they are; **en ~** *ou* **voici un** here's one, there's one; **~** *ou* **voici deux ans** two years ago; **~** *ou* **voici deux ans que** it's two years since; **et ~!** there we are!; **~ tout** that's all; **"~** *ou* **voici"** (*en offrant etc*) "there *ou* here you are"

voilage [vwalaʒ] *nm* (*rideau*) net curtain; (*tissu*) net

voile [vwal] *nm* veil; (*tissu léger*) net ▷ *nf* sail; (*sport*) sailing; **prendre le ~** to take the veil; **mettre à la ~** to make way under sail; **~ du palais** *nm* soft palate, velum; **~ au poumon** *nm* shadow on the lung

voiler [vwale] *vt* to veil; (*Photo*) to fog; (*fausser: roue*) to buckle; (: *bois*) to warp; **se voiler** *vi* (*lune, regard*) to mist over; (*ciel*) to grow hazy; (*voix*) to become husky; (*roue, disque*) to buckle; (*planche*) to warp; **se ~ la face** to hide one's face

voilette [vwalɛt] *nf* (hat) veil

voilier [vwalje] *nm* sailing ship; (*de plaisance*) sailing boat

voilure [vwalyʀ] *nf* (*de voilier*) sails *pl*; (*d'avion*) aerofoils *pl* (*Brit*), airfoils *pl* (*US*); (*de parachute*) canopy

voir [vwaʀ] *vi, vt* to see; **se voir**: **se ~ critiquer/transformer** to be criticized/transformed; **cela se voit** (*cela arrive*) it happens; (*c'est visible*) that's obvious, it shows; **~ à faire qch** to see to it that sth is done; **~ loin** (*fig*) to be far-sighted; **~ venir** (*fig*) to wait and see; **faire ~ qch à qn** to show sb sth; **en faire ~ à qn** (*fig*) to give sb a hard time; **ne pas pouvoir ~ qn** (*fig*) not to be able to stand sb; **regardez ~** just look; **montrez ~** show (me); **dites ~** tell me; **voyons!** let's see now; (*indignation etc*) come (along) now!; **c'est à ~!** we'll see!; **c'est ce qu'on va ~!** we'll see about that!; **avoir quelque chose à ~ avec** to have something to do with; **ça n'a rien à ~ avec lui** that has nothing to do with him

voire [vwaʀ] *adv* indeed; nay; or even

voirie [vwaʀi] *nf* highway maintenance; (*administration*) highways department; (*enlèvement des ordures*) refuse (*Brit*) *ou* garbage (*US*) collection

vois [vwa] *vb voir* **voir**

voisin, e [vwazɛ̃, -in] *adj* (*proche*) neighbouring (*Brit*), neighboring (*US*); (*contigu*) next; (*ressemblant*) connected ▷ *nm/f* neighbo(u)r; (*de table, de dortoir etc*) person next to me (*ou* him *etc*); **~ de palier** neighbo(u)r across the landing (*Brit*) *ou* hall (*US*)

voisinage [vwazinaʒ] *nm* (*proximité*) proximity; (*environs*) vicinity; (*quartier, voisins*) neighbourhood (*Brit*), neighborhood (*US*); **relations de bon ~** neighbo(u)rly terms

voisiner [vwazine] *vi*: **~ avec** to be side by side with

voit [vwa] *vb voir* **voir**

voiture [vwatyʀ] *nf* car; (*wagon*) coach, carriage; **en ~!** all aboard!; **~ à bras** handcart; **~ d'enfant** pram (*Brit*), baby carriage (*US*); **~ d'infirme** invalid carriage; **~ de sport** sports car

voiture-lit [vwatyʀli] (*pl* **voitures-lits**) *nf* sleeper

voiture-restaurant [vwatyʀʀɛstɔʀɑ̃] (*pl* **voitures-restaurants**) *nf* dining car

voix [vwa] *nf* voice; (*Pol*) vote; **la ~ de la conscience/raison** the voice of conscience/reason; **à haute ~** aloud; **à ~ basse** in a low voice; **faire la grosse ~** to speak gruffly; **avoir de la ~** to have a good voice; **rester sans ~** to be speechless; **~ de basse/ténor** *etc* bass/tenor *etc* voice; **à deux/quatre ~** (*Mus*) in two/four parts; **avoir ~ au chapitre** to have a say in the matter; **mettre aux ~** to put to the vote; **~ off** voice-over

vol [vɔl] *nm* (*mode de locomotion*) flying; (*trajet, voyage, groupe d'oiseaux*) flight; (*mode d'appropriation*) theft, stealing; (*larcin*) theft; **à ~ d'oiseau** as the crow flies; **au ~: attraper qch au ~** to catch sth as it flies past; **saisir une remarque au ~** to pick up a passing remark; **prendre son ~** to take flight; **de haut ~** (*fig*) of the highest order; **en ~** in flight; **~ avec effraction** breaking and entering *no pl*, break-in; **à l'étalage** shoplifting *no pl*; **~ libre** hang-gliding; **~ à main armée** armed robbery; **~ de nuit** night flight; **~ plané** (*Aviat*) glide, gliding *no pl*; **à la tire** pickpocketing *no pl*; **~ à voile** gliding

vol. *abr* (= *volume*) vol

volage [vɔlaʒ] *adj* fickle

volaille [vɔlaj] *nf* (*oiseaux*) poultry *pl*; (*viande*) poultry *no pl*; (*oiseau*) fowl

volailler [vɔlaje] *nm* poulterer

volant, e [vɔlɑ̃, -ɑ̃t] *adj voir* **feuille** *etc* ▷ *nm* (*d'automobile*) (steering) wheel; (*de commande*) wheel; (*objet lancé*) shuttlecock; (*jeu*) battledore and shuttlecock; (*bande de tissu*) flounce; (*feuillet détachable*) tear-off portion; **le personnel ~**, **les ~s** (*Aviat*) the flight staff; **~ de sécurité** (*fig*) reserve, margin, safeguard

volatil, e [vɔlatil] *adj* volatile

volatile [vɔlatil] *nm* (*volaille*) bird; (*tout oiseau*) winged creature

volatiliser [vɔlatilize]: **se volatiliser** *vi* (*Chimie*) to volatilize; (*fig*) to vanish into thin air

vol-au-vent [vɔlovɑ̃] *nm inv* vol-au-vent

volcan [vɔlkɑ̃] *nm* volcano; (*fig: personne*) hothead

volcanique [vɔlkanik] *adj* volcanic; (*fig: tempérament*) volatile

volcanologie [vɔlkanɔlɔʒi] *nf* vulcanology

volcanologue [vɔlkanɔlɔg] *nm/f* vulcanologist

volée [vɔle] *nf* (*groupe d'oiseaux*) flight, flock; (*Tennis*) volley; **~ de coups/de flèches** volley of blows/arrows; **à la ~: rattraper à la ~** to catch in midair; **lancer à la ~** to fling about; **semer à la ~** to (sow) broadcast; **à toute ~** (*sonner les cloches*) vigorously; (*lancer un projectile*) with full force; **de haute ~** (*fig*) of the highest order

voler [vɔle] *vi* (*avion, oiseau, fig*) to fly; (*voleur*) to steal ▷ *vt* (*objet*) to steal; (*personne*) to rob; ~ **en éclats** to smash to smithereens; ~ **de ses propres ailes** (*fig*) to stand on one's own two feet; ~ **au vent** to fly in the wind; ~ **qch à qn** to steal sth from sb

volet [vɔlɛ] *nm* (*de fenêtre*) shutter; (*Aviat*) flap; (*de feuillet, document*) section; (*fig: d'un plan*) facet; **trié sur le** ~ hand-picked

voleter [vɔlte] *vi* to flutter (about)

voleur, -euse [vɔlœʀ, -øz] *nm/f* thief ▷ *adj* thieving; "**au ~!**" "stop thief!"

volière [vɔljɛʀ] *nf* aviary

volley [vɔlɛ], **volley-ball** [vɔlɛbol] *nm* volleyball

volleyeur, -euse [vɔlɛjœʀ, -øz] *nm/f* volleyball player

volontaire [vɔlɔ̃tɛʀ] *adj* (*acte, activité*) voluntary; (*délibéré*) deliberate; (*caractère, personne: décidé*) self-willed ▷ *nm/f* volunteer

volontairement [vɔlɔ̃tɛʀmɑ̃] *adv* voluntarily; deliberately

volontariat [vɔlɔ̃taʀja] *nm* voluntary service

volontarisme [vɔlɔ̃taʀism(ə)] *nm* voluntarism

volontariste [vɔlɔ̃taʀist(ə)] *adj, nm/f* voluntarist

volonté [vɔlɔ̃te] *nf* (*faculté de vouloir*) will; (*énergie, fermeté*) will(power); (*souhait, désir*) wish; **se servir/boire à** ~ to take/drink as much as one likes; **bonne** ~ goodwill, willingness; **mauvaise** ~ lack of goodwill, unwillingness

volontiers [vɔlɔ̃tje] *adv* (*de bonne grâce*) willingly; (*avec plaisir*) willingly, gladly; (*habituellement, souvent*) readily, willingly; "**~**" "with pleasure", "I'd be glad to"

volt [vɔlt] *nm* volt

voltage [vɔltaʒ] *nm* voltage

volte-face [vɔltəfas] *nf inv* about-turn; (*fig*) about-turn, U-turn; **faire** ~ to do an about-turn; to do a U-turn

voltige [vɔltiʒ] *nf* (*Équitation*) trick riding; (*au cirque*) acrobatics *sg*; (*Aviat*) (aerial) acrobatics *sg*; **numéro de haute** ~ acrobatic act

voltiger [vɔltiʒe] *vi* to flutter (about)

voltigeur [vɔltiʒœʀ] *nm* (*au cirque*) acrobat; (*Mil*) light infantryman

voltmètre [vɔltmɛtʀ(ə)] *nm* voltmeter

volubile [vɔlybil] *adj* voluble

volubilis [vɔlybilis] *nm* convolvulus

volume [vɔlym] *nm* volume; (*Géom: solide*) solid

volumineux, -euse [vɔyminø, -øz] *adj* voluminous, bulky

volupté [vɔlypte] *nf* sensual delight *ou* pleasure

voluptueusement [vɔlyptɥøzmɑ̃] *adv* voluptuously

voluptueux, -euse [vɔlyptɥø, -øz] *adj* voluptuous

volute [vɔlyt] *nf* (*Archit*) volute; ~ **de fumée** curl of smoke

vomi [vɔmi] *nm* vomit

vomir [vɔmiʀ] *vi* to vomit, be sick ▷ *vt* to vomit, bring up; (*fig*) to belch out, spew out; (*exécrer*) to loathe, abhor

vomissements [vɔmismɑ̃] *nmpl* (*action*) vomiting *no pl*; **des** ~ vomit *sg*

vomissure [vɔmisyʀ] *nf* vomit *no pl*

vomitif [vɔmitif] *nm* emetic

vont [vɔ̃] *vb voir* **aller**

vorace [vɔʀas] *adj* voracious

voracement [vɔʀasmɑ̃] *adv* voraciously

voracité [vɔʀasite] *nf* voracity

vos [vo] *adj poss voir* **votre**

Vosges [voʒ] *nfpl*: **les** ~ the Vosges

vosgien, ne [voʒjɛ̃, -ɛn] *adj* of *ou* from the Vosges ▷ *nm/f* inhabitant *ou* native of the Vosges

VOST *sigle f* (*Ciné*: = *version originale sous-titrée*) sub-titled version

votant, e [vɔtɑ̃, -ɑ̃t] *nm/f* voter

vote [vɔt] *nm* vote; ~ **par correspondance/procuration** postal/proxy vote; ~ **à main levée** vote by show of hands; ~ **secret**, ~ **à bulletins secrets** secret ballot

voter [vɔte] *vi* to vote ▷ *vt* (*loi, décision*) to vote for

votre [vɔtʀ(ə)] (*pl* **vos** [vo]) *adj poss* your

vôtre [votʀ(ə)] *pron*: **le** ~, **la** ~, **les** ~**s** yours; **les** ~**s** (*fig*) your family *ou* folks; **à la** ~ (*toast*) your (good) health!

voudrai *etc* [vudʀe] *vb voir* **vouloir**

voué, e [vwe] *adj*: ~ **à** doomed to, destined for

vouer [vwe] *vt*: ~ **qch à** (*Dieu/un saint*) to dedicate sth to; ~ **sa vie/son temps à** (*étude, cause etc*) to devote one's life/time to; ~ **une haine/amitié éternelle à qn** to vow undying hatred/friendship to sb

 MOT-CLÉ

vouloir [vulwaʀ] *nm*: **le bon vouloir de qn** sb's goodwill; sb's pleasure

▷ *vt* **1** (*exiger, désirer*) to want; **vouloir faire/que qn fasse** to want to do/sb to do; **voulez-vous du thé?** would you like *ou* do you want some tea?; **vouloir qch à qn** to wish sth for sb; **que me veut-il?** what does he want with me?; **que veux-tu que je te dise?** what do you want me to say?; **sans le vouloir** (*involontairement*) without meaning to, unintentionally; **je voudrais ceci/faire** I would *ou* I'd like this/to do; **le hasard a voulu que ...** as fate would have it, ...; **la tradition veut que ...** tradition demands that ...; **... qui se veut moderne ...** which purports to be modern

2 (*consentir*): **je veux bien** (*bonne volonté*) I'll be happy to; (*concession*) fair enough, that's fine; **oui, si on veut** (*en quelque sorte*) yes, if you like; **comme tu veux** as you wish; (*en quelque sorte*) if you like; **veuillez attendre** please wait; **veuillez agréer ...** (*formule épistolaire*) yours faithfully

3: **en vouloir** (*être ambitieux*) to be out to win; **en vouloir à qn** to bear sb a grudge; **je lui en veux d'avoir fait ça** I resent his having done that; **s'en vouloir (de)** to be annoyed with o.s. (for);

il en veut à mon argent he's after my money
4: **vouloir de** to want; **la compagnie ne veut plus de lui** the firm doesn't want him any more; **elle ne veut pas de son aide** she doesn't want his help
5: **vouloir dire** to mean

voulu, e [vuly] *pp de* **vouloir** ▷ *adj* (*requis*) required, requisite; (*délibéré*) deliberate, intentional
voulus *etc* [vuly] *vb voir* **vouloir**
vous [vu] *pron* you; (*objet indirect*) (to) you; (*réfléchi*) yourself; (*réciproque*) each other ▷ *nm*: **employer le ~** (*vouvoyer*) to use the "vous" form; **~-même** yourself; **~-mêmes** yourselves
voûte [vut] *nf* vault; **la ~ céleste** the vault of heaven; **~ du palais** (*Anat*) roof of the mouth; **~ plantaire** arch (of the foot)
voûté, e [vute] *adj* vaulted, arched; (*dos, personne*) bent, stooped
voûter [vute] *vt* (*Archit*) to arch, vault; **se voûter** *vi* (*dos, personne*) to become stooped
vouvoiement [vuvwamã] *nm* use of formal "vous" form
vouvoyer [vuvwaje] *vt*: **~ qn** to address sb as "vous"
voyage [vwajaʒ] *nm* journey, trip; (*fait de voyager*): **le ~** travel(ling); **partir/être en ~** to go off/be away on a journey *ou* trip; **faire un ~** to go on *ou* make a trip *ou* journey; **faire bon ~** to have a good journey; **les gens du ~** travelling people; **~ d'agrément/d'affaires** pleasure/ business trip; **~ de noces** honeymoon; **~ organisé** package tour
voyager [vwajaʒe] *vi* to travel
voyageur, -euse [vwajaʒœʀ, -øz] *nm/f* traveller; (*passager*) passenger ▷ *adj* (*tempérament*) nomadic, wayfaring; **~ (de commerce)** commercial traveller
voyagiste [vwajaʒist(ə)] *nm* tour operator
voyais *etc* [vwaje] *vb voir* **voir**
voyance [vwajãs] *nf* clairvoyance
voyant, e [vwajã, -ãt] *adj* (*couleur*) loud, gaudy ▷ *nm/f* (*personne qui voit*) sighted person ▷ *nm* (*signal*) (warning) light ▷ *nf* clairvoyant
voyelle [vwajɛl] *nf* vowel
voyeur, -euse [vwajœʀ, -øz] *nm/f* voyeur; peeping Tom
voyeurisme [vwajœʀism(ə)] *nm* voyeurism
voyons *etc* [vwajõ] *vb voir* **voir**
voyou [vwaju] *nm* lout, hoodlum; (*enfant*) guttersnipe
VPC *sigle f* (= *vente par correspondance*) mail order selling
vrac [vʀak]: **en ~** *adv* higgledy-piggledy; (*Comm*) in bulk
vrai, e [vʀɛ] *adj* (*véridique: récit, faits*) true; (*non factice, authentique*) real ▷ *nm*: **le ~** the truth; **à ~ dire** to tell the truth; **il est ~ que** it is true that; **être dans le ~** to be right
vraiment [vʀɛmã] *adv* really

vraisemblable [vʀɛsãblabl(ə)] *adj* (*plausible*) likely, plausible; (*probable*) likely, probable
vraisemblablement [vʀɛsãblabləmã] *adv* in all likelihood, very likely
vraisemblance [vʀɛsãblãs] *nf* likelihood, plausibility; (*romanesque*) verisimilitude; **selon toute ~** in all likelihood
vraquier [vʀakje] *nm* freighter
vrille [vʀij] *nf* (*de plante*) tendril; (*outil*) gimlet; (*spirale*) spiral; (*Aviat*) spin
vriller [vʀije] *vt* to bore into, pierce
vrombir [vʀõbiʀ] *vi* to hum
vrombissant, e [vʀõbisã, -ãt] *adj* humming
vrombissement [vʀõbismã] *nm* hum(ming)
VRP *sigle m* (= *voyageur, représentant, placier*) (sales) rep
VTT *sigle m* (= *vélo tout-terrain*) mountain bike
vu¹ [vy] *prép* (*en raison de*) in view of; **vu que** in view of the fact that
vu², e¹ [vy] *pp de* **voir** ▷ *adj*: **bien/mal vu** (*personne*) well-/poorly thought of; (*conduite*) good/bad form ▷ *nm*: **au vu et au su de tous** openly and publicly; **ni vu ni connu** what the eye doesn't see …!, no one will be any the wiser; **c'est tout vu** it's a foregone conclusion
vue² [vy] *nf* (*fait de voir*): **la ~ de** the sight of; (*sens, faculté*) (eye)sight; (*panorama, image, photo*) view; (*spectacle*) sight; **vues** *nfpl* (*idées*) views; (*dessein*) designs; **perdre la ~** to lose one's (eye)sight; **perdre de ~** to lose sight of; **à la ~ de tous** in full view of everybody; **hors de ~** out of sight; **à première ~** at first sight; **connaître de ~** to know by sight; **à ~** (*Comm*) at sight; **tirer à ~** to shoot on sight; **à ~ d'œil** *adv* visibly; (*à première vue*) at a quick glance; **avoir ~ sur** to have a view of; **en ~** (*visible*) in sight; (*Comm*) in the public eye; **avoir qch en ~** (*intentions*) to have one's sights on sth; **en ~ de faire** with the intention of doing, with a view to doing; **~ d'ensemble** overall view; **~ de l'esprit** theoretical view
vulcanisation [vylkanizasjõ] *nf* vulcanization
vulcaniser [vylkanize] *vt* to vulcanize
vulcanologie [vylkanɔlɔʒi] *nf* = **volcanologie**
vulcanologue [vylkanɔlɔg] *nm/f* = **volcanologue**
vulgaire [vylgɛʀ] *adj* (*grossier*) vulgar, coarse; (*trivial*) commonplace, mundane; (*péj: quelconque*): **de ~s touristes/chaises de cuisine** common tourists/kitchen chairs; (*Bot, Zool: non latin*) common
vulgairement [vylgɛʀmã] *adv* vulgarly, coarsely; (*communément*) commonly
vulgariser [vylgaʀize] *vt* to popularize
vulgarité [vylgaʀite] *nf* vulgarity, coarseness
vulnérabilité [vylneʀabilite] *nf* vulnerability
vulnérable [vylneʀabl(ə)] *adj* vulnerable
vulve [vylv(ə)] *nf* vulva
Vve *abr* = **veuve**
VVF *sigle m* (= *village vacances famille*) state-subsidized holiday village
vx *abr* = **vieux**

W, w [dubləve] *nm inv* W, w ▷ *abr* (= *watt*) W; **W comme William** W for William

wagon [vagɔ̃] *nm* (*de voyageurs*) carriage; (*de marchandises*) truck, wagon

wagon-citerne [vagɔ̃sitɛʀn(ə)] (*pl* **wagons-citernes**) *nm* tanker

wagon-lit [vagɔ̃li] (*pl* **wagons-lits**) *nm* sleeper, sleeping car

wagonnet [vagɔnɛ] *nm* small truck

wagon-poste [vagɔ̃pɔst(ə)] (*pl* **wagons-postes**) *nm* mail van

wagon-restaurant [vagɔ̃ʀɛstɔʀɑ̃] (*pl* **wagons-restaurants**) *nm* restaurant *ou* dining car

Walkman® [wɔkman] *nm* Walkman®, personal stereo

Wallis et Futuna [walisefytyna]: **les îles** ~ the Wallis and Futuna Islands

wallon, ne [walɔ̃, -ɔn] *adj* Walloon ▷ *nm* (*Ling*) Walloon ▷ *nm/f*: **Wallon, ne** Walloon

Wallonie [walɔni] *nf*: **la** ~ French-speaking (part of) Belgium

water-polo [watɛʀpɔlo] *nm* water polo

waters [watɛʀ] *nmpl* toilet *sg*, loo *sg* (Brit)

watt [wat] *nm* watt

WC [vese] *nmpl* toilet *sg*, lavatory *sg*

Web [wɛb] *nm inv*: **le** ~ the (World Wide) Web

webcam [wɛbkam] *nf* webcam

webmaster [-mastœʀ], **webmestre** [-mɛstʀ] *nm/f* webmaster

week-end [wikɛnd] *nm* weekend

western [wɛstɛʀn] *nm* western

Westphalie [vɛsfali] *nf*: **la** ~ Westphalia

whisky [wiski] (*pl* **whiskies**) *nm* whisky

white-spirit [wajtspiʀit] *nm* white spirit

wifi, Wi-Fi [wifi] *nm inv* (= *wireless fidelity*) wifi, Wi-Fi

wok [wɔk] *nm* wok

WWW *sigle m*: **World Wide Web** WWW

X, x [iks] *nm inv* X, x ▷ *sigle m* = **(École) polytechnique**; **plainte contre X** (*Jur*) action against person or persons unknown; **X comme Xavier** X for Xmas

xénophobe [gzenɔfɔb] *adj* xenophobic ▷ *nm/f* xenophobe

xénophobie [gzenɔfɔbi] *nf* xenophobia

xérès [gzeʀɛs] *nm* sherry

xylographie [ksilɔgʀafi] *nf* xylography; (*image*) xylograph

xylophone [ksilɔfɔn] *nm* xylophone

Yy

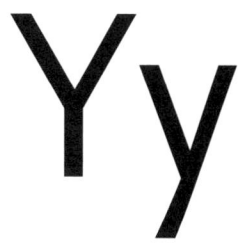

Y, y [igʀɛk] *nm inv* Y, y; **Y comme Yvonne** Y for Yellow (*Brit*) *ou* Yoke (*US*)

y [i] *adv* (*à cet endroit*) there; (*dessus*) on it (*ou* them); (*dedans*) in it (*ou* them) ▷ *pron* (about *ou* on *ou* of) it (*vérifier la syntaxe du verbe employé*); **j'y pense** I'm thinking about it; *voir aussi* **aller**; **avoir**

yacht [jɔt] *nm* yacht

yaourt [jauʀt] *nm* yoghurt

yaourtière [jauʀtjɛʀ] *nf* yoghurt-maker

Yémen [jemɛn] *nm*: **le ~** Yemen

yéménite [jemenit] *adj* Yemeni

yeux [jø] *nmpl de* **œil**

yoga [jɔga] *nm* yoga

yoghourt [jɔguʀt] *nm* = **yaourt**

yole [jɔl] *nf* skiff

yougoslave [jugɔslav] *adj* Yugoslav(ian) ▷ *nm/f*: **Yougoslave** Yugoslav(ian)

Yougoslavie [jugɔslavi] *nf*: **la ~** Yugoslavia

youyou [juju] *nm* dinghy

yo-yo [jojo] *nm inv* yo-yo

yucca [juka] *nm* yucca (tree *ou* plant)

Zz

Z, z [zɛd] *nm inv* Z, z; **Z comme Zoé** Z for Zebra

ZAC [zak] *sigle f* (= *zone d'aménagement concerté*) urban development zone

ZAD [zad] *sigle f* (= *zone d'aménagement différé*) future development zone

Zaïre [zaiʀ] *nm*: **le ~** Zaïre

zaïrois, e [zaiʀwa, -waz] *adj* Zairian

Zambèze [zãbɛz] *nm*: **le ~** the Zambezi

Zambie [zãbi] *nf*: **la ~** Zambia

zambien, ne [zãbjɛ̃, -ɛn] *adj* Zambian

zapper [zape] *vi* to zap

zapping [zapiŋ] *nm*: **faire du ~** to flick through the channels

zébré, e [zebʀe] *adj* striped, streaked

zèbre [zɛbʀ(ə)] *nm* (*Zool*) zebra

zébrure [zebʀyʀ] *nf* stripe, streak

zélateur, -trice [zelatœʀ, -tʀis] *nm/f* partisan, zealot

zélé, e [zele] *adj* zealous

zèle [zɛl] *nm* diligence, assiduousness; **faire du ~** (*péj*) to be over-zealous

zénith [zenit] *nm* zenith

ZEP [zɛp] *sigle f* (= *zone d'éducation prioritaire*) area targeted for special help in education

zéro [zeʀo] *nm* zero, nought (*Brit*); **au-dessous de ~** below zero (Centigrade), below freezing; **partir de ~** to start from scratch; **réduire à ~** to reduce to nothing; **trois (buts) à ~** three (goals to) nil

zeste [zɛst(ə)] *nm* peel, zest; **un ~ de citron** a piece of lemon peel

zézaiement [zezɛmã] *nm* lisp

zézayer [zezeje] *vi* to have a lisp

ZI *sigle f* = **zone industrielle**

zibeline [ziblin] *nf* sable

ZIF [zif] *sigle f* (= *zone d'intervention foncière*) intervention zone

zigouiller [ziguje] *vt* (*fam*) to do in

zigzag [zigzag] *nm* zigzag

zigzaguer [zigzage] *vi* to zigzag (along)

Zimbabwe [zimbabwe] *nm*: **le ~** Zimbabwe

zimbabwéen, ne [zimbabweɛ̃, -ɛn] *adj* Zimbabwean

zinc [zɛ̃g] *nm* (*Chimie*) zinc; (*comptoir*) bar, counter

zinguer [zɛ̃ge] *vt* to cover with zinc

zipper [zipe] *vt* (*Inform*) to zip

zircon [ziʀkɔ̃] *nm* zircon

zizanie [zizani] *nf*: **semer la ~** to stir up ill-feeling

zizi [zizi] *nm* (*fam*) willy (*Brit*), peter (*US*)

zodiacal, e, -aux [zɔdjakal, -o] *adj* (*signe*) of the zodiac

zodiaque [zɔdjak] *nm* zodiac

zona [zona] *nm* shingles *sg*

zonage [zonaʒ] *nm* (*Admin*) zoning

zonard, e [zonaʀ, -aʀd] *nm/f* (*fam*) (young) hooligan *ou* thug

zone [zon] *nf* zone, area; (*quartiers*): **la ~** the slum belt; **de seconde ~** (*fig*) second-rate; **~ d'action** (*Mil*) sphere of activity; **~ bleue** ≈ restricted parking area; **~ d'extension** *ou* **d'urbanisation** urban development area; **~ franche** free zone; **~ industrielle (ZI)** industrial estate; **~ piétonne** pedestrian precinct; **~ résidentielle** residential area; **~ tampon** buffer zone

zoner [zone] *vi* (*fam*) to hang around

zoo [zoo] *nm* zoo

zoologie [zɔɔlɔʒi] *nf* zoology

zoologique [zɔɔlɔʒik] *adj* zoological

zoologiste [zɔɔlɔʒist(ə)] *nm/f* zoologist

zoom [zum] *nm* (*Photo*) zoom (lens)

ZUP [zyp] *sigle f* = **zone à urbaniser en priorité**; = **ZAC**

Zurich [zyʀik] *n* Zürich

zut [zyt] *excl* dash (it)! (*Brit*), nuts! (*US*)

L'anglais en situation
French in action

Collaborateurs / Contributors
Rose Rociola   Daphne Day

Coordination / Coordination
Isobel Gordon

Introduction

The aim of **French in action** is to help you express yourself simply but correctly in fluent, natural French.

The **Sentence builder** section provides hundreds of phrases in which the key elements have been translated, providing an invaluable point of reference when you then construct your own sentences.

The section on correspondence provides practical models of personal and business letters, job applications and CVs, together with examples of standard opening and closing formulae and information on how to address an envelope.This section also offers guidance notes to help the user adapt these models to his/her needs.

A separate section covers fax and e-mail correspondence as well as all the expressions you might need to make different types of phone calls.

We hope you will find **French in action** both relevant and useful and that, used in conjunction with the dictionary, it will improve your understanding and enjoyment of French.

Contents

Introduction

L'anglais en situation a pour objectif de vous aider à vous exprimer en anglais, dans un style simple et naturel.

Dans le **Mémo des tournures essentielles**, vous trouverez des centaines d'expressions anglaises de base, qui vous permettront de construire vos propres phrases dans toutes sortes de contextes.

La partie correspondance contient des modèles de lettres de tous genres, dont vous pourrez vous inspirer pour rédiger à votre tour vos lettres, que ce soit dans un contexte privé ou professionnel. Si vous êtes à la recherche d'un travail, vous y trouverez également des exemples de curriculum vitæ et de lettres de candidature. Pour vous permettre d'adapter ces modèles à vos besoins, nous vous donnons en outre une liste des formules de politesse employées en début et en fin de lettre.

La dernière partie est consacrée à la communication par télécopie, par courrier électronique et par téléphone, et comprend une liste des expressions de base les plus couramment utilisées au téléphone.

L'anglais en situation, complément indispensable de votre dictionnaire, vous permettra de vous exprimer avec aisance dans toutes les situations.

Table des matières

Likes, dislikes and preferences

Saying what you like

J'aime les gâteaux.	I like …
J'aime que les choses soient à leur place.	I like …
J'ai bien aimé le film.	I liked …
J'adore sortir en boîte.	I love …
Ce que je préfère chez Laurent, c'est son enthousiasme.	What I like most …
Ce que j'aime par-dessus tout, c'est son sourire.	What I like most of all is …
La visite des vignobles **m'a beaucoup plu.**	I very much enjoyed …
J'ai un faible pour le chocolat.	I've got a weakness for …
Rien ne vaut un bon café.	You can't beat …
Rien de tel qu'un bon bain chaud !	There's nothing better than …
Le couscous est **mon** plat **favori.**	My favourite …
La lecture est **une de mes** activités **préférées.**	… one of my favourite …
Cela ne me déplaît pas de sortir seule.	I don't mind …

Saying what you dislike

Je n'aime pas le poisson.	I don't like …
Je n'aime pas beaucoup parler en public.	I'm not very keen on …
Je ne l'aime pas du tout.	I don't like … at all.
Cette idée **ne m'emballe pas.**	I'm not particularly keen on …
Je déteste la chimie.	I hate …
J'ai horreur du sport.	I loathe …
Je ne supporte pas qu'on me mente.	I can't stand …
Sa façon d'agir **ne me plaît pas du tout.**	I don't like … at all.
Ce que je déteste le plus, c'est le repassage.	What I hate most is …

Saying what you prefer

Je préfère le rock **à** la musique classique.	I prefer … to …
Je préférerais vivre à Paris.	I would rather …
J'aimerais mieux mourir de faim **que de** lui demander un service.	I'd sooner … than …

Expressing indifference

Ça m'est égal. It's all the same to me.
Je n'ai pas de préférence. I have no preference either way.

C'est comme vous voudrez. As you wish.
Cela n'a aucune importance. It doesn't matter in the least.

Peu importe. I don't mind.

Asking what someone likes

Est-ce que vous aimez les frites ? Do you like ...
Est-ce que vous aimez faire la cuisine ? Do you like ...
Est-ce que cela vous plaît de vivre en ville ? Do you like ...
Qu'est-ce que vous préférez : la mer ou la montagne ? Which do you like better ...
Vous préférez lequel, le rouge ou le noir ? Which do you prefer ...
Est-ce que vous préférez vivre à la campagne ou en ville ? Do you prefer ...
Qu'est-ce que vous aimez le plus à la télévision ? What do you like best ...

Opinions

Asking for opinions

Qu'en pensez-vous ? What do you think about it?
Que pensez-vous de sa façon d'agir ? What do you think of ...
Je voudrais savoir ce que vous pensez de son travail. I'd like to know what you think of ...
J'aimerais connaître votre avis sur ce problème. I would like to know your views on ...

Est-ce que vous pourriez me donner votre opinion sur cette émission ? What do you think of ...
Quelle est votre opinion sur la peine de mort ? What is your opinion on ...
À votre avis, hommes et femmes sont-ils égaux ? In your opinion ...
Selon vous, faut-il donner plus de liberté aux jeunes ? In your opinion ...

Expressing opinions

Vous avez raison.	You are right.
Il a tort.	He is wrong.
Il a eu tort de démissionner.	He was wrong to ...
Je pense que ce sera possible.	I think ...
Je crois que c'est un peu prématuré.	I think ...
Je trouve que c'est normal.	I think ...
Personnellement, je pense que c'est trop cher.	Personally, I think that ...
Il me semble que vous vous trompez.	I think ...
J'ai l'impression que ses parents ne la comprennent pas.	I get the impression that ...
Je suis certain qu'il est tout à fait sincère.	I'm sure ...
Je suis sûr que Marc va gagner.	I'm sure ...
Je suis persuadé qu'il y a d'autres solutions.	I am convinced that ...
À mon avis, il n'a pas changé.	In my opinion ...
D'après moi, il a fait une erreur.	In my view ...
Selon moi, c'est impossible.	In my view ...

Being noncommittal

Ça dépend.	It depends.
Tout dépend de ce que vous entendez par là.	It all depends what you mean by ...
Je ne peux pas me prononcer.	I'd rather not express an opinion.
Je n'ai pas d'opinion bien précise à ce sujet.	I have no definite opinion on this.
Je ne me suis jamais posé la question.	I have never thought about it.

Approval and agreement

Je trouve que c'est une excellente idée.	I think it's an excellent idea.
Quelle bonne idée !	What a good idea!
J'ai beaucoup apprécié son article.	I was very impressed by ...
C'est une très bonne chose.	It's a very good thing.
Je trouve que vous avez raison de vous méfier.	I think you're right to ...
Les journaux **ont raison de** publier ces informations.	... are right to ...

Vous avez bien fait de laisser vos bagages à la consigne.	You were right to ...
Vous n'avez pas tort de critiquer le gouvernement.	You're quite justified in ...
Je partage cette opinion.	I share this view.
Je partage votre inquiétude.	I fully share your ...
Nous sommes favorables à la création d'emplois.	We are in favour of ...
Nous sommes en faveur d'une Europe unie.	We are in favour of ...
Il est exact que c'est un risque à prendre.	It is true that ...
Il est vrai que cette erreur aurait pu être évitée.	It is true that ...
Je suis d'accord avec vous.	I agree with you.
Je suis entièrement d'accord avec toi.	I entirely agree with you.

Disapproval and disagreement

Je trouve qu'il a eu tort d'emprunter autant d'argent.	I think he was wrong to ...
Il est dommage qu'il ait réagi ainsi.	It's a pity that ...
Il est regrettable qu'ils ne nous aient pas prévenus.	It is regrettable that ...
Cette idée **me déplaît profondément.**	I dislike ... intensely.
Je ne supporte pas le mensonge.	I can't stand ...
Nous sommes contre la chasse.	We are against ...
Je refuse cette solution.	I reject ...
Je suis opposé à toute forme de censure.	I am opposed to ...
Je ne partage pas ce point de vue.	I don't share this point of view.
Je suis déçu par son attitude.	I am disappointed by ...
Je suis profondément déçu.	I am deeply disappointed.
Tu n'aurais pas dû lui parler sur ce ton.	You shouldn't have ...
Nous ne pouvons accepter de voir la situation se dégrader.	We can't stand by and ...
De quel droit agit-**il** de la sorte ?	What gives him the right to ...
Je ne suis pas d'accord.	I disagree.
Nous ne sommes pas d'accord avec eux.	We don't agree with ...
Je ne suis absolument pas d'accord avec ce qu'il a dit.	I totally disagree with ...
C'est faux de dire que cette erreur était inévitable.	It is wrong to say that ...
Vous vous trompez !	You're wrong!

Apologies

How to say sorry

Excusez-moi.	Sorry.
Excusez-moi de vous déranger.	Sorry to bother you.
Oh, pardon ! J'ai dû faire un faux numéro.	Oh, sorry!
Je suis désolé de vous avoir réveillé.	I am sorry I ...
Je suis désolé pour tout ce qui s'est passé.	I am sorry about ...
Je vous prie de m'excuser.	I do apologize.
Nous prions nos lecteurs de bien vouloir excuser cette omission.	We hope ... will excuse ...

Admitting responsibility

C'est (de) ma faute : j'aurais dû partir plus tôt.	It's my fault, I should have ...
Je n'aurais pas dû me moquer d'elle.	I shouldn't have ...
Nous avons eu tort de ne pas vérifier cette information.	We were wrong not to ...
J'assume seul l'entière responsabilité de cette erreur.	I take full responsibility for ...
Si seulement j'avais préparé ma leçon !	If only I had ...

Disclaiming responsibility

Ce n'est pas (de) ma faute.	It's not my fault.
Ce n'est pas (de) ma faute si nous sommes en retard.	It isn't my fault if ...
Je ne l'ai pas fait exprès.	I didn't do it on purpose.
Je ne pouvais pas faire autrement.	I had no other option.
J'avais pourtant cru comprendre que je pouvais me garer là.	But I thought that ...
J'avais cru bien faire en le prévenant.	I thought I was doing the right thing in ...

Apologizing for being unable to do something

Je regrette, mais ce n'est pas possible.	I'm sorry, but ...
Je suis désolé, mais je ne peux pas vous aider.	I'm sorry, but ...
Il nous est malheureusement impossible d'accéder à votre demande.	Unfortunately, it's impossible for us to ...

Explanations

Causes

Je n'ai rien acheté **parce que** je n'ai pas d'argent.	... because ...
Je suis arrivé en retard **à cause des** embouteillages.	... because of ...
Puisque tu insistes, je rentre dans une semaine.	Since ...
Comme j'habitais près de la bibliothèque, j'y allais souvent.	As ...
J'ai réussi à m'en sortir **grâce au** soutien de . mes amis	... thanks to ...
Je ne pourrai pas venir **car** je n'ai pas fini.	... as ...
Vu la situation actuelle, nous ne pouvons pas nous prononcer.	Given ...
Étant donné la crise, il est difficile de trouver du travail.	Given ...
C'est une rupture d'essieu **qui a provoqué** le déraillement.	It was ... that caused ...
Le théâtre va fermer **faute de** moyens.	... due to lack of ...
Il a donné sa démission **pour des raisons de** santé.	... for ... reasons.
Le projet a été abandonné **en raison de** problèmes juridiques.	... owing to ...
Le malaise des enseignants **est lié à** la difficulté de leur métier.	... is linked to ...
Le problème vient de ce que les gens ont peur des ordinateurs.	The problem is that ...
Le ralentissement des exportations **provient de** la chute de la demande européenne.	... is the result of ...
La haine **résulte de** l'incompréhension.	... results from ...

Consequences

Je dois partir ce soir. Je ne pourrai **donc** pas venir avec vous.	... so ...
La distribution a été améliorée, **de telle sorte que** les lecteurs trouveront leur journal plus tôt.	... so that ...
Le cidre nouveau est très peu fermenté et **par conséquent** très peu alcoolisé.	... consequently ...
Ce manque de concertation **a eu pour conséquence** une duplication inutile de nos efforts.	... has resulted in ...
Voilà pourquoi on s'en souvient.	That's why ...

Comparisons

On peut comparer la télévision **à** une drogue.	... can be compared to ...
C'est une très belle performance **que l'on peut comparer à** celle des meilleurs athlètes.	... which can be compared to ...
Le Centre Pompidou **est souvent comparé à** un paquebot.	... is often compared to ...
Le bruit **était comparable à** celui d'une moto dépourvue de silencieux.	... was comparable to ...
L'Afrique reste un continent sous-peuplé **comparé à** l'Asie.	... compared with ...
Par comparaison avec l'Islande, l'Irlande a un climat tropical.	Compared to ...
Les investissements publicitaires ont connu une légère progression **par rapport à** l'année dernière.	... compared to ...
Cette histoire **ressemble à** un conte de fées.	... is like ...
Il adorait cette campagne qui **lui rappelait** l'Irlande.	... reminded him of ...
Des taux de chômage effrayants, **rappelant ceux** des années 30.	... reminiscent of those ...
Il me fait penser à mon frère.	He reminds me of ...
Le surf des neiges **est l'équivalent** sur neige **de** la planche à roulettes.	... is the equivalent ... of ...
Cette somme **correspond à** six mois de salaire.	... corresponds to ...
C'est la même chose.	It's the same thing.
Cela revient au même.	It comes to the same thing.
Ce disque **n'est ni meilleur ni moins bon que** les autres.	... is no better and no worse than ...

Stressing differences

Aucune catastrophe **ne peut être comparée au** tsunami de 2004.	No ... can compare with ...
On ne peut pas comparer les usines modernes **à** celles où travaillaient nos grands-parents.	... cannot be compared with ...
Les actions de ce groupe **n'ont rien de comparable avec** les agissements des terroristes.	... are in no way comparable to ...
Sa démarche le **différencie de** son frère.	... distinguishes ... from ...
L'histoire des États-Unis **ne ressemble en rien à** la nôtre.	... in no way resembles ...
Il y a des événements bien plus tragiques que de perdre une finale de Coupe d'Europe.	There are worse things than ...
Le gruyère **est meilleur que** le comté.	... is better than ...

Son deuxième film **est moins** réussi **que** le premier.	... is less ... than ...
L'espérance de vie des femmes est de 81 ans, **tandis que** celle des hommes est de 72 ans.	... while ...
Alors que la consommation de vin et de bière diminue, l'eau minérale est un marché en expansion.	While ...

Requests and offers

Requests

Je voudrais trois tartelettes.	I'd like ...
Je voudrais connaître les horaires des trains pour Lille.	I'd like to ...
Pourriez-vous nous donner un coup de main ?	Could you ...
Est-ce que vous pouvez annoncer la bonne nouvelle à Éliane ?	Can you ...
Est-ce que vous pourriez venir me chercher ?	Could you ...
Sois gentille, fais un saut chez le boulanger.	Be an angel ...
Auriez-vous l'amabilité de m'indiquer la sortie ?	Could you please ...
Auriez-vous la gentillesse de nous donner la recette ?	Would you be so kind as to ...
Auriez-vous l'obligeance de me garder ma place ?	Would you be very kind and ...
Puis-je vous demander de m'accorder un instant ?	Could you ...
Merci de bien vouloir patienter.	If you wouldn't mind ...
Est-ce que cela vous dérangerait d'ouvrir la fenêtre ?	Would you mind ...
Je vous serais reconnaissant de me prévenir dès que possible.	I would be grateful if you would ...
Je vous serais reconnaissant de bien vouloir me communiquer votre décision d'ici vendredi.	I would be grateful if you would ...

Offers

Je peux passer vous prendre, **si** vous voulez.	I can ... if ...
Je pourrais vous accompagner.	I could ...
Ça te dirait, une glace ?	Do you fancy ...
Ça vous dirait d'aller faire un tour ?	Would you like to ...
Que diriez-vous d'une balade en forêt ?	How do you fancy ...
Est-ce que vous voulez que j'aille chercher votre voiture ?	Do you want me to ...
Est-ce que vous voulez dîner avec nous un soir ?	Would you like to ...

Advice and suggestions

Asking for advice or suggestions

À ma place, que feriez-vous ?	What would you do, if you were me?
Quel est votre avis sur la question ?	What's your opinion on the matter?
Qu'est-ce que vous me conseillez, les Baléares ou les Canaries ?	Which would you recommend ...
Que me conseillez-vous de faire ?	What would you advise me to do?
Parmi les excursions à faire, laquelle nous conseilleriez-vous ?	... which would you recommend?
Quelle stratégie proposez-vous ?	What ... do you suggest?
Que proposez-vous pour réduire la pollution ?	What, in your opinion, should be done to ...
Qu'est-ce que vous proposez contre le chômage ?	How would you deal with ...

Offering advice or suggestions

À votre place, je me méfierais.	If I were you ...
Si j'étais toi, je ne dirais rien.	If I were you ...
Je peux vous donner un conseil : achetez votre billet à l'avance.	If I may give you a bit of advice ...
Un conseil : lisez le mode d'emploi.	A word of advice ...
Un bon conseil : n'attendez pas le dernier moment pour faire votre réservation.	A useful tip ...
Vous devriez voir un spécialiste.	You should ...
Vous feriez bien de consulter un avocat.	You would do well to ...
Vous feriez mieux d'acheter une nouvelle voiture.	You would do better to ...
Vous pourriez peut-être demander à quelqu'un de vous le traduire.	You could perhaps ...
Vous pourriez montrer un peu plus de compréhension.	You could ...
Pourquoi ne pas lui téléphoner ?	Why don't you ...
Il faudrait peut-être essayer autre chose.	Perhaps we ought to ...
Et si on allait au cinéma ?	How about ...
Je vous propose le 3 mars à 10 h 30.	How about ...
Il vaudrait mieux lui offrir de l'argent qu'un bijou.	It might be better to ...
Il serait préférable d'attendre le résultat.	It would be better to ...

Warnings

Je vous préviens, je ne me laisserai pas faire.
Je te préviens que ça ne sera pas facile.
N'oubliez pas de conserver le double de votre déclaration d'impôts.
Méfiez-vous des apparences.

Surtout, n'y allez jamais le samedi.
Si tu ne viens pas, **tu risques de** le regretter.

I warn you ...
I'd better warn you that ...
Don't forget to ...

Remember: appearances can be deceptive.

Whatever you do, don't ...
... you risk ...

Intentions and desires

Asking what someone intends to do

Qu'est-ce que vous allez faire ?
Qu'est-ce que tu vas faire si tu rates ton examen ?
Qu'allez-vous faire en rentrant? **Avez-vous des projets ?**

Quels sont vos projets ?
Est-ce que tu comptes passer tes vacances ici ?
Vous comptez rester longtemps ?
Que comptez-vous faire de votre collection ?

Comment comptez-vous faire ?

Tu as l'intention de passer des concours ?
Songez-vous à refaire un film en Europe ?

What are you going to do?
What will you do if ...
What are you going to do ... ? Do you have anything planned?

What are your plans?
Are you planning to ...
Are you planning on ...
What are you planning to do with ...

What are you thinking of doing?

Do you intend to ...
Are you thinking of ...

Talking about intentions

Je comptais m'envoler pour Ajaccio le 8 juillet.
Elle prévoit de voyager pendant un an.
Il est prévu de construire un nouveau stade.
Ils envisagent d'avoir plusieurs enfants.
Cette banque **a l'intention de** fermer un grand nombre de succursales.
Je songe à abandonner la politique.
J'ai décidé de changer de carrière.
Je suis décidée à arrêter de fumer.

I was planning to ...
She plans to ...
There are plans to ...
They are thinking of ...
... intends to ...

I am thinking of ...
I have decided to ...
I have made up my mind to ...

Je me suis décidée à y aller.	I have decided to ...
C'est décidé, nous partons à la campagne.	That's settled ...
Il n'a jamais été dans nos intentions de lui cacher la vérité.	We never had any intention of ...
Il n'est pas question pour moi **de** renoncer à ce projet.	There is no question of ...

Wishes

Je veux faire du cinéma.	I want to ...
Je voudrais savoir jouer aussi bien que lui.	I'd like to ...
J'aimerais faire du deltaplane.	I'd like to ...
J'aimerais que mes photos soient publiées dans la presse.	I would like ...
J'aurais aimé avoir un frère.	I would have liked to ...
Lionel **voulait à tout prix** partir le soir-même.	... wanted at all costs ...
Nous souhaitons préserver notre indépendance.	We wish to ...
J'espère avoir des enfants.	I hope to ...
Nous espérons que les enfants regarderont cette émission avec leurs parents.	We hope that ...
Vous rêvez de faire le tour du monde ?	Do you dream of ...
Mon rêve serait d'avoir une grande maison.	My dream would be to ...

Obligation

Il faut que je me trouve un logement.	I must ...
Il faut absolument qu'on se revoie avant le 23 !	We really must ...
Si vous allez en Pologne, **vous devez** venir nous voir.	... you must ...
Les auteurs du détournement **ont exigé que** l'avion reparte vers New York.	... demanded that ...
Ça **me force à** faire de l'exercice.	... makes me ...
Une violente crise d'asthme **m'a obligé à** consulter un médecin.	... forced me to ...
Je suis obligé de partir.	I have to ...
Il est obligé de travailler, **il n'a pas le choix.**	He has to ... he has no other option.
On ne peut pas faire autrement que d'accepter.	You have no choice but to ...
L'école **est obligatoire** jusqu'à seize ans.	... is compulsory ...
Il est indispensable de voyager pour comprendre les autres.	It is essential to ...

Permission

Asking for permission

Je peux téléphoner ?	Can I …
Je peux vous demander quelque chose ?	Can I …
Est-ce que je peux passer vous dire un petit bonjour tout à l'heure ?	Can I …
Ça ne vous dérange pas si j'arrive en avance ?	Is it alright if …
Ça ne vous dérange pas que je fume ?	Do you mind if …
Est-ce que ça vous dérange si j'ouvre la fenêtre ?	Do you mind if …
Vous permettez, Madame, **que** je regarde ce qu'il y a dans votre sac ?	Would you mind if …

Giving permission

(Vous) faites comme vous voulez.	Do as you please.
Allez-y !	Go ahead!
Je n'y vois pas d'inconvénient.	I have nothing against it.
Vous avez le droit de porter plainte.	You have the right to …

Saying something is not allowed

Je te défends de sortir !	I forbid you to …
C'est défendu.	It's forbidden.
Il est interdit de fumer dans les toilettes.	… is forbidden.
Le travail des enfants **est formellement interdit par** une convention de l'ONU.	… is strictly forbidden by …
Défense d'entrer.	No entry.
Stationnement interdit.	No parking.
Interdiction de stationner.	No parking.
C'est interdit.	It's not allowed.
Elle interdit à ses enfants **d'**ouvrir la porte.	She forbids … to …
Tu n'as pas le droit.	You're not allowed.
On n'avait pas le droit de manger ni de boire pendant le service.	We weren't allowed to …
Il n'en est pas question.	That's out of the question.

Certainty, probability and possibility

Certainty

Il est certain qu'il y aura des problèmes.	Undoubtedly ...
Il ne fait aucun doute que ce produit connaîtra un réel succès.	There is no doubt that ...
Il est évident qu'il traverse une période difficile.	Clearly ...
C'est **de toute évidence** la seule chose à faire.	Quite obviously ...
Il est indéniable qu'il a eu tort d'agir ainsi.	It is undeniable that ...
Je suis sûre que mon frère te plaira.	I am sure that ...
Je suis sûr de gagner.	I am sure that I ...
Je suis certain que nous sommes sur la bonne voie.	I am certain that ...
J'ai la certitude qu'en travaillant avec lui, je ne m'ennuierai pas.	I am sure that ...
Je suis persuadé qu'il y a d'autres solutions.	I am convinced that ...

Probability

Il est probable que le prix du pétrole va continuer d'augmenter.	... probably ...
Le taux d'inflation dépassera **très probablement** les 10 %.	... very probably ...
80 % des problèmes de peau sont **sans doute** d'origine psychique.	... undoubtedly ...
Ils avaient **sans doute** raison.	... no doubt ...
Les travaux **devraient** débuter au mois d'avril.	... should ...
Il se pourrait bien qu'ils cherchent à tester nos réactions.	It is quite possible that ...
On dirait que tout lui est égal.	It's as if ...
Il a dû oublier d'ouvrir les fenêtres.	He must have ...

Possibility

C'est possible.	It is possible.
Il est possible que cela coûte plus cher.	That might ...
Il n'est pas impossible qu'il soit parti à Paris.	It is not impossible that ...
Il se pourrait que l'Amérique ait été découverte par des Chinois.	It is possible that ...
Il se peut que ce virus soit particulièrement virulent.	... may ...
En quelques mois tout **peut** changer.	... could ...
Il a **peut-être** mal compris.	Maybe ...
Peut-être que je me trompe.	Perhaps ...

Doubt, improbability and impossibility

Doubt

Je ne suis pas sûr que ce soit utile.	I'm not sure ...
Je ne suis pas sûre d'y arriver.	I'm not sure I'll ...
Je ne suis pas certain d'avoir raison.	I'm not sure I'm ...
Il n'est pas certain que cela soit une bonne idée.	I'm not sure that ...
Il n'est pas certain qu'un vaccin puisse être mis au point.	I'm not sure that ...
Je me demande si nous avons fait beaucoup de progrès dans ce domaine.	I wonder if ...
Est-ce sage ? **J'en doute.**	I doubt it.
Il se mit à **douter de** la compétence de son médecin.	... to have doubts about ...
Je doute fort qu'il accepte de rester inactif.	I very much doubt ...
On ne sait pas exactement ce qui s'est passé.	Nobody knows exactly ...

Improbability

Il **ne** changera **probablement pas** d'avis.	... probably won't ...
Il est peu probable qu'il reste encore des places.	It is unlikely that ...
Ça m'étonnerait qu'ils aient ta pointure.	I'd be surprised if ...
Il serait étonnant que tout se passe conformément aux prévisions.	It would be amazing if ...
Nous ne risquons pas de nous ennuyer.	There's no danger of ...
Elles ne risquent pas d'avoir le prix Nobel d'économie.	They are not likely to ...
Il y a peu de chances que le taux de croissance dépasse 1,5 %.	There is not much chance of ...

Impossibility

C'est impossible.	It's impossible.
Il n'est pas possible qu'il n'y ait rien à faire.	It is not possible that ...
Il est impossible que ces renseignements soient faux.	... cannot ...
Il n'y a aucune chance qu'ils viennent à notre secours.	There is no chance of ...

Greetings

Bonjour !	Hello!
Bonsoir !	Good evening!
Salut !	Hi!
Comment allez-vous ?	How are you?
Comment ça va ?	How's things?

What to say in reply

Très bien, merci, et vous ?	Fine thanks, and you?
Ça va, et toi ?	Fine thanks, and you?
Super bien !	Great!
On fait aller.	So-so.
Couci-couça.	So-so.

Introductions

Je vous présente Charles.	This is …
Je vous présente mon amie.	May I introduce …
Marc ; Laurent	Marc, this is Laurent; Laurent, Marc.
Je ne crois pas que vous vous connaissiez.	I don't believe you know one another.

Replying to an introduction

Enchanté.	Pleased to meet you.
Enchanté or **Ravi de faire votre connaissance.**	Pleased to meet you.
Salut, moi c'est Dominique.	Hi, I'm …

Leavetaking

Au revoir !	Goodbye!
Bonne nuit !	Good night!
Salut !	Bye!
Ciao !	See you!
À bientôt !	See you later!
À demain !	See you tomorrow!
À la semaine prochaine !	See you next week!
À jeudi !	See you Thursday!

Best wishes

Bon anniversaire !	Happy Birthday!
Joyeux Noël !	Merry Christmas!
Bonne année !	Happy New Year!
Félicitations !	Congratulations!
Bon voyage !	Safe journey!
Bonne chance !	Good luck!
Bienvenue !	Welcome!
Amusez-vous bien !	Have fun!
Bon appétit !	Enjoy your meal!
(À votre) santé !	Cheers!
Tchin-tchin !	Cheers!

Correspondence

How to address an envelope

On the front

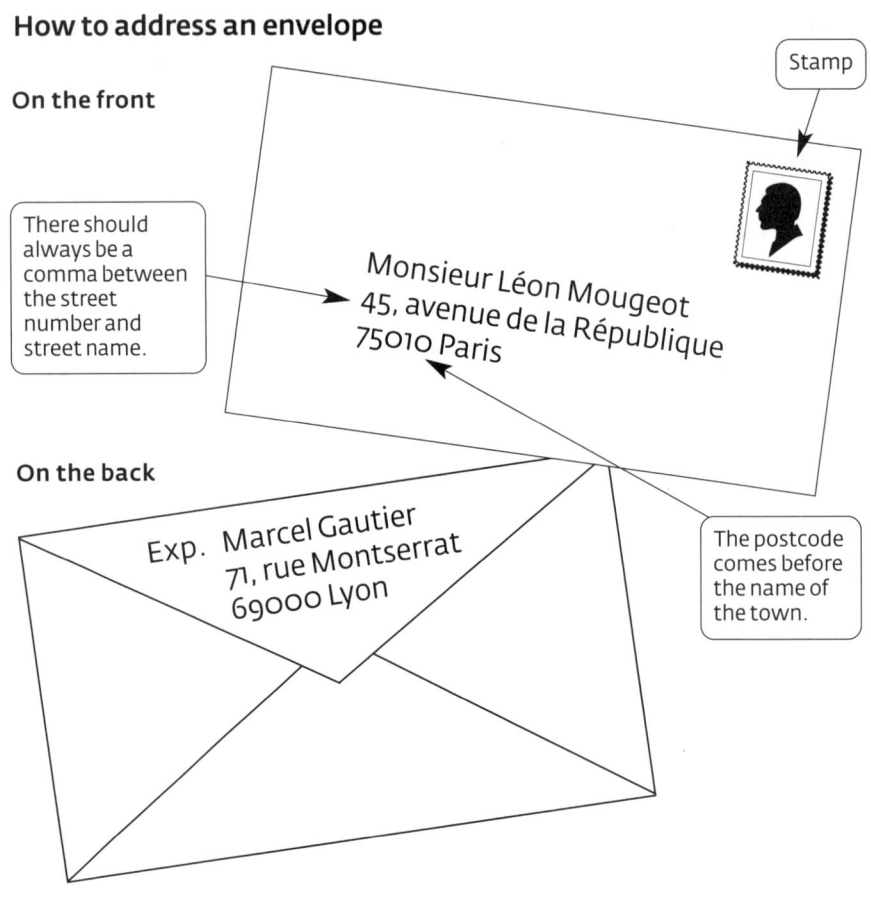

Stamp

There should always be a comma between the street number and street name.

Monsieur Léon Mougeot
45, avenue de la République
75010 Paris

The postcode comes before the name of the town.

On the back

Exp. Marcel Gautier
71, rue Montserrat
69000 Lyon

Common abbreviations used in addresses

av. = avenue	bd = boulevard	Exp. = expéditeur
fg = faubourg	pas. = passage	pl. = place

Standard opening and closing formulae
In personal correspondence

Cher Monsieur	Je vous envoie mes bien amicales pensées *(fairly formal)*
Chers Jean et Sylvie	**Bien amicalement**
Chère tante Laure	**Je t'embrasse bien affectueusement**
Mon cher Laurent	**Grosses bises** *(very informal)*

In formal correspondence

Monsieur le Directeur
  (or le Maire etc)
Madame le Directeur
	Je vous prie d'agréer, [...], l'assurance de ma
	  considération distinguée

Messieurs
Monsieur
Madame
	Je vous prie d'agréer, [...], l'assurance de mes
	  sentiments distingués or
	  Veuillez accepter, [...], l'expression de mes
	  sentiments distingués

Cher Monsieur Chère Madame	Croyez, [...], à l'expression de mes sentiments les meilleurs

Starting a personal letter

Je te remercie de ta lettre ...	Thanks for your letter ...
J'ai été très content d'avoir de tes nouvelles.	It was lovely to hear from you.
Je suis désolé de ne pas vous avoir répondu plus vite.	I'm sorry I didn't reply sooner.

Starting a formal letter

Suite à ... je vous écris pour ...	Further to ... I am writing to ...
Je vous serais reconnaissant de ...	I would be grateful if you would ...
Je vous prie de ...	Please ...
Nous vous remercions de votre lettre ...	Thank you for your letter ...

Ending a personal letter

Transmettez mes amitiés à ...	Give my regards to ...
Dis bonjour à ... de ma part.	Say hello to ... for me.
... t'embrasse ...	... sends you his love ...
Embrasse ... pour moi.	Give my love to ...

Ending a formal letter

Dans l'attente de votre réponse ...	I look forward to hearing from you ...

Je demeure à votre entière disposition
  pour toute information complémentaire.
	I will be happy to supply any
	  further information you may
	  require.

Je vous remercie dès à présent de ...	Thank you in advance for ...

Thank you letter

Name and address of sender.

The town or city from which the letter is being sent should be included along with the date. The article **le** should be included in the date.

Anne et Cyrille Legendre
25, rue des Grillons
69000 LYON

Lyon, le 24 octobre 2007

Chers oncle et tante,

Le grand jour, c'était il y a presqu'un mois déjà ...
Ce fut une merveilleuse fête et nous étions très heureux
de vous avoir parmi nous.

Nous tenons à vous remercier chaleureusement de votre
gentil cadeau et nous vous inviterons bientôt pour
inaugurer ce superbe service à raclette comme
il se doit.

Vous trouverez aussi ci-joint une photo-souvenir.

Nous vous embrassons tous les deux,

Anne et Cyrille

For alternatives see p20.

Hotel booking

Name and address of letter's recipient.

Jeanne Judon
89, bd des Tertres
75008 PARIS

Hôtel Renoir
15, rue de Beaumanoir
59000 LILLE

Paris, le 3 novembre 2007

Madame ou Monsieur,

For alternatives see p21.

Me rendant à Lille le mois prochain à l'occasion du Salon de l'esthétique, j'aimerais réserver une chambre avec salle de bains pour deux nuits le mercredi 5 et le jeudi 6 décembre 2007.

Je vous saurais gré de me communiquer vos tarifs et de me confirmer que vous avez bien une chambre libre à cette époque.

Je vous prie de croire, Madame, Monsieur, à l'assurance de mes sentiments distingués.

Jeanne Judon

Letter of complaint

M et Mme DAUNAY
La Longue Haie
35135 CHANTEPIE

Hôtel "Au Bon Accueil "
17, rue Nationale
86000 POITIERS

Chantepie, le 29 décembre 2007

Madame, Monsieur,

Mon mari et moi avons passé la nuit du 23 décembre dans votre hôtel, où nous avions préalablement réservé une chambre. Nous tenons à vous faire savoir que nous avons été très déçus par vos services, en particulier par le bruit – nous avons pourtant demandé une chambre calme – et l'impossibilité de se faire servir un petit déjeuner avant notre départ à 6 h 30.

Cet arrêt dans votre hôtel qui devait nous permettre de nous reposer au cours d'un long voyage en voiture n'a fait que nous fatiguer davantage. Sachez que nous prendrons bien soin de déconseiller votre établissement à nos amis.

Je vous prie d'agréer, Madame, Monsieur, mes salutations distinguées.

For alternatives see p21.

Curriculum Vitæ

The words **courriel** or **mél** can also be used.

CURRICULUM VITÆ

LEGUEN Maxime
29, rue de Vannes
35000 RENNES
Tél : 56 02 71 28

29 ans
célibataire
nationalité française

Adresse électronique : mleguen@agriventes.com.fr

EXPÉRIENCE PROFESSIONNELLE

Du 10.3.05 à ce jour :   Adjointe du directeur à l'exportation,
Agriventes, Rennes

Du 8.10.03 au 30.1.05 :   Secrétaire de direction,
France-Exportations, Cognac

DIPLÔMES

2003 :   Diplôme de secrétaire bilingue, délivré par l'École de
commerce de Poitiers

2002 :   Licence de langues étrangères appliquées (anglais et russe),
Université de Poitiers – plusieurs mentions

1998 :   Baccalauréat (langues) – mention assez bien

AUTRES RENSEIGNEMENTS

Langues étrangères : anglais et russe (courant), allemand (bonnes
connaissances)

Stage d'information dans le cadre de la formation continue, 2005

Permis de conduire

Nombreux voyages en Europe et aux États-Unis

If you have British or American etc qualifications you should use wording such as "**équivalence baccalauréat (3 A-levels), équivalence licence de lettres (BA Hons)**" etc.

Job application

This is appropriate if you are writing to a company. However, if you are writing to the holder of a particular post use the following:
Monsieur (or **Madame**) **le Directeur des ressources humaines**
Société GERBAULT etc and begin the letter:
Monsieur le Directeur des ressources humaines,
If you know the name of the person you should use the following:
Monsieur Alain Dupont
Directeur des ressources humaines
Société GERBAULT etc and begin the letter:
Monsieur,

Maxime LEGUEN
29, rue de Vannes
35000 RENNES

Service du Personnel
Société GERBAULT
85, bd de la Liberté
35000 RENNES

Rennes, le 12 juillet 2007

Madame, Monsieur,

Votre annonce parue dans le Monde du 8 juillet concernant un poste d'assistante de direction dans votre service Import-Export m'a particulièrement intéressée.

Mon expérience de quatre ans en tant qu'assistante de direction dans le service d'exportation d'une petite entreprise m'a permis d'acquérir un sens des responsabilités ainsi qu'une grande capacité d'adaptation. Le poste que vous proposez m'intéresse tout particulièrement car j'aimerais beaucoup pouvoir utiliser ma connaissance de la langue et de la culture russe dans le cadre de mon travail.

Je me tiens à votre disposition pour vous apporter de plus amples renseignements sur ma formation et mon expérience.

Je vous prie, Madame, Monsieur, de bien vouloir agréer mes salutations distinguées.

Maxime Leguen

Maxime Leguen
P.J. : CV

= **pièces jointes.** You should add this if you are enclosing any other information with your letter eg a CV.

Invitation to interview

SOCIÉTÉ GERBAULT

85, bd de la Liberté
35000 RENNES
TÉLÉPHONE : **02 99 45 32 88** • *TÉLÉCOPIE :* **02 99 45 32 90**

Maxime LEGUEN
29, rue de Vannes
35000 RENNES

Rennes, le 19 juillet

Madame,

Votre candidature au poste d'assistante de direction au sein de notre Compagnie a retenu notre attention.

Nous vous proposons, dans le but de faire plus ample connaissance de part et d'autre, de rencontrer :

Monsieur LAURENT

notre Directeur Régional, le 26 juillet prochain, à 9 h, à l'adresse suivante :

2, bd de Lattre de Tassigny
35000 RENNES

Si cette date ne vous convenait pas, vous seriez aimable d'avertir notre secrétariat (Tél : 02 99 45 32 88) afin de convenir d'un autre rendez-vous.

Nous vous prions de croire, Madame, à l'expression de nos sentiments distingués.

Jean Minet
Jean Minet

For alternatives see p21.

Fax

France-Sanitaires S.A.

55, rue de Strasbourg
75012 Paris
Téléphone : 01 63 13 84 20
Télécopie : 01 63 13 84 32

TÉLÉCOPIE

À : Mme Robin

Date : le 7 janvier 2007

De : M. Edmond
Service clientèle

Nombre de pages à suivre : 1

Réf. : Devis pour installation salle de bains.

Madame,

Suite à notre visite d'avant-hier, veuillez trouver ci-joint notre devis pour l'installation d'une salle de bains dans votre appartement. Les prix comprennent la fourniture du matériel ainsi que la main d'oeuvre.

Dans l'attente de votre réponse, je vous prie, Madame, d'agréer l'expression de mes meilleurs sentiments,

Y. Edmond

E-Mail

Sending messages

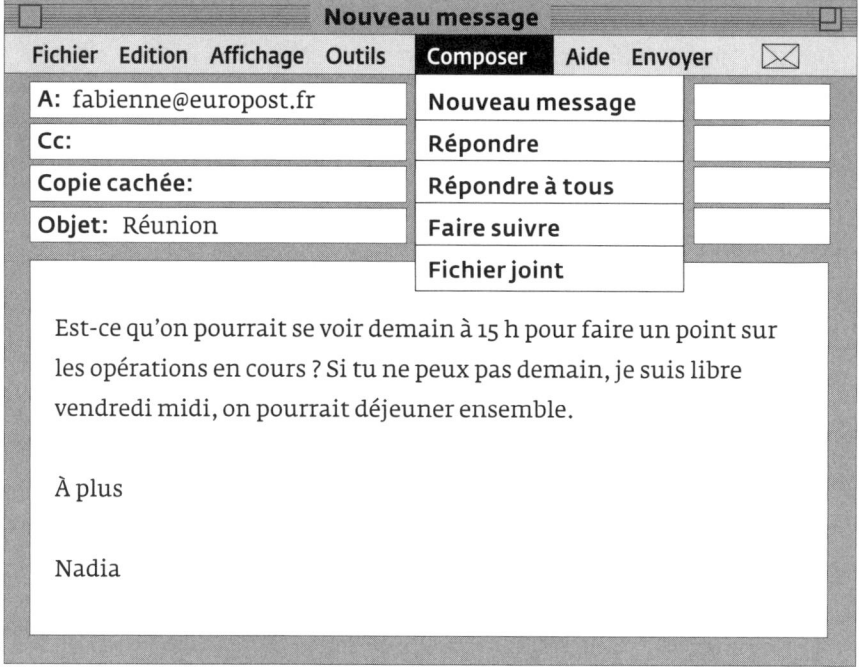

Fichier	File
Édition	Edit
Affichage	View
Outils	Tools
Composer	Compose
Aide	Help
Envoyer	Send
Nouveau message	New
Répondre	Reply to Sender

E-Mail

Receiving messages

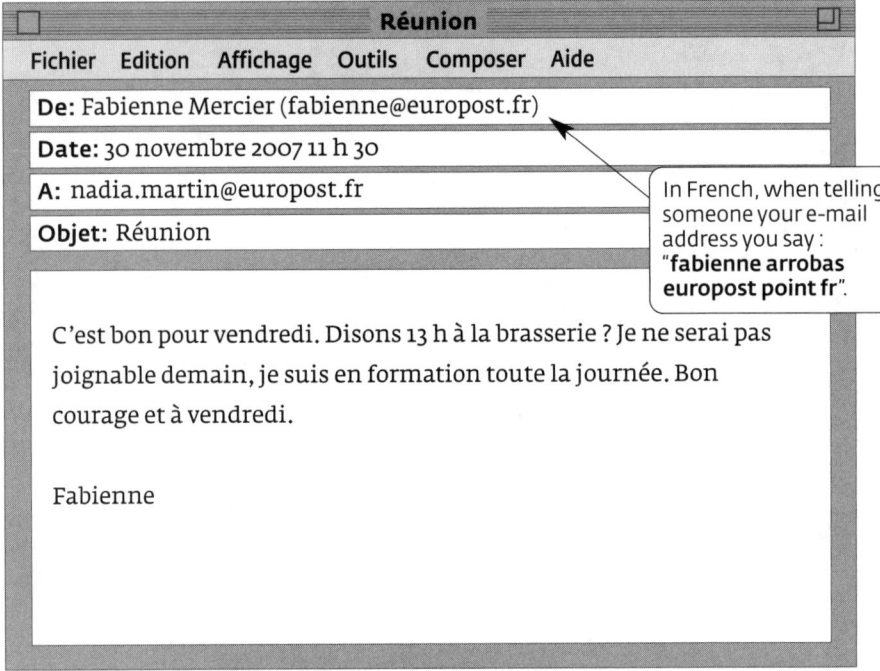

Répondre à tous	Reply to All
Faire suivre	Forward
Fichier joint	Attachment
À	To
Cc	Cc (carbon copy)
Copie cachée	Bcc (blind carbon copy)
Objet	Subject
De	From
Date	Sent

TELEPHONE

Different types of call

Communication locale/interurbaine.

Local/national call.

Je voudrais appeler l'étranger.

I want to make an international call.

Je voudrais appeler Londres **en PCV.**

I want to make a reverse charge call *(Brit)* to a ... number *or* I want to call a ... number collect *(US)*.

Comment est-ce que je peux téléphoner à l'extérieur ?

How do I get an outside line?

Asking for information

Quel est le numéro des renseignements ?

What is the number for directory enquiries *(Brit)* or directory assistance *(US)*?

Je voudrais le numéro de la société Europost, 20, rue de la Marelle, à Pierrefitte.

Can you give me the number of ...

Quel est l'indicatif de la Martinique ?

What is the code for ...

Quel est le numéro de l'horloge parlante ?

What is the number for the speaking clock?

Receiving information

Le numéro que vous avez demandé est le 01 40 32 37 12. (zéro-un quarante trente-deux trente-sept douze)

The number you require is ...

Je regrette, mais il n'y a pas d'abonné à ce nom.

I'm sorry, there's no listing under that name.

Le numéro que vous avez demandé est sur liste rouge.

The number you require is ex-directory *(Brit)* or unlisted *(US)*.

When your number answers

Je voudrais parler à *or* Pourrais-je parler à M. Wolff, s'il vous plaît ?

Could I speak to ...

Pourriez-vous me passer le docteur Henderson, s'il vous plaît ?

Could you put me through to ...

Pourriez-vous me passer le poste 52 64, s'il vous plaît ?

Can I have extension ...

Je rappellerai dans une demi-heure.

I'll call back in ...

Pourriez-vous lui demander de me rappeler à son retour ?

Would you ask him to ring me when he gets back?

The switchboard operator speaks

C'est de la part de qui ?	Who shall I say is calling?
Je vous le passe.	I'm putting you through.
J'ai un appel de Tokyo pour Mme Thomson.	I have a call from ... for ...
J'ai Mlle Martin en ligne.	I've got ... on the line.
Le docteur Roberts est en ligne, vous patientez ?	... is on another line. Do you want to wait?
Ne quittez pas.	Please hold.
Ça ne répond pas.	There's no reply.
Voulez-vous laisser un message ?	Would you like to leave a message?

Recorded messages

Le numéro de votre correspondant n'est plus attribué. Veuillez consulter l'annuaire ou votre centre de renseignements.	The number you have dialled has not been recognized. Please consult the directory or directory enquiries.
Le numéro de votre correspondant a changé. Veuillez composer désormais le 33 42 21 70.	The number you have dialled has been changed to ...
Par suite de l'encombrement des lignes, votre appel ne peut aboutir. Veuillez rappeler ultérieurement.	All the lines are busy right now. Please try again later.
Bonjour, vous êtes en communication avec le service des ventes. Veuillez patienter, nous allons donner suite à votre appel dans quelques instants.	Hello, you have reached ... Please wait, your call will be answered shortly.
Bonjour, vous êtes bien chez M. et Mme Martin. Laissez un message après le bip sonore et nous vous rappellerons dès notre retour. Merci.	Hello, you are through to ... Leave a message after the tone and we'll get back to you.

Answering the telephone

Allô, c'est Anne à l'appareil.	Hello, it's ... speaking.
C'est moi or lui-même (or elle-même).	Speaking.
Qui est à l'appareil ?	Who's speaking?

When in trouble

Je n'arrive pas à avoir le numéro.	I can't get through.
Leur téléphone est en dérangement.	Their phone is out of order.
Nous avons été coupés.	We have been cut off.
J'ai dû faire un faux numéro.	I must have dialled the wrong number.
La ligne est très mauvaise.	This is a very bad line.

Goûts et préférences

Pour dire ce que l'on aime

I like cakes.	J'aime …
I like things to be in their proper place.	J'aime que …
I really liked the film.	J'ai bien aimé …
I love going to clubs.	J'adore …
What I like best about Matthew are his eyes.	Ce que je préfère …
What I enjoy most is an evening with friends.	Ce que j'aime par-dessus tout, c'est …
I very much enjoyed the trip to the vineyards.	… m'a beaucoup plu.
I've never tasted **anything better than** this chicken.	… rien … de meilleur que …
I've got a weakness for chocolate cakes.	J'ai un faible pour …
You can't beat a good cup of tea.	Rien ne vaut …
There's nothing quite like a nice hot bath!	Rien de tel que …
My favourite dish is lasagne.	… mon … favori.
Reading is **one of my favourite** pastimes.	… une de mes … préférées.
I don't mind being alone.	Cela ne me déplaît pas de …

Pour dire ce que l'on n'aime pas

I don't like fish.	Je n'aime pas …
I don't like him **at all**.	Je ne … aime pas du tout.
I'm not very keen on speaking in public.	Je n'aime pas beaucoup …
I'm not particularly keen on the idea.	… ne m'emballe pas.
I hate chemistry.	Je déteste …
I loathe sport.	J'ai horreur du …
I can't stand being lied to.	Je ne supporte pas que …
If there's one thing I hate it's ironing.	Ce que je déteste le plus, c'est de …

Préférences

I prefer pop **to** classical music.	Je préfère … à …
I would rather live in Paris.	Je préférerais …
I'd rather starve **than** ask him a favour.	J'aimerais mieux … que de …

Indifférence

It's all the same to me.	Ça m'est égal.
I have no particular preference.	Je n'ai pas de préférence.
As you like.	C'est comme vous voudrez.

It doesn't matter in the least.	Cela n'a aucune importance.
I don't mind.	Peu importe.

Comment demander à quelqu'un ce qu'il aime

Do you like chocolate?	Est-ce que vous aimez ...
Do you like cooking?	Est-ce que vous aimez ...
Which do you like better: football or cricket?	Qu'est-ce que vous préférez : ...
Which would you rather have: the red one or the black one?	Lequel préférez-vous : ...
Do you prefer living in the town or in the country?	Est-ce que vous préférez ...
What do you like best on television?	Qu'est-ce que vous aimez le plus ...

Opinions

Comment demander l'avis de quelqu'un

What do you think about it?	Qu'en pensez-vous ?
What do you think about divorce?	Que pensez-vous du ...
What do you think of his behaviour?	Que pensez-vous de ...
I'd like to know what you think of his work.	Je voudrais savoir ce que vous pensez de ...
I would like to know your views on this.	J'aimerais connaître votre avis sur ...
What is your opinion on the team's chances of success?	Quelle est votre opinion sur ...
Could you give me your opinion on this proposal?	Est-ce que vous pourriez me donner votre avis sur ...
In your opinion, are men and women equal?	À votre avis ...
In your view, is this the best solution?	Selon vous ...

Comment donner son avis

You are right.	Vous avez raison.
He is wrong.	Il a tort.
He was wrong to resign.	Il a eu tort de ...
I think it ought to be possible.	Je pense que ...

I **think** it's a bit premature.	Je crois que …
I **think** it's quite natural.	Je trouve que …
Personally, I think that it's a waste of money.	Personnellement, je pense que …
I **have the impression that** her parents don't understand her.	J'ai l'impression que …
I'**m sure** he is completely sincere.	Je suis certain que …
I'**m convinced that** there are other possibilities.	Je suis persuadé que …
In my opinion, he hasn't changed.	À mon avis …
In my view, he's their best player.	Selon moi …

Comment éviter de donner son avis

It depends.	Ça dépend.
It all depends on what you mean by patriotism.	Tout dépend de ce que vous entendez par …
I'**d rather not express an opinion.**	Je préfère ne pas me prononcer.
Actually, I've never thought about it.	À vrai dire, je ne me suis jamais posé la question.

Approbation et accord

I **think it's an excellent idea.**	Je trouve que c'est une excellente idée.
What a good idea!	Quelle bonne idée !
I **was very impressed by** his speech.	J'ai beaucoup apprécié …
It's a very good thing.	C'est une très bonne chose.
I **think you're right to** be wary.	Je trouve que vous avez raison de …
Newspapers **are right to** publish these stories.	… ont raison de …
You were right to leave your bags in left-luggage.	Vous avez bien fait de …
Third World countries **rightly believe that** most pollution comes from developed countries.	… estiment à juste titre que …
You're quite justified in complaining.	Vous avez bien raison de …
I **share this view.**	Je partage cette opinion.
I **fully share** your concern.	Je partage …
We support the creation of jobs.	Nous sommes favorables à …
We are in favour of a united Europe.	Nous sommes en faveur de …

It is true that mistakes were made.	Il est vrai que ...
I agree with you.	Je suis d'accord avec vous.
I entirely agree with you.	Je suis entièrement d'accord avec toi.

Désapprobation et désaccord

I think he was wrong to borrow so much money.	Je trouve qu'il a eu tort de ...
It's a pity that you didn't tell me.	Il est dommage que ...
It is regrettable that they allowed this to happen.	Il est regrettable que ...
I dislike the idea **intensely.**	... me déplaît profondément.
I can't stand lies.	Je ne supporte pas ...
We are against hunting.	Nous sommes contre ...
We do not condone violence.	Nous ne tolérons pas ...
I am opposed to compulsory screening.	Je suis opposé au ...
I don't share this point of view.	Je ne partage pas ce point de vue.
I am disappointed by his attitude.	Je suis déçu par ...
I am deeply disappointed.	Je suis profondément déçu.
You shouldn't have said that.	Tu n'aurais pas dû ...
What gives him **the right to** act like this?	De quel droit ...
I disagree.	Je ne suis pas d'accord.
We don't agree with them.	Nous ne sommes pas d'accord avec ...
I totally disagree with what he said.	Je ne suis absolument pas d'accord avec ...
It is not true to say that the disaster was inevitable.	C'est faux de dire que ...
You are wrong!	Vous vous trompez !

Excuses

Pour s'excuser

Sorry.	Excusez-moi.
Oh, sorry! I've got the wrong number.	Oh, pardon !
Sorry to bother you.	Excusez-moi de vous déranger.

I'm sorry I woke you.	Je suis désolé de ...
I'm terribly sorry about the misunderstanding.	Je suis navré de ...
I do apologize.	Je vous prie de m'excuser.
We hope our readers **will excuse** this oversight.	Nous prions ... de bien vouloir excuser ...

En assumant la responsabilité de ce qui s'est passé

It's my fault; I should have left earlier.	C'est (de) ma faute : j'aurais dû ...
I shouldn't have laughed at her.	Je n'aurais pas dû ...
We were wrong not to check this information.	Nous avons eu tort de ne pas ...
I take full responsibility for what I did.	J'assume seul l'entière responsabilité de ...
If only I had done my homework!	Si seulement j'avais ...

En niant toute responsabilité

It's not my fault.	Ce n'est pas (de) ma faute.
It isn't my fault if we're late.	Ce n'est pas (de) ma faute si ...
I didn't do it on purpose.	Je ne l'ai pas fait exprès.
I had no option.	Je ne pouvais pas faire autrement.
But I thought that it was okay to park here.	J'avais pourtant cru comprendre que ...
I thought I was doing the right thing in warning him.	J'avais cru bien faire en ...

En exprimant ses regrets

I'm sorry, but it's impossible.	Je regrette, mais ...
I'm afraid we're fully booked.	Je regrette, mais ...
Unfortunately we are unable to meet your request.	Il nous est malheureusement impossible de ...

Explications

Causes

I didn't buy anything **because** I had no money.	... parce que ...
I arrived late **because of** the traffic.	... à cause de ...
Since you insist, I'll come again tomorrow.	Puisque ...
As I lived near the library, I used it a lot.	Comme ...
I got through it **thanks to** the support of my friends.	... grâce à ...
Given the present situation, finding a job will be difficult.	Vu ...
Given that there is an economic crisis, it is difficult to find work.	Étant donné ...
Considering how many problems we had, we did well.	Étant donné ...
It was a broken axle **that caused** the derailment.	C'est ... qui a provoqué ...
He resigned **for** health **reasons.**	... pour des raisons de ...
The theatre is closing, **due to lack of** funds.	... faute de ...
The project was abandoned **owing to** legal problems.	... en raison de ...
Many cancers **are linked to** smoking.	... sont dus à ...
The problem is that people are afraid of computers.	Le problème vient de ce que ...
The drop in sales **is the result of** high interest rates.	... est due à ...
The quarrel **resulted from** a misunderstanding.	... a pour origine ...

Conséquences

I have to leave tonight; **so** I can't come with you.	... donc ...
Distribution has been improved **so that** readers now get their newspaper earlier.	... de telle sorte que ...
This cider is fermented for a very short time and is **consequently** low in alcohol.	... par conséquent ...
Our lack of consultation **has resulted in** a duplication of effort.	... a eu pour conséquence ...
That's why they are easy to remember.	Voilà pourquoi ...

Comparaisons

Gambling **can be compared to** a drug.	On peut comparer ... à ...
The gas has a smell **that can be compared to** rotten eggs.	... que l'on peut comparer à ...

The shape of Italy **is often compared to** a boot.	... est souvent comparé à ...
The noise **was comparable to** that of a large motorbike.	... était comparable à ...
Africa is still underpopulated **compared with** Asia.	... comparé à ...
In the UK, the rate of inflation increased slightly **compared to** the previous year.	... par rapport à ...
What is so special about a holiday in Florida **as compared to** one in Spain?	... par rapport à ...
This story **is like** a fairy tale.	... ressemble à ...
He loved this countryside, which **reminded him of** Ireland.	... lui rappelait ...
Frightening levels of unemployment, **reminiscent of those** of the 30s.	... rappelant ceux ...
The snowboard **is the equivalent** on snow **of** the skateboard.	... est l'équivalent ... de ...
This sum **corresponds to** six months' salary.	... correspond à ...
A 'bap'? **It's the same thing as** a bread roll.	C'est la même chose que ...
It comes to the same thing in terms of calories.	Ça revient au même ...
This record **is no better and no worse than** the others.	... n'est ni meilleur ni moins bon que ...

Pour souligner une différence

No catastrophe **can compare with** the tsunami of 2004.	Aucune ... ne peut être comparée à ...
Modern factories **cannot be compared with** those our grandparents worked in.	On ne peut pas comparer ... à ...
The actions of this group **are in no way comparable to** those of terrorists.	... n'ont rien de comparable avec ...
The newspaper reports **differ** on this point.	... divergent ...
The history of the United States **in no way resembles** our own.	... ne ressemble en rien à ...
There are worse things than losing a European cup final.	Il y a des événements bien plus tragiques que ...
This film **is less** interesting **than** his first one.	... est moins ... que ...
Women's life expectancy is 81 years, **while** men's is 72.	... tandis que ...
While the consumption of wine and beer is decreasing, the consumption of bottled water is increasing.	Alors que ...

Demandes et propositions

Demandes

I'd like another beer.	Je voudrais ...
I'd like to know the times of trains to Lille.	Je voudrais ...
Could you give us a hand?	Pourriez-vous ...
Can you tell Eleanor the good news?	Est-ce que vous pouvez ...
Could you please show me the way out?	Auriez-vous l'obligeance de ...
Could I ask you for a few minutes of your time?	Puis-je vous demander de ...
Be an angel, pop to the baker's for me.	Sois gentille ...
If you wouldn't mind waiting for a moment.	Merci de bien vouloir ...
Would you mind opening the window?	Est-ce que cela vous dérangerait de ...
Would you be very kind and save my seat for me?	Auriez-vous l'obligeance de ...
I would be grateful if you could reply as soon as possible.	Je vous serais reconnaissant de ...

Propositions

I can come and pick you up **if** you like.	Je peux ... si ...
I could go with you.	Je pourrais ...
Do you fancy a bit of Stilton?	Ça te dit ...
How about a pear tart?	Que diriez-vous de ...
Would you like to see my photos?	Ça vous dirait de ...
Would you like to have dinner with me one evening?	Est-ce que vous voulez ...
Do you want me to go and get your car?	Est-ce que vous voulez que ...

Conseils et suggestions

Comment demander conseil

What would you do, if you were me?	À ma place, que feriez-vous ?
Would you accept, **if you were me?**	À ma place ...
What's your opinion on this?	Quel est votre avis sur la question ?
What, in your opinion, should be done to reduce pollution?	Que proposez-vous pour ...
What would you advise?	Que me conseillez-vous ?

What would you advise me to do?	Que me conseillez-vous de faire ?
Which would you recommend, Majorca or Ibiza?	Qu'est-ce que vous me conseillez ...
If we were to sponsor a player, **who would you recommend?**	... lequel nous conseilleriez-vous ?
What strategy **do you suggest?**	Quelle ... proposez-vous ?
How would you deal with unemployment?	Qu'est-ce que vous proposez contre ...

Comment donner un conseil

If I were you, I'd be a bit wary.	À votre place ...
If I were you I wouldn't say anything.	À ta place ...
Take my advice, buy your tickets in advance.	Je vous conseille de ...
A word of advice: read the instructions.	Un conseil ...
A useful tip: always have some pasta in your cupboard.	Un bon conseil ...
As you like languages, **you ought to** study as a translator.	... vous devriez ...
You should see a specialist.	Vous devriez ...
You would do well to see a solicitor.	Vous feriez bien de ...
You would do better to spend the money on a new car.	Vous feriez mieux de ...
You could perhaps ask someone to go with you.	Vous pourriez peut-être ...
You could try being a little more understanding.	Vous pourriez ...
Perhaps you should speak to a plumber about it.	Il faudrait peut-être que ...
Perhaps we ought to try a different approach.	Il faudrait peut-être ...
Why don't you phone him?	Pourquoi ne pas ...
How about renting a video?	Et si on ...
How about 3 March at 10.30am?	... ça vous va ?
It might be better to give her money rather than jewellery.	Il vaudrait peut-être mieux ...
It would be better to wait a bit.	Il serait préférable de ...

Mises en garde

I warn you, I intend to get my own back.	Je vous préviens ...
I'd better warn you that he knows you did it.	Mieux vaut que je te prévienne ...
Don't forget to keep a copy of your income tax return.	N'oubliez pas de ...

Remember: appearances can be deceptive.	Méfiez-vous des apparences.
Beware of buying tickets from touts.	Attention ...
Whatever you do, don't leave your camera in the car.	Surtout, ne ... jamais ...
If you don't book early you risk being disappointed.	... tu risques de ...

Intentions et souhaits

Pour demander à quelqu'un ce qu'il compte faire

What are you going to do?	Qu'est-ce que vous allez faire ?
What will you do if you fail your exams?	Qu'est-ce que tu vas faire si ...
What are you going to do when you get back?	Qu'allez-vous faire ...
Do you have anything planned?	Avez-vous des projets ?
Can we expect you next Sunday?	On compte sur vous ...
Are you planning to spend all of the holiday here?	Est-ce que tu comptes ...
Are you planning on staying long?	Vous comptez ...
What are you planning to do with your collection?	Que comptez-vous faire de ...
What are you thinking of doing?	Que comptez-vous faire ?
Do you intend to go into teaching?	Est-ce que tu as l'intention de ...
Are you thinking of making another film in Europe?	Songez-vous à ...

Pour dire ce qu'on a l'intention de faire

I was planning to go to Ajaccio on 8 July.	Je comptais ...
She plans to go to India for a year.	Elle prévoit de ...
There are plans to build a new stadium.	Il est prévu de ...
The bank intends to close a hundred branches.	... a l'intention de ...
I am thinking of giving up politics.	Je songe à ...
I have decided to get a divorce.	J'ai décidé de ...
I have made up my mind to stop smoking.	Je suis décidé à ...
We never had any intention of talking to the press.	Il n'a jamais été dans nos intentions de ...
That's settled, we'll go to Florida in May.	C'est décidé ...
For me, living abroad is out of the question.	Il n'est pas question ... de ...

Souhaits

I'd like to be able to play as well as him.	Je voudrais …
I'd like to go hang-gliding.	J'aimerais …
I would like my photos to be published.	J'aimerais que …
I would like to have had a brother.	J'aurais aimé …
I want to act in films.	Je veux …
Ian **wanted at all costs** to prevent his boss finding out.	… voulait à tout prix …
We wish to preserve our independence.	Nous souhaitons …
I hope to have children.	J'espère …
We hope that children will watch this programme with their parents.	Nous espérons que …
Do you dream of winning the lottery?	Vous rêvez de …
I dream of having a big house.	Mon rêve serait de …

Obligation

I must find somewhere to live.	Il faut que je …
We really must see each other more often!	Il faut absolument qu'on …
If you're going to Poland, **you must** learn Polish.	… vous devez …
He **made** his secretary answer all his calls.	… exigeait que …
My mother **makes me** eat spinach.	… me force à …
The hijackers **demanded that** the plane fly to New York.	… ont exigé que …
A serious illness **forced me to** cancel my holiday.	… m'a obligé à …
He **was obliged to** borrow more and more money.	… a été obligé de …
Mary **had no choice but to** invite him.	… n'avait pas pu faire autrement que de …
The only thing you can do is say no.	Tu ne peux pas faire autrement que de …
Many mothers **have to** work; **they have no other option.**	… sont obligées de … elles n'ont pas le choix.
She had the baby adopted because **she had no other option.**	… elle ne pouvait pas faire autrement.
School **is compulsory** until the age of sixteen.	… est obligatoire …
It is essential to know some history, if we are to understand the situation.	Il est indispensable de …

Permission

Comment demander la permission de faire quelque chose

Can I use the phone?	Je peux ...
Can I ask you something?	Je peux ...
Is it okay if I come now, or is it too early?	Ça ne vous dérange pas si ...
Do you mind if I smoke?	Ça ne vous dérange pas que ...
Do you mind if I open the window?	Est-ce que ça vous dérange si ...
Would you mind if I had a look in your briefcase, madam?	Vous permettez que ...
Could I have permission to leave early?	Est-ce que je peux vous demander la permission de ...

Autorisation

Do as you please.	(Vous) faites comme vous voulez.
Go ahead!	Allez-y !
No, of course I don't mind.	Bien sûr que non.
I have nothing against it.	Je n'y vois pas d'inconvénient.
Pupils **are allowed to** wear what they like.	... ont le droit de ...

Défense

I forbid you to go out!	Je te défends de ...
It's forbidden.	C'est défendu.
Smoking in the toilet **is forbidden.**	Il est interdit de ...
Child labour is **strictly forbidden by** a UN convention.	... formellement interdit par ...
No entry!	Défense d'entrer !
No parking.	Stationnement interdit.
It's not allowed.	C'est interdit.
You are not allowed to swim in the lake.	Il est interdit de ...
We weren't allowed to eat or drink while on duty.	On n'avait pas le droit de ...
That's out of the question.	Il n'en est pas question.

Certitude, probabilité et possibilité

Certitude

Undoubtedly, there will be problems.	Il est certain que ...
There is no doubt that the country's image has suffered.	Il ne fait aucun doute que ...
It's bound to cause trouble.	Cela va sûrement ...
Clearly the company is in difficulties.	Il est évident que ...
A foreign tourist is **quite obviously** a rare sight here.	... de toute évidence ...
It is undeniable that she was partly to blame.	Il est indéniable que ...
I **am sure** you will like my brother.	Je suis sûre que ...
I **am sure that** I will win.	Je suis sûr de ...
I'm **sure that** I won't get bored working with him.	J'ai la certitude que ...
I am **certain that** we are on the right track.	Je suis certain que ...
I am **convinced that** there are other solutions.	Je suis persuadé que ...

Probabilité

The price of petrol will **probably** rise.	Il est probable que ...
Inflation will **very probably** exceed 10%.	... très probablement ...
It is highly probable that they will abandon the project.	Il est fort probable que ...
The trend **is likely** to continue.	Il est probable que ...
80% of skin problems **undoubtedly** have psychological origins.	... sans doute ...
They were **no doubt** right.	... sans doute ...
The construction work **should** start in April.	... devrait ...
He **must have** forgotten to open the windows.	Il a dû ...

Possibilité

It's possible.	C'est possible.
It is possible that they got your name from the electoral register.	Il est possible que ...
It is not impossible that he has gone to Paris.	Il n'est pas impossible que ...
That might be more expensive.	Il se peut que ...
He **may have** misunderstood.	Il a peut-être ...
This virus **may** be extremely infectious.	Il se peut que ...
It may be that it will take time to achieve peace.	Il se peut que ...
In a few months everything **could** change.	... peut ...
Perhaps I am mistaken.	Peut-être que ...

Incertitude, improbabilité et impossibilité

Incertitude

I'm **not sure** it's useful.	Je ne suis pas sûr que …
I'm **not sure** I'll manage.	Je ne suis pas certain de …
I'm **not sure that** it's a good idea.	Je ne suis pas sûr que …
We **cannot be sure that** the problem will be solved.	Il n'est pas sûr que …
I **very much doubt** he'll adapt to not working.	Je doute fort que …
Is it wise? **I doubt it.**	J'en doute.
He began to **have doubts about** his doctor's competence.	… douter de …
I wonder if we've made much progress in this area.	Je me demande si …
There is no guarantee that a vaccine can be developed.	Il n'est pas certain que …
Nobody knows exactly what happened.	Personne ne sait exactement …

Improbabilité

He **probably won't** change his mind.	… ne … probablement pas …
It is unlikely that there'll be any tickets left.	Il est peu probable que …
I'd be surprised if they had your size.	Ça m'étonnerait que …
They are not likely to get the Nobel prize for Economics!	Ils ne risquent pas de …
There is not much chance the growth rate will exceed 1.5%.	Il y a peu de chances que …
There's no danger we'll get bored.	Nous ne risquons pas de …
It would be amazing if everything went according to plan.	Il serait étonnant que …

Impossibilité

It's impossible.	C'est impossible.
It is not possible for the government to introduce this Bill before the recess.	Il n'est pas possible que …
This information **cannot be** wrong.	Il est impossible que …
There is no chance of their helping us.	Il n'y a aucune chance que …

Salutations

Hello!	Bonjour !
Hi!	Salut !
Good morning!	Bonjour !
Good afternoon!	Bonjour !
Good evening!	Bonsoir !
How's it going?	Comment ça va ?
How's things?	Comment (ça) va ?
How's life?	Comment (ça) va ?
How are you?	Comment allez-vous ?

Réponses

Very well, and you?	Très bien, merci, et vous ?
Fine, thanks.	Bien, merci.
Great!	Super bien !
So-so.	Comme ci comme ça.
Could be worse.	On fait aller.

Présentations

This is Charles.	Je te présente …
Let me introduce you to my girlfriend.	Je vous présente …
I'd like you to meet my husband.	Je vous présente …
I don't believe you know one another.	Je ne crois pas que vous vous connaissiez.

Une fois qu'on a été présenté

Pleased to meet you.	Enchanté.
Hello, how do you do?	Enchanté de faire votre connaissance.
Hi, I'm Jane.	Salut, moi c'est …

Pour prendre congé

Bye!	Au revoir !
Goodbye!	Au revoir !
Good night!	Bonne nuit !
See you!	Ciao !
See you later!	À tout à l'heure !

See you soon!	À bientôt !
See you tomorrow!	À demain !
See you next week!	À la semaine prochaine !
See you Thursday!	À jeudi !

Vœux et félicitations

Happy Birthday!	Bon anniversaire !
Many happy returns!	Bon anniversaire !
Merry Christmas!	Joyeux Noël !
Happy New Year!	Bonne année !
Happy Anniversary!	Bon anniversaire de mariage !
Congratulations!	Félicitations !
Welcome!	Soyez les bienvenus !
Good luck!	Bonne chance !
Safe journey!	Bon voyage !
Have fun!	Amusez-vous bien !
Get well soon!	Bon rétablissement !
Take care!	Fais bien attention à toi !
Cheers!	(À votre) santé !
Enjoy your meal!	Bon appétit !

Correspondance

La rédaction de l'adresse en Grande-Bretagne

Timbre

Le code postal vient après le nom de la ville ou du département.

Mrs J.M. Mackintosh
129 Strathmore Ave
EDINBURGH
EH11 2AD
UK

La rédaction de l'adresse aux États-Unis

Timbre

MARK SMITH
968 MICHIGAN ST
SEATTLE WA   98060-1024
USA

Le code postal (**zip code**) vient après le nom de la ville et de l'État (en abrégé).

Abréviations couramment employées dans les adresses

Ave = avenue	Dr = drive	Pl = place	Sq = square
Cres = crescent	Gdns = gardens	Rd = road	St = street

Les formes d'adresse et les formules de politesse
Dans les lettres personnelles

Dear Mr and Mrs Roberts	**Yours** (*assez soutenu*)
Dear Kate and Jeremy	**With best wishes**
Dear Aunt Jane and Uncle Alan	**Love from**
Dear Granny	**Lots of love from** (*familier*)

Dans les lettres d'affaires

Dear Sirs	Yours faithfully
Dear Sir	
Dear Madam	
Dear Sir or Madam	
Dear Professor Meldrum	Yours sincerely
Dear Ms Gilmour	

Pour commencer une lettre personnelle

It was lovely to hear from you.	Cela m'a fait plaisir d'avoir de vos nouvelles.
Thanks for your letter ...	Merci pour ta lettre ...
Sorry I haven't written sooner.	Je suis désolé de ne pas t'avoir écrit plus tôt.

Pour commencer une lettre d'affaires

Thank you for your letter of ...	Je vous remercie de votre lettre du ...
In reply to your letter of ...	En réponse à votre lettre du ...
With reference to ...	Suite à ...
We are writing to you to ...	Nous vous écrivons pour ...
We are pleased to inform you ...	Nous avons le plaisir de vous informer ...
We regret to inform you ...	Nous sommes au regret de vous informer ...

Pour terminer une lettre personnelle

Write soon.	Écris-moi vite.
Give my regards to ...	Transmettez mes amitiés à ...
... sends his/her best wishes.	... me charge de transmettre ses amitiés.
Give my love to ...	Embrasse ... de ma part.

Pour terminer une lettre d'affaires

I look forward to hearing from you.	Dans l'attente de votre réponse.
Thanking you in advance for your help.	En vous remerciant à l'avance pour votre aide.
If you require any further information please do not hesitate to contact me.	N'hésitez pas à me contacter pour toute information complémentaire.

Lettre de remerciement

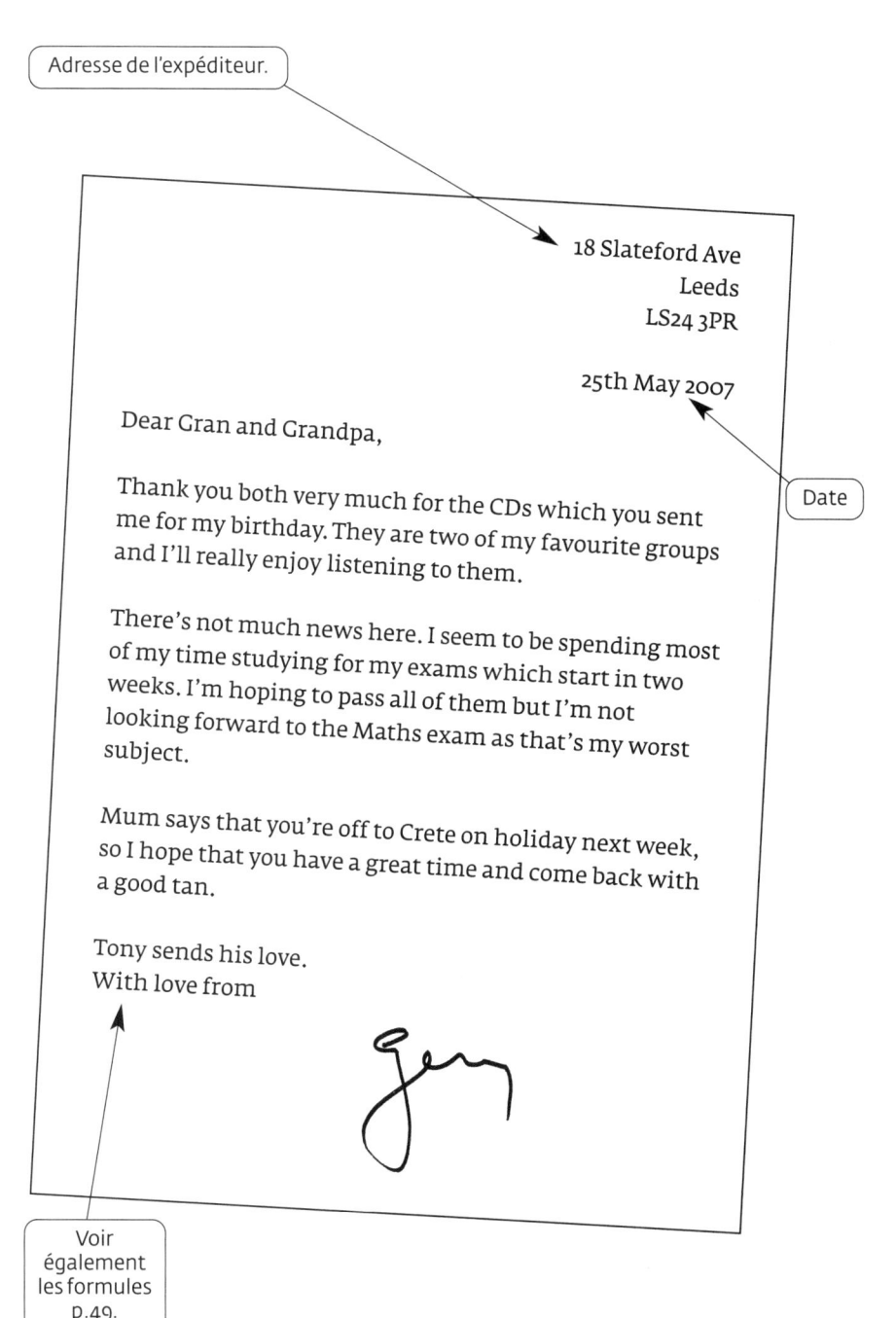

Adresse de l'expéditeur.

18 Slateford Ave
Leeds
LS24 3PR

25th May 2007

Dear Gran and Grandpa,

Thank you both very much for the CDs which you sent me for my birthday. They are two of my favourite groups and I'll really enjoy listening to them.

There's not much news here. I seem to be spending most of my time studying for my exams which start in two weeks. I'm hoping to pass all of them but I'm not looking forward to the Maths exam as that's my worst subject.

Mum says that you're off to Crete on holiday next week, so I hope that you have a great time and come back with a good tan.

Tony sends his love.
With love from

Date

Voir également les formules p.49.

Pour réserver une chambre d'hôtel

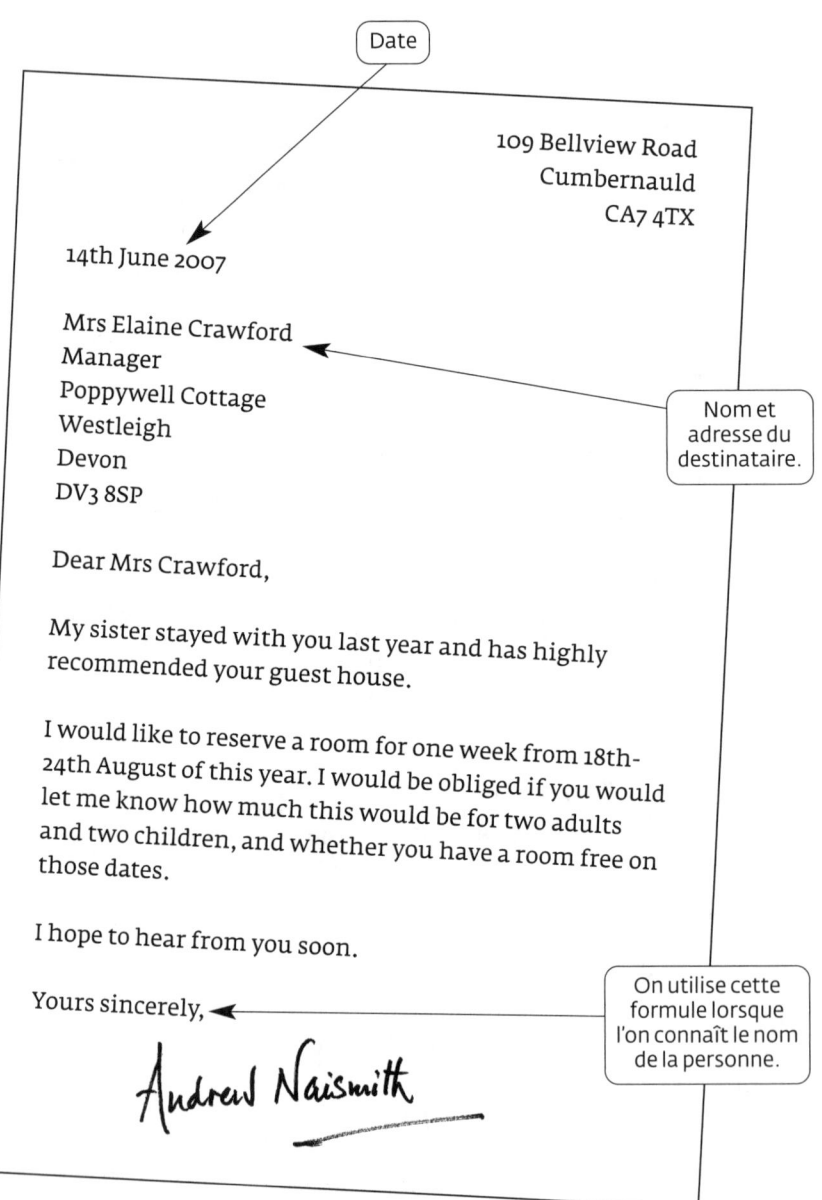

Date

109 Bellview Road
Cumbernauld
CA7 4TX

14th June 2007

Mrs Elaine Crawford
Manager
Poppywell Cottage
Westleigh
Devon
DV3 8SP

Nom et adresse du destinataire.

Dear Mrs Crawford,

My sister stayed with you last year and has highly recommended your guest house.

I would like to reserve a room for one week from 18th-24th August of this year. I would be obliged if you would let me know how much this would be for two adults and two children, and whether you have a room free on those dates.

I hope to hear from you soon.

Yours sincerely,

On utilise cette formule lorsque l'on connaît le nom de la personne.

Andrew Naismith

Lettre de réclamation

Voir également les formules p.50.

85 Rush Lane
Triptown
Lancs
LC4 2DT

20th February 2007

Woodpecker Restaurant
145 Main Street
Triptown
Lancs
LC4 3EF

Dear Sir/Madam

I was to have dined in your restaurant last Thursday by way of celebrating my wedding anniversary with my wife and young son but am writing to let you know of our great dissatisfaction.

I had reserved a corner table for two with a view of the lake. However, when we arrived we had to wait for more than 20 minutes for a table and even then, not in the area which I had chosen. There was no highchair for my son as was promised and your staff made no effort whatsoever to accommodate our needs. In fact, they were downright discourteous. Naturally we went elsewhere, and not only have you lost any future custom from me, but I will be sure to advise my friends and colleagues against your establishment.

Yours faithfully

T. Greengage

On utilise cette formule lorsque l'on commence la lettre par **Dear Sir** etc.

Curriculum Vitæ

CURRICULUM VITÆ

Name:	Rosalind A. Williamson
Address:	11 North Street, Barnton NE6 2BT
Telephone:	01294 476230
E-mail:	rosalind@metalcomp.co.uk
Date of Birth:	18/4/1981
Nationality:	British
Marital Status:	Single

> Pour les diplômes obtenus en France, mettre le nom du diplôme suivi d'une brève description en anglais entre parenthèses.

CAREER

2/05 to date: Sales and Marketing Executive, Metal Company plc, Barnton

11/03-1/05: Marketing Assistant, Metal Company plc

QUALIFICATIONS

1999-2003: University of Newby BA (Hons) Italian with French – 2:1

1992-1999: Barnton Comprehensive School
A-levels: English Literature (D), French (B), Italian (A)
GCSEs: Art, Chemistry, English Language, English Literature, French, German, Italian, Maths

OTHER SKILLS

Computer literate (Word for Windows, Excel, QuarkXPress), good keyboarding skills, full, clean driving licence.

INTERESTS

Travel (have travelled extensively throughout Europe and North Amercia), riding and sailing.

REFEREES

Ms Alice Bluegown
Sales and Marketing Manager
Metal Company plc
Barnton
NE4 3KL

Dr I.O. Sono
Department of Italian
University of Newby
Newby
S13 2RR

> Il est d'usage d'indiquer sur son C.V. les noms de deux personnes prêtes à fournir une recommandation à l'employeur potentiel. L'une d'entre elles doit normalement être un ancien employeur, ou, pour les étudiants, un professeur.

Lettre de candidature

11 North Street
Barnton
NE6 2BY

18 August 2007

The Personnel Director
Clifton Manufacturing Ltd
Firebrick House
Clifton
MK45 6RB

Dear Sir or Madam

> Lorsqu'on ignore si le destinataire est un homme ou une femme, il convient d'utiliser la formule ci–contre. Toutefois, si l'on connaît le nom de la personne, on utilise la présentation suivante :
> **Mrs Lynn Kerr**
> **Personnel Director**
> **Clifton Manufacturing Ltd** etc.
> Pour commencer votre lettre, la formule à employer est la suivante :
> **Dear Mrs Kerr**

With reference to your advertisement in the Guardian of 15 August, I wish to apply for the position of Marketing Manager in your company.

I am currently employed as a Sales and Marketing Executive for the Metal Company in Barnton where my main role is maintaining and developing links with our customers within the UK and producing material for marketing purposes.

I am interested in this position as it offers an opportunity to apply my sales and marketing skills in a new and challenging direction. I enclose my Curriculum Vitae for your consideration. Please do not hesitate to contact me if you require any further details.

Yours faithfully

Rosalind Williamson

Enc.

> On utilise cette formule lorsque l'on commence la lettre par **Dear Sir or Madam** etc.

> = **enclosures.** On ajoute ceci lorsque l'on joint d'autres pièces à la lettre, un C.V. par exemple.

Pour proposer un entretien

Clifton Manufacturing Ltd.

Firebrick House • Clifton MK45 6RB
Tel: (01367) 345 900 • Fax: (01367) 345 901
E-mail: personnel@cliftman.co.uk

Ref: RW/LK

27 August 2007

Ms Rosalind Williamson
11 North Street
Barnton
NE6 2BT

Dear Ms Williamson
Following your recent application for the position of Marketing Manager, I would like to invite you to attend an interview at the above office on Friday 3 September at 11am.

The interview will be conducted by the Sales and Marketing Director and myself and should last approximately one hour.

If this date does not suit please notify Jane Simpson on extension 3287 to arrange an alternative date.

We look forward to meeting you.

Yours sincerely

Lynn Kerr

Lynn Kerr (Mrs)
Personnel Director

Télécopie

Brown & Sons

Northport Enterprise Park
Birmingham B45 6JH
Tel: 0121 346 3287
Fax: 0121 346 3288
E-mail: orders@brownandsons.co.uk

FAX

To: Emma Scott, Westcott Hotel

Date: 6 November 2007

From: Malcolm Marshall

No. of pages to follow: 1

Re your order of 23 October for 100 tablecloths (Catalogue number 435789), I regret to inform you that these items are currently out of stock.

The next delivery will be in approximately four weeks' time. However, if this delay is unacceptable to you, please can you let me know so that I can cancel the order.

I am sorry for any inconvenience this may cause.

Regards

Malcolm Marshall

Courrier électronique

Envoyer des messages

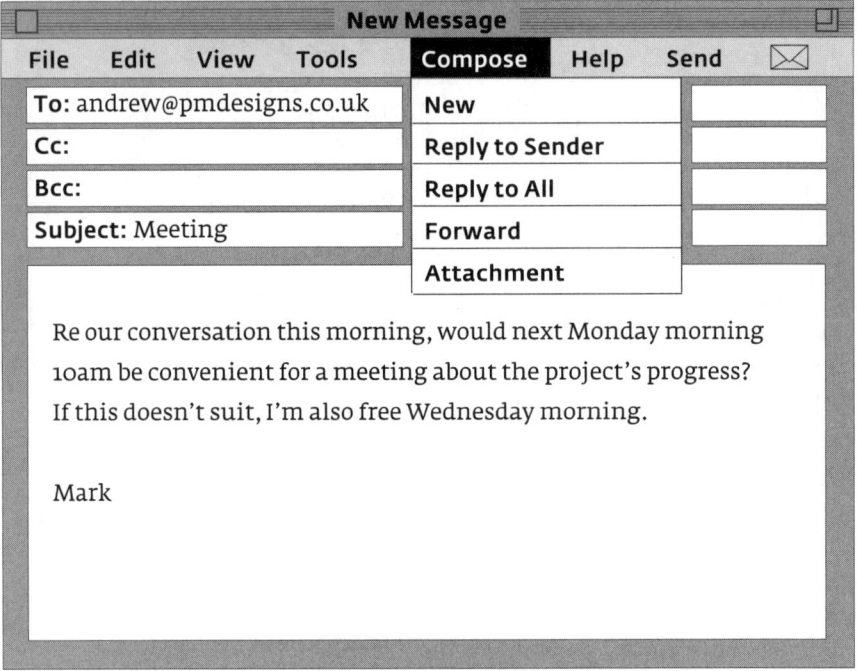

New Message	Nouveau message
File	Fichier
Edit	Édition
View	Affichage
Tools	Outils
Compose	Composer
Help	Aide
Send	Envoyer
New	Nouveau message
Reply to Sender	Répondre

Courrier électronique

Recevoir des messages

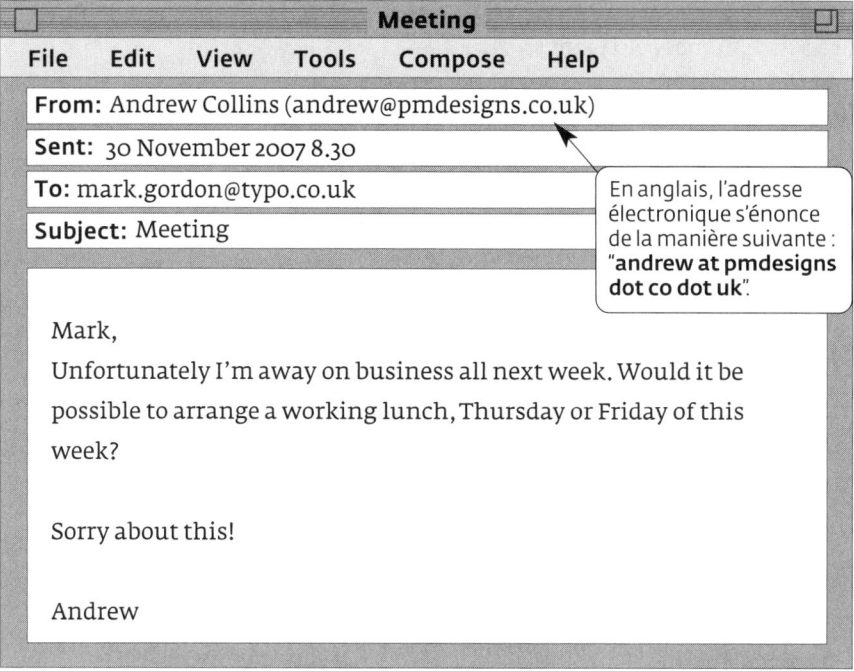

	Meeting	
File Edit View Tools Compose Help		

From: Andrew Collins (andrew@pmdesigns.co.uk)

Sent: 30 November 2007 8.30

To: mark.gordon@typo.co.uk

Subject: Meeting

> En anglais, l'adresse électronique s'énonce de la manière suivante : **"andrew at pmdesigns dot co dot uk"**.

Mark,

Unfortunately I'm away on business all next week. Would it be possible to arrange a working lunch, Thursday or Friday of this week?

Sorry about this!

Andrew

Reply to All	Répondre à tous
Forward	Faire suivre
Attachment	Fichier joint
To	À
Cc (carbon copy)	Cc
Bcc (blind carbon copy)	Copie cachée
Subject	Objet
From	De
Sent	Date

Téléphone

Les différents types de communication

Local/national call.

Communication locale/ interurbaine.

I want to make an international call.

Je voudrais appeler l'étranger.

I want to make a reverse charge call *(Brit)* to a Paris number *ou* I want to call a Paris number collect *(US)*.

Je voudrais appeler ... en PCV.

How do I get an outside line?

Comment est-ce que je peux téléphoner à l'extérieur ?

Les renseignements

What is the number for directory enquiries *(Brit) ou* directory assistance *(US)*?

Quel est le numéro des renseignements ?

Can you give me the number of Europost, 20 Cumberland Street, Newquay?

Je voudrais le numéro de ...

What is the code for Martinique?

Quel est l'indicatif de ...

What is the number for the speaking clock?

Quel est le numéro de l'horloge parlante ?

Réponses

The number you require is 0181-613 3297. *(o-one-eight-one six-one-three three-two-nine-seven)*

Le numéro que vous avez demandé est le ...

I'm sorry, there's no listing under that name.

Je regrette, mais il n'y a pas d'abonné à ce nom.

The number you require is ex-directory *(Brit) ou* unlisted *(US)*.

Le numéro que vous avez demandé est sur liste rouge.

Lorsque l'abonné répond

Could I speak to Mr Sanderson, please?

Pourrais-je parler à ...

Could you put me through to Dr Evans, please?

Pourriez-vous me passer ...

Can I have extension 6578, please?

Pourriez-vous me passer le poste ...

I'll call back in half an hour.

Je rappellerai dans ...

Would you ask him to ring me when he gets back?

Pourriez-vous lui demander de me rappeler à son retour ?

Au standard

Who shall I say is calling?	C'est de la part de qui ?
I'm putting you through.	Je vous le passe.
I have a call from Tokyo for Mrs Thomson.	J'ai un appel de … pour …
I've got Miss Martin on the line.	J'ai … en ligne.
Dr Roberts is on another line. Do you want to wait?	… est en ligne, vous patientez ?
Please hold.	Ne quittez pas.
There's no reply.	Ça ne répond pas.
Would you like to leave a message?	Voulez-vous laisser un message ?

Messages enregistrés

The number you have dialled has not been recognized. Please hang up.	Le numéro de votre correspondant n'est plus attribué. Veuillez raccrocher.
The number you have dialled has been changed to 020-7789 0044.	Le numéro de votre correspondant a changé. Veuillez composer désormais le …
All the lines are busy right now. Please try again later.	Par suite de l'encombrement des lignes, votre appel ne peut aboutir. Veuillez rappeler ultérieurement.
Hello, you have reached Sunspot Insurance. Please wait, your call will be answered shortly.	Bonjour, vous êtes en communication avec … Veuillez patienter, nous allons donner suite à votre appel dans quelques instants.
Hello, you are through to Emma and Matthew Hargreaves. Please leave a message after the tone and we'll get back to you. Thanks.	Bonjour, vous êtes bien chez … Laissez un message après le bip sonore et nous vous rappellerons dès notre retour.

Pour répondre au téléphone

Hello, it's Anne speaking.	Allô, c'est … à l'appareil.
Speaking.	C'est moi.
Who's speaking?	Qui est à l'appareil ?

En cas de difficulté

I can't get through.	Je n'arrive pas à avoir le numéro.
Their phone is out of order.	Leur téléphone est en dérangement.
We have been cut off.	Nous avons été coupés.
I must have dialled the wrong number.	J'ai dû faire un faux numéro.
We've got a crossed line.	Il y a quelqu'un d'autre sur la ligne.
This is a very bad line.	La ligne est très mauvaise.

Aa

A, a¹ [eɪ] *n* (*letter*) A, a *m*; (*Scol: mark*) A; (*Mus*) la *m*;
A for Andrew, A for Able (*US*) A comme
Anatole; **A shares** *npl* (*Brit Stock Exchange*)
actions *fpl* prioritaires

 KEYWORD

a² [eɪ, ə] (*before vowel and silent h* **an**) *indef art* **1**
un(e); **a book** un livre; **an apple** une pomme;
she's a doctor elle est médecin
2 (*instead of the number "one"*) un(e); **a year ago** il
y a un an; **a hundred/thousand** *etc* **pounds**
cent/mille *etc* livres
3 (*in expressing ratios, prices etc*): **three a day/week**
trois par jour/semaine; **10 km an hour** 10 km à
l'heure; **£5 a person** 5£ par personne; **30p a
kilo** 30p le kilo

a. *abbr* = **acre**
A2 *n* (*Brit: Scol*) deuxième partie de l'examen équivalent
au baccalauréat
A.A. *n abbr* (*Brit:* = *Automobile Association*) ≈ ACF *m*;
(*US:* = *Associate in/of Arts*) diplôme universitaire;
(= *Alcoholics Anonymous*) AA; (= *anti-aircraft*) AA
A.A.A. *n abbr* (= *American Automobile Association*)
≈ ACF *m*; (*Brit*) = **Amateur Athletics Association**
A & R *n abbr* (*Mus*) = **artists and repertoire**; ~
man découvreur *m* de talent
AAUP *n abbr* (= *American Association of University
Professors*) syndicat universitaire
AB *abbr* (*Brit*) = **able-bodied seaman**; (*Canada*)
= **Alberta**
aback [ə'bæk] *adv*: **to be taken ~** être
décontenancé(e)
abacus (*pl* **abaci**) ['æbəkəs, -saɪ] *n* boulier *m*
abandon [ə'bændən] *vt* abandonner ⊳ *n*
abandon *m*; **to ~ ship** évacuer le navire
abandoned [ə'bændənd] *adj* (*child, house etc*)
abandonné(e); (*unrestrained*) sans retenue
abase [ə'beɪs] *vt*: **to ~ o.s. (so far as to do)**
s'abaisser (à faire)
abashed [ə'bæʃt] *adj* confus(e), embarrassé(e)
abate [ə'beɪt] *vi* s'apaiser, se calmer
abatement [ə'beɪtmənt] *n*: **noise ~** lutte *f*
contre le bruit
abattoir ['æbətwɑːʳ] *n* (*Brit*) abattoir *m*

abbey ['æbɪ] *n* abbaye *f*
abbot ['æbət] *n* père supérieur
abbreviate [ə'briːvɪeɪt] *vt* abréger
abbreviation [əbriːvɪ'eɪʃən] *n* abréviation *f*
ABC *n abbr* (= *American Broadcasting Company*) chaîne
de télévision
abdicate ['æbdɪkeɪt] *vt, vi* abdiquer
abdication [æbdɪ'keɪʃən] *n* abdication *f*
abdomen ['æbdəmən] *n* abdomen *m*
abdominal [æb'dɔmɪnl] *adj* abdominal(e)
abduct [æb'dʌkt] *vt* enlever
abduction [æb'dʌkʃən] *n* enlèvement *m*
Aberdonian [æbə'dəunɪən] *adj* d'Aberdeen ⊳ *n*
habitant(e) d'Aberdeen, natif(-ive) d'Aberdeen
aberration [æbə'reɪʃən] *n* anomalie *f*; **in a
moment of mental ~** dans un moment
d'égarement
abet [ə'bɛt] *vt see* **aid**
abeyance [ə'beɪəns] *n*: **in ~** (*law*) en désuétude;
(*matter*) en suspens
abhor [əb'hɔːʳ] *vt* abhorrer, exécrer
abhorrent [əb'hɔrənt] *adj* odieux(-euse),
exécrable
abide [ə'baɪd] *vt* souffrir, supporter; **I can't ~ it/
him** je ne le supporte pas
▶ **abide by** *vt fus* observer, respecter
abiding [ə'baɪdɪŋ] *adj* (*memory etc*) durable
ability [ə'bɪlɪtɪ] *n* compétence *f*; capacité *f*; (*skill*)
talent *m*; **to the best of my ~** de mon mieux
abject ['æbdʒɛkt] *adj* (*poverty*) sordide; (*coward*)
méprisable; **an ~ apology** les excuses les plus
plates
ablaze [ə'bleɪz] *adj* en feu, en flammes; **~ with
light** resplendissant de lumière
able ['eɪbl] *adj* compétent(e); **to be ~ to do sth**
pouvoir faire qch, être capable de faire qch
able-bodied ['eɪbl'bɔdɪd] *adj* robuste; **~ seaman**
(*Brit*) matelot breveté
ably ['eɪblɪ] *adv* avec compétence *or* talent,
habilement
ABM *n abbr* = **anti-ballistic missile**
abnormal [æb'nɔːməl] *adj* anormal(e)
abnormality [æbnɔː'mælɪtɪ] *n* (*condition*)
caractère anormal; (*instance*) anomalie *f*
aboard [ə'bɔːd] *adv* à bord ⊳ *prep* à bord de;
(*train*) dans

abode [ə'bəud] *n* (*old*) demeure *f*; (*Law*): **of no fixed ~** sans domicile fixe

abolish [ə'bɔlɪʃ] *vt* abolir

abolition [æbə'lɪʃən] *n* abolition *f*

abominable [ə'bɔmɪnəbl] *adj* abominable

aborigine [æbə'rɪdʒɪnɪ] *n* aborigène *m/f*

abort [ə'bɔːt] *vt* (*Med*) faire avorter; (*Comput, fig*) abandonner

abortion [ə'bɔːʃən] *n* avortement *m*; **to have an ~** se faire avorter

abortionist [ə'bɔːʃənɪst] *n* avorteur(-euse)

abortive [ə'bɔːtɪv] *adj* manqué(e)

abound [ə'baund] *vi* abonder; **to ~ in** abonder en, regorger de

O **KEYWORD**

about [ə'baut] *adv* **1** (*approximately*) environ, à peu près; **about a hundred/thousand** *etc* environ cent/mille *etc*, une centaine (de)/un millier (de) *etc*; **it takes about 10 hours** ça prend environ *or* à peu près 10 heures; **at about 2 o'clock** vers 2 heures; **I've just about finished** j'ai presque fini

2 (*referring to place*) çà et là, de-ci de-là; **to run about** courir çà et là; **to walk about** se promener, aller et venir; **is Paul about?** (*Brit*) est-ce que Paul est là?; **it's about here** c'est par ici, c'est dans les parages; **they left all their things lying about** ils ont laissé traîner toutes leurs affaires

3: **to be about to do sth** être sur le point de faire qch; **I'm not about to do all that for nothing** (*inf*) je ne vais quand même pas faire tout ça pour rien

4 (*opposite*): **it's the other way about** (*Brit*) c'est l'inverse

▷ *prep* **1** (*relating to*) au sujet de, à propos de; **a book about London** un livre sur Londres; **what is it about?** de quoi s'agit-il?; **we talked about it** nous en avons parlé; **do something about it!** faites quelque chose!; **what** *or* **how about doing this?** et si nous faisions ceci?

2 (*referring to place*) dans; **to walk about the town** se promener dans la ville

above [ə'bʌv] *adv* au-dessus ▷ *prep* au-dessus de; (*more than*) plus de; **mentioned ~** mentionné ci-dessus; **costing ~ £10** coûtant plus de 10 livres; **~ all** par-dessus tout, surtout

aboveboard [ə'bʌv'bɔːd] *adj* franc (franche), loyal(e); honnête

abrasion [ə'breɪʒən] *n* frottement *m*; (*on skin*) écorchure *f*

abrasive [ə'breɪzɪv] *adj* abrasif(-ive); (*fig*) caustique, agressif(-ive)

abreast [ə'brɛst] *adv* de front; **to keep ~ of** se tenir au courant de

abridge [ə'brɪdʒ] *vt* abréger

abroad [ə'brɔːd] *adv* à l'étranger; **there is a rumour ~ that ...** (*fig*) le bruit court que ...

abrupt [ə'brʌpt] *adj* (*steep, blunt*) abrupt(e); (*sudden, gruff*) brusque

abruptly [ə'brʌptlɪ] *adv* (*speak, end*) brusquement

abscess ['æbsɪs] *n* abcès *m*

abscond [əb'skɔnd] *vi* disparaître, s'enfuir

absence ['æbsəns] *n* absence *f*; **in the ~ of** (*person*) en l'absence de; (*thing*) faute de

absent ['æbsənt] *adj* absent(e); **~ without leave (AWOL)** (*Mil*) en absence irrégulière

absentee [æbsən'tiː] *n* absent(e)

absenteeism [æbsən'tiːɪzəm] *n* absentéisme *m*

absent-minded ['æbsənt'maɪndɪd] *adj* distrait(e)

absent-mindedness ['æbsənt'maɪndɪdnɪs] *n* distraction *f*

absolute ['æbsəluːt] *adj* absolu(e)

absolutely [æbsə'luːtlɪ] *adv* absolument

absolve [əb'zɔlv] *vt*: **to ~ sb (from)** (*sin etc*) absoudre qn (de); **to ~ sb from** (*oath*) délier qn de

absorb [əb'zɔːb] *vt* absorber; **to be ~ed in a book** être plongé(e) dans un livre

absorbent [əb'zɔːbənt] *adj* absorbant(e)

absorbent cotton [əb'zɔːbənt-] *n* (*US*) coton *m* hydrophile

absorbing [əb'zɔːbɪŋ] *adj* absorbant(e); (*book, film etc*) captivant(e)

absorption [əb'sɔːpʃən] *n* absorption *f*

abstain [əb'steɪn] *vi*: **to ~ (from)** s'abstenir (de)

abstemious [əb'stiːmɪəs] *adj* sobre, frugal(e)

abstention [əb'stɛnʃən] *n* abstention *f*

abstinence ['æbstɪnəns] *n* abstinence *f*

abstract ['æbstrækt] *adj* abstrait(e) ▷ *n* (*summary*) résumé *m* ▷ *vt* [æb'strækt] extraire

absurd [əb'səːd] *adj* absurde

absurdity [əb'səːdɪtɪ] *n* absurdité *f*

ABTA ['æbtə] *n abbr* = **Association of British Travel Agents**

Abu Dhabi ['æbuː'dɑːbɪ] *n* Ab(o)u Dhabî *m*

abundance [ə'bʌndəns] *n* abondance *f*

abundant [ə'bʌndənt] *adj* abondant(e)

abuse *n* [ə'bjuːs] (*insults*) insultes *fpl*, injures *fpl*; (*ill-treatment*) mauvais traitements *mpl*; (*of power etc*) abus *m* ▷ *vt* [ə'bjuːz] (*insult*) insulter; (*ill-treat*) malmener; (*power etc*) abuser de; **to be open to ~** se prêter à des abus

abusive [ə'bjuːsɪv] *adj* grossier(-ière), injurieux(-euse)

abysmal [ə'bɪzməl] *adj* exécrable; (*ignorance etc*) sans bornes

abyss [ə'bɪs] *n* abîme *m*, gouffre *m*

AC *n abbr* (*US*) = **athletic club**

a/c *abbr* (*Banking etc*) = **account**; **account current**

academic [ækə'dɛmɪk] *adj* universitaire; (*person: scholarly*) intellectuel(-le); (*pej: issue*) oiseux(-euse), purement théorique ▷ *n* universitaire *m/f*; **~ freedom** liberté *f* académique

academic year *n* (*University*) année *f* universitaire; (*Scol*) année scolaire

academy [ə'kædəmɪ] *n* (*learned body*) académie *f*; (*school*) collège *m*; **military/naval ~** école militaire/navale; **~ of music** conservatoire *m*

ACAS ['eɪkæs] *n abbr* (Brit: = *Advisory, Conciliation and Arbitration Service*) *organisme de conciliation et d'arbitrage des conflits du travail*
accede [æk'siːd] *vi*: **to ~ to** (*request, throne*) accéder à
accelerate [æk'sɛləreɪt] *vt, vi* accélérer
acceleration [æksɛlə'reɪʃən] *n* accélération *f*
accelerator [æk'sɛləreɪtəʳ] *n* (*Brit*) accélérateur *m*
accent ['æksɛnt] *n* accent *m*
accentuate [æk'sɛntjueɪt] *vt* (*syllable*) accentuer; (*need, difference etc*) souligner
accept [ək'sɛpt] *vt* accepter
acceptable [ək'sɛptəbl] *adj* acceptable
acceptance [ək'sɛptəns] *n* acceptation *f*; **to meet with general ~** être favorablement accueilli par tous
access ['æksɛs] *n* accès *m* ▷ *vt* (*Comput*) accéder à; **to have ~ to** (*information, library etc*) avoir accès à, pouvoir utiliser *or* consulter; (*person*) avoir accès auprès de; **the burglars gained ~ through a window** les cambrioleurs sont entrés par une fenêtre
accessible [æk'sɛsəbl] *adj* accessible
accession [æk'sɛʃən] *n* accession *f*; (*of king*) avènement *m*; (*to library*) acquisition *f*
accessory [æk'sɛsərɪ] *n* accessoire *m*; **toilet accessories** (*Brit*) articles *mpl* de toilette; **~ to** (*Law*) accessoire à
access road *n* voie *f* d'accès; (*to motorway*) bretelle *f* de raccordement
access time *n* (*Comput*) temps *m* d'accès
accident ['æksɪdənt] *n* accident *m*; (*chance*) hasard *m*; **to meet with** *or* **to have an ~** avoir un accident; **I've had an ~** j'ai eu un accident; **~s at work** accidents du travail; **by ~** (*by chance*) par hasard; (*not deliberately*) accidentellement
accidental [æksɪ'dɛntl] *adj* accidentel(le)
accidentally [æksɪ'dɛntəlɪ] *adv* accidentellement
Accident and Emergency Department *n* (*Brit*) service *m* des urgences
accident insurance *n* assurance *f* accident
accident-prone ['æksɪdənt'prəun] *adj* sujet(te) aux accidents
acclaim [ə'kleɪm] *vt* acclamer ▷ *n* acclamations *fpl*
acclamation [æklə'meɪʃən] *n* (*approval*) acclamation *f*; (*applause*) ovation *f*
acclimatize [ə'klaɪmətaɪz] (*US*), **acclimate** [ə'klaɪmət] *vt*: **to become ~d** s'acclimater
accolade ['ækəleɪd] *n* accolade *f*; (*fig*) marque *f* d'honneur
accommodate [ə'kɔmədeɪt] *vt* loger, recevoir; (*oblige, help*) obliger; (*car etc*) contenir; (*adapt*): **to ~ one's plans to** adapter ses projets à
accommodating [ə'kɔmədeɪtɪŋ] *adj* obligeant(e), arrangeant(e)
accommodation, (*US*) **accommodations** [əkɔmə'deɪʃən(z)] *n(pl)* logement *m*; **he's found ~** il a trouvé à se loger; **"~ to let"** (*Brit*) "appartement *or* studio *etc* à louer"; **they have**

~ for 500 ils peuvent recevoir 500 personnes, il y a de la place pour 500 personnes; **the hall has seating ~ for 600** (*Brit*) la salle contient 600 places assises
accompaniment [ə'kʌmpənɪmənt] *n* accompagnement *m*
accompanist [ə'kʌmpənɪst] *n* accompagnateur(-trice)
accompany [ə'kʌmpənɪ] *vt* accompagner
accomplice [ə'kʌmplɪs] *n* complice *m/f*
accomplish [ə'kʌmplɪʃ] *vt* accomplir
accomplished [ə'kʌmplɪʃt] *adj* accompli(e)
accomplishment [ə'kʌmplɪʃmənt] *n* (*skill: gen pl*) talent *m*; (*completion*) accomplissement *m*; (*achievement*) réussite *f*
accord [ə'kɔːd] *n* accord *m* ▷ *vt* accorder; **of his own ~** de son plein gré; **with one ~** d'un commun accord
accordance [ə'kɔːdəns] *n*: **in ~ with** conformément à
according [ə'kɔːdɪŋ]: **~ to** (*prep*) selon; **~ to plan** comme prévu
accordingly [ə'kɔːdɪŋlɪ] *adv* (*appropriately*) en conséquence; (*as a result*) par conséquent
accordion [ə'kɔːdɪən] *n* accordéon *m*
accost [ə'kɔst] *vt* accoster, aborder
account [ə'kaunt] *n* (*Comm*) compte *m*; (*report*) compte rendu, récit *m*; **accounts** *npl* (*Comm: records*) comptabilité *f*, comptes; **"~ payee only"** (*Brit*) "chèque non endossable"; **to keep an ~ of** noter; **to bring sb to ~ for sth/for having done sth** amener qn à rendre compte de qch/ d'avoir fait qch; **by all ~s** au dire de tous; **of little ~** de peu d'importance; **of no ~** sans importance; **on ~** en acompte; **to buy sth on ~** acheter qch à crédit; **on no ~** en aucun cas; **on ~ of** à cause de; **to take into ~, take ~ of** tenir compte de
▶ **account for** *vt fus* (*explain*) expliquer, rendre compte de; (*represent*) représenter; **all the children were ~ed for** aucun enfant ne manquait; **four people are still not ~ed for** on n'a toujours pas retrouvé quatre personnes
accountability [əkauntə'bɪlɪtɪ] *n* responsabilité *f*; (*financial, political*) transparence *f*
accountable [ə'kauntəbl] *adj*: **~ (for/to)** responsable (de/devant)
accountancy [ə'kauntənsɪ] *n* comptabilité *f*
accountant [ə'kauntənt] *n* comptable *m/f*
accounting [ə'kauntɪŋ] *n* comptabilité *f*
accounting period *n* exercice financier, période *f* comptable
account number *n* numéro *m* de compte
account payable *n* compte *m* fournisseurs
account receivable *n* compte *m* clients
accredited [ə'krɛdɪtɪd] *adj* (*person*) accrédité(e)
accretion [ə'kriːʃən] *n* accroissement *m*
accrue [ə'kruː] *vi* s'accroître; (*mount up*) s'accumuler; **to ~ to** s'ajouter à; **~d interest** intérêt couru
accumulate [ə'kjuːmjuleɪt] *vt* accumuler,

amasser ⊳ *vi* s'accumuler, s'amasser

accumulation [əkju:mju'leɪʃən] *n*
accumulation *f*

accuracy ['ækjurəsɪ] *n* exactitude *f*, précision *f*

accurate ['ækjurɪt] *adj* exact(e), précis(e);
(*device*) précis

accurately ['ækjurɪtlɪ] *adv* avec précision

accusation [ækju'zeɪʃən] *n* accusation *f*

accusative [ə'kju:zətɪv] *n* (*Ling*) accusatif *m*

accuse [ə'kju:z] *vt*: **to ~ sb (of sth)** accuser qn
(de qch)

accused [ə'kju:zd] *n* (*Law*) accusé(e)

accuser [ə'kju:zər] *n* accusateur(-trice)

accustom [ə'kʌstəm] *vt* accoutumer, habituer;
to ~ o.s. to sth s'habituer à qch

accustomed [ə'kʌstəmd] *adj* (*usual*)
habituel(le); **~ to** habitué(e) *or* accoutumé(e) à

AC/DC *abbr* = **alternating current/direct current**

ACE [eɪs] *n abbr* = **American Council on Education**

ace [eɪs] *n* as *m*; **within an ~ of** (*Brit*) à deux
doigts *or* un cheveu de

acerbic [ə'sə:bɪk] *adj* (*also fig*) acerbe

acetate ['æsɪteɪt] *n* acétate *m*

ache [eɪk] *n* mal *m*, douleur *f* ⊳ *vi* (*be sore*) faire
mal, être douloureux(-euse); (*yearn*): **to ~ to do
sth** mourir d'envie de faire qch; **I've got
stomach ~** *or* (US) **a stomach ~** j'ai mal à
l'estomac; **my head ~s** j'ai mal à la tête; **I'm
aching all over** j'ai mal partout

achieve [ə'tʃi:v] *vt* (*aim*) atteindre; (*victory,
success*) remporter, obtenir; (*task*) accomplir

achievement [ə'tʃi:vmənt] *n* exploit *m*, réussite
f; (*of aims*) réalisation *f*

Achilles heel [ə'kɪli:z-] *n* talon *m* d'Achille

acid ['æsɪd] *adj, n* acide (*m*)

acidity [ə'sɪdɪtɪ] *n* acidité *f*

acid rain *n* pluies *fpl* acides

acid test *n* (*fig*) épreuve décisive

acknowledge [ək'nɔlɪdʒ] *vt* (*also*: **acknowledge
receipt of**) accuser réception de; (*fact*)
reconnaître

acknowledgement [ək'nɔlɪdʒmənt] *n* (*of letter*)
accusé *m* de réception; **acknowledgements** (*in
book*) remerciements *mpl*

ACLU *n abbr* (= *American Civil Liberties Union*) ligue *des
droits de l'homme*

acme ['ækmɪ] *n* point culminant

acne ['æknɪ] *n* acné *m*

acorn ['eɪkɔ:n] *n* gland *m*

acoustic [ə'ku:stɪk] *adj* acoustique

acoustics [ə'ku:stɪks] *n, npl* acoustique *f*

acquaint [ə'kweɪnt] *vt*: **to ~ sb with sth** mettre
qn au courant de qch; **to be ~ed with** (*person*)
connaître; (*fact*) savoir

acquaintance [ə'kweɪntəns] *n* connaissance *f*;
to make sb's ~ faire la connaissance de qn

acquiesce [ækwɪ'ɛs] *vi* (*agree*): **to ~ (in)**
acquiescer (à)

acquire [ə'kwaɪər] *vt* acquérir

acquired [ə'kwaɪəd] *adj* acquis(e); **an ~ taste** un

goût acquis

acquisition [ækwɪ'zɪʃən] *n* acquisition *f*

acquisitive [ə'kwɪzɪtɪv] *adj* qui a l'instinct de
possession *or* le goût de la propriété

acquit [ə'kwɪt] *vt* acquitter; **to ~ o.s. well** s'en
tirer très honorablement

acquittal [ə'kwɪtl] *n* acquittement *m*

acre ['eɪkər] *n* acre *f* (= 4047 *m"*)

acreage ['eɪkərɪdʒ] *n* superficie *f*

acrid ['ækrɪd] *adj* (*smell*) âcre; (*fig*) mordant(e)

acrimonious [ækrɪ'məunɪəs] *adj*
acrimonieux(-euse), aigre

acrobat ['ækrəbæt] *n* acrobate *m/f*

acrobatic [ækrə'bætɪk] *adj* acrobatique

acrobatics [ækrə'bætɪks] *n, npl* acrobatie *f*

acronym ['ækrənɪm] *n* acronyme *m*

Acropolis [ə'krɔpəlɪs] *n*: **the ~** l'Acropole *f*

across [ə'krɔs] *prep* (*on the other side*) de l'autre
côté de; (*crosswise*) en travers de ⊳ *adv* de l'autre
côté; en travers; **to walk ~ (the road)** traverser
(la route); **to run/swim ~** traverser en courant/
à la nage; **to take sb ~ the road** faire traverser
la route à qn; **a road ~ the wood** une route qui
traverse le bois; **the lake is 12 km ~** le lac fait 12
km de large; **~ from** en face de; **to get sth ~ (to
sb)** faire comprendre qch (à qn)

acrylic [ə'krɪlɪk] *adj, n* acrylique (*m*)

ACT *n abbr* (= *American College Test*) examen de fin
d'études secondaires

act [ækt] *n* acte *m*, action *f*; (*Theat: part of play*)
acte; (*: of performer*) numéro *m*; (*Law*) loi *f* ⊳ *vi*
agir; (*Theat*) jouer; (*pretend*) jouer la comédie
⊳ *vt* (*role*) jouer, tenir; **~ of God** (*Law*)
catastrophe naturelle; **to catch sb in the ~**
prendre qn sur le fait *or* en flagrant délit; **it's
only an ~** c'est du cinéma; **to ~ Hamlet** (*Brit*)
tenir *or* jouer le rôle d'Hamlet; **to ~ the fool**
(*Brit*) faire l'idiot; **to ~ as** servir de; **it ~s as a
deterrent** cela a un effet dissuasif; **~ing in my
capacity as chairman, I ...** en ma qualité de
président, je ...
   ▶ **act on** *vt*: **to ~ on sth** agir sur la base de qch
   ▶ **act out** *vt* (*event*) raconter en mimant;
   (*fantasies*) réaliser
   ▶ **act up** (*inf*) *vi* (*person*) se conduire mal; (*knee,
   back, injury*) jouer des tours; (*machine*) être
   capricieux(-ieuse)

acting ['æktɪŋ] *adj* suppléant(e), par intérim ⊳ *n*
(*of actor*) jeu *m*; (*activity*): **to do some ~** faire du
théâtre (*or* du cinéma); **he is the ~ manager** il
remplace (provisoirement) le directeur

action ['ækʃən] *n* action *f*; (*Mil*) combat(s) *m(pl)*;
(*Law*) procès *m*, action en justice; **to bring an ~
against sb** (*Law*) poursuivre qn en justice,
intenter un procès contre qn; **killed in ~** (*Mil*)
tué au champ d'honneur; **out of ~** hors de
combat; (*machine etc*) hors d'usage; **to take ~**
agir, prendre des mesures; **to put a plan into ~**
mettre un projet à exécution

action replay *n* (*Brit TV*) ralenti *m*

activate ['æktɪveɪt] *vt* (*mechanism*) actionner,
faire fonctionner; (*Chem, Physics*) activer

active ['æktɪv] *adj* actif(-ive); *(volcano)* en activité; **to play an ~ part in** jouer un rôle actif dans

active duty *n* *(US Mil)* campagne *f*

actively ['æktɪvlɪ] *adv* activement; *(discourage)* vivement

active partner *n* *(Comm)* associé(e) *m/f*

active service *n* *(Brit Mil)* campagne *f*

activist ['æktɪvɪst] *n* activiste *m/f*

activity [æk'tɪvɪtɪ] *n* activité *f*

activity holiday *n* vacances actives

actor ['æktə^r] *n* acteur *m*

actress ['æktrɪs] *n* actrice *f*

actual ['æktjuəl] *adj* réel(le), véritable; *(emphatic use)* lui-même (elle-même)

actually ['æktjuəlɪ] *adv* réellement, véritablement; *(in fact)* en fait

actuary ['æktjuərɪ] *n* actuaire *m*

actuate ['æktjueɪt] *vt* déclencher, actionner

acuity [ə'kju:ɪtɪ] *n* acuité *f*

acumen ['ækjumən] *n* perspicacité *f*; **business ~ sens** *m* des affaires

acupuncture ['ækjupʌŋktʃə^r] *n* acuponcture *f*

acute [ə'kju:t] *adj* aigu(ë); *(mind, observer)* pénétrant(e)

A.D. *adv abbr* (= *Anno Domini*) ap. J.-C. ▷ *n abbr* *(US Mil)* = **active duty**

ad [æd] *n abbr* = **advertisement**

adamant ['ædəmənt] *adj* inflexible

Adam's apple ['ædəmz-] *n* pomme *f* d'Adam

adapt [ə'dæpt] *vt* adapter ▷ *vi*: **to ~ (to)** s'adapter (à)

adaptability [ədæptə'bɪlɪtɪ] *n* faculté *f* d'adaptation

adaptable [ə'dæptəbl] *adj* *(device)* adaptable; *(person)* qui s'adapte facilement

adaptation [ædæp'teɪʃən] *n* adaptation *f*

adapter, adaptor [ə'dæptə^r] *n* *(Elec)* adaptateur *m*; *(for several plugs)* prise *f* multiple

ADC *n abbr* *(Mil)* = **aide-de-camp**; *(US: = Aid to Dependent Children)* aide pour enfants assistés

add [æd] *vt* ajouter; *(figures: also: **to add up**)* additionner ▷ *vi*: **to ~ to** *(increase)* ajouter à, accroître

▸ **add on** *vt* ajouter ▷ *vi* *(fig)*: **it doesn't ~ up** cela ne rime à rien

▸ **add up to** *vt fus* *(Math)* s'élever à; *(fig: mean)* signifier; **it doesn't ~ up to much** ça n'est pas grand'chose

adder ['ædə^r] *n* vipère *f*

addict ['ædɪkt] *n* toxicomane *m/f*; *(fig)* fanatique *m/f*; **heroin ~** héroïnomane *m/f*; **drug ~** drogué(e) *m/f*

addicted [ə'dɪktɪd] *adj*: **to be ~ to** *(drink, drugs)* être adonné(e) à; *(fig: football etc)* être un(e) fanatique de

addiction [ə'dɪkʃən] *n* *(Med)* dépendance *f*

addictive [ə'dɪktɪv] *adj* qui crée une dépendance

adding machine ['ædɪŋ-] *n* machine *f* à calculer

Addis Ababa ['ædɪs'æbəbə] *n* Addis Abeba, Addis Ababa

addition [ə'dɪʃən] *n* *(adding up)* addition *f*; *(thing*

added) ajout *m*; **in ~** de plus, de surcroît; **in ~ to** en plus de

additional [ə'dɪʃənl] *adj* supplémentaire

additive ['ædɪtɪv] *n* additif *m*

address [ə'drɛs] *n* adresse *f*; *(talk)* discours *m*, allocution *f* ▷ *vt* adresser; *(speak to)* s'adresser à; **my ~ is ...** mon adresse, c'est ...; **form of ~** titre *m*; **what form of ~ do you use for ...?** comment s'adresse-t-on à ...?; **to ~ (o.s. to)** sth *(problem, issue)* aborder qch; **absolute/relative ~** *(Comput)* adresse absolue/relative

address book *n* carnet *m* d'adresses

addressee [ædrɛ'si:] *n* destinataire *m/f*

Aden ['eɪdən] *n*: **Gulf of ~** Golfe *m* d'Aden

adenoids ['ædɪnɔɪdz] *npl* végétations *fpl*

adept ['ædɛpt] *adj*: **~ at** expert(e) à *or* en

adequate ['ædɪkwɪt] *adj* *(enough)* suffisant(e); *(satisfactory)* satisfaisant(e); **to feel ~ to the task** se sentir à la hauteur de la tâche

adequately ['ædɪkwɪtlɪ] *adv* de façon adéquate

adhere [əd'hɪə^r] *vi*: **to ~ to** adhérer à; *(fig: rule, decision)* se tenir à

adhesion [əd'hi:ʒən] *n* adhésion *f*

adhesive [əd'hi:zɪv] *adj* adhésif(-ive) ▷ *n* adhésif *m*

adhesive tape *n* *(Brit)* ruban *m* adhésif; *(US Med)* sparadrap *m*

ad hoc [æd'hɔk] *adj* *(decision)* de circonstance; *(committee)* ad hoc

ad infinitum ['ædɪnfɪ'naɪtəm] *adv* à l'infini

adjacent [ə'dʒeɪsənt] *adj* adjacent(e), contigu(ë); **~ to** adjacent à

adjective ['ædʒɛktɪv] *n* adjectif *m*

adjoin [ə'dʒɔɪn] *vt* jouxter

adjoining [ə'dʒɔɪnɪŋ] *adj* voisin(e), adjacent(e), attenant(e) ▷ *prep* voisin de, adjacent à

adjourn [ə'dʒə:n] *vt* ajourner ▷ *vi* suspendre la séance; lever la séance; clore la session; *(go)* se retirer; **to ~ a meeting till the following week** reporter une réunion à la semaine suivante; **they ~ed to the pub** *(Brit inf)* ils ont filé au pub

adjournment [ə'dʒə:nmənt] *n* *(period)* ajournement *m*

Adjt *abbr* *(Mil: = adjutant)* Adj

adjudicate [ə'dʒu:dɪkeɪt] *vt* *(contest)* juger; *(claim)* statuer (sur) ▷ *vi* se prononcer

adjudication [ədʒu:dɪ'keɪʃən] *n* *(Law)* jugement *m*

adjust [ə'dʒʌst] *vt* *(machine)* ajuster, régler; *(prices, wages)* rajuster ▷ *vi*: **to ~ (to)** s'adapter (à)

adjustable [ə'dʒʌstəbl] *adj* réglable

adjuster [ə'dʒʌstə^r] *n see* **loss**

adjustment [ə'dʒʌstmənt] *n* *(of machine)* ajustage *m*, réglage *m*; *(of prices, wages)* rajustement *m*; *(of person)* adaptation *f*

adjutant ['ædʒətənt] *n* adjudant *m*

ad-lib [æd'lɪb] *vt, vi* improviser ▷ *n* improvisation *f* ▷ *adv*: **ad lib** à volonté, à discrétion

adman ['ædmæn] *(irreg)* *n* *(inf)* publicitaire *m*

admin ['ædmɪn] *n abbr* *(inf)* = **administration**

administer [əd'mɪnɪstə^r] *vt* administrer;

(justice) rendre

administration [ədmɪnɪs'treɪʃən] n
(management) administration f; (government)
gouvernement m

administrative [əd'mɪnɪstrətɪv] adj
administratif(-ive)

administrator [əd'mɪnɪstreɪtər] n
administrateur(-trice)

admirable ['ædmərəbl] adj admirable

admiral ['ædmərəl] n amiral m

Admiralty ['ædmərəltɪ] n (Brit: also: **Admiralty
Board**) ministère m de la Marine

admiration [ædmə'reɪʃən] n admiration f

admire [əd'maɪər] vt admirer

admirer [əd'maɪərər] n (fan) admirateur(-trice)

admiring [əd'maɪrɪŋ] adj admiratif(-ive)

admissible [əd'mɪsəbl] adj acceptable,
admissible; (evidence) recevable

admission [əd'mɪʃən] n admission f; (to
exhibition, night club etc) entrée f; (confession) aveu
m; "**~ free**", "**free ~**" "entrée libre"; **by his own**
~ de son propre aveu

admission charge n droits mpl d'admission

admit [əd'mɪt] vt laisser entrer; admettre;
(agree) reconnaître, admettre; (crime)
reconnaître avoir commis; "**children not
~ted**" "entrée interdite aux enfants"; **this
ticket ~s two** ce billet est valable pour deux
personnes; **I must ~ that ...** je dois admettre or
reconnaître que ...

▸ **admit of** vt fus admettre, permettre

▸ **admit to** vt fus reconnaître, avouer

admittance [əd'mɪtəns] n admission f, (droit m
d')entrée f; "**no ~**" "défense d'entrer"

admittedly [əd'mɪtɪdlɪ] adv il faut en convenir

admonish [əd'mɔnɪʃ] vt donner un
avertissement à; réprimander

ad nauseam [æd'nɔːsɪæm] adv à satiété

ado [ə'duː] n: **without (any) more ~** sans plus
de cérémonies

adolescence [ædəu'lɛsns] n adolescence f

adolescent [ædəu'lɛsnt] adj, n adolescent(e)

adopt [ə'dɔpt] vt adopter

adopted [ə'dɔptɪd] adj adoptif(-ive), adopté(e)

adoption [ə'dɔpʃən] n adoption f

adore [ə'dɔːr] vt adorer

adoring [ə'dɔːrɪŋ] adj: **his ~ wife** sa femme qui
est en adoration devant lui

adoringly [ə'dɔːrɪŋlɪ] adv avec adoration

adorn [ə'dɔːn] vt orner

adornment [ə'dɔːnmənt] n ornement m

ADP n abbr = **automatic data processing**

adrenalin [ə'drɛnəlɪn] n adrénaline f; **to get
the ~ going** faire monter le taux d'adrénaline

Adriatic [eɪdrɪ'ætɪk]

Adriatic Sea n: **the Adriatic (Sea)** la mer
Adriatique, l'Adriatique f

adrift [ə'drɪft] adv à la dérive; **to come ~** (boat)
aller à la dérive; (wire, rope, fastening etc) se défaire

adroit [ə'drɔɪt] adj adroit(e), habile

ADT abbr (US: = Atlantic Daylight Time) heure d'été de
New York

adult ['ædʌlt] n adulte m/f ▷ adj (grown-up)
adulte; (for adults) pour adultes

adult education n éducation f des adultes

adulterate [ə'dʌltəreɪt] vt frelater, falsifier

adulterer [ə'dʌltərər] n homme m adultère

adulteress [ə'dʌltərɪs] n femme f adultère

adultery [ə'dʌltərɪ] n adultère m

adulthood ['ædʌlthud] n âge m adulte

advance [əd'vɑːns] n avance f ▷ vt avancer ▷ vi
s'avancer; **in ~** en avance, d'avance; **to make
~s to sb** (gen) faire des propositions à qn;
(amorously) faire des avances à qn; **~ booking**
location f; **~ notice, ~ warning** préavis m;
(verbal) avertissement m; **do I need to book in
~?** est-ce qu'il faut réserver à l'avance?

advanced [əd'vɑːnst] adj avancé(e); (Scol: studies)
supérieur(e); **~ in years** d'un âge avancé

advancement [əd'vɑːnsmənt] n avancement m

advantage [əd'vɑːntɪdʒ] n (also Tennis) avantage
m; **to take ~ of** (person) exploiter; (opportunity)
profiter de; **it's to our ~** c'est notre intérêt; **it's
to our ~ to ...** nous avons intérêt à ...

advantageous [ædvən'teɪdʒəs] adj
avantageux(-euse)

advent ['ædvənt] n avènement m, venue f; **A~**
(Rel) avent m

Advent calendar n calendrier m de l'avent

adventure [əd'vɛntʃər] n aventure f

adventure playground n aire f de jeux

adventurous [əd'vɛntʃərəs] adj
aventureux(-euse)

adverb ['ædvəːb] n adverbe m

adversary ['ædvəsərɪ] n adversaire m/f

adverse ['ædvəːs] adj adverse; (effect)
négatif(-ive); (weather, publicity) mauvais(e);
(wind) contraire; **~ to** hostile à; **in ~
circumstances** dans l'adversité

adversity [əd'vəːsɪtɪ] n adversité f

advert ['ædvəːt] n abbr (Brit) = **advertisement**

advertise ['ædvətaɪz] vi faire de la publicité or
de la réclame; (in classified ads etc) mettre une
annonce ▷ vt faire de la publicité or de la
réclame pour; (in classified ads etc) mettre une
annonce pour vendre; **to ~ for** (staff) recruter
par (voie d')annonce

advertisement [əd'vəːtɪsmənt] n (Comm)
publicité f, réclame f; (in classified ads etc)
annonce f

advertiser ['ædvətaɪzər] n annonceur m

advertising ['ædvətaɪzɪŋ] n publicité f

advertising agency n agence f de publicité

advertising campaign n campagne f de
publicité

advice [əd'vaɪs] n conseils mpl; (notification) avis
m; **a piece of ~** un conseil; **to ask (sb) for ~**
demander conseil (à qn); **to take legal ~**
consulter un avocat

advice note n (Brit) avis m d'expédition

advisable [əd'vaɪzəbl] adj recommandable,
indiqué(e)

advise [əd'vaɪz] vt conseiller; **to ~ sb of sth**
aviser or informer qn de qch; **to ~ against sth/**

doing sth déconseiller qch/conseiller de ne pas faire qch; **you would be well/ill ~d to go** vous feriez mieux d'y aller/de ne pas y aller, vous auriez intérêt à y aller/à ne pas y aller

advisedly [əd'vaɪzɪdlɪ] adv (deliberately) délibérément

adviser, advisor [əd'vaɪzər] n conseiller(-ère)

advisory [əd'vaɪzərɪ] adj consultatif(-ive); **in an ~ capacity** à titre consultatif

advocate n ['ædvəkɪt] (lawyer) avocat (plaidant); (upholder) défenseur m, avocat(e) ⊳ vt ['ædvəkeɪt] recommander, prôner; **to be an ~ of** être partisan(e) de

advt. abbr = **advertisement**

AEA n abbr (Brit: = Atomic Energy Authority) ≈ AEN f (= Agence pour l'énergie nucléaire)

AEC n abbr (US: = Atomic Energy Commission) CEA m (= Commissariat à l'énergie atomique)

AEEU n abbr (Brit: = Amalgamated Engineering and Electrical Union) syndicat de techniciens et d'électriciens

Aegean [i:'dʒi:ən] n, adj: **the ~ (Sea)** la mer Égée, l'Égée f

aegis ['i:dʒɪs] n: **under the ~ of** sous l'égide de

aeon ['i:ən] n éternité f

aerial ['ɛərɪəl] n antenne f ⊳ adj aérien(ne)

aerobatics ['ɛərəu'bætɪks] npl acrobaties aériennes

aerobics [ɛə'rəubɪks] n aérobic m

aerodrome ['ɛərədrəum] n (Brit) aérodrome m

aerodynamic ['ɛərəudaɪ'næmɪk] adj aérodynamique

aeronautics [ɛərə'nɔ:tɪks] n aéronautique f

aeroplane ['ɛərəpleɪn] n (Brit) avion m

aerosol ['ɛərəsɔl] n aérosol m

aerospace industry ['ɛərəuspeɪs-] n (industrie) aérospatiale f

aesthetic [ɪs'θɛtɪk] adj esthétique

afar [ə'fɑ:ʳ] adv: **from ~** de loin

AFB n abbr (US) = **Air Force Base**

AFDC n abbr (US: = Aid to Families with Dependent Children) aide pour enfants assistés

affable ['æfəbl] adj affable

affair [ə'fɛəʳ] n affaire f; (also: **love affair**) liaison f; aventure f; **affairs** (business) affaires

affect [ə'fɛkt] vt affecter; (subj: disease) atteindre

affectation [æfɛk'teɪʃən] n affectation f

affected [ə'fɛktɪd] adj affecté(e)

affection [ə'fɛkʃən] n affection f

affectionate [ə'fɛkʃənɪt] adj affectueux(-euse)

affectionately [ə'fɛkʃənɪtlɪ] adv affectueusement

affidavit [æfɪ'deɪvɪt] n (Law) déclaration écrite sous serment

affiliated [ə'fɪlɪeɪtɪd] adj affilié(e); **~ company** filiale f

affinity [ə'fɪnɪtɪ] n affinité f

affirm [ə'fə:m] vt affirmer

affirmation [æfə'meɪʃən] n affirmation f, assertion f

affirmative [ə'fə:mətɪv] adj affirmatif(-ive) ⊳ n: **in the ~** dans or par l'affirmative

affix [ə'fɪks] vt apposer, ajouter

afflict [ə'flɪkt] vt affliger

affliction [ə'flɪkʃən] n affliction f

affluence ['æfluəns] n aisance f, opulence f

affluent ['æfluənt] adj opulent(e); (person, family, surroundings) aisé(e), riche; **the ~ society** la société d'abondance

afford [ə'fɔ:d] vt (goods etc) avoir les moyens d'acheter or d'entretenir; (behaviour) se permettre; (provide) fournir, procurer; **can we ~ a car?** avons-nous de quoi acheter or les moyens d'acheter une voiture?; **I can't ~ the time** je n'ai vraiment pas le temps

affordable [ə'fɔ:dəbl] adj abordable

affray [ə'freɪ] n (Brit Law) échauffourée f, rixe f

affront [ə'frʌnt] n affront m

affronted [ə'frʌntɪd] adj insulté(e)

Afghan ['æfgæn] adj afghan(e) ⊳ n Afghan(e)

Afghanistan [æf'gænɪstæn] n Afghanistan m

afield [ə'fi:ld] adv: **far ~** loin

AFL-CIO n abbr (= American Federation of Labor and Congress of Industrial Organizations) confédération syndicale

afloat [ə'fləut] adj à flot ⊳ adv: **to stay ~** surnager; **to keep/get a business ~** maintenir à flot/lancer une affaire

afoot [ə'fut] adv: **there is something ~** il se prépare quelque chose

aforementioned [ə'fɔ:mɛnʃənd] adj, **aforesaid** [ə'fɔ:sɛd] ⊳ adj susdit(e), susmentionné(e)

afraid [ə'freɪd] adj effrayé(e); **to be ~ of** or **to** avoir peur de; **I am ~ that** je crains que + sub; **I'm ~ so/not** oui/non, malheureusement

afresh [ə'frɛʃ] adv de nouveau

Africa ['æfrɪkə] n Afrique f

African ['æfrɪkən] adj africain(e) ⊳ n Africain(e)

African-American ['æfrɪkənə'mɛrɪkən] adj afro-américain(e) ⊳ n Afro-Américain(e)

Afrikaans [æfrɪ'kɑ:ns] n afrikaans m

Afrikaner [æfrɪ'kɑ:nəʳ] n Afrikaner m/f

Afro-American ['æfrəuə'mɛrɪkən] adj afro-américain(e)

AFT n abbr (= American Federation of Teachers) syndicat enseignant

aft [ɑ:ft] adv à l'arrière, vers l'arrière

after ['ɑ:ftəʳ] prep, adv après ⊳ conj après que, après avoir or être + pp; **~ dinner** après (le) dîner; **the day ~ tomorrow** après demain; **it's quarter ~ two** (US) il est deux heures et quart; **~ having done/~ he left** après avoir fait/après son départ; **to name sb ~ sb** donner à qn le nom de qn; **to ask ~ sb** demander des nouvelles de qn; **what/who are you ~?** que/qui cherchez-vous?; **the police are ~ him** la police est à ses trousses; **~ you!** après vous!; **~ all** après tout

afterbirth ['ɑ:ftəbə:θ] n placenta m

aftercare ['ɑ:ftəkɛəʳ] n (Brit Med) post-cure f

after-effects ['ɑ:ftərɪfɛkts] npl (of disaster, radiation, drink etc) répercussions fpl; (of illness) séquelles fpl, suites fpl

afterlife ['ɑ:ftəlaɪf] n vie future

aftermath ['ɑ:ftəmɑ:θ] n conséquences fpl; **in the ~ of** dans les mois or années etc qui suivirent, au lendemain de

afternoon ['ɑːftə'nuːn] n après-midi m or f; **good ~!** bonjour!; (goodbye) au revoir!

afters ['ɑːftəz] n (Brit inf: dessert) dessert m

after-sales service [ɑːftə'seɪlz-] n service m après-vente, SAV m

after-shave ['ɑːftəʃeɪv], **after-shave lotion** n lotion f après-rasage

aftershock ['ɑːftəʃɔk] n réplique f (sismique)

aftersun ['ɑːftəsʌn], **aftersun cream, aftersun lotion** n après-soleil m inv

aftertaste ['ɑːftəteɪst] n arrière-goût m

afterthought ['ɑːftəθɔːt] n: **I had an ~** il m'est venu une idée après coup

afterwards ['ɑːftəwədz], (US) **afterward** ['ɑːftəwəd] adv après

again [ə'gɛn] adv de nouveau, encore (une fois); **to do sth ~** refaire qch; **not ... ~** ne ... plus; **~ and ~** à plusieurs reprises; **he's opened it ~** il l'a rouvert, il l'a de nouveau or l'a encore ouvert; **now and ~** de temps à autre

against [ə'gɛnst] prep contre; (compared to) par rapport à; **~ a blue background** sur un fond bleu; **(as) ~** (Brit) contre

age [eɪdʒ] n âge m ▷ vt, vi vieillir; **what ~ is he?** quel âge a-t-il?; **he is 20 years of ~** il a 20 ans; **under ~** mineur(e); **to come of ~** atteindre sa majorité; **it's been ~s since I saw you** ça fait une éternité que je ne t'ai pas vu

aged ['eɪdʒd] adj âgé(e); **~ 10** âgé de 10 ans; **the ~** ['eɪdʒɪd] ▷ npl les personnes âgées

age group n tranche f d'âge; **the 40 to 50 ~** la tranche d'âge des 40 à 50 ans

ageing ['eɪdʒɪŋ] adj vieillissant(e)

ageless ['eɪdʒlɪs] adj sans âge

age limit n limite f d'âge

agency ['eɪdʒənsɪ] n agence f; **through** or **by the ~ of** par l'entremise or l'action de

agenda [ə'dʒɛndə] n ordre m du jour; **on the ~** à l'ordre du jour

agent ['eɪdʒənt] n agent m; (firm) concessionnaire m

aggravate ['ægrəveɪt] vt (situation) aggraver; (annoy) exaspérer, agacer

aggravation [ægrə'veɪʃən] n agacements mpl

aggregate ['ægrɪgɪt] n ensemble m, total m; **on ~** (Sport) au total des points

aggression [ə'grɛʃən] n agression f

aggressive [ə'grɛsɪv] adj agressif(-ive)

aggressiveness [ə'grɛsɪvnɪs] n agressivité f

aggressor [ə'grɛsər] n agresseur m

aggrieved [ə'griːvd] adj chagriné(e), affligé(e)

aggro ['ægrəu] n (inf: physical) grabuge m; (: hassle) embêtements mpl

aghast [ə'gɑːst] adj consterné(e), atterré(e)

agile ['ædʒaɪl] adj agile

agility [ə'dʒɪlɪtɪ] n agilité f, souplesse f

agitate ['ædʒɪteɪt] vt rendre inquiet(-ète) or agité(e) ▷ vi faire de l'agitation (politique); **to ~ for** faire campagne pour

agitator ['ædʒɪteɪtər] n agitateur(-trice) (politique)

AGM n abbr (= annual general meeting) AG f

ago [ə'gəu] adv: **two days ~** il y a deux jours; **not long ~** il n'y a pas longtemps; **as long ~ as 1960** déjà en 1960; **how long ~?** il y a combien de temps (de cela)?

agog [ə'gɔg] adj: **(all) ~** en émoi

agonize ['ægənaɪz] vi: **he ~d over the problem** ce problème lui a causé bien du tourment

agonizing ['ægənaɪzɪŋ] adj angoissant(e); (cry) déchirant(e)

agony ['ægənɪ] n (pain) douleur f atroce; (distress) angoisse f; **to be in ~** souffrir le martyre

agony aunt n (Brit inf) journaliste qui tient la rubrique du courrier du cœur

agony column n courrier m du cœur

agree [ə'griː] vt (price) convenir de ▷ vi: **to ~ with** (person) être d'accord avec; (statements etc) concorder avec; (Ling) s'accorder avec; **to ~ to do** accepter or consentir à faire; **to ~ to sth** consentir à qch; **to ~ that** (admit) convenir or reconnaître que; **it was ~d that ...** il a été convenu que ...; **they ~ on this** ils sont d'accord sur ce point; **they ~d on going/a price** ils se mirent d'accord pour y aller/sur un prix; **garlic doesn't ~ with me** je ne supporte pas l'ail

agreeable [ə'griːəbl] adj (pleasant) agréable; (willing) consentant(e), d'accord; **are you ~ to this?** est-ce que vous êtes d'accord?

agreed [ə'griːd] adj (time, place) convenu(e); **to be ~** être d'accord

agreement [ə'griːmənt] n accord m; **in ~** d'accord; **by mutual ~** d'un commun accord

agricultural [ægrɪ'kʌltʃərəl] adj agricole

agriculture ['ægrɪkʌltʃər] n agriculture f

aground [ə'graund] adv: **to run ~** s'échouer

ahead [ə'hɛd] adv en avant; devant; **go right** or **straight ~** (direction) allez tout droit; **go ~!** (permission) allez-y!; **~ of** devant; (fig: schedule etc) en avance sur; **~ of time** en avance; **they were (right) ~ of us** ils nous précédaient (de peu), ils étaient (juste) devant nous

AI n abbr = **Amnesty International**; (Comput) = **artificial intelligence**

AIB n abbr (Brit: = Accident Investigation Bureau) commission d'enquête sur les accidents

AID n abbr (= artificial insemination by donor) IAD f; (US: = Agency for International Development) agence pour le développement international

aid [eɪd] n aide f; (device) appareil m ▷ vt aider; **with the ~ of** avec l'aide de; **in ~ of** en faveur de; **to ~ and abet** (Law) se faire le complice de

aide [eɪd] n (person) assistant(e)

AIDS [eɪdz] n abbr (= acquired immune (or immuno-)deficiency syndrome) SIDA m

AIH n abbr (= artificial insemination by husband) IAC f

ailing ['eɪlɪŋ] adj (person) souffreteux(euse); (economy) malade

ailment ['eɪlmənt] n affection f

aim [eɪm] vt: **to ~ sth (at)** (gun, camera) braquer or pointer qch (sur); (missile) lancer qch (à or contre or en direction de); (remark, blow) destiner or adresser qch (à) ▷ vi (also: **to take aim**) viser ▷ n

(*objective*) but *m*; (*skill*): **his ~ is bad** il vise mal;
to ~ at viser; (*fig*) viser (à); avoir pour but *or*
ambition; **to ~ to do** avoir l'intention de faire
aimless ['eɪmlɪs] *adj* sans but
aimlessly ['eɪmlɪslɪ] *adv* sans but
ain't [eɪnt] (*inf*) = **am not**; **aren't**; **isn't**
air [ɛəʳ] *n* air *m* ▷ *vt* aérer; (*idea, grievance, views*)
mettre sur le tapis; (*knowledge*) faire étalage de
▷ *cpd* (*currents, attack etc*) aérien(ne); **to throw**
sth into the ~ (*ball etc*) jeter qch en l'air; **by ~**
par avion; **to be on the ~** (*Radio, TV: programme*)
être diffusé(e); (: *station*) émettre
airbag ['ɛəbæg] *n* airbag *m*
air base *n* base aérienne
airbed ['ɛəbɛd] *n* (*Brit*) matelas *m* pneumatique
airborne ['ɛəbɔːn] *adj* (*plane*) en vol; (*troops*)
aéroporté(e); (*particles*) dans l'air; **as soon as**
the plane was ~ dès que l'avion eut décollé
air cargo *n* fret aérien
air-conditioned ['ɛəkən'dɪʃənd] *adj*
climatisé(e), à air conditionné
air conditioning [-kən'dɪʃnɪŋ] *n* climatisation *f*
air-cooled ['ɛəkuːld] *adj* à refroidissement à air
aircraft ['ɛəkrɑːft] *n inv* avion *m*
aircraft carrier *n* porte-avions *m inv*
air cushion *n* coussin *m* d'air
airdrome ['ɛədrəum] *n* (*US*) aérodrome *m*
airfield ['ɛəfiːld] *n* terrain *m* d'aviation
Air Force *n* Armée *f* de l'air
air freight *n* fret aérien
air freshener [-'frɛʃnəʳ] *n* désodorisant *m*
airgun ['ɛəgʌn] *n* fusil *m* à air comprimé
air hostess *n* (*Brit*) hôtesse *f* de l'air
airily ['ɛərɪlɪ] *adv* d'un air dégagé
airing ['ɛərɪŋ] *n*: **to give an ~ to** aérer; (*fig: ideas,*
views etc) mettre sur le tapis
airing cupboard *n* (*Brit*) placard qui contient la
chaudière et dans lequel on met le linge à sécher
air letter *n* (*Brit*) aérogramme *m*
airlift ['ɛəlɪft] *n* pont aérien
airline ['ɛəlaɪn] *n* ligne aérienne, compagnie
aérienne
airliner ['ɛəlaɪnəʳ] *n* avion *m* de ligne
airlock ['ɛəlɔk] *n* sas *m*
airmail ['ɛəmeɪl] *n*: **by ~** par avion
air mattress *n* matelas *m* pneumatique
air mile *n* air mile *m*
airplane ['ɛəpleɪn] *n* (*US*) avion *m*
air pocket *n* trou *m* d'air
airport ['ɛəpɔːt] *n* aéroport *m*
air raid *n* attaque aérienne
air rifle *n* carabine *f* à air comprimé
airsick ['ɛəsɪk] *adj*: **to be ~** avoir le mal de l'air
airspace ['ɛəspeɪs] *n* espace *m* aérien
airspeed ['ɛəspiːd] *n* vitesse relative
airstrip ['ɛəstrɪp] *n* terrain *m* d'atterrissage
air terminal *n* aérogare *f*
airtight ['ɛətaɪt] *adj* hermétique
air time *n* (*Radio, TV*) temps *m* d'antenne
air traffic control *n* contrôle *m* de la navigation
aérienne
air-traffic controller *n* aiguilleur *m* du ciel

airway ['ɛəweɪ] *n* (*Aviat*) voie aérienne; **airways**
(*Anat*) voies aériennes
airy ['ɛərɪ] *adj* bien aéré(e); (*manners*) dégagé(e)
aisle [aɪl] *n* (*of church: central*) allée *f* centrale;
(: *side*) nef *f* latérale, bas-côté *m*; (*in theatre,*
supermarket) allée; (*on plane*) couloir *m*
aisle seat *n* place *f* côté couloir
ajar [ə'dʒɑːʳ] *adj* entrouvert(e)
AK *abbr* (*US*) = **Alaska**
aka *abbr* (= *also known as*) alias
akin [ə'kɪn] *adj*: **~ to** semblable à, du même
ordre que
AL *abbr* (*US*) = **Alabama**
ALA *n abbr* = **American Library Association**
Ala. *abbr* (*US*) = **Alabama**
à la carte [ælæ'kɑːt] *adv* à la carte
alacrity [ə'lækrɪtɪ] *n*: **with ~** avec
empressement, promptement
alarm [ə'lɑːm] *n* alarme *f* ▷ *vt* alarmer
alarm call *n* coup *m* de fil pour réveiller; **could I**
have an ~ at 7 am, please? pouvez-vous me
réveiller à 7 heures, s'il vous plaît?
alarm clock *n* réveille-matin *m inv*, réveil *m*
alarmed [ə'lɑːmd] *adj* (*frightened*) alarmé(e);
(*protected by an alarm*) protégé(e) par un système
d'alarme; **to become ~** prendre peur
alarming [ə'lɑːmɪŋ] *adj* alarmant(e)
alarmingly [ə'lɑːmɪŋlɪ] *adv* d'une manière
alarmante; **~ close** dangereusement proche; **~**
quickly à une vitesse inquiétante
alarmist [ə'lɑːmɪst] *n* alarmiste *m/f*
alas [ə'læs] *excl* hélas
Alas. *abbr* (*US*) = **Alaska**
Alaska [ə'læskə] *n* Alaska *m*
Albania [æl'beɪnɪə] *n* Albanie *f*
Albanian [æl'beɪnɪən] *adj* albanais(e) ▷ *n*
Albanais(e); (*Ling*) albanais *m*
albatross ['ælbətrɔs] *n* albatros *m*
albeit [ɔːl'biːɪt] *conj* bien que + *sub*, encore que +
sub
album ['ælbəm] *n* album *m*
albumen ['ælbjumɪn] *n* albumine *f*; (*of egg*)
albumen *m*
alchemy ['ælkɪmɪ] *n* alchimie *f*
alcohol ['ælkəhɔl] *n* alcool *m*
alcohol-free ['ælkəhɔlfriː] *adj* sans alcool
alcoholic [ælkə'hɔlɪk] *adj, n* alcoolique (*m/f*)
alcoholism ['ælkəhɔlɪzəm] *n* alcoolisme *m*
alcove ['ælkəuv] *n* alcôve *f*
Ald. *abbr* = **alderman**
alderman ['ɔːldəmən] *n* conseiller municipal
(*en Angleterre*)
ale [eɪl] *n* bière *f*
alert [ə'ləːt] *adj* alerte, vif (vive); (*watchful*)
vigilant(e) ▷ *n* alerte *f* ▷ *vt* alerter; **to ~ sb (to**
sth) attirer l'attention de qn (sur qch); **to ~ sb**
to the dangers of sth avertir qn des dangers de
qch; **on the ~** sur le qui-vive; (*Mil*) en état
d'alerte
Aleutian Islands [ə'luːʃən-] *npl* îles
Aléoutiennes
A levels *npl* ≈ baccalauréat *msg*

Alexandria [ælɪg'zɑ:ndrɪə] *n* Alexandrie
alfresco [æl'frɛskəu] *adj, adv* en plein air
algebra ['ældʒɪbrə] *n* algèbre *m*
Algeria [æl'dʒɪərɪə] *n* Algérie *f*
Algerian [æl'dʒɪərɪən] *adj* algérien(ne) ▷ *n* Algérien(ne)
Algiers [æl'dʒɪəz] *n* Alger
algorithm ['ælgərɪðəm] *n* algorithme *m*
alias ['eɪlɪəs] *adv* alias ▷ *n* faux nom, nom d'emprunt
alibi ['ælɪbaɪ] *n* alibi *m*
alien ['eɪlɪən] *n (from abroad)* étranger(-ère); *(from outer space)* extraterrestre ▷ *adj*: **~ (to)** étranger(-ère) (à)
alienate ['eɪlɪəneɪt] *vt* aliéner; *(subj: person)* s'aliéner
alienation [eɪlɪə'neɪʃən] *n* aliénation *f*
alight [ə'laɪt] *adj, adv* en feu ▷ *vi* mettre pied à terre; *(passenger)* descendre; *(bird)* se poser
align [ə'laɪn] *vt* aligner
alignment [ə'laɪnmənt] *n* alignement *m*; **it's out of ~ (with)** ce n'est pas aligné (avec)
alike [ə'laɪk] *adj* semblable, pareil(le) ▷ *adv* de même; **to look ~** se ressembler
alimony ['ælɪmənɪ] *n (payment)* pension *f* alimentaire
alive [ə'laɪv] *adj* vivant(e); *(active)* plein(e) de vie; **~ with** grouillant(e) de; **~ to** sensible à
alkali ['ælkəlaɪ] *n* alcali *m*

 KEYWORD

all [ɔ:l] *adj (singular)* tout(e); *(plural)* tous (toutes); **all day** toute la journée; **all night** toute la nuit; **all men** tous les hommes; **all five** tous les cinq; **all the food** toute la nourriture; **all the books** tous les livres; **all the time** tout le temps; **all his life** toute sa vie
▷ *pron* **1** tout; **I ate it all, I ate all of it** j'ai tout mangé; **all of us went** nous y sommes tous allés; **all of the boys went** tous les garçons y sont allés; **is that all?** c'est tout?; *(in shop)* ce sera tout?
2 *(in phrases)*: **above all** surtout, par-dessus tout; **after all** après tout; **at all**: **not at all** *(in answer to question)* pas du tout; *(in answer to thanks)* je vous en prie!; **I'm not at all tired** je ne suis pas du tout fatigué(e); **anything at all will do** n'importe quoi fera l'affaire; **all in all** tout bien considéré, en fin de compte
▷ *adv*: **all alone** tout(e) seul(e); **it's not as hard as all that** ce n'est pas si difficile que ça; **all the more/the better** d'autant plus/mieux; **all but** presque, pratiquement; **to be all in** *(Brit inf)* être complètement à plat; **the score is 2 all** le score est de 2 partout

Allah ['ælə] *n* Allah *m*
all-around [ɔːlə'raund] *adj (US)* = **all-round**
allay [ə'leɪ] *vt (fears)* apaiser, calmer
all clear *n (also fig)* fin *f* d'alerte
allegation [ælɪ'geɪʃən] *n* allégation *f*

allege [ə'lɛdʒ] *vt* alléguer, prétendre; **he is ~d to have said** il aurait dit
alleged [ə'lɛdʒd] *adj* prétendu(e)
allegedly [ə'lɛdʒɪdlɪ] *adv* à ce que l'on prétend, paraît-il
allegiance [ə'li:dʒəns] *n* fidélité *f*, obéissance *f*
allegory ['ælɪgərɪ] *n* allégorie *f*
all-embracing ['ɔːlɪm'breɪsɪŋ] *adj* universel(le)
allergic [ə'lə:dʒɪk] *adj*: **~ to** allergique à; **I'm ~ to penicillin** je suis allergique à la pénicilline
allergy ['ælədʒɪ] *n* allergie *f*
alleviate [ə'li:vɪeɪt] *vt* soulager, adoucir
alley ['ælɪ] *n* ruelle *f*; *(in garden)* allée *f*
alleyway ['ælɪweɪ] *n* ruelle *f*
alliance [ə'laɪəns] *n* alliance *f*
allied ['ælaɪd] *adj* allié(e)
alligator ['ælɪgeɪtər] *n* alligator *m*
all-important ['ɔːlɪm'pɔːtənt] *adj* capital(e), crucial(e)
all-in ['ɔːlɪn] *adj, adv (Brit: charge)* tout compris
all-in wrestling *n (Brit)* catch *m*
alliteration [əlɪtə'reɪʃən] *n* allitération *f*
all-night ['ɔːl'naɪt] *adj* ouvert(e) *or* qui dure toute la nuit
allocate ['æləkeɪt] *vt (share out)* répartir, distribuer; **to ~ sth to** *(duties)* assigner *or* attribuer qch à; *(sum, time)* allouer qch à; **to ~ sth for** affecter qch à
allocation [æləu'keɪʃən] *n (see vb)* répartition *f*; attribution *f*; allocation *f*; affectation *f*; *(money)* crédit(s) *m(pl)*, somme(s) allouée(s)
allot [ə'lɔt] *vt (share out)* répartir, distribuer; **to ~ sth to** *(time)* allouer qch à; *(duties)* assigner qch à; **in the ~ted time** dans le temps imparti
allotment [ə'lɔtmənt] *n (share)* part *f*; *(garden)* lopin *m* de terre *(loué à la municipalité)*
all-out ['ɔːlaut] *adj (effort etc)* total(e)
allow [ə'lau] *vt (practice, behaviour)* permettre, autoriser; *(sum to spend etc)* accorder, allouer; *(sum, time estimated)* compter, prévoir; *(claim, goal)* admettre; *(concede)*: **to ~ that** convenir que; **to ~ sb to do** permettre à qn de faire, autoriser qn à faire; **he is ~ed to ...** on lui permet de ...; **smoking is not ~ed** il est interdit de fumer; **we must ~ three days for the journey** il faut compter trois jours pour le voyage
▷ **allow for** *vt fus* tenir compte de
allowance [ə'lauəns] *n (money received)* allocation *f*; *(: from parent etc)* subside *m*; *(: for expenses)* indemnité *f*; *(US: pocket money)* argent *m* de poche; *(Tax)* somme *f* déductible du revenu imposable, abattement *m*; **to make ~s for** *(person)* essayer de comprendre; *(thing)* tenir compte de
alloy ['ælɔɪ] *n* alliage *m*
all right *adv (feel, work)* bien; *(as answer)* d'accord
all-round ['ɔːl'raund] *adj* compétent(e) dans tous les domaines; *(athlete etc)* complet(-ète)
all-rounder [ɔːl'raundər] *n (Brit)*: **to be a good ~** être doué(e) en tout
allspice ['ɔːlspaɪs] *n* poivre *m* de la Jamaïque
all-time ['ɔːl'taɪm] *adj (record)* sans précédent,

absolu(e)

allude [ə'luːd] *vi*: **to ~ to** faire allusion à

alluring [ə'ljuərɪŋ] *adj* séduisant(e),
alléchant(e)

allusion [ə'luːʒən] *n* allusion *f*

alluvium [ə'luːvɪəm] *n* alluvions *fpl*

ally ['ælaɪ] *n* allié *m* ▷ *vt* [ə'laɪ]: **to ~ o.s. with**
s'allier avec

almighty [ɔːl'maɪtɪ] *adj* tout(e)-puissant(e);
(*tremendous*) énorme

almond ['ɑːmənd] *n* amande *f*

almost ['ɔːlməust] *adv* presque; **he ~ fell** il a
failli tomber

alms [ɑːmz] *n* aumône(s) *f(pl)*

aloft [ə'lɔft] *adv* en haut, en l'air; (*Naut*) dans la
mâture

alone [ə'ləun] *adj*, *adv* seul(e); **to leave sb ~**
laisser qn tranquille; **to leave sth ~** ne pas
toucher à qch; **let ~ ...** sans parler de ...; encore
moins ...

along [ə'lɔŋ] *prep* le long de ▷ *adv*: **is he coming
~ with us?** vient-il avec nous?; **he was
hopping/limping ~** il venait *or* avançait en
sautillant/boitant; **~ with** avec, en plus de;
(*person*) en compagnie de; **all ~** (*all the time*)
depuis le début

alongside [ə'lɔŋ'saɪd] *prep* (*along*) le long de;
(*beside*) à côté de ▷ *adv* bord à bord; côte à côte;
we brought our boat ~ (*of a pier, shore etc*) nous
avons accosté

aloof [ə'luːf] *adj* distant(e) ▷ *adv* à distance, à
l'écart; **to stand ~** se tenir à l'écart *or* à distance

aloofness [ə'luːfnɪs] *n* réserve (hautaine),
attitude distante

aloud [ə'laud] *adv* à haute voix

alphabet ['ælfəbɛt] *n* alphabet *m*

alphabetical [ælfə'bɛtɪkl] *adj* alphabétique; **in
~ order** par ordre alphabétique

alphanumeric [ælfənjuː'mɛrɪk] *adj*
alphanumérique

alpine ['ælpaɪn] *adj* alpin(e), alpestre; **~ hut**
cabane *f* or refuge *m* de montagne; **~ pasture**
pâturage *m* (de montagne); **~ skiing** ski alpin

Alps [ælps] *npl*: **the ~** les Alpes *fpl*

already [ɔːl'rɛdɪ] *adv* déjà

alright ['ɔːl'raɪt] *adv* (*Brit*) = **all right**

Alsace [æl'sæs] *n* Alsace *f*

Alsatian [æl'seɪʃən] *adj* alsacien(ne), d'Alsace
▷ *n* Alsacien(ne); (*Brit*: *dog*) berger allemand

also ['ɔːlsəu] *adv* aussi

Alta. *abbr* (*Canada*) = **Alberta**

altar ['ɔltəʳ] *n* autel *m*

alter ['ɔltəʳ] *vt*, *vi* changer

alteration [ɔltə'reɪʃən] *n* changement *m*,
modification *f*; **alterations** *npl* (*Sewing*)
retouches *fpl*; (*Archit*) modifications *fpl*;
timetable subject to ~ horaires sujets à
modifications

altercation [ɔltə'keɪʃən] *n* altercation *f*

alternate *adj* [ɔl'təːnɪt] alterné(e), alternant(e),
alternatif(-ive); (*US*) = **alternative** ▷ *vi*
['ɔltəːneɪt] alterner; **to ~ with** alterner avec; **on**

~ days un jour sur deux, tous les deux jours

alternately [ɔl'təːnɪtlɪ] *adv* alternativement, en
alternant

alternating ['ɔltə:neɪtɪŋ] *adj* (*current*)
alternatif(-ive)

alternative [ɔl'təːnətɪv] *adj* (*solution, plan*) autre,
de remplacement; (*energy*) doux (douce);
(*lifestyle*) parallèle ▷ *n* (*choice*) alternative *f*; (*other
possibility*) autre possibilité *f*; **~ medicine**
médecine alternative, médecine douce

alternatively [ɔl'təːnətɪvlɪ] *adv*: **~ one could ...**
une autre *or* l'autre solution serait de ...

alternative medicine *n* médecines *fpl*
parallèles *or* douces

alternator ['ɔltə:neɪtəʳ] *n* (*Aut*) alternateur *m*

although [ɔːl'ðəu] *conj* bien que + *sub*

altitude ['æltɪtjuːd] *n* altitude *f*

alto ['æltəu] *n* (*female*) contralto *m*; (*male*) haute-
contre *f*

altogether [ɔːltə'gɛðəʳ] *adv* entièrement, tout à
fait; (*on the whole*) tout compte fait; (*in all*) en
tout; **how much is that ~?** ça fait combien en
tout?

altruism ['æltruɪzəm] *n* altruisme *m*

altruistic [æltru'ɪstɪk] *adj* altruiste

aluminium [ælju'mɪnɪəm] (*US*), **aluminum**
[ə'luːmɪnəm] *n* aluminium *m*

alumna (*pl* **-e**) [ə'lʌmnə, -niː] *n* (*US Scol*)
ancienne élève; (*University*) ancienne étudiante

alumnus (*pl* **alumni**) [ə'lʌmnəs, -naɪ] *n* (*US Scol*)
ancien élève; (*University*) ancien étudiant

always ['ɔːlweɪz] *adv* toujours

Alzheimer's ['æltshaɪməz], **Alzheimer's
disease** *n* maladie *f* d'Alzheimer

AM *abbr* = **amplitude modulation** ▷ *n abbr*
(= *Assembly Member*) député *m* au Parlement
gallois

am [æm] *vb see* **be**

a.m. *adv abbr* (= *ante meridiem*) du matin

AMA *n abbr* = **American Medical Association**

amalgam [ə'mælgəm] *n* amalgame *m*

amalgamate [ə'mælgəmeɪt] *vt*, *vi* fusionner

amalgamation [əmælgə'meɪʃən] *n* fusion *f*;
(*Comm*) fusionnement *m*

amass [ə'mæs] *vt* amasser

amateur ['æmətəʳ] *n* amateur *m* ▷ *adj* (*Sport*)
amateur *inv*; **~ dramatics** le théâtre amateur

amateurish ['æmətərɪʃ] *adj* (*pej*) d'amateur, un
peu amateur

amaze [ə'meɪz] *vt* stupéfier; **to be ~d (at)** être
stupéfait(e) (de)

amazed [ə'meɪzd] *adj* stupéfait(e)

amazement [ə'meɪzmənt] *n* surprise *f*,
étonnement *m*

amazing [ə'meɪzɪŋ] *adj* étonnant(e), incroyable;
(*bargain, offer*) exceptionnel(le)

amazingly [ə'meɪzɪŋlɪ] *adv* incroyablement

Amazon ['æməzən] *n* (*Geo, Mythology*) Amazone *f*
▷ *cpd* amazonien(ne), de l'Amazone; **the ~
basin** le bassin de l'Amazone; **the ~ jungle** la
forêt amazonienne

Amazonian [æmə'zəunɪən] *adj* amazonien(ne)

ambassador [æm'bæsədər] n ambassadeur m
amber ['æmbər] n ambre m; **at ~** (Brit Aut) à
l'orange
ambidextrous [æmbɪ'dɛkstrəs] adj ambidextre
ambience ['æmbɪəns] n ambiance f
ambiguity [æmbɪ'gjuɪtɪ] n ambiguïté f
ambiguous [æm'bɪgjuəs] adj ambigu(ë)
ambition [æm'bɪʃən] n ambition f
ambitious [æm'bɪʃəs] adj ambitieux(-euse)
ambivalent [æm'bɪvələnt] adj (attitude)
ambivalent(e)
amble ['æmbl] vi (also: **to amble along**) aller
d'un pas tranquille
ambulance ['æmbjuləns] n ambulance f; **call
an ~!** appelez une ambulance!
ambush ['æmbuʃ] n embuscade f ▷ vt tendre
une embuscade à
ameba [ə'mi:bə] n (US) = **amoeba**
ameliorate [ə'mi:lɪəreɪt] vt améliorer
amen ['ɑ:'mɛn] excl amen
amenable [ə'mi:nəbl] adj: **~ to** (advice etc)
disposé(e) à écouter or suivre; **~ to the law**
responsable devant la loi
amend [ə'mɛnd] vt (law) amender; (text)
corriger; (habits) réformer ▷ vi s'amender, se
corriger; **to make ~s** réparer ses torts, faire
amende honorable
amendment [ə'mɛndmənt] n (to law)
amendement m; (to text) correction f
amenities [ə'mi:nɪtɪz] npl aménagements mpl,
équipements mpl
amenity [ə'mi:nɪtɪ] n charme m, agrément m
America [ə'mɛrɪkə] n Amérique f
American [ə'mɛrɪkən] adj américain(e) ▷ n
Américain(e)
American football n (Brit) football m américain
americanize [ə'mɛrɪkənaɪz] vt américaniser
amethyst ['æmɪθɪst] n améthyste f
Amex ['æmɛks] n abbr = **American Stock
Exchange**
amiable ['eɪmɪəbl] adj aimable, affable
amicable ['æmɪkəbl] adj amical(e); (Law) à
l'amiable
amicably ['æmɪkəblɪ] adv amicalement
amid [ə'mɪd], **amidst** [ə'mɪdst] prep parmi, au
milieu de
amiss [ə'mɪs] adj, adv: **there's something ~** il y
a quelque chose qui ne va pas or qui cloche; **to
take sth ~** prendre qch mal or de travers
ammo ['æməu] n abbr (inf) = **ammunition**
ammonia [ə'məunɪə] n (gas) ammoniac m;
(liquid) ammoniaque f
ammunition [æmju'nɪʃən] n munitions fpl; (fig)
arguments mpl
ammunition dump n dépôt m de munitions
amnesia [æm'ni:zɪə] n amnésie f
amnesty ['æmnɪstɪ] n amnistie f; **to grant an ~
to** accorder une amnistie à
Amnesty International n Amnesty
International
amoeba, (US) **ameba** [ə'mi:bə] n amibe f
amok [ə'mɔk] adv: **to run ~** être pris(e) d'un

accès de folie furieuse
among [ə'mʌŋ], **amongst** [ə'mʌŋst] prep
parmi, entre
amoral [æ'mɔrəl] adj amoral(e)
amorous ['æmərəs] adj amoureux(-euse)
amorphous [ə'mɔ:fəs] adj amorphe
amortization [əmɔ:taɪ'zeɪʃən] n (Comm)
amortissement m
amount [ə'maunt] n (sum of money) somme f;
(total) montant m; (quantity) quantité f; nombre
m ▷ vi: **to ~ to** (total) s'élever à; (be same as)
équivaloir à, revenir à; **this ~s to a refusal** cela
équivaut à un refus; **the total ~** (of money) le
montant total
amp ['æmp], **ampère** ['æmpɛər] n ampère m; **a
13 ~ plug** une fiche de 13 A
ampersand ['æmpəsænd] n signe &, "et"
commercial
amphetamine [æm'fɛtəmi:n] n amphétamine f
amphibian [æm'fɪbɪən] n batracien m
amphibious [æm'fɪbɪəs] adj amphibie
amphitheatre, (US) **amphitheater**
['æmfɪθɪətər] n amphithéâtre m
ample ['æmpl] adj ample, spacieux(-euse);
(enough): **this is ~** c'est largement suffisant; **to
have ~ time/room** avoir bien assez de temps/
place, avoir largement le temps/la place
amplifier ['æmplɪfaɪər] n amplificateur m
amplify ['æmplɪfaɪ] vt amplifier
amply ['æmplɪ] adv amplement, largement
ampoule, (US) **ampule** ['æmpu:l] n (Med)
ampoule f
amputate ['æmpjuteɪt] vt amputer
amputee [æmpju'ti:] n amputé(e)
Amsterdam ['æmstədæm] n Amsterdam
amt abbr = **amount**
Amtrak ['æmtræk] (US) n société mixte de transports
ferroviaires interurbains pour voyageurs
amuck [ə'mʌk] adv = **amok**
amuse [ə'mju:z] vt amuser; **to ~ o.s. with sth/
by doing sth** se divertir avec qch/à faire qch; **to
be ~d at** être amusé par; **he was not ~d** il n'a
pas apprécié
amusement [ə'mju:zmənt] n amusement m;
(pastime) distraction f
amusement arcade n salle f de jeu
amusement park n parc m d'attractions
amusing [ə'mju:zɪŋ] adj amusant(e),
divertissant(e)
an [æn, ən, n] indef art see **a**
ANA n abbr = **American Newspaper Association;
American Nurses Association**
anachronism [ə'nækrənɪzəm] n
anachronisme m
anaemia, (US) **anemia** [ə'ni:mɪə] n anémie f
anaemic, (US) **anemic** [ə'ni:mɪk] adj anémique
anaesthetic, (US) **anesthetic** [ænɪs'θɛtɪk] adj, n
anesthésique m; **under the ~** sous anesthésie;
local/general ~ anesthésie locale/générale
anaesthetist [æ'ni:sθɪtɪst] n anesthésiste m/f
anagram ['ænəgræm] n anagramme m
anal ['eɪnl] adj anal(e)

analgesic [ænæl'dʒiːsɪk] *adj, n* analgésique (*m*)

analogous [ə'næləgəs] *adj:* ~ **(to** *or* **with)** analogue (à)

analogue, analog ['ænəlɔg] *adj* (*watch, computer*) analogique

analogy [ə'nælədʒɪ] *n* analogie *f*; **to draw an ~ between** établir une analogie entre

analyse, (*US*) **analyze** ['ænəlaɪz] *vt* analyser

analysis (*pl* **analyses**) [ə'næləsɪs, -siːz] *n* analyse *f*; **in the last ~** en dernière analyse

analyst ['ænəlɪst] *n* (*political analyst etc*) analyste *m/f*; (*US*) psychanalyste *m/f*

analytic [ænə'lɪtɪk], **analytical** [ænə'lɪtɪkəl] *adj* analytique

analyze ['ænəlaɪz] *vt* (*US*) = **analyse**

anarchic [æ'nɑːkɪk] *adj* anarchique

anarchist ['ænəkɪst] *adj, n* anarchiste (*m/f*)

anarchy ['ænəkɪ] *n* anarchie *f*

anathema [ə'næθɪmə] *n*: **it is ~ to him** il a cela en abomination

anatomical [ænə'tɔmɪkəl] *adj* anatomique

anatomy [ə'nætəmɪ] *n* anatomie *f*

ANC *n abbr* (= *African National Congress*) ANC *m*

ancestor ['ænsɪstəʳ] *n* ancêtre *m*, aïeul *m*

ancestral [æn'sɛstrəl] *adj* ancestral(e)

ancestry ['ænsɪstrɪ] *n* ancêtres *mpl*; ascendance *f*

anchor ['æŋkəʳ] *n* ancre *f* ⊳ *vi* (*also:* **to drop anchor**) jeter l'ancre, mouiller ⊳ *vt* mettre à l'ancre; (*fig*): **to ~ sth to** fixer qch à; **to weigh ~** lever l'ancre

anchorage ['æŋkərɪdʒ] *n* mouillage *m*, ancrage *m*

anchor man, anchor woman (*irreg*) *n* (TV, *Radio*) présentateur(-trice)

anchovy ['æntʃəvɪ] *n* anchois *m*

ancient ['eɪnʃənt] *adj* ancien(ne), antique; (*person*) d'un âge vénérable; (*car*) antédiluvien(ne); **~ monument** monument *m* historique

ancillary [æn'sɪlərɪ] *adj* auxiliaire

and [ænd] *conj* et; ~ **so on** et ainsi de suite; **try ~ come** tâchez de venir; **come ~ sit here** venez vous asseoir ici; **he talked ~ talked** il a parlé pendant des heures; **better ~ better** de mieux en mieux; **more ~ more** de plus en plus

Andes ['ændiːz] *npl*: **the ~** les Andes *fpl*

Andorra [æn'dɔːrə] *n* (principauté *f* d')Andorre *f*

anecdote ['ænɪkdəʊt] *n* anecdote *f*

anemia *etc* [ə'niːmɪə] *n* (*US*) = **anaemia** *etc*

anemic [ə'niːmɪk] *adj* = **anaemic**

anemone [ə'nɛmənɪ] *n* (*Bot*) anémone *f*; **sea ~** anémone de mer

anesthesiologist [ænɪsθiːzɪ'ɔlədʒɪst] *n* (*US*) anesthésiste *m/f*

anesthetic [ænɪs'θɛtɪk] *n, adj* (*US*) = **anaesthetic**

anesthetist [æ'niːsθɪtɪst] *n* = **anaesthetist**

anew [ə'njuː] *adv* à nouveau

angel ['eɪndʒəl] *n* ange *m*

angel dust *n* poussière *f* d'ange

anger ['æŋgəʳ] *n* colère *f* ⊳ *vt* mettre en colère,

irriter

angina [æn'dʒaɪnə] *n* angine *f* de poitrine

angle ['æŋgl] *n* angle *m* ⊳ *vi:* **to ~ for** (*trout*) pêcher; (*compliments*) chercher, quêter; **from their ~** de leur point de vue

angler ['æŋgləʳ] *n* pêcheur(-euse) à la ligne

Anglican ['æŋglɪkən] *adj, n* anglican(e)

anglicize ['æŋglɪsaɪz] *vt* angliciser

angling ['æŋglɪŋ] *n* pêche *f* à la ligne

Anglo- ['æŋgləʊ] *prefix* anglo(-)

Anglo-French ['æŋgləʊ'frɛntʃ] *adj* anglo-français(e)

Anglo-Saxon ['æŋgləʊ'sæksən] *adj, n* anglo-saxon(ne)

Angola [æŋ'gəʊlə] *n* Angola *m*

Angolan [æŋ'gəʊlən] *adj* angolais(e) ⊳ *n* Angolais(e)

angrily ['æŋgrɪlɪ] *adv* avec colère

angry ['æŋgrɪ] *adj* en colère, furieux(-euse); (*wound*) enflammé(e); **to be ~ with sb/at sth** être furieux contre qn/de qch; **to get ~** se fâcher, se mettre en colère; **to make sb ~** mettre qn en colère

anguish ['æŋgwɪʃ] *n* angoisse *f*

anguished ['æŋgwɪʃt] *adj* (*mentally*) angoissé(e); (*physically*) plein(e) de souffrance

angular ['æŋgjuləʳ] *adj* anguleux(-euse)

animal ['ænɪməl] *n* animal *m* ⊳ *adj* animal(e)

animal rights *npl* droits *mpl* de l'animal

animate *vt* ['ænɪmeɪt] animer ⊳ *adj* ['ænɪmɪt] animé(e), vivant(e)

animated ['ænɪmeɪtɪd] *adj* animé(e)

animation [ænɪ'meɪʃən] *n* (*of person*) entrain *m*; (*of street, Cine*) animation *f*

animosity [ænɪ'mɔsɪtɪ] *n* animosité *f*

aniseed ['ænɪsiːd] *n* anis *m*

Ankara ['æŋkərə] *n* Ankara

ankle ['æŋkl] *n* cheville *f*

ankle socks *npl* socquettes *fpl*

annex ['ænɛks] *n* (*Brit: also:* **annexe**) annexe *f* ⊳ *vt* [ə'nɛks] annexer

annexation [ænɛks'eɪʃən] *n* annexion *f*

annihilate [ə'naɪəleɪt] *vt* annihiler, anéantir

annihilation [ənaɪə'leɪʃən] *n* anéantissement *m*

anniversary [ænɪ'vəːsərɪ] *n* anniversaire *m*

anniversary dinner *n* dîner commémoratif *or* anniversaire

annotate ['ænəuteɪt] *vt* annoter

announce [ə'naʊns] *vt* annoncer; (*birth, death*) faire part de; **he ~d that he wasn't going** il a déclaré qu'il n'irait pas

announcement [ə'naʊnsmənt] *n* annonce *f*; (*for births etc: in newspaper*) avis *m* de faire-part; (: *letter, card*) faire-part *m*; **I'd like to make an ~** j'ai une communication à faire

announcer [ə'naʊnsəʳ] *n* (*Radio, TV: between programmes*) speaker(ine); (: *in a programme*) présentateur(-trice)

annoy [ə'nɔɪ] *vt* agacer, ennuyer, contrarier; **to be ~ed (at sth/with sb)** être en colère *or* irrité (contre qch/qn); **don't get ~ed!** ne vous fâchez pas!

annoyance [ə'nɔɪəns] *n* mécontentement *m*, contrariété *f*

annoying [ə'nɔɪɪŋ] *adj* agaçant(e), contrariant(e)

annual ['ænjuəl] *adj* annuel(le) ▷ *n* (*Bot*) plante annuelle; (*book*) album *m*

annual general meeting *n* (*Brit*) assemblée générale annuelle

annually ['ænjuəlɪ] *adv* annuellement

annual report *n* rapport annuel

annuity [ə'njuːɪtɪ] *n* rente *f*; **life ~** rente viagère

annul [ə'nʌl] *vt* annuler; (*law*) abroger

annulment [ə'nʌlmənt] *n* (*see vb*) annulation *f*; abrogation *f*

annum ['ænəm] *n see* **per**

Annunciation [ənʌnsɪ'eɪʃən] *n* Annonciation *f*

anode ['ænəud] *n* anode *f*

anoint [ə'nɔɪnt] *vt* oindre

anomalous [ə'nɔmələs] *adj* anormal(e)

anomaly [ə'nɔməlɪ] *n* anomalie *f*

anon. [ə'nɔn] *abbr* = **anonymous**

anonymity [ænə'nɪmɪtɪ] *n* anonymat *m*

anonymous [ə'nɔnɪməs] *adj* anonyme; **to remain ~** garder l'anonymat

anorak ['ænəræk] *n* anorak *m*

anorexia [ænə'rɛksɪə] *n* (*also:* **anorexia nervosa**) anorexie *f*

anorexic [ænə'rɛksɪk] *adj, n* anorexique (*m/f*)

another [ə'nʌðə'] *adj*: **~ book** (*one more*) un autre livre, encore un livre, un livre de plus; (*a different one*) un autre livre ▷ *pron* un(e) autre, encore un(e), un(e) de plus; **~ drink?** encore un verre?; **in ~ five years** dans cinq ans; *see also* **one**

ANSI ['ænsɪ] *n abbr* (= *American National Standards Institution*) ANSI *m* (= *Institut américain de normalisation*)

answer ['ɑːnsə'] *n* réponse *f*; (*to problem*) solution *f* ▷ *vi* répondre ▷ *vt* (*reply to*) répondre à; (*problem*) résoudre; (*prayer*) exaucer; **in ~ to your letter** suite à *or* en réponse à votre lettre; **to ~ the phone** répondre (au téléphone); **to ~ the bell** *or* **the door** aller *or* venir ouvrir (la porte)

▸ **answer back** *vi* répondre, répliquer

▸ **answer for** *vt fus* répondre de, se porter garant de; (*crime, one's actions*) répondre de

▸ **answer to** *vt fus* (*description*) répondre *or* correspondre à

answerable ['ɑːnsərəbl] *adj*: **~ (to sb/for sth)** responsable (devant qn/de qch); **I am ~ to no-one** je n'ai de comptes à rendre à personne

answering machine ['ɑːnsərɪŋ-] *n* répondeur *m*

answerphone ['ɑːnsərfəun] *n* (*esp Brit*) répondeur *m* (téléphonique)

ant [ænt] *n* fourmi *f*

ANTA *n abbr* = **American National Theater and Academy**

antagonism [æn'tægənɪzəm] *n* antagonisme *m*

antagonist [æn'tægənɪst] *n* antagoniste *m/f*, adversaire *m/f*

antagonistic [æntægə'nɪstɪk] *adj* (*attitude, feelings*) hostile

antagonize [æn'tægənaɪz] *vt* éveiller l'hostilité de, contrarier

Antarctic [ænt'ɑːktɪk] *adj* antarctique, austral(e) ▷ *n*: **the ~** l'Antarctique *m*

Antarctica [ænt'ɑːktɪkə] *n* Antarctique *m*, Terres Australes

Antarctic Circle *n* cercle *m* Antarctique

Antarctic Ocean *n* océan *m* Antarctique *or* Austral

ante ['æntɪ] *n*: **to up the ~** faire monter les enjeux

ante... ['æntɪ] *prefix* anté..., anti..., pré...

anteater ['ænti:tə'] *n* fourmilier *m*, tamanoir *m*

antecedent [æntɪ'si:dənt] *n* antécédent *m*

antechamber ['æntɪtʃeɪmbə'] *n* antichambre *f*

antelope ['æntɪləup] *n* antilope *f*

antenatal ['æntɪ'neɪtl] *adj* prénatal(e)

antenatal clinic *n* service *m* de consultation prénatale

antenna (*pl* **-e**) [æn'tɛnə, -niː] *n* antenne *f*

anthem ['ænθəm] *n* motet *m*; **national ~** hymne national

ant-hill ['ænthɪl] *n* fourmilière *f*

anthology [æn'θɔlədʒɪ] *n* anthologie *f*

anthrax ['ænθræks] *n* anthrax *m*

anthropologist [ænθrə'pɔlədʒɪst] *n* anthropologue *m/f*

anthropology [ænθrə'pɔlədʒɪ] *n* anthropologie *f*

anti ['æntɪ] *prefix* anti-

anti-aircraft ['æntɪ'ɛəkrɑːft] *adj* antiaérien(ne)

anti-aircraft defence *n* défense *f* contre avions, DCA *f*

antiballistic ['æntɪbə'lɪstɪk] *adj* antibalistique

antibiotic ['æntɪbaɪ'ɔtɪk] *adj, n* antibiotique *m*

antibody ['æntɪbɔdɪ] *n* anticorps *m*

anticipate [æn'tɪsɪpeɪt] *vt* s'attendre à, prévoir; (*wishes, request*) aller au devant de, devancer; **this is worse than I ~d** c'est pire que je ne pensais; **as ~d** comme prévu

anticipation [æntɪsɪ'peɪʃən] *n* attente *f*; **thanking you in ~** en vous remerciant d'avance, avec mes remerciements anticipés

anticlimax ['æntɪ'klaɪmæks] *n* déception *f*

anticlockwise ['æntɪ'klɔkwaɪz] (*Brit*) *adv* dans le sens inverse des aiguilles d'une montre

antics ['æntɪks] *npl* singeries *fpl*

anticyclone ['æntɪ'saɪkləun] *n* anticyclone *m*

antidepressant ['æntɪ'prɛsnt] *n* antidépresseur *m*

antidote ['æntɪdəut] *n* antidote *m*, contrepoison *m*

antifreeze ['æntɪfriːz] *n* antigel *m*

anti-globalization [æntɪgləubəlaɪ'zeɪʃən] *n* antimondialisation *f*

antihistamine [æntɪ'hɪstəmɪn] *n* antihistaminique *m*

Antilles [æn'tɪliːz] *npl*: **the ~** les Antilles *fpl*

antipathy [æn'tɪpəθɪ] *n* antipathie *f*

antiperspirant [æntɪ'pəːspɪrənt] *n* déodorant *m*

Antipodean [æntɪpə'diːən] *adj* australien(ne) et néozélandais(e), d'Australie et de Nouvelle-Zélande

Antipodes [æn'tɪpədiːz] *npl*: **the ~** l'Australie *f*

et la Nouvelle-Zélande

antiquarian [æntɪˈkwɛərɪən] *adj*: ~ **bookshop** librairie *f* d'ouvrages anciens ▷ *n* expert *m* en objets *or* livres anciens; amateur *m* d'antiquités

antiquated [ˈæntɪkweɪtɪd] *adj* vieilli(e), suranné(e), vieillot(te)

antique [ænˈtiːk] *n* (*ornament*) objet *m* d'art ancien; (*furniture*) meuble ancien ▷ *adj* ancien(ne); (*pre-mediaeval*) antique

antique dealer *n* antiquaire *m/f*

antique shop *n* magasin *m* d'antiquités

antiquity [ænˈtɪkwɪtɪ] *n* antiquité *f*

anti-Semitic [ˈæntɪsɪˈmɪtɪk] *adj* antisémite

anti-Semitism [ˈæntɪˈsɛmɪtɪzəm] *n* antisémitisme *m*

antiseptic [æntɪˈsɛptɪk] *adj*, *n* antiseptique (*m*)

antisocial [ˈæntɪˈsəʊfəl] *adj* (*unfriendly*) peu liant(e), insociable; (*against society*) antisocial(e)

antitank [æntɪˈtæŋk] *adj* antichar

antithesis (*pl* **antitheses**) [ænˈtɪθɪsɪs, -siːz] *n* antithèse *f*

antitrust [æntɪˈtrʌst] *adj*: ~ **legislation** loi *f* anti-trust

antivirus [æntɪˈvaɪərəs] *adj* antivirus *inv*; ~ **software** (logiciel *m*) antivírus *m*

antlers [ˈæntləz] *npl* bois *mpl*, ramure *f*

Antwerp [ˈæntwəːp] *n* Anvers

anus [ˈeɪnəs] *n* anus *m*

anvil [ˈænvɪl] *n* enclume *f*

anxiety [æŋˈzaɪətɪ] *n* anxiété *f*, (*keenness*): ~ **to do** grand désir *or* impatience *f* de faire

anxious [ˈæŋkʃəs] *adj* (très) inquiet(-ète), (*always worried*) anxieux(-euse); (*worrying*) angoissant(e); (*keen*): ~ **to do/that** qui tient beaucoup à faire/à ce que + *sub*; impatient(e) de faire/que + *sub*; **I'm very ~ about you** je me fais beaucoup de souci pour toi

anxiously [ˈæŋkʃəslɪ] *adv* anxieusement

🔘 **KEYWORD**

any [ˈenɪ] *adj* **1** (*in questions etc*: *singular*) du, de l', de la; (: *plural*) des; **do you have any butter/children/ink?** avez-vous du beurre/des enfants/de l'encre?

2 (*with negative*) de, d'; **I don't have any money/books** je n'ai pas d'argent/de livres; **without any difficulty** sans la moindre difficulté

3 (*no matter which*) n'importe quel(le); (*each and every*) tout(e), chaque; **choose any book you like** vous pouvez choisir n'importe quel livre; **any teacher you ask will tell you** n'importe quel professeur vous le dira

4 (*in phrases*): **in any case** de toute façon; **any day now** d'un jour à l'autre; **at any moment** à tout moment, d'un instant à l'autre; **at any rate** en tout cas; **any time** n'importe quand; **he might come (at) any time** il pourrait venir n'importe quand; **come (at) any time** venez quand vous voulez

▷ *pron* **1** (*in questions etc*) en; **have you got any?** est-ce que vous en avez?; **can any of you sing?**

est-ce que parmi vous il y en a qui savent chanter?

2 (*with negative*) en; **I don't have any (of them)** je n'en ai pas, je n'en ai aucun

3 (*no matter which one(s)*) n'importe lequel (*or* laquelle); (*anybody*) n'importe qui; **take any of those books (you like)** vous pouvez prendre n'importe lequel de ces livres

▷ *adv* **1** (*in questions etc*): **do you want any more soup/sandwiches?** voulez-vous encore de la soupe/des sandwichs?; **are you feeling any better?** est-ce que vous vous sentez mieux?

2 (*with negative*): **I can't hear him any more** je ne l'entends plus; **don't wait any longer** n'attendez pas plus longtemps

anybody [ˈenɪbɔdɪ] *pron* n'importe qui; (*in interrogative sentences*) quelqu'un; (*in negative sentences*): **I don't see ~** je ne vois personne; **if ~ should phone ...** si quelqu'un téléphone ...

anyhow [ˈenɪhaʊ] *adv* quoi qu'il en soit; (*haphazardly*) n'importe comment; **do it ~ you like** faites-le comme vous voulez; **she leaves things just ~** elle laisse tout traîner; **I shall go ~** j'irai de toute façon

anyone [ˈenɪwʌn] *pron* = **anybody**

anyplace [ˈenɪpleɪs] *adv* (*US*) = **anywhere**

anything [ˈenɪθɪŋ] *pron* (*no matter what*) n'importe quoi; (*in questions*) quelque chose; (*with negative*) ne ... rien; **I don't want ~** je ne veux rien; **can you see ~?** tu vois quelque chose?; **if ~ happens to me ...** s'il m'arrive quoi que ce soit ...; **you can say ~ you like** vous pouvez dire ce que vous voulez; **~ will do** n'importe quoi fera l'affaire; **he'll eat ~** il mange de tout; **~ else?** (*in shop*) avec ceci?; **it can cost ~ between £15 and £20** (*Brit*) ça peut coûter n'importe quoi entre 15 et 20 livres

anytime [ˈenɪtaɪm] *adv* (*at any moment*) d'un moment à l'autre; (*whenever*) n'importe quand

anyway [ˈenɪweɪ] *adv* de toute façon; **~, I couldn't come even if I wanted to** de toute façon, je ne pouvais pas venir même si je le voulais; **I shall go ~** j'irai quand même; **why are you phoning, ~?** au fait, pourquoi tu me téléphones?

anywhere [ˈenɪwɛəʳ] *adv* n'importe où; (*in interrogative sentences*) quelque part; (*in negative sentences*): **I can't see him ~** je ne le vois nulle part; **can you see him ~?** tu le vois quelque part?; **put the books down ~** pose les livres n'importe où; **~ in the world** (*no matter where*) n'importe où dans le monde

Anzac [ˈænzæk] *n abbr* (= *Australia-New Zealand Army Corps*) soldat du corps ANZAC

Anzac Day *n voir article*

⬤ **ANZAC DAY**
⬤
⬤ *Anzac Day* est le 25 avril, jour férié en
⬤ Australie et en Nouvelle-Zélande
⬤ commémorant le débarquement des soldats

● du corps "ANZAC" à Gallipoli en 1915,
● pendant la Première Guerre mondiale. Ce
● fut la plus célèbre des campagnes du corps
● "ANZAC".

apart [ə'pɑːt] *adv* (*to one side*) à part; de côté; à
l'écart; (*separately*) séparément; **to take/pull ~**
démonter; **10 miles/a long way ~** à 10 miles/
très éloignés l'un de l'autre; **they are living ~**
ils sont séparés; **~ from** (*prep*) à part, excepté

apartheid [ə'pɑːteɪt] *n* apartheid *m*

apartment [ə'pɑːtmənt] *n* (*US*) appartement *m*,
logement *m*; (*room*) chambre *f*

apartment building *n* (*US*) immeuble *m*;
maison divisée en appartements

apathetic [æpə'θɛtɪk] *adj* apathique,
indifférent(e)

apathy ['æpəθɪ] *n* apathie *f*, indifférence *f*

APB *n abbr* (*US: = all points bulletin*) *expression de la*
police signifiant "découvrir et appréhender le suspect"

ape [eɪp] *n* (grand) singe ▷ *vt* singer

Apennines ['æpənaɪnz] *npl*: **the ~** les Apennins
mpl

aperitif [ə'pɛrɪtɪf] *n* apéritif *m*

aperture ['æpətʃjuə^r] *n* orifice *m*, ouverture *f*;
(*Phot*) ouverture (du diaphragme)

APEX ['eɪpɛks] *n abbr* (*Aviat: = advance purchase*
excursion) APEX *m*

apex ['eɪpɛks] *n* sommet *m*

aphid ['eɪfɪd] *n* puceron *m*

aphrodisiac [æfrəʊ'dɪzɪæk] *adj*, *n*
aphrodisiaque (*m*)

API *n abbr* = **American Press Institute**

apiece [ə'piːs] *adv* (*for each person*) chacun(e), par
tête; (*for each item*) chacun(e), la pièce

aplomb [ə'plɔm] *n* sang-froid *m*, assurance *f*

APO *n abbr* (*US: = Army Post Office*) *service postal de*
l'armée

apocalypse [ə'pɔkəlɪps] *n* apocalypse *f*

apolitical [eɪpə'lɪtɪkl] *adj* apolitique

apologetic [əpɔlə'dʒɛtɪk] *adj* (*tone, letter*)
d'excuse; **to be very ~ about** s'excuser
vivement de

apologetically [əpɔlə'dʒɛtɪkəlɪ] *adv* (*say*) en
s'excusant

apologize [ə'pɔlədʒaɪz] *vi*: **to ~ (for sth to sb)**
s'excuser (de qch auprès de qn), présenter des
excuses (à qn pour qch)

apology [ə'pɔlədʒɪ] *n* excuses *fpl*; **to send one's**
apologies envoyer une lettre *or* un mot
d'excuse, s'excuser (de ne pas pouvoir venir);
please accept my apologies vous voudrez bien
m'excuser

apoplectic [æpə'plɛktɪk] *adj* (*Med*)
apoplectique; (*inf*): **~ with rage** fou (folle) de
rage

apoplexy ['æpəplɛksɪ] *n* apoplexie *f*

apostle [ə'pɔsl] *n* apôtre *m*

apostrophe [ə'pɔstrəfɪ] *n* apostrophe *f*

appal, (*US*) **appall** [ə'pɔːl] *vt* consterner,
atterrer; horrifier

Appalachian Mountains [æpə'leɪʃən-] *npl*: **the**

~ les (monts *mpl*) Appalaches *mpl*

appalling [ə'pɔːlɪŋ] *adj* épouvantable; (*stupidity*)
consternant(e); **she's an ~ cook** c'est une très
mauvaise cuisinière

apparatus [æpə'reɪtəs] *n* appareil *m*, dispositif
m; (*in gymnasium*) agrès *mpl*

apparel [ə'pærl] *n* (*US*) habillement *m*,
confection *f*

apparent [ə'pærənt] *adj* apparent(e); **it is ~**
that il est évident que

apparently [ə'pærəntlɪ] *adv* apparemment

apparition [æpə'rɪʃən] *n* apparition *f*

appeal [ə'piːl] *vi* (*Law*) faire *or* interjeter appel
▷ *n* (*Law*) appel *m*; (*request*) appel; prière *f*;
(*charm*) attrait *m*, charme *m*; **to ~ for** demander
(instamment); implorer; **to ~ to** (*beg*) faire
appel à; (*be attractive*) plaire à; **to ~ to sb for**
mercy implorer la pitié de qn, prier *or* adjurer
qn d'avoir pitié; **it doesn't ~ to me** cela ne
m'attire pas; **right of ~** droit *m* de recours

appealing [ə'piːlɪŋ] *adj* (*attractive*) attrayant(e);
(*touching*) attendrissant(e)

appear [ə'pɪə^r] *vi* apparaître, se montrer; (*Law*)
comparaître; (*publication*) paraître, sortir, être
publié(e); (*seem*) paraître, sembler; **it would ~**
that il semble que; **to ~ in Hamlet** jouer dans
Hamlet; **to ~ on TV** passer à la télé

appearance [ə'pɪərəns] *n* apparition *f*; parution
f; (*look, aspect*) apparence *f*, aspect *m*; **to put in** *or*
make an ~ faire acte de présence; (*Theat*): **by**
order of ~ par ordre d'entrée en scène; **to keep**
up ~s sauver les apparences; **to all ~s** selon
toute apparence

appease [ə'piːz] *vt* apaiser, calmer

appeasement [ə'piːzmənt] *n* (*Pol*)
apaisement *m*

append [ə'pɛnd] *vt* (*Comput*) ajouter (à la fin
d'un fichier)

appendage [ə'pɛndɪdʒ] *n* appendice *m*

appendices [ə'pɛndɪsiːz] *npl of* **appendix**

appendicitis [əpɛndɪ'saɪtɪs] *n* appendicite *f*

appendix (*pl* **appendices**) [ə'pɛndɪks, -siːz] *n*
appendice *m*; **to have one's ~ out** se faire
opérer de l'appendicite

appetite ['æpɪtaɪt] *n* appétit *m*; **that walk has**
given me an ~ cette promenade m'a ouvert
l'appétit

appetizer ['æpɪtaɪzə^r] *n* (*food*) amuse-gueule *m*;
(*drink*) apéritif *m*

appetizing ['æpɪtaɪzɪŋ] *adj* appétissant(e)

applaud [ə'plɔːd] *vt*, *vi* applaudir

applause [ə'plɔːz] *n* applaudissements *mpl*

apple ['æpl] *n* pomme *f*; (*also*: **apple tree**)
pommier *m*; **it's the ~ of my eye** j'y tiens
comme à la prunelle de mes yeux

apple pie *n* tarte *f* aux pommes

apple turnover *n* chausson *m* aux pommes

appliance [ə'plaɪəns] *n* appareil *m*; **electrical**
~s l'électroménager *m*

applicable [ə'plɪkəbl] *adj* applicable; **the law is**
~ from January la loi entre en vigueur au mois
de janvier; **to be ~ to** (*relevant*) valoir pour

applicant ['æplɪkənt] n: ~ **(for)** (Admin: for benefit etc) demandeur(-euse) (de); (for post) candidat(e) (à)

application [æplɪ'keɪʃən] n application f; (for a job, a grant etc) demande f; candidature f; **on** ~ sur demande

application form n formulaire m de demande

application program n (Comput) programme m d'application

applications package n (Comput) progiciel m d'application

applied [ə'plaɪd] adj appliqué(e); ~ **arts** npl arts décoratifs

apply [ə'plaɪ] vt: **to** ~ **(to)** (paint, ointment) appliquer (sur); (law, etc) appliquer (à) ▷ vi: **to** ~ **to** (ask) s'adresser à; (be suitable for, relevant to) s'appliquer à, être valable pour; **to** ~ **(for)** (permit, grant) faire une demande (en vue d'obtenir); (job) poser sa candidature (pour), faire une demande d'emploi (concernant); **to** ~ **the brakes** actionner les freins, freiner; **to** ~ **o.s. to** s'appliquer à

appoint [ə'pɔɪnt] vt (to post) nommer, engager; (date, place) fixer, désigner

appointee [əpɔɪn'tiː] n personne nommée; candidat retenu

appointment [ə'pɔɪntmənt] n (to post) nomination f; (job) poste m; (arrangement to meet) rendez-vous m; **to have an** ~ avoir un rendez-vous; **to make an** ~ **(with)** prendre rendez-vous (avec); **I'd like to make an** ~ je voudrais prendre rendez-vous; **"~s (vacant)"** (Press) "offres d'emploi"; **by** ~ sur rendez-vous

apportion [ə'pɔːʃən] vt (share out) répartir, distribuer; **to** ~ **sth to sb** attribuer or assigner or allouer qch à qn

appraisal [ə'preɪzl] n évaluation f

appraise [ə'preɪz] vt (value) estimer; (situation etc) évaluer

appreciable [ə'priːʃəbl] adj appréciable

appreciably [ə'priːʃəblɪ] adv sensiblement, de façon appréciable

appreciate [ə'priːʃɪeɪt] vt (like) apprécier, faire cas de; (be grateful for) être reconnaissant(e) de; (assess) évaluer; (be aware of) comprendre, se rendre compte de ▷ vi (Finance) prendre de la valeur; **I** ~ **your help** je vous remercie pour votre aide

appreciation [əpriːʃɪ'eɪʃən] n appréciation f; (gratitude) reconnaissance f; (Finance) hausse f, valorisation f

appreciative [ə'priːʃɪətɪv] adj (person) sensible; (comment) élogieux(-euse)

apprehend [æprɪ'hend] vt appréhender, arrêter; (understand) comprendre

apprehension [æprɪ'henʃən] n appréhension f, inquiétude f

apprehensive [æprɪ'hensɪv] adj inquiet(-ète), appréhensif(-ive)

apprentice [ə'prentɪs] n apprenti m ▷ vt: **to be** ~**d to** être en apprentissage chez

apprenticeship [ə'prentɪsʃɪp] n apprentissage

m; **to serve one's** ~ faire son apprentissage

appro. ['æprəu] abbr (Brit Comm: inf) = **approval**

approach [ə'prəutʃ] vi approcher ▷ vt (come near) approcher de; (ask, apply to) s'adresser à; (subject, passer-by) aborder ▷ n approche f; accès m, abord m; démarche f (auprès de qn); démarche f (intellectuelle); **to** ~ **sb about sth** aller or venir voir qn pour qch

approachable [ə'prəutʃəbl] adj accessible

approach road n voie f d'accès

approbation [æprə'beɪʃən] n approbation f

appropriate adj [ə'prəuprɪɪt] (tool etc) qui convient, approprié(e); (moment, remark) opportun(e) ▷ vt [ə'prəuprɪeɪt] (take) s'approprier; (allot): **to** ~ **sth for** affecter qch à; ~ **for** or **to** approprié à; **it would not be** ~ **for me to comment** il ne me serait pas approprié de commenter

appropriately [ə'prəuprɪɪtlɪ] adv pertinemment, avec à-propos

appropriation [əprəuprɪ'eɪʃən] n dotation f, affectation f

approval [ə'pruːvəl] n approbation f; **to meet with sb's** ~ (proposal etc) recueillir l'assentiment de qn; **on** ~ (Comm) à l'examen

approve [ə'pruːv] vt approuver
▶ **approve of** vt fus (thing) approuver; (person): **they don't** ~ **of her** ils n'ont pas bonne opinion d'elle

approved school [ə'pruːvd-] n (Brit) centre m d'éducation surveillée

approvingly [ə'pruːvɪŋlɪ] adv d'un air approbateur

approx. abbr (= approximately) env

approximate [ə'prɔksɪmɪt] adj approximatif(-ive) ▷ vt [ə'prɔksɪmeɪt] se rapprocher de; être proche de

approximately [ə'prɔksɪmətlɪ] adv approximativement

approximation [ə'prɔksɪ'meɪʃən] n approximation f

Apr. abbr = **April**

apr n abbr (= annual percentage rate) taux (d'intérêt) annuel

apricot ['eɪprɪkɔt] n abricot m

April ['eɪprəl] n avril m; ~ **fool!** poisson d'avril!; for phrases see also **July**

April Fools' Day n le premier avril; voir article

● **APRIL FOOLS' DAY**
●
● April Fools' Day est le 1er avril, à l'occasion
● duquel on fait des farces de toutes sortes. Les
● victimes de ces farces sont les "April fools".
● Traditionnellement, on n'est censé faire des
● farces que jusqu'à midi.

apron ['eɪprən] n tablier m; (Aviat) aire f de stationnement

apse [æps] n (Archit) abside f

APT n abbr (Brit: = advanced passenger train) ≈ TGV m

Apt. abbr (= apartment) appt

apt [æpt] *adj (suitable)* approprié(e); *(able)*: ~ **(at)** doué(e) (pour); apte (à); *(likely)*: ~ **to do** susceptible de faire; ayant tendance à faire
aptitude ['æptɪtjuːd] *n* aptitude *f*
aptitude test *n* test *m* d'aptitude
aptly ['æptlɪ] *adv* (fort) à propos
aqualung ['ækwəlʌŋ] *n* scaphandre *m* autonome
aquarium [ə'kwɛərɪəm] *n* aquarium *m*
Aquarius [ə'kwɛərɪəs] *n* le Verseau; **to be ~** être du Verseau
aquatic [ə'kwætɪk] *adj* aquatique; *(sport)* nautique
aqueduct ['ækwɪdʌkt] *n* aqueduc *m*
AR *abbr (US)* = **Arkansas**
ARA *n abbr (Brit)* = **Associate of the Royal Academy**
Arab ['ærəb] *n* Arabe *m/f* ▷ *adj* arabe
Arabia [ə'reɪbɪə] *n* Arabie *f*
Arabian [ə'reɪbɪən] *adj* arabe
Arabian Desert *n* désert *m* d'Arabie
Arabian Sea *n* mer *f* d'Arabie
Arabic ['ærəbɪk] *adj, n* arabe *(m)*
Arabic numerals *npl* chiffres *mpl* arabes
arable ['ærəbl] *adj* arable
ARAM *n abbr (Brit)* = **Associate of the Royal Academy of Music**
arbiter ['ɑːbɪtər] *n* arbitre *m*
arbitrary ['ɑːbɪtrərɪ] *adj* arbitraire
arbitrate ['ɑːbɪtreɪt] *vi* arbitrer; trancher
arbitration [ɑːbɪ'treɪʃən] *n* arbitrage *m*; **the dispute went to ~** le litige a été soumis à arbitrage
arbitrator ['ɑːbɪtreɪtər] *n* arbitre *m*, médiateur(-trice)
ARC *n abbr* = **American Red Cross**
arc [ɑːk] *n* arc *m*
arcade [ɑː'keɪd] *n* arcade *f*; *(passage with shops)* passage *m*, galerie *f*; *(with games)* salle *f* de jeu
arch [ɑːtʃ] *n* arche *f*; *(of foot)* cambrure *f*, voûte *f* plantaire ▷ *vt* arquer, cambrer ▷ *adj* malicieux(-euse) ▷ *prefix*: ~(-) achevé(e); par excellence; **pointed ~** ogive *f*
archaeological [ɑːkɪə'lɔdʒɪkl] *adj* archéologique
archaeologist [ɑːkɪ'ɔlədʒɪst] *n* archéologue *m/f*
archaeology, (US) **archeology** [ɑːkɪ'ɔlədʒɪ] *n* archéologie *f*
archaic [ɑː'keɪɪk] *adj* archaïque
archangel ['ɑːkeɪndʒəl] *n* archange *m*
archbishop [ɑːtʃ'bɪʃəp] *n* archevêque *m*
archenemy ['ɑːtʃ'ɛnɪmɪ] *n* ennemi *m* de toujours *or* par excellence
archeology [ɑːkɪ'ɔlədʒɪ] (US) = **archaeology**
archer ['ɑːtʃər] *n* archer *m*
archery ['ɑːtʃərɪ] *n* tir *m* à l'arc
archetypal ['ɑːkɪtaɪpəl] *adj* archétype
archetype ['ɑːkɪtaɪp] *n* prototype *m*, archétype *m*
archipelago [ɑːkɪ'pɛlɪgəu] *n* archipel *m*
architect ['ɑːkɪtɛkt] *n* architecte *m*
architectural [ɑːkɪ'tɛktʃərəl] *adj* architectural(e)

architecture ['ɑːkɪtɛktʃər] *n* architecture *f*
archive ['ɑːkaɪv] *n (often pl)* archives *fpl*
archive file *n (Comput)* fichier *m* d'archives
archives ['ɑːkaɪvz] *npl* archives *fpl*
archivist ['ɑːkɪvɪst] *n* archiviste *m/f*
archway ['ɑːtʃweɪ] *n* voûte *f*, porche voûté *or* cintré
ARCM *n abbr (Brit)* = **Associate of the Royal College of Music**
Arctic ['ɑːktɪk] *adj* arctique ▷ *n*: **the ~** l'Arctique *m*
Arctic Circle *n* cercle *m* Arctique
Arctic Ocean *n* océan *m* Arctique
ARD *n abbr (US Med)* = **acute respiratory disease**
ardent ['ɑːdənt] *adj* fervent(e)
ardour, (US) **ardor** ['ɑːdər] *n* ardeur *f*
arduous ['ɑːdjuəs] *adj* ardu(e)
are [ɑːr] *vb see* **be**
area ['ɛərɪə] *n (Geom)* superficie *f*; *(zone)* région *f*; (: *smaller*) secteur *m*; *(in room)* coin *m*; *(knowledge, research)* domaine *m*; **the London ~** la région Londonienne
area code (US) *n (Tel)* indicatif *m* de zone
arena [ə'riːnə] *n* arène *f*
aren't [ɑːnt] = **are not**
Argentina [ɑːdʒən'tiːnə] *n* Argentine *f*
Argentinian [ɑːdʒən'tɪnɪən] *adj* argentin(e) ▷ *n* Argentin(e)
arguable ['ɑːgjuəbl] *adj* discutable, contestable; **it is ~ whether** on peut se demander si
arguably ['ɑːgjuəblɪ] *adv*: **it is ~ ...** on peut soutenir que c'est ...
argue ['ɑːgjuː] *vi (quarrel)* se disputer; *(reason)* argumenter ▷ *vt (debate: case, matter)* débattre; **to ~ about sth (with sb)** se disputer (avec qn) au sujet de qch; **to ~ that** objecter *or* alléguer que, donner comme argument que
argument ['ɑːgjumənt] *n (quarrel)* dispute *f*, discussion *f*; *(reasons)* argument *m*; *(debate)* discussion, controverse *f*; **~ for/against** argument pour/contre
argumentative [ɑːgju'mɛntətɪv] *adj* ergoteur(-euse), raisonneur(-euse)
aria ['ɑːrɪə] *n* aria *f*
ARIBA [ə'riːbə] *n abbr (Brit)* = **Associate of the Royal Institute of British Architects**
arid ['ærɪd] *adj* aride
aridity [ə'rɪdɪtɪ] *n* aridité *f*
Aries ['ɛərɪz] *n* le Bélier; **to be ~** être du Bélier
arise (*pt* **arose**, *pp* **-n**) [ə'raɪz, ə'rəuz, ə'rɪzn] *vi* survenir, se présenter; **to ~ from** résulter de; **should the need ~** en cas de besoin
aristocracy [ærɪs'tɔkrəsɪ] *n* aristocratie *f*
aristocrat ['ærɪstəkræt] *n* aristocrate *m/f*
aristocratic [ærɪstə'krætɪk] *adj* aristocratique
arithmetic [ə'rɪθmətɪk] *n* arithmétique *f*
arithmetical [ærɪθ'mɛtɪkl] *adj* arithmétique
Ariz. *abbr (US)* = **Arizona**
ark [ɑːk] *n*: **Noah's A~** l'Arche *f* de Noé
Ark. *abbr (US)* = **Arkansas**

arm [ɑ:m] n bras m ▷ vt armer; **arms** npl
(weapons, Heraldry) armes fpl; ~ **in** ~ bras dessus
bras dessous

armaments ['ɑ:məmənts] npl (weapons)
armement m

armband ['ɑ:mbænd] n brassard m

armchair ['ɑ:mtʃɛəʳ] n fauteuil m

armed [ɑ:md] adj armé(e)

armed forces npl: **the ~** les forces armées

armed robbery n vol m à main armée

Armenia [ɑ:'mi:nɪə] n Arménie f

Armenian [ɑ:'mi:nɪən] adj arménien(ne) ▷ n
Arménien(ne); (Ling) arménien m

armful ['ɑ:mful] n brassée f

armistice ['ɑ:mɪstɪs] n armistice m

armour, (US) **armor** ['ɑ:məʳ] n armure f; (also:
armour-plating) blindage m; (Mil: tanks)
blindés mpl

armoured car, (US) **armored car** ['ɑ:məd-] n
véhicule blindé

armoury, (US) **armory** ['ɑ:mərɪ] n arsenal m

armpit ['ɑ:mpɪt] n aisselle f

armrest ['ɑ:mrɛst] n accoudoir m

arms control n contrôle m des armements

arms race n course f aux armements

army ['ɑ:mɪ] n armée f

A road n (Brit) ≈ route nationale

aroma [ə'rəumə] n arôme m

aromatherapy [ərəumə'θɛrəpɪ] n
aromathérapie f

aromatic [ærə'mætɪk] adj aromatique

arose [ə'rəuz] pt of **arise**

around [ə'raund] adv (tout) autour; (nearby)
dans les parages ▷ prep autour de; (near) près de;
(fig: about) environ; (: date, time) vers; **is he ~?** est-
il dans les parages or là?

arousal [ə'rauzəl] n (sexual) excitation sexuelle,
éveil m

arouse [ə'rauz] vt (sleeper) éveiller; (curiosity,
passions) éveiller, susciter; (anger) exciter

arrange [ə'reɪndʒ] vt arranger; (programme)
arrêter, convenir de ▷ vi: **we have ~d for a car
to pick you up** nous avons prévu qu'une
voiture vienne vous prendre; **it was ~d that ...**
il a été convenu que ..., il a été décidé que ...; **to
~ to do sth** prévoir de faire qch

arrangement [ə'reɪndʒmənt] n arrangement
m; **to come to an ~ (with sb)** se mettre d'accord
(avec qn); **home deliveries by ~** livraison à
domicile sur demande; **arrangements** npl
(plans etc) arrangements mpl, dispositions fpl;
I'll make ~s for you to be met je vous enverrai
chercher

arrant ['ærənt] adj: **he's talking ~ nonsense** il
raconte vraiment n'importe quoi

array [ə'reɪ] n (of objects) déploiement m, étalage
m; (Math, Comput) tableau m

arrears [ə'rɪəz] npl arriéré m; **to be in ~ with
one's rent** devoir un arriéré de loyer, être en
retard pour le paiement de son loyer

arrest [ə'rɛst] vt arrêter; (sb's attention) retenir,
attirer ▷ n arrestation f; **under ~** en état

d'arrestation

arresting [ə'rɛstɪŋ] adj (fig: beauty) saisissant(e);
(: charm, candour) désarmant(e)

arrival [ə'raɪvl] n arrivée f; (Comm) arrivage m;
(person) arrivant(e); **new ~** nouveau venu/
nouvelle venue; (baby) nouveau-né(e)

arrive [ə'raɪv] vi arriver
▶ **arrive at** vt fus (decision, solution) parvenir à

arrogance ['ærəgəns] n arrogance f

arrogant ['ærəgənt] adj arrogant(e)

arrow ['ærəu] n flèche f

arse [ɑ:s] n (Brit inf!) cul m (!)

arsenal ['ɑ:sɪnl] n arsenal m

arsenic ['ɑ:snɪk] n arsenic m

arson ['ɑ:sn] n incendie criminel

art [ɑ:t] n art m; (craft) métier m; **work of ~**
œuvre f d'art; **Arts** npl (Scol) les lettres fpl

art college n école f des beaux-arts

artefact ['ɑ:tɪfækt] n objet fabriqué

arterial [ɑ:'tɪərɪəl] adj (Anat) artériel(le); (road
etc) à grande circulation

artery ['ɑ:tərɪ] n artère f

artful ['ɑ:tful] adj rusé(e)

art gallery n musée m d'art; (saleroom) galerie f
de peinture

arthritis [ɑ:'θraɪtɪs] n arthrite f

artichoke ['ɑ:tɪtʃəuk] n artichaut m; **Jerusalem
~** topinambour m

article ['ɑ:tɪkl] n article m; (Brit Law: training):
articles npl ≈ stage m; **~s of clothing**
vêtements mpl

articles of association npl (Comm) statuts mpl
d'une société

articulate [adj ɑ:'tɪkjulɪt, vb ɑ:'tɪkjuleɪt] adj
(person) qui s'exprime clairement et aisément;
(speech) bien articulé(e), prononcé(e) clairement
▷ vi articuler, parler distinctement ▷ vt
articuler

articulated lorry [ɑ:'tɪkjuleɪtɪd-] n (Brit)
(camion m) semi-remorque m

artifact ['ɑ:tɪfækt] n (US) objet fabriqué

artifice ['ɑ:tɪfɪs] n ruse f

artificial [ɑ:tɪ'fɪʃəl] adj artificiel(le)

artificial insemination [-ɪnsɛmɪ'neɪʃən] n
insémination artificielle

artificial intelligence n intelligence
artificielle

artificial respiration n respiration artificielle

artillery [ɑ:'tɪlərɪ] n artillerie f

artisan ['ɑ:tɪzæn] n artisan(e)

artist ['ɑ:tɪst] n artiste m/f

artistic [ɑ:'tɪstɪk] adj artistique

artistry ['ɑ:tɪstrɪ] n art m, talent m

artless ['ɑ:tlɪs] adj naïf (naïve), simple,
ingénu(e)

arts [ɑ:ts] npl (Scol) lettres fpl

art school n ≈ école f des beaux-arts

artwork ['ɑ:twə:k] n maquette f (prête pour la
photogravure)

ARV n abbr (= American Revised Version) traduction
américaine de la Bible

AS n abbr (US Scol: = Associate in/of Science) diplôme

universitaire ▷ *abbr* (US) = **American Samoa**

🔘 KEYWORD

as [æz] *conj* **1** (*time: moment*) comme, alors que; à mesure que; (: *duration*) tandis que; **he came in as I was leaving** il est arrivé comme je partais; **as the years went by** à mesure que les années passaient; **as from tomorrow** à partir de demain

2 (*since, because*) comme, puisque; **he left early as he had to be home by 10** comme il *or* puisqu'il devait être de retour avant 10h, il est parti de bonne heure

3 (*referring to manner, way*) comme; **do as you wish** faites comme vous voudrez; **as she said** comme elle disait

▷ *adv* **1** (*in comparisons*): **as big as** aussi grand que; **twice as big as** deux fois plus grand que; **big as it is** si grand que ce soit; **much as I like them, I ...** je les aime bien, mais je ...; **as much** *or* **many as** autant que; **as much money/many books as** autant d'argent/de livres que; **as soon as** dès que

2 (*concerning*): **as for** *or* **to that** quant à cela, pour ce qui est de cela

3: **as if** *or* **though** comme si; **he looked as if he was ill** il avait l'air d'être malade; *see also* **long**; **such**; **well**

▷ *prep* (*in the capacity of*) en tant que, en qualité de; **he works as a driver** il travaille comme chauffeur; **as chairman of the company, he ...** en tant que président de la société, il ...; **dressed up as a cowboy** déguisé en cowboy; **he gave me it as a present** il me l'a offert, il m'en a fait cadeau

ASA *n abbr* (= *American Standards Association*) *association de normalisation*

a.s.a.p. *abbr* = **as soon as possible**

asbestos [æz'bestəs] *n* asbeste *m*, amiante *m*

ascend [ə'send] *vt* gravir

ascendancy [ə'sendənsɪ] *n* ascendant *m*

ascendant [ə'sendənt] *n*: **to be in the ~** monter

ascension [ə'senʃən] *n*: **the A~** (*Rel*) l'Ascension *f*

Ascension Island *n* île *f* de l'Ascension

ascent [ə'sent] *n* (*climb*) ascension *f*

ascertain [æsə'teɪn] *vt* s'assurer de, vérifier; établir

ascetic [ə'setɪk] *adj* ascétique

asceticism [ə'setɪsɪzəm] *n* ascétisme *m*

ASCII ['æskiː] *n abbr* (= *American Standard Code for Information Interchange*) ASCII

ascribe [ə'skraɪb] *vt*: **to ~ sth to** attribuer qch à; (*blame*) imputer qch à

ASCU *n abbr* (US) = **Association of State Colleges and Universities**

ASE *n abbr* = **American Stock Exchange**

ASH [æʃ] *n abbr* (Brit: = *Action on Smoking and Health*) *ligue anti-tabac*

ash [æʃ] *n* (*dust*) cendre *f*; (*also*: **ash tree**) frêne *m*

ashamed [ə'ʃeɪmd] *adj* honteux(-euse),

confus(e); **to be ~ of** avoir honte de; **to be ~ (of o.s.) for having done** avoir honte d'avoir fait

ashen ['æʃən] *adj* (*pale*) cendreux(-euse), blême

ashore [ə'ʃɔːʳ] *adv* à terre; **to go ~** aller à terre, débarquer

ashtray ['æʃtreɪ] *n* cendrier *m*

Ash Wednesday *n* mercredi *m* des Cendres

Asia ['eɪʃə] *n* Asie *f*

Asia Minor *n* Asie Mineure

Asian ['eɪʃən] *n* (*from Asia*) Asiatique *m/f*; (Brit: *from Indian subcontinent*) Indo-Pakistanais(-e) ▷ *adj* asiatique; indo-pakistanais(-e)

Asiatic [eɪsɪ'ætɪk] *adj* asiatique

aside [ə'saɪd] *adv* de côté; à l'écart ▷ *n* aparté *m*; **~ from** *prep* à part, excepté

ask [ɑːsk] *vt* demander; (*invite*) inviter; **to ~ sb sth/to do sth** demander à qn qch/de faire qch; **to ~ sb the time** demander l'heure à qn; **to ~ sb about sth** questionner qn au sujet de qch; se renseigner auprès de qn au sujet de qch; **to ~ about the price** s'informer du prix, se renseigner au sujet du prix; **to ~ (sb) a question** poser une question (à qn); **to ~ sb out to dinner** inviter qn au restaurant

▸ **ask after** *vt fus* demander des nouvelles de

▸ **ask for** *vt fus* demander; **it's just ~ing for trouble** *or* **for it** ce serait chercher des ennuis

askance [ə'skɑːns] *adv*: **to look ~ at sb** regarder qn de travers *or* d'un œil désapprobateur

askew [ə'skjuː] *adv* de travers, de guinguois

asking price ['ɑːskɪŋ-] *n* prix demandé

asleep [ə'sliːp] *adj* endormi(e); **to be ~** dormir, être endormi; **to fall ~** s'endormir

ASLEF ['æzlɛf] *n abbr* (Brit: = *Associated Society of Locomotive Engineers and Firemen*) *syndicat de cheminots*

AS level *n abbr* (= *Advanced Subsidiary level*) *première partie de l'examen équivalent au baccalauréat*

asp [æsp] *n* aspic *m*

asparagus [əs'pærəgəs] *n* asperges *fpl*

asparagus tips *npl* pointes *fpl* d'asperges

ASPCA *n abbr* (= *American Society for the Prevention of Cruelty to Animals*) ≈ SPA *f*

aspect ['æspekt] *n* aspect *m*; (*direction in which a building etc faces*) orientation *f*, exposition *f*

aspersions [əs'pəːʃənz] *npl*: **to cast ~ on** dénigrer

asphalt ['æsfælt] *n* asphalte *m*

asphyxiate [æs'fɪksɪeɪt] *vt* asphyxier

asphyxiation [æsfɪksɪ'eɪʃən] *n* asphyxie *f*

aspiration [æspə'reɪʃən] *n* aspiration *f*

aspire [əs'paɪəʳ] *vi*: **to ~ to** aspirer à

aspirin ['æsprɪn] *n* aspirine *f*

aspiring [əs'paɪərɪŋ] *adj* (*artist, writer*) en herbe; (*manager*) potentiel(le)

ass [æs] *n* âne *m*; (*inf*) imbécile *m/f*; (US inf!) cul *m* (!)

assail [ə'seɪl] *vt* assaillir

assailant [ə'seɪlənt] *n* agresseur *m*; assaillant *m*

assassin [ə'sæsɪn] *n* assassin *m*

assassinate [ə'sæsɪneɪt] *vt* assassiner

assassination [əsæsɪ'neɪʃən] *n* assassinat *m*

assault [ə'sɔːlt] *n* (*Mil*) assaut *m*; (*gen: attack*) agression *f*; (*Law*): ~ **(and battery)** voies *fpl* de fait, coups *mpl* et blessures *fpl* ▷ *vt* attaquer; (*sexually*) violenter

assemble [ə'sɛmbl] *vt* assembler ▷ *vi* s'assembler, se rassembler

assembly [ə'sɛmblɪ] *n* (*meeting*) rassemblement *m*; (*parliament*) assemblée *f*; (*construction*) assemblage *m*

assembly language *n* (*Comput*) langage *m* d'assemblage

assembly line *n* chaîne *f* de montage

assent [ə'sɛnt] *n* assentiment *m*, consentement *m* ▷ *vi*: **to** ~ **(to sth)** donner son assentiment (à qch), consentir (à qch)

assert [ə'sɜːt] *vt* affirmer, déclarer; établir; (*authority*) faire valoir; (*innocence*) protester de; **to** ~ **o.s.** s'imposer

assertion [ə'sɜːʃən] *n* assertion *f*, affirmation *f*

assertive [ə'sɜːtɪv] *adj* assuré(e); péremptoire

assess [ə'sɛs] *vt* évaluer, estimer; (*tax, damages*) établir *or* fixer le montant de; (*property etc: for tax*) calculer la valeur imposable de; (*person*) juger la valeur de

assessment [ə'sɛsmənt] *n* évaluation *f*, estimation *f*; (*of tax*) fixation *f*; (*of property*) calcul *m* de la valeur imposable; (*judgment*): ~ **(of)** jugement *m or* opinion *f* (sur)

assessor [ə'sɛsər] *n* expert *m* (*en matière d'impôt et d'assurance*)

asset ['æsɛt] *n* avantage *m*, atout *m*; (*person*) atout; **assets** *npl* (*Comm*) capital *m*; avoir(s) *m(pl)*; actif *m*

asset-stripping ['æsɛt'strɪpɪŋ] *n* (*Comm*) récupération *f* (et démantèlement *m*) d'une entreprise en difficulté

assiduous [ə'sɪdjuəs] *adj* assidu(e)

assign [ə'saɪn] *vt* (*date*) fixer, arrêter; **to** ~ **sth to** (*task*) assigner qch à; (*resources*) affecter qch à; (*cause, meaning*) attribuer qch à

assignment [ə'saɪnmənt] *n* (*task*) mission *f*; (*homework*) devoir *m*

assimilate [ə'sɪmɪleɪt] *vt* assimiler

assimilation [əsɪmɪ'leɪʃən] *n* assimilation *f*

assist [ə'sɪst] *vt* aider, assister; (*injured person etc*) secourir

assistance [ə'sɪstəns] *n* aide *f*, assistance *f*; secours *mpl*

assistant [ə'sɪstənt] *n* assistant(e), adjoint(e); (*Brit: also*: **shop assistant**) vendeur(-euse)

assistant manager *n* sous-directeur *m*

assizes [ə'saɪzɪz] *npl* assises *fpl*

associate [*adj, n* ə'səʊʃɪɪt, *vb* ə'səʊʃɪeɪt] *adj, n* associé(e) ▷ *vt* associer ▷ *vi*: **to** ~ **with sb** fréquenter qn; ~ **director** directeur adjoint; ~**d company** société affiliée

association [əsəʊsɪ'eɪʃən] *n* association *f*; **in** ~ **with** en collaboration avec

association football *n* (*Brit*) football *m*

assorted [ə'sɔːtɪd] *adj* assorti(e); **in** ~ **sizes** en plusieurs tailles

assortment [ə'sɔːtmənt] *n* assortiment *m*; (*of people*) mélange *m*

Asst. *abbr* = **assistant**

assuage [ə'sweɪdʒ] *vt* (*grief, pain*) soulager; (*thirst, appetite*) assouvir

assume [ə'sjuːm] *vt* supposer; (*responsibilities etc*) assumer; (*attitude, name*) prendre, adopter

assumed name [ə'sjuːmd-] *n* nom *m* d'emprunt

assumption [ə'sʌmpʃən] *n* supposition *f*, hypothèse *f*; (*of power*) assomption *f*, prise *f*; **on the** ~ **that** dans l'hypothèse où; (*on condition that*) à condition que

assurance [ə'ʃuərəns] *n* assurance *f*; **I can give you no** ~**s** je ne peux rien vous garantir

assure [ə'ʃuər] *vt* assurer

assured [ə'ʃuəd] *adj* assuré(e)

AST *abbr* (*US*: = *Atlantic Standard Time*) heure d'hiver de New York

asterisk ['æstərɪsk] *n* astérisque *m*

astern [ə'stɜːn] *adv* à l'arrière

asteroid ['æstərɔɪd] *n* astéroïde *m*

asthma ['æsmə] *n* asthme *m*

asthmatic [æs'mætɪk] *adj, n* asthmatique *m/f*

astigmatism [ə'stɪgmətɪzəm] *n* astigmatisme *m*

astir [ə'stɜːr] *adv* en émoi

astonish [ə'stɔnɪʃ] *vt* étonner, stupéfier

astonished [ə'stɔnɪʃd] *adj* étonné(e); **to be** ~ **at** être étonné(e) de

astonishing [ə'stɔnɪʃɪŋ] *adj* étonnant(e), stupéfiant(e); **I find it** ~ **that** ... je trouve incroyable que ... + *sub*

astonishingly [ə'stɔnɪʃɪŋlɪ] *adv* incroyablement

astonishment [ə'stɔnɪʃmənt] *n* (grand) étonnement, stupéfaction *f*

astound [ə'staund] *vt* stupéfier, sidérer

astray [ə'streɪ] *adv*: **to go** ~ s'égarer; (*fig*) quitter le droit chemin; **to lead** ~ (*morally*) détourner du droit chemin; **to go** ~ **in one's calculations** faire fausse route dans ses calculs

astride [ə'straɪd] *adv* à cheval ▷ *prep* à cheval sur

astringent [əs'trɪndʒənt] *adj* astringent(e) ▷ *n* astringent *m*

astrologer [əs'trɔlədʒər] *n* astrologue *m*

astrology [əs'trɔlədʒɪ] *n* astrologie *f*

astronaut ['æstrənɔːt] *n* astronaute *m/f*

astronomer [əs'trɔnəmər] *n* astronome *m*

astronomical [æstrə'nɔmɪkl] *adj* astronomique

astronomy [əs'trɔnəmɪ] *n* astronomie *f*

astrophysics ['æstrəu'fɪzɪks] *n* astrophysique *f*

astute [əs'tjuːt] *adj* astucieux(-euse), malin(-igne)

asunder [ə'sʌndər] *adv*: **to tear** ~ déchirer

ASV *n abbr* (= *American Standard Version*) traduction de la Bible

asylum [ə'saɪləm] *n* asile *m*; **to seek political** ~ demander l'asile politique

asylum seeker [-siːkər] *n* demandeur(-euse) d'asile

asymmetric [eɪsɪ'mɛtrɪk], **asymmetrical**

[eɪsɪ'mɛtrɪkl] *adj* asymétrique

🔵 **KEYWORD**

at [æt] *prep* **1** (*referring to position, direction*) à; **at the top** au sommet; **at home/school** à la maison *or* chez soi/à l'école; **at the baker's** à la boulangerie, chez le boulanger; **to look at sth** regarder qch
2 (*referring to time*): **at 4 o'clock** à 4 heures; **at Christmas** à Noël; **at night** la nuit; **at times** par moments, parfois
3 (*referring to rates, speed etc*) à; **at £1 a kilo** une livre le kilo; **two at a time** deux à la fois; **at 50 km/h** à 50 km/h; **at full speed** à toute vitesse
4 (*referring to manner*): **at a stroke** d'un seul coup; **at peace** en paix
5 (*referring to activity*): **to be at work** (*in the office etc*) être au travail; (*working*) travailler; **to play at cowboys** jouer aux cowboys; **to be good at sth** être bon en qch
6 (*referring to cause*): **shocked/surprised/ annoyed at sth** choqué par/étonné de/agacé par qch; **I went at his suggestion** j'y suis allé sur son conseil
7 (*@ symbol*) arobase *f*

ate [eɪt] *pt of* **eat**
atheism ['eɪθɪɪzəm] *n* athéisme *m*
atheist ['eɪθɪɪst] *n* athée *m/f*
Athenian [ə'θiːnɪən] *adj* athénien(ne) ▷ *n* Athénien(ne)
Athens ['æθɪnz] *n* Athènes
athlete ['æθliːt] *n* athlète *m/f*
athletic [æθ'lɛtɪk] *adj* athlétique
athletics [æθ'lɛtɪks] *n* athlétisme *m*
Atlantic [ət'læntɪk] *adj* atlantique ▷ *n*: **the ~ (Ocean)** l'(océan *m*) Atlantique *m*
atlas ['ætləs] *n* atlas *m*
Atlas Mountains *npl*: **the ~** les monts *mpl* de l'Atlas, l'Atlas *m*
A.T.M. *n abbr* (= *Automated Telling Machine*) guichet *m* automatique
atmosphere ['ætməsfɪə'] *n* (*air*) atmosphère *f*; (*fig: of place etc*) atmosphère, ambiance *f*
atmospheric [ætməs'fɛrɪk] *adj* atmosphérique
atmospherics [ætməs'fɛrɪks] *n* (*Radio*) parasites *mpl*
atoll ['ætɔl] *n* atoll *m*
atom ['ætəm] *n* atome *m*
atom bomb *n* bombe *f* atomique
atomic [ə'tɔmɪk] *adj* atomique
atom bomb *n* bombe *f* atomique
atomizer ['ætəmaɪzə'] *n* atomiseur *m*
atone [ə'təun] *vi*: **to ~ for** expier, racheter
atonement [ə'təunmənt] *n* expiation *f*
ATP *n abbr* (= *Association of Tennis Professionals*) ATP *f* (= *Association des tennismen professionnels*)
atrocious [ə'trəuʃəs] *adj* (*very bad*) atroce, exécrable
atrocity [ə'trɔsɪtɪ] *n* atrocité *f*
atrophy ['ætrəfɪ] *n* atrophie *f* ▷ *vt* atrophier ▷ *vi*

s'atrophier
attach [ə'tætʃ] *vt* (*gen*) attacher; (*document, letter*) joindre; (*employee, troops*) affecter; **to be ~ed to sb/sth** (*to like*) être attaché à qn/qch; **the ~ed letter** la lettre ci-jointe
attaché [ə'tæʃeɪ] *n* attaché *m*
attaché case *n* mallette *f*, attaché-case *m*
attachment [ə'tætʃmənt] *n* (*tool*) accessoire *m*; (*Comput*) fichier *m* joint; (*love*): **~ (to)** affection *f* (pour), attachement *m* (à)
attack [ə'tæk] *vt* attaquer; (*task etc*) s'attaquer à ▷ *n* attaque *f*; **heart ~** crise *f* cardiaque
attacker [ə'tækə'] *n* attaquant *m*; agresseur *m*
attain [ə'teɪn] *vt* (*also*: **to attain to**) parvenir à, atteindre; (*knowledge*) acquérir
attainments [ə'teɪnmənts] *npl* connaissances *fpl*, résultats *mpl*
attempt [ə'tɛmpt] *n* tentative *f* ▷ *vt* essayer, tenter; **~ed theft** *etc* (*Law*) tentative de vol *etc*; **to make an ~ on sb's life** attenter à la vie de qn; **he made no ~ to help** il n'a rien fait pour m'aider *or* l'aider *etc*
attempted [ə'tɛmptɪd] *adj*: **~ murder/suicide** tentative *f* de meurtre/suicide
attend [ə'tɛnd] *vt* (*course*) suivre; (*meeting, talk*) assister à; (*school, church*) aller à, fréquenter; (*patient*) soigner, s'occuper de; **to ~ (up)on** servir; être au service de
▶ **attend to** *vt fus* (*needs, affairs etc*) s'occuper de; (*customer*) s'occuper de, servir
attendance [ə'tɛndəns] *n* (*being present*) présence *f*; (*people present*) assistance *f*
attendant [ə'tɛndənt] *n* employé(e); gardien(ne) ▷ *adj* concomitant(e), qui accompagne *or* s'ensuit
attention [ə'tɛnʃən] *n* attention *f*; **attentions** attentions *fpl*, prévenances *fpl* ▷ *excl* (*Mil*) garde-à-vous!; **at ~** (*Mil*) au garde-à-vous; **for the ~ of** (*Admin*) à l'attention de; **it has come to my ~ that ...** je constate que ...
attentive [ə'tɛntɪv] *adj* attentif(-ive); (*kind*) prévenant(e)
attentively [ə'tɛntɪvlɪ] *adv* attentivement, avec attention
attenuate [ə'tɛnjueɪt] *vt* atténuer ▷ *vi* s'atténuer
attest [ə'tɛst] *vi*: **to ~ to** témoigner de attester (de)
attic ['ætɪk] *n* grenier *m*, combles *mpl*
attire [ə'taɪə'] *n* habit *m*, atours *mpl*
attitude ['ætɪtjuːd] *n* (*behaviour*) attitude *f*, manière *f*; (*posture*) pose *f*, attitude; (*view*): **~ (to)** attitude (envers)
attorney [ə'təːnɪ] *n* (*US: lawyer*) avocat *m*; (*having proxy*) mandataire *m*; **power of ~** procuration *f*
Attorney General *n* (*Brit*) ≈ procureur général; (*US*) ≈ garde *m* des Sceaux, ministre *m* de la Justice
attract [ə'trækt] *vt* attirer
attraction [ə'trækʃən] *n* (*gen pl: pleasant things*) attraction *f*, attrait *m*; (*Physics*) attraction; (*fig: towards sb, sth*) attirance *f*

attractive [ə'træktɪv] *adj* séduisant(e), attrayant(e)

attribute ['ætrɪbjuːt] *n* attribut *m* ▷ *vt* [ə'trɪbjuːt]: **to ~ sth to** attribuer qch à

attrition [ə'trɪʃən] *n*: **war of ~** guerre *f* d'usure

Atty. Gen. *abbr* = **Attorney General**

ATV *n abbr* (= *all terrain vehicle*) véhicule *m* tout-terrain

atypical [eɪ'tɪpɪkl] *adj* atypique

aubergine ['əubəʒiːn] *n* aubergine *f*

auburn ['ɔːbən] *adj* auburn *inv*, châtain roux *inv*

auction ['ɔːkʃən] *n* (*also*: **sale by auction**) vente *f* aux enchères ▷ *vt* (*also*: **to sell by auction**) vendre aux enchères; (*also*: **to put up for auction**) mettre aux enchères

auctioneer [ɔːkʃə'nɪəʳ] *n* commissaire-priseur *m*

auction room *n* salle *f* des ventes

audacious [ɔː'deɪʃəs] *adj* impudent(e); audacieux(-euse), intrépide

audacity [ɔː'dæsɪtɪ] *n* impudence *f*; audace *f*

audible ['ɔːdɪbl] *adj* audible

audience ['ɔːdɪəns] *n* (*people*) assistance *f*, public *m*; (*on radio*) auditeurs *mpl*; (*at theatre*) spectateurs *mpl*; (*interview*) audience *f*

audiovisual [ɔːdɪəu'vɪzjuəl] *adj* audio-visuel(le); **~ aids** supports *or* moyens audiovisuels

audit ['ɔːdɪt] *n* vérification *f* des comptes, apurement *m* ▷ *vt* vérifier, apurer

audition [ɔː'dɪʃən] *n* audition *f* ▷ *vi* auditionner

auditor ['ɔːdɪtəʳ] *n* vérificateur *m* des comptes

auditorium [ɔːdɪ'tɔːrɪəm] *n* auditorium *m*, salle *f* de concert *or* de spectacle

Aug. *abbr* = **August**

augment [ɔːg'mɛnt] *vt*, *vi* augmenter

augur ['ɔːgəʳ] *vt* (*be a sign of*) présager, annoncer ▷ *vi*: **it ~s well** c'est bon signe *or* de bon augure, cela s'annonce bien

August ['ɔːgəst] *n* août *m*; *for phrases see also* **July**

august [ɔː'gʌst] *adj* majestueux(-euse), imposant(e)

aunt [ɑːnt] *n* tante *f*

auntie, aunty ['ɑːntɪ] *n diminutive of* **aunt**

au pair ['əu'pɛəʳ] *n* (*also*: **au pair girl**) jeune fille *f* au pair

aura ['ɔːrə] *n* atmosphère *f*; (*of person*) aura *f*

auspices ['ɔːspɪsɪz] *npl*: **under the ~ of** sous les auspices de

auspicious [ɔːs'pɪʃəs] *adj* de bon augure, propice

austere [ɔs'tɪəʳ] *adj* austère

austerity [ɔs'tɛrɪtɪ] *n* austérité *f*

Australasia [ɔːstrə'leɪzɪə] *n* Australasie *f*

Australia [ɔs'treɪlɪə] *n* Australie *f*

Australian [ɔs'treɪlɪən] *adj* australien(ne) ▷ *n* Australien(ne)

Austria ['ɔstrɪə] *n* Autriche *f*

Austrian ['ɔstrɪən] *adj* autrichien(ne) ▷ *n* Autrichien(ne)

AUT *n abbr* (Brit: = *Association of University Teachers*) *syndicat universitaire*

authentic [ɔː'θɛntɪk] *adj* authentique

authenticate [ɔː'θɛntɪkeɪt] *vt* établir l'authenticité de

authenticity [ɔːθɛn'tɪsɪtɪ] *n* authenticité *f*

author ['ɔːθəʳ] *n* auteur *m*

authoritarian [ɔːθɔrɪ'tɛərɪən] *adj* autoritaire

authoritative [ɔː'θɔrɪtətɪv] *adj* (*account*) digne de foi; (*study, treatise*) qui fait autorité; (*manner*) autoritaire

authority [ɔː'θɔrɪtɪ] *n* autorité *f*; (*permission*) autorisation (formelle); **the authorities** les autorités *fpl*, l'administration *f*; **to have ~ to do sth** être habilité à faire qch

authorization [ɔːθəraɪ'zeɪʃən] *n* autorisation *f*

authorize ['ɔːθəraɪz] *vt* autoriser

authorized capital ['ɔːθəraɪzd-] *n* (*Comm*) capital social

authorship ['ɔːθəʃɪp] *n* paternité *f* (*littéraire etc*)

autistic [ɔː'tɪstɪk] *adj* autistique

auto ['ɔːtəu] *n* (US) auto *f*, voiture *f*

autobiography [ɔːtəbaɪ'ɔgrəfɪ] *n* autobiographie *f*

autocratic [ɔːtə'krætɪk] *adj* autocratique

autograph ['ɔːtəgrɑːf] *n* autographe *m* ▷ *vt* signer, dédicacer

autoimmune [ɔːtəʊɪ'mjuːn] *adj* auto-immune

automat ['ɔːtəmæt] *n* (*vending machine*) distributeur *m* (automatique); (US: *place*) cafétéria *f* avec distributeurs automatiques

automated ['ɔːtəmeɪtɪd] *adj* automatisé(e)

automatic [ɔːtə'mætɪk] *adj* automatique ▷ *n* (*gun*) automatique *m*; (*washing machine*) lave-linge *m* automatique; (*car*) voiture *f* à transmission automatique

automatically [ɔːtə'mætɪklɪ] *adv* automatiquement

automatic data processing *n* traitement *m* automatique des données

automation [ɔːtə'meɪʃən] *n* automatisation *f*

automaton (*pl* **automata**) [ɔː'tɔmətən, -tə] *n* automate *m*

automobile ['ɔːtəməbiːl] *n* (US) automobile *f*

autonomous [ɔː'tɔnəməs] *adj* autonome

autonomy [ɔː'tɔnəmɪ] *n* autonomie *f*

autopsy ['ɔːtɔpsɪ] *n* autopsie *f*

autumn ['ɔːtəm] *n* automne *m*

auxiliary [ɔːg'zɪlɪərɪ] *adj*, *n* auxiliaire (*m/f*)

AV *n abbr* (= *Authorized Version*) *traduction anglaise de la Bible* ▷ *abbr* = **audiovisual**

Av. *abbr* (= *avenue*) Av

avail [ə'veɪl] *vt*: **to ~ o.s. of** user de; profiter de ▷ *n*: **to no ~** sans résultat, en vain, en pure perte

availability [əveɪlə'bɪlɪtɪ] *n* disponibilité *f*

available [ə'veɪləbl] *adj* disponible; **every ~ means** tous les moyens possibles *or* à sa (*or* notre *etc*) disposition; **is the manager ~?** est-ce que le directeur peut (me) recevoir?; (*on phone*) pourrais-je parler au directeur?; **to make sth ~ to sb** mettre qch à la disposition de qn

avalanche ['ævəlɑːnʃ] *n* avalanche *f*

avant-garde ['ævɑ̃ŋ'gɑːd] *adj* d'avant-garde

avaricious [ævə'rɪʃəs] *adj* âpre au gain

avdp. *abbr* = **avoirdupoids**

Ave. *abbr* = **avenue**

avenge [ə'vɛndʒ] *vt* venger

avenue ['ævənjuː] *n* avenue *f*; (*fig*) moyen *m*

average ['ævərɪdʒ] *n* moyenne *f* ▷ *adj* moyen(ne) ▷ *vt* (*a certain figure*) atteindre *or* faire *etc* en moyenne; **on** ~ en moyenne; **above/ below (the)** ~ au-dessus/en-dessous de la moyenne

  ▶ **average out** *vi*: **to** ~ **out at** représenter en moyenne, donner une moyenne de

averse [ə'vəːs] *adj*: **to be** ~ **to sth/doing** éprouver une forte répugnance envers qch/à faire; **I wouldn't be** ~ **to a drink** un petit verre ne serait pas de refus, je ne dirais pas non à un petit verre

aversion [ə'vəːʃən] *n* aversion *f*, répugnance *f*

avert [ə'vəːt] *vt* (*danger*) prévenir, écarter; (*one's eyes*) détourner

aviary ['eɪvɪərɪ] *n* volière *f*

aviation [eɪvɪ'eɪʃən] *n* aviation *f*

avid ['ævɪd] *adj* avide

avidly ['ævɪdlɪ] *adv* avidement, avec avidité

avocado [ævə'kɑːdəu] *n* (*Brit: also:* **avocado pear**) avocat *m*

avoid [ə'vɔɪd] *vt* éviter

avoidable [ə'vɔɪdəbl] *adj* évitable

avoidance [ə'vɔɪdəns] *n* le fait d'éviter

avowed [ə'vaud] *adj* déclaré(e)

AVP *n abbr* (*US*) = **assistant vice-president**

AWACS ['eɪwæks] *n abbr* (= *airborne warning and control system*) AWACS (*système aéroporté d'alerte et de contrôle*)

await [ə'weɪt] *vt* attendre; ~**ing attention/ delivery** (*Comm*) en souffrance; **long** ~**ed** tant attendu(e)

awake [ə'weɪk] (*pt* **awoke** [ə'wəuk] (*pp* **awoken**) [ə'wəukən] *adj* éveillé(e); (*fig*) en éveil ▷ *vt* éveiller ▷ *vi* s'éveiller; ~ **to** conscient de; **to be** ~ être réveillé(e); **he was still** ~ il ne dormait pas encore

awakening [ə'weɪknɪŋ] *n* réveil *m*

award [ə'wɔːd] *n* (*for bravery*) récompense *f*; (*prize*) prix *m*; (*Law: damages*) dommages-intérêts *mpl* ▷ *vt* (*prize*) décerner; (*Law: damages*) accorder

aware [ə'wɛər] *adj*: ~ **of** (*conscious*) conscient(e) de; (*informed*) au courant de; **to become** ~ **of/ that** prendre conscience de/que; se rendre compte de/que; **politically/socially** ~ sensibilisé(e) aux *or* ayant pris conscience des problèmes politiques/sociaux; **I am fully** ~ **that** je me rends parfaitement compte que

awareness [ə'wɛənɪs] *n* conscience *f*, connaissance *f*; **to develop people's** ~ (**of**) sensibiliser le public (à)

awash [ə'wɔʃ] *adj* recouvert(e) (d'eau); ~ **with** inondé(e) de

away [ə'weɪ] *adv* (au) loin; (*movement*): **she went** ~ elle est partie ▷ *adj* (*not in, not here*) absent(e); **far** ~ (au) loin; **two kilometres** ~ à (une

distance de) deux kilomètres, à deux kilomètres de distance; **two hours** ~ **by car** à deux heures de voiture *or* de route; **the holiday was two weeks** ~ il restait deux semaines jusqu'aux vacances; ~ **from** loin de; **he's** ~ **for a week** il est parti (pour) une semaine; **he's** ~ **in Milan** il est (parti) à Milan; **to take sth** ~ **from sb** prendre qch à qn; **to take sth** ~ **from sth** (*subtract*) ôter qch de qch; **to work/pedal** ~ travailler/pédaler à cœur joie; **to fade** ~ (*colour*) s'estomper; (*sound*) s'affaiblir

away game *n* (*Sport*) match *m* à l'extérieur

awe [ɔː] *n* respect mêlé de crainte, effroi mêlé d'admiration

awe-inspiring ['ɔːɪnspaɪərɪŋ], **awesome** ['ɔːsəm] *adj* impressionnant(e)

awesome ['ɔːsəm] (*US*) *adj* (*inf: excellent*) génial(e)

awestruck ['ɔːstrʌk] *adj* frappé(e) d'effroi

awful ['ɔːfəl] *adj* affreux(-euse); **an** ~ **lot of** énormément de

awfully ['ɔːfəlɪ] *adv* (*very*) terriblement, vraiment

awhile [ə'waɪl] *adv* un moment, quelque temps

awkward ['ɔːkwəd] *adj* (*clumsy*) gauche, maladroit(e); (*inconvenient*) peu pratique; (*embarrassing*) gênant; **I can't talk just now, it's a bit** ~ je ne peux pas parler tout de suite, c'est un peu difficile

awkwardness ['ɔːkwədnɪs] *n* (*embarrassment*) gêne *f*

awl [ɔːl] *n* alêne *f*

awning ['ɔːnɪŋ] *n* (*of tent*) auvent *m*; (*of shop*) store *m*; (*of hotel etc*) marquise *f* (de toile)

awoke [ə'wəuk] *pt of* **awake**

awoken [ə'wəukən] *pp of* **awake**

AWOL ['eɪwɔl] *abbr* (*Mil*) = **absent without leave**

awry [ə'raɪ] *adv, adj* de travers; **to go** ~ mal tourner

axe, (*US*) **ax** [æks] *n* hache *f* ▷ *vt* (*employee*) renvoyer; (*project etc*) abandonner; (*jobs*) supprimer; **to have an** ~ **to grind** (*fig*) prêcher pour son saint

axes ['æksiːz] *npl of* **axis**

axiom ['æksɪəm] *n* axiome *m*

axiomatic [æksɪəu'mætɪk] *adj* axiomatique

axis (*pl* **axes**) ['æksɪs, -siːz] *n* axe *m*

axle ['æksl] *n* (*also:* **axle-tree**) essieu *m*

ay, aye [aɪ] *excl* (*yes*) oui ▷ *n*: **the ay(e)s** les oui

AYH *n abbr* = **American Youth Hostels**

AZ (*US*) = **Arizona**

azalea [ə'zeɪlɪə] *n* azalée *f*

Azerbaijan [æzəbaɪ'dʒɑːn] *n* Azerbaïdjan *m*

Azerbaijani, Azeri [æzəbaɪ'dʒɑːnɪ, ə'zɛərɪ] *adj* azerbaïdjanais(e) ▷ *n* Azerbaïdjanais(e)

Azores [ə'zɔːz] *npl*: **the** ~ les Açores *fpl*

AZT *n abbr* (= *azidothymidine*) AZT *f*

Aztec ['æztɛk] *adj* aztèque ▷ *n* Aztèque *m/f*

azure ['eɪʒər] *adj* azuré(e)

Bb

B, b [biː] n (letter) B, b m; (Scol: mark) B; (Mus): **B** si m; **B for Benjamin**, (US) **B for Baker** B comme Berthe; **B road** n (Brit Aut) route départementale

b. abbr = **born**

B.A. abbr = **British Academy**; (Scol) = **Bachelor of Arts**

babble ['bæbl] vi babiller ▷ n babillage m

baboon [bə'buːn] n babouin m

baby ['beɪbɪ] n bébé m

baby carriage n (US) voiture f d'enfant

baby food n aliments mpl pour bébé(s)

baby grand n (also: **baby grand piano**) (piano m) demi-queue m

babyish ['beɪbɪɪʃ] adj enfantin(e), de bébé

baby-minder ['beɪbɪmaɪndə'] n (Brit) gardienne f (d'enfants)

baby-sit ['beɪbɪsɪt] vi garder les enfants

baby-sitter ['beɪbɪsɪtə'] n baby-sitter m/f

baby wipe n lingette f (pour bébé)

bachelor ['bætʃələ'] n célibataire m; **B~ of Arts/Science (BA/BSc)** ≈ licencié(e) ès or en lettres/sciences; **B~ of Arts/Science degree (BA/BSc)** n ≈ licence f ès or en lettres/sciences; voir article

BACHELOR'S DEGREE

Un *Bachelor's degree* est un diplôme accordé après trois ou quatre années d'université. Les *Bachelor's degrees* les plus courants sont le "BA" (Bachelor of Arts), le "BSc" (Bachelor of Science), le "BEd" (Bachelor of Education) et le "LLB" (Bachelor of Laws).

bachelor party n (US) enterrement m de vie de garçon

back [bæk] n (of person, horse) dos m; (of hand) dos, revers m; (of house) derrière m; (of car, train) arrière m; (of chair) dossier m; (of page) verso m; (of crowd): **can the people at the ~ hear me properly?** est-ce que les gens du fond peuvent m'entendre?; (Football) arrière m; **to have one's ~ to the wall** (fig) être au pied du mur; **to break the ~ of a job** (Brit) faire le gros d'un travail; **~ to front** à l'envers ▷ vt (financially) soutenir (financièrement); (candidate: also: **back up**)

soutenir, appuyer; (horse: at races) parier or miser sur; (car) (faire) reculer ▷ vi reculer; (car etc) faire marche arrière ▷ adj (in compounds) de derrière, à l'arrière; **~ seat/wheel** (Aut) siège m/roue f arrière inv; **~ payments/rent** arriéré m de paiements/loyer; **~ garden/room** jardin/pièce sur l'arrière; **to take a ~ seat** (fig) se contenter d'un second rôle, être relégué(e) au second plan ▷ adv (not forward) en arrière; (returned): **he's ~** il est rentré, il est de retour; **when will you be ~?** quand seras-tu de retour?; **he ran ~** il est revenu en courant; (restitution): **throw the ball ~** renvoie la balle; **can I have it ~?** puis-je le ravoir?, peux-tu me le rendre?; (again): **he called ~** il a rappelé

▶ **back down** vi rabattre de ses prétentions

▶ **back on to** vt fus: **the house ~s on to the golf course** la maison donne derrière sur le terrain de golf

▶ **back out** vi (of promise) se dédire

▶ **back up** vt (person) soutenir; (Comput) faire une copie de sauvegarde de

backache ['bækeɪk] n mal m au dos

backbencher [bæk'bentʃə'] (Brit) n membre du parlement sans portefeuille

back benches npl (Brit) voir article

BACK BENCHES

Le terme *back benches* désigne les bancs les plus éloignés de l'allée centrale de la Chambre des communes. Les députés qui occupent ces bancs sont les "backbenchers" et ils n'ont pas de portefeuille ministériel.

backbiting ['bækbaɪtɪŋ] n médisance(s) f(pl)

backbone ['bækbəun] n colonne vertébrale, épine dorsale; **he's the ~ of the organization** c'est sur lui que repose l'organisation

backchat ['bæktʃæt] n (Brit inf) impertinences fpl

backcloth ['bækklɔθ] n (Brit) toile f de fond

backcomb ['bækkəum] vt (Brit) crêper

backdate [bæk'deɪt] vt (letter) antidater; **~d pay rise** augmentation f avec effet rétroactif

back door n porte f de derrière

backdrop ['bækdrɔp] n = **backcloth**

backer ['bækə^r] n partisan m; (Comm) commanditaire m

backfire [bæk'faɪə^r] vi (Aut) pétarader; (plans) mal tourner

backgammon ['bækgæmən] n trictrac m

background ['bækgraund] n arrière-plan m; (of events) situation f, conjoncture f; (basic knowledge) éléments mpl de base; (experience) formation f ▷ cpd (noise, music) de fond; ~ **reading** lecture(s) générale(s) (sur un sujet); **family ~** milieu familial

backhand ['bækhænd] n (Tennis: also: **backhand stroke**) revers m

backhanded ['bæk'hændɪd] adj (fig) déloyal(e); équivoque

backhander ['bæk'hændə^r] n (Brit: bribe) pot-de-vin m

backing ['bækɪŋ] n (fig) soutien m, appui m; (Comm) soutien (financier); (Mus) accompagnement m

backlash ['bæklæʃ] n contre-coup m, répercussion f

backlog ['bæklɔg] n: ~ **of work** travail m en retard

back number n (of magazine etc) vieux numéro

backpack ['bækpæk] n sac m à dos

backpacker ['bækpækə^r] n randonneur(-euse)

back pain n mal m de dos

back pay n rappel m de salaire

backpedal ['bækpɛdl] vi (fig) faire marche arrière

backseat driver ['bæksi:t-] n passager qui donne des conseils au conducteur

backside ['bæksaɪd] n (inf) derrière m, postérieur m

backslash ['bækslæʃ] n barre oblique inversée

backslide ['bækslaɪd] vi retomber dans l'erreur

backspace ['bækspeɪs] vi (in typing) appuyer sur la touche retour

backstage [bæk'steɪdʒ] adv dans les coulisses

back-street ['bækstri:t] adj (abortion) clandestin(e); ~ **abortionist** avorteur(-euse) (clandestin)

backstroke ['bækstrəuk] n dos crawlé

backtrack ['bæktræk] vi (fig) = **backpedal**

backup ['bækʌp] adj (train, plane) supplémentaire, de réserve; (Comput) de sauvegarde ▷ n (support) appui m, soutien m; (Comput: also: **backup file**) sauvegarde f

backward ['bækwəd] adj (movement) en arrière; (measure) rétrograde; (person, country) arriéré(e), attardé(e); (shy) hésitant(e); ~ **and forward movement** mouvement de va-et-vient

backwards ['bækwədz] adv (move, go) en arrière; (read a list) à l'envers, à rebours; (fall) à la renverse; (walk) à reculons; (in time) en arrière, vers le passé; **to know sth ~** or (US) ~ **and forwards** (inf) connaître qch sur le bout des doigts

backwater ['bækwɔ:tə^r] n (fig) coin reculé; bled perdu

backyard [bæk'jɑ:d] n arrière-cour f

bacon ['beɪkən] n bacon m, lard m

bacteria [bæk'tɪərɪə] npl bactéries fpl

bacteriology [bæktɪərɪ'ɔlədʒɪ] n bactériologie f

bad [bæd] adj mauvais(e); (child) vilain(e); (mistake, accident) grave; (meat, food) gâté(e), avarié(e); **his ~ leg** sa jambe malade; **to go ~** (meat, food) se gâter; (milk) tourner; **to have a ~ time of it** traverser une mauvaise passe; **I feel ~ about it** (guilty) j'ai un peu mauvaise conscience; ~ **debt** créance douteuse; **in ~ faith** de mauvaise foi

baddie, baddy ['bædɪ] n (inf: Cine etc) méchant m

bade [bæd] pt of **bid**

badge [bædʒ] n insigne m; (of policeman) plaque f; (stick-on, sew-on) badge m

badger ['bædʒə^r] n blaireau m ▷ vt harceler

badly ['bædlɪ] adv (work, dress etc) mal; **to reflect ~ on sb** donner une mauvaise image de qn; ~ **wounded** grièvement blessé; **he needs it ~** il en a absolument besoin; **things are going ~** les choses vont mal; ~ **off** (adj, adv) dans la gêne

bad-mannered ['bæd'mænəd] adj mal élevé(e)

badminton ['bædmɪntən] n badminton m

bad-mouth ['bæd'mauθ] vt (US inf) débiner

bad-tempered ['bæd'tɛmpəd] adj (by nature) ayant mauvais caractère; (on one occasion) de mauvaise humeur

baffle ['bæfl] vt (puzzle) déconcerter

baffling ['bæflɪŋ] adj déroutant(e), déconcertant(e)

bag [bæg] n sac m; (of hunter) gibecière f, chasse f ▷ vt (inf: take) empocher; s'approprier; (Tech) mettre en sacs; ~s **of** (inf: lots of) des tas de; **to pack one's ~s** faire ses valises or bagages; ~s **under the eyes** poches fpl sous les yeux

bagful ['bægful] n plein sac

baggage ['bægɪdʒ] n bagages mpl

baggage allowance n franchise f de bagages

baggage reclaim n (at airport) livraison f des bagages

baggy ['bægɪ] adj avachi(e), qui fait des poches

Baghdad [bæg'dæd] n Baghdâd, Bagdad

bag lady n (inf) clocharde f

bagpipes ['bægpaɪps] npl cornemuse f

bag-snatcher ['bægsnætʃə^r] n (Brit) voleur m à l'arraché

bag-snatching ['bægsnætʃɪŋ] n (Brit) vol m à l'arraché

Bahamas [bə'hɑːməz] npl: **the ~** les Bahamas fpl

Bahrain [bɑː'reɪn] n BahreÔn m

bail [beɪl] n caution f ▷ vt (prisoner: also: **grant bail to**) mettre en liberté sous caution; (boat: also: **bail out**) écoper; **to be released on ~** être libéré(e) sous caution; see **bale**
▶ **bail out** vt (prisoner) payer la caution de

bailiff ['beɪlɪf] n huissier m

bait [beɪt] n appât m ▷ vt appâter; (fig: tease) tourmenter

bake [beɪk] vt (faire) cuire au four ▷ vi (bread etc) cuire (au four); (make cakes etc) faire de la pâtisserie

baked beans [beɪkt-] *npl* haricots blancs à la sauce tomate

baked potato *n* pomme *f* de terre en robe des champs

baker ['beɪkər] *n* boulanger *m*

bakery ['beɪkərɪ] *n* boulangerie *f*; boulangerie industrielle

baking ['beɪkɪŋ] *n* (*process*) cuisson *f*

baking powder *n* levure *f* (chimique)

baking tin *n* (*for cake*) moule *m* à gâteaux; (*for meat*) plat *m* pour le four

baking tray *n* plaque *f* à gâteaux

balaclava [bælə'klɑ:və] *n* (*also:* **balaclava helmet**) passe-montagne *m*

balance ['bæləns] *n* équilibre *m*; (*Comm: sum*) solde *m*; (*remainder*) reste *m*; (*scales*) balance *f* ▷ *vt* mettre *or* faire tenir en équilibre; (*pros and cons*) peser; (*budget*) équilibrer; (*account*) balancer; (*compensate*) compenser, contrebalancer; **~ of trade/payments** balance commerciale/des comptes *or* paiements; **~ carried forward** solde *m* à reporter; **~ brought forward** solde reporté; **to ~ the books** arrêter les comptes, dresser le bilan

balanced ['bælənst] *adj* (*personality, diet*) équilibré(e); (*report*) objectif(-ive)

balance sheet *n* bilan *m*

balcony ['bælkənɪ] *n* balcon *m*; **do you have a room with a ~?** avez-vous une chambre avec balcon?

bald [bɔ:ld] *adj* chauve; (*tyre*) lisse

baldness ['bɔ:ldnɪs] *n* calvitie *f*

bale [beɪl] *n* balle *f*, ballot *m*
▶ **bale out** *vi* (*of a plane*) sauter en parachute ▷ *vt* (*Naut: water, boat*) écoper

Balearic Islands [bælɪ'ærɪk-] *npl*: **the ~** les (îles *fpl*) Baléares *fpl*

baleful ['beɪlful] *adj* funeste, maléfique

balk [bɔ:k] *vi*: **to ~ (at)** (*person*) regimber (contre); (*horse*) se dérober (devant)

Balkan ['bɔ:lkən] *adj* balkanique ▷ *n*: **the ~s** les Balkans *mpl*

ball [bɔ:l] *n* boule *f*; (*football*) ballon *m*; (*for tennis, golf*) balle *f*; (*dance*) bal *m*; **to play ~** jouer au ballon (*or* à la balle); (*fig*) coopérer; **to be on the ~** (*fig: competent*) être à la hauteur; (*: alert*) être éveillé(e), être vif (vive); **to start the ~ rolling** (*fig*) commencer; **the ~ is in their court** (*fig*) la balle est dans leur camp

ballad ['bæləd] *n* ballade *f*

ballast ['bæləst] *n* lest *m*

ball bearings *n* roulement *m* à billes

ball cock *n* robinet *m* à flotteur

ballerina [bælə'ri:nə] *n* ballerine *f*

ballet ['bæleɪ] *n* ballet *m*; (*art*) danse *f* (classique)

ballet dancer *n* danseur(-euse) de ballet

ballet shoe *n* chausson *m* de danse

ballistic [bə'lɪstɪk] *adj* balistique

ballistics [bə'lɪstɪks] *n* balistique *f*

balloon [bə'lu:n] *n* ballon *m*; (*in comic strip*) bulle *f* ▷ *vi* gonfler

balloonist [bə'lu:nɪst] *n* aéronaute *m/f*

ballot ['bælət] *n* scrutin *m*

ballot box *n* urne (électorale)

ballot paper *n* bulletin *m* de vote

ballpark ['bɔ:lpɑ:k] *n* (*US*) stade *m* de base-ball

ballpark figure *n* (*inf*) chiffre approximatif

ballpoint ['bɔ:lpɔɪnt], **ballpoint pen** *n* stylo *m* à bille

ballroom ['bɔ:lrum] *n* salle *f* de bal

balls [bɔ:lz] *npl* (*inf!*) couilles *fpl* (!)

balm [bɑ:m] *n* baume *m*

balmy ['bɑ:mɪ] *adj* (*breeze, air*) doux (douce); (*Brit inf*) = **barmy**

BALPA ['bælpə] *n abbr* (= *British Airline Pilots' Association*) syndicat des pilotes de ligne

balsa ['bɔ:lsə], **balsa wood** *n* balsa *m*

balsam ['bɔ:lsəm] *n* baume *m*

Baltic [bɔ:ltɪk] *adj, n*: **the ~ (Sea)** la (mer) Baltique

balustrade [bæləs'treɪd] *n* balustrade *f*

bamboo [bæm'bu:] *n* bambou *m*

bamboozle [bæm'bu:zl] *vt* (*inf*) embobiner

ban [bæn] *n* interdiction *f* ▷ *vt* interdire; **he was ~ned from driving** (*Brit*) on lui a retiré le permis (de conduire)

banal [bə'nɑ:l] *adj* banal(e)

banana [bə'nɑ:nə] *n* banane *f*

band [bænd] *n* bande *f*; (*at a dance*) orchestre *m*; (*Mil*) musique *f*, fanfare *f*
▶ **band together** *vi* se liguer

bandage ['bændɪdʒ] *n* bandage *m*, pansement *m* ▷ *vt* (*wound, leg*) mettre un pansement *or* un bandage sur; (*person*) mettre un pansement *or* un bandage à

Band-Aid® ['bændeɪd] *n* (*US*) pansement adhésif

B. & B. *n abbr* = **bed and breakfast**

bandit ['bændɪt] *n* bandit *m*

bandstand ['bændstænd] *n* kiosque *m* (à musique)

bandwagon ['bændwægən] *n*: **to jump on the ~** (*fig*) monter dans *or* prendre le train en marche

bandy ['bændɪ] *vt* (*jokes, insults*) échanger
▶ **bandy about** *vt* employer à tout bout de champ *or* à tort et à travers

bandy-legged ['bændɪ'lɛgɪd] *adj* aux jambes arquées

bane [beɪn] *n*: **it** (*or* **he** *etc*) **is the ~ of my life** c'est (*or* il est *etc*) le drame de ma vie

bang [bæŋ] *n* détonation *f*; (*of door*) claquement *m*; (*blow*) coup (violent) ▷ *vt* frapper (violemment); (*door*) claquer ▷ *vi* détoner; claquer ▷ *adv*: **to be ~ on time** (*Brit inf*) être à l'heure pile; **to ~ at the door** cogner à la porte; **to ~ into sth** se cogner contre qch

banger ['bæŋər] *n* (*Brit: car: also:* **old banger**) (vieux) tacot; (*Brit inf: sausage*) saucisse *f*; (*firework*) pétard *m*

Bangkok [bæŋ'kɔk] *n* Bangkok

Bangladesh [bæŋglə'dɛʃ] *n* Bangladesh *m*

Bangladeshi [bæŋglə'dɛʃɪ] *adj* du Bangladesh ▷ *n* habitant(e) du Bangladesh

bangle ['bæŋgl] n bracelet m
bangs [bæŋz] npl (US: fringe) frange f
banish ['bænɪʃ] vt bannir
banister ['bænɪstə'] n, **banisters** ['bænɪstəz] npl rampe f (d'escalier)
banjo (pl -es or -s) ['bændʒəu] n banjo m
bank [bæŋk] n banque f; (of river, lake) bord m, rive f; (of earth) talus m, remblai m ▷ vi (Aviat) virer sur l'aile; (Comm): **they ~ with Pitt's** leur banque or banquier est Pitt's
  ▶ **bank on** vt fus miser or tabler sur
bank account n compte m en banque
bank balance n solde m bancaire
bank card (Brit) n carte f d'identité bancaire
bank charges npl (Brit) frais mpl de banque
bank draft n traite f bancaire
banker ['bæŋkə'] n banquier m; **~'s card** (Brit) carte f d'identité bancaire; **~'s order** (Brit) ordre m de virement
bank giro n paiement m par virement
bank holiday n (Brit) jour férié (où les banques sont fermées); voir article

  ● **BANK HOLIDAY**
  ●
  ● Le terme bank holiday s'applique au
  ● Royaume-Uni aux jours fériés pendant
  ● lesquels banques et commerces sont fermés.
  ● Les principaux bank holidays à part Noël et
  ● Pâques se situent au mois de mai et fin août,
  ● et contrairement aux pays de tradition
  ● catholique, ne coïncident pas
  ● nécessairement avec une fête religieuse.

banking ['bæŋkɪŋ] n opérations fpl bancaires; profession f de banquier
banking hours npl heures fpl d'ouverture des banques
bank loan n prêt m bancaire
bank manager n directeur m d'agence (bancaire)
banknote ['bæŋknəut] n billet m de banque
bank rate n taux m de l'escompte
bankrupt ['bæŋkrʌpt] n failli(e) ▷ adj en faillite; **to go ~** faire faillite
bankruptcy ['bæŋkrʌptsɪ] n faillite f
bank statement n relevé m de compte
banner ['bænə'] n bannière f
bannister ['bænɪstə'] n, **bannisters** ['bænɪstəz] npl = **banister; banisters**
banns [bænz] npl bans mpl (de mariage)
banquet ['bæŋkwɪt] n banquet m, festin m
bantam-weight ['bæntəmweɪt] n poids m coq inv
banter ['bæntə'] n badinage m
baptism ['bæptɪzəm] n baptême m
Baptist ['bæptɪst] n baptiste m/f
baptize [bæp'taɪz] vt baptiser
bar [ba:'] n (pub) bar m; (counter) comptoir m, bar; (rod: of metal etc) barre f; (of window etc) barreau m; (of chocolate) tablette f, plaque f; (fig: obstacle) obstacle m; (prohibition) mesure f d'exclusion;

(Mus) mesure f ▷ vt (road) barrer; (window) munir de barreaux; (person) exclure; (activity) interdire; **~ of soap** savonnette f; **behind ~s** (prisoner) derrière les barreaux; **the B~** (Law) le barreau; **~ none** sans exception
Barbados [ba:'beɪdɔs] n Barbade f
barbaric [ba:'bærɪk] adj barbare
barbarous ['ba:bərəs] adj barbare, cruel(le)
barbecue ['ba:bɪkju:] n barbecue m
barbed wire ['ba:bd-] n fil m de fer barbelé
barber ['ba:bə'] n coiffeur m (pour hommes)
barber's ['ba:bə'z], **barber's shop**, (US) **barber shop** n salon m de coiffure (pour hommes); **to go to the barber's** aller chez le coiffeur
barbiturate [ba:'bɪtjurɪt] n barbiturique m
Barcelona [ba:sə'ləunə] n Barcelone f
bar chart n diagramme m en bâtons
bar code n code m à barres, code-barre m
bare [bɛə'] adj nu(e) ▷ vt mettre à nu, dénuder; (teeth) montrer; **the ~ essentials** le strict nécessaire
bareback ['bɛəbæk] adv à cru, sans selle
barefaced ['bɛəfeɪst] adj impudent(e), effronté(e)
barefoot ['bɛəfut] adj, adv nu-pieds, (les) pieds nus
bareheaded [bɛə'hɛdɪd] adj, adv nu-tête, (la) tête nue
barely ['bɛəlɪ] adv à peine
Barents Sea ['bærənts-] n: **the ~** la mer de Barents
bargain ['ba:gɪn] n (transaction) marché m; (good buy) affaire f, occasion f ▷ vi (haggle) marchander; (negotiate) négocier, traiter; **into the ~** par-dessus le marché
  ▶ **bargain for** vt fus (inf): **he got more than he ~ed for!** il en a eu pour son argent!
bargaining ['ba:gənɪŋ] n marchandage m; négociations fpl
bargaining position n: **to be in a weak/strong ~** être en mauvaise/bonne position pour négocier
barge [ba:dʒ] n péniche f
  ▶ **barge in** vi (walk in) faire irruption; (interrupt talk) intervenir mal à propos
  ▶ **barge into** vt fus rentrer dans
baritone ['bærɪtəun] n baryton m
barium meal ['bɛərɪəm-] n (bouillie f de) sulfate m de baryum
bark [ba:k] n (of tree) écorce f; (of dog) aboiement m ▷ vi aboyer
barley ['ba:lɪ] n orge f
barley sugar n sucre m d'orge
barmaid ['ba:meɪd] n serveuse f (de bar), barmaid f
barman ['ba:mən] (irreg) n serveur m (de bar), barman m
bar meal n repas m de bistrot; **to go for a ~** aller manger au bistrot
barmy ['ba:mɪ] adj (Brit inf) timbré(e), cinglé(e)
barn [ba:n] n grange f
barnacle ['ba:nəkl] n anatife m, bernache f
barn owl n chouette-effraie f, chat-huant m

barometer [bəˈrɔmɪtəʳ] *n* baromètre *m*
baron [ˈbærən] *n* baron *m*; **the press/oil ~s** les magnats *mpl or* barons *mpl* de la presse/du pétrole
baroness [ˈbærənɪs] *n* baronne *f*
barrack [ˈbærək] *vt* (*Brit*) chahuter
barracking [ˈbærəkɪŋ] *n* (*Brit*): **to give sb a ~** chahuter qn
barracks [ˈbærəks] *npl* caserne *f*
barrage [ˈbærɑːʒ] *n* (*Mil*) tir *m* de barrage; (*dam*) barrage *m*; (*of criticism*) feu *m*
barrel [ˈbærəl] *n* tonneau *m*; (*of gun*) canon *m*
barrel organ *n* orgue *m* de Barbarie
barren [ˈbærən] *adj* stérile; (*hills*) aride
barrette [bəˈrɛt] (*US*) *n* barrette *f*
barricade [bærɪˈkeɪd] *n* barricade *f* ▷ *vt* barricader
barrier [ˈbærɪəʳ] *n* barrière *f*; (*Brit: also*: **crash barrier**) rail *m* de sécurité
barrier cream *n* (*Brit*) crème protectrice
barring [ˈbɑːrɪŋ] *prep* sauf
barrister [ˈbærɪstəʳ] *n* (*Brit*) avocat (plaidant); *voir article*

⬤ **BARRISTER**
⬤
⬤ En Angleterre, un *barrister*, que l'on appelle
⬤ également "barrister-at-law", est un avocat
⬤ qui représente ses clients devant la cour et
⬤ plaide pour eux. Le client doit d'abord passer
⬤ par l'intermédiaire d'un "solicitor". On
⬤ obtient le diplôme de *barrister* après avoir fait
⬤ des études dans l'une des "Inns of Court", les
⬤ quatre écoles de droit londoniennes.

barrow [ˈbærəu] *n* (*cart*) charrette *f* à bras
barstool [ˈbɑːstuːl] *n* tabouret *m* de bar
Bart. *abbr* = **baronet**
bartender [ˈbɑːtɛndəʳ] *n* (*US*) serveur *m* (*de bar*), barman *m*
barter [ˈbɑːtəʳ] *n* échange *m*, troc *m* ▷ *vt*: **to ~ sth for** échanger qch contre
base [beɪs] *n* base *f* ▷ *vt* (*troops*): **to be ~d at** être basé(e) à; (*opinion, belief*): **to ~ sth on** baser *or* fonder qch sur ▷ *adj* vil(e), bas(se); **coffee-~d** à base de café; **a Paris-~d firm** une maison opérant de Paris *or* dont le siège est à Paris; **I'm ~d in London** je suis basé(e) à Londres
baseball [ˈbeɪsbɔːl] *n* base-ball *m*
baseball cap *n* casquette *f* de base-ball
baseboard [ˈbeɪsbɔːd] *n* (*US*) plinthe *f*
base camp *n* camp *m* de base
Basel [bɑːl] *n* = **Basle**
baseline [ˈbeɪslaɪn] *n* (*Tennis*) ligne *f* de fond
basement [ˈbeɪsmənt] *n* sous-sol *m*
base rate *n* taux *m* de base
bases [ˈbeɪsiːz] *npl of* **basis** [ˈbeɪsɪz] ▷ *npl of* **base**
bash [bæʃ] *vt* (*inf*) frapper, cogner ▷ *n*: **I'll have a ~ (at it)** (*Brit inf*) je vais essayer un coup; **~ed in** *adj* enfoncé(e), défoncé(e)
▶ **bash up** *vt* (*inf: car*) bousiller; (: *Brit: person*) tabasser

bashful [ˈbæʃful] *adj* timide; modeste
bashing [ˈbæʃɪŋ] *n* (*inf*) raclée *f*; **Paki-~** ≈ ratonnade *f*; **queer-~** chasse *f* aux pédés
BASIC [ˈbeɪsɪk] *n* (*Comput*) BASIC *m*
basic [ˈbeɪsɪk] *adj* (*precautions, rules*) élémentaire; (*principles, research*) fondamental(e); (*vocabulary, salary*) de base; (*minimal*) réduit(e) au minimum, rudimentaire
basically [ˈbeɪsɪklɪ] *adv* (*in fact*) en fait; (*essentially*) fondamentalement
basic rate *n* (*of tax*) première tranche d'imposition
basics [ˈbeɪsɪks] *npl*: **the ~** l'essentiel *m*
basil [ˈbæzl] *n* basilic *m*
basin [ˈbeɪsn] *n* (*vessel, also Geo*) cuvette *f*, bassin *m*; (*Brit: for food*) bol *m*; (: *bigger*) saladier *m*; (*also:* **washbasin**) lavabo *m*
basis (*pl* **bases**) [ˈbeɪsɪs, -siːz] *n* base *f*; **on a part-time/trial ~** à temps partiel/à l'essai; **on the ~ of what you've said** d'après *or* compte tenu de ce que vous dites
bask [bɑːsk] *vi*: **to ~ in the sun** se chauffer au soleil
basket [ˈbɑːskɪt] *n* corbeille *f*; (*with handle*) panier *m*
basketball [ˈbɑːskɪtbɔːl] *n* basket-ball *m*
basketball player *n* basketteur(-euse)
Basle [bɑːl] *n* Bâle
basmati rice [bəzˈmætɪ-] *n* riz *m* basmati
Basque [bæsk] *adj* basque ▷ *n* Basque *m/f*; **the ~ Country** le Pays basque
bass [beɪs] *n* (*Mus*) basse *f*
bass clef *n* clé *f* de fa
bass drum *n* grosse caisse *f*
bassoon [bəˈsuːn] *n* basson *m*
bastard [ˈbɑːstəd] *n* enfant naturel(le), bâtard(e); (*inf!*) salaud *m* (!)
baste [beɪst] *vt* (*Culin*) arroser; (*Sewing*) bâtir, faufiler
bat [bæt] *n* chauve-souris *f*; (*for baseball etc*) batte *f*; (*Brit: for table tennis*) raquette *f* ▷ *vt*: **he didn't ~ an eyelid** il n'a pas sourcillé *or* bronché; **off one's own ~** de sa propre initiative
batch [bætʃ] *n* (*of bread*) fournée *f*; (*of papers*) liasse *f*; (*of applicants, letters*) paquet *m*; (*of work*) monceau *m*; (*of goods*) lot *m*
bated [ˈbeɪtɪd] *adj*: **with ~ breath** en retenant son souffle
bath (*pl* **-s**) [bɑːθ, bɑːðz] *n* bain *m*; (*bathtub*) baignoire *f* ▷ *vt* baigner, donner un bain à; **to have a ~** prendre un bain; *see also* **baths**
bathe [beɪð] *vi* se baigner ▷ *vt* baigner; (*wound etc*) laver
bather [ˈbeɪðəʳ] *n* baigneur(-euse)
bathing [ˈbeɪðɪŋ] *n* baignade *f*
bathing cap *n* bonnet *m* de bain
bathing costume, (*US*) **bathing suit** *n* maillot *m* (de bain)
bathmat [ˈbɑːθmæt] *n* tapis *m* de bain
bathrobe [ˈbɑːθrəub] *n* peignoir *m* de bain
bathroom [ˈbɑːθrum] *n* salle *f* de bains
baths [bɑːðz] *npl* (*Brit: also*: **swimming baths**)

piscine f

bath towel n serviette f de bain

bathtub [ˈbɑːθtʌb] n baignoire f

batman [ˈbætmən] (irreg) n (Brit Mil) ordonnance f

baton [ˈbætən] n bâton m; (Mus) baguette f; (club) matraque f

battalion [bəˈtælɪən] n bataillon m

batten [ˈbætn] n (Carpentry) latte f; (Naut: on sail) latte de voile

▶ **batten down** vt (Naut): **to ~ down the hatches** fermer les écoutilles

batter [ˈbætəʳ] vt battre ▷ n pâte f à frire

battered [ˈbætəd] adj (hat, pan) cabossé(e); **~ wife/child** épouse/enfant maltraité(e) or martyr(e)

battering ram [ˈbætərɪŋ-] n bélier m; (fig)

battery [ˈbætərɪ] n (for torch, radio) pile f; (Aut, Mil) batterie f

battery charger n chargeur m

battery farming n élevage m en batterie

battle [ˈbætl] n bataille f, combat m ▷ vi se battre, lutter; **that's half the ~** (fig) c'est déjà bien; **it's a** or **we're fighting a losing ~** (fig) c'est perdu d'avance, c'est peine perdue

battle dress n tenue f de campagne or d'assaut

battlefield [ˈbætlfiːld] n champ m de bataille

battlements [ˈbætlmənts] npl remparts mpl

battleship [ˈbætlʃɪp] n cuirassé m

batty [ˈbætɪ] adj (inf: person) toqué(e); (: idea, behaviour) loufoque

bauble [ˈbɔːbl] n babiole f

baulk [bɔːlk] vi = **balk**

bauxite [ˈbɔːksaɪt] n bauxite f

Bavaria [bəˈvɛərɪə] n Bavière f

Bavarian [bəˈvɛərɪən] adj bavarois(e) ▷ n Bavarois(e)

bawdy [ˈbɔːdɪ] adj paillard(e)

bawl [bɔːl] vi hurler, brailler

bay [beɪ] n (of sea) baie f; (Brit: for parking) place f de stationnement; (: for loading) aire f de chargement; (horse) bai(e) m/f; **B~ of Biscay** golfe m de Gascogne; **to hold sb at ~** tenir qn à distance or en échec

bay leaf n laurier m

bayonet [ˈbeɪənɪt] n baïonnette f

bay tree n laurier m

bay window n baie vitrée

bazaar [bəˈzɑːʳ] n (shop, market) bazar m; (sale) vente f de charité

bazooka [bəˈzuːkə] n bazooka m

BB n abbr (Brit: = Boys' Brigade) mouvement de garçons

BBB n abbr (US: = Better Business Bureau) organisme de défense du consommateur

BBC n abbr (= British Broadcasting Corporation) office de la radiodiffusion et télévision britannique; voir article

BBC

La BBC est un organisme centralisé dont les membres, nommés par l'État, gèrent les chaînes de télévision publiques (BBC1, qui présente des émissions d'intérêt général, et BBC2, qui est plutôt orientée vers les émissions plus culturelles, et les chaînes numériques) et les stations de radio publiques. Bien que non contrôlée par l'État, la BBC est responsable devant le "Parliament" quant au contenu des émissions qu'elle diffuse. Par ailleurs, la BBC offre un service mondial de diffusion d'émissions, en anglais et dans 43 autres langues, appelé "BBC World Service". La BBC est financée par la redevance télévision et par l'exportation d'émissions.

B.C. adv abbr (= before Christ) av. J.-C. ▷ abbr (Canada) = **British Columbia**

BCG n abbr (= Bacillus Calmette-Guérin) BCG m

BD n abbr (= Bachelor of Divinity) diplôme universitaire

B/D abbr = **bank draft**

BDS n abbr (= Bachelor of Dental Surgery) diplôme universitaire

◯ KEYWORD

be [biː] (pt **was, were**, pp **been**) aux vb **1** (with present participle: forming continuous tenses): **what are you doing?** que faites-vous?; **they're coming tomorrow** ils viennent demain; **I've been waiting for you for 2 hours** je t'attends depuis 2 heures

2 (with pp: forming passives) être; **to be killed** être tué(e); **the box had been opened** la boîte avait été ouverte; **he was nowhere to be seen** on ne le voyait nulle part

3 (in tag questions): **it was fun, wasn't it?** c'était drôle, n'est-ce pas?; **he's good-looking, isn't he?** il est beau, n'est-ce pas?; **she's back, is she?** elle est rentrée, n'est-ce pas or alors?

4 (+to +infinitive): **the house is to be sold** (necessity) la maison doit être vendue; (future) la maison va être vendue; **he's not to open it** il ne doit pas l'ouvrir; **am I to understand that ...?** dois-je comprendre que ...?; **he was to have come yesterday** il devait venir hier

5 (possibility, supposition): **if I were you, I ...** à votre place, je ..., si j'étais vous, je ...

▷ vb + complement **1** (gen) être; **I'm English** je suis anglais(e); **I'm tired** je suis fatigué(e); **I'm hot/cold** j'ai chaud/froid; **he's a doctor** il est médecin; **be careful/good/quiet!** faites attention/soyez sages/taisez-vous!; **2 and 2 are 4** 2 et 2 font 4

2 (of health) aller; **how are you?** comment allez-vous?; **I'm better now** je vais mieux maintenant; **he's fine now** il va bien maintenant; **he's very ill** il est très malade

3 (of age) avoir; **how old are you?** quel âge avez-vous?; **I'm sixteen (years old)** j'ai seize ans

4 (cost) coûter; **how much was the meal?** combien a coûté le repas?; **that'll be £5, please** ça fera 5 livres, s'il vous plaît; **this shirt is £17** cette chemise coûte 17 livres

▷ vi **1** (*exist, occur etc*) être, exister; **the prettiest girl that ever was** la fille la plus jolie qui ait jamais existé; **is there a God?** y a-t-il un dieu?; **be that as it may** quoi qu'il en soit; **so be it** soit

2 (*referring to place*) être, se trouver; **I won't be here tomorrow** je ne serai pas là demain; **Edinburgh is in Scotland** Édimbourg est or se trouve en Écosse

3 (*referring to movement*) aller; **where have you been?** où êtes-vous allé(s)?

▷ impers vb **1** (*referring to time*) être; **it's 5 o'clock** il est 5 heures; **it's the 28th of April** c'est le 28 avril

2 (*referring to distance*): **it's 10 km to the village** le village est à 10 km

3 (*referring to the weather*) faire; **it's too hot/cold** il fait trop chaud/froid; **it's windy today** il y a du vent aujourd'hui

4 (*emphatic*): **it's me/the postman** c'est moi/le facteur; **it was Maria who paid the bill** c'est Maria qui a payé la note

B/E *abbr* = **bill of exchange**
beach [biːtʃ] *n* plage *f* ▷ *vt* échouer
beachcomber ['biːtʃkəʊməʳ] *n* ramasseur *m* d'épaves; (*fig*) bon(-ne) *m/f* à rien
beachwear ['biːtʃwɛəʳ] *n* tenues *fpl* de plage
beacon ['biːkən] *n* (*lighthouse*) fanal *m*; (*marker*) balise *f*; (*also*: **radio beacon**) radiophare *m*
bead [biːd] *n* perle *f*; (*of dew, sweat*) goutte *f*; **beads** *npl* (*necklace*) collier *m*
beady ['biːdɪ] *adj*: **~ eyes** yeux *mpl* de fouine
beagle ['biːgl] *n* beagle *m*
beak [biːk] *n* bec *m*
beaker ['biːkəʳ] *n* gobelet *m*
beam [biːm] *n* (*Archit*) poutre *f*; (*of light*) rayon *m*; (*Radio*) faisceau *m* radio ▷ *vi* rayonner; **to drive on full** or **main** or (*US*) **high ~** rouler en pleins phares
beaming ['biːmɪŋ] *adj* (*sun, smile*) radieux(-euse)
bean [biːn] *n* haricot *m*; (*of coffee*) grain *m*
beanpole ['biːnpəʊl] *n* (*inf*) perche *f*
beansprouts ['biːnsprauts] *npl* pousses *fpl* or germes *mpl* de soja
bear [bɛəʳ] (*pt* **bore**, *pp* **borne**) [bɔːʳ, bɔːn] *n* ours *m*; (*Stock Exchange*) baissier *m* ▷ *vt* porter; (*endure*) supporter; (*traces, signs*) porter; (*Comm: interest*) rapporter ▷ *vi*: **to ~ right/left** obliquer à droite/gauche, se diriger vers la droite/gauche; **to ~ the responsibility of** assumer la responsabilité de; **to ~ comparison with** soutenir la comparaison avec; **I can't ~ him** je ne peux pas le supporter or souffrir; **to bring pressure to ~ on sb** faire pression sur qn
▶ **bear out** *vt* (*theory, suspicion*) confirmer
▶ **bear up** *vi* supporter, tenir le coup; **he bore up well** il a tenu le coup
▶ **bear with** *vt fus* (*sb's moods, temper*) supporter; **~ with me a minute** un moment, s'il vous plaît
bearable ['bɛərəbl] *adj* supportable
beard [bɪəd] *n* barbe *f*

bearded ['bɪədɪd] *adj* barbu(e)
bearer ['bɛərəʳ] *n* porteur *m*; (*of passport etc*) titulaire *m/f*
bearing ['bɛərɪŋ] *n* maintien *m*, allure *f*; (*connection*) rapport *m*; (*Tech*): **(ball) bearings** *npl* roulement *m* (à billes); **to take a ~** faire le point; **to find one's ~s** s'orienter
beast [biːst] *n* bête *f*; (*inf: person*) brute *f*
beastly ['biːstlɪ] *adj* infect(e)
beat [biːt] *n* battement *m*; (*Mus*) temps *m*, mesure *f*; (*of policeman*) ronde *f* ▷ *vt*, *vi* (*pt* **-**, *pp* **-en**) battre; **off the ~en track** hors des chemins or sentiers battus; **to ~ it** (*inf*) ficher le camp; **to ~ about the bush** tourner autour du pot; **that ~s everything!** c'est le comble!
▶ **beat down** *vt* (*door*) enfoncer; (*price*) faire baisser; (*seller*) faire descendre ▷ *vi* (*rain*) tambouriner; (*sun*) taper
▶ **beat off** *vt* repousser
▶ **beat up** *vt* (*eggs*) battre; (*inf: person*) tabasser
beater ['biːtəʳ] *n* (*for eggs, cream*) fouet *m*, batteur *m*
beating ['biːtɪŋ] *n* raclée *f*
beat-up ['biːt'ʌp] *adj* (*inf*) déglingué(e)
beautician [bjuː'tɪʃən] *n* esthéticien(ne)
beautiful ['bjuːtɪful] *adj* beau (belle)
beautifully ['bjuːtɪflɪ] *adv* admirablement
beautify ['bjuːtɪfaɪ] *vt* embellir
beauty ['bjuːtɪ] *n* beauté *f*; **the ~ of it is that …** le plus beau, c'est que …
beauty contest *n* concours *m* de beauté
beauty parlour, (*US*) **beauty parlor** [-'pɑːləʳ] *n* institut *m* de beauté
beauty queen *n* reine *f* de beauté
beauty salon *n* institut *m* de beauté
beauty sleep *n*: **I need my ~** j'ai besoin de faire un gros dodo
beauty spot *n* (*on skin*) grain *m* de beauté; (*Brit Tourism*) site naturel (d'une grande beauté)
beaver ['biːvəʳ] *n* castor *m*
becalmed [bɪ'kɑːmd] *adj* immobilisé(e) par le calme plat
became [bɪ'keɪm] *pt of* **become**
because [bɪ'kɔz] *conj* parce que; **~ of** (*prep*) à cause de
beck [bɛk] *n*: **to be at sb's ~ and call** être à l'entière disposition de qn
beckon ['bɛkən] *vt* (*also*: **beckon to**) faire signe (de venir) à
become [bɪ'kʌm] *vi* devenir; **to ~ fat/thin** grossir/maigrir; **to ~ angry** se mettre en colère; **it became known that** on apprit que; **what has ~ of him?** qu'est-il devenu?
becoming [bɪ'kʌmɪŋ] *adj* (*behaviour*) convenable, bienséant(e); (*clothes*) seyant(e)
BECTU ['bɛktu] *n abbr* (*Brit*) = **Broadcasting, Entertainment, Cinematographic and Theatre Union**
BEd *n abbr* (= *Bachelor of Education*) diplôme d'aptitude à l'enseignement
bed [bɛd] *n* lit *m*; (*of flowers*) parterre *m*; (*of coal, clay*) couche *f*; (*of sea, lake*) fond *m*; **to go to ~**

aller se coucher
▶ **bed down** vi se coucher
bed and breakfast n (terms) chambre et petit
déjeuner; (place) ≈ chambre f d'hôte; voir article

● **BED AND BREAKFAST**
●
● Un bed and breakfast est une petite pension
● dans une maison particulière ou une ferme
● où l'on peut louer une chambre avec petit
● déjeuner compris pour un prix modique par
● rapport à ce que l'on paierait dans un hôtel.
● Ces établissements sont communément
● appelés "B & B", et sont signalés par une
● pancarte dans le jardin ou au-dessus de la
● porte.

bedbug ['bɛdbʌg] n punaise f
bedclothes ['bɛdkləuðz] npl couvertures fpl et
draps mpl
bedcover ['bɛdkʌvəʳ] n couvre-lit m, dessus-de-
lit m
bedding ['bɛdɪŋ] n literie f
bedevil [bɪ'dɛvl] vt (harass) harceler; **to be ~led
by** être victime de
bedfellow ['bɛdfɛləu] n: **they are strange ~s**
(fig) ça fait un drôle de mélange
bedlam ['bɛdləm] n chahut m, cirque m
bed linen n draps mpl de lit (et taies fpl
d'oreillers), literie f
bedpan ['bɛdpæn] n bassin m (hygiénique)
bedpost ['bɛdpəust] n colonne f de lit
bedraggled [bɪ'drægld] adj dépenaillé(e), les
vêtements en désordre
bedridden ['bɛdrɪdn] adj cloué(e) au lit
bedrock ['bɛdrɔk] n (fig) principes essentiels or
de base, essentiel m; (Geo) roche f en place,
socle m
bedroom ['bɛdrum] n chambre f (à coucher)
Beds abbr (Brit) = **Bedfordshire**
bed settee n canapé-lit m
bedside ['bɛdsaɪd] n: **at sb's ~** au chevet de qn
▷ cpd (book, lamp) de chevet
bedside lamp n lampe f de chevet
bedside table n table f de chevet
bedsit ['bɛdsɪt], **bedsitter** ['bɛdsɪtəʳ] n (Brit)
chambre meublée, studio m
bedspread ['bɛdsprɛd] n couvre-lit m, dessus-
de-lit m
bedtime ['bɛdtaɪm] n: **it's ~** c'est l'heure de se
coucher
bee [bi:] n abeille f; **to have a ~ in one's bonnet
(about sth)** être obnubilé(e) (par qch)
beech [bi:tʃ] n hêtre m
beef [bi:f] n bœuf m; **roast ~** rosbif m
▶ **beef up** vt (inf: support) renforcer; (: essay)
étoffer
beefburger ['bi:fbə:gəʳ] n hamburger m
beehive ['bi:haɪv] n ruche f
bee-keeping ['bi:ki:pɪŋ] n apiculture f
beeline ['bi:laɪn] n: **to make a ~ for** se diriger
tout droit vers

been [bi:n] pp of **be**
beep [bi:p] n bip m
beeper ['bi:pəʳ] n (pager) bip m
beer [bɪəʳ] n bière f
beer belly n (inf) bedaine f (de buveur de bière)
beer can n canette f de bière
beer garden n (Brit) jardin m d'un pub (où l'on
peut emmener ses consommations)
beet [bi:t] n (vegetable) betterave f; (US: also: **red
beet**) betterave (potagère)
beetle ['bi:tl] n scarabée m, coléoptère m
beetroot ['bi:tru:t] n (Brit) betterave f
befall [bɪ'fɔ:l] vi, vt (irreg: like **fall**) advenir (à)
befit [bɪ'fɪt] vt seoir à
before [bɪ'fɔ:ʳ] prep (of time) avant; (of space)
devant ▷ conj avant que + sub; avant de ▷ adv
avant; **~ going** avant de partir; **~ she goes**
avant qu'elle (ne) parte; **the week ~** la semaine
précédente or d'avant; **I've seen it ~** je l'ai déjà
vu; **I've never seen it ~** c'est la première fois
que je le vois
beforehand [bɪ'fɔ:hænd] adv au préalable, à
l'avance
befriend [bɪ'frɛnd] vt venir en aide à; traiter en
ami
befuddled [bɪ'fʌdld] adj: **to be ~** avoir les idées
brouillées
beg [bɛg] vi mendier ▷ vt mendier; (favour)
quémander, solliciter; (forgiveness, mercy etc)
demander; (entreat) supplier; **to ~ sb to do sth**
supplier qn de faire qch; **I ~ your pardon**
(apologising) excusez-moi; (: not hearing) pardon?;
that ~s the question of ... cela soulève la
question de ..., cela suppose réglée la question
de ...; see also **pardon**
began [bɪ'gæn] pt of **begin**
beggar ['bɛgəʳ] n (also: **beggarman,
beggarwoman**) mendiant(e)
begin [bɪ'gɪn] (pt **began**, pp **begun** [bɪ'gɪn, -'gæn,
-'gʌn]) vt, vi commencer; **to ~ doing** or **to do
sth** commencer à faire qch; **~ning (from)
Monday** à partir de lundi; **I can't ~ to thank
you** je ne saurais vous remercier; **to ~ with**
d'abord, pour commencer
beginner [bɪ'gɪnəʳ] n débutant(e)
beginning [bɪ'gɪnɪŋ] n commencement m,
début m; **right from the ~** dès le début
begrudge [bɪ'grʌdʒ] vt: **to ~ sb sth** envier qch à
qn; donner qch à contrecœur or à regret à qn
beguile [bɪ'gaɪl] vt (enchant) enjôler
beguiling [bɪ'gaɪlɪŋ] adj (charming) séduisant(e),
enchanteur(eresse)
begun [bɪ'gʌn] pp of **begin**
behalf [bɪ'hɑ:f] n: **on ~ of**, (US) **in ~ of**
(representing) de la part de; au nom de; (for benefit
of) pour le compte de; **on my/his ~** de ma/sa
part
behave [bɪ'heɪv] vi se conduire, se comporter;
(well: also: **behave o.s.**) se conduire bien or
comme il faut
behaviour, (US) **behavior** [bɪ'heɪvjəʳ] n
comportement m, conduite f

behead [bɪˈhɛd] vt décapiter

beheld [bɪˈhɛld] pt, pp of **behold**

behind [bɪˈhaɪnd] prep derrière; (time) en retard sur; (supporting): **to be ~ sb** soutenir qn ▷ adv derrière; en retard ▷ n derrière m; **~ the scenes** dans les coulisses; **to leave sth ~** (forget) oublier de prendre qch; **to be ~ (schedule) with sth** être en retard dans qch

behold [bɪˈhəʊld] vt (irreg: like **hold**) apercevoir, voir

beige [beɪʒ] adj beige

Beijing [ˈbeɪˈdʒɪŋ] n Pékin

being [ˈbiːɪŋ] n être m; **to come into ~** prendre naissance

Beirut [beɪˈruːt] n Beyrouth

Belarus [bɛləˈrus] n Biélorussie f, Bélarus m

Belarussian [bɛləˈrʌʃən] adj biélorusse ▷ n Biélorusse m/f; (Ling) biélorusse m

belated [bɪˈleɪtɪd] adj tardif(-ive)

belch [bɛltʃ] vi avoir un renvoi, roter ▷ vt (also: **belch out**: smoke etc) vomir, cracher

beleaguered [bɪˈliːgɪd] adj (city) assiégé(e); (army) cerné(e); (fig) sollicité(e) de toutes parts

Belfast [ˈbɛlfɑːst] n Belfast

belfry [ˈbɛlfrɪ] n beffroi m

Belgian [ˈbɛldʒən] adj belge, de Belgique ▷ n Belge m/f

Belgium [ˈbɛldʒəm] n Belgique f

Belgrade [bɛlˈgreɪd] n Belgrade

belie [bɪˈlaɪ] vt démentir; (give false impression of) occulter

belief [bɪˈliːf] n (opinion) conviction f; (trust, faith) foi f; (acceptance as true) croyance f; **it's beyond ~** c'est incroyable; **in the ~ that** dans l'idée que

believable [bɪˈliːvəbl] adj croyable

believe [bɪˈliːv] vt, vi croire, estimer; **to ~ in** (God) croire en; (ghosts, method) croire à; **I don't ~ in corporal punishment** je ne suis pas partisan des châtiments corporels; **he is ~d to be abroad** il serait à l'étranger

believer [bɪˈliːvəʳ] n (in idea, activity) partisan(e); **~ in** partisan(e) de; (Rel) croyant(e)

belittle [bɪˈlɪtl] vt déprécier, rabaisser

Belize [bɛˈliːz] n Bélize m

bell [bɛl] n cloche f; (small) clochette f, grelot m; (on door) sonnette f; (electric) sonnerie f; **that rings a ~** (fig) cela me rappelle qch

bell-bottoms [ˈbɛlbɔtəmz] npl pantalon m à pattes d'éléphant

bellboy [ˈbɛlbɔɪ], (US) **bellhop** [ˈbɛlhɔp] n groom m, chasseur m

belligerent [bɪˈlɪdʒərənt] adj (at war) belligérant(e); (fig) agressif(-ive)

bellow [ˈbɛləʊ] vi (bull) meugler; (person) brailler ▷ vt (orders) hurler

bellows [ˈbɛləʊz] npl soufflet m

bell pepper n (esp US) poivron m

bell push n (Brit) bouton m de sonnette

belly [ˈbɛlɪ] n ventre m

bellyache [ˈbɛlɪeɪk] (inf) n colique f ▷ vi ronchonner

belly button (inf) n nombril m

bellyful [ˈbɛlɪful] n (inf): **I've had a ~** j'en ai ras le bol

belong [bɪˈlɔŋ] vi: **to ~ to** appartenir à; (club etc) faire partie de; **this book ~s here** ce livre va ici, la place de ce livre est ici

belongings [bɪˈlɔŋɪŋz] npl affaires fpl, possessions fpl; **personal ~** effets personnels

Belorussia [bɛləˈrʌʃə] n Biélorussie f

Belorussian [bɛləˈrʌʃən] adj, n = **Belarussian**

beloved [bɪˈlʌvɪd] adj (bien-)aimé(e), chéri(e) ▷ n bien-aimé(e)

below [bɪˈləʊ] prep sous, au-dessous de ▷ adv en dessous; en contre-bas; **see ~** voir plus bas or plus loin or ci-dessous; **temperatures ~ normal** températures inférieures à la normale

belt [bɛlt] n ceinture f; (Tech) courroie f ▷ vt (thrash) donner une raclée à ▷ vi (Brit inf) filer (à toutes jambes); **industrial ~** zone industrielle

▶ **belt out** vt (song) chanter à tue-tête or à pleins poumons

▶ **belt up** vi (Brit inf) la boucler

beltway [ˈbɛltweɪ] n (US Aut) route f de ceinture; (: motorway) périphérique m

bemoan [bɪˈməʊn] vt se lamenter sur

bemused [bɪˈmjuːzd] adj médusé(e)

bench [bɛntʃ] n banc m; (in workshop) établi m; **the B~** (Law: judges) la magistrature, la Cour

bench mark n repère m

bend [bɛnd] (pt, pp **bent** [bɛnt]) vt courber; (leg, arm) plier ▷ vi se courber ▷ n (Brit: in road) virage m, tournant m; (in pipe, river) coude m

▶ **bend down** vi se baisser

▶ **bend over** vi se pencher

bends [bɛndz] npl (Med) maladie f des caissons

beneath [bɪˈniːθ] prep sous, au-dessous de; (unworthy of) indigne de ▷ adv dessous, au-dessous, en bas

benefactor [ˈbɛnɪfæktəʳ] n bienfaiteur m

benefactress [ˈbɛnɪfæktrɪs] n bienfaitrice f

beneficial [bɛnɪˈfɪʃəl] adj: **~ (to)** salutaire (pour), bénéfique (à)

beneficiary [bɛnɪˈfɪʃərɪ] n (Law) bénéficiaire m/f

benefit [ˈbɛnɪfɪt] n avantage m, profit m; (allowance of money) allocation f ▷ vt faire du bien à, profiter à ▷ vi: **he'll ~ from it** cela lui fera du bien, il y gagnera or s'en trouvera bien

benefit performance n représentation f or gala m de bienfaisance

Benelux [ˈbɛnɪlʌks] n Bénélux m

benevolent [bɪˈnɛvələnt] adj bienveillant(e)

BEng n abbr (= Bachelor of Engineering) diplôme universitaire

benign [bɪˈnaɪn] adj (person, smile) bienveillant(e), affable; (Med) bénin(-igne)

bent [bɛnt] pt, pp of **bend** ▷ n inclination f, penchant m ▷ adj (wire, pipe) coudé(e); (inf: dishonest) véreux(-euse); **to be ~ on** être résolu(e) à

bequeath [bɪˈkwiːð] vt léguer

bequest [bɪˈkwɛst] n legs m

bereaved [bɪˈriːvd] n: **the ~** la famille du disparu ▷ adj endeuillé(e)

bereavement [bɪˈriːvmənt] *n* deuil *m*
beret [ˈbɛreɪ] *n* béret *m*
Bering Sea [ˈbeɪrɪŋ-] *n*: **the ~** la mer de Béring
berk [bəːk] *n* (*Brit inf*) andouille *m/f*
Berks *abbr* (*Brit*) = **Berkshire**
Berlin [bəːˈlɪn] *n* Berlin; **East/West ~** Berlin Est/Ouest
berm [bəːm] *n* (*US Aut*) accotement *m*
Bermuda [bəːˈmjuːdə] *n* Bermudes *fpl*
Bermuda shorts *npl* bermuda *m*
Bern [bəːn] *n* Berne
berry [ˈbɛrɪ] *n* baie *f*
berserk [bəˈsəːk] *adj*: **to go ~** être pris(e) d'une rage incontrôlable; se déchaîner
berth [bəːθ] *n* (*bed*) couchette *f*; (*for ship*) poste *m* d'amarrage, mouillage *m* ▷ *vi* (*in harbour*) venir à quai; (*at anchor*) mouiller; **to give sb a wide ~** (*fig*) éviter qn
beseech (*pt, pp* **besought**) [bɪˈsiːtʃ, -ˈsɔːt] *vt* implorer, supplier
beset (*pt, pp* -) [bɪˈsɛt] *vt* assaillir ▷ *adj*: **~ with** semé(e) de
besetting [bɪˈsɛtɪŋ] *adj*: **his ~ sin** son vice, son gros défaut
beside [bɪˈsaɪd] *prep* à côté de; (*compared with*) par rapport à; **that's ~ the point** ça n'a rien à voir; **to be ~ o.s. (with anger)** être hors de soi
besides [bɪˈsaɪdz] *adv* en outre, de plus ▷ *prep* en plus de; (*except*) excepté
besiege [bɪˈsiːdʒ] *vt* (*town*) assiéger; (*fig*) assaillir
besotted [bɪˈsɔtɪd] *adj* (*Brit*): **~ with** entiché(e) de
besought [bɪˈsɔːt] *pt, pp of* **beseech**
bespectacled [bɪˈspɛktɪkld] *adj* à lunettes
bespoke [bɪˈspəuk] *adj* (*Brit: garment*) fait(e) sur mesure; **~ tailor** tailleur *m* à façon
best [bɛst] *adj* meilleur(e) ▷ *adv* le mieux; **the ~ part of** (*quantity*) le plus clair de, la plus grande partie de; **at ~** au mieux; **to make the ~ of sth** s'accommoder de qch (du mieux que l'on peut); **to do one's ~** faire de son mieux; **to the ~ of my knowledge** pour autant que je sache; **to the ~ of my ability** du mieux que je pourrai; **he's not exactly patient at the ~ of times** il n'est jamais spécialement patient; **the ~ thing to do is ...** le mieux, c'est de ...
best-before date *n* date *f* de limite d'utilisation *or* de consommation
best man (*irreg*) *n* garçon *m* d'honneur
bestow [bɪˈstəu] *vt* accorder; (*title*) conférer
bestseller [ˈbɛstˈsɛləʳ] *n* best-seller *m*, succès *m* de librairie
bet [bɛt] *n* pari *m* ▷ *vt, vi* (*pt, pp* - *or* -**ted**) parier; **it's a safe ~** (*fig*) il y a de fortes chances; **to ~ sb sth** parier qch à qn
Bethlehem [ˈbɛθlɪhɛm] *n* Bethléem
betray [bɪˈtreɪ] *vt* trahir
betrayal [bɪˈtreɪəl] *n* trahison *f*
better [ˈbɛtəʳ] *adj* meilleur(e) ▷ *adv* mieux ▷ *vt* améliorer ▷ *n*: **to get the ~ of** triompher de, l'emporter sur; **a change for the ~** une amélioration; **I had ~ go** il faut que je m'en

aille; **you had ~ do it** vous feriez mieux de le faire; **he thought ~ of it** il s'est ravisé; **to get ~** (*Med*) aller mieux; (*improve*) s'améliorer; **that's ~!** c'est mieux!; **~ off** *adj* plus à l'aise financièrement; (*fig*): **you'd be ~ off this way** vous vous en trouveriez mieux ainsi, ce serait mieux *or* plus pratique ainsi
betting [ˈbɛtɪŋ] *n* paris *mpl*
betting shop *n* (*Brit*) bureau *m* de paris
between [bɪˈtwiːn] *prep* entre ▷ *adv* au milieu, dans l'intervalle; **the road ~ here and London** la route d'ici à Londres; **we only had 5 ~ us** nous n'en avions que 5 en tout
bevel [ˈbɛvəl] *n* (*also:* **bevel edge**) biseau *m*
beverage [ˈbɛvərɪdʒ] *n* boisson *f* (*gén sans alcool*)
bevy [ˈbɛvɪ] *n*: **a ~ of** un essaim *or* une volée de
bewail [bɪˈweɪl] *vt* se lamenter sur
beware [bɪˈwɛəʳ] *vt, vi*: **to ~ (of)** prendre garde (à); **"~ of the dog"** "(attention) chien méchant"
bewildered [bɪˈwɪldəd] *adj* dérouté(e), ahuri(e)
bewildering [bɪˈwɪldrɪŋ] *adj* déroutant(e), ahurissant(e)
bewitching [bɪˈwɪtʃɪŋ] *adj* enchanteur(-teresse)
beyond [bɪˈjɔnd] *prep* (*in space, time*) au-delà de; (*exceeding*) au-dessus de ▷ *adv* au-delà; **~ doubt** hors de doute; **~ repair** irréparable
b/f *abbr* = **brought forward**
BFPO *n abbr* (= *British Forces Post Office*) *service postal de l'armée*
bhp *n abbr* (*Aut*: = *brake horsepower*) puissance *f* aux freins
bi... [baɪ] *prefix* bi...
biannual [baɪˈænjuəl] *adj* semestriel(le)
bias [ˈbaɪəs] *n* (*prejudice*) préjugé *m*, parti pris; (*preference*) prévention *f*
biased, biassed [ˈbaɪəst] *adj* partial(e), montrant un parti pris; **to be bias(s)ed against** avoir un préjugé contre
biathlon [baɪˈæθlən] *n* biathlon *m*
bib [bɪb] *n* bavoir *m*, bavette *f*
Bible [ˈbaɪbl] *n* Bible *f*
bibliography [bɪblɪˈɔɡrəfɪ] *n* bibliographie *f*
bicarbonate of soda [baɪˈkɑːbənɪt] *n* bicarbonate *m* de soude
bicentenary [baɪsɛnˈtiːnərɪ] *n*, **bicentennial** [baɪsɛnˈtɛnɪəl] ▷ *n* bicentenaire *m*
biceps [ˈbaɪsɛps] *n* biceps *m*
bicker [ˈbɪkəʳ] *vi* se chamailler
bicycle [ˈbaɪsɪkl] *n* bicyclette *f*
bicycle path *n*, **bicycle track** *n* piste *f* cyclable
bicycle pump *n* pompe *f* à vélo
bid [bɪd] *n* offre *f*; (*at auction*) enchère *f*; (*attempt*) tentative *f* ▷ *vi* (*pt, pp* -) faire une enchère *or* offre ▷ *vt* (*pt* **bade**) [bæd] (*pp* -**den**) [ˈbɪdn] faire une enchère *or* offre de; **to ~ sb good day** souhaiter le bonjour à qn
bidden [ˈbɪdn] *pp of* **bid**
bidder [ˈbɪdəʳ] *n*: **the highest ~** le plus offrant
bidding [ˈbɪdɪŋ] *n* enchères *fpl*
bide [baɪd] *vt*: **to ~ one's time** attendre son heure

bidet ['biːdeɪ] n bidet m

bidirectional ['baɪdɪ'rɛkʃənl] adj bidirectionnel(le)

biennial [baɪ'ɛnɪəl] adj biennal(e), bisannuel(le) ▷ n biennale f; (plant) plante bisannuelle

bier [bɪəʳ] n bière f (cercueil)

bifocals [baɪ'fəuklz] npl lunettes fpl à double foyer

big [bɪg] adj (in height: person, building, tree) grand(e); (in bulk, amount: person, parcel, book) gros(se); **to do things in a ~ way** faire les choses en grand

bigamy ['bɪgəmɪ] n bigamie f

big dipper [-'dɪpəʳ] n montagnes fpl russes

big end n (Aut) tête f de bielle

biggish ['bɪgɪʃ] adj (see big) assez grand(e), assez gros(se)

bigheaded ['bɪg'hɛdɪd] adj prétentieux(-euse)

big-hearted ['bɪg'hɑːtɪd] adj au grand cœur

bigot ['bɪgət] n fanatique m/f, sectaire m/f

bigoted ['bɪgətɪd] adj fanatique, sectaire

bigotry ['bɪgətrɪ] n fanatisme m, sectarisme m

big toe n gros orteil

big top n grand chapiteau

big wheel n (at fair) grande roue

bigwig ['bɪgwɪg] n (inf) grosse légume, huile f

bike [baɪk] n vélo m, bécane f

bike lane n piste f cyclable

bikini [bɪ'kiːnɪ] n bikini m

bilateral [baɪ'lætərl] adj bilatéral(e)

bile [baɪl] n bile f

bilingual [baɪ'lɪŋgwəl] adj bilingue

bilious ['bɪlɪəs] adj bilieux(-euse); (fig) maussade, irritable

bill [bɪl] n note f, facture f; (in restaurant) addition f, note f; (Pol) projet m de loi; (US: banknote) billet m (de banque); (notice) affiche f; (of bird) bec m; (Theat): **on the ~** à l'affiche ▷ vt (item) facturer; (customer) remettre la facture à; **may I have the ~ please?** (est-ce que je peux avoir) l'addition, s'il vous plaît?; **put it on my ~** mettez-le sur mon compte; **"post no ~s"** "défense d'afficher"; **to fit** or **fill the ~** (fig) faire l'affaire; **~ of exchange** lettre f de change; **~ of lading** connaissement m; **~ of sale** contrat m de vente

billboard ['bɪlbɔːd] (US) n panneau m d'affichage

billet ['bɪlɪt] n cantonnement m (chez l'habitant) ▷ vt (troops) cantonner

billfold ['bɪlfəuld] n (US) portefeuille m

billiards ['bɪljədz] n (jeu m de) billard m

billion ['bɪljən] n (Brit) billion m (million de millions); (US) milliard m

billow ['bɪləu] n nuage m ▷ vi (smoke) s'élever en nuage; (sail) se gonfler

billy goat ['bɪlɪgəut] n bouc m

bimbo ['bɪmbəu] n (inf) ravissante idiote f

bin [bɪn] n boîte f; (Brit: also: **dustbin, litter bin**) poubelle f; (for coal) coffre m

binary ['baɪnərɪ] adj binaire

bind (pt, pp **bound**) [baɪnd, baund] vt attacher; (book) relier; (oblige) obliger, contraindre ▷ n (inf: nuisance) scie f

▶ **bind over** vt (Law) mettre en liberté conditionnelle

▶ **bind up** vt (wound) panser; **to be bound up in** (work, research etc) être complètement absorbé par, être accroché par; **to be bound up with** (person) être accroché à

binder ['baɪndəʳ] n (file) classeur m

binding ['baɪndɪŋ] n (of book) reliure f ▷ adj (contract) qui constitue une obligation

binge [bɪndʒ] n (inf): **to go on a ~** faire la bringue

bingo ['bɪŋgəu] n sorte de jeu de loto pratiqué dans des établissements publics

bin liner n sac m poubelle

binoculars [bɪ'nɔkjuləz] npl jumelles fpl [baɪə'] prefix

biochemistry [baɪə'kɛmɪstrɪ] n biochimie f

biodegradable ['baɪəudɪ'greɪdəbl] adj biodégradable

biodiversity ['baɪəudaɪ'vəːsɪtɪ] n biodiversité f

biofuel ['baɪəufjuəl] n combustible m organique

biographer [baɪ'ɔgrəfəʳ] n biographe m

biographic [baɪə'græfɪk], **biographical** [baɪə'græfɪkl] adj biographique

biography [baɪ'ɔgrəfɪ] n biographie f

biological [baɪə'lɔdʒɪkl] adj biologique

biological clock n horloge f physiologique

biologist [baɪ'ɔlədʒɪst] n biologiste m/f

biology [baɪ'ɔlədʒɪ] n biologie f

biometric [baɪə'mɛtrɪk] adj biométrique

biophysics ['baɪəu'fɪzɪks] n biophysique f

biopic ['baɪəupɪk] n film m biographique

biopsy ['baɪɔpsɪ] n biopsie f

biosphere ['baɪəsfɪəʳ] n biosphère f

biotechnology ['baɪəutɛk'nɔlədʒɪ] n biotechnologie f

birch [bəːtʃ] n bouleau m

bird [bəːd] n oiseau m; (Brit inf: girl) nana f

bird flu n grippe f aviaire

bird of prey n oiseau m de proie

bird's-eye view ['bəːdzaɪ-] n vue f à vol d'oiseau; (fig) vue d'ensemble or générale

bird watcher [-wɔtʃəʳ] n ornithologue m/f amateur

birdwatching ['bəːdwɔtʃɪŋ] n ornithologie f (d'amateur)

Biro® ['baɪərəu] n stylo m à bille

birth [bəːθ] n naissance f; **to give ~ to** donner naissance à, mettre au monde; (subj: animal) mettre bas

birth certificate n acte m de naissance

birth control n (policy) limitation f des naissances; (methods) méthode(s) contraceptive(s)

birthday ['bəːθdeɪ] n anniversaire m ▷ cpd (cake, card etc) d'anniversaire

birthmark ['bəːθmɑːk] n envie f, tache f de vin

birthplace ['bəːθpleɪs] n lieu m de naissance

birth rate n (taux m de) natalité f

Biscay ['bɪskeɪ] n: **the Bay of ~** le golfe de

Gascogne

biscuit ['bɪskɪt] *n* (*Brit*) biscuit *m*; (*US*) petit pain au lait

bisect [baɪ'sɛkt] *vt* couper *or* diviser en deux

bisexual ['baɪ'sɛksjuəl] *adj, n* bisexuel(le)

bishop ['bɪʃəp] *n* évêque *m*; (*Chess*) fou *m*

bistro ['bi:strəu] *n* petit restaurant *m*, bistrot *m*

bit [bɪt] *pt of* **bite** ▷ *n* morceau *m*; (*Comput*) bit *m*, élément *m* binaire; (*of tool*) mèche *f*; (*of horse*) mors *m*; **a ~ of** un peu de; **a ~ mad/dangerous** un peu fou/risqué; **~ by ~** petit à petit; **to come to ~s** (*break*) tomber en morceaux, se déglinguer; **bring all your ~s and pieces** apporte toutes tes affaires; **to do one's ~** y mettre du sien

bitch [bɪtʃ] *n* (*dog*) chienne *f*; (*inf!*) salope *f* (*!*), garce *f*

bite [baɪt] *vt, vi* (*pt* **bit**, *pp* **bitten** [bɪt, 'bɪtn]) mordre; (*insect*) piquer ▷ *n* morsure *f*; (*insect bite*) piqûre *f*; (*mouthful*) bouchée *f*; **let's have a ~ (to eat)** mangeons un morceau; **to ~ one's nails** se ronger les ongles

biting ['baɪtɪŋ] *adj* mordant(e)

bit part *n* (*Theat*) petit rôle

bitten ['bɪtn] *pp of* **bite**

bitter ['bɪtər] *adj* amer(-ère); (*criticism*) cinglant(e); (*icy: weather, wind*) glacial(e) ▷ *n* (*Brit: beer*) bière *f* (*à forte teneur en houblon*); **to the ~ end** jusqu'au bout

bitterly ['bɪtəlɪ] *adv* (*complain, weep*) amèrement; (*oppose, criticise*) durement, âprement; (*jealous, disappointed*) horriblement; **it's ~ cold** il fait un froid de loup

bitterness ['bɪtənɪs] *n* amertume *f*; goût amer

bittersweet ['bɪtəswi:t] *adj* aigre-doux (douce)

bitty ['bɪtɪ] *adj* (*Brit inf*) décousu(e)

bitumen ['bɪtjumɪn] *n* bitume *m*

bivouac ['bɪvuæk] *n* bivouac *m*

bizarre [bɪ'zɑ:r] *adj* bizarre

bk *abbr* = **bank; book**

BL *n abbr* (= *Bachelor of Law(s), Bachelor of Letters*) diplôme universitaire; (*US*: = *Bachelor of Literature*) diplôme universitaire

bl *abbr* = **bill of lading**

blab [blæb] *vi* jaser, trop parler ▷ *vt* (*also*: **blab out**) laisser échapper, aller raconter

black [blæk] *adj* noir(e) ▷ *n* (*colour*) noir *m*; (*person*): **B~** noir(e) ▷ *vt* (*shoes*) cirer; (*Brit Industry*) boycotter; **to give sb a ~ eye** pocher l'œil à qn, faire un œil au beurre noir à qn; **there it is in ~ and white** (*fig*) c'est écrit noir sur blanc; **to be in the ~** (*in credit*) avoir un compte créditeur; **~ and blue** (*bruised*) couvert(e) de bleus

▸ **black out** *vi* (*faint*) s'évanouir

black belt *n* (*Judo etc*) ceinture noire; **he's a ~** il est ceinture noire

blackberry ['blækbərɪ] *n* mûre *f*

blackbird ['blækbə:d] *n* merle *m*

blackboard ['blækbɔ:d] *n* tableau noir

black box *n* (*Aviat*) boîte noire

black coffee *n* café noir

Black Country *n* (*Brit*): **the ~** le Pays Noir (*dans les Midlands*)

blackcurrant ['blæk'kʌrənt] *n* cassis *m*

black economy *n* (*Brit*) travail *m* au noir

blacken ['blækn] *vt* noircir

Black Forest *n*: **the ~** la Forêt Noire

blackhead ['blækhɛd] *n* point noir

black hole *n* (*Astronomy*) trou noir

black ice *n* verglas *m*

blackjack ['blækdʒæk] *n* (*Cards*) vingt-et-un *m*; (*US: truncheon*) matraque *f*

blackleg ['blæklɛg] *n* (*Brit*) briseur *m* de grève, jaune *m*

blacklist ['blæklɪst] *n* liste noire ▷ *vt* mettre sur la liste noire

blackmail ['blækmeɪl] *n* chantage *m* ▷ *vt* faire chanter, soumettre au chantage

blackmailer ['blækmeɪlər] *n* maître-chanteur *m*

black market *n* marché noir

blackout ['blækaut] *n* panne *f* d'électricité; (*in wartime*) black-out *m*; (*TV*) interruption *f* d'émission; (*fainting*) syncope *f*

black pepper *n* poivre noir

black pudding *n* boudin (noir)

Black Sea *n*: **the ~** la mer Noire

black sheep *n* brebis galeuse

blacksmith ['blæksmɪθ] *n* forgeron *m*

black spot *n* (*Aut*) point noir

bladder ['blædər] *n* vessie *f*

blade [bleɪd] *n* lame *f*; (*of oar*) plat *m*; (*of propeller*) pale *f*; **a ~ of grass** un brin d'herbe

blame [bleɪm] *n* faute *f*, blâme *m* ▷ *vt*: **to ~ sb/sth for sth** attribuer à qn/qch la responsabilité de qch; reprocher qch à qn/qch; **who's to ~?** qui est le fautif *or* coupable *or* responsable?; **I'm not to ~** ce n'est pas ma faute

blameless ['bleɪmlɪs] *adj* irréprochable

blanch [blɑ:ntʃ] *vi* (*person, face*) blêmir ▷ *vt* (*Culin*) blanchir

bland [blænd] *adj* affable; (*taste, food*) doux (douce), fade

blank [blæŋk] *adj* blanc (blanche); (*look*) sans expression, dénué(e) d'expression ▷ *n* espace *m* vide, blanc *m*; (*cartridge*) cartouche *f* à blanc; **his mind was a ~** il avait la tête vide; **we drew a ~** (*fig*) nous n'avons abouti à rien

blank cheque, (*US*) **blank check** *n* chèque *m* en blanc; **to give sb a ~ to do ...** (*fig*) donner carte blanche à qn pour faire ...

blanket ['blæŋkɪt] *n* couverture *f*; (*of snow, cloud*) couche *f* ▷ *adj* (*statement, agreement*) global(e), de portée générale; **to give ~ cover** (*insurance policy*) couvrir tous les risques

blare [blɛər] *vi* (*brass band, horns, radio*) beugler

blasé ['blɑ:zeɪ] *adj* blasé(e)

blasphemous ['blæsfɪməs] *adj* (*words*) blasphématoire; (*person*) blasphémateur(-trice)

blasphemy ['blæsfɪmɪ] *n* blasphème *m*

blast [blɑ:st] *n* explosion *f*; (*shock wave*) souffle *m*; (*of air, steam*) bouffée *f* ▷ *vt* faire sauter *or* exploser ▷ *excl* (*Brit inf*) zut!; **(at) full ~** (*play music etc*) à plein volume

▸ **blast off** vi (Space) décoller

blast-off ['blɑːstɔf] n (Space) lancement m

blatant ['bleɪtənt] adj flagrant(e), criant(e)

blatantly ['bleɪtəntlɪ] adv (lie) ouvertement; **it's ~ obvious** c'est l'évidence même

blaze [bleɪz] n (fire) incendie m; (flames: of fire, sun etc) embrasement m; (: in hearth) flamme f, flambée f; (fig) flamboiement m ▷ vi (fire) flamber; (fig) flamboyer, resplendir ▷ vt: **to ~ a trail** (fig) montrer la voie; **in a ~ of publicity** à grand renfort de publicité

blazer ['bleɪzə'] n blazer m

bleach [bliːtʃ] n (also: **household bleach**) eau f de Javel ▷ vt (linen) blanchir

bleached [bliːtʃt] adj (hair) oxygéné(e), décoloré(e)

bleachers ['bliːtʃəz] npl (US Sport) gradins mpl (en plein soleil)

bleak [bliːk] adj morne, désolé(e); (weather) triste, maussade; (smile) lugubre; (prospect, future) morose

bleary-eyed ['blɪərɪ'aɪd] adj aux yeux pleins de sommeil

bleat [bliːt] n bêlement m ▷ vi bêler

bled [blɛd] pt, pp of **bleed**

bleed (pt, pp bled) [bliːd, blɛd] vt saigner; (brakes, radiator) purger ▷ vi saigner; **my nose is ~ing** je saigne du nez

bleep [bliːp] n (Radio, TV) top m; (of pocket device) bip m ▷ vi émettre des signaux ▷ vt (doctor etc) appeler (au moyen d'un bip)

bleeper ['bliːpə'] n (of doctor etc) bip m

blemish ['blɛmɪʃ] n défaut m; (on reputation) tache f

blend [blɛnd] n mélange m ▷ vt mélanger ▷ vi (colours etc: also: **blend in**) se mélanger, se fondre, s'allier

blender ['blɛndə'] n (Culin) mixeur m

bless (pt, pp **-ed** or **blest**) [blɛs, blɛst] vt bénir; **to be ~ed with** avoir le bonheur de jouir de or d'avoir; **~ you!** (after sneeze) à tes souhaits!

blessed ['blɛsɪd] adj (Rel: holy) béni(e); (happy) bienheureux(-euse); **it rains every ~ day** il ne se passe pas de jour sans qu'il ne pleuve

blessing ['blɛsɪŋ] n bénédiction f; (godsend) bienfait m; **to count one's ~s** s'estimer heureux; **it was a ~ in disguise** c'est un bien pour un mal

blew [bluː] pt of **blow**

blight [blaɪt] n (of plants) rouille f ▷ vt (hopes etc) anéantir, briser

blimey ['blaɪmɪ] excl (Brit inf) mince alors!

blind [blaɪnd] adj aveugle ▷ n (for window) store m ▷ vt aveugler; **to turn a ~ eye (on or to)** fermer les yeux (sur); **the blind** npl les aveugles mpl

blind alley n impasse f

blind corner n (Brit) virage m sans visibilité

blind date n rendez-vous galant (avec un(e) inconnu(e))

blindfold ['blaɪndfəuld] n bandeau m ▷ adj, adv les yeux bandés ▷ vt bander les yeux à

blindly ['blaɪndlɪ] adv aveuglément

blindness ['blaɪndnɪs] n cécité f; (fig) aveuglement m

blind spot n (Aut etc) angle m aveugle; (fig) angle mort

blink [blɪŋk] vi cligner des yeux; (light) clignoter ▷ n: **the TV's on the ~** (inf) la télé ne va pas tarder à nous lâcher

blinkers ['blɪŋkəz] npl œillères fpl

blinking ['blɪŋkɪŋ] adj (Brit inf): **this ~ ...** ce fichu or sacré ...

blip [blɪp] n (on radar etc) spot m; (on graph) petite aberration; (fig) petite anomalie (passagère)

bliss [blɪs] n félicité f, bonheur m sans mélange

blissful ['blɪsful] adj (event, day) merveilleux(-euse); (smile) de bonheur; **a ~ sigh** un soupir d'aise; **in ~ ignorance** dans une ignorance béate

blissfully ['blɪsfulɪ] adv (smile) béatement; (happy) merveilleusement

blister ['blɪstə'] n (on skin) ampoule f, cloque f; (on paintwork) boursouflure f ▷ vi (paint) se boursoufler, se cloquer

BLit, BLitt n abbr (= Bachelor of Literature) diplôme universitaire

blithely ['blaɪðlɪ] adv (unconcernedly) tranquillement; (joyfully) gaiement

blithering ['blɪðərɪŋ] adj (inf): **this ~ idiot** cet espèce d'idiot

blitz [blɪts] n bombardement (aérien); **to have a ~ on sth** (fig) s'attaquer à qch

blizzard ['blɪzəd] n blizzard m, tempête f de neige

BLM n abbr (US: = Bureau of Land Management) ≈ les domaines

bloated ['bləutɪd] adj (face) bouffi(e); (stomach, person) gonflé(e)

blob [blɔb] n (drop) goutte f; (stain, spot) tache f

bloc [blɔk] n (Pol) bloc m

block [blɔk] n bloc m; (in pipes) obstruction f; (toy) cube m; (of buildings) pâté m (de maisons) ▷ vt bloquer; (fig) faire obstacle à; (Comput) grouper; **the sink is ~ed** l'évier est bouché; **~ of flats** (Brit) immeuble (locatif); **3 ~s from here** à trois rues d'ici; **mental ~** blocage m; **~ and tackle** (Tech) palan m

▸ **block up** vt boucher

blockade [blɔ'keɪd] n blocus m ▷ vt faire le blocus de

blockage ['blɔkɪdʒ] n obstruction f

block booking n réservation f en bloc

blockbuster ['blɔkbʌstə'] n (film, book) grand succès

block capitals npl majuscules fpl d'imprimerie

blockhead ['blɔkhɛd] n imbécile m/f

block letters npl majuscules fpl

block release n (Brit) congé m de formation

block vote n (Brit) vote m de délégation

blog [blɔg] n blog m, blogue m ▷ vi blogger

blogger ['blɔgə'] (inf) n (person) blogueur(-euse) m/f

bloke [bləuk] n (Brit inf) type m

blond, blonde [blɔnd] adj, n blond(e)

blood [blʌd] *n* sang *m*
blood bank *n* banque *f* du sang
blood count *n* numération *f* globulaire
bloodcurdling ['blʌdkə:dlɪŋ] *adj* à vous glacer le sang
blood donor *n* donneur(-euse) de sang
blood group *n* groupe sanguin
bloodhound ['blʌdhaund] *n* limier *m*
bloodless ['blʌdlɪs] *adj* (*victory*) sans effusion de sang; (*pale*) anémié(e)
bloodletting ['blʌdlɛtɪŋ] *n* (*Med*) saignée *f*; (*fig*) effusion *f* de sang, représailles *fpl*
blood poisoning *n* empoisonnement *m* du sang
blood pressure *n* tension (artérielle); **to have high/low ~** faire de l'hypertension/l'hypotension
bloodshed ['blʌdʃɛd] *n* effusion *f* de sang, carnage *m*
bloodshot ['blʌdʃɔt] *adj*: **~ eyes** yeux injectés de sang
blood sports *npl* sports *mpl* sanguinaires
bloodstained ['blʌdsteɪnd] *adj* taché(e) de sang
bloodstream ['blʌdstri:m] *n* sang *m*, système sanguin
blood test *n* analyse *f* de sang
bloodthirsty ['blʌdθə:stɪ] *adj* sanguinaire
blood transfusion *n* transfusion *f* de sang
blood type *n* groupe sanguin
blood vessel *n* vaisseau sanguin
bloody ['blʌdɪ] *adj* sanglant(e); (*Brit inf!*): **this ~ ...** ce foutu ..., ce putain de ... (!) ▷ *adv*: **~ strong/good** (*Brit: inf!*) vachement *or* sacrément fort/bon
bloody-minded ['blʌdɪ'maɪndɪd] *adj* (*Brit inf*) contrariant(e), obstiné(e)
bloom [blu:m] *n* fleur *f*; (*fig*) épanouissement *m* ▷ *vi* être en fleur; (*fig*) s'épanouir; être florissant(e)
blooming ['blu:mɪŋ] *adj* (*inf*): **this ~ ...** ce fichu *or* sacré ...
blossom ['blɔsəm] *n* fleur(s) *f(pl)* ▷ *vi* être en fleurs; (*fig*) s'épanouir; **to ~ into** (*fig*) devenir
blot [blɔt] *n* tache *f* ▷ *vt* tacher; (*ink*) sécher; **to be a ~ on the landscape** gâcher le paysage; **to ~ one's copy book** (*fig*) faire un impair
▶ **blot out** *vt* (*memories*) effacer; (*view*) cacher, masquer; (*nation, city*) annihiler
blotchy ['blɔtʃɪ] *adj* (*complexion*) couvert(e) de marbrures
blotting paper ['blɔtɪŋ-] *n* buvard *m*
blotto ['blɔtəu] *adj* (*inf*) bourré(e)
blouse [blauz] *n* (*feminine garment*) chemisier *m*, corsage *m*
blow [bləu] (*pt* **blew**, *pp* **-n**) [blu:, bləun] *n* coup *m* ▷ *vi* souffler ▷ *vt* (*glass*) souffler; (*instrument*) jouer de; (*fuse*) faire sauter; **to ~ one's nose** se moucher; **to ~ a whistle** siffler; **to come to ~s** en venir aux coups
▶ **blow away** *vi* s'envoler ▷ *vt* chasser, faire s'envoler
▶ **blow down** *vt* faire tomber, renverser
▶ **blow off** *vi* s'envoler ▷ *vt* (*hat*) emporter;

(*ship*): **to ~ off course** faire dévier
▶ **blow out** *vi* (*fire, flame*) s'éteindre; (*tyre*) éclater; (*fuse*) sauter
▶ **blow over** *vi* s'apaiser
▶ **blow up** *vi* exploser, sauter ▷ *vt* faire sauter; (*tyre*) gonfler; (*Phot*) agrandir
blow-dry ['bləudraɪ] *n* (*hairstyle*) brushing *m* ▷ *vt* faire un brushing à
blowlamp ['bləulæmp] *n* (*Brit*) chalumeau *m*
blown [bləun] *pp of* **blow**
blow-out ['bləuaut] *n* (*of tyre*) éclatement *m*; (*Brit: inf: big meal*) gueuleton *m*
blowtorch ['bləutɔ:tʃ] *n* chalumeau *m*
blowzy ['blauzɪ] *adj* (*Brit*) peu soigné(e)
BLS *n abbr* (*US*) = **Bureau of Labor Statistics**
blubber ['blʌbəʳ] *n* blanc *m* de baleine ▷ *vi* (*pej*) pleurer comme un veau
bludgeon ['blʌdʒən] *n* gourdin *m*, trique *f*
blue [blu:] *adj* bleu(e); (*depressed*) triste; **~ film/joke** film *m*/histoire *f* pornographique; **(only) once in a ~ moon** tous les trente-six du mois; **out of the ~** (*fig*) à l'improviste, sans qu'on s'y attende
blue baby *n* enfant bleu(e)
bluebell ['blu:bɛl] *n* jacinthe *f* des bois
blueberry ['blu:bərɪ] *n* myrtille *f*, airelle *f*
bluebottle ['blu:bɔtl] *n* mouche *f* à viande
blue cheese *n* (fromage) bleu *m*
blue-chip ['blu:tʃɪp] *adj*: **~ investment** investissement *m* de premier ordre
blue-collar worker ['blu:kɔlə'-] *n* ouvrier(-ère) col bleu
blue jeans *npl* blue-jeans *mpl*
blueprint ['blu:prɪnt] *n* bleu *m*; (*fig*) projet *m*, plan directeur
blues [blu:z] *npl*: **the ~** (*Mus*) le blues; **to have the ~** (*inf: feeling*) avoir le cafard
bluff [blʌf] *vi* bluffer ▷ *n* bluff *m*; (*cliff*) promontoire *m*, falaise *f* ▷ *adj* (*person*) bourru(e), brusque; **to call sb's ~** mettre qn au défi d'exécuter ses menaces
blunder ['blʌndəʳ] *n* gaffe *f*, bévue *f* ▷ *vi* faire une gaffe *or* une bévue; **to ~ into sb/sth** buter contre qn/qch
blunt [blʌnt] *adj* (*knife*) émoussé(e), peu tranchant(e); (*pencil*) mal taillé(e); (*person*) brusque, ne mâchant pas ses mots ▷ *vt* émousser; **~ instrument** (*Law*) instrument contondant
bluntly ['blʌntlɪ] *adv* carrément, sans prendre de gants
bluntness ['blʌntnɪs] *n* (*of person*) brusquerie *f*, franchise brutale
blur [blə:ʳ] *n* (*shape*): **to become a ~** devenir flou ▷ *vt* brouiller, rendre flou(e)
blurb [blə:b] *n* (*for book*) texte *m* de présentation; (*pej*) baratin *m*
blurred [blə:d] *adj* flou(e)
blurt [blə:t]: **to ~ out** *vt* (*reveal*) lâcher; (*say*) balbutier, dire d'une voix entrecoupée
blush [blʌʃ] *vi* rougir ▷ *n* rougeur *f*
blusher ['blʌʃəʳ] *n* rouge *m* à joues

bluster ['blʌstə^r] n paroles fpl en l'air; (boasting) fanfaronnades fpl; (threats) menaces fpl en l'air ▷ vi parler en l'air; fanfaronner

blustering ['blʌstərɪŋ] adj fanfaron(ne)

blustery ['blʌstərɪ] adj (weather) à bourrasques

Blvd abbr (= boulevard) Bd

BM n abbr = **British Museum**; (Scol: = Bachelor of Medicine) diplôme universitaire

BMA n abbr = **British Medical Association**

BMJ n abbr = **British Medical Journal**

BMus n abbr (= Bachelor of Music) diplôme universitaire

BMX n abbr (= bicycle motorcross) BMX m

BO n abbr (inf: = body odour) odeurs corporelles; (US) = **box office**

boar [bɔː^r] n sanglier m

board [bɔːd] n (wooden) planche f; (on wall) panneau m; (for chess etc) plateau m; (cardboard) carton m; (committee) conseil m, comité m; (in firm) conseil d'administration; (Naut, Aviat): **on ~** à bord ▷ vt (ship) monter à bord de; (train) monter dans; **full ~** (Brit) pension complète; **half ~** (Brit) demi-pension f; **~ and lodging** (n) chambre f avec pension; **with ~ and lodging** logé nourri; **above ~** (fig) régulier(-ère); **across the ~** (fig: adv) systématiquement; (: adj) de portée générale; **to go by the ~** (hopes, principles) être abandonné(e); (be unimportant) compter pour rien, n'avoir aucune importance
▸ **board up** vt (door) condamner (au moyen de planches, de tôle)

boarder ['bɔːdə^r] n pensionnaire m/f; (Scol) interne m/f, pensionnaire

board game n jeu m de société

boarding card ['bɔːdɪŋ-] n (Aviat, Naut) carte f d'embarquement

boarding house ['bɔːdɪŋ-] n pension f

boarding party ['bɔːdɪŋ-] n section f d'abordage

boarding pass ['bɔːdɪŋ-] n (Brit) = **boarding card**

boarding school ['bɔːdɪŋ-] n internat m, pensionnat m

board meeting n réunion f du conseil d'administration

board room n salle f du conseil d'administration

boardwalk ['bɔːdwɔːk] n (US) cheminement m en planches

boast [bəust] vi: **to ~ (about or of)** se vanter (de) ▷ vt s'enorgueillir de ▷ n vantardise f; sujet m d'orgueil or de fierté

boastful ['bəustful] adj vantard(e)

boastfulness ['bəustfulnɪs] n vantardise f

boat [bəut] n bateau m; (small) canot m; barque f; **to go by ~** aller en bateau; **to be in the same ~** (fig) être logé à la même enseigne

boater ['bəutə^r] n (hat) canotier m

boating ['bəutɪŋ] n canotage m

boat people npl boat people mpl

boatswain ['bəusn] n maître m d'équipage

bob [bɔb] vi (boat, cork on water: also: **bob up and down**) danser, se balancer ▷ n (Brit inf) = **shilling**

▸ **bob up** vi surgir or apparaître brusquement

bobbin ['bɔbɪn] n bobine f; (of sewing machine) navette f

bobby ['bɔbɪ] n (Brit inf) ≈ agent m (de police)

bobby pin ['bɔbɪ-] n (US) pince f à cheveux

bobsleigh ['bɔbsleɪ] n bob m

bode [bəud] vi: **to ~ well/ill (for)** être de bon/mauvais augure (pour)

bodice ['bɔdɪs] n corsage m

bodily ['bɔdɪlɪ] adj corporel(le); (pain, comfort) physique; (needs) matériel(le) ▷ adv (carry, lift) dans ses bras

body ['bɔdɪ] n corps m; (of car) carrosserie f; (of plane) fuselage m; (also: **body stocking**) body m, justaucorps m; (fig: society) organe m, organisme m; (: quantity) ensemble m, masse f; (of wine) corps m; **ruling ~** organe directeur; **in a ~** en masse, ensemble; (speak) comme un seul et même homme

body blow n (fig) coup dur, choc m

body-building ['bɔdɪbɪldɪŋ] n body-building m, culturisme m

bodyguard ['bɔdɪgɑːd] n garde m du corps

body language n langage m du corps

body repairs npl travaux mpl de carrosserie

body search n fouille f (corporelle); **to carry out a ~ on sb** fouiller qn; **to submit to or undergo a ~** se faire fouiller

bodywork ['bɔdɪwəːk] n carrosserie f

boffin ['bɔfɪn] n (Brit) savant m

bog [bɔg] n tourbière f ▷ vt: **to get ~ged down (in)** (fig) s'enliser (dans)

boggle ['bɔgl] vi: **the mind ~s** c'est incroyable, on en reste sidéré

bogie ['bəugɪ] n bogie m

Bogotá [bəugə'tɑː] n Bogotá

bogus ['bəugəs] adj bidon inv; fantôme

Bohemia [bəu'hiːmɪə] n Bohême f

Bohemian [bəu'hiːmɪən] adj bohémien(ne) ▷ n Bohémien(ne); (gipsy: also: **bohemian**) bohémien(ne)

boil [bɔɪl] vt (faire) bouillir ▷ vi bouillir ▷ n (Med) furoncle m; **to come to the** or (US) **a ~** bouillir; **to bring to the** or (US) **a ~** porter à ébullition
▸ **boil down** vi (fig): **to ~ down to** se réduire or ramener à
▸ **boil over** vi déborder

boiled egg n œuf m à la coque

boiler ['bɔɪlə^r] n chaudière f

boiler suit n (Brit) bleu m de travail, combinaison f

boiling ['bɔɪlɪŋ] adj: **I'm ~ (hot)** (inf) je crève de chaud

boiling point n point m d'ébullition

boil-in-the-bag [bɔɪlɪnðə'bæg] adj (rice etc) en sachet cuisson

boisterous ['bɔɪstərəs] adj bruyant(e), tapageur(-euse)

bold [bəuld] adj hardi(e), audacieux(-euse); (pej) effronté(e); (outline, colour) franc (franche), tranché(e), marqué(e)

boldness ['bəuldnɪs] *n* hardiesse *f*, audace *f*; aplomb *m*, effronterie *f*

bold type *n* (*Typ*) caractères *mpl* gras

Bolivia [bə'lɪvɪə] *n* Bolivie *f*

Bolivian [bə'lɪvɪən] *adj* bolivien(ne) ▷ *n* Bolivien(ne)

bollard ['bɔləd] *n* (*Naut*) bitte *f* d'amarrage; (*Brit Aut*) borne lumineuse *or* de signalisation

bolshy ['bɔlʃɪ] *adj* râleur(-euse); **to be in a ~ mood** être peu coopératif(-ive)

bolster ['bəulstə^r] *n* traversin *m*
  ▶ **bolster up** *vt* soutenir

bolt [bəult] *n* verrou *m*; (*with nut*) boulon *m* ▷ *adv*: **~ upright** droit(e) comme un piquet ▷ *vt* (*door*) verrouiller; (*food*) engloutir ▷ *vi* se sauver, filer (comme une flèche); **a ~ from the blue** (*horse*) s'emballer; (*fig*) un coup de tonnerre dans un ciel bleu

bomb [bɔm] *n* bombe *f* ▷ *vt* bombarder

bombard [bɔm'baːd] *vt* bombarder

bombardment [bɔm'baːdmənt] *n* bombardement *m*

bombastic [bɔm'bæstɪk] *adj* grandiloquent(e), pompeux(-euse)

bomb disposal *n*: **~ unit** section *f* de déminage; **~ expert** artificier *m*

bomber ['bɔmə^r] *n* caporal *m* d'artillerie; (*Aviat*) bombardier *m*; (*terrorist*) poseur *m* de bombes

bombing ['bɔmɪŋ] *n* bombardement *m*

bomb scare *n* alerte *f* à la bombe

bombshell ['bɔmʃɛl] *n* obus *m*; (*fig*) bombe *f*

bomb site *n* zone *f* de bombardement

bona fide ['bəunə'faɪdɪ] *adj* de bonne foi; (*offer*) sérieux(-euse)

bonanza [bə'nænzə] *n* filon *m*

bond [bɔnd] *n* lien *m*; (*binding promise*) engagement *m*, obligation *f*; (*Finance*) obligation; **bonds** *npl* (*chains*) chaînes *fpl*; **in ~** (*of goods*) en entrepôt

bondage ['bɔndɪdʒ] *n* esclavage *m*

bonded warehouse ['bɔndɪd-] *n* entrepôt *m* sous douanes

bone [bəun] *n* os *m*; (*of fish*) arête *f* ▷ *vt* désosser; ôter les arêtes de

bone china *n* porcelaine *f* tendre

bone-dry ['bəun'draɪ] *adj* absolument sec (sèche)

bone idle *adj* fainéant(e)

bone marrow *n* moelle osseuse

boner ['bəunə^r] *n* (*US*) gaffe *f*, bourde *f*

bonfire ['bɔnfaɪə^r] *n* feu *m* (de joie); (*for rubbish*) feu

bonk [bɔŋk] (*inf!*) *vt* s'envoyer (!), sauter (!) ▷ *vi* s'envoyer en l'air (!)

bonkers ['bɔŋkəz] *adj* (*Brit inf*) cinglé(e), dingue

Bonn [bɔn] *n* Bonn

bonnet ['bɔnɪt] *n* bonnet *m*; (*Brit: of car*) capot *m*

bonny [bɔnɪ] *adj* (*Scottish*) joli(e)

bonus ['bəunəs] *n* (*money*) prime *f*; (*advantage*) avantage *m*

bony ['bəunɪ] *adj* (*arm, face*; *Med: tissue*) osseux(-euse); (*thin: person*) squelettique; (*meat*) plein(e) d'os; (*fish*) plein d'arêtes

boo [buː] *excl* hou!, peuh! ▷ *vt* huer ▷ *n* huée *f*

boob [buːb] *n* (*inf: breast*) nichon *m*; (: *Brit: mistake*) gaffe *f*

booby prize ['buːbɪ-] *n* timbale *f* (ironique)

booby trap ['buːbɪ-] *n* guet-apens *m*

booby-trapped ['buːbɪtræpt] *adj* piégé(e)

book [buk] *n* livre *m*; (*of stamps, tickets etc*) carnet *m*; (*Comm*): **books** *npl* comptes *mpl*, comptabilité *f* ▷ *vt* (*ticket*) prendre; (*seat, room*) réserver; (*driver*) dresser un procès-verbal à; (*football player*) prendre le nom de, donner un carton à; **I ~ed a table in the name of ...** j'ai réservé une table au nom de ...; **to keep the ~s** tenir la comptabilité; **by the ~** à la lettre, selon les règles; **to throw the ~ at sb** passer un savon à qn
  ▶ **book in** *vi* (*Brit: at hotel*) prendre sa chambre
  ▶ **book up** *vt* réserver; **all seats are ~ed up** tout est pris, c'est complet; **the hotel is ~ed up** l'hôtel est complet

bookable ['bukəbl] *adj*: **seats are ~** on peut réserver ses places

bookcase ['bukkeɪs] *n* bibliothèque *f* (meuble)

book ends *npl* serre-livres *m inv*

booking ['bukɪŋ] *n* (*Brit*) réservation *f*; **I confirmed my ~ by fax/email** j'ai confirmé ma réservation par fax/e-mail

booking office *n* (*Brit*) bureau *m* de location

book-keeping ['buk'kiːpɪŋ] *n* comptabilité *f*

booklet ['buklɪt] *n* brochure *f*

bookmaker ['bukmeɪkə^r] *n* bookmaker *m*

bookmark ['bukmaːk] *n* (*for book*) marque-page *m*; (*Comput*) signet *m*

bookseller ['buksɛlə^r] *n* libraire *m/f*

bookshelf ['bukʃɛlf] *n* (*single*) étagère *f* (à livres); (*bookcase*) bibliothèque *f*; **bookshelves** rayons *mpl* (de bibliothèque)

bookshop ['bukʃɔp], **bookstore** *n* librairie *f*

bookstall ['bukstɔːl] *n* kiosque *m* à journaux

book store ['bukstɔː^r] *n* = **bookshop**

book token *n* bon-cadeau *m* (pour un livre)

book value *n* valeur *f* comptable

bookworm ['bukwəːm] *n* dévoreur(-euse) de livres

boom [buːm] *n* (*noise*) grondement *m*; (*in prices, population*) forte augmentation; (*busy period*) boom *m*, vague *f* de prospérité ▷ *vi* gronder; prospérer

boomerang ['buːməræŋ] *n* boomerang *m*

boom town *n* ville *f* en plein essor

boon [buːn] *n* bénédiction *f*, grand avantage

boorish ['buərɪʃ] *adj* grossier(-ère), rustre

boost [buːst] *n* stimulant *m*, remontant *m* ▷ *vt* stimuler; **to give a ~ to sb's spirits** *or* **to sb** remonter le moral à qn

booster ['buːstə^r] *n* (*TV*) amplificateur *m* (de signal); (*Elec*) survolteur *m*; (*also*: **booster rocket**) booster *m*; (*Med: vaccine*) rappel *m*

booster seat *n* (*Aut: for children*) siège *m* rehausseur

boot [buːt] *n* botte *f*; (*for hiking*) chaussure *f* (de marche); (*ankle boot*) bottine *f*; (*Brit: of car*) coffre *m* ▷ *vt* (*Comput*) lancer, mettre en route; **to ~** (*in addition*) par-dessus le marché, en plus; **to give sb the ~** (*inf*) flanquer qn dehors, virer qn

booth [buːð] *n* (*at fair*) baraque (foraine); (*of telephone etc*) cabine *f*; (*also:* **voting booth**) isoloir *m*

bootleg ['buːtlɛg] *adj* de contrebande; **~ record** enregistrement *m* pirate

booty ['buːtɪ] *n* butin *m*

booze [buːz] (*inf*) *n* boissons *fpl* alcooliques, alcool *m* ▷ *vi* boire, picoler

boozer ['buːzəʳ] *n* (*inf: person*): **he's a ~** il picole pas mal; (*Brit inf: pub*) pub *m*

border ['bɔːdəʳ] *n* bordure *f*; bord *m*; (*of a country*) frontière *f*; **the B~s** *la région frontière entre l'Écosse et l'Angleterre*

▸ **border on** *vt fus* être voisin(e) de, toucher à

borderline ['bɔːdəlaɪn] *n* (*fig*) ligne *f* de démarcation ▷ *adj*: **~ case** cas *m* limite

bore [bɔːʳ] *pt of* **bear** ▷ *vt* (*person*) ennuyer, raser; (*hole*) percer; (*well, tunnel*) creuser ▷ *n* (*person*) raseur(-euse); (*boring thing*) barbe *f*; (*of gun*) calibre *m*

bored ['bɔːd] *adj*: **to be ~** s'ennuyer; **he's ~ to tears** *or* **to death** *or* **stiff** il s'ennuie à mourir

boredom ['bɔːdəm] *n* ennui *m*

boring ['bɔːrɪŋ] *adj* ennuyeux(-euse)

born [bɔːn] *adj*: **to be ~** naître; **I was ~ in 1960** je suis né en 1960; **~ blind** aveugle de naissance; **a ~ comedian** un comédien-né

born-again [bɔːnə'gɛn] *adj*: **~ Christian** ≈ évangeliste *m/f*

borne [bɔːn] *pp of* **bear**

Borneo ['bɔːnɪəu] *n* Bornéo *f*

borough ['bʌrə] *n* municipalité *f*

borrow ['bɔrəu] *vt*: **to ~ sth (from sb)** emprunter qch (à qn); **may I ~ your car?** est-ce que je peux vous emprunter votre voiture?

borrower ['bɔrəuəʳ] *n* emprunteur(-euse)

borrowing ['bɔrəuɪŋ] *n* emprunt(s) *mpl*

borstal ['bɔːstl] *n* (*Brit*) ≈ maison *f* de correction

Bosnia ['bɔznɪə] *n* Bosnie *f*

Bosnia-Herzegovina ['bɔznɪə-hɛrzə'gəuviːnə] *n*, **Bosnia-Hercegovina** Bosnie-Herzégovine *f*

Bosnian ['bɔznɪən] *adj* bosniaque, bosnien(ne) ▷ *n* Bosniaque *m/f*, Bosnien(ne)

bosom ['buzəm] *n* poitrine *f*; (*fig*) sein *m*

bosom friend *n* ami(e) intime

boss [bɔs] *n* patron(ne) ▷ *vt* (*also:* **boss about, boss around**) mener à la baguette

bossy ['bɔsɪ] *adj* autoritaire

bosun ['bəusn] *n* maître *m* d'équipage

botanical [bə'tænɪkl] *adj* botanique

botanist ['bɔtənɪst] *n* botaniste *m/f*

botany ['bɔtənɪ] *n* botanique *f*

botch [bɔtʃ] *vt* (*also:* **botch up**) saboter, bâcler

both [bəuθ] *adj* les deux, l'un(e) et l'autre ▷ *pron*: **~ (of them)** les deux, tous (toutes) (les) deux, l'un(e) et l'autre; **~ of us went, we ~ went** nous y sommes allés tous les deux ▷ *adv*: **~ A and B** A et B; **they sell ~ the fabric and the finished**

curtains ils vendent (et) le tissu et les rideaux (finis), ils vendent à la fois le tissu et les rideaux (finis)

bother ['bɔðəʳ] *vt* (*worry*) tracasser; (*needle, bait*) importuner, ennuyer; (*disturb*) déranger ▷ *vi* (*also:* **bother o.s.**) se tracasser, se faire du souci ▷ *n* (*trouble*) ennuis *mpl*; **it is a ~ to have to do** c'est vraiment ennuyeux d'avoir à faire ▷ *excl* zut!; **to ~ doing** prendre la peine de faire; **I'm sorry to ~ you** excusez-moi de vous déranger; **please don't ~** ne vous dérangez pas; **don't ~** ce n'est pas la peine; **it's no ~** aucun problème

Botswana [bɔt'swaːnə] *n* Botswana *m*

bottle ['bɔtl] *n* bouteille *f*; (*baby's*) biberon *m*; (*of perfume, medicine*) flacon *m* ▷ *vt* mettre en bouteille(s); **~ of wine/milk** bouteille de vin/lait; **wine/milk ~** bouteille à vin/lait

▸ **bottle up** *vt* refouler, contenir

bottle bank *n* conteneur *m* (de bouteilles)

bottleneck ['bɔtlnɛk] *n* (*in traffic*) bouchon *m*; (*in production*) goulet *m* d'étranglement

bottle-opener ['bɔtləupnəʳ] *n* ouvre-bouteille *m*

bottom ['bɔtəm] *n* (*of container, sea etc*) fond *m*; (*buttocks*) derrière *m*; (*of page, list*) bas *m*; (*of chair*) siège *m*; (*of mountain, tree, hill*) pied *m* ▷ *adj* (*shelf, step*) du bas; **to get to the ~ of sth** (*fig*) découvrir le fin fond de qch

bottomless ['bɔtəmlɪs] *adj* sans fond, insondable

bottom line *n*: **the ~ is that ...** l'essentiel, c'est que ...

botulism ['bɔtjulɪzəm] *n* botulisme *m*

bough [bau] *n* branche *f*, rameau *m*

bought [bɔːt] *pt, pp of* **buy**

boulder ['bəuldəʳ] *n* gros rocher (*gén lisse, arrondi*)

bounce [bauns] *vi* (*ball*) rebondir; (*cheque*) être refusé (*étant sans provision*); (*also:* **to bounce forward/out etc**) bondir, s'élancer ▷ *vt* faire rebondir ▷ *n* (*rebound*) rebond *m*; **he's got plenty of ~** (*fig*) il est plein d'entrain *or* d'allant

bouncer ['baunsəʳ] *n* (*inf: at dance, club*) videur *m*

bound [baund] *pt, pp of* **bind** ▷ *n* (*gen pl*) limite *f*; (*leap*) bond *m* ▷ *vi* (*leap*) bondir ▷ *vt* (*limit*) borner ▷ *adj*: **to be ~ to do sth** (*obliged*) être obligé(e) *or* avoir obligation de faire qch; **he's ~ to fail** (*likely*) il est sûr d'échouer, son échec est inévitable *or* assuré; **~ by** (*law, regulation*) engagé(e) par; **~ for** à destination de; **out of ~s** dont l'accès est interdit

boundary ['baundrɪ] *n* frontière *f*

boundless ['baundlɪs] *adj* illimité(e), sans bornes

bountiful ['bauntɪful] *adj* (*person*) généreux(-euse); (*God*) bienfaiteur(-trice); (*supply*) ample

bounty ['bauntɪ] *n* (*generosity*) générosité *f*

bouquet ['bukeɪ] *n* bouquet *m*

bourbon ['buəbən] *n* (*US: also:* **bourbon whiskey**) bourbon *m*

bourgeois ['buəʒwaː] *adj, n* bourgeois(e)

bout [baut] *n* période *f*; (*of malaria etc*) accès *m*, crise f, attaque f; (Boxing etc) combat m, match m

boutique [buːˈtiːk] n boutique f

bow¹ [bəu] n nœud m; (weapon) arc m; (Mus) archet m

bow² [bau] n (with body) révérence f, inclination f (du buste or corps); (Naut: also: **bows**) proue f ▷ vi faire une révérence, s'incliner; (yield): **to ~ to** or **before** s'incliner devant, se soumettre à; **to ~ to the inevitable** accepter l'inévitable or l'inéluctable

bowels [bauəlz] npl intestins mpl; (fig) entrailles fpl

bowl [bəul] n (for eating) bol m; (for washing) cuvette f; (ball) boule f; (of pipe) fourneau m ▷ vi (Cricket) lancer (la balle)

▶ **bowl over** vt (fig) renverser

bow-legged [ˈbəuˈlɛgɪd] adj aux jambes arquées

bowler [ˈbəuləʳ] n joueur m de boules; (Cricket) lanceur m (de la balle); (Brit: also: **bowler hat**) (chapeau m) melon m

bowling [ˈbəulɪŋ] n (game) jeu m de boules, jeu de quilles

bowling alley n bowling m

bowling green n terrain m de boules (gazonné et carré)

bowls [bəulz] n (jeu m de) boules fpl

bow tie [bəu-] n nœud m papillon

box [bɔks] n boîte f; (also: **cardboard box**) carton m; (crate) caisse f; (Theat) loge f ▷ vt mettre en boîte; (Sport) boxer avec ▷ vi boxer, faire de la boxe

boxer [ˈbɔksəʳ] n (person) boxeur m; (dog) boxer m

boxer shorts [ˈbɔksəfɔːts] npl caleçon m

boxing [ˈbɔksɪŋ] n (sport) boxe f

Boxing Day n (Brit) le lendemain de Noël; voir article

⬤ **BOXING DAY**
⬤
⬤ Boxing Day est le lendemain de Noël, férié en
⬤ Grande-Bretagne. Ce nom vient d'une
⬤ coutume du XIXe siècle qui consistait à
⬤ donner des cadeaux de Noël (dans des
⬤ boîtes) à ses employés etc le 26 décembre.

boxing gloves npl gants mpl de boxe

boxing ring n ring m

box number n (for advertisements) numéro m d'annonce

box office n bureau m de location

box room n débarras m; chambrette f

boy [bɔɪ] n garçon m

boy band n boys band m

boycott [ˈbɔɪkɔt] n boycottage m ▷ vt boycotter

boyfriend [ˈbɔɪfrɛnd] n (petit) ami

boyish [ˈbɔɪɪʃ] adj d'enfant, de garçon; **to look ~** (man: appear youthful) faire jeune

Bp abbr = **bishop**

BR abbr = **British Rail**

Br. abbr (Rel) = **brother**

bra [brɑː] n soutien-gorge m

brace [breɪs] n (support) attache f, agrafe f; (Brit: also: **braces**: on teeth) appareil m (dentaire); (tool)

vilebrequin m; (Typ: also: **brace bracket**) accolade f ▷ vt (support) consolider, soutenir; **braces** npl (Brit: for trousers) bretelles fpl; **to ~ o.s.** (fig) se préparer mentalement

bracelet [ˈbreɪslɪt] n bracelet m

bracing [ˈbreɪsɪŋ] adj tonifiant(e), tonique

bracken [ˈbrækən] n fougère f

bracket [ˈbrækɪt] n (Tech) tasseau m, support m; (group) classe f, tranche f; (also: **brace bracket**) accolade f; (also: **round bracket**) parenthèse f; (also: **square bracket**) crochet m ▷ vt mettre entre parenthèses; (fig: also: **bracket together**) regrouper; **income ~** tranche f des revenus; **in ~s** entre parenthèses or crochets

brackish [ˈbrækɪʃ] adj (water) saumâtre

brag [bræg] vi se vanter

braid [breɪd] n (trimming) galon m; (of hair) tresse f, natte f

Braille [breɪl] n braille m

brain [breɪn] n cerveau m; **brains** npl (intellect, food) cervelle f; **he's got ~s** il est intelligent

brainchild [ˈbreɪntʃaɪld] n trouvaille (personnelle), invention f

braindead [ˈbreɪndɛd] adj (Med) dans un coma dépassé; (inf) demeuré(e)

brainless [ˈbreɪnlɪs] adj sans cervelle, stupide

brainstorm [ˈbreɪnstɔːm] n (fig) moment m d'égarement; (US: brainwave) idée f de génie

brainwash [ˈbreɪnwɔʃ] vt faire subir un lavage de cerveau à

brainwave [ˈbreɪnweɪv] n idée f de génie

brainy [ˈbreɪnɪ] adj intelligent(e), doué(e)

braise [breɪz] vt braiser

brake [breɪk] n frein m ▷ vt, vi freiner

brake light n feu m de stop

brake pedal n pédale f de frein

bramble [ˈbræmbl] n ronces fpl; (fruit) mûre f

bran [bræn] n son m

branch [brɑːntʃ] n branche f; (Comm) succursale f; (: of bank) agence f; (of association) section locale ▷ vi bifurquer

▶ **branch off** vi (road) bifurquer

▶ **branch out** vi diversifier ses activités; **to ~ out into** étendre ses activités à

branch line n (Rail) bifurcation f, embranchement m

branch manager n directeur(-trice) de succursale (or d'agence)

brand [brænd] n marque (commerciale) ▷ vt (cattle) marquer (au fer rouge); (fig: pej): **to ~ sb a communist** etc traiter or qualifier qn de communiste etc

brandish [ˈbrændɪʃ] vt brandir

brand name n nom m de marque

brand-new [ˈbrændˈnjuː] adj tout(e) neuf (neuve), flambant neuf (neuve)

brandy [ˈbrændɪ] n cognac m, fine f

brash [bræʃ] adj effronté(e)

Brasilia [brəˈzɪlɪə] n Brasilia

brass [brɑːs] n cuivre m (jaune), laiton m; **the ~** (Mus) les cuivres

brass band n fanfare f

brass tacks *npl*: **to get down to ~** en venir au fait

brat [bræt] *n* (*pej*) mioche *m/f*, môme *m/f*

bravado [brə'vɑːdəʊ] *n* bravade *f*

brave [breɪv] *adj* courageux(-euse), brave ▷ *n* guerrier indien ▷ *vt* braver, affronter

bravery ['breɪvərɪ] *n* bravoure *f*, courage *m*

brawl [brɔːl] *n* rixe *f*, bagarre *f* ▷ *vi* se bagarrer

brawn [brɔːn] *n* muscle *m*; (*meat*) fromage *m* de tête

brawny ['brɔːnɪ] *adj* musclé(e), costaud(e)

bray [breɪ] *n* braiement *m* ▷ *vi* braire

brazen ['breɪzn] *adj* impudent(e), effronté(e) ▷ *vt*: **to ~ it out** payer d'effronterie, crâner

brazier ['breɪzɪə'] *n* brasero *m*

Brazil [brə'zɪl] *n* Brésil *m*

Brazilian [brə'zɪljən] *adj* brésilien(ne) ▷ *n* Brésilien(ne)

Brazil nut *n* noix *f* du Brésil

breach [briːtʃ] *vt* ouvrir une brèche dans ▷ *n* (*gap*) brèche *f*; (*estrangement*) brouille *f*; (*breaking*): **~ of contract** rupture *f* de contrat; **~ of the peace** attentat *m* à l'ordre public; **~ of trust** abus *m* de confiance

bread [brɛd] *n* pain *m*; (*inf: money*) fric *m*; **~ and butter** (*n*) tartines (beurrées); (*fig*) subsistance *f*; **to earn one's daily ~** gagner son pain; **to know which side one's ~ is buttered (on)** savoir où est son avantage *or* intérêt

breadbin ['brɛdbɪn] *n* (*Brit*) boîte *f or* huche *f* à pain

breadboard ['brɛdbɔːd] *n* planche *f* à pain; (*Comput*) montage expérimental

breadbox ['brɛdbɔks] *n* (*US*) boîte *f or* huche *f* à pain

breadcrumbs ['brɛdkrʌmz] *npl* miettes *fpl* de pain; (*Culin*) chapelure *f*, panure *f*

breadline ['brɛdlaɪn] *n*: **to be on the ~** être sans le sou *or* dans l'indigence

breadth [brɛtθ] *n* largeur *f*

breadwinner ['brɛdwɪnə'] *n* soutien *m* de famille

break [breɪk] (*pt* **broke**, *pp* **broken** ['brəʊk, 'brəʊkən]) *vt* casser, briser; (*promise*) rompre; (*law*) violer ▷ *vi* se casser, se briser; (*weather*) tourner; (*storm*) éclater; (*day*) se lever ▷ *n* (*gap*) brèche *f*; (*fracture*) cassure *f*; (*rest*) interruption *f*, arrêt *m*; (*: short*) pause *f*; (*: at school*) récréation *f*; (*chance*) chance *f*, occasion *f* favorable; **to ~ one's leg** *etc* se casser la jambe *etc*; **to ~ a record** battre un record; **to ~ the news to sb** annoncer la nouvelle à qn; **to ~ with sb** rompre avec qn; **to ~ even** *vi* rentrer dans ses frais; **to ~ free** *or* **loose** *vi* se dégager, s'échapper; **to take a ~** (*few minutes*) faire une pause, s'arrêter cinq minutes; (*holiday*) prendre un peu de repos; **without a ~** sans interruption, sans arrêt

▶ **break down** *vt* (*door etc*) enfoncer; (*resistance*) venir à bout de; (*figures, data*) décomposer, analyser ▷ *vi* s'effondrer; (*Med*) faire une dépression (nerveuse); (*Aut*) tomber en panne; **my car has broken down** ma voiture est en panne

▶ **break in** *vt* (*horse etc*) dresser ▷ *vi* (*burglar*) entrer par effraction; (*interrupt*) interrompre

▶ **break into** *vt fus* (*house*) s'introduire *or* pénétrer par effraction dans

▶ **break off** *vi* (*speaker*) s'interrompre; (*branch*) se rompre ▷ *vt* (*talks, engagement*) rompre

▶ **break open** *vt* (*door etc*) forcer, fracturer

▶ **break out** *vi* éclater, se déclarer; (*prisoner*) s'évader; **to ~ out in spots** se couvrir de boutons

▶ **break through** *vi*: **the sun broke through** le soleil a fait son apparition ▷ *vt fus* (*defences, barrier*) franchir; (*crowd*) se frayer un passage à travers

▶ **break up** *vi* (*partnership*) cesser, prendre fin; (*marriage*) se briser; (*crowd, meeting*) se séparer; (*ship*) se disloquer; (*Scol: pupils*) être en vacances; (*line*) couper; **the line's** *or* **you're ~ing up** ça coupe ▷ *vt* fracasser, casser; (*fight etc*) interrompre, faire cesser; (*marriage*) désunir

breakable ['breɪkəbl] *adj* cassable, fragile ▷ *n*: **~s** objets *mpl* fragiles

breakage ['breɪkɪdʒ] *n* casse *f*; **to pay for ~s** payer la casse

breakaway ['breɪkəweɪ] *adj* (*group etc*) dissident(e)

breakdown ['breɪkdaʊn] *n* (*Aut*) panne *f*; (*in communications, marriage*) rupture *f*; (*Med: also*: **nervous breakdown**) dépression (nerveuse); (*of figures*) ventilation *f*, répartition *f*

breakdown service *n* (*Brit*) service *m* de dépannage

breakdown truck, (*US*) **breakdown van** *n* dépanneuse *f*

breaker ['breɪkə'] *n* brisant *m*

breakeven ['breɪk'iːvn] *cpd*: **~ chart** graphique *m* de rentabilité; **~ point** seuil *m* de rentabilité

breakfast ['brɛkfəst] *n* petit déjeuner *m*; **what time is ~?** le petit déjeuner est à quelle heure?

breakfast cereal *n* céréales *fpl*

break-in ['breɪkɪn] *n* cambriolage *m*

breaking and entering *n* (*Law*) effraction *f*

breaking point ['breɪkɪŋ-] *n* limites *fpl*

breakthrough ['breɪkθruː] *n* percée *f*

break-up ['breɪkʌp] *n* (*of partnership, marriage*) rupture *f*

break-up value *n* (*Comm*) valeur *f* de liquidation

breakwater ['breɪkwɔːtə'] *n* brise-lames *m inv*, digue *f*

breast [brɛst] *n* (*of woman*) sein *m*; (*chest*) poitrine *f*; (*of chicken, turkey*) blanc *m*

breast-feed ['brɛstfiːd] *vt, vi* (*irreg: like* **feed**) allaiter

breast pocket *n* poche *f* (de) poitrine

breast-stroke ['brɛststrəʊk] *n* brasse *f*

breath [brɛθ] *n* haleine *f*, souffle *m*; **to go out for a ~ of air** sortir prendre l'air; **to take a deep ~** respirer à fond; **out of ~** à bout de souffle, essoufflé(e)

breathalyse ['brɛθəlaɪz] *vt* faire subir l'alcootest à

Breathalyser® ['brεθəlaɪzəʳ] (*Brit*) *n* alcootest *m*
breathe [bri:ð] *vt, vi* respirer; **I won't ~ a word about it** je n'en soufflerai pas mot, je n'en dirai rien à personne
  ▸ **breathe in** *vi* inspirer ▷ *vt* aspirer
  ▸ **breathe out** *vt, vi* expirer
breather ['bri:ðəʳ] *n* moment *m* de repos or de répit
breathing ['bri:ðɪŋ] *n* respiration *f*
breathing space *n* (*fig*) (moment *m* de) répit *m*
breathless ['brεθlɪs] *adj* essoufflé(e), haletant(e), oppressé(e); **~ with excitement** le souffle coupé par l'émotion
breathtaking ['brεθteɪkɪŋ] *adj* stupéfiant(e), à vous couper le souffle
breath test *n* alcootest *m*
bred [brεd] *pt, pp of* **breed**
-bred [brεd] *suffix*: **well/ill~** bien/mal élevé(e)
breed [bri:d] (*pt, pp* **bred**) [brεd] *vt* élever, faire l'élevage de; (*fig*: *hate, suspicion*) engendrer ▷ *vi* se reproduire ▷ *n* race *f*, variété *f*
breeder ['bri:dəʳ] *n* (*person*) éleveur *m*; (*Physics: also*: **breeder reactor**) (réacteur *m*) surrégénérateur *m*
breeding ['bri:dɪŋ] *n* reproduction *f*; élevage *m*; (*upbringing*) éducation *f*
breeze [bri:z] *n* brise *f*
breeze-block ['bri:zblɔk] *n* (*Brit*) parpaing *m*
breezy ['bri:zɪ] *adj* (*day, weather*) venteux(-euse); (*manner*) désinvolte; (*person*) jovial(e)
Breton ['brεtən] *adj* breton(ne) ▷ *n* Breton(ne); (*Ling*) breton *m*
brevity ['brεvɪtɪ] *n* brièveté *f*
brew [bru:] *vt* (*tea*) faire infuser; (*beer*) brasser; (*plot*) tramer, préparer ▷ *vi* (*tea*) infuser; (*beer*) fermenter; (*fig*) se préparer, couver
brewer ['bru:əʳ] *n* brasseur *m*
brewery ['bru:ərɪ] *n* brasserie *f* (*fabrique*)
briar ['braɪəʳ] *n* (*thorny bush*) ronces *fpl*; (*wild rose*) églantine *f*
bribe [braɪb] *n* pot-de-vin *m* ▷ *vt* acheter; soudoyer; **to ~ sb to do sth** soudoyer qn pour qu'il fasse qch
bribery ['braɪbərɪ] *n* corruption *f*
bric-a-brac ['brɪkəbræk] *n* bric-à-brac *m*
brick [brɪk] *n* brique *f*
bricklayer ['brɪkleɪəʳ] *n* maçon *m*
brickwork ['brɪkwə:k] *n* briquetage *m*, maçonnerie *f*
brickworks ['brɪkwə:ks] *n* briqueterie *f*
bridal ['braɪdl] *adj* nuptial(e); **~ party** noce *f*
bride [braɪd] *n* mariée *f*, épouse *f*
bridegroom ['braɪdgru:m] *n* marié *m*, époux *m*
bridesmaid ['braɪdzmeɪd] *n* demoiselle *f* d'honneur
bridge [brɪdʒ] *n* pont *m*; (*Naut*) passerelle *f* (de commandement); (*of nose*) arête *f*; (*Cards, Dentistry*) bridge *m* ▷ *vt* (*river*) construire un pont sur; (*gap*) combler
bridging loan ['brɪdʒɪŋ-] *n* (*Brit*) prêt *m* relais
bridle ['braɪdl] *n* bride *f* ▷ *vt* refréner, mettre la bride à; (*horse*) brider

bridle path *n* piste or allée cavalière
brief [bri:f] *adj* bref (brève) ▷ *n* (*Law*) dossier *m*, cause *f*; (*gen*) tâche *f* ▷ *vt* mettre au courant; (*Mil*) donner des instructions à; **briefs** *npl* slip *m*; **in ~ ...** (en) bref ...
briefcase ['bri:fkeɪs] *n* serviette *f*; porte-documents *m inv*
briefing ['bri:fɪŋ] *n* instructions *fpl*; (*Press*) briefing *m*
briefly ['bri:flɪ] *adv* brièvement; (*visit*) en coup de vent; **to glimpse ~** entrevoir
briefness ['bri:fnɪs] *n* brièveté *f*
Brig. *abbr* = **brigadier**
brigade [brɪ'geɪd] *n* (*Mil*) brigade *f*
brigadier [brɪgə'dɪəʳ] *n* brigadier général
bright [braɪt] *adj* brillant(e); (*room, weather*) clair(e); (*person: clever*) intelligent(e), doué(e); (: *cheerful*) gai(e); (*idea*) génial(e); (*colour*) vif (vive); **to look on the ~ side** regarder le bon côté des choses
brighten ['braɪtn] (*also*: **brighten up**) *vt* (*room*) éclaircir; égayer ▷ *vi* s'éclaircir; (*person*) retrouver un peu de sa gaieté
brightly ['braɪtlɪ] *adv* brillamment
brill [brɪl] *adj* (*Brit inf*) super *inv*
brilliance ['brɪljəns] *n* éclat *m*; (*fig: of person*) brio *m*
brilliant ['brɪljənt] *adj* brillant(e); (*light, sunshine*) éclatant(e); (*inf: great*) super
brim [brɪm] *n* bord *m*
brimful ['brɪm'ful] *adj* plein(e) à ras bord; (*fig*) débordant(e)
brine [braɪn] *n* eau salée; (*Culin*) saumure *f*
bring (*pt, pp* **brought**) [brɪŋ, brɔ:t] *vt* (*thing*) apporter; (*person*) amener; **to ~ sth to an end** mettre fin à qch; **I can't ~ myself to fire him** je ne peux me résoudre à le mettre à la porte
  ▸ **bring about** *vt* provoquer, entraîner
  ▸ **bring back** *vt* rapporter; (*person*) ramener
  ▸ **bring down** *vt* (*lower*) abaisser; (*shoot down*) abattre; (*government*) faire s'effondrer
  ▸ **bring forward** *vt* avancer; (*Book-Keeping*) reporter
  ▸ **bring in** *vt* (*person*) faire entrer; (*object*) rentrer; (*Pol: legislation*) introduire; (*Law: verdict*) rendre; (*produce: income*) rapporter
  ▸ **bring off** *vt* (*task, plan*) réussir, mener à bien; (*deal*) mener à bien
  ▸ **bring on** *vt* (*illness, attack*) provoquer; (*player, substitute*) amener
  ▸ **bring out** *vt* sortir; (*meaning*) faire ressortir, mettre en relief; (*new product, book*) sortir
  ▸ **bring round, bring to** *vt* (*unconscious person*) ranimer
  ▸ **bring up** *vt* élever; (*carry up*) monter; (*question*) soulever; (*food: vomit*) vomir, rendre
brink [brɪŋk] *n* bord *m*; **on the ~ of doing** sur le point de faire, à deux doigts de faire; **she was on the ~ of tears** elle était au bord des larmes
brisk [brɪsk] *adj* vif (vive); (*abrupt*) brusque; (*trade etc*) actif(-ive); **to go for a ~ walk** se promener d'un bon pas; **business is ~** les

bristle ['brɪsl] *n* poil *m* ▷ *vi* se hérisser;
bristling with hérissé(e) de

bristly ['brɪslɪ] *adj (beard, hair)* hérissé(e); **your
chin's all ~** ton menton gratte

Brit [brɪt] *n abbr (inf:* = *British person)* Britannique
m/f

Britain ['brɪtən] *n (also:* **Great Britain)** la
Grande-Bretagne; **in ~** en Grande-Bretagne

British ['brɪtɪʃ] *adj* britannique ▷ *npl:* **the ~** les
Britanniques *mpl*

British Isles *npl:* **the ~** les îles *fpl* Britanniques

British Rail *n compagnie ferroviaire britannique,*
≈ SNCF *f*

British Summer Time *n* heure *f* d'été
britannique

Briton ['brɪtən] *n* Britannique *m/f*

Brittany ['brɪtənɪ] *n* Bretagne *f*

brittle ['brɪtl] *adj* cassant(e), fragile

Bro. *abbr (Rel)* = **brother**

broach [brəutʃ] *vt (subject)* aborder

B road *n (Brit)* ≈ route départementale

broad [brɔːd] *adj* large; *(distinction)* général(e);
(accent) prononcé(e) ▷ *n (US inf)* nana *f;* **~ hint**
allusion transparente; **in ~ daylight** en plein
jour; **the ~ outlines** les grandes lignes

broadband ['brɔːdbænd] *n* transmission *f* à
haut débit

broad bean *n* fève *f*

broadcast ['brɔːdkɑːst] *(pt, pp* **-)** *n* émission *f* ▷ *vt*
(Radio) radiodiffuser; *(TV)* téléviser ▷ *vi* émettre

broadcaster ['brɔːdkɑːstər] *n* personnalité *f* de
la radio *or* de la télévision

broadcasting ['brɔːdkɑːstɪŋ] *n* radiodiffusion *f;*
télévision *f*

broadcasting station *n* station *f* de radio *(or* de
télévision)

broaden ['brɔːdn] *vt* élargir; **to ~ one's mind**
élargir ses horizons ▷ *vi* s'élargir

broadly ['brɔːdlɪ] *adv* en gros, généralement

broad-minded ['brɔːd'maɪndɪd] *adj* large
d'esprit

broadsheet ['brɔːdʃiːt] *n (Brit)* journal *m* grand
format

broccoli ['brɔkəlɪ] *n* brocoli *m*

brochure ['brəuʃjuər] *n* prospectus *m*, dépliant *m*

brogue ['brəug] *n (accent)* accent régional; *(shoe)*
(sorte de) chaussure basse de cuir épais

broil [brɔɪl] *(US) vt* rôtir

broke [brəuk] *pt of* **break** ▷ *adj (inf)* fauché(e); **to
go ~** *(business)* faire faillite

broken ['brəukn] *pp of* **break** ▷ *adj (stick, leg etc)*
cassé(e); *(machine: also:* **broken down)** fichu(e);
(promise, vow) rompu(e); **a ~ marriage** un couple
dissocié; **a ~ home** un foyer désuni; **in ~
French/English** dans un français/anglais
approximatif *or* hésitant

broken-down ['brəukn'daun] *adj (car)* en panne;
(machine) fichu(e); *(house)* en ruines

broken-hearted ['brəukn'hɑːtɪd] *adj* (ayant) le
cœur brisé

broker ['brəukər] *n* courtier *m*

brokerage ['brəukrɪdʒ] *n* courtage *m*

brolly ['brɔlɪ] *n (Brit inf)* pépin *m*, parapluie *m*

bronchitis [brɔŋ'kaɪtɪs] *n* bronchite *f*

bronze [brɔnz] *n* bronze *m*

bronzed ['brɔnzd] *adj* bronzé(e), hâlé(e)

brooch [brəutʃ] *n* broche *f*

brood [bruːd] *n* couvée *f* ▷ *vi (hen, storm)* couver;
(person) méditer (sombrement), ruminer

broody ['bruːdɪ] *adj (fig)* taciturne,
mélancolique

brook [bruk] *n* ruisseau *m*

broom [brum] *n* balai *m; (Bot)* genêt *m*

broomstick ['brumstɪk] *n* manche *m* à balai

Bros. *abbr (Comm:* = *brothers)* Frères

broth [brɔθ] *n* bouillon *m* de viande et de
légumes

brothel ['brɔθl] *n* maison close, bordel *m*

brother ['brʌðər] *n* frère *m*

brotherhood ['brʌðəhud] *n* fraternité *f*

brother-in-law ['brʌðərɪn'lɔːʳ] *n* beau-frère *m*

brotherly ['brʌðəlɪ] *adj* fraternel(le)

brought [brɔːt] *pt, pp of* **bring**

brow [brau] *n* front *m; (rare: gen: eyebrow)* sourcil
m; (of hill) sommet *m*

browbeat ['braubiːt] *vt* intimider, brusquer

brown [braun] *adj* brun(e), marron *inv; (hair)*
châtain *inv; (tanned)* bronzé(e); *(rice, bread, flour)*
complet(-ète) ▷ *n (colour)* brun *m*, marron *m* ▷ *vt*
brunir; *(Culin)* faire dorer, faire roussir; **to go ~**
(person) bronzer; *(leaves)* jaunir

brown bread *n* pain *m* bis

Brownie ['braunɪ] *n* jeannette *f* éclaireuse
(cadette)

brown paper *n* papier *m* d'emballage, papier
kraft

brown rice *n* riz *m* complet

brown sugar *n* cassonade *f*

browse [brauz] *vi (in shop)* regarder *(sans acheter);*
(among books) bouquiner, feuilleter les livres;
(animal) paître; **to ~ through a book** feuilleter
un livre

browser [brauzər] *n (Comput)* navigateur *m*

bruise [bruːz] *n* bleu *m*, ecchymose *f*, contusion *f*
▷ *vt* contusionner, meurtrir ▷ *vi (fruit)* se taler,
se meurtrir; **to ~ one's arm** se faire un bleu au
bras

Brum [brʌm] *n abbr,* **Brummagem**
['brʌmədʒəm] *n (inf)* Birmingham

Brummie ['brʌmɪ] *n (inf)* habitant(e) de
Birmingham; natif(-ive) de Birmingham

brunch [brʌntʃ] *n* brunch *m*

brunette [bruː'nɛt] *n (femme)* brune

brunt [brʌnt] *n:* **the ~ of** *(attack, criticism etc)* le
plus gros de

brush [brʌʃ] *n* brosse *f; (for painting)* pinceau *m;*
(for shaving) blaireau *m; (quarrel)* accrochage *m,*
prise *f* de bec ▷ *vt* brosser; *(also:* **brush past,
brush against)** effleurer, frôler; **to have a ~
with sb** s'accrocher avec qn; **to have a ~ with
the police** avoir maille à partir avec la police

▶ **brush aside** *vt* écarter, balayer

▶ **brush up** *vt (knowledge)* rafraîchir, réviser

brushed [brʌʃt] *adj* (*Tech: steel, chrome etc*) brossé(e); (*nylon, denim etc*) gratté(e)

brush-off ['brʌʃɔf] *n* (*inf*): **to give sb the ~** envoyer qn promener

brushwood ['brʌʃwud] *n* broussailles *fpl*, taillis *m*

brusque [bru:sk] *adj* (*person, manner*) brusque, cassant(e); (*tone*) sec (sèche), cassant(e)

Brussels ['brʌslz] *n* Bruxelles

Brussels sprout [-sprawt] *n* chou *m* de Bruxelles

brutal ['bru:tl] *adj* brutal(e)

brutality [bru:'tælɪtɪ] *n* brutalité *f*

brutalize ['bru:təlaɪz] *vt* (*harden*) rendre brutal(e); (*ill-treat*) brutaliser

brute [bru:t] *n* brute *f* ▷ *adj*: **by ~ force** par la force

brutish ['bru:tɪʃ] *adj* grossier(-ère), brutal(e)

BS *n abbr* (*US:* = *Bachelor of Science*) diplôme universitaire

bs *abbr* = **bill of sale**

BSA *n abbr* = **Boy Scouts of America**

B.Sc. *n abbr* = **Bachelor of Science**

BSE *n abbr* (= *bovine spongiform encephalopathy*) ESB *f*, BSE *f*

BSI *n abbr* (= *British Standards Institution*) association de normalisation

BST *abbr* (= *British Summer Time*) heure *f* d'été

Bt. *abbr* (*Brit*) = **baronet**

btu *n abbr* (= *British thermal unit*) btu (= 1054,2 *joules*)

bubble ['bʌbl] *n* bulle *f* ▷ *vi* bouillonner, faire des bulles; (*sparkle, fig*) pétiller

bubble bath *n* bain moussant

bubble gum *n* chewing-gum *m*

bubblejet printer ['bʌbldʒɛt-] *n* imprimante *f* à bulle d'encre

bubbly ['bʌblɪ] *adj* (*drink*) pétillant(e); (*person*) plein(e) de vitalité ▷ *n* (*inf*) champ *m*

Bucharest [bu:kə'rɛst] *n* Bucarest

buck [bʌk] *n* mâle *m* (*d'un lapin, lièvre, daim etc*); (*US inf*) dollar *m* ▷ *vi* ruer, lancer une ruade; **to pass the ~ (to sb)** se décharger de la responsabilité (sur qn)

▶ **buck up** *vi* (*cheer up*) reprendre du poil de la bête, se remonter ▷ *vt*: **to ~ one's ideas up** se reprendre

bucket ['bʌkɪt] *n* seau *m* ▷ *vi* (*Brit inf*): **the rain is ~ing (down)** il pleut à verse

Buckingham Palace ['bʌkɪŋhəm-] *n* le palais de Buckingham; *voir article*

● **BUCKINGHAM PALACE**

●
● *Buckingham Palace* est la résidence officielle
● londonienne du souverain britannique
● depuis 1762. Construit en 1703, il fut à
● l'origine le palais du duc de Buckingham. Il
● a été partiellement reconstruit au début du
● XXe siècle.

buckle ['bʌkl] *n* boucle *f* ▷ *vt* (*belt etc*) boucler, attacher ▷ *vi* (*warp*) tordre, gauchir; (: *wheel*) se

voiler

▶ **buckle down** *vi* s'y mettre

Bucks [bʌks] *abbr* (*Brit*) = **Buckinghamshire**

bud [bʌd] *n* bourgeon *m*; (*of flower*) bouton *m* ▷ *vi* bourgeonner; (*flower*) éclore

Buddha ['budə] *n* Bouddha *m*

Buddhism ['budɪzəm] *n* bouddhisme *m*

Buddhist ['budɪst] *adj* bouddhiste ▷ *n* Bouddhiste *m/f*

budding ['bʌdɪŋ] *adj* (*flower*) en bouton; (*poet etc*) en herbe; (*passion etc*) naissant(e)

buddy ['bʌdɪ] *n* (*US*) copain *m*

budge [bʌdʒ] *vt* faire bouger ▷ *vi* bouger

budgerigar ['bʌdʒərɪgɑːʳ] *n* perruche *f*

budget ['bʌdʒɪt] *n* budget *m* ▷ *vi*: **to ~ for sth** inscrire qch au budget; **I'm on a tight ~** je dois faire attention à mon budget

budgie ['bʌdʒɪ] *n* = **budgerigar**

Buenos Aires ['bweɪnɔs'aɪrɪz] *n* Buenos Aires

buff [bʌf] *adj* (couleur *f*) chamois *m* ▷ *n* (*inf: enthusiast*) mordu(e)

buffalo (*pl* - *or* -**es**) ['bʌfələu] *n* (*Brit*) buffle *m*; (*US*) bison *m*

buffer ['bʌfəʳ] *n* tampon *m*; (*Comput*) mémoire *f* tampon

buffering ['bʌfərɪŋ] *n* (*Comput*) mise *f* en mémoire tampon

buffer state *n* état *m* tampon

buffer zone *n* zone *f* tampon

buffet *n* ['bufeɪ] (*food Brit: bar*) buffet *m* ▷ *vt* ['bʌfɪt] gifler, frapper; secouer, ébranler

buffet car *n* (*Brit Rail*) voiture-bar *f*

buffet lunch *n* lunch *m*

buffoon [bə'fu:n] *n* buffon *m*, pitre *m*

bug [bʌg] *n* (*bedbug etc*) punaise *f*; (*esp US: any insect*) insecte *m*, bestiole *f*; (*fig: germ*) virus *m*, microbe *m*; (*spy device*) dispositif *m* d'écoute (électronique), micro clandestin; (*Comput: of program*) erreur *f*; (: *of equipment*) défaut *m* ▷ *vt* (*room*) poser des micros dans; (*inf: annoy*) embêter; **I've got the travel ~** (*fig*) j'ai le virus du voyage

bugbear ['bʌgbɛəʳ] *n* cauchemar *m*, bête noire *f*

bugger ['bʌgəʳ] (*inf!*) *n* salaud *m* (!), connard *m* (!) ▷ *vb*: **~ off!** tire-toi! (!); **~ (it)!** merde! (!)

buggy ['bʌgɪ] *n* poussette *f*

bugle ['bju:gl] *n* clairon *m*

build [bɪld] *n* (*of person*) carrure *f*, charpente *f* ▷ *vt* (*pt, pp* **built**) [bɪlt] construire, bâtir

▶ **build on** *vt fus* (*fig*) tirer parti de, partir de

▶ **build up** *vt* accumuler, amasser; (*business*) développer; (*reputation*) bâtir

builder ['bɪldəʳ] *n* entrepreneur *m*

building ['bɪldɪŋ] *n* (*trade*) construction *f*; (*structure*) bâtiment *m*, construction; (: *residential, offices*) immeuble *m*

building contractor *n* entrepreneur *m* (en bâtiment)

building industry *n* (industrie *f* du) bâtiment *m*

building site *n* chantier *m* (de construction)

building society *n* (*Brit*) société *f* de crédit

immobilier; *voir article*

● Une *building society* est une mutuelle dont les
● épargnants et emprunteurs sont les
● propriétaires. Ces mutuelles offrent deux
● services principaux: on peut y avoir un
● compte d'épargne duquel on peut retirer son
● argent sur demande ou moyennant un
● court préavis et on peut également y faire
● des emprunts à long terme, par exemple
● pour acheter une maison. Les *building societies*
● ont eu jusqu'en 1985 le quasi-monopole des
● comptes d'épargne et des prêts immobiliers,
● mais les banques ont maintenant une part
● importante de ce marché.

building trade *n* = **building industry**
build-up ['bɪldʌp] *n* (*of gas etc*) accumulation *f*;
(*publicity*): **to give sb/sth a good ~** faire de la
pub pour qn/qch
built [bɪlt] *pt, pp of* **build**
built-in ['bɪlt'ɪn] *adj* (*cupboard*) encastré(e);
(*device*) incorporé(e); intégré(e)
built-up ['bɪlt'ʌp] *adj*: **~ area** agglomération
(urbaine); zone urbanisée
bulb [bʌlb] *n* (*Bot*) bulbe *m*, oignon *m*; (*Elec*)
ampoule *f*
bulbous ['bʌlbəs] *adj* bulbeux(-euse)
Bulgaria [bʌl'gɛərɪə] *n* Bulgarie *f*
Bulgarian [bʌl'gɛərɪən] *adj* bulgare ▷ *n* Bulgare
m/f; (*Ling*) bulgare *m*
bulge [bʌldʒ] *n* renflement *m*, gonflement *m*; (*in
birth rate, sales*) brusque augmentation *f* ▷ *vi*
faire saillie; présenter un renflement; (*pocket,
file*): **to be bulging with** être plein(e) à
craquer de
bulimia [bə'lɪmɪə] *n* boulimie *f*
bulimic [bju:'lɪmɪk] *adj, n* boulimique *m/f*
bulk [bʌlk] *n* masse *f*, volume *m*; **in ~** (*Comm*) en
gros, en vrac; **the ~ of** la plus grande *or* grosse
partie de
bulk buying [-'baɪɪŋ] *n* achat *m* en gros
bulk carrier *n* cargo *m*
bulkhead ['bʌlkhɛd] *n* cloison *f* (étanche)
bulky ['bʌlkɪ] *adj* volumineux(-euse),
encombrant(e)
bull [bul] *n* taureau *m*; (*male elephant, whale*) mâle
m; (*Stock Exchange*) haussier *m*; (*Rel*) bulle *f*
bulldog ['buldɔg] *n* bouledogue *m*
bulldoze ['buldəuz] *vt* passer *or* raser au
bulldozer; **I was ~d into doing it** (*fig: inf*) on
m'a forcé la main
bulldozer ['buldəuzə'] *n* bulldozer *m*
bullet ['bulɪt] *n* balle *f* (*de fusil etc*)
bulletin ['bulɪtɪn] *n* bulletin *m*, communiqué *m*;
(*also*: **news bulletin**) (bulletin d')informations *fpl*
bulletin board *n* (*Comput*) messagerie *f*
(électronique)
bulletproof ['bulɪtpru:f] *adj* à l'épreuve des
balles; **~ vest** gilet *m* pare-balles

bullfight ['bulfaɪt] *n* corrida *f*, course *f* de
taureaux
bullfighter ['bulfaɪtə'] *n* torero *m*
bullfighting ['bulfaɪtɪŋ] *n* tauromachie *f*
bullion ['buljən] *n* or *m or* argent *m* en lingots
bullock ['bulək] *n* bœuf *m*
bullring ['bulrɪŋ] *n* arène *f*
bull's-eye ['bulzaɪ] *n* centre *m* (*de la cible*)
bullshit ['bulʃɪt] (*inf!*) *n* connerie(s) *f(pl)* (!) ▷ *vt*
raconter des conneries à (!) ▷ *vi* déconner (!)
bully ['bulɪ] *n* brute *f*, tyran *m* ▷ *vt* tyranniser,
rudoyer; (*frighten*) intimider
bullying ['bulɪɪŋ] *n* brimades *fpl*
bum [bʌm] *n* (*inf: Brit: backside*) derrière *m*; (: *esp
US: tramp*) vagabond(e), traîne-savates *m/f inv*;
(: *idler*) glandeur *m*
▶ **bum around** *vi* (*inf*) vagabonder
bumblebee ['bʌmblbi:] *n* bourdon *m*
bumf [bʌmf] *n* (*inf: forms etc*) paperasses *fpl*
bump [bʌmp] *n* (*blow*) coup *m*, choc *m*; (*jolt*)
cahot *m*; (*on road etc, on head*) bosse *f* ▷ *vt* heurter,
cogner; (*car*) emboutir
▶ **bump along** *vi* avancer en cahotant
▶ **bump into** *vt fus* rentrer dans, tamponner;
(*inf: meet*) tomber sur
bumper ['bʌmpə'] *n* pare-chocs *m inv* ▷ *adj*: **~
crop/harvest** récolte/moisson exceptionnelle
bumper cars *npl* (*US*) autos tamponneuses
bumph [bʌmf] *n* = **bumf**
bumptious ['bʌmpʃəs] *adj* suffisant(e),
prétentieux(-euse)
bumpy ['bʌmpɪ] *adj* (*road*) cahoteux(-euse); **it
was a ~ flight/ride** on a été secoués dans
l'avion/la voiture
bun [bʌn] *n* (*cake*) petit gâteau; (*bread*) petit pain
au lait; (*of hair*) chignon *m*
bunch [bʌntʃ] *n* (*of flowers*) bouquet *m*; (*of keys*)
trousseau *m*; (*of bananas*) régime *m*; (*of people*)
groupe *m*; **bunches** *npl* (*in hair*) couettes *fpl*; **~ of
grapes** grappe *f* de raisin
bundle ['bʌndl] *n* paquet *m* ▷ *vt* (*also*: **bundle up**)
faire un paquet de; (*put*): **to ~ sth/sb into**
fourrer *or* enfourner qch/qn dans
▶ **bundle off** *vt* (*person*) faire sortir (en toute
hâte); expédier
▶ **bundle out** *vt* éjecter, sortir (sans
ménagements)
bun fight *n* (*Brit inf*) réception *f*; (*tea party*) thé *m*
bung [bʌŋ] *n* bonde *f*, bouchon *m* ▷ *vt* (*Brit:
throw: also*: **bung into**) flanquer; (*also*: **bung up**:
pipe, hole) boucher; **my nose is ~ed up** j'ai le nez
bouché
bungalow ['bʌŋgələu] *n* bungalow *m*
bungee jumping ['bʌndʒi:'dʒʌmpɪŋ] *n* saut *m* à
l'élastique
bungle ['bʌŋgl] *vt* bâcler, gâcher
bunion ['bʌnjən] *n* oignon *m* (*au pied*)
bunk [bʌŋk] *n* couchette *f*; (*Brit inf*): **to do a ~**
mettre les bouts *or* les voiles
▶ **bunk off** *vi* (*Brit inf: Scol*) sécher (les cours); **I'll
~ off at 3 o'clock this afternoon** je vais mettre
les bouts *or* les voiles à 3 heures cet après-midi

bunk beds *npl* lits superposés
bunker ['bʌŋkəʳ] *n* (*coal store*) soute *f* à charbon; (*Mil, Golf*) bunker *m*
bunny ['bʌnɪ] *n* (*also*: **bunny rabbit**) lapin *m*
bunny girl *n* (*Brit*) *hôtesse de cabaret*
bunny hill *n* (*US Ski*) piste *f* pour débutants
bunting ['bʌntɪŋ] *n* pavoisement *m*, drapeaux *mpl*
buoy [bɔɪ] *n* bouée *f*
▸ **buoy up** *vt* faire flotter; (*fig*) soutenir, épauler
buoyancy ['bɔɪənsɪ] *n* (*of ship*) flottabilité *f*
buoyant ['bɔɪənt] *adj* (*ship*) flottable; (*carefree*) gai(e), plein(e) d'entrain; (*Comm: market, economy*) actif(-ive); (: *prices, currency*) soutenu(e)
burden ['bə:dn] *n* fardeau *m*, charge *f* ▸ *vt* charger; (*oppress*) accabler, surcharger; **to be a ~ to sb** être un fardeau pour qn
bureau (*pl* -**x**) ['bjuərəu, -z] *n* (*Brit: writing desk*) bureau *m*, secrétaire *m*; (*US: chest of drawers*) commode *f*; (*office*) bureau, office *m*
bureaucracy [bjuə'rɔkrəsɪ] *n* bureaucratie *f*
bureaucrat ['bjuərəkræt] *n* bureaucrate *m/f*, rond-de-cuir *m*
bureaucratic [bjuərə'krætɪk] *adj* bureaucratique
bureau de change [-də'ʃãʒ] (*pl* **bureaux de change**) *n* bureau *m* de change
bureaux ['bjuərəuz] *npl of* **bureau**
burgeon ['bə:dʒən] *vi* (*fig*) être en expansion rapide
burger ['bə:gəʳ] *n* hamburger *m*
burglar ['bə:gləʳ] *n* cambrioleur *m*
burglar alarm *n* sonnerie *f* d'alarme
burglarize ['bə:gləraɪz] *vt* (*US*) cambrioler
burglary ['bə:glərɪ] *n* cambriolage *m*
burgle ['bə:gl] *vt* cambrioler
Burgundy ['bə:gəndɪ] *n* Bourgogne *f*
burial ['bɛrɪəl] *n* enterrement *m*
burial ground *n* cimetière *m*
burly ['bə:lɪ] *adj* de forte carrure, costaud(e)
Burma ['bə:mə] *n* Birmanie *f*; *see also* **Myanmar**
Burmese [bə:'mi:z] *adj* birman(e), de Birmanie ▸ *n* (*pl inv*) Birman(e); (*Ling*) birman *m*
burn [bə:n] *vt, vi* (*pt, pp* -**ed** *or* -**t**) [bə:nt] brûler ▸ *n* brûlure *f*; **the cigarette ~t a hole in her dress** la cigarette a fait un trou dans sa robe; **I've ~t myself!** je me suis brûlé(e)!
▸ **burn down** *vt* incendier, détruire par le feu
▸ **burn out** *vt* (*writer etc*): **to ~ o.s. out** s'user (à force de travailler)
burner ['bə:nəʳ] *n* brûleur *m*
burning ['bə:nɪŋ] *adj* (*building, forest*) en flammes; (*issue, question*) brûlant(e); (*ambition*) dévorant(e)
burnish ['bə:nɪʃ] *vt* polir
Burns' Night [bə:nz-] *n* *fête écossaise à la mémoire du poète Robert Burns*; *voir article*

⬤ **BURNS' NIGHT**

⬤
⬤ *Burns' Night est une fête qui a lieu le 25*
⬤ *janvier, à la mémoire du poète écossais*
⬤ *Robert Burns (1759–1796), à l'occasion de*
⬤ *laquelle les Écossais partout dans le monde*
⬤ *organisent un souper, en général arrosé de*
⬤ *whisky. Le plat principal est toujours le*
⬤ *haggis, servi avec de la purée de pommes de*
⬤ *terre et de la purée de rutabagas. On apporte*
⬤ *le haggis au son des cornemuses et au cours*
⬤ *du repas on lit des poèmes de Burns et on*
⬤ *chante ses chansons.*

burnt [bə:nt] *pt, pp of* **burn**
burnt sugar *n* (*Brit*) caramel *m*
burp [bə:p] (*inf*) *n* rot *m* ▸ *vi* roter
burrow ['bʌrəu] *n* terrier *m* ▸ *vt* creuser ▸ *vi* (*rabbit*) creuser un terrier; (*rummage*) fouiller
bursar ['bə:səʳ] *n* économe *m/f*; (*Brit: student*) boursier(-ère)
bursary ['bə:sərɪ] *n* (*Brit*) bourse *f* (d'études)
burst [bə:st] (*pt, pp* -) *vt* faire éclater; (*river: banks etc*) rompre ▸ *vi* éclater; (*tyre*) crever ▸ *n* explosion *f*; (*also*: **burst pipe**) fuite *f* (*due à une rupture*); **a ~ of enthusiasm/energy** un accès d'enthousiasme/d'énergie; **~ of laughter** éclat *m* de rire; **a ~ of applause** une salve d'applaudissement; **a ~ of gunfire** une rafale de tir; **a ~ of speed** une pointe de vitesse; **~ blood vessel** rupture *f* de vaisseau sanguin; **the river has ~ its banks** le cours d'eau est sorti de son lit; **to ~ into flames** s'enflammer soudainement; **to ~ out laughing** éclater de rire; **to ~ into tears** fondre en larmes; **to ~ open** (*vi*) s'ouvrir violemment *or* soudainement; **to be ~ing with** (*container*) être plein(e) (à craquer) de, regorger de; (*fig*) être débordant(e) de
▸ **burst into** *vt fus* (*room etc*) faire irruption dans
▸ **burst out of** *vt fus* sortir précipitamment de
bury ['bɛrɪ] *vt* enterrer; **to ~ one's face in one's hands** se couvrir le visage de ses mains; **to ~ one's head in the sand** (*fig*) pratiquer la politique de l'autruche; **to ~ the hatchet** (*fig*) enterrer la hache de guerre
bus (*pl* -**es**) [bʌs, 'bʌsɪz] *n* autobus *m*
busboy ['bʌsbɔɪ] *n* (*US*) aide-serveur *m*
bus conductor *n* receveur(-euse) *m/f* de bus
bush [buʃ] *n* buisson *m*; (*scrub land*) brousse *f*; **to beat about the ~** tourner autour du pot
bushed [buʃt] *adj* (*inf*) crevé(e), claqué(e)
bushel ['buʃl] *n* boisseau *m*
bushfire ['buʃfaɪəʳ] *n* feu *m* de brousse
bushy ['buʃɪ] *adj* broussailleux(-euse), touffu(e)
busily ['bɪzɪlɪ] *adv*: **to be ~ doing sth** s'affairer à faire qch
business ['bɪznɪs] *n* (*matter, firm*) affaire *f*; (*trading*) affaires *fpl*; (*job, duty*) travail *m*; **to be away on ~** être en déplacement d'affaires; **I'm here on ~** je suis là pour affaires; **he's in the insurance ~** il est dans les assurances; **to do ~ with sb** traiter avec qn; **it's none of my ~** cela ne me regarde pas, ce ne sont pas mes affaires; **he means ~** il ne plaisante pas, il est sérieux
business address *n* adresse professionnelle *or* au bureau

business card n carte f de visite (professionnelle)

business class n (on plane) classe f affaires

businesslike ['bɪznɪslaɪk] adj sérieux(-euse), efficace

businessman ['bɪznɪsmən] (irreg) n homme m d'affaires

business trip n voyage m d'affaires

businesswoman ['bɪznɪswumən] (irreg) n femme f d'affaires

busker ['bʌskəʳ] n (Brit) artiste ambulant(e)

bus lane n (Brit) voie réservée aux autobus

bus pass n carte f de bus

bus shelter n abribus m

bus station n gare routière

bus stop n arrêt m d'autobus

bust [bʌst] n buste m; (measurement) tour m de poitrine ▷ adj (inf: broken) fichu(e), fini(e) ▷ vt (inf: Police: arrest) pincer; **to go ~** faire faillite

bustle ['bʌsl] n remue-ménage m, affairement m ▷ vi s'affairer, se démener

bustling ['bʌslɪŋ] adj (person) affairé(e); (town) très animé(e)

bust-up ['bʌstʌp] n (Brit inf) engueulade f

busty ['bʌstɪ] adj (inf) à la poitrine plantureuse

busy ['bɪzɪ] adj occupé(e); (shop, street) très fréquenté(e); (US: telephone, line) occupé ▷ vt: **to ~ o.s.** s'occuper; **he's a ~ man** (normally) c'est un homme très pris; (temporarily) il est très pris

busybody ['bɪzɪbɔdɪ] n mouche f du coche, âme f charitable

busy signal n (US) tonalité f occupé inv

 KEYWORD

but [bʌt] conj mais; **I'd love to come, but I'm busy** j'aimerais venir mais je suis occupé; **he's not English but French** il n'est pas anglais mais français; **but that's far too expensive!** mais c'est bien trop cher!
▷ prep (apart from, except) sauf, excepté; **nothing but** rien d'autre que; **we've had nothing but trouble** nous n'avons eu que des ennuis; **no-one but him can do it** lui seul peut le faire; **who but a lunatic would do such a thing?** qui sinon un fou ferait une chose pareille?; **but for you/your help** sans toi/ton aide; **anything but that** tout sauf or excepté ça, tout mais pas ça; **the last but one** (Brit) l'avant-dernier(-ère)
▷ adv (just, only) ne … que; **she's but a child** elle n'est qu'une enfant; **had I but known** si seulement j'avais su; **I can but try** je peux toujours essayer; **all but finished** pratiquement terminé; **anything but finished** tout sauf fini, très loin d'être fini

butane ['bju:teɪn] n (also: **butane gas**) butane m

butch [butʃ] adj (inf: man) costaud, viril; (: woman) costaude, masculine

butcher ['butʃəʳ] n boucher m ▷ vt massacrer; (cattle etc for meat) tuer

butcher's ['butʃəʳz], **butcher's shop** n

boucherie f

butler ['bʌtləʳ] n maître m d'hôtel

butt [bʌt] n (cask) gros tonneau; (thick end) (gros) bout; (of gun) crosse f; (of cigarette) mégot m; (Brit fig: target) cible f ▷ vt donner un coup de tête à
▶ **butt in** vi (interrupt) interrompre

butter ['bʌtəʳ] n beurre m ▷ vt beurrer

buttercup ['bʌtəkʌp] n bouton m d'or

butter dish n beurrier m

butterfingers ['bʌtəfɪŋɡəz] n (inf) maladroit(e)

butterfly ['bʌtəflaɪ] n papillon m; (Swimming: also: **butterfly stroke**) brasse f papillon

buttocks ['bʌtəks] npl fesses fpl

button ['bʌtn] n bouton m; (US: badge) pin m ▷ vt (also: **button up**) boutonner ▷ vi se boutonner

buttonhole ['bʌtnhəul] n boutonnière f ▷ vt accrocher, arrêter, retenir

buttress ['bʌtrɪs] n contrefort m

buxom ['bʌksəm] adj aux formes avantageuses or épanouies, bien galbé(e)

buy [baɪ] (pt, pp bought [bɔ:t]) vt acheter; (Comm: company) (r)acheter ▷ n achat m; **that was a good/bad ~** c'était un bon/mauvais achat; **to ~ sb sth/sth from sb** acheter qch à qn; **to ~ sb a drink** offrir un verre or à boire à qn; **can I ~ you a drink?** je vous offre un verre?; **where can I ~ some postcards?** où est-ce que je peux acheter des cartes postales?
▶ **buy back** vt racheter
▶ **buy in** vt (Brit: goods) acheter, faire venir
▶ **buy into** vt fus (Brit Comm) acheter des actions de
▶ **buy off** vt (bribe) acheter
▶ **buy out** vt (partner) désintéresser; (business) racheter
▶ **buy up** vt acheter en bloc, rafler

buyer ['baɪəʳ] n acheteur(-euse) m/f; **~'s market** marché m favorable aux acheteurs

buy-out ['baɪaut] n (Comm) rachat m (d'entreprise)

buzz [bʌz] n bourdonnement m; (inf: phone call): **to give sb a ~** passer un coup de fil à qn ▷ vi bourdonner ▷ vt (call on intercom) appeler; (with buzzer) sonner; (Aviat: plane, building) raser; **my head is ~ing** j'ai la tête qui bourdonne
▶ **buzz off** vi (inf) s'en aller, ficher le camp

buzzard ['bʌzəd] n buse f

buzzer ['bʌzəʳ] n timbre m électrique

buzz word n (inf) mot m à la mode or dans le vent

 KEYWORD

by [baɪ] prep **1** (referring to cause, agent) par, de; **killed by lightning** tué par la foudre; **surrounded by a fence** entouré d'une barrière; **a painting by Picasso** un tableau de Picasso
2 (referring to method, manner, means): **by bus/car** en autobus/voiture; **by train** par le or en train; **to pay by cheque** payer par chèque; **by moonlight/candlelight** à la lueur de la lune/d'une bougie; **by saving hard, he …** à force d'économiser, il …

3 (*via, through*) par; **we came by Dover** nous sommes venus par Douvres

4 (*close to, past*) à côté de; **the house by the school** la maison à côté de l'école; **a holiday by the sea** des vacances au bord de la mer; **she sat by his bed** elle était assise à son chevet; **she went by me** elle est passée à côté de moi; **I go by the post office every day** je passe devant la poste tous les jours

5 (*with time: not later than*) avant; (: *during*): **by daylight** à la lumière du jour; **by night** la nuit, de nuit; **by 4 o'clock** avant 4 heures; **by this time tomorrow** d'ici demain à la même heure; **by the time I got here it was too late** lorsque je suis arrivé il était déjà trop tard

6 (*amount*) à; **by the kilo/metre** au kilo/au mètre; **paid by the hour** payé à l'heure; **to increase** *etc* **by the hour** augmenter *etc* d'heure en heure

7 (*Math: measure*): **to divide/multiply by 3** diviser/multiplier par 3; **a room 3 metres by 4** une pièce de 3 mètres sur 4; **it's broader by a metre** c'est plus large d'un mètre; **the bullet missed him by inches** la balle est passée à quelques centimètres de lui; **one by one** un à un; **little by little** petit à petit, peu à peu

8 (*according to*) d'après, selon; **it's 3 o'clock by my watch** il est 3 heures à ma montre; **it's all right by me** je n'ai rien contre

9: **(all) by oneself** *etc* tout(e) seul(e)
▷ *adv* **1** *see* **go**; **pass** *etc*

2: **by and by** un peu plus tard, bientôt; **by and large** dans l'ensemble

bye ['baɪ], **bye-bye** ['baɪ'baɪ] *excl* au revoir!, salut!

bye-law ['baɪlɔː] *n* = **by-law**

by-election ['baɪɪlɛkʃən] *n* (*Brit*) élection (législative) partielle

Byelorussia [bjɛləu'rʌʃə] *n* Biélorussie *f*

Byelorussian [bjɛləu'rʌʃən] *adj*, *n* = **Belorussian**

bygone ['baɪgɔn] *adj* passé(e) ▷ *n*: **let ~s be ~s** passons l'éponge, oublions le passé

by-law ['baɪlɔː] *n* arrêté municipal

bypass ['baɪpɑːs] *n* rocade *f*; (*Med*) pontage *m* ▷ *vt* éviter

by-product ['baɪprɔdʌkt] *n* sous-produit *m*, dérivé *m*; (*fig*) conséquence *f* secondaire, retombée *f*

byre ['baɪəʳ] *n* (*Brit*) étable *f* (à vaches)

bystander ['baɪstændəʳ] *n* spectateur(-trice), badaud(e)

byte [baɪt] *n* (*Comput*) octet *m*

byway ['baɪweɪ] *n* chemin détourné

byword ['baɪwəːd] *n*: **to be a ~ for** être synonyme de (*fig*)

by-your-leave ['baɪjɔː'liːv] *n*: **without so much as a ~** sans même demander la permission

Cc

C¹, c¹ [siː] *n* (*letter*) C, c *m*; (*Scol: mark*) C; (*Mus*): **C** do *m*; **C for Charlie** C comme Célestin

C² *abbr* (= *Celsius, centigrade*) C

c² *abbr* (= *century*) s.; (= *circa*) v.; (*US etc*) = **cent(s)**

CA *n abbr* = **Central America**; (*Brit*) = **chartered accountant** ▷ *abbr* (*US*) = **California**

ca. *abbr* (= *circa*) v

c/a *abbr* = **capital account; credit account; current account**

CAA *n abbr* (*Brit*) = **Civil Aviation Authority**; (*US*: = *Civil Aeronautics Authority*) *direction de l'aviation civile*

CAB *n abbr* (*Brit*) = **Citizens' Advice Bureau**

cab [kæb] *n* taxi *m*; (*of train, truck*) cabine *f*; (*horse-drawn*) fiacre *m*

cabaret ['kæbəreɪ] *n* attractions *fpl*; (*show*) spectacle *m* de cabaret

cabbage ['kæbɪdʒ] *n* chou *m*

cabbie, cabby ['kæbɪ], **cab driver** *n* (*inf*) taxi *m*, chauffeur *m* de taxi

cabin ['kæbɪn] *n* (*house*) cabane *f*, hutte *f*; (*on ship*) cabine *f*; (*on plane*) compartiment *m*

cabin crew *n* (*Aviat*) équipage *m*

cabin cruiser *n* yacht *m* (à moteur)

cabinet ['kæbɪnɪt] *n* (*Pol*) cabinet *m*; (*furniture*) petit meuble à tiroirs et rayons; (*also*: **display cabinet**) vitrine *f*, petite armoire vitrée

cabinet-maker ['kæbɪnɪt'meɪkəʳ] *n* ébéniste *m*

cabinet minister *n* ministre *m* (*membre du cabinet*)

cable ['keɪbl] *n* câble *m* ▷ *vt* câbler, télégraphier

cable car *n* ['keɪblkaːʳ] *n* téléphérique *m*

cablegram ['keɪblgræm] *n* câblogramme *m*

cable railway *n* (*Brit*) funiculaire *m*

cable television *n* télévision *f* par câble

cache [kæʃ] *n* cachette *f*; **a ~ of food** *etc* un dépôt secret de provisions *etc*, une cachette contenant des provisions *etc*

cackle ['kækl] *vi* caqueter

cactus (*pl* **cacti**) ['kæktəs, -taɪ] *n* cactus *m*

CAD *n abbr* (= *computer-aided design*) CAO *f*

caddie ['kædɪ] *n* caddie *m*

cadet [kə'dɛt] *n* (*Mil*) élève *m* officier; **police ~** élève agent de police

cadge [kædʒ] *vt* (*inf*) se faire donner; **to ~ a meal (off sb)** se faire inviter à manger (par qn)

cadre ['kædrɪ] *n* cadre *m*

Caesarean, (*US*) **Cesarean** [siː'zɛərɪən] *adj*: **~ (section)** césarienne *f*

CAF *abbr* (*Brit*: = *cost and freight*) C et F

café ['kæfeɪ] *n* ≈ café(-restaurant) *m* (*sans alcool*)

cafeteria [kæfɪ'tɪərɪə] *n* cafétéria *f*

caffeine ['kæfiːn] *n* caféine *f*

cage [keɪdʒ] *n* cage *f* ▷ *vt* mettre en cage

cagey ['keɪdʒɪ] *adj* (*inf*) réticent(e), méfiant(e)

cagoule [kə'guːl] *n* K-way® *m*

cahoots [kə'huːts] *n*: **to be in ~ (with)** être de mèche (avec)

CAI *n abbr* (= *computer-aided instruction*) EAO *m*

Cairo ['kaɪərəʊ] *n* le Caire

cajole [kə'dʒəʊl] *vt* couvrir de flatteries *or* de gentillesses

cake [keɪk] *n* gâteau *m*; **~ of soap** savonnette *f*; **it's a piece of ~** (*inf*) c'est un jeu d'enfant; **he wants to have his ~ and eat it (too)** (*fig*) il veut tout avoir

caked [keɪkt] *adj*: **~ with** raidi(e) par, couvert(e) d'une croûte de

cake shop *n* pâtisserie *f*

Cal. *abbr* (*US*) = **California**

calamitous [kə'læmɪtəs] *adj* catastrophique, désastreux(-euse)

calamity [kə'læmɪtɪ] *n* calamité *f*, désastre *m*

calcium ['kælsɪəm] *n* calcium *m*

calculate ['kælkjuleɪt] *vt* calculer; (*estimate: chances, effect*) évaluer

▶ **calculate on** *vt fus*: **to ~ on sth/on doing sth** compter sur qch/faire qch

calculated ['kælkjuleɪtɪd] *adj* (*insult, action*) délibéré(e); **a ~ risk** un risque pris en toute connaissance de cause

calculating ['kælkjuleɪtɪŋ] *adj* calculateur(-trice)

calculation [kælkju'leɪʃən] *n* calcul *m*

calculator ['kælkjuleɪtəʳ] *n* machine *f* à calculer, calculatrice *f*

calculus ['kælkjuləs] *n* analyse *f* (mathématique), calcul infinitésimal; **integral/differential ~** calcul intégral/différentiel

calendar ['kæləndəʳ] *n* calendrier *m*

calendar year *n* année civile

calf (pl **calves**) [kɑːf, kɑːvz] n (of cow) veau m; (of other animals) petit m; (also: **calfskin**) veau m, vachette f; (Anat) mollet m

caliber ['kælɪbəʳ] n (US) = **calibre**

calibrate ['kælɪbreɪt] vt (gun etc) calibrer; (scale of measuring instrument) étalonner

calibre, (US) **caliber** ['kælɪbəʳ] n calibre m

calico ['kælɪkəu] n (Brit) calicot m; (US) indienne f

Calif. abbr (US) = **California**

California [kælɪ'fɔːnɪə] n Californie f

calipers ['kælɪpəz] npl (US) = **callipers**

call [kɔːl] vt (gen, also Tel) appeler; (announce: flight) annoncer; (meeting) convoquer; (strike) lancer ▷ vi appeler; (visit: also: **call in, call round**) passer ▷ n (shout) appel m, cri m; (summons: for flight etc, fig: lure) appel; (visit) visite f; (also: **telephone call**) coup m de téléphone; communication f; **to be on ~** être de permanence; **to be ~ed** s'appeler; **she's ~ed Suzanne** elle s'appelle Suzanne; **who is ~ing?** (Tel) qui est à l'appareil?; **London ~ing** (Radio) ici Londres; **please give me a ~ at 7** appelez-moi à 7 heures; **to make a ~** téléphoner, passer un coup de fil; **can I make a ~ from here?** est-ce que je peux téléphoner d'ici?; **to pay a ~ on sb** rendre visite à qn, passer voir qn; **there's not much ~ for these items** ces articles ne sont pas très demandés

▶ **call at** vt fus (ship) faire escale à; (train) s'arrêter à

▶ **call back** vi (return) repasser; (Tel) rappeler ▷ vt (Tel) rappeler; **can you ~ back later?** pouvez-vous rappeler plus tard?

▶ **call for** vt fus (demand) demander; (fetch) passer prendre

▶ **call in** vt (doctor, expert, police) appeler, faire venir

▶ **call off** vt annuler; **the strike was ~ed off** l'ordre de grève a été rapporté

▶ **call on** vt fus (visit) rendre visite à, passer voir; (request): **to ~ on sb to do** inviter qn à faire

▶ **call out** vi pousser un cri or des cris ▷ vt (doctor, police, troops) appeler

▶ **call up** vt (Mil) appeler, mobiliser; (Tel) appeler

call box ['kɔːlbɔks] n (Brit) cabine f téléphonique

call centre, (US) **call center** n centre m d'appels

caller ['kɔːləʳ] n (Tel) personne f qui appelle; (visitor) visiteur m; **hold the line, ~!** (Tel) ne quittez pas, Monsieur (or Madame)!

call girl n call-girl f

call-in ['kɔːlɪn] n (US Radio, TV) programme m à ligne ouverte

calling ['kɔːlɪŋ] n vocation f; (trade, occupation) état m

calling card n (US) carte f de visite

callipers, (US) **calipers** ['kælɪpəz] npl (Math) compas m; (Med) appareil m orthopédique; gouttière f; étrier m

callous ['kæləs] adj dur(e), insensible

callousness ['kæləsnɪs] n dureté f, manque m de cœur, insensibilité f

callow ['kæləu] adj sans expérience (de la vie)

calm [kɑːm] adj calme ▷ n calme m ▷ vt calmer, apaiser

▶ **calm down** vi se calmer, s'apaiser ▷ vt calmer, apaiser

calmly ['kɑːmlɪ] adv calmement, avec calme

calmness ['kɑːmnɪs] n calme m

Calor gas® ['kælə-] n (Brit) butane m, butagaz® m

calorie ['kælərɪ] n calorie f; **low ~ product** produit m pauvre en calories

calve [kɑːv] vi vêler, mettre bas

calves [kɑːvz] npl of **calf**

CAM n abbr (= computer-aided manufacturing) FAO f

camber ['kæmbəʳ] n (of road) bombement m

Cambodia [kæm'bəudɪə] n Cambodge m

Cambodian [kæm'bəudɪən] adj cambodgien(ne) ▷ n Cambodgien(ne)

Cambs abbr (Brit) = **Cambridgeshire**

camcorder ['kæmkɔːdəʳ] n caméscope m

came [keɪm] pt of **come**

camel ['kæməl] n chameau m

cameo ['kæmɪəu] n camée m

camera ['kæmərə] n appareil-photo m; (Cine, TV) caméra f; **35mm ~** appareil 24 x 36 or petit format; **in ~** à huis clos, en privé

cameraman ['kæmərəmæn] (irreg) n caméraman m

camera phone n téléphone m avec appareil photo

Cameroon, Cameroun [kæmə'ruːn] n Cameroun m

camouflage ['kæməflɑːʒ] n camouflage m ▷ vt camoufler

camp [kæmp] n camp m ▷ vi camper ▷ adj (man) efféminé(e)

campaign [kæm'peɪn] n (Mil, Pol) campagne f ▷ vi (also fig) faire campagne; **to ~ for/against** militer pour/contre

campaigner [kæm'peɪnəʳ] n: **~ for** partisan(e) de; **~ against** opposant(e) à

camp bed ['kæmp'bɛd] n (Brit) lit m de camp

camper ['kæmpəʳ] n campeur(-euse); (vehicle) camping-car m

camping ['kæmpɪŋ] n camping m; **to go ~** faire du camping

camping gas® n butane m

campsite ['kæmpsaɪt] n (terrain m de) camping m

campus ['kæmpəs] n campus m

camshaft ['kæmʃɑːft] n arbre m à came

can¹ [kæn] n (of milk, oil, water) bidon m; (tin) boîte f (de conserve) ▷ vt mettre en conserve; **a ~ of beer** une canette de bière; **he had to carry the ~** (Brit inf) on lui a fait porter le chapeau; see also **keyword**

 KEYWORD

can² [kæn] (negative **cannot, can't**, conditional and pt **could**) aux vb **1** (be able to) pouvoir; **you can do**

it if you try vous pouvez le faire si vous essayez; **I can't hear you** je ne t'entends pas
2 (*know how to*) savoir; **I can swim/play tennis/ drive** je sais nager/jouer au tennis/conduire; **can you speak French?** parlez-vous français?
3 (*may*) pouvoir; **can I use your phone?** puis-je me servir de votre téléphone?
4 (*expressing disbelief, puzzlement etc*): **it can't be true!** ce n'est pas possible!; **what CAN he want?** qu'est-ce qu'il peut bien vouloir?
5 (*expressing possibility, suggestion etc*): **he could be in the library** il est peut-être dans la bibliothèque; **she could have been delayed** il se peut qu'elle ait été retardée; **they could have forgotten** ils ont pu oublier

Canada ['kænədə] *n* Canada *m*
Canadian [kə'neɪdɪən] *adj* canadien(ne) ▷ *n* Canadien(ne)
canal [kə'næl] *n* canal *m*
canary [kə'nɛərɪ] *n* canari *m*, serin *m*
Canary Islands, Canaries [kə'nɛərɪz] *npl*: **the ~** les (îles *fpl*) Canaries *fpl*
Canberra ['kænbərə] *n* Canberra
cancel ['kænsəl] *vt* annuler; (*train*) supprimer; (*party, appointment*) décommander; (*cross out*) barrer, rayer; (*stamp*) oblitérer; (*cheque*) faire opposition à; **I would like to ~ my booking** je voudrais annuler ma réservation
▶ **cancel out** *vt* annuler; **they ~ each other out** ils s'annulent
cancellation [kænsə'leɪʃən] *n* annulation *f*; suppression *f*; oblitération *f*; (*Tourism*) réservation annulée, client *etc* qui s'est décommandé
Cancer ['kænsə'] *n* (*Astrology*) le Cancer; **to be ~** être du Cancer
cancer ['kænsə'] *n* cancer *m*
cancerous ['kænsrəs] *adj* cancéreux(-euse)
cancer patient *n* cancéreux(-euse)
cancer research *n* recherche *f* contre le cancer
C and F *abbr* (*Brit*: = *cost and freight*) C et F
candid ['kændɪd] *adj* (très) franc (franche), sincère
candidacy ['kændɪdəsɪ] *n* candidature *f*
candidate ['kændɪdeɪt] *n* candidat(e)
candidature ['kændɪdətʃə'] *n* (*Brit*) = **candidacy**
candied ['kændɪd] *adj* confit(e); **~ apple** (*US*) pomme caramélisée
candle ['kændl] *n* bougie *f*; (*of tallow*) chandelle *f*; (*in church*) cierge *m*
candlelight ['kændlaɪt] *n*: **by ~** à la lumière d'une bougie; (*dinner*) aux chandelles
candlestick ['kændlstɪk] *n* (*also*: **candle holder**) bougeoir *m*; (*bigger, ornate*) chandelier *m*
candour, (*US*) **candor** ['kændə'] *n* (grande) franchise *or* sincérité
C & W *n abbr* = **country and western**
candy ['kændɪ] *n* sucre candi; (*US*) bonbon *m*
candy bar (*US*) *n* barre *f* chocolatée
candyfloss ['kændɪflɔs] *n* (*Brit*) barbe *f* à papa
candy store *n* (*US*) confiserie *f*

cane [keɪn] *n* canne *f*; (*for baskets, chairs etc*) rotin *m* ▷ *vt* (*Brit Scol*) administrer des coups de bâton à
canine ['kænaɪn] *adj* canin(e)
canister ['kænɪstə'] *n* boîte *f* (*gén en métal*); (*of gas*) bombe *f*
cannabis ['kænəbɪs] *n* (*drug*) cannabis *m*; (*cannabis plant*) chanvre indien
canned ['kænd] *adj* (*food*) en boîte, en conserve; (*inf: music*) enregistré(e); (*Brit inf: drunk*) bourré(e); (*US inf: worker*) mis(e) à la porte
cannibal ['kænɪbəl] *n* cannibale *m/f*, anthropophage *m/f*
cannibalism ['kænɪbəlɪzəm] *n* cannibalisme *m*, anthropophagie *f*
cannon (*pl* - *or* -**s**) ['kænən] *n* (*gun*) canon *m*
cannonball ['kænənbɔːl] *n* boulet *m* de canon
cannon fodder *n* chair *f* à canon
cannot ['kænɔt] = **can not**
canny ['kænɪ] *adj* madré(e), finaud(e)
canoe [kə'nuː] *n* pirogue *f*; (*Sport*) canoë *m*
canoeing [kə'nuːɪŋ] *n* (*sport*) canoë *m*
canoeist [kə'nuːɪst] *n* canoéiste *m/f*
canon ['kænən] *n* (*clergyman*) chanoine *m*; (*standard*) canon *m*
canonize ['kænənaɪz] *vt* canoniser
can-opener [-'əupnə'] *n* ouvre-boîte *m*
canopy ['kænəpɪ] *n* baldaquin *m*; dais *m*
cant [kænt] *n* jargon *m* ▷ *vt*, *vi* pencher
can't [kɑːnt] = **can not**
Cantab. *abbr* (*Brit*: = *cantabrigiensis*) of Cambridge
cantankerous [kæn'tæŋkərəs] *adj* querelleur(-euse), acariâtre
canteen [kæn'tiːn] *n* (*eating place*) cantine *f*; (*Brit: of cutlery*) ménagère *f*
canter ['kæntə'] *n* petit galop ▷ *vi* aller au petit galop
cantilever ['kæntɪliːvə'] *n* porte-à-faux *m inv*
canvas ['kænvəs] *n* (*gen*) toile *f*; **under ~** (*camping*) sous la tente; (*Naut*) toutes voiles dehors
canvass ['kænvəs] *vi* (*Pol*): **to ~ for** faire campagne pour ▷ *vt* (*Pol: district*) faire la tournée électorale dans; (: *person*) solliciter le suffrage de; (*Comm: district*) prospecter; (*citizens, opinions*) sonder
canvasser ['kænvəsə'] *n* (*Pol*) agent électoral; (*Comm*) démarcheur *m*
canvassing ['kænvəsɪŋ] *n* (*Pol*) prospection électorale, démarchage électoral; (*Comm*) démarchage, prospection
canyon ['kænjən] *n* cañon *m*, gorge (profonde)
CAP *n abbr* (= *Common Agricultural Policy*) PAC *f*
cap [kæp] *n* casquette *f*; (*for swimming*) bonnet *m* de bain; (*of pen*) capuchon *m*; (*of bottle*) capsule *f*; (*Brit: contraceptive: also*: **Dutch cap**) diaphragme *m*; (*Football*) sélection *f* pour l'équipe nationale ▷ *vt* capsuler; (*outdo*) surpasser; (*put limit on*) plafonner; **~ped with** coiffé(e) de; **and to ~ it all, he ...** (*Brit*) pour couronner le tout, il ...
capability [keɪpə'bɪlɪtɪ] *n* aptitude *f*, capacité *f*
capable ['keɪpəbl] *adj* capable; **~ of** (*interpretation*

etc) susceptible de

capacious [kə'peɪʃəs] *adj* vaste

capacity [kə'pæsɪtɪ] *n* (*of container*) capacité *f*, contenance *f*; (*ability*) aptitude *f*; **filled to ~** plein(e); **in his ~ as** en sa qualité de; **in an advisory ~** à titre consultatif; **to work at full ~** travailler à plein rendement

cape [keɪp] *n* (*garment*) cape *f*; (*Geo*) cap *m*

Cape of Good Hope *n* cap *m* de Bonne Espérance

caper ['keɪpə^r] *n* (*Culin: gen pl*) câpre *f*; (*prank*) farce *f*

Cape Town *n* Le Cap

capita ['kæpɪtə] *see* **per capita**

capital ['kæpɪtl] *n* (*also:* **capital city**) capitale *f*; (*money*) capital *m*; (*also:* **capital letter**) majuscule *f*

capital account *n* balance *f* des capitaux; (*of country*) compte capital

capital allowance *n* provision *f* pour amortissement

capital assets *npl* immobilisations *fpl*

capital expenditure *n* dépenses *fpl* d'équipement

capital gains tax *n* impôt *m* sur les plus-values

capital goods *n* biens *mpl* d'équipement

capital-intensive ['kæpɪtlɪn'tɛnsɪv] *adj* à forte proportion de capitaux

capitalism ['kæpɪtəlɪzəm] *n* capitalisme *m*

capitalist ['kæpɪtəlɪst] *adj, n* capitaliste *m/f*

capitalize ['kæpɪtəlaɪz] *vt* (*provide with capital*) financer

▶ **capitalize on** *vt fus* (*fig*) profiter de

capital punishment *n* peine capitale

capital transfer tax *n* (*Brit*) impôt *m* sur le transfert de propriété

Capitol ['kæpɪtl] *n*: **the ~** le Capitole; *voir article*

⬤ **Capitol**
⬤
⬤ Le *Capitol* est le siège du "Congress", à
⬤ Washington. Il est situé sur Capitol Hill.

capitulate [kə'pɪtjuleɪt] *vi* capituler

capitulation [kəpɪtju'leɪʃən] *n* capitulation *f*

capricious [kə'prɪʃəs] *adj* capricieux(-euse), fantasque

Capricorn ['kæprɪkɔːn] *n* le Capricorne; **to be ~** être du Capricorne

caps [kæps] *abbr* = **capital letters**

capsize [kæp'saɪz] *vt* faire chavirer ▷ *vi* chavirer

capstan ['kæpstən] *n* cabestan *m*

capsule ['kæpsjuːl] *n* capsule *f*

Capt. *abbr* (= *captain*) Cne

captain ['kæptɪn] *n* capitaine *m* ▷ *vt* commander, être le capitaine de

caption ['kæpʃən] *n* légende *f*

captivate ['kæptɪveɪt] *vt* captiver, fasciner

captive ['kæptɪv] *adj, n* captif(-ive)

captivity [kæp'tɪvɪtɪ] *n* captivité *f*

captor ['kæptə^r] *n* (*unlawful*) ravisseur *m*; (*lawful*): **his ~s** les gens (*or* ceux *etc*) qui l'ont

arrêté

capture ['kæptʃə^r] *vt* (*prisoner, animal*) capturer; (*town*) prendre; (*attention*) capter; (*Comput*) saisir ▷ *n* capture *f*; (*of data*) saisie *f* de données

car [kɑː^r] *n* voiture *f*, auto *f*; (*US Rail*) wagon *m*, voiture; **by ~** en voiture

carafe [kə'ræf] *n* carafe *f*

carafe wine *n* (*in restaurant*) ≈ vin ouvert

caramel ['kærəməl] *n* caramel *m*

carat ['kærət] *n* carat *m*; **18 ~ gold** or *m* à 18 carats

caravan ['kærəvæn] *n* caravane *f*

caravan site *n* (*Brit*) camping *m* pour caravanes

caraway ['kærəweɪ] *n*: **~ seed** graine *f* de cumin, cumin *m*

carbohydrate [kɑːbəu'haɪdreɪt] *n* hydrate *m* de carbone; (*food*) féculent *m*

carbolic acid [kɑː'bɔlɪk-] *n* phénol *m*

car bomb *n* voiture piégée

carbon ['kɑːbən] *n* carbone *m*

carbonated ['kɑːbəneɪtɪd] *adj* (*drink*) gazeux(-euse)

carbon copy *n* carbone *m*

carbon dioxide [-daɪ'ɔksaɪd] *n* gaz *m* carbonique, dioxyde *m* de carbone

carbon monoxide [-mɔ'nɔksaɪd] *n* oxyde *m* de carbone

carbon paper *n* papier *m* carbone

carbon ribbon *n* ruban *m* carbone

car boot sale *n* marché aux puces où des particuliers vendent des objets entreposés dans le coffre de leur voiture

carburettor, (*US*) **carburetor** [kɑːbju'rɛtə^r] *n* carburateur *m*

carcass ['kɑːkəs] *n* carcasse *f*

carcinogenic [kɑːsɪnə'dʒɛnɪk] *adj* cancérigène

card [kɑːd] *n* carte *f*; (*material*) carton *m*; (*membership card*) carte d'adhérent; **to play ~s** jouer aux cartes

cardamom ['kɑːdəməm] *n* cardamome *f*

cardboard ['kɑːdbɔːd] *n* carton *m*

cardboard box *n* (boîte *f* en) carton *m*

cardboard city *n* endroit de la ville où dorment les SDF dans des boîtes en carton

card-carrying member ['kɑːdkærɪɪŋ-] *n* membre actif

card game *n* jeu *m* de cartes

cardiac ['kɑːdɪæk] *adj* cardiaque

cardigan ['kɑːdɪgən] *n* cardigan *m*

cardinal ['kɑːdɪnl] *adj* cardinal(e); (*importance*) capital(e) ▷ *n* cardinal *m*

card index *n* fichier *m* (alphabétique)

cardphone ['kɑːdfəun] *n* téléphone *m* à carte (magnétique)

cardsharp ['kɑːdʃɑːp] *n* tricheur(-euse) professionnel(le)

card vote *n* (*Brit*) vote *m* de délégués

CARE [kɛə^r] *n abbr* (= *Cooperative for American Relief Everywhere*) association charitable

care [kɛə^r] *n* soin *m*, attention *f*; (*worry*) souci *m* ▷ *vi*: **to ~ about** (*feel interest for*) se soucier de, s'intéresser à; (*person: love*) être attaché(e) à; **in sb's ~** à la garde de qn, confié à qn; **~ of** (*on letter*) chez; **"with ~"** "fragile"; **to take ~ (to do)** faire attention (à faire); **to take ~ of** (vt) s'occuper de; **the child has been taken into ~** l'enfant a été placé en institution; **would you ~ to/for ...?** voulez-vous ...?; **I wouldn't ~ to do it** je n'aimerais pas le faire; **I don't ~** ça m'est bien égal, peu m'importe; **I couldn't ~ less** cela m'est complètement égal, je m'en fiche complètement

▶ **care for** vt fus s'occuper de; (like) aimer

careen [kə'ri:n] vi (ship) donner de la bande ▷ vt caréner, mettre en carène

career [kə'rɪə^r] n carrière f ▷ vi (also: **career along**) aller à toute allure

career girl n jeune fille f or femme f qui veut faire carrière

careers officer n conseiller(-ère) d'orientation (professionnelle)

career woman (irreg) n femme ambitieuse

carefree ['kɛəfri:] adj sans souci, insouciant(e)

careful ['kɛəful] adj soigneux(-euse); (cautious) prudent(e); **(be) ~!** (fais) attention!; **to be ~ with one's money** regarder à la dépense

carefully ['kɛəfəlɪ] adv avec soin, soigneusement; prudemment

caregiver ['kɛəgɪvə^r] (US) n (professional) travailleur social; (unpaid) personne qui s'occupe d'un proche qui est malade

careless ['kɛəlɪs] adj négligent(e); (heedless) insouciant(e)

carelessly ['kɛəlɪslɪ] adv négligemment; avec insouciance

carelessness ['kɛəlɪsnɪs] n manque m de soin, négligence f; insouciance f

carer ['kɛərə^r] n (professional) travailleur social; (unpaid) personne qui s'occupe d'un proche qui est malade

caress [kə'rɛs] n caresse f ▷ vt caresser

caretaker ['kɛəteɪkə^r] n gardien(ne), concierge m/f

caretaker government n (Brit) gouvernement m intérimaire

car-ferry ['ka:fɛrɪ] n (on sea) ferry(-boat) m; (on river) bac m

cargo (pl **-es**) ['ka:gəu] n cargaison f, chargement m

cargo boat n cargo m

cargo plane n avion-cargo m

car hire n (Brit) location f de voitures

Caribbean [kærɪ'bi:ən] adj, n: **the ~ (Sea)** la mer des Antilles or des Caraïbes

caricature ['kærɪkətjuə^r] n caricature f

caring ['kɛərɪŋ] adj (person) bienveillant(e); (society, organization) humanitaire

carnage ['ka:nɪdʒ] n carnage m

carnal ['ka:nl] adj charnel(le)

carnation [ka:'neɪʃən] n œillet m

carnival ['ka:nɪvl] n (public celebration) carnaval m; (US: funfair) fête foraine

carnivorous [ka:'nɪvərəs] adj carnivore, carnassier(-ière)

carol ['kærəl] n: **(Christmas) ~** chant m de Noël

carouse [kə'rauz] vi faire la bringue

carousel [kærə'sɛl] n (for luggage) carrousel m; (US) manège m

carp [ka:p] n (fish) carpe f

▶ **carp at** vt fus critiquer

car park (Brit) n parking m, parc m de stationnement

carpenter ['ka:pɪntə^r] n charpentier m; (joiner) menuisier m

carpentry ['ka:pɪntrɪ] n charpenterie f, métier m de charpentier; (woodwork: at school etc) menuiserie f

carpet ['ka:pɪt] n tapis m ▷ vt recouvrir (d'un tapis); **fitted ~** (Brit) moquette f

carpet bombing n bombardement intensif

carpet slippers npl pantoufles fpl

carpet sweeper [-'swi:pə^r] n balai m mécanique

car phone n téléphone m de voiture

car rental n (US) location f de voitures

carriage ['kærɪdʒ] n (Brit Rail) wagon m; (horse-drawn) voiture f; (of goods) transport m; (: cost) port m; (of typewriter) chariot m; (bearing) maintien m, port m; **~ forward** port dû; **~ free** franco de port; **~ paid** (en) port payé

carriage return n retour m à la ligne

carriageway ['kærɪdʒweɪ] n (Brit: part of road) chaussée f

carrier ['kærɪə^r] n transporteur m, camionneur m; (company) entreprise f de transport; (Med) porteur(-euse); (Naut) porte-avions m inv

carrier bag n (Brit) sac m en papier or en plastique

carrier pigeon n pigeon voyageur

carrion ['kærɪən] n charogne f

carrot ['kærət] n carotte f

carry ['kærɪ] vt (subj: person) porter; (: vehicle) transporter; (a motion, bill) voter, adopter; (Math: figure) retenir; (Comm: interest) rapporter; (involve: responsibilities etc) comporter, impliquer; (Med: disease) être porteur de ▷ vi (sound) porter; **to get carried away** (fig) s'emballer, s'enthousiasmer; **this loan carries 10% interest** ce prêt est à 10% (d'intérêt)

▶ **carry forward** vt (gen, Book-Keeping) reporter

▶ **carry on** vi (continue) continuer; (inf: make a fuss) faire des histoires ▷ vt (conduct: business) diriger; (conversation) entretenir; (continue: business, conversation) continuer; **to ~ on with sth/doing** continuer qch/à faire

▶ **carry out** vt (orders) exécuter; (investigation) effectuer; (idea, threat) mettre à exécution

carrycot ['kærɪkɔt] n (Brit) porte-bébé m

carry-on ['kærɪ'ɔn] n (inf: fuss) histoires fpl; (: annoying behaviour) cirque m, cinéma m

cart [ka:t] n charrette f ▷ vt (inf) transporter

carte blanche ['ka:t'blɔnʃ] n: **to give sb ~** donner carte blanche à qn

cartel [ka:'tɛl] n (Comm) cartel m

cartilage ['ka:tɪlɪdʒ] n cartilage m

cartographer [ka:'tɔgrəfə^r] n cartographe m/f

cartography [ka:'tɔgrəfɪ] n cartographie f

carton ['ka:tən] n (box) carton m; (of yogurt) pot m (en carton); (of cigarettes) cartouche f

cartoon [kɑː'tuːn] n (Press) dessin m (humoristique); (satirical) caricature f; (comic strip) bande dessinée; (Cine) dessin animé

cartoonist [kɑː'tuːnɪst] n dessinateur(-trice) humoristique; caricaturiste m/f; auteur m de dessins animés; auteur de bandes dessinées

cartridge ['kɑːtrɪdʒ] n (for gun, pen) cartouche f; (for camera) chargeur m; (music tape) cassette f; (of record player) cellule f

cartwheel ['kɑːtwiːl] n roue f; **to turn a ~** faire la roue

carve [kɑːv] vt (meat: also: **carve up**) découper; (wood, stone) tailler, sculpter

carving ['kɑːvɪŋ] n (in wood etc) sculpture f

carving knife n couteau m à découper

car wash n station f de lavage (de voitures)

Casablanca [kæsə'blæŋkə] n Casablanca

cascade [kæs'keɪd] n cascade f ▷ vi tomber en cascade

case [keɪs] n cas m; (Law) affaire f, procès m; (box) caisse f, boîte f; (for glasses) étui m; (Brit: also: **suitcase**) valise f; (Typ): **lower/upper ~** minuscule f/majuscule f; **to have a good ~** avoir de bons arguments; **there's a strong ~ for reform** il y aurait lieu d'engager une réforme; **in ~ of** en cas de; **in ~ he** au cas où il; **just in ~** à tout hasard; **in any ~** en tout cas, de toute façon

case history n (Med) dossier médical, antécédents médicaux

case study n étude f de cas

cash [kæʃ] n argent m; (Comm) (argent m) liquide m, numéraire m; liquidités fpl; (: in payment) argent comptant, espèces fpl ▷ vt encaisser; **to pay (in) ~** payer (en argent) comptant or en espèces; **~ with order/on delivery** (Comm) payable or paiement à la commande/livraison; **to be short of ~** être à court d'argent; **I haven't got any ~** je n'ai pas de liquide

▶ **cash in** vt (insurance policy etc) toucher

▶ **cash in on** vt fus profiter de

cash account n compte m caisse

cash and carry n libre-service m de gros, cash and carry m inv

cashback ['kæʃbæk] n (discount) remise f; (at supermarket etc) retrait m (à la caisse)

cashbook ['kæʃbuk] n livre m de caisse

cash box n caisse f

cash card n carte f de retrait

cash desk n (Brit) caisse f

cash discount n escompte m de caisse (pour paiement au comptant), remise f au comptant

cash dispenser n distributeur m automatique de billets

cashew [kæ'ʃuː] n (also: **cashew nut**) noix f de cajou

cash flow n cash-flow m, marge brute d'autofinancement

cashier [kæ'ʃɪər] n caissier(-ère) ▷ vt (Mil) destituer, casser

cashmere ['kæʃmɪər] n cachemire m

cash payment n paiement comptant,

versement m en espèces

cash point n distributeur m automatique de billets

cash price n prix comptant

cash register n caisse enregistreuse

cash sale n vente f au comptant

casing ['keɪsɪŋ] n revêtement (protecteur), enveloppe (protectrice)

casino [kə'siːnəu] n casino m

cask [kɑːsk] n tonneau m

casket ['kɑːskɪt] n coffret m; (US: coffin) cercueil m

Caspian Sea ['kæspɪən-] n: **the ~** la mer Caspienne

casserole ['kæsərəul] n (pot) cocotte f; (food) ragoût m (en cocotte)

cassette [kæ'sɛt] n cassette f

cassette deck n platine f cassette

cassette player n lecteur m de cassettes

cassette recorder n magnétophone m à cassettes

cast [kɑːst] (vb: pt, pp ~) vt (throw) jeter; (shadow: lit) projeter; (: fig) jeter; (glance) jeter; (shed) perdre; se dépouiller de; (metal) couler, fondre ▷ n (Theat) distribution f; (also: **plaster cast**) plâtre m; **to ~ sb as Hamlet** attribuer à qn le rôle d'Hamlet; **to ~ one's vote** voter, exprimer son suffrage; **to ~ doubt on** jeter un doute sur

▶ **cast aside** vt (reject) rejeter

▶ **cast off** vi (Naut) larguer les amarres; (Knitting) arrêter les mailles ▷ vt (Knitting) arrêter

▶ **cast on** (Knitting) vt monter ▷ vi monter les mailles

castanets [kæstə'nɛts] npl castagnettes fpl

castaway ['kɑːstəweɪ] n naufragé(e)

caste [kɑːst] n caste f, classe sociale

caster sugar ['kɑːstə-] n (Brit) sucre m semoule

casting vote ['kɑːstɪŋ-] n (Brit) voix prépondérante (pour départager)

cast-iron ['kɑːstaɪən] adj (lit) de or en fonte; (fig: will) de fer; (alibi) en béton

cast iron n fonte f

castle ['kɑːsl] n château m; (fortress) château-fort m; (Chess) tour f

cast-offs ['kɑːstɔfs] npl vêtements mpl dont on ne veut plus

castor ['kɑːstər] n (wheel) roulette f

castor oil n huile f de ricin

castrate [kæs'treɪt] vt châtrer

casual ['kæʒjul] adj (by chance) de hasard, fait(e) au hasard, fortuit(e); (irregular: work etc) temporaire; (unconcerned) désinvolte; **~ wear** vêtements mpl sport inv

casual labour n main-d'œuvre f temporaire

casually ['kæʒjulɪ] adv avec désinvolture, négligemment; (by chance) fortuitement

casualty ['kæʒjultɪ] n accidenté(e), blessé(e); (dead) victime f, mort(e); (Brit: Med: department) urgences fpl; **heavy casualties** lourdes pertes

casualty ward n (Brit) service m des urgences

cat [kæt] *n* chat *m*

catacombs ['kætəku:mz] *npl* catacombes *fpl*

Catalan ['kætəlæn] *adj* catalan(e)

catalogue, *(US)* **catalog** ['kætəlɔg] *n* catalogue *m* ▷ *vt* cataloguer

catalyst ['kætəlɪst] *n* catalyseur *m*

catalytic converter [kætə'lɪtɪkkən'və:tə^r] *n* pot *m* catalytique

catapult ['kætəpʌlt] *n* lance-pierres *m inv*, fronde *f*; *(History)* catapulte *f*

cataract ['kætərækt] *n* *(also Med)* cataracte *f*

catarrh [kə'tɑ:^r] *n* rhume *m* chronique, catarrhe *f*

catastrophe [kə'tæstrəfɪ] *n* catastrophe *f*

catastrophic [kætə'strɔfɪk] *adj* catastrophique

catcall ['kætkɔ:l] *n* *(at meeting etc)* sifflet *m*

catch [kætʃ] *(pt, pp* **caught** [kɔ:t]*) vt* *(ball, train, thief, cold)* attraper; *(person: by surprise)* prendre, surprendre; *(understand)* saisir; *(get entangled)* accrocher ▷ *vi* *(fire)* prendre; *(get entangled)* s'accrocher ▷ *n* *(fish etc)* prise *f*; *(thief etc)* capture *f*; *(hidden problem)* attrape *f*; *(Tech)* loquet *m*; cliquet *m*; **to ~ sb's attention** *or* **eye** attirer l'attention de qn; **to ~ fire** prendre feu; **to ~ sight of** apercevoir; **to play ~** jouer à chat; *(with ball)* jouer à attraper le ballon

▸ **catch on** *vi* *(become popular)* prendre; *(understand)*: **to ~ on (to sth)** saisir (qch)

▸ **catch out** *vt* *(Brit: fig: with trick question)* prendre en défaut

▸ **catch up** *vi* *(with work)* se rattraper, combler son retard ▷ *vt* *(also:* **catch up with**) rattraper

catch-22 ['kætʃtwentɪ'tu:] *n*: **it's a ~ situation** c'est (une situation) sans issue

catching ['kætʃɪŋ] *adj* *(Med)* contagieux(-euse)

catchment area ['kætʃmənt-] *n* *(Brit Scol)* aire *f* de recrutement; *(Geo)* bassin *m* hydrographique

catch phrase *n* slogan *m*, expression toute faite

catchy ['kætʃɪ] *adj* *(tune)* facile à retenir

catechism ['kætɪkɪzəm] *n* catéchisme *m*

categoric [kætɪ'gɔrɪk], **categorical** [kætɪ'gɔrɪkl] *adj* catégorique

categorize ['kætɪgəraɪz] *vt* classer par catégories

category ['kætɪgərɪ] *n* catégorie *f*

cater ['keɪtə^r] *vi*: **to ~ for** *(Brit: needs)* satisfaire, pourvoir à; *(: readers, consumers)* s'adresser à, pourvoir aux besoins de; *(Comm: parties etc)* préparer des repas pour

caterer ['keɪtərə^r] *n* traiteur *m*; fournisseur *m*

catering ['keɪtərɪŋ] *n* restauration *f*; approvisionnement *m*, ravitaillement *m*

caterpillar ['kætəpɪlə^r] *n* chenille *f* ▷ *cpd* *(vehicle)* à chenille; **~ track** *n* chenille *f*

cat flap *n* chatière *f*

cathedral [kə'θi:drəl] *n* cathédrale *f*

cathode ['kæθəud] *n* cathode *f*

cathode ray tube *n* tube *m* cathodique

Catholic ['kæθəlɪk] *(Rel) adj* catholique ▷ *n* catholique *m/f*

catholic ['kæθəlɪk] *adj* *(wide-ranging)* éclectique; universel(le); libéral(e)

catsup ['kætsəp] *n* *(US)* ketchup *m*

cattle ['kætl] *npl* bétail *m*, bestiaux *mpl*

catty ['kætɪ] *adj* méchant(e)

catwalk ['kætwɔ:k] *n* passerelle *f*; *(for models)* podium *m* *(de défilé de mode)*

Caucasian [kɔ:'keɪzɪən] *adj, n* caucasien(ne)

Caucasus ['kɔ:kəsəs] *n* Caucase *m*

caucus ['kɔ:kəs] *n* *(US Pol)* comité électoral (pour désigner des candidats); *voir article*; *(Brit Pol: group)* comité local *(d'un parti politique)*

● **CAUCUS**
●
● Un *caucus* aux États-Unis est une réunion
● restreinte des principaux dirigeants d'un
● parti politique, précédant souvent une
● assemblée générale, dans le but de choisir
● des candidats ou de définir une ligne
● d'action. Par extension, ce terme désigne
● également l'état-major d'un parti politique.

caught [kɔ:t] *pt, pp of* **catch**

cauliflower ['kɔlɪflauə^r] *n* chou-fleur *m*

cause [kɔ:z] *n* cause *f* ▷ *vt* causer; **there is no ~ for concern** il n'y a pas lieu de s'inquiéter; **to ~ sth to be done** faire faire qch; **to ~ sb to do sth** faire faire qch à qn

causeway ['kɔ:zweɪ] *n* chaussée (surélevée)

caustic ['kɔ:stɪk] *adj* caustique

caution ['kɔ:ʃən] *n* prudence *f*; *(warning)* avertissement *m* ▷ *vt* avertir, donner un avertissement à

cautious ['kɔ:ʃəs] *adj* prudent(e)

cautiously ['kɔ:ʃəslɪ] *adv* prudemment, avec prudence

cautiousness ['kɔ:ʃəsnɪs] *n* prudence *f*

cavalier [kævə'lɪə^r] *adj* cavalier(-ère), désinvolte ▷ *n* *(knight)* cavalier *m*

cavalry ['kævəlrɪ] *n* cavalerie *f*

cave [keɪv] *n* caverne *f*, grotte *f* ▷ *vi*: **to go caving** faire de la spéléo(logie)

▸ **cave in** *vi* *(roof etc)* s'effondrer

caveman ['keɪvmæn] *(irreg) n* homme *m* des cavernes

cavern ['kævən] *n* caverne *f*

caviar, caviare ['kævɪɑ:^r] *n* caviar *m*

cavity ['kævɪtɪ] *n* cavité *f*; *(Med)* carie *f*

cavity wall insulation *n* isolation *f* des murs creux

cavort [kə'vɔ:t] *vi* cabrioler, faire des cabrioles

cayenne [keɪ'ɛn] *n* *(also:* **cayenne pepper**) poivre *m* de cayenne

CB *n abbr* (= *Citizens' Band (Radio)*) CB *f*; *(Brit*: = *Companion of (the Order of) the Bath)* titre honorifique

CBC *n abbr* (= *Canadian Broadcasting Corporation*) organisme de radiodiffusion

CBE *n abbr* (= *Companion of (the Order of) the British Empire*) titre honorifique

CBI *n abbr* (= *Confederation of British Industry*) ≈ CNPF *m* (= *Conseil national du patronat français*)

CBS *n abbr* (*US*: = *Columbia Broadcasting System*) chaîne de télévision

CC *abbr* (*Brit*) = **county council**
cc *abbr* (= *cubic centimetre*) cm³; (*on letter etc*) = **carbon copy**
CCA *n abbr* (*US*: = *Circuit Court of Appeals*) cour d'appel itinérante
CCTV *n abbr* = **closed-circuit television**
CCU *n abbr* (*US*: = *coronary care unit*) unité *f* de soins cardiologiques
CD *n abbr* (= *compact disc*) CD *m*; (*Mil: Brit*) = **Civil Defence (Corps)**; (: *US*) = **Civil Defense** ▷ *abbr* (*Brit*: = *Corps Diplomatique*) CD
CD burner *n* graveur *m* de CD
CDC *n abbr* (*US*) = **center for disease control**
CD player *n* platine *f* laser
Cdr. *abbr* (= *commander*) Cdt
CD-ROM [si:di:'rɔm] *n abbr* (= *compact disc read-only memory*) CD-ROM *m inv*
CDT *abbr* (*US*: = *Central Daylight Time*) heure d'été du centre
CDW *n abbr* = **collision damage waiver**
CD writer *n* graveur *m* de CD
cease [si:s] *vt, vi* cesser
ceasefire ['si:sfaɪəʳ] *n* cessez-le-feu *m*
ceaseless ['si:slɪs] *adj* incessant(e), continuel(le)
CED *n abbr* (*US*) = **Committee for Economic Development**
cedar ['si:dəʳ] *n* cèdre *m*
cede [si:d] *vt* céder
cedilla [sɪ'dɪlə] *n* cédille *f*
CEEB *n abbr* (*US*: = *College Entrance Examination Board*) commission d'admission dans l'enseignement supérieur
ceilidh ['keɪlɪ] *n* bal *m* folklorique écossais *or* irlandais
ceiling ['si:lɪŋ] *n* (*also fig*) plafond *m*
celebrate ['sɛlɪbreɪt] *vt, vi* célébrer
celebrated ['sɛlɪbreɪtɪd] *adj* célèbre
celebration [sɛlɪ'breɪʃən] *n* célébration *f*
celebrity [sɪ'lɛbrɪtɪ] *n* célébrité *f*
celeriac [sə'lɛrɪæk] *n* céleri(-rave) *m*
celery ['sɛlərɪ] *n* céleri *m* (en branches)
celestial [sɪ'lɛstɪəl] *adj* céleste
celibacy ['sɛlɪbəsɪ] *n* célibat *m*
cell [sɛl] *n* (*gen*) cellule *f*; (*Elec*) élément *m* (de pile)
cellar ['sɛləʳ] *n* cave *f*
'cellist ['tʃɛlɪst] *n* violoncelliste *m/f*
cello ['tʃɛləu] *n* violoncelle *m*
Cellophane® ['sɛləfeɪn] *n* cellophane® *f*
cellphone ['sɛlfəun] *n* (téléphone *m*) portable *m*, mobile *m*
cellular ['sɛljuləʳ] *adj* cellulaire
cellulose ['sɛljuləus] *n* cellulose *f*
Celsius ['sɛlsɪəs] *adj* Celsius *inv*
Celt [kɛlt, sɛlt] *n* Celte *m/f*
Celtic ['kɛltɪk, 'sɛltɪk] *adj* celte, celtique ▷ *n* (*Ling*) celtique *m*
cement [sə'mɛnt] *n* ciment *m* ▷ *vt* cimenter
cement mixer *n* bétonnière *f*
cemetery ['sɛmɪtrɪ] *n* cimetière *m*
cenotaph ['sɛnətɑːf] *n* cénotaphe *m*
censor ['sɛnsəʳ] *n* censeur *m* ▷ *vt* censurer

censorship ['sɛnsəʃɪp] *n* censure *f*
censure ['sɛnʃəʳ] *vt* blâmer, critiquer
census ['sɛnsəs] *n* recensement *m*
cent [sɛnt] *n* (*unit of dollar, euro*) cent *m* (= *un centième du dollar, de l'euro*); *see also* **per**
centenary [sɛn'ti:nərɪ], (*US*) **centennial** [sɛn'tɛnɪəl] *n* centenaire *m*
center ['sɛntəʳ] *n, vt* (*US*) = **centre** [sɛntɪ] *prefix*
centigrade ['sɛntɪɡreɪd] *adj* centigrade
centilitre, (*US*) **centiliter** ['sɛntɪli:təʳ] *n* centilitre *m*
centimetre, (*US*) **centimeter** ['sɛntɪmi:təʳ] *n* centimètre *m*
centipede ['sɛntɪpi:d] *n* mille-pattes *m inv*
central ['sɛntrəl] *adj* central(e)
Central African Republic *n* République Centrafricaine
Central America *n* Amérique centrale
central heating *n* chauffage central
centralize ['sɛntrəlaɪz] *vt* centraliser
central processing unit *n* (*Comput*) unité centrale (de traitement)
central reservation *n* (*Brit Aut*) terre-plein central
centre, (*US*) **center** ['sɛntəʳ] *n* centre *m* ▷ *vt* centrer; (*Phot*) cadrer; (*concentrate*): **to ~ (on)** centrer (sur)
centrefold, (*US*) **centerfold** ['sɛntəfəuld] *n* (*Press*) pages centrales détachables (*avec photo de pin up*)
centre-forward ['sɛntə'fɔ:wəd] *n* (*Sport*) avant-centre *m*
centre-half ['sɛntə'hɑːf] *n* (*Sport*) demi-centre *m*
centrepiece, (*US*) **centerpiece** ['sɛntəpi:s] *n* milieu *m* de table; (*fig*) pièce maîtresse
centre spread *n* (*Brit*) publicité *f* en double page
centre-stage [sɛntə'steɪdʒ] *n*: **to take ~** occuper le centre de la scène
centrifugal [sɛn'trɪfjugl] *adj* centrifuge
centrifuge ['sɛntrɪfju:ʒ] *n* centrifugeuse *f*
century ['sɛntjurɪ] *n* siècle *m*; **in the twentieth ~** au vingtième siècle
CEO *n abbr* (*US*) = **chief executive officer**
ceramic [sɪ'ræmɪk] *adj* céramique
cereal ['si:rɪəl] *n* céréale *f*
cerebral ['sɛrɪbrəl] *adj* cérébral(e)
ceremonial [sɛrɪ'məunɪəl] *n* cérémonial *m*; (*rite*) rituel *m*
ceremony ['sɛrɪmənɪ] *n* cérémonie *f*; **to stand on ~** faire des façons
cert [sə:t] *n* (*Brit inf*): **it's a dead ~** ça ne fait pas un pli
certain ['sə:tən] *adj* certain(e); **to make ~ of** s'assurer de; **for ~** certainement, sûrement
certainly ['sə:tənlɪ] *adv* certainement
certainty ['sə:təntɪ] *n* certitude *f*
certificate [sə'tɪfɪkɪt] *n* certificat *m*
certified letter ['sə:tɪfaɪd-] *n* (*US*) lettre recommandée
certified public accountant ['sə:tɪfaɪd-] *n* (*US*) expert-comptable *m*
certify ['sə:tɪfaɪ] *vt* certifier; (*award diploma to*) certifier

conférer un diplôme *etc* à; *(declare insane)* déclarer malade mental(e) ▷ *vi:* **to ~ to** attester

cervical ['sə:vɪkl] *adj:* **~ cancer** cancer *m* du col de l'utérus; **~ smear** frottis vaginal

cervix ['sə:vɪks] *n* col *m* de l'utérus

Cesarean [si:'zɛərɪən] *adj, n* (US) = **Caesarean**

cessation [sə'seɪʃən] *n* cessation *f*, arrêt *m*

cesspit ['sɛspɪt] *n* fosse *f* d'aisance

CET *n abbr* (= *Central European Time*) heure d'Europe centrale

Ceylon [sɪ'lɔn] *n* Ceylan *m*

cf. *abbr* (= *compare*) cf., voir

c/f *abbr* (*Comm*) = **carried forward**

CFC *n abbr* (= *chlorofluorocarbon*) CFC *m*

CG *n abbr* (US) = **coastguard**

cg *abbr* (= *centigram*) cg

CH *n abbr* (Brit: = *Companion of Honour*) titre honorifique

ch *abbr* (Brit: = *central heating*) cc

ch. *abbr* (= *chapter*) chap

Chad [tʃæd] *n* Tchad *m*

chafe [tʃeɪf] *vt* irriter, frotter contre ▷ *vi* (*fig*): **to ~ against** se rebiffer contre, regimber contre

chaffinch ['tʃæfɪntʃ] *n* pinson *m*

chagrin ['ʃægrɪn] *n* contrariété *f*, déception *f*

chain [tʃeɪn] *n* (*gen*) chaîne *f* ▷ *vt* (*also:* **chain up**) enchaîner, attacher (avec une chaîne)

chain reaction *n* réaction *f* en chaîne

chain-smoke ['tʃeɪnsməʊk] *vi* fumer cigarette sur cigarette

chain store *n* magasin *m* à succursales multiples

chair [tʃɛəʳ] *n* chaise *f*; (*armchair*) fauteuil *m*; (*of university*) chaire *f*; (*of meeting*) présidence *f* ▷ *vt* (*meeting*) présider; **the ~** (US: *electric chair*) la chaise électrique

chairlift ['tʃɛəlɪft] *n* télésiège *m*

chairman ['tʃɛəmən] (*irreg*) *n* président *m*

chairperson ['tʃɛəpə:sn] (*irreg*) *n* président(e)

chairwoman ['tʃɛəwumən] *n* présidente *f*

chalet ['ʃæleɪ] *n* chalet *m*

chalice ['tʃælɪs] *n* calice *m*

chalk [tʃɔ:k] *n* craie *f*

▶ **chalk up** *vt* écrire à la craie; (*fig: success etc*) remporter

challenge ['tʃælɪndʒ] *n* défi *m* ▷ *vt* défier; (*statement, right*) mettre en question, contester; **to ~ sb to a fight/game** inviter qn à se battre/à jouer (*sous forme d'un défi*); **to ~ sb to do** mettre qn au défi de faire

challenger ['tʃælɪndʒəʳ] *n* (*Sport*) challenger *m*

challenging ['tʃælɪndʒɪŋ] *adj* (*task, career*) qui représente un défi *or* une gageure; (*tone, look*) de défi, provocateur(-trice)

chamber ['tʃeɪmbəʳ] *n* chambre *f*; (Brit Law: *gen pl*) cabinet *m*; **~ of commerce** chambre de commerce

chambermaid ['tʃeɪmbəmeɪd] *n* femme *f* de chambre

chamber music *n* musique *f* de chambre

chamberpot ['tʃeɪmbəpɔt] *n* pot *m* de chambre

chameleon [kə'mi:lɪən] *n* caméléon *m*

chamois ['ʃæmwɑ:] *n* chamois *m*

chamois leather ['ʃæmɪ-] *n* peau *f* de chamois

champagne [ʃæm'peɪn] *n* champagne *m*

champers ['ʃæmpəz] *n* (*inf*) champ *m*

champion ['tʃæmpɪən] *n* (*also of cause*) champion(ne) ▷ *vt* défendre

championship ['tʃæmpɪənʃɪp] *n* championnat *m*

chance [tʃɑ:ns] *n* (*luck*) hasard *m*; (*opportunity*) occasion *f*, possibilité *f*; (*hope, likelihood*) chance *f*; (*risk*) risque *m* ▷ *vt* (*risk*) risquer; (*happen*): **to ~ to do** faire par hasard ▷ *adj* fortuit(e), de hasard; **there is little ~ of his coming** il est peu probable *or* il y a peu de chances qu'il vienne; **to take a ~** prendre un risque; **it's the ~ of a lifetime** c'est une occasion unique; **by ~** par hasard; **to ~ doing sth** se risquer à faire qch; **to ~ it** risquer le coup, essayer

▶ **chance on, chance upon** *vt fus* (*person*) tomber sur, rencontrer par hasard; (*thing*) trouver par hasard

chancel ['tʃɑ:nsəl] *n* chœur *m*

chancellor ['tʃɑ:nsələʳ] *n* chancelier *m*

Chancellor of the Exchequer [-ɪks'tʃɛkəʳ] (Brit) *n* chancelier *m* de l'Échiquier

chandelier [ʃændə'lɪəʳ] *n* lustre *m*

change [tʃeɪndʒ] *vt* (*alter, replace:* Comm: *money*) changer; (*switch, substitute: hands, trains, clothes, one's name etc*) changer de; (*transform*): **to ~ sb into** changer *or* transformer qn en ▷ *vi* (*gen*) changer; (*change clothes*) se changer; (*be transformed*): **to ~ into** se changer *or* transformer en ▷ *n* changement *m*; (*money*) monnaie *f*; **to ~ gear** (Aut) changer de vitesse; **to ~ one's mind** changer d'avis; **she ~d into an old skirt** elle (s'est changée et) a enfilé une vieille jupe; **a ~ of clothes** des vêtements de rechange; **for a ~** pour changer; **small ~** petite monnaie; **to give sb ~ for** *or* **of £10** faire à qn la monnaie de 10 livres; **do you have ~ for £10?** vous avez la monnaie de 10 livres?; **where can I ~ some money?** où est-ce que je peux changer de l'argent?; **keep the ~!** gardez la monnaie!

▶ **change over** *vi* (*swap*) échanger; (*change: drivers etc*) changer; (*change sides: players etc*) changer de côté; **to ~ over from sth to sth** passer de qch à qch

changeable ['tʃeɪndʒəbl] *adj* (*weather*) variable; (*person*) d'humeur changeante

change machine *n* distributeur *m* de monnaie

changeover ['tʃeɪndʒəʊvəʳ] *n* (*to new system*) changement *m*, passage *m*

changing ['tʃeɪndʒɪŋ] *adj* changeant(e)

changing room *n* (Brit: *in shop*) salon *m* d'essayage; (: *Sport*) vestiaire *m*

channel ['tʃænl] *n* (TV) chaîne *f*; (*waveband, groove, fig: medium*) canal *m*; (*of river, sea*) chenal *m* ▷ *vt* canaliser; (*fig: interest, energies*): **to ~ into** diriger vers; **through the usual ~s** en suivant la filière habituelle; **green/red ~** (Customs) couloir *m* *or* sortie *f* "rien à déclarer"/ "marchandises à déclarer"; **the (English) C~** la

Manche

channel-hopping ['tsʃænl'hɔpɪŋ] *n* (TV) zapping *m*

Channel Islands *npl*: **the ~** les îles *fpl* Anglo-Normandes

Channel Tunnel *n*: **the ~** le tunnel sous la Manche

chant [tʃɑːnt] *n* chant *m*; mélopée *f*; (*Rel*) psalmodie *f* ▷ *vt* chanter, scander; psalmodier

chaos ['keɪɔs] *n* chaos *m*

chaos theory *n* théorie *f* du chaos

chaotic [keɪ'ɔtɪk] *adj* chaotique

chap [tʃæp] *n* (*Brit inf*: *man*) type *m*; (*term of address*): **old ~** mon vieux ▷ *vt* (*skin*) gercer, crevasser

chapel ['tʃæpl] *n* chapelle *f*

chaperon ['ʃæpərəun] *n* chaperon *m* ▷ *vt* chaperonner

chaplain ['tʃæplɪn] *n* aumônier *m*

chapped [tʃæpt] *adj* (*skin, lips*) gercé(e)

chapter ['tʃæptə^r] *n* chapitre *m*

char [tʃɑː^r] *vt* (*burn*) carboniser ▷ *vi* (*Brit*: *cleaner*) faire des ménages ▷ *n* (*Brit*) = **charlady**

character ['kærɪktə^r] *n* caractère *m*; (*in novel, film*) personnage *m*; (*eccentric person*) numéro *m*, phénomène *m*; **a person of good ~** une personne bien

character code *n* (*Comput*) code *m* de caractère

characteristic ['kærɪktə'rɪstɪk] *adj, n* caractéristique (*f*)

characterize ['kærɪktəraɪz] *vt* caractériser; **to ~ (as)** définir (comme)

charade [ʃə'rɑːd] *n* charade *f*

charcoal ['tʃɑːkəul] *n* charbon *m* de bois; (*Art*) charbon

charge [tʃɑːdʒ] *n* (*accusation*) accusation *f*; (*Law*) inculpation *f*; (*cost*) prix (demandé); (*of gun, battery, Mil: attack*) charge *f* ▷ *vt* (*gun, battery, Mil: enemy*) charger; (*customer, sum*) faire payer ▷ *vi* (*gen with: up, along etc*) foncer; **charges** *npl* (*costs*) frais *mpl*; (*Brit Tel*): **to reverse the ~s** téléphoner en PCV; **bank/labour ~s** frais *mpl* de banque/main-d'œuvre; **is there a ~?** doit-on payer?; **there's no ~** c'est gratuit, on ne fait pas payer; **extra ~** supplément *m*; **to take ~ of** se charger de; **to be in ~ of** être responsable de, s'occuper de; **to ~ in/out** entrer/sortir en trombe; **to ~ down/up** dévaler/ grimper à toute allure; **to ~ sb (with)** (*Law*) inculper qn (de); **to have ~ of sb** avoir la charge de qn; **they ~d us £10 for the meal** ils nous ont fait payer le repas 10 livres, ils nous ont compté 10 livres pour le repas; **how much do you ~ for this repair?** combien demandez-vous pour cette réparation?; **to ~ an expense (up) to sb** mettre une dépense sur le compte de qn; **~ it to my account** facturez-le sur mon compte

charge account *n* compte *m* client

charge card *n* carte *f* de client (*émise par un grand magasin*)

chargehand ['tʃɑːdʒhænd] *n* (*Brit*) chef *m* d'équipe

charger ['tʃɑːdʒə^r] *n* (*also*: **battery charger**) chargeur *m*; (*old: warhorse*) cheval *m* de bataille

charismatic [kærɪz'mætɪk] *adj* charismatique

charitable ['tʃærɪtəbl] *adj* charitable

charity ['tʃærɪtɪ] *n* charité *f*; (*organization*) institution *f* charitable *or* de bienfaisance, œuvre *f* (de charité)

charity shop *n* (*Brit*) boutique vendant des articles d'occasion au profit d'une organisation caritative

charlady ['tʃɑːleɪdɪ] *n* (*Brit*) femme *f* de ménage

charm [tʃɑːm] *n* charme *m*; (*on bracelet*) breloque *f* ▷ *vt* charmer, enchanter

charm bracelet *n* bracelet *m* à breloques

charming ['tʃɑːmɪŋ] *adj* charmant(e)

chart [tʃɑːt] *n* tableau *m*, diagramme *m*; graphique *m*; (*map*) carte marine; (*weather chart*) carte *f* du temps ▷ *vt* dresser *or* établir la carte de; (*sales, progress*) établir la courbe de; **charts** *npl* (*Mus*) hit-parade *m*; **to be in the ~s** (*record, pop group*) figurer au hit-parade

charter ['tʃɑːtə^r] *vt* (*plane*) affréter ▷ *n* (*document*) charte *f*; **on ~** (*plane*) affrété(e)

chartered accountant ['tʃɑːtəd-] *n* (*Brit*) expert-comptable *m*

charter flight *n* charter *m*

charwoman ['tʃɑːwumən] *n* (*irreg*) = **charlady**

chase [tʃeɪs] *vt* poursuivre, pourchasser; (*also*: **chase away**) chasser ▷ *n* poursuite *f*, chasse *f*
  ▶ **chase down** *vt* (US) = **chase up**
  ▶ **chase up** *vt* (*Brit*: *person*) relancer; (: *information*) rechercher

chasm ['kæzəm] *n* gouffre *m*, abîme *m*

chassis ['ʃæsɪ] *n* châssis *m*

chastened ['tʃeɪsnd] *adj* assagi(e), rappelé(e) à la raison

chastening ['tʃeɪsnɪŋ] *adj* qui fait réfléchir

chastise [tʃæs'taɪz] *vt* punir, châtier; corriger

chastity ['tʃæstɪtɪ] *n* chasteté *f*

chat [tʃæt] *vi* (*also*: **have a chat**) bavarder, causer; (*on Internet*) chatter ▷ *n* conversation *f*
  ▶ **chat up** *vt* (*Brit inf*: *girl*) baratiner

chatline ['tʃætlaɪn] *n* numéro téléphonique qui permet de bavarder avec plusieurs personnes en même temps

chat room *n* (*Internet*) salon *m* de discussion

chat show *n* (*Brit*) talk-show *m*

chattel ['tʃætl] *n see* **good**

chatter ['tʃætə^r] *vi* (*person*) bavarder, papoter ▷ *n* bavardage *m*, papotage *m*; **my teeth are ~ing** je claque des dents

chatterbox ['tʃætəbɔks] *n* moulin *m* à paroles, babillard(e)

chattering classes ['tʃætərɪŋ-] *npl*: **the ~** (*inf, pej*) les intellos *mpl*

chatty ['tʃætɪ] *adj* (*style*) familier(-ière); (*person*) enclin(e) à bavarder *or* au papotage

chauffeur ['ʃəufə^r] *n* chauffeur *m* (de maître)

chauvinism ['ʃəuvɪnɪzəm] *n* (*also*: **male chauvinism**) phallocratie *f*, machisme *m*; (*nationalism*) chauvinisme *m*

chauvinist ['ʃəuvɪnɪst] *n* (*also*: **male chauvinist**) phallocrate *m*, macho *m*; (*nationalist*) chauvin(e)

ChE *abbr* = **chemical engineer**

cheap [tʃiːp] *adj* bon marché *inv*, pas cher (chère); (*reduced: ticket*) à prix réduit; (: *fare*) réduit(e); (*joke*) facile, d'un goût douteux; (*poor quality*) à bon marché, de qualité médiocre ▷ *adv* à bon marché, pour pas cher; **~er** *adj* moins cher (chère); **can you recommend a ~ hotel/restaurant, please?** pourriez-vous m'indiquer un hôtel/restaurant bon marché?

cheap day return *n* billet *m* d'aller et retour réduit (*valable pour la journée*)

cheapen ['tʃiːpn] *vt* rabaisser, déprécier

cheaply ['tʃiːplɪ] *adv* à bon marché, à bon compte

cheat [tʃiːt] *vi* tricher; (*in exam*) copier ▷ *vt* tromper, duper; (*rob*): **to ~ sb out of sth** escroquer qch à qn ▷ *n* tricheur(-euse) *m/f*; escroc *m*; (*trick*) duperie *f*, tromperie *f*
  ▶ **cheat on** *vt fus* tromper

cheating ['tʃiːtɪŋ] *n* tricherie *f*

Chechnya [tʃitʃˈnjaː] *n* Tchétchénie *f*

check [tʃɛk] *vt* vérifier; (*passport, ticket*) contrôler; (*halt*) enrayer; (*restrain*) maîtriser ▷ *vi* (*official etc*) se renseigner ▷ *n* vérification *f*; contrôle *m*; (*curb*) frein *m*; (*Brit: bill*) addition *f*; (*US*) = **cheque**; (*pattern: gen pl*) carreaux *mpl* ▷ *adj* (*also:* **checked**: *pattern, cloth*) à carreaux; **to ~ with sb** demander à qn; **to keep a ~ on sb/sth** surveiller qn/qch
  ▶ **check in** *vi* (*in hotel*) remplir sa fiche (d'hôtel); (*at airport*) se présenter à l'enregistrement ▷ *vt* (*luggage*) (faire) enregistrer
  ▶ **check off** *vt* (*tick off*) cocher
  ▶ **check out** *vi* (*in hotel*) régler sa note ▷ *vt* (*luggage*) retirer; (*investigate: story*) vérifier; (*person*) prendre des renseignements sur
  ▶ **check up** *vi*: **to ~ up (on sth)** vérifier (qch); **to ~ up on sb** se renseigner sur le compte de qn

checkbook ['tʃɛkbuk] *n* (*US*) = **chequebook**

checked ['tʃɛkt] *adj* (*pattern, cloth*) à carreaux

checkered ['tʃɛkəd] *adj* (*US*) = **chequered**

checkers ['tʃɛkəz] *n* (*US*) jeu *m* de dames

check guarantee card *n* (*US*) carte *f* (d'identité) bancaire

check-in ['tʃɛkin] *n* (*also:* **check-in desk**: *at airport*) enregistrement *m*

checking account ['tʃɛkɪŋ-] *n* (*US*) compte courant

checklist ['tʃɛklɪst] *n* liste *f* de contrôle

checkmate ['tʃɛkmeɪt] *n* échec et mat *m*

checkout ['tʃɛkaut] *n* (*in supermarket*) caisse *f*

checkpoint ['tʃɛkpɔɪnt] *n* contrôle *m*

checkroom ['tʃɛkruːm] (*US*) *n* consigne *f*

checkup ['tʃɛkʌp] *n* (*Med*) examen médical, check-up *m*

cheddar ['tʃedəʳ] *n* (*also:* **cheddar cheese**) cheddar *m*

cheek [tʃiːk] *n* joue *f*; (*impudence*) toupet *m*, culot *m*; **what a ~!** quel toupet!

cheekbone ['tʃiːkbəun] *n* pommette *f*

cheeky ['tʃiːkɪ] *adj* effronté(e), culotté(e)

cheep [tʃiːp] *n* (*of bird*) piaulement *m* ▷ *vi* piauler

cheer [tʃɪəʳ] *vt* acclamer, applaudir; (*gladden*) réjouir, réconforter ▷ *vi* applaudir ▷ *n* (*gen pl*) acclamations *fpl*, applaudissements *mpl*; bravos *mpl*, hourras *mpl*; **~s!** à la vôtre!
  ▶ **cheer on** *vt* encourager (par des cris *etc*)
  ▶ **cheer up** *vi* se dérider, reprendre courage ▷ *vt* remonter le moral à *or* de, dérider, égayer

cheerful ['tʃɪəful] *adj* gai(e), joyeux(-euse)

cheerfulness ['tʃɪəfulnɪs] *n* gaieté *f*, bonne humeur

cheerio [tʃɪərɪˈəu] *excl* (*Brit*) salut!, au revoir!

cheerleader ['tʃɪəliːdəʳ] *n* membre d'un groupe de majorettes qui chantent et dansent pour soutenir leur équipe pendant les matchs de football américain

cheerless ['tʃɪəlɪs] *adj* sombre, triste

cheese [tʃiːz] *n* fromage *m*

cheeseboard ['tʃiːzbɔːd] *n* plateau *m* à fromages; (*with cheese on it*) plateau *m* de fromages

cheeseburger ['tʃiːzbəgəʳ] *n* cheeseburger *m*

cheesecake ['tʃiːzkeɪk] *n* tarte *f* au fromage

cheetah ['tʃiːtə] *n* guépard *m*

chef [ʃɛf] *n* chef (cuisinier)

chemical ['kɛmɪkl] *adj* chimique ▷ *n* produit *m* chimique

chemist ['kɛmɪst] *n* (*Brit: pharmacist*) pharmacien(ne); (*scientist*) chimiste *m/f*

chemistry ['kɛmɪstrɪ] *n* chimie *f*

chemist's ['kɛmɪsts], **chemist's shop** *n* (*Brit*) pharmacie *f*

chemotherapy [kiːməuˈθɛrəpɪ] *n* chimiothérapie *f*

cheque, (*US*) **check** [tʃɛk] *n* chèque *m*; **to pay by ~** payer par chèque

chequebook, (*US*) **checkbook** ['tʃɛkbuk] *n* chéquier *m*, carnet *m* de chèques

cheque card *n* (*Brit*) carte *f* (d'identité) bancaire

chequered, (*US*) **checkered** ['tʃɛkəd] *adj* (*fig*) varié(e)

cherish ['tʃɛrɪʃ] *vt* chérir; (*hope etc*) entretenir

cheroot [ʃəˈruːt] *n* cigare *m* de Manille

cherry ['tʃɛrɪ] *n* cerise *f*; (*also:* **cherry tree**) cerisier *m*

Ches *abbr* (*Brit*) = **Cheshire**

chess [tʃɛs] *n* échecs *mpl*

chessboard ['tʃɛsbɔːd] *n* échiquier *m*

chessman ['tʃɛsmən] (*irreg*) *n* pièce *f* (de jeu d'échecs)

chessplayer ['tʃɛspleɪəʳ] *n* joueur(-euse) d'échecs

chest [tʃɛst] *n* poitrine *f*; (*box*) coffre *m*, caisse *f*; **to get sth off one's ~** (*inf*) vider son sac

chest measurement *n* tour *m* de poitrine

chestnut ['tʃɛsnʌt] *n* châtaigne *f*; (*also:* **chestnut tree**) châtaignier *m*; (*colour*) châtain *m* ▷ *adj* (*hair*) châtain *inv*; (*horse*) alezan

chest of drawers *n* commode *f*

chesty ['tʃɛstɪ] *adj* (*cough*) de poitrine

chew [tʃuː] *vt* mâcher

chewing gum ['tʃuːɪŋ-] *n* chewing-gum *m*

chic [ʃiːk] *adj* chic *inv*, élégant(e)

chick [tʃɪk] *n* poussin *m*; (*inf*) pépée *f*

chicken ['tʃɪkɪn] n poulet m; (inf: coward) poule mouillée
▶ **chicken out** vi (inf) se dégonfler
chicken feed n (fig) broutilles fpl, bagatelle f
chickenpox ['tʃɪkɪnpɔks] n varicelle f
chickpea ['tʃɪkpi:] n pois m chiche
chicory ['tʃɪkərɪ] n chicorée f; (salad) endive f
chide [tʃaɪd] vt réprimander, gronder
chief [tʃi:f] n chef m ▷ adj principal(e); **C~ of Staff** (Mil) chef d'État-major
chief constable n (Brit) ≈ préfet m de police
chief executive, (US) **chief executive officer** n directeur(-trice) général(e)
chiefly ['tʃi:flɪ] adv principalement, surtout
chiffon ['ʃɪfɔn] n mousseline f de soie
chilblain ['tʃɪlbleɪn] n engelure f
child (pl **children**) [tʃaɪld, 'tʃɪldrən] n enfant m/f
child abuse n maltraitance f d'enfants; (sexual) abus mpl sexuels sur des enfants
child benefit n (Brit) ≈ allocations familiales
childbirth ['tʃaɪldbə:θ] n accouchement m
childcare ['tʃaɪldkɛər] n (for working parents) garde f des enfants (pour les parents qui travaillent)
childhood ['tʃaɪldhud] n enfance f
childish ['tʃaɪldɪʃ] adj puéril(e), enfantin(e)
childless ['tʃaɪldlɪs] adj sans enfants
childlike ['tʃaɪldlaɪk] adj innocent(e), pur(e)
child minder n (Brit) garde f d'enfants
child prodigy n enfant m/f prodige
children ['tʃɪldrən] npl of **child**
children's home ['tʃɪldrənz-] n ≈ foyer m d'accueil (pour enfants)
Chile ['tʃɪlɪ] n Chili m
Chilean ['tʃɪlɪən] adj chilien(ne) ▷ n Chilien(ne)
chill [tʃɪl] n (of water) froid m; (of air) fraîcheur f; (Med) refroidissement m, coup m de froid ▷ adj froid(e), glacial(e) ▷ vt (person) faire frissonner; refroidir; (Culin) mettre au frais, rafraîchir; **"serve ~ed"** "à servir frais"
▶ **chill out** vi (inf: esp US) se relaxer
chilli, chili ['tʃɪlɪ] n piment m (rouge)
chilling ['tʃɪlɪŋ] adj (wind) frais (fraîche), froid(e); (look, smile) glacé(e); (thought) qui donne le frisson
chilly ['tʃɪlɪ] adj froid(e), glacé(e); (sensitive to cold) frileux(-euse); **to feel ~** avoir froid
chime [tʃaɪm] n carillon m ▷ vi carillonner, sonner
chimney ['tʃɪmnɪ] n cheminée f
chimney sweep n ramoneur m
chimpanzee [tʃɪmpæn'zi:] n chimpanzé m
chin [tʃɪn] n menton m
China ['tʃaɪnə] n Chine f
china ['tʃaɪnə] n (material) porcelaine f; (crockery) (vaisselle f en) porcelaine
Chinese [tʃaɪ'ni:z] adj chinois(e) ▷ n (pl inv) Chinois(e); (Ling) chinois m
chink [tʃɪŋk] n (opening) fente f, fissure f; (noise) tintement m
chinwag ['tʃɪnwæg] n (Brit inf): **to have a ~** tailler une bavette
chip [tʃɪp] n (gen pl: Culin: Brit) frite f; (: US: also:

potato chip) chip m; (of wood) copeau m; (of glass, stone) éclat m; (also: **microchip**) puce f; (in gambling) fiche f ▷ vt (cup, plate) ébrécher; **when the ~s are down** (fig) au moment critique
▶ **chip in** vi (inf) mettre son grain de sel
chipboard ['tʃɪpbɔ:d] n aggloméré m, panneau m de particules
chipmunk ['tʃɪpmʌŋk] n suisse m (animal)
chippings ['tʃɪpɪŋz] npl: **loose ~** gravillons mpl
chip shop n (Brit) friterie f; voir article

● **CHIP SHOP**
●
● Un chip shop, que l'on appelle également un
● "fish-and-chip shop", est un magasin où
● l'on vend des plats à emporter. Les chip shops
● sont d'ailleurs à l'origine des "takeaways".
● On y achète en particulier du poisson frit et
● des frites, mais on y trouve également des
● plats traditionnels britanniques ("steak
● pies", saucisses, etc). Tous les plats étaient à
● l'origine emballés dans du papier journal.
● Dans certains de ces magasins, on peut
● s'asseoir pour consommer sur place.

chiropodist [kɪ'rɔpədɪst] n (Brit) pédicure m/f
chirp [tʃə:p] n pépiement m, gazouillis m; (of crickets) stridulation f ▷ vi pépier, gazouiller; chanter, striduler
chirpy ['tʃə:pɪ] adj (inf) plein(e) d'entrain, tout guilleret(te)
chisel ['tʃɪzl] n ciseau m
chit [tʃɪt] n mot m, note f
chitchat ['tʃɪttʃæt] n bavardage m, papotage m
chivalrous ['ʃɪvəlrəs] adj chevaleresque
chivalry ['ʃɪvəlrɪ] n chevalerie f; esprit m chevaleresque
chives [tʃaɪvz] npl ciboulette f, civette f
chloride ['klɔ:raɪd] n chlorure m
chlorinate ['klɔrɪneɪt] vt chlorer
chlorine ['klɔ:ri:n] n chlore m
choc-ice ['tʃɔkaɪs] n (Brit) esquimau® m
chock [tʃɔk] n cale f
chock-a-block ['tʃɔkə'blɔk], **chock-full** [tʃɔk'ful] adj plein(e) à craquer
chocolate ['tʃɔklɪt] n chocolat m
choice [tʃɔɪs] n choix m ▷ adj de choix; **by** or **from ~** par choix; **a wide ~** un grand choix
choir ['kwaɪər] n chœur m, chorale f
choirboy ['kwaɪəbɔɪ] n jeune choriste m, petit chanteur
choke [tʃəuk] vi étouffer ▷ vt étrangler; étouffer; (block) boucher, obstruer ▷ n (Aut) starter m
cholera ['kɔlərə] n choléra m
cholesterol [kə'lɛstərɔl] n cholestérol m
choose (pt **chose**, pp **chosen**) [tʃu:z, tʃəuz, 'tʃəuzn] vt choisir ▷ vi: **to ~ between** choisir entre; **to ~ from** choisir parmi; **to ~ to do** décider de faire, juger bon de faire
choosy ['tʃu:zɪ] adj: **(to be) ~** (faire le) difficile
chop [tʃɔp] vt (wood) couper (à la hache); (Culin:

also: **chop up**) couper (fin), émincer, hacher (en morceaux) ▷ *n* coup *m* (*de hache, du tranchant de la main*); (*Culin*) côtelette *f*; **to get the ~** (*Brit inf*: *project*) tomber à l'eau; (: *person*: *be sacked*) se faire renvoyer
▶ **chop down** *vt* (*tree*) abattre
▶ **chop off** *vt* trancher
chopper ['tʃɔpər] *n* (*helicopter*) hélicoptère *m*, hélico *m*
choppy ['tʃɔpɪ] *adj* (*sea*) un peu agité(e)
chops [tʃɔps] *npl* (*jaws*) mâchoires *fpl*; babines *fpl*
chopsticks ['tʃɔpstɪks] *npl* baguettes *fpl*
choral ['kɔːrəl] *adj* choral(e), chanté(e) en chœur
chord [kɔːd] *n* (*Mus*) accord *m*
chore [tʃɔːr] *n* travail *m* de routine; **household ~s** travaux *mpl* du ménage
choreographer [kɔrɪˈɔgrəfər] *n* chorégraphe *m/f*
choreography [kɔrɪˈɔgrəfɪ] *n* chorégraphie *f*
chorister ['kɔrɪstər] *n* choriste *m/f*
chortle ['tʃɔːtl] *vi* glousser
chorus ['kɔːrəs] *n* chœur *m*; (*repeated part of song, also fig*) refrain *m*
chose [tʃəuz] *pt of* **choose**
chosen ['tʃəuzn] *pp of* **choose**
chow [tʃau] *n* (*dog*) chow-chow *m*
chowder ['tʃaudər] *n* soupe *f* de poisson
Christ [kraɪst] *n* Christ *m*
christen ['krɪsn] *vt* baptiser
christening ['krɪsnɪŋ] *n* baptême *m*
Christian ['krɪstɪən] *adj, n* chrétien(ne)
Christianity [krɪstɪˈænɪtɪ] *n* christianisme *m*
Christian name *n* prénom *m*
Christmas ['krɪsməs] *n* Noël *m or f*; **happy** *or* **merry ~!** joyeux Noël!
Christmas card *n* carte *f* de Noël
Christmas carol *n* chant *m* de Noël
Christmas Day *n* le jour de Noël
Christmas Eve *n* la veille de Noël; la nuit de Noël
Christmas Island *n* île *f* Christmas
Christmas pudding *n* (*esp Brit*) Christmas *m* pudding
Christmas tree *n* arbre *m* de Noël
chrome [krəum] *n* chrome *m*
chromium ['krəumɪəm] *n* chrome *m*; (*also*: **chromium plating**) chromage *m*
chromosome ['krəuməsəum] *n* chromosome *m*
chronic ['krɔnɪk] *adj* chronique; (*fig: liar, smoker*) invétéré(e)
chronicle ['krɔnɪkl] *n* chronique *f*
chronological [krɔnə'lɔdʒɪkl] *adj* chronologique
chrysanthemum [krɪ'sænθəməm] *n* chrysanthème *m*
chubby ['tʃʌbɪ] *adj* potelé(e), rondelet(te)
chuck [tʃʌk] *vt* (*inf*) lancer, jeter; (*Brit: also*: **chuck up**: *job*) lâcher; (: *person*) plaquer
▶ **chuck out** *vt* (*inf: person*) flanquer dehors *or* à la porte; (: *rubbish etc*) jeter
chuckle ['tʃʌkl] *vi* glousser
chuffed [tʃʌft] *adj* (*Brit inf*): **to be ~ about sth** être content(e) de qch

chug [tʃʌg] *vi* faire teuf-teuf; souffler
chum [tʃʌm] *n* copain (copine)
chump ['tʃʌmp] *n* (*inf*) imbécile *m/f*, crétin(e)
chunk [tʃʌŋk] *n* gros morceau; (*of bread*) quignon *m*
chunky ['tʃʌŋkɪ] *adj* (*furniture etc*) massif(-ive); (*person*) trapu(e); (*knitwear*) en grosse laine
Chunnel ['tʃʌnəl] *n* = **Channel Tunnel**
church [tʃəːtʃ] *n* église *f*; **the C~ of England** l'Église anglicane
churchyard ['tʃəːtʃjɑːd] *n* cimetière *m*
churlish ['tʃəːlɪʃ] *adj* grossier(-ère); hargneux(-euse)
churn [tʃəːn] *n* (*for butter*) baratte *f*; (*also*: **milk churn**) (grand) bidon à lait
▶ **churn out** *vt* débiter
chute [ʃuːt] *n* goulotte *f*; (*also*: **rubbish chute**) vide-ordures *m inv*; (*Brit: children's slide*) toboggan *m*
chutney ['tʃʌtnɪ] *n* chutney *m*
CIA *n abbr* (= *Central Intelligence Agency*) CIA *f*
CID *n abbr* (= *Criminal Investigation Department*) ≈ P. J. *f*
cider ['saɪdər] *n* cidre *m*
CIF *abbr* (= *cost, insurance and freight*) CAF
cigar [sɪ'gɑːr] *n* cigare *m*
cigarette [sɪgə'rɛt] *n* cigarette *f*
cigarette case *n* étui *m* à cigarettes
cigarette end *n* mégot *m*
cigarette holder *n* fume-cigarettes *m inv*
cigarette lighter *n* briquet *m*
C-in-C *abbr* = **commander-in-chief**
cinch [sɪntʃ] *n* (*inf*): **it's a ~** c'est du gâteau, c'est l'enfance de l'art
Cinderella [sɪndə'rɛlə] *n* Cendrillon
cine-camera ['sɪnɪ'kæmərə] *n* (*Brit*) caméra *f*
cine-film ['sɪnɪfɪlm] *n* (*Brit*) film *m*
cinema ['sɪnəmə] *n* cinéma *m*
cine-projector ['sɪnɪprə'dʒɛktər] *n* (*Brit*) projecteur *m* de cinéma
cinnamon ['sɪnəmən] *n* cannelle *f*
cipher ['saɪfər] *n* code secret; (*fig: faceless employee etc*) numéro *m*; **in ~** codé(e)
circa ['səːkə] *prep* circa, environ
circle ['səːkl] *n* cercle *m*; (*in cinema*) balcon *m* ▷ *vi* faire *or* décrire des cercles ▷ *vt* (*surround*) entourer, encercler; (*move round*) faire le tour de, tourner autour de
circuit ['səːkɪt] *n* circuit *m*; (*lap*) tour *m*
circuit board *n* plaquette *f*
circuitous [səː'kjuɪtəs] *adj* indirect(e), qui fait un détour
circular ['səːkjulər] *adj* circulaire ▷ *n* circulaire *f*; (*as advertisement*) prospectus *m*
circulate ['səːkjuleɪt] *vi* circuler ▷ *vt* faire circuler
circulation [səːkju'leɪʃən] *n* circulation *f*; (*of newspaper*) tirage *m*
circumcise ['səːkəmsaɪz] *vt* circoncire
circumference [sə'kʌmfərəns] *n* circonférence *f*
circumflex ['səːkəmflɛks] *n* (*also*: **circumflex accent**) accent *m* circonflexe

circumscribe ['sɔ:kəmskraɪb] vt circonscrire

circumspect ['sɔ:kəmspɛkt] adj circonspect(e)

circumstances ['sɔ:kəmstənsız] npl circonstances fpl; (financial condition) moyens mpl, situation financière; **in** or **under the ~** dans ces conditions; **under no ~** en aucun cas, sous aucun prétexte

circumstantial [sɔ:kəm'stænʃl] adj (report, statement) circonstancié(e); **~ evidence** preuve indirecte

circumvent [sɔ:kəm'vɛnt] vt (rule etc) tourner

circus ['sɔ:kəs] n cirque m; (also: **Circus**: in place names) place f

cirrhosis [sɪ'rəusɪs] n (also: **cirrhosis of the liver**) cirrhose f (du foie)

CIS n abbr (= Commonwealth of Independent States) CEI f

cissy ['sɪsɪ] n = **sissy**

cistern ['sɪstən] n réservoir m (d'eau); (in toilet) réservoir de la chasse d'eau

citation [saɪ'teɪʃən] n citation f; (US) P.-V m

cite [saɪt] vt citer

citizen ['sɪtɪzn] n (Pol) citoyen(ne); (resident): **the ~s of this town** les habitants de cette ville

Citizens' Advice Bureau ['sɪtɪznz-] n (Brit) ≈ Bureau m d'aide sociale

citizenship ['sɪtɪznʃɪp] n citoyenneté f; (Brit: Scol) ≈ éducation f civique

citric ['sɪtrɪk] adj: **~ acid** acide m citrique

citrus fruits ['sɪtrəs-] npl agrumes mpl

city ['sɪtɪ] n (grande) ville f; **the C~** la Cité de Londres (centre des affaires)

city centre n centre ville m

City Hall n (US) ≈ hôtel m de ville

city technology college n (Brit) établissement m d'enseignement technologique (situé dans un quartier défavorisé)

civic ['sɪvɪk] adj civique; (authorities) municipal(e)

civic centre n (Brit) centre administratif (municipal)

civil ['sɪvɪl] adj civil(e); (polite) poli(e), civil(e)

civil engineer n ingénieur civil

civil engineering n génie civil, travaux publics

civilian [sɪ'vɪlɪən] adj, n civil(e)

civilization [sɪvɪlaɪ'zeɪʃən] n civilisation f

civilized ['sɪvɪlaɪzd] adj civilisé(e); (fig) où règnent les bonnes manières, empreint(e) d'une courtoisie de bon ton

civil law n code civil; (study) droit civil

civil liberties npl libertés fpl civiques

civil rights npl droits mpl civiques

civil servant n fonctionnaire m/f

Civil Service n fonction publique, administration f

civil war n guerre civile

civvies ['sɪvɪz] npl: **in ~** (inf) en civil

CJD n abbr (= Creutzfeldt-Jakob disease) MCJ f

cl abbr (= centilitre) cl

clad [klæd] adj: **~ (in)** habillé(e) de, vêtu(e) de

claim [kleɪm] vt (rights etc) revendiquer; (compensation) réclamer; (assert) déclarer, prétendre ▷ vi (for insurance) faire une déclaration de sinistre ▷ n revendication f; prétention f; (right) droit m; (for expenses) note f de frais; **(insurance) ~** demande f d'indemnisation, déclaration f de sinistre; **to put in a ~ for** (pay rise etc) demander

claimant ['kleɪmənt] n (Admin, Law) requérant(e)

claim form n (gen) formulaire m de demande

clairvoyant [klɛə'vɔɪənt] n voyant(e), extra-lucide m/f

clam [klæm] n palourde f
  ▶ **clam up** vi (inf) la boucler

clamber ['klæmbər] vi grimper, se hisser

clammy ['klæmɪ] adj humide et froid(e) (au toucher), moite

clamour, (US) **clamor** ['klæmər] n (noise) clameurs fpl; (protest) protestations bruyantes ▷ vi: **to ~ for sth** réclamer qch à grands cris

clamp [klæmp] n crampon m; (on workbench) valet m; (on car) sabot m de Denver ▷ vt attacher; (car) mettre un sabot à
  ▶ **clamp down on** vt fus sévir contre, prendre des mesures draconiennes à l'égard de

clampdown ['klæmpdaun] n: **there has been a ~ on ...** des mesures énergiques ont été prises contre ...

clan [klæn] n clan m

clandestine [klæn'dɛstɪn] adj clandestin(e)

clang [klæŋ] n bruit m or fracas m métallique ▷ vi émettre un bruit or fracas métallique

clanger ['klæŋər] n: **to drop a ~** (Brit inf) faire une boulette

clansman ['klænzmən] (irreg) n membre m d'un clan (écossais)

clap [klæp] vi applaudir ▷ vt: **to ~ (one's hands)** battre des mains ▷ n claquement m; tape f; **a ~ of thunder** un coup de tonnerre

clapping ['klæpɪŋ] n applaudissements mpl

claptrap ['klæptræp] n (inf) baratin m

claret ['klærət] n (vin m de) bordeaux m (rouge)

clarification [klærɪfɪ'keɪʃən] n (fig) clarification f, éclaircissement m

clarify ['klærɪfaɪ] vt clarifier

clarinet [klærɪ'nɛt] n clarinette f

clarity ['klærɪtɪ] n clarté f

clash [klæʃ] n (sound) choc m, fracas m; (with police) affrontement m; (fig) conflit m ▷ vi se heurter; être or entrer en conflit; (colours) jurer; (dates, events) tomber en même temps

clasp [klɑːsp] n (of necklace, bag) fermoir m ▷ vt serrer, étreindre

class [klɑːs] n (gen) classe f; (group, category) catégorie f ▷ vt classer, classifier

class-conscious ['klɑːs'kɔnʃəs] adj conscient(e) de son appartenance sociale

class consciousness n conscience f de classe

classic ['klæsɪk] adj classique ▷ n (author, work) classique m; (race etc) classique f

classical ['klæsɪkl] adj classique

classics ['klæsɪks] npl (Scol) lettres fpl classiques

classification [klæsɪfɪ'keɪʃən] n classification f

classified ['klæsɪfaɪd] *adj* (*information*)
secret(-ète); **~ ads** petites annonces
classify ['klæsɪfaɪ] *vt* classifier, classer
classless society ['klɑ:slɪs-] *n* société *f* sans
classes
classmate ['klɑ:smeɪt] *n* camarade *m/f* de classe
classroom ['klɑ:srum] *n* (salle *f* de) classe *f*
classroom assistant *n* assistant(-e)
d'éducation
classy ['klɑ:sɪ] (*inf*) *adj* classe (*inf*)
clatter ['klætər] *n* cliquetis *m* ▷ *vi* cliqueter
clause [klɔ:z] *n* clause *f*; (*Ling*) proposition *f*
claustrophobia [klɔ:strə'fəubɪə] *n*
claustrophobie *f*
claustrophobic [klɔ:strə'fəubɪk] *adj* (*person*)
claustrophobe; (*place*) où l'on se sent
claustrophobe
claw [klɔ:] *n* griffe *f*; (*of bird of prey*) serre *f*; (*of
lobster*) pince *f* ▷ *vt* griffer; déchirer
clay [kleɪ] *n* argile *f*
clean [kli:n] *adj* propre; (*clear, smooth*) net(te);
(*record, reputation*) sans tache; (*joke, story*)
correct(e) ▷ *vt* nettoyer ▷ *adv*: **he ~ forgot** il a
complètement oublié; **to come ~** (*inf: admit
guilt*) se mettre à table; **to ~ one's teeth** se laver
les dents; **~ driving licence** *or* (*US*) **record**
permis où n'est portée aucune indication de contravention
▶ **clean off** *vt* enlever
▶ **clean out** *vt* nettoyer (à fond)
▶ **clean up** *vt* nettoyer; (*fig*) remettre de l'ordre
dans ▷ *vi* (*fig: make profit*): **to ~ up on** faire son
beurre avec
clean-cut ['kli:n'kʌt] *adj* (*man*) soigné; (*situation
etc*) bien délimité(e), net(te), clair(e)
cleaner ['kli:nər] *n* (*person*) nettoyeur(-euse),
femme *f* de ménage; (*also*: **dry cleaner**)
teinturier(-ière); (*product*) détachant *m*
cleaner's ['kli:nərz] *n* (*also*: **dry cleaner's**)
teinturier *m*
cleaning ['kli:nɪŋ] *n* nettoyage *m*
cleaning lady *n* femme *f* de ménage
cleanliness ['klɛnlɪnɪs] *n* propreté *f*
cleanly ['kli:nlɪ] *adv* proprement; nettement
cleanse [klɛnz] *vt* nettoyer; purifier
cleanser ['klɛnzər] *n* détergent *m*; (*for face*)
démaquillant *m*
clean-shaven ['kli:n'ʃeɪvn] *adj* rasé(e) de près
cleansing department ['klɛnzɪŋ-] *n* (*Brit*)
service *m* de voirie
clean sweep *n*: **to make a ~** (*Sport*) rafler tous les
prix
clean-up ['kli:nʌp] *n* nettoyage *m*
clear [klɪər] *adj* clair(e); (*glass, plastic*)
transparent(e); (*road, way*) libre, dégagé(e);
(*profit, majority*) net(te); (*conscience*) tranquille;
(*skin*) frais (fraîche); (*sky*) dégagé(e) ▷ *vt* (*road*)
dégager, déblayer; (*table*) débarrasser; (*room etc*:
of people) faire évacuer; (*woodland*) défricher;
(*cheque*) compenser; (*Comm: goods*) liquider;
(*Law: suspect*) innocenter; (*obstacle*) franchir *or*
sauter sans heurter ▷ *vi* (*weather*) s'éclaircir;
(*fog*) se dissiper ▷ *adv*: **~ of** à distance de, à

l'écart de ▷ *n*: **to be in the ~** (*out of debt*) être
dégagé(e) de toute dette; (*out of suspicion*) être
lavé(e) de tout soupçon; (*out of danger*) être hors
de danger; **to ~ the table** débarrasser la table,
desservir; **to ~ one's throat** s'éclaircir la gorge;
to ~ a profit faire un bénéfice net; **to make
o.s. ~** se faire bien comprendre; **to make it ~ to
sb that ...** bien faire comprendre à qn que ...; **I
have a ~ day tomorrow** (*Brit*) je n'ai rien de
prévu demain; **to keep ~ of sb/sth** éviter qn/
qch
▶ **clear away** *vt* (*things, clothes etc*) enlever,
retirer; **to ~ away the dishes** débarrasser la
table
▶ **clear off** *vi* (*inf: leave*) dégager
▶ **clear up** *vi* s'éclaircir, se dissiper ▷ *vt* ranger,
mettre en ordre; (*mystery*) éclaircir, résoudre
clearance ['klɪərəns] *n* (*removal*) déblayage *m*;
(*free space*) dégagement *m*; (*permission*)
autorisation *f*
clearance sale *n* (*Comm*) liquidation *f*
clear-cut ['klɪə'kʌt] *adj* précis(e), nettement
défini(e)
clearing ['klɪərɪŋ] *n* (*in forest*) clairière *f*; (*Brit
Banking*) compensation *f*, clearing *m*
clearing bank *n* (*Brit*) banque *f* qui appartient à
une chambre de compensation
clearly ['klɪəlɪ] *adv* clairement; (*obviously*) de
toute évidence
clearway ['klɪəweɪ] *n* (*Brit*) route *f* à
stationnement interdit
cleavage ['kli:vɪdʒ] *n* (*of dress*) décolleté *m*
cleaver ['kli:vər] *n* fendoir *m*, couperet *m*
clef [klɛf] *n* (*Mus*) clé *f*
cleft [klɛft] *n* (*in rock*) crevasse *f*, fissure *f*
clemency ['klɛmənsɪ] *n* clémence *f*
clement ['klɛmənt] *adj* (*weather*) clément(e)
clementine ['klɛməntaɪn] *n* clémentine *f*
clench [klɛntʃ] *vt* serrer
clergy ['klə:dʒɪ] *n* clergé *m*
clergyman ['klə:dʒɪmən] (*irreg*) *n*
ecclésiastique *m*
clerical ['klɛrɪkl] *adj* de bureau, d'employé de
bureau; (*Rel*) clérical(e), du clergé
clerk [klɑ:k] (*US*) [klə:rk] *n* (*Brit*) employé(e) de
bureau; (*US: salesman/woman*) vendeur(-euse);
C~ of Court (*Law*) greffier *m* (du tribunal)
clever ['klɛvər] *adj* (*intelligent*) intelligent(e);
(*skilful*) habile, adroit(e); (*device, arrangement*)
ingénieux(-euse), astucieux(-euse)
cleverly ['klɛvəlɪ] *adv* (*skilfully*) habilement;
(*craftily*) astucieusement
clew [klu:] *n* (*US*) = **clue**
cliché ['kli:ʃeɪ] *n* cliché *m*
click [klɪk] *vi* faire un bruit sec *or* un déclic;
(*Comput*) cliquer ▷ *vt*: **to ~ one's tongue** faire
claquer sa langue; **to ~ one's heels** claquer des
talons; **to ~ on an icon** cliquer sur une icône
client ['klaɪənt] *n* client(e)
clientele [kli:ã:n'tɛl] *n* clientèle *f*
cliff [klɪf] *n* falaise *f*
cliffhanger ['klɪfhæŋər] *n* (*TV, fig*) histoire

pleine de suspense

climactic [klaɪˈmæktɪk] *adj* à son point culminant, culminant(e)

climate [ˈklaɪmɪt] *n* climat *m*

climate change *n* changement *m* climatique

climax [ˈklaɪmæks] *n* apogée *m*, point culminant; (*sexual*) orgasme *m*

climb [klaɪm] *vi* grimper, monter; (*plane*) prendre de l'altitude ▷ *vt* (*stairs*) monter; (*mountain*) escalader; (*tree*) grimper à ▷ *n* montée *f*, escalade *f*; **to ~ over a wall** passer par dessus un mur
  ▸ **climb down** *vi* (re)descendre; (*Brit fig*) rabattre de ses prétentions

climb-down [ˈklaɪmdaun] *n* (*Brit*) reculade *f*

climber [ˈklaɪmər] *n* (*also*: **rock climber**) grimpeur(-euse), varappeur(-euse); (*plant*) plante grimpante

climbing [ˈklaɪmɪŋ] *n* (*also*: **rock climbing**) escalade *f*, varappe *f*

clinch [klɪntʃ] *vt* (*deal*) conclure, sceller

clincher [ˈklɪntʃər] *n*: **that was the ~** c'est ce qui a fait pencher la balance

cling (*pt, pp* **clung**) [klɪŋ, klʌŋ] *vi*: **to ~ (to)** se cramponner (à), s'accrocher (à); (*clothes*) coller (à)

Clingfilm® [ˈklɪŋfɪlm] *n* film *m* alimentaire

clinic [ˈklɪnɪk] *n* clinique *f*; centre médical; (*session: Med*) consultation(s) *f(pl)*, séance(s) *f(pl)*; (*Sport*) séance(s) de perfectionnement

clinical [ˈklɪnɪkl] *adj* clinique; (*fig*) froid(e)

clink [klɪŋk] *vi* tinter, cliqueter

clip [klɪp] *n* (*for hair*) barrette *f*; (*also*: **paper clip**) trombone *m*; (*Brit: also*: **bulldog clip**) pince *f* de bureau; (*holding hose etc*) collier *m or* bague *f* (métallique) de serrage; (*TV, Cinema*) clip *m* ▷ *vt* (*also*: **clip together**: *papers*) attacher; (*hair, nails*) couper; (*hedge*) tailler

clippers [ˈklɪpəz] *npl* tondeuse *f*; (*also*: **nail clippers**) coupe-ongles *m inv*

clipping [ˈklɪpɪŋ] *n* (*from newspaper*) coupure *f* de journal

clique [kliːk] *n* clique *f*, coterie *f*

cloak [kləuk] *n* grande cape ▷ *vt* (*fig*) masquer, cacher

cloakroom [ˈkləukrum] *n* (*for coats etc*) vestiaire *m*; (*Brit: W.C.*) toilettes *fpl*

clock [klɔk] *n* (*large*) horloge *f*; (*small*) pendule *f*; **round the ~** (*work etc*) vingt-quatre heures sur vingt-quatre; **to sleep round the ~** *or* **the ~ round** faire le tour du cadran; **30,000 on the ~** (*Brit Aut*) 30 000 milles au compteur; **to work against the ~** faire la course contre la montre
  ▸ **clock in** *or* **on** (*Brit*) *vi* (*with card*) pointer (en arrivant); (*start work*) commencer à travailler
  ▸ **clock off** *or* **out** (*Brit*) *vi* (*with card*) pointer (en partant); (*leave work*) quitter le travail
  ▸ **clock up** *vt* (*miles, hours etc*) faire

clockwise [ˈklɔkwaɪz] *adv* dans le sens des aiguilles d'une montre

clockwork [ˈklɔkwəːk] *n* rouages *mpl*, mécanisme *m*; (*of clock*) mouvement *m*

(d'horlogerie) ▷ *adj* (*toy, train*) mécanique

clog [klɔg] *n* sabot *m* ▷ *vt* boucher, encrasser ▷ *vi* (*also*: **clog up**) se boucher, s'encrasser

cloister [ˈklɔɪstər] *n* cloître *m*

clone [kləun] *n* clone *m* ▷ *vt* cloner

close¹ [kləus] *adj* (*near*): **~ (to)** près (de), proche (de); (*writing, texture*) serré(e); (*contact, link, watch*) étroit(e); (*examination*) attentif(-ive), minutieux(-euse); (*contest*) très serré(e); (*weather*) lourd(e), étouffant(e); (*room*) mal aéré(e) ▷ *adv* près, à proximité; **~ to** (*prep*) près de; **~ by, ~ at hand** (*adj, adv*) tout(e) près; **how ~ is Edinburgh to Glasgow?** combien de kilomètres y-a-t-il entre Édimbourg et Glasgow?; **a ~ friend** un ami intime; **to have a ~ shave** (*fig*) l'échapper belle; **at ~ quarters** tout près, à côté

close² [kləuz] *vt* fermer; (*bargain, deal*) conclure ▷ *vi* (*shop etc*) fermer; (*lid, door etc*) se fermer; (*end*) se terminer, se conclure ▷ *n* (*end*) conclusion *f*; **to bring sth to a ~** mettre fin à qch; **what time do you ~?** à quelle heure fermez-vous?
  ▸ **close down** *vt, vi* fermer (*définitivement*)
  ▸ **close in** *vi* (*hunters*) approcher; (*night, fog*) tomber; **the days are closing in** les jours raccourcissent; **to ~ in on sb** cerner qn
  ▸ **close off** *vt* (*area*) boucler

closed [kləuzd] *adj* (*shop etc*) fermé(e); (*road*) fermé à la circulation

closed-circuit [ˈkləuzdˈsəːkɪt] *adj*: **~ television** télévision *f* en circuit fermé

closed shop *n* organisation *f* qui n'admet que des travailleurs syndiqués

close-knit [ˈkləusˈnɪt] *adj* (*family, community*) très uni(e)

closely [ˈkləuslɪ] *adv* (*examine, watch*) de près; **we are ~ related** nous sommes proches parents; **a ~ guarded secret** un secret bien gardé

close season [kləus-] *n* (*Brit: Hunting*) fermeture *f* de la chasse/pêche; (: *Football*) trêve *f*

closet [ˈklɔzɪt] *n* (*cupboard*) placard *m*, réduit *m*

close-up [ˈkləusʌp] *n* gros plan

closing [ˈkləuzɪŋ] *adj* (*stages, remarks*) final(e); **~ price** (*Stock Exchange*) cours *m* de clôture

closing time *n* heure *f* de fermeture

closure [ˈkləuʒər] *n* fermeture *f*

clot [klɔt] *n* (*of blood, milk*) caillot *m*; (*inf: person*) ballot *m* ▷ *vi* (*blood*) former des caillots; (: *external bleeding*) se coaguler

cloth [klɔθ] *n* (*material*) tissu *m*, étoffe *f*; (*Brit: also*: **tea cloth**) torchon *m*; lavette *f*; (*also*: **tablecloth**) nappe *f*

clothe [kləuð] *vt* habiller, vêtir

clothes [kləuðz] *npl* vêtements *mpl*, habits *mpl*; **to put one's ~ on** s'habiller; **to take one's ~ off** enlever ses vêtements

clothes brush *n* brosse *f* à habits

clothes line *n* corde *f* (à linge)

clothes peg, (*US*) **clothes pin** *n* pince *f* à linge

clothing [ˈkləuðɪŋ] *n* = **clothes**

clotted cream [ˈklɔtɪd-] *n* (*Brit*) crème caillée

cloud [klaud] *n* nuage *m* ▷ *vt* (*liquid*) troubler; **to**

~ **the issue** brouiller les cartes; **every ~ has a silver lining** (*proverb*) à quelque chose malheur est bon (*proverbe*)

▸ **cloud over** *vi* se couvrir; (*fig*) s'assombrir

cloudburst ['klaudbə:st] *n* violente averse

cloud-cuckoo-land ['klaud'kuku:'lænd] *n* (*Brit*) monde *m* imaginaire

cloudy ['klaudı] *adj* nuageux(-euse), couvert(e); (*liquid*) trouble

clout [klaut] *n* (*blow*) taloche *f*; (*fig*) pouvoir *m* ▸ *vt* flanquer une taloche à

clove [kləuv] *n* clou *m* de girofle; **a ~ of garlic** une gousse d'ail

clover ['kləuvə^r] *n* trèfle *m*

cloverleaf ['kləuvəli:f] *n* feuille *f* de trèfle; (*Aut*) croisement *m* en trèfle

clown [klaun] *n* clown *m* ▸ *vi* (*also*: **clown about, clown around**) faire le clown

cloying ['klɔıın] *adj* (*taste, smell*) écœurant(e)

club [klʌb] *n* (*society*) club *m*; (*weapon*) massue *f*, matraque *f*; (*also*: **golf club**) club ▸ *vt* matraquer ▸ *vi*: **to ~ together** s'associer; **clubs** *npl* (*Cards*) trèfle *m*

club car *n* (*US Rail*) wagon-restaurant *m*

club class *n* (*Aviat*) classe *f* club

clubhouse ['klʌbhaus] *n* pavillon *m*

club soda *n* (*US*) eau *f* de seltz

cluck [klʌk] *vi* glousser

clue [klu:] *n* indice *m*; (*in crosswords*) définition *f*; **I haven't a ~** je n'en ai pas la moindre idée

clued up, (*US*) **clued in** [klu:d-] *adj* (*inf*) (vachement) calé(e)

clump [klʌmp] *n*: ~ **of trees** bouquet *m* d'arbres

clumsy ['klʌmzı] *adj* (*person*) gauche, maladroit(e); (*object*) malcommode, peu maniable

clung [klʌŋ] *pt, pp of* **cling**

cluster ['klʌstə^r] *n* (petit) groupe; (*of flowers*) grappe *f* ▸ *vi* se rassembler

clutch [klʌtʃ] *n* (*Aut*) embrayage *m*; (*grasp*): ~**es** étreinte *f*, prise *f* ▸ *vt* (*grasp*) agripper; (*hold tightly*) serrer fort; (*hold on to*) se cramponner à

clutter ['klʌtə^r] *vt* (*also*: **clutter up**) encombrer ▸ *n* désordre *m*, fouillis *m*

cm *abbr* (= *centimetre*) cm

CNAA *n abbr* (*Brit*: = *Council for National Academic Awards*) organisme non universitaire délivrant des diplômes

CND *n abbr* = **Campaign for Nuclear Disarmament**

CO *n abbr* (= *commanding officer*) Cdt; (*Brit*) = **Commonwealth Office** ▸ *abbr* (*US*) = **Colorado**

Co. *abbr* = **company, county**

c/o *abbr* (= *care of*) c/o, aux bons soins de

coach [kəutʃ] *n* (*bus*) autocar *m*; (*horse-drawn*) diligence *f*; (*of train*) voiture *f*, wagon *m*; (*Sport: trainer*) entraîneur(-euse); (*school: tutor*) répétiteur(-trice) ▸ *vt* (*Sport*) entraîner; (*student*) donner des leçons particulières à

coach station (*Brit*) *n* gare routière

coach trip *n* excursion *f* en car

coagulate [kəu'ægjuleıt] *vt* coaguler ▸ *vi* se coaguler

coal [kəul] *n* charbon *m*

coal face *n* front *m* de taille

coalfield ['kəulfi:ld] *n* bassin houiller

coalition [kəuə'lıʃən] *n* coalition *f*

coalman ['kəulmən] (*irreg*) *n* charbonnier *m*, marchand *m* de charbon

coal mine *n* mine *f* de charbon

coarse [kɔ:s] *adj* grossier(-ère), rude; (*vulgar*) vulgaire

coast [kəust] *n* côte *f* ▸ *vi* (*car, cycle*) descendre en roue libre

coastal ['kəustl] *adj* côtier(-ère)

coaster ['kəustə^r] *n* (*Naut*) caboteur *m*; (*for glass*) dessous *m* de verre

coastguard ['kəustgɑ:d] *n* garde-côte *m*

coastline ['kəustlaın] *n* côte *f*, littoral *m*

coat [kəut] *n* manteau *m*; (*of animal*) pelage *m*, poil *m*; (*of paint*) couche *f* ▸ *vt* couvrir, enduire; ~ **of arms** *n* blason *m*, armoiries *fpl*

coat hanger *n* cintre *m*

coating ['kəutıŋ] *n* couche *f*, enduit *m*

co-author ['kəu'ɔ:θə^r] *n* co-auteur *m*

coax [kəuks] *vt* persuader par des cajoleries

cob [kɔb] *n see* **corn**

cobbled ['kɔbld] *adj* pavé(e)

cobbler ['kɔblə^r] *n* cordonnier *m*

cobbles, cobblestones ['kɔblz, 'kɔblstəunz] *npl* pavés (ronds)

COBOL ['kəubɔl] *n* COBOL *m*

cobra ['kəubrə] *n* cobra *m*

cobweb ['kɔbweb] *n* toile *f* d'araignée

cocaine [kə'keın] *n* cocaïne *f*

cock [kɔk] *n* (*rooster*) coq *m*; (*male bird*) mâle *m* ▸ *vt* (*gun*) armer; **to ~ one's ears** (*fig*) dresser l'oreille

cock-a-hoop [kɔkə'hu:p] *adj* jubilant(e)

cockerel ['kɔkərl] *n* jeune coq *m*

cock-eyed ['kɔkaıd] *adj* (*fig*) de travers; qui louche; qui ne tient pas debout (*fig*)

cockle ['kɔkl] *n* coque *f*

cockney ['kɔknı] *n* cockney *m/f* (*habitant des quartiers populaires de l'East End de Londres*), ≈ faubourien(ne)

cockpit ['kɔkpıt] *n* (*in aircraft*) poste *m* de pilotage, cockpit *m*

cockroach ['kɔkrəutʃ] *n* cafard *m*, cancrelat *m*

cocktail ['kɔkteıl] *n* cocktail *m*; **prawn ~**, (*US*) **shrimp ~** cocktail de crevettes

cocktail cabinet *n* (meuble-)bar *m*

cocktail party *n* cocktail *m*

cocktail shaker [-'ʃeıkə^r] *n* shaker *m*

cocky ['kɔkı] *adj* trop sûr(e) de soi

cocoa ['kəukəu] *n* cacao *m*

coconut ['kəukənʌt] *n* noix *f* de coco

cocoon [kə'ku:n] *n* cocon *m*

C.O.D. *abbr* = **cash on delivery**; (*US*) = **collect on delivery**

cod [kɔd] *n* morue fraîche, cabillaud *m*

code [kəud] *n* code *m*; (*Tel: area code*) indicatif *m*; ~ **of behaviour** règles *fpl* de conduite; ~ **of practice** déontologie *f*

codeine ['kəudi:n] *n* codéine *f*
codger ['kɔdʒəʳ] *n*: **an old ~** (*Brit inf*) un drôle de vieux bonhomme
codicil ['kɔdɪsɪl] *n* codicille *m*
codify ['kəudɪfaɪ] *vt* codifier
cod-liver oil ['kɔdlɪvər-] *n* huile *f* de foie de morue
co-driver ['kəu'draɪvəʳ] *n* (*in race*) copilote *m*; (*of lorry*) deuxième chauffeur *m*
co-ed ['kəu'ɛd] *adj abbr* = **coeducational** ▷ *n abbr* (*US: female student*) étudiante *d'une université mixte*; (*Brit: school*) école *f* mixte
coeducational ['kəuɛdju'keɪʃənl] *adj* mixte
coerce [kəu'ə:s] *vt* contraindre
coercion [kəu'ə:ʃən] *n* contrainte *f*
coexistence ['kəuɪg'zɪstəns] *n* coexistence *f*
C. of C. *n abbr* = **chamber of commerce**
C of E *n abbr* = **Church of England**
coffee ['kɔfɪ] *n* café *m*; **white ~**, (*US*) **~ with cream** (café-)crème *m*
coffee bar *n* (*Brit*) café *m*
coffee bean *n* grain *m* de café
coffee break *n* pause-café *f*
coffee cake ['kɔfɪkeɪk] *n* (*US*) ≈ petit pain aux raisins
coffee cup *n* tasse *f* à café
coffee maker *n* cafetière *f*
coffeepot ['kɔfɪpɔt] *n* cafetière *f*
coffee shop *n* café *m*
coffee table *n* (petite) table basse
coffin ['kɔfɪn] *n* cercueil *m*
C of I *n abbr* = **Church of Ireland**
C of S *n abbr* = **Church of Scotland**
cog [kɔg] *n* (*wheel*) roue dentée; (*tooth*) dent *f* (d'engrenage)
cogent ['kəudʒənt] *adj* puissant(e), convaincant(e)
cognac ['kɔnjæk] *n* cognac *m*
cogwheel ['kɔgwi:l] *n* roue dentée
cohabit [kəu'hæbɪt] *vi* (*formal*): **to ~ (with sb)** cohabiter (avec qn)
coherent [kəu'hɪərənt] *adj* cohérent(e)
cohesion [kəu'hi:ʒən] *n* cohésion *f*
cohesive [kəu'hi:sɪv] *adj* (*fig*) cohésif(-ive)
COI *n abbr* (*Brit*: = *Central Office of Information*) service d'information gouvernemental
coil [kɔɪl] *n* rouleau *m*, bobine *f*; (*one loop*) anneau *m*, spire *f*; (*of smoke*) volute *f*; (*contraceptive*) stérilet *m* ▷ *vt* enrouler
coin [kɔɪn] *n* pièce *f* (de monnaie) ▷ *vt* (*word*) inventer
coinage ['kɔɪnɪdʒ] *n* monnaie *f*, système *m* monétaire
coinbox ['kɔɪnbɔks] *n* (*Brit*) cabine *f* téléphonique
coincide [kəuɪn'saɪd] *vi* coïncider
coincidence [kəu'ɪnsɪdəns] *n* coïncidence *f*
coin-operated ['kɔɪn'ɔpəreɪtɪd] *adj* (*machine, launderette*) automatique
Coke® [kəuk] *n* coca *m*
coke [kəuk] *n* (*coal*) coke *m*
Col. *abbr* (= *colonel*) Col; (*US*) = **Colorado**

COLA *n abbr* (*US*: = *cost-of-living adjustment*) réajustement (*des salaires, indemnités etc*) en fonction du coût de la vie
colander ['kɔləndəʳ] *n* passoire *f* (à légumes)
cold [kəuld] *adj* froid(e) ▷ *n* froid *m*; (*Med*) rhume *m*; **it's ~** il fait froid; **to be ~** (*person*) avoir froid; **to catch ~** prendre *or* attraper froid; **to catch a ~** s'enrhumer, attraper un rhume; **in ~ blood** de sang-froid; **to have ~ feet** avoir froid aux pieds; (*fig*) avoir la frousse *or* la trouille; **to give sb the ~ shoulder** battre froid à qn
cold-blooded ['kəuld'blʌdɪd] *adj* (*Zool*) à sang froid
cold cream *n* crème *f* de soins
coldly ['kəuldlɪ] *adv* froidement
cold sore *n* bouton *m* de fièvre
cold sweat *n*: **to be in a ~ (about sth)** avoir des sueurs froides (au sujet de qch)
cold turkey *n* (*inf*) manque *m*; **to go ~** être en manque
Cold War *n*: **the ~** la guerre froide
coleslaw ['kəulslɔ:] *n* sorte de salade de chou cru
colic ['kɔlɪk] *n* colique(s) *f(pl)*
colicky ['kɔlɪkɪ] *adj* qui souffre de coliques
collaborate [kə'læbəreɪt] *vi* collaborer
collaboration [kəlæbə'reɪʃən] *n* collaboration *f*
collaborator [kə'læbəreɪtəʳ] *n* collaborateur(-trice)
collage [kɔ'lɑ:ʒ] *n* (*Art*) collage *m*
collagen ['kɔlədʒən] *n* collagène *m*
collapse [kə'læps] *vi* s'effondrer, s'écrouler; (*Med*) avoir un malaise ▷ *n* effondrement *m*, écroulement *m*; (*of government*) chute *f*
collapsible [kə'læpsəbl] *adj* pliant(e), télescopique
collar ['kɔləʳ] *n* (*of coat, shirt*) col *m*; (*for dog*) collier *m*; (*Tech*) collier, bague *f* ▷ *vt* (*inf: person*) pincer
collarbone ['kɔləbəun] *n* clavicule *f*
collate [kɔ'leɪt] *vt* collationner
collateral [kə'lætərl] *n* nantissement *m*
collation [kə'leɪʃən] *n* collation *f*
colleague ['kɔli:g] *n* collègue *m/f*
collect [kə'lɛkt] *vt* rassembler; (*pick up*) ramasser; (*as a hobby*) collectionner; (*Brit: call for*) (passer) prendre; (*mail*) faire la levée de, ramasser; (*money owed*) encaisser; (*donations, subscriptions*) recueillir ▷ *vi* (*people*) se rassembler; (*dust, dirt*) s'amasser; **to ~ one's thoughts** réfléchir, réunir ses idées; **~ on delivery (COD)** (*US Comm*) payable *or* paiement à la livraison; **to call ~** (*US Tel*) téléphoner en PCV
collected [kə'lɛktɪd] *adj*: **~ works** œuvres complètes
collection [kə'lɛkʃən] *n* collection *f*; (*of mail*) levée *f*; (*for money*) collecte *f*, quête *f*
collective [kə'lɛktɪv] *adj* collectif(-ive) ▷ *n* collectif *m*
collective bargaining *n* convention collective
collector [kə'lɛktəʳ] *n* collectionneur *m*; (*of taxes*) percepteur *m*; (*of rent, cash*) encaisseur *m*; **~'s item** *or* **piece** pièce *f* de collection
college ['kɔlɪdʒ] *n* collège *m*; (*of technology,*

agriculture etc) institut *m*; **to go to ~** faire des études supérieures; **~ of education** ≈ école normale

collide [kə'laɪd] *vi*: **to ~ (with)** entrer en collision (avec)

collie ['kɔlɪ] *n* (*dog*) colley *m*

colliery ['kɔlɪərɪ] *n* (*Brit*) mine *f* de charbon, houillère *f*

collision [kə'lɪʒən] *n* collision *f*, heurt *m*; **to be on a ~ course** aller droit à la collision; (*fig*) aller vers l'affrontement

collision damage waiver *n* (*Insurance*) rachat *m* de franchise

colloquial [kə'ləʊkwɪəl] *adj* familier(-ère)

collusion [kə'luːʒən] *n* collusion *f*; **in ~ with** en complicité avec

Colo. *abbr* (*US*) = **Colorado**

cologne [kə'ləʊn] *n* (*also:* **eau de cologne**) eau *f* de cologne

Colombia [kə'lɔmbɪə] *n* Colombie *f*

Colombian [kə'lɔmbɪən] *adj* colombien(ne) ▷ *n* Colombien(ne)

colon ['kəʊlən] *n* (*sign*) deux-points *mpl*; (*Med*) côlon *m*

colonel ['kəːnl] *n* colonel *m*

colonial [kə'ləʊnɪəl] *adj* colonial(e)

colonize ['kɔlənaɪz] *vt* coloniser

colony ['kɔlənɪ] *n* colonie *f*

color ['kʌlər] *n* (*US*) = **colour**

Colorado beetle [kɔlə'rɑːdəʊ-] *n* doryphore *m*

colossal [kə'lɔsl] *adj* colossal(e)

colour, (*US*) **color** ['kʌlər] *n* couleur *f* ▷ *vt* colorer; (*dye*) teindre; (*paint*) peindre; (*with crayons*) colorier; (*news*) fausser, exagérer ▷ *vi* (*blush*) rougir ▷ *cpd* (*film, photograph, television*) en couleur; **colours** *npl* (*of party, club*) couleurs *fpl*; **I'd like a different ~** je le voudrais dans un autre coloris
▶ **colour in** *vt* colorier

colour bar, (*US*) **color bar** *n* discrimination raciale (*dans un établissement etc*)

colour-blind, (*US*) **color-blind** ['kʌləblaɪnd] *adj* daltonien(ne)

coloured, (*US*) **colored** ['kʌləd] *adj* coloré(e); (*photo*) en couleur

colour film, (*US*) **color film** *n* (*for camera*) pellicule *f* (en) couleur

colourful, (*US*) **colorful** ['kʌləful] *adj* coloré(e), vif (vive); (*personality*) pittoresque, haut(e) en couleurs

colouring, (*US*) **coloring** ['kʌlərɪŋ] *n* colorant *m*; (*complexion*) teint *m*

colour scheme, (*US*) **color scheme** *n* combinaison *f* de(s) couleur(s)

colour supplement *n* (*Brit Press*) supplément *m* magazine

colour television, (*US*) **color television** *n* télévision *f* (en) couleur

colt [kəʊlt] *n* poulain *m*

column ['kɔləm] *n* colonne *f*; (*fashion column, sports column etc*) rubrique *f*; **the editorial ~** l'éditorial *m*

columnist ['kɔləmnɪst] *n* rédacteur(-trice) d'une rubrique

coma ['kəʊmə] *n* coma *m*

comb [kəʊm] *n* peigne *m* ▷ *vt* (*hair*) peigner; (*area*) ratisser, passer au peigne fin

combat ['kɔmbæt] *n* combat *m* ▷ *vt* combattre, lutter contre

combination [kɔmbɪ'neɪʃən] *n* (*gen*) combinaison *f*

combination lock *n* serrure *f* à combinaison

combine [kəm'baɪn] *vt* combiner ▷ *vi* s'associer; (*Chem*) se combiner ▷ *n* ['kɔmbaɪn] association *f*; (*Econ*) trust *m*; (*also:* **combine harvester**) moissonneuse-batteuse(-lieuse) *f*; **to ~ sth with sth** (*one quality with another*) joindre *ou* allier qch à qch; **a ~d effort** un effort conjugué

combine harvester *n* moissonneuse-batteuse(-lieuse) *f*

combo ['kɔmbəʊ] *n* (*Jazz etc*) groupe *m* de musiciens

combustible [kəm'bʌstɪbl] *adj* combustible

combustion [kəm'bʌstʃən] *n* combustion *f*

 KEYWORD

come (*pt* **came,** *pp* **-**) [kʌm, keɪm] *vi* **1** (*movement towards*) venir; **to ~ running** arriver en courant; **he's ~ here to work** il est venu ici pour travailler; **~ with me** suivez-moi; **to ~ into sight** *or* **view** apparaître

2 (*arrive*) arriver; **to ~ home** rentrer (chez soi *or* à la maison); **we've just ~ from Paris** nous arrivons de Paris; **coming!** j'arrive!

3 (*reach*): **to ~ to** (*decision etc*) parvenir à, arriver à; **the bill came to £40** la note s'est élevée à 40 livres; **if it ~s to it** s'il le faut, dans le pire des cas

4 (*occur*): **an idea came to me** il m'est venu une idée; **what might ~ of it** ce qui pourrait en résulter, ce qui pourrait advenir *ou* se produire

5 (*be, become*): **to ~ loose/undone** se défaire/desserrer; **I've ~ to like him** j'ai fini par bien l'aimer

6 (*inf: sexually*) jouir

▶ **come about** *vi* se produire, arriver

▶ **come across** *vt fus* rencontrer par hasard, tomber sur ▷ *vi*: **to ~ across well/badly** faire une bonne/mauvaise impression

▶ **come along** *vi* (*Brit: pupil, work*) faire des progrès, avancer; **~ along!** viens!; allons!, allez!

▶ **come apart** *vi* s'en aller en morceaux; se détacher

▶ **come away** *vi* partir, s'en aller; (*become detached*) se détacher

▶ **come back** *vi* revenir; (*reply*): **can I ~ back to you on that one?** est-ce qu'on peut revenir là-dessus plus tard?

▶ **come by** *vt fus* (*acquire*) obtenir, se procurer

▶ **come down** *vi* descendre; (*prices*) baisser; (*buildings*) s'écrouler; (: *be demolished*) être démoli(e)

▶ **come forward** *vi* s'avancer; (*make o.s. known*) se présenter, s'annoncer

▶ **come from** vt fus (source) venir de; (place) venir de, être originaire de

▶ **come in** vi entrer; (train) arriver; (fashion) entrer en vogue; (on deal etc) participer

▶ **come in for** vt fus (criticism etc) être l'objet de

▶ **come into** vt fus (money) hériter de

▶ **come off** vi (button) se détacher; (attempt) réussir

▶ **come on** vi (lights, electricity) s'allumer; (central heating) se mettre en marche; (pupil, work, project) faire des progrès, avancer; ~ **on!** viens!; allons!, allez!

▶ **come out** vi sortir; (sun) se montrer; (book) paraître; (stain) s'enlever; (strike) cesser le travail, se mettre en grève

▶ **come over** vt fus: **I don't know what's ~ over him!** je ne sais pas ce qui lui a pris!

▶ **come round** vi (after faint, operation) revenir à soi, reprendre connaissance

▶ **come through** vi (survive) s'en sortir; (telephone call): **the call came through** l'appel est bien parvenu

▶ **come to** vi revenir à soi ▷ vt (add up to: amount): **how much does it ~ to?** ça fait combien?

▶ **come under** vt fus (heading) se trouver sous; (influence) subir

▶ **come up** vi monter; (sun) se lever; (problem) se poser; (event) survenir; (in conversation) être soulevé

▶ **come up against** vt fus (resistance, difficulties) rencontrer

▶ **come up to** vt fus arriver à; **the film didn't ~ up to our expectations** le film nous a déçu

▶ **come up with** vt fus (money) fournir; **he came up with an idea** il a eu une idée, il a proposé quelque chose

▶ **come upon** vt fus tomber sur

comeback ['kʌmbæk] n (Theat) rentrée f; (reaction) réaction f; (response) réponse f

Comecon ['kɔmɪkɔn] n abbr (= Council for Mutual Economic Aid) COMECON m

comedian [kə'mi:dɪən] n (comic) comique m; (Theat) comédien m

comedienne [kəmi:dɪ'ɛn] n comique f

comedown ['kʌmdaun] n déchéance f

comedy ['kɔmɪdɪ] n comédie f; (humour) comique m

comet ['kɔmɪt] n comète f

comeuppance [kʌm'ʌpəns] n: **to get one's ~** recevoir ce qu'on mérite

comfort ['kʌmfət] n confort m, bien-être m; (solace) consolation f, réconfort m ▷ vt consoler, réconforter

comfortable ['kʌmfətəbl] adj confortable; (person) à l'aise; (financially) aisé(e); (patient) dont l'état est stationnaire; **I don't feel very ~ about it** cela m'inquiète un peu

comfortably ['kʌmfətəbli] adv (sit) confortablement; (live) à l'aise

comforter ['kʌmfətər] n (US) édredon m

comforts ['kʌmfəts] npl aises fpl

comfort station n (US) toilettes fpl

comic ['kɔmɪk] adj (also: **comical**) comique ▷ n (person) comique m; (Brit: magazine: for children) magazine m de bandes dessinées or de BD; (: for adults) illustré m

comical ['kɔmɪkl] adj amusant(e)

comic book (US) n (for children) magazine m de bandes dessinées or de BD; (for adults) illustré m

comic strip n bande dessinée

coming ['kʌmɪŋ] n arrivée f ▷ adj (next) prochain(e); (future) à venir; **in the ~ weeks** dans les prochaines semaines

Comintern ['kɔmɪntə:n] n Comintern m

comma ['kɔmə] n virgule f

command [kə'mɑ:nd] n ordre m, commandement m; (Mil: authority) commandement m; (mastery) maîtrise f; (Comput) commande f ▷ vt (troops) commander; (be able to get) (pouvoir) disposer de, avoir à sa disposition; (deserve) avoir droit à; **to ~ sb to do** donner l'ordre or commander à qn de faire; **to have/take ~ of** avoir/prendre le commandement de; **to have at one's ~** (money, resources etc) disposer de

command economy n économie planifiée

commandeer [kɔmən'dɪər] vt réquisitionner (par la force)

commander [kə'mɑ:ndər] n chef m; (Mil) commandant m

commander-in-chief [kə'mɑ:ndərɪn'tʃi:f] n (Mil) commandant m en chef

commanding [kə'mɑ:ndɪŋ] adj (appearance) imposant(e); (voice, tone) autoritaire; (lead, position) dominant(e)

commanding officer n commandant m

commandment [kə'mɑ:ndmənt] n (Rel) commandement m

command module n (Space) module m de commande

commando [kə'mɑ:ndəu] n commando m; membre m d'un commando

commemorate [kə'mɛməreɪt] vt commémorer

commemoration [kəmɛmə'reɪʃən] n commémoration f

commemorative [kə'mɛmərətɪv] adj commémoratif(-ive)

commence [kə'mɛns] vt, vi commencer

commend [kə'mɛnd] vt louer; (recommend) recommander

commendable [kə'mɛndəbl] adj louable

commendation [kɔmɛn'deɪʃən] n éloge m; recommandation f

commensurate [kə'mɛnʃərɪt] adj: **~ with/to** en rapport avec/selon

comment ['kɔmɛnt] n commentaire m ▷ vi faire des remarques or commentaires; **to ~ on** faire des remarques sur; **to ~ that** faire remarquer que; **"no ~"** "je n'ai rien à déclarer"

commentary ['kɔməntərɪ] n commentaire m; (Sport) reportage m (en direct)

commentator ['kɔmənteɪtər] n commentateur m; (Sport) reporter m

commerce ['kɔmə:s] n commerce m

commercial [kə'mə:ʃəl] adj commercial(e) ▷ n

(*Radio, TV*) annonce *f* publicitaire, spot *m* (publicitaire)

commercial bank *n* banque *f* d'affaires

commercial break *n* (*Radio, TV*) spot *m* (publicitaire)

commercial college *n* école *f* de commerce

commercialism [kə'mə:fəlɪzəm] *n* mercantilisme *m*

commercial television *n* publicité *f* à la télévision, chaînes privées (financées par la publicité)

commercial traveller *n* voyageur *m* de commerce

commercial vehicle *n* véhicule *m* utilitaire

commiserate [kə'mɪzəreɪt] *vi*: **to ~ with sb** témoigner de la sympathie pour qn

commission [kə'mɪʃən] *n* (*committee, fee*) commission *f*; (*order for work of art etc*) commande *f* ▷ *vt* (*Mil*) nommer (à un commandement); (*work of art*) commander, charger un artiste de l'exécution de; **out of ~** (*Naut*) hors de service; (*machine*) hors service; **I get 10% ~** je reçois une commission de 10%; **~ of inquiry** (*Brit*) commission d'enquête

commissionaire [kəmɪʃə'nɛəʳ] *n* (*Brit: at shop, cinema etc*) portier *m* (en uniforme)

commissioner [kə'mɪʃənəʳ] *n* membre *m* d'une commission; (*Police*) préfet *m* (de police)

commit [kə'mɪt] *vt* (*act*) commettre; (*resources*) consacrer; (*to sb's care*) confier (à); **to ~ o.s. (to do)** s'engager (à faire); **to ~ suicide** se suicider; **to ~ to writing** coucher par écrit; **to ~ sb for trial** traduire qn en justice

commitment [kə'mɪtmənt] *n* engagement *m*; (*obligation*) responsabilité(s) (*fpl*)

committed [kə'mɪtɪd] *adj* (*writer, politician etc*) engagé(e)

committee [kə'mɪtɪ] *n* comité *m*; commission *f*; **to be on a ~** siéger dans un comité *or* une commission)

committee meeting *n* réunion *f* de comité *or* commission

commodity [kə'mɔdɪtɪ] *n* produit *m*, marchandise *f*, article *m*; (*food*) denrée *f*

commodity exchange *n* bourse *f* de marchandises

common ['kɔmən] *adj* (*gen*) commun(e); (*usual*) courant(e) ▷ *n* terrain communal; **in ~** en commun; **in ~ use** d'un usage courant; **it's ~ knowledge that** il est bien connu *or* notoire que; **to the ~ good** pour le bien de tous, dans l'intérêt général

common cold *n*: **the ~** le rhume

common denominator *n* dénominateur commun

commoner ['kɔmənəʳ] *n* roturier(-ière)

common ground *n* (*fig*) terrain *m* d'entente

common land *n* terrain communal

common law *n* droit coutumier

common-law ['kɔmənlɔ:] *adj*: **~ wife** épouse *f* de facto

commonly ['kɔmənlɪ] *adv* communément,

généralement; couramment

Common Market *n* Marché commun

commonplace ['kɔmənpleɪs] *adj* banal(e), ordinaire

commonroom ['kɔmənrum] *n* salle commune; (*Scol*) salle des professeurs

Commons ['kɔmənz] *npl* (*Brit Pol*): **the (House of) ~** la chambre des Communes

common sense *n* bon sens

Commonwealth ['kɔmənwɛlθ] *n*: **the ~** le Commonwealth; *voir article*

● **COMMONWEALTH**
●
● Le *Commonwealth* regroupe 50 États
● indépendants et plusieurs territoires qui
● reconnaissent tous le souverain britannique
● comme chef de cette association.

commotion [kə'məuʃən] *n* désordre *m*, tumulte *m*

communal ['kɔmju:nl] *adj* (*life*) communautaire; (*for common use*) commun(e)

commune *n* ['kɔmju:n] *n* (*group*) communauté *f* ▷ *vi* [kə'mju:n]: **to ~ with** (*nature*) converser intimement avec; communier avec

communicate [kə'mju:nɪkeɪt] *vt* communiquer, transmettre ▷ *vi*: **to ~ (with)** communiquer (avec)

communication [kəmju:nɪ'keɪʃən] *n* communication *f*

communication cord *n* (*Brit*) sonnette *f* d'alarme

communications network *n* réseau *m* de communications

communications satellite *n* satellite *m* de télécommunications

communicative [kə'mju:nɪkətɪv] *adj* communicatif(-ive)

communion [kə'mju:nɪən] *n* (*also:* **Holy Communion**) communion *f*

communism ['kɔmjunɪzəm] *n* communisme *m*

communist ['kɔmjunɪst] *adj, n* communiste *m/f*

community [kə'mju:nɪtɪ] *n* communauté *f*

community centre, (*US*) **community center** *n* foyer socio-éducatif, centre *m* de loisirs

community chest *n* (*US*) fonds commun

community health centre *n* centre médico-social

community service *n* ≈ travail *m* d'intérêt général, TIG *m*

community spirit *n* solidarité *f*

commutation ticket [kɔmju'teɪʃən-] *n* (*US*) carte *f* d'abonnement

commute [kə'mju:t] *vi* faire le trajet journalier (*de son domicile à un lieu de travail assez éloigné*) ▷ *vt* (*Law*) commuer; (*Math: terms etc*) opérer la commutation de

commuter [kə'mju:təʳ] *n* banlieusard(e) (*qui fait un trajet journalier pour se rendre à son travail*)

compact *adj* [kəm'pækt] compact(e) ▷ *n* ['kɔmpækt] contrat *m*, entente *f*; (*also:* **powder**

515

compact) poudrier m

compact disc n disque compact

compact disc player n lecteur m de disques compacts

companion [kəm'pænjən] n compagnon (compagne)

companionship [kəm'pænjənʃɪp] n camaraderie f

companionway [kəm'pænjənweɪ] n (Naut) escalier m des cabines

company ['kʌmpənɪ] n (also Comm, Mil, Theat) compagnie f; he's good ~ il est d'une compagnie agréable; we have ~ nous avons de la visite; to keep sb ~ tenir compagnie à qn; to part ~ with se séparer de; Smith and C~ Smith et Compagnie

company car n voiture f de fonction

company director n administrateur(-trice)

company secretary n (Brit Comm) secrétaire général (d'une société)

comparable ['kɔmpərəbl] adj comparable

comparative [kəm'pærətɪv] adj (study) comparatif(-ive); (relative) relatif(-ive)

comparatively [kəm'pærətɪvlɪ] adv (relatively) relativement

compare [kəm'pɛər] vt: to ~ sth/sb with or to comparer qch/qn avec or à ▷ vi: to ~ (with) se comparer (à); être comparable (à); how do the prices ~? comment sont les prix?, est-ce que les prix sont comparables?; ~d with or to par rapport à

comparison [kəm'pærɪsn] n comparaison f; in ~ (with) en comparaison (de)

compartment [kəm'pɑːtmənt] n (also Rail) compartiment m; a non-smoking ~ un compartiment non-fumeurs

compass ['kʌmpəs] n boussole f; compasses npl (Math) compas m; within the ~ of dans les limites de

compassion [kəm'pæʃən] n compassion f, humanité f

compassionate [kəm'pæʃənɪt] adj accessible à la compassion, au cœur charitable et bienveillant; on ~ grounds pour raisons personnelles or de famille

compassionate leave n congé exceptionnel (pour raisons de famille)

compatibility [kəmpætɪ'bɪlɪtɪ] n compatibilité f

compatible [kəm'pætɪbl] adj compatible

compel [kəm'pɛl] vt contraindre, obliger

compelling [kəm'pɛlɪŋ] adj (fig: argument) irrésistible

compendium [kəm'pɛndɪəm] n (summary) abrégé m

compensate ['kɔmpənseɪt] vt indemniser, dédommager ▷ vi: to ~ for compenser

compensation [kɔmpən'seɪʃən] n compensation f; (money) dédommagement m, indemnité f

compere ['kɔmpɛər] n présentateur(-trice), animateur(-trice)

compete [kəm'piːt] vi (take part) concourir; (vie):

to ~ (with) rivaliser (avec), faire concurrence (à)

competence ['kɔmpɪtəns] n compétence f, aptitude f

competent ['kɔmpɪtənt] adj compétent(e), capable

competing [kəm'piːtɪŋ] adj (ideas, theories) opposé(e); (companies) concurrent(e)

competition [kɔmpɪ'tɪʃən] n (contest) compétition f, concours m; (Econ) concurrence f; in ~ en concurrence avec

competitive [kəm'pɛtɪtɪv] adj (Econ) concurrentiel(le); (sports) de compétition; (person) qui a l'esprit de compétition

competitive examination n concours m

competitor [kəm'pɛtɪtər] n concurrent(e)

compile [kəm'paɪl] vt compiler

complacency [kəm'pleɪsnsɪ] n contentement m de soi, autosatisfaction f

complacent [kəm'pleɪsnt] adj (trop) content(e) de soi

complain [kəm'pleɪn] vi: to ~ (about) se plaindre (de); (in shop etc) réclamer (au sujet de)
▶ complain of vt fus (Med) se plaindre de

complaint [kəm'pleɪnt] n plainte f; (in shop etc) réclamation f; (Med) affection f

complement ['kɔmplɪmənt] n complément m; (esp of ship's crew etc) effectif complet ▷ vt (enhance) compléter

complementary [kɔmplɪ'mɛntərɪ] adj complémentaire

complete [kəm'pliːt] adj complet(-ète); (finished) achevé(e) ▷ vt achever, parachever; (set, group) compléter; (a form) remplir

completely [kəm'pliːtlɪ] adv complètement

completion [kəm'pliːʃən] n achèvement m; (of contract) exécution f; to be nearing ~ être presque terminé

complex ['kɔmplɛks] adj complexe ▷ n (Psych, buildings etc) complexe m

complexion [kəm'plɛkʃən] n (of face) teint m; (of event etc) aspect m, caractère m

complexity [kəm'plɛksɪtɪ] n complexité f

compliance [kəm'plaɪəns] n (submission) docilité f; (agreement): ~ with le fait de se conformer à; in ~ with en conformité avec, conformément à

compliant [kəm'plaɪənt] adj docile, très accommodant(e)

complicate ['kɔmplɪkeɪt] vt compliquer

complicated ['kɔmplɪkeɪtɪd] adj compliqué(e)

complication [kɔmplɪ'keɪʃən] n complication f

compliment n ['kɔmplɪmənt] compliment m
▷ vt ['kɔmplɪmənt] complimenter;

compliments npl compliments mpl, hommages mpl; vœux mpl; to pay sb a ~ faire or adresser un compliment à qn; to ~ sb (on sth/on doing sth) féliciter qn (pour qch/de faire qch)

complimentary [kɔmplɪ'mɛntərɪ] adj flatteur(-euse); (free) à titre gracieux

complimentary ticket n billet m de faveur

compliments slip n fiche f de transmission

comply [kəm'plaɪ] vi: to ~ with se soumettre à, se conformer à

component [kəm'pəunənt] *adj* composant(e), constituant(e) ▷ *n* composant *m*, élément *m*
compose [kəm'pəuz] *vt* composer; *(form)*: **to ~d of** se composer de; **to ~ o.s.** se calmer, se maîtriser; **to ~ one's features** prendre une contenance
composed [kəm'pəuzd] *adj* calme, posé(e)
composer [kəm'pəuzə^r] *n* (*Mus*) compositeur *m*
composite ['kɔmpəzɪt] *adj* composite; (*Bot, Math*) composé(e)
composition [kɔmpə'zɪʃən] *n* composition *f*
compost ['kɔmpɔst] *n* compost *m*
composure [kəm'pəuʒə^r] *n* calme *m*, maîtrise *f* de soi
compound ['kɔmpaund] *n* (*Chem, Ling*) composé *m*; (*enclosure*) enclos *m*, enceinte *f* ▷ *adj* composé(e); (*fracture*) compliqué(e) ▷ *vt* [kəm'paund] (*fig: problem etc*) aggraver
compound fracture *n* fracture compliquée
compound interest *n* intérêt composé
comprehend [kɔmprɪ'hɛnd] *vt* comprendre
comprehension [kɔmprɪ'hɛnʃən] *n* compréhension *f*
comprehensive [kɔmprɪ'hɛnsɪv] *adj* (très) complet(-ète); **~ policy** (*Insurance*) assurance *f* tous risques
comprehensive [kɔmprɪ'hɛnsɪv], **comprehensive school** *n* (*Brit*) *école secondaire non sélective avec libre circulation d'une section à l'autre*, ≈ CES *m*
compress *vt* [kəm'prɛs] comprimer; (*text, information*) condenser ▷ *n* ['kɔmprɛs] (*Med*) compresse *f*
compression [kəm'prɛʃən] *n* compression *f*
comprise [kəm'praɪz] *vt* (*also:* **be comprised of**) comprendre; (*constitute*) constituer, représenter
compromise ['kɔmprəmaɪz] *n* compromis *m* ▷ *vt* compromettre ▷ *vi* transiger, accepter un compromis ▷ *cpd* (*decision, solution*) de compromis
compulsion [kəm'pʌlʃən] *n* contrainte *f*, force *f*; **under ~** sous la contrainte
compulsive [kəm'pʌlsɪv] *adj* (*Psych*) compulsif(-ive); (*book, film etc*) captivant(e); **he's a ~ smoker** c'est un fumeur invétéré
compulsory [kəm'pʌlsərɪ] *adj* obligatoire
compulsory purchase *n* expropriation *f*
compunction [kəm'pʌŋkʃən] *n* scrupule *m*; **to have no ~ about doing sth** n'avoir aucun scrupule à faire qch
computer [kəm'pju:tə^r] *n* ordinateur *m*; (*mechanical*) calculatrice *f*
computer game *n* jeu *m* vidéo
computer-generated [kəm'pju:tə^rdʒɛnəreɪtɪd] *adj* de synthèse
computerize [kəm'pju:təraɪz] *vt* (*data*) traiter par ordinateur; (*system, office*) informatiser
computer language *n* langage *m* machine *or* informatique
computer literate *adj* initié(e) à l'informatique
computer peripheral *n* périphérique *m*
computer program *n* programme *m* informatique
computer programmer *n* programmeur(-euse)
computer programming *n* programmation *f*
computer science *n* informatique *f*
computer scientist *n* informaticien(ne)
computer studies *npl* informatique *f*
computing [kəm'pju:tɪŋ] *n* informatique *f*
comrade ['kɔmrɪd] *n* camarade *m/f*
comradeship ['kɔmrɪdʃɪp] *n* camaraderie *f*
Comsat ['kɔmsæt] *n abbr* = **communications satellite**
con [kɔn] *vt* duper; (*cheat*) escroquer ▷ *n* escroquerie *f*; **to ~ sb into doing sth** tromper qn pour lui faire faire qch
concave ['kɔn'keɪv] *adj* concave
conceal [kən'si:l] *vt* cacher, dissimuler
concede [kən'si:d] *vt* concéder ▷ *vi* céder
conceit [kən'si:t] *n* vanité *f*, suffisance *f*, prétention *f*
conceited [kən'si:tɪd] *adj* vaniteux(-euse), suffisant(e)
conceivable [kən'si:vəbl] *adj* concevable, imaginable; **it is ~ that** il est concevable que
conceivably [kən'si:vəblɪ] *adv*: **he may ~ be right** il n'est pas impossible qu'il ait raison
conceive [kən'si:v] *vt, vi* concevoir; **to ~ of sth/ of doing sth** imaginer qch/de faire qch
concentrate ['kɔnsəntreɪt] *vi* se concentrer ▷ *vt* concentrer
concentration [kɔnsən'treɪʃən] *n* concentration *f*
concentration camp *n* camp *m* de concentration
concentric [kɔn'sɛntrɪk] *adj* concentrique
concept ['kɔnsɛpt] *n* concept *m*
conception [kən'sɛpʃən] *n* conception *f*; (*idea*) idée *f*
concern [kən'sə:n] *n* affaire *f*; (*Comm*) entreprise *f*, firme *f*; (*anxiety*) inquiétude *f*, souci *m* ▷ *vt* (*worry*) inquiéter; (*involve*) concerner; (*relate to*) se rapporter à; **to be ~ed (about)** s'inquiéter (de), être inquiet(-ète) (au sujet de); **"to whom it may ~"** "à qui de droit"; **as far as I am ~ed** en ce qui me concerne; **to be ~ed with** (*person: involved with*) s'occuper de; **the department ~ed** (*under discussion*) le service en question; (*involved*) le service concerné
concerning [kən'sə:nɪŋ] *prep* en ce qui concerne, à propos de
concert ['kɔnsət] *n* concert *m*; **in ~** à l'unisson, en chœur; ensemble
concerted [kən'sə:tɪd] *adj* concerté(e)
concert hall *n* salle *f* de concert
concertina [kɔnsə'ti:nə] *n* concertina *m* ▷ *vi* se télescoper, se caramboler
concerto [kən'tʃə:təu] *n* concerto *m*
concession [kən'sɛʃən] *n* (*compromise*) concession *f*; (*reduced price*) réduction *f*; **tax ~** dégrèvement fiscal; **"~s"** tarif réduit
concessionaire [kənsɛʃə'nɛə^r] *n* concessionnaire *m/f*

concessionary [kən'sɛʃənrɪ] *adj* (*ticket, fare*) à tarif réduit

conciliation [kənsɪlɪ'eɪʃən] *n* conciliation *f*, apaisement *m*

conciliatory [kən'sɪlɪətrɪ] *adj* conciliateur(-trice); conciliant(e)

concise [kən'saɪs] *adj* concis(e)

conclave ['kɒnkleɪv] *n* assemblée secrète; (*Rel*) conclave *m*

conclude [kən'klu:d] *vt* conclure ▷ *vi* (*speaker*) conclure; (*events*): **to ~ (with)** se terminer (par)

concluding [kən'klu:dɪŋ] *adj* (*remarks etc*) final(e)

conclusion [kən'klu:ʒən] *n* conclusion *f*; **to come to the ~ that** (en) conclure que

conclusive [kən'klu:sɪv] *adj* concluant(e), définitif(-ive)

concoct [kən'kɒkt] *vt* confectionner, composer

concoction [kən'kɒkʃən] *n* (*food, drink*) mélange *m*

concord ['kɒnkɔ:d] *n* (*harmony*) harmonie *f*; (*treaty*) accord *m*

concourse ['kɒnkɔ:s] *n* (*hall*) hall *m*, salle *f* des pas perdus; (*crowd*) affluence *f*; multitude *f*

concrete ['kɒnkri:t] *n* béton *m* ▷ *adj* concret(-ète); (*Constr*) en béton

concrete mixer *n* bétonnière *f*

concur [kən'kə:ʳ] *vi* être d'accord

concurrently [kən'kʌrntlɪ] *adv* simultanément

concussion [kən'kʌʃən] *n* (*Med*) commotion (cérébrale)

condemn [kən'dɛm] *vt* condamner

condemnation [kɒndɛm'neɪʃən] *n* condamnation *f*

condensation [kɒndɛn'seɪʃən] *n* condensation *f*

condense [kən'dɛns] *vi* se condenser ▷ *vt* condenser

condensed milk [kən'dɛnst-] *n* lait concentré (sucré)

condescend [kɒndɪ'sɛnd] *vi* condescendre, s'abaisser; **to ~ to do sth** daigner faire qch

condescending [kɒndɪ'sɛndɪŋ] *adj* condescendant(e)

condition [kən'dɪʃən] *n* condition *f*; (*disease*) maladie *f* ▷ *vt* déterminer, conditionner; **in good/poor ~** en bon/mauvais état; **a heart ~** une maladie cardiaque; **weather ~s** conditions *fpl* météorologiques; **on ~ that** à condition que +*sub*, à condition de

conditional [kən'dɪʃənl] *adj* conditionnel(le); **to be ~ upon** dépendre de

conditioner [kən'dɪʃənəʳ] *n* (*for hair*) baume démêlant; (*for fabrics*) assouplissant *m*

condo ['kɒndəu] *n* (*US inf*) = **condominium**

condolences [kən'dəulənsɪz] *npl* condoléances *fpl*

condom ['kɒndəm] *n* préservatif *m*

condominium [kɒndə'mɪnɪəm] *n* (*US: building*) immeuble *m* (en copropriété); (*: rooms*) appartement *m* (dans un immeuble en copropriété)

condone [kən'dəun] *vt* fermer les yeux sur, approuver (tacitement)

conducive [kən'dju:sɪv] *adj*: **~ to** favorable à, qui contribue à

conduct *n* ['kɒndʌkt] conduite *f* ▷ *vt* [kən'dʌkt] conduire; (*manage*) mener, diriger; (*Mus*) diriger; **to ~ o.s.** se conduire, se comporter

conductor [kən'dʌktəʳ] *n* (*of orchestra*) chef *m* d'orchestre; (*on bus*) receveur *m*; (*US: on train*) chef *m* de train; (*Elec*) conducteur *m*

conductress [kən'dʌktrɪs] *n* (*on bus*) receveuse *f*

conduit ['kɒndɪt] *n* conduit *m*, tuyau *m*; tube *m*

cone [kəun] *n* cône *m*; (*for ice-cream*) cornet *m*; (*Bot*) pomme *f* de pin, cône

confectioner [kən'fɛkʃənəʳ] *n* (*of cakes*) pâtissier(-ière); (*of sweets*) confiseur(-euse); **~'s (shop)** confiserie(-pâtisserie) *f*

confectionery [kən'fɛkʃənrɪ] *n* (*sweets*) confiserie *f*; (*cakes*) pâtisserie *f*

confederate [kən'fɛdrɪt] *adj* confédéré(e) ▷ *n* (*pej*) acolyte *m*; (*US History*) confédéré(e)

confederation [kənfɛdə'reɪʃən] *n* confédération *f*

confer [kən'fə:ʳ] *vt*: **to ~ sth on** conférer qch à ▷ *vi* conférer, s'entretenir; **to ~ (with sb about sth)** s'entretenir (de qch avec qn)

conference ['kɒnfərns] *n* conférence *f*; **to be in ~** être en réunion *or* en conférence

conference room *n* salle *f* de conférence

confess [kən'fɛs] *vt* confesser, avouer ▷ *vi* (*admit sth*) avouer; (*Rel*) se confesser

confession [kən'fɛʃən] *n* confession *f*

confessional [kən'fɛʃənl] *n* confessional *m*

confessor [kən'fɛsəʳ] *n* confesseur *m*

confetti [kən'fɛtɪ] *n* confettis *mpl*

confide [kən'faɪd] *vi*: **to ~ in** s'ouvrir à, se confier à

confidence ['kɒnfɪdns] *n* confiance *f*; (*also*: **self-confidence**) assurance *f*, confiance en soi; (*secret*) confidence *f*; **to have (every) ~ that** être certain que; **motion of no ~** motion *f* de censure; **in ~** (*speak, write*) en confidence, confidentiellement; **to tell sb sth in strict ~** dire qch à qn en toute confidence

confidence trick *n* escroquerie *f*

confident ['kɒnfɪdənt] *adj* (*self-assured*) sûr(e) de soi; (*sure*) sûr

confidential [kɒnfɪ'dɛnʃəl] *adj* confidentiel(le); (*secretary*) particulier(-ère)

confidentiality ['kɒnfɪdɛnʃɪ'ælɪtɪ] *n* confidentialité *f*

configuration [kən'fɪgju'reɪʃən] *n* (*also Comput*) configuration *f*

confine [kən'faɪn] *vt* limiter, borner; (*shut up*) confiner, enfermer; **to ~ o.s. to doing sth/to sth** se contenter de faire qch/se limiter à qch

confined [kən'faɪnd] *adj* (*space*) restreint(e), réduit(e)

confinement [kən'faɪnmənt] *n* emprisonnement *m*, détention *f*; (*Mil*) consigne *f* (au quartier); (*Med*) accouchement *m*

confines ['kɒnfaɪnz] *npl* confins *mpl*, bornes *fpl*

confirm [kən'fə:m] *vt* (*report, Rel*) confirmer; (*appointment*) ratifier

confirmation [kɔnfə'meɪʃən] *n* confirmation *f*; ratification *f*

confirmed [kən'fə:md] *adj* invétéré(e), incorrigible

confiscate ['kɔnfɪskeɪt] *vt* confisquer

confiscation [kɔnfɪs'keɪʃən] *n* confiscation *f*

conflagration [kɔnflə'greɪʃən] *n* incendie *m*; (*fig*) conflagration *f*

conflict *n* ['kɔnflɪkt] conflit *m*, lutte *f* ▷ *vi* [kən'flɪkt] être *or* entrer en conflit; (*opinions*) s'opposer, se heurter

conflicting [kən'flɪktɪŋ] *adj* contradictoire

conform [kən'fɔ:m] *vi*: **to ~ (to)** se conformer (à)

conformist [kən'fɔ:mɪst] *n* (*gen*, *Rel*) conformiste *m/f*

confound [kən'faund] *vt* confondre; (*amaze*) rendre perplexe

confounded [kən'faundɪd] *adj* maudit(e), sacré(e)

confront [kən'frʌnt] *vt* (*two people*) confronter; (*enemy*, *danger*) affronter, faire face à; (*problem*) faire face à

confrontation [kɔnfrən'teɪʃən] *n* confrontation *f*

confrontational [kɔnfrən'teɪʃənl] *adj* conflictuel(le)

confuse [kən'fju:z] *vt* (*person*) troubler; (*situation*) embrouiller; (*one thing with another*) confondre

confused [kən'fju:zd] *adj* (*person*) dérouté(e), désorienté(e); (*situation*) embrouillé(e)

confusing [kən'fju:zɪŋ] *adj* peu clair(e), déroutant(e)

confusion [kən'fju:ʒən] *n* confusion *f*

congeal [kən'dʒi:l] *vi* (*oil*) se figer; (*blood*) se coaguler

congenial [kən'dʒi:nɪəl] *adj* sympathique, agréable

congenital [kən'dʒenɪtl] *adj* congénital(e)

conger eel ['kɔngər-] *n* congre *m*, anguille *f* de roche

congested [kən'dʒestɪd] *adj* (*Med*) congestionné(e); (*fig*) surpeuplé(e); congestionné; bloqué(e); (*telephone lines*) encombré(e)

congestion [kən'dʒestʃən] *n* (*Med*) congestion *f*; (*fig*: *traffic*) encombrement *m*

conglomerate [kən'glɔmərɪt] *n* (*Comm*) conglomérat *m*

conglomeration [kənglɔmə'reɪʃən] *n* groupement *m*; agglomération *f*

Congo ['kɔngəu] *n* (*state*) (république *f* du) Congo

congratulate [kən'grætjuleɪt] *vt*: **to ~ sb (on)** féliciter qn (de)

congratulations [kəngrætju'leɪʃənz] *npl*: **~ (on)** félicitations *fpl* (pour) ▷ *excl*: **~!** (toutes mes) félicitations!

congregate ['kɔngrɪgeɪt] *vi* se rassembler, se réunir

congregation [kɔngrɪ'geɪʃən] *n* assemblée *f* (des fidèles)

congress ['kɔngres] *n* congrès *m*; (*Pol*): **C~**

Congrès *m*; *voir article*

congressman ['kɔngresmən] (*irreg*) *n* membre *m* du Congrès

congresswoman ['kɔngreswumən] (*irreg*) *n* membre *m* du Congrès

conical ['kɔnɪkl] *adj* (de forme) conique

conifer ['kɔnɪfər] *n* conifère *m*

coniferous [kə'nɪfərəs] *adj* (*forest*) de conifères

conjecture [kən'dʒɛktʃər] *n* conjecture *f* ▷ *vt*, *vi* conjecturer

conjugal ['kɔndʒugl] *adj* conjugal(e)

conjugate ['kɔndʒugeɪt] *vt* conjuguer

conjugation [kɔndʒə'geɪʃən] *n* conjugaison *f*

conjunction [kən'dʒʌŋkʃən] *n* conjonction *f*; **in ~ with** (conjointement) avec

conjunctivitis [kəndʒʌŋktɪ'vaɪtɪs] *n* conjonctivite *f*

conjure ['kʌndʒər] *vt* faire apparaître (par la prestidigitation) [kən'dʒuər] conjurer, supplier ▷ *vi* faire des tours de passe-passe
  ▶ **conjure up** *vt* (*ghost*, *spirit*) faire apparaître; (*memories*) évoquer

conjurer ['kʌndʒərər] *n* prestidigitateur *m*, illusionniste *m/f*

conjuring trick ['kʌndʒərɪŋ-] *n* tour *m* de prestidigitation

conker ['kɔŋkər] *n* (*Brit*) marron *m* (d'Inde)

conk out [kɔŋk-] *vi* (*inf*) tomber *or* rester en panne

conman ['kɔnmæn] (*irreg*) *n* escroc *m*

Conn. *abbr* (*US*) = **Connecticut**

connect [kə'nɛkt] *vt* joindre, relier; (*Elec*) connecter; (*Tel*: *caller*) mettre en connexion; (: *subscriber*) brancher; (*fig*) établir un rapport entre, faire un rapprochement entre ▷ *vi* (*train*): **to ~ with** assurer la correspondance avec; **to be ~ed with** avoir un rapport avec; (*have dealings with*) avoir des rapports avec, être en relation avec; **I am trying to ~ you** (*Tel*) j'essaie d'obtenir votre communication

connecting flight *n* (vol *m* de) correspondance *f*

connection [kə'nɛkʃən] *n* relation *f*, lien *m*; (*Elec*) connexion *f*; (*Tel*) communication *f*; (*train etc*) correspondance *f*; **in ~ with** à propos de; **what is the ~ between them?** quel est le lien entre eux?; **business ~s** relations d'affaires; **to miss/get one's ~** (*train etc*) rater/avoir sa correspondance

connexion [kə'nɛkʃən] *n* (*Brit*) = **connection**

conning tower ['kɔnɪŋ-] *n* kiosque *m* (de sous-marin)

connive [kə'naɪv] *vi*: **to ~ at** se faire le complice de

connoisseur [kɔnɪ'sə:ʳ] n connaisseur m
connotation [kɔnə'teɪʃən] n connotation f, implication f
connubial [kə'nju:bɪəl] adj conjugal(e)
conquer ['kɔŋkəʳ] vt conquérir; (feelings) vaincre, surmonter
conqueror ['kɔŋkərəʳ] n conquérant m, vainqueur m
conquest ['kɔŋkwɛst] n conquête f
cons [kɔnz] npl see **convenience**; **pro**
conscience ['kɔnʃəns] n conscience f; **in all ~** en conscience
conscientious [kɔnʃɪ'ɛnʃəs] adj consciencieux(-euse); (scruple, objection) de conscience
conscientious objector n objecteur m de conscience
conscious ['kɔnʃəs] adj conscient(e); (deliberate: insult, error) délibéré(e); **to become ~ of sth/ that** prendre conscience de qch/que
consciousness ['kɔnʃəsnɪs] n conscience f; (Med) connaissance f; **to lose/regain ~** perdre/ reprendre connaissance
conscript ['kɔnskrɪpt] n conscrit m
conscription [kən'skrɪpʃən] n conscription f
consecrate ['kɔnsɪkreɪt] vt consacrer
consecutive [kən'sɛkjutɪv] adj consécutif(-ive); **on three ~ occasions** trois fois de suite
consensus [kən'sɛnsəs] n consensus m; **the ~ (of opinion)** le consensus (d'opinion)
consent [kən'sɛnt] n consentement m ▷ vi: **to ~ (to)** consentir (à); **age of ~** âge nubile (légal); **by common ~** d'un commun accord
consenting adults [kən'sɛntɪŋ-] npl personnes consentantes
consequence ['kɔnsɪkwəns] n suites fpl, conséquence f; (significance) importance f; **in ~** en conséquence, par conséquent
consequently ['kɔnsɪkwəntlɪ] adv par conséquent, donc
conservation [kɔnsə'veɪʃən] n préservation f, protection f; (also: **nature conservation**) défense f de l'environnement; **energy ~** économies fpl d'énergie
conservationist [kɔnsə'veɪʃnɪst] n protecteur(-trice) de la nature
conservative [kən'sə:vətɪv] adj conservateur(-trice); (cautious) prudent(e)
Conservative [kən'sə:vətɪv] adj, n (Brit Pol) conservateur(-trice); **the ~ Party** le parti conservateur
conservatory [kən'sə:vətrɪ] n (room) jardin m d'hiver; (Mus) conservatoire m
conserve [kən'sə:v] vt conserver, préserver; (supplies, energy) économiser ▷ n confiture f, conserve f (de fruits)
consider [kən'sɪdəʳ] vt (study) considérer, réfléchir à; (take into account) penser à, prendre en considération; (regard, judge) considérer, estimer; **to ~ doing sth** envisager de faire qch; **~ yourself lucky** estimez-vous heureux; **all things ~ed** (toute) réflexion faite

considerable [kən'sɪdərəbl] adj considérable
considerably [kən'sɪdərəblɪ] adv nettement
considerate [kən'sɪdərɪt] adj prévenant(e), plein(e) d'égards
consideration [kənsɪdə'reɪʃən] n considération f; (reward) rétribution f, rémunération f; **out of ~ for** par égard pour; **under ~** à l'étude; **my first ~ is my family** ma famille passe avant tout le reste
considered [kən'sɪdəd] adj: **it is my ~ opinion that ...** après avoir mûrement réfléchi, je pense que ...
considering [kən'sɪdərɪŋ] prep: **~ (that)** étant donné (que)
consign [kən'saɪn] vt expédier, livrer
consignee [kɔnsaɪ'ni:] n destinataire m/f
consignment [kən'saɪnmənt] n arrivage m, envoi m
consignment note n (Comm) bordereau m d'expédition
consignor [kən'saɪnəʳ] n expéditeur(-trice)
consist [kən'sɪst] vi: **to ~ of** consister en, se composer de
consistency [kən'sɪstənsɪ] n (thickness) consistance f; (fig) cohérence f
consistent [kən'sɪstənt] adj logique, cohérent(e); **~ with** compatible avec, en accord avec
consolation [kɔnsə'leɪʃən] n consolation f
console¹ [kən'səul] vt consoler
console² ['kɔnsəul] n console f
consolidate [kən'sɔlɪdeɪt] vt consolider
consols ['kɔnsɔlz] npl (Brit Stock Exchange) rente f d'État
consommé [kən'sɔmeɪ] n consommé m
consonant ['kɔnsənənt] n consonne f
consort ['kɔnsɔ:t] n époux (épouse); **prince ~** prince m consort ▷ vi (often pej): **to ~ with sb** frayer avec qn
consortium [kən'sɔ:tɪəm] n consortium m, comptoir m
conspicuous [kən'spɪkjuəs] adj voyant(e), qui attire l'attention; **to make o.s. ~** se faire remarquer
conspiracy [kən'spɪrəsɪ] n conspiration f, complot m
conspiratorial [kən'spɪrə'tɔ:rɪəl] adj (behaviour) de conspirateur; (glance) conspirateur(-trice)
conspire [kən'spaɪəʳ] vi conspirer, comploter
constable ['kʌnstəbl] n (Brit) ≈ agent m de police, gendarme m; **chief ~** ≈ préfet m de police
constabulary [kən'stæbjulərɪ] n ≈ police f, gendarmerie f
constant ['kɔnstənt] adj constant(e); incessant(e)
constantly ['kɔnstəntlɪ] adv constamment, sans cesse
constellation [kɔnstə'leɪʃən] n constellation f
consternation [kɔnstə'neɪʃən] n consternation f
constipated ['kɔnstɪpeɪtɪd] adj constipé(e)
constipation [kɔnstɪ'peɪʃən] n constipation f

constituency [kən'stɪtjuənsɪ] n (Pol: area) circonscription électorale; (: electors) électorat m; voir article

● CONSTITUENCY
●
● Une constituency est à la fois une région qui
● élit un député au parlement et l'ensemble
● des électeurs dans cette région. En Grande-
● Bretagne, les députés font régulièrement
● des "permanences" dans leur
● circonscription électorale lors desquelles les
● électeurs peuvent venir les voir pour parler
● de leurs problèmes de logement etc.

constituency party n section locale (d'un parti)
constituent [kən'stɪtjuənt] n électeur(-trice); (part) élément constitutif, composant m
constitute ['kɔnstɪtjuːt] vt constituer
constitution [kɔnstɪ'tjuːʃən] n constitution f
constitutional [kɔnstɪ'tjuːʃənl] adj constitutionnel(le)
constitutional monarchy n monarchie constitutionnelle
constrain [kən'streɪn] vt contraindre, forcer
constrained [kən'streɪnd] adj contraint(e), gêné(e)
constraint [kən'streɪnt] n contrainte f; (embarrassment) gêne f
constrict [kən'strɪkt] vt rétrécir, resserrer; gêner, limiter
construct [kən'strʌkt] vt construire
construction [kən'strʌkʃən] n construction f; (fig: interpretation) interprétation f; **under ~** (building etc) en construction
construction industry n (industrie f du) bâtiment
constructive [kən'strʌktɪv] adj constructif(-ive)
construe [kən'struː] vt analyser, expliquer
consul ['kɔnsl] n consul m
consulate ['kɔnsjulɪt] n consulat m
consult [kən'sʌlt] vt consulter; **to ~ sb (about sth)** consulter qn (à propos de qch)
consultancy [kən'sʌltənsɪ] n service m de conseils
consultancy fee n honoraires mpl d'expert
consultant [kən'sʌltənt] n (Med) médecin consultant; (other specialist) consultant m, (expert-)conseil m ▷ cpd: **~ engineer** n ingénieur-conseil m; **~ paediatrician** n pédiatre m; **legal/management ~** conseiller m juridique/en gestion
consultation [kɔnsəl'teɪʃən] n consultation f; **in ~ with** en consultation avec
consultative [kən'sʌltətɪv] adj consultatif(-ive)
consulting room [kən'sʌltɪŋ-] n (Brit) cabinet m de consultation
consume [kən'sjuːm] vt consommer; (subj: flames, hatred, desire) consumer; **to be ~d with hatred** être dévoré par la haine; **to be ~d with desire** brûler de désir

consumer [kən'sjuːməʳ] n consommateur(-trice); (of electricity, gas etc) usager m
consumer credit n crédit m aux consommateurs
consumer durables npl biens mpl de consommation durables
consumer goods npl biens mpl de consommation
consumerism [kən'sjuːmərɪzəm] n (consumer protection) défense f du consommateur; (Econ) consumérisme m
consumer society n société f de consommation
consumer watchdog n organisme m pour la défense des consommateurs
consummate ['kɔnsʌmeɪt] vt consommer
consumption [kən'sʌmpʃən] n consommation f; **not fit for human ~** non comestible
cont. abbr (= continued) suite
contact ['kɔntækt] n contact m; (person) connaissance f, relation f ▷ vt se mettre en contact or en rapport avec; **to be in ~ with sb/sth** être en contact avec qn/qch; **business ~s** relations fpl d'affaires, contacts mpl
contact lenses npl verres mpl de contact
contagious [kən'teɪdʒəs] adj contagieux(-euse)
contain [kən'teɪn] vt contenir; **to ~ o.s.** se contenir, se maîtriser
container [kən'teɪnəʳ] n récipient m; (for shipping etc) conteneur m
containerize [kən'teɪnəraɪz] vt conteneuriser
container ship n porte-conteneurs m inv
contaminate [kən'tæmɪneɪt] vt contaminer
contamination [kəntæmɪ'neɪʃən] n contamination f
cont'd abbr (= continued) suite
contemplate ['kɔntəmpleɪt] vt contempler; (consider) envisager
contemplation [kɔntəm'pleɪʃən] n contemplation f
contemporary [kən'tempərərɪ] adj contemporain(e); (design, wallpaper) moderne ▷ n contemporain(e)
contempt [kən'tempt] n mépris m, dédain m; **~ of court** (Law) outrage m à l'autorité de la justice
contemptible [kən'temptəbl] adj méprisable, vil(e)
contemptuous [kən'temptjuəs] adj dédaigneux(-euse), méprisant(e)
contend [kən'tend] vt: **to ~ that** soutenir or prétendre que ▷ vi: **to ~ with** (compete) rivaliser avec; (struggle) lutter avec; **to have to ~ with** (be faced with) avoir affaire à, être aux prises avec
contender [kən'tendəʳ] n prétendant(e); candidat(e)
content [kən'tent] adj content(e), satisfait(e) ▷ vt contenter, satisfaire ▷ n ['kɔntent] contenu m; (of fat, moisture) teneur f; **contents** npl (of container etc) contenu m; **(table of) ~s** table f des matières; **to be ~ with** se contenter de; **to ~ o.s. with sth/with doing sth** se contenter de

qch/de faire qch

contented [kən'tɛntɪd] *adj* content(e), satisfait(e)

contentedly [kən'tɛntɪdlɪ] *adv* avec un sentiment de (profonde) satisfaction

contention [kən'tɛnʃən] *n* dispute *f*, contestation *f*; *(argument)* assertion *f*, affirmation *f*; **bone of ~** sujet *m* de discorde

contentious [kən'tɛnʃəs] *adj* querelleur(-euse); litigieux(-euse)

contentment [kən'tɛntmənt] *n* contentement *m*, satisfaction *f*

contest *n* ['kɔntɛst] combat *m*, lutte *f*; *(competition)* concours *m* ▷ *vt* [kən'tɛst] contester, discuter; *(compete for)* disputer; *(Law)* attaquer

contestant [kən'tɛstənt] *n* concurrent(e); *(in fight)* adversaire *m/f*

context ['kɔntɛkst] *n* contexte *m*; **in/out of ~** dans le/hors contexte

continent ['kɔntɪnənt] *n* continent *m*; **the C~** *(Brit)* l'Europe continentale; **on the C~** en Europe (continentale)

continental [kɔntɪ'nɛntl] *adj* continental(e) ▷ *n* *(Brit)* Européen(ne) (continental(e))

continental breakfast *n* café *(or* thé*)* complet

continental quilt *n* *(Brit)* couette *f*

contingency [kən'tɪndʒənsɪ] *n* éventualité *f*, événement imprévu

contingency plan *n* plan *m* d'urgence

contingent [kən'tɪndʒənt] *adj* contingent(e) ▷ *n* contingent *m*; **to be ~ upon** dépendre de

continual [kən'tɪnjuəl] *adj* continuel(le)

continually [kən'tɪnjuəlɪ] *adv* continuellement, sans cesse

continuation [kəntɪnju'eɪʃən] *n* continuation *f*; *(after interruption)* reprise *f*; *(of story)* suite *f*

continue [kən'tɪnju:] *vi* continuer ▷ *vt* continuer; *(start again)* reprendre; **to be ~d** *(story)* à suivre; **~d on page 10** suite page 10

continuing education [kən'tɪnjuɪŋ-] *n* formation permanente *or* continue

continuity [kɔntɪ'nju:ɪtɪ] *n* continuité *f*; *(TV)* enchaînement *m*; *(Cine)* script *m*

continuity girl *n* *(Cine)* script-girl *f*

continuous [kən'tɪnjuəs] *adj* continu(e), permanent(e); *(Ling)* progressif(-ive); **~ performance** *(Cine)* séance permanente; **~ stationery** *(Comput)* papier *m* en continu

continuous assessment *(Brit)* *n* contrôle continu

continuously [kən'tɪnjuəslɪ] *adv* *(repeatedly)* continuellement; *(uninterruptedly)* sans interruption

contort [kən'tɔ:t] *vt* tordre, crisper

contortion [kən'tɔ:ʃən] *n* crispation *f*, torsion *f*; *(of acrobat)* contorsion *f*

contortionist [kən'tɔ:ʃənɪst] *n* contorsionniste *m/f*

contour ['kɔntuəʳ] *n* contour *m*, profil *m*; *(also:* **contour line***)* courbe *f* de niveau

contraband ['kɔntrəbænd] *n* contrebande *f*

▷ *adj* de contrebande

contraception [kɔntrə'sɛpʃən] *n* contraception *f*

contraceptive [kɔntrə'sɛptɪv] *adj* contraceptif(-ive), anticonceptionnel(le) ▷ *n* contraceptif *m*

contract [*n, cpd* 'kɔntrækt, *vb* kən'trækt] *n* contrat *m* ▷ *cpd* *(price, date)* contractuel(le); *(work)* à forfait ▷ *vi* *(become smaller)* se contracter, se resserrer ▷ *vt* contracter; *(Comm)*: **to ~ to do sth** s'engager (par contrat) à faire qch; **~ of employment/service** contrat de travail/de service

▶ **contract in** *vi* s'engager (par contrat); *(Brit Admin)* s'affilier au régime de retraite complémentaire

▶ **contract out** *vi* se dégager; *(Brit Admin)* opter pour la non-affiliation au régime de retraite complémentaire

contraction [kən'trækʃən] *n* contraction *f*; *(Ling)* forme contractée

contractor [kən'træktəʳ] *n* entrepreneur *m*

contractual [kən'træktʃuəl] *adj* contractuel(le)

contradict [kɔntrə'dɪkt] *vt* contredire; *(be contrary to)* démentir, être en contradiction avec

contradiction [kɔntrə'dɪkʃən] *n* contradiction *f*; **to be in ~ with** contredire, être en contradiction avec

contradictory [kɔntrə'dɪktərɪ] *adj* contradictoire

contraflow ['kɔntrəfləu] *n* *(Aut)*: **~ lane** voie *f* à contresens; **there's a ~ system in operation on ...** une voie a été mise en sens inverse sur ...

contralto [kən'træltəu] *n* contralto *m*

contraption [kən'træpʃən] *n* *(pej)* machin *m*, truc *m*

contrary¹ ['kɔntrərɪ] *adj* contraire, opposé(e) ▷ *n* contraire *m*; **on the ~** au contraire; **unless you hear to the ~** sauf avis contraire; **~ to what we thought** contrairement à ce que nous pensions

contrary² [kən'trɛərɪ] *adj* *(perverse)* contrariant(e), entêté(e)

contrast *n* ['kɔntrɑ:st] contraste *m* ▷ *vt* [kən'trɑ:st] mettre en contraste, contraster; **in ~ to** *or* **with** contrairement à, par opposition à

contrasting [kən'trɑ:stɪŋ] *adj* opposé(e), contrasté(e)

contravene [kɔntrə'vi:n] *vt* enfreindre, violer, contrevenir à

contravention [kɔntrə'vɛnʃən] *n*: **~ (of)** infraction *f* (à)

contribute [kən'trɪbju:t] *vi* contribuer ▷ *vt*: **to ~ £10/an article to** donner 10 livres/un article à; **to ~ to** *(gen)* contribuer à; *(newspaper)* collaborer à; *(discussion)* prendre part à

contribution [kɔntrɪ'bju:ʃən] *n* contribution *f*; *(Brit: for social security)* cotisation *f*; *(to publication)* article *m*

contributor [kən'trɪbjutəʳ] *n* *(to newspaper)* collaborateur(-trice); *(of money, goods)* donateur(-trice)

contributory [kən'trɪbjutərɪ] *adj* *(cause)* annexe;

it was a ~ factor in ... ce facteur a contribué à ...
contributory pension scheme n (Brit)
régime m de retraite salariale
contrite ['kɔntraɪt] adj contrit(e)
contrivance [kən'traɪvəns] n (scheme)
machination f, combinaison f; (device) appareil
m, dispositif m
contrive [kən'traɪv] vt combiner, inventer ▷ vi:
to ~ to do s'arranger pour faire, trouver le
moyen de faire
control [kən'trəul] vt (process, machinery)
commander; (temper) maîtriser; (disease)
enrayer; (check) contrôler ▷ n maîtrise f; (power)
autorité f; **controls** npl (of machine etc)
commandes fpl; (on radio) boutons mpl de
réglage; **to take ~ of** se rendre maître de;
(Comm) acquérir une participation majoritaire
dans; **to be in ~ of** être maître de, maîtriser; (in
charge of) être responsable de; **to ~ o.s.** se
contrôler; **everything is under ~** j'ai (or il a etc)
la situation en main; **the car went out of ~** j'ai
(or il a etc) perdu le contrôle du véhicule;
beyond our ~ indépendant(e) de notre volonté
control key n (Comput) touche f de commande
controller [kən'trəulər] n contrôleur m
controlling interest [kən'trəulɪŋ-] n (Comm)
participation f majoritaire
control panel n (on aircraft, ship, TV etc) tableau m
de commandes
control point n (poste m de) contrôle m
control room n (Naut Mil) salle f des
commandes; (Radio, TV) régie f
control tower n (Aviat) tour f de contrôle
control unit n (Comput) unité f de contrôle
controversial [kɔntrə'və:ʃl] adj discutable,
controversé(e)
controversy ['kɔntrəvə:sɪ] n controverse f,
polémique f
conurbation [kɔnə'beɪʃən] n conurbation f
convalesce [kɔnvə'lɛs] vi relever de maladie, se
remettre (d'une maladie)
convalescence [kɔnvə'lɛsns] n convalescence f
convalescent [kɔnvə'lɛsnt] adj, n
convalescent(e)
convector [kən'vɛktər] n radiateur m à
convection, appareil m de chauffage par
convection
convene [kən'vi:n] vt convoquer, assembler ▷ vi
se réunir, s'assembler
convener [kən'vi:nər] n organisateur m
convenience [kən'vi:nɪəns] n commodité f; **at
your ~** quand or comme cela vous convient; **at
your earliest ~** (Comm) dans les meilleurs
délais, le plus tôt possible; **all modern ~s, all
mod cons** (Brit) avec tout le confort moderne,
tout confort
convenience foods npl plats cuisinés
convenient [kən'vi:nɪənt] adj commode; **if it is
~ to you** si cela vous convient, si cela ne vous
dérange pas
conveniently [kən'vi:nɪəntlɪ] adv (happen) à pic;
(situated) commodément

convent ['kɔnvənt] n couvent m
convention [kən'vɛnʃən] n convention f;
(custom) usage m
conventional [kən'vɛnʃənl] adj
conventionnel(le)
convent school n couvent m
converge [kən'və:dʒ] vi converger
conversant [kən'və:snt] adj: **to be ~ with** s'y
connaître en; être au courant de
conversation [kɔnvə'seɪʃən] n conversation f
conversational [kɔnvə'seɪʃənl] adj de la
conversation; (Comput) conversationnel(le)
conversationalist [kɔnvə'seɪʃnəlɪst] n
brillant(e) causeur(-euse)
converse ['kɔnvə:s] n contraire m, inverse m ▷ vi
[kən'və:s]: **to ~ (with sb about sth)**
s'entretenir (avec qn de qch)
conversely [kɔn'və:slɪ] adv inversement,
réciproquement
conversion [kən'və:ʃən] n conversion f; (Brit: of
house) transformation f, aménagement m;
(Rugby) transformation f
conversion table n table f de conversion
convert vt [kən'və:t] (Rel, Comm) convertir; (alter)
transformer; (house) aménager; (Rugby)
transformer ▷ n ['kɔnvə:t] converti(e)
convertible [kən'və:təbl] adj convertible ▷ n
(voiture f) décapotable f
convex ['kɔn'vɛks] adj convexe
convey [kən'veɪ] vt transporter; (thanks)
transmettre; (idea) communiquer
conveyance [kən'veɪəns] n (of goods) transport
m de marchandises; (vehicle) moyen m de
transport
conveyancing [kən'veɪənsɪŋ] n (Law)
rédaction f des actes de cession de propriété
conveyor belt [kən'veɪər-] n convoyeur m tapis
roulant
convict vt [kən'vɪkt] déclarer (or reconnaître)
coupable ▷ n ['kɔnvɪkt] forçat m, convict m
conviction [kən'vɪkʃən] n (Law) condamnation
f; (belief) conviction f
convince [kən'vɪns] vt convaincre, persuader;
to ~ sb (of sth/that) persuader qn (de qch/que)
convinced [kən'vɪnst] adj: **~ of/that**
convaincu(e) de/que
convincing [kən'vɪnsɪŋ] adj persuasif(-ive),
convaincant(e)
convincingly [kən'vɪnsɪŋlɪ] adv de façon
convaincante
convivial [kən'vɪvɪəl] adj joyeux(-euse), plein(e)
d'entrain
convoluted ['kɔnvəlu:tɪd] adj (shape)
tarabiscoté(e); (argument) compliqué(e)
convoy ['kɔnvɔɪ] n convoi m
convulse [kən'vʌls] vt ébranler; **to be ~d with
laughter** se tordre de rire
convulsion [kən'vʌlʃən] n convulsion f
coo [ku:] vi roucouler
cook [kuk] vt (faire) cuire ▷ vi cuire; (person)
faire la cuisine ▷ n cuisinier(-ière)
▶ **cook up** vt (inf: excuse, story) inventer

cookbook ['kukbuk] n livre m de cuisine
cooker ['kukə^r] n cuisinière f
cookery ['kukərı] n cuisine f
cookery book n (Brit) = **cookbook**
cookie ['kukı] n (US) biscuit m, petit gâteau sec
cooking ['kukıŋ] n cuisine f ▷ cpd (apples, chocolate) à cuire; (utensils, salt) de cuisine
cookout ['kukaut] n (US) barbecue m
cool [ku:l] adj frais (fraîche); (not afraid) calme; (unfriendly) froid(e); (impertinent) effronté(e); (inf: trendy) cool inv (inf); (: great) super inv (inf) ▷ vt, vi rafraîchir, refroidir; **it's ~** (weather) il fait frais; **to keep sth ~** or **in a ~ place** garder or conserver qch au frais
▶ **cool down** vi refroidir; (fig: person, situation) se calmer
▶ **cool off** vi (become calmer) se calmer; (lose enthusiasm) perdre son enthousiasme
coolant ['ku:lənt] n liquide m de refroidissement
cool box, (US) **cooler** ['ku:lə^r] n boîte f isotherme
cooling ['ku:lıŋ] adj (breeze) rafraîchissant(e)
cooling tower n refroidisseur m
coolly ['ku:lı] adv (calmly) calmement; (audaciously) sans se gêner; (unenthusiastically) froidement
coolness ['ku:lnıs] n fraîcheur f; sang-froid m, calme m; froideur f
coop [ku:p] n poulailler m ▷ vt: **to ~ up** (fig) cloîtrer, enfermer
co-op ['kəuɔp] n abbr (= cooperative (society)) coop f
cooperate [kəu'ɔpəreıt] vi coopérer, collaborer
cooperation [kəuɔpə'reıʃən] n coopération f, collaboration f
cooperative [kəu'ɔpərətıv] adj coopératif(-ive) ▷ n coopérative f
coopt [kəu'ɔpt] vt: **to ~ sb onto a committee** coopter qn pour faire partie d'un comité
coordinate vt [kəu'ɔ:dıneıt] coordonner ▷ n [kəu'ɔdınət] (Math) coordonnée f; **coordinates** npl (clothes) ensemble m, coordonnés mpl
coordination [kəuɔ:dı'neıʃən] n coordination f
coot [ku:t] n foulque f
co-ownership ['kəu'əunəʃıp] n copropriété f
cop [kɔp] n (inf) flic m
cope [kəup] vi s'en sortir, tenir le coup; **to ~ with** (problem) faire face à; (take care of) s'occuper de
Copenhagen ['kəupn'heıgən] n Copenhague
copier ['kɔpıə^r] n (also: **photocopier**) copieur m
co-pilot ['kəu'paılət] n copilote m
copious ['kəupıəs] adj copieux(-euse), abondant(e)
copper ['kɔpə^r] n cuivre m; (Brit: inf: policeman) flic m; **coppers** npl petite monnaie
coppice ['kɔpıs], **copse** [kɔps] n taillis m
copulate ['kɔpjuleıt] vi copuler
copy ['kɔpı] n copie f; (book etc) exemplaire m; (material: for printing) copie ▷ vt copier; (imitate) imiter; **rough ~** (gen) premier jet; (Scol) brouillon m; **fair ~** version définitive; propre m;

to make good ~ (Press) faire un bon sujet d'article
▶ **copy out** vt copier
copycat ['kɔpıkæt] n (pej) copieur(-euse)
copyright ['kɔpıraıt] n droit m d'auteur, copyright m; **~ reserved** tous droits (de reproduction) réservés
copy typist n dactylo m/f
copywriter ['kɔpıraıtə^r] n rédacteur(-trice) publicitaire
coral ['kɔrəl] n corail m
coral reef n récif m de corail
Coral Sea n: **the ~** la mer de Corail
cord [kɔ:d] n corde f; (fabric) velours côtelé; whipcord m; corde f; (Elec) cordon m (d'alimentation), fil m (électrique); **cords** npl (trousers) pantalon m de velours côtelé
cordial ['kɔ:dıəl] adj cordial(e), chaleureux(-euse) ▷ n sirop m; cordial m
cordless ['kɔ:dlıs] adj sans fil
cordon ['kɔ:dn] n cordon m
▶ **cordon off** vt (area) interdire l'accès à; (crowd) tenir à l'écart
corduroy ['kɔ:dərɔı] n velours côtelé
CORE [kɔ:^r] n abbr (US) = **Congress of Racial Equality**
core [kɔ:^r] n (of fruit) trognon m, cœur m; (Tech: also of earth) noyau m; cœur ▷ vt enlever le trognon or le cœur de; **rotten to the ~** complètement pourri
Corfu [kɔ:'fu:] n Corfou
coriander [kɔrı'ændə^r] n coriandre f
cork [kɔ:k] n (material) liège m; (of bottle) bouchon m
corkage ['kɔ:kıdʒ] n droit payé par le client qui apporte sa propre bouteille de vin
corked [kɔ:kt], (US) **corky** ['kɔ:kı] adj (wine) qui sent le bouchon
corkscrew ['kɔ:kskru:] n tire-bouchon m
cormorant ['kɔ:mərnt] n cormoran m
corn [kɔ:n] n (Brit: wheat) blé m; (US: maize) maïs m; (on foot) cor m; **~ on the cob** (Culin) épi m de maïs au naturel
cornea ['kɔ:nıə] n cornée f
corned beef ['kɔ:nd-] n corned-beef m
corner ['kɔ:nə^r] n coin m; (in road) tournant m, virage m; (Football: also: **corner kick**) corner m ▷ vt (trap: prey) acculer; (fig) coincer; (Comm: market) accaparer ▷ vi prendre un virage; **to cut ~s** (fig) prendre des raccourcis
corner flag n (Football) piquet m de coin
corner kick n (Football) corner m
corner shop (Brit) n magasin m du coin
cornerstone ['kɔ:nəstəun] n pierre f angulaire
cornet ['kɔ:nıt] n (Mus) cornet m à pistons; (Brit: of ice-cream) cornet (de glace)
cornflakes ['kɔ:nfleıks] npl cornflakes mpl
cornflour ['kɔ:nflauə^r] n (Brit) farine f de maïs, maïzena® f
cornice ['kɔ:nıs] n corniche f
Cornish ['kɔ:nıʃ] adj de Cornouailles, cornouaillais(e)

corn oil n huile f de maïs

cornstarch ['kɔːnstɑːtʃ] n (US) farine f de maïs, maïzena® f

cornucopia [kɔːnjuˈkəupɪə] n corne f d'abondance

Cornwall ['kɔːnwəl] n Cornouailles f

corny ['kɔːnɪ] adj (inf) rebattu(e), galvaudé(e)

corollary [kəˈrɔlərɪ] n corollaire m

coronary ['kɔrənərɪ] n: ~ **(thrombosis)** infarctus m (du myocarde), thrombose f coronaire

coronation [kɔrəˈneɪʃən] n couronnement m

coroner ['kɔrənəʳ] n coroner m, officier de police judiciaire chargé de déterminer les causes d'un décès

coronet ['kɔrənɪt] n couronne f

Corp. abbr = **corporation**

corporal ['kɔːpərl] n caporal m, brigadier m
▷ adj: ~ **punishment** châtiment corporel

corporate ['kɔːpərɪt] adj (action, ownership) en commun; (Comm) de la société

corporate hospitality n arrangement selon lequel une société offre des places de théâtre, concert etc à ses clients

corporate identity, corporate image n (of organization) image f de la société

corporation [kɔːpəˈreɪʃən] n (of town) municipalité f, conseil municipal; (Comm) société f

corporation tax n ≈ impôt m sur les bénéfices

corps [kɔːʳ] (pl - [kɔːz]) n corps m; **the diplomatic ~** le corps diplomatique; **the press ~** la presse

corpse [kɔːps] n cadavre m

corpuscle ['kɔːpʌsl] n corpuscule m

corral [kəˈrɑːl] n corral m

correct [kəˈrɛkt] adj (accurate) correct(e), exact(e); (proper) correct, convenable ▷ vt corriger; **you are ~** vous avez raison

correction [kəˈrɛkʃən] n correction f

correlate ['kɔrɪleɪt] vt mettre en corrélation ▷ vi: **to ~ with** correspondre à

correlation [kɔrɪˈleɪʃən] n corrélation f

correspond [kɔrɪsˈpɔnd] vi correspondre; **to ~ to** sth (be equivalent to) correspondre à qch

correspondence [kɔrɪsˈpɔndəns] n correspondance f

correspondence course n cours m par correspondance

correspondent [kɔrɪsˈpɔndənt] n correspondant(e)

corresponding [kɔrɪsˈpɔndɪŋ] adj correspondant(e)

corridor ['kɔrɪdɔːʳ] n couloir m, corridor m

corroborate [kəˈrɔbəreɪt] vt corroborer, confirmer

corrode [kəˈrəud] vt corroder, ronger ▷ vi se corroder

corrosion [kəˈrəuʒən] n corrosion f

corrosive [kəˈrəuzɪv] adj corrosif(-ive)

corrugated ['kɔrəgeɪtɪd] adj plissé(e); ondulé(e)

corrugated iron n tôle ondulée

corrupt [kəˈrʌpt] adj corrompu(e); (Comput)

altéré(e) ▷ vt corrompre; (Comput) altérer; ~ **practices** (dishonesty, bribery) malversation f

corruption [kəˈrʌpʃən] n corruption f; (Comput) altération f (de données)

corset ['kɔːsɪt] n corset m

Corsica ['kɔːsɪkə] n Corse f

Corsican ['kɔːsɪkən] adj corse ▷ n Corse m/f

cortège [kɔːˈteɪʒ] n cortège m (gén funèbre)

cortisone ['kɔːtɪzəun] n cortisone f

coruscating ['kɔrəskeɪtɪŋ] adj scintillant(e)

cosh [kɔʃ] n (Brit) matraque f

cosignatory ['kəuˈsɪgnətərɪ] n cosignataire m/f

cosiness ['kəuzɪnɪs] n atmosphère douillette, confort m

cos lettuce ['kɔs-] n (laitue f) romaine f

cosmetic [kɔzˈmɛtɪk] n produit m de beauté, cosmétique m ▷ adj (preparation) cosmétique; (fig: reforms) symbolique, superficiel(le)

cosmetic surgery n chirurgie f esthétique

cosmic ['kɔzmɪk] adj cosmique

cosmonaut ['kɔzmənɔːt] n cosmonaute m/f

cosmopolitan [kɔzməˈpɔlɪtn] adj cosmopolite

cosmos ['kɔzmɔs] n cosmos m

cosset ['kɔsɪt] vt choyer, dorloter

cost [kɔst] (pt, pp -) n coût m ▷ vi coûter ▷ vt établir or calculer le prix de revient de; **costs** npl (Comm) frais mpl; (Law) dépens mpl; **how much does it ~?** combien ça coûte?; **it ~s £5/too much** cela coûte 5 livres/trop cher; **what will it ~ to have it repaired?** combien cela coûtera de le faire réparer?; **to ~ sb time/effort** demander du temps/un effort à qn; **it ~ him his life/job** ça lui a coûté la vie/son emploi; **at all ~s** coûte que coûte, à tout prix

cost accountant n analyste m/f de coûts

co-star ['kəustɑːʳ] n partenaire m/f

Costa Rica ['kɔstəˈriːkə] n Costa Rica m

cost centre n centre m de coût

cost control n contrôle m des coûts

cost-effective ['kɔstɪˈfɛktɪv] adj rentable

cost-effectiveness ['kɔstɪˈfɛktɪvnɪs] n rentabilité f

costing ['kɔstɪŋ] n calcul m du prix de revient

costly ['kɔstlɪ] adj coûteux(-euse)

cost of living ['kɔstəvˈlɪvɪŋ] n coût m de la vie ▷ adj: ~ **allowance** indemnité f de vie chère; ~ **index** indice m du coût de la vie

cost price n (Brit) prix coûtant or de revient

costume ['kɔstjuːm] n costume m; (lady's suit) tailleur m; (Brit: also: **swimming costume**) maillot m (de bain)

costume jewellery n bijoux mpl de fantaisie

cosy, (US) **cozy** ['kəuzɪ] adj (room, bed) douillet(te); (scarf, gloves) bien chaud(e); (atmosphere) chaleureux(-euse); **to be ~** (person) être bien (au chaud)

cot [kɔt] n (Brit: child's) lit m d'enfant, petit lit; (US: campbed) lit de camp

cot death n mort subite du nourrisson

Cotswolds ['kɔtswəuldz] npl: **the ~** région de collines du Gloucestershire

cottage ['kɔtɪdʒ] n petite maison (à la

campagne), cottage *m*
cottage cheese *n* fromage blanc (*maigre*)
cottage industry *n* industrie familiale *or* artisanale
cottage pie *n* ≈ hachis *m* Parmentier
cotton ['kɔtn] *n* coton *m*; (*thread*) fil *m* (de coton); ~ **dress** *etc* robe *etc* en *or* de coton
▸ **cotton on** *vi* (*inf*): **to ~ on (to sth)** piger (qch)
cotton bud (*Brit*) *n* coton-tige ® *m*
cotton candy (*US*) *n* barbe *f* à papa
cotton wool *n* (*Brit*) ouate *f*, coton *m* hydrophile
couch [kautʃ] *n* canapé *m*; divan *m*; (*doctor's*) table *f* d'examen; (*psychiatrist's*) divan ▷ *vt* formuler, exprimer
couchette [ku:'ʃɛt] *n* couchette *f*
couch potato *n* (*inf*) mollasson(ne) (*qui passe son temps devant la télé*)
cough [kɔf] *vi* tousser ▷ *n* toux *f*; **I've got a ~** j'ai la toux
cough drop *n* pastille *f* pour *or* contre la toux
cough mixture, cough syrup *n* sirop *m* pour la toux
cough sweet *n* pastille *f* pour *or* contre la toux
could [kud] *pt of* **can²**
couldn't ['kudnt] = **could not**
council ['kaunsl] *n* conseil *m*; **city** *or* **town ~** conseil municipal; **C~ of Europe** Conseil de l'Europe
council estate *n* (*Brit*) (quartier *m or* zone *f* de) logements loués à/par la municipalité
council house *n* (*Brit*) maison *f* (à loyer modéré) louée par la municipalité
councillor, (*US*) **councilor** ['kaunslə^r] *n* conseiller(-ère)
council tax *n* (*Brit*) impôts locaux
counsel ['kaunsl] *n* conseil *m*; (*lawyer*) avocat(e) ▷ *vt*: **to ~ (sb to do sth)** conseiller (à qn de faire qch); ~ **for the defence/the prosecution** (avocat de la) défense/ avocat du ministère public
counselling, (*US*) **counseling** ['kaunslɪŋ] *n* (*Psych*) aide psychosociale
counsellor, (*US*) **counselor** ['kaunslə^r] *n* conseiller(-ère); (*US Law*) avocat *m*
count [kaunt] *vt, vi* compter ▷ *n* compte *m*; (*nobleman*) comte *m*; **to ~ (up) to 10** compter jusqu'à 10; **to keep ~ of sth** tenir le compte de qch; **not ~ing the children** sans compter les enfants; **10 ~ing him** 10 avec lui, 10 en le comptant; **to ~ the cost of** établir le coût de; **it ~s for very little** cela n'a pas beaucoup d'importance; ~ **yourself lucky** estimez-vous heureux
▸ **count in** *vt* (*inf*): **to ~ sb in on sth** inclure qn dans qch
▸ **count on** *vt fus* compter sur; **to ~ on doing sth** compter faire qch
▸ **count up** *vt* compter, additionner
countdown ['kauntdaun] *n* compte *m* à rebours
countenance ['kauntɪnəns] *n* expression *f* ▷ *vt* approuver
counter ['kauntə^r] *n* comptoir *m*; (*in post office,*

bank) guichet *m*; (*in game*) jeton *m* ▷ *vt* aller à l'encontre de, opposer; (*blow*) parer ▷ *adv*: ~ **to** à l'encontre de; contrairement à; **to buy under the ~** (*fig*) acheter sous le manteau *or* en sousmain; **to ~ sth with sth/by doing sth** contrer *or* riposter à qch par qch/en faisant qch
counteract ['kauntər'ækt] *vt* neutraliser, contrebalancer
counterattack ['kauntərə'tæk] *n* contreattaque *f* ▷ *vi* contre-attaquer
counterbalance ['kauntə'bæləns] *vt* contrebalancer, faire contrepoids à
counterclockwise ['kauntə'klɔkwaɪz] (*US*) *adv* en sens inverse des aiguilles d'une montre
counter-espionage ['kauntər'ɛspɪənɑ:ʒ] *n* contre-espionnage *m*
counterfeit ['kauntəfɪt] *n* faux *m*, contrefaçon *f* ▷ *vt* contrefaire ▷ *adj* faux (fausse)
counterfoil ['kauntəfɔɪl] *n* talon *m*, souche *f*
counterintelligence ['kauntərɪn'tɛlɪdʒəns] *n* contre-espionnage *m*
countermand ['kauntəmɑ:nd] *vt* annuler
countermeasure ['kauntəmɛʒə^r] *n* contremesure *f*
counteroffensive ['kauntərə'fɛnsɪv] *n* contreoffensive *f*
counterpane ['kauntəpeɪn] *n* dessus-de-lit *m*
counterpart ['kauntəpɑ:t] *n* (*of document etc*) double *m*; (*of person*) homologue *m/f*
counterproductive ['kauntəprə'dʌktɪv] *adj* contre-productif(-ive)
counterproposal ['kauntəprə'pəuzl] *n* contreproposition *f*
countersign ['kauntəsaɪn] *vt* contresigner
countersink ['kauntəsɪŋk] *vt* (*hole*) fraiser
countess ['kauntɪs] *n* comtesse *f*
countless ['kauntlɪs] *adj* innombrable
countrified ['kʌntrɪfaɪd] *adj* rustique, à l'air campagnard
country ['kʌntrɪ] *n* pays *m*; (*native land*) patrie *f*; (*as opposed to town*) campagne *f*; (*region*) région *f*, pays; **in the ~** à la campagne; **mountainous ~** pays de montagne, région montagneuse
country and western, country and western music *n* musique *f* country
country dancing *n* (*Brit*) danse *f* folklorique
country house *n* manoir *m*, (petit) château
countryman ['kʌntrɪmən] (*irreg*) *n* (*national*) compatriote *m*; (*rural*) habitant *m* de la campagne, campagnard *m*
countryside ['kʌntrɪsaɪd] *n* campagne *f*
countrywide ['kʌntrɪ'waɪd] *adj* s'étendant à l'ensemble du pays; (*problem*) à l'échelle nationale ▷ *adv* à travers *or* dans tout le pays
county ['kauntɪ] *n* comté *m*
county council *n* (*Brit*) ≈ conseil régional
county town *n* (*Brit*) chef-lieu *m*
coup [ku:] (*pl* -**s**) [ku:z] *n* (*achievement*) beau coup; (*also:* **coup d'état**) coup d'État
coupé [ku:'peɪ] *n* (*Aut*) coupé *m*
couple ['kʌpl] *n* couple *m* ▷ *vt* (*carriages*) atteler; (*Tech*) coupler; (*ideas, names*) associer; **a ~ of** (*two*)

deux; (*a few*) deux ou trois

couplet ['kʌplɪt] *n* distique *m*

coupling ['kʌplɪŋ] *n* (*Rail*) attelage *m*

coupon ['ku:pɔn] *n* (*voucher*) bon *m* de réduction; (*detachable form*) coupon *m* détachable, coupon-réponse *m*; (*Finance*) coupon

courage ['kʌrɪdʒ] *n* courage *m*

courageous [kə'reɪdʒəs] *adj* courageux(-euse)

courgette [kuə'ʒɛt] *n* (*Brit*) courgette *f*

courier ['kurɪər] *n* messager *m*, courrier *m*; (*for tourists*) accompagnateur(-trice)

course [kɔːs] *n* cours *m*; (*of ship*) route *f*; (*for golf*) terrain *m*; (*part of meal*) plat *m*; **first ~** entrée *f*; **of ~** (*adv*) bien sûr; **(no,) of ~ not!** bien sûr que non!, évidemment que non!; **in the ~ of** au cours de; **in the ~ of the next few days** au cours des prochains jours; **in due ~** en temps utile *or* voulu; **~ (of action)** parti *m*, ligne *f* de conduite; **the best ~ would be to ...** le mieux serait de ...; **we have no other ~ but to ...** nous n'avons pas d'autre solution que de ...; **~ of lectures** série *f* de conférences; **~ of treatment** (*Med*) traitement *m*

court [kɔːt] *n* cour *f*; (*Law*) cour, tribunal *m*; (*Tennis*) court *m* ▷ *vt* (*woman*) courtiser, faire la cour à; (*fig: favour, popularity*) rechercher; (: *death, disaster*) courir après, flirter avec; **out of ~** (*Law: settle*) à l'amiable; **to take to ~** actionner *or* poursuivre en justice; **~ of appeal** cour d'appel

courteous ['kəːtɪəs] *adj* courtois(e), poli(e)

courtesan [kɔːtɪ'zæn] *n* courtisane *f*

courtesy ['kəːtəsɪ] *n* courtoisie *f*, politesse *f*; **(by) ~ of** avec l'aimable autorisation de

courtesy bus, courtesy coach *n* navette gratuite

courtesy light *n* (*Aut*) plafonnier *m*

court-house ['kɔːthaus] *n* (*US*) palais *m* de justice

courtier ['kɔːtɪər] *n* courtisan *m*, dame *f* de cour

court martial (*pl* **courts martial**) *n* cour martiale, conseil *m* de guerre

courtroom ['kɔːtrum] *n* salle *f* de tribunal

court shoe *n* escarpin *m*

courtyard ['kɔːtjɑːd] *n* cour *f*

cousin ['kʌzn] *n* cousin(e); **first ~** cousin(e) germain(e)

cove [kəuv] *n* petite baie, anse *f*

covenant ['kʌvənənt] *n* contrat *m*, engagement *m* ▷ *vt*: **to ~ £200 per year to a charity** s'engager à verser 200 livres par an à une œuvre de bienfaisance

Coventry ['kɔvəntrɪ] *n*: **to send sb to ~** (*fig*) mettre qn en quarantaine

cover ['kʌvər] *vt* couvrir; (*Press: report on*) faire un reportage sur; (*feelings, mistake*) cacher; (*include*) englober; (*discuss*) traiter ▷ *n* (*of book, Comm*) couverture *f*; (*of pan*) couvercle *m*; (*over furniture*) housse *f*; (*shelter*) abri *m*; **covers** *npl* (*on bed*) couvertures; **to take ~** se mettre à l'abri; **under ~** à l'abri; **under ~ of darkness** à la faveur de la nuit; **under separate ~** (*Comm*) sous pli séparé; **£10 will ~ everything** 10 livres suffiront (pour

tout payer)

▶ **cover up** *vt* (*person, object*): **to ~ up (with)** couvrir (de); (*fig: truth, facts*) occulter ▷ *vi*: **to ~ up for sb** (*fig*) couvrir qn

coverage ['kʌvərɪdʒ] *n* (*in media*) reportage *m*; (*Insurance*) couverture *f*

cover charge *n* couvert *m* (*supplément à payer*)

covering ['kʌvərɪŋ] *n* couverture *f*, enveloppe *f*

covering letter, (*US*) **cover letter** *n* lettre explicative

cover note *n* (*Insurance*) police *f* provisoire

cover price *n* prix *m* de l'exemplaire

covert ['kʌvət] *adj* (*threat*) voilé(e), caché(e); (*attack*) indirect(e); (*glance*) furtif(-ive)

cover-up ['kʌvərʌp] *n* tentative *f* pour étouffer une affaire

covet ['kʌvɪt] *vt* convoiter

cow [kau] *n* vache *f* ▷ *cpd* femelle ▷ *vt* effrayer, intimider

coward ['kauəd] *n* lâche *m/f*

cowardice ['kauədɪs] *n* lâcheté *f*

cowardly ['kauədlɪ] *adj* lâche

cowboy ['kaubɔɪ] *n* cow-boy *m*

cower ['kauər] *vi* se recroqueviller; trembler

cowshed ['kauʃɛd] *n* étable *f*

cowslip ['kauslɪp] *n* (*Bot*) (fleur *f* de) coucou *m*

coy [kɔɪ] *adj* faussement effarouché(e) *or* timide

coyote [kɔɪ'əutɪ] *n* coyote *m*

cozy ['kəuzɪ] *adj* (*US*) = **cosy**

CP *n abbr* (= *Communist Party*) PC *m*

cp. *abbr* (= *compare*) cf

CPA *n abbr* (*US*) = **certified public accountant**

CPI *n abbr* (= *Consumer Price Index*) IPC *m*

Cpl. *abbr* (= *corporal*) C/C

CP/M *n abbr* (= *Central Program for Microprocessors*) CP/M *m*

c.p.s. *abbr* (= *characters per second*) caractères/seconde

CPSA *n abbr* (*Brit*: = *Civil and Public Services Association*) *syndicat de la fonction publique*

CPU *n abbr* = **central processing unit**

cr. *abbr* = **credit**; **creditor**

crab [kræb] *n* crabe *m*

crab apple *n* pomme *f* sauvage

crack [kræk] *n* (*split*) fente *f*, fissure *f*; (*in cup, bone*) fêlure *f*; (*in wall*) lézarde *f*; (*noise*) craquement *m*, coup (sec); (*joke*) plaisanterie *f*; (*inf: attempt*): **to have a ~ (at sth)** essayer (qch); (*Drugs*) crack *m* ▷ *vt* fendre, fissurer; fêler; lézarder; (*whip*) faire claquer; (*nut*) casser; (*problem*) résoudre, trouver la clef de; (*code*) déchiffrer ▷ *cpd* (*athlete*) de première classe, d'élite; **to ~ jokes** (*inf*) raconter des blagues; **to get ~ing** (*inf*) s'y mettre, se magner

▶ **crack down on** *vt fus* (*crime*) sévir contre, réprimer; (*spending*) mettre un frein à

▶ **crack up** *vi* être au bout de son rouleau, flancher

crackdown ['krækdaun] *n*: **~ (on)** (*on crime*) répression *f* (de); (*on spending*) restrictions *fpl* (de)

cracked [krækt] *adj* (*cup, bone*) fêlé(e); (*broken*) cassé(e); (*wall*) lézardé(e); (*surface*) craquelé(e);

(*inf*) toqué(e), timbré(e)

cracker ['krækə'] *n* (*also*: **Christmas cracker**) pétard *m*; (*biscuit*) biscuit (salé), craquelin *m*; **a ~ of a ...** (*Brit inf*) un(e) ... formidable; **he's ~s** (*Brit inf*) il est cinglé

crackle ['krækl] *vi* crépiter, grésiller

crackling ['kræklɪŋ] *n* crépitement *m*, grésillement *m*; (*on radio, telephone*) grésillement, friture *f*; (*of pork*) couenne *f*

crackpot ['krækpɔt] *n* (*inf*) tordu(e)

cradle ['kreɪdl] *n* berceau *m* ▷ *vt* (*child*) bercer; (*object*) tenir dans ses bras

craft [krɑːft] *n* métier (artisanal); (*cunning*) ruse *f*, astuce *f*; (*boat: pl inv*) embarcation *f*, barque *f*; (*plane: pl inv*) appareil *m*

craftsman (*irreg*) ['krɑːftsmən] (*irreg*) *n* artisan *m* ouvrier (qualifié)

craftsmanship ['krɑːftsmənʃɪp] *n* métier *m*, habileté *f*

crafty ['krɑːftɪ] *adj* rusé(e), malin(-igne), astucieux(-euse)

crag [kræg] *n* rocher escarpé

cram [kræm] *vt* (*fill*): **to ~ sth with** bourrer qch de; (*put*): **to ~ sth into** fourrer qch dans ▷ *vi* (*for exams*) bachoter

cramming ['kræmɪŋ] *n* (*for exams*) bachotage *m*

cramp [kræmp] *n* crampe *f* ▷ *vt* gêner, entraver; **I've got ~ in my leg** j'ai une crampe à la jambe

cramped [kræmpt] *adj* à l'étroit, très serré(e)

crampon ['kræmpən] *n* crampon *m*

cranberry ['krænbərɪ] *n* canneberge *f*

crane [kreɪn] *n* grue *f* ▷ *vt, vi*: **to ~ forward, to ~ one's neck** allonger le cou

cranium (*pl* **crania**) ['kreɪnɪəm, 'kreɪnɪə] *n* boîte crânienne

crank [kræŋk] *n* manivelle *f*; (*person*) excentrique *m/f*

crankshaft ['kræŋkʃɑːft] *n* vilebrequin *m*

cranky ['kræŋkɪ] *adj* excentrique, loufoque; (*bad-tempered*) grincheux(-euse), revêche

cranny ['krænɪ] *n see* **nook**

crap [kræp] *n* (*inf!: nonsense*) conneries *fpl* (!); (: *excrement*) merde *f* (!); **the party was ~** la fête était merdique (!); **to have a ~** chier (!)

crappy ['kræpɪ] *adj* (*inf*) merdique (!)

crash [kræʃ] *n* (*noise*) fracas *m*; (*of car, plane*) collision *f*; (*of business*) faillite *f*; (*Stock Exchange*) krach *m* ▷ *vt* (*plane*) écraser ▷ *vi* (*plane*) s'écraser; (*two cars*) se percuter, s'emboutir; (*business*) s'effondrer; **to ~ into** se jeter *or* se fracasser contre; **he ~ed the car into a wall** il s'est écrasé contre un mur avec sa voiture

crash barrier *n* (*Brit Aut*) rail *m* de sécurité

crash course *n* cours intensif

crash helmet *n* casque (protecteur)

crash landing *n* atterrissage forcé *or* en catastrophe

crass [kræs] *adj* grossier(-ière), crasse

crate [kreɪt] *n* cageot *m*; (*for bottles*) caisse *f*

crater ['kreɪtə'] *n* cratère *m*

cravat [krə'væt] *n* foulard (*noué autour du cou*)

crave [kreɪv] *vt, vi*: **to ~ (for)** désirer

violemment, avoir un besoin physiologique de, avoir une envie irrésistible de

craving ['kreɪvɪŋ] *n*: **~ (for)** (*for food, cigarettes etc*) envie *f* irrésistible (de)

crawl [krɔːl] *vi* ramper; (*vehicle*) avancer au pas ▷ *n* (*Swimming*) crawl *m*; **to ~ on one's hands and knees** aller à quatre pattes; **to ~ to sb** (*inf*) faire de la lèche à qn

crawler lane ['krɔːlə-] *n* (*Brit Aut*) file *f or* voie *f* pour véhicules lents

crayfish ['kreɪfɪʃ] *n* (*pl inv: freshwater*) écrevisse *f*; (*saltwater*) langoustine *f*

crayon ['kreɪən] *n* crayon *m* (de couleur)

craze [kreɪz] *n* engouement *m*

crazed [kreɪzd] *adj* (*look, person*) affolé(e); (*pottery, glaze*) craquelé(e)

crazy ['kreɪzɪ] *adj* fou (folle); **to go ~** devenir fou; **to be ~ about sb/sth** (*inf*) être fou de qn/qch

crazy paving *n* (*Brit*) dallage irrégulier (en pierres plates)

creak [kriːk] *vi* (*hinge*) grincer; (*floor, shoes*) craquer

cream [kriːm] *n* crème *f* ▷ *adj* (*colour*) crème *inv*; **whipped ~** crème fouettée

▶ **cream off** *vt* (*fig*) prélever

cream cake *n* (petit) gâteau à la crème

cream cheese *n* fromage *m* à la crème, fromage blanc

creamery ['kriːmərɪ] *n* (*shop*) crémerie *f*; (*factory*) laiterie *f*

creamy ['kriːmɪ] *adj* crémeux(-euse)

crease [kriːs] *n* pli *m* ▷ *vt* froisser, chiffonner ▷ *vi* se froisser, se chiffonner

crease-resistant ['kriːsrɪzɪstənt] *adj* infroissable

create [kriːˈeɪt] *vt* créer; (*impression, fuss*) faire

creation [kriːˈeɪʃən] *n* création *f*

creative [kriːˈeɪtɪv] *adj* créatif(-ive)

creativity [kriːeɪˈtɪvɪtɪ] *n* créativité *f*

creator [kriːˈeɪtə'] *n* créateur(-trice)

creature ['kriːtʃə'] *n* créature *f*

creature comforts *npl* petit confort

crèche [krɛʃ] *n* garderie *f*, crèche *f*

credence ['kriːdns] *n* croyance *f*, foi *f*

credentials [krɪˈdɛnʃlz] *npl* (*references*) références *fpl*; (*identity papers*) pièce *f* d'identité; (*letters of reference*) pièces justificatives

credibility [krɛdɪˈbɪlɪtɪ] *n* crédibilité *f*

credible ['krɛdɪbl] *adj* digne de foi, crédible

credit ['krɛdɪt] *n* crédit *m*; (*recognition*) honneur *m*; (*Scol*) unité *f* de valeur ▷ *vt* (*Comm*) créditer; (*believe: also*: **give credit to**) ajouter foi à, croire; **credits** *npl* (*Cine*) générique *m*; **to be in ~** (*person, bank account*) être créditeur(-trice); **on ~** à crédit; **to one's ~** à son honneur; à son actif; **to take the ~ for** s'attribuer le mérite de; **it does him ~** cela lui fait honneur; **to ~ sb with** (*fig*) prêter *or* attribuer à qn; **to ~ £5 to sb** créditer (le compte de) qn de 5 livres

creditable ['krɛdɪtəbl] *adj* honorable, estimable

credit account *n* compte *m* client

credit agency *n* (*Brit*) agence *f* de

renseignements commerciaux
credit balance n solde créditeur
credit bureau n (US) agence f de
renseignements commerciaux
credit card n carte f de crédit; **do you take ~s?**
acceptez-vous les cartes de crédit?
credit control n suivi m des factures
credit facilities npl facilités fpl de paiement
credit limit n limite f de crédit
credit note n (Brit) avoir m
creditor ['krɛdɪtəʳ] n créancier(-ière)
credit transfer n virement m
creditworthy ['krɛdɪtwə:ðɪ] adj solvable
credulity [krɪ'dju:lɪtɪ] n crédulité f
creed [kri:d] n croyance f; credo m, principes mpl
creek [kri:k] n (inlet) crique f, anse f; (US: stream)
ruisseau m, petit cours d'eau
creel ['kri:l] n panier m de pêche; (also: **lobster
creel**) panier à homards
creep (pt, pp crept) [kri:p, krɛpt] vi ramper;
(silently) se faufiler, se glisser; (plant) grimper
▷ n (inf: flatterer) lèche-botte m; **he's a ~** c'est un
type puant; **it gives me the ~s** cela me fait
froid dans le dos; **to ~ up on sb** s'approcher
furtivement de qn
creeper ['kri:pəʳ] n plante grimpante
creepers ['kri:pəz] npl (US: for baby) barboteuse f
creepy ['kri:pɪ] adj (frightening) qui fait
frissonner, qui donne la chair de poule
creepy-crawly ['kri:pɪ'krɔ:lɪ] n (inf) bestiole f
cremate [krɪ'meɪt] vt incinérer
cremation [krɪ'meɪʃən] n incinération f
crematorium (pl crematoria) [krɛmə'tɔ:rɪəm,
-'tɔ:rɪə] n four m crématoire
creosote ['krɪəsəut] n créosote f
crepe [kreɪp] n crêpe m
crepe bandage n (Brit) bande f Velpeau®
crepe paper n papier m crépon
crept [krɛpt] pt, pp of **creep**
crescendo [krɪ'ʃɛndəu] n crescendo m
crescent ['krɛsnt] n croissant m; (street) rue f (en
arc de cercle)
cress [krɛs] n cresson m
crest [krɛst] n crête f; (of helmet) cimier m; (of coat
of arms) timbre m
crestfallen ['krɛstfɔ:lən] adj déconfit(e),
découragé(e)
Crete ['kri:t] n Crète f
crevasse [krɪ'væs] n crevasse f
crevice ['krɛvɪs] n fissure f, lézarde f, fente f
crew [kru:] n équipage m; (Cine) équipe f (de
tournage); (gang) bande f
crew-cut ['kru:kʌt] n: **to have a ~** avoir les
cheveux en brosse
crew-neck ['kru:nɛk] n col ras
crib [krɪb] n lit m d'enfant; (for baby) berceau m
▷ vt (inf) copier
cribbage ['krɪbɪdʒ] n sorte de jeu de cartes
crick [krɪk] n crampe f; **~ in the neck**
torticolis m
cricket ['krɪkɪt] n (insect) grillon m, cri-cri m inv;
(game) cricket m

cricketer ['krɪkɪtəʳ] n joueur m de cricket
crime [kraɪm] n crime m; **minor ~** délit mineur,
infraction mineure
crime wave n poussée f de la criminalité
criminal ['krɪmɪnl] adj, n criminel(le)
crimp [krɪmp] vt friser, frisotter
crimson ['krɪmzn] adj cramoisi(e)
cringe [krɪndʒ] vi avoir un mouvement de recul;
(fig) s'humilier, ramper
crinkle ['krɪŋkl] vt froisser, chiffonner
cripple ['krɪpl] n boiteux(-euse), infirme m/f ▷ vt
(person) estropier, paralyser; (ship, plane)
immobiliser; (production, exports) paralyser; **~d
with rheumatism** perclus(e) de rhumatismes
crippling ['krɪplɪŋ] adj (disease) handicapant(e);
(taxation, debts) écrasant(e)
crisis (pl crises) ['kraɪsɪs, -si:z] n crise f
crisp [krɪsp] adj croquant(e); (weather) vif (vive);
(manner etc) brusque
crisps [krɪsps] (Brit) npl (pommes fpl) chips fpl
crispy ['krɪspɪ] adj croustillant(e)
crisscross ['krɪskrɔs] adj entrecroisé(e), en
croisillons ▷ vt sillonner; **~ pattern** croisillons
mpl
criterion (pl criteria) [kraɪ'tɪərɪən, -'tɪərɪə] n
critère m
critic ['krɪtɪk] n critique m/f
critical ['krɪtɪkl] adj critique; **to be ~ of sb/sth**
critiquer qn/qch
critically ['krɪtɪklɪ] adv (examine) d'un œil
critique; (speak) sévèrement; **~ ill** gravement
malade
criticism ['krɪtɪsɪzəm] n critique f
criticize ['krɪtɪsaɪz] vt critiquer
croak [krəuk] vi (frog) coasser; (raven) croasser
Croat ['krəuæt] adj, n = **Croatian**
Croatia [krəu'eɪʃə] n Croatie f
Croatian [krəu'eɪʃən] adj croate ▷ n Croate m/f;
(Ling) croate m
crochet ['krəuʃeɪ] n travail m au crochet
crock [krɔk] n cruche f; (inf: also: **old crock**)
épave f
crockery ['krɔkərɪ] n vaisselle f
crocodile ['krɔkədaɪl] n crocodile m
crocus ['krəukəs] n crocus m
croft [krɔft] n (Brit) petite ferme
crofter ['krɔftəʳ] n (Brit) fermier m
croissant ['krwasɑ̃] n croissant m
crone [krəun] n vieille bique, (vieille) sorcière f
crony ['krəunɪ] n copain (copine)
crook [kruk] n escroc m; (of shepherd) houlette f
crooked ['krukɪd] adj courbé(e), tordu(e);
(action) malhonnête
crop [krɔp] n (produce) culture f; (amount produced)
récolte f; (riding crop) cravache f; (of bird) jabot m
▷ vt (hair) tondre; (animals: grass) brouter
▶ **crop up** vi surgir, se présenter, survenir
cropper ['krɔpəʳ] n: **to come a ~** (inf) faire la
culbute, s'étaler
crop spraying [-spreɪɪŋ] n pulvérisation f des
cultures
croquet ['krəukeɪ] n croquet m

cross [krɔs] n croix f; (Biol) croisement m ▷ vt (street etc) traverser; (arms, legs, Biol) croiser; (cheque) barrer; (thwart: person, plan) contrarier ▷ vi: **the boat ~es from ... to ...** le bateau fait la traversée de ... à ... ▷ adj en colère, fâché(e); **to ~ o.s.** se signer, faire le signe de (la) croix; **we have a ~ed line** (Brit: on telephone) il y a des interférences; **they've got their lines ~ed** (fig) il y a un malentendu entre eux; **to be/get ~ with sb (about sth)** être en colère/(se) fâcher contre qn (à propos de qch)
  ▶ **cross off** or **out** vt barrer, rayer
  ▶ **cross over** vi traverser
crossbar ['krɔsbɑːʳ] n barre transversale
crossbow ['krɔsbəu] n arbalète f
crossbreed ['krɔsbriːd] n hybride m, métis(se)
cross-Channel ferry ['krɔs'tʃænl-] n ferry m qui fait la traversée de la Manche
cross-check ['krɔstʃɛk] n recoupement m ▷ vi vérifier par recoupement
cross-country ['krɔs'kʌntrɪ], **cross-country race** n cross(-country) m
cross-dressing [krɔs'drɛsɪŋ] n travestisme m
cross-examination ['krɔsɪgzæmɪ'neɪʃən] n (Law) examen m contradictoire (d'un témoin)
cross-examine ['krɔsɪg'zæmɪn] vt (Law) faire subir un examen contradictoire à
cross-eyed ['krɔsaɪd] adj qui louche
crossfire ['krɔsfaɪəʳ] n feux croisés
crossing ['krɔsɪŋ] n croisement m, carrefour m; (sea passage) traversée f; (also: **pedestrian crossing**) passage clouté; **how long does the ~ take?** combien de temps dure la traversée?
crossing guard (US) n contractuel qui fait traverser la rue aux enfants
crossing point n poste frontalier
cross-purposes ['krɔs'pəːpəsɪz] npl: **to be at ~ with sb** comprendre qn de travers; **we're (talking) at ~** on ne parle pas de la même chose
cross-question ['krɔs'kwɛstʃən] vt faire subir un interrogatoire à
cross-reference ['krɔs'rɛfrəns] n renvoi m, référence f
crossroads ['krɔsrəudz] n carrefour m
cross section n (Biol) coupe transversale; (in population) échantillon m
crosswalk ['krɔswɔːk] n (US) passage clouté
crosswind ['krɔswɪnd] n vent m de travers
crosswise ['krɔswaɪz] adv en travers
crossword ['krɔswəːd] n mots mpl croisés
crotch [krɔtʃ] n (of garment) entrejambe m; (Anat) entrecuisse m
crotchet ['krɔtʃɪt] n (Mus) noire f
crotchety ['krɔtʃɪtɪ] adj (person) grognon(ne), grincheux(-euse)
crouch [krautʃ] vi s'accroupir; (hide) se tapir; (before springing) se ramasser
croup [kruːp] n (Med) croup m
crouton ['kruːtɔn] n croûton m
crow [krəu] n (bird) corneille f; (of cock) chant m du coq, cocorico m ▷ vi (cock) chanter; (fig) pavoiser, chanter victoire

crowbar ['krəubɑːʳ] n levier m
crowd [kraud] n foule f ▷ vt bourrer, remplir ▷ vi affluer, s'attrouper, s'entasser; **~s of people** une foule de gens
crowded ['kraudɪd] adj bondé(e), plein(e); **~ with** plein de
crowd scene n (Cine, Theat) scène f de foule
crown [kraun] n couronne f; (of head) sommet m de la tête, calotte crânienne; (of hat) fond m; (of hill) sommet m ▷ vt (also tooth) couronner
crown court n (Brit) ≈ Cour f d'assises; voir article

● **CROWN COURT**
●
● En Angleterre et au pays de Galles, une crown
● court est une cour de justice où sont jugées
● les affaires très graves, telles que le meurtre,
● l'homicide, le viol et le vol, en présence d'un
● jury. Tous les crimes et délits, quel que soit
● leur degré de gravité, doivent d'abord passer
● devant une "magistrates' court". Il existe
● environ 90 crown courts.

crowning ['kraunɪŋ] adj (achievement, glory) suprême
crown jewels npl joyaux mpl de la Couronne
crown prince n prince héritier
crow's-feet ['krəuzfiːt] npl pattes fpl d'oie (fig)
crow's-nest ['krəuznɛst] n (on sailing-ship) nid m de pie
crucial ['kruːʃl] adj crucial(e), décisif(-ive); (also: **crucial to**) essentiel(le) à
crucifix ['kruːsɪfɪks] n crucifix m
crucifixion [kruːsɪ'fɪkʃən] n crucifiement m, crucifixion f
crucify ['kruːsɪfaɪ] vt crucifier, mettre en croix; (fig) crucifier
crude [kruːd] adj (materials) brut(e); non raffiné(e); (basic) rudimentaire, sommaire; (vulgar) cru(e), grossier(-ière) ▷ n (also: **crude oil**) (pétrole m) brut m
cruel ['kruəl] adj cruel(le)
cruelty ['kruəltɪ] n cruauté f
cruet ['kruːɪt] n huilier m; vinaigrier m
cruise [kruːz] n croisière f ▷ vi (ship) croiser; (car) rouler; (aircraft) voler; (taxi) être en maraude
cruise missile n missile m de croisière
cruiser ['kruːzəʳ] n croiseur m
cruising speed ['kruːzɪŋ-] n vitesse f de croisière
crumb [krʌm] n miette f
crumble ['krʌmbl] vt émietter ▷ vi s'émietter; (plaster etc) s'effriter; (land, earth) s'ébouler; (building) s'écrouler, crouler; (fig) s'effondrer
crumbly ['krʌmblɪ] adj friable
crummy ['krʌmɪ] adj (inf) minable; (: unwell) mal fichu(e), patraque
crumpet ['krʌmpɪt] n petite crêpe (épaisse)
crumple ['krʌmpl] vt froisser, friper
crunch [krʌntʃ] vt croquer; (underfoot) faire craquer, écraser; faire crisser ▷ n (fig) instant m or moment m critique, moment de vérité
crunchy ['krʌntʃɪ] adj croquant(e),

croustillant(e)

crusade [kruː'seɪd] n croisade f ▷ vi (fig): **to ~ for/against** partir en croisade pour/contre

crusader [kruː'seɪdər] n croisé m; (fig): **~ (for)** champion m (de)

crush [krʌʃ] n (crowd) foule f, cohue f; (love): **to have a ~ on sb** avoir le béguin pour qn; (drink): **lemon ~** citron pressé ▷ vt écraser; (crumple) froisser; (grind, break up: garlic, ice) piler; (: grapes) presser; (hopes) anéantir

crush barrier n (Brit) barrière f de sécurité

crushing ['krʌʃɪŋ] adj écrasant(e)

crust [krʌst] n croûte f

crustacean [krʌs'teɪʃən] n crustacé m

crusty ['krʌstɪ] adj (bread) croustillant(e); (inf: person) revêche, bourru(e); (: remark) irrité(e)

crutch [krʌtʃ] n béquille f; (Tech) support m; (also: **crotch**) entrejambe m

crux [krʌks] n point crucial

cry [kraɪ] vi pleurer; (shout: also: **cry out**) crier ▷ n cri m; **why are you ~ing?** pourquoi pleures-tu?; **to ~ for help** appeler à l'aide; **she had a good ~** elle a pleuré un bon coup; **it's a far ~ from …** (fig) on est loin de …
  ▶ **cry off** vi se dédire; se décommander
  ▶ **cry out** vi (call out, shout) pousser un cri ▷ vt crier

crying ['kraɪɪŋ] adj (fig) criant(e), flagrant(e)

crypt [krɪpt] n crypte f

cryptic ['krɪptɪk] adj énigmatique

crystal ['krɪstl] n cristal m

crystal-clear ['krɪstl'klɪər] adj clair(e) comme de l'eau de roche

crystallize ['krɪstəlaɪz] vt cristalliser ▷ vi (se) cristalliser; **~d fruits** (Brit) fruits confits

CSA n abbr = **Confederate States of America**; (Brit: = Child Support Agency) organisme pour la protection des enfants de parents séparés, qui contrôle le versement des pensions alimentaires.

CSC n abbr (= Civil Service Commission) commission de recrutement des fonctionnaires

CS gas n (Brit) gaz m C.S.

CST abbr (US: = Central Standard Time) fuseau horaire

CT abbr (US) = **Connecticut**

ct abbr = **carat**

CTC n abbr (Brit) = **city technology college**

CT scanner n abbr (Med: = computerized tomography scanner) scanner m, tomodensitomètre m

cu. abbr = **cubic**

cub [kʌb] n petit m (d'un animal); (also: **cub scout**) louveteau m

Cuba ['kjuːbə] n Cuba m

Cuban ['kjuːbən] adj cubain(e) ▷ n Cubain(e)

cubbyhole ['kʌbɪhəul] n cagibi m

cube [kjuːb] n cube m ▷ vt (Math) élever au cube

cube root n racine f cubique

cubic ['kjuːbɪk] adj cubique; **~ metre** etc mètre m etc cube; **~ capacity** (Aut) cylindrée f

cubicle ['kjuːbɪkl] n (in hospital) box m; (at pool) cabine f

cuckoo ['kukuː] n coucou m

cuckoo clock n (pendule f à) coucou m

cucumber ['kjuːkʌmbər] n concombre m

cud [kʌd] n: **to chew the ~** ruminer

cuddle ['kʌdl] vt câliner, caresser ▷ vi se blottir l'un contre l'autre

cuddly ['kʌdlɪ] adj câlin(e)

cudgel ['kʌdʒl] n gourdin m ▷ vt: **to ~ one's brains** se creuser la tête

cue [kjuː] n queue f de billard; (Theat etc) signal m

cuff [kʌf] n (Brit: of shirt, coat etc) poignet m, manchette f; (US: on trousers) revers m; (blow) gifle f ▷ vt gifler; **off the ~** (adv) à l'improviste

cufflinks ['kʌflɪŋks] n boutons m de manchette

cu. in. abbr = **cubic inches**

cuisine [kwɪ'ziːn] n cuisine f, art m culinaire

cul-de-sac ['kʌldəsæk] n cul-de-sac m, impasse f

culinary ['kʌlɪnərɪ] adj culinaire

cull [kʌl] vt sélectionner; (kill selectively) pratiquer l'abattage sélectif de ▷ n (of animals) abattage sélectif

culminate ['kʌlmɪneɪt] vi: **to ~ in** finir or se terminer par; (lead to) mener à

culmination [kʌlmɪ'neɪʃən] n point culminant

culottes [kjuː'lɔts] npl jupe-culotte f

culpable ['kʌlpəbl] adj coupable

culprit ['kʌlprɪt] n coupable m/f

cult [kʌlt] n culte m

cult figure n idole f

cultivate ['kʌltɪveɪt] vt (also fig) cultiver

cultivation [kʌltɪ'veɪʃən] n culture f

cultural ['kʌltʃərəl] adj culturel(le)

culture ['kʌltʃər] n (also fig) culture f

cultured ['kʌltʃəd] adj cultivé(e) (fig)

cumbersome ['kʌmbəsəm] adj encombrant(e), embarrassant(e)

cumin ['kʌmɪn] n (spice) cumin m

cumulative ['kjuːmjulətɪv] adj cumulatif(-ive)

cunning ['kʌnɪŋ] n ruse f, astuce f ▷ adj rusé(e), malin(-igne); (clever: device, idea) astucieux(-euse)

cunt [kʌnt] n (inf!) chatte f (!); (insult) salaud m (!), salope f (!)

cup [kʌp] n tasse f; (prize, event) coupe f; (of bra) bonnet m; **a ~ of tea** une tasse de thé

cupboard ['kʌbəd] n placard m

cup final n (Brit Football) finale f de la coupe

Cupid ['kjuːpɪd] n Cupidon m; (figurine) amour m

cupidity [kjuː'pɪdɪtɪ] n cupidité f

cupola ['kjuːpələ] n coupole f

cuppa ['kʌpə] n (Brit inf) tasse f de thé

cup tie n (Brit Football) match m de coupe

curable ['kjuərəbl] adj guérissable, curable

curate ['kjuərɪt] n vicaire m

curator [kjuə'reɪtər] n conservateur m (d'un musée etc)

curb [kəːb] vt refréner, mettre un frein à; (expenditure) limiter, juguler ▷ n (fig) frein m; (US) bord m du trottoir

curd cheese n ≈ fromage blanc

curdle ['kəːdl] vi (se) cailler

curds [kəːdz] npl lait caillé

cure [kjuəʳ] vt guérir; (Culin: salt) saler; (: smoke) fumer; (: dry) sécher ▷ n remède m; **to be ~d of sth** être guéri de qch
cure-all ['kjuərɔːl] n (also fig) panacée f
curfew ['kəːfjuː] n couvre-feu m
curio ['kjuərɪəu] n bibelot m, curiosité f
curiosity [kjuərɪ'ɔsɪtɪ] n curiosité f
curious ['kjuərɪəs] adj curieux(-euse); **I'm ~ about him** m'intrigue
curiously ['kjuərɪəslɪ] adv curieusement; (inquisitively) avec curiosité; **~ enough, ...** bizarrement, ...
curl [kəːl] n boucle f (de cheveux); (of smoke etc) volute f ▷ vt, vi boucler; (tightly) friser
▶ **curl up** vi s'enrouler; (person) se pelotonner
curler ['kəːləʳ] n bigoudi m, rouleau m; (Sport) joueur(-euse) de curling
curlew ['kəːluː] n courlis m
curling ['kəːlɪŋ] n (sport) curling m
curling tongs, (US) **curling irons** npl fer m à friser
curly ['kəːlɪ] adj bouclé(e); (tightly curled) frisé(e)
currant ['kʌrnt] n raisin m de Corinthe, raisin sec; (fruit) groseille f
currency ['kʌrnsɪ] n monnaie f; **foreign ~** devises étrangères, monnaie étrangère; **to gain ~** (fig) s'accréditer
current ['kʌrnt] n courant m ▷ adj (common) courant(e); (tendency, price, event) actuel(le); **direct/alternating ~** (Elec) courant continu/alternatif; **the ~ issue of a magazine** le dernier numéro d'un magazine; **in ~ use** d'usage courant
current account n (Brit) compte courant
current affairs npl (questions fpl d')actualité f
current assets npl (Comm) actif m disponible
current liabilities npl (Comm) passif m exigible
currently ['kʌrntlɪ] adv actuellement
curriculum (pl **-s** or **curricula**) [kə'rɪkjuləm, -lə] n programme m d'études
curriculum vitae [-'viːtaɪ] n curriculum vitae (CV) m
curry ['kʌrɪ] n curry m ▷ vt: **to ~ favour with** chercher à gagner la faveur or à s'attirer les bonnes grâces de; **chicken ~** curry de poulet, poulet m au curry
curry powder n poudre f de curry
curse [kəːs] vi jurer, blasphémer ▷ vt maudire ▷ n (spell) malédiction f; (problem, scourge) fléau m; (swearword) juron m
cursor ['kəːsəʳ] n (Comput) curseur m
cursory ['kəːsərɪ] adj superficiel(le), hâtif(-ive)
curt [kəːt] adj brusque, sec(-sèche)
curtail [kəː'teɪl] vt (visit etc) écourter; (expenses etc) réduire
curtain ['kəːtn] n rideau m; **to draw the ~s** (together) fermer or tirer les rideaux; (apart) ouvrir les rideaux
curtain call n (Theat) rappel m
curtsey, curtsy ['kəːtsɪ] n révérence f ▷ vi faire une révérence
curvature ['kəːvətʃəʳ] n courbure f

curve [kəːv] n courbe f; (in the road) tournant m, virage m ▷ vt courber ▷ vi se courber; (road) faire une courbe
curved [kəːvd] adj courbe
cushion ['kuʃən] n coussin m ▷ vt (seat) rembourrer; (fall, shock) amortir
cushy ['kuʃɪ] adj (inf): **a ~ job** un boulot de tout repos; **to have a ~ time** se la couler douce
custard ['kʌstəd] n (for pouring) crème anglaise
custard powder n (Brit) ≈ crème pâtissière instantanée
custodial sentence [kʌs'təudɪəl-] n peine f de prison
custodian [kʌs'təudɪən] n gardien(ne); (of collection etc) conservateur(-trice)
custody ['kʌstədɪ] n (of child) garde f; (for offenders) détention préventive; **to take sb into ~** placer qn en détention préventive; **in the ~ of** sous la garde de
custom ['kʌstəm] n coutume f, usage m; (Law) droit coutumier, coutume; (Comm) clientèle f
customary ['kʌstəmərɪ] adj habituel(le); **it is ~ to do it** l'usage veut qu'on le fasse
custom-built ['kʌstəm'bɪlt] adj see **custom-made**
customer ['kʌstəməʳ] n client(e); **he's an awkward ~** (inf) ce n'est pas quelqu'un de facile
customer profile n profil m du client
customized ['kʌstəmaɪzd] adj personnalisé(e); (car etc) construit(e) sur commande
custom-made ['kʌstəm'meɪd] adj (clothes) fait(e) sur mesure; (other goods: also: **custom-built**) hors série, fait(e) sur commande
customs ['kʌstəmz] npl douane f; **to go through (the) ~** passer la douane
Customs and Excise n (Brit) administration f des douanes
customs officer n douanier m
cut [kʌt] (pt, pp **-**) vt couper; (meat) découper; (shape, make) tailler; couper; creuser; graver; (reduce) réduire; (inf: lecture, appointment) manquer ▷ vi couper; (intersect) se couper ▷ n (gen) coupure f; (of clothes) coupe f; (of jewel) taille f; (in salary etc) réduction f; (of meat) morceau m; **to ~ teeth** (baby) faire ses dents; **to ~ a tooth** percer une dent; **to ~ one's finger** se couper le doigt; **to get one's hair ~** se faire couper les cheveux; **I've ~ myself** je me suis coupé; **to ~ sth short** couper court à qch; **to ~ sb dead** ignorer (complètement) qn
▶ **cut back** vt (plants) tailler; (production, expenditure) réduire
▶ **cut down** vt (tree) abattre; (reduce) réduire; **to ~ sb down to size** (fig) remettre qn à sa place
▶ **cut down on** vt fus réduire
▶ **cut in** vi (interrupt: conversation): **to ~ in (on)** couper la parole (à); (Aut) faire une queue de poisson
▶ **cut off** vt couper; (fig) isoler; **we've been ~ off** (Tel) nous avons été coupés
▶ **cut out** vt (picture etc) découper; (remove) supprimer

▶ **cut up** *vt* découper

cut-and-dried ['kʌtən'draɪd] *adj* (*also*: **cut-and-dry**) tout(e) fait(e), tout(e) décidé(e)

cutaway ['kʌtəweɪ] *adj, n*: ~ **(drawing)** écorché *m*

cutback ['kʌtbæk] *n* réduction *f*

cute [kju:t] *adj* mignon(ne), adorable; (*clever*) rusé(e), astucieux(-euse)

cut glass *n* cristal taillé

cuticle ['kju:tɪkl] *n* (*on nail*): ~ **remover** repousse-peaux *m inv*

cutlery ['kʌtlərɪ] *n* couverts *mpl*; (*trade*) coutellerie *f*

cutlet ['kʌtlɪt] *n* côtelette *f*

cutoff ['kʌtɔf] *n* (*also*: **cutoff point**) seuil-limite *m*

cutoff switch *n* interrupteur *m*

cutout ['kʌtaut] *n* coupe-circuit *m inv*; (*paper figure*) découpage *m*

cut-price ['kʌt'praɪs], (US) **cut-rate** ['kʌt'reɪt] *adj* au rabais, à prix réduit

cut-throat ['kʌtθrəut] *n* assassin *m* ▷ *adj*: ~ **competition** concurrence *f* sauvage

cutting ['kʌtɪŋ] *adj* tranchant(e), coupant(e); (*fig*) cinglant(e) ▷ *n* (*Brit: from newspaper*) coupure *f* (de journal); (*from plant*) bouture *f*; (*Rail*) tranchée *f*; (*Cine*) montage *m*

cutting edge *n* (*of knife*) tranchant *m*; **on** *or* **at the ~ of** à la pointe de

cuttlefish ['kʌtlfɪʃ] *n* seiche *f*

cut-up ['kʌtʌp] *adj* affecté(e), démoralisé(e)

CV *n abbr* = **curriculum vitae**

cwo *abbr* (*Comm*) = **cash with order**

cwt *abbr* = **hundredweight**

cyanide ['saɪənaɪd] *n* cyanure *m*

cybernetics [saɪbə'nɛtɪks] *n* cybernétique *f*

cyberspace ['saɪbəspeɪs] *n* cyberespace *m*

cyclamen ['sɪkləmən] *n* cyclamen *m*

cycle ['saɪkl] *n* cycle *m*; (*bicycle*) bicyclette *f*, vélo *m* ▷ *vi* faire de la bicyclette

cycle hire *n* location *f* de vélos

cycle lane, cycle path *n* piste *f* cyclable

cycle race *n* course *f* cycliste

cycle rack *n* râtelier *m* à bicyclette

cycling ['saɪklɪŋ] *n* cyclisme *m*; **to go on a ~ holiday** (*Brit*) faire du cyclotourisme

cyclist ['saɪklɪst] *n* cycliste *m/f*

cyclone ['saɪkləun] *n* cyclone *m*

cygnet ['sɪgnɪt] *n* jeune cygne *m*

cylinder ['sɪlɪndəʳ] *n* cylindre *m*

cylinder capacity *n* cylindrée *f*

cylinder head *n* culasse *f*

cymbals ['sɪmblz] *npl* cymbales *fpl*

cynic ['sɪnɪk] *n* cynique *m/f*

cynical ['sɪnɪkl] *adj* cynique

cynicism ['sɪnɪsɪzəm] *n* cynisme *m*

CYO *n abbr* (US: = *Catholic Youth Organization*) ≈ JC *f*

cypress ['saɪprɪs] *n* cyprès *m*

Cypriot ['sɪprɪət] *adj* cypriote, chypriote ▷ *n* Cypriote *m/f*, Chypriote *m/f*

Cyprus ['saɪprəs] *n* Chypre *f*

cyst [sɪst] *n* kyste *m*

cystitis [sɪs'taɪtɪs] *n* cystite *f*

CZ *n abbr* (US: = *Central Zone*) zone du canal de Panama

czar [zɑːʳ] *n* tsar *m*

Czech [tʃɛk] *adj* tchèque ▷ *n* Tchèque *m/f*; (*Ling*) tchèque *m*

Czechoslovak [tʃɛkə'sləuvæk] *adj, n* = **Czechoslovakian**

Czechoslovakia [tʃɛkəslə'vækɪə] *n* Tchécoslovaquie *f*

Czechoslovakian [tʃɛkəslə'vækɪən] *adj* tchécoslovaque ▷ *n* Tchécoslovaque *m/f*

Czech Republic *n*: **the ~** la République tchèque

Dd

D¹, d¹ [di:] *n* (*letter*) D, d *m*; (*Mus*): **D** ré *m*; **D for David**, (*US*) **D for Dog** D comme Désirée

D² *abbr* (*US Pol*) = **democrat; democratic**

d² *abbr* (*Brit: old*) = **penny**

d. *abbr* = **died**

DA *n abbr* (*US*) = **district attorney**

dab [dæb] *vt* (*eyes, wound*) tamponner; (*paint, cream*) appliquer (par petites touches *or* rapidement); **a ~ of paint** un petit coup de peinture

dabble ['dæbl] *vi*: **to ~ in** faire *or* se mêler *or* s'occuper un peu de

Dacca ['dækə] *n* Dacca

dachshund ['dækʃhund] *n* teckel *m*

dad, daddy [dæd, 'dædɪ] *n* papa *m*

daddy-long-legs [dædɪ'lɔŋlɛgz] *n* tipule *f*; faucheux *m*

daffodil ['dæfədɪl] *n* jonquille *f*

daft [dɑ:ft] *adj* (*inf*) idiot(e), stupide; **to be ~ about** être toqué(e) *or* mordu(e) de

dagger ['dægə'] *n* poignard *m*; **to be at ~s drawn with sb** être à couteaux tirés avec qn; **to look ~s at sb** foudroyer qn du regard

dahlia ['deɪljə] *n* dahlia *m*

daily ['deɪlɪ] *adj* quotidien(ne), journalier(-ière) ▷ *n* quotidien *m*; (*Brit: servant*) femme *f* de ménage (*à la journée*) ▷ *adv* tous les jours; **twice ~** deux fois par jour

dainty ['deɪntɪ] *adj* délicat(e), mignon(ne)

dairy ['dɛərɪ] *n* (*shop*) crémerie *f*, laiterie *f*; (*on farm*) laiterie ▷ *adj* laitier(-ière)

dairy cow *n* vache laitière

dairy farm *n* exploitation *f* pratiquant l'élevage laitier

dairy produce *n* produits laitiers

dairy products *npl* produits laitier

dais ['deɪɪs] *n* estrade *f*

daisy ['deɪzɪ] *n* pâquerette *f*

daisy wheel *n* (*on printer*) marguerite *f*

daisy-wheel printer ['deɪzɪwi:l-] *n* imprimante *f* à marguerite

Dakar ['dækə] *n* Dakar

dale [deɪl] *n* vallon *m*

dally ['dælɪ] *vi* musarder, flâner

dalmatian [dæl'meɪʃən] *n* (*dog*) dalmatien(ne)

dam [dæm] *n* (*wall*) barrage *m*; (*water*) réservoir *m*, lac *m* de retenue ▷ *vt* endiguer

damage ['dæmɪdʒ] *n* dégâts *mpl*, dommages *mpl*; (*fig*) tort *m* ▷ *vt* endommager, abîmer; (*fig*) faire du tort à; **damages** *npl* (*Law*) dommages-intérêts *mpl*; **to pay £5000 in ~s** payer 5000 livres de dommages-intérêts; **~ to property** dégâts matériels

damaging ['dæmɪdʒɪŋ] *adj*: **~ (to)** préjudiciable (à), nuisible (à)

Damascus [də'mɑ:skəs] *n* Damas

dame [deɪm] *n* (*title*) titre porté par une femme décorée de l'ordre de l'Empire Britannique ou d'un ordre de chevalerie, titre porté par la femme ou la veuve d'un chevalier ou baronnet; (*US inf*) nana *f*; (*Theat*) vieille dame (*rôle comique joué par un homme*)

damn [dæm] *vt* condamner; (*curse*) maudire ▷ *n* (*inf*): **I don't give a ~** je m'en fous ▷ *adj* (*inf: also*: **damned**): **this ~ ...** ce sacré *or* foutu ...; **~ (it)!** zut!

damnable ['dæmnəbl] *adj* (*inf: behaviour*) odieux(-euse), détestable; (: *weather*) épouvantable, abominable

damnation [dæm'neɪʃən] *n* (*Rel*) damnation *f* ▷ *excl* (*inf*) malédiction!, merde!

damning ['dæmɪŋ] *adj* (*evidence*) accablant(e)

damp [dæmp] *adj* humide ▷ *n* humidité *f* ▷ *vt* (*also*: **dampen**: *cloth, rag*) humecter; (: *enthusiasm etc*) refroidir

dampcourse ['dæmpkɔ:s] *n* couche isolante (contre l'humidité)

damper ['dæmpə'] *n* (*Mus*) étouffoir *m*; (*of fire*) registre *m*; **to put a ~ on** (*fig: atmosphere, enthusiasm*) refroidir

dampness ['dæmpnɪs] *n* humidité *f*

damson ['dæmzən] *n* prune *f* de Damas

dance [dɑ:ns] *n* danse *f*; (*ball*) bal *m* ▷ *vi* danser; **to ~ about** sautiller, gambader

dance floor *n* piste *f* de danse

dance hall *n* salle *f* de bal, dancing *m*

dancer ['dɑ:nsə'] *n* danseur(-euse)

dancing ['dɑ:nsɪŋ] *n* danse *f*

D and C *n abbr* (*Med*: = *dilation and curettage*) curetage *m*

dandelion ['dændɪlaɪən] *n* pissenlit *m*

dandruff ['dændrəf] *n* pellicules *fpl*

D & T *n abbr* (*Brit: Scol*) = **design and technology**

dandy ['dændɪ] *n* dandy *m*, élégant *m* ▷ *adj* (*US inf*) fantastique, super
Dane [deɪn] *n* Danois(e)
danger ['deɪndʒəʳ] *n* danger *m*; **~!** (*on sign*) danger!; **there is a ~ of fire** il y a (un) risque d'incendie; **in ~** en danger; **he was in ~ of falling** il risquait de tomber; **out of ~** hors de danger
danger list *n* (*Med*): **on the ~** dans un état critique
danger money *n* (*Brit*) prime *f* de risque
dangerous ['deɪndʒrəs] *adj* dangereux(-euse)
dangerously ['deɪndʒrəslɪ] *adv* dangereusement; **~ ill** très gravement malade, en danger de mort
danger zone *n* zone dangereuse
dangle ['dæŋgl] *vt* balancer; (*fig*) faire miroiter ▷ *vi* pendre, se balancer
Danish ['deɪnɪʃ] *adj* danois(e) ▷ *n* (*Ling*) danois *m*
Danish pastry *n* feuilleté *m* (*recouvert d'un glaçage et fourré aux fruits etc*)
dank [dæŋk] *adj* froid(e) et humide
Danube ['dænjuːb] *n*: **the ~** le Danube
dapper ['dæpəʳ] *adj* pimpant(e)
Dardanelles [dɑːdə'nɛlz] *npl* Dardanelles *fpl*
dare [dɛəʳ] *vt*: **to ~ sb to do** défier qn *or* mettre qn au défi de faire ▷ *vi*: **to ~ (to) do sth** oser faire qch; **I ~n't tell him** (*Brit*) je n'ose pas le lui dire; **I ~ say he'll turn up** il est probable qu'il viendra
daredevil ['dɛədɛvl] *n* casse-cou *m inv*
Dar-es-Salaam ['dɑːrɛssə'lɑːm] *n* Dar-es-Salaam, Dar-es-Salam
daring ['dɛərɪŋ] *adj* hardi(e), audacieux(-euse) ▷ *n* audace *f*, hardiesse *f*
dark [dɑːk] *adj* (*night, room*) obscur(e), sombre; (*colour, complexion*) foncé(e), sombre; (*fig*) sombre ▷ *n*: **in the ~** dans le noir; **to be in the ~ about** (*fig*) ignorer tout de; **after ~** après la tombée de la nuit; **it is/is getting ~** il fait nuit/commence à faire nuit
darken [dɑːkn] *vt* obscurcir, assombrir ▷ *vi* s'obscurcir, s'assombrir
dark glasses *npl* lunettes noires
dark horse *n* (*fig*): **he's a ~** on ne sait pas grand-chose de lui
darkly ['dɑːklɪ] *adv* (*gloomily*) mélancoliquement; (*in a sinister way*) lugubrement
darkness ['dɑːknɪs] *n* obscurité *f*
darkroom ['dɑːkrʊm] *n* chambre noire
darling ['dɑːlɪŋ] *adj*, *n* chéri(e)
darn [dɑːn] *vt* repriser
dart [dɑːt] *n* fléchette *f*; (*in sewing*) pince *f* ▷ *vi*: **to ~ towards** (*also*: **make a dart towards**) se précipiter *or* s'élancer vers; **to ~ away/along** partir/passer comme une flèche
dartboard ['dɑːtbɔːd] *n* cible *f* (de jeu de fléchettes)
darts [dɑːts] *n* jeu *m* de fléchettes
dash [dæʃ] *n* (*sign*) tiret *m*; (*small quantity*) goutte *f*, larme *f* ▷ *vt* (*throw*) jeter *or* lancer violemment; (*hopes*) anéantir ▷ *vi*: **to ~ towards** (*also*: **make a dash towards**) se précipiter *or* se ruer vers; **a ~ of soda** un peu d'eau gazeuse
▶ **dash away** *vi* partir à toute allure
dashboard ['dæʃbɔːd] *n* (*Aut*) tableau *m* de bord
dashing ['dæʃɪŋ] *adj* fringant(e)
▶ **dash off** *vi* = **dash away**
dastardly ['dæstədlɪ] *adj* lâche
DAT *n abbr* (= *digital audio tape*) cassette *f* audio digitale
data ['deɪtə] *npl* données *fpl*
database ['deɪtəbeɪs] *n* base *f* de données
data capture *n* saisie *f* de données
data processing *n* traitement *m* (électronique) de l'information
data transmission *n* transmission *f* de données
date [deɪt] *n* date *f*; (*with sb*) rendez-vous *m*; (*fruit*) datte *f* ▷ *vt* dater; (*person*) sortir avec; **what's the ~ today?** quelle date sommes-nous aujourd'hui?; **~ of birth** date de naissance; **closing ~** date de clôture; **to ~** (*adv*) à ce jour; **out of ~** périmé(e); **up to ~** à la page, mis(e) à jour, moderne; **to bring up to ~** (*correspondence, information*) mettre à jour; (*method*) moderniser; (*person*) mettre au courant; **letter ~d 5th July** *or* (*US*) **July 5th** lettre (datée) du 5 juillet
dated ['deɪtɪd] *adj* démodé(e)
dateline ['deɪtlaɪn] *n* ligne *f* de changement de date
date rape *n* viol *m* (à l'issue d'un rendez-vous galant)
date stamp *n* timbre-dateur *m*
daub [dɔːb] *vt* barbouiller
daughter ['dɔːtəʳ] *n* fille *f*
daughter-in-law ['dɔːtərɪnlɔː] *n* belle-fille *f*, bru *f*
daunt [dɔːnt] *vt* intimider, décourager
daunting ['dɔːntɪŋ] *adj* décourageant(e), intimidant(e)
dauntless ['dɔːntlɪs] *adj* intrépide
dawdle ['dɔːdl] *vi* traîner, lambiner; **to ~ over one's work** traînasser *or* lambiner sur son travail
dawn [dɔːn] *n* aube *f*, aurore *f* ▷ *vi* (*day*) se lever, poindre; (*fig*) naître, se faire jour; **at ~** à l'aube; **from ~ to dusk** du matin au soir; **it ~ed on him that ...** il lui vint à l'esprit que ...
dawn chorus *n* (*Brit*) chant *m* des oiseaux à l'aube
day [deɪ] *n* jour *m*; (*as duration*) journée *f*; (*period of time, age*) époque *f*, temps *m*; **the ~ before** la veille, le jour précédent; **the ~ after, the following ~** le lendemain, le jour suivant; **the ~ before yesterday** avant-hier; **the ~ after tomorrow** après-demain; **(on) the ~ that ...** le jour où ...; **~ by ~** jour après jour; **by ~** de jour; **paid by the ~** payé(e) à la journée; **these ~s, in the present ~** de nos jours, à l'heure actuelle
daybook ['deɪbuk] *n* (*Brit*) main courante, brouillard *m*, journal *m*
day boy *n* (*Scol*) externe *m*
daybreak ['deɪbreɪk] *n* point *m* du jour
day-care centre ['deɪkɛə-] *n* (*for elderly etc*)

centre m d'accueil de jour; (for children) garderie f

daydream ['deɪdriːm] n rêverie f ▷ vi rêver (tout éveillé)

day girl n (Scol) externe f

daylight ['deɪlaɪt] n (lumière f du) jour m

daylight robbery n: **it's ~** (fig: inf) c'est du vol caractérisé or manifeste

daylight saving time n (US) heure f d'été

day release n: **to be on ~** avoir une journée de congé pour formation professionnelle

day return n (Brit) billet m d'aller-retour (valable pour la journée)

day shift n équipe f de jour

daytime ['deɪtaɪm] n jour m, journée f

day-to-day ['deɪtə'deɪ] adj (routine, expenses) journalier(-ière); **on a ~ basis** au jour le jour

day trip n excursion f (d'une journée)

day tripper n excursionniste m/f

daze [deɪz] vt (drug) hébéter; (blow) étourdir ▷ n: **in a ~** hébété(e), étourdi(e)

dazed [deɪzd] adj abruti(e)

dazzle ['dæzl] vt éblouir, aveugler

dazzling ['dæzlɪŋ] adj (light) aveuglant(e), éblouissant(e); (fig) éblouissant(e)

DC abbr (Elec) = **direct current**; (US) = **District of Columbia**

DD n abbr (= Doctor of Divinity) titre universitaire

dd. abbr (Comm) = **delivered**

D/D abbr = **direct debit**

D-day ['diːdeɪ] n le jour J

DDS n abbr (US: = Doctor of Dental Science; Brit: = Doctor of Dental Surgery) titres universitaires

DDT n abbr (= dichlorodiphenyl trichloroethane) DDT m

DE abbr (US) = **Delaware**

DEA n abbr (US: = Drug Enforcement Administration) ≈ brigade f des stupéfiants

deacon ['diːkən] n diacre m

dead [dɛd] adj mort(e); (numb) engourdi(e), insensible; (battery) à plat ▷ adv (completely) absolument, complètement; (exactly) juste; **the dead** npl les morts; **he was shot ~** il a été tué d'un coup de revolver; **~ on time** à l'heure pile; **~ tired** éreinté(e), complètement fourbu(e); **to stop ~** s'arrêter pile or net; **the line is ~** (Tel) la ligne est coupée

dead beat adj (inf) claqué(e), crevé(e)

deaden [dɛdn] vt (blow, sound) amortir; (make numb) endormir, rendre insensible

dead end n impasse f

dead-end ['dɛdɛnd] adj: **a ~ job** un emploi or poste sans avenir

dead heat n (Sport): **to finish in a ~** terminer ex aequo

dead-letter office [dɛd'lɛtər-] n ≈ centre m de recherche du courrier

deadline ['dɛdlaɪn] n date f or heure f limite; **to work to a ~** avoir des délais stricts à respecter

deadlock ['dɛdlɔk] n impasse f; (fig)

dead loss n (inf): **to be a ~** (person) n'être bon (bonne à rien); (thing) ne rien valoir

deadly ['dɛdlɪ] adj mortel(le); (weapon) meurtrier(-ière); **~ dull** ennuyeux(-euse) à

mourir, mortellement ennuyeux

deadpan ['dɛdpæn] adj impassible; (humour) pince-sans-rire inv

Dead Sea n: **the ~** la mer Morte

deaf [dɛf] adj sourd(e); **to turn a ~ ear to sth** faire la sourde oreille à qch

deaf-aid ['dɛfeɪd] n (Brit) appareil auditif

deaf-and-dumb ['dɛfən'dʌm] adj sourd(e)-muet(te); **~ alphabet** alphabet m des sourds-muets

deafen ['dɛfn] vt rendre sourd(e); (fig) assourdir

deafening ['dɛfnɪŋ] adj assourdissant(e)

deaf-mute ['dɛfmjuːt] n sourd/e-muet/te

deafness ['dɛfnɪs] n surdité f

deal [diːl] n affaire f, marché m ▷ vt (pt, pp **-t**) [dɛlt] (blow) porter; (cards) donner, distribuer; **to strike a ~ with sb** faire or conclure un marché avec qn; **it's a ~!** (inf) marché conclu!, tope-là!, topez-là!; **he got a bad ~ from them** ils ont mal agi envers lui; **he got a fair ~ from them** ils ont agi loyalement envers lui; **a good ~** (a lot) beaucoup; **a good ~ of, a great ~ of** beaucoup de, énormément de

▶ **deal in** vt fus (Comm) faire le commerce de, être dans le commerce de

▶ **deal with** vt fus (Comm) traiter avec; (handle) s'occuper or se charger de; (be about: book etc) traiter de

dealer ['diːlər] n (Comm) marchand m; (Cards) donneur m

dealership ['diːləʃɪp] n concession f

dealings ['diːlɪŋz] npl (in goods, shares) opérations fpl, transactions fpl; (relations) relations fpl, rapports mpl

dealt [dɛlt] pt, pp of **deal**

dean [diːn] n (Rel, Brit Scol) doyen m; (US Scol) conseiller principal (conseillère principale) d'éducation

dear [dɪər] adj cher (chère); (expensive) cher, coûteux(-euse) ▷ n: **my ~** mon cher (ma chère) ▷ excl: **~ me!** mon Dieu!; **D~ Sir/Madam** (in letter) Monsieur/Madame; **D~ Mr/Mrs X** Cher Monsieur/Chère Madame X

dearly ['dɪəlɪ] adv (love) tendrement; (pay) cher

dearth [dəːθ] n disette f, pénurie f

death [dɛθ] n mort f; (Admin) décès m

deathbed ['dɛθbɛd] n lit m de mort

death certificate n acte m de décès

deathly ['dɛθlɪ] adj de mort ▷ adv comme la mort

death penalty n peine f de mort

death rate n taux m de mortalité

death row [-'rəu] n (US) quartier m des condamnés à mort; **to be on ~** être condamné à la peine de mort

death sentence n condamnation f à mort

death squad n escadron m de la mort

death toll n nombre m de morts

deathtrap ['dɛθtræp] n endroit or véhicule etc dangereux

deb [dɛb] n abbr (inf) = **debutante**

debar [dɪ'bɑːr] vt: **to ~ sb from a club** etc exclure

qn d'un club *etc*; **to ~ sb from doing** interdire à qn de faire

debase [dɪ'beɪs] *vt* (*currency*) déprécier, dévaloriser; (*person*) abaisser, avilir

debatable [dɪ'beɪtəbl] *adj* discutable, contestable; **it is ~ whether ...** il est douteux que ...

debate [dɪ'beɪt] *n* discussion *f*, débat *m* ▷ *vt* discuter, débattre ▷ *vi* (*consider*): **to ~ whether** se demander si

debauchery [dɪ'bɔ:tʃərɪ] *n* débauche *f*

debenture [dɪ'bɛntʃər] *n* (*Comm*) obligation *f*

debilitate [dɪ'bɪlɪteɪt] *vt* débiliter

debit ['dɛbɪt] *n* débit *m* ▷ *vt*: **to ~ a sum to sb** *or* **to sb's account** porter une somme au débit de qn, débiter qn d'une somme

debit balance *n* solde débiteur

debit card *n* carte *f* de paiement

debit note *n* note *f* de débit

debrief [di:'bri:f] *vt* demander un compte rendu de fin de mission à

debriefing [di:'bri:fɪŋ] *n* compte rendu *m*

debris ['dɛbri:] *n* débris *mpl*, décombres *mpl*

debt [dɛt] *n* dette *f*; **to be in ~** avoir des dettes, être endetté(e); **bad ~** créance *f* irrécouvrable

debt collector *n* agent *m* de recouvrements

debtor ['dɛtər] *n* débiteur(-trice)

debug ['di:'bʌg] *vt* (*Comput*) déverminer

debunk [di:'bʌŋk] *vt* (*theory, claim*) montrer le ridicule de

debut ['deɪbju:] *n* début(s) *m(pl)*

debutante ['dɛbjutænt] *n* débutante *f*

Dec. *abbr* (= *December*) déc

decade ['dɛkeɪd] *n* décennie *f*, décade *f*

decadence ['dɛkədəns] *n* décadence *f*

decadent ['dɛkədənt] *adj* décadent(e)

decaf ['di:kæf] *n* (*inf*) déca *m*

decaffeinated [dɪ'kæfɪneɪtɪd] *adj* décaféiné(e)

decamp [dɪ'kæmp] *vi* (*inf*) décamper, filer

decant [dɪ'kænt] *vt* (*wine*) décanter

decanter [dɪ'kæntər] *n* carafe *f*

decarbonize [di:'kɑ:bənaɪz] *vt* (*Aut*) décalaminer

decathlon [dɪ'kæθlən] *n* décathlon *m*

decay [dɪ'keɪ] *n* (*of food, wood etc*) décomposition *f*, pourriture *f*; (*of building*) délabrement *m*; (*fig*) déclin *m*; (*also*: **tooth decay**) carie *f* (dentaire) ▷ *vi* (*rot*) se décomposer, pourrir; (: *teeth*) se carier; (*fig*: *city, district, building*) se délabrer; (: *civilization*) décliner; (: *system*) tomber en ruine

decease [dɪ'si:s] *n* décès *m*

deceased [dɪ'si:st] *n*: **the ~** le (la) défunt(e)

deceit [dɪ'si:t] *n* tromperie *f*, supercherie *f*

deceitful [dɪ'si:tful] *adj* trompeur(-euse)

deceive [dɪ'si:v] *vt* tromper; **to ~ o.s.** s'abuser

decelerate [di:'sɛləreɪt] *vt, vi* ralentir

December [dɪ'sɛmbər] *n* décembre *m*; *for phrases see also* **July**

decency ['di:sənsɪ] *n* décence *f*

decent ['di:sənt] *adj* (*proper*) décent(e), convenable; **they were very ~ about it** ils se sont montrés très chics

decently ['di:səntlɪ] *adv* (*respectably*) décemment, convenablement; (*kindly*) décemment

decentralization [di:sɛntrəlaɪ'zeɪʃən] *n* décentralisation *f*

decentralize [di:'sɛntrəlaɪz] *vt* décentraliser

deception [dɪ'sɛpʃən] *n* tromperie *f*

deceptive [dɪ'sɛptɪv] *adj* trompeur(-euse)

decibel ['dɛsɪbɛl] *n* décibel *m*

decide [dɪ'saɪd] *vt* (*subj: person*) décider; (*question, argument*) trancher, régler ▷ *vi* se décider, décider; **to ~ to do/that** décider de faire/que; **to ~ on** décider, se décider pour; **to ~ on doing** décider de faire; **to ~ against doing** décider de ne pas faire

decided [dɪ'saɪdɪd] *adj* (*resolute*) résolu(e), décidé(e); (*clear, definite*) net(te), marqué(e)

decidedly [dɪ'saɪdɪdlɪ] *adv* résolument; incontestablement, nettement

deciding [dɪ'saɪdɪŋ] *adj* décisif(-ive)

deciduous [dɪ'sɪdjuəs] *adj* à feuilles caduques

decimal ['dɛsɪməl] *adj* décimal(e) ▷ *n* décimale *f*; **to three ~ places** (jusqu')à la troisième décimale

decimalize ['dɛsɪməlaɪz] *vt* (*Brit*) décimaliser

decimal point *n* ≈ virgule *f*

decimate ['dɛsɪmeɪt] *vt* décimer

decipher [dɪ'saɪfər] *vt* déchiffrer

decision [dɪ'sɪʒən] *n* décision *f*; **to make a ~** prendre une décision

decisive [dɪ'saɪsɪv] *adj* décisif(-ive); (*influence*) décisif, déterminant(e); (*manner, person*) décidé(e), catégorique; (*reply*) ferme, catégorique

deck [dɛk] *n* (*Naut*) pont *m*; (*of cards*) jeu *m*; (*record deck*) platine *f*; (*of bus*): **top ~** impériale *f*; **to go up on ~** monter sur le pont; **below ~** dans l'entrepont

deckchair ['dɛktʃɛər] *n* chaise longue

deck hand *n* matelot *m*

declaration [dɛklə'reɪʃən] *n* déclaration *f*

declare [dɪ'klɛər] *vt* déclarer

declassify [di:'klæsɪfaɪ] *vt* rendre accessible au public *or* à tous

decline [dɪ'klaɪn] *n* (*decay*) déclin *m*; (*lessening*) baisse *f* ▷ *vt* refuser, décliner ▷ *vi* décliner; (*business*) baisser; **~ in living standards** baisse du niveau de vie; **to ~ to do sth** refuser (poliment) de faire qch

declutch ['di:'klʌtʃ] *vi* (*Brit*) débrayer

decode [di:'kəud] *vt* décoder

decoder [di:'kəudər] *n* (*Comput, TV*) décodeur *m*

decompose [di:kəm'pəuz] *vi* se décomposer

decomposition [di:kɔmpə'zɪʃən] *n* décomposition *f*

decompression [di:kəm'prɛʃən] *n* décompression *f*

decompression chamber *n* caisson *m* de décompression

decongestant [di:kən'dʒɛstənt] *n* décongestif *m*

decontaminate [di:kən'tæmɪneɪt] *vt*

décontaminer

decontrol [di:kən'trəul] *vt* (*prices etc*) libérer

décor ['deɪkɔːʳ] *n* décor *m*

decorate ['dɛkəreɪt] *vt* (*adorn, give a medal to*) décorer; (*paint and paper*) peindre et tapisser

decoration [dɛkə'reɪʃən] *n* (*medal etc, adornment*) décoration *f*

decorative ['dɛkərətɪv] *adj* décoratif(-ive)

decorator ['dɛkəreɪtəʳ] *n* peintre *m* en bâtiment

decorum [dɪ'kɔːrəm] *n* décorum *m*, bienséance *f*

decoy ['diːkɔɪ] *n* piège *m*; **they used him as a ~ for the enemy** ils se sont servis de lui pour attirer l'ennemi

decrease *n* ['diːkriːs] diminution *f* ▷ *vt, vi* [diː'kriːs] diminuer; **to be on the ~** diminuer, être en diminution

decreasing [diː'kriːsɪŋ] *adj* en voie de diminution

decree [dɪ'kriː] *n* (*Pol, Rel*) décret *m*; (*Law*) arrêt *m*, jugement *m* ▷ *vt*: **to ~ (that)** décréter (que), ordonner (que); **~ absolute** jugement définitif (de divorce); **~ nisi** jugement provisoire de divorce

decrepit [dɪ'krɛpɪt] *adj* (*person*) décrépit(e); (*building*) délabré(e)

decry [dɪ'kraɪ] *vt* condamner ouvertement, déplorer; (*disparage*) dénigrer, décrier

dedicate ['dɛdɪkeɪt] *vt* consacrer; (*book etc*) dédier

dedicated ['dɛdɪkeɪtɪd] *adj* (*person*) dévoué(e); (*Comput*) spécialisé(e), dédié(e); **~ word processor** station *f* de traitement de texte

dedication [dɛdɪ'keɪʃən] *n* (*devotion*) dévouement *m*; (*in book*) dédicace *f*

deduce [dɪ'djuːs] *vt* déduire, conclure

deduct [dɪ'dʌkt] *vt*: **to ~ sth (from)** déduire qch (de), retrancher qch (de); (*from wage etc*) prélever qch (sur), retenir qch (sur)

deduction [dɪ'dʌkʃən] *n* (*deducting, deducing*) déduction *f*; (*from wage etc*) prélèvement *m*, retenue *f*

deed [diːd] *n* action *f*, acte *m*; (*Law*) acte notarié, contrat *m*; **~ of covenant** (acte *m* de) donation *f*

deem [diːm] *vt* (*formal*) juger, estimer; **to ~ it wise to do** juger bon de faire

deep [diːp] *adj* (*water, sigh, sorrow, thoughts*) profond(e); (*voice*) grave ▷ *adv*: **~ in snow** recouvert(e) d'une épaisse couche de neige; **spectators stood 20 ~** il y avait 20 rangs de spectateurs; **knee-~ in water** dans l'eau jusqu'aux genoux; **4 metres ~** de 4 mètres de profondeur; **how ~ is the water?** l'eau a quelle profondeur?; **he took a ~ breath** il inspira profondément, il prit son souffle

deepen [diːpn] *vt* (*hole*) approfondir ▷ *vi* s'approfondir; (*darkness*) s'épaissir

deepfreeze ['diːp'friːz] *n* congélateur *m* ▷ *vt* surgeler

deep-fry ['diːp'fraɪ] *vt* faire frire (dans une friteuse)

deeply ['diːplɪ] *adv* profondément; (*dig*) en profondeur; (*regret, interested*) vivement

deep-rooted ['diːp'ruːtɪd] *adj* (*prejudice*) profondément enraciné(e); (*affection*) profond(e); (*habit*) invétéré(e)

deep-sea ['diːp'siː] *adj*: **~ diver** plongeur sous-marin; **~ diving** plongée sous-marine; **~ fishing** pêche hauturière

deep-seated ['diːp'siːtɪd] *adj* (*belief*) profondément enraciné(e)

deep-set ['diːpsɛt] *adj* (*eyes*) enfoncé(e)

deep vein thrombosis *n* thrombose *f* veineuse profonde

deer [dɪəʳ] *n* (*pl inv*): **the ~** les cervidés *mpl*; (*Zool*): **(red) ~** cerf *m*; **(fallow) ~** daim *m*; **(roe) ~** chevreuil *m*

deerskin ['dɪəskɪn] *n* peau *f* de daim

deerstalker ['dɪəstɔːkəʳ] *n* (*person*) chasseur *m* de cerf; (*hat*) casquette *f* à la Sherlock Holmes

deface [dɪ'feɪs] *vt* dégrader; barbouiller; rendre illisible

defamation [dɛfə'meɪʃən] *n* diffamation *f*

defamatory [dɪ'fæmətrɪ] *adj* diffamatoire, diffamant(e)

default [dɪ'fɔːlt] *vi* (*Law*) faire défaut; (*gen*) manquer à ses engagements ▷ *n* (*Comput: also*: **default value**) valeur *f* par défaut; **by ~** (*Law*) par défaut, par contumace; (*Sport*) par forfait; **to ~ on a debt** ne pas s'acquitter d'une dette

defaulter [dɪ'fɔːltəʳ] *n* (*on debt*) débiteur défaillant

default option *n* (*Comput*) option *f* par défaut

defeat [dɪ'fiːt] *n* défaite *f* ▷ *vt* (*team, opponents*) battre; (*fig: plans, efforts*) faire échouer

defeatism [dɪ'fiːtɪzəm] *n* défaitisme *m*

defeatist [dɪ'fiːtɪst] *adj, n* défaitiste *m/f*

defecate ['dɛfəkeɪt] *vi* déféquer

defect ['diːfɛkt] *n* défaut *m* ▷ *vi* [dɪ'fɛkt]: **to ~ to the enemy/the West** passer à l'ennemi/ l'Ouest; **physical ~** malformation *f*, vice *m* de conformation; **mental ~** anomalie *or* déficience mentale

defective [dɪ'fɛktɪv] *adj* défectueux(-euse)

defector [dɪ'fɛktəʳ] *n* transfuge *m/f*

defence, (*US*) **defense** [dɪ'fɛns] *n* défense *f*; **in ~ of** pour défendre; **witness for the ~** témoin *m* à décharge; **the Ministry of D~**, (*US*) **the Department of Defense** le ministère de la Défense nationale

defenceless [dɪ'fɛnslɪs] *adj* sans défense

defend [dɪ'fɛnd] *vt* défendre; (*decision, action, opinion*) justifier, défendre

defendant [dɪ'fɛndənt] *n* défendeur(-deresse); (*in criminal case*) accusé(e), prévenu(e)

defender [dɪ'fɛndəʳ] *n* défenseur *m*

defending champion [dɪ'fɛndɪŋ-] *n* (*Sport*) champion(ne) en titre

defending counsel [dɪ'fɛndɪŋ-] *n* (*Law*) avocat *m* de la défense

defense [dɪ'fɛns] *n* (*US*) = **defence**

defensive [dɪ'fɛnsɪv] *adj* défensif(-ive) ▷ *n* défensive *f*; **on the ~** sur la défensive

defer [dɪ'fəːʳ] *vt* (*postpone*) différer, ajourner ▷ *vi* (*submit*): **to ~ to sb/sth** déférer à qn/qch, s'en remettre à qn/qch

deference ['dɛfərəns] n déférence f, égards mpl;
out of or **in ~ to** par déférence or égards pour

defiance [dɪ'faɪəns] n défi m; **in ~ of** au mépris
de

defiant [dɪ'faɪənt] adj provocant(e), de défi;
(person) rebelle, intraitable

defiantly [dɪ'faɪəntlɪ] adv d'un air (or d'un ton)
de défi

deficiency [dɪ'fɪʃənsɪ] n (lack) insuffisance f;
(: Med) carence f; (flaw) faiblesse f; (Comm)
déficit m, découvert m

deficiency disease n maladie f de carence

deficient [dɪ'fɪʃənt] adj (inadequate)
insuffisant(e); (defective) défectueux(-euse); **to
be ~ in** manquer de

deficit ['dɛfɪsɪt] n déficit m

defile [dɪ'faɪl] vt souiller ▷ vi défiler ▷ n ['di:faɪl]
défilé m

define [dɪ'faɪn] vt définir

definite ['dɛfɪnɪt] adj (fixed) défini(e), (bien)
déterminé(e); (clear, obvious) net(te), manifeste;
(Ling) défini(e); (certain) sûr(e); **he was ~ about
it** il a été catégorique; il était sûr de son fait

definitely ['dɛfɪnɪtlɪ] adv sans aucun doute

definition [dɛfɪ'nɪʃən] n définition f; (clearness)
netteté f

definitive [dɪ'fɪnɪtɪv] adj définitif(-ive)

deflate [di:'fleɪt] vt dégonfler; (pompous person)
rabattre le caquet à; (Econ) provoquer la
déflation de; (: prices) faire tomber or baisser

deflation [di:'fleɪʃən] n (Econ) déflation f

deflationary [di:'fleɪʃənrɪ] adj (Econ)
déflationniste

deflect [dɪ'flɛkt] vt détourner, faire dévier

defog ['di:'fɒg] vt (US Aut) désembuer

defogger ['di:'fɒgəʳ] n (US Aut) dispositif m anti-
buée inv

deform [dɪ'fɔːm] vt déformer

deformed [dɪ'fɔːmd] adj difforme

deformity [dɪ'fɔːmɪtɪ] n difformité f

defraud [dɪ'frɔːd] vt frauder; **to ~ sb of sth**
soutirer qch malhonnêtement à qn; escroquer
qch à qn; frustrer qn de qch

defray [dɪ'freɪ] vt: **to ~ sb's expenses** défrayer
qn (de ses frais), rembourser or payer à qn ses
frais

defrost [di:'frɒst] vt (fridge) dégivrer; (frozen food)
décongeler

deft [dɛft] adj adroit(e), preste

defunct [dɪ'fʌŋkt] adj défunt(e)

defuse [di:'fjuːz] vt désamorcer

defy [dɪ'faɪ] vt défier; (efforts etc) résister à; **it
defies description** cela défie toute description

degenerate vi [dɪ'dʒɛnəreɪt] dégénérer ▷ adj
[dɪ'dʒɛnərɪt] dégénéré(e)

degradation [dɛgrə'deɪʃən] n dégradation f

degrade [dɪ'greɪd] vt dégrader

degrading [dɪ'greɪdɪŋ] adj dégradant(e)

degree [dɪ'griː] n degré m; (Scol) diplôme m
(universitaire); **10 ~s below (zero)** 10 degrés
au-dessous de zéro; **a (first) ~ in maths** (Brit)

une licence en maths; **a considerable ~ of risk**
un considérable facteur or élément de risque;
by ~s (gradually) par degrés; **to some ~, to a
certain ~** jusqu'à un certain point, dans une
certaine mesure

dehydrated [di:haɪ'dreɪtɪd] adj déshydraté(e);
(milk, eggs) en poudre

dehydration [di:haɪ'dreɪʃən] n déshydratation f

de-ice ['di:'aɪs] vt (windscreen) dégivrer

de-icer ['di:'aɪsəʳ] n dégivreur m

deign [deɪn] vi: **to ~ to do** daigner faire

deity ['di:ɪtɪ] n divinité f; dieu m, déesse f

déjà vu [deɪʒɑ:'vuː] n: **I had a sense of ~** j'ai eu
une impression de déjà-vu

dejected [dɪ'dʒɛktɪd] adj abattu(e), déprimé(e)

dejection [dɪ'dʒɛkʃən] n abattement m,
découragement m

Del. abbr (US) = **Delaware**

del. abbr = **delete**

delay [dɪ'leɪ] vt (journey, operation) retarder,
différer; (traveller, train) retarder; (payment)
différer ▷ vi s'attarder ▷ n délai m, retard m; **to
be ~ed** être en retard; **without ~** sans délai,
sans tarder

delayed-action [dɪ'leɪd'ækʃən] adj à
retardement

delectable [dɪ'lɛktəbl] adj délicieux(-euse)

delegate n ['dɛlɪgɪt] délégué(e) ▷ vt ['dɛlɪgeɪt]
déléguer; **to ~ sth to sb/sb to do sth** déléguer
qch à qn/qn pour faire qch

delegation [dɛlɪ'geɪʃən] n délégation f

delete [dɪ'liːt] vt rayer, supprimer; (Comput)
effacer

Delhi ['dɛlɪ] n Delhi

deli ['dɛlɪ] n épicerie fine

deliberate adj [dɪ'lɪbərɪt] (intentional) délibéré(e);
(slow) mesuré(e) ▷ vi [dɪ'lɪbəreɪt] délibérer,
réfléchir

deliberately [dɪ'lɪbərɪtlɪ] adv (on purpose) exprès,
délibérément

deliberation [dɪlɪbə'reɪʃən] n délibération f,
réflexion f; (gen pl: discussion) délibérations,
débats mpl

delicacy ['dɛlɪkəsɪ] n délicatesse f; (choice food)
mets fin or délicat, friandise f

delicate ['dɛlɪkɪt] adj délicat(e)

delicately ['dɛlɪkɪtlɪ] adv délicatement; (act,
express) avec délicatesse, avec tact

delicatessen [dɛlɪkə'tɛsn] n épicerie fine

delicious [dɪ'lɪʃəs] adj délicieux(-euse), exquis(e)

delight [dɪ'laɪt] n (grande) joie, grand plaisir
▷ vt enchanter; **she's a ~ to work with** c'est un
plaisir de travailler avec elle; **a ~ to the eyes** un
régal or plaisir pour les yeux; **to take ~ in**
prendre grand plaisir à; **to be the ~ of** faire les
délices or la joie de

delighted [dɪ'laɪtɪd] adj: **~ (at** or **with sth)**
ravi(e) (de qch); **to be ~ to do sth/that** être
enchanté(e) or ravi(e) de faire qch/que; **I'd be ~**
j'en serais enchanté or ravi

delightful [dɪ'laɪtful] adj (person) absolument
charmant(e), adorable; (meal, evening)

merveilleux(-euse)

delimit [diːˈlɪmɪt] *vt* délimiter

delineate [dɪˈlɪnɪeɪt] *vt* tracer, esquisser; *(fig)* dépeindre, décrire

delinquency [dɪˈlɪŋkwənsɪ] *n* délinquance *f*

delinquent [dɪˈlɪŋkwənt] *adj, n* délinquant(e)

delirious [dɪˈlɪrɪəs] *adj* (*Med: fig*) délirant(e); **to be ~** délirer

delirium [dɪˈlɪrɪəm] *n* délire *m*

deliver [dɪˈlɪvə^r] *vt* (*mail*) distribuer; (*goods*) livrer; (*message*) remettre; (*speech*) prononcer; (*warning, ultimatum*) lancer; (*free*) délivrer; (*Med: baby*) mettre au monde; (: *woman*) accoucher; **to ~ the goods** (*fig*) tenir ses promesses

deliverance [dɪˈlɪvrəns] *n* délivrance *f*, libération *f*

delivery [dɪˈlɪvərɪ] *n* (*of mail*) distribution *f*; (*of goods*) livraison *f*; (*of speaker*) élocution *f*; (*Med*) accouchement *m*; **to take ~ of** prendre livraison de

delivery note *n* bon *m* de livraison

delivery van, (*US*) **delivery truck** *n* fourgonnette *f or* camionnette *f* de livraison

delta [ˈdɛltə] *n* delta *m*

delude [dɪˈluːd] *vt* tromper, leurrer; **to ~ o.s.** se leurrer, se faire des illusions

deluge [ˈdɛljuːdʒ] *n* déluge *m* ▷ *vt* (*fig*): **to ~ (with)** inonder (de)

delusion [dɪˈluːʒən] *n* illusion *f*; **to have ~s of grandeur** être un peu mégalomane

de luxe [dəˈlʌks] *adj* de luxe

delve [dɛlv] *vi*: **to ~ into** fouiller dans

Dem. *abbr* (*US Pol*) = **democrat; democratic**

demagogue [ˈdɛməgɔg] *n* démagogue *m/f*

demand [dɪˈmɑːnd] *vt* réclamer, exiger; (*need*) exiger, requérir ▷ *n* exigence *f*; (*claim*) revendication *f*; (*Econ*) demande *f*; **to ~ sth (from *or* of sb)** exiger qch (de qn), réclamer qch (à qn); **in ~** demandé(e), recherché(e); **on ~** sur demande

demanding [dɪˈmɑːndɪŋ] *adj* (*person*) exigeant(e); (*work*) astreignant(e)

demarcation [diːmɑːˈkeɪʃən] *n* démarcation *f*

demarcation dispute *n* (*Industry*) conflit *m* d'attributions

demean [dɪˈmiːn] *vt*: **to ~ o.s.** s'abaisser

demeanour, (*US*) **demeanor** [dɪˈmiːnə^r] *n* comportement *m*; maintien *m*

demented [dɪˈmɛntɪd] *adj* dément(e), fou (folle)

demilitarized zone [diːˈmɪlɪtəraɪzd-] *n* zone démilitarisée

demise [dɪˈmaɪz] *n* décès *m*

demist [diːˈmɪst] *vt* (*Brit Aut*) désembuer

demister [diːˈmɪstə^r] *n* (*Brit Aut*) dispositif *m* anti-buée *inv*

demo [ˈdɛməu] *n abbr* (*inf*) = **demonstration**; (*protest*) manif *f*; (*Comput*) démonstration *f*

demobilize [diːˈməubɪlaɪz] *vt* démobiliser

democracy [dɪˈmɔkrəsɪ] *n* démocratie *f*

democrat [ˈdɛməkræt] *n* démocrate *m/f*

democratic [dɛməˈkrætɪk] *adj* démocratique; **the D~ Party** (*US*) le parti démocrate

demography [dɪˈmɔgrəfɪ] *n* démographie *f*

demolish [dɪˈmɔlɪʃ] *vt* démolir

demolition [dɛməˈlɪʃən] *n* démolition *f*

demon [ˈdiːmən] *n* démon *m* ▷ *cpd*: **a ~ squash player** un crack en squash; **a ~ driver** un fou du volant

demonstrate [ˈdɛmənstreɪt] *vt* démontrer, prouver; (*show*) faire une démonstration de ▷ *vi*: **to ~ (for/against)** manifester (en faveur de/contre)

demonstration [dɛmənˈstreɪʃən] *n* démonstration *f*; (*Pol etc*) manifestation *f*; **to hold a ~** (*Pol etc*) organiser une manifestation, manifester

demonstrative [dɪˈmɔnstrətɪv] *adj* démonstratif(-ive)

demonstrator [ˈdɛmənstreɪtə^r] *n* (*Pol etc*) manifestant(e); (*Comm: sales person*) vendeur(-euse); (: *car, computer etc*) modèle *m* de démonstration

demoralize [dɪˈmɔrəlaɪz] *vt* démoraliser

demote [dɪˈməut] *vt* rétrograder

demotion [dɪˈməuʃən] *n* rétrogradation *f*

demur [dɪˈməː^r] *vi*: **to ~ (at sth)** hésiter (devant qch); (*object*) élever des objections (contre qch) ▷ *n*: **without ~** sans hésiter; sans faire de difficultés

demure [dɪˈmjuə^r] *adj* sage, réservé(e), d'une modestie affectée

demurrage [dɪˈmʌrɪdʒ] *n* droits *mpl* de magasinage; surestarie *f*

den [dɛn] *n* (*of lion*) tanière *f*; (*room*) repaire *m*

denationalization [diːnæʃnəlaɪˈzeɪʃən] *n* dénationalisation *f*

denationalize [diːˈnæʃnəlaɪz] *vt* dénationaliser

denial [dɪˈnaɪəl] *n* (*of accusation*) démenti *m*; (*of rights, guilt, truth*) dénégation *f*

denier [ˈdɛnɪə^r] *n* denier *m*; **15 ~ stockings** bas de 15 deniers

denigrate [ˈdɛnɪgreɪt] *vt* dénigrer

denim [ˈdɛnɪm] *n* jean *m*; **denims** *npl* (blue-)jeans *mpl*

denim jacket *n* veste *f* en jean

denizen [ˈdɛnɪzn] *n* (*inhabitant*) habitant(e); (*foreigner*) étranger(-ère)

Denmark [ˈdɛnmɑːk] *n* Danemark *m*

denomination [dɪnɔmɪˈneɪʃən] *n* (*money*) valeur *f*; (*Rel*) confession *f*; culte *m*

denominator [dɪˈnɔmɪneɪtə^r] *n* dénominateur *m*

denote [dɪˈnəut] *vt* dénoter

denounce [dɪˈnauns] *vt* dénoncer

dense [dɛns] *adj* dense; (*inf: stupid*) obtus(e), dur(e) *or* lent(e) à la comprenette

densely [ˈdɛnslɪ] *adv*: **~ wooded** couvert(e) d'épaisses forêts; **~ populated** à forte densité (de population), très peuplé(e)

density [ˈdɛnsɪtɪ] *n* densité *f*

dent [dɛnt] *n* bosse *f* ▷ *vt* (*also*: **make a dent in**) cabosser; **to make a ~ in** (*fig*) entamer

dental [ˈdɛntl] *adj* dentaire

dental floss [-flɔs] *n* fil *m* dentaire

dental surgeon n (chirurgien(ne)) dentiste
dental surgery n cabinet m de dentiste
dentist ['dɛntɪst] n dentiste m/f; **~'s surgery** (Brit) cabinet m de dentiste
dentistry ['dɛntɪstrɪ] n art m dentaire
dentures ['dɛntʃəz] npl dentier msg
denunciation [dɪnʌnsɪ'eɪʃən] n dénonciation f
deny [dɪ'naɪ] vt nier; (refuse) refuser; (disown) renier; **he denies having said it** il nie l'avoir dit
deodorant [diː'əudərənt] n désodorisant m, déodorant m
depart [dɪ'paːt] vi partir; **to ~ from** (leave) quitter, partir de; (fig: differ from) s'écarter de
departed [dɪ'paːtɪd] adj (dead) défunt(e); **the (dear) ~** le défunt/la défunte/les défunts
department [dɪ'paːtmənt] n (Comm) rayon m; (Scol) section f; (Pol) ministère m, département m; **that's not my ~** (fig) ce n'est pas mon domaine or ma compétence, ce n'est pas mon rayon; **D~ of State** (US) Département d'État
departmental [diːpaːt'mɛntl] adj d'une or de la section; d'un or du ministère, d'un or du département; **~ manager** chef m de service; (in shop) chef de rayon
department store n grand magasin
departure [dɪ'paːtʃər] n départ m; (fig): **~ from** écart m par rapport à; **a new ~** une nouvelle voie
departure lounge n salle f de départ
depend [dɪ'pɛnd] vi: **to ~ (up)on** dépendre de; (rely on) compter sur; (financially) dépendre (financièrement) de, être à la charge de; **it ~s** cela dépend; **~ing on the result ...** selon le résultat ...
dependable [dɪ'pɛndəbl] adj sûr(e), digne de confiance
dependant [dɪ'pɛndənt] n personne f à charge
dependence [dɪ'pɛndəns] n dépendance f
dependent [dɪ'pɛndənt] adj: **to be ~ (on)** dépendre (de) ▷ n = **dependant**
depict [dɪ'pɪkt] vt (in picture) représenter; (in words) (dé)peindre, décrire
depilatory [dɪ'pɪlətrɪ] n (also: **depilatory cream**) dépilatoire m, crème f à épiler
depleted [dɪ'pliːtɪd] adj (considérablement) réduit(e) or diminué(e)
deplorable [dɪ'plɔːrəbl] adj déplorable, lamentable
deplore [dɪ'plɔːr] vt déplorer
deploy [dɪ'plɔɪ] vt déployer
depopulate [diː'pɔpjuleɪt] vt dépeupler
depopulation ['diːpɔpju'leɪʃən] n dépopulation f, dépeuplement m
deport [dɪ'pɔːt] vt déporter, expulser
deportation [diːpɔː'teɪʃən] n déportation f, expulsion f
deportation order n arrêté m d'expulsion
deportee [diːpɔː'tiː] n déporté(e)
deportment [dɪ'pɔːtmənt] n maintien m, tenue f
depose [dɪ'pəuz] vt déposer
deposit [dɪ'pɔzɪt] n (Chem, Comm, Geo) dépôt m;

(of ore, oil) gisement m; (part payment) arrhes fpl, acompte m; (on bottle etc) consigne f; (for hired goods etc) cautionnement m, garantie f ▷ vt déposer; (valuables) mettre or laisser en dépôt; **to put down a ~ of £50** verser 50 livres d'arrhes or d'acompte; laisser 50 livres en garantie
deposit account n compte m sur livret
depositor [dɪ'pɔzɪtər] n déposant(e)
depository [dɪ'pɔzɪtərɪ] n (person) dépositaire m/f; (place) dépôt m
depot ['dɛpəu] n dépôt m; (US: Rail) gare f
depraved [dɪ'preɪvd] adj dépravé(e), perverti(e)
depravity [dɪ'prævɪtɪ] n dépravation f
deprecate ['dɛprɪkeɪt] vt désapprouver
deprecating ['dɛprɪkeɪtɪŋ] adj (disapproving) désapprobateur(-trice); (apologetic): **a ~ smile** un sourire d'excuse
depreciate [dɪ'priːʃɪeɪt] vt déprécier ▷ vi se déprécier, se dévaloriser
depreciation [dɪpriːʃɪ'eɪʃən] n dépréciation f
depress [dɪ'prɛs] vt déprimer; (press down) appuyer sur, abaisser; (wages etc) faire baisser
depressant [dɪ'prɛsnt] n (Med) dépresseur m
depressed [dɪ'prɛst] adj (person) déprimé(e), abattu(e); (area) en déclin, touché(e) par le sous-emploi; (Comm: market, trade) maussade; **to get ~** se démoraliser, se laisser abattre
depressing [dɪ'prɛsɪŋ] adj déprimant(e)
depression [dɪ'prɛʃən] n (Econ) dépression f
deprivation [dɛprɪ'veɪʃən] n privation f; (loss) perte f
deprive [dɪ'praɪv] vt: **to ~ sb of** priver qn de
deprived [dɪ'praɪvd] adj déshérité(e)
dept. abbr (= department) dép, dépt
depth [dɛpθ] n profondeur f; **in the ~s of** au fond de; au cœur de; au plus profond de; **to be in the ~s of despair** être au plus profond du désespoir; **at a ~ of 3 metres** à 3 mètres de profondeur; **to be out of one's ~** (Brit: swimmer) ne plus avoir pied; (fig) être dépassé(e), nager; **to study sth in ~** étudier qch en profondeur
depth charge n grenade sous-marine
deputation [dɛpju'teɪʃən] n députation f, délégation f
deputize ['dɛpjutaɪz] vi: **to ~ for** assurer l'intérim de
deputy ['dɛpjutɪ] n (replacement) suppléant(e), intérimaire m/f; (second in command) adjoint(e); (Pol) député m; (US: also: **deputy sheriff**) shérif adjoint ▷ adj: **~ chairman** vice-président m; **~ head** (Scol) directeur(-trice) adjoint(e), sous-directeur(-trice); **~ leader** (Brit Pol) vice-président(e), secrétaire adjoint(e)
derail [dɪ'reɪl] vt faire dérailler; **to be ~ed** dérailler
derailment [dɪ'reɪlmənt] n déraillement m
deranged [dɪ'reɪndʒd] adj: **to be (mentally) ~** avoir le cerveau dérangé
derby ['dəːrbɪ] n (US) (chapeau m) melon m
deregulate [dɪ'rɛgjuleɪt] vt libérer, dérégler
deregulation [dɪrɛgju'leɪʃən] n libération f, dérèglement m

derelict ['dɛrɪlɪkt] *adj* abandonné(e), à l'abandon

deride [dɪ'raɪd] *vt* railler

derision [dɪ'rɪʒən] *n* dérision *f*

derisive [dɪ'raɪsɪv] *adj* moqueur(-euse), railleur(-euse)

derisory [dɪ'raɪsərɪ] *adj* (*sum*) dérisoire; (*smile, person*) moqueur(-euse), railleur(-euse)

derivation [dɛrɪ'veɪʃən] *n* dérivation *f*

derivative [dɪ'rɪvətɪv] *n* dérivé *m* ▷ *adj* dérivé(e)

derive [dɪ'raɪv] *vt*: **to ~ sth from** tirer qch de; trouver qch dans ▷ *vi*: **to ~ from** provenir de, dériver de

dermatitis [də:mə'taɪtɪs] *n* dermatite *f*

dermatology [də:mə'tɔlədʒɪ] *n* dermatologie *f*

derogatory [dɪ'rɔgətərɪ] *adj* désobligeant(e), péjoratif(-ive)

derrick ['dɛrɪk] *n* mât *m* de charge, derrick *m*

derv [də:v] *n* (*Brit*) gas-oil *m*, diesel *m*

DES *n abbr* (*Brit*: = *Department of Education and Science*) *ministère de l'éducation nationale et des sciences*

desalination [di:sælɪ'neɪʃən] *n* dessalement *m*, dessalage *m*

descend [dɪ'sɛnd] *vt, vi* descendre; **to ~ from** descendre de, être issu(e) de; **to ~ to** s'abaisser à; **in ~ing order of importance** par ordre d'importance décroissante

▸ **descend on** *vt fus* (*enemy, angry person*) tomber *or* sauter sur; (*misfortune*) s'abattre sur; (*gloom, silence*) envahir; **visitors ~ed (up)on us** des gens sont arrivés chez nous à l'improviste

descendant [dɪ'sɛndənt] *n* descendant(e)

descent [dɪ'sɛnt] *n* descente *f*; (*origin*) origine *f*

describe [dɪs'kraɪb] *vt* décrire

description [dɪs'krɪpʃən] *n* description *f*; (*sort*) sorte *f*, espèce *f*; **of every ~** de toutes sortes

descriptive [dɪs'krɪptɪv] *adj* descriptif(-ive)

desecrate ['dɛsɪkreɪt] *vt* profaner

desert [*n* 'dɛzət, *vb* dɪ'zə:t] *n* désert *m* ▷ *vt* déserter, abandonner ▷ *vi* (*Mil*) déserter

deserted [dɪ'zə:tɪd] *adj* désert(e)

deserter [dɪ'zə:tə^r] *n* déserteur *m*

desertion [dɪ'zɔ:ʃən] *n* désertion *f*

desert island *n* île déserte

deserts [dɪ'zə:ts] *npl*: **to get one's just ~** n'avoir que ce qu'on mérite

deserve [dɪ'zə:v] *vt* mériter

deservedly [dɪ'zə:vɪdlɪ] *adv* à juste titre, à bon droit

deserving [dɪ'zə:vɪŋ] *adj* (*person*) méritant(e); (*action, cause*) méritoire

desiccated ['dɛsɪkeɪtɪd] *adj* séché(e)

design [dɪ'zaɪn] *n* (*sketch*) plan *m*, dessin *m*; (*layout, shape*) conception *f*, ligne *f*; (*pattern*) dessin, motif(s) *m*(*pl*); (*of dress, car*) modèle *m*; (*art*) design *m*, stylisme *m*; (*intention*) dessein *m* ▷ *vt* dessiner; (*plan*) concevoir; **to have ~s on** avoir des visées sur; **well-~ed** *adj* bien conçu(e); **industrial ~** esthétique industrielle

design and technology *n* (*Brit: Scol*) technologie *f*

designate *vt* ['dɛzɪgneɪt] désigner ▷ *adj* ['dɛzɪgnɪt] désigné(e)

designation [dɛzɪg'neɪʃən] *n* désignation *f*

designer [dɪ'zaɪnə^r] *n* (*Archit, Art*) dessinateur(-trice); (*Industry*) concepteur *m*, designer *m*; (*Fashion*) styliste *m/f*

desirability [dɪzaɪərə'bɪlɪtɪ] *n* avantage *m*; attrait *m*

desirable [dɪ'zaɪərəbl] *adj* (*property, location, purchase*) attrayant(e); **it is ~ that** il est souhaitable que

desire [dɪ'zaɪə^r] *n* désir *m* ▷ *vt* désirer, vouloir; **to ~ to do sth/that** désirer faire qch/que

desirous [dɪ'zaɪərəs] *adj*: **~ of** désireux(-euse) de

desk [dɛsk] *n* (*in office*) bureau *m*; (*for pupil*) pupitre *m*; (*Brit: in shop, restaurant*) caisse *f*; (*in hotel, at airport*) réception *f*

desktop computer ['dɛsktɔp-] *n* ordinateur *m* de bureau *or* de table

desk-top publishing ['dɛsktɔp-] *n* publication assistée par ordinateur, PAO *f*

desolate ['dɛsəlɪt] *adj* désolé(e)

desolation [dɛsə'leɪʃən] *n* désolation *f*

despair [dɪs'pɛə^r] *n* désespoir *m* ▷ *vi*: **to ~ of** désespérer de; **to be in ~** être au désespoir

despatch [dɪs'pætʃ] *n, vt* = **dispatch**

desperate ['dɛspərɪt] *adj* désespéré(e); (*fugitive*) prêt(e) à tout; (*measures*) désespéré, extrême; **to be ~ for sth/to do sth** avoir désespérément besoin de qch/de faire qch; **we are getting ~** nous commençons à désespérer

desperately ['dɛspərɪtlɪ] *adv* désespérément; (*very*) terriblement, extrêmement; **~ ill** très gravement malade

desperation [dɛspə'reɪʃən] *n* désespoir *m*; **in (sheer) ~** en désespoir de cause

despicable [dɪs'pɪkəbl] *adj* méprisable

despise [dɪs'paɪz] *vt* mépriser, dédaigner

despite [dɪs'paɪt] *prep* malgré, en dépit de

despondent [dɪs'pɔndənt] *adj* découragé(e), abattu(e)

despot ['dɛspɔt] *n* despote *m/f*

dessert [dɪ'zə:t] *n* dessert *m*

dessertspoon [dɪ'zə:tspu:n] *n* cuiller *f* à dessert

destabilize [di:'steɪbɪlaɪz] *vt* déstabiliser

destination [dɛstɪ'neɪʃən] *n* destination *f*

destine ['dɛstɪn] *vt* destiner

destined ['dɛstɪnd] *adj*: **to be ~ to do sth** être destiné(e) à faire qch; **~ for London** à destination de Londres

destiny ['dɛstɪnɪ] *n* destinée *f*, destin *m*

destitute ['dɛstɪtju:t] *adj* indigent(e), dans le dénuement; **~ of** dépourvu(e) *or* dénué(e) de

destroy [dɪs'trɔɪ] *vt* détruire; (*injured horse*) abattre; (*dog*) faire piquer

destroyer [dɪs'trɔɪə^r] *n* (*Naut*) contre-torpilleur *m*

destruction [dɪs'trʌkʃən] *n* destruction *f*

destructive [dɪs'trʌktɪv] *adj* destructeur(-trice)

desultory ['dɛsəltərɪ] *adj* (*reading, conversation*) décousu(e); (*contact*) irrégulier(-ière)

detach [dɪ'tætʃ] *vt* détacher

detachable [dɪ'tætʃəbl] *adj* amovible,

détachable
detached [dɪ'tætʃt] *adj* (*attitude*) détaché(e)
detached house *n* pavillon *m* maison(nette) (individuelle)
detachment [dɪ'tætʃmənt] *n* (*Mil*) détachement *m*; (*fig*) détachement, indifférence *f*
detail ['diːteɪl] *n* détail *m*; (*Mil*) détachement *m* ▷ *vt* raconter en détail, énumérer; (*Mil*): **to ~ sb (for)** affecter qn (à), détacher qn (pour); **in ~** en détail; **to go into ~(s)** entrer dans les détails
detailed ['diːteɪld] *adj* détaillé(e)
detain [dɪ'teɪn] *vt* retenir; (*in captivity*) détenir; (*in hospital*) hospitaliser
detainee [diːteɪ'niː] *n* détenu(e)
detect [dɪ'tɛkt] *vt* déceler, percevoir; (*Med, Police*) dépister; (*Mil, Radar, Tech*) détecter
detection [dɪ'tɛkʃən] *n* découverte *f*; (*Med, Police*) dépistage *m*; (*Mil, Radar, Tech*) détection *f*; **to escape ~** échapper aux recherches, éviter d'être découvert(e); (*mistake*) passer inaperçu(e); **crime ~** le dépistage des criminels
detective [dɪ'tɛktɪv] *n* agent *m* de la sûreté, policier *m*; **private ~** détective privé
detective story *n* roman policier
detector [dɪ'tɛktər] *n* détecteur *m*
détente [deɪ'tɑːnt] *n* détente *f*
detention [dɪ'tɛnʃən] *n* détention *f*; (*Scol*) retenue *f*, consigne *f*
deter [dɪ'təːr] *vt* dissuader
detergent [dɪ'təːdʒənt] *n* détersif *m*, détergent *m*
deteriorate [dɪ'tɪərɪəreɪt] *vi* se détériorer, se dégrader
deterioration [dɪtɪərɪə'reɪʃən] *n* détérioration *f*
determination [dɪtəːmɪ'neɪʃən] *n* détermination *f*
determine [dɪ'təːmɪn] *vt* déterminer; **to ~ to do** résoudre de faire, se déterminer à faire
determined [dɪ'təːmɪnd] *adj* (*person*) déterminé(e), décidé(e); (*quantity*) déterminé, établi(e); (*effort*) très gros(se); **~ to do** bien décidé à faire
deterrence [dɪ'tɛrns] *n* dissuasion *f*
deterrent [dɪ'tɛrənt] *n* effet *m* de dissuasion; force *f* de dissuasion; **to act as a ~** avoir un effet dissuasif
detest [dɪ'tɛst] *vt* détester, avoir horreur de
detestable [dɪ'tɛstəbl] *adj* détestable, odieux(-euse)
detonate ['dɛtəneɪt] *vi* exploser ▷ *vt* faire exploser *or* détoner
detonator ['dɛtəneɪtər] *n* détonateur *m*
detour ['diːtuər] *n* détour *m*; (*US Aut*: *diversion*) déviation *f*
detract [dɪ'trækt] *vt*: **to ~ from** (*quality, pleasure*) diminuer; (*reputation*) porter atteinte à
detractor [dɪ'træktər] *n* détracteur(-trice)
detriment ['dɛtrɪmənt] *n*: **to the ~ of** au détriment de, au préjudice de; **without ~ to** sans porter atteinte *or* préjudice à, sans conséquences fâcheuses pour
detrimental [dɛtrɪ'mɛntl] *adj*: **~ to**

préjudiciable *or* nuisible à
deuce [djuːs] *n* (*Tennis*) égalité *f*
devaluation [dɪvælju'eɪʃən] *n* dévaluation *f*
devalue ['diː'vælju:] *vt* dévaluer
devastate ['dɛvəsteɪt] *vt* dévaster; **he was ~d by the news** cette nouvelle lui a porté un coup terrible
devastating ['dɛvəsteɪtɪŋ] *adj* dévastateur(-trice); (*news*) accablant(e)
devastation [dɛvəs'teɪʃən] *n* dévastation *f*
develop [dɪ'vɛləp] *vt* (*gen*) développer; (*disease*) commencer à souffrir de; (*habit*) contracter; (*resources*) mettre en valeur, exploiter; (*land*) aménager ▷ *vi* se développer; (*situation, disease*: *evolve*) évoluer; (*facts, symptoms*: *appear*) se manifester, se produire; **can you ~ this film?** pouvez-vous développer cette pellicule?; **to ~ a taste for sth** prendre goût à qch; **to ~ into** devenir
developer [dɪ'vɛləpər] *n* (*Phot*) révélateur *m*; (*of land*) promoteur *m*; (*also*: **property developer**) promoteur immobilier
developing country [dɪ'vɛləpɪŋ-] *n* pays *m* en voie de développement
development [dɪ'vɛləpmənt] *n* développement *m*; (*of land*) exploitation *f*; (*new fact, event*) rebondissement *m*, fait(s) nouveau(x)
development area *n* zone *f* à urbaniser
deviate ['diːvɪeɪt] *vi*: **to ~ (from)** dévier (de)
deviation [diːvɪ'eɪʃən] *n* déviation *f*
device [dɪ'vaɪs] *n* (*scheme*) moyen *m*, expédient *m*; (*apparatus*) appareil *m*, dispositif *m*; **explosive ~** engin explosif
devil ['dɛvl] *n* diable *m*; démon *m*
devilish ['dɛvlɪʃ] *adj* diabolique
devil-may-care ['dɛvlmeɪ'kɛər] *adj* je-m'en-foutiste
devil's advocate *n*: **to play devil's advocate** se faire avocat du diable
devious ['diːvɪəs] *adj* (*means*) détourné(e); (*person*) sournois(e), dissimulé(e)
devise [dɪ'vaɪz] *vt* imaginer, concevoir
devoid [dɪ'vɔɪd] *adj*: **~ of** dépourvu(e) de, dénué(e) de
devolution [diːvə'luːʃən] *n* (*Pol*) décentralisation *f*
devolve [dɪ'vɔlv] *vi*: **to ~ (up)on** retomber sur
devote [dɪ'vəut] *vt*: **to ~ sth to** consacrer qch à
devoted [dɪ'vəutɪd] *adj* dévoué(e); **to be ~ to** être dévoué(e) *or* très attaché(e) à; (*book etc*) être consacré(e) à
devotee [dɛvəu'tiː] *n* (*Rel*) adepte *m/f*; (*Mus, Sport*) fervent(e)
devotion [dɪ'vəuʃən] *n* dévouement *m*, attachement *m*; (*Rel*) dévotion *f*, piété *f*
devour [dɪ'vauər] *vt* dévorer
devout [dɪ'vaut] *adj* pieux(-euse), dévot(e)
dew [djuː] *n* rosée *f*
dexterity [dɛks'tɛrɪtɪ] *n* dextérité *f*, adresse *f*
DfEE *n abbr* (*Brit*: = *Department for Education and Employment*) Ministère de l'éducation et de l'emploi

dg *abbr* (= *decigram*) dg

diabetes [daɪə'biːtiːz] *n* diabète *m*

diabetic [daɪə'bɛtɪk] *n* diabétique *m/f* ▷ *adj* (*person*) diabétique; (*chocolate, jam*) pour diabétiques

diabolical [daɪə'bɔlɪkl] *adj* diabolique; (*inf*: *dreadful*) infernal(e), atroce

diagnose [daɪəg'nəuz] *vt* diagnostiquer

diagnosis (*pl* **diagnoses**) [daɪəg'nəusɪs, -siːz] *n* diagnostic *m*

diagonal [daɪ'ægənl] *adj* diagonal(e) ▷ *n* diagonale *f*

diagram ['daɪəgræm] *n* diagramme *m*, schéma *m*

dial ['daɪəl] *n* cadran *m* ▷ *vt* (*number*) faire, composer; **to ~ a wrong number** faire un faux numéro; **can I ~ London direct?** puis-je *or* est-ce-que je peux avoir Londres par l'automatique?

dial. *abbr* = **dialect**

dialect ['daɪəlɛkt] *n* dialecte *m*

dialling code ['daɪəlɪŋ-], (*US*) **dial code** *n* indicatif *m* (téléphonique); **what's the ~ for Paris?** quel est l'indicatif de Paris?

dialling tone ['daɪəlɪŋ-], (*US*) **dial tone** *n* tonalité *f*

dialogue, (*US*) **dialog** ['daɪəlɔg] *n* dialogue *m*

dialysis [daɪ'ælɪsɪs] *n* dialyse *f*

diameter [daɪ'æmɪtə'] *n* diamètre *m*

diametrically [daɪə'mɛtrɪklɪ] *adv*: **~ opposed** (**to**) diamétralement opposé(e) (à)

diamond ['daɪəmənd] *n* diamant *m*; (*shape*) losange *m*; **diamonds** *npl* (*Cards*) carreau *m*

diamond ring *n* bague *f* de diamant(s)

diaper ['daɪəpə'] *n* (*US*) couche *f*

diaphragm ['daɪəfræm] *n* diaphragme *m*

diarrhoea, (*US*) **diarrhea** [daɪə'riːə] *n* diarrhée *f*

diary ['daɪərɪ] *n* (*daily account*) journal *m*; (*book*) agenda *m*; **to keep a ~** tenir un journal

diatribe ['daɪətraɪb] *n* diatribe *f*

dice [daɪs] *n* (*pl inv*) dé *m* ▷ *vt* (*Culin*) couper en dés *or* en cubes

dicey ['daɪsɪ] *adj* (*inf*): **it's a bit ~** c'est un peu risqué

dichotomy [daɪ'kɔtəmɪ] *n* dichotomie *f*

dickhead ['dɪkhɛd] *n* (*Brit inf!*) tête *f* de nœud (!)

Dictaphone® ['dɪktəfəun] *n* Dictaphone® *m*

dictate [*vb* dɪk'teɪt, *n* 'dɪkteɪt] *vt* dicter ▷ *vi*: **to ~ to** (*person*) imposer sa volonté à, régenter; **I won't be ~d to** je n'ai d'ordres à recevoir de personne ▷ *n* injonction *f*

dictation [dɪk'teɪʃən] *n* dictée *f*; **at ~ speed** à une vitesse de dictée

dictator [dɪk'teɪtə'] *n* dictateur *m*

dictatorship [dɪk'teɪtəʃɪp] *n* dictature *f*

diction ['dɪkʃən] *n* diction *f*, élocution *f*

dictionary ['dɪkʃənrɪ] *n* dictionnaire *m*

did [dɪd] *pt of* **do**

didactic [daɪ'dæktɪk] *adj* didactique

didn't [dɪdnt] = **did not**

die [daɪ] *n* (*pl* **dice**) dé *m*; (*pl* **-s**) coin *m*; matrice *f*;

étampe *f* ▷ *vi* mourir; **to ~ of** *or* **from** mourir de; **to be dying** être mourant(e); **to be dying for sth** avoir une envie folle de qch; **to be dying to do sth** mourir d'envie de faire qch

▸ **die away** *vi* s'éteindre

▸ **die down** *vi* se calmer, s'apaiser

▸ **die out** *vi* disparaître, s'éteindre

diehard ['daɪhɑːd] *n* réactionnaire *m/f*, jusqu'au-boutiste *m/f*

diesel ['diːzl] *n* (*vehicle*) diesel *m*; (*also*: **diesel oil**) carburant *m* diesel, gas-oil *m*

diesel engine *n* moteur *m* diesel

diesel fuel, diesel oil *n* carburant *m* diesel

diet ['daɪət] *n* alimentation *f*; (*restricted food*) régime *m* ▷ *vi* (*also*: **be on a diet**) suivre un régime; **to live on a ~ of** se nourrir de

dietician [daɪə'tɪʃən] *n* diététicien(ne)

differ ['dɪfə'] *vi*: **to ~ from sth** (*be different*) être différent(e) de qch, différer de qch; **to ~ from sb over sth** ne pas être d'accord avec qn au sujet de qch

difference ['dɪfrəns] *n* différence *f*; (*quarrel*) différend *m*, désaccord *m*; **it makes no ~ to me** cela m'est égal, cela m'est indifférent; **to settle one's ~s** résoudre la situation

different ['dɪfrənt] *adj* différent(e)

differential [dɪfə'rɛnʃəl] *n* (*Aut, wages*) différentiel *m*

differentiate [dɪfə'rɛnʃɪeɪt] *vt* différencier ▷ *vi* se différencier; **to ~ between** faire une différence entre

differently ['dɪfrəntlɪ] *adv* différemment

difficult ['dɪfɪkəlt] *adj* difficile; **~ to understand** difficile à comprendre

difficulty ['dɪfɪkəltɪ] *n* difficulté *f*; **to have difficulties with** avoir des ennuis *or* problèmes avec; **to be in ~** avoir des difficultés, avoir des problèmes

diffidence ['dɪfɪdəns] *n* manque *m* de confiance en soi, manque d'assurance

diffident ['dɪfɪdənt] *adj* qui manque de confiance *or* d'assurance, peu sûr(e) de soi

diffuse *adj* [dɪ'fjuːs] diffus(e) ▷ *vt* [dɪ'fjuːz] diffuser, répandre

dig [dɪg] *vt* (*pt, pp* **dug** [dʌg]) (*hole*) creuser; (*garden*) bêcher ▷ *n* (*prod*) coup *m* de coude; (*fig*: *remark*) coup de griffe *or* de patte; (*Archaeology*) fouille *f*; **to ~ into** (*snow, soil*) creuser; **to ~ into one's pockets for sth** fouiller dans ses poches pour chercher *or* prendre qch; **to ~ one's nails into** enfoncer ses ongles dans

▸ **dig in** *vi* (*also*: **dig o.s. in**: *Mil*) se retrancher; (: *fig*) tenir bon, se braquer; (*inf*: *eat*) attaquer (un repas *or* un plat *etc*) ▷ *vt* (*compost*) bien mélanger à la bêche; (*knife, claw*) enfoncer; **to ~ in one's heels** (*fig*) se braquer, se buter

▸ **dig out** *vt* (*survivors, car from snow*) sortir *or* dégager (à coups de pelles *or* pioches)

▸ **dig up** *vt* déterrer

digest *vt* [daɪ'dʒɛst] digérer ▷ *n* ['daɪdʒɛst] sommaire *m*, résumé *m*

digestible [dɪ'dʒɛstəbl] *adj* digestible

digestion [dɪ'dʒɛstʃən] *n* digestion *f*
digestive [dɪ'dʒɛstɪv] *adj* digestif(-ive)
digit ['dɪdʒɪt] *n* (*number*) chiffre *m* (*de o à 9*); (*finger*) doigt *m*
digital ['dɪdʒɪtl] *adj* (*system, recording, radio*) numérique, digital(e); (*watch*) à affichage numérique *or* digital
digital camera *n* appareil *m* photo numérique
digital compact cassette *n* cassette *f* numérique
digital TV *n* télévision *f* numérique
dignified ['dɪgnɪfaɪd] *adj* digne
dignitary ['dɪgnɪtərɪ] *n* dignitaire *m*
dignity ['dɪgnɪtɪ] *n* dignité *f*
digress [daɪ'grɛs] *vi*: **to ~ from** s'écarter de, s'éloigner de
digression [daɪ'grɛʃən] *n* digression *f*
digs [dɪgz] *npl* (*Brit inf*) piaule *f*, chambre meublée
dilapidated [dɪ'læpɪdeɪtɪd] *adj* délabré(e)
dilate [daɪ'leɪt] *vt* dilater ▷ *vi* se dilater
dilatory ['dɪlətərɪ] *adj* dilatoire
dilemma [daɪ'lɛmə] *n* dilemme *m*; **to be in a ~** être pris dans un dilemme
diligent ['dɪlɪdʒənt] *adj* appliqué(e), assidu(e)
dill [dɪl] *n* aneth *m*
dilly-dally ['dɪlɪ'dælɪ] *vi* hésiter, tergiverser; traînasser, lambiner
dilute [daɪ'lu:t] *vt* diluer ▷ *adj* dilué(e)
dim [dɪm] *adj* (*light, eyesight*) faible; (*memory, outline*) vague, indécis(e); (*room*) sombre; (*inf: stupid*) borné(e), obtus(e) ▷ *vt* (*light*) réduire, baisser; (*US Aut*) mettre en code, baisser; **to take a ~ view of sth** voir qch d'un mauvais œil
dime [daɪm] *n* (*US*) pièce *f* de 10 cents
dimension [daɪ'mɛnʃən] *n* dimension *f*
-dimensional [dɪ'mɛnʃənl] *adj suffix*: **two~** à deux dimensions
diminish [dɪ'mɪnɪʃ] *vt, vi* diminuer
diminished [dɪ'mɪnɪʃt] *adj*: **~ responsibility** (*Law*) responsabilité atténuée
diminutive [dɪ'mɪnjutɪv] *adj* minuscule, tout(e) petit(e) ▷ *n* (*Ling*) diminutif *m*
dimly ['dɪmlɪ] *adv* faiblement; vaguement
dimmer ['dɪmə'] *n* (*also*: **dimmer switch**) variateur *m*; **dimmers** *npl* (*US Aut*: *dipped headlights*) phares *mpl*, code *inv*; (*parking lights*) feux *mpl* de position
dimple ['dɪmpl] *n* fossette *f*
dim-witted ['dɪm'wɪtɪd] *adj* (*inf*) stupide, borné(e)
din [dɪn] *n* vacarme *m* ▷ *vt*: **to ~ sth into sb** (*inf*) enfoncer qch dans la tête *or* la caboche de qn
dine [daɪn] *vi* dîner
diner ['daɪnə'] *n* (*person*) dîneur(-euse); (*Rail*) = **dining car**; (*US: eating place*) petit restaurant
dinghy ['dɪŋgɪ] *n* youyou *m*; (*inflatable*) canot *m* pneumatique; (*also*: **sailing dinghy**) voilier *m*, dériveur *m*
dingy ['dɪndʒɪ] *adj* miteux(-euse), minable
dining car ['daɪnɪŋ-] *n* (*Brit*) voiture-restaurant *f*, wagon-restaurant *m*

dining room ['daɪnɪŋ-] *n* salle *f* à manger
dining table [daɪnɪŋ-] *n* table *f* de (la) salle à manger
dinner ['dɪnə'] *n* (*evening meal*) dîner *m*; (*lunch*) déjeuner *m*; (*public*) banquet *m*; **~'s ready!** à table!
dinner jacket *n* smoking *m*
dinner party *n* dîner *m*
dinner time *n* (*evening*) heure *f* du dîner; (*midday*) heure du déjeuner
dinosaur ['daɪnəsɔ:'] *n* dinosaure *m*
dint [dɪnt] *n*: **by ~ of (doing) sth** à force de (faire) qch
diocese ['daɪəsɪs] *n* diocèse *m*
dioxide [daɪ'ɔksaɪd] *n* dioxyde *m*
Dip. *abbr* (*Brit*) = **diploma**
dip [dɪp] *n* (*slope*) déclivité *f*; (*in sea*) baignade *f*, bain *m*; (*Culin*) ≈ sauce *f* ▷ *vt* tremper, plonger; (*Brit Aut: lights*) mettre en code, baisser ▷ *vi* plonger
diphtheria [dɪf'θɪərɪə] *n* diphtérie *f*
diphthong ['dɪfθɔŋ] *n* diphtongue *f*
diploma [dɪ'pləumə] *n* diplôme *m*
diplomacy [dɪ'pləuməsɪ] *n* diplomatie *f*
diplomat ['dɪpləmæt] *n* diplomate *m*
diplomatic [dɪplə'mætɪk] *adj* diplomatique; **to break off ~ relations (with)** rompre les relations diplomatiques (avec)
diplomatic corps *n* corps *m* diplomatique
diplomatic immunity *n* immunité *f* diplomatique
dipstick ['dɪpstɪk] *n* (*Brit Aut*) jauge *f* de niveau d'huile
dipswitch ['dɪpswɪtʃ] *n* (*Brit Aut*) commutateur *m* de code
dire [daɪə'] *adj* (*poverty*) extrême; (*awful*) affreux(-euse)
direct [daɪ'rɛkt] *adj* direct(e); (*manner, person*) direct, franc (franche) ▷ *vt* (*tell way*) diriger, orienter; (*letter, remark*) adresser; (*Cine, TV*) réaliser; (*Theat*) mettre en scène; (*order*): **to ~ sb to do sth** ordonner à qn de faire qch ▷ *adv* directement; **can you ~ me to ...?** pouvez-vous m'indiquer le chemin de ...?
direct cost *n* (*Comm*) coût *m* variable
direct current *n* (*Elec*) courant continu
direct debit *n* (*Brit Banking*) prélèvement *m* automatique
direct dialling *n* (*Tel*) automatique *m*
direct hit *n* (*Mil*) coup *m* au but, touché *m*
direction [dɪ'rɛkʃən] *n* direction *f*; (*Theat*) mise *f* en scène; (*Cine, TV*) réalisation *f*; **directions** *npl* (*to a place*) indications *fpl*; **~s for use** mode *m* d'emploi; **to ask for ~s** demander sa route *or* son chemin; **sense of ~** sens *m* de l'orientation; **in the ~ of** dans la direction de, vers
directive [dɪ'rɛktɪv] *n* directive *f*; **a government ~** une directive du gouvernement
direct labour *n* main-d'œuvre directe; employés municipaux
directly [dɪ'rɛktlɪ] *adv* (*in straight line*) directement, tout droit; (*at once*) tout de suite,

immédiatement

direct mail *n* vente *f* par publicité directe

direct mailshot *n* (*Brit*) publicité postale

directness [daɪ'rɛktnɪs] *n* (*of person, speech*) franchise *f*

director [dɪ'rɛktəʳ] *n* directeur *m*; (*board member*) administrateur *m*; (*Theat*) metteur *m* en scène; (*Cine*, TV) réalisateur(-trice); **D~ of Public Prosecutions** (*Brit*) ≈ procureur général

directory [dɪ'rɛktərɪ] *n* annuaire *m*; (*also*: **street directory**) indicateur *m* de rues; (*also*: **trade directory**) annuaire du commerce; (*Comput*) répertoire *m*

directory enquiries, (US) **directory assistance** *n* (*Tel*: *service*) renseignements *mpl*

dirt [dəːt] *n* saleté *f*; (*mud*) boue *f*; **to treat sb like ~** traiter qn comme un chien

dirt-cheap ['dəːt'tʃiːp] *adj* (ne) coûtant presque rien

dirt road *n* chemin non macadamisé *or* non revêtu

dirty ['dəːtɪ] *adj* sale; (*joke*) cochon(ne) ▷ *vt* salir; **~ story** histoire cochonne; **~ trick** coup tordu

disability [dɪsə'bɪlɪtɪ] *n* invalidité *f*, infirmité *f*

disability allowance *n* allocation *f* d'invalidité *or* d'infirmité

disable [dɪs'eɪbl] *vt* (*illness, accident*) rendre *or* laisser infirme; (*tank, gun*) mettre hors d'action

disabled [dɪs'eɪbld] *adj* handicapé(e); (*maimed*) mutilé(e); (*through illness, old age*) impotent(e)

disadvantage [dɪsəd'vɑːntɪdʒ] *n* désavantage *m*, inconvénient *m*

disadvantaged [dɪsəd'vɑːntɪdʒd] *adj* (*person*) désavantagé(e)

disadvantageous [dɪsædvɑːn'teɪdʒəs] *adj* désavantageux(-euse)

disaffected [dɪsə'fɛktɪd] *adj*: **~ (to** *or* **towards)** mécontent(e) (de)

disaffection [dɪsə'fɛkʃən] *n* désaffection *f*, mécontentement *m*

disagree [dɪsə'griː] *vi* (*differ*) ne pas concorder; (*be against, think otherwise*): **to ~ (with)** ne pas être d'accord (avec); **garlic ~s with me** l'ail ne me convient pas, je ne supporte pas l'ail

disagreeable [dɪsə'griːəbl] *adj* désagréable

disagreement [dɪsə'griːmənt] *n* désaccord *m*, différend *m*

disallow ['dɪsə'lau] *vt* rejeter, désavouer; (*Brit Football: goal*) refuser

disappear [dɪsə'pɪəʳ] *vi* disparaître

disappearance [dɪsə'pɪərəns] *n* disparition *f*

disappoint [dɪsə'pɔɪnt] *vt* décevoir

disappointed [dɪsə'pɔɪntɪd] *adj* déçu(e)

disappointing [dɪsə'pɔɪntɪŋ] *adj* décevant(e)

disappointment [dɪsə'pɔɪntmənt] *n* déception *f*

disapproval [dɪsə'pruːvəl] *n* désapprobation *f*

disapprove [dɪsə'pruːv] *vi*: **to ~ of** désapprouver

disapproving [dɪsə'pruːvɪŋ] *adj* désapprobateur(-trice), de désapprobation

disarm [dɪs'ɑːm] *vt* désarmer

disarmament [dɪs'ɑːməmənt] *n*

désarmement *m*

disarming [dɪs'ɑːmɪŋ] *adj* (*smile*) désarmant(e)

disarray [dɪsə'reɪ] *n* désordre *m*, confusion *f*; **in ~** (*troops*) en déroute; (*thoughts*) embrouillé(e); (*clothes*) en désordre; **to throw into ~** semer la confusion *or* le désordre dans (*or* parmi)

disaster [dɪ'zɑːstəʳ] *n* catastrophe *f*, désastre *m*

disastrous [dɪ'zɑːstrəs] *adj* désastreux(-euse)

disband [dɪs'bænd] *vt* démobiliser; disperser ▷ *vi* se séparer; se disperser

disbelief ['dɪsbə'liːf] *n* incrédulité *f*; **in ~** avec incrédulité

disbelieve ['dɪsbə'liːv] *vt* (*person*) ne pas croire; (*story*) mettre en doute; **I don't ~ you** je veux bien vous croire

disc [dɪsk] *n* disque *m*; (*Comput*) = **disk**

disc. *abbr* (*Comm*) = **discount**

discard [dɪs'kɑːd] *vt* (*old things*) se débarrasser de, mettre au rencart *or* au rebut; (*fig*) écarter, renoncer à

disc brake *n* frein *m* à disque

discern [dɪ'səːn] *vt* discerner, distinguer

discernible [dɪ'səːnəbl] *adj* discernable, perceptible; (*object*) visible

discerning [dɪ'səːnɪŋ] *adj* judicieux(-euse), perspicace

discharge *vt* [dɪs'tʃɑːdʒ] (*duties*) s'acquitter de; (*settle: debt*) s'acquitter de, régler; (*waste etc*) déverser; décharger; (*Elec, Med*) émettre; (*patient*) renvoyer (chez lui); (*employee, soldier*) congédier, licencier; (*defendant*) relaxer, élargir ▷ *n* ['dɪstʃɑːdʒ] (*Elec, Med*) émission *f*; (*also*: **vaginal discharge**) pertes blanches; (*dismissal*) renvoi *m*; licenciement *m*; élargissement *m*; **to ~ one's gun** faire feu; **~d bankrupt** failli(e), réhabilité(e)

disciple [dɪ'saɪpl] *n* disciple *m*

disciplinary ['dɪsɪplɪnərɪ] *adj* disciplinaire; **to take ~ action against sb** prendre des mesures disciplinaires à l'encontre de qn

discipline ['dɪsɪplɪn] *n* discipline *f* ▷ *vt* discipliner; (*punish*) punir; **to ~ o.s. to do sth** s'imposer *or* s'astreindre à une discipline pour faire qch

disc jockey *n* disque-jockey *m* (DJ)

disclaim [dɪs'kleɪm] *vt* désavouer, dénier

disclaimer [dɪs'kleɪməʳ] *n* démenti *m*, dénégation *f*; **to issue a ~** publier un démenti

disclose [dɪs'kləuz] *vt* révéler, divulguer

disclosure [dɪs'kləuʒəʳ] *n* révélation *f*, divulgation *f*

disco ['dɪskəu] *n abbr* discothèque *f*

discolour, (US) **discolor** [dɪs'kʌləʳ] *vt* décolorer; (*sth white*) jaunir ▷ *vi* se décolorer; jaunir

discolouration, (US) **discoloration** [dɪskʌlə'reɪʃən] *n* décoloration *f*; jaunissement *m*

discoloured, (US) **discolored** [dɪs'kʌləd] *adj* décoloré(e), jauni(e)

discomfort [dɪs'kʌmfət] *n* malaise *m*, gêne *f*; (*lack of comfort*) manque *m* de confort

disconcert [dɪskən'səːt] *vt* déconcerter,

décontenancer

disconnect [dɪskə'nɛkt] *vt* détacher; (*Elec, Radio*) débrancher; (*gas, water*) couper

disconnected [dɪskə'nɛktɪd] *adj* (*speech, thoughts*) décousu(e), peu cohérent(e)

disconsolate [dɪs'kɔnsəlɪt] *adj* inconsolable

discontent [dɪskən'tɛnt] *n* mécontentement *m*

discontented [dɪskən'tɛntɪd] *adj* mécontent(e)

discontinue [dɪskən'tɪnjuː] *vt* cesser, interrompre; **"~d"** (*Comm*) "fin de série"

discord ['dɪskɔːd] *n* discorde *f*, dissension *f*; (*Mus*) dissonance *f*

discordant [dɪs'kɔːdənt] *adj* discordant(e), dissonant(e)

discount *n* ['dɪskaunt] remise *f*, rabais *m* ▷ *vt* [dɪs'kaunt] (*report etc*) ne pas tenir compte de; **to give sb a ~ on sth** faire une remise *or* un rabais à qn sur qch; **~ for cash** escompte *f* au comptant; **at a ~** avec une remise *or* réduction, au rabais

discount house *n* (*Finance*) banque *f* d'escompte; (*Comm: also:* **discount store**) magasin *m* de discount

discount rate *n* taux *m* de remise

discourage [dɪs'kʌrɪdʒ] *vt* décourager; (*dissuade, deter*) dissuader, décourager

discouragement [dɪs'kʌrɪdʒmənt] *n* (*depression*) découragement *m*; **to act as a ~ to sb** dissuader qn

discouraging [dɪs'kʌrɪdʒɪŋ] *adj* décourageant(e)

discourteous [dɪs'kəːtɪəs] *adj* incivil(e), discourtois(e)

discover [dɪs'kʌvər] *vt* découvrir

discovery [dɪs'kʌvərɪ] *n* découverte *f*

discredit [dɪs'krɛdɪt] *vt* (*idea*) mettre en doute; (*person*) discréditer ▷ *n* discrédit *m*

discreet [dɪ'skriːt] *adj* discret(-ète)

discreetly [dɪ'skriːtlɪ] *adv* discrètement

discrepancy [dɪ'skrɛpənsɪ] *n* divergence *f*, contradiction *f*

discretion [dɪ'skrɛʃən] *n* discrétion *f*; **at the ~ of** à la discrétion de; **use your own ~** à vous de juger

discretionary [dɪ'skrɛʃənrɪ] *adj* (*powers*) discrétionnaire

discriminate [dɪ'skrɪmɪneɪt] *vi*: **to ~ between** établir une distinction entre, faire la différence entre; **to ~ against** pratiquer une discrimination contre

discriminating [dɪ'skrɪmɪneɪtɪŋ] *adj* qui a du discernement

discrimination [dɪskrɪmɪ'neɪʃən] *n* discrimination *f*; (*judgment*) discernement *m*; **racial/sexual ~** discrimination raciale/sexuelle

discus ['dɪskəs] *n* disque *m*

discuss [dɪ'skʌs] *vt* discuter de; (*debate*) discuter

discussion [dɪ'skʌʃən] *n* discussion *f*; **under ~** en discussion

disdain [dɪs'deɪn] *n* dédain *m*

disease [dɪ'ziːz] *n* maladie *f*

diseased [dɪ'ziːzd] *adj* malade

disembark [dɪsɪm'bɑːk] *vt, vi* débarquer

disembarkation [dɪsɛmbɑː'keɪʃən] *n* débarquement *m*

disembodied ['dɪsɪm'bɔdɪd] *adj* désincarné(e)

disembowel ['dɪsɪm'bauəl] *vt* éviscérer, étriper

disenchanted ['dɪsɪn'tʃɑːntɪd] *adj*: **~ (with)** désenchanté(e) (de), désabusé(e) (de)

disenfranchise ['dɪsɪn'fræntʃaɪz] *vt* priver du droit de vote; (*Comm*) retirer la franchise à

disengage [dɪsɪn'geɪdʒ] *vt* dégager; (*Tech*) déclencher; **to ~ the clutch** (*Aut*) débrayer

disentangle [dɪsɪn'tæŋgl] *vt* démêler

disfavour, (*US*) **disfavor** [dɪs'feɪvər] *n* défaveur *f*; disgrâce *f*

disfigure [dɪs'fɪgər] *vt* défigurer

disgorge [dɪs'gɔːdʒ] *vt* déverser

disgrace [dɪs'greɪs] *n* honte *f*; (*disfavour*) disgrâce *f* ▷ *vt* déshonorer, couvrir de honte

disgraceful [dɪs'greɪsful] *adj* scandaleux(-euse), honteux(-euse)

disgruntled [dɪs'grʌntld] *adj* mécontent(e)

disguise [dɪs'gaɪz] *n* déguisement *m* ▷ *vt* déguiser; (*voice*) déguiser, contrefaire; (*feelings etc*) masquer, dissimuler; **in ~** déguisé(e); **to ~ o.s. as** se déguiser en; **there's no disguising the fact that ...** on ne peut pas se dissimuler que ...

disgust [dɪs'gʌst] *n* dégoût *m*, aversion *f* ▷ *vt* dégoûter, écœurer

disgusted [dɪs'gʌstɪd] *adj* dégoûté(e), écœuré(e)

disgusting [dɪs'gʌstɪŋ] *adj* dégoûtant(e), révoltant(e)

dish [dɪʃ] *n* plat *m*; **to do** *or* **wash the ~es** faire la vaisselle
▶ **dish out** *vt* distribuer
▶ **dish up** *vt* servir; (*facts, statistics*) sortir, débiter

dishcloth ['dɪʃklɔθ] *n* (*for drying*) torchon *m*; (*for washing*) lavette *f*

dishearten [dɪs'hɑːtn] *vt* décourager

dishevelled, (*US*) **disheveled** [dɪ'ʃɛvəld] *adj* ébouriffé(e), décoiffé(e), débraillé(e)

dishonest [dɪs'ɔnɪst] *adj* malhonnête

dishonesty [dɪs'ɔnɪstɪ] *n* malhonnêteté *f*

dishonour, (*US*) **dishonor** [dɪs'ɔnər] *n* déshonneur *m*

dishonourable, (*US*) **dishonorable** [dɪs'ɔnərəbl] *adj* déshonorant(e)

dish soap *n* (*US*) produit *m* pour la vaisselle

dishtowel ['dɪʃtauəl] *n* (*US*) torchon *m* (à vaisselle)

dishwasher ['dɪʃwɔʃər] *n* lave-vaisselle *m*; (*person*) plongeur(-euse)

dishy ['dɪʃɪ] *adj* (*Brit inf*) séduisant(e), sexy *inv*

disillusion [dɪsɪ'luːʒən] *vt* désabuser, désenchanter ▷ *n* désenchantement *m*; **to become ~ed (with)** perdre ses illusions (en ce qui concerne)

disillusionment [dɪsɪ'luːʒənmənt] *n* désillusionnement *m*, désillusion *f*

disincentive [dɪsɪn'sɛntɪv] *n*: **it's a ~** c'est démotivant; **to be a ~ to sb** démotiver qn

disinclined ['dɪsɪn'klaɪnd] *adj*: **to be ~ to do sth**

être peu disposé(e) *or* peu enclin(e) à faire qch

disinfect [dɪsɪn'fɛkt] *vt* désinfecter

disinfectant [dɪsɪn'fɛktənt] *n* désinfectant *m*

disinflation [dɪsɪn'fleɪʃən] *n* désinflation *f*

disinformation [dɪsɪnfə'meɪʃən] *n* désinformation *f*

disinherit [dɪsɪn'hɛrɪt] *vt* déshériter

disintegrate [dɪs'ɪntɪgreɪt] *vi* se désintégrer

disinterested [dɪs'ɪntrəstɪd] *adj* désintéressé(e)

disjointed [dɪs'dʒɔɪntɪd] *adj* décousu(e), incohérent(e)

disk [dɪsk] *n* (*Comput*) disquette *f*; **single-/double-sided ~** disquette une face/double face

disk drive *n* lecteur *m* de disquette

diskette [dɪs'kɛt] *n* (*Comput*) disquette *f*

disk operating system *n* système *m* d'exploitation à disques

dislike [dɪs'laɪk] *n* aversion *f*, antipathie *f* ▷ *vt* ne pas aimer; **to take a ~ to sb/sth** prendre qn/qch en grippe; **I ~ the idea** l'idée me déplaît

dislocate ['dɪsləkeɪt] *vt* disloquer, déboîter; (*services etc*) désorganiser; **he has ~d his shoulder** il s'est disloqué l'épaule

dislodge [dɪs'lɔdʒ] *vt* déplacer, faire bouger; (*enemy*) déloger

disloyal [dɪs'lɔɪəl] *adj* déloyal(e)

dismal ['dɪzml] *adj* (*gloomy*) lugubre, maussade; (*very bad*) lamentable

dismantle [dɪs'mæntl] *vt* démonter; (*fort, warship*) démanteler

dismast [dɪs'mɑːst] *vt* démâter

dismay [dɪs'meɪ] *n* consternation *f* ▷ *vt* consterner; **much to my ~** à ma grande consternation, à ma grande inquiétude

dismiss [dɪs'mɪs] *vt* congédier, renvoyer; (*idea*) écarter; (*Law*) rejeter ▷ *vi* (*Mil*) rompre les rangs

dismissal [dɪs'mɪsl] *n* renvoi *m*

dismount [dɪs'maunt] *vi* mettre pied à terre

disobedience [dɪsə'biːdɪəns] *n* désobéissance *f*

disobedient [dɪsə'biːdɪənt] *adj* désobéissant(e), indiscipliné(e)

disobey [dɪsə'beɪ] *vt* désobéir à; (*rule*) transgresser, enfreindre

disorder [dɪs'ɔːdə^r] *n* désordre *m*; (*rioting*) désordres *mpl*; (*Med*) troubles *mpl*

disorderly [dɪs'ɔːdəlɪ] *adj* (*room*) en désordre; (*behaviour, retreat, crowd*) désordonné(e)

disorderly conduct *n* (*Law*) conduite *f* contraire aux bonnes mœurs

disorganized [dɪs'ɔːgənaɪzd] *adj* désorganisé(e)

disorientated [dɪs'ɔːrɪenteɪtɪd] *adj* désorienté(e)

disown [dɪs'əun] *vt* renier

disparaging [dɪs'pærɪdʒɪŋ] *adj* désobligeant(e); **to be ~ about sb/sth** faire des remarques désobligeantes sur qn/qch

disparate ['dɪspərɪt] *adj* disparate

disparity [dɪs'pærɪtɪ] *n* disparité *f*

dispassionate [dɪs'pæʃənət] *adj* calme, froid(e), impartial(e), objectif(-ive)

dispatch [dɪs'pætʃ] *vt* expédier, envoyer; (*deal with: business*) régler, en finir avec ▷ *n* envoi *m*, expédition *f*; (*Mil, Press*) dépêche *f*

dispatch department *n* service *m* des expéditions

dispatch rider *n* (*Mil*) estafette *f*

dispel [dɪs'pɛl] *vt* dissiper, chasser

dispensary [dɪs'pɛnsərɪ] *n* pharmacie *f*; (*in chemist's*) officine *f*

dispense [dɪs'pɛns] *vt* distribuer, administrer; (*medicine*) préparer (et vendre); **to ~ sb from** dispenser qn de
  ▶ **dispense with** *vt fus* se passer de; (*make unnecessary*) rendre superflu(e)

dispenser [dɪs'pɛnsə^r] *n* (*device*) distributeur *m*

dispensing chemist [dɪs'pɛnsɪŋ-] *n* (*Brit*) pharmacie *f*

dispersal [dɪs'pəːsl] *n* dispersion *f*; (*Admin*) déconcentration *f*

disperse [dɪs'pəːs] *vt* disperser; (*knowledge*) disséminer ▷ *vi* se disperser

dispirited [dɪs'pɪrɪtɪd] *adj* découragé(e), déprimé(e)

displace [dɪs'pleɪs] *vt* déplacer

displaced person [dɪs'pleɪst-] *n* (*Pol*) personne déplacée

displacement [dɪs'pleɪsmənt] *n* déplacement *m*

display [dɪs'pleɪ] *n* (*of goods*) étalage *m*; affichage *m*; (*Comput: information*) visualisation *f*; (*: device*) visuel *m*; (*of feeling*) manifestation *f*; (*pej*) ostentation *f*; (*show, spectacle*) spectacle *m*; (*military display*) parade *f* militaire ▷ *vt* montrer; (*goods*) mettre à l'étalage, exposer; (*results, departure times*) afficher; (*pej*) faire étalage de; **on ~** (*exhibits*) exposé(e), exhibé(e); (*goods*) à l'étalage

display advertising *n* publicité rédactionnelle

displease [dɪs'pliːz] *vt* mécontenter, contrarier; **~d** mécontent(e) de

displeasure [dɪs'plɛʒə^r] *n* mécontentement *m*

disposable [dɪs'pəuzəbl] *adj* (*pack etc*) jetable; (*income*) disponible; **~ nappy** (*Brit*) couche *f* à jeter, couche-culotte *f*

disposal [dɪs'pəuzl] *n* (*of rubbish*) évacuation *f*, destruction *f*; (*of property etc: by selling*) vente *f*; (*: by giving away*) cession *f*; (*availability, arrangement*) disposition *f*; **at one's ~** à sa disposition; **to put sth at sb's ~** mettre qch à la disposition de qn

dispose [dɪs'pəuz] *vt* disposer ▷ *vi*: **to ~ of** (*time, money*) disposer de; (*unwanted goods*) se débarrasser de, se défaire de; (*Comm: stock*) écouler, vendre; (*problem*) expédier

disposed [dɪs'pəuzd] *adj*: **~ to do** disposé(e) à faire

disposition [dɪspə'zɪʃən] *n* disposition *f*; (*temperament*) naturel *m*

dispossess ['dɪspə'zɛs] *vt*: **to ~ sb (of)** déposséder qn (de)

disproportion [dɪsprə'pɔːʃən] *n* disproportion *f*

disproportionate [dɪsprə'pɔːʃənət] *adj* disproportionné(e)

disprove [dɪs'pruːv] *vt* réfuter

dispute [dɪs'pjuːt] *n* discussion *f*; (*also*: **industrial dispute**) conflit *m* ▷ *vt* (*question*) contester; (*matter*) discuter; (*victory*) disputer; **to be in** *or* **under** ~ (*matter*) être en discussion; (*territory*) être contesté(e)

disqualification [dɪskwɔlɪfɪ'keɪʃən] *n* disqualification *f*; ~ **(from driving)** (*Brit*) retrait *m* du permis (de conduire)

disqualify [dɪs'kwɔlɪfaɪ] *vt* (*Sport*) disqualifier; **to** ~ **sb for sth/from doing** (*status, situation*) rendre qn inapte à qch/à faire; (*authority*) signifier à qn l'interdiction de faire; **to** ~ **sb (from driving)** (*Brit*) retirer à qn son permis (de conduire)

disquiet [dɪs'kwaɪət] *n* inquiétude *f*, trouble *m*

disquieting [dɪs'kwaɪətɪŋ] *adj* inquiétant(e), alarmant(e)

disregard [dɪsrɪ'gɑːd] *vt* ne pas tenir compte de ▷ *n* (*indifference*): ~ **(for)** (*feelings*) indifférence *f* (pour), insensibilité *f* (à); (*danger, money*) mépris *m* (pour)

disrepair ['dɪsrɪ'pɛəʳ] *n* mauvais état; **to fall into** ~ (*building*) tomber en ruine; (*street*) se dégrader

disreputable [dɪs'rɛpjutəbl] *adj* (*person*) de mauvaise réputation, peu recommandable; (*behaviour*) déshonorant(e); (*area*) mal famé(e), louche

disrepute ['dɪsrɪ'pjuːt] *n* déshonneur *m*, discrédit *m*; **to bring into** ~ faire tomber dans le discrédit

disrespectful [dɪsrɪ'spɛktful] *adj* irrespectueux(-euse)

disrupt [dɪs'rʌpt] *vt* (*plans, meeting, lesson*) perturber, déranger

disruption [dɪs'rʌpʃən] *n* perturbation *f*, dérangement *m*

disruptive [dɪs'rʌptɪv] *adj* perturbateur(-trice)

dissatisfaction [dɪssætɪs'fækʃən] *n* mécontentement *m*, insatisfaction *f*

dissatisfied [dɪs'sætɪsfaɪd] *adj*: ~ **(with)** insatisfait(e) (de)

dissect [dɪ'sɛkt] *vt* disséquer; (*fig*) disséquer, éplucher

disseminate [dɪ'sɛmɪneɪt] *vt* disséminer

dissent [dɪ'sɛnt] *n* dissentiment *m*, différence *f* d'opinion

dissenter [dɪ'sɛntəʳ] *n* (*Rel, Pol etc*) dissident(e)

dissertation [dɪsə'teɪʃən] *n* (*Scol*) mémoire *m*

disservice [dɪs'sə:vɪs] *n*: **to do sb a** ~ rendre un mauvais service à qn; desservir qn

dissident ['dɪsɪdnt] *adj, n* dissident(e)

dissimilar [dɪ'sɪmɪləʳ] *adj*: ~ **(to)** dissemblable (à), différent(e) (de)

dissipate ['dɪsɪpeɪt] *vt* dissiper; (*energy, efforts*) disperser

dissipated ['dɪsɪpeɪtɪd] *adj* dissolu(e), débauché(e)

dissociate [dɪ'səuʃɪeɪt] *vt* dissocier; **to** ~ **o.s. from** se désolidariser de

dissolute ['dɪsəluːt] *adj* débauché(e), dissolu(e)

dissolve [dɪ'zɔlv] *vt* dissoudre ▷ *vi* se dissoudre, fondre; (*fig*) disparaître; **to** ~ **in(to) tears** fondre en larmes

dissuade [dɪ'sweɪd] *vt*: **to** ~ **sb (from)** dissuader qn (de)

distance ['dɪstns] *n* distance *f*; **what's the** ~ **to London?** à quelle distance se trouve Londres?; **it's within walking** ~ on peut y aller à pied; **in the** ~ au loin

distant ['dɪstnt] *adj* lointain(e), éloigné(e); (*manner*) distant(e), froid(e)

distaste [dɪs'teɪst] *n* dégoût *m*

distasteful [dɪs'teɪstful] *adj* déplaisant(e), désagréable

Dist. Atty. *abbr* (*US*) = **district attorney**

distemper [dɪs'tɛmpəʳ] *n* (*paint*) détrempe *f*, badigeon *m*; (*of dogs*) maladie *f* de Carré

distended [dɪs'tɛndɪd] *adj* (*stomach*) dilaté(e)

distil, (*US*) **distill** [dɪs'tɪl] *vt* distiller

distillery [dɪs'tɪlərɪ] *n* distillerie *f*

distinct [dɪs'tɪŋkt] *adj* distinct(e); (*clear*) marqué(e); **as** ~ **from** par opposition à, en contraste avec

distinction [dɪs'tɪŋkʃən] *n* distinction *f*; (*in exam*) mention *f* très bien; **to draw a** ~ **between** faire une distinction entre; **a writer of** ~ un écrivain réputé

distinctive [dɪs'tɪŋktɪv] *adj* distinctif(-ive)

distinctly [dɪs'tɪŋktlɪ] *adv* distinctement; (*specify*) expressément

distinguish [dɪs'tɪŋgwɪʃ] *vt* distinguer ▷ *vi*: **to** ~ **between** (*concepts*) distinguer entre, faire une distinction entre; **to** ~ **o.s.** se distinguer

distinguished [dɪs'tɪŋgwɪʃt] *adj* (*eminent, refined*) distingué(e); (*career*) remarquable, brillant(e)

distinguishing [dɪs'tɪŋgwɪʃɪŋ] *adj* (*feature*) distinctif(-ive), caractéristique

distort [dɪs'tɔːt] *vt* déformer

distortion [dɪs'tɔːʃən] *n* déformation *f*

distract [dɪs'trækt] *vt* distraire, déranger

distracted [dɪs'træktɪd] *adj* (*not concentrating*) distrait(e); (*worried*) affolé(e)

distraction [dɪs'trækʃən] *n* distraction *f*, dérangement *m*; **to drive sb to** ~ rendre qn fou (folle)

distraught [dɪs'trɔːt] *adj* éperdu(e)

distress [dɪs'trɛs] *n* détresse *f*; (*pain*) douleur *f* ▷ *vt* affliger; **in** ~ (*ship*) en perdition; (*plane*) en détresse; ~**ed area** (*Brit*) zone sinistrée

distressing [dɪs'trɛsɪŋ] *adj* douloureux(-euse), pénible, affligeant(e)

distress signal *n* signal *m* de détresse

distribute [dɪs'trɪbjuːt] *vt* distribuer

distribution [dɪstrɪ'bjuːʃən] *n* distribution *f*

distribution cost *n* coût *m* de distribution

distributor [dɪs'trɪbjutəʳ] *n* (*gen: Tech*) distributeur *m*; (*Comm*) concessionnaire *m/f*

district ['dɪstrɪkt] *n* (*of country*) région *f*; (*of town*) quartier *m*; (*Admin*) district *m*

district attorney *n* (*US*) ≈ procureur *m* de la République

district council n (Brit) ≈ conseil municipal; voir article

district nurse n (Brit) infirmière visiteuse

distrust [dɪs'trʌst] n méfiance f, doute m ▷ vt se méfier de

distrustful [dɪs'trʌstful] adj méfiant(e)

disturb [dɪs'təːb] vt troubler; (inconvenience) déranger; **sorry to ~ you** excusez-moi de vous déranger

disturbance [dɪs'təːbəns] n dérangement m; (political etc) troubles mpl; (by drunks etc) tapage m; **to cause a ~** troubler l'ordre public; **~ of the peace** (Law) tapage injurieux or nocturne

disturbed [dɪs'təːbd] adj (worried, upset) agité(e), troublé(e); **to be emotionally ~** avoir des problèmes affectifs

disturbing [dɪs'təːbɪŋ] adj troublant(e), inquiétant(e)

disuse [dɪs'juːs] n: **to fall into ~** tomber en désuétude

disused [dɪs'juːzd] adj désaffecté(e)

ditch [dɪtʃ] n fossé m; (for irrigation) rigole f ▷ vt (inf) abandonner; (person) plaquer

dither ['dɪðər] vi hésiter

ditto ['dɪtəu] adv idem

divan [dɪ'væn] n divan m

divan bed n divan-lit m

dive [daɪv] n plongeon m; (of submarine) plongée f; (Aviat) piqué m; (pej: café, bar etc) bouge m ▷ vi plonger; **to ~ into** (bag etc) plonger la main dans; (place) se précipiter dans

diver ['daɪvər] n plongeur m

diverge [daɪ'vəːdʒ] vi diverger

diverse [daɪ'vəːs] adj divers(e)

diversification [daɪvəːsɪfɪ'keɪʃən] n diversification f

diversify [daɪ'vəːsɪfaɪ] vt diversifier

diversion [daɪ'vəːʃən] n (Brit Aut) déviation f; (distraction, Mil) diversion f

diversionary tactics [daɪ'vəːʃənɪ-] npl tactique fsg de diversion

diversity [daɪ'vəːsɪtɪ] n diversité f, variété f

divert [daɪ'vəːt] vt (Brit: traffic) dévier; (plane) dérouter; (train, river) détourner; (amuse) divertir

divest [daɪ'vɛst] vt: **to ~ sb of** dépouiller qn de

divide [dɪ'vaɪd] vt diviser; (separate) séparer ▷ vi se diviser; **to ~ (between or among)** répartir or diviser (entre); **40 ~d by 5** 40 divisé par 5
▶ **divide out** vt: **to ~ out (between or among)** distribuer or répartir (entre)

divided [dɪ'vaɪdɪd] adj (fig: country, couple) désuni(e); (opinions) partagé(e)

divided highway (US) n route f à quatre voies

divided skirt n jupe-culotte f

dividend ['dɪvɪdɛnd] n dividende m

dividend cover n rapport m dividendes-résultat

dividers [dɪ'vaɪdəz] npl compas m à pointes sèches; (between pages) feuillets mpl intercalaires

divine [dɪ'vaɪn] adj divin(e) ▷ vt (future) prédire; (truth) deviner, entrevoir; (water, metal) détecter la présence de (par l'intermédiaire de la radiesthésie)

diving ['daɪvɪŋ] n plongée (sous-marine)

diving board n plongeoir m

diving suit n scaphandre m

divinity [dɪ'vɪnɪtɪ] n divinité f; (as study) théologie f

division [dɪ'vɪʒən] n division f; (Brit: Football) division f; (separation) séparation f; (Comm) service m; (Brit: Pol) vote m; (also: **division of labour**) division du travail

divisive [dɪ'vaɪsɪv] adj qui entraîne la division, qui crée des dissensions

divorce [dɪ'vɔːs] n divorce m ▷ vt divorcer d'avec

divorced [dɪ'vɔːst] adj divorcé(e)

divorcee [dɪvɔː'siː] n divorcé(e)

divot ['dɪvət] n (Golf) motte f de gazon

divulge [daɪ'vʌldʒ] vt divulguer, révéler

DIY adj, n abbr (Brit) = **do-it-yourself**

dizziness ['dɪzɪnɪs] n vertige m, étourdissement m

dizzy ['dɪzɪ] adj (height) vertigineux(-euse); **to make sb ~** donner le vertige à qn; **I feel ~** la tête me tourne, j'ai la tête qui tourne

DJ n abbr = **disc jockey**

d.j. n abbr = **dinner jacket**

Djakarta [dʒə'kɑːtə] n Djakarta

DJIA n abbr (US Stock Exchange) = **Dow-Jones Industrial Average**

dl abbr (= decilitre) dl

DLit, DLitt n abbr (= Doctor of Literature, Doctor of Letters) titre universitaire

DMus n abbr (= Doctor of Music) titre universitaire

DMZ n abbr = **demilitarized zone**

DNA n abbr (= deoxyribonucleic acid) ADN m

DNA fingerprinting [-'fɪŋgəprɪntɪŋ] n technique f des empreintes génétiques

do abbr (= ditto) d

 KEYWORD

do [duː] (pt **did**, pp **done**) n (inf: party etc) soirée f, fête f; (: formal gathering) réception f
▷ vb **1** (in negative constructions) non traduit; **I don't understand** je ne comprends pas
2 (to form questions) non traduit; **didn't you know?** vous ne le saviez pas?; **what do you think?** qu'en pensez-vous?; **why didn't you come?** pourquoi n'êtes-vous pas venu?
3 (for emphasis, in polite expressions): **people do make mistakes sometimes** on peut toujours se tromper; **she does seem rather late** je trouve qu'elle est bien en retard; **do sit down/ help yourself** asseyez-vous/servez-vous je vous

en prie; **do take care!** faites bien attention à vous!; **I do wish I could go** j'aimerais tant y aller; **but I do like it!** mais si, je l'aime!
4 (*used to avoid repeating vb*): **she swims better than I do** elle nage mieux que moi; **do you agree? — yes, I do/no I don't** vous êtes d'accord? — oui/non; **she lives in Glasgow — so do I** elle habite Glasgow — moi aussi; **he didn't like it and neither did we** il n'a pas aimé ça, et nous non plus; **who broke it? — I did** qui l'a cassé? — c'est moi; **he asked me to help him and I did** il m'a demandé de l'aider, et c'est ce que j'ai fait
5 (*in question tags*): **you like him, don't you?** vous l'aimez bien, n'est-ce pas?; **he laughed, didn't he?** il a ri, n'est-ce pas?; **I don't know him, do I?** je ne crois pas le connaître
▷ *vt* **1** (*gen: carry out, perform etc*) faire; (*visit: city, museum*) faire, visiter; **what are you doing tonight?** qu'est-ce que vous faites ce soir?; **what do you do?** (*job*) que faites-vous dans la vie?; **what did he do with the cat?** qu'a-t-il fait du chat?; **what can I do for you?** que puis-je faire pour vous?; **to do the cooking/ washing-up** faire la cuisine/la vaisselle; **to do one's teeth/hair/nails** se brosser les dents/se coiffer/se faire les ongles
2 (*Aut etc: distance*) faire; (: *speed*) faire du; **we've done 200 km already** nous avons déjà fait 200 km; **the car was doing 100** la voiture faisait du 100 (à l'heure); **he can do 100 in that car** il peut faire du 100 (à l'heure) dans cette voiture-là
▷ *vi* **1** (*act, behave*) faire; **do as I do** faites comme moi
2 (*get on, fare*) marcher; **the firm is doing well** l'entreprise marche bien; **he's doing well/ badly at school** ça marche bien/mal pour lui à l'école; **how do you do?** comment allez-vous?; (*on being introduced*) enchanté(e)!
3 (*suit*) aller; **will it do?** est-ce que ça ira?
4 (*be sufficient*) suffire, aller; **will £10 do?** est-ce que 10 livres suffiront?; **that'll do** ça suffit, ça ira; **that'll do!** (*in annoyance*) ça va *or* suffit comme ça!; **to make do (with)** se contenter (de)
▶ **do away with** *vt fus* abolir; (*kill*) supprimer
▶ **do for** *vt fus* (*Brit inf: clean for*) faire le ménage chez
▶ **do up** *vt* (*laces, dress*) attacher; (*buttons*) boutonner; (*zip*) fermer; (*renovate: room*) refaire; (: *house*) remettre à neuf; **to do o.s. up** se faire beau (belle)
▶ **do with** *vt fus* (*need*): **I could do with a drink/ some help** quelque chose à boire/un peu d'aide ne serait pas de refus; **it could do with a wash** ça ne lui ferait pas de mal d'être lavé; (*be connected with*): **that has nothing to do with you** cela ne vous concerne pas; **I won't have anything to do with it** je ne veux pas m'en mêler; **what has that got to do with it?** quel est le rapport?, qu'est-ce que cela vient faire là-dedans?

▶ **do without** *vi* s'en passer; **if you're late for tea then you'll do without** si vous êtes en retard pour le dîner il faudra vous en passer ▷ *vt fus* se passer de; **I can do without a car** je peux me passer de voiture

DOA *abbr* (= *dead on arrival*) décédé(e) à l'admission
d.o.b. *abbr* = **date of birth**
doc [dɔk] *n* (*inf*) toubib *m*
docile ['dəusaɪl] *adj* docile
dock [dɔk] *n* dock *m*; (*wharf*) quai *m*; (*Law*) banc *m* des accusés ▷ *vi* se mettre à quai; (*Space*) s'arrimer ▷ *vt*: **they ~ed a third of his wages** ils lui ont retenu *or* décompté un tiers de son salaire; **docks** *npl* (*Naut*) docks
dock dues *npl* droits *mpl* de bassin
docker ['dɔkə^r] *n* docker *m*
docket ['dɔkɪt] *n* bordereau *m*; (*on parcel etc*) étiquette *f or* fiche *f* (*décrivant le contenu d'un paquet etc*)
dockyard ['dɔkjɑːd] *n* chantier *m* de construction navale
doctor ['dɔktə^r] *n* médecin *m*, docteur *m*; (*PhD etc*) docteur ▷ *vt* (*cat*) couper; (*interfere with: food*) altérer; (: *drink*) frelater; (: *text, document*) arranger; **~'s office** (*US*) cabinet *m* de consultation; **call a ~!** appelez un docteur *or* un médecin!
doctorate ['dɔktərɪt] *n* doctorat *m*; *voir article*

⬤ **DOCTORATE**
⬤
⬤ Le *doctorate* est le diplôme universitaire le
⬤ plus prestigieux. Il est le résultat d'au
⬤ minimum trois années de recherche et est
⬤ accordé après soutenance d'une thèse
⬤ devant un jury. Le "doctorat" le plus courant
⬤ est le "PhD" (Doctor of Philosophy), accordé
⬤ en lettres, en sciences et en ingénierie, bien
⬤ qu'il existe également d'autres doctorats
⬤ spécialisés (en musique, en droit, etc); voir
⬤ "Bachelor's degree", "Master's degree"

Doctor of Philosophy *n* (*degree*) doctorat *m*; (*person*) titulaire *m/f* d'un doctorat
docudrama ['dɔkjudrɑːmə] *n* (*TV*) docudrame *m*
document ['dɔkjumənt] *n* document *m* ▷ *vt* ['dɔkjumɛnt] documenter
documentary [dɔkju'mɛntərɪ] *adj, n* documentaire (*m*)
documentation [dɔkjumən'teɪʃən] *n* documentation *f*
DOD *n abbr* (*US*) = **Department of Defense**
doddering ['dɔdərɪŋ] *adj* (*senile*) gâteux(-euse)
doddery ['dɔdərɪ] *adj* branlant(e)
doddle ['dɔdl] *n*: **it's a ~** (*inf*) c'est simple comme bonjour, c'est du gâteau
Dodecanese [dəudɪkə'niːz] *n*, **Dodecanese Islands** *npl* Dodécanèse *m*
dodge [dɔdʒ] *n* truc *m*; combine *f* ▷ *vt* esquiver,

éviter ▷ *vi* faire un saut de côté; (*Sport*) faire une esquive; **to ~ out of the way** s'esquiver; **to ~ through the traffic** se faufiler *or* faire de savantes manœuvres entre les voitures

dodgems ['dɔdʒəmz] *npl* (*Brit*) autos tamponneuses

dodgy ['dɔdʒɪ] *adj* (*inf: uncertain*) douteux(-euse); (: *shady*) louche

DOE *n abbr* (*Brit*) = **Department of the Environment**; (*US*) = **Department of Energy**

doe [dəu] *n* (*deer*) biche *f*; (*rabbit*) lapine *f*

does [dʌz] *vb see* **do**

doesn't ['dʌznt] = **does not**

dog [dɔg] *n* chien(ne) ▷ *vt* (*follow closely*) suivre de près, ne pas lâcher d'une semelle; (*fig: memory etc*) poursuivre, harceler; **to go to the ~s** (*nation etc*) aller à vau-l'eau

dog biscuits *npl* biscuits *mpl* pour chien

dog collar *n* collier *m* de chien; (*fig*) faux-col *m* d'ecclésiastique

dog-eared ['dɔgɪəd] *adj* corné(e)

dog food *n* nourriture *f* pour les chiens *or* le chien

dogged ['dɔgɪd] *adj* obstiné(e), opiniâtre

doggy ['dɔgɪ] *n* (*inf*) toutou *m*

doggy bag ['dɔgɪ-] *n petit sac pour emporter les restes*

dogma ['dɔgmə] *n* dogme *m*

dogmatic [dɔg'mætɪk] *adj* dogmatique

do-gooder [du:'gudəʳ] *n* (*pej*) faiseur(-euse) de bonnes œuvres

dogsbody ['dɔgzbɔdɪ] *n* (*Brit*) bonne *f* à tout faire, tâcheron *m*

doily ['dɔɪlɪ] *n* dessus *m* d'assiette

doing ['duɪŋ] *n*: **this is your ~** c'est votre travail, c'est vous qui avez fait ça

doings ['duɪŋz] *npl* activités *fpl*

do-it-yourself ['du:ɪtjɔː'sɛlf] *n* bricolage *m*

doldrums ['dɔldrəmz] *npl*: **to be in the ~** avoir le cafard; être dans le marasme

dole [dəul] *n* (*Brit: payment*) allocation *f* de chômage; **on the ~** au chômage

▶ **dole out** *vt* donner au compte-goutte

doleful ['dəulful] *adj* triste, lugubre

doll [dɔl] *n* poupée *f*

▶ **doll up** *vt*: **to ~ o.s. up** se faire beau (belle)

dollar ['dɔləʳ] *n* dollar *m*

dollop ['dɔləp] *n* (*of butter, cheese*) bon morceau; (*of cream*) bonne cuillerée

dolly ['dɔlɪ] *n* poupée *f*

dolphin ['dɔlfɪn] *n* dauphin *m*

domain [də'meɪn] *n* (*also fig*) domaine *m*

dome [dəum] *n* dôme *m*

domestic [də'mɛstɪk] *adj* (*duty, happiness*) familial(e); (*policy, affairs, flight*) intérieur(e); (*news*) national(e); (*animal*) domestique

domesticated [də'mɛstɪkeɪtɪd] *adj* domestiqué(e); (*pej*) d'intérieur; **he's very ~** il participe volontiers aux tâches ménagères; question ménage, il est très organisé

domesticity [dəumɛs'tɪsɪtɪ] *n* vie *f* de famille

domestic servant *n* domestique *m/f*

domicile ['dɔmɪsaɪl] *n* domicile *m*

dominant ['dɔmɪnənt] *adj* dominant(e)

dominate ['dɔmɪneɪt] *vt* dominer

domination [dɔmɪ'neɪʃən] *n* domination *f*

domineering [dɔmɪ'nɪərɪŋ] *adj* dominateur(-trice), autoritaire

Dominican Republic [də'mɪnɪkən-] *n* République Dominicaine

dominion [də'mɪnɪən] *n* domination *f*; territoire *m*; dominion *m*

domino ['dɔmɪnəu] (*pl* **-es**) *n* domino *m*

dominoes ['dɔmɪnəuz] *n* (*game*) dominos *mpl*

don [dɔn] *n* (*Brit*) professeur *m* d'université ▷ *vt* revêtir

donate [də'neɪt] *vt* faire don de, donner

donation [də'neɪʃən] *n* donation *f*, don *m*

done [dʌn] *pp of* **do**

donkey ['dɔŋkɪ] *n* âne *m*

donkey-work ['dɔŋkɪwəːk] *n* (*Brit inf*) le gros du travail, le plus dur (du travail)

donor ['dəunəʳ] *n* (*of blood etc*) donneur(-euse); (*to charity*) donateur(-trice)

donor card *n* carte *f* de don d'organes

don't [dəunt] = **do not**

donut ['dəunʌt] (*US*) *n* = **doughnut**

doodle ['du:dl] *n* griffonnage *m*, gribouillage *m* ▷ *vi* griffonner, gribouiller

doom [du:m] *n* (*fate*) destin *m*; (*ruin*) ruine *f* ▷ *vt*: **to be ~ed to failure** être voué(e) à l'échec

doomsday ['du:mzdeɪ] *n* le Jugement dernier

door [dɔːʳ] *n* porte *f*; (*Rail, car*) portière *f*; **to go from ~ to ~** aller de porte en porte

doorbell ['dɔːbɛl] *n* sonnette *f*

door handle *n* poignée *f* de porte; (*of car*) poignée de portière

doorknob ['dɔːnɔb] *n* poignée *f or* bouton *m* de porte

doorman ['dɔːmən] (*irreg*) *n* (*in hotel*) portier *m*; (*in block of flats*) concierge *m*

doormat ['dɔːmæt] *n* paillasson *m*

doorpost ['dɔːpəust] *n* montant *m* de porte

doorstep ['dɔːstɛp] *n* pas *m* de (la) porte, seuil *m*

door-to-door ['dɔːtə'dɔːʳ] *adj*: **~ selling** vente *f* à domicile

doorway ['dɔːweɪ] *n* (*embrasure f de*) porte *f*

dope [dəup] *n* (*inf: drug*) drogue *f*; (: *person*) andouille *f*; (: *information*) tuyaux *mpl*, rancards *mpl* ▷ *vt* (*horse etc*) doper

dopey ['dəupɪ] *adj* (*inf*) à moitié endormi(e)

dormant ['dɔːmənt] *adj* assoupi(e), en veilleuse; (*rule, law*) inappliqué(e)

dormer ['dɔːməʳ] *n* (*also*: **dormer window**) lucarne *f*

dormice ['dɔːmaɪs] *npl of* **dormouse**

dormitory ['dɔːmɪtrɪ] *n* (*Brit*) dortoir *m*; (*US: hall of residence*) résidence *f* universitaire

dormouse (*pl* **dormice**) ['dɔːmaus, -maɪs] *n* loir *m*

DOS [dɔs] *n abbr* (= *disk operating system*) DOS *m*

dosage ['dəusɪdʒ] *n* dose *f*; dosage *m*; (*on label*) posologie *f*

dose [dəus] *n* dose *f*; (*Brit: bout*) attaque *f* ▷ *vt*: **to ~ o.s.** se bourrer de médicaments; **a ~ of flu** une belle *or* bonne grippe

dosh [dɔʃ] (inf) n fric m
dosser ['dɔsəʳ] n (Brit inf) clochard(e)
doss house ['dɔs-] n (Brit) asile m de nuit
DOT n abbr (US) = **Department of Transportation**
dot [dɔt] n point m; (on material) pois m ▷ vt: ~**ted with** parsemé(e) de; **on the** ~ à l'heure tapante
dotcom [dɔt'kɔm] n point com m, pointcom m
dot command n (Comput) commande précédée d'un point
dote [dəut]: **to** ~ **on** vt fus être fou (folle de)
dot-matrix printer [dɔt'meɪtrɪks-] n imprimante matricielle
dotted line ['dɔtɪd-] n ligne pointillée; (Aut) ligne discontinue; **to sign on the** ~ signer à l'endroit indiqué or sur la ligne pointillée; (fig) donner son consentement
dotty ['dɔtɪ] adj (inf) loufoque, farfelu(e)
double ['dʌbl] adj double ▷ adv (fold) en deux; (twice): **to cost** ~ (**sth**) coûter le double (de qch) or deux fois plus (que qch) ▷ n double m; (Cine) doublure f ▷ vt doubler; (fold) plier en deux ▷ vi doubler; (have two uses): **to** ~ **as** servir aussi de; ~ **five two six (5526)** (Brit Tel) cinquante-cinq – vingt-six; **it's spelt with a** – "**l**" ça s'écrit avec deux "l"; **on the** ~, **at the** ~ au pas de course
▶ **double back** vi (person) revenir sur ses pas
▶ **double up** vi (bend over) se courber, se plier; (share room) partager la chambre
double bass n contrebasse f
double bed n grand lit
double-breasted ['dʌbl'brɛstɪd] adj croisé(e)
double-check ['dʌbl'tʃɛk] vt, vi revérifier
double-click ['dʌbl'klɪk] vi (Comput) double-cliquer
double-clutch ['dʌbl'klʌtʃ] vi (US) faire un double débrayage
double cream n (Brit) crème fraîche épaisse
double-cross ['dʌbl'krɔs] vt doubler, trahir
double-decker ['dʌbl'dɛkəʳ] n autobus m à impériale
double declutch vi (Brit) faire un double débrayage
double exposure n (Phot) surimpression f
double glazing n (Brit) double vitrage m
double-page ['dʌblpeɪdʒ] adj: ~ **spread** publicité f en double page
double parking n stationnement m en double file
double room n chambre f pour deux
doubles ['dʌblz] n (Tennis) double m
double whammy [-'wæmɪ] n (inf) double contretemps m
double yellow lines npl (Brit: Aut) double bande jaune marquant l'interdiction de stationner
doubly ['dʌblɪ] adv doublement, deux fois plus
doubt [daut] n doute m ▷ vt douter de; **no** ~ sans doute; **without (a)** ~ sans aucun doute; **beyond** ~ adv indubitablement ▷ adj indubitable; **to** ~ **that** douter que + sub; **I** ~ **it very much** j'en doute fort
doubtful ['dautful] adj douteux(-euse); (person)

incertain(e); **to be** ~ **about sth** avoir des doutes sur qch, ne pas être convaincu de qch; **I'm a bit** ~ je n'en suis pas certain or sûr
doubtless ['dautlɪs] adv sans doute, sûrement
dough [dəu] n pâte f; (inf: money) fric m, pognon m
doughnut ['dəunʌt], (US) **donut** n beignet m
dour [duəʳ] adj austère
douse [dauz] vt (with water) tremper, inonder; (flames) éteindre
dove [dʌv] n colombe f
Dover ['dəuvəʳ] n Douvres
dovetail ['dʌvteɪl] n: ~ **joint** assemblage m à queue d'aronde ▷ vi (fig) concorder
dowager ['dauədʒəʳ] n douairière f
dowdy ['daudɪ] adj démodé(e), mal fagoté(e)
Dow-Jones average ['dau'dʒəunz-] n (US) indice m Dow-Jones
down [daun] n (fluff) duvet m; (hill) colline (dénudée) ▷ adv en bas, vers le bas; (on the ground) par terre ▷ prep en bas de; (along) le long de ▷ vt (enemy) abattre; (inf: drink) siffler; **to fall** ~ tomber; **she's going** ~ **to Bristol** elle descend à Bristol; **to write sth** ~ écrire qch; ~ **there** là-bas (en bas), là au fond; ~ **here** ici en bas; **the price of meat is** ~ le prix de la viande a baissé; **I've got it** ~ **in my diary** c'est inscrit dans mon agenda; **to pay £2** ~ verser 2 livres d'arrhes or en acompte; **England is two goals** ~ l'Angleterre a deux buts de retard; **to walk** ~ **a hill** descendre une colline; **to run** ~ **the street** descendre la rue en courant; **to** ~ **tools** (Brit) cesser le travail; ~ **with X!** à bas X!
down-and-out ['daunəndaut] n (tramp) clochard(e)
down-at-heel ['daunət'hi:l] adj (fig) miteux(-euse)
downbeat ['daunbi:t] n (Mus) temps frappé ▷ adj sombre, négatif(-ive)
downcast ['daunkɑ:st] adj démoralisé(e)
downer ['daunəʳ] n (inf: drug) tranquillisant m; **to be on a** ~ (depressed) flipper
downfall ['daunfɔ:l] n chute f; ruine f
downgrade ['daungreɪd] vt déclasser
downhearted ['daun'hɑ:tɪd] adj découragé(e)
downhill ['daun'hɪl] adv (face, look) en aval, vers l'aval; (roll, go) vers le bas, en bas ▷ n (Ski: also: **downhill race**) descente f; **to go** ~ descendre; (business) péricliter, aller à vau-l'eau
Downing Street ['daunɪŋ-] n (Brit): **10** ~ résidence du Premier ministre; voir article

● **DOWNING STREET**
●
● Downing Street est une rue de Westminster (à
● Londres) où se trouvent la résidence
● officielle du Premier ministre et celle du
● ministre des Finances. Le nom Downing Street
● est souvent utilisé pour désigner le
● gouvernement britannique.

download ['daunləud] n téléchargement m ▷ vt

(*Comput*) télécharger
down-market ['daun'mɑːkɪt] *adj* (*product*) bas de gamme *inv*
down payment *n* acompte *m*
downplay ['daunpleɪ] *vt* (*US*) minimiser (l'importance de)
downpour ['daunpɔːᵊ] *n* pluie torrentielle, déluge *m*
downright ['daunraɪt] *adj* (*lie etc*) effronté(e); (*refusal*) catégorique
Downs [daunz] *npl* (*Brit*): **the ~** collines crayeuses du sud-est de l'Angleterre
downsize [daun'saɪz] *vt* réduire l'effectif de
Down's syndrome [daunz-] *n* mongolisme *m*, trisomie *f*; **a ~ baby** un bébé mongolien *or* trisomique
downstairs ['daun'stɛəz] *adv* (*on or to ground floor*) au rez-de-chaussée; (*on or to floor below*) à l'étage inférieur; **to come ~, to go ~** descendre (l'escalier)
downstream ['daunstriːm] *adv* en aval
downtime ['dauntaɪm] *n* (*of machine etc*) temps mort; (*of person*) temps d'arrêt
down-to-earth ['dauntu'ə:θ] *adj* terre à terre *inv*
downtown ['daun'taun] *adv* en ville ▷ *adj* (*US*): **~ Chicago** le centre commerçant de Chicago
downtrodden ['dauntrɔdn] *adj* opprimé(e)
down under *adv* en Australie *or* Nouvelle Zélande
downward ['daunwəd] *adj, adv* vers le bas; **a ~ trend** une tendance à la baisse, une diminution progressive
downwards ['daunwədz] *adv* vers le bas
dowry ['dauri] *n* dot *f*
doz. *abbr* = **dozen**
doze [dəuz] *vi* sommeiller
▸ **doze off** *vi* s'assoupir
dozen ['dʌzn] *n* douzaine *f*; **a ~ books** une douzaine de livres; **8op a ~** 8op la douzaine; **~s of** des centaines de
DPh, DPhil *n abbr* (= *Doctor of Philosophy*) titre universitaire
DPP *n abbr* (*Brit*) = **Director of Public Prosecutions**
DPT *n abbr* (*Med*: = *diphtheria, pertussis, tetanus*) DCT *m*
DPW *n abbr* (*US*) = **Department of Public Works**
Dr. *abbr* (= *doctor*) Dr; (*in street names*) = **drive**
dr *abbr* (*Comm*) = **debtor**
drab [dræb] *adj* terne, morne
draft [drɑːft] *n* (*of letter, school work*) brouillon *m*; (*of literary work*) ébauche *f*; (*of contract, document*) version *f* préliminaire; (*Comm*) traite *f*; (*US Mil*) contingent *m*; (: *call-up*) conscription *f* ▷ *vt* faire le brouillon de; (*document, report*) rédiger une version préliminaire de; (*Mil: send*) détacher; *see also* **draught**
drag [dræg] *vt* traîner; (*river*) draguer ▷ *vi* traîner ▷ *n* (*Aviat, Naut*) résistance *f*; (*inf*) casse-pieds *m/f*; (*women's clothing*): **in ~** (en) travesti; **to ~ and drop** (*Comput*) glisser-poser
▸ **drag away** *vt*: **to ~ away (from)** arracher *or*

emmener de force (de)
▸ **drag on** *vi* s'éterniser
dragnet ['drægnɛt] *n* drège *f*; (*fig*) piège *m*, filets *mpl*
dragon ['drægn] *n* dragon *m*
dragonfly ['drægənflaɪ] *n* libellule *f*
dragoon [drə'guːn] *n* (*cavalryman*) dragon *m* ▷ *vt*: **to ~ sb into doing sth** (*Brit*) forcer qn à faire qch
drain [dreɪn] *n* égout *m*; (*on resources*) saignée *f* ▷ *vt* (*land, marshes*) drainer, assécher; (*vegetables*) égoutter; (*reservoir etc*) vider ▷ *vi* (*water*) s'écouler; **to feel ~ed (of energy** *or* **emotion)** être miné(e)
drainage ['dreɪnɪdʒ] *n* (*system*) système *m* d'égouts; (*act*) drainage *m*
draining board ['dreɪnɪŋ-] (*US*), **drainboard** ['dreɪnbɔːd] *n* égouttoir *m*
drainpipe ['dreɪnpaɪp] *n* tuyau *m* d'écoulement
drake [dreɪk] *n* canard *m* (mâle)
dram [dræm] *n* petit verre
drama ['drɑːmə] *n* (*art*) théâtre *m*, art *m* dramatique; (*play*) pièce *f*; (*event*) drame *m*
dramatic [drə'mætɪk] *adj* (*Theat*) dramatique; (*impressive*) spectaculaire
dramatically [drə'mætɪklɪ] *adv* de façon spectaculaire
dramatist ['dræmətɪst] *n* auteur *m* dramatique
dramatize ['dræmətaɪz] *vt* (*events etc*) dramatiser; (*adapt*) adapter pour la télévision (*or* pour l'écran)
drank [dræŋk] *pt of* **drink**
drape [dreɪp] *vt* draper; **drapes** *npl* (*US*) rideaux *mpl*
draper ['dreɪpəʳ] *n* (*Brit*) marchand(e) de nouveautés
drastic ['dræstɪk] *adj* (*measures*) d'urgence, énergique; (*change*) radical(e)
drastically ['dræstɪklɪ] *adv* radicalement
draught, (*US*) **draft** [drɑːft] *n* courant *m* d'air; (*of chimney*) tirage *m*; (*Naut*) tirant *m* d'eau; **on ~** (*beer*) à la pression
draught beer *n* bière *f* (à la) pression
draughtboard ['drɑːftbɔːd] *n* (*Brit*) damier *m*
draughts [drɑːfts] *n* (*Brit: game*) (jeu *m* de) dames *fpl*
draughtsman, (*US*) **draftsman** ['drɑːftsmən] (*irreg*) *n* dessinateur(-trice) (industriel(le))
draughtsmanship, (*US*) **draftsmanship** ['drɑːftsmənʃɪp] *n* (*technique*) dessin industriel; (*art*) graphisme *m*
draw [drɔː] (*vb: pt* **drew**, *pp* **~n**) [druː, drɔːn] *vt* tirer; (*picture*) dessiner; (*attract*) attirer; (*line, circle*) tracer; (*money*) retirer; (*wages*) toucher; (*comparison, distinction*): **to ~ (between)** faire (entre) ▷ *vi* (*Sport*) faire match nul ▷ *n* match nul; (*lottery*) loterie *f*; (: *picking of ticket*) tirage *m* au sort; **to ~ to a close** toucher à *or* tirer à sa fin; **to ~ near** *vi* s'approcher; approcher
▸ **draw back** *vi* (*move back*): **to ~ back (from)** reculer (de)
▸ **draw in** *vi* (*Brit: car*) s'arrêter le long du trottoir; (: *train*) entrer en gare *or* dans la station

▶ **draw on** vt (resources) faire appel à; (imagination, person) avoir recours à, faire appel à

▶ **draw out** vi (lengthen) s'allonger ▷ vt (money) retirer

▶ **draw up** vi (stop) s'arrêter ▷ vt (document) établir, dresser; (plan) formuler, dessiner; (chair) approcher

drawback ['drɔːbæk] n inconvénient m, désavantage m

drawbridge ['drɔːbrɪdʒ] n pont-levis m

drawee [drɔːˈiː] n tiré m

drawer [drɔːʳ] n tiroir m ['drɔːəʳ] (of cheque) tireur m

drawing ['drɔːɪŋ] n dessin m

drawing board n planche f à dessin

drawing pin n (Brit) punaise f

drawing room n salon m

drawl [drɔːl] n accent traînant

drawn [drɔːn] pp of **draw** ▷ adj (haggard) tiré(e), crispé(e)

drawstring ['drɔːstrɪŋ] n cordon m

dread [drɛd] n épouvante f, effroi m ▷ vt redouter, appréhender

dreadful ['drɛdful] adj épouvantable, affreux(-euse)

dream [driːm] n rêve m ▷ vt, vi (pt, pp **-ed** or **-t**) [drɛmt] rêver; **to have a ~ about sb/sth** rêver à qn/qch; **sweet ~s!** faites de beaux rêves!

▶ **dream up** vt inventer

dreamer ['driːməʳ] n rêveur(-euse)

dreamt [drɛmt] pt, pp of **dream**

dreamy ['driːmɪ] adj (absent-minded) rêveur(-euse)

dreary ['drɪərɪ] adj triste; monotone

dredge [drɛdʒ] vt draguer

▶ **dredge up** vt draguer; (fig: unpleasant facts) (faire) ressortir

dredger ['drɛdʒəʳ] n (ship) dragueur m; (machine) drague f; (Brit: also: **sugar dredger**) saupoudreuse f

dregs [drɛgz] npl lie f

drench [drɛntʃ] vt tremper; **~ed to the skin** trempé(e) jusqu'aux os

dress [drɛs] n robe f; (clothing) habillement m, tenue f ▷ vt habiller; (wound) panser; (food) préparer ▷ vi: **she ~es very well** elle s'habille très bien; **to ~ o.s., to get ~ed** s'habiller; **to ~ a shop window** faire l'étalage or la vitrine

▶ **dress up** vi s'habiller; (in fancy dress) se déguiser

dress circle n (Brit) premier balcon

dress designer n modéliste m/f, dessinateur(-trice) de mode

dresser ['drɛsəʳ] n (Theat) habilleur(-euse); (also: **window dresser**) étalagiste m/f; (furniture) vaisselier m; (: US) coiffeuse f, commode f

dressing ['drɛsɪŋ] n (Med) pansement m; (Culin) sauce f, assaisonnement m

dressing gown n (Brit) robe f de chambre

dressing room n (Theat) loge f; (Sport) vestiaire m

dressing table n coiffeuse f

dressmaker ['drɛsmeɪkəʳ] n couturière f

dressmaking ['drɛsmeɪkɪŋ] n couture f; travaux mpl de couture

dress rehearsal n (répétition f) générale f

dress shirt n chemise f à plastron

dressy ['drɛsɪ] adj (inf: clothes) (qui fait) habillé(e)

drew [druː] pt of **draw**

dribble ['drɪbl] vi tomber goutte à goutte; (baby) baver ▷ vt (ball) dribbler

dried [draɪd] adj (fruit, beans) sec (sèche); (eggs, milk) en poudre

drier ['draɪəʳ] n = **dryer**

drift [drɪft] n (of current etc) force f; direction f; (of sand etc) amoncellement m; (of snow) rafale f; coulée f; (: on ground) congère f; (general meaning) sens général ▷ vi (boat) aller à la dérive, dériver; (sand, snow) s'amonceler, s'entasser; **to let things ~** laisser les choses aller à la dérive; **to ~ apart** (friends, lovers) s'éloigner l'un de l'autre; **I get** or **catch your ~** je vois en gros ce que vous voulez dire

drifter ['drɪftəʳ] n personne f sans but dans la vie

driftwood ['drɪftwud] n bois flotté

drill [drɪl] n perceuse f; (bit) foret m; (of dentist) roulette f, fraise f; (Mil) exercice m ▷ vt percer; (troops) entraîner; (pupils: in grammar) faire faire des exercices à ▷ vi (for oil) faire un or des forage(s)

drilling ['drɪlɪŋ] n (for oil) forage m

drilling rig n (on land) tour f (de forage), derrick m; (at sea) plate-forme f de forage

drily ['draɪlɪ] adv = **dryly**

drink [drɪŋk] n boisson f; (alcoholic) verre m ▷ vt, vi (pt **drank**, pp **drunk** [dræŋk, drʌŋk]) boire; **to have a ~** boire quelque chose, boire un verre; **a ~ of water** un verre d'eau; **would you like a ~?** tu veux boire quelque chose?; **we had ~s before lunch** on a pris l'apéritif

▶ **drink in** vt (fresh air) inspirer profondément; (story) avaler, ne pas perdre une miette de; (sight) se remplir la vue de

drinkable ['drɪŋkəbl] adj (not dangerous) potable; (palatable) buvable

drink-driving ['drɪŋk'draɪvɪŋ] n conduite f en état d'ivresse

drinker ['drɪŋkəʳ] n buveur(-euse)

drinking ['drɪŋkɪŋ] n (drunkenness) boisson f, alcoolisme m

drinking fountain n (in park etc) fontaine publique; (in building) jet m d'eau potable

drinking water n eau f potable

drip [drɪp] n (drop) goutte f; (sound: of water etc) bruit m de l'eau qui tombe goutte à goutte; (Med: device) goutte-à-goutte m inv; (: liquid) perfusion f; (inf: person) lavette f, nouille f ▷ vi tomber goutte à goutte; (tap) goutter; (washing) s'égoutter; (wall) suinter

drip-dry ['drɪp'draɪ] adj (shirt) sans repassage

drip-feed ['drɪpfiːd] vt alimenter au goutte-à-goutte or par perfusion

dripping ['drɪpɪŋ] n graisse f de rôti ▷ adj: **~ wet** trempé(e)

drive [draɪv] (pt **drove**, pp **driven** [drəuv, 'drɪvn])
n promenade f or trajet m en voiture; (also:
driveway) allée f; (energy) dynamisme m,
énergie f; (Psych) besoin m; pulsion f; (push)
effort (concerté); campagne f; (Sport) drive m;
(Tech) entraînement m; traction f; transmission
f; (Comput: also: **disk drive**) lecteur m de
disquette ▷ vt conduire; (nail) enfoncer; (push)
chasser, pousser; (Tech: motor) actionner;
entraîner ▷ vi (be at the wheel) conduire; (travel by
car) aller en voiture; **to go for a ~** aller faire une
promenade en voiture; **it's 3 hours' ~ from
London** Londres est à 3 heures de route; **left-/
right-hand ~** (Aut) conduite f à gauche/droite;
front-/rear-wheel ~ (Aut) traction f avant/
arrière; **to ~ sb to (do) sth** pousser or conduire
qn à (faire) qch; **to ~ sb mad** rendre qn fou
(folle)
▶ **drive at** vt fus (fig: intend, mean) vouloir dire, en
venir à
▶ **drive on** vi poursuivre sa route, continuer;
(after stopping) reprendre sa route, repartir ▷ vt
(incite, encourage) inciter
▶ **drive out** vt (force out) chasser
drive-by ['draɪvbaɪ] n (also: **drive-by shooting**)
tentative d'assassinat par coups de feu tirés d'une voiture
drive-in ['draɪvɪn] adj, n (esp US) drive-in m
drive-in window n (US) guichet-auto m
drivel ['drɪvl] n (inf) idioties fpl, imbécillités fpl
driven ['drɪvn] pp of **drive**
driver ['draɪvə^r] n conducteur(-trice); (of taxi,
bus) chauffeur m
driver's license n (US) permis m de conduire
driveway ['draɪvweɪ] n allée f
driving ['draɪvɪŋ] adj: **~ rain** n pluie battante
▷ n conduite f
driving force n locomotive f, élément m
dynamique
driving instructor n moniteur m d'auto-école
driving lesson n leçon f de conduite
driving licence n (Brit) permis m de conduire
driving school n auto-école f
driving test n examen m du permis de conduire
drizzle ['drɪzl] n bruine f, crachin m ▷ vi bruiner
droll [drəul] adj drôle
dromedary ['drɒmədərɪ] n dromadaire m
drone [drəun] vi (bee) bourdonner; (engine etc)
ronronner; (also: **drone on**) parler d'une voix
monocorde ▷ n bourdonnement m;
ronronnement m; (male bee) faux-bourdon m
drool [druːl] vi baver; **to ~ over sb/sth** (fig) baver
d'admiration or être en extase devant qn/qch
droop [druːp] vi (flower) commencer à se faner;
(shoulders, head) tomber
drop [drɒp] n (of liquid) goutte f; (fall) baisse f; (: in
salary) réduction f; (also: **parachute drop**) saut
m; (of cliff) dénivellation f; à-pic m ▷ vt laisser
tomber; (voice, eyes, price) baisser; (passenger)
déposer ▷ vi (wind, temperature, price, voice)
tomber; (numbers, attendance) diminuer; **drops**
npl (Med) gouttes; **cough ~s** pastilles fpl pour la
toux; **a ~ of 10%** une baisse or réduction) de 10%;

to ~ anchor jeter l'ancre; **to ~ sb a line** mettre
un mot à qn
▶ **drop in** vi (inf: visit): **to ~ in (on)** faire un saut
(chez), passer (chez)
▶ **drop off** vi (sleep) s'assoupir ▷ vt (passenger)
déposer; **to ~ sb off** déposer qn
▶ **drop out** vi (withdraw) se retirer; (student etc)
abandonner, décrocher
droplet ['drɒplɪt] n gouttelette f
dropout ['drɒpaut] n (from society) marginal(e);
(from university) drop-out m/f, dropé(e)
dropper ['drɒpə^r] n (Med etc) compte-gouttes
m inv
droppings ['drɒpɪŋz] npl crottes fpl
dross [drɒs] n déchets mpl; rebut m
drought [draut] n sécheresse f
drove [drəuv] pt of **drive** ▷ n: **~s of people** une
foule de gens
drown [draun] vt noyer; (also: **drown out**: sound)
couvrir, étouffer ▷ vi se noyer
drowse [drauz] vi somnoler
drowsy ['drauzɪ] adj somnolent(e)
drudge [drʌdʒ] n bête f de somme (fig)
drudgery ['drʌdʒərɪ] n corvée f
drug [drʌg] n médicament m; (narcotic) drogue f
▷ vt droguer; **to be on ~s** se droguer; **he's on ~s**
il se drogue; (Med) il est sous médication
drug addict n toxicomane m/f
drug dealer n revendeur(-euse) de drogue
druggist ['drʌgɪst] n (US) pharmacien(ne)-
droguiste
drug peddler n revendeur(-euse) de drogue
drugstore ['drʌgstɔː^r] n (US) pharmacie-
droguerie f, drugstore m
drum [drʌm] n tambour m; (for oil, petrol) bidon m
▷ vt: **to ~ one's fingers on the table** pianoter or
tambouriner sur la table; **drums** npl (Mus)
batterie f
▶ **drum up** vt (enthusiasm, support) susciter,
rallier
drummer ['drʌmə^r] n (joueur m de) tambour m
drum roll n roulement m de tambour
drumstick ['drʌmstɪk] n (Mus) baguette f de
tambour; (of chicken) pilon m
drunk [drʌŋk] pp of **drink** ▷ adj ivre, soûl(e) ▷ n
(also: **drunkard**) ivrogne m/f; **to get ~** s'enivrer,
se soûler
drunkard ['drʌŋkəd] n ivrogne m/f
drunken ['drʌŋkən] adj ivre, soûl(e); (rage, stupor)
ivrogne, d'ivrogne; **~ driving** conduite f en état
d'ivresse
drunkenness ['drʌŋkənnɪs] n ivresse f;
ivrognerie f
dry [draɪ] adj sec (sèche); (day) sans pluie;
(humour) pince-sans-rire; (uninteresting) aride,
rébarbatif(-ive) ▷ vt sécher; (clothes) faire
sécher ▷ vi sécher; **on ~ land** sur la terre ferme;
to ~ one's hands/hair/eyes se sécher les
mains/les cheveux/les yeux
▶ **dry off** vi, vt sécher
▶ **dry up** vi (river, supplies) se tarir; (: speaker)
sécher, rester sec

dry-clean ['draɪ'kliːn] vt nettoyer à sec
dry-cleaner ['draɪ'kliːnəʳ] n teinturier m
dry-cleaner's ['draɪ'kliːnəz] n teinturerie f
dry-cleaning ['draɪ'kliːnɪŋ] n (process) nettoyage m à sec
dry dock n (Naut) cale sèche, bassin m de radoub
dryer ['draɪəʳ] n (tumble-dryer) sèche-linge m inv; (for hair) sèche-cheveux m inv
dry goods npl (Comm) textiles mpl, mercerie f
dry goods store n (US) magasin m de nouveautés
dry ice n neige f carbonique
dryly ['draɪlɪ] adv sèchement, d'un ton sec
dryness ['draɪnɪs] n sécheresse f
dry rot n pourriture sèche (du bois)
dry run n (fig) essai m
dry ski slope n piste (de ski) artificielle
DSc n abbr (= Doctor of Science) titre universitaire
DSS n abbr (Brit) = **Department of Social Security**
DST abbr (US: = Daylight Saving Time) heure d'été
DT n abbr (Comput) = **data transmission**
DTI n abbr (Brit) = **Department of Trade and Industry**
DTP n abbr (= desktop publishing) PAO f
DT's [diː'tiːz] n abbr (inf: = delirium tremens) delirium tremens m
dual ['djuəl] adj double
dual carriageway n (Brit) route f à quatre voies
dual-control ['djuəlkən'trəul] adj à doubles commandes
dual nationality n double nationalité f
dual-purpose ['djuəl'pə:pəs] adj à double emploi
dubbed [dʌbd] adj (Cine) doublé(e); (nicknamed) surnommé(e)
dubious ['djuːbɪəs] adj hésitant(e), incertain(e); (reputation, company) douteux(-euse); (also: **I'm very dubious about it**) j'ai des doutes sur la question, je n'en suis pas sûr du tout
Dublin ['dʌblɪn] n Dublin
Dubliner ['dʌblɪnəʳ] n habitant(e) de Dublin, originaire m/f de Dublin
duchess ['dʌtʃɪs] n duchesse f
duck [dʌk] n canard m ▷ vi se baisser vivement, baisser subitement la tête ▷ vt plonger dans l'eau
duckling ['dʌklɪŋ] n caneton m
duct [dʌkt] n conduite f, canalisation f; (Anat) conduit m
dud [dʌd] n (shell) obus non éclaté; (object, tool): **it's a ~** c'est de la camelote, ça ne marche pas ▷ adj (Brit: cheque) sans provision; (: note, coin) faux (fausse)
due [djuː] adj (money, payment) dû (due); (expected) attendu(e); (fitting) qui convient ▷ adv: **~ north** droit vers le nord; **dues** npl (for club, union) cotisation f; (in harbour) droits mpl (de port); **~ to** (because of) en raison de; (caused by) dû à; **in ~ course** en temps utile or voulu; (in the end) finalement; **the rent is ~ on the 30th** il faut payer le loyer le 30; **the train is ~ at 8 a.m.** le train est attendu à 8 h; **she is ~ back**

tomorrow elle doit rentrer demain; **he is ~ £10** on lui doit 10 livres; **I am ~ 6 days' leave** j'ai droit à 6 jours de congé; **to give sb his** or **her ~** être juste envers qn
due date n date f d'échéance
duel ['djuəl] n duel m
duet [djuː'ɛt] n duo m
duff [dʌf] adj (Brit inf) nullard(e), nul(le)
duffel bag, duffle bag ['dʌfl-] n sac marin
duffel coat, duffle coat ['dʌfl-] n duffel-coat m
duffer ['dʌfəʳ] n (inf) nullard(e)
dug [dʌg] pt, pp of **dig**
dugout ['dʌgaut] n (Sport) banc m de touche
duke [djuːk] n duc m
dull [dʌl] adj (boring) ennuyeux(-euse); (slow) borné(e); (not bright) morne, terne; (sound, pain) sourd(e); (weather, day) gris(e), maussade; (blade) émoussé(e) ▷ vt (pain, grief) atténuer; (mind, senses) engourdir
duly ['djuːlɪ] adv (on time) en temps voulu; (as expected) comme il se doit
dumb [dʌm] adj muet(te); (stupid) bête; **to be struck ~** (fig) rester abasourdi(e), être sidéré(e)
dumbbell ['dʌmbɛl] n (Sport) haltère m
dumbfounded [dʌm'faundɪd] adj sidéré(e)
dummy ['dʌmɪ] n (tailor's model) mannequin m; (mock-up) factice m, maquette f; (Sport) feinte f; (Brit: for baby) tétine f ▷ adj faux (fausse), factice
dummy run n essai m
dump [dʌmp] n tas m d'ordures; (also: **rubbish dump**) décharge (publique); (Mil) dépôt m; (Comput) listage m (de la mémoire); (inf: place) trou m ▷ vt (put down) déposer; déverser; (get rid of) se débarrasser de; (Comput) lister; (Comm: goods) vendre à perte (sur le marché extérieur); **to be (down) in the ~s** (inf) avoir le cafard, broyer du noir
dumping ['dʌmpɪŋ] n (Econ) dumping m; (of rubbish): **"no ~"** "décharge interdite"
dumpling ['dʌmplɪŋ] n boulette f (de pâte)
dumpy ['dʌmpɪ] adj courtaud(e), boulot(te)
dunce [dʌns] n âne m, cancre m
dune [djuːn] n dune f
dung [dʌŋ] n fumier m
dungarees [dʌŋgə'riːz] npl bleu(s) m(pl); (for child, woman) salopette f
dungeon ['dʌndʒən] n cachot m
dunk [dʌŋk] vt tremper
Dunkirk [dʌn'kə:k] n Dunkerque
duo ['djuːəu] n (gen: Mus) duo m
duodenal [djuː·əu'diːnl] adj duodénal(e); **~ ulcer** ulcère m du duodénum
dupe [djuːp] n dupe f ▷ vt duper, tromper
duplex ['djuːplɛks] n (US: also: **duplex apartment**) duplex m
duplicate n ['djuːplɪkət] double m, copie exacte; (copy of letter etc) duplicata m ▷ adj (copy) en double ▷ vt ['djuːplɪkeɪt] faire un double de; (on machine) polycopier; **in ~** en deux exemplaires, en double; **~ key** double m de la (or d'une) clé
duplicating machine ['djuːplɪkeɪtɪŋ-], **duplicator** ['djuːplɪkeɪtəʳ] n duplicateur m

duplicity [djuː'plɪsɪtɪ] n duplicité f, fausseté f
durability [djuərə'bɪlɪtɪ] n solidité f; durabilité f
durable ['djuərəbl] adj durable; (clothes, metal) résistant(e), solide
duration [djuə'reɪʃən] n durée f
duress [djuə'rɛs] n: **under ~** sous la contrainte
Durex® ['djuərɛks] n (Brit) préservatif (masculin)
during ['djuərɪŋ] prep pendant, au cours de
dusk [dʌsk] n crépuscule m
dusky ['dʌskɪ] adj sombre
dust [dʌst] n poussière f ▷ vt (furniture) essuyer, épousseter; (cake etc): **to ~ with** saupoudrer de
  ▶ **dust off** vt (also fig) dépoussiérer
dustbin ['dʌstbɪn] n (Brit) poubelle f
duster ['dʌstə'] n chiffon m
dust jacket n jacquette f
dustman ['dʌstmən] (irreg) n (Brit) boueux m, éboueur m
dustpan ['dʌstpæn] n pelle f à poussière
dusty ['dʌstɪ] adj poussiéreux(-euse)
Dutch [dʌtʃ] adj hollandais(e), néerlandais(e)
  ▷ n (Ling) hollandais m, néerlandais m ▷ adv: **to go ~** or **dutch** (inf) partager les frais; **the Dutch**
  npl les Hollandais, les Néerlandais
Dutch auction n enchères fpl à la baisse
Dutchman ['dʌtʃmən] (irreg) n Hollandais m
Dutchwoman ['dʌtʃwumən] (irreg) n Hollandaise f
dutiable ['djuːtɪəbl] adj taxable, soumis(e) à des droits de douane
dutiful ['djuːtɪful] adj (child) respectueux(-euse); (husband, wife) plein(e) d'égards, prévenant(e); (employee) consciencieux(-euse)
duty ['djuːtɪ] n devoir m; (tax) droit m, taxe f;
  duties npl fonctions fpl; **to make it one's ~ to do sth** se faire un devoir de faire qch; **to pay ~ on sth** payer un droit or une taxe sur qch; **on ~** de service; (at night etc) de garde; **off ~** libre, pas de service or de garde
duty-free ['djuːtɪ'friː] adj exempté(e) de douane,

hors-taxe; **~ shop** boutique f hors-taxe
duty officer n (Mil etc) officier m de permanence
duvet ['duːveɪ] n (Brit) couette f
DV abbr (= Deo volente) si Dieu le veut
DVD n abbr (= digital versatile or video disc) DVD m
DVD burner n graveur m de DVD
DVD player n lecteur m de DVD
DVD writer n graveur m de DVD
DVLA n abbr (Brit: = Driver and Vehicle Licensing Agency) service qui délivre les cartes grises et les permis de conduire
DVM n abbr (US: = Doctor of Veterinary Medicine) titre universitaire
DVT n abbr = **deep vein thrombosis**
dwarf (pl **dwarves**) [dwɔːf, dwɔːvz] n nain(e)
  ▷ vt écraser
dwell (pt, pp **dwelt**) [dwɛl, dwɛlt] vi demeurer
  ▶ **dwell on** vt fus s'étendre sur
dweller ['dwɛlə'] n habitant(e)
dwelling ['dwɛlɪŋ] n habitation f, demeure f
dwelt [dwɛlt] pt, pp of **dwell**
dwindle ['dwɪndl] vi diminuer, décroître
dwindling ['dwɪndlɪŋ] adj décroissant(e), en diminution
dye [daɪ] n teinture f ▷ vt teindre; **hair ~** teinture pour les cheveux
dyestuffs ['daɪstʌfs] npl colorants mpl
dying ['daɪɪŋ] adj mourant(e), agonisant(e)
dyke [daɪk] n (embankment) digue f
dynamic [daɪ'næmɪk] adj dynamique
dynamics [daɪ'næmɪks] n or npl dynamique f
dynamite ['daɪnəmaɪt] n dynamite f ▷ vt dynamiter, faire sauter à la dynamite
dynamo ['daɪnəməu] n dynamo f
dynasty ['dɪnəstɪ] n dynastie f
dysentery ['dɪsntrɪ] n dysenterie f
dyslexia [dɪs'lɛksɪə] n dyslexie f
dyslexic [dɪs'lɛksɪk] adj, n dyslexique m/f
dyspepsia [dɪs'pɛpsɪə] n dyspepsie f
dystrophy ['dɪstrəfɪ] n dystrophie f; **muscular ~** dystrophie musculaire

Ee

E¹, e [iː] *n (letter)* E, e *m*; *(Mus)*: **E** mi *m*; **E for Edward**, *(US)* **E for Easy** E comme Eugène

E² *abbr (= east)* E ▷ *n abbr (Drugs)* = **ecstasy**

ea. *abbr* = **each**

E.A. *n abbr (US: = educational age)* niveau scolaire

each [iːtʃ] *adj* chaque ▷ *pron* chacun(e); **~ one** chacun(e); **~ other** l'un l'autre; **they hate ~ other** ils se détestent (mutuellement); **you are jealous of ~ other** vous êtes jaloux l'un de l'autre; **~ day** chaque jour, tous les jours; **they have 2 books ~** ils ont 2 livres chacun; **they cost £5 ~** ils coûtent 5 livres (la) pièce; **~ of us** chacun(e) de nous

eager ['iːgəʳ] *adj (person, buyer)* empressé(e); *(lover)* ardent(e), passionné(e); *(keen: pupil, worker)* enthousiaste; **to be ~ to do sth** *(impatient)* brûler de faire qch; *(keen)* désirer vivement faire qch; **to be ~ for** *(event)* désirer vivement; *(vengeance, affection, information)* être avide de

eagle ['iːgl] *n* aigle *m*

E and OE *abbr* = **errors and omissions excepted**

ear [ɪəʳ] *n* oreille *f*; *(of corn)* épi *m*; **up to one's ~s in debt** endetté(e) jusqu'au cou

earache ['ɪəreɪk] *n* mal *m* aux oreilles

eardrum ['ɪədrʌm] *n* tympan *m*

earful ['ɪəful] *n (inf)*: **to give sb an ~** passer un savon à qn

earl [əːl] *n* comte *m*

earlier ['əːlɪəʳ] *adj (date etc)* plus rapproché(e); *(edition etc)* plus ancien(ne), antérieur(e) ▷ *adv* plus tôt

early ['əːlɪ] *adv* tôt, de bonne heure; *(ahead of time)* en avance; *(near the beginning)* au début ▷ *adj* précoce, qui se manifeste *(or se fait)* tôt *or* de bonne heure; *(Christians, settlers)* premier(-ière); *(reply)* rapide; *(death)* prématuré(e); *(work)* de jeunesse; **to have an ~ night/start** se coucher/partir tôt *or* de bonne heure; **take the ~ train** prenez le premier train; **in the ~** *or* **~ in the spring/19th century** au début *or* commencement du printemps/19ème siècle; **you're ~!** tu es en avance!; **~ in the morning** tôt le matin; **she's in her ~ forties** elle a un peu plus de quarante ans *or* de la quarantaine; **at your earliest convenience** *(Comm)* dans les meilleurs délais

early retirement *n* retraite anticipée

early warning system *n* système *m* de première alerte

earmark ['ɪəmɑːk] *vt*: **to ~ sth for** réserver *or* destiner qch à

earn [əːn] *vt* gagner; *(Comm: yield)* rapporter; **to ~ one's living** gagner sa vie; **this ~ed him much praise, he ~ed much praise for this** ceci lui a valu de nombreux éloges; **he's ~ed his rest/reward** il mérite *or* a bien mérité *or* a bien gagné son repos/sa récompense

earned income [əːnd-] *n* revenu *m* du travail

earnest ['əːnɪst] *adj* sérieux(-euse) ▷ *n (also:* **earnest money)** acompte *m*, arrhes *fpl*; **in ~** *(adv)* sérieusement, pour de bon

earnings ['əːnɪŋz] *npl* salaire *m*; gains *mpl*; *(of company etc)* profits *mpl*, bénéfices *mpl*

ear, nose and throat specialist *n* oto-rhino-laryngologiste *m/f*

earphones ['ɪəfəunz] *npl* écouteurs *mpl*

earplugs ['ɪəplʌgz] *npl* boules *fpl* Quiès®; *(to keep out water)* protège-tympans *mpl*

earring ['ɪərɪŋ] *n* boucle *f* d'oreille

earshot ['ɪəʃɔt] *n*: **out of/within ~** hors de portée/à portée de voix

earth [əːθ] *n (gen, also Brit Elec)* terre *f*; *(of fox etc)* terrier *m* ▷ *vt (Brit Elec)* relier à la terre

earthenware ['əːθnwɛəʳ] *n* poterie *f*; faïence *f* ▷ *adj* de *or* en faïence

earthly ['əːθlɪ] *adj* terrestre; *(also:* **earthly paradise)** paradis *m* terrestre; **there is no ~ reason to think that ...** il n'y a absolument aucune raison *or* pas la moindre raison de penser que ...

earthquake ['əːθkweɪk] *n* tremblement *m* de terre, séisme *m*

earth-shattering ['əːθʃætərɪŋ] *adj* stupéfiant(e)

earth tremor *n* secousse *f* sismique

earthworks ['əːθwəːks] *npl* travaux *mpl* de terrassement

earthy ['əːθɪ] *adj (fig)* terre à terre *inv*, truculent(e)

earwax ['ɪəwæks] *n* cérumen *m*

earwig ['ɪəwɪg] *n* perce-oreille *m*

ease [iːz] *n* facilité *f*, aisance *f*; *(comfort)* bien-être *m* ▷ *vt (soothe: mind)* tranquilliser; *(reduce:*

pain, problem) atténuer; (: *tension*) réduire; (*loosen*) relâcher, détendre; (*help pass*): **to ~ sth in/out** faire pénétrer/sortir qch délicatement *or* avec douceur, faciliter la pénétration/la sortie de qch ▷ *vi* (*situation*) se détendre; **with ~** sans difficulté, aisément; **life of ~** vie oisive; **at ~** à l'aise; (*Mil*) au repos
▶ **ease off, ease up** *vi* diminuer; (*slow down*) ralentir; (*relax*) se détendre

easel ['iːzl] *n* chevalet *m*

easily ['iːzɪlɪ] *adv* facilement; (*by far*) de loin

easiness ['iːsɪnɪs] *n* facilité *f*; (*of manner*) aisance *f*; nonchalance *f*

east [iːst] *n* est *m* ▷ *adj* (*wind*) d'est; (*side*) est *inv* ▷ *adv* à l'est, vers l'est; **the E~** l'Orient *m*; (*Pol*) les pays *mpl* de l'Est

eastbound ['iːstbaund] *adj* en direction de l'est; (*carriageway*) est *inv*

Easter ['iːstəʳ] *n* Pâques *fpl* ▷ *adj* (*holidays*) de Pâques, pascal(e)

Easter egg *n* œuf *m* de Pâques

Easter Island *n* île *f* de Pâques

easterly ['iːstəlɪ] *adj* d'est

Easter Monday *n* le lundi de Pâques

eastern ['iːstən] *adj* de l'est, oriental(e); **E~ Europe** l'Europe de l'Est; **the E~ bloc** (*Pol*) les pays *mpl* de l'est

Easter Sunday *n* le dimanche de Pâques

East Germany *n* (*formerly*) Allemagne *f* de l'Est

eastward ['iːstwəd], **eastwards** ['iːstwədz] *adv* vers l'est, à l'est

easy ['iːzɪ] *adj* facile; (*manner*) aisé(e) ▷ *adv*: **to take it** *or* **things ~** (*rest*) ne pas se fatiguer; (*not worry*) ne pas (trop) s'en faire; **to have an ~ life** avoir la vie facile; **payment on ~ terms** (*Comm*) facilités *fpl* de paiement; **that's easier said than done** c'est plus facile à dire qu'à faire, c'est vite dit; **I'm ~** (*inf*) ça m'est égal

easy chair *n* fauteuil *m*

easy-going ['iːzɪˈgəʊɪŋ] *adj* accommodant(e), facile à vivre

easy touch *n* (*inf*): **he's an ~** c'est une bonne poire

eat (*pt* **ate**, *pp* **-en**) [iːt, eɪt, 'iːtn] *vt, vi* manger; **can we have something to ~?** est-ce qu'on peut manger quelque chose?
▶ **eat away** *vt* (*sea*) saper, éroder; (*acid*) ronger, corroder
▶ **eat away at, eat into** *vt fus* ronger, attaquer
▶ **eat out** *vi* manger au restaurant
▶ **eat up** *vt* (*food*) finir (de manger); **it ~s up electricity** ça bouffe du courant, ça consomme beaucoup d'électricité

eatable ['iːtəbl] *adj* mangeable; (*safe to eat*) comestible

eaten ['iːtn] *pp of* **eat**

eau de Cologne ['əʊdəkə'ləʊn] *n* eau *f* de Cologne

eaves [iːvz] *npl* avant-toit *m*

eavesdrop ['iːvzdrɔp] *vi*: **to ~ (on)** écouter de façon indiscrète

ebb [ɛb] *n* reflux *m* ▷ *vi* refluer; (*fig: also*: **ebb away**) décliner; **the ~ and flow** le flux et le reflux; **to be at a low ~** (*fig*) être bien bas(se), ne pas aller bien fort

ebb tide *n* marée descendante, reflux *m*

ebony ['ɛbənɪ] *n* ébène *f*

e-book ['iːbuk] *n* livre *m* électronique

ebullient [ɪ'bʌlɪənt] *adj* exubérant(e)

e-business ['iːbɪznɪs] *n* (*company*) entreprise *f* électronique; (*commerce*) commerce *m* électronique

ECB *n abbr* (= *European Central Bank*) BCE *f* (= *Banque centrale européenne*)

eccentric [ɪk'sɛntrɪk] *adj, n* excentrique *m/f*

ecclesiastic [ɪkliːzɪ'æstɪk], **ecclesiastical** [ɪkliːzɪ'æstɪkl] *adj* ecclésiastique

ECG *n abbr* = **electrocardiogram**

echo ['ɛkəʊ] (*pl* **-es**) *n* écho *m* ▷ *vt* répéter; faire chorus avec ▷ *vi* résonner; faire écho

éclair ['eɪklɛəʳ] *n* éclair *m* (*Culin*)

eclipse [ɪ'klɪps] *n* éclipse *f* ▷ *vt* éclipser

eco- ['iːkəʊ] *prefix* éco-

eco-friendly [iːkəʊ'frɛndlɪ] *adj* non nuisible à *or* qui ne nuit pas à l'environnement

ecological [iːkə'lɔdʒɪkəl] *adj* écologique

ecologist [ɪ'kɔlədʒɪst] *n* écologiste *m/f*

ecology [ɪ'kɔlədʒɪ] *n* écologie *f*

e-commerce [iːkɔmə:s] *n* commerce *m* électronique

economic [iːkə'nɔmɪk] *adj* économique; (*profitable*) rentable

economical [iːkə'nɔmɪkl] *adj* économique; (*person*) économe

economically [iːkə'nɔmɪklɪ] *adv* économiquement

economics [iːkə'nɔmɪks] *n* (*Scol*) économie *f* politique ▷ *npl* (*of project etc*) côté *m or* aspect *m* économique

economist [ɪ'kɔnəmɪst] *n* économiste *m/f*

economize [ɪ'kɔnəmaɪz] *vi* économiser, faire des économies

economy [ɪ'kɔnəmɪ] *n* économie *f*; **economies of scale** économies d'échelle

economy class *n* (*Aviat*) classe *f* touriste

economy class syndrome *n* syndrome *m* de la classe économique

economy size *n* taille *f* économique

ecosystem ['iːkəʊsɪstəm] *n* écosystème *m*

eco-tourism [iːkəʊ'tuərɪzəm] *n* écotourisme *m*

ECSC *n abbr* (= *European Coal & Steel Community*) CECA *f* (= *Communauté européenne du charbon et de l'acier*)

ecstasy ['ɛkstəsɪ] *n* extase *f*; (*Drugs*) ecstasy *m*; **to go into ecstasies over** s'extasier sur

ecstatic [ɛks'tætɪk] *adj* extatique, en extase

ECT *n abbr* = **electroconvulsive therapy**

Ecuador ['ɛkwədɔːʳ] *n* Équateur *m*

ecumenical [iːkjuˈmɛnɪkl] *adj* œcuménique

eczema ['ɛksɪmə] *n* eczéma *m*

eddy ['ɛdɪ] *n* tourbillon *m*

edge [ɛdʒ] *n* bord *m*; (*of knife etc*) tranchant *m*, fil *m* ▷ *vt* border ▷ *vi*: **to ~ forward** avancer petit à petit; **to ~ away from** s'éloigner furtivement de; **on** ~ (fig) crispé(e), tendu(e); **to have the ~ on** (fig) l'emporter (de justesse) sur, être légèrement meilleur que

edgeways ['ɛdʒweɪz] adv latéralement; **he couldn't get a word in** ~ il ne pouvait pas placer un mot

edging ['ɛdʒɪŋ] n bordure f

edgy ['ɛdʒɪ] adj crispé(e), tendu(e)

edible ['ɛdɪbl] adj comestible; (meal) mangeable

edict ['iːdɪkt] n décret m

edifice ['ɛdɪfɪs] n édifice m

edifying ['ɛdɪfaɪɪŋ] adj édifiant(e)

Edinburgh ['ɛdɪnbərə] n Édimbourg

edit ['ɛdɪt] vt (text, book) éditer; (report) préparer; (film) monter; (broadcast) réaliser; (magazine) diriger; (newspaper) être le rédacteur or la rédactrice en chef de

edition [ɪ'dɪʃən] n édition f

editor ['ɛdɪtə'] n (of newspaper) rédacteur(-trice), rédacteur(-trice) en chef; (of sb's work) éditeur(-trice); (also: **film editor**) monteur(-euse); **political/ foreign** ~ rédacteur politique/au service étranger

editorial [ɛdɪ'tɔːrɪəl] adj de la rédaction, éditorial(e) ▷ n éditorial m; **the ~ staff** la rédaction

EDP n abbr = **electronic data processing**

EDT abbr (US: = Eastern Daylight Time) heure d'été de New York

educate ['ɛdjukeɪt] vt (teach) instruire; (bring up) éduquer; **~d at ...** qui a fait ses études à ...

educated ['ɛdjukeɪtɪd] adj (person) cultivé(e)

educated guess n supposition éclairée

education [ɛdju'keɪʃən] n éducation f; (studies) études fpl; (teaching) enseignement m, instruction f; (at university: subject etc) pédagogie f; **primary** or (US) **elementary/secondary ~** instruction f primaire/secondaire

educational [ɛdju'keɪʃənl] adj pédagogique; (institution) scolaire; (useful) instructif(-ive); (game, toy) éducatif(-ive); **~ technology** technologie f de l'enseignement

Edwardian [ɛd'wɔːdɪən] adj de l'époque du roi Édouard VII, des années 1900

EE abbr = **electrical engineer**

EEG n abbr = **electroencephalogram**

eel [iːl] n anguille f

EENT n abbr (US Med) = **eye, ear, nose and throat**

EEOC n abbr (US) = **Equal Employment Opportunity Commission**

eerie ['ɪərɪ] adj inquiétant(e), spectral(e), surnaturel(le)

EET abbr (= Eastern European Time) HEO (= heure d'Europe orientale)

effect [ɪ'fɛkt] n effet m ▷ vt effectuer; **effects** npl (Theat) effets mpl; (property) effets, affaires fpl; **to take ~** (Law) entrer en vigueur, prendre effet; (drug) agir, faire son effet; **to put into ~** (plan) mettre en application or à exécution; **to have an ~ on sb/sth** avoir or produire un effet sur qn/ qch; **in ~** en fait; **his letter is to the ~ that ...** sa lettre nous apprend que ...

effective [ɪ'fɛktɪv] adj efficace; (striking: display, outfit) frappant(e), qui produit or fait de l'effet; (actual) véritable; **to become ~** (Law) entrer en vigueur, prendre effet; **~ date** date f d'effet or d'entrée en vigueur

effectively [ɪ'fɛktɪvlɪ] adv efficacement; (strikingly) d'une manière frappante, avec beaucoup d'effet; (in reality) effectivement, en fait

effectiveness [ɪ'fɛktɪvnɪs] n efficacité f

effeminate [ɪ'fɛmɪnɪt] adj efféminé(e)

effervescent [ɛfə'vɛsnt] adj effervescent(e)

efficacy ['ɛfɪkəsɪ] n efficacité f

efficiency [ɪ'fɪʃənsɪ] n efficacité f; (of machine, car) rendement m

efficiency apartment n (US) studio m avec coin cuisine

efficient [ɪ'fɪʃənt] adj efficace; (machine, car) d'un bon rendement

efficiently [ɪ'fɪʃəntlɪ] adv efficacement

effigy ['ɛfɪdʒɪ] n effigie f

effluent ['ɛfluənt] n effluent m

effort ['ɛfət] n effort m; **to make an ~ to do sth** faire or fournir un effort pour faire qch

effortless ['ɛfətlɪs] adj sans effort, aisé(e); (achievement) facile

effrontery [ɪ'frʌntərɪ] n effronterie f

effusive [ɪ'fjuːsɪv] adj (person) expansif(-ive); (welcome) chaleureux(-euse)

EFL n abbr (Scol) = **English as a Foreign Language**

EFTA ['ɛftə] n abbr (= European Free Trade Association) AELE f (= Association européenne de libre-échange)

e.g. adv abbr (= exempli gratia) par exemple, p. ex.

egalitarian [ɪgælɪ'tɛərɪən] adj égalitaire

egg [ɛg] n œuf m; **hard-boiled/soft-boiled ~** œuf dur/à la coque

  ▶ **egg on** vt pousser

eggcup ['ɛgkʌp] n coquetier m

egg plant ['ɛgplɑːnt] (US) n aubergine f

eggshell ['ɛgʃɛl] n coquille f d'œuf ▷ adj (colour) blanc cassé inv

egg-timer ['ɛgtaɪmə'] n sablier m

egg white n blanc m d'œuf

egg yolk n jaune m d'œuf

ego ['iːgəu] n (self-esteem) amour-propre m; (Psych) moi m

egoism ['ɛgəuɪzəm] n égoïsme m

egoist ['ɛgəuɪst] n égoïste m/f

egotism ['ɛgəutɪzəm] n égotisme m

egotist ['ɛgəutɪst] n égocentrique m/f

ego trip n: **to be on an ~** être en plein délire d'autosatisfaction

Egypt ['iːdʒɪpt] n Égypte f

Egyptian [ɪ'dʒɪpʃən] adj égyptien(ne) ▷ n Égyptien(ne)

EHIC n abbr (= European Health Insurance Card) CEAM f

eiderdown ['aɪdədaun] n édredon m

Eiffel Tower ['aɪfəl-] n tour f Eiffel

eight [eɪt] num huit

eighteen [eɪ'tiːn] num dix-huit

eighteenth [eɪ'tiːnθ] num dix-huitième

eighth [eɪtθ] *num* huitième

eightieth ['eɪtɪɪθ] *num* quatre-vingtième

eighty ['eɪtɪ] *num* quatre-vingt(s)

Eire ['ɛərə] *n* République f d'Irlande

EIS *n abbr* (= *Educational Institute of Scotland*) syndicat enseignant

either ['aɪðəʳ] *adj* l'un ou l'autre; (*both, each*) chaque ▷ *pron:* ~ **(of them)** l'un ou l'autre ▷ *adv* non plus ▷ *conj:* ~ **good or bad** ou bon ou mauvais, soit bon soit mauvais; **I haven't seen ~ one or the other** je n'ai vu ni l'un ni l'autre; **on ~ side** de chaque côté; **I don't like ~** je n'aime ni l'un ni l'autre; **no, I don't ~** moi non plus; **which bike do you want? — ~ will do** quel vélo voulez-vous? — n'importe lequel; **answer with ~ yes or no** répondez par oui ou par non

ejaculation [ɪdʒækju'leɪʃən] *n* (*Physiol*) éjaculation f

eject [ɪ'dʒɛkt] *vt* (*tenant etc*) expulser; (*object*) éjecter ▷ *vi* (*pilot*) s'éjecter

ejector seat [ɪ'dʒɛktə-] *n* siège m éjectable

eke [i:k]: **to ~ out** *vt* faire durer; augmenter

EKG *n abbr* (*US*) = **electrocardiogram**

el [ɛl] *n abbr* (*US inf*) = **elevated railroad**

elaborate [*adj* ɪ'læbərɪt, *vb* ɪ'læbəreɪt] *adj* compliqué(e), recherché(e), minutieux(-euse) ▷ *vt* élaborer ▷ *vi* entrer dans les détails

elapse [ɪ'læps] *vi* s'écouler, passer

elastic [ɪ'læstɪk] *adj, n* élastique (m)

elastic band *n* (*Brit*) élastique m

elasticity [ɪlæs'tɪsɪtɪ] *n* élasticité f

elated [ɪ'leɪtɪd] *adj* transporté(e) de joie

elation [ɪ'leɪʃən] *n* (grande) joie, allégresse f

elbow ['ɛlbəu] *n* coude m ▷ *vt:* **to ~ one's way through the crowd** se frayer un passage à travers la foule (en jouant des coudes)

elbow grease *n:* **to use a bit of ~** mettre de l'huile de coude

elder ['ɛldəʳ] *adj* aîné(e) ▷ *n* (*tree*) sureau m; **one's ~s** ses aînés

elderly ['ɛldəlɪ] *adj* âgé(e) ▷ *npl:* **the ~** les personnes âgées

elder statesman (*irreg*) *n* vétéran m de la politique

eldest ['ɛldɪst] *adj, n:* **the ~ (child)** l'aîné(e) (des enfants)

elect [ɪ'lɛkt] *vt* élire; (*choose*): **to ~ to do** choisir de faire ▷ *adj:* **the president ~** le président désigné

election [ɪ'lɛkʃən] *n* élection f; **to hold an ~** procéder à une élection

election campaign *n* campagne électorale

electioneering [ɪlɛkʃə'nɪərɪŋ] *n* propagande électorale, manœuvres électorales

elector [ɪ'lɛktəʳ] *n* électeur(-trice)

electoral [ɪ'lɛktərəl] *adj* électoral(e)

electoral college *n* collège électoral

electoral roll *n* (*Brit*) liste électorale

electorate [ɪ'lɛktərɪt] *n* électorat m

electric [ɪ'lɛktrɪk] *adj* électrique

electrical [ɪ'lɛktrɪkl] *adj* électrique

electrical engineer *n* ingénieur électricien

electrical failure *n* panne f d'électricité *or* de courant

electric blanket *n* couverture chauffante

electric chair *n* chaise f électrique

electric cooker *n* cuisinière f électrique

electric current *n* courant m électrique

electric fire *n* (*Brit*) radiateur m électrique

electrician [ɪlɛk'trɪʃən] *n* électricien m

electricity [ɪlɛk'trɪsɪtɪ] *n* électricité f; **to switch on/off the ~** rétablir/couper le courant

electricity board *n* (*Brit*) ≈ agence régionale de l'E.D.F.

electric light *n* lumière f électrique

electric shock *n* choc m *or* décharge f électrique

electrify [ɪ'lɛktrɪfaɪ] *vt* (*Rail*) électrifier; (*audience*) électriser

electro... [ɪ'lɛktrəu] *prefix* électro...

electrocardiogram [ɪ'lɛktrə] *n* électrocardiogramme m

electro-convulsive therapy [ɪ'lɛktrə] *n* électrochocs mpl

electrocute [ɪ'lɛktrəkju:t] *vt* électrocuter

electrode [ɪ'lɛktrəud] *n* électrode f

electroencephalogram [ɪ'lɛktrəu] *n* électroencéphalogramme m

electrolysis [ɪlɛk'trɔlɪsɪs] *n* électrolyse f

electromagnetic [ɪ'lɛktrəmæg'nɛtɪk] *adj* électromagnétique

electron [ɪ'lɛktrɔn] *n* électron m

electronic [ɪlɛk'trɔnɪk] *adj* électronique

electronic data processing *n* traitement m électronique des données

electronic mail *n* courrier m électronique

electronics [ɪlɛk'trɔnɪks] *n* électronique f

electron microscope *n* microscope m électronique

electroplated [ɪ'lɛktrə'pleɪtɪd] *adj* plaqué(e) *or* doré(e) *or* argenté(e) par galvanoplastie

electrotherapy [ɪ'lɛktrə'θɛrəpɪ] *n* électrothérapie f

elegance ['ɛlɪgəns] *n* élégance f

elegant ['ɛlɪgənt] *adj* élégant(e)

element ['ɛlɪmənt] *n* (*gen*) élément m; (*of heater, kettle etc*) résistance f

elementary [ɛlɪ'mɛntərɪ] *adj* élémentaire; (*school, education*) primaire

elementary school *n* (*US*) école f primaire; *voir article*

● ELEMENTARY SCHOOL

● Aux États-Unis et au Canada, une *elementary school* (également appelée "grade school" ou "grammar school" aux États-Unis) est une école publique où les enfants passent les six à huit premières années de leur scolarité.

elephant ['ɛlɪfənt] *n* éléphant m

elevate ['ɛlɪveɪt] *vt* élever

elevated railroad ['ɛlɪveɪtɪd-] *n* (*US*) métro m aérien

elevation [ɛlɪ'veɪʃən] n élévation f; (height) altitude f

elevator ['ɛlɪveɪtəʳ] n (in warehouse etc) élévateur m, monte-charge m inv; (US: lift) ascenseur m

eleven [ɪ'lɛvn] num onze

elevenses [ɪ'lɛvnzɪz] npl (Brit) ≈ pause-café f

eleventh [ɪ'lɛvnθ] num onzième; **at the ~ hour** (fig) à la dernière minute

elf (pl **elves**) [ɛlf, ɛlvz] n lutin m

elicit [ɪ'lɪsɪt] vt: **to ~ (from)** obtenir (de); tirer (de)

eligible ['ɛlɪdʒəbl] adj éligible; (for membership) admissible; **an ~ young man** un beau parti; **to be ~ for sth** remplir les conditions requises pour qch; **~ for a pension** ayant droit à la retraite

eliminate [ɪ'lɪmɪneɪt] vt éliminer

elimination [ɪlɪmɪ'neɪʃən] n élimination f; **by process of ~** par élimination

elitist [eɪ'liːtɪst] adj (pej) élitiste

Elizabethan [ɪlɪzə'biːθən] adj élisabéthain(e)

ellipse [ɪ'lɪps] n ellipse f

elliptical [ɪ'lɪptɪkl] adj elliptique

elm [ɛlm] n orme m

elocution [ɛlə'kjuːʃən] n élocution f

elongated ['iːlɔŋgeɪtɪd] adj étiré(e), allongé(e)

elope [ɪ'ləup] vi (lovers) s'enfuir (ensemble)

elopement [ɪ'ləupmənt] n fugue amoureuse

eloquence ['ɛləkwəns] n éloquence f

eloquent ['ɛləkwənt] adj éloquent(e)

else [ɛls] adv d'autre; **something ~** quelque chose d'autre, autre chose; **somewhere ~** ailleurs, autre part; **everywhere ~** partout ailleurs, autre part; **everyone ~** tous les autres; **nothing ~** rien d'autre; **is there anything ~ I can do?** est-ce que je peux faire quelque chose d'autre?; **where ~?** à quel autre endroit?; **little ~** pas grand-chose d'autre

elsewhere [ɛls'wɛəʳ] adv ailleurs, autre part

ELT n abbr (Scol) = **English Language Teaching**

elucidate [ɪ'luːsɪdeɪt] vt élucider

elude [ɪ'luːd] vt échapper à; (question) éluder

elusive [ɪ'luːsɪv] adj insaisissable; (answer) évasif(-ive)

elves [ɛlvz] npl of **elf**

emaciated [ɪ'meɪsɪeɪtɪd] adj émacié(e), décharné(e)

email ['iːmeɪl] n abbr (= electronic mail) (e-)mail m, courriel m ▷ vt: **to ~ sb** envoyer un (e-)mail or un courriel à qn

email account n compte m (e-)mail

email address n adresse f (e-)mail or électronique

emanate ['ɛməneɪt] vi: **to ~ from** émaner de

emancipate [ɪ'mænsɪpeɪt] vt émanciper

emancipation [ɪmænsɪ'peɪʃən] n émancipation f

emasculate [ɪ'mæskjuleɪt] vt émasculer

embalm [ɪm'bɑːm] vt embaumer

embankment [ɪm'bæŋkmənt] n (of road, railway) remblai m, talus m; (of river) berge f, quai m; (dyke) digue f

embargo [ɪm'bɑːgəu] (pl **-es**) n (Comm, Naut) embargo m; (prohibition) interdiction f ▷ vt frapper d'embargo, mettre l'embargo sur; **to put an ~ on sth** mettre l'embargo sur qch

embark [ɪm'bɑːk] vi embarquer; **to ~ on** (s')embarquer à bord de or sur ▷ vt embarquer; **to ~ on** (journey etc) commencer, entreprendre; (fig) se lancer or s'embarquer dans

embarkation [ɛmbɑː'keɪʃən] n embarquement m

embarkation card n carte f d'embarquement

embarrass [ɪm'bærəs] vt embarrasser, gêner

embarrassed [ɪm'bærəst] adj gêné(e); **to be ~** être gêné(e)

embarrassing [ɪm'bærəsɪŋ] adj gênant(e), embarrassant(e)

embarrassment [ɪm'bærəsmənt] n embarras m, gêne f; (embarrassing thing, person) source f d'embarras

embassy ['ɛmbəsɪ] n ambassade f; **the French E~** l'ambassade de France

embed [ɪm'bɛd] vt enfoncer; sceller

embellish [ɪm'bɛlɪʃ] vt embellir; enjoliver

embers ['ɛmbəz] npl braise f

embezzle [ɪm'bɛzl] vt détourner

embezzlement [ɪm'bɛzlmənt] n détournement m (de fonds)

embezzler [ɪm'bɛzləʳ] n escroc m

embitter [ɪm'bɪtəʳ] vt aigrir; envenimer

emblem ['ɛmbləm] n emblème m

embodiment [ɪm'bɔdɪmənt] n personnification f, incarnation f

embody [ɪm'bɔdɪ] vt (features) réunir, comprendre; (ideas) formuler, exprimer

embolden [ɪm'bəuldn] vt enhardir

embolism ['ɛmbəlɪzəm] n embolie f

embossed [ɪm'bɔst] adj repoussé(e), gaufré(e); **~ with** où figure(nt) en relief

embrace [ɪm'breɪs] vt embrasser, étreindre; (include) embrasser, couvrir, comprendre ▷ vi s'embrasser, s'étreindre ▷ n étreinte f

embroider [ɪm'brɔɪdəʳ] vt broder; (fig: story) enjoliver

embroidery [ɪm'brɔɪdərɪ] n broderie f

embroil [ɪm'brɔɪl] vt: **to become ~ed (in sth)** se retrouver mêlé(e) (à qch), se laisser entraîner (dans qch)

embryo ['ɛmbrɪəu] n (also fig) embryon m

emcee [ɛm'siː] n maître m de cérémonie

emend [ɪ'mɛnd] vt (text) corriger

emerald ['ɛmərəld] n émeraude f

emerge [ɪ'məːdʒ] vi apparaître; (from room, car) surgir; (from sleep, imprisonment) sortir; **it ~s that** (Brit) il ressort que

emergence [ɪ'məːdʒəns] n apparition f; (of nation) naissance f

emergency [ɪ'məːdʒənsɪ] n (crisis) cas m d'urgence; (Med) urgence f; **in an ~** en cas d'urgence; **state of ~** état m d'urgence

emergency brake (US) n frein m à main

emergency exit n sortie f de secours

emergency landing n atterrissage forcé

emergency lane n (US Aut) accotement stabilisé

emergency road service n (US) service m de dépannage

emergency room n (US: Med) urgences fpl

emergency services npl: **the ~** (fire, police, ambulance) les services mpl d'urgence

emergency stop n (Brit Aut) arrêt m d'urgence

emergent [ɪ'mɜːdʒənt] adj: **~ nation** pays m en voie de développement

emery board ['ɛmərɪ-] n lime f à ongles (en carton émerisé)

emery paper ['ɛmərɪ-] n papier m (d')émeri

emetic [ɪ'mɛtɪk] n vomitif m, émétique m

emigrant ['ɛmɪɡrənt] n émigrant(e)

emigrate ['ɛmɪɡreɪt] vi émigrer

emigration [ɛmɪ'ɡreɪʃən] n émigration f

émigré ['ɛmɪɡreɪ] n émigré(e)

eminence ['ɛmɪnəns] n éminence f

eminent ['ɛmɪnənt] adj éminent(e)

eminently ['ɛmɪnəntlɪ] adv éminemment, admirablement

emissions [ɪ'mɪʃənz] npl émissions fpl

emit [ɪ'mɪt] vt émettre

emolument [ɪ'mɔljumənt] n (often pl: formal) émoluments mpl; (fee) honoraires mpl; (salary) traitement m

emotion [ɪ'məuʃən] n sentiment m; (as opposed to reason) émotion f, sentiments

emotional [ɪ'məuʃənl] adj (person) émotif(-ive), très sensible; (needs) affectif(-ive); (scene) émouvant(e); (tone, speech) qui fait appel aux sentiments

emotionally [ɪ'məuʃnəlɪ] adv (behave) émotivement; (be involved) affectivement; (speak) avec émotion; **~ disturbed** qui souffre de troubles de l'affectivité

emotive [ɪ'məutɪv] adj émotif(-ive); **~ power** capacité f d'émouvoir or de toucher

empathy ['ɛmpəθɪ] n communion f d'idées or de sentiments, empathie f; **to feel ~ with sb** se mettre à la place de qn

emperor ['ɛmpərər] n empereur m

emphasis (pl **-ases**) ['ɛmfəsɪs, -siːz] n accent m; **to lay** or **place ~ on sth** (fig) mettre l'accent sur, insister sur; **the ~ is on reading** la lecture tient une place primordiale, on accorde une importance particulière à la lecture

emphasize ['ɛmfəsaɪz] vt (syllable, word, point) appuyer or insister sur; (feature) souligner, accentuer

emphatic [ɛm'fætɪk] adj (strong) énergique, vigoureux(-euse); (unambiguous, clear) catégorique

emphatically [ɛm'fætɪklɪ] adv avec vigueur or énergie; catégoriquement

empire ['ɛmpaɪər] n empire m

empirical [ɛm'pɪrɪkl] adj empirique

employ [ɪm'plɔɪ] vt employer; **he's ~ed in a bank** il est employé de banque, il travaille dans une banque

employee [ɪmplɔɪ'iː] n employé(e)

employer [ɪm'plɔɪər] n employeur(-euse)

employment [ɪm'plɔɪmənt] n emploi m; **to find ~** trouver un emploi or du travail; **without ~** au chômage, sans emploi; **place of ~** lieu m de travail

employment agency n agence f or bureau m de placement

employment exchange n (Brit) agence f pour l'emploi

empower [ɪm'pauər] vt: **to ~ sb to do** autoriser or habiliter qn à faire

empress ['ɛmprɪs] n impératrice f

emptiness ['ɛmptɪnɪs] n vide m; (of area) aspect m désertique

empty ['ɛmptɪ] adj vide; (street, area) désert(e); (threat, promise) en l'air, vain(e) ▷ n (bottle) bouteille f vide ▷ vt vider ▷ vi se vider; (liquid) s'écouler; **on an ~ stomach** à jeun; **to ~ into** (river) se jeter dans, se déverser dans

empty-handed ['ɛmptɪ'hændɪd] adj les mains vides

empty-headed ['ɛmptɪ'hɛdɪd] adj écervelé(e), qui n'a rien dans la tête

EMS n abbr (= European Monetary System) SME m

EMT n abbr = **emergency medical technician**

EMU n abbr (= European Monetary Union) UME f

emulate ['ɛmjuleɪt] vt rivaliser avec, imiter

emulsion [ɪ'mʌlʃən] n émulsion f; (also: **emulsion paint**) peinture mate

enable [ɪ'neɪbl] vt: **to ~ sb to do** permettre à qn de faire, donner à qn la possibilité de faire

enact [ɪ'nækt] vt (Law) promulguer; (play, scene) jouer, représenter

enamel [ɪ'næməl] n émail m; (also: **enamel paint**) (peinture f) laque f

enamoured [ɪ'næməd] adj: **~ of** amoureux(-euse) de; (idea) enchanté(e) par

encampment [ɪn'kæmpmənt] n campement m

encased [ɪn'keɪst] adj: **~ in** enfermé(e) dans, recouvert(e) de

enchant [ɪn'tʃɑːnt] vt enchanter

enchanting [ɪn'tʃɑːntɪŋ] adj ravissant(e), enchanteur(-eresse)

encircle [ɪn'sɜːkl] vt entourer, encercler

encl. abbr (on letters etc: = enclosed) ci-joint(e); (= enclosure) PJ f

enclose [ɪn'kləuz] vt (land) clôturer; (space, object) entourer; (letter etc): **to ~ (with)** joindre (à); **please find ~d** veuillez trouver ci-joint

enclosure [ɪn'kləuʒər] n enceinte f; (in letter etc) annexe f

encoder [ɪn'kəudər] n (Comput) encodeur m

encompass [ɪn'kʌmpəs] vt encercler, entourer; (include) contenir, inclure

encore [ɔŋ'kɔːr] excl, n bis (m)

encounter [ɪn'kauntər] n rencontre f ▷ vt rencontrer

encourage [ɪn'kʌrɪdʒ] vt encourager; (industry, growth) favoriser; **to ~ sb to do sth** encourager qn à faire qch

encouragement [ɪn'kʌrɪdʒmənt] n encouragement m

encouraging [ɪn'kʌrɪdʒɪŋ] *adj* encourageant(e)
encroach [ɪn'krəutʃ] *vi*: **to ~ (up)on** empiéter sur
encrusted [ɪn'krʌstɪd] *adj*: **~ (with)** incrusté(e) (de)
encyclopaedia, encyclopedia [ɛnsaɪkləu-'piːdɪə] *n* encyclopédie *f*
end [ɛnd] *n* fin *f*; (*of table, street, rope etc*) bout *m*, extrémité *f*; (*of pointed object*) pointe *f*; (*of town*) bout; (*Sport*) côté *m* ▷ *vt* terminer; (*also*: **bring to an end, put an end to**) mettre fin à ▷ *vi* se terminer, finir; **from ~ to ~** d'un bout à l'autre; **to come to an ~** prendre fin; **to be at an ~** être fini(e), être terminé(e); **in the ~** finalement; **on ~** (*object*) debout, dressé(e); **to stand on ~** (*hair*) se dresser sur la tête; **for 5 hours on ~** durant 5 heures d'affilée *or* de suite; **for hours on ~** pendant des heures (et des heures); **at the ~ of the day** (*Brit fig*) en fin de compte; **to this ~, with this ~ in view** à cette fin, dans ce but
▶ **end up** *vi*: **to ~ up in** (*condition*) finir *or* se terminer par; (*place*) finir *or* aboutir à
endanger [ɪn'deɪndʒər] *vt* mettre en danger; **an ~ed species** une espèce en voie de disparition
endear [ɪn'dɪər] *vt*: **to ~ o.s. to sb** se faire aimer de qn
endearing [ɪn'dɪərɪŋ] *adj* attachant(e)
endearment [ɪn'dɪəmənt] *n*: **to whisper ~s** murmurer des mots *or* choses tendres; **term of ~** terme *m* d'affection
endeavour, (*US*) **endeavor** [ɪn'dɛvər] *n* effort *m*; (*attempt*) tentative *f* ▷ *vt*: **to ~ to do** tenter *or* s'efforcer de faire
endemic [ɛn'dɛmɪk] *adj* endémique
ending ['ɛndɪŋ] *n* dénouement *m*, conclusion *f*; (*Ling*) terminaison *f*
endive ['ɛndaɪv] *n* (*curly*) chicorée *f*; (*smooth, flat*) endive *f*
endless ['ɛndlɪs] *adj* sans fin, interminable; (*patience, resources*) inépuisable, sans limites; (*possibilities*) illimité(e)
endorse [ɪn'dɔːs] *vt* (*cheque*) endosser; (*approve*) appuyer, approuver, sanctionner
endorsee [ɪndɔː'siː] *n* bénéficiaire *m/f*, endossataire *m/f*
endorsement [ɪn'dɔːsmənt] *n* (*approval*) appui *m*, aval *m*; (*signature*) endossement *m*; (*Brit: on driving licence*) contravention *f* (*portée au permis de conduire*)
endorser [ɪn'dɔːsər] *n* avaliste *m*, endosseur *m*
endow [ɪn'dau] *vt* (*provide with money*) faire une donation à, doter; (*equip*): **to ~ with** gratifier de, doter de
endowment [ɪn'daumənt] *n* dotation *f*
endowment mortgage *n* hypothèque liée à une assurance-vie
endowment policy *n* assurance *f* à capital différé
end product *n* (*Industry*) produit fini; (*fig*) résultat *m*, aboutissement *m*
end result *n* résultat final
endurable [ɪn'djuərəbl] *adj* supportable

endurance [ɪn'djuərəns] *n* endurance *f*
endurance test *m* test *m* d'endurance
endure [ɪn'djuər] *vt* (*bear*) supporter, endurer ▷ *vi* (*last*) durer
end user *n* (*Comput*) utilisateur final
enema ['ɛnɪmə] *n* (*Med*) lavement *m*
enemy ['ɛnəmɪ] *adj, n* ennemi(e); **to make an ~ of sb** se faire un(e) ennemi(e) de qn, se mettre qn à dos
energetic [ɛnə'dʒɛtɪk] *adj* énergique; (*activity*) très actif(-ive), qui fait se dépenser (physiquement)
energy ['ɛnədʒɪ] *n* énergie *f*; **Department of E~** ministère *m* de l'Énergie
energy crisis *n* crise *f* de l'énergie
energy-saving ['ɛnədʒɪ'seɪvɪŋ] *adj* (*policy*) d'économie d'énergie; (*device*) qui permet de réaliser des économies d'énergie
enervating ['ɛnəveɪtɪŋ] *adj* débilitant(e), affaiblissant(e)
enforce [ɪn'fɔːs] *vt* (*law*) appliquer, faire respecter
enforced [ɪn'fɔːst] *adj* forcé(e)
enfranchise [ɪn'fræntʃaɪz] *vt* accorder le droit de vote à; (*set free*) affranchir
engage [ɪn'geɪdʒ] *vt* engager; (*Mil*) engager le combat avec; (*lawyer*) prendre ▷ *vi* (*Tech*) s'enclencher, s'engrener; **to ~ in** se lancer dans; **to ~ sb in conversation** engager la conversation avec qn
engaged [ɪn'geɪdʒd] *adj* (*Brit: busy, in use*) occupé(e); (*betrothed*) fiancé(e); **to get ~** se fiancer; **the line's ~** la ligne est occupée; **he is ~ in research/a survey** il fait de la recherche/ une enquête
engaged tone *n* (*Brit Tel*) tonalité *f* occupé *inv*
engagement [ɪn'geɪdʒmənt] *n* (*undertaking*) obligation *f*, engagement *m*; (*appointment*) rendez-vous *m inv*; (*to marry*) fiançailles *fpl*; (*Mil*) combat *m*; **I have a previous ~** j'ai déjà un rendez-vous, je suis déjà pris(e)
engagement ring *n* bague *f* de fiançailles
engaging [ɪn'geɪdʒɪŋ] *adj* engageant(e), attirant(e)
engender [ɪn'dʒɛndər] *vt* produire, causer
engine ['ɛndʒɪn] *n* (*Aut*) moteur *m*; (*Rail*) locomotive *f*
engine driver *n* (*Brit: of train*) mécanicien *m*
engineer [ɛndʒɪ'nɪər] *n* ingénieur *m*; (*Brit: repairer*) dépanneur *m*; (*Navy, US Rail*) mécanicien *m*; **civil/mechanical ~** ingénieur des Travaux Publics *or* des Ponts et Chaussées/ mécanicien
engineering [ɛndʒɪ'nɪərɪŋ] *n* engineering *m*, ingénierie *f*; (*of bridges, ships*) génie *m*; (*of machine*) mécanique *f* ▷ *cpd*: **~ works** *or* **factory** atelier *m* de construction mécanique
engine failure *n* panne *f*
engine trouble *n* ennuis *mpl* mécaniques
England ['ɪŋglənd] *n* Angleterre *f*
English ['ɪŋglɪʃ] *adj* anglais(e) ▷ *n* (*Ling*) anglais *m*; **the ~** (*npl*) les Anglais; **an ~ speaker** un

anglophone
English Channel *n*: **the ~** la Manche
Englishman ['ɪŋglɪʃmən] (*irreg*) *n* Anglais *m*
English-speaking ['ɪŋglɪʃ'spi:kɪŋ] *adj* qui parle anglais; anglophone
Englishwoman ['ɪŋglɪʃwumən] (*irreg*) *n* Anglaise *f*
engrave [ɪn'greɪv] *vt* graver
engraving [ɪn'greɪvɪŋ] *n* gravure *f*
engrossed [ɪn'grəust] *adj*: **~ in** absorbé(e) par, plongé(e) dans
engulf [ɪn'gʌlf] *vt* engloutir
enhance [ɪn'hɑ:ns] *vt* rehausser, mettre en valeur; (*position*) améliorer; (*reputation*) accroître
enigma [ɪ'nɪgmə] *n* énigme *f*
enigmatic [ɛnɪg'mætɪk] *adj* énigmatique
enjoy [ɪn'dʒɔɪ] *vt* aimer, prendre plaisir à; (*have benefit of: health, fortune*) jouir de; (*: success*) connaître; **to ~ o.s.** s'amuser
enjoyable [ɪn'dʒɔɪəbl] *adj* agréable
enjoyment [ɪn'dʒɔɪmənt] *n* plaisir *m*
enlarge [ɪn'lɑ:dʒ] *vt* accroître; (*Phot*) agrandir ▷ *vi*: **to ~ on** (*subject*) s'étendre sur
enlarged [ɪn'lɑ:dʒd] *adj* (*edition*) augmenté(e); (*Med: organ, gland*) anormalement gros(se), hypertrophié(e)
enlargement [ɪn'lɑ:dʒmənt] *n* (*Phot*) agrandissement *m*
enlighten [ɪn'laɪtn] *vt* éclairer
enlightened [ɪn'laɪtnd] *adj* éclairé(e)
enlightening [ɪn'laɪtnɪŋ] *adj* instructif(-ive), révélateur(-trice)
enlightenment [ɪn'laɪtnmənt] *n* édification *f*; éclaircissements *mpl*; (*History*): **the E~** ≈ le Siècle des lumières
enlist [ɪn'lɪst] *vt* recruter; (*support*) s'assurer ▷ *vi* s'engager; **~ed man** (*US Mil*) simple soldat *m*
enliven [ɪn'laɪvn] *vt* animer, égayer
enmity ['ɛnmɪtɪ] *n* inimitié *f*
ennoble [ɪ'nəubl] *vt* (*with title*) anoblir
enormity [ɪ'nɔ:mɪtɪ] *n* énormité *f*
enormous [ɪ'nɔ:məs] *adj* énorme
enormously [ɪ'nɔ:məslɪ] *adv* (*increase*) dans des proportions énormes; (*rich*) extrêmement
enough [ɪ'nʌf] *adj*: **~ time/books** assez *or* suffisamment de temps/livres ▷ *adv*: **big ~** assez *or* suffisamment grand ▷ *pron*: **have you got ~?** (en) avez-vous assez?; **will five be ~?** est-ce que cinq suffiront?, est-ce qu'il y en aura assez avec cinq?; **~ to eat** assez à manger; **that's ~!** ça suffit!, assez!; **that's ~, thanks** cela suffit *or* c'est assez, merci; **I've had ~!** je n'en peux plus!; **I've had ~ of him** j'en ai assez de lui; **he has not worked ~** il n'a pas assez *or* suffisamment travaillé, il n'a pas travaillé assez *or* suffisamment; **~!** assez!, ça suffit!; **it's hot ~ (as it is)!** il fait assez chaud comme ça!; **he was kind ~ to lend me the money** il a eu la gentillesse de me prêter l'argent; **... which, funnily** *or* **oddly ~ ...** qui, chose curieuse, ...
enquire [ɪn'kwaɪə'] *vt, vi* = **inquire**
enquiry [ɪn'kwaɪərɪ] *n* = **inquiry**

enrage [ɪn'reɪdʒ] *vt* mettre en fureur *or* en rage, rendre furieux(-euse)
enrich [ɪn'rɪtʃ] *vt* enrichir
enrol, (*US*) **enroll** [ɪn'rəul] *vt* inscrire ▷ *vi* s'inscrire
enrolment, (*US*) **enrollment** [ɪn'rəulmənt] *n* inscription *f*
en route [ɔn'ru:t] *adv* en route, en chemin; **~ for** *or* **to** en route vers, à destination de
ensconced [ɪn'skɒnst] *adj*: **~ in** bien calé(e) dans
enshrine [ɪn'ʃraɪn] *vt* (*fig*) préserver
ensign *n* (*Naut*) ['ɛnsən] enseigne *f*, pavillon *m*; (*Mil*) ['ɛnsaɪn] porte-étendard *m*
enslave [ɪn'sleɪv] *vt* asservir
ensue [ɪn'sju:] *vi* s'ensuivre, résulter
en suite ['ɒnswi:t] *adj*: **with ~ bathroom** avec salle de bains en attenante
ensure [ɪn'ʃuə'] *vt* assurer, garantir; **to ~ that** s'assurer que
ENT *n abbr* (= *Ear, Nose and Throat*) ORL *f*
entail [ɪn'teɪl] *vt* entraîner, nécessiter
entangle [ɪn'tæŋgl] *vt* emmêler, embrouiller; **to become ~d in sth** (*fig*) se laisser entraîner *or* empêtrer dans qch
enter ['ɛntə'] *vt* (*room*) entrer dans, pénétrer dans; (*club, army*) entrer à; (*profession*) embrasser; (*competition*) s'inscrire à *or* pour; (*sb for a competition*) (faire) inscrire; (*write down*) inscrire, noter; (*Comput*) entrer, introduire ▷ *vi* entrer
  ▶ **enter for** *vt fus* s'inscrire à, se présenter pour *or* à
  ▶ **enter into** *vt fus* (*explanation*) se lancer dans; (*negotiations*) entamer; (*debate*) prendre part à; (*agreement*) conclure
  ▶ **enter on** *vt fus* commencer
  ▶ **enter up** *vt* inscrire
  ▶ **enter upon** *vt fus* = **enter on**
enteritis [ɛntə'raɪtɪs] *n* entérite *f*
enterprise ['ɛntəpraɪz] *n* (*company, undertaking*) entreprise *f*; (*initiative*) (esprit *m* d')initiative *f*; **free ~** libre entreprise; **private ~** entreprise privée
enterprising ['ɛntəpraɪzɪŋ] *adj* entreprenant(e), dynamique; (*scheme*) audacieux(-euse)
entertain [ɛntə'teɪn] *vt* amuser, distraire; (*invite*) recevoir (à dîner); (*idea, plan*) envisager
entertainer [ɛntə'teɪnə'] *n* artiste *m/f* de variétés
entertaining [ɛntə'teɪnɪŋ] *adj* amusant(e), distrayant(e) ▷ *n*: **to do a lot of ~** beaucoup recevoir
entertainment [ɛntə'teɪnmənt] *n* (*amusement*) distraction *f*, divertissement *m*, amusement *m*; (*show*) spectacle *m*
entertainment allowance *n* frais *mpl* de représentation
enthralled [ɪn'θrɔ:ld] *adj* captivé(e)
enthralling [ɪn'θrɔ:lɪŋ] *adj* captivant(e), enchanteur(-eresse)
enthuse [ɪn'θu:z] *vi*: **to ~ about** *or* **over** parler avec enthousiasme de
enthusiasm [ɪn'θu:zɪæzəm] *n* enthousiasme *m*

enthusiast [ɪn'θuːzɪæst] n enthousiaste m/f; **a jazz** etc ~ un fervent or passionné du jazz etc
enthusiastic [ɪnθuːzɪ'æstɪk] adj enthousiaste; **to be ~ about** être enthousiasmé(e) par
entice [ɪn'taɪs] vt attirer, séduire
enticing [ɪn'taɪsɪŋ] adj (person, offer) séduisant(e); (food) alléchant(e)
entire [ɪn'taɪə'] adj (tout) entier(-ère)
entirely [ɪn'taɪəlɪ] adv entièrement, complètement
entirety [ɪn'taɪərətɪ] n: **in its ~** dans sa totalité
entitle [ɪn'taɪtl] vt (allow): **to ~ sb to do** donner (le) droit à qn de faire; **to ~ sb to sth** donner droit à qch à qn
entitled [ɪn'taɪtld] adj (book) intitulé(e); **to be ~ to do** avoir le droit de faire
entity [ˈɛntɪtɪ] n entité f
entrails [ˈɛntreɪlz] npl entrailles fpl
entrance n [ˈɛntrns] entrée f ▷ vt [ɪn'trɑːns] enchanter, ravir; **where's the ~?** où est l'entrée?; **to gain ~ to** (university etc) être admis à
entrance examination n examen m d'entrée or d'admission
entrance fee n (to museum etc) prix m d'entrée; (to join club etc) droit m d'inscription
entrance ramp n (US Aut) bretelle f d'accès
entrancing [ɪn'trɑːnsɪŋ] adj enchanteur(-eresse), ravissant(e)
entrant [ˈɛntrnt] n (in race etc) participant(e), concurrent(e); (Brit: in exam) candidat(e)
entreat [ɛn'triːt] vt supplier
entreaty [ɛn'triːtɪ] n supplication f, prière f
entrée [ˈɔntreɪ] n (Culin) entrée f
entrenched [ɛn'trɛntʃt] adj retranché(e)
entrepreneur [ˈɔntrəprə'nəː'] n entrepreneur m
entrepreneurial [ˈɔntrəprə'nəːrɪəl] adj animé(e) d'un esprit d'entreprise
entrust [ɪn'trʌst] vt: **to ~ sth to** confier qch à
entry [ˈɛntrɪ] n entrée f; (in register, diary) inscription f; (in ledger) écriture f; **"no ~"** "défense d'entrer", "entrée interdite"; (Aut) "sens interdit"; **single/double ~ book-keeping** comptabilité f en partie simple/double
entry form n feuille f d'inscription
entry phone n (Brit) interphone m (à l'entrée d'un immeuble)
entwine [ɪn'twaɪn] vt entrelacer
E-number [ˈiːnʌmbə'] n additif m (alimentaire)
enumerate [ɪ'njuːməreɪt] vt énumérer
enunciate [ɪ'nʌnsɪeɪt] vt énoncer; prononcer
envelop [ɪn'vɛləp] vt envelopper
envelope [ˈɛnvələup] n enveloppe f
enviable [ˈɛnvɪəbl] adj enviable
envious [ˈɛnvɪəs] adj envieux(-euse)
environment [ɪn'vaɪərnmənt] n (social, moral) milieu m; (natural world): **the ~** l'environnement m; **Department of the E~** (Brit) ministère de l'Équipement et de l'Aménagement du territoire
environmental [ɪnvaɪərn'mɛntl] adj (of surroundings) du milieu; (issue, disaster) écologique; **~ studies** (in school etc) écologie f
environmentalist [ɪnvaɪərn'mɛntlɪst] n

écologiste m/f
environmentally [ɪnvaɪərn'mɛntlɪ] adv: **~ sound/friendly** qui ne nuit pas à l'environnement
Environmental Protection Agency n (US) ≈ ministère m de l'Environnement
envisage [ɪn'vɪzɪdʒ] vt (imagine) envisager; (foresee) prévoir
envision [ɪn'vɪʒən] vt envisager, concevoir
envoy [ˈɛnvɔɪ] n envoyé(e); (diplomat) ministre m plénipotentiaire
envy [ˈɛnvɪ] n envie f ▷ vt envier; **to ~ sb sth** envier qch à qn
enzyme [ˈɛnzaɪm] n enzyme m
EPA n abbr (US) = **Environmental Protection Agency**
ephemeral [ɪ'fɛmərl] adj éphémère
epic [ˈɛpɪk] n épopée f ▷ adj épique
epicentre, (US) **epicenter** [ˈɛpɪsɛntə'] n épicentre m
epidemic [ɛpɪ'dɛmɪk] n épidémie f
epilepsy [ˈɛpɪlɛpsɪ] n épilepsie f
epileptic [ɛpɪ'lɛptɪk] adj, n épileptique m/f
epileptic fit [ɛpɪ'lɛptɪk-] n crise f d'épilepsie
epilogue [ˈɛpɪlɔg] n épilogue m
episcopal [ɪ'pɪskəpl] adj épiscopal(e)
episode [ˈɛpɪsəud] n épisode m
epistle [ɪ'pɪsl] n épître f
epitaph [ˈɛpɪtɑːf] n épitaphe f
epithet [ˈɛpɪθɛt] n épithète f
epitome [ɪ'pɪtəmɪ] n (fig) quintessence f, type m
epitomize [ɪ'pɪtəmaɪz] vt (fig) illustrer, incarner
epoch [ˈiːpɔk] n époque f, ère f
epoch-making [ˈiːpɔkmeɪkɪŋ] adj qui fait époque
eponymous [ɪ'pɔnɪməs] adj de ce or du même nom, éponyme
equable [ˈɛkwəbl] adj égal(e), de tempérament égal
equal [ˈiːkwl] adj égal(e) ▷ n égal(e) ▷ vt égaler; **~ to** (task) à la hauteur de; **~ to doing** de taille à or capable de faire
equality [iː'kwɔlɪtɪ] n égalité f
equalize [ˈiːkwəlaɪz] vt, vi (Sport) égaliser
equalizer [ˈiːkwəlaɪzə'] n but égalisateur
equally [ˈiːkwəlɪ] adv également; (share) en parts égales; (treat) de la même façon; (pay) autant; (just as) tout aussi; **they are ~ clever** ils sont tout aussi intelligents
Equal Opportunities Commission, (US) **Equal Employment Opportunity Commission** n commission pour la non discrimination dans l'emploi
equal sign, equals sign n signe m d'égalité
equanimity [ɛkwə'nɪmɪtɪ] n égalité f d'humeur
equate [ɪ'kweɪt] vt: **to ~ sth with** comparer qch à; assimiler qch à; **to ~ sth to** mettre qch en équation avec; égaler qch à
equation [ɪ'kweɪʃən] n (Math) équation f
equator [ɪ'kweɪtə'] n équateur m
Equatorial Guinea [ˌɛkwə'tɔːrɪəl 'gɪnɪ] n Guinée équatoriale
equestrian [ɪ'kwɛstrɪən] adj équestre ▷ n

écuyer(-ère), cavalier(-ère)

equilibrium [iːkwɪˈlɪbrɪəm] *n* équilibre *m*

equinox [ˈiːkwɪnɔks] *n* équinoxe *m*

equip [ɪˈkwɪp] *vt* équiper; **to ~ sb/sth with** équiper *or* munir qn/qch de; **he is well ~ped for the job** il a les compétences *or* les qualités requises pour ce travail

equipment [ɪˈkwɪpmənt] *n* équipement *m*; *(electrical etc)* appareillage *m*, installation *f*

equitable [ˈɛkwɪtəbl] *adj* équitable

equities [ˈɛkwɪtɪz] *npl (Brit Comm)* actions cotées en Bourse

equity [ˈɛkwɪtɪ] *n* équité *f*

equity capital *n* capitaux *mpl* propres

equivalent [ɪˈkwɪvəlnt] *adj* équivalent(e) ▷ *n* équivalent *m*; **to be ~ to** équivaloir à, être équivalent(e) à

equivocal [ɪˈkwɪvəkl] *adj* équivoque; *(open to suspicion)* douteux(-euse)

equivocate [ɪˈkwɪvəkeɪt] *vi* user de faux-fuyants; éviter de répondre

equivocation [ɪkwɪvəˈkeɪʃən] *n* équivoque *f*

ER *abbr (Brit: = Elizabeth Regina)* la reine Élisabeth; *(US: Med: = emergency room)* urgences *fpl*

ERA *n abbr (US Pol: = Equal Rights Amendment)* amendement sur l'égalité des droits des femmes

era [ˈɪərə] *n* ère *f*, époque *f*

eradicate [ɪˈrædɪkeɪt] *vt* éliminer

erase [ɪˈreɪz] *vt* effacer

eraser [ɪˈreɪzər] *n* gomme *f*

erect [ɪˈrɛkt] *adj* droit(e) ▷ *vt* construire; *(monument)* ériger, élever; *(tent etc)* dresser

erection [ɪˈrɛkʃən] *n (Physiol)* érection *f*; *(of building)* construction *f*; *(of machinery etc)* installation *f*

ergonomics [əːɡəˈnɔmɪks] *n* ergonomie *f*

ERISA *n abbr (US: = Employee Retirement Income Security Act)* loi sur les pensions de retraite

Eritrea [ɛrɪˈtreɪə] *n* Érythrée *f*

ERM *n abbr (= Exchange Rate Mechanism)* mécanisme *m* des taux de change

ermine [ˈəːmɪn] *n* hermine *f*

ERNIE [ˈəːnɪ] *n abbr (Brit: = Electronic Random Number Indicator Equipment)* ordinateur servant au tirage des bons à lots gagnants

erode [ɪˈrəud] *vt* éroder; *(metal)* ronger

erogenous zone [ɪˈrɔdʒənəs-] *n* zone *f* érogène

erosion [ɪˈrəuʒən] *n* érosion *f*

erotic [ɪˈrɔtɪk] *adj* érotique

eroticism [ɪˈrɔtɪsɪzəm] *n* érotisme *m*

err [əːr] *vi* se tromper; *(Rel)* pécher

errand [ˈɛrnd] *n* course *f*, commission *f*; **to run ~s** faire des courses; **~ of mercy** mission *f* de charité, acte *m* charitable

errand boy *n* garçon *m* de courses

erratic [ɪˈrætɪk] *adj* irrégulier(-ière), inconstant(e)

erroneous [ɪˈrəunɪəs] *adj* erroné(e)

error [ˈɛrər] *n* erreur *f*; **typing/spelling ~** faute *f* de frappe/d'orthographe; **in ~** par erreur, par méprise; **~s and omissions excepted** sauf erreur ou omission

error message *n (Comput)* message *m* d'erreur

erstwhile [ˈəːstwaɪl] *adj* précédent(e), d'autrefois

erudite [ˈɛrjudaɪt] *adj* savant(e)

erupt [ɪˈrʌpt] *vi* entrer en éruption; *(fig)* éclater, exploser

eruption [ɪˈrʌpʃən] *n* éruption *f*; *(of anger, violence)* explosion *f*

ESA *n abbr (= European Space Agency)* ASE *f (= Agence spatiale européenne)*

escalate [ˈɛskəleɪt] *vi* s'intensifier; *(costs)* monter en flèche

escalation [ɛskəˈleɪʃən] *n* escalade *f*

escalation clause *n* clause *f* d'indexation

escalator [ˈɛskəleɪtər] *n* escalier roulant

escapade [ɛskəˈpeɪd] *n* fredaine *f*; équipée *f*

escape [ɪˈskeɪp] *n* évasion *f*, fuite *f*; *(of gas etc)* fuite; *(Tech)* échappement *m* ▷ *vi* s'échapper, fuir; *(from jail)* s'évader; *(fig)* s'en tirer, en réchapper; *(leak)* fuir; s'échapper ▷ *vt* échapper à; **to ~ from** *(person)* échapper à; *(place)* s'échapper de; *(fig)* fuir; **to ~ to** *(another place)* fuir à, s'enfuir à; **to ~ to safety** se réfugier dans *or* gagner un endroit sûr; **to ~ notice** passer inaperçu(e); **his name ~s me** son nom m'échappe

escape artist *n* virtuose *m/f* de l'évasion

escape clause *n* clause *f* dérogatoire

escapee [ɪskeɪˈpiː] *n* évadé(e)

escape key *n (Comput)* touche *f* d'échappement

escape route *n (from fire)* issue *f* de secours; *(of prisoners etc)* voie empruntée pour s'échapper

escapism [ɪˈskeɪpɪzəm] *n* évasion *f (fig)*

escapist [ɪˈskeɪpɪst] *adj (literature)* d'évasion ▷ *n* personne *f* qui se réfugie hors de la réalité

escapologist [ɛskəˈpɔlədʒɪst] *n (Brit)* = **escape artist**

escarpment [ɪsˈkɑːpmənt] *n* escarpement *m*

eschew [ɪsˈtʃuː] *vt* éviter

escort *vt* [ɪˈskɔːt] escorter ▷ *n* [ˈɛskɔːt] *(Mil)* escorte *f*; *(to dance etc)*: **her ~** son compagnon *or* cavalier; **his ~** sa compagne

escort agency *n* bureau *m* d'hôtesses

Eskimo [ˈɛskɪməu] *adj* esquimau(de), eskimo ▷ *n* Esquimau(de); *(Ling)* esquimau *m*

ESL *n abbr (Scol)* = **English as a Second Language**

esophagus [iːˈsɔfəgəs] *n (US)* = **oesophagus**

esoteric [ɛsəˈtɛrɪk] *adj* ésotérique

ESP *n abbr* = **extrasensory perception**; *(Scol)* = **English for Special Purposes**

esp. *abbr* = **especially**

especially [ɪˈspɛʃlɪ] *adv (particularly)* particulièrement; *(above all)* surtout

espionage [ˈɛspɪənɑːʒ] *n* espionnage *m*

esplanade [ɛspləˈneɪd] *n* esplanade *f*

espouse [ɪˈspauz] *vt* épouser, embrasser

Esquire [ɪˈskwaɪər] *n (Brit: abbr Esq.)*: **J. Brown, ~** Monsieur J. Brown

essay [ˈɛseɪ] *n (Scol)* dissertation *f*; *(Literature)* essai *m*; *(attempt)* tentative *f*

essence [ˈɛsns] *n* essence *f*; *(Culin)* extrait *m*; **in ~** en substance; **speed is of the ~** l'essentiel, c'est la rapidité

essential [ɪ'sɛnʃl] *adj* essentiel(le); (*basic*) fondamental(e); **essentials** *npl* éléments essentiels; **it is ~ that** il est essentiel or primordial que

essentially [ɪ'sɛnʃlɪ] *adv* essentiellement

EST *abbr* (US: = *Eastern Standard Time*) heure d'hiver de New York

est. *abbr* = **established, estimate(d)**

establish [ɪ'stæblɪʃ] *vt* établir; (*business*) fonder, créer; (*one's power etc*) asseoir, affermir

established [ɪ'stæblɪʃt] *adj* bien établi(e)

establishment [ɪ'stæblɪʃmənt] *n* établissement *m*; (*founding*) création *f*; (*institution*) établissement; **the E~** les pouvoirs établis; l'ordre établi

estate [ɪ'steɪt] *n* (*land*) domaine *m*, propriété *f*; (*Law*) biens *mpl*, succession *f*; (*Brit: also:* **housing estate**) lotissement *m*

estate agency *n* (Brit) agence immobilière

estate agent *n* (Brit) agent immobilier

estate car *n* (Brit) break *m*

esteem [ɪ'stiːm] *n* estime *f* ▷ *vt* estimer; apprécier; **to hold sb in high ~** tenir qn en haute estime

esthetic [ɪs'θɛtɪk] *adj* (US) = **aesthetic**

estimate [*n* 'ɛstɪmət, *vb* 'ɛstɪmeɪt] *n* estimation *f*; (*Comm*) devis *m* ▷ *vt* estimer ▷ *vi* (Brit Comm): **to ~ for** estimer, faire une estimation de; (*bid for*) faire un devis pour; **to give sb an ~ of** faire or donner un devis à qn pour; **at a rough ~** approximativement

estimation [ɛstɪ'meɪʃən] *n* opinion *f*; estime *f*; **in my ~** à mon avis, selon moi

Estonia [ɛ'stəʊnɪə] *n* Estonie *f*

Estonian [ɛ'stəʊnɪən] *adj* estonien(ne) ▷ *n* Estonien(ne); (*Ling*) estonien *m*

estranged [ɪs'treɪndʒd] *adj* (*couple*) séparé(e); (*husband, wife*) dont on s'est séparé(e)

estrangement [ɪs'treɪndʒmənt] *n* (*from wife, family*) séparation *f*

estrogen ['iːstrəudʒən] *n* (US) = **oestrogen**

estuary ['ɛstjʊərɪ] *n* estuaire *m*

ET *n abbr* (Brit: = *Employment Training*) formation professionnelle pour les demandeurs d'emploi ▷ *abbr* (US: = *Eastern Time*) heure de New York

ETA *n abbr* (= *estimated time of arrival*) HPA *f* (= *heure probable d'arrivée*)

et al. *abbr* (= *et alii: and others*) et coll

etc *abbr* (= *et cetera*) etc

etch [ɛtʃ] *vt* graver à l'eau forte

etching ['ɛtʃɪŋ] *n* eau-forte *f*

ETD *n abbr* (= *estimated time of departure*) HPD *f* (= *heure probable de départ*)

eternal [ɪ'təːnl] *adj* éternel(le)

eternity [ɪ'təːnɪtɪ] *n* éternité *f*

ether ['iːθəʳ] *n* éther *m*

ethereal [ɪ'θɪərɪəl] *adj* éthéré(e)

ethical ['ɛθɪkl] *adj* moral(e)

ethics ['ɛθɪks] *n* éthique *f* ▷ *npl* moralité *f*

Ethiopia [iːθɪ'əʊpɪə] *n* Éthiopie *f*

Ethiopian [iːθɪ'əʊpɪən] *adj* éthiopien(ne) ▷ *n*

Éthiopien(ne)

ethnic ['ɛθnɪk] *adj* ethnique; (*clothes, food*) folklorique, exotique, *propre aux minorités ethniques non-occidentales*

ethnic cleansing [-'klɛnzɪŋ] *n* purification *f* ethnique

ethnic minority *n* minorité *f* ethnique

ethnology [ɛθ'nɔlədʒɪ] *n* ethnologie *f*

ethos ['iːθɔs] *n* (système *m* de) valeurs *fpl*

e-ticket ['iːtɪkɪt] *n* billet *m* électronique

etiquette ['ɛtɪkɛt] *n* convenances *fpl*, étiquette *f*

ETV *n abbr* (US: = *Educational Television*) télévision scolaire

etymology [ɛtɪ'mɔlədʒɪ] *n* étymologie *f*

EU *n abbr* (= *European Union*) UE *f*

eucalyptus [juːkə'lɪptəs] *n* eucalyptus *m*

eulogy ['juːlədʒɪ] *n* éloge *m*

euphemism ['juːfəmɪzəm] *n* euphémisme *m*

euphemistic [juːfə'mɪstɪk] *adj* euphémique

euphoria [juː'fɔːrɪə] *n* euphorie *f*

Eurasia [jʊə'reɪʃə] *n* Eurasie *f*

Eurasian [jʊə'reɪʃən] *adj* eurasien(ne); (*continent*) eurasiatique ▷ *n* Eurasien(ne)

Euratom [jʊə'rætəm] *n abbr* (= *European Atomic Energy Community*) EURATOM *f*

euro ['jʊərəu] *n* (*currency*) euro *m*

Euro- ['jʊərəu] *prefix* euro-

Eurocrat ['jʊərəukræt] *n* eurocrate *m/f*

Euroland ['jʊərəulænd] *n* Euroland *m*

Europe ['jʊərəp] *n* Europe *f*

European [jʊərə'piːən] *adj* européen(ne) ▷ *n* Européen(ne)

European Community *n* Communauté européenne

European Court of Justice *n* Cour *f* de Justice de la CEE

European Union *n* Union européenne

Euro-sceptic ['jʊərəuskɛptɪk] *n* eurosceptique *m/f*

Eurostar® ['jʊərəustaːʳ] *n* Eurostar® *m*

euthanasia [juːθə'neɪzɪə] *n* euthanasie *f*

evacuate [ɪ'vækjueɪt] *vt* évacuer

evacuation [ɪvækju'eɪʃən] *n* évacuation *f*

evacuee [ɪvækju'iː] *n* évacué(e)

evade [ɪ'veɪd] *vt* échapper à; (*question etc*) éluder; (*duties*) se dérober

evaluate [ɪ'væljueɪt] *vt* évaluer

evangelist [ɪ'vændʒəlɪst] *n* évangéliste *m*

evangelize [ɪ'vændʒəlaɪz] *vt* évangéliser, prêcher l'Évangile à

evaporate [ɪ'væpəreɪt] *vi* s'évaporer; (*fig: hopes, fear*) s'envoler; (*anger*) se dissiper ▷ *vt* faire évaporer

evaporated milk [ɪ'væpəreɪtɪd-] *n* lait condensé (non sucré)

evaporation [ɪvæpə'reɪʃən] *n* évaporation *f*

evasion [ɪ'veɪʒən] *n* dérobade *f*; (*excuse*) faux-fuyant *m*

evasive [ɪ'veɪsɪv] *adj* évasif(-ive)

eve [iːv] *n*: **on the ~ of** à la veille de

even ['iːvn] *adj* (*level, smooth*) régulier(-ière);

(equal) égal(e); *(number)* pair(e) ▷ *adv* même; **~ if** même si + *indic*; **~ though** quand (bien) même + *cond*, alors même que + *cond*; **~ more** encore plus; **~ faster** encore plus vite; **~ so** quand même; **not ~** pas même; **~ he was there** même lui était là; **~ on Sundays** même le dimanche; **to break ~** s'y retrouver, équilibrer ses comptes; **to get ~ with sb** prendre sa revanche sur qn
  ▶ **even out** *vi* s'égaliser
even-handed [iːvnˈhændɪd] *adj* équitable
evening [ˈiːvnɪŋ] *n* soir *m*; *(as duration, event)* soirée *f*; **in the ~** le soir; **this ~** ce soir; **tomorrow/yesterday ~** demain/hier soir
evening class *n* cours *m* du soir
evening dress *n* *(man's)* tenue *f* de soirée, smoking *m*; *(woman's)* robe *f* de soirée
evenly [ˈiːvnlɪ] *adv* uniformément, également; *(space)* régulièrement
evensong [ˈiːvnsɔŋ] *n* office *m* du soir
event [ɪˈvɛnt] *n* événement *m*; *(Sport)* épreuve *f*; **in the course of ~s** par la suite; **in the ~ of** en cas de; **in the ~** en réalité, en fait; **at all ~s** *(Brit)*: **in any ~** en tout cas, de toute manière
eventful [ɪˈvɛntful] *adj* mouvementé(e)
eventing [ɪˈvɛntɪŋ] *n* *(Horse-Riding)* concours complet *(équitation)*
eventual [ɪˈvɛntʃuəl] *adj* final(e)
eventuality [ɪvɛntʃuˈælɪtɪ] *n* possibilité *f*, éventualité *f*
eventually [ɪˈvɛntʃuəlɪ] *adv* finalement
ever [ˈɛvəʳ] *adv* jamais; *(at all times)* toujours; *(in questions)*: **why ~ not?** mais enfin, pourquoi pas?; **the best ~** le meilleur qu'on ait jamais vu; **have you ~ seen it?** l'as-tu déjà vu?, as-tu eu l'occasion *or* t'est-il arrivé de le voir?; **did you ~ meet him?** est-ce qu'il vous est arrivé de le rencontrer?; **have you ~ been there?** y êtes-vous déjà allé?; **for ~** pour toujours; **hardly ~** ne … presque jamais; **~ since** *(as adv)* depuis; *(as conj)* depuis que; **~ so pretty** si joli; **thank you ~ so much** merci mille fois
Everest [ˈɛvərɪst] *n* *(also:* **Mount Everest***)* le mont Everest, l'Everest *m*
evergreen [ˈɛvəgriːn] *n* arbre *m* à feuilles persistantes
everlasting [ɛvəˈlɑːstɪŋ] *adj* éternel(le)

 KEYWORD

every [ˈɛvrɪ] *adj* **1** *(each)* chaque; **every one of them** tous (sans exception); **every shop in town was closed** tous les magasins en ville étaient fermés
2 *(all possible)* tous (toutes) les; **I gave you every assistance** j'ai fait tout mon possible pour vous aider; **I have every confidence in him** j'ai entièrement *or* pleinement confiance en lui; **we wish you every success** nous vous souhaitons beaucoup de succès
3 *(showing recurrence)* tous les; **every day** tous les jours, chaque jour; **every other car** une

voiture sur deux; **every other/third day** tous les deux/trois jours; **every now and then** de temps en temps

everybody [ˈɛvrɪbɔdɪ] *pron* = **everyone**
everyday [ˈɛvrɪdeɪ] *adj* *(expression)* courant(e), d'usage courant; *(use)* courant; *(clothes, life)* de tous les jours; *(occurrence, problem)* quotidien(ne)
everyone [ˈɛvrɪwʌn] *pron* tout le monde, tous *pl*; **~ knows about it** tout le monde le sait; **~ else** tous les autres
everything [ˈɛvrɪθɪŋ] *pron* tout; **~ is ready** tout est prêt; **he did ~ possible** il a fait tout son possible
everywhere [ˈɛvrɪwɛəʳ] *adv* partout; **~ you go you meet …** où qu'on aille on rencontre …
evict [ɪˈvɪkt] *vt* expulser
eviction [ɪˈvɪkʃən] *n* expulsion *f*
eviction notice *n* préavis *m* d'expulsion
evidence [ˈɛvɪdns] *n* *(proof)* preuve(s) *f(pl)*; *(of witness)* témoignage *m*; *(sign)*: **to show ~ of** donner des signes de; **to give ~** témoigner, déposer; **in ~** *(obvious)* en évidence; en vue
evident [ˈɛvɪdnt] *adj* évident(e)
evidently [ˈɛvɪdntlɪ] *adv* de toute évidence; *(apparently)* apparemment
evil [ˈiːvl] *adj* mauvais(e) ▷ *n* mal *m*
evince [ɪˈvɪns] *vt* manifester
evocative [ɪˈvɔkətɪv] *adj* évocateur(-trice)
evoke [ɪˈvəuk] *vt* évoquer; *(admiration)* susciter
evolution [iːvəˈluːʃən] *n* évolution *f*
evolve [ɪˈvɔlv] *vt* élaborer ▷ *vi* évoluer, se transformer
ewe [juː] *n* brebis *f*
ex [ɛks] *n* *(inf)*: **my ex** mon ex
ex- [ɛks] *prefix* *(former: husband, president etc)* ex-; *(out of)*: **the price ~works** le prix départ usine
exacerbate [ɛksˈæsəbeɪt] *vt* *(pain)* exacerber, accentuer; *(fig)* aggraver
exact [ɪgˈzækt] *adj* exact(e) ▷ *vt*: **to ~ sth (from)** *(signature, confession)* extorquer qch (à); *(apology)* exiger qch (de)
exacting [ɪgˈzæktɪŋ] *adj* exigeant(e); *(work)* fatigant(e)
exactitude [ɪgˈzæktɪtjuːd] *n* exactitude *f*, précision *f*
exactly [ɪgˈzæktlɪ] *adv* exactement; **~!** parfaitement!, précisément!
exaggerate [ɪgˈzædʒəreɪt] *vt, vi* exagérer
exaggeration [ɪgzædʒəˈreɪʃən] *n* exagération *f*
exalted [ɪgˈzɔːltɪd] *adj* *(rank)* élevé(e); *(person)* haut placé(e); *(elated)* exalté(e)
exam [ɪgˈzæm] *n abbr* *(Scol)* = **examination**
examination [ɪgzæmɪˈneɪʃən] *n* *(Scol, Med)* examen *m*; **to take** *or* **sit an ~** *(Brit)* passer un examen; **the matter is under ~** la question est à l'examen
examine [ɪgˈzæmɪn] *vt* *(gen)* examiner; *(Scol, Law: person)* interroger; *(inspect: machine, premises)* inspecter; *(passport)* contrôler; *(luggage)* fouiller
examiner [ɪgˈzæmɪnəʳ] *n* examinateur(-trice)
example [ɪgˈzɑːmpl] *n* exemple *m*; **for ~** par

exemple; **to set a good/bad ~** donner le bon/ mauvais exemple

exasperate [ɪg'zɑːspəreɪt] vt exaspérer, agacer

exasperated [ɪg'zɑːspəreɪtɪd] adj exaspéré(e)

exasperation [ɪgzɑːspə'reɪʃən] n exaspération f, irritation f

excavate ['ɛkskəveɪt] vt (site) fouiller, excaver; (object) mettre au jour

excavation [ɛkskə'veɪʃən] n excavation f

excavator ['ɛkskəveɪtər] n excavateur m, excavatrice f

exceed [ɪk'siːd] vt dépasser; (one's powers) outrepasser

exceedingly [ɪk'siːdɪŋlɪ] adv extrêmement

excel [ɪk'sɛl] vi exceller ▷ vt surpasser; **to ~ o.s.** se surpasser

excellence ['ɛksələns] n excellence f

Excellency ['ɛksələnsɪ] n: **His ~** son Excellence f

excellent ['ɛksələnt] adj excellent(e)

except [ɪk'sɛpt] prep (also: **except for, excepting**) sauf, excepté, à l'exception de ▷ vt excepter; **~ if/when** sauf si/quand; **~ that** excepté que, si ce n'est que

exception [ɪk'sɛpʃən] n exception f; **to take ~ to** s'offusquer de; **with the ~ of** à l'exception de

exceptional [ɪk'sɛpʃənl] adj exceptionnel(le)

exceptionally [ɪk'sɛpʃənəlɪ] adv exceptionnellement

excerpt ['ɛksəːpt] n extrait m

excess [ɪk'sɛs] n excès m; **in ~ of** plus de

excess baggage n excédent m de bagages

excess fare n supplément m

excessive [ɪk'sɛsɪv] adj excessif(-ive)

excess supply n suroffre f, offre f excédentaire

exchange [ɪks'tʃeɪndʒ] n échange m; (also: **telephone exchange**) central m ▷ vt: **to ~ (for)** échanger (contre); **could I ~ this, please?** est- ce que je peux échanger ceci, s'il vous plaît?; **in ~ for** en échange de; **foreign ~** (Comm) change m

exchange control n contrôle m des changes

exchange market n marché m des changes

exchange rate n taux m de change

excisable [ɪk'saɪzəbl] adj taxable

excise n ['ɛksaɪz] taxe f ▷ vt [ɛk'saɪz] exciser

excise duties npl impôts indirects

excitable [ɪk'saɪtəbl] adj excitable, nerveux(-euse)

excite [ɪk'saɪt] vt exciter

excited [ɪk'saɪtəd] adj (tout (toute)) excité(e); **to get ~** s'exciter

excitement [ɪk'saɪtmənt] n excitation f

exciting [ɪk'saɪtɪŋ] adj passionnant(e)

excl. abbr = **excluding; exclusive (of)**

exclaim [ɪk'skleɪm] vi s'exclamer

exclamation [ɛksklə'meɪʃən] n exclamation f

exclamation mark, (US) **exclamation point** n point m d'exclamation

exclude [ɪk'skluːd] vt exclure

excluding [ɪk'skluːdɪŋ] prep: **~ VAT** la TVA non comprise

exclusion [ɪk'skluːʒən] n exclusion f; **to the ~ of** à l'exclusion de

exclusion clause n clause f d'exclusion

exclusion zone n zone interdite

exclusive [ɪk'skluːsɪv] adj exclusif(-ive); (club, district) sélect(e); (item of news) en exclusivité ▷ adv (Comm) exclusivement, non inclus; **~ of VAT** TVA non comprise; **~ of postage** (les) frais de poste non compris; **from 1st to 15th March ~** du 1er au 15 mars exclusivement or exclu; **~ rights** (Comm) exclusivité f

exclusively [ɪk'skluːsɪvlɪ] adv exclusivement

excommunicate [ɛkskə'mjuːnɪkeɪt] vt excommunier

excrement ['ɛkskrəmənt] n excrément m

excruciating [ɪk'skruːʃɪeɪtɪŋ] adj (pain) atroce, déchirant(e); (embarrassing) pénible

excursion [ɪk'skəːʃən] n excursion f

excursion ticket n billet m tarif excursion

excusable [ɪk'skjuːzəbl] adj excusable

excuse n [ɪk'skjuːs] excuse f ▷ vt [ɪk'skjuːz] (forgive) excuser; (justify) excuser, justifier; **to ~ sb from** (activity) dispenser qn de; **~ me!** excusez-moi!, pardon!; **now if you will ~ me, …** maintenant, si vous (le) permettez …; **to make ~s for sb** trouver des excuses à qn; **to ~ o.s. for sth/for doing sth** s'excuser de/d'avoir fait qch

ex-directory ['ɛksdɪ'rɛktərɪ] adj (Brit) sur la liste rouge

execute ['ɛksɪkjuːt] vt exécuter

execution [ɛksɪ'kjuːʃən] n exécution f

executioner [ɛksɪ'kjuːʃnər] n bourreau m

executive [ɪg'zɛkjutɪv] n (person) cadre m; (managing group) bureau m; (Pol) exécutif m ▷ adj exécutif(-ive); (position, job) de cadre; (secretary) de direction; (offices) de la direction; (car, plane) de fonction

executive director n administrateur(-trice)

executor [ɪg'zɛkjutər] n exécuteur(-trice) testamentaire

exemplary [ɪg'zɛmplərɪ] adj exemplaire

exemplify [ɪg'zɛmplɪfaɪ] vt illustrer

exempt [ɪg'zɛmpt] adj: **~ from** exempté(e) or dispensé(e) de ▷ vt: **to ~ sb from** exempter or dispenser qn de

exemption [ɪg'zɛmpʃən] n exemption f, dispense f

exercise ['ɛksəsaɪz] n exercice m ▷ vt exercer; (patience etc) faire preuve de; (dog) promener ▷ vi (also: **to take exercise**) prendre de l'exercice

exercise bike n vélo m d'appartement

exercise book n cahier m

exert [ɪg'zəːt] vt exercer, employer; (strength, force) employer; **to ~ o.s.** se dépenser

exertion [ɪg'zəːʃən] n effort m

ex gratia ['ɛks'greɪʃə] adj: **~ payment** gratification f

exhale [ɛks'heɪl] vt (breathe out) expirer; exhaler ▷ vi expirer

exhaust [ɪg'zɔːst] n (also: **exhaust fumes**) gaz mpl d'échappement; (also: **exhaust pipe**) tuyau m d'échappement ▷ vt épuiser; **to ~ o.s.** s'épuiser exhausted [ɪgˈzɔːstɪd] *adj* épuisé(e)

exhausting [ɪgˈzɔːstɪŋ] *adj* épuisant(e)

exhaustion [ɪgˈzɔːstʃən] *n* épuisement *m*; **nervous ~** fatigue nerveuse

exhaustive [ɪgˈzɔːstɪv] *adj* très complet(-ète)

exhibit [ɪgˈzɪbɪt] *n* (*Art*) objet exposé, pièce exposée; (*Law*) pièce à conviction ▷ *vt* (*Art*) exposer; (*courage, skill*) faire preuve de

exhibition [ɛksɪˈbɪʃən] *n* exposition *f*; **~ of temper** manifestation *f* de colère

exhibitionist [ɛksɪˈbɪʃənɪst] *n* exhibitionniste *m/f*

exhibitor [ɪgˈzɪbɪtəʳ] *n* exposant(e)

exhilarating [ɪgˈzɪləreɪtɪŋ] *adj* grisant(e), stimulant(e)

exhilaration [ɪgzɪləˈreɪʃən] *n* euphorie *f*, ivresse *f*

exhort [ɪgˈzɔːt] *vt* exhorter

ex-husband [ˈɛksˈhʌzbənd] *n* ex-mari *m*

exile [ˈɛksaɪl] *n* exil *m*; (*person*) exilé(e) ▷ *vt* exiler; **in ~** en exil

exist [ɪgˈzɪst] *vi* exister

existence [ɪgˈzɪstəns] *n* existence *f*; **to be in ~** exister

existentialism [ɛgzɪsˈtɛnʃlɪzəm] *n* existentialisme *m*

existing [ɪgˈzɪstɪŋ] *adj* (*laws*) existant(e); (*system, regime*) actuel(le)

exit [ˈɛksɪt] *n* sortie *f* ▷ *vi* (*Comput, Theat*) sortir; **where's the ~?** où est la sortie?

exit poll *n* sondage *m* (*fait à la sortie de l'isoloir*)

exit ramp *n* (*US Aut*) bretelle *f* d'accès

exit visa *n* visa *m* de sortie

exodus [ˈɛksədəs] *n* exode *m*

ex officio [ˈɛksəˈfɪʃɪəu] *adj, adv* d'office, de droit

exonerate [ɪgˈzɔnəreɪt] *vt*: **to ~ from** disculper de

exorbitant [ɪgˈzɔːbɪtnt] *adj* (*price*) exorbitant(e), excessif(-ive); (*demands*) exorbitant, démesuré(e)

exorcize [ˈɛksɔːsaɪz] *vt* exorciser

exotic [ɪgˈzɔtɪk] *adj* exotique

expand [ɪkˈspænd] *vt* (*area*) agrandir; (*quantity*) accroître; (*influence etc*) étendre ▷ *vi* (*population, production*) s'accroître; (*trade, etc*) se développer, s'accroître; (*gas, metal*) se dilater, dilater; **to ~ on** (*notes, story etc*) développer

expanse [ɪkˈspæns] *n* étendue *f*

expansion [ɪkˈspænʃən] *n* (*territorial, economic*) expansion *f*; (*of trade, influence etc*) développement *m*; (*of production*) accroissement *m*; (*of population*) croissance *f*; (*of gas, metal*) expansion, dilatation *f*

expansionism [ɪkˈspænʃənɪzəm] *n* expansionnisme *m*

expansionist [ɪkˈspænʃənɪst] *adj* expansionniste

expatriate *n* [ɛksˈpætrɪət] expatrié(e) ▷ *vt* [ɛksˈpætrɪeɪt] expatrier, exiler

expect [ɪkˈspɛkt] *vt* (*anticipate*) s'attendre à, s'attendre à ce que + *sub*; (*count on*) compter sur, escompter; (*hope for*) espérer; (*require*) demander,

exiger; (*suppose*) supposer; (*await: also baby*) attendre ▷ *vi*: **to be ~ing** (*pregnant woman*) être enceinte; **to ~ sb to do** (*anticipate*) s'attendre à ce que qn fasse; (*demand*) attendre de qn qu'il fasse; **to ~ to do sth** penser *or* compter faire qch, s'attendre à faire qch; **as ~ed** comme prévu; **I ~ so** je crois que oui, je crois bien

expectancy [ɪksˈpɛktənsɪ] *n* attente *f*; **life ~** espérance *f* de vie

expectant [ɪkˈspɛktənt] *adj* qui attend (quelque chose); **~ mother** future maman

expectantly [ɪkˈspɛktəntlɪ] *adv* (*look, listen*) avec l'air d'attendre quelque chose

expectation [ɛkspɛkˈteɪʃən] *n* (*hope*) attente *f*, espérance(s) *f(pl)*; (*belief*) attente; **in ~ of** dans l'attente de, en prévision de; **against** *or* **contrary to all ~(s)** contre toute attente, contrairement à ce qu'on attendait; **to come** *or* **live up to sb's ~s** répondre à l'attente *or* aux espérances de qn

expedience, expediency [ɪkˈspiːdɪəns, ɪkˈspiːdɪənsɪ] *n* opportunité *f*; convenance *f* (du moment); **for the sake of ~** parce que c'est (*or* c'était) plus simple *or* plus commode

expedient [ɪkˈspiːdɪənt] *adj* indiqué(e), opportun(e), commode ▷ *n* expédient *m*

expedite [ˈɛkspədaɪt] *vt* hâter; expédier

expedition [ɛkspəˈdɪʃən] *n* expédition *f*

expeditionary force [ɛkspəˈdɪʃənrɪ-] *n* corps *m* expéditionnaire

expeditious [ɛkspəˈdɪʃəs] *adj* expéditif(-ive), prompt(e)

expel [ɪkˈspɛl] *vt* chasser, expulser; (*Scol*) renvoyer, exclure

expend [ɪkˈspɛnd] *vt* consacrer; (*use up*) dépenser

expendable [ɪkˈspɛndəbl] *adj* remplaçable

expenditure [ɪkˈspɛndɪtʃəʳ] *n* (*act of spending*) dépense *f*; (*money spent*) dépenses *fpl*

expense [ɪkˈspɛns] *n* (*high cost*) coût *m*; (*spending*) dépense *f*, frais *mpl*; **expenses** *npl* frais *mpl*; dépenses; **to go to the ~ of** faire la dépense de; **at great/little ~** à grands/peu de frais; **at the ~ of** aux frais de; (*fig*) aux dépens de

expense account *n* (note *f* de) frais *mpl*

expensive [ɪkˈspɛnsɪv] *adj* cher (chère), coûteux(-euse); **to be ~** coûter cher; **it's too ~** ça coûte trop cher; **~ tastes** goûts *mpl* de luxe

experience [ɪkˈspɪərɪəns] *n* expérience *f* ▷ *vt* connaître; (*feeling*) éprouver; **to know by ~** savoir par expérience

experienced [ɪkˈspɪərɪənst] *adj* expérimenté(e)

experiment [ɪkˈspɛrɪmənt] *n* expérience *f* ▷ *vi* faire une expérience; **to ~ with** expérimenter; **to perform** *or* **carry out an ~** faire une expérience; **as an ~** à titre d'expérience

experimental [ɪkspɛrɪˈmɛntl] *adj* expérimental(e)

expert [ˈɛkspəːt] *adj* expert(e) ▷ *n* expert *m*; **~ in** *or* **at doing sth** spécialiste de qch; **an ~ on sth** un spécialiste de qch; **~ witness** (*Law*) expert *m*

expertise [ɛkspəːˈtiːz] *n* (grande) compétence

expire [ɪk'spaɪəʳ] vi expirer
expiry [ɪk'spaɪərɪ] n expiration f
expiry date n date f d'expiration; (on label) à utiliser avant …
explain [ɪk'spleɪn] vt expliquer
▸ **explain away** vt justifier, excuser
explanation [ɛksplə'neɪʃən] n explication f; **to find an ~ for sth** trouver une explication à qch
explanatory [ɪk'splænətrɪ] adj explicatif(-ive)
expletive [ɪk'spliːtɪv] n juron m
explicit [ɪk'splɪsɪt] adj explicite; (definite) formel(le)
explode [ɪk'spləud] vi exploser ▷ vt faire exploser; (fig: theory) démolir; **to ~ a myth** détruire un mythe
exploit n ['eksplɔɪt] exploit m ▷ vt [ɪk'splɔɪt] exploiter
exploitation [ɛksplɔɪ'teɪʃən] n exploitation f
exploration [ɛksplə'reɪʃən] n exploration f
exploratory [ɪk'splɔrətrɪ] adj (fig: talks) préliminaire; **~ operation** (Med) intervention f (à visée) exploratrice
explore [ɪk'splɔːʳ] vt explorer; (possibilities) étudier, examiner
explorer [ɪk'splɔːrəʳ] n explorateur(-trice)
explosion [ɪk'spləuʒən] n explosion f
explosive [ɪk'spləusɪv] adj explosif(-ive) ▷ n explosif m
exponent [ɪk'spəunənt] n (of school of thought etc) interprète m, représentant m; (Math) exposant m
export vt [ɛk'spɔːt] exporter ▷ n ['ekspɔːt] exportation f ▷ cpd ['ekspɔːt] d'exportation
exportation [ekspɔː'teɪʃən] n exportation f
exporter [ɛk'spɔːtəʳ] n exportateur m
export licence n licence f d'exportation
expose [ɪk'spəuz] vt exposer; (unmask) démasquer, dévoiler; **to ~ o.s.** (Law) commettre un outrage à la pudeur
exposed [ɪk'spəuzd] adj (land, house) exposé(e); (Elec: wire) à nu; (pipe, beam) apparent(e)
exposition [ɛkspə'zɪʃən] n exposition f
exposure [ɪk'spəuʒəʳ] n exposition f; (publicity) couverture f; (Phot: speed) (temps m de) pose f; (: shot) pose; **suffering from ~** (Med) souffrant des effets du froid et de l'épuisement; **to die of ~** (Med) mourir de froid
exposure meter n posemètre m
expound [ɪk'spaund] vt exposer, expliquer
express [ɪk'spres] adj (definite) formel(le), exprès(-esse); (Brit: letter etc) exprès inv ▷ n (train) rapide m ▷ adv (send) exprès ▷ vt exprimer; **to ~ o.s.** s'exprimer
expression [ɪk'spreʃən] n expression f
expressionism [ɪk'spreʃənɪzəm] n expressionnisme m
expressive [ɪk'spresɪv] adj expressif(-ive)
expressly [ɪk'spresli] adv expressément, formellement
expressway [ɪk'spreswei] n (US) voie f express (à plusieurs files)
expropriate [ɛks'prəuprieit] vt exproprier

expulsion [ɪk'spʌlʃən] n expulsion f; renvoi m
exquisite [ɛk'skwɪzɪt] adj exquis(e)
ex-serviceman ['ɛks'sə:vɪsmən] (irreg) n ancien combattant
ext. abbr (Tel) = **extension**
extemporize [ɪk'stempəraɪz] vi improviser
extend [ɪk'stɛnd] vt (visit, street) prolonger; (deadline) reporter, remettre; (building) agrandir; (offer) présenter, offrir; (Comm: credit) accorder; (hand, arm) tendre ▷ vi (land) s'étendre
extension [ɪk'stɛnʃən] n (of visit, street) prolongation f; (of building) agrandissement m; (building) annexe f; (to wire, table) rallonge f; (telephone: in offices) poste m; (: in private house) téléphone m supplémentaire; **~ 3718** (Tel) poste 3718
extension cable, extension lead n (Elec) rallonge f
extensive [ɪk'stɛnsɪv] adj étendu(e), vaste; (damage, alterations) considérable; (inquiries) approfondi(e); (use) largement répandu(e)
extensively [ɪk'stɛnsɪvlɪ] adv (altered, damaged etc) considérablement; **he's travelled ~** il a beaucoup voyagé
extent [ɪk'stɛnt] n étendue f; (degree: of damage, loss) importance f; **to some ~** dans une certaine mesure; **to a certain ~** dans une certaine mesure, jusqu'à un certain point; **to a large ~** en grande partie; **to the ~ of …** au point de …; **to what ~?** dans quelle mesure?, jusqu'à quel point?; **to such an ~ that …** à tel point que …
extenuating [ɪk'stɛnjueitɪŋ] adj: **~ circumstances** circonstances atténuantes
exterior [ɛk'stɪərɪəʳ] adj extérieur(e) ▷ n extérieur m
exterminate [ɪk'stə:mineit] vt exterminer
extermination [ɪkstə:mɪ'neɪʃən] n extermination f
external [ɛk'stə:nl] adj externe ▷ n: **the ~s** les apparences fpl; **for ~ use only** (Med) à usage externe
externally [ɛk'stə:nəlɪ] adv extérieurement
extinct [ɪk'stɪŋkt] adj (volcano) éteint(e); (species) disparu(e)
extinction [ɪk'stɪŋkʃən] n extinction f
extinguish [ɪk'stɪŋgwɪʃ] vt éteindre
extinguisher [ɪk'stɪŋgwɪʃəʳ] n extincteur m
extol, (US) **extoll** [ɪk'stəul] vt (merits) chanter, prôner; (person) chanter les louanges de
extort [ɪk'stɔːt] vt: **to ~ sth (from)** extorquer qch (à)
extortion [ɪk'stɔːʃən] n extorsion f
extortionate [ɪk'stɔːʃnɪt] adj exorbitant(e)
extra ['ekstrə] adj supplémentaire, de plus ▷ adv (in addition) en plus ▷ n supplément m; (perk) à-coté m; (Cine, Theat) figurant(e); **wine will cost ~** le vin sera en supplément; **~ large sizes** très grandes tailles
extra… ['ekstrə] prefix extra…
extract vt [ɪk'strækt] extraire; (tooth) arracher; (money, promise) soutirer ▷ n ['ekstrækt] extrait m
extraction [ɪk'strækʃən] n extraction f

extractor fan [ɪkˈstræktə-] *n* exhausteur *m*,
ventilateur *m* extracteur

extracurricular [ˈɛkstrəkəˈrɪkjuləʳ] *adj* (*Scol*)
parascolaire

extradite [ˈɛkstrədaɪt] *vt* extrader

extradition [ɛkstrəˈdɪʃən] *n* extradition *f*

extramarital [ˈɛkstrəˈmærɪtl] *adj*
extraconjugal(e)

extramural [ˈɛkstrəˈmjuərl] *adj* hors-faculté *inv*

extraneous [ɛkˈstreɪnɪəs] *adj*: **~ to**
étranger(-ère) à

extraordinary [ɪkˈstrɔːdnrɪ] *adj* extraordinaire;
the ~ thing is that ... le plus étrange *or*
étonnant c'est que ...

extraordinary general meeting *n* assemblée *f*
générale extraordinaire

extrapolation [ɛkstræpəˈleɪʃən] *n*
extrapolation *f*

extrasensory perception [ˈɛkstrəˈsɛnsərɪ-] *n*
perception *f* extrasensorielle

extra time *n* (*Football*) prolongations *fpl*

extravagance [ɪkˈstrævəgəns] *n* (*excessive
spending*) prodigalités *fpl*; (*thing bought*) folie *f*,
dépense excessive

extravagant [ɪkˈstrævəgənt] *adj*
extravagant(e); (*in spending: person*) prodigue,
dépensier(-ière); (: *tastes*) dispendieux(-euse)

extreme [ɪkˈstriːm] *adj, n* extrême (*m*); **the ~
left/right** (*Pol*) l'extrême gauche *f*/droite *f*; **~s
of temperature** différences *fpl* extrêmes de
température

extremely [ɪkˈstriːmlɪ] *adv* extrêmement

extremist [ɪkˈstriːmɪst] *adj, n* extrémiste *m/f*

extremity [ɪkˈstrɛmɪtɪ] *n* extrémité *f*

extricate [ˈɛkstrɪkeɪt] *vt*: **to ~ sth (from)**
dégager qch (de)

extrovert [ˈɛkstrəvəːt] *n* extraverti(e)

exuberance [ɪɡˈzjuːbərns] *n* exubérance *f*

exuberant [ɪɡˈzjuːbərnt] *adj* exubérant(e)

exude [ɪɡˈzjuːd] *vt* exsuder; (*fig*) respirer; **the**

charm *etc* **he ~s** le charme *etc* qui émane de lui

exult [ɪɡˈzʌlt] *vi* exulter, jubiler

exultant [ɪɡˈzʌltənt] *adj* (*shout, expression*) de
triomphe; **to be ~** jubiler, triompher

exultation [ɛɡzʌlˈteɪʃən] *n* exultation *f*,
jubilation *f*

ex-wife [ˈɛkswaɪf] *n* ex-femme *f*

eye [aɪ] *n* œil *m*; (*of needle*) trou *m*, chas *m* ▷ *vt*
examiner; **as far as the ~ can see** à perte de
vue; **to keep an ~ on** surveiller; **to have an ~
for sth** avoir l'œil pour qch; **in the public ~** en
vue; **with an ~ to doing sth** (*Brit*) en vue de
faire qch; **there's more to this than meets
the ~** ce n'est pas aussi simple que cela paraît

eyeball [ˈaɪbɔːl] *n* globe *m* oculaire

eyebath [ˈaɪbaːθ] *n* (*Brit*) œillère *f* (*pour bains d'œil*)

eyebrow [ˈaɪbrau] *n* sourcil *m*

eyebrow pencil *n* crayon *m* à sourcils

eye-catching [ˈaɪkætʃɪŋ] *adj* voyant(e),
accrocheur(-euse)

eye cup *n* (*US*) = **eyebath**

eye drops [ˈaɪdrɒps] *npl* gouttes *fpl* pour les yeux

eyeful [ˈaɪful] *n*: **to get an ~ (of sth)** se rincer
l'œil (en voyant qch)

eyeglass [ˈaɪɡlaːs] *n* monocle *m*

eyelash [ˈaɪlæʃ] *n* cil *m*

eyelet [ˈaɪlɪt] *n* œillet *m*

eye-level [ˈaɪlɛvl] *adj* en hauteur

eyelid [ˈaɪlɪd] *n* paupière *f*

eyeliner [ˈaɪlaɪnəʳ] *n* eye-liner *m*

eye-opener [ˈaɪəupnəʳ] *n* révélation *f*

eye shadow [ˈaɪʃædəu] *n* ombre *f* à paupières

eyesight [ˈaɪsaɪt] *n* vue *f*

eyesore [ˈaɪsɔːʳ] *n* horreur *f*, chose *f* qui dépare *or*
enlaidit

eyestrain [ˈaɪstreɪn] *adj*: **to get ~** se fatiguer la
vue *or* les yeux

eyewash [ˈaɪwɒʃ] *n* bain *m* d'œil; (*fig*) frime *f*

eye witness *n* témoin *m* oculaire

eyrie [ˈɪərɪ] *n* aire *f*

Ff

F¹, f [ɛf] *n* (*letter*) F, f m; (*Mus*): **F** fa m; **F for Frederick**, (US) **F for Fox** F comme François

F² *abbr* (= Fahrenheit) F

FA *n abbr* (Brit: = Football Association) fédération de football

FAA *n abbr* (US) = **Federal Aviation Administration**

fable ['feɪbl] *n* fable f

fabric ['fæbrɪk] *n* tissu m ▷ *cpd*: **~ ribbon** (for typewriter) ruban m (en) tissu

fabricate ['fæbrɪkeɪt] *vt* fabriquer, inventer

fabrication [fæbrɪ'keɪʃən] *n* fabrication f, invention f

fabulous ['fæbjuləs] *adj* fabuleux(-euse); (*inf*: super) formidable, sensationnel(le)

façade [fə'sɑːd] *n* façade f

face [feɪs] *n* visage m, figure f; (*expression*) air m; grimace f; (*of clock*) cadran m; (*of cliff*) paroi f; (*of mountain*) face f; (*of building*) façade f; (*side, surface*) face f ▷ *vt* faire face à; (*facts etc*) accepter; **~ down** (*person*) à plat ventre; (*card*) face en dessous; **to lose/save ~** perdre/sauver la face; **to pull a ~** faire une grimace; **in the ~ of** (*difficulties etc*) face à, devant; **on the ~ of it** à première vue; **~ to ~** face à face
  ▸ **face up to** *vt fus* faire face à, affronter

face cloth *n* (Brit) gant m de toilette

face cream *n* crème f pour le visage

face lift *n* lifting m; (*of façade etc*) ravalement m, retapage m

face pack *n* (Brit) masque m (de beauté)

face powder *n* poudre f (pour le visage)

face-saving ['feɪsseɪvɪŋ] *adj* qui sauve la face

facet ['fæsɪt] *n* facette f

facetious [fə'siːʃəs] *adj* facétieux(-euse)

face-to-face ['feɪstə'feɪs] *adv* face à face

face value ['feɪs'væljuː] *n* (*of coin*) valeur nominale; **to take sth at ~** (*fig*) prendre qch pour argent comptant

facia ['feɪʃə] *n* = **fascia**

facial ['feɪʃl] *adj* facial(e) ▷ *n* soin complet du visage

facile ['fæsaɪl] *adj* facile

facilitate [fə'sɪlɪteɪt] *vt* faciliter

facilities [fə'sɪlɪtɪz] *npl* installations fpl, équipement m; **credit ~** facilités de paiement

facility [fə'sɪlɪtɪ] *n* facilité f

facing ['feɪsɪŋ] *prep* face à, en face de ▷ *n* (*of wall etc*) revêtement m; (*Sewing*) revers m

facsimile [fæk'sɪmɪlɪ] *n* (*exact replica*) facsimilé m; (*also*: **facsimile machine**) télécopieur m; (*transmitted document*) télécopie f

fact [fækt] *n* fait m; **in ~** en fait; **to know for a ~ that ...** savoir pertinemment que ...

fact-finding ['fæktfaɪndɪŋ] *adj*: **a ~ tour** or **mission** une mission d'enquête

faction ['fækʃən] *n* faction f

factional ['fækʃnl] *adj* de factions

factor ['fæktə'] *n* facteur m; (*of sun cream*) indice m (de protection); (*Comm*) factor m, société f d'affacturage; (: agent) dépositaire m/f ▷ *vi* faire du factoring; **safety ~** facteur de sécurité; **I'd like a ~ 15 suntan lotion** je voudrais une crème solaire d'indice 15

factory ['fæktərɪ] *n* usine f, fabrique f

factory farming *n* (Brit) élevage industriel

factory floor *n*: **the ~** (*workers*) les ouvriers mpl; (*workshop*) l'usine f; **on the ~** dans les ateliers

factory ship *n* navire-usine m

factual ['fæktjuəl] *adj* basé(e) sur les faits

faculty ['fækəltɪ] *n* faculté f; (US: teaching staff) corps enseignant

fad [fæd] *n* (*personal*) manie f; (*craze*) engouement m

fade [feɪd] *vi* se décolorer, passer; (*light, sound*) s'affaiblir, disparaître; (*flower*) se faner
  ▸ **fade away** *vi* (*sound*) s'affaiblir
  ▸ **fade in** *vt* (*picture*) ouvrir en fondu; (*sound*) monter progressivement
  ▸ **fade out** *vt* (*picture*) fermer en fondu; (*sound*) baisser progressivement

faeces, (US) **feces** ['fiːsiːz] *npl* fèces fpl

fag [fæg] *n* (Brit inf: cigarette) clope f; (: chore): **what a ~!** quelle corvée!; (US inf: homosexual) pédé m

fag end *n* (Brit inf) mégot m

fagged out [fægd-] *adj* (Brit inf) crevé(e)

Fahrenheit ['fɑːrənhaɪt] *n* Fahrenheit m inv

fail [feɪl] *vt* (*exam*) échouer à; (*candidate*) recaler; (*subj: courage, memory*) faire défaut à ▷ *vi* échouer; (*supplies*) manquer; (*eyesight, health, light: also: be failing*) baisser, s'affaiblir; (*brakes*) lâcher; **to ~**

to do sth (*neglect*) négliger de *or* ne pas faire qch; (*be unable*) ne pas arriver *or* parvenir à faire qch; **without ~** à coup sûr; sans faute

failing ['feɪlɪŋ] *n* défaut *m* ▷ *prep* faute de; **~ that** à défaut, sinon

failsafe ['feɪlseɪf] *adj* (*device etc*) à sûreté intégrée

failure ['feɪljər] *n* échec *m*; (*person*) raté(e); (*mechanical etc*) défaillance *f*; **his ~ to turn up** le fait de n'être pas venu *or* qu'il ne soit pas venu

faint [feɪnt] *adj* faible; (*recollection*) vague; (*mark*) à peine visible; (*smell, breeze, trace*) léger(-ère) ▷ *n* évanouissement *m* ▷ *vi* s'évanouir; **to feel ~** défaillir

faintest ['feɪntɪst] *adj*: **I haven't the ~ idea** je n'en ai pas la moindre idée

faint-hearted ['feɪnt'hɑːtɪd] *adj* pusillanime

faintly ['feɪntlɪ] *adv* faiblement; (*vaguely*) vaguement

faintness ['feɪntnɪs] *n* faiblesse *f*

fair [fɛər] *adj* équitable, juste; (*reasonable*) correct(e), honnête; (*hair*) blond(e); (*skin, complexion*) pâle, blanc (blanche); (*weather*) beau (belle); (*good enough*) assez bon(ne); (*sizeable*) considérable ▷ *adv*: **to play ~** jouer franc jeu ▷ *n* foire *f*; (*Brit: funfair*) fête (foraine); (*also*: **trade fair**) foire(-exposition) commerciale; **it's not ~!** ce n'est pas juste!; **a ~ amount of** une quantité considérable de

fair copy *n* copie *f* au propre, corrigé *m*

fair game *n*: **to be ~ (for)** être une cible légitime (pour)

fairground ['fɛəgraund] *n* champ *m* de foire

fair-haired [fɛə'hɛəd] *adj* (*person*) aux cheveux clairs, blond(e)

fairly ['fɛəlɪ] *adv* (*justly*) équitablement; (*quite*) assez; **I'm ~ sure** j'en suis quasiment *or* presque sûr

fairness ['fɛənɪs] *n* (*of trial etc*) justice *f*, équité *f*; (*of person*) sens *m* de la justice; **in all ~** en toute justice

fair play *n* fair play *m*

fair trade *n* commerce *m* équitable

fairway ['fɛəweɪ] *n* (*Golf*) fairway *m*

fairy ['fɛərɪ] *n* fée *f*

fairy godmother *n* bonne fée

fairy lights *npl* (*Brit*) guirlande *f* électrique

fairy tale *n* conte *m* de fées

faith [feɪθ] *n* foi *f*; (*trust*) confiance *f*; (*sect*) culte *m*, religion *f*; **to have ~ in sb/sth** avoir confiance en qn/qch

faithful ['feɪθful] *adj* fidèle

faithfully ['feɪθfəlɪ] *adv* fidèlement; **yours ~** (*Brit: in letters*) veuillez agréer l'expression de mes salutations les plus distinguées

faith healer [-hiːlər] *n* guérisseur(-euse)

fake [feɪk] *n* (*painting etc*) faux *m*; (*photo*) trucage *m*; (*person*) imposteur *m* ▷ *adj* faux (fausse) ▷ *vt* (*emotions*) simuler; (*painting*) faire un faux de; (*photo*) truquer; (*story*) fabriquer; **his illness is a ~** sa maladie est une comédie *or* de la simulation

falcon ['fɔːlkən] *n* faucon *m*

Falkland Islands ['fɔːlklənd-] *npl*: **the ~** les Malouines *fpl*, les îles *fpl* Falkland

fall [fɔːl] *n* chute *f*; (*decrease*) baisse *f*; (*US: autumn*) automne *m* ▷ *vi* (*pt* **fell**, *pp* **-en** [fɛl, 'fɔːlən]) tomber; (*price, temperature, dollar*) baisser; **falls** *npl* (*waterfall*) chute *f* d'eau, cascade *f*; **to ~ flat** (*vi: on one's face*) tomber de tout son long, s'étaler; (*joke*) tomber à plat; (*plan*) échouer; **to ~ short of** (*sb's expectations*) ne pas répondre à; **a ~ of snow** (*Brit*) une chute de neige

▶ **fall apart** *vi* (*object*) tomber en morceaux; (*inf: emotionally*) craquer

▶ **fall back** *vi* reculer, se retirer

▶ **fall back on** *vt fus* se rabattre sur; **to have something to ~ back on** (*money etc*) avoir quelque chose en réserve; (*job etc*) avoir une solution de rechange

▶ **fall behind** *vi* prendre du retard

▶ **fall down** *vi* (*person*) tomber; (*building*) s'effondrer, s'écrouler

▶ **fall for** *vt fus* (*trick*) se laisser prendre à; (*person*) tomber amoureux(-euse) de

▶ **fall in** *vi* s'effondrer; (*Mil*) se mettre en rangs

▶ **fall in with** *vt fus* (*sb's plans etc*) accepter

▶ **fall off** *vi* tomber; (*diminish*) baisser, diminuer

▶ **fall out** *vi* (*friends etc*) se brouiller; (*hair, teeth*) tomber

▶ **fall over** *vi* tomber (par terre)

▶ **fall through** *vi* (*plan, project*) tomber à l'eau

fallacy ['fæləsɪ] *n* erreur *f*, illusion *f*

fallback ['fɔːlbæk] *adj*: **~ position** position *f* de repli

fallen ['fɔːlən] *pp of* **fall**

fallible ['fæləbl] *adj* faillible

fallopian tube [fə'ləupɪən-] *n* (*Anat*) trompe *f* de Fallope

fallout ['fɔːlaut] *n* retombées (radioactives)

fallout shelter *n* abri *m* anti-atomique

fallow ['fæləu] *adj* en jachère; en friche

false [fɔːls] *adj* faux (fausse); **under ~ pretences** sous un faux prétexte

false alarm *n* fausse alerte

falsehood ['fɔːlshud] *n* mensonge *m*

falsely ['fɔːlslɪ] *adv* (*accuse*) à tort

false teeth *npl* (*Brit*) fausses dents, dentier *m*

falsify ['fɔːlsɪfaɪ] *vt* falsifier; (*accounts*) maquiller

falter ['fɔːltər] *vi* chanceler, vaciller

fame [feɪm] *n* renommée *f*, renom *m*

familiar [fə'mɪlɪər] *adj* familier(-ière); **to be ~ with sth** connaître qch; **to make o.s. ~ with sth** se familiariser avec qch; **to be on ~ terms with sb** bien connaître qn

familiarity [fəmɪlɪ'ærɪtɪ] *n* familiarité *f*

familiarize [fə'mɪlɪəraɪz] *vt* familiariser; **to ~ o.s. with** se familiariser avec

family ['fæmɪlɪ] *n* famille *f*

family allowance *n* (*Brit*) allocations familiales

family business *n* entreprise familiale

family credit *n* (*Brit*) complément familial

family doctor *n* médecin *m* de famille

family life *n* vie *f* de famille

family man (irreg) n père m de famille
family planning n planning familial
family planning clinic n centre m de planning familial
family tree n arbre m généalogique
famine ['fæmɪn] n famine f
famished ['fæmɪʃt] adj affamé(e); **I'm ~!** (inf) je meurs de faim!
famous ['feɪməs] adj célèbre
famously ['feɪməslɪ] adv (get on) fameusement, à merveille
fan [fæn] n (folding) éventail m; (Elec) ventilateur m; (person) fan m, admirateur(-trice); (Sport) supporter m/f ▷ vt éventer; (fire, quarrel) attiser
  ▶ **fan out** vi se déployer (en éventail)
fanatic [fə'nætɪk] n fanatique m/f
fanatical [fə'nætɪkl] adj fanatique
fan belt n courroie f de ventilateur
fancied ['fænsɪd] adj imaginaire
fanciful ['fænsɪful] adj fantaisiste
fan club n fan-club m
fancy ['fænsɪ] n (whim) fantaisie f, envie f; (imagination) imagination f ▷ adj (luxury) de luxe; (elaborate: jewellery, packaging) fantaisie inv; (showy) tape-à-l'œil inv; (pretentious: words) recherché(e) ▷ vt (feel like, want) avoir envie de; (imagine) imaginer; **to take a ~ to** se prendre d'affection pour; s'enticher de; **it took** or **caught my ~** ça m'a plu; **when the ~ takes him** quand ça lui prend; **to ~ that ...** se figurer or s'imaginer que ...; **he fancies her** elle lui plaît
fancy dress n déguisement m, travesti m
fancy-dress ball [fænsɪ'drɛs-] n bal masqué or costumé
fancy goods npl articles mpl (de) fantaisie
fanfare ['fænfɛəʳ] n fanfare f (musique)
fanfold paper ['fænfəuld-] n papier m à pliage accordéon
fang [fæŋ] n croc m; (of snake) crochet m
fan heater n (Brit) radiateur soufflant
fanlight ['fænlaɪt] n imposte f
fanny ['fænɪ] n (Brit inf!) chatte f (!); (US inf) cul m (!)
fantasize ['fæntəsaɪz] vi fantasmer
fantastic [fæn'tæstɪk] adj fantastique
fantasy ['fæntəsɪ] n imagination f, fantaisie f; (unreality) fantasme m
fanzine ['fænziːn] n fanzine m
FAO n abbr (= Food and Agriculture Organization) FAO f
FAQ n abbr (= frequently asked question) FAQ f inv, faq f inv ▷ abbr (= free alongside quay) FLQ
far [fɑːʳ] adj (distant) lointain(e), éloigné(e) ▷ adv loin; **the ~ side/end** l'autre côté/bout; **the ~ left/right** (Pol) l'extrême gauche f/droite f; **is it ~ to London?** est-ce qu'on est loin de Londres?; **it's not ~ (from here)** ce n'est pas loin (d'ici); **~ away, ~ off** au loin, dans le lointain; **~ better** beaucoup mieux; **~ from** loin de; **by ~** de loin, de beaucoup; **as ~ back as the 13th century** dès le 13e siècle; **go as ~ as the bridge** allez jusqu'au pont; **as ~ as I know** pour autant que

je sache; **how ~ is it to ...?** combien y a-t-il jusqu'à ...?; **as ~ as possible** dans la mesure du possible; **how ~ have you got with your work?** où en êtes-vous dans votre travail?
faraway ['fɑːrəweɪ] adj lointain(e); (look) absent(e)
farce [fɑːs] n farce f
farcical ['fɑːsɪkl] adj grotesque
fare [fɛəʳ] n (on trains, buses) prix m du billet; (in taxi) prix de la course; (passenger in taxi) client m; (food) table f, chère f ▷ vi se débrouiller; **half ~** demi-tarif; **full ~** plein tarif
Far East n: **the ~** l'Extrême-Orient m
farewell [fɛə'wɛl] excl, n adieu m ▷ cpd (party etc) d'adieux
far-fetched ['fɑː'fɛtʃt] adj exagéré(e), poussé(e)
farm [fɑːm] n ferme f ▷ vt cultiver
  ▶ **farm out** vt (work etc) distribuer
farmer ['fɑːməʳ] n fermier(-ière), cultivateur(-trice)
farmhand ['fɑːmhænd] n ouvrier(-ière) agricole
farmhouse ['fɑːmhaus] n (maison f de) ferme f
farming ['fɑːmɪŋ] n agriculture f; (of animals) élevage m; **intensive ~** culture intensive; **sheep ~** élevage du mouton
farm labourer n = **farmhand**
farmland ['fɑːmlænd] n terres cultivées or arables
farm produce n produits mpl agricoles
farm worker n = **farmhand**
farmyard ['fɑːmjɑːd] n cour f de ferme
Faroe Islands ['fɛərəu-] npl, **Faroes** ['fɛərəuz] npl: **the ~** les îles fpl Féroé or Faeroe
far-reaching ['fɑː'riːtʃɪŋ] adj d'une grande portée
far-sighted ['fɑː'saɪtɪd] adj presbyte; (fig) prévoyant(e), qui voit loin
fart [fɑːt] (inf!) n pet m ▷ vi péter
farther ['fɑːðəʳ] adv plus loin ▷ adj plus éloigné(e), plus lointain(e)
farthest ['fɑːðɪst] superlative of **far**
FAS abbr (Brit: = free alongside ship) FLB
fascia ['feɪʃə] n (Aut) (garniture f du) tableau m de bord
fascinate ['fæsɪneɪt] vt fasciner, captiver
fascinating ['fæsɪneɪtɪŋ] adj fascinant(e)
fascination [fæsɪ'neɪʃən] n fascination f
fascism ['fæʃɪzəm] n fascisme m
fascist ['fæʃɪst] adj, n fasciste m/f
fashion ['fæʃən] n mode f; (manner) façon f, manière f ▷ vt façonner; **in ~** à la mode; **out of ~** démodé(e); **in the Greek ~** à la grecque; **after a ~** (finish, manage etc) tant bien que mal
fashionable ['fæʃnəbl] adj à la mode
fashion designer n (grand(e)) couturier(-ière)
fashion show n défilé m de mannequins or de mode
fast [fɑːst] adj rapide; (clock): **to be ~** avancer; (dye, colour) grand or bon teint inv ▷ adv vite, rapidement; (stuck, held) solidement ▷ n jeûne m ▷ vi jeûner; **my watch is 5 minutes ~** ma montre avance de 5 minutes; **~ asleep**

profondément endormi; **as ~ as I can** aussi vite que je peux; **to make a boat ~** (*Brit*) amarrer un bateau

fasten ['fɑːsn] *vt* attacher, fixer; (*coat*) attacher, fermer ▷ *vi* se fermer, s'attacher

▸ **fasten on, fasten upon** *vt fus* (*idea*) se cramponner à

fastener ['fɑːsnər], **fastening** ['fɑːsnɪŋ] *n* fermeture *f*, attache *f*; (*Brit: zip fastener*) fermeture éclair® *inv or* à glissière

fast food *n* fast food *m*, restauration *f* rapide

fastidious [fæs'tɪdɪəs] *adj* exigeant(e), difficile

fast lane *n* (*Aut: in Britain*) voie *f* de droite

fat [fæt] *adj* gros(se) ▷ *n* graisse *f*; (*on meat*) gras *m*; (*for cooking*) matière grasse; **to live off the ~ of the land** vivre grassement

fatal ['feɪtl] *adj* (*mistake*) fatal(e); (*injury*) mortel(le)

fatalism ['feɪtlɪzəm] *n* fatalisme *m*

fatality [fə'tælɪtɪ] *n* (*road death etc*) victime *f*, décès *m*

fatally ['feɪtəlɪ] *adv* fatalement; (*injured*) mortellement

fate [feɪt] *n* destin *m*; (*of person*) sort *m*; **to meet one's ~** trouver la mort

fated ['feɪtɪd] *adj* (*person*) condamné(e); (*project*) voué(e) à l'échec

fateful ['feɪtful] *adj* fatidique

fat-free ['fæt'friː] *adj* sans matières grasses

father ['fɑːðər] *n* père *m*

Father Christmas *n* le Père Noël

fatherhood ['fɑːðəhud] *n* paternité *f*

father-in-law ['fɑːðərɪnlɔː] *n* beau-père *m*

fatherland ['fɑːðəlænd] *n* (mère *f*) patrie *f*

fatherly ['fɑːðəlɪ] *adj* paternel(le)

fathom ['fæðəm] *n* brasse *f* (= 1828 *mm*) ▷ *vt* (*mystery*) sonder, pénétrer

fatigue [fə'tiːg] *n* fatigue *f*; (*Mil*) corvée *f*; **metal ~** fatigue du métal

fatness ['fætnɪs] *n* corpulence *f*, grosseur *f*

fatten ['fætn] *vt, vi* engraisser

fattening ['fætnɪŋ] *adj* (*food*) qui fait grossir; **chocolate is ~** le chocolat fait grossir

fatty ['fætɪ] *adj* (*food*) gras(se) ▷ *n* (*inf*) gros (grosse)

fatuous ['fætjuəs] *adj* stupide

faucet ['fɔːsɪt] *n* (*US*) robinet *m*

fault [fɔːlt] *n* faute *f*; (*defect*) défaut *m*; (*Geo*) faille *f* ▷ *vt* trouver des défauts à, prendre en défaut; **it's my ~** c'est de ma faute; **to find ~ with** trouver à redire *or* à critiquer à; **at ~** fautif(-ive), coupable; **to a ~** à l'excès

faultless ['fɔːltlɪs] *adj* impeccable; irréprochable

faulty ['fɔːltɪ] *adj* défectueux(-euse)

fauna ['fɔːnə] *n* faune *f*

faux pas ['fəu'pɑː] *n* impair *m*, bévue *f*, gaffe *f*

favour, (*US*) **favor** ['feɪvər] *n* faveur *f*; (*help*) service *m* ▷ *vt* (*proposition*) être en faveur de; (*pupil etc*) favoriser; (*team, horse*) donner gagnant; **to do sb a ~** rendre un service à qn; **in ~ of** en faveur de; **to be in ~ of sth/of doing sth** être partisan de qch/de faire qch; **to find ~**

with sb trouver grâce aux yeux de qn

favourable, (*US*) **favorable** ['feɪvrəbl] *adj* favorable; (*price*) avantageux(-euse)

favourably, (*US*) **favorably** ['feɪvrəblɪ] *adv* favorablement

favourite, (*US*) **favorite** ['feɪvrɪt] *adj, n* favori(te)

favouritism, (*US*) **favoritism** ['feɪvrɪtɪzəm] *n* favoritisme *m*

fawn [fɔːn] *n* (*deer*) faon *m* ▷ *adj* (*also*: **fawn-coloured**) fauve ▷ *vi*: **to ~ (up)on** flatter servilement

fax [fæks] *n* (*document*) télécopie *f*; (*machine*) télécopieur *m* ▷ *vt* envoyer par télécopie

FBI *n abbr* (*US: = Federal Bureau of Investigation*) FBI *m*

FCC *n abbr* (*US*) = **Federal Communications Commission**

FCO *n abbr* (*Brit: = Foreign and Commonwealth Office*) ministère des Affaires étrangères et du Commonwealth

FD *n abbr* (*US*) = **fire department**

FDA *n abbr* (*US: = Food and Drug Administration*) office de contrôle des produits pharmaceutiques et alimentaires

FE *n abbr* = **further education**

fear [fɪər] *n* crainte *f*, peur *f* ▷ *vt* craindre ▷ *vi*: **to ~ for** craindre pour; **to ~ that** craindre que; **~ of heights** vertige *m*; **for ~ of** de peur que + *sub* or de + *infinitive*

fearful ['fɪəful] *adj* craintif(-ive); (*sight, noise*) affreux(-euse), épouvantable; **to be ~ of** avoir peur de, craindre

fearfully ['fɪəfəlɪ] *adv* (*timidly*) craintivement; (*inf: very*) affreusement

fearless ['fɪəlɪs] *adj* intrépide, sans peur

fearsome ['fɪəsəm] *adj* (*opponent*) redoutable; (*sight*) épouvantable

feasibility [fiːzə'bɪlɪtɪ] *n* (*of plan*) possibilité *f* de réalisation, faisabilité *f*

feasibility study *n* étude *f* de faisabilité

feasible ['fiːzəbl] *adj* faisable, réalisable

feast [fiːst] *n* festin *m*, banquet *m*; (*Rel: also*: **feast day**) fête *f* ▷ *vi* festoyer; **to ~ on** se régaler de

feat [fiːt] *n* exploit *m*, prouesse *f*

feather ['fɛðər] *n* plume *f* ▷ *vt*: **to ~ one's nest** (*fig*) faire sa pelote ▷ *cpd* (*bed etc*) de plumes

feather-weight ['fɛðəweɪt] *n* poids *m* plume *inv*

feature ['fiːtʃər] *n* caractéristique *f*; (*article*) chronique *f*, rubrique *f* ▷ *vt* (*film*) avoir pour vedette(s) ▷ *vi* figurer (en bonne place); **features** *npl* (*of face*) traits *mpl*; **a (special) ~ on sth/sb** un reportage sur qch/qn; **it ~d prominently in ...** cela a figuré en bonne place sur *or* dans ...

feature film *n* long métrage

featureless ['fiːtʃəlɪs] *adj* anonyme, sans traits distinctifs

Feb. *abbr* (= *February*) fév

February ['fɛbruərɪ] *n* février *m*; *for phrases see also* **July**

feces ['fiːsiːz] *npl* (*US*) = **faeces**

feckless ['fɛklɪs] *adj* inepte

Fed *abbr* (*US*) = **federal; federation**

fed [fɛd] *pt, pp of* **feed**

Fed. [fɛd] *n abbr* (*US inf*) = **Federal Reserve Board**

federal ['fɛdərəl] *adj* fédéral(e)

Federal Reserve Board *n* (*US*) *organe de contrôle de la banque centrale américaine*

Federal Trade Commission *n* (*US*) *organisme de protection contre les pratiques commerciales abusives*

federation [fɛdə'reɪʃən] *n* fédération *f*

fed up [fɛd'ʌp] *adj*: **to be ~ (with)** en avoir marre *or* plein le dos (de)

fee [fi:] *n* rémunération *f*; (*of doctor, lawyer*) honoraires *mpl*; (*of school, college etc*) frais *mpl* de scolarité; (*for examination*) droits *mpl*; **entrance/membership ~** droit d'entrée/d'inscription; **for a small ~** pour une somme modique

feeble ['fi:bl] *adj* faible; (*attempt, excuse*) pauvre; (*joke*) piteux(-euse)

feeble-minded ['fi:bl'maɪndɪd] *adj* faible d'esprit

feed [fi:d] *n* (*of baby*) tétée *f*; (*of animal*) nourriture *f*, pâture *f*; (*on printer*) mécanisme *m* d'alimentation ▷ *vt* (*pt, pp* **fed** [fɛd]) (*person*) nourrir; (*Brit: baby: breastfeed*) allaiter; (*: with bottle*) donner le biberon à; (*horse etc*) donner à manger à; (*machine*) alimenter; (*data etc*) **to ~ sth into** enregistrer qch dans
▶ **feed back** *vt* (*results*) donner en retour
▶ **feed on** *vt fus* se nourrir de

feedback ['fi:dbæk] *n* (*Elec*) effet *m* Larsen; (*from person*) réactions *fpl*

feeder ['fi:dər] *n* (*bib*) bavette *f*

feeding bottle ['fi:dɪŋ-] *n* (*Brit*) biberon *m*

feel [fi:l] *n* (*sensation*) sensation *f*; (*impression*) impression *f* ▷ *vt* (*pt, pp* **felt** [fɛlt]) (*touch*) toucher; (*explore*) tâter, palper; (*cold, pain*) sentir; (*grief, anger*) ressentir, éprouver; (*think, believe*): **to ~ (that)** trouver que; **I ~ that you ought to do it** il me semble que vous devriez le faire; **to ~ hungry/cold** avoir faim/froid; **to ~ lonely/better** se sentir seul/mieux; **I don't ~ well** je ne me sens pas bien; **to ~ sorry for** avoir pitié de; **it ~s soft** c'est doux au toucher; **it ~s colder here** je trouve qu'il fait plus froid ici; **it ~s like velvet** on dirait du velours, ça ressemble au velours; **to ~ like** (*want*) avoir envie de; **to ~ about** *or* **around** fouiller, tâtonner; **to get the ~ of sth** (*fig*) s'habituer à qch

feeler ['fi:lər] *n* (*of insect*) antenne *f*; (*fig*): **to put out a ~** *or* **~s** tâter le terrain

feeling ['fi:lɪŋ] *n* (*physical*) sensation *f*; (*emotion, impression*) sentiment *m*; **to hurt sb's ~s** froisser qn; **~s ran high about it** cela a déchaîné les passions; **what are your ~s about the matter?** quel est votre sentiment sur cette question?; **my ~ is that ...** j'estime que ...; **I have a ~ that ...** j'ai l'impression que ...

fee-paying school ['fi:peɪɪŋ-] *n* établissement (d'enseignement) privé

feet [fi:t] *npl of* **foot**

feign [feɪn] *vt* feindre, simuler

felicitous [fɪ'lɪsɪtəs] *adj* heureux(-euse)

fell [fɛl] *pt of* **fall** ▷ *vt* (*tree*) abattre ▷ *n* (*Brit: mountain*) montagne *f*; (*: moorland*): **the ~s** la lande ▷ *adj*: **with one ~ blow** d'un seul coup

fellow ['fɛləu] *n* type *m*; (*comrade*) compagnon *m*; (*of learned society*) membre *m*; (*of university*) universitaire *m/f* (*membre du conseil*) ▷ *cpd*: **their ~ prisoners/students** leurs camarades prisonniers/étudiants; **his ~ workers** ses collègues *mpl* (de travail)

fellow citizen *n* concitoyen(ne)

fellow countryman (*irreg*) *n* compatriote *m*

fellow feeling *n* sympathie *f*

fellow men *npl* semblables *mpl*

fellowship ['fɛləuʃɪp] *n* (*society*) association *f*; (*comradeship*) amitié *f*, camaraderie *f*; (*Scol*) sorte de bourse universitaire

fellow traveller *n* compagnon (compagne) de route; (*Pol*) communisant(e)

fell-walking ['fɛlwɔ:kɪŋ] *n* (*Brit*) randonnée *f* en montagne

felon ['fɛlən] *n* (*Law*) criminel(le)

felony ['fɛlənɪ] *n* crime *m*, forfait *m*

felt [fɛlt] *pt, pp of* **feel** ▷ *n* feutre *m*

felt-tip ['fɛlttɪp-] *n* (*also:* **felt-tip pen**) stylofeutre *m*

female ['fi:meɪl] *n* (*Zool*) femelle *f*; (*pej: woman*) bonne femme ▷ *adj* (*Biol, Elec*) femelle; (*sex, character*) féminin(e); (*vote etc*) des femmes; (*child etc*) du sexe féminin; **male and ~ students** étudiants et étudiantes

female impersonator *n* (*Theat*) travesti *m*

feminine ['fɛmɪnɪn] *adj* féminin(e) ▷ *n* féminin *m*

femininity [fɛmɪ'nɪnɪtɪ] *n* féminité *f*

feminism ['fɛmɪnɪzəm] *n* féminisme *m*

feminist ['fɛmɪnɪst] *n* féministe *m/f*

fen [fɛn] *n* (*Brit*): **the F~s** les plaines *fpl* du Norfolk (*anciennement marécageuses*)

fence [fɛns] *n* barrière *f*; (*Sport*) obstacle *m*; (*inf: person*) receleur(-euse) ▷ *vt* (*also:* **fence in**) clôturer ▷ *vi* faire de l'escrime; **to sit on the ~** (*fig*) ne pas se mouiller

fencing ['fɛnsɪŋ] *n* (*sport*) escrime *m*

fend [fɛnd] *vi*: **to ~ for o.s.** se débrouiller (tout seul)
▶ **fend off** *vt* (*attack etc*) parer; (*questions*) éluder

fender ['fɛndər] *n* garde-feu *m inv*; (*on boat*) défense *f*; (*US: of car*) aile *f*

fennel ['fɛnl] *n* fenouil *m*

ferment *vi* [fə'mɛnt] fermenter ▷ *n* ['fə:mɛnt] (*fig*) agitation *f*, effervescence *f*

fermentation [fə:mɛn'teɪʃən] *n* fermentation *f*

fern [fə:n] *n* fougère *f*

ferocious [fə'rəuʃəs] *adj* féroce

ferocity [fə'rɔsɪtɪ] *n* férocité *f*

ferret ['fɛrɪt] *n* furet *m*
▶ **ferret about, ferret around** *vi* fureter
▶ **ferret out** *vt* dénicher

ferry ['fɛrɪ] *n* (*small*) bac *m*; (*large: also:* **ferryboat**) ferry(-boat) *m* ▷ *vt* transporter; **to ~ sth/sb across** *or* **over** faire traverser qch/qn

ferryman ['fɛrɪmən] (*irreg*) *n* passeur *m*

fertile ['fə:taɪl] *adj* fertile; (*Biol*) fécond(e); ~ **period** période *f* de fécondité

fertility [fə'tɪlɪtɪ] *n* fertilité *f*; fécondité *f*

fertility drug *n* médicament *m* contre la stérilité

fertilize ['fə:tɪlaɪz] *vt* fertiliser; (*Biol*) féconder

fertilizer ['fə:tɪlaɪzəʳ] *n* engrais *m*

fervent ['fə:vənt] *adj* fervent(e), ardent(e)

fervour, (US) **fervor** ['fə:vəʳ] *n* ferveur *f*

fester ['fɛstəʳ] *vi* suppurer

festival ['fɛstɪvəl] *n* (*Rel*) fête *f*; (*Art, Mus*) festival *m*

festive ['fɛstɪv] *adj* de fête; **the ~ season** (*Brit: Christmas*) la période des fêtes

festivities [fɛs'tɪvɪtɪz] *npl* réjouissances *fpl*

festoon [fɛs'tu:n] *vt*: **to ~ with** orner de

fetch [fɛtʃ] *vt* aller chercher; (*Brit: sell for*) rapporter; **how much did it ~?** ça a atteint quel prix?

▸ **fetch up** *vi* (*Brit*) se retrouver

fetching ['fɛtʃɪn] *adj* charmant(e)

fête [feɪt] *n* fête *f*, kermesse *f*

fetid ['fɛtɪd] *adj* fétide

fetish ['fɛtɪʃ] *n* fétiche *m*

fetter ['fɛtəʳ] *vt* entraver

fetters ['fɛtəz] *npl* chaînes *fpl*

fettle ['fɛtl] *n* (*Brit*): **in fine ~** en bonne forme

fetus ['fi:təs] *n* (US) = **foetus**

feud [fju:d] *n* querelle *f*, dispute *f* ▷ *vi* se quereller, se disputer; **a family ~** une querelle de famille

feudal ['fju:dl] *adj* féodal(e)

feudalism ['fju:dlɪzəm] *n* féodalité *f*

fever ['fi:vəʳ] *n* fièvre *f*; **he has a ~** il a de la fièvre

feverish ['fi:vərɪʃ] *adj* fiévreux(-euse), fébrile

few [fju:] *adj* (*not many*) peu de ▷ *pron* peu; ~ **succeed** il y en a peu qui réussissent, (bien) peu réussissent; **they were ~** ils étaient peu (nombreux), il y en avait peu; **a ~** (*as adj*) quelques; (*as pron*) quelques-uns(-unes); **I know a ~** j'en connais quelques-uns; **quite a ~ ...** (*adj*) un certain nombre de ..., pas mal de ...; **in the next ~ days** dans les jours qui viennent; **in the past ~ days** ces derniers jours; **every ~ days/ months** tous les deux ou trois jours/mois; **a ~ more ...** encore quelques ..., quelques ... de plus

fewer ['fju:əʳ] *adj* moins de ▷ *pron* moins; **they are ~ now** il y en a moins maintenant, ils sont moins (nombreux) maintenant

fewest ['fju:ɪst] *adj* le moins nombreux

FFA *n abbr* = **Future Farmers of America**

FH *abbr* (*Brit*) = **fire hydrant**

FHA *n abbr* (US: = *Federal Housing Administration*) office fédéral du logement

fiancé [fɪ'ã:ŋseɪ] *n* fiancé *m*

fiancée [fɪ'ã:ŋseɪ] *n* fiancée *f*

fiasco [fɪ'æskəu] *n* fiasco *m*

fib [fɪb] *n* bobard *m*

fibre, (US) **fiber** ['faɪbəʳ] *n* fibre *f*

fibreboard, (US) **fiberboard** ['faɪbəbɔ:d] *n* panneau *m* de fibres

fibreglass, (US) **Fiberglass**® ['faɪbəɡlɑ:s] *n* fibre *f* de verre

fibrositis [faɪbrə'saɪtɪs] *n* aponévrosite *f*

FICA *n abbr* (US) = **Federal Insurance Contributions Act**

fickle ['fɪkl] *adj* inconstant(e), volage, capricieux(-euse)

fiction ['fɪkʃən] *n* romans *mpl*, littérature *f* romanesque; (*invention*) fiction *f*

fictional ['fɪkʃənl] *adj* fictif(-ive)

fictionalize ['fɪkʃnəlaɪz] *vt* romancer

fictitious [fɪk'tɪʃəs] *adj* fictif(-ive), imaginaire

fiddle ['fɪdl] *n* (*Mus*) violon *m*; (*cheating*) combine *f*; escroquerie *f* ▷ *vt* (*Brit: accounts*) falsifier, maquiller; **tax ~** fraude fiscale, combine *f* pour échapper au fisc; **to work a ~** traficoter

▸ **fiddle with** *vt fus* tripoter

fiddler ['fɪdləʳ] *n* violoniste *m/f*

fiddly ['fɪdlɪ] *adj* (*task*) minutieux(-euse)

fidelity [fɪ'dɛlɪtɪ] *n* fidélité *f*

fidget ['fɪdʒɪt] *vi* se trémousser, remuer

fidgety ['fɪdʒɪtɪ] *adj* agité(e), qui a la bougeotte

fiduciary [fɪ'dju:ʃɪərɪ] *n* agent *m* fiduciaire

field [fi:ld] *n* champ *m*; (*fig*) domaine *m*, champ; (*Sport: ground*) terrain *m*; (*Comput*) champ, zone *f*; **to lead the ~** (*Sport, Comm*) dominer; **the children had a ~ day** (*fig*) c'était un grand jour pour les enfants

field glasses *npl* jumelles *fpl*

field hospital *n* antenne chirurgicale

field marshal *n* maréchal *m*

fieldwork ['fi:ldwə:k] *n* travaux *mpl* pratiques (*or* recherches *fpl*) sur le terrain

fiend [fi:nd] *n* démon *m*

fiendish ['fi:ndɪʃ] *adj* diabolique

fierce [fɪəs] *adj* (*look, animal*) féroce, sauvage; (*wind, attack, person*) (très) violent(e); (*fighting, enemy*) acharné(e)

fiery ['faɪərɪ] *adj* ardent(e), brûlant(e), fougueux(-euse)

FIFA ['fi:fə] *n abbr* (= *Fédération Internationale de Football Association*) FIFA *f*

fifteen [fɪf'ti:n] *num* quinze

fifteenth [fɪf'ti:nθ] *num* quinzième

fifth [fɪfθ] *num* cinquième

fiftieth ['fɪftɪɪθ] *num* cinquantième

fifty ['fɪftɪ] *num* cinquante

fifty-fifty ['fɪftɪ'fɪftɪ] *adv* moitié-moitié; **to share ~ with sb** partager moitié-moitié avec qn ▷ *adj*: **to have a ~ chance (of success)** avoir une chance sur deux (de réussir)

fig [fɪɡ] *n* figue *f*

fight [faɪt] (*pt, pp* **fought** [fɔ:t]) *n* (*between persons*) bagarre *f*; (*argument*) dispute *f*; (*Mil*) combat *m*; (*against cancer etc*) lutte *f* ▷ *vt* se battre contre; (*cancer, alcoholism, emotion*) combattre, lutter contre; (*election*) se présenter à; (*Law: case*) défendre ▷ *vi* se battre; (*argue*) se disputer; (*fig*): **to ~ (for/against)** lutter (pour/contre)

▸ **fight back** *vi* rendre les coups; (*after illness*) reprendre le dessus ▷ *vt* (*tears*) réprimer

▸ **fight off** *vt* repousser; (*disease, sleep, urge*) lutter contre

fighter ['faɪtə'] n lutteur m; (fig: plane) chasseur m

fighter pilot n pilote m de chasse

fighting ['faɪtɪŋ] n combats mpl; (brawls) bagarres fpl

figment ['fɪgmənt] n: **a ~ of the imagination** une invention

figurative ['fɪgjʊrətɪv] adj figuré(e)

figure ['fɪgə'] n (Drawing, Geom) figure f; (number) chiffre m; (body, outline) silhouette f; (person's shape) ligne f, formes fpl; (person) personnage m ▷ vt (US: think) supposer ▷ vi (appear) figurer; (US: make sense) s'expliquer; **public ~** personnalité f; **~ of speech** figure f de rhétorique

▶ **figure on** vt fus (US): **to ~ on doing** compter faire

▶ **figure out** vt (understand) arriver à comprendre; (plan) calculer

figurehead ['fɪgəhɛd] n (Naut) figure f de proue; (pej) prête-nom m

figure skating n figures imposées (en patinage), patinage m artistique

Fiji ['fiːdʒiː] n, **Fiji Islands** npl (îles fpl) Fi(d)ji fpl

filament ['fɪləmənt] n filament m

filch [fɪltʃ] vt (inf: steal) voler, chiper

file [faɪl] n (tool) lime f; (dossier) dossier m; (folder) dossier, chemise f; (: binder) classeur m; (Comput) fichier m; (row) file f ▷ vt (nails, wood) limer; (papers) classer; (Law: claim) faire enregistrer; déposer ▷ vi: **to ~ in/out** entrer/sortir l'un derrière l'autre; **to ~ past** défiler devant; **to ~ a suit against sb** (Law) intenter un procès à qn

file name n (Comput) nom m de fichier

filibuster ['fɪlɪbʌstə'] (esp US Pol) n (also: **filibusterer**) obstructionniste m/f ▷ vi faire de l'obstructionnisme

filing ['faɪlɪŋ] n (travaux mpl de) classement m; **filings** npl limaille f

filing cabinet n classeur m (meuble)

filing clerk n documentaliste m/f

Filipino [fɪlɪ'piːnəu] adj philippin(e) ▷ n (person) Philippin(e); (Ling) tagalog m

fill [fɪl] vt remplir; (vacancy) pourvoir à ▷ n: **to eat one's ~** manger à sa faim; **to ~ with** remplir de

▶ **fill in** vt (hole) boucher; (form) remplir; (details, report) compléter

▶ **fill out** vt (form, receipt) remplir

▶ **fill up** vt remplir ▷ vi (Aut) faire le plein; **~ it up, please** (Aut) le plein, s'il vous plaît

fillet ['fɪlɪt] n filet m ▷ vt préparer en filets

fillet steak n filet m de bœuf, tournedos m

filling ['fɪlɪŋ] n (Culin) garniture f, farce f; (for tooth) plombage m

filling station n station-service f, station f d'essence

fillip ['fɪlɪp] n coup m de fouet (fig)

filly ['fɪlɪ] n pouliche f

film [fɪlm] n film m; (Phot) pellicule f, film; (of powder, liquid) couche f, pellicule ▷ vt (scene) filmer ▷ vi tourner; **I'd like a 36-exposure ~** je voudrais une pellicule de 36 poses

film star n vedette f de cinéma

filmstrip ['fɪlmstrɪp] n (film m pour) projection f fixe

film studio n studio m (de cinéma)

Filofax® ['faɪləufæks] n Filofax® m

filter ['fɪltə'] n filtre m ▷ vt filtrer

filter coffee n café m filtre

filter lane n (Brit Aut: at traffic lights) voie f de dégagement; (: on motorway) voie f de sortie

filter tip n bout m filtre

filth [fɪlθ] n saleté f

filthy ['fɪlθɪ] adj sale, dégoûtant(e); (language) ordurier(-ière), grossier(-ière)

fin [fɪn] n (of fish) nageoire f; (of shark) aileron m; (of diver) palme f

final ['faɪnl] adj final(e), dernier(-ière); (decision, answer) définitif(-ive) ▷ n (Brit Sport) finale f; **finals** npl (Scol) examens mpl de dernière année; (US Sport) finale f; **~ demand** (on invoice etc) dernier rappel

finale [fɪ'nɑːlɪ] n finale m

finalist ['faɪnəlɪst] n (Sport) finaliste m/f

finalize ['faɪnəlaɪz] vt mettre au point

finally ['faɪnəlɪ] adv (eventually) enfin, finalement; (lastly) en dernier lieu; (irrevocably) définitivement

finance [faɪ'næns] n finance f ▷ vt financer; **finances** npl finances fpl

financial [faɪ'nænʃəl] adj financier(-ière); **~ statement** bilan m, exercice financier

financially [faɪ'nænʃəlɪ] adv financièrement

financial year n année f budgétaire

financier [faɪ'nænsɪə'] n financier m

find [faɪnd] vt (pt, pp **found** [faund]) trouver; (lost object) retrouver ▷ n trouvaille f, découverte f; **to ~ sb guilty** (Law) déclarer qn coupable; **to ~ (some) difficulty in doing sth** avoir du mal à faire qch

▶ **find out** vt se renseigner sur; (truth, secret) découvrir; (person) démasquer ▷ vi: **to ~ out about** (make enquiries) se renseigner sur; (by chance) apprendre

findings ['faɪndɪŋz] npl (Law) conclusions fpl, verdict m; (of report) constatations fpl

fine [faɪn] adj (weather) beau (belle); (excellent) excellent(e); (thin, subtle, not coarse) fin(e); (acceptable) bien inv ▷ adv (well) très bien; (small) fin, finement ▷ n (Law) amende f; contravention f ▷ vt (Law) condamner à une amende; donner une contravention à; **he's ~** il va bien; **the weather is ~** il fait beau; **you're doing ~** c'est bien, vous vous débrouillez bien; **to cut it ~** calculer un peu juste

fine arts npl beaux-arts mpl

fine print n: **the ~** ce qui est imprimé en tout petit

finery ['faɪnərɪ] n parure f

finesse [fɪ'nɛs] n finesse f, élégance f

fine-tooth comb ['faɪntuːθ-] n: **to go through sth with a ~** (fig) passer qch au peigne fin or au crible

finger ['fɪŋgəʳ] n doigt m ▷ vt palper, toucher; **index ~** index m

fingernail ['fɪŋgəneɪl] n ongle m (de la main)

fingerprint ['fɪŋgəprɪnt] n empreinte digitale ▷ vt (person) prendre les empreintes digitales de

fingerstall ['fɪŋgəstɔːl] n doigtier m

fingertip ['fɪŋgətɪp] n bout m du doigt; (fig): **to have sth at one's ~s** avoir qch à sa disposition; (knowledge) savoir qch sur le bout du doigt

finicky ['fɪnɪkɪ] adj tatillon(ne), méticuleux(-euse), minutieux(-euse)

finish ['fɪnɪʃ] n fin f; (Sport) arrivée f; (polish etc) finition f ▷ vt finir, terminer ▷ vi finir, se terminer; (session) s'achever; **to ~ doing sth** finir de faire qch; **to ~ third** arriver or terminer troisième; **when does the show ~?** quand est-ce que le spectacle se termine?
  ▶ **finish off** vt finir, terminer; (kill) achever
  ▶ **finish up** vi, vt finir

finishing line ['fɪnɪʃɪŋ-] n ligne f d'arrivée

finishing school ['fɪnɪʃɪŋ-] n institution privée (pour jeunes filles)

finite ['faɪnaɪt] adj fini(e); (verb) conjugué(e)

Finland ['fɪnlənd] n Finlande f

Finn [fɪn] n Finnois(e), Finlandais(e)

Finnish ['fɪnɪʃ] adj finnois(e), finlandais(e) ▷ n (Ling) finnois m

fiord [fjɔːd] n fjord m

fir [fəːʳ] n sapin m

fire ['faɪəʳ] n feu m; (accidental) incendie m; (heater) radiateur m ▷ vt (discharge): **to ~ a gun** tirer un coup de feu; (fig: interest) enflammer, animer; (inf: dismiss) mettre à la porte, renvoyer ▷ vi (shoot) tirer, faire feu ▷ cpd: **~ hazard, ~ risk: that's a ~ hazard** or **risk** cela présente un risque d'incendie; **~! au feu!; on ~** en feu; **to set ~ to sth, set sth on ~** mettre le feu à qch; **insured against ~** assuré contre l'incendie

fire alarm n avertisseur m d'incendie

firearm ['faɪərɑːm] n arme f à feu

fire brigade n (régiment m de sapeurs-) pompiers mpl

fire chief n (US) = **fire master**

fire department n (US) = **fire brigade**

fire door n porte f coupe-feu

fire engine n (Brit) pompe f à incendie

fire escape n escalier m de secours

fire exit n issue f or sortie f de secours

fire extinguisher n extincteur m

fireguard ['faɪəgɑːd] n (Brit) garde-feu m inv

fire insurance n assurance f incendie

fireman (irreg) ['faɪəmən] n pompier m

fire master n (Brit) capitaine m des pompiers

fireplace ['faɪəpleɪs] n cheminée f

fireproof ['faɪəpruːf] adj ignifuge

fire regulations npl consignes fpl en cas d'incendie

fire screen n (decorative) écran m de cheminée; (for protection) garde-feu m inv

fireside ['faɪəsaɪd] n foyer m, coin m du feu

fire station n caserne f de pompiers

fire truck n (US) = **fire engine**

firewall ['faɪəwɔːl] n (Internet) pare-feu m

firewood ['faɪəwud] n bois m de chauffage

fireworks ['faɪəwəːks] npl (display) feu(x) m(pl) d'artifice

firing ['faɪərɪŋ] n (Mil) feu m, tir m

firing squad n peloton m d'exécution

firm [fəːm] adj ferme ▷ n compagnie f, firme f; **it is my ~ belief that ...** je crois fermement que ...

firmly ['fəːmlɪ] adv fermement

firmness ['fəːmnɪs] n fermeté f

first [fəːst] adj premier(-ière) ▷ adv (before other people) le premier, la première; (before other things) en premier, d'abord; (when listing reasons etc) en premier lieu, premièrement; (in the beginning) au début ▷ n (person: in race) premier(-ière); (Brit Scol) mention f très bien; (Aut) première f; **the ~ of January** le premier janvier; **at ~** au commencement, au début; **~ of all** tout d'abord, pour commencer; **in the ~ instance** en premier lieu; **I'll do it ~ thing tomorrow** je le ferai tout de suite demain matin

first aid n premiers secours or soins

first-aid kit [fəːst'eɪd-] n trousse f à pharmacie

first-class ['fəːst'klɑːs] adj (ticket etc) de première classe; (excellent) excellent(e), exceptionnel(le); (post) en tarif prioritaire

first-class mail n courrier m rapide

first-hand ['fəːst'hænd] adj de première main

first lady n (US) femme f du président

firstly ['fəːstlɪ] adv premièrement, en premier lieu

first name n prénom m

first night n (Theat) première f

first-rate ['fəːst'reɪt] adj excellent(e)

first-time buyer ['fəːsttaɪm-] n personne achetant une maison ou un appartement pour la première fois

fir tree n sapin m

fiscal ['fɪskl] adj fiscal(e)

fiscal year n exercice financier

fish [fɪʃ] n (pl inv) poisson m; poissons mpl ▷ vt, vi pêcher; **to ~ a river** pêcher dans une rivière; **~ and chips** poisson frit et frites

fisherman (irreg) ['fɪʃəmən] n pêcheur m

fishery ['fɪʃərɪ] n pêcherie f

fish factory n (Brit) conserverie f de poissons

fish farm n établissement m piscicole

fish fingers npl (Brit) bâtonnets mpl de poisson (congelés)

fish hook n hameçon m

fishing ['fɪʃɪŋ] n pêche f; **to go ~** aller à la pêche

fishing boat ['fɪʃɪŋ-] n barque f de pêche

fishing industry ['fɪʃɪŋ-] n industrie f de la pêche

fishing line ['fɪʃɪŋ-] n ligne f (de pêche)

fishing rod ['fɪʃɪŋ-] n canne f à pêche

fishing tackle ['fɪʃɪŋ-] n attirail m de pêche

fish market n marché m au poisson

fishmonger ['fɪʃmʌŋgəʳ] n (Brit) marchand m de poisson

fishmonger's ['fɪʃmʌŋgəz], **fishmonger's shop** n (Brit) poissonnerie f

fish slice n (Brit) pelle f à poisson
fish sticks npl (US) = **fish fingers**
fishy ['fɪʃɪ] adj (inf) suspect(e), louche
fission ['fɪʃən] n fission f; **atomic** or **nuclear ~** fission nucléaire
fissure ['fɪʃəʳ] n fissure f
fist [fɪst] n poing m
fistfight ['fɪstfaɪt] n pugilat m, bagarre f (à coups de poing)
fit [fɪt] adj (Med, Sport) en (bonne) forme; (proper) convenable; approprié(e) ▷ vt (subj: clothes) aller à; (adjust) ajuster; (put in, attach) installer, poser; adapter; (equip) équiper, garnir, munir; (suit) convenir à ▷ vi (clothes) aller; (parts) s'adapter; (in space, gap) entrer, s'adapter ▷ n (Med) accès m, crise f; (of anger) accès; (of hysterics, jealousy) crise; **~ to** (ready to) en état de; **~ for** (worthy) digne de; (capable) apte à; **to keep ~** se maintenir en forme; **this dress is a tight/good ~** cette robe est un peu juste/(me) va très bien; **a ~ of coughing** une quinte de toux; **to have a ~** (Med) faire or avoir une crise; (inf) piquer une crise; **by ~s and starts** par à-coups
▶ **fit in** vi (add up) cadrer; (integrate) s'intégrer; (to new situation) s'adapter
▶ **fit out** vt (Brit: also: **fit up**) équiper
fitful ['fɪtful] adj intermittent(e)
fitment ['fɪtmənt] n meuble encastré, élément m
fitness ['fɪtnɪs] n (Med) forme f physique; (of remark) à-propos m, justesse f
fitted ['fɪtɪd] adj (jacket, shirt) ajusté(e)
fitted carpet ['fɪtɪd-] n moquette f
fitted kitchen ['fɪtɪd-] n (Brit) cuisine équipée
fitted sheet ['fɪtɪd-] n drap-housse m
fitter ['fɪtəʳ] n monteur m; (Dressmaking) essayeur(-euse)
fitting ['fɪtɪŋ] adj approprié(e) ▷ n (of dress) essayage m; (of piece of equipment) pose f, installation f
fitting room n (in shop) cabine f d'essayage
fittings ['fɪtɪŋz] npl installations fpl
five [faɪv] num cinq
five-day week ['faɪvdeɪ-] n semaine f de cinq jours
fiver ['faɪvəʳ] n (inf: Brit) billet m de cinq livres; (: US) billet de cinq dollars
fix [fɪks] vt (date, amount etc) fixer; (sort out) arranger; (mend) réparer; (make ready: meal, drink) préparer; (inf: game etc) truquer ▷ n: **to be in a ~** être dans le pétrin
▶ **fix up** vt (meeting) arranger; **to ~ sb up with sth** faire avoir qch à qn
fixation [fɪk'seɪʃən] n (Psych) fixation f; (fig) obsession f
fixed [fɪkst] adj (prices etc) fixe; **there's a ~ charge** il y a un prix forfaitaire; **how are you ~ for money?** (inf) question fric, ça va?
fixed assets npl immobilisations fpl
fixture ['fɪkstʃəʳ] n installation f (fixe); (Sport) rencontre f (au programme)
fizz [fɪz] vi pétiller

fizzle ['fɪzl] vi pétiller
▶ **fizzle out** vi rater
fizzy ['fɪzɪ] adj pétillant(e), gazeux(-euse)
fjord [fjɔ:d] n = **fiord**
FL, Fla. abbr (US) = **Florida**
flabbergasted ['flæbəgɑ:stɪd] adj sidéré(e), ahuri(e)
flabby ['flæbɪ] adj mou (molle)
flag [flæg] n drapeau m; (also: **flagstone**) dalle f ▷ vi faiblir; fléchir; **~ of convenience** pavillon m de complaisance
▶ **flag down** vt héler, faire signe (de s'arrêter) à
flagon ['flægən] n bonbonne f
flagpole ['flægpəul] n mât m
flagrant ['fleɪgrənt] adj flagrant(e)
flagship ['flægʃɪp] n vaisseau m amiral; (fig) produit m vedette
flag stop n (US: for bus) arrêt facultatif
flair [flɛəʳ] n flair m
flak [flæk] n (Mil) tir antiaérien; (inf: criticism) critiques fpl
flake [fleɪk] n (of rust, paint) écaille f; (of snow, soap powder) flocon m ▷ vi (also: **flake off**) s'écailler
flaky ['fleɪkɪ] adj (paintwork) écaillé(e); (skin) desquamé(e); (pastry) feuilleté(e)
flamboyant [flæm'bɔɪənt] adj flamboyant(e), éclatant(e); (person) haut(e) en couleur
flame [fleɪm] n flamme f
flamingo [flə'mɪŋgəu] n flamant m (rose)
flammable ['flæməbl] adj inflammable
flan [flæn] n (Brit) tarte f
Flanders ['flɑ:ndəz] n Flandre(s) f(pl)
flange [flændʒ] n boudin m; collerette f
flank [flæŋk] n flanc m ▷ vt flanquer
flannel ['flænl] n (Brit: also: **face flannel**) gant m de toilette; (fabric) flanelle f; (Brit inf) baratin m; **flannels** npl pantalon m de flanelle
flap [flæp] n (of pocket, envelope) rabat m ▷ vt (wings) battre (de) ▷ vi (sail, flag) claquer; (inf: also: **be in a flap**) paniquer
flapjack ['flæpdʒæk] n (US: pancake) ≈ crêpe f; (Brit: biscuit) galette f
flare [flɛəʳ] n (signal) signal lumineux; (Mil) fusée éclairante; (in skirt etc) évasement m; **flares** npl (trousers) pantalon m à pattes d'éléphant
▶ **flare up** vi s'embraser; (fig: person) se mettre en colère, s'emporter; (: revolt) éclater
flared ['flɛəd] adj (trousers) à jambes évasées; (skirt) évasé(e)
flash [flæʃ] n éclair m; (also: **news flash**) flash m (d'information); (Phot) flash ▷ vt (switch on) allumer; (brièvement); (direct): **to ~ sth at** braquer qch sur; (flaunt) étaler, exhiber; (send: message) câbler; (smile) lancer ▷ vi briller; jeter des éclairs; (light on ambulance etc) clignoter; **a ~ of lightning** un éclair; **in a ~** en un clin d'œil; **to ~ one's headlights** faire un appel de phares; **he ~ed by** or **past** il passa (devant nous) comme un éclair
flashback ['flæʃbæk] n flashback m, retour m en arrière

flashbulb ['flæʃbʌlb] n ampoule f de flash
flash card n (Scol) carte f (support visuel)
flashcube ['flæʃkjuːb] n cube-flash m
flasher ['flæʃəʳ] n (Aut) clignotant m
flashlight ['flæʃlaɪt] n lampe f de poche
flashpoint ['flæʃpɔɪnt] n point m d'ignition;
(fig): **to be at ~** être sur le point d'exploser
flashy ['flæʃɪ] adj (pej) tape-à-l'œil inv,
tapageur(-euse)
flask [flɑːsk] n flacon m, bouteille f; (Chem)
ballon m; (also: **vacuum flask**) bouteille f
thermos®
flat [flæt] adj plat(e); (tyre) dégonflé(e), à plat;
(beer) éventé(e); (battery) à plat; (denial)
catégorique; (Mus) bémol inv; (: voice) faux
(fausse) ▷ n (Brit: apartment) appartement m;
(Aut) crevaison f, pneu crevé; (Mus) bémol m; ~
out (work) sans relâche; (race) à fond; **~ rate of
pay** (Comm) salaire m fixe
flat-footed ['flæt'futɪd] adj: **to be ~** avoir les
pieds plats
flatly ['flætlɪ] adv catégoriquement
flatmate ['flætmeɪt] n (Brit): **he's my ~** il
partage l'appartement avec moi
flatness ['flætnɪs] n (of land) absence f de relief,
aspect plat
flat-screen ['flætskriːn] adj à écran plat
flatten ['flætn] vt (also: **flatten out**) aplatir;
(crop) coucher; (house, city) raser
flatter ['flætəʳ] vt flatter
flatterer ['flætərəʳ] n flatteur m
flattering ['flætərɪŋ] adj flatteur(-euse); (clothes
etc) seyant(e)
flattery ['flætərɪ] n flatterie f
flatulence ['flætjuləns] n flatulence f
flaunt [flɔːnt] vt faire étalage de
flavour, (US) **flavor** ['fleɪvəʳ] n goût m, saveur f;
(of ice cream etc) parfum m ▷ vt parfumer,
aromatiser; **vanilla-~ed** à l'arôme de vanille,
vanillé(e); **what ~s do you have?** quels
parfums avez-vous?; **to give** or **add ~ to** donner
du goût à, relever
flavouring, (US) **flavoring** ['fleɪvərɪŋ] n
arôme m (synthétique)
flaw [flɔː] n défaut m
flawless ['flɔːlɪs] adj sans défaut
flax [flæks] n lin m
flaxen ['flæksən] adj blond(e)
flea [fliː] n puce f
flea market n marché m aux puces
fleck [flɛk] n (of dust) particule f; (of mud, paint,
colour) tacheture f, moucheture f ▷ vt tacher,
éclabousser; **brown ~ed with white** brun
moucheté de blanc
fled [flɛd] pt, pp of **flee**
fledgeling, fledgling ['flɛdʒlɪŋ] n oisillon m
flee (pt, pp **fled**) [fliː, flɛd] vt fuir, s'enfuir de ▷ vi
fuir, s'enfuir
fleece [fliːs] n (of sheep) toison f; (top) (laine f)
polaire f ▷ vt (inf) voler, filouter
fleecy ['fliːsɪ] adj (blanket) moelleux(-euse);
(cloud) floconneux(-euse)

fleet [fliːt] n flotte f; (of lorries, cars etc) parc m;
convoi m
fleeting ['fliːtɪŋ] adj fugace, fugitif(-ive); (visit)
très bref (brève)
Flemish ['flɛmɪʃ] adj flamand(e) ▷ n (Ling)
flamand m; **the ~** (npl) les Flamands
flesh [flɛʃ] n chair f
flesh wound [-wuːnd] n blessure superficielle
flew [fluː] pt of **fly**
flex [flɛks] n fil m or câble m électrique (souple)
▷ vt (knee) fléchir; (muscles) tendre
flexibility [flɛksɪ'bɪlɪtɪ] n flexibilité f
flexible ['flɛksəbl] adj flexible; (person, schedule)
souple
flexitime ['flɛksɪtaɪm], (US) **flextime**
['flɛkstaɪm] n horaire m variable or à la carte
flick [flɪk] n petit coup; (with finger) chiquenaude
f ▷ vt donner un petit coup à; (switch) appuyer
sur
▶ **flick through** vt fus feuilleter
flicker ['flɪkəʳ] vi (light, flame) vaciller ▷ n
vacillement m; **a ~ of light** une brève lueur
flick knife n (Brit) couteau m à cran d'arrêt
flicks [flɪks] npl (inf) ciné m
flier ['flaɪəʳ] n aviateur m
flies [flaɪz] npl of **fly**
flight [flaɪt] n vol m; (escape) fuite f; (also: **flight
of steps**) escalier m; **to take ~** prendre la fuite;
to put to ~ mettre en fuite
flight attendant n steward m, hôtesse f de l'air
flight crew n équipage m
flight deck n (Aviat) poste m de pilotage; (Naut)
pont m d'envol
flight path n trajectoire f (de vol)
flight recorder n enregistreur m de vol
flimsy ['flɪmzɪ] adj peu solide; (clothes) trop
léger(-ère); (excuse) pauvre, mince
flinch [flɪntʃ] vi tressaillir; **to ~ from** se dérober
à, reculer devant
fling [flɪŋ] vt (pt, pp **flung** [flʌŋ]) jeter, lancer ▷ n
(love affair) brève liaison, passade f
flint [flɪnt] n silex m; (in lighter) pierre f (à
briquet)
flip [flɪp] n chiquenaude f ▷ vt (throw) donner
une chiquenaude à; (switch) appuyer sur; (US:
pancake) faire sauter; **to ~ sth over** retourner
qch ▷ vi: **to ~ for sth** (US) jouer qch à pile ou
face
▶ **flip through** vt fus feuilleter
flip-flops ['flɪpflɔps] npl (esp Brit) tongs fpl
flippant ['flɪpənt] adj désinvolte,
irrévérencieux(-euse)
flipper ['flɪpəʳ] n (of animal) nageoire f; (for
swimmer) palme f
flip side n (of record) deuxième face f
flirt [fləːt] vi flirter ▷ n flirteur(-euse)
flirtation [fləː'teɪʃən] n flirt m
flit [flɪt] vi voleter
float [fləut] n flotteur m; (in procession) char m;
(sum of money) réserve f ▷ vi flotter; (bather)
flotter, faire la planche ▷ vt faire flotter; (loan,
business, idea) lancer

floating ['fləʊtɪŋ] *adj* flottant(e); **~ vote** voix flottante; **~ voter** électeur indécis

flock [flɔk] *n* (*of sheep*) troupeau *m*; (*of birds*) vol *m*; (*of people*) foule *f*

floe [fləʊ] *n* (*also*: **ice floe**) iceberg *m*

flog [flɔg] *vt* fouetter

flood [flʌd] *n* inondation *f*; (*of letters, refugees etc*) flot *m* ▷ *vt* inonder; (*Aut: carburettor*) noyer ▷ *vi* (*place*) être inondé; (*people*): **to ~ into** envahir; **to ~ the market** (*Comm*) inonder le marché; **in ~** en crue

flooding ['flʌdɪŋ] *n* inondation *f*

floodlight ['flʌdlaɪt] *n* projecteur *m* ▷ *vt* éclairer aux projecteurs, illuminer

floodlit ['flʌdlɪt] *pt, pp of* **floodlight** ▷ *adj* illuminé(e)

flood tide *n* marée montante

floodwater ['flʌdwɔ:tə^r] *n* eau *f* de la crue

floor [flɔ:^r] *n* sol *m*; (*storey*) étage *m*; (*of sea, valley*) fond *m*; (*fig: at meeting*): **the ~** l'assemblée *f*, les membres *mpl* de l'assemblée ▷ *vt* (*knock down*) terrasser; (*baffle*) désorienter; **on the ~** par terre; **ground ~**, (*US*) **first ~** rez-de-chaussée *m*; **first ~**, (*US*) **second ~** premier étage; **top ~** dernier étage; **what ~ is it on?** c'est à quel étage?; **to have the ~** (*speaker*) avoir la parole

floorboard ['flɔ:bɔ:d] *n* planche *f* (*du plancher*)

flooring ['flɔ:rɪŋ] *n* sol *m*; (*wooden*) plancher *m*; (*material to make floor*) matériau(x) *m(pl)* pour planchers; (*covering*) revêtement *m* de sol

floor lamp *n* (*US*) lampadaire *m*

floor show *n* spectacle *m* de variétés

floorwalker ['flɔ:wɔ:kə^r] *n* (*esp US*) surveillant *m* (de grand magasin)

flop [flɔp] *n* fiasco *m* ▷ *vi* (*fail*) faire fiasco; (*fall*) s'affaler, s'effondrer

floppy ['flɔpɪ] *adj* lâche, flottant(e) ▷ *n* (*Comput: also*: **floppy disk**) disquette *f*; **~ hat** chapeau *m* à bords flottants

floppy disk *n* disquette *f*, disque *m* souple

flora ['flɔ:rə] *n* flore *f*

floral ['flɔ:rl] *adj* floral(e); (*dress*) à fleurs

Florence ['flɔrəns] *n* Florence

florid ['flɔrɪd] *adj* (*complexion*) fleuri(e); (*style*) plein(e) de fioritures

florist ['flɔrɪst] *n* fleuriste *m/f*

florist's ['flɔrɪsts], **florist's shop** *n* magasin *m* or boutique *f* de fleuriste

flotation [fləʊ'teɪʃən] *n* (*of shares*) émission *f*; (*of company*) lancement *m* (en Bourse)

flounce [flaʊns] *n* volant *m*
▶ **flounce out** *vi* sortir dans un mouvement d'humeur

flounder ['flaʊndə^r] *n* (*Zool*) flet *m* ▷ *vi* patauger

flour ['flaʊə^r] *n* farine *f*

flourish ['flʌrɪʃ] *vi* prospérer ▷ *vt* brandir ▷ *n* (*gesture*) moulinet *m*; (*decoration*) fioriture *f*; (*of trumpets*) fanfare *f*

flourishing ['flʌrɪʃɪŋ] *adj* prospère, florissant(e)

flout [flaʊt] *vt* se moquer de, faire fi de

flow [fləʊ] *n* (*of water, traffic etc*) écoulement *m*; (*tide, influx*) flux *m*; (*of orders, letters etc*) flot *m*; (*of blood, Elec*) circulation *f*; (*of river*) courant *m* ▷ *vi* couler; (*traffic*) s'écouler; (*robes, hair*) flotter

flow chart, flow diagram *n* organigramme *m*

flower ['flaʊə^r] *n* fleur *f* ▷ *vi* fleurir; **in ~** en fleur

flower bed *n* plate-bande *f*

flowerpot ['flaʊəpɔt] *n* pot *m* (à fleurs)

flowery ['flaʊərɪ] *adj* fleuri(e)

flown [fləʊn] *pp of* **fly**

fl. oz. *abbr* = **fluid ounce**

flu [flu:] *n* grippe *f*

fluctuate ['flʌktjueɪt] *vi* varier, fluctuer

fluctuation [flʌktju'eɪʃən] *n* fluctuation *f*, variation *f*

flue [flu:] *n* conduit *m*

fluency ['flu:ənsɪ] *n* facilité *f*, aisance *f*

fluent ['flu:ənt] *adj* (*speech, style*) coulant(e), aisé(e); **he's a ~ speaker/reader** il s'exprime/lit avec aisance *or* facilité; **he speaks ~ French**, **he's ~ in French** il parle le français couramment

fluently ['flu:əntlɪ] *adv* couramment; avec aisance *or* facilité

fluff [flʌf] *n* duvet *m*; (*on jacket, carpet*) peluche *f*

fluffy ['flʌfɪ] *adj* duveteux(-euse); (*jacket, carpet*) pelucheux(-euse); (*toy*) en peluche

fluid ['flu:ɪd] *n* fluide *m*; (*in diet*) liquide *m* ▷ *adj* fluide

fluid ounce *n* (*Brit*) = 0.028 l; 0.05 pints

fluke [flu:k] *n* coup *m* de veine

flummox ['flʌməks] *vt* dérouter, déconcerter

flung [flʌŋ] *pt, pp of* **fling**

flunky ['flʌŋkɪ] *n* larbin *m*

fluorescent [flʊə'rɛsnt] *adj* fluorescent(e)

fluoride ['flʊəraɪd] *n* fluor *m*

fluorine ['flʊəri:n] *n* fluor *m*

flurry ['flʌrɪ] *n* (*of snow*) rafale *f*, bourrasque *f*; **a ~ of activity** un affairement soudain; **a ~ of excitement** une excitation soudaine

flush [flʌʃ] *n* (*on face*) rougeur *f*; (*fig: of youth etc*) éclat *m*; (*of blood*) afflux *m* ▷ *vt* nettoyer à grande eau; (*also*: **flush out**) débusquer ▷ *vi* rougir ▷ *adj* (*inf*) en fonds; (*level*): **~ with** au ras de, de niveau avec; **to ~ the toilet** tirer la chasse (d'eau); **hot ~es** (*Med*) bouffées *fpl* de chaleur

flushed ['flʌʃt] *adj* (*tout*)e) rouge

fluster ['flʌstə^r] *n* agitation *f*, trouble *m*

flustered ['flʌstəd] *adj* énervé(e)

flute [flu:t] *n* flûte *f*

flutter ['flʌtə^r] *n* (*of panic, excitement*) agitation *f*; (*of wings*) battement *m* ▷ *vi* (*bird*) battre des ailes, voleter; (*person*) aller et venir dans une grande agitation

flux [flʌks] *n*: **in a state of ~** fluctuant sans cesse

fly [flaɪ] (*pt* **flew**, *pp* **flown** [flu:, fləʊn]) *n* (*insect*) mouche *f*; (*on trousers: also*: **flies**) braguette *f* ▷ *vt* (*plane*) piloter; (*passengers, cargo*) transporter (par avion); (*distance*) parcourir ▷ *vi* voler; (*passengers*) aller en avion; (*escape*) s'enfuir, fuir; (*flag*) se déployer; **to ~ open** s'ouvrir brusquement; **to ~ off the handle** s'énerver, s'emporter
▶ **fly away, fly off** *vi* s'envoler

▶ **fly in** vi (plane) atterrir; **he flew in yesterday** il est arrivé hier (par avion)

▶ **fly out** vi partir (par avion)

fly-drive ['flaɪdraɪv] n formule f avion plus voiture

fly-fishing ['flaɪfɪʃɪŋ] n pêche f à la mouche

flying ['flaɪɪŋ] n (activity) aviation f; (action) vol m ▷ adj: ~ **visit** visite f éclair inv; **with ~ colours** haut la main; **he doesn't like ~** il n'aime pas voyager en avion

flying buttress n arc-boutant m

flying picket n piquet m de grève volant

flying saucer n soucoupe volante

flying squad n (Police) brigade volante

flying start n: **to get off to a ~** faire un excellent départ

flyleaf ['flaɪliːf] n page f de garde

flyover ['flaɪəuvə'] n (Brit: overpass) pont routier, saut-de-mouton m (Canada)

flypast ['flaɪpɑːst] n défilé aérien

flysheet ['flaɪʃiːt] n (for tent) double toit m

flyweight ['flaɪweɪt] n (Sport) poids m mouche

flywheel ['flaɪwiːl] n volant m (de commande)

FM abbr (Brit Mil) = **field marshal**; (Radio: = frequency modulation) FM

FMB n abbr (US) = **Federal Maritime Board**

FMCS n abbr (US: = Federal Mediation and Conciliation Services) organisme de conciliation en cas de conflits du travail

FO n abbr (Brit) = **Foreign Office**

foal [fəul] n poulain m

foam [fəum] n écume f; (on beer) mousse f; (also: **foam rubber**) caoutchouc m mousse; (also: **plastic foam**) mousse cellulaire or de plastique ▷ vi (liquid) écumer; (soapy water) mousser

foam rubber n caoutchouc m mousse

FOB abbr (= free on board) fob

fob [fɔb] n (also: **watch fob**) chaîne f, ruban m ▷ vt: **to ~ sb off with sth** refiler qch à qn

foc abbr (Brit) = **free of charge**

focal ['fəukl] adj (also fig) focal(e)

focal point n foyer m; (fig) centre m de l'attention, point focal

focus ['fəukəs] n (pl **-es**) foyer m; (of interest) centre m ▷ vt (field glasses etc) mettre au point; (light rays) faire converger ▷ vi: **to ~ (on)** (with camera) régler la mise au point (sur); (with eyes) fixer son regard (sur); (fig: concentrate) se concentrer; **out of/in ~** (picture) flou(e)/net(te); (camera) pas au point/au point

fodder ['fɔdə'] n fourrage m

FOE n abbr (= Friends of the Earth) AT mpl (= Amis de la Terre); (US: = Fraternal Order of Eagles) organisation charitable

foe [fəu] n ennemi m

foetus, (US) **fetus** ['fiːtəs] n fœtus m

fog [fɔg] n brouillard m

fogbound ['fɔgbaund] adj bloqué(e) par le brouillard

foggy ['fɔgɪ] adj: **it's ~** il y a du brouillard

fog lamp, (US) **fog light** n (Aut) phare m anti-brouillard

foible ['fɔɪbl] n faiblesse f

foil [fɔɪl] vt déjouer, contrecarrer ▷ n feuille f de métal; (kitchen foil) papier m d'alu(minium); (Fencing) fleuret m; **to act as a ~ to** (fig) servir de repoussoir or de faire-valoir à

foist [fɔɪst] vt: **to ~ sth on sb** imposer qch à qn

fold [fəuld] n (bend, crease) pli m; (Agr) parc m à moutons; (fig) bercail m ▷ vt plier; **to ~ one's arms** croiser les bras

▶ **fold up** vi (map etc) se plier, se replier; (business) fermer boutique ▷ vt (map etc) plier, replier

folder ['fəuldə'] n (for papers) chemise f; (: binder) classeur m; (brochure) dépliant m; (Comput) dossier m

folding ['fəuldɪŋ] adj (chair, bed) pliant(e)

foliage ['fəuliɪdʒ] n feuillage m

folk [fəuk] npl gens mpl ▷ cpd folklorique; **folks** npl (inf: parents) famille f, parents mpl

folklore ['fəuklɔːr] n folklore m

folk music n musique f folklorique; (contemporary) musique folk, folk m

folk song ['fəuksɔŋ] n chanson f folklorique; (contemporary) chanson folk inv

follow ['fɔləu] vt suivre ▷ vi suivre; (result) s'ensuivre; **to ~ sb's advice** suivre les conseils de qn; **I don't quite ~ you** je ne vous suis plus; **to ~ in sb's footsteps** emboîter le pas à qn; (fig) suivre les traces de qn; **it ~s that ...** de ce fait, il s'ensuit que ...; **to ~ suit** (fig) faire de même

▶ **follow out** vt (idea, plan) poursuivre, mener à terme

▶ **follow through** vt = **follow out**

▶ **follow up** vt (victory) tirer parti de; (letter, offer) donner suite à; (case) suivre

follower ['fɔləuə'] n disciple m/f, partisan(e)

following ['fɔləuɪŋ] adj suivant(e) ▷ n partisans mpl, disciples mpl

follow-up ['fɔləuʌp] n suite f; (on file, case) suivi m

folly ['fɔlɪ] n inconscience f; sottise f; (building) folie f

fond [fɔnd] adj (memory, look) tendre, affectueux(-euse); (hopes, dreams) un peu fou (folle); **to be ~ of** aimer beaucoup

fondle ['fɔndl] vt caresser

fondly ['fɔndlɪ] adv (lovingly) tendrement; (naïvely) naïvement

fondness ['fɔndnɪs] n (for things) attachement m; (for people) sentiments affectueux; **a special ~ for** une prédilection pour

font [fɔnt] n (Rel) fonts baptismaux; (Typ) police f de caractères

food [fuːd] n nourriture f

food chain n chaîne f alimentaire

food mixer n mixeur m

food poisoning n intoxication f alimentaire

food processor n robot m de cuisine

food stamp n (US) bon m de nourriture (pour indigents)

foodstuffs ['fuːdstʌfs] npl denrées fpl alimentaires

fool [fuːl] n idiot(e); (History: of king) bouffon m,

fou *m*; (*Culin*) mousse *f* de fruits ▷ *vt* berner,
duper ▷ *vi* (*also*: **fool around**) faire l'idiot *or*
l'imbécile; **to make a ~ of sb** (*ridicule*)
ridiculiser qn; (*trick*) avoir *or* duper qn; **to make
a ~ of o.s.** se couvrir de ridicule; **you can't ~ me**
vous (ne) me la ferez pas, on (ne) me la fait pas
▶ **fool about, fool around** *vi* (*pej*: *waste time*)
traînailler, glandouiller; (: *behave foolishly*) faire
l'idiot *or* l'imbécile

foolhardy ['fuːlhɑːdɪ] *adj* téméraire,
imprudent(e)

foolish ['fuːlɪʃ] *adj* idiot(e), stupide; (*rash*)
imprudent(e)

foolishly ['fuːlɪʃlɪ] *adv* stupidement

foolishness ['fuːlɪʃnɪs] *n* idiotie *f*, stupidité *f*

foolproof ['fuːlpruːf] *adj* (*plan etc*) infaillible

foolscap ['fuːlskæp] *n* ≈ papier *m* ministre

foot (*pl* **feet**) [fut, fiːt] *n* pied *m*; (*measure*) pied (= 30.48 cm; 12 inches) ▷ *vt* (*bill*)
casquer, payer; **on** ~ à pied; **to find one's feet**
(*fig*) s'acclimater; **to put one's ~ down** (*Aut*)
appuyer sur le champignon; (*say no*) s'imposer

footage ['futɪdʒ] *n* (*Cine*: *length*) ≈ métrage *m*;
(: *material*) séquences *fpl*

foot-and-mouth [futənd'mauθ], **foot-and-
mouth disease** *n* fièvre aphteuse

football ['futbɔːl] *n* (*ball*) ballon *m* (de football);
(*sport*: *Brit*) football *m*; (: *US*) football américain

footballer ['futbɔːlə^r] *n* (*Brit*) = **football player**

football ground *n* terrain *m* de football

football match *n* (*Brit*) match *m* de foot(ball)

football player *n* footballeur(-euse),
joueur(-euse) de football; (*US*) joueur(-euse) de
football américain

football pools *npl* (*US*) ≈ loto *m* sportif,
≈ pronostics *mpl* (sur les matchs de football)

footbrake ['futbreɪk] *n* frein *m* à pédale

footbridge ['futbrɪdʒ] *n* passerelle *f*

foothills ['futhɪlz] *npl* contreforts *mpl*

foothold ['futhəuld] *n* prise *f* (de pied)

footing ['futɪŋ] *n* (*fig*) position *f*; **to lose one's ~**
perdre pied; **on an equal ~** sur pied d'égalité

footlights ['futlaɪts] *npl* rampe *f*

footman ['futmən] (*irreg*) *n* laquais *m*

footnote ['futnəut] *n* note *f* (en bas de page)

footpath ['futpɑːθ] *n* sentier *m*; (*in street*)
trottoir *m*

footprint ['futprɪnt] *n* trace *f* (de pied)

footrest ['futrest] *n* marchepied *m*

footsie ['futsɪ] *n* (*inf*): **to play ~ with sb** faire du
pied à qn

footsore ['futsɔː^r] *adj*: **to be ~** avoir mal aux
pieds

footstep ['futstep] *n* pas *m*

footwear ['futwɛə^r] *n* chaussures *fpl*

FOR *abbr* (= *free on rail*) franco wagon

 KEYWORD

for [fɔː^r] *prep* **1** (*indicating destination, intention,
purpose*) pour; **the train for London** le train
pour (*or* à destination de) Londres; **he left for**

Rome il est parti pour Rome; **he went for the
paper** il est allé chercher le journal; **is this for
me?** c'est pour moi?; **it's time for lunch** c'est
l'heure du déjeuner; **what's it for?** ça sert à
quoi?; **what for?** (*why*) pourquoi?; (*to what end*)
pour quoi faire?, à quoi bon?; **for sale** à vendre;
to pray for peace prier pour la paix

2 (*on behalf of, representing*) pour; **the MP for
Hove** le député de Hove; **to work for sb/sth**
travailler pour qn/qch; **I'll ask him for you** je
vais lui demander pour toi; **G for George** G
comme Georges

3 (*because of*) pour; **for this reason** pour cette
raison; **for fear of being criticized** de peur
d'être critiqué

4 (*with regard to*) pour; **it's cold for July** il fait
froid pour juillet; **a gift for languages** un don
pour les langues

5 (*in exchange for*): **I sold it for £5** je l'ai vendu 5
livres; **to pay 50 pence for a ticket** payer un
billet 50 pence

6 (*in favour of*) pour; **are you for or against us?**
êtes-vous pour ou contre nous?; **I'm all for it** je
suis tout à fait pour; **vote for X** votez pour X

7 (*referring to distance*) pendant, sur; **there are
roadworks for 5 km** il y a des travaux sur *or*
pendant 5 km; **we walked for miles** nous
avons marché pendant des kilomètres

8 (*referring to time*) pendant; depuis; pour; **he
was away for 2 years** il a été absent pendant 2
ans; **she will be away for a month** elle sera
absente (pendant) un mois; **it hasn't rained
for 3 weeks** ça fait 3 semaines qu'il ne pleut
pas, il ne pleut pas depuis 3 semaines; **I have
known her for years** je la connais depuis des
années; **can you do it for tomorrow?** est-ce
que tu peux le faire pour demain?

9 (*with infinitive clauses*): **it is not for me to
decide** ce n'est pas à moi de décider; **it would
be best for you to leave** le mieux serait que
vous partiez; **there is still time for you to do
it** vous avez encore le temps de le faire; **for this
to be possible ...** pour que cela soit possible ..

10 (*in spite of*): **for all that** malgré cela,
néanmoins; **for all his work/efforts** malgré
tout son travail/tous ses efforts; **for all his
complaints, he's very fond of her** il a beau se
plaindre, il l'aime beaucoup
▷ *conj* (*since, as*: *formal*) car

forage ['fɔrɪdʒ] *n* fourrage *m* ▷ *vi* fourrager,
fouiller

forage cap *n* calot *m*

foray ['fɔreɪ] *n* incursion *f*

forbad, forbade [fə'bæd] *pt of* **forbid**

forbearing [fɔː'bɛərɪŋ] *adj* patient(e),
tolérant(e)

forbid (*pt* **forbad(e)**, *pp* **-den**) [fə'bɪd, -'bæd,
-'bɪdn] *vt* défendre, interdire; **to ~ sb to do**
défendre *or* interdire à qn de faire

forbidden [fə'bɪdn] *adj* défendu(e)

forbidding [fə'bɪdɪŋ] *adj* d'aspect *or* d'allure

sévère or sombre

force [fɔːs] n force f ▷ vt forcer; (push) pousser (de force); **Forces** npl: **the F~s** (Brit Mil) les forces armées; **to ~ o.s. to do** se forcer à faire; **to ~ sb to do sth** forcer qn à faire qch; **in ~** (being used: rule, law, prices) en vigueur; (in large numbers) en force; **to come into ~** entrer en vigueur; **a ~ 5 wind** un vent de force 5; **the sales ~** (Comm) la force de vente; **to join ~s** unir ses forces

▶ **force back** vt (crowd, enemy) repousser; (tears) refouler

▶ **force down** vt (food) se forcer à manger

forced [fɔːst] adj forcé(e)

force-feed ['fɔːsfiːd] vt nourrir de force

forceful ['fɔːsful] adj énergique

forcemeat ['fɔːsmiːt] n (Brit Culin) farce f

forceps ['fɔːsɛps] npl forceps m

forcibly ['fɔːsəblɪ] adv par la force, de force; (vigorously) énergiquement

ford [fɔːd] n gué m ▷ vt passer à gué

fore [fɔːʳ] n: **to the ~** en évidence; **to come to the ~** se faire remarquer

forearm ['fɔːrɑːm] n avant-bras m inv

forebear ['fɔːbɛəʳ] n ancêtre m

foreboding [fɔː'bəudɪŋ] n pressentiment m (néfaste)

forecast ['fɔːkɑːst] n prévision f; (also: **weather forecast**) prévisions fpl météorologiques, météo f ▷ vt (irreg: like **cast**) prévoir

foreclose [fɔː'kləuz] vt (Law: also: **foreclose on**) saisir

foreclosure [fɔː'kləuʒəʳ] n saisie f du bien hypothéqué

forecourt ['fɔːkɔːt] n (of garage) devant m

forefathers ['fɔːfɑːðəz] npl ancêtres mpl

forefinger ['fɔːfɪŋgəʳ] n index m

forefront ['fɔːfrʌnt] n: **in the ~ of** au premier rang or plan de

forego (pt **forewent**, pp **foregone**) [fɔː'gəu, -'wɛnt, -'gɔn] vt renoncer à

foregoing ['fɔːgəuɪŋ] adj susmentionné(e) ▷ n: **the ~** ce qui précède

foregone ['fɔːgɔn] adj: **it's a ~ conclusion** c'est à prévoir, c'est couru d'avance

foreground ['fɔːgraund] n premier plan ▷ cpd (Comput) prioritaire

forehand ['fɔːhænd] n (Tennis) coup droit

forehead ['fɔrɪd] n front m

foreign ['fɔrɪn] adj étranger(-ère); (trade) extérieur(e); (travel) à l'étranger

foreign body n corps étranger

foreign currency n devises étrangères

foreigner ['fɔrɪnəʳ] n étranger(-ère)

foreign exchange n (system) change m; (money) devises fpl

foreign exchange market n marché m des devises

foreign exchange rate n cours m des devises

foreign investment n investissement m à l'étranger

Foreign Office n (Brit) ministère m des Affaires étrangères

Foreign Secretary n (Brit) ministre m des Affaires étrangères

foreleg ['fɔːlɛg] n patte f de devant, jambe antérieure

foreman (irreg) ['fɔːmən] n (in construction) contremaître m; (Law: of jury) président m (du jury)

foremost ['fɔːməust] adj le (la) plus en vue, premier(-ière) ▷ adv: **first and ~** avant tout, tout d'abord

forename ['fɔːneɪm] n prénom m

forensic [fə'rɛnsɪk] adj: **~ medicine** médecine légale; **~ expert** expert m de la police, expert légiste

foreplay ['fɔːpleɪ] n stimulation f érotique, prélude m

forerunner ['fɔːrʌnəʳ] n précurseur m

foresee (pt **foresaw**, pp **foreseen**) [fɔː'siː, -'sɔː, -'siːn] vt prévoir

foreseeable [fɔː'siːəbl] adj prévisible

foreseen [fɔː'siːn] pp of **foresee**

foreshadow [fɔː'ʃædəu] vt présager, annoncer, laisser prévoir

foreshorten [fɔː'ʃɔːtn] vt (figure, scene) réduire, faire en raccourci

foresight ['fɔːsaɪt] n prévoyance f

foreskin ['fɔːskɪn] n (Anat) prépuce m

forest ['fɔrɪst] n forêt f

forestall [fɔː'stɔːl] vt devancer

forestry ['fɔrɪstrɪ] n sylviculture f

foretaste ['fɔːteɪst] n avant-goût m

foretell (pt, pp **foretold**) [fɔː'tɛl, -'təuld] vt prédire

forethought ['fɔːθɔːt] n prévoyance f

foretold [fɔː'təuld] pt, pp of **foretell**

forever [fə'rɛvəʳ] adv pour toujours; (fig: endlessly) continuellement

forewarn [fɔː'wɔːn] vt avertir

forewent [fɔː'wɛnt] pt of **forego**

foreword ['fɔːwəːd] n avant-propos m inv

forfeit ['fɔːfɪt] n prix m, rançon f ▷ vt perdre; (one's life, health) payer de

forgave [fə'geɪv] pt of **forgive**

forge [fɔːdʒ] n forge f ▷ vt (signature) contrefaire; (wrought iron) forger; **to ~ documents/a will** fabriquer de faux papiers/un faux testament; **to ~ money** (Brit) fabriquer de la fausse monnaie

▶ **forge ahead** vi pousser de l'avant, prendre de l'avance

forged [fɔːdʒd] adj faux (fausse)

forger ['fɔːdʒəʳ] n faussaire m

forgery ['fɔːdʒərɪ] n faux m, contrefaçon f

forget (pt **forgot**, pp **forgotten**) [fə'gɛt, -'gɔt, -'gɔtn] vt, vi oublier; **to ~ to do sth** oublier de faire qch; **to ~ about sth** (accidentally) oublier qch; (on purpose) ne plus penser à qch; **I've forgotten my key/passport** j'ai oublié ma clé/mon passeport

forgetful [fə'gɛtful] adj distrait(e), étourdi(e); **~ of** oublieux(-euse) de

forgetfulness [fə'gɛtfulnɪs] n tendance f aux

oublis; (*oblivion*) oubli m

forget-me-not [fə'gɛtmɪnɔt] n myosotis m

forgive (*pt* **forgave**, *pp* **forgiven**) [fə'gɪv, -'geɪv, -'gɪvn] vt pardonner; **to ~ sb for sth/for doing sth** pardonner qch à qn/à qn de faire qch

forgiveness [fə'gɪvnɪs] n pardon m

forgiving [fə'gɪvɪŋ] adj indulgent(e)

forgo (*pt* **forwent**, *pp* **forgone**) [fɔ:'gəu, -'wɛnt, -'gɒn] vt = **forego**

forgot [fə'gɒt] *pt of* **forget**

forgotten [fə'gɒtn] *pp of* **forget**

fork [fɔ:k] n (*for eating*) fourchette f; (*for gardening*) fourche f; (*of roads*) bifurcation f; (*of railways*) embranchement m ▷ vi (*road*) bifurquer
  ▶ **fork out** (*inf: pay*) vt allonger, se fendre de ▷ vi casquer

forked [fɔ:kt] adj (*lightning*) en zigzags, ramifié(e)

fork-lift truck ['fɔ:klɪft-] n chariot élévateur

forlorn [fə'lɔ:n] adj (*person*) délaissé(e); (*deserted*) abandonné(e); (*hope, attempt*) désespéré(e)

form [fɔ:m] n forme f; (*Scol*) classe f; (*questionnaire*) formulaire m ▷ vt former; (*habit*) contracter; **in the ~ of** sous forme de; **to ~ part of sth** faire partie de qch; **to be on good ~** (*Sport: fig*) être en forme; **on top ~** en pleine forme

formal ['fɔ:məl] adj (*offer, receipt*) en bonne et due forme; (*person*) cérémonieux(-euse), à cheval sur les convenances; (*occasion, dinner*) officiel(le); (*garden*) à la française; (*Art, Philosophy*) formel(le); (*clothes*) de soirée

formality [fɔ:'mælɪtɪ] n formalité f, cérémonie(s) f(pl)

formalize ['fɔ:məlaɪz] vt officialiser

formally ['fɔ:məlɪ] adv officiellement; formellement; cérémonieusement

format ['fɔ:mæt] n format m ▷ vt (*Comput*) formater

formation [fɔ:'meɪʃən] n formation f

formative ['fɔ:mətɪv] adj: **~ years** années fpl d'apprentissage (*fig*) or de formation (*d'un enfant, d'un adolescent*)

former ['fɔ:mər] adj ancien(ne); (*before n*) précédent(e); **the ~ ... the latter** le premier ... le second, celui-là ... celui-ci; **the ~ president** l'ex-président; **the ~ Yugoslavia/Soviet Union** l'ex Yougoslavie/Union Soviétique

formerly ['fɔ:məlɪ] adv autrefois

form feed n (*on printer*) alimentation f en feuilles

formidable ['fɔ:mɪdəbl] adj redoutable

formula ['fɔ:mjulə] n formule f; **F~ One** (*Aut*) Formule un

formulate ['fɔ:mjuleɪt] vt formuler

fornicate ['fɔ:nɪkeɪt] vi forniquer

forsake (*pt* **forsook**, *pp* **forsaken**) [fə'seɪk, -'suk, -'seɪkən] vt abandonner

fort [fɔ:t] n fort m; **to hold the ~** (*fig*) assurer la permanence

forte ['fɔ:tɪ] n (point) fort m

forth [fɔ:θ] adv en avant; **to go back and ~** aller et venir; **and so ~** et ainsi de suite

forthcoming [fɔ:θ'kʌmɪŋ] adj qui va paraître or avoir lieu prochainement; (*character*) ouvert(e), communicatif(-ive); (*available*) disponible

forthright ['fɔ:θraɪt] adj franc (franche), direct(e)

forthwith ['fɔ:θ'wɪθ] adv sur le champ

fortieth ['fɔ:tɪɪθ] num quarantième

fortification [fɔ:tɪfɪ'keɪʃən] n fortification f

fortified wine ['fɔ:tɪfaɪd-] n vin liquoreux or de liqueur

fortify ['fɔ:tɪfaɪ] vt (*city*) fortifier; (*person*) remonter

fortitude ['fɔ:tɪtju:d] n courage m, force f d'âme

fortnight ['fɔ:tnaɪt] n (*Brit*) quinzaine f, quinze jours mpl; **it's a ~ since ...** il y a quinze jours que ...

fortnightly ['fɔ:tnaɪtlɪ] adj bimensuel(le) ▷ adv tous les quinze jours

FORTRAN ['fɔ:træn] n FORTRAN m

fortress ['fɔ:trɪs] n forteresse f

fortuitous [fɔ:'tju:ɪtəs] adj fortuit(e)

fortunate ['fɔ:tʃənɪt] adj heureux(-euse); (*person*) chanceux(-euse); **to be ~** avoir de la chance; **it is ~ that** c'est une chance que, il est heureux que

fortunately ['fɔ:tʃənɪtlɪ] adv heureusement, par bonheur

fortune ['fɔ:tʃən] n chance f; (*wealth*) fortune f; **to make a ~** faire fortune

fortune-teller ['fɔ:tʃəntɛlər] n diseuse f de bonne aventure

forty ['fɔ:tɪ] num quarante

forum ['fɔ:rəm] n forum m, tribune f

forward ['fɔ:wəd] adj (*movement, position*) en avant, vers l'avant; (*not shy*) effronté(e); (*in time*) en avance; (*Comm: delivery, sales, exchange*) à terme ▷ adv (*also:* **forwards**) en avant ▷ n (*Sport*) avant m ▷ vt (*letter*) faire suivre; (*parcel, goods*) expédier; (*fig*) promouvoir, favoriser; **to look ~ to sth** attendre qch avec impatience; **to move ~** avancer; **"please ~"** "prière de faire suivre"; **~ planning** planification f à long terme

forwarding address n adresse f de réexpédition

forward slash n barre f oblique

forwent [fɔ:'wɛnt] *pt of* **forgo**

fossil ['fɒsl] adj, n fossile m; **~ fuel** combustible m fossile

foster ['fɒstər] vt (*encourage*) encourager, favoriser; (*child*) élever (*sans adopter*)

foster brother n frère adoptif; frère de lait

foster child n enfant élevé dans une famille d'accueil

foster mother n mère adoptive; mère nourricière

foster parent n parent qui élève un enfant sans l'adopter

fought [fɔ:t] *pt, pp of* **fight**

foul [faul] adj (*weather, smell, food*) infect(e); (*language*) ordurier(-ière); (*deed*) infâme ▷ n (*Football*) faute f ▷ vt (*dirty*) salir, encrasser; (*football player*) commettre une faute sur; (*entangle: anchor, propeller*) emmêler; **he's got a ~ temper** il a un caractère de chien

foul play n (Sport) jeu déloyal; (Law) acte criminel; ~ **is not suspected** la mort (or l'incendie etc) n'a pas de causes suspectes, on écarte l'hypothèse d'un meurtre (or d'un acte criminel)

found [faund] pt, pp of **find** ▷ vt (establish) fonder

foundation [faun'deɪʃən] n (act) fondation f; (base) fondement m; (also: **foundation cream**) fond m de teint; **foundations** npl (of building) fondations fpl; **to lay the ~s** (fig) poser les fondements

foundation stone n première pierre

founder ['faundər] n fondateur m ▷ vi couler, sombrer

founding ['faundɪŋ] adj: ~ **fathers** (esp US) pères mpl fondateurs; ~ **member** membre m fondateur

foundry ['faundrɪ] n fonderie f

fount [faunt] n source f; (Typ) fonte f

fountain ['fauntɪn] n fontaine f

fountain pen n stylo m (à encre)

four [fɔːʳ] num quatre; **on all ~s** à quatre pattes

four-letter word ['fɔːlɛtə-] n obscénité f, gros mot

four-poster ['fɔː'pəustəʳ] n (also: **four-poster bed**) lit m à baldaquin

foursome ['fɔːsəm] n partie f à quatre; sortie f à quatre

fourteen ['fɔː'tiːn] num quatorze

fourteenth ['fɔː'tiːnθ] num quatorzième

fourth ['fɔːθ] num quatrième ▷ n (Aut: also: **fourth gear**) quatrième f

four-wheel drive ['fɔːwiːl-] n (Aut: car) voiture f à quatre roues motrices; **with ~** à quatre roues motrices

fowl [faul] n volaille f

fox [fɔks] n renard m ▷ vt mystifier

fox fur n renard m

foxglove ['fɔksglʌv] n (Bot) digitale f

fox-hunting ['fɔkshʌntɪŋ] n chasse f au renard

foyer ['fɔɪeɪ] n (in hotel) vestibule m; (Theat) foyer m

FP n abbr (Brit) = **former pupil**; (US) = **fireplug**

FPA n abbr (Brit) = **Family Planning Association**

Fr. abbr (Rel = **father**) P; (= friar) F

fr. abbr (= franc) F

fracas ['fræka:] n bagarre f

fraction ['frækʃən] n fraction f

fractionally ['frækʃnəlɪ] adv: ~ **smaller** etc un poil plus petit etc

fractious ['frækʃəs] adj grincheux(-euse)

fracture ['fræktʃəʳ] n fracture f ▷ vt fracturer

fragile ['frædʒaɪl] adj fragile

fragment ['frægmənt] n fragment m

fragmentary ['frægməntərɪ] adj fragmentaire

fragrance ['freɪgrəns] n parfum m

fragrant ['freɪgrənt] adj parfumé(e), odorant(e)

frail [freɪl] adj fragile, délicat(e); (person) frêle

frame [freɪm] n (of building) charpente f; (of human, animal) charpente f, ossature f; (of picture) cadre m; (of door, window) encadrement m, chambranle m; (of spectacles: also: **frames**) monture f ▷ vt (picture) encadrer; (theory, plan) construire, élaborer; **to ~ sb** (inf) monter un coup contre qn; ~ **of mind** disposition f d'esprit

framework ['freɪmwəːk] n structure f

France [frɑːns] n la France; **in** ~ en France

franchise ['fræntʃaɪz] n (Pol) droit m de vote; (Comm) franchise f

franchisee [fræntʃaɪ'ziː] n franchisé m

franchiser ['fræntʃaɪzəʳ] n franchiseur m

frank [fræŋk] adj franc (franche) ▷ vt (letter) affranchir

Frankfurt ['fræŋkfəːt] n Francfort

franking machine ['fræŋkɪŋ-] n machine f à affranchir

frankly ['fræŋklɪ] adv franchement

frankness ['fræŋknɪs] n franchise f

frantic ['fræntɪk] adj (hectic) frénétique; (need, desire) effréné(e); (distraught) hors de soi

frantically ['fræntɪklɪ] adv frénétiquement

fraternal [frə'təːnl] adj fraternel(le)

fraternity [frə'təːnɪtɪ] n (club) communauté f, confrérie f; (spirit) fraternité f

fraternize ['frætənaɪz] vi fraterniser

fraud [frɔːd] n supercherie f, fraude f, tromperie f; (person) imposteur m

fraudulent ['frɔːdjulənt] adj frauduleux(-euse)

fraught [frɔːt] adj (tense: person) très tendu(e); (: situation) pénible; ~ **with** (difficulties etc) chargé(e) de, plein(e) de

fray [freɪ] n bagarre f; (Mil) combat m ▷ vt effilocher ▷ vi s'effilocher; **tempers were ~ed** les gens commençaient à s'énerver; **her nerves were ~ed** elle était à bout de nerfs

FRB n abbr (US) = **Federal Reserve Board**

FRCM n abbr (Brit) = **Fellow of the Royal College of Music**

FRCO n abbr (Brit) = **Fellow of the Royal College of Organists**

FRCP n abbr (Brit) = **Fellow of the Royal College of Physicians**

FRCS n abbr (Brit) = **Fellow of the Royal College of Surgeons**

freak [friːk] n (eccentric person) phénomène m; (unusual event) hasard m extraordinaire; (pej: fanatic): **health food** ~ fana m/f or obsédé(e) de l'alimentation saine ▷ adj (storm) exceptionnel(le); (accident) bizarre

▶ **freak out** vi (inf: drop out) se marginaliser; (: on drugs) se défoncer

freakish ['friːkɪʃ] adj insolite, anormal(e)

freckle ['frɛkl] n tache f de rousseur

free [friː] adj libre; (gratis) gratuit(e); (liberal) généreux(-euse), large ▷ vt (prisoner etc) libérer; (jammed object or person) dégager; **is this seat ~?** la place est libre?; **to give sb a ~ hand** donner carte blanche à qn; ~ **and easy** sans façon, décontracté(e); **admission** ~ entrée libre; ~ **(of charge)** gratuitement

freebie ['friːbɪ] n (inf): **it's a** ~ c'est gratuit

freedom ['friːdəm] n liberté f

freedom fighter n combattant m de la liberté

free enterprise n libre entreprise f

Freefone® ['fri:fəun] *n* numéro vert
free-for-all ['fri:fərɔ:l] *n* mêlée générale
free gift *n* prime *f*
freehold ['fri:həuld] *n* propriété foncière libre
free kick *n* (*Sport*) coup franc
freelance ['fri:lɑ:ns] *adj* (*journalist etc*)
  indépendant(e), free-lance *inv*; (*work*) en free-
  lance ▷ *adv* en free-lance
freeloader ['fri:ləudə'] *n* (*pej*) parasite *m*
freely ['fri:lɪ] *adv* librement; (*liberally*)
  libéralement
free-market economy [fri:'mɑ:kɪt-] *n*
  économie *f* de marché
freemason ['fri:meɪsn] *n* franc-maçon *m*
freemasonry ['fri:meɪsnrɪ] *n* franc-
  maçonnerie *f*
Freepost® ['fri:pəust] *n* (*Brit*) port payé
free-range ['fri:'reɪndʒ] *adj* (*egg*) de ferme;
  (*chicken*) fermier
free sample *n* échantillon gratuit
free speech *n* liberté *f* d'expression
free trade *n* libre-échange *m*
freeway ['fri:weɪ] *n* (*US*) autoroute *f*
freewheel [fri:'wi:l] *vi* descendre en roue libre
freewheeling [fri:'wi:lɪŋ] *adj* indépendant(e),
  libre
free will *n* libre arbitre *m*; **of one's own ~** de son
  plein gré
freeze [fri:z] (*pt* **froze**, *pp* **frozen** [frəuz, 'frəuzn])
  vi geler ▷ *vt* geler; (*food*) congeler; (*prices,*
  salaries) bloquer, geler ▷ *n* gel *m*; (*of prices, salaries*)
  blocage *m*
  ▸ **freeze over** *vi* (*river*) geler; (*windscreen*) se
  couvrir de givre *or* de glace
  ▸ **freeze up** *vi* geler
freeze-dried ['fri:zdraɪd] *adj* lyophilisé(e)
freezer ['fri:zə'] *n* congélateur *m*
freezing ['fri:zɪŋ] *adj*: **~ (cold)** (*room etc*)
  glacial(e); (*person, hands*) gelé(e), glacé(e) ▷ *n*: **3**
  degrees below ~ 3 degrés au-dessous de zéro;
  it's ~ il fait un froid glacial
freezing point *n* point *m* de congélation
freight [freɪt] *n* (*goods*) fret *m*, cargaison *f*; (*money*
  charged) fret, prix *m* du transport; **~ forward**
  port dû; **~ inward** port payé par le destinataire
freighter ['freɪtə'] *n* (*Naut*) cargo *m*
freight forwarder [-fɔ:wədə'] *n* transitaire *m*
freight train *n* (*US*) train *m* de marchandises
French [frentʃ] *adj* français(e) ▷ *n* (*Ling*) français
  m; **the ~** (*npl*) les Français; **what's the ~ (word)**
  for ...? comment dit-on ... en français?
French bean *n* (*Brit*) haricot vert
French bread *n* pain *m* français
French Canadian *adj* canadien(ne) français(e)
  ▷ *n* Canadien(ne) français(e)
French dressing *n* (*Culin*) vinaigrette *f*
French fried potatoes, (*US*) **French fries** *npl*
  (pommes de terre *fpl*) frites *fpl*
French Guiana [-gaɪ'ænə] *n* Guyane française
French horn *n* (*Mus*) cor *m* (d'harmonie)
French kiss *n* baiser profond
French loaf *n* ≈ pain *m*, ≈ parisien *m*

Frenchman ['frentʃmən] (*irreg*) *n* Français *m*
French Riviera *n*: **the ~** la Côte d'Azur
French stick *n* ≈ baguette *f*
French window *n* porte-fenêtre *f*
Frenchwoman ['frentʃwumən] (*irreg*) *n*
  Française *f*
frenetic [frə'nɛtɪk] *adj* frénétique
frenzy ['frɛnzɪ] *n* frénésie *f*
frequency ['fri:kwənsɪ] *n* fréquence *f*
frequency modulation *n* modulation *f* de
  fréquence
frequent *adj* ['fri:kwənt] fréquent(e) ▷ *vt*
  [frɪ'kwɛnt] fréquenter
frequently ['fri:kwəntlɪ] *adv* fréquemment
fresco ['frɛskəu] *n* fresque *f*
fresh [frɛʃ] *adj* frais (fraîche); (*new*) nouveau
  (nouvelle); (*cheeky*) familier(-ière), culotté(e);
  to make a ~ start prendre un nouveau départ
freshen ['frɛʃən] *vi* (*wind, air*) fraîchir
  ▸ **freshen up** *vi* faire un brin de toilette
freshener ['frɛʃnə'] *n*: **skin ~** astringent *m*; **air ~**
  désodorisant *m*
fresher ['frɛʃə'] *n* (*Brit University*: *inf*) bizuth *m*,
  étudiant(e) de première année
freshly ['frɛʃlɪ] *adv* nouvellement, récemment
freshman (*US*: *irreg*) ['frɛʃmən] *n* = **fresher**
freshness ['frɛʃnɪs] *n* fraîcheur *f*
freshwater ['frɛʃwɔ:tə'] *adj* (*fish*) d'eau douce
fret [frɛt] *vi* s'agiter, se tracasser
fretful ['frɛtful] *adj* (*child*) grincheux(-euse)
Freudian ['frɔɪdɪən] *adj* freudien(ne); **~ slip**
  lapsus *m*
FRG *n abbr* (= *Federal Republic of Germany*) RFA *f*
friar ['fraɪə'] *n* moine *m*, frère *m*
friction ['frɪkʃən] *n* friction *f*, frottement *m*
friction feed *n* (*on printer*) entraînement *m* par
  friction
Friday ['fraɪdɪ] *n* vendredi *m*; *for phrases see also*
  Tuesday
fridge [frɪdʒ] *n* (*Brit*) frigo *m*, frigidaire® *m*
fridge-freezer ['frɪdʒ'fri:zə'] *n* réfrigérateur-
  congélateur *m*
fried [fraɪd] *pt, pp of* **fry** ▷ *adj* frit(e); **~ egg** œuf *m*
  sur le plat
friend [frɛnd] *n* ami(e); **to make ~s with** se lier
  (d'amitié) avec
friendliness ['frɛndlɪnɪs] *n* attitude amicale
friendly ['frɛndlɪ] *adj* amical(e); (*kind*)
  sympathique, gentil(le); (*place*) accueillant(e);
  (*Pol: country*) ami(e) ▷ *n* (*also*: **friendly match**)
  match amical; **to be ~ with** être ami(e) avec; **to**
  be ~ to être bien disposé(e) à l'égard de
friendly fire *n*: **they were killed by ~** ils sont
  morts sous les tirs de leur propre camp
friendly society *n* société *f* mutualiste
friendship ['frɛndʃɪp] *n* amitié *f*
fries [fraɪz] (*esp US*) *npl* = **French fried potatoes**
frieze [fri:z] *n* frise *f*, bordure *f*
frigate ['frɪgɪt] *n* (*Naut: modern*) frégate *f*
fright [fraɪt] *n* peur *f*, effroi *m*; **to give sb a ~**
  faire peur à qn; **to take ~** prendre peur,
  s'effrayer; **she looks a ~** elle a l'air d'un

épouvantail

frighten ['fraitn] *vt* effrayer, faire peur à
▸ **frighten away**, **frighten off** *vt* (*birds, children etc*) faire fuir, effaroucher

frightened ['fraitnd] *adj*: **to be ~ (of)** avoir peur (de)

frightening ['fraitniŋ] *adj* effrayant(e)

frightful ['fraitful] *adj* affreux(-euse)

frightfully ['fraitfəli] *adv* affreusement

frigid ['fridʒid] *adj* frigide

frigidity [fri'dʒiditi] *n* frigidité *f*

frill [fril] *n* (*of dress*) volant *m*; (*of shirt*) jabot *m*; **without ~s** (*fig*) sans manières

frilly ['frili] *adj* à fanfreluches

fringe [frindʒ] *n* (*Brit: of hair*) frange *f*; (*edge: of forest etc*) bordure *f*; (*fig*): **on the ~** en marge

fringe benefits *npl* avantages sociaux *or* en nature

fringe theatre *n* théâtre *m* d'avant-garde

Frisbee® ['frizbi] *n* Frisbee® *m*

frisk [frisk] *vt* fouiller

frisky ['friski] *adj* vif (vive), sémillant(e)

fritter ['fritəʳ] *n* beignet *m*
▸ **fritter away** *vt* gaspiller

frivolity [fri'vɔliti] *n* frivolité *f*

frivolous ['frivələs] *adj* frivole

frizzy ['frizi] *adj* crépu(e)

fro [frəu] *adv see* **to**

frock [frɔk] *n* robe *f*

frog [frɔg] *n* grenouille *f*; **to have a ~ in one's throat** avoir un chat dans la gorge

frogman (*irreg*) ['frɔgmən] *n* homme-grenouille *m*

frogmarch ['frɔgmɑːtʃ] *vt* (*Brit*): **to ~ sb in/out** faire entrer/sortir qn de force

frolic ['frɔlik] *n* ébats *mpl* ▷ *vi* folâtrer, batifoler

 KEYWORD

from [frɔm] *prep* **1** (*indicating starting place, origin etc*) de; **where do you come from?**, **where are you from?** d'où venez-vous?; **where has he come from?** d'où arrive-t-il?; **from London to Paris** de Londres à Paris; **to escape from sb/ sth** échapper à qn/qch; **a letter/telephone call from my sister** une lettre/un appel de ma sœur; **to drink from the bottle** boire à (même) la bouteille; **tell him from me that ...** dites-lui de ma part que ...
2 (*indicating time*) (à partir) de; **from one o'clock to** *or* **until** *or* **till two** d'une heure à deux heures; **from January (on)** à partir de janvier
3 (*indicating distance*) de; **the hotel is one kilometre from the beach** l'hôtel est à un kilomètre de la plage
4 (*indicating price, number etc*) de; **prices range from £10 to £50** les prix varient entre 10 livres et 50 livres; **the interest rate was increased from 9% to 10%** le taux d'intérêt est passé de 9% à 10%
5 (*indicating difference*) de; **he can't tell red from green** il ne peut pas distinguer le rouge du vert;

to be different from sb/sth être différent de qn/qch
6 (*because of, on the basis of*): **from what he says** d'après ce qu'il dit; **weak from hunger** affaibli par la faim

frond [frɔnd] *n* fronde *f*

front [frʌnt] *n* (*of house, dress*) devant *m*; (*of coach, train*) avant *m*; (*of book*) couverture *f*; (*promenade: also*: **sea front**) bord *m* de mer; (*Mil, Pol, Meteorology*) front *m*; (*fig: appearances*) contenance *f*, façade *f* ▷ *adj* de devant; (*page, row*) premier(-ière); (*seat, wheel*) avant *inv* ▷ *vi*: **to ~ onto sth** donner sur qch; **in ~ (of)** devant

frontage ['frʌntidʒ] *n* façade *f*; (*of shop*) devanture *f*

frontal ['frʌntl] *adj* frontal(e)

front bench *n* (*Brit: Pol*) *voir article*

● FRONT BENCH

● Le *front bench* est le banc du gouvernement,
● placé à la droite du "Speaker", ou celui du
● cabinet fantôme, placé à sa gauche. Ils se
● font face dans l'enceinte de la Chambre des
● communes. Par extension, *front bench*
● désigne les dirigeants des groupes
● parlementaires de la majorité et de
● l'opposition, qui sont appelés
● "frontbenchers" par opposition aux autres
● députés qui sont appelés "backbenchers".

front desk *n* (*US: in hotel, at doctor's*) réception *f*

front door *n* porte *f* d'entrée; (*of car*) portière *f* avant

frontier ['frʌntiəʳ] *n* frontière *f*

frontispiece ['frʌntispiːs] *n* frontispice *m*

front page *n* première page

front room *n* (*Brit*) pièce *f* de devant, salon *m*

front runner *n* (*fig*) favori(te)

front-wheel drive ['frʌntwiːl-] *n* traction *f* avant

frost [frɔst] *n* gel *m*, gelée *f*; (*also*: **hoarfrost**) givre *m*

frostbite ['frɔstbait] *n* gelures *fpl*

frosted ['frɔstid] *adj* (*glass*) dépoli(e); (*esp US: cake*) glacé(e)

frosting ['frɔstiŋ] *n* (*esp US: on cake*) glaçage *m*

frosty ['frɔsti] *adj* (*window*) couvert(e) de givre; (*weather, welcome*) glacial(e)

froth [frɔθ] *n* mousse *f*; écume *f*

frown [fraun] *n* froncement *m* de sourcils ▷ *vi* froncer les sourcils
▸ **frown on** *vt* (*fig*) désapprouver

froze [frəuz] *pt of* **freeze**

frozen ['frəuzn] *pp of* **freeze** ▷ *adj* (*food*) congelé(e); (*very cold: person: Comm: assets*) gelé(e)

FRS *n abbr* (*Brit*: = *Fellow of the Royal Society*) membre de l'Académie des sciences; (*US*: = *Federal Reserve System*) banque centrale américaine

frugal ['fruːgl] *adj* frugal(e)

fruit [fruːt] *n* (*pl inv*) fruit *m*

fruiterer ['fru:tərə'] *n* fruitier *m*, marchand(e) de fruits; **~'s (shop)** fruiterie *f*

fruit fly *n* mouche *f* du vinaigre, drosophile *f*

fruitful ['fru:tful] *adj* fructueux(-euse); (*plant, soil*) fécond(e)

fruition [fru:'ɪʃən] *n*: **to come to ~** se réaliser

fruit juice *n* jus *m* de fruit

fruitless ['fru:tlɪs] *adj* (*fig*) vain(e), infructueux(-euse)

fruit machine *n* (*Brit*) machine *f* à sous

fruit salad *n* salade *f* de fruits

frump [frʌmp] *n* mocheté *f*

frustrate [frʌs'treɪt] *vt* frustrer; (*plot, plans*) faire échouer

frustrated [frʌs'treɪtɪd] *adj* frustré(e)

frustrating [frʌs'treɪtɪŋ] *adj* (*job*) frustrant(e); (*day*) démoralisant(e)

frustration [frʌs'treɪʃən] *n* frustration *f*

fry (*pt, pp* **fried**) [fraɪ, -d] *vt* (faire) frire ▷ *n*: **small ~** le menu fretin

frying pan ['fraɪɪŋ-] *n* poêle *f* (à frire)

FT *n abbr* (*Brit*: = *Financial Times*) *journal financier*

ft. *abbr* = **foot**; **feet**

FTC *n abbr* (*US*) = **Federal Trade Commission**

FTSE 100 (Share) Index *n abbr* (= *Financial Times Stock Exchange 100 (Share) Index*) indice *m* Footsie des cent grandes valeurs

fuchsia ['fju:ʃə] *n* fuchsia *m*

fuck [fʌk] *vt, vi* (*inf!*) baiser (!); **~ off!** fous le camp! (!)

fuddled ['fʌdld] *adj* (*muddled*) embrouillé(e), confus(e)

fuddy-duddy ['fʌdɪdʌdɪ] *adj* (*pej*) vieux jeu *inv*, ringard(e)

fudge [fʌdʒ] *n* (*Culin*) sorte de confiserie à base de sucre, de beurre et de lait ▷ *vt* (*issue, problem*) esquiver

fuel [fjuəl] *n* (*for heating*) combustible *m*; (*for engine*) carburant *m*

fuel oil *n* mazout *m*

fuel pump *n* (*Aut*) pompe *f* d'alimentation

fuel tank *n* cuve *f* à mazout, citerne *f*; (*in vehicle*) réservoir *m* de *or* à carburant

fug [fʌg] *n* (*Brit*) puanteur *f*, odeur *f* de renfermé

fugitive ['fju:dʒɪtɪv] *n* fugitif(-ive)

fulfil, (*US*) **fulfill** [ful'fɪl] *vt* (*function, condition*) remplir; (*order*) exécuter; (*wish, desire*) satisfaire, réaliser

fulfilled [ful'fɪld] *adj* (*person*) comblé(e), épanoui(e)

fulfilment, (*US*) **fulfillment** [ful'fɪlmənt] *n* (*of wishes*) réalisation *f*

full [ful] *adj* plein(e); (*details, hotel, bus*) complet(-ète); (*price*) fort(e), normal(e); (*busy: day*) chargé(e); (*skirt*) ample, large ▷ *adv*: **to know ~ well that** savoir fort bien que; **~ (up)** (*hotel etc*) complet(-ète); **I'm ~ (up)** j'ai bien mangé; **~ employment/fare** plein emploi/tarif; **a ~ two hours** deux bonnes heures; **at ~ speed** à toute vitesse; **in ~** (*reproduce, quote, pay*) intégralement; (*write name etc*) en toutes lettres

fullback ['fulbæk] *n* (*Rugby, Football*) arrière *m*

full-blooded ['ful'blʌdɪd] *adj* (*vigorous*) vigoureux(-euse)

full-cream ['ful'kri:m] *adj*: **~ milk** (*Brit*) lait entier

full-grown ['ful'grəun] *adj* arrivé(e) à maturité, adulte

full-length ['ful'lɛŋθ] *adj* (*portrait*) en pied; (*coat*) long(ue); **~ film** long métrage

full moon *n* pleine lune

full-scale ['fulskeɪl] *adj* (*model*) grandeur nature *inv*; (*search, retreat*) complet(-ète), total(e)

full-sized ['ful'saɪzd] *adj* (*portrait etc*) grandeur nature *inv*

full stop *n* point *m*

full-time ['ful'taɪm] *adj, adv* (*work*) à plein temps ▷ *n* (*Sport*) fin *f* du match

fully ['fulɪ] *adv* entièrement, complètement; (*at least*): **~ as big** au moins aussi grand

fully-fledged ['fulɪ'flɛdʒd] *adj* (*teacher, barrister*) diplômé(e); (*citizen, member*) à part entière

fulsome ['fulsəm] *adj* (*pej: praise*) excessif(-ive); (: *manner*) exagéré(e)

fumble ['fʌmbl] *vi* fouiller, tâtonner ▷ *vt* (*ball*) mal réceptionner, cafouiller

▸ **fumble with** *vt fus* tripoter

fume [fju:m] *vi* (*rage*) rager

fumes [fju:mz] *npl* vapeurs *fpl*, émanations *fpl*, gaz *mpl*

fumigate ['fju:mɪgeɪt] *vt* désinfecter (par fumigation)

fun [fʌn] *n* amusement *m*, divertissement *m*; **to have ~** s'amuser; **for ~** pour rire; **it's not much ~** ce n'est pas très drôle *or* amusant; **to make ~ of** se moquer de

function ['fʌŋkʃən] *n* fonction *f*; (*reception, dinner*) cérémonie *f*, soirée officielle ▷ *vi* fonctionner; **to ~ as** faire office de

functional ['fʌŋkʃənl] *adj* fonctionnel(le)

function key *n* (*Comput*) touche *f* de fonction

fund [fʌnd] *n* caisse *f*, fonds *m*; (*source, store*) source *f*, mine *f*; **funds** *npl* (*money*) fonds *mpl*

fundamental [fʌndə'mɛntl] *adj* fondamental(e); **fundamentals** *npl* principes *mpl* de base

fundamentalism [fʌndə'mɛntəlɪzəm] *n* intégrisme *m*

fundamentalist [fʌndə'mɛntəlɪst] *n* intégriste *m/f*

fundamentally [fʌndə'mɛntəlɪ] *adv* fondamentalement

funding ['fʌndɪŋ] *n* financement *m*

fund-raising ['fʌndreɪzɪŋ] *n* collecte *f* de fonds

funeral ['fju:nərəl] *n* enterrement *m*, obsèques *fpl* (*more formal occasion*)

funeral director *n* entrepreneur *m* des pompes funèbres

funeral parlour [-'pɑːlə'] *n* (*Brit*) dépôt *m* mortuaire

funeral service *n* service *m* funèbre

funereal [fju:'nɪərɪəl] *adj* lugubre, funèbre

funfair ['fʌnfɛə'] *n* (*Brit*) fête (foraine)

fungus (*pl* **fungi**) ['fʌŋgəs, -gaɪ] *n* champignon *m*; (*mould*) moisissure *f*

funicular [fjuː'nɪkjuləʳ] n (also: **funicular railway**) funiculaire m

funky ['fʌŋkɪ] adj (music) funky inv; (inf: excellent) super inv

funnel ['fʌnl] n entonnoir m; (of ship) cheminée f

funnily ['fʌnɪlɪ] adv drôlement; (strangely) curieusement

funny ['fʌnɪ] adj amusant(e), drôle; (strange) curieux(-euse), bizarre

funny bone n endroit sensible du coude

fun run n course f de fond (pour amateurs)

fur [fəːʳ] n fourrure f; (Brit: in kettle etc) (dépôt m de) tartre m

fur coat n manteau m de fourrure

furious ['fjuərɪəs] adj furieux(-euse); (effort) acharné(e); **to be ~ with sb** être dans une fureur noire contre qn

furiously ['fjuərɪəslɪ] adv furieusement; avec acharnement

furl [fəːl] vt rouler; (Naut) ferler

furlong ['fəːlɔŋ] n = 201.17 m (terme d'hippisme)

furlough ['fəːləu] n permission f, congé m

furnace ['fəːnɪs] n fourneau m

furnish ['fəːnɪʃ] vt meubler; (supply) fournir; **~ed flat** or (US) **apartment** meublé m

furnishings ['fəːnɪʃɪŋz] npl mobilier m, articles mpl d'ameublement

furniture ['fəːnɪtʃəʳ] n meubles mpl, mobilier m; **piece of ~** meuble m

furniture polish n encaustique f

furore [fjuə'rɔːrɪ] n (protests) protestations fpl

furrier ['fʌrɪəʳ] n fourreur m

furrow ['fʌrəu] n sillon m

furry ['fəːrɪ] adj (animal) à fourrure; (toy) en peluche

further ['fəːðəʳ] adj supplémentaire, autre; nouveau (nouvelle) ▷ adv plus loin; (more) davantage; (moreover) de plus ▷ vt faire avancer or progresser, promouvoir; **how much ~ is it?** quelle distance or combien reste-t-il à parcourir?; **until ~ notice** jusqu'à nouvel ordre or avis; **~ to your letter of ...** (Comm) suite à votre lettre du ...

further education n enseignement m postscolaire (recyclage, formation professionnelle)

furthermore [fəːðə'mɔːʳ] adv de plus, en outre

furthermost ['fəːðəməust] adj le (la) plus éloigné(e)

furthest ['fəːðɪst] superlative of **far**

furtive ['fəːtɪv] adj furtif(-ive)

fury ['fjuərɪ] n fureur f

fuse, (US) **fuze** [fjuːz] n fusible m; (for bomb etc) amorce f, détonateur m ▷ vt, vi (metal) fondre; (fig) fusionner; (Brit: Elec): **to ~ the lights** faire sauter les fusibles or les plombs; **a ~ has blown** un fusible a sauté

fuse box n boîte f à fusibles

fuselage ['fjuːzəlɑːʒ] n fuselage m

fuse wire n fusible m

fusillade [fjuːzɪ'leɪd] n fusillade f; (fig) feu roulant

fusion ['fjuːʒən] n fusion f

fuss [fʌs] n (anxiety, excitement) chichis mpl, façons fpl; (commotion) tapage m; (complaining, trouble) histoire(s) f(pl) ▷ vi faire des histoires ▷ vt (person) embêter; **to make a ~** faire des façons (or des histoires); **to make a ~ of sb** dorloter qn

▶ **fuss over** vt fus (person) dorloter

fusspot ['fʌspɔt] n (inf): **don't be such a ~!** ne fais pas tant d'histoires!

fussy ['fʌsɪ] adj (person) tatillon(ne), difficile, chichiteux(-euse); (dress, style) tarabiscoté(e); **I'm not ~** (inf) ça m'est égal

fusty ['fʌstɪ] adj (old-fashioned) vieillot(te); (smell) de renfermé or moisi

futile ['fjuːtaɪl] adj futile

futility [fjuː'tɪlɪtɪ] n futilité f

futon ['fuːtɔn] n futon m

future ['fjuːtʃəʳ] adj futur(e) ▷ n avenir m; (Ling) futur m; **futures** npl (Comm) opérations fpl à terme; **in (the) ~** à l'avenir; **in the near/immediate ~** dans un avenir proche/immédiat

futuristic [fjuːtʃə'rɪstɪk] adj futuriste

fuze [fjuːz] n, vt, vi (US) = **fuse**

fuzzy ['fʌzɪ] adj (Phot) flou(e); (hair) crépu(e)

fwd. abbr = **forward**

fwy abbr (US) = **freeway**

FY abbr = **fiscal year**

FYI abbr = **for your information**

Gg

G¹, g [dʒiː] n (letter) G, g m; (Mus): **G** sol m; **G for George** G comme Gaston

G² n abbr (Brit Scol: = good) b (= bien); (US Cine: = general (audience)) ≈ tous publics; (Pol: = G8) G8 m

g. abbr (= gram) g; (= gravity) g

G8 abbr (Pol): **the G8 nations** le G8

GA abbr (US) = **Georgia**

gab [gæb] n (inf): **to have the gift of the ~** avoir la langue bien pendue

gabble ['gæbl] vi bredouiller; jacasser

gaberdine [gæbə'diːn] n gabardine f

gable ['geɪbl] n pignon m

Gabon [gə'bɔn] n Gabon m

gad about ['gædə'baut] vi (inf) se balader

gadget ['gædʒɪt] n gadget m

Gaelic ['geɪlɪk] adj, n (Ling) gaélique (m)

gaffe [gæf] n gaffe f

gaffer ['gæfəʳ] n (Brit: foreman) contremaître m; (Brit inf: boss) patron m

gag [gæg] n (on mouth) bâillon m; (joke) gag m ▷ vt (prisoner etc) bâillonner ▷ vi (choke) étouffer

gaga ['gɑːgɑː] adj: **to go ~** devenir gaga or gâteux(-euse)

gaiety ['geɪtɪ] n gaieté f

gaily ['geɪlɪ] adv gaiement

gain [geɪn] n (improvement) gain m; (profit) gain, profit m ▷ vt gagner ▷ vi (watch) avancer; **to ~ from/by** gagner de/à; **to ~ on sb** (catch up) rattraper qn; **to ~ 3lbs (in weight)** prendre 3 livres; **to ~ ground** gagner du terrain

gainful ['geɪnful] adj profitable, lucratif(-ive)

gainfully ['geɪnfəlɪ] adv: **to be ~ employed** avoir un emploi rémunéré

gainsay [geɪn'seɪ] vt (irreg: like **say**) contredire; nier

gait [geɪt] n démarche f

gal. abbr = **gallon**

gala ['gɑːlə] n gala m; **swimming ~** grand concours de natation

Galápagos [gə'læpəgəs], **Galápagos Islands** npl: **the ~ (Islands)** les îles fpl Galapagos fpl

galaxy ['gæləksɪ] n galaxie f

gale [geɪl] n coup m de vent; **~ force 10** vent m de force 10

gall [gɔːl] n (Anat) bile f; (fig) effronterie f ▷ vt ulcérer, irriter

gall. abbr = **gallon**

gallant ['gælənt] adj vaillant(e), brave; (towards ladies) empressé(e), galant(e)

gallantry ['gæləntrɪ] n bravoure f, vaillance f; empressement m, galanterie f

gall bladder ['gɔːl-] n vésicule f biliaire

galleon ['gælɪən] n galion m

gallery ['gælərɪ] n galerie f; (also: **art gallery**) musée m; (: private) galerie; (for spectators) tribune f; (: in theatre) dernier balcon

galley ['gælɪ] n (ship's kitchen) cambuse f; (ship) galère f; (also: **galley proof**) placard m, galée f

Gallic ['gælɪk] adj (of Gaul) gaulois(e); (French) français(e)

galling ['gɔːlɪŋ] adj irritant(e)

gallon ['gæln] n gallon m (Brit = 4.543 l; US = 3.785 l), = 8 pints

gallop ['gæləp] n galop m ▷ vi galoper; **~ing inflation** inflation galopante

gallows ['gæləuz] n potence f

gallstone ['gɔːlstəun] n calcul m (biliaire)

Gallup Poll ['gæləp-] n sondage m Gallup

galore [gə'lɔːʳ] adv en abondance, à gogo

galvanize ['gælvənaɪz] vt galvaniser; (fig): **to ~ sb into action** galvaniser qn

Gambia ['gæmbɪə] n Gambie f

gambit ['gæmbɪt] n (fig): **(opening) ~** manœuvre f stratégique

gamble ['gæmbl] n pari m, risque calculé ▷ vt, vi jouer; **to ~ on the Stock Exchange** jouer en or à la Bourse; **to ~ on** (fig) miser sur

gambler ['gæmbləʳ] n joueur m

gambling ['gæmblɪŋ] n jeu m

gambol ['gæmbl] vi gambader

game [geɪm] n jeu m; (event) match m; (of tennis, chess, cards) partie f; (Hunting) gibier m ▷ adj brave; (willing): **to be ~ (for)** être prêt(e) (à or pour); **a ~ of football/tennis** une partie de football/tennis; **big ~** gros gibier; **games** npl (Scol) sport m; (sport event) jeux

game bird n gibier m à plume

gamekeeper ['geɪmkiːpəʳ] n garde-chasse m

gamely ['geɪmlɪ] adv vaillamment

game reserve n réserve animalière

games console ['geɪmz-] n console f de jeux vidéo

game show ['geɪmʃəu] n jeu télévisé
gamesmanship ['geɪmzmənʃɪp] n roublardise f
gaming ['geɪmɪŋ] n jeu m, jeux mpl d'argent
gammon ['gæmən] n (bacon) quartier m de lard fumé; (ham) jambon fumé or salé
gamut ['gæmət] n gamme f
gang [gæŋ] n bande f, groupe m; (of workmen) équipe f
▶ **gang up** vi: **to ~ up on sb** se liguer contre qn
Ganges ['gændʒiːz] n: **the ~** le Gange
gangland ['gæŋlænd] adj: **~ killer** tueur professionnel du milieu; **~ boss** chef m de gang
gangling ['gæŋglɪŋ], **gangly** ['gæŋglɪ] adj dégingandé(e)
gangplank ['gæŋplæŋk] n passerelle f
gangrene ['gæŋgriːn] n gangrène f
gangster ['gæŋstəʳ] n gangster m, bandit m
gangway ['gæŋweɪ] n passerelle f; (Brit: of bus) couloir central
gantry ['gæntrɪ] n portique m; (for rocket) tour f de lancement
GAO n abbr (US: = General Accounting Office) ≈ Cour f des comptes
gaol [dʒeɪl] n, vt (Brit) = **jail**
gap [gæp] n trou m; (in time) intervalle m; (fig) lacune f; vide m; (difference): **~ (between)** écart m (entre)
gape [geɪp] vi (person) être or rester bouche bée; (hole, shirt) être ouvert(e)
gaping ['geɪpɪŋ] adj (hole) béant(e)
gap year n année que certains étudiants prennent pour voyager ou pour travailler avant d'entrer à l'université
garage ['gæraːʒ] n garage m
garage sale n vide-grenier m
garb [gaːb] n tenue f, costume m
garbage ['gaːbɪdʒ] n (US: rubbish) ordures fpl, détritus mpl; (inf: nonsense) âneries fpl
garbage can n (US) poubelle f, boîte f à ordures
garbage collector n (US) éboueur m
garbage disposal, garbage disposal unit n broyeur m d'ordures
garbage truck n (US) camion m (de ramassage des ordures), benne f à ordures
garbled ['gaːbld] adj déformé(e), faussé(e)
garden ['gaːdn] n jardin m ▷ vi jardiner;
   gardens npl (public) jardin public; (private) parc m
garden centre (Brit) n pépinière f, jardinerie f
garden city n (Brit) cité-jardin f
gardener ['gaːdnəʳ] n jardinier m
gardening ['gaːdnɪŋ] n jardinage m
gargle ['gaːgl] vi se gargariser ▷ n gargarisme m
gargoyle ['gaːgɔɪl] n gargouille f
garish ['gɛərɪʃ] adj criard(e), voyant(e)
garland ['gaːlənd] n guirlande f; couronne f
garlic ['gaːlɪk] n ail m
garment ['gaːmənt] n vêtement m
garner ['gaːnəʳ] vt engranger, amasser
garnish ['gaːnɪʃ] (Culin) vt garnir ▷ n décoration f
garret ['gærɪt] n mansarde f
garrison ['gærɪsn] n garnison f ▷ vt mettre en garnison, stationner
garrulous ['gærjuləs] adj volubile, loquace
garter ['gaːtəʳ] n jarretière f; (US: suspender) jarretelle f
garter belt n (US) porte-jarretelles m inv
gas [gæs] n gaz m; (used as anaesthetic): **to be given ~** se faire endormir; (US: gasoline) essence f ▷ vt asphyxier; (Mil) gazer; **I can smell ~** ça sent le gaz
Gascony ['gæskənɪ] n Gascogne f
gas cooker n (Brit) cuisinière f à gaz
gas cylinder n bouteille f de gaz
gaseous ['gæsɪəs] adj gazeux(-euse)
gas fire n (Brit) radiateur m à gaz
gas-fired ['gæsfaɪəd] adj au gaz
gash [gæʃ] n entaille f; (on face) balafre f ▷ vt taillader; balafrer
gasket ['gæskɪt] n (Aut) joint m de culasse
gas mask n masque m à gaz
gas meter n compteur m à gaz
gasoline ['gæsəliːn] n (US) essence f
gasp [gaːsp] n halètement m; (of shock etc): **she gave a small ~ of pain** la douleur lui coupa le souffle ▷ vi haleter; (fig) avoir le souffle coupé
▶ **gasp out** vt (say) dire dans un souffle or d'une voix entrecoupée
gas pedal n (US) accélérateur m
gas ring n brûleur m
gas station n (US) station-service f
gas stove n réchaud m à gaz; (cooker) cuisinière f à gaz
gassy ['gæsɪ] adj gazeux(-euse)
gas tank n (US Aut) réservoir m d'essence
gas tap n bouton m (de cuisinière à gaz); (on pipe) robinet m à gaz
gastric ['gæstrɪk] adj gastrique
gastric ulcer n ulcère m de l'estomac
gastroenteritis ['gæstrəuɛntə'raɪtɪs] n gastroentérite f
gastronomy [gæs'trɔnəmɪ] n gastronomie f
gasworks ['gæswəːks] n, npl usine f à gaz
gate [geɪt] n (of garden) portail m; (of field, at level crossing) barrière f; (of building, town, at airport) porte f; (of lock) vanne f
gateau (pl -x) ['gætəu, -z] n gros gâteau à la crème
gatecrash ['geɪtkræʃ] vt s'introduire sans invitation dans
gatecrasher ['geɪtkræʃəʳ] n intrus(e)
gatehouse ['geɪthaus] n loge f
gateway ['geɪtweɪ] n porte f
gather ['gæðəʳ] vt (flowers, fruit) cueillir; (pick up) ramasser; (assemble: objects) rassembler; (: people) réunir; (: information) recueillir; (understand) comprendre; (Sewing) froncer ▷ vi (assemble) rassembler; (dust) s'amasser; (clouds) s'amonceler; **to ~ (from/that)** conclure or déduire (de/que); **as far as I can ~** d'après ce que je comprends; **to ~ speed** prendre de la vitesse
gathering ['gæðərɪŋ] n rassemblement m
GATT [gæt] n abbr (= General Agreement on Tariffs and

Trade) GATT *m*

gauche [gəʊʃ] *adj* gauche, maladroit(e)

gaudy ['gɔːdɪ] *adj* voyant(e)

gauge [geɪdʒ] *n* (*standard measure*) calibre *m*; (*Rail*) écartement *m*; (*instrument*) jauge *f* ▷ *vt* jauger; (*fig: sb's capabilities, character*) juger de; **to ~ the right moment** calculer le moment propice; **petrol ~**, (*US*) **gas ~** jauge d'essence

Gaul [gɔːl] *n* (*country*) Gaule *f*; (*person*) Gaulois(e)

gaunt [gɔːnt] *adj* décharné(e); (*grim, desolate*) désolé(e)

gauntlet ['gɔːntlɪt] *n* (*fig*) **to throw down the ~** jeter le gant; **to run the ~ through an angry crowd** se frayer un passage à travers une foule hostile *or* entre deux haies de manifestants *etc* hostiles

gauze [gɔːz] *n* gaze *f*

gave [geɪv] *pt of* **give**

gawky ['gɔːkɪ] *adj* dégingandé(e), godiche

gawp [gɔːp] *vi*: **to ~ at** regarder bouche bée

gay [geɪ] *adj* (*homosexual*) homosexuel(le); (*slightly old-fashioned: cheerful*) gai(e), réjoui(e); (*colour*) gai, vif (vive)

gaze [geɪz] *n* regard *m* fixe ▷ *vi*: **to ~ at** (*vt*) fixer du regard

gazelle [gə'zɛl] *n* gazelle *f*

gazette [gə'zɛt] *n* (*newspaper*) gazette *f*; (*official publication*) journal officiel

gazetteer [gæzə'tɪər] *n* dictionnaire *m* géographique

gazump [gə'zʌmp] *vi* (*Brit*) *revenir sur une promesse de vente pour accepter un prix plus élevé*

GB *abbr* = **Great Britain**

GBH *n abbr* (*Brit Law: inf*) = **grievous bodily harm**

GC *n abbr* (*Brit*: = *George Cross*) *distinction honorifique*

GCE *n abbr* (*Brit*) = **General Certificate of Education**

GCHQ *n abbr* (*Brit*: = *Government Communications Headquarters*) *centre d'interception des télécommunications étrangères*

GCSE *n abbr* (*Brit*: = *General Certificate of Secondary Education*) *examen passé à l'âge de 16 ans sanctionnant les connaissances de l'élève*; **she's got eight ~s** elle a réussi dans huit matières aux épreuves du GCSE

Gdns. *abbr* = **gardens**

GDP *n abbr* = **gross domestic product**

GDR *n abbr* (*old*: = *German Democratic Republic*) RDA *f*

gear [gɪər] *n* matériel *m*, équipement *m*; (*Tech*) engrenage *m*; (*Aut*) vitesse *f* ▷ *vt* (*fig: adapt*) adapter; **top** *or* (*US*) **high/low ~** quatrième (*or* cinquième)/première vitesse; **in ~** en prise; **out of ~** au point mort; **our service is ~ed to meet the needs of the disabled** notre service répond de façon spécifique aux besoins des handicapés

▶ **gear up** *vi*: **to ~ up (to do)** se préparer (à faire)

gear box *n* boîte *f* de vitesse

gear lever *n* levier *m* de vitesse

gear shift (*US*) *n* = **gear lever**

gear stick (*Brit*) *n* = **gear lever**

GED *n abbr* (*US Scol*) = **general educational**
development

geese [giːs] *npl of* **goose**

geezer ['giːzər] *n* (*Brit inf*) mec *m*

Geiger counter ['gaɪgə-] *n* compteur *m* Geiger

gel [dʒɛl] *n* gelée *f*; (*Chem*) colloïde *m*

gelatin, gelatine ['dʒɛlətiːn] *n* gélatine *f*

gelignite ['dʒɛlɪgnaɪt] *n* plastic *m*

gem [dʒɛm] *n* pierre précieuse

Gemini ['dʒɛmɪnaɪ] *n* les Gémeaux *mpl*; **to be ~** être des Gémeaux

gen [dʒɛn] *n* (*Brit inf*): **to give sb the ~ on sth** mettre qn au courant de qch

Gen. *abbr* (*Mil*: = *general*) Gal

gen. *abbr* (= *general, generally*) gén

gender ['dʒɛndər] *n* genre *m*; (*person's sex*) sexe *m*

gene [dʒiːn] *n* (*Biol*) gène *m*

genealogy [dʒiːnɪ'ælədʒɪ] *n* généalogie *f*

general ['dʒɛnərl] *n* général *m* ▷ *adj* général(e); **in ~** en général; **the ~ public** le grand public; **~ audit** (*Comm*) vérification annuelle

general anaesthetic, (*US*) **general anesthetic** *n* anesthésie générale

general delivery *n* poste restante

general election *n* élection(s) législative(s)

generalization ['dʒɛnrəlaɪ'zeɪʃən] *n* généralisation *f*

generalize ['dʒɛnrəlaɪz] *vi* généraliser

general knowledge *n* connaissances générales

generally ['dʒɛnrəlɪ] *adv* généralement

general manager *n* directeur général

general practitioner *n* généraliste *m/f*

general store *n* épicerie *f*

general strike *n* grève générale

generate ['dʒɛnəreɪt] *vt* engendrer; (*electricity*) produire

generation [dʒɛnə'reɪʃən] *n* génération *f*; (*of electricity etc*) production *f*

generator ['dʒɛnəreɪtər] *n* générateur *m*

generic [dʒɪ'nɛrɪk] *adj* générique

generosity [dʒɛnə'rɔsɪtɪ] *n* générosité *f*

generous ['dʒɛnərəs] *adj* généreux(-euse); (*copious*) copieux(-euse)

genesis ['dʒɛnɪsɪs] *n* genèse *f*

genetic [dʒɪ'nɛtɪk] *adj* génétique; **~ engineering** ingénierie *m* génétique; **~ fingerprinting** système *m* d'empreinte génétique

genetically modified *adj* (*food etc*) génétiquement modifié(e)

genetics [dʒɪ'nɛtɪks] *n* génétique *f*

Geneva [dʒɪ'niːvə] *n* Genève; **Lake ~** le lac Léman

genial ['dʒiːnɪəl] *adj* cordial(e), chaleureux(-euse); (*climate*) clément(e)

genitals ['dʒɛnɪtlz] *npl* organes génitaux

genitive ['dʒɛnɪtɪv] *n* génitif *m*

genius ['dʒiːnɪəs] *n* génie *m*

Genoa ['dʒɛnəuə] *n* Gênes

genocide ['dʒɛnəusaɪd] *n* génocide *m*

gent [dʒɛnt] *n abbr* (*Brit inf*) = **gentleman**

genteel [dʒɛn'tiːl] *adj* de bon ton, distingué(e)

gentle ['dʒɛntl] *adj* doux (douce); (*breeze, touch*)

léger(-ère)

gentleman (irreg) ['dʒɛntlmən] n monsieur m; (well-bred man) gentleman m; ~'s **agreement** gentleman's agreement m

gentlemanly ['dʒɛntlmənlɪ] adj bien élevé(e)

gentleness ['dʒɛntlnɪs] n douceur f

gently ['dʒɛntlɪ] adv doucement

gentry ['dʒɛntrɪ] n petite noblesse

gents [dʒɛnts] n W.-C. mpl (pour hommes)

genuine ['dʒɛnjuɪn] adj véritable, authentique; (person, emotion) sincère

genuinely ['dʒɛnjuɪnlɪ] adv sincèrement, vraiment

geographer [dʒɪ'ɒgrəfəʳ] n géographe m/f

geographic [dʒɪə'græfɪk], **geographical** [dʒɪə'græfɪkl] adj géographique

geography [dʒɪ'ɒgrəfɪ] n géographie f

geological [dʒɪə'lɒdʒɪkl] adj géologique

geologist [dʒɪ'ɔlədʒɪst] n géologue m/f

geology [dʒɪ'ɔlədʒɪ] n géologie f

geometric [dʒɪə'mɛtrɪk], **geometrical** [dʒɪə'mɛtrɪkl] adj géométrique

geometry [dʒɪ'ɔmətrɪ] n géométrie f

Geordie ['dʒɔːdɪ] n (inf) habitant(e) de Tyneside, originaire m/f de Tyneside.

Georgia ['dʒɔːdʒə] n Géorgie f

Georgian ['dʒɔːdʒən] adj (Geo) géorgien(ne) ▷ n Géorgien(ne); (Ling) géorgien m

geranium [dʒɪ'reɪnɪəm] n géranium m

geriatric [dʒɛrɪ'ætrɪk] adj gériatrique ▷ n patient(e) gériatrique

germ [dʒəːm] n (Med) microbe m; (Biol: fig) germe m

German ['dʒəːmən] adj allemand(e) ▷ n Allemand(e); (Ling) allemand m

germane [dʒəː'meɪn] adj (formal): ~ **(to)** se rapportant (à)

German measles n rubéole f

Germany ['dʒəːmənɪ] n Allemagne f

germination [dʒəːmɪ'neɪʃən] n germination f

germ warfare n guerre f bactériologique

gerrymandering ['dʒɛrɪmændərɪŋ] n tripotage m du découpage électoral

gestation [dʒɛs'teɪʃən] n gestation f

gesticulate [dʒɛs'tɪkjuleɪt] vi gesticuler

gesture ['dʒɛstjəʳ] n geste m; **as a ~ of friendship** en témoignage d'amitié

⬤ **KEYWORD**

get [gɛt] (pt, pp **got**, pp **gotten**) (US) vi 1 (become, be) devenir; **to get old/tired** devenir vieux/ fatigué, vieillir/se fatiguer; **to get drunk** s'enivrer; **to get ready/washed/shaved** etc se préparer/laver/raser etc; **to get killed** se faire tuer; **to get dirty** se salir; **to get married** se marier; **when do I get paid?** quand est-ce que je serai payé?; **it's getting late** il se fait tard

2 (go): **to get to/from** aller à/de; **to get home** rentrer chez soi; **how did you get here?** comment es-tu arrivé ici?; **he got across the bridge/under the fence** il a traversé le pont/ est passé au-dessous de la barrière

3 (begin) commencer or se mettre à; **to get to know sb** apprendre à connaître qn; **I'm getting to like him** je commence à l'apprécier; **let's get going** or **started** allons-y

4 (modal aux vb): **you've got to do it** il faut que vous le fassiez; **I've got to tell the police** je dois le dire à la police

▷ vt 1: **to get sth done** (do) faire qch; (have done) faire faire qch; **to get sth/sb ready** préparer qch/qn; **to get one's hair cut** se faire couper les cheveux; **to get the car going** or **to go** (faire) démarrer la voiture; **to get sb to do sth** faire faire qch à qn; **to get sb drunk** enivrer qn

2 (obtain: money, permission, results) obtenir, avoir; (buy) acheter; (find: job, flat) trouver; (fetch: person, doctor, object) aller chercher; **to get sth for sb** procurer qch à qn; **get me Mr Jones, please** (on phone) passez-moi Mr Jones, s'il vous plaît; **can I get you a drink?** est-ce que je peux vous servir à boire?

3 (receive: present, letter) recevoir, avoir; (acquire: reputation) avoir; (prize) obtenir; **what did you get for your birthday?** qu'est-ce que tu as eu pour ton anniversaire?; **how much did you get for the painting?** combien avez-vous vendu le tableau?

4 (catch) prendre, saisir, attraper; (hit: target etc) atteindre; **to get sb by the arm/throat** prendre or saisir or attraper qn par le bras/à la gorge; **get him!** arrête-le!; **the bullet got him in the leg** il a pris la balle dans la jambe; **he really gets me!** il me porte sur les nerfs!

5 (take, move): **to get sth to sb** faire parvenir qch à qn; **do you think we'll get it through the door?** on arrivera à le faire passer par la porte?; **I'll get you there somehow** je me débrouillerai pour t'y emmener

6 (catch, take: plane, bus etc) prendre; **where do I get the train for Birmingham?** où prend-on le train pour Birmingham?

7 (understand) comprendre, saisir; (hear) entendre; **I've got it!** j'ai compris!; **I don't get your meaning** je ne vois or comprends pas ce que vous voulez dire; **I didn't get your name** je n'ai pas entendu votre nom

8 (have, possess): **to have got** avoir; **how many have you got?** vous en avez combien?

9 (illness) avoir; **I've got a cold** j'ai le rhume; **she got pneumonia and died** elle a fait une pneumonie et elle en est morte

▶ **get about** vi se déplacer; (news) se répandre

▶ **get across** vt: **to get across (to)** (message, meaning) faire passer (à) ▷ vi: **to get across (to)** (speaker) se faire comprendre (par)

▶ **get along** vi (agree) s'entendre; (depart) s'en aller; (manage) = **get by**

▶ **get at** vt fus (attack) s'en prendre à; (reach) attraper, atteindre; **what are you getting at?** à quoi voulez-vous en venir?

▶ **get away** vi partir, s'en aller; (escape) s'échapper

▶ **get away with** vt fus (punishment) en être quitte pour; (crime etc) se faire pardonner
▶ **get back** vi (return) rentrer ▷ vt récupérer, recouvrer; **to get back to** (start again) retourner or revenir à; (contact again) recontacter; **when do we get back?** quand serons-nous de retour?
▶ **get back at** vt fus (inf): **to get back at sb** rendre la monnaie de sa pièce à qn
▶ **get by** vi (pass) passer; (manage) se débrouiller; **I can get by in Dutch** je me débrouille en hollandais
▶ **get down** vi, vt fus descendre ▷ vt descendre; (depress) déprimer
▶ **get down to** vt fus (work) se mettre à (faire); **to get down to business** passer aux choses sérieuses
▶ **get in** vi entrer; (arrive home) rentrer; (train) arriver ▷ vt (bring in: harvest) rentrer; (: coal) faire rentrer; (: supplies) faire des provisions de
▶ **get into** vt fus entrer dans; (car, train etc) monter dans; (clothes) mettre, enfiler, endosser; **to get into bed/a rage** se mettre au lit/en colère
▶ **get off** vi (from train etc) descendre; (depart: person, car) s'en aller; (escape) s'en tirer ▷ vt (remove: clothes, stain) enlever; (send off) expédier; (have as leave: day, time): **we got 2 days off** nous avons eu 2 jours de congé ▷ vt fus (train, bus) descendre de; **where do I get off?** où est-ce que je dois descendre?; **to get off to a good start** (fig) prendre un bon départ
▶ **get on** vi (at exam etc) se débrouiller; (agree): **to get on (with)** s'entendre (avec); **how are you getting on?** comment ça va? ▷ vt fus monter dans; (horse) monter sur
▶ **get on to** vt fus (Brit: deal with: problem) s'occuper de; (contact: person) contacter
▶ **get out** vi sortir; (of vehicle) descendre; (news etc) s'ébruiter ▷ vt sortir
▶ **get out of** vt fus sortir de; (duty etc) échapper à, se soustraire à
▶ **get over** vt fus (illness) se remettre de ▷ vt (communicate: idea etc) communiquer; (finish): **let's get it over (with)** finissons-en
▶ **get round** vi: **to get round to doing sth** se mettre (finalement) à faire qch ▷ vt fus contourner; (fig: person) entortiller
▶ **get through** vi (Tel) avoir la communication; **to get through to sb** atteindre qn ▷ vt fus (finish: work, book) finir, terminer
▶ **get together** vi se réunir ▷ vt rassembler
▶ **get up** vi (rise) se lever ▷ vt fus monter
▶ **get up to** vt fus (reach) arriver à; (prank etc) faire

getaway ['gɛtəweɪ] n fuite f
getaway car n voiture prévue pour prendre la fuite
get-together ['gɛttəgɛðə^r] n petite réunion, petite fête
get-up ['gɛtʌp] n (inf: outfit) accoutrement m
get-well card [gɛt'wɛl-] n carte f de vœux de bon rétablissement

geyser ['giːzə^r] n chauffe-eau m inv; (Geo) geyser m
Ghana ['gɑːnə] n Ghana m
Ghanaian [gɑːˈneɪən] adj ghanéen(ne) ▷ n Ghanéen(ne)
ghastly ['gɑːstlɪ] adj atroce, horrible; (pale) livide, blême
gherkin ['gəːkɪn] n cornichon m
ghetto ['gɛtəu] n ghetto m
ghetto blaster [-blɑːstə^r] n (inf) gros radiocassette
ghost [gəust] n fantôme m, revenant m ▷ vt (sb else's book) écrire
ghostly ['gəustlɪ] adj fantomatique
ghostwriter ['gəustraɪtə^r] n nègre m (fig)
ghoul [guːl] n (ghost) vampire m
ghoulish ['guːlɪʃ] adj (tastes etc) morbide
GHQ n abbr (Mil: = general headquarters) GQG m
GI n abbr (US inf: = government issue) soldat de l'armée américaine, GI m
giant ['dʒaɪənt] n géant(e) ▷ adj géant(e), énorme; **~ (size) packet** paquet géant
giant killer n (Sport) équipe inconnue qui remporte un match contre une équipe renommée
gibber ['dʒɪbə^r] vi émettre des sons inintelligibles
gibberish ['dʒɪbərɪʃ] n charabia m
gibe [dʒaɪb] n sarcasme m ▷ vi: **to ~ at** railler
giblets ['dʒɪblɪts] npl abats mpl
Gibraltar [dʒɪˈbrɔːltə^r] n Gibraltar m
giddiness ['gɪdɪnɪs] n vertige m
giddy ['gɪdɪ] adj (dizzy): **to be (or feel) ~** avoir le vertige; (height) vertigineux(-euse); (thoughtless) sot(te), étourdi(e)
gift [gɪft] n cadeau m, présent m; (donation, talent) don m; (Comm: also: **free gift**) cadeau(-réclame) m; **to have a ~ for sth** avoir des dons pour or le don de qch
gifted ['gɪftɪd] adj doué(e)
gift shop, (US) **gift store** n boutique f de cadeaux
gift token, gift voucher n chèque-cadeau m
gig [gɪg] n (inf: concert) concert m
gigabyte ['dʒɪgəbaɪt] n gigaoctet m
gigantic [dʒaɪˈgæntɪk] adj gigantesque
giggle ['gɪgl] vi pouffer, ricaner sottement ▷ n petit rire sot, ricanement m
GIGO ['gaɪgəu] abbr (Comput: inf: = garbage in, garbage out) qualité d'entrée = qualité de sortie
gild [gɪld] vt dorer
gill [dʒɪl] n (measure) = 0.25 pints (Brit = 0.148 l; US = 0.118 l)
gills [gɪlz] npl (of fish) ouïes fpl, branchies fpl
gilt [gɪlt] n dorure f ▷ adj doré(e)
gilt-edged ['gɪltɛdʒd] adj (stocks, securities) de premier ordre
gimlet ['gɪmlɪt] n vrille f
gimmick ['gɪmɪk] n truc m; **sales ~** offre promotionnelle
gin [dʒɪn] n gin m
ginger ['dʒɪndʒə^r] n gingembre m
▶ **ginger up** vt secouer; animer

ginger ale, ginger beer *n* boisson gazeuse au gingembre

gingerbread ['dʒɪndʒəbrɛd] *n* pain *m* d'épices

ginger group *n* (*Brit*) groupe *m* de pression

ginger-haired ['dʒɪndʒə'hɛəd] *adj* roux (rousse)

gingerly ['dʒɪndʒəlɪ] *adv* avec précaution

gingham ['gɪŋəm] *n* vichy *m*

ginseng ['dʒɪnsɛŋ] *n* ginseng *m*

gipsy ['dʒɪpsɪ] *n* = **gypsy**

giraffe [dʒɪ'rɑːf] *n* girafe *f*

girder ['gəːdə] *n* poutrelle *f*

girdle ['gəːdl] *n* (*corset*) gaine *f* ▷ *vt* ceindre

girl [gəːl] *n* fille *f*, fillette *f*; (*young unmarried woman*) jeune fille; (*daughter*) fille; **an English ~** une jeune Anglaise; **a little English ~** une petite Anglaise

girl band *n* girls band *m*

girlfriend ['gəːlfrɛnd] *n* (*of girl*) amie *f*; (*of boy*) petite amie

Girl Guide *n* (*Brit*) éclaireuse *f*; (*Roman Catholic*) guide *f*

girlish ['gəːlɪʃ] *adj* de jeune fille

Girl Scout *n* (*US*) = **Girl Guide**

Giro ['dʒaɪrəu] *n*: **the National ~** (*Brit*) ≈ les comptes chèques postaux

giro ['dʒaɪrəu] *n* (*bank giro*) virement *m* bancaire; (*post office giro*) mandat *m*

girth [gəːθ] *n* circonférence *f*; (*of horse*) sangle *f*

gist [dʒɪst] *n* essentiel *m*

give [gɪv] (*pt* **gave**, *pp* **given** [geɪv, 'gɪvn]) *n* (*of fabric*) élasticité *f* ▷ *vt* donner ▷ *vi* (*break*) céder; (*stretch: fabric*) se prêter; **to ~ sb sth, ~ sth to sb** donner qch à qn; (*gift*) offrir qch à qn; (*message*) transmettre qch à qn; **to ~ sb a call/kiss** appeler/embrasser qn; **to ~ a cry/sigh** pousser un cri/un soupir; **how much did you ~ for it?** combien (l')avez-vous payé?; **12 o'clock, ~ or take a few minutes** midi, à quelques minutes près; **to ~ way** céder; (*Brit Aut*) donner la priorité

▶ **give away** *vt* donner; (*give free*) faire cadeau de; (*betray*) donner, trahir; (*disclose*) révéler; (*bride*) conduire à l'autel

▶ **give back** *vt* rendre

▶ **give in** *vi* céder ▷ *vt* donner

▶ **give off** *vt* dégager

▶ **give out** *vt* (*food etc*) distribuer; (*news*) annoncer ▷ *vi* (*be exhausted: supplies*) s'épuiser; (*fail*) lâcher

▶ **give up** *vi* renoncer ▷ *vt* renoncer à; **to ~ up smoking** arrêter de fumer; **to ~ o.s. up** se rendre

give-and-take ['gɪvənd'teɪk] *n* concessions mutuelles

giveaway ['gɪvəweɪ] *n* (*inf*): **her expression was a ~** son expression la trahissait; **the exam was a ~!** cet examen, c'était du gâteau! ▷ *cpd*: **~ prices** prix sacrifiés

given ['gɪvn] *pp of* **give** ▷ *adj* (*fixed: time, amount*) donné(e), déterminé(e) ▷ *conj*: **~ the circumstances ...** étant donné les circonstances ...; vu les circonstances ...; **~ that ...** étant donné que ...

glacial ['gleɪsɪəl] *adj* (*Geo*) glaciaire; (*wind, weather*) glacial(e)

glacier ['glæsɪə] *n* glacier *m*

glad [glæd] *adj* content(e); **to be ~ about sth/ that** être heureux(-euse) *or* bien content de qch/que; **I was ~ of his help** j'étais bien content de (pouvoir compter sur) son aide *or* qu'il m'aide

gladden ['glædn] *vt* réjouir

glade [gleɪd] *n* clairière *f*

gladioli [glædɪ'əulaɪ] *npl* glaïeuls *mpl*

gladly ['glædlɪ] *adv* volontiers

glamorous ['glæmərəs] *adj* (*person*) séduisant(e); (*job*) prestigieux(-euse)

glamour, (*US*) **glamor** ['glæmə] *n* éclat *m*, prestige *m*

glance [glɑːns] *n* coup *m* d'œil ▷ *vi*: **to ~ at** jeter un coup d'œil à

▶ **glance off** *vt fus* (*bullet*) ricocher sur

glancing ['glɑːnsɪŋ] *adj* (*blow*) oblique

gland [glænd] *n* glande *f*

glandular ['glændjulə] *adj*: **~ fever** (*Brit*) mononucléose infectieuse

glare [glɛə] *n* (*of anger*) regard furieux; (*of light*) lumière éblouissante; (*of publicity*) feux *mpl* ▷ *vi* briller d'un éclat aveuglant; **to ~ at** lancer un regard *or* des regards furieux à

glaring ['glɛərɪŋ] *adj* (*mistake*) criant(e), qui saute aux yeux

glasnost ['glæznɔst] *n* glasnost *f*

glass [glɑːs] *n* verre *m*; (*also*: **looking glass**) miroir *m*; **glasses** *npl* (*spectacles*) lunettes *fpl*

glass-blowing ['glɑːsbləuɪŋ] *n* soufflage *m* (du verre)

glass ceiling *n* (*fig*) plafond *dans l'échelle hiérarchique au-dessus duquel les femmes ou les membres d'une minorité ethnique ne semblent pouvoir s'élever*

glass fibre *n* fibre *f* de verre

glasshouse ['glɑːshaus] *n* serre *f*

glassware ['glɑːswɛə] *n* verrerie *f*

glassy ['glɑːsɪ] *adj* (*eyes*) vitreux(-euse)

Glaswegian [glæs'wiːdʒən] *adj* de Glasgow ▷ *n* habitant(e) de Glasgow, natif(-ive) de Glasgow

glaze [gleɪz] *vt* (*door*) vitrer; (*pottery*) vernir; (*Culin*) glacer ▷ *n* vernis *m*; (*Culin*) glaçage *m*

glazed [gleɪzd] *adj* (*eye*) vitreux(-euse); (*pottery*) verni(e); (*tiles*) vitrifié(e)

glazier ['gleɪzɪə] *n* vitrier *m*

gleam [gliːm] *n* lueur *f* ▷ *vi* luire, briller; **a ~ of hope** une lueur d'espoir

gleaming ['gliːmɪŋ] *adj* luisant(e)

glean [gliːn] *vt* (*information*) recueillir

glee [gliː] *n* joie *f*

gleeful ['gliːful] *adj* joyeux(-euse)

glen [glɛn] *n* vallée *f*

glib [glɪb] *adj* qui a du bagou; facile

glide [glaɪd] *vi* glisser; (*Aviat, bird*) planer ▷ *n* glissement *m*; vol plané

glider ['glaɪdə] *n* (*Aviat*) planeur *m*

gliding ['glaɪdɪŋ] *n* (*Aviat*) vol *m* à voile

glimmer ['glɪmə] *vi* luire ▷ *n* lueur *f*

glimpse [glɪmps] *n* vision passagère, aperçu *m* ▷ *vt* entrevoir, apercevoir; **to catch a ~ of** entrevoir

glint [glɪnt] *n* éclair *m* ▷ *vi* étinceler

glisten ['glɪsn] *vi* briller, luire

glitter ['glɪtə'] *vi* scintiller, briller ▷ *n* scintillement *m*

glitz [glɪts] *n* (*inf*) clinquant *m*

gloat [gləʊt] *vi*: **to ~ (over)** jubiler (à propos de)

global ['gləʊbl] *adj* (*world-wide*) mondial(e); (*overall*) global(e)

globalization [gləʊblaɪz'eɪʃən] *n* mondialisation *f*

global warming [-'wɔ:mɪŋ] *n* réchauffement *m* de la planète

globe [gləʊb] *n* globe *m*

globe-trotter ['gləʊbtrɒtə'] *n* globe-trotter *m*

globule ['glɒbju:l] *n* (*Anat*) globule *m*; (*of water etc*) gouttelette *f*

gloom [glu:m] *n* obscurité *f*; (*sadness*) tristesse *f*, mélancolie *f*

gloomy ['glu:mɪ] *adj* (*person*) morose; (*place, outlook*) sombre; **to feel ~** avoir *or* se faire des idées noires

glorification [glɔ:rɪfɪ'keɪʃən] *n* glorification *f*

glorify ['glɔ:rɪfaɪ] *vt* glorifier

glorious ['glɔ:rɪəs] *adj* glorieux(-euse); (*beautiful*) splendide

glory ['glɔ:rɪ] *n* gloire *f*; splendeur *f* ▷ *vi*: **to ~ in** se glorifier de

glory hole *n* (*inf*) capharnaüm *m*

Glos *abbr* (*Brit*) = **Gloucestershire**

gloss [glɒs] *n* (*shine*) brillant *m*, vernis *m*; (*also*: **gloss paint**) peinture brillante *or* laquée
  ▸ **gloss over** *vt fus* glisser sur

glossary ['glɒsərɪ] *n* glossaire *m*, lexique *m*

glossy ['glɒsɪ] *adj* brillant(e), luisant(e) ▷ *n* (*also*: **glossy magazine**) revue *f* de luxe

glove [glʌv] *n* gant *m*

glove compartment *n* (*Aut*) boîte *f* à gants, vide-poches *m inv*

glow [gləʊ] *vi* rougeoyer; (*face*) rayonner; (*eyes*) briller ▷ *n* rougeoiement *m*

glower ['glauə'] *vi* lancer des regards mauvais

glowing ['gləʊɪŋ] *adj* (*fire*) rougeoyant(e); (*complexion*) éclatant(e); (*report, description etc*) dithyrambique

glow-worm ['gləʊwə:m] *n* ver luisant

glucose ['glu:kəʊs] *n* glucose *m*

glue [glu:] *n* colle *f* ▷ *vt* coller

glue-sniffing ['glu:snɪfɪŋ] *n* inhalation *f* de colle

glum [glʌm] *adj* maussade, morose

glut [glʌt] *n* surabondance *f* ▷ *vt* rassasier; (*market*) encombrer

glutinous ['glu:tɪnəs] *adj* visqueux(-euse)

glutton ['glʌtn] *n* glouton(ne); **a ~ for work** un bourreau de travail

gluttonous ['glʌtənəs] *adj* glouton(ne)

gluttony ['glʌtənɪ] *n* gloutonnerie *f*; (*sin*) gourmandise *f*

glycerin, glycerine ['glɪsəri:n] *n* glycérine *f*

GM *abbr* (= *genetically modified*) génétiquement modifié(e)

gm *abbr* (= *gram*) g

GMAT *n abbr* (*US*: = *Graduate Management Admissions Test*) examen d'admission dans le 2e cycle de l'enseignement supérieur

GMO *n abbr* (= *genetically modified organism*) OGM *m*

GMT *abbr* (= *Greenwich Mean Time*) GMT

gnarled [nɑ:ld] *adj* noueux(-euse)

gnash [næʃ] *vt*: **to ~ one's teeth** grincer des dents

gnat [næt] *n* moucheron *m*

gnaw [nɔ:] *vt* ronger

gnome [nəʊm] *n* gnome *m*, lutin *m*

GNP *n abbr* = **gross national product**

go [gəʊ] (*pt* **went**, *pp* **gone** [wɛnt, gɒn]) *vi* aller; (*depart*) partir, s'en aller; (*work*) marcher; (*break*) céder; (*time*) passer; (*be sold*): **to go for £10** se vendre 10 livres; (*become*): **to go pale/mouldy** pâlir/moisir ▷ *n* (*pl* **goes**): **to have a go (at)** essayer (de faire); **to be on the go** être en mouvement; **whose go is it?** à qui est-ce de jouer?; **to go by car/on foot** aller en voiture/à pied; **he's going to do it** il va le faire, il est sur le point de le faire; **to go for a walk** aller se promener; **to go dancing/shopping** aller danser/faire les courses; **to go looking for sb/sth** aller *or* partir à la recherche de qn/qch; **to go to sleep** s'endormir; **to go and see sb, go to see sb** aller voir qn; **how is it going?** comment ça marche?; **how did it go?** comment est-ce que ça s'est passé?; **to go round the back/by the shop** passer par derrière/devant le magasin; **my voice has gone** j'ai une extinction de voix; **the cake is all gone** il n'y a plus de gâteau; **I'll take whatever is going** (*Brit*) je prendrai ce qu'il y a (*or* ce que vous avez); **... to go** (*US*: *food*) ... à emporter
  ▸ **go about** *vi* (*also*: **go around**) aller çà et là; (*rumour*) se répandre ▷ *vt fus*: **how do I go about this?** comment dois-je m'y prendre (pour faire ceci)?; **to go about one's business** s'occuper de ses affaires
  ▸ **go after** *vt fus* (*pursue*) poursuivre, courir après; (*job, record etc*) essayer d'obtenir
  ▸ **go against** *vt fus* (*be unfavourable to*) être défavorable à; (*be contrary to*) être contraire à
  ▸ **go ahead** *vi* (*make progress*) avancer; (*take place*) avoir lieu; (*get going*) y aller
  ▸ **go along** *vi* aller, avancer ▷ *vt fus* longer, parcourir; **as you go along (with your work)** au fur et à mesure (de votre travail); **to go along with** (*accompany*) accompagner; (*agree with: idea*) être d'accord sur; (: *person*) suivre
  ▸ **go away** *vi* partir, s'en aller
  ▸ **go back** *vi* rentrer; revenir; (*go again*) retourner
  ▸ **go back on** *vt fus* (*promise*) revenir sur
  ▸ **go by** *vi* (*years, time*) passer, s'écouler ▷ *vt fus* s'en tenir à; (*believe*) en croire
  ▸ **go down** *vi* descendre; (*number, price, amount*) baisser; (*ship*) couler; (*sun*) se coucher ▷ *vt fus*

descendre; **that should go down well with him** (*fig*) ça devrait lui plaire
▸ **go for** *vt fus* (*fetch*) aller chercher; (*like*) aimer; (*attack*) s'en prendre à; attaquer
▸ **go in** *vi* entrer
▸ **go in for** *vt fus* (*competition*) se présenter à; (*like*) aimer
▸ **go into** *vt fus* entrer dans; (*investigate*) étudier, examiner; (*embark on*) se lancer dans
▸ **go off** *vi* partir, s'en aller; (*food*) se gâter; (*milk*) tourner; (*bomb*) sauter; (*alarm clock*) sonner; (*alarm*) se déclencher; (*lights etc*) s'éteindre; (*event*) se dérouler ▷ *vt fus* ne plus aimer, ne plus avoir envie de; **the gun went off** le coup est parti; **to go off to sleep** s'endormir; **the party went off well** la fête s'est bien passée *or* était très réussie
▸ **go on** *vi* continuer; (*happen*) se passer; (*lights*) s'allumer ▷ *vt fus* (*be guided by: evidence etc*) se fonder sur; **to go on doing** continuer à faire; **what's going on here?** qu'est-ce qui se passe ici?
▸ **go on at** *vt fus* (*nag*) tomber sur le dos de
▸ **go on with** *vt fus* poursuivre, continuer
▸ **go out** *vi* sortir; (*fire, light*) s'éteindre; (*tide*) descendre; **to go out with sb** sortir avec qn
▸ **go over** *vi* (*ship*) chavirer ▷ *vt fus* (*check*) revoir, vérifier; **to go over sth in one's mind** repasser qch dans son esprit
▸ **go past** *vt fus*: **to go past sth** passer devant qch
▸ **go round** *vi* (*circulate: news, rumour*) circuler; (*revolve*) tourner; (*suffice*) suffire (pour tout le monde); (*visit*): **to go round to sb's** passer chez qn; aller chez qn; (*make a detour*): **to go round (by)** faire un détour (par)
▸ **go through** *vt fus* (*town etc*) traverser; (*search through*) fouiller; (*suffer*) subir; (*examine: list, book*) lire *or* regarder en détail, éplucher; (*perform: lesson*) réciter; (*: formalities*) remplir; (*: programme*) exécuter
▸ **go through with** *vt fus* (*plan, crime*) aller jusqu'au bout de
▸ **go under** *vi* (*sink: also fig*) couler; (*: person*) succomber
▸ **go up** *vi* monter; (*price*) augmenter ▷ *vt fus* gravir; (*also*: **go up in flames**) flamber, s'enflammer brusquement
▸ **go with** *vt fus* aller avec
▸ **go without** *vt fus* se passer de
goad [gəud] *vt* aiguillonner
go-ahead ['gəuəhɛd] *adj* dynamique, entreprenant(e) ▷ *n* feu vert
goal [gəul] *n* but *m*
goal difference *n* différence *f* de buts
goalie ['gəulɪ] *n* (*inf*) goal *m*
goalkeeper ['gəulki:pər] *n* gardien *m* de but
goal-post ['gəulpəust] *n* poteau *m* de but
goat [gəut] *n* chèvre *f*
gobble ['gɔbl] *vt* (*also*: **gobble down, gobble up**) engloutir
go-between ['gəubɪtwi:n] *n* médiateur *m*

Gobi Desert ['gəubɪ-] *n* désert *m* de Gobi
goblet ['gɔblɪt] *n* coupe *f*
goblin ['gɔblɪn] *n* lutin *m*
go-cart ['gəuka:t] *n* kart *m* ▷ *cpd*: ~ **racing** karting *m*
god [gɔd] *n* dieu *m*; **G~** Dieu
god-awful [gɔd'ɔ:fəl] *adj* (*inf*) franchement atroce
godchild ['gɔdtʃaɪld] *n* filleul(e)
goddamn ['gɔddæm], **goddamned** ['gɔddæmd] *excl* (*esp US inf*): ~ **(it)!** nom de Dieu! ▷ *adj* satané(e), sacré(e) ▷ *adv* sacrément
goddaughter ['gɔddɔ:tər] *n* filleule *f*
goddess ['gɔdɪs] *n* déesse *f*
godfather ['gɔdfɑ:ðər] *n* parrain *m*
god-fearing ['gɔdfɪərɪŋ] *adj* croyant(e)
god-forsaken ['gɔdfəseɪkən] *adj* maudit(e)
godmother ['gɔdmʌðər] *n* marraine *f*
godparents ['gɔdpɛərənts] *npl*: **the** ~ le parrain et la marraine
godsend ['gɔdsɛnd] *n* aubaine *f*
godson ['gɔdsʌn] *n* filleul *m*
goes [gəuz] *vb see* **go**
gofer ['gəufər] *n* coursier(-ière)
go-getter ['gəugɛtər] *n* arriviste *m/f*
goggle ['gɔgl] *vi*: **to ~ at** regarder avec des yeux ronds
goggles ['gɔglz] *npl* (*for skiing etc*) lunettes (protectrices); (*for swimming*) lunettes de piscine
going ['gəuɪŋ] *n* (*conditions*) état *m* du terrain ▷ *adj*: **the ~ rate** le tarif (en vigueur); **a ~ concern** une affaire prospère; **it was slow ~** les progrès étaient lents, ça n'avançait pas vite
going-over [gəuɪŋ'əuvər] *n* vérification *f*, révision *f*; (*inf: beating*) passage *m* à tabac
goings-on ['gəuɪŋz'ɔn] *npl* (*inf*) manigances *fpl*
go-kart ['gəuka:t] *n* = **go-cart**
gold [gəuld] *n or m* ▷ *adj* en or; (*reserves*) d'or
golden ['gəuldən] *adj* (*made of gold*) en or; (*gold in colour*) doré(e)
golden age *n* âge *m* d'or
golden handshake *n* (*Brit*) prime *f* de départ
golden rule *n* règle *f* d'or
goldfish ['gəuldfɪʃ] *n* poisson *m* rouge
gold leaf *n or m* en feuille
gold medal *n* (*Sport*) médaille *f* d'or
goldmine ['gəuldmaɪn] *n* mine *f* d'or
gold-plated ['gəuld'pleɪtɪd] *adj* plaqué(e) or *inv*
goldsmith ['gəuldsmɪθ] *n* orfèvre *m*
gold standard *n* étalon-or *m*
golf [gɔlf] *n* golf *m*
golf ball *n* balle *f* de golf; (*on typewriter*) boule *f*
golf club *n* club *m* de golf; (*stick*) club *m*, crosse *f* de golf
golf course *n* terrain *m* de golf
golfer ['gɔlfər] *n* joueur(-euse) de golf
golfing ['gɔlfɪŋ] *n* golf *m*
gondola ['gɔndələ] *n* gondole *f*
gondolier [gɔndə'lɪər] *n* gondolier *m*
gone [gɔn] *pp of* **go** ▷ *adj* parti(e)
goner ['gɔnər] *n* (*inf*): **to be a** ~ être fichu(e) *or* foutu(e)

gong [gɒŋ] *n* gong *m*

good [gud] *adj* bon(ne); (*kind*) gentil(le); (*child*) sage; (*weather*) beau (belle) ▷ *n* bien *m*; **goods** *npl* marchandise *f*, articles *mpl*; (*Comm etc*) marchandises; ~! bon!, très bien!; **to be ~ at** être bon en; **to be ~ for** être bon pour; **it's ~ for you** c'est bon pour vous; **it's a ~ thing you were there** heureusement que vous étiez là; **she is ~ with children/her hands** elle sait bien s'occuper des enfants/sait se servir de ses mains; **to feel ~** se sentir bien; **it's ~ to see you** ça me fait plaisir de vous voir, je suis content de vous voir; **he's up to no ~** il prépare quelque mauvais coup; **it's no ~ complaining** cela ne sert à rien de se plaindre; **to make ~** (*deficit*) combler; (*losses*) compenser; **for the common ~** dans l'intérêt commun; **for ~** (*for ever*) pour de bon, une fois pour toutes; **would you be ~ enough to ...?** auriez-vous la bonté *or* l'amabilité de ...?; **that's very ~ of you** c'est très gentil de votre part; **is this any ~?** (*will it do?*) est-ce que ceci fera l'affaire?, est-ce que cela peut vous rendre service?; (*what's it like?*) qu'est-ce que ça vaut?; **~s and chattels** biens *mpl* et effets *mpl*; **a ~ deal (of)** beaucoup (de); **a ~ many** beaucoup (de); **~ morning/afternoon!** bonjour!; **~ evening!** bonsoir!; **~ night!** bonsoir!; (*on going to bed*) bonne nuit!

goodbye [gud'baɪ] *excl* au revoir!; **to say ~ to sb** dire au revoir à qn

good faith *n* bonne foi

good-for-nothing ['gudfənʌθɪŋ] *adj* bon(ne) *or* propre à rien

Good Friday *n* Vendredi saint

good-humoured ['gud'hju:məd] *adj* (*person*) jovial(e); (*remark, joke*) sans malice

good-looking ['gud'lukɪŋ] *adj* beau (belle), bien *inv*

good-natured ['gud'neɪtʃəd] *adj* (*person*) qui a un bon naturel; (*discussion*) enjoué(e)

goodness ['gudnɪs] *n* (*of person*) bonté *f*; **for ~ sake!** je vous en prie!; **~ gracious!** mon Dieu!

goods train *n* (*Brit*) train *m* de marchandises

goodwill [gud'wɪl] *n* bonne volonté; (*Comm*) réputation *f* (auprès de la clientèle)

goody-goody ['gudɪgudɪ] *n* (*pej*) petit saint, sainte nitouche

gooey ['gu:ɪ] *adj* (*Brit inf*) gluant(e)

Google® ['gugl] *vi, vt* googler®

goose (*pl* **geese**) [gu:s, gi:s] *n* oie *f*

gooseberry ['guzbərɪ] *n* groseille *f* à maquereau; **to play ~** (*Brit*) tenir la chandelle

goose bumps, goose pimples *npl* chair *f* de poule

gooseflesh ['gu:sflɛʃ] *n*, **goosepimples** ['gu:spɪmplz] ▷ *npl* chair *f* de poule

goose step *n* (*Mil*) pas *m* de l'oie

GOP *n abbr* (*US Pol: inf: = Grand Old Party*) parti républicain

gopher ['gəufər] *n* = **gofer**

gore [gɔ:r] *vt* encorner ▷ *n* sang *m*

gorge [gɔ:dʒ] *n* gorge *f* ▷ *vt*: **to ~ o.s. (on)** se gorger (de)

gorgeous ['gɔ:dʒəs] *adj* splendide, superbe

gorilla [gə'rɪlə] *n* gorille *m*

gormless ['gɔ:mlɪs] *adj* (*Brit inf*) lourdaud(e)

gorse [gɔ:s] *n* ajoncs *mpl*

gory ['gɔ:rɪ] *adj* sanglant(e)

gosh [gɒʃ] (*inf*) *excl* mince alors!

go-slow ['gəu'sləu] *n* (*Brit*) grève perlée

gospel ['gɒspl] *n* évangile *m*

gossamer ['gɒsəmər] *n* (*cobweb*) fils *mpl* de la vierge; (*light fabric*) étoffe très légère

gossip ['gɒsɪp] *n* (*chat*) bavardages *mpl*; (*malicious*) commérage *m*, cancans *mpl*; (*person*) commère *f* ▷ *vi* bavarder; cancaner, faire des commérages; **a piece of ~** un ragot, un racontar

gossip column *n* (*Press*) échos *mpl*

got [gɒt] *pt, pp of* **get**

Gothic ['gɒθɪk] *adj* gothique

gotten ['gɒtn] (*US*) *pp of* **get**

gouge [gaudʒ] *vt* (*also*: **gouge out**: *hole etc*) évider; (: *initials*) tailler; **to ~ sb's eyes out** crever les yeux à qn

gourd [guəd] *n* calebasse *f*, gourde *f*

gourmet ['guəmeɪ] *n* gourmet *m*, gastronome *m/f*

gout [gaut] *n* goutte *f*

govern ['gʌvən] *vt* (*gen: Ling*) gouverner; (*influence*) déterminer

governess ['gʌvənɪs] *n* gouvernante *f*

governing ['gʌvənɪŋ] *adj* (*Pol*) au pouvoir, au gouvernement; **~ body** conseil *m* d'administration

government ['gʌvnmənt] *n* gouvernement *m*; (*Brit: ministers*) ministère *m* ▷ *cpd* de l'État

governmental [gʌvn'mɛntl] *adj* gouvernemental(e)

government housing *n* (*US*) logements sociaux

government stock *n* titres *mpl* d'État

governor ['gʌvənər] *n* (*of colony, state, bank*) gouverneur *m*; (*of school, hospital etc*) administrateur(-trice); (*Brit: of prison*) directeur(-trice)

Govt *abbr* (*= government*) gvt

gown [gaun] *n* robe *f*; (*of teacher, Brit: of judge*) toge *f*

GP *n abbr* (*Med*) = **general practitioner**; **who's your GP?** qui est votre médecin traitant?

GPMU *n abbr* (*Brit*) = **Graphical, Paper and Media Union**

GPO *n abbr* (*Brit: old*) = **General Post Office**; (*US*) = **Government Printing Office**

GPS *n abbr* (*= global positioning system*) GPS *m*

gr. *abbr* (*Comm*) = **gross**

grab [græb] *vt* saisir, empoigner; (*property, power*) se saisir de ▷ *vi*: **to ~ at** essayer de saisir

grace [greɪs] *n* grâce *f* ▷ *vt* (*honour*) honorer; (*adorn*) orner; **5 days' ~** un répit de 5 jours; **to say ~** dire le bénédicité; (*after meal*) dire les grâces; **with a good/bad ~** de bonne/mauvaise grâce; **his sense of humour is his saving ~** il se rachète par son sens de l'humour

graceful ['greɪsful] *adj* gracieux(-euse), élégant(e)

gracious ['greɪʃəs] *adj* (*kind*) charmant(e), bienveillant(e); (*elegant*) plein(e) d'élégance, d'une grande élégance; (*formal: pardon etc*) miséricordieux(-euse) ▷ *excl*: (**good**) ~! mon Dieu!

gradation [grə'deɪʃən] *n* gradation *f*

grade [greɪd] *n* (*Comm: quality*) qualité *f*; (*size*) calibre *m*; (*type*) catégorie *f*; (*in hierarchy*) grade *m*, échelon *m*; (*Scol*) note *f*; (*US: school class*) classe *f*; (: *gradient*) pente *f* ▷ *vt* classer; (*by size*) calibrer; graduer; **to make the** ~ (*fig*) réussir

grade crossing *n* (*US*) passage *m* à niveau

grade school *n* (*US*) école *f* primaire

gradient ['greɪdɪənt] *n* inclinaison *f*, pente *f*; (*Geom*) gradient *m*

gradual ['grædjuəl] *adj* graduel(le), progressif(-ive)

gradually ['grædjuəlɪ] *adv* peu à peu, graduellement

graduate *n* ['grædjuɪt] diplômé(e) d'université; (*US: of high school*) diplômé(e) de fin d'études ▷ *vi* ['grædjueɪt] obtenir un diplôme d'université (*or* de fin d'études)

graduated pension ['grædjueɪtɪd-] *n* retraite calculée en fonction des derniers salaires

graduation [grædju'eɪʃən] *n* cérémonie *f* de remise des diplômes

graffiti [grə'fi:tɪ] *npl* graffiti *mpl*

graft [grɑːft] *n* (*Agr, Med*) greffe *f*; (*bribery*) corruption *f* ▷ *vt* greffer; **hard** ~ (*Brit: inf*) boulot acharné

grain [greɪn] *n* (*single piece*) grain *m*; (*no pl: cereals*) céréales *fpl*; (*US: corn*) blé *m*; (*of wood*) fibre *f*; **it goes against the** ~ cela va à l'encontre de sa (*or* ma *etc*) nature

gram [græm] *n* gramme *m*

grammar ['græmə^r] *n* grammaire *f*

grammar school *n* (*Brit*) ≈ lycée *m*

grammatical [grə'mætɪkl] *adj* grammatical(e)

gramme [græm] *n* = **gram**

gramophone ['græməfəun] *n* (*Brit*) gramophone *m*

gran [græn] (*inf*) *n* (*Brit*) mamie *f* (*inf*), mémé *f* (*inf*); **my** ~ (*young child speaking*) ma mamie *or* mémé; (*older child or adult speaking*) ma grand-mère

granary ['grænərɪ] *n* grenier *m*

grand [grænd] *adj* magnifique, splendide; (*terrific*) magnifique, formidable; (*gesture etc*) noble ▷ *n* (*inf: thousand*) mille livres *fpl* (*or* dollars *mpl*)

grandad ['grændæd] (*inf*) *n* = **granddad**

grandchild (*pl* **grandchildren**) ['græntʃaɪld, 'græntʃɪldrən] *n* petit-fils *m*, petite-fille *f*; **grandchildren** *npl* petits-enfants

granddad ['grændæd] *n* (*inf*) papy *m* (*inf*), papi *m* (*inf*), pépé *m* (*inf*); **my** ~ (*young child speaking*) mon papy *or* papi *or* pépé; (*older child or adult speaking*) mon grand-père

granddaughter ['grændɔːtə^r] *n* petite-fille *f*

grandeur ['grændjə^r] *n* magnificence *f*, splendeur *f*; (*of position etc*) éminence *f*

grandfather ['grændfɑːðə^r] *n* grand-père *m*

grandiose ['grændɪəus] *adj* grandiose; (*pej*) pompeux(-euse)

grand jury *n* (*US*) jury *m* d'accusation (*formé de 12 à 23 jurés*)

grandma ['grænmɑː] *n* (*inf*) = **gran**

grandmother ['grænmʌðə^r] *n* grand-mère *f*

grandpa ['grænpɑː] *n* (*inf*) = **granddad**

grandparents ['grændpɛərənts] *npl* grands-parents *mpl*

grand piano *n* piano *m* à queue

Grand Prix ['grɑ̃:'priː] *n* (*Aut*) grand prix automobile

grandson ['grænsʌn] *n* petit-fils *m*

grandstand ['grændstænd] *n* (*Sport*) tribune *f*

grand total *n* total général

granite ['grænɪt] *n* granit *m*

granny ['grænɪ] *n* (*inf*) = **gran**

grant [grɑːnt] *vt* accorder; (*a request*) accéder à; (*admit*) concéder ▷ *n* (*Scol*) bourse *f*; (*Admin*) subside *m*, subvention *f*; **to take sth for ~ed** considérer qch comme acquis; **to take sb for ~ed** considérer qn comme faisant partie du décor; **to ~ that** admettre que

granulated ['grænjuleɪtɪd] *adj*: ~ **sugar** sucre *m* en poudre

granule ['grænjuːl] *n* granule *m*

grape [greɪp] *n* raisin *m*; **a bunch of ~s** une grappe de raisin

grapefruit ['greɪpfruːt] *n* pamplemousse *m*

grapevine ['greɪpvaɪn] *n* vigne *f*; **I heard it on the** ~ (*fig*) je l'ai appris par le téléphone arabe

graph [grɑːf] *n* graphique *m*, courbe *f*

graphic ['græfɪk] *adj* graphique; (*vivid*) vivant(e)

graphic designer *n* graphiste *m/f*

graphic equalizer *n* égaliseur *m* graphique

graphics ['græfɪks] *n* (*art*) arts *mpl* graphiques; (*process*) graphisme *m* ▷ *npl* (*drawings*) illustrations *fpl*

graphite ['græfaɪt] *n* graphite *m*

graph paper *n* papier millimétré

grapple ['græpl] *vi*: **to ~ with** être aux prises avec

grappling iron ['græplɪŋ-] *n* (*Naut*) grappin *m*

grasp [grɑːsp] *vt* saisir, empoigner; (*understand*) saisir, comprendre ▷ *n* (*grip*) prise *f*; (*fig*) compréhension *f*, connaissance *f*; **to have sth within one's** ~ avoir qch à sa portée; **to have a good ~ of sth** (*fig*) bien comprendre qch
  ▶ **grasp at** *vt fus* (*rope etc*) essayer de saisir; (*fig: opportunity*) sauter sur

grasping ['grɑːspɪŋ] *adj* avide

grass [grɑːs] *n* herbe *f*; (*lawn*) gazon *m*; (*Brit inf: informer*) mouchard(e), (: *ex-terrorist*) balanceur(-euse)

grasshopper ['grɑːshɔpə^r] *n* sauterelle *f*

grassland ['grɑːslænd] *n* prairie *f*

grass roots *npl* (*fig*) base *f*

grass snake *n* couleuvre *f*

grassy ['grɑːsɪ] *adj* herbeux(-euse)
grate [greɪt] *n* grille *f* de cheminée ▷ *vi* grincer ▷ *vt* (*Culin*) râper
grateful ['greɪtful] *adj* reconnaissant(e)
gratefully ['greɪtfəlɪ] *adv* avec reconnaissance
grater ['greɪtə^r] *n* râpe *f*
gratification [grætɪfɪ'keɪʃən] *n* satisfaction *f*
gratify ['grætɪfaɪ] *vt* faire plaisir à; (*whim*) satisfaire
gratifying ['grætɪfaɪɪŋ] *adj* agréable, satisfaisant(e)
grating ['greɪtɪŋ] *n* (*iron bars*) grille *f* ▷ *adj* (*noise*) grinçant(e)
gratitude ['grætɪtjuːd] *n* gratitude *f*
gratuitous [grə'tjuːɪtəs] *adj* gratuit(e)
gratuity [grə'tjuːɪtɪ] *n* pourboire *m*
grave [greɪv] *n* tombe *f* ▷ *adj* grave, sérieux(-euse)
gravedigger ['greɪvdɪgə^r] *n* fossoyeur *m*
gravel ['grævl] *n* gravier *m*
gravely ['greɪvlɪ] *adv* gravement, sérieusement; **~ ill** gravement malade
gravestone ['greɪvstəun] *n* pierre tombale
graveyard ['greɪvjɑːd] *n* cimetière *m*
gravitate ['grævɪteɪt] *vi* graviter
gravity ['grævɪtɪ] *n* (*Physics*) gravité *f*; pesanteur *f*; (*seriousness*) gravité, sérieux *m*
gravy ['greɪvɪ] *n* jus *m* (de viande), sauce *f* (au jus de viande)
gravy boat *n* saucière *f*
gravy train *n* (*inf*): **to ride the ~** avoir une bonne planque
gray [greɪ] *adj* (*US*) = **grey**
graze [greɪz] *vi* paître, brouter ▷ *vt* (*touch lightly*) frôler, effleurer; (*scrape*) écorcher ▷ *n* écorchure *f*
grazing ['greɪzɪŋ] *n* (*pasture*) pâturage *m*
grease [griːs] *n* (*fat*) graisse *f*; (*lubricant*) lubrifiant *m* ▷ *vt* graisser; lubrifier; **to ~ the skids** (*US: fig*) huiler les rouages
grease gun *n* graisseur *m*
greasepaint ['griːspeɪnt] *n* produits *mpl* de maquillage
greaseproof paper ['griːspruːf-] *n* (*Brit*) papier sulfurisé
greasy ['griːsɪ] *adj* gras(se), graisseux(-euse); (*hands, clothes*) graisseux; (*Brit: road, surface*) glissant(e)
great [greɪt] *adj* grand(e); (*heat, pain etc*) très fort(e), intense; (*inf*) formidable; **they're ~ friends**, ils sont très amis, ce sont de grands amis; **we had a ~ time** nous nous sommes bien amusés; **it was ~!** c'était fantastique *or* super!; **the ~ thing is that ...** ce qu'il y a de vraiment bien c'est que ...
Great Barrier Reef *n*: **the ~** la Grande Barrière
Great Britain *n* Grande-Bretagne *f*
great-grandchild (*pl* **-children**) [greɪt'græntʃaɪld, -tʃɪldrən] *n* arrière-petit(e)-enfant
great-grandfather [greɪt'grænfɑːðə^r] *n* arrière-grand-père *m*

great-grandmother [greɪt'grænmʌðə^r] *n* arrière-grand-mère *f*
Great Lakes *npl*: **the ~** les Grands Lacs
greatly ['greɪtlɪ] *adv* très, grandement; (*with verbs*) beaucoup
greatness ['greɪtnɪs] *n* grandeur *f*
Grecian ['griːʃən] *adj* grec (grecque)
Greece [griːs] *n* Grèce *f*
greed [griːd] *n* (*also*: **greediness**) avidité *f*; (*for food*) gourmandise *f*
greedily ['griːdɪlɪ] *adv* avidement; avec gourmandise
greedy ['griːdɪ] *adj* avide; (*for food*) gourmand(e)
Greek [griːk] *adj* grec (grecque) ▷ *n* Grec (Grecque); (*Ling*) grec *m*; **ancient/modern ~** grec classique/moderne
green [griːn] *adj* vert(e); (*inexperienced*) (bien) jeune, naïf(-ïve); (*ecological: product etc*) écologique ▷ *n* (*colour*) vert *m*; (*on golf course*) green *m*; (*stretch of grass*) pelouse *f*; (*also*: **village green**) ≈ place *f* du village; **greens** *npl* (*vegetables*) légumes verts; **to have ~ fingers** *or* (*US*) **a ~ thumb** (*fig*) avoir le pouce vert; **G~** (*Pol*) écologiste *m/f*; **the G~ Party** le parti écologiste
green belt *n* (*round town*) ceinture verte
green card *n* (*Aut*) carte verte; (*US: work permit*) permis *m* de travail
greenery ['griːnərɪ] *n* verdure *f*
greenfly ['griːnflaɪ] *n* (*Brit*) puceron *m*
greengage ['griːngeɪdʒ] *n* reine-claude *f*
greengrocer ['griːngrəusə^r] *n* (*Brit*) marchand *m* de fruits et légumes
greengrocer's ['griːngrəusə^r z], **greengrocer's shop** *n* magasin *m* de fruits et légumes
greenhouse ['griːnhaus] *n* serre *f*
greenhouse effect *n*: **the ~** l'effet *m* de serre
greenhouse gas *n* gaz *m* contribuant à l'effet de serre
greenish ['griːnɪʃ] *adj* verdâtre
Greenland ['griːnlənd] *n* Groenland *m*
Greenlander ['griːnləndə^r] *n* Groenlandais(e)
green light *n*: **to give sb/sth the ~** donner le feu vert à qn/qch
green pepper *n* poivron (vert)
green pound *n* (*Econ*) livre verte
green salad *n* salade verte
greet [griːt] *vt* accueillir
greeting ['griːtɪŋ] *n* salutation *f*; **Christmas/birthday ~s** souhaits *mpl* de Noël/de bon anniversaire
greeting card, greetings card *n* carte *f* de vœux
gregarious [grə'gɛərɪəs] *adj* grégaire; sociable
grenade [grə'neɪd] *n* (*also*: **hand grenade**) grenade *f*
grew [gruː] *pt of* **grow**
grey, (*US*) **gray** [greɪ] *adj* gris(e); (*dismal*) sombre; **to go ~** (commencer à) grisonner
grey-haired, (*US*) **gray-haired** [greɪ'hɛəd] *adj* aux cheveux gris
greyhound ['greɪhaund] *n* lévrier *m*
grid [grɪd] *n* grille *f*; (*Elec*) réseau *m*; (*US Aut*)

intersection f (*matérialisée par des marques au sol*)
griddle [ɡrɪdl] n (*on cooker*) plaque chauffante
gridiron [ˈɡrɪdaɪən] n gril m
gridlock [ˈɡrɪdlɔk] n (*traffic jam*) embouteillage m
gridlocked [ˈɡrɪdlɔkt] adj: **to be ~** (*roads*) être bloqué par un embouteillage; (*talks etc*) être suspendu
grief [ɡriːf] n chagrin m, douleur f; **to come to ~** (*plan*) échouer; (*person*) avoir un malheur
grievance [ˈɡriːvəns] n doléance f, grief m; (*cause for complaint*) grief
grieve [ɡriːv] vi avoir du chagrin; se désoler ▷ vt faire de la peine à, affliger; **to ~ for sb** pleurer qn; **to ~ at** se désoler de; pleurer
grievous [ˈɡriːvəs] adj grave, cruel(le); **~ bodily harm** (*Law*) coups mpl et blessures fpl
grill [ɡrɪl] n (*on cooker*) gril m; (*also:* **mixed grill**) grillade(s) f(pl); (*also:* **grillroom**) rôtisserie f ▷ vt (*Brit*) griller; (*inf: question*) interroger longuement, cuisiner
grille [ɡrɪl] n grillage m; (*Aut*) calandre f
grillroom [ˈɡrɪlrum] n rôtisserie f
grim [ɡrɪm] adj sinistre, lugubre; (*serious, stern*) sévère
grimace [ɡrɪˈmeɪs] n grimace f ▷ vi grimacer, faire une grimace
grime [ɡraɪm] n crasse f
grimy [ˈɡraɪmɪ] adj crasseux(-euse)
grin [ɡrɪn] n large sourire m ▷ vi sourire; **to ~ (at)** faire un grand sourire (à)
grind [ɡraɪnd] (*pt, pp* **ground** [ɡraund]) vt écraser; (*coffee, pepper etc*) moudre; (*US: meat*) hacher; (*make sharp*) aiguiser; (*polish: gem, lens*) polir ▷ vi (*car gears*) grincer ▷ n (*work*) corvée f; **to ~ one's teeth** grincer des dents; **to ~ to a halt** (*vehicle*) s'arrêter dans un grincement de freins; (*fig*) s'arrêter, s'immobiliser; **the daily ~** (*inf*) le train-train quotidien
grinder [ˈɡraɪndər] n (*machine: for coffee*) moulin m (à café); (: *for waste disposal etc*) broyeur m
grindstone [ˈɡraɪndstəun] n: **to keep one's nose to the ~** travailler sans relâche
grip [ɡrɪp] n (*handclasp*) poigne f; (*control*) prise f; (*handle*) poignée f; (*holdall*) sac m de voyage ▷ vt saisir, empoigner; (*viewer, reader*) captiver; **to come to ~s with** se colleter avec, en venir aux prises avec; **to ~ the road** (*Aut*) adhérer à la route; **to lose one's ~** lâcher prise; (*fig*) perdre les pédales, être dépassé(e)
gripe [ɡraɪp] n (*Med*) coliques fpl; (*inf: complaint*) ronchonnement m, rouspétance f ▷ vi (*inf*) râler
gripping [ˈɡrɪpɪŋ] adj prenant(e), palpitant(e)
grisly [ˈɡrɪzlɪ] adj sinistre, macabre
grist [ɡrɪst] n (*fig*): **it's (all) ~ to his mill** ça l'arrange, ça apporte de l'eau à son moulin
gristle [ˈɡrɪsl] n cartilage m (*de poulet etc*)
grit [ɡrɪt] n gravillon m; (*courage*) cran m ▷ vt (*road*) sabler; **to ~ one's teeth** serrer les dents; **to have a piece of ~ in one's eye** avoir une poussière or saleté dans l'œil
grits [ɡrɪts] npl (*US*) gruau m de maïs
grizzle [ˈɡrɪzl] vi (*Brit*) pleurnicher

grizzly [ˈɡrɪzlɪ] n (*also:* **grizzly bear**) grizzli m, ours gris
groan [ɡrəun] n (*of pain*) gémissement m; (*of disapproval, dismay*) grognement m ▷ vi gémir; grogner
grocer [ˈɡrəusər] n épicier m
groceries [ˈɡrəusərɪz] npl provisions fpl
grocer's [ˈɡrəusəz], **grocer's shop**, **grocery** [ˈɡrəusərɪ] n épicerie f
grog [ɡrɔɡ] n grog m
groggy [ˈɡrɔɡɪ] adj groggy inv
groin [ɡrɔɪn] n aine f
groom [ɡruːm] n (*for horses*) palefrenier m; (*also:* **bridegroom**) marié m ▷ vt (*horse*) panser; (*fig*): **to ~ sb for** former qn pour
groove [ɡruːv] n sillon m, rainure f
grope [ɡrəup] vi tâtonner; **to ~ for** chercher à tâtons
gross [ɡrəus] adj grossier(-ière); (*Comm*) brut(e) ▷ n (*pl inv: twelve dozen*) grosse f ▷ vt (*Comm*): **to ~ £500,000** gagner 500 000 livres avant impôt
gross domestic product n produit brut intérieur
grossly [ˈɡrəuslɪ] adv (*greatly*) très, grandement
gross national product n produit national brut
grotesque [ɡrəˈtɛsk] adj grotesque
grotto [ˈɡrɔtəu] n grotte f
grotty [ˈɡrɔtɪ] adj (*Brit inf*) minable
grouch [ɡrautʃ] (*inf*) vi rouspéter ▷ n (*person*) rouspéteur(-euse)
ground [ɡraund] *pt, pp* of **grind** ▷ n sol m, terre f; (*land*) terrain m, terres fpl; (*Sport*) terrain; (*reason: gen pl*) raison f; (*US: also:* **ground wire**) terre f ▷ vt (*plane*) empêcher de décoller, retenir au sol; (*US Elec*) équiper d'une prise de terre, mettre à la terre ▷ vi (*ship*) s'échouer ▷ adj (*coffee etc*) moulu(e); (*US: meat*) haché(e); **grounds** npl (*gardens etc*) parc m, domaine m; (*of coffee*) marc m; **on the ~, to the ~** par terre; **below ~** sous terre; **to gain/lose ~** gagner/perdre du terrain; **common ~** terrain d'entente; **he covered a lot of ~ in his lecture** sa conférence a traité un grand nombre de questions or la question en profondeur
ground cloth n (*US*) = **groundsheet**
ground control n (*Aviat, Space*) centre m de contrôle (au sol)
ground floor n (*Brit*) rez-de-chaussée m
grounding [ˈɡraundɪŋ] n (*in education*) connaissances fpl de base
groundless [ˈɡraundlɪs] adj sans fondement
groundnut [ˈɡraundnʌt] n arachide f
ground rent n (*Brit*) fermage m
ground rules npl: **the ~** les principes mpl de base
groundsheet [ˈɡraundʃiːt] n (*Brit*) tapis m de sol
groundsman [ˈɡraundzmən] (*irreg*), (*US*) **groundskeeper** [ˈɡraundzkiːpər] n (*Sport*) gardien m de stade
ground staff n équipage m au sol
groundswell [ˈɡraundswɛl] n lame f or vague f de fond

ground-to-air ['grauntu'ɛə^r] adj (Mil) sol-air inv
ground-to-ground ['grauntə'graund] adj (Mil) sol-sol inv
groundwork ['graundwə:k] n préparation f
group [gru:p] n groupe m ▷ vt (also: **group together**) grouper ▷ vi (also: **group together**) se grouper
groupie ['gru:pɪ] n groupie f
group therapy n thérapie f de groupe
grouse [graus] n (pl inv: bird) grouse f (sorte de coq de bruyère) ▷ vi (complain) rouspéter, râler
grove [grəuv] n bosquet m
grovel ['grɔvl] vi (fig): **to ~ (before)** ramper (devant)
grow (pt **grew**, pp **-n**) [grəu, gru:, grəun] vi (plant) pousser, croître; (person) grandir; (increase) augmenter, se développer; (become) devenir; **to ~ rich/weak** s'enrichir/s'affaiblir ▷ vt cultiver, faire pousser; (hair, beard) laisser pousser
▸ **grow apart** vi (fig) se détacher (l'un de l'autre)
▸ **grow away from** vt fus (fig) s'éloigner de
▸ **grow on** vt fus: **that painting is ~ing on me** je finirai par aimer ce tableau
▸ **grow out of** vt fus (clothes) devenir trop grand pour; (habit) perdre (avec le temps); **he'll ~ out of it** ça lui passera
▸ **grow up** vi grandir
grower ['grəuə^r] n producteur m; (Agr) cultivateur(-trice)
growing ['grəuɪŋ] adj (fear, amount) croissant(e), grandissant(e); **~ pains** (Med) fièvre f de croissance; (fig) difficultés fpl de croissance
growl [graul] vi grogner
grown [grəun] pp of **grow** ▷ adj adulte
grown-up [grəun'ʌp] n adulte m/f, grande personne
growth [grəuθ] n croissance f, développement m; (what has grown) pousse f; poussée f; (Med) grosseur f, tumeur f
growth rate n taux m de croissance
GRSM n abbr (Brit) = **Graduate of the Royal Schools of Music**
grub [grʌb] n larve f; (inf: food) bouffe f
grubby ['grʌbɪ] adj crasseux(-euse)
grudge [grʌdʒ] n rancune f ▷ vt: **to ~ sb sth** (in giving) donner qch à qn à contre-cœur; (resent) reprocher qch à qn; **to bear sb a ~ (for)** garder rancune or en vouloir à qn (de); **he ~s spending** il rechigne à dépenser
grudgingly ['grʌdʒɪŋlɪ] adv à contre-cœur, de mauvaise grâce
gruelling, (US) **grueling** ['gruəlɪŋ] adj exténuant(e)
gruesome ['gru:səm] adj horrible
gruff [grʌf] adj bourru(e)
grumble ['grʌmbl] vi rouspéter, ronchonner
grumpy ['grʌmpɪ] adj grincheux(-euse)
grunge [grʌndʒ] n (Mus: style) grunge m
grunt [grʌnt] vi grogner ▷ n grognement m
G-string ['dʒi:strɪŋ] n (garment) cache-sexe m inv
GSUSA n abbr = **Girl Scouts of the United States of America**

GU abbr (US) = **Guam**
guarantee [gærən'ti:] n garantie f ▷ vt garantir; **he can't ~ (that) he'll come** il n'est pas absolument certain de pouvoir venir
guarantor [gærən'tɔ:^{r}] n garant(e)
guard [gɑ:d] n garde f, surveillance f; (squad: Boxing, Fencing) garde f; (one man) garde m; (Brit Rail) chef m de train; (safety device: on machine) dispositif m de sûreté; (also: **fireguard**) garde-feu m inv ▷ vt garder, surveiller; (protect): **to ~ sb/sth (against** or **from)** protéger qn/qch (contre); **to be on one's ~** (fig) être sur ses gardes
▸ **guard against** vi: **to ~ against doing sth** se garder de faire qch
guard dog n chien m de garde
guarded ['gɑ:dɪd] adj (fig) prudent(e)
guardian ['gɑ:dɪən] n gardien(ne); (of minor) tuteur(-trice)
guard's van ['gɑ:dz-] n (Brit Rail) fourgon m
Guatemala [gwɑ:tɪ'mɑ:lə] n Guatémala m
Guernsey ['gə:nzɪ] n Guernesey m or f
guerrilla [gə'rɪlə] n guérillero m
guerrilla warfare n guérilla f
guess [gɛs] vi deviner ▷ vt deviner; (estimate) évaluer; (US) croire, penser ▷ n supposition f, hypothèse f; **to take** or **have a ~** essayer de deviner; **to keep sb ~ing** laisser qn dans le doute or l'incertitude, tenir qn en haleine
guesstimate ['gɛstɪmɪt] n (inf) estimation f
guesswork ['gɛswə:k] n hypothèse f; **I got the answer by ~** j'ai deviné la réponse
guest [gɛst] n invité(e); (in hotel) client(e); **be my ~** faites comme chez vous
guest house ['gɛsthaus] n pension f
guest room n chambre f d'amis
guff [gʌf] n (inf) bêtises fpl
guffaw [gʌ'fɔ:] n gros rire ▷ vi pouffer de rire
guidance ['gaɪdəns] n (advice) conseils mpl; **under the ~ of** conseillé(e) or encadré(e) par, sous la conduite de; **vocational ~** orientation professionnelle; **marriage ~** conseils conjugaux
guide [gaɪd] n (person) guide m/f; (book) guide m; (also: **Girl Guide**) éclaireuse f; (Roman Catholic) guide f ▷ vt guider; **to be ~d by sb/sth** se laisser guider par qn/qch; **is there an English-speaking ~?** est-ce que l'un des guides parle anglais?
guidebook ['gaɪdbuk] n guide m; **do you have a ~ in English?** est-ce que vous avez un guide en anglais?
guided missile ['gaɪdɪd-] n missile téléguidé
guide dog n chien m d'aveugle
guided tour n visite guidée; **what time does the ~ start?** la visite guidée commence à quelle heure?
guidelines ['gaɪdlaɪnz] npl (advice) instructions générales, conseils mpl
guild [gɪld] n (History) corporation f; (sharing interests) cercle m, association f

guildhall ['gɪldhɔːl] n (Brit) hôtel m de ville
guile [gaɪl] n astuce f
guileless ['gaɪllɪs] adj candide
guillotine ['gɪləti:n] n guillotine f; (for paper) massicot m
guilt [gɪlt] n culpabilité f
guilty ['gɪltɪ] adj coupable; **to plead ~/not ~** plaider coupable/non coupable; **to feel ~ about doing sth** avoir mauvaise conscience à faire qch
Guinea ['gɪnɪ] n: **Republic of ~** (République f de) Guinée f
guinea ['gɪnɪ] n (Brit: formerly) guinée f (= 21 shillings)
guinea pig ['gɪnɪ-] n cobaye m
guise [gaɪz] n aspect m, apparence f
guitar [gɪ'tɑːʳ] n guitare f
guitarist [gɪ'tɑːrɪst] n guitariste m/f
gulch [gʌltʃ] n (US) ravin m
gulf [gʌlf] n golfe m; (abyss) gouffre m; **the (Persian) G~** le golfe Persique
Gulf States npl: **the ~** (in Middle East) les pays mpl du Golfe
Gulf Stream n: **the ~** le Gulf Stream
gull [gʌl] n mouette f
gullet ['gʌlɪt] n gosier m
gullibility [gʌlɪ'bɪlɪtɪ] n crédulité f
gullible ['gʌlɪbl] adj crédule
gully ['gʌlɪ] n ravin m; ravine f; couloir m
gulp [gʌlp] vi avaler sa salive; (from emotion) avoir la gorge serrée, s'étrangler ▷ vt (also: **gulp down**) avaler ▷ n (of drink) gorgée f; **at one ~** d'un seul coup
gum [gʌm] n (Anat) gencive f; (glue) colle f; (sweet) boule f de gomme; (also: **chewing-gum**) chewing-gum m ▷ vt coller
gumboil ['gʌmbɔɪl] n abcès m dentaire
gumboots ['gʌmbu:ts] npl (Brit) bottes fpl en caoutchouc
gumption ['gʌmpʃən] n bon sens, jugeote f
gun [gʌn] n (small) revolver m, pistolet m; (rifle) fusil m, carabine f; (cannon) canon m ▷ vt (also: **gun down**) abattre; **to stick to one's ~s** (fig) ne pas en démordre
gunboat ['gʌnbəut] n canonnière f
gun dog n chien m de chasse
gunfire ['gʌnfaɪəʳ] n fusillade f
gunk [gʌŋk] n (inf) saleté f
gunman (irreg) ['gʌnmən] n bandit armé
gunner ['gʌnəʳ] n artilleur m
gunpoint ['gʌnpɔɪnt] n: **at ~** sous la menace du pistolet (or fusil)
gunpowder ['gʌnpaudəʳ] n poudre f à canon
gunrunner ['gʌnrʌnəʳ] n trafiquant m d'armes
gunrunning ['gʌnrʌnɪŋ] n trafic m d'armes
gunshot ['gʌnʃɔt] n coup m de feu; **within ~** à portée de fusil
gunsmith ['gʌnsmɪθ] n armurier m
gurgle ['gə:gl] n gargouillis m ▷ vi gargouiller
guru ['guru:] n gourou m
gush [gʌʃ] n jaillissement m, jet m ▷ vi jaillir; (fig) se répandre en effusions
gushing ['gʌʃɪŋ] adj (person) trop exubérant(e) or

expansif(-ive); (compliments) exagéré(e)
gusset ['gʌsɪt] n gousset m, soufflet m; (in tights, pants) entre-jambes m
gust [gʌst] n (of wind) rafale f; (of smoke) bouffée f
gusto ['gʌstəu] n enthousiasme m
gusty ['gʌstɪ] adj venteux(-euse); **~ winds** des rafales de vent
gut [gʌt] n intestin m, boyau m; (Mus etc) boyau ▷ vt (poultry, fish) vider; (building) ne laisser que les murs de; **guts** npl (Anat) boyaux mpl; (inf: courage) cran m; **to hate sb's ~s** ne pas pouvoir voir qn en peinture or sentir qn
gut reaction n réaction instinctive
gutsy ['gʌtsɪ] adj (person) qui a du cran; (style) qui a du punch
gutted ['gʌtɪd] adj: **I was ~** (inf: disappointed) j'étais carrément dégoûté
gutter ['gʌtəʳ] n (of roof) gouttière f; (in street) caniveau m; (fig) ruisseau m
gutter press n: **the ~** la presse de bas étage or à scandale
guttural ['gʌtərl] adj guttural(e)
guy [gaɪ] n (inf: man) type m; (also: **guyrope**) corde f; (figure) effigie de Guy Fawkes
Guyana [gaɪ'ænə] n Guyane f
Guy Fawkes' Night [gaɪ'fɔ:ks-] n voir article

● **GUY FAWKES' NIGHT**
●
● Guy Fawkes' Night, que l'on appelle
● également "bonfire night", commémore
● l'échec du complot (le "Gunpowder Plot")
● contre James Ist et son parlement le 5
● novembre 1605. L'un des conspirateurs,
● Guy Fawkes, avait été surpris dans les caves
● du parlement alors qu'il s'apprêtait à y
● mettre le feu. Chaque année pour le 5
● novembre, les enfants préparent à l'avance
● une effigie de Guy Fawkes et ils demandent
● aux passants "un penny pour le guy" avec
● lequel ils pourront s'acheter des fusées de
● feu d'artifice. Beaucoup de gens font
● encore un feu dans leur jardin sur lequel ils
● brûlent le "guy".

guzzle ['gʌzl] vi s'empiffrer ▷ vt avaler gloutonnement
gym [dʒɪm] n (also: **gymnasium**) gymnase m; (also: **gymnastics**) gym f
gymkhana [dʒɪm'kɑːnə] n gymkhana m
gymnasium [dʒɪm'neɪzɪəm] n gymnase m
gymnast ['dʒɪmnæst] n gymnaste m/f
gymnastics [dʒɪm'næstɪks] n, npl gymnastique f
gym shoes npl chaussures fpl de gym(nastique)
gynaecologist, (US) **gynecologist** [gaɪnɪ'kɔlədʒɪst] n gynécologue m/f
gynaecology, (US) **gynecology** [gaɪnə'kɔlədʒɪ] n gynécologie f
gypsy ['dʒɪpsɪ] n gitan(e), bohémien(ne) ▷ cpd: **~ caravan** n roulotte f
gyrate [dʒaɪ'reɪt] vi tournoyer

Hh

H, h [eɪtʃ] n (letter) H, h m; **H for Harry**, (US) **H for How** H comme Henri

habeas corpus ['heɪbɪəs'kɔ:pəs] n (Law) habeas corpus m

haberdashery [hæbə'dæʃərɪ] n (Brit) mercerie f

habit ['hæbɪt] n habitude f; (costume: Rel) habit m; (for riding) tenue f d'équitation; **to get out of/into the ~ of doing sth** perdre/prendre l'habitude de faire qch

habitable ['hæbɪtəbl] adj habitable

habitat ['hæbɪtæt] n habitat m

habitation [hæbɪ'teɪʃən] n habitation f

habitual [hə'bɪtjuəl] adj habituel(le); (drinker, liar) invétéré(e)

habitually [hə'bɪtjuəlɪ] adv habituellement, d'habitude

hack [hæk] vt hacher, tailler ▷ n (cut) entaille f; (blow) coup m; (pej: writer) nègre m; (old horse) canasson m

hacker ['hækə'] n (Comput) pirate m (informatique); (: enthusiast) passionné(e) m/f des ordinateurs

hackles ['hæklz] npl: **to make sb's ~ rise** (fig) mettre qn hors de soi

hackney cab ['hæknɪ-] n fiacre m

hackneyed ['hæknɪd] adj usé(e), rebattu(e)

hacksaw ['hæksɔ:] n scie f à métaux

had [hæd] pt, pp of **have**

haddock (pl - or -s) ['hædək] n églefin m; **smoked ~** haddock m

hadn't ['hædnt] = **had not**

haematology, (US) **hematology** ['hi:mə'tɔlədʒɪ] n hématologie f

haemoglobin, (US) **hemoglobin** ['hi:mə'gləubɪn] n hémoglobine f

haemophilia, (US) **hemophilia** ['hi:mə'fɪlɪə] n hémophilie f

haemorrhage, (US) **hemorrhage** ['hɛmərɪdʒ] n hémorragie f

haemorrhoids, (US) **hemorrhoids** ['hɛmərɔɪdz] npl hémorroïdes fpl

hag [hæg] n (ugly) vieille sorcière; (nasty) chameau m, harpie f; (witch) sorcière

haggard ['hægəd] adj hagard(e), égaré(e)

haggis ['hægɪs] n haggis m

haggle ['hægl] vi marchander; **to ~ over** chicaner sur

haggling ['hæglɪŋ] n marchandage m

Hague [heɪg] n: **The ~** La Haye

hail [heɪl] n grêle f ▷ vt (call) héler; (greet) acclamer ▷ vi grêler; (originate): **he ~s from Scotland** il est originaire d'Écosse

hailstone ['heɪlstəun] n grêlon m

hailstorm ['heɪlstɔ:m] n averse f de grêle

hair [hɛə'] n cheveux mpl; (on body) poils mpl, pilosité f; (of animal) pelage m; (single hair: on head) cheveu m; (: on body, of animal) poil m; **to do one's ~** se coiffer

hairband ['hɛəbænd] n (elasticated) bandeau m; (plastic) serre-tête m

hairbrush ['hɛəbrʌʃ] n brosse f à cheveux

haircut ['hɛəkʌt] n coupe f (de cheveux)

hairdo ['hɛədu:] n coiffure f

hairdresser ['hɛədrɛsə'] n coiffeur(-euse)

hairdresser's ['hɛədrɛsə'z] n salon m de coiffure, coiffeur m

hair dryer ['hɛədraɪə'] n sèche-cheveux m, séchoir m

-haired [hɛəd] suffix: **fair/long~** aux cheveux blonds/longs

hair gel n gel m pour cheveux

hairgrip ['hɛəgrɪp] n pince f à cheveux

hairline ['hɛəlaɪn] n naissance f des cheveux

hairline fracture n fêlure f

hairnet ['hɛənɛt] n résille f

hair oil n huile f capillaire

hairpiece ['hɛəpi:s] n postiche m

hairpin ['hɛəpɪn] n épingle f à cheveux

hairpin bend, (US) **hairpin curve** n virage m en épingle à cheveux

hair-raising ['hɛəreɪzɪŋ] adj à (vous) faire dresser les cheveux sur la tête

hair remover n dépilateur m

hair removing cream n crème f dépilatoire

hair spray n laque f (pour les cheveux)

hairstyle ['hɛəstaɪl] n coiffure f

hairy ['hɛərɪ] adj poilu(e), chevelu(e); (inf: frightening) effrayant(e)

Haiti ['heɪtɪ] n Haïti m

hake (pl - or -s) [heɪk] n colin m, merlu m

halcyon ['hælsɪən] adj merveilleux(-euse)

hale [heɪl] adj: **~ and hearty** robuste, en

pleine santé

half [hɑ:f] n (pl **halves** [hɑ:vz]) moitié f; (of beer: also: **half pint**) ≈ demi m; (Rail, bus: also: **half fare**) demi-tarif m; (Sport: of match) mi-temps f; (: of ground) moitié (du terrain) ▷ adj demi(e) ▷ adv (à) moitié, à demi; ~ **an hour** une demi-heure; ~ **a dozen** une demi-douzaine; ~ **a pound** une demi-livre, ≈ 250 g; **two and a** ~ deux et demi; **a week and a** ~ une semaine et demie; ~ **(of it)** la moitié; ~ **(of)** la moitié de; ~ **the amount of** la moitié de; **to cut sth in** ~ couper qch en deux; ~ **past three** trois heures et demie; ~ **empty/closed** à moitié vide/fermé; **to go halves (with sb)** se mettre de moitié avec qn

half-back ['hɑ:fbæk] n (Sport) demi m

half-baked ['hɑ:f'beɪkt] adj (inf: idea, scheme) qui ne tient pas debout

half board n (Brit: in hotel) demi-pension f

half-breed ['hɑ:fbri:d] n (pej) = **half-caste**

half-brother ['hɑ:fbrʌðə^r] n demi-frère m

half-caste ['hɑ:fkɑ:st] n (pej) métis(se)

half day n demi-journée f

half fare n demi-tarif m

half-hearted ['hɑ:f'hɑ:tɪd] adj tiède, sans enthousiasme

half-hour [hɑ:f'auə^r] n demi-heure f

half-mast ['hɑ:f'mɑ:st] n: **at** ~ (flag) en berne, à mi-mât

halfpenny ['heɪpnɪ] n demi-penny m

half-price ['hɑ:f'praɪs] adj à moitié prix ▷ adv (also: **at half-price**) à moitié prix

half term n (Brit Scol) vacances fpl (de demi-trimestre)

half-time [hɑ:f'taɪm] n mi-temps f

halfway ['hɑ:f'weɪ] adv à mi-chemin; **to meet sb** ~ (fig) parvenir à un compromis avec qn; ~ **through sth** au milieu de qch

halfway house n (hostel) centre m de réadaptation (pour anciens prisonniers, malades mentaux etc); (fig): **a** ~ **(between)** une étape intermédiaire (entre)

half-wit ['hɑ:fwɪt] n (inf) idiot(e), imbécile m/f

half-yearly [hɑ:'fjɪəlɪ] adv deux fois par an ▷ adj semestriel(le)

halibut ['hælɪbət] n (pl inv) flétan m

halitosis [hælɪ'təusɪs] n mauvaise haleine

hall [hɔ:l] n salle f; (entrance way: big) hall m; (small) entrée f; (US: corridor) couloir m; (mansion) château m, manoir m

hallmark ['hɔ:lmɑ:k] n poinçon m; (fig) marque f

hallo [hə'ləu] excl = **hello**

hall of residence n (Brit) pavillon m or résidence f universitaire

Hallowe'en, Halloween ['hæləu'i:n] n veille f de la Toussaint; voir article

● **HALLOWE'EN**
●
● Selon la tradition, Hallowe'en est la nuit des
● fantômes et des sorcières. En Écosse et aux
● États-Unis surtout (et de plus en plus en
● Angleterre) les enfants, pour fêter

● Hallowe'en, se déguisent ce soir-là et ils vont
● ainsi de porte en porte en demandant de
● petits cadeaux (du chocolat, etc).

hallucination [həlu:sɪ'neɪʃən] n hallucination f

hallucinogenic [həlu:sɪnəu'dʒenɪk] adj hallucinogène

hallway ['hɔ:lweɪ] n (entrance) vestibule m; (corridor) couloir m

halo ['heɪləu] n (of saint etc) auréole f; (of sun) halo m

halt [hɔ:lt] n halte f, arrêt m ▷ vt faire arrêter; (progress etc) interrompre ▷ vi faire halte, s'arrêter; **to call a** ~ **to sth** (fig) mettre fin à qch

halter ['hɔ:ltə^r] n (for horse) licou m

halterneck ['hɔ:ltənɛk] adj (dress) (avec) dos nu inv

halve [hɑ:v] vt (apple etc) partager or diviser en deux; (reduce by half) réduire de moitié

halves [hɑ:vz] npl of **half**

ham [hæm] n jambon m; (inf: also: **radio ham**) radio-amateur m; (also: **ham actor**) cabotin(e)

Hamburg ['hæmbə:g] n Hambourg

hamburger ['hæmbə:gə^r] n hamburger m

ham-fisted ['hæm'fɪstɪd], (US) **ham-handed** ['hæm'hændɪd] adj maladroit(e)

hamlet ['hæmlɪt] n hameau m

hammer ['hæmə^r] n marteau m ▷ vt (nail) enfoncer; (fig) éreinter, démolir ▷ vi (at door) frapper à coups redoublés; **to** ~ **a point home to sb** faire rentrer qch dans la tête de qn
  ▶ **hammer out** vt (metal) étendre au marteau; (fig: solution) élaborer

hammock ['hæmək] n hamac m

hamper ['hæmpə^r] vt gêner ▷ n panier m (d'osier)

hamster ['hæmstə^r] n hamster m

hamstring ['hæmstrɪŋ] n (Anat) tendon m du jarret

hand [hænd] n main f; (of clock) aiguille f; (handwriting) écriture f; (at cards) jeu m; (measurement: of horse) paume f; (worker) ouvrier(-ière) ▷ vt passer, donner; **to give sb a** ~ donner un coup de main à qn; **at** ~ à portée de la main; **in** ~ (situation) en main; (work) en cours; **we have the situation in** ~ nous avons la situation bien en main; **to be on** ~ (person) être disponible; (emergency services) se tenir prêt(e) (à intervenir); **to** ~ (information etc) sous la main, à portée de la main; **to force sb's** ~ forcer la main à qn; **to have a free** ~ avoir carte blanche; **to have sth in one's** ~ tenir qch à la main; **on the one** ~ ..., **on the other** ~ d'une part ..., d'autre part
  ▶ **hand down** vt passer; (tradition, heirloom) transmettre; (US: sentence, verdict) prononcer
  ▶ **hand in** vt remettre
  ▶ **hand out** vt distribuer
  ▶ **hand over** vt remettre; (powers etc) transmettre
  ▶ **hand round** vt (Brit: information) faire circuler; (: chocolates etc) faire passer

handbag ['hændbæg] n sac m à main
hand baggage n = **hand luggage**
handball ['hændbɔːl] n handball m
handbasin ['hændbeɪsn] n lavabo m
handbook ['hændbuk] n manuel m
handbrake ['hændbreɪk] n frein m à main
h & c abbr (Brit) = **hot and cold (water)**
hand cream n crème f pour les mains
handcuffs ['hændkʌfs] npl menottes fpl
handful ['hændful] n poignée f
hand-held ['hænd'hɛld] adj à main
handicap ['hændɪkæp] n handicap m ▷ vt
handicaper; **mentally/physically ~ped**
handicapé(e) mentalement/physiquement
handicraft ['hændɪkrɑːft] n travail m
d'artisanat, technique artisanale
handiwork ['hændɪwəːk] n ouvrage m; **this**
looks like his ~ (pej) ça a tout l'air d'être son
œuvre
handkerchief ['hæŋkətʃɪf] n mouchoir m
handle ['hændl] n (of door etc) poignée f; (of cup
etc) anse f; (of knife etc) manche m; (of saucepan)
queue f; (for winding) manivelle f ▷ vt toucher,
manier; (deal with) s'occuper de; (treat: people)
prendre; **"~ with care"** "fragile"; **to fly off the**
~ s'énerver
handlebar ['hændlbɑːʳ] n, **handlebars**
['hændlbɑːz] npl guidon m
handling ['hændlɪŋ] n (Aut) maniement m;
(treatment): **his ~ of the matter** la façon dont il
a traité l'affaire
handling charges npl frais mpl de
manutention; (Banking) agios mpl
hand luggage ['hændlʌgɪdʒ] n bagages mpl à
main; **one item of ~** un bagage à main
handmade ['hænd'meɪd] adj fait(e) à la main
handout ['hændaut] n (money) aide f, don m;
(leaflet) prospectus m; (press handout)
communiqué m de presse; (at lecture)
polycopié m
hand-picked ['hænd'pɪkt] adj (produce) cueilli(e)
à la main; (staff etc) trié(e) sur le volet
handrail ['hændreɪl] n (on staircase etc) rampe f,
main courante
handset ['hændsɛt] n (Tel) combiné m
hands-free ['hændz'friː] adj mains libres inv ▷ n
(also: **hands-free kit**) kit m mains libres inv
handshake ['hændʃeɪk] n poignée f de main;
(Comput) établissement m de la liaison
handsome ['hænsəm] adj beau (belle); (gift)
généreux(-euse); (profit) considérable
hands-on ['hændz'ɔn] adj (training, experience) sur
le tas; **she has a very ~ approach** sa politique
est de mettre la main à la pâte
handstand ['hændstænd] n: **to do a ~** faire
l'arbre droit
hand-to-mouth ['hændtə'mauθ] adj (existence)
au jour le jour
handwriting ['hændraɪtɪŋ] n écriture f
handwritten ['hændrɪtn] adj manuscrit(e),
écrit(e) à la main
handy ['hændɪ] adj (person) adroit(e); (close at

hand) sous la main; (convenient) pratique; **to**
come in ~ être (or s'avérer) utile
handyman ['hændɪmæn] (irreg) n bricoleur m;
(servant) homme m à tout faire
hang (pt, pp **hung**) [hæŋ, hʌŋ] vt accrocher;
(criminal: pt, pp **-ed**) pendre ▷ vi pendre; (hair,
drapery) tomber ▷ n: **to get the ~ of (doing) sth**
(inf) attraper le coup pour faire qch
  ▸ **hang about, hang around** vi flâner, traîner
  ▸ **hang back** vi (hesitate): **to ~ back (from**
doing) être réticent(e) (pour faire)
  ▸ **hang down** vi pendre
  ▸ **hang on** vi (wait) attendre ▷ vt fus (depend on)
dépendre de; **to ~ on to** (keep hold of) ne pas
lâcher; (keep) garder
  ▸ **hang out** vt (washing) étendre (dehors) ▷ vi
pendre; (inf: live) habiter, percher; (: spend time)
traîner
  ▸ **hang round** vi = **hang around**
  ▸ **hang together** vi (argument etc) se tenir, être
cohérent(e)
  ▸ **hang up** vi (Tel) raccrocher ▷ vt (coat, painting
etc) accrocher, suspendre; **to ~ up on sb** (Tel)
raccrocher au nez de qn
hangar ['hæŋəʳ] n hangar m
hangdog ['hæŋdɔg] adj (look, expression) de chien
battu
hanger ['hæŋəʳ] n cintre m, portemanteau m
hanger-on [hæŋər'ɔn] n parasite m
hang-glider ['hæŋglaɪdəʳ] n deltaplane m
hang-gliding ['hæŋglaɪdɪŋ] n vol m libre or sur
aile delta
hanging ['hæŋɪŋ] n (execution) pendaison f
hangman ['hæŋmən] (irreg) n bourreau m
hangover ['hæŋəuvəʳ] n (after drinking) gueule f
de bois
hang-up ['hæŋʌp] n complexe m
hank [hæŋk] n écheveau m
hanker ['hæŋkəʳ] vi: **to ~ after** avoir envie de
hankering ['hæŋkərɪŋ] n: **to have a ~ for/to do**
sth avoir une grande envie de/de faire qch
hankie, hanky ['hæŋkɪ] n abbr = **handkerchief**
Hants abbr (Brit) = **Hampshire**
haphazard [hæp'hæzəd] adj fait(e) au hasard,
fait(e) au petit bonheur
hapless ['hæplɪs] adj malheureux(-euse)
happen ['hæpən] vi arriver, se passer, se
produire; **what's ~ing?** que se passe-t-il?; **she**
~ed to be free il s'est trouvé (or se trouvait)
qu'elle était libre; **if anything ~ed to him** s'il
lui arrivait quoi que ce soit; **as it ~s** justement
  ▸ **happen on, happen upon** vt fus tomber sur
happening ['hæpnɪŋ] n événement m
happily ['hæpɪlɪ] adv heureusement; (cheerfully)
joyeusement
happiness ['hæpɪnɪs] n bonheur m
happy ['hæpɪ] adj heureux(-euse); **~ with**
(arrangements etc) satisfait(e) de; **to be ~ to do**
faire volontiers; **yes, I'd be ~ to** oui, avec plaisir
or (bien) volontiers; **~ birthday!** bon
anniversaire!; **~ Christmas/New Year!** joyeux
Noël/bonne année!

happy-go-lucky ['hæpɪgəu'lʌkɪ] *adj* insouciant(e)

happy hour *n* l'heure *f* de l'apéritif, *heure pendant laquelle les consommations sont à prix réduit*

harangue [hə'ræŋ] *vt* haranguer

harass ['hærəs] *vt* accabler, tourmenter

harassed ['hærəst] *adj* tracassé(e)

harassment ['hærəsmənt] *n* tracasseries *fpl*; **sexual ~** harcèlement sexuel

harbour, (*US*) **harbor** ['hɑ:bə^r] *n* port *m* ▷ *vt* héberger, abriter; (*hopes, suspicions*) entretenir; **to ~ a grudge against sb** en vouloir à qn

harbour dues, (*US*) **harbor dues** *npl* droits *mpl* de port

harbour master, (*US*) **harbor master** *n* capitaine *m* du port

hard [hɑ:d] *adj* dur(e); (*question, problem*) difficile; (*facts, evidence*) concret(-ète) ▷ *adv* (*work*) dur; (*think, try*) sérieusement; **to look ~ at** regarder fixement; (*thing*) regarder de près; **to drink ~** boire sec; **~ luck!** pas de veine!; **no ~ feelings!** sans rancune!; **to be ~ of hearing** être dur(e) d'oreille; **to be ~ done by** être traité(e) injustement; **to be ~ on sb** être dur(e) avec qn; **I find it ~ to believe that ...** je n'arrive pas à croire que ...

hard-and-fast ['hɑ:dən'fɑ:st] *adj* strict(e), absolu(e)

hardback ['hɑ:dbæk] *n* livre relié

hardboard ['hɑ:dbɔ:d] *n* Isorel® *m*

hard-boiled egg ['hɑ:d'bɔɪld-] *n* œuf dur

hard cash *n* espèces *fpl*

hard copy *n* (*Comput*) sortie *f or* copie *f* papier

hard-core ['hɑ:d'kɔ:^r] *adj* (*pornography*) (dit(e)) dur(e); (*supporters*) inconditionnel(le)

hard court *n* (*Tennis*) court *m* en dur

hard disk *n* (*Comput*) disque dur

harden ['hɑ:dn] *vt* durcir; (*steel*) tremper; (*fig*) endurcir ▷ *vi* (*substance*) durcir

hardened ['hɑ:dnd] *adj* (*criminal*) endurci(e); **to be ~ to sth** s'être endurci(e) à qch, être (devenu(e)) insensible à qch

hard-headed ['hɑ:d'hedɪd] *adj* réaliste; décidé(e)

hard-hearted ['hɑ:d'hɑ:tɪd] *adj* dur(e), impitoyable

hard-hitting ['hɑ:d'hɪtɪŋ] *adj* (*speech, article*) sans complaisances

hard labour *n* travaux forcés

hardliner [hɑ:d'laɪnə^r] *n* intransigeant(e), dur(e)

hard-luck story [hɑ:d'lʌk-] *n* histoire larmoyante

hardly ['hɑ:dlɪ] *adv* (*scarcely*) à peine; (*harshly*) durement; **it's ~ the case** ce n'est guère le cas; **~ anywhere/ever** presque nulle part/jamais; **I can ~ believe it** j'ai du mal à le croire

hardness ['hɑ:dnɪs] *n* dureté *f*

hard-nosed ['hɑ:d'nəuzd] *adj* impitoyable, dur(e)

hard-pressed ['hɑ:d'prest] *adj* sous pression

hard sell *n* vente agressive

hardship ['hɑ:dʃɪp] *n* (*difficulties*) épreuves *fpl*; (*deprivation*) privations *fpl*

hard shoulder *n* (*Brit Aut*) accotement stabilisé

hard-up [hɑ:d'ʌp] *adj* (*inf*) fauché(e)

hardware ['hɑ:dwɛə^r] *n* quincaillerie *f*; (*Comput, Mil*) matériel *m*

hardware shop, (*US*) **hardware store** *n* quincaillerie *f*

hard-wearing [hɑ:d'wɛərɪŋ] *adj* solide

hard-won ['hɑ:d'wʌn] *adj* (*si*) durement gagné(e)

hard-working [hɑ:d'wə:kɪŋ] *adj* travailleur(-euse), consciencieux(-euse)

hardy ['hɑ:dɪ] *adj* robuste; (*plant*) résistant(e) au gel

hare [hɛə^r] *n* lièvre *m*

hare-brained ['hɛəbreɪnd] *adj* farfelu(e), écervelé(e)

harelip ['hɛəlɪp] *n* (*Med*) bec-de-lièvre *m*

harem [hɑ:'ri:m] *n* harem *m*

hark back [hɑ:k-] *vi*: **to ~ to** (en) revenir toujours à

harm [hɑ:m] *n* mal *m*; (*wrong*) tort *m* ▷ *vt* (*person*) faire du mal *or* du tort à; (*thing*) endommager; **to mean no ~** ne pas avoir de mauvaises intentions; **there's no ~ in trying** on peut toujours essayer; **out of ~'s way** à l'abri du danger, en lieu sûr

harmful ['hɑ:mful] *adj* nuisible

harmless [hɑ:mlɪs] *adj* inoffensif(-ive)

harmonic [hɑ:'mɔnɪk] *adj* harmonique

harmonica [hɑ:'mɔnɪkə] *n* harmonica *m*

harmonics [hɑ:'mɔnɪks] *npl* harmoniques *mpl or fpl*

harmonious [hɑ:'məunɪəs] *adj* harmonieux(-euse)

harmonium [hɑ:'məunɪəm] *n* harmonium *m*

harmonize ['hɑ:mənaɪz] *vt* harmoniser ▷ *vi* s'harmoniser

harmony ['hɑ:mənɪ] *n* harmonie *f*

harness ['hɑ:nɪs] *n* harnais *m* ▷ *vt* (*horse*) harnacher; (*resources*) exploiter

harp [hɑ:p] *n* harpe *f* ▷ *vi*: **to ~ on about** revenir toujours sur

harpist ['hɑ:pɪst] *n* harpiste *m/f*

harpoon [hɑ:'pu:n] *n* harpon *m*

harpsichord ['hɑ:psɪkɔ:d] *n* clavecin *m*

harrowing ['hærəuɪŋ] *adj* déchirant(e)

harsh [hɑ:ʃ] *adj* (*hard*) dur(e); (*severe*) sévère; (*rough: surface*) rugueux(-euse); (*unpleasant: sound*) discordant(e); (*: light*) cru(e); (*: taste*) âpre

harshly ['hɑ:ʃlɪ] *adv* durement, sévèrement

harshness ['hɑ:ʃnɪs] *n* dureté *f*, sévérité *f*

harvest ['hɑ:vɪst] *n* (*of corn*) moisson *f*; (*of fruit*) récolte *f*; (*of grapes*) vendange *f* ▷ *vi, vt* moissonner; récolter; vendanger

harvester ['hɑ:vɪstə^r] *n* (*machine*) moissonneuse *f*; (*also*: **combine harvester**) moissonneuse-batteuse(-lieuse *f*) *f*

has [hæz] *vb see* **have**

has-been ['hæzbi:n] *n* (*inf: person*): **he/she's a ~** il/elle a fait son temps *or* est fini(e)

hash [hæʃ] n (Culin) hachis m; (fig: mess) gâchis m
▷ n abbr (inf) = **hashish**
hashish ['hæʃɪʃ] n haschisch m
hasn't ['hæznt] = **has not**
hassle ['hæsl] n (inf: fuss) histoire(s) f(pl)
haste [heɪst] n hâte f, précipitation f; **in ~** à la
hâte, précipitamment
hasten ['heɪsn] vt hâter, accélérer ▷ vi se hâter,
s'empresser; **I ~ to add that ...** je m'empresse
d'ajouter que ...
hastily ['heɪstɪlɪ] adv à la hâte; (leave)
précipitamment
hasty ['heɪstɪ] adj (decision, action) hâtif(-ive);
(departure, escape) précipité(e)
hat [hæt] n chapeau m
hatbox ['hætbɔks] n carton m à chapeau
hatch [hætʃ] n (Naut: also: **hatchway**) écoutille f;
(Brit: also: **service hatch**) passe-plats m inv ▷ vi
éclore ▷ vt faire éclore; (fig: scheme) tramer,
ourdir
hatchback ['hætʃbæk] n (Aut) modèle m avec
hayon arrière
hatchet ['hætʃɪt] n hachette f
hatchet job n (inf) démolissage m
hatchet man (irreg) n (inf) homme m de main
hate [heɪt] vt haïr, détester ▷ n haine f; **to ~ to
do** or **doing** détester faire; **I ~ to trouble you,
but ...** désolé de vous déranger, mais ...
hateful ['heɪtful] adj odieux(-euse), détestable
hatred ['heɪtrɪd] n haine f
hat trick n (Brit Sport, also fig): **to get a ~** réussir
trois coups (or gagner trois matchs etc)
consécutifs
haughty ['hɔːtɪ] adj hautain(e), arrogant(e)
haul [hɔːl] vt traîner, tirer; (by lorry) camionner;
(Naut) haler ▷ n (of fish) prise f; (of stolen goods etc)
butin m
haulage ['hɔːlɪdʒ] n transport routier
haulage contractor n (Brit: firm) entreprise f de
transport (routier); (: person) transporteur
routier
haulier ['hɔːlɪəʳ], (US) **hauler** ['hɔːləʳ] n
transporteur (routier), camionneur m
haunch [hɔːntʃ] n hanche f; **~ of venison**
cuissot m de chevreuil
haunt [hɔːnt] vt (subj: ghost, fear) hanter; (: person)
fréquenter ▷ n repaire m
haunted ['hɔːntɪd] adj (castle etc) hanté(e); (look)
égaré(e), hagard(e)
haunting ['hɔːntɪŋ] adj (sight, music) obsédant(e)
Havana [hə'vænə] n La Havane

○ KEYWORD

have [hæv] (pt, pp **had**) aux vb **1** (gen) avoir; être;
to have eaten/slept avoir mangé/dormi; **to
have arrived/gone** être arrivé(e)/allé(e); **he
has been promoted** il a eu une promotion;
having finished or **when he had finished, he
left** quand il a eu fini, il est parti; **we'd already
eaten** nous avions déjà mangé
2 (in tag questions): **you've done it, haven't you?**

vous l'avez fait, n'est-ce pas?
3 (in short answers and questions): **no I haven't!/yes
we have!** mais non!/mais si!; **so I have!** ah oui!,
oui c'est vrai!; **I've been there before, have
you?** j'y suis déjà allé, et vous?
▷ modal aux vb (be obliged): **to have (got) to do
sth** devoir faire qch, être obligé(e) de faire qch;
she has (got) to do it elle doit le faire, il faut
qu'elle le fasse; **you haven't to tell her** vous
n'êtes pas obligé de le lui dire; (must not) ne le
lui dites surtout pas; **do you have to book?** il
faut réserver?
▷ vt **1** (possess) avoir; **he has (got) blue eyes/
dark hair** il a les yeux bleus/les cheveux bruns
2 (referring to meals etc): **to have breakfast**
prendre le petit déjeuner; **to have dinner/
lunch** dîner/déjeuner; **to have a drink**
prendre un verre; **to have a cigarette** fumer
une cigarette
3 (receive) avoir, recevoir; (obtain) avoir; **may I
have your address?** puis-je avoir votre
adresse?; **you can have it for £5** vous pouvez
l'avoir pour 5 livres; **I must have it for
tomorrow** il me le faut pour demain; **to have a
baby** avoir un bébé
4 (maintain, allow): **I won't have it!** ça ne se
passera pas comme ça!; **we can't have that**
nous ne tolérerons pas ça
5 (by sb else): **to have sth done** faire faire qch;
to have one's hair cut se faire couper les
cheveux; **to have sb do sth** faire faire qch à qn
6 (experience, suffer) avoir; **to have a cold/flu**
avoir un rhume/la grippe; **to have an
operation** se faire opérer; **she had her bag
stolen** elle s'est fait voler son sac
7 (+noun): **to have a swim/walk** nager/se
promener; **to have a bath/shower** prendre un
bain/une douche; **let's have a look** regardons;
to have a meeting se réunir; **to have a party**
organiser une fête; **let me have a try** laissez-
moi essayer
8 (inf: dupe) avoir; **he's been had** il s'est fait
avoir or rouler
▶ **have out** vt: **to have it out with sb** (settle a
problem etc) s'expliquer (franchement) avec qn

haven ['heɪvn] n port m; (fig) havre m
haven't ['hævnt] = **have not**
haversack ['hævəsæk] n sac m à dos
haves [hævz] npl (inf): **the ~ and have-nots** les
riches et les pauvres
havoc ['hævək] n ravages mpl, dégâts mpl; **to
play ~ with** (fig) désorganiser complètement;
détraquer
Hawaii [hə'waɪː] n (îles fpl) Hawaï m
Hawaiian [hə'waɪjən] adj hawaïen(ne) ▷ n
Hawaïen(ne); (Ling) hawaïen m
hawk [hɔːk] n faucon m ▷ vt (goods for sale)
colporter
hawker ['hɔːkəʳ] n colporteur m
hawkish ['hɔːkɪʃ] adj belliciste
hawthorn ['hɔːθɔːn] n aubépine f

hay [heɪ] n foin m
hay fever n rhume m des foins
haystack ['heɪstæk] n meule f de foin
haywire ['heɪwaɪəʳ] adj (inf): **to go ~** perdre la tête; mal tourner
hazard ['hæzəd] n (risk) danger m, risque m; (chance) hasard m, chance f ▷ vt risquer, hasarder; **to be a health/fire ~** présenter un risque pour la santé/d'incendie; **to ~ a guess** émettre or hasarder une hypothèse
hazardous ['hæzədəs] adj hasardeux(-euse), risqué(e)
hazard pay n (US) prime f de risque
hazard warning lights npl (Aut) feux mpl de détresse
haze [heɪz] n brume f
hazel [heɪzl] n (tree) noisetier m ▷ adj (eyes) noisette inv
hazelnut ['heɪzlnʌt] n noisette f
hazy ['heɪzɪ] adj brumeux(-euse); (idea) vague; (photograph) flou(e)
H-bomb ['eɪtʃbɔm] n bombe f H
HE abbr = **high explosive**; (Rel, Diplomacy) = **His (or Her) Excellency**
he [hi:] pron il; **it is he who ...** c'est lui qui ...; **here he is** le voici; **he-bear** etc ours etc mâle
head [hɛd] n tête f; (leader) chef m; (of school) directeur(-trice); (of secondary school) proviseur m ▷ vt (list) être en tête de; (group, company) être à la tête de; **heads** pl (on coin) (le côté) face; **~s or tails** pile ou face; **~ first** la tête la première; **~ over heels in love** follement or éperdument amoureux(-euse); **to ~ the ball** faire une tête; **10 euros a** or **per ~** 10 euros par personne; **to sit at the ~ of the table** présider la tablée; **to have a ~ for business** avoir des dispositions pour les affaires; **to have no ~ for heights** être sujet(te) au vertige; **to come to a ~** (fig: situation etc) devenir critique
  ▶ **head for** vt fus se diriger vers; (disaster) aller à
  ▶ **head off** vt (threat, danger) détourner
headache ['hɛdeɪk] n mal m de tête; **to have a ~** avoir mal à la tête
headband ['hɛdbænd] n bandeau m
headboard ['hɛdbɔːd] n dosseret m
head cold n rhume m de cerveau
headdress ['hɛddrɛs] n coiffure f
headed notepaper ['hɛdɪd-] n papier m à lettres à en-tête
header ['hɛdəʳ] n (Brit inf: Football) (coup m de) tête f; (: fall) chute f (or plongeon m) la tête la première
head-first ['hɛd'fəːst] adv (lit) la tête la première
headhunt ['hɛdhʌnt] vt: **she was ~ed** elle a été recrutée par un chasseur de têtes
headhunter ['hɛdhʌntəʳ] n chasseur m de têtes
heading ['hɛdɪŋ] n titre m; (subject title) rubrique f
headlamp ['hɛdlæmp] (Brit) n = **headlight**
headland ['hɛdlənd] n promontoire m, cap m
headlight ['hɛdlaɪt] n phare m
headline ['hɛdlaɪn] n titre m

headlong ['hɛdlɔŋ] adv (fall) la tête la première; (rush) tête baissée
headmaster [hɛd'mɑːstəʳ] n directeur m, proviseur m
headmistress [hɛd'mɪstrɪs] n directrice f
head office n siège m, bureau m central
head-on [hɛd'ɔn] adj (collision) de plein fouet
headphones ['hɛdfəunz] npl casque m (à écouteurs)
headquarters ['hɛdkwɔːtəz] npl (of business) bureau or siège central; (Mil) quartier général
headrest ['hɛdrɛst] n appui-tête m
headroom ['hɛdrum] n (in car) hauteur f de plafond; (under bridge) hauteur limite; dégagement m
headscarf ['hɛdskɑːf] (pl **headscarves** [-skɑːvz]) n foulard m
headset ['hɛdsɛt] n = **headphones**
headstone ['hɛdstəun] n pierre tombale
headstrong ['hɛdstrɔŋ] adj têtu(e), entêté(e)
headteacher [hɛd'tɪtʃəʳ] n directeur(-trice); (of secondary school) proviseur m
head waiter n maître m d'hôtel
headway ['hɛdweɪ] n: **to make ~** avancer, faire des progrès
headwind ['hɛdwɪnd] n vent m contraire
heady ['hɛdɪ] adj capiteux(-euse), enivrant(e)
heal [hi:l] vt, vi guérir
health [hɛlθ] n santé f; **Department of H~** (Brit, US) ≈ ministère m de la Santé
health care n services médicaux
health centre n (Brit) centre m de santé
health food n aliment(s) naturel(s)
health food shop n magasin m diététique
health hazard n risque m pour la santé
Health Service n: **the ~** (Brit) ≈ la Sécurité Sociale
healthy ['hɛlθɪ] adj (person) en bonne santé; (climate, food, attitude etc) sain(e)
heap [hi:p] n tas m, monceau m ▷ vt (also: **heap up**) entasser, amonceler; **she ~ed her plate with cakes** elle a chargé son assiette de gâteaux; **~s (of)** (inf: lots) des tas (de); **to ~ favours/praise/gifts** etc **on sb** combler qn de faveurs/d'éloges/de cadeaux etc
hear (pt, pp **heard**) [hɪəʳ, həːd] vt entendre; (news) apprendre; (lecture) assister à, écouter ▷ vi entendre; **to ~ about** entendre parler de; (have news of) avoir des nouvelles de; **did you ~ about the move?** tu es au courant du déménagement?; **to ~ from sb** recevoir des nouvelles de qn; **I've never ~d of that book** je n'ai jamais entendu parler de ce livre
  ▶ **hear out** vt écouter jusqu'au bout
heard [həːd] pt, pp of **hear**
hearing ['hɪərɪŋ] n (sense) ouïe f; (of witnesses) audition f; (of a case) audience f; (of committee) séance f; **to give sb a ~** (Brit) écouter ce que qn a à dire
hearing aid n appareil m acoustique
hearsay ['hɪəseɪ] n on-dit mpl, rumeurs fpl; **by ~** adv par ouï-dire

hearse [hə:s] n corbillard m
heart [hɑ:t] n cœur m; **hearts** npl (Cards) cœur; **at ~** au fond; **by ~** (learn, know) par cœur; **to have a weak ~** avoir le cœur malade, avoir des problèmes de cœur; **to lose/take ~** perdre/prendre courage; **to set one's ~ on sth/on doing sth** vouloir absolument qch/faire qch; **the ~ of the matter** le fond du problème
heartache ['hɑ:teɪk] n chagrin m, douleur f
heart attack n crise f cardiaque
heartbeat ['hɑ:tbi:t] n battement m de cœur
heartbreak ['hɑ:tbreɪk] n immense chagrin m
heartbreaking ['hɑ:tbreɪkɪŋ] adj navrant(e), déchirant(e)
heartbroken ['hɑ:trəʊkən] adj: **to be ~** avoir beaucoup de chagrin
heartburn ['hɑ:tbə:n] n brûlures fpl d'estomac
heart disease n maladie f cardiaque
-hearted ['hɑ:tɪd] suffix: **kind~** généreux(-euse), qui a bon cœur
heartening ['hɑ:tnɪŋ] adj encourageant(e), réconfortant(e)
heart failure n (Med) arrêt m du cœur
heartfelt ['hɑ:tfɛlt] adj sincère
hearth [hɑ:θ] n foyer m, cheminée f
heartily ['hɑ:tɪlɪ] adv chaleureusement; (laugh) de bon cœur; (eat) de bon appétit; **to agree ~** être entièrement d'accord; **to be ~ sick of** (Brit) en avoir ras le bol de
heartland ['hɑ:tlænd] n centre m, cœur m; **France's ~s** la France profonde
heartless ['hɑ:tlɪs] adj (person) sans cœur, insensible; (treatment) cruel(le)
heartstrings ['hɑ:tstrɪŋz] npl: **to tug (at) sb's ~** toucher or faire vibrer les cordes sensibles de qn
heartthrob ['hɑ:tθrɔb] n idole f
heart-to-heart ['hɑ:t'tə'hɑ:t] adj, adv à cœur ouvert
heart transplant n greffe f du cœur
heartwarming ['hɑ:twɔ:mɪŋ] adj réconfortant(e)
hearty ['hɑ:tɪ] adj chaleureux(-euse); (appetite) solide; (dislike) cordial(e); (meal) copieux(-euse)
heat [hi:t] n chaleur f; (fig) ardeur f; feu m; (Sport: also: **qualifying heat**) éliminatoire f; (Zool): **in** or **on ~** (Brit) en chaleur ▷ vt chauffer
▶ **heat up** vi (liquid) chauffer; (room) se réchauffer ▷ vt réchauffer
heated ['hi:tɪd] adj chauffé(e); (fig) passionné(e), échauffé(e), excité(e)
heater ['hi:tər] n appareil m de chauffage; radiateur m; (in car) chauffage m; (water heater) chauffe-eau m
heath [hi:θ] n (Brit) lande f
heathen ['hi:ðn] adj, n païen(ne)
heather ['hɛðər] n bruyère f
heating ['hi:tɪŋ] n chauffage m
heat-resistant ['hi:trɪzɪstənt] adj résistant(e) à la chaleur
heat-seeking ['hi:tsi:kɪŋ] adj guidé(e) par infrarouge
heatstroke ['hi:tstrəʊk] n coup m de chaleur

heatwave ['hi:tweɪv] n vague f de chaleur
heave [hi:v] vt soulever (avec effort) ▷ vi se soulever; (retch) avoir des haut-le-cœur ▷ n (push) poussée f; **to ~ a sigh** pousser un gros soupir
heaven ['hɛvn] n ciel m, paradis m; (fig) paradis; **~ forbid!** surtout pas!; **thank ~!** Dieu merci!; **for ~`s sake!** (pleading) je vous en prie!; (protesting) mince alors!
heavenly ['hɛvnlɪ] adj céleste, divin(e)
heavily ['hɛvɪlɪ] adv lourdement; (drink, smoke) beaucoup; (sleep, sigh) profondément
heavy ['hɛvɪ] adj lourd(e); (work, rain, user, eater) gros(se); (drinker, smoker) grand(e); (schedule, week) chargé(e); **it's too ~** c'est trop lourd; **it's ~ going** ça ne va pas tout seul, c'est pénible
heavy cream n (US) crème fraîche épaisse
heavy-duty ['hɛvɪdju:tɪ] adj à usage intensif
heavy goods vehicle n (Brit) poids lourd m
heavy-handed ['hɛvɪhændɪd] adj (fig) maladroit(e), qui manque de tact
heavy metal n (Mus) heavy metal m
heavy-set ['hɛvɪ'sɛt] adj (esp US) costaud(e)
heavyweight ['hɛvɪweɪt] n (Sport) poids lourd
Hebrew ['hi:bru:] adj hébraïque ▷ n (Ling) hébreu m
Hebrides ['hɛbrɪdi:z] npl: **the ~** les Hébrides fpl
heck [hɛk] n (inf): **why the ~ ...?** pourquoi diable ...?; **a ~ of a lot** une sacrée quantité; **he has done a ~ of a lot for us** il a vraiment beaucoup fait pour nous
heckle ['hɛkl] vt interpeller (un orateur)
heckler ['hɛklər] n interrupteur m; élément perturbateur
hectare ['hɛktɑ:r] n (Brit) hectare m
hectic ['hɛktɪk] adj (schedule) très chargé(e); (day) mouvementé(e); (activity) fiévreux(-euse); (lifestyle) trépidant(e)
he'd [hi:d] = **he would; he had**
hedge [hɛdʒ] n haie f ▷ vi se dérober ▷ vt: **to ~ one's bets** (fig) se couvrir; **as a ~ against inflation** pour se prémunir contre l'inflation
▶ **hedge in** vt entourer d'une haie
hedgehog ['hɛdʒhɔg] n hérisson m
hedgerow ['hɛdʒrəʊ] n haie(s) f(pl)
hedonism ['hi:dənɪzəm] n hédonisme m
heed [hi:d] vt (also: **take heed of**) tenir compte de, prendre garde à
heedless ['hi:dlɪs] adj insouciant(e)
heel [hi:l] n talon m ▷ vt (shoe) retalonner; **to bring to ~** (dog) faire venir à ses pieds; (fig: person) rappeler à l'ordre; **to take to one's ~s** prendre ses jambes à son cou
hefty ['hɛftɪ] adj (person) costaud(e); (parcel) lourd(e); (piece, price) gros(se)
heifer ['hɛfər] n génisse f
height [haɪt] n (of person) taille f, grandeur f; (of object) hauteur f; (of plane, mountain) altitude f; (high ground) hauteur, éminence f; (fig: of glory, fame, power) sommet m; (: of luxury, stupidity) comble m; **at the ~ of summer** au cœur de l'été; **what ~ are you?** combien mesurez-vous?,

quelle est votre taille?; **of average ~** de taille moyenne; **to be afraid of ~s** être sujet(te) au vertige; **it's the ~ of fashion** c'est le dernier cri

heighten ['haɪtn] *vt* hausser, surélever; *(fig)* augmenter

heinous ['heɪnəs] *adj* odieux(-euse), atroce

heir [ɛə^r] *n* héritier *m*

heir apparent *n* héritier présomptif

heiress ['ɛərɛs] *n* héritière *f*

heirloom ['ɛəlu:m] *n* meuble *m* (*or* bijou *m or* tableau *m*) de famille

heist [haɪst] *n* (*US inf: hold-up*) casse *m*

held [hɛld] *pt, pp of* **hold**

helicopter ['hɛlɪkɔptə^r] *n* hélicoptère *m*

heliport ['hɛlɪpɔ:t] *n* (*Aviat*) héliport *m*

helium ['hi:lɪəm] *n* hélium *m*

hell [hɛl] *n* enfer *m*; **a ~ of a ...** (*inf*) un(e) sacré(e) ...; **oh ~!** (*inf*) merde!

he'll [hi:l] = **he will; he shall**

hell-bent [hɛl'bɛnt] *adj* (*inf*): **to be ~ on doing sth** vouloir à tout prix faire qch

hellish ['hɛlɪʃ] *adj* infernal(e)

hello [hə'ləu] *excl* bonjour!; (*to attract attention*) hé!; (*surprise*) tiens!

helm [hɛlm] *n* (*Naut*) barre *f*

helmet ['hɛlmɪt] *n* casque *m*

helmsman ['hɛlmzmən] (*irreg*) *n* timonier *m*

help [hɛlp] *n* aide *f*; (*cleaner etc*) femme *f* de ménage; (*assistant etc*) employé(e) ▷ *vt, vi* aider; **~! au secours!**; **~ yourself** servez-vous; **can you ~ me?** pouvez-vous m'aider?; **can I ~ you?** (*in shop*) vous désirez?; **with the ~ of** (*person*) avec l'aide de; (*tool etc*) à l'aide de; **to be of ~ to sb** être utile à qn; **to ~ sb (to) do sth** aider qn à faire qch; **I can't ~ saying** je ne peux pas m'empêcher de dire; **he can't ~ it** il n'y peut rien

▶ **help out** *vi* aider ▷ *vt*: **to ~ sb out** aider qn

helper ['hɛlpə^r] *n* aide *m/f*, assistant(e)

helpful ['hɛlpful] *adj* serviable, obligeant(e); (*useful*) utile

helping ['hɛlpɪŋ] *n* portion *f*

helping hand *n* coup *m* de main; **to give sb a ~** prêter main-forte à qn

helpless ['hɛlplɪs] *adj* impuissant(e); (*baby*) sans défense

helplessly ['hɛlplɪslɪ] *adv* (*watch*) sans pouvoir rien faire

helpline ['hɛlplaɪn] *n* service *m* d'assistance téléphonique; (*free*) ≈ numéro vert

Helsinki ['hɛlsɪŋkɪ] *n* Helsinki

helter-skelter ['hɛltə'skɛltə^r] *n* (*Brit: at amusement park*) toboggan *m*

hem [hɛm] *n* ourlet *m* ▷ *vt* ourler

▶ **hem in** *vt* cerner; **to feel ~med in** (*fig*) avoir l'impression d'étouffer, se sentir oppressé(e) *or* écrasé(e)

he-man ['hi:mæn] (*irreg*) *n* (*inf*) macho *m*

hematology ['hi:mə'tɔlədʒɪ] *n* (*US*) = **haematology**

hemisphere ['hɛmɪsfɪə^r] *n* hémisphère *m*

hemlock ['hɛmlɔk] *n* ciguë *f*

hemoglobin ['hi:mə'gləubɪn] *n* (*US*) = **haemoglobin**

hemophilia ['hi:mə'fɪlɪə] *n* (*US*) = **haemophilia**

hemorrhage ['hɛmərɪdʒ] *n* (*US*) = **haemorrhage**

hemorrhoids ['hɛmərɔɪdz] *npl* (*US*) = **haemorrhoids**

hemp [hɛmp] *n* chanvre *m*

hen [hɛn] *n* poule *f*; (*female bird*) femelle *f*

hence [hɛns] *adv* (*therefore*) d'où, de là; **2 years ~** d'ici 2 ans

henceforth [hɛns'fɔ:θ] *adv* dorénavant

henchman ['hɛntʃmən] (*irreg*) *n* (*pej*) acolyte *m*, séide *m*

henna ['hɛnə] *n* henné *m*

hen night, hen party *n* soirée *f* entre filles (*avant le mariage de l'une d'elles*)

henpecked ['hɛnpɛkt] *adj* dominé par sa femme

hepatitis [hɛpə'taɪtɪs] *n* hépatite *f*

her [hə:^r] *pron* (*direct*) la, l' + *vowel or h mute*; (*indirect*) lui; (*stressed, after prep*) elle ▷ *adj* son (sa), ses *pl*; **I see ~** je la vois; **give ~ a book** donne-lui un livre; **after ~** après elle; *see also* **me; my**

herald ['hɛrəld] *n* héraut *m* ▷ *vt* annoncer

heraldic [hɛ'rældɪk] *adj* héraldique

heraldry ['hɛrəldrɪ] *n* héraldique *f*; (*coat of arms*) blason *m*

herb [hə:b] *n* herbe *f*; **herbs** *npl* fines herbes

herbaceous [hə:'beɪʃəs] *adj* herbacé(e)

herbal ['hə:bl] *adj* à base de plantes

herbal tea *n* tisane *f*

herbicide ['hə:bɪsaɪd] *n* herbicide *m*

herd [hə:d] *n* troupeau *m*; (*of wild animals, swine*) troupeau, troupe *f* ▷ *vt* (*drive: animals, people*) mener, conduire; (*gather*) rassembler; **~ed together** parqués (comme du bétail)

here [hɪə^r] *adv* ici; (*time*) alors ▷ *excl* tiens!, tenez!; **~!** (*present*) présent!; **~ is, ~ are** voici; **~'s my sister** voici ma sœur; **~ he/she is** le (la) voici; **~ she comes** la voici qui vient; **come ~!** viens ici!; **~ and there** ici et là

hereabouts ['hɪərə'bauts] *adv* par ici, dans les parages

hereafter [hɪər'ɑ:ftə^r] *adv* après, plus tard; ci-après ▷ *n*: **the ~** l'au-delà *m*

hereby [hɪə'baɪ] *adv* (*in letter*) par la présente

hereditary [hɪ'rɛdɪtrɪ] *adj* héréditaire

heredity [hɪ'rɛdɪtɪ] *n* hérédité *f*

heresy ['hɛrəsɪ] *n* hérésie *f*

heretic ['hɛrətɪk] *n* hérétique *m/f*

heretical [hɪ'rɛtɪkl] *adj* hérétique

herewith [hɪə'wɪð] *adv* avec ceci, ci-joint

heritage ['hɛrɪtɪdʒ] *n* héritage *m*, patrimoine *m*; **our national ~** notre patrimoine national

hermetically [hə:'mɛtɪklɪ] *adv* hermétique

hermit ['hə:mɪt] *n* ermite *m*

hernia ['hə:nɪə] *n* hernie *f*

hero ['hɪərəu] (*pl ~es*) *n* héros *m*

heroic [hɪ'rəuɪk] *adj* héroïque

heroin ['hɛrəuɪn] *n* héroïne *f* (*drogue*)

heroin addict *n* héroïnomane *m/f*

heroine ['hɛrəuɪn] *n* héroïne *f (femme)*
heroism ['hɛrəuɪzəm] *n* héroïsme *m*
heron ['hɛrən] *n* héron *m*
hero worship *n* culte *m* (du héros)
herring ['hɛrɪŋ] *n* hareng *m*
hers [hə:z] *pron* le (la) sien(ne), les siens (siennes); **a friend of ~** un(e) ami(e) à elle, un(e) de ses ami(e)s; *see also* **mine¹**
herself [hə:'sɛlf] *pron (reflexive)* se; *(emphatic)* elle-même; *(after prep)* elle; *see also* **oneself**
Herts [hɑ:ts] *abbr (Brit)* = **Hertfordshire**
he's [hi:z] = **he is; he has**
hesitant ['hɛzɪtənt] *adj* hésitant(e), indécis(e); **to be ~ about doing sth** hésiter à faire qch
hesitate ['hɛzɪteɪt] *vi*: **to ~ (about/to do)** hésiter (sur/à faire)
hesitation [hɛzɪ'teɪʃən] *n* hésitation *f*; **I have no ~ in saying (that)** ... je n'hésiterais pas à dire (que) ...
hessian ['hɛsɪən] *n* (toile *f* de) jute *m*
heterogeneous ['hɛtərə'dʒi:nɪəs] *adj* hétérogène
heterosexual ['hɛtərəu'sɛksjuəl] *adj, n* hétérosexuel(le)
het up [hɛt'ʌp] *adj (inf)* agité(e), excité(e)
HEW *n abbr (US* = *Department of Health, Education and Welfare)* ministère de la santé publique, de l'enseignement et du bien-être
hew [hju:] *vt* tailler *(à la hache)*
hex [hɛks] *(US)* *n* sort *m* ▷ *vt* jeter un sort sur
hexagon ['hɛksəgən] *n* hexagone *m*
hexagonal [hɛk'sægənl] *adj* hexagonal(e)
hey [heɪ] *excl* hé!
heyday ['heɪdeɪ] *n*: **the ~ of** l'âge *m* d'or de, les beaux jours de
HF *n abbr* (= *high frequency*) HF *f*
HGV *n abbr* = **heavy goods vehicle**
HI *abbr (US)* = **Hawaii**
hi [haɪ] *excl* salut!; *(to attract attention)* hé!
hiatus [haɪ'eɪtəs] *n* trou *m*, lacune *f*; *(Ling)* hiatus *m*
hibernate ['haɪbəneɪt] *vi* hiberner
hibernation [haɪbə'neɪʃən] *n* hibernation *f*
hiccough, hiccup ['hɪkʌp] *vi* hoqueter ▷ *n* hoquet *m*; **to have (the) ~s** avoir le hoquet
hick [hɪk] *n (US inf)* plouc *m*, péquenaud(e)
hid [hɪd] *pt of* **hide**
hidden ['hɪdn] *pp of* **hide** ▷ *adj*: **there are no ~ extras** absolument tout est compris dans le prix; **~ agenda** intentions non déclarées
hide [haɪd] *(pt* **hid**, *pp* **hidden** [hɪd, 'hɪdn]) *n (skin)* peau *f* ▷ *vt* cacher; *(feelings, truth)* dissimuler; **to ~ sth from sb** cacher qch à qn ▷ *vi*: **to ~ (from sb)** se cacher (de qn)
hide-and-seek ['haɪdən'si:k] *n* cache-cache *m*
hideaway ['haɪdəweɪ] *n* cachette *f*
hideous ['hɪdɪəs] *adj* hideux(-euse), atroce
hide-out ['haɪdaut] *n* cachette *f*
hiding ['haɪdɪŋ] *n (beating)* correction *f*, volée *f* de coups; **to be in ~** *(concealed)* se tenir caché(e)
hiding place *n* cachette *f*
hierarchy ['haɪərɑ:kɪ] *n* hiérarchie *f*

hieroglyphic [haɪərə'glɪfɪk] *adj* hiéroglyphique; **hieroglyphics** *npl* hiéroglyphes *mpl*
hi-fi ['haɪfaɪ] *adj, n abbr* (= *high fidelity*) hi-fi *f inv*
higgledy-piggledy ['hɪgldɪ'pɪgldɪ] *adv* pêle-mêle, dans le plus grand désordre
high [haɪ] *adj* haut(e); *(speed, respect, number)* grand(e); *(price)* élevé(e); *(wind)* fort(e), violent(e); *(voice)* aigu(ë); *(inf: person: on drugs)* défoncé(e), fait(e); *(: on drink)* soûl(e), bourré(e); *(Brit Culin: meat, game)* faisandé(e); *(: spoilt)* avarié(e) ▷ *adv* haut, en haut ▷ *n (weather)* zone *f* de haute pression; **exports have reached a new ~** les exportations ont atteint un nouveau record; **20 m ~** haut(e) de 20 m; **to pay a ~ price for sth** payer cher pour qch; **~ in the air** haut dans le ciel
highball ['haɪbɔ:l] *n (US)* whisky *m* à l'eau avec des glaçons
highboy ['haɪbɔɪ] *n (US)* grande commode
highbrow ['haɪbrau] *adj, n* intellectuel(le)
highchair ['haɪtʃɛəʳ] *n (child's)* chaise haute
high-class ['haɪ'klɑ:s] *adj (neighbourhood, hotel)* chic *inv*, de grand standing; *(performance etc)* de haut niveau
High Court *n (Law)* cour *f* suprême; *voir article*

● **HIGH COURT**
●
● Dans le système juridique anglais et gallois,
● la *High Court* est une cour de droit civil
● chargée des affaires plus importantes et
● complexes que celles traitées par les "county
● courts". En Écosse en revanche, la *High Court*
● *(of Justiciary)* est la plus haute cour de justice
● à laquelle les affaires les plus graves telles
● que le meurtre et le viol sont soumises et où
● elles sont jugées devant un jury.

higher ['haɪəʳ] *adj (form of life, study etc)* supérieur(e) ▷ *adv* plus haut
higher education *n* études supérieures
highfalutin [haɪfə'lu:tɪn] *adj (inf)* affecté(e)
high finance *n* la haute finance
high-flier, high-flyer ['haɪ'flaɪəʳ] *n (fig: ambitious)* ambitieux(-euse); *(: gifted)* personne particulièrement douée et promise à un avenir brillant
high-flying ['haɪ'flaɪɪŋ] *adj (fig)* ambitieux(-euse), de haut niveau
high-handed ['haɪ'hændɪd] *adj* très autoritaire; très cavalier(-ière)
high-heeled ['haɪ'hi:ld] *adj* à hauts talons
high heels *npl* talons hauts, hauts talons
high jump *n (Sport)* saut *m* en hauteur
highlands ['haɪləndz] *npl* région montagneuse; **the H~** *(in Scotland)* les Highlands *mpl*
high-level ['haɪlɛvl] *adj (talks etc)* à un haut niveau; **~ language** *(Comput)* langage évolué
highlight ['haɪlaɪt] *n (fig: of event)* point culminant ▷ *vt (emphasize)* faire ressortir, souligner; **highlights** *npl (in hair)* reflets *mpl*
highlighter ['haɪlaɪtəʳ] *n (pen)* surligneur (lumineux)

highly ['haɪlɪ] adv extrêmement, très; (unlikely) fort; (recommended, skilled, qualified) hautement; ~ **paid** très bien payé(e); **to speak ~ of** dire beaucoup de bien de

highly strung adj nerveux(-euse), toujours tendu(e)

High Mass n grand-messe f

highness ['haɪnɪs] n hauteur f; **His/Her H~** son Altesse f

high-pitched [haɪ'pɪtʃt] adj aigu(ë)

high point n: **the ~ (of)** le clou (de), le point culminant (de)

high-powered ['haɪ'pauəd] adj (engine) performant(e); (fig: person) dynamique; (: job, businessman) très important(e)

high-pressure ['haɪprɛʃəʳ] adj à haute pression

high-rise ['haɪraɪz] n (also: **high-rise block, high-rise building**) tour f (d'habitation)

high school n lycée m; (US) établissement m d'enseignement supérieur; voir article

● **HIGH SCHOOL**
●
● Une high school est un établissement
● d'enseignement secondaire. Aux États-
● Unis, il y a la "Junior High School", qui
● correspond au collège, et la "Senior High
● School", qui correspond au lycée. En Grande-
● Bretagne, c'est un nom que l'on donne
● parfois aux écoles secondaires; voir
● "elementary school".

high season n (Brit) haute saison

high spirits npl pétulance f; **to be in ~** être plein(e) d'entrain

high street n (Brit) grand-rue f

high-tech ['haɪ'tɛk] (inf) adj de pointe

highway ['haɪweɪ] n (Brit) route f; (US) route nationale; **the information ~** l'autoroute f de l'information

Highway Code n (Brit) code m de la route

highwayman ['haɪweɪmən] (irreg) n voleur m de grand chemin

hijack ['haɪdʒæk] vt détourner (par la force) ▷ n (also: **hijacking**) détournement m (d'avion)

hijacker ['haɪdʒækəʳ] n auteur m d'un détournement d'avion, pirate m de l'air

hike [haɪk] vi faire des excursions à pied ▷ n excursion f à pied, randonnée f; (inf: in prices etc) augmentation f ▷ vt (inf) augmenter

hiker ['haɪkəʳ] n promeneur(-euse), excursionniste m/f

hiking ['haɪkɪŋ] n excursions fpl à pied, randonnée f

hilarious [hɪ'lɛərɪəs] adj (behaviour, event) désopilant(e)

hilarity [hɪ'lærɪtɪ] n hilarité f

hill [hɪl] n colline f; (fairly high) montagne f; (on road) côte f

hillbilly ['hɪlbɪlɪ] n (US) montagnard(e) du sud des USA; (pej) péquenaud m

hillock ['hɪlək] n petite colline, butte f

hillside ['hɪlsaɪd] n (flanc m de) coteau m

hill start n (Aut) démarrage m en côte

hill walking ['hɪl'wɔːkɪŋ] n randonnée f de basse montagne

hilly ['hɪlɪ] adj vallonné(e), montagneux(-euse); (road) à fortes côtes

hilt [hɪlt] n (of sword) garde f; **to the ~** (fig: support) à fond

him [hɪm] pron (direct) le, l' + vowel or h mute; (stressed, indirect, after prep) lui; **I see ~** je le vois; **give ~ a book** donne-lui un livre; **after ~** après lui; see also **me**

Himalayas [hɪmə'leɪəz] npl: **the ~** l'Himalaya m

himself [hɪm'sɛlf] pron (reflexive) se; (emphatic) lui-même; (after prep) lui; see also **oneself**

hind [haɪnd] adj de derrière ▷ n biche f

hinder ['hɪndəʳ] vt gêner; (delay) retarder; (prevent): **to ~ sb from doing** empêcher qn de faire

hindquarters ['haɪnd'kwɔːtəz] npl (Zool) arrière-train m

hindrance ['hɪndrəns] n gêne f, obstacle m

hindsight ['haɪndsaɪt] n bon sens après coup; **with (the benefit of) ~** avec du recul, rétrospectivement

Hindu ['hɪnduː] n Hindou(e)

Hinduism ['hɪnduɪzəm] n (Rel) hindouisme m

hinge [hɪndʒ] n charnière f ▷ vi (fig): **to ~ on** dépendre de

hint [hɪnt] n allusion f; (advice) conseil m; (clue) indication f ▷ vt: **to ~ that** insinuer que ▷ vi: **to ~ at** faire une allusion à; **to drop a ~** faire une allusion or insinuation; **give me a ~** (clue) mettez-moi sur la voie, donnez-moi une indication

hip [hɪp] n hanche f; (Bot) fruit m de l'églantier or du rosier

hip flask n flacon m (pour la poche)

hip hop n hip hop m

hippie, hippy ['hɪpɪ] n hippie m/f

hippo ['hɪpəu] (pl **-s**) n hippopotame m

hippopotamus [hɪpə'pɔtəməs] (pl **-es** or **hippopotami** [hɪpə'pɔtəmɪ]) n hippopotame m

hippy ['hɪpɪ] n = **hippie**

hire ['haɪəʳ] vt (Brit: car, equipment) louer; (worker) embaucher, engager ▷ n location f; **for ~** à louer; (taxi) libre; **on ~** en location; **I'd like to ~ a car** je voudrais louer une voiture
▶ **hire out** vt louer

hire car, hired car ['haɪəd-] n (Brit) voiture f de location

hire purchase n (Brit) achat m (or vente f) à tempérament or crédit; **to buy sth on ~** acheter qch en location-vente

his [hɪz] pron le (la) sien(ne), les siens (siennes) ▷ adj son (sa), ses pl; **this is ~** c'est à lui, c'est le sien; **a friend of ~** un(e) de ses ami(e)s, un(e) ami(e) à lui; see also **mine**[1]; see also **my**

Hispanic [hɪs'pænɪk] adj (in US) hispano-américain(e) ▷ n Hispano-Américain(e)

hiss [hɪs] vi siffler ▷ n sifflement m

histogram ['hɪstəgræm] n histogramme m

historian [hɪ'stɔːrɪən] n historien(ne)
historic [hɪ'stɔrɪk], **historical** [hɪ'stɔrɪkl] adj historique
history ['hɪstərɪ] n histoire f; **medical ~** (of patient) passé médical
histrionics [hɪstrɪ'ɔnɪks] n gestes mpl dramatiques, cinéma m (fig)
hit [hɪt] vt (pt, pp **-**) frapper; (knock against) cogner; (reach: target) atteindre, toucher; (collide with: car) entrer en collision avec, heurter; (fig: affect) toucher; (find) tomber sur ▷ n coup m; (success) coup réussi; succès m; (song) chanson f à succès, tube m; (to website) visite f; (on search engine) résultat m de recherche; **to ~ it off with sb** bien s'entendre avec qn; **to ~ the headlines** être à la une des journaux; **to ~ the road** (inf) se mettre en route
▸ **hit back** vi: **to ~ back at sb** prendre sa revanche sur qn
▸ **hit on** vt fus (answer) trouver (par hasard); (solution) tomber sur (par hasard)
▸ **hit out at** vt fus envoyer un coup à; (fig) attaquer
▸ **hit upon** vt fus = **hit on**
hit-and-miss ['hɪtænd'mɪs] adj au petit bonheur (la chance)
hit-and-run driver ['hɪtænd'rʌn-] n chauffard m
hitch [hɪtʃ] vt (fasten) accrocher, attacher; (also: **hitch up**) remonter d'une saccade ▷ vi faire de l'autostop ▷ n (knot) nœud m; (difficulty) anicroche f, contretemps m; **to ~ a lift** faire du stop; **technical ~** incident m technique
▸ **hitch up** vt (horse, cart) atteler; see also **hitch**
hitch-hike ['hɪtʃhaɪk] vi faire de l'auto-stop
hitch-hiker ['hɪtʃhaɪkəʳ] n auto-stoppeur(-euse)
hitch-hiking ['hɪtʃhaɪkɪŋ] n auto-stop m, stop m (inf)
hi-tech ['haɪ'tɛk] adj de pointe ▷ n high-tech m
hitherto [hɪðə'tuː] adv jusqu'ici, jusqu'à présent
hit list n liste noire
hitman ['hɪtmæn] (irreg) n (inf) tueur m à gages
hit-or-miss ['hɪtə'mɪs] adj au petit bonheur (la chance); **it's ~ whether ...** il est loin d'être certain que ... + sub
hit parade n hit parade m
HIV n abbr (= human immunodeficiency virus) HIV m, VIH m; **~-negative/positive** séronégatif(-ive)/positif(-ive)
hive [haɪv] n ruche f; **the shop was a ~ of activity** (fig) le magasin était une véritable ruche
▸ **hive off** vt (inf) mettre à part, séparer
hl abbr (= hectolitre) hl
HM abbr (= His (or Her) Majesty) SM
HMG abbr (Brit) = **His (or Her) Majesty's Government**
HMI n abbr (Brit Scol) = **His (or Her) Majesty's Inspector**
HMO n abbr (US: = health maintenance organization) organisme médical assurant un forfait entretien de santé

HMS abbr (Brit) = **His (or Her) Majesty's Ship**
HMSO n abbr (Brit: = His (or Her) Majesty's Stationery Office) ≈ Imprimerie nationale
HNC n abbr (Brit: = Higher National Certificate) ≈ DUT m
HND n abbr (Brit: = Higher National Diploma) ≈ licence f de sciences et techniques
hoard [hɔːd] n (of food) provisions fpl, réserves fpl; (of money) trésor m ▷ vt amasser
hoarding ['hɔːdɪŋ] n (Brit) panneau m d'affichage or publicitaire
hoarfrost ['hɔːfrɔst] n givre m
hoarse [hɔːs] adj enroué(e)
hoax [həuks] n canular m
hob [hɔb] n plaque chauffante
hobble ['hɔbl] vi boitiller
hobby ['hɔbɪ] n passe-temps favori
hobby-horse ['hɔbɪhɔːs] n cheval m à bascule; (fig) dada m
hobnob ['hɔbnɔb] vi: **to ~ with** frayer avec, fréquenter
hobo ['həubəu] n (US) vagabond m
hock [hɔk] n (Brit: wine) vin m du Rhin; (of animal: Culin) jarret m
hockey ['hɔkɪ] n hockey m
hockey stick n crosse f de hockey
hocus-pocus ['həukəs'pəukəs] n (trickery) supercherie f; (words: of magician) formules fpl magiques; (: jargon) galimatias m
hod [hɔd] n oiseau m, hotte f
hodgepodge ['hɔdʒpɔdʒ] n = **hotchpotch**
hoe [həu] n houe f, binette f ▷ vt (ground) biner; (plants etc) sarcler
hog [hɔg] n porc (châtré) ▷ vt (fig) accaparer; **to go the whole ~** aller jusqu'au bout
Hogmanay [hɔgmə'neɪ] n réveillon m du jour de l'An, Saint-Sylvestre f; voir article

▸ **HOGMANAY**

La Saint-Sylvestre ou "New Year's Eve" se nomme Hogmanay en Écosse. En cette occasion, la famille et les amis se réunissent pour entendre sonner les douze coups de minuit et pour fêter le "first-footing", une coutume qui veut qu'on se rende chez ses amis et voisins en apportant quelque chose à boire (du whisky en général) et un morceau de charbon en gage de prospérité pour la nouvelle année.

hogwash ['hɔgwɔʃ] n (inf) foutaises fpl
hoist [hɔɪst] n palan m ▷ vt hisser
hoity-toity [hɔɪtɪ'tɔɪtɪ] adj (inf) prétentieux(-euse), qui se donne
hold [həuld] (pt, pp **held** [hɛld]) vt tenir; (contain) contenir; (meeting) tenir; (keep back) retenir; (believe) maintenir; considérer; (possess) avoir; détenir ▷ vi (withstand pressure) tenir (bon); (be valid) valoir; (on telephone) attendre ▷ n prise f; (find) influence f; (Naut) cale f; **to catch** or **get (a) ~ of** saisir; **to get ~ of** (find) trouver; **to get ~**

of o.s. se contrôler; **~ the line!** (Tel) ne quittez pas!; **to ~ one's own** (fig) (bien) se défendre; **to ~ office** (Pol) avoir un portefeuille; **to ~ firm** or **fast** tenir bon; **he ~s the view that ...** il pense or estime que ..., d'après lui ...; **to ~ sb responsible for sth** tenir qn pour responsable de qch

▶ **hold back** vt retenir; (secret) cacher; **to ~ sb back from doing sth** empêcher qn de faire qch

▶ **hold down** vt (person) maintenir à terre; (job) occuper

▶ **hold forth** vi pérorer

▶ **hold off** vt tenir à distance ▷ vi: **if the rain ~s off** s'il ne pleut pas, s'il ne se met pas à pleuvoir

▶ **hold on** vi tenir bon; (wait) attendre; **~ on!** (Tel) ne quittez pas!; **to ~ on to sth** (grasp) se cramponner à qch; (keep) conserver or garder qch

▶ **hold out** vt offrir ▷ vi (resist): **to ~ out (against)** résister (devant), tenir bon (devant)

▶ **hold over** vt (meeting etc) ajourner, reporter

▶ **hold up** vt (raise) lever; (support) soutenir; (delay) retarder; (: traffic) ralentir; (rob) braquer

holdall ['həʊldɔːl] n (Brit) fourre-tout m inv

holder ['həʊldə'] n (container) support m; (of ticket, record) détenteur(-trice); (of office, title, passport etc) titulaire m/f

holding ['həʊldɪŋ] n (share) intérêts mpl; (farm) ferme f

holding company n holding m

hold-up ['həʊldʌp] n (robbery) hold-up m; (delay) retard m; (Brit: in traffic) embouteillage m

hole [həʊl] n trou m ▷ vt trouer, faire un trou dans; **~ in the heart** (Med) communication f interventriculaire; **to pick ~s (in)** (fig) chercher des poux (dans)

▶ **hole up** vi se terrer

holiday ['hɔlədɪ] n (Brit: vacation) vacances fpl; (day off) jour m de congé; (public) jour férié; **to be on ~** être en vacances; **I'm here on ~** je suis ici en vacances; **tomorrow is a ~** demain c'est fête, on a congé demain

holiday camp n (Brit: for children) colonie f de vacances; (also: **holiday centre**) camp m de vacances

holiday job n (Brit) boulot m (inf) de vacances

holiday-maker ['hɔlədɪmeɪkə'] n (Brit) vacancier(-ière)

holiday pay n paie f des vacances

holiday resort n centre m de villégiature or de vacances

holiday season n période f des vacances

holiness ['həʊlɪnɪs] n sainteté f

holistic [həʊ'lɪstɪk] adj holiste, holistique

Holland ['hɔlənd] n Hollande f

holler ['hɔlə'] vi (inf) brailler

hollow ['hɔləʊ] adj creux(-euse); (fig) faux (fausse) ▷ n creux m; (in land) dépression f (de terrain), cuvette f ▷ vt: **to ~ out** creuser, évider

holly ['hɔlɪ] n houx m

hollyhock ['hɔlɪhɔk] n rose trémière

holocaust ['hɔləkɔːst] n holocauste m

hologram ['hɔləgræm] n hologramme m

hols [hɔlz] npl (inf) vacances fpl

holster ['həʊlstə'] n étui m de revolver

holy ['həʊlɪ] adj saint(e); (bread, water) bénit(e); (ground) sacré(e)

Holy Communion n la (sainte) communion

Holy Ghost, Holy Spirit n Saint-Esprit m

Holy Land n: **the ~** la Terre Sainte

holy orders npl ordres (majeurs)

homage ['hɔmɪdʒ] n hommage m; **to pay ~ to** rendre hommage à

home [həʊm] n foyer m, maison f; (country) pays natal, patrie f; (institution) maison ▷ adj de famille; (Econ, Pol) national(e), intérieur(e); (Sport: team) qui reçoit; (: match, win) sur leur (or notre) terrain ▷ adv chez soi, à la maison; au pays natal; (right in: nail etc) à fond; **at ~** chez soi, à la maison; **to go (or come) ~** rentrer (chez soi), rentrer à la maison (or au pays); **I'm going ~ on Tuesday** je rentre mardi; **make yourself at ~** faites comme chez vous; **near my ~** près de chez moi

▶ **home in on** vt fus (missile) se diriger automatiquement vers or sur

home address n domicile permanent

home-brew [həʊm'bruː] n vin m (or bière f) maison

homecoming ['həʊmkʌmɪŋ] n retour m (au bercail)

home computer n ordinateur m domestique

Home Counties npl les comtés autour de Londres

home economics n économie f domestique

home ground n: **to be on ~** être sur son terrain

home-grown ['həʊmgrəʊn] adj (not foreign) du pays; (from garden) du jardin

home help n (Brit) aide-ménagère f

homeland ['həʊmlænd] n patrie f

homeless ['həʊmlɪs] adj sans foyer, sans abri; **the homeless** npl les sans-abri mpl

home loan n prêt m sur hypothèque

homely ['həʊmlɪ] adj (plain) simple, sans prétention; (welcoming) accueillant(e)

home-made [həʊm'meɪd] adj fait(e) à la maison

home match n match m à domicile

Home Office n (Brit) ministère m de l'Intérieur

homeopathy etc [həʊmɪ'ɔpəθɪ] (US) = **homoeopathy** etc

home owner ['həʊməʊnə'] n propriétaire occupant

home page n (Comput) page f d'accueil

home rule n autonomie f

Home Secretary n (Brit) ministre m de l'Intérieur

homesick ['həʊmsɪk] adj: **to be ~** avoir le mal du pays; (missing one's family) s'ennuyer de sa famille

homestead ['həʊmstɛd] n propriété f; (farm) ferme f

home town n ville natale

home truth n: **to tell sb a few ~s** dire ses quatre vérités à qn

homeward ['həʊmwəd] *adj* (*journey*) du retour
 ▷ *adv* = **homewards**
homewards ['həʊmwədz] *adv* vers la maison
homework ['həʊmwəːk] *n* devoirs *mpl*
homicidal [hɒmɪˈsaɪdl] *adj* homicide
homicide ['hɒmɪsaɪd] *n* (*US*) homicide *m*
homily ['hɒmɪlɪ] *n* homélie *f*
homing ['həʊmɪŋ] *adj* (*device, missile*) à tête
 chercheuse; ~ **pigeon** pigeon voyageur
homoeopath ['həʊmɪəʊpæθ], (*US*) **homeopath**
 n homéopathe *m/f*
homoeopathic, (*US*) **homeopathic**
 [həʊmɪɔ'pəθɪk] *adj* (*medicine*) homéopathique;
 (*doctor*) homéopathe
homoeopathy, (*US*) **homeopathy**
 [həʊmɪˈɔpəθɪ] *n* homéopathie *f*
homogeneous [hɒməʊˈdʒiːnɪəs] *adj* homogène
homogenize [həˈmɔdʒənaɪz] *vt* homogénéiser
homosexual [hɒməʊˈsɛksjʊəl] *adj, n*
 homosexuel(le)
Hon. *abbr* (= *honourable, honorary*) *dans un titre*
Honduras [hɒnˈdjʊərəs] *n* Honduras *m*
hone [həʊn] *n* pierre *f* à aiguiser ▷ *vt* affûter,
 aiguiser
honest ['ɔnɪst] *adj* honnête; (*sincere*) franc
 (franche); **to be quite ~ with you ...** à dire
 vrai ...
honestly ['ɔnɪstlɪ] *adv* honnêtement;
 franchement
honesty ['ɔnɪstɪ] *n* honnêteté *f*
honey ['hʌnɪ] *n* miel *m*; (*inf: darling*) chéri(e)
honeycomb ['hʌnɪkəʊm] *n* rayon *m* de miel;
 (*pattern*) nid *m* d'abeilles, motif alvéolé ▷ *vt* (*fig*):
 to ~ with cribler de
honeymoon ['hʌnɪmuːn] *n* lune *f* de miel,
 voyage *m* de noces; **we're on ~** nous sommes en
 voyage de noces
honeysuckle ['hʌnɪsʌkl] *n* chèvrefeuille *m*
Hong Kong ['hɔŋ'kɔŋ] *n* Hong Kong
honk [hɔŋk] *n* (*Aut*) coup *m* de klaxon ▷ *vi*
 klaxonner
Honolulu [hɔnə'luːluː] *n* Honolulu
honorary ['ɔnərərɪ] *adj* honoraire; (*duty, title*)
 honorifique; ~ **degree** diplôme *m* honoris
 causa
honour, (*US*) **honor** ['ɔnə^r] *vt* honorer ▷ *n*
 honneur *m*; **in ~ of** en l'honneur de; **to**
 graduate with ~s obtenir sa licence avec
 mention
honourable, (*US*) **honorable** ['ɔnərəbl] *adj*
 honorable
honour-bound, (*US*) **honor-bound** ['ɔnə'baʊnd]
 adj: **to be ~ to do** se devoir de faire
honours degree ['ɔnəz-] *n* (*Scol*) ≈ licence *f* avec
 mention; *voir article*

⊕ **HONOURS DEGREE**
⊕
⊕ Un *honours degree* est un diplôme
⊕ universitaire que l'on reçoit après trois
⊕ années d'études en Angleterre et quatre
⊕ années en Écosse. Les mentions qui

⊕ l'accompagnent sont, par ordre décroissant:
⊕ "first class" (très bien/bien), "upper second
⊕ class" (assez bien), "lower second class"
⊕ (passable), et "third class" (diplôme sans
⊕ mention). Le titulaire d'un *honours degree* a
⊕ un titre qu'il peut mettre à la suite de son
⊕ nom, par exemple: Peter Jones BA Hons; voir
⊕ "ordinary degree".

honours list *n* (*Brit*): *voir article*

⊕ **HONOURS LIST**
⊕
⊕ L' *honours list* est la liste des citoyens du
⊕ Royaume-Uni et du Commonwealth
⊕ auxquels le souverain confère un titre ou
⊕ une décoration. Cette liste est préparée par
⊕ le Premier ministre et paraît deux fois par
⊕ an, au Nouvel An et lors de l'anniversaire
⊕ officiel du règne du souverain. Des
⊕ personnes qui se sont distinguées dans le
⊕ monde des affaires, des sports et des médias,
⊕ ainsi que dans les forces armées, mais
⊕ également des citoyens "ordinaires" qui se
⊕ consacrent à des œuvres de charité sont
⊕ ainsi récompensées.

Hons. *abbr* (*Scol*) = **honours degree**
hood [hʊd] *n* capuchon *m*; (*of cooker*) hotte *f*; (*Brit*
 Aut) capote *f*; (*US Aut*) capot *m*; (*inf*) truand *m*
hoodie ['hʊdɪ] *n* (*top*) sweat *m* à capuche; (*youth*)
 jeune *m* à capuche
hoodlum ['huːdləm] *n* truand *m*
hoodwink ['hʊdwɪŋk] *vt* tromper
hoof (*pl* **-s** *or* **hooves**) [huːf, huːvz] *n* sabot *m*
hook [hʊk] *n* crochet *m*; (*on dress*) agrafe *f*; (*for*
 fishing) hameçon *m* ▷ *vt* accrocher; (*dress*)
 agrafer; **off the ~** (*Tel*) décroché; **~ and eye**
 agrafe; **by ~ or by crook** de gré ou de force,
 coûte que coûte; **to be ~ed (on)** (*inf*) être
 accroché(e) (par); (*person*) être dingue (de)
 ▶ **hook up** *vt* (*Radio, TV etc*) faire un duplex entre
hooligan ['huːlɪɡən] *n* voyou *m*
hoop [huːp] *n* cerceau *m*; (*of barrel*) cercle *m*
hoot [huːt] *vi* (*Brit: Aut*) klaxonner; (*siren*) mugir;
 (*owl*) hululer ▷ *vt* (*jeer at*) huer ▷ *n* huée *f*; coup
 m de klaxon; mugissement *m*; hululement *m*;
 to ~ with laughter rire aux éclats
hooter ['huːtə^r] *n* (*Brit Aut*) klaxon *m*; (*Naut,*
 factory) sirène *f*
Hoover® ['huːvə^r] *n* (*Brit*) aspirateur *m* ▷ *vt*: **to**
 hoover (*room*) passer l'aspirateur dans; (*carpet*)
 passer l'aspirateur sur
hooves [huːvz] *npl of* **hoof**
hop [hɔp] *vi* sauter; (*on one foot*) sauter à cloche-
 pied; (*bird*) sautiller ▷ *n* saut *m*
hope [həʊp] *vt, vi* espérer ▷ *n* espoir *m*; **I ~ so** je
 l'espère; **I ~ not** j'espère que non
hopeful ['həʊpful] *adj* (*person*) plein(e) d'espoir;
 (*situation*) prometteur(-euse), encourageant(e);
 I'm ~ that she'll manage to come j'ai bon
 espoir qu'elle pourra venir

hopefully ['həupfulɪ] adv (expectantly) avec espoir, avec optimisme; (one hopes) avec un peu de chance; ~, **they'll come back** espérons bien qu'ils reviendront

hopeless ['həuplɪs] adj désespéré(e), sans espoir; (useless) nul(le)

hopelessly ['həuplɪslɪ] adv (live etc) sans espoir; ~ **confused** etc complètement désorienté etc

hops [hɔps] npl houblon m

horizon [hə'raɪzn] n horizon m

horizontal [hɔrɪ'zɔntl] adj horizontal(e)

hormone ['hɔːməun] n hormone f

hormone replacement therapy n hormonothérapie substitutive, traitement hormono-supplétif

horn [hɔːn] n corne f; (Mus) cor m; (Aut) klaxon m

horned [hɔːnd] adj (animal) à cornes

hornet ['hɔːnɪt] n frelon m

horny ['hɔːnɪ] adj corné(e); (hands) calleux(-euse); (inf: aroused) excité(e)

horoscope ['hɔrəskəup] n horoscope m

horrendous [hə'rɛndəs] adj horrible, affreux(-euse)

horrible ['hɔrɪbl] adj horrible, affreux(-euse)

horrid ['hɔrɪd] adj (person) détestable; (weather, place, smell) épouvantable

horrific [hɔ'rɪfɪk] adj horrible

horrify ['hɔrɪfaɪ] vt horrifier

horrifying ['hɔrɪfaɪɪŋ] adj horrifiant(e)

horror ['hɔrəʳ] n horreur f

horror film n film m d'épouvante

horror-struck ['hɔrəstrʌk], **horror-stricken** ['hɔrəstrɪkn] adj horrifié(e)

hors d'œuvre [ɔː'dəːvrə] n hors d'œuvre m

horse [hɔːs] n cheval m

horseback ['hɔːsbæk]: **on ~** (adj, adv) à cheval

horsebox ['hɔːsbɔks] n van m

horse chestnut n (nut) marron m (d'Inde); (tree) marronnier m (d'Inde)

horse-drawn ['hɔːsdrɔːn] adj tiré(e) par des chevaux

horsefly ['hɔːsflaɪ] n taon m

horseman ['hɔːsmən] (irreg) n cavalier m

horsemanship ['hɔːsmənʃɪp] n talents mpl de cavalier

horseplay ['hɔːspleɪ] n chahut m (blagues etc)

horsepower ['hɔːspauəʳ] n puissance f (en chevaux); (unit) cheval-vapeur m (CV)

horse-racing ['hɔːsreɪsɪŋ] n courses fpl de chevaux

horseradish ['hɔːsrædɪʃ] n raifort m

horse riding n (Brit) équitation f

horseshoe ['hɔːsʃuː] n fer m à cheval

horse show n concours m hippique

horse-trading ['hɔːstreɪdɪŋ] n maquignonnage m

horse trials npl = **horse show**

horsewhip ['hɔːswɪp] vt cravacher

horsewoman ['hɔːswumən] (irreg) n cavalière f

horsey ['hɔːsɪ] adj féru(e) d'équitation or de cheval; (appearance) chevalin(e)

horticulture ['hɔːtɪkʌltʃəʳ] n horticulture f

hose [həuz] n (also: **hosepipe**) tuyau m; (also: **garden hose**) tuyau d'arrosage
▸ **hose down** vt laver au jet

hosepipe ['həuzpaɪp] n tuyau m; (in garden) tuyau d'arrosage; (for fire) tuyau d'incendie

hosiery ['həuzɪərɪ] n (rayon m des) bas mpl

hospice ['hɔspɪs] n hospice m

hospitable ['hɔspɪtəbl] adj hospitalier(-ière)

hospital ['hɔspɪtl] n hôpital m; **in ~**, (US) **in the ~** à l'hôpital; **where's the nearest ~?** où est l'hôpital le plus proche?

hospitality [hɔspɪ'tælɪtɪ] n hospitalité f

hospitalize ['hɔspɪtəlaɪz] vt hospitaliser

host [həust] n hôte m; (in hotel etc) patron m; (TV, Radio) présentateur(-trice), animateur(-trice); (large number): **a ~ of** une foule de; (Rel) hostie f
▹ vt (TV programme) présenter, animer

hostage ['hɔstɪdʒ] n otage m

host country n pays m d'accueil, pays-hôte m

hostel ['hɔstl] n foyer m; (also: **youth hostel**) auberge f de jeunesse

hostelling ['hɔstlɪŋ] n: **to go (youth) ~** faire une virée or randonnée en séjournant dans des auberges de jeunesse

hostess ['həustɪs] n hôtesse f; (Brit: also: **air hostess**) hôtesse de l'air; (TV, Radio) animatrice f; (in nightclub) entraîneuse f

hostile ['hɔstaɪl] adj hostile

hostility [hɔ'stɪlɪtɪ] n hostilité f

hot [hɔt] adj chaud(e); (as opposed to only warm) très chaud; (spicy) fort(e); (fig: contest) acharné(e); (topic) brûlant(e); (temper) violent(e), passionné(e); **to be ~** (person) avoir chaud; (thing) être (très) chaud; (weather) faire chaud
▸ **hot up** (Brit inf) vi (situation) devenir tendu(e); (party) s'animer ▹ vt (pace) accélérer, forcer; (engine) gonfler

hot-air balloon [hɔt'ɛə-] n montgolfière f, ballon m

hotbed ['hɔtbɛd] n (fig) foyer m, pépinière f

hotchpotch ['hɔtʃpɔtʃ] n (Brit) mélange m hétéroclite

hot dog n hot-dog m

hotel [həu'tɛl] n hôtel m

hotelier [həu'tɛlɪəʳ] n hôtelier(-ière)

hotel industry n industrie hôtelière

hotel room n chambre f d'hôtel

hot flush n (Brit) bouffée f de chaleur

hotfoot ['hɔtfut] adv à toute vitesse

hothead ['hɔthɛd] n (fig) tête brûlée

hotheaded [hɔt'hɛdɪd] adj impétueux(-euse)

hothouse ['hɔthaus] n serre chaude

hotline ['hɔtlaɪn] n (Pol) téléphone m rouge, ligne directe

hotly ['hɔtlɪ] adv passionnément, violemment

hotplate ['hɔtpleɪt] n (on cooker) plaque chauffante

hotpot ['hɔtpɔt] n (Brit Culin) ragoût m

hot potato n (Brit inf) sujet brûlant; **to drop sb/ sth like a ~** laisser tomber qn/qch brusquement

hot seat *n* (*fig*) poste chaud

hot spot *n* point chaud

hot spring *n* source thermale

hot-tempered ['hɔt'tɛmpəd] *adj* emporté(e)

hot-water bottle [hɔt'wɔːtə-] *n* bouillotte *f*

hot-wire ['hɔtwaɪəʳ] *vt* (*inf: car*) démarrer en faisant se toucher les fils de contact

hound [haund] *vt* poursuivre avec acharnement ▷ *n* chien courant; **the ~s** la meute

hour ['auəʳ] *n* heure *f*; **at 30 miles an ~** ≈ à 50 km à l'heure; **lunch ~** heure du déjeuner; **to pay sb by the ~** payer qn à l'heure

hourly ['auəlɪ] *adj* toutes les heures; (*rate*) horaire; **~ paid** *adj* payé(e) à l'heure

house *n* [haus] (*pl* **-s** ['hauzɪz]) maison *f*; (*Pol*) chambre *f*; (*Theat*) salle *f*; auditoire *m* ▷ *vt* [hauz] (*person*) loger, héberger; **at** (*or* **to**) **my ~** chez moi; **the H~ of Commons/of Lords** (*Brit*) la Chambre des communes/des lords; *voir article*; **the H~ (of Representatives)** (*US*) la Chambre des représentants; *voir article*; **on the ~** (*fig*) aux frais de la maison

● **HOUSE OF COMMONS/OF LORDS**
●
● Le parlement en Grande-Bretagne est
● constitué de deux assemblées: la *House of*
● *Commons*, présidée par le "Speaker" et
● composée de plus de 600 députés (les "MP")
● élus au suffrage universel direct. Ceux-ci
● reçoivent tous un salaire. La Chambre des
● communes siège environ 175 jours par an.
● La *House of Lords*, présidée par le "Lord
● Chancellor" et composée de membres du
● haut clergé et de lords séculiers dont le titre
● est, soit héréditaire, soit attribué par le
● souverain (dans ce dernier cas, il peut être
● héréditaire ou à vie); elle peut amender
● certains projets de loi votés par la *House of*
● *Commons*, mais elle n'est pas habilitée à
● débattre des projets de lois de finances. La
● *House of Lords* fait également office de la
● juridiction suprême en Angleterre et au
● pays de Galles.

● **HOUSE OF REPRESENTATIVES**
●
● Aux États-Unis, le parlement, appelé le
● "Congress", est constitué du "Senate" et de
● la *House of Representatives*. Cette dernière
● comprend 435 membres, le nombre de ces
● représentants par État étant proportionnel
● à la densité de population de cet État. Ils
● sont élus pour deux ans au suffrage
● universel direct et siègent au "Capitol", à
● Washington D.C.

house arrest *n* assignation *f* à domicile

houseboat ['hausbəut] *n* bateau (aménagé en habitation)

housebound ['hausbaund] *adj* confiné(e)

chez soi

housebreaking ['hausbreɪkɪŋ] *n* cambriolage *m* (avec effraction)

house-broken ['hausbrəukn] *adj* (*US*) = **house-trained**

housecoat ['hauskəut] *n* peignoir *m*

household ['haushəuld] *n* (*Admin etc*) ménage *m*; (*people*) famille *f*, maisonnée *f*; **~ name** nom connu de tout le monde

householder ['haushəuldəʳ] *n* propriétaire *m/f*; (*head of house*) chef *m* de famille

househunting ['haushʌntɪŋ] *n*: **to go ~** se mettre en quête d'une maison (*or* d'un appartement)

housekeeper ['hauskiːpəʳ] *n* gouvernante *f*

housekeeping ['hauskiːpɪŋ] *n* (*work*) ménage *m*; (*also*: **housekeeping money**) argent *m* du ménage; (*Comput*) gestion *f* (des disques)

houseman ['hausmən] (*irreg*) *n* (*Brit Med*) ≈ interne *m*

house-owner ['hausəunəʳ] *n* propriétaire *m/f* (*de maison ou d'appartement*)

house-proud ['hauspraud] *adj* qui tient à avoir une maison impeccable

house-to-house ['haustə'haus] *adj* (*enquiries etc*) chez tous les habitants (du quartier *etc*)

house-train ['haustreɪn] *vt* (*pet*) apprendre à être propre à

house-trained ['haustreɪnd] *adj* (*pet*) propre

house-warming ['hauswɔːmɪŋ] *n* (*also*: **house-warming party**) pendaison *f* de crémaillère

housewife (*irreg*) ['hauswaɪf] *n* ménagère *f*; femme *f* au foyer

house wine *n* cuvée *f* maison *or* du patron

housework ['hauswəːk] *n* (travaux *mpl* du) ménage *m*

housing ['hauzɪŋ] *n* logement *m* ▷ *cpd* (*problem, shortage*) de *or* du logement

housing association *n* fondation *f* charitable fournissant des logements

housing benefit *n* (*Brit*) ≈ allocations *fpl* logement

housing development, (*Brit*) **housing estate** *n* (*blocks of flats*) cité *f*; (*houses*) lotissement *m*

hovel ['hɔvl] *n* taudis *m*

hover ['hɔvəʳ] *vi* planer; **to ~ round sb** rôder *or* tourner autour de qn

hovercraft ['hɔvəkrɑːft] *n* aéroglisseur *m*, hovercraft *m*

hoverport ['hɔvəpɔːt] *n* hoverport *m*

how [hau] *adv* comment; **~ are you?** comment allez-vous?; **~ do you do?** bonjour; (*on being introduced*) enchanté(e); **~ far is it to …?** combien y a-t-il jusqu'à …?; **~ long have you been here?** depuis combien de temps êtes-vous là?; **~ lovely/awful!** que *or* comme c'est joli/affreux!; **~ many/much?** combien?; **~ much time/many people?** combien de temps/gens?; **~ much does it cost?** ça coûte combien?; **~ old are you?** quel âge avez-vous?; **~ tall is he?** combien mesure-t-il?; **~ is school?** ça va à l'école?; **~ was the film?** comment était le film?; **~'s life?** (*inf*) comment ça va?; **~ about a drink?** si on buvait quelque chose?; **~ is it that ...?** comment se fait-il que ... + *sub*?

however [hau'εvə'] *conj* pourtant, cependant ▷ *adv* de quelque façon *or* manière que + *sub*; (+ *adjective*) quelque *or* si ... que + *sub*; (*in questions*) comment; **~ I do it** de quelque manière que je m'y prenne; **~ cold it is** même s'il fait très froid; **~ did you do it?** comment y êtes-vous donc arrivé?

howitzer ['hautsə'] *n* (*Mil*) obusier *m*

howl [haul] *n* hurlement *m* ▷ *vi* hurler; (*wind*) mugir

howler ['haulə'] *n* gaffe *f*, bourde *f*

howling ['haulɪŋ] *adj*: **a ~ wind** *or* **gale** un vent à décorner les bœufs

H.P. *n abbr* (*Brit*) = **hire purchase**

h.p. *abbr* (*Aut*) = **horsepower**

HQ *n abbr* (= *headquarters*) QG *m*

HR *n abbr* (*US*) = **House of Representatives**

hr *abbr* (= *hour*) h

HRH *abbr* (= *His* (*or Her*) *Royal Highness*) SAR

hrs *abbr* (= *hours*) h

HRT *n abbr* = **hormone replacement therapy**

HS *abbr* (*US*) = **high school**

HST *abbr* (*US*: = *Hawaiian Standard Time*) heure de Hawaii

HTML *n abbr* (= *hypertext markup language*) HTML *m*

hub [hʌb] *n* (*of wheel*) moyeu *m*; (*fig*) centre *m*, foyer *m*

hubbub ['hʌbʌb] *n* brouhaha *m*

hubcap [hʌbkæp] *n* (*Aut*) enjoliveur *m*

HUD *n abbr* (*US*: = *Department of Housing and Urban Development*) ministère de l'urbanisme et du logement

huddle ['hʌdl] *vi*: **to ~ together** se blottir les uns contre les autres

hue [hju:] *n* teinte *f*, nuance *f*; **~ and cry** *n* tollé (général), clameur *f*

huff [hʌf] *n*: **in a ~** fâché(e); **to take the ~** prendre la mouche

huffy ['hʌfɪ] *adj* (*inf*) froissé(e)

hug [hʌg] *vt* serrer dans ses bras; (*shore, kerb*) serrer ▷ *n* étreinte *f*; **to give sb a ~** serrer qn dans ses bras

huge [hju:dʒ] *adj* énorme, immense

hulk [hʌlk] *n* (*ship*) vieux rafiot; (*car, building*) carcasse *f*; (*person*) mastodonte *m*, malabar *m*

hulking ['hʌlkɪŋ] *adj* balourd(e)

hull [hʌl] *n* (*of ship*) coque *f*; (*of nuts*) coque; (*of peas*) cosse *f*

hullabaloo ['hʌləbə'lu:] *n* (*inf: noise*) tapage *m*, raffut *m*

hullo [hə'ləu] *excl* = **hello**

hum [hʌm] *vt* (*tune*) fredonner ▷ *vi* fredonner; (*insect*) bourdonner; (*plane, tool*) vrombir ▷ *n* fredonnement *m*; bourdonnement *m*; vrombissement *m*

human ['hju:mən] *adj* humain(e) ▷ *n* (*also*: **human being**) être humain

humane [hju:'meɪn] *adj* humain(e), humanitaire

humanism ['hju:mənɪzəm] *n* humanisme *m*

humanitarian [hju:mænɪ'tɛərɪən] *adj* humanitaire

humanity [hju:'mænɪtɪ] *n* humanité *f*

humanly ['hju:mənlɪ] *adv* humainement

humanoid ['hju:mənɔɪd] *adj, n* humanoïde *m/f*

human rights *npl* droits *mpl* de l'homme

humble ['hʌmbl] *adj* humble, modeste ▷ *vt* humilier

humbly ['hʌmblɪ] *adv* humblement, modestement

humbug ['hʌmbʌg] *n* fumisterie *f*; (*Brit: sweet*) bonbon *m* à la menthe

humdrum ['hʌmdrʌm] *adj* monotone, routinier(-ière)

humid ['hju:mɪd] *adj* humide

humidifier [hju:'mɪdɪfaɪə'] *n* humidificateur *m*

humidity [hju:'mɪdɪtɪ] *n* humidité *f*

humiliate [hju:'mɪlɪeɪt] *vt* humilier

humiliating [hju:'mɪlɪeɪtɪŋ] *adj* humiliant(e)

humiliation [hju:mɪlɪ'eɪʃən] *n* humiliation *f*

humility [hju:'mɪlɪtɪ] *n* humilité *f*

hummus ['huməs] *n* houm(m)ous *m*

humorist ['hju:mərɪst] *n* humoriste *m/f*

humorous ['hju:mərəs] *adj* humoristique; (*person*) plein(e) d'humour

humour, (*US*) **humor** ['hju:mə'] *n* humour *m*; (*mood*) humeur *f* ▷ *vt* (*person*) faire plaisir à; se prêter aux caprices de; **sense of ~** sens *m* de l'humour; **to be in a good/bad ~** être de bonne/mauvaise humeur

humourless, (*US*) **humorless** ['hu:məlɪs] *adj* dépourvu(e) d'humour

hump [hʌmp] *n* bosse *f*

humpback ['hʌmpbæk] *n* bossu(e); (*Brit: also*: **humpback bridge**) dos-d'âne *m*

humus ['hju:məs] *n* humus *m*

hunch [hʌntʃ] *n* bosse *f*; (*premonition*) intuition *f*; **I have a ~ that** j'ai (comme une vague) idée que

hunchback ['hʌntʃbæk] *n* bossu(e)

hunched [hʌntʃt] *adj* arrondi(e), voûté(e)

hundred ['hʌndrəd] *num* cent; **about a ~ people** une centaine de personnes; **~s of** des centaines de; **I'm a ~ per cent sure** j'en suis absolument certain

hundredth [-ɪdθ] *num* centième

hundredweight ['hʌndrɪdweɪt] *n* (*Brit*) =50.8 kg; 112 lb; (*US*) = 45.3 kg; 100 lb

hung [hʌŋ] *pt, pp of* **hang**

Hungarian [hʌŋ'gɛərɪən] *adj* hongrois(e) ▷ *n* Hongrois(e); (*Ling*) hongrois *m*

Hungary ['hʌŋgərɪ] *n* Hongrie *f*

hunger ['hʌŋgə'] *n* faim *f* ▷ *vi*: **to ~ for** avoir faim de, désirer ardemment

hunger strike *n* grève *f* de la faim

hungover [hʌŋ'əuvə'] *adj* (*inf*): **to be ~** avoir la gueule de bois

hungrily ['hʌŋgrəlɪ] *adv* voracement; (*fig*) avidement

hungry ['hʌŋgrɪ] *adj* affamé(e); **to be ~** avoir faim; **~ for** (*fig*) avide de

hung up *adj* (*inf*) complexé(e), bourré(e) de complexes

hunk [hʌŋk] *n* gros morceau; (*inf: man*) beau mec

hunt [hʌnt] *vt* (*seek*) chercher; (*criminal*) pourchasser; (*Sport*) chasser ▷ *vi* (*search*): **to ~ for** chercher (partout); (*Sport*) chasser ▷ *n* (*Sport*) chasse *f*
▶ **hunt down** *vt* pourchasser

hunter ['hʌntə'] *n* chasseur *m*; (*Brit: horse*) cheval *m* de chasse

hunting ['hʌntɪŋ] *n* chasse *f*

hurdle ['hə:dl] *n* (*for fences*) claie *f*; (*Sport*) haie *f*; (*fig*) obstacle *m*

hurl [hə:l] *vt* lancer (avec violence); (*abuse, insults*) lancer

hurling ['hə:lɪŋ] *n* (*Sport*) genre de hockey joué en Irlande

hurly-burly ['hə:lɪ'bə:lɪ] *n* tohu-bohu *m inv*; brouhaha *m*

hurrah, hurray [hu'rɑ:, hu'reɪ] *excl* hourra!

hurricane ['hʌrɪkən] *n* ouragan *m*

hurried ['hʌrɪd] *adj* pressé(e), précipité(e); (*work*) fait(e) à la hâte

hurriedly ['hʌrɪdlɪ] *adv* précipitamment, à la hâte

hurry ['hʌrɪ] *n* hâte *f*, précipitation *f* ▷ *vi* se presser, se dépêcher ▷ *vt* (*person*) faire presser, faire se dépêcher; (*work*) presser; **to be in a ~** être pressé(e); **to do sth in a ~** faire qch en vitesse; **to ~ in/out** entrer/sortir précipitamment; **to ~ home** se dépêcher de rentrer
▶ **hurry along** *vi* marcher d'un pas pressé
▶ **hurry away, hurry off** *vi* partir précipitamment
▶ **hurry up** *vi* se dépêcher

hurt [hə:t] (*pt, pp* **-**) *vt* (*cause pain to*) faire mal à; (*injure, fig*) blesser; (*damage: business, interests etc*) nuire à; faire du tort à ▷ *vi* faire mal ▷ *adj* blessé(e); **my arm ~s** j'ai mal au bras; **I ~ my arm** je me suis fait mal au bras; **to ~ o.s.** se faire mal; **where does it ~?** où avez-vous mal?, où est-ce que ça vous fait mal?

hurtful ['hə:tful] *adj* (*remark*) blessant(e)

hurtle ['hə:tl] *vt* lancer (de toutes ses forces) ▷ *vi*: **to ~ past** passer en trombe; **to ~ down** dégringoler

husband ['hʌzbənd] *n* mari *m*

hush [hʌʃ] *n* calme *m*, silence *m* ▷ *vt* faire taire; **~!** chut!
▶ **hush up** *vt* (*fact*) étouffer

hush-hush [hʌʃ'hʌʃ] *adj* (*inf*) ultra-secret(-ète)

husk [hʌsk] *n* (*of wheat*) balle *f*; (*of rice, maize*) enveloppe *f*; (*of peas*) cosse *f*

husky ['hʌskɪ] *adj* (*voice*) rauque; (*burly*) costaud(e) ▷ *n* chien *m* esquimau *or* de traîneau

hustings ['hʌstɪŋz] *npl* (*Brit Pol*) plate-forme électorale

hustle ['hʌsl] *vt* pousser, bousculer ▷ *n* bousculade *f*; **~ and bustle** *n* tourbillon *m* (d'activité)

hut [hʌt] *n* hutte *f*; (*shed*) cabane *f*

hutch [hʌtʃ] *n* clapier *m*

hyacinth ['haɪəsɪnθ] *n* jacinthe *f*

hybrid ['haɪbrɪd] *adj, n* hybride (*m*)

hydrant ['haɪdrənt] *n* prise *f* d'eau; (*also*: **fire hydrant**) bouche *f* d'incendie

hydraulic [haɪ'drɔ:lɪk] *adj* hydraulique

hydraulics [haɪ'drɔ:lɪks] *n* hydraulique *f*

hydrochloric ['haɪdrəu'klɔrɪk] *adj*: **~ acid** acide *m* chlorhydrique

hydroelectric ['haɪdrəuɪ'lɛktrɪk] *adj* hydro-électrique

hydrofoil ['haɪdrəfɔɪl] *n* hydrofoil *m*

hydrogen ['haɪdrədʒən] *n* hydrogène *m*

hydrogen bomb *n* bombe *f* à hydrogène

hydrophobia ['haɪdrə'fəubɪə] *n* hydrophobie *f*

hydroplane ['haɪdrəpleɪn] *n* (*seaplane*) hydravion *m*; (*jetfoil*) hydroglisseur *m*

hyena [haɪ'i:nə] *n* hyène *f*

hygiene ['haɪdʒi:n] *n* hygiène *f*

hygienic [haɪ'dʒi:nɪk] *adj* hygiénique

hymn [hɪm] *n* hymne *m*; cantique *m*

hype [haɪp] *n* (*inf*) matraquage *m* publicitaire *or* médiatique

hyperactive ['haɪpər'æktɪv] *adj* hyperactif(-ive)

hypermarket ['haɪpəmɑ:kɪt] (*Brit*) *n* hypermarché *m*

hypertension ['haɪpə'tɛnʃən] *n* (*Med*) hypertension *f*

hypertext ['haɪpətɛkst] *n* (*Comput*) hypertexte *m*

hyphen ['haɪfn] *n* trait *m* d'union

hypnosis [hɪp'nəusɪs] *n* hypnose *f*

hypnotic [hɪp'nɔtɪk] *adj* hypnotique

hypnotism ['hɪpnətɪzəm] *n* hypnotisme *m*

hypnotist ['hɪpnətɪst] *n* hypnotiseur(-euse)

hypnotize ['hɪpnətaɪz] *vt* hypnotiser

hypoallergenic ['haɪpəuælə'dʒɛnɪk] *adj* hypoallergénique

hypochondriac [haɪpə'kɔndrɪæk] *n* hypocondriaque *m/f*

hypocrisy [hɪ'pɔkrɪsɪ] *n* hypocrisie *f*

hypocrite ['hɪpəkrɪt] *n* hypocrite *m/f*

hypocritical [hɪpə'krɪtɪkl] *adj* hypocrite

hypodermic [haɪpə'də:mɪk] *adj* hypodermique ▷ *n* (*syringe*) seringue *f* hypodermique

hypotenuse [haɪ'pɔtɪnju:z] *n* hypoténuse *f*

hypothermia [haɪpə'θə:mɪə] *n* hypothermie *f*

hypothesis (*pl* **hypotheses**) [haɪ'pɔθɪsɪs, -si:z] *n* hypothèse *f*

hysterectomy [hɪstə'rɛktəmɪ] *n* hystérectomie *f*

hysteria [hɪ'stɪərɪə] *n* hystérie *f*

hysterical [hɪ'stɛrɪkl] *adj* hystérique; (*funny*) hilarant(e); **to become ~** avoir une crise de nerfs

hysterics [hɪ'stɛrɪks] *npl* (violente) crise de nerfs; (*laughter*) crise de rire; **to be in/have ~** (*anger, panic*) avoir une crise de nerfs; (*laughter*) attraper un fou rire

Hz *abbr* (= *hertz*) Hz

I i

I¹, i [aɪ] n (letter) I, i m; **I for Isaac,** (US) **I for Item** I comme Irma

I² [aɪ] pron je; (before vowel) j'; (stressed) moi ▷ abbr (= island, isle) I

IA, Ia. abbr (US) = **Iowa**

IAEA n abbr = **International Atomic Energy Agency**

IBA n abbr (Brit: = Independent Broadcasting Authority) ≈ CNCL f (= Commission nationale de la communication audio-visuelle)

Iberian [aɪˈbɪərɪən] adj ibérique, ibérien(ne)

Iberian Peninsula n: the ~ la péninsule Ibérique

IBEW n abbr (US: = International Brotherhood of Electrical Workers) syndicat international des électriciens

i/c abbr (Brit) = **in charge**

ICBM n abbr (= intercontinental ballistic missile) ICBM m, engin m balistique à portée intercontinentale

ICC n abbr (= International Chamber of Commerce) CCI f; (US) = **Interstate Commerce Commission**

ice [aɪs] n glace f; (on road) verglas m ▷ vt (cake) glacer; (drink) faire rafraîchir ▷ vi (also: **ice over**) geler; (also: **ice up**) se givrer; **to put sth on ~** (fig) mettre qch en attente

Ice Age n ère f glaciaire

ice axe, (US) **ice ax** n piolet m

iceberg [ˈaɪsbəːg] n iceberg m; **the tip of the ~** (also fig) la partie émergée de l'iceberg

icebox [ˈaɪsbɔks] n (US) réfrigérateur m; (Brit) compartiment m à glace; (insulated box) glacière f

icebreaker [ˈaɪsbreɪkər] n brise-glace m

ice bucket n seau m à glace

ice-cap [ˈaɪskæp] n calotte f glaciaire

ice-cold [aɪsˈkəuld] adj glacé(e)

ice cream n glace f

ice cube n glaçon m

iced [aɪst] adj (drink) frappé(e); (coffee, tea, also cake) glacé(e)

ice hockey n hockey m sur glace

Iceland [ˈaɪslənd] n Islande f

Icelander [ˈaɪsləndər] n Islandais(e)

Icelandic [aɪsˈlændɪk] adj islandais(e) ▷ n (Ling) islandais m

ice lolly n (Brit) esquimau m

ice pick n pic m à glace

ice rink n patinoire f

ice-skate [ˈaɪsskeɪt] n patin m à glace ▷ vi faire du patin à glace

ice skating [ˈaɪsskeɪtɪŋ] n patinage m (sur glace)

icicle [ˈaɪsɪkl] n glaçon m (naturel)

icing [ˈaɪsɪŋ] n (Aviat etc) givrage m; (Culin) glaçage m

icing sugar n (Brit) sucre m glace

ICJ n abbr = **International Court of Justice**

icon [ˈaɪkɔn] n icône f

ICR n abbr (US) = **Institute for Cancer Research**

ICRC n abbr (= International Committee of the Red Cross) CICR m

ICT n abbr (Brit: Scol: = information and communications technology) TIC fpl

ICU n abbr = **intensive care unit**

icy [ˈaɪsɪ] adj glacé(e); (road) verglacé(e); (weather, temperature) glacial(e)

ID abbr (US) = **Idaho**

I'd [aɪd] = **I would; I had**

Ida. abbr (US) = **Idaho**

ID card n carte f d'identité

IDD n abbr (Brit Tel: = international direct dialling) automatique international

idea [aɪˈdɪə] n idée f; **good ~!** bonne idée!; **to have an ~ that ...** avoir idée que ...; **I have no ~** je n'ai pas la moindre idée

ideal [aɪˈdɪəl] n idéal m ▷ adj idéal(e)

idealist [aɪˈdɪəlɪst] n idéaliste m/f

ideally [aɪˈdɪəlɪ] adv (preferably) dans l'idéal; (perfectly): **he is ~ suited to the job** il est parfait pour ce poste; **~ the book should have ...** l'idéal serait que le livre ait ...

identical [aɪˈdɛntɪkl] adj identique

identification [aɪdɛntɪfɪˈkeɪʃən] n identification f; **means of ~** pièce f d'identité

identify [aɪˈdɛntɪfaɪ] vt identifier ▷ vi: **to ~ with** s'identifier à

Identikit® [aɪˈdɛntɪkɪt] n: **~ (picture)** portrait-robot m

identity [aɪˈdɛntɪtɪ] n identité f

identity card n carte f d'identité

identity parade n (Brit) parade f d'identification

identity theft n usurpation f d'identité

ideological [aɪdɪə'lɔdʒɪkl] *adj* idéologique
ideology [aɪdɪ'ɔlədʒɪ] *n* idéologie *f*
idiocy ['ɪdɪəsɪ] *n* idiotie *f*, stupidité *f*
idiom ['ɪdɪəm] *n* (*language*) langue *f*, idiome *m*; (*phrase*) expression *f* idiomatique; (*style*) style *m*
idiomatic [ɪdɪə'mætɪk] *adj* idiomatique
idiosyncrasy [ɪdɪəu'sɪŋkrəsɪ] *n* particularité *f*, caractéristique *f*
idiot ['ɪdɪət] *n* idiot(e), imbécile *m/f*
idiotic [ɪdɪ'ɔtɪk] *adj* idiot(e), bête, stupide
idle ['aɪdl] *adj* (*doing nothing*) sans occupation, désœuvré(e); (*lazy*) oisif(-ive), paresseux(-euse); (*unemployed*) au chômage; (*machinery*) au repos; (*question, pleasures*) vain(e), futile ▷ *vi* (*engine*) tourner au ralenti; **to lie ~** être arrêté, ne pas fonctionner
  ▸ **idle away** *vt*: **to ~ away one's time** passer son temps à ne rien faire
idleness ['aɪdlnɪs] *n* désœuvrement *m*; oisiveté *f*
idler ['aɪdlə^r] *n* désœuvré(e), oisif(-ive)
idle time *n* (*Comm*) temps mort
idol ['aɪdl] *n* idole *f*
idolize ['aɪdəlaɪz] *vt* idolâtrer, adorer
idyllic [ɪ'dɪlɪk] *adj* idyllique
i.e. *abbr* (= *id est: that is*) c. à d., c'est-à-dire
if [ɪf] *conj* si ▷ *n*: **there are a lot of ifs and buts** il y a beaucoup de si *mpl* et de mais *mpl*; **I'd be pleased if you could do it** je serais très heureux si vous pouviez le faire; **if necessary** si nécessaire, le cas échéant; **if so** si c'est le cas; **if not** sinon; **if only I could!** si seulement je pouvais!; **if only he were here** si seulement il était là; **if only to show him my gratitude** ne serait-ce que pour lui témoigner ma gratitude; *see also* **as**; **even**
iffy ['ɪfɪ] *adj* (*inf*) douteux(-euse)
igloo ['ɪglu:] *n* igloo *m*
ignite [ɪg'naɪt] *vt* mettre le feu à, enflammer ▷ *vi* s'enflammer
ignition [ɪg'nɪʃən] *n* (*Aut*) allumage *m*; **to switch on/off the ~** mettre/couper le contact
ignition key *n* (*Aut*) clé *f* de contact
ignoble [ɪg'nəubl] *adj* ignoble, indigne
ignominious [ɪgnə'mɪnɪəs] *adj* honteux(-euse), ignominieux(-euse)
ignoramus [ɪgnə'reɪməs] *n* personne *f* ignare
ignorance ['ɪgnərəns] *n* ignorance *f*; **to keep sb in ~ of sth** tenir qn dans l'ignorance de qch
ignorant ['ɪgnərənt] *adj* ignorant(e); **to be ~ of** (*subject*) ne rien connaître en; (*events*) ne pas être au courant de
ignore [ɪg'nɔ:^r] *vt* ne tenir aucun compte de; (*mistake*) ne pas relever; (*person: pretend to not see*) faire semblant de ne pas reconnaître; (: *pay no attention to*) ignorer
ikon ['aɪkɔn] *n* = **icon**
IL *abbr* (*US*) = **Illinois**
ILA *n abbr* (*US*: = *International Longshoremen's Association*) syndicat international des dockers
ill [ɪl] *adj* (*sick*) malade; (*bad*) mauvais(e) ▷ *n* mal *m* ▷ *adv*: **to speak/think ~ of sb** dire/penser du mal de qn; **to be taken ~** tomber malade

Ill. *abbr* (*US*) = **Illinois**
I'll [aɪl] = **I will**; **I shall**
ill-advised [ɪləd'vaɪzd] *adj* (*decision*) peu judicieux(-euse); (*person*) malavisé(e)
ill-at-ease [ɪlət'i:z] *adj* mal à l'aise
ill-considered [ɪlkən'sɪdəd] *adj* (*plan*) inconsidéré(e), irréfléchi(e)
ill-disposed [ɪldɪs'pəuzd] *adj*: **to be ~ towards sb/sth** être mal disposé(e) envers qn/qch
illegal [ɪ'li:gl] *adj* illégal(e)
illegally [ɪ'li:gəlɪ] *adv* illégalement
illegible [ɪ'lɛdʒɪbl] *adj* illisible
illegitimate [ɪlɪ'dʒɪtɪmət] *adj* illégitime
ill-fated [ɪl'feɪtɪd] *adj* malheureux(-euse); (*day*) néfaste
ill-favoured, (*US*) **ill-favored** [ɪl'feɪvəd] *adj* déplaisant(e)
ill feeling *n* ressentiment *m*, rancune *f*
ill-gotten ['ɪlgɔtn] *adj* (*gains etc*) mal acquis(e)
ill health *n* mauvaise santé
illicit [ɪ'lɪsɪt] *adj* illicite
ill-informed [ɪlɪn'fɔ:md] *adj* (*judgment*) erroné(e); (*person*) mal renseigné(e)
illiterate [ɪ'lɪtərət] *adj* illettré(e); (*letter*) plein(e) de fautes
ill-mannered [ɪl'mænəd] *adj* impoli(e), grossier(-ière)
illness ['ɪlnɪs] *n* maladie *f*
illogical [ɪ'lɔdʒɪkl] *adj* illogique
ill-suited [ɪl'su:tɪd] *adj* (*couple*) mal assorti(e); **he is ~ to the job** il n'est pas vraiment fait pour ce travail
ill-timed [ɪl'taɪmd] *adj* inopportun(e)
ill-treat [ɪl'tri:t] *vt* maltraiter
ill-treatment [ɪl'tri:tmənt] *n* mauvais traitement
illuminate [ɪ'lu:mɪneɪt] *vt* (*room, street*) éclairer; (*for special effect*) illuminer; **~d sign** enseigne lumineuse
illuminating [ɪ'lu:mɪneɪtɪŋ] *adj* éclairant(e)
illumination [ɪlu:mɪ'neɪʃən] *n* éclairage *m*; illumination *f*
illusion [ɪ'lu:ʒən] *n* illusion *f*; **to be under the ~ that** avoir l'illusion que
illusive [ɪ'lu:sɪv], **illusory** [ɪ'lu:sərɪ] *adj* illusoire
illustrate ['ɪləstreɪt] *vt* illustrer
illustration [ɪlə'streɪʃən] *n* illustration *f*
illustrator ['ɪləstreɪtə^r] *n* illustrateur(-trice)
illustrious [ɪ'lʌstrɪəs] *adj* illustre
ill will *n* malveillance *f*
ILO *n abbr* (= *International Labour Organization*) OIT *f*
ILWU *n abbr* (*US*: = *International Longshoremen's and Warehousemen's Union*) syndicat international des dockers et des magasiniers
I'm [aɪm] = **I am**
image ['ɪmɪdʒ] *n* image *f*; (*public face*) image de marque
imagery ['ɪmɪdʒərɪ] *n* images *fpl*
imaginable [ɪ'mædʒɪnəbl] *adj* imaginable
imaginary [ɪ'mædʒɪnərɪ] *adj* imaginaire
imagination [ɪmædʒɪ'neɪʃən] *n* imagination *f*
imaginative [ɪ'mædʒɪnətɪv] *adj*

imaginatif(-ive); (person) plein(e)
d'imagination
imagine [ɪ'mædʒɪn] vt s'imaginer; (suppose)
imaginer, supposer
imbalance [ɪm'bæləns] n déséquilibre m
imbecile ['ɪmbəsiːl] n imbécile m/f
imbue [ɪm'bjuː] vt: **to ~ sth with** imprégner qch
de
IMF n abbr = **International Monetary Fund**
imitate ['ɪmɪteɪt] vt imiter
imitation [ɪmɪ'teɪʃən] n imitation f
imitator ['ɪmɪteɪtəʳ] n imitateur(-trice)
immaculate [ɪ'mækjulət] adj impeccable; (Rel)
immaculé(e)
immaterial [ɪmə'tɪərɪəl] adj sans importance,
insignifiant(e)
immature [ɪmə'tjuəʳ] adj (fruit) qui n'est pas
mûr(e); (person) qui manque de maturité
immaturity [ɪmə'tjuərɪtɪ] n immaturité f
immeasurable [ɪ'mɛʒrəbl] adj
incommensurable
immediacy [ɪ'miːdɪəsɪ] n (of events etc) caractère
or rapport immédiat; (of needs) urgence f
immediate [ɪ'miːdɪət] adj immédiat(e)
immediately [ɪ'miːdɪətlɪ] adv (at once)
immédiatement; **~ next to** juste à côté de
immense [ɪ'mɛns] adj immense, énorme
immensity [ɪ'mɛnsɪtɪ] n immensité f
immerse [ɪ'məːs] vt immerger, plonger; **to ~
sth in** plonger qch dans; **to be ~d in** (fig) être
plongé dans
immersion heater [ɪ'məːʃən-] n (Brit) chauffe-
eau m électrique
immigrant ['ɪmɪgrənt] n immigrant(e); (already
established) immigré(e)
immigration [ɪmɪ'greɪʃən] n immigration f
immigration authorities npl service m de
l'immigration
immigration laws npl lois fpl sur l'immigration
imminent ['ɪmɪnənt] adj imminent(e)
immobile [ɪ'məubaɪl] adj immobile
immobilize [ɪ'məubɪlaɪz] vt immobiliser
immoderate [ɪ'mɔdərət] adj immodéré(e),
démesuré(e)
immodest [ɪ'mɔdɪst] adj (indecent) indécent(e);
(boasting) pas modeste, présomptueux(-euse)
immoral [ɪ'mɔrl] adj immoral(e)
immorality [ɪmə'rælɪtɪ] n immoralité f
immortal [ɪ'mɔːtl] adj, n immortel(le)
immortalize [ɪ'mɔːtlaɪz] vt immortaliser
immovable [ɪ'muːvəbl] adj (object) fixe;
immobilier(-ière); (person) inflexible; (opinion)
immuable
immune [ɪ'mjuːn] adj: **~ (to)** immunisé(e)
(contre)
immune system n système m immunitaire
immunity [ɪ'mjuːnɪtɪ] n immunité f;
diplomatic ~ immunité diplomatique
immunization [ɪmjunaɪ'zeɪʃən] n
immunisation f
immunize ['ɪmjunaɪz] vt immuniser
imp [ɪmp] n (small devil) lutin m; (child) petit

diable
impact ['ɪmpækt] n choc m, impact m; (fig)
impact
impair [ɪm'pɛəʳ] vt détériorer, diminuer
impaired [ɪm'pɛəd] adj (organ, vision) abimé(e),
détérioré(e); **his memory/circulation is ~** il a
des problèmes de mémoire/circulation;
visually ~ malvoyant(e); **hearing ~**
malentendant(e); **mentally/physically ~**
intellectuellement/physiquement diminué(e)
impale [ɪm'peɪl] vt empaler
impart [ɪm'pɑːt] vt (make known) communiquer,
transmettre; (bestow) confier, donner
impartial [ɪm'pɑːʃl] adj impartial(e)
impartiality [ɪmpɑːʃɪ'ælɪtɪ] n impartialité f
impassable [ɪm'pɑːsəbl] adj infranchissable;
(road) impraticable
impasse [æm'pɑːs] n (fig) impasse f
impassioned [ɪm'pæʃənd] adj passionné(e)
impassive [ɪm'pæsɪv] adj impassible
impatience [ɪm'peɪʃəns] n impatience f
impatient [ɪm'peɪʃənt] adj impatient(e); **to get**
or **grow ~** s'impatienter
impatiently [ɪm'peɪʃəntlɪ] adv avec impatience
impeach [ɪm'piːtʃ] vt accuser, attaquer; (public
official) mettre en accusation
impeachment [ɪm'piːtʃmənt] n (Law) (mise f
en) accusation f
impeccable [ɪm'pɛkəbl] adj impeccable,
parfait(e)
impecunious [ɪmpɪ'kjuːnɪəs] adj sans
ressources
impede [ɪm'piːd] vt gêner
impediment [ɪm'pɛdɪmənt] n obstacle m; (also:
speech impediment) défaut m d'élocution
impel [ɪm'pɛl] vt (force): **to ~ sb (to do sth)**
forcer qn (à faire qch)
impending [ɪm'pɛndɪŋ] adj imminent(e)
impenetrable [ɪm'pɛnɪtrəbl] adj impénétrable
imperative [ɪm'pɛrətɪv] adj nécessaire; (need)
urgent(e), pressant(e); (tone) impérieux(-euse)
▷ n (Ling) impératif m
imperceptible [ɪmpə'sɛptɪbl] adj imperceptible
imperfect [ɪm'pəːfɪkt] adj imparfait(e); (goods
etc) défectueux(-euse) ▷ n (Ling: also: **imperfect
tense**) imparfait m
imperfection [ɪmpə'fɛkʃən] n imperfection f;
défectuosité f
imperial [ɪm'pɪərɪəl] adj impérial(e); (Brit:
measure) légal(e)
imperialism [ɪm'pɪərɪəlɪzəm] n impérialisme m
imperil [ɪm'pɛrɪl] vt mettre en péril
imperious [ɪm'pɪərɪəs] adj impérieux(-euse)
impersonal [ɪm'pəːsənl] adj impersonnel(le)
impersonate [ɪm'pəːsəneɪt] vt se faire passer
pour; (Theat) imiter
impersonation [ɪmpəːsə'neɪʃən] n (Law)
usurpation f d'identité; (Theat) imitation f
impersonator [ɪm'pəːsəneɪtəʳ] n imposteur m;
(Theat) imitateur(-trice)
impertinence [ɪm'pəːtɪnəns] n impertinence f,
insolence f

impertinent [ɪm'pə:tɪnənt] *adj* impertinent(e), insolent(e)

imperturbable [ɪmpə'tə:bəbl] *adj* imperturbable

impervious [ɪm'pə:vɪəs] *adj* imperméable; (*fig*): ~ **to** insensible à; inaccessible à

impetuous [ɪm'pɛtjuəs] *adj* impétueux(-euse), fougueux(-euse)

impetus ['ɪmpətəs] *n* impulsion *f*; (*of runner*) élan *m*

impinge [ɪm'pɪndʒ]: **to ~ on** *vt fus* (*person*) affecter, toucher; (*rights*) empiéter sur

impish ['ɪmpɪʃ] *adj* espiègle

implacable [ɪm'plækəbl] *adj* implacable

implant [ɪm'plɑ:nt] *vt* (*Med*) implanter; (*fig*: *idea*, *principle*) inculquer

implausible [ɪm'plɔ:zɪbl] *adj* peu plausible

implement *n* ['ɪmplɪmənt] outil *m*, instrument *m*; (*for cooking*) ustensile *m* ▷ *vt* ['ɪmplɪmɛnt] exécuter, mettre à effet

implicate ['ɪmplɪkeɪt] *vt* impliquer, compromettre

implication [ɪmplɪ'keɪʃən] *n* implication *f*; **by ~** indirectement

implicit [ɪm'plɪsɪt] *adj* implicite; (*complete*) absolu(e), sans réserve

implicitly [ɪm'plɪsɪtlɪ] *adv* implicitement; absolument, sans réserve

implore [ɪm'plɔ:ʳ] *vt* implorer, supplier

imply [ɪm'plaɪ] *vt* (*hint*) suggérer, laisser entendre; (*mean*) indiquer, supposer

impolite [ɪmpə'laɪt] *adj* impoli(e)

imponderable [ɪm'pɔndərəbl] *adj* impondérable

import *vt* [ɪm'pɔ:t] importer ▷ *n* ['ɪmpɔ:t] (*Comm*) importation *f*; (*meaning*) portée *f*, signification *f* ▷ *cpd* ['ɪmpɔ:t] (*duty, licence etc*) d'importation

importance [ɪm'pɔ:tns] *n* importance *f*; **to be of great/little ~** avoir beaucoup/peu d'importance

important [ɪm'pɔ:tnt] *adj* important(e); **it is ~ that** il importe que, il est important que; **it's not ~** c'est sans importance, ce n'est pas important

importantly [ɪm'pɔ:tntlɪ] *adv* (*with an air of importance*) d'un air important; (*essentially*): **but, more ~ ...** mais, (ce qui est) plus important encore ...

importation [ɪmpɔ:'teɪʃən] *n* importation *f*

imported [ɪm'pɔ:tɪd] *adj* importé(e), d'importation

importer [ɪm'pɔ:təʳ] *n* importateur(-trice)

impose [ɪm'pəuz] *vt* imposer ▷ *vi*: **to ~ on sb** abuser de la gentillesse de qn

imposing [ɪm'pəuzɪŋ] *adj* imposant(e), impressionnant(e)

imposition [ɪmpə'zɪʃən] *n* (*of tax etc*) imposition *f*; **to be an ~ on** (*person*) abuser de la gentillesse or la bonté de

impossibility [ɪmpɔsə'bɪlɪtɪ] *n* impossibilité *f*

impossible [ɪm'pɔsɪbl] *adj* impossible; **it is ~**

for me to leave il m'est impossible de partir

impostor [ɪm'pɔstəʳ] *n* imposteur *m*

impotence ['ɪmpətns] *n* impuissance *f*

impotent ['ɪmpətnt] *adj* impuissant(e)

impound [ɪm'paund] *vt* confisquer, saisir

impoverished [ɪm'pɔvərɪʃt] *adj* pauvre, appauvri(e)

impracticable [ɪm'præktɪkəbl] *adj* impraticable

impractical [ɪm'præktɪkl] *adj* pas pratique; (*person*) qui manque d'esprit pratique

imprecise [ɪmprɪ'saɪs] *adj* imprécis(e)

impregnable [ɪm'prɛgnəbl] *adj* (*fortress*) imprenable; (*fig*) inattaquable, irréfutable

impregnate ['ɪmprɛgneɪt] *vt* imprégner; (*fertilize*) féconder

impresario [ɪmprɪ'sɑ:rɪəu] *n* impresario *m*

impress [ɪm'prɛs] *vt* impressionner, faire impression sur; (*mark*) imprimer, marquer; **to ~ sth on sb** faire bien comprendre qch à qn

impressed [ɪm'prɛst] *adj* impressionné(e)

impression [ɪm'prɛʃən] *n* impression *f*; (*of stamp, seal*) empreinte *f*; (*imitation*) imitation *f*; **to make a good/bad ~ on sb** faire bonne/mauvaise impression sur qn; **to be under the ~ that** avoir l'impression que

impressionable [ɪm'prɛʃnəbl] *adj* impressionnable, sensible

impressionist [ɪm'prɛʃənɪst] *n* impressionniste *m/f*

impressive [ɪm'prɛsɪv] *adj* impressionnant(e)

imprint ['ɪmprɪnt] *n* empreinte *f*; (*Publishing*) notice *f*; (*: label*) nom *m* (de collection or d'éditeur)

imprinted [ɪm'prɪntɪd] *adj*: **~ on** imprimé(e) sur; (*fig*) imprimé(e) or gravé(e) dans

imprison [ɪm'prɪzn] *vt* emprisonner, mettre en prison

imprisonment [ɪm'prɪznmənt] *n* emprisonnement *m*; (*period*): **to sentence sb to 10 years' ~** condamner qn à 10 ans de prison

improbable [ɪm'prɔbəbl] *adj* improbable; (*excuse*) peu plausible

impromptu [ɪm'prɔmptju:] *adj* impromptu(e) ▷ *adv* impromptu

improper [ɪm'prɔpəʳ] *adj* (*wrong*) incorrect(e); (*unsuitable*) déplacé(e), de mauvais goût; (*indecent*) indécent(e); (*dishonest*) malhonnête

impropriety [ɪmprə'praɪətɪ] *n* inconvenance *f*; (*of expression*) impropriété *f*

improve [ɪm'pru:v] *vt* améliorer ▷ *vi* s'améliorer; (*pupil etc*) faire des progrès
  ▶ **improve on, improve upon** *vt fus* (*offer*) enchérir sur

improvement [ɪm'pru:vmənt] *n* amélioration *f*; (*of pupil etc*) progrès *m*; **to make ~s to** apporter des améliorations à

improvisation [ɪmprəvaɪ'zeɪʃən] *n* improvisation *f*

improvise ['ɪmprəvaɪz] *vt, vi* improviser

imprudence [ɪm'pru:dns] *n* imprudence *f*

imprudent [ɪm'pru:dnt] *adj* imprudent(e)

impudent ['ɪmpjudnt] *adj* impudent(e)

impugn [ɪmˈpjuːn] *vt* contester, attaquer
impulse [ˈɪmpʌls] *n* impulsion *f*; **on ~**
impulsivement, sur un coup de tête
impulse buy *n* achat *m* d'impulsion
impulsive [ɪmˈpʌlsɪv] *adj* impulsif(-ive)
impunity [ɪmˈpjuːnɪtɪ] *n*: **with ~** impunément
impure [ɪmˈpjuə^r] *adj* impur(e)
impurity [ɪmˈpjuərɪtɪ] *n* impureté *f*
IN *abbr* (US) = **Indiana**

 KEYWORD

in [ɪn] *prep* **1** (*indicating place, position*) dans; **in the house/the fridge** dans la maison/le frigo; **in the garden** dans le *or* au jardin; **in town** en ville; **in the country** à la campagne; **in school** à l'école; **in here/there** ici/là
2 (*with place names: of town, region, country*): **in London** à Londres; **in England** en Angleterre; **in Japan** au Japon; **in the United States** aux États-Unis
3 (*indicating time: during*): **in spring** au printemps; **in summer** en été; **in May/2005** en mai/2005; **in the afternoon** (dans) l'après-midi; **at 4 o'clock in the afternoon** à 4 heures de l'après-midi
4 (*indicating time: in the space of*) en; (: *future*) dans; **I did it in 3 hours/days** je l'ai fait en 3 heures/jours; **I'll see you in 2 weeks** *or* **in 2 weeks' time** je te verrai dans 2 semaines; **once in a hundred years** une fois tous les cent ans
5 (*indicating manner etc*) à; **in a loud/soft voice** à voix haute/basse; **in pencil** au crayon; **in writing** par écrit; **in French** en français; **to pay in dollars** payer en dollars; **the boy in the blue shirt** le garçon à *or* avec la chemise bleue
6 (*indicating circumstances*): **in the sun** au soleil; **in the shade** à l'ombre; **in the rain** sous la pluie; **a change in policy** un changement de politique
7 (*indicating mood, state*): **in tears** en larmes; **in anger** sous le coup de la colère; **in despair** au désespoir; **in good condition** en bon état; **to live in luxury** vivre dans le luxe
8 (*with ratios, numbers*): **1 in 10 households, 1 household in 10** 1 ménage sur 10; **20 pence in the pound** 20 pence par livre sterling; **they lined up in twos** ils se mirent en rangs (deux) par deux; **in hundreds** par centaines
9 (*referring to people, works*) chez; **the disease is common in children** c'est une maladie courante chez les enfants; **in (the works of) Dickens** chez Dickens, dans (l'œuvre de) Dickens
10 (*indicating profession etc*) dans; **to be in teaching** être dans l'enseignement
11 (*after superlative*) de; **the best pupil in the class** le meilleur élève de la classe
12 (*with present participle*): **in saying this** en disant ceci
▷ *adv*: **to be in** (*person: at home, work*) être là; (*train, ship, plane*) être arrivé(e); (*in fashion*) être à

la mode; **to ask sb in** inviter qn à entrer; **to run/limp** *etc* **in** entrer en courant/boitant *etc*; **their party is in** leur parti est au pouvoir
▷ *n*: **the ins and outs (of)** (*of proposal, situation etc*) les tenants et aboutissants (de)

in. *abbr* = **inch; inches**
inability [ɪnəˈbɪlɪtɪ] *n* incapacité *f*; **~ to pay** incapacité de payer
inaccessible [ɪnəkˈsɛsɪbl] *adj* inaccessible
inaccuracy [ɪnˈækjurəsɪ] *n* inexactitude *f*; manque *m* de précision
inaccurate [ɪnˈækjurət] *adj* inexact(e); (*person*) qui manque de précision
inaction [ɪnˈækʃən] *n* inaction *f*, inactivité *f*
inactivity [ɪnækˈtɪvɪtɪ] *n* inactivité *f*
inadequacy [ɪnˈædɪkwəsɪ] *n* insuffisance *f*
inadequate [ɪnˈædɪkwət] *adj* insuffisant(e), inadéquat(e)
inadmissible [ɪnədˈmɪsəbl] *adj* (*behaviour*) inadmissible; (*Law: evidence*) irrecevable
inadvertent [ɪnədˈvəːtnt] *adj* (*mistake*) commis(e) par inadvertance
inadvertently [ɪnədˈvəːtntlɪ] *adv* par mégarde
inadvisable [ɪnədˈvaɪzəbl] *adj* à déconseiller; **it is ~ to** il est déconseillé de
inane [ɪˈneɪn] *adj* inepte, stupide
inanimate [ɪnˈænɪmət] *adj* inanimé(e)
inapplicable [ɪnˈæplɪkəbl] *adj* inapplicable
inappropriate [ɪnəˈprəuprɪət] *adj* inopportun(e), mal à propos; (*word, expression*) impropre
inapt [ɪnˈæpt] *adj* inapte; peu approprié(e)
inaptitude [ɪnˈæptɪtjuːd] *n* inaptitude *f*
inarticulate [ɪnɑːˈtɪkjulət] *adj* (*person*) qui s'exprime mal; (*speech*) indistinct(e)
inasmuch [ɪnəzˈmʌtʃ] *adv*: **~ as** vu que, en ce sens que
inattention [ɪnəˈtɛnʃən] *n* manque *m* d'attention
inattentive [ɪnəˈtɛntɪv] *adj* inattentif(-ive), distrait(e); négligent(e)
inaudible [ɪnˈɔːdɪbl] *adj* inaudible
inaugural [ɪˈnɔːgjurəl] *adj* inaugural(e)
inaugurate [ɪˈnɔːgjureɪt] *vt* inaugurer; (*president, official*) investir de ses fonctions
inauguration [ɪnɔːgjuˈreɪʃən] *n* inauguration *f*; investiture *f*
inauspicious [ɪnɔːsˈpɪʃəs] *adj* peu propice
in-between [ɪnbɪˈtwiːn] *adj* entre les deux
inborn [ɪnˈbɔːn] *adj* (*feeling*) inné(e); (*defect*) congénital(e)
inbred [ɪnˈbrɛd] *adj* inné(e), naturel(le); (*family*) consanguin(e)
inbreeding [ɪnˈbriːdɪŋ] *n* croisement *m* d'animaux de même souche; unions consanguines
Inc. *abbr* = **incorporated**
Inca [ˈɪŋkə] *adj* (*also:* **Incan**) inca *inv* ▷ *n* Inca *m/f*
incalculable [ɪnˈkælkjuləbl] *adj* incalculable
incapability [ɪnkeɪpəˈbɪlɪtɪ] *n* incapacité *f*
incapable [ɪnˈkeɪpəbl] *adj*: **~ (of)** incapable (de)

incapacitate [ɪnkə'pæsɪteɪt] *vt*: **to ~ sb from doing** rendre qn incapable de faire

incapacitated [ɪnkə'pæsɪteɪtɪd] *adj* (*Law*) frappé(e) d'incapacité

incapacity [ɪnkə'pæsɪtɪ] *n* incapacité *f*

incarcerate [ɪn'kɑːsəreɪt] *vt* incarcérer

incarnate *adj* [ɪn'kɑːnɪt] incarné(e) ▷ *vt* ['ɪnkɑːneɪt] incarner

incarnation [ɪnkɑː'neɪʃən] *n* incarnation *f*

incendiary [ɪn'sɛndɪərɪ] *adj* incendiaire ▷ *n* (*bomb*) bombe *f* incendiaire

incense *n* ['ɪnsɛns] encens *m* ▷ *vt* [ɪn'sɛns] (*anger*) mettre en colère

incense burner *n* encensoir *m*

incentive [ɪn'sɛntɪv] *n* encouragement *m*, raison *f* de se donner de la peine

incentive scheme *n* système *m* de primes d'encouragement

inception [ɪn'sɛpʃən] *n* commencement *m*, début *m*

incessant [ɪn'sɛsnt] *adj* incessant(e)

incessantly [ɪn'sɛsntlɪ] *adv* sans cesse, constamment

incest ['ɪnsɛst] *n* inceste *m*

inch [ɪntʃ] *n* pouce *m* (=25 mm; 12 in a foot); **within an ~ of** à deux doigts de; **he wouldn't give an ~** (*fig*) il n'a pas voulu céder d'un pouce
▸ **inch forward** *vi* avancer petit à petit

inch tape *n* (*Brit*) centimètre *m* (de couturière)

incidence ['ɪnsɪdns] *n* (*of crime, disease*) fréquence *f*

incident ['ɪnsɪdnt] *n* incident *m*; (*in book*) péripétie *f*

incidental [ɪnsɪ'dɛntl] *adj* accessoire; (*unplanned*) accidentel(le); **~ to** qui accompagne; **~ expenses** faux frais *mpl*

incidentally [ɪnsɪ'dɛntəlɪ] *adv* (*by the way*) à propos

incidental music *n* musique *f* de fond

incident room *n* (*Police*) salle *f* d'opérations

incinerate [ɪn'sɪnəreɪt] *vt* incinérer

incinerator [ɪn'sɪnəreɪtəʳ] *n* incinérateur *m*

incipient [ɪn'sɪpɪənt] *adj* naissant(e)

incision [ɪn'sɪʒən] *n* incision *f*

incisive [ɪn'saɪsɪv] *adj* incisif(-ive), mordant(e)

incisor [ɪn'saɪzəʳ] *n* incisive *f*

incite [ɪn'saɪt] *vt* inciter, pousser

incl. *abbr* = **including; inclusive (of)**

inclement [ɪn'klɛmənt] *adj* inclément(e), rigoureux(-euse)

inclination [ɪnklɪ'neɪʃən] *n* inclination *f*; (*desire*) envie *f*

incline *n* ['ɪnklaɪn, *vb* ɪn'klaɪn] *n* pente *f*, plan incliné ▷ *vt* incliner ▷ *vi* (*surface*) s'incliner; **to ~ to** avoir tendance à; **to be ~d to do** (*want to*) être enclin(e) à faire; (*have a tendency to do*) avoir tendance à faire; **to be well ~d towards sb** être bien disposé(e) à l'égard de qn

include [ɪn'kluːd] *vt* inclure, comprendre; **service is/is not ~d** le service est compris/n'est pas compris

including [ɪn'kluːdɪŋ] *prep* y compris; **~ service** service compris

inclusion [ɪn'kluːʒən] *n* inclusion *f*

inclusive [ɪn'kluːsɪv] *adj* inclus(e), compris(e); **~ of tax** taxes comprises; **£50 ~ of all surcharges** 50 livres tous frais compris

inclusive terms *npl* (*Brit*) prix tout compris

incognito [ɪnkɔg'niːtəu] *adv* incognito

incoherent [ɪnkəu'hɪərənt] *adj* incohérent(e)

income ['ɪnkʌm] *n* revenu *m*; (*from property etc*) rentes *fpl*; **gross/net ~** revenu brut/net; **~ and expenditure account** compte *m* de recettes et de dépenses

income support *n* (*Brit*) ≈ revenu *m* minimum d'insertion, RMI *m*

income tax *n* impôt *m* sur le revenu

income tax inspector *n* inspecteur *m* des contributions directes

income tax return *n* déclaration *f* des revenus

incoming ['ɪnkʌmɪŋ] *adj* (*passengers, mail*) à l'arrivée; (*government, tenant*) nouveau (nouvelle); **~ tide** marée montante

incommunicado ['ɪnkəmjunɪ'kɑːdəu] *adj*: **to hold sb ~** tenir qn au secret

incomparable [ɪn'kɔmpərəbl] *adj* incomparable

incompatible [ɪnkəm'pætɪbl] *adj* incompatible

incompetence [ɪn'kɔmpɪtns] *n* incompétence *f*, incapacité *f*

incompetent [ɪn'kɔmpɪtnt] *adj* incompétent(e), incapable

incomplete [ɪnkəm'pliːt] *adj* incomplet(-ète)

incomprehensible [ɪnkɔmprɪ'hɛnsɪbl] *adj* incompréhensible

inconceivable [ɪnkən'siːvəbl] *adj* inconcevable

inconclusive [ɪnkən'kluːsɪv] *adj* peu concluant(e); (*argument*) peu convaincant(e)

incongruous [ɪn'kɔŋgruəs] *adj* peu approprié(e); (*remark, act*) incongru(e), déplacé(e)

inconsequential [ɪnkɔnsɪ'kwɛnʃl] *adj* sans importance

inconsiderable [ɪnkən'sɪdərəbl] *adj*: **not ~** non négligeable

inconsiderate [ɪnkən'sɪdərət] *adj* (*action*) inconsidéré(e); (*person*) qui manque d'égards

inconsistency [ɪnkən'sɪstənsɪ] *n* (*of actions etc*) inconséquence *f*; (*of work*) irrégularité *f*; (*of statement etc*) incohérence *f*

inconsistent [ɪnkən'sɪstnt] *adj* qui manque de constance; (*work*) irrégulier(-ière); (*statement*) peu cohérent(e); **~ with** en contradiction avec

inconsolable [ɪnkən'səuləbl] *adj* inconsolable

inconspicuous [ɪnkən'spɪkjuəs] *adj* qui passe inaperçu(e); (*colour, dress*) discret(-ète); **to make o.s. ~** ne pas se faire remarquer

inconstant [ɪn'kɔnstnt] *adj* inconstant(e), variable

incontinence [ɪn'kɔntɪnəns] *n* incontinence *f*

incontinent [ɪn'kɔntɪnənt] *adj* incontinent(e)

incontrovertible [ɪnkɔntrə'vəːtəbl] *adj* irréfutable

inconvenience [ɪnkən'viːnjəns] *n* inconvénient

m; (trouble) dérangement m ▷ vt déranger;
don't ~ yourself ne vous dérangez pas
inconvenient [ɪnkən'viːnjənt] adj
malcommode; (time, place) mal choisi(e), qui ne
convient pas; (visitor) importun(e); **that time is
very ~ for me** c'est un moment qui ne me
convient pas du tout
incorporate [ɪn'kɔːpəreɪt] vt incorporer;
(contain) contenir ▷ vi fusionner; (two firms) se
constituer en société
incorporated [ɪn'kɔːpəreɪtɪd] adj: **~ company**
(US) ≈ société f anonyme
incorrect [ɪnkə'rɛkt] adj incorrect(e); (opinion,
statement) inexact(e)
incorrigible [ɪn'kɔrɪdʒɪbl] adj incorrigible
incorruptible [ɪnkə'rʌptɪbl] adj incorruptible
increase n ['ɪnkriːs] augmentation f ▷ vi, vt
[ɪn'kriːs] augmenter; **an ~ of 5%** une
augmentation de 5%; **to be on the ~** être en
augmentation
increasing [ɪn'kriːsɪŋ] adj croissant(e)
increasingly [ɪn'kriːsɪŋlɪ] adv de plus en plus
incredible [ɪn'krɛdɪbl] adj incroyable
incredibly [ɪn'krɛdɪblɪ] adv incroyablement
incredulous [ɪn'krɛdjuləs] adj incrédule
increment ['ɪnkrɪmənt] n augmentation f
incriminate [ɪn'krɪmɪneɪt] vt incriminer,
compromettre
incriminating [ɪn'krɪmɪneɪtɪŋ] adj
compromettant(e)
incubate ['ɪnkjubeɪt] vt (egg) couver, incuber
▷ vi (eggs) couver; (disease) couver
incubation [ɪnkju'beɪʃən] n incubation f
incubation period n période f d'incubation
incubator ['ɪnkjubeɪtəʳ] n incubateur m; (for
babies) couveuse f
inculcate ['ɪnkʌlkeɪt] vt: **to ~ sth in sb**
inculquer qch à qn
incumbent [ɪn'kʌmbənt] adj: **it is ~ on him
to ...** il lui appartient de ... ▷ n titulaire m/f
incur [ɪn'kəːʳ] vt (expenses) encourir; (anger, risk)
s'exposer à; (debt) contracter; (loss) subir
incurable [ɪn'kjuərəbl] adj incurable
incursion [ɪn'kəːʃən] n incursion f
Ind. abbr (US) = **Indiana**
indebted [ɪn'dɛtɪd] adj: **to be ~ to sb (for)** être
redevable à qn (de)
indecency [ɪn'diːsnsɪ] n indécence f
indecent [ɪn'diːsnt] adj indécent(e),
inconvenant(e)
indecent assault n (Brit) attentat m à la pudeur
indecent exposure n outrage m public à la
pudeur
indecipherable [ɪndɪ'saɪfərəbl] adj
indéchiffrable
indecision [ɪndɪ'sɪʒən] n indécision f
indecisive [ɪndɪ'saɪsɪv] adj indécis(e); (discussion)
peu concluant(e)
indeed [ɪn'diːd] adv (confirming, agreeing) en effet,
effectivement; (for emphasis) vraiment;
(furthermore) d'ailleurs; **yes ~!** certainement!
indefatigable [ɪndɪ'fætɪgəbl] adj infatigable

indefensible [ɪndɪ'fɛnsɪbl] adj (conduct)
indéfendable
indefinable [ɪndɪ'faɪnəbl] adj indéfinissable
indefinite [ɪn'dɛfɪnɪt] adj indéfini(e); (answer)
vague; (period, number) indéterminé(e)
indefinitely [ɪn'dɛfɪnɪtlɪ] adv (wait)
indéfiniment; (speak) vaguement, avec
imprécision
indelible [ɪn'dɛlɪbl] adj indélébile
indelicate [ɪn'dɛlɪkɪt] adj (tactless) indélicat(e),
grossier(-ière); (not polite) inconvenant(e),
malséant(e)
indemnify [ɪn'dɛmnɪfaɪ] vt indemniser,
dédommager
indemnity [ɪn'dɛmnɪtɪ] n (insurance) assurance f,
garantie f; (compensation) indemnité f
indent [ɪn'dɛnt] vt (text) commencer en retrait
indentation [ɪndɛn'teɪʃən] n découpure f; (Typ)
alinéa m; (on metal) bosse f
indenture [ɪn'dɛntʃəʳ] n contrat m d'emploi-
formation
independence [ɪndɪ'pɛndns] n indépendance f
Independence Day n (US) fête de l'Indépendance
américaine; voir article

● **INDEPENDENCE DAY**
●
● L'Independence Day est la fête nationale aux
● États-Unis, le 4 juillet. Il commémore
● l'adoption de la déclaration
● d'Indépendance, en 1776, écrite par Thomas
● Jefferson et proclamant la séparation des 13
● colonies américaines de la Grande-
● Bretagne.

independent [ɪndɪ'pɛndnt] adj indépendant(e);
(radio) libre; **to become ~** s'affranchir
independently [ɪndɪ'pɛndntlɪ] adv de façon
indépendante; **~ of** indépendamment de
independent school n (Brit) école privée
in-depth ['ɪndɛpθ] adj approfondi(e)
indescribable [ɪndɪ'skraɪbəbl] adj
indescriptible
indeterminate [ɪndɪ'təːmɪnɪt] adj
indéterminé(e)
index ['ɪndɛks] n (pl -es) (in book) index m; (: in
library etc) catalogue m (pl **indices** ['ɪndɪsiːz])
(ratio, sign) indice m
index card n fiche f
index finger n index m
index-linked ['ɪndɛks'lɪŋkt], (US) **indexed**
['ɪndɛkst] adj indexé(e) (sur le coût de la vie etc)
India ['ɪndɪə] n Inde f
Indian ['ɪndɪən] adj indien(ne) ▷ n Indien(ne);
(American) ~ Indien(ne) (d'Amérique)
Indian ink n encre f de Chine
Indian Ocean n: **the ~** l'océan Indien
Indian summer n (fig) été indien, beaux jours
en automne
India paper n papier m bible
India rubber n gomme f
indicate ['ɪndɪkeɪt] vt indiquer ▷ vi (Brit Aut): **to**

~ left/right mettre son clignotant à gauche/à droite

indication [ɪndɪ'keɪʃən] n indication f, signe m

indicative [ɪn'dɪkətɪv] adj indicatif(-ive); **to be ~ of sth** être symptomatique de qch ▷ n (Ling) indicatif m

indicator ['ɪndɪkeɪtər] n (sign) indicateur m; (Aut) clignotant m

indices ['ɪndɪsi:z] npl of **index**

indict [ɪn'daɪt] vt accuser

indictable [ɪn'daɪtəbl] adj (person) passible de poursuites; **~ offence** délit m tombant sous le coup de la loi

indictment [ɪn'daɪtmənt] n accusation f

indifference [ɪn'dɪfrəns] n indifférence f

indifferent [ɪn'dɪfrənt] adj indifférent(e); (poor) médiocre, quelconque

indigenous [ɪn'dɪdʒɪnəs] adj indigène

indigestible [ɪndɪ'dʒɛstɪbl] adj indigeste

indigestion [ɪndɪ'dʒɛstʃən] n indigestion f, mauvaise digestion

indignant [ɪn'dɪgnənt] adj: **~ (at sth/with sb)** indigné (e) (de qch/contre qn)

indignation [ɪndɪg'neɪʃən] n indignation f

indignity [ɪn'dɪgnɪtɪ] n indignité f, affront m

indigo ['ɪndɪgəu] adj indigo inv ▷ n indigo m

indirect [ɪndɪ'rɛkt] adj indirect(e)

indirectly [ɪndɪ'rɛktlɪ] adv indirectement

indiscreet [ɪndɪ'skri:t] adj indiscret(-ète); (rash) imprudent(e)

indiscretion [ɪndɪ'skrɛʃən] n indiscrétion f; (rashness) imprudence f

indiscriminate [ɪndɪ'skrɪmɪnət] adj (person) qui manque de discernement; (admiration) aveugle; (killings) commis(e) au hasard

indispensable [ɪndɪ'spɛnsəbl] adj indispensable

indisposed [ɪndɪ'spəuzd] adj (unwell) indisposé(e), souffrant(e)

indisposition [ɪndɪspə'zɪʃən] n (illness) indisposition f, malaise m

indisputable [ɪndɪ'spju:təbl] adj incontestable, indiscutable

indistinct [ɪndɪ'stɪŋkt] adj indistinct(e); (memory, noise) vague

indistinguishable [ɪndɪ'stɪŋgwɪʃəbl] adj impossible à distinguer

individual [ɪndɪ'vɪdjuəl] n individu m ▷ adj individuel(le); (characteristic) particulier(-ière), original(e)

individualist [ɪndɪ'vɪdjuəlɪst] n individualiste m/f

individuality [ɪndɪvɪdju'ælɪtɪ] n individualité f

individually [ɪndɪ'vɪdjuəlɪ] adv individuellement

indivisible [ɪndɪ'vɪzɪbl] adj indivisible; (Math) insécable

Indo-China ['ɪndəu'tʃaɪnə] n Indochine f

indoctrinate [ɪn'dɔktrɪneɪt] vt endoctriner

indoctrination [ɪndɔktrɪ'neɪʃən] n endoctrinement m

indolent ['ɪndələnt] adj indolent(e),

nonchalant(e)

Indonesia [ɪndə'ni:zɪə] n Indonésie f

Indonesian [ɪndə'ni:zɪən] adj indonésien(ne) ▷ n Indonésien(ne); (Ling) indonésien m

indoor ['ɪndɔ:ʳ] adj d'intérieur; (plant) d'appartement; (swimming pool) couvert(e); (sport, games) pratiqué(e) en salle

indoors [ɪn'dɔ:z] adv à l'intérieur; (at home) à la maison

indubitable [ɪn'dju:bɪtəbl] adj indubitable, incontestable

induce [ɪn'dju:s] vt (persuade) persuader; (bring about) provoquer; (labour) déclencher; **to ~ sb to do sth** inciter or pousser qn à faire qch

inducement [ɪn'dju:smənt] n incitation f; (incentive) but m; (pej: bribe) pot-de-vin m

induct [ɪn'dʌkt] vt établir dans ses fonctions; (fig) initier

induction [ɪn'dʌkʃən] n (Med: of birth) accouchement provoqué

induction course n (Brit) stage m de mise au courant

indulge [ɪn'dʌldʒ] vt (whim) céder à, satisfaire; (child) gâter ▷ vi: **to ~ in sth** (luxury) s'offrir qch, se permettre qch; (fantasies etc) se livrer à qch

indulgence [ɪn'dʌldʒəns] n fantaisie f (que l'on s'offre); (leniency) indulgence f

indulgent [ɪn'dʌldʒənt] adj indulgent(e)

industrial [ɪn'dʌstrɪəl] adj industriel(le); (injury) du travail; (dispute) ouvrier(-ière)

industrial action n action revendicative

industrial estate n (Brit) zone industrielle

industrialist [ɪn'dʌstrɪəlɪst] n industriel m

industrialize [ɪn'dʌstrɪəlaɪz] vt industrialiser

industrial park n (US) zone industrielle

industrial relations npl relations fpl dans l'entreprise

industrial tribunal n (Brit) ≈ conseil m de prud'hommes

industrious [ɪn'dʌstrɪəs] adj travailleur(-euse)

industry ['ɪndəstrɪ] n industrie f; (diligence) zèle m, application f

inebriated [ɪ'ni:brɪeɪtɪd] adj ivre

inedible [ɪn'ɛdɪbl] adj immangeable; (plant etc) non comestible

ineffective [ɪnɪ'fɛktɪv], **ineffectual** [ɪnɪ'fɛktʃuəl] adj inefficace; incompétent(e)

inefficiency [ɪnɪ'fɪʃənsɪ] n inefficacité f

inefficient [ɪnɪ'fɪʃənt] adj inefficace

inelegant [ɪn'ɛlɪgənt] adj peu élégant(e), inélégant(e)

ineligible [ɪn'ɛlɪdʒɪbl] adj (candidate) inéligible; **to be ~ for sth** ne pas avoir droit à qch

inept [ɪ'nɛpt] adj inepte

ineptitude [ɪ'nɛptɪtju:d] n ineptie f

inequality [ɪnɪ'kwɔlɪtɪ] n inégalité f

inequitable [ɪn'ɛkwɪtəbl] adj inéquitable, inique

ineradicable [ɪnɪ'rædɪkəbl] adj indéracinable, tenace

inert [ɪ'nə:t] adj inerte

inertia [ɪ'nə:ʃə] n inertie f

inertia-reel seat belt [ɪˈnəːʃəˈriːl-] n ceinture f de sécurité à enrouleur
inescapable [ɪnɪˈskeɪpəbl] adj inéluctable, inévitable
inessential [ɪnɪˈsɛnʃl] adj superflu(e)
inestimable [ɪnˈɛstɪməbl] adj inestimable, incalculable
inevitable [ɪnˈɛvɪtəbl] adj inévitable
inevitably [ɪnˈɛvɪtəblɪ] adv inévitablement, fatalement
inexact [ɪnɪgˈzækt] adj inexact(e)
inexcusable [ɪnɪksˈkjuːzəbl] adj inexcusable
inexhaustible [ɪnɪgˈzɔːstɪbl] adj inépuisable
inexorable [ɪnˈɛksərəbl] adj inexorable
inexpensive [ɪnɪkˈspɛnsɪv] adj bon marché inv
inexperience [ɪnɪkˈspɪərɪəns] n inexpérience f, manque m d'expérience
inexperienced [ɪnɪkˈspɪərɪənst] adj inexpérimenté(e); **to be ~ in sth** manquer d'expérience dans qch
inexplicable [ɪnɪkˈsplɪkəbl] adj inexplicable
inexpressible [ɪnɪkˈsprɛsɪbl] adj inexprimable; indicible
inextricable [ɪnɪkˈstrɪkəbl] adj inextricable
infallibility [ɪnfæləˈbɪlɪtɪ] n infaillibilité f
infallible [ɪnˈfælɪbl] adj infaillible
infamous [ˈɪnfəməs] adj infâme, abominable
infamy [ˈɪnfəmɪ] n infamie f
infancy [ˈɪnfənsɪ] n petite enfance, bas âge; (fig) enfance, débuts mpl
infant [ˈɪnfənt] n (baby) nourrisson m; (young child) petit(e) enfant
infantile [ˈɪnfəntaɪl] adj infantile
infant mortality n mortalité f infantile
infantry [ˈɪnfəntrɪ] n infanterie f
infantryman [ˈɪnfəntrɪmən] (irreg) n fantassin m
infant school n (Brit) classes fpl préparatoires (entre 5 et 7 ans)
infatuated [ɪnˈfætjueɪtɪd] adj: **~ with** entiché(e) de; **to become ~ (with sb)** s'enticher (de qn)
infatuation [ɪnfætjuˈeɪʃən] n toquade f; engouement m
infect [ɪnˈfɛkt] vt (wound) infecter; (person, blood) contaminer; (fig pej) corrompre; **~ed with** (illness) atteint(e) de; **to become ~ed** (wound) s'infecter
infection [ɪnˈfɛkʃən] n infection f; (contagion) contagion f
infectious [ɪnˈfɛkʃəs] adj infectieux(-euse); (also fig) contagieux(-euse)
infer [ɪnˈfəː] vt: **to ~ (from)** conclure (de), déduire (de)
inference [ˈɪnfərəns] n conclusion f, déduction f
inferior [ɪnˈfɪərɪə] adj inférieur(e); (goods) de qualité inférieure ▷ n inférieur(e); (in rank) subalterne m/f; **to feel ~** avoir un sentiment d'infériorité
inferiority [ɪnfɪərɪˈɔrətɪ] n infériorité f
inferiority complex n complexe m d'infériorité
infernal [ɪnˈfəːnl] adj infernal(e)
inferno [ɪnˈfəːnəu] n enfer m; brasier m

infertile [ɪnˈfəːtaɪl] adj stérile
infertility [ɪnfəːˈtɪlɪtɪ] n infertilité f, stérilité f
infested [ɪnˈfɛstɪd] adj: **~ (with)** infesté(e) (de)
infidelity [ɪnfɪˈdɛlɪtɪ] n infidélité f
in-fighting [ˈɪnfaɪtɪŋ] n querelles fpl internes
infiltrate [ˈɪnfɪltreɪt] vt (troops etc) faire s'infiltrer; (enemy line etc) s'infiltrer dans ▷ vi s'infiltrer
infinite [ˈɪnfɪnɪt] adj infini(e); (time, money) illimité(e)
infinitely [ˈɪnfɪnɪtlɪ] adv infiniment
infinitesimal [ɪnfɪnɪˈtɛsɪməl] adj infinitésimal(e)
infinitive [ɪnˈfɪnɪtɪv] n infinitif m
infinity [ɪnˈfɪnɪtɪ] n infinité f; (also Math) infini m
infirm [ɪnˈfəːm] adj infirme
infirmary [ɪnˈfəːmərɪ] n hôpital m; (in school, factory) infirmerie f
infirmity [ɪnˈfəːmɪtɪ] n infirmité f
inflamed [ɪnˈfleɪmd] adj enflammé(e)
inflammable [ɪnˈflæməbl] adj (Brit) inflammable
inflammation [ɪnfləˈmeɪʃən] n inflammation f
inflammatory [ɪnˈflæmətərɪ] adj (speech) incendiaire
inflatable [ɪnˈfleɪtəbl] adj gonflable
inflate [ɪnˈfleɪt] vt (tyre, balloon) gonfler; (fig: exaggerate) grossir, gonfler; (: increase) gonfler
inflated [ɪnˈfleɪtɪd] adj (style) enflé(e); (value) exagéré(e)
inflation [ɪnˈfleɪʃən] n (Econ) inflation f
inflationary [ɪnˈfleɪʃənərɪ] adj inflationniste
inflexible [ɪnˈflɛksɪbl] adj inflexible, rigide
inflict [ɪnˈflɪkt] vt: **to ~ on** infliger à
infliction [ɪnˈflɪkʃən] n: **without the ~ of pain** sans infliger de douleurs
in-flight [ˈɪnflaɪt] adj (refuelling) en vol; (service etc) à bord
inflow [ˈɪnfləu] n afflux m
influence [ˈɪnfluəns] n influence f ▷ vt influencer; **under the ~ of** sous l'effet de; **under the ~ of alcohol** en état d'ébriété
influential [ɪnfluˈɛnʃl] adj influent(e)
influenza [ɪnfluˈɛnzə] n grippe f
influx [ˈɪnflʌks] n afflux m
info (inf) [ˈɪnfəu] n (= information) renseignements mpl
infomercial [ˈɪnfəuməːʃl] (US) n (for product) publi-information f; (Pol) émission où un candidat présente son programme électoral
inform [ɪnˈfɔːm] vt: **to ~ sb (of)** informer or avertir qn (de) ▷ vi: **to ~ on sb** dénoncer qn, informer contre qn; **to ~ sb about** renseigner qn sur, mettre qn au courant de
informal [ɪnˈfɔːml] adj (person, manner, party) simple, sans cérémonie; (visit, discussion) dénué(e) de formalités; (announcement, invitation) non officiel(le); (colloquial) familier(-ère); **"dress ~"** "tenue de ville"
informality [ɪnfɔːˈmælɪtɪ] n simplicité f, absence f de cérémonie; caractère non officiel

informally [ɪnˈfɔːməlɪ] *adv* sans cérémonie, en toute simplicité; non officiellement

informant [ɪnˈfɔːmənt] *n* informateur(-trice)

information [ɪnfəˈmeɪʃən] *n* information(s) *f(pl)*; renseignements *mpl*; (*knowledge*) connaissances *fpl*; **to get ~ on** se renseigner sur; **a piece of ~** un renseignement; **for your ~** à titre d'information

information bureau *n* bureau *m* de renseignements

information desk *n* accueil *m*

information office *n* bureau *m* de renseignements

information processing *n* traitement *m* de l'information

information technology *n* informatique *f*

informative [ɪnˈfɔːmətɪv] *adj* instructif(-ive)

informed [ɪnˈfɔːmd] *adj* (bien) informé(e); **an ~ guess** une hypothèse fondée sur la connaissance des faits

informer [ɪnˈfɔːmə^r] *n* dénonciateur(-trice); (*also*: **police informer**) indicateur(-trice)

infra dig [ˈɪnfrəˈdɪg] *adj abbr* (*inf*: = *infra dignitatem*) au-dessous de ma (*or* sa *etc*) dignité

infra-red [ɪnfrəˈred] *adj* infrarouge

infrastructure [ˈɪnfrəstrʌktʃə^r] *n* infrastructure *f*

infrequent [ɪnˈfriːkwənt] *adj* peu fréquent(e), rare

infringe [ɪnˈfrɪndʒ] *vt* enfreindre ▷ *vi*: **to ~ on** empiéter sur

infringement [ɪnˈfrɪndʒmənt] *n*: **~ (of)** infraction *f* (à)

infuriate [ɪnˈfjuərɪeɪt] *vt* mettre en fureur

infuriating [ɪnˈfjuərɪeɪtɪŋ] *adj* exaspérant(e)

infuse [ɪnˈfjuːz] *vt*: **to ~ sb with sth** (*fig*) insuffler qch à qn

infusion [ɪnˈfjuːʒən] *n* (*tea etc*) infusion *f*

ingenious [ɪnˈdʒiːnjəs] *adj* ingénieux(-euse)

ingenuity [ɪndʒɪˈnjuːɪtɪ] *n* ingéniosité *f*

ingenuous [ɪnˈdʒenjuəs] *adj* franc (franche), ouvert(e)

ingot [ˈɪŋgət] *n* lingot *m*

ingrained [ɪnˈgreɪnd] *adj* enraciné(e)

ingratiate [ɪnˈgreɪʃɪeɪt] *vt*: **to ~ o.s. with** s'insinuer dans les bonnes grâces de, se faire bien voir de

ingratiating [ɪnˈgreɪʃɪeɪtɪŋ] *adj* (*smile, speech*) insinuant(e); (*person*) patelin(e)

ingratitude [ɪnˈgrætɪtjuːd] *n* ingratitude *f*

ingredient [ɪnˈgriːdɪənt] *n* ingrédient *m*; (*fig*) élément *m*

ingrowing [ˈɪngrəuɪŋ], **ingrown** [ˈɪngrəun] *adj*: **~ toenail** ongle incarné

inhabit [ɪnˈhæbɪt] *vt* habiter

inhabitable [ɪnˈhæbɪtəbl] *adj* habitable

inhabitant [ɪnˈhæbɪtnt] *n* habitant(e)

inhale [ɪnˈheɪl] *vt* inhaler; (*perfume*) respirer; (*smoke*) avaler ▷ *vi* (*breathe in*) aspirer; (*in smoking*) avaler la fumée

inhaler [ɪnˈheɪlə^r] *n* inhalateur *m*

inherent [ɪnˈhɪərənt] *adj*: **~ (in** *or* **to)**

inhérent(e) (à)

inherently [ɪnˈhɪərəntlɪ] *adv* (*easy, difficult*) en soi; (*lazy*) fondamentalement

inherit [ɪnˈherɪt] *vt* hériter (de)

inheritance [ɪnˈherɪtəns] *n* héritage *m*; (*fig*): **the situation that was his ~ as president** la situation dont il a hérité en tant que président; **law of ~** droit *m* de la succession

inhibit [ɪnˈhɪbɪt] *vt* (*Psych*) inhiber; (*growth*) freiner; **to ~ sb from doing** empêcher *or* retenir qn de faire

inhibited [ɪnˈhɪbɪtɪd] *adj* (*person*) inhibé(e)

inhibiting [ɪnˈhɪbɪtɪŋ] *adj* gênant(e)

inhibition [ɪnhɪˈbɪʃən] *n* inhibition *f*

inhospitable [ɪnhɔsˈpɪtəbl] *adj* inhospitalier(-ière)

in-house [ˈɪnˈhaus] *adj* (*system*) interne; (*training*) effectué(e) sur place *or* dans le cadre de la compagnie ▷ *adv* (*train, produce*) sur place

inhuman [ɪnˈhjuːmən] *adj* inhumain(e)

inhumane [ɪnhjuːˈmeɪn] *adj* inhumain(e)

inimitable [ɪˈnɪmɪtəbl] *adj* inimitable

iniquity [ɪˈnɪkwɪtɪ] *n* iniquité *f*

initial [ɪˈnɪʃl] *adj* initial(e) ▷ *n* initiale *f* ▷ *vt* parafer; **initials** *npl* initiales *fpl*; (*as signature*) parafe *m*

initialize [ɪˈnɪʃəlaɪz] *vt* (*Comput*) initialiser

initially [ɪˈnɪʃəlɪ] *adv* initialement, au début

initiate [ɪˈnɪʃɪeɪt] *vt* (*start*) entreprendre; amorcer; (*enterprise*) lancer; (*person*) initier; **to ~ sb into a secret** initier qn à un secret; **to ~ proceedings against sb** (*Law*) intenter une action à qn, engager des poursuites contre qn

initiation [ɪnɪʃɪˈeɪʃən] *n* (*into secret etc*) initiation *f*

initiative [ɪˈnɪʃətɪv] *n* initiative *f*; **to take the ~** prendre l'initiative

inject [ɪnˈdʒekt] *vt* (*liquid, fig: money*) injecter; (*person*): **to ~ sb with sth** faire une piqûre de qch à qn

injection [ɪnˈdʒekʃən] *n* injection *f*, piqûre *f*; **to have an ~** se faire faire une piqûre

injudicious [ɪndʒuˈdɪʃəs] *adj* peu judicieux(-euse)

injunction [ɪnˈdʒʌŋkʃən] *n* (*Law*) injonction *f*, ordre *m*

injure [ˈɪndʒə^r] *vt* blesser; (*wrong*) faire du tort à; (*damage: reputation etc*) compromettre; (*feelings*) heurter; **to ~ o.s.** se blesser

injured [ˈɪndʒəd] *adj* (*person, leg etc*) blessé(e); (*tone, feelings*) offensé(e); **~ party** (*Law*) partie lésée

injurious [ɪnˈdʒuərɪəs] *adj*: **~ (to)** préjudiciable (à)

injury [ˈɪndʒərɪ] *n* blessure *f*; (*wrong*) tort *m*; **to escape without ~** s'en sortir sain et sauf

injury time *n* (*Sport*) arrêts *mpl* de jeu

injustice [ɪnˈdʒʌstɪs] *n* injustice *f*; **you do me an ~** vous êtes injuste envers moi

ink [ɪŋk] *n* encre *f*

ink-jet printer [ˈɪŋkdʒet-] *n* imprimante *f* à jet d'encre

inkling [ˈɪŋklɪŋ] *n* soupçon *m*, vague idée *f*

inkpad ['ɪŋkpæd] *n* tampon *m* encreur
inky ['ɪŋkɪ] *adj* taché(e) d'encre
inlaid ['ɪnleɪd] *adj* incrusté(e); (*table etc*) marqueté(e)
inland *adj* ['ɪnlənd] intérieur(e) ▷ *adv* [ɪn'lænd] à l'intérieur, dans les terres; ~ **waterways** canaux *mpl* et rivières *fpl*
Inland Revenue *n* (*Brit*) fisc *m*
in-laws ['ɪnlɔːz] *npl* beaux-parents *mpl*; belle famille
inlet ['ɪnlɛt] *n* (*Geo*) crique *f*
inlet pipe *n* (*Tech*) tuyau *m* d'arrivée
inmate ['ɪnmeɪt] *n* (*in prison*) détenu(e); (*in asylum*) interné(e)
inmost ['ɪnməust] *adj* le (la) plus profond(e)
inn [ɪn] *n* auberge *f*
innards ['ɪnədz] *npl* (*inf*) entrailles *fpl*
innate [ɪ'neɪt] *adj* inné(e)
inner ['ɪnə^r] *adj* intérieur(e)
inner city *n* centre *m* urbain (*souffrant souvent de délabrement, d'embouteillages etc*)
inner-city ['ɪnə^rsɪtɪ] *adj* (*schools, problems*) de quartiers déshérités
innermost ['ɪnəməust] *adj* le (la) plus profond(e)
inner tube *n* (*of tyre*) chambre *f* à air
inning ['ɪnɪŋ] *n* (*US: Baseball*) tour *m* de batte; **innings** *npl* (*Cricket*) tour de batte; (*Brit fig*): **he has had a good ~s** il (en) a bien profité
innocence ['ɪnəsns] *n* innocence *f*
innocent ['ɪnəsnt] *adj* innocent(e)
innocuous [ɪ'nɔkjuəs] *adj* inoffensif(-ive)
innovation [ɪnəu'veɪʃən] *n* innovation *f*
innovative ['ɪnəu'veɪtɪv] *adj* novateur(-trice); (*product*) innovant(e)
innuendo (*pl* **-es** [ɪnju'ɛndəu]) *n* insinuation *f*, allusion (*malveillante*)
innumerable [ɪ'njuːmrəbl] *adj* innombrable
inoculate [ɪ'nɔkjuleɪt] *vt*: **to ~ sb with sth** inoculer qch à qn; **to ~ sb against sth** vacciner qn contre qch
inoculation [ɪnɔkju'leɪʃən] *n* inoculation *f*
inoffensive [ɪnə'fɛnsɪv] *adj* inoffensif(-ive)
inopportune [ɪn'ɔpətjuːn] *adj* inopportun(e)
inordinate [ɪ'nɔːdɪnət] *adj* démesuré(e)
inordinately [ɪ'nɔːdɪnətlɪ] *adv* démesurément
inorganic [ɪnɔː'gænɪk] *adj* inorganique
in-patient ['ɪnpeɪʃənt] *n* malade hospitalisé(e)
input ['ɪnput] *n* (*contribution*) contribution *f*; (*resources*) ressources *fpl*; (*Elec*) énergie *f*, puissance *f*; (*of machine*) consommation *f*; (*Comput*) entrée *f* (de données); (: *data*) données *fpl* ▷ *vt* (*Comput*) introduire, entrer
inquest ['ɪnkwɛst] *n* enquête (*criminelle*); (*coroner's*) enquête judiciaire
inquire [ɪn'kwaɪə^r] *vi* demander ▷ *vt* demander, s'informer de; **to ~ about** s'informer de, se renseigner sur; **to ~ when/where/whether** demander quand/où/si
▶ **inquire after** *vt fus* demander des nouvelles de
▶ **inquire into** *vt fus* faire une enquête sur

inquiring [ɪn'kwaɪərɪŋ] *adj* (*mind*) curieux(-euse), investigateur(-trice)
inquiry [ɪn'kwaɪərɪ] *n* demande *f* de renseignements; (*Law*) enquête *f*, investigation *f*; **"inquiries"** "renseignements"; **to hold an ~ into sth** enquêter sur qch
inquiry desk *n* (*Brit*) guichet *m* de renseignements
inquiry office *n* (*Brit*) bureau *m* de renseignements
inquisition [ɪnkwɪ'zɪʃən] *n* enquête *f*, investigation *f*; (*Rel*): **the I~** l'Inquisition *f*
inquisitive [ɪn'kwɪzɪtɪv] *adj* curieux(-euse)
inroads ['ɪnrəudz] *npl*: **to make ~ into** (*savings, supplies*) entamer
ins. *abbr* = **inches**
insane [ɪn'seɪn] *adj* fou (folle); (*Med*) aliéné(e)
insanitary [ɪn'sænɪtərɪ] *adj* insalubre
insanity [ɪn'sænɪtɪ] *n* folie *f*; (*Med*) aliénation (*mentale*)
insatiable [ɪn'seɪʃəbl] *adj* insatiable
inscribe [ɪn'skraɪb] *vt* inscrire; (*book etc*): **to ~ (to sb)** dédicacer (à qn)
inscription [ɪn'skrɪpʃən] *n* inscription *f*; (*in book*) dédicace *f*
inscrutable [ɪn'skruːtəbl] *adj* impénétrable
inseam ['ɪnsiːm] *n* (*US*): ~ **measurement** hauteur *f* d'entre-jambe
insect ['ɪnsɛkt] *n* insecte *m*
insect bite *n* piqûre *f* d'insecte
insecticide [ɪn'sɛktɪsaɪd] *n* insecticide *m*
insect repellent *n* crème *f* anti-insectes
insecure [ɪnsɪ'kjuə^r] *adj* (*person*) anxieux(-euse); (*job*) précaire; (*building etc*) peu sûr(e)
insecurity [ɪnsɪ'kjuərɪtɪ] *n* insécurité *f*
insensible [ɪn'sɛnsɪbl] *adj* insensible; (*unconscious*) sans connaissance
insensitive [ɪn'sɛnsɪtɪv] *adj* insensible
insensitivity [ɪnsɛnsɪ'tɪvɪtɪ] *n* insensibilité *f*
inseparable [ɪn'sɛprəbl] *adj* inséparable
insert *vt* [ɪn'səːt] insérer ▷ *n* ['ɪnsəːt] insertion *f*
insertion [ɪn'səːʃən] *n* insertion *f*
in-service ['ɪn'səːvɪs] *adj* (*training*) continu(e); (*course*) d'initiation; de perfectionnement; de recyclage
inshore [ɪn'ʃɔː^r] *adj* côtier(-ière) ▷ *adv* près de la côte; vers la côte
inside ['ɪn'saɪd] *n* intérieur *m*; (*of road: Brit*) côté *m* gauche (*de la route*); (: *US, Europe etc*) côté droit (*de la route*) ▷ *adj* intérieur(e) ▷ *adv* à l'intérieur, dedans ▷ *prep* à l'intérieur de; (*of time*): ~ **10 minutes** en moins de 10 minutes; **insides** *npl* (*inf*) intestins *mpl*; ~ **information** renseignements *mpl* à la source; ~ **story** histoire racontée par un témoin; **to go ~** rentrer
inside forward *n* (*Sport*) intérieur *m*
inside lane *n* (*Aut: in Britain*) voie *f* de gauche; (: *in US, Europe*) voie *f* de droite
inside leg measurement *n* (*Brit*) hauteur *f* d'entre-jambe
inside out *adv* à l'envers; (*know*) à fond; **to turn**

sth ~ retourner qch
insider [ɪn'saɪdə^r] *n* initié(e)
insider dealing, insider trading *n* (*Stock Exchange*) délit *m* d'initiés
insidious [ɪn'sɪdɪəs] *adj* insidieux(-euse)
insight ['ɪnsaɪt] *n* perspicacité *f*; (*glimpse, idea*) aperçu *m*; **to gain (an)** ~ **into** parvenir à comprendre
insignia [ɪn'sɪɡnɪə] *npl* insignes *mpl*
insignificant [ɪnsɪɡ'nɪfɪknt] *adj* insignifiant(e)
insincere [ɪnsɪn'sɪə^r] *adj* hypocrite
insincerity [ɪnsɪn'sɛrɪtɪ] *n* manque *m* de sincérité, hypocrisie *f*
insinuate [ɪn'sɪnjueɪt] *vt* insinuer
insinuation [ɪnsɪnju'eɪʃən] *n* insinuation *f*
insipid [ɪn'sɪpɪd] *adj* insipide, fade
insist [ɪn'sɪst] *vi* insister; **to** ~ **on doing** insister pour faire; **to** ~ **on sth** exiger qch; **to** ~ **that** insister pour que + *sub*; (*claim*) maintenir *or* soutenir que
insistence [ɪn'sɪstəns] *n* insistance *f*
insistent [ɪn'sɪstənt] *adj* insistant(e), pressant(e); (*noise, action*) ininterrompu(e)
insofar [ɪnsəu'fɑː^r]: ~ **as** *conj* dans la mesure où
insole ['ɪnsəul] *n* semelle intérieure; (*fixed part of shoe*) première *f*
insolence ['ɪnsələns] *n* insolence *f*
insolent ['ɪnsələnt] *adj* insolent(e)
insoluble [ɪn'sɔljubl] *adj* insoluble
insolvency [ɪn'sɔlvənsɪ] *n* insolvabilité *f*; faillite *f*
insolvent [ɪn'sɔlvənt] *adj* insolvable; (*bankrupt*) en faillite
insomnia [ɪn'sɔmnɪə] *n* insomnie *f*
insomniac [ɪn'sɔmnɪæk] *n* insomniaque *m/f*
inspect [ɪn'spɛkt] *vt* inspecter; (*Brit: ticket*) contrôler
inspection [ɪn'spɛkʃən] *n* inspection *f*; (*Brit: of tickets*) contrôle *m*
inspector [ɪn'spɛktə^r] *n* inspecteur(-trice); (*Brit: on buses, trains*) contrôleur(-euse)
inspiration [ɪnspə'reɪʃən] *n* inspiration *f*
inspire [ɪn'spaɪə^r] *vt* inspirer
inspired [ɪn'spaɪəd] *adj* (*writer, book etc*) inspiré(e); **in an** ~ **moment** dans un moment d'inspiration
inspiring [ɪn'spaɪərɪŋ] *adj* inspirant(e)
inst. *abbr* (*Brit Comm*) = **instant**; **of the 16th** ~ du 16 courant
instability [ɪnstə'bɪlɪtɪ] *n* instabilité *f*
install, (*US*) **instal** [ɪn'stɔːl] *vt* installer
installation [ɪnstə'leɪʃən] *n* installation *f*
installment plan *n* (*US*) achat *m* (*or* vente *f*) à tempérament *or* crédit
instalment, (*US*) **installment** [ɪn'stɔːlmənt] *n* (*payment*) acompte *m*, versement partiel; (*of TV serial etc*) épisode *m*; **in** ~**s** (*pay*) à tempérament; (*receive*) en plusieurs fois
instance ['ɪnstəns] *n* exemple *m*; **for** ~ par exemple; **in many** ~**s** dans bien des cas; **in that** ~ dans ce cas; **in the first** ~ tout d'abord, en premier lieu

instant ['ɪnstənt] *n* instant *m* ▷ *adj* immédiat(e), urgent(e); (*coffee, food*) instantané(e), en poudre; **the 10th** ~ le 10 courant
instantaneous [ɪnstən'teɪnɪəs] *adj* instantané(e)
instantly ['ɪnstəntlɪ] *adv* immédiatement, tout de suite
instant messaging *n* messagerie *f* instantanée
instant replay *n* (*US TV*) retour *m* sur une séquence
instead [ɪn'stɛd] *adv* au lieu de cela; ~ **of** au lieu de; ~ **of sb** à la place de qn
instep ['ɪnstɛp] *n* cou-de-pied *m*; (*of shoe*) cambrure *f*
instigate ['ɪnstɪɡeɪt] *vt* (*rebellion, strike, crime*) inciter à; (*new ideas etc*) susciter
instigation [ɪnstɪ'ɡeɪʃən] *n* instigation *f*; **at sb's** ~ à l'instigation de qn
instil [ɪn'stɪl] *vt*: **to** ~ (**into**) inculquer (à); (*courage*) insuffler (à)
instinct ['ɪnstɪŋkt] *n* instinct *m*
instinctive [ɪn'stɪŋktɪv] *adj* instinctif(-ive)
instinctively [ɪn'stɪŋktɪvlɪ] *adv* instinctivement
institute ['ɪnstɪtjuːt] *n* institut *m* ▷ *vt* instituer, établir; (*inquiry*) ouvrir; (*proceedings*) entamer
institution [ɪnstɪ'tjuːʃən] *n* institution *f*; (*school*) établissement *m* (scolaire); (*for care*) établissement (psychiatrique *etc*)
institutional [ɪnstɪ'tjuːʃənl] *adj* institutionnel(le); ~ **care** soins fournis par un établissement médico-social
instruct [ɪn'strʌkt] *vt* instruire, former; **to** ~ **sb in sth** enseigner qch à qn; **to** ~ **sb to do** charger qn *or* ordonner à qn de faire
instruction [ɪn'strʌkʃən] *n* instruction *f*; **instructions** *npl* (*orders*) directives *fpl*; ~**s for use** mode *m* d'emploi
instruction book *n* manuel *m* d'instructions
instructive [ɪn'strʌktɪv] *adj* instructif(-ive)
instructor [ɪn'strʌktə^r] *n* professeur *m*; (*for skiing, driving*) moniteur *m*
instrument ['ɪnstrumənt] *n* instrument *m*
instrumental [ɪnstru'mɛntl] *adj* (*Mus*) instrumental(e); **to be** ~ **in sth/in doing sth** contribuer à qch/à faire qch
instrumentalist [ɪnstru'mɛntəlɪst] *n* instrumentiste *m/f*
instrument panel *n* tableau *m* de bord
insubordinate [ɪnsə'bɔːdənɪt] *adj* insubordonné(e)
insubordination [ɪnsəbɔːdə'neɪʃən] *n* insubordination *f*
insufferable [ɪn'sʌfrəbl] *adj* insupportable
insufficient [ɪnsə'fɪʃənt] *adj* insuffisant(e)
insufficiently [ɪnsə'fɪʃəntlɪ] *adv* insuffisamment
insular ['ɪnsjulə^r] *adj* insulaire; (*outlook*) étroit(e); (*person*) aux vues étroites
insulate ['ɪnsjuleɪt] *vt* isoler; (*against sound*) insonoriser

insulating tape ['ɪnsjuleɪtɪŋ-] n ruban isolant
insulation [ɪnsju'leɪʃən] n isolation f; (against sound) insonorisation f
insulin ['ɪnsjulɪn] n insuline f
insult n ['ɪnsʌlt] insulte f, affront m ▷ vt [ɪn'sʌlt] insulter, faire un affront à
insulting [ɪn'sʌltɪŋ] adj insultant(e), injurieux(-euse)
insuperable [ɪn'sju:prəbl] adj insurmontable
insurance [ɪn'ʃuərəns] n assurance f; **fire/life ~** assurance-incendie/-vie; **to take out ~ (against)** s'assurer (contre)
insurance agent n agent m d'assurances
insurance broker n courtier m en assurances
insurance company n compagnie f or société f d'assurances
insurance policy n police f d'assurance
insurance premium n prime f d'assurance
insure [ɪn'ʃuəʳ] vt assurer; **to ~** (fig) parer à; **to ~ sb/sb's life** assurer qn/la vie de qn; **to be ~d for £5000** être assuré(e) pour 5000 livres
insured [ɪn'ʃuəd] n: **the ~** l'assuré(e)
insurer [ɪn'ʃuərəʳ] n assureur m
insurgent [ɪn'sə:dʒənt] adj, n insurgé(e)
insurmountable [ɪnsə'mauntəbl] adj insurmontable
insurrection [ɪnsə'rɛkʃən] n insurrection f
intact [ɪn'tækt] adj intact(e)
intake ['ɪnteɪk] n (Tech) admission f; (consumption) consommation f; (Brit Scol): **an ~ of 200 a year** 200 admissions par an
intangible [ɪn'tændʒɪbl] adj intangible; (assets) immatériel(le)
integral ['ɪntɪgrəl] adj (whole) intégral(e); (part) intégrant(e)
integrate ['ɪntɪgreɪt] vt intégrer ▷ vi s'intégrer
integrated circuit ['ɪntɪgreɪtɪd-] n (Comput) circuit intégré
integration [ɪntɪ'greɪʃən] n intégration f; **racial ~** intégration raciale
integrity [ɪn'tɛgrɪtɪ] n intégrité f
intellect ['ɪntəlɛkt] n intelligence f
intellectual [ɪntə'lɛktjuəl] adj, n intellectuel(le)
intelligence [ɪn'tɛlɪdʒəns] n intelligence f; (Mil) informations fpl, renseignements mpl
intelligence quotient n quotient intellectuel
Intelligence Service n services mpl de renseignements
intelligence test n test m d'intelligence
intelligent [ɪn'tɛlɪdʒənt] adj intelligent(e)
intelligently [ɪn'tɛlɪdʒəntlɪ] adv intelligemment
intelligible [ɪn'tɛlɪdʒɪbl] adj intelligible
intemperate [ɪn'tɛmpərət] adj immodéré(e); (drinking too much) adonné(e) à la boisson
intend [ɪn'tɛnd] vt (gift etc): **to ~ sth for** destiner qch à; **to ~ to do** avoir l'intention de faire
intended [ɪn'tɛndɪd] adj (insult) intentionnel(le); (journey) projeté(e); (effect) voulu(e)
intense [ɪn'tɛns] adj intense; (person) véhément(e)

intensely [ɪn'tɛnslɪ] adv intensément; (moving) profondément
intensify [ɪn'tɛnsɪfaɪ] vt intensifier
intensity [ɪn'tɛnsɪtɪ] n intensité f
intensive [ɪn'tɛnsɪv] adj intensif(-ive)
intensive care n: **to be in ~** être en réanimation
intensive care unit n service m de réanimation
intent [ɪn'tɛnt] n intention f ▷ adj attentif(-ive), absorbé(e); **to all ~s and purposes** en fait, pratiquement; **to be ~ on doing sth** être (bien) décidé à faire qch
intention [ɪn'tɛnʃən] n intention f
intentional [ɪn'tɛnʃənl] adj intentionnel(le), délibéré(e)
intently [ɪn'tɛntlɪ] adv attentivement
inter [ɪn'tə:ʳ] vt enterrer
interact [ɪntər'ækt] vi avoir une action réciproque; (people) communiquer
interaction [ɪntər'ækʃən] n interaction f
interactive [ɪntər'æktɪv] adj (group) interactif(-ive); (Comput) interactif, conversationnel(le)
intercede [ɪntə'si:d] vi: **to ~ with sb/on behalf of sb** intercéder auprès de qn/en faveur de qn
intercept [ɪntə'sɛpt] vt intercepter; (person) arrêter au passage
interception [ɪntə'sɛpʃən] n interception f
interchange n ['ɪntətʃeɪndʒ] (exchange) échange m; (on motorway) échangeur m ▷ vt [ɪntə'tʃeɪndʒ] échanger; mettre à la place l'un(e) de l'autre
interchangeable [ɪntə'tʃeɪndʒəbl] adj interchangeable
intercity [ɪntə'sɪtɪ] adj: **~ (train)** train m rapide
intercom ['ɪntəkɔm] n interphone m
interconnect [ɪntəkə'nɛkt] vi (rooms) communiquer
intercontinental ['ɪntəkɔntɪ'nɛntl] adj intercontinental(e)
intercourse ['ɪntəkɔ:s] n rapports mpl; **sexual ~** rapports sexuels
interdependent [ɪntədɪ'pɛndənt] adj interdépendant(e)
interest ['ɪntrɪst] n intérêt m; (Comm: stake, share) participation f, intérêts mpl ▷ vt intéresser; **compound/simple ~** intérêt composé/simple; **British ~s in the Middle East** les intérêts britanniques au Moyen-Orient; **his main ~ is ...** ce qui l'intéresse le plus est ...
interested ['ɪntrɪstɪd] adj intéressé(e); **to be ~ in sth** s'intéresser à qch; **I'm ~ in going** ça m'intéresse d'y aller
interest-free ['ɪntrɪst'fri:] adj sans intérêt
interesting ['ɪntrɪstɪŋ] adj intéressant(e)
interest rate n taux m d'intérêt
interface ['ɪntəfeɪs] n (Comput) interface f
interfere [ɪntə'fɪəʳ] vi: **to ~ in** (quarrel) s'immiscer dans; (other people's business) se mêler de; **to ~ with** (object) tripoter, toucher à; (plans) contrecarrer; (duty) être en conflit avec; **don't ~** mêlez-vous de vos affaires
interference [ɪntə'fɪərəns] n (gen) ingérence f; (Physics) interférence f; (Radio, TV) parasites mpl

interfering [ɪntə'fɪərɪŋ] *adj* importun(e)
interim ['ɪntərɪm] *adj* provisoire; (*post*) intérimaire ▷ *n*: **in the ~** dans l'intérim
interior [ɪn'tɪərɪə^r] *n* intérieur *m* ▷ *adj* intérieur(e); (*minister, department*) de l'intérieur
interior decorator, interior designer *n* décorateur(-trice) d'intérieur
interior design *n* architecture *f* d'intérieur
interjection [ɪntə'dʒɛkʃən] *n* interjection *f*
interlock [ɪntə'lɔk] *vi* s'enclencher ▷ *vt* enclencher
interloper ['ɪntələupə^r] *n* intrus(e)
interlude ['ɪntəlu:d] *n* intervalle *m*; (*Theat*) intermède *m*
intermarry [ɪntə'mærɪ] *vi* former des alliances entre familles (*or* tribus); former des unions consanguines
intermediary [ɪntə'mi:dɪərɪ] *n* intermédiaire *m/f*
intermediate [ɪntə'mi:dɪət] *adj* intermédiaire; (*Scol: course, level*) moyen(ne)
interment [ɪn'tə:mənt] *n* inhumation *f*, enterrement *m*
interminable [ɪn'tə:mɪnəbl] *adj* sans fin, interminable
intermission [ɪntə'mɪʃən] *n* pause *f*; (*Theat, Cine*) entracte *m*
intermittent [ɪntə'mɪtnt] *adj* intermittent(e)
intermittently [ɪntə'mɪtntlɪ] *adv* par intermittence, par intervalles
intern *vt* [ɪn'tə:n] interner ▷ *n* ['ɪntə:n] (*US*) interne *m/f*
internal [ɪn'tə:nl] *adj* interne; (*dispute, reform etc*) intérieur(e); **~ injuries** lésions *fpl* internes
internally [ɪn'tə:nəlɪ] *adv* intérieurement; **"not to be taken ~"** "pour usage externe"
Internal Revenue Service *n* (*US*) fisc *m*
international [ɪntə'næʃənl] *adj* international(e) ▷ *n* (*Brit Sport*) international *m*
International Atomic Energy Agency *n* Agence Internationale de l'Énergie Atomique
International Court of Justice *n* Cour internationale de justice
international date line *n* ligne *f* de changement de date
internationally [ɪntə'næʃnəlɪ] *adv* dans le monde entier
International Monetary Fund *n* Fonds monétaire international
international relations *npl* relations internationales
internecine [ɪntə'ni:saɪn] *adj* mutuellement destructeur(-trice)
internee [ɪntə:'ni:] *n* interné(e)
Internet [ɪntə'nɛt] *n*: **the ~** l'Internet *m*
Internet café *n* cybercafé *m*
Internet Service Provider *n* fournisseur *m* d'accès à Internet
Internet user *n* internaute *m/f*
internment [ɪn'tə:nmənt] *n* internement *m*
interplay ['ɪntəpleɪ] *n* effet *m* réciproque, jeu *m*
Interpol ['ɪntəpɔl] *n* Interpol *m*

interpret [ɪn'tə:prɪt] *vt* interpréter ▷ *vi* servir d'interprète
interpretation [ɪntə:prɪ'teɪʃən] *n* interprétation *f*
interpreter [ɪn'tə:prɪtə^r] *n* interprète *m/f*; **could you act as an ~ for us?** pourriez-vous nous servir d'interprète?
interpreting [ɪn'tə:prɪtɪŋ] *n* (*profession*) interprétariat *m*
interrelated [ɪntərɪ'leɪtɪd] *adj* en corrélation, en rapport étroit
interrogate [ɪn'tɛrəugeɪt] *vt* interroger; (*suspect etc*) soumettre à un interrogatoire
interrogation [ɪntɛrəu'geɪʃən] *n* interrogation *f*; (*by police*) interrogatoire *m*
interrogative [ɪntə'rɔgətɪv] *adj* interrogateur(-trice) ▷ *n* (*Ling*) interrogatif *m*
interrogator [ɪn'tɛrəgeɪtə^r] *n* interrogateur(-trice)
interrupt [ɪntə'rʌpt] *vt*, *vi* interrompre
interruption [ɪntə'rʌpʃən] *n* interruption *f*
intersect [ɪntə'sɛkt] *vt* couper, croiser; (*Math*) intersecter ▷ *vi* se croiser, se couper; s'intersecter
intersection [ɪntə'sɛkʃən] *n* intersection *f*; (*of roads*) croisement *m*
intersperse [ɪntə'spə:s] *vt*: **to ~ with** parsemer de
interstate ['ɪntəsteɪt] (*US*) *n* autoroute *f* (qui relie plusieurs États)
intertwine [ɪntə'twaɪn] *vt* entrelacer ▷ *vi* s'entrelacer
interval ['ɪntəvl] *n* intervalle *m*; (*Brit: Theat*) entracte *m*; (: *Sport*) mi-temps *f*; **bright ~s** (*in weather*) éclaircies *fpl*; **at ~s** par intervalles
intervene [ɪntə'vi:n] *vi* (*time*) s'écouler (entre-temps); (*event*) survenir; (*person*) intervenir
intervention [ɪntə'vɛnʃən] *n* intervention *f*
interview ['ɪntəvju:] *n* (*Radio, TV*) interview *f*; (*for job*) entrevue *f* ▷ *vt* interviewer, avoir une entrevue avec
interviewee [ɪntəvju'i:] *n* (*for job*) candidat *m* (qui passe un entretien); (*TV etc*) invité(e), personne interviewée
interviewer ['ɪntəvjuə^r] *n* (*Radio, TV*) interviewer *m*
intestate [ɪn'tɛsteɪt] *adj* intestat *f inv*
intestinal [ɪn'tɛstɪnl] *adj* intestinal(e)
intestine [ɪn'tɛstɪn] *n* intestin *m*; **large ~** gros intestin; **small ~** intestin grêle
intimacy ['ɪntɪməsɪ] *n* intimité *f*
intimate *adj* ['ɪntɪmət] intime; (*friendship*) profond(e); (*knowledge*) approfondi(e) ▷ *vt* ['ɪntɪmeɪt] suggérer, laisser entendre; (*announce*) faire savoir
intimately ['ɪntɪmətlɪ] *adv* intimement
intimation [ɪntɪ'meɪʃən] *n* annonce *f*
intimidate [ɪn'tɪmɪdeɪt] *vt* intimider
intimidating [ɪn'tɪmɪdeɪtɪŋ] *adj* intimidant(e)
intimidation [ɪntɪmɪ'deɪʃən] *n* intimidation *f*
into ['ɪntu] *prep* dans; **~ pieces/French** en morceaux/français; **to change pounds ~**

dollars changer des livres en dollars; **3 ~ 9 goes 3** 9 divisé par 3 donne 3; **she's ~ opera** c'est une passionnée d'opéra
intolerable [ɪn'tɔlərəbl] *adj* intolérable
intolerance [ɪn'tɔlərns] *n* intolérance *f*
intolerant [ɪn'tɔlərnt] *adj*: **~ (of)** intolérant(e) (de); *(Med)* intolérant (à)
intonation [ɪntəu'neɪʃən] *n* intonation *f*
intoxicate [ɪn'tɔksɪkeɪt] *vt* enivrer
intoxicated [ɪn'tɔksɪkeɪtɪd] *adj* ivre
intoxication [ɪntɔksɪ'keɪʃən] *n* ivresse *f*
intractable [ɪn'træktəbl] *adj* (*child, temper*) indocile, insoumis(e); (*problem*) insoluble; (*illness*) incurable
intranet [ɪn'trənɛt] *n* intranet *m*
intransigent [ɪn'trænsɪdʒənt] *adj* intransigeant(e)
intransitive [ɪn'trænsɪtɪv] *adj* intransitif(-ive)
intra-uterine device ['ɪntrə'juːtərɑɪn-] *n* dispositif intra-utérin, stérilet *m*
intravenous [ɪntrə'viːnəs] *adj* intraveineux(-euse)
in-tray ['ɪntreɪ] *n* courrier *m* "arrivée"
intrepid [ɪn'trɛpɪd] *adj* intrépide
intricacy ['ɪntrɪkəsɪ] *n* complexité *f*
intricate ['ɪntrɪkət] *adj* complexe, compliqué(e)
intrigue [ɪn'triːg] *n* intrigue *f* ▷ *vt* intriguer ▷ *vi* intriguer, comploter
intriguing [ɪn'triːgɪŋ] *adj* fascinant(e)
intrinsic [ɪn'trɪnsɪk] *adj* intrinsèque
introduce [ɪntrə'djuːs] *vt* introduire; (*TV show etc*) présenter; **to ~ sb (to sb)** présenter qn (à qn); **to ~ sb to** (*pastime, technique*) initier qn à; **may I ~ ...?** je vous présente ...
introduction [ɪntrə'dʌkʃən] *n* introduction *f*; (*of person*) présentation *f*; (*to new experience*) initiation *f*; **a letter of ~** une lettre de recommandation
introductory [ɪntrə'dʌktərɪ] *adj* préliminaire, introductif(-ive); **~ remarks** remarques *fpl* liminaires; **an ~ offer** une offre de lancement
introspection [ɪntrəu'spɛkʃən] *n* introspection *f*
introspective [ɪntrəu'spɛktɪv] *adj* introspectif(-ive)
introvert ['ɪntrəuvəːt] *adj, n* introverti(e)
intrude [ɪn'truːd] *vi* (*person*) être importun(e); **to ~ on** *or* **into** (*conversation etc*) s'immiscer dans; **am I intruding?** est-ce que je vous dérange?
intruder [ɪn'truːdəʳ] *n* intrus(e)
intrusion [ɪn'truːʒən] *n* intrusion *f*
intrusive [ɪn'truːsɪv] *adj* importun(e), gênant(e)
intuition [ɪntjuː'ɪʃən] *n* intuition *f*
intuitive [ɪn'tjuːɪtɪv] *adj* intuitif(-ive)
inundate ['ɪnʌndeɪt] *vt*: **to ~ with** inonder de
inure [ɪn'juəʳ] *vt*: **to ~ (to)** habituer (à)
invade [ɪn'veɪd] *vt* envahir
invader [ɪn'veɪdəʳ] *n* envahisseur *m*
invalid *n* ['ɪnvəlɪd] malade *m/f*; (*with disability*) invalide *m/f* ▷ *adj* [ɪn'vælɪd] (*not valid*) invalide, non valide
invalidate [ɪn'vælɪdeɪt] *vt* invalider, annuler

invalid chair ['ɪnvəlɪd-] *n* (*Brit*) fauteuil *m* d'infirme
invaluable [ɪn'væljuəbl] *adj* inestimable, inappréciable
invariable [ɪn'vɛərɪəbl] *adj* invariable; (*fig*) immanquable
invariably [ɪn'vɛərɪəblɪ] *adv* invariablement; **she is ~ late** elle est toujours en retard
invasion [ɪn'veɪʒən] *n* invasion *f*
invective [ɪn'vɛktɪv] *n* invective *f*
inveigle [ɪn'viːgl] *vt*: **to ~ sb into (doing) sth** amener qn à (faire) qch (par la ruse *or* la flatterie)
invent [ɪn'vɛnt] *vt* inventer
invention [ɪn'vɛnʃən] *n* invention *f*
inventive [ɪn'vɛntɪv] *adj* inventif(-ive)
inventiveness [ɪn'vɛntɪvnɪs] *n* esprit inventif *or* d'invention
inventor [ɪn'vɛntəʳ] *n* inventeur(-trice)
inventory ['ɪnvəntrɪ] *n* inventaire *m*
inventory control *n* (*Comm*) contrôle *m* des stocks
inverse [ɪn'vəːs] *adj* inverse ▷ *n* inverse *m*, contraire *m*; **in ~ proportion (to)** inversement proportionnel(le) (à)
inversely [ɪn'vəːslɪ] *adv* inversement
invert [ɪn'vəːt] *vt* intervertir; (*cup, object*) retourner
invertebrate [ɪn'vəːtɪbrət] *n* invertébré *m*
inverted commas [ɪn'vəːtɪd-] *npl* (*Brit*) guillemets *mpl*
invest [ɪn'vɛst] *vt* investir; (*endow*): **to ~ sb with sth** conférer qch à qn ▷ *vi* faire un investissement, investir; **to ~ in** placer de l'argent *or* investir dans; (*fig: acquire*) s'offrir, faire l'acquisition de
investigate [ɪn'vɛstɪgeɪt] *vt* étudier, examiner; (*crime*) faire une enquête sur
investigation [ɪnvɛstɪ'geɪʃən] *n* examen *m*; (*of crime*) enquête *f*, investigation *f*
investigative [ɪn'vɛstɪgeɪtɪv] *adj*: **~ journalism** enquête-reportage *f*, journalisme *m* d'enquête
investigator [ɪn'vɛstɪgeɪtəʳ] *n* investigateur(-trice); **private ~** détective privé
investiture [ɪn'vɛstɪtʃəʳ] *n* investiture *f*
investment [ɪn'vɛstmənt] *n* investissement *m*, placement *m*
investment income *n* revenu *m* de placement
investment trust *n* société *f* d'investissements
investor [ɪn'vɛstəʳ] *n* épargnant(e); (*shareholder*) actionnaire *m/f*
inveterate [ɪn'vɛtərət] *adj* invétéré(e)
invidious [ɪn'vɪdɪəs] *adj* injuste; (*task*) déplaisant(e)
invigilate [ɪn'vɪdʒɪleɪt] (*Brit*) *vt* surveiller ▷ *vi* être de surveillance
invigilator [ɪn'vɪdʒɪleɪtəʳ] *n* (*Brit*) surveillant *m* (d'examen)
invigorating [ɪn'vɪgəreɪtɪŋ] *adj* vivifiant(e), stimulant(e)
invincible [ɪn'vɪnsɪbl] *adj* invincible
inviolate [ɪn'vaɪələt] *adj* inviolé(e)

invisible [ɪnˈvɪzɪbl] *adj* invisible
invisible assets *npl* (*Brit*) actif incorporel
invisible ink *n* encre *f* sympathique
invisible mending *n* stoppage *m*
invitation [ɪnvɪˈteɪʃən] *n* invitation *f*; **by ~ only** sur invitation; **at sb's ~** à la demande de qn
invite [ɪnˈvaɪt] *vt* inviter; (*opinions etc*) demander; (*trouble*) chercher; **to ~ sb (to do)** inviter qn (à faire); **to ~ sb to dinner** inviter qn à dîner
  ▶ **invite out** *vt* inviter (à sortir)
  ▶ **invite over** *vt* inviter (chez soi)
inviting [ɪnˈvaɪtɪŋ] *adj* engageant(e), attrayant(e); (*gesture*) encourageant(e)
invoice [ˈɪnvɔɪs] *n* facture *f* ▷ *vt* facturer; **to ~ sb for goods** facturer des marchandises à qn
invoke [ɪnˈvəuk] *vt* invoquer
involuntary [ɪnˈvɔləntrɪ] *adj* involontaire
involve [ɪnˈvɔlv] *vt* (*entail*) impliquer; (*concern*) concerner; (*require*) nécessiter; **to ~ sb in** (*theft etc*) impliquer qn dans; (*activity, meeting*) faire participer qn à
involved [ɪnˈvɔlvd] *adj* (*complicated*) complexe; **to be ~ in** (*take part*) participer à; (*be engrossed*) être plongé(e) dans; **to feel ~** se sentir concerné(e); **to become ~** (*in love etc*) s'engager
involvement [ɪnˈvɔlvmənt] *n* (*personal role*) rôle *m*; (*participation*) participation *f*; (*enthusiasm*) enthousiasme *m*; (*of resources, funds*) mise *f* en jeu
invulnerable [ɪnˈvʌlnərəbl] *adj* invulnérable
inward [ˈɪnwəd] *adj* (*movement*) vers l'intérieur; (*thought, feeling*) profond(e), intime ▷ *adv* = **inwards**
inwardly [ˈɪnwədlɪ] *adv* (*feel, think etc*) secrètement, en son for intérieur
inwards [ˈɪnwədz] *adv* vers l'intérieur
I/O *abbr* (*Comput*: = *input/output*) E/S
IOC *n abbr* (= *International Olympic Committee*) CIO *m* (= *Comité international olympique*)
iodine [ˈaɪəudiːn] *n* iode *m*
IOM *abbr* = **Isle of Man**
ion [ˈaɪən] *n* ion *m*
Ionian Sea [aɪˈəunɪən-] *n*: **the ~** la mer Ionienne
ioniser [ˈaɪənaɪzəʳ] *n* ioniseur *m*
iota [aɪˈəutə] *n* (*fig*) brin *m*, grain *m*
IOU *n abbr* (= *I owe you*) reconnaissance *f* de dette
IOW *abbr* (*Brit*) = **Isle of Wight**
IPA *n abbr* (= *International Phonetic Alphabet*) A.P.I *m*
IQ *n abbr* (= *intelligence quotient*) Q.I. *m*
IRA *n abbr* (= *Irish Republican Army*) IRA *f*; (*US*) = **individual retirement account**
Iran [ɪˈrɑːn] *n* Iran *m*
Iranian [ɪˈreɪnɪən] *adj* iranien(ne) ▷ *n* Iranien(ne); (*Ling*) iranien *m*
Iraq [ɪˈrɑːk] *n* Irak *m*
Iraqi [ɪˈrɑːkɪ] *adj* irakien(ne) ▷ *n* Irakien(ne)
irascible [ɪˈræsɪbl] *adj* irascible
irate [aɪˈreɪt] *adj* courroucé(e)
Ireland [ˈaɪələnd] *n* Irlande *f*; **Republic of ~** République *f* d'Irlande
iris, irises [ˈaɪrɪs, -ɪz] *n* iris *m*
Irish [ˈaɪrɪʃ] *adj* irlandais(e) ▷ *npl*: **the ~** les

Irlandais ▷ *n* (*Ling*) irlandais *m*; **the Irish** *npl* les Irlandais
Irishman [ˈaɪrɪʃmən] (*irreg*) *n* Irlandais *m*
Irish Sea *n*: **the ~** la mer d'Irlande
Irishwoman [ˈaɪrɪʃwumən] (*irreg*) *n* Irlandaise *f*
irk [əːk] *vt* ennuyer
irksome [ˈəːksəm] *adj* ennuyeux(-euse)
IRN *n abbr* (= *Independent Radio News*) agence de presse radiophonique
IRO *n abbr* (*US*) = **International Refugee Organization**
iron [ˈaɪən] *n* fer *m*; (*for clothes*) fer *m* à repasser ▷ *adj* de or en fer ▷ *vt* (*clothes*) repasser; **irons** *npl* (*chains*) fers *mpl*, chaînes *fpl*
  ▶ **iron out** *vt* (*crease*) faire disparaître au fer; (*fig*) aplanir; faire disparaître
Iron Curtain *n*: **the ~** le rideau de fer
iron foundry *n* fonderie *f* de fonte
ironic [aɪˈrɔnɪk], **ironical** [aɪˈrɔnɪkl] *adj* ironique
ironically [aɪˈrɔnɪklɪ] *adv* ironiquement
ironing [ˈaɪənɪŋ] *n* (*activity*) repassage *m*; (*clothes*: *ironed*) linge repassé; (: *to be ironed*) linge à repasser
ironing board *n* planche *f* à repasser
ironmonger [ˈaɪənmʌŋgəʳ] *n* (*Brit*) quincaillier *m*; **~'s (shop)** quincaillerie *f*
iron ore *n* minerai *m* de fer
ironworks [ˈaɪənwəːks] *n* usine *f* sidérurgique
irony [ˈaɪrənɪ] *n* ironie *f*
irrational [ɪˈræʃənl] *adj* irrationnel(le); (*person*) qui n'est pas rationnel
irreconcilable [ɪrɛkənˈsaɪləbl] *adj* irréconciliable; (*opinion*): **~ with** inconciliable avec
irredeemable [ɪrɪˈdiːməbl] *adj* (*Comm*) non remboursable
irrefutable [ɪrɪˈfjuːtəbl] *adj* irréfutable
irregular [ɪˈrɛgjuləʳ] *adj* irrégulier(-ière); (*surface*) inégal(e); (*action, event*) peu orthodoxe
irregularity [ɪrɛgjuˈlærɪtɪ] *n* irrégularité *f*
irrelevance [ɪˈrɛləvəns] *n* manque *m* de rapport or d'à-propos
irrelevant [ɪˈrɛləvənt] *adj* sans rapport, hors de propos
irreligious [ɪrɪˈlɪdʒəs] *adj* irréligieux(-euse)
irreparable [ɪˈrɛprəbl] *adj* irréparable
irreplaceable [ɪrɪˈpleɪsəbl] *adj* irremplaçable
irrepressible [ɪrɪˈprɛsɪbl] *adj* irrépressible
irreproachable [ɪrɪˈprəutʃəbl] *adj* irréprochable
irresistible [ɪrɪˈzɪstɪbl] *adj* irrésistible
irresolute [ɪˈrɛzəluːt] *adj* irrésolu(e), indécis(e)
irrespective [ɪrɪˈspɛktɪv] *adj*: **~ of** *prep* sans tenir compte de
irresponsible [ɪrɪˈspɔnsɪbl] *adj* (*act*) irréfléchi(e); (*person*) qui n'a pas le sens des responsabilités
irretrievable [ɪrɪˈtriːvəbl] *adj* irréparable, irrémédiable; (*object*) introuvable
irreverent [ɪˈrɛvərnt] *adj* irrévérencieux(-euse)
irrevocable [ɪˈrɛvəkəbl] *adj* irrévocable
irrigate [ˈɪrɪgeɪt] *vt* irriguer

irrigation [ɪrɪˈɡeɪʃən] *n* irrigation *f*
irritable [ˈɪrɪtəbl] *adj* irritable
irritate [ˈɪrɪteɪt] *vt* irriter
irritating [ˈɪrɪteɪtɪŋ] *adj* irritant(e)
irritation [ɪrɪˈteɪʃən] *n* irritation *f*
IRS *n abbr* (*US*) = **Internal Revenue Service**
is [ɪz] *vb see* **be**
ISA *n abbr* (*Brit*: = *Individual Savings Account*) plan *m* d'épargne défiscalisé
ISBN *n abbr* (= *International Standard Book Number*) ISBN *m*
ISDN *n abbr* (= *Integrated Services Digital Network*) RNIS *m*
Islam [ˈɪzlɑːm] *n* Islam *m*
Islamic [ɪzˈlɑːmɪk] *adj* islamique; **~ fundamentalists** intégristes *mpl* musulmans
island [ˈaɪlənd] *n* île *f*; (*also*: **traffic island**) refuge *m* (pour piétons)
islander [ˈaɪləndəʳ] *n* habitant(e) d'une île, insulaire *m/f*
isle [aɪl] *n* île *f*
isn't [ˈɪznt] = **is not**
isolate [ˈaɪsəleɪt] *vt* isoler
isolated [ˈaɪsəleɪtɪd] *adj* isolé(e)
isolation [aɪsəˈleɪʃən] *n* isolement *m*
ISP *n abbr* = **Internet Service Provider**
Israel [ˈɪzreɪl] *n* Israël *m*
Israeli [ɪzˈreɪlɪ] *adj* israélien(ne) ▷ *n* Israélien(ne)
issue [ˈɪʃuː] *n* question *f*, problème *m*; (*outcome*) résultat *m*, issue *f*; (*of banknotes*) émission *f*; (*of newspaper*) numéro *m*; (*of book*) publication *f*, parution *f*; (*offspring*) descendance *f* ▷ *vt* (*rations, equipment*) distribuer; (*orders*) donner; (*statement*) publier, faire; (*certificate, passport*) délivrer; (*book*) faire paraître; publier; (*banknotes, cheques, stamps*) émettre, mettre en circulation ▷ *vi*: **to ~ from** provenir de; **at ~** en jeu, en cause; **to avoid the ~** éluder le problème; **to take ~ with sb (over sth)** exprimer son désaccord avec qn (sur qch); **to make an ~ of sth** faire de qch un problème; **to confuse** *or* **obscure the ~** embrouiller la question
Istanbul [ɪstænˈbuːl] *n* Istamboul, Istanbul
isthmus [ˈɪsməs] *n* isthme *m*
IT *n abbr* = **information technology**

 KEYWORD

it [ɪt] *pron* **1** (*specific: subject*) il (elle); (*: direct object*) le (la, l'); (*: indirect object*) lui; **it's on the table** c'est *or* il (*or* elle) est sur la table; **I can't find it** je n'arrive pas à le trouver; **give it to me** donne-le-moi
2 (*after prep*): **about/from/of it** en; **I spoke to him about it** je lui en ai parlé; **what did you learn from it?** qu'est-ce que vous en avez retiré?; **I'm proud of it** j'en suis fier; **I've come from it** j'en viens; **in/to it** y; **put the book in it** mettez-y le livre; **it's on it** c'est dessus; **he agreed to it** il y a consenti; **did you go to it?** (*party, concert etc*) est-ce que vous y êtes

allé(s)?; **above it, over it** (au-)dessus; **below it, under it** (en-)dessous; **in front of/behind it** devant/derrière
3 (*impersonal*) il; ce, cela, ça; **it's raining** il pleut; **it's Friday tomorrow** demain, c'est vendredi *or* nous sommes, vendredi; **it's 6 o'clock** il est 6 heures; **how far is it?** — **it's 10 miles** c'est loin? — c'est à 10 miles; **it's 2 hours by train** c'est à 2 heures de train; **who is it?** — **it's me** qui est-ce? — c'est moi

ITA *n abbr* (*Brit*: = *initial teaching alphabet*) alphabet en partie phonétique utilisé pour l'enseignement de la lecture
Italian [ɪˈtæljən] *adj* italien(ne) ▷ *n* Italien(ne); (*Ling*) italien *m*
italic [ɪˈtælɪk] *adj* italique
italics [ɪˈtælɪks] *npl* italique *m*
Italy [ˈɪtəlɪ] *n* Italie *f*
itch [ɪtʃ] *n* démangeaison *f* ▷ *vi* (*person*) éprouver des démangeaisons; (*part of body*) démanger; **I'm ~ing to do** l'envie me démange de faire
itchy [ˈɪtʃɪ] *adj* qui démange; **my back is ~** j'ai le dos qui me démange
it'd [ˈɪtd] = **it would; it had**
item [ˈaɪtəm] *n* (*gen*) article *m*; (*on agenda*) question *f*, point *m*; (*in programme*) numéro *m*; (*also*: **news item**) nouvelle *f*; **~s of clothing** articles vestimentaires
itemize [ˈaɪtəmaɪz] *vt* détailler, spécifier
itemized bill [ˈaɪtəmaɪzd-] *n* facture détaillée
itinerant [ɪˈtɪnərənt] *adj* itinérant(e); (*musician*) ambulant(e)
itinerary [aɪˈtɪnərərɪ] *n* itinéraire *m*
it'll [ˈɪtl] = **it will; it shall**
ITN *n abbr* (*Brit*: = *Independent Television News*) chaîne de télévision commerciale
its [ɪts] *adj* son (sa), ses *pl* ▷ *pron* le (la) sien(ne), les siens (siennes)
it's [ɪts] = **it is; it has**
itself [ɪtˈsɛlf] *pron* (*reflexive*) se; (*emphatic*) lui-même (elle-même)
ITV *n abbr* (*Brit*: = *Independent Television*) chaîne de télévision commerciale
IUD *n abbr* = **intra-uterine device**
I've [aɪv] = **I have**
ivory [ˈaɪvərɪ] *n* ivoire *m*
Ivory Coast *n* Côte *f* d'Ivoire
ivy [ˈaɪvɪ] *n* lierre *m*
Ivy League *n* (*US*) *voir article*

IVY LEAGUE

L'*Ivy League* regroupe les huit universités les plus prestigieuses du nord-est des États-Unis, ainsi surnommées à cause de leurs murs recouverts de lierre. Elles organisent des compétitions sportives entre elles. Ces universités sont: Brown, Columbia, Cornell, Dartmouth College, Harvard, Princeton, l'université de Pennsylvanie et Yale.

J j

J, j [dʒeɪ] *n* (*letter*) J, j *m*; **J for Jack**, (US) **J for Jig** J comme Joseph

JA *n abbr* = **judge advocate**

J/A *n abbr* = **joint account**

jab [dʒæb] *vt*: **to ~ sth into** enfoncer *or* planter qch dans ▷ *n* coup *m*; (*Med: inf*) piqûre *f*

jabber ['dʒæbəʳ] *vt, vi* bredouiller, baragouiner

jack [dʒæk] *n* (*Aut*) cric *m*; (*Bowls*) cochonnet *m*; (*Cards*) valet *m*
  ▸ **jack in** *vt* (*inf*) laisser tomber
  ▸ **jack up** *vt* soulever (au cric)

jackal ['dʒækl] *n* chacal *m*

jackass ['dʒækæs] *n* (*also fig*) âne *m*

jackdaw ['dʒækdɔ:] *n* choucas *m*

jacket ['dʒækɪt] *n* veste *f*, veston *m*; (*of boiler etc*) enveloppe *f*; (*of book*) couverture *f*, jaquette *f*

jacket potato *n* pomme *f* de terre en robe des champs

jack-in-the-box ['dʒækɪnðəbɔks] *n* diable *m* à ressort

jackknife ['dʒæknaɪf] *n* couteau *m* de poche ▷ *vi*: **the lorry ~d** la remorque (du camion) s'est mise en travers

jack-of-all-trades ['dʒækəv'ɔ:ltreɪdz] *n* bricoleur *m*

jack plug *n* (*Brit*) jack *m*

jackpot ['dʒækpɔt] *n* gros lot

Jacuzzi® [dʒə'ku:zɪ] *n* jacuzzi® *m*

jaded ['dʒeɪdɪd] *adj* éreinté(e), fatigué(e)

JAG *n abbr* = **Judge Advocate General**

jagged ['dʒægɪd] *adj* dentelé(e)

jaguar ['dʒægjuəʳ] *n* jaguar *m*

jail [dʒeɪl] *n* prison *f* ▷ *vt* emprisonner, mettre en prison

jailbird ['dʒeɪlbə:d] *n* récidiviste *m/f*

jailbreak ['dʒeɪlbreɪk] *n* évasion *f*

jailer ['dʒeɪləʳ] *n* geôlier(-ière)

jail sentence *n* peine *f* de prison

jalopy [dʒə'lɔpɪ] *n* (*inf*) vieux clou

jam [dʒæm] *n* confiture *f*; (*of shoppers etc*) cohue *f*; (*also*: **traffic jam**) embouteillage *m* ▷ *vt* (*passage etc*) encombrer, obstruer; (*mechanism, drawer etc*) bloquer, coincer; (*Radio*) brouiller ▷ *vi* (*mechanism, sliding part*) se coincer, se bloquer; (*gun*) s'enrayer; **to be in a ~** (*inf*) être dans le pétrin; **to get sb out of a ~** (*inf*) sortir qn du pétrin; **to ~ sth into** (*stuff*) entasser *or* comprimer qch dans; (*thrust*) enfoncer qch dans; **the telephone lines are ~med** les lignes (téléphoniques) sont encombrées

Jamaica [dʒə'meɪkə] *n* Jamaïque *f*

Jamaican [dʒə'meɪkən] *adj* jamaïquain(e) ▷ *n* Jamaïquain(e)

jamb ['dʒæm] *n* jambage *m*

jam jar *n* pot *m* à confiture

jammed [dʒæmd] *adj* (*window etc*) coincé(e)

jam-packed [dʒæm'pækt] *adj*: **~ (with)** bourré(e) (de)

jam session *n* jam session *f*

jangle ['dʒæŋgl] *vi* cliqueter

janitor ['dʒænɪtəʳ] *n* (*caretaker*) concierge *m*

January ['dʒænjuərɪ] *n* janvier *m*; *for phrases see also* **July**

Japan [dʒə'pæn] *n* Japon *m*

Japanese [dʒæpə'ni:z] *adj* japonais(e) ▷ *n* (*pl inv*) Japonais(e); (*Ling*) japonais *m*

jar [dʒɑ:ʳ] *n* (*stone, earthenware*) pot *m*; (*glass*) bocal *m* ▷ *vi* (*sound*) produire un son grinçant *or* discordant; (*colours etc*) détonner, jurer ▷ *vt* (*shake*) ébranler, secouer

jargon ['dʒɑ:gən] *n* jargon *m*

jarring ['dʒɑ:rɪŋ] *adj* (*sound, colour*) discordant(e)

Jas. *abbr* = **James**

jasmin, jasmine ['dʒæzmɪn] *n* jasmin *m*

jaundice ['dʒɔ:ndɪs] *n* jaunisse *f*

jaundiced ['dʒɔ:ndɪst] *adj* (*fig*) envieux(-euse), désapprobateur(-trice)

jaunt [dʒɔ:nt] *n* balade *f*

jaunty ['dʒɔ:ntɪ] *adj* enjoué(e), désinvolte

Java ['dʒɑ:və] *n* Java *f*

javelin ['dʒævlɪn] *n* javelot *m*

jaw [dʒɔ:] *n* mâchoire *f*

jawbone ['dʒɔ:bəun] *n* maxillaire *m*

jay [dʒeɪ] *n* geai *m*

jaywalker ['dʒeɪwɔ:kəʳ] *n* piéton indiscipliné

jazz [dʒæz] *n* jazz *m*
  ▸ **jazz up** *vt* animer, égayer

jazz band *n* orchestre *m or* groupe *m* de jazz

jazzy ['dʒæzɪ] *adj* bariolé(e), tapageur(-euse); (*beat*) de jazz

JCB® *n* excavatrice *f*

JCS *n abbr* (US) = **Joint Chiefs of Staff**

JD n abbr (US: = Doctor of Laws) titre universitaire; (= Justice Department) ministère de la Justice

jealous ['dʒɛləs] adj jaloux(-ouse)

jealously ['dʒɛləslɪ] adv jalousement

jealousy ['dʒɛləsɪ] n jalousie f

jeans [dʒiːnz] npl jean m

Jeep® [dʒiːp] n jeep f

jeer [dʒɪə'] vi: **to ~ (at)** huer; se moquer cruellement (de), railler

jeering ['dʒɪərɪŋ] adj railleur(-euse), moqueur(-euse) ▷ n huées fpl

jeers ['dʒɪəz] npl huées fpl; sarcasmes mpl

Jehovah's Witness [dʒɪ'həuvəz-] n témoin m de Jéhovah

Jello® ['dʒɛləu] (US) n gelée f

jelly ['dʒɛlɪ] n (dessert) gelée f; (US: jam) confiture f

jellyfish ['dʒɛlɪfɪʃ] n méduse f

jeopardize ['dʒɛpədaɪz] vt mettre en danger or péril

jeopardy ['dʒɛpədɪ] n: **in ~** en danger or péril

jerk [dʒəːk] n secousse f, saccade f; (of muscle) spasme m; (inf) pauvre type m ▷ vt (shake) donner une secousse à; (pull) tirer brusquement ▷ vi (vehicles) cahoter

jerkin ['dʒəːkɪn] n blouson m

jerky ['dʒəːkɪ] adj saccadé(e), cahotant(e)

jerry-built ['dʒɛrɪbɪlt] adj de mauvaise qualité

jerry can ['dʒɛrɪ-] n bidon m

Jersey ['dʒəːzɪ] n Jersey f

jersey ['dʒəːzɪ] n tricot m; (fabric) jersey m

Jerusalem [dʒə'ruːsləm] n Jérusalem

jest [dʒɛst] n plaisanterie f; **in ~** en plaisantant

jester ['dʒɛstə'] n (History) plaisantin m

Jesus ['dʒiːzəs] n Jésus; **~ Christ** Jésus-Christ

jet [dʒɛt] n (of gas, liquid) jet m; (Aut) gicleur m; (Aviat) avion m à réaction, jet m

jet-black ['dʒɛt'blæk] adj (d'un noir) de jais

jet engine n moteur m à réaction

jet lag n décalage m horaire

jetsam ['dʒɛtsəm] n objets jetés à la mer (et rejetés sur la côte)

jet-setter ['dʒɛtsɛtə'] n membre m du or de la jet set

jet-ski vi faire du jet-ski or scooter des mers

jettison ['dʒɛtɪsn] vt jeter par-dessus bord

jetty ['dʒɛtɪ] n jetée f, digue f

Jew [dʒuː] n Juif m

jewel ['dʒuːəl] n bijou m, joyau m; (in watch) rubis m

jeweller, (US) **jeweler** ['dʒuːələ'] n bijoutier(-ière), joaillier m

jeweller's, jeweller's shop n (Brit) bijouterie f, joaillerie f

jewellery, (US) **jewelry** ['dʒuːəlrɪ] n bijoux mpl

Jewess ['dʒuːɪs] n Juive f

Jewish ['dʒuːɪʃ] adj juif (juive)

JFK n abbr (US) = **John Fitzgerald Kennedy International Airport**

jib [dʒɪb] n (Naut) foc m; (of crane) flèche f ▷ vi (horse) regimber; **to ~ at doing sth** rechigner à faire qch

jibe [dʒaɪb] n sarcasme m

jiffy ['dʒɪfɪ] n (inf): **in a ~** en un clin d'œil

jig [dʒɪg] n (dance, tune) gigue m

jigsaw ['dʒɪgsɔː] n (also: **jigsaw puzzle**) puzzle m; (tool) scie sauteuse

jilt [dʒɪlt] vt laisser tomber, plaquer

jingle ['dʒɪŋgl] n (advertising jingle) couplet m publicitaire ▷ vi cliqueter, tinter

jingoism ['dʒɪŋgəuɪzəm] n chauvinisme m

jinx [dʒɪŋks] n (inf) (mauvais) sort

jitters ['dʒɪtəz] npl (inf): **to get the ~** avoir la trouille or la frousse

jittery ['dʒɪtərɪ] adj (inf) nerveux(-euse); **to be ~** avoir les nerfs en pelote

jiujitsu [dʒuː'dʒɪtsuː] n jiu-jitsu m

job [dʒɔb] n (chore, task) travail m, tâche f; (employment) emploi m, poste m, place f; **a part-time/full-time ~** un emploi à temps partiel/à plein temps; **he's only doing his ~** il fait son boulot; **it's a good ~ that ...** c'est heureux or c'est une chance que ... + sub; **just the ~!** (c'est) juste or exactement ce qu'il faut!

jobber ['dʒɔbə'] n (Brit Stock Exchange) négociant m en titres

jobbing ['dʒɔbɪŋ] adj (Brit: workman) à la tâche, à la journée

job centre ['dʒɔbsɛntə'] (Brit) n ≈ ANPE f, ≈ Agence nationale pour l'emploi

job creation scheme n plan m pour la création d'emplois

job description n description f du poste

jobless ['dʒɔblɪs] adj sans travail, au chômage ▷ npl: **the ~** les sans-emploi m inv, les chômeurs mpl

job lot n lot m (d'articles divers)

job satisfaction n satisfaction professionnelle

job security n sécurité f de l'emploi

job specification n caractéristiques fpl du poste

Jock [dʒɔk] n (inf: Scotsman) Écossais m

jockey ['dʒɔkɪ] n jockey m ▷ vi: **to ~ for position** manœuvrer pour être bien placé

jockey box n (US Aut) boîte f à gants, vide-poches m inv

jockstrap ['dʒɔkstræp] n slip m de sport

jocular ['dʒɔkjulə'] adj jovial(e), enjoué(e); facétieux(-euse)

jog [dʒɔg] vt secouer ▷ vi (Sport) faire du jogging; **to ~ along** cahoter; trotter; **to ~ sb's memory** rafraîchir la mémoire de qn

jogger ['dʒɔgə'] n jogger m/f

jogging ['dʒɔgɪŋ] n jogging m

john [dʒɔn] n (US inf): **the ~** (toilet) les cabinets mpl

join [dʒɔɪn] vt (put together) unir, assembler; (become member of) s'inscrire à; (meet) rejoindre, retrouver; (queue) se joindre à ▷ vi (roads, rivers) se rejoindre, se rencontrer ▷ n raccord m; **will you ~ us for dinner?** vous dînerez bien avec nous?; **I'll ~ you later** je vous rejoindrai plus tard; **to ~ forces (with)** s'associer (à)

▶ **join in** vi se mettre de la partie ▷ vt fus se mêler à

▶ **join up** vi (meet) se rejoindre; (Mil) s'engager

joiner ['dʒɔɪnəʳ] (*Brit*) *n* menuisier *m*
joinery ['dʒɔɪnərɪ] *n* menuiserie *f*
joint [dʒɔɪnt] *n* (*Tech*) jointure *f*; joint *m*; (*Anat*) articulation *f*, jointure; (*Brit Culin*) rôti *m*; (*inf: place*) boîte *f*; (*of cannabis*) joint ▷ *adj* commun(e); (*committee*) mixte, paritaire; (*winner*) ex aequo; **~ responsibility** coresponsabilité *f*
joint account *n* compte joint
jointly ['dʒɔɪntlɪ] *adv* ensemble, en commun
joint ownership *n* copropriété *f*
joint-stock company ['dʒɔɪntstɔk-] *n* société *f* par actions
joint venture *n* entreprise commune
joist [dʒɔɪst] *n* solive *f*
joke [dʒəuk] *n* plaisanterie *f*; (*also:* **practical joke**) farce *f* ▷ *vi* plaisanter; **to play a ~ on** jouer un tour à, faire une farce à
joker ['dʒəukəʳ] *n* plaisantin *m*, blagueur(-euse); (*Cards*) joker *m*
joking ['dʒəukɪŋ] *n* plaisanterie *f*
jollity ['dʒɔlɪtɪ] *n* réjouissances *fpl*, gaieté *f*
jolly ['dʒɔlɪ] *adj* gai(e), enjoué(e); (*enjoyable*) amusant(e), plaisant(e) ▷ *adv* (*Brit inf*) rudement, drôlement ▷ *vt* (*Brit*): **to ~ sb along** amadouer qn, convaincre *or* entraîner qn à force d'encouragements; **~ good!** (*Brit*) formidable!
jolt [dʒəult] *n* cahot *m*, secousse *f*; (*shock*) choc *m* ▷ *vt* cahoter, secouer
Jordan [dʒɔː.dən] *n* (*country*) Jordanie *f*; (*river*) Jourdain *m*
Jordanian [dʒɔː'deɪnɪən] *adj* jordanien(ne) ▷ *n* Jordanien(ne)
joss stick ['dʒɔsstɪk] *n* bâton *m* d'encens
jostle ['dʒɔsl] *vt* bousculer, pousser ▷ *vi* jouer des coudes
jot [dʒɔt] *n*: **not one ~** pas un brin
▶**jot down** *vt* inscrire rapidement, noter
jotter ['dʒɔtəʳ] *n* (*Brit*) cahier *m* (de brouillon); bloc-notes *m*
journal ['dʒə:nl] *n* journal *m*
journalese [dʒə:nə'li:z] *n* (*pej*) style *m* journalistique
journalism ['dʒə:nəlɪzəm] *n* journalisme *m*
journalist ['dʒə:nəlɪst] *n* journaliste *m/f*
journey ['dʒə:nɪ] *n* voyage *m*; (*distance covered*) trajet *m* ▷ *vi* voyager; **the ~ takes two hours** le trajet dure deux heures; **a 5-hour ~** un voyage de 5 heures; **how was your ~?** votre voyage s'est bien passé?
jovial ['dʒəuvɪəl] *adj* jovial(e)
jowl [dʒaul] *n* mâchoire *f* (*inférieure*); bajoue *f*
joy [dʒɔɪ] *n* joie *f*
joyful ['dʒɔɪful], **joyous** ['dʒɔɪəs] *adj* joyeux(-euse)
joyride ['dʒɔɪraɪd] *vi*: **to go joyriding** faire une virée dans une voiture volée
joyrider ['dʒɔɪraɪdəʳ] *n* voleur(-euse) de voiture (*qui fait une virée dans le véhicule volé*)
joy stick ['dʒɔɪstɪk] *n* (*Aviat*) manche *m* à balai; (*Comput*) manche à balai, manette *f* (de jeu)
JP *n abbr* = **Justice of the Peace**

Jr *abbr* = **junior**
JTPA *n abbr* (*US*: = *Job Training Partnership Act*) programme gouvernemental de formation
jubilant ['dʒu:bɪlnt] *adj* triomphant(e), réjoui(e)
jubilation [dʒu:bɪ'leɪʃən] *n* jubilation *f*
jubilee ['dʒu:bɪli:] *n* jubilé *m*; **silver ~** (jubilé du) vingt-cinquième anniversaire
judge [dʒʌdʒ] *n* juge *m* ▷ *vt* juger; (*estimate: weight, size etc*) apprécier; (*consider*) estimer ▷ *vi*: **judging** *or* **to ~ by his expression** d'après son expression; **as far as I can ~** autant que je puisse en juger
judge advocate *n* (*Mil*) magistrat *m* militaire
judgment, judgement ['dʒʌdʒmənt] *n* jugement *m*; (*punishment*) châtiment *m*; **in my ~** à mon avis; **to pass ~ on** (*Law*) prononcer un jugement (sur)
judicial [dʒu:'dɪʃl] *adj* judiciaire; (*fair*) impartial(e)
judiciary [dʒu:'dɪʃɪərɪ] *n* (pouvoir *m*) judiciaire *m*
judicious [dʒu:'dɪʃəs] *adj* judicieux(-euse)
judo ['dʒu:dəu] *n* judo *m*
jug [dʒʌg] *n* pot *m*, cruche *f*
jugged hare ['dʒʌgd-] *n* (*Brit*) civet *m* de lièvre
juggernaut ['dʒʌgənɔ:t] *n* (*Brit: huge truck*) mastodonte *m*
juggle ['dʒʌgl] *vi* jongler
juggler ['dʒʌgləʳ] *n* jongleur *m*
Jugoslav ['ju:gəu'slɑ:v] *adj, n* = **Yugoslav**
jugular ['dʒʌgjuləʳ] *adj*: **~ (vein)** veine *f* jugulaire
juice [dʒu:s] *n* jus *m*; (*inf: petrol*): **we've run out of ~** c'est la panne sèche
juicy ['dʒu:sɪ] *adj* juteux(-euse)
jukebox ['dʒu:kbɔks] *n* juke-box *m*
July [dʒu:'laɪ] *n* juillet *m*; **the first of ~** le premier juillet; **(on) the eleventh of ~** le onze juillet; **in the month of ~** au mois de juillet; **at the beginning/end of ~** au début/à la fin (du mois) de juillet, début/fin juillet; **in the middle of ~** au milieu (du mois) de juillet, à la mi-juillet; **during ~** pendant le mois de juillet; **in ~ of next year** en juillet de l'année prochaine; **each** *or* **every ~** tous les ans *or* chaque année en juillet; **~ was wet this year** il a beaucoup plu cette année en juillet
jumble ['dʒʌmbl] *n* fouillis *m* ▷ *vt* (*also:* **jumble up, jumble together**) mélanger, brouiller
jumble sale *n* (*Brit*) vente *f* de charité
jumbo ['dʒʌmbəu] *adj* (*also:* **jumbo jet**) (avion) gros porteur (à réaction); **~ size** format maxi *or* extra-grand
jump [dʒʌmp] *vi* sauter, bondir; (*with fear etc*) sursauter; (*increase*) monter en flèche ▷ *vt* sauter, franchir ▷ *n* saut *m*, bond *m*; (*with fear etc*) sursaut *m*; (*fence*) obstacle *m*; **to ~ the queue** (*Brit*) passer avant son tour
▶**jump about** *vi* sautiller
▶**jump at** *vt fus* (*fig*) sauter sur; **he ~ed at the offer** il s'est empressé d'accepter la proposition
▶**jump down** *vi* sauter (pour descendre)
▶**jump up** *vi* se lever (d'un bond)
jumped-up ['dʒʌmptʌp] *adj* (*Brit pej*) parvenu(e)

jumper ['dʒʌmpə^r] n (Brit: pullover) pull-over m; (US: pinafore dress) robe-chasuble f; (Sport) sauteur(-euse)

jump leads, (US) **jumper cables** npl câbles mpl de démarrage

jump-start ['dʒʌmpstɑ:t] vt (car: push) démarrer en poussant; (: with jump leads) démarrer avec des câbles (de démarrage); (fig: project, situation) faire redémarrer promptement

jumpy ['dʒʌmpɪ] adj nerveux(-euse), agité(e)

Jun. abbr = **June**; **junior**

junction ['dʒʌŋkʃən] n (Brit: of roads) carrefour m; (of rails) embranchement m

juncture ['dʒʌŋktʃə^r] n: **at this ~** à ce moment-là, sur ces entrefaites

June [dʒu:n] n juin m; for phrases see also **July**

jungle ['dʒʌŋgl] n jungle f

junior ['dʒu:nɪə^r] adj, n: **he's ~ to me (by two years), he's my ~ (by two years)** il est mon cadet (de deux ans), il est plus jeune que moi (de deux ans); **he's ~ to me** (seniority) il est en dessous de moi (dans la hiérarchie), j'ai plus d'ancienneté que lui

junior executive n cadre moyen

junior high school n (US) ≈ collège m d'enseignement secondaire; see also **high school**

junior minister n (Brit) ministre m sous tutelle

junior partner n associé(-adjoint) m

junior school n (Brit) école f primaire

junior sizes npl (Comm) tailles fpl fillettes/garçonnets

juniper ['dʒu:nɪpə^r] n: **~ berry** baie f de genièvre

junk [dʒʌŋk] n (rubbish) camelote f; (cheap goods) bric-à-brac m inv; (ship) jonque f ▷ vt (inf) abandonner, mettre au rancart

junk bond n (Comm) obligation hautement spéculative utilisée dans les OPA agressives

junk dealer n brocanteur(-euse)

junket ['dʒʌŋkɪt] n (Culin) lait caillé; (Brit inf): **to go on a ~, go ~ing** voyager aux frais de la princesse

junk food n snacks vite prêts (sans valeur nutritive)

junkie ['dʒʌŋkɪ] n (inf) junkie m, drogué(e)

junk mail n prospectus mpl; (Comput) messages mpl publicitaires

junk room n (US) débarras m

junk shop n (boutique f de) brocanteur m

Junr abbr = **junior**

junta ['dʒʌntə] n junte f

Jupiter ['dʒu:pɪtə^r] n (planet) Jupiter f

jurisdiction [dʒuərɪs'dɪkʃən] n juridiction f; **it falls** or **comes within/outside our ~** cela est/n'est pas de notre compétence or ressort

jurisprudence [dʒuərɪs'pru:dəns] n jurisprudence f

juror ['dʒuərə^r] n juré m

jury ['dʒuərɪ] n jury m

jury box n banc m des jurés

juryman ['dʒuərɪmən] (irreg) n = **juror**

just [dʒʌst] adj juste ▷ adv: **he's ~ done it/left** il vient de le faire/partir; **~ as I expected** exactement or précisément comme je m'y attendais; **~ right/two o'clock** exactement or juste ce qu'il faut/deux heures; **we were ~ going** nous partions; **I was ~ about to phone** j'allais téléphoner; **~ as he was leaving** au moment or à l'instant précis où il partait; **~ before/enough/here** juste avant/assez/là; **it's ~ me/a mistake** ce n'est que moi/(rien) qu'une erreur; **~ missed/caught** manqué/attrapé de justesse; **~ listen to this!** écoutez un peu ça!; **~ ask someone the way** vous n'avez qu'à demander votre chemin à quelqu'un; **it's ~ as good** c'est (vraiment) aussi bon; **she's ~ as clever as you** elle est tout aussi intelligente que vous; **it's ~ as well that you ...** heureusement que vous ...; **not ~ now** pas tout de suite; **~ a minute!, ~ one moment!** un instant (s'il vous plaît)!

justice ['dʒʌstɪs] n justice f; (US: judge) juge m de la Cour suprême; **Lord Chief J~** (Brit) premier président de la cour d'appel; **this photo doesn't do you ~** cette photo ne vous avantage pas

Justice of the Peace n juge m de paix

justifiable [dʒʌstɪ'faɪəbl] adj justifiable

justifiably [dʒʌstɪ'faɪəblɪ] adv légitimement, à juste titre

justification [dʒʌstɪfɪ'keɪʃən] n justification f

justify ['dʒʌstɪfaɪ] vt justifier; **to be justified in doing sth** être en droit de faire qch

justly ['dʒʌstlɪ] adv avec raison, justement

justness ['dʒʌstnɪs] n justesse f

jut [dʒʌt] vi (also: **jut out**) dépasser, faire saillie

jute [dʒu:t] n jute m

juvenile ['dʒu:vənaɪl] adj juvénile; (court, books) pour enfants ▷ n adolescent(e)

juvenile delinquency n délinquance f juvénile

juxtapose ['dʒʌkstəpəuz] vt juxtaposer

juxtaposition ['dʒʌkstəpə'zɪʃən] n juxtaposition f

Kk

K, k [keɪ] n (letter) K, k m; **K for King** K comme Kléber ▷ abbr (= one thousand) K; (Brit: = Knight) titre honorifique
kaftan ['kæftæn] n cafetan m
Kalahari Desert [kælə'hɑːrɪ-] n désert m de Kalahari
kale [keɪl] n chou frisé
kaleidoscope [kə'laɪdəskəup] n kaléidoscope m
kamikaze [kæmɪ'kɑːzɪ] adj kamikaze
Kampala [kæm'pɑːlə] n Kampala
Kampuchea [kæmpu'tʃɪə] n Kampuchéa m
kangaroo [kæŋgə'ruː] n kangourou m
Kans. abbr (US) = **Kansas**
kaput [kə'put] adj (inf) kaput
karaoke [kɑːrə'əukɪ] n karaoké m
karate [kə'rɑːtɪ] n karaté m
Kashmir [kæʃ'mɪəʳ] n Cachemire m
Kazakhstan [kɑːzɑːk'stæn] n Kazakhstan m
kB n abbr (= kilobyte) Ko m
KC n abbr (Brit Law: = King's Counsel) titre donné à certains avocats; see also **QC**
kd abbr (US: = knocked down) en pièces détachées
kebab [kə'bæb] n kebab m
keel [kiːl] n quille f; **on an even ~** (fig) à flot
  ▶ **keel over** vi (Naut) chavirer, dessaler; (person) tomber dans les pommes
keen [kiːn] adj (eager) plein(e) d'enthousiasme; (interest, desire, competition) vif (vive); (eye, intelligence) pénétrant(e); (edge) effilé(e); **to be ~ to do** or **on doing sth** désirer vivement faire qch, tenir beaucoup à faire qch; **to be ~ on sth/ sb** aimer beaucoup qch/qn; **I'm not ~ on going** je ne suis pas chaud pour y aller, je n'ai pas très envie d'y aller
keenly ['kiːnlɪ] adv (enthusiastically) avec enthousiasme; (feel) vivement, profondément; (look) intensément
keenness ['kiːnnɪs] n (eagerness) enthousiasme m; ~ **to do** vif désir de faire
keep [kiːp] (pt, pp **kept** [kɛpt]) vt (retain, preserve) garder; (hold back) retenir; (shop, accounts, promise, diary) tenir; (support) entretenir, assurer la subsistance de; (a promise) tenir; (chickens, bees, pigs etc) élever ▷ vi (food) se conserver; (remain: in a certain state or place) rester ▷ n (of castle) donjon m; (food etc): **enough for his ~** assez pour

(assurer) sa subsistance; **to ~ doing sth** (continue) continuer à faire qch; (repeatedly) ne pas arrêter de faire qch; **to ~ sb from doing/ sth from happening** empêcher qn de faire or que qn (ne) fasse/que qch (n')arrive; **to ~ sb happy/a place tidy** faire que qn soit content/ qu'un endroit reste propre; **to ~ sb waiting** faire attendre qn; **to ~ an appointment** ne pas manquer un rendez-vous; **to ~ a record of sth** prendre note de qch; **to ~ sth to o.s.** garder qch pour soi, tenir qch secret; **to ~ sth from sb** cacher qch à qn; **to ~ time** (clock) être à l'heure, ne pas retarder; **for ~s** (inf) pour de bon, pour toujours
  ▶ **keep away** vt: **to ~ sth/sb away from sb** tenir qch/qn éloigné de qn ▷ vi: **to ~ away (from)** ne pas s'approcher (de)
  ▶ **keep back** vt (crowds, tears, money) retenir; (conceal: information): **to ~ sth back from sb** cacher qch à qn ▷ vi rester en arrière
  ▶ **keep down** vt (control: prices, spending) empêcher d'augmenter, limiter; (retain: food) garder ▷ vi (person) rester assis(e); rester par terre
  ▶ **keep in** vt (invalid, child) garder à la maison; (Scol) consigner ▷ vi (inf): **to ~ in with sb** rester en bons termes avec qn
  ▶ **keep off** vt (dog, person) éloigner ▷ vi ne pas s'approcher; **if the rain ~s off** s'il ne pleut pas; **~ your hands off!** pas touche! (inf); **"~ off the grass"** "pelouse interdite"
  ▶ **keep on** vi continuer; **to ~ on doing** continuer à faire; **don't ~ on about it!** arrête (d'en parler)!
  ▶ **keep out** vt empêcher d'entrer ▷ vi (stay out) rester en dehors; **"~ out"** "défense d'entrer"
  ▶ **keep up** vi (fig: in comprehension) suivre ▷ vt continuer, maintenir; **to ~ up with sb** (in work etc) se maintenir au même niveau que qn; (in race etc) aller aussi vite que qn
keeper ['kiːpəʳ] n gardien(ne)
keep-fit [kiːp'fɪt] n gymnastique f (d'entretien)
keeping ['kiːpɪŋ] n (care) garde f; **in ~ with** en harmonie avec
keeps [kiːps] n: **for ~** (inf) pour de bon, pour toujours

keepsake ['ki:pseɪk] n souvenir m

keg [kɛg] n barrique f, tonnelet m

Ken. abbr (US) = **Kentucky**

kennel ['kɛnl] n niche f; **kennels** npl (for boarding) chenil m

Kenya ['kɛnjə] n Kenya m

Kenyan ['kɛnjən] adj kényan(ne) ▷ n Kényan(ne)

kept [kɛpt] pt, pp of **keep**

kerb [kə:b] n (Brit) bordure f du trottoir

kerb crawler [-krɔ:ləʳ] n personne qui accoste les prostitué(e)s en voiture

kernel ['kə:nl] n amande f; (fig) noyau m

kerosene ['kɛrəsi:n] n kérosène m

ketchup ['kɛtʃəp] n ketchup m

kettle ['kɛtl] n bouilloire f

key [ki:] n; clé f; (of piano, typewriter) touche f; (on map) légende f ▷ adj (factor, role, area) clé inv ▷ cpd (-)clé ▷ vt (also: **key in**: text) saisir; **can I have my ~?** je peux avoir ma clé?; **a ~ issue** un problème fondamental

keyboard ['ki:bɔ:d] n clavier m ▷ vt (text) saisir

keyboarder ['ki:bɔ:dəʳ] n claviste m/f

keyed up [ki:d'ʌp] adj: **to be (all) ~** être surexcité(e)

keyhole ['ki:həul] n trou m de la serrure

keyhole surgery n chirurgie très minutieuse où l'incision est minimale

keynote ['ki:nəut] n (Mus) tonique f; (fig) note dominante

keypad ['ki:pæd] n pavé m numérique

keyring ['ki:rɪŋ] n porte-clés m

keystroke ['ki:strəuk] n frappe f

kg abbr (= kilogram) K

KGB n abbr KGB m

khaki ['kɑ:kɪ] adj, n kaki m

kibbutz [kɪ'buts] n kibboutz m

kick [kɪk] vt donner un coup de pied à ▷ vi (horse) ruer ▷ n coup m de pied; (of rifle) recul m; (inf: thrill): **he does it for ~s** il le fait parce que ça l'excite, il le fait pour le plaisir; **to ~ the habit** (inf) arrêter

▶ **kick around** vi (inf) traîner

▶ **kick off** vi (Sport) donner le coup d'envoi

kick-off ['kɪkɔf] n (Sport) coup m d'envoi

kick-start ['kɪkstɑ:t] n (also: **kick-starter**) lanceur m au pied

kid [kɪd] n (inf: child) gamin(e), gosse m/f; (animal, leather) chevreau m ▷ vi (inf) plaisanter, blaguer

kid gloves npl: **to treat sb with ~** traiter qn avec ménagement

kidnap ['kɪdnæp] vt enlever, kidnapper

kidnapper ['kɪdnæpəʳ] n ravisseur(-euse)

kidnapping ['kɪdnæpɪŋ] n enlèvement m

kidney ['kɪdnɪ] n (Anat) rein m; (Culin) rognon m

kidney bean n haricot m rouge

kidney machine n (Med) rein artificiel

Kilimanjaro [kɪlɪmən'dʒɑ:rəu] n: **Mount ~** Kilimandjaro m

kill [kɪl] vt tuer; (fig) faire échouer; détruire; supprimer ▷ n mise f à mort; **to ~ time** tuer le temps

▶ **kill off** vt exterminer; (fig) éliminer

killer ['kɪləʳ] n tueur(-euse); (murderer) meurtrier(-ière)

killer instinct n combativité f; **to have the ~** avoir un tempérament de battant

killing ['kɪlɪŋ] n meurtre m; (of group of people) tuerie f, massacre m; (inf): **to make a ~** se remplir les poches, réussir un beau coup ▷ adj (inf) tordant(e)

killjoy ['kɪldʒɔɪ] n rabat-joie m inv

kiln [kɪln] n four m

kilo ['ki:ləu] n kilo m

kilobyte ['ki:ləubaɪt] n (Comput) kilo-octet m

kilogram, kilogramme ['kɪləugræm] n kilogramme m

kilometre, (US) **kilometer** ['kɪləmi:təʳ] n kilomètre m

kilowatt ['kɪləuwɔt] n kilowatt m

kilt [kɪlt] n kilt m

kilter ['kɪltəʳ] n: **out of ~** déréglé(e), détraqué(e)

kimono [kɪ'məunəu] n kimono m

kin [kɪn] n see **next-of-kin**; **kith**

kind [kaɪnd] adj gentil(le), aimable ▷ n sorte f, espèce f; (species) genre m; **would you be ~ enough to …?, would you be so ~ as to …?** auriez-vous la gentillesse or l'obligeance de …?; **it's very ~ of you (to do)** c'est très aimable à vous (de faire); **to be two of a ~** se ressembler; **in ~** (Comm) en nature; (fig): **to repay sb in ~** rendre la pareille à qn; **~ of** (inf: rather) plutôt; **a ~ of** une sorte de; **what ~ of …?** quelle sorte de …?

kindergarten ['kɪndəgɑ:tn] n jardin m d'enfants

kind-hearted [kaɪnd'hɑ:tɪd] adj bon (bonne)

kindle ['kɪndl] vt allumer, enflammer

kindling ['kɪndlɪŋ] n petit bois

kindly ['kaɪndlɪ] adj bienveillant(e), plein(e) de gentillesse ▷ adv avec bonté; **will you ~ …** auriez-vous la bonté or l'obligeance de …; **he didn't take it ~** il l'a mal pris

kindness ['kaɪndnɪs] n (quality) bonté f, gentillesse f

kindred ['kɪndrɪd] adj apparenté(e); **~ spirit** âme f sœur

kinetic [kɪ'nɛtɪk] adj cinétique

king [kɪŋ] n roi m

kingdom ['kɪŋdəm] n royaume m

kingfisher ['kɪŋfɪʃəʳ] n martin-pêcheur m

kingpin ['kɪŋpɪn] n (Tech) pivot m; (fig) cheville ouvrière

king-size ['kɪŋsaɪz], **king-sized** ['kɪŋsaɪzd] adj (cigarette) (format) extra-long (longue)

king-size bed, king-sized bed n grand lit (de 1,95 m de large)

kink [kɪŋk] n (of rope) entortillement m; (in hair) ondulation f; (inf: fig) aberration f

kinky ['kɪŋkɪ] adj (fig) excentrique; (pej) aux goûts spéciaux

kinship ['kɪnʃɪp] n parenté f

kinsman ['kɪnzmən] (irreg) n parent m

kinswoman ['kɪnzwumən] (irreg) n parente f

kiosk ['ki:ɔsk] *n* kiosque *m*; (*Brit: also:* **telephone kiosk**) cabine *f* (téléphonique); (*also:* **newspaper kiosk**) kiosque à journaux
kipper ['kɪpəʳ] *n* hareng fumé et salé
Kirghizia [kə:'gɪzɪə] *n* Kirghizistan *m*
kiss [kɪs] *n* baiser *m* ▷ *vt* embrasser; **to ~ (each other)** s'embrasser; **to ~ sb goodbye** dire au revoir à qn en l'embrassant
kissagram ['kɪsəgræm] *n* baiser envoyé à l'occasion d'une célébration par l'intermédiaire d'une personne employée à cet effet
kiss of life *n* (*Brit*) bouche à bouche *m*
kit [kɪt] *n* équipement *m*, matériel *m*; (*set of tools etc*) trousse *f*; (*for assembly*) kit *m*; **tool ~** nécessaire *m* à outils
  ▸ **kit out** *vt* (*Brit*) équiper
kitbag ['kɪtbæg] *n* sac *m* de voyage *or* de marin
kitchen ['kɪtʃɪn] *n* cuisine *f*
kitchen garden *n* jardin *m* potager
kitchen sink *n* évier *m*
kitchen unit *n* (*Brit*) élément *m* de cuisine
kitchenware ['kɪtʃɪnwɛəʳ] *n* vaisselle *f*; ustensiles *mpl* de cuisine
kite [kaɪt] *n* (*toy*) cerf-volant *m*; (*Zool*) milan *m*
kith [kɪθ] *n*: **~ and kin** parents et amis *mpl*
kitten ['kɪtn] *n* petit chat, chaton *m*
kitty ['kɪtɪ] *n* (*money*) cagnotte *f*
kiwi ['ki:wi:] *n* (*also:* **kiwi fruit**) kiwi *m*
KKK *n abbr* (*US*) = **Ku Klux Klan**
Kleenex® ['kli:nɛks] *n* Kleenex® *m*
kleptomaniac [klɛptəu'meɪnɪæk] *n* kleptomane *m/f*
km *abbr* (= *kilometre*) km
km/h *abbr* (= *kilometres per hour*) km/h
knack [næk] *n*: **to have the ~ (of doing)** avoir le coup (pour faire); **there's a ~** il y a un coup à prendre *or* une combine
knackered ['nækəd] *adj* (*inf*) crevé(e), nase
knapsack ['næpsæk] *n* musette *f*
knave [neɪv] *n* (*Cards*) valet *m*
knead [ni:d] *vt* pétrir
knee [ni:] *n* genou *m*
kneecap ['ni:kæp] *n* rotule *f* ▷ *vt* tirer un coup de feu dans la rotule de
knee-deep ['ni:'di:p] *adj*: **the water was ~** l'eau arrivait aux genoux
kneel (*pt, pp* **knelt**) [ni:l, nɛlt] *vi* (*also:* **kneel down**) s'agenouiller
kneepad ['ni:pæd] *n* genouillère *f*
knell [nɛl] *n* glas *m*
knelt [nɛlt] *pt, pp of* **kneel**
knew [nju:] *pt of* **know**
knickers ['nɪkəz] *npl* (*Brit*) culotte *f* (de femme)
knick-knack ['nɪknæk] *n* colifichet *m*
knife [naɪf] *n* (*pl* **knives** [naɪvz]) couteau *m* ▷ *vt* poignarder, frapper d'un coup de couteau; **~, fork and spoon** couvert *m*
knife-edge ['naɪfɛdʒ] *n*: **to be on a ~** être sur le fil du rasoir
knight [naɪt] *n* chevalier *m*; (*Chess*) cavalier *m*
knighthood ['naɪthud] *n* chevalerie *f*; (*title*): **to get a ~** être fait chevalier

knit [nɪt] *vt* tricoter; (*fig*): **to ~ together** unir ▷ *vi* tricoter; (*broken bones*) se ressouder; **to ~ one's brows** froncer les sourcils
knitted ['nɪtɪd] *adj* en tricot
knitting ['nɪtɪŋ] *n* tricot *m*
knitting machine *n* machine *f* à tricoter
knitting needle *n* aiguille *f* à tricoter
knitting pattern *n* modèle *m* (pour tricot)
knitwear ['nɪtwɛəʳ] *n* tricots *mpl*, lainages *mpl*
knives [naɪvz] *npl of* **knife**
knob [nɔb] *n* bouton *m*; (*Brit*): **a ~ of butter** une noix de beurre
knobbly ['nɔblɪ], (*US*) **knobby** ['nɔbɪ] *adj* (*wood, surface*) noueux(-euse); (*knees*) noueux
knock [nɔk] *vt* frapper; (*bump into*) heurter; (*make: hole etc*): **to ~ a hole in** faire un trou dans, trouer; (*for: nail etc*): **to ~ a nail into** enfoncer un clou dans; (*fig: col*) dénigrer ▷ *vi* (*engine*) cogner; (*at door etc*): **to ~ at/on** frapper à/sur ▷ *n* coup *m*; **he ~ed at the door** il frappa à la porte
  ▸ **knock down** *vt* renverser; (*price*) réduire
  ▸ **knock off** *vi* (*inf: finish*) s'arrêter (de travailler) ▷ *vt* (*vase, object*) faire tomber; (*inf: steal*) piquer; (*fig: from price etc*): **to ~ off £10** faire une remise de 10 livres
  ▸ **knock out** *vt* assommer; (*Boxing*) mettre k.-o.; (*in competition*) éliminer
  ▸ **knock over** *vt* (*object*) faire tomber; (*pedestrian*) renverser
knockdown ['nɔkdaun] *adj* (*price*) sacrifié(e)
knocker ['nɔkəʳ] *n* (*on door*) heurtoir *m*
knocking ['nɔkɪŋ] *n* coups *mpl*
knock-kneed [nɔk'ni:d] *adj* aux genoux cagneux
knockout ['nɔkaut] *n* (*Boxing*) knock-out *m*, K.-O. *m*; **~ competition** (*Brit*) compétition *f* avec épreuves éliminatoires
knock-up ['nɔkʌp] *n* (*Tennis*): **to have a ~** faire des balles
knot [nɔt] *n* (*gen*) nœud *m* ▷ *vt* nouer; **to tie a ~** faire un nœud
knotty ['nɔtɪ] *adj* (*fig*) épineux(-euse)
know [nəu] *vt* (*pt* **knew**, *pp* **known** [nju:, nəun]) savoir; (*person, place*) connaître; **to ~ that** savoir que; **to ~ how to do** savoir faire; **to ~ how to swim** savoir nager; **to ~ about/of sth** (*event*) être au courant de qch; (*subject*) connaître qch; **to get to ~ sth** (*fact*) apprendre qch; (*place*) apprendre à connaître qch; **I don't ~** je ne sais pas; **I don't ~ him** je ne le connais pas; **do you ~ where I can ...?** savez-vous où je peux ...?; **to ~ right from wrong** savoir distinguer le bon du mauvais; **as far as I ~ ...** à ma connaissance ..., autant que je sache ...
know-all ['nəuɔ:l] *n* (*Brit pej*) je-sais-tout *m/f*
know-how ['nəuhau] *n* savoir-faire *m*, technique *f*, compétence *f*
knowing ['nəuɪŋ] *adj* (*look etc*) entendu(e)
knowingly ['nəuɪŋlɪ] *adv* (*on purpose*) sciemment; (*smile, look*) d'un air entendu
know-it-all ['nəuɪtɔ:l] *n* (*US*) = **know-all**
knowledge ['nɔlɪdʒ] *n* connaissance *f*; (*learning*)

connaissances, savoir *m*; **to have no ~ of** ignorer; **not to my ~** pas à ma connaissance; **without my ~** à mon insu; **to have a working ~ of French** se débrouiller en français; **it is common ~ that ...** chacun sait que ...; **it has come to my ~ that ...** j'ai appris que ...
knowledgeable ['nɔlɪdʒəbl] *adj* bien informé(e)
known [nəun] *pp of* **know** ▷ *adj* (*thief, facts*) notoire; (*expert*) célèbre
knuckle ['nʌkl] *n* articulation *f* (des phalanges), jointure *f*
▶ **knuckle down** *vi* (*inf*) s'y mettre
▶ **knuckle under** *vi* (*inf*) céder
knuckleduster ['nʌkldʌstər] *n* coup-de-poing américain
KO *abbr* = **knock out** ▷ *n* K.-O. *m* ▷ *vt* mettre K.-O.
koala [kəu'ɑːlə] *n* (*also:* **koala bear**) koala *m*
kook [kuːk] *n* (*US inf*) loufoque *m/f*
Koran [kɔ'rɑːn] *n* Coran *m*

Korea [kə'rɪə] *n* Corée *f*; **North/South ~** Corée du Nord/Sud
Korean [kə'rɪən] *adj* coréen(ne) ▷ *n* Coréen(ne)
kosher ['kəuʃər] *adj* kascher *inv*
Kosovar, Kosovan ['kɔsəvɑːr, 'kɔsəvən] *adj* kosovar(e)
Kosovo ['kɔsɔvəu] *n* Kosovo *m*
kowtow ['kau'tau] *vi*: **to ~ to sb** s'aplatir devant qn
Kremlin ['krɛmlɪn] *n*: **the ~** le Kremlin
KS *abbr* (*US*) = **Kansas**
Kt *abbr* (*Brit*: = *Knight*) *titre honorifique*
Kuala Lumpur ['kwɑːlə'lumpuər] *n* Kuala Lumpur
kudos ['kjuːdɔs] *n* gloire *f*, lauriers *mpl*
Kurd [kəːd] *n* Kurde *m/f*
Kuwait [ku'weɪt] *n* Koweït *m*
Kuwaiti [ku'weɪtɪ] *adj* koweïtien(ne) ▷ *n* Koweïtien(ne)
kW *abbr* (= *kilowatt*) kW
KY, Ky. *abbr* (*US*) = **Kentucky**

Ll

L¹, l [ɛl] *n (letter)* L, l *m;* **L for Lucy,** (US) **L for Love** L comme Louis
L² *abbr* (= *lake, large*) L; (= *left*) g; (*Brit Aut:* = *learner*) *signale un conducteur débutant*
l. *abbr* (= *litre*) l
LA *n abbr* (US) = **Los Angeles** ▷ *abbr* (US) = **Louisiana**
La. *abbr* (US) = **Louisiana**
lab [læb] *n abbr* (= *laboratory*) labo *m*
Lab. *abbr* (*Canada*) = **Labrador**
label ['leɪbl] *n* étiquette *f;* (*brand: of record*) marque *f* ▷ *vt* étiqueter; **to ~ sb a ...** qualifier qn de ...
labor *etc* ['leɪbə'] (US) = **labour** *etc*
laboratory [lə'bɔrətərɪ] *n* laboratoire *m*
Labor Day *n* (US, Canada) fête *f* du travail (*le premier lundi de septembre*); *voir article*

⬤ LABOR DAY
⬤
⬤ *Labor Day aux États-Unis et au Canada est*
⬤ fixée au premier lundi de septembre.
⬤ Instituée par le Congrès en 1894 après avoir
⬤ été réclamée par les mouvements ouvriers
⬤ pendant douze ans, elle a perdu une grande
⬤ partie de son caractère politique pour
⬤ devenir un jour férié assez ordinaire et
⬤ l'occasion de partir pour un long week-end
⬤ avant la rentrée des classes.

laborious [lə'bɔːrɪəs] *adj* laborieux(-euse)
labor union *n* (US) syndicat *m*
Labour ['leɪbə'] *n* (*Brit Pol: also:* **the Labour Party**) le parti travailliste, les travaillistes *mpl*
labour, (US) **labor** ['leɪbə'] *n* (*work*) travail *m;* (*workforce*) main-d'œuvre *f;* (*Med*) travail, accouchement *m* ▷ *vi:* **to ~ (at)** travailler dur (à), peiner (sur) ▷ *vt:* **to ~ a point** insister sur un point; **in ~** (*Med*) en travail
labour camp, (US) **labor camp** *n* camp *m* de travaux forcés
labour cost, (US) **labor cost** *n* coût *m* de la main-d'œuvre; coût de la façon
laboured, (US) **labored** ['leɪbəd] *adj* lourd(e), laborieux(-euse); (*breathing*) difficile, pénible; (*style*) lourd, embarrassé(e)

labourer, (US) **laborer** ['leɪbərə'] *n* manœuvre *m;* **farm ~** ouvrier *m* agricole
labour force, (US) **labor force** *n* main-d'œuvre *f*
labour-intensive, (US) **labor-intensive** [leɪbərɪn'tɛnsɪv] *adj* intensif(-ive) en main-d'œuvre
labour market, (US) **labor market** *n* marché *m* du travail
labour pains, (US) **labor pains** *npl* douleurs *fpl* de l'accouchement
labour relations, (US) **labor relations** *npl* relations *fpl* dans l'entreprise
labour-saving, (US) **labor-saving** ['leɪbəseɪvɪŋ] *adj* qui simplifie le travail
labour unrest, (US) **labor unrest** *n* agitation sociale
labyrinth ['læbɪrɪnθ] *n* labyrinthe *m,* dédale *m*
lace [leɪs] *n* dentelle *f;* (*of shoe etc*) lacet *m* ▷ *vt* (*shoe: also:* **lace up**) lacer; (*drink*) arroser, corser
lacemaking ['leɪsmeɪkɪŋ] *n* fabrication *f* de dentelle
laceration [læsə'reɪʃən] *n* lacération *f*
lace-up ['leɪsʌp] *adj* (*shoes etc*) à lacets
lack [læk] *n* manque *m* ▷ *vt* manquer de; **through** *or* **for ~ of** faute de, par manque de; **to be ~ing** manquer, faire défaut; **to be ~ing in** manquer de
lackadaisical [lækə'deɪzɪkl] *adj* nonchalant(e), indolent(e)
lackey ['lækɪ] *n* (*also fig*) laquais *m*
lacklustre ['læklʌstə'] *adj* terne
laconic [lə'kɔnɪk] *adj* laconique
lacquer ['lækə'] *n* laque *f*
lacy ['leɪsɪ] *adj* (*made of lace*) en dentelle; (*like lace*) comme de la dentelle, qui ressemble à de la dentelle
lad [læd] *n* garçon *m,* gars *m;* (*Brit: in stable etc*) lad *m*
ladder ['lædə'] *n* échelle *f;* (*Brit: in tights*) maille filée *f* ▷ *vt, vi* (*Brit: tights*) filer
laden ['leɪdn] *adj:* **~ (with)** chargé(e) (de); **fully ~** (*truck, ship*) en pleine charge
ladle ['leɪdl] *n* louche *f*
lady ['leɪdɪ] *n* dame *f;* **"ladies and gentlemen ..."** "Mesdames (et) Messieurs ..."; **young ~** jeune fille *f;* (*married*) jeune femme *f;*

L~ Smith lady Smith; **the ladies' (room)** les toilettes *fpl* des dames; **a ~ doctor** une doctoresse, une femme médecin
ladybird ['leɪdɪbəːd], *(US)* **ladybug** ['leɪdɪbʌg] *n* coccinelle *f*
lady-in-waiting ['leɪdɪɪn'weɪtɪŋ] *n* dame *f* d'honneur
lady-killer ['leɪdɪkɪləʳ] *n* don Juan *m*
ladylike ['leɪdɪlaɪk] *adj* distingué(e)
ladyship ['leɪdɪʃɪp] *n*: **your L~** Madame la comtesse (*or* la baronne *etc*)
lag [læg] *n* retard *m* ▷ *vi* (*also*: **lag behind**) rester en arrière, traîner; (*fig*) rester à la traîne ▷ *vt* (*pipes*) calorifuger
lager ['lɑːgəʳ] *n* bière blonde
lager lout *n* (*Brit inf*) jeune voyou *m* (*porté sur la boisson*)
lagging ['lægɪŋ] *n* enveloppe isolante, calorifuge *m*
lagoon [lə'guːn] *n* lagune *f*
Lagos ['leɪgɔs] *n* Lagos
laid [leɪd] *pt, pp of* **lay**
laid back *adj* (*inf*) relaxe, décontracté(e)
laid up *adj* alité(e)
lain [leɪn] *pp of* **lie**
lair [lɛəʳ] *n* tanière *f*, gîte *m*
laissez-faire [lɛseɪ'fɛəʳ] *n* libéralisme *m*
laity ['leɪətɪ] *n* laïques *mpl*
lake [leɪk] *n* lac *m*
Lake District *n*: **the ~** (*Brit*) la région des lacs
lamb [læm] *n* agneau *m*
lamb chop *n* côtelette *f* d'agneau
lambskin ['læmskɪn] *n* (peau *f* d')agneau *m*
lambswool ['læmzwul] *n* laine *f* d'agneau
lame [leɪm] *adj* (*also fig*) boiteux(-euse); **~ duck** (*fig*) canard boiteux
lamely ['leɪmlɪ] *adv* (*fig*) sans conviction
lament [lə'mɛnt] *n* lamentation *f* ▷ *vt* pleurer, se lamenter sur
lamentable ['læməntəbl] *adj* déplorable, lamentable
laminated ['læmɪneɪtɪd] *adj* laminé(e); (*windscreen*) (en verre) feuilleté
lamp [læmp] *n* lampe *f*
lamplight ['læmplaɪt] *n*: **by ~** à la lumière de la (*or* d'une) lampe
lampoon [læm'puːn] *n* pamphlet *m*
lamppost ['læmppəust] *n* (*Brit*) réverbère *m*
lampshade ['læmpʃeɪd] *n* abat-jour *m inv*
lance [lɑːns] *n* lance *f* ▷ *vt* (*Med*) inciser
lance corporal *n* (*Brit*) (soldat *m* de) première classe *m*
lancet ['lɑːnsɪt] *n* (*Med*) bistouri *m*
Lancs [læŋks] *abbr* (*Brit*) = **Lancashire**
land [lænd] *n* (*as opposed to sea*) terre *f* (ferme); (*country*) pays *m*; (*soil*) terre; (*piece of land*) terrain *m*; (*estate*) terre(s), domaine(s) *m(pl)* ▷ *vi* (*from ship*) débarquer; (*Aviat*) atterrir; (*fig: fall*) (re)tomber ▷ *vt* (*passengers, goods*) débarquer; (*obtain*) décrocher; **to go/travel by ~** se déplacer par voie de terre; **to own ~** être propriétaire foncier; **to ~ on one's feet** (*also fig*)

retomber sur ses pieds; **to ~ sb with sth** (*inf*) coller qch à qn
▶ **land up** *vi* atterrir, (finir par) se retrouver
landed gentry ['lændɪd-] *n* (*Brit*) propriétaires terriens *or* fonciers
landfill site ['lændfɪl-] *n* centre *m* d'enfouissement des déchets
landing ['lændɪŋ] *n* (*from ship*) débarquement *m*; (*Aviat*) atterrissage *m*; (*of staircase*) palier *m*
landing card *n* carte *f* de débarquement
landing craft *n* péniche *f* de débarquement
landing gear *n* train *m* d'atterrissage
landing stage *n* (*Brit*) débarcadère *m*, embarcadère *m*
landing strip *n* piste *f* d'atterrissage
landlady ['lændleɪdɪ] *n* propriétaire *f*, logeuse *f*; (*of pub*) patronne *f*
landlocked ['lændlɔkt] *adj* entouré(e) de terre(s), sans accès à la mer
landlord ['lændlɔːd] *n* propriétaire *m*, logeur *m*; (*of pub etc*) patron *m*
landlubber ['lændlʌbəʳ] *n* terrien(ne)
landmark ['lændmɑːk] *n* (point *m* de) repère *m*; **to be a ~** (*fig*) faire date *or* époque
landowner ['lændəunəʳ] *n* propriétaire foncier *or* terrien
landscape ['lænskeɪp] *n* paysage *m*
landscape architect, landscape gardener *n* paysagiste *m/f*
landscape painting *n* (*Art*) paysage *m*
landslide ['lændslaɪd] *n* (*Geo*) glissement *m* (de terrain); (*fig: Pol*) raz-de-marée (électoral)
lane [leɪn] *n* (*in country*) chemin *m*; (*in town*) ruelle *f*; (*Aut: of road*) voie *f*; (: *line of traffic*) file *f*; (*in race*) couloir *m*; **shipping ~** route *f* maritime *or* de navigation
language ['læŋgwɪdʒ] *n* langue *f*; (*way one speaks*) langage *m*; **what ~s do you speak?** quelles langues parlez-vous?; **bad ~** grossièretés *fpl*, langage grossier
language laboratory *n* laboratoire *m* de langues
language school *n* école *f* de langue
languid ['læŋgwɪd] *adj* languissant(e), langoureux(-euse)
languish ['læŋgwɪʃ] *vi* languir
lank [læŋk] *adj* (*hair*) raide et terne
lanky ['læŋkɪ] *adj* grand(e) et maigre, efflanqué(e)
lanolin, lanoline ['lænəlɪn] *n* lanoline *f*
lantern ['læntn] *n* lanterne *f*
Laos [laus] *n* Laos *m*
lap [læp] *n* (*of track*) tour *m* (de piste); (*of body*): **in** *or* **on one's ~** sur les genoux ▷ *vt* (*also*: **lap up**) laper ▷ *vi* (*waves*) clapoter
▶ **lap up** *vt* (*fig*) boire comme du petit-lait, se gargariser de; (: *lies etc*) gober
La Paz [læ'pæz] *n* La Paz
lapdog ['læpdɔg] *n* chien *m* d'appartement
lapel [lə'pɛl] *n* revers *m*
Lapland ['læplænd] *n* Laponie *f*
lapse [læps] *n* défaillance *f*; (*in behaviour*) écart *m*

(de conduite) ▷ *vi* (*Law*) cesser d'être en vigueur; (*contract*) expirer; (*pass*) être périmé; (*subscription*) prendre fin; **to ~ into bad habits** prendre de mauvaises habitudes; **~ of time** laps *m* de temps, intervalle *m*; **a ~ of memory** un trou de mémoire

laptop ['læptɔp], **laptop computer** *n* portable *m*

larceny ['lɑːsənɪ] *n* vol *m*

larch [lɑːtʃ] *n* mélèze *m*

lard [lɑːd] *n* saindoux *m*

larder ['lɑːdə^r] *n* garde-manger *m inv*

large [lɑːdʒ] *adj* grand(e); (*person, animal*) gros (grosse); **to make ~r** agrandir; **a ~ number of people** beaucoup de gens; **by and ~** en général; **on a ~ scale** sur une grande échelle; **at ~** (*free*) en liberté; (*generally*) en général; **pour la plupart**; *see also* **by**

largely ['lɑːdʒlɪ] *adv* en grande partie; (*principally*) surtout

large-scale ['lɑːdʒ'skeɪl] *adj* (*map, drawing etc*) à grande échelle; (*fig*) important(e)

lark [lɑːk] *n* (*bird*) alouette *f*; (*joke*) blague *f*, farce *f*

▸ **lark about** *vi* faire l'idiot, rigoler

larva (*pl* **-e**) ['lɑːvə, -iː] *n* larve *f*

laryngitis [lærɪn'dʒaɪtɪs] *n* laryngite *f*

larynx ['lærɪŋks] *n* larynx *m*

lasagne [lə'zænjə] *n* lasagne *f*

lascivious [lə'sɪvɪəs] *adj* lascif(-ive)

laser ['leɪzə^r] *n* laser *m*

laser beam *n* rayon *m* laser

laser printer *n* imprimante *f* laser

lash [læʃ] *n* coup *m* de fouet; (*also*: **eyelash**) cil *m* ▷ *vt* fouetter; (*tie*) attacher

▸ **lash down** *vt* attacher; amarrer; arrimer ▷ *vi* (*rain*) tomber avec violence

▸ **lash out** *vi*: **to ~ out** (**at** *or* **against sb/sth**) attaquer violemment (qn/qch); **to ~ out** (**on sth**) (*inf: spend*) se fendre (de qch)

lashing ['læʃɪŋ] *n*: **~s of** (*Brit inf: cream etc*) des masses de

lass [læs] (*Brit*) *n* (jeune) fille *f*

lasso [læ'suː] *n* lasso *m* ▷ *vt* prendre au lasso

last [lɑːst] *adj* dernier(-ière) ▷ *adv* en dernier; (*most recently*) la dernière fois; (*finally*) finalement ▷ *vi* durer; **~ week** la semaine dernière; **~ night** (*evening*) hier soir; (*night*) la nuit dernière; **at ~** enfin; **~ but one** avant-dernier(-ière); **the ~ time** la dernière fois; **it ~s (for) 2 hours** ça dure 2 heures

last-ditch ['lɑːst'dɪtʃ] *adj* ultime, désespéré(e)

lasting ['lɑːstɪŋ] *adj* durable

lastly ['lɑːstlɪ] *adv* en dernier lieu, pour finir

last-minute ['lɑːstmɪnɪt] *adj* de dernière minute

latch [lætʃ] *n* loquet *m*

▸ **latch onto** *vt fus* (*cling to: person, group*) s'accrocher à; (*idea*) se mettre en tête

latchkey ['lætʃkiː] *n* clé *f* (de la porte d'entrée)

late [leɪt] *adj* (*not on time*) en retard; (*far on in day etc*) tardif(-ive); (: *edition, delivery*) dernier(-ière); (*recent*) récent(e), dernier; (*former*) ancien(ne); (*dead*) défunt(e) ▷ *adv* tard; (*behind time, schedule*) en retard; **to be ~** avoir du retard; **to be 10 minutes ~** avoir 10 minutes de retard; **sorry I'm ~** désolé d'être en retard; **it's too ~** il est trop tard; **to work ~** travailler tard; **~ in life** sur le tard, à un âge avancé; **of ~** dernièrement; **in ~ May** vers la fin (du mois) de mai, fin mai; **the ~ Mr X** feu M. X

latecomer ['leɪtkʌmə^r] *n* retardataire *m/f*

lately ['leɪtlɪ] *adv* récemment

lateness ['leɪtnɪs] *n* (*of person*) retard *m*; (*of event*) heure tardive

latent ['leɪtnt] *adj* latent(e); **~ defect** vice caché

later ['leɪtə^r] *adj* (*date etc*) ultérieur(e); (*version etc*) plus récent(e) ▷ *adv* plus tard; **~ on today** plus tard dans la journée

lateral ['lætərl] *adj* latéral(e)

latest ['leɪtɪst] *adj* tout(e) dernier(-ière); **the ~ news** les dernières nouvelles; **at the ~** au plus tard

latex ['leɪtɛks] *n* latex *m*

lath (*pl* **-s**) [læθ, læðz] *n* latte *f*

lathe [leɪð] *n* tour *m*

lather ['lɑːðə^r] *n* mousse *f* (de savon) ▷ *vt* savonner ▷ *vi* mousser

Latin ['lætɪn] *n* latin *m* ▷ *adj* latin(e)

Latin America *n* Amérique latine

Latin American *adj* latino-américain(e), d'Amérique latine ▷ *n* Latino-Américain(e)

latitude ['lætɪtjuːd] *n* (*also fig*) latitude *f*

latrine [lə'triːn] *n* latrines *fpl*

latter ['lætə^r] *adj* deuxième, dernier(-ière) ▷ *n*: **the ~** ce dernier, celui-ci

latterly ['lætəlɪ] *adv* dernièrement, récemment

lattice ['lætɪs] *n* treillis *m*; treillage *m*

lattice window *n* fenêtre treillissée, fenêtre à croisillons

Latvia ['lætvɪə] *n* Lettonie *f*

Latvian ['lætvɪən] *adj* letton(ne) ▷ *n* Letton(ne); (*Ling*) letton *m*

laudable ['lɔːdəbl] *adj* louable

laudatory ['lɔːdətrɪ] *adj* élogieux(-euse)

laugh [lɑːf] *n* rire *m* ▷ *vi* rire; (**to do sth**) **for a ~** (faire qch) pour rire

▸ **laugh at** *vt fus* se moquer de; (*joke*) rire de

▸ **laugh off** *vt* écarter *or* rejeter par une plaisanterie *or* par une boutade

laughable ['lɑːfəbl] *adj* risible, ridicule

laughing ['lɑːfɪŋ] *adj* rieur(-euse); **this is no ~ matter** il n'y a pas de quoi rire, ça n'a rien d'amusant

laughing gas *n* gaz hilarant

laughing stock *n*: **the ~ of** la risée de

laughter ['lɑːftə^r] *n* rire *m*; (*of several people*) rires *mpl*

launch [lɔːntʃ] *n* lancement *m*; (*boat*) chaloupe *f*; (*also*: **motor launch**) vedette *f* ▷ *vt* (*ship, rocket, plan*) lancer

▸ **launch into** *vt fus* se lancer dans

▸ **launch out** *vi*: **to ~ out** (**into**) se lancer (dans)

launching ['lɔːntʃɪŋ] *n* lancement *m*

launder ['lɔ:ndə'] vt laver; (fig: money) blanchir
Launderette® [lɔ:n'dret], (US) **Laundromat**® ['lɔ:ndrəmæt] n laverie f (automatique)
laundry ['lɔ:ndrɪ] n (clothes) linge m; (business) blanchisserie f; (room) buanderie f; **to do the ~** faire la lessive
laureate ['lɔ:rɪət] adj see **poet laureate**
laurel ['lɔrl] n laurier m; **to rest on one's ~s** se reposer sur ses lauriers
lava ['lɑ:və] n lave f
lavatory ['lævətərɪ] n toilettes fpl
lavatory paper n (Brit) papier m hygiénique
lavender ['lævəndə'] n lavande f
lavish ['lævɪʃ] adj (amount) copieux(-euse); (meal) somptueux(-euse); (hospitality) généreux(-euse); (person: giving freely): **~ with** prodigue de ▷ vt: **to ~ sth on sb** prodiguer qch à qn; (money) dépenser qch sans compter pour qn
lavishly ['lævɪʃlɪ] adv (give, spend) sans compter; (furnished) luxueusement
law [lɔ:] n loi f; (science) droit m; **against the ~** contraire à la loi; **to study ~** faire du droit; **to go to ~** (Brit) avoir recours à la justice; **~ and order** (n) l'ordre public
law-abiding ['lɔ:əbaɪdɪŋ] adj respectueux(-euse) des lois
lawbreaker ['lɔ:breɪkə'] n personne f qui transgresse la loi
law court n tribunal m, cour f de justice
lawful ['lɔ:ful] adj légal(e), permis(e)
lawfully ['lɔ:fəlɪ] adv légalement
lawless ['lɔ:lɪs] adj (action) illégal(e); (place) sans loi
Law Lord n (Brit) juge siégant à la Chambre des Lords
lawmaker ['lɔ:meɪkə'] n législateur(-trice)
lawn [lɔ:n] n pelouse f
lawnmower ['lɔ:nməuə'] n tondeuse f à gazon
lawn tennis n tennis m
law school n faculté f de droit
law student n étudiant(e) en droit
lawsuit ['lɔ:su:t] n procès m; **to bring a ~ against** engager des poursuites contre
lawyer ['lɔ:jə'] n (consultant, with company) juriste m; (for sales, wills etc) ≈ notaire m; (partner, in court) ≈ avocat m
lax [læks] adj relâché(e)
laxative ['læksətɪv] n laxatif m
laxity ['læksɪtɪ] n relâchement m
lay [leɪ] pt of **lie** ▷ adj laïque; (not expert) profane ▷ vt (pt, pp **laid** [leɪd]) poser, mettre; (eggs) pondre; (trap) tendre; (plans) élaborer; **to ~ the table** mettre la table; **to ~ the facts/one's proposals before sb** présenter les faits/ses propositions à qn; **to get laid** (inf!) baiser (!), se faire baiser (!)
▸ **lay aside, lay by** vt mettre de côté
▸ **lay down** vt poser; (rules etc) établir; **to ~ down the law** (fig) faire la loi
▸ **lay in** vt accumuler, s'approvisionner en
▸ **lay into** vi (inf: attack) tomber sur; (: scold) passer une engueulade à
▸ **lay off** vt (workers) licencier

▸ **lay on** vt (water, gas) mettre, installer; (provide: meal etc) fournir; (paint) étaler
▸ **lay out** vt (design) dessiner, concevoir; (display) disposer; (spend) dépenser
▸ **lay up** vt (store) amasser; (car) remiser; (ship) désarmer; (illness) forcer à s'aliter
layabout ['leɪəbaut] n fainéant(e)
lay-by ['leɪbaɪ] n (Brit) aire f de stationnement (sur le bas-côté)
lay days npl (Naut) estarie f
layer ['leɪə'] n couche f
layette [leɪ'ɛt] n layette f
layman ['leɪmən] (irreg) n (Rel) laïque m; (non-expert) profane m
lay-off ['leɪɔf] n licenciement m
layout ['leɪaut] n disposition f, plan m, agencement m; (Press) mise f en page
laze [leɪz] vi paresser
laziness ['leɪzɪnɪs] n paresse f
lazy ['leɪzɪ] adj paresseux(-euse)
LB abbr (Canada) = **Labrador**
lb. abbr (weight) = **pound**
lbw abbr (Cricket: = leg before wicket) faute dans laquelle le joueur a la jambe devant le guichet
LC n abbr (US) = **Library of Congress**
lc abbr (Typ: = lower case) b.d.c.
L/C abbr = **letter of credit**
LCD n abbr = **liquid crystal display**
Ld abbr (Brit: = lord) titre honorifique
LDS n abbr (= Licentiate in Dental Surgery) diplôme universitaire; (= Latter-day Saints) Église de Jésus-Christ des Saints du dernier jour
LEA n abbr (Brit: = local education authority) services locaux de l'enseignement
lead¹ [li:d] (pt, pp **led** [lɛd]) n (front position) tête f; (distance, time ahead) avance f; (clue) piste f; (to battery) raccord m; (Elec) fil m; (for dog) laisse f; (Theat) rôle principal ▷ vt (guide) mener, conduire; (induce) amener; (be leader of) être à la tête de; (Sport) être en tête de; (orchestra: Brit) être le premier violon; (: US) diriger ▷ vi (Sport) mener, être en tête; **to ~ to** (road, pipe) mener à, conduire à; (result in) conduire à; aboutir à; **to ~ sb astray** détourner qn du droit chemin; **to be in the ~** (Sport: in race) mener, être en tête; (: in match) mener (à la marque); **to take the ~** (Sport) passer en tête, prendre la tête; mener; (fig) prendre l'initiative; **to ~ sb to believe that ...** amener qn à croire que ...; **to ~ sb to do sth** amener qn à faire qch; **to ~ the way** montrer le chemin
▸ **lead away** vt emmener
▸ **lead back** vt ramener
▸ **lead off** vi (in game etc) commencer
▸ **lead on** vt (tease) faire marcher; **to ~ sb on to** (induce) amener qn à
▸ **lead up to** vt conduire à; (in conversation) en venir à
lead² [lɛd] n (metal) plomb m; (in pencil) mine f
leaded ['lɛdɪd] adj (windows) à petits carreaux
leaded petrol n essence f au plomb
leaden ['lɛdn] adj de or en plomb

leader ['li:dəʳ] n (of team) chef m; (of party etc) dirigeant(e), leader m; (Sport: in league) leader; (: in race) coureur m de tête; (in newspaper) éditorial m; **they are ~s in their field** (fig) ils sont à la pointe du progrès dans leur domaine; **the L~ of the House** (Brit) le chef de la majorité ministérielle

leadership ['li:dəʃɪp] n (position) direction f; **under the ~ of ...** sous la direction de ...; **qualities of ~** qualités fpl de chef or de meneur

lead-free ['lɛdfri:] adj sans plomb

leading ['li:dɪŋ] adj de premier plan; (main) principal(e); (in race) de tête; **a ~ question** une question tendancieuse; **~ role** rôle prépondérant or de premier plan

leading lady n (Theat) vedette (féminine)

leading light n (person) sommité f, personnalité f de premier plan

leading man (irreg) n (Theat) vedette (masculine)

lead pencil [lɛd-] n crayon noir or à papier

lead poisoning [lɛd-] n saturnisme m

lead singer [li:d-] n (in pop group) (chanteur m) vedette f

lead time [li:d-] n (Comm) délai m de livraison

lead weight [lɛd-] n plomb m

leaf (pl **leaves**) [li:f, li:vz] n feuille f; (of table) rallonge f; **to turn over a new ~** (fig) changer de conduite or d'existence; **to take a ~ out of sb's book** (fig) prendre exemple sur qn
  ▶ **leaf through** vt (book) feuilleter

leaflet ['li:flɪt] n prospectus m, brochure f; (Pol, Rel) tract m

leafy ['li:fɪ] adj feuillu(e)

league [li:g] n ligue f; (Football) championnat m; (measure) lieue f; **to be in ~ with** avoir partie liée avec, être de mèche avec

league table n classement m

leak [li:k] n (out: also fig) fuite f; (in) infiltration f ▷ vi (pipe, liquid etc) fuir; (shoes) prendre l'eau; (ship) faire eau ▷ vt (liquid) répandre; (information) divulguer
  ▶ **leak out** vi fuir; (information) être divulgué(e)

leakage ['li:kɪdʒ] n (also fig) fuite f

leaky ['li:kɪ] adj (pipe, bucket) qui fuit, percé(e); (roof) qui coule; (shoe) qui prend l'eau; (boat) qui fait eau

lean [li:n] (pt, pp **-ed** or **leant** [lɛnt]) adj maigre ▷ n (of meat) maigre m ▷ vt: **to ~ sth on** appuyer qch sur ▷ vi (slope) pencher; (rest): **to ~ against** s'appuyer contre; être appuyé(e) contre; **to ~ on** s'appuyer sur
  ▶ **lean back** vi se pencher en arrière
  ▶ **lean forward** vi se pencher en avant
  ▶ **lean out** vi: **to ~ out (of)** se pencher au dehors (de)
  ▶ **lean over** vi se pencher

leaning ['li:nɪŋ] adj penché(e) ▷ n: **~ (towards)** penchant m (pour); **the L~ Tower of Pisa** la tour penchée de Pise

leant [lɛnt] pt, pp of **lean**

lean-to ['li:ntu:] n appentis m

leap [li:p] n bond m, saut m ▷ vi (pt, pp **-ed** or **leapt** [lɛpt]) bondir, sauter; **to ~ at an offer** saisir une offre
  ▶ **leap up** vi (person) faire un bond; se lever d'un bond

leapfrog ['li:pfrɔg] n jeu m de saute-mouton

leapt [lɛpt] pt, pp of **leap**

leap year n année f bissextile

learn (pt, pp **-ed** or **-t**) [lə:n, -t] vt, vi apprendre; **to ~ (how) to do sth** apprendre à faire qch; **we were sorry to ~ that ...** nous avons appris avec regret que ...; **to ~ about sth** (Scol) étudier qch; (hear, read) apprendre qch

learned ['lə:nɪd] adj érudit(e), savant(e)

learner ['lə:nəʳ] n débutant(e); (Brit: also: **learner driver**) (conducteur(-trice)) débutant(e)

learning ['lə:nɪŋ] n savoir m

learnt [lə:nt] pp of **learn**

lease [li:s] n bail m ▷ vt louer à bail; **on ~** en location
  ▶ **lease back** vt vendre en cession-bail

leaseback ['li:sbæk] n cession-bail f

leasehold ['li:shəuld] n (contract) bail m ▷ adj loué(e) à bail

leash [li:ʃ] n laisse f

least [li:st] adj: **the ~** (+ noun) le (la) plus petit(e), le (la) moindre; (smallest amount of) le moins de ▷ pron: **(the) ~** le moins ▷ adv (+ verb) le moins; (+ adj): **the ~** le (la) moins; **the ~ money** le moins d'argent; **the ~ expensive** le (la) moins cher (chère); **the ~ possible effort** le moins d'effort possible; **at ~** au moins; (or rather) du moins; **you could at ~ have written** tu aurais au moins pu écrire; **not in the ~** pas le moins du monde

leather ['lɛðəʳ] n cuir m ▷ cpd en or de cuir; **~ goods** maroquinerie f

leave [li:v] (vb: pt, pp **left** [lɛft]) vt laisser; (go away from) quitter; (forget) oublier ▷ vi partir, s'en aller ▷ n (time off) congé m; (Mil, also: consent) permission f; **what time does the train/bus ~?** le train/le bus part à quelle heure?; **to ~ sth to sb** (money etc) laisser qch à qn; **to be left** rester; **there's some milk left over** il reste du lait; **to ~ school** quitter l'école, terminer sa scolarité; **~ it to me!** laissez-moi faire!, je m'en occupe!; **on ~** en permission; **to take one's ~ of** prendre congé de; **~ of absence** n congé exceptionnel; (Mil) permission spéciale
  ▶ **leave behind** vt (also fig) laisser; (opponent in race) distancer; (forget) laisser, oublier
  ▶ **leave off** vt (cover, lid, heating) ne pas (re)mettre; (light) ne pas (r)allumer, laisser éteint(e); (Brit inf: stop): **to ~ off (doing sth)** s'arrêter (de faire qch)
  ▶ **leave on** vt (coat etc) garder, ne pas enlever; (lid) laisser dessus; (light, fire, cooker) laisser allumé(e)
  ▶ **leave out** vt oublier, omettre

leaves [li:vz] npl of **leaf**

leavetaking ['li:vteɪkɪŋ] n adieux mpl

Lebanese [lɛbə'ni:z] adj libanais(e) ▷ n (pl inv)

Libanais(e)

Lebanon ['lɛbənən] *n* Liban *m*

lecherous ['lɛtʃərəs] *adj* lubrique

lectern ['lɛktə:n] *n* lutrin *m*, pupitre *m*

lecture ['lɛktʃəʳ] *n* conférence *f*; (*Scol*) cours (magistral) ▷ *vi* donner des cours; enseigner ▷ *vt* (*scold*) sermonner, réprimander; **to ~ on** faire un cours (*or* son cours) sur; **to give a ~ (on)** faire une conférence (sur), faire un cours (sur)

lecture hall *n* amphithéâtre *m*

lecturer ['lɛktʃərəʳ] *n* (*speaker*) conférencier(-ière); (*Brit: at university*) professeur *m* (d'université), prof *m/f* de fac (*inf*); **assistant ~** (*Brit*) ≈ assistant(e); **senior ~** (*Brit*) ≈ chargé(e) d'enseignement

lecture theatre *n* = **lecture hall**

LED *n abbr* (= *light-emitting diode*) LED *f*, diode électroluminescente

led [lɛd] *pt, pp of* **lead**[1]

ledge [lɛdʒ] *n* (*of window, on wall*) rebord *m*; (*of mountain*) saillie *f*, corniche *f*

ledger ['lɛdʒəʳ] *n* registre *m*, grand livre

lee [li:] *n* côté *m* sous le vent; **in the ~ of** à l'abri de

leech [li:tʃ] *n* sangsue *f*

leek [li:k] *n* poireau *m*

leer [lɪəʳ] *vi*: **to ~ at sb** regarder qn d'un air mauvais *or* concupiscent, lorgner qn

leeward ['li:wəd] *adj, adv* sous le vent ▷ *n* côté *m* sous le vent; **to ~** sous le vent

leeway ['li:weɪ] *n* (*fig*) **to make up ~** rattraper son retard; **to have some ~** avoir une certaine liberté d'action

left [lɛft] *pt, pp of* **leave** ▷ *adj* gauche ▷ *adv* à gauche ▷ *n* gauche *f*; **there are two ~** il en reste deux; **on the ~**, **to the ~** à gauche; **the L~** (*Pol*) la gauche

left-hand ['lɛfthænd] *adj*: **the ~ side** la gauche, le côté gauche

left-hand drive ['lɛfthænd-] *n* (*Brit*) conduite *f* à gauche; (*vehicle*) véhicule *m* avec la conduite à gauche

left-handed [lɛft'hændɪd] *adj* gaucher(-ère); (*scissors etc*) pour gauchers

leftie ['lɛftɪ] *n* (*inf*) gaucho *m/f*, gauchiste *m/f*

leftist ['lɛftɪst] *adj* (*Pol*) gauchiste, de gauche

left-luggage [lɛft'lʌgɪdʒ], **left-luggage office** *n* (*Brit*) consigne *f*

left-luggage locker [lɛft'lʌgɪdʒ-] *n* (*Brit*) (casier *m* à) consigne *f* automatique

left-overs ['lɛftəuvəz] *npl* restes *mpl*

left wing *n* (*Mil, Sport*) aile *f* gauche; (*Pol*) gauche *f*

left-wing ['lɛft'wɪŋ] *adj* (*Pol*) de gauche

left-winger ['lɛft'wɪŋgəʳ] *n* (*Pol*) membre *m* de la gauche; (*Sport*) ailier *m* gauche

lefty ['lɛftɪ] *n* (*inf*) = **leftie**

leg [lɛg] *n* jambe *f*; (*of animal*) patte *f*; (*of furniture*) pied *m*; (*Culin: of chicken*) cuisse *f*; (*of journey*) étape *f*; **1st/2nd ~** (*Sport*) match *m* aller/retour; (*of journey*) 1ère/2ème étape; **~ of lamb** (*Culin*) gigot *m* d'agneau; **to stretch one's ~s** se

dégourdir les jambes

legacy ['lɛgəsɪ] *n* (*also fig*) héritage *m*, legs *m*

legal ['li:gl] *adj* (*permitted by law*) légal(e); (*relating to law*) juridique; **to take ~ action** *or* **proceedings against sb** poursuivre qn en justice

legal adviser *n* conseiller(-ère) juridique

legal holiday (*US*) *n* jour férié

legality [lɪ'gælɪtɪ] *n* légalité *f*

legalize ['li:gəlaɪz] *vt* légaliser

legally ['li:gəlɪ] *adv* légalement; **~ binding** juridiquement contraignant(e)

legal tender *n* monnaie légale

legation [lɪ'geɪʃən] *n* légation *f*

legend ['lɛdʒənd] *n* légende *f*

legendary ['lɛdʒəndərɪ] *adj* légendaire

-legged ['lɛgɪd] *suffix*: **two~** à deux pattes (*or* jambes *or* pieds)

leggings ['lɛgɪŋz] *npl* caleçon *m*

leggy ['lɛgɪ] *adj* aux longues jambes

legibility [lɛdʒɪ'bɪlɪtɪ] *n* lisibilité *f*

legible ['lɛdʒəbl] *adj* lisible

legibly ['lɛdʒəblɪ] *adv* lisiblement

legion ['li:dʒən] *n* légion *f*

legionnaire [li:dʒə'nɛəʳ] *n* légionnaire *m*; **~'s disease** maladie *f* du légionnaire

legislate ['lɛdʒɪsleɪt] *vi* légiférer

legislation [lɛdʒɪs'leɪʃən] *n* législation *f*; **a piece of ~** un texte de loi

legislative ['lɛdʒɪslətɪv] *adj* législatif(-ive)

legislator ['lɛdʒɪsleɪtəʳ] *n* législateur(-trice)

legislature ['lɛdʒɪslətʃəʳ] *n* corps législatif

legitimacy [lɪ'dʒɪtɪməsɪ] *n* légitimité *f*

legitimate [lɪ'dʒɪtɪmət] *adj* légitime

legitimize [lɪ'dʒɪtɪmaɪz] *vt* légitimer

legless ['lɛglɪs] *adj* (*Brit inf*) bourré(e)

leg-room ['lɛgru:m] *n* place *f* pour les jambes

Leics *abbr* (*Brit*) = **Leicestershire**

leisure ['lɛʒəʳ] *n* (*free time*) temps libre, loisirs *mpl*; **at ~** (tout) à loisir; **at your ~** (*later*) à tête reposée

leisure centre *n* (*Brit*) centre *m* de loisirs

leisurely ['lɛʒəlɪ] *adj* tranquille, fait(e) sans se presser

leisure suit *n* (*Brit*) survêtement *m* (mode)

lemon ['lɛmən] *n* citron *m*

lemonade [lɛmə'neɪd] *n* (*fizzy*) limonade *f*

lemon cheese, lemon curd *n* crème *f* de citron

lemon juice *n* jus *m* de citron

lemon squeezer [-skwi:zəʳ] *n* presse-citron *m* inv

lemon tea *n* thé *m* au citron

lend (*pt, pp* **lent**) [lɛnd, lɛnt] *vt*: **to ~ sth (to sb)** prêter qch (à qn); **could you ~ me some money?** pourriez-vous me prêter de l'argent?; **to ~ a hand** donner un coup de main

lender ['lɛndəʳ] *n* prêteur(-euse)

lending library ['lɛndɪŋ-] *n* bibliothèque *f* de prêt

length [lɛŋθ] *n* longueur *f*; (*section: of road, pipe etc*) morceau *m*, bout *m*; **~ of time** durée *f*; **what ~ is it?** quelle longueur fait-il?; **it is 2 metres**

in ~ cela fait 2 mètres de long; **to fall full ~** tomber de tout son long; **at ~** (at last) enfin, à la fin; (lengthily) longuement; **to go to any ~(s) to do sth** faire n'importe quoi pour faire qch, ne reculer devant rien pour faire qch

lengthen ['lɛŋθn] vt allonger, prolonger ▷ vi s'allonger

lengthways ['lɛŋθweɪz] adv dans le sens de la longueur, en long

lengthy ['lɛŋθɪ] adj (très) long (longue)

leniency ['li:nɪənsɪ] n indulgence f, clémence f

lenient ['li:nɪənt] adj indulgent(e), clément(e)

leniently ['li:nɪəntlɪ] adv avec indulgence or clémence

lens [lɛnz] n lentille f; (of spectacles) verre m; (of camera) objectif m

Lent [lɛnt] n carême m

lent [lɛnt] pt, pp of **lend**

lentil ['lɛntl] n lentille f

Leo ['li:əu] n le Lion; **to be ~** être du Lion

leopard ['lɛpəd] n léopard m

leotard ['li:əta:d] n justaucorps m

leper ['lɛpər] n lépreux(-euse)

leper colony n léproserie f

leprosy ['lɛprəsɪ] n lèpre f

lesbian ['lɛzbɪən] n lesbienne f ▷ adj lesbien(ne)

lesion ['li:ʒən] n (Med) lésion f

Lesotho [lɪ'su:tu:] n Lesotho m

less [lɛs] adj moins de ▷ pron, adv moins ▷ prep: ~ **tax/10% discount** avant impôt/moins 10% de remise; ~ **than that/you** moins que cela/vous; ~ **than half** moins de la moitié; ~ **than one/a kilo/3 metres** moins de un/d'un kilo/de 3 mètres; ~ **than ever** moins que jamais; ~ **and ~** de moins en moins; **the ~ he works ...** moins il travaille ...

lessee [lɛ'si:] n locataire m/f (à bail), preneur(-euse) du bail

lessen ['lɛsn] vi diminuer, s'amoindrir, s'atténuer ▷ vt diminuer, réduire, atténuer

lesser ['lɛsər] adj moindre; **to a ~ extent or degree** à un degré moindre

lesson ['lɛsn] n leçon f; **a maths ~** une leçon or un cours de maths; **to give ~s in** donner des cours de; **to teach sb a ~** (fig) donner une bonne leçon à qn; **it taught him a ~** (fig) cela lui a servi de leçon

lessor ['lɛsɔ:ʳ, lɛ'sɔ:ʳ] n bailleur(-eresse)

lest [lɛst] conj de peur de + infinitive, de peur que + sub

let (pt, pp ~) [lɛt] vt laisser; (Brit: lease) louer; **to ~ sb do sth** laisser qn faire qch; **to ~ sb know sth** faire savoir qch à qn, prévenir qn de qch; **he ~ me go** il m'a laissé partir; ~ **the water boil and ...** faites bouillir l'eau et ...; **to ~ go** lâcher prise; **to ~ go of sth, to ~ sth go** lâcher qch; ~'**s go** allons-y; ~ **him come** qu'il vienne; **"to ~"** (Brit) "à louer"

▶ **let down** vt (lower) baisser; (dress) rallonger; (hair) défaire; (Brit: tyre) dégonfler; (disappoint) décevoir

▶ **let go** vi lâcher prise ▷ vt lâcher

▶ **let in** vt laisser entrer; (visitor etc) faire entrer; **what have you ~ yourself in for?** à quoi t'es-tu engagé?

▶ **let off** vt (allow to leave) laisser partir; (not punish) ne pas punir; (taxi driver, bus driver) déposer; (firework etc) faire partir; (bomb) faire exploser; (smell etc) dégager; **to ~ off steam** (fig: inf) se défouler, décharger sa rate or bile

▶ **let on** vi (inf): **to ~ on that ....** révéler que ..., dire que ...

▶ **let out** vt laisser sortir; (dress) élargir; (scream) laisser échapper; (Brit: rent out) louer

▶ **let up** vi diminuer, s'arrêter

let-down ['lɛtdaun] n (disappointment) déception f

lethal ['li:θl] adj mortel(le), fatal(e); (weapon) meurtrier(-ère)

lethargic [lɛ'θɑ:dʒɪk] adj léthargique

lethargy ['lɛθədʒɪ] n léthargie f

letter ['lɛtəʳ] n lettre f; **letters** npl (Literature) lettres; **small/capital ~** minuscule f/majuscule f; ~ **of credit** lettre f de crédit

letter bomb n lettre piégée

letterbox ['lɛtəbɔks] n (Brit) boîte f aux or à lettres

letterhead ['lɛtəhɛd] n en-tête m

lettering ['lɛtərɪŋ] n lettres fpl; caractères mpl

letter opener n coupe-papier m

letterpress ['lɛtəprɛs] n (method) typographie f

letter quality n qualité f "courrier"

letters patent npl brevet m d'invention

lettuce ['lɛtɪs] n laitue f, salade f

let-up ['lɛtʌp] n répit m, détente f

leukaemia, (US) **leukemia** [lu:'ki:mɪə] n leucémie f

level ['lɛvl] adj (flat) plat(e), plan(e), uni(e); (horizontal) horizontal(e) ▷ n niveau m; (flat place) terrain plat; (also: spirit level) niveau à bulle ▷ vt niveler, aplanir; (gun) pointer, braquer; (accusation): **to ~ (against)** lancer or porter (contre) ▷ vi (inf): **to ~ with sb** être franc (franche) avec qn; **"A" ~s** (npl: Brit) ≈ baccalauréat m; **"O" ~s** npl (Brit: formerly) examens passés à l'âge de 16 ans sanctionnant les connaissances de l'élève, ≈ brevet m des collèges; **a ~ spoonful** (Culin) une cuillerée rase; **to be ~ with** être au même niveau que; **to draw ~ with** (team) arriver à égalité de points avec, égaliser avec; arriver au même classement que; (runner, car) arriver à la hauteur de, rattraper; **on the ~** à l'horizontale; (fig: honest) régulier(-ière)

▶ **level off, level out** vi (prices etc) se stabiliser ▷ vt (ground) aplanir, niveler

level crossing n (Brit) passage m à niveau

level-headed [lɛvl'hɛdɪd] adj équilibré(e)

levelling, (US) **leveling** ['lɛvlɪŋ] adj (process, effect) de nivellement

level playing field n: **to compete on a ~** jouer sur un terrain d'égalité

lever ['li:vəʳ] n levier m ▷ vt: **to ~ up/out** soulever/extraire au moyen d'un levier

leverage ['li:vərɪdʒ] n (influence): ~ **(on or with)**

prise f (sur)
levity ['lɛvɪtɪ] n manque m de sérieux, légèreté f
levy ['lɛvɪ] n taxe f, impôt m ⊳ vt (tax) lever; (fine) infliger
lewd [lu:d] adj obscène, lubrique
lexicographer [lɛksɪ'kɔgrəfər] n lexicographe m/f
lexicography [lɛksɪ'kɔgrəfɪ] n lexicographie f
LGV n abbr (= Large Goods Vehicle) poids lourd
LI abbr (US) = **Long Island**
liabilities [laɪə'bɪlətɪz] npl (Comm) obligations fpl, engagements mpl; (on balance sheet) passif m
liability [laɪə'bɪlətɪ] n responsabilité f; (handicap) handicap m
liable ['laɪəbl] adj (subject): ~ **to** sujet(te) à, passible de; (responsible): ~ **(for)** responsable (de); (likely): ~ **to do** susceptible de faire; **to be ~ to a fine** être passible d'une amende
liaise [li:'eɪz] vi: **to ~ with** assurer la liaison avec
liaison [li:'eɪzɔn] n liaison f
liar ['laɪər] n menteur(-euse)
libel ['laɪbl] n diffamation f; (document) écrit m diffamatoire ⊳ vt diffamer
libellous ['laɪbləs] adj diffamatoire
liberal ['lɪbərl] adj libéral(e); (generous): ~ **with** prodigue de, généreux(-euse) avec ⊳ n: **L~** (Pol) libéral(e)
Liberal Democrat n (Brit) libéral(e)-démocrate m/f
liberality [lɪbə'rælɪtɪ] n (generosity) générosité f, libéralité f
liberalize ['lɪbərəlaɪz] vt libéraliser
liberal-minded ['lɪbərl'maɪndɪd] adj libéral(e), tolérant(e)
liberate ['lɪbəreɪt] vt libérer
liberation [lɪbə'reɪʃən] n libération f
liberation theology n théologie f de libération
Liberia [laɪ'bɪərɪə] n Libéria m, Liberia m
Liberian [laɪ'bɪərɪən] adj libérien(ne) ⊳ n Libérien(ne)
liberty ['lɪbətɪ] n liberté f; **to be at ~** (criminal) être en liberté; **at ~ to do** libre de faire; **to take the ~ of** prendre la liberté de, se permettre de
libido [lɪ'bi:dəu] n libido f
Libra ['li:brə] n la Balance; **to be ~** être de la Balance
librarian [laɪ'brɛərɪən] n bibliothécaire m/f
library ['laɪbrərɪ] n bibliothèque f
library book n livre m de bibliothèque
libretto [lɪ'brɛtəu] n livret m
Libya ['lɪbɪə] n Libye f
Libyan ['lɪbɪən] adj libyen(ne), de Libye ⊳ n Libyen(ne)
lice [laɪs] npl of **louse**
licence, (US) **license** ['laɪsns] n autorisation f, permis m; (Comm) licence f; (Radio, TV) redevance f; (also: **driving licence**; US: also: **driver's license**) permis m (de conduire); (excessive freedom) licence f; **import ~** licence d'importation; **produced under ~** fabriqué(e) sous licence
licence number n (Brit Aut) numéro m

d'immatriculation
license ['laɪsns] n (US) = **licence** ⊳ vt donner une licence à; (car) acheter la vignette de; délivrer la vignette de
licensed ['laɪsnst] adj (for alcohol) patenté(e) pour la vente des spiritueux, qui a une patente de débit de boissons; (car) muni(e) de la vignette
licensee [laɪsən'si:] n (Brit: of pub) patron(ne), gérant(e)
license plate n (US Aut) plaque f minéralogique
licensing hours (Brit) npl heures fpl d'ouvertures (des pubs)
licentious [laɪ'sɛnʃəs] adj licencieux(-euse)
lichen ['laɪkən] n lichen m
lick [lɪk] vt lécher; (inf: defeat) écraser, flanquer une piquette or raclée à ⊳ n coup m de langue; **a ~ of paint** un petit coup de peinture; **to ~ one's lips** (fig) se frotter les mains
licorice ['lɪkərɪs] n = **liquorice**
lid [lɪd] n couvercle m; (eyelid) paupière f; **to take the ~ off sth** (fig) exposer or étaler qch au grand jour
lido ['laɪdəu] n piscine f en plein air, complexe m balnéaire
lie [laɪ] n mensonge m ⊳ vi (pt, pp **-d**) (tell lies) mentir; (pt **lay**, pp **lain** [leɪ, leɪn]) (rest) être étendu(e) or allongé(e) or couché(e); (in grave) être enterré(e), reposer; (object: be situated) se trouver, être; **to ~ low** (fig) se cacher, rester caché(e); **to tell ~s** mentir
  ▶ **lie about, lie around** vi (things) traîner; (Brit: person) traînasser, flemmarder
  ▶ **lie back** vi se renverser en arrière
  ▶ **lie down** vi se coucher, s'étendre
  ▶ **lie up** vi (hide) se cacher
Liechtenstein ['lɪktənstaɪn] n Liechtenstein m
lie detector n détecteur m de mensonges
lie-down ['laɪdaun] n (Brit): **to have a ~** s'allonger, se reposer
lie-in ['laɪɪn] n (Brit): **to have a ~** faire la grasse matinée
lieu [lu:]: **in ~ of** prep au lieu de, à la place de
Lieut. abbr (= lieutenant) Lt
lieutenant [lɛf'tɛnənt, (US) lu:'tɛnənt] n lieutenant m
lieutenant-colonel [lɛf'tɛnənt'kɜːnl, (US) lu:'tɛnənt'kɜːnl] n lieutenant-colonel m
life (pl **lives**) [laɪf, laɪvz] n vie f; **to come to ~** (fig) s'animer ⊳ cpd de vie; de la vie; à vie; **true to ~** réaliste, fidèle à la réalité; **to paint from ~** peindre d'après nature; **to be sent to prison for ~** être condamné(e) (à la réclusion criminelle) à perpétuité; **country/city ~** la vie à la campagne/à la ville
life annuity n pension f, rente viagère
life assurance n (Brit) = **life insurance**
lifebelt ['laɪfbɛlt] n (Brit) bouée f de sauvetage
lifeblood ['laɪfblʌd] n (fig) élément moteur
lifeboat ['laɪfbəut] n canot m or chaloupe f de sauvetage
lifebuoy ['laɪfbɔɪ] n bouée f de sauvetage
life expectancy n espérance f de vie

lifeguard ['laɪfgɑːd] n surveillant m de baignade
life imprisonment n prison f à vie; (Law) réclusion f à perpétuité
life insurance n assurance-vie f
life jacket n gilet m or ceinture f de sauvetage
lifeless ['laɪflɪs] adj sans vie, inanimé(e); (dull) qui manque de vie or de vigueur
lifelike ['laɪflaɪk] adj qui semble vrai(e) or vivant(e), ressemblant(e); (painting) réaliste
lifeline ['laɪflaɪn] n corde f de sauvetage
lifelong ['laɪflɒŋ] adj de toute une vie, de toujours
life preserver [-prɪ'zɜːvəʳ] n (US) gilet m or ceinture f de sauvetage
lifer ['laɪfəʳ] n (inf) condamné(e) à perpète
life-raft ['laɪfrɑːft] n radeau m de sauvetage
life-saver ['laɪfseɪvəʳ] n surveillant m de baignade
life-saving ['laɪfseɪvɪŋ] n sauvetage m
life sentence n condamnation f à vie or à perpétuité
life-size ['laɪfsaɪz], **life-sized** ['laɪfsaɪzd] adj grandeur nature inv
life span n (durée f de) vie f
lifestyle ['laɪfstaɪl] n style m de vie
life-support system n (Med) respirateur artificiel
lifetime ['laɪftaɪm] n: **in his ~** de son vivant; **the chance of a ~** la chance de ma (or sa etc) vie, une occasion unique
lift [lɪft] vt soulever, lever; (end) supprimer, lever; (steal) prendre, voler ▷ vi (fog) se lever ▷ n (Brit: elevator) ascenseur m; **to give sb a ~** (Brit) emmener or prendre qn en voiture; **can you give me a ~ to the station?** pouvez-vous m'emmener à la gare?
  ▶ **lift off** vi (rocket, helicopter) décoller
  ▶ **lift out** vt sortir; (troops, evacuees etc) évacuer par avion or hélicoptère
  ▶ **lift up** vt soulever
lift-off ['lɪftɒf] n décollage m
ligament ['lɪgəmənt] n ligament m
light [laɪt] n lumière f; (daylight) lumière, jour m; (lamp) lampe f; (Aut: rear light) feu m; (: headlamp) phare m; (for cigarette etc): **have you got a ~?** avez-vous du feu? ▷ vt (pt, pp **-ed**, pt, pp **lit** [lɪt]) (candle, cigarette, fire) allumer; (room) éclairer ▷ adj (room, colour) clair(e); (not heavy, also fig) léger(-ère); (not strenuous) peu fatigant(e) ▷ adv (travel) avec peu de bagages; **lights** npl (traffic lights) feux mpl; **to turn the ~ on/off** allumer/éteindre; **to cast** or **shed** or **throw ~ on** éclaircir; **to come to ~** être dévoilé(e) or découvert(e); **in the ~ of** à la lumière de; étant donné; **to make ~ of sth** (fig) prendre qch à la légère, faire peu de cas de qch
  ▶ **light up** vi s'allumer; (face) s'éclairer; (smoke) allumer une cigarette or une pipe etc ▷ vt (illuminate) éclairer, illuminer
light bulb n ampoule f
lighten ['laɪtn] vi s'éclairer ▷ vt (light up) éclairer; (make lighter) éclaircir; (make less heavy)

alléger
lighter ['laɪtəʳ] n (also: **cigarette lighter**) briquet m; (: in car) allume-cigare m inv; (boat) péniche f
light-fingered [laɪt'fɪŋgəd] adj chapardeur(-euse)
light-headed [laɪt'hɛdɪd] adj étourdi(e), écervelé(e)
light-hearted [laɪt'hɑːtɪd] adj gai(e), joyeux(-euse), enjoué(e)
lighthouse ['laɪthaus] n phare m
lighting ['laɪtɪŋ] n éclairage m; (in theatre) éclairages
lighting-up time [laɪtɪŋ'ʌp-] n (Brit) heure officielle de la tombée du jour
lightly ['laɪtlɪ] adv légèrement; **to get off ~** s'en tirer à bon compte
light meter n (Phot) photomètre m, cellule f
lightness ['laɪtnɪs] n clarté f; (in weight) légèreté f
lightning ['laɪtnɪŋ] n foudre f; (flash) éclair m
lightning conductor, (US) **lightning rod** n paratonnerre m
lightning strike n (Brit) grève f surprise
light pen n crayon m optique
lightship ['laɪtʃɪp] n bateau-phare m
lightweight ['laɪtweɪt] adj (suit) léger(-ère) ▷ n (Boxing) poids léger
light year ['laɪtjɪəʳ] n année-lumière f
like [laɪk] vt aimer (bien) ▷ prep comme ▷ adj semblable, pareil(le) ▷ n: **the ~** un(e) pareil(e) or semblable; le (la) pareil(le); (pej) (d')autres du même genre or acabit; **his ~s and dislikes** ses goûts mpl or préférences fpl; **I would ~**, **I'd ~** je voudrais, j'aimerais; **would you ~ a coffee?** voulez-vous du café?; **to be/look ~ sb/sth** ressembler à qn/qch; **what's he ~?** comment est-il?; **what's the weather ~?** quel temps fait-il?; **what does it look ~?** de quoi est-ce que ça a l'air?; **what does it taste ~?** quel goût est-ce que ça a?; **that's just ~ him** c'est bien de lui, ça lui ressemble; **something ~ that** quelque chose comme ça; **do it ~ this** fais-le comme ceci; **I feel ~ a drink** je boirais bien quelque chose; **if you ~** si vous voulez; **it's nothing ~ ...** ce n'est pas du tout comme ...; **there's nothing ~ ...** il n'y a rien de tel que ...
likeable ['laɪkəbl] adj sympathique, agréable
likelihood ['laɪklɪhud] n probabilité f; **in all ~** selon toute vraisemblance
likely ['laɪklɪ] adj (result, outcome) probable; (excuse) plausible; **he's ~ to leave** il va sûrement partir, il risque fort de partir; **not ~!** (inf) pas de danger!
like-minded [laɪk'maɪndɪd] adj de même opinion
liken ['laɪkən] vt: **to ~ sth to** comparer qch à
likeness ['laɪknɪs] n ressemblance f
likewise ['laɪkwaɪz] adv de même, pareillement
liking ['laɪkɪŋ] n (for person) affection f; (for thing) penchant m, goût m; **to take a ~ to sb** se prendre d'amitié pour qn; **to be to sb's ~** être au goût de qn, plaire à qn
lilac ['laɪlək] n lilas m ▷ adj lilas inv

Lilo® ['laɪləu] *n* matelas *m* pneumatique

lilt [lɪlt] *n* rythme *m*, cadence *f*

lilting ['lɪltɪŋ] *adj* aux cadences mélodieuses; chantant(e)

lily ['lɪlɪ] *n* lis *m*; ~ **of the valley** muguet *m*

Lima ['li:mə] *n* Lima

limb [lɪm] *n* membre *m*; **to be out on a** ~ (*fig*) être isolé(e)

limber ['lɪmbə^r]: **to** ~ **up** *vi* se dégourdir, se mettre en train

limbo ['lɪmbəu] *n*: **to be in** ~ (*fig*) être tombé(e) dans l'oubli

lime [laɪm] *n* (*tree*) tilleul *m*; (*fruit*) citron vert, lime *f*; (*Geo*) chaux *f*

lime juice *n* jus *m* de citron vert

limelight ['laɪmlaɪt] *n*: **in the** ~ (*fig*) en vedette, au premier plan

limerick ['lɪmərɪk] *n* petit poème humoristique

limestone ['laɪmstəun] *n* pierre *f* à chaux; (*Geo*) calcaire *m*

limit ['lɪmɪt] *n* limite *f* ▷ *vt* limiter; **weight/ speed** ~ limite de poids/de vitesse

limitation [lɪmɪ'teɪʃən] *n* limitation *f*, restriction *f*

limited ['lɪmɪtɪd] *adj* limité(e), restreint(e); ~ **edition** édition *f* à tirage limité; **to be** ~ **to** se limiter à, ne concerner que

limited company, limited liability company *n* (*Brit*) ≈ société *f* anonyme

limitless ['lɪmɪtlɪs] *adj* illimité(e)

limousine ['lɪməzi:n] *n* limousine *f*

limp [lɪmp] *n*: **to have a** ~ boiter ▷ *vi* boiter ▷ *adj* mou (molle)

limpet ['lɪmpɪt] *n* patelle *f*; **like a** ~ (*fig*) comme une ventouse

limpid ['lɪmpɪd] *adj* limpide

linchpin ['lɪntʃpɪn] *n* esse *f*; (*fig*) pivot *m*

Lincs [lɪŋks] *abbr* (*Brit*) = **Lincolnshire**

line [laɪn] *n* (*gen*) ligne *f*; (*stroke*) trait *m*; (*wrinkle*) ride *f*; (*rope*) corde *f*; (*wire*) fil *m*; (*of poem*) vers *m*; (*row, series*) rangée *f*; (*of people*) file *f*, queue *f*; (*railway track*) voie *f*; (*Comm: series of goods*) article(s) *m(pl)*, ligne de produits; (*work*) métier *m* ▷ *vt*: **to** ~ (**with**) (*clothes*) doubler (de); (*box*) garnir *or* tapisser (de); (*subj: trees, crowd*) border; **to stand in** ~ (*US*) faire la queue; **to cut in** ~ (*US*) passer avant son tour; **in his** ~ **of business** dans sa partie, dans son rayon; **on the right** ~s sur la bonne voie; **a new** ~ **in cosmetics** une nouvelle ligne de produits de beauté; **hold the** ~ **please** (*Brit Tel*) ne quittez pas; **to be in** ~ **for sth** (*fig*) être en lice pour qch; **in** ~ **with** en accord avec, en conformité avec; **in a** ~ aligné(e); **to bring sth into** ~ **with sth** aligner qch sur qch; **to draw the** ~ **at** (**doing**) **sth** (*fig*) se refuser à (faire) qch; ne pas tolérer *or* admettre (qu'on fasse) qch; **to take the** ~ **that** ... être d'avis *or* de l'opinion que ...

▶ **line up** *vi* s'aligner, se mettre en rang(s); (*in queue*) faire la queue ▷ *vt* aligner; (*event*) prévoir; (*find*) trouver; **to have sb/sth** ~**d up** avoir qn/qch en vue *or* de prévu(e)

linear ['lɪnɪə^r] *adj* linéaire

lined [laɪnd] *adj* (*paper*) réglé(e); (*face*) marqué(e), ridé(e); (*clothes*) doublé(e)

lineman ['laɪnmən] (*irreg*) *n* (US: *Rail*) poseur *m* de rails; (: *Tel*) ouvrier *m* de ligne; (: *Football*) avant *m*

linen ['lɪnɪn] *n* linge *m* (de corps *or* de maison); (*cloth*) lin *m*

line printer *n* imprimante *f* (ligne par) ligne

liner ['laɪnə^r] *n* (*ship*) paquebot *m* de ligne; (*for bin*) sac-poubelle *m*

linesman ['laɪnzmən] (*irreg*) *n* (*Tennis*) juge *m* de ligne; (*Football*) juge de touche

line-up ['laɪnʌp] *n* (US: *queue*) file *f*; (*also*: **police line-up**) parade *f* d'identification; (*Sport*) (composition *f* de l')équipe *f*

linger ['lɪŋgə^r] *vi* s'attarder; traîner; (*smell, tradition*) persister

lingerie ['lænʒəri:] *n* lingerie *f*

lingering ['lɪŋgərɪŋ] *adj* persistant(e); qui subsiste; (*death*) lent(e)

lingo ['lɪŋgəu] (*pl* -**es**) *n* (*pej*) jargon *m*

linguist ['lɪŋgwɪst] *n* linguiste *m/f*; **to be a good** ~ être doué(e) pour les langues

linguistic [lɪŋ'gwɪstɪk] *adj* linguistique

linguistics [lɪŋ'gwɪstɪks] *n* linguistique *f*

lining ['laɪnɪŋ] *n* doublure *f*; (*Tech*) revêtement *m*; (: *of brakes*) garniture *f*

link [lɪŋk] *n* (*connection*) lien *m*, rapport *m*; (*Internet*) lien; (*of a chain*) maillon *m* ▷ *vt* relier, lier, unir; **links** *npl* (*Golf*) (terrain *m* de) golf *m*; **rail** ~ liaison *f* ferroviaire

▶ **link up** *vt* relier ▷ *vi* (*people*) se rejoindre; (*companies etc*) s'associer

link-up ['lɪŋkʌp] *n* lien *m*, rapport *m*; (*of roads*) jonction *f*, raccordement *m*; (*of spaceships*) arrimage *m*; (*Radio, TV*) liaison *f*; (: *programme*) duplex *m*

lino ['laɪnəu] *n* = **linoleum**

linoleum [lɪ'nəulɪəm] *n* linoléum *m*

linseed oil ['lɪnsi:d-] *n* huile *f* de lin

lint [lɪnt] *n* tissu ouaté (*pour pansements*)

lintel ['lɪntl] *n* linteau *m*

lion ['laɪən] *n* lion *m*

lion cub *n* lionceau *m*

lioness ['laɪənɪs] *n* lionne *f*

lip [lɪp] *n* lèvre *f*; (*of cup etc*) rebord *m*; (*insolence*) insolences *fpl*

liposuction ['lɪpəusʌkʃən] *n* liposuccion *f*

lipread ['lɪpri:d] *vi* (*irreg*: *like* **read**) lire sur les lèvres

lip salve [-sælv] *n* pommade *f* pour les lèvres, pommade rosat

lip service *n*: **to pay** ~ **sth** ne reconnaître le mérite de qch que pour la forme *or* qu'en paroles

lipstick ['lɪpstɪk] *n* rouge *m* à lèvres

liquefy ['lɪkwɪfaɪ] *vt* liquéfier ▷ *vi* se liquéfier

liqueur [lɪ'kjuə^r] *n* liqueur *f*

liquid ['lɪkwɪd] *n* liquide *m* ▷ *adj* liquide

liquid assets *npl* liquidités *fpl*, disponibilités *fpl*

liquidate ['lɪkwɪdeɪt] *vt* liquider

liquidation [lɪkwɪ'deɪʃən] *n* liquidation *f*; **to go**

into ~ déposer son bilan
liquidator ['lɪkwɪdeɪtər] n liquidateur m
liquid crystal display n affichage m à cristaux liquides
liquidize ['lɪkwɪdaɪz] vt (Brit Culin) passer au mixer
liquidizer ['lɪkwɪdaɪzər] n (Brit Culin) mixer m
liquor ['lɪkər] n spiritueux m, alcool m
liquorice ['lɪkərɪs] n (Brit) réglisse m
liquor store (US) n magasin m de vins et spiritueux
Lisbon ['lɪzbən] n Lisbonne
lisp [lɪsp] n zézaiement m ▷ vi zézayer
lissom ['lɪsəm] adj souple, agile
list [lɪst] n liste f; (of ship) inclinaison f ▷ vt (write down) inscrire; (make list of) faire la liste de; (enumerate) énumérer; (Comput) lister ▷ vi (ship) gîter, donner de la bande; **shopping** ~ liste des courses
listed building ['lɪstɪd-] n (Archit) monument classé
listed company ['lɪstɪd-] n société cotée en Bourse
listen ['lɪsn] vi écouter; **to** ~ **to** écouter
listener ['lɪsnər] n auditeur(-trice)
listeria [lɪs'tɪərɪə] n listéria f
listing ['lɪstɪŋ] n (Comput) listage m; (: hard copy) liste f, listing m
listless ['lɪstlɪs] adj indolent(e), apathique
listlessly ['lɪstlɪslɪ] adv avec indolence or apathie
list price n prix m de catalogue
lit [lɪt] pt, pp of **light**
litany ['lɪtənɪ] n litanie f
liter ['liːtər] n (US) = **litre**
literacy ['lɪtərəsɪ] n degré m d'alphabétisation, fait m de savoir lire et écrire; (Brit: Scol) enseignement m de la lecture et de l'écriture
literal ['lɪtərl] adj littéral(e)
literally ['lɪtrəlɪ] adv littéralement; (really) réellement
literary ['lɪtərərɪ] adj littéraire
literate ['lɪtərət] adj qui sait lire et écrire; (educated) instruit(e)
literature ['lɪtrɪtʃər] n littérature f; (brochures etc) copie f publicitaire, prospectus mpl
lithe [laɪð] adj agile, souple
lithography [lɪ'θɔgrəfɪ] n lithographie f
Lithuania [lɪθju'eɪnɪə] n Lituanie f
Lithuanian [lɪθju'eɪnɪən] adj lituanien(ne) ▷ n Lituanien(ne); (Ling) lituanien m
litigate ['lɪtɪgeɪt] vt mettre en litige ▷ vi plaider
litigation [lɪtɪ'geɪʃən] n litige m; contentieux m
litmus ['lɪtməs] n: ~ **paper** papier m de tournesol
litre, (US) **liter** ['liːtər] n litre m
litter ['lɪtər] n (rubbish) détritus mpl; (dirtier) ordures fpl; (young animals) portée f ▷ vt éparpiller; laisser des détritus dans; **~ed with** jonché(e) de, couvert(e) de
litter bin n (Brit) poubelle f
litter lout, (US) **litterbug** ['lɪtəbʌg] n personne qui jette des détritus par terre
little ['lɪtl] adj (small) petit(e); (not much): ~ **milk**

peu de lait ▷ adv peu; **a** ~ un peu (de); **a** ~ **milk** un peu de lait; **a** ~ **bit** un peu; **for a** ~ **while** pendant un petit moment; **with** ~ **difficulty** sans trop de difficulté; **as** ~ **as possible** le moins possible; ~ **by** ~ petit à petit, peu à peu; **to make** ~ **of** faire peu de cas de
little finger n auriculaire m, petit doigt
little-known ['lɪtl'nəun] adj peu connu(e)
liturgy ['lɪtədʒɪ] n liturgie f
live¹ [laɪv] adj (animal) vivant(e), en vie; (wire) sous tension; (broadcast) (transmis(e)) en direct; (issue) d'actualité, brûlant(e); (unexploded) non explosé(e); ~ **ammunition** munitions fpl de combat
live² [lɪv] vi vivre; (reside) vivre, habiter; **to** ~ **in London** habiter (à) Londres; **where do you** ~? où habitez-vous?
  ▶ **live down** vt faire oublier (avec le temps)
  ▶ **live in** vi être logé(e) et nourri(e); être interne
  ▶ **live off** vt (land, fish etc) vivre de; (pej: parents etc) vivre aux crochets de
  ▶ **live on** vt fus (food) vivre de ▷ vi survivre; **to** ~ **on £50 a week** vivre avec 50 livres par semaine
  ▶ **live out** vi (Brit: students) être externe ▷ vt: **to** ~ **out one's days** or **life** passer sa vie
  ▶ **live together** vi vivre ensemble, cohabiter
  ▶ **live up** vt: **to** ~ **it up** (inf) faire la fête; mener la grande vie
  ▶ **live up to** vt fus se montrer à la hauteur de
live-in ['lɪvɪn] adj (nanny) à demeure; ~ **partner** concubin(e)
livelihood ['laɪvlɪhud] n moyens mpl d'existence
liveliness ['laɪvlɪnəs] n vivacité f, entrain m
lively ['laɪvlɪ] adj vif (vive), plein(e) d'entrain; (place, book) vivant(e)
liven up ['laɪvn-] vt (room etc) égayer; (discussion, evening) animer ▷ vi s'animer
liver ['lɪvər] n foie m
liverish ['lɪvərɪʃ] adj qui a mal au foie; (fig) grincheux(-euse)
Liverpudlian [lɪvə'pʌdlɪən] adj de Liverpool ▷ n habitant(e) de Liverpool, natif(-ive) de Liverpool
livery ['lɪvərɪ] n livrée f
lives [laɪvz] npl of **life**
livestock ['laɪvstɔk] n cheptel m, bétail m
live wire [laɪv-] n (inf, fig): **to be a (real)** ~ péter le feu
livid ['lɪvɪd] adj livide, blafard(e); (furious) furieux(-euse), furibond(e)
living ['lɪvɪŋ] adj vivant(e), en vie ▷ n: **to earn** or **make a** ~ gagner sa vie; **within** ~ **memory** de mémoire d'homme
living conditions npl conditions fpl de vie
living expenses npl dépenses courantes
living room n salle f de séjour
living standards npl niveau m de vie
living wage n salaire m permettant de vivre (décemment)
lizard ['lɪzəd] n lézard m
llama ['lɑːmə] n lama m
LLB n abbr (= Bachelor of Laws) titre universitaire

LLD *n abbr* (= *Doctor of Laws*) *titre universitaire*
LMT *abbr* (*US*: = *Local Mean Time*) *heure locale*
load [ləud] *n* (*weight*) poids *m*; (*thing carried*)
chargement *m*, charge *f*; (*Elec, Tech*) charge ▷ *vt*:
to ~ (with) (*also*: **load up**: *lorry, ship*) charger (de);
(*gun, camera*) charger (avec); (*Comput*) charger; **a
~ of, ~s of** (*fig*) un *or* des tas de, des masses de; **to
talk a ~ of rubbish** (*inf*) dire des bêtises
loaded [ləudɪd] *adj* (*dice*) pipé(e); (*question*)
insidieux(-euse); (*inf: rich*) bourré(e) de fric;
(*: drunk*) bourré
loading bay [ləudɪŋ-] *n* aire *f* de chargement
loaf (*pl* **loaves**) [ləuf, ləuvz] *n* pain *m*, miche *f*
▷ *vi* (*also*: **loaf about, loaf around**) fainéanter,
traîner
loam [ləum] *n* terreau *m*
loan [ləun] *n* prêt *m* ▷ *vt* prêter; **on ~** prêté(e),
en prêt; **public ~** emprunt public
loan account *n* compte *m* de prêt
loan capital *n* capital *m* d'emprunt
loan shark *n* (*inf, pej*) usurier *m*
loath [ləuθ] *adj*: **to be ~ to do** répugner à faire
loathe [ləuð] *vt* détester, avoir en horreur
loathing [ləuðɪŋ] *n* dégoût *m*, répugnance *f*
loathsome [ləuðsəm] *adj* répugnant(e),
détestable
loaves [ləuvz] *npl of* **loaf**
lob [lɔb] *vt* (*ball*) lober
lobby [lɔbɪ] *n* hall *m*, entrée *f*; (*Pol*) groupe *m* de
pression, lobby *m* ▷ *vt* faire pression sur
lobbyist [lɔbɪɪst] *n* membre *m/f* d'un groupe de
pression
lobe [ləub] *n* lobe *m*
lobster [lɔbstər] *n* homard *m*
lobster pot *n* casier *m* à homards
local [ləukl] *adj* local(e) ▷ *n* (*Brit*: *pub*) pub *m or*
café *m* du coin; **the locals** *npl* les gens *mpl* du
pays *or* du coin
local anaesthetic, (*US*) **local anesthetic** *n*
anesthésie locale
local authority *n* collectivité locale,
municipalité *f*
local call *n* (*Tel*) communication urbaine
local government *n* administration locale *or*
municipale
locality [ləu'kælɪtɪ] *n* région *f*, environs *mpl*;
(*position*) lieu *m*
localize [ləukəlaɪz] *vt* localiser
locally [ləukəlɪ] *adv* localement; dans les
environs *or* la région
locate [ləu'keɪt] *vt* (*find*) trouver, repérer;
(*situate*) situer; **to be ~d in** être situé à *or* en
location [ləu'keɪʃən] *n* emplacement *m*; **on ~**
(*Cine*) en extérieur
loch [lɔx] *n* lac *m*, loch *m*
lock [lɔk] *n* (*of door, box*) serrure *f*; (*of canal*) écluse
f; (*of hair*) mèche *f*, boucle *f* ▷ *vt* (*with key*) fermer
à clé; (*immobilize*) bloquer ▷ *vi* (*door etc*) fermer à
clé; (*wheels*) se bloquer; **~ stock and barrel** (*fig*)
en bloc; **on full ~** (*Brit Aut*) le volant tourné à
fond
▶ **lock away** *vt* (*valuables*) mettre sous clé;

(*criminal*) mettre sous les verrous, enfermer
▶ **lock in** *vt* enfermer
▶ **lock out** *vt* enfermer dehors; (*on purpose*)
mettre à la porte; (: *workers*) lock-outer
▶ **lock up** *vt* (*person*) enfermer; (*house*) fermer à
clé ▷ *vi* tout fermer (à clé)
locker [lɔkər] *n* casier *m*; (*in station*) consigne *f*
automatique
locker-room [lɔkərru:m] (*US*) *n* (*Sport*)
vestiaire *m*
locket [lɔkɪt] *n* médaillon *m*
lockjaw [lɔkdʒɔ:] *n* tétanos *m*
lockout [lɔkaut] *n* (*Industry*) lock-out *m*, grève
patronale
locksmith [lɔksmɪθ] *n* serrurier *m*
lock-up [lɔkʌp] *n* (*prison*) prison *f*; (*cell*) cellule *f*
provisoire; (*also*: **lock-up garage**) box *m*
locomotive [ləukə'məutɪv] *n* locomotive *f*
locum [ləukəm] *n* (*Med*) suppléant(e) de
médecin *etc*
locust [ləukəst] *n* locuste *f*, sauterelle *f*
lodge [lɔdʒ] *n* pavillon *m* (de gardien); (*also*:
hunting lodge) pavillon de chasse; (*Freemasonry*)
loge *f* ▷ *vi* (*person*): **to ~ with** être logé(e) chez,
être en pension chez; (*bullet*) se loger ▷ *vt* (*appeal
etc*) présenter; déposer; **to ~ a complaint** porter
plainte; **to ~ (itself) in/between** se loger dans/
entre
lodger [lɔdʒər] *n* locataire *m/f*; (*with room and
meals*) pensionnaire *m/f*
lodging [lɔdʒɪŋ] *n* logement *m*; *see also* **board**
lodging house *n* (*Brit*) pension *f* de famille
lodgings [lɔdʒɪŋz] *npl* chambre *f*, meublé *m*
loft [lɔft] *n* grenier *m*; (*apartment*) grenier
aménagé (en appartement) (*gén dans ancien
entrepôt ou fabrique*)
lofty [lɔftɪ] *adj* élevé(e); (*haughty*) hautain(e);
(*sentiments, aims*) noble
log [lɔg] *n* (*of wood*) bûche *f*; (*Naut*) livre *m or*
journal *m* de bord; (*of car*) ≈ carte grise ▷ *n abbr*
(= *logarithm*) log *m* ▷ *vt* enregistrer
▶ **log in, log on** *vi* (*Comput*) ouvrir une session,
entrer dans le système
▶ **log off, log out** *vi* (*Comput*) clore une session,
sortir du système
logarithm [lɔgərɪðm] *n* logarithme *m*
logbook [lɔgbuk] *n* (*Naut*) livre *m or* journal *m* de
bord; (*Aviat*) carnet *m* de vol; (*of lorry driver*)
carnet de route; (*of movement of goods etc*) registre
m; (*of car*) ≈ carte grise
log cabin *n* cabane *f* en rondins
log fire *n* feu *m* de bois
logger [lɔgər] *n* bûcheron *m*
loggerheads [lɔgəhɛdz] *npl*: **at ~ (with)** à
couteaux tirés (avec)
logic [lɔdʒɪk] *n* logique *f*
logical [lɔdʒɪkl] *adj* logique
logically [lɔdʒɪkəlɪ] *adv* logiquement
logistics [lɔ'dʒɪstɪks] *n* logistique *f*
logjam [lɔgdʒæm] *n*: **to break the ~** créer une
ouverture dans l'impasse
logo [ləugəu] *n* logo *m*

loin [lɔɪn] *n* (*Culin*) filet *m*, longe *f*; **loins** *npl* reins *mpl*

loin cloth *n* pagne *m*

Loire [lwa:] *n*: **the (River)** ~ la Loire

loiter ['lɔɪtəʳ] *vi* s'attarder; **to** ~ **(about)** traîner, musarder; (*pej*) rôder

loll [lɔl] *vi* (*also*: **loll about**) se prélasser, fainéanter

lollipop ['lɔlɪpɔp] *n* sucette *f*

lollipop man/lady (*Brit*: *irreg*) *n contractuel(le) qui fait traverser la rue aux enfants*; *voir article*

⬤ **LOLLIPOP MEN/LADIES**
⬤
⬤ Les *lollipop men/ladies* sont employés pour
⬤ aider les enfants à traverser la rue à
⬤ proximité des écoles à l'heure où ils entrent
⬤ en classe et à la sortie. On les repère
⬤ facilement à cause de leur long ciré jaune et
⬤ ils portent une pancarte ronde pour faire
⬤ signe aux automobilistes de s'arrêter. On les
⬤ appelle ainsi car la forme circulaire de cette
⬤ pancarte rappelle une sucette.

lollop ['lɔləp] *vi* (*Brit*) avancer (*or* courir) maladroitement

lolly ['lɔlɪ] *n* (*inf*: *ice*) esquimau *m*; (: *lollipop*) sucette *f*; (: *money*) fric *m*

Lombardy ['lɔmbədɪ] *n* Lombardie *f*

London ['lʌndən] *n* Londres

Londoner ['lʌndənəʳ] *n* Londonien(ne)

lone [ləun] *adj* solitaire

loneliness ['ləunlɪnɪs] *n* solitude *f*, isolement *m*

lonely ['ləunlɪ] *adj* seul(e); (*childhood etc*) solitaire; (*place*) solitaire, isolé(e)

lonely hearts *adj*: ~ **ad** petite annonce (personnelle); ~ **club** club *m* de rencontres (*pour personnes seules*)

lone parent *n* parent *m* unique

loner ['ləunəʳ] *n* solitaire *m/f*

lonesome ['ləunsəm] *adj* seul(e), solitaire

long [lɔŋ] *adj* long (longue) ▷ *adv* longtemps ▷ *n*: **the** ~ **and the short of it is that** ... (*fig*) le fin mot de l'histoire c'est que ... ▷ *vi*: **to** ~ **for sth/to do sth** avoir très envie de qch/de faire qch, attendre qch avec impatience/attendre avec impatience de faire qch; **he had** ~ **understood that** ... il avait compris depuis longtemps que ...; **how** ~ **is this river/course?** quelle est la longueur de ce fleuve/la durée de ce cours?; **6 metres** ~ (long) de 6 mètres; **6 months** ~ qui dure 6 mois, de 6 mois; **all night** ~ toute la nuit; **he no** ~**er comes** il ne vient plus; **I can't stand it any** ~**er** je ne peux plus le supporter; ~ **before** longtemps avant; **before** ~ (+*future*) avant peu, dans peu de temps; (+*past*) peu de temps après; ~ **ago** il y a longtemps; **don't be** ~! fais vite!, dépêche-toi!; **I shan't be** ~ je n'en ai pas pour longtemps; **at** ~ **last** enfin; **in the** ~ **run** à la longue; finalement; **so** *or* **as** ~ **as** à condition que + *sub*

long-distance [lɔŋ'dɪstəns] *adj* (*race*) de fond; (*call*) interurbain(e)

longer ['lɔŋgəʳ] *adv see* **long**

long-haired ['lɔŋ'hɛəd] *adj* (*person*) aux cheveux longs; (*animal*) aux longs poils

longhand ['lɔŋhænd] *n* écriture normale *or* courante

long-haul ['lɔŋhɔ:l] *adj* (*flight*) long-courrier

longing ['lɔŋɪŋ] *n* désir *m*, envie *f*; (*nostalgia*) nostalgie *f* ▷ *adj* plein(e) d'envie *or* de nostalgie

longingly ['lɔŋɪŋlɪ] *adv* avec désir *or* nostalgie

longitude ['lɔŋgɪtju:d] *n* longitude *f*

long johns [-dʒɔnz] *npl* caleçons longs

long jump *n* saut *m* en longueur

long-life [lɔŋ'laɪf] *adj* (*batteries etc*) longue durée *inv*; (*milk*) longue conservation

long-lost ['lɔŋlɔst] *adj* perdu(e) depuis longtemps

long-playing ['lɔŋpleɪɪŋ] *adj*: ~ **record (LP)** (disque *m*) 33 tours *m inv*

long-range ['lɔŋ'reɪndʒ] *adj* à longue portée; (*weather forecast*) à long terme

longshoreman ['lɔŋʃɔ:mən] (*irreg*) *n* (*US*) docker *m*, débardeur *m*

long-sighted ['lɔŋ'saɪtɪd] *adj* (*Brit*) presbyte; (*fig*) prévoyant(e)

long-standing ['lɔŋ'stændɪŋ] *adj* de longue date

long-suffering [lɔŋ'sʌfərɪŋ] *adj* empreint(e) d'une patience résignée; extrêmement patient(e)

long-term ['lɔŋtə:m] *adj* à long terme

long wave *n* (*Radio*) grandes ondes, ondes longues

long-winded [lɔŋ'wɪndɪd] *adj* intarissable, interminable

loo [lu:] *n* (*Brit inf*) w.-c *mpl*, petit coin

loofah ['lu:fə] *n sorte d'éponge végétale*

look [luk] *vi* regarder; (*seem*) sembler, paraître, avoir l'air; (*building etc*): **to** ~ **south/on to the sea** donner au sud/sur la mer ▷ *n* regard *m*; (*appearance*) air *m*, allure *f*, aspect *m*; **looks** *npl* (*good looks*) physique *m*, beauté *f*; **to** ~ **like** ressembler à; **it** ~**s like him** on dirait que c'est lui; **it** ~**s about 4 metres long** je dirais que ça fait 4 mètres de long; **it** ~**s all right to me** ça me paraît bien; **to have a** ~ regarder; **to have a** ~ **at sth** jeter un coup d'œil à qch; **to have a** ~ **for sth** chercher qch; **to** ~ **ahead** regarder devant soi; (*fig*) envisager l'avenir; ~ **(here)!** (*annoyance*) écoutez!

▶ **look after** *vt fus* s'occuper de, prendre soin de; (*luggage etc*: *watch over*) garder, surveiller

▶ **look around** *vi* regarder autour de soi

▶ **look at** *vt fus* regarder; (*problem etc*) examiner

▶ **look back** *vi*: **to** ~ **back at sth/sb** se retourner pour regarder qch/qn; **to** ~ **back on** (*event, period*) évoquer, repenser à

▶ **look down on** *vt fus* (*fig*) regarder de haut, dédaigner

▶ **look for** *vt fus* chercher; **we're** ~**ing for a hotel/restaurant** nous cherchons un hôtel/ restaurant

▶ **look forward to** *vt fus* attendre avec

impatience; **I'm not ~ing forward to it** cette perspective ne me réjouit guère; **~ing forward to hearing from you** (in letter) dans l'attente de vous lire

▶ **look in** vi: **to ~ in on sb** passer voir qn

▶ **look into** vt fus (matter, possibility) examiner, étudier

▶ **look on** vi regarder (en spectateur)

▶ **look out** vi (beware): **to ~ out (for)** prendre garde (à), faire attention (à); **~ out!** attention!

▶ **look out for** vt fus (seek) être à la recherche de; (try to spot) guetter

▶ **look over** vt (essay) jeter un coup d'œil à; (town, building) visiter (rapidement); (person) jeter un coup d'œil à; examiner de la tête aux pieds

▶ **look round** vt fus (house, shop) faire le tour de ▷ vi (turn) regarder derrière soi, se retourner; **to ~ round for sth** chercher qch

▶ **look through** vt fus (papers, book) examiner; (: briefly) parcourir; (telescope) regarder à travers

▶ **look to** vt fus veiller à; (rely on) compter sur

▶ **look up** vi lever les yeux; (improve) s'améliorer ▷ vt (word) chercher; (friend) passer voir

▶ **look up to** vt fus avoir du respect pour

lookout ['lukaut] n (tower etc) poste m de guet; (person) guetteur m; **to be on the ~ (for)** guetter

look-up table ['lukʌp-] n (Comput) table f à consulter

loom [lu:m] n métier m à tisser ▷ vi (also: **loom up**) surgir; (event) paraître imminent(e); (threaten) menacer

loony ['lu:nɪ] adj, n (inf) timbré(e), cinglé(e) m/f

loop [lu:p] n boucle f; (contraceptive) stérilet m ▷ vt: **to ~ sth round sth** passer qch autour de qch

loophole ['lu:phəul] n (fig) porte f de sortie; échappatoire f

loose [lu:s] adj (knot, screw) desserré(e); (stone) branlant(e); (clothes) vague, ample, lâche; (hair) dénoué(e), épars(e); (not firmly fixed) pas solide; (animal) en liberté, échappé(e); (life) dissolu(e); (morals, discipline) relâché(e); (thinking) peu rigoureux(-euse), vague; (translation) approximatif(-ive) ▷ n: **to be on the ~** être en liberté ▷ vt (free: animal) lâcher; (: prisoner) relâcher, libérer; (slacken) détendre, relâcher; desserrer; défaire; donner du mou a; donner du ballant à; (Brit: arrow) tirer; **~ connection** (Elec) mauvais contact; **to be at a ~ end** or (US) **at ~ ends** (fig) ne pas trop savoir quoi faire; **to tie up ~ ends** (fig) mettre au point or régler les derniers détails

loose change n petite monnaie

loose chippings [-'tʃɪpɪŋz] npl (on road) gravillons mpl

loose-fitting ['lu:sfɪtɪŋ] adj (clothes) ample

loose-leaf ['lu:sli:f] adj: **~ binder** or **folder** classeur m à feuilles or feuillets mobiles

loose-limbed [lu:s'lɪmd] adj agile, souple

loosely ['lu:slɪ] adv sans serrer; (imprecisely) approximativement

loosely-knit ['lu:slɪ'nɪt] adj élastique

loosen ['lu:sn] vt desserrer, relâcher, défaire

▶ **loosen up** vi (before game) s'échauffer; (inf: relax) se détendre, se laisser aller

loot [lu:t] n butin m ▷ vt piller

looter ['lu:tər] n pillard m, casseur m

looting ['lu:tɪŋ] n pillage m

lop [lɔp]: **to ~ off** vt couper, trancher

lop-sided ['lɔp'saɪdɪd] adj de travers, asymétrique

lord [lɔ:d] n seigneur m; **L~ Smith** lord Smith; **the L~** (Rel) le Seigneur; **my L~** (to noble) Monsieur le comte/le baron; (to judge) Monsieur le juge; (to bishop) Monseigneur; **good L~!** mon Dieu!

lordly ['lɔ:dlɪ] adj noble, majestueux(-euse); (arrogant) hautain(e)

Lords ['lɔ:dz] npl (Brit: Pol): **the (House of) ~** (Brit) la Chambre des Lords

lordship ['lɔ:dʃɪp] n (Brit): **your L~** Monsieur le comte (or le baron or le Juge)

lore [lɔ:r] n tradition(s) f(pl)

lorry ['lɔrɪ] n (Brit) camion m

lorry driver n (Brit) camionneur m, routier m

lose (pt, pp **lost**) [lu:z, lɔst] vt perdre; (opportunity) manquer, perdre; (pursuers) distancer, semer ▷ vi perdre; **I've lost my wallet/passport** j'ai perdu mon portefeuille/passeport; **to ~ (time)** (clock) retarder; **to ~ no time (in doing sth)** ne pas perdre de temps (à faire qch); **to get lost** (vi: person) se perdre; **my watch has got lost** ma montre est perdue

▶ **lose out** vi être perdant(e)

loser ['lu:zər] n perdant(e); **to be a good/bad ~** être beau/mauvais joueur

loss [lɔs] n perte f; **to cut one's ~es** limiter les dégâts; **to make a ~** enregistrer une perte; **to sell sth at a ~** vendre qch à perte; **to be at a ~** être perplexe or embarrassé(e); **to be at a ~ to do** se trouver incapable de faire

loss adjuster n (Insurance) responsable m/f de l'évaluation des dommages

loss leader n (Comm) article sacrifié

lost [lɔst] pt, pp of **lose** ▷ adj perdu(e); **to get ~** (vi) se perdre; **I'm ~** je me suis perdu; **~ in thought** perdu dans ses pensées; **~ and found property** (n: US) objets trouvés; **~ and found** (n: US) (bureau m des) objets trouvés

lost property n (Brit) objets trouvés; **~ office** or **department** (bureau m des) objets trouvés

lot [lɔt] n (at auctions, set) lot m; (destiny) sort m, destinée f; **the ~** (everything) le tout; (everyone) tous mpl, toutes fpl; **a ~** beaucoup; **a ~ of** beaucoup de; **~s of** des tas de; **to draw ~s (for sth)** tirer (qch) au sort

lotion ['ləuʃən] n lotion f

lottery ['lɔtərɪ] n loterie f

loud [laud] adj bruyant(e), sonore; (voice) fort(e); (condemnation etc) vigoureux(-euse); (gaudy) voyant(e), tapageur(-euse) ▷ adv (speak etc) fort; **out ~** tout haut

loud-hailer [laud'heɪlər] n porte-voix m inv

loudly ['laudlɪ] *adv* fort, bruyamment
loudspeaker [laud'spi:kəʳ] *n* haut-parleur *m*
lounge [laundʒ] *n* salon *m*; (*of airport*) salle *f*;
  (*Brit: also*: **lounge bar**) (salle de) café *m* or bar *m*
  ▷ *vi* (*also*: **lounge about, lounge around**) se
  prélasser, paresser
lounge-bar *n* (salle *f* de) bar *m*
lounge suit *n* (*Brit*) complet *m*; (: *on invitation*)
  "tenue de ville"
louse (*pl* **lice**) [laus, laɪs] *n* pou *m*
  ▸ **louse up** [lauz-] *vt* (*inf*) gâcher
lousy ['lauzɪ] (*inf*) *adj* (*bad quality*) infect(e),
  moche; **I feel ~** je suis mal fichu(e)
lout [laut] *n* rustre *m*, butor *m*
louvre, (*US*) **louver** ['lu:vəʳ] *adj* (*door, window*) à
  claire-voie
lovable ['lʌvəbl] *adj* très sympathique; adorable
love [lʌv] *n* amour *m* ▷ *vt* aimer; (*caringly, kindly*)
  aimer beaucoup; **I ~ chocolate** j'adore le
  chocolat; **to ~ to do** aimer beaucoup or adorer
  faire; **I'd ~ to come** cela me ferait très plaisir
  (de venir); **"15 ~"** (*Tennis*) "15 à rien or zéro"; **to
  be/fall in ~ with** être/tomber amoureux(-euse)
  de; **to make ~** faire l'amour; **~ at first sight** le
  coup de foudre; **to send one's ~ to sb** adresser
  ses amitiés à qn; **~ from Anne, ~, Anne**
  affectueusement, Anne; **I ~ you** je t'aime
love affair *n* liaison (amoureuse)
love child *n* (*irreg*) enfant *m/f* illégitime or
  naturel(le)
loved ones ['lʌvdwʌnz] *npl* proches *mpl* et amis
  chers
love-hate relationship [lʌv'heɪt-] *n* rapport
  ambigu; **they have a ~** ils s'aiment et se
  détestent à la fois
love life *n* vie sentimentale
lovely ['lʌvlɪ] *adj* (*pretty*) ravissant(e); (*friend, wife*)
  charmant(e); (*holiday, surprise*) très agréable,
  merveilleux(-euse); **we had a ~ time** c'était
  vraiment très bien, nous avons eu beaucoup de
  plaisir
lover ['lʌvəʳ] *n* amant *m*; (*person in love*)
  amoureux(-euse); (*amateur*): **a ~ of** un(e) ami(e)
  de, un(e) amoureux(-euse) de
lovesick ['lʌvsɪk] *adj* qui se languit d'amour
love song ['lʌvsɒŋ] *n* chanson *f* d'amour
loving ['lʌvɪŋ] *adj* affectueux(-euse), tendre,
  aimant(e)
low [ləu] *adj* bas (basse); (*quality*) mauvais(e),
  inférieur(e) ▷ *adv* bas ▷ *n* (*Meteorology*)
  dépression *f* ▷ *vi* (*cow*) mugir; **to feel ~** se sentir
  déprimé(e); **he's very ~** (*ill*) il est bien bas or très
  affaibli; **to turn (down) ~** (*vt*) baisser; **to be ~
  on** (*supplies etc*) être à court de; **to reach a new** or
  an all-time ~ tomber au niveau le plus bas
low-alcohol [ləu'ælkəhɒl] *adj* à faible teneur en
  alcool, peu alcoolisé(e)
lowbrow ['ləubrau] *adj* sans prétentions
  intellectuelles
low-calorie ['ləu'kælərɪ] *adj* hypocalorique
low-cut ['ləukʌt] *adj* (*dress*) décolleté(e)
low-down ['ləudaun] *n* (*inf*): **he gave me the ~**

(**on it**) il m'a mis au courant ▷ *adj* (*mean*)
  méprisable
lower *adj* ['ləuəʳ] inférieur(e) ▷ *vt* ['ləuəʳ]
  baisser; (*resistance*) diminuer ▷ *vi* ['ləuəʳ]
  (*person*): **to ~ at sb** jeter un regard mauvais or
  noir à qn; (*sky, clouds*) être menaçant; **to ~ o.s.
  to** s'abaisser à
lower sixth (*Brit*) *n* (*Scol*) première *f*
low-fat ['ləu'fæt] *adj* maigre
low-key ['ləu'ki:] *adj* modéré(e), discret(-ète)
lowland, lowlands ['ləulənd(z)] *n(pl)*
  plaine(s) *f(pl)*
low-level ['ləulɛvl] *adj* bas (basse); (*flying*) à
  basse altitude
low-loader ['ləuləudəʳ] *n* semi-remorque *f* à
  plate-forme surbaissée
lowly ['ləulɪ] *adj* humble, modeste
low-lying [ləu'laɪɪŋ] *adj* à faible altitude
low-paid [ləu'peɪd] *adj* mal payé(e), aux salaires
  bas
low-rise ['ləuraɪz] *adj* bas(se), de faible hauteur
low-tech ['ləutɛk] *adj* sommaire
loyal ['lɔɪəl] *adj* loyal(e), fidèle
loyalist ['lɔɪəlɪst] *n* loyaliste *m/f*
loyalty ['lɔɪəltɪ] *n* loyauté *f*, fidélité *f*
loyalty card *n* carte *f* de fidélité
lozenge ['lɒzɪndʒ] *n* (*Med*) pastille *f*; (*Geom*)
  losange *m*
LP *n abbr* = **long-playing record**
LPG *n abbr* (= *liquid petroleum gas*) GPL *m*
L-plates ['ɛlpleɪts] *npl* (*Brit*) plaques *fpl*
  (obligatoires) d'apprenti conducteur
LPN *n abbr* (*US*: = *Licensed Practical Nurse*)
  infirmier(-ière) diplômé(e)
LRAM *n abbr* (*Brit*) = **Licentiate of the Royal
  Academy of Music**
LSAT *n abbr* (*US*) = **Law School Admissions Test**
LSD *n abbr* (= *lysergic acid diethylamide*) LSD *m*; (*Brit*:
  = *pounds, shillings and pence*) *système monétaire en
  usage en GB jusqu'en 1971*
LSE *n abbr* = **London School of Economics**
LT *abbr* (*Elec*: = *low tension*) BT
Lt *abbr* (= *lieutenant*) Lt.
Ltd *abbr* (*Comm*: *company*: = *limited*) ≈ S.A.
lubricant ['lu:brɪkənt] *n* lubrifiant *m*
lubricate ['lu:brɪkeɪt] *vt* lubrifier, graisser
lucid ['lu:sɪd] *adj* lucide
lucidity [lu:'sɪdɪtɪ] *n* lucidité *f*
luck [lʌk] *n* chance *f*; **bad ~** malchance *f*,
  malheur *m*; **to be in ~** avoir de la chance; **to be
  out of ~** ne pas avoir de chance; **good ~!** bonne
  chance!; **bad** or **hard** or **tough ~!** pas de chance!
luckily ['lʌkɪlɪ] *adv* heureusement, par bonheur
luckless ['lʌklɪs] *adj* (*person*)
  malchanceux(-euse); (*trip*) marqué(e) par la
  malchance
lucky ['lʌkɪ] *adj* (*person*) qui a de la chance;
  (*coincidence*) heureux(-euse); (*number etc*) qui
  porte bonheur
lucrative ['lu:krətɪv] *adj* lucratif(-ive), rentable,
  qui rapporte
ludicrous ['lu:dɪkrəs] *adj* ridicule, absurde

ludo ['luːdəʊ] *n* jeu *m* des petits chevaux
lug [lʌg] *vt* traîner, tirer
luggage ['lʌgɪdʒ] *n* bagages *mpl*; **our ~ hasn't arrived** nos bagages ne sont pas arrivés; **could you send someone to collect our ~?** pourriez-vous envoyer quelqu'un chercher nos bagages?
luggage lockers *npl* consigne *f* automatique
luggage rack *n* (*in train*) porte-bagages *m inv*; (: *made of string*) filet *m* à bagages; (*on car*) galerie *f*
luggage van, (US) **luggage car** *n* (*Rail*) fourgon *m* (à bagages)
lugubrious [luˈguːbrɪəs] *adj* lugubre
lukewarm ['luːkwɔːm] *adj* tiède
lull [lʌl] *n* accalmie *f*; (*in conversation*) pause *f* ▷ *vt*: **to ~ sb to sleep** bercer qn pour qu'il s'endorme; **to be ~ed into a false sense of security** s'endormir dans une fausse sécurité
lullaby ['lʌləbaɪ] *n* berceuse *f*
lumbago [lʌmˈbeɪgəʊ] *n* lumbago *m*
lumber ['lʌmbər] *n* (*wood*) bois *m* de charpente; (*junk*) bric-à-brac *m inv* ▷ *vt* (*Brit inf*): **to ~ sb with sth/sb** coller *or* refiler qch/qn à qn ▷ *vi* (*also*: **lumber about, lumber along**) marcher pesamment
lumberjack ['lʌmbədʒæk] *n* bûcheron *m*
lumber room *n* (*Brit*) débarras *m*
lumber yard *n* entrepôt *m* de bois
luminous ['luːmɪnəs] *adj* lumineux(-euse)
lump [lʌmp] *n* morceau *m*; (*in sauce*) grumeau *m*; (*swelling*) grosseur *f* ▷ *vt* (*also*: **lump together**) réunir, mettre en tas
lump sum *n* somme globale *or* forfaitaire
lumpy ['lʌmpɪ] *adj* (*sauce*) qui a des grumeaux; (*bed*) défoncé(e), peu confortable
lunacy ['luːnəsɪ] *n* démence *f*, folie *f*
lunar ['luːnər] *adj* lunaire
lunatic ['luːnətɪk] *n* fou (folle), dément(e) ▷ *adj* fou (folle), dément(e)
lunatic asylum *n* asile *m* d'aliénés
lunch [lʌntʃ] *n* déjeuner *m* ▷ *vi* déjeuner; **it is his ~ hour** c'est l'heure où il déjeune; **to invite sb to** *or* **for ~** inviter qn à déjeuner
lunch break, lunch hour *n* pause *f* de midi, heure *f* du déjeuner
luncheon ['lʌntʃən] *n* déjeuner *m*
luncheon meat *n* sorte de saucisson
luncheon voucher *n* chèque-repas *m*, ticket-repas *m*
lunchtime ['lʌntʃtaɪm] *n*: **it's ~** c'est l'heure du déjeuner
lung [lʌŋ] *n* poumon *m*
lung cancer *n* cancer *m* du poumon
lunge [lʌndʒ] *vi* (*also*: **lunge forward**) faire un mouvement brusque en avant; **to ~ at sb** envoyer *or* assener un coup à qn
lupin ['luːpɪn] *n* lupin *m*
lurch [ləːtʃ] *vi* vaciller, tituber ▷ *n* écart *m* brusque, embardée *f*; **to leave sb in the ~** laisser qn se débrouiller *or* se dépêtrer tout(e) seul(e)
lure [luər] *n* (*attraction*) attrait *m*, charme *m*; (*in hunting*) appât *m*, leurre *m* ▷ *vt* attirer *or* persuader par la ruse
lurid ['luərɪd] *adj* affreux(-euse), atroce
lurk [ləːk] *vi* se tapir, se cacher
luscious ['lʌʃəs] *adj* succulent(e), appétissant(e)
lush [lʌʃ] *adj* luxuriant(e)
lust [lʌst] *n* (*sexual*) désir (sexuel); (*Rel*) luxure *f*; (*fig*): **~ for** soif *f* de
  ▶ **lust after** *vt fus* convoiter, désirer
luster ['lʌstər] *n* (US) = **lustre**
lustful ['lʌstful] *adj* lascif(-ive)
lustre, (US) **luster** ['lʌstər] *n* lustre *m*, brillant *m*
lusty ['lʌstɪ] *adj* vigoureux(-euse), robuste
lute [luːt] *n* luth *m*
Luxembourg ['lʌksəmbəːg] *n* Luxembourg *m*
luxuriant [lʌgˈzjuərɪənt] *adj* luxuriant(e)
luxurious [lʌgˈzjuərɪəs] *adj* luxueux(-euse)
luxury ['lʌkʃərɪ] *n* luxe *m* ▷ *cpd* de luxe
LV *n abbr* (*Brit*) = **luncheon voucher**
LW *abbr* (*Radio*: = *long wave*) GO
Lycra® ['laɪkrə] *n* Lycra® *m*
lying ['laɪɪŋ] *n* mensonge(s) *m(pl)* ▷ *adj* (*statement, story*) mensonger(-ère), faux (fausse); (*person*) menteur(-euse)
lynch [lɪntʃ] *vt* lyncher
lynx [lɪŋks] *n* lynx *m inv*
Lyons ['ljɔ̃] *n* Lyon
lyre ['laɪər] *n* lyre *f*
lyric ['lɪrɪk] *adj* lyrique
lyrical ['lɪrɪkl] *adj* lyrique
lyrics ['lɪrɪks] *npl* (*of song*) paroles *fpl*
lyricism ['lɪrɪsɪzəm] *n* lyrisme *m*

Mm

M, m [ɛm] *n* (*letter*) M, m *m*; **M for Mary**, (US) **M for Mike** M comme Marcel

M *n abbr* (*Brit*) = **motorway**; (= *the M8*) ≈ l'A8
▷ *abbr* (= *medium*) M

m. *abbr* (= *metre*) m; (= *million*) M; (= *mile*) mi

M.A. *n abbr* (*Scol*) = **Master of Arts** ▷ *abbr* (US) = **military academy**; (US) = **Massachusetts**

ma [mɑ:] (*inf*) *n* maman *f*

mac [mæk] *n* (*Brit*) imper(méable *m*) *m*

macabre [mə'kɑ:brə] *adj* macabre

macaroni [mækə'rəʊnɪ] *n* macaronis *mpl*

macaroon [mækə'ru:n] *n* macaron *m*

mace [meɪs] *n* masse *f*; (*spice*) macis *m*

Macedonia [mæsɪ'dəʊnɪə] *n* Macédoine *f*

Macedonian [mæsɪ'dəʊnɪən] *adj* macédonien(ne) ▷ *n* Macédonien(ne); (*Ling*) macédonien *m*

machinations [mækɪ'neɪʃənz] *npl* machinations *fpl*, intrigues *fpl*

machine [mə'ʃi:n] *n* machine *f* ▷ *vt* (*dress etc*) coudre à la machine; (*Tech*) usiner

machine code *n* (*Comput*) code *m* machine

machine gun *n* mitrailleuse *f*

machine language *n* (*Comput*) langage *m* machine

machine-readable [mə'ʃi:nri:dəbl] *adj* (*Comput*) exploitable par une machine

machinery [mə'ʃi:nərɪ] *n* machinerie *f*, machines *fpl*; (*fig*) mécanisme(s) *m(pl)*

machine shop *n* atelier *m* d'usinage

machine tool *n* machine-outil *f*

machine washable *adj* (*garment*) lavable en machine

machinist [mə'ʃi:nɪst] *n* machiniste *m/f*

macho ['mætʃəʊ] *adj* macho *inv*

mackerel ['mækrl] *n* (*pl inv*) maquereau *m*

mackintosh ['mækɪntɔʃ] *n* (*Brit*) imperméable *m*

macro... ['mækrəʊ] *prefix* macro...

macro-economics ['mækrəʊi:kə'nɔmɪks] *n* macro-économie *f*

mad [mæd] *adj* fou (folle); (*foolish*) insensé(e); (*angry*) furieux(-euse); **to go ~** devenir fou; **to be ~ (keen) about** *or* **on sth** (*inf*) être follement passionné de qch, être fou de qch

Madagascar [mædə'gæskəʳ] *n* Madagascar *m*

madam ['mædəm] *n* madame *f*; **yes ~** oui Madame; **M~ Chairman** Madame la Présidente

madcap ['mædkæp] *adj* (*inf*) écervelé(e)

mad cow disease *n* maladie *f* des vaches folles

madden ['mædn] *vt* exaspérer

maddening ['mædnɪŋ] *adj* exaspérant(e)

made [meɪd] *pt, pp of* **make**

Madeira [mə'dɪərə] *n* (*Geo*) Madère *f*; (*wine*) madère *m*

made-to-measure ['meɪdtə'mɛʒəʳ] *adj* (*Brit*) fait(e) sur mesure

made-up ['meɪdʌp] *adj* (*story*) inventé(e), fabriqué(e)

madhouse ['mædhaus] *n* (*also fig*) maison *f* de fous

madly ['mædlɪ] *adv* follement; **~ in love** éperdument amoureux(-euse)

madman ['mædmən] (*irreg*) *n* fou *m*, aliéné *m*

madness ['mædnɪs] *n* folie *f*

Madrid [mə'drɪd] *n* Madrid

Mafia ['mæfɪə] *n* maf(f)ia *f*

mag [mæg] *n abbr* (*Brit inf*: = *magazine*) magazine *m*

magazine [mægə'zi:n] *n* (*Press*) magazine *m*, revue *f*; (*Radio, TV*) magazine; (*Mil: store*) dépôt *m*, arsenal *m*; (*of firearm*) magasin *m*

maggot ['mægət] *n* ver *m*, asticot *m*

magic ['mædʒɪk] *n* magie *f* ▷ *adj* magique

magical ['mædʒɪkl] *adj* magique; (*experience, evening*) merveilleux(-euse)

magician [mə'dʒɪʃən] *n* magicien(ne)

magistrate ['mædʒɪstreɪt] *n* magistrat *m*; juge *m*; **~s' court** (*Brit*) ≈ tribunal *m* d'instance

magnanimous [mæg'nænɪməs] *adj* magnanime

magnate ['mægneɪt] *n* magnat *m*

magnesium [mæg'ni:zɪəm] *n* magnésium *m*

magnet ['mægnɪt] *n* aimant *m*

magnetic [mæg'nɛtɪk] *adj* magnétique

magnetic disk *n* (*Comput*) disque *m* magnétique

magnetic tape *n* bande *f* magnétique

magnetism ['mægnɪtɪzəm] *n* magnétisme *m*

magnification [mægnɪfɪ'keɪʃən] *n* grossissement *m*

magnificence [mæg'nɪfɪsns] *n* magnificence *f*

magnificent [mæg'nɪfɪsnt] *adj* superbe,

magnifique; (*splendid*: *robe, building*)
somptueux(-euse), magnifique
magnify ['mægnɪfaɪ] *vt* grossir; (*sound*)
amplifier
magnifying glass ['mægnɪfaɪɪŋ-] *n* loupe *f*
magnitude ['mægnɪtjuːd] *n* ampleur *f*
magnolia [mæg'nəʊlɪə] *n* magnolia *m*
magpie ['mægpaɪ] *n* pie *f*
mahogany [mə'hɔgənɪ] *n* acajou *m* ▷ *cpd* en
(bois d')acajou
maid [meɪd] *n* bonne *f*; (*in hotel*) femme *f* de
chambre; **old ~** (*pej*) vieille fille
maiden ['meɪdn] *n* jeune fille *f* ▷ *adj* (*aunt etc*)
non mariée; (*speech, voyage*) inaugural(e)
maiden name *n* nom *m* de jeune fille
mail [meɪl] *n* poste *f*; (*letters*) courrier *m* ▷ *vt*
envoyer (par la poste); **by ~** par la poste
mailbag ['meɪlbæg] *n* (*US*) sac postal; (*postman's*)
sacoche *f*
mailbox ['meɪlbɔks] *n* (*US: also Comput*) boîte *f*
aux lettres
mailing list ['meɪlɪŋ-] *n* liste *f* d'adresses
mailman ['meɪlmæn] (*irreg*) *n* (*US*) facteur *m*
mail-order ['meɪlɔːdəʳ] *n* vente *f* or achat *m* par
correspondance ▷ *cpd*: **~ firm** or **house** maison *f*
de vente par correspondance
mailshot ['meɪlʃɔt] *n* (*Brit*) mailing *m*
mail train *n* train postal
mail truck *n* (*US Aut*) = **mail van**
mail van *n* (*Brit Aut*) voiture *f* or fourgonnette *f*
des postes; (*: Rail*) wagon-poste *m*
maim [meɪm] *vt* mutiler
main [meɪn] *adj* principal(e) ▷ *n* (*pipe*) conduite
principale, canalisation *f*; **the ~s** (*Elec*) le
secteur; **the ~ thing** l'essentiel *m*; **in the ~**
dans l'ensemble
main course *n* (*Culin*) plat *m* de résistance
mainframe ['meɪnfreɪm] *n* (*also*: **mainframe**
computer) (gros) ordinateur, unité centrale
mainland ['meɪnlənd] *n* continent *m*
mainline ['meɪnlaɪn] *adj* (*Rail*) de grande ligne
▷ *vt* (*drugs slang*) se shooter à ▷ *vi* (*drugs slang*) se
shooter
main line *n* (*Rail*) grande ligne
mainly ['meɪnlɪ] *adv* principalement, surtout
main road *n* grand axe, route nationale
mainstay ['meɪnsteɪ] *n* (*fig*) pilier *m*
mainstream ['meɪnstriːm] *n* (*fig*) courant
principal
main street *n* rue *f* principale
maintain [meɪn'teɪn] *vt* entretenir; (*continue*)
maintenir, préserver; (*affirm*) soutenir; **to ~**
that ... soutenir que ...
maintenance ['meɪntənəns] *n* entretien *m*;
(*Law: alimony*) pension *f* alimentaire
maintenance contract *n* contrat *m* d'entretien
maintenance order *n* (*Law*) obligation *f*
alimentaire
maisonette [meɪzə'nɛt] *n* (*Brit*) appartement *m*
en duplex
maize [meɪz] *n* (*Brit*) maïs *m*
Maj. *abbr* (*Mil*) = **major**

majestic [mə'dʒɛstɪk] *adj* majestueux(-euse)
majesty ['mædʒɪstɪ] *n* majesté *f*; (*title*): **Your**
M~ Votre Majesté
major ['meɪdʒəʳ] *n* (*Mil*) commandant *m* ▷ *adj*
(*important*) important(e); (*most important*)
principal(e); (*Mus*) majeur(e) ▷ *vi* (*US Scol*): **to ~**
(in) se spécialiser (en); **a ~ operation** (*Med*) une
grosse opération
Majorca [mə'jɔːkə] *n* Majorque *f*
major general *n* (*Mil*) général *m* de division
majority [mə'dʒɔrɪtɪ] *n* majorité *f* ▷ *cpd* (*verdict,*
holding) majoritaire
make [meɪk] *vt* (*pt, pp* **made**) [meɪd] faire;
(*manufacture*) faire, fabriquer; (*earn*) gagner;
(*decision*) prendre; (*friend*) se faire; (*speech*) faire,
prononcer; (*cause to be*): **to ~ sb sad** *etc* rendre qn
triste *etc*; (*force*): **to ~ sb do sth** obliger qn à
faire qch, faire faire qch à qn; (*equal*): **2 and 2 ~ 4**
2 et 2 font 4 ▷ *n* (*manufacture*) fabrication *f*;
(*brand*) marque *f*; **to ~ the bed** faire le lit; **to ~ a**
fool of sb (*ridicule*) ridiculiser qn; (*trick*) avoir or
duper qn; **to ~ a profit** faire un or des
bénéfice(s); **to ~ a loss** essuyer une perte; **to ~**
it (*in time etc*) y arriver; (*succeed*) réussir; **what**
time do you ~ it? quelle heure avez-vous?; **I ~ it**
£249 d'après mes calculs ça fait 249 livres; **to be**
made of être en; **to ~ good** *vi* (*succeed*) faire son
chemin, réussir ▷ *vt* (*deficit*) combler; (*losses*)
compenser; **to ~ do with** se contenter de; se
débrouiller avec
▶ **make for** *vt fus* (*place*) se diriger vers
▶ **make off** *vi* filer
▶ **make out** *vt* (*write out*: *cheque*) faire; (*decipher*)
déchiffrer; (*understand*) comprendre; (*see*)
distinguer; (*claim, imply*) prétendre, vouloir faire
croire; **to ~ out a case for sth** présenter des
arguments solides en faveur de qch
▶ **make over** *vt* (*assign*): **to ~ over (to)** céder (à),
transférer (au nom de)
▶ **make up** *vt* (*invent*) inventer, imaginer;
(*constitute*) constituer; (*parcel, bed*) faire ▷ *vi* se
réconcilier; (*with cosmetics*) se maquiller, se
farder; **to be made up of** se composer de
▶ **make up for** *vt fus* compenser; (*lost time*)
rattraper
make-believe ['meɪkbɪliːv] *n*: **a world of ~** un
monde de chimères or d'illusions; **it's just ~**
c'est de la fantaisie; c'est une illusion
makeover ['meɪkəʊvəʳ] *n* (*by beautician*) soins *mpl*
de maquillage; (*change of image*) changement *m*
d'image
maker ['meɪkəʳ] *n* fabricant *m*; (*of film,*
programme) réalisateur(-trice)
makeshift ['meɪkʃɪft] *adj* provisoire,
improvisé(e)
make-up ['meɪkʌp] *n* maquillage *m*
make-up bag *n* trousse *f* de maquillage
make-up remover *n* démaquillant *m*
making ['meɪkɪŋ] *n* (*fig*): **in the ~** en formation
or gestation; **to have the ~s of** (*actor, athlete*)
avoir l'étoffe de
maladjusted [mælə'dʒʌstɪd] *adj* inadapté(e)

malaise [mæˈleɪz] *n* malaise *m*
malaria [məˈlɛərɪə] *n* malaria *f*, paludisme *m*
Malawi [məˈlɑːwɪ] *n* Malawi *m*
Malay [məˈleɪ] *adj* malais(e) ▷ *n* (*person*) Malais(e); (*language*) malais *m*
Malaya [məˈleɪə] *n* Malaisie *f*
Malayan [məˈleɪən] *adj, n* = **Malay**
Malaysia [məˈleɪzɪə] *n* Malaisie *f*
Malaysian [məˈleɪzɪən] *adj* malaisien(ne) ▷ *n* Malaisien(ne)
Maldives [ˈmɔːldaɪvz] *npl*: **the ~** les Maldives *fpl*
male [meɪl] *n* (*Biol, Elec*) mâle *m* ▷ *adj* (*sex, attitude*) masculin(e); (*animal*) mâle; (*child etc*) du sexe masculin; **~ and female students** étudiants et étudiantes
male chauvinist *n* phallocrate *m*
male nurse *n* infirmier *m*
malevolence [məˈlɛvələns] *n* malveillance *f*
malevolent [məˈlɛvələnt] *adj* malveillant(e)
malfunction [mælˈfʌŋkʃən] *n* fonctionnement défectueux
malice [ˈmælɪs] *n* méchanceté *f*, malveillance *f*
malicious [məˈlɪʃəs] *adj* méchant(e), malveillant(e); (*Law*) avec intention criminelle
malign [məˈlaɪn] *vt* diffamer, calomnier
malignant [məˈlɪgnənt] *adj* (*Med*) malin(-igne)
malingerer [məˈlɪŋgərəʳ] *n* simulateur(-trice)
mall [mɔːl] *n* (*also*: **shopping mall**) centre commercial
malleable [ˈmælɪəbl] *adj* malléable
mallet [ˈmælɪt] *n* maillet *m*
malnutrition [mælnjuːˈtrɪʃən] *n* malnutrition *f*
malpractice [mælˈpræktɪs] *n* faute professionnelle; négligence *f*
malt [mɔːlt] *n* malt *m* ▷ *cpd* (*whisky*) pur malt
Malta [ˈmɔːltə] *n* Malte *f*
Maltese [mɔːlˈtiːz] *adj* maltais(e) ▷ *n* (*pl inv*) Maltais(e); (*Ling*) maltais *m*
maltreat [mælˈtriːt] *vt* maltraiter
mammal [ˈmæml] *n* mammifère *m*
mammoth [ˈmæməθ] *n* mammouth *m* ▷ *adj* géant(e), monstre
man (*pl* **men**) [mæn, mɛn] *n* homme *m*; (*Sport*) joueur *m*; (*Chess*) pièce *f*; (*Draughts*) pion *m* ▷ *vt* (*Naut: ship*) garnir d'hommes; (*machine*) assurer le fonctionnement de; (*Mil: gun*) servir; (: *post*) être de service à; **an old ~** un vieillard; **~ and wife** mari et femme
Man. *abbr* (*Canada*) = **Manitoba**
manacles [ˈmænəklz] *npl* menottes *fpl*
manage [ˈmænɪdʒ] *vi* se débrouiller; (*succeed*) y arriver, réussir ▷ *vt* (*business*) gérer; (*team, operation*) diriger; (*control: ship*) manier, manœuvrer; (: *person*) savoir s'y prendre avec; (*device, things to do, carry etc*) arriver à se débrouiller avec, s'en tirer avec; **to ~ to do** se débrouiller pour faire; (*succeed*) réussir à faire
manageable [ˈmænɪdʒəbl] *adj* maniable; (*task etc*) faisable; (*number*) raisonnable
management [ˈmænɪdʒmənt] *n* (*running*) administration *f*, direction *f*; (*people in charge: of business, firm*) dirigeants *mpl*, cadres *mpl*; (: *of*

hotel, shop, theatre) direction; **"under new ~"** "changement de gérant", "changement de propriétaire"
management accounting *n* comptabilité *f* de gestion
management consultant *n* conseiller(-ère) de direction
manager [ˈmænɪdʒəʳ] *n* (*of business*) directeur *m*; (*of institution etc*) administrateur *m*; (*of department, unit*) responsable *m/f*, chef *m*; (*of hotel etc*) gérant *m*; (*Sport*) manager *m*; (*of artist*) impresario *m*; **sales ~** responsable *or* chef des ventes
manageress [mænɪdʒəˈrɛs] *n* directrice *f*; (*of hotel etc*) gérante *f*
managerial [mænɪˈdʒɪərɪəl] *adj* directorial(e); (*skills*) de cadre, de gestion; **~ staff** cadres *mpl*
managing director [ˈmænɪdʒɪŋ-] *n* directeur général
Mancunian [mænˈkjuːnɪən] *adj* de Manchester ▷ *n* habitant(e) de Manchester; natif(-ive) de Manchester
mandarin [ˈmændərɪn] *n* (*also*: **mandarin orange**) mandarine *f*; (*person*) mandarin *m*
mandate [ˈmændeɪt] *n* mandat *m*
mandatory [ˈmændətərɪ] *adj* obligatoire; (*powers etc*) mandataire
mandolin, mandoline [ˈmændəlɪn] *n* mandoline *f*
mane [meɪn] *n* crinière *f*
maneuver [məˈnuːvəʳ] (*US*) = **manoeuvre**
manfully [ˈmænfəlɪ] *adv* vaillamment
manganese [mæŋgəˈniːz] *n* manganèse *m*
mangetout [ˈmɔnʒˈtuː] *n* mange-tout *m inv*
mangle [ˈmæŋgl] *vt* déchiqueter; mutiler ▷ *n* essoreuse *f*; calandre *f*
mango (*pl* **-es**) [ˈmæŋgəu] *n* mangue *f*
mangrove [ˈmæŋgrəuv] *n* palétuvier *m*
mangy [ˈmeɪndʒɪ] *adj* galeux(-euse)
manhandle [ˈmænhændl] *vt* (*mistreat*) maltraiter, malmener; (*move by hand*) manutentionner
manhole [ˈmænhəul] *n* trou *m* d'homme
manhood [ˈmænhud] *n* (*age*) âge *m* d'homme; (*manliness*) virilité *f*
man-hour [ˈmænauəʳ] *n* heure-homme *f*, heure *f* de main-d'œuvre
manhunt [ˈmænhʌnt] *n* chasse *f* à l'homme
mania [ˈmeɪnɪə] *n* manie *f*
maniac [ˈmeɪnɪæk] *n* maniaque *m/f*; (*fig*) fou (folle)
manic [ˈmænɪk] *adj* maniaque
manic-depressive [ˈmænɪkdɪˈprɛsɪv] *adj, n* (*Psych*) maniaco-dépressif(-ive)
manicure [ˈmænɪkjuəʳ] *n* manucure *f* ▷ *vt* (*person*) faire les mains à
manicure set *n* trousse *f* à ongles
manifest [ˈmænɪfɛst] *vt* manifester ▷ *adj* manifeste, évident(e) ▷ *n* (*Aviat, Naut*) manifeste *m*
manifestation [mænɪfɛsˈteɪʃən] *n* manifestation *f*

manifesto [mænɪˈfɛstəu] *n* (*Pol*) manifeste *m*
manifold [ˈmænɪfəuld] *adj* multiple, varié(e)
▷ *n* (*Aut etc*): **exhaust** ~ collecteur *m*
d'échappement
Manila [məˈnɪlə] *n* Manille, Manila
manila [məˈnɪlə] *adj*: ~ **paper** papier *m* bulle
manipulate [məˈnɪpjuleɪt] *vt* manipuler;
(*system, situation*) exploiter
manipulation [mənɪpjuˈleɪʃən] *n*
manipulation *f*
mankind [mænˈkaɪnd] *n* humanité *f*, genre
humain
manliness [ˈmænlɪnɪs] *n* virilité *f*
manly [ˈmænlɪ] *adj* viril(e)
man-made [ˈmænˈmeɪd] *adj* artificiel(le); (*fibre*)
synthétique
manna [ˈmænə] *n* manne *f*
mannequin [ˈmænɪkɪn] *n* mannequin *m*
manner [ˈmænəʳ] *n* manière *f*, façon *f*;
(*behaviour*) attitude *f*, comportement *m*;
manners *npl*: (**good**) ~**s** (bonnes) manières;
bad ~**s** mauvaises manières; **all** ~ **of** toutes
sortes de
mannerism [ˈmænərɪzəm] *n* particularité *f* de
langage (*or* de comportement), tic *m*
mannerly [ˈmænəlɪ] *adj* poli(e), courtois(e)
manoeuvrable, (US) **maneuverable** [məˈnu:
vrəbl] *adj* facile à manœuvrer
manoeuvre, (US) **maneuver** [məˈnu:vəʳ] *vt*
(*move*) manœuvrer; (*manipulate: person*)
manipuler; (: *situation*) exploiter ▷ *n* manœuvre
f; **to** ~ **sb into doing sth** manipuler qn pour lui
faire faire qch
manor [ˈmænəʳ] *n* (*also*: **manor house**) manoir *m*
manpower [ˈmænpauəʳ] *n* main-d'œuvre *f*
manservant (*pl* **menservants**) [ˈmænsə:vənt,
ˈmɛn-] *n* domestique *m*
mansion [ˈmænʃən] *n* château *m*, manoir *m*
manslaughter [ˈmænslɔ:təʳ] *n* homicide *m*
involontaire
mantelpiece [ˈmæntlpi:s] *n* cheminée *f*
mantle [ˈmæntl] *n* cape *f*; (*fig*) manteau *m*
man-to-man [ˈmæntəˈmæn] *adj*, *adv* d'homme
à homme
manual [ˈmænjuəl] *adj* manuel(le) ▷ *n*
manuel *m*
manual worker *n* travailleur manuel
manufacture [mænjuˈfæktʃəʳ] *vt* fabriquer ▷ *n*
fabrication *f*
manufactured goods [mænjuˈfæktʃəd-] *npl*
produits manufacturés
manufacturer [mænjuˈfæktʃərəʳ] *n* fabricant *m*
manufacturing industries [mænju] *npl*
industries *fpl* de transformation
manure [məˈnjuəʳ] *n* fumier *m*; (*artificial*)
engrais *m*
manuscript [ˈmænjuskrɪpt] *n* manuscrit *m*
many [ˈmɛnɪ] *adj* beaucoup de, de
nombreux(-euses) ▷ *pron* beaucoup, un grand
nombre; **how** ~? combien?; **a great** ~ un grand
nombre (de); **too** ~ **difficulties** trop de
difficultés; **twice as** ~ deux fois plus; ~ **a** ...

bien des ..., plus d'un(e) ...
Maori [ˈmaurɪ] *n* Maori(e) ▷ *adj* maori(e)
map [mæp] *n* carte *f*; (*of town*) plan *m* ▷ *vt*
dresser la carte de; **can you show it to me on
the** ~? pouvez-vous me l'indiquer sur la carte?
▶ **map out** *vt* tracer; (*fig: task*) planifier; (*career,
holiday*) organiser, préparer (à l'avance); (: *essay*)
faire le plan de
maple [ˈmeɪpl] *n* érable *m*
mar [mɑ:ʳ] *vt* gâcher, gâter
marathon [ˈmærəθən] *n* marathon *m* ▷ *adj*: **a** ~
session une séance-marathon
marathon runner *n* coureur(-euse) de
marathon, marathonien(ne)
marauder [məˈrɔ:dəʳ] *n* maraudeur(-euse)
marble [ˈmɑ:bl] *n* marbre *m*; (*toy*) bille *f*;
marbles *npl* (*game*) billes
March [mɑ:tʃ] *n* mars *m*
march [mɑ:tʃ] *vi* marcher au pas; (*demonstrators*)
défiler ▷ *n* marche *f*; (*demonstration*)
manifestation *f*; **to** ~ **out of/into** *etc* sortir de/
entrer dans *etc* (*de manière décidée ou impulsive*)
marcher [ˈmɑ:tʃəʳ] *n* (*demonstrator*)
manifestant(e), marcheur(-euse)
marching [ˈmɑ:tʃɪŋ] *n*: **to give sb his** ~ **orders**
(*fig*) renvoyer qn; envoyer promener qn
march-past [ˈmɑ:tʃpɑ:st] *n* défilé *m*
mare [mɛəʳ] *n* jument *f*
marg. [mɑ:dʒ] *n abbr* (*inf*) = **margarine**
margarine [mɑ:dʒəˈri:n] *n* margarine *f*
margin [ˈmɑ:dʒɪn] *n* marge *f*
marginal [ˈmɑ:dʒɪnl] *adj* marginal(e); ~ **seat**
(*Pol*) siège disputé
marginally [ˈmɑ:dʒɪnəlɪ] *adv* très légèrement,
sensiblement
marigold [ˈmærɪgəuld] *n* souci *m*
marijuana [mærɪˈwɑ:nə] *n* marijuana *f*
marina [məˈri:nə] *n* marina *f*
marinade *n* [mærɪˈneɪd] marinade *f* ▷ *vt*
[ˈmærɪneɪd] = **marinate**
marinate [ˈmærɪneɪt] *vt* (faire) mariner
marine [məˈri:n] *adj* marin(e) ▷ *n* fusilier
marin; (US) marine *m*
marine insurance *n* assurance *f* maritime
marital [ˈmærɪtl] *adj* matrimonial(e)
marital status *n* situation *f* de famille
maritime [ˈmærɪtaɪm] *adj* maritime
maritime law *n* droit *m* maritime
marjoram [ˈmɑ:dʒərəm] *n* marjolaine *f*
mark [mɑ:k] *n* marque *f*; (*of skid etc*) trace *f*; (*Brit
Scol*) note *f*; (*Sport*) cible *f*; (*currency*) mark *m*; (*Brit
Tech*): **M~ 2/3** 2ème/3ème série *f* or version *f*;
(*oven temperature*): (**gas**) ~ **4** thermostat *m* 4 ▷ *vt*
(*also Sport: player*) marquer; (*stain*) tacher; (*Brit
Scol*) corriger, noter; (*also*: **punctuation marks**)
signes *mpl* de ponctuation; **to** ~ **time** marquer
le pas; **to be quick off the** ~ (**in doing**) (*fig*) ne
pas perdre de temps (pour faire); **up to the** ~ (*in
efficiency*) à la hauteur
▶ **mark down** *vt* (*prices, goods*) démarquer,
réduire le prix de
▶ **mark off** *vt* (*tick off*) cocher, pointer

▶ **mark out** vt désigner
▶ **mark up** vt (price) majorer
marked [mɑ:kt] adj (obvious) marqué(e), net(te)
markedly ['mɑ:kɪdlɪ] adv visiblement, manifestement
marker ['mɑ:kər] n (sign) jalon m; (bookmark) signet m
market ['mɑ:kɪt] n marché m ▷ vt (Comm) commercialiser; **to be on the ~** être sur le marché; **on the open ~** en vente libre; **to play the ~** jouer à la or spéculer en Bourse
marketable ['mɑ:kɪtəbl] adj commercialisable
market analysis n analyse f de marché
market day n jour m de marché
market demand n besoins mpl du marché
market economy n économie f de marché
market forces npl tendances fpl du marché
market garden n (Brit) jardin maraîcher
marketing ['mɑ:kɪtɪŋ] n marketing m
marketplace ['mɑ:kɪtpleɪs] n place f du marché; (Comm) marché m
market price n prix marchand
market research n étude f de marché
market value n valeur marchande; valeur du marché
marking ['mɑ:kɪŋ] n (on animal) marque f, tache f; (on road) signalisation f
marksman ['mɑ:ksmən] (irreg) n tireur m d'élite
marksmanship ['mɑ:ksmənʃɪp] n adresse f au tir
mark-up ['mɑ:kʌp] n (Comm: margin) marge f (bénéficiaire); (: increase) majoration f
marmalade ['mɑ:məleɪd] n confiture f d'oranges
maroon [mə'ru:n] vt: **to be ~ed** être abandonné(e); (fig) être bloqué(e) ▷ adj (colour) bordeaux inv
marquee [mɑ:'ki:] n chapiteau m
marquess, marquis ['mɑ:kwɪs] n marquis m
Marrakech, Marrakesh [mærə'kɛʃ] n Marrakech
marriage ['mærɪdʒ] n mariage m
marriage bureau n agence matrimoniale
marriage certificate n extrait m d'acte de mariage
marriage guidance, (US) **marriage counseling** n conseils conjugaux
marriage of convenience n mariage m de convenance
married ['mærɪd] adj marié(e); (life, love) conjugal(e)
marrow ['mærəu] n (of bone) moelle f; (vegetable) courge f
marry ['mærɪ] vt épouser, se marier avec; (subj: father, priest etc) marier ▷ vi (also: **get married**) se marier
Mars [mɑ:z] n (planet) Mars f
Marseilles [mɑ:'seɪ] n Marseille
marsh [mɑ:ʃ] n marais m, marécage m
marshal ['mɑ:ʃl] n maréchal m; (US: fire, police) ≈ capitaine m; (for demonstration, meeting) membre m du service d'ordre ▷ vt rassembler

marshalling yard ['mɑ:ʃlɪŋ-] n (Rail) gare f de triage
marshmallow [mɑ:ʃ'mæləu] n (Bot) guimauve f; (sweet) (pâte f de) guimauve
marshy ['mɑ:ʃɪ] adj marécageux(-euse)
marsupial [mɑ:'su:pɪəl] adj marsupial(e) ▷ n marsupial m
martial ['mɑ:ʃl] adj martial(e)
martial arts npl arts martiaux
martial law n loi martiale
Martian ['mɑ:ʃən] n Martien(ne)
martin ['mɑ:tɪn] n (also: **house martin**) martinet m
martyr ['mɑ:tər] n martyr(e) ▷ vt martyriser
martyrdom ['mɑ:tədəm] n martyre m
marvel ['mɑ:vl] n merveille f ▷ vi: **to ~ (at)** s'émerveiller (de)
marvellous, (US) **marvelous** ['mɑ:vləs] adj merveilleux(-euse)
Marxism ['mɑ:ksɪzəm] n marxisme m
Marxist ['mɑ:ksɪst] adj, n marxiste (m/f)
marzipan ['mɑ:zɪpæn] n pâte f d'amandes
mascara [mæs'kɑ:rə] n mascara m
mascot ['mæskət] n mascotte f
masculine ['mæskjulɪn] adj masculin(e) ▷ n masculin m
masculinity [mæskju'lɪnɪtɪ] n masculinité f
MASH [mæʃ] n abbr (US Mil) = **mobile army surgical hospital**
mash [mæʃ] vt (Culin) faire une purée de
mashed potato n, **mashed potatoes** npl purée f de pommes de terre
mask [mɑ:sk] n masque m ▷ vt masquer
masochism ['mæsəukɪzəm] n masochisme m
masochist ['mæsəukɪst] n masochiste m/f
mason ['meɪsn] n (also: **stonemason**) maçon m; (also: **freemason**) franc-maçon m
masonic [mə'sɔnɪk] adj maçonnique
masonry ['meɪsnrɪ] n maçonnerie f
masquerade [mæskə'reɪd] n bal masqué; (fig) mascarade f ▷ vi: **to ~ as** se faire passer pour
mass [mæs] n multitude f, masse f; (Physics) masse; (Rel) messe f ▷ cpd (communication) de masse; (unemployment) massif(-ive) ▷ vi se masser; **masses** npl: **the ~es** les masses; **~es of** (inf) des tas de; **to go to ~** aller à la messe
Mass. abbr (US) = **Massachusetts.**
massacre ['mæsəkər] n massacre m ▷ vt massacrer
massage ['mæsɑ:ʒ] n massage m ▷ vt masser
massive ['mæsɪv] adj énorme, massif(-ive)
mass market n marché m grand public
mass media npl mass-media mpl
mass meeting n rassemblement m de masse
mass-produce ['mæsprə'dju:s] vt fabriquer en série
mass production n fabrication f en série
mast [mɑ:st] n mât m; (Radio, TV) pylône m
mastectomy [mæs'tɛktəmɪ] n mastectomie f
master ['mɑ:stər] n maître m; (in secondary school) professeur m; (in primary school) instituteur m; (title for boys): **M~ X** Monsieur X ▷ vt maîtriser;

(learn) apprendre à fond; (understand) posséder parfaitement or à fond; **~ of ceremonies (MC)** n maître des cérémonies; **M~ of Arts/Science (MA/MSc)** (n) ≈ titulaire m/f d'une maîtrise (en lettres/science); **M~ of Arts/Science degree (MA/MSc)** (n) ≈ maîtrise f; **M~'s degree** (n) ≈ maîtrise; *voir article*

● MASTER'S DEGREE

●
● Le *Master's degree* est un diplôme que l'on
● prépare en général après le "Bachelor's
● degree", bien que certaines universités
● décernent un *Master's* au lieu d'un
● "Bachelor's". Il consiste soit à suivre des
● cours, soit à rédiger un mémoire à partir
● d'une recherche personnelle, soit encore les
● deux. Les principaux masters sont le "MA"
● (Master of Arts), et le "MSc" (Master of
● Science), qui comprennent cours et
● mémoire, et le "MLitt "(Master of Letters) et
● le "MPhil" (Master of Philosophy), qui
● reposent uniquement sur le mémoire; voir
● "doctorate".

master disk n (Comput) disque original
masterful ['mɑːstəful] adj autoritaire, impérieux(-euse)
master key n passe-partout m inv
masterly ['mɑːstəlɪ] adj magistral(e)
mastermind ['mɑːstəmaɪnd] n esprit supérieur ▷ vt diriger, être le cerveau de
masterpiece ['mɑːstəpiːs] n chef-d'œuvre m
master plan n stratégie f d'ensemble
master stroke n coup m de maître
mastery ['mɑːstərɪ] n maîtrise f; connaissance parfaite
mastiff ['mæstɪf] n mastiff m
masturbate ['mæstəbeɪt] vi se masturber
masturbation [mæstə'beɪʃən] n masturbation f
mat [mæt] n petit tapis; (also: **doormat**) paillasson m; (also: **tablemat**) set m de table ▷ adj – **matt**
match [mætʃ] n allumette f; (game) match m, partie f; (fig) égal(e); mariage m; parti m ▷ vt (also: **match up**) assortir; (go well with) aller bien avec, s'assortir à; (equal) égaler, valoir ▷ vi être assorti(e); **to be a good ~** être bien assorti(e)
▶ **match up** vt assortir
matchbox ['mætʃbɔks] n boîte f d'allumettes
matching ['mætʃɪŋ] adj assorti(e)
matchless ['mætʃlɪs] adj sans égal
mate [meɪt] n camarade m/f de travail; (inf) copain (copine); (animal) partenaire m/f, mâle (femelle); (in merchant navy) second m ▷ vi s'accoupler ▷ vt accoupler
material [mə'tɪərɪəl] n (substance) matière f, matériau m; (cloth) tissu m, étoffe f; (information, data) données fpl ▷ adj matériel(le); (relevant: evidence) pertinent(e); (important) essentiel(le); **materials** npl (equipment) matériaux mpl; **reading ~** de quoi lire, de la lecture

materialistic [mətɪərɪə'lɪstɪk] adj matérialiste
materialize [mə'tɪərɪəlaɪz] vi se matérialiser, se réaliser
materially [mə'tɪərɪəlɪ] adv matériellement; essentiellement
maternal [mə'təːnl] adj maternel(le)
maternity [mə'təːnɪtɪ] n maternité f ▷ cpd de maternité, de grossesse
maternity benefit n prestation f de maternité
maternity dress n robe f de grossesse
maternity hospital n maternité f
maternity leave n congé m de maternité
matey ['meɪtɪ] adj (Brit inf) copain-copain inv
math [mæθ] n (US: = mathematics) maths fpl
mathematical [mæθə'mætɪkl] adj mathématique
mathematician [mæθəmə'tɪʃən] n mathématicien(ne)
mathematics [mæθə'mætɪks] n mathématiques fpl
maths [mæθs] n abbr (Brit: = mathematics) maths fpl
matinée ['mætɪneɪ] n matinée f
mating ['meɪtɪŋ] n accouplement m
mating call n appel m du mâle
mating season n saison f des amours
matriarchal [meɪtrɪ'ɑːkl] adj matriarcal(e)
matrices ['meɪtrɪsiːz] npl of **matrix**
matriculation [mətrɪkju'leɪʃən] n inscription f
matrimonial [mætrɪ'məunɪəl] adj matrimonial(e), conjugal(e)
matrimony ['mætrɪmənɪ] n mariage m
matrix (pl **matrices**) ['meɪtrɪks, 'meɪtrɪsiːz] n matrice f
matron ['meɪtrən] n (in hospital) infirmière-chef f; (in school) infirmière f
matronly ['meɪtrənlɪ] adj de matrone; imposant(e)
matt [mæt] adj mat(e)
matted ['mætɪd] adj emmêlé(e)
matter ['mætər] n question f; (Physics) matière f, substance f; (content) contenu m, fond m; (Med: pus) pus m ▷ vi importer; **matters** npl (affairs, situation) la situation; **it doesn't ~** cela n'a pas d'importance; (I don't mind) cela ne fait rien; **what's the ~?** qu'est-ce qu'il y a?, qu'est-ce qui ne va pas?; **no ~ what** quoi qu'il arrive; **that's another ~** c'est une autre affaire; **as a ~ of course** tout naturellement; **as a ~ of fact** en fait; **it's a ~ of habit** c'est une question d'habitude; **printed ~** imprimés mpl; **reading ~** (Brit) de quoi lire, de la lecture
matter-of-fact ['mætərəv'fækt] adj terre à terre, neutre
matting ['mætɪŋ] n natte f
mattress ['mætrɪs] n matelas m
mature [mə'tjuər] adj mûr(e); (cheese) fait(e); (wine) arrive(e) à maturité ▷ vi mûrir; (cheese, wine) se faire
mature student n étudiant(e) plus âgé(e) que la moyenne
maturity [mə'tjuərɪtɪ] n maturité f

maudlin ['mɔːdlɪn] *adj* larmoyant(e)

maul [mɔːl] *vt* lacérer

Mauritania [mɔːrɪ'teɪnɪə] *n* Mauritanie *f*

Mauritius [mə'rɪʃəs] *n* l'île *f* Maurice

mausoleum [mɔːsə'lɪəm] *n* mausolée *m*

mauve [məʊv] *adj* mauve

maverick ['mævrɪk] *n* (*fig*) franc-tireur *m*, non-conformiste *m/f*

mawkish ['mɔːkɪʃ] *adj* mièvre; fade

max *abbr* = **maximum**

maxim ['mæksɪm] *n* maxime *f*

maxima ['mæksɪmə] *npl of* **maximum**

maximize ['mæksɪmaɪz] *vt* (*profits etc, chances*) maximiser

maximum ['mæksɪməm] (*pl* **maxima**) ['mæksɪmə] *adj* maximum ▷ *n* maximum *m*

May [meɪ] *n* mai *m*; *for phrases see also* **July**

may [meɪ] (*conditional* **might**) *vi* (*indicating possibility*): **he ~ come** il se peut qu'il vienne; (*be allowed to*): **~ I smoke?** puis-je fumer?; (*wishes*): **~ God bless you!** (que) Dieu vous bénisse!; **~ I sit here?** vous permettez que je m'assoie ici?; **he might be there** il pourrait bien y être, il se pourrait qu'il y soit; **you ~ as well go** vous feriez aussi bien d'y aller; **I might as well go** je ferais aussi bien d'y aller, autant y aller; **you might like to try** vous pourriez (peut-être) essayer

maybe ['meɪbiː] *adv* peut-être; **~ he'll ...** peut-être qu'il ...; **~ not** peut-être pas

May Day *n* le Premier mai

mayday ['meɪdeɪ] *n* S.O.S *m*

mayhem ['meɪhɛm] *n* grabuge *m*

mayonnaise [meɪə'neɪz] *n* mayonnaise *f*

mayor [mɛə^r] *n* maire *m*

mayoress ['mɛərɛs] *n* (*female mayor*) maire *m*; (*wife of mayor*) épouse *f* du maire

maypole ['meɪpəʊl] *n* mât enrubanné (*autour duquel on danse*)

maze [meɪz] *n* labyrinthe *m*, dédale *m*

MB *abbr* (*Comput*) = **megabyte**; (*Canada*) = **Manitoba**

MBA *n abbr* (= *Master of Business Administration*) titre universitaire

MBBS, MBChB *n abbr* (*Brit*: = *Bachelor of Medicine and Surgery*) titre universitaire

MBE *n abbr* (*Brit*: = *Member of the Order of the British Empire*) titre honorifique

MBO *n abbr* (*Brit*) = **management buyout**

MC *n abbr* = **master of ceremonies**

MCAT *n abbr* (*US*) = **Medical College Admissions Test**

MD *n abbr* (= *Doctor of Medicine*) titre universitaire; (*Comm*) = **managing director** ▷ *abbr* (*US*) = **Maryland**

Md. *abbr* (*US*) = **Maryland**

MDT *abbr* (*US*: = *Mountain Daylight Time*) heure d'été des Montagnes Rocheuses

ME *n abbr* (*US*: = *medical examiner*) médecin légiste *m/f*; (*Med*: = *myalgic encephalomyelitis*) encéphalomyélite *f* myalgique ▷ *abbr* (*US*) = **Maine**

me [miː] *pron* me, m' + *vowel or h mute*; (*stressed, after prep*) moi; **it's me** c'est moi; **he heard me** il m'a entendu; **give me a book** donnez-moi un livre; **it's for me** c'est pour moi

meadow ['mɛdəʊ] *n* prairie *f*, pré *m*

meagre, (*US*) **meager** ['miːgə^r] *adj* maigre

meal [miːl] *n* repas *m*; (*flour*) farine *f*; **to go out for a ~** sortir manger

meals on wheels *npl* (*Brit*) repas livrés à domicile aux personnes âgées ou handicapées

mealtime ['miːltaɪm] *n* heure *f* du repas

mealy-mouthed ['miːlɪmaʊðd] *adj* mielleux(-euse)

mean [miːn] *adj* (*with money*) avare, radin(e); (*unkind*) mesquin(e), méchant(e); (*shabby*) misérable; (*US inf: animal*) méchant, vicieux(-euse); (: *person*) vache; (*average*) moyen(ne) ▷ *vt* (*pt, pp* **-t**) [mɛnt] (*signify*) signifier, vouloir dire; (*refer to*) faire allusion à, parler de; (*intend*): **to ~ to do** avoir l'intention de faire ▷ *n* moyenne *f*; **means** *npl* (*way, money*) moyens *mpl*; **by ~s of** (*instrument*) au moyen de; **by all ~s** je vous en prie; **to be ~t for** être destiné(e) à; **do you ~ it?** vous êtes sérieux?; **what do you ~?** que voulez-vous dire?

meander [mɪ'ændə^r] *vi* faire des méandres; (*fig*) flâner

meaning ['miːnɪŋ] *n* signification *f*, sens *m*

meaningful ['miːnɪŋful] *adj* significatif(-ive); (*relationship*) valable

meaningless ['miːnɪŋlɪs] *adj* dénué(e) de sens

meanness ['miːnnɪs] *n* avarice *f*; mesquinerie *f*

means test *n* (*Admin*) contrôle *m* des conditions de ressources

meant [mɛnt] *pt, pp of* **mean**

meantime ['miːntaɪm] *adv* (*also*: **in the meantime**) pendant ce temps

meanwhile ['miːnwaɪl] *adv* = **meantime**

measles ['miːzlz] *n* rougeole *f*

measly ['miːzlɪ] *adj* (*inf*) minable

measurable ['mɛʒərəbl] *adj* mesurable

measure ['mɛʒə^r] *vt, vi* mesurer ▷ *n* mesure *f*; (*ruler*) règle (graduée); **a litre ~** un litre; **some ~ of success** un certain succès; **to take ~s to do sth** prendre des mesures pour faire qch ▶ **measure up** *vi*: **to ~ up (to)** être à la hauteur (de)

measured ['mɛʒəd] *adj* mesuré(e)

measurements ['mɛʒəməntz] *npl* mesures *fpl*; **chest/hip ~** tour *m* de poitrine/hanches; **to take sb's ~** prendre les mesures de qn

meat [miːt] *n* viande *f*; **I don't eat ~** je ne mange pas de viande; **cold ~s** (*Brit*) viandes froides; **crab ~** crabe *f*

meatball ['miːtbɔːl] *n* boulette *f* de viande

meat pie *n* pâté *m* en croûte

meaty ['miːtɪ] *adj* (*flavour*) de viande; (*fig: argument, book*) étoffé(e), substantiel(le)

Mecca ['mɛkə] *n* la Mecque; (*fig*): **a ~ (for)** la Mecque (de)

mechanic [mɪ'kænɪk] *n* mécanicien *m*; **can you send a ~?** pouvez-vous nous envoyer un mécanicien?

mechanical [mɪ'kænɪkl] *adj* mécanique

mechanical engineering *n* (*science*) mécanique *f*; (*industry*) construction *f* mécanique

mechanics [mə'kænɪks] *n* mécanique *f* ▷ *npl* mécanisme *m*

mechanism ['mɛkənɪzəm] *n* mécanisme *m*

mechanization [mɛkənaɪ'zeɪʃən] *n* mécanisation *f*

MEd *n abbr* (= *Master of Education*) *titre universitaire*

medal ['mɛdl] *n* médaille *f*

medallion [mɪ'dælɪən] *n* médaillon *m*

medallist, (US) **medalist** ['mɛdlɪst] *n* (*Sport*) médaillé(e)

meddle ['mɛdl] *vi*: **to ~ in** se mêler de, s'occuper de; **to ~ with** toucher à

meddlesome ['mɛdlsəm], **meddling** ['mɛdlɪŋ] *adj* indiscret(-ète), qui se mêle de ce qui ne le (*or* la) regarde pas; touche-à-tout *inv*

media ['mi:dɪə] *npl* media *mpl* ▷ *npl of* **medium**

media circus *n* (*event*) battage *m* médiatique; (*group of journalists*) cortège *m* médiatique

mediaeval [mɛdɪ'i:vl] *adj* = **medieval**

median ['mi:dɪən] *n* (US: *also*: **median strip**) bande médiane

media research *n* étude *f* de l'audience

mediate ['mi:dɪeɪt] *vi* servir d'intermédiaire

mediation [mi:dɪ'eɪʃən] *n* médiation *f*

mediator ['mi:dɪeɪtəʳ] *n* médiateur(-trice)

Medicaid ['mɛdɪkeɪd] *n* (US) *assistance médicale aux indigents*

medical ['mɛdɪkl] *adj* médical(e) ▷ *n* (*also*: **medical examination**) visite médicale; (*private*) examen médical

medical certificate *n* certificat médical

medical student *n* étudiant(e) en médecine

Medicare ['mɛdɪkɛəʳ] *n* (US) *régime d'assurance maladie*

medicated ['mɛdɪkeɪtɪd] *adj* traitant(e), médicamenteux(-euse)

medication [mɛdɪ'keɪʃən] *n* (*drugs etc*) médication *f*

medicinal [mɛ'dɪsɪnl] *adj* médicinal(e)

medicine ['mɛdsɪn] *n* médecine *f*; (*drug*) médicament *m*

medicine chest *n* pharmacie *f* (*murale ou portative*)

medicine man (*irreg*) *n* sorcier *m*

medieval [mɛdɪ'i:vl] *adj* médiéval(e)

mediocre [mi:dɪ'əukəʳ] *adj* médiocre

mediocrity [mi:dɪ'ɔkrɪtɪ] *n* médiocrité *f*

meditate ['mɛdɪteɪt] *vi*: **to ~ (on)** méditer (sur)

meditation [mɛdɪ'teɪʃən] *n* méditation *f*

Mediterranean [mɛdɪtə'reɪnɪən] *adj* méditerranéen(ne); **the ~ (Sea)** la (mer) Méditerranée

medium ['mi:dɪəm] *adj* moyen(ne) ▷ *n* (*pl* **media**) (*means*) moyen *m* (*pl* **-s**) (*person*) médium *m*; **the happy ~** le juste milieu

medium-dry ['mi:dɪəm'draɪ] *adj* demi-sec

medium-sized ['mi:dɪəm'saɪzd] *adj* de taille moyenne

medium wave *n* (*Radio*) ondes moyennes, petites ondes

medley ['mɛdlɪ] *n* mélange *m*

meek [mi:k] *adj* doux (douce), humble

meet (*pt, pp* **met**) [mi:t, mɛt] *vt* rencontrer; (*by arrangement*) retrouver, rejoindre; (*for the first time*) faire la connaissance de; (*go and fetch*): **I'll ~ you at the station** j'irai te chercher à la gare; (*opponent, danger, problem*) faire face à; (*requirements*) satisfaire à, répondre à; (*bill, expenses*) régler, honorer ▷ *vi* (*friends*) se rencontrer; se retrouver; (*in session*) se réunir; (*join: lines, roads*) se joindre ▷ *n* (*Brit Hunting*) rendez-vous *m* de chasse; (*US Sport*) rencontre *f*, meeting *m*; **pleased to ~ you!** enchanté!; **nice ~ing you** ravi d'avoir fait votre connaissance
 ▶ **meet up** *vi*: **to ~ up with sb** rencontrer qn
 ▶ **meet with** *vt fus* (*difficulty*) rencontrer; **to ~ with success** être couronné(e) de succès

meeting ['mi:tɪŋ] *n* (*of group of people*) réunion *f*; (*between individuals*) rendez-vous *m*; (*formal*) assemblée *f*; (*Sport: rally*) rencontre, meeting *m*; (*interview*) entrevue *f*; **she's at** *or* **in a ~** (*Comm*) elle est en réunion; **to call a ~** convoquer une réunion

meeting place *n* lieu *m* de (la) réunion; (*for appointment*) lieu de rendez-vous

mega ['mɛgə] (*inf*) *adv*: **he's ~ rich** il est hyper-riche

megabyte ['mɛgəbaɪt] *n* (*Comput*) méga-octet *m*

megaphone ['mɛgəfəun] *n* porte-voix *m inv*

megapixel ['mɛgəpɪksl] *n* mégapixel *m*

melancholy ['mɛlənkəlɪ] *n* mélancolie *f* ▷ *adj* mélancolique

mellow ['mɛləu] *adj* velouté(e), doux (douce); (*colour*) riche et profond(e); (*fruit*) mûr(e) ▷ *vi* (*person*) s'adoucir

melodious [mɪ'ləudɪəs] *adj* mélodieux(-euse)

melodrama ['mɛləudrɑːmə] *n* mélodrame *m*

melodramatic [mɛlədrə'mætɪk] *adj* mélodramatique

melody ['mɛlədɪ] *n* mélodie *f*

melon ['mɛlən] *n* melon *m*

melt [mɛlt] *vi* fondre; (*become soft*) s'amollir; (*fig*) s'attendrir ▷ *vt* faire fondre
 ▶ **melt away** *vi* fondre complètement
 ▶ **melt down** *vt* fondre

meltdown ['mɛltdaun] *n* fusion *f* (du cœur d'un réacteur nucléaire)

melting point ['mɛltɪŋ-] *n* point *m* de fusion

melting pot ['mɛltɪŋ-] *n* (*fig*) creuset *m*; **to be in the ~** être encore en discussion

member ['mɛmbəʳ] *n* membre *m*; (*of club, political party*) membre, adhérent(e) ▷ *cpd*: **~ country/ state** *n* pays *m*/état *m* membre

membership ['mɛmbəʃɪp] *n* (*becoming a member*) adhésion *f*; admission *f*; (*being a member*) qualité *f* de membre, fait *m* d'être membre; (*members*) membres *mpl*, adhérents *mpl*; (*number of members*) nombre *m* des membres *or* adhérents

membership card *n* carte *f* de membre

membrane ['mɛmbreɪn] *n* membrane *f*

memento [mə'mɛntəu] *n* souvenir *m*
memo ['mɛməu] *n* note *f* (de service)
memoir ['mɛmwɑː'] *n* mémoire *m*, étude *f*;
  memoirs *npl* mémoires
memo pad *n* bloc-notes *m*
memorable ['mɛmərəbl] *adj* mémorable
memorandum (*pl* **memoranda**)
  [mɛmə'rændəm, -də] *n* note *f* (de service);
  (*Diplomacy*) mémorandum *m*
memorial [mɪ'mɔːrɪəl] *n* mémorial *m* ▷ *adj*
  commémoratif(-ive)
Memorial Day *n* (US) *voir article*

⬤ **MEMORIAL DAY**
⬤
⬤ *Memorial Day* est un jour férié aux États-Unis,
⬤ le dernier lundi de mai dans la plupart des
⬤ États, à la mémoire des soldats américains
⬤ morts au combat.

memorize ['mɛməraɪz] *vt* apprendre *or* retenir
  par cœur
memory ['mɛmərɪ] *n* (*also Comput*) mémoire *f*;
  (*recollection*) souvenir *m*; **to have a good/bad ~**
  avoir une bonne/mauvaise mémoire; **loss of ~**
  perte *f* de mémoire; **in ~ of** à la mémoire de
memory card *n* (*for digital camera*) carte *f*
  mémoire
men [mɛn] *npl of* **man**
menace ['mɛnɪs] *n* menace *f*; (*inf: nuisance*) peste
  f, plaie *f* ▷ *vt* menacer; **a public ~** un danger
  public
menacing ['mɛnɪsɪŋ] *adj* menaçant(e)
menagerie [mɪ'nædʒərɪ] *n* ménagerie *f*
mend [mɛnd] *vt* réparer; (*darn*) raccommoder,
  repriser ▷ *n* reprise *f*; **on the ~** en voie de
  guérison; **to ~ one's ways** s'amender
mending ['mɛndɪŋ] *n* raccommodages *mpl*
menial ['miːnɪəl] *adj* de domestique,
  inférieur(e); subalterne
meningitis [mɛnɪn'dʒaɪtɪs] *n* méningite *f*
menopause ['mɛnəupɔːz] *n* ménopause *f*
menservants ['mɛnsəːvənts] *npl of* **manservant**
men's room (US) *n*: **the men's room** les
  toilettes *fpl* pour hommes
menstruate ['mɛnstrueɪt] *vi* avoir ses règles
menstruation [mɛnstru'eɪʃən] *n*
  menstruation *f*
menswear ['mɛnzwɛə'] *n* vêtements *mpl*
  d'hommes
mental ['mɛntl] *adj* mental(e); **~ illness**
  maladie mentale
mental hospital *n* hôpital *m* psychiatrique
mentality [mɛn'tælɪtɪ] *n* mentalité *f*
mentally ['mɛntlɪ] *adv*: **to be ~ handicapped**
  être handicapé(e) mental(e); **the ~ ill** les
  malades mentaux
menthol ['mɛnθɔl] *n* menthol *m*
mention ['mɛnʃən] *n* mention *f* ▷ *vt*
  mentionner, faire mention de; **don't ~ it!** je
  vous en prie, il n'y a pas de quoi!; **I need hardly
  ~ that** ... est-il besoin de rappeler que ...?; **not**

to ~ ..., **without ~ing** ... sans parler de ..., sans
  compter ...
mentor ['mɛntɔː'] *n* mentor *m*
menu ['mɛnjuː] *n* (*set menu, Comput*) menu *m*; (*list
  of dishes*) carte *f*; **could we see the ~?** est-ce
  qu'on peut voir la carte?
menu-driven ['mɛnjuːdrɪvn] *adj* (*Comput*)
  piloté(e) par menu
MEP *n abbr* = **Member of the European
  Parliament**
mercantile ['məːkəntaɪl] *adj* marchand(e);
  (*law*) commercial(e)
mercenary ['məːsɪnərɪ] *adj* (*person*) intéressé(e),
  mercenaire ▷ *n* mercenaire *m*
merchandise ['məːtʃəndaɪz] *n* marchandises *fpl*
  ▷ *vt* commercialiser
merchandiser ['məːtʃəndaɪzə'] *n*
  marchandiseur *m*
merchant ['məːtʃənt] *n* négociant *m*, marchand
  m; **timber/wine ~** négociant en bois/vins,
  marchand de bois/vins
merchant bank *n* (*Brit*) banque *f* d'affaires
merchantman ['məːtʃəntmən] (*irreg*) *n* navire
  marchand
merchant navy, (US) **merchant marine** *n*
  marine marchande
merciful ['məːsɪful] *adj* miséricordieux(-euse),
  clément(e)
mercifully ['məːsɪflɪ] *adv* avec clémence;
  (*fortunately*) par bonheur, Dieu merci
merciless ['məːsɪlɪs] *adj* impitoyable, sans pitié
mercurial [məː'kjuərɪəl] *adj* changeant(e);
  (*lively*) vif (vive)
mercury ['məːkjurɪ] *n* mercure *m*
mercy ['məːsɪ] *n* pitié *f*, merci *f*; (*Rel*)
  miséricorde *f*; **to have ~ on sb** avoir pitié de qn;
  at the ~ of à la merci de
mercy killing *n* euthanasie *f*
mere [mɪə'] *adj* simple; (*chance*) pur(e); **a ~ two
  hours** seulement deux heures
merely ['mɪəlɪ] *adv* simplement, purement
merge [məːdʒ] *vt* unir; (*Comput*) fusionner,
  interclasser ▷ *vi* (*colours, shapes, sounds*) se mêler;
  (*roads*) se joindre; (*Comm*) fusionner
merger ['məːdʒə'] *n* (*Comm*) fusion *f*
meridian [mə'rɪdɪən] *n* méridien *m*
meringue [mə'ræŋ] *n* meringue *f*
merit ['mɛrɪt] *n* mérite *m*, valeur *f* ▷ *vt* mériter
meritocracy [mɛrɪ'tɔkrəsɪ] *n* méritocratie *f*
mermaid ['məːmeɪd] *n* sirène *f*
merriment ['mɛrɪmənt] *n* gaieté *f*
merry ['mɛrɪ] *adj* gai(e); **M~ Christmas!** joyeux
  Noël!
merry-go-round ['mɛrɪɡəuraund] *n* manège *m*
mesh [mɛʃ] *n* mailles *fpl* ▷ *vi* (*gears*) s'engrener;
  wire ~ grillage *m* (métallique), treillis *m*
  (métallique)
mesmerize ['mɛzməraɪz] *vt* hypnotiser;
  fasciner
mess [mɛs] *n* désordre *m*, fouillis *m*, pagaille *f*;
  (*muddle: of life*) gâchis *m*; (: *of economy*) pagaille *f*;
  (*dirt*) saleté *f*; (*Mil*) mess *m*, cantine *f*; **to be (in)**

a ~ être en désordre; **to be/get o.s. in a ~** (fig) être/se mettre dans le pétrin
▶ **mess about** or **around** (inf) vi perdre son temps
▶ **mess about** or **around with** vt fus (inf) chambarder, tripoter
▶ **mess up** vt (dirty) salir; (spoil) gâcher
▶ **mess with** (inf) vt fus (challenge, confront) se frotter à; (interfere with) toucher à
message ['mɛsɪdʒ] n message m; **can I leave a ~?** est-ce que je peux laisser un message?; **are there any ~s for me?** est-ce que j'ai des messages?; **to get the ~** (fig: inf) saisir, piger
message switching [-swɪtʃɪŋ] n (Comput) commutation f de messages
messenger ['mɛsɪndʒəʳ] n messager m
Messiah [mɪ'saɪə] n Messie m
Messrs, Messrs. ['mɛsəz] abbr (on letters: = messieurs) MM
messy ['mɛsɪ] adj (dirty) sale; (untidy) en désordre
Met [mɛt] n abbr (US) = **Metropolitan Opera**
met [mɛt] pt, pp of **meet** ▷ adj abbr (= meteorological) météo inv
metabolism [mɛ'tæbəlɪzəm] n métabolisme m
metal ['mɛtl] n métal m ▷ cpd en métal ▷ vt empierrer
metallic [mɛ'tælɪk] adj métallique
metallurgy [mɛ'tælədʒɪ] n métallurgie f
metalwork ['mɛtlwə:k] n (craft) ferronnerie f
metamorphosis (pl **-ses**) [mɛtə'mɔ:fəsɪs, -si:z] n métamorphose f
metaphor ['mɛtəfəʳ] n métaphore f
metaphysics [mɛtə'fɪzɪks] n métaphysique f
mete [mi:t] **to ~ out** vt fus infliger
meteor ['mi:tɪəʳ] n météore m
meteoric [mi:tɪ'ɔrɪk] adj (fig) fulgurant(e)
meteorite ['mi:tɪəraɪt] n météorite m or f
meteorological [mi:tɪərə'lɔdʒɪkl] adj météorologique
meteorology [mi:tɪə'rɔlədʒɪ] n météorologie f
meter ['mi:təʳ] n (instrument) compteur m; (also: **parking meter**) parc(o)mètre m; (US: unit) = **metre** ▷ vt (US Post) affranchir à la machine
methane ['mi:θeɪn] n méthane m
method ['mɛθəd] n méthode f; **~ of payment** mode m or modalité f de paiement
methodical [mɪ'θɔdɪkl] adj méthodique
Methodist ['mɛθədɪst] adj, n méthodiste (m/f)
methylated spirit ['mɛθɪleɪtɪd-] n (Brit: also: **meths**) alcool m à brûler
meticulous [mɛ'tɪkjuləs] adj méticuleux(-euse)
Met Office ['mɛt'ɔfɪs] n (Brit): **the ~** ≈ la Météorologie nationale
metre, (US) **meter** ['mi:təʳ] n mètre m
metric ['mɛtrɪk] adj métrique; **to go ~** adopter le système métrique
metrical ['mɛtrɪkl] adj métrique
metrication [mɛtrɪ'keɪʃən] n conversion f au système métrique
metric system n système m métrique
metric ton n tonne f
metro ['mɛtrəu] n métro m

metronome ['mɛtrənəum] n métronome m
metropolis [mɪ'trɔpəlɪs] n métropole f
metropolitan [mɛtrə'pɔlɪtən] adj métropolitain(e); **the M~ Police** (Brit) la police londonienne
mettle ['mɛtl] n courage m
mew [mju:] vi (cat) miauler
mews [mju:z] n (Brit): **~ cottage** maisonnette aménagée dans une ancienne écurie ou remise
Mexican ['mɛksɪkən] adj mexicain(e) ▷ n Mexicain(e)
Mexico ['mɛksɪkəu] n Mexique m
Mexico City n Mexico
mezzanine ['mɛtsəni:n] n mezzanine f; (of shops, offices) entresol m
MFA n abbr (US: = Master of Fine Arts) titre universitaire
mfr abbr = **manufacture; manufacturer**
mg abbr (= milligram) mg
Mgr abbr (= Monseigneur, Monsignor) Mgr; (= manager) dir
MHR n abbr (US) = **Member of the House of Representatives**
MHz abbr (= megahertz) MHz
MI abbr (US) = **Michigan**
MI5 n abbr (Brit: = Military Intelligence 5) ≈ DST f
MI6 n abbr (Brit: = Military Intelligence 6) ≈ DGSE f
MIA abbr (= missing in action) disparu au combat
miaow [mi:'au] vi miauler
mice [maɪs] npl of **mouse**
Mich. abbr (US) = **Michigan**
micro ['maɪkrəu] n (also: **microcomputer**) micro(-ordinateur m) m
micro... [maɪkrəu] prefix
microbe ['maɪkrəub] n microbe m
microbiology [maɪkrəbaɪ'ɔlədʒɪ] n microbiologie f
microchip ['maɪkrəutʃɪp] n (Elec) puce f
microcomputer ['maɪkrəukəm'pju:təʳ] n micro-ordinateur m
microcosm ['maɪkrəukɔzəm] n microcosme m
microeconomics ['maɪkrəui:kə'nɔmɪks] n micro-économie f
microfiche ['maɪkrəufi:ʃ] n microfiche f
microfilm ['maɪkrəufɪlm] n microfilm m ▷ vt microfilmer
microlight ['maɪkrəulaɪt] n ULM m
micrometer [maɪ'krɔmɪtəʳ] n palmer m, micromètre m
microphone ['maɪkrəfəun] n microphone m
microprocessor ['maɪkrəu'prəusɛsəʳ] n microprocesseur m
microscope ['maɪkrəskəup] n microscope m; **under the ~** au microscope
microscopic [maɪkrə'skɔpɪk] adj microscopique ▷ n
mid [mɪd] adj: **~ May** la mi-mai; **~ afternoon** le milieu de l'après-midi; **in ~ air** en plein ciel; **he's in his ~ thirties** il a dans les trente-cinq ans
midday [mɪd'deɪ] n midi m
middle ['mɪdl] n milieu m; (waist) ceinture f,

taille f ▷ adj du milieu; (average) moyen(ne); **in the ~ of the night** au milieu de la nuit; **I'm in the ~ of reading it** je suis (justement) en train de le lire

middle age n tranche d'âge aux limites floues, entre la quarantaine et le début du troisième âge

middle-aged [mɪdl'eɪdʒd] adj d'un certain âge, ni vieux ni jeune; (pej: values, outlook) conventionnel(le), rassis(e)

Middle Ages npl: **the ~** le moyen âge

middle-class [mɪdl'klɑːs] adj bourgeois(e)

middle class n, **middle classes** npl: **the ~(es)** ≈ les classes moyennes

Middle East n: **the ~** le Proche-Orient, le Moyen-Orient

middleman ['mɪdlmæn] (irreg) n intermédiaire m

middle management n cadres moyens

middle name n second prénom

middle-of-the-road ['mɪdləvðə'rəud] adj (policy) modéré(e), du juste milieu; (music etc) plutôt classique, assez traditionnel(le)

middle school n (US) école pour les enfants de 12 à 14 ans, ≈ collège m; (Brit) école pour les enfants de 8 à 14 ans

middleweight ['mɪdlweɪt] n (Boxing) poids moyen

middling ['mɪdlɪŋ] adj moyen(ne)

midge [mɪdʒ] n moucheron m

midget ['mɪdʒɪt] n nain(e) ▷ adj minuscule

midi system ['mɪdɪ-] n chaîne f midi

Midlands ['mɪdləndz] npl comtés du centre de l'Angleterre

midnight ['mɪdnaɪt] n minuit m; **at ~** à minuit

midriff ['mɪdrɪf] n estomac m, taille f

midst [mɪdst] n: **in the ~ of** au milieu de

midsummer [mɪd'sʌmər] n milieu m de l'été

midway [mɪd'weɪ] adj, adv: **~ (between)** à mi-chemin (entre); **~ through ...** au milieu de ..., en plein(e) ...

midweek [mɪd'wiːk] adj du milieu de la semaine ▷ adv au milieu de la semaine, en pleine semaine

midwife (pl **midwives**) ['mɪdwaɪf, -vz] n sage-femme f

midwifery ['mɪdwɪfərɪ] n obstétrique f

midwinter [mɪd'wɪntər] n milieu m de l'hiver

miffed [mɪft] adj (inf) fâché(e), vexé(e)

might [maɪt] vb see **may** ▷ n puissance f, force f

mighty ['maɪtɪ] adj puissant(e) ▷ adv (inf) rudement

migraine ['miːɡreɪn] n migraine f

migrant ['maɪɡrənt] n (bird, animal) migrateur m; (person) migrant(e); nomade m/f ▷ adj migrateur(-trice); migrant(e); nomade; (worker) saisonnier(-ière)

migrate [maɪ'ɡreɪt] vi migrer

migration [maɪ'ɡreɪʃən] n migration f

mike [maɪk] n abbr (= microphone) micro m

Milan [mɪ'læn] n Milan

mild [maɪld] adj doux (douce); (reproach, infection) léger(-ère); (illness) bénin(-igne); (interest)

modéré(e); (taste) peu relevé(e) ▷ n bière légère

mildew ['mɪldjuː] n mildiou m

mildly ['maɪldlɪ] adv doucement; légèrement; **to put it ~** (inf) c'est le moins qu'on puisse dire

mildness ['maɪldnɪs] n douceur f

mile [maɪl] n mil(l)e m (= 1609 m); **to do 30 ~s per gallon** ≈ faire 9, 4 litres aux cent

mileage ['maɪlɪdʒ] n distance f en milles, ≈ kilométrage m

mileage allowance n ≈ indemnité f kilométrique

mileometer [maɪ'lɔmɪtər] n compteur m kilométrique

milestone ['maɪlstəun] n borne f; (fig) jalon m

milieu ['miːljəː] n milieu m

militant ['mɪlɪtnt] adj, n militant(e)

militarism ['mɪlɪtərɪzəm] n militarisme m

militaristic [mɪlɪtə'rɪstɪk] adj militariste

military ['mɪlɪtərɪ] adj militaire ▷ n: **the ~** l'armée f, les militaires mpl

military service n service m (militaire ou national)

militate ['mɪlɪteɪt] vi: **to ~ against** militer contre

militia [mɪ'lɪʃə] n milice f

milk [mɪlk] n lait m ▷ vt (cow) traire; (fig: person) dépouiller, plumer; (: situation) exploiter à fond

milk chocolate n chocolat m au lait

milk float n (Brit) voiture f or camionnette f du or de laitier

milking ['mɪlkɪŋ] n traite f

milkman ['mɪlkmən] (irreg) n laitier m

milk shake n milk-shake m

milk tooth n dent f de lait

milk truck n (US) = **milk float**

milky ['mɪlkɪ] adj (drink) au lait; (colour) laiteux(-euse)

Milky Way n Voie lactée

mill [mɪl] n moulin m; (factory) usine f, fabrique f; (spinning mill) filature f; (flour mill) minoterie f; (steel mill) aciérie f ▷ vt moudre, broyer ▷ vi (also: **mill about**) grouiller

millennium (pl **-s** or **millennia**) [mɪ'lɛnɪəm, -'lɛnɪə] n millénaire m

millennium bug [mɪ'lɛnɪəm-] n bogue m or bug m de l'an 2000

miller ['mɪlər] n meunier m

millet ['mɪlɪt] n millet m

milli... ['mɪlɪ] prefix milli...

milligram, milligramme ['mɪlɪɡræm] n milligramme m

millilitre, (US) **milliliter** ['mɪlɪliːtər] n millilitre m

millimetre, (US) **millimeter** ['mɪlɪmiːtər] n millimètre m

milliner ['mɪlɪnər] n modiste f

millinery ['mɪlɪnərɪ] n modes fpl

million ['mɪljən] n million m; **a ~ pounds** un million de livres sterling

millionaire [mɪljə'nɛər] n millionnaire m

millionth [-θ] num millionième

millipede ['mɪlɪpiːd] n mille-pattes m inv

millstone ['mɪlstəun] n meule f
millwheel ['mɪlwiːl] n roue f de moulin
milometer [maɪˈlɒmɪtəʳ] n = **mileometer**
mime [maɪm] n mime m ▷ vt, vi mimer
mimic ['mɪmɪk] n imitateur(-trice) ▷ vt, vi
imiter, contrefaire
mimicry ['mɪmɪkrɪ] n imitation f; (Zool)
mimétisme m
Min. abbr (Brit Pol) = **ministry**
min. abbr (= minute(s)) mn.; (= minimum) min.
minaret [mɪnəˈrɛt] n minaret m
mince [mɪns] vt hacher ▷ vi (in walking) marcher
à petits pas maniérés ▷ n (Brit Culin) viande
hachée, hachis m; **he does not ~ (his) words** il
ne mâche pas ses mots
mincemeat ['mɪnsmiːt] n hachis de fruits secs
utilisés en pâtisserie; (US) viande hachée, hachis m
mince pie n sorte de tarte aux fruits secs
mincer ['mɪnsəʳ] n hachoir m
mincing ['mɪnsɪŋ] adj affecté(e)
mind [maɪnd] n esprit m ▷ vt (attend to, look after)
s'occuper de; (be careful) faire attention à; (object
to): **I don't ~ the noise** je ne crains pas le bruit,
le bruit ne me dérange pas; **it is on my ~** cela
me préoccupe; **to change one's ~** changer
d'avis; **to be in two ~s about sth** (Brit) être
indécis(e) or irrésolu(e) en ce qui concerne qch;
to my ~ à mon avis, selon moi; **to be out of
one's ~** ne plus avoir toute sa raison; **to keep
sth in ~** ne pas oublier qch; **to bear sth in ~**
tenir compte de qch; **to have sb/sth in ~** avoir
qn/qch en tête; **to have in ~ to do** avoir
l'intention de faire; **it went right out of my ~**
ça m'est complètement sorti de la tête; **to
bring** or **call sth to ~** se rappeler qch; **to make
up one's ~** se décider; **do you ~ if ...?** est-ce que
cela vous gêne si ...?; **I don't ~** cela ne me
dérange pas; (don't care) ça m'est égal; **~ you, ...**
remarquez, ...; **never ~** peu importe, ça ne fait
rien; (don't worry) ne vous en faîtes pas; **"~ the
step"** "attention à la marche"
mind-boggling ['maɪndbɒglɪŋ] adj (inf)
époustouflant(e), ahurissant(e)
-minded ['maɪndɪd] adj: **fair-** impartial(e); **an
industrially~ nation** une nation orientée vers
l'industrie
minder ['maɪndəʳ] n (child minder) gardienne f;
(bodyguard) ange gardien (fig)
mindful ['maɪndful] adj: **~ of** attentif(-ive) à,
soucieux(-euse) de
mindless ['maɪndlɪs] adj irréfléchi(e); (violence,
crime) insensé(e); (boring: job) idiot(e)
mine[1] [maɪn] pron le (la) mien(ne), les miens
(miennes); **a friend of ~** un de mes amis, un
ami à moi; **this book is ~** ce livre est à moi
mine[2] [maɪn] n mine f ▷ vt (coal) extraire; (ship,
beach) miner
mine detector n détecteur m de mines
minefield ['maɪnfiːld] n champ m de mines
miner ['maɪnəʳ] n mineur m
mineral ['mɪnərəl] adj minéral(e) ▷ n minéral
m; **minerals** npl (Brit: soft drinks) boissons

gazeuses (sucrées)
mineralogy [mɪnəˈrælədʒɪ] n minéralogie f
mineral water n eau minérale
minesweeper ['maɪnswiːpəʳ] n dragueur m de
mines
mingle ['mɪŋgl] vt mêler, mélanger ▷ vi: **to ~
with** se mêler à
mingy ['mɪndʒɪ] adj (inf) radin(e)
miniature ['mɪnətʃəʳ] adj (en) miniature ▷ n
miniature f
minibar ['mɪnɪbɑːʳ] n minibar m
minibus ['mɪnɪbʌs] n minibus m
minicab ['mɪnɪkæb] n (Brit) taxi m indépendant
minicomputer ['mɪnɪkəmˈpjuːtəʳ] n mini-
ordinateur m
minim ['mɪnɪm] n (Mus) blanche f
minima ['mɪnɪmə] npl of **minimum**
minimal ['mɪnɪml] adj minimal(e)
minimalist ['mɪnɪməlɪst] adj, n minimaliste
(m/f)
minimize ['mɪnɪmaɪz] vt (reduce) réduire au
minimum; (play down) minimiser
minimum ['mɪnɪməm] n (pl **minima**) [-mə]
minimum m ▷ adj minimum; **to reduce to a ~**
réduire au minimum
minimum lending rate n (Econ) taux m de
crédit minimum
mining ['maɪnɪŋ] n exploitation minière ▷ adj
minier(-ière); de mineurs
minion ['mɪnjən] n (pej) laquais m; favori(te)
mini-series ['mɪnɪsɪəriːz] n téléfilm m en
plusieurs parties
miniskirt ['mɪnɪskəːt] n mini-jupe f
minister ['mɪnɪstəʳ] n (Brit Pol) ministre m; (Rel)
pasteur m ▷ vi: **to ~ to sb** donner ses soins à qn;
to ~ to sb's needs pourvoir aux besoins de qn
ministerial [mɪnɪsˈtɪərɪəl] adj (Brit Pol)
ministériel(le)
ministry ['mɪnɪstrɪ] n (Brit Pol) ministère m;
(Rel): **to go into the ~** devenir pasteur
mink [mɪŋk] n vison m
mink coat n manteau m de vison
Minn. abbr (US) = **Minnesota**
minnow ['mɪnəu] n vairon m
minor ['maɪnəʳ] adj petit(e), de peu
d'importance; (Mus, poet, problem) mineur(e) ▷ n
(Law) mineur(e)
Minorca [mɪˈnɔːkə] n Minorque f
minority [maɪˈnɔrɪtɪ] n minorité f; **to be in a ~**
être en minorité
minster ['mɪnstəʳ] n église abbatiale
minstrel ['mɪnstrəl] n trouvère m, ménestrel m
mint [mɪnt] n (plant) menthe f; (sweet) bonbon m
à la menthe ▷ vt (coins) battre; **the (Royal) M~,
the (US) M~** ≈ l'hôtel m de la Monnaie; **in ~
condition** à l'état de neuf
mint sauce n sauce f à la menthe
minuet [mɪnjuˈɛt] n menuet m
minus ['maɪnəs] n (also: **minus sign**) signe m
moins ▷ prep moins; **12 ~ 6 equals 6** 12 moins 6
égal 6; **~ 24°C** moins 24°C
minuscule ['mɪnəskjuːl] adj minuscule

minute[1] *n* ['mɪnɪt] minute *f*; (*official record*) procès-verbal *m*, compte rendu; **minutes** *npl* (*of meeting*) procès-verbal *m*, compte rendu; **it is 5 ~s past 3** il est 3 heures 5; **wait a ~!** (attendez) un instant!; **at the last ~** à la dernière minute; **up to the ~** (*fashion*) dernier cri; (*news*) de dernière minute; (*machine, technology*) de pointe

minute[2] *adj* [maɪ'njuːt] minuscule; (*detailed*) minutieux(-euse); **in ~ detail** par le menu

minute book *n* registre *m* des procès-verbaux

minute hand *n* aiguille *f* des minutes

minutely [maɪ'njuːtlɪ] *adv* (*by a small amount*) de peu, de manière infime; (*in detail*) minutieusement, dans les moindres détails

minutiae [mɪ'njuːʃiː] *npl* menus détails

miracle ['mɪrəkl] *n* miracle *m*

miraculous [mɪ'rækjuləs] *adj* miraculeux(-euse)

mirage ['mɪrɑːʒ] *n* mirage *m*

mire ['maɪərʳ] *n* bourbe *f*, boue *f*

mirror ['mɪrəʳ] *n* miroir *m*, glace *f*; (*in car*) rétroviseur *m* ▷ *vt* refléter

mirror image *n* image inversée

mirth [məːθ] *n* gaieté *f*

misadventure [mɪsəd'vɛntʃəʳ] *n* mésaventure *f*; **death by ~** (*Brit*) décès accidentel

misanthropist [mɪ'zænθrəpɪst] *n* misanthrope *m/f*

misapply [mɪsə'plaɪ] *vt* mal employer

misapprehension ['mɪsæprɪ'hɛnʃən] *n* malentendu *m*, méprise *f*

misappropriate [mɪsə'prəuprɪeɪt] *vt* détourner

misappropriation ['mɪsəprəuprɪ'eɪʃən] *n* escroquerie *f*, détournement *m*

misbehave [mɪsbɪ'heɪv] *vi* mal se conduire

misbehaviour, (*US*) **misbehavior** [mɪsbɪ'heɪvjəʳ] *n* mauvaise conduite

misc. *abbr* = **miscellaneous**

miscalculate [mɪs'kælkjuleɪt] *vt* mal calculer

miscalculation ['mɪskælkju'leɪʃən] *n* erreur *f* de calcul

miscarriage ['mɪskærɪdʒ] *n* (*Med*) fausse couche; **~ of justice** erreur *f* judiciaire

miscarry [mɪs'kærɪ] *vi* (*Med*) faire une fausse couche; (*fail: plans*) échouer, mal tourner

miscellaneous [mɪsɪ'leɪnɪəs] *adj* (*items, expenses*) divers(es); (*selection*) varié(e)

miscellany [mɪ'sɛlənɪ] *n* recueil *m*

mischance [mɪs'tʃɑːns] *n* malchance *f*; **by (some) ~** par malheur

mischief ['mɪstʃɪf] *n* (*naughtiness*) sottises *fpl*; (*fun*) farce *f*; (*playfulness*) espièglerie *f*; (*harm*) mal *m*, dommage *m*; (*maliciousness*) méchanceté *f*

mischievous ['mɪstʃɪvəs] *adj* (*playful, naughty*) coquin(e), espiègle; (*harmful*) méchant(e)

misconception ['mɪskən'sɛpʃən] *n* idée fausse

misconduct [mɪs'kɔndʌkt] *n* inconduite *f*; **professional ~** faute professionnelle

misconstrue [mɪskən'struː] *vt* mal interpréter

miscount [mɪs'kaunt] *vt*, *vi* mal compter

misdeed ['mɪs'diːd] *n* méfait *m*

misdemeanour, (*US*) **misdemeanor** [mɪsdɪ'miː-

nəʳ] *n* écart *m* de conduite; infraction *f*

misdirect [mɪsdɪ'rɛkt] *vt* (*person*) mal renseigner; (*letter*) mal adresser

miser ['maɪzəʳ] *n* avare *m/f*

miserable ['mɪzərəbl] *adj* (*person, expression*) malheureux(-euse); (*conditions*) misérable; (*weather*) maussade; (*offer, donation*) minable; (*failure*) pitoyable; **to feel ~** avoir le cafard

miserably ['mɪzərəblɪ] *adv* (*smile, answer*) tristement; (*live, pay*) misérablement; (*fail*) lamentablement

miserly ['maɪzəlɪ] *adj* avare

misery ['mɪzərɪ] *n* (*unhappiness*) tristesse *f*; (*pain*) souffrances *fpl*; (*wretchedness*) misère *f*

misfire [mɪs'faɪəʳ] *vi* rater; (*car engine*) avoir des ratés

misfit ['mɪsfɪt] *n* (*person*) inadapté(e)

misfortune [mɪs'fɔːtʃən] *n* malchance *f*, malheur *m*

misgiving [mɪs'gɪvɪŋ] *n* (*apprehension*) craintes *fpl*; **to have ~s about sth** avoir des doutes quant à qch

misguided [mɪs'gaɪdɪd] *adj* malavisé(e)

mishandle [mɪs'hændl] *vt* (*treat roughly*) malmener; (*mismanage*) mal s'y prendre pour faire *or* résoudre *etc*

mishap ['mɪshæp] *n* mésaventure *f*

mishear [mɪs'hɪəʳ] *vt*, *vi* (*irreg: like* **hear**) mal entendre

mishmash ['mɪʃmæʃ] *n* (*inf*) fatras *m*, méli-mélo *m*

misinform [mɪsɪn'fɔːm] *vt* mal renseigner

misinterpret [mɪsɪn'təːprɪt] *vt* mal interpréter

misinterpretation ['mɪsɪntəːprɪ'teɪʃən] *n* interprétation erronée, contresens *m*

misjudge [mɪs'dʒʌdʒ] *vt* méjuger, se méprendre sur le compte de

mislay [mɪs'leɪ] *vt* (*irreg: like* **lay**) égarer

mislead [mɪs'liːd] *vt* (*irreg: like* **lead**) induire en erreur

misleading [mɪs'liːdɪŋ] *adj* trompeur(-euse)

misled [mɪs'lɛd] *pt*, *pp of* **mislead**

mismanage [mɪs'mænɪdʒ] *vt* mal gérer; mal s'y prendre pour faire *or* résoudre *etc*

mismanagement [mɪs'mænɪdʒmənt] *n* mauvaise gestion

misnomer [mɪs'nəuməʳ] *n* terme *or* qualificatif trompeur *or* peu approprié

misogynist [mɪ'sɔdʒɪnɪst] *n* misogyne *m/f*

misplace [mɪs'pleɪs] *vt* égarer; **to be ~d** (*trust etc*) être mal placé(e)

misprint ['mɪsprɪnt] *n* faute *f* d'impression

mispronounce [mɪsprə'nauns] *vt* mal prononcer

misquote [mɪs'kwəut] *vt* citer erronément *or* inexactement

misread [mɪs'riːd] *vt* (*irreg: like* **read**) mal lire

misrepresent [mɪsrɛprɪ'zɛnt] *vt* présenter sous un faux jour

Miss [mɪs] *n* Mademoiselle; **Dear ~ Smith** Chère Mademoiselle Smith

miss [mɪs] *vt* (*fail to get, attend, see*) manquer,

rater; (*appointment, class*) manquer; (*escape, avoid*) échapper à, éviter; (*notice loss of: money etc*) s'apercevoir de l'absence de; (*regret the absence of*): **I ~ him/it** il/cela me manque ▷ *vi* manquer ▷ *n* (*shot*) coup manqué; **we ~ed our train** nous avons raté notre train; **the bus just ~ed the wall** le bus a évité le mur de justesse; **you're ~ing the point** vous êtes à côté de la question; **you can't ~ it** vous ne pouvez pas vous tromper
▶ **miss out** *vt* (*Brit*) oublier
▶ **miss out on** *vt fus* (*fun, party*) rater, manquer; (*chance, bargain*) laisser passer

Miss. *abbr* (*US*) = **Mississippi**

missal ['mɪsl] *n* missel *m*

misshapen [mɪs'ʃeɪpən] *adj* difforme

missile ['mɪsaɪl] *n* (*Aviat*) missile *m*; (*object thrown*) projectile *m*

missile base *n* base *f* de missiles

missile launcher [-lɔːntʃə^r] *n* lance-missiles *m*

missing ['mɪsɪŋ] *adj* manquant(e); (*after escape, disaster: person*) disparu(e); **to go ~** disparaître; **~ person** personne disparue, disparu(e); **~ in action** (*Mil*) porté(e) disparu(e)

mission ['mɪʃən] *n* mission *f*; **on a ~ to sb** en mission auprès de qn

missionary ['mɪʃənrɪ] *n* missionnaire *m/f*

mission statement *n* déclaration *f* d'intention

missive ['mɪsɪv] *n* missive *f*

misspell ['mɪs'spɛl] *vt* (*irreg: like* **spell**) mal orthographier

misspent ['mɪs'spɛnt] *adj*: **his ~ youth** sa folle jeunesse

mist [mɪst] *n* brume *f* ▷ *vi* (*also*: **mist over, mist up**) devenir brumeux(-euse); (*Brit: windows*) s'embuer

mistake [mɪs'teɪk] *n* erreur *f*, faute *f* ▷ *vt* (*irreg: like* **take**); (*meaning*) mal comprendre; (*intentions*) se méprendre sur; **to ~ for** prendre pour; **by ~** par erreur, par inadvertance; **to make a ~** (*in writing*) faire une faute; (*in calculating etc*) faire une erreur; **there must be some ~** il doit y avoir une erreur, se tromper; **to make a ~ about sb/sth** se tromper sur le compte de qn/ sur qch

mistaken [mɪs'teɪkən] *pp of* **mistake** ▷ *adj* (*idea etc*) erroné(e); **to be ~** faire erreur, se tromper

mistaken identity *n* erreur *f* d'identité

mistakenly [mɪs'teɪkənlɪ] *adv* par erreur, par mégarde

mister ['mɪstə^r] *n* (*inf*) Monsieur *m*; *see* **Mr**

mistletoe ['mɪsltəu] *n* gui *m*

mistook [mɪs'tuk] *pt of* **mistake**

mistranslation [mɪstræns'leɪʃən] *n* erreur *f* de traduction, contresens *m*

mistreat [mɪs'triːt] *vt* maltraiter

mistress ['mɪstrɪs] *n* maîtresse *f*; (*Brit: in primary school*) institutrice *f*; (: *in secondary school*) professeur *m*

mistrust [mɪs'trʌst] *vt* se méfier de ▷ *n*: **~ (of)** méfiance *f* (à l'égard de)

mistrustful [mɪs'trʌstful] *adj*: **~ (of)** méfiant(e) (à l'égard de)

misty ['mɪstɪ] *adj* brumeux(-euse); (*glasses, window*) embué(e)

misty-eyed ['mɪstɪ'aɪd] *adj* les yeux embués de larmes; (*fig*) sentimental(e)

misunderstand [mɪsʌndə'stænd] *vt, vi* (*irreg: like* **stand**) mal comprendre

misunderstanding ['mɪsʌndə'stændɪŋ] *n* méprise *f*, malentendu *m*; **there's been a ~** il y a eu un malentendu

misunderstood [mɪsʌndə'stud] *pt, pp of* **misunderstand** ▷ *adj* (*person*) incompris(e)

misuse *n* [mɪs'juːs] mauvais emploi; (*of power*) abus *m* ▷ *vt* [mɪs'juːz] mal employer; abuser de

MIT *n abbr* (*US*) = **Massachusetts Institute of Technology**

mite [maɪt] *n* (*small quantity*) grain *m*, miette *f*; (*Brit: small child*) petit(e)

mitigate ['mɪtɪgeɪt] *vt* atténuer; **mitigating circumstances** circonstances atténuantes

mitigation [mɪtɪ'geɪʃən] *n* atténuation *f*

mitre, (*US*) **miter** ['maɪtə^r] *n* mitre *f*; (*Carpentry*) onglet *m*

mitt ['mɪt], **mitten** ['mɪtn] *n* moufle *f*; (*fingerless*) mitaine *f*

mix [mɪks] *vt* mélanger; (*sauce, drink etc*) préparer ▷ *vi* se mélanger; (*socialize*): **he doesn't ~ well** il est peu sociable ▷ *n* mélange *m*; **to ~ sth with sth** mélanger qch à qch; **to ~ business with pleasure** unir l'utile à l'agréable; **cake ~** préparation *f* pour gâteau
▶ **mix in** *vt* incorporer, mélanger
▶ **mix up** *vt* mélanger; (*confuse*) confondre; **to be ~ed up in sth** être mêlé(e) à qch *or* impliqué(e) dans qch

mixed [mɪkst] *adj* (*feelings, reactions*) contradictoire; (*school, marriage*) mixte

mixed-ability ['mɪkstə'bɪlɪtɪ] *adj* (*class etc*) sans groupes de niveaux

mixed bag *n*: **it's a (bit of a) ~** il y a (un peu) de tout

mixed blessing *n*: **it's a ~** cela a du bon et du mauvais

mixed doubles *npl* (*Sport*) double *m* mixte

mixed economy *n* économie *f* mixte

mixed grill *n* (*Brit*) assortiment *m* de grillades

mixed marriage *n* mariage *m* mixte

mixed salad *n* salade *f* de crudités

mixed-up [mɪkst'ʌp] *adj* (*person*) désorienté(e), embrouillé(e)

mixer ['mɪksə^r] *n* (*for food*) batteur *m*, mixeur *m*; (*drink*) boisson gazeuse (*servant à couper un alcool*); (*person*): **he is a good ~** il est très sociable

mixer tap *n* (robinet *m*) mélangeur *m*

mixture ['mɪkstʃə^r] *n* assortiment *m*, mélange *m*; (*Med*) préparation *f*

mix-up ['mɪksʌp] *n*: **there was a ~** il y a eu confusion

MK *abbr* (*Brit Tech*) = **mark**

mk *abbr* = **mark**

mkt *abbr* = **market**

ml *abbr* (= *millilitre(s)*) ml

MLitt *n abbr* (= *Master of Literature, Master of Letters*) *titre universitaire*

MLR *n abbr* (*Brit*) = **minimum lending rate**

mm *abbr* (= *millimetre*) mm

MN *abbr* (*Brit*) = **Merchant Navy**; (*US*) = **Minnesota**

MO *n abbr* (*Med*) = **medical officer**; (*US inf*: = *modus operandi*) méthode *f* ▷ *abbr* (*US*) = **Missouri**

m.o. *abbr* = **money order**

moan [məun] *n* gémissement *m* ▷ *vi* gémir; (*inf*: *complain*): **to ~ (about)** se plaindre (de)

moaner ['məunə^r] *n* (*inf*) rouspéteur(-euse), râleur(-euse)

moaning ['məunɪŋ] *n* gémissements *mpl*

moat [məut] *n* fossé *m*, douves *fpl*

mob [mɔb] *n* foule *f*; (*disorderly*) cohue *f*; (*pej*): **the ~** la populace ▷ *vt* assaillir

mobile ['məubaɪl] *adj* mobile ▷ *n* (*Art*) mobile *m*; (*Brit inf*: *mobile phone*) (téléphone *m*) portable *m*, mobile *m*; **applicants must be ~** (*Brit*) les candidats devront être prêts à accepter tout déplacement

mobile home *n* caravane *f*

mobile phone *n* (téléphone *m*) portable *m*, mobile *m*

mobile shop *n* (*Brit*) camion *m* magasin

mobility [məu'bɪlɪtɪ] *n* mobilité *f*

mobilize ['məubɪlaɪz] *vt*, *vi* mobiliser

moccasin ['mɔkəsɪn] *n* mocassin *m*

mock [mɔk] *vt* ridiculiser; (*laugh at*) se moquer de ▷ *adj* faux (fausse); **mocks** *npl* (*Brit*: *Scol*) examens blancs

mockery ['mɔkərɪ] *n* moquerie *f*, raillerie *f*; **to make a ~ of** ridiculiser, tourner en dérision

mocking ['mɔkɪŋ] *adj* moqueur(-euse)

mockingbird ['mɔkɪŋbə:d] *n* moqueur *m*

mock-up ['mɔkʌp] *n* maquette *f*

MOD *n abbr* (*Brit*) = **Ministry of Defence**; *see* **defence**

mod [mɔd] *adj see* **convenience**

mod cons ['mɔd'kɔnz] *npl abbr* (*Brit*) = **modern conveniences**; *see* **convenience**

mode [məud] *n* mode *m*; (*of transport*) moyen *m*

model ['mɔdl] *n* modèle *m*; (*person: for fashion*) mannequin *m*; (: *for artist*) modèle ▷ *vt* (*with clay etc*) modeler ▷ *vi* travailler comme mannequin ▷ *adj* (*railway: toy*) modèle réduit *inv*; (*child, factory*) modèle; **to ~ clothes** présenter des vêtements; **to ~ o.s. on** imiter; **to ~ sb/sth on** modeler qn/qch sur

modem ['məudɛm] *n* modem *m*

moderate [*adj, n* 'mɔdərət, *vb* 'mɔdəreɪt] *adj* modéré(e); (*amount, change*) peu important(e) ▷ *n* (*Pol*) modéré(e) ▷ *vi* se modérer, se calmer ▷ *vt* modérer

moderately ['mɔdərətlɪ] *adv* (*act*) avec modération *or* mesure; (*expensive, difficult*) moyennement; (*pleased, happy*) raisonnablement, assez; **~ priced** à un prix raisonnable

moderation [mɔdə'reɪʃən] *n* modération *f*, mesure *f*; **in ~** à dose raisonnable, pris(e) *or*

pratiqué(e) modérément

moderator ['mɔdəreɪtə^r] *n* (*Rel*): **M~** président *m* (de l'Assemblée générale de l'Église presbytérienne); (*Pol*) modérateur *m*

modern ['mɔdən] *adj* moderne

modernization [mɔdənaɪ'zeɪʃən] *n* modernisation *f*

modernize ['mɔdənaɪz] *vt* moderniser

modern languages *npl* langues vivantes

modest ['mɔdɪst] *adj* modeste

modesty ['mɔdɪstɪ] *n* modestie *f*

modicum ['mɔdɪkəm] *n*: **a ~ of** un minimum de

modification [mɔdɪfɪ'keɪʃən] *n* modification *f*; **to make ~s** faire *or* apporter des modifications

modify ['mɔdɪfaɪ] *vt* modifier

modish ['məudɪʃ] *adj* à la mode

Mods [mɔdz] *n abbr* (*Brit*: = (*Honour*) *Moderations*) *premier examen universitaire* (*à Oxford*)

modular ['mɔdjulə^r] *adj* (*filing, unit*) modulaire

modulate ['mɔdjuleɪt] *vt* moduler

modulation [mɔdju'leɪʃən] *n* modulation *f*

module ['mɔdju:l] *n* module *m*

mogul ['məugl] *n* (*fig*) nabab *m*; (*Ski*) bosse *f*

MOH *n abbr* (*Brit*) = **Medical Officer of Health**

mohair ['məuhɛə^r] *n* mohair *m*

Mohammed [mə'hæmɛd] *n* Mahomet *m*

moist [mɔɪst] *adj* humide, moite

moisten ['mɔɪsn] *vt* humecter, mouiller légèrement

moisture ['mɔɪstʃə^r] *n* humidité *f*; (*on glass*) buée *f*

moisturize ['mɔɪstʃəraɪz] *vt* (*skin*) hydrater

moisturizer ['mɔɪstʃəraɪzə^r] *n* crème hydratante

molar ['məulə^r] *n* molaire *f*

molasses [məu'læsɪz] *n* mélasse *f*

mold *etc* [məuld] (*US*) = **mould** *etc*

Moldavia [mɔl'deɪvɪə], **Moldova** [mɔl'dəuvə] *n* Moldavie *f*

Moldavian [mɔl'deɪvɪən], **Moldovan** [mɔl'dəuvən] *adj* moldave

mole [məul] *n* (*animal, spy*) taupe *f*; (*spot*) grain *m* de beauté

molecule ['mɔlɪkju:l] *n* molécule *f*

molehill ['məulhɪl] *n* taupinière *f*

molest [məu'lɛst] *vt* (*assault sexually*) attenter à la pudeur de; (*attack*) molester; (*harass*) tracasser

mollusc ['mɔləsk] *n* mollusque *m*

mollycoddle ['mɔlɪkɔdl] *vt* chouchouter, couver

Molotov cocktail ['mɔlətɔf-] *n* cocktail *m* Molotov

molt [məult] *vi* (*US*) = **moult**

molten ['məultən] *adj* fondu(e); (*rock*) en fusion

mom [mɔm] *n* (*US*) = **mum**

moment ['məumənt] *n* moment *m*, instant *m*; (*importance*) importance *f*; **at the ~** en ce moment; **for the ~** pour l'instant; **in a ~** dans un instant; **"one ~ please"** (*Tel*) "ne quittez pas"

momentarily ['məuməntrɪlɪ] *adv* momentanément; (*US: soon*) bientôt

momentary ['məuməntərɪ] *adj* momentané(e), passager(-ère)

momentous [məu'mɛntəs] *adj* important(e), capital(e)

momentum [məu'mɛntəm] *n* élan *m*, vitesse acquise; (*fig*) dynamique *f*; **to gather** ~ prendre de la vitesse; (*fig*) gagner du terrain

mommy ['mɔmɪ] *n* (*US: mother*) maman *f*

Monaco ['mɔnəkəu] *n* Monaco *f*

monarch ['mɔnək] *n* monarque *m*

monarchist ['mɔnəkɪst] *n* monarchiste *m/f*

monarchy ['mɔnəkɪ] *n* monarchie *f*

monastery ['mɔnəstərɪ] *n* monastère *m*

monastic [mə'næstɪk] *adj* monastique

Monday ['mʌndɪ] *n* lundi *m*; *for phrases see also* **Tuesday**

monetarist ['mʌnɪtərɪst] *n* monétariste *m/f*

monetary ['mʌnɪtərɪ] *adj* monétaire

money ['mʌnɪ] *n* argent *m*; **to make** ~ (*person*) gagner de l'argent; (*business*) rapporter; **I've got no ~ left** je n'ai plus d'argent, je n'ai plus un sou

money belt *n* ceinture-portefeuille *f*

moneyed ['mʌnɪd] *adj* riche

moneylender ['mʌnɪlɛndə^r] *n* prêteur(-euse)

moneymaker ['mʌnɪmeɪkə^r] *n* (*Brit: col: business*) affaire lucrative

moneymaking ['mʌnɪmeɪkɪŋ] *adj* lucratif(-ive), qui rapporte (de l'argent)

money market *n* marché financier

money order *n* mandat *m*

money-spinner ['mʌnɪspɪnə^r] *n* (*inf*) mine *f* d'or (*fig*)

money supply *n* masse *f* monétaire

Mongol ['mɔŋgəl] *n* Mongol(e); (*Ling*) mongol *m*

mongol ['mɔŋgəl] *adj, n* (*Med*) mongolien(ne)

Mongolia [mɔŋ'gəulɪə] *n* Mongolie *f*

Mongolian [mɔŋ'gəulɪən] *adj* mongol(e) ▷ *n* Mongol(e); (*Ling*) mongol *m*

mongoose ['mɔŋguːs] *n* mangouste *f*

mongrel ['mʌŋgrəl] *n* (*dog*) bâtard *m*

monitor ['mɔnɪtə^r] *n* (*TV, Comput*) écran *m*, moniteur *m*; (*Brit Scol*) chef *m* de classe; (*US Scol*) surveillant *m* (d'examen) ▷ *vt* contrôler; (*foreign station*) être à l'écoute de; (*progress*) suivre de près

monk [mʌŋk] *n* moine *m*

monkey ['mʌŋkɪ] *n* singe *m*

monkey nut *n* (*Brit*) cacahuète *f*

monkey wrench *n* clé *f* à molette

mono ['mɔnəu] *adj* mono *inv*

mono... ['mɔnəu] *prefix* mono...

monochrome ['mɔnəkrəum] *adj* monochrome

monocle ['mɔnəkl] *n* monocle *m*

monogamous [mɔ'nɔgəməs] *adj* monogame

monogamy [mɔ'nɔgəmɪ] *n* monogamie *f*

monogram ['mɔnəgræm] *n* monogramme *m*

monolith ['mɔnəlɪθ] *n* monolithe *m*

monologue ['mɔnəlɔg] *n* monologue *m*

monoplane ['mɔnəpleɪn] *n* monoplan *m*

monopolize [mə'nɔpəlaɪz] *vt* monopoliser

monopoly [mə'nɔpəlɪ] *n* monopole *m*; **Monopolies and Mergers Commission** (*Brit*) *commission britannique d'enquête sur les monopoles*

monorail ['mɔnəureɪl] *n* monorail *m*

monosodium glutamate [mɔnə'səudɪəm 'gluː təmeɪt] *n* glutamate *m* de sodium

monosyllabic [mɔnəsɪ'læbɪk] *adj* monosyllabique; (*person*) laconique

monosyllable ['mɔnəsɪləbl] *n* monosyllabe *m*

monotone ['mɔnətəun] *n* ton *m* (*or* voix *f*) monocorde; **to speak in a** ~ parler sur un ton monocorde

monotonous [mə'nɔtənəs] *adj* monotone

monotony [mə'nɔtənɪ] *n* monotonie *f*

monoxide [mɔ'nɔksaɪd] *n*: **carbon** ~ oxyde *m* de carbone

monsoon [mɔn'suːn] *n* mousson *f*

monster ['mɔnstə^r] *n* monstre *m*

monstrosity [mɔns'trɔsɪtɪ] *n* monstruosité *f*, atrocité *f*

monstrous ['mɔnstrəs] *adj* (*huge*) gigantesque; (*atrocious*) monstrueux(-euse), atroce

Mont. *abbr* (*US*) = **Montana**

montage [mɔn'taːʒ] *n* montage *m*

Mont Blanc [mɔ̃blã] *n* Mont Blanc *m*

month [mʌnθ] *n* mois *m*; **every** ~ tous les mois; **300 dollars a** ~ 300 dollars par mois

monthly ['mʌnθlɪ] *adj* mensuel(le) ▷ *adv* mensuellement ▷ *n* (*magazine*) mensuel *m*, publication mensuelle; **twice** ~ deux fois par mois

Montreal [mɔntrɪ'ɔːl] *n* Montréal

monument ['mɔnjumənt] *n* monument *m*

monumental [mɔnju'mɛntl] *adj* monumental(e)

monumental mason *n* marbrier *m*

moo [muː] *vi* meugler, beugler

mood [muːd] *n* humeur *f*, disposition *f*; **to be in a good/bad** ~ être de bonne/mauvaise humeur; **to be in the** ~ **for** être d'humeur à, avoir envie de

moody ['muːdɪ] *adj* (*variable*) d'humeur changeante, lunatique; (*sullen*) morose, maussade

moon [muːn] *n* lune *f*

moonbeam ['muːnbiːm] *n* rayon *m* de lune

moon landing *n* alunissage *m*

moonlight ['muːnlaɪt] *n* clair *m* de lune ▷ *vi* travailler au noir

moonlighting ['muːnlaɪtɪŋ] *n* travail *m* au noir

moonlit ['muːnlɪt] *adj* éclairé(e) par la lune; **a** ~ **night** une nuit de lune

moonshot ['muːnʃɔt] *n* (*Space*) tir *m* lunaire

moonstruck ['muːnstrʌk] *adj* fou (folle), dérangé(e)

moony ['muːnɪ] *adj*: **to have** ~ **eyes** avoir l'air dans la lune *or* rêveur

Moor [muə^r] *n* Maure (Mauresque)

moor [muə^r] *n* lande *f* ▷ *vt* (*ship*) amarrer ▷ *vi* mouiller

moorings ['muərɪŋz] *npl* (*chains*) amarres *fpl*; (*place*) mouillage *m*

Moorish ['muərɪʃ] *adj* maure, mauresque

moorland ['muələnd] *n* lande *f*

moose [muːs] *n* (*pl inv*) élan *m*

moot [muːt] *vt* soulever ▷ *adj*: ~ **point** point *m* discutable

mop [mɔp] n balai m à laver; (for dishes) lavette f à vaisselle ▷ vt éponger, essuyer; ~ **of hair** tignasse f
  ▶ **mop up** vt éponger

mope [məup] vi avoir le cafard, se morfondre
  ▶ **mope about, mope around** vi broyer du noir, se morfondre

moped ['məupɛd] n cyclomoteur m

MOR adj abbr (Mus: = middle-of-the-road) tous publics

moral ['mɔrl] adj moral(e) ▷ n morale f; **morals** npl moralité f

morale [mɔ'rɑːl] n moral m

morality [mə'rælɪtɪ] n moralité f

moralize ['mɔrəlaɪz] vi: **to ~ (about)** moraliser (sur)

morally ['mɔrəlɪ] adv moralement

moral victory n victoire morale

morass [mə'ræs] n marais m, marécage m

moratorium [mɔrə'tɔːrɪəm] n moratoire m

morbid ['mɔːbɪd] adj morbide

⭕ KEYWORD

more [mɔːr] adj **1** (greater in number etc) plus (de), davantage (de); **more people/work (than)** plus de gens/de travail (que)
2 (additional) encore (de); **do you want (some) more tea?** voulez-vous encore du thé?; **is there any more wine?** reste-t-il du vin?; **I have no** or **I don't have any more money** je n'ai plus d'argent; **it'll take a few more weeks** ça prendra encore quelques semaines
▷ pron plus, davantage; **more than 10** plus de 10; **it cost more than we expected** cela a coûté plus que prévu; **I want more** j'en veux plus or davantage; **is there any more?** est-ce qu'il en reste?; **there's no more** il n'y en a plus; **a little more** un peu plus; **many/much more** beaucoup plus, bien davantage
▷ adv plus; **more dangerous/easily (than)** plus dangereux/facilement (que); **more and more expensive** de plus en plus cher; **more or less** plus ou moins; **more than ever** plus que jamais; **once more** encore une fois, une fois de plus; **and what's more ...** et de plus ..., et qui plus est ...

moreover [mɔː'rəuvər] adv de plus

morgue [mɔːg] n morgue f

MORI ['mɔːrɪ] n abbr (Brit: = Market & Opinion Research Institute) institut de sondage

moribund ['mɔrɪbʌnd] adj moribond(e)

morning ['mɔːnɪŋ] n matin m; (as duration) matinée f ▷ cpd matinal(e); (paper) du matin; **in the ~** le matin; **7 o'clock in the ~** 7 heures du matin; **this ~** ce matin

morning-after pill ['mɔːnɪŋ'ɑːftə-] n pilule f du lendemain

morning sickness n nausées matinales

Moroccan [mə'rɔkən] adj marocain(e) ▷ n

Marocain(e)

Morocco [mə'rɔkəu] n Maroc m

moron ['mɔːrɔn] n idiot(e), minus m/f

moronic [mə'rɔnɪk] adj idiot(e), imbécile

morose [mə'rəus] adj morose, maussade

morphine ['mɔːfiːn] n morphine f

morris dancing ['mɔrɪs-] n (Brit) danses folkloriques anglaises

Morse [mɔːs] n (also: **Morse code**) morse m

morsel ['mɔːsl] n bouchée f

mortal ['mɔːtl] adj, n mortel(le)

mortality [mɔː'tælɪtɪ] n mortalité f

mortality rate n (taux m de) mortalité f

mortar ['mɔːtər] n mortier m

mortgage ['mɔːgɪdʒ] n hypothèque f; (loan) prêt m (or crédit m) hypothécaire ▷ vt hypothéquer; **to take out a ~** prendre une hypothèque, faire un emprunt

mortgage company n (US) société f de crédit immobilier

mortgagee [mɔːgə'dʒiː] n prêteur(-euse) (sur hypothèque)

mortgagor ['mɔːgədʒər] n emprunteur(-euse) (sur hypothèque)

mortician [mɔː'tɪʃən] n (US) entrepreneur m de pompes funèbres

mortified ['mɔːtɪfaɪd] adj mort(e) de honte

mortise lock ['mɔːtɪs-] n serrure encastrée

mortuary ['mɔːtjuərɪ] n morgue f

mosaic [məu'zeɪɪk] n mosaïque f

Moscow ['mɔskəu] n Moscou

Moslem ['mɔzləm] adj, n = **Muslim**

mosque [mɔsk] n mosquée f

mosquito (pl **-es**) [mɔs'kiːtəu] n moustique m

mosquito net n moustiquaire f

moss [mɔs] n mousse f

mossy ['mɔsɪ] adj moussu(e)

most [məust] adj (majority of) la plupart de; (greatest amount of) le plus de ▷ pron la plupart ▷ adv le plus; (very) très, extrêmement; **the ~** le plus; **~ fish** la plupart des poissons; **the ~ beautiful woman in the world** la plus belle femme du monde; **~ of** (with plural) la plupart de; (with singular) la plus grande partie de; **~ of them** la plupart d'entre eux; **~ of the time** la plupart du temps; **I saw ~** (a lot but not all) j'en ai vu la plupart; (more than anyone else) c'est moi qui en ai vu le plus; **at the (very) ~** au plus; **to make the ~ of** profiter au maximum de

mostly ['məustlɪ] adv (chiefly) surtout, principalement; (usually) généralement

MOT n abbr (Brit) = **Ministry of Transport**; **the ~ (test)** visite technique (annuelle) obligatoire des véhicules à moteur

motel [məu'tɛl] n motel m

moth [mɔθ] n papillon m de nuit; (in clothes) mite f

mothball ['mɔθbɔːl] n boule f de naphtaline

moth-eaten ['mɔθiːtn] adj mité(e)

mother ['mʌðər] n mère f ▷ vt (pamper, protect) dorloter

mother board n (Comput) carte-mère f

motherhood ['mʌðəhud] n maternité f
mother-in-law ['mʌðərɪnlɔ:] n belle-mère f
motherly ['mʌðəlɪ] adj maternel(le)
mother-of-pearl ['mʌðərəv'pə:l] n nacre f
Mother's Day n fête f des Mères
mother's help n aide f or auxiliaire f familiale
mother-to-be ['mʌðətə'bi:] n future maman
mother tongue n langue maternelle
mothproof ['mɔθpru:f] adj traité(e) à l'antimite
motion ['məuʃən] n mouvement m; (gesture) geste m; (at meeting) motion f; (Brit: also: **bowel motion**) selles fpl ▷ vt, vi: **to ~ (to) sb to do** faire signe à qn de faire; **to be in ~** (vehicle) être en marche; **to set in ~** mettre en marche; **to go through the ~s of doing sth** (fig) faire qch machinalement or sans conviction
motionless ['məuʃənlɪs] adj immobile, sans mouvement
motion picture n film m
motivate ['məutɪveɪt] vt motiver
motivated ['məutɪveɪtɪd] adj motivé(e)
motivation [məutɪ'veɪʃən] n motivation f
motive ['məutɪv] n motif m, mobile m ▷ adj moteur(-trice); **from the best (of) ~s** avec les meilleures intentions (du monde)
motley ['mɔtlɪ] adj hétéroclite; bigarré(e), bariolé(e)
motor ['məutər] n moteur m; (Brit inf: vehicle) auto f ▷ adj moteur(-trice)
motorbike ['məutəbaɪk] n moto f
motorboat ['məutəbəut] n bateau m à moteur
motorcade ['məutəkeɪd] n cortège m d'automobiles or de voitures
motorcar ['məutəkɑː] n (Brit) automobile f
motorcoach ['məutəkəutʃ] n (Brit) car m
motorcycle ['məutəsaɪkl] n moto f
motorcycle racing n course f de motos
motorcyclist ['məutəsaɪklɪst] n motocycliste m/f
motoring ['məutərɪŋ] (Brit) n tourisme m automobile ▷ adj (accident) de voiture, de la route; ~ **holiday** vacances fpl en voiture; ~ **offence** infraction f au code de la route
motorist ['məutərɪst] n automobiliste m/f
motorize ['məutəraɪz] vt motoriser
motor mechanic n mécanicien m garagiste
motor oil n huile f de graissage
motor racing n (Brit) course f automobile
motor scooter n scooter m
motor trade n secteur m de l'automobile
motor vehicle n véhicule m automobile
motorway ['məutəweɪ] n (Brit) autoroute f
mottled ['mɔtld] adj tacheté(e), marbré(e)
motto (pl **-es**) ['mɔtəu] n devise f
mould, (US) **mold** [məuld] n moule m; (mildew) moisissure f ▷ vt mouler, modeler; (fig) façonner
moulder, (US) **molder** ['məuldər] vi (decay) moisir
moulding, (US) **mold** ['məuldɪŋ] n (Archit) moulure f

mouldy, (US) **moldy** ['məuldɪ] adj moisi(e); (smell) de moisi
moult, (US) **molt** [məult] vi muer
mound [maund] n monticule m, tertre m
mount [maunt] n (hill) mont m, montagne f; (horse) monture f; (for picture) carton m de montage; (for jewel etc) monture ▷ vt monter; (horse) monter à; (bike) monter sur; (exhibition) organiser, monter; (picture) monter sur carton; (stamp) coller dans un album ▷ vi (inflation, tension) augmenter
▶ **mount up** vi s'élever, monter; (bills, problems, savings) s'accumuler
mountain ['mauntɪn] n montagne f ▷ cpd de (la) montagne; **to make a ~ out of a molehill** (fig) se faire une montagne d'un rien
mountain bike n VTT m, vélo m tout terrain
mountaineer [mauntɪ'nɪər] n alpiniste m/f
mountaineering [mauntɪ'nɪərɪŋ] n alpinisme m; **to go ~** faire de l'alpinisme
mountainous ['mauntɪnəs] adj montagneux(-euse)
mountain range n chaîne f de montagnes
mountain rescue team n colonne f de secours
mountainside ['mauntɪnsaɪd] n flanc m or versant m de la montagne
mounted ['mauntɪd] adj monté(e)
mourn [mɔ:n] vt pleurer ▷ vi: **to ~ for sb** pleurer qn; **to ~ for sth** se lamenter sur qch
mourner ['mɔ:nər] n parent(e) or ami(e) du défunt; personne f en deuil or venue rendre hommage au défunt
mourning ['mɔ:nɪŋ] n deuil m ▷ cpd (dress) de deuil; **in ~** en deuil
mouse (pl **mice**) [maus, maɪs] n (also Comput) souris f
mouse mat n (Comput) tapis m de souris
mousetrap ['maustræp] n souricière f
moussaka [mu'sɑ:kə] n moussaka f
mousse [mu:s] n mousse f
moustache, (US) **mustache** [məs'tɑ:ʃ] n moustache(s) f(pl)
mousy ['mausɪ] adj (person) effacé(e); (hair) d'un châtain terne
mouth [mauθ, pl mauðz] n bouche f; (of dog, cat) gueule f; (of river) embouchure f; (of hole, cave) ouverture f; (of bottle) goulot m; (opening) orifice m
mouthful ['mauθful] n bouchée f
mouth organ n harmonica m
mouthpiece ['mauθpi:s] n (of musical instrument) bec m, embouchure f; (spokesperson) porte-parole m inv
mouth-to-mouth ['mauθtə'mauθ] adj: ~ **resuscitation** bouche à bouche m
mouthwash ['mauθwɔʃ] n eau f dentifrice
mouth-watering ['mauθwɔ:tərɪŋ] adj qui met l'eau à la bouche
movable ['mu:vəbl] adj mobile
move [mu:v] n (movement) mouvement m; (in game) coup m; (: turn to play) tour m; (change of house) déménagement m; (change of job)

changement m d'emploi ▷ vt déplacer, bouger; (emotionally) émouvoir; (Pol: resolution etc) proposer ▷ vi (gen) bouger, remuer; (traffic) circuler; (also: **move house**) déménager; (in game) jouer; **can you ~ your car, please?** pouvez-vous déplacer votre voiture, s'il vous plaît?; **to ~ towards** se diriger vers; **to ~ sb to do sth** pousser or inciter qn à faire qch; **to get a ~ on** se dépêcher, se remuer

▶ **move about, move around** vi (fidget) remuer; (travel) voyager, se déplacer

▶ **move along** vi se pousser

▶ **move away** vi s'en aller, s'éloigner

▶ **move back** vi revenir, retourner

▶ **move forward** vi avancer ▷ vt avancer; (people) faire avancer

▶ **move in** vi (to a house) emménager; (police, soldiers) intervenir

▶ **move off** vi s'éloigner, s'en aller

▶ **move on** vi se remettre en route ▷ vt (onlookers) faire circuler

▶ **move out** vi (of house) déménager

▶ **move over** vi se pousser, se déplacer

▶ **move up** vi avancer; (employee) avoir de l'avancement; (pupil) passer dans la classe supérieure

moveable ['muːvəbl] adj = **movable**

movement ['muːvmənt] n mouvement m; **~ (of the bowels)** (Med) selles fpl

mover ['muːvə^r] n auteur m d'une proposition

movie ['muːvɪ] n film m; **movies** npl: **the ~s** le cinéma

movie camera n caméra f

moviegoer ['muːvɪɡəʊə^r] n (US) cinéphile m/f

movie theater (US) n cinéma m

moving ['muːvɪŋ] adj en mouvement; (touching) émouvant(e) ▷ n (US) déménagement m

mow (pt **-ed**, pp **-ed** or **-n**) [məʊ, -d, -n] vt faucher; (lawn) tondre

▶ **mow down** vt faucher

mower ['məʊə^r] n (also: **lawnmower**) tondeuse f à gazon

mown [məʊn] pp of **mow**

Mozambique [məʊzəm'biːk] n Mozambique m

MP n abbr (= Military Police) PM; (Brit) = **Member of Parliament**; (Canada) = **Mounted Police**

MP3 n mp3 m

MP3 player n baladeur m numérique, lecteur m mp3

mpg n abbr (= miles per gallon) (30 mpg = 9,4 l. aux 100 km)

m.p.h. abbr (= miles per hour) (60 mph = 96 km/h)

MPhil n abbr (US: = Master of Philosophy) titre universitaire

MPS n abbr (Brit) = **Member of the Pharmaceutical Society**

Mr, (US) **Mr.** ['mɪstə^r] n: **Mr X** Monsieur X, M. X

MRC n abbr (Brit: = Medical Research Council) conseil de la recherche médicale

MRCP n abbr (Brit) = **Member of the Royal College of Physicians**

MRCS n abbr (Brit) = **Member of the Royal College of Surgeons**

MRCVS n abbr (Brit) = **Member of the Royal College of Veterinary Surgeons**

Mrs, (US) **Mrs.** ['mɪsɪz] n: **~ X** Madame X, Mme X

MS n abbr (= manuscript) ms; (= multiple sclerosis) SEP f; (US: = Master of Science) titre universitaire ▷ abbr (US) = **Mississippi**

Ms, (US) **Ms.** [mɪz] n (Miss or Mrs): **Ms X** Madame X, Mme X; voir article

⬤ **M s**

⬤
⬤ Ms est un titre utilisé à la place de "Mrs"
⬤ (Mme) ou de "Miss" (Mlle) pour éviter la
⬤ distinction traditionnelle entre femmes
⬤ mariées et femmes non mariées.

MSA n abbr (US: = Master of Science in Agriculture) titre universitaire

MSc n abbr = **Master of Science**

MSG n abbr = **monosodium glutamate**

MSP n abbr (= Member of the Scottish Parliament) député m au Parlement écossais

MST abbr (US: = Mountain Standard Time) heure d'hiver des Montagnes Rocheuses

MT n abbr (= machine translation) TM ▷ abbr (US) = **Montana**

Mt abbr (Geo: = mount) Mt

mth abbr (= month) m

MTV n abbr = **music television**

much [mʌtʃ] adj beaucoup de ▷ adv, n or pron beaucoup; **~ milk** beaucoup de lait; **we don't have ~ time** nous n'avons pas beaucoup de temps; **how ~ is it?** combien est-ce que ça coûte?; **it's not ~** ce n'est pas beaucoup; **too ~** trop (de); **so ~** tant (de); **I like it very/so ~** j'aime beaucoup/tellement ça; **as ~ as** autant de; **thank you very ~** merci beaucoup; **that's ~ better** c'est beaucoup mieux; **~ to my amazement ...** à mon grand étonnement ...

muck [mʌk] n (mud) boue f; (dirt) ordures fpl

▶ **muck about** vi (inf) faire l'imbécile; (: waste time) traînasser; (: tinker) bricoler; tripoter

▶ **muck in** vi (Brit inf) donner un coup de main

▶ **muck out** vt (stable) nettoyer

▶ **muck up** vt (inf: ruin) gâcher, esquinter; (: dirty) salir; (: exam, interview) se planter à

muckraking ['mʌkreɪkɪŋ] n (fig: inf) déterrement m d'ordures

mucky ['mʌkɪ] adj (dirty) boueux(-euse), sale

mucus ['mjuːkəs] n mucus m

mud [mʌd] n boue f

muddle ['mʌdl] n (mess) pagaille f, fouillis m; (mix-up) confusion f ▷ vt (also: **muddle up**) brouiller, embrouiller; **to be in a ~** (person) ne plus savoir où l'on en est; **to get in a ~** (while explaining etc) s'embrouiller

▶ **muddle along** vi aller son chemin tant bien que mal

▶ **muddle through** vi se débrouiller

muddle-headed [mʌdl'hɛdɪd] adj (person) à l'esprit embrouillé or confus, dans le brouillard

muddy ['mʌdɪ] *adj* boueux(-euse)

mud flats *npl* plage *f* de vase

mudguard ['mʌdgɑːd] *n* garde-boue *m inv*

mudpack ['mʌdpæk] *n* masque *m* de beauté

mud-slinging ['mʌdslɪŋɪŋ] *n* médisance *f*, dénigrement *m*

muesli ['mjuːzlɪ] *n* muesli *m*

muff [mʌf] *n* manchon *m* ▷ *vt* (*inf*: *shot, catch etc*) rater, louper; **to ~ it** rater *or* louper son coup

muffin ['mʌfɪn] *n* (*roll*) petit pain rond et plat; (*cake*) petit gâteau au chocolat ou aux fruits

muffle ['mʌfl] *vt* (*sound*) assourdir, étouffer; (*against cold*) emmitoufler

muffled ['mʌfld] *adj* étouffé(e), voilé(e)

muffler ['mʌflər] *n* (*scarf*) cache-nez *m inv*; (*US Aut*) silencieux *m*

mufti ['mʌftɪ] *n*: **in ~** en civil

mug [mʌg] *n* (*cup*) tasse *f* (*sans soucoupe*); (: *for beer*) chope *f*; (*inf*: *face*) bouille *f*; (: *fool*) poire *f* ▷ *vt* (*assault*) agresser; **it's a ~'s game** (*Brit*) c'est bon pour les imbéciles

   ▶ **mug up** *vt* (*Brit inf*: *also*: **mug up on**) bosser, bûcher

mugger ['mʌgər] *n* agresseur *m*

mugging ['mʌgɪŋ] *n* agression *f*

muggins ['mʌgɪnz] *n* (*inf*) ma pomme

muggy ['mʌgɪ] *adj* lourd(e), moite

mug shot *n* (*inf*: *Police*) photo *f* de criminel; (: *gen*: *photo*) photo d'identité

mulatto (*pl* **-es**) [mjuːˈlætəu] *n* mulâtre(-esse)

mulberry ['mʌlbrɪ] *n* (*fruit*) mûre *f*; (*tree*) mûrier *m*

mule [mjuːl] *n* mule *f*

mull [mʌl]: **to ~ over** *vt* réfléchir à, ruminer

mulled [mʌld] *adj*: **~ wine** vin chaud

multi... ['mʌltɪ] *prefix* multi...

multi-access ['mʌltɪˈæksɛs] *adj* (*Comput*) à accès multiple

multicoloured, (*US*) **multicolored** ['mʌltɪkʌləd] *adj* multicolore

multifarious [mʌltɪˈfɛərɪəs] *adj* divers(es), varié(e)

multilateral [mʌltɪˈlætərl] *adj* (*Pol*) multilatéral(e)

multi-level ['mʌltɪlɛvl] *adj* (*US*) = **multistorey**

multimedia ['mʌltɪˈmiːdɪə] *adj* multimédia *inv*

multimillionaire [mʌltɪmɪljəˈnɛər] *n* milliardaire *m/f*

multinational [mʌltɪˈnæʃənl] *n* multinationale *f* ▷ *adj* multinational(e)

multiple ['mʌltɪpl] *adj* multiple ▷ *n* multiple *m*; (*Brit*: *also*: **multiple store**) magasin *m* à succursales (multiples)

multiple choice, multiple choice test *n* QCM *m*, questionnaire *m* à choix multiple

multiple crash *n* carambolage *m*

multiple sclerosis [-sklɪˈrəusɪs] *n* sclérose *f* en plaques

multiplex ['mʌltɪplɛks], **multiplex cinema** *n* (cinéma *m*) multisalles *m*

multiplication [mʌltɪplɪˈkeɪʃən] *n* multiplication *f*

multiplication table *n* table *f* de multiplication

multiplicity [mʌltɪˈplɪsɪtɪ] *n* multiplicité *f*

multiply ['mʌltɪplaɪ] *vt* multiplier ▷ *vi* se multiplier

multiracial [mʌltɪˈreɪʃl] *adj* multiracial(e)

multistorey ['mʌltɪˈstɔːrɪ] *adj* (*Brit*: *building*) à étages; (: *car park*) à étages *or* niveaux multiples

multitude ['mʌltɪtjuːd] *n* multitude *f*

mum [mʌm] *n* (*Brit*) maman *f* ▷ *adj*: **to keep ~** ne pas souffler mot; **~'s the word!** motus et bouche cousue!

mumble ['mʌmbl] *vt*, *vi* marmotter, marmonner

mumbo jumbo ['mʌmbəu-] *n* (*inf*) baragouin *m*, charabia *m*

mummify ['mʌmɪfaɪ] *vt* momifier

mummy ['mʌmɪ] *n* (*Brit*: *mother*) maman *f*; (*embalmed*) momie *f*

mumps [mʌmps] *n* oreillons *mpl*

munch [mʌntʃ] *vt*, *vi* mâcher

mundane [mʌnˈdeɪn] *adj* banal(e), terre à terre *inv*

municipal [mjuːˈnɪsɪpl] *adj* municipal(e)

municipality [mjuːnɪsɪˈpælɪtɪ] *n* municipalité *f*

munitions [mjuːˈnɪʃənz] *npl* munitions *fpl*

mural ['mjuərl] *n* peinture murale

murder ['məːdər] *n* meurtre *m*, assassinat *m* ▷ *vt* assassiner; **to commit ~** commettre un meurtre

murderer ['məːdərər] *n* meurtrier *m*, assassin *m*

murderess ['məːdərɪs] *n* meurtrière *f*

murderous ['məːdərəs] *adj* meurtrier(-ière)

murk [məːk] *n* obscurité *f*

murky ['məːkɪ] *adj* sombre, ténébreux(-euse); (*water*) trouble

murmur ['məːmər] *n* murmure *m* ▷ *vt*, *vi* murmurer; **heart ~** (*Med*) souffle *m* au cœur

MusB, MusBac *n abbr* (= *Bachelor of Music*) titre universitaire

muscle ['mʌsl] *n* muscle *m*; (*fig*) force *f*
   ▶ **muscle in** *vi* s'imposer, s'immiscer

muscular ['mʌskjulər] *adj* musculaire; (*person, arm*) musclé(e)

muscular dystrophy *n* dystrophie *f* musculaire

MusD, MusDoc *n abbr* (= *Doctor of Music*) titre universitaire

muse [mjuːz] *vi* méditer, songer ▷ *n* muse *f*

museum [mjuːˈzɪəm] *n* musée *m*

mush [mʌʃ] *n* bouillie *f*; (*pej*) sentimentalité *f* à l'eau de rose

mushroom ['mʌʃrum] *n* champignon *m* ▷ *vi* (*fig*) pousser comme un (*or* des) champignon(s)

mushy ['mʌʃɪ] *adj* (*vegetables, fruit*) en bouillie; (*movie etc*) à l'eau de rose

music ['mjuːzɪk] *n* musique *f*

musical ['mjuːzɪkl] *adj* musical(e); (*person*) musicien(ne) ▷ *n* (*show*) comédie musicale

musical box *n* = **music box**

musical chairs *npl* chaises musicales; (*fig*): **to play ~** faire des permutations

musical instrument *n* instrument *m* de musique

music box n boîte f à musique
music centre n chaîne compacte
music hall n music-hall m
musician [mjuː'zɪʃən] n musicien(ne)
music stand n pupitre m à musique
musk [mʌsk] n musc m
musket ['mʌskɪt] n mousquet m
muskrat ['mʌskræt] n rat musqué
musk rose n (Bot) rose f muscade
Muslim ['mʌzlɪm] adj, n musulman(e)
muslin ['mʌzlɪn] n mousseline f
musquash ['mʌskwɔʃ] n loutre f; (fur) rat m
  d'Amérique, ondatra m
mussel ['mʌsl] n moule f
must [mʌst] aux vb (obligation): **I ~ do it** je dois le
  faire, il faut que je le fasse; (probability): **he ~ be
  there by now** il doit y être maintenant, il y est
  probablement maintenant; (suggestion,
  invitation): **you ~ come and see me** il faut que
  vous veniez me voir ▷ n nécessité f, impératif
  m; **it's a ~** c'est indispensable; **I ~ have made a
  mistake** j'ai dû me tromper
mustache ['mʌstæʃ] n (US) = **moustache**
mustard ['mʌstəd] n moutarde f
mustard gas n ypérite f, gaz m moutarde
muster ['mʌstər] vt rassembler; (also: **muster
  up**: strength, courage) rassembler
mustiness ['mʌstɪnɪs] n goût m de moisi;
  odeur f de moisi or de renfermé
mustn't ['mʌsnt] = **must not**
musty ['mʌstɪ] adj qui sent le moisi or le
  renfermé
mutant ['mjuːtənt] adj mutant(e) ▷ n mutant m
mutate [mjuː'teɪt] vi subir une mutation
mutation [mjuː'teɪʃən] n mutation f
mute [mjuːt] adj, n muet(te)
muted ['mjuːtɪd] adj (noise) sourd(e), assourdi(e);
  (criticism) voilé(e); (Mus) en sourdine; (: trumpet)
  bouché(e)
mutilate ['mjuːtɪleɪt] vt mutiler

mutilation [mjuːtɪ'leɪʃən] n mutilation f
mutinous ['mjuːtɪnəs] adj (troops) mutiné(e);
  (attitude) rebelle
mutiny ['mjuːtɪnɪ] n mutinerie f ▷ vi se
  mutiner
mutter ['mʌtər] vt, vi marmonner, marmotter
mutton ['mʌtn] n mouton m
mutual ['mjuːtʃuəl] adj mutuel(le), réciproque;
  (benefit, interest) commun(e)
mutually ['mjuːtʃuəlɪ] adv mutuellement,
  réciproquement
Muzak® ['mjuːzæk] n (often pej) musique f
  d'ambiance
muzzle ['mʌzl] n museau m; (protective device)
  muselière f; (of gun) gueule f ▷ vt museler
MVP n abbr (US Sport) = **most valuable player**
MW abbr (= medium wave) PO
my [maɪ] adj mon (ma), mes pl; **my house/car/
  gloves** ma maison/ma voiture/mes gants; **I've
  washed my hair/cut my finger** je me suis lavé
  les cheveux/coupé le doigt; **is this my pen or
  yours?** c'est mon stylo ou c'est le vôtre?
Myanmar ['maɪænmɑːr] n Myanmar m
myopic [maɪ'ɔpɪk] adj myope
myriad ['mɪrɪəd] n myriade f
myself [maɪ'sɛlf] pron (reflexive) me; (emphatic)
  moi-même; (after prep) moi; see also **oneself**
mysterious [mɪs'tɪərɪəs] adj mystérieux(-euse)
mystery ['mɪstərɪ] n mystère m
mystery story n roman m à suspense
mystic ['mɪstɪk] n mystique m/f ▷ adj (mysterious)
  ésotérique
mystical ['mɪstɪkl] adj mystique
mystify ['mɪstɪfaɪ] vt (deliberately) mystifier;
  (puzzle) ébahir
mystique [mɪs'tiːk] n mystique f
myth [mɪθ] n mythe m
mythical ['mɪθɪkl] adj mythique
mythological [mɪθə'lɔdʒɪkl] adj mythologique
mythology [mɪ'θɔlədʒɪ] n mythologie f

Nn

N, n [ɛn] *n* (*letter*) N, n *m*; **N for Nellie**, (*US*) **N for Nan** N comme Nicolas

N *abbr* (= *north*) N

NA *n abbr* (*US*: = *Narcotics Anonymous*) *association d'aide aux drogués*; (*US*) = **National Academy**

n/a *abbr* (= *not applicable*) n.a.; (*Comm etc*) = **no account**

NAACP *n abbr* (*US*) = **National Association for the Advancement of Colored People**

NAAFI ['næfɪ] *n abbr* (*Brit*: = *Navy, Army & Air Force Institute*) *organisme responsable des magasins et cantines de l'armée*

nab [næb] *vt* (*inf*) pincer, attraper

NACU *n abbr* (*US*) = **National Association of Colleges and Universities**

nadir ['neɪdɪəʳ] *n* (*Astronomy*) nadir *m*; (*fig*) fond *m*, point *m* extrême

naff [næf] (*Brit: inf*) *adj* nul(le)

nag [næg] *vt* (*scold*) être toujours après, reprendre sans arrêt ▷ *n* (*pej: horse*) canasson *m*; (*person*): **she's an awful ~** elle est constamment après lui (*or eux etc*), elle est très casse-pieds

nagging ['nægɪŋ] *adj* (*doubt, pain*) persistant(e) ▷ *n* remarques continuelles

nail [neɪl] *n* (*human*) ongle *m*; (*metal*) clou *m* ▷ *vt* clouer; **to ~ sth to sth** clouer qch à qch; **to ~ sb down to a date/price** contraindre qn à accepter *or* donner une date/un prix; **to pay cash on the ~** (*Brit*) payer rubis sur l'ongle

nailbrush ['neɪlbrʌʃ] *n* brosse *f* à ongles

nailfile ['neɪlfaɪl] *n* lime *f* à ongles

nail polish *n* vernis *m* à ongles

nail polish remover *n* dissolvant *m*

nail scissors *npl* ciseaux *mpl* à ongles

nail varnish *n* (*Brit*) = **nail polish**

Nairobi [naɪ'rəubɪ] *n* Nairobi

naïve [naɪ'iːv] *adj* naïf(-ive)

naïveté [naɪ'iːvteɪ], **naivety** [naɪ'iːvɪtɪ] *n* naïveté *f*

naked ['neɪkɪd] *adj* nu(e); **with the ~ eye** à l'œil nu

nakedness ['neɪkɪdnɪs] *n* nudité *f*

NAM *n abbr* (*US*) = **National Association of Manufacturers**

name [neɪm] *n* nom *m*; (*reputation*) réputation *f* ▷ *vt* nommer; (*identify: accomplice etc*) citer; (*price,*

date) fixer, donner; **by ~** par son nom; de nom; **in the ~ of** au nom de; **what's your ~?** comment vous appelez-vous?, quel est votre nom?; **my ~ is Peter** je m'appelle Peter; **to take sb's ~ and address** relever l'identité de qn *or* les nom et adresse de qn; **to make a ~ for o.s.** se faire un nom; **to get (o.s.) a bad ~** se faire une mauvaise réputation; **to call sb ~s** traiter qn de tous les noms

name dropping *n* mention (*pour se faire valoir*) *du nom de personnalités qu'on connaît (ou prétend connaître*)

nameless ['neɪmlɪs] *adj* sans nom; (*witness, contributor*) anonyme

namely ['neɪmlɪ] *adv* à savoir

nameplate ['neɪmpleɪt] *n* (*on door etc*) plaque *f*

namesake ['neɪmseɪk] *n* homonyme *m*

nan bread [nɑːn-] *n* nan *m*

nanny ['nænɪ] *n* bonne *f* d'enfants

nanny goat *n* chèvre *f*

nap [næp] *n* (*sleep*) (petit) somme ▷ *vi*: **to be caught ~ping** être pris(e) à l'improviste *or* en défaut

NAPA *n abbr* (*US*: = *National Association of Performing Artists*) *syndicat des gens du spectacle*

napalm ['neɪpɑːm] *n* napalm *m*

nape [neɪp] *n*: **~ of the neck** nuque *f*

napkin ['næpkɪn] *n* serviette *f* (de table)

Naples ['neɪplz] *n* Naples

Napoleonic [nəpəulɪ'ɔnɪk] *adj* napoléonien(ne)

nappy ['næpɪ] *n* (*Brit*) couche *f*

nappy liner *n* (*Brit*) protège-couche *m*

nappy rash *n*: **to have ~** avoir les fesses rouges

narcissistic [nɑːsɪ'sɪstɪk] *adj* narcissique

narcissus (*pl* **narcissi**) [nɑː'sɪsəs, -saɪ] *n* narcisse *m*

narcotic [nɑː'kɔtɪk] *n* (*Med*) narcotique *m*

narcotics [nɑː'kɔtɪks] *npl* (*illegal drugs*) stupéfiants *mpl*

nark [nɑːk] *vt* (*Brit inf*) mettre en rogne

narrate [nə'reɪt] *vt* raconter, narrer

narration [nə'reɪʃən] *n* narration *f*

narrative ['nærətɪv] *n* récit *m* ▷ *adj* narratif(-ive)

narrator [nə'reɪtəʳ] *n* narrateur(-trice)

narrow ['nærəu] *adj* étroit(e); (*fig*) restreint(e),

limité(e) ▷ vi (road) devenir plus étroit, se rétrécir; (gap, difference) se réduire; **to have a ~ escape** l'échapper belle
  ▶ **narrow down** vt restreindre
narrow gauge adj (Rail) à voie étroite
narrowly ['nærəʊlɪ] adv: **he ~ missed injury/ the tree** il a failli se blesser/rentrer dans l'arbre; **he only ~ missed the target** il a manqué la cible de peu or de justesse
narrow-minded [nærəʊ'maɪndɪd] adj à l'esprit étroit, borné(e); (attitude) borné(e)
NAS n abbr (US) = **National Academy of Sciences**
NASA ['næsə] n abbr (US: = National Aeronautics and Space Administration) NASA f
nasal ['neɪzl] adj nasal(e)
Nassau ['næsɔ:] n (in Bahamas) Nassau
nastily ['nɑ:stɪlɪ] adv (say, act) méchamment
nastiness ['nɑ:stɪnɪs] n (of person, remark) méchanceté f
nasturtium [nəs'tə:ʃəm] n capucine f
nasty ['nɑ:stɪ] adj (person: malicious) méchant(e); (: rude) très désagréable; (smell) dégoûtant(e); (wound, situation) mauvais(e), vilain(e); (weather) affreux(-euse); **to turn ~** (situation) mal tourner; (weather) se gâter; (person) devenir méchant; **it's a ~ business** c'est une sale affaire
NAS/UWT n abbr (Brit: = National Association of Schoolmasters/Union of Women Teachers) syndicat enseignant
nation ['neɪʃən] n nation f
national ['næʃənl] adj national(e) ▷ n (abroad) ressortissant(e); (when home) national(e)
national anthem n hymne national
National Curriculum n (Brit) programme scolaire commun à toutes les écoles publiques en Angleterre et au Pays de Galles comprenant dix disciplines
national debt n dette publique
national dress n costume national
National Guard n (US) milice f (de volontaires)
National Health Service n (Brit) service national de santé, ≈ Sécurité Sociale
National Insurance n (Brit) ≈ Sécurité Sociale
nationalism ['næʃnəlɪzəm] n nationalisme m
nationalist ['næʃnəlɪst] adj, n nationaliste m/f
nationality [næʃə'nælɪtɪ] n nationalité f
nationalization [næʃnəlaɪ'zeɪʃən] n nationalisation f
nationalize ['næʃnəlaɪz] vt nationaliser
nationally ['næʃnəlɪ] adv du point de vue national; dans le pays entier
national park n parc national
national press n presse nationale
National Security Council n (US) conseil national de sécurité
national service n (Mil) service m militaire
National Trust n (Brit) ≈ Caisse f nationale des monuments historiques et des sites; voir article

● **NATIONAL TRUST**
●
● Le National Trust est un organisme
● indépendant, à but non lucratif, dont la

● mission est de protéger et de mettre en
● valeur les monuments et les sites
● britanniques en raison de leur intérêt
● historique ou de leur beauté naturelle.

nationwide ['neɪʃənwaɪd] adj s'étendant à l'ensemble du pays; (problem) à l'échelle du pays entier ▷ adv à travers or dans tout le pays
native ['neɪtɪv] n habitant(e) du pays, autochtone m/f; (in colonies) indigène m/f ▷ adj du pays, indigène; (country) natal(e); (language) maternel(le); (ability) inné(e); **a ~ of Russia** une personne originaire de Russie; **a ~ speaker of French** une personne de langue maternelle française
Native American n Indien(ne) d'Amérique ▷ adj amérindien(ne)
native speaker n locuteur natif
Nativity [nə'tɪvɪtɪ] n (Rel): **the ~** la Nativité
nativity play n mystère m or miracle m de la Nativité
NATO ['neɪtəʊ] n abbr (= North Atlantic Treaty Organization) OTAN f
natter ['nætəʳ] vi (Brit) bavarder
natural ['nætʃrəl] adj naturel(le); **to die of ~ causes** mourir d'une mort naturelle
natural childbirth n accouchement m sans douleur
natural gas n gaz naturel
natural history n histoire naturelle
naturalist ['nætʃrəlɪst] n naturaliste m/f
naturalization ['nætʃrəlaɪ'zeɪʃən] n naturalisation f; acclimatation f
naturalize ['nætʃrəlaɪz] vt naturaliser; (plant) acclimater; **to become ~d** (person) se faire naturaliser
naturally ['nætʃrəlɪ] adv naturellement
natural resources npl ressources naturelles
natural selection n sélection naturelle
natural wastage n (Industry) départs naturels et volontaires
nature ['neɪtʃəʳ] n nature f; **by ~** par tempérament, de nature; **documents of a confidential ~** documents à caractère confidentiel
-natured ['neɪtʃəd] suffix: **ill~** qui a mauvais caractère
nature reserve n (Brit) réserve naturelle
nature trail n sentier de découverte de la nature
naturist ['neɪtʃərɪst] n naturiste m/f
naught [nɔ:t] n = **nought**
naughtiness ['nɔ:tɪnɪs] n (of child) désobéissance f; (of story etc) grivoiserie f
naughty ['nɔ:tɪ] adj (child) vilain(e), pas sage; (story, film) grivois(e)
nausea ['nɔ:sɪə] n nausée f
nauseate ['nɔ:sɪeɪt] vt écœurer, donner la nausée à
nauseating ['nɔ:sɪeɪtɪŋ] adj écœurant(e), dégoûtant(e)
nauseous ['nɔ:sɪəs] adj nauséabond(e), écœurant(e); (feeling sick): **to be ~** avoir des

nausées

nautical ['nɔːtɪkl] *adj* nautique

nautical mile *n* mille marin (= 1853 m)

naval ['neɪvl] *adj* naval(e)

naval officer *n* officier *m* de marine

nave [neɪv] *n* nef *f*

navel ['neɪvl] *n* nombril *m*

navigable ['nævɪɡəbl] *adj* navigable

navigate ['nævɪɡeɪt] *vt* (*steer*) diriger, piloter ▷ *vi* naviguer; (*Aut*) indiquer la route à suivre

navigation [nævɪ'ɡeɪʃən] *n* navigation *f*

navigator ['nævɪɡeɪtə^r] *n* navigateur *m*

navvy ['nævɪ] *n* (*Brit*) terrassier *m*

navy ['neɪvɪ] *n* marine *f*; **Department of the N~** (*US*) ministère *m* de la Marine

navy-blue ['neɪvɪ'bluː] *adj* bleu marine *inv*

Nazi ['nɑːtsɪ] *adj* nazi(e) ▷ *n* Nazi(e)

NB *abbr* (= *nota bene*) NB; (*Canada*) = **New Brunswick**

NBA *n abbr* (*US*) = **National Basketball Association; National Boxing Association**

NBC *n abbr* (*US*: = *National Broadcasting Company*) chaîne de télévision

NBS *n abbr* (*US*: = *National Bureau of Standards*) office de normalisation

NC *abbr* (*Comm etc*) = **no charge**; (*US*) = **North Carolina**

NCC *n abbr* (*Brit*: = *Nature Conservancy Council*) organisme de protection de la nature; (*US*) = **National Council of Churches**

NCO *n abbr* = **non-commissioned officer**

ND, N. Dak. *abbr* (*US*) = **North Dakota**

NE *abbr* (*US*) = **Nebraska; New England**

NEA *n abbr* (*US*) = **National Education Association**

neap [niːp] *n* (*also:* **neaptide**) mortes-eaux *fpl*

near [nɪə^r] *adj* proche ▷ *adv* près ▷ *prep* (*also:* **near to**) près de ▷ *vt* approcher de; **~ here/there** près d'ici/non loin de là; **£25,000 or ~est offer** (*Brit*) 25 000 livres à débattre; **in the ~ future** dans un proche avenir; **to come ~** *vi* s'approcher

nearby [nɪə'baɪ] *adj* proche ▷ *adv* tout près, à proximité

Near East *n*: **the ~** le Proche-Orient

nearer ['nɪərə^r] *adj* plus proche ▷ *adv* plus près

nearly ['nɪəlɪ] *adv* presque; **I ~ fell** j'ai failli tomber; **it's not ~ big enough** ce n'est vraiment pas assez grand, c'est loin d'être assez grand

near miss *n* collision évitée de justesse; (*when aiming*) coup manqué de peu *or* de justesse

nearness ['nɪənɪs] *n* proximité *f*

nearside ['nɪəsaɪd] (*Aut*) *n* (*right-hand drive*) côté *m* gauche; (*left-hand drive*) côté droit ▷ *adj* de gauche; de droite

near-sighted [nɪə'saɪtɪd] *adj* myope

neat [niːt] *adj* (*person, work*) soigné(e); (*room etc*) bien tenu(e) *or* rangé(e); (*solution, plan*) habile; (*spirits*) pur(e); **I drink it ~** je le bois sec *or* sans eau

neatly ['niːtlɪ] *adv* avec soin *or* ordre; (*skilfully*) habilement

neatness ['niːtnɪs] *n* (*tidiness*) netteté *f*; (*skilfulness*) habileté *f*

Nebr. *abbr* (*US*) = **Nebraska**

nebulous ['nɛbjuləs] *adj* nébuleux(-euse)

necessarily ['nɛsɪsrɪlɪ] *adv* nécessairement; **not ~** pas nécessairement *or* forcément

necessary ['nɛsɪsrɪ] *adj* nécessaire; **if ~** si besoin est, le cas échéant

necessitate [nɪ'sɛsɪteɪt] *vt* nécessiter

necessity [nɪ'sɛsɪtɪ] *n* nécessité *f*; chose nécessaire *or* essentielle; **in case of ~** en cas d'urgence

neck [nɛk] *n* cou *m*; (*of horse, garment*) encolure *f*; (*of bottle*) goulot *m* ▷ *vi* (*inf*) se peloter; **~ and ~** à égalité; **to stick one's ~ out** (*inf*) se mouiller

necklace ['nɛklɪs] *n* collier *m*

neckline ['nɛklaɪn] *n* encolure *f*

necktie ['nɛktaɪ] *n* (*esp US*) cravate *f*

nectar ['nɛktə^r] *n* nectar *m*

nectarine ['nɛktərɪn] *n* brugnon *m*, nectarine *f*

née [neɪ] *adj*: **~ Scott** née Scott

need [niːd] *n* besoin *m* ▷ *vt* avoir besoin de; **to ~ to do** devoir faire; avoir besoin de faire; **you don't ~ to go** vous n'avez pas besoin *or* vous n'êtes pas obligé de partir; **a signature is ~ed** il faut une signature; **to be in ~ of** *or* **have ~ of** avoir besoin de; **£10 will meet my immediate ~s** 10 livres suffiront pour mes besoins immédiats; **in case of ~** en cas de besoin, au besoin; **there's no ~ to do ....** il n'y a pas lieu de faire ..., il n'est pas nécessaire de faire ...; **there's no ~ for that** ce n'est pas la peine, cela n'est pas nécessaire

needle ['niːdl] *n* aiguille *f*; (*on record player*) saphir *m* ▷ *vt* (*inf*) asticoter, tourmenter

needlecord ['niːdlkɔːd] *n* (*Brit*) velours *m* milleraies

needless ['niːdlɪs] *adj* inutile; **~ to say, ...** inutile de dire que ...

needlessly ['niːdlɪslɪ] *adv* inutilement

needlework ['niːdlwəːk] *n* (*activity*) travaux *mpl* d'aiguille; (*object*) ouvrage *m*

needn't ['niːdnt] = **need not**

needy ['niːdɪ] *adj* nécessiteux(-euse)

negation [nɪ'ɡeɪʃən] *n* négation *f*

negative ['nɛɡətɪv] *n* (*Phot, Elec*) négatif *m*; (*Ling*) terme *m* de négation ▷ *adj* négatif(-ive); **to answer in the ~** répondre par la négative

negative equity *n* situation dans laquelle la valeur d'une maison est inférieure à celle du prêt immobilier contracté pour la payer

neglect [nɪ'ɡlɛkt] *vt* négliger; (*garden*) ne pas entretenir; (*duty*) manquer à ▷ *n* (*of person, duty, garden*) le fait de négliger; (**state of**) **~** abandon *m*; **to ~ to do sth** négliger *or* omettre de faire qch; **to ~ one's appearance** se négliger

neglected [nɪ'ɡlɛktɪd] *adj* négligé(e), à l'abandon

neglectful [nɪ'ɡlɛktful] *adj* (*gen*) négligent(e); **to be ~ of sb/sth** négliger qn/qch

negligee ['nɛɡlɪʒeɪ] *n* déshabillé *m*

negligence ['nɛglɪdʒəns] n négligence f
negligent ['nɛglɪdʒənt] adj négligent(e)
negligently ['nɛglɪdʒəntlɪ] adv par négligence;
(offhandedly) négligemment
negligible ['nɛglɪdʒɪbl] adj négligeable
negotiable [nɪ'gəuʃɪəbl] adj négociable; **not ~**
(cheque) non négociable
negotiate [nɪ'gəuʃɪeɪt] vi négocier ▷ vt
négocier; (Comm) négocier; (obstacle) franchir,
négocier; (bend in road) négocier; **to ~ with sb
for sth** négocier avec qn en vue d'obtenir qch
negotiating table [nɪ'gəuʃɪeɪtɪŋ-] n table f des
négociations
negotiation [nɪgəuʃɪ'eɪʃən] n négociation f,
pourparlers mpl; **to enter into ~s with sb**
engager des négociations avec qn
negotiator [nɪ'gəuʃɪeɪtər] n négociateur(-trice)
Negress ['niːgrɪs] n négresse f
Negro ['niːgrəu] adj (gen) noir(e); (music, arts)
nègre, noir ▷ n (pl **-es**) Noir(e)
neigh [neɪ] vi hennir
neighbour, (US) **neighbor** ['neɪbər] n voisin(e)
neighbourhood, (US) **neighborhood**
['neɪbəhud] n (place) quartier m; (people)
voisinage m
neighbourhood watch n (Brit: also:
neighbourhood watch scheme) système de
surveillance, assuré par les habitants d'un même quartier
neighbouring, (US) **neighboring** ['neɪbərɪŋ] adj
voisin(e), avoisinant(e)
neighbourly, (US) **neighborly** ['neɪbəlɪ] adj
obligeant(e); (relations) de bon voisinage
neither ['naɪðər] adj, pron aucun(e) (des deux), ni
l'un(e) ni l'autre ▷ conj: **~ do I** moi non plus; **I
didn't move and ~ did Claude** je n'ai pas
bougé, (et) Claude non plus ▷ adv: **~ good nor
bad** ni bon ni mauvais; **~ did I refuse** (et or
mais) je n'ai pas non plus refusé; **~ of them** ni
l'un ni l'autre
neo... ['niːəu] prefix néo-
neolithic [niːəu'lɪθɪk] adj néolithique
neologism [nɪ'ɔlədʒɪzəm] n néologisme m
neon ['niːɔn] n néon m
neon light n lampe f au néon
neon sign n enseigne (lumineuse) au néon
Nepal [nɪ'pɔːl] n Népal m
nephew ['nɛvjuː] n neveu m
nepotism ['nɛpətɪzəm] n népotisme m
nerd [nəːd] n (inf) pauvre mec m, ballot m
nerve [nəːv] n nerf m; (bravery) sang-froid m,
courage m; (cheek) aplomb m, toupet m; **nerves**
npl (nervousness) nervosité f; **he gets on my ~s** il
m'énerve; **to have a fit of ~s** avoir le trac; **to
lose one's ~** (self-confidence) perdre son sang-
froid
nerve centre n (Anat) centre nerveux; (fig)
centre névralgique
nerve gas n gaz m neuroplégique
nerve-racking ['nəːvrækɪŋ] adj angoissant(e)
nervous ['nəːvəs] adj nerveux(-euse); (anxious)
inquiet(-ète), plein(e) d'appréhension; (timid)
intimidé(e)

nervous breakdown n dépression nerveuse
nervously ['nəːvəslɪ] adv nerveusement
nervousness ['nəːvəsnɪs] n nervosité f;
inquiétude f, appréhension f
nervous wreck n: **to be a ~** être une boule de
nerfs
nervy ['nəːvɪ] adj: **he`s very ~** il a les nerfs à
fleur de peau or à vif
nest [nɛst] n nid m ▷ vi (se) nicher, faire son nid;
~ of tables table f gigogne
nest egg n (fig) bas m de laine, magot m
nestle ['nɛsl] vi se blottir
nestling ['nɛstlɪŋ] n oisillon m
Net [nɛt] n (Comput): **the ~** (Internet) le Net
net [nɛt] n filet m; (fabric) tulle f ▷ adj net(te) ▷ vt
(fish etc) prendre au filet; (money: person) toucher;
(: deal, sale) rapporter; **~ of tax** net d'impôt; **he
earns £10,000 ~ per year** il gagne 10 000 livres
net par an
netball ['nɛtbɔːl] n netball m
net curtains npl voilages mpl
Netherlands ['nɛðələndz] npl: **the ~** les Pays-
Bas mpl
net profit n bénéfice net
nett [nɛt] adj = **net**
netting ['nɛtɪŋ] n (for fence etc) treillis m, grillage
m; (fabric) voile m
nettle ['nɛtl] n ortie f
network ['nɛtwəːk] n réseau m ▷ vt (Radio, TV)
diffuser sur l'ensemble du réseau; (computers)
interconnecter; **there's no ~ coverage here**
(Tel) il n'y a pas de réseau ici
neuralgia [njuə'rældʒə] n névralgie f
neurological [njuərə'lɔdʒɪkl] adj neurologique
neurosis (pl **neuroses**) [njuə'rəusɪs, -siːz] n
névrose f
neurotic [njuə'rɔtɪk] adj, n névrosé(e)
neuter ['njuːtər] adj neutre ▷ n neutre m ▷ vt
(cat etc) châtrer, couper
neutral ['njuːtrəl] adj neutre ▷ n (Aut) point
mort
neutrality [njuː'trælɪtɪ] n neutralité f
neutralize ['njuːtrəlaɪz] vt neutraliser
neutron bomb ['njuːtrɔn-] n bombe f à
neutrons
Nev. abbr (US) = **Nevada**
never ['nɛvər] adv (ne ...) jamais; **I ~ went** je n'y
suis pas allé; **I've ~ been to Spain** je ne suis
jamais allé en Espagne; **~ again** plus jamais; **~
in my life** jamais de ma vie; see also **mind**
never-ending [nɛvər'ɛndɪŋ] adj interminable
nevertheless [nɛvəðə'lɛs] adv néanmoins,
malgré tout
new [njuː] adj nouveau (nouvelle); (brand new)
neuf (neuve); **as good as ~** comme neuf
New Age n New Age m
newborn ['njuːbɔːn] adj nouveau-né(e)
newcomer ['njuːkʌmər] n nouveau venu
(nouvelle venue)
new-fangled ['njuːfæŋgld] adj (pej)
ultramoderne (et farfelu(e))
new-found ['njuːfaund] adj de fraîche date;

(*friend*) nouveau (nouvelle)
Newfoundland ['njuːfənlənd] *n* Terre-Neuve *f*
New Guinea *n* Nouvelle-Guinée *f*
newly ['njuːlɪ] *adv* nouvellement, récemment
newly-weds ['njuːlɪwɛdz] *npl* jeunes mariés *mpl*
new moon *n* nouvelle lune
newness ['njuːnɪs] *n* nouveauté *f*; (*of fabric, clothes etc*) état neuf
New Orleans [-'ɔːliːənz] *n* la Nouvelle-Orléans
news [njuːz] *n* nouvelle(s) *f(pl)*; (*Radio, TV*) informations *fpl*, actualités *fpl*; **a piece of** ~ une nouvelle; **good/bad** ~ bonne/mauvaise nouvelle; **financial** ~ (*Press, Radio, TV*) page financière
news agency *n* agence *f* de presse
newsagent ['njuːzeɪdʒənt] *n* (*Brit*) marchand *m* de journaux
news bulletin *n* (*Radio TV*) bulletin *m* d'informations
newscaster ['njuːzkɑːstər] *n* (*Radio, TV*) présentateur(-trice)
news flash *n* flash *m* d'information
newsletter ['njuːzlɛtər] *n* bulletin *m*
newspaper ['njuːzpeɪpər] *n* journal *m*; **daily** ~ quotidien *m*; **weekly** ~ hebdomadaire *m*
newsprint ['njuːzprɪnt] *n* papier *m* (de) journal
newsreader ['njuːzriːdər] *n* = **newscaster**
newsreel ['njuːzriːl] *n* actualités (filmées)
newsroom ['njuːzruːm] *n* (*Press*) salle *f* de rédaction; (*Radio, TV*) studio *m*
news stand *n* kiosque *m* à journaux
newsworthy ['njuːzwəːðɪ] *adj*: **to be** ~ valoir la peine d'être publié
newt [njuːt] *n* triton *m*
new town *n* (*Brit*) ville nouvelle
New Year *n* Nouvel An; **Happy** ~! Bonne Année!; **to wish sb a happy** ~ souhaiter la Bonne Année à qn
New Year's Day *n* le jour de l'An
New Year's Eve *n* la Saint-Sylvestre
New York [-'jɔːk] *n* New York; (*also*: **New York State**) New York *m*
New Zealand [-'ziːlənd] *n* Nouvelle-Zélande *f* ▷ *adj* néo-zélandais(e)
New Zealander [-'ziːləndər] *n* Néo-Zélandais(e)
next [nɛkst] *adj* (*in time*) prochain(e); (*seat, room*) voisin(e), d'à côté; (*meeting, bus stop*) suivant(e) ▷ *adv* la fois suivante; la prochaine fois; (*afterwards*) ensuite; ~ **to** (*prep*) à côté de; ~ **to nothing** presque rien; ~ **time** (*adv*) la prochaine fois; **the** ~ **day** le lendemain, le jour suivant *or* d'après; ~ **week** la semaine prochaine; **the** ~ **week** la semaine suivante; ~ **year** l'année prochaine; **"turn to the** ~ **page"** "voir page suivante"; ~ **please!** (*at doctor's etc*) au suivant!; **who's** ~? c'est à qui?; **the week after** ~ dans deux semaines; **when do we meet** ~? quand nous revoyons-nous?
next door *adv* à côté ▷ *adj* (*neighbour*) d'à côté
next-of-kin ['nɛkstəv'kɪn] *n* parent *m* le plus proche
NF *n abbr* (*Brit Pol*: = *National Front*) ≈ FN ▷ *abbr*

(*Canada*) = **Newfoundland**
NFL *n abbr* (*US*) = **National Football League**
Nfld. *abbr* (*Canada*) = **Newfoundland**
NG *abbr* (*US*) = **National Guard**
NGO *n abbr* (*US*: = *non-governmental organization*) ONG *f*
NH *abbr* (*US*) = **New Hampshire**
NHL *n abbr* (*US*) = **National Hockey League**
NHS *n abbr* (*Brit*) = **National Health Service**
NI *abbr* = **Northern Ireland**; (*Brit*) = **National Insurance**
Niagara Falls [naɪ'ægərə-] *npl*: **the** ~ les chutes *fpl* du Niagara
nib [nɪb] *n* (*of pen*) (bec *m* de) plume *f*
nibble ['nɪbl] *vt* grignoter
Nicaragua [nɪkə'rægjuə] *n* Nicaragua *m*
Nicaraguan [nɪkə'rægjuən] *adj* nicaraguayen(ne) ▷ *n* Nicaraguayen(ne)
nice [naɪs] *adj* (*holiday, trip, taste*) agréable; (*flat, picture*) joli(e); (*person*) gentil(le); (*distinction, point*) subtil(e)
nice-looking ['naɪslukɪŋ] *adj* joli(e)
nicely ['naɪslɪ] *adv* agréablement; joliment; gentiment; subtilement; **that will do** ~ ce sera parfait
niceties ['naɪsɪtɪz] *npl* subtilités *fpl*
niche [niːʃ] *n* (*Archit*) niche *f*
nick [nɪk] *n* (*indentation*) encoche *f*; (*wound*) entaille *f*; (*Brit inf*): **in good** ~ en bon état ▷ *vt* (*cut*): **to** ~ **o.s.** se couper; (*inf: steal*) faucher, piquer; (: *Brit: arrest*) choper, pincer; **in the** ~ **of time** juste à temps
nickel ['nɪkl] *n* nickel *m*; (*US*) pièce *f* de 5 cents
nickname ['nɪkneɪm] *n* surnom *m* ▷ *vt* surnommer
Nicosia [nɪkə'siːə] *n* Nicosie
nicotine ['nɪkətiːn] *n* nicotine *f*
nicotine patch *n* timbre *m* anti-tabac, patch *m*
niece [niːs] *n* nièce *f*
nifty ['nɪftɪ] *adj* (*inf: car, jacket*) qui a du chic *or* de la classe; (: *gadget, tool*) astucieux(-euse)
Niger ['naɪdʒər] *n* (*country, river*) Niger *m*
Nigeria [naɪ'dʒɪərɪə] *n* Nigéria *m or f*
Nigerian [naɪ'dʒɪərɪən] *adj* nigérien(ne) ▷ *n* Nigérien(ne)
niggardly ['nɪgədlɪ] *adj* (*person*) parcimonieux(-euse), pingre; (*allowance, amount*) misérable
nigger ['nɪgər] *n* (*inf!: highly offensive*) nègre (négresse)
niggle ['nɪgl] *vt* tracasser ▷ *vi* (*find fault*) trouver toujours à redire; (*fuss*) n'être jamais content(e)
niggling ['nɪglɪŋ] *adj* tatillon(ne); (*detail*) insignifiant(e); (*doubt, pain*) persistant(e)
night [naɪt] *n* nuit *f*; (*evening*) soir *m*; **at** ~ la nuit; **by** ~ de nuit; **in the** ~, **during the** ~ pendant la nuit; **last** ~ (*evening*) hier soir; (*night-time*) la nuit dernière; **the** ~ **before last** avant-hier soir
night-bird ['naɪtbəːd] *n* oiseau *m* nocturne; (*fig*) couche-tard *m inv*, noctambule *m/f*
nightcap ['naɪtkæp] *n* boisson prise avant le coucher
night club *n* boîte *f* de nuit

nightdress ['naɪtdrɛs] n chemise f de nuit
nightfall ['naɪtfɔ:l] n tombée f de la nuit
nightie ['naɪtɪ] n chemise f de nuit
nightingale ['naɪtɪŋgeɪl] n rossignol m
nightlife ['naɪtlaɪf] n vie f nocturne
nightly ['naɪtlɪ] adj (news) du soir; (by night) nocturne ▷ adv (every evening) tous les soirs; (every night) toutes les nuits
nightmare ['naɪtmɛəʳ] n cauchemar m
night porter n gardien m de nuit, concierge m de service la nuit
night safe n coffre m de nuit
night school n cours mpl du soir
nightshade ['naɪtʃeɪd] n: **deadly ~** (Bot) belladone f
night shift ['naɪtʃɪft] n équipe f de nuit
night-time ['naɪttaɪm] n nuit f
night watchman (irreg) n veilleur m de nuit; poste m de nuit
nihilism ['naɪɪlɪzəm] n nihilisme m
nil [nɪl] n rien m; (Brit Sport) zéro m
Nile [naɪl] n: **the ~** le Nil
nimble ['nɪmbl] adj agile
nine [naɪn] num neuf
nineteen ['naɪn'ti:n] num dix-neuf
nineteenth [naɪn'ti:nθ] num dix-neuvième
ninetieth ['naɪntɪɪθ] num quatre-vingt-dixième
ninety ['naɪntɪ] num quatre-vingt-dix
ninth [naɪnθ] num neuvième
nip [nɪp] vt pincer ▷ vi (Brit inf): **to ~ out/down/ up** sortir/descendre/monter en vitesse ▷ n pincement m; (drink) petit verre; **to ~ into a shop** faire un saut dans un magasin
nipple ['nɪpl] n (Anat) mamelon m, bout m du sein
nippy ['nɪpɪ] adj (Brit: person) alerte, leste; (: car) nerveux(-euse)
nit [nɪt] n (in hair) lente f; (inf: idiot) imbécile m/f, crétin(e)
nit-pick ['nɪtpɪk] vi (inf) être tatillon(ne)
nitrogen ['naɪtrədʒən] n azote m
nitroglycerin, nitroglycerine ['naɪtrəu'glɪsəri:n] n nitroglycérine f
nitty-gritty ['nɪtɪ'grɪtɪ] n (fam): **to get down to the ~** en venir au fond du problème
nitwit ['nɪtwɪt] n (inf) nigaud(e)
NJ abbr (US) = **New Jersey**
NLF n abbr (= National Liberation Front) FLN m
NLQ abbr (= near letter quality) qualité f courrier
NLRB n abbr (US: = National Labor Relations Board) organisme de protection des travailleurs
NM, N. Mex. abbr (US) = **New Mexico**

 KEYWORD

no [nəu] (pl **noes**) adv (opposite of "yes") non; **are you coming? — no (I'm not)** est-ce que vous venez? — non; **would you like some more? — no thank you** vous en voulez encore? — non merci
▷ adj (not any) (ne ...) pas de, (ne ...) aucun(e); **I have no money/books** je n'ai pas d'argent/de livres; **no student would have done it** aucun étudiant ne l'aurait fait; **"no smoking"** "défense de fumer"; **"no dogs"** "les chiens ne sont pas admis"
▷ n non m; **I won't take no for an answer** il n'est pas question de refuser

no. abbr (= number) nᵒ
nobble ['nɔbl] vt (Brit inf: bribe: person) soudoyer, acheter; (: person: to speak to) mettre le grappin sur; (Racing: horse, dog) droguer (pour l'empêcher de gagner)
Nobel prize [nəu'bɛl-] n prix m Nobel
nobility [nəu'bɪlɪtɪ] n noblesse f
noble ['nəubl] adj noble
nobleman ['nəublmən] (irreg) n noble m
nobly ['nəublɪ] adv noblement
nobody ['nəubədɪ] pron (ne ...) personne
no-claims bonus ['nəukleɪmz-] n bonus m
nocturnal [nɔk'tə:nl] adj nocturne
nod [nɔd] vi faire un signe de (la) tête (affirmatif ou amical); (sleep) somnoler ▷ vt: **to ~ one's head** faire un signe de (la) tête; (in agreement) faire signe que oui ▷ n signe m de (la) tête; **they ~ded their agreement** ils ont acquiescé d'un signe de la tête
▶ **nod off** vi s'assoupir
no-fly zone [nəu'flaɪ-] n zone interdite (aux avions et hélicoptères)
noise [nɔɪz] n bruit m; **I can't sleep for the ~** je n'arrive pas à dormir à cause du bruit
noiseless ['nɔɪzlɪs] adj silencieux(-euse)
noisily ['nɔɪzɪlɪ] adv bruyamment
noisy ['nɔɪzɪ] adj bruyant(e)
nomad ['nəumæd] n nomade m/f
nomadic [nəu'mædɪk] adj nomade
no man's land n no man's land m
nominal ['nɔmɪnl] adj (rent, fee) symbolique; (value) nominal(e)
nominate ['nɔmɪneɪt] vt (propose) proposer; (appoint) nommer
nomination [nɔmɪ'neɪʃən] n nomination f
nominee [nɔmɪ'ni:] n candidat agréé; personne nommée
non- [nɔn] prefix non-
nonalcoholic [nɔnælkə'hɔlɪk] adj non alcoolisé(e)
nonbreakable [nɔn'breɪkəbl] adj incassable
nonce word ['nɔns-] n mot créé pour l'occasion
nonchalant ['nɔnʃələnt] adj nonchalant(e)
non-commissioned [nɔnkə'mɪʃənd] adj: **~ officer** sous-officier m
noncommittal [nɔnkə'mɪtl] adj évasif(-ive)
nonconformist [nɔnkən'fɔ:mɪst] n non-conformiste m/f ▷ adj non-conformiste, dissident(e)
noncooperation ['nɔnkəuɔpə'reɪʃən] n refus m de coopérer, non-coopération f
nondescript ['nɔndɪskrɪpt] adj quelconque, indéfinissable
none [nʌn] pron aucun(e); **~ of you** aucun d'entre vous, personne parmi vous; **I have ~** je

n'en ai pas; **I have ~ left** je n'en ai plus; **~ at all** (*not one*) aucun(e); **how much milk? — ~ at all** combien de lait? — pas du tout; **he's ~ the worse for it** il ne s'en porte pas plus mal

nonentity [nɔ'nɛntɪtɪ] *n* personne insignifiante

nonessential [nɔnɪ'sɛnʃl] *adj* accessoire, superflu(e) ▷ *n*: **~s** le superflu

nonetheless ['nʌnðə'lɛs] *adv* néanmoins

nonevent [nɔnɪ'vɛnt] *n* événement manqué

nonexecutive [nɔnɪg'zɛkjutɪv] *adj*: **~ director** administrateur(-trice), conseiller(-ère) de direction

nonexistent [nɔnɪg'zɪstənt] *adj* inexistant(e)

non-fiction [nɔn'fɪkʃən] *n* littérature *f* non romanesque

nonintervention ['nɔnɪntə'vɛnʃən] *n* non-intervention *f*

no-no ['nəunəu] *n* (*inf*): **it's a ~** il n'en est pas question

non obst. *abbr* (= *non obstante: notwithstanding*) nonobstant

no-nonsense [nəu'nɔnsəns] *adj* (*manner, person*) plein(e) de bon sens

nonpayment [nɔn'peɪmənt] *n* non-paiement *m*

nonplussed [nɔn'plʌst] *adj* perplexe

non-profit-making [nɔn'prɔfɪtmeɪkɪŋ] *adj* à but non lucratif

nonsense ['nɔnsəns] *n* absurdités *fpl*, idioties *fpl*; **~!** ne dites pas d'idioties!; **it is ~ to say that** ... il est absurde de dire que ....

nonsensical [nɔn'sɛnsɪkl] *adj* absurde, qui n'a pas de sens

non-smoker ['nɔn'sməukə^r] *n* non-fumeur *m*

non-smoking ['nɔn'sməukɪŋ] *adj* non-fumeur

nonstarter [nɔn'stɑːtə^r] *n*: **it`s a ~** c'est voué à l'échec

non-stick ['nɔn'stɪk] *adj* qui n'attache pas

nonstop ['nɔn'stɔp] *adj* direct(e), sans arrêt (*or* escale) ▷ *adv* sans arrêt

nontaxable [nɔn'tæksəbl] *adj*: **~ income** revenu *m* non imposable

non-U ['nɔnjuː] *adj abbr* (*Brit inf*: = *non-upper class*) qui ne se dit (*or* se fait) pas

nonvolatile [nɔn'vɔlətaɪl] *adj*: **~ memory** (*Comput*) mémoire rémanente *or* non volatile

nonvoting [nɔn'vəutɪŋ] *adj*: **~ shares** actions *fpl* sans droit de vote

non-white ['nɔn'waɪt] *adj* de couleur ▷ *n* personne *f* de couleur

noodles ['nuːdlz] *npl* nouilles *fpl*

nook [nuk] *n*: **~s and crannies** recoins *mpl*

noon [nuːn] *n* midi *m*

no-one ['nəuwʌn] *pron* = **nobody**

noose [nuːs] *n* nœud coulant; (*hangman's*) corde *f*

nor [nɔː^r] *conj* = **neither** ▷ *adv see* **neither**

norm [nɔːm] *n* norme *f*

normal ['nɔːml] *adj* normal(e) ▷ *n*: **to return to ~** redevenir normal(e)

normality [nɔː'mælɪtɪ] *n* normalité *f*

normally ['nɔːməlɪ] *adv* normalement

Normandy ['nɔːməndɪ] *n* Normandie *f*

north [nɔːθ] *n* nord *m* ▷ *adj* nord *inv*; (*wind*) du nord ▷ *adv* au *or* vers le nord

North Africa *n* Afrique *f* du Nord

North African *adj* nord-africain(e), d'Afrique du Nord ▷ *n* Nord-Africain(e)

North America *n* Amérique *f* du Nord

North American *n* Nord-Américain(e) ▷ *adj* nord-américain(e), d'Amérique du Nord

Northants [nɔː'θænts] *abbr* (*Brit*) = **Northamptonshire**

northbound ['nɔːθbaund] *adj* (*traffic*) en direction du nord; (*carriageway*) nord *inv*

north-east [nɔːθ'iːst] *n* nord-est *m*

northerly ['nɔːðəlɪ] *adj* (*wind, direction*) du nord

northern ['nɔːðən] *adj* du nord, septentrional(e)

Northern Ireland *n* Irlande *f* du Nord

North Korea *n* Corée *f* du Nord

North Pole *n*: **the ~** le pôle Nord

North Sea *n*: **the ~** la mer du Nord

North Sea oil *n* pétrole *m* de la mer du Nord

northward ['nɔːθwəd], **northwards** ['nɔːθwədz] *adv* vers le nord

north-west [nɔːθ'wɛst] *n* nord-ouest *m*

Norway ['nɔːweɪ] *n* Norvège *f*

Norwegian [nɔː'wiːdʒən] *adj* norvégien(ne) ▷ *n* Norvégien(ne); (*Ling*) norvégien *m*

nos. *abbr* (= *numbers*) n^{os}

nose [nəuz] *n* nez *m*; (*of dog, cat*) museau *m*; (*fig*) flair *m* ▷ *vi* (*also*: **nose one's way**) avancer précautionneusement; **to pay through the ~** (**for sth**) (*inf*) payer un prix excessif (pour qch)
   ▶ **nose about, nose around** *vi* fouiner *or* fureter (partout)

nosebleed ['nəuzbliːd] *n* saignement *m* de nez

nose-dive ['nəuzdaɪv] *n* (descente *f* en) piqué *m*

nose drops *npl* gouttes *fpl* pour le nez

nosey ['nəuzɪ] *adj* (*inf*) curieux(-euse)

nostalgia [nɔs'tældʒɪə] *n* nostalgie *f*

nostalgic [nɔs'tældʒɪk] *adj* nostalgique

nostril ['nɔstrɪl] *n* narine *f*; (*of horse*) naseau *m*

nosy ['nəuzɪ] (*inf*) *adj* = **nosey**

not [nɔt] *adv* (ne ...) pas; **he is ~** *or* **isn't here** il n'est pas ici; **you must ~** *or* **mustn't do that** tu ne dois pas faire ça; **I hope ~** j'espère que non; **~ at all** pas du tout; (*after thanks*) de rien; **it's too late, isn't it?** c'est trop tard, n'est-ce pas?; **~ yet/now** pas encore/maintenant; *see also* **only**

notable ['nəutəbl] *adj* notable

notably ['nəutəblɪ] *adv* (*particularly*) en particulier; (*markedly*) spécialement

notary ['nəutərɪ] *n* (*also*: **notary public**) notaire *m*

notation [nəu'teɪʃən] *n* notation *f*

notch [nɔtʃ] *n* encoche *f*
   ▶ **notch up** *vt* (*score*) marquer; (*victory*) remporter

note [nəut] *n* note *f*; (*letter*) mot *m*; (*banknote*) billet *m* ▷ *vt* (*also*: **note down**) noter; (*notice*) constater; **just a quick ~ to let you know ...** juste un mot pour vous dire ...; **to take ~s** prendre des notes; **to compare ~s** (*fig*) échanger des (or leurs etc) impressions; **to take ~ of** prendre note de; **a person of ~** une personne éminente

notebook ['nəʊtbʊk] n carnet m; (for shorthand etc) bloc-notes m

note-case ['nəʊtkeɪs] n (Brit) porte-feuille m

noted ['nəʊtɪd] adj réputé(e)

notepad ['nəʊtpæd] n bloc-notes m

notepaper ['nəʊtpeɪpəʳ] n papier m à lettres

noteworthy ['nəʊtwəːðɪ] adj remarquable

nothing ['nʌθɪŋ] n rien m; he does ~ il ne fait rien; **~ new** rien de nouveau; for ~ (free) pour rien, gratuitement; (in vain) pour rien; **~ at all** rien du tout; **~ much** pas grand-chose

notice ['nəʊtɪs] n (announcement, warning) avis m; (of leaving) congé m; (Brit: review: of play etc) critique f, compte rendu m ▷ vt remarquer, s'apercevoir de; **without ~** sans préavis; **advance ~** préavis m; **to give sb ~ of sth** notifier qn de qch; **at short ~** dans un délai très court; **until further ~** jusqu'à nouvel ordre; **to give ~, hand in one's ~** (employee) donner sa démission, démissionner; **to take ~ of** prêter attention à; **to bring sth to sb's ~** porter qch à la connaissance de qn; **it has come to my ~ that ...** on m'a signalé que ...; **to escape** or **avoid ~** (essayer de) passer inaperçu or ne pas se faire remarquer

noticeable ['nəʊtɪsəbl] adj visible

notice board n (Brit) panneau m d'affichage

notification [nəʊtɪfɪ'keɪʃən] n notification f

notify ['nəʊtɪfaɪ] vt: **to ~ sth to sb** notifier qch à qn; **to ~ sb of sth** avertir qn de qch

notion ['nəʊʃən] n idée f; (concept) notion f; **notions** npl (US: haberdashery) mercerie f

notoriety [nəʊtə'raɪətɪ] n notoriété f

notorious [nəʊ'tɔːrɪəs] adj notoire (souvent en mal)

notoriously [nəʊ'tɔːrɪəslɪ] adj notoirement

Notts [nɔts] abbr (Brit) = **Nottinghamshire**

notwithstanding [nɔtwɪθ'stændɪŋ] adv néanmoins ▷ prep en dépit de

nougat ['nuːgɑː] n nougat m

nought [nɔːt] n zéro m

noun [naʊn] n nom m

nourish ['nʌrɪʃ] vt nourrir

nourishing ['nʌrɪʃɪŋ] adj nourrissant(e)

nourishment ['nʌrɪʃmənt] n nourriture f

Nov. abbr (= November) nov

Nova Scotia ['nəʊvə'skəʊʃə] n Nouvelle-Écosse f

novel ['nɔvl] n roman m ▷ adj nouveau (nouvelle), original(e)

novelist ['nɔvəlɪst] n romancier m

novelty ['nɔvəltɪ] n nouveauté f

November [nəʊ'vɛmbəʳ] n novembre m; for phrases see also **July**

novice ['nɔvɪs] n novice m/f

NOW [naʊ] n abbr (US) = **National Organization for Women**

now [naʊ] adv maintenant ▷ conj: **~ (that)** maintenant (que); **right ~** tout de suite; **by ~** à l'heure qu'il est; **just ~** (:): **that's the fashion**

just ~ c'est la mode en ce moment or maintenant; **I saw her just ~** je viens de la voir, je l'ai vue à l'instant; **I'll read it just ~** je vais le lire à l'instant or dès maintenant; **~ and then, ~ and again** de temps en temps; **from ~ on** dorénavant; **in 3 days from ~** dans or d'ici trois jours; **between ~ and Monday** d'ici (à) lundi; **that's all for ~** c'est tout pour l'instant

nowadays ['naʊədeɪz] adv de nos jours

nowhere ['nəʊwɛəʳ] adv (ne ...) nulle part; **~ else** nulle part ailleurs

no-win situation [nəʊ'wɪn-] n impasse f; **we're in a ~** nous sommes dans l'impasse

noxious ['nɔkʃəs] adj toxique

nozzle ['nɔzl] n (of hose) jet m, lance f; (of vacuum cleaner) suceur m

NP n abbr = **notary public**

nr abbr (Brit) = **near**

NS abbr (Canada) = **Nova Scotia**

NSC n abbr (US) = **National Security Council**

NSF n abbr (US) = **National Science Foundation**

NSPCC n abbr (Brit) = **National Society for the Prevention of Cruelty to Children**

NSW abbr (Australia) = **New South Wales**

NT n abbr (= New Testament) NT m ▷ abbr (Canada) = **Northwest Territories**

nth [ɛnθ] adj: **for the ~ time** (inf) pour la énième fois

nuance ['njuːɑːns] n nuance f

nubile ['njuːbaɪl] adj nubile; (attractive) jeune et désirable

nuclear ['njuːklɪəʳ] adj nucléaire

nuclear disarmament n désarmement m nucléaire

nuclear family n famille f nucléaire

nuclear-free zone ['njuːklɪə'friː-] n zone f où le nucléaire est interdit

nucleus (pl **nuclei**) ['njuːklɪəs, 'njuːklɪaɪ] n noyau m

NUCPS n abbr (Brit: = National Union of Civil and Public Servants) syndicat des fonctionnaires

nude [njuːd] adj nu(e) ▷ n (Art) nu m; **in the ~** (tout(e)) nu(e)

nudge [nʌdʒ] vt donner un (petit) coup de coude à

nudist ['njuːdɪst] n nudiste m/f

nudist colony n colonie f de nudistes

nudity ['njuːdɪtɪ] n nudité f

nugget ['nʌgɪt] n pépite f

nuisance ['njuːsns] n: **it's a ~** c'est (très) ennuyeux or gênant; **he's a ~** il est assommant or casse-pieds; **what a ~!** quelle barbe!

NUJ n abbr (Brit: = National Union of Journalists) syndicat des journalistes

nuke [njuːk] n (inf) bombe f atomique

null [nʌl] adj: **~ and void** nul(le) et non avenu(e)

nullify ['nʌlɪfaɪ] vt invalider

NUM n abbr (Brit: = National Union of Mineworkers) syndicat des mineurs

numb [nʌm] adj engourdi(e); (with fear) paralysé(e) ▷ vt engourdir; **~ with cold** engourdi(e) par le froid, transi(e) (de froid); **~**

with fear transi de peur, paralysé(e) par la peur

number ['nʌmbə^r] *n* nombre *m*; *(numeral)* chiffre *m*; *(of house, car, telephone, newspaper)* numéro *m* ▷ *vt* numéroter; *(amount to)* compter; **a ~ of** un certain nombre de; **they were seven in ~** ils étaient (au nombre de) sept; **to be ~ed among** compter parmi; **the staff ~s 20** le nombre d'employés s'élève à *or* est de 20; **wrong ~** *(Tel)* mauvais numéro

numbered account ['nʌmbəd-] *n* *(in bank)* compte numéroté

number plate *n* *(Brit Aut)* plaque *f* minéralogique *or* d'immatriculation

Number Ten *n* *(Brit: 10 Downing Street)* résidence du Premier ministre

numbness ['nʌmnɪs] *n* torpeur *f*; *(due to cold)* engourdissement *m*

numbskull ['nʌmskʌl] *n* *(inf)* gourde *f*

numeral ['njuːmərəl] *n* chiffre *m*

numerate ['njuːmərɪt] *adj* *(Brit)*: **to be ~** avoir des notions d'arithmétique

numerical [njuː'mɛrɪkl] *adj* numérique

numerous ['njuːmərəs] *adj* nombreux(-euse)

nun [nʌn] *n* religieuse *f*, sœur *f*

nunnery ['nʌnərɪ] *n* couvent *m*

nuptial ['nʌpʃəl] *adj* nuptial(e)

nurse [nəːs] *n* infirmière *f*; *(also: **nursemaid**)* bonne *f* d'enfants ▷ *vt* *(patient, cold)* soigner; *(baby: Brit)* bercer (dans ses bras); *(: US)* allaiter, nourrir; *(hope)* nourrir

nursery ['nəːsərɪ] *n* *(room)* nursery *f*; *(institution)* crèche *f*, garderie *f*; *(for plants)* pépinière *f*

nursery rhyme *n* comptine *f*, chansonnette *f* pour enfants

nursery school *n* école maternelle

nursery slope *n* *(Brit Ski)* piste *f* pour débutants

nursing ['nəːsɪŋ] *n* *(profession)* profession *f* d'infirmière; *(care)* soins *mpl* ▷ *adj* *(mother)* qui allaite

nursing home *n* clinique *f*; *(for convalescence)* maison *f* de convalescence *or* de repos; *(for old people)* maison de retraite

nurture ['nəːtʃə^r] *vt* élever

NUS *n abbr* *(Brit: = National Union of Students)* syndicat des étudiants

NUT *n abbr* *(Brit: = National Union of Teachers)* syndicat enseignant

nut [nʌt] *n* *(of metal)* écrou *m*; *(fruit: walnut)* noix *f*; *(: hazelnut)* noisette *f*; *(: peanut)* cacahuète *f* *(terme générique en anglais)* ▷ *adj* *(chocolate etc)* aux noisettes; **he's ~s** *(inf)* il est dingue

nutcase ['nʌtkeɪs] *n* *(inf)* dingue *m/f*

nutcrackers ['nʌtkrækəz] *npl* casse-noix *m inv*, casse-noisette(s) *m*

nutmeg ['nʌtmɛg] *n* *(noix f)* muscade *f*

nutrient ['njuːtrɪənt] *adj* nutritif(-ive) ▷ *n* substance nutritive

nutrition [njuː'trɪʃən] *n* nutrition *f*, alimentation *f*

nutritionist [njuː'trɪʃənɪst] *n* nutritionniste *m/f*

nutritious [njuː'trɪʃəs] *adj* nutritif(-ive), nourrissant(e)

nuts [nʌts] *(inf)* *adj* dingue

nutshell ['nʌtʃɛl] *n* coquille *f* de noix; **in a ~** en un mot

nutter ['nʌtə^r] *(Brit: inf)* *n*: **he's a complete ~** il est complètement cinglé

nutty ['nʌtɪ] *adj* *(flavour)* à la noisette; *(inf: person)* cinglé(e), dingue

nuzzle ['nʌzl] *vi*: **to ~ up to** fourrer son nez contre

NV *abbr* *(US)* = **Nevada**

NVQ *n abbr* *(Brit)* = **National Vocational Qualification**

NWT *abbr* *(Canada)* = **Northwest Territories**

NY *abbr* *(US)* = **New York**

NYC *abbr* *(US)* = **New York City**

nylon ['naɪlɔn] *n* nylon *m* ▷ *adj* de *or* en nylon; **nylons** *npl* bas *mpl* nylon

nymph [nɪmf] *n* nymphe *f*

nymphomaniac ['nɪmfəu'meɪnɪæk] *adj, n* nymphomane *f*

NYSE *n abbr* *(US)* = **New York Stock Exchange**

NZ *abbr* = **New Zealand**

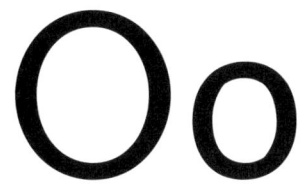

Oo

O, o [əu] *n* (letter) O, o *m*; (US Scol: = outstanding) tb (= *très bien*); **O for Oliver**, (US) **O for Oboe** O comme Oscar

oaf [əuf] *n* balourd *m*

oak [əuk] *n* chêne *m* ▷ *cpd* de *or* en (bois de) chêne

O&M *n abbr* = **organization and method**

O.A.P. *n abbr* (Brit) = **old age pensioner**

oar [ɔːʳ] *n* aviron *m*, rame *f*; **to put** *or* **shove one's ~ in** (fig: inf) mettre son grain de sel

oarsman ['ɔːzmən], **oarswoman** ['ɔːzwumən] (irreg) *n* rameur(-euse); (Naut, Sport) nageur(-euse)

OAS *n abbr* (= Organization of American States) OEA *f* (= Organisation des États américains)

oasis (pl **oases**) [əu'eisis, əu'eisi:z] *n* oasis *f*

oath [əuθ] *n* serment *m*; (swear word) juron *m*; **to take the ~** prêter serment; **on** (Brit) *or* **under ~** sous serment; assermenté(e)

oatmeal ['əutmi:l] *n* flocons *mpl* d'avoine

oats [əuts] *n* avoine *f*

OAU *n abbr* (= Organization of African Unity) OUA *f* (= Organisation de l'unité africaine)

obdurate ['ɔbdjurit] *adj* obstiné(e), impénitent(e); intraitable

OBE *n abbr* (Brit: = Order of the British Empire) distinction honorifique

obedience [ə'bi:diəns] *n* obéissance *f*; **in ~ to** conformément à

obedient [ə'bi:diənt] *adj* obéissant(e); **to be ~ to sb/sth** obéir à qn/qch

obelisk ['ɔbilisk] *n* obélisque *m*

obese [əu'bi:s] *adj* obèse

obesity [əu'bi:siti] *n* obésité *f*

obey [ə'bei] *vt* obéir à; (instructions, regulations) se conformer à ▷ *vi* obéir

obituary [ə'bitjuəri] *n* nécrologie *f*

object *n* ['ɔbdʒikt] objet *m*; (purpose) but *m*, objet; (Ling) complément *m* d'objet ▷ *vi* [əb'dʒɛkt]: **to ~ to** (attitude) désapprouver; (proposal) protester contre, élever une objection contre; **I ~!** je proteste!; **he ~ed that ...** il a fait valoir *or* a objecté que ...; **do you ~ to my smoking?** est-ce que cela vous gêne si je fume?; **what's the ~ of doing that?** quel est l'intérêt de faire cela?; **money is no ~** l'argent n'est pas un problème

objection [əb'dʒɛkʃən] *n* objection *f*; (drawback) inconvénient *m*; **if you have no ~** si vous n'y voyez pas d'inconvénient; **to make** *or* **raise an ~** élever une objection

objectionable [əb'dʒɛkʃənəbl] *adj* très désagréable; choquant(e)

objective [əb'dʒɛktiv] *n* objectif *m* ▷ *adj* objectif(-ive)

objectivity [ɔbdʒik'tiviti] *n* objectivité *f*

object lesson *n* (fig) (bonne) illustration

objector [əb'dʒɛktəʳ] *n* opposant(e)

obligation [ɔbli'geiʃən] *n* obligation *f*, devoir *m*; (debt) dette *f* (de reconnaissance); **"without ~"** "sans engagement"

obligatory [ə'bligətəri] *adj* obligatoire

oblige [ə'blaidʒ] *vt* (force): **to ~ sb to do** obliger *or* forcer qn à faire; (do a favour) rendre service à, obliger; **to be ~d to sb for sth** être obligé(e) à qn de qch; **anything to ~!** (inf) (toujours prêt à rendre) service!

obliging [ə'blaidʒiŋ] *adj* obligeant(e), serviable

oblique [ə'bli:k] *adj* oblique; (allusion) indirect(e) ▷ *n* (Brit Typ): **~ (stroke)** barre *f* oblique

obliterate [ə'blitəreit] *vt* effacer

oblivion [ə'bliviən] *n* oubli *m*

oblivious [ə'bliviəs] *adj*: **~ of** oublieux(-euse) de

oblong ['ɔblɔŋ] *adj* oblong(ue) ▷ *n* rectangle *m*

obnoxious [əb'nɔkʃəs] *adj* odieux(-euse); (smell) nauséabond(e)

o.b.o. *abbr* (US) = **or best offer**; (in classified ads) ≈ à débattre

oboe ['əubəu] *n* hautbois *m*

obscene [əb'si:n] *adj* obscène

obscenity [əb'sɛniti] *n* obscénité *f*

obscure [əb'skjuəʳ] *adj* obscur(e) ▷ *vt* obscurcir; (hide: sun) cacher

obscurity [əb'skjuəriti] *n* obscurité *f*

obsequious [əb'si:kwiəs] *adj* obséquieux(-euse)

observable [əb'zə:vəbl] *adj* observable; (appreciable) notable

observance [əb'zə:vns] *n* observance *f*, observation *f*; **religious ~s** observances religieuses

observant [əb'zə:vnt] *adj* observateur(-trice)

observation [ɔbzə'veiʃən] *n* observation *f*; (by police etc) surveillance *f*

observation post n (Mil) poste m d'observation
observatory [əb'zɜːvətrɪ] n observatoire m
observe [əb'zɜːv] vt observer; (remark) faire observer or remarquer
observer [əb'zɜːvəʳ] n observateur(-trice)
obsess [əb'sɛs] vt obséder; **to be ~ed by** or **with sb/sth** être obsédé(e) par qn/qch
obsession [əb'sɛʃən] n obsession f
obsessive [əb'sɛsɪv] adj obsédant(e)
obsolescence [ɔbsə'lɛsns] n vieillissement m; obsolescence f; **built-in** or **planned ~** (Comm) désuétude calculée
obsolescent [ɔbsə'lɛsnt] adj obsolescent(e), en voie d'être périmé(e)
obsolete [ɔbsəliːt] adj dépassé(e), périmé(e)
obstacle ['ɔbstəkl] n obstacle m
obstacle race n course f d'obstacles
obstetrician [ɔbstə'trɪʃən] n obstétricien(ne)
obstetrics [ɔb'stɛtrɪks] n obstétrique f
obstinacy ['ɔbstɪnəsɪ] n obstination f
obstinate ['ɔbstɪnɪt] adj obstiné(e); (pain, cold) persistant(e)
obstreperous [əb'strɛpərəs] adj turbulent(e)
obstruct [əb'strʌkt] vt (block) boucher, obstruer; (halt) arrêter; (hinder) entraver
obstruction [əb'strʌkʃən] n obstruction f; (to plan, progress) obstacle m
obstructive [əb'strʌktɪv] adj obstructionniste
obtain [əb'teɪn] vt obtenir ▷ vi avoir cours
obtainable [əb'teɪnəbl] adj qu'on peut obtenir
obtrusive [əb'truːsɪv] adj (person) importun(e); (smell) pénétrant(e); (building etc) trop en évidence
obtuse [əb'tjuːs] adj obtus(e)
obverse ['ɔbvɜːs] n (of medal, coin) côté m face; (fig) contrepartie f
obviate ['ɔbvɪeɪt] vt parer à, obvier à
obvious ['ɔbvɪəs] adj évident(e), manifeste
obviously ['ɔbvɪəslɪ] adv manifestement; (of course): **~, he ...** or **he ~ ...** il est bien évident qu'il ...; **~!** bien sûr!; **~ not!** évidemment pas!, bien sûr que non!
OCAS n abbr (= Organization of Central American States) ODEAC f (= Organisation des États d'Amérique centrale)
occasion [ə'keɪʒən] n occasion f; (event) événement m ▷ vt occasionner, causer; **on that ~** à cette occasion; **to rise to the ~** se montrer à la hauteur de la situation
occasional [ə'keɪʒənl] adj pris(e) (or fait(e) etc) de temps en temps; (worker, spending) occasionnel(le)
occasionally [ə'keɪʒənəlɪ] adv de temps en temps, quelquefois; **very ~** (assez) rarement
occasional table n table décorative
occult [ɔ'kʌlt] adj occulte ▷ n: **the ~** le surnaturel
occupancy ['ɔkjupənsɪ] n occupation f
occupant ['ɔkjupənt] n occupant m
occupation [ɔkju'peɪʃən] n occupation f; (job) métier m, profession f; **unfit for ~** (house) impropre à l'habitation

occupational [ɔkju'peɪʃənl] adj (accident, disease) du travail; (hazard) du métier
occupational guidance n (Brit) orientation professionnelle
occupational hazard n risque m du métier
occupational pension n retraite professionnelle
occupational therapy n ergothérapie f
occupier ['ɔkjupaɪəʳ] n occupant(e)
occupy ['ɔkjupaɪ] vt occuper; **to ~ o.s. with** or **by doing** s'occuper à faire; **to be occupied with sth** être occupé avec qch
occur [ə'kɜːʳ] vi se produire; (difficulty, opportunity) se présenter; (phenomenon, error) se rencontrer; **to ~ to sb** venir à l'esprit de qn
occurrence [ə'kʌrəns] n (existence) présence f, existence f; (event) cas m, fait m
ocean ['əuʃən] n océan m; **~s of** (inf) des masses de
ocean bed n fond (sous-)marin
ocean-going ['əuʃəngəuɪŋ] adj de haute mer
Oceania [əuʃɪ'eɪnɪə] n Océanie f
ocean liner n paquebot m
ochre ['əukəʳ] adj ocre
o'clock [ə'klɔk] adv: **it is 5 o'clock** il est 5 heures
OCR n abbr = **optical character reader; optical character recognition**
Oct. abbr (= October) oct
octagonal [ɔk'tægənl] adj octogonal(e)
octane ['ɔkteɪn] n octane m; **high-~ petrol** or (US) **gas** essence f à indice d'octane élevé
octave ['ɔktɪv] n octave f
October [ɔk'təubəʳ] n octobre m; for phrases see also **July**
octogenarian ['ɔktəudʒɪ'nɛərɪən] n octogénaire m/f
octopus ['ɔktəpəs] n pieuvre f
odd [ɔd] adj (strange) bizarre, curieux(-euse); (number) impair(e); (left over) qui reste, en plus; (not of a set) dépareillé(e); **60-~** 60 et quelques; **at ~ times** de temps en temps; **the ~ one out** l'exception f
oddball ['ɔdbɔːl] n (inf) excentrique m/f
oddity ['ɔdɪtɪ] n bizarrerie f; (person) excentrique m/f
odd-job man [ɔd'dʒɔb-] (irreg) n homme m à tout faire
odd jobs npl petits travaux divers
oddly ['ɔdlɪ] adv bizarrement, curieusement
oddments ['ɔdmənts] npl (Brit Comm) fins fpl de série
odds [ɔdz] npl (in betting) cote f; **the ~ are against his coming** il y a peu de chances qu'il vienne; **it makes no ~** cela n'a pas d'importance; **to succeed against all the ~** réussir contre toute attente; **~ and ends** de petites choses; **at ~** en désaccord
odds-on [ɔdz'ɔn] adj: **the ~ favourite** le grand favori; **it's ~ that he'll come** il y a toutes les chances or gros à parier qu'il vienne
ode [əud] n ode f
odious ['əudɪəs] adj odieux(-euse), détestable

odometer [ɔ'dɒmɪtə^r] *n* (*US*) odomètre *m*
odour, (*US*) **odor** ['əudə^r] *n* odeur *f*
odourless, (*US*) **odorless** ['əudəlɪs] *adj* inodore
OECD *n abbr* (= *Organization for Economic Cooperation and Development*) OCDE *f* (= *Organisation de coopération et de développement économique*)
oesophagus, (*US*) **esophagus** [iː'sɔfəgəs] *n* œsophage *m*
oestrogen, (*US*) **estrogen** ['iːstrəudʒən] *n* œstrogène *m*

 KEYWORD

of [ɔv, əv] *prep* **1** (*gen*) de; **a friend of ours** un de nos amis; **a boy of 10** un garçon de 10 ans; **that was kind of you** c'était gentil de votre part
2 (*expressing quantity, amount, dates etc*) de; **a kilo of flour** un kilo de farine; **how much of this do you need?** combien vous en faut-il?; **there were three of them** (*people*) ils étaient 3; (*objects*) il y en avait 3; **three of us went** 3 d'entre nous y sont allé(e)s; **the 5th of July** le 5 juillet; **a quarter of 4** (*US*) 4 heures moins le quart
3 (*from, out of*) en, de; **a statue of marble** une statue de *or* en marbre; **made of wood** (fait) en bois

Ofcom ['ɔfkɔm] *n abbr* (*Brit*: = *Office of Communications Regulation*) *organe de régulation de télécommunications*
off [ɔf] *adj, adv* (*engine*) coupé(e); (*light, TV*) éteint(e); (*tap*) fermé(e); (*Brit: food*) mauvais(e), avancé(e); (: *milk*) tourné(e); (*absent*) absent(e); (*cancelled*) annulé(e); (*removed*): **the lid was ~** le couvercle était retiré *or* n'était pas mis; (*away*): **to run/drive ~** partir en courant/en voiture ▷ *prep* de; **to be ~** (*to leave*) partir, s'en aller; **I must be ~** il faut que je file; **to be ~ sick** être absent pour cause de maladie; **a day ~** un jour de congé; **to have an ~ day** n'être pas en forme; **he had his coat ~** il avait enlevé son manteau; **the hook is ~** le crochet s'est détaché; le crochet n'est pas mis; **10% ~** (*Comm*) 10% de rabais; **5 km ~ (the road)** à 5 km (de la route); **~ the coast** au large de la côte; **a house ~ the main road** une maison à l'écart de la grand-route; **it's a long way ~** c'est loin (d'ici); **I'm ~ meat** je ne mange plus de viande; je n'aime plus la viande; **on the ~ chance** à tout hasard; **to be well/badly ~** être bien/mal loti; (*financially*) être aisé/dans la gêne; **~ and on, on and ~** de temps à autre; **I'm afraid the chicken is ~** (*Brit: not available*) je regrette, il n'y a plus de poulet; **that's a bit ~** (*fig: inf*) c'est un peu fort
offal ['ɔfl] *n* (*Culin*) abats *mpl*
offbeat ['ɔfbiːt] *adj* excentrique
off-centre [ɔf'sɛntə^r] *adj* décentré(e), excentré(e)
off-colour ['ɔf'kʌlə^r] *adj* (*Brit: ill*) malade, mal fichu(e); **to feel ~** être mal fichu
offence, (*US*) **offense** [ə'fɛns] *n* (*crime*) délit *m*,

infraction *f*; **to give ~ to** blesser, offenser; **to take ~ at** se vexer de, s'offenser de; **to commit an ~** commettre une infraction
offend [ə'fɛnd] *vt* (*person*) offenser, blesser ▷ *vi*: **to ~ against** (*law, rule*) contrevenir à, enfreindre
offender [ə'fɛndə^r] *n* délinquant(e); (*against regulations*) contrevenant(e)
offending [ə'fɛndɪŋ] *adj* incriminé(e)
offense [ə'fɛns] *n* (*US*) = **offence**
offensive [ə'fɛnsɪv] *adj* offensant(e), choquant(e); (*smell etc*) très déplaisant(e); (*weapon*) offensif(-ive) ▷ *n* (*Mil*) offensive *f*
offer ['ɔfə^r] *n* offre *f*, proposition *f* ▷ *vt* offrir, proposer; **to make an ~ for sth** faire une offre pour qch; **to ~ sth to sb, ~ sb sth** offrir qch à qn; **to ~ to do sth** proposer de faire qch; **"on ~"** (*Comm*) "en promotion"
offering ['ɔfərɪŋ] *n* offrande *f*
offhand [ɔf'hænd] *adj* désinvolte ▷ *adv* spontanément; **I can't tell you ~** je ne peux pas vous le dire comme ça
office ['ɔfɪs] *n* (*place*) bureau *m*; (*position*) charge *f*, fonction *f*; **doctor's ~** (*US*) cabinet (médical); **to take ~** entrer en fonctions; **through his good ~s** (*fig*) grâce à ses bons offices; **O~ of Fair Trading** (*Brit*) organisme de protection contre les pratiques commerciales abusives
office automation *n* bureautique *f*
office bearer *n* (*of club etc*) membre *m* du bureau
office block, (*US*) **office building** *n* immeuble *m* de bureaux
office boy *n* garçon *m* de bureau
office hours *npl* heures *fpl* de bureau; (*US Med*) heures de consultation
office manager *n* responsable administratif(-ive)
officer ['ɔfɪsə^r] *n* (*Mil etc*) officier *m*; (*also*: **police officer**) agent *m* (de police); (*of organization*) membre *m* du bureau directeur
office work *n* travail *m* de bureau
office worker *n* employé(e) de bureau
official [ə'fɪʃl] *adj* (*authorized*) officiel(le) ▷ *n* officiel *m*; (*civil servant*) fonctionnaire *m/f*; (*of railways, post office, town hall*) employé(e)
officialdom [ə'fɪʃldəm] *n* bureaucratie *f*
officially [ə'fɪʃəlɪ] *adv* officiellement
official receiver *n* administrateur *m* judiciaire, syndic *m* de faillite
officiate [ə'fɪʃɪeɪt] *vi* (*Rel*) officier; **to ~ as Mayor** exercer les fonctions de maire; **to ~ at a marriage** célébrer un mariage
officious [ə'fɪʃəs] *adj* trop empressé(e)
offing ['ɔfɪŋ] *n*: **in the ~** (*fig*) en perspective
off-key [ɔf'kiː] *adj* faux (fausse) ▷ *adv* faux
off-licence ['ɔflaɪsns] *n* (*Brit: shop*) débit *m* de vins et de spiritueux
off-limits [ɔf'lɪmɪts] *adj* (*esp US*) dont l'accès est interdit
off-line [ɔf'laɪn] *adj* (*Comput*) (en mode) autonome; (: *switched off*) non connecté(e)
off-load ['ɔfləud] *vt*: **to ~ sth (onto)** (*goods*) décharger qch (sur); (*job*) se décharger de qch

(sur)

off-peak [ɔfˈpiːk] *adj* aux heures creuses; (*electricity, ticket*) au tarif heures creuses

off-putting [ˈɔfputɪŋ] *adj* (*Brit: remark*) rébarbatif(-ive); (*person*) rebutant(e), peu engageant(e)

off-road vehicle [ˈɔfrəud-] *n* véhicule *m* tout-terrain

off-season [ˈɔfˈsiːzn] *adj, adv* hors-saison *inv*

offset [ˈɔfsɛt] *vt* (*irreg: like* **set**); (*counteract*) contrebalancer, compenser ▷ *n* (*also:* **offset printing**) offset *m*

offshoot [ˈɔfʃuːt] *n* (*fig*) ramification *f*, antenne *f*; (*: of discussion etc*) conséquence *f*

offshore [ɔfˈʃɔːʳ] *adj* (*breeze*) de terre; (*island*) proche du littoral; (*fishing*) côtier(-ière); ~ **oilfield** gisement *m* pétrolifère en mer

offside [ˈɔfˈsaɪd] *n* (*Aut: with right-hand drive*) côté droit; (*: with left-hand drive*) côté gauche ▷ *adj* (*Sport*) hors jeu; (*Aut: in Britain*) de droite; (*: in US, Europe*) de gauche

offspring [ˈɔfsprɪŋ] *n* progéniture *f*

offstage [ɔfˈsteɪdʒ] *adv* dans les coulisses

off-the-cuff [ɔfðəˈkʌf] *adv* au pied levé; de chic

off-the-job [ɔfðəˈdʒɔb] *adj*: ~ **training** formation professionnelle extérieure

off-the-peg [ˈɔfðəˈpɛg], (*US*) **off-the-rack** [ˈɔfðəˈræk] *adv* en prêt-à-porter

off-the-record [ˈɔfðəˈrɛkɔːd] *adj* (*remark*) confidentiel(le), sans caractère officiel ▷ *adv* officieusement

off-white [ˈɔfwaɪt] *adj* blanc cassé *inv*

often [ˈɔfn] *adv* souvent; **how ~ do you go?** vous y allez tous les combien?; **every so ~** de temps en temps, de temps à autre; **as ~ as not** la plupart du temps

Ofwat [ˈɔfwɔt] *n abbr* (*Brit: = Office of Water Services*) *organisme qui surveille les activités des compagnies des eaux*

ogle [ˈəugl] *vt* lorgner

ogre [ˈəugəʳ] *n* ogre *m*

OH *abbr* (*US*) = **Ohio**

oh [əu] *excl* ô!, oh!, ah!

OHMS *abbr* (*Brit*) = **On His (or Her) Majesty's Service**

oil [ɔɪl] *n* huile *f*; (*petroleum*) pétrole *m*; (*for central heating*) mazout *m* ▷ *vt* (*machine*) graisser

oilcan [ˈɔɪlkæn] *n* burette *f* de graissage; (*for storing*) bidon *m* à huile

oil change *n* vidange *f*

oilfield [ˈɔɪlfiːld] *n* gisement *m* de pétrole

oil filter *n* (*Aut*) filtre *m* à huile

oil-fired [ˈɔɪlfaɪəd] *adj* au mazout

oil gauge *n* jauge *f* de niveau d'huile

oil industry *n* industrie pétrolière

oil level *n* niveau *m* d'huile

oil painting *n* peinture *f* à l'huile

oil refinery *n* raffinerie *f* de pétrole

oil rig *n* derrick *m*; (*at sea*) plate-forme pétrolière

oilskins [ˈɔɪlskɪnz] *npl* ciré *m*

oil slick *n* nappe *f* de mazout

oil tanker *n* (*ship*) pétrolier *m*; (*truck*) camion-citerne *m*

oil well *n* puits *m* de pétrole

oily [ˈɔɪlɪ] *adj* huileux(-euse); (*food*) gras(se)

ointment [ˈɔɪntmənt] *n* onguent *m*

OK *abbr* (*US*) = **Oklahoma**

O.K., okay [ˈəuˈkeɪ] (*inf*) *excl* d'accord! ▷ *vt* approuver, donner son accord à ▷ *n*: **to give sth one's O.K.** donner son accord à qch ▷ *adj* (*not bad*) pas mal, en règle; en bon état; sain et sauf; acceptable; **is it O.K.?, are you O.K.?** ça va?; **are you O.K. for money?** ça va *or* ira question argent?; **it's O.K. with** *or* **by me** ça me va, c'est d'accord en ce qui me concerne

Okla. *abbr* (*US*) = **Oklahoma**

old [əuld] *adj* vieux (vieille); (*person*) vieux, âgé(e); (*former*) ancien(ne), vieux; **how ~ are you?** quel âge avez-vous?; **he's 10 years ~** il a 10 ans, il est âgé de 10 ans; **~er brother/sister** frère/sœur aîné(e); **any ~ thing will do** n'importe quoi fera l'affaire

old age *n* vieillesse *f*

old-age pensioner *n* (*Brit*) retraité(e)

old-fashioned [ˈəuldˈfæʃnd] *adj* démodé(e); (*person*) vieux jeu *inv*

old maid *n* vieille fille

old people's home *n* (*esp Brit*) maison *f* de retraite

old-style [ˈəuldstaɪl] *adj* à l'ancienne (mode)

old-time [ˈəuldtaɪm] *adj* du temps jadis, d'autrefois

old-timer [əuldˈtaɪməʳ] *n* ancien *m*

old wives' tale *n* conte *m* de bonne femme

O-level [ˈəulɛvl] *n* (*in England and Wales: formerly*) *examen passé à l'âge de 16 ans sanctionnant les connaissances de l'élève*, ≈ brevet *m* des collèges

olive [ˈɔlɪv] *n* (*fruit*) olive *f*; (*tree*) olivier *m* ▷ *adj* (*also:* **olive-green**) (vert) olive *inv*

olive oil *n* huile *f* d'olive

Olympic [əuˈlɪmpɪk] *adj* olympique; **the ~ Games, the ~s** les Jeux *mpl* olympiques

OM *n abbr* (*Brit: = Order of Merit*) *titre honorifique*

Oman [əuˈmɑːn] *n* Oman *m*

OMB *n abbr* (*US: = Office of Management and Budget*) *service conseillant le président en matière budgétaire*

omelette, omelet [ˈɔmlɪt] *n* omelette *f*; **ham/ cheese omelet(te)** omelette au jambon/ fromage

omen [ˈəumən] *n* présage *m*

ominous [ˈɔmɪnəs] *adj* menaçant(e), inquiétant(e); (*event*) de mauvais augure

omission [əuˈmɪʃən] *n* omission *f*

omit [əuˈmɪt] *vt* omettre; **to ~ to do sth** négliger de faire qch

omnivorous [ɔmˈnɪvrəs] *adj* omnivore

ON *abbr* (*Canada*) = **Ontario**

 KEYWORD

on [ɔn] *prep* **1** (*indicating position*) sur; **on the table** sur la table; **on the wall** sur le *or* au mur; **on the left** à gauche; **I haven't any money on me** je n'ai pas d'argent sur moi

2 (*indicating means, method, condition etc*): **on foot** à pied; **on the train/plane** (*be*) dans le train/ l'avion; (*go*) en train/avion; **on the telephone/ radio/television** au téléphone/à la radio/à la télévision; **to be on drugs** se droguer; **on holiday** (*Brit*): **on vacation** (*US*) en vacances; **on the continent** sur le continent
3 (*referring to time*): **on Friday** vendredi; **on Fridays** le vendredi; **on June 20th** le 20 juin; **a week on Friday** vendredi en huit; **on arrival** à l'arrivée; **on seeing this** en voyant cela
4 (*about, concerning*) sur, de; **a book on Balzac/ physics** un livre sur Balzac/de physique
5 (*at the expense of*): **this round is on me** c'est ma tournée
▷ *adv* **1** (*referring to dress*): **to have one's coat on** avoir (mis) son manteau; **to put one's coat on** mettre son manteau; **what's she got on?** qu'est-ce qu'elle porte?
2 (*referring to covering*): **screw the lid on tightly** vissez bien le couvercle
3 (*further, continuously*): **to walk** *etc* **on** continuer à marcher *etc*; **on and off** de temps à autre; **from that day on** depuis ce jour
▷ *adj* **1** (*in operation: machine*) en marche; (: *radio, TV, light*) allumé(e); (: *tap, gas*) ouvert(e); (: *brakes*) mis(e); **is the meeting still on?** (*not cancelled*) est-ce que la réunion a bien lieu?; **it was well on in the evening** c'était tard dans la soirée; **when is this film on?** quand passe ce film?
2 (*inf*): **that's not on!** (*not acceptable*) cela ne se fait pas!; (*not possible*) pas question!

ONC *n abbr* (*Brit*: = *Ordinary National Certificate*) ≈ BT *m*

once [wʌns] *adv* une fois; (*formerly*) autrefois
▷ *conj* une fois que + *sub*; **~ he had left/it was done** une fois qu'il fut parti/ que ce fut terminé; **at ~** tout de suite, immédiatement; (*simultaneously*) à la fois; **all at ~** (*adv*) tout d'un coup; **~ a week** une fois par semaine; **~ more** encore une fois; **I knew him ~** je l'ai connu autrefois; **~ and for all** une fois pour toutes; **~ upon a time there was ...** il y avait une fois ..., il était une fois ...

oncoming [ˈɒnkʌmɪŋ] *adj* (*traffic*) venant en sens inverse

OND *n abbr* (*Brit*: = *Ordinary National Diploma*) ≈ BTS *m*

 KEYWORD

one [wʌn] *num* un(e); **one hundred and fifty** cent cinquante; **one by one** un(e) à *or* par un(e); **one day** un jour
▷ *adj* **1** (*sole*) seul(e), unique; **the one book which** l'unique *or* le seul livre qui; **the one man who** le seul (homme) qui
2 (*same*) même; **they came in the one car** ils sont venus dans la même voiture
▷ *pron* **1**: **this one** celui-ci (celle-ci); **that one** celui-là (celle-là); **I've already got one/a red**

one j'en ai déjà un(e)/un(e) rouge; **which one do you want?** lequel voulez-vous?
2: **one another** l'un(e) l'autre; **to look at one another** se regarder
3 (*impersonal*) on; **one never knows** on ne sait jamais; **to cut one's finger** se couper le doigt; **one needs to eat** il faut manger
4 (*phrases*): **to be one up on sb** avoir l'avantage sur qn; **to be at one (with sb)** être d'accord (avec qn)

one-armed bandit [ˈwʌnɑːmd-] *n* machine *f* à sous
one-day excursion [ˈwʌndeɪ-] *n* (*US*) billet *m* d'aller-retour (valable pour la journée)
One-hundred share index [ˈwʌnhʌndrəd-] *n* indice *m* Footsie des cent grandes valeurs
one-man [ˈwʌnˈmæn] *adj* (*business*) dirigé(e) *etc* par un seul homme
one-man band *n* homme-orchestre *m*
one-off [wʌnˈɒf] *n* (*Brit inf*) exemplaire *m* unique
▷ *adj* unique
one-parent family [ˈwʌnpɛərənt-] *n* famille monoparentale
one-piece [ˈwʌnpiːs] *adj*: **~ bathing suit** maillot *m* une pièce
onerous [ˈɒnərəs] *adj* (*task, duty*) pénible; (*responsibility*) lourd(e)
oneself [wʌnˈsɛlf] *pron* se; (*after prep, also emphatic*) soi-même; **to hurt ~** se faire mal; **to keep sth for ~** garder qch pour soi; **to talk to ~** se parler à soi-même; **by ~** tout seul
one-shot [wʌnˈʃɒt] (*US*) *n* = **one-off**
one-sided [wʌnˈsaɪdɪd] *adj* (*argument, decision*) unilatéral(e); (*judgment, account*) partial(e); (*contest*) inégal(e)
one-time [ˈwʌntaɪm] *adj* d'autrefois
one-to-one [ˈwʌntəwʌn] *adj* (*relationship*) univoque
one-upmanship [wʌnˈʌpmənʃɪp] *n*: **the art of ~** l'art de faire mieux que les autres
one-way [ˈwʌnweɪ] *adj* (*street, traffic*) à sens unique
ongoing [ˈɒngəuɪŋ] *adj* en cours; (*relationship*) suivi(e)
onion [ˈʌnjən] *n* oignon *m*
on-line [ˈɒnlaɪn] *adj* (*Comput*) en ligne; (: *switched on*) connecté(e)
onlooker [ˈɒnlukəʳ] *n* spectateur(-trice)
only [ˈəunlɪ] *adv* seulement ▷ *adj* seul(e), unique ▷ *conj* seulement, mais; **an ~ child** un enfant unique; **not ~ ... but also** non seulement ... mais aussi; **I ~ took one** j'en ai seulement pris un, je n'en ai pris qu'un; **I saw her ~ yesterday** je l'ai vue hier encore; **I'd be ~ too pleased to help** je ne serais que trop content de vous aider; **I would come, ~ I'm very busy** je viendrais bien mais j'ai beaucoup à faire
ono *abbr* (*Brit*) = **or nearest offer**; (*in classified ads*) ≈ à débattre
on-screen [ɒnˈskriːn] *adj* à l'écran
onset [ˈɒnsɛt] *n* début *m*; (*of winter, old age*)

approche f

onshore ['ɒnʃɔːʳ] adj (wind) du large

onslaught ['ɒnslɔːt] n attaque f, assaut m

Ont. abbr (Canada) = **Ontario**

on-the-job ['ɒnðə'dʒɒb] adj: ~ **training** formation f sur place

onto ['ɒntu] prep = **on to**

onus ['əunəs] n responsabilité f; **the ~ is upon him to prove it** c'est à lui de le prouver

onward ['ɒnwəd], **onwards** ['ɒnwədz] adv (move) en avant; **from that time ~s** à partir de ce moment

oops [ups] excl houp!; ~-**a-daisy!** houp-là!

ooze [uːz] vi suinter

opacity [əu'pæsɪtɪ] n opacité f

opal ['əupl] n opale f

opaque [əu'peɪk] adj opaque

OPEC ['əupɛk] n abbr (= Organization of Petroleum-Exporting Countries) OPEP f

open ['əupn] adj ouvert(e); (car) découvert(e); (road, view) dégagé(e); (meeting) public(-ique); (admiration) manifeste; (question) non résolu(e); (enemy) déclaré(e) ▷ vt ouvrir ▷ vi (flower, eyes, door, debate) s'ouvrir; (shop, bank, museum) ouvrir; (book etc: commence) commencer, débuter; **is it ~ to public?** est-ce ouvert au public?; **what time do you ~?** à quelle heure ouvrez-vous?; **in the ~ (air)** en plein air; **the ~ sea** le large; **~ ground** (among trees) clairière f; (waste ground) terrain m vague; **to have an ~ mind (on sth)** avoir l'esprit ouvert (sur qch)

▶ **open on to** vt fus (room, door) donner sur

▶ **open out** vt ouvrir ▷ vi s'ouvrir

▶ **open up** vt ouvrir; (blocked road) dégager ▷ vi s'ouvrir

open-air [əupn'ɛəʳ] adj en plein air

open-and-shut ['əupnən'ʃʌt] adj: ~ **case** cas m limpide

open day n journée f portes ouvertes

open-ended [əupn'ɛndɪd] adj (fig) non limité(e)

opener ['əupnəʳ] n (also: **can opener, tin opener**) ouvre-boîtes m

open-heart surgery [əupn'hɑːt-] n chirurgie f à cœur ouvert

opening ['əupnɪŋ] n ouverture f; (opportunity) occasion f; (work) débouché m; (job) poste vacant

opening hours npl heures fpl d'ouverture

opening night n (Theat) première f

open learning n enseignement universitaire à la carte, notamment par correspondance; (distance learning) télé-enseignement m

open learning centre n centre ouvert à tous où l'on dispense un enseignement général à temps partiel

openly ['əupnlɪ] adv ouvertement

open-minded [əupn'maɪndɪd] adj à l'esprit ouvert

open-necked ['əupnnɛkt] adj à col ouvert

openness ['əupnnɪs] n (frankness) franchise f

open-plan ['əupn'plæn] adj sans cloisons

open prison n prison ouverte

open sandwich n canapé m

open shop n entreprise qui admet les travailleurs non syndiqués

Open University n (Brit) cours universitaires par correspondance

opera ['ɒpərə] n opéra m

opera glasses npl jumelles fpl de théâtre

opera house n opéra m

opera singer n chanteur(-euse) d'opéra

operate ['ɒpəreɪt] vt (machine) faire marcher, faire fonctionner; (system) pratiquer ▷ vi fonctionner; (drug) faire effet; **to ~ on sb (for)** (Med) opérer qn (de)

operatic [ɒpə'rætɪk] adj d'opéra

operating ['ɒpəreɪtɪŋ] adj (Comm: costs, profit) d'exploitation; (Med): ~ **table** table f d'opération

operating room n (US: Med) salle f d'opération

operating system n (Comput) système m d'exploitation

operating theatre n (Brit: Med) salle f d'opération

operation [ɒpə'reɪʃən] n opération f; (of machine) fonctionnement m; **to have an ~ (for)** se faire opérer (de); **to be in ~** (machine) être en service; (system) être en vigueur

operational [ɒpə'reɪʃənl] adj opérationnel(le); (ready for use) en état de marche; **when the service is fully ~** lorsque le service fonctionnera pleinement

operative ['ɒpərətɪv] adj (measure) en vigueur ▷ n (in factory) ouvrier(-ière); **the ~ word** le mot clef

operator ['ɒpəreɪtəʳ] n (of machine) opérateur(-trice); (Tel) téléphoniste m/f

operetta [ɒpə'rɛtə] n opérette f

ophthalmologist [ɒfθæl'mɒlədʒɪst] n ophtalmologiste m/f, ophtalmologue m/f

opinion [ə'pɪnjən] n opinion f, avis m; **in my ~** à mon avis; **to seek a second ~** demander un deuxième avis

opinionated [ə'pɪnjəneɪtɪd] adj aux idées bien arrêtées

opinion poll n sondage m d'opinion

opium ['əupɪəm] n opium m

opponent [ə'pəunənt] n adversaire m/f

opportune ['ɒpətjuːn] adj opportun(e)

opportunist [ɒpə'tjuːnɪst] n opportuniste m/f

opportunity [ɒpə'tjuːnɪtɪ] n occasion f; **to take the ~ to do** or **of doing** profiter de l'occasion pour faire

oppose [ə'pəuz] vt s'opposer à; **to be ~d to sth** être opposé(e) à qch; **as ~d to** par opposition à

opposing [ə'pəuzɪŋ] adj (side) opposé(e)

opposite ['ɒpəzɪt] adj opposé(e); (house etc) d'en face ▷ adv en face ▷ prep en face de ▷ n opposé m, contraire m; (of word) contraire m; **"see ~ page"** "voir ci-contre"

opposite number n (Brit) homologue m/f

opposite sex n: **the ~** l'autre sexe

opposition [ɒpə'zɪʃən] n opposition f

oppress [ə'prɛs] vt opprimer

oppression [ə'prɛʃən] n oppression f

oppressive [ə'prɛsɪv] *adj* oppressif(-ive)
opprobrium [ə'prəʊbrɪəm] *n* (*formal*) opprobre *m*
opt [ɔpt] *vi*: **to ~ for** opter pour; **to ~ to do** choisir de faire
  ▶ **opt out** *vi* (*school, hospital*) devenir autonome; (*health service*) devenir privé(e); **to ~ out of** choisir de ne pas participer à *or* de ne pas faire
optical ['ɔptɪkl] *adj* optique; (*instrument*) d'optique
optical character reader *n* lecteur *m* optique
optical character recognition *n* lecture *f* optique
optical fibre *n* fibre *f* optique
optician [ɔp'tɪʃən] *n* opticien(ne)
optics ['ɔptɪks] *n* optique *f*
optimism ['ɔptɪmɪzəm] *n* optimisme *m*
optimist ['ɔptɪmɪst] *n* optimiste *m/f*
optimistic [ɔptɪ'mɪstɪk] *adj* optimiste
optimum ['ɔptɪməm] *adj* optimum
option ['ɔpʃən] *n* choix *m*, option *f*; (*Scol*) matière *f* à option; (*Comm*) option; **to keep one's ~s open** (*fig*) ne pas s'engager; **I have no ~** je n'ai pas le choix
optional ['ɔpʃənl] *adj* facultatif(-ive); (*Comm*) en option; **~ extras** accessoires *mpl* en option, options *fpl*
opulence ['ɔpjuləns] *n* opulence *f*; abondance *f*
opulent ['ɔpjulənt] *adj* opulent(e); abondant(e)
OR *abbr* (*US*) = **Oregon**
or [ɔːʳ] *conj* ou; (*with negative*): **he hasn't seen or heard anything** il n'a rien vu ni entendu; **or else** sinon; ou bien
oracle ['ɔrəkl] *n* oracle *m*
oral ['ɔːrəl] *adj* oral(e) ▷ *n* oral *m*
orange ['ɔrɪndʒ] *n* (*fruit*) orange *f* ▷ *adj* orange *inv*
orangeade [ɔrɪndʒ'eɪd] *n* orangeade *f*
orange juice *n* jus *m* d'orange
oration [ɔː'reɪʃən] *n* discours solennel
orator ['ɔrətəʳ] *n* orateur(-trice)
oratorio [ɔrə'tɔːrɪəʊ] *n* oratorio *m*
orb [ɔːb] *n* orbe *m*
orbit ['ɔːbɪt] *n* orbite *f* ▷ *vt* graviter autour de; **to be in/go into ~ (round)** être/entrer en orbite (autour de)
orbital ['ɔːbɪtl] *n* (*also*: **orbital motorway**) périphérique *f*
orchard ['ɔːtʃəd] *n* verger *m*; **apple ~** verger de pommiers
orchestra ['ɔːkɪstrə] *n* orchestre *m*; (*US: seating*) (fauteuils *mpl* d')orchestre
orchestral [ɔː'kɛstrəl] *adj* orchestral(e); (*concert*) symphonique
orchestrate ['ɔːkɪstreɪt] *vt* (*Mus, fig*) orchestrer
orchid ['ɔːkɪd] *n* orchidée *f*
ordain [ɔː'deɪn] *vt* (*Rel*) ordonner; (*decide*) décréter
ordeal [ɔː'diːl] *n* épreuve *f*
order ['ɔːdəʳ] *n* ordre *m*; (*Comm*) commande *f* ▷ *vt* ordonner; (*Comm*) commander; **in ~** en ordre; (*of document*) en règle; **out of ~** (*not in correct order*) en désordre; (*machine*) hors service; (*telephone*)

en dérangement; **a machine in working ~** une machine en état de marche; **in ~ of size** par ordre de grandeur; **in ~ to do/that** pour faire/que + *sub*; **to place an ~ for sth with sb** commander qch auprès de qn, passer commande de qch à qn; **could I ~ now, please?** je peux commander, s'il vous plaît?; **to be on ~** être en commande; **made to ~** fait sur commande; **to be under ~s to do sth** avoir ordre de faire qch; **a point of ~** un point de procédure; **to the ~ of** (*Banking*) à l'ordre de; **to ~ sb to do** ordonner à qn de faire
order book *n* carnet *m* de commandes
order form *n* bon *m* de commande
orderly ['ɔːdəlɪ] *n* (*Mil*) ordonnance *f*; (*Med*) garçon *m* de salle ▷ *adj* (*room*) en ordre; (*mind*) méthodique; (*person*) qui a de l'ordre
order number *n* (*Comm*) numéro *m* de commande
ordinal ['ɔːdɪnl] *adj* (*number*) ordinal(e)
ordinary ['ɔːdnrɪ] *adj* ordinaire, normal(e); (*pej*) ordinaire, quelconque; **out of the ~** exceptionnel(le)
ordinary degree *n* (*Scol*) ≈ licence *f* libre; *voir article*

  ● **ORDINARY DEGREE**
  ●
  ● Un *ordinary degree* est un diplôme inférieur à
  ● l'"honours degree" que l'on obtient en
  ● général après trois années d'études
  ● universitaires. Il peut aussi être décerné en
  ● cas d'échec à l'"honours degree".

ordinary seaman *n* (*Brit*) matelot *m*
ordinary shares *npl* actions *fpl* ordinaires
ordination [ɔːdɪ'neɪʃən] *n* ordination *f*
ordnance ['ɔːdnəns] *n* (*Mil: unit*) service *m* du matériel
Ordnance Survey map *n* (*Brit*) ≈ carte *f* d'État-major
ore [ɔːʳ] *n* minerai *m*
Ore., Oreg. *abbr* (*US*) = **Oregon**
oregano [ɔrɪ'gɑːnəʊ] *n* origan *m*
organ ['ɔːgən] *n* organe *m*; (*Mus*) orgue *m*, orgues *fpl*
organic [ɔː'gænɪk] *adj* organique; (*crops etc*) biologique, naturel(le)
organism ['ɔːgənɪzəm] *n* organisme *m*
organist ['ɔːgənɪst] *n* organiste *m/f*
organization [ɔːgənaɪ'zeɪʃən] *n* organisation *f*
organization chart *n* organigramme *m*
organize ['ɔːgənaɪz] *vt* organiser; **to get ~d** s'organiser
organized ['ɔːgənaɪzd] *adj* (*planned*) organisé(e); (*efficient*) bien organisé
organized crime ['ɔːgənaɪzd-] *n* crime organisé, grand banditisme
organized labour ['ɔːgənaɪzd-] *n* main-d'œuvre syndiquée
organizer ['ɔːgənaɪzəʳ] *n* organisateur(-trice)
orgasm ['ɔːgæzəm] *n* orgasme *m*

orgy ['ɔːdʒɪ] n orgie f
Orient ['ɔːrɪənt] n: **the ~** l'Orient m
oriental [ɔːrɪ'ɛntl] adj oriental(e) ▷ n Oriental(e)
orientate ['ɔːrɪənteɪt] vt orienter
orientation [ɔːrɪən'teɪʃən] n (attitudes) tendance f; (in job) orientation f; (of building) orientation, exposition f
orifice ['ɒrɪfɪs] n orifice m
origin ['ɒrɪdʒɪn] n origine f; **country of ~** pays m d'origine
original [ə'rɪdʒɪnl] adj original(e); (earliest) originel(le) ▷ n original m
originality [ərɪdʒɪ'nælɪtɪ] n originalité f
originally [ə'rɪdʒɪnəlɪ] adv (at first) à l'origine
originate [ə'rɪdʒɪneɪt] vi: **to ~ from** être originaire de; (suggestion) provenir de; **to ~ in** (custom) prendre naissance dans, avoir son origine dans
originator [ə'rɪdʒɪneɪtər] n auteur m
Orkney ['ɔːknɪ] n (also: **the Orkneys, the Orkney Islands**) les Orcades fpl
ornament ['ɔːnəmənt] n ornement m; (trinket) bibelot m
ornamental [ɔːnə'mɛntl] adj décoratif(-ive); (garden) d'agrément
ornamentation [ɔːnəmɛn'teɪʃən] n ornementation f
ornate [ɔː'neɪt] adj très orné(e)
ornithologist [ɔːnɪ'θɒlədʒɪst] n ornithologue m/f
ornithology [ɔːnɪ'θɒlədʒɪ] n ornithologie f
orphan ['ɔːfn] n orphelin(e) ▷ vt: **to be ~ed** devenir orphelin
orphanage ['ɔːfənɪdʒ] n orphelinat m
orthodox ['ɔːθədɔks] adj orthodoxe
orthopaedic, (US) **orthopedic** [ɔːθə'piːdɪk] adj orthopédique
OS abbr (Brit: = Ordnance Survey) ≈ IGN m (= Institut géographique national); (: Naut) = **ordinary seaman**; (: Dress) = **outsize**
O/S abbr = **out of stock**
Oscar ['ɒskər] n oscar m
oscillate ['ɒsɪleɪt] vi osciller
OSHA n abbr (US: = Occupational Safety and Health Administration) office de l'hygiène et de la sécurité au travail
Oslo ['ɒzləu] n Oslo
ostensible [ɒs'tɛnsɪbl] adj prétendu(e); apparent(e)
ostensibly [ɒs'tɛnsɪblɪ] adv en apparence
ostentation [ɒstɛn'teɪʃən] n ostentation f
ostentatious [ɒstɛn'teɪʃəs] adj prétentieux(-euse); ostentatoire
osteopath ['ɒstɪəpæθ] n ostéopathe m/f
ostracize ['ɒstrəsaɪz] vt frapper d'ostracisme
ostrich ['ɒstrɪtʃ] n autruche f
OT n abbr (= Old Testament) AT m
OTB n abbr (US: = off-track betting) paris pris en dehors du champ de course
O.T.E. abbr (= on-target earnings) primes fpl sur objectifs inclus

other ['ʌðər] adj autre ▷ pron: **the ~ (one)** l'autre; **~s** (other people) d'autres ▷ adv: **~ than** autrement que; à part; **some actor or ~** un certain acteur, je ne sais quel acteur; **somebody or ~** quelqu'un; **some ~ people have still to arrive** on attend encore quelques personnes; **the ~ day** l'autre jour; **the car was none ~ than John's** la voiture n'était autre que celle de John
otherwise ['ʌðəwaɪz] adv, conj autrement; **an ~ good piece of work** par ailleurs, un beau travail
OTT abbr (inf) = **over the top**; see **top**
Ottawa ['ɒtəwə] n Ottawa
otter ['ɒtər] n loutre f
OU n abbr (Brit) = **Open University**
ouch [autʃ] excl aïe!
ought (pt -) [ɔːt] aux vb: **I ~ to do it** je devrais le faire, il faudrait que je le fasse; **this ~ to have been corrected** cela aurait dû être corrigé; **he ~ to win** (probability) il devrait gagner; **you ~ to go and see it** vous devriez aller le voir
ounce [auns] n once f (28.35g; 16 in a pound)
our ['auər] adj notre, nos pl; see also **my**
ours [auəz] pron le (la) nôtre, les nôtres; see also **mine¹**
ourselves [auə'sɛlvz] pron pl (reflexive, after preposition) nous; (emphatic) nous-mêmes; **we did it (all) by ~** nous avons fait ça tout seuls; see also **oneself**
oust [aust] vt évincer
out [aut] adv dehors; (published, not at home etc) sorti(e); (light, fire) éteint(e); (on strike) en grève ▷ vt: **to ~ sb** révéler l'homosexualité de qn; **~ here** ici; **~ there** là-bas; **he's ~** (absent) il est sorti; (unconscious) il est sans connaissance; **to be ~ in one's calculations** s'être trompé dans ses calculs; **to run/back** etc **~** sortir en courant/ en reculant etc; **to be ~ and about** or (US) **around again** être de nouveau sur pied; **before the week was ~** avant la fin de la semaine; **the journey ~** l'aller m; **the boat was 10 km ~** le bateau était à 10 km du rivage; **~ loud** (adv) à haute voix; **~ of** (prep: outside) en dehors de; (because of: anger etc) par; (from among): **10 ~ of 10** 10 sur 10; (without): **~ of petrol** sans essence, à court d'essence; **made ~ of wood** en or de bois; **~ of order** (machine) en panne; (Tel: line) en dérangement; **~ of stock** (Comm: article) épuisé(e); (: shop) en rupture de stock
outage ['autɪdʒ] n (esp US: power failure) panne f or coupure f de courant
out-and-out ['autəndaut] adj véritable
outback ['autbæk] n campagne isolée; (in Australia) intérieur m
outbid [aut'bɪd] vt (irreg: like **bid**) surenchérir
outboard ['autbɔːd] n: **~ (motor)** (moteur m) hors-bord m
outbound ['autbaund] adj: **~ (from/for)** en partance (de/pour)
outbreak ['autbreɪk] n (of violence) éruption f, explosion f; (of disease) de nombreux cas; **the ~**

of war south of the border la guerre qui s'est déclarée au sud de la frontière

outbuilding ['autbɪldɪŋ] n dépendance f

outburst ['autbə:st] n explosion f, accès m

outcast ['autka:st] n exilé(e); (socially) paria m

outclass [aut'kla:s] vt surclasser

outcome ['autkʌm] n issue f, résultat m

outcrop ['autkrɔp] n affleurement m

outcry ['autkraɪ] n tollé (général)

outdated [aut'deɪtɪd] adj démodé(e)

outdistance [aut'dɪstəns] vt distancer

outdo [aut'du:] vt (irreg: like **do**) surpasser

outdoor [aut'dɔ:ʳ] adj de or en plein air

outdoors [aut'dɔ:z] adv dehors; au grand air

outer ['autəʳ] adj extérieur(e); **~ suburbs** grande banlieue

outer space n espace m cosmique

outfit ['autfɪt] n équipement m; (clothes) tenue f; (inf: Comm) organisation f, boîte f

outfitter ['autfɪtəʳ] n (Brit): **"(gent's) ~'s"** "confection pour hommes"

outgoing ['autgəuɪŋ] adj (president, tenant) sortant(e); (character) ouvert(e), extraverti(e)

outgoings ['autgəuɪŋz] npl (Brit: expenses) dépenses fpl

outgrow [aut'grəu] vt (irreg: like **grow**); (clothes) devenir trop grand(e) pour

outhouse ['authaus] n appentis m, remise f

outing ['autɪŋ] n sortie f; excursion f

outlandish [aut'lændɪʃ] adj étrange

outlast [aut'la:st] vt survivre à

outlaw ['autlɔ:] n hors-la-loi m inv ▷ vt (person) mettre hors la loi; (practice) proscrire

outlay ['autleɪ] n dépenses fpl; (investment) mise f de fonds

outlet ['autlɛt] n (for liquid etc) issue f, sortie f; (for emotion) exutoire m; (for goods) débouché m; (also: **retail outlet**) point m de vente; (US: Elec) prise f de courant

outline ['autlaɪn] n (shape) contour m; (summary) esquisse f, grandes lignes ▷ vt (fig: theory, plan) exposer à grands traits

outlive [aut'lɪv] vt survivre à

outlook ['autluk] n perspective f; (point of view) attitude f

outlying ['autlaɪɪŋ] adj écarté(e)

outmanoeuvre [autmə'nu:vəʳ] vt (rival etc) avoir au tournant

outmoded [aut'məudɪd] adj démodé(e); dépassé(e)

outnumber [aut'nʌmbəʳ] vt surpasser en nombre

out-of-court [autəv'kɔ:t] adj, adv à l'aimable

out-of-date [autəv'deɪt] adj (passport, ticket) périmé(e); (theory, idea) dépassé(e); (custom) désuet(-ète); (clothes) démodé(e)

out-of-doors [autəv'dɔ:z] adv = **outdoors**

out-of-the-way [autəvðə'weɪ] adj loin de tout; (fig) insolite

out-of-town [autəv'taun] adj (shopping centre etc) en périphérie

outpatient ['autpeɪʃənt] n malade m/f en

consultation externe

outpost ['autpəust] n avant-poste m

outpouring ['autpɔ:rɪŋ] n (fig) épanchement(s) m(pl)

output ['autput] n rendement m, production f; (Comput) sortie f ▷ vt (Comput) sortir

outrage ['autreɪdʒ] n (anger) indignation f; (violent act) atrocité f, acte m de violence; (scandal) scandale m ▷ vt outrager

outrageous [aut'reɪdʒəs] adj atroce; (scandalous) scandaleux(-euse)

outrider ['autraɪdəʳ] n (on motorcycle) motard m

outright adv [aut'raɪt] complètement; (deny, refuse) catégoriquement; (ask) carrément; (kill) sur le coup ▷ adj ['autraɪt] complet(-ète); catégorique

outrun [aut'rʌn] vt (irreg: like **run**) dépasser

outset ['autsɛt] n début m

outshine [aut'ʃaɪn] vt (irreg: like **shine**); (fig) éclipser

outside [aut'saɪd] n extérieur m ▷ adj extérieur(e); (remote, unlikely): **an ~ chance** une (très) faible chance ▷ adv (au) dehors, à l'extérieur ▷ prep hors de, à l'extérieur de; (in front of) devant; **at the ~** (fig) au plus or maximum; **~ left/right** n (Football) ailier gauche/droit

outside broadcast n (Radio, TV) reportage m

outside lane n (Aut: in Britain) voie f de droite; (: in US, Europe) voie de gauche

outside line n (Tel) ligne extérieure

outsider [aut'saɪdəʳ] n (in race etc) outsider m; (stranger) étranger(-ère)

outsize ['autsaɪz] adj énorme; (clothes) grande taille inv

outskirts ['autskə:ts] npl faubourgs mpl

outsmart [aut'sma:t] vt se montrer plus malin(-igne) or futé(e) que

outspoken [aut'spəukən] adj très franc (franche)

outspread [aut'sprɛd] adj (wings) déployé(e)

outstanding [aut'stændɪŋ] adj remarquable, exceptionnel(le); (unfinished: work, business) en suspens, en souffrance; (debt) impayé(e); (problem) non réglé(e); **your account is still ~** vous n'avez pas encore tout remboursé

outstay [aut'steɪ] vt: **to ~ one's welcome** abuser de l'hospitalité de son hôte

outstretched [aut'strɛtʃt] adj (hand) tendu(e); (body) étendu(e)

outstrip [aut'strɪp] vt (also fig) dépasser

out-tray ['auttreɪ] n courrier m "départ"

outvote [aut'vəut] vt: **to ~ sb (by)** mettre qn en minorité (par); **to ~ sth (by)** rejeter qch (par)

outward ['autwəd] adj (sign, appearances) extérieur(e); (journey) (d')aller

outwardly ['autwədlɪ] adv extérieurement; en apparence

outwards ['autwədz] adv (esp Brit) = **outward**

outweigh [aut'weɪ] vt l'emporter sur

outwit [aut'wɪt] vt se montrer plus malin que

oval ['əuvl] adj, n ovale m

Oval Office n (US: Pol) voir article

● OVAL OFFICE
●
● L'Oval Office est le bureau personnel du
● président des États-Unis à la Maison-
● Blanche, ainsi appelé du fait de sa forme
● ovale. Par extension, ce terme désigne la
● présidence elle-même.

ovarian [əu'vɛərɪən] adj ovarien(ne); (cancer) des
ovaires
ovary ['əuvərɪ] n ovaire m
ovation [əu'veɪʃən] n ovation f
oven ['ʌvn] n four m
oven glove n gant m de cuisine
ovenproof ['ʌvnpru:f] adj allant au four
oven-ready ['ʌvnrɛdɪ] adj prêt(e) à cuire
ovenware ['ʌvnwɛər] n plats mpl allant au four
over ['əuvər] adv (par-)dessus; (excessively) trop
▷ adj (or adv) (finished) fini(e), terminé(e); (too
much) en plus ▷ prep sur; par-dessus; (above) au-
dessus de; (on the other side of) de l'autre côté de;
(more than) plus de; (during) pendant; (about,
concerning): **they fell out ~ money/her** ils se
sont brouillés pour des questions d'argent/à
cause d'elle; **~ here** ici; **~ there** là-bas; **all ~**
(everywhere) partout; (finished) fini(e); **~ and ~**
(again) à plusieurs reprises; **~ and above** en
plus de; **to ask sb ~** inviter qn (à passer); **to go
~ to sb's** passer chez qn; **to fall ~** tomber; **to
turn sth ~** retourner qch; **now ~ to our Paris
correspondent** nous passons l'antenne à
notre correspondant à Paris; **the world ~** dans
le monde entier; **she's not ~ intelligent** (Brit)
elle n'est pas particulièrement intelligente
over... ['əuvər] prefix: **overabundant**
surabondant(e)
overact [əuvər'ækt] vi (Theat) outrer son rôle
overall ['əuvərɔ:l] adj (length) total(e); (study,
impression) d'ensemble ▷ n (Brit) blouse f ▷ adv
[əuvər'ɔ:l] dans l'ensemble, en général;
overalls npl (boiler suit) bleus mpl (de travail)
overall majority n majorité absolue
overanxious [əuvər'æŋkʃəs] adj trop
anxieux(-euse)
overawe [əuvər'ɔ:] vt impressionner
overbalance [əuvə'bæləns] vi basculer
overbearing [əuvə'bɛərɪŋ] adj
impérieux(-euse), autoritaire
overboard ['əuvəbɔ:d] adv (Naut) par-dessus
bord; **to go ~ for sth** (fig) s'emballer (pour qch)
overbook [əuvə'buk] vi faire du surbooking
overcame [əuvə'keɪm] pt of **overcome**
overcapitalize [əuvə'kæpɪtəlaɪz] vt
surcapitaliser
overcast ['əuvəkɑ:st] adj couvert(e)
overcharge [əuvə'tʃɑ:dʒ] vt: **to ~ sb for sth** faire
payer qch trop cher à qn
overcoat ['əuvəkəut] n pardessus m
overcome [əuvə'kʌm] vt (irreg: like **come**);
(defeat) triompher de; (difficulty) surmonter ▷ adj

(emotionally) bouleversé(e); **~ with grief**
accablé(e) de douleur
overconfident [əuvə'kɔnfɪdənt] adj trop sûr(e)
de soi
overcrowded [əuvə'kraudɪd] adj bondé(e); (city,
country) surpeuplé(e)
overcrowding [əuvə'kraudɪŋ] n
surpeuplement m; (in bus) encombrement m
overdo [əuvə'du:] vt (irreg: like **do**) exagérer;
(overcook) trop cuire; **to ~ it, to ~ things** (work too
hard) en faire trop, se surmener
overdone [əuvə'dʌn] adj (vegetables, steak) trop
cuit(e)
overdose ['əuvədəus] n dose excessive
overdraft ['əuvədrɑ:ft] n découvert m
overdrawn [əuvə'drɔ:n] adj (account) à découvert
overdrive ['əuvədraɪv] n (Aut) (vitesse f)
surmultipliée f
overdue [əuvə'dju:] adj en retard; (bill)
impayé(e); (change) qui tarde; **that change was
long ~** ce changement n'avait que trop tardé
overemphasis [əuvər'ɛmfəsɪs] n: **to put an ~
on** accorder trop d'importance à
overestimate [əuvər'ɛstɪmeɪt] vt surestimer
overexcited [əuvərɪk'saɪtɪd] adj surexcité(e)
overexertion [əuvərɪg'zə:ʃən] n surmenage m
(physique)
overexpose [əuvərɪk'spəuz] vt (Phot) surexposer
overflow vi [əuvə'fləu] déborder ▷ n ['əuvəfləu]
trop-plein m; (also: **overflow pipe**) tuyau m
d'écoulement, trop-plein m
overfly [əuvə'flaɪ] vt (irreg: like **fly**) survoler
overgenerous [əuvə'dʒɛnərəs] adj (person)
prodigue; (offer) excessif(-ive)
overgrown [əuvə'grəun] adj (garden) envahi(e)
par la végétation; **he's just an ~ schoolboy** (fig)
c'est un écolier attardé
overhang ['əuvəhæŋ] vt (irreg: like **hang**)
surplomber ▷ vi faire saillie
overhaul vt [əuvə'hɔ:l] réviser ▷ n ['əuvəhɔ:l]
révision f
overhead adv [əuvə'hɛd] au-dessus ▷ adj, n
['əuvəhɛd] ▷ adj aérien(ne); (lighting) vertical(e)
▷ n (US) = **overheads**
overhead projector n rétroprojecteur m
overheads ['əuvəhɛdz] npl (Brit) frais généraux
overhear [əuvə'hɪər] vt (irreg: like **hear**) entendre
(par hasard)
overheat [əuvə'hi:t] vi devenir surchauffé(e);
(engine) chauffer
overjoyed [əuvə'dʒɔɪd] adj ravi(e), enchanté(e)
overkill ['əuvəkɪl] n (fig): **it would be ~** ce serait
de trop
overland ['əuvəlænd] adj, adv par voie de terre
overlap vi [əuvə'læp] se chevaucher ▷ n
['əuvəlæp] chevauchement m
overleaf [əuvə'li:f] adv au verso
overload [əuvə'ləud] vt surcharger
overlook [əuvə'luk] vt (have view of) donner sur;
(miss) oublier, négliger; (forgive) fermer les yeux
sur
overlord ['əuvəlɔ:d] n chef m suprême

overmanning [əuvə'mænɪŋ] *n* sureffectif *m*,
main-d'œuvre *f* pléthorique

overnight *adv* [əuvə'naɪt] (*happen*) durant la
nuit; (*fig*) soudain ▷ *adj* ['əuvənaɪt] d'une (*or* de)
nuit; soudain(e); **to stay ~ (with sb)** passer la
nuit (chez qn); **he stayed there ~** il y a passé la
nuit; **if you travel ~ ...** si tu fais le voyage de
nuit ...; **he'll be away ~** il ne rentrera pas ce
soir

overnight bag *n* nécessaire *m* de voyage

overpass ['əuvəpɑːs] *n* (*US*: *for cars*) pont
autoroutier; (: *for pedestrians*) passerelle *f*, pont *m*

overpay [əuvə'peɪ] *vt* (*irreg*: *like* **pay**); **to ~ sb by
£50** donner à qn 50 livres de trop

overplay [əuvə'pleɪ] *vt* exagérer; **to ~ one's
hand** trop présumer de sa situation

overpower [əuvə'pauə'] *vt* vaincre; (*fig*)
accabler

overpowering [əuvə'pauərɪŋ] *adj* irrésistible;
(*heat, stench*) suffocant(e)

overproduction ['əuvəprə'dʌkʃən] *n*
surproduction *f*

overrate [əuvə'reɪt] *vt* surestimer

overreact [əuvəriː'ækt] *vi* réagir de façon
excessive

override [əuvə'raɪd] *vt* (*irreg*: *like* **ride**); (*order,
objection*) passer outre à; (*decision*) annuler

overriding [əuvə'raɪdɪŋ] *adj* prépondérant(e)

overrule [əuvə'ruːl] *vt* (*decision*) annuler; (*claim*)
rejeter; (*person*) rejeter l'avis de

overrun [əuvə'rʌn] *vt* (*irreg*: *like* **run**); (*Mil*: *country
etc*) occuper; (*time limit etc*) dépasser ▷ *vi*
dépasser le temps imparti; **the town is ~ with
tourists** la ville est envahie de touristes

overseas [əuvə'siːz] *adv* outre-mer; (*abroad*) à
l'étranger ▷ *adj* (*trade*) extérieur(e); (*visitor*)
étranger(-ère)

oversee [əuvə'siː] *vt* (*irreg*: *like* **see**) surveiller

overseer ['əuvəsɪə'] *n* (*in factory*) contremaître *m*

overshadow [əuvə'ʃædəu] *vt* (*fig*) éclipser

overshoot [əuvə'ʃuːt] *vt* (*irreg*: *like* **shoot**)
dépasser

oversight ['əuvəsaɪt] *n* omission *f*, oubli *m*; **due
to an ~** par suite d'une inadvertance

oversimplify [əuvə'sɪmplɪfaɪ] *vt* simplifier à
l'excès

oversleep [əuvə'sliːp] *vi* (*irreg*: *like* **sleep**) se
réveiller (trop) tard

overspend [əuvə'spɛnd] *vi* (*irreg*: *like* **spend**)
dépenser de trop; **we have overspent by 5,000
dollars** nous avons dépassé notre budget de
5 000 dollars, nous avons dépensé 5 000 dollars
de trop

overspill ['əuvəspɪl] *n* excédent *m* de
population

overstaffed [əuvə'stɑːft] *adj*: **to be ~** avoir trop
de personnel, être en surnombre

overstate [əuvə'steɪt] *vt* exagérer

overstatement [əuvə'steɪtmənt] *n*
exagération *f*

overstay [əuvə'steɪ] *vt*: **to ~ one's welcome (at
sb's)** abuser de l'hospitalité de qn

overstep [əuvə'stɛp] *vt*: **to ~ the mark** dépasser
la mesure

overstock [əuvə'stɔk] *vt* stocker en
surabondance

overstretched [əuvə'strɛtʃt] *adj* (*person*)
débordé(e); **my budget is ~** j'ai atteint les
limites de mon budget

overstrike *n* ['əuvəstraɪk] (*on printer*)
superposition *f*, double frappe *f* ▷ *vt* (*irreg*: *like*
strike) [əuvə'straɪk] surimprimer

overt [əu'vəːt] *adj* non dissimulé(e)

overtake [əuvə'teɪk] *vt* (*irreg*: *like* **take**) dépasser;
(*Brit*: *Aut*) dépasser, doubler

overtaking [əuvə'teɪkɪŋ] *n* (*Aut*)
dépassement *m*

overtax [əuvə'tæks] *vt* (*Econ*) surimposer; (*fig*:
strength, patience) abuser de; **to ~ o.s.** se
surmener

overthrow [əuvə'θrəu] *vt* (*irreg*: *like* **throw**);
(*government*) renverser

overtime ['əuvətaɪm] *n* heures *fpl*
supplémentaires; **to do** *or* **work ~** faire des
heures supplémentaires

overtime ban *n* refus *m* de faire des heures
supplémentaires

overtone ['əuvətəun] *n* (*also*: **overtones**) note *f*,
sous-entendus *mpl*

overtook [əuvə'tuk] *pt* *of* **overtake**

overture ['əuvətʃuə'] *n* (*Mus, fig*) ouverture *f*

overturn [əuvə'təːn] *vt* renverser; (*decision, plan*)
annuler ▷ *vi* se retourner

overview ['əuvəvjuː] *n* vue *f* d'ensemble

overweight [əuvə'weɪt] *adj* (*person*) trop
gros(se); (*luggage*) trop lourd(e)

overwhelm [əuvə'wɛlm] *vt* (*subj*: *emotion*)
accabler, submerger; (*enemy, opponent*) écraser

overwhelming [əuvə'wɛlmɪŋ] *adj* (*victory, defeat*)
écrasant(e); (*desire*) irrésistible; **one's ~
impression is of heat** on a une impression
dominante de chaleur

overwhelmingly [əuvə'wɛlmɪŋlɪ] *adv* (*vote*) en
masse; (*win*) d'une manière écrasante

overwork [əuvə'wəːk] *n* surmenage *m* ▷ *vt*
surmener ▷ *vi* se surmener

overwrite [əuvə'raɪt] *vt* (*irreg*: *like* **write**);
(*Comput*) écraser

overwrought [əuvə'rɔːt] *adj* excédé(e)

ovulation [ɔvju'leɪʃən] *n* ovulation *f*

owe [əu] *vt* devoir; **to ~ sb sth**, **to ~ sth to sb**
devoir qch à qn; **how much do I ~ you?**
combien est-ce que je vous dois?

owing to ['əuɪŋtuː] *prep* à cause de, en raison de

owl [aul] *n* hibou *m*

own [əun] *vt* posséder ▷ *vi* (*Brit*): **to ~ to sth**
reconnaître *or* avouer qch; **to ~ to having done
sth** avouer avoir fait qch ▷ *adj* propre; **a room
of my ~** une chambre à moi, ma propre
chambre; **can I have it for my (very) ~?** puis-je
l'avoir pour moi (tout) seul?; **to get one's ~
back** prendre sa revanche; **on one's ~** tout(e)
seul(e); **to come into one's ~** trouver sa voie;
trouver sa justification

▶**own up** vi avouer

own brand n (Comm) marque f de distributeur

owner ['əunəʳ] n propriétaire m/f

owner-occupier ['əunərˈɔkjupaɪəʳ] n propriétaire occupant

ownership ['əunəʃɪp] n possession f; **it's under new** ~ (shop etc) il y a eu un changement de propriétaire

own goal n: **he scored an** ~ (Sport) il a marqué un but contre son camp; (fig) cela s'est retourné contre lui

ox (pl **oxen**) [ɔks, 'ɔksn] n bœuf m

Oxbridge ['ɔksbrɪdʒ] n (Brit) les universités d'Oxford et de Cambridge; voir article

● **OXBRIDGE**
●
● Oxbridge, nom formé à partir des mots
● Ox(ford) et (Cam)bridge, s'utilise pour
● parler de ces deux universités comme
● formant un tout, dans la mesure où elles
● sont toutes deux les universités
● britanniques les plus prestigieuses et
● mondialement connues.

oxen ['ɔksən] npl of **ox**

Oxfam ['ɔksfæm] n abbr (Brit: = Oxford Committee for Famine Relief) association humanitaire

oxide ['ɔksaɪd] n oxyde m

Oxon. ['ɔksn] abbr (Brit: Oxoniensis) = **of Oxford**

oxtail ['ɔksteɪl] n: ~ **soup** soupe f à la queue de bœuf

oxygen ['ɔksɪdʒən] n oxygène m

oxygen mask n masque m à oxygène

oxygen tent n tente f à oxygène

oyster ['ɔɪstəʳ] n huître f

oz. abbr = **ounce**; **ounces**

ozone ['əuzəun] n ozone m

ozone friendly ['əuzəunfrɛndlɪ] adj qui n'attaque pas or qui préserve la couche d'ozone

ozone hole n trou m d'ozone

ozone layer n couche f d'ozone

Pp

P, p [piː] *n* (*letter*) P, p *m*; **P for Peter** P comme Pierre

P *abbr* = **president; prince**

p *abbr* (= *page*) p; (*Brit*) = **penny; pence**

P.A. *n abbr* = **personal assistant; public address system** ▷ *abbr* (*US*) = **Pennsylvania**

pa [pɑː] *n* (*inf*) papa *m*

Pa. *abbr* (*US*) = **Pennsylvania**

p.a. *abbr* = **per annum**

PAC *n abbr* (*US*) = **political action committee**

pace [peɪs] *n* pas *m*; (*speed*) allure *f*; vitesse *f* ▷ *vi*: **to ~ up and down** faire les cent pas; **to keep ~ with** aller à la même vitesse que; (*events*) se tenir au courant de; **to set the ~** (*running*) donner l'allure; (*fig*) donner le ton; **to put sb through his ~s** (*fig*) mettre qn à l'épreuve

pacemaker ['peɪsmeɪkəʳ] *n* (*Med*) stimulateur *m* cardiaque; (*Sport: also:* **pacesetter**) meneur(-euse) de train

Pacific [pə'sɪfɪk] *n*: **the ~ (Ocean)** le Pacifique, l'océan *m* Pacifique

pacific [pə'sɪfɪk] *adj* pacifique

pacification [pæsɪfɪ'keɪʃən] *n* pacification *f*

pacifier ['pæsɪfaɪəʳ] *n* (*US: dummy*) tétine *f*

pacifist ['pæsɪfɪst] *n* pacifiste *m/f*

pacify ['pæsɪfaɪ] *vt* pacifier; (*soothe*) calmer

pack [pæk] *n* paquet *m*; (*bundle*) ballot *m*; (*of hounds*) meute *f*; (*of thieves, wolves etc*) bande *f*; (*of cards*) jeu *m*; (*US: of cigarettes*) paquet; (*back pack*) sac *m* à dos ▷ *vt* (*goods*) empaqueter, emballer; (*in suitcase etc*) emballer; (*box*) remplir; (*cram*) entasser; (*press down*) tasser; damer; (*Comput*) grouper, tasser ▷ *vi*: **to ~ (one's bags)** faire ses bagages; **to ~ into** (*room, stadium*) s'entasser dans; **to send sb ~ing** (*inf*) envoyer promener qn

▶ **pack in** (*Brit inf*) *vi* (*machine*) tomber en panne ▷ *vt* (*boyfriend*) plaquer; **~ it in!** laisse tomber!

▶ **pack off** *vt*: **to ~ sb off to** expédier qn à

▶ **pack up** *vi* (*Brit inf: machine*) tomber en panne; (: *person*) se tirer ▷ *vt* (*belongings*) ranger; (*goods, presents*) empaqueter, emballer

package ['pækɪdʒ] *n* paquet *m*; (*of goods*) emballage *m*, conditionnement *m*; (*also:* **package deal**: *agreement*) marché global; (: *purchase*) forfait *m*; (*Comput*) progiciel *m* ▷ *vt* (*goods*) conditionner

package holiday *n* (*Brit*) vacances organisées

package tour *n* voyage organisé

packaging ['pækɪdʒɪŋ] *n* (*wrapping materials*) emballage *m*; (*of goods*) conditionnement *m*

packed [pækt] *adj* (*crowded*) bondé(e)

packed lunch (*Brit*) *n* repas froid

packer ['pækəʳ] *n* (*person*) emballeur(-euse); conditionneur(-euse)

packet ['pækɪt] *n* paquet *m*

packet switching [-swɪtʃɪŋ] *n* (*Comput*) commutation *f* de paquets

pack ice ['pækaɪs] *n* banquise *f*

packing ['pækɪŋ] *n* emballage *m*

packing case *n* caisse *f* (d'emballage)

pact [pækt] *n* pacte *m*, traité *m*

pad [pæd] *n* bloc(-notes *m*) *m*; (*to prevent friction*) tampon *m*; (*for inking*) tampon *m* encreur; (*inf: flat*) piaule *f* ▷ *vt* rembourrer ▷ *vi*: **to ~ in/about** *etc* entrer/aller etc *etc* à pas feutrés

padded ['pædɪd] *adj* (*jacket*) matelassé(e); (*bra*) rembourré(e); **~ cell** cellule capitonnée

padding ['pædɪŋ] *n* rembourrage *m*; (*fig*) délayage *m*

paddle ['pædl] *n* (*oar*) pagaie *f*; (*US: for table tennis*) raquette *f* de ping-pong ▷ *vi* (*with feet*) barboter, faire trempette ▷ *vt*: **to ~ a canoe** *etc* pagayer

paddle steamer *n* bateau *m* à aubes

paddling pool ['pædlɪŋ-] *n* petit bassin

paddock ['pædək] *n* enclos *m*; (*Racing*) paddock *m*

paddy ['pædɪ] *n* (*also:* **paddy field**) rizière *f*

padlock ['pædlɔk] *n* cadenas *m* ▷ *vt* cadenasser

padre ['pɑːdrɪ] *n* aumônier *m*

paediatrician, (*US*) **pediatrician** [piːdɪə'trɪʃən] *n* pédiatre *m/f*

paediatrics, (*US*) **pediatrics** [piːdɪ'ætrɪks] *n* pédiatrie *f*

paedophile, (*US*) **pedophile** ['piːdəufaɪl] *n* pédophile *m*

pagan ['peɪgən] *adj, n* païen(ne)

page [peɪdʒ] *n* (*of book*) page *f*; (*also:* **page boy**) groom *m*, chasseur *m*; (*at wedding*) garçon *m* d'honneur ▷ *vt* (*in hotel etc*) (faire) appeler

pageant ['pædʒənt] *n* spectacle *m* historique; grande cérémonie

pageantry ['pædʒəntrı] n apparat m, pompe f
page break n fin f or saut m de page
pager ['peɪdʒə^r] n bip m (inf), Alphapage® m
paginate ['pædʒɪneɪt] vt paginer
pagination [pædʒɪ'neɪʃən] n pagination f
pagoda [pə'gəudə] n pagode f
paid [peɪd] pt, pp of **pay** ▷ adj (work, official)
rémunéré(e); (holiday) payé(e); **to put ~ to** (Brit)
mettre fin à, mettre par terre
paid-up ['peɪdʌp], (US) **paid-in** ['peɪdɪn] adj
(member) à jour de sa cotisation; (shares)
libéré(e); **~ capital** capital versé
pail [peɪl] n seau m
pain [peɪn] n douleur f; (inf: nuisance) plaie f; **to
be in ~** souffrir, avoir mal; **to have a ~ in** avoir
mal à or une douleur à or dans; **to take ~s to do**
se donner du mal pour faire; **on ~ of death** sous
peine de mort
pained ['peɪnd] adj peiné(e), chagrin(e)
painful ['peɪnful] adj douloureux(-euse);
(difficult) difficile, pénible
painfully ['peɪnfəlɪ] adv (fig: very) terriblement
painkiller ['peɪnkɪlə^r] n calmant m,
analgésique m
painless ['peɪnlɪs] adj indolore
painstaking ['peɪnzteɪkɪŋ] adj (person)
soigneux(-euse); (work) soigné(e)
paint [peɪnt] n peinture f ▷ vt peindre; (fig)
dépeindre; **to ~ the door blue** peindre la porte
en bleu; **to ~ in oils** faire de la peinture à
l'huile
paintbox ['peɪntbɔks] n boîte f de couleurs
paintbrush ['peɪntbrʌʃ] n pinceau m
painter ['peɪntə^r] n peintre m
painting ['peɪntɪŋ] n peinture f; (picture)
tableau m
paint-stripper ['peɪntstrɪpə^r] n décapant m
paintwork ['peɪntwə:k] n (Brit) peintures fpl;
(: of car) peinture f
pair [peə^r] n (of shoes, gloves etc) paire f; (of people)
couple m; (twosome) duo m; **~ of scissors** (paire
de) ciseaux mpl; **~ of trousers** pantalon m
▶ **pair off** vi se mettre par deux
pajamas [pə'dʒɑːməz] npl (US) pyjama(s) m(pl)
Pakistan [pɑːkɪ'stɑːn] n Pakistan m
Pakistani [pɑːkɪ'stɑːnɪ] adj pakistanais(e) ▷ n
Pakistanais(e)
PAL [pæl] n abbr (TV: = phase alternation line) PAL m
pal [pæl] n (inf) copain (copine)
palace ['pæləs] n palais m
palatable ['pælɪtəbl] adj bon (bonne), agréable
au goût
palate ['pælɪt] n palais m (Anat)
palatial [pə'leɪʃəl] adj grandiose, magnifique
palaver [pə'lɑːvə^r] n palabres fpl or mpl;
histoire(s) f(pl)
pale [peɪl] adj pâle ▷ vi pâlir ▷ n: **to be beyond
the ~** être au ban de la société; **to grow** or **turn
~** (person) pâlir; **~ blue** (adj) bleu pâle inv; **to ~
into insignificance (beside)** perdre beaucoup
d'importance (par rapport à)
paleness ['peɪlnɪs] n pâleur f

Palestine ['pælɪstaɪn] n Palestine f
Palestinian [pælɪs'tɪnɪən] adj palestinien(ne)
▷ n Palestinien(ne)
palette ['pælɪt] n palette f
paling ['peɪlɪŋ] n (stake) palis m; (fence)
palissade f
palisade [pælɪ'seɪd] n palissade f
pall [pɔːl] n (of smoke) voile m ▷ vi: **to ~ (on)**
devenir lassant (pour)
pallet ['pælɪt] n (for goods) palette f
pallid ['pælɪd] adj blême
pallor ['pælə^r] n pâleur f
pally ['pælɪ] adj (inf) copain (copine)
palm [pɑːm] n (Anat) paume f; (also: **palm tree**)
palmier m; (leaf, symbol) palme f ▷ vt: **to ~ sth off
on sb** (inf) refiler qch à qn
palmist ['pɑːmɪst] n chiromancien(ne)
Palm Sunday n le dimanche des Rameaux
palpable ['pælpəbl] adj évident(e), manifeste
palpitation [pælpɪ'teɪʃən] n palpitation f
paltry ['pɔːltrɪ] adj dérisoire; piètre
pamper ['pæmpə^r] vt gâter, dorloter
pamphlet ['pæmflət] n brochure f; (political etc)
tract m
pan [pæn] n (also: **saucepan**) casserole f; (also:
frying pan) poêle f; (of lavatory) cuvette f ▷ vi
(Cine) faire un panoramique ▷ vt (inf: book, film)
éreinter; **to ~ for gold** laver du sable aurifère
panacea [pænə'sɪə] n panacée f
Panama ['pænəmɑː] n Panama m
Panama Canal n canal m de Panama
pancake ['pænkeɪk] n crêpe f
Pancake Day n (Brit) mardi gras
pancake roll n rouleau m de printemps
pancreas ['pæŋkrɪəs] n pancréas m
panda ['pændə] n panda m
panda car n (Brit) ≈ voiture f pie inv
pandemonium [pændɪ'məunɪəm] n tohu-
bohu m
pander ['pændə^r] vi: **to ~ to** flatter bassement;
obéir servilement à
p&h abbr (US: = postage and handling) frais mpl de
port
P&L abbr = **profit and loss**
p&p abbr (Brit: = postage and packing) frais mpl de
port
pane [peɪn] n carreau m (de fenêtre), vitre f
panel ['pænl] n (of wood, cloth etc) panneau m;
(Radio, TV) panel m, invités mpl; (for interview,
exams) jury m; (official: of experts) table ronde,
comité m
panel game n (Brit) jeu m (radiophonique/
télévisé)
panelling, (US) **paneling** ['pænəlɪŋ] n boiseries
fpl
panellist, (US) **panelist** ['pænəlɪst] n invité(e)
(d'un panel), membre d'un panel
pang [pæŋ] n: **~s of remorse** pincements mpl de
remords; **~s of hunger/conscience**
tiraillements mpl d'estomac/de la conscience
panhandler ['pænhændlə^r] n (US inf)
mendiant(e)

panic ['pænɪk] n panique f, affolement m ▷ vi s'affoler, paniquer
panic buying [-baɪɪŋ] n achats mpl de précaution
panicky ['pænɪkɪ] adj (person) qui panique or s'affole facilement
panic-stricken ['pænɪkstrɪkən] adj affolé(e)
pannier ['pænɪəʳ] n (on animal) bât m; (on bicycle) sacoche f
panorama [pænə'rɑːmə] n panorama m
panoramic [pænə'ræmɪk] adj panoramique
pansy ['pænzɪ] n (Bot) pensée f; (inf) tapette f, pédé m
pant [pænt] vi haleter
pantechnicon [pæn'tɛknɪkən] n (Brit) (grand) camion de déménagement
panther ['pænθəʳ] n panthère f
panties ['pæntɪz] npl slip m, culotte f
pantihose ['pæntɪhəuz] n (US) collant m
panto ['pæntəu] n = **pantomime**
pantomime ['pæntəmaɪm] n (Brit) spectacle m de Noël
pantry ['pæntrɪ] n garde-manger m inv; (room) office m
pants [pænts] n (Brit: woman's) culotte f, slip m; (: man's) slip, caleçon m; (US: trousers) pantalon m
pantsuit ['pæntsuːt] n (US) tailleur-pantalon m
pantyhose ['pæntɪhəuz] (US) npl collant m
papacy ['peɪpəsɪ] n papauté f
papal ['peɪpəl] adj papal(e), pontifical(e)
paparazzi [pæpə'rætsiː] npl paparazzi mpl
paper ['peɪpəʳ] n papier m; (also: **wallpaper**) papier peint; (also: **newspaper**) journal m; (academic essay) article m; (exam) épreuve écrite ▷ adj en or de papier ▷ vt tapisser (de papier peint); **papers** npl (also: **identity papers**) papiers mpl (d'identité); **a piece of ~** (odd bit) un bout de papier; (sheet) une feuille de papier; **to put sth down on ~** mettre qch par écrit
paper advance n (on printer) avance f (du) papier
paperback ['peɪpəbæk] n livre broché or non relié; (small) livre m de poche ▷ adj: **~ edition** édition brochée
paper bag n sac m en papier
paperboy ['peɪpəbɔɪ] n (selling) vendeur m de journaux; (delivering) livreur m de journaux
paper clip n trombone m
paper handkerchief n, **paper hankie** n (inf) mouchoir m en papier
paper mill n papeterie f
paper money n papier-monnaie m
paper profit n profit m théorique
paper shop n (Brit) marchand m de journaux
paperweight ['peɪpəweɪt] n presse-papiers m inv
paperwork ['peɪpəwəːk] n papiers mpl; (pej) paperasserie f
papier-mâché ['pæpɪeɪ'mæʃeɪ] n papier mâché m
paprika ['pæprɪkə] n paprika m
Pap test, Pap smear n (Med) frottis m
par [pɑːʳ] n pair m; (Golf) normale f du parcours; **on a ~ with** à égalité avec, au même niveau que;

at ~ au pair; **above/below ~** au-dessus/au-dessous du pair; **to feel below** or **under** or **not up to ~** ne pas se sentir en forme
parable ['pærəbl] n parabole f (Rel)
parabola [pə'ræbələ] n parabole f (Math)
paracetamol [pærə'siːtəmɔl] (Brit) n paracétamol m
parachute ['pærəʃuːt] n parachute m ▷ vi sauter en parachute
parachute jump n saut m en parachute
parachutist ['pærəʃuːtɪst] n parachutiste m/f
parade [pə'reɪd] n défilé m; (inspection) revue f; (street) boulevard m ▷ vt (fig) faire étalage de ▷ vi défiler; **a fashion ~** (Brit) un défilé de mode
parade ground n terrain m de manœuvre
paradise ['pærədaɪs] n paradis m
paradox ['pærədɔks] n paradoxe m
paradoxical [pærə'dɔksɪkl] adj paradoxal(e)
paradoxically [pærə'dɔksɪklɪ] adv paradoxalement
paraffin ['pærəfɪn] n (Brit): **~ (oil)** pétrole (lampant); **liquid ~** huile f de paraffine
paraffin heater n (Brit) poêle m à mazout
paraffin lamp n (Brit) lampe f à pétrole
paragon ['pærəgən] n parangon m
paragraph ['pærəgrɑːf] n paragraphe m; **to begin a new ~** aller à la ligne
Paraguay ['pærəgwaɪ] n Paraguay m
Paraguayan [pærə'gwaɪən] adj paraguayen(ne) ▷ n Paraguayen(ne)
parallel ['pærəlɛl] adj: **~ (with** or **to)** parallèle (à); (fig) analogue (à) ▷ n (line) parallèle f; (fig, Geo) parallèle m
paralysed ['pærəlaɪzd] adj paralysé(e)
paralysis (pl **paralyses**) [pə'rælɪsɪs, -siːz] n paralysie f
paralytic [pærə'lɪtɪk] adj paralytique; (Brit inf: drunk) ivre mort(e)
paralyze ['pærəlaɪz] vt paralyser
paramedic [pærə'mɛdɪk] n auxiliaire m/f médical(e)
parameter [pə'ræmɪtəʳ] n paramètre m
paramilitary [pærə'mɪlɪtərɪ] adj paramilitaire
paramount ['pærəmaunt] adj: **of ~ importance** de la plus haute or grande importance
paranoia [pærə'nɔɪə] n paranoïa f
paranoid ['pærənɔɪd] adj (Psych) paranoïaque; (neurotic) paranoïde
paranormal [pærə'nɔːml] adj paranormal(e)
paraphernalia [pærəfə'neɪlɪə] n attirail m, affaires fpl
paraphrase ['pærəfreɪz] vt paraphraser
paraplegic [pærə'pliːdʒɪk] n paraplégique m/f
parapsychology [pærəsaɪ'kɔlədʒɪ] n parapsychologie f
parasite ['pærəsaɪt] n parasite m
parasol ['pærəsɔl] n ombrelle f; (at café etc) parasol m
paratrooper ['pærətruːpəʳ] n parachutiste m (soldat)
parcel ['pɑːsl] n paquet m, colis m ▷ vt (also: **parcel up**) empaqueter

▶ **parcel out** vt répartir
parcel bomb n (Brit) colis piégé
parcel post n service m de colis postaux
parch [pɑːtʃ] vt dessécher
parched [pɑːtʃt] adj (person) assoiffé(e)
parchment ['pɑːtʃmənt] n parchemin m
pardon ['pɑːdn] n pardon m; (Law) grâce f ▷ vt
pardonner à; (Law) gracier; ~! pardon!; ~ **me!**
(after burping etc) excusez-moi!; **I beg your ~!** (I'm
sorry) pardon!, je suis désolé!; (**I beg your**) ~?,
(US) ~ **me?** (what did you say?) pardon?
pare [pɛəʳ] vt (Brit: nails) couper; (fruit etc) peler;
(fig: costs etc) réduire
parent ['pɛərənt] n (father) père m; (mother) mère
f; **parents** npl parents mpl
parentage ['pɛərəntɪdʒ] n naissance f; **of
unknown ~** de parents inconnus
parental [pə'rɛntl] adj parental(e), des parents
parent company n société f mère
parenthesis (pl **parentheses**) [pə'rɛnθɪsɪs, -siːz]
n parenthèse f; **in parentheses** entre
parenthèses
parenthood ['pɛərənthud] n paternité f or
maternité f
parenting ['pɛərəntɪŋ] n le métier de parent, le
travail d'un parent
Paris ['pærɪs] n Paris
parish ['pærɪʃ] n paroisse f; (Brit: civil)
≈ commune f ▷ adj paroissial(e)
parish council n (Brit) ≈ conseil municipal
parishioner [pə'rɪʃənəʳ] n paroissien(ne)
Parisian [pə'rɪzɪən] adj parisien(ne), de Paris ▷ n
Parisien(ne)
parity ['pærɪtɪ] n parité f
park [pɑːk] n parc m, jardin public ▷ vt garer
▷ vi se garer; **can I ~ here?** est-ce que je peux
me garer ici?
parka ['pɑːkə] n parka m
parking ['pɑːkɪŋ] n stationnement m; **"no ~"**
"stationnement interdit"
parking lights npl feux mpl de stationnement
parking lot n (US) parking m, parc m de
stationnement
parking meter n parc(o)mètre m
parking offence, (US) **parking violation** n
infraction f au stationnement
parking place n place f de stationnement
parking ticket n P.-V. m
Parkinson's ['pɑːkɪnsənz] n (also: **Parkinson's
disease**) maladie f de Parkinson, parkinson m
parkway ['pɑːkweɪ] n (US) route f express (en site
vert ou aménagé)
parlance ['pɑːləns] n: **in common/modern ~**
dans le langage courant/actuel
parliament ['pɑːləmənt] n parlement m; voir
article

● **PARLIAMENT**
●
● Le Parliament est l'assemblée législative
● britannique; elle est composée de deux
● chambres: la "House of Commons" et la

● "House of Lords". Ses bureaux sont les
● "Houses of Parliament" au palais de
● Westminster à Londres. Chaque Parliament
● est en général élu pour cinq ans. Les débats
● du Parliament sont maintenant retransmis à
● la télévision.

parliamentary [pɑːlə'mɛntərɪ] adj
parlementaire
parlour, (US) **parlor** ['pɑːləʳ] n salon m
parlous ['pɑːləs] adj (formal) précaire
Parmesan [pɑːmɪ'zæn] n (also: **Parmesan
cheese**) Parmesan m
parochial [pə'rəukɪəl] adj paroissial(e); (pej) à
l'esprit de clocher
parody ['pærədɪ] n parodie f
parole [pə'rəul] n: **on ~** en liberté conditionnelle
paroxysm ['pærəksɪzəm] n (Med, of grief)
paroxysme m; (of anger) accès m
parquet ['pɑːkeɪ] n: ~ **floor(ing)** parquet m
parrot ['pærət] n perroquet m
parrot fashion adv comme un perroquet
parry ['pærɪ] vt esquiver, parer à
parsimonious [pɑːsɪ'məunɪəs] adj
parcimonieux(-euse)
parsley ['pɑːslɪ] n persil m
parsnip ['pɑːsnɪp] n panais m
parson ['pɑːsn] n ecclésiastique m; (Church of
England) pasteur m
part [pɑːt] n partie f; (of machine) pièce f; (Theat)
rôle m; (Mus) voix f; partie; (of serial) épisode m;
(US: in hair) raie f ▷ adj partiel(le) ▷ adv = **partly**
▷ vt séparer ▷ vi (people) se séparer; (crowd)
s'ouvrir; (roads) se diviser; **to take ~ in**
participer à, prendre part à; **to take sb's ~**
prendre le parti de qn, prendre parti pour qn;
on his ~ de sa part; **for my ~** en ce qui me
concerne; **for the most ~** en grande partie;
dans la plupart des cas; **for the better ~ of the
day** pendant la plus grande partie de la
journée; **to be ~ and parcel of** faire partie de;
in ~ en partie; **to take sth in good/bad ~**
prendre qch du bon/mauvais côté
▶ **part with** vt fus (person) se séparer de;
(possessions) se défaire de
partake [pɑː'teɪk] vi (irreg: like **take**); (formal): **to
~ of sth** prendre part à qch, partager qch
part exchange n (Brit): **in ~** en reprise
partial ['pɑːʃl] adj (incomplete) partiel(le); (unjust)
partial(e); **to be ~ to** aimer, avoir un faible pour
partially ['pɑːʃəlɪ] adv en partie, partiellement;
partialement
participant [pɑː'tɪsɪpənt] n (in competition,
campaign) participant(e)
participate [pɑː'tɪsɪpeɪt] vi: **to ~ (in)** participer
(à), prendre part (à)
participation [pɑːtɪsɪ'peɪʃən] n participation f
participle ['pɑːtɪsɪpl] n participe m
particle ['pɑːtɪkl] n particule f; (of dust) grain m
particular [pə'tɪkjuləʳ] adj (specific)
particulier(-ière); (special) particulier,
spécial(e); (fussy) difficile, exigeant(e); (careful)

méticuleux(-euse); **in ~** en particulier, surtout

particularly [pə'tɪkjʊləlɪ] *adv* particulièrement; (*in particular*) en particulier

particulars [pə'tɪkjʊlaz] *npl* détails *mpl*; (*information*) renseignements *mpl*

parting ['pɑːtɪŋ] *n* séparation *f*; (*Brit: in hair*) raie *f* ▷ *adj* d'adieu; **his ~ shot was ...** il lança en partant ....

partisan [pɑːtɪ'zæn] *n* partisan(e) ▷ *adj* partisan(e); de parti

partition [pɑː'tɪʃən] *n* (*Pol*) partition *f*, division *f*; (*wall*) cloison *f*

partly ['pɑːtlɪ] *adv* en partie, partiellement

partner ['pɑːtnəʳ] *n* (*Comm*) associé(e); (*Sport*) partenaire *m/f*; (*spouse*) conjoint(e); (*lover*) ami(e); (*at dance*) cavalier(-ière) ▷ *vt* être l'associé *or* le partenaire *or* le cavalier de

partnership ['pɑːtnəʃɪp] *n* association *f*; **to go into ~ (with), form a ~ (with)** s'associer (avec)

part payment *n* acompte *m*

partridge ['pɑːtrɪdʒ] *n* perdrix *f*

part-time ['pɑːt'taɪm] *adj*, *adv* à mi-temps, à temps partiel

part-timer [pɑːt'taɪməʳ] *n* (*also:* **part-time worker**) travailleur(-euse) à temps partiel

party ['pɑːtɪ] *n* (*Pol*) parti *m*; (*celebration*) fête *f*; (*: formal*) réception *f*; (*: in evening*) soirée *f*; (*team*) équipe *f*; (*group*) groupe *m*; (*Law*) partie *f*; **dinner ~** dîner *m*; **to give** *or* **throw a ~** donner une réception; **we're having a ~ next Saturday** nous organisons une soirée *or* réunion entre amis samedi prochain; **it's for our son's birthday ~** c'est pour la fête (*or* le goûter) d'anniversaire de notre garçon; **to be a ~ to a crime** être impliqué(e) dans un crime

party dress *n* robe habillée

party line *n* (*Pol*) ligne *f* politique; (*Tel*) ligne partagée

party piece *n* numéro habituel

party political broadcast *n* émission réservée à un parti politique.

pass [pɑːs] *vt* (*time, object*) passer; (*place*) passer devant; (*friend*) croiser; (*exam*) être reçu(e) à, réussir; (*candidate*) admettre; (*overtake*) dépasser; (*approve*) approuver, accepter; (*law*) promulguer ▷ *vi* passer; (*Scol*) être reçu(e) *or* admis(e), réussir ▷ *n* (*permit*) laissez-passer *m inv*; (*membership card*) carte *f* d'accès *or* d'abonnement; (*in mountains*) col *m*; (*Sport*) passe *f*; (*Scol: also:* **pass mark**): **to get a ~** être reçu(e) (sans mention); **to ~ sb sth** passer qch à qn; **could you ~ the salt/oil, please?** pouvez-vous me passer le sel/l'huile, s'il vous plaît?; **she could ~ for 25** on lui donnerait 25 ans; **to ~ sth through a ring** *etc* (faire) passer qch dans un anneau *etc*; **could you ~ the vegetables round?** pourriez-vous faire passer les légumes?; **things have come to a pretty ~** (*Brit*) voilà où on en est!; **to make a ~ at sb** (*inf*) faire des avances à qn

▶ **pass away** *vi* mourir

▶ **pass by** *vi* passer ▷ *vt* (*ignore*) négliger

▶ **pass down** *vt* (*customs, inheritance*) transmettre

▶ **pass on** *vi* (*die*) s'éteindre, décéder ▷ *vt* (*hand on*): **to ~ on (to)** transmettre (à); (*: illness*) passer (à); (*: price rises*) répercuter (sur)

▶ **pass out** *vi* s'évanouir; (*Brit Mil*) sortir (*d'une école militaire*)

▶ **pass over** *vt* (*ignore*) passer sous silence

▶ **pass up** *vt* (*opportunity*) laisser passer

passable ['pɑːsəbl] *adj* (*road*) praticable; (*work*) acceptable

passage ['pæsɪdʒ] *n* (*also:* **passageway**) couloir *m*; (*gen, in book*) passage *m*; (*by boat*) traversée *f*

passbook ['pɑːsbʊk] *n* livret *m*

passenger ['pæsɪndʒəʳ] *n* passager(-ère)

passer-by [pɑːsə'baɪ] *n* passant(e)

passing ['pɑːsɪŋ] *adj* (*fig*) passager(-ère); **in ~** en passant

passing place *n* (*Aut*) aire *f* de croisement

passion ['pæʃən] *n* passion *f*; **to have a ~ for sth** avoir la passion de qch

passionate ['pæʃənɪt] *adj* passionné(e)

passion fruit *n* fruit *m* de la passion

passion play *n* mystère *m* de la Passion

passive ['pæsɪv] *adj* (*also Ling*) passif(-ive)

passive smoking *n* tabagisme passif

passkey ['pɑːskiː] *n* passe *m*

Passover ['pɑːsəʊvəʳ] *n* Pâque juive

passport ['pɑːspɔːt] *n* passeport *m*

passport control *n* contrôle *m* des passeports

passport office *n* bureau *m* de délivrance des passeports

password ['pɑːswəːd] *n* mot *m* de passe

past [pɑːst] *prep* (*in front of*) devant; (*further than*) au delà de, plus loin que; après; (*later than*) après ▷ *adv*: **to run ~** passer en courant ▷ *adj* passé(e); (*president etc*) ancien(ne) ▷ *n* passé *m*; **he's ~ forty** il a dépassé la quarantaine, il a plus de *or* passé quarante ans; **ten/quarter ~ eight** huit heures dix/un *or* et quart; **it's ~ midnight** il est plus de minuit, il est passé minuit; **he ran ~ me** il m'a dépassé en courant, il a passé devant moi en courant; **for the ~ few/3 days** depuis quelques/3 jours; ces derniers/3 derniers jours; **in the ~** (*gen*) dans le temps, autrefois; (*Ling*) au passé; **I'm ~ caring** je ne m'en fais plus; **to be ~ it** (*Brit inf: person*) avoir passé l'âge

pasta ['pæstə] *n* pâtes *fpl*

paste [peɪst] *n* pâte *f*; (*Culin: meat*) pâté *m* (à tartiner); (*: tomato*) purée *f*, concentré *m*; (*glue*) colle *f* (de pâte); (*jewellery*) strass *m* ▷ *vt* coller

pastel ['pæstl] *adj* pastel *inv* ▷ *n* (*Art: pencil*) (crayon *m*) pastel *m*; (*: drawing*) (dessin *m* au) pastel; (*colour*) ton *m* pastel *inv*

pasteurized ['pæstəraɪzd] *adj* pasteurisé(e)

pastille ['pæstl] *n* pastille *f*

pastime ['pɑːstaɪm] *n* passe-temps *m inv*, distraction *f*

past master *n* (*Brit*): **to be a ~ at** être expert en

pastor ['pɑːstəʳ] *n* pasteur *m*

pastoral ['pɑːstərl] *adj* pastoral(e)

pastry ['peɪstrɪ] *n* pâte *f*; (*cake*) pâtisserie *f*

pasture ['pɑːstʃəʳ] *n* pâturage *m*

pasty¹ *n* ['pæstɪ] petit pâté (en croûte)
pasty² ['peɪstɪ] *adj* pâteux(-euse); (*complexion*) terreux(-euse)
pat [pæt] *vt* donner une petite tape à; (*dog*) caresser ▷ *n*: **a ~ of butter** une noisette de beurre; **to give sb/o.s. a ~ on the back** (*fig*) congratuler qn/se congratuler; **he knows it (off) ~**, (*US*) **he has it down ~** il sait cela sur le bout des doigts
patch [pætʃ] *n* (*of material*) pièce *f*; (*eye patch*) cache *m*; (*spot*) tache *f*; (*of land*) parcelle *f*; (*on tyre*) rustine *f* ▷ *vt* (*clothes*) rapiécer; **a bad ~** (*Brit*) une période difficile
▶ **patch up** *vt* réparer
patchwork ['pætʃwɜːk] *n* patchwork *m*
patchy ['pætʃɪ] *adj* inégal(e); (*incomplete*) fragmentaire
pate [peɪt] *n*: **a bald ~** un crâne chauve *or* dégarni
pâté ['pæteɪ] *n* pâté *m*, terrine *f*
patent ['peɪtnt] (*US*) ['pætnt] *n* brevet *m* (d'invention) ▷ *vt* faire breveter ▷ *adj* patent(e), manifeste
patent leather *n* cuir verni
patently ['peɪtntlɪ] *adv* manifestement
patent medicine *n* spécialité *f* pharmaceutique
patent office *n* bureau *m* des brevets
paternal [pə'tɜːnl] *adj* paternel(le)
paternity [pə'tɜːnɪtɪ] *n* paternité *f*
paternity leave [pə'tɜːnɪtɪ-] *n* congé *m* de paternité
paternity suit *n* (*Law*) action *f* en recherche de paternité
path [pɑːθ] *n* chemin *m*, sentier *m*; (*in garden*) allée *f*; (*of planet*) course *f*; (*of missile*) trajectoire *f*
pathetic [pə'θɛtɪk] *adj* (*pitiful*) pitoyable; (*very bad*) lamentable, minable; (*moving*) pathétique
pathological [pæθə'lɔdʒɪkl] *adj* pathologique
pathologist [pə'θɔlədʒɪst] *n* pathologiste *m/f*
pathology [pə'θɔlədʒɪ] *n* pathologie *f*
pathos ['peɪθɔs] *n* pathétique *m*
pathway ['pɑːθweɪ] *n* chemin *m*, sentier *m*; (*in garden*) allée *f*
patience ['peɪʃns] *n* patience *f*; (*Brit: Cards*) réussite *f*; **to lose (one's)** **~** perdre patience
patient ['peɪʃnt] *n* malade *m/f*; (*of dentist etc*) patient(e) ▷ *adj* patient(e)
patiently ['peɪʃntlɪ] *adv* patiemment
patio ['pætɪəu] *n* patio *m*
patriot ['peɪtrɪət] *n* patriote *m/f*
patriotic [pætrɪ'ɔtɪk] *adj* patriotique; (*person*) patriote
patriotism ['pætrɪətɪzəm] *n* patriotisme *m*
patrol [pə'trəul] *n* patrouille *f* ▷ *vt* patrouiller dans; **to be on ~** être de patrouille
patrol boat *n* patrouilleur *m*
patrol car *n* voiture *f* de police
patrolman [pə'trəulmən] (*irreg*) *n* (*US*) agent *m* de police
patron ['peɪtrən] *n* (*in shop*) client(e); (*of charity*) patron(ne); **~ of the arts** mécène *m*
patronage ['pætrənɪdʒ] *n* patronage *m*, appui *m*

patronize ['pætrənaɪz] *vt* être (un) client *or* un habitué de; (*fig*) traiter avec condescendance
patronizing ['pætrənaɪzɪŋ] *adj* condescendant(e)
patron saint *n* saint(e) patron(ne)
patter ['pætər] *n* crépitement *m*, tapotement *m*; (*sales talk*) boniment *m* ▷ *vi* crépiter, tapoter
pattern ['pætən] *n* modèle *m*; (*Sewing*) patron *m*; (*design*) motif *m*; (*sample*) échantillon *m*; **behaviour ~** mode *m* de comportement
patterned ['pætənd] *adj* à motifs
paucity ['pɔːsɪtɪ] *n* pénurie *f*, carence *f*
paunch [pɔːntʃ] *n* gros ventre, bedaine *f*
pauper ['pɔːpər] *n* indigent(e); **~'s grave** fosse commune
pause [pɔːz] *n* pause *f*, arrêt *m*; (*Mus*) silence *m* ▷ *vi* faire une pause, s'arrêter; **to ~ for breath** reprendre son souffle; (*fig*) faire une pause
pave [peɪv] *vt* paver, daller; **to ~ the way for** ouvrir la voie à
pavement ['peɪvmənt] *n* (*Brit*) trottoir *m*; (*US*) chaussée *f*
pavilion [pə'vɪlɪən] *n* pavillon *m*; tente *f*; (*Sport*) stand *m*
paving ['peɪvɪŋ] *n* (*material*) pavé *m*, dalle *f*; (*area*) pavage *m*, dallage *m*
paving stone *n* pavé *m*
paw [pɔː] *n* patte *f* ▷ *vt* donner un coup de patte à; (*person: pej*) tripoter
pawn [pɔːn] *n* gage *m*; (*Chess, also fig*) pion *m* ▷ *vt* mettre en gage
pawnbroker ['pɔːnbrəukər] *n* prêteur *m* sur gages
pawnshop ['pɔːnʃɔp] *n* mont-de-piété *m*
pay [peɪ] (*pt, pp* **paid**) [peɪd] *n* salaire *m*; (*of manual worker*) paie *f* ▷ *vt* payer; (*be profitable to: also fig*) rapporter à ▷ *vi* payer; (*be profitable*) être rentable; **how much did you ~ for it?** combien l'avez-vous payé?, vous l'avez payé combien?; **I paid £5 for that ticket** j'ai payé ce billet 5 livres; **can I ~ by credit card?** est-ce que je peux payer par carte de crédit?; **to ~ one's way** payer sa part; (*company*) couvrir ses frais; **to ~ dividends** (*fig*) porter ses fruits, s'avérer rentable; **it won't ~ you to do that** vous ne gagnerez rien à faire cela; **to ~ attention (to)** prêter attention (à); **to ~ sb a visit** rendre visite à qn; **to ~ one's respects to sb** présenter ses respects à qn
▶ **pay back** *vt* rembourser
▶ **pay for** *vt fus* payer
▶ **pay in** *vt* verser
▶ **pay off** *vt* (*debts*) régler, acquitter; (*person*) rembourser; (*workers*) licencier ▷ *vi* (*scheme, decision*) se révéler payant(e); **to ~ sth off in instalments** payer qch à tempérament
▶ **pay out** *vt* (*money*) payer, sortir de sa poche; (*rope*) laisser filer
▶ **pay up** *vt* (*debts*) régler; (*amount*) payer
payable ['peɪəbl] *adj* payable; **to make a cheque ~ to sb** établir un chèque à l'ordre de qn
pay-as-you-go [ˌpeɪəzjə'gəu] *adj* (*mobile phone*) à

carte prépayée
pay award n augmentation f
pay day n jour m de paie
PAYE n abbr (Brit: = pay as you earn) système de retenue des impôts à la source
payee [peɪˈiː] n bénéficiaire m/f
pay envelope n (US) paie f
paying [ˈpeɪɪŋ] adj payant(e); ~ **guest** hôte payant
payload [ˈpeɪləud] n charge f utile
payment [ˈpeɪmənt] n paiement m; (of bill) règlement m; (of deposit, cheque) versement m; **advance** ~ (part sum) acompte m; (total sum) paiement anticipé; **deferred** ~, ~ **by instalments** paiement par versements échelonnés; **monthly** ~ mensualité f; **in** ~ **for**, **in** ~ **of** en règlement de; **on** ~ **of £5** pour 5 livres
payout [ˈpeɪaut] n (from insurance) dédommagement m; (in competition) prix m
pay packet n (Brit) paie f
pay phone n cabine f téléphonique, téléphone public
pay raise n (US) = **pay rise**
pay rise n (Brit) augmentation f (de salaire)
payroll [ˈpeɪrəul] n registre m du personnel; **to be on a firm's** ~ être employé par une entreprise
pay slip n (Brit) bulletin m de paie, feuille f de paie
pay station n (US) cabine f téléphonique
pay television n chaînes fpl payantes
PBS n abbr (US: = Public Broadcasting Service) groupement d'aide à la réalisation d'émissions pour la TV publique
PBX n abbr (Brit: = private branch exchange) PBX m, commutateur m privé
PC n abbr = **personal computer**; (Brit) = **police constable** ▷ adj abbr = **politically correct** ▷ abbr (Brit) = **Privy Councillor**
p.c. abbr = **per cent**; **postcard**
p/c abbr = **petty cash**
PCB n abbr = **printed circuit board**
pcm n abbr (= per calender month) par mois
PD n abbr (US) = **police department**
pd abbr = **paid**
PDA n abbr (= personal digital assistant) agenda m électronique
PDQ n abbr = **pretty damn quick**
PDSA n abbr (Brit) = **People's Dispensary for Sick Animals**
PDT abbr (US: = Pacific Daylight Time) heure d'été du Pacifique
PE n abbr (= physical education) EPS f ▷ abbr (Canada) = **Prince Edward Island**
pea [piː] n (petit) pois
peace [piːs] n paix f; (calm) calme m, tranquillité f; **to be at** ~ **with sb/sth** être en paix avec qn/qch; **to keep the** ~ (policeman) assurer le maintien de l'ordre; (citizen) ne pas troubler l'ordre
peaceable [ˈpiːsəbl] adj paisible, pacifique
peaceful [ˈpiːsful] adj paisible, calme

peacekeeper [ˈpiːskiːpər] n (force) force gardienne de la paix
peacekeeping [ˈpiːskiːpɪŋ] n maintien m de la paix
peacekeeping force n forces fpl qui assurent le maintien de la paix
peace offering n gage m de réconciliation; (humorous) gage de paix
peach [piːtʃ] n pêche f
peacock [ˈpiːkɔk] n paon m
peak [piːk] n (mountain) pic m, cime f; (of cap) visière f; (fig: highest level) maximum m; (: of career, fame) apogée m
peak-hour [ˈpiːkauər] adj (traffic etc) de pointe
peak hours npl heures fpl d'affluence or de pointe
peak period n période f de pointe
peak rate n plein tarif
peaky [ˈpiːkɪ] adj (Brit inf) fatigué(e)
peal [piːl] n (of bells) carillon m; ~**s of laughter** éclats mpl de rire
peanut [ˈpiːnʌt] n arachide f, cacahuète f
peanut butter n beurre m de cacahuète
pear [pɛər] n poire f
pearl [pəːl] n perle f
peasant [ˈpɛznt] n paysan(ne)
peat [piːt] n tourbe f
pebble [ˈpɛbl] n galet m, caillou m
peck [pɛk] vt (also: **peck at**) donner un coup de bec à; (food) picorer ▷ n coup m de bec; (kiss) bécot m
pecking order [ˈpɛkɪŋ-] n ordre m hiérarchique
peckish [ˈpɛkɪʃ] adj (Brit inf): **I feel** ~ je mangerais bien quelque chose, j'ai la dent
peculiar [pɪˈkjuːlɪər] adj (odd) étrange, bizarre, curieux(-euse); (particular) particulier(-ière); ~ **to** particulier à
peculiarity [pɪkjuːlɪˈærɪtɪ] n bizarrerie f; particularité f
pecuniary [pɪˈkjuːnɪərɪ] adj pécuniaire
pedal [ˈpɛdl] n pédale f ▷ vi pédaler
pedal bin n (Brit) poubelle f à pédale
pedantic [pɪˈdæntɪk] adj pédant(e)
peddle [ˈpɛdl] vt colporter; (drugs) faire le trafic de
peddler [ˈpɛdlər] n colporteur m; camelot m
pedestal [ˈpɛdəstl] n piédestal m
pedestrian [pɪˈdɛstrɪən] n piéton m ▷ adj piétonnier(-ière); (fig) prosaïque, terre à terre inv
pedestrian crossing n (Brit) passage clouté
pedestrianized [pɪˈdɛstrɪənaɪzd] adj: **a** ~ **street** une rue piétonne
pedestrian precinct, (US) **pedestrian zone** n (Brit) zone piétonne
pediatrics [piːdɪˈætrɪks] n (US) = **paediatrics**
pedigree [ˈpɛdɪgriː] n ascendance f; (of animal) pedigree m ▷ cpd (animal) de race
pedlar [ˈpɛdlər] n = **peddler**
pedophile [ˈpiːdəufaɪl] (US) n = **paedophile**
pee [piː] vi (inf) faire pipi, pisser
peek [piːk] vi jeter un coup d'œil (furtif)

peel [piːl] *n* pelure *f*, épluchure *f*; (*of orange, lemon*) écorce *f* ▷ *vt* peler, éplucher ▷ *vi* (*paint etc*) s'écailler; (*wallpaper*) se décoller; (*skin*) peler
▶ **peel back** *vt* décoller
peeler ['piːləʳ] *n* (*potato etc peeler*) éplucheur *m*
peelings ['piːlɪŋz] *npl* pelures *fpl*, épluchures *fpl*
peep [piːp] *n* (*Brit: look*) coup d'œil furtif; (*sound*) pépiement *m* ▷ *vi* (*Brit*) jeter un coup d'œil (furtif)
▶ **peep out** *vi* (*Brit*) se montrer (furtivement)
peephole ['piːphəul] *n* judas *m*
peer [pɪəʳ] *vi*: **to ~ at** regarder attentivement, scruter ▷ *n* (*noble*) pair *m*; (*equal*) pair, égal(e)
peerage ['pɪərɪdʒ] *n* pairie *f*
peerless ['pɪəlɪs] *adj* incomparable, sans égal
peeved [piːvd] *adj* irrité(e), ennuyé(e)
peevish ['piːvɪʃ] *adj* grincheux(-euse), maussade
peg [pɛg] *n* cheville *f*; (*for coat etc*) patère *f*; (*Brit: also*: **clothes peg**) pince *f* à linge ▷ *vt* (*clothes*) accrocher; (*Brit: groundsheet*) fixer (avec des piquets); (*fig: prices, wages*) contrôler, stabiliser
pejorative [pɪ'dʒɔrətɪv] *adj* péjoratif(-ive)
Pekin [piː'kɪn] *n*, **Peking** [piː'kɪŋ] ▷ *n* Pékin
Pekinese, Pekingese [piːkɪ'niːz] *n* pékinois *m*
pelican ['pɛlɪkən] *n* pélican *m*
pelican crossing *n* (*Brit Aut*) feu *m* à commande manuelle
pellet ['pɛlɪt] *n* boulette *f*; (*of lead*) plomb *m*
pell-mell ['pɛl'mɛl] *adv* pêle-mêle
pelmet ['pɛlmɪt] *n* cantonnière *f*; lambrequin *m*
pelt [pɛlt] *vt*: **to ~ sb (with)** bombarder qn (de) ▷ *vi* (*rain*) tomber à seaux; (*inf: run*) courir à toutes jambes ▷ *n* peau *f*
pelvis ['pɛlvɪs] *n* bassin *m*
pen [pɛn] *n* (*for writing*) stylo *m*; (*for sheep*) parc *m*; (*US inf: prison*) taule *f*; **to put ~ to paper** prendre la plume
penal ['piːnl] *adj* pénal(e)
penalize ['piːnəlaɪz] *vt* pénaliser; (*fig*) désavantager
penal servitude [-'səːvɪtjuːd] *n* travaux forcés
penalty ['pɛnltɪ] *n* pénalité *f*; sanction *f*; (*fine*) amende *f*; (*Sport*) pénalisation *f*; (*also*: **penalty kick**: *Football*) penalty *m*; (: *Rugby*) pénalité *f*; **to pay the ~ for** être pénalisé(e) pour
penalty area *n* (*Brit Sport*) surface *f* de réparation
penalty clause *n* clause pénale
penalty kick *n* (*Football*) penalty *m*
penalty shoot-out [-'ʃuːtaut] *n* (*Football*) épreuve *f* des penalties
penance ['pɛnəns] *n* pénitence *f*
pence [pɛns] *npl of* **penny**
penchant ['pɑ̃ːʃɑ̃ːŋ] *n* penchant *m*
pencil ['pɛnsl] *n* crayon *m*
▶ **pencil in** *vt* noter provisoirement
pencil case *n* trousse *f* (d'écolier)
pencil sharpener *n* taille-crayon(s) *m inv*
pendant ['pɛndnt] *n* pendentif *m*
pending ['pɛndɪŋ] *prep* en attendant ▷ *adj* en suspens
pendulum ['pɛndjuləm] *n* pendule *m*; (*of clock*) balancier *m*

penetrate ['pɛnɪtreɪt] *vt* pénétrer dans; (*enemy territory*) entrer en; (*sexually*) pénétrer
penetrating ['pɛnɪtreɪtɪŋ] *adj* pénétrant(e)
penetration [pɛnɪ'treɪʃən] *n* pénétration *f*
penfriend ['pɛnfrɛnd] *n* (*Brit*) correspondant(e)
penguin ['pɛŋgwɪn] *n* pingouin *m*
penicillin [pɛnɪ'sɪlɪn] *n* pénicilline *f*
peninsula [pə'nɪnsjulə] *n* péninsule *f*
penis ['piːnɪs] *n* pénis *m*, verge *f*
penitence ['pɛnɪtns] *n* repentir *m*
penitent ['pɛnɪtnt] *adj* repentant(e)
penitentiary [pɛnɪ'tɛnʃərɪ] *n* (*US*) prison *f*
penknife ['pɛnnaɪf] *n* canif *m*
Penn., Penna. *abbr* (*US*) = **Pennsylvania**
pen name *n* nom *m* de plume, pseudonyme *m*
pennant ['pɛnənt] *n* flamme *f*, banderole *f*
penniless ['pɛnɪlɪs] *adj* sans le sou
Pennines ['pɛnaɪnz] *npl*: **the ~** les Pennines *fpl*
penny (*pl* **pennies** *or* **pence**) ['pɛnɪ, 'pɛnɪz, pɛns] *n* (*Brit*) penny *m*; (*US*) cent *m*
penpal ['pɛnpæl] *n* correspondant(e)
penpusher ['pɛnpuʃɛʳ] *n* (*pej*) gratte-papier *m inv*
pension ['pɛnʃən] *n* (*from company*) retraite *f*; (*Mil*) pension *f*
▶ **pension off** *vt* mettre à la retraite
pensionable ['pɛnʃnəbl] *adj* qui a droit à une retraite
pensioner ['pɛnʃənəʳ] *n* (*Brit*) retraité(e)
pension fund *n* caisse *f* de retraite
pension plan *n* plan *m* de retraite
pensive ['pɛnsɪv] *adj* pensif(-ive)
pentagon ['pɛntəgən] *n* pentagone *m*; **the P~** (*US Pol*) le Pentagone; *voir article*

● **PENTAGON**
●
● Le *Pentagon* est le nom donné aux bureaux du
● ministère de la Défense américain, situés à
● Arlington en Virginie, à cause de la forme
● pentagonale du bâtiment dans lequel ils se
● trouvent. Par extension, ce terme est
● également utilisé en parlant du ministère
● lui-même.

pentathlon [pɛn'tæθlən] *n* pentathlon *m*
Pentecost ['pɛntɪkɔst] *n* Pentecôte *f*
penthouse ['pɛnthaus] *n* appartement *m* (de luxe) en attique
pent-up ['pɛntʌp] *adj* (*feelings*) refoulé(e)
penultimate [pɪ'nʌltɪmət] *adj* pénultième, avant-dernier(-ière)
penury ['pɛnjurɪ] *n* misère *f*
people ['piːpl] *npl* gens *mpl*; personnes *fpl*; (*inhabitants*) population *f*; (*Pol*) peuple *m* ▷ *n* (*nation, race*) peuple *m* ▷ *vt* peupler; **I know ~ who ...** je connais des gens qui ...; **the room was full of ~** la salle était pleine de monde *or* de gens; **several ~ came** plusieurs personnes sont venues; **~ say that ...** on dit *or* les gens disent que ...; **old ~** les personnes âgées; **young ~** les jeunes; **a man of the ~** un homme du peuple
PEP [pɛp] *n* (= *personal equity plan*) ≈ CEA *m*

(= *compte d'épargne en actions*)

pep [pɛp] *n* (*inf*) entrain *m*, dynamisme *m*
▶ **pep up** *vt* (*inf*) remonter

pepper ['pɛpə'] *n* poivre *m*; (*vegetable*) poivron *m*
▷ *vt* (*Culin*) poivrer

pepper mill *n* moulin *m* à poivre

peppermint ['pɛpəmɪnt] *n* (*plant*) menthe
poivrée; (*sweet*) pastille *f* de menthe

pepperoni [pɛpə'rəʊnɪ] *n* *saucisson sec de porc et de
bœuf très poivré.*

pepperpot ['pɛpəpɔt] *n* poivrière *f*

pep talk ['pɛptɔːk] *n* (*inf*) (petit) discours
d'encouragement

per [pəː'] *prep* par; ~ **hour** (*miles etc*) à l'heure;
(*fee*) (de) l'heure; ~ **kilo** *etc* le kilo *etc*; ~ **day/
person** par jour/personne; ~ **annum** per an; **as
~ your instructions** conformément à vos
instructions

per annum *adv* par an

per capita *adj, adv* par habitant, par personne

perceive [pə'siːv] *vt* percevoir; (*notice*)
remarquer, s'apercevoir de

per cent *adv* pour cent; **a 20 ~ discount** une
réduction de 20 pour cent

percentage [pə'sɛntɪdʒ] *n* pourcentage *m*; **on a
~ basis** au pourcentage

percentage point *n*: **ten ~s** dix pour cent

perceptible [pə'sɛptɪbl] *adj* perceptible

perception [pə'sɛpʃən] *n* perception *f*; (*insight*)
sensibilité *f*

perceptive [pə'sɛptɪv] *adj* (*remark, person*)
perspicace

perch [pəːtʃ] *n* (*fish*) perche *f*; (*for bird*) perchoir *m*
▷ *vi* (se) percher

percolate ['pəːkəleɪt] *vt, vi* passer

percolator ['pəːkəleɪtə'] *n* percolateur *m*;
cafetière *f* électrique

percussion [pə'kʌʃən] *n* percussion *f*

peremptory [pə'rɛmptərɪ] *adj* péremptoire

perennial [pə'rɛnɪəl] *adj* perpétuel(le); (*Bot*)
vivace ▷ *n* (*Bot*) (plante *f*) vivace *f*, plante
pluriannuelle

perfect ['pəːfɪkt] *adj* parfait(e) ▷ *n* (*also:* **perfect
tense**) parfait *m* ▷ *vt* [pə'fɛkt] (*technique, skill,
work of art*) parfaire; (*method, plan*) mettre au
point; **he's a ~ stranger to me** il m'est
totalement inconnu

perfection [pə'fɛkʃən] *n* perfection *f*

perfectionist [pə'fɛkʃənɪst] *n* perfectionniste
m/f

perfectly ['pəːfɪktlɪ] *adv* parfaitement; **I'm ~
happy with the situation** cette situation me
convient parfaitement; **you know ~ well** vous
le savez très bien

perforate ['pəːfəreɪt] *vt* perforer, percer

perforated ulcer ['pəːfəreɪtɪd-] *n* (*Med*) ulcère
perforé

perforation [pəːfə'reɪʃən] *n* perforation *f*; (*line of
holes*) pointillé *m*

perform [pə'fɔːm] *vt* (*carry out*) exécuter,
remplir; (*concert etc*) jouer, donner ▷ *vi* (*actor,
musician*) jouer; (*machine, car*) marcher,

fonctionner; (*company, economy*): **to ~ well/
badly** produire de bons/mauvais résultats

performance [pə'fɔːməns] *n* représentation *f*,
spectacle *m*; (*of an artist*) interprétation *f*; (*Sport:
of car, engine*) performance *f*; (*of company, economy*)
résultats *mpl*; **the team put up a good ~**
l'équipe a bien joué

performer [pə'fɔːmə'] *n* artiste *m/f*

performing [pə'fɔːmɪŋ] *adj* (*animal*) savant(e)

performing arts *npl*: **the ~** les arts *mpl* du
spectacle

perfume ['pəːfjuːm] *n* parfum *m* ▷ *vt* parfumer

perfunctory [pə'fʌŋktərɪ] *adj* négligent(e), pour
la forme

perhaps [pə'hæps] *adv* peut-être; ~ **he'll ...**
peut-être qu'il ...; ~ **so/not** peut-être que oui/
que non

peril ['pɛrɪl] *n* péril *m*

perilous ['pɛrɪləs] *adj* périlleux(-euse)

perilously ['pɛrɪləslɪ] *adv*: **they came ~ close to
being caught** ils ont été à deux doigts de se
faire prendre

perimeter [pə'rɪmɪtə'] *n* périmètre *m*

perimeter wall *n* mur *m* d'enceinte

period ['pɪərɪəd] *n* période *f*; (*History*) époque *f*;
(*Scol*) cours *m*; (*full stop*) point *m*; (*Med*) règles *fpl*
▷ *adj* (*costume, furniture*) d'époque; **for a ~ of
three weeks** pour (une période de) trois
semaines; **the holiday ~** (*Brit*) la période des
vacances

periodic [pɪərɪ'ɔdɪk] *adj* périodique

periodical [pɪərɪ'ɔdɪkl] *adj* périodique ▷ *n*
périodique *m*

periodically [pɪərɪ'ɔdɪklɪ] *adv* périodiquement

period pains *npl* (*Brit*) douleurs menstruelles

peripatetic [pɛrɪpə'tɛtɪk] *adj* (*salesman*)
ambulant; (*Brit: teacher*) qui travaille dans
plusieurs établissements

peripheral [pə'rɪfərəl] *adj* périphérique ▷ *n*
(*Comput*) périphérique *m*

periphery [pə'rɪfərɪ] *n* périphérie *f*

periscope ['pɛrɪskəʊp] *n* périscope *m*

perish ['pɛrɪʃ] *vi* périr, mourir; (*decay*) se
détériorer

perishable ['pɛrɪʃəbl] *adj* périssable

perishables ['pɛrɪʃəblz] *npl* denrées *fpl*
périssables

perishing ['pɛrɪʃɪŋ] *adj* (*Brit inf: cold*) glacial(e)

peritonitis [pɛrɪtə'naɪtɪs] *n* péritonite *f*

perjure ['pəːdʒə'] *vt*: **to ~ o.s.** se parjurer

perjury ['pəːdʒərɪ] *n* (*Law: in court*) faux
témoignage; (*breach of oath*) parjure *m*

perk [pəːk] *n* (*inf*) avantage *m*, à-côté *m*
▶ **perk up** *vi* (*inf: cheer up*) se ragaillardir

perky ['pəːkɪ] *adj* (*cheerful*) guilleret(te), gai(e)

perm [pəːm] *n* (*for hair*) permanente *f* ▷ *vt*: **to
have one's hair ~ed** se faire faire une
permanente

permanence ['pəːmənəns] *n* permanence *f*

permanent ['pəːmənənt] *adj* permanent(e);
(*job, position*) permanent, fixe; (*dye, ink*)
indélébile; **I'm not ~ here** je ne suis pas ici à

titre définitif; ~ **address** adresse habituelle

permanently ['pəːmənəntlɪ] *adv* de façon permanente; (*move abroad*) définitivement; (*open, closed*) en permanence; (*tired, unhappy*) constamment

permeable ['pəːmɪəbl] *adj* perméable

permeate ['pəːmɪeɪt] *vi* s'infiltrer ▷ *vt* s'infiltrer dans; pénétrer

permissible [pə'mɪsɪbl] *adj* permis(e), acceptable

permission [pə'mɪʃən] *n* permission*f*, autorisation*f*; **to give sb ~ to do sth** donner à qn la permission de faire qch

permissive [pə'mɪsɪv] *adj* tolérant(e); **the ~ society** la société de tolérance

permit *n* ['pəːmɪt] permis *m*; (*entrance pass*) autorisation*f*, laissez-passer *m*; (*for goods*) licence*f* ▷ *vt* [pə'mɪt] permettre; **to ~ sb to do** autoriser qn à faire, permettre à qn de faire; **weather ~ting** si le temps le permet

permutation [pəːmju'teɪʃən] *n* permutation*f*

pernicious [pəː'nɪʃəs] *adj* pernicieux(-euse), nocif(-ive)

pernickety [pə'nɪkɪtɪ] *adj* (*inf*) pointilleux(-euse), tatillon(ne); (*task*) minutieux(-euse)

perpendicular [pəːpən'dɪkjuləʳ] *adj*, *n* perpendiculaire*f*

perpetrate ['pəːpɪtreɪt] *vt* perpétrer, commettre

perpetual [pə'pɛtjuəl] *adj* perpétuel(le)

perpetuate [pə'pɛtjueɪt] *vt* perpétuer

perpetuity [pəːpɪ'tjuːɪtɪ] *n*: **in ~** à perpétuité

perplex [pə'plɛks] *vt* (*person*) rendre perplexe; (*complicate*) embrouiller

perplexing [pəː'plɛksɪŋ] *adj* embarrassant(e)

perquisites ['pəːkwɪzɪts] *npl* (*also*: **perks**) avantages *mpl* annexes

persecute ['pəːsɪkjuːt] *vt* persécuter

persecution [pəːsɪ'kjuːʃən] *n* persécution*f*

perseverance [pəːsɪ'vɪərns] *n* persévérance*f*, ténacité*f*

persevere [pəːsɪ'vɪəʳ] *vi* persévérer

Persia ['pəːʃə] *n* Perse*f*

Persian ['pəːʃən] *adj* persan(e) ▷ *n* (*Ling*) persan *m*; **the ~ Gulf** le golfe Persique

Persian cat *n* chat persan

persist [pə'sɪst] *vi*: **to ~ (in doing)** persister (à faire), s'obstiner (à faire)

persistence [pə'sɪstəns] *n* persistance*f*, obstination*f*; opiniâtreté*f*

persistent [pə'sɪstənt] *adj* persistant(e), tenace; (*lateness, rain*) persistant; **~ offender** (*Law*) multirécidiviste *m/f*

persnickety [pə'snɪkɪtɪ] *adj* (*US inf*) = **pernickety**

person ['pəːsn] *n* personne*f*; **in ~** en personne; **on** *or* **about one's ~** sur soi; **~ to ~ call** (*Tel*) appel *m* avec préavis

personable ['pəːsnəbl] *adj* de belle prestance, au physique attrayant

personal ['pəːsnl] *adj* personnel(le); **~ belongings, ~ effects** effets personnels; **~**

hygiene hygiène*f* intime; **a ~ interview** un entretien

personal allowance *n* (*Tax*) part*f* du revenu non imposable

personal assistant *n* secrétaire personnel(le)

personal call *n* (*Tel*) communication*f* avec préavis

personal column *n* annonces personnelles

personal computer *n* ordinateur individuel, PC *m*

personal details *npl* (*on form etc*) coordonnées*fpl*

personal identification number *n* (*Comput, Banking*) numéro *m* d'identification personnel

personality [pəːsə'nælɪtɪ] *n* personnalité*f*

personally ['pəːsnəlɪ] *adv* personnellement; **to take sth ~** se sentir visé(e) par qch

personal organizer *n* agenda (personnel); (*electronic*) agenda électronique

personal property *n* biens personnels

personal stereo *n* Walkman® *m*, baladeur *m*

personify [pə'sɔnɪfaɪ] *vt* personnifier

personnel [pəːsə'nɛl] *n* personnel *m*

personnel department *n* service *m* du personnel

personnel manager *n* chef *m* du personnel

perspective [pə'spɛktɪv] *n* perspective*f*; **to get sth into ~** ramener qch à sa juste mesure

perspex® ['pəːspɛks] *n* (*Brit*) Plexiglas® *m*

perspicacity [pəːspɪ'kæsɪtɪ] *n* perspicacité*f*

perspiration [pəːspɪ'reɪʃən] *n* transpiration*f*

perspire [pə'spaɪəʳ] *vi* transpirer

persuade [pə'sweɪd] *vt*: **to ~ sb to do sth** persuader qn de faire qch, amener *or* décider qn à faire qch; **to ~ sb of sth/that** persuader qn de qch/que

persuasion [pə'sweɪʒən] *n* persuasion*f*; (*creed*) conviction*f*

persuasive [pə'sweɪsɪv] *adj* persuasif(-ive)

pert [pəːt] *adj* coquin(e), mutin(e)

pertaining [pəː'teɪnɪŋ]: **~ to** *prep* relatif(-ive) à

pertinent ['pəːtɪnənt] *adj* pertinent(e)

perturb [pə'təːb] *vt* troubler, inquiéter

perturbing [pə'təːbɪŋ] *adj* troublant(e)

Peru [pə'ruː] *n* Pérou *m*

perusal [pə'ruːzl] *n* lecture (attentive)

Peruvian [pə'ruːvjən] *adj* péruvien(ne) ▷ *n* Péruvien(ne)

pervade [pə'veɪd] *vt* se répandre dans, envahir

pervasive [pə'veɪsɪv] *adj* (*smell*) pénétrant(e); (*influence*) insidieux(-euse); (*gloom, ideas*) diffus(e)

perverse [pə'vəːs] *adj* pervers(e); (*contrary*) entêté(e), contrariant(e)

perversion [pə'vəːʃən] *n* perversion*f*

perversity [pə'vəːsɪtɪ] *n* perversité*f*

pervert *n* ['pəːvəːt] perverti(e) ▷ *vt* [pə'vəːt] pervertir; (*words*) déformer

pessimism ['pɛsɪmɪzəm] *n* pessimisme *m*

pessimist ['pɛsɪmɪst] *n* pessimiste *m/f*

pessimistic [pɛsɪ'mɪstɪk] *adj* pessimiste

pest [pɛst] *n* animal *m* (*or* insecte *m*) nuisible; (*fig*) fléau *m*

pest control n lutte f contre les nuisibles

pester ['pɛstə^r] vt importuner, harceler

pesticide ['pɛstɪsaɪd] n pesticide m

pestilence ['pɛstɪləns] n peste f

pestle ['pɛsl] n pilon m

pet [pɛt] n animal familier; (favourite) chouchou m ▷ cpd (favourite) favori(e) ▷ vt choyer; (stroke) caresser, câliner ▷ vi (inf) se peloter; ~ **lion** etc lion etc apprivoisé; **teacher's** ~ chouchou m du professeur; ~ **hate** bête noire

petal ['pɛtl] n pétale m

peter ['piːtə^r]: **to ~ out** vi s'épuiser; s'affaiblir

petite [pə'tiːt] adj menu(e)

petition [pə'tɪʃən] n pétition f ▷ vt adresser une pétition à ▷ vi: **to ~ for divorce** demander le divorce

pet name n (Brit) petit nom

petrified ['pɛtrɪfaɪd] adj (fig) mort(e) de peur

petrify ['pɛtrɪfaɪ] vt pétrifier

petrochemical [pɛtrə'kɛmɪkl] adj pétrochimique

petrodollars ['pɛtrəudɔləz] npl pétrodollars mpl

petrol ['pɛtrəl] n (Brit) essence f; **I've run out of** ~ je suis en panne d'essence

petrol bomb n cocktail m Molotov

petrol can n (Brit) bidon m à essence

petrol engine n (Brit) moteur m à essence

petroleum [pə'trəulɪəm] n pétrole m

petroleum jelly n vaseline f

petrol pump n (Brit: in car, at garage) pompe f à essence

petrol station n (Brit) station-service f

petrol tank n (Brit) réservoir m d'essence

petticoat ['pɛtɪkəut] n jupon m

pettifogging ['pɛtɪfɔgɪŋ] adj chicanier(-ière)

pettiness ['pɛtɪnɪs] n mesquinerie f

petty ['pɛtɪ] adj (mean) mesquin(e); (unimportant) insignifiant(e), sans importance

petty cash n caisse f des dépenses courantes, petite caisse

petty officer n second-maître m

petulant ['pɛtjulənt] adj irritable

pew [pjuː] n banc m (d'église)

pewter ['pjuːtə^r] n étain m

Pfc abbr (US Mil) = **private first class**

PG n abbr (Cine: = parental guidance) avis des parents recommandé

PGA n abbr = **Professional Golfers Association**

PH n abbr (US Mil: = Purple Heart) décoration accordée aux blessés de guerre

PHA n abbr (US: = Public Housing Administration) organisme d'aide à la construction

phallic ['fælɪk] adj phallique

phantom ['fæntəm] n fantôme m; (vision) fantasme m

Pharaoh ['fɛərəu] n pharaon m

pharmaceutical [faːmə'sjuːtɪkl] adj pharmaceutique ▷ n: ~**s** produits mpl pharmaceutiques

pharmacist ['faːməsɪst] n pharmacien(ne)

pharmacy ['faːməsɪ] n pharmacie f

phase [feɪz] n phase f, période f

▶ **phase in** vt introduire progressivement

▶ **phase out** vt supprimer progressivement

Ph.D. abbr = **Doctor of Philosophy**

pheasant ['fɛznt] n faisan m

phenomena [fə'nɔmɪnə] npl of **phenomenon**

phenomenal [fɪ'nɔmɪnl] adj phénoménal(e)

phenomenon (pl **phenomena**) [fə'nɔmɪnən, -nə] n phénomène m

phew [fjuː] excl ouf!

phial ['faɪəl] n fiole f

philanderer [fɪ'lændərə^r] n don Juan m

philanthropic [fɪlən'θrɔpɪk] adj philanthropique

philanthropist [fɪ'lænθrəpɪst] n philanthrope m/f

philatelist [fɪ'lætəlɪst] n philatéliste m/f

philately [fɪ'lætəlɪ] n philatélie f

Philippines ['fɪlɪpiːnz] npl (also: **Philippine Islands**): **the** ~ les Philippines fpl

philosopher [fɪ'lɔsəfə^r] n philosophe m

philosophical [fɪlə'sɔfɪkl] adj philosophique

philosophy [fɪ'lɔsəfɪ] n philosophie f

phishing ['fɪʃɪŋ] n phishing m

phlegm [flɛm] n flegme m

phlegmatic [flɛg'mætɪk] adj flegmatique

phobia ['fəubjə] n phobie f

phone [fəun] n téléphone m ▷ vt téléphoner à ▷ vi téléphoner; **to be on the** ~ avoir le téléphone; (be calling) être au téléphone

▶ **phone back** vt, vi rappeler

▶ **phone up** vt téléphoner à ▷ vi téléphoner

phone bill n facture f de téléphone

phone book n annuaire m

phone box, (US) **phone booth** n cabine f téléphonique

phone call n coup m de fil or de téléphone

phonecard ['fəunkaːd] n télécarte f

phone-in ['fəunɪn] n (Brit Radio, TV) programme m à ligne ouverte

phone number n numéro m de téléphone

phone tapping [-tæpɪŋ] n mise f sur écoutes téléphoniques

phonetics [fə'nɛtɪks] n phonétique f

phoney ['fəunɪ] adj faux (fausse), factice; (person) pas franc (franche) ▷ n (person) charlatan m; fumiste m/f

phonograph ['fəunəgraːf] n (US) électrophone m

phony ['fəunɪ] adj, n = **phoney**

phosphate ['fɔsfeɪt] n phosphate m

phosphorus ['fɔsfərəs] n phosphore m

photo ['fəutəu] n photo f; **to take a** ~ **of** prendre en photo

photo... ['fəutəu] prefix photo...

photo album n album m de photos

photocall ['fəutəukɔːl] n séance f de photos pour la presse

photocopier ['fəutəukɔpɪə^r] n copieur m

photocopy ['fəutəukɔpɪ] n photocopie f ▷ vt photocopier

photoelectric [fəutəu'lɛktrɪk] adj photoélectrique; ~ **cell** cellule f photoélectrique

Photofit® ['fəutəufɪt] *n* portrait-robot *m*

photogenic [fəutəu'dʒɛnɪk] *adj* photogénique

photograph ['fəutəgræf] *n* photographie *f* ▷ *vt* photographier; **to take a ~ of sb** prendre qn en photo

photographer [fə'tɔgrəfə'] *n* photographe *m/f*

photographic [fəutə'græfɪk] *adj* photographique

photography [fə'tɔgrəfɪ] *n* photographie *f*

photo opportunity *n* occasion, souvent arrangée, pour prendre des photos d'une personnalité.

Photostat® ['fəutəustæt] *n* photocopie *f*, photostat *m*

photosynthesis [fəutəu'sɪnθəsɪs] *n* photosynthèse *f*

phrase [freɪz] *n* expression *f*; (*Ling*) locution *f* ▷ *vt* exprimer; (*letter*) rédiger

phrase book *n* recueil *m* d'expressions (pour touristes)

physical ['fɪzɪkl] *adj* physique; **~ examination** examen médical; **~ exercises** gymnastique *f*

physical education *n* éducation *f* physique

physically ['fɪzɪklɪ] *adv* physiquement

physician [fɪ'zɪʃən] *n* médecin *m*

physicist ['fɪzɪsɪst] *n* physicien(ne)

physics ['fɪzɪks] *n* physique *f*

physiological [fɪzɪə'lɔdʒɪkl] *adj* physiologique

physiology [fɪzɪ'ɔlədʒɪ] *n* physiologie *f*

physiotherapist [fɪzɪəu'θɛrəpɪst] *n* kinésithérapeute *m/f*

physiotherapy [fɪzɪəu'θɛrəpɪ] *n* kinésithérapie *f*

physique [fɪ'ziːk] *n* (*appearance*) physique *m*; (*health etc*) constitution *f*

pianist ['piːənɪst] *n* pianiste *m/f*

piano [pɪ'ænəu] *n* piano *m*

piano accordion *n* (*Brit*) accordéon *m* à touches

Picardy ['pɪkədɪ] *n* Picardie *f*

piccolo ['pɪkələu] *n* piccolo *m*

pick [pɪk] *n* (*tool: also*: **pick-axe**) pic *m*, pioche *f* ▷ *vt* choisir; (*gather*) cueillir; (*remove*) prendre; (*lock*) forcer; (*scab, spot*) gratter, écorcher; **take your ~** faites votre choix; **the ~ of** le (la) meilleur(e) de; **to ~ a bone** ronger un os; **to ~ one's nose** se mettre les doigts dans le nez; **to ~ one's teeth** se curer les dents; **to ~ sb's brains** faire appel aux lumières de qn; **to ~ pockets** pratiquer le vol à la tire; **to ~ a quarrel with sb** chercher noise à qn

▶ **pick at** *vt fus*: **to ~ at one's food** manger du bout des dents, chipoter

▶ **pick off** *vt* (*kill*) (viser soigneusement et) abattre

▶ **pick on** *vt fus* (*person*) harceler

▶ **pick out** *vt* choisir; (*distinguish*) distinguer

▶ **pick up** *vi* (*improve*) remonter, s'améliorer ▷ *vt* ramasser; (*telephone*) décrocher; (*collect*) passer prendre; (*Aut: give lift to*) prendre; (*learn*) apprendre; (*Radio*) capter; **to ~ up speed** prendre de la vitesse; **to ~ o.s. up** se relever; **to ~ up where one left off** reprendre là où l'on s'est arrêté

pickaxe, (US) **pickax** ['pɪkæks] *n* pioche *f*

picket ['pɪkɪt] *n* (*in strike*) gréviste *m/f* participant à un piquet de grève; piquet *m* de grève ▷ *vt* mettre un piquet de grève devant

picket line *n* piquet *m* de grève

pickings ['pɪkɪŋz] *npl*: **there are rich ~ to be had in ...** il y a gros à gagner dans ...

pickle ['pɪkl] *n* (*also*: **pickles**: *as condiment*) pickles *mpl* ▷ *vt* conserver dans du vinaigre *or* dans de la saumure; **in a ~** (*fig*) dans le pétrin

pick-me-up ['pɪkmiːʌp] *n* remontant *m*

pickpocket ['pɪkpɔkɪt] *n* pickpocket *m*

pick-up ['pɪkʌp] *n* (*also*: **pick-up truck**) pick-up *m inv*; (*Brit: on record player*) bras *m* pick-up

picnic ['pɪknɪk] *n* pique-nique *m* ▷ *vi* pique-niquer

picnic area *n* aire *f* de pique-nique

picnicker ['pɪknɪkə'] *n* pique-niqueur(-euse)

pictorial [pɪk'tɔːrɪəl] *adj* illustré(e)

picture ['pɪktʃə'] *n* (*also TV*) image *f*; (*painting*) peinture *f*, tableau *m*; (*photograph*) photo(graphie) *f*; (*drawing*) dessin *m*; (*film*) film *m*; (*fig: description*) description *f* ▷ *vt* (*imagine*) se représenter; (*describe*) dépeindre, représenter; **pictures** *npl*: **the ~s** (*Brit*) le cinéma; **to take a ~ of sb/sth** prendre qn/qch en photo; **would you take a ~ of us, please?** pourriez-vous nous prendre en photo, s'il vous plaît?; **the overall ~** le tableau d'ensemble; **to put sb in the ~** mettre qn au courant

picture book *n* livre *m* d'images

picture frame *n* cadre *m*

picture messaging *n* picture messaging *m*, messagerie *f* d'images

picturesque [pɪktʃə'rɛsk] *adj* pittoresque

picture window *n* baie vitrée, fenêtre *f* panoramique

piddling ['pɪdlɪŋ] *adj* (*inf*) insignifiant(e)

pie [paɪ] *n* tourte *f*; (*of fruit*) tarte *f*; (*of meat*) pâté *m* en croûte

piebald ['paɪbɔːld] *adj* pie *inv*

piece [piːs] *n* morceau *m*; (*of land*) parcelle *f*; (*item*): **a ~ of furniture/advice** un meuble/conseil; (*Draughts*) pion *m* ▷ *vt*: **to ~ together** rassembler; **in ~s** (*broken*) en morceaux, en miettes; (*not yet assembled*) en pièces détachées; **to take to ~s** démonter; **in one ~** (*object*) intact(e); **to get back all in one ~** (*person*) rentrer sain et sauf; **a 10p ~** (*Brit*) une pièce de 10p; **~ by ~** morceau par morceau; **a six-~ band** un orchestre de six musiciens; **to say one's ~** réciter son morceau

piecemeal ['piːsmiːl] *adv* par bouts

piece rate *n* taux *m* *or* tarif *m* à la pièce

piecework ['piːswəːk] *n* travail *m* aux pièces *or* à la pièce

pie chart *n* graphique *m* à secteurs, camembert *m*

Piedmont ['piːdmɔnt] *n* Piémont *m*

pier [pɪə'] *n* jetée *f*; (*of bridge etc*) pile *f*

pierce [pɪəs] *vt* percer, transpercer; **to have one's ears ~d** se faire percer les oreilles

pierced [pɪəst] *adj* (*ears*) percé(e)
piercing ['pɪəsɪŋ] *adj* (*cry*) perçant(e)
piety ['paɪətɪ] *n* piété *f*
piffling ['pɪflɪŋ] *adj* insignifiant(e)
pig [pɪg] *n* cochon *m*, porc *m*; (*pej: unkind person*) mufle *m*; (: *greedy person*) goinfre *m*
pigeon ['pɪdʒən] *n* pigeon *m*
pigeonhole ['pɪdʒənhəʊl] *n* casier *m*
pigeon-toed ['pɪdʒəntəʊd] *adj* marchant les pieds en dedans
piggy bank ['pɪgɪ-] *n* tirelire *f*
pigheaded ['pɪg'hɛdɪd] *adj* entêté(e), têtu(e)
piglet ['pɪglɪt] *n* petit cochon, porcelet *m*
pigment ['pɪgmənt] *n* pigment *m*
pigmentation [pɪgmən'teɪʃən] *n* pigmentation *f*
pigmy ['pɪgmɪ] *n* = **pygmy**
pigskin ['pɪgskɪn] *n* (peau *f* de) porc *m*
pigsty ['pɪgstaɪ] *n* porcherie *f*
pigtail ['pɪgteɪl] *n* natte *f*, tresse *f*
pike [paɪk] *n* (*spear*) pique *f*; (*fish*) brochet *m*
pilchard ['pɪltʃəd] *n* pilchard *m* (*sorte de sardine*)
pile [paɪl] *n* (*pillar, of books*) pile *f*; (*heap*) tas *m*; (*of carpet*) épaisseur *f*; **in a ~** en tas
  ▶ **pile on** *vt*: **to ~ it on** (*inf*) exagérer
  ▶ **pile up** *vi* (*accumulate*) s'entasser, s'accumuler ▷ *vt* (*put in heap*) empiler, entasser; (*accumulate*) accumuler
piles [paɪlz] *npl* hémorroïdes *fpl*
pile-up ['paɪlʌp] *n* (*Aut*) télescopage *m*, collision *f* en série
pilfer ['pɪlfə'] *vt* chaparder ▷ *vi* commettre des larcins
pilfering ['pɪlfərɪŋ] *n* chapardage *m*
pilgrim ['pɪlgrɪm] *n* pèlerin *m*; *voir article*

● PILGRIM FATHERS

Les *Pilgrim Fathers* ("Pères pèlerins") sont un groupe de puritains qui quittèrent l'Angleterre en 1620 pour fuir les persécutions religieuses. Ayant traversé l'Atlantique à bord du "Mayflower", ils fondèrent New Plymouth en Nouvelle-Angleterre, dans ce qui est aujourd'hui le Massachusetts. Ces Pères pèlerins sont considérés comme les fondateurs des États-Unis, et l'on commémore chaque année, le jour de "Thanksgiving", la réussite de leur première récolte.

pilgrimage ['pɪlgrɪmɪdʒ] *n* pèlerinage *m*
pill [pɪl] *n* pilule *f*; **the ~** la pilule; **to be on the ~** prendre la pilule
pillage ['pɪlɪdʒ] *vt* piller
pillar ['pɪlə'] *n* pilier *m*
pillar box *n* (*Brit*) boîte *f* aux lettres (*publique*)
pillion ['pɪljən] *n* (*of motor cycle*) siège *m* arrière; **to ride ~** être derrière; (*on horse*) être en croupe
pillory ['pɪlərɪ] *n* pilori *m* ▷ *vt* mettre au pilori
pillow ['pɪləʊ] *n* oreiller *m*
pillowcase ['pɪləʊkeɪs], **pillowslip** ['pɪləʊslɪp]

n taie *f* d'oreiller
pilot ['paɪlət] *n* pilote *m* ▷ *cpd* (*scheme etc*) pilote, expérimental(e) ▷ *vt* piloter
pilot boat *n* bateau-pilote *m*
pilot light *n* veilleuse *f*
pimento [pɪ'mɛntəʊ] *n* piment *m*
pimp [pɪmp] *n* souteneur *m*, maquereau *m*
pimple ['pɪmpl] *n* bouton *m*
pimply ['pɪmplɪ] *adj* boutonneux(-euse)
PIN *n abbr* (= *personal identification number*) code *m* confidentiel
pin [pɪn] *n* épingle *f*; (*Tech*) cheville *f*; (*Brit: drawing pin*) punaise *f*; (*in grenade*) goupille *f*; (*Brit Elec: of plug*) broche *f* ▷ *vt* épingler; **~s and needles** fourmis *fpl*; **to ~ sb against/to** clouer qn contre/à; **to ~ sb down** (*fig*) coincer qn; **to ~ sth on sb** (*fig*) mettre qch sur le dos de qn
  ▶ **pin down** *vt* (*fig*): **to ~ sb down** obliger qn à répondre; **there's something strange here but I can't quite ~ it down** il y a quelque chose d'étrange ici, mais je n'arrive pas exactement à savoir quoi
pinafore ['pɪnəfɔ:'] *n* tablier *m*
pinafore dress *n* robe-chasuble *f*
pinball ['pɪnbɔ:l] *n* flipper *m*
pincers ['pɪnsəz] *npl* tenailles *fpl*
pinch [pɪntʃ] *n* pincement *m*; (*of salt etc*) pincée *f* ▷ *vt* pincer; (*inf: steal*) piquer, chiper ▷ *vi* (*shoe*) serrer; **at a ~** à la rigueur; **to feel the ~** (*fig*) se ressentir des restrictions (*or de la récession etc*)
pinched [pɪntʃt] *adj* (*drawn*) tiré(e); **~ with cold** transi(e) de froid; **~ for** (*short of*): **~ for money** à court d'argent; **~ for space** à l'étroit
pincushion ['pɪnkʊʃən] *n* pelote *f* à épingles
pine [paɪn] *n* (*also*: **pine tree**) pin *m* ▷ *vi*: **to ~ for** aspirer à, désirer ardemment
  ▶ **pine away** *vi* dépérir
pineapple ['paɪnæpl] *n* ananas *m*
pine cone *n* pomme *f* de pin
ping [pɪŋ] *n* (*noise*) tintement *m*
ping-pong® ['pɪŋpɔŋ] *n* ping-pong® *m*
pink [pɪŋk] *adj* rose ▷ *n* (*colour*) rose *m*; (*Bot*) œillet *m*, mignardise *f*
pinking shears ['pɪŋkɪŋ-] *npl* ciseaux *mpl* à denteler
pin money *n* (*Brit*) argent *m* de poche
pinnacle ['pɪnəkl] *n* pinacle *m*
pinpoint ['pɪnpɔɪnt] *vt* indiquer (avec précision)
pinstripe ['pɪnstraɪp] *n* rayure très fine
pint [paɪnt] *n* pinte *f* (*Brit* = 0,57 l; *US* = 0,47 l); (*Brit inf*) ≈ demi *m*, ≈ pot *m*
pinup ['pɪnʌp] *n* pin-up *f inv*
pioneer [paɪə'nɪə'] *n* explorateur(-trice); (*early settler*) pionnier *m*; (*fig*) pionnier, précurseur *m* ▷ *vt* être un pionnier de
pious ['paɪəs] *adj* pieux(-euse)
pip [pɪp] *n* (*seed*) pépin *m*; **pips** *npl*: **the ~s** (*Brit: time signal on radio*) le top
pipe [paɪp] *n* tuyau *m*, conduite *f*; (*for smoking*) pipe *f*; (*Mus*) pipeau *m* ▷ *vt* amener par tuyau; **pipes** *npl* (*also*: **bagpipes**) cornemuse *f*
  ▶ **pipe down** *vi* (*inf*) se taire

pipe cleaner n cure-pipe m

piped music [paɪpt-] n musique f de fond

pipe dream n chimère f, utopie f

pipeline ['paɪplaɪn] n (for gas) gazoduc m, pipeline m; (for oil) oléoduc m, pipeline; **it is in the ~** (fig) c'est en route, ça va se faire

piper ['paɪpəʳ] n (flautist) joueur(-euse) de pipeau; (of bagpipes) joueur(-euse) de cornemuse

pipe tobacco n tabac m pour la pipe

piping ['paɪpɪŋ] adv: **~ hot** très chaud(e)

piquant ['piːkənt] adj piquant(e)

pique [piːk] n dépit m

piracy ['paɪərəsɪ] n piraterie f

pirate ['paɪərət] n pirate m ▷ vt (CD, video, book) pirater

pirated ['paɪərətɪd] adj pirate

pirate radio n (Brit) radio f pirate

pirouette [pɪruˈɛt] n pirouette f ▷ vi faire une or des pirouette(s)

Pisces ['paɪsiːz] n les Poissons mpl; **to be ~** être des Poissons

piss [pɪs] vi (inf!) pisser (!); **~ off!** tire-toi! (!)

pissed [pɪst] (inf!) adj (Brit: drunk) bourré(e); (US: angry) furieux(-euse)

pistol ['pɪstl] n pistolet m

piston ['pɪstən] n piston m

pit [pɪt] n trou m, fosse f; (also: **coal pit**) puits m de mine; (also: **orchestra pit**) fosse d'orchestre; (US: fruit stone) noyau m ▷ vt: **to ~ sb against sb** opposer qn à qn; **to ~ o.s.** or **one's wits against** se mesurer à; **pits** npl (in motor racing) aire f de service

pitapat ['pɪtəˈpæt] adv (Brit): **to go ~** (heart) battre la chamade; (rain) tambouriner

pitch [pɪtʃ] n (Brit Sport) terrain m; (throw) lancement m; (Mus) ton m; (of voice) hauteur f; (fig: degree) degré m; (also: **sales pitch**) baratin m, boniment m; (Naut) tangage m; (tar) poix f ▷ vt (throw) lancer; (tent) dresser; (set: price, message) adapter, positionner ▷ vi (Naut) tanguer; (fall): **to ~ into/off** tomber dans/de; **to be ~ed forward** être projeté(e) en avant; **at this ~** à ce rythme

pitch-black ['pɪtʃ'blæk] adj noir(e) comme poix

pitched battle [pɪtʃt-] n bataille rangée

pitcher ['pɪtʃəʳ] n cruche f

pitchfork ['pɪtʃfɔːk] n fourche f

piteous ['pɪtɪəs] adj pitoyable

pitfall ['pɪtfɔːl] n trappe f, piège m

pith [pɪθ] n (of plant) moelle f; (of orange etc) intérieur m de l'écorce; (fig) essence f; vigueur f

pithead ['pɪthɛd] n (Brit) bouche f de puits

pithy ['pɪθɪ] adj piquant(e); vigoureux(-euse)

pitiable ['pɪtɪəbl] adj pitoyable

pitiful ['pɪtɪful] adj (touching) pitoyable; (contemptible) lamentable

pitifully ['pɪtɪfəlɪ] adv pitoyablement; lamentablement

pitiless ['pɪtɪlɪs] adj impitoyable

pittance ['pɪtns] n salaire m de misère

pitted ['pɪtɪd] adj: **~ with** (chickenpox) grêlé(e) par; (rust) piqué(e) de

pity ['pɪtɪ] n pitié f ▷ vt plaindre; **what a ~!** quel dommage!; **it is a ~ that you can't come** c'est dommage que vous ne puissiez venir; **to have** or **take ~ on sb** avoir pitié de qn

pitying ['pɪtɪɪŋ] adj compatissant(e)

pivot ['pɪvət] n pivot m ▷ vi pivoter

pixel ['pɪksl] n (Comput) pixel m

pixie ['pɪksɪ] n lutin m

pizza ['piːtsə] n pizza f

placard ['plækɑːd] n affiche f; (in march) pancarte f

placate [plə'keɪt] vt apaiser, calmer

placatory [plə'keɪtərɪ] adj d'apaisement, lénifiant(e)

place [pleɪs] n endroit m, lieu m; (proper position, job, rank, seat) place f; (house) maison f, logement m; (in street names): **Laurel ~ ≈** rue des Lauriers; (home): **at/to his ~** chez lui ▷ vt (position) placer, mettre; (identify) situer; reconnaître; **to take ~** avoir lieu; (occur) se produire; **to take sb's ~** remplacer qn; **to change ~s with sb** changer de place avec qn; **from ~ to ~** d'un endroit à l'autre; **all over the ~** partout; **out of ~** (not suitable) déplacé(e), inopportun(e); **I feel out of ~ here** je ne me sens pas à ma place ici; **in the first ~** d'abord, en premier; **to put sb in his ~** (fig) remettre qn à sa place; **he's going ~s** (fig: inf) il fait son chemin; **it is not my ~ to do it** ce n'est pas à moi de le faire; **to ~ an order with sb (for)** (Comm) passer commande à qn (de); **to be ~d** (in race, exam) se placer; **how are you ~d next week?** comment ça se présente pour la semaine prochaine?

placebo [plə'siːbəu] n placebo m

place mat n set m de table; (in linen etc) napperon m

placement ['pleɪsmənt] n placement m; (during studies) stage m

place name n nom m de lieu

placenta [plə'sɛntə] n placenta m

placid ['plæsɪd] adj placide

placidity [plə'sɪdɪtɪ] n placidité f

plagiarism ['pleɪdʒərɪzəm] n plagiat m

plagiarist ['pleɪdʒərɪst] n plagiaire m/f

plagiarize ['pleɪdʒəraɪz] vt plagier

plague [pleɪg] n fléau m; (Med) peste f ▷ vt (fig) tourmenter; **to ~ sb with questions** harceler qn de questions

plaice [pleɪs] n (pl inv) carrelet m

plaid [plæd] n tissu écossais

plain [pleɪn] adj (in one colour) uni(e); (clear) clair(e), évident(e); (simple) simple, ordinaire; (frank) franc (franche); (not handsome) quelconque, ordinaire; (cigarette) sans filtre; (without seasoning etc) nature inv ▷ adv franchement, carrément ▷ n plaine f; **in ~ clothes** (police) en civil; **to make sth ~ to sb** faire clairement comprendre qch à qn

plain chocolate n chocolat m à croquer

plainly ['pleɪnlɪ] adv clairement; (frankly) carrément, sans détours

plainness ['pleɪnnɪs] n simplicité f

plain speaking n propos mpl sans équivoque; **she has a reputation for ~** elle est bien connue pour son franc parler or sa franchise

plaintiff ['pleɪntɪf] n plaignant(e)

plaintive ['pleɪntɪv] adj plaintif(-ive)

plait [plæt] n tresse f, natte f ▷ vt tresser, natter

plan [plæn] n plan m; (scheme) projet m ▷ vt (think in advance) projeter; (prepare) organiser ▷ vi faire des projets; **to ~ to do** projeter de faire; **how long do you ~ to stay?** combien de temps comptez-vous rester?

plane [pleɪn] n (Aviat) avion m; (also: **plane tree**) platane m; (tool) rabot m; (Art, Math etc) plan m; (fig) niveau m, plan ▷ adj plan(e); plat(e) ▷ vt (with tool) raboter

planet ['plænɪt] n planète f

planetarium [plænɪ'tɛərɪəm] n planétarium m

plank [plæŋk] n planche f; (Pol) point m d'un programme

plankton ['plæŋktən] n plancton m

planned economy [plænd-] n économie planifiée

planner ['plænər] n planificateur(-trice); (chart) planning m; **town** or (US) **city ~** urbaniste m/f

planning ['plænɪŋ] n planification f; **family ~** planning familial

planning permission n (Brit) permis m de construire

plant [plɑːnt] n plante f; (machinery) matériel m; (factory) usine f ▷ vt planter; (bomb) déposer, poser; (microphone, evidence) cacher

plantation [plæn'teɪʃən] n plantation f

plant pot n (Brit) pot m de fleurs

plaque [plæk] n plaque f

plasma ['plæzmə] n plasma m

plaster ['plɑːstər] n plâtre m; (also: **plaster of Paris**) plâtre à mouler; (Brit: also: **sticking plaster**) pansement adhésif ▷ vt plâtrer; (cover): **to ~ with** couvrir de; **in ~** (Brit: leg etc) dans le plâtre

plasterboard ['plɑːstəbɔːd] n Placoplâtre® m

plaster cast n (Med) plâtre m; (model, statue) moule m

plastered ['plɑːstəd] adj (inf) soûl(e)

plasterer ['plɑːstərər] n plâtrier m

plastic ['plæstɪk] n plastique m ▷ adj (made of plastic) en plastique; (flexible) plastique, malléable; (art) plastique

plastic bag n sac m en plastique

plastic bullet n balle f de plastique

plastic explosive n plastic m

plasticine® ['plæstɪsiːn] n pâte f à modeler

plastic surgery n chirurgie f esthétique

plate [pleɪt] n (dish) assiette f; (sheet of metal, on door: Phot) plaque f; (Typ) cliché m; (in book) gravure f; (dental) dentier m; (Aut: number plate) plaque minéralogique; **gold/silver ~** (dishes) vaisselle f d'or/d'argent

plateau (pl **-s** or **-x**) ['plætəu, -z] n plateau m

plateful ['pleɪtful] n assiette f, assiettée f

plate glass n verre m à vitre, vitre f

platen ['plætən] n (on typewriter, printer) rouleau m

plate rack n égouttoir m

platform ['plætfɔːm] n (at meeting) tribune f; (Brit: of bus) plate-forme f; (stage) estrade f; (Rail) quai m; (Pol) plateforme f; **the train leaves from ~ 7** le train part de la voie 7

platform ticket n (Brit) billet m de quai

platinum ['plætɪnəm] n platine m

platitude ['plætɪtjuːd] n platitude f, lieu commun

platoon [plə'tuːn] n peloton m

platter ['plætər] n plat m

plaudits ['plɔːdɪts] npl applaudissements mpl

plausible ['plɔːzɪbl] adj plausible; (person) convaincant(e)

play [pleɪ] n jeu m; (Theat) pièce f (de théâtre) ▷ vt (game) jouer à; (team, opponent) jouer contre; (instrument) jouer de; (part, piece of music, note) jouer; (CD etc) passer ▷ vi jouer; **to bring** or **call into ~** faire entrer en jeu; **~ on words** jeu de mots; **to ~ safe** ne prendre aucun risque; **to ~ a trick on sb** jouer un tour à qn; **they're ~ing at soldiers** ils jouent aux soldats; **to ~ for time** (fig) chercher à gagner du temps; **to ~ into sb's hands** (fig) faire le jeu de qn
  ▸ **play about, play around** vi (person) s'amuser
  ▸ **play along** vi (fig): **to ~ along with** (person) entrer dans le jeu de ▷ vt (fig): **to ~ sb along** faire marcher qn
  ▸ **play back** vt repasser, réécouter
  ▸ **play down** vt minimiser
  ▸ **play on** vt fus (sb's feelings, credulity) jouer sur; **to ~ on sb's nerves** porter sur les nerfs de qn
  ▸ **play up** vi (cause trouble) faire des siennes

playact ['pleɪækt] vi jouer la comédie

playboy ['pleɪbɔɪ] n playboy m

played-out ['pleɪd'aut] adj épuisé(e)

player ['pleɪər] n joueur(-euse); (Theat) acteur(-trice); (Mus) musicien(ne)

playful ['pleɪful] adj enjoué(e)

playgoer ['pleɪgəuər] n amateur(-trice) de théâtre, habitué(e) des théâtres

playground ['pleɪgraund] n cour f de récréation; (in park) aire f de jeux

playgroup ['pleɪgruːp] n garderie f

playing card ['pleɪɪŋ-] n carte f à jouer

playing field ['pleɪɪŋ-] n terrain m de sport

playmaker ['pleɪmeɪkər] n (Sport) joueur qui crée des occasions de marquer des buts pour ses coéquipiers.

playmate ['pleɪmeɪt] n camarade m/f, copain (copine)

play-off ['pleɪɔf] n (Sport) belle f

playpen ['pleɪpɛn] n parc m (pour bébé)

playroom ['pleɪruːm] n salle f de jeux

playschool ['pleɪskuːl] n = **playgroup**

plaything ['pleɪθɪŋ] n jouet m

playtime ['pleɪtaɪm] n (Scol) récréation f

playwright ['pleɪraɪt] n dramaturge m

plc abbr (Brit: = public limited company) ≈ SARL f

plea [pliː] n (request) appel m; (excuse) excuse f; (Law) défense f

plea bargaining n (Law) négociations entre le procureur, l'avocat de la défense et parfois le juge, pour *réduire la gravité des charges.*

plead [pli:d] *vt* plaider; (*give as excuse*) invoquer ▷ *vi* (*Law*) plaider; (*beg*): **to ~ with sb (for sth)** implorer qn (d'accorder qch); **to ~ for sth** implorer qch; **to ~ guilty/not guilty** plaider coupable/non coupable

pleasant ['plɛznt] *adj* agréable

pleasantly ['plɛzntlɪ] *adv* agréablement

pleasantry ['plɛzntrɪ] *n* (*joke*) plaisanterie *f*; **pleasantries** *npl* (*polite remarks*) civilités *fpl*

please [pli:z] *excl* s'il te (*or* vous) plaît ▷ *vt* plaire à ▷ *vi* (*think fit*): **do as you ~** faites comme il vous plaira; **my bill, ~** l'addition, s'il vous plaît; **~ don't cry!** je t'en prie, ne pleure pas!; **~ yourself!** (*inf*) (faites) comme vous voulez!

pleased [pli:zd] *adj*: **~ (with)** content(e) (de); **~ to meet you** enchanté (de faire votre connaissance); **we are ~ to inform you that ...** nous sommes heureux de vous annoncer que ...

pleasing ['pli:zɪŋ] *adj* plaisant(e), qui fait plaisir

pleasurable ['plɛʒərəbl] *adj* très agréable

pleasure ['plɛʒəʳ] *n* plaisir *m*; **"it's a ~"** "je vous en prie"; **with ~** avec plaisir; **is this trip for business or ~?** est-ce un voyage d'affaires ou d'agrément?

pleasure cruise *n* croisière *f*

pleat [pli:t] *n* pli *m*

plebiscite ['plɛbɪsɪt] *n* plébiscite *m*

plebs [plɛbz] *npl* (*pej*) bas peuple

plectrum ['plɛktrəm] *n* plectre *m*

pledge [plɛdʒ] *n* gage *m*; (*promise*) promesse *f* ▷ *vt* engager; promettre; **to ~ support for sb** s'engager à soutenir qn; **to ~ sb to secrecy** faire promettre à qn de garder le secret

plenary ['pli:nərɪ] *adj*: **in ~ session** en séance plénière

plentiful ['plɛntɪful] *adj* abondant(e), copieux(-euse)

plenty ['plɛntɪ] *n* abondance *f*; **~ of** beaucoup de; (*sufficient*) (bien) assez de; **we've got ~ of time** nous avons largement le temps

pleurisy ['pluərɪsɪ] *n* pleurésie *f*

pliable ['plaɪəbl] *adj* flexible; (*person*) malléable

pliers ['plaɪəz] *npl* pinces *fpl*

plight [plaɪt] *n* situation *f* critique

plimsolls ['plɪmsəlz] *npl* (*Brit*) (chaussures *fpl*) tennis *fpl*

plinth [plɪnθ] *n* socle *m*

PLO *n abbr* (= *Palestine Liberation Organization*) OLP *f*

plod [plɔd] *vi* avancer péniblement; (*fig*) peiner

plodder ['plɔdəʳ] *n* bûcheur(-euse)

plodding ['plɔdɪŋ] *adj* pesant(e)

plonk [plɔŋk] (*inf*) *n* (*Brit*: *wine*) pinard *m*, piquette *f* ▷ *vt*: **to ~ sth down** poser brusquement qch

plot [plɔt] *n* complot *m*, conspiration *f*; (*of story, play*) intrigue *f*; (*of land*) lot *m* de terrain, lopin *m* ▷ *vt* (*mark out*) tracer point par point; (*Naut*) pointer; (*make graph of*) faire le graphique de; (*conspire*) comploter ▷ *vi* comploter; **a vegetable ~** (*Brit*) un carré de légumes

plotter ['plɔtəʳ] *n* conspirateur(-trice); (*Comput*)

traceur *m*

plough, (*US*) **plow** [plau] *n* charrue *f* ▷ *vt* (*earth*) labourer; **to ~ money into** investir dans
▸ **plough back** *vt* (*Comm*) réinvestir
▸ **plough through** *vt fus* (*snow etc*) avancer péniblement dans

ploughing, (*US*) **plowing** ['plauɪŋ] *n* labourage *m*

ploughman, (*US*) **plowman** ['plaumən] (*irreg*) *n* laboureur *m*

plow [plau] (*US*) = **plough**

ploy [plɔɪ] *n* stratagème *m*

pls *abbr* (= *please*) SVP *m*

pluck [plʌk] *vt* (*fruit*) cueillir; (*musical instrument*) pincer; (*bird*) plumer ▷ *n* courage *m*, cran *m*; **to ~ one's eyebrows** s'épiler les sourcils; **to ~ up courage** prendre son courage à deux mains

plucky ['plʌkɪ] *adj* courageux(-euse)

plug [plʌg] *n* (*stopper*) bouchon *m*, bonde *f*; (*Elec*) prise *f* de courant; (*Aut*: *also*: **spark(ing) plug**) bougie *f* ▷ *vt* (*hole*) boucher; (*inf*: *advertise*) faire du battage pour, matraquer; **to give sb/sth a ~** (*inf*) faire de la pub pour qn/qch
▸ **plug in** *vt* (*Elec*) brancher ▷ *vi* (*Elec*) se brancher

plughole ['plʌghəul] *n* (*Brit*) trou *m* (d'écoulement)

plum [plʌm] *n* (*fruit*) prune *f* ▷ *adj*: **~ job** (*inf*) travail *m* en or

plumb [plʌm] *adj* vertical(e) ▷ *n* plomb *m* ▷ *adv* (*exactly*) en plein ▷ *vt* sonder
▸ **plumb in** *vt* (*washing machine*) faire le raccordement de

plumber ['plʌməʳ] *n* plombier *m*

plumbing ['plʌmɪŋ] *n* (*trade*) plomberie *f*; (*piping*) tuyauterie *f*

plumbline ['plʌmlaɪn] *n* fil *m* à plomb

plume [plu:m] *n* plume *f*, plumet *m*

plummet ['plʌmɪt] *vi* (*person, object*) plonger; (*sales, prices*) dégringoler

plump [plʌmp] *adj* rondelet(te), dodu(e), bien en chair ▷ *vt*: **to ~ sth (down) on** laisser tomber qch lourdement sur
▸ **plump for** *vt fus* (*inf*: *choose*) se décider pour
▸ **plump up** *vt* (*cushion*) battre (pour lui redonner forme)

plunder ['plʌndəʳ] *n* pillage *m* ▷ *vt* piller

plunge [plʌndʒ] *n* plongeon *m*; (*fig*) chute *f* ▷ *vt* plonger ▷ *vi* (*fall*) tomber, dégringoler; (*dive*) plonger; **to take the ~** se jeter à l'eau

plunger ['plʌndʒəʳ] *n* piston *m*; (*for blocked sink*) (débouchoir *m* à) ventouse *f*

plunging ['plʌndʒɪŋ] *adj* (*neckline*) plongeant(e)

pluperfect [plu:'pə:fɪkt] *n* (*Ling*) plus-que-parfait *m*

plural ['pluərl] *adj* pluriel(le) ▷ *n* pluriel *m*

plus [plʌs] *n* (*also*: **plus sign**) signe *m* plus; (*advantage*) atout *m* ▷ *prep* plus; **ten/twenty ~** plus de dix/vingt; **it's a ~** c'est un atout

plus fours *npl* pantalon *m* (de) golf

plush [plʌʃ] *adj* somptueux(-euse) ▷ *n* peluche *f*

ply [plaɪ] *n* (*of wool*) fil *m*; (*of wood*) feuille *f*,

épaisseur f ▷ vt (tool) manier; (a trade) exercer
▷ vi (ship) faire la navette; **three ~ (wool)** n
laine f trois fils; **to ~ sb with drink** donner
continuellement à boire à qn
plywood ['plaɪwʊd] n contreplaqué m
P.M. n abbr (Brit) = **prime minister**
p.m. adv abbr (= post meridiem) de l'après-midi
PMS n abbr (= premenstrual syndrome) syndrome
prémenstruel
PMT n abbr (= premenstrual tension) syndrome
prémenstruel
pneumatic [njuː'mætɪk] adj pneumatique
pneumatic drill [njuː'mætɪk-] n marteau-
piqueur m
pneumonia [njuː'məunɪə] n pneumonie f
PO n abbr (= Post Office) PTT fpl; (Mil) = **petty
officer**
po abbr = **postal order**
POA n abbr (Brit) = **Prison Officers' Association**
poach [pəutʃ] vt (cook) pocher; (steal) pêcher (or
chasser) sans permis ▷ vi braconner
poached [pəutʃt] adj (egg) poché(e)
poacher ['pəutʃəʳ] n braconnier m
poaching ['pəutʃɪŋ] n braconnage m
P.O. Box n abbr = **post office box**
pocket ['pɔkɪt] n poche f ▷ vt empocher; **to be
(£5) out of ~** (Brit) en être de sa poche (pour 5
livres)
pocketbook ['pɔkɪtbuk] n (notebook) carnet m;
(US: wallet) portefeuille m; (: handbag) sac m à
main
pocket knife n canif m
pocket money n argent m de poche
pockmarked ['pɔkmɑːkt] adj (face) grêlé(e)
pod [pɔd] n cosse f ▷ vt écosser
podcast n podcast m
podcasting ['pɔdkɑːstɪŋ] n podcasting m,
baladodiffusion f
podgy ['pɔdʒɪ] adj rondelet(te)
podiatrist [pɔ'diːətrɪst] n (US) pédicure m/f
podiatry [pɔ'diːətrɪ] n (US) pédicurie f
podium ['pəudɪəm] n podium m
POE n abbr = **port of embarkation; port of entry**
poem ['pəuɪm] n poème m
poet ['pəuɪt] n poète m
poetic [pəu'ɛtɪk] adj poétique
poet laureate n poète lauréat; voir article

poetry ['pəuɪtrɪ] n poésie f
poignant ['pɔɪnjənt] adj poignant(e); (sharp) vif
(vive)

point [pɔɪnt] n (Geom, Scol, Sport, on scale) point m;
(tip) pointe f; (in time) moment m; (in space)
endroit m; (subject, idea) point, sujet m; (purpose)
but m; (also: **decimal point**): **2 ~ 3 (2.3)** 2 virgule 3
(2,3); (Brit Elec: also: **power point**) prise f (de
courant) ▷ vt (show) indiquer; (wall, window)
jointoyer; (gun etc): **to ~ sth at** braquer or
diriger qch sur ▷ vi: **to ~ at** montrer du doigt;
points npl (Aut) vis platinées; (Rail) aiguillage
m; **good ~s** fpl; **the train stops at
Carlisle and all ~s south** le train dessert
Carlisle et toutes les gares vers le sud; **to make
a ~** faire une remarque; **to make a ~ of doing
sth** ne pas manquer de faire qch; **to make
one's ~** se faire comprendre; **to get/miss the ~**
comprendre/ne pas comprendre; **to come to
the ~** en venir au fait; **when it comes to the ~**
le moment venu; **there's no ~ (in doing)** cela
ne sert à rien (de faire); **what's the ~?** à quoi ça
sert?; **to be on the ~ of doing sth** être sur le
point de faire qch; **that's the whole ~!**
précisément!; **to be beside the ~** être à côté de
la question; **you've got a ~ there!** (c'est) juste!;
in ~ of fact en fait, en réalité; **~ of departure**
(also fig) point de départ; **~ of order** point de
procédure; **~ of sale** (Comm) point de vente; **to ~
to sth** (fig) signaler
▸ **point out** vt (show) montrer, indiquer;
(mention) faire remarquer, souligner
point-blank ['pɔɪnt'blæŋk] adv (fig)
catégoriquement; (also: **at point-blank range**) à
bout portant ▷ adj (fig) catégorique
point duty n (Brit): **to be on ~** diriger la
circulation
pointed ['pɔɪntɪd] adj (shape) pointu(e); (remark)
plein(e) de sous-entendus
pointedly ['pɔɪntɪdlɪ] adv d'une manière
significative
pointer ['pɔɪntəʳ] n (stick) baguette f; (needle)
aiguille f; (dog) chien m d'arrêt; (clue) indication
f; (advice) tuyau m
pointless ['pɔɪntlɪs] adj inutile, vain(e)
point of view n point m de vue
poise [pɔɪz] n (balance) équilibre m; (of head, body)
port m; (calmness) calme m ▷ vt placer en
équilibre; **to be ~d for** (fig) être prêt à
poison ['pɔɪzn] n poison m ▷ vt empoisonner
poisoning ['pɔɪznɪŋ] n empoisonnement m
poisonous ['pɔɪznəs] adj (snake)
venimeux(-euse); (substance, plant)
vénéneux(-euse); (fumes) toxique; (fig)
pernicieux(-euse)
poke [pəuk] vt (fire) tisonner; (jab with finger, stick
etc) piquer; pousser du doigt; (put): **to ~ sth
in(to)** fourrer or enfoncer qch dans ▷ n (jab)
(petit) coup; (to fire) coup m de tisonnier; **to ~
fun at sb** se moquer de qn
▸ **poke about** vi fureter
▸ **poke out** vi (stick out) sortir ▷ vt: **to ~ one's
head out of the window** passer la tête par la
fenêtre
poker ['pəukəʳ] n tisonnier m; (Cards) poker m

poker-faced ['pəukə'feɪst] *adj* au visage impassible
poky ['pəukɪ] *adj* exigu(ë)
Poland ['pəulənd] *n* Pologne *f*
polar ['pəulə'] *adj* polaire
polar bear *n* ours blanc
polarize ['pəulərɑɪz] *vt* polariser
Pole [pəul] *n* Polonais(e)
pole [pəul] *n* (*of wood*) mât *m*, perche *f*; (*Elec*) poteau *m*; (*Geo*) pôle *m*
poleaxe ['pəulæks] *vt* (*fig*) terrasser
pole bean *n* (*US*) haricot *m* (à rames)
polecat ['pəulkæt] *n* putois *m*
Pol. Econ. ['pɒlɪkɒn] *n abbr* = **political economy**
polemic [pɒ'lɛmɪk] *n* polémique *f*
pole star ['pəulstɑ:'] *n* étoile *f* polaire
pole vault ['pəulvɔ:lt] *n* saut *m* à la perche
police [pə'li:s] *npl* police *f* ▷ *vt* maintenir l'ordre dans; **a large number of ~ were hurt** de nombreux policiers ont été blessés
police car *n* voiture *f* de police
police constable *n* (*Brit*) agent *m* de police
police department *n* (*US*) services *mpl* de police
police force *n* police *f*, forces *fpl* de l'ordre
policeman [pə'li:smən] (*irreg*) *n* agent *m* de police, policier *m*
police officer *n* agent *m* de police
police record *n* casier *m* judiciaire
police state *n* état policier
police station *n* commissariat *m* de police
policewoman [pə'li:swumən] (*irreg*) *n* femme-agent *f*
policy ['pɒlɪsɪ] *n* politique *f*; (*also:* **insurance policy**) police *f* (d'assurance); (*of newspaper, company*) politique générale; **to take out a ~** (*Insurance*) souscrire une police d'assurance
policy holder *n* assuré(e)
policy-making ['pɒlɪsɪmeɪkɪŋ] *n* élaboration *f* de nouvelles lignes d'action
polio ['pəulɪəu] *n* polio *f*
Polish ['pəulɪʃ] *adj* polonais(e) ▷ *n* (*Ling*) polonais *m*
polish ['pɒlɪʃ] *n* (*for shoes*) cirage *m*; (*for floor*) cire *f*, encaustique *f*; (*for nails*) vernis *m*; (*shine*) éclat *m*, poli *m*; (*fig: refinement*) raffinement *m* ▷ *vt* (*put polish on: shoes, wood*) cirer; (*make shiny*) astiquer, faire briller; (*fig: improve*) perfectionner
 ▸ **polish off** *vt* (*work*) expédier; (*food*) liquider
polished ['pɒlɪʃt] *adj* (*fig*) raffiné(e)
polite [pə'laɪt] *adj* poli(e); **it's not ~ to do that** ça ne se fait pas
politely [pə'laɪtlɪ] *adv* poliment
politeness [pə'laɪtnɪs] *n* politesse *f*
politic ['pɒlɪtɪk] *adj* diplomatique
political [pə'lɪtɪkl] *adj* politique
political asylum *n* asile *m* politique
politically [pə'lɪtɪklɪ] *adv* politiquement; **~ correct** politiquement correct(e)
politician [pɒlɪ'tɪʃən] *n* homme/femme politique, politicien(ne)
politics ['pɒlɪtɪks] *n* politique *f*
polka ['pɒlkə] *n* polka *f*

polka dot *n* pois *m*
poll [pəul] *n* scrutin *m*, vote *m*; (*also:* **opinion poll**) sondage *m* (d'opinion) ▷ *vt* (*votes*) obtenir; **to go to the ~s** (*voters*) aller aux urnes; (*government*) tenir des élections
pollen ['pɒlən] *n* pollen *m*
pollen count *n* taux *m* de pollen
pollination [pɒlɪ'neɪʃən] *n* pollinisation *f*
polling ['pəulɪŋ] *n* (*Brit Pol*) élections *fpl*; (*Tel*) invitation *f* à émettre
polling booth *n* (*Brit*) isoloir *m*
polling day *n* (*Brit*) jour *m* des élections
polling station *n* (*Brit*) bureau *m* de vote
pollster ['pəulstə'] *n* sondeur *m*, enquêteur(-euse)
poll tax *n* (*Brit: formerly*) ≈ impôts locaux.
pollutant [pə'lu:tənt] *n* polluant *m*
pollute [pə'lu:t] *vt* polluer
pollution [pə'lu:ʃən] *n* pollution *f*
polo ['pəuləu] *n* polo *m*
polo-neck ['pəuləunɛk] *adj* à col roulé ▷ *n* (*sweater*) pull *m* à col roulé
polo shirt *n* polo *m*
poly ['pɒlɪ] *n abbr* (*Brit*) = **polytechnic**
poly bag *n* (*Brit inf*) sac *m* en plastique
polyester [pɒlɪ'ɛstə'] *n* polyester *m*
polygamy [pə'lɪɡəmɪ] *n* polygamie *f*
polygraph ['pɒlɪɡrɑ:f] *n* détecteur *m* de mensonges
Polynesia [pɒlɪ'ni:zɪə] *n* Polynésie *f*
Polynesian [pɒlɪ'ni:zɪən] *adj* polynésien(ne) ▷ *n* Polynésien(ne)
polyp ['pɒlɪp] *n* (*Med*) polype *m*
polystyrene [pɒlɪ'staɪri:n] *n* polystyrène *m*
polytechnic [pɒlɪ'tɛknɪk] *n* (*college*) IUT *m*, Institut *m* universitaire de technologie
polythene ['pɒlɪθi:n] *n* (*Brit*) polyéthylène *m*
polythene bag *n* sac *m* en plastique
polyurethane [pɒlɪ'juərɪθeɪn] *n* polyuréthane *m*
pomegranate ['pɒmɪɡrænɪt] *n* grenade *f*
pommel ['pɒml] *n* pommeau *m* ▷ *vt* = **pummel**
pomp [pɒmp] *n* pompe *f*, faste *f*, apparat *m*
pompom ['pɒmpɒm] *n* pompon *m*
pompous ['pɒmpəs] *adj* pompeux(-euse)
pond [pɒnd] *n* étang *m*; (*stagnant*) mare *f*
ponder ['pɒndə'] *vi* réfléchir ▷ *vt* considérer, peser
ponderous ['pɒndərəs] *adj* pesant(e), lourd(e)
pong [pɒŋ] (*Brit inf*) *n* puanteur *f* ▷ *vi* schlinguer
pontiff ['pɒntɪf] *n* pontife *m*
pontificate [pɒn'tɪfɪkeɪt] *vi* (*fig*): **to ~ (about)** pontifier (sur)
pontoon [pɒn'tu:n] *n* ponton *m*; (*Brit Cards*) vingt-et-un *m*
pony ['pəunɪ] *n* poney *m*
ponytail ['pəunɪteɪl] *n* queue *f* de cheval
pony trekking [-trɛkɪŋ] *n* (*Brit*) randonnée *f* équestre *or* à cheval
poodle ['pu:dl] *n* caniche *m*
pooh-pooh ['pu:'pu:] *vt* dédaigner
pool [pu:l] *n* (*of rain*) flaque *f*; (*pond*) mare *f*;

(*artificial*) bassin *m*; (*also:* **swimming pool**) piscine *f*; (*sth shared*) fonds commun; (*money at cards*) cagnotte *f*; (*billiards*) poule *f*; (*Comm: consortium*) pool *m*; (*US: monopoly trust*) trust *m* ▷ *vt* mettre en commun; **pools** *npl* (*football*) ≈ loto sportif; **typing ~**, (US) **secretary ~** pool *m* dactylographique; **to do the (football) ~s** (*Brit*) ≈ jouer au loto sportif; *see also* **football pools**

poor [puə^r] *adj* pauvre; (*mediocre*) médiocre, faible, mauvais(e) ▷ *npl*: **the ~** les pauvres *mpl*

poorly ['puəlɪ] *adv* pauvrement; (*badly*) mal, médiocrement ▷ *adj* souffrant(e), malade

pop [pɔp] *n* (*noise*) bruit sec; (*Mus*) musique *f* pop; (*inf: drink*) soda *m*; (*US inf: father*) papa *m* ▷ *vt* (*put*) fourrer, mettre (rapidement) ▷ *vi* éclater; (*cork*) sauter; **she ~ped her head out of the window** elle lui passa la tête par la fenêtre
  ▶ **pop in** *vi* entrer en passant
  ▶ **pop out** *vi* sortir
  ▶ **pop up** *vi* apparaître, surgir

pop concert *n* concert *m* pop

popcorn ['pɔpkɔːn] *n* pop-corn *m*

pope [pəup] *n* pape *m*

poplar ['pɔplə^r] *n* peuplier *m*

poplin ['pɔplɪn] *n* popeline *f*

popper ['pɔpə^r] *n* (*Brit*) bouton-pression *m*

poppy ['pɔpɪ] *n* (*wild*) coquelicot *m*; (*cultivated*) pavot *m*

poppycock ['pɔpɪkɔk] *n* (*inf*) balivernes *fpl*

Popsicle® ['pɔpsɪkl] *n* (*US*) esquimau *m* (*glace*)

pop star *n* pop star *f*

populace ['pɔpjuləs] *n* peuple *m*

popular ['pɔpjulə^r] *adj* populaire; (*fashionable*) à la mode; **to be ~ (with)** (*person*) avoir du succès (auprès de); (*decision*) être bien accueilli(e) (par)

popularity [pɔpju'lærɪtɪ] *n* popularité *f*

popularize ['pɔpjuləraɪz] *vt* populariser; (*science*) vulgariser

populate ['pɔpjuleɪt] *vt* peupler

population [pɔpju'leɪʃən] *n* population *f*

population explosion *n* explosion *f* démographique

populous ['pɔpjuləs] *adj* populeux(-euse)

pop-up *adj* (*Comput: menu, window*) pop up *inv* ▷ *n* pop up *m inv*, fenêtre *f* pop up

porcelain ['pɔːslɪn] *n* porcelaine *f*

porch [pɔːtʃ] *n* porche *m*; (*US*) véranda *f*

porcupine ['pɔːkjupaɪn] *n* porc-épic *m*

pore [pɔː^r] *n* pore *m* ▷ *vi*: **to ~ over** s'absorber dans, être plongé(e) dans

pork [pɔːk] *n* porc *m*

pork chop *n* côte *f* de porc

pork pie *n* pâté *m* de porc en croûte

porn [pɔːn] *adj* (*inf*) porno ▷ *n* (*inf*) porno *m*

pornographic [pɔːnə'græfɪk] *adj* pornographique

pornography [pɔː'nɔɡrəfɪ] *n* pornographie *f*

porous ['pɔːrəs] *adj* poreux(-euse)

porpoise ['pɔːpəs] *n* marsouin *m*

porridge ['pɔrɪdʒ] *n* porridge *m*

port [pɔːt] *n* (*harbour*) port *m*; (*opening in ship*) sabord *m*; (*Naut: left side*) bâbord *m*; (*wine*) porto *m*; (*Comput*) port *m*, accès *m* ▷ *cpd* portuaire, du port; **to ~** (*Naut*) à bâbord; **~ of call** (port d')escale *f*

portable ['pɔːtəbl] *adj* portatif(-ive)

portal ['pɔːtl] *n* portail *m*

portcullis [pɔːt'kʌlɪs] *n* herse *f*

portent ['pɔːtɛnt] *n* présage *m*

porter ['pɔːtə^r] *n* (*for luggage*) porteur *m*; (*doorkeeper*) gardien(ne); portier *m*

portfolio [pɔːt'fəulɪəu] *n* portefeuille *m*; (*of artist*) portfolio *m*

porthole ['pɔːthəul] *n* hublot *m*

portico ['pɔːtɪkəu] *n* portique *m*

portion ['pɔːʃən] *n* portion *f*, part *f*

portly ['pɔːtlɪ] *adj* corpulent(e)

portrait ['pɔːtreɪt] *n* portrait *m*

portray [pɔː'treɪ] *vt* faire le portrait de; (*in writing*) dépeindre, représenter; (*subj: actor*) jouer

portrayal [pɔː'treɪəl] *n* portrait *m*, représentation *f*

Portugal ['pɔːtjuɡl] *n* Portugal *m*

Portuguese [pɔːtju'ɡiːz] *adj* portugais(e) ▷ *n* (*pl inv*) Portugais(e); (*Ling*) portugais *m*

Portuguese man-of-war [-mænəv'wɔː^r] *n* (*jellyfish*) galère *f*

pose [pəuz] *n* pose *f*; (*pej*) affectation *f* ▷ *vi* poser; (*pretend*): **to ~ as** se faire passer pour ▷ *vt* poser; (*problem*) créer; **to strike a ~** poser (pour la galerie)

poser ['pəuzə^r] *n* question difficile *or* embarrassante; (*person*) = **poseur**

poseur [pəu'zəː^r] *n* (*pej*) poseur(-euse)

posh [pɔʃ] *adj* (*inf*) chic *inv*; **to talk ~** parler d'une manière affectée

position [pə'zɪʃən] *n* position *f*; (*job, situation*) situation *f* ▷ *vt* mettre en place *or* en position; **to be in a ~ to do sth** être en mesure de faire qch

positive ['pɔzɪtɪv] *adj* positif(-ive); (*certain*) sûr(e), certain(e); (*definite*) formel(le), catégorique; (*clear*) indéniable, réel(le)

positively ['pɔzɪtɪvlɪ] *adv* (*affirmatively, enthusiastically*) de façon positive; (*inf: really*) carrément; **to think ~** être positif(-ive)

posse ['pɔsɪ] *n* (*US*) détachement *m*

possess [pə'zɛs] *vt* posséder; **like one ~ed** comme un fou; **whatever can have ~ed you?** qu'est-ce qui vous a pris?

possession [pə'zɛʃən] *n* possession *f*; **possessions** *npl* (*belongings*) affaires *fpl*; **to take ~ of sth** prendre possession de qch

possessive [pə'zɛsɪv] *adj* possessif(-ive)

possessiveness [pə'zɛsɪvnɪs] *n* possessivité *f*

possessor [pə'zɛsə^r] *n* possesseur *m*

possibility [pɔsɪ'bɪlɪtɪ] *n* possibilité *f*; (*event*) éventualité *f*; **he's a ~ for the part** c'est un candidat possible pour le rôle

possible ['pɔsɪbl] *adj* possible; (*solution*) envisageable, éventuel(le); **it is ~ to do it** il est possible de le faire; **as far as ~** dans la mesure du possible, autant que possible; **if ~** si possible; **as big as ~** aussi gros que possible

possibly ['pɒsɪblɪ] *adv* (*perhaps*) peut-être; **if you ~ can** si cela vous est possible; **I cannot ~ come** il m'est impossible de venir

post [pəust] *n* (*Brit: mail*) poste *f*; (*: collection*) levée *f*; (*: letters, delivery*) courrier *m*; (*job, situation*) poste *m*; (*pole*) poteau *m*; (*trading post*) comptoir (commercial) ▷ *vt* (*Brit: send by post, Mil*) poster; (*: appoint*): **to ~ to** affecter à; (*notice*) afficher; **by ~** (*Brit*) par la poste; **by return of ~** (*Brit*) par retour du courrier; **where can I ~ these cards?** où est-ce que je peux poster ces cartes postales?; **to keep sb ~ed** tenir qn au courant

post... [pəust] *prefix* post...; **post 1990** *adj* d'après 1990 ▷ *adv* après 1990

postage ['pəustɪdʒ] *n* tarifs *mpl* d'affranchissement; **~ paid** port payé; **~ prepaid** (*US*) franco (de port)

postage stamp *n* timbre-poste *m*

postal ['pəustl] *adj* postal(e)

postal order *n* mandat(-poste *m*) *m*

postbag ['pəustbæg] *n* (*Brit*) sac postal; (*postman's*) sacoche *f*

postbox ['pəustbɒks] *n* (*Brit*) boîte *f* aux lettres (*publique*)

postcard ['pəustkɑːd] *n* carte postale

postcode ['pəustkəud] *n* (*Brit*) code postal

postdate ['pəust'deɪt] *vt* (*cheque*) postdater

poster ['pəustəʳ] *n* affiche *f*

poste restante [pəust'rɛstɑ̃ːnt] *n* (*Brit*) poste restante

posterior [pɒs'tɪərɪəʳ] *n* (*inf*) postérieur *m*, derrière *m*

posterity [pɒs'tɛrɪtɪ] *n* postérité *f*

poster paint *n* gouache *f*

post exchange *n* (*US Mil*) magasin *m* de l'armée

post-free [pəust'friː] *adj* (*Brit*) franco (de port)

postgraduate ['pəust'grædjuət] *n* ≈ étudiant(e) de troisième cycle

posthumous ['pɒstjuməs] *adj* posthume

posthumously ['pɒstjuməslɪ] *adv* après la mort de l'auteur, à titre posthume

posting ['pəustɪŋ] *n* (*Brit*) affectation *f*

postman ['pəustmən] (*Brit: irreg*) *n* facteur *m*

postmark ['pəustmɑːk] *n* cachet *m* (de la poste)

postmaster ['pəustmɑːstəʳ] *n* receveur *m* des postes

Postmaster General *n* ≈ ministre *m* des Postes et Télécommunications

postmistress ['pəustmɪstrɪs] *n* receveuse *f* des postes

post-mortem [pəust'mɔːtəm] *n* autopsie *f*

postnatal ['pəust'neɪtl] *adj* postnatal(e)

post office *n* (*building*) poste *f*; (*organization*): **the Post Office** les postes *fpl*

post office box *n* boîte postale

post-paid ['pəust'peɪd] *adj* (*Brit*) port payé

postpone [pəs'pəun] *vt* remettre (à plus tard), reculer

postponement [pəs'pəunmənt] *n* ajournement *m*, renvoi *m*

postscript ['pəustskrɪpt] *n* post-scriptum *m*

postulate ['pɒstjuleɪt] *vt* postuler

posture ['pɒstʃəʳ] *n* posture *f*; (*fig*) attitude *f* ▷ *vi* poser

postwar [pəust'wɔːʳ] *adj* d'après-guerre

postwoman [pəust'wumən] (*Brit: irreg*) *n* factrice *f*

posy ['pəuzɪ] *n* petit bouquet

pot [pɒt] *n* (*for cooking*) marmite *f*; casserole *f*; (*teapot*) théière *f*; (*for coffee*) cafetière *f*; (*for plants, jam*) pot *m*; (*piece of pottery*) poterie *f*; (*inf: marijuana*) herbe *f* ▷ *vt* (*plant*) mettre en pot; **to go to ~** (*inf*) aller à vau-l'eau; **~s of** (*Brit inf*) beaucoup de, plein de

potash ['pɒtæʃ] *n* potasse *f*

potassium [pə'tæsɪəm] *n* potassium *m*

potato (*pl -es*) [pə'teɪtəu] *n* pomme *f* de terre

potato crisps, (*US*) **potato chips** *npl* chips *mpl*

potato flour *n* fécule *f*

potato peeler *n* épluche-légumes *m*

potbellied ['pɒtbɛlɪd] *adj* (*from overeating*) bedonnant(e); (*from malnutrition*) au ventre ballonné

potency ['pəutnsɪ] *n* puissance *f*, force *f*; (*of drink*) degré *m* d'alcool

potent ['pəutnt] *adj* puissant(e); (*drink*) fort(e), très alcoolisé(e); (*man*) viril

potentate ['pəutnteɪt] *n* potentat *m*

potential [pə'tɛnʃl] *adj* potentiel(le) ▷ *n* potentiel *m*; **to have ~** être prometteur(-euse); ouvrir des possibilités

potentially [pə'tɛnʃəlɪ] *adv* potentiellement; **it's ~ dangerous** ça pourrait se révéler dangereux, il y a possibilité de danger

pothole ['pɒthəul] *n* (*in road*) nid *m* de poule; (*Brit: underground*) gouffre *m*, caverne *f*

potholer ['pɒthəuləʳ] *n* (*Brit*) spéléologue *m/f*

potholing ['pɒthəulɪŋ] *n* (*Brit*): **to go ~** faire de la spéléologie

potion ['pəuʃən] *n* potion *f*

potluck [pɒt'lʌk] *n*: **to take ~** tenter sa chance

pot plant *n* plante *f* d'appartement

potpourri [pəu'puːriː] *n* pot-pourri *m*

pot roast *n* rôti *m* à la cocotte

pot shot ['pɒtʃɒt] *n*: **to take ~s at** canarder

potted ['pɒtɪd] *adj* (*food*) en conserve; (*plant*) en pot; (*fig: shortened*) abrégé(e)

potter ['pɒtəʳ] *n* potier *m* ▷ *vi* (*Brit*): **to ~ around** *or* **about** bricoler; **~'s wheel** tour *m* de potier

pottery ['pɒtərɪ] *n* poterie *f*; **a piece of ~** une poterie

potty ['pɒtɪ] *adj* (*Brit inf: mad*) dingue ▷ *n* (*child's*) pot *m*

potty-training ['pɒtɪtreɪnɪŋ] *n* apprentissage *m* de la propreté

pouch [pautʃ] *n* (*Zool*) poche *f*; (*for tobacco*) blague *f*; (*for money*) bourse *f*

pouf, pouffe [puːf] *n* (*stool*) pouf *m*

poultice ['pəultɪs] *n* cataplasme *m*

poultry ['pəultrɪ] *n* volaille *f*

poultry farm *n* élevage *m* de volaille

poultry farmer *n* aviculteur *m*

pounce [pauns] *vi*: **to ~ (on)** bondir (sur), fondre (sur) ▷ *n* bond *m*, attaque *f*

pound [paund] *n* livre *f* (*weight* = 453g, 16 ounces; *money* = 100 pence); (*for dogs, cars*) fourrière *f* ▷ *vt* (*beat*) bourrer de coups, marteler; (*crush*) piler, pulvériser; (*with guns*) pilonner ▷ *vi* (*heart*) battre violemment, taper; **half a ~ (of)** une demi-livre (de); **a five-~ note** un billet de cinq livres

pounding ['paundɪŋ] *n*: **to take a ~** (*fig*) prendre une râclée

pound sterling *n* livre *f* sterling

pour [pɔːʳ] *vt* verser ▷ *vi* couler à flots; (*rain*) pleuvoir à verse; **to ~ sb a drink** verser *or* servir à boire à qn; **to come ~ing in** (*water*) entrer à flots; (*letters*) arriver par milliers; (*cars, people*) affluer
  ▶ **pour away, pour off** *vt* vider
  ▶ **pour in** *vi* (*people*) affluer, se précipiter; (*news, letters*) arriver en masse
  ▶ **pour out** *vi* (*people*) sortir en masse ▷ *vt* vider; (*fig*) déverser; (*serve: a drink*) verser

pouring ['pɔːrɪŋ] *adj*: **~ rain** pluie torrentielle

pout [paut] *n* moue *f* ▷ *vi* faire la moue

poverty ['pɔvətɪ] *n* pauvreté *f*, misère *f*

poverty line *n* seuil *m* de pauvreté

poverty-stricken ['pɔvətɪstrɪkn] *adj* pauvre, déshérité(e)

poverty trap *n* (*Brit*) piège *m* de la pauvreté

POW *n abbr* = **prisoner of war**

powder ['paudəʳ] *n* poudre *f* ▷ *vt* poudrer; **to ~ one's nose** se poudrer; (*euphemism*) aller à la salle de bain

powder compact *n* poudrier *m*

powdered milk *n* lait *m* en poudre

powder keg *n* (*fig*) poudrière *f*

powder puff *n* houppette *f*

powder room *n* toilettes *fpl* (pour dames)

powdery ['paudərɪ] *adj* poudreux(-euse)

power ['pauəʳ] *n* (*strength, nation*) puissance *f*, force *f*; (*ability, Pol: of party, leader*) pouvoir *m*; (*Math*) puissance; (*of speech, thought*) faculté *f*; (*Elec*) courant *m* ▷ *vt* faire marcher, actionner; **to do all in one's ~ to help sb** faire tout ce qui est en son pouvoir pour aider qn; **the world ~s** les grandes puissances; **to be in ~** être au pouvoir

powerboat ['pauəbəut] *n* (*Brit*) hors-bord *m*

power cut *n* (*Brit*) coupure *f* de courant

powered ['pauəd] *adj*: **~ by** actionné(e) par, fonctionnant à; **nuclear-~ submarine** sous-marin *m* (à propulsion) nucléaire

power failure *n* panne *f* de courant

powerful ['pauəful] *adj* puissant(e); (*performance etc*) très fort(e)

powerhouse ['pauəhaus] *n* (*fig: person*) fonceur *m*; **a ~ of ideas** une mine d'idées

powerless ['pauəlɪs] *adj* impuissant(e)

power line *n* ligne *f* électrique

power of attorney *n* procuration *f*

power point *n* (*Brit*) prise *f* de courant

power station *n* centrale *f* électrique

power steering *n* direction assistée

power struggle *n* lutte *f* pour le pouvoir

powwow ['pauwau] *n* conciliabule *m*

p.p. *abbr* (= *per procurationem: by proxy*) p.p.

PPE *n abbr* (*Brit Scol*) = **philosophy, politics and economics**

PPS *n abbr* (= *post postscriptum*) PPS; (*Brit: = parliamentary private secretary*) parlementaire chargé de mission auprès d'un ministre

PQ *abbr* (*Canada: = Province of Quebec*) PQ

PR *n abbr* = **proportional representation**; **public relations** ▷ *abbr* (*US*) = **Puerto Rico**

Pr. *abbr* (= *prince*) Pce

practicability [præktɪkə'bɪlɪtɪ] *n* possibilité *f* de réalisation

practicable ['præktɪkəbl] *adj* (*scheme*) réalisable

practical ['præktɪkl] *adj* pratique

practicality [præktɪ'kælɪtɪ] *n* (*of plan*) aspect *m* pratique; (*of person*) sens *m* pratique; **practicalities** *npl* détails *mpl* pratiques

practical joke *n* farce *f*

practically ['præktɪklɪ] *adv* (*almost*) pratiquement

practice ['præktɪs] *n* pratique *f*; (*of profession*) exercice *m*; (*at football etc*) entraînement *m*; (*business*) cabinet *m*; clientèle *f* ▷ *vt, vi* (*US*) = **practise**; **in ~** (*in reality*) en pratique; **out of ~** rouillé(e); **2 hours' piano ~** 2 heures de travail *or* d'exercices au piano; **target ~** exercices de tir; **it's common ~** c'est courant, ça se fait couramment; **to put sth into ~** mettre qch en pratique

practice match *n* match *m* d'entraînement

practise, (US) **practice** ['præktɪs] *vt* (*work at: piano, backhand etc*) s'exercer à, travailler; (*train for: sport*) s'entraîner à; (*a sport, religion, method*) pratiquer; (*profession*) exercer ▷ *vi* s'exercer, travailler; (*train*) s'entraîner; (*lawyer, doctor*) exercer; **to ~ for a match** s'entraîner pour un match

practised, (US) **practiced** ['præktɪst] *adj* (*person*) expérimenté(e); (*performance*) impeccable; (*liar*) invétéré(e); **with a ~ eye** d'un œil exercé

practising, (US) **practicing** ['præktɪsɪŋ] *adj* (*Christian etc*) pratiquant(e); (*lawyer*) en exercice; (*homosexual*) déclaré

practitioner [præk'tɪʃənəʳ] *n* praticien(ne)

pragmatic [præg'mætɪk] *adj* pragmatique

Prague [prɑːg] *n* Prague

prairie ['prɛərɪ] *n* savane *f*; (*US*): **the ~s** la Prairie

praise [preɪz] *n* éloge(s) *m(pl)*, louange(s) *f(pl)* ▷ *vt* louer, faire l'éloge de

praiseworthy ['preɪzwə:ðɪ] *adj* digne de louanges

pram [præm] *n* (*Brit*) landau *m*, voiture *f* d'enfant

prance [prɑːns] *vi* (*horse*) caracoler

prank [præŋk] *n* farce *f*

prat [præt] *n* (*Brit inf*) imbécile *m*, andouille *f*

prattle ['prætl] *vi* jacasser

prawn [prɔːn] *n* crevette *f* (rose)

prawn cocktail *n* cocktail *m* de crevettes

pray [preɪ] *vi* prier

prayer [prɛəʳ] *n* prière *f*

prayer book n livre m de prières
pre... ['priː] prefix pré...; **pre-1970** adj d'avant 1970 ▷ adv avant 1970
preach [priːtʃ] vt, vi prêcher; **to ~ at sb** faire la morale à qn
preacher ['priːtʃə^r] n prédicateur m; (US: clergyman) pasteur m
preamble [prɪ'æmbl] n préambule m
prearranged [priːə'reɪndʒd] adj organisé(e) or fixé(e) à l'avance
precarious [prɪ'kɛərɪəs] adj précaire
precaution [prɪ'kɔːʃən] n précaution f
precautionary [prɪ'kɔːʃənrɪ] adj (measure) de précaution
precede [prɪ'siːd] vt, vi précéder
precedence ['prɛsɪdəns] n préséance f
precedent ['prɛsɪdənt] n précédent m; **to establish** or **set a ~** créer un précédent
preceding [prɪ'siːdɪŋ] adj qui précède (or précédait)
precept ['priːsɛpt] n précepte m
precinct ['priːsɪŋkt] n (round cathedral) pourtour m, enceinte f; (US: district) circonscription f, arrondissement m; **precincts** npl (neighbourhood) alentours mpl, environs mpl; **pedestrian ~** (Brit) zone piétonnière; **shopping ~** (Brit) centre commercial
precious ['prɛʃəs] adj précieux(-euse) ▷ adv (inf): **~ little** or **few** fort peu; **your ~ dog** (ironic) ton chien chéri, ton chéri chien
precipice ['prɛsɪpɪs] n précipice m
precipitate [prɪ'sɪpɪtɪt] adj (hasty) précipité(e) ▷ vt [prɪ'sɪpɪteɪt] précipiter
precipitation [prɪsɪpɪ'teɪʃən] n précipitation f
precipitous [prɪ'sɪpɪtəs] adj (steep) abrupt(e), à pic
précis (pl ~) ['preɪsiː, -z] n résumé m
precise [prɪ'saɪs] adj précis(e)
precisely [prɪ'saɪslɪ] adv précisément
precision [prɪ'sɪʒən] n précision f
preclude [prɪ'kluːd] vt exclure, empêcher; **to ~ sb from doing** empêcher qn de faire
precocious [prɪ'kəuʃəs] adj précoce
preconceived [priːkən'siːvd] adj (idea) préconçu(e)
preconception [priːkən'sɛpʃən] n idée préconçue
precondition ['priːkən'dɪʃən] n condition f nécessaire
precursor [priː'kəːsə^r] n précurseur m
predate ['priː'deɪt] vt (precede) antidater
predator ['prɛdətə^r] n prédateur m, rapace m
predatory ['prɛdətərɪ] adj rapace
predecessor ['priːdɪsɛsə^r] n prédécesseur m
predestination [priːdɛstɪ'neɪʃən] n prédestination f
predetermine [priːdɪ'təːmɪn] vt déterminer à l'avance
predicament [prɪ'dɪkəmənt] n situation f difficile
predicate ['prɛdɪkɪt] n (Ling) prédicat m
predict [prɪ'dɪkt] vt prédire

predictable [prɪ'dɪktəbl] adj prévisible
predictably [prɪ'dɪktəblɪ] adv (behave, react) de façon prévisible; **~ she didn't arrive** comme on pouvait s'y attendre, elle n'est pas venue
prediction [prɪ'dɪkʃən] n prédiction f
predispose [priːdɪs'pəuz] vt prédisposer
predominance [prɪ'dɔmɪnəns] n prédominance f
predominant [prɪ'dɔmɪnənt] adj prédominant(e)
predominantly [prɪ'dɔmɪnəntlɪ] adv en majeure partie; (especially) surtout
predominate [prɪ'dɔmɪneɪt] vi prédominer
pre-eminent [priː'ɛmɪnənt] adj prééminent(e)
pre-empt [priː'ɛmt] vt (Brit) acquérir par droit de préemption; (fig) anticiper sur; **to ~ the issue** conclure avant même d'ouvrir les débats
pre-emptive [prɪ'ɛmtɪv] adj: **~ strike** attaque (or action) préventive
preen [priːn] vt: **to ~ itself** (bird) se lisser les plumes; **to ~ o.s.** s'admirer
prefab ['priːfæb] n abbr (= prefabricated building) bâtiment préfabriqué
prefabricated [priː'fæbrɪkeɪtɪd] adj préfabriqué(e)
preface ['prɛfəs] n préface f
prefect ['priːfɛkt] n (Brit: in school) élève chargé de certaines fonctions de discipline; (in France) préfet m
prefer [prɪ'fəː^r] vt préférer; (Law): **to ~ charges** procéder à une inculpation; **to ~ coffee to tea** préférer le café au thé; **to ~ doing** or **to do sth** préférer faire qch
preferable ['prɛfrəbl] adj préférable
preferably ['prɛfrəblɪ] adv de préférence
preference ['prɛfrəns] n préférence f; **in ~ to sth** plutôt que qch, de préférence à qch
preference shares npl (Brit) actions privilégiées
preferential [prɛfə'rɛnʃəl] adj préférentiel(le); **~ treatment** traitement m de faveur
preferred stock [prɪ'fəːd-] npl (US) = **preference shares**
prefix ['priːfɪks] n préfixe m
pregnancy ['prɛgnənsɪ] n grossesse f
pregnancy test n test m de grossesse
pregnant ['prɛgnənt] adj enceinte adj f; (animal) pleine; **3 months ~** enceinte de 3 mois
prehistoric ['priːhɪs'tɔrɪk] adj préhistorique
prehistory [priː'hɪstərɪ] n préhistoire f
prejudge [priː'dʒʌdʒ] vt préjuger de
prejudice ['prɛdʒudɪs] n préjugé m; (harm) tort m, préjudice m ▷ vt porter préjudice à; (bias): **to ~ sb in favour of/against** prévenir qn en faveur de/contre; **racial ~** préjugés raciaux
prejudiced ['prɛdʒudɪst] adj (person) plein(e) de préjugés; (in a matter) partial(e); (view) préconçu(e), partial(e); **to be ~ against sb/sth** avoir un parti-pris contre qn/qch; **to be racially ~** avoir des préjugés raciaux
prelate ['prɛlət] n prélat m
preliminaries [prɪ'lɪmɪnərɪz] npl préliminaires mpl
preliminary [prɪ'lɪmɪnərɪ] adj préliminaire

prelude ['prɛljuːd] n prélude m
premarital ['priːˈmærɪtl] adj avant le mariage; ~ **contract** contrat m de mariage
premature ['prɛmətʃuəʳ] adj prématuré(e); **to be ~ (in doing sth)** aller un peu (trop) vite (en faisant qch)
premeditated [priːˈmɛdɪteɪtɪd] adj prémédité(e)
premeditation [priːmɛdɪˈteɪʃən] n préméditation f
premenstrual [priːˈmɛnstruəl] adj prémenstruel(le)
premenstrual tension n irritabilité f avant les règles
premier ['prɛmɪəʳ] adj premier(-ière), principal(e) ▷ n (Pol: Prime Minister) premier ministre; (Pol: President) chef m de l'État
premiere ['prɛmɪɛəʳ] n première f
Premier League n première division
premise ['prɛmɪs] n prémisse f
premises ['prɛmɪsɪz] npl locaux mpl; **on the ~** sur les lieux; sur place; **business ~** locaux commerciaux
premium ['priːmɪəm] n prime f; **to be at a ~** (fig: housing etc) être très demandé(e), être rarissime; **to sell at a ~** (shares) vendre au-dessus du pair
premium bond n (Brit) obligation f à prime, bon m à lots
premium deal n (Comm) offre spéciale
premium fuel, (US) **premium gasoline** n super m
premonition [prɛməˈnɪʃən] n prémonition f
preoccupation [priːɔkjuˈpeɪʃən] n préoccupation f
preoccupied [priːˈɔkjupaɪd] adj préoccupé(e)
prep [prɛp] adj abbr: ~ **school**; = **preparatory school** ▷ n abbr (Scol: = preparation) étude f
prepackaged [priːˈpækɪdʒd] adj préempaqueté(e)
prepaid [priːˈpeɪd] adj payé(e) d'avance
preparation [prɛpəˈreɪʃən] n préparation f; **preparations** npl (for trip, war) préparatifs mpl; **in ~ for** en vue de
preparatory [prɪˈpærətərɪ] adj préparatoire; ~ **to sth/to doing sth** en prévision de qch/avant de faire qch
preparatory school n (Brit) école primaire privée; (US) lycée privé; voir article

● **PREPARATORY SCHOOL**
●
● En Grande-Bretagne, une preparatory school –
● ou, plus familièrement, une prep school – est
● une école payante qui prépare les enfants de
● 7 à 13 ans aux "public schools".

prepare [prɪˈpɛəʳ] vt préparer ▷ vi: **to ~ for** se préparer à
prepared [prɪˈpɛəd] adj: ~ **for** préparé(e) à; ~ **to** prêt(e) à
preponderance [prɪˈpɔndərns] n prépondérance f
preposition [prɛpəˈzɪʃən] n préposition f

prepossessing [priːpəˈzɛsɪŋ] adj avenant(e), engageant(e)
preposterous [prɪˈpɔstərəs] adj ridicule, absurde
prep school n = **preparatory school**
prerecord ['priːrɪˈkɔːd] vt: ~**ed broadcast** émission f en différé; ~**ed cassette** cassette enregistrée
prerequisite [priːˈrɛkwɪzɪt] n condition f préalable
prerogative [prɪˈrɔgətɪv] n prérogative f
presbyterian [prɛzbɪˈtɪərɪən] adj, n presbytérien(ne)
presbytery ['prɛzbɪtərɪ] n presbytère m
preschool ['priːˈskuːl] adj préscolaire; (child) d'âge préscolaire
prescribe [prɪˈskraɪb] vt prescrire; ~**d books** (Brit Scol) œuvres fpl au programme
prescription [prɪˈskrɪpʃən] n prescription f; (Med) ordonnance f; (: medicine) médicament m (obtenu sur ordonnance); **to make up** or (US) **fill a ~** faire une ordonnance; **could you write me a ~?** pouvez-vous me faire une ordonnance?; **"only available on ~"** "uniquement sur ordonnance"
prescription charges npl (Brit) participation f fixe au coût de l'ordonnance
prescriptive [prɪˈskrɪptɪv] adj normatif(-ive)
presence ['prɛzns] n présence f; **in sb's ~** en présence de qn; ~ **of mind** présence d'esprit
present ['prɛznt] adj présent(e); (current) présent, actuel(le) ▷ n cadeau m; (actuality, also: **present tense**) présent m ▷ vt [prɪˈzɛnt] présenter; (prize, medal) remettre; (give): **to ~ sb with sth** offrir qch à qn; **to be ~ at** assister à; **those ~** les présents; **at ~** en ce moment; **to give sb a ~** offrir un cadeau à qn; **to ~ sb (to sb)** présenter qn (à qn)
presentable [prɪˈzɛntəbl] adj présentable
presentation [prɛznˈteɪʃən] n présentation f; (gift) cadeau m, présent m; (ceremony) remise f du cadeau (or de la médaille etc); **on ~ of** (voucher etc) sur présentation de
present-day ['prɛzntdeɪ] adj contemporain(e), actuel(le)
presenter [prɪˈzɛntəʳ] n (Brit Radio, TV) présentateur(-trice)
presently ['prɛzntlɪ] adv (soon) tout à l'heure, bientôt; (with verb in past) peu après; (at present) en ce moment; (US: now) maintenant
preservation [prɛzəˈveɪʃən] n préservation f, conservation f
preservative [prɪˈzəːvətɪv] n agent m de conservation
preserve [prɪˈzəːv] vt (keep safe) préserver, protéger; (maintain) conserver, garder; (food) mettre en conserve ▷ n (for game, fish) réserve f; (often pl: jam) confiture f; (: fruit) fruits mpl en conserve
preshrunk [priːˈʃrʌŋk] adj irrétrécissable
preside [prɪˈzaɪd] vi présider
presidency ['prɛzɪdənsɪ] n présidence f

president ['prɛzɪdənt] n président(e); (US: of
company) président-directeur général, PDG m
presidential [prɛzɪ'dɛnʃl] adj présidentiel(le)
press [prɛs] n (tool, machine, newspapers) presse f;
(for wine) pressoir m; (crowd) cohue f, foule f ▷ vt
(push) appuyer sur; (squeeze) presser, serrer;
(clothes: iron) repasser; (pursue) talonner; (insist):
to ~ sth on sb presser qn d'accepter qch; (urge,
entreat): **to ~ sb to do** or **into doing sth** pousser
qn à faire qch ▷ vi appuyer, peser; se presser;
we are ~ed for time le temps nous manque; **to
~ for sth** faire pression pour obtenir qch; **to ~
sb for an answer** presser qn de répondre; **to ~
charges against sb** (Law) engager des
poursuites contre qn; **to go to ~** (newspaper) aller
à l'impression; **to be in the ~** (being printed) être
sous presse; (in the newspapers) être dans le
journal
▶ **press ahead** vi = **press on**
▶ **press on** vi continuer
press agency n agence f de presse
press clipping n coupure f de presse
press conference n conférence f de presse
press cutting n = **press clipping**
press-gang ['prɛsgæŋ] vt (fig): **to ~ sb into
doing sth** faire pression sur qn pour qu'il fasse
qch
pressing ['prɛsɪŋ] adj urgent(e), pressant(e) ▷ n
repassage m
press officer n attaché(e) de presse
press release n communiqué m de presse
press stud n (Brit) bouton-pression m
press-up ['prɛsʌp] n (Brit) traction f
pressure ['prɛʃər] n pression f; (stress) tension f
▷ vt = **to put pressure on**; **to put ~ on sb (to do
sth)** faire pression sur qn (pour qu'il fasse qch)
pressure cooker n cocotte-minute f
pressure gauge n manomètre m
pressure group n groupe m de pression
pressurize ['prɛʃəraɪz] vt pressuriser; (Brit fig):
to ~ sb (into doing sth) faire pression sur qn
(pour qu'il fasse qch)
pressurized ['prɛʃəraɪzd] adj pressurisé(e)
prestige [prɛs'tiːʒ] n prestige m
prestigious [prɛs'tɪdʒəs] adj prestigieux(-euse)
presumably [prɪ'zjuːməblɪ] adv
vraisemblablement; **~ he did it** c'est sans
doute lui (qui a fait cela)
presume [prɪ'zjuːm] vt présumer, supposer; **to
~ to do** (dare) se permettre de faire
presumption [prɪ'zʌmpʃən] n supposition f,
présomption f; (boldness) audace f
presumptuous [prɪ'zʌmpʃəs] adj
présomptueux(-euse)
presuppose [priːsə'pəuz] vt présupposer
pre-tax [priː'tæks] adj avant impôt(s)
pretence, (US) **pretense** [prɪ'tɛns] n (claim)
prétention f; (pretext) prétexte m; **she is devoid
of all ~** elle n'est pas du tout prétentieuse; **to
make a ~ of doing** faire semblant de faire; **on**
or **under the ~ of doing sth** sous prétexte de
faire qch; **under false ~s** sous des prétextes

fallacieux
pretend [prɪ'tɛnd] vt (feign) feindre, simuler ▷ vi
(feign) faire semblant; (claim): **to ~ to sth**
prétendre à qch; **to ~ to do** faire semblant de
faire
pretense [prɪ'tɛns] n (US) = **pretence**
pretension [prɪ'tɛnʃən] n (claim) prétention f; **to
have no ~s to sth/to being sth** n'avoir aucune
prétention à qch/à être qch
pretentious [prɪ'tɛnʃəs] adj prétentieux(-euse)
preterite ['prɛtərɪt] n prétérit m
pretext ['priːtɛkst] n prétexte m; **on** or **under
the ~ of doing sth** sous prétexte de faire qch
pretty ['prɪtɪ] adj joli(e) ▷ adv assez
prevail [prɪ'veɪl] vi (win) l'emporter, prévaloir;
(be usual) avoir cours; (persuade): **to ~ (up)on sb
to do** persuader qn de faire
prevailing [prɪ'veɪlɪŋ] adj (widespread) courant(e),
répandu(e); (wind) dominant(e)
prevalent ['prɛvələnt] adj répandu(e),
courant(e); (fashion) en vogue
prevarication [prɪværɪ'keɪʃən] n (usage m de)
faux-fuyants mpl
prevent [prɪ'vɛnt] vt: **to ~ (from doing)**
empêcher (de faire)
preventable [prɪ'vɛntəbl] adj évitable
preventative [prɪ'vɛntətɪv] adj préventif(-ive)
prevention [prɪ'vɛnʃən] n prévention f
preventive [prɪ'vɛntɪv] adj préventif(-ive)
preview ['priːvjuː] n (of film) avant-première f;
(fig) aperçu m
previous ['priːvɪəs] adj (last) précédent(e);
(earlier) antérieur(e); (question, experience)
préalable; **I have a ~ engagement** je suis déjà
pris(e); **~ to doing** avant de faire
previously ['priːvɪəslɪ] adv précédemment,
auparavant
prewar [priː'wɔːr] adj d'avant-guerre
prey [preɪ] n proie f ▷ vi: **to ~ on** s'attaquer à; **it
was ~ing on his mind** ça le rongeait or minait
price [praɪs] n prix m; (Betting: odds) cote f ▷ vt
(goods) fixer le prix de; tarifer; **what is the ~ of
…?** combien coûte …?, quel est le prix de …?; **to
go up** or **rise in ~** augmenter; **to put a ~ on sth**
chiffrer qch; **to be ~d out of the market**
(article) être trop cher pour soutenir la
concurrence; (producer, nation) ne pas pouvoir
soutenir la concurrence; **what ~ his promises
now?** (Brit) que valent maintenant toutes ses
promesses?; **he regained his freedom, but at
a ~** il a retrouvé sa liberté, mais cela lui a coûté
cher
price control n contrôle m des prix
price-cutting ['praɪskʌtɪŋ] n réductions fpl de
prix
priceless ['praɪslɪs] adj sans prix, inestimable;
(inf: amusing) impayable
price list n tarif m
price range n gamme f de prix; **it's within my
~** c'est dans mes prix
price tag n étiquette f
price war n guerre f des prix

pricey ['praɪsɪ] *adj* (*inf*) chérot *inv*
prick [prɪk] *n* (*sting*) piqûre *f*; (*inf!*) bitte *f* (!);
 connard *m* (!) ▷ *vt* piquer; **to ~ up one's ears**
 dresser *or* tendre l'oreille
prickle ['prɪkl] *n* (*of plant*) épine *f*; (*sensation*)
 picotement *m*
prickly ['prɪklɪ] *adj* piquant(e), épineux(-euse);
 (*fig: person*) irritable
prickly heat *n* fièvre *f* miliaire
prickly pear *n* figue *f* de Barbarie
pride [praɪd] *n* (*feeling proud*) fierté *f*; (*pej*) orgueil
 m; (*self-esteem*) amour-propre *m* ▷ *vt*: **to ~ o.s.**
 on se flatter de; s'enorgueillir de; **to take (a) ~**
 in être (très) fier(-ère) de; **to take a ~ in doing**
 mettre sa fierté à faire; **to have ~ of place** (*Brit*)
 avoir la place d'honneur
priest [pri:st] *n* prêtre *m*
priestess ['pri:stɪs] *n* prêtresse *f*
priesthood ['pri:sthud] *n* prêtrise *f*, sacerdoce *m*
prig [prɪg] *n* poseur(-euse), fat *m*
prim [prɪm] *adj* collet monté *inv*, guindé(e)
prima facie ['praɪmə'feɪʃɪ] *adj*: **to have a ~ case**
 (*Law*) avoir une affaire recevable
primal ['praɪməl] *adj* (*first in time*) primitif(-ive);
 (*first in importance*) primordial(e)
primarily ['praɪmərɪlɪ] *adv* principalement,
 essentiellement
primary ['praɪmərɪ] *adj* primaire; (*first in*
 importance) premier(-ière), primordial(e) ▷ *n*
 (*US: election*) (élection *f*) primaire *f*; *voir article*

primary colour *n* couleur fondamentale
primary school *n* (*Brit*) école *f* primaire; *voir article*

 primate *n* (*Rel*) ['praɪmɪt] primat *m*; (*Zool*)

['praɪmeɪt] primate *m*
prime [praɪm] *adj* primordial(e),
 fondamental(e); (*excellent*) excellent(e) ▷ *vt*
 (*gun, pump*) amorcer; (*fig*) mettre au courant ▷ *n*:
 in the ~ of life dans la fleur de l'âge
Prime Minister *n* Premier ministre
primer ['praɪmə'] *n* (*book*) premier livre, manuel
 m élémentaire; (*paint*) apprêt *m*
prime time *n* (*Radio, TV*) heure(s) *f(pl)* de grande
 écoute
primeval [praɪ'mi:vl] *adj* primitif(-ive)
primitive ['prɪmɪtɪv] *adj* primitif(-ive)
primrose ['prɪmrəuz] *n* primevère *f*
primus® ['praɪməs], **primus® stove** *n* (*Brit*)
 réchaud *m* de camping
prince [prɪns] *n* prince *m*
princess [prɪn'sɛs] *n* princesse *f*
principal ['prɪnsɪpl] *adj* principal(e) ▷ *n* (*head*
 teacher) directeur *m*, principal *m*; (*in play*) rôle
 principal; (*money*) principal *m*
principality [prɪnsɪ'pælɪtɪ] *n* principauté *f*
principally ['prɪnsɪplɪ] *adv* principalement
principle ['prɪnsɪpl] *n* principe *m*; **in ~** en
 principe; **on ~** par principe
print [prɪnt] *n* (*mark*) empreinte *f*; (*letters*)
 caractères *mpl*; (*fabric*) imprimé *m*; (*Art*) gravure
 f, estampe *f*; (*Phot*) épreuve *f* ▷ *vt* imprimer;
 (*publish*) publier; (*write in capitals*) écrire en
 majuscules; **out of ~** épuisé(e)
 ▶ **print out** *vt* (*Comput*) imprimer
printed circuit board ['prɪntɪd-] *n* carte *f* à
 circuit imprimé
printed matter ['prɪntɪd-] *n* imprimés *mpl*
printer ['prɪntə'] *n* (*machine*) imprimante *f*;
 (*person*) imprimeur *m*
printhead ['prɪnthɛd] *n* tête *f* d'impression
printing ['prɪntɪŋ] *n* impression *f*
printing press *n* presse *f* typographique
printout ['prɪntaut] *n* (*Comput*) sortie *f*
 imprimante
print wheel *n* marguerite *f*
prior ['praɪə'] *adj* antérieur(e), précédent(e);
 (*more important*) prioritaire ▷ *n* (*Rel*) prieur *m*
 ▷ *adv*: **~ to doing** avant de faire; **without ~**
 notice sans préavis; **to have a ~ claim to sth**
 avoir priorité pour qch
priority [praɪ'ɔrɪtɪ] *n* priorité *f*; **to have** *or* **take ~**
 over sth/sb avoir la priorité sur qch/qn
priory ['praɪərɪ] *n* prieuré *m*
prise [praɪz] *vt*: **to ~ open** forcer
prism ['prɪzəm] *n* prisme *m*
prison ['prɪzn] *n* prison *f* ▷ *cpd* pénitentiaire
prison camp *n* camp *m* de prisonniers
prisoner ['prɪznə'] *n* prisonnier(-ière); **the ~ at**
 the bar l'accusé(e); **to take sb ~** faire qn
 prisonnier
prisoner of war *n* prisonnier(-ière) de guerre
prissy ['prɪsɪ] *adj* bégueule
pristine ['prɪsti:n] *adj* virginal(e)
privacy ['prɪvəsɪ] *n* intimité *f*, solitude *f*
private ['praɪvɪt] *adj* (*not public*) privé(e);
 (*personal*) personnel(le); (*house, car, lesson*)

particulier(-ière); (*quiet: place*) tranquille ▷ *n* soldat *m* de deuxième classe; **"~"** (*on envelope*) "personnelle"; (*on door*) "privé"; **in** ~ en privé; **in (his)** ~ **life** dans sa vie privée; **he is a very ~ person** il est très secret; **to be in ~ practice** être médecin (*or* dentiste *etc*) non conventionné; ~ **hearing** (*Law*) audience *f* à huis-clos

private detective *n* détective privé
private enterprise *n* entreprise privée
private eye *n* détective privé
private limited company *n* (*Brit*) société *f* à participation restreinte (*non cotée en Bourse*)
privately ['praɪvɪtlɪ] *adv* en privé; (*within oneself*) intérieurement
private parts *npl* parties (génitales)
private property *n* propriété privée
private school *n* école privée
privatize ['praɪvɪtaɪz] *vt* privatiser
privet ['prɪvɪt] *n* troène *m*
privilege ['prɪvɪlɪdʒ] *n* privilège *m*
privileged ['prɪvɪlɪdʒd] *adj* privilégié(e); **to be ~ to do sth** avoir le privilège de faire qch
privy ['prɪvɪ] *adj*: **to be ~ to** être au courant de
privy council *n* conseil privé; *voir article*

⬤ **PRIVY COUNCIL**
⬤
⬤ Le *privy council* existe en Angleterre depuis
⬤ l'avènement des Normands. À l'époque, ses
⬤ membres étaient les conseillers privés du
⬤ roi, mais en 1688 le cabinet les a supplantés.
⬤ Les ministres du cabinet sont aujourd'hui
⬤ automatiquement conseillers du roi, et ce
⬤ titre est également accordé aux personnes
⬤ qui ont occupé de hautes fonctions en
⬤ politique, dans le clergé ou dans les milieux
⬤ juridiques. Les pouvoirs de ces conseillers en
⬤ tant que tels sont maintenant limités.

prize [praɪz] *n* prix *m* ▷ *adj* (*example, idiot*) parfait(e); (*bull, novel*) primé(e) ▷ *vt* priser, faire grand cas de
prize-fighter ['praɪzfaɪtə^r] *n* boxeur professionnel
prize-giving ['praɪzgɪvɪŋ] *n* distribution *f* des prix
prize money *n* argent *m* du prix
prizewinner ['praɪzwɪnə^r] *n* gagnant(e)
prizewinning ['praɪzwɪnɪŋ] *adj* gagnant(e); (*novel, essay etc*) primé(e)
PRO *n abbr* = **public relations officer**
pro [prəu] *n* (*inf: Sport*) professionnel(le) ▷ *prep* pro; **pros** *npl*: **the ~s and cons** le pour et le contre
pro- [prəu] *prefix* (*in favour of*) pro-
pro-active [prəu'æktɪv] *adj* dynamique
probability [prɔbə'bɪlɪtɪ] *n* probabilité *f*; **in all ~** très probablement
probable ['prɔbəbl] *adj* probable; **it is ~/hardly ~ that ...** il est probable/peu probable que ...
probably ['prɔbəblɪ] *adv* probablement

probate ['prəubɪt] *n* (*Law*) validation *f*, homologation *f*
probation [prə'beɪʃən] *n* (*in employment*) (période *f* d')essai *m*; (*Law*) liberté surveillée; (*Rel*) noviciat *m*, probation *f*; **on** ~ (*employee*) à l'essai; (*Law*) en liberté surveillée
probationary [prə'beɪʃənrɪ] *adj* (*period*) d'essai
probe [prəub] *n* (*Med, Space*) sonde *f*; (*enquiry*) enquête *f*, investigation *f* ▷ *vt* sonder, explorer
probity ['prəubɪtɪ] *n* probité *f*
problem ['prɔbləm] *n* problème *m*; **to have ~s with the car** avoir des ennuis avec la voiture; **what's the ~?** qu'y a-t-il?, quel est le problème?; **I had no ~ in finding her** je n'ai pas eu de mal à la trouver; **no ~!** pas de problème!
problematic [prɔblə'mætɪk] *adj* problématique
problem-solving ['prɔbləmsɔlvɪŋ] *n* résolution *f* de problèmes; **an approach to ~** une approche en matière de résolution de problèmes
procedure [prə'si:dʒə^r] *n* (*Admin, Law*) procédure *f*; (*method*) marche *f* à suivre, façon *f* de procéder
proceed [prə'si:d] *vi* (*go forward*) avancer; (*act*) procéder; (*continue*): **to ~ (with)** continuer, poursuivre; **to ~ to** aller à; passer à; **to ~ to do** se mettre à faire; **I am not sure how to ~** je ne sais pas exactement comment m'y prendre; **to ~ against sb** (*Law*) intenter des poursuites contre qn
proceedings [prə'si:dɪŋz] *npl* (*measures*) mesures *fpl*; (*Law: against sb*) poursuites *fpl*; (*meeting*) réunion *f*, séance *f*; (*records*) compte rendu; actes *mpl*
proceeds ['prəusi:dz] *npl* produit *m*, recette *f*
process ['prəusɛs] *n* processus *m*; (*method*) procédé *m* ▷ *vt* traiter ▷ *vi* [prə'sɛs] (*Brit formal: go in procession*) défiler; **in** ~ en cours; **we are in the ~ of doing** nous sommes en train de faire
processed cheese ['prəusɛst-] *n* ≈ fromage fondu
processing ['prəusɛsɪŋ] *n* traitement *m*
procession [prə'sɛʃən] *n* défilé *m*, cortège *m*; **funeral ~** (*on foot*) cortège funèbre; (*in cars*) convoi *m* mortuaire
pro-choice [prəu'tʃɔɪs] *adj* en faveur de l'avortement
proclaim [prə'kleɪm] *vt* déclarer, proclamer
proclamation [prɔklə'meɪʃən] *n* proclamation *f*
proclivity [prə'klɪvɪtɪ] *n* inclination *f*
procrastinate [prəu'kræstɪneɪt] *vi* faire traîner les choses, vouloir tout remettre au lendemain
procrastination [prəukræstɪ'neɪʃən] *n* procrastination *f*
procreation [prəukrɪ'eɪʃən] *n* procréation *f*
Procurator Fiscal ['prɔkjureɪtə-] *n* (*Scottish*) ≈ procureur *m* (*de la République*)
procure [prə'kjuə^r] *vt* (*for o.s.*) se procurer; (*for sb*) procurer
procurement [prə'kjuəmənt] *n* achat *m*, approvisionnement *m*
prod [prɔd] *vt* pousser ▷ *n* (*push, jab*) petit coup, poussée *f*
prodigal ['prɔdɪgl] *adj* prodigue

prodigious [prə'dɪdʒəs] *adj* prodigieux(-euse)
prodigy ['prɔdɪdʒɪ] *n* prodige *m*
produce *n* ['prɔdjuːs] (*Agr*) produits *mpl* ▷ *vt*
[prə'djuːs] produire; (*show*) présenter; (*cause*)
provoquer, causer; (*Theat*) monter, mettre en
scène; (*TV: programme*) réaliser; (*: play, film*)
mettre en scène; (*Radio: programme*) réaliser;
(*: play*) mettre en ondes
producer [prə'djuːsəʳ] *n* (*Theat*) metteur *m* en
scène; (*Agr, Comm, Cine*) producteur *m*; (*TV: of
programme*) réalisateur *m*; (*: of play, film*) metteur
en scène; (*Radio: of programme*) réalisateur; (*: of
play*) metteur en ondes
product ['prɔdʌkt] *n* produit *m*
production [prə'dʌkʃən] *n* production *f*; (*Theat*)
mise *f* en scène; **to put into ~** (*goods*)
entreprendre la fabrication de
production agreement *n* (*US*) accord *m* de
productivité
production line *n* chaîne *f* (de fabrication)
production manager *n* directeur(-trice) de la
production
productive [prə'dʌktɪv] *adj* productif(-ive)
productivity [prɔdʌk'tɪvɪtɪ] *n* productivité *f*
productivity agreement *n* (*Brit*) accord *m* de
productivité
productivity bonus *n* prime *f* de rendement
Prof. [prɔf] *abbr* (= *professor*) Prof
profane [prə'feɪn] *adj* sacrilège; (*lay*) profane
profess [prə'fɛs] *vt* professer; **I do not ~ to be
an expert** je ne prétends pas être spécialiste
professed [prə'fɛst] *adj* (*self-declared*) déclaré(e)
profession [prə'fɛʃən] *n* profession *f*; **the ~s** les
professions libérales
professional [prə'fɛʃənl] *n* professionnel(le)
▷ *adj* professionnel(le); (*work*) de professionnel;
he's a ~ man il exerce une profession libérale;
to take ~ advice consulter un spécialiste
professionalism [prə'fɛʃnəlɪzəm] *n*
professionnalisme *m*
professionally [prə'fɛʃnəlɪ] *adv*
professionnellement; (*Sport: play*) en
professionnel; **I only know him ~** je n'ai avec
lui que des relations de travail
professor [prə'fɛsəʳ] *n* professeur *m* (*titulaire
d'une chaire*); (*US: teacher*) professeur *m*
professorship [prə'fɛsəʃɪp] *n* chaire *f*
proffer ['prɔfəʳ] *vt* (*hand*) tendre; (*remark*) faire;
(*apologies*) présenter
proficiency [prə'fɪʃənsɪ] *n* compétence *f*,
aptitude *f*
proficient [prə'fɪʃənt] *adj* compétent(e), capable
profile ['prəufaɪl] *n* profil *m*; **to keep a high/
low ~** (*fig*) rester *or* être très en évidence/
discret(-ète)
profit ['prɔfɪt] *n* (*from trading*) bénéfice *m*;
(*advantage*) profit *m* ▷ *vi*: **to ~ (by** *or* **from)**
profiter (de); **~ and loss account** compte *m* de
profits et pertes; **to make a ~** faire un *or* des
bénéfice(s); **to sell sth at a ~** vendre qch à
profit
profitability [prɔfɪtə'bɪlɪtɪ] *n* rentabilité *f*

profitable ['prɔfɪtəbl] *adj* lucratif(-ive),
rentable; (*fig: beneficial*) avantageux(-euse);
(*: meeting*) fructueux(-euse)
profit centre *n* centre *m* de profit
profiteering [prɔfɪ'tɪərɪŋ] *n* (*pej*)
mercantilisme *m*
profit-making ['prɔfɪtmeɪkɪŋ] *adj* à but lucratif
profit margin *n* marge *f* bénéficiaire
profit-sharing ['prɔfɪtʃɛərɪŋ] *n* intéressement *m*
aux bénéfices
profits tax *n* (*Brit*) impôt *m* sur les bénéfices
profligate ['prɔflɪgɪt] *adj* (*behaviour, act*)
dissolu(e); (*person*) débauché(e); (*extravagant*): **~
(with)** prodigue (de)
pro forma ['prəu'fɔːmə] *adj*: **~ invoice** facture *f*
pro-forma
profound [prə'faund] *adj* profond(e)
profuse [prə'fjuːs] *adj* abondant(e)
profusely [prə'fjuːslɪ] *adv* abondamment;
(*thank etc*) avec effusion
profusion [prə'fjuːʒən] *n* profusion *f*,
abondance *f*
progeny ['prɔdʒɪnɪ] *n* progéniture *f*;
descendants *mpl*
prognosis [prɔg'nəusɪs] (*pl* **prognoses**) *n*
pronostic *m*
programme, (*US*) **program** ['prəugræm] *n*
(*Comput: also Brit*) programme *m*; (*Radio, TV*)
émission *f* ▷ *vt* programmer
programmer ['prəugræməʳ] *n*
programmeur(-euse)
programming, (*US*) **programing**
['prəugræmɪŋ] *n* programmation *f*
programming language, (*US*) **programing
language** *n* langage *m* de programmation
progress *n* ['prəugrɛs] progrès *m(pl)* ▷ *vi*
[prə'grɛs] progresser, avancer; **in ~** en cours; **to
make ~** progresser, faire des progrès, être en
progrès; **as the match ~ed** au fur et à mesure
que la partie avançait
progression [prə'grɛʃən] *n* progression *f*
progressive [prə'grɛsɪv] *adj* progressif(-ive);
(*person*) progressiste
progressively [prə'grɛsɪvlɪ] *adv*
progressivement
progress report *n* (*Med*) bulletin *m* de santé;
(*Admin*) rapport *m* d'activité; rapport sur l'état
(d'avancement) des travaux
prohibit [prə'hɪbɪt] *vt* interdire, défendre; **to ~
sb from doing sth** défendre *or* interdire à qn de
faire qch; **"smoking ~ed"** "défense de fumer"
prohibition [prəuɪ'bɪʃən] *n* prohibition *f*
prohibitive [prə'hɪbɪtɪv] *adj* (*price etc*)
prohibitif(-ive)
project [*n* 'prɔdʒɛkt, *vb* prə'dʒɛkt] *n* (*plan*) projet
m, plan *m*; (*venture*) opération *f*, entreprise *f*;
(*Scol: research*) étude *f*, dossier *m* ▷ *vt* projeter ▷ *vi*
(*stick out*) faire saillie, s'avancer
projectile [prə'dʒɛktaɪl] *n* projectile *m*
projection [prə'dʒɛkʃən] *n* projection *f*;
(*overhang*) saillie *f*
projectionist [prə'dʒɛkʃənɪst] *n* (*Cine*)

projectionniste *m/f*

projection room *n* (*Cine*) cabine *f* de projection

projector [prə'dʒɛktər] *n* (*Cine etc*) projecteur *m*

proletarian [prəʊlɪ'tɛərɪən] *adj* prolétarien(ne) ▷ *n* prolétaire *m/f*

proletariat [prəʊlɪ'tɛərɪət] *n* prolétariat *m*

pro-life [prəʊ'laɪf] *adj* contre l'avortement

proliferate [prə'lɪfəreɪt] *vi* proliférer

proliferation [prəlɪfə'reɪʃən] *n* prolifération *f*

prolific [prə'lɪfɪk] *adj* prolifique

prologue ['prəʊlɔg] *n* prologue *m*

prolong [prə'lɔŋ] *vt* prolonger

prom [prɔm] *n abbr* = **promenade; promenade concert**; (*US: ball*) bal *m* d'étudiants; **the P~s** *série de concerts de musique classique*; *voir article*

● **PROM**
●
● En Grande-Bretagne, un *promenade concert* ou
● *prom* est un concert de musique classique,
● ainsi appelé car, à l'origine, le public restait
● debout et se promenait au lieu de rester
● assis. De nos jours, une partie du public
● reste debout, mais il y a également des
● places assises (plus chères). Les *Proms* les
● plus connus sont les Proms londoniens. La
● dernière séance (the "Last Night of the
● Proms") est un grand événement
● médiatique où se jouent des airs
● traditionnels et patriotiques.
● Aux États-Unis et au Canada, le *prom* ou
● *promenade* est un bal organisé par le lycée.

promenade [prɔmə'nɑːd] *n* (*by sea*) esplanade *f*, promenade *f*

promenade concert *n* concert *m* (de musique classique)

promenade deck *n* (*Naut*) pont *m* promenade

prominence ['prɔmɪnəns] *n* proéminence *f*; importance *f*

prominent ['prɔmɪnənt] *adj* (*standing out*) proéminent(e); (*important*) important(e); **he is ~ in the field of** ... il est très connu dans le domaine de ...

prominently ['prɔmɪnəntlɪ] *adv* (*display, set*) bien en évidence; **he figured ~ in the case** il a joué un rôle important dans l'affaire

promiscuity [prɔmɪs'kjuːɪtɪ] *n* (*sexual*) légèreté *f* de mœurs

promiscuous [prə'mɪskjuəs] *adj* (*sexually*) de mœurs légères

promise ['prɔmɪs] *n* promesse *f* ▷ *vt, vi* promettre; **to make sb a ~** faire une promesse à qn; **a young man of ~** un jeune homme plein d'avenir; **to ~ well** *vi* promettre

promising ['prɔmɪsɪŋ] *adj* prometteur(-euse)

promissory note ['prɔmɪsərɪ-] *n* billet *m* à ordre

promontory ['prɔməntrɪ] *n* promontoire *m*

promote [prə'məʊt] *vt* promouvoir; (*venture, event*) organiser, mettre sur pied; (*new product*) lancer; **the team was ~d to the second division** (*Brit Football*) l'équipe est montée en 2ᵉ division

promoter [prə'məʊtər] *n* (*of event*) organisateur(-trice)

promotion [prə'məʊʃən] *n* promotion *f*

prompt [prɔmpt] *adj* rapide ▷ *n* (*Comput*) message *m* (de guidage) ▷ *vt* inciter; (*cause*) entraîner, provoquer; (*Theat*) souffler (son rôle *or* ses répliques) à; **they're very ~** (*punctual*) ils sont ponctuels; **at 8 o'clock ~** à 8 heures précises; **he was ~ to accept** il a tout de suite accepté; **to ~ sb to do** inciter *or* pousser qn à faire

prompter ['prɔmptər] *n* (*Theat*) souffleur *m*

promptly ['prɔmptlɪ] *adv* (*quickly*) rapidement, sans délai; (*on time*) ponctuellement

promptness ['prɔmptnɪs] *n* rapidité *f*; promptitude *f*; ponctualité *f*

prone [prəʊn] *adj* (*lying*) couché(e) (face contre terre); (*liable*): **~ to** enclin(e) à; **to be ~ to illness** être facilement malade; **to be ~ to an illness** être sujet à une maladie; **she is ~ to burst into tears if** ... elle a tendance à tomber en larmes si ...

prong [prɔŋ] *n* pointe *f*; (*of fork*) dent *f*

pronoun ['prəʊnaʊn] *n* pronom *m*

pronounce [prə'naʊns] *vt* prononcer ▷ *vi*: **to ~ (up)on** se prononcer sur; **how do you ~ it?** comment est-ce que ça se prononce?; **they ~d him unfit to drive** ils l'ont déclaré inapte à la conduite

pronounced [prə'naʊnst] *adj* (*marked*) prononcé(e)

pronouncement [prə'naʊnsmənt] *n* déclaration *f*

pronunciation [prənʌnsɪ'eɪʃən] *n* prononciation *f*

proof [pruːf] *n* preuve *f*; (*test, of book, Phot*) épreuve *f*; (*of alcohol*) degré *m* ▷ *adj*: **~ against** à l'épreuve de ▷ *vt* (*Brit: tent, anorak*) imperméabiliser; **to be 70° ~** = titrer 40 degrés

proofreader ['pruːfriːdər] *n* correcteur(-trice) (d'épreuves)

prop [prɔp] *n* support *m*, étai *m*; (*fig*) soutien *m* ▷ *vt* (*also*: **prop up**) étayer, soutenir; **props** *npl* accessoires *mpl*; (*lean*): **to ~ sth against** appuyer qch contre *or* à

Prop. *abbr* (*Comm*) = **proprietor**

propaganda [prɔpə'gændə] *n* propagande *f*

propagation [prɔpə'geɪʃən] *n* propagation *f*

propel [prə'pɛl] *vt* propulser, faire avancer

propeller [prə'pɛlər] *n* hélice *f*

propelling pencil [prə'pɛlɪŋ-] *n* (*Brit*) porte-mine *m inv*

propensity [prə'pɛnsɪtɪ] *n* propension *f*

proper ['prɔpər] *adj* (*suited, right*) approprié(e), bon (bonne); (*seemly*) correct(e), convenable; (*authentic*) vrai(e), véritable; (*inf: real*) fini(e), vrai(e); (*referring to place*): **the village ~** le village proprement dit; **to go through the ~ channels** (*Admin*) passer par la voie officielle

properly ['prɔpəlɪ] *adv* correctement, convenablement; (*really*) bel et bien

proper noun *n* nom *m* propre
property ['prɔpətɪ] *n* (*possessions*) biens *mpl*; (*house etc*) propriété *f*; (*land*) terres *fpl*, domaine *m*; (*Chem etc: quality*) propriété *f*; **it's their** ~ cela leur appartient, c'est leur propriété
property developer *n* (*Brit*) promoteur immobilier
property owner *n* propriétaire *m*
property tax *n* impôt foncier
prophecy ['prɔfɪsɪ] *n* prophétie *f*
prophesy ['prɔfɪsaɪ] *vt* prédire ▷ *vi* prophétiser
prophet ['prɔfɪt] *n* prophète *m*
prophetic [prə'fɛtɪk] *adj* prophétique
proportion [prə'pɔːʃən] *n* proportion *f*; (*share*) part *f*; partie *f* ▷ *vt* proportionner; **proportions** *npl* (*size*) dimensions *fpl*; **to be in/out of ~ to** *or* **with sth** être à la mesure de/hors de proportion avec qch; **to see sth in ~** (*fig*) ramener qch à de justes proportions
proportional [prə'pɔːʃənl], **proportionate** [prə'pɔːʃənɪt] *adj* proportionnel(le)
proportional representation *n* (*Pol*) représentation proportionnelle
proposal [prə'pəuzl] *n* proposition *f*, offre *f*; (*plan*) projet *m*; (*of marriage*) demande *f* en mariage
propose [prə'pəuz] *vt* proposer, suggérer; (*have in mind*): **to ~ sth/to do** *or* **doing sth** envisager qch/de faire qch ▷ *vi* faire sa demande en mariage; **to ~ to do** avoir l'intention de faire
proposer [prə'pəuzər] *n* (*Brit: of motion etc*) auteur *m*
proposition [prɔpə'zɪʃən] *n* proposition *f*; **to make sb a ~** faire une proposition à qn
propound [prə'paund] *vt* proposer, soumettre
proprietary [prə'praɪətərɪ] *adj* de marque déposée; **~ article** article *m or* produit *m* de marque; **~ brand** marque déposée
proprietor [prə'praɪətər] *n* propriétaire *m/f*
propriety [prə'praɪətɪ] *n* (*seemliness*) bienséance *f*, convenance *f*
propulsion [prə'pʌlʃən] *n* propulsion *f*
pro rata [prəu'rɑːtə] *adv* au prorata
prosaic [prəu'zeɪɪk] *adj* prosaïque
Pros. Atty. *abbr* (*US*) = **prosecuting attorney**
proscribe [prə'skraɪb] *vt* proscrire
prose [prəuz] *n* prose *f*; (*Scol: translation*) thème *m*
prosecute ['prɔsɪkjuːt] *vt* poursuivre
prosecuting attorney ['prɔsɪkjuːtɪŋ-] *n* (*US*) procureur *m*
prosecution [prɔsɪ'kjuːʃən] *n* poursuites *fpl* judiciaires; (*accusing side: in criminal case*) accusation *f*; (: *in civil case*) la partie plaignante
prosecutor ['prɔsɪkjuːtər] *n* (*lawyer*) procureur *m*; (*also*: **public prosecutor**) ministère public; (*US: plaintiff*) plaignant(e)
prospect *n* ['prɔspɛkt] perspective *f*; (*hope*) espoir *m*, chances *fpl* ▷ *vt*, *vi* [prə'spɛkt] prospecter; **prospects** *npl* (*for work etc*) possibilités *fpl* d'avenir, débouchés *mpl*; **we are faced with the ~ of leaving** nous risquons de devoir partir; **there is every ~ of an early**

victory tout laisse prévoir une victoire rapide
prospecting [prə'spɛktɪŋ] *n* prospection *f*
prospective [prə'spɛktɪv] *adj* (*possible*) éventuel(le); (*future*) futur(e)
prospector [prə'spɛktər] *n* prospecteur *m*; **gold ~** chercheur *m* d'or
prospectus [prə'spɛktəs] *n* prospectus *m*
prosper ['prɔspər] *vi* prospérer
prosperity [prɔ'spɛrɪtɪ] *n* prospérité *f*
prosperous ['prɔspərəs] *adj* prospère
prostate ['prɔsteɪt] *n* (*also*: **prostate gland**) prostate *f*
prostitute ['prɔstɪtjuːt] *n* prostituée *f*; **male ~** prostitué *m*
prostitution [prɔstɪ'tjuːʃən] *n* prostitution *f*
prostrate *adj* ['prɔstreɪt] prosterné(e); (*fig*) prostré(e) ▷ *vt* [prɔ'streɪt]: **to ~ o.s. (before sb)** se prosterner (devant qn)
protagonist [prə'tægənɪst] *n* protagoniste *m*
protect [prə'tɛkt] *vt* protéger
protection [prə'tɛkʃən] *n* protection *f*; **to be under sb's ~** être sous la protection de qn
protectionism [prə'tɛkʃənɪzəm] *n* protectionnisme *m*
protection racket *n* racket *m*
protective [prə'tɛktɪv] *adj* protecteur(-trice); (*clothing*) de protection; **~ custody** (*Law*) détention préventive
protector [prə'tɛktər] *n* protecteur(-trice)
protégé ['prəutɛʒeɪ] *n* protégé *m*
protégée ['prəutɛʒeɪ] *n* protégée *f*
protein ['prəutiːn] *n* protéine *f*
pro tem [prəu'tɛm] *adv abbr* (= *pro tempore: for the time being*) provisoirement
protest [*n* 'prəutɛst, *vb* prə'tɛst] *n* protestation *f* ▷ *vi*: **to ~ against/about** protester contre/à propos de ▷ *vt* protester de; **to ~ (that)** protester que
Protestant ['prɔtɪstənt] *adj*, *n* protestant(e)
protester, protestor [prə'tɛstər] *n* (*in demonstration*) manifestant(e)
protest march *n* manifestation *f*
protocol ['prəutəkɔl] *n* protocole *m*
prototype ['prəutətaɪp] *n* prototype *m*
protracted [prə'træktɪd] *adj* prolongé(e)
protractor [prə'træktər] *n* (*Geom*) rapporteur *m*
protrude [prə'truːd] *vi* avancer, dépasser
protuberance [prə'tjuːbərəns] *n* protubérance *f*
proud [praud] *adj* fier(-ère); (*pej*) orgueilleux(-euse); **to be ~ to do sth** être fier de faire qch; **to do sb ~** (*inf*) faire honneur à qn; **to do o.s. ~** (*inf*) ne se priver de rien
proudly ['praudlɪ] *adv* fièrement
prove [pruːv] *vt* prouver, démontrer ▷ *vi*: **to ~ correct** *etc* s'avérer juste *etc*; **to ~ o.s.** montrer ce dont on est capable; **to ~ o.s./itself (to be) useful** *etc* se montrer *or* se révéler utile *etc*; **he was ~d right in the end** il s'est avéré qu'il avait raison
proverb ['prɔvəːb] *n* proverbe *m*
proverbial [prə'vəːbɪəl] *adj* proverbial(e)
provide [prə'vaɪd] *vt* fournir; **to ~ sb with sth**

fournir qch à qn; **to be ~d with** (person) disposer de; (thing) être équipé(e) or muni(e) de
▶ **provide for** vt fus (person) subvenir aux besoins de; (future event) prévoir
provided [prə'vaɪdɪd] conj: ~ **(that)** à condition que + sub
Providence ['prɒvɪdəns] n la Providence
providing [prə'vaɪdɪŋ] conj à condition que + sub
province ['prɒvɪns] n province f; (fig) domaine m
provincial [prə'vɪnʃəl] adj provincial(e)
provision [prə'vɪʒən] n (supply) provision f; (supplying) fourniture f; approvisionnement m; (stipulation) disposition f; **provisions** npl (food) provisions fpl; **to make ~ for** (one's future) assurer; (one's family) assurer l'avenir de; **there's no ~ for this in the contract** le contrat ne prévoit pas cela
provisional [prə'vɪʒənl] adj provisoire ▷ n: **P~** (Irish Pol) Provisional m (membre de la tendance activiste de l'IRA)
provisional licence n (Brit Aut) permis m provisoire
provisionally [prə'vɪʒnəlɪ] adv provisoirement
proviso [prə'vaɪzəu] n condition f; **with the ~ that** à la condition (expresse) que
Provo ['prɒvəu] n abbr (inf) = **Provisional**
provocation [prɒvə'keɪʃən] n provocation f
provocative [prə'vɒkətɪv] adj provocateur(-trice), provocant(e)
provoke [prə'vəuk] vt provoquer; **to ~ sb to sth/ to do** or **into doing sth** pousser qn à qch/à faire qch
provoking [prə'vəukɪŋ] adj énervant(e), exaspérant(e)
provost ['prɒvəst] n (Brit: of university) principal m; (Scottish) maire m
prow [prau] n proue f
prowess ['prauɪs] n prouesse f
prowl [praul] vi (also: **prowl about, prowl around**) rôder ▷ n: **to be on the ~** rôder
prowler ['praulər] n rôdeur(-euse)
proximity [prɒk'sɪmɪtɪ] n proximité f
proxy ['prɒksɪ] n procuration f; **by ~** par procuration
PRP n abbr (= performance related pay) salaire m au rendement
prude [pru:d] n prude f
prudence ['pru:dns] n prudence f
prudent ['pru:dnt] adj prudent(e)
prudish ['pru:dɪʃ] adj prude, pudibond(e)
prune [pru:n] n pruneau m ▷ vt élaguer
pry [praɪ] vi: **to ~ into** fourrer son nez dans
PS n abbr (= postscript) PS m
psalm [sɑ:m] n psaume m
PSAT n abbr (US) = **Preliminary Scholastic Aptitude Test**
PSBR n abbr (Brit: = public sector borrowing requirement) besoins mpl d'emprunts des pouvoirs publics
pseud [sju:d] n (Brit inf: intellectually) pseudo-intello m; (: socially) snob m/f
pseudo- ['sju:dəu] prefix pseudo-

pseudonym ['sju:dənɪm] n pseudonyme m
PSHE n abbr (Brit: Scol: = personal, social and health education) cours d'éducation personnelle, sanitaire et sociale préparant à la vie adulte
PST abbr (US: = Pacific Standard Time) heure d'hiver du Pacifique
PSV n abbr (Brit) = **public service vehicle**
psyche ['saɪkɪ] n psychisme m
psychiatric [saɪkɪ'ætrɪk] adj psychiatrique
psychiatrist [saɪ'kaɪətrɪst] n psychiatre m/f
psychiatry [saɪ'kaɪətrɪ] n psychiatrie f
psychic ['saɪkɪk] adj (also: **psychical**) (méta)psychique; (person) doué(e) de télépathie or d'un sixième sens
psycho ['saɪkəu] n (inf) psychopathe m/f
psychoanalysis (pl **-ses**) [saɪkəuə'nælɪsɪs, -si:z] n psychanalyse f
psychoanalyst [saɪkəu'ænəlɪst] n psychanalyste m/f
psychological [saɪkə'lɔdʒɪkl] adj psychologique
psychologist [saɪ'kɔlədʒɪst] n psychologue m/f
psychology [saɪ'kɔlədʒɪ] n psychologie f
psychopath ['saɪkəupæθ] n psychopathe m/f
psychosis (pl **psychoses**) [saɪ'kəusɪs, -si:z] n psychose f
psychosomatic [saɪkəusə'mætɪk] adj psychosomatique
psychotherapy [saɪkəu'θɛrəpɪ] n psychothérapie f
psychotic [saɪ'kɔtɪk] adj, n psychotique m/f
PT n abbr (Brit: = physical training) EPS f
Pt. abbr (in place names: = Point) Pte
pt abbr = **pint; pints; point; points**
PTA n abbr = **Parent-Teacher Association**
Pte. abbr (Brit Mil) = **private**
PTO abbr (= please turn over) TSVP
PTV abbr (US) = **pay television**
pub [pʌb] n abbr (= public house) pub m
pub crawl n (Brit inf): **to go on a ~** faire la tournée des bars
puberty ['pju:bətɪ] n puberté f
pubic ['pju:bɪk] adj pubien(ne), du pubis
public ['pʌblɪk] adj public(-ique) ▷ n public m; **in ~** en public; **the general ~** le grand public; **to be ~ knowledge** être de notoriété publique; **to go ~** (Comm) être coté(e) en Bourse; **to make ~ rendre public**
public address system n (système m de) sonorisation f, sono f (col)
publican ['pʌblɪkən] n patron m or gérant m de pub
publication [pʌblɪ'keɪʃən] n publication f
public company n société f anonyme
public convenience n (Brit) toilettes fpl
public holiday n (Brit) jour férié
public house n (Brit) pub m
publicity [pʌb'lɪsɪtɪ] n publicité f
publicize ['pʌblɪsaɪz] vt (make known) faire connaître, rendre public; (advertise) faire de la publicité pour
public limited company n ≈ société f anonyme (SA) (cotée en Bourse)

publicly ['pʌblɪklɪ] adv publiquement, en public
public opinion n opinion publique
public ownership n: **to be taken into** ~ être nationalisé(e), devenir propriété de l'État
public prosecutor n ≈ procureur m (de la République); **~'s office** parquet m
public relations n or npl relations publiques (RP)
public relations officer n responsable m/f des relations publiques
public school n (Brit) école privée; (US) école publique; voir article

● **PUBLIC SCHOOL**

● Une public school est un établissement
● d'enseignement secondaire privé. Bon
● nombre d'entre elles sont des pensionnats.
● Beaucoup ont également une école primaire
● qui leur est rattachée (une "prep" ou
● "preparatory school") pour préparer les
● élèves au cycle secondaire. Ces écoles sont
● en général prestigieuses, et les frais de
● scolarité sont très élevés dans les plus
● connues (Westminster, Eton, Harrow).
● Beaucoup d'élèves vont ensuite à
● l'université, et un grand nombre entre à
● Oxford ou à Cambridge. Les grands
● industriels, les députés et les hauts
● fonctionnaires sortent souvent de ces
● écoles. Aux États-Unis, le terme "public
● school" désigne tout simplement une école
● publique gratuite.

public sector n secteur public
public service vehicle n (Brit) véhicule affecté au transport de personnes
public-spirited [pʌblɪk'spɪrɪtɪd] adj qui fait preuve de civisme
public transport, (US) **public transportation** n transports mpl en commun
public utility n service public
public works npl travaux publics
publish ['pʌblɪʃ] vt publier
publisher ['pʌblɪʃə'] n éditeur m
publishing ['pʌblɪʃɪŋ] n (industry) édition f; (of a book) publication f
publishing company n maison f d'édition
pub lunch n repas m de bistrot
puce [pju:s] adj puce
puck [pʌk] n (elf) lutin m; (Ice Hockey) palet m
pucker ['pʌkə'] vt plisser
pudding ['pudɪŋ] n (Brit: dessert) dessert m, entremets m; (sweet dish) pudding m, gâteau m; (sausage) boudin m; **rice ~** ≈ riz m au lait; **black ~**, (US) **blood ~** boudin (noir)
puddle ['pʌdl] n flaque f d'eau
puerile ['pjuəraɪl] adj puéril(e)
Puerto Rico ['pwə:təu'ri:kəu] n Porto Rico f
puff [pʌf] n bouffée f ▷ vt: **to ~ one's pipe** tirer sur sa pipe; (also: **puff out**: sails, cheeks) gonfler ▷ vi sortir par bouffées; (pant) haleter; **to ~ out smoke** envoyer des bouffées de fumée

puffed [pʌft] adj (inf: out of breath) tout(e) essoufflé(e)
puffin ['pʌfɪn] n macareux m
puff pastry, (US) **puff paste** n pâte feuilletée
puffy ['pʌfɪ] adj bouffi(e), boursouflé(e)
pugnacious [pʌg'neɪʃəs] adj pugnace, batailleur(-euse)
pull [pul] n (tug): **to give sth a ~** tirer sur qch; (of moon, magnet, the sea etc) attraction f; (fig) influence f ▷ vt tirer; (trigger) presser; (strain: muscle, tendon) se claquer ▷ vi tirer; **to ~ a face** faire une grimace; **to ~ to pieces** mettre en morceaux; **to ~ one's punches** (also fig) ménager son adversaire; **to ~ one's weight** y mettre du sien; **to ~ o.s. together** se ressaisir; **to ~ sb's leg** faire marcher qn; **to ~ strings (for sb)** intervenir (en faveur de qn)
▶ **pull about** vt (Brit: handle roughly: object) maltraiter; (: person) malmener
▶ **pull apart** vt séparer; (break) mettre en pièces, démantibuler
▶ **pull away** vi (vehicle: move off) partir; (draw back) s'éloigner
▶ **pull back** vt (lever etc) tirer sur; (curtains) ouvrir ▷ vi (refrain) s'abstenir; (Mil: withdraw) se retirer
▶ **pull down** vt baisser, abaisser; (house) démolir; (tree) abattre
▶ **pull in** vi (Aut) se ranger; (Rail) entrer en gare
▶ **pull off** vt enlever, ôter; (deal etc) conclure
▶ **pull out** vi démarrer, partir; (withdraw) se retirer; (Aut: come out of line) déboîter ▷ vt (from bag, pocket) sortir; (remove) arracher; (withdraw) retirer
▶ **pull over** vi (Aut) se ranger
▶ **pull round** vi (unconscious person) revenir à soi; (sick person) se rétablir
▶ **pull through** vi s'en sortir
▶ **pull up** vi (stop) s'arrêter ▷ vt remonter; (uproot) déraciner, arracher; (stop) arrêter
pulley ['pulɪ] n poulie f
pull-out ['pulaut] n (of forces etc) retrait m ▷ cpd (magazine, pages) détachable
pullover ['puləuvə'] n pull-over m, tricot m
pulp [pʌlp] n (of fruit) pulpe f; (for paper) pâte f à papier; (pej: also: **pulp magazines** etc) presse f à sensation or de bas étage; **to reduce sth to (a) ~** réduire qch en purée
pulpit ['pulpɪt] n chaire f
pulsate [pʌl'seɪt] vi battre, palpiter; (music) vibrer
pulse [pʌls] n (of blood) pouls m; (of heart) battement m; (of music, engine) vibrations fpl; **pulses** npl (Culin) légumineuses fpl; **to feel** or **take sb's ~** prendre le pouls à qn
pulverize ['pʌlvəraɪz] vt pulvériser
puma ['pju:mə] n puma m
pumice ['pʌmɪs] n (also: **pumice stone**) pierre f ponce
pummel ['pʌml] vt rouer de coups
pump [pʌmp] n pompe f; (shoe) escarpin m ▷ vt pomper; (fig: inf) faire parler; **to ~ sb for information** essayer de soutirer des

renseignements à qn
▶ **pump up** vt gonfler
pumpkin ['pʌmpkɪn] n potiron m, citrouille f
pun [pʌn] n jeu m de mots, calembour m
punch [pʌntʃ] n (blow) coup m de poing; (fig: force) vivacité f, mordant m; (tool) poinçon m; (drink) punch m ▷ vt (make a hole in) poinçonner, perforer; (hit): **to ~ sb/sth** donner un coup de poing à qn/sur qch; **to ~ a hole (in)** faire un trou (dans)
▶ **punch in** vi (US) pointer (en arrivant)
▶ **punch out** vi (US) pointer (en partant)
punch card, punched card [pʌntʃt-] n carte perforée
punch-drunk ['pʌntʃdrʌŋk] adj (Brit) sonné(e)
punch line n (of joke) conclusion f
punch-up ['pʌntʃʌp] n (Brit inf) bagarre f
punctual ['pʌŋktjuəl] adj ponctuel(le)
punctuality [pʌŋktju'ælɪtɪ] n ponctualité f
punctually ['pʌŋktjuəlɪ] adv ponctuellement; **it will start ~ at 6** cela commencera à 6 heures précises
punctuate ['pʌŋktjueɪt] vt ponctuer
punctuation [pʌŋktju'eɪʃən] n ponctuation f
punctuation mark n signe m de ponctuation
puncture ['pʌŋktʃər] n (Brit) crevaison f ▷ vt crever; **I have a ~** (Aut) j'ai (un pneu) crevé
pundit ['pʌndɪt] n individu m qui pontifie, pontife m
pungent ['pʌndʒənt] adj piquant(e); (fig) mordant(e), caustique
punish ['pʌnɪʃ] vt punir; **to ~ sb for sth/for doing sth** punir qn de qch/d'avoir fait qch
punishable ['pʌnɪʃəbl] adj punissable
punishing ['pʌnɪʃɪŋ] adj (fig: exhausting) épuisant(e) ▷ n punition f
punishment ['pʌnɪʃmənt] n punition f, châtiment m; (fig: inf): **to take a lot of ~** (boxer) encaisser; (car, person etc) être mis(e) à dure épreuve
punk [pʌŋk] n (person: also: **punk rocker**) punk m/f; (music: also: **punk rock**) le punk; (US inf: hoodlum) voyou m
punt [pʌnt] n (boat) bachot m; (Irish) livre irlandaise f ▷ vi (Brit: bet) parier
punter ['pʌntər] n (Brit: gambler) parieur(-euse); (: inf) Monsieur m tout le monde; type m
puny ['pju:nɪ] adj chétif(-ive)
pup [pʌp] n chiot m
pupil ['pju:pl] n élève m/f; (of eye) pupille f
puppet ['pʌpɪt] n marionnette f, pantin m
puppet government n gouvernement m fantoche
puppy ['pʌpɪ] n chiot m, petit chien
purchase ['pə:tʃɪs] n achat m; (grip) prise f ▷ vt acheter; **to get a ~ on** trouver appui sur
purchase order n ordre m d'achat
purchase price n prix m d'achat
purchaser ['pə:tʃɪsər] n acheteur(-euse)
purchase tax n (Brit) taxe f à l'achat
purchasing power ['pə:tʃɪsɪŋ-] n pouvoir m d'achat

pure [pjuər] adj pur(e); **a ~ wool jumper** un pull en pure laine; **~ and simple** pur(e) et simple
purebred ['pjuəbred] adj de race
purée ['pjuəreɪ] n purée f
purely ['pjuəlɪ] adv purement
purge [pə:dʒ] n (Med) purge f; (Pol) épuration f, purge ▷ vt purger; (fig) épurer, purger
purification [pjuərɪfɪ'keɪʃən] n purification f
purify ['pjuərɪfaɪ] vt purifier, épurer
purist ['pjuərɪst] n puriste m/f
puritan ['pjuərɪtən] n puritain(e)
puritanical [pjuərɪ'tænɪkl] adj puritain(e)
purity ['pjuərɪtɪ] n pureté f
purl [pə:l] n maille f à l'envers ▷ vt tricoter à l'envers
purloin [pə:'lɔɪn] vt dérober
purple ['pə:pl] adj violet(te); (face) cramoisi(e)
purport [pə:'pɔ:t] vi: **to ~ to be/do** prétendre être/faire
purpose ['pə:pəs] n intention f, but m; **on ~** exprès; **for illustrative ~s** à titre d'illustration; **for teaching ~s** dans un but pédagogique; **for the ~s of this meeting** pour cette réunion; **to no ~** en pure perte
purpose-built ['pə:pəs'bɪlt] adj (Brit) fait(e) sur mesure
purposeful ['pə:pəsful] adj déterminé(e), résolu(e)
purposely ['pə:pəslɪ] adv exprès
purr [pə:r] n ronronnement m ▷ vi ronronner
purse [pə:s] n (Brit: for money) porte-monnaie m inv, bourse f; (US: handbag) sac m (à main) ▷ vt serrer, pincer
purser ['pə:sər] n (Naut) commissaire m du bord
purse snatcher [-'snætʃər] n (US) voleur m à l'arraché
pursue [pə'sju:] vt poursuivre; (pleasures) rechercher; (inquiry, matter) approfondir
pursuer [pə'sju:ər] n poursuivant(e)
pursuit [pə'sju:t] n poursuite f; (occupation) occupation f, activité f; **scientific ~s** recherches fpl scientifiques; **in (the) ~ of sth** à la recherche de qch
purveyor [pə'veɪər] n fournisseur m
pus [pʌs] n pus m
push [puʃ] n poussée f; (effort) gros effort; (drive) énergie f ▷ vt pousser; (button) appuyer sur; (thrust): **to ~ sth (into)** enfoncer qch (dans); (fig: product) mettre en avant, faire de la publicité pour ▷ vi pousser; appuyer; **to ~ a door open/shut** pousser une porte pour l'ouvrir/pour la fermer; **"~"** (on door) "pousser"; (on bell) "appuyer"; **to ~ for** (better pay, conditions) réclamer; **to be ~ed for time/money** être à court de temps/d'argent; **she is ~ing fifty** (inf) elle frise la cinquantaine; **at a ~** (Brit inf) à la limite, à la rigueur
▶ **push aside** vt écarter
▶ **push in** vi s'introduire de force
▶ **push off** vi (inf) filer, ficher le camp
▶ **push on** vi (continue) continuer
▶ **push over** vt renverser

▶ **push through** vt (measure) faire voter ▷ vi (in crowd) se frayer un chemin

▶ **push up** vt (total, prices) faire monter

push-bike ['puʃbaɪk] n (Brit) vélo m

push-button ['puʃbʌtn] n bouton(-poussoir m) m

pushchair ['puʃtʃɛəʳ] n (Brit) poussette f

pusher ['puʃəʳ] n (also: **drug pusher**) revendeur(-euse) (de drogue), ravitailleur(-euse) (en drogue)

pushover ['puʃəuvəʳ] n (inf): **it's a ~** c'est un jeu d'enfant

push-up ['puʃʌp] n (US) traction f

pushy ['puʃɪ] adj (pej) arriviste

pussy ['pusɪ], **pussy-cat** n (inf) minet m

put (pt, pp ~) [put] vt mettre; (place) poser, placer; (say) dire, exprimer; (a question) poser; (case, view) exposer, présenter; (estimate) estimer; **to ~ sb in a good/bad mood** mettre qn de bonne/mauvaise humeur; **to ~ sb to bed** mettre qn au lit, coucher qn; **to ~ sb to a lot of trouble** déranger qn; **how shall I ~ it?** comment dirais-je?, comment dire?; **to ~ a lot of time into sth** passer beaucoup de temps à qch; **to ~ money on a horse** miser sur un cheval; **I ~ it to you that ...** (Brit) je (vous) suggère que ..., je suis d'avis que ...; **to stay ~** ne pas bouger

▶ **put about** vi (Naut) virer de bord ▷ vt (rumour) faire courir

▶ **put across** vt (ideas etc) communiquer; faire comprendre

▶ **put aside** vt mettre de côté

▶ **put away** vt (store) ranger

▶ **put back** vt (replace) remettre, replacer; (postpone) remettre; (delay, watch, clock) retarder; **this will ~ us back ten years** cela nous ramènera dix ans en arrière

▶ **put by** vt (money) mettre de côté, économiser

▶ **put down** vt (parcel etc) poser, déposer; (pay) verser; (in writing) mettre par écrit, inscrire; (suppress: revolt etc) réprimer, écraser; (attribute) attribuer; (animal) abattre; (cat, dog) faire piquer

▶ **put forward** vt (ideas) avancer, proposer; (date, watch, clock) avancer

▶ **put in** vt (gas, electricity) installer; (complaint) soumettre; (time, effort) consacrer

▶ **put in for** vt fus (job) poser sa candidature pour; (promotion) solliciter

▶ **put off** vt (light etc) éteindre; (postpone) remettre à plus tard, ajourner; (discourage) dissuader

▶ **put on** vt (clothes, lipstick, CD) mettre; (light etc) allumer; (play etc) monter; (extra bus, train etc) mettre en service; (food, meal: provide) servir; (: cook) mettre à cuire or à chauffer; (weight) prendre; (assume: accent, manner) prendre; (: airs)

se donner, prendre; (inf: tease) faire marcher; (inform, indicate): **to ~ sb on to sb/sth** indiquer qn/qch à qn; **to ~ the brakes on** freiner

▶ **put out** vt (take outside) mettre dehors; (one's hand) tendre; (news, rumour) faire courir, répandre; (light etc) éteindre; (person: inconvenience) déranger, gêner; (Brit: dislocate) se démettre ▷ vi (Naut): **to ~ out to sea** prendre le large; **to ~ out from Plymouth** quitter Plymouth

▶ **put through** vt (Tel: caller) mettre en communication; (: call) passer; (plan) faire accepter; **~ me through to Miss Blair** passez-moi Miss Blair

▶ **put together** vt mettre ensemble; (assemble: furniture) monter, assembler; (meal) préparer

▶ **put up** vt (raise) lever, relever, remonter; (pin up) afficher; (hang) accrocher; (build) construire, ériger; (tent) monter; (umbrella) ouvrir; (increase) augmenter; (accommodate) loger; (incite): **to ~ sb up to doing sth** pousser qn à faire qch; **to ~ sth up for sale** mettre qch en vente

▶ **put upon** vt fus: **to be ~ upon** (imposed on) se laisser faire

▶ **put up with** vt fus supporter

putrid ['pjuːtrɪd] adj putride

putt [pʌt] vt, vi putter ▷ n putt m

putter ['pʌtəʳ] n (Golf) putter m

putting green ['pʌtɪŋ-] n green m

putty ['pʌtɪ] n mastic m

put-up ['putʌp] adj: **~ job** coup monté

puzzle ['pʌzl] n énigme f, mystère m; (game) jeu m, casse-tête m; (jigsaw) puzzle m; (also: **crossword puzzle**) mots croisés ▷ vt intriguer, rendre perplexe ▷ vi se creuser la tête; **to ~ over** chercher à comprendre

puzzled ['pʌzld] adj perplexe; **to be ~ about sth** être perplexe au sujet de qch

puzzling ['pʌzlɪŋ] adj déconcertant(e), inexplicable

PVC n abbr (= polyvinyl chloride) PVC m

Pvt. abbr (US Mil) = **private**

POW abbr = **prisoner of war**

pw abbr (= per week) p. sem.

PX n abbr (US Mil) = **post exchange**

pygmy ['pɪgmɪ] n pygmée m/f

pyjamas [pɪ'dʒɑːməz] npl (Brit) pyjama m; **a pair of ~** un pyjama

pylon ['paɪlən] n pylône m

pyramid ['pɪrəmɪd] n pyramide f

Pyrenean [pɪrə'niːən] adj pyrénéen(ne), des Pyrénées

Pyrenees [pɪrə'niːz] npl Pyrénées fpl

Pyrex® ['paɪrɛks] n Pyrex® m ▷ cpd: **Pyrex dish** plat m en Pyrex

python ['paɪθən] n python m

Qq

Q, q [kjuː] n (letter) Q, q m; **Q for Queen** Q
comme Quintal
Qatar [kæˈtɑːʳ] n Qatar m, Katar m
QC n abbr = **Queen's Counsel**; voir article

● **QC**
●
● En Angleterre, un QC ou Queen's Counsel (ou
● "KC" pour "King's Counsel", sous le règne
● d'un roi) est un avocat qui reçoit un poste de
● haut fonctionnaire sur recommandation du
● "Lord Chancellor". Il fait alors souvent
● suivre son nom des lettres QC, et lorsqu'il va
● au tribunal, il est toujours accompagné par
● un autre avocat (un "junior barrister").

QED abbr (= quod erat demonstrandum) CQFD
q.t. n abbr (inf) = **quiet**; **on the q.t.** discrètement
qty abbr (= quantity) qté
quack [kwæk] n (of duck) coin-coin m inv; (pej:
doctor) charlatan m ▷ vi faire coin-coin
quad [kwɔd] n abbr = **quadruplet; quadrangle**
quadrangle [ˈkwɔdræŋgl] n (Math) quadrilatère
m; (courtyard: abbr: quad) cour f
quadruped [ˈkwɔdrupɛd] n quadrupède m
quadruple [kwɔˈdruːpl] adj, n quadruple m ▷ vt,
vi quadrupler
quadruplet [kwɔˈdruːplɪt] n quadruplé(e)
quagmire [ˈkwægmaɪəʳ] n bourbier m
quail [kweɪl] n (Zool) caille f ▷ vi: **to ~ at** or
before reculer devant
quaint [kweɪnt] adj bizarre; (old-fashioned)
désuet(-ète); (picturesque) au charme vieillot,
pittoresque
quake [kweɪk] vi trembler ▷ n abbr = **earthquake**
Quaker [ˈkweɪkəʳ] n quaker(esse)
qualification [kwɔlɪfɪˈkeɪʃən] n (often pl: degree
etc) diplôme m; (training) qualification(s) f(pl);
(ability) compétence(s) f(pl); (limitation) réserve f,
restriction f; **what are your ~s?** qu'avez-vous
comme diplômes?; quelles sont vos
qualifications?
qualified [ˈkwɔlɪfaɪd] adj (trained) qualifié(e);
(professionally) diplômé(e); (fit, competent)
compétent(e), qualifié(e); (limited)
conditionnel(le); **it was a ~ success** ce fut un

succès mitigé; **~ for/to do** qui a les diplômes
requis pour/pour faire; qualifié pour/pour faire
qualify [ˈkwɔlɪfaɪ] vt qualifier; (modify) atténuer,
nuancer; (limit: statement) apporter des réserves
à ▷ vi: **to ~ (as)** obtenir son diplôme (de); **to ~
(for)** remplir les conditions requises (pour);
(Sport) se qualifier (pour)
qualifying [ˈkwɔlɪfaɪɪŋ] adj: **~ exam** examen m
d'entrée; **~ round** éliminatoires fpl
qualitative [ˈkwɔlɪtətɪv] adj qualitatif(-ive)
quality [ˈkwɔlɪtɪ] n qualité f ▷ cpd de qualité; **of
good/poor ~** de bonne/mauvaise qualité
quality control n contrôle m de qualité

● **QUALITY PRESS**
●
● La quality press ou les "quality (news)papers"
● englobent les journaux sérieux, quotidiens
● ou hebdomadaires, par opposition aux
● journaux populaires ("tabloid press"). Ces
● journaux visent un public qui souhaite des
● informations détaillées sur un éventail très
● vaste de sujets et qui est prêt à consacrer
● beaucoup de temps à leur lecture. Les
● "quality newspapers" sont en général de
● grand format.

quality time n moments privilégiés
qualm [kwɑːm] n doute m; scrupule m; **to have
~s about sth** avoir des doutes sur qch; éprouver
des scrupules à propos de qch
quandary [ˈkwɔndrɪ] n: **in a ~** devant un
dilemme, dans l'embarras
quango [ˈkwæŋgəu] n abbr (Brit: = quasi-
autonomous non-governmental organization)
commission nommée par le gouvernement
quantify [ˈkwɔntɪfaɪ] vt quantifier
quantitative [ˈkwɔntɪtətɪv] adj
quantitatif(-ive)
quantity [ˈkwɔntɪtɪ] n quantité f; **in ~** en
grande quantité
quantity surveyor n (Brit) métreur vérificateur
quantum leap [ˈkwɔntəm-] n (fig) bond m en
avant
quarantine [ˈkwɔrntiːn] n quarantaine f
quark [kwɑːk] n quark m

quarrel ['kwɔrl] *n* querelle *f*, dispute *f* ▷ *vi* se disputer, se quereller; **to have a ~ with sb** se quereller avec qn; **I've no ~ with him** je n'ai rien contre lui; **I can't ~ with that** je ne vois rien à redire à cela

quarrelsome ['kwɔrəlsəm] *adj* querelleur(-euse)

quarry ['kwɔrı] *n* (*for stone*) carrière *f*; (*animal*) proie *f*, gibier *m* ▷ *vt* (*marble etc*) extraire

quart [kwɔːt] *n* ≈ litre *m*

quarter ['kwɔːtər] *n* quart *m*; (*of year*) trimestre *m*; (*district*) quartier *m*; (*US, Canada: 25 cents*) (pièce *f* de) vingt-cinq cents *mpl* ▷ *vt* partager en quartiers *or* en quatre; (*Mil*) caserner, cantonner; **quarters** *npl* logement *m*; (*Mil*) quartiers *mpl*, cantonnement *m*; **a ~ of an hour** un quart d'heure; **it's a ~ to 3**, (*US*) **it's a ~ of 3** il est 3 heures moins le quart; **it's a ~ past 3**, (*US*) **it's a ~ after 3** il est 3 heures et quart; **from all ~s** de tous côtés

quarterback ['kwɔːtəbæk] *n* (*US Football*) quarterback *m/f*

quarter-deck ['kwɔːtədɛk] *n* (*Naut*) plage *f* arrière

quarter final *n* quart *m* de finale

quarterly ['kwɔːtəlı] *adj* trimestriel(le) ▷ *adv* tous les trois mois ▷ *n* (*Press*) revue trimestrielle

quartermaster ['kwɔːtəmɑːstər] *n* (*Mil*) intendant *m* militaire de troisième classe; (*Naut*) maître *m* de manœuvre

quartet, quartette [kwɔːˈtɛt] *n* quatuor *m*; (*jazz players*) quartette *m*

quarto ['kwɔːtəu] *adj*, *n* in-quarto *m inv*

quartz [kwɔːts] *n* quartz *m* ▷ *cpd* de *or* en quartz; (*watch, clock*) à quartz

quash [kwɔʃ] *vt* (*verdict*) annuler, casser

quasi- ['kweɪzaɪ] *prefix* quasi- + *noun*; quasi, presque + *adjective*

quaver ['kweɪvər] *n* (*Brit Mus*) croche *f* ▷ *vi* trembler

quay [kiː] *n* (*also*: **quayside**) quai *m*

Que. *abbr* (*Canada*) = **Quebec**

queasy ['kwiːzı] *adj* (*stomach*) délicat(e); **to feel ~** avoir mal au cœur

Quebec [kwɪˈbɛk] *n* (*city*) Québec; (*province*) Québec *m*

queen [kwiːn] *n* (*gen*) reine *f*; (*Cards etc*) dame *f*

queen mother *n* reine mère *f*

Queen's speech *n* (*Brit*) discours *m* de la reine; *voir article*

◉ QUEEN'S SPEECH

◉ Le *Queen's speech* (ou "King's speech") est le
◉ discours lu par le souverain à l'ouverture du
◉ "Parliament", dans la "House of Lords", en
◉ présence des lords et des députés. Il contient
◉ le programme de politique générale que
◉ propose le gouvernement pour la session, et
◉ il est préparé par le Premier ministre en
◉ consultation avec le cabinet.

queer [kwɪər] *adj* étrange, curieux(-euse);

(*suspicious*) louche; (*Brit: sick*): **I feel ~** je ne me sens pas bien ▷ *n* (*inf: highly offensive*) homosexuel *m*

quell [kwɛl] *vt* réprimer, étouffer

quench [kwɛntʃ] *vt* (*flames*) éteindre; **to ~ one's thirst** se désaltérer

querulous ['kwɛruləs] *adj* (*person*) récriminateur(-trice); (*voice*) plaintif(-ive)

query ['kwɪərı] *n* question *f*; (*doubt*) doute *m*; (*question mark*) point *m* d'interrogation ▷ *vt* (*disagree with, dispute*) mettre en doute, questionner

quest [kwɛst] *n* recherche *f*, quête *f*

question ['kwɛstʃən] *n* question *f* ▷ *vt* (*person*) interroger; (*plan, idea*) mettre en question *or* en doute; **to ask sb a ~**, **to put a ~ to sb** poser une question à qn; **to bring** *or* **call sth into ~** remettre qch en question; **the ~ is ...** la question est de savoir ...; **it's a ~ of doing** il s'agit de faire; **there's some ~ of doing** il est question de faire; **beyond ~** sans aucun doute; **out of the ~** hors de question

questionable ['kwɛstʃənəbl] *adj* discutable

questioner ['kwɛstʃənər] *n* personne *f* qui pose une question (*or* qui a posé la question *etc*)

questioning ['kwɛstʃənıŋ] *adj* interrogateur(-trice) ▷ *n* interrogatoire *m*

question mark *n* point *m* d'interrogation

questionnaire [kwɛstʃəˈnɛər] *n* questionnaire *m*

queue [kjuː] (*Brit*) *n* queue *f*, file *f* ▷ *vi* (*also*: **queue up**) faire la queue; **to jump the ~** passer avant son tour

quibble ['kwɪbl] *vi* ergoter, chicaner

quiche [kiːʃ] *n* quiche *f*

quick [kwɪk] *adj* rapide; (*reply*) prompt(e), rapide; (*mind*) vif (vive); (*agile*) agile, vif (vive) ▷ *adv* vite, rapidement ▷ *n*: **cut to the ~** (*fig*) touché(e) au vif; **be ~!** dépêche-toi!; **to be ~ to act** agir tout de suite

quicken ['kwɪkən] *vt* accélérer, presser; (*rouse*) stimuler ▷ *vi* s'accélérer, devenir plus rapide

quick fix *n* solution *f* de fortune

quicklime ['kwɪklaɪm] *n* chaux vive

quickly ['kwɪklı] *adv* (*fast*) vite, rapidement; (*immediately*) tout de suite

quickness ['kwɪknɪs] *n* rapidité *f*, promptitude *f*; (*of mind*) vivacité *f*

quicksand ['kwɪksænd] *n* sables mouvants

quickstep ['kwɪkstɛp] *n* fox-trot *m*

quick-tempered [kwɪkˈtɛmpəd] *adj* emporté(e)

quick-witted [kwɪkˈwɪtɪd] *adj* à l'esprit vif

quid [kwɪd] *n* (*pl inv*: *Brit inf*) livre *f*

quid pro quo ['kwɪdprəuˈkwəu] *n* contrepartie *f*

quiet ['kwaɪət] *adj* tranquille, calme; (*not noisy*: *engine*) silencieux(-euse); (*reserved*) réservé(e); (*voice*) bas(se); (*not busy*: *day, business*) calme; (*ceremony, colour*) discret(-ète) ▷ *n* tranquillité *f*, calme *m*; (*silence*) silence *m* ▷ *vt*, *vi* (*US*) = **quieten**; **keep ~!** tais-toi!; **on the ~** en secret, discrètement; **I'll have a ~ word with him** je lui en parlerai discrètement

quieten ['kwaɪətn] (*also*: **quieten down**) *vi* se

calmer, s'apaiser ▷ vt calmer, apaiser

quietly ['kwaɪətlɪ] adv tranquillement; (silently) silencieusement; (discreetly) discrètement

quietness ['kwaɪətnɪs] n tranquillité f, calme m; silence m

quill [kwɪl] n plume f (d'oie)

quilt [kwɪlt] n édredon m; (continental quilt) couette f

quin [kwɪn] n abbr = **quintuplet**

quince [kwɪns] n coing m; (tree) cognassier m

quinine [kwɪ'niːn] n quinine f

quintet, quintette [kwɪn'tɛt] n quintette m

quintuplet [kwɪn'tjuːplɪt] n quintuplé(e)

quip [kwɪp] n remarque piquante or spirituelle, pointe f ▷ vt: ... **he ~ped** ... lança-t-il

quire ['kwaɪər] n ≈ main f (de papier)

quirk [kwəːk] n bizarrerie f; **by some ~ of fate** par un caprice du hasard

quirky ['kwɜːkɪ] adj singulier(-ère)

quit [kwɪt] (pt, pp - or **-ted**) vt quitter ▷ vi (give up) abandonner, renoncer; (resign) démissionner; **to ~ doing** arrêter de faire; **~ stalling!** (US inf) arrête de te dérober!; **notice to ~** (Brit) congé m (signifié au locataire)

quite [kwaɪt] adv (rather) assez, plutôt; (entirely) complètement, tout à fait; **~ new** plutôt neuf; tout à fait neuf; **she's ~ pretty** elle est plutôt jolie; **I ~ understand** je comprends très bien; **~ a few of them** un assez grand nombre d'entre eux; **that's not ~ right** ce n'est pas tout à fait juste; **not ~ as many as last time** pas tout à fait autant que la dernière fois; **~ (so)!** exactement!

Quito ['kiːtəu] n Quito

quits [kwɪts] adj: **~ (with)** quitte (envers); **let's call it ~** restons-en là

quiver ['kwɪvər] vi trembler, frémir ▷ n (for arrows) carquois m

quiz [kwɪz] n (on TV) jeu-concours m (télévisé); (in magazine etc) test m de connaissances ▷ vt interroger

quizzical ['kwɪzɪkl] adj narquois(e)

quoits [kwɔɪts] npl jeu m du palet

quorum ['kwɔːrəm] n quorum m

quota ['kwəutə] n quota m

quotation [kwəu'teɪʃən] n citation f; (of shares etc) cote f, cours m; (estimate) devis m

quotation marks npl guillemets mpl

quote [kwəut] n citation f; (estimate) devis m ▷ vt (sentence, author) citer; (price) donner, soumettre; (shares) coter ▷ vi: **to ~ from** citer; **to ~ for a job** établir un devis pour des travaux; **quotes** npl (inverted commas) guillemets mpl; **in ~s** entre guillemets; **~ ... unquote** (in dictation) ouvrez les guillemets ... fermez les guillemets

quotient ['kwəuʃənt] n quotient m

qv abbr (= quod vide: which see) voir

qwerty keyboard ['kwəːtɪ-] n clavier m QWERTY

Rr

R, r [ɑːʳ] *n* (letter) R, r *m*; **R for Robert**, (US) **R for Roger** R comme Raoul

R *abbr* (= *right*) dr; (= *river*) riv., fl; (= *Réaumur* (*scale*)) R; (*US Cine*: = *restricted*) interdit aux moins de 17 ans; (*US Pol*) = **republican**; (*Brit*) Rex, Regina

RA *abbr* = **rear admiral** ▷ *n abbr* (*Brit*) = **Royal Academy** = **Royal Academician**

RAAF *n abbr* = **Royal Australian Air Force**

Rabat [rə'bɑːt] *n* Rabat

rabbi ['ræbaɪ] *n* rabbin *m*

rabbit ['ræbɪt] *n* lapin *m* ▷ *vi*: **to ~ (on)** (*Brit*) parler à n'en plus finir

rabbit hole *n* terrier *m* (de lapin)

rabbit hutch *n* clapier *m*

rabble ['ræbl] *n* (*pej*) populace *f*

rabid ['ræbɪd] *adj* enragé(e)

rabies ['reɪbiːz] *n* rage *f*

RAC *n abbr* (*Brit*: = *Royal Automobile Club*) ≈ ACF *m*

raccoon, racoon [rə'kuːn] *n* raton *m* laveur

race [reɪs] *n* (*species*) race *f*; (*competition, rush*) course *f* ▷ *vt* (*person*) faire la course avec; (*horse*) faire courir; (*engine*) emballer ▷ *vi* (*compete*) faire la course, courir; (*hurry*) aller à toute vitesse, courir; (*engine*) s'emballer; (*pulse*) battre très vite; **the human ~** la race humaine; **to ~ in/out** *etc* entrer/sortir *etc* à toute vitesse

race car *n* (US) = **racing car**

race car driver *n* (US) = **racing driver**

racecourse ['reɪskɔːs] *n* champ *m* de courses

racehorse ['reɪshɔːs] *n* cheval *m* de course

racer ['reɪsəʳ] *n* (*bike*) vélo *m* de course

race relations *npl* rapports *mpl* entre les races

racetrack ['reɪstræk] *n* piste *f*

racial ['reɪʃl] *adj* racial(e)

racialism ['reɪʃlɪzəm] *n* racisme *m*

racialist ['reɪʃlɪst] *adj, n* raciste (*m/f*)

racing ['reɪsɪŋ] *n* courses *fpl*

racing car *n* (*Brit*) voiture *f* de course

racing driver *n* (*Brit*) pilote *m* de course

racism ['reɪsɪzəm] *n* racisme *m*

racist ['reɪsɪst] *adj, n* raciste *m/f*

rack [ræk] *n* (*for guns, tools*) râtelier *m*; (*for clothes*) portant *m*; (*for bottles*) casier *m*; (*also*: **luggage rack**) filet *m* à bagages; (*also*: **roof rack**) galerie *f*; (*also*: **dish rack**) égouttoir *m* ▷ *vt* tourmenter; **magazine ~** porte-revues *m inv*; **shoe ~** étagère *f*

à chaussures; **toast ~** porte-toast *m*; **to ~ one's brains** se creuser la cervelle; **to go to ~ and ruin** (*building*) tomber en ruine; (*business*) péricliter

▸ **rack up** *vt* accumuler

racket ['rækɪt] *n* (*for tennis*) raquette *f*; (*noise*) tapage *m*, vacarme *m*; (*swindle*) escroquerie *f*; (*organized crime*) racket *m*

racketeer [rækɪ'tɪəʳ] *n* (*esp US*) racketteur *m*

racquet ['rækɪt] *n* raquette *f*

racy ['reɪsɪ] *adj* plein(e) de verve, osé(e)

RADA [rɑːdə] *n abbr* (*Brit*) = **Royal Academy of Dramatic Art**

radar ['reɪdɑːʳ] *n* radar *m* ▷ *cpd* radar *inv*

radar trap *n* (*Aut*: *police*) contrôle *m* radar

radial ['reɪdɪəl] *adj* (*also*: **radial-ply**) à carcasse radiale

radiance ['reɪdɪəns] *n* éclat *m*, rayonnement *m*

radiant ['reɪdɪənt] *adj* rayonnant(e); (*Physics*) radiant(e)

radiate ['reɪdɪeɪt] *vt* (*heat*) émettre, dégager ▷ *vi* (*lines*) rayonner

radiation [reɪdɪ'eɪʃən] *n* rayonnement *m*; (*radioactive*) radiation *f*

radiation sickness *n* mal *m* des rayons

radiator ['reɪdɪeɪtəʳ] *n* radiateur *m*

radiator cap *n* bouchon *m* de radiateur

radiator grill *n* (*Aut*) calandre *f*

radical ['rædɪkl] *adj* radical(e)

radii ['reɪdɪaɪ] *npl of* **radius**

radio ['reɪdɪəu] *n* radio *f* ▷ *vi*: **to ~ to sb** envoyer un message radio à qn ▷ *vt* (*information*) transmettre par radio; (*one's position*) signaler par radio; (*person*) appeler par radio; **on the ~** à la radio

radioactive ['reɪdɪəu'æktɪv] *adj* radioactif(-ive)

radioactivity ['reɪdɪəuæk'tɪvɪtɪ] *n* radioactivité *f*

radio announcer *n* annonceur *m*

radio cassette *n* radiocassette *m*

radio-controlled ['reɪdɪəukən'trəuld] *adj* radioguidé(e)

radiographer [reɪdɪ'ɔgrəfəʳ] *n* radiologue *m/f* (*technicien*)

radiography [reɪdɪ'ɔgrəfɪ] *n* radiographie *f*

radiologist [reɪdɪ'ɔlədʒɪst] *n* radiologue *m/f*

(*médecin*)

radiology [reɪdɪ'ɔlədʒɪ] *n* radiologie *f*

radio station *n* station *f* de radio

radio taxi *n* radio-taxi *m*

radiotelephone ['reɪdɪəu'tɛlɪfəun] *n*
radiotéléphone *m*

radiotherapist ['reɪdɪəu'θɛrəpɪst] *n*
radiothérapeute *m/f*

radiotherapy ['reɪdɪəu'θɛrəpɪ] *n* radiothérapie *f*

radish ['rædɪʃ] *n* radis *m*

radium ['reɪdɪəm] *n* radium *m*

radius (*pl* **radii**) ['reɪdɪəs, -ɪaɪ] *n* rayon *m*; (*Anat*)
radius *m*; **within a ~ of 50 miles** dans un rayon
de 50 milles

RAF *n abbr* (*Brit*) = **Royal Air Force**

raffia ['ræfɪə] *n* raphia *m*

raffish ['ræfɪʃ] *adj* dissolu(e), canaille

raffle ['ræfl] *n* tombola *f* ▷ *vt* mettre comme lot
dans une tombola

raft [rɑːft] *n* (*craft: also:* **life raft**) radeau *m*; (*logs*)
train *m* de flottage

rafter ['rɑːftə'] *n* chevron *m*

rag [ræg] *n* chiffon *m*; (*pej: newspaper*) feuille *f*,
torchon *m*; (*for charity*) attractions organisées par les
étudiants au profit d'œuvres de charité ▷ *vt* (*Brit*)
chahuter, mettre en boîte; **rags** *npl* haillons
mpl; **in ~s** (*person*) en haillons; (*clothes*) en
lambeaux

rag-and-bone man [rægən'bəunmæn] (*irreg*) *n*
chiffonnier *m*

ragbag ['rægbæg] *n* (*fig*) ramassis *m*

rag doll *n* poupée *f* de chiffon

rage [reɪdʒ] *n* (*fury*) rage *f*, fureur *f* ▷ *vi* (*person*)
être fou (folle) de rage; (*storm*) faire rage, être
déchaîné(e); **to fly into a ~** se mettre en rage;
it's all the ~ cela fait fureur

ragged ['rægɪd] *adj* (*edge*) inégal(e), qui
accroche; (*clothes*) en loques; (*cuff*) effiloché(e);
(*appearance*) déguenillé(e)

raging ['reɪdʒɪŋ] *adj* (*sea, storm*) en furie; (*fever,
pain*) violent(e); **~ toothache** rage *f* de dents; **in
a ~ temper** dans une rage folle

rag trade *n* (*inf*): **the ~** la confection

⬤ **RAG WEEK**
⬤
⬤
⬤ *Rag Week*, est une semaine où les étudiants
⬤ se déguisent et collectent de l'argent pour
⬤ les œuvres de charité. Toutes sortes
⬤ d'animations sont organisées à cette
⬤ occasion (marches sponsorisées, spectacles
⬤ de rue etc). Des magazines (les "rag mags")
⬤ contenant des plaisanteries osées sont
⬤ vendus dans les rues, également au profit
⬤ des œuvres. Enfin, la plupart des universités
⬤ organisent un bal (le "rag ball").

raid [reɪd] *n* (*Mil*) raid *m*; (*criminal*) hold-up *m inv*;
(*by police*) descente *f*, rafle *f* ▷ *vt* faire un raid sur
or un hold-up dans *or* une descente dans

raider ['reɪdə'] *n* malfaiteur *m*

rail [reɪl] *n* (*on stair*) rampe *f*; (*on bridge, balcony*)

balustrade *f*; (*of ship*) bastingage *m*; (*for train*) rail
m; **rails** *npl* rails *mpl*, voie ferrée; **by ~** en train,
par le train

railcard ['reɪlkɑːd] *n* (*Brit*) carte *f* de chemin de
fer; **young person's ~** carte *f* jeune

railing ['reɪlɪŋ] *n*, **railings** ['reɪlɪŋz] ▷ *npl* grille *f*

railway ['reɪlweɪ], (*US*) **railroad** ['reɪlrəud] *n*
chemin *m* de fer; (*track*) voie *f* ferrée

railway engine *n* locomotive *f*

railway line *n* (*Brit*) ligne *f* de chemin de fer;
(*track*) voie ferrée

railwayman ['reɪlweɪmən] (*irreg*) *n* cheminot *m*

railway station *n* (*Brit*) gare *f*

rain [reɪn] *n* pluie *f* ▷ *vi* pleuvoir; **in the ~** sous
la pluie; **it's ~ing** il pleut; **it's ~ing cats and
dogs** il pleut à torrents

rainbow ['reɪnbəu] *n* arc-en-ciel *m*

raincoat ['reɪnkəut] *n* imperméable *m*

raindrop ['reɪndrɔp] *n* goutte *f* de pluie

rainfall ['reɪnfɔːl] *n* chute *f* de pluie;
(*measurement*) hauteur *f* des précipitations

rainforest ['reɪnfɔrɪst] *n* forêt tropicale

rainproof ['reɪnpruːf] *adj* imperméable

rainstorm ['reɪnstɔːm] *n* pluie torrentielle

rainwater ['reɪnwɔːtə'] *n* eau *f* de pluie

rainy ['reɪnɪ] *adj* pluvieux(-euse)

raise [reɪz] *n* augmentation *f* ▷ *vt* (*lift*) lever;
hausser; (*end: siege, embargo*) lever; (*build*) ériger;
(*increase*) augmenter; (*morale*) remonter;
(*standards*) améliorer; (*a protest, doubt*) provoquer,
causer; (*a question*) soulever; (*cattle, family*)
élever; (*crop*) faire pousser; (*army, funds*)
rassembler; (*loan*) obtenir; **to ~ one's glass to
sb/sth** porter un toast en l'honneur de qn/qch;
to ~ one's voice élever la voix; **to ~ sb's hopes**
donner de l'espoir à qn; **to ~ a laugh/a smile**
faire rire/sourire

raisin ['reɪzn] *n* raisin sec

Raj [rɑːdʒ] *n*: **the ~** l'empire *m* (*aux Indes*)

rajah ['rɑːdʒə] *n* radja(h) *m*

rake [reɪk] *n* (*tool*) râteau *m*; (*person*) débauché *m*
▷ *vt* (*garden*) ratisser; (*fire*) tisonner; (*with
machine gun*) balayer ▷ *vi*: **to ~ through** (*fig:
search*) fouiller (dans)

rake-off ['reɪkɔf] *n* (*inf*) pourcentage *m*

rakish ['reɪkɪʃ] *adj* dissolu(e); cavalier(-ière)

rally ['rælɪ] *n* (*Pol etc*) meeting *m*, rassemblement
m; (*Aut*) rallye *m*; (*Tennis*) échange *m* ▷ *vt*
rassembler, rallier; (*support*) gagner ▷ *vi* se
rallier; (*sick person*) aller mieux; (*Stock Exchange*)
reprendre

▶ **rally round** *vi* venir en aide ▷ *vt fus* se rallier
à; venir en aide à

rallying point ['rælɪɪŋ-] *n* (*Mil*) point *m* de
ralliement

RAM [ræm] *n abbr* (*Comput: =* random access
memory) mémoire vive

ram [ræm] *n* bélier *m* ▷ *vt* (*push*) enfoncer; (*soil*)
tasser; (*crash into: vehicle*) emboutir; (: *lamppost
etc*) percuter; (*in battle*) éperonner

Ramadan [ræmə'dæn] *n* Ramadan *m*

ramble ['ræmbl] *n* randonnée *f* ▷ *vi* (*walk*) se

promener, faire une randonnée; (pej: also:
ramble on) discourir, pérorer
rambler ['ræmblə^r] n promeneur(-euse),
randonneur(-euse); (Bot) rosier grimpant
rambling ['ræmblɪŋ] adj (speech) décousu(e);
(house) plein(e) de coins et de recoins; (Bot)
grimpant(e)
RAMC n abbr (Brit) = **Royal Army Medical Corps**
ramification [ræmɪfɪ'keɪʃən] n ramification f
ramp [ræmp] n (incline) rampe f; (Aut)
dénivellation f; (in garage) pont m; **on/off** ~ (US
Aut) bretelle f d'accès
rampage [ræm'peɪdʒ] n: **to be on the** ~ se
déchaîner ▷ vi: **they went rampaging
through the town** ils ont envahi les rues et ont
tout saccagé sur leur passage
rampant ['ræmpənt] adj (disease etc) qui sévit
rampart ['ræmpɑːt] n rempart m
ram raiding [-reɪdɪŋ] n pillage d'un magasin en
enfonçant la vitrine avec une voiture volée
ramshackle ['ræmʃækl] adj (house) délabré(e);
(car etc) déglingué(e)
RAN n abbr = **Royal Australian Navy**
ran [ræn] pt of **run**
ranch [rɑːntʃ] n ranch m
rancher ['rɑːntʃə^r] n (owner) propriétaire m de
ranch; (ranch hand) cowboy m
rancid ['rænsɪd] adj rance
rancour, (US) **rancor** ['ræŋkə^r] n rancune f,
rancœur f
R&B n abbr = **rhythm and blues**
R&D n abbr (= research and development) R-D f
random ['rændəm] adj fait(e) or établi(e) au
hasard; (Comput, Math) aléatoire ▷ n: **at** ~ au
hasard
random access memory n (Comput) mémoire
vive, RAM f
R&R n abbr (US Mil) = **rest and recreation**
randy ['rændɪ] adj (Brit inf) excité(e); lubrique
rang [ræŋ] pt of **ring**
range [reɪndʒ] n (of mountains) chaîne f; (of missile,
voice) portée f; (of products) choix m, gamme f;
(also: **shooting range**) champ m de tir; (: indoor)
stand m de tir; (also: **kitchen range**) fourneau m
(de cuisine) ▷ vt (place) mettre en rang, placer;
(roam) parcourir ▷ vi: **to** ~ **over** couvrir; **to** ~
from ... to aller de ... à; **price** ~ éventail m des
prix; **do you have anything else in this price**
~? avez-vous autre chose dans ces prix?; **within
(firing)** ~ à portée (de tir); ~**d left/right** (text)
justifié à gauche/à droite
ranger ['reɪndʒə^r] n garde m forestier
Rangoon [ræŋ'guːn] n Rangoon
rank [ræŋk] n rang m; (Mil) grade m; (Brit: also:
taxi rank) station f de taxis ▷ vi: **to** ~ **among**
compter or se classer parmi ▷ vt: **I** ~ **him sixth**
je le place sixième ▷ adj (smell) nauséabond(e);
(hypocrisy, injustice etc) flagrant(e); **he's a** ~
outsider il n'est vraiment pas dans la course;
the ~**s** (Mil) la troupe; **the** ~ **and file** (fig) la
masse, la base; **to close** ~**s** (Mil: fig) serrer les
rangs

rankle ['ræŋkl] vi (insult) rester sur le cœur
ransack ['rænsæk] vt fouiller (à fond); (plunder)
piller
ransom ['rænsəm] n rançon f; **to hold sb to** ~
(fig) exercer un chantage sur qn
rant [rænt] vi fulminer
ranting ['ræntɪŋ] n invectives fpl
rap [ræp] n petit coup sec; tape f; (music) rap m
▷ vt (door) frapper sur or à; (table etc) taper sur
rape [reɪp] n viol m; (Bot) colza m ▷ vt violer
rape oil, **rapeseed oil** ['reɪp(siː)d] n huile f de
colza
rapid ['ræpɪd] adj rapide
rapidity [rə'pɪdɪtɪ] n rapidité f
rapidly ['ræpɪdlɪ] adv rapidement
rapids ['ræpɪdz] npl (Geo) rapides mpl
rapist ['reɪpɪst] n auteur m d'un viol
rapport [ræ'pɔː^r] n entente f
rapt [ræpt] adj (attention) extrême; **to be** ~ **in
contemplation** être perdu(e) dans la
contemplation
rapture ['ræptʃə^r] n extase f, ravissement m; **to
go into** ~**s over** s'extasier sur
rapturous ['ræptʃərəs] adj extasié(e); frénétique
rare [reə^r] adj rare; (Culin: steak) saignant(e)
rarebit ['reəbɪt] n see **Welsh rarebit**
rarefied ['reərɪfaɪd] adj (air, atmosphere) raréfié(e)
rarely ['reəlɪ] adv rarement
raring ['reərɪŋ] adj: **to be** ~ **to go** (inf) être très
impatient(e) de commencer
rarity ['reərɪtɪ] n rareté f
rascal ['rɑːskl] n vaurien m
rash [ræʃ] adj imprudent(e), irréfléchi(e) ▷ n
(Med) rougeur f, éruption f; (of events) série f
(noire); **to come out in a** ~ avoir une éruption
rasher ['ræʃə^r] n fine tranche (de lard)
rasp [rɑːsp] n (tool) lime f ▷ vt (speak: also: **rasp
out**) dire d'une voix grinçante
raspberry ['rɑːzbərɪ] n framboise f
raspberry bush n framboisier m
rasping ['rɑːspɪŋ] adj: ~ **noise** grincement m
Rastafarian [ræstə'fɛərɪən] adj, n rastafari (m/f)
rat [ræt] n rat m
ratable ['reɪtəbl] adj see **rateable value**
ratchet ['rætʃɪt] n: ~ **wheel** roue f à rochet
rate [reɪt] n (ratio) taux m, pourcentage m; (speed)
vitesse f, rythme m; (price) tarif m ▷ vt (price)
évaluer, estimer; (people) classer; (deserve)
mériter; **rates** npl (Brit: property tax) impôts
locaux; **to** ~ **sb/sth as** considérer qn/qch
comme; **to** ~ **sb/sth among** classer qn/qch
parmi; **to** ~ **sb/sth highly** avoir une haute
opinion de qn/qch; **at a** ~ **of 60 kph** à une
vitesse de 60 km/h; **at any** ~ en tout cas; ~ **of
exchange** taux or cours m du change; ~ **of flow**
débit m; ~ **of return** (taux de) rendement m;
pulse ~ fréquence f des pulsations
rateable value ['reɪtəbl-] n (Brit) valeur locative
imposable
ratepayer ['reɪtpeɪə^r] n (Brit) contribuable m/f
(payant les impôts locaux)
rather ['rɑːðə^r] adv (somewhat) assez, plutôt; (to

some extent) un peu; **it's ~ expensive** c'est assez cher; (*too much*) c'est un peu cher; **there's ~ a lot** il y en a beaucoup; **I would** *or* **I'd ~ go** j'aimerais mieux *or* je préférerais partir; **I had ~ go** il vaudrait mieux que je parte; **I'd ~ not leave** j'aimerais mieux ne pas partir; **or ~** (*more accurately*) ou plutôt; **I ~ think he won't come** je crois bien qu'il ne viendra pas

ratification [rætɪfɪ'keɪʃən] *n* ratification *f*

ratify ['rætɪfaɪ] *vt* ratifier

rating ['reɪtɪŋ] *n* (*assessment*) évaluation *f*; (*score*) classement *m*; (*Finance*) cote *f*; (*Naut: category*) classe *f*; (*: sailor: Brit*) matelot *m*; **ratings** *npl* (*Radio*) indice(s) *m(pl)* d'écoute; (*TV*) Audimat® *m*

ratio ['reɪʃɪəu] *n* proportion *f*; **in the ~ of 100 to 1** dans la proportion de 100 contre 1

ration ['ræʃən] *n* ration *f* ▷ *vt* rationner; **rations** *npl* (*food*) vivres *mpl*

rational ['ræʃənl] *adj* raisonnable, sensé(e); (*solution, reasoning*) logique; (*Med: person*) lucide

rationale [ræʃə'nɑːl] *n* raisonnement *m*; justification *f*

rationalization [ræʃnəlaɪ'zeɪʃən] *n* rationalisation *f*

rationalize ['ræʃnəlaɪz] *vt* rationaliser; (*conduct*) essayer d'expliquer *or* de motiver

rationally ['ræʃnəlɪ] *adv* raisonnablement; logiquement

rationing ['ræʃnɪŋ] *n* rationnement *m*

rat pack ['rætpæk] *n* (*Brit inf*) journalistes *mpl* de la presse à sensation

rat poison *n* mort-aux-rats *f inv*

rat race *n* foire *f* d'empoigne

rattan [ræ'tæn] *n* rotin *m*

rattle ['rætl] *n* (*of door, window*) battement *m*; (*of coins, chain*) cliquetis *m*; (*of train, engine*) bruit *m* de ferraille; (*for baby*) hochet *m*; (*of sports fan*) crécelle *f* ▷ *vi* cliqueter; (*car, bus*): **to ~ along** rouler en faisant un bruit de ferraille ▷ *vt* agiter (bruyamment); (*inf: disconcert*) décontenancer; (*: annoy*) embêter

rattlesnake ['rætlsneɪk] *n* serpent *m* à sonnettes

ratty ['rætɪ] *adj* (*inf*) en rogne

raucous ['rɔːkəs] *adj* rauque

raucously ['rɔːkəslɪ] *adv* d'une voix rauque

raunchy ['rɔːntʃɪ] *adj* (*inf: voice, image, act*) sexy; (*scenes, film*) lubrique

ravage ['rævɪdʒ] *vt* ravager

ravages ['rævɪdʒɪz] *npl* ravages *mpl*

rave [reɪv] *vi* (*in anger*) s'emporter; (*with enthusiasm*) s'extasier; (*Med*) délirer ▷ *n* (*inf: party*) rave *f*, soirée *f* techno ▷ *adj* (*scene, culture, music*) rave, techno ▷ *cpd*: **~ review** (*inf*) critique *f* dithyrambique

raven ['reɪvən] *n* grand corbeau

ravenous ['rævənəs] *adj* affamé(eè)

ravine [rə'viːn] *n* ravin *m*

raving ['reɪvɪŋ] *adj*: **he's ~ mad** il est complètement cinglé

ravings ['reɪvɪŋz] *npl* divagations *fpl*

ravioli [rævɪ'əulɪ] *n* ravioli *mpl*

ravish ['rævɪʃ] *vt* ravir

ravishing ['rævɪʃɪŋ] *adj* enchanteur(-eresse)

raw [rɔː] *adj* (*uncooked*) cru(e); (*not processed*) brut(e); (*sore*) à vif, irrité(e); (*inexperienced*) inexpérimenté(e); (*weather, day*) froid(e) et humide; **~ deal** (*inf: bad bargain*) sale coup *m*; (*: unfair treatment*): **to get a ~ deal** être traité(e) injustement; **~ materials** matières premières

Rawalpindi [rɔːl'pɪndɪ] *n* Rawalpindi

raw material *n* matière première

ray [reɪ] *n* rayon *m*; **~ of hope** lueur *f* d'espoir

rayon ['reɪɔn] *n* rayonne *f*

raze [reɪz] *vt* (*also*: **raze to the ground**) raser

razor ['reɪzər] *n* rasoir *m*

razor blade *n* lame *f* de rasoir

razzle ['ræzl], **razzle-dazzle** ['ræzl'dæzl] *n* (*Brit inf*): **to go on the ~(-dazzle)** faire la bringue

razzmatazz ['ræzmə'tæz] *n* (*inf*) tralala *m*, tapage *m*

RC *abbr* = **Roman Catholic**

RCAF *n abbr* = **Royal Canadian Air Force**

RCMP *n abbr* = **Royal Canadian Mounted Police**

RCN *n abbr* = **Royal Canadian Navy**

RD *abbr* (*US*) = **rural delivery**

Rd *abbr* = **road**

RDC *n abbr* (*Brit*) = **rural district council**

RE *n abbr* (*Brit*) = **religious education**; (*Brit Mil*) = **Royal Engineers**

re [riː] *prep* concernant

reach [riːtʃ] *n* portée *f*, atteinte *f*; (*of river etc*) étendue *f* ▷ *vt* atteindre, arriver à; (*conclusion, decision*) parvenir à ▷ *vi* s'étendre; (*stretch out hand*): **to ~ up/down** *etc* (**for sth**) lever/baisser *etc* le bras (pour prendre qch); **to ~ sb by phone** joindre qn par téléphone; **out of/within ~** (*object*) hors de/à portée; **within easy ~ (of)** (*place*) à proximité (de), proche (de)

▶ **reach out** *vt* tendre ▷ *vi*: **to ~ out (for)** allonger le bras (pour prendre)

react [riː'ækt] *vi* réagir

reaction [riː'ækʃən] *n* réaction *f*

reactionary [riː'ækʃənrɪ] *adj*, *n* réactionnaire (*m/f*)

reactor [riː'æktər] *n* réacteur *m*

read (*pt, pp* -) [riːd, rɛd] *vi* lire ▷ *vt* lire; (*understand*) comprendre, interpréter; (*study*) étudier; (*meter*) relever; (*subj: instrument etc*) indiquer, marquer; **to take sth as ~** (*fig*) considérer qch comme accepté; **do you ~ me?** (*Tel*) est-ce que vous me recevez?

▶ **read out** *vt* lire à haute voix

▶ **read over** *vt* relire

▶ **read through** *vt* (*quickly*) parcourir; (*thoroughly*) lire jusqu'au bout

▶ **read up** *vt*, **read up on** *vt fus* étudier

readable ['riːdəbl] *adj* facile *or* agréable à lire

reader ['riːdər] *n* lecteur(-trice); (*book*) livre *m* de lecture; (*Brit: at university*) maître *m* de conférences

readership ['riːdəʃɪp] *n* (*of paper etc*) (nombre *m* de) lecteurs *mpl*

readily ['rɛdɪlɪ] *adv* volontiers, avec empressement; (*easily*) facilement

readiness ['rɛdɪnɪs] *n* empressement *m*; **in ~** (*prepared*) prêt(e)

reading ['ri:dɪŋ] *n* lecture *f*; (*understanding*) interprétation *f*; (*on instrument*) indications *fpl*

reading lamp *n* lampe *f* de bureau

reading room *n* salle *f* de lecture

readjust [ri:ə'dʒʌst] *vt* rajuster; (*instrument*) régler de nouveau ▷ *vi* (*person*): **to ~ (to)** se réadapter (à)

ready ['rɛdɪ] *adj* prêt(e); (*willing*) prêt, disposé(e); (*quick*) prompt(e); (*available*) disponible ▷ *n*: **at the ~** (*Mil*) prêt à faire feu; (*fig*) tout(e) prêt(e); **~ for use** prêt à l'emploi; **to be ~ to do sth** être prêt à faire qch; **when will my photos be ~?** quand est-ce que mes photos seront prêtes?; **to get ~** (*as vi*) se préparer; (*as vt*) préparer

ready cash *n* (argent *m*) liquide *m*

ready-cooked ['rɛdɪ'kukd] *adj* précuit(e)

ready-made ['rɛdɪ'meɪd] *adj* tout(e) faite(e)

ready-mix ['rɛdɪmɪks] *n* (*for cakes etc*) préparation *f* en sachet

ready reckoner [-'rɛknər] *n* (*Brit*) barème *m*

ready-to-wear ['rɛdɪtə'wɛər] *adj* (en) prêt-à-porter

reagent [ri:'eɪdʒənt] *n* réactif *m*

real [rɪəl] *adj* (*world, life*) réel(le); (*genuine*) véritable; (*proper*) vrai(e) ▷ *adv* (*US inf: very*) vraiment; **in ~ life** dans la réalité

real ale *n* bière traditionnelle

real estate *n* biens fonciers *or* immobiliers

realism ['rɪəlɪzəm] *n* réalisme *m*

realist ['rɪəlɪst] *n* réaliste *m/f*

realistic [rɪə'lɪstɪk] *adj* réaliste

reality [ri:'ælɪtɪ] *n* réalité *f*; **in ~** en réalité, en fait

reality TV *n* téléréalité *f*

realization [rɪəlaɪ'zeɪʃən] *n* (*awareness*) prise *f* de conscience; (*fulfilment: also: of asset*) réalisation *f*

realize ['rɪəlaɪz] *vt* (*understand*) se rendre compte de, prendre conscience de; (*a project, Comm: asset*) réaliser

really ['rɪəlɪ] *adv* vraiment; **~?** vraiment?, c'est vrai?

realm [rɛlm] *n* royaume *m*; (*fig*) domaine *m*

real-time ['ri:ltaɪm] *adj* (*Comput*) en temps réel

realtor ['rɪəltɔ:ʳ] *n* (*US*) agent immobilier

ream [ri:m] *n* rame *f* (*de papier*); **reams** *npl* (*fig: inf*) des pages et des pages

reap [ri:p] *vt* moissonner; (*fig*) récolter

reaper ['ri:pəʳ] *n* (*machine*) moissonneuse *f*

reappear [ri:ə'pɪəʳ] *vi* réapparaître, reparaître

reappearance [ri:ə'pɪərəns] *n* réapparition *f*

reapply [ri:ə'plaɪ] *vi*: **to ~ for** (*job*) faire une nouvelle demande d'emploi concernant; reposer sa candidature à; (*loan, grant*) faire une nouvelle demande de

reappraisal [ri:ə'preɪzl] *n* réévaluation *f*

rear [rɪəʳ] *adj* de derrière, arrière *inv*; (*Aut: wheel etc*) arrière ▷ *n* arrière *m*, derrière *m* ▷ *vt* (*cattle, family*) élever ▷ *vi* (*also*: **rear up**: *animal*) se cabrer

rear admiral *n* vice-amiral *m*

rear-engined ['rɪər'ɛndʒɪnd] *adj* (*Aut*) avec moteur à l'arrière

rearguard ['rɪəɡɑ:d] *n* arrière-garde *f*

rearmament [ri:'ɑ:məmənt] *n* réarmement *m*

rearrange [ri:ə'reɪndʒ] *vt* réarranger

rear-view mirror *n* (*Aut*) rétroviseur *m*

rear-wheel drive *n* (*Aut*) traction *f* arrière

reason ['ri:zn] *n* raison *f* ▷ *vi*: **to ~ with sb** raisonner qn, faire entendre raison à qn; **the ~ for/why** la raison de/pour laquelle; **to have ~ to think** avoir lieu de penser; **it stands to ~ that** il va sans dire que; **she claims with good ~ that …** elle affirme à juste titre que …; **all the more ~ why** raison de plus pour + *infinitive or* pour que + *sub*; **within ~** dans les limites du raisonnable

reasonable ['ri:znəbl] *adj* raisonnable; (*not bad*) acceptable

reasonably ['ri:znəblɪ] *adv* (*behave*) raisonnablement; (*fairly*) assez; **one can ~ assume that …** on est fondé à *or* il est permis de supposer que …

reasoned ['ri:znd] *adj* (*argument*) raisonné(e)

reasoning ['ri:znɪŋ] *n* raisonnement *m*

reassemble [ri:ə'sɛmbl] *vt* rassembler; (*machine*) remonter

reassert [ri:ə'sə:t] *vt* réaffirmer

reassurance [ri:ə'ʃuərəns] *n* (*factual*) assurance *f*, garantie *f*; (*emotional*) réconfort *m*

reassure [ri:ə'ʃuəʳ] *vt* rassurer; **to ~ sb of** donner à qn l'assurance répétée de

reassuring [ri:ə'ʃuərɪŋ] *adj* rassurant(e)

reawakening [ri:ə'weɪknɪŋ] *n* réveil *m*

rebate ['ri:beɪt] *n* (*on product*) rabais *m*; (*on tax etc*) dégrèvement *m*; (*repayment*) remboursement *m*

rebel *n* ['rɛbl] rebelle *m/f* ▷ *vi* [rɪ'bɛl] se rebeller, se révolter

rebellion [rɪ'bɛljən] *n* rébellion *f*, révolte *f*

rebellious [rɪ'bɛljəs] *adj* rebelle

rebirth [ri:'bə:θ] *n* renaissance *f*

rebound *vi* [rɪ'baund] (*ball*) rebondir ▷ *n* ['ri:baund] rebond *m*

rebuff [rɪ'bʌf] *n* rebuffade *f* ▷ *vt* repousser

rebuild [ri:'bɪld] *vt* (*irreg: like* **build**) reconstruire

rebuke [rɪ'bju:k] *n* réprimande *f*, reproche *m* ▷ *vt* réprimander

rebut [rɪ'bʌt] *vt* réfuter

rebuttal [rɪ'bʌtl] *n* réfutation *f*

recalcitrant [rɪ'kælsɪtrənt] *adj* récalcitrant(e)

recall *vt* [rɪ'kɔ:l] rappeler; (*remember*) se rappeler, se souvenir de ▷ *n* [rɪ'kɔ:l] rappel *m*; (*ability to remember*) mémoire *f*; **beyond ~** *adj* irrévocable

recant [rɪ'kænt] *vi* se rétracter; (*Rel*) abjurer

recap ['ri:kæp] *n* récapitulation *f* ▷ *vt, vi* récapituler

recapture [ri:'kæptʃəʳ] *vt* reprendre; (*atmosphere*) recréer

recede [rɪ'si:d] *vi* s'éloigner; reculer

receding [rɪ'si:dɪŋ] *adj* (*forehead, chin*) fuyant(e); **~ hairline** front dégarni

receipt [rɪ'si:t] *n* (*document*) reçu *m*; (*for parcel etc*) accusé *m* de réception; (*act of receiving*) réception *f*; **receipts** *npl* (*Comm*) recettes *fpl*; **to acknowledge ~ of** accuser réception de; **we are in ~ of ...** nous avons reçu ...; **can I have a ~, please?** je peux avoir un reçu, s'il vous plaît?

receivable [rɪ'si:vəbl] *adj* (*Comm*) recevable; (: *owing*) à recevoir

receive [rɪ'si:v] *vt* recevoir; (*guest*) recevoir, accueillir; **"~d with thanks"** (*Comm*) "pour acquit"; **R~d Pronunciation**: *voir article*

● **RECEIVED PRONUNCIATION**
●
● En Grande-Bretagne, la *Received Pronunciation*
● ou "RP" est une prononciation de la langue
● anglaise qui, récemment encore, était
● surtout associée à l'aristocratie et à la
● bourgeoisie, mais qui maintenant est en
● général considérée comme la prononciation
● correcte.

receiver [rɪ'si:vəʳ] *n* (*Tel*) récepteur *m*, combiné *m*; (*Radio*) récepteur; (*of stolen goods*) receleur *m*; (*for bankruptcies*) administrateur *m* judiciaire

receivership [rɪ'si:vəʃɪp] *n*: **to go into ~** être placé sous administration judiciaire

recent ['ri:snt] *adj* récent(e); **in ~ years** au cours de ces dernières années

recently ['ri:sntlɪ] *adv* récemment; **as ~ as** pas plus tard que; **until ~** jusqu'à il y a peu de temps encore

receptacle [rɪ'sɛptɪkl] *n* récipient *m*

reception [rɪ'sɛpʃən] *n* réception *f*; (*welcome*) accueil *m*, réception

reception centre *n* (*Brit*) centre *m* d'accueil

reception desk *n* réception *f*

receptionist [rɪ'sɛpʃənɪst] *n* réceptionniste *m/f*

receptive [rɪ'sɛptɪv] *adj* réceptif(-ive)

recess [rɪ'sɛs] *n* (*in room*) renfoncement *m*; (*for bed*) alcôve *f*; (*secret place*) recoin *m*; (*Pol etc*: *holiday*) vacances *fpl*; (*US Law*: *short break*) suspension *f* d'audience; (*Scol*: *esp US*) récréation *f*

recession [rɪ'sɛʃən] *n* (*Econ*) récession *f*

recharge [ri:'tʃɑ:dʒ] *vt* (*battery*) recharger

rechargeable [ri:'tʃɑ:dʒəbl] *adj* rechargeable

recipe ['rɛsɪpɪ] *n* recette *f*

recipient [rɪ'sɪpɪənt] *n* (*of payment*) bénéficiaire *m/f*; (*of letter*) destinataire *m/f*

reciprocal [rɪ'sɪprəkl] *adj* réciproque

reciprocate [rɪ'sɪprəkeɪt] *vt* retourner, offrir en retour ▷ *vi* en faire autant

recital [rɪ'saɪtl] *n* récital *m*

recite [rɪ'saɪt] *vt* (*poem*) réciter; (*complaints etc*) énumérer

reckless ['rɛkləs] *adj* (*driver etc*) imprudent(e); (*spender etc*) insouciant(e)

recklessly ['rɛkləslɪ] *adv* imprudemment; avec insouciance

reckon ['rɛkən] *vt* (*count*) calculer, compter; (*consider*) considérer, estimer; (*think*): **I ~ (that)** ... je pense (que) ..., j'estime (que) ... ▷ *vi*: **he is**

somebody to be ~ed with il ne faut pas le sous-estimer; **to ~ without sb/sth** ne pas tenir compte de qn/qch
▶ **reckon on** *vt fus* compter sur, s'attendre à

reckoning ['rɛknɪŋ] *n* compte *m*, calcul *m*; estimation *f*; **the day of ~** le jour du Jugement

reclaim [rɪ'kleɪm] *vt* (*land*: *from sea*) assécher; (: *from forest*) défricher; (: *with fertilizer*) amender; (*demand back*) réclamer (le remboursement *or* la restitution de); (*waste materials*) récupérer

reclamation [rɛklə'meɪʃən] *n* (*of land*) amendement *m*; assèchement *m*; défrichement *m*

recline [rɪ'klaɪn] *vi* être allongé(e) *or* étendu(e)

reclining [rɪ'klaɪnɪŋ] *adj* (*seat*) à dossier réglable

recluse [rɪ'klu:s] *n* reclus(e), ermite *m*

recognition [rɛkəg'nɪʃən] *n* reconnaissance *f*; **in ~ of** en reconnaissance de; **to gain ~** être reconnu(e); **transformed beyond ~** méconnaissable

recognizable ['rɛkəgnaɪzəbl] *adj*: **~ (by)** reconnaissable (à)

recognize ['rɛkəgnaɪz] *vt*: **to ~ (by/as)** reconnaître (à/comme étant)

recoil [rɪ'kɔɪl] *vi* (*person*): **to ~ (from)** reculer (devant) ▷ *n* (*of gun*) recul *m*

recollect [rɛkə'lɛkt] *vt* se rappeler, se souvenir de

recollection [rɛkə'lɛkʃən] *n* souvenir *m*; **to the best of my ~** autant que je m'en souvienne

recommend [rɛkə'mɛnd] *vt* recommander; **can you ~ a good restaurant?** pouvez-vous me conseiller un bon restaurant?; **she has a lot to ~ her** elle a beaucoup de choses en sa faveur

recommendation [rɛkəmɛn'deɪʃən] *n* recommandation *f*

recommended retail price [rɛkə'mɛndɪd-] *n* (*Brit*) prix conseillé

recompense ['rɛkəmpɛns] *vt* récompenser; (*compensate*) dédommager ▷ *n* récompense *f*; dédommagement *m*

reconcilable ['rɛkənsaɪləbl] *adj* (*ideas*) conciliable

reconcile ['rɛkənsaɪl] *vt* (*two people*) réconcilier; (*two facts*) concilier, accorder; **to ~ o.s. to** se résigner à

reconciliation [rɛkənsɪlɪ'eɪʃən] *n* réconciliation *f*; conciliation *f*

recondite [rɪ'kɔndaɪt] *adj* abstrus(e), obscur(e)

recondition [ri:kən'dɪʃən] *vt* remettre à neuf; réviser entièrement

reconnaissance [rɪ'kɔnɪsns] *n* (*Mil*) reconnaissance *f*

reconnoitre, (*US*) **reconnoiter** [rɛkə'nɔɪtəʳ] (*Mil*) *vt* reconnaître ▷ *vi* faire une reconnaissance

reconsider [ri:kən'sɪdəʳ] *vt* reconsidérer

reconstitute [ri:'kɔnstɪtju:t] *vt* reconstituer

reconstruct [ri:kən'strʌkt] *vt* (*building*) reconstruire; (*crime, system*) reconstituer

reconstruction [ri:kən'strʌkʃən] *n* reconstruction *f*; reconstitution *f*

reconvene [ri:kən'vi:n] vt reconvoquer ▷ vi se réunir or s'assembler de nouveau

record n ['rɛkɔ:d] rapport m, récit m; (of meeting etc) procès-verbal m; (register) registre m; (file) dossier m; (Comput) article m; (also: **police record**) casier m judiciaire; (Mus: disc) disque m; (Sport) record m ▷ adj record inv ▷ vt [ri'kɔ:d] (set down) noter; (relate) rapporter; (Mus: song etc) enregistrer; **public ~s** archives fpl; **to keep a ~ of** noter; **to keep the ~ straight** (fig) mettre les choses au point; **he is on ~ as saying that …** il a déclaré en public que …; **Italy's excellent ~** les excellents résultats obtenus par l'Italie; **off the ~** adj officieux(-euse) ▷ adv officieusement; **in ~ time** dans un temps record

record card n (in file) fiche f

recorded delivery [ri'kɔ:dɪd-] n (Brit Post): **to send sth ~** ≈ envoyer qch en recommandé

recorded delivery letter [ri'kɔ:dɪd-] n (Brit Post) ≈ lettre recommandée

recorder [ri'kɔ:də^r] n (Law) avocat nommé à la fonction de juge; (Mus) flûte f à bec

record holder n (Sport) détenteur(-trice) du record

recording [ri'kɔ:dɪŋ] n (Mus) enregistrement m

recording studio n studio m d'enregistrement

record library n discothèque f

record player n tourne-disque m

recount [ri'kaunt] vt raconter

re-count n ['ri:kaunt] (Pol: of votes) nouveau décompte (des suffrages) ▷ vt [ri:'kaunt] recompter

recoup [ri'ku:p] vt: **to ~ one's losses** récupérer ce qu'on a perdu, se refaire

recourse [ri'kɔ:s] n recours m; expédient m; **to have ~ to** recourir à, avoir recours à

recover [ri'kʌvə^r] vt récupérer ▷ vi (from illness) se rétablir; (from shock) se remettre; (country) se redresser

re-cover [ri:'kʌvə^r] vt (chair etc) recouvrir

recovery [ri'kʌvəri] n récupération f; rétablissement m; (Econ) redressement m

recreate [ri:kri'eit] vt recréer

recreation [rɛkri'eiʃən] n (leisure) récréation f, détente f

recreational [rɛkri'eiʃnl] adj pour la détente, récréatif(-ive)

recreational drug [rɛkri'eiʃənl-] n drogue récréative

recreational vehicle [rɛkri'eiʃənl-] n (US) camping-car m

recrimination [rikrimi'neiʃən] n récrimination f

recruit [ri'kru:t] n recrue f ▷ vt recruter

recruiting office [ri'kru:tiŋ-] n bureau m de recrutement

recruitment [ri'kru:tmənt] n recrutement m

rectangle ['rɛktæŋgl] n rectangle m

rectangular [rɛk'tæŋgjulə^r] adj rectangulaire

rectify ['rɛktifai] vt (error) rectifier, corriger; (omission) réparer

rector ['rɛktə^r] n (Rel) pasteur m; (in Scottish

universities) personnalité élue par les étudiants pour les représenter

rectory ['rɛktəri] n presbytère m

rectum ['rɛktəm] n (Anat) rectum m

recuperate [ri'kju:pəreit] vi (from illness) se rétablir

recur [ri'kə:^r] vi se reproduire; (idea, opportunity) se retrouver; (symptoms) réapparaître

recurrence [ri'kə:rns] n répétition f; réapparition f

recurrent [ri'kə:rnt] adj périodique, fréquent(e)

recurring [ri'kə:riŋ] adj (problem) périodique, fréquent(e); (Math) périodique

recyclable [ri:'saikləbl] adj recyclable

recycle [ri:'saikl] vt, vi recycler

recycling [ri:'saikliŋ] n recyclage m

red [rɛd] n rouge m; (Pol: pej) rouge m/f ▷ adj rouge; (hair) roux (rousse); **in the ~** (account) à découvert; (business) en déficit

red alert n alerte f rouge

red-blooded [rɛd'blʌdid] adj (inf) viril(e), vigoureux(-euse)

⬤ **REDBRICK UNIVERSITY**

⬤ Une *redbrick university*, ainsi nommée à cause ⬤ du matériau de construction répandu à ⬤ l'époque (la brique), est une université ⬤ britannique provinciale construite assez ⬤ récemment, en particulier fin XIXe-début ⬤ XXe siècle. Il y en a notamment une à ⬤ Manchester, une à Liverpool et une à Bristol. ⬤ Ce terme est utilisé pour établir une ⬤ distinction avec les universités les plus ⬤ anciennes et traditionnelles.

red carpet treatment n réception f en grande pompe

Red Cross n Croix-Rouge f

redcurrant ['rɛdkʌrənt] n groseille f (rouge)

redden ['rɛdn] vt, vi rougir

reddish ['rɛdiʃ] adj rougeâtre; (hair) plutôt roux (rousse)

redecorate [ri:'dɛkəreit] vt refaire à neuf, repeindre et retapisser

redeem [ri'di:m] vt (debt) rembourser; (sth in pawn) dégager; (fig, also Rel) racheter

redeemable [ri'di:məbl] adj rachetable; remboursable, amortissable

redeeming [ri'di:miŋ] adj (feature) qui sauve, qui rachète (le reste)

redefine [ri:di'fain] vt redéfinir

redemption [ri'dɛmʃən] n (Rel) rédemption f; **past** or **beyond ~** (situation) irrémédiable; (place) qui ne peut plus être sauvé(e); (person) irrécupérable

redeploy [ri:di'plɔi] vt (Mil) redéployer; (staff, resources) reconvertir

redeployment [ri:di'plɔimənt] n redéploiement m; reconversion f

redevelop [ri:di'vɛləp] vt rénover

redevelopment [ri:di'vɛləpmənt] n

rénovation f

red-haired [rɛdˈhɛəʳd] adj roux (rousse)

red-handed [rɛdˈhændɪd] adj: **to be caught ~** être pris(e) en flagrant délit or la main dans le sac

redhead [ˈrɛdhɛd] n roux (rousse)

red herring n (fig) diversion f, fausse piste

red-hot [rɛdˈhɔt] adj chauffé(e) au rouge, brûlant(e)

redirect [riːdaɪˈrɛkt] vt (mail) faire suivre

redistribute [riːdɪˈstrɪbjuːt] vt redistribuer

red-letter day [ˈrɛdlɛtə-] n grand jour, jour mémorable

red light n: **to go through a ~** (Aut) brûler un feu rouge

red-light district [ˈrɛdlaɪt-] n quartier mal famé

red meat n viande f rouge

redness [ˈrɛdnɪs] n rougeur f; (of hair) rousseur f

redo [riːˈduː] vt (irreg: like **do**) refaire

redolent [ˈrɛdələnt] adj: **~ of** qui sent; (fig) qui évoque

redouble [riːˈdʌbl] vt: **to ~ one's efforts** redoubler d'efforts

redraft [riːˈdrɑːft] vt remanier

redress [rɪˈdrɛs] n réparation f ▷ vt redresser; **to ~ the balance** rétablir l'équilibre

Red Sea n: **the ~** la mer Rouge

redskin [ˈrɛdskɪn] n Peau-Rouge m/f

red tape n (fig) paperasserie (administrative)

reduce [rɪˈdjuːs] vt réduire; (lower) abaisser; **"~ speed now"** (Aut) "ralentir"; **to ~ sth by/to** réduire qch de/à; **to ~ sb to tears** faire pleurer qn

reduced [rɪˈdjuːst] adj réduit(e); **"greatly ~ prices"** "gros rabais"; **at a ~ price** (goods) au rabais; (ticket etc) à prix réduit

reduction [rɪˈdʌkʃən] n réduction f; (of price) baisse f; (discount) rabais m; réduction; **is there a ~ for children/students?** y a-t-il une réduction pour les enfants/les étudiants?

redundancy [rɪˈdʌndənsɪ] n (Brit) licenciement m, mise f au chômage; **compulsory ~** licenciement; **voluntary ~** départ m volontaire

redundancy payment n (Brit) indemnité f de licenciement

redundant [rɪˈdʌndnt] adj (Brit: worker) licencié(e), mis(e) au chômage; (detail, object) superflu(e); **to be made ~** (worker) être licencié, être mis au chômage

reed [riːd] n (Bot) roseau m; (Mus: of clarinet etc) anche f

re-educate [riːˈedjukeɪt] vt rééduquer

reedy [ˈriːdɪ] adj (voice, instrument) ténu(e)

reef [riːf] n (at sea) récif m, écueil m

reek [riːk] vi: **to ~ (of)** puer, empester

reel [riːl] n bobine f; (Tech) dévidoir m; (Fishing) moulinet m; (Cine) bande f; (dance) quadrille écossais m; (Tech) bobiner; (also: **reel up**) enrouler ▷ vi (sway) chanceler; **my head is ~ing** j'ai la tête qui tourne

▸ **reel in** vt (fish, line) ramener

▸ **reel off** vt (say) énumérer, débiter

re-election [riːɪˈlɛkʃən] n réélection f

re-enter [riːˈɛntəʳ] vt (also Space) rentrer dans

re-entry [riːˈɛntrɪ] n (also Space) rentrée f

re-export vt [ˈriːiksˈpɔːt] réexporter ▷ n [riːˈɛkspɔːt] marchandise réexportée; (act) réexportation f

ref [rɛf] n abbr (inf: = referee) arbitre m

ref. abbr (Comm: = with reference to) réf

refectory [rɪˈfɛktərɪ] n réfectoire m

refer [rɪˈfəːʳ] vt: **to ~ sth to** (dispute, decision) soumettre qch à; **to ~ sb to** (inquirer, patient) adresser qn à; (reader: to text) renvoyer qn à ▷ vi: **to ~ to** (allude to) parler de, faire allusion à; (consult) se reporter à; (apply to) s'appliquer à; **~ring to your letter** (Comm) en réponse à votre lettre; **he ~red me to the manager** il m'a dit de m'adresser au directeur

referee [rɛfəˈriː] n arbitre m; (Tennis) juge-arbitre m; (Brit: for job application) répondant(e) ▷ vt arbitrer

reference [ˈrɛfrəns] n référence f, renvoi m; (mention) allusion f, mention f; (for job application: letter) références; lettre f de recommandation; (: person) répondant(e); **with ~ to** en ce qui concerne; (Comm: in letter) me référant à; **"please quote this ~"** (Comm) "prière de rappeler cette référence"

reference book n ouvrage m de référence

reference library n bibliothèque f d'ouvrages à consulter

reference number n (Comm) numéro m de référence

referendum (pl **referenda**) [rɛfəˈrɛndəm, -də] n référendum m

referral [rɪˈfəːrəl] n soumission f; **she got a ~ to a specialist** elle a été adressée à un spécialiste

refill vt [riːˈfɪl] remplir à nouveau; (pen, lighter etc) recharger ▷ n [ˈriːfɪl] (for pen etc) recharge f

refine [rɪˈfaɪn] vt (sugar, oil) raffiner; (taste) affiner; (idea, theory) peaufiner

refined [rɪˈfaɪnd] adj (person, taste) raffiné(e)

refinement [rɪˈfaɪnmənt] n (of person) raffinement m

refinery [rɪˈfaɪnərɪ] n raffinerie f

refit (Naut) n [ˈriːfɪt] remise f en état ▷ vt [riːˈfɪt] remettre en état

reflate [riːˈfleɪt] vt (economy) relancer

reflation [riːˈfleɪʃən] n relance f

reflationary [riːˈfleɪʃənrɪ] adj de relance

reflect [rɪˈflɛkt] vt (light, image) réfléchir, refléter; (fig) refléter ▷ vi (think) réfléchir, méditer; **it ~s badly on him** cela le discrédite; **it ~s well on him** c'est tout à son honneur

reflection [rɪˈflɛkʃən] n réflexion f; (image) reflet m; (criticism): **~ on** critique f de; atteinte f à; **on ~** réflexion faite

reflector [rɪˈflɛktəʳ] n (also Aut) réflecteur m

reflex [ˈriːflɛks] adj, n réflexe (m)

reflexive [rɪˈflɛksɪv] adj (Ling) réfléchi(e)

reform [rɪˈfɔːm] n réforme f ▷ vt réformer

reformat [riːˈfɔːmæt] vt (Comput) reformater

Reformation [rɛfə'meɪʃən] *n*: **the ~** la Réforme
reformatory [rɪ'fɔ:mətərɪ] *n* (*US*) centre *m* d'éducation surveillée
reformed [rɪ'fɔ:md] *adj* amendé(e), assagi(e)
reformer [rɪ'fɔ:məʳ] *n* réformateur(-trice)
refrain [rɪ'freɪn] *vi*: **to ~ from doing** s'abstenir de faire ▷ *n* refrain *m*
refresh [rɪ'frɛʃ] *vt* rafraîchir; (*subj: food, sleep etc*) redonner des forces à
refresher course [rɪ'frɛʃə-] *n* (*Brit*) cours *m* de recyclage
refreshing [rɪ'frɛʃɪŋ] *adj* (*drink*) rafraîchissant(e); (*sleep*) réparateur(-trice); (*fact, idea etc*) qui réjouit par son originalité *or* sa rareté
refreshment [rɪ'frɛʃmənt] *n*: **for some ~** (*eating*) pour se restaurer *or* sustenter; **in need of ~** (*resting etc*) ayant besoin de refaire ses forces
refreshments [rɪ'frɛʃmənts] *npl* rafraîchissements *mpl*
refrigeration [rɪfrɪdʒə'reɪʃən] *n* réfrigération *f*
refrigerator [rɪ'frɪdʒəreɪtəʳ] *n* réfrigérateur *m*, frigidaire *m*
refuel [ri:'fjuəl] *vt* ravitailler en carburant ▷ *vi* se ravitailler en carburant
refuge ['rɛfju:dʒ] *n* refuge *m*; **to take ~ in** se réfugier dans
refugee [rɛfju'dʒi:] *n* réfugié(e)
refugee camp *n* camp *m* de réfugiés
refund *n* ['ri:fʌnd] remboursement *m* ▷ *vt* [rɪ'fʌnd] rembourser
refurbish [ri:'fə:bɪʃ] *vt* remettre à neuf
refurnish [ri:'fə:nɪʃ] *vt* remeubler
refusal [rɪ'fju:zəl] *n* refus *m*; **to have first ~ on sth** avoir droit de préemption sur qch
refuse¹ ['rɛfju:s] *n* ordures *fpl*, détritus *mpl*
refuse² [rɪ'fju:z] *vt, vi* refuser; **to ~ to do sth** refuser de faire qch
refuse collection *n* ramassage *m* d'ordures
refuse disposal *n* élimination *f* des ordures
refusenik [rɪ'fju:znɪk] *n* refuznik *m/f*
refute [rɪ'fju:t] *vt* réfuter
regain [rɪ'geɪn] *vt* (*lost ground*) regagner; (*strength*) retrouver
regal ['ri:gl] *adj* royal(e)
regale [rɪ'geɪl] *vt*: **to ~ sb with sth** régaler qn de qch
regalia [rɪ'geɪlɪə] *n* insignes *mpl* de la royauté
regard [rɪ'gɑ:d] *n* respect *m*, estime *f*, considération *f* ▷ *vt* considérer; **to give one's ~s to** faire ses amitiés à; **"with kindest ~s"** "bien amicalement"; **as ~s, with ~ to** en ce qui concerne
regarding [rɪ'gɑ:dɪŋ] *prep* en ce qui concerne
regardless [rɪ'gɑ:dlɪs] *adv* quand même; **~ of** sans se soucier de
regatta [rɪ'gætə] *n* régate *f*
regency ['ri:dʒənsɪ] *n* régence *f*
regenerate [rɪ'dʒɛnəreɪt] *vt* régénérer ▷ *vi* se régénérer
regent ['ri:dʒənt] *n* régent(e)
reggae ['rɛgeɪ] *n* reggae *m*
régime [reɪ'ʒi:m] *n* régime *m*

regiment ['rɛdʒɪmənt] *n* régiment *m* ▷ *vt* ['rɛdʒɪmɛnt] imposer une discipline trop stricte à
regimental [rɛdʒɪ'mɛntl] *adj* d'un régiment
regimentation [rɛdʒɪmɛn'teɪʃən] *n* réglementation excessive
region ['ri:dʒən] *n* région *f*; **in the ~ of** (*fig*) aux alentours de
regional ['ri:dʒənl] *adj* régional(e)
regional development *n* aménagement *m* du territoire
register ['rɛdʒɪstəʳ] *n* registre *m*; (*also*: **electoral register**) liste électorale ▷ *vt* enregistrer, inscrire; (*birth*) déclarer; (*vehicle*) immatriculer; (*luggage*) enregistrer; (*letter*) envoyer en recommandé; (*subj: instrument*) marquer ▷ *vi* s'inscrire; (*at hotel*) signer le registre; (*make impression*) être (bien) compris(e); **to ~ for a course** s'inscrire à un cours; **to ~ a protest** protester
registered ['rɛdʒɪstəd] *adj* (*design*) déposé(e); (*Brit: letter*) recommandé(e); (*student, voter*) inscrit(e)
registered company *n* société immatriculée
registered nurse *n* (*US*) infirmier(-ière) diplômé(e) d'État
registered office *n* siège social
registered trademark *n* marque déposée
registrar ['rɛdʒɪstrɑ:ʳ] *n* officier *m* de l'état civil; secrétaire *m/f* général
registration [rɛdʒɪs'treɪʃən] *n* (*act*) enregistrement *m*; (*of student*) inscription *f*; (*Brit Aut: also*: **registration number**) numéro *m* d'immatriculation
registry ['rɛdʒɪstrɪ] *n* bureau *m* de l'enregistrement
registry office ['rɛdʒɪstrɪ-] *n* (*Brit*) bureau *m* de l'état civil; **to get married in a ~** ≈ se marier à la mairie
regret [rɪ'grɛt] *n* regret *m* ▷ *vt* regretter; **to ~ that** regretter que + *sub*; **we ~ to inform you that ...** nous sommes au regret de vous informer que ...
regretfully [rɪ'grɛtfəlɪ] *adv* à *or* avec regret
regrettable [rɪ'grɛtəbl] *adj* regrettable, fâcheux(-euse)
regrettably [rɪ'grɛtəblɪ] *adv* (*drunk, late*) fâcheusement; **~, he ...** malheureusement, il ...
regroup [ri:'gru:p] *vt* regrouper ▷ *vi* se regrouper
regt *abbr* = **regiment**
regular ['rɛgjuləʳ] *adj* régulier(-ière); (*usual*) habituel(le), normal(e); (*listener, reader*) fidèle; (*soldier*) de métier; (*Comm: size*) ordinaire ▷ *n* (*client etc*) habitué(e)
regularity [rɛgju'lærɪtɪ] *n* régularité *f*
regularly ['rɛgjuləlɪ] *adv* régulièrement
regulate ['rɛgjuleɪt] *vt* régler
regulation [rɛgju'leɪʃən] *n* (*rule*) règlement *m*; (*adjustment*) réglage *m* ▷ *cpd* réglementaire
rehabilitate [ri:ə'bɪlɪteɪt] *vt* (*criminal*) réinsérer; (*drug addict*) désintoxiquer; (*invalid*) rééduquer

rehabilitation ['ri:əbɪlɪ'teɪʃən] n (of offender) réhabilitation f; (of addict) réadaptation f; (of disabled) rééducation f, réadaptation f
rehash [ri:'hæʃ] vt (inf) remanier
rehearsal [rɪ'hə:səl] n répétition f; **dress ~** (répétition) générale f
rehearse [rɪ'hə:s] vt répéter
rehouse [ri:'hauz] vt reloger
reign [reɪn] n règne m ▷ vi régner
reigning ['reɪnɪŋ] adj (monarch) régnant(e); (champion) actuel(le)
reimburse [ri:ɪm'bə:s] vt rembourser
rein [reɪn] n (for horse) rêne f; **to give sb free ~** (fig) donner carte blanche à qn
reincarnation [ri:ɪnkɑ:'neɪʃən] n réincarnation f
reindeer ['reɪndɪər] n (pl inv) renne m
reinforce [ri:ɪn'fɔ:s] vt renforcer
reinforced concrete [ri:ɪn'fɔst-] n béton armé
reinforcement [ri:ɪn'fɔ:smənt] n (action) renforcement m
reinforcements [ri:ɪn'fɔ:smənts] npl (Mil) renfort(s) m(pl)
reinstate [ri:ɪn'steɪt] vt rétablir, réintégrer
reinstatement [ri:ɪn'steɪtmənt] n réintégration f
reissue [ri:'ɪʃju:] vt (book) rééditer; (film) ressortir
reiterate [ri:'ɪtəreɪt] vt réitérer, répéter
reject n ['ri:dʒɛkt] (Comm) article m de rebut ▷ vt [rɪ'dʒɛkt] refuser; (Comm: goods) mettre au rebut; (idea) rejeter
rejection [rɪ'dʒɛkʃən] n rejet m, refus m
rejoice [rɪ'dʒɔɪs] vi: **to ~ (at or over)** se réjouir (de)
rejoinder [rɪ'dʒɔɪndər] n (retort) réplique f
rejuvenate [rɪ'dʒu:vəneɪt] vt rajeunir
rekindle [ri:'kɪndl] vt rallumer; (fig) raviver
relapse [rɪ'læps] n (Med) rechute f
relate [rɪ'leɪt] vt (tell) raconter; (connect) établir un rapport entre ▷ vi: **to ~ to** (connect) se rapporter à; **to ~ to sb** (interact) entretenir des rapports avec qn
related [rɪ'leɪtɪd] adj apparenté(e), **~ to** (subject) lié(e) à
relating to [rɪ'leɪtɪŋ-] prep concernant
relation [rɪ'leɪʃən] n (person) parent(e); (link) rapport m, lien m; **relations** npl (relatives) famille f; **diplomatic/international ~s** relations diplomatiques/internationales; **in ~ to** en ce qui concerne; par rapport à; **to bear no ~ to** être sans rapport avec
relationship [rɪ'leɪʃənʃɪp] n rapport m, lien m; (personal ties) relations fpl, rapports; (also: **family relationship**) lien de parenté; (affair) liaison f; **they have a good ~** ils s'entendent bien
relative ['rɛlətɪv] n parent(e) ▷ adj relatif(-ive); (respective) respectif(-ive); **all her ~s** toute sa famille
relatively ['rɛlətɪvlɪ] adv relativement
relax [rɪ'læks] vi (muscle) se relâcher; (person: unwind) se détendre; (calm down) se calmer ▷ vt relâcher; (mind, person) détendre

relaxation [ri:læk'seɪʃən] n relâchement m; (of mind) détente f; (recreation) détente, délassement m; (entertainment) distraction f
relaxed [rɪ'lækst] adj relâché(e); détendu(e)
relaxing [rɪ'læksɪŋ] adj délassant(e)
relay ['ri:leɪ] n (Sport) course f de relais ▷ vt (message) retransmettre, relayer
release [rɪ'li:s] n (from prison, obligation) libération f; (of gas etc) émission f; (of film etc) sortie f; (new recording) disque m; (device) déclencheur m ▷ vt (prisoner) libérer; (book, film) sortir; (report, news) rendre public, publier; (gas etc) émettre, dégager; (free: from wreckage etc) dégager; (Tech: catch, spring etc) déclencher; (let go: person, animal) relâcher; (: hand, object) lâcher; (: grip, brake) desserrer; **to ~ one's grip** or **hold** lâcher prise; **to ~ the clutch** (Aut) débrayer
relegate ['rɛləgeɪt] vt reléguer; (Brit Sport): **to be ~d** descendre dans une division inférieure
relent [rɪ'lɛnt] vi se laisser fléchir
relentless [rɪ'lɛntlɪs] adj implacable; (non-stop) continuel(le)
relevance ['rɛləvəns] n pertinence f; **~ of sth to sth** rapport m entre qch et qch
relevant ['rɛləvənt] adj (question) pertinent(e); (corresponding) approprié(e); (fact) significatif(-ive); (information) utile; **~ to** ayant rapport à, approprié à
reliability [rɪlaɪə'bɪlɪtɪ] n sérieux m; fiabilité f
reliable [rɪ'laɪəbl] adj (person, firm) sérieux(-euse), fiable; (method, machine) fiable; (news, information) sûr(e)
reliably [rɪ'laɪəblɪ] adv: **to be ~ informed** savoir de source sûre
reliance [rɪ'laɪəns] n: **~ (on)** (trust) confiance f (en); (dependence) besoin m (de), dépendance f (de)
reliant [rɪ'laɪənt] adj: **to be ~ on sth/sb** dépendre de qch/qn
relic ['rɛlɪk] n (Rel) relique f; (of the past) vestige m
relief [rɪ'li:f] n (from pain, anxiety) soulagement m; (help, supplies) secours m(pl); (of guard) relève f; (Art, Geo) relief m; **by way of light ~** pour faire diversion
relief map n carte f en relief
relief road n (Brit) route f de délestage
relieve [rɪ'li:v] vt (pain, patient) soulager; (fear, worry) dissiper; (bring help) secourir; (take over from: gen) relayer; (: guard) relever; **to ~ sb of sth** débarrasser qn de qch; **to ~ sb of his command** (Mil) relever qn de ses fonctions; **to ~ o.s.** (euphemism) se soulager, faire ses besoins
relieved [rɪ'li:vd] adj soulagé(e); **to be ~ that ...** être soulagé que ...; **I'm ~ to hear it** je suis soulagé de l'entendre
religion [rɪ'lɪdʒən] n religion f
religious [rɪ'lɪdʒəs] adj religieux(-euse); (book) de piété
religious education n instruction religieuse
relinquish [rɪ'lɪŋkwɪʃ] vt abandonner; (plan, habit) renoncer à
relish ['rɛlɪʃ] n (Culin) condiment m; (enjoyment)

délectation f ⊳ vt (food etc) savourer; **to ~ doing** se délecter à faire
relive [riː'lɪv] vt revivre
reload [riː'ləud] vt recharger
relocate [riːləu'keɪt] vt (business) transférer ⊳ vi se transférer, s'installer or s'établir ailleurs; **to ~ in** (déménager et) s'installer or s'établir à, se transférer à
reluctance [rɪ'lʌktəns] n répugnance f
reluctant [rɪ'lʌktənt] adj peu disposé(e), qui hésite; **to be ~ to do sth** hésiter à faire qch
reluctantly [rɪ'lʌktəntlɪ] adv à contrecœur, sans enthousiasme
rely on [rɪ'laɪ-] vt fus (be dependent on) dépendre de; (trust) compter sur
remain [rɪ'meɪn] vi rester; **to ~ silent** garder le silence; **I ~, yours faithfully** (Brit: in letters) je vous prie d'agréer, Monsieur etc l'assurance de mes sentiments distingués
remainder [rɪ'meɪndə^r] n reste m; (Comm) fin f de série
remaining [rɪ'meɪnɪŋ] adj qui reste
remains [rɪ'meɪnz] npl restes mpl
remake ['riːmeɪk] n (Cine) remake m
remand [rɪ'mɑːnd] n: **on ~** en détention préventive ⊳ vt: **to be ~ed in custody** être placé(e) en détention préventive
remand home n (Brit) centre m d'éducation surveillée
remark [rɪ'mɑːk] n remarque f, observation f ⊳ vt (faire) remarquer, dire; (notice) remarquer; **to ~ on sth** faire une or des remarque(s) sur qch
remarkable [rɪ'mɑːkəbl] adj remarquable
remarkably [rɪ'mɑːkəblɪ] adv remarquablement
remarry [riː'mærɪ] vi se remarier
remedial [rɪ'miːdɪəl] adj (tuition, classes) de rattrapage
remedy ['rɛmədɪ] n: **~ (for)** remède m (contre or à) ⊳ vt remédier à
remember [rɪ'mɛmbə^r] vt se rappeler, se souvenir de; (send greetings): **~ me to him** saluez-le de ma part; **I ~ seeing it, I ~ having seen it** je me rappelle l'avoir vu or que je l'ai vu; **she ~ed to do it** elle a pensé à le faire; **~ me to your wife** rappelez-moi au bon souvenir de votre femme
remembrance [rɪ'mɛmbrəns] n souvenir m; mémoire f
Remembrance Day [rɪ'mɛmbrəns-] n (Brit) ≈ (le jour de) l'Armistice m, ≈ le 11 novembre; voir article

● **REMEMBRANCE DAY**
●
● Remembrance Day ou Remembrance Sunday est le
● dimanche le plus proche du 11 novembre,
● jour où la Première Guerre mondiale a
● officiellement pris fin. Il rend hommage
● aux victimes des deux guerres mondiales. À
● cette occasion, on observe deux minutes de
● silence à 11h, heure de la signature de

● l'armistice avec l'Allemagne en 1918;
● certaines membres de la famille royale et du
● gouvernement déposent des gerbes de
● coquelicots au cénotaphe de Whitehall, et
● des couronnes sont placées sur les
● monuments aux morts dans toute la
● Grande-Bretagne; par ailleurs, les gens
● portent des coquelicots artificiels fabriqués
● et vendus par des membres de la légion
● britannique blessés au combat, au profit des
● blessés de guerre et de leur famille.

remind [rɪ'maɪnd] vt: **to ~ sb of sth** rappeler qch à qn; **to ~ sb to do** faire penser à qn à faire, rappeler à qn qu'il doit faire; **that ~s me!** j'y pense!
reminder [rɪ'maɪndə^r] n (Comm: letter) rappel m; (note etc) pense-bête m; (souvenir) souvenir m
reminisce [rɛmɪ'nɪs] vi: **to ~ (about)** évoquer ses souvenirs (de)
reminiscences [rɛmɪ'nɪsnsɪz] npl réminiscences fpl, souvenirs mpl
reminiscent [rɛmɪ'nɪsnt] adj: **~ of** qui rappelle, qui fait penser à
remiss [rɪ'mɪs] adj négligent(e); **it was ~ of me** c'était une négligence de ma part
remission [rɪ'mɪʃən] n rémission f; (of debt, sentence) remise f; (of fee) exemption f
remit [rɪ'mɪt] vt (send: money) envoyer
remittance [rɪ'mɪtns] n envoi m, paiement m
remnant ['rɛmnənt] n reste m, restant m; (of cloth) coupon m; **remnants** npl (Comm) fins fpl de série
remonstrate ['rɛmənstreɪt] vi: **to ~ (with sb about sth)** se plaindre (à qn de qch)
remorse [rɪ'mɔːs] n remords m
remorseful [rɪ'mɔːsful] adj plein(e) de remords
remorseless [rɪ'mɔːslɪs] adj (fig) impitoyable
remote [rɪ'məut] adj éloigné(e), lointain(e); (person) distant(e); (possibility) vague; **there is a ~ possibility that ...** il est tout juste possible que ...
remote control n télécommande f
remote-controlled [rɪ'məutkən'trəuld] adj téléguidé(e)
remotely [rɪ'məutlɪ] adv au loin; (slightly) très vaguement
remould ['riːməuld] n (Brit: tyre) pneu m rechapé
removable [rɪ'muːvəbl] adj (detachable) amovible
removal [rɪ'muːvəl] n (taking away) enlèvement m; suppression f; (Brit: from house) déménagement m; (from office: dismissal) renvoi m; (of stain) nettoyage m; (Med) ablation f
removal man (irreg) n (Brit) déménageur m
removal van n (Brit) camion m de déménagement
remove [rɪ'muːv] vt enlever, retirer; (employee) renvoyer; (stain) faire partir; (abuse) supprimer; (doubt) chasser; **first cousin once ~d** cousin(e) au deuxième degré
remover [rɪ'muːvə^r] n (for paint) décapant m; (for

varnish) dissolvant *m*; **make-up ~** démaquillant *m*

remunerate [rɪˈmjuːnəreɪt] *vt* rémunérer

remuneration [rɪmjuːnəˈreɪʃən] *n* rémunération *f*

Renaissance [rɪˈneɪsɑ̃s] *n*: **the ~** la Renaissance

rename [riːˈneɪm] *vt* rebaptiser

rend *(pt, pp* **rent)** [rɛnd, rɛnt] *vt* déchirer

render [ˈrɛndəʳ] *vt* rendre; *(Culin: fat)* clarifier

rendering [ˈrɛndərɪŋ] *n (Mus etc)* interprétation *f*

rendezvous [ˈrɒndɪvuː] *n* rendez-vous *m inv* ▷ *vi* opérer une jonction, se rejoindre; **to ~ with sb** rejoindre qn

renegade [ˈrɛnɪgeɪd] *n* renégat(e)

renew [rɪˈnjuː] *vt* renouveler; *(negotiations)* reprendre; *(acquaintance)* renouer

renewable [rɪˈnjuːəbl] *adj* renouvelable; **~ energy, ~s** énergies renouvelables

renewal [rɪˈnjuːəl] *n* renouvellement *m*; reprise *f*

renounce [rɪˈnauns] *vt* renoncer à; *(disown)* renier

renovate [ˈrɛnəveɪt] *vt* rénover; *(work of art)* restaurer

renovation [rɛnəˈveɪʃən] *n* rénovation *f*; restauration *f*

renown [rɪˈnaun] *n* renommée *f*

renowned [rɪˈnaund] *adj* renommé(e)

rent [rɛnt] *pt, pp of* **rend** ▷ *n* loyer *m* ▷ *vt* louer; *(car, TV)* louer, prendre en location; *(also:* **rent out**: *car, TV)* louer, donner en location

rental [ˈrɛntl] *n (for television, car)* (prix *m* de) location *f*

rent boy *n (Brit inf)* jeune prostitué

renunciation [rɪnʌnsɪˈeɪʃən] *n* renonciation *f*; *(self-denial)* renoncement *m*

reopen [riːˈəupən] *vt* rouvrir

reorder [riːˈɔːdəʳ] *vt* commander de nouveau; *(rearrange)* réorganiser

reorganize [riːˈɔːgənaɪz] *vt* réorganiser

rep [rɛp] *n abbr (Comm)* = **representative**; *(Theat)* = **repertory**

Rep. *abbr (US Pol)* = **representative**; **republican**

repair [rɪˈpɛəʳ] *n* réparation *f* ▷ *vt* réparer; **in good/bad ~** en bon/mauvais état; **under ~** en réparation; **where can I get this ~ed?** où est-ce que je peux faire réparer ceci?

repair kit *n* trousse *f* de réparations

repair man *(irreg) n* réparateur *m*

repair shop *n (Aut etc)* atelier *m* de réparations

repartee [rɛpɑːˈtiː] *n* repartie *f*

repast [rɪˈpɑːst] *n (formal)* repas *m*

repatriate [riːˈpætrɪeɪt] *vt* rapatrier

repay [riːˈpeɪ] *vt (irreg: like* **pay***)*; *(money, creditor)* rembourser; *(sb's efforts)* récompenser

repayment [riːˈpeɪmənt] *n* remboursement *m*; récompense *f*

repeal [rɪˈpiːl] *n (of law)* abrogation *f*; *(of sentence)* annulation *f* ▷ *vt* abroger; annuler

repeat [rɪˈpiːt] *n (Radio, TV)* reprise *f* ▷ *vt* répéter; *(pattern)* reproduire; *(promise, attack, also Comm:*

order) renouveler; *(Scol: a class)* redoubler ▷ *vi* répéter; **can you ~ that, please?** pouvez-vous répéter, s'il vous plaît?

repeatedly [rɪˈpiːtɪdlɪ] *adv* souvent, à plusieurs reprises

repeat prescription *n (Brit)*: **I'd like a ~** je voudrais renouveler mon ordonnance

repel [rɪˈpɛl] *vt* repousser

repellent [rɪˈpɛlənt] *adj* repoussant(e) ▷ *n*: **insect ~** insectifuge *m*; **moth ~** produit *m* antimite(s)

repent [rɪˈpɛnt] *vi*: **to ~ (of)** se repentir (de)

repentance [rɪˈpɛntəns] *n* repentir *m*

repercussions [riːpəˈkʌʃənz] *npl* répercussions *fpl*

repertoire [ˈrɛpətwɑːʳ] *n* répertoire *m*

repertory [ˈrɛpətərɪ] *n (also:* **repertory theatre***)* théâtre *m* de répertoire

repertory company *n* troupe théâtrale permanente

repetition [rɛpɪˈtɪʃən] *n* répétition *f*

repetitious [rɛpɪˈtɪʃəs] *adj (speech)* plein(e) de redites

repetitive [rɪˈpɛtɪtɪv] *adj (movement, work)* répétitif(-ive); *(speech)* plein(e) de redites

replace [rɪˈpleɪs] *vt (put back)* remettre, replacer; *(take the place of)* remplacer; *(Tel)*: **"~ the receiver"** "raccrochez"

replacement [rɪˈpleɪsmənt] *n* replacement *m*; *(substitution)* remplacement *m*; *(person)* remplaçant(e)

replacement part *n* pièce *f* de rechange

replay [ˈriːpleɪ] *n (of match)* match rejoué; *(of tape, film)* répétition *f*

replenish [rɪˈplɛnɪʃ] *vt (glass)* remplir (de nouveau); *(stock etc)* réapprovisionner

replete [rɪˈpliːt] *adj* rempli(e); *(well-fed)*: **~ (with)** rassasié(e) (de)

replica [ˈrɛplɪkə] *n* réplique *f*, copie exacte

reply [rɪˈplaɪ] *n* réponse *f* ▷ *vi* répondre; **in ~ (to)** en réponse (à); **there's no ~** *(Tel)* ça ne répond pas

reply coupon *n* coupon-réponse *m*

report [rɪˈpɔːt] *n* rapport *m*; *(Press etc)* reportage *m*; *(Brit: also:* **school report***)* bulletin *m* (scolaire); *(of gun)* détonation *f* ▷ *vt* rapporter, faire un compte rendu de; *(Press etc)* faire un reportage sur; *(notify: accident)* signaler; *(: culprit)* dénoncer ▷ *vi (make a report)* faire un rapport; *(for newspaper)* faire un reportage (sur); **I'd like to ~ a theft** je voudrais signaler un vol; *(present o.s.)*: **to ~ (to sb)** se présenter (chez qn); **it is ~ed that** on dit *or* annonce que; **it is ~ed from Berlin that** on nous apprend de Berlin que

report card *n (US, Scottish)* bulletin *m* (scolaire)

reportedly [rɪˈpɔːtɪdlɪ] *adv*: **she is ~ living in Spain** elle habiterait en Espagne; **he ~ told them to ...** il leur aurait dit de ...

reported speech *n (Ling)* discours indirect

reporter [rɪˈpɔːtəʳ] *n* reporter *m*

repose [rɪˈpəuz] *n*: **in ~** en *or* au repos

repossess [riːpəˈzɛs] *vt* saisir

repossession order [ri:pə'zɛʃən-] n ordre m de reprise de possession

reprehensible [rɛprɪ'hɛnsɪbl] adj répréhensible

represent [rɛprɪ'zɛnt] vt représenter; (view, belief) présenter, expliquer; (describe): **to ~ sth as** présenter or décrire qch comme; **to ~ to sb that** expliquer à qn que

representation [rɛprɪzɛn'teɪʃən] n représentation f; **representations** npl (protest) démarche f

representative [rɛprɪ'zɛntətɪv] n représentant(e); (Comm) représentant(e) (de commerce); (US Pol) député m ▷ adj représentatif(-ive), caractéristique

repress [rɪ'prɛs] vt réprimer

repression [rɪ'prɛʃən] n répression f

repressive [rɪ'prɛsɪv] adj répressif(-ive)

reprieve [rɪ'pri:v] n (Law) grâce f; (fig) sursis m, délai m ▷ vt gracier; accorder un sursis or un délai à

reprimand ['rɛprɪmɑ:nd] n réprimande f ▷ vt réprimander

reprint n ['ri:prɪnt] réimpression f ▷ vt [ri:'prɪnt] réimprimer

reprisal [rɪ'praɪzl] n représailles fpl; **to take ~s** user de représailles

reproach [rɪ'prəutʃ] n reproche m ▷ vt: **to ~ sb with sth** reprocher qch à qn; **beyond ~** irréprochable

reproachful [rɪ'prəutʃful] adj de reproche

reproduce [ri:prə'dju:s] vt reproduire ▷ vi se reproduire

reproduction [ri:prə'dʌkʃən] n reproduction f

reproductive [ri:prə'dʌktɪv] adj reproducteur(-trice)

reproof [rɪ'pru:f] n reproche m

reprove [rɪ'pru:v] vt (action) réprouver; (person): **to ~ (for)** blâmer (de)

reproving [rɪ'pru:vɪŋ] adj réprobateur(-trice)

reptile ['rɛptaɪl] n reptile m

Repub. abbr (US Pol) = **republican**

republic [rɪ'pʌblɪk] n république f

republican [rɪ'pʌblɪkən] adj, n républicain(e)

repudiate [rɪ'pju:dɪeɪt] vt (ally, behaviour) désavouer; (accusation) rejeter; (wife) répudier

repugnant [rɪ'pʌgnənt] adj répugnant(e)

repulse [rɪ'pʌls] vt repousser

repulsion [rɪ'pʌlʃən] n répulsion f

repulsive [rɪ'pʌlsɪv] adj repoussant(e), répulsif(-ive)

reputable ['rɛpjutəbl] adj de bonne réputation; (occupation) honorable

reputation [rɛpju'teɪʃən] n réputation f; **to have a ~ for** être réputé(e) pour; **he has a ~ for being awkward** il a la réputation de ne pas être commode

repute [rɪ'pju:t] n (bonne) réputation

reputed [rɪ'pju:tɪd] adj réputé(e); **he is ~ to be rich/intelligent** etc on dit qu'il est riche/intelligent etc

reputedly [rɪ'pju:tɪdlɪ] adv d'après ce qu'on dit

request [rɪ'kwɛst] n demande f; (formal) requête f ▷ vt: **to ~ (of or from sb)** demander (à qn); **at the ~ of** à la demande de

request stop n (Brit: for bus) arrêt facultatif

requiem ['rɛkwɪəm] n requiem m

require [rɪ'kwaɪəʳ] vt (need: subj: person) avoir besoin de; (: thing, situation) nécessiter, demander; (want) exiger; (order): **to ~ sb to do sth/sth of sb** exiger que qn fasse qch/qch de qn; **if ~d** s'il le faut; **what qualifications are ~d?** quelles sont les qualifications requises?; **~d by law** requis par la loi

required [rɪ'kwaɪəd] adj requis(e), voulu(e)

requirement [rɪ'kwaɪəmənt] n (need) exigence f; besoin m; (condition) condition f (requise)

requisite ['rɛkwɪzɪt] n chose f nécessaire ▷ adj requis(e), nécessaire; **toilet ~s** accessoires mpl de toilette

requisition [rɛkwɪ'zɪʃən] n: **~ (for)** demande f (de) ▷ vt (Mil) réquisitionner

reroute [ri:'ru:t] vt (train etc) dérouter

resale ['ri:'seɪl] n revente f

resale price maintenance n vente au détail à prix imposé

resat [ri:'sæt] pt, pp of **resit**

rescind [rɪ'sɪnd] vt annuler; (law) abroger; (judgment) rescinder

rescue ['rɛskju:] n (from accident) sauvetage m; (help) secours mpl ▷ vt sauver; **to come to sb's ~** venir au secours de qn

rescue party n équipe f de sauvetage

rescuer ['rɛskjuəʳ] n sauveteur m

research [rɪ'sə:tʃ] n recherche(s) f(pl) ▷ vt faire des recherches sur ▷ vi: **to ~ (into sth)** faire des recherches (sur qch); **a piece of ~** un travail de recherche; **~ and development (R & D)** recherche-développement (R-D)

researcher [rɪ'sə:tʃəʳ] n chercheur(-euse)

research work n recherches fpl

resell [ri:'sɛl] vt (irreg: like **sell**) revendre

resemblance [rɪ'zɛmbləns] n ressemblance f; **to bear a strong ~ to** ressembler beaucoup à

resemble [rɪ'zɛmbl] vt ressembler à

resent [rɪ'zɛnt] vt éprouver du ressentiment de, être contrarié(e) par

resentful [rɪ'zɛntful] adj irrité(e), plein(e) de ressentiment

resentment [rɪ'zɛntmənt] n ressentiment m

reservation [rɛzə'veɪʃən] n (booking) réservation f; (doubt, protected area) réserve f; (Brit Aut: also: **central reservation**) bande médiane; **to make a ~ (in an hotel/a restaurant/on a plane)** réserver or retenir une chambre/une table/une place; **with ~s** (doubts) avec certaines réserves

reservation desk n (US: in hotel) réception f

reserve [rɪ'zə:v] n réserve f; (Sport) remplaçant(e) ▷ vt (seats etc) réserver, retenir; **reserves** npl (Mil) réservistes mpl; **in ~** en réserve

reserve currency n monnaie f de réserve

reserved [rɪ'zə:vd] adj réservé(e)

reserve price n (Brit) mise f à prix, prix m de départ

reserve team n (Brit Sport) deuxième équipe f
reservist [rɪ'zəːvɪst] n (Mil) réserviste m
reservoir ['rɛzəvwɑːʳ] n réservoir m
reset [riː'sɛt] vt (irreg: like **set**) remettre; (clock, watch) mettre à l'heure; (Comput) remettre à zéro
reshape [riː'ʃeɪp] vt (policy) réorganiser
reshuffle [riː'ʃʌfl] n: **Cabinet ~** (Pol) remaniement ministériel
reside [rɪ'zaɪd] vi résider
residence ['rɛzɪdəns] n résidence f; **to take up ~** s'installer; **in ~** (queen etc) en résidence; (doctor) résidant(e)
residence permit n (Brit) permis m de séjour
resident ['rɛzɪdənt] n (of country) résident(e); (of area, house) habitant(e); (in hotel) pensionnaire ▷ adj résidant(e)
residential [rɛzɪ'dɛnʃəl] adj de résidence; (area) résidentiel(le); (course) avec hébergement sur place
residential school n internat m
residue ['rɛzɪdjuː] n reste m; (Chem, Physics) résidu m
resign [rɪ'zaɪn] vt (one's post) se démettre de ▷ vi démissionner; **to ~ o.s. to** (endure) se résigner à
resignation [rɛzɪg'neɪʃən] n (from post) démission f; (state of mind) résignation f; **to tender one's ~** donner sa démission
resigned [rɪ'zaɪnd] adj résigné(e)
resilience [rɪ'zɪlɪəns] n (of material) élasticité f; (of person) ressort m
resilient [rɪ'zɪlɪənt] adj (person) qui réagit, qui a du ressort
resin ['rɛzɪn] n résine f
resist [rɪ'zɪst] vt résister à
resistance [rɪ'zɪstəns] n résistance f
resistant [rɪ'zɪstənt] adj: **~ (to)** résistant(e) (à)
resit vt [riː'sɪt] (Brit: pt, pp **resat**) (exam) repasser ▷ n ['riːsɪt] deuxième session f (d'un examen)
resolute ['rɛzəluːt] adj résolu(e)
resolution [rɛzə'luːʃən] n résolution f; **to make a ~** prendre une résolution
resolve [rɪ'zɔlv] n résolution f ▷ vt (decide): **to ~ to do** résoudre or décider de faire; (problem) résoudre
resolved [rɪ'zɔlvd] adj résolu(e)
resonance ['rɛzənəns] n résonance f
resonant ['rɛzənənt] adj résonnant(e)
resort [rɪ'zɔːt] n (seaside town) station f balnéaire; (for skiing) station de ski; (recourse) recours m ▷ vi: **to ~ to** avoir recours à; **in the last ~** en dernier ressort
resound [rɪ'zaund] vi: **to ~ (with)** retentir (de)
resounding [rɪ'zaundɪŋ] adj retentissant(e)
resource [rɪ'sɔːs] n ressource f; **resources** npl ressources; **natural ~s** ressources naturelles; **to leave sb to his (or her) own ~s** (fig) livrer qn à lui-même (or elle-même)
resourceful [rɪ'sɔːsful] adj ingénieux(-euse), débrouillard(e)
resourcefulness [rɪ'sɔːsfəlnɪs] n ressource f
respect [rɪs'pɛkt] n respect m; (point, detail): **in**

some ~s à certains égards ▷ vt respecter;
respects npl respects, hommages mpl; **to have** or **show ~ for sb/sth** respecter qn/qch; **out of ~ for** par respect pour; **with ~ to** en ce qui concerne; **in ~ of** sous le rapport de, quant à; **in this ~** sous ce rapport, à cet égard; **with due ~ I** ... malgré le respect que je vous dois, je ...
respectability [rɪspɛktə'bɪlɪtɪ] n respectabilité f
respectable [rɪs'pɛktəbl] adj respectable; (quite good: result etc) honorable; (player) assez bon (bonne)
respectful [rɪs'pɛktful] adj respectueux(-euse)
respective [rɪs'pɛktɪv] adj respectif(-ive)
respectively [rɪs'pɛktɪvlɪ] adv respectivement
respiration [rɛspɪ'reɪʃən] n respiration f
respirator ['rɛspɪreɪtəʳ] n respirateur m
respiratory ['rɛspərətərɪ] adj respiratoire
respite ['rɛspaɪt] n répit m
resplendent [rɪs'plɛndənt] adj resplendissant(e)
respond [rɪs'pɔnd] vi répondre; (react) réagir
respondent [rɪs'pɔndənt] n (Law) défendeur(-deresse)
response [rɪs'pɔns] n réponse f; (reaction) réaction f; **in ~ to** en réponse à
responsibility [rɪspɔnsɪ'bɪlɪtɪ] n responsabilité f; **to take ~ for sth/sb** accepter la responsabilité de qch/d'être responsable de qn
responsible [rɪs'pɔnsɪbl] adj (liable): **~ (for)** responsable (de); (person) digne de confiance; (job) qui comporte des responsabilités; **to be ~ to sb (for sth)** être responsable devant qn (de qch)
responsibly [rɪs'pɔnsɪblɪ] adv avec sérieux
responsive [rɪs'pɔnsɪv] adj (student, audience) réceptif(-ive); (brakes, steering) sensible
rest [rɛst] n repos m; (stop) arrêt m, pause f; (Mus) silence m; (support) support m, appui m; (remainder) reste m, restant m ▷ vi se reposer; (be supported): **to ~ on** appuyer or reposer sur; (remain) rester ▷ vt (lean): **to ~ sth on/against** appuyer qch sur/contre; **the ~ of them** les autres; **to set sb's mind at ~** tranquilliser qn; **it ~s with him to** c'est à lui de; **~ assured that** ... soyez assuré que ...
restart [riː'stɑːt] vt (engine) remettre en marche; (work) reprendre
restaurant ['rɛstərɔŋ] n restaurant m
restaurant car n (Brit Rail) wagon-restaurant m
rest cure n cure f de repos
restful ['rɛstful] adj reposant(e)
rest home n maison f de repos
restitution [rɛstɪ'tjuːʃən] n (act) restitution f; (reparation) réparation f
restive ['rɛstɪv] adj agité(e), impatient(e); (horse) rétif(-ive)
restless ['rɛstlɪs] adj agité(e); **to get ~** s'impatienter
restlessly ['rɛstlɪslɪ] adv avec agitation
restock [riː'stɔk] vt réapprovisionner
restoration [rɛstə'reɪʃən] n (of building) restauration f; (of stolen goods) restitution f

restorative [rɪˈstɔrətɪv] *adj* reconstituant(e) ▷ *n* reconstituant *m*

restore [rɪˈstɔːʳ] *vt* (*building*) restaurer; (*sth stolen*) restituer; (*peace, health*) rétablir; **to ~ to** (*former state*) ramener à

restorer [rɪˈstɔːrəʳ] *n* (*Art etc*) restaurateur(-trice) (d'œuvres d'art)

restrain [rɪsˈtreɪn] *vt* (*feeling*) contenir; (*person*): **to ~ (from doing)** retenir (de faire)

restrained [rɪsˈtreɪnd] *adj* (*style*) sobre; (*manner*) mesuré(e)

restraint [rɪsˈtreɪnt] *n* (*restriction*) contrainte *f*; (*moderation*) retenue *f*; (*of style*) sobriété *f*; **wage ~** limitations salariales

restrict [rɪsˈtrɪkt] *vt* restreindre, limiter

restricted area [rɪsˈtrɪktɪd-] *n* (*Aut*) zone *f* à vitesse limitée

restriction [rɪsˈtrɪkʃən] *n* restriction *f*, limitation *f*

restrictive [rɪsˈtrɪktɪv] *adj* restrictif(-ive)

restrictive practices *npl* (*Industry*) pratiques *fpl* entravant la libre concurrence

rest room *n* (*US*) toilettes *fpl*

restructure [riːˈstrʌktʃəʳ] *vt* restructurer

result [rɪˈzʌlt] *n* résultat *m* ▷ *vi*: **to ~ (from)** résulter (de); **to ~ in** aboutir à, se terminer par; **as a ~ it is too expensive** il en résulte que c'est trop cher; **as a ~ of** à la suite de

resultant [rɪˈzʌltənt] *adj* résultant(e)

resume [rɪˈzjuːm] *vt* (*work, journey*) reprendre; (*sum up*) résumer ▷ *vi* (*work etc*) reprendre

résumé [ˈreɪzjuːmeɪ] *n* (*summary*) résumé *m*; (*US: curriculum vitae*) curriculum vitae *m inv*

resumption [rɪˈzʌmpʃən] *n* reprise *f*

resurgence [rɪˈsəːdʒəns] *n* réapparition *f*

resurrection [rɛzəˈrɛkʃən] *n* résurrection *f*

resuscitate [rɪˈsʌsɪteɪt] *vt* (*Med*) réanimer

resuscitation [rɪsʌsɪˈteɪʃən] *n* réanimation *f*

retail [ˈriːteɪl] *n* (*vente f au*) détail *m* ▷ *adj* de or au détail ▷ *adv* au détail ▷ *vt* vendre au détail ▷ *vi*: **to ~ at 10 euros** se vendre au détail à 10 euros

retailer [ˈriːteɪləʳ] *n* détaillant(e)

retail outlet *n* point *m* de vente

retail price *n* prix *m* de détail

retail price index *n* ≈ indice *m* des prix

retain [rɪˈteɪn] *vt* (*keep*) garder, conserver; (*employ*) engager

retainer [rɪˈteɪnəʳ] *n* (*servant*) serviteur *m*; (*fee*) acompte *m*, provision *f*

retaliate [rɪˈtælɪeɪt] *vi*: **to ~ (against)** se venger (de); **to ~ (on sb)** rendre la pareille (à qn)

retaliation [rɪtælɪˈeɪʃən] *n* représailles *fpl*, vengeance *f*; **in ~ for** par représailles pour

retaliatory [rɪˈtælɪətərɪ] *adj* de représailles

retarded [rɪˈtɑːdɪd] *adj* retardé(e)

retch [rɛtʃ] *vi* avoir des haut-le-cœur

retentive [rɪˈtɛntɪv] *adj*: **~ memory** excellente mémoire

rethink [ˈriːˈθɪŋk] *vt* repenser

reticence [ˈrɛtɪsns] *n* réticence *f*

reticent [ˈrɛtɪsnt] *adj* réticent(e)

retina [ˈrɛtɪnə] *n* rétine *f*

retinue [ˈrɛtɪnjuː] *n* suite *f*, cortège *m*

retire [rɪˈtaɪəʳ] *vi* (*give up work*) prendre sa retraite; (*withdraw*) se retirer, partir; (*go to bed*) (aller) se coucher

retired [rɪˈtaɪəd] *adj* (*person*) retraité(e)

retirement [rɪˈtaɪəmənt] *n* retraite *f*

retirement age *n* âge *m* de la retraite

retiring [rɪˈtaɪərɪŋ] *adj* (*person*) réservé(e); (*chairman etc*) sortant(e)

retort [rɪˈtɔːt] *n* (*reply*) riposte *f*; (*container*) cornue *f* ▷ *vi* riposter

retrace [riːˈtreɪs] *vt* reconstituer; **to ~ one's steps** revenir sur ses pas

retract [rɪˈtrækt] *vt* (*statement, claws*) rétracter; (*undercarriage, aerial*) rentrer, escamoter ▷ *vi* se rétracter; rentrer

retractable [rɪˈtræktəbl] *adj* escamotable

retrain [riːˈtreɪn] *vt* recycler ▷ *vi* se recycler

retraining [riːˈtreɪnɪŋ] *n* recyclage *m*

retread *vt* [riːˈtrɛd] (*Aut: tyre*) rechaper ▷ *n* [ˈriːtrɛd] pneu rechapé

retreat [rɪˈtriːt] *n* retraite *f* ▷ *vi* battre en retraite; (*flood*) reculer; **to beat a hasty ~** (*fig*) partir avec précipitation

retrial [riːˈtraɪəl] *n* nouveau procès

retribution [rɛtrɪˈbjuːʃən] *n* châtiment *m*

retrieval [rɪˈtriːvəl] *n* récupération *f*; réparation *f*; recherche *f* et extraction *f*

retrieve [rɪˈtriːv] *vt* (*sth lost*) récupérer; (*situation, honour*) sauver; (*error, loss*) réparer; (*Comput*) rechercher

retriever [rɪˈtriːvəʳ] *n* chien *m* d'arrêt

retroactive [rɛtrəuˈæktɪv] *adj* rétroactif(-ive)

retrograde [ˈrɛtrəgreɪd] *adj* rétrograde

retrospect [ˈrɛtrəspɛkt] *n*: **in ~** rétrospectivement, après coup

retrospective [rɛtrəˈspɛktɪv] *adj* rétrospectif(-ive); (*law*) rétroactif(-ive) ▷ *n* (*Art*) rétrospective *f*

return [rɪˈtəːn] *n* (*going or coming back*) retour *m*; (*of sth stolen etc*) restitution *f*; (*recompense*) récompense *f*; (*Finance: from land, shares*) rapport *m*; (*report*) relevé *m*, rapport ▷ *cpd* (*journey*) de retour; (*Brit: ticket*) aller et retour; (*match*) retour ▷ *vi* (*person etc: come back*) revenir; (: *go back*) retourner ▷ *vt* rendre; (*bring back*) rapporter; (*send back*) renvoyer; (*put back*) remettre; (*Pol: candidate*) élire; **returns** *npl* (*Comm*) recettes *fpl*; (*Finance*) bénéfices *mpl*; (: *returned goods*) marchandises renvoyées; **many happy ~s (of the day)!** bon anniversaire!; **by ~ (of post)** par retour (du courrier); **in ~ (for)** en échange (de); **a ~ (ticket) for ...** un billet aller et retour pour ...

returnable [rɪˈtəːnəbl] *adj* (*bottle etc*) consigné(e)

returner [rɪˈtəːnəʳ] *n* femme qui reprend un travail après avoir élevé ses enfants

returning officer [rɪˈtəːnɪŋ-] *n* (*Brit Pol*) président *m* de bureau de vote

return key *n* (*Comput*) touche *f* de retour

return ticket *n* (*esp Brit*) billet *m* aller-retour

reunion [ri:'ju:nɪən] *n* réunion *f*
reunite [ri:ju:'naɪt] *vt* réunir
reuse [ri:'ju:z] *vt* réutiliser
rev [rɛv] *n abbr* = **revolution**; (*Aut*) tour *m* ▷ *vt*
(*also*: **rev up**) emballer ▷ *vi* (*also*: **rev up**)
s'emballer
Rev. *abbr* = **reverend**
revaluation [ri:væljuˈeɪʃən] *n* réévaluation *f*
revamp [ri:ˈvæmp] *vt* (*house*) retaper; (*firm*)
réorganiser
rev counter *n* (*Brit*) compte-tours *m inv*
Revd. *abbr* = **reverend**
reveal [rɪˈviːl] *vt* (*make known*) révéler; (*display*)
laisser voir
revealing [rɪˈviːlɪŋ] *adj* révélateur(-trice); (*dress*)
au décolleté généreux *or* suggestif
reveille [rɪˈvælɪ] *n* (*Mil*) réveil *m*
revel ['rɛvl] *vi*: **to ~ in sth/in doing** se délecter
de qch/à faire
revelation [rɛvəˈleɪʃən] *n* révélation *f*
reveller ['rɛvləʳ] *n* fêtard *m*
revelry ['rɛvlrɪ] *n* festivités *fpl*
revenge [rɪˈvɛndʒ] *n* vengeance *f*; (*in game etc*)
revanche *f* ▷ *vt* venger; **to take ~ (on)** se venger
(sur)
revengeful [rɪˈvɛndʒful] *adj* vengeur(-eresse),
vindicatif(-ive)
revenue ['rɛvənjuː] *n* revenu *m*
reverberate [rɪˈvəːbəreɪt] *vi* (*sound*) retentir, se
répercuter; (*light*) se réverbérer
reverberation [rɪvəːbəˈreɪʃən] *n* répercussion *f*;
réverbération *f*
revere [rɪˈvɪəʳ] *vt* vénérer, révérer
reverence ['rɛvərəns] *n* vénération *f*, révérence *f*
Reverend ['rɛvərənd] *adj* vénérable; (*in titles*):
the ~ John Smith (*Anglican*) le révérend John
Smith; (*Catholic*) l'abbé (John) Smith;
(*Protestant*) le pasteur (John) Smith
reverent ['rɛvərənt] *adj* respectueux(-euse)
reverie ['rɛvərɪ] *n* rêverie *f*
reversal [rɪˈvəːsl] *n* (*of opinion*) revirement *m*; (*of
order*) renversement *m*; (*of direction*)
changement *m*
reverse [rɪˈvəːs] *n* contraire *m*, opposé *m*; (*back*)
dos *m*, envers *m*; (*of paper*) verso *m*; (*of coin*) revers
m; (*Aut: also*: **reverse gear**) marche *f* arrière ▷ *adj*
(*order, direction*) opposé(e), inverse ▷ *vt* (*order,
position*) changer, inverser; (*direction, policy*)
changer complètement de; (*decision*) annuler;
(*roles*) renverser; (*car*) faire marche arrière avec;
(*Law: judgment*) réformer ▷ *vi* (*Brit Aut*) faire
marche arrière; **to go into ~** faire marche
arrière; **in ~ order** en ordre inverse
reverse video *n* vidéo *m* inverse
reversible [rɪˈvəːsəbl] *adj* (*garment*) réversible;
(*procedure*) révocable
reversing lights [rɪˈvəːsɪŋ-] *npl* (*Brit Aut*) feux
mpl de marche arrière *or* de recul
reversion [rɪˈvəːʃən] *n* retour *m*
revert [rɪˈvəːt] *vi*: **to ~ to** revenir à, retourner à
review [rɪˈvjuː] *n* revue *f*; (*of book, film*) critique *f*;
(*of situation, policy*) examen *m*, bilan *m*; (*US*:

examination) examen ▷ *vt* passer en revue; faire
la critique de; examiner; **to come under ~** être
révisé(e)
reviewer [rɪˈvjuːəʳ] *n* critique *m*
revile [rɪˈvaɪl] *vt* injurier
revise [rɪˈvaɪz] *vt* réviser, modifier; (*manuscript*)
revoir, corriger ▷ *vi* (*study*) réviser; **~d edition**
édition revue et corrigée
revision [rɪˈvɪʒən] *n* révision *f*; (*revised version*)
version corrigée
revitalize [riːˈvaɪtəlaɪz] *vt* revitaliser
revival [rɪˈvaɪvəl] *n* reprise *f*; (*recovery*)
rétablissement *m*; (*of faith*) renouveau *m*
revive [rɪˈvaɪv] *vt* (*person*) ranimer; (*custom*)
rétablir; (*economy*) relancer; (*hope, courage*)
raviver, faire renaître; (*play, fashion*) reprendre
▷ *vi* (*person*) reprendre connaissance; (: *from ill
health*) se rétablir; (*hope etc*) renaître; (*activity*)
reprendre
revoke [rɪˈvəuk] *vt* révoquer; (*promise, decision*)
revenir sur
revolt [rɪˈvəult] *n* révolte *f* ▷ *vi* se révolter, se
rebeller ▷ *vt* révolter, dégoûter
revolting [rɪˈvəultɪŋ] *adj* dégoûtant(e)
revolution [rɛvəˈluːʃən] *n* révolution *f*; (*of wheel*
etc) tour *m*, révolution
revolutionary [rɛvəˈluːʃənrɪ] *adj, n*
révolutionnaire (*m/f*)
revolutionize [rɛvəˈluːʃənaɪz] *vt* révolutionner
revolve [rɪˈvɔlv] *vi* tourner
revolver [rɪˈvɔlvəʳ] *n* revolver *m*
revolving [rɪˈvɔlvɪŋ] *adj* (*chair*) pivotant(e);
(*light*) tournant(e)
revolving door *n* (*porte f à*) tambour *m*
revue [rɪˈvjuː] *n* (*Theat*) revue *f*
revulsion [rɪˈvʌlʃən] *n* dégoût *m*, répugnance *f*
reward [rɪˈwɔːd] *n* récompense *f* ▷ *vt*: **to ~ (for)**
récompenser (de)
rewarding [rɪˈwɔːdɪŋ] *adj* (*fig*) qui (en) vaut la
peine, gratifiant(e); **financially ~**
financièrement intéressant(e)
rewind [riːˈwaɪnd] *vt* (*irreg: like* **wind**); (*watch*)
remonter; (*tape*) réembobiner
rewire [riːˈwaɪəʳ] *vt* (*house*) refaire l'installation *m*
électrique de
reword [riːˈwəːd] *vt* formuler *or* exprimer
différemment
rewritable [riːˈraɪtəbl] *adj* (CD, DVD)
réinscriptible
rewrite [riːˈraɪt] (*pt* **rewrote**, *pp* **rewritten**) *vt*
récrire
Reykjavik ['reɪkjəviːk] *n* Reykjavik
RFD *abbr* (*US Post*) = **rural free delivery**
Rh *abbr* (= *rhesus*) Rh
rhapsody ['ræpsədɪ] *n* (*Mus*) rhapsodie *f*; (*fig*)
éloge délirant
rhesus negative [ˈriːsəs-] *adj* (*Med*) de rhésus
négatif
rhesus positive [ˈriːsəs-] *adj* (*Med*) de rhésus
positif
rhetoric ['rɛtərɪk] *n* rhétorique *f*
rhetorical [rɪˈtɔrɪkl] *adj* rhétorique

rheumatic [ruːˈmætɪk] *adj* rhumatismal(e)
rheumatism [ˈruːmətɪzəm] *n* rhumatisme *m*
rheumatoid arthritis [ˈruːmətɔɪd-] *n* polyarthrite *f* chronique
Rhine [raɪn] *n*: **the (River)** ~ le Rhin
rhinestone [ˈraɪnstəun] *n* faux diamant
rhinoceros [raɪˈnɔsərəs] *n* rhinocéros *m*
Rhodes [rəudz] *n* Rhodes *f*
Rhodesia [rəuˈdiːʒə] *n* Rhodésie *f*
Rhodesian [rəuˈdiːʒən] *adj* rhodésien(ne) ▷ *n* Rhodésien(ne)
rhododendron [rəudəˈdɛndrn] *n* rhododendron *m*
rhubarb [ˈruːbɑːb] *n* rhubarbe *f*
rhyme [raɪm] *n* rime *f*; (*verse*) vers *mpl* ▷ *vi*: **to ~ (with)** rimer (avec); **without ~ or reason** sans rime ni raison
rhythm [ˈrɪðm] *n* rythme *m*
rhythmic [ˈrɪðmɪk], **rhythmical** [ˈrɪðmɪkl] *adj* rythmique
rhythmically [ˈrɪðmɪklɪ] *adv* avec rythme
rhythm method *n* méthode *f* des températures
RI *n abbr* (*Brit*) = **religious instruction** ▷ *abbr* (*US*) = **Rhode Island**
rib [rɪb] *n* (*Anat*) côte *f* ▷ *vt* (*mock*) taquiner
ribald [ˈrɪbəld] *adj* paillard(e)
ribbed [rɪbd] *adj* (*knitting*) à côtes; (*shell*) strié(e)
ribbon [ˈrɪbən] *n* ruban *m*; **in ~s** (*torn*) en lambeaux
rice [raɪs] *n* riz *m*
rice field [ˈraɪsfiːld] *n* rizière *f*
rice pudding *n* riz *m* au lait
rich [rɪtʃ] *adj* riche; (*gift, clothes*) somptueux(-euse); **the ~** (*npl*) les riches *mpl*; **riches** *npl* richesses *fpl*; **to be ~ in sth** être riche en qch
richly [ˈrɪtʃlɪ] *adv* richement; (*deserved, earned*) largement, grandement
rickets [ˈrɪkɪts] *n* rachitisme *m*
rickety [ˈrɪkɪtɪ] *adj* branlant(e)
rickshaw [ˈrɪkʃɔ:] *n* pousse(-pousse) *m inv*
ricochet [ˈrɪkəʃeɪ] *n* ricochet *m* ▷ *vi* ricocher
rid [rɪd] (*pt, pp* -) *vt*: **to ~ sb of** débarrasser qn de; **to get ~ of** se débarrasser de
riddance [ˈrɪdns] *n*: **good ~!** bon débarras!
ridden [ˈrɪdn] *pp of* **ride**
riddle [ˈrɪdl] *n* (*puzzle*) énigme *f* ▷ *vt*: **to be ~d with** être criblé(e) de; (*fig*) être en proie à
ride [raɪd] (*pt* **rode**, *pp* **ridden**) [rəud, ˈrɪdn] *n* promenade *f*, tour *m*; (*distance covered*) trajet *m* ▷ *vi* (*as sport*) monter (à cheval), faire du cheval; (*go somewhere: on horse, bicycle*) aller (à cheval or bicyclette *etc*); (*travel: on bicycle, motor cycle, bus*) rouler ▷ *vt* (*a horse*) monter; (*distance*) parcourir, faire; **we rode all day/all the way** nous sommes restés toute la journée en selle/avons fait tout le chemin en selle *or* à cheval; **to ~ a horse/bicycle** monter à cheval/à bicyclette; **can you ~ a bike?** est-ce que tu sais monter à bicyclette?; **to ~ at anchor** (*Naut*) être à l'ancre; **horse/car ~** promenade *or* tour à cheval/en voiture; **to go for a ~** faire une promenade (en

voiture *or* à bicyclette *etc*); **to take sb for a ~** (*fig*) faire marcher qn; (*cheat*) rouler qn
▶ **ride out** *vt*: **to ~ out the storm** (*fig*) surmonter les difficultés
rider [ˈraɪdə^r] *n* cavalier(-ière); (*in race*) jockey *m*; (*on bicycle*) cycliste *m/f*; (*on motorcycle*) motocycliste *m/f*; (*in document*) annexe *f*, clause additionnelle
ridge [rɪdʒ] *n* (*of hill*) faîte *m*; (*of roof, mountain*) arête *f*; (*on object*) strie *f*
ridicule [ˈrɪdɪkjuːl] *n* ridicule *m*; dérision *f* ▷ *vt* ridiculiser, tourner en dérision; **to hold sb/sth up to ~** tourner qn/qch en ridicule
ridiculous [rɪˈdɪkjuləs] *adj* ridicule
riding [ˈraɪdɪŋ] *n* équitation *f*
riding school *n* manège *m*, école *f* d'équitation
rife [raɪf] *adj* répandu(e); **~ with** abondant(e) en
riffraff [ˈrɪfræf] *n* racaille *f*
rifle [ˈraɪfl] *n* fusil *m* (à canon rayé) ▷ *vt* vider, dévaliser
▶ **rifle through** *vt fus* fouiller dans
rifle range *n* champ *m* de tir; (*indoor*) stand *m* de tir
rift [rɪft] *n* fente *f*, fissure *f*; (*fig: disagreement*) désaccord *m*
rig [rɪg] *n* (*also*: **oil rig**: *on land*) derrick *m*; (: *at sea*) plate-forme pétrolière ▷ *vt* (*election etc*) truquer
▶ **rig out** *vt* (*Brit*) habiller; (: *pej*) fringuer, attifer
▶ **rig up** *vt* arranger, faire avec des moyens de fortune
rigging [ˈrɪgɪŋ] *n* (*Naut*) gréement *m*
right [raɪt] *adj* (*true*) juste, exact(e); (*correct*) bon (bonne); (*suitable*) approprié(e), convenable; (*just*) juste, équitable; (*morally good*) bien *inv*; (*not left*) droit(e) ▷ *n* (*moral good*) bien *m*; (*title, claim*) droit *m*; (*not left*) droite *f* ▷ *adv* (*answer*) correctement; (*treat*) bien, comme il faut; (*not on the left*) à droite ▷ *vt* redresser ▷ *excl* bon!; **rights** *npl* (*Comm*) droits *mpl*; **the ~ time** (*precise*) l'heure exacte; (*not wrong*) la bonne heure; **do you have the ~ time?** avez-vous l'heure juste *or* exacte?; **to be ~** (*person*) avoir raison; (*answer*) être juste *or* correct(e); **to get sth ~** ne pas se tromper sur qch; **let's get it ~ this time!** essayons de ne pas nous tromper cette fois-ci!; **you did the ~ thing** vous avez bien fait; **to put a mistake ~** (*Brit*) rectifier une erreur; **by ~s** en toute justice; **on the ~** à droite; **~ and wrong** le bien et le mal; **to be in the ~** avoir raison; **film ~s** droits d'adaptation cinématographique; **~ now** en ce moment même; (*immediately*) tout de suite; **~ before/after** juste avant/après; **~ against the wall** tout contre le mur; **~ ahead** tout droit; droit devant; **~ in the middle** en plein milieu; **~ away** immédiatement; **to go ~ to the end of sth** aller jusqu'au bout de qch
right angle *n* (*Math*) angle droit
righteous [ˈraɪtʃəs] *adj* droit(e), vertueux(-euse); (*anger*) justifié(e)
righteousness [ˈraɪtʃəsnɪs] *n* droiture *f*, vertu *f*
rightful [ˈraɪtful] *adj* (*heir*) légitime
rightfully [ˈraɪtfəlɪ] *adv* à juste titre,

légitimement

right-hand ['raɪthænd] *adj*: **the ~ side** la droite

right-hand drive *n* (*Brit*) conduite *f* à droite; (*vehicle*) véhicule *m* avec la conduite à droite

right-handed [raɪt'hændɪd] *adj* (*person*) droitier(-ière)

right-hand man ['raɪthænd-] (*irreg*) *n* bras droit (*fig*)

rightly ['raɪtlɪ] *adv* bien, correctement; (*with reason*) à juste titre; **if I remember ~** (*Brit*) si je me souviens bien

right-minded ['raɪt'maɪndɪd] *adj* sensé(e), sain(e) d'esprit

right of way *n* (*on path etc*) droit *m* de passage; (*Aut*) priorité *f*

rights issue *n* (*Stock Exchange*) émission préférentielle *or* de droit de souscription

right wing *n* (*Mil, Sport*) aile droite; (*Pol*) droite *f*

right-wing [raɪt'wɪŋ] *adj* (*Pol*) de droite

right-winger [raɪt'wɪŋər] *n* (*Pol*) membre *m* de la droite; (*Sport*) ailier droit

rigid ['rɪdʒɪd] *adj* rigide; (*principle, control*) strict(e)

rigidity [rɪ'dʒɪdɪtɪ] *n* rigidité *f*

rigidly ['rɪdʒɪdlɪ] *adv* rigidement; (*behave*) inflexiblement

rigmarole ['rɪgmərəʊl] *n* galimatias *m*, comédie *f*

rigor ['rɪgər] *n* (*US*) = **rigour**

rigor mortis ['rɪgə'mɔːtɪs] *n* rigidité *f* cadavérique

rigorous ['rɪgərəs] *adj* rigoureux(-euse)

rigorously ['rɪgərəslɪ] *adv* rigoureusement

rigour, (*US*) **rigor** ['rɪgər] *n* rigueur *f*

rig-out ['rɪgaʊt] *n* (*Brit inf*) tenue *f*

rile [raɪl] *vt* agacer

rim [rɪm] *n* bord *m*; (*of spectacles*) monture *f*; (*of wheel*) jante *f*

rimless ['rɪmlɪs] *adj* (*spectacles*) à monture invisible

rind [raɪnd] *n* (*of bacon*) couenne *f*; (*of lemon etc*) écorce *f*, zeste *m*; (*of cheese*) croûte *f*

ring [rɪŋ] (*pt* **rang**, *pp* **rung**) [ræŋ, rʌŋ] *n* anneau *m*; (*on finger*) bague *f*; (*also*: **wedding ring**) alliance *f*; (*for napkin*) rond *m*; (*of people, objects*) cercle *m*; (*of spies*) réseau *m*; (*of smoke etc*) rond *m*; (*arena*) piste *f*, arène *f*; (*for boxing*) ring *m*; (*sound of bell*) sonnerie *f*; (*telephone call*) coup *m* de téléphone ▷ *vi* (*telephone, bell*) sonner; (*person: by telephone*) téléphoner; (*ears*) bourdonner; (*also*: **ring out**: *voice, words*) retentir ▷ *vt* (*Brit Tel*: *also*: **ring up**) téléphoner à, appeler; **to ~ the bell** sonner; **to give sb a ~** (*Tel*) passer un coup de téléphone *or* de fil à qn; **that has the ~ of truth about it** cela sonne vrai; **the name doesn't ~ a bell (with me)** ce nom ne me dit rien

▸ **ring back** *vt, vi* (*Brit Tel*) rappeler

▸ **ring off** *vi* (*Brit Tel*) raccrocher

▸ **ring up** (*Brit*) *vt* (*Tel*) téléphoner à, appeler

ring binder *n* classeur *m* à anneaux

ring finger *n* annulaire *m*

ringing ['rɪŋɪŋ] *n* (*of bell*) tintement *m*; (*louder: also*: **of telephone**) sonnerie *f*; (*in ears*)

bourdonnement *m*

ringing tone *n* (*Brit Tel*) tonalité *f* d'appel

ringleader ['rɪŋliːdər] *n* (*of gang*) chef *m*, meneur *m*

ringlets ['rɪŋlɪts] *npl* anglaises *fpl*

ring road *n* (*Brit*) rocade *f*; (*motorway*) périphérique *m*

ring tone ['rɪŋtəʊn] *n* (*on mobile*) sonnerie *f* (*de téléphone portable*)

rink [rɪŋk] *n* (*also*: **ice rink**) patinoire *f*; (*for roller-skating*) skating *m*

rinse [rɪns] *n* rinçage *m* ▷ *vt* rincer

Rio ['riːəʊ], **Rio de Janeiro** ['riːəʊdədʒə'nɪərəʊ] *n* Rio de Janeiro

riot ['raɪət] *n* émeute *f*, bagarres *fpl* ▷ *vi* (*demonstrators*) manifester avec violence; (*population*) se soulever, se révolter; **a ~ of colours** une débauche *or* orgie de couleurs; **to run ~** se déchaîner

rioter ['raɪətər] *n* émeutier(-ière), manifestant(e)

riot gear *n*: **in ~** casqué et portant un bouclier

riotous ['raɪətəs] *adj* tapageur(-euse); tordant(e)

riotously ['raɪətəslɪ] *adv*: **~ funny** tordant(e)

riot police *n* forces *fpl* de police intervenant en cas d'émeute; **hundreds of ~** des centaines de policiers casqués et armés

RIP *abbr* (= *rest in peace*) RIP

rip [rɪp] *n* déchirure *f* ▷ *vt* déchirer ▷ *vi* se déchirer

▸ **rip off** *vt* (*inf*: *cheat*) arnaquer

▸ **rip up** *vt* déchirer

ripcord ['rɪpkɔːd] *n* poignée *f* d'ouverture

ripe [raɪp] *adj* (*fruit*) mûr(e); (*cheese*) fait(e)

ripen ['raɪpn] *vt* mûrir ▷ *vi* mûrir; se faire

ripeness ['raɪpnɪs] *n* maturité *f*

rip-off ['rɪpɔf] *n* (*inf*): **it's a ~!** c'est du vol manifeste!, c'est de l'arnaque!

riposte [rɪ'pɔst] *n* riposte *f*

ripple ['rɪpl] *n* ride *f*, ondulation *f*; (*of applause, laughter*) cascade *f* ▷ *vi* se rider, onduler ▷ *vt* rider, faire onduler

rise [raɪz] *n* (*slope*) côte *f*, pente *f*; (*hill*) élévation *f*; (*increase: in wages*: *Brit*) augmentation *f*; (: *in prices, temperature*) hausse *f*, augmentation; (*fig: to power etc*) ascension *f* ▷ *vi* (*pt* **rose**, *pp* **-n**) [rəʊz, rɪzn] s'élever, monter; (*prices, numbers*) augmenter, monter; (*waters, river*) monter; (*sun, wind, person: from chair, bed*) se lever; (*also*: **rise up**: *tower, building*) s'élever; (: *rebel*) se révolter; se rebeller; (*in rank*) s'élever; **~ to power** montée *f* au pouvoir; **to give ~ to** donner lieu à; **to ~ to the occasion** se montrer à la hauteur

risen ['rɪzn] *pp of* **rise**

rising ['raɪzɪŋ] *adj* (*increasing: number, prices*) en hausse; (*tide*) montant(e); (*sun, moon*) levant(e) ▷ *n* (*uprising*) soulèvement *m*, insurrection *f*

rising damp *n* humidité *f* (montant des fondations)

rising star *n* (*also fig*) étoile montante

risk [rɪsk] *n* risque *m*, danger *m*; (*deliberate*) risque ▷ *vt* risquer; **to take** *or* **run the ~ of**

doing courir le risque de faire; **at ~** en danger; **at one's own ~** à ses risques et périls; **it's a fire/health ~** cela présente un risque d'incendie/pour la santé; **I'll ~ it** je vais risquer le coup

risk capital n capital-risque m

risky ['rɪskɪ] adj risqué(e)

risqué ['riːskeɪ] adj (joke) risqué(e)

rissole ['rɪsəʊl] n croquette f

rite [raɪt] n rite m; **the last ~s** les derniers sacrements

ritual ['rɪtjʊəl] adj rituel(le) ▷ n rituel m

rival ['raɪvl] n rival(e); (in business) concurrent(e) ▷ adj rival(e); qui fait concurrence ▷ vt (match) égaler; (compete with) être en concurrence avec; **to ~ sb/sth in** rivaliser avec qn/qch de

rivalry ['raɪvlrɪ] n rivalité f; (in business) concurrence f

river ['rɪvər] n rivière f; (major: also fig) fleuve m ▷ cpd (port, traffic) fluvial(e); **up/down ~** en amont/aval

riverbank ['rɪvəbæŋk] n rive f, berge f

riverbed ['rɪvəbɛd] n lit m (de rivière or de fleuve)

riverside ['rɪvəsaɪd] n bord m de la rivière or du fleuve

rivet ['rɪvɪt] n rivet m ▷ vt riveter; (fig) river, fixer

riveting ['rɪvɪtɪŋ] adj (fig) fascinant(e)

Riviera [rɪvɪ'ɛərə] n: **the (French) ~** la Côte d'Azur; **the Italian ~** la Riviera (italienne)

Riyadh [rɪ'jaːd] n Riyad

RMT n abbr (= Rail, Maritime and Transport) syndicat des transports

RN n abbr = **registered nurse**; (Brit) = **Royal Navy**

RNA n abbr (= ribonucleic acid) ARN m

RNLI n abbr (Brit: = Royal National Lifeboat Institution) ≈ SNSM f

RNZAF n abbr = **Royal New Zealand Air Force**

RNZN n abbr = **Royal New Zealand Navy**

road [rəʊd] n route f; (in town) rue f; (fig) chemin, voie f ▷ cpd (accident) de la route; **main ~** grande route; **major/minor ~** route principale or à priorité/voie secondaire; **it takes four hours by ~** il y a quatre heures de route; **which ~ do I take for …?** quelle route dois-je prendre pour aller à …?; **"~ up"** (Brit) "attention travaux"

road accident n accident m de la circulation

roadblock ['rəʊdblɔk] n barrage routier

road haulage n transports routiers

roadhog ['rəʊdhɔg] n chauffard m

road map n carte routière

road rage n comportement très agressif de certains usagers de la route

road safety n sécurité routière

roadside ['rəʊdsaɪd] n bord m de la route, bas-côté m ▷ cpd (situé(e) etc) au bord de la route; **by the ~** au bord de la route

road sign ['rəʊdsaɪn] n panneau m de signalisation

road sweeper ['rəʊdswiːpər] n (Brit: person) balayeur(-euse)

road tax n (Brit Aut) taxe f sur les automobiles

road user n usager m de la route

roadway ['rəʊdweɪ] n chaussée f

roadworks ['rəʊdwəːks] npl travaux mpl (de réfection des routes)

roadworthy ['rəʊdwəːðɪ] adj en bon état de marche

roam [rəʊm] vi errer, vagabonder ▷ vt parcourir, errer par

roar [rɔːr] n rugissement m; (of crowd) hurlements mpl; (of vehicle, thunder, storm) grondement m ▷ vi rugir; hurler; gronder; **to ~ with laughter** rire à gorge déployée

roaring ['rɔːrɪŋ] adj: **a ~ fire** une belle flambée; **a ~ success** un succès fou; **to do a ~ trade** faire des affaires en or

roast [rəʊst] n rôti m ▷ vt (meat) (faire) rôtir; (coffee) griller, torréfier

roast beef n rôti m de bœuf, rosbif m

roasting ['rəʊstɪŋ] n (inf): **to give sb a ~** sonner les cloches à qn

rob [rɔb] vt (person) voler; (bank) dévaliser; **to ~ sb of sth** voler or dérober qch à qn; (fig: deprive) priver qn de qch

robber ['rɔbər] n bandit m, voleur m

robbery ['rɔbərɪ] n vol m

robe [rəʊb] n (for ceremony etc) robe f; (also: **bathrobe**) peignoir m; (US: rug) couverture f ▷ vt revêtir (d'une robe)

robin ['rɔbɪn] n rouge-gorge m

robot ['rəʊbɔt] n robot m

robotics [rə'bɔtɪks] n robotique m

robust [rəʊ'bʌst] adj robuste; (material, appetite) solide

rock [rɔk] n (substance) roche f, roc m; (boulder) rocher m, roche; (US: small stone) caillou m; (Brit: sweet) ≈ sucre m d'orge ▷ vt (swing gently: cradle) balancer; (: child) bercer; (shake) ébranler, secouer ▷ vi se balancer, être ébranlé(e) or secoué(e); **on the ~s** (drink) avec des glaçons; (ship) sur les écueils; (marriage etc) en train de craquer; **to ~ the boat** (fig) jouer les trouble-fête

rock and roll n rock (and roll) m, rock'n'roll m

rock-bottom ['rɔk'bɔtəm] n (fig) niveau le plus bas ▷ adj (fig: prices) sacrifié(e); **to reach** or **touch ~** (price, person) tomber au plus bas

rock climber n varappeur(-euse)

rock climbing n varappe f

rockery ['rɔkərɪ] n (jardin m de) rocaille f

rocket ['rɔkɪt] n fusée f; (Mil) fusée, roquette f; (Culin) roquette ▷ vi (prices) monter en flèche

rocket launcher [-lɔːnʃər] n lance-roquettes m inv

rock face n paroi rocheuse

rock fall n chute f de pierres

rocking chair ['rɔkɪŋ-] n fauteuil m à bascule

rocking horse ['rɔkɪŋ-] n cheval m à bascule

rocky ['rɔkɪ] adj (hill) rocheux(-euse); (path) rocailleux(-euse); (unsteady: table) branlant(e)

Rocky Mountains npl: **the ~** les (montagnes fpl) Rocheuses fpl

rod [rɔd] n (metallic) tringle f; (Tech) tige f;

(*wooden*) baguette *f*; (*also:* **fishing rod**) canne *f* à pêche
rode [rəud] *pt of* **ride**
rodent ['rəudnt] *n* rongeur *m*
rodeo ['rəudɪəu] *n* rodéo *m*
roe [rəu] *n* (*species: also:* **roe deer**) chevreuil *m*; (*of fish: also:* **hard roe**) œufs *mpl* de poisson; **soft ~** laitance *f*
roe deer *n* chevreuil *m*; chevreuil femelle
rogue [rəug] *n* coquin(e)
roguish ['rəugɪʃ] *adj* coquin(e)
role [rəul] *n* rôle *m*
role-model ['rəulmɔdl] *n* modèle *m* à émuler
role play, role playing *n* jeu *m* de rôle
roll [rəul] *n* rouleau *m*; (*of banknotes*) liasse *f*; (*also:* **bread roll**) petit pain; (*register*) liste *f*; (*sound: of drums etc*) roulement *m*; (*movement: of ship*) roulis *m* ▷ *vt* rouler; (*also:* **roll up**: *string*) enrouler; (*also:* **roll out**: *pastry*) étendre au rouleau, abaisser ▷ *vi* rouler; (*wheel*) tourner; **cheese ~** ≈ sandwich *m* au fromage (*dans un petit pain*)
▶ **roll about, roll around** *vi* rouler çà et là; (*person*) se rouler par terre
▶ **roll by** *vi* (*time*) s'écouler, passer
▶ **roll in** *vi* (*mail, cash*) affluer
▶ **roll over** *vi* se retourner
▶ **roll up** *vi* (*inf: arrive*) arriver, s'amener ▷ *vt* (*carpet, cloth, map*) rouler; (*sleeves*) retrousser; **to ~ o.s. up into a ball** se rouler en boule
roll call *n* appel *m*
roller ['rəulə'] *n* rouleau *m*; (*wheel*) roulette *f*; (*for road*) rouleau compresseur; (*for hair*) bigoudi *m*
Rollerblades® ['rəulə'bleɪdz] *npl* patins *mpl* en ligne
roller blind *n* (*Brit*) store *m*
roller coaster *n* montagnes *fpl* russes
roller skates *npl* patins *mpl* à roulettes
roller-skating ['rəulə'skeɪtɪŋ] *n* patin *m* à roulettes; **to go ~** faire du patin à roulettes
rollicking ['rɔlɪkɪŋ] *adj* bruyant(e) et joyeux(-euse); (*play*) bouffon(ne); **to have a ~ time** s'amuser follement
rolling ['rəulɪŋ] *adj* (*landscape*) onduleux(-euse)
rolling mill *n* laminoir *m*
rolling pin *n* rouleau *m* à pâtisserie
rolling stock *n* (*Rail*) matériel roulant
roll-on-roll-off ['rəulɔn'rəulɔf] *adj* (*Brit: ferry*) roulier(-ière)
roly-poly ['rəulɪ'pəulɪ] *n* (*Brit Culin*) roulé *m* à la confiture
ROM [rɔm] *n abbr* (*Comput:* = *read-only memory*) mémoire morte, ROM *f*
Roman ['rəumən] *adj* romain(e) ▷ *n* Romain(e)
Roman Catholic *adj, n* catholique (*m/f*)
romance [rə'mæns] *n* (*love affair*) idylle *f*; (*charm*) poésie *f*; (*novel*) roman *m* à l'eau de rose
Romanesque [rəumə'nɛsk] *adj* roman(e)
Romania [rəu'meɪnɪə] = **Rumania**
Romanian [rəu'meɪnɪən] *adj, n see* **Rumanian**
Roman numeral *n* chiffre romain
romantic [rə'mæntɪk] *adj* romantique; (*novel,*

attachment) sentimental(e)
romanticism [rə'mæntɪsɪzəm] *n* romantisme *m*
Romany ['rɔmənɪ] *adj* de bohémien ▷ *n* bohémien(ne); (*Ling*) romani *m*
Rome [rəum] *n* Rome
romp [rɔmp] *n* jeux bruyants ▷ *vi* (*also:* **romp about**) s'ébattre, jouer bruyamment; **to ~ home** (*horse*) arriver bon premier
rompers ['rɔmpəz] *npl* barboteuse *f*
rondo ['rɔndəu] *n* (*Mus*) rondeau *m*
roof [ru:f] *n* toit *m*; (*of tunnel, cave*) plafond *m* ▷ *vt* couvrir (d'un toit); **the ~ of the mouth** la voûte du palais
roof garden *n* toit-terrasse *m*
roofing ['ru:fɪŋ] *n* toiture *f*
roof rack *n* (*Aut*) galerie *f*
rook [ruk] *n* (*bird*) freux *m*; (*Chess*) tour *f* ▷ *vt* (*inf: cheat*) rouler, escroquer
rookie ['rukɪ] *n* (*inf: esp Mil*) bleu *m*
room [ru:m] *n* (*in house*) pièce *f*; (*also:* **bedroom**) chambre *f* (à coucher); (*in school etc*) salle *f*; (*space*) place *f*; **rooms** *npl* (*lodging*) meublé *m*; **"~s to let"**, (*US*) **"~s for rent"** "chambres à louer"; **is there ~ for this?** est-ce qu'il y a de la place pour ceci?; **to make ~ for sb** faire de la place à qn; **there is ~ for improvement** on peut faire mieux
rooming house ['ru:mɪŋ-] *n* (*US*) maison *f* de rapport
roommate ['ru:mmeɪt] *n* camarade *m/f* de chambre
room service *n* service *m* des chambres (*dans un hôtel*)
room temperature *n* température ambiante; **"serve at ~"** (*wine*) "servir chambré"
roomy ['ru:mɪ] *adj* spacieux(-euse); (*garment*) ample
roost [ru:st] *n* juchoir *m* ▷ *vi* se jucher
rooster ['ru:stə'] *n* coq *m*
root [ru:t] *n* (*Bot, Math*) racine *f*; (*fig: of problem*) origine *f*, fond *m* ▷ *vi* (*plant*) s'enraciner; **to take ~** (*plant, idea*) prendre racine
▶ **root about** *vi* (*fig*) fouiller
▶ **root for** *vt fus* (*inf*) applaudir
▶ **root out** *vt* extirper
root beer *n* (*US*) *sorte de limonade à base d'extraits végétaux*
rope [rəup] *n* corde *f*; (*Naut*) cordage *m* ▷ *vt* (*box*) corder; (*tie up or together*) attacher; (*climbers: also:* **rope together**) encorder; (*area: also:* **rope off**) interdire l'accès de; (: *divide off*) séparer; **to ~ sb in** (*fig*) embringuer qn; **to know the ~s** (*fig*) être au courant, connaître les ficelles
rope ladder *n* échelle *f* de corde
ropey ['rəupɪ] *adj* (*inf*) pas fameux(-euse) *or* brillant(e); **I feel a bit ~ today** c'est pas la forme aujourd'hui
rosary ['rəuzərɪ] *n* chapelet *m*
rose [rəuz] *pt of* **rise** ▷ *n* rose *f*; (*also:* **rosebush**) rosier *m*; (*on watering can*) pomme *f* ▷ *adj* rose
rosé ['rəuzeɪ] *n* rosé *m*
rosebed ['rəuzbɛd] *n* massif *m* de rosiers

rosebud ['rəuzbʌd] n bouton m de rose
rosebush ['rəuzbuʃ] n rosier m
rosemary ['rəuzmərɪ] n romarin m
rosette [rəu'zɛt] n rosette f; (larger) cocarde f
ROSPA ['rɔspə] n abbr (Brit) = **Royal Society for the Prevention of Accidents**
roster ['rɔstər] n: **duty** ~ tableau m de service
rostrum ['rɔstrəm] n tribune f (pour un orateur etc)
rosy ['rəuzɪ] adj rose; **a ~ future** un bel avenir
rot [rɔt] n (decay) pourriture f; (fig: pej: nonsense) idioties fpl, balivernes fpl ▷ vt, vi pourrir; **to stop the ~** (Brit fig) rétablir la situation; **dry ~** pourriture sèche (du bois); **wet ~** pourriture (du bois)
rota ['rəutə] n liste f, tableau m de service; **on a ~ basis** par roulement
rotary ['rəutərɪ] adj rotatif(-ive)
rotate [rəu'teɪt] vt (revolve) faire tourner; (change round: crops) alterner; (: jobs) faire à tour de rôle ▷ vi (revolve) tourner
rotating [rəu'teɪtɪŋ] adj (movement) tournant(e)
rotation [rəu'teɪʃən] n rotation f; **in ~** à tour de rôle
rote [rəut] n: **by ~** machinalement, par cœur
rotor ['rəutər] n rotor m
rotten ['rɔtn] adj (decayed) pourri(e); (dishonest) corrompu(e); (inf: bad) mauvais(e), moche; **to feel ~** (ill) être mal fichu(e)
rotting ['rɔtɪŋ] adj pourrissant(e)
rotund [rəu'tʌnd] adj rondelet(te); arrondi(e)
rouble, (US) **ruble** ['ru:bl] n rouble m
rouge [ru:ʒ] n rouge m (à joues)
rough [rʌf] adj (cloth, skin) rêche, rugueux(-euse); (terrain) accidenté(e); (path) rocailleux(-euse); (voice) rauque, rude; (person, manner: coarse) rude, fruste; (: violent) brutal(e); (district, weather) mauvais(e); (sea) houleux(-euse); (plan) ébauché(e); (guess) approximatif(-ive) ▷ n (Golf) rough m ▷ vt: **to ~ it** vivre à la dure; **the sea is ~ today** la mer est agitée aujourd'hui; **to have a ~ time (of it)** en voir de dures; **~ estimate** approximation f; **to play ~** jouer avec brutalité; **to sleep ~** (Brit) coucher à la dure; **to feel ~** (Brit) être mal fichu(e)
▸ **rough out** vt (draft) ébaucher
roughage ['rʌfɪdʒ] n fibres fpl diététiques
rough-and-ready ['rʌfən'rɛdɪ] adj (accommodation, method) rudimentaire
rough-and-tumble ['rʌfən'tʌmbl] n agitation f
roughcast ['rʌfkɑ:st] n crépi m
rough copy, rough draft n brouillon m
roughen ['rʌfn] vt (a surface) rendre rude or rugueux(-euse)
rough justice n justice f sommaire
roughly ['rʌflɪ] adv (handle) rudement, brutalement; (speak) avec brusquerie; (make) grossièrement; (approximately) à peu près, en gros; **~ speaking** en gros
roughness ['rʌfnɪs] n (of cloth, skin) rugosité f; (of person) rudesse f; brutalité f
roughshod ['rʌfʃɔd] adv: **to ride ~ over** ne tenir aucun compte de

rough work n (at school etc) brouillon m
roulette [ru:'lɛt] n roulette f
Roumania etc [ru:'meɪnɪə] n = **Romania** etc
round [raund] adj rond(e) ▷ n rond m, cercle m; (Brit: of toast) tranche f; (duty: of policeman, milkman etc) tournée f; (: of doctor) visites fpl; (game: of cards, in competition) partie f; (Boxing) round m; (of talks) série f ▷ vt (corner) tourner; (bend) prendre; (cape) doubler ▷ prep autour de ▷ adv: **right ~**, **all ~** tout autour; **in ~ figures** en chiffres ronds; **to go the ~s** (disease, story) circuler; **the daily ~** (fig) la routine quotidienne; **~ of ammunition** cartouche f; **~ of applause** applaudissements mpl; **~ of drinks** tournée f; **~ of sandwiches** (Brit) sandwich m; **the long way ~** (par) le chemin le plus long; **all (the) year ~** toute l'année; **it's just ~ the corner** c'est juste après le coin; (fig) c'est tout près; **to ask sb ~** inviter qn (chez soi); **I'll be ~ at 6 o'clock** je serai là à 6 heures; **to go ~** faire le tour or un détour; **to go ~ to sb's (house)** aller chez qn; **to go ~ an obstacle** contourner un obstacle; **go ~ the back** passez par derrière; **to go ~ a house** visiter une maison, faire le tour d'une maison; **enough to go ~** assez pour tout le monde; **she arrived ~ (about) noon** (Brit) elle est arrivée vers midi; **~ the clock** 24 heures sur 24
▸ **round off** vt (speech etc) terminer
▸ **round up** vt rassembler; (criminals) effectuer une rafle de; (prices) arrondir (au chiffre supérieur)
roundabout ['raundəbaut] n (Brit Aut) rond-point m (à sens giratoire); (at fair) manège m (de chevaux de bois) ▷ adj (route, means) détourné(e)
rounded ['raundɪd] adj arrondi(e); (style) harmonieux(-euse)
rounders ['raundəz] npl (game) ≈ balle f au camp
roundly ['raundlɪ] adv (fig) tout net, carrément
round-shouldered ['raund'ʃəuldəd] adj au dos rond
round trip n (voyage m) aller et retour m
roundup ['raundʌp] n rassemblement m; (of criminals) rafle f; **a ~ of the latest news** un rappel des derniers événements
rouse [rauz] vt (wake up) réveiller; (stir up) susciter, provoquer; (interest) éveiller; (suspicions) susciter, éveiller
rousing ['rauzɪŋ] adj (welcome) enthousiaste
rout [raut] n (Mil) déroute f ▷ vt mettre en déroute
route [ru:t] n itinéraire m; (of bus) parcours m; (of trade, shipping) route f; **"all ~s"** (Aut) "toutes directions"; **the best ~ to London** le meilleur itinéraire pour aller à Londres
route map n (Brit: for journey) croquis m d'itinéraire; (for trains etc) carte f du réseau
routine [ru:'ti:n] adj (work) ordinaire, courant(e); (procedure) d'usage ▷ n (habits) habitudes fpl; (pej) train-train m; (Theat) numéro m; **daily ~** occupations journalières
roving ['rəuvɪŋ] adj (life) vagabond(e)
roving reporter n reporter volant

row¹ [rəu] n (line) rangée f; (of people, seats, Knitting) rang m; (behind one another: of cars, people) file f ▷ vi (in boat) ramer; (as sport) faire de l'aviron ▷ vt (boat) faire aller à la rame or à l'aviron; **in a ~** (fig) d'affilée

row² [rau] n (noise) vacarme m; (dispute) dispute f, querelle f; (scolding) réprimande f, savon m ▷ vi (also: **to have a row**) se disputer, se quereller

rowboat ['rəubəut] n (US) canot m (à rames)

rowdiness ['raudinis] n tapage m, chahut m; (fighting) bagarre f

rowdy ['raudi] adj chahuteur(-euse); bagarreur(-euse) ▷ n voyou m

rowdyism ['raudiizəm] n tapage m, chahut m

rowing ['rəuiŋ] n canotage m; (as sport) aviron m

rowing boat n (Brit) canot m (à rames)

rowlock ['rɔlək] n (Brit) dame f de nage, tolet m

royal ['rɔiəl] adj royal(e)

Royal Academy, Royal Academy of Arts n (Brit) l'Académie f royale des Beaux-Arts; voir article

● **ROYAL ACADEMY (OF ARTS)**

● La Royal Academy ou Royal Academy of Arts,
● fondée en 1768 par George III pour
● encourager la peinture, la sculpture et
● l'architecture, est située à Burlington
● House, sur Piccadilly. Une exposition des
● œuvres d'artistes contemporains a lieu tous
● les étés. L'Académie dispense également des
● cours en peinture, sculpture et architecture.

Royal Air Force n (Brit) armée de l'air britannique

royal blue adj bleu roi inv

royalist ['rɔiəlist] adj, n royaliste m/f

Royal Navy n (Brit) marine de guerre britannique

royalty ['rɔiəlti] n (royal persons) (membres mpl de la) famille royale; (payment: to author) droits mpl d'auteur; (: to inventor) royalties fpl

RP n abbr (Brit: = received pronunciation) prononciation f standard

RPI n abbr = **retail price index**

rpm abbr (= revolutions per minute) t/mn (= = tours/minute)

RR abbr (US) = **railroad**

RRP abbr = **recommended retail price**

RSA n abbr (Brit) = **Royal Society of Arts; Royal Scottish Academy**

RSI n abbr (Med: = repetitive strain injury) microtraumatisme permanent

RSPB n abbr (Brit: = Royal Society for the Protection of Birds) ≈ LPO f

RSPCA n abbr (Brit: = Royal Society for the Prevention of Cruelty to Animals) ≈ SPA f

R.S.V.P. abbr (= répondez s'il vous plaît) RSVP

RTA n abbr (= road traffic accident) accident m de la route

Rt. Hon. abbr (Brit: = Right Honourable) titre donné aux députés de la Chambre des communes

Rt Rev. abbr (= Right Reverend) très révérend

rub [rʌb] n (with cloth) coup m de chiffon or de torchon; (on person) friction f; **to give sth a ~** donner un coup de chiffon or de torchon à qch ▷ vt frotter; (person) frictionner; (hands) se frotter; **to ~ sb up** (Brit) or **to ~ sb** (US) **the wrong way** prendre qn à rebrousse-poil

▶ **rub down** vt (body) frictionner; (horse) bouchonner

▶ **rub in** vt (ointment) faire pénétrer

▶ **rub off** vi partir; **to ~ off on** déteindre sur

▶ **rub out** vt effacer ▷ vi s'effacer

rubber ['rʌbər] n caoutchouc m; (Brit: eraser) gomme f (à effacer)

rubber band n élastique m

rubber bullet n balle f en caoutchouc

rubber gloves npl gants mpl en caoutchouc

rubber plant n caoutchouc m (plante verte)

rubber ring n (for swimming) bouée f (de natation)

rubber stamp n tampon m

rubber-stamp [rʌbə'stæmp] vt (fig) approuver sans discussion

rubbery ['rʌbəri] adj caoutchouteux(-euse)

rubbish ['rʌbiʃ] n (from household) ordures fpl; (fig: pej) choses fpl sans valeur; camelote f; (nonsense) bêtises fpl, idioties fpl ▷ vt (Brit inf) dénigrer, rabaisser; **what you've just said is ~** tu viens de dire une bêtise

rubbish bin n (Brit) boîte f à ordures, poubelle f

rubbish dump n (Brit: in town) décharge publique, dépotoir m

rubbishy ['rʌbiʃi] adj (Brit inf) qui ne vaut rien, moche

rubble ['rʌbl] n décombres mpl; (smaller) gravats mpl; (Constr) blocage m

ruble ['ru:bl] n (US) = **rouble**

ruby ['ru:bi] n rubis m

RUC n abbr (Brit) = **Royal Ulster Constabulary**

rucksack ['rʌksæk] n sac m à dos

ructions ['rʌkʃənz] npl grabuge m

rudder ['rʌdər] n gouvernail m

ruddy ['rʌdi] adj (face) coloré(e); (inf: damned) sacré(e), fichu(e)

rude [ru:d] adj (impolite: person) impoli(e); (: word, manners) grossier(-ière); (shocking) indécent(e), inconvenant(e); **to be ~ to sb** être grossier envers qn

rudely ['ru:dli] adv impoliment; grossièrement

rudeness ['ru:dnis] n impolitesse f; grossièreté f

rudiment ['ru:dimənt] n rudiment m

rudimentary [ru:di'mɛntəri] adj rudimentaire

rue [ru:] vt se repentir de, regretter amèrement

rueful ['ru:ful] adj triste

ruff [rʌf] n fraise f, collerette f

ruffian ['rʌfiən] n brute f, voyou m

ruffle ['rʌfl] vt (hair) ébouriffer; (clothes) chiffonner; (water) agiter; (fig: person) émouvoir, faire perdre son flegme à; **to get ~d** s'énerver

rug [rʌg] n petit tapis; (Brit: blanket) couverture f

rugby ['rʌgbi] n (also: **rugby football**) rugby m

rugged ['rʌgid] adj (landscape) accidenté(e); (features, character) rude; (determination) farouche

rugger ['rʌgər] n (Brit inf) rugby m

ruin ['ru:in] n ruine f ▷ vt ruiner; (spoil: clothes)

abîmer; (: *event*) gâcher; **ruins** *npl* (*of building*) ruine(s); **in ~s** en ruine

ruination [ruːɪˈneɪʃən] *n* ruine *f*

ruinous [ˈruːɪnəs] *adj* ruineux(-euse)

rule [ruːl] *n* règle *f*; (*regulation*) règlement *m*; (*government*) autorité *f*, gouvernement *m*; (*dominion etc*): **under British ~** sous l'autorité britannique ▷ *vt* (*country*) gouverner; (*person*) dominer; (*decide*) décider ▷ *vi* commander; décider; (*Law*): **to ~ against/in favour of/on** statuer contre/en faveur de/sur; **to ~ that** (*umpire, judge etc*) décider que; **it's against the ~s** c'est contraire au règlement; **by ~ of thumb** à vue de nez; **as a ~** normalement, en règle générale
▶ **rule out** *vt* exclure; **murder cannot be ~d out** l'hypothèse d'un meurtre ne peut être exclue

ruled [ruːld] *adj* (*paper*) réglé(e)

ruler [ˈruːlər] *n* (*sovereign*) souverain(e); (*leader*) chef *m* (d'État); (*for measuring*) règle *f*

ruling [ˈruːlɪŋ] *adj* (*party*) au pouvoir; (*class*) dirigeant(e) ▷ *n* (*Law*) décision *f*

rum [rʌm] *n* rhum *m* ▷ *adj* (*Brit inf*) bizarre

Rumania [ruːˈmeɪnɪə] *n* Roumanie *f*

Rumanian [ruːˈmeɪnɪən] *adj* roumain(e) ▷ *n* Roumain(e); (*Ling*) roumain *m*

rumble [ˈrʌmbl] *n* grondement *m*; (*of stomach, pipe*) gargouillement *m* ▷ *vi* gronder; (*stomach, pipe*) gargouiller

rumbustious [rʌmˈbʌstʃəs], **rumbunctious** [rʌmˈbʌŋkʃəs] *adj* (*US: person*) exubérant(e)

rummage [ˈrʌmɪdʒ] *vi* fouiller

rumour, (*US*) **rumor** [ˈruːmər] *n* rumeur *f*, bruit *m* (qui court) ▷ *vt*: **it is ~ed that** le bruit court que

rump [rʌmp] *n* (*of animal*) croupe *f*

rumple [ˈrʌmpl] *vt* (*hair*) ébouriffer; (*clothes*) chiffonner, friper

rump steak *n* romsteck *m*

rumpus [ˈrʌmpəs] *n* (*inf*) tapage *m*, chahut *m*; (*quarrel*) prise *f* de bec; **to kick up a ~** faire toute une histoire

run [rʌn] (*pt* **ran**, *pp* **-**) [ræn, rʌn] *n* (*race*) course *f*; (*outing*) tour *m* or promenade *f* (en voiture); (*distance travelled*) parcours *m*, trajet *m*; (*series*) suite *f*, série *f*; (*Theat*) série de représentations; (*Ski*) piste *f*; (*Cricket, Baseball*) point *m*; (*in tights, stockings*) maille filée, échelle *f* ▷ *vt* (*business*) diriger; (*competition, course*) organiser; (*hotel, house*) tenir; (*race*) participer à; (*Comput: program*) exécuter; (*force through: rope, pipe*): **to ~ sth through** faire passer qch à travers; (*to pass: hand, finger*): **to ~ sth over** promener or passer qch sur; (*water, bath*) faire couler; (*Press: feature*) publier ▷ *vi* courir; (*pass: road etc*) passer; (*work: machine, factory*) marcher; (*bus, train*) circuler; (*continue: play*) se jouer, être à l'affiche; (: *contract*) être valide or en vigueur; (*slide: drawer etc*) glisser; (*flow: river, bath, nose*) couler; (*colours, washing*) déteindre; (*in election*) être candidat, se présenter; **at a ~** au pas de course; **to go for a ~**

aller courir or faire un peu de course à pied; (*in car*) faire un tour or une promenade (en voiture); **to break into a ~** se mettre à courir; **a ~ of luck** une série de coups de chance; **to have the ~ of sb's house** avoir la maison de qn à sa disposition; **there was a ~ on** (*meat, tickets*) les gens se sont rués sur; **in the long ~** à la longue, à longue échéance; **in the short ~** à brève échéance, à court terme; **on the ~** en fuite; **to make a ~ for it** s'enfuir; **I'll ~ you to the station** je vais vous emmener or conduire à la gare; **to ~ errands** faire des commissions; **the train ~s between Gatwick and Victoria** le train assure le service entre Gatwick et Victoria; **the bus ~s every 20 minutes** il y a un autobus toutes les 20 minutes; **it's very cheap to ~** (*car, machine*) c'est très économique; **to ~ on petrol** or (*US*) **gas/on diesel/off batteries** marcher à l'essence/au diesel/sur piles; **to ~ for president** être candidat à la présidence; **to ~ a risk** courir un risque; **their losses ran into millions** leurs pertes se sont élevées à plusieurs millions; **to be ~ off one's feet** (*Brit*) ne plus savoir où donner de la tête
▶ **run about** *vi* (*children*) courir çà et là
▶ **run across** *vt fus* (*find*) trouver par hasard
▶ **run after** *vt fus* (*to catch up*) courir après; (*chase*) poursuivre
▶ **run around** *vi* = **run about**
▶ **run away** *vi* s'enfuir
▶ **run down** *vi* (*clock*) s'arrêter (faute d'avoir été remonté) ▷ *vt* (*Aut: knock over*) renverser; (*Brit: reduce: production*) réduire progressivement; (: *factory/shop*) réduire progressivement la production/l'activité de; (*criticize*) critiquer, dénigrer; **to be ~ down** (*tired*) être fatigué(e) or à plat
▶ **run in** *vt* (*Brit: car*) roder
▶ **run into** *vt fus* (*meet: person*) rencontrer par hasard; (: *trouble*) se heurter à; (*collide with*) heurter; **to ~ into debt** contracter des dettes
▶ **run off** *vi* s'enfuir ▷ *vt* (*water*) laisser s'écouler; (*copies*) tirer
▶ **run out** *vi* (*person*) sortir en courant; (*liquid*) couler; (*lease*) expirer; (*money*) être épuisé(e)
▶ **run out of** *vt fus* se trouver à court de; **I've ~ out of petrol** or (*US*) **gas** je suis en panne d'essence
▶ **run over** *vt* (*Aut*) écraser ▷ *vt fus* (*revise*) revoir, reprendre
▶ **run through** *vt fus* (*recap*) reprendre, revoir; (*play*) répéter
▶ **run up** *vi*: **to ~ up against** (*difficulties*) se heurter à ▷ *vt*: **to ~ up a debt** s'endetter

runaround [ˈrʌnəraund] *n* (*inf*): **to give sb the ~** rester très évasif

runaway [ˈrʌnəweɪ] *adj* (*horse*) emballé(e); (*truck*) fou (folle); (*person*) fugitif(-ive); (*child*) fugueur(-euse); (*inflation*) galopant(e)

rundown [ˈrʌndaun] *n* (*Brit: of industry etc*) réduction progressive

rung [rʌŋ] *pp of* **ring** ▷ *n* (*of ladder*) barreau *m*

run-in ['rʌnɪn] n (inf) accrochage m, prise f de bec

runner ['rʌnəʳ] n (in race: person) coureur(-euse); (: horse) partant m; (on sledge) patin m; (for drawer etc) coulisseau m; (carpet: in hall etc) chemin m

runner bean n (Brit) haricot m (à rames)

runner-up [rʌnər'ʌp] n second(e)

running ['rʌnɪŋ] n (in race etc) course f; (of business, organization) direction f, gestion f; (of event) organisation f; (of machine etc) marche f, fonctionnement m ▷ adj (water) courant(e); (commentary) suivi(e); **6 days ~** 6 jours de suite; **to be in/out of the ~ for sth** être/ne pas être sur les rangs pour qch

running commentary n commentaire détaillé

running costs npl (of business) frais mpl de gestion; (of car): **the ~ are high** elle revient cher

running head n (Typ, Comput) titre courant

running mate n (US Pol) candidat à la vice-présidence

runny ['rʌnɪ] adj qui coule

run-off ['rʌnɔf] n (in contest, election) deuxième tour m; (extra race etc) épreuve f supplémentaire

run-of-the-mill ['rʌnəvðə'mɪl] adj ordinaire, banal(e)

runt [rʌnt] n avorton m

run-through ['rʌnθru:] n répétition f, essai m

run-up ['rʌnʌp] n (Brit): **~ to sth** période f précédant qch

runway ['rʌnweɪ] n (Aviat) piste f (d'envol or d'atterrissage)

rupee [ru:'pi:] n roupie f

rupture ['rʌptʃəʳ] n (Med) hernie f ▷ vt: **to ~ o.s.** se donner une hernie

rural ['ruərl] adj rural(e)

ruse [ru:z] n ruse f

rush [rʌʃ] n course précipitée; (of crowd, Comm: sudden demand) ruée f; (hurry) hâte f; (of anger, joy) accès m; (current) flot m; (Bot) jonc m; (for chair) paille f ▷ vt (hurry) transporter or envoyer d'urgence; (attack: town etc) prendre d'assaut; (Brit inf: overcharge) estamper; faire payer ▷ vi se précipiter; **don't ~ me!** laissez-moi le temps de souffler!; **to ~ sth off** (do quickly) faire qch à la hâte; (send) envoyer qch d'urgence; **is there any ~ for this?** est-ce urgent?; **we've had a ~ of orders** nous avons reçu une avalanche de commandes; **I'm in a ~ (to do)** je suis vraiment pressé (de faire); **gold ~** ruée vers l'or

  ▸ **rush through** vt fus (work) exécuter à la hâte ▷ vt (Comm: order) exécuter d'urgence

rush hour n heures fpl de pointe or d'affluence

rush job n travail urgent

rush matting n natte f de paille

rusk [rʌsk] n biscotte f

Russia ['rʌʃə] n Russie f

Russian ['rʌʃən] adj russe ▷ n Russe m/f; (Ling) russe m

rust [rʌst] n rouille f ▷ vi rouiller

rustic ['rʌstɪk] adj rustique ▷ n (pej) rustaud(e)

rustle ['rʌsl] vi bruire, produire un bruissement ▷ vt (paper) froisser; (US: cattle) voler

rustproof ['rʌstpru:f] adj inoxydable

rustproofing ['rʌstpru:fɪŋ] n traitement m antirouille

rusty ['rʌstɪ] adj rouillé(e)

rut [rʌt] n ornière f; (Zool) rut m; **to be in a ~** (fig) suivre l'ornière, s'encroûter

rutabaga [ru:tə'beɪgə] n (US) rutabaga m

ruthless ['ru:θlɪs] adj sans pitié, impitoyable

ruthlessness ['ru:θlɪsnɪs] n dureté f, cruauté f

RV abbr (= revised version) traduction anglaise de la Bible de 1885 ▷ n abbr (US) = **recreational vehicle**

rye [raɪ] n seigle m

rye bread n pain m de seigle

Ss

S, s [εs] n (letter) S, s m; (US Scol: satisfactory)
≈ assez bien; **S for Sugar** S comme Suzanne
S abbr (= south, small) S; (= saint) St
SA n abbr = **South Africa**; **South America**
Sabbath ['sæbəθ] n (Jewish) sabbat m; (Christian)
dimanche m
sabbatical [sə'bætɪkl] adj: **~ year** année f
sabbatique
sabotage ['sæbətɑːʒ] n sabotage m ▷ vt saboter
saccharin, saccharine ['sækərɪn] n
saccharine f
sachet ['sæʃeɪ] n sachet m
sack [sæk] n (bag) sac m ▷ vt (dismiss) renvoyer,
mettre à la porte; (plunder) piller, mettre à sac;
to give sb the ~ renvoyer qn, mettre qn à la
porte; **to get the ~** être renvoyé(e) or mis(e) à la
porte
sackful ['sækful] n: **a ~ of** un (plein) sac de
sacking ['sækɪŋ] n toile f à sac; (dismissal)
renvoi m
sacrament ['sækrəmənt] n sacrement m
sacred ['seɪkrɪd] adj sacré(e)
sacred cow n (fig) chose sacro-sainte
sacrifice ['sækrɪfaɪs] n sacrifice m ▷ vt sacrifier;
to make ~s (for sb) se sacrifier or faire des
sacrifices (pour qn)
sacrilege ['sækrɪlɪdʒ] n sacrilège m
sacrosanct ['sækrəusæŋkt] adj sacro-saint(e)
sad [sæd] adj (unhappy) triste; (deplorable) triste,
fâcheux(-euse); (inf: pathetic: thing) triste,
lamentable; (: person) minable
sadden ['sædn] vt attrister, affliger
saddle ['sædl] n selle f ▷ vt (horse) seller; **to be
~d with sth** (inf) avoir qch sur les bras
saddlebag ['sædlbæg] n sacoche f
sadism ['seɪdɪzəm] n sadisme m
sadist ['seɪdɪst] n sadique m/f
sadistic [sə'dɪstɪk] adj sadique
sadly ['sædlɪ] adv tristement; (unfortunately)
malheureusement; (seriously) fort
sadness ['sædnɪs] n tristesse f
sado-masochism [seɪdəu'mæsəkɪzəm] n
sadomasochisme m
s.a.e. n abbr (Brit: = stamped addressed envelope)
enveloppe affranchie pour la réponse
safari [sə'fɑːrɪ] n safari m

safari park n réserve f
safe [seɪf] adj (out of danger) hors de danger, en
sécurité; (not dangerous) sans danger; (cautious)
prudent(e); (sure: bet) assuré(e) ▷ n coffre-fort
m; **~ from** à l'abri de; **~ and sound** sain(e) et
sauf (sauve); **(just) to be on the ~ side** pour
plus de sûreté, par précaution; **to play ~** ne
prendre aucun risque; **it is ~ to say that ...** on
peut dire sans crainte que ...; **~ journey!** bon
voyage!
safe bet n: **it was a ~** ça ne comportait pas trop
de risques; **it's a ~ that he'll be late** il y a
toutes les chances pour qu'il soit en retard
safe-breaker ['seɪfbreɪkə^r] n (Brit) perceur m de
coffre-fort
safe-conduct [seɪf'kɔndʌkt] n sauf-conduit m
safe-cracker ['seɪfkrækə^r] n = **safe-breaker**
safe-deposit ['seɪfdɪpɔzɪt] n (vault) dépôt m de
coffres-forts; (box) coffre-fort m
safeguard ['seɪfgɑːd] n sauvegarde f, protection
f ▷ vt sauvegarder, protéger
safe haven n zone f de sécurité
safekeeping ['seɪf'kiːpɪŋ] n bonne garde
safely ['seɪflɪ] adv (assume, say) sans risque
d'erreur; (drive, arrive) sans accident; **I can ~
say ...** je peux dire à coup sûr ...
safe passage n: **to grant sb ~** accorder un
laissez-passer à qn
safe sex n rapports sexuels protégés
safety ['seɪftɪ] n sécurité f; **~ first!** la sécurité
d'abord!
safety belt n ceinture f de sécurité
safety catch n cran m de sûreté or sécurité
safety net n filet m de sécurité
safety pin n épingle f de sûreté or de nourrice
safety valve n soupape f de sûreté
saffron ['sæfrən] n safran m
sag [sæg] vi s'affaisser, fléchir; (hem, breasts)
pendre
saga ['sɑːgə] n saga f; (fig) épopée f
sage [seɪdʒ] n (herb) sauge f; (person) sage m
Sagittarius [sædʒɪ'tɛərɪəs] n le Sagittaire; **to be
~** être du Sagittaire
sago ['seɪgəu] n sagou m
Sahara [sə'hɑːrə] n: **the ~ (Desert)** le (désert du)
Sahara m

Sahel [sæ'hɛl] n Sahel m
said [sɛd] pt, pp of **say**
Saigon [saɪ'gɒn] n Saigon
sail [seɪl] n (on boat) voile f; (trip): **to go for a ~**
faire un tour en bateau ▷ vt (boat) manœuvrer,
piloter ▷ vi (travel: ship) avancer, naviguer;
(: passenger) aller or se rendre (en bateau); (set off)
partir, prendre la mer; (Sport) faire de la voile;
they ~ed into Le Havre ils sont entrés dans le
port du Havre
▶ **sail through** vi, vt fus (fig) réussir haut la main
sailboat ['seɪlbəut] n (US) bateau m à voiles,
voilier m
sailing ['seɪlɪŋ] n (Sport) voile f; **to go ~** faire de la
voile
sailing boat n bateau m à voiles, voilier m
sailing ship n grand voilier
sailor ['seɪlə^r] n marin m, matelot m
saint [seɪnt] n saint(e)
saintly ['seɪntlɪ] adj saint(e), plein(e) de bonté
sake [seɪk] n: **for the ~ of** (out of concern for) pour
(l'amour de), dans l'intérêt de; (out of
consideration for) par égard pour; (in order to achieve)
pour plus de, par souci de; **arguing for**
arguing's ~ discuter pour (le plaisir de)
discuter; **for heaven's ~!** pour l'amour du ciel!;
for the ~ of argument à titre d'exemple
salad ['sæləd] n salade f; **tomato ~** salade de
tomates
salad bowl n saladier m
salad cream n (Brit) (sorte f de) mayonnaise f
salad dressing n vinaigrette f
salad oil n huile f de table
salami [sə'lɑːmɪ] n salami m
salaried ['sælərɪd] adj (staff) salarié(e), qui
touche un traitement
salary ['sælərɪ] n salaire m, traitement m
salary scale n échelle f des traitements
sale [seɪl] n vente f; (at reduced prices) soldes mpl;
sales npl (total amount sold) chiffre m de ventes;
"for ~" "à vendre"; **on ~** en vente; **on ~ or**
return vendu(e) avec faculté de retour;
closing-down or **liquidation ~** (US) liquidation
f (avant fermeture); **~ and lease back** n cession-
bail f
saleroom ['seɪlruːm] n salle f des ventes
sales assistant, (US) **sales clerk** n
vendeur(-euse)
sales conference n réunion f de vente
sales drive n campagne commerciale,
animation f des ventes
sales force n (ensemble m du) service des ventes
salesman ['seɪlzmən] (irreg) n (in shop) vendeur
m; (representative) représentant m de commerce
sales manager n directeur commercial
salesmanship ['seɪlzmənʃɪp] n art m de la vente
salesperson ['seɪlzpəːsn] (irreg) n (in shop)
vendeur(-euse)
sales rep n (Comm) représentant(e) m/f
sales tax n (US) taxe f à l'achat
saleswoman ['seɪlzwumən] (irreg) n (in shop)
vendeuse f

salient ['seɪlɪənt] adj saillant(e)
saline ['seɪlaɪn] adj salin(e)
saliva [sə'laɪvə] n salive f
sallow ['sæləu] adj cireux(-euse)
sally forth, sally out ['sælɪ-] vi partir plein(e)
d'entrain
salmon ['sæmən] n (pl inv) saumon m
salmon trout n truite saumonée
salon ['sælɒn] n salon m
saloon [sə'luːn] n (US) bar m; (Brit Aut) berline f;
(ship's lounge) salon m
SALT [sɔːlt] n abbr (= Strategic Arms Limitation Talks/
Treaty) SALT m
salt [sɔːlt] n sel m ▷ vt saler ▷ cpd de sel; (Culin)
salé(e); **an old ~** un vieux loup de mer
▶ **salt away** vt mettre de côté
salt cellar n salière f
salt-free ['sɔːlt'friː] adj sans sel
saltwater ['sɔːlt'wɔːtə^r] adj (fish etc) (d'eau) de
mer
salty ['sɔːltɪ] adj salé(e)
salubrious [sə'luːbrɪəs] adj salubre
salutary ['sæljutərɪ] adj salutaire
salute [sə'luːt] n salut m; (of guns) salve f ▷ vt
saluer
salvage ['sælvɪdʒ] n (saving) sauvetage m; (things
saved) biens sauvés or récupérés ▷ vt sauver,
récupérer
salvage vessel n bateau m de sauvetage
salvation [sæl'veɪʃən] n salut m
Salvation Army [sæl'veɪʃən-] n Armée f du
Salut
salver ['sælvə^r] n plateau m de métal
salvo ['sælvəu] n salve f
Samaritan [sə'mærɪtən] n: **the ~s** (organization)
≈ S.O.S. Amitié
same [seɪm] adj même ▷ pron: **the ~** le (la)
même, les mêmes; **the ~ book as** le même livre
que; **on the ~ day** le même jour; **at the ~ time**
en même temps; (yet) néanmoins; **all** or **just**
the ~ tout de même, quand même; **they're one**
and the ~ (person/thing) c'est une seule et même
personne/chose; **to do the ~** faire de même, en
faire autant; **to do the ~ as sb** faire comme qn;
and the ~ to you! et à vous de même!; (after
insult) toi-même!; **~ here!** moi aussi!; **the ~**
again! (in bar etc) la même chose!
sample ['sɑːmpl] n échantillon m; (Med)
prélèvement m ▷ vt (food, wine) goûter; **to take a**
~ prélever un échantillon; **free ~** échantillon
gratuit
sanatorium (pl **sanatoria**) [sænə'tɔːrɪəm, -rɪə] n
sanatorium m
sanctify ['sæŋktɪfaɪ] vt sanctifier
sanctimonious [sæŋktɪ'məunɪəs] adj
moralisateur(-trice)
sanction ['sæŋkʃən] n approbation f, sanction f
▷ vt cautionner, sanctionner; **sanctions** npl
(Pol) sanctions; **to impose economic ~s on** or
against prendre des sanctions économiques
contre
sanctity ['sæŋktɪtɪ] n sainteté f, caractère sacré

sanctuary ['sæŋktjuərɪ] n (holy place) sanctuaire m; (refuge) asile m; (for wildlife) réserve f

sand [sænd] n sable m ▷ vt sabler; (also: **sand down**: wood etc) poncer

sandal ['sændl] n sandale f

sandbag ['sændbæg] n sac m de sable

sandblast ['sændblɑːst] vt décaper à la sableuse

sandbox ['sændbɒks] n (US: for children) tas m de sable

sand castle ['sændkɑːsl] n château m de sable

sand dune n dune f de sable

sander ['sændər] n ponceuse f

S&M n abbr (= sadomasochism) sadomasochisme m

sandpaper ['sændpeɪpər] n papier m de verre

sandpit ['sændpɪt] n (Brit: for children) tas m de sable

sands [sændz] npl plage f (de sable)

sandstone ['sændstəun] n grès m

sandstorm ['sændstɔːm] n tempête f de sable

sandwich ['sændwɪtʃ] n sandwich m ▷ vt (also: **sandwich in**) intercaler; **~ed between** pris en sandwich entre; **cheese/ham ~** sandwich au fromage/jambon

sandwich board n panneau m publicitaire (porté par un homme-sandwich)

sandwich course n (Brit) cours m de formation professionnelle

sandy ['sændɪ] adj sablonneux(-euse); couvert(e) de sable; (colour) sable inv, blond roux inv

sane [seɪn] adj (person) sain(e) d'esprit; (outlook) sensé(e), sain(e)

sang [sæŋ] pt of **sing**

sanguine ['sæŋgwɪn] adj optimiste

sanitarium (pl **sanitaria**) [sænɪ'tɛərɪəm, -rɪə] n (US) = **sanatorium**

sanitary ['sænɪtərɪ] adj (system, arrangements) sanitaire; (clean) hygiénique

sanitary towel, (US) **sanitary napkin** ['sænɪtərɪ-] n serviette f hygiénique

sanitation [sænɪ'teɪʃən] n (in house) installations fpl sanitaires; (in town) système m sanitaire

sanitation department n (US) service m de voirie

sanity ['sænɪtɪ] n santé mentale; (common sense) bon sens

sank [sæŋk] pt of **sink**

San Marino ['sænmə'riːnəu] n Saint-Marin m

Santa Claus [sæntə'klɔːz] n le Père Noël

Santiago [sæntɪ'ɑːgəu] n (also: **Santiago de Chile**) Santiago (du Chili)

sap [sæp] n (of plants) sève f ▷ vt (strength) saper, miner

sapling ['sæplɪŋ] n jeune arbre m

sapphire ['sæfaɪər] n saphir m

sarcasm ['sɑːkæzm] n sarcasme m, raillerie f

sarcastic [sɑː'kæstɪk] adj sarcastique

sarcophagus (pl **sarcophagi**) [sɑː'kɒfəgəs, -gaɪ] n sarcophage m

sardine [sɑː'diːn] n sardine f

Sardinia [sɑː'dɪnɪə] n Sardaigne f

Sardinian [sɑː'dɪnɪən] adj sarde ▷ n Sarde m/f; (Ling) sarde m

sardonic [sɑː'dɒnɪk] adj sardonique

sari ['sɑːrɪ] n sari m

SARS ['sɑːrz] n abbr = **severe acute respiratory syndrome**

sartorial [sɑː'tɔːrɪəl] adj vestimentaire

SAS n abbr (Brit Mil: = Special Air Service) ≈ GIGN m

SASE n abbr (US: = self-addressed stamped envelope) enveloppe affranchie pour la réponse

sash [sæʃ] n écharpe f

sash window n fenêtre f à guillotine

Sask. abbr (Canada) = **Saskatchewan**

sat [sæt] pt, pp of **sit**

Sat. abbr (= Saturday) sa

Satan ['seɪtn] n Satan m

satanic [sə'tænɪk] adj satanique, démoniaque

satchel ['sætʃl] n cartable m

sated ['seɪtɪd] adj repu(e); blasé(e)

satellite ['sætəlaɪt] adj, n satellite m

satellite dish n antenne f parabolique

satellite navigation system n système m de navigation par satellite

satellite television n télévision f par satellite

satiate ['seɪʃɪeɪt] vt rassasier

satin ['sætɪn] n satin m ▷ adj en or de satin, satiné(e); **with a ~ finish** satiné(e)

satire ['sætaɪər] n satire f

satirical [sə'tɪrɪkl] adj satirique

satirist ['sætɪrɪst] n (writer) auteur m satirique; (cartoonist) caricaturiste m/f

satirize ['sætɪraɪz] vt faire la satire de, satiriser

satisfaction [sætɪs'fækʃən] n satisfaction f

satisfactory [sætɪs'fæktərɪ] adj satisfaisant(e)

satisfied ['sætɪsfaɪd] adj satisfait(e); **to be ~ with sth** être satisfait de qch

satisfy ['sætɪsfaɪ] vt satisfaire, contenter; (convince) convaincre, persuader; **to ~ the requirements** remplir les conditions; **to ~ sb (that)** convaincre qn (que); **to ~ o.s. of sth** vérifier qch, s'assurer de qch

satisfying ['sætɪsfaɪɪŋ] adj satisfaisant(e)

SAT(s) n abbr (US) = **Scholastic Aptitude Test(s)**

satsuma [sæt'suːmə] n satsuma f

saturate ['sætʃəreɪt] vt: **to ~ (with)** saturer (de)

saturated fat ['sætʃəreɪtɪd-] n graisse saturée

saturation [sætʃə'reɪʃən] n saturation f

Saturday ['sætədɪ] n samedi m; for phrases see also **Tuesday**

sauce [sɔːs] n sauce f

saucepan ['sɔːspən] n casserole f

saucer ['sɔːsər] n soucoupe f

saucy ['sɔːsɪ] adj impertinent(e)

Saudi Arabia n Arabie f Saoudite

Saudi (Arabian) ['saudi] adj saoudien(ne) ▷ n Saoudien(ne)

sauna ['sɔːnə] n sauna m

saunter ['sɔːntər] vi: **to ~ to** aller en flânant or se balader jusqu'à

sausage ['sɒsɪdʒ] n saucisse f; (salami etc) saucisson m

sausage roll n friand m

sauté ['səuteɪ] adj (Culin: potatoes) sauté(e);

(: *onions*) revenu(e) ▷ *vt* faire sauter; faire revenir

sautéed ['səuteɪd] *adj* sauté(e)

savage ['sævɪdʒ] *adj* (*cruel, fierce*) brutal(e), féroce; (*primitive*) primitif(-ive), sauvage ▷ *n* sauvage *m/f* ▷ *vt* attaquer férocement

savagery ['sævɪdʒrɪ] *n* sauvagerie *f*, brutalité *f*, férocité *f*

save [seɪv] *vt* (*person, belongings*) sauver; (*money*) mettre de côté, économiser; (*time*) (faire) gagner; (*keep*) garder; (*Comput*) sauvegarder; (*Sport: stop*) arrêter; (*avoid: trouble*) éviter ▷ *vi* (*also*: **save up**) mettre de l'argent de côté ▷ *n* (*Sport*) arrêt *m* (du ballon) ▷ *prep* sauf, à l'exception de; **it will ~ me an hour** ça me fera gagner une heure; **to ~ face** sauver la face; **God ~ the Queen!** vive la Reine!

saving ['seɪvɪŋ] *n* économie *f* ▷ *adj*: **the ~ grace of** ce qui rachète; **savings** *npl* économies *fpl*; **to make ~s** faire des économies

savings account *n* compte *m* d'épargne

savings and loan association (US) *n* ≈ société *f* de crédit immobilier

savings bank *n* caisse *f* d'épargne

saviour, (US) **savior** ['seɪvjə^r] *n* sauveur *m*

savour, (US) **savor** ['seɪvə^r] *n* saveur *f*, goût *m* ▷ *vt* savourer

savoury, (US) **savory** ['seɪvərɪ] *adj* savoureux(-euse); (*dish: not sweet*) salé(e)

savvy ['sævɪ] *n* (*inf*) jugeote *f*

saw [sɔː] *pt of* **see** ▷ *n* (*tool*) scie *f* ▷ *vt* (*pt* -**ed**, *pp* -**ed** *or* -**n** [sɔːn]) scier; **to ~ sth up** débiter qch à la scie

sawdust ['sɔːdʌst] *n* sciure *f*

sawmill ['sɔːmɪl] *n* scierie *f*

sawn [sɔːn] *pp of* **saw**

sawn-off ['sɔːnɔf], **sawed-off** ['sɔːdɔf] (US) *adj*: **~ shotgun** carabine *f* à canon scié

sax [sæks] (*inf*) *n* saxo *m*

saxophone ['sæksəfəun] *n* saxophone *m*

say [seɪ] *n*: **to have one's ~** dire ce qu'on a à dire ▷ *vt* (*pt, pp* **said**) [sɛd] dire; **to have a ~** avoir voix au chapitre; **could you ~ that again?** pourriez-vous répéter ce que vous venez de dire?; **to ~ yes/no** dire oui/non; **she said (that) I was to give you this** elle m'a chargé de vous remettre ceci; **my watch ~s 3 o'clock** ma montre indique 3 heures, il est 3 heures à ma montre; **shall we ~ Tuesday?** disons mardi?; **that doesn't ~ much for him** ce n'est pas vraiment à son honneur; **when all is said and done** en fin de compte, en définitive; **there is something** *or* **a lot to be said for it** cela a des avantages; **that is to ~** c'est-à-dire; **to ~ nothing of** sans compter; **~ that ...** mettons *or* disons que ...; **that goes without ~ing** cela va sans dire, cela va de soi

saying ['seɪɪŋ] *n* dicton *m*, proverbe *m*

SBA *n abbr* (US: = *Small Business Administration*) *organisme d'aide aux PME*

SC *n abbr* (US) = **supreme court** ▷ *abbr* (US) = **South Carolina**

s/c *abbr* = **self-contained**

scab [skæb] *n* croûte *f*; (*pej*) jaune *m*

scabby ['skæbɪ] *adj* croûteux(-euse)

scaffold ['skæfəld] *n* échafaud *m*

scaffolding ['skæfəldɪŋ] *n* échafaudage *m*

scald [skɔːld] *n* brûlure *f* ▷ *vt* ébouillanter

scalding ['skɔːldɪŋ] *adj* (*also*: **scalding hot**) brûlant(e), bouillant(e)

scale [skeɪl] *n* (*of fish*) écaille *f*; (*Mus*) gamme *f*; (*of ruler, thermometer etc*) graduation *f*, échelle (graduée); (*of salaries, fees etc*) barème *m*; (*of map, also size, extent*) échelle ▷ *vt* (*mountain*) escalader; (*fish*) écailler; **scales** *npl* balance *f*; (*larger*) bascule *f*; (*also*: **bathroom scales**) pèse-personne *m inv*; **pay ~** échelle des salaires; **~ of charges** tableau *m* des tarifs; **on a large ~** sur une grande échelle, en grand; **to draw sth to ~** dessiner qch à l'échelle; **small-~ model** modèle réduit

▶ **scale down** *vt* réduire

scaled-down [skeɪld'daun] *adj* à échelle réduite

scale drawing *n* dessin *m* à l'échelle

scale model *n* modèle *m* à l'échelle

scallion ['skæljən] *n* oignon *m*; (US: *salad onion*) ciboule *f*; (: *shallot*) échalote *f*; (: *leek*) poireau *m*

scallop ['skɔləp] *n* coquille *f* Saint-Jacques; (*Sewing*) feston *m*

scalp [skælp] *n* cuir chevelu ▷ *vt* scalper

scalpel ['skælpl] *n* scalpel *m*

scalper ['skælpə^r] *n* (*US inf: of tickets*) revendeur *m* de billets

scam [skæm] *n* (*inf*) arnaque *f*

scamp [skæmp] *vt* bâcler

scamper ['skæmpə^r] *vi*: **to ~ away, ~ off** détaler

scampi ['skæmpɪ] *npl* langoustines (frites), scampi *mpl*

scan [skæn] *vt* (*examine*) scruter, examiner; (*glance at quickly*) parcourir; (*poetry*) scander; (*TV, Radar*) balayer ▷ *n* (*Med*) scanographie *f*

scandal ['skændl] *n* scandale *m*; (*gossip*) ragots *mpl*

scandalize ['skændəlaɪz] *vt* scandaliser, indigner

scandalous ['skændələs] *adj* scandaleux(-euse)

Scandinavia [skændɪ'neɪvɪə] *n* Scandinavie *f*

Scandinavian [skændɪ'neɪvɪən] *adj* scandinave ▷ *n* Scandinave *m/f*

scanner ['skænə^r] *n* (*Radar, Med*) scanner *m*, scanographe *m*; (*Comput*) scanner

scant [skænt] *adj* insuffisant(e)

scantily ['skæntɪlɪ] *adv*: **~ clad** *or* **dressed** vêtu(e) du strict minimum

scanty ['skæntɪ] *adj* peu abondant(e), insuffisant(e), maigre

scapegoat ['skeɪpgəut] *n* bouc *m* émissaire

scar [skɑː^r] *n* cicatrice *f* ▷ *vt* laisser une cicatrice *or* une marque à

scarce [skɛəs] *adj* rare, peu abondant(e); **to make o.s. ~** (*inf*) se sauver

scarcely ['skɛəslɪ] *adv* à peine, presque pas; **~ anybody** pratiquement personne; **I can ~ believe it** j'ai du mal à le croire

scarcity ['skɛəsɪtɪ] n rareté f, manque m, pénurie f

scarcity value n valeur f de rareté

scare [skɛəʳ] n peur f, panique f ▷ vt effrayer, faire peur à; **to ~ sb stiff** faire une peur bleue à qn; **bomb ~** alerte f à la bombe
▸ **scare away, scare off** vt faire fuir

scarecrow ['skɛəkrəʊ] n épouvantail m

scared ['skɛəd] adj: **to be ~** avoir peur

scaremonger ['skɛəmʌŋgəʳ] n alarmiste m/f

scarf (pl **scarves**) [skɑːf, skɑːvz] n (long) écharpe f; (square) foulard m

scarlet ['skɑːlɪt] adj écarlate

scarlet fever n scarlatine f

scarper ['skɑːpəʳ] vi (Brit inf) ficher le camp

scarves [skɑːvz] npl of **scarf**

scary ['skɛərɪ] adj (inf) effrayant(e); (film) qui fait peur

scathing ['skeɪðɪŋ] adj cinglant(e), acerbe; **to be ~ about sth** être très critique vis-à-vis de qch

scatter ['skætəʳ] vt éparpiller, répandre; (crowd) disperser ▷ vi se disperser

scatterbrained ['skætəbreɪnd] adj écervelé(e), étourdi(e)

scattered ['skætəd] adj épars(e), dispersé(e)

scatty ['skætɪ] adj (Brit inf) loufoque

scavenge ['skævəndʒ] vi (person): **to ~ (for)** faire les poubelles (pour trouver); **to ~ for food** (hyenas etc) se nourrir de charognes

scavenger ['skævəndʒəʳ] n éboueur m

SCE n abbr = **Scottish Certificate of Education**

scenario [sɪ'nɑːrɪəu] n scénario m

scene [siːn] n (Theat, fig etc) scène f; (of crime, accident) lieu(x) m(pl), endroit m; (sight, view) spectacle m, vue f; **behind the ~s** (also fig) dans les coulisses; **to make a ~** (inf: fuss) faire une scène or toute une histoire; **to appear on the ~** (also fig) faire son apparition, arriver; **the political ~** la situation politique

scenery ['siːnərɪ] n (Theat) décor(s) m(pl); (landscape) paysage m

scenic ['siːnɪk] adj scénique; offrant de beaux paysages or panoramas

scent [sɛnt] n parfum m, odeur f; (fig: track) piste f; (sense of smell) odorat m ▷ vt parfumer; (smell: also fig) flairer; (also: **to put** or **throw sb off the scent**: fig) mettre qn sur une mauvaise piste

sceptic, (US) **skeptic** ['skɛptɪk] n sceptique m/f

sceptical, (US) **skeptical** ['skɛptɪkl] adj sceptique

scepticism, (US) **skepticism** ['skɛptɪsɪzəm] n scepticisme m

sceptre, (US) **scepter** ['sɛptəʳ] n sceptre m

schedule ['ʃɛdjuːl] (US) ['skɛdjuːl] n programme m, plan m; (of trains) horaire m; (of prices etc) barème m, tarif m ▷ vt prévoir; **as ~d** comme prévu; **on ~** à l'heure (prévue); à la date prévue; **to be ahead of/behind ~** avoir de l'avance/du retard; **we are working to a very tight ~** notre programme de travail est très serré or intense; **everything went according to ~** tout s'est passé comme prévu

scheduled ['ʃɛdjuːld, (US) 'skɛdjuːld] adj (date, time) prévu(e), indiqué(e); (visit, event) programmé(e), prévu; (train, bus, stop, flight) régulier(-ière)

scheduled flight n vol régulier

schematic [skɪ'mætɪk] adj schématique

scheme [skiːm] n plan m, projet m; (method) procédé m; (plot) complot m, combine f; (arrangement) arrangement m, classification f; (pension scheme etc) régime m ▷ vt, vi comploter, manigancer; **colour ~** combinaison f de(s) couleurs

scheming ['skiːmɪŋ] adj rusé(e), intrigant(e) ▷ n manigances fpl, intrigues fpl

schism ['skɪzəm] n schisme m

schizophrenia [skɪtsə'friːnɪə] n schizophrénie f

schizophrenic [skɪtsə'frɛnɪk] adj schizophrène

scholar ['skɔlə] n érudit(e); (pupil) boursier(-ère)

scholarly ['skɔləlɪ] adj érudit(e), savant(e)

scholarship ['skɔləʃɪp] n érudition f; (grant) bourse f (d'études)

school [skuːl] n (gen) école f; (secondary school) collège m; lycée m; (in university) faculté f; (US: university) université f; (of fish) banc m ▷ cpd scolaire ▷ vt (animal) dresser

school age n âge m scolaire

schoolbook ['skuːlbuk] n livre m scolaire or de classe

schoolboy ['skuːlbɔɪ] n écolier m; (at secondary school) collégien m; lycéen m

schoolchildren ['skuːltʃɪldrən] npl écoliers mpl; (at secondary school) collégiens mpl; lycéens mpl

schooldays ['skuːldeɪz] npl années fpl de scolarité

schoolgirl ['skuːlgəːl] n écolière f; (at secondary school) collégienne f; lycéenne f

schooling ['skuːlɪŋ] n instruction f, études fpl

school-leaver ['skuːlliːvəʳ] n (Brit) jeune qui vient de terminer ses études secondaires

schoolmaster ['skuːlmɑːstəʳ] n (primary) instituteur m; (secondary) professeur m

schoolmistress ['skuːlmɪstrɪs] n (primary) institutrice f; (secondary) professeur m

school report n (Brit) bulletin m (scolaire)

schoolroom ['skuːlruːm] n (salle f de) classe f

schoolteacher ['skuːltiːtʃəʳ] n (primary) instituteur(-trice); (secondary) professeur m

schoolyard ['skuːljɑːd] n (US) cour f de récréation

schooner ['skuːnəʳ] n (ship) schooner m, goélette f; (glass) grand verre (à xérès)

sciatica [saɪ'ætɪkə] n sciatique f

science ['saɪəns] n science f; **the ~s** les sciences; (Scol) les matières fpl scientifiques

science fiction n science-fiction f

scientific [saɪən'tɪfɪk] adj scientifique

scientist ['saɪəntɪst] n scientifique m/f; (eminent) savant m

sci-fi ['saɪfaɪ] n abbr (inf: = science fiction) SF f

Scilly Isles ['sɪlɪ'aɪlz], **Scillies** ['sɪlɪz] npl: **the ~** les Sorlingues fpl, les îles fpl Scilly

scintillating ['sıntıleıtıŋ] *adj* scintillant(e), étincelant(e); (*wit etc*) brillant(e)

scissors ['sɪzəz] *npl* ciseaux *mpl*; **a pair of** ~ une paire de ciseaux

sclerosis [sklı'rəusıs] *n* sclérose *f*

scoff [skɔf] *vt* (*Brit inf: eat*) avaler, bouffer ▷ *vi*: **to** ~ **(at)** (*mock*) se moquer (de)

scold [skəuld] *vt* gronder, attraper, réprimander

scolding ['skəuldıŋ] *n* réprimande *f*

scone [skɔn] *n* sorte de petit pain rond au lait

scoop [sku:p] *n* pelle *f* (à main); (*for ice cream*) boule *f* à glace; (*Press*) reportage exclusif *or* à sensation

▶ **scoop out** *vt* évider, creuser

▶ **scoop up** *vt* ramasser

scooter ['sku:tə^r] *n* (*motor cycle*) scooter *m*; (*toy*) trottinette *f*

scope [skəup] *n* (*capacity: of plan, undertaking*) portée *f*, envergure *f*; (: *of person*) compétence *f*, capacités *fpl*; (*opportunity*) possibilités *fpl*; **within the** ~ **of** dans les limites de; **there is plenty of** ~ **for improvement** (*Brit*) cela pourrait être beaucoup mieux

scorch [skɔːtʃ] *vt* (*clothes*) brûler (légèrement), roussir; (*earth, grass*) dessécher, brûler

scorched earth policy ['skɔːtʃt-] *n* politique *f* de la terre brûlée

scorcher ['skɔːtʃə^r] *n* (*inf: hot day*) journée *f* torride

scorching ['skɔːtʃıŋ] *adj* torride, brûlant(e)

score [skɔː^r] *n* score *m*, décompte *m* des points; (*Mus*) partition *f* ▷ *vt* (*goal, point*) marquer; (*success*) remporter; (*cut: leather, wood, card*) entailler, inciser ▷ *vi* marquer des points; (*Football*) marquer un but; (*keep score*) compter les points; **on that** ~ sur ce chapitre, à cet égard; **to have an old** ~ **to settle with sb** (*fig*) avoir un (vieux) compte à régler avec qn; **a** ~ **of** (*twenty*) vingt; ~**s of** (*fig*) des tas de; **to** ~ **6 out of 10** obtenir 6 sur 10

▶ **score out** *vt* rayer, barrer, biffer

scoreboard ['skɔːbɔːd] *n* tableau *m*

scorecard ['skɔːkɑːd] *n* (*Sport*) carton *m*, feuille *f* de marque

scoreline ['skɔːlaın] *n* (*Sport*) score *m*

scorer ['skɔːrə^r] *n* (*Football*) auteur *m* du but; buteur *m*; (*keeping score*) marqueur *m*

scorn [skɔːn] *n* mépris *m*, dédain *m* ▷ *vt* mépriser, dédaigner

scornful ['skɔːnful] *adj* méprisant(e), dédaigneux(-euse)

Scorpio ['skɔːpıəu] *n* le Scorpion; **to be** ~ être du Scorpion

scorpion ['skɔːpıən] *n* scorpion *m*

Scot [skɔt] *n* Écossais(e)

Scotch [skɔtʃ] *n* whisky *m*, scotch *m*

scotch [skɔtʃ] *vt* faire échouer; enrayer; étouffer

Scotch tape® (*US*) *n* scotch® *m*, ruban adhésif

scot-free ['skɔt'friː] *adj*: **to get off** ~ s'en tirer sans être puni(e); s'en sortir indemne

Scotland ['skɔtlənd] *n* Écosse *f*

Scots [skɔts] *adj* écossais(e)

Scotsman ['skɔtsmən] (*irreg*) *n* Écossais *m*

Scotswoman ['skɔtswumən] (*irreg*) *n* Écossaise *f*

Scottish ['skɔtıʃ] *adj* écossais(e); **the** ~ **National Party** le parti national écossais; **the** ~ **Parliament** le Parlement écossais

scoundrel ['skaundrl] *n* vaurien *m*

scour ['skauə^r] *vt* (*clean*) récurer; frotter; décaper; (*search*) battre, parcourir

scourer ['skauərə^r] *n* tampon abrasif *or* à récurer; (*powder*) poudre *f* à récurer

scourge [skə:dʒ] *n* fléau *m*

scout [skaut] *n* (*Mil*) éclaireur *m*; (*also:* **boy scout**) scout *m*; **girl** ~ (*US*) guide *f*

▶ **scout around** *vi* chercher

scowl [skaul] *vi* se renfrogner, avoir l'air maussade; **to** ~ **at** regarder de travers

scrabble ['skræbl] *vi* (*claw*): **to** ~ **(at)** gratter; **to** ~ **about** *or* **around for sth** chercher qch à tâtons ▷ *n*: **S**~® Scrabble® *m*

scraggy ['skrægı] *adj* décharné(e), efflanqué(e), famélique

scram [skræm] *vi* (*inf*) ficher le camp

scramble ['skræmbl] *n* (*rush*) bousculade *f*, ruée *f* ▷ *vi* grimper/descendre tant bien que mal; **to** ~ **for** se bousculer *or* se disputer pour (avoir); **to go scrambling** (*Sport*) faire du trial

scrambled eggs ['skræmbld-] *npl* œufs brouillés

scrap [skræp] *n* bout *m*, morceau *m*; (*fight*) bagarre *f*; (*also:* **scrap iron**) ferraille *f* ▷ *vt* jeter, mettre au rebut; (*fig*) abandonner, laisser tomber ▷ *vi* se bagarrer; **scraps** *npl* (*waste*) déchets *mpl*; **to sell sth for** ~ vendre qch à la casse *or* à la ferraille

scrapbook ['skræpbuk] *n* album *m*

scrap dealer *n* marchand *m* de ferraille

scrape [skreıp] *vt, vi* gratter, racler ▷ *n*: **to get into a** ~ s'attirer des ennuis

▶ **scrape through** *vi* (*exam etc*) réussir de justesse

▶ **scrape together** *vt* (*money*) racler ses fonds de tiroir pour réunir

scraper ['skreıpə^r] *n* grattoir *m*, racloir *m*

scrap heap *n* tas *m* de ferraille; (*fig*): **on the** ~ au rancart *or* rebut

scrap merchant *n* (*Brit*) marchand *m* de ferraille

scrap metal *n* ferraille *f*

scrap paper *n* papier *m* brouillon

scrappy ['skræpı] *adj* fragmentaire, décousu(e)

scrap yard *n* parc *m* à ferrailles; (*for cars*) cimetière *m* de voitures

scratch [skrætʃ] *n* égratignure *f*, rayure *f*; (*on paint*) éraflure *f*; (*from claw*) coup *m* de griffe ▷ *adj*: ~ **team** équipe de fortune *or* improvisée ▷ *vt* (*rub*) (se) gratter; (*record*) rayer; (*paint etc*) érafler; (*with claw, nail*) griffer; (*Comput*) effacer ▷ *vi* (se) gratter; **to start from** ~ partir de zéro; **to be up to** ~ être à la hauteur

scratch card *n* carte *f* à gratter

scrawl [skrɔːl] *n* gribouillage *m* ▷ *vi* gribouiller

scrawny ['skrɔːnı] *adj* décharné(e)

scream [skri:m] *n* cri perçant, hurlement *m* ▷ *vi* crier, hurler; **to be a ~** (*inf*) être impayable; **to ~ at sb to do sth** crier *or* hurler à qn de faire qch

scree [skri:] *n* éboulis *m*

screech [skri:tʃ] *n* cri strident, hurlement *m*; (*of tyres, brakes*) crissement *m*, grincement *m* ▷ *vi* hurler; crisser, grincer

screen [skri:n] *n* écran *m*; (*in room*) paravent *m*; (*Cine, TV*) écran; (*fig*) écran, rideau *m* ▷ *vt* masquer, cacher; (*from the wind etc*) abriter, protéger; (*film*) projeter; (*candidates etc*) filtrer; (*for illness*): **to ~ sb for sth** faire subir un test de dépistage de qch à qn

screen editing [-'ɛdɪtɪŋ] *n* (*Comput*) édition *f or* correction *f* sur écran

screening ['skri:nɪŋ] *n* (*of film*) projection *f*; (*Med*) test *m* (*or* tests) de dépistage; (*for security*) filtrage *m*

screen memory *n* (*Comput*) mémoire *f* écran

screenplay ['skri:npleɪ] *n* scénario *m*

screen saver *n* (*Comput*) économiseur *m* d'écran

screen test *n* bout *m* d'essai

screw [skru:] *n* vis *f*; (*propeller*) hélice *f* ▷ *vt* (*also*: **screw in**) visser; (*inf!: woman*) baiser (!); **to ~ sth to the wall** visser qch au mur; **to have one's head ~ed on** (*fig*) avoir la tête sur les épaules
▶ **screw up** *vt* (*paper etc*) froisser; (*inf: ruin*) bousiller; **to ~ up one's eyes** se plisser les yeux; **to ~ up one's face** faire la grimace

screwdriver ['skru:draɪvə^r] *n* tournevis *m*

screwed-up ['skru:d'ʌp] *adj* (*inf*): **to be ~** être paumé(e)

screwy ['skru:ɪ] *adj* (*inf*) dingue, cinglé(e)

scribble ['skrɪbl] *n* gribouillage *m* ▷ *vt* gribouiller, griffonner; **to ~ sth down** griffonner qch

scribe [skraɪb] *n* scribe *m*

script [skrɪpt] *n* (*Cine etc*) scénario *m*, texte *m*; (*in exam*) copie *f*; (*writing*) (écriture *f*) script *m*

scripted ['skrɪptɪd] *adj* (*Radio, TV*) préparé(e) à l'avance

Scripture ['skrɪptʃə^r] *n* Écriture sainte

scriptwriter ['skrɪptraɪtə^r] *n* scénariste *m/f*, dialoguiste *m/f*

scroll [skrəul] *n* rouleau *m* ▷ *vt* (*Comput*) faire défiler (sur l'écran)

scrotum ['skrəutəm] *n* scrotum *m*

scrounge ['skraundʒ] (*inf*) *vt*: **to ~ sth (off or from sb)** se faire payer qch (par qn), emprunter qch (à qn) ▷ *vi*: **to ~ on sb** vivre aux crochets de qn

scrounger ['skraundʒə^r] *n* parasite *m*

scrub [skrʌb] *n* (*clean*) nettoyage *m* (à la brosse); (*land*) broussailles *fpl* ▷ *vt* (*floor*) nettoyer à la brosse; (*pan*) récurer; (*washing*) frotter; (*reject*) annuler

scrubbing brush ['skrʌbɪŋ-] *n* brosse dure

scruff [skrʌf] *n*: **by the ~ of the neck** par la peau du cou

scruffy ['skrʌfɪ] *adj* débraillé(e)

scrum ['skrʌm], **scrummage** ['skrʌmɪdʒ] *n* mêlée *f*

scruple ['skru:pl] *n* scrupule *m*; **to have no ~s about doing sth** n'avoir aucun scrupule à faire qch

scrupulous ['skru:pjuləs] *adj* scrupuleux(-euse)

scrupulously ['skru:pjuəslɪ] *adv* scrupuleusement; **to be ~ honest** être d'une honnêteté scrupuleuse

scrutinize ['skru:tɪnaɪz] *vt* scruter, examiner minutieusement

scrutiny ['skru:tɪnɪ] *n* examen minutieux; **under the ~ of sb** sous la surveillance de qn

scuba ['sku:bə] *n* scaphandre *m* (autonome)

scuba diving ['sku:bə-] *n* plongée sous-marine

scuff [skʌf] *vt* érafler

scuffle ['skʌfl] *n* échauffourée *f*, rixe *f*

scullery ['skʌlərɪ] *n* arrière-cuisine *f*

sculptor ['skʌlptə^r] *n* sculpteur *m*

sculpture ['skʌlptʃə^r] *n* sculpture *f*

scum [skʌm] *n* écume *f*, mousse *f*; (*pej: people*) rebut *m*, lie *f*

scupper ['skʌpə^r] *vt* (*Brit*) saborder

scurrilous ['skʌrɪləs] *adj* haineux(-euse), virulent(e); calomnieux(-euse)

scurry ['skʌrɪ] *vi* filer à toute allure; **to ~ off** détaler, se sauver

scurvy ['skə:vɪ] *n* scorbut *m*

scuttle ['skʌtl] *n* (*Naut*) écoutille *f*; (*also*: **coal scuttle**) seau *m* (à charbon) ▷ *vt* (*ship*) saborder ▷ *vi* (*scamper*): **to ~ away, ~ off** détaler

scythe [saɪð] *n* faux *f*

SD, S. Dak. *abbr* (*US*) = **South Dakota**

SDI *n abbr* (= *Strategic Defense Initiative*) IDS *f*

SDLP *n abbr* (*Brit Pol*) = **Social Democratic and Labour Party**

sea [si:] *n* mer *f* ▷ *cpd* marin(e), de (la) mer, maritime; **on the ~** (*boat*) en mer; (*town*) au bord de la mer; **by** *or* **beside the ~** (*holiday, town*) au bord de la mer; **by ~** par mer, en bateau; **out to ~** au large; (**out**) **at ~** en mer; **heavy** *or* **rough ~(s)** grosse mer, mer agitée; **a ~ of faces** (*fig*) une multitude de visages; **to be all at ~** (*fig*) nager complètement

sea bed *n* fond *m* de la mer

sea bird *n* oiseau *m* de mer

seaboard ['si:bɔ:d] *n* côte *f*

sea breeze *n* brise *f* de mer

seafarer ['si:fɛərə^r] *n* marin *m*

seafaring ['si:fɛərɪŋ] *adj* (*life*) de marin; **~ people** les gens *mpl* de mer

seafood ['si:fu:d] *n* fruits *mpl* de mer

sea front ['si:frʌnt] *n* bord *m* de mer

seagoing ['si:gəuɪŋ] *adj* (*ship*) de haute mer

seagull ['si:gʌl] *n* mouette *f*

seal [si:l] *n* (*animal*) phoque *m*; (*stamp*) sceau *m*, cachet *m*; (*impression*) cachet, estampille *f* ▷ *vt* sceller; (*envelope*) coller; (*: with seal*) cacheter; (*decide: sb's fate*) décider (de); (*: bargain*) conclure; **~ of approval** approbation *f*
▶ **seal off** *vt* (*close*) condamner; (*forbid entry to*) interdire l'accès de

sea level *n* niveau *m* de la mer

sealing wax ['si:lɪŋ-] *n* cire *f* à cacheter

sea lion *n* lion *m* de mer

sealskin ['siːlskɪn] *n* peau *f* de phoque

seam [siːm] *n* couture *f*; (*of coal*) veine *f*, filon *m*; **the hall was bursting at the ~s** la salle était pleine à craquer

seaman ['siːmən] (*irreg*) *n* marin *m*

seamanship ['siːmənʃɪp] *n* qualités *fpl* de marin

seamless ['siːmlɪs] *adj* sans couture(s)

seamy ['siːmɪ] *adj* louche, mal famé(e)

seance ['seɪɔns] *n* séance *f* de spiritisme

seaplane ['siːpleɪn] *n* hydravion *m*

seaport ['siːpɔːt] *n* port *m* de mer

search [səːtʃ] *n* (*for person, thing, Comput*) recherche(s) *f(pl)*; (*of drawer, pockets*) fouille *f*; (*Law: at sb's home*) perquisition *f* ▷ *vt* fouiller; (*examine*) examiner minutieusement; scruter ▷ *vi*: **to ~ for** chercher; **in ~ of** à la recherche de ▶**search through** *vt fus* fouiller

search engine *n* (*Comput*) moteur *m* de recherche

searcher ['səːtʃər] *n* chercheur(-euse)

searching ['səːtʃɪŋ] *adj* (*look, question*) pénétrant(e); (*examination*) minutieux(-euse)

searchlight ['səːtʃlaɪt] *n* projecteur *m*

search party *n* expédition *f* de secours

search warrant *n* mandat *m* de perquisition

searing ['sɪərɪŋ] *adj* (*heat*) brûlant(e); (*pain*) aigu(ë)

seashore ['siːʃɔːr] *n* rivage *m*, plage *f*, bord *m* de (la) mer; **on the ~** sur le rivage

seasick ['siːsɪk] *adj*: **to be ~** avoir le mal de mer

seaside ['siːsaɪd] *n* bord *m* de mer

seaside resort *n* station *f* balnéaire

season ['siːzn] *n* saison *f* ▷ *vt* assaisonner, relever; **to be in/out of ~** être/ne pas être de saison; **the busy ~** (*for shops*) la période de pointe; (*for hotels etc*) la pleine saison; **the open ~** (*Hunting*) la saison de la chasse

seasonal ['siːznl] *adj* saisonnier(-ière)

seasoned ['siːznd] *adj* (*wood*) séché(e); (*fig: worker, actor, troops*) expérimenté(e); **a ~ campaigner** un vieux militant, un vétéran

seasoning ['siːznɪŋ] *n* assaisonnement *m*

season ticket *n* carte *f* d'abonnement

seat [siːt] *n* siège *m*; (*in bus, train: place*) place *f*; (*Parliament*) siège; (*buttocks*) postérieur *m*; (*of trousers*) fond *m* ▷ *vt* faire asseoir, placer; (*have room for*) avoir des places assises pour, pouvoir accueillir; **are there any ~s left?** est-ce qu'il reste des places?; **to take one's ~** prendre place; **to be ~ed** être assis; **please be ~ed** veuillez vous asseoir

seat belt *n* ceinture *f* de sécurité

seating ['siːtɪŋ] *n* sièges *fpl*, places assises

seating capacity ['siːtɪŋ-] *n* nombre *m* de places assises

sea urchin *n* oursin *m*

sea water *n* eau *f* de mer

seaweed ['siːwiːd] *n* algues *fpl*

seaworthy ['siːwəːðɪ] *adj* en état de naviguer

SEC *n abbr* (*US: = Securities and Exchange Commission*) ≈ COB *f* (= *Commission des opérations de Bourse*)

sec. *abbr* (= *second*) sec

secateurs [sɛkə'təːz] *npl* sécateur *m*

secede [sɪ'siːd] *vi* faire sécession

secluded [sɪ'kluːdɪd] *adj* retiré(e), à l'écart

seclusion [sɪ'kluːʒən] *n* solitude *f*

second¹ ['sɛkənd] *num* deuxième, second(e) ▷ *adv* (*in race etc*) en seconde position ▷ *n* (*unit of time*) seconde *f*; (*Aut: also:* **second gear**) seconde; (*in series, position*) deuxième *m/f*, second(e); (*Comm: imperfect*) article *m* de second choix; (*Brit Scol*) ≈ licence *f* avec mention ▷ *vt* (*motion*) appuyer; **seconds** *npl* (*inf: food*) rab *m* (*inf*); **Charles the S~** Charles II; **just a ~!** une seconde!, un instant!; (*stopping sb*) pas si vite!; **~ floor** (*Brit*) deuxième (étage) *m*; (*US*) premier (étage) *m*; **to ask for a ~ opinion** (*Med*) demander l'avis d'un autre médecin

second² [sɪ'kɔnd] *vt* (*employee*) détacher, mettre en détachement

secondary ['sɛkəndərɪ] *adj* secondaire

secondary school *n* (*age 11 to 15*) collège *m*; (*age 15 to 18*) lycée *m*

second-best [sɛkənd'bɛst] *n* deuxième choix *m*; **as a ~** faute de mieux

second-class ['sɛkənd'klɑːs] *adj* de deuxième classe; (*Rail*) de seconde (classe); (*Post*) au tarif réduit; (*pej*) de qualité inférieure ▷ *adv* (*Rail*) en seconde; (*Post*) au tarif réduit; **~ citizen** citoyen(ne) de deuxième classe

second cousin *n* cousin(e) issu(e) de germains

seconder ['sɛkəndər] *n* personne *f* qui appuie une motion

second-guess ['sɛkənd'gɛs] *vt* (*predict*) (essayer d')anticiper; **they're still trying to ~ his motives** ils essaient toujours de comprendre ses raisons

second hand *n* (*on clock*) trotteuse *f*

secondhand ['sɛkənd'hænd] *adj* d'occasion; (*information*) de seconde main ▷ *adv* (*buy*) d'occasion; **to hear sth ~** apprendre qch indirectement

second-in-command ['sɛkəndɪnkə'mɑːnd] *n* (*Mil*) commandant *m* en second; (*Admin*) adjoint(e), sous-chef *m*

secondly ['sɛkəndlɪ] *adv* deuxièmement; **firstly ... ~ ...** d'abord ... ensuite ... or de plus ...

secondment [sɪ'kɔndmənt] *n* (*Brit*) détachement *m*

second-rate ['sɛkənd'reɪt] *adj* de deuxième ordre, de qualité inférieure

second thoughts *npl*: **to have ~** changer d'avis; **on ~** *or* **thought** (*US*) à la réflexion

secrecy ['siːkrəsɪ] *n* secret *m*; **in ~** en secret

secret ['siːkrɪt] *adj* secret(-ète) ▷ *n* secret *m*; **in ~** (*adv*) en secret, secrètement, en cachette; **to keep sth ~ from sb** cacher qch à qn, ne pas révéler qch à qn; **to make no ~ of sth** ne pas cacher qch; **keep it ~** n'en parle à personne

secret agent *n* agent secret

secretarial [sɛkrɪ'tɛərɪəl] *adj* de secrétaire, de secrétariat

secretariat [sɛkrɪ'tɛərɪət] *n* secrétariat *m*

secretary ['sɛkrətrɪ] n secrétaire m/f; (Comm) secrétaire général; **S~ of State** (US Pol) ≈ ministre m des Affaires étrangères; **S~ of State (for)** (Brit Pol) ministre m (de)

secretary-general ['sɛkrətrɪ'dʒɛnərl] n secrétaire général

secrete [sɪ'kri:t] vt (Anat, Biol, Med) sécréter; (hide) cacher

secretion [sɪ'kri:ʃən] n sécrétion f

secretive ['si:krətɪv] adj réservé(e); (pej) cachottier(-ière), dissimulé(e)

secretly ['si:krɪtlɪ] adv en secret, secrètement, en cachette

secret police n police secrète

secret service n services secrets

sect [sɛkt] n secte f

sectarian [sɛk'tɛərɪən] adj sectaire

section ['sɛkʃən] n section f; (department) section; (Comm) rayon m; (of document) section, article m, paragraphe m; (cut) coupe f ▷ vt sectionner; **the business** etc ~ (Press) la page des affaires etc

sector ['sɛktər] n secteur m

secular ['sɛkjulər] adj laïque

secure [sɪ'kjuər] adj (free from anxiety) sans inquiétude, sécurisé(e); (firmly fixed) solide, bien attaché(e) (or fermé(e) etc); (in safe place) en lieu sûr, en sûreté ▷ vt (fix) fixer, attacher; (get) obtenir, se procurer; (Comm: loan) garantir; **to make sth ~** bien fixer or attacher qch; **to ~ sth for sb** obtenir qch pour qn, procurer qch à qn

secured creditor [sɪ'kjuəd-] n créancier(-ière), privilégié(e)

security [sɪ'kjuərɪtɪ] n sécurité f, mesures fpl de sécurité; (for loan) caution f, garantie f; **securities** npl (Stock Exchange) valeurs fpl, titres mpl; **to increase** or **tighten ~** renforcer les mesures de sécurité; **~ of tenure** stabilité f d'un emploi, titularisation f

Security Council n: **the ~** le Conseil de sécurité

security forces npl forces fpl de sécurité

security guard n garde chargé de la sécurité; (transporting money) convoyeur m de fonds

security risk n menace f pour la sécurité de l'état (or d'une entreprise etc)

sedan [sə'dæn] n (US Aut) berline f

sedate [sɪ'deɪt] adj calme; posé(e) ▷ vt donner des sédatifs à

sedation [sɪ'deɪʃən] n (Med) sédation f; **to be under ~** être sous calmants

sedative ['sɛdɪtɪv] n calmant m, sédatif m

sedentary ['sɛdntrɪ] adj sédentaire

sediment ['sɛdɪmənt] n sédiment m, dépôt m

sedition [sɪ'dɪʃən] n sédition f

seduce [sɪ'dju:s] vt séduire

seduction [sɪ'dʌkʃən] n séduction f

seductive [sɪ'dʌktɪv] adj séduisant(e); (smile) séducteur(-trice); (fig: offer) alléchant(e)

see [si:] (pt **saw**, pp **seen** [sɔ:, si:n]) vt (gen) voir; (accompany): **to ~ sb to the door** reconduire or raccompagner qn jusqu'à la porte ▷ vi voir ▷ n évêché m; **to ~ that** (ensure) veiller à ce que + sub,

faire en sorte que + sub, s'assurer que; **there was nobody to be ~n** il n'y avait pas un chat; **let me ~** (show me) fais(-moi) voir; (let me think) voyons (un peu); **to go and ~ sb** aller voir qn; ~ **for yourself** voyez vous-même; **I don't know what she ~s in him** je ne sais pas ce qu'elle lui trouve; **as far as I can ~** pour autant que je puisse en juger; **~ you!** au revoir!, à bientôt!; ~ **you soon/later/tomorrow!** à bientôt/plus tard/demain!

▸ **see about** vt fus (deal with) s'occuper de

▸ **see off** vt accompagner (à l'aéroport etc)

▸ **see out** vt (take to door) raccompagner à la porte

▸ **see through** vt mener à bonne fin ▷ vt fus voir clair dans

▸ **see to** vt fus s'occuper de, se charger de

seed [si:d] n graine f; (fig) germe m; (Tennis etc) tête f de série; **to go to ~** (plant) monter en graine; (fig) se laisser aller

seedless ['si:dlɪs] adj sans pépins

seedling ['si:dlɪŋ] n jeune plant m, semis m

seedy ['si:dɪ] adj (shabby) minable, miteux(-euse)

seeing ['si:ɪŋ] conj: ~ **(that)** vu que, étant donné que

seek [si:k] (pt, pp **sought** [sɔ:t]) vt chercher, rechercher; **to ~ advice/help from sb** demander conseil/de l'aide à qn

▸ **seek out** vt (person) chercher

seem [si:m] vi sembler, paraître; **there ~s to be ...** il semble qu'il y a ..., on dirait qu'il y a ...; **it ~s (that) ...** il semble que ...; **what ~s to be the trouble?** qu'est-ce qui ne va pas?

seemingly ['si:mɪŋlɪ] adv apparemment

seen [si:n] pp of **see**

seep [si:p] vi suinter, filtrer

seer [sɪər] n prophète (prophétesse) voyant(e)

seersucker ['sɪəsʌkər] n cloqué m, étoffe cloquée

seesaw ['si:sɔ:] n (jeu m de) bascule f

seethe [si:ð] vi être en effervescence; **to ~ with anger** bouillir de colère

see-through ['si:θru:] adj transparent(e)

segment ['sɛgmənt] n segment m; (of orange) quartier m

segregate ['sɛgrɪgeɪt] vt séparer, isoler

segregation [sɛgrɪ'geɪʃən] n ségrégation f

Seine [seɪn] n: **the (River) ~** la Seine

seismic ['saɪzmɪk] adj sismique

seize [si:z] vt (grasp) saisir, attraper; (take possession of) s'emparer de; (opportunity) saisir; (Law) saisir

▸ **seize on** vt fus saisir, sauter sur

▸ **seize up** vi (Tech) se gripper

▸ **seize upon** vt fus = **seize on**

seizure ['si:ʒər] n (Med) crise f, attaque f; (of power) prise f; (Law) saisie f

seldom ['sɛldəm] adv rarement

select [sɪ'lɛkt] adj choisi(e), d'élite; (hotel, restaurant, club) chic inv, sélect inv ▷ vt sélectionner, choisir; **a ~ few** quelques privilégiés

selection [sɪ'lɛkʃən] n sélection f, choix m

selection committee *n* comité *m* de sélection
selective [sɪˈlɛktɪv] *adj* sélectif(-ive); *(school)* à recrutement sélectif
selector [sɪˈlɛktə^r] *n (person)* sélectionneur(-euse); *(Tech)* sélecteur *m*
self [sɛlf] *n (pl selves)* [sɛlvz]: **the ~** le moi *inv* ▷ *prefix* auto-
self-addressed [ˈsɛlfəˈdrɛst] *adj*: **~ envelope** enveloppe *f* à mon *(or votre etc)* nom
self-adhesive [sɛlfədˈhiːzɪv] *adj* autocollant(e)
self-assertive [sɛlfəˈsɜːtɪv] *adj* autoritaire
self-assurance [sɛlfəˈʃuərəns] *n* assurance *f*
self-assured [sɛlfəˈʃuəd] *adj* sûr(e) de soi, plein(e) d'assurance
self-catering [sɛlfˈkeɪtərɪŋ] *adj (Brit: flat)* avec cuisine, où l'on peut faire sa cuisine; *(: holiday)* en appartement *(or* chalet *etc)* loué
self-centred, (US) self-centered [sɛlfˈsɛntəd] *adj* égocentrique
self-cleaning [sɛlfˈkliːnɪŋ] *adj* autonettoyant(e).
self-confessed [sɛlfkənˈfɛst] *adj (alcoholic etc)* déclaré(e), qui ne s'en cache pas
self-confidence [sɛlfˈkɒnfɪdns] *n* confiance *f* en soi
self-confident [sɛlfˈkɒnfɪdnt] *adj* sûr(e) de soi, plein(e) d'assurance
self-conscious [sɛlfˈkɒnʃəs] *adj* timide, qui manque d'assurance
self-contained [sɛlfkənˈteɪnd] *adj (Brit: flat)* avec entrée particulière, indépendant(e)
self-control [sɛlfkənˈtrəul] *n* maîtrise *f* de soi
self-defeating [sɛlfdɪˈfiːtɪŋ] *adj* qui a un effet contraire à l'effet recherché
self-defence, (US) self-defense [sɛlfdɪˈfɛns] *n* autodéfense *f*; *(Law)* légitime défense *f*
self-discipline [sɛlfˈdɪsɪplɪn] *n* discipline personnelle
self-drive [sɛlfˈdraɪv] *adj (Brit)*: **~ car** voiture *f* de location
self-employed [sɛlfɪmˈplɔɪd] *adj* qui travaille à son compte
self-esteem [sɛlfɪˈstiːm] *n* amour-propre *m*
self-evident [sɛlfˈɛvɪdnt] *adj* évident(e), qui va de soi
self-explanatory [sɛlfɪkˈsplænətrɪ] *adj* qui se passe d'explication
self-governing [sɛlfˈɡʌvənɪŋ] *adj* autonome
self-help [ˈsɛlfˈhɛlp] *n* initiative personnelle, efforts personnels
self-importance [sɛlfɪmˈpɔːtns] *n* suffisance *f*
self-indulgent [sɛlfɪnˈdʌldʒənt] *adj* qui ne se refuse rien
self-inflicted [sɛlfɪnˈflɪktɪd] *adj* volontaire
self-interest [sɛlfˈɪntrɪst] *n* intérêt personnel
selfish [ˈsɛlfɪʃ] *adj* égoïste
selfishness [ˈsɛlfɪʃnɪs] *n* égoïsme *m*
selfless [ˈsɛlflɪs] *adj* désintéressé(e)
selflessly [ˈsɛlflɪslɪ] *adv* sans penser à soi
self-made man [ˈsɛlfmeɪd-] *n* self-made man *m*
self-pity [sɛlfˈpɪtɪ] *n* apitoiement *m* sur soi-même

self-portrait [sɛlfˈpɔːtreɪt] *n* autoportrait *m*
self-possessed [sɛlfpəˈzɛst] *adj* assuré(e)
self-preservation [ˈsɛlfprɛzəˈveɪʃən] *n* instinct *m* de conservation
self-raising [sɛlfˈreɪzɪŋ], (US) **self-rising** [sɛlfˈraɪzɪŋ] *adj*: **~ flour** farine *f* pour gâteaux *(avec levure incorporée)*
self-reliant [sɛlfrɪˈlaɪənt] *adj* indépendant(e)
self-respect [sɛlfrɪsˈpɛkt] *n* respect *m* de soi, amour-propre *m*
self-respecting [sɛlfrɪsˈpɛktɪŋ] *adj* qui se respecte
self-righteous [sɛlfˈraɪtʃəs] *adj* satisfait(e) de soi, pharisaïque
self-rising [sɛlfˈraɪzɪŋ] *adj (US)* = **self-raising**
self-sacrifice [sɛlfˈsækrɪfaɪs] *n* abnégation *f*
self-same [ˈsɛlfseɪm] *adj* même
self-satisfied [sɛlfˈsætɪsfaɪd] *adj* content(e) de soi, suffisant(e)
self-sealing [sɛlfˈsiːlɪŋ] *adj (envelope)* autocollant(e)
self-service [sɛlfˈsɜːvɪs] *adj, n* libre-service *(m)*, self-service *(m)*
self-styled [ˈsɛlfstaɪld] *adj* soi-disant *inv*
self-sufficient [sɛlfsəˈfɪʃənt] *adj* indépendant(e)
self-supporting [sɛlfsəˈpɔːtɪŋ] *adj* financièrement indépendant(e)
self-tanning [ˈsɛlftænɪŋ] *adj*: **~ cream** *or* **lotion** *etc* autobronzant *m*
self-taught [sɛlfˈtɔːt] *adj* autodidacte
sell *(pt, pp sold)* [sɛl, səuld] *vt* vendre ▷ *vi* se vendre; **to ~ at** *or* **for 10 euros** se vendre 10 euros; **to ~ sb an idea** *(fig)* faire accepter une idée à qn
  ▶ **sell off** *vt* liquider
  ▶ **sell out** *vi*: **to ~ out (of sth)** *(use up stock)* vendre tout son stock (de qch); **to ~ out (to)** *(Comm)* vendre son fonds *or* son affaire (à) ▷ *vt* vendre tout son stock de; **the tickets are all sold out** il ne reste plus de billets
  ▶ **sell up** *vi* vendre son fonds *or* son affaire
sell-by date [ˈsɛlbaɪ-] *n* date *f* limite de vente
seller [ˈsɛlə^r] *n* vendeur(-euse), marchand(e); **~'s market** marché *m* à la hausse
selling price [ˈsɛlɪŋ-] *n* prix *m* de vente
Sellotape® [ˈsɛləuteɪp] *n (Brit)* scotch® *m*
sellout [ˈsɛlaut] *n* trahison *f*, capitulation *f*; *(of tickets)*: **it was a ~** tous les billets ont été vendus
selves [sɛlvz] *npl of* **self**
semantic [sɪˈmæntɪk] *adj* sémantique
semantics [sɪˈmæntɪks] *n* sémantique *f*
semaphore [ˈsɛməfɔː^r] *n* signaux *mpl* à bras; *(Rail)* sémaphore *m*
semblance [ˈsɛmblns] *n* semblant *m*
semen [ˈsiːmən] *n* sperme *m*
semester [sɪˈmɛstə^r] *n (esp US)* semestre *m*
semi... [ˈsɛmɪ] *prefix* semi-, demi-; à demi, à moitié ▷ *n*: **semi** = **semidetached house**
semi-breve [ˈsɛmɪbriːv] *n (Brit)* ronde *f*
semicircle [ˈsɛmɪsɜːkl] *n* demi-cercle *m*
semicircular [ˈsɛmɪˈsɜːkjulə^r] *adj* en demi-cercle, semi-circulaire

semicolon [sɛmɪ'kəulən] *n* point-virgule *m*
semiconductor [sɛmɪkən'dʌktəʳ] *n* semi-conducteur *m*
semiconscious [sɛmɪ'kɔnʃəs] *adj* à demi conscient(e)
semidetached [sɛmɪdɪ'tætʃt], **semidetached house** *n* (*Brit*) maison jumelée *or* jumelle
semi-final [sɛmɪ'faɪnl] *n* demi-finale *f*
seminar ['sɛmɪnɑːʳ] *n* séminaire *m*
seminary ['sɛmɪnərɪ] *n* (*Rel: for priests*) séminaire *m*
semiprecious [sɛmɪ'prɛʃəs] *adj* semi-précieux(-euse)
semiquaver ['sɛmɪkweɪvəʳ] *n* (*Brit*) double croche *f*
semiskilled [sɛmɪ'skɪld] *adj*: ~ **worker** ouvrier(-ière) spécialisé(e)
semi-skimmed ['sɛmɪ'skɪmd] *adj* demi-écrémé(e)
semitone ['sɛmɪtəun] *n* (*Mus*) demi-ton *m*
semolina [sɛmə'liːnə] *n* semoule *f*
SEN *n abbr* (*Brit*) = **State Enrolled Nurse**
Sen., sen. *abbr* = **senator; senior**
senate ['sɛnɪt] *n* sénat *m*; (*US*): **the S~** le Sénat; *voir article*

⬤ **S E N A T E**
⬤
⬤ Le *Senate* est la chambre haute du
⬤ "Congress", le parlement des États-Unis. Il
⬤ est composé de 100 sénateurs, 2 par État,
⬤ élus au suffrage universel direct tous les 6
⬤ ans, un tiers d'entre eux étant renouvelé
⬤ tous les 2 ans.

senator ['sɛnɪtəʳ] *n* sénateur *m*
send (*pt, pp* **sent**) [sɛnd, sɛnt] *vt* envoyer; **to ~ by post** *or* (*US*) **mail** envoyer *or* expédier par la poste; **to ~ sb for sth** envoyer qn chercher qch; **to ~ word that ...** faire dire que ...; **she ~s (you) her love** elle vous adresse ses amitiés; **to ~ sb to Coventry** (*Brit*) mettre qn en quarantaine; **to ~ sb to sleep** endormir qn; **to ~ sb into fits of laughter** faire rire qn aux éclats; **to ~ sth flying** envoyer valser qch
▶ **send away** *vt* (*letter, goods*) envoyer, expédier
▶ **send away for** *vt fus* commander par correspondance, se faire envoyer
▶ **send back** *vt* renvoyer
▶ **send for** *vt fus* envoyer chercher; faire venir; (*by post*) se faire envoyer, commander par correspondance
▶ **send in** *vt* (*report, application, resignation*) remettre
▶ **send off** *vt* (*goods*) envoyer, expédier; (*Brit Sport: player*) expulser *or* renvoyer du terrain
▶ **send on** *vt* (*Brit: letter*) faire suivre; (*luggage etc: in advance*) (faire) expédier à l'avance
▶ **send out** *vt* (*invitation*) envoyer (par la poste); (*emit: light, heat, signal*) émettre
▶ **send round** *vt* (*letter, document etc*) faire circuler

▶ **send up** *vt* (*person, price*) faire monter; (*Brit: parody*) mettre en boîte, parodier
sender ['sɛndəʳ] *n* expéditeur(-trice)
send-off ['sɛndɔf] *n*: **a good ~** des adieux chaleureux
Senegal [sɛnɪ'gɔːl] *n* Sénégal *m*
Senegalese [sɛnɪgə'liːz] *adj* sénégalais(e) ▷ *n* (*pl inv*) Sénégalais(e)
senile ['siːnaɪl] *adj* sénile
senility [sɪ'nɪlɪtɪ] *n* sénilité *f*
senior ['siːnɪəʳ] *adj* (*older*) aîné(e), plus âgé(e); (*high-ranking*) de haut niveau; (*of higher rank*): **to be ~ to sb** être le supérieur de qn ▷ *n* (*older*): **she is 15 years his ~** elle est son aînée de 15 ans, elle est plus âgée que lui de 15 ans; (*in service*) personne *f* qui a plus d'ancienneté; **P. Jones ~** P. Jones père
senior citizen *n* personne *f* du troisième âge
senior high school *n* (*US*) ≈ lycée *m*
seniority [siːnɪ'ɔrɪtɪ] *n* priorité *f* d'âge, ancienneté *f*; (*in rank*) supériorité *f* (hiérarchique)
sensation [sɛn'seɪʃən] *n* sensation *f*; **to create a ~** faire sensation
sensational [sɛn'seɪʃənl] *adj* qui fait sensation; (*marvellous*) sensationnel(le)
sense [sɛns] *n* sens *m*; (*feeling*) sentiment *m*; (*meaning*) sens, signification *f*; (*wisdom*) bon sens ▷ *vt* sentir, pressentir; **senses** *npl* raison *f*; **it makes ~** c'est logique; **there is no ~ in (doing) that** cela n'a pas de sens; **to come to one's ~s** (*regain consciousness*) reprendre conscience; (*become reasonable*) revenir à la raison; **to take leave of one's ~s** perdre la tête
senseless ['sɛnslɪs] *adj* insensé(e), stupide; (*unconscious*) sans connaissance
sense of humour, (*US*) **sense of humor** *n* sens *m* de l'humour
sensibility [sɛnsɪ'bɪlɪtɪ] *n* sensibilité *f*; **sensibilities** *npl* susceptibilité *f*
sensible ['sɛnsɪbl] *adj* sensé(e), raisonnable; (*shoes etc*) pratique
sensitive ['sɛnsɪtɪv] *adj*: ~ **(to)** sensible (à); **he is very ~ about it** c'est un point très sensible (chez lui)
sensitivity [sɛnsɪ'tɪvɪtɪ] *n* sensibilité *f*
sensual ['sɛnsjuəl] *adj* sensuel(le)
sensuous ['sɛnsjuəs] *adj* voluptueux(-euse), sensuel(le)
sent [sɛnt] *pt, pp of* **send**
sentence ['sɛntns] *n* (*Ling*) phrase *f*; (*Law: judgment*) condamnation *f*, sentence *f*; (*: punishment*) peine *f* ▷ *vt*: **to ~ sb to death/to 5 years** condamner qn à mort/à 5 ans; **to pass ~ on sb** prononcer une peine contre qn
sentiment ['sɛntɪmənt] *n* sentiment *m*; (*opinion*) opinion *f*, avis *m*
sentimental [sɛntɪ'mɛntl] *adj* sentimental(e)
sentimentality [sɛntɪmɛn'tælɪtɪ] *n* sentimentalité *f*, sensiblerie *f*
sentry ['sɛntrɪ] *n* sentinelle *f*, factionnaire *m*
sentry duty *n*: **to be on ~** être de faction

Seoul [səul] n Séoul
separable ['sɛprəbl] adj séparable
separate [adj 'sɛprɪt, vb 'sɛpəreɪt] adj séparé(e); (organization) indépendant(e); (day, occasion, issue) différent(e) ▷ vt séparer; (distinguish) distinguer ▷ vi se séparer; **~ from** distinct(e) de; **under ~ cover** (Comm) sous pli séparé; **to ~ into** diviser en
separately ['sɛprɪtlɪ] adv séparément
separates ['sɛprɪts] npl (clothes) coordonnés mpl
separation [sɛpə'reɪʃən] n séparation f
Sept. abbr (= September) sept
September [sɛp'tɛmbə^r] n septembre m; for phrases see also **July**
septic ['sɛptɪk] adj septique; (wound) infecté(e); **to go ~** s'infecter
septicaemia [sɛptɪ'siːmɪə] n septicémie f
septic tank n fosse f septique
sequel ['siːkwl] n conséquence f; séquelles fpl; (of story) suite f
sequence ['siːkwəns] n ordre m, suite f; (in film) séquence f; (dance) numéro m; **in ~** par ordre, dans l'ordre, les uns après les autres; **~ of tenses** concordance f des temps
sequential [sɪ'kwɛnʃəl] adj: **~ access** (Comput) accès séquentiel
sequin ['siːkwɪn] n paillette f
Serb [səːb] adj, n = **Serbian**
Serbia ['səːbɪə] n Serbie f
Serbian ['səːbɪən] adj serbe ▷ n Serbe m/f; (Ling) serbe m
Serbo-Croat ['səːbəu'krəuæt] n (Ling) serbo-croate m
serenade [sɛrə'neɪd] n sérénade f ▷ vt donner une sérénade à
serene [sɪ'riːn] adj serein(e), calme, paisible
serenity [sə'rɛnɪtɪ] n sérénité f, calme m
sergeant ['saːdʒənt] n sergent m; (Police) brigadier m
sergeant major n sergent-major m
serial ['sɪərɪəl] n feuilleton m ▷ adj (Comput: interface, printer) série inv; (: access) séquentiel(le)
serialize ['sɪərɪəlaɪz] vt publier (or adapter) en feuilleton
serial killer n meurtrier m tuant en série
serial number n numéro m de série
series ['sɪərɪz] n série f; (Publishing) collection f
serious ['sɪərɪəs] adj sérieux(-euse); (accident etc) grave; **are you ~ (about it)?** parlez-vous sérieusement?
seriously ['sɪərɪəslɪ] adv sérieusement; (hurt) gravement; **~ rich/difficult** (inf: extremely) drôlement riche/difficile; **to take sth/sb ~** prendre qch/qn au sérieux
seriousness ['sɪərɪəsnɪs] n sérieux m, gravité f
sermon ['səːmən] n sermon m
serrated [sɪ'reɪtɪd] adj en dents de scie
serum ['sɪərəm] n sérum m
servant ['səːvənt] n domestique m/f; (fig) serviteur (servante)
serve [səːv] vt (employer etc) servir, être au service de; (purpose) servir à; (customer, food, meal) servir;

(subj: train) desservir; (apprenticeship) faire, accomplir; (prison term) faire; purger ▷ vi (Tennis) servir; (be useful): **to ~ as/for/to do** servir de/à/à faire ▷ n (Tennis) service m; **are you being ~d?** est-ce qu'on s'occupe de vous?; **to ~ on a committee/jury** faire partie d'un comité/jury; **it ~s him right** c'est bien fait pour lui; **it ~s my purpose** cela fait mon affaire
▸ **serve out, serve up** vt (food) servir
server [səːvə^r] n (Comput) serveur m
service ['səːvɪs] n (gen) service m; (Aut) révision f; (Rel) office m ▷ vt (car etc) réviser; **services** npl (Econ: tertiary sector) (secteur m) tertiaire m, secteur des services; (Brit: on motorway) station-service f; (Mil): **the S~s** (npl) les forces armées; **to be of ~ to sb, to do sb a ~** rendre service à qn; **~ included/not included** service compris/non compris; **to put one's car in for ~** donner sa voiture à réviser; **dinner ~** service de table
serviceable ['səːvɪsəbl] adj pratique, commode
service area n (on motorway) aire f de services
service charge n (Brit) service m
service industries npl les industries fpl de service, les services mpl
serviceman ['səːvɪsmən] (irreg) n militaire m
service station n station-service f
serviette [səːvɪ'ɛt] n (Brit) serviette f (de table)
servile ['səːvaɪl] adj servile
session ['sɛʃən] n (sitting) séance f; (Scol) année f scolaire (or universitaire); **to be in ~** siéger, être en session or en séance
session musician n musicien(ne) de studio
set [sɛt] (pt, pp **set**) n série f, assortiment m; (of tools etc) jeu m; (Radio, TV) poste m; (Tennis) set m; (group of people) cercle m, milieu m; (Cine) plateau m; (Theat: stage) scène f; (: scenery) décor m; (Math) ensemble m; (Hairdressing) mise f en plis ▷ adj (fixed) fixe, déterminé(e); (ready) prêt(e) ▷ vt (place) mettre, poser, placer; (fix, establish) fixer; (: record) établir; (assign: task, homework) donner; (exam) composer; (adjust) régler; (decide: rules etc) fixer, choisir; (Typ) composer ▷ vi (sun) se coucher; (jam, jelly, concrete) prendre; (bone) se ressouder; **to be ~ on doing** être résolu(e) à faire; **to be all ~ to do** être (fin) prêt(e) pour faire; **to be (dead) ~ against** être (totalement) opposé à; **he's ~ in his ways** il n'est pas très souple, il tient à ses habitudes; **to ~ to music** mettre en musique; **to ~ on fire** mettre le feu à; **to ~ free** libérer; **to ~ sth going** déclencher qch; **to ~ the alarm clock for seven o'clock** mettre le réveil à sonner à sept heures; **to ~ sail** partir, prendre la mer; **a ~ phrase** une expression toute faite, une locution; **a ~ of false teeth** un dentier; **a ~ of dining-room furniture** une salle à manger
▸ **set about** vt fus (task) entreprendre, se mettre à; **to ~ about doing sth** se mettre à faire qch
▸ **set aside** vt mettre de côté; (time) garder
▸ **set back** vt (in time): **to ~ back (by)** retarder (de); (place): **a house ~ back from the road** une maison située en retrait de la route

▶ **set down** *vt* (*subj: bus, train*) déposer
▶ **set in** *vi* (*infection, bad weather*) s'installer; (*complications*) survenir, surgir; **the rain has ~ in for the day** c'est parti pour qu'il pleuve toute la journée
▶ **set off** *vi* se mettre en route, partir ▷ *vt* (*bomb*) faire exploser; (*cause to start*) déclencher; (*show up well*) mettre en valeur, faire valoir
▶ **set out** *vi*: **to ~ out (from)** partir (de) ▷ *vt* (*arrange*) disposer; (*state*) présenter, exposer; **to ~ out to do** entreprendre de faire; avoir pour but *or* intention de faire
▶ **set up** *vt* (*organization*) fonder, créer; (*monument*) ériger; **to ~ up shop** (*fig*) s'établir, s'installer
setback ['sɛtbæk] *n* (*hitch*) revers *m*, contretemps *m*; (*in health*) rechute *f*
set menu *n* menu *m*
set square *n* équerre *f*
settee [sɛ'ti:] *n* canapé *m*
setting ['sɛtɪŋ] *n* cadre *m*; (*of jewel*) monture *f*; (*position: of controls*) réglage *m*
setting lotion *n* lotion *f* pour mise en plis
settle ['sɛtl] *vt* (*argument, matter, account*) régler; (*problem*) résoudre; (*Med: calm*) calmer; (*colonize: land*) coloniser ▷ *vi* (*bird, dust etc*) se poser; (*sediment*) se déposer; **to ~ to sth** se mettre sérieusement à qch; **to ~ for sth** accepter qch, se contenter de qch; **to ~ on sth** opter *or* se décider pour qch; **that's ~d then** alors, c'est d'accord!; **to ~ one's stomach** calmer des maux d'estomac
▶ **settle down** *vi* (*get comfortable*) s'installer; (*become calmer*) se calmer; se ranger
▶ **settle in** *vi* s'installer
▶ **settle up** *vi*: **to ~ up with sb** régler (ce que l'on doit à) qn
settlement ['sɛtlmənt] *n* (*payment*) règlement *m*; (*agreement*) accord *m*; (*colony*) colonie *f*; (*village etc*) village *m*, hameau *m*; **in ~ of our account** (*Comm*) en règlement de notre compte
settler ['sɛtlə'] *n* colon *m*
setup ['sɛtʌp] *n* (*arrangement*) manière *f* dont les choses sont organisées; (*situation*) situation *f*, allure *f* des choses
seven ['sɛvn] *num* sept
seventeen [sɛvn'ti:n] *num* dix-sept
seventeenth [sɛvn'ti:nθ] *num* dix-septième
seventh ['sɛvnθ] *num* septième
seventieth ['sɛvntɪɪθ] *num* soixante-dixième
seventy ['sɛvntɪ] *num* soixante-dix
sever ['sɛvə'] *vt* couper, trancher; (*relations*) rompre
several ['sɛvərl] *adj, pron* plusieurs *pl*; **~ of us** plusieurs d'entre nous; **~ times** plusieurs fois
severance ['sɛvərəns] *n* (*of relations*) rupture *f*
severance pay *n* indemnité *f* de licenciement
severe [sɪ'vɪə'] *adj* (*stern*) sévère, strict(e); (*serious*) grave, sérieux(-euse); (*hard*) rigoureux(-euse), dur(e); (*plain*) sévère, austère
severely [sɪ'vɪəlɪ] *adv* sévèrement; (*wounded, ill*) gravement

severity [sɪ'vɛrɪtɪ] *n* sévérité *f*; gravité *f*; rigueur *f*
sew (*pt* **-ed**, *pp* **-n**) [səu, səud, səun] *vt, vi* coudre
▶ **sew up** *vt* (re)coudre; **it is all ~n up** (*fig*) c'est dans le sac *or* dans la poche
sewage ['su:ɪdʒ] *n* vidange(s) *f(pl)*
sewage works *n* champ *m* d'épandage
sewer ['su:ə'] *n* égout *m*
sewing ['səuɪŋ] *n* couture *f*; (*item(s)*) ouvrage *m*
sewing machine *n* machine *f* à coudre
sewn [səun] *pp* of **sew**
sex [sɛks] *n* sexe *m*; **to have ~ with** avoir des rapports (sexuels) avec
sex act *n* acte sexuel
sex appeal *n* sex-appeal *m*
sex education *n* éducation sexuelle
sexism ['sɛksɪzəm] *n* sexisme *m*
sexist ['sɛksɪst] *adj* sexiste
sex life *n* vie sexuelle
sex object *n* femme-objet *f*, objet sexuel
sextet [sɛks'tɛt] *n* sextuor *m*
sexual ['sɛksjuəl] *adj* sexuel(le); **~ assault** attentat *m* à la pudeur; **~ harassment** harcèlement sexuel
sexual intercourse *n* rapports sexuels
sexuality [sɛksju'ælɪtɪ] *n* sexualité *f*
sexy ['sɛksɪ] *adj* sexy *inv*
Seychelles [seɪ'ʃɛl(z)] *npl*: **the ~** les Seychelles *fpl*
SF *n abbr* (= *science fiction*) SF *f*
SG *n abbr* (US) = **Surgeon General**
Sgt *abbr* (= *sergeant*) Sgt
shabbiness ['ʃæbɪnɪs] *n* aspect miteux; mesquinerie *f*
shabby ['ʃæbɪ] *adj* miteux(-euse); (*behaviour*) mesquin(e), méprisable
shack [ʃæk] *n* cabane *f*, hutte *f*
shackles ['ʃæklz] *npl* chaînes *fpl*, entraves *fpl*
shade [ʃeɪd] *n* ombre *f*; (*for lamp*) abat-jour *m inv*; (*of colour*) nuance *f*, ton *m*; (US: *window shade*) store *m*; (*small quantity*): **a ~ of** un soupçon de ▷ *vt* abriter du soleil, ombrager; **shades** *npl* (US: *sunglasses*) lunettes *fpl* de soleil; **in the ~** à l'ombre; **a ~ smaller** un tout petit peu plus petit
shadow ['ʃædəu] *n* ombre *f* ▷ *vt* (*follow*) filer; **without** *or* **beyond a ~ of doubt** sans l'ombre d'un doute
shadow cabinet *n* (Brit Pol) cabinet parallèle formé par le parti qui n'est pas au pouvoir
shadowy ['ʃædəuɪ] *adj* ombragé(e); (*dim*) vague, indistinct(e)
shady ['ʃeɪdɪ] *adj* ombragé(e); (*fig: dishonest*) louche, véreux(-euse)
shaft [ʃɑ:ft] *n* (*of arrow, spear*) hampe *f*; (Aut, Tech) arbre *m*; (*of mine*) puits *m*; (*of lift*) cage *f*; (*of light*) rayon *m*, trait *m*; **ventilator ~** conduit *m* d'aération *or* de ventilation
shaggy ['ʃægɪ] *adj* hirsute; en broussaille
shake [ʃeɪk] (*pt* **shook**, *pp* **shaken** [ʃuk, 'ʃeɪkn]) *vt* secouer; (*bottle, cocktail*) agiter; (*house, confidence*) ébranler ▷ *vi* trembler ▷ *n* secousse *f*; **to ~ one's head** (*in refusal etc*) dire *or* faire non de la

tête; (in dismay) secouer la tête; **to ~ hands with sb** serrer la main à qn
▶ **shake off** vt secouer; (pursuer) se débarrasser de
▶ **shake up** vt secouer
shake-up ['ʃeɪkʌp] n grand remaniement
shakily ['ʃeɪkɪlɪ] adv (reply) d'une voix tremblante; (walk) d'un pas mal assuré; (write) d'une main tremblante
shaky ['ʃeɪkɪ] adj (hand, voice) tremblant(e); (building) branlant(e), peu solide; (memory) chancelant(e); (knowledge) incertain(e)
shale [ʃeɪl] n schiste argileux
shall [ʃæl] aux vb: **I ~ go** j'irai; **~ I open the door?** j'ouvre la porte?; **I'll get the coffee, ~ I?** je vais chercher le café, d'accord?
shallot [ʃə'lɒt] n (Brit) échalote f
shallow ['ʃæləu] adj peu profond(e); (fig) superficiel(le), qui manque de profondeur
sham [ʃæm] n frime f; (jewellery, furniture) imitation f ▷ adj feint(e), simulé(e) ▷ vt feindre, simuler
shambles ['ʃæmblz] n confusion f, pagaïe f, fouillis m; **the economy is (in) a complete ~** l'économie est dans la confusion la plus totale
shambolic [ʃæm'bɒlɪk] adj (inf) bordélique
shame [ʃeɪm] n honte f ▷ vt faire honte à; **it is a ~ (that/to do)** c'est dommage (que + sub/de faire); **what a ~!** quel dommage!; **to put sb/sth to ~** (fig) faire honte à qn/qch
shamefaced ['ʃeɪmfeɪst] adj honteux(-euse), penaud(e)
shameful ['ʃeɪmful] adj honteux(-euse), scandaleux(-euse)
shameless ['ʃeɪmlɪs] adj éhonté(e), effronté(e); (immodest) impudique
shampoo [ʃæm'pu:] n shampooing m ▷ vt faire un shampooing à; **~ and set** shampooing et mise f en plis
shamrock ['ʃæmrɒk] n trèfle m (emblème national de l'Irlande)
shandy ['ʃændɪ] n bière panachée
shan't [ʃɑ:nt] = **shall not**
shantytown ['ʃæntɪtaun] n bidonville m
SHAPE [ʃeɪp] n abbr (= Supreme Headquarters Allied Powers, Europe) quartier général des forces alliées en Europe
shape [ʃeɪp] n forme f ▷ vt façonner, modeler; (clay, stone) donner forme à; (statement) formuler; (sb's ideas, character) former; (sb's life) déterminer; (course of events) influer sur le cours de ▷ vi (also: **shape up**: events) prendre tournure; (: person) faire des progrès, s'en sortir; **to take ~** prendre forme or tournure; **in the ~ of a heart** en forme de cœur; **I can't bear gardening in any ~ or form** je déteste le jardinage sous quelque forme que ce soit; **to get o.s. into ~** (re)trouver la forme
-shaped [ʃeɪpt] suffix: **heart~** en forme de cœur
shapeless ['ʃeɪplɪs] adj informe, sans forme
shapely ['ʃeɪplɪ] adj bien proportionné(e), beau (belle)

share [ʃɛəʳ] n (thing received, contribution) part f; (Comm) action f ▷ vt partager; (have in common) avoir en commun; **to ~ out (among** or **between)** partager (entre); **to ~ in** (joy, sorrow) prendre part à; (profits) participer à, avoir part à; (work) partager
share capital n capital social
share certificate n certificat m or titre m d'action
shareholder ['ʃɛəhəuldəʳ] n (Brit) actionnaire m/f
share index n indice m de la Bourse
shark [ʃɑ:k] n requin m
sharp [ʃɑ:p] adj (razor, knife) tranchant(e), bien aiguisé(e); (point, voice) aigu(ë); (nose, chin) pointu(e); (outline, increase) net(te); (curve, bend) brusque; (cold, pain) vif (vive); (taste) piquant(e), âcre; (Mus) dièse; (person: quick-witted) vif (vive), éveillé(e); (: unscrupulous) malhonnête ▷ n (Mus) dièse m ▷ adv: **at 2 o'clock ~** à 2 heures pile or tapantes; **turn ~ left** tournez immédiatement à gauche; **to be ~ with sb** être brusque avec qn; **look ~!** dépêche-toi!
sharpen ['ʃɑ:pn] vt aiguiser; (pencil) tailler; (fig) aviver
sharpener ['ʃɑ:pnəʳ] n (also: **pencil sharpener**) taille-crayon(s) m inv; (also: **knife sharpener**) aiguisoir m
sharp-eyed [ʃɑ:p'aɪd] adj à qui rien n'échappe
sharpish ['ʃɑ:pɪʃ] adv (Brit inf: quickly) en vitesse
sharply ['ʃɑ:plɪ] adv (turn, stop) brusquement; (stand out) nettement; (criticize, retort) sèchement, vertement
sharp-tempered [ʃɑ:p'tɛmpəd] adj prompt(e) à se mettre en colère
sharp-witted [ʃɑ:p'wɪtɪd] adj à l'esprit vif, malin(-igne)
shatter ['ʃætəʳ] vt fracasser, briser, faire voler en éclats; (fig: upset) bouleverser; (: ruin) briser, ruiner ▷ vi voler en éclats, se briser, se fracasser
shattered ['ʃætəd] adj (overwhelmed, grief-stricken) bouleversé(e); (inf: exhausted) éreinté(e)
shatterproof ['ʃætəpru:f] adj incassable
shave [ʃeɪv] vt raser ▷ vi se raser ▷ n: **to have a ~** se raser
shaven ['ʃeɪvn] adj (head) rasé(e)
shaver ['ʃeɪvəʳ] n (also: **electric shaver**) rasoir m électrique
shaving ['ʃeɪvɪŋ] n (action) rasage m
shaving brush n blaireau m
shaving cream n crème f à raser
shaving foam n mousse f à raser
shavings ['ʃeɪvɪŋz] npl (of wood etc) copeaux mpl
shaving soap n savon m à barbe
shawl [ʃɔ:l] n châle m
she [ʃi:] pron elle; **there ~ is** la voilà; **~-elephant** etc éléphant m etc femelle
sheaf (pl **sheaves**) [ʃi:f, ʃi:vz] n gerbe f
shear [ʃɪəʳ] vt (pt **-ed**, pp **-ed** or **shorn** [ʃɔ:n]) (sheep) tondre
▶ **shear off** vt tondre; (branch) élaguer
shears ['ʃɪəz] npl (for hedge) cisaille(s) f(pl)

sheath [ʃi:θ] *n* gaine *f*, fourreau *m*, étui *m*; (*contraceptive*) préservatif *m*

sheathe [ʃi:ð] *vt* gainer; (*sword*) rengainer

sheath knife *n* couteau *m* à gaine

sheaves [ʃi:vz] *npl* of **sheaf**

shed [ʃed] *n* remise *f*, resserre *f*; (*Industry*, *Rail*) hangar *m* ▷ *vt* (*pt, pp -*) (*leaves, fur etc*) perdre; (*tears*) verser, répandre; (*workers*) congédier; **to ~ light on** (*problem, mystery*) faire la lumière sur

she'd [ʃi:d] = **she had; she would**

sheen [ʃi:n] *n* lustre *m*

sheep [ʃi:p] *n* (*pl inv*) mouton *m*

sheepdog ['ʃi:pdɔg] *n* chien *m* de berger

sheep farmer *n* éleveur *m* de moutons

sheepish ['ʃi:pɪʃ] *adj* penaud(e), timide

sheepskin ['ʃi:pskɪn] *n* peau *f* de mouton

sheepskin jacket *n* canadienne *f*

sheer [ʃɪəʳ] *adj* (*utter*) pur(e), pur et simple; (*steep*) à pic, abrupt(e); (*almost transparent*) extrêmement fin(e) ▷ *adv* à pic, abruptement; **by ~ chance** par pur hasard

sheet [ʃi:t] *n* (*on bed*) drap *m*; (*of paper*) feuille *f*; (*of glass, metal etc*) feuille, plaque *f*

sheet feed *n* (*on printer*) alimentation *f* en papier (feuille à feuille)

sheet lightning *n* éclair *m* en nappe(s)

sheet metal *n* tôle *f*

sheet music *n* partition(s) *f(pl)*

sheik, sheikh [ʃeɪk] *n* cheik *m*

shelf (*pl* **shelves**) [ʃelf, ʃelvz] *n* étagère *f*, rayon *m*; **set of shelves** rayonnage *m*

shelf life *n* (*Comm*) durée *f* de conservation (avant la vente)

shell [ʃel] *n* (*on beach*) coquillage *m*; (*of egg, nut etc*) coquille *f*; (*explosive*) obus *m*; (*of building*) carcasse *f* ▷ *vt* (*crab, prawn etc*) décortiquer; (*peas*) écosser; (*Mil*) bombarder (d'obus)

▶ **shell out** *vi* (*inf*): **to ~ out (for)** casquer (pour)

she'll [ʃi:l] = **she will; she shall**

shellfish ['ʃelfɪʃ] *n* (*pl inv*: *crab etc*) crustacé *m*; (*: scallop etc*) coquillage *m* ▷ *npl* (*as food*) fruits *mpl* de mer

shell suit *n* survêtement *m*

shelter ['ʃeltəʳ] *n* abri *m*, refuge *m* ▷ *vt* abriter, protéger; (*give lodging to*) donner asile à ▷ *vi* s'abriter, se mettre à l'abri; **to take ~ (from)** s'abriter (de)

sheltered ['ʃeltəd] *adj* (*life*) retiré(e), à l'abri des soucis; (*spot*) abrité(e)

sheltered housing *n* foyers *mpl* (*pour personnes âgées ou handicapées*)

shelve [ʃelv] *vt* (*fig*) mettre en suspens *or* en sommeil

shelves ['ʃelvz] *npl* of **shelf**

shelving ['ʃelvɪŋ] *n* (*shelves*) rayonnage(s) *m(pl)*

shepherd ['ʃepəd] *n* berger *m* ▷ *vt* (*guide*) guider, escorter

shepherdess ['ʃepədɪs] *n* bergère *f*

shepherd's pie ['ʃepədz-] *n* ≈ hachis *m* Parmentier

sherbet ['ʃə:bət] *n* (*Brit*: *powder*) poudre acidulée; (*US*: *water ice*) sorbet *m*

sheriff ['ʃerɪf] (*US*) *n* shérif *m*

sherry ['ʃeri] *n* xérès *m*, sherry *m*

she's [ʃi:z] = **she is; she has**

Shetland ['ʃetlənd] *n* (*also*: **the Shetlands, the Shetland Isles** *or* **Islands**) les îles *fpl* Shetland

Shetland pony *n* poney *m* des îles Shetland

shield [ʃi:ld] *n* bouclier *m*; (*protection*) écran *m* de protection ▷ *vt*: **to ~ (from)** protéger (de *or* contre)

shift [ʃɪft] *n* (*change*) changement *m*; (*work period*) période *f* de travail; (*of workers*) équipe *f*, poste *m* ▷ *vt* déplacer, changer de place; (*remove*) enlever ▷ *vi* changer de place, bouger; **the wind has ~ed to the south** le vent a tourné au sud; **a ~ in demand** (*Comm*) un déplacement de la demande

shift key *n* (*on typewriter*) touche *f* de majuscule

shiftless ['ʃɪftlɪs] *adj* fainéant(e)

shift work *n* travail *m* par roulement; **to do ~** travailler par roulement

shifty ['ʃɪftɪ] *adj* sournois(e); (*eyes*) fuyant(e)

Shiite ['ʃi:aɪt] *n* Chiite *m/f* ▷ *adj* chiite

shilling ['ʃɪlɪŋ] *n* (*Brit*) shilling *m* (= 12 old pence; 20 in a pound)

shilly-shally ['ʃɪlɪʃælɪ] *vi* tergiverser, atermoyer

shimmer ['ʃɪməʳ] *n* miroitement *m*, chatoiement *m* ▷ *vi* miroiter, chatoyer

shin [ʃɪn] *n* tibia *m* ▷ *vi*: **to ~ up/down a tree** grimper dans un/descendre d'un arbre

shindig ['ʃɪndɪg] *n* (*inf*) bamboula *f*

shine [ʃaɪn] *n* (*pt, pp* **shone**) [ʃɔn] *n* éclat *m*, brillant *m* ▷ *vi* briller ▷ *vt* (*torch*): **to ~ on** braquer sur; (*polish*) (*pt, pp* **-d**) faire briller *or* reluire

shingle ['ʃɪŋgl] *n* (*on beach*) galets *mpl*; (*on roof*) bardeau *m*

shingles ['ʃɪŋglz] *n* (*Med*) zona *m*

shining ['ʃaɪnɪŋ] *adj* brillant(e)

shiny ['ʃaɪnɪ] *adj* brillant(e)

ship [ʃɪp] *n* bateau *m*; (*large*) navire *m* ▷ *vt* transporter (par mer); (*send*) expédier (par mer); (*load*) charger, embarquer; **on board ~** à bord

shipbuilder ['ʃɪpbɪldəʳ] *n* constructeur *m* de navires

shipbuilding ['ʃɪpbɪldɪŋ] *n* construction navale

ship chandler [-'tʃɑ:ndləʳ] *n* fournisseur *m* maritime, shipchandler *m*

shipment ['ʃɪpmənt] *n* cargaison *f*

shipowner ['ʃɪpəunəʳ] *n* armateur *m*

shipper ['ʃɪpəʳ] *n* affréteur *m*, expéditeur *m*

shipping ['ʃɪpɪŋ] *n* (*ships*) navires *mpl*; (*traffic*) navigation *f*; (*the industry*) industrie navale; (*transport*) transport *m*

shipping agent *n* agent *m* maritime

shipping company *n* compagnie *f* de navigation

shipping lane *n* couloir *m* de navigation

shipping line *n* = **shipping company**

shipshape ['ʃɪpʃeɪp] *adj* en ordre impeccable

shipwreck ['ʃɪprek] *n* épave *f*; (*event*) naufrage *m* ▷ *vt*: **to be ~ed** faire naufrage

shipyard ['ʃɪpjɑ:d] *n* chantier naval

shire ['ʃaɪəʳ] *n* (*Brit*) comté *m*

shirk [ʃəːk] *vt* esquiver, se dérober à

shirt [ʃəːt] *n* chemise *f*; (*woman's*) chemisier *m*; **in ~ sleeves** en bras de chemise

shirty ['ʃəːtɪ] *adj* (*Brit inf*) de mauvais poil

shit [ʃɪt] *excl* (*inf!*) merde (!)

shiver ['ʃɪvə'] *n* frisson *m* ▷ *vi* frissonner

shoal [ʃəul] *n* (*of fish*) banc *m*

shock [ʃɔk] *n* (*impact*) choc *m*, heurt *m*; (*Elec*) secousse *f*, décharge *f*; (*emotional*) choc; (*Med*) commotion *f*, choc ▷ *vt* (*scandalize*) choquer, scandaliser; (*upset*) bouleverser; **suffering from ~** (*Med*) commotionné(e); **it gave us a ~** ça nous a fait un choc; **it came as a ~ to hear that** ... nous avons appris avec stupeur que ...

shock absorber [-əbzɔːbə'] *n* amortisseur *m*

shocker ['ʃɔkə'] *n* (*inf*): **the news was a real ~ to him** il a vraiment été choqué par cette nouvelle

shocking ['ʃɔkɪŋ] *adj* (*outrageous*) choquant(e), scandaleux(-euse); (*awful*) épouvantable

shockproof ['ʃɔkpruːf] *adj* anti-choc *inv*

shock therapy, shock treatment *n* (*Med*) (traitement *m* par) électrochoc(s) *m(pl)*

shock wave *n* (*also fig*) onde *f* de choc

shod [ʃɔd] *pt, pp of* **shoe**; **well-~** bien chaussé(e)

shoddy ['ʃɔdɪ] *adj* de mauvaise qualité, mal fait(e)

shoe [ʃuː] *n* chaussure *f*, soulier *m*; (*also:* **horseshoe**) fer *m* à cheval; (*also:* **brake shoe**) mâchoire *f* de frein ▷ *vt* (*pt, pp* **shod**) [ʃɔd] (*horse*) ferrer

shoebrush ['ʃuːbrʌʃ] *n* brosse *f* à chaussures

shoehorn ['ʃuːhɔːn] *n* chausse-pied *m*

shoelace ['ʃuːleɪs] *n* lacet *m* (de soulier)

shoemaker ['ʃuːmeɪkə'] *n* cordonnier *m*, fabricant *m* de chaussures

shoe polish *n* cirage *m*

shoeshop ['ʃuːʃɔp] *n* magasin *m* de chaussures

shoestring ['ʃuːstrɪŋ] *n*: **on a ~** (*fig*) avec un budget dérisoire; avec des moyens très restreints

shoetree ['ʃuːtriː] *n* embauchoir *m*

shone [ʃɔn] *pt, pp of* **shine**

shoo [ʃuː] *excl* allez, ouste! ▷ *vt* (*also:* **shoo away, shoo off**) chasser

shook [ʃuk] *pt of* **shake**

shoot [ʃuːt] *(pt, pp* **shot**) [ʃɔt] *n* (*on branch, seedling*) pousse *f*; (*shooting party*) partie *f* de chasse ▷ *vt* (*game: hunt*) chasser; (: *aim at*) tirer; (: *kill*) abattre; (*person*) blesser/tuer d'un coup de fusil (*or* de revolver); (*execute*) fusiller; (*arrow*) tirer; (*gun*) tirer un coup de; (*Cine*) tourner ▷ *vi* (*with gun, bow*): **to ~ (at)** tirer (sur); (*Football*) shooter, tirer; **to ~ past sb** passer en flèche devant qn; **to ~ in/out** entrer/sortir comme une flèche
▶ **shoot down** *vt* (*plane*) abattre
▶ **shoot up** *vi* (*fig: prices etc*) monter en flèche

shooting ['ʃuːtɪŋ] *n* (*shots*) coups *mpl* de feu; (*attack*) fusillade *f*; (*murder*) homicide *m* (à l'aide d'une arme à feu); (*Hunting*) chasse *f*; (*Cine*) tournage *m*

shooting range *n* stand *m* de tir

shooting star *n* étoile filante

shop [ʃɔp] *n* magasin *m*; (*workshop*) atelier *m* ▷ *vi* (*also:* **go shopping**) faire ses courses *or* ses achats; **repair ~** atelier de réparations; **to talk ~** (*fig*) parler boutique
▶ **shop around** *vi* faire le tour des magasins (pour comparer les prix); (*fig*) se renseigner avant de choisir *or* décider

shopaholic [ʃɔpə'hɔlɪk] *n* (*inf*) *personne qui achète sans pouvoir s'arrêter*

shop assistant *n* (*Brit*) vendeur(-euse)

shop floor *n* (*Brit: fig*) ouvriers *mpl*

shopkeeper ['ʃɔpkiːpə'] *n* marchand(e), commerçant(e)

shoplift ['ʃɔplɪft] *vi* voler à l'étalage

shoplifter ['ʃɔplɪftə'] *n* voleur(-euse) à l'étalage

shoplifting ['ʃɔplɪftɪŋ] *n* vol *m* à l'étalage

shopper ['ʃɔpə'] *n* personne *f* qui fait ses courses, acheteur(-euse)

shopping ['ʃɔpɪŋ] *n* (*goods*) achats *mpl*, provisions *fpl*

shopping bag *n* sac *m* (à provisions)

shopping centre, (*US*) **shopping center** *n* centre commercial

shopping mall *n* centre commercial

shopping trolley *n* (*Brit*) Caddie® *m*

shop-soiled ['ʃɔpsɔɪld] *adj* défraîchi(e), qui a fait la vitrine

shop window *n* vitrine *f*

shore [ʃɔː'] *n* (*of sea, lake*) rivage *m*, rive *f* ▷ *vt*: **to ~ (up)** étayer; **on ~** à terre

shore leave *n* (*Naut*) permission *f* à terre

shorn [ʃɔːn] *pp of* **shear** ▷ *adj*: **~ of** dépouillé(e) de

short [ʃɔːt] *adj* (*not long*) court(e); (*soon finished*) court, bref (brève); (*person, step*) petit(e); (*curt*) brusque, sec (sèche); (*insufficient*) insuffisant(e) ▷ *n* (*also:* **short film**) court métrage; (*Elec*) court-circuit *m*; **to be ~ of sth** être à court de *or* manquer de qch; **to be in ~ supply** manquer, être difficile à trouver; **I'm 3 ~** il m'en manque 3; **in ~** bref; en bref; **~ of doing** à moins de faire; **everything ~ of** tout sauf; **it is ~ for** c'est l'abréviation *or* le diminutif de; **a ~ time ago** il y a peu de temps; **in the ~ term** à court terme; **to cut ~** (*speech, visit*) abréger, écourter; (*person*) couper la parole à; **to fall ~ of** ne pas être à la hauteur de; **to run ~ of** arriver à court de, venir à manquer de; **to stop ~** s'arrêter net; **to stop ~ of** ne pas aller jusqu'à

shortage ['ʃɔːtɪdʒ] *n* manque *m*, pénurie *f*

shortbread ['ʃɔːtbrɛd] *n* ≈ sablé *m*

short-change [ʃɔːt'tʃeɪndʒ] *vt*: **to ~ sb** ne pas rendre assez à qn

short-circuit [ʃɔːt'səːkɪt] *n* court-circuit *m* ▷ *vt* court-circuiter ▷ *vi* se mettre en court-circuit

shortcoming ['ʃɔːtkʌmɪŋ] *n* défaut *m*

shortcrust pastry ['ʃɔːtkrʌst-], **short pastry** *n* (*Brit*) pâte brisée

shortcut ['ʃɔːtkʌt] *n* raccourci *m*

shorten ['ʃɔːtn] *vt* raccourcir; (*text, visit*) abréger

shortening ['ʃɔːtnɪŋ] *n* (*Culin*) matière grasse

shortfall ['ʃɔːtfɔːl] *n* déficit *m*

shorthand ['ʃɔ:thænd] *n* (*Brit*) sténo(graphie) *f*;
  to take sth down in ~ prendre qch en sténo
shorthand notebook *n* bloc *m* sténo
shorthand typist *n* (*Brit*) sténodactylo *m/f*
shortlist ['ʃɔ:tlɪst] *n* (*Brit*: *for job*) liste *f* des
  candidats sélectionnés
short-lived ['ʃɔ:t'lɪvd] *adj* de courte durée
shortly ['ʃɔ:tlɪ] *adv* bientôt, sous peu
shortness ['ʃɔ:tnɪs] *n* brièveté *f*
short notice *n*: **at ~** au dernier moment
shorts [ʃɔ:ts] *npl*: **(a pair of) ~** un short
short-sighted [ʃɔ:t'saitɪd] *adj* (*Brit*) myope; (*fig*)
  qui manque de clairvoyance
short-sleeved [ʃɔ:t'sli:vd] *adj* à manches
  courtes
short-staffed [ʃɔ:t'stɑ:ft] *adj* à court de
  personnel
short-stay [ʃɔ:t'steɪ] *adj* (*car park*) de courte
  durée
short story *n* nouvelle *f*
short-tempered [ʃɔ:t'tɛmpəd] *adj* qui
  s'emporte facilement
short-term ['ʃɔ:ttə:m] *adj* (*effect*) à court terme
short time *n*: **to work ~, to be on ~** (*Industry*) être
  en chômage partiel, travailler à horaire réduit
short wave *n* (*Radio*) ondes courtes
shot [ʃɔt] *pt, pp of* **shoot** ▷ *n* coup *m* (de feu);
  (*shotgun pellets*) plombs *mpl*; (*try*) coup, essai *m*;
  (*injection*) piqûre *f*; (*Phot*) photo *f*; **to be a good/**
  poor ~ (*person*) tirer bien/mal; **to fire a ~ at sb/**
  sth tirer sur qn/qch; **to have a ~ at (doing) sth**
  essayer de faire qch; **like a ~** comme une flèche;
  (*very readily*) sans hésiter; **to get ~ of sb/sth** (*inf*)
  se débarrasser de qn/qch; **a big ~** (*inf*) un gros
  bonnet
shotgun ['ʃɔtgʌn] *n* fusil *m* de chasse
should [ʃud] *aux vb*: **I ~ go now** je devrais partir
  maintenant; **he ~ be there now** il devrait être
  arrivé maintenant; **I ~ go if I were you** si j'étais
  vous j'irais; **I ~ like to** volontiers, j'aimerais
  bien; **~ he phone ...** si jamais il téléphone ...
shoulder ['ʃəuldəʳ] *n* épaule *f*; (*Brit*: *of road*): **hard**
  ~ accotement *m* ▷ *vt* (*fig*) endosser, se charger
  de; **to look over one's ~** regarder derrière soi
  (en tournant la tête); **to rub ~s with sb** (*fig*)
  côtoyer qn; **to give sb the cold ~** (*fig*) battre
  froid à qn
shoulder bag *n* sac *m* à bandoulière
shoulder blade *n* omoplate *f*
shoulder strap *n* bretelle *f*
shouldn't ['ʃudnt] = **should not**
shout [ʃaut] *n* cri *m* ▷ *vt* crier ▷ *vi* crier, pousser
  des cris; **to give sb a ~** appeler qn
  ▶ **shout down** *vt* huer
shouting ['ʃautɪŋ] *n* cris *mpl*
shouting match *n* (*inf*) engueulade *f*,
  empoignade *f*
shove [ʃʌv] *vt* pousser; (*inf*: *put*): **to ~ sth in**
  fourrer *or* ficher qch dans ▷ *n* poussée *f*; **he ~d**
  me out of the way il m'a écarté en me
  poussant
  ▶ **shove off** *vi* (*Naut*) pousser au large; (*fig*: *col*)

ficher le camp
shovel ['ʃʌvl] *n* pelle *f* ▷ *vt* pelleter, enlever (*or*
  enfourner) à la pelle
show [ʃəu] (*pt* **-ed**, *pp* **-n**) [ʃəun] *n* (*of emotion*)
  manifestation *f*, démonstration *f*; (*semblance*)
  semblant *m*, apparence *f*; (*exhibition*) exposition
  f, salon *m*; (*Theat, TV*) spectacle *m*; (*Cine*) séance *f*
  ▷ *vt* montrer; (*film*) passer; (*courage etc*) faire
  preuve de, manifester; (*exhibit*) exposer ▷ *vi* se
  voir, être visible; **can you ~ me where it is,**
  please? pouvez-vous me montrer où c'est?; **to**
  ask for a ~ of hands demander que l'on vote à
  main levée; **to be on ~** être exposé(e); **it's just**
  for ~ c'est juste pour l'effet; **who's running**
  the ~ here? (*inf*) qui est-ce qui commande ici?;
  to ~ sb to his seat/to the door accompagner
  qn jusqu'à sa place/la porte; **to ~ a profit/loss**
  (*Comm*) indiquer un bénéfice/une perte; **it just**
  goes to ~ that ... ça prouve bien que ...
  ▶ **show in** *vt* faire entrer
  ▶ **show off** *vi* (*pej*) crâner ▷ *vt* (*display*) faire
  valoir; (*pej*) faire étalage de
  ▶ **show out** *vt* reconduire à la porte
  ▶ **show up** *vi* (*stand out*) ressortir; (*inf*: *turn up*) se
  montrer ▷ *vt* démontrer; (*unmask*) démasquer,
  dénoncer; (*flaw*) faire ressortir
showbiz ['ʃəubɪz] *n* (*inf*) showbiz *m*
show business *n* le monde du spectacle
showcase ['ʃəukeɪs] *n* vitrine *f*
showdown ['ʃəudaun] *n* épreuve *f* de force
shower ['ʃauəʳ] *n* (*for washing*) douche *f*; (*rain*)
  averse *f*; (*of stones etc*) pluie *f*, grêle *f*; (*US*: *party*)
  réunion organisée pour la remise de cadeaux ▷ *vi*
  prendre une douche, se doucher ▷ *vt*: **to ~ sb**
  with (*gifts etc*) combler qn de; (*abuse etc*) accabler
  qn de; (*missiles*) bombarder qn de; **to have** *or*
  take a ~ prendre une douche, se doucher
shower cap *n* bonnet *m* de douche
shower gel *n* gel *m* douche
showerproof ['ʃauəpru:f] *adj* imperméable
showery ['ʃauərɪ] *adj* (*weather*) pluvieux(-euse)
showground ['ʃəugraund] *n* champ *m* de foire
showing ['ʃəuɪŋ] *n* (*of film*) projection *f*
show jumping [-dʒʌmpɪŋ] *n* concours *m*
  hippique
showman ['ʃəumən] (*irreg*) *n* (*at fair, circus*) forain
  m; (*fig*) comédien *m*
showmanship ['ʃəumənʃɪp] *n* art *m* de la mise
  en scène
shown [ʃəun] *pp of* **show**
show-off ['ʃəuɔf] *n* (*inf*: *person*) crâneur(-euse),
  m'as-tu-vu(e)
showpiece ['ʃəupi:s] *n* (*of exhibition etc*) joyau *m*,
  clou *m*; **that hospital is a ~** cet hôpital est un
  modèle du genre
showroom ['ʃəurum] *n* magasin *m* *or* salle *f*
  d'exposition
show trial *n* grand procès *m* médiatique (*qui fait*
  un exemple)
showy ['ʃəuɪ] *adj* tapageur(-euse)
shrank [ʃræŋk] *pt of* **shrink**
shrapnel ['ʃræpnl] *n* éclats *mpl* d'obus

shred [ʃrɛd] n (gen pl) lambeau m, petit morceau; (fig: of truth, evidence) parcelle f ▷ vt mettre en lambeaux, déchirer; (documents) détruire; (Culin: grate) râper; (: lettuce etc) couper en lanières
shredder [ˈʃrɛdər] n (for vegetables) râpeur m; (for documents, papers) déchiqueteuse f
shrewd [ʃruːd] adj astucieux(-euse), perspicace; (business person) habile
shrewdness [ˈʃruːdnɪs] n perspicacité f
shriek [ʃriːk] n cri perçant or aigu, hurlement m ▷ vt, vi hurler, crier
shrift [ʃrɪft] n: **to give sb short ~** expédier qn sans ménagements
shrill [ʃrɪl] adj perçant(e), aigu(ë), strident(e)
shrimp [ʃrɪmp] n crevette grise
shrine [ʃraɪn] n châsse f; (place) lieu m de pèlerinage
shrink (pt **shrank**, pp **shrunk**) [ʃrɪŋk, ʃræŋk, ʃrʌŋk] vi rétrécir; (fig) diminuer; (also: **shrink away**) reculer ▷ vt (wool) (faire) rétrécir ▷ n (inf: pej) psychanalyste m/f; **to ~ from (doing) sth** reculer devant (la pensée de faire) qch
shrinkage [ˈʃrɪŋkɪdʒ] n (of clothes) rétrécissement m
shrink-wrap [ˈʃrɪŋkræp] vt emballer sous film plastique
shrivel [ˈʃrɪvl] (also: **shrivel up**) vt ratatiner, flétrir ▷ vi se ratatiner, se flétrir
shroud [ʃraud] n linceul m ▷ vt: **~ed in mystery** enveloppé(e) de mystère
Shrove Tuesday [ˈʃrəuv-] n (le) Mardi gras
shrub [ʃrʌb] n arbuste m
shrubbery [ˈʃrʌbərɪ] n massif m d'arbustes
shrug [ʃrʌg] n haussement m d'épaules ▷ vt, vi: **to ~ (one's shoulders)** hausser les épaules
▶ **shrug off** vt faire fi de; (cold, illness) se débarrasser de
shrunk [ʃrʌŋk] pp of **shrink**
shrunken [ˈʃrʌŋkn] adj ratatiné(e)
shudder [ˈʃʌdər] n frisson m, frémissement m ▷ vi frissonner, frémir
shuffle [ˈʃʌfl] vt (cards) battre; **to ~ (one's feet)** traîner les pieds
shun [ʃʌn] vt éviter, fuir
shunt [ʃʌnt] vt (Rail: direct) aiguiller; (: divert) détourner ▷ vi: **to ~ (to and fro)** faire la navette
shunting yard [ˈʃʌntɪŋ-] n voies fpl de garage or de triage
shush [ʃuʃ] excl chut!
shut (pt, pp **-**) [ʃʌt] vt fermer ▷ vi (se) fermer
▶ **shut down** vt fermer définitivement; (machine) arrêter ▷ vi fermer définitivement
▶ **shut off** vt couper, arrêter
▶ **shut out** vt (person, cold) empêcher d'entrer; (noise) éviter d'entendre; (block: view) boucher; (: memory of sth) chasser de son esprit
▶ **shut up** vi (inf: keep quiet) se taire ▷ vt (close) fermer; (silence) faire taire
shutdown [ˈʃʌtdaun] n fermeture f
shutter [ˈʃʌtər] n volet m; (Phot) obturateur m
shuttle [ˈʃʌtl] n navette f; (also: **shuttle service**) (service m de) navette f ▷ vi (vehicle, person) faire

la navette ▷ vt (passengers) transporter par un système de navette
shuttlecock [ˈʃʌtlkɔk] n volant m (de badminton)
shuttle diplomacy n navettes fpl diplomatiques
shy [ʃaɪ] adj timide; **to fight ~ of** se dérober devant; **to be ~ of doing sth** hésiter à faire qch, ne pas oser faire qch ▷ vi: **to ~ away from doing sth** (fig) craindre de faire qch
shyness [ˈʃaɪnɪs] n timidité f
Siam [saɪˈæm] n Siam m
Siamese [saɪəˈmiːz] adj: **~ cat** chat siamois mpl; **~ twins** (frères mpl) siamois mpl, (sœurs fpl) siamoises fpl
Siberia [saɪˈbɪərɪə] n Sibérie f
siblings [ˈsɪblɪŋz] npl (formal) frères et sœurs mpl (de mêmes parents)
Sicilian [sɪˈsɪlɪən] adj sicilien(ne) ▷ n Sicilien(ne)
Sicily [ˈsɪsɪlɪ] n Sicile f
sick [sɪk] adj (ill) malade; (Brit: vomiting): **to be ~** vomir; (humour) noir(e), macabre; **to feel ~** avoir envie de vomir, avoir mal au cœur; **to fall ~** tomber malade; **to be (off) ~** être absent(e) pour cause de maladie; **a ~ person** un(e) malade; **to be ~ of** (fig) en avoir assez de
sick bag n sac m vomitoire
sick bay n infirmerie f
sick building syndrome n maladie dûe à la climatisation, l'éclairage artificiel etc des bureaux
sicken [ˈsɪkn] vt écœurer ▷ vi: **to be ~ing for sth** (cold, flu etc) couver qch
sickening [ˈsɪknɪŋ] adj (fig) écœurant(e), révoltant(e), répugnant(e)
sickle [ˈsɪkl] n faucille f
sick leave n congé m de maladie
sickle-cell anaemia [ˈsɪklsɛl-] n anémie f à hématies falciformes, drépanocytose f
sickly [ˈsɪklɪ] adj maladif(-ive), souffreteux(-euse); (causing nausea) écœurant(e)
sickness [ˈsɪknɪs] n maladie f; (vomiting) vomissement(s) m(pl)
sickness benefit n (prestations fpl de l')assurance-maladie f
sick note n (from parents) mot m d'absence; (from doctor) certificat médical
sick pay n indemnité f de maladie (versée par l'employeur)
sickroom [ˈsɪkruːm] n infirmerie f
side [saɪd] n côté m; (of animal) flanc m; (of lake, road) bord m; (of mountain) versant m; (fig: aspect) côté, aspect m; (team: Sport) équipe f; (TV: channel) chaîne f ▷ adj (door, entrance) latéral(e) ▷ vi: **to ~ with sb** prendre le parti de qn, se ranger du côté de qn; **by the ~ of** au bord de; **~ by ~** côte à côte; **the right/wrong ~** le bon/mauvais côté, l'endroit/l'envers m; **they are on our ~** ils sont avec nous; **from all ~s** de tous côtés; **to rock from ~ to ~** se balancer; **to take ~s (with)** prendre parti (pour); **a ~ of beef** ≈ un quartier de bœuf
sideboard [ˈsaɪdbɔːd] n buffet m
sideboards [ˈsaɪdbɔːdz] (Brit), **sideburns**

['saɪdbə:nz] *npl* (*whiskers*) pattes *fpl*
sidecar ['saɪdkɑːʳ] *n* side-car *m*
side dish *n* (*plat m d'*)accompagnement *m*
side drum *n* (*Mus*) tambour plat, caisse claire
side effect *n* effet *m* secondaire
sidekick ['saɪdkɪk] *n* (*inf*) sous-fifre *m*
sidelight ['saɪdlaɪt] *n* (*Aut*) veilleuse *f*
sideline ['saɪdlaɪn] *n* (*Sport*) (ligne *f* de) touche *f*;
(*fig*) activité *f* secondaire
sidelong ['saɪdlɔŋ] *adj*: **to give sb a ~ glance**
regarder qn du coin de l'œil
side order *n* garniture *f*
side plate *n* petite assiette
side road *n* petite route, route transversale
sidesaddle ['saɪdsædl] *adv* en amazone
sideshow ['saɪdʃəu] *n* attraction *f*
sidestep ['saɪdstɛp] *vt* (*question*) éluder; (*problem*)
éviter ▷ *vi* (*Boxing etc*) esquiver
side street *n* rue transversale
sidetrack ['saɪdtræk] *vt* (*fig*) faire dévier de son
sujet
sidewalk ['saɪdwɔːk] *n* (*US*) trottoir *m*
sideways ['saɪdweɪz] *adv* de côté
siding ['saɪdɪŋ] *n* (*Rail*) voie *f* de garage
sidle ['saɪdl] *vi*: **to ~ up (to)** s'approcher
furtivement (de)
SIDS [sɪdz] *n abbr* (= *sudden infant death syndrome*)
mort subite du nourrisson, mort *f* au berceau
siege [siːdʒ] *n* siège *m*; **to lay ~ to** assiéger
siege economy *n* économie *f* de (temps de)
siège
Sierra Leone [sɪˈɛrəlɪˈəun] *n* Sierra Leone *f*
sieve [sɪv] *n* tamis *m*, passoire *f* ▷ *vt* tamiser,
passer (au tamis)
sift [sɪft] *vt* passer au tamis *or* au crible; (*fig*)
passer au crible ▷ *vi* (*fig*): **to ~ through** passer
en revue
sigh [saɪ] *n* soupir *m* ▷ *vi* soupirer, pousser un
soupir
sight [saɪt] *n* (*faculty*) vue *f*; (*spectacle*) spectacle
m; (*on gun*) mire *f* ▷ *vt* apercevoir; **in ~** visible;
(*fig*) en vue; **out of ~** hors de vue; **at ~** (*Comm*) à
vue; **at first ~** à première vue, au premier
abord; **I know her by ~** je la connais de vue; **to
catch ~ of sb/sth** apercevoir qn/qch; **to lose ~
of sb/sth** perdre qn/qch de vue; **to set one's ~s
on sth** jeter son dévolu sur qch
sighted ['saɪtɪd] *adj* qui voit; **partially ~** qui a
un certain degré de vision
sightseeing ['saɪtsiːɪŋ] *n* tourisme *m*; **to go ~**
faire du tourisme
sightseer ['saɪtsiːəʳ] *n* touriste *m/f*
sign [saɪn] *n* (*gen*) signe *m*; (*with hand etc*) signe,
geste *m*; (*notice*) panneau *m*, écriteau *m*; (*also*:
road sign) panneau de signalisation ▷ *vt*
signer; **as a ~ of** en signe de; **it's a good/bad ~**
c'est bon/mauvais signe; **plus/minus ~** signe
plus/moins; **there's no ~ of a change of mind**
rien ne laisse présager un revirement; **he was
showing ~s of improvement** il commençait
visiblement à faire des progrès; **to ~ one's
name** signer; **where do I ~?** où dois-je signer?

▶ **sign away** *vt* (*rights etc*) renoncer
officiellement à
▶ **sign for** *vt fus* (*item*) signer le reçu pour
▶ **sign in** *vi* signer le registre (en arrivant)
▶ **sign off** *vi* (*Radio, TV*) terminer l'émission
▶ **sign on** *vi* (*Mil*) s'engager; (*Brit: as unemployed*)
s'inscrire au chômage; (*enrol*) s'inscrire ▷ *vt*
(*Mil*) engager; (*employee*) embaucher; **to ~ on
for a course** s'inscrire pour un cours
▶ **sign out** *vi* signer le registre (en partant)
▶ **sign over** *vt*: **to ~ sth over to sb** céder qch par
écrit à qn
▶ **sign up** *vt* (*Mil*) engager ▷ *vi* (*Mil*) s'engager;
(*for course*) s'inscrire
signal ['sɪgnl] *n* signal *m* ▷ *vi* (*Aut*) mettre son
clignotant ▷ *vt* (*person*) faire signe à; (*message*)
communiquer par signaux; **to ~ a left/right
turn** (*Aut*) indiquer *or* signaler que l'on tourne à
gauche/droite; **to ~ to sb (to do sth)** faire signe
à qn (de faire qch)
signal box *n* (*Rail*) poste *m* d'aiguillage
signalman [ˈsɪgnlmən] *n* (*Rail*) aiguilleur *m*
signatory [ˈsɪgnətərɪ] *n* signataire *m/f*
signature [ˈsɪgnətʃəʳ] *n* signature *f*
signature tune *n* indicatif musical
signet ring [ˈsɪgnət-] *n* chevalière *f*
significance [sɪgˈnɪfɪkəns] *n* signification *f*;
importance *f*; **that is of no ~** ceci n'a pas
d'importance
significant [sɪgˈnɪfɪkənt] *adj* significatif(-ive);
(*important*) important(e), considérable
significantly [sɪgˈnɪfɪkəntlɪ] *adv* (*improve,
increase*) sensiblement; (*smile*) d'un air entendu,
éloquemment; **~, ...** fait significatif, ...
signify [ˈsɪgnɪfaɪ] *vt* signifier
sign language *n* langage *m* par signes
signpost [ˈsaɪnpəust] *n* poteau indicateur
Sikh [siːk] *adj, n* Sikh *m/f*
silage [ˈsaɪlɪdʒ] *n* (*fodder*) fourrage vert; (*method*)
ensilage *m*
silence [ˈsaɪlns] *n* silence *m* ▷ *vt* faire taire,
réduire au silence
silencer [ˈsaɪlənsəʳ] *n* (*Brit: on gun, Aut*)
silencieux *m*
silent [ˈsaɪlnt] *adj* silencieux(-euse); (*film*)
muet(te); **to keep** *or* **remain ~** garder le silence,
ne rien dire
silently [ˈsaɪlntlɪ] *adv* silencieusement
silent partner *n* (*Comm*) bailleur *m* de fonds,
commanditaire *m*
silhouette [sɪluːˈɛt] *n* silhouette *f* ▷ *vt*: **~d
against** se profilant sur, se découpant contre
silicon [ˈsɪlɪkən] *n* silicium *m*
silicon chip [ˈsɪlɪkən-] *n* puce *f* électronique
silicone [ˈsɪlɪkəun] *n* silicone *f*
silk [sɪlk] *n* soie *f* ▷ *cpd* de *or* en soie
silky [ˈsɪlkɪ] *adj* soyeux(-euse)
sill [sɪl] *n* (*also*: **windowsill**) rebord *m* (de la
fenêtre); (*of door*) seuil *m*; (*Aut*) bas *m* de marche
silly [ˈsɪlɪ] *adj* stupide, sot(te), bête; **to do
something ~** faire une bêtise
silo [ˈsaɪləu] *n* silo *m*

silt [sɪlt] n vase f; limon m
silver ['sɪlvə^r] n argent m; (money) monnaie f (en pièces d'argent); (also: **silverware**) argenterie f ▷ adj (made of silver) d'argent, en argent; (in colour) argenté(e); (car) gris métallisé inv
silver-plated [sɪlvə'pleɪtɪd] adj plaqué(e) argent
silversmith ['sɪlvəsmɪθ] n orfèvre m/f
silverware ['sɪlvəwɛə^r] n argenterie f
silver wedding, silver wedding anniversary n noces fpl d'argent
silvery ['sɪlvrɪ] adj argenté(e)
SIM card abbr (= subscriber identity module card) carte f SIM
similar ['sɪmɪlə^r] adj: ~ (to) semblable (à)
similarity [sɪmɪ'lærɪtɪ] n ressemblance f, similarité f
similarly ['sɪmɪləlɪ] adv de la même façon, de même
simile ['sɪmɪlɪ] n comparaison f
simmer ['sɪmə^r] vi cuire à feu doux, mijoter
▸ **simmer down** vi (fig: inf) se calmer
simper ['sɪmpə^r] vi minauder
simpering ['sɪmprɪŋ] adj stupide
simple ['sɪmpl] adj simple; **the ~ truth** la vérité pure et simple
simple interest n (Math, Comm) intérêts mpl simples
simple-minded [sɪmpl'maɪndɪd] adj simplet(te), simple d'esprit
simpleton ['sɪmpltən] n nigaud(e), niais(e)
simplicity [sɪm'plɪsɪtɪ] n simplicité f
simplification [sɪmplɪfɪ'keɪʃən] n simplification f
simplify ['sɪmplɪfaɪ] vt simplifier
simply ['sɪmplɪ] adv simplement; (without fuss) avec simplicité; (absolutely) absolument
simulate ['sɪmjuleɪt] vt simuler, feindre
simulation [sɪmju'leɪʃən] n simulation f
simultaneous [sɪməl'teɪnɪəs] adj simultané(e)
simultaneously [sɪməl'teɪnɪəslɪ] adv simultanément
sin [sɪn] n péché m ▷ vi pécher
Sinai ['saɪneɪaɪ] n Sinaï m
since [sɪns] adv, prep depuis ▷ conj (time) depuis que; (because) puisque, étant donné que, comme; ~ **then, ever ~** depuis ce moment-là; ~ **Monday** depuis lundi; **(ever) ~ I arrived** depuis mon arrivée, depuis que je suis arrivé
sincere [sɪn'sɪə^r] adj sincère
sincerely [sɪn'sɪəlɪ] adv sincèrement; **Yours ~** (at end of letter) veuillez agréer, Monsieur (or Madame) l'expression de mes sentiments distingués or les meilleurs
sincerity [sɪn'sɛrɪtɪ] n sincérité f
sine [saɪn] n (Math) sinus m
sinew ['sɪnju:] n tendon m; **sinews** npl muscles mpl
sinful ['sɪnful] adj coupable
sing (pt **sang**, pp **sung**) [sɪŋ, sæŋ, sʌŋ] vt, vi chanter
Singapore [sɪŋgə'pɔ:^r] n Singapour m
singe [sɪndʒ] vt brûler légèrement; (clothes)

roussir
singer ['sɪŋə^r] n chanteur(-euse)
Singhalese [sɪŋə'li:z] adj = **Sinhalese**
singing ['sɪŋɪŋ] n (of person, bird) chant m; façon f de chanter; (of kettle, bullet, in ears) sifflement m
single ['sɪŋgl] adj seul(e), unique; (unmarried) célibataire; (not double) simple ▷ n (Brit: also: **single ticket**) aller m (simple); (record) 45 tours m; **singles** npl (Tennis) simple m; (US: single people) célibataires m/fpl; **not a ~ one was left** il n'en est pas resté un(e), seul(e); **every ~ day** chaque jour sans exception
▸ **single out** vt choisir; (distinguish) distinguer
single bed n lit m d'une personne or à une place
single-breasted ['sɪŋglbrɛstɪd] adj droit(e)
Single European Market n: **the ~** le marché unique européen
single file n: **in ~** en file indienne
single-handed [sɪŋgl'hændɪd] adv tout(e) seul(e), sans (aucune) aide
single-minded [sɪŋgl'maɪndɪd] adj résolu(e), tenace
single parent n parent unique (or célibataire); **single-parent family** famille monoparentale
single room n chambre f à un lit or pour une personne
singles bar n (esp US) bar m de rencontres pour célibataires
single-sex school [sɪŋgl'sɛks-] n école f non mixte
singlet ['sɪŋglɪt] n tricot m de corps
single-track road [sɪŋgl'træk-] n route f à voie unique
singly ['sɪŋglɪ] adv séparément
singsong ['sɪŋsɔŋ] adj (tone) chantant(e) ▷ n (songs): **to have a ~** chanter quelque chose (ensemble)
singular ['sɪŋgjulə^r] adj singulier(-ière); (odd) singulier, étrange; (outstanding) remarquable; (Ling) (au) singulier, du singulier ▷ n (Ling) singulier m; **in the feminine ~** au féminin singulier
singularly ['sɪŋgjuləlɪ] adv singulièrement; étrangement
Sinhalese [sɪnhə'li:z] adj cingalais(e)
sinister ['sɪnɪstə^r] adj sinistre
sink [sɪŋk] (pt **sank**, pp **sunk**) [sæŋk, sʌŋk] n évier m; (washbasin) lavabo m ▷ vt (ship) (faire) couler, faire sombrer; (foundations) creuser; (piles etc): **to ~ sth into** enfoncer qch dans ▷ vi couler, sombrer; (ground etc) s'affaisser; **to ~ into sth** (chair) s'enfoncer dans qch; **he sank into a chair/the mud** il s'est enfoncé dans un fauteuil/la boue; **a ~ing feeling** un serrement de cœur
▸ **sink in** vi s'enfoncer, pénétrer; (explanation) rentrer (inf), être compris; **it took a long time to ~ in** il a fallu longtemps pour que ça rentre
sinking fund n fonds mpl d'amortissement
sink unit n bloc-évier m
sinner ['sɪnə^r] n pécheur(-eresse)
Sinn Féin [ʃɪn'feɪn] n Sinn Féin m (parti politique

irlandais qui soutient l'IRA)
Sino- ['saɪnəu] *prefix* sino-
sinuous ['sɪnjuəs] *adj* sinueux(-euse)
sinus ['saɪnəs] *n* (*Anat*) sinus *m inv*
sip [sɪp] *n* petite gorgée ▷ *vt* boire à petites gorgées
siphon ['saɪfən] *n* siphon *m* ▷ *vt* (*also*: **siphon off**) siphonner; (: *fig*: *funds*) transférer; (: *illegally*) détourner
sir [sə^r] *n* monsieur *m*; **S~ John Smith** sir John Smith; **yes ~** oui Monsieur; **Dear S~** (*in letter*) Monsieur
siren ['saɪərn] *n* sirène *f*
sirloin ['sə:lɔɪn] *n* (*also*: **sirloin steak**) aloyau *m*
sirloin steak *n* bifteck *m* dans l'aloyau
sirocco [sɪ'rɔkəu] *n* sirocco *m*
sisal ['saɪsəl] *n* sisal *m*
sissy ['sɪsɪ] *n* (*inf*: *coward*) poule mouillée
sister ['sɪstə^r] *n* sœur *f*; (*nun*) religieuse *f*, (bonne) sœur; (*Brit*: *nurse*) infirmière *f* en chef ▷ *cpd*: **~ organization** organisation *f* sœur; **~ ship** sister(-)ship *m*
sister-in-law ['sɪstərɪnlɔ:] *n* belle-sœur *f*
sit (*pt*, *pp* **sat**) [sɪt, sæt] *vi* s'asseoir; (*be sitting*) être assis(e); (*assembly*) être en séance, siéger; (*for painter*) poser; (*dress etc*) tomber ▷ *vt* (*exam*) passer, se présenter à; **to ~ tight** ne pas bouger
▶ **sit about, sit around** *vi* être assis(e) *or* rester à ne rien faire
▶ **sit back** *vi* (*in seat*) bien s'installer, se carrer
▶ **sit down** *vi* s'asseoir; **to be ~ting down** être assis(e)
▶ **sit in** *vi*: **to ~ in on a discussion** assister à une discussion
▶ **sit on** *vt fus* (*jury, committee*) faire partie de
▶ **sit up** *vi* s'asseoir; (*straight*) se redresser; (*not go to bed*) rester debout, ne pas se coucher
sitcom ['sɪtkɔm] *n abbr* (*TV*: = *situation comedy*) sitcom *f*, comédie *f* de situation
sit-down ['sɪtdaun] *adj*: **a ~ strike** une grève sur le tas; **a ~ meal** un repas assis
site [saɪt] *n* emplacement *m*, site *m*; (*also*: **building site**) chantier *m* ▷ *vt* placer
sit-in ['sɪtɪn] *n* (*demonstration*) sit-in *m inv*, occupation *f* de locaux
siting ['saɪtɪŋ] *n* (*location*) emplacement *m*
sitter ['sɪtə^r] *n* (*for painter*) modèle *m*; (*also*: **babysitter**) baby-sitter *m/f*
sitting ['sɪtɪŋ] *n* (*of assembly etc*) séance *f*; (*in canteen*) service *m*
sitting member *n* (*Pol*) parlementaire *m/f* en exercice
sitting room *n* salon *m*
sitting tenant *n* (*Brit*) locataire occupant(e)
situate ['sɪtjueɪt] *vt* situer
situated ['sɪtjueɪtɪd] *adj* situé(e)
situation [sɪtju'eɪʃən] *n* situation *f*; **"~s vacant/wanted"** (*Brit*) "offres/demandes d'emploi"
situation comedy *n* (*Theat*) comédie *f* de situation
six [sɪks] *num* six
six-pack ['sɪkspæk] *n* (*esp US*) pack *m* de six

canettes
sixteen [sɪks'ti:n] *num* seize
sixteenth [sɪks'ti:nθ] *num* seizième
sixth ['sɪksθ] *num* sixième ▷ *n*: **the upper/lower ~** (*Brit Scol*) la terminale/la première
sixth form *n* (*Brit*) ≈ classes *fpl* de première et de terminale
sixth-form college *n* lycée n'ayant que des classes de première et de terminale
sixtieth ['sɪkstɪɪθ] *num* soixantième
sixty ['sɪkstɪ] *num* soixante
size [saɪz] *n* dimensions *fpl*; (*of person*) taille *f*; (*of clothing*) taille *f*; (*of shoes*) pointure *f*; (*of estate, area*) étendue *f*; (*of problem*) ampleur *f*; (*of company*) importance *f*; (*glue*) colle *f*; **I take ~ 14** (*of dress etc*) ≈ je prends du 42 *or* la taille 42; **the small/large ~** (*of soap powder etc*) le petit/grand modèle; **it's the ~ of ...** c'est de la taille (*or* grosseur) de ..., c'est grand (*or* gros) comme ...; **cut to ~** découpé(e) aux dimensions voulues
▶ **size up** *vt* juger, jauger
sizeable ['saɪzəbl] *adj* (*object, building, estate*) assez grand(e); (*amount, problem, majority*) assez important(e)
sizzle ['sɪzl] *vi* grésiller
SK *abbr* (*Canada*) = **Saskatchewan**
skate [skeɪt] *n* patin *m*; (*fish*: *pl inv*) raie *f* ▷ *vi* patiner
▶ **skate over, skate around** *vt* (*problem, issue*) éluder
skateboard ['skeɪtbɔ:d] *n* skateboard *m*, planche *f* à roulettes
skateboarding ['skeɪtbɔ:dɪŋ] *n* skateboard *m*
skater ['skeɪtə^r] *n* patineur(-euse)
skating ['skeɪtɪŋ] *n* patinage *m*
skating rink *n* patinoire *f*
skeleton ['skɛlɪtn] *n* squelette *m*; (*outline*) schéma *m*
skeleton key *n* passe-partout *m*
skeleton staff *n* effectifs réduits
skeptic ['skɛptɪk] (*US*) = **sceptic**
skeptical ['skɛptɪkl] (*US*) = **sceptical**
sketch [skɛtʃ] *n* (*drawing*) croquis *m*, esquisse *f*; (*outline plan*) aperçu *m*; (*Theat*) sketch *m*, saynète *f* ▷ *vt* esquisser, faire un croquis *or* une esquisse de; (*plan etc*) esquisser
sketch book *n* carnet *m* à dessin
sketch pad *n* bloc *m* à dessin
sketchy ['skɛtʃɪ] *adj* incomplet(-ète), fragmentaire
skew [skju:] *n* (*Brit*): **on the ~** de travers, en biais
skewer ['skju:ə^r] *n* brochette *f*
ski [ski:] *n* ski *m* ▷ *vi* skier, faire du ski
ski boot *n* chaussure *f* de ski
skid [skɪd] *n* dérapage *m* ▷ *vi* déraper; **to go into a ~** déraper
skid mark *n* trace *f* de dérapage
skier ['ski:ə^r] *n* skieur(-euse)
skiing ['ski:ɪŋ] *n* ski *m*; **to go ~** (aller) faire du ski
ski instructor *n* moniteur(-trice) de ski
ski jump *n* (*ramp*) tremplin *m*; (*event*) saut *m* à skis

skilful, (US) **skillful** ['skɪlful] adj habile, adroit(e)

skilfully, (US) **skillfully** ['skɪlfəlɪ] adv habilement, adroitement

ski lift n remonte-pente m inv

skill [skɪl] n (ability) habileté f, adresse f, talent m; (requiring training) compétences fpl

skilled [skɪld] adj habile, adroit(e); (worker) qualifié(e)

skillet ['skɪlɪt] n poêlon m

skillful etc ['skɪlful] (US) = **skilful** etc

skim [skɪm] vt (milk) écrémer; (soup) écumer; (glide over) raser, effleurer ▷ vi: **to ~ through** (fig) parcourir

skimmed milk [skɪmd-], (US) **skim milk** n lait écrémé

skimp [skɪmp] vt (work) bâcler, faire à la va-vite; (cloth etc) lésiner sur

skimpy ['skɪmpɪ] adj étriqué(e); maigre

skin [skɪn] n peau f ▷ vt (fruit etc) éplucher; (animal) écorcher; **wet** or **soaked to the ~** trempé(e) jusqu'aux os

skin cancer n cancer m de la peau

skin-deep ['skɪn'diːp] adj superficiel(le)

skin diver n plongeur(-euse) sous-marin(e)

skin diving n plongée sous-marine

skinflint ['skɪnflɪnt] n grippe-sou m

skin graft n greffe f de peau

skinhead ['skɪnhɛd] n skinhead m

skinny ['skɪnɪ] adj maigre, maigrichon(ne)

skin test n cuti f(-réaction) f

skintight ['skɪntaɪt] adj (dress etc) collant(e), ajusté(e)

skip [skɪp] n petit bond or saut; (Brit: container) benne f ▷ vi gambader, sautiller; (with rope) sauter à la corde ▷ vt (pass over) sauter; **to ~ school** (esp US) faire l'école buissonnière

ski pants npl pantalon m de ski

ski pass n forfait-skieur(s) m

ski pole n bâton m de ski

skipper ['skɪpə'] n (Naut, Sport) capitaine m; (in race) skipper m ▷ vt (boat) commander; (team) être le chef de

skipping rope ['skɪpɪŋ-], (US) **skip rope** n corde f à sauter

ski resort n station f de sports d'hiver

skirmish ['skəːmɪʃ] n escarmouche f, accrochage m

skirt [skəːt] n jupe f ▷ vt longer, contourner

skirting board ['skəːtɪŋ-] n (Brit) plinthe f

ski run n piste f de ski

ski slope n piste f de ski

ski suit n combinaison f de ski

skit [skɪt] n sketch m satirique

ski tow n = **ski lift**

skittle ['skɪtl] n quille f; **skittles** (game) (jeu m de) quilles fpl

skive [skaɪv] vi (Brit inf) tirer au flanc

skulk [skʌlk] vi rôder furtivement

skull [skʌl] n crâne m

skullcap ['skʌlkæp] n calotte f

skunk [skʌŋk] n mouffette f; (fur) sconse m

sky [skaɪ] n ciel m; **to praise sb to the skies** porter qn aux nues

sky-blue [skaɪ'bluː] adj bleu ciel inv

skydiving ['skaɪdaɪvɪŋ] n parachutisme m (en chute libre)

sky-high ['skaɪ'haɪ] adv très haut ▷ adj exorbitant(e); **prices are ~** les prix sont exorbitants

skylark ['skaɪlɑːk] n (bird) alouette f (des champs)

skylight ['skaɪlaɪt] n lucarne f

skyline ['skaɪlaɪn] n (horizon) (ligne f d')horizon m; (of city) ligne des toits

skyscraper ['skaɪskreɪpə'] n gratte-ciel m inv

slab [slæb] n plaque f; (of stone) dalle f; (of wood) bloc m; (of meat, cheese) tranche épaisse

slack [slæk] adj (loose) lâche, desserré(e); (slow) stagnant(e); (careless) négligent(e), peu sérieux(-euse) or consciencieux(-euse); (Comm: market) peu actif(-ive); (: demand) faible; (period) creux(-euse) ▷ n (in rope etc) mou m; **business is ~** les affaires vont mal

slacken ['slækn] (also: **slacken off**) vi ralentir, diminuer ▷ vt relâcher

slacks [slæks] npl pantalon m

slag [slæg] n scories fpl

slag heap n crassier m

slag off (Brit: inf) vt dire du mal de

slain [sleɪn] pp of **slay**

slake [sleɪk] vt (one's thirst) étancher

slalom ['slɑːləm] n slalom m

slam [slæm] vt (door) (faire) claquer; (throw) jeter violemment, flanquer; (inf: criticize) éreinter, démolir ▷ vi claquer

slammer ['slæmə'] n (inf): **the ~** la taule

slander ['slɑːndə'] n calomnie f; (Law) diffamation f ▷ vt calomnier; diffamer

slanderous ['slɑːndrəs] adj calomnieux(-euse); diffamatoire

slang [slæŋ] n argot m

slanging match ['slæŋɪŋ-] n (Brit inf) engueulade f, empoignade f

slant [slɑːnt] n inclinaison f; (fig) angle m, point m de vue

slanted ['slɑːntɪd] adj tendancieux(-euse)

slanting ['slɑːntɪŋ] adj en pente, incliné(e); couché(e)

slap [slæp] n claque f, gifle f; (on the back) tape f ▷ vt donner une claque or une gifle (or une tape) à; **to ~ on** (paint) appliquer rapidement ▷ adv (directly) tout droit, en plein

slapdash ['slæpdæʃ] adj (work) fait(e) sans soin or à la va-vite; (person) insouciant(e), négligent(e)

slaphead ['slæphɛd] n (Brit inf) chauve

slapstick ['slæpstɪk] n (comedy) grosse farce (style tarte à la crème)

slap-up ['slæpʌp] adj (Brit): **a ~ meal** un repas extra or fameux

slash [slæʃ] vt entailler, taillader; (fig: prices) casser

slat [slæt] n (of wood) latte f, lame f

slate [sleɪt] n ardoise f ▷ vt (fig: criticize) éreinter, démolir

slaughter ['slɔːtəʳ] n carnage m, massacre m; (of animals) abattage m ▷ vt (animal) abattre; (people) massacrer

slaughterhouse ['slɔːtəhaus] n abattoir m

Slav [slɑːv] adj slave

slave [sleɪv] n esclave m/f ▷ vi (also: **slave away**) trimer, travailler comme un forçat; **to ~ (away) at sth/at doing sth** se tuer à qch/à faire qch

slave driver n (inf: pej) négrier(-ière)

slave labour n travail m d'esclave; **it's just ~** (fig) c'est de l'esclavage

slaver ['slævəʳ] vi (dribble) baver

slavery ['sleɪvərɪ] n esclavage m

Slavic ['slævɪk] adj slave

slavish ['sleɪvɪʃ] adj servile

slavishly ['sleɪvɪʃlɪ] adv (copy) servilement

Slavonic [sləˈvɔnɪk] adj slave

slay (pt **slew**, pp **slain**) [sleɪ, sluː, sleɪn] vt (literary) tuer

sleazy ['sliːzɪ] adj miteux(-euse), minable

sled [slɛd] (US) = **sledge**

sledge [slɛdʒ] n luge f

sledgehammer ['slɛdʒhæməʳ] n marteau m de forgeron

sleek [sliːk] adj (hair, fur) brillant(e), luisant(e); (car, boat) aux lignes pures or élégantes

sleep [sliːp] n sommeil m ▷ vi (pt, pp **slept**) [slɛpt] dormir; (spend night) dormir, coucher ▷ vt: **we can ~ 4** on peut coucher or loger 4 personnes; **to go to ~** s'endormir; **to have a good night's ~** passer une bonne nuit; **to put to ~** (patient) endormir; (animal: euphemism: kill) piquer; **to ~ lightly** avoir le sommeil léger; **to ~ with sb** (have sex) coucher avec qn
  ▶ **sleep around** vi coucher à droite et à gauche
  ▶ **sleep in** vi (oversleep) se réveiller trop tard; (on purpose) faire la grasse matinée
  ▶ **sleep together** vi (have sex) coucher ensemble

sleeper ['sliːpəʳ] n (person) dormeur(-euse); (Brit Rail: on track) traverse f; (: train) train-couchettes m; (: carriage) wagon-lits m, voiture-lits f; (: berth) couchette f

sleepily ['sliːpɪlɪ] adv d'un air endormi

sleeping ['sliːpɪŋ] adj qui dort, endormi(e)

sleeping bag n sac m de couchage

sleeping car n wagon-lits m, voiture-lits f

sleeping partner n (Brit Comm) = **silent partner**

sleeping pill n somnifère m

sleeping sickness n maladie f du sommeil

sleepless ['sliːplɪs] adj: **a ~ night** une nuit blanche

sleeplessness ['sliːplɪsnɪs] n insomnie f

sleepover ['sliːpəuvəʳ] n nuit f chez un copain or une copine; **we're having a ~ at Jo's** nous allons passer la nuit chez Jo

sleepwalk ['sliːpwɔːk] vi marcher en dormant

sleepwalker ['sliːpwɔːkəʳ] n somnambule m/f

sleepy ['sliːpɪ] adj qui a envie de dormir; (fig) endormi(e); **to be** or **feel ~** avoir sommeil, avoir envie de dormir

sleet [sliːt] n neige fondue

sleeve [sliːv] n manche f; (of record) pochette f

sleeveless ['sliːvlɪs] adj (garment) sans manches

sleigh [sleɪ] n traîneau m

sleight [slaɪt] n: **~ of hand** tour m de passe-passe

slender ['slɛndəʳ] adj svelte, mince; (fig) faible, ténu(e)

slept [slɛpt] pt, pp of **sleep**

sleuth [sluːθ] n (inf) détective (privé)

slew [sluː] vi (also: **slew round**) virer, pivoter ▷ pt of **slay**

slice [slaɪs] n tranche f; (round) rondelle f; (utensil) spatule f; (also: **fish slice**) pelle f à poisson ▷ vt couper en tranches (or en rondelles); **~d bread** pain m en tranches

slick [slɪk] adj (skilful) bien ficelé(e); (salesperson) qui a du bagout, mielleux(-euse) ▷ n (also: **oil slick**) nappe f de pétrole, marée noire

slid [slɪd] pt, pp of **slide**

slide [slaɪd] (pt, pp **slid**) [slɪd] n (in playground) toboggan m; (Phot) diapositive f; (Brit: also: **hair slide**) barrette f; (microscope slide) (lame f) porte-objet m; (in prices) chute f, baisse f ▷ vt (faire) glisser ▷ vi glisser; **to let things ~** (fig) laisser les choses aller à la dérive

slide projector n (Phot) projecteur m de diapositives

slide rule n règle f à calcul

sliding ['slaɪdɪŋ] adj (door) coulissant(e); **~ roof** (Aut) toit ouvrant

sliding scale n échelle f mobile

slight [slaɪt] adj (slim) mince, menu(e); (frail) frêle; (trivial) faible, insignifiant(e); (small) petit(e), léger(-ère); (before n) ▷ n offense f, affront m ▷ vt (offend) blesser, offenser; **the ~est** le (or la) moindre; **not in the ~est** pas le moins du monde, pas du tout

slightly ['slaɪtlɪ] adv légèrement, un peu; **~ built** fluet(te)

slim [slɪm] adj mince ▷ vi maigrir; (diet) suivre un régime amaigrissant

slime [slaɪm] n vase f; substance visqueuse

slimming ['slɪmɪŋ] n amaigrissement m ▷ adj (diet, pills) amaigrissant(e), pour maigrir; (food) qui ne fait pas grossir

slimy ['slaɪmɪ] adj visqueux(-euse), gluant(e); (covered with mud) vaseux(-euse)

sling [slɪŋ] n (Med) écharpe f; (for baby) porte-bébé m; (weapon) fronde f, lance-pierre m ▷ vt (pt, pp **slung**) [slʌŋ] lancer, jeter; **to have one's arm in a ~** avoir le bras en écharpe

slink (pt, pp **slunk**) [slɪŋk, slʌŋk] vi: **to ~ away** or **off** s'en aller furtivement

slinky ['slɪŋkɪ] adj (clothes) moulant(e)

slip [slɪp] n faux pas; (mistake) erreur f, bévue f; (underskirt) combinaison f; (of paper) petite feuille, fiche f ▷ vt (slide) glisser ▷ vi (slide) glisser; (decline) baisser; (move smoothly): **to ~ into/out of** se glisser or se faufiler dans/hors de; **to let a chance ~ by** laisser passer une occasion; **to ~ sth on/off** enfiler/enlever qch; **it ~ped from her hand** cela lui a glissé des mains; **to give sb the ~** fausser compagnie à

qn; **a ~ of the tongue** un lapsus
▸ **slip away** vi s'esquiver
▸ **slip in** vt glisser
▸ **slip out** vi sortir
▸ **slip up** vi faire une erreur, gaffer
slip-on ['slɪpɒn] adj facile à enfiler; **~ shoes** mocassins mpl
slipped disc [slɪpt-] n déplacement m de vertèbre
slipper ['slɪpər] n pantoufle f
slippery ['slɪpərɪ] adj glissant(e); (fig: person) insaisissable
slip road n (Brit: to motorway) bretelle f d'accès
slipshod ['slɪpʃɒd] adj négligé(e), peu soigné(e)
slip-up ['slɪpʌp] n bévue f
slipway ['slɪpweɪ] n cale f (de construction or de lancement)
slit [slɪt] n fente f; (cut) incision f; (tear) déchirure f ▷ vt (pt, pp -) fendre; couper, inciser; déchirer; **to ~ sb's throat** trancher la gorge à qn
slither ['slɪðər] vi glisser, déraper
sliver ['slɪvər] n (of glass, wood) éclat m; (of cheese, sausage) petit morceau
slob [slɒb] n (inf) rustaud(e)
slog [slɒg] n (Brit: effort) gros effort; (: work) tâche fastidieuse ▷ vi travailler très dur
slogan ['sləʊgən] n slogan m
slop [slɒp] vi (also: **slop over**) se renverser; déborder ▷ vt répandre; renverser
slope [sləʊp] n pente f, côte f; (side of mountain) versant m; (slant) inclinaison f ▷ vi: **to ~ down** être or descendre en pente; **to ~ up** monter
sloping ['sləʊpɪŋ] adj en pente, incliné(e); (handwriting) penché(e)
sloppy ['slɒpɪ] adj (work) peu soigné(e), bâclé(e); (appearance) négligé(e), débraillé(e); (film etc) sentimental(e)
slosh [slɒʃ] vi (inf): **to ~ about** or **around** (children) patauger; (liquid) clapoter
sloshed [slɒʃt] adj (inf: drunk) bourré(e)
slot [slɒt] n fente f; (fig: in timetable, Radio, TV) créneau m, plage f ▷ vt: **to ~ sth into** encastrer or insérer qch dans ▷ vi: **to ~ into** s'encastrer or s'insérer dans
sloth [sləʊθ] n (vice) paresse f; (Zool) paresseux m
slot machine n (Brit: vending machine) distributeur m (automatique), machine f à sous; (for gambling) appareil m or machine à sous
slot meter n (Brit) compteur m à pièces
slouch [slaʊtʃ] vi avoir le dos rond, être voûté(e)
▸ **slouch about, slouch around** vi traîner à ne rien faire
Slovak ['sləʊvæk] adj slovaque ▷ n Slovaque m/f; (Ling) slovaque m; **the ~ Republic** la République slovaque
Slovakia [sləʊ'vækɪə] n Slovaquie f
Slovakian [sləʊ'vækɪən] adj, n = **Slovak**
Slovene [sləʊ'viːn] adj slovène ▷ n Slovène m/f; (Ling) slovène m
Slovenia [sləʊ'viːnɪə] n Slovénie f
Slovenian [sləʊ'viːnɪən] adj, n = **Slovene**

slovenly ['slʌvənlɪ] adj sale, débraillé(e), négligé(e)
slow [sləʊ] adj lent(e); (watch): **to be ~** retarder ▷ adv lentement ▷ vt, vi ralentir; **"~"** (road sign) "ralentir"; **at a ~ speed** à petite vitesse; **to be ~ to act/decide** être lent à agir/décider; **my watch is 20 minutes ~** ma montre retarde de 20 minutes; **business is ~** les affaires marchent au ralenti; **to go ~** (driver) rouler lentement; (in industrial dispute) faire la grève perlée
▸ **slow down** vi ralentir
slow-acting [sləʊ'æktɪŋ] adj qui agit lentement, à action lente
slowcoach ['sləʊkəʊtʃ] n (Brit inf) lambin(e)
slowly ['sləʊlɪ] adv lentement
slow motion n: **in ~** au ralenti
slowness ['sləʊnɪs] n lenteur f
slowpoke ['sləʊpəʊk] n (US inf) = **slowcoach**
sludge [slʌdʒ] n boue f
slug [slʌg] n limace f; (bullet) balle f
sluggish ['slʌgɪʃ] adj (person) mou (molle), lent(e); (stream, engine, trading) lent(e); (business, sales) stagnant(e)
sluice [sluːs] n écluse f; (also: **sluice gate**) vanne f ▷ vt: **to ~ down** or **out** laver à grande eau
slum [slʌm] n (house) taudis m; **slums** npl (area) quartiers mpl pauvres
slumber ['slʌmbər] n sommeil m
slump [slʌmp] n baisse soudaine, effondrement m; (Econ) crise f ▷ vi s'effondrer, s'affaisser
slung [slʌŋ] pt, pp of **sling**
slunk [slʌŋk] pt, pp of **slink**
slur [sləːr] n bredouillement m; (smear): **~ (on)** atteinte f (à); insinuation f (contre) ▷ vt mal articuler; **to be a ~ on** porter atteinte à
slurp [sləːp] vt, vi boire à grand bruit
slurred [sləːd] adj (pronunciation) inarticulé(e), indistinct(e)
slush [slʌʃ] n neige fondue
slush fund n caisse noire, fonds secrets
slushy ['slʌʃɪ] adj (snow) fondu(e); (street) couvert(e) de neige fondue; (Brit: fig) à l'eau de rose
slut [slʌt] n souillon f
sly [slaɪ] adj (person) rusé(e); (smile, expression, remark) sournois(e); **on the ~** en cachette
smack [smæk] n (slap) tape f; (on face) gifle f ▷ vt donner une tape à; (on face) gifler; (on bottom) donner la fessée à ▷ vi: **to ~ of** avoir des relents de, sentir ▷ adv (inf): **it fell ~ in the middle** c'est tombé en plein milieu or en plein dedans; **to ~ one's lips** se lécher les babines
smacker ['smækər] n (inf: kiss) bisou m or bise f sonore; (: Brit: pound note) livre f; (: US: dollar bill) dollar m
small [smɔːl] adj petit(e); (letter) minuscule ▷ n: **the ~ of the back** le creux des reins; **to get** or **grow ~er** diminuer; **to make ~er** (amount, income) diminuer; (object, garment) rapetisser; **a ~ shopkeeper** un petit commerçant
small ads npl (Brit) petites annonces

small arms *npl* armes individuelles

small business *n* petit commerce, petite affaire

small change *n* petite *or* menue monnaie

smallholder ['smɔ:lhəuldər] *n* (*Brit*) petit cultivateur

smallholding ['smɔ:lhəuldɪŋ] *n* (*Brit*) petite ferme

small hours *npl*: **in the ~** au petit matin

smallish ['smɔ:lɪʃ] *adj* plutôt *or* assez petit(e)

small-minded [smɔ:l'maɪndɪd] *adj* mesquin(e)

smallpox ['smɔ:lpɔks] *n* variole *f*

small print *n* (*in contract etc*) clause(s) imprimée(s) en petits caractères

small-scale ['smɔ:lskeɪl] *adj* (*map, model*) à échelle réduite, à petite échelle; (*business, farming*) peu important(e), modeste

small talk *n* menus propos

small-time ['smɔ:ltaɪm] *adj* (*farmer etc*) petit(e); **a ~ thief** un voleur à la petite semaine

small-town ['smɔ:ltaun] *adj* provincial(e)

smarmy ['smɑ:mɪ] *adj* (*Brit pej*) flagorneur(-euse), lécheur(-euse)

smart [smɑ:t] *adj* élégant(e), chic *inv*; (*clever*) intelligent(e); (*pej*) futé(e); (*quick*) vif (vive), prompt(e) ⊳ *vi* faire mal, brûler; **the ~ set** le beau monde; **to look ~** être élégant(e); **my eyes are ~ing** j'ai les yeux irrités *or* qui me piquent

smart card ['smɑ:t'kɑ:d] *n* carte *f* à puce

smarten up ['smɑ:tn-] *vi* devenir plus élégant(e), se faire beau (belle) ⊳ *vt* rendre plus élégant(e)

smash [smæʃ] *n* (*also*: **smash-up**) collision *f*, accident *m*; (*Mus*) succès foudroyant; (*sound*) fracas *m* ⊳ *vt* casser, briser, fracasser; (*opponent*) écraser; (*hopes*) ruiner, détruire; (*Sport: record*) pulvériser ⊳ *vi* se briser, se fracasser; s'écraser dans
▸ **smash up** *vt* (*car*) bousiller; (*room*) tout casser dans

smashing ['smæʃɪŋ] *adj* (*inf*) formidable

smattering ['smætərɪŋ] *n*: **a ~ of** quelques notions de

smear [smɪər] *n* (*stain*) tache *f*; (*mark*) trace *f*; (*Med*) frottis *m*; (*insult*) calomnie *f* ⊳ *vt* enduire; (*make dirty*) salir; (*fig*) porter atteinte à; **his hands were ~ed with oil/ink** il avait les mains maculées de cambouis/d'encre

smear campaign *n* campagne *f* de dénigrement

smear test *n* (*Brit Med*) frottis *m*

smell [smɛl] (*pt, pp* **smelt** *or* **-ed**) *n* odeur *f*; (*sense*) odorat *m* ⊳ *vt* sentir ⊳ *vi* (*pej*) sentir mauvais; (*food etc*) **to ~ (of)** sentir; **it ~s good** ça sent bon

smelly ['smɛlɪ] *adj* qui sent mauvais, malodorant(e)

smelt [smɛlt] *pt, pp of* **smell** ⊳ *vt* (*ore*) fondre

smile [smaɪl] *n* sourire *m* ⊳ *vi* sourire

smiling ['smaɪlɪŋ] *adj* souriant(e)

smirk [smə:k] *n* petit sourire suffisant *or* affecté

smith [smɪθ] *n* maréchal-ferrant *m*; forgeron *m*

smithy ['smɪðɪ] *n* forge *f*

smitten ['smɪtn] *adj*: **~ with** pris(e) de;

frappé(e) de

smock [smɔk] *n* blouse *f*, sarrau *m*

smog [smɔg] *n* brouillard mêlé de fumée

smoke [sməuk] *n* fumée *f* ⊳ *vt, vi* fumer; **to have a ~** fumer une cigarette; **do you ~?** est-ce que vous fumez?; **do you mind if I ~?** ça ne vous dérange pas que je fume?; **to go up in ~** (*house etc*) brûler; (*fig*) partir en fumée

smoke alarm *n* détecteur *m* de fumée

smoked ['sməukt] *adj* (*bacon, glass*) fumé(e)

smokeless fuel ['sməuklɪs-] *n* combustible non polluant

smokeless zone ['sməuklɪs-] *n* (*Brit*) zone *f* où l'usage du charbon est réglementé

smoker ['sməukər] *n* (*person*) fumeur(-euse); (*Rail*) wagon *m* fumeurs

smoke screen *n* rideau *m* *or* écran *m* de fumée; (*fig*) paravent *m*

smoke shop *n* (*US*) (bureau *m* de) tabac *m*

smoking ['sməukɪŋ] *n*: **"no ~"** (*sign*) "défense de fumer"; **to give up ~** arrêter de fumer

smoking compartment, (*US*) **smoking car** *n* wagon *m* fumeurs

smoky ['sməukɪ] *adj* enfumé(e); (*taste*) fumé(e)

smolder ['sməuldər] *vi* (*US*) = **smoulder**

smoochy ['smu:tʃɪ] *adj* (*inf*) langoureux(-euse)

smooth [smu:ð] *adj* lisse; (*sauce*) onctueux(-euse); (*flavour, whisky*) moelleux(-euse); (*cigarette*) doux (douce); (*movement*) régulier(-ière), sans à-coups *or* heurts; (*landing, takeoff*) en douceur; (*flight*) sans secousses; (*pej: person*) doucereux(-euse), mielleux(-euse) ⊳ *vt* (*also*: **smooth out**) lisser, défroisser; (*creases, difficulties*) faire disparaître
▸ **smooth over** *vt*: **to ~ things over** (*fig*) arranger les choses

smoothly ['smu:ðlɪ] *adv* (*easily*) facilement, sans difficulté(s); **everything went ~** tout s'est bien passé

smother ['smʌðər] *vt* étouffer

smoulder, (*US*) **smolder** ['sməuldər] *vi* couver

SMS *n abbr* (= *short message service*) SMS *m*

SMS message *n* (message *m*) SMS *m*

smudge [smʌdʒ] *n* tache *f*, bavure *f* ⊳ *vt* salir, maculer

smug [smʌg] *adj* suffisant(e), content(e) de soi

smuggle ['smʌgl] *vt* passer en contrebande *or* en fraude; **to ~ in/out** (*goods etc*) faire entrer/sortir clandestinement *or* en fraude

smuggler ['smʌglər] *n* contrebandier(-ière)

smuggling ['smʌglɪŋ] *n* contrebande *f*

smut [smʌt] *n* (*grain of soot*) grain *m* de suie; (*mark*) tache *f* de suie; (*in conversation etc*) obscénités *fpl*

smutty ['smʌtɪ] *adj* (*fig*) grossier(-ière), obscène

snack [snæk] *n* casse-croûte *m inv*; **to have a ~** prendre un en-cas, manger quelque chose (de léger)

snack bar *n* snack(-bar) *m*

snag [snæg] *n* inconvénient *m*, difficulté *f*

snail [sneɪl] *n* escargot *m*

snake [sneɪk] *n* serpent *m*

snap [snæp] *n* (*sound*) claquement *m*, bruit sec; (*photograph*) photo *f*, instantané *m*; (*game*) sorte de jeu de bataille ▷ *adj* subit(e), fait(e) sans réfléchir ▷ *vt* (*fingers*) faire claquer; (*break*) casser net; (*photograph*) prendre un instantané de ▷ *vi* se casser net *or* avec un bruit sec; (*fig: person*) craquer; (*speak sharply*) parler d'un ton brusque; **to ~ open/shut** s'ouvrir/se refermer brusquement; **to ~ one's fingers at** (*fig*) se moquer de; **a cold ~** (*of weather*) un refroidissement soudain de la température
 ▸ **snap at** *vt fus* (*subj: dog*) essayer de mordre
 ▸ **snap off** *vt* (*break*) casser net
 ▸ **snap up** *vt* sauter sur, saisir
snap fastener *n* bouton-pression *m*
snappy ['snæpɪ] *adj* prompt(e); (*slogan*) qui a du punch; **make it ~!** (*inf: hurry up*) grouille-toi!, magne-toi!
snapshot ['snæpʃɒt] *n* photo *f*, instantané *m*
snare [snɛə^r] *n* piège *m* ▷ *vt* attraper, prendre au piège
snarl [snɑ:l] *n* grondement *m or* grognement *m* féroce ▷ *vi* gronder ▷ *vt*: **to get ~ed up** (*wool, plans*) s'emmêler; (*traffic*) se bloquer
snatch [snætʃ] *n* (*fig*) vol *m*; (*small amount*): **~es of** des fragments *mpl or* bribes *fpl* de ▷ *vt* saisir (*d'un geste vif*); (*steal*) voler ▷ *vi*: **don't ~!** doucement!; **to ~ a sandwich** manger *or* avaler un sandwich à la hâte; **to ~ some sleep** arriver à dormir un peu
 ▸ **snatch up** *vt* saisir, s'emparer de
snazzy ['snæzɪ] *adj* (*inf: clothes*) classe *inv*, chouette
sneak [sni:k] (*US: pt* **snuck**) *vi*: **to ~ in/out** entrer/sortir furtivement *or* à la dérobée ▷ *vt*: **to ~ a look at sth** regarder furtivement qch ▷ *n* (*inf: pej: informer*) faux jeton; **to ~ up on sb** s'approcher de qn sans faire de bruit
sneakers ['sni:kəz] *npl* tennis *mpl*, baskets *fpl*
sneaking ['sni:kɪŋ] *adj*: **to have a ~ feeling** *or* **suspicion that …** avoir la vague impression que …
sneaky ['sni:kɪ] *adj* sournois(e)
sneer [snɪə^r] *n* ricanement *m* ▷ *vi* ricaner, sourire d'un air sarcastique; **to ~ at sb/sth** se moquer de qn/qch avec mépris
sneeze [sni:z] *n* éternuement *m* ▷ *vi* éternuer
snide [snaɪd] *adj* sarcastique, narquois(e)
sniff [snɪf] *n* reniflement *m* ▷ *vi* renifler ▷ *vt* renifler, flairer; (*glue, drug*) sniffer, respirer
 ▸ **sniff at** *vt fus*: **it's not to be ~ed at** il ne faut pas cracher dessus, ce n'est pas à dédaigner
sniffer dog ['snɪfə-] *n* (*Police*) chien dressé pour la recherche d'explosifs et de stupéfiants
snigger ['snɪgə^r] *n* ricanement *m*; rire moqueur ▷ *vi* ricaner
snip [snɪp] *n* (*cut*) entaille *f*; (*piece*) petit bout; (*Brit: inf: bargain*) (bonne) occasion *or* affaire ▷ *vt* couper
sniper ['snaɪpə^r] *n* (*marksman*) tireur embusqué
snippet ['snɪpɪt] *n* bribes *fpl*
snivelling ['snɪvlɪŋ] *adj* larmoyant(e),

pleurnicheur(-euse)
snob [snɒb] *n* snob *m/f*
snobbery ['snɒbərɪ] *n* snobisme *m*
snobbish ['snɒbɪʃ] *adj* snob *inv*
snog [snɒg] *vi* (*inf*) se bécoter
snooker ['snu:kə^r] *n* sorte de jeu de billard
snoop [snu:p] *vi*: **to ~ on sb** espionner qn; **to ~ about** fureter
snooper ['snu:pə^r] *n* fureteur(-euse)
snooty ['snu:tɪ] *adj* snob *inv*, prétentieux(-euse)
snooze [snu:z] *n* petit somme ▷ *vi* faire un petit somme
snore [snɔ:^r] *vi* ronfler ▷ *n* ronflement *m*
snoring ['snɔ:rɪŋ] *n* ronflement(s) *m(pl)*
snorkel ['snɔ:kl] *n* (*of swimmer*) tuba *m*
snort [snɔ:t] *n* grognement *m* ▷ *vi* grogner; (*horse*) renâcler ▷ *vt* (*inf: drugs*) sniffer
snotty ['snɒtɪ] *adj* morveux(-euse)
snout [snaut] *n* museau *m*
snow [snəu] *n* neige *f* ▷ *vi* neiger ▷ *vt*: **to be ~ed under with work** être débordé(e) de travail
snowball ['snəubɔ:l] *n* boule *f* de neige
snowbound ['snəubaund] *adj* enneigé(e), bloqué(e) par la neige
snow-capped ['snəukæpt] *adj* (*peak, mountain*) couvert(e) de neige
snowdrift ['snəudrɪft] *n* congère *f*
snowdrop ['snəudrɒp] *n* perce-neige *m*
snowfall ['snəufɔ:l] *n* chute *f* de neige
snowflake ['snəufleɪk] *n* flocon *m* de neige
snowman ['snəumæn] (*irreg*) *n* bonhomme *m* de neige
snowplough, (*US*) **snowplow** ['snəuplau] *n* chasse-neige *m inv*
snowshoe ['snəuʃu:] *n* raquette *f* (*pour la neige*)
snowstorm ['snəustɔ:m] *n* tempête *f* de neige
snowy ['snəuɪ] *adj* neigeux(-euse); (*covered with snow*) enneigé(e)
SNP *n abbr* (*Brit Pol*) = **Scottish National Party**
snub [snʌb] *vt* repousser, snober ▷ *n* rebuffade *f*
snub-nosed [snʌb'nəuzd] *adj* au nez retroussé
snuck [snʌk] (*US*) *pt, pp of* **sneak**
snuff [snʌf] *n* tabac *m* à priser ▷ *vt* (*also*: **snuff out**: *candle*) moucher
snuff movie *n* (*inf*) film pornographique qui se termine par le meurtre réel de l'un des acteurs
snug [snʌg] *adj* douillet(te), confortable; (*person*) bien au chaud; **it's a ~ fit** c'est bien ajusté(e)
snuggle ['snʌgl] *vi*: **to ~ down in bed/up to sb** se pelotonner dans son lit/contre qn
SO *abbr* (*Banking*) = **standing order**

 KEYWORD

so [səu] *adv* **1** (*thus, likewise*) ainsi, de cette façon; **if so** si oui; **so do** *or* **have I** moi aussi; **it's 5 o'clock — so it is!** il est 5 heures — en effet! *or* c'est vrai!; **I hope/think so** je l'espère/le crois; **so far** jusqu'ici, jusqu'à maintenant; (*in past*) jusque-là; **quite so!** exactement!, c'est bien ça!; **even so** quand même, tout de même
 2 (*in comparisons etc: to such a degree*) si, tellement;

so big (that) si *or* tellement grand (que); **she's not so clever as her brother** elle n'est pas aussi intelligente que son frère
3: **so much** (*adj, adv*) tant (de); **I've got so much work** j'ai tant de travail; **I love you so much** je vous aime tant; **so many** tant (de)
4 (*phrases*): **10 or so** à peu près *or* environ 10; **so long!** (*inf: goodbye*) au revoir!, à un de ces jours!; **so to speak** pour ainsi dire; **so (what)?** (*inf*) (bon) et alors?, et après?
▷ *conj* **1** (*expressing purpose*): **so as to do** pour faire, afin de faire; **so (that)** pour que *or* afin que + *sub*
2 (*expressing result*) donc, par conséquent; **so that** si bien que, de (telle) sorte que; **so that's the reason!** c'est donc (pour) ça!; **so you see, I could have gone** alors tu vois, j'aurais pu y aller

soak [səuk] *vt* faire *or* laisser tremper; (*drench*) tremper ▷ *vi* tremper; **to be ~ed through** être trempé jusqu'aux os
▶ **soak in** *vi* pénétrer, être absorbé(e)
▶ **soak up** *vt* absorber
soaking ['səukɪŋ] *adj* (*also:* **soaking wet**) trempé(e)
so-and-so ['səuənsəu] *n* (*somebody*) un(e) tel(le)
soap [səup] *n* savon *m*
soapbox ['səupbɔks] *n* tribune improvisée (en plein air)
soapflakes ['səupfleɪks] *npl* paillettes *fpl* de savon
soap opera *n* feuilleton télévisé (*quotidienneté réaliste ou embellie*)
soap powder *n* lessive *f*, détergent *m*
soapsuds ['səupsʌds] *npl* mousse *f* de savon
soapy ['səupɪ] *adj* savonneux(-euse)
soar [sɔː^r] *vi* monter (en flèche), s'élancer; (*building*) s'élancer; **~ing prices** prix qui grimpent
sob [sɔb] *n* sanglot *m* ▷ *vi* sangloter
s.o.b. *n abbr* (*US inf!:* = son of a bitch) salaud *m* (!)
sober ['səubə^r] *adj* qui n'est pas (*or* plus) ivre; (*serious*) sérieux(-euse), sensé(e); (*moderate*) mesuré(e); (*colour, style*) sobre, discret(-ète)
▶ **sober up** *vt* dégriser ▷ *vi* se dégriser
sobriety [sə'braɪətɪ] *n* (*not being drunk*) sobriété *f*; (*seriousness, sedateness*) sérieux *m*
sob story *n* (*inf: pej*) histoire larmoyante
Soc. *abbr* (= *society*) Soc
so-called ['səu'kɔːld] *adj* soi-disant *inv*
soccer ['sɔkə^r] *n* football *m*
soccer pitch *n* terrain *m* de football
soccer player *n* footballeur *m*
sociable ['səuʃəbl] *adj* sociable
social ['səuʃl] *adj* social(e); (*sociable*) sociable ▷ *n* (petite) fête
social climber *n* arriviste *m/f*
social club *n* amicale *f*, foyer *m*
Social Democrat *n* social-démocrate *m/f*
social insurance *n* (*US*) sécurité sociale
socialism ['səuʃəlɪzəm] *n* socialisme *m*

socialist ['səuʃəlɪst] *adj, n* socialiste (*m/f*)
socialite ['səuʃəlaɪt] *n* personnalité mondaine
socialize ['səuʃəlaɪz] *vi* voir *or* rencontrer des gens, se faire des amis; **to ~ with** (*meet often*) fréquenter; (*get to know*) lier connaissance *or* parler avec
social life *n* vie sociale; **how's your ~?** est-ce que tu sors beaucoup?
socially ['səuʃəlɪ] *adv* socialement, en société
social science *n* sciences humaines
social security *n* aide sociale
social services *npl* services sociaux
social welfare *n* sécurité sociale
social work *n* assistance sociale
social worker *n* assistant(e) sociale(e)
society [sə'saɪətɪ] *n* société *f*; (*club*) société, association *f*; (*also:* **high society**) (haute) société, grand monde ▷ *cpd* (*party*) mondain(e)
socio-economic ['səusɪəui:kə'nɔmɪk] *adj* socioéconomique
sociological [səusɪə'lɔdʒɪkl] *adj* sociologique
sociologist [səusɪ'ɔlədʒɪst] *n* sociologue *m/f*
sociology [səusɪ'ɔlədʒɪ] *n* sociologie *f*
sock [sɔk] *n* chaussette *f* ▷ *vt* (*inf: hit*) flanquer un coup à; **to pull one's ~s up** (*fig*) se secouer (les puces)
socket ['sɔkɪt] *n* cavité *f*; (*Elec: also:* **wall socket**) prise *f* de courant; (*: for light bulb*) douille *f*
sod [sɔd] *n* (*of earth*) motte *f*; (*Brit inf!*) con *m* (!), salaud *m* (!)
▶ **sod off** *vi*: ~ **off!** (*Brit inf!*) fous le camp!, va te faire foutre! (!)
soda ['səudə] *n* (*Chem*) soude *f*; (*also:* **soda water**) eau *f* de Seltz; (*US: also:* **soda pop**) soda *m*
sodden ['sɔdn] *adj* trempé(e), détrempé(e)
sodium ['səudɪəm] *n* sodium *m*
sodium chloride *n* chlorure *m* de sodium
sofa ['səufə] *n* sofa *m*, canapé *m*
sofa bed *n* canapé-lit *m*
Sofia ['səufɪə] *n* Sofia
soft [sɔft] *adj* (*not rough*) doux (douce); (*not hard*) doux, mou (molle); (*not loud*) doux, léger(-ère); (*kind*) doux, gentil(le); (*weak*) indulgent(e); (*stupid*) stupide, débile
soft-boiled ['sɔftbɔɪld] *adj* (*egg*) à la coque
soft drink *n* boisson non alcoolisée
soft drugs *npl* drogues douces
soften ['sɔfn] *vt* (r)amollir; (*fig*) adoucir ▷ *vi* se ramollir; (*fig*) s'adoucir
softener ['sɔfnə^r] *n* (*water softener*) adoucisseur *m*; (*fabric softener*) produit assouplissant
soft fruit *n* (*Brit*) baies *fpl*
soft furnishings *npl* tissus *mpl* d'ameublement
soft-hearted [sɔft'hɑːtɪd] *adj* au cœur tendre
softly ['sɔftlɪ] *adv* doucement; (*touch*) légèrement; (*kiss*) tendrement
softness ['sɔftnɪs] *n* douceur *f*
soft option *n* solution *f* de facilité
soft sell *n* promotion *f* de vente discrète
soft target *n* cible *f* facile
soft toy *n* jouet *m* en peluche
software ['sɔftwɛə^r] *n* (*Comput*) logiciel *m*,

software *m*

software package *n* (*Comput*) progiciel *m*

soggy ['sɒgɪ] *adj* (*clothes*) trempé(e); (*ground*) détrempé(e)

soil [sɔɪl] *n* (*earth*) sol *m*, terre *f* ▷ *vt* salir; (*fig*) souiller

soiled [sɔɪld] *adj* sale; (*Comm*) défraîchi(e)

sojourn ['sɒdʒəːn] *n* (*formal*) séjour *m*

solace ['sɒlɪs] *n* consolation *f*, réconfort *m*

solar ['səʊləʳ] *adj* solaire

solarium (*pl* **solaria**) [sə'lɛərɪəm, -rɪə] *n* solarium *m*

solar panel *n* panneau *m* solaire

solar plexus [-'plɛksəs] *n* (*Anat*) plexus *m* solaire

solar power *n* énergie *f* solaire

solar system *n* système *m* solaire

sold [səʊld] *pt, pp of* **sell**

solder ['səʊldəʳ] *vt* souder (*au fil à souder*) ▷ *n* soudure *f*

soldier ['səʊldʒəʳ] *n* soldat *m*, militaire *m* ▷ *vi*: **to ~ on** persévérer, s'accrocher; **toy ~** petit soldat

sold out *adj* (*Comm*) épuisé(e)

sole [səʊl] *n* (*of foot*) plante *f*; (*of shoe*) semelle *f*; (*fish: pl inv*) sole *f* ▷ *adj* seul(e), unique; **the ~ reason** la seule et unique raison

solely ['səʊllɪ] *adv* seulement, uniquement; **I will hold you ~ responsible** je vous en tiendrai pour seul responsable

solemn ['sɒləm] *adj* solennel(le); (*person*) sérieux(-euse), grave

sole trader *n* (*Comm*) chef *m* d'entreprise individuelle

solicit [sə'lɪsɪt] *vt* (*request*) solliciter ▷ *vi* (*prostitute*) racoler

solicitor [sə'lɪsɪtəʳ] *n* (*Brit: for wills etc*) ≈ notaire *m*; (: *in court*) ≈ avocat *m*

solid ['sɒlɪd] *adj* (*strong, sound, reliable: not liquid*) solide; (*not hollow: mass*) compact(e); (: *metal, rock, wood*) massif(-ive); (*meal*) consistant(e), substantiel(le); (*vote*) unanime ▷ *n* solide *m*; **to be on ~ ground** être sur la terre ferme; (*fig*) être en terrain sûr; **we waited two ~ hours** nous avons attendu deux heures entières

solidarity [sɒlɪ'dærɪtɪ] *n* solidarité *f*

solid fuel *n* combustible *m* solide

solidify [sə'lɪdɪfaɪ] *vi* se solidifier ▷ *vt* solidifier

solidity [sə'lɪdɪtɪ] *n* solidité *f*

solid-state ['sɒlɪdsteɪt] *adj* (*Elec*) à circuits intégrés

soliloquy [sə'lɪləkwɪ] *n* monologue *m*

solitaire [sɒlɪ'tɛəʳ] *n* (*gem, Brit: game*) solitaire *m*; (*US: card game*) réussite *f*

solitary ['sɒlɪtərɪ] *adj* solitaire

solitary confinement *n* (*Law*) isolement *m* (cellulaire)

solitude ['sɒlɪtjuːd] *n* solitude *f*

solo ['səʊləʊ] *n* solo *m* ▷ *adv* (*fly*) en solitaire

soloist ['səʊləʊɪst] *n* soliste *m/f*

Solomon Islands ['sɒləmən-] *npl*: **the ~** les (îles *fpl*) Salomon *fpl*

solstice ['sɒlstɪs] *n* solstice *m*

soluble ['sɒljʊbl] *adj* soluble

solution [sə'luːʃən] *n* solution *f*

solve [sɒlv] *vt* résoudre

solvency ['sɒlvənsɪ] *n* (*Comm*) solvabilité *f*

solvent ['sɒlvənt] *adj* (*Comm*) solvable ▷ *n* (*Chem*) (dis)solvant *m*

solvent abuse *n* usage *m* de solvants hallucinogènes

Somali [səʊ'mɑːlɪ] *adj* somali(e), somalien(ne) ▷ *n* Somali(e), Somalien(ne)

Somalia [səʊ'mɑːlɪə] *n* (République *f* de) Somalie *f*

Somaliland [səʊ'mɑːlɪlænd] *n* Somaliland *m*

sombre, (*US*) **somber** ['sɒmbəʳ] *adj* sombre, morne

 KEYWORD

some [sʌm] *adj* **1** (*a certain amount or number of*): **some tea/water/ice cream** du thé/de l'eau/de la glace; **some children/apples** des enfants/pommes; **I've got some money but not much** j'ai de l'argent mais pas beaucoup

2 (*certain: in contrasts*): **some people say that ...** il y a des gens qui disent que ...; **some films were excellent, but most were mediocre** certains films étaient excellents, mais la plupart étaient médiocres

3 (*unspecified*): **some woman was asking for you** il y avait une dame qui vous demandait; **he was asking for some book (or other)** il demandait un livre quelconque; **some day** un de ces jours; **some day next week** un jour la semaine prochaine; **after some time** après un certain temps; **at some length** assez longuement; **in some form or other** sous une forme ou une autre, sous une forme quelconque

▷ *pron* **1** (*a certain number*) quelques-un(e)s, certain(e)s; **I've got some** (*books etc*) j'en ai (quelques-uns); **some (of them) have been sold** certains ont été vendus

2 (*a certain amount*) un peu; **I've got some** (*money, milk*) j'en ai (un peu); **would you like some?** est-ce que vous en voulez?, en voulez-vous?; **could I have some of that cheese?** pourrais-je avoir un peu de ce fromage?; **I've read some of the book** j'ai lu une partie du livre

▷ *adv*: **some 10 people** quelque 10 personnes, 10 personnes environ

somebody ['sʌmbədɪ] *pron* = **someone**

someday ['sʌmdeɪ] *adv* un de ces jours, un jour ou l'autre

somehow ['sʌmhaʊ] *adv* d'une façon ou d'une autre; (*for some reason*) pour une raison ou une autre

someone ['sʌmwʌn] *pron* quelqu'un; **~ or other** quelqu'un, je ne sais qui

someplace ['sʌmpleɪs] *adv* (*US*) = **somewhere**

somersault ['sʌməsɔːlt] *n* culbute *f*, saut périlleux ▷ *vi* faire la culbute *or* un saut périlleux; (*car*) faire un tonneau

something ['sʌmθɪŋ] *pron* quelque chose *m*; ~ **interesting** quelque chose d'intéressant; ~ **to do** quelque chose à faire; **he's ~ like me** il est un peu comme moi; **it's ~ of a problem** il y a là un problème

sometime ['sʌmtaɪm] *adv* (*in future*) un de ces jours, un jour ou l'autre; (*in past*): ~ **last month** au cours du mois dernier

sometimes ['sʌmtaɪmz] *adv* quelquefois, parfois

somewhat ['sʌmwɔt] *adv* quelque peu, un peu

somewhere ['sʌmwɛər] *adv* quelque part; ~ **else** ailleurs, autre part

son [sʌn] *n* fils *m*

sonar ['səʊnɑːr] *n* sonar *m*

sonata [sə'nɑːtə] *n* sonate *f*

song [sɔŋ] *n* chanson *f*; (*of bird*) chant *m*

songbook ['sɔŋbʊk] *n* chansonnier *m*

songwriter ['sɔŋraɪtər] *n* auteur-compositeur *m*

sonic ['sɔnɪk] *adj* (*boom*) supersonique

son-in-law ['sʌnɪnlɔː] *n* gendre *m*, beau-fils *m*

sonnet ['sɔnɪt] *n* sonnet *m*

sonny ['sʌnɪ] *n* (*inf*) fiston *m*

soon [suːn] *adv* bientôt; (*early*) tôt; ~ **afterwards** peu après; **quite ~** sous peu; **how ~ can you do it?** combien de temps vous faut-il pour le faire, au plus pressé?; **how ~ can you come back?** quand *or* dans combien de temps pouvez-vous revenir, au plus tôt?; **see you ~!** à bientôt!; *see also* **as**

sooner ['suːnər] *adv* (*time*) plus tôt; (*preference*): **I would ~ do that** j'aimerais autant *or* je préférerais faire ça; ~ **or later** tôt ou tard; **no ~ said than done** sitôt dit, sitôt fait; **the ~ the better** le plus tôt sera le mieux; **no ~ had we left than ...** à peine étions-nous partis que ...

soot [sʊt] *n* suie *f*

soothe [suːð] *vt* calmer, apaiser

soothing ['suːðɪŋ] *adj* (*ointment etc*) lénitif(-ive), lénifiant(e); (*tone, words etc*) apaisant(e); (*drink, bath*) relaxant(e)

SOP *n abbr* = **standard operating procedure**

sop [sɔp] *n*: **that's only a ~** c'est pour nous (*or* les *etc*) amadouer

sophisticated [sə'fɪstɪkeɪtɪd] *adj* raffiné(e), sophistiqué(e); (*machinery*) hautement perfectionné(e), très complexe; (*system etc*) très perfectionné(e), sophistiqué

sophistication [səfɪstɪ'keɪʃən] *n* raffinement *m*, niveau *m* (de) perfectionnement *m*

sophomore ['sɔfəmɔːr] *n* (*US*) étudiant(e) de seconde année

soporific [sɔpə'rɪfɪk] *adj* soporifique ▷ *n* somnifère *m*

sopping ['sɔpɪŋ] *adj* (*also*: **sopping wet**) tout(e) trempé(e)

soppy ['sɔpɪ] *adj* (*pej*) sentimental(e)

soprano [sə'prɑːnəʊ] *n* (*voice*) soprano *m*; (*singer*) soprano *m/f*

sorbet ['sɔːbeɪ] *n* sorbet *m*

sorcerer ['sɔːsərər] *n* sorcier *m*

sordid ['sɔːdɪd] *adj* sordide

sore [sɔːr] *adj* (*painful*) douloureux(-euse), sensible; (*offended*) contrarié(e), vexé(e) ▷ *n* plaie *f*; **to have a ~ throat** avoir mal à la gorge; **it's a ~ point** (*fig*) c'est un point délicat

sorely ['sɔːlɪ] *adv* (*tempted*) fortement

sorrel ['sɔrəl] *n* oseille *f*

sorrow ['sɔrəʊ] *n* peine *f*, chagrin *m*

sorrowful ['sɔrəʊful] *adj* triste

sorry ['sɔrɪ] *adj* désolé(e); (*condition, excuse, tale*) triste, déplorable; (*sight*) désolant(e); **~!** pardon!, excusez-moi!; **~?** pardon?; **to feel ~ for sb** plaindre qn; **I'm ~ to hear that ...** je suis désolé(e) *or* navré(e) d'apprendre que ...; **to be ~ about sth** regretter qch

sort [sɔːt] *n* genre *m*, espèce *f*, sorte *f*; (*make: of coffee, car etc*) marque *f* ▷ *vt* (*also*: **sort out**: *select which to keep*) trier; (*classify*) classer; (*tidy*) ranger; (*letters etc*) trier; (*Comput*) trier; **what ~ do you want?** quelle sorte *or* quel genre voulez-vous?; **what ~ of car?** quelle marque de voiture?; **I'll do nothing of the ~!** je ne ferai rien de tel!; **it's ~ of awkward** (*inf*) c'est plutôt gênant
  ▶ **sort out** *vt* (*problem*) résoudre, régler

sortie ['sɔːtɪ] *n* sortie *f*

sorting office ['sɔːtɪŋ-] *n* (*Post*) bureau *m* de tri

SOS *n* SOS *m*

so-so ['səʊsəʊ] *adv* comme ci comme ça

soufflé ['suːfleɪ] *n* soufflé *m*

sought [sɔːt] *pt*, *pp* of **seek**

sought-after ['sɔːtɑːftər] *adj* recherché(e)

soul [səʊl] *n* âme *f*; **the poor ~ had nowhere to sleep** le pauvre n'avait nulle part où dormir; **I didn't see a ~** je n'ai vu (absolument) personne

soul-destroying ['səʊldɪstrɔɪɪŋ] *adj* démoralisant(e)

soulful ['səʊlful] *adj* plein(e) de sentiment

soulless ['səʊllɪs] *adj* sans cœur, inhumain(e)

soul mate *n* âme *f* sœur

soul-searching ['səʊlsəːtʃɪŋ] *n*: **after much ~, I decided ...** j'ai longuement réfléchi avant de décider ...

sound [saʊnd] *adj* (*healthy*) en bonne santé, sain(e); (*safe, not damaged*) solide, en bon état; (*reliable, not superficial*) sérieux(-euse), solide; (*sensible*) sensé(e) ▷ *adv*: ~ **asleep** profondément endormi(e) ▷ *n* (*noise, volume*) son *m*; (*louder*) bruit *m*; (*Geo*) détroit *m*, bras *m* de mer ▷ *vt* (*alarm*) sonner; (*also*: **sound out**: *opinions*) sonder ▷ *vi* sonner, retentir; (*fig: seem*) sembler (être); **to be of ~ mind** être sain(e) d'esprit; **I don't like the ~ of it** ça ne me dit rien qui vaille; **to ~ one's horn** (*Aut*) klaxonner, actionner son avertisseur; **to ~ like** ressembler à; **it ~s as if ...** il semblerait que ..., j'ai l'impression que ...
  ▶ **sound off** *vi* (*inf*): **to ~ off (about)** la ramener (sur)

sound barrier *n* mur *m* du son

sound bite *n* phrase toute faite (*pour être citée dans les médias*)

sound effects *npl* bruitage *m*

sound engineer *n* ingénieur *m* du son

sounding ['saʊndɪŋ] *n* (*Naut etc*) sondage *m*

sounding board n (Mus) table f d'harmonie; (fig): **to use sb as a ~ for one's ideas** essayer ses idées sur qn

soundly ['saundlɪ] adv (sleep) profondément; (beat) complètement, à plate couture

soundproof ['saundpru:f] vt insonoriser ▷ adj insonorisé(e)

sound system n sono(risation) f

soundtrack ['saundtræk] n (of film) bande f sonore

sound wave n (Physics) onde f sonore

soup [su:p] n soupe f, potage m; **in the ~** (fig) dans le pétrin

soup course n potage m

soup kitchen n soupe f populaire

soup plate n assiette creuse or à soupe

soupspoon ['su:pspu:n] n cuiller f à soupe

sour ['sauər] adj aigre, acide; (milk) tourné(e), aigre; (fig) acerbe, aigre; revêche; **to go** or **turn ~** (milk, wine) tourner; (fig: relationship, plans) mal tourner; **it's ~ grapes** c'est du dépit

source [sɔːs] n source f; **I have it from a reliable ~ that** je sais de source sûre que

south [sauθ] n sud m ▷ adj sud inv; (wind) du sud ▷ adv au sud, vers le sud; **(to the) ~ of** au sud de; **to travel ~** aller en direction du sud

South Africa n Afrique f du Sud

South African adj sud-africain(e) ▷ n Sud-Africain(e)

South America n Amérique f du Sud

South American adj sud-américain(e) ▷ n Sud-Américain(e)

southbound ['sauθbaund] adj en direction du sud; (carriageway) sud inv

south-east [sauθ'i:st] n sud-est m

South-East Asia n le Sud-Est asiatique

southerly ['sʌðəlɪ] adj du sud; au sud

southern ['sʌðən] adj (du) sud; méridional(e); **with a ~ aspect** orienté(e) or exposé(e) au sud; **the ~ hemisphere** l'hémisphère sud or austral

South Korea n Corée f du Sud

South of France n: **the ~** le Sud de la France, le Midi

South Pole n Pôle m Sud

South Sea Islands npl: **the ~** l'Océanie f

South Seas npl: **the ~** les mers fpl du Sud

South Vietnam n Viêt-Nam m du Sud

South Wales n sud m du Pays de Galles

southward ['sauθwəd], **southwards** ['sauθwədz] adv vers le sud

south-west [sauθ'wɛst] n sud-ouest m

souvenir [su:və'nɪər] n souvenir m (objet)

sovereign ['sɔvrɪn] adj, n souverain(e)

sovereignty ['sɔvrɪntɪ] n souveraineté f

soviet ['səuvɪət] adj soviétique

Soviet Union n: **the ~** l'Union f soviétique

sow[1] [səu] (pt **-ed**, pp **-n**) [səun] vt semer

sow[2] [sau] n truie f

soya ['sɔɪə], (US) **soy** [sɔɪ] n: **~ bean** graine f de soja; **~ sauce** sauce f au soja

sozzled ['sɔzld] adj (Brit inf) paf inv

spa [spa:] n (town) station thermale; (US: also:

health spa) établissement m de cure de rajeunissement

space [speɪs] n (gen) espace m; (room) place f; espace; (length of time) laps m de temps ▷ cpd spatial(e) ▷ vt (also: **space out**) espacer; **to clear a ~ for sth** faire de la place pour qch; **in a confined ~** dans un espace réduit or restreint; **in a short ~ of time** dans peu de temps; **(with)in the ~ of an hour** en l'espace d'une heure

space bar n (on typewriter) barre f d'espacement

spacecraft ['speɪskrɑːft] n engin or vaisseau spatial

spaceman ['speɪsmæn] (irreg) n astronaute m, cosmonaute m

spaceship ['speɪsʃɪp] n = **spacecraft**

space shuttle n navette spatiale

spacesuit ['speɪssuːt] n combinaison spatiale

spacewoman ['speɪswumən] (irreg) n astronaute f, cosmonaute f

spacing ['speɪsɪŋ] n espacement m; **single/double ~** (Typ etc) interligne m simple/double

spacious ['speɪʃəs] adj spacieux(-euse), grand(e)

spade [speɪd] n (tool) bêche f, pelle f; (child's) pelle; **spades** npl (Cards) pique m

spadework ['speɪdwəːk] n (fig) gros m du travail

spaghetti [spə'gɛtɪ] n spaghetti mpl

Spain [speɪn] n Espagne f

spam [spæm] n (Comput) spam m

span [spæn] n (of bird, plane) envergure f; (of arch) portée f; (in time) espace m de temps, durée f ▷ vt enjamber, franchir; (fig) couvrir, embrasser

Spaniard ['spænjəd] n Espagnol(e)

spaniel ['spænjəl] n épagneul m

Spanish ['spænɪʃ] adj espagnol(e), d'Espagne ▷ n (Ling) espagnol m; **the Spanish** npl les Espagnols; **~ omelette** omelette f à l'espagnole

spank [spæŋk] vt donner une fessée à

spanner ['spænər] n (Brit) clé f (de mécanicien)

spar [spa:r] n espar m ▷ vi (Boxing) s'entraîner

spare [spɛər] adj de réserve, de rechange; (surplus) de or en trop, de reste ▷ n (part) pièce f de rechange, pièce détachée ▷ vt (do without) se passer de; (afford to give) donner, accorder, passer; (not hurt) épargner; (not use) ménager; **to ~ (surplus)** en surplus, de trop; **there are 2 going ~** (Brit) il y en a 2 de disponible; **to ~ no expense** ne pas reculer devant la dépense; **can you ~ the time?** est-ce que vous avez le temps?; **there is no time to ~** il n'y a pas de temps à perdre; **I've a few minutes to ~** je dispose de quelques minutes

spare part n pièce f de rechange, pièce détachée

spare room n chambre f d'ami

spare time n moments mpl de loisir

spare tyre, (US) **spare tire** n (Aut) pneu m de rechange

spare wheel n (Aut) roue f de secours

sparing ['spɛərɪŋ] adj: **to be ~ with** ménager

sparingly ['spɛərɪŋlɪ] adv avec modération

spark [spa:k] n étincelle f; (fig) étincelle, lueur f

sparkle ['spa:kl] n scintillement m,

étincellement *m*, éclat *m* ▷ *vi* étinceler, scintiller; (*bubble*) pétiller

sparkler ['spɑːklə^r] *n* cierge *m* magique

sparkling ['spɑːklɪŋ] *adj* étincelant(e), scintillant(e); (*wine*) mousseux(-euse), pétillant(e); (*water*) pétillant(e), gazeux(-euse)

spark plug *n* bougie *f*

sparring partner ['spɑːrɪŋ-] *n* sparring-partner *m*; (*fig*) vieil(le) ennemi(e)

sparrow ['spærəu] *n* moineau *m*

sparse [spɑːs] *adj* clairsemé(e)

spartan ['spɑːtən] *adj* (*fig*) spartiate

spasm ['spæzəm] *n* (*Med*) spasme *m*; (*fig*) accès *m*

spasmodic [spæz'mɔdɪk] *adj* (*fig*) intermittent(e)

spastic ['spæstɪk] *n* handicapé(e) moteur

spat [spæt] *pt, pp of* **spit** ▷ *n* (*US*) prise *f* de bec

spate [speɪt] *n* (*fig*): ~ **of** avalanche *f or* torrent *m* de; **in** ~ (*river*) en crue

spatial ['speɪʃl] *adj* spatial(e)

spatter ['spætə^r] *n* éclaboussure(s) *f(pl)* ▷ *vt* éclabousser ▷ *vi* gicler

spatula ['spætjulə] *n* spatule *f*

spawn [spɔːn] *vt* pondre; (*pej*) engendrer ▷ *vi* frayer ▷ *n* frai *m*

SPCA *n abbr* (*US*: = *Society for the Prevention of Cruelty to Animals*) ≈ SPA *f*

SPCC *n abbr* (*US*) = **Society for the Prevention of Cruelty to Children**

speak (*pt* **spoke**, *pp* **spoken**) [spiːk, spəuk, 'spəukn] *vt* (*language*) parler; (*truth*) dire ▷ *vi* parler; (*make a speech*) prendre la parole; **to** ~ **to sb/of** *or* **about sth** parler à qn/de qch; **I don't** ~ **French** je ne parle pas français; **do you** ~ **English?** parlez-vous anglais?; **can I** ~ **to ...?** est-ce que je peux parler à ...?; **~ing!** (*on telephone*) c'est moi-même!; **to** ~ **one's mind** dire ce que l'on pense; **it ~s for itself** c'est évident; ~ **up!** parle plus fort!; **he has no money to** ~ **of** il n'a pas d'argent
▶ **speak for** *vt fus*: **to** ~ **for sb** parler pour qn; **that picture is already spoken for** (*in shop*) ce tableau est déjà réservé

speaker ['spiːkə^r] *n* (*in public*) orateur *m*; (*also:* **loudspeaker**) haut-parleur *m*; (*for stereo etc*) baffle *m*, enceinte *f*; (*Pol*): **the S~** (*Brit*) le président de la Chambre des communes *or* des représentants; (*US*) le président de la Chambre; **are you a Welsh ~?** parlez-vous gallois?

speaking ['spiːkɪŋ] *adj* parlant(e); **French-~ people** les francophones; **to be on ~ terms** se parler

spear [spɪə^r] *n* lance *f* ▷ *vt* transpercer

spearhead ['spɪəhɛd] *n* fer *m* de lance; (*Mil*) colonne *f* d'attaque ▷ *vt* (*attack etc*) mener

spearmint ['spɪəmɪnt] *n* (*Bot etc*) menthe verte

spec [spɛk] *n* (*Brit inf*): **on** ~ à tout hasard; **to buy on** ~ acheter avec l'espoir de faire une bonne affaire

special ['spɛʃl] *adj* spécial(e) ▷ *n* (*train*) train spécial; **take** ~ **care** soyez particulièrement prudents; **nothing** ~ rien de spécial; **today's** ~ (*at restaurant*) le plat du jour

special agent *n* agent secret

special correspondent *n* envoyé spécial

special delivery *n* (*Post*): **by** ~ en express

special effects *npl* (*Cine*) effets spéciaux

specialist ['spɛʃəlɪst] *n* spécialiste *m/f*; **heart** ~ cardiologue *m/f*

speciality [spɛʃɪ'ælɪtɪ] *n* (*Brit*) spécialité *f*

specialize ['spɛʃəlaɪz] *vi*: **to** ~ **(in)** se spécialiser (dans)

specially ['spɛʃlɪ] *adv* spécialement, particulièrement

special needs *npl* (*Brit*) difficultés *fpl* d'apprentissage scolaire

special offer *n* (*Comm*) réclame *f*

special school *n* (*Brit*) établissement *m* d'enseignement spécialisé

specialty ['spɛʃəltɪ] *n* (*US*) = **speciality**

species ['spiːʃiːz] *n* (*pl inv*) espèce *f*

specific [spə'sɪfɪk] *adj* (*not vague*) précis(e), explicite; (*particular*) particulier(-ière); (*Bot, Chem etc*) spécifique; **to be ~ to** être particulier à, être le *or* un caractère (*or* les caractères) spécifique(s) de

specifically [spə'sɪfɪklɪ] *adv* explicitement, précisément; (*intend, ask, design*) expressément, spécialement; (*exclusively*) exclusivement, spécifiquement

specification [spɛsɪfɪ'keɪʃən] *n* spécification *f*; stipulation *f*; **specifications** *npl* (*of car, building etc*) spécification

specify ['spɛsɪfaɪ] *vt* spécifier, préciser; **unless otherwise specified** sauf indication contraire

specimen ['spɛsɪmən] *n* spécimen *m*, échantillon *m*; (*Med: of blood*) prélèvement *m*; (: *of urine*) échantillon *m*

specimen copy *n* spécimen *m*

specimen signature *n* spécimen *m* de signature

speck [spɛk] *n* petite tache, petit point; (*particle*) grain *m*

speckled ['spɛkld] *adj* tacheté(e), moucheté(e)

specs [spɛks] *npl* (*inf*) lunettes *fpl*

spectacle ['spɛktəkl] *n* spectacle *m*; **spectacles** *npl* (*Brit*) lunettes *fpl*

spectacle case *n* (*Brit*) étui *m* à lunettes

spectacular [spɛk'tækjulə^r] *adj* spectaculaire ▷ *n* (*Cine etc*) superproduction *f*

spectator [spɛk'teɪtə^r] *n* spectateur(-trice)

spectator sport *n*: **football is a great** ~ le football est un sport qui passionne les foules

spectra ['spɛktrə] *npl of* **spectrum**

spectre, (*US*) **specter** ['spɛktə^r] *n* spectre *m*, fantôme *m*

spectrum (*pl* **spectra**) ['spɛktrəm, -rə] *n* spectre *m*; (*fig*) gamme *f*

speculate ['spɛkjuleɪt] *vi* spéculer; (*try to guess*): **to** ~ **about** s'interroger sur

speculation [spɛkju'leɪʃən] *n* spéculation *f*; conjectures *fpl*

speculative ['spɛkjulətɪv] *adj* spéculatif(-ive)

speculator ['spɛkjuleɪtə^r] *n* spéculateur(-trice)

sped [spɛd] *pt, pp of* **speed**

speech [spi:tʃ] *n* (*faculty*) parole *f*; (*talk*) discours *m*, allocution *f*; (*manner of speaking*) façon *f* de parler, langage *m*; (*language*) langage *m*; (*enunciation*) élocution *f*

speech day *n* (*Brit Scol*) distribution *f* des prix

speech impediment *n* défaut *m* d'élocution

speechless ['spi:tʃlɪs] *adj* muet(te)

speech therapy *n* orthophonie *f*

speed [spi:d] *n* vitesse *f*; (*promptness*) rapidité *f* ▷ *vi* (*pt, pp* **sped**) [spɛd] (*Aut: exceed speed limit*) faire un excès de vitesse; **to ~ along/by** *etc* aller/ passer *etc* à toute vitesse; **at ~** (*Brit*) rapidement; **at full** *or* **top ~** à toute vitesse *or* allure; **at a ~ of 70 km/h** à une vitesse de 70 km/h; **shorthand/ typing ~s** nombre *m* de mots à la minute en sténographie/dactylographie; **a five-~ gearbox** une boîte cinq vitesses

▶ **speed up** (*pt, pp* **-ed up**) *vi* aller plus vite, accélérer ▷ *vt* accélérer

speedboat ['spi:dbəut] *n* vedette *f*, hors-bord *m inv*

speedily ['spi:dɪlɪ] *adv* rapidement, promptement

speeding ['spi:dɪŋ] *n* (*Aut*) excès *m* de vitesse

speed limit *n* limitation *f* de vitesse, vitesse maximale permise

speedometer [spɪ'dɔmɪtə'] *n* compteur *m* (de vitesse)

speed trap *n* (*Aut*) piège *m* de police pour contrôle de vitesse

speedway *n* (*Sport*) piste *f* de vitesse pour motos; (*also:* **speedway racing**) épreuve(s) *f(pl)* de vitesse de motos

speedy ['spi:dɪ] *adj* rapide, prompt(e)

speleologist [spɛlɪ'ɔlədʒɪst] *n* spéléologue *m/f*

spell [spɛl] *n* (*also:* **magic spell**) sortilège *m*, charme *m*; (*period of time*) (courte) période ▷ *vt* (*pt, pp* **spelt** *or* **-ed**) [spɛlt, spɛld] (*in writing*) écrire, orthographier; (*aloud*) épeler; (*fig*) signifier; **to cast a ~ on sb** jeter un sort à qn; **he can't ~** il fait des fautes d'orthographe; **how do you ~ your name?** comment écrivez-vous votre nom?; **can you ~ it for me?** pouvez-vous me l'épeler?

▶ **spell out** *vt* (*explain*): **to ~ sth out for sb** expliquer qch clairement à qn

spellbound ['spɛlbaund] *adj* envoûté(e), subjugué(e)

spellchecker ['spɛltʃɛkə'] *n* (*Comput*) correcteur *m or* vérificateur *m* orthographique

spelling ['spɛlɪŋ] *n* orthographe *f*

spelt [spɛlt] *pt, pp of* **spell**

spend (*pt, pp* **spent**) [spɛnd, spɛnt] *vt* (*money*) dépenser; (*time, life*) passer; (*devote*) consacrer; **to ~ time/money/effort on sth** consacrer du temps/de l'argent/de l'énergie à qch

spending ['spɛndɪŋ] *n* dépenses *fpl*; **government ~** les dépenses publiques

spending money *n* argent *m* de poche

spending power *n* pouvoir *m* d'achat

spendthrift ['spɛndθrɪft] *n* dépensier(-ière)

spent [spɛnt] *pt, pp of* **spend** ▷ *adj* (*patience*) épuisé(e), à bout; (*cartridge, bullets*) vide; **~ matches** vieilles allumettes

sperm [spə:m] *n* spermatozoïde *m*; (*semen*) sperme *m*

sperm bank *n* banque *f* du sperme

sperm whale *n* cachalot *m*

spew [spju:] *vt* vomir

sphere [sfɪə'] *n* sphère *f*; (*fig*) sphère, domaine *m*

spherical ['sfɛrɪkl] *adj* sphérique

sphinx [sfɪŋks] *n* sphinx *m*

spice [spaɪs] *n* épice *f* ▷ *vt* épicer

spick-and-span ['spɪkən'spæn] *adj* impeccable

spicy ['spaɪsɪ] *adj* épicé(e), relevé(e); (*fig*) piquant(e)

spider ['spaɪdə'] *n* araignée *f*; **~'s web** toile *f* d'araignée

spiel [spi:l] *n* laïus *m inv*

spike [spaɪk] *n* pointe *f*; (*Elec*) pointe de tension; (*Bot*) épi *m*; **spikes** *npl* (*Sport*) chaussures *fpl* à pointes

spike heel *n* (*US*) talon *m* aiguille

spiky ['spaɪkɪ] *adj* (*bush, branch*) épineux(-euse); (*animal*) plein(e) de piquants

spill (*pt, pp* **spilt** *or* **-ed**) [spɪl, -t, -d] *vt* renverser; répandre ▷ *vi* se répandre; **to ~ the beans** (*inf*) vendre la mèche; (*: confess*) lâcher le morceau

▶ **spill out** *vi* sortir à flots, se répandre

▶ **spill over** *vi* déborder

spillage ['spɪlɪdʒ] *n* (*of oil*) déversement *m* (accidentel)

spilt [spɪlt] *pt, pp of* **spill**

spin [spɪn] (*pt, pp* **spun**) [spʌn] *n* (*revolution of wheel*) tour *m*; (*Aviat*) (chute *f* en) vrille *f*; (*trip in car*) petit tour, balade *f*; (*on ball*) effet *m* ▷ *vt* (*wool etc*) filer; (*wheel*) faire tourner; (*Brit: clothes*) essorer ▷ *vi* (*turn*) tourner, tournoyer; **to ~ a yarn** débiter une longue histoire; **to ~ a coin** (*Brit*) jouer à pile ou face

▶ **spin out** *vt* faire durer

spina bifida ['spaɪnə'bɪfɪdə] *n* spina-bifida *m inv*

spinach ['spɪnɪtʃ] *n* épinard *m*; (*as food*) épinards *mpl*

spinal ['spaɪnl] *adj* vertébral(e), spinal(e)

spinal column *n* colonne vertébrale

spinal cord *n* moelle épinière

spindly ['spɪndlɪ] *adj* grêle, filiforme

spin doctor *n* (*inf*) personne employée pour présenter un parti politique sous un jour favorable

spin-dry ['spɪn'draɪ] *vt* essorer

spin-dryer [spɪn'draɪə'] *n* (*Brit*) essoreuse *f*

spine [spaɪn] *n* colonne vertébrale; (*thorn*) épine *f*, piquant *m*

spine-chilling ['spaɪntʃɪlɪŋ] *adj* terrifiant(e)

spineless ['spaɪnlɪs] *adj* invertébré(e); (*fig*) mou (molle), sans caractère

spinner ['spɪnə'] *n* (*of thread*) fileur(-euse)

spinning ['spɪnɪŋ] *n* (*of thread*) filage *m*; (*by machine*) filature *f*

spinning top *n* toupie *f*

spinning wheel *n* rouet *m*

spin-off ['spɪnɔf] *n* sous-produit *m*; avantage

inattendu

spinster ['spɪnstər] n célibataire f; vieille fille

spiral ['spaɪərl] n spirale f ▷ adj en spirale ▷ vi (fig: prices etc) monter en flèche; **the inflationary** ~ la spirale inflationniste

spiral staircase n escalier m en colimaçon

spire ['spaɪər] n flèche f, aiguille f

spirit ['spɪrɪt] n (soul) esprit m, âme f; (ghost) esprit, revenant m; (mood) esprit, état m d'esprit; (courage) courage m, énergie f; **spirits** npl (drink) spiritueux mpl, alcool m; **in good ~s** de bonne humeur; **in low ~s** démoralisé(e); **community** ~ solidarité f; **public** ~ civisme m

spirit duplicator n duplicateur m à alcool

spirited ['spɪrɪtɪd] adj vif (vive), fougueux(-euse), plein(e) d'allant

spirit level n niveau m à bulle

spiritual ['spɪrɪtjuəl] adj spirituel(le); (religious) religieux(-euse) ▷ n (also: **Negro spiritual**) spiritual m

spiritualism ['spɪrɪtjuəlɪzəm] n spiritisme m

spit [spɪt] n (for roasting) broche f; (spittle) crachat m; (saliva) salive f ▷ vi (pt, pp **spat**) [spæt] cracher; (sound) crépiter; (rain) crachiner

spite [spaɪt] n rancune f, dépit m ▷ vt contrarier, vexer; **in** ~ **of** en dépit de, malgré

spiteful ['spaɪtful] adj malveillant(e), rancunier(-ière)

spitroast ['spɪt'rəust] vt faire rôtir à la broche

spitting ['spɪtɪŋ] n: **"~ prohibited"** "défense de cracher" ▷ adj: **to be the** ~ **image of sb** être le portrait tout craché de qn

spittle ['spɪtl] n salive f; bave f; crachat m

spiv [spɪv] n (Brit inf) chevalier m d'industrie, aigrefin m

splash [splæʃ] n (sound) plouf m; (of colour) tache f ▷ vt éclabousser ▷ vi (also: **splash about**) barboter, patauger
▶ **splash out** vi (Brit) faire une folie

splashdown ['splæʃdaun] n amerrissage m

splay [spleɪ] adj: **~footed** marchant les pieds en dehors

spleen [spli:n] n (Anat) rate f

splendid ['splɛndɪd] adj splendide, superbe, magnifique

splendour, (US) **splendor** ['splɛndər] n splendeur f, magnificence f

splice [splaɪs] vt épisser

splint [splɪnt] n attelle f, éclisse f

splinter ['splɪntər] n (wood) écharde f; (metal) éclat m ▷ vi (wood) se fendre; (glass) se briser

splinter group n groupe dissident

split [splɪt] (pt, pp **split**) n fente f, déchirure f; (fig: Pol) scission f ▷ vt fendre, déchirer; (party) diviser; (work, profits) partager, répartir ▷ vi (break) se fendre, se briser; (divide) se diviser; **let's** ~ **the difference** coupons la poire en deux; **to do the ~s** faire le grand écart
▶ **split up** vi (couple) se séparer, rompre; (meeting) se disperser

split-level ['splɪtlɛvl] adj (house) à deux or plusieurs niveaux

split peas npl pois cassés

split personality n double personnalité f

split second n fraction f de seconde

splitting ['splɪtɪŋ] adj: **a** ~ **headache** un mal de tête atroce

splutter ['splʌtər] vi bafouiller; postillonner

spoil (pt, pp **-ed** or **spoilt**) [spɔɪl, -d, -t] vt (damage) abîmer; (mar) gâcher; (child) gâter; (ballot paper) rendre nul ▷ vi: **to be ~ing for a fight** chercher la bagarre

spoils [spɔɪlz] npl butin m

spoilsport ['spɔɪlspɔ:t] n trouble-fête m/f inv, rabat-joie m inv

spoilt [spɔɪlt] pt, pp of **spoil** ▷ adj (child) gâté(e); (ballot paper) nul(le)

spoke [spəuk] pt of **speak** ▷ n rayon m

spoken ['spəukn] pp of **speak**

spokesman ['spəuksmən] (irreg) n porte-parole m inv

spokesperson ['spəukspə:sn] (irreg) n porte-parole m inv

spokeswoman ['spəukswumən] (irreg) n porte-parole m inv

sponge [spʌndʒ] n éponge f; (Culin: also: **sponge cake**) ≈ biscuit m de Savoie ▷ vt éponger ▷ vi: **to** ~ **off** or **on** vivre aux crochets de

sponge bag n (Brit) trousse f de toilette

sponge cake n ≈ biscuit m de Savoie

sponger ['spʌndʒər] n (pej) parasite m

spongy ['spʌndʒɪ] adj spongieux(-euse)

sponsor ['sponsər] n (Radio, TV, Sport) sponsor m; (for application) parrain m, marraine f; (Brit: for fund-raising event) donateur(-trice) ▷ vt (programme, competition etc) parrainer, patronner, sponsoriser; (Pol: bill) présenter; (new member) parrainer; (fund-raiser) faire un don à; **I ~ed him at 3p a mile** (in fund-raising race) je me suis engagé à lui donner 3p par mile

sponsorship ['sponsəʃɪp] n sponsoring m; patronage m, parrainage m; dons mpl

spontaneity [spontə'neɪɪtɪ] n spontanéité f

spontaneous [spon'teɪnɪəs] adj spontané(e)

spoof [spu:f] n (parody) parodie f; (trick) canular m

spooky ['spu:kɪ] adj (inf) qui donne la chair de poule

spool [spu:l] n bobine f

spoon [spu:n] n cuiller f

spoon-feed ['spu:nfi:d] vt nourrir à la cuiller; (fig) mâcher le travail à

spoonful ['spu:nful] n cuillerée f

sporadic [spə'rædɪk] adj sporadique

sport [spɔ:t] n sport m; (amusement) divertissement m; (person) chic type m/chic fille f ▷ vt (wear) arborer; **indoor/outdoor ~s** sports en salle/de plein air; **to say sth in** ~ dire qch pour rire

sporting ['spɔ:tɪŋ] adj sportif(-ive); **to give sb a** ~ **chance** donner sa chance à qn

sport jacket n (US) = **sports jacket**

sports car n voiture f de sport

sports centre (Brit) n centre sportif

sports ground n terrain m de sport
sports jacket n (Brit) veste f de sport
sportsman ['spɔːtsmən] (irreg) n sportif m
sportsmanship ['spɔːtsmənʃɪp] n esprit sportif, sportivité f
sports page n page f des sports
sports utility vehicle n véhicule m de loisirs (de type SUV)
sportswear ['spɔːtswɛə'] n vêtements mpl de sport
sportswoman ['spɔːtswumən] (irreg) n sportive f
sporty ['spɔːtɪ] adj sportif(-ive)
spot [spɔt] n tache f; (dot: on pattern) pois m; (pimple) bouton m; (place) endroit m, coin m; (also: **spot advertisement**) message m publicitaire; (small amount): **a ~ of** un peu de ⊳ vt (notice) apercevoir, repérer; **on the ~** sur place, sur les lieux; (immediately) sur le champ; **to put sb on the ~** (fig) mettre qn dans l'embarras; **to come out in ~s** se couvrir de boutons, avoir une éruption de boutons
spot check n contrôle intermittent
spotless ['spɔtlɪs] adj immaculé(e)
spotlight ['spɔtlaɪt] n projecteur m; (Aut) phare m auxiliaire
spot-on [spɔt'ɔn] adj (Brit inf) en plein dans le mille
spot price n prix m sur place
spotted ['spɔtɪd] adj tacheté(e), moucheté(e); à pois; **~ with** tacheté(e) de
spotty ['spɔtɪ] adj (face) boutonneux(-euse)
spouse [spauz] n époux (épouse)
spout [spaut] n (of jug) bec m; (of liquid) jet m ⊳ vi jaillir
sprain [spreɪn] n entorse f, foulure f ⊳ vt: **to ~ one's ankle** se fouler or se tordre la cheville
sprang [spræŋ] pt of **spring**
sprawl [sprɔːl] vi s'étaler ⊳ n: **urban ~** expansion urbaine; **to send sb ~ing** envoyer qn rouler par terre
spray [spreɪ] n jet m (en fines gouttelettes); (from sea) embruns mpl; (aerosol) vaporisateur m, bombe f; (for garden) pulvérisateur m; (of flowers) petit bouquet ⊳ vt vaporiser, pulvériser; (crops) traiter ⊳ cpd (deodorant etc) en bombe or atomiseur
spread [sprɛd] (pt, pp **spread**) n (distribution) répartition f; (Culin) pâte f à tartiner; (inf: meal) festin m; (Press, Typ: two pages) double page f ⊳ vt (paste, contents) étendre, étaler; (rumour, disease) répandre, propager; (repayments) échelonner, étaler; (wealth) répartir ⊳ vi s'étendre; se répandre; se propager; (stain) s'étaler; **middle-age ~** embonpoint m (pris avec l'âge)
▶ **spread out** vi (people) se disperser
spread-eagled ['sprɛdiːgld] adj: **to be** or **lie ~** être étendu(e) bras et jambes écartés
spreadsheet ['sprɛdʃiːt] n (Comput) tableur m
spree [spriː] n: **to go on a ~** faire la fête
sprig [sprɪg] n rameau m
sprightly ['spraɪtlɪ] adj alerte

spring [sprɪŋ] (pt **sprang**, pp **sprung** [spræŋ, sprʌŋ]) n (season) printemps m; (leap) bond m, saut m; (coiled metal) ressort m; (bounciness) élasticité f; (of water) source f ⊳ vi bondir, sauter ⊳ vt: **to ~ a leak** (pipe etc) se mettre à fuir; **he sprang the news on me** il m'a annoncé la nouvelle de but en blanc; **in ~, in the ~** au printemps; **to ~ from** provenir de; **to ~ into action** passer à l'action; **to walk with a ~ in one's step** marcher d'un pas souple
▶ **spring up** vi (problem) se présenter, surgir; (plant, buildings) surgir de terre
springboard ['sprɪŋbɔːd] n tremplin m
spring-clean [sprɪŋ'kliːn] n (also: **spring-cleaning**) grand nettoyage de printemps
spring onion n (Brit) ciboule f, cive f
spring roll n rouleau m de printemps
springtime ['sprɪŋtaɪm] n printemps m
springy ['sprɪŋɪ] adj élastique, souple
sprinkle ['sprɪŋkl] vt (pour) répandre; verser; **~ water etc on, ~ with water etc** asperger d'eau etc; **to ~ sugar etc on, ~ with sugar etc** saupoudrer de sucre etc; **~d with** (fig) parsemé(e) de
sprinkler ['sprɪŋklə'] n (for lawn etc) arroseur m; (to put out fire) diffuseur m d'extincteur automatique d'incendie
sprinkling ['sprɪŋklɪŋ] n (of water) quelques gouttes fpl; (of salt) pincée f; (of sugar) légère couche
sprint [sprɪnt] n sprint m ⊳ vi courir à toute vitesse; (Sport) sprinter
sprinter ['sprɪntə'] n sprinteur(-euse)
sprite [spraɪt] n lutin m
spritzer ['sprɪtsə'] n boisson à base de vin blanc et d'eau de Seltz
sprocket ['sprɔkɪt] n (on printer etc) picot m
sprout [spraut] vi germer, pousser
sprouts [sprauts] npl (also: **Brussels sprouts**) choux mpl de Bruxelles
spruce [spruːs] n épicéa m ⊳ adj net(te), pimpant(e)
▶ **spruce up** vt (smarten up: room etc) apprêter; **to ~ o.s. up** se faire beau (belle)
sprung [sprʌŋ] pp of **spring**
spry [spraɪ] adj alerte, vif (vive)
SPUC n abbr = **Society for the Protection of Unborn Children**
spud [spʌd] n (inf: potato) patate f
spun [spʌn] pt, pp of **spin**
spur [spəː'] n éperon m; (fig) aiguillon m ⊳ vt (also: **spur on**) éperonner; aiguillonner; **on the ~ of the moment** sous l'impulsion du moment
spurious ['spjuərɪəs] adj faux (fausse)
spurn [spəːn] vt repousser avec mépris
spurt [spəːt] n jet m; (of blood) jaillissement m; (of energy) regain m, sursaut m ⊳ vi jaillir, gicler; **to put in** or **on a ~** (runner) piquer un sprint; (fig: in work etc) donner un coup de collier
sputter ['spʌtə'] vi = **splutter**
spy [spaɪ] n espion(ne) ⊳ vi: **to ~ on** espionner, épier ⊳ vt (see) apercevoir ⊳ cpd (film, story)

d'espionnage

spying ['spaɪɪŋ] n espionnage m

Sq. abbr (in address) = **square**

sq. abbr (Math etc) = **square**

squabble ['skwɔbl] n querelle f, chamaillerie f
▷ vi se chamailler

squad [skwɔd] n (Mil, Police) escouade f, groupe
m; (Football) contingent m; **flying ~** (Police)
brigade volante

squad car n (Brit Police) voiture f de police

squaddie ['skwɔdɪ] n (Mil: inf) troufion m,
bidasse m

squadron ['skwɔdrn] n (Mil) escadron m; (Aviat,
Naut) escadrille f

squalid ['skwɔlɪd] adj sordide, ignoble

squall [skwɔ:l] n rafale f, bourrasque f

squalor ['skwɔləʳ] n conditions fpl sordides

squander ['skwɔndəʳ] vt gaspiller, dilapider

square [skwɛəʳ] n carré m; (in town) place f; (US:
block of houses) îlot m, pâté m de maisons;
(instrument) équerre f ▷ adj carré(e); (honest)
honnête, régulier(-ière); (inf: ideas, tastes) vieux
jeu inv, qui retarde ▷ vt (arrange) régler;
arranger; (Math) élever au carré; (reconcile)
concilier ▷ vi (agree) cadrer, s'accorder; **all ~**
quitte; à égalité; **a ~ meal** un repas convenable;
2 metres ~ (de) 2 mètres sur 2; **1 ~ metre** 1
mètre carré; **we're back to ~ one** (fig) on se
retrouve à la case départ
  ▸ **square up** vi (Brit: settle) régler; **to ~ up with
  sb** régler ses comptes avec qn

square bracket n (Typ) crochet m

squarely ['skwɛəlɪ] adv carrément; (honestly,
fairly) honnêtement, équitablement

square root n racine carrée

squash [skwɔʃ] n (Brit: drink): **lemon/orange ~**
citronnade f/orangeade f; (Sport) squash m; (US:
vegetable) courge f ▷ vt écraser

squat [skwɔt] adj petit(e) et épais(se),
ramassé(e) ▷ vi (also: **squat down**) s'accroupir;
(on property) squatter, squattériser

squatter ['skwɔtəʳ] n squatter m

squawk [skwɔ:k] vi pousser un or des
gloussement(s)

squeak [skwi:k] n (of hinge, wheel etc) grincement
m; (of shoes) craquement m; (of mouse etc) petit cri
aigu ▷ vi (hinge, wheel) grincer; (mouse) pousser
un petit cri

squeaky ['skwi:kɪ] adj grinçant(e); **to be ~
clean** (fig) être au-dessus de tout soupçon

squeal [skwi:l] vi pousser un or des cri(s) aigu(s)
or perçant(s); (brakes) grincer

squeamish ['skwi:mɪʃ] adj facilement
dégoûté(e); facilement scandalisé(e)

squeeze [skwi:z] n pression f; (also: **credit
squeeze**) encadrement m du crédit, restrictions
fpl de crédit ▷ vt presser; (hand, arm) serrer ▷ vi:
to ~ past/under sth se glisser avec (beaucoup
de) difficulté devant/sous qch; **a ~ of lemon**
quelques gouttes de citron
  ▸ **squeeze out** vt exprimer; (fig) soutirer

squelch [skwɛltʃ] vi faire un bruit de succion;

patauger

squib [skwɪb] n pétard m

squid [skwɪd] n calmar m

squiggle ['skwɪgl] n gribouillis m

squint [skwɪnt] vi loucher ▷ n: **he has a ~** il
louche, il souffre de strabisme; **to ~ at sth**
regarder qch du coin de l'œil; (quickly) jeter un
coup d'œil à qch

squire ['skwaɪəʳ] n (Brit) propriétaire terrien

squirm [skwə:m] vi se tortiller

squirrel ['skwɪrəl] n écureuil m

squirt [skwə:t] n jet m ▷ vi jaillir, gicler ▷ vt
faire gicler

Sr abbr = **senior**; = **sister**

SRC n abbr (Brit: = Students' Representative Council)
≈ CROUS m

Sri Lanka [srɪ'læŋkə] n Sri Lanka m

SRN n abbr (Brit) = **State Registered Nurse**

SRO abbr (US) = **standing room only**

SS abbr (= steamship) S/S

SSA n abbr (US: = Social Security Administration)
organisme de sécurité sociale

SST n abbr (US) = **supersonic transport**

ST abbr (US: = Standard Time) heure officielle

St abbr = **saint**; **street**

stab [stæb] n (with knife etc) coup m (de couteau
etc); (of pain) lancée f; (inf: try): **to have a ~ at
(doing) sth** s'essayer à (faire) qch ▷ vt
poignarder; **to ~ sb to death** tuer qn à coups de
couteau

stabbing ['stæbɪŋ] n: **there's been a ~**
quelqu'un a été attaqué à coups de couteau
▷ adj (pain, ache) lancinant(e)

stability [stə'bɪlɪtɪ] n stabilité f

stabilization [steɪbəlaɪ'zeɪʃən] n stabilisation f

stabilize ['steɪbəlaɪz] vt stabiliser ▷ vi se
stabiliser

stabilizer ['steɪbəlaɪzəʳ] n stabilisateur m

stable ['steɪbl] n écurie f ▷ adj stable; **riding ~s**
centre m d'équitation

staccato [stə'kɑːtəu] adv staccato ▷ adj (Mus)
piqué(e); (noise, voice) saccadé(e)

stack [stæk] n tas m, pile f ▷ vt empiler,
entasser; **there's ~s of time** (Brit inf) on a tout
le temps

stadium ['steɪdɪəm] n stade m

staff [stɑːf] n (work force) personnel m; (Brit Scol:
also: **teaching staff**) professeurs mpl,
enseignants mpl, personnel enseignant;
(servants) domestiques mpl; (Mil) état-major m;
(stick) perche f, bâton m ▷ vt pourvoir en
personnel

staffroom ['stɑːfruːm] n salle f des professeurs

Staffs abbr (Brit) = **Staffordshire**

stag [stæg] n cerf m; (Brit Stock Exchange) loup m

stage [steɪdʒ] n scène f; (platform) estrade f;
(point) étape f, stade m; (profession): **the ~** le
théâtre ▷ vt (play) monter, mettre en scène;
(demonstration) organiser; (fig: recovery etc)
effectuer; **in ~s** par étapes, par degrés; **to go
through a difficult ~** traverser une période
difficile; **in the early ~s** au début; **in the final**

~s à la fin

stagecoach ['steɪdʒkəʊtʃ] n diligence f

stage door n entrée f des artistes

stage fright n trac m

stagehand ['steɪdʒhænd] n machiniste m

stage-manage ['steɪdʒmænɪdʒ] vt (fig)
orchestrer

stage manager n régisseur m

stagger ['stægə˞] vi chanceler, tituber ▷ vt
(person: amaze) stupéfier; bouleverser; (hours,
holidays) étaler, échelonner

staggering ['stægərɪŋ] adj (amazing)
stupéfiant(e), renversant(e)

staging post ['steɪdʒɪŋ-] n relais m

stagnant ['stægnənt] adj stagnant(e)

stagnate [stæg'neɪt] vi stagner, croupir

stagnation [stæg'neɪʃən] n stagnation f

stag night, stag party n enterrement m de vie
de garçon

staid [steɪd] adj posé(e), rassis(e)

stain [steɪn] n tache f; (colouring) colorant m ▷ vt
tacher; (wood) teindre

stained glass [steɪnd-] n (decorative) verre coloré;
(in church) vitraux mpl; ~ **window** vitrail m

stainless ['steɪnlɪs] adj (steel) inoxydable

stainless steel n inox m, acier m inoxydable

stain remover n détachant m

stair [stɛə˞] n (step) marche f

staircase ['stɛəkeɪs] n = **stairway**

stairs [stɛəz] npl escalier m; **on the** ~ dans
l'escalier

stairway ['stɛəweɪ] n escalier m

stairwell ['stɛəwɛl] n cage f d'escalier

stake [steɪk] n pieu m, poteau m; (Comm: interest)
intérêts mpl; (Betting) enjeu m ▷ vt risquer,
jouer; (also: **stake out**: area) marquer, délimiter;
to be at ~ être en jeu; **to have a** ~ **in sth** avoir
des intérêts (en jeu) dans qch; **to** ~ **a claim (to
sth)** revendiquer (qch)

stakeout ['steɪkaʊt] n surveillance f; **to be on a**
~ effectuer une surveillance

stalactite ['stæləktaɪt] n stalactite f

stalagmite ['stæləgmaɪt] n stalagmite f

stale [steɪl] adj (bread) rassis(e); (food) pas frais
(fraîche); (beer) éventé(e); (smell) de renfermé;
(air) confiné(e)

stalemate ['steɪlmeɪt] n pat m; (fig) impasse f

stalk [stɔːk] n tige f ▷ vt traquer ▷ vi: **to** ~ **out/
off** sortir/partir d'un air digne

stall [stɔːl] n (Brit: in street, market etc) éventaire m,
étal m; (in stable) stalle f ▷ vt (Aut) caler; (fig:
delay) retarder ▷ vi (Aut) caler; (fig) essayer de
gagner du temps; **stalls** npl (Brit: in cinema,
theatre) orchestre m; **a newspaper/flower** ~ un
kiosque à journaux/de fleuriste

stallholder ['stɔːlhəʊldə˞] n (Brit) marchand(e)
en plein air

stallion ['stæljən] n étalon m (cheval)

stalwart ['stɔːlwət] n partisan m fidèle

stamen ['steɪmɛn] n étamine f

stamina ['stæmɪnə] n vigueur f, endurance f

stammer ['stæmə˞] n bégaiement m ▷ vi

bégayer

stamp [stæmp] n timbre m; (also: **rubber
stamp**) tampon m; (mark, also fig) empreinte f;
(on document) cachet m ▷ vi (also: **stamp one's
foot**) taper du pied ▷ vt (letter) timbrer; (with
rubber stamp) tamponner

 ▶ **stamp out** vt (fire) piétiner; (crime) éradiquer;
(opposition) éliminer

stamp album n album m de timbres(-poste)

stamp collecting [-kəlɛktɪŋ] n philatélie f

stamp duty n (Brit) droit m de timbre

stamped addressed envelope n (Brit)
enveloppe affranchie pour la réponse

stampede [stæm'piːd] n ruée f; (of cattle)
débandade f

stamp machine n distributeur m de timbres

stance [stæns] n position f

stand [stænd] (pt, pp **stood**) [stʊd] n (position)
position f; (for taxis) station f (de taxis); (Mil)
résistance f; (structure) guéridon m; support m;
(Comm) étalage m, stand m; (Sport: also: **stands**)
tribune f; (also: **music stand**) pupitre m ▷ vi être
or se tenir (debout); (rise) se lever, se mettre
debout; (be placed) se trouver; (remain: offer etc)
rester valable ▷ vt (place) mettre, poser; (tolerate,
withstand) supporter; (treat, invite) offrir, payer;
to make a ~ prendre position; **to take a** ~ **on
an issue** prendre position sur un problème; **to**
~ **for parliament** (Brit) se présenter aux
élections (comme candidat à la députation); **to** ~
guard or **watch** (Mil) monter la garde; **it** ~**s to
reason** c'est logique; cela va de soi; **as things** ~
dans l'état actuel des choses; **to** ~ **sb a drink/
meal** payer à boire/à manger à qn; **I can't** ~
him je ne peux pas le voir

 ▶ **stand aside** vi s'écarter

 ▶ **stand back** vi (move back) reculer, s'écarter

 ▶ **stand by** vi (be ready) se tenir prêt(e) ▷ vt fus
(opinion) s'en tenir à; (person) ne pas abandonner,
soutenir

 ▶ **stand down** vi (withdraw) se retirer; (Law)
renoncer à ses droits

 ▶ **stand for** vt fus (signify) représenter, signifier;
(tolerate) supporter, tolérer

 ▶ **stand in for** vt fus remplacer

 ▶ **stand out** vi (be prominent) ressortir

 ▶ **stand up** vi (rise) se lever, se mettre debout

 ▶ **stand up for** vt fus défendre

 ▶ **stand up to** vt fus tenir tête à, résister à

stand-alone ['stændələun] adj (Comput)
autonome

standard ['stændəd] n (norm) norme f, étalon m;
(level) niveau m (voulu); (criterion) critère m; (flag)
étendard m ▷ adj (size etc) ordinaire, normal(e);
(model, feature) standard inv; (practice) courant(e);
(text) de base; **standards** npl (morals) morale f,
principes mpl; **to be** or **come up to** ~ être du
niveau voulu or à la hauteur; **to apply a double**
~ avoir or appliquer deux poids deux mesures

standardization [stændədaɪ'zeɪʃən] n
standardisation f

standardize ['stændədaɪz] vt standardiser

standard lamp n (Brit) lampadaire m
standard of living n niveau m de vie
standard time n heure légale
stand-by ['stændbaɪ] n remplaçant(e) ▷ adj (provisions) de réserve; **to be on ~** se tenir prêt(e) (à intervenir); (doctor) être de garde
stand-by generator n générateur m de secours
stand-by passenger n passager(-ère) en stand-by or en attente
stand-by ticket n (Aviat) billet m stand-by
stand-in ['stændɪn] n remplaçant(e); (Cine) doublure f
standing ['stændɪŋ] adj debout inv; (permanent) permanent(e); (rule) immuable; (army) de métier; (grievance) constant(e), de longue date ▷ n réputation f, rang m, standing m; (duration): **of 6 months'** ~ qui dure depuis 6 mois; **of many years'** ~ qui dure or existe depuis longtemps; **he was given a ~ ovation** on s'est levé pour l'acclamer; **it's a ~ joke** c'est un vieux sujet de plaisanterie; **a man of some ~** un homme estimé
standing committee n commission permanente
standing order n (Brit: at bank) virement m automatique, prélèvement m bancaire; **standing orders** npl (Mil) règlement m
standing room n places fpl debout
stand-off ['stændɔf] n (esp US: stalemate) impasse f
stand-offish [stænd'ɔfɪʃ] adj distant(e), froid(e)
standpat ['stændpæt] adj (US) inflexible, rigide
standpipe ['stændpaɪp] n colonne f d'alimentation
standpoint ['stændpɔɪnt] n point m de vue
standstill ['stændstɪl] n: **at a ~** à l'arrêt; (fig) au point mort; **to come to a ~** s'immobiliser, s'arrêter
stank [stæŋk] pt of **stink**
stanza ['stænzə] n strophe f; couplet m
staple ['steɪpl] n (for papers) agrafe f; (chief product) produit m de base ▷ adj (food, crop, industry etc) de base principal(e) ▷ vt agrafer
stapler ['steɪplər] n agrafeuse f
star [stɑːʳ] n étoile f; (celebrity) vedette f ▷ vi: **to ~ (in)** être la vedette (de) ▷ vt (Cine) avoir pour vedette; **4-~ hotel** hôtel m 4 étoiles; **2-~ petrol** (Brit) essence f ordinaire; **4-~ petrol** (Brit) super m; **stars** npl: **the ~s** (Astrology) l'horoscope m
star attraction n grande attraction
starboard ['stɑːbəd] n tribord m; **to ~** à tribord
starch [stɑːtʃ] n amidon m; (in food) fécule f
starched ['stɑːtʃt] adj (collar) amidonné(e), empesé(e)
starchy ['stɑːtʃɪ] adj riche en féculents; (person) guindé(e)
stardom ['stɑːdəm] n célébrité f
stare [stɛəʳ] n regard m fixe ▷ vi: **to ~ at** regarder fixement
starfish ['stɑːfɪʃ] n étoile f de mer
stark [stɑːk] adj (bleak) désolé(e), morne; (simplicity, colour) austère; (reality, poverty) nu(e)
▷ adv: **~ naked** complètement nu(e)
starkers ['stɑːkəz] adj: **to be ~** (Brit inf) être à poil
starlet ['stɑːlɪt] n (Cine) starlette f
starlight ['stɑːlaɪt] n: **by ~** à la lumière des étoiles
starling ['stɑːlɪŋ] n étourneau m
starlit ['stɑːlɪt] adj étoilé(e); illuminé(e) par les étoiles
starry ['stɑːrɪ] adj étoilé(e)
starry-eyed [stɑːrɪ'aɪd] adj (innocent) ingénu(e)
Stars and Stripes npl: **the ~** la bannière étoilée
star sign n signe zodiacal or du zodiaque
star-studded ['stɑːstʌdɪd] adj: **a ~ cast** une distribution prestigieuse
start [stɑːt] n commencement m, début m; (of race) départ m; (sudden movement) sursaut m; (advantage) avance f, avantage m ▷ vt commencer; (cause: fight) déclencher; (rumour) donner naissance à; (fashion) lancer; (found: business, newspaper) lancer, créer; (engine) mettre en marche ▷ vi (begin) commencer; (begin journey) partir, se mettre en route; (jump) sursauter; **when does the film ~?** à quelle heure est-ce que le film commence?; **at the ~** au début; **for a ~** d'abord, pour commencer; **to make an early ~** partir or commencer de bonne heure; **to ~ doing** or **to do sth** se mettre à faire qch; **to ~ (off) with ...** (firstly) d'abord ...; (at the beginning) au commencement ...
▶ **start off** vi commencer; (leave) partir
▶ **start out** vi (begin) commencer; (set out) partir
▶ **start over** vi (US) recommencer
▶ **start up** vi commencer; (car) démarrer ▷ vt (fight) déclencher; (business) créer; (car) mettre en marche
starter ['stɑːtəʳ] n (Aut) démarreur m; (Sport: official) starter m; (: runner, horse) partant m; (Brit Culin) entrée f
starting handle ['stɑːtɪŋ-] n (Brit) manivelle f
starting point ['stɑːtɪŋ-] n point m de départ
starting price ['stɑːtɪŋ-] n prix initial
startle ['stɑːtl] vt faire sursauter; donner un choc à
startling ['stɑːtlɪŋ] adj surprenant(e), saisissant(e)
star turn n (Brit) vedette f
starvation [stɑː'veɪʃən] n faim f, famine f; **to die of ~** mourir de faim or d'inanition
starve [stɑːv] vi mourir de faim ▷ vt laisser mourir de faim; **I'm starving** je meurs de faim
stash [stæʃ] vt (inf): **to ~ sth away** planquer qch
state [steɪt] n état m; (Pol) État; (pomp): **in ~** en grande pompe ▷ vt (declare) déclarer, affirmer; (specify) indiquer, spécifier; **States** npl: **the S~s** les États-Unis; **to be in a ~** être dans tous ses états; **~ of emergency** état d'urgence; **~ of mind** état d'esprit; **the ~ of the art** l'état actuel de la technologie (or des connaissances)
state control n contrôle m de l'État
stated ['steɪtɪd] adj fixé(e), prescrit(e)
State Department n (US) Département m d'État, ≈ ministère m des Affaires étrangères

state education n (Brit) enseignement public

stateless ['steɪtlɪs] adj apatride

stately ['steɪtlɪ] adj majestueux(-euse), imposant(e)

stately home ['steɪtlɪ-] n manoir m or château m (ouvert au public)

statement ['steɪtmənt] n déclaration f; (Law) déposition f; (Econ) relevé m; **official ~** communiqué officiel; **~ of account, bank ~** relevé de compte

state-owned ['steɪtəund] adj étatisé(e)

States [steɪts] npl: **the ~** les États-Unis mpl

state school n école publique

statesman ['steɪtsmən] (irreg) n homme m d'État

statesmanship ['steɪtsmənʃɪp] n qualités fpl d'homme d'État

static ['stætɪk] n (Radio) parasites mpl; (also: **static electricity**) électricité f statique ▷ adj statique

station ['steɪʃən] n gare f; (also: **police station**) poste m or commissariat m (de police); (Mil) poste m (militaire); (rank) condition f, rang m ▷ vt placer, poster; **action ~s** postes de combat; **to be ~ed in** (Mil) être en garnison à

stationary ['steɪʃnərɪ] adj à l'arrêt, immobile

stationer ['steɪʃənər] n papetier(-ière)

stationer's, stationer's shop n (Brit) papeterie f

stationery ['steɪʃnərɪ] n papier m à lettres, petit matériel de bureau

station wagon n (US) break m

statistic [stə'tɪstɪk] n statistique f

statistical [stə'tɪstɪkl] adj statistique

statistics [stə'tɪstɪks] n (science) statistique f

statue ['stætjuː] n statue f

statuesque [stætju'ɛsk] adj sculptural(e)

statuette [stætju'ɛt] n statuette f

stature ['stætʃər] n stature f; (fig) envergure f

status ['steɪtəs] n position f, situation f; (prestige) prestige m; (Admin, official position) statut m

status quo [-'kwəu] n: **the ~** le statu quo

status symbol n marque f de standing, signe extérieur de richesse

statute ['stætjuːt] n loi f; **statutes** npl (of club etc) statuts mpl

statute book n ≈ code m, textes mpl de loi

statutory ['stætjutrɪ] adj statutaire, prévu(e) par un article de loi; **~ meeting** assemblée constitutive or statutaire

staunch [stɔːntʃ] adj sûr(e), loyal(e) ▷ vt étancher

stave [steɪv] n (Mus) portée f ▷ vt: **to ~ off** (attack) parer; (threat) conjurer

stay [steɪ] n (period of time) séjour m; (Law): **~ of execution** sursis m à statuer ▷ vi rester; (reside) loger; (spend some time) séjourner; **to ~ put** ne pas bouger; **to ~ with friends** loger chez des amis; **to ~ the night** passer la nuit

▶ **stay away** vi (from person, building) ne pas s'approcher; (from event) ne pas venir

▶ **stay behind** vi rester en arrière

▶ **stay in** vi (at home) rester à la maison

▶ **stay on** vi rester

▶ **stay out** vi (of house) ne pas rentrer; (strikers) rester en grève

▶ **stay up** vi (at night) ne pas se coucher

staying power ['steɪɪŋ-] n endurance f

STD n abbr (= sexually transmitted disease) MST f; (Brit: = subscriber trunk dialling) l'automatique m

stead [stɛd] n (Brit): **in sb's ~** à la place de qn; **to stand sb in good ~** être très utile or servir beaucoup à qn

steadfast ['stɛdfɑːst] adj ferme, résolu(e)

steadily ['stɛdɪlɪ] adv (regularly) progressivement; (firmly) fermement; (walk) d'un pas ferme; (fixedly: look) sans détourner les yeux

steady ['stɛdɪ] adj stable, solide, ferme; (regular) constant(e), régulier(-ière); (person) calme, pondéré(e) ▷ vt assurer, stabiliser; (nerves) calmer; (voice) assurer; **a ~ boyfriend** un petit ami; **to ~ oneself** reprendre son aplomb

steak [steɪk] n (meat) bifteck m, steak m; (fish, pork) tranche f

steakhouse ['steɪkhaus] n ≈ grill-room m

steal (pt **stole**, pp **stolen**) [stiːl, stəul, 'stəuln] vt, vi voler; (move) se faufiler, se déplacer furtivement; **my wallet has been stolen** on m'a volé mon portefeuille

▶ **steal away, steal off** vi s'esquiver

stealth [stɛlθ] n: **by ~** furtivement

stealthy ['stɛlθɪ] adj furtif(-ive)

steam [stiːm] n vapeur f ▷ vt passer à la vapeur; (Culin) cuire à la vapeur ▷ vi fumer; (ship): **to ~ along** filer; **under one's own ~** (fig) par ses propres moyens; **to run out of ~** (fig: person) caler; être à bout; **to let off ~** (fig: inf) se défouler

▶ **steam up** vi (window) se couvrir de buée; **to get ~ed up about sth** (fig: inf) s'exciter à propos de qch

steam engine n locomotive f à vapeur

steamer ['stiːmər] n (bateau m à) vapeur m; (Culin) ≈ couscoussier m

steam iron n fer m à repasser à vapeur

steamroller ['stiːmrəulər] n rouleau compresseur

steamship ['stiːmʃɪp] n = **steamer**

steamy ['stiːmɪ] adj humide; (window) embué(e); (sexy) torride

steed [stiːd] n (literary) coursier m

steel [stiːl] n acier m ▷ cpd d'acier

steel band n steel band m

steel industry n sidérurgie f

steel mill n aciérie f, usine f sidérurgique

steelworks ['stiːlwəːks] n aciérie f

steely ['stiːlɪ] adj (determination) inflexible; (eyes, gaze) d'acier

steep [stiːp] adj raide, escarpé(e); (price) très élevé(e), excessif(-ive) ▷ vt (faire) tremper

steeple ['stiːpl] n clocher m

steeplechase ['stiːpltʃeɪs] n steeple(-chase) m

steeplejack ['stiːpldʒæk] n réparateur m de

clochers et de hautes cheminées

steeply ['sti:plɪ] *adv* en pente raide

steer [stɪə^r] *n* bœuf *m* ▷ *vt* diriger; (*boat*) gouverner; (*lead: person*) guider, conduire ▷ *vi* tenir le gouvernail; **to ~ clear of sb/sth** (*fig*) éviter qn/qch

steering ['stɪərɪŋ] *n* (*Aut*) conduite *f*

steering column *n* (*Aut*) colonne *f* de direction

steering committee *n* comité *m* d'organisation

steering wheel *n* volant *m*

stellar ['stɛlə^r] *adj* stellaire

stem [stɛm] *n* (*of plant*) tige *f*; (*of leaf, fruit*) queue *f*; (*of glass*) pied *m* ▷ *vt* contenir, endiguer; (*attack, spread of disease*) juguler

▸ **stem from** *vt fus* provenir de, découler de

stem cell *n* cellule *f* souche

stench [stɛntʃ] *n* puanteur *f*

stencil ['stɛnsl] *n* stencil *m*; pochoir *m* ▷ *vt* polycopier

stenographer [stɛ'nɔɡrəfə^r] *n* (*US*) sténographe *m/f*

stenography [stɛ'nɔɡrəfɪ] *n* (*US*) sténo(graphie) *f*

step [stɛp] *n* pas *m*; (*stair*) marche *f*; (*action*) mesure *f*, disposition *f* ▷ *vi*: **to ~ forward/back** faire un pas en avant/arrière, avancer/reculer; **steps** *npl* (*Brit*) = **stepladder**; **~ by ~** pas à pas; (*fig*) petit à petit; **to be in/out of ~ (with)** (*fig*) aller dans le sens (de)/être déphasé(e) (par rapport à)

▸ **step down** *vi* (*fig*) se retirer, se désister

▸ **step in** *vi* (*fig*) intervenir

▸ **step off** *vt fus* descendre de

▸ **step over** *vt fus* enjamber

▸ **step up** *vt* (*production, sales*) augmenter; (*campaign, efforts*) intensifier

step aerobics® *npl* step® *m*

stepbrother ['stɛpbrʌðə^r] *n* demi-frère *m*

stepchild ['stɛptʃaɪld] (*pl* **-ren**) *n* beau-fils *m*, belle-fille *f*

stepdaughter ['stɛpdɔːtə^r] *n* belle-fille *f*

stepfather ['stɛpfɑːðə^r] *n* beau-père *m*

stepladder ['stɛplædə^r] *n* (*Brit*) escabeau *m*

stepmother ['stɛpmʌðə^r] *n* belle-mère *f*

stepping stone ['stɛpɪŋ-] *n* pierre *f* de gué; (*fig*) tremplin *m*

stepsister ['stɛpsɪstə^r] *n* demi-sœur *f*

stepson ['stɛpsʌn] *n* beau-fils *m*

stereo ['stɛrɪəu] *n* (*sound*) stéréo *f*; (*hi-fi*) chaîne *f* stéréo ▷ *adj* (*also*: **stereophonic**) stéréo(phonique); **in ~** en stéréo

stereotype ['stɪərɪətaɪp] *n* stéréotype *m* ▷ *vt* stéréotyper

sterile ['stɛraɪl] *adj* stérile

sterility [stɛ'rɪlɪtɪ] *n* stérilité *f*

sterilization [stɛrɪlaɪ'zeɪʃən] *n* stérilisation *f*

sterilize ['stɛrɪlaɪz] *vt* stériliser

sterling ['stəːlɪŋ] *adj* sterling *inv*; (*silver*) de bon aloi, fin(e); (*fig*) à toute épreuve, excellent(e) ▷ *n* (*currency*) livre *f* sterling *inv*; **a pound ~** une livre sterling

sterling area *n* zone *f* sterling *inv*

stern [stəːn] *adj* sévère ▷ *n* (*Naut*) arrière *m*, poupe *f*

sternum ['stəːnəm] *n* sternum *m*

steroid ['stɪərɔɪd] *n* stéroïde *m*

stethoscope ['stɛθəskəup] *n* stéthoscope *m*

stevedore ['stiːvədɔː^r] *n* docker *m*, débardeur *m*

stew [stjuː] *n* ragoût *m* ▷ *vt, vi* cuire à la casserole; **~ed tea** thé trop infusé; **~ed fruit** fruits cuits *or* en compote

steward ['stjuːəd] *n* (*Aviat, Naut, Rail*) steward *m*; (*in club etc*) intendant *m*; (*also*: **shop steward**) délégué syndical

stewardess ['stjuːədɛs] *n* hôtesse *f*

stewardship ['stjuːədʃɪp] *n* intendance *f*

stewing steak ['stjuːɪŋ-], (*US*) **stew meat** *n* bœuf *m* à braiser

St. Ex. *abbr* = **stock exchange**

stg *abbr* = **sterling**

stick [stɪk] (*pt, pp* **stuck**) [stʌk] *n* bâton *m*; (*for walking*) canne *f*; (*of chalk etc*) morceau *m* ▷ *vt* (*glue*) coller; (*thrust*): **to ~ sth into** piquer *or* planter *or* enfoncer qch dans; (*inf: put*) mettre, fourrer; (: *tolerate*) supporter ▷ *vi* (*adhere*) tenir, coller; (*remain*) rester; (*get jammed: door, lift*) se bloquer; **to get hold of the wrong end of the ~** (*Brit fig*) comprendre de travers; **to ~ to** (*one's promise*) s'en tenir à; (*principles*) rester fidèle à

▸ **stick around** *vi* (*inf*) rester (dans les parages)

▸ **stick out** *vi* dépasser, sortir ▷ *vt*: **to ~ it out** (*inf*) tenir le coup

▸ **stick up** *vi* dépasser, sortir

▸ **stick up for** *vt fus* défendre

sticker ['stɪkə^r] *n* auto-collant *m*

sticking plaster ['stɪkɪŋ-] *n* sparadrap *m*, pansement adhésif

sticking point ['stɪkɪŋ-] *n* (*fig*) point *m* de friction

stick insect *n* phasme *m*

stickleback ['stɪklbæk] *n* épinoche *f*

stickler ['stɪklə^r] *n*: **to be a ~ for** être pointilleux(-euse) sur

stick shift *n* (*US Aut*) levier *m* de vitesses

stick-up ['stɪkʌp] *n* (*inf*) braquage *m*, hold-up *m*

sticky ['stɪkɪ] *adj* poisseux(-euse); (*label*) adhésif(-ive); (*fig: situation*) délicat(e)

stiff [stɪf] *adj* (*gen*) raide, rigide; (*door, brush*) dur(e); (*difficult*) difficile, ardu(e); (*cold*) froid(e), distant(e); (*strong, high*) fort(e), élevé(e) ▷ *adv*: **to be bored/scared/frozen ~** s'ennuyer à mourir/être mort(e) de peur/froid; **to be** *or* **feel ~** (*person*) avoir des courbatures; **to have a ~ back** avoir mal au dos; **~ upper lip** (*Brit: fig*) flegme *m* (typiquement britannique)

stiffen ['stɪfn] *vt* raidir, renforcer ▷ *vi* se raidir; se durcir

stiff neck *n* torticolis *m*

stiffness ['stɪfnɪs] *n* raideur *f*

stifle ['staɪfl] *vt* étouffer, réprimer

stifling ['staɪflɪŋ] *adj* (*heat*) suffocant(e)

stigma ['stɪɡmə] *n* (*Bot, Med, Rel*) (*pl* **-ta**) ['stɪɡˈmɑː] (*fig*), **stigmas** *n* stigmate *m*

stile [staɪl] *n* échalier *m*

stiletto [stɪ'lɛtəu] n (Brit: also: **stiletto heel**) talon m aiguille

still [stɪl] adj (motionless) immobile; (calm) calme, tranquille; (Brit: mineral water etc) non gazeux(-euse) ▷ adv (up to this time) encore, toujours; (even) encore; (nonetheless) quand même, tout de même ▷ n (Cine) photo f; **to stand ~** rester immobile, ne pas bouger; **keep ~!** ne bouge pas!; **he ~ hasn't arrived** il n'est pas encore arrivé, il n'est toujours pas arrivé

stillborn ['stɪlbɔːn] adj mort-né(e)

still life n nature morte

stilt [stɪlt] n échasse f; (pile) pilotis m

stilted ['stɪltɪd] adj guindé(e), emprunté(e)

stimulant ['stɪmjulənt] n stimulant m

stimulate ['stɪmjuleɪt] vt stimuler

stimulating ['stɪmjuleɪtɪŋ] adj stimulant(e)

stimulation [stɪmju'leɪʃən] n stimulation f

stimulus (pl **stimuli**) ['stɪmjuləs, 'stɪmjulaɪ] n stimulant m; (Biol, Psych) stimulus m

sting [stɪŋ] n piqûre f; (organ) dard m; (inf: confidence trick) arnaque m ▷ vt, vi (pt, pp **stung**) [stʌŋ] piquer; **my eyes are ~ing** j'ai les yeux qui piquent

stingy ['stɪndʒɪ] adj avare, pingre, chiche

stink [stɪŋk] n puanteur f ▷ vi (pt **stank**, pp **stunk**) [stæŋk, stʌŋk] puer, empester

stinker ['stɪŋkər] n (inf: problem, exam) vacherie f; (person) dégueulasse m/f

stinking ['stɪŋkɪŋ] adj (fig: inf) infect(e); **~ rich** bourré(e) de pognon

stint [stɪnt] n part f de travail ▷ vi: **to ~ on** lésiner sur, être chiche de

stipend ['staɪpɛnd] n (of vicar etc) traitement m

stipendiary [staɪ'pɛndɪərɪ] adj: **~ magistrate** juge m de tribunal d'instance

stipulate ['stɪpjuleɪt] vt stipuler

stipulation [stɪpju'leɪʃən] n stipulation f, condition f

stir [stəːr] n agitation f, sensation f ▷ vt remuer ▷ vi remuer, bouger; **to give sth a ~** remuer qch; **to cause a ~** faire sensation
  ▶ **stir up** vt exciter; (trouble) fomenter, provoquer

stir-fry ['stəː'fraɪ] vt faire sauter ▷ n: **vegetable ~** légumes sautés à la poêle

stirring ['stəːrɪŋ] adj excitant(e); émouvant(e)

stirrup ['stɪrəp] n étrier m

stitch [stɪtʃ] n (Sewing) point m; (Knitting) maille f; (Med) point de suture; (pain) point de côté ▷ vt coudre, piquer; (Med) suturer

stoat [stəut] n hermine f (avec son pelage d'été)

stock [stɒk] n réserve f, provision f; (Comm) stock m; (Agr) cheptel m, bétail m; (Culin) bouillon m; (Finance) valeurs fpl, titres mpl; (Rail: also: **rolling stock**) matériel roulant; (descent, origin) souche f ▷ adj (fig: reply etc) courant(e); classique ▷ vt (have in stock) avoir, vendre; **well-~ed** bien approvisionné(e) or fourni(e); **in ~** en stock, en magasin; **out of ~** épuisé(e); **to take ~** (fig) faire le point; **~s and shares** valeurs (mobilières), titres; **government ~** fonds publics

  ▶ **stock up** vi: **to ~ up (with)** s'approvisionner (en)

stockade [stɒ'keɪd] n palissade f

stockbroker ['stɒkbrəukər] n agent m de change

stock control n (Comm) gestion f des stocks

stock cube n (Brit Culin) bouillon-cube m

stock exchange n Bourse f (des valeurs)

stockholder ['stɒkhəuldər] n (US) actionnaire m/f

Stockholm ['stɒkhəum] n Stockholm

stocking ['stɒkɪŋ] n bas m

stock-in-trade ['stɒkɪn'treɪd] n (fig): **it's his ~** c'est sa spécialité

stockist ['stɒkɪst] n (Brit) stockiste m

stock market n Bourse f, marché financier

stock phrase n cliché m

stockpile ['stɒkpaɪl] n stock m, réserve f ▷ vt stocker, accumuler

stockroom ['stɒkruːm] n réserve f, magasin m

stocktaking ['stɒkteɪkɪŋ] n (Brit Comm) inventaire m

stocky ['stɒkɪ] adj trapu(e), râblé(e)

stodgy ['stɒdʒɪ] adj bourratif(-ive), lourd(e)

stoic ['stəuɪk] n stoïque m/f

stoical ['stəuɪkl] adj stoïque

stoke [stəuk] vt garnir, entretenir; chauffer

stoker ['stəukər] n (Rail, Naut etc) chauffeur m

stole [stəul] pt of **steal** ▷ n étole f

stolen ['stəuln] pp of **steal**

stolid ['stɒlɪd] adj impassible, flegmatique

stomach ['stʌmək] n estomac m; (abdomen) ventre m ▷ vt supporter, digérer

stomachache ['stʌməkeɪk] n mal m à l'estomac or au ventre

stomach pump n pompe stomacale

stomach ulcer n ulcère m à l'estomac

stomp [stɒmp] vi: **to ~ in/out** entrer/sortir d'un pas bruyant

stone [stəun] n pierre f; (pebble) caillou m, galet m; (in fruit) noyau m; (Med) calcul m; (Brit: weight) = 6.348 kg; 14 pounds ▷ cpd de or en pierre ▷ vt (person) lancer des pierres sur, lapider; (fruit) dénoyauter; **within a ~'s throw of the station** à deux pas de la gare

Stone Age n: **the ~** l'âge m de pierre

stone-cold ['stəun'kəuld] adj complètement froid(e)

stoned [stəund] adj (inf: drunk) bourré(e); (: on drugs) défoncé(e)

stone-deaf ['stəun'dɛf] adj sourd(e) comme un pot

stonemason ['stəunmeɪsn] n tailleur m de pierre(s)

stonewall [stəun'wɔːl] vi faire de l'obstruction ▷ vt faire obstruction à

stonework ['stəunwəːk] n maçonnerie f

stony ['stəunɪ] adj pierreux(-euse), rocailleux(-euse)

stood [stud] pt, pp of **stand**

stooge [stuːdʒ] n (inf) larbin m

stool [stuːl] n tabouret m

stoop [stuːp] vi (also: **have a stoop**) être voûté(e);

(*also*: **stoop down**: *bend*) se baisser, se courber; (*fig*): **to ~ to sth/doing sth** s'abaisser jusqu'à qch/jusqu'à faire qch

stop [stɔp] *n* arrêt *m*; (*short stay*) halte *f*; (*in punctuation*) point *m* ▷ *vt* arrêter; (*break off*) interrompre; (*also*: **put a stop to**) mettre fin à; (*prevent*) empêcher ▷ *vi* s'arrêter; (*rain, noise etc*) cesser, s'arrêter; **could you ~ here/at the corner?** arrêtez-vous ici/au coin, s'il vous plaît; **to ~ doing sth** cesser *or* arrêter de faire qch; **to ~ sb (from) doing sth** empêcher qn de faire qch; **to ~ dead** *vi* s'arrêter net; **~ it!** arrête!
▶ **stop by** *vi* s'arrêter (au passage)
▶ **stop off** *vi* faire une courte halte
▶ **stop up** *vt* (*hole*) boucher

stopcock ['stɔpkɔk] *n* robinet *m* d'arrêt

stopgap ['stɔpgæp] *n* (*person*) bouche-trou *m*; (*also*: **stopgap measure**) mesure *f* intérimaire

stoplights ['stɔplaɪts] *npl* (*Aut*) signaux *mpl* de stop, feux *mpl* arrière

stopover ['stɔpəuvəʳ] *n* halte *f*; (*Aviat*) escale *f*

stoppage ['stɔpɪdʒ] *n* arrêt *m*; (*of pay*) retenue *f*; (*strike*) arrêt *m* de travail; (*obstruction*) obstruction *f*

stopper ['stɔpəʳ] *n* bouchon *m*

stop press *n* nouvelles *fpl* de dernière heure

stopwatch ['stɔpwɔtʃ] *n* chronomètre *m*

storage ['stɔ:rɪdʒ] *n* emmagasinage *m*; (*of nuclear waste etc*) stockage *m*; (*in house*) rangement *m*; (*Comput*) mise *f* en mémoire *or* réserve

storage heater *n* (*Brit*) radiateur *m* électrique par accumulation

store [stɔ:ʳ] *n* (*stock*) provision *f*, réserve *f*; (*depot*) entrepôt *m*; (*Brit: large shop*) grand magasin; (*US: shop*) magasin *m* ▷ *vt* emmagasiner; (*nuclear waste etc*) stocker; (*information*) enregistrer; (*in filing system*) classer, ranger; (*Comput*) mettre en mémoire; **stores** *npl* (*food*) provisions; **who knows what is in ~ for us?** qui sait ce que l'avenir nous réserve *or* ce qui nous attend?; **to set great/little ~ by sth** faire grand cas/peu de cas de qch
▶ **store up** *vt* mettre en réserve, emmagasiner

storehouse ['stɔ:haus] *n* entrepôt *m*

storekeeper ['stɔ:ki:pəʳ] *n* (*US*) commerçant(e)

storeroom ['stɔ:ru:m] *n* réserve *f*, magasin *m*

storey, (*US*) **story** ['stɔ:rɪ] *n* étage *m*

stork [stɔ:k] *n* cigogne *f*

storm [stɔ:m] *n* tempête *f*; (*thunderstorm*) orage *m* ▷ *vi* (*fig*) fulminer ▷ *vt* prendre d'assaut

storm cloud *n* nuage *m* d'orage

storm door *n* double-porte (extérieure)

stormy ['stɔ:mɪ] *adj* orageux(-euse)

story ['stɔ:rɪ] *n* histoire *f*; récit *m*; (*Press: article*) article *m*; (*: subject*) affaire *f*; (*US*) = **storey**

storybook ['stɔ:rɪbuk] *n* livre *m* d'histoires *or* de contes

storyteller ['stɔ:rɪtɛləʳ] *n* conteur(-euse)

stout [staut] *adj* (*strong*) solide; (*brave*) intrépide; (*fat*) gros(se), corpulent(e) ▷ *n* bière brune

stove [stəuv] *n* (*for cooking*) fourneau *m*; (*: small*)

réchaud *m*; (*for heating*) poêle *m*; **gas/electric ~** (*cooker*) cuisinière *f* à gaz/électrique

stow [stəu] *vt* ranger; cacher

stowaway ['stəuəweɪ] *n* passager(-ère) clandestin(e)

straddle ['strædl] *vt* enjamber, être à cheval sur

strafe [strɑ:f] *vt* mitrailler

straggle ['strægl] *vi* être (*or* marcher) en désordre; **~d along the coast** disséminé(e) tout au long de la côte

straggler [strægləʳ] *n* traînard(e)

straggling ['stræglɪŋ], **straggly** ['stræglɪ] *adj* (*hair*) en désordre

straight [streɪt] *adj* droit(e); (*hair*) raide; (*frank*) honnête, franc (franche); (*simple*) simple; (*Theat: part, play*) sérieux(-euse); (*inf: heterosexual*) hétéro *inv* ▷ *adv* (tout) droit; (*drink*) sec, sans eau ▷ *n*: **the ~** (*Sport*) la ligne droite; **to put** *or* **get ~** mettre en ordre, mettre de l'ordre dans; (*fig*) mettre au clair; **let's get this ~** mettons les choses au point; **10 ~ wins** 10 victoires d'affilée; **to go ~ home** rentrer directement à la maison; **~ away, ~ off** (*at once*) tout de suite; **~ off, ~ out** sans hésiter

straighten ['streɪtn] *vt* ajuster; (*bed*) arranger
▶ **straighten out** *vt* (*fig*) débrouiller; **to ~ things out** arranger les choses
▶ **straighten up** *vi* (*stand up*) se redresser; (*tidy*) ranger

straight-faced [streɪt'feɪst] *adj* impassible ▷ *adv* en gardant son sérieux

straightforward [streɪt'fɔ:wəd] *adj* simple; (*frank*) honnête, direct(e)

strain [streɪn] *n* (*Tech*) tension *f*; pression *f*; (*physical*) effort *m*; (*mental*) tension (nerveuse); (*Med*) entorse *f*; (*streak, trace*) tendance *f*; élément *m*; (*breed: of plants*) variété *f*; (*: of animals*) race *f*; (*of virus*) souche *f* ▷ *vt* (*stretch*) tendre fortement; (*fig: resources etc*) mettre à rude épreuve, grever; (*hurt: back etc*) se faire mal à; (*filter*) passer, filtrer; (*vegetables*) égoutter ▷ *vi* peiner, fournir un gros effort; **strains** *npl* (*Mus*) accords *mpl*, accents *mpl*; **he's been under a lot of ~** il a traversé des moments difficiles, il est très éprouvé nerveusement

strained [streɪnd] *adj* (*muscle*) froissé(e); (*laugh etc*) forcé(e), contraint(e); (*relations*) tendu(e)

strainer ['streɪnəʳ] *n* passoire *f*

strait [streɪt] *n* (*Geo*) détroit *m*; **straits** *npl*: **to be in dire ~s** (*fig*) avoir de sérieux ennuis

straitjacket ['streɪtdʒækɪt] *n* camisole *f* de force

strait-laced [streɪt'leɪst] *adj* collet monté *inv*

strand [strænd] *n* (*of thread*) fil *m*, brin *m*; (*of rope*) toron *m*; (*of hair*) mèche *f* ▷ *vt* (*boat*) échouer

stranded ['strændɪd] *adj* en rade, en plan

strange [streɪndʒ] *adj* (*not known*) inconnu(e); (*odd*) étrange, bizarre

strangely ['streɪndʒlɪ] *adv* étrangement, bizarrement; *see also* **enough**

stranger ['streɪndʒəʳ] *n* (*unknown*) inconnu(e); (*from somewhere else*) étranger(-ère); **I'm a ~ here** je ne suis pas d'ici

strangle ['stræŋgl] *vt* étrangler

stranglehold ['stræŋglhəuld] *n* (*fig*) emprise totale, mainmise *f*

strangulation [stræŋgju'leɪʃən] *n* strangulation *f*

strap [stræp] *n* lanière *f*, courroie *f*, sangle *f*; (*of slip, dress*) bretelle *f* ▷ *vt* attacher (avec une courroie *etc*)

straphanging ['stræphæŋɪŋ] *n* (fait *m* de) voyager debout (dans le métro *etc*)

strapless ['stræplɪs] *adj* (*bra, dress*) sans bretelles

strapped [stræpt] *adj*: **to be ~ for cash** (*inf*) être à court d'argent

strapping ['stræpɪŋ] *adj* bien découplé(e), costaud(e)

strappy [stræpɪ] *adj* (*dress*) à bretelles; (*sandals*) à lanières

Strasbourg ['stræzbɜːg] *n* Strasbourg

strata ['strɑːtə] *npl of* **stratum**

stratagem ['strætɪdʒəm] *n* stratagème *m*

strategic [strə'tiːdʒɪk] *adj* stratégique

strategist ['strætɪdʒɪst] *n* stratège *m*

strategy ['strætɪdʒɪ] *n* stratégie *f*

stratosphere ['strætəsfɪər] *n* stratosphère *f*

stratum (*pl* **strata**) ['strɑːtəm, 'strɑːtə] *n* strate *f*, couche *f*

straw [strɔː] *n* paille *f*; **that's the last ~!** ça c'est le comble!

strawberry ['strɔːbərɪ] *n* fraise *f*; (*plant*) fraisier *m*

stray [streɪ] *adj* (*animal*) perdu(e), errant(e); (*scattered*) isolé(e) ▷ *vi* s'égarer; **~ bullet** balle perdue

streak [striːk] *n* bande *f*, filet *m*; (*in hair*) raie *f*; (*fig: of madness etc*): **a ~ of** une *or* des tendance(s) à ▷ *vt* zébrer, strier ▷ *vi*: **to ~ past** passer à toute allure; **to have ~s in one's hair** s'être fait faire des mèches; **a winning/losing ~** une bonne/mauvaise série *or* période

streaker ['striːkər] *n* streaker(-euse)

streaky ['striːkɪ] *adj* zébré(e), strié(e)

streaky bacon *n* (*Brit*) ≈ lard *m* (maigre)

stream [striːm] *n* (*brook*) ruisseau *m*; (*current*) courant *m*, flot *m*; (*of people*) défilé ininterrompu, flot ▷ *vt* (*Scol*) répartir par niveau ▷ *vi* ruisseler; **to ~ in/out** entrer/sortir à flots; **against the ~** à contre courant; **on ~** (*new power plant etc*) en service

streamer ['striːmər] *n* serpentin *m*, banderole *f*

stream feed *n* (*on photocopier etc*) alimentation *f* en continu

streamline ['striːmlaɪn] *vt* donner un profil aérodynamique à; (*fig*) rationaliser

streamlined ['striːmlaɪnd] *adj* (*Aviat*) fuselé(e), profilé(e); (*Aut*) aérodynamique; (*fig*) rationalisé(e)

street [striːt] *n* rue *f*; **the back ~s** les quartiers pauvres; **to be on the ~s** (*homeless*) être à la rue *or* sans abri

streetcar ['striːtkɑːr] *n* (*US*) tramway *m*

street cred [-krɛd] *n* (*inf*): **to have ~** être branché(e)

street lamp *n* réverbère *m*

street light *n* réverbère *m*

street lighting *n* éclairage public

street map, street plan *n* plan *m* des rues

street market *n* marché *m* à ciel ouvert

streetwise ['striːtwaɪz] *adj* (*inf*) futé(e), réaliste

strength [strɛŋθ] *n* force *f*; (*of girder, knot etc*) solidité *f*; (*of chemical solution*) titre *m*; (*of wine*) degré *m* d'alcool; **on the ~ of** en vertu de; **at full ~** au grand complet; **below ~** à effectifs réduits

strengthen ['strɛŋθn] *vt* renforcer; (*muscle*) fortifier; (*building, Econ*) consolider

strenuous ['strɛnjuəs] *adj* vigoureux(-euse), énergique; (*tiring*) ardu(e), fatigant(e)

stress [strɛs] *n* (*force, pressure*) pression *f*; (*mental strain*) tension (nerveuse), stress *m*; (*accent*) accent *m*; (*emphasis*) insistance *f* ▷ *vt* insister sur, souligner; (*syllable*) accentuer; **to lay great ~ on sth** insister beaucoup sur qch; **to be under ~** être stressé(e)

stressed [strɛst] *adj* (*tense*) stressé(e); (*syllable*) accentué(e)

stressful ['strɛsful] *adj* (*job*) stressant(e)

stretch [strɛtʃ] *n* (*of sand etc*) étendue *f*; (*of time*) période *f* ▷ *vi* s'étirer; (*extend*): **to ~ to** *or* **as far as** s'étendre jusqu'à; (*be enough: money, food*): **to ~ to** aller pour ▷ *vt* tendre, étirer; (*spread*) étendre; (*fig*) pousser (au maximum); **at a ~** d'affilée; **to ~ a muscle** se distendre un muscle; **to ~ one's legs** se dégourdir les jambes
▶ **stretch out** *vi* s'étendre ▷ *vt* (*arm etc*) allonger, tendre; (*to spread*) étendre; **to ~ out for sth** allonger la main pour prendre qch

stretcher ['strɛtʃər] *n* brancard *m*, civière *f*

stretcher-bearer ['strɛtʃəbɛərər] *n* brancardier *m*

stretch marks *npl* (*on skin*) vergetures *fpl*

stretchy ['strɛtʃɪ] *adj* élastique

strewn [struːn] *adj*: **~ with** jonché(e) de

stricken ['strɪkən] *adj* très éprouvé(e); dévasté(e); (*ship*) très endommagé(e); **~ with** frappé(e) *or* atteint(e) de

strict [strɪkt] *adj* strict(e); **in ~ confidence** tout à fait confidentiellement

strictly ['strɪktlɪ] *adv* strictement; **~ confidential** strictement confidentiel(le); **~ speaking** à strictement parler

stride [straɪd] *n* grand pas, enjambée *f* ▷ *vi* (*pt* **strode**) [strəud] marcher à grands pas; **to take in one's ~** (*fig: changes etc*) accepter sans sourciller

strident ['straɪdnt] *adj* strident(e)

strife [straɪf] *n* conflit *m*, dissensions *fpl*

strike [straɪk] (*pt, pp* **struck**) [strʌk] *n* grève *f*; (*of oil etc*) découverte *f*; (*attack*) raid *m* ▷ *vt* frapper; (*oil etc*) trouver, découvrir; (*make: agreement, deal*) conclure ▷ *vi* faire grève; (*attack*) attaquer; (*clock*) sonner; **to go on** *or* **come out on ~** se mettre en grève, faire grève; **to ~ a match** frotter une allumette; **to ~ a balance** (*fig*) trouver un juste milieu

▶ **strike back** vi (Mil, fig) contre-attaquer
▶ **strike down** vt (fig) terrasser
▶ **strike off** vt (from list) rayer; (: doctor etc) radier
▶ **strike out** vt rayer
▶ **strike up** vt (Mus) se mettre à jouer; **to ~ up a friendship with** se lier d'amitié avec
strikebreaker ['straɪkbreɪkəʳ] n briseur m de grève
striker ['straɪkəʳ] n gréviste m/f; (Sport) buteur m
striking ['straɪkɪŋ] adj frappant(e), saisissant(e); (attractive) éblouissant(e)
strimmer® ['strɪməʳ] n (Brit) coupe-bordures m
string [strɪŋ] n ficelle f, fil m; (row: of beads) rang m; (: of onions, excuses) chapelet m; (: of people, cars) file f; (Mus) corde f; (Comput) chaîne f ▷ vt (pt, pp **strung**) [strʌŋ]: **to ~ out** échelonner; **to ~ together** enchaîner; **the strings** npl (Mus) les instruments mpl à cordes; **to pull ~s** (fig) faire jouer le piston; **to get a job by pulling ~s** obtenir un emploi en faisant jouer le piston; **with no ~s attached** (fig) sans conditions
string bean n haricot vert
stringed instrument [strɪŋ(d)-], **string instrument** n (Mus) instrument m à cordes
stringent ['strɪndʒənt] adj rigoureux(-euse); (need) impérieux(-euse)
string quartet n quatuor m à cordes
strip [strɪp] n bande f; (Sport) tenue f ▷ vt (undress) déshabiller; (paint) décaper; (fig) dégarnir, dépouiller; (also: **strip down**: machine) démonter ▷ vi se déshabiller; **wearing the Celtic ~** en tenue du Celtic
▶ **strip off** vt (paint etc) décaper ▷ vi (person) se déshabiller
strip cartoon n bande dessinée
stripe [straɪp] n raie f, rayure f; (Mil) galon m
striped ['straɪpt] adj rayé(e), à rayures
strip light n (Brit) (tube m au) néon m
stripper ['strɪpəʳ] n strip-teaseuse f
strip-search ['strɪpsəːtʃ] n fouille corporelle (en faisant se déshabiller la personne) ▷ vt: **to ~ sb** fouiller qn (en le faisant se déshabiller)
striptease ['strɪptiːz] n strip-tease m
stripy ['straɪpɪ] adj rayé(e)
strive (pt **strove**, pp **striven**) [straɪv, strəuv, 'strɪvn] vi: **to ~ to do/for sth** s'efforcer de faire/ d'obtenir qch
strobe [strəub] n (also: **strobe light**) stroboscope m
strode [strəud] pt of **stride**
stroke [strəuk] n coup m; (Med) attaque f; (caress) caresse f; (Swimming: style) (sorte f de) nage f; (of piston) course f ▷ vt caresser; **at a ~** d'un (seul) coup; **on the ~ of 5** à 5 heures sonnantes; **a ~ of luck** un coup de chance; **a 2-~ engine** un moteur à 2 temps
stroll [strəul] n petite promenade ▷ vi flâner, se promener nonchalamment; **to go for a ~** aller se promener or faire un tour
stroller ['strəuləʳ] n (US: for child) poussette f
strong [strɔŋ] adj (gen) fort(e); (healthy) vigoureux(-euse); (heart, nerves) solide; (distaste, desire) vif (vive); (drugs, chemicals) puissant(e) ▷ adv: **to be going ~** (company) marcher bien; (person) être toujours solide; **they are 50 ~** ils sont au nombre de 50
strong-arm ['strɔŋɑːm] adj (tactics, methods) musclé(e)
strongbox ['strɔŋbɔks] n coffre-fort m
stronghold ['strɔŋhəuld] n forteresse f, fort m; (fig) bastion m
strongly ['strɔŋlɪ] adv fortement, avec force; vigoureusement; solidement; **I feel ~ about it** c'est une question qui me tient particulièrement à cœur; (negatively) j'y suis profondément opposé(e)
strongman ['strɔŋmæn] (irreg) n hercule m, colosse m; (fig) homme m à poigne
strongroom ['strɔŋruːm] n chambre forte
stroppy ['strɔpɪ] adj (Brit inf) contrariant(e), difficile
strove [strəuv] pt of **strive**
struck [strʌk] pt, pp of **strike**
structural ['strʌktʃrəl] adj structural(e); (Constr) de construction; affectant les parties portantes
structurally ['strʌktʃrəlɪ] adv du point de vue de la construction
structure ['strʌktʃəʳ] n structure f; (building) construction f
struggle ['strʌgl] n lutte f ▷ vi lutter, se battre; **to have a ~ to do sth** avoir beaucoup de mal à faire qch
strum [strʌm] vt (guitar) gratter de
strung [strʌŋ] pt, pp of **string**
strut [strʌt] n étai m, support m ▷ vi se pavaner
strychnine ['strɪkniːn] n strychnine f
stub [stʌb] n (of cigarette) bout m, mégot m; (of ticket etc) talon m ▷ vt: **to ~ one's toe (on sth)** se heurter le doigt de pied (contre qch)
▶ **stub out** vt écraser
stubble ['stʌbl] n chaume m; (on chin) barbe f de plusieurs jours
stubborn ['stʌbən] adj têtu(e), obstiné(e), opiniâtre
stubby ['stʌbɪ] adj trapu(e); gros(se) et court(e)
stucco ['stʌkəu] n stuc m
stuck [stʌk] pt, pp of **stick** ▷ adj (jammed) bloqué(e), coincé(e); **to get ~** se bloquer or coincer
stuck-up [stʌk'ʌp] adj prétentieux(-euse)
stud [stʌd] n (on boots etc) clou m; (collar stud) bouton m de col; (earring) petite boucle d'oreille; (of horses: also: **stud farm**) écurie f, haras m; (also: **stud horse**) étalon m ▷ vt (fig): **~ded with** parsemé(e) or criblé(e) de
student ['stjuːdənt] n étudiant(e) ▷ adj (life) estudiantin(e), étudiant(e), d'étudiant; (residence, restaurant) universitaire; (loan, movement) étudiant, universitaire d'étudiant; **law/medical ~** étudiant en droit/ médecine
student driver n (US) (conducteur(-trice)) débutant(e)
students' union n (Brit: association) ≈ union f des étudiants; (: building) ≈ foyer m des étudiants

studied ['stʌdɪd] *adj* étudié(e), calculé(e)

studio ['stju:dɪəu] *n* studio *m*, atelier *m*; (*TV etc*) studio

studio flat, (*US*) **studio apartment** *n* studio *m*

studious ['stju:dɪəs] *adj* studieux(-euse), appliqué(e); (*studied*) étudié(e)

studiously ['stju:dɪəslɪ] *adv* (*carefully*) soigneusement

study ['stʌdɪ] *n* étude *f*; (*room*) bureau *m* ▷ *vt* étudier; (*examine*) examiner ▷ *vi* étudier, faire ses études; **to make a ~ of sth** étudier qch, faire une étude de qch; **to ~ for an exam** préparer un examen

stuff [stʌf] *n* (*gen*) chose(s) *f(pl)*, truc *m*; (*belongings*) affaires *fpl*, trucs; (*substance*) substance *f* ▷ *vt* rembourrer; (*Culin*) farcir; (*inf: push*) fourrer; (*animal: for exhibition*) empailler; **my nose is ~ed up** j'ai le nez bouché; **get ~ed!** (*inf!*) va te faire foutre! (*!*); **~ed toy** jouet *m* en peluche

stuffing ['stʌfɪŋ] *n* bourre *f*, rembourrage *m*; (*Culin*) farce *f*

stuffy ['stʌfɪ] *adj* (*room*) mal ventilé(e) or aéré(e); (*ideas*) vieux jeu *inv*

stumble ['stʌmbl] *vi* trébucher; **to ~ across** or **on** (*fig*) tomber sur

stumbling block ['stʌmblɪŋ-] *n* pierre *f* d'achoppement

stump [stʌmp] *n* souche *f*; (*of limb*) moignon *m* ▷ *vt*: **to be ~ed** sécher, ne pas savoir que répondre

stun [stʌn] *vt* (*blow*) étourdir; (*news*) abasourdir, stupéfier

stung [stʌŋ] *pt*, *pp of* **sting**

stunk [stʌŋk] *pp of* **stink**

stunned [stʌnd] *adj* assommé(e); (*fig*) sidéré(e)

stunning ['stʌnɪŋ] *adj* (*beautiful*) étourdissant(e); (*news etc*) stupéfiant(e)

stunt [stʌnt] *n* tour *m* de force; (*in film*) cascade *f*, acrobatie *f*; (*publicity*) truc *m* publicitaire; (*Aviat*) acrobatie *f* ▷ *vt* retarder, arrêter

stunted ['stʌntɪd] *adj* rabougri(e)

stuntman ['stʌntmæn] (*irreg*) *n* cascadeur *m*

stupefaction [stju:pɪ'fækʃən] *n* stupéfaction *f*, stupeur *f*

stupefy ['stju:pɪfaɪ] *vt* étourdir; abrutir; (*fig*) stupéfier

stupendous [stju:'pɛndəs] *adj* prodigieux(-euse), fantastique

stupid ['stju:pɪd] *adj* stupide, bête

stupidity [stju:'pɪdɪtɪ] *n* stupidité *f*, bêtise *f*

stupidly ['stju:pɪdlɪ] *adv* stupidement, bêtement

stupor ['stju:pə^r] *n* stupeur *f*

sturdy ['stə:dɪ] *adj* (*person, plant*) robuste, vigoureux(-euse); (*object*) solide

sturgeon ['stə:dʒən] *n* esturgeon *m*

stutter ['stʌtə^r] *n* bégaiement *m* ▷ *vi* bégayer

sty [staɪ] *n* (*of pigs*) porcherie *f*

stye [staɪ] *n* (*Med*) orgelet *m*

style [staɪl] *n* style *m*; (*of dress etc*) genre *m*; (*distinction*) allure *f*, cachet *m*, style (*design*)

modèle *m*; **in the latest ~** à la dernière mode; **hair ~** coiffure *f*

stylish ['staɪlɪʃ] *adj* élégant(e), chic *inv*

stylist ['staɪlɪst] *n* (*hair stylist*) coiffeur(-euse); (*literary stylist*) styliste *m/f*

stylized ['staɪlaɪzd] *adj* stylisé(e)

stylus (*pl* **styli** *or* **-es**) ['staɪləs, -laɪ] *n* (*of record player*) pointe *f* de lecture

Styrofoam® ['staɪrəfəum] *n* (*US*) polystyrène expansé ▷ *adj* en polystyrène

suave [swɑ:v] *adj* doucereux(-euse), onctueux(-euse)

sub [sʌb] *n abbr* = **submarine**; **subscription**

sub... [sʌb] *prefix* sub..., sous-

subcommittee ['sʌbkəmɪtɪ] *n* sous-comité *m*

subconscious [sʌb'kɒnʃəs] *adj* subconscient(e) ▷ *n* subconscient *m*

subcontinent [sʌb'kɒntɪnənt] *n*: **the (Indian) ~** le sous-continent indien

subcontract *n* ['sʌb'kɒntrækt] contrat *m* de sous-traitance ▷ *vt* [sʌbkən'trækt] sous-traiter

subcontractor ['sʌbkən'træktə^r] *n* sous-traitant *m*

subdivide [sʌbdɪ'vaɪd] *vt* subdiviser

subdivision ['sʌbdɪvɪʒən] *n* subdivision *f*

subdue [səb'dju:] *vt* subjuguer, soumettre

subdued [səb'dju:d] *adj* contenu(e), atténué(e); (*light*) tamisé(e); (*person*) qui a perdu de son entrain

sub-editor ['sʌb'ɛdɪtə^r] *n* (*Brit*) secrétaire *m/f* de (la) rédaction

subject *n* ['sʌbdʒɪkt] sujet *m*; (*Scol*) matière *f* ▷ *vt* [səb'dʒɛkt]: **to ~ to** soumettre à; exposer à; **to be ~ to** (*law*) être soumis(e) à; (*disease*) être sujet(te) à; **~ to confirmation in writing** sous réserve de confirmation écrite; **to change the ~** changer de conversation

subjection [səb'dʒɛkʃən] *n* soumission *f*, sujétion *f*

subjective [səb'dʒɛktɪv] *adj* subjectif(-ive)

subject matter *n* sujet *m*; (*content*) contenu *m*

sub judice [sʌb'dju:dɪsɪ] *adj* (*Law*) devant les tribunaux

subjugate ['sʌbdʒugeɪt] *vt* subjuguer

subjunctive [səb'dʒʌŋktɪv] *adj* subjonctif(-ive) ▷ *n* subjonctif *m*

sublet [sʌb'lɛt] *vt* sous-louer

sublime [sə'blaɪm] *adj* sublime

subliminal [sʌb'lɪmɪnl] *adj* subliminal(e)

submachine gun ['sʌbmə'ʃi:n-] *n* mitraillette *f*

submarine [sʌbmə'ri:n] *n* sous-marin *m*

submerge [səb'mə:dʒ] *vt* submerger; immerger ▷ *vi* plonger

submersion [səb'mə:ʃən] *n* submersion *f*; immersion *f*

submission [səb'mɪʃən] *n* soumission *f*; (*to committee etc*) présentation *f*

submissive [səb'mɪsɪv] *adj* soumis(e)

submit [səb'mɪt] *vt* soumettre ▷ *vi* se soumettre

subnormal [sʌb'nɔ:ml] *adj* au-dessous de la normale; (*person*) arriéré(e)

subordinate [sə'bɔ:dɪnət] *adj* (*junior*) subalterne;

(*Grammar*) subordonné(e) ▷ *n* subordonné(e)

subpoena [səb'pi:nə] (*Law*) *n* citation *f*, assignation *f* ▷ *vt* citer *or* assigner (à comparaître)

subroutine [sʌbru:'ti:n] *n* (*Comput*) sous-programme *m*

subscribe [səb'skraɪb] *vi* cotiser; **to ~ to** (*opinion, fund*) souscrire à; (*newspaper*) s'abonner à; être abonné(e) à

subscriber [səb'skraɪbər] *n* (*to periodical, telephone*) abonné(e)

subscript ['sʌbskrɪpt] *n* (*Typ*) indice inférieur

subscription [səb'skrɪpʃən] *n* (*to fund*) souscription *f*; (*to magazine etc*) abonnement *m*; (*membership dues*) cotisation *f*; **to take out a ~ to** s'abonner à

subsequent ['sʌbsɪkwənt] *adj* ultérieur(e), suivant(e); **~ to** *prep* à la suite de

subsequently ['sʌbsɪkwəntlɪ] *adv* par la suite

subservient [səb'sə:vɪənt] *adj* obséquieux(-euse)

subside [səb'saɪd] *vi* (*land*) s'affaisser; (*flood*) baisser; (*wind, feelings*) tomber

subsidence [səb'saɪdns] *n* affaissement *m*

subsidiarity [səbsɪdɪ'ærɪtɪ] *n* (*Pol*) subsidiarité *f*

subsidiary [səb'sɪdɪərɪ] *adj* subsidiaire; accessoire; (*Brit Scol: subject*) complémentaire ▷ *n* filiale *f*

subsidize ['sʌbsɪdaɪz] *vt* subventionner

subsidy ['sʌbsɪdɪ] *n* subvention *f*

subsist [səb'sɪst] *vi*: **to ~ on sth** (arriver à) vivre avec *or* subsister avec qch

subsistence [səb'sɪstəns] *n* existence *f*, subsistance *f*

subsistence allowance *n* indemnité *f* de séjour

subsistence level *n* niveau *m* de vie minimum

substance ['sʌbstəns] *n* substance *f*; (*fig*) essentiel *m*; **a man of ~** un homme jouissant d'une certaine fortune; **to lack ~** être plutôt mince (*fig*)

substance abuse *n* abus *m* de substances toxiques

substandard [sʌb'stændəd] *adj* (*goods*) de qualité inférieure, qui laisse à désirer; (*housing*) inférieur(e) aux normes requises

substantial [səb'stænʃl] *adj* substantiel(le); (*fig*) important(e)

substantially [səb'stænʃəlɪ] *adv* considérablement; en grande partie

substantiate [səb'stænʃɪeɪt] *vt* étayer, fournir des preuves à l'appui de

substitute ['sʌbstɪtju:t] *n* (*person*) remplaçant(e); (*thing*) succédané *m* ▷ *vt*: **to ~ sth/sb for** substituer qch/qn à, remplacer par qch/qn

substitute teacher *n* (*US*) suppléant(e)

substitution [sʌbstɪ'tju:ʃən] *n* substitution *f*

subterfuge ['sʌbtəfju:dʒ] *n* subterfuge *m*

subterranean [sʌbtə'reɪnɪən] *adj* souterrain(e)

subtitled ['sʌbtaɪtld] *adj* sous-titré(e)

subtitles ['sʌbtaɪtlz] *npl* (*Cine*) sous-titres *mpl*

subtle ['sʌtl] *adj* subtil(e)

subtlety ['sʌtltɪ] *n* subtilité *f*

subtly ['sʌtlɪ] *adv* subtilement

subtotal [sʌb'təutl] *n* total partiel

subtract [səb'trækt] *vt* soustraire, retrancher

subtraction [səb'trækʃən] *n* soustraction *f*

subtropical [sʌb'trɔpɪkl] *adj* subtropical(e)

suburb ['sʌbə:b] *n* faubourg *m*; **the ~s** la banlieue

suburban [sə'bə:bən] *adj* de banlieue, suburbain(e)

suburbia [sə'bə:bɪə] *n* la banlieue

subvention [səb'vɛnʃən] *n* (*subsidy*) subvention *f*

subversion [səb'və:ʃən] *n* subversion *f*

subversive [səb'və:sɪv] *adj* subversif(-ive)

subway ['sʌbweɪ] *n* (*Brit: underpass*) passage souterrain; (*US: railway*) métro *m*

sub-zero [sʌb'zɪərəu] *adj* au-dessous de zéro

succeed [sək'si:d] *vi* réussir ▷ *vt* succéder à; **to ~ in doing** réussir à faire

succeeding [sək'si:dɪŋ] *adj* suivant(e), qui suit (*or* suivent *or* suivront *etc*)

success [sək'sɛs] *n* succès *m*; réussite *f*

successful [sək'sɛsful] *adj* qui a du succès; (*candidate*) choisi(e), agréé(e); (*business*) prospère, qui réussit; (*attempt*) couronné(e) de succès; **to be ~ (in doing)** réussir (à faire)

successfully [sək'sɛsfəlɪ] *adv* avec succès

succession [sək'sɛʃən] *n* succession *f*; **in ~** successivement; **3 years in ~** 3 ans de suite

successive [sək'sɛsɪv] *adj* successif(-ive); **on 3 ~ days** 3 jours de suite *or* consécutifs

successor [sək'sɛsər] *n* successeur *m*

succinct [sək'sɪŋkt] *adj* succinct(e), bref (brève)

succulent ['sʌkjulənt] *adj* succulent(e) ▷ *n* (*Bot*): **~s** plantes grasses

succumb [sə'kʌm] *vi* succomber

such [sʌtʃ] *adj* tel (telle); (*of that kind*): **~ a book** un livre de ce genre *or* pareil, un tel livre; (*so much*): **~ courage** un tel courage ▷ *adv* si; **~ books** des livres de ce genre *or* pareils, de tels livres; **~ a long trip** un si long voyage; **~ good books** de si bons livres; **~ a long trip that** un voyage si *or* tellement long que; **~ a lot of** tellement *or* tant de; **making ~ a noise that** faisant un tel bruit que *or* tellement de bruit que; **~ a long time ago** il y a si *or* tellement longtemps; **~ as** (*like*) tel (telle) que, comme; **a noise ~ as to** un bruit de nature à; **~ books as I have** les quelques livres que j'ai; **as ~** (*adv*) en tant que tel (telle), à proprement parler

such-and-such ['sʌtʃənsʌtʃ] *adj* tel ou tel (telle ou telle)

suchlike ['sʌtʃlaɪk] *pron* (*inf*): **and ~** et le reste

suck [sʌk] *vt* sucer; (*breast, bottle*) téter; (*pump, machine*) aspirer

sucker ['sʌkər] *n* (*Bot, Zool, Tech*) ventouse *f*; (*inf*) naïf(-ïve), poire *f*

suckle ['sʌkl] *vt* allaiter

sucrose ['su:krəuz] *n* saccharose *m*

suction ['sʌkʃən] *n* succion *f*

suction pump *n* pompe aspirante

Sudan [su'dɑ:n] *n* Soudan *m*

Sudanese [suːdəˈniːz] *adj* soudanais(e) ▷ *n* Soudanais(e)

sudden ['sʌdn] *adj* soudain(e), subit(e); **all of a ~** soudain, tout à coup

sudden-death [sʌdn'dɛθ] *n*: **~ play-off** *partie supplémentaire pour départager les adversaires*

suddenly ['sʌdnlɪ] *adv* brusquement, tout à coup, soudain

sudoku [suˈdəʊkuː] *n* sudoku *m*

suds [sʌdz] *npl* eau savonneuse

sue [suː] *vt* poursuivre en justice, intenter un procès à ▷ *vi*: **to ~ (for)** intenter un procès (pour); **to ~ for divorce** engager une procédure de divorce; **to ~ sb for damages** poursuivre qn en dommages-intérêts

suede [sweɪd] *n* daim *m*, cuir suédé ▷ *cpd* de daim

suet ['suɪt] *n* graisse *f* de rognon *or* de bœuf

Suez Canal ['suːɪz-] *n* canal *m* de Suez

suffer ['sʌfə^r] *vt* souffrir, subir; *(bear)* tolérer, supporter, subir ▷ *vi* souffrir; **to ~ from** *(illness)* souffrir de, avoir; **to ~ from the effects of alcohol/a fall** se ressentir des effets de l'alcool/des conséquences d'une chute

sufferance ['sʌfərns] *n*: **he was only there on ~** sa présence était seulement tolérée

sufferer ['sʌfərə^r] *n* malade *m/f*; victime *m/f*

suffering ['sʌfərɪŋ] *n* souffrance(s) *f(pl)*

suffice [sə'faɪs] *vi* suffire

sufficient [sə'fɪʃənt] *adj* suffisant(e); **~ money** suffisamment d'argent

sufficiently [sə'fɪʃəntlɪ] *adv* suffisamment, assez

suffix ['sʌfɪks] *n* suffixe *m*

suffocate ['sʌfəkeɪt] *vi* suffoquer; étouffer

suffocation [sʌfə'keɪʃən] *n* suffocation *f*; *(Med)* asphyxie *f*

suffrage ['sʌfrɪdʒ] *n* suffrage *m*; droit *m* de suffrage *or* de vote

suffuse [sə'fjuːz] *vt* baigner, imprégner; **the room was ~d with light** la pièce baignait dans la lumière *or* était imprégnée de lumière

sugar ['ʃugə^r] *n* sucre *m* ▷ *vt* sucrer

sugar beet *n* betterave sucrière

sugar bowl *n* sucrier *m*

sugar cane *n* canne *f* à sucre

sugar-coated ['ʃugə'kəutɪd] *adj* dragéifié(e)

sugar lump *n* morceau *m* de sucre

sugar refinery *n* raffinerie *f* de sucre

sugary ['ʃugərɪ] *adj* sucré(e)

suggest [sə'dʒɛst] *vt* suggérer, proposer; *(indicate)* sembler indiquer; **what do you ~ I do?** que vous me suggérez de faire?

suggestion [sə'dʒɛstʃən] *n* suggestion *f*

suggestive [sə'dʒɛstɪv] *adj* suggestif(-ive)

suicidal [suɪ'saɪdl] *adj* suicidaire

suicide ['suɪsaɪd] *n* suicide *m*; **to commit ~** se suicider; **~ bombing** attentat *m* suicide; *see also* **commit**

suicide bomber *n* kamikaze *m/f*

suit [suːt] *n* *(man's)* costume *m*, complet *m*; *(woman's)* tailleur *m*, ensemble *m*; *(Cards)* couleur *f*; *(lawsuit)* procès *m* ▷ *vt* *(subj: clothes, hairstyle)* aller à; *(be convenient for)* convenir à; *(adapt)*: **to ~ sth to** adapter *or* approprier qch à; **to be ~ed to sth** *(suitable for)* être adapté(e) *or* approprié(e) à qch; **well ~ed** *(couple)* faits l'un pour l'autre, très bien assortis; **to bring a ~ against sb** intenter un procès contre qn; **to follow ~** *(fig)* faire de même

suitable ['suːtəbl] *adj* qui convient; approprié(e), adéquat(e); **would tomorrow be ~?** est-ce que demain vous conviendrait?; **we found somebody ~** nous avons trouvé la personne qu'il nous faut

suitably ['suːtəblɪ] *adv* comme il se doit *(or* se devait *etc)*, convenablement

suitcase ['suːtkeɪs] *n* valise *f*

suite [swiːt] *n* *(of rooms, also Mus)* suite *f*; *(furniture)*: **bedroom/dining room ~** (ensemble *m* de) chambre *f* à coucher/salle *f* à manger; **a three-piece ~** un salon (canapé et deux fauteuils)

suitor ['suːtə^r] *n* soupirant *m*, prétendant *m*

sulfate ['sʌlfeɪt] *n* *(US)* = **sulphate**

sulfur ['sʌlfə^r] *(US)* *n* = **sulphur**

sulk [sʌlk] *vi* bouder

sulky ['sʌlkɪ] *adj* boudeur(-euse), maussade

sullen ['sʌlən] *adj* renfrogné(e), maussade; morne

sulphate, *(US)* **sulfate** ['sʌlfeɪt] *n* sulfate *m*; **copper ~** sulfate de cuivre

sulphur, *(US)* **sulfur** ['sʌlfə^r] *n* soufre *m*

sulphur dioxide *n* anhydride sulfureux

sulphuric, *(US)* **sulfuric** [sʌl'fjuərɪk] *adj*: **~ acid** acide *m* sulfurique

sultan ['sʌltən] *n* sultan *m*

sultana [sʌl'tɑːnə] *n* *(fruit)* raisin (sec) de Smyrne

sultry ['sʌltrɪ] *adj* étouffant(e)

sum [sʌm] *n* somme *f*; *(Scol etc)* calcul *m*
▶ **sum up** *vt* résumer; *(evaluate rapidly)* récapituler ▷ *vi* résumer

Sumatra [su'mɑːtrə] *n* Sumatra

summarize ['sʌməraɪz] *vt* résumer

summary ['sʌmərɪ] *n* résumé *m* ▷ *adj* *(justice)* sommaire

summer ['sʌmə^r] *n* été *m* ▷ *cpd* d'été, estival(e); **in (the) ~** en été, pendant l'été

summer camp *n* *(US)* colonie *f* de vacances

summer holidays *npl* grandes vacances

summerhouse ['sʌməhaus] *n* *(in garden)* pavillon *m*

summertime ['sʌmətaɪm] *n* *(season)* été *m*

summer time *n* *(by clock)* heure *f* d'été

summery ['sʌmərɪ] *adj* estival(e); d'été

summing-up [sʌmɪŋ'ʌp] *n* résumé *m*, récapitulation *f*

summit ['sʌmɪt] *n* sommet *m*; *(also:* **summit conference)** (conférence *f* au) sommet *m*

summon ['sʌmən] *vt* appeler, convoquer; **to ~ a witness** citer *or* assigner un témoin
▶ **summon up** *vt* rassembler, faire appel à

summons ['sʌmənz] *n* citation *f*, assignation *f*

▷ *vt* citer, assigner; **to serve a ~ on sb** remettre une assignation à qn

sumo ['su:məu] *n*: **~ wrestling** sumo *m*

sump [sʌmp] *n* (*Brit Aut*) carter *m*

sumptuous ['sʌmptjuəs] *adj* somptueux(-euse)

Sun. *abbr* (= *Sunday*) dim

sun [sʌn] *n* soleil *m*; **in the ~** au soleil; **to catch the ~** prendre le soleil; **everything under the ~** absolument tout

sunbathe ['sʌnbeɪð] *vi* prendre un bain de soleil

sunbeam ['sʌnbi:m] *n* rayon *m* de soleil

sunbed ['sʌnbɛd] *n* lit pliant; (*with sun lamp*) lit à ultra-violets

sunblock ['sʌnblɔk] *n* écran *m* total

sunburn ['sʌnbə:n] *n* coup *m* de soleil

sunburned ['sʌnbə:nd], **sunburnt** ['sʌnbə:nt] *adj* bronzé(e), hâlé(e); (*painfully*) brûlé(e) par le soleil

sun cream *n* crème *f* (anti-)solaire

sundae ['sʌndeɪ] *n* sundae *m*, coupe glacée

Sunday ['sʌndɪ] *n* dimanche *m*; *for phrases see also* **Tuesday**

Sunday paper *n* journal *m* du dimanche; *voir article*

● **SUNDAY PAPER**
●
● Les *Sunday papers* sont une véritable
● institution en Grande-Bretagne. Il y a des
● "quality Sunday papers" et des "popular
● Sunday papers", et la plupart des quotidiens
● ont un journal du dimanche qui leur est
● associé, bien que leurs équipes de rédacteurs
● soient différentes. Les quality Sunday
● papers ont plusieurs suppléments et
● magazines; voir "quality press" et "tabloid
● press".

Sunday school *n* ≈ catéchisme *m*

sundial ['sʌndaɪəl] *n* cadran *m* solaire

sundown ['sʌndaun] *n* coucher *m* du soleil

sundries ['sʌndrɪz] *npl* articles divers

sundry ['sʌndrɪ] *adj* divers(e), différent(e); **all and ~** tout le monde, n'importe qui

sunflower ['sʌnflauəʳ] *n* tournesol *m*

sung [sʌŋ] *pp of* **sing**

sunglasses ['sʌnglɑ:sɪz] *npl* lunettes *fpl* de soleil

sunk [sʌŋk] *pp of* **sink**

sunken ['sʌŋkn] *adj* (*rock, ship*) submergé(e); (*cheeks*) creux(-euse); (*bath*) encastré(e)

sunlamp ['sʌnlæmp] *n* lampe *f* à rayons ultra-violets

sunlight ['sʌnlaɪt] *n* (lumière *f* du) soleil *m*

sunlit ['sʌnlɪt] *adj* ensoleillé(e)

sun lounger *n* chaise longue

sunny ['sʌnɪ] *adj* ensoleillé(e); (*fig*) épanoui(e), radieux(-euse); **it is ~** il fait (du) soleil, il y a du soleil

sunrise ['sʌnraɪz] *n* lever *m* du soleil

sun roof *n* (*Aut*) toit ouvrant

sunscreen ['sʌnskri:n] *n* crème *f* solaire

sunset ['sʌnsɛt] *n* coucher *m* du soleil

sunshade ['sʌnʃeɪd] *n* (*lady's*) ombrelle *f*; (*over table*) parasol *m*

sunshine ['sʌnʃaɪn] *n* (lumière *f* du) soleil *m*

sunspot ['sʌnspɔt] *n* tache *f* solaire

sunstroke ['sʌnstrəuk] *n* insolation *f*, coup *m* de soleil

suntan ['sʌntæn] *n* bronzage *m*

suntan lotion *n* lotion *f* or lait *m* solaire

suntanned ['sʌntænd] *adj* bronzé(e)

suntan oil *n* huile *f* solaire

suntrap ['sʌntræp] *n* coin très ensoleillé

super ['su:pəʳ] *adj* (*inf*) formidable

superannuation [su:pərænju'eɪʃən] *n* cotisations *fpl* pour la pension

superb [su:'pə:b] *adj* superbe, magnifique

Super Bowl *n* (*US Sport*) Super Bowl *m*

supercilious [su:pə'sɪlɪəs] *adj* hautain(e), dédaigneux(-euse)

superconductor [su:pəkən'dʌktəʳ] *n* supraconducteur *m*

superficial [su:pə'fɪʃəl] *adj* superficiel(le)

superficially [su:pə'fɪʃəlɪ] *adv* superficiellement

superfluous [su'pə:fluəs] *adj* superflu(e)

superglue ['su:pəglu:] *n* colle forte

superhighway ['su:pəhaɪweɪ] *n* (*US*) voie *f* express (à plusieurs files); **the information ~** la super-autoroute de l'information

superhuman [su:pə'hju:mən] *adj* surhumain(e)

superimpose ['su:pərɪm'pəuz] *vt* superposer

superintend [su:pərɪn'tɛnd] *vt* surveiller

superintendent [su:pərɪn'tɛndənt] *n* directeur(-trice); (*Police*) ≈ commissaire *m*

superior [su'pɪərɪəʳ] *adj* supérieur(e); (*Comm: goods, quality*) de qualité supérieure; (*smug*) condescendant(e), méprisant(e) ▷ *n* supérieur(e); **Mother S~** (*Rel*) Mère supérieure

superiority [supɪərɪ'ɔrɪtɪ] *n* supériorité *f*

superlative [su'pə:lətɪv] *adj* sans pareil(le), suprême ▷ *n* (*Ling*) superlatif *m*

superman ['su:pəmæn] (*irreg*) *n* surhomme *m*

supermarket ['su:pəmɑ:kɪt] *n* supermarché *m*

supermodel ['su:pəmɔdl] *n* top model *m*

supernatural [su:pə'nætʃərəl] *adj* surnaturel(le) ▷ *n*: **the ~** le surnaturel

supernova [su:pə'nəuvə] *n* supernova *f*

superpower ['su:pəpauəʳ] *n* (*Pol*) superpuissance *f*

supersede [su:pə'si:d] *vt* remplacer, supplanter

supersonic ['su:pə'sɔnɪk] *adj* supersonique

superstar ['su:pəstɑ:ʳ] *n* (*Cine etc*) superstar *f*; (*Sport*) superchampion(ne) ▷ *adj* (*status, lifestyle*) de superstar

superstition [su:pə'stɪʃən] *n* superstition *f*

superstitious [su:pə'stɪʃəs] *adj* superstitieux(-euse)

superstore ['su:pəstɔ:ʳ] *n* (*Brit*) hypermarché *m*, grande surface

supertanker ['su:pətæŋkəʳ] *n* pétrolier géant, superpétrolier *m*

supertax ['su:pətæks] *n* tranche supérieure de l'impôt

supervise ['su:pəvaɪz] *vt* (*children etc*) surveiller; (*organization, work*) diriger

supervision [su:pə'vɪʒən] *n* surveillance *f*; (*monitoring*) contrôle *m*; (*management*) direction *f*; **under medical ~** sous contrôle du médecin

supervisor ['su:pəvaɪzə^r] *n* surveillant(e); (*in shop*) chef *m* de rayon; (*Scol*) directeur(-trice) de thèse

supervisory ['su:pəvaɪzərɪ] *adj* de surveillance

supine ['su:paɪn] *adj* couché(e) *or* étendu(e) sur le dos

supper ['sʌpə^r] *n* dîner *m*; (*late*) souper *m*; **to have ~** dîner; souper

supplant [sə'plɑ:nt] *vt* supplanter

supple ['sʌpl] *adj* souple

supplement *n* ['sʌplɪmənt] supplément *m* ▷ *vt* [sʌplɪ'mɛnt] ajouter à, compléter

supplementary [sʌplɪ'mɛntərɪ] *adj* supplémentaire

supplementary benefit *n* (*Brit*) allocation *f* supplémentaire d'aide sociale

supplier [sə'plaɪə^r] *n* fournisseur *m*

supply [sə'plaɪ] *vt* (*provide*) fournir; (*equip*): **to ~ (with)** approvisionner *or* ravitailler (en); fournir (en); (*system, machine*): **to ~ sth (with sth)** alimenter qch (en qch); (*a need*) répondre à ▷ *n* provision *f*, réserve *f*; (*supplying*) approvisionnement *m*; (*Tech*) alimentation *f*; **supplies** *npl* (*food*) vivres *mpl*; (*Mil*) subsistances *fpl*; **office supplies** fournitures *fpl* de bureau; **to be in short ~** être rare, manquer; **the electricity/water/gas ~** l'alimentation *f* en électricité/eau/gaz; **~ and demand** l'offre *f* et la demande; **it comes supplied with an adaptor** il (*or* elle) est pourvu(e) d'un adaptateur

supply teacher *n* (*Brit*) suppléant(e)

support [sə'pɔ:t] *n* (*moral, financial etc*) soutien *m*, appui *m*; (*Tech*) support *m*, soutien ▷ *vt* soutenir, supporter; (*financially*) subvenir aux besoins de; (*uphold*) être pour, être partisan de, appuyer; (*Sport: team*) être pour; **to ~ o.s.** (*financially*) gagner sa vie

supporter [sə'pɔ:tə^r] *n* (*Pol etc*) partisan(e); (*Sport*) supporter *m*

supporting [sə'pɔ:tɪŋ] *adj* (*wall*) d'appui

supporting role *n* second rôle *m*

supportive [sə'pɔ:tɪv] *adj*: **my family were very ~** ma famille m'a été d'un grand soutien

suppose [sə'pəuz] *vt, vi* supposer; imaginer; **to be ~d to do/be** être censé(e) faire/être; **I don't ~ she'll come** je suppose qu'elle ne viendra pas, cela m'étonnerait qu'elle vienne

supposedly [sə'pəuzɪdlɪ] *adv* soi-disant

supposing [sə'pəuzɪŋ] *conj* si, à supposer que + *sub*

supposition [sʌpə'zɪʃən] *n* supposition *f*, hypothèse *f*

suppository [sə'pɔzɪtrɪ] *n* suppositoire *m*

suppress [sə'prɛs] *vt* (*revolt, feeling*) réprimer; (*information*) faire disparaître; (*scandal, yawn*) étouffer

suppression [sə'prɛʃən] *n* suppression *f*,

répression *f*

suppressor [sə'prɛsə^r] *n* (*Elec etc*) dispositif *m* antiparasite

supremacy [su'prɛməsɪ] *n* suprématie *f*

supreme [su'pri:m] *adj* suprême

Supreme Court *n* (*US*) Cour *f* suprême

supremo [su'pri:məu] *n* grand chef

Supt. *abbr* (*Police*) = **superintendent**

surcharge ['sə:tʃɑ:dʒ] *n* surcharge *f*; (*extra tax*) surtaxe *f*

sure [ʃuə^r] *adj* (*gen*) sûr(e); (*definite, convinced*) sûr, certain(e) ▷ *adv* (*inf: US*): **that ~ is pretty, that's ~ pretty** c'est drôlement joli(e); **~!** (*of course*) bien sûr!; **~ enough** effectivement; **I'm not ~ how/why/when** je ne sais pas très bien comment/pourquoi/quand; **to be ~ of o.s.** être sûr de soi; **to make ~ of sth/that** s'assurer de qch/que, vérifier qch/que

sure-fire ['ʃuəfaɪə^r] *adj* (*inf*) certain(e), infaillible

sure-footed [ʃuə'futɪd] *adj* au pied sûr

surely ['ʃuəlɪ] *adv* sûrement; certainement; **~ you don't mean that!** vous ne parlez pas sérieusement!

surety ['ʃuərətɪ] *n* caution *f*; **to go** *or* **stand ~ for sb** se porter caution pour qn

surf [sə:f] *n* (*waves*) ressac *m* ▷ *vt*: **to ~ the Net** surfer sur Internet, surfer sur le net

surface ['sə:fɪs] *n* surface *f* ▷ *vt* (*road*) poser un revêtement sur ▷ *vi* remonter à la surface; (*fig*) faire surface; **on the ~** (*fig*) au premier abord; **by ~ mail** par voie de terre; (*by sea*) par voie maritime

surface area *n* superficie *f*, aire *f*

surface mail *n* courrier *m* par voie de terre (*or* maritime)

surface-to-surface ['sə:fɪstə'sə:fɪs] *adj* (*Mil*) sol-sol *inv*

surfboard ['sə:fbɔ:d] *n* planche *f* de surf

surfeit ['sə:fɪt] *n*: **a ~ of** un excès de; une indigestion de

surfer ['sə:fə^r] *n* (*in sea*) surfeur(-euse); **web** *or* **net ~** internaute *m/f*

surfing ['sə:fɪŋ] *n* surf *m*

surge [sə:dʒ] *n* (*of emotion*) vague *f*; (*Elec*) pointe *f* de courant ▷ *vi* déferler; **to ~ forward** se précipiter (en avant)

surgeon ['sə:dʒən] *n* chirurgien *m*

Surgeon General *n* (*US*) chef *m* du service fédéral de la santé publique

surgery ['sə:dʒərɪ] *n* chirurgie *f*; (*Brit: room*) cabinet *m* (de consultation); (*also:* **surgery hours**) heures *fpl* de consultation; (*of MP etc*) permanence *f* (*où le député etc reçoit les électeurs etc*); **to undergo ~** être opéré(e)

surgery hours *npl* (*Brit*) heures *fpl* de consultation

surgical ['sə:dʒɪkl] *adj* chirurgical(e)

surgical spirit *n* (*Brit*) alcool *m* à 90°

surly ['sə:lɪ] *adj* revêche, maussade

surmise [sə:'maɪz] *vt* présumer, conjecturer

surmount [sə:'maunt] *vt* surmonter

surname ['sə:neɪm] *n* nom *m* de famille

surpass [sə:ˈpɑːs] *vt* surpasser, dépasser

surplus [ˈsə:pləs] *n* surplus *m*, excédent *m* ▷ *adj* en surplus, de trop; (*Comm*) excédentaire; **it is ~ to our requirements** cela dépasse nos besoins; **~ stock** surplus *m*

surprise [səˈpraɪz] *n* (*gen*) surprise *f*; (*astonishment*) étonnement *m* ▷ *vt* surprendre, étonner; **to take by ~** (*person*) prendre au dépourvu; (*Mil: town, fort*) prendre par surprise

surprised [səˈpraɪzd] *adj* (*look, smile*) surpris(e), étonné(e); **to be ~** être surpris

surprising [səˈpraɪzɪŋ] *adj* surprenant(e), étonnant(e)

surprisingly [səˈpraɪzɪŋlɪ] *adv* (*easy, helpful*) étonnamment, étrangement; **(somewhat) ~, he agreed** curieusement, il a accepté

surrealism [səˈrɪəlɪzəm] *n* surréalisme *m*

surrealist [səˈrɪəlɪst] *adj, n* surréaliste (*m/f*)

surrender [səˈrɛndəʳ] *n* reddition *f*, capitulation *f* ▷ *vi* se rendre, capituler ▷ *vt* (*claim, right*) renoncer à

surrender value *n* valeur *f* de rachat

surreptitious [sʌrəpˈtɪʃəs] *adj* subreptice, furtif(-ive)

surrogate [ˈsʌrəgɪt] *n* (*Brit: substitute*) substitut *m* ▷ *adj* de substitution, de remplacement; **a food ~** un succédané alimentaire; **~ coffee** ersatz *m* or succédané *m* de café

surrogate mother *n* mère porteuse or de substitution

surround [səˈraund] *vt* entourer; (*Mil etc*) encercler

surrounding [səˈraundɪŋ] *adj* environnant(e)

surroundings [səˈraundɪŋz] *npl* environs *mpl*, alentours *mpl*

surtax [ˈsə:tæks] *n* surtaxe *f*

surveillance [sə:ˈveɪləns] *n* surveillance *f*

survey *n* [ˈsə:veɪ] enquête *f*, étude *f*; (*in house buying etc*) inspection *f*, (*rapport m* d')expertise *f*; (*of land*) levé *m*; (*comprehensive view: of situation etc*) vue *f* d'ensemble ▷ *vt* [sə:ˈveɪ] (*situation*) passer en revue; (*examine carefully*) inspecter; (*building*) expertiser; (*land*) faire le levé de; (*look at*) embrasser du regard

surveying [səˈveɪɪŋ] *n* arpentage *m*

surveyor [səˈveɪəʳ] *n* (*of building*) expert *m*; (*of land*) (arpenteur *m*) géomètre *m*

survival [səˈvaɪvl] *n* survie *f*; (*relic*) vestige *m* ▷ *cpd* (*course, kit*) de survie

survive [səˈvaɪv] *vi* survivre; (*custom etc*) subsister ▷ *vt* (*accident etc*) survivre à, réchapper de; (*person*) survivre à

survivor [səˈvaɪvəʳ] *n* survivant(e)

susceptible [səˈsɛptəbl] *adj*; **~ (to)** sensible (à); (*disease*) prédisposé(e) (à)

suspect *adj, n* [ˈsʌspɛkt] suspect(e) ▷ *vt* [səsˈpɛkt] soupçonner, suspecter

suspected [səsˈpɛktɪd] *adj*: **a ~ terrorist** une personne soupçonnée de terrorisme; **he had a ~ broken arm** il avait une supposée fracture du bras

suspend [səsˈpɛnd] *vt* suspendre

suspended animation [səsˈpɛndɪd-] *n*: **in a state of ~** en hibernation

suspended sentence [səsˈpɛndɪd-] *n* (*Law*) condamnation *f* avec sursis

suspender belt [səsˈpɛndə-] *n* (*Brit*) porte-jarretelles *m inv*

suspenders [səsˈpɛndəz] *npl* (*Brit*) jarretelles *fpl*; (*US*) bretelles *fpl*

suspense [səsˈpɛns] *n* attente *f*, incertitude *f*; (*in film etc*) suspense *m*; **to keep sb in ~** tenir qn en suspens, laisser qn dans l'incertitude

suspension [səsˈpɛnʃən] *n* (*gen, Aut*) suspension *f*; (*of driving licence*) retrait *m* provisoire

suspension bridge *n* pont suspendu

suspicion [səsˈpɪʃən] *n* soupçon(s) *m(pl)*; **to be under ~** être considéré(e) comme suspect(e), être suspecté(e); **arrested on ~ of murder** arrêté sur présomption de meurtre

suspicious [səsˈpɪʃəs] *adj* (*suspecting*) soupçonneux(-euse), méfiant(e); (*causing suspicion*) suspect(e); **to be ~ of** or **about sb/sth** avoir des doutes à propos de qn/sur qch, trouver qn/qch suspect(e)

suss out [ˈsʌsˈaut] *vt* (*Brit inf: discover*) supputer; (*: understand*) piger

sustain [səsˈteɪn] *vt* soutenir; supporter; corroborer; (*subj: food*) nourrir, donner des forces à; (*damage*) subir; (*injury*) recevoir

sustainable [səsˈteɪnəbl] *adj* (*rate, growth*) qui peut être maintenu(e); (*development*) durable

sustained [səsˈteɪnd] *adj* (*effort*) soutenu(e), prolongé(e)

sustenance [ˈsʌstɪnəns] *n* nourriture *f*; moyens *mpl* de subsistance

suture [ˈsuːtʃəʳ] *n* suture *f*

SUV *n abbr* (*esp US:* = *sports utility vehicle*) SUV *m*, véhicule *m* de loisirs

SW *abbr* (= *short wave*) OC

swab [swɔb] *n* (*Med*) tampon *m*; prélèvement *m* ▷ *vt* (*Naut: also:* **swab down**) nettoyer

swagger [ˈswægəʳ] *vi* plastronner, parader

swallow [ˈswɔləu] *n* (*bird*) hirondelle *f*; (*of food etc*) gorgée *f* ▷ *vt* avaler; (*fig: story*) gober
▶ **swallow up** *vt* engloutir

swam [swæm] *pt of* **swim**

swamp [swɔmp] *n* marais *m*, marécage *m* ▷ *vt* submerger

swampy [ˈswɔmpɪ] *adj* marécageux(-euse)

swan [swɔn] *n* cygne *m*

swank [swæŋk] *vi* (*inf*) faire de l'épate

swan song *n* (*fig*) chant *m* du cygne

swap [swɔp] *n* échange *m*, troc *m* ▷ *vt*: **to ~ (for)** échanger (contre), troquer (contre)

SWAPO [ˈswɑːpəu] *n abbr* (= *South-West Africa People's Organization*) SWAPO *f*

swarm [swɔ:m] *n* essaim *m* ▷ *vi* (*bees*) essaimer; (*people*) grouiller; **to be ~ing with** grouiller de

swarthy [ˈswɔ:ðɪ] *adj* basané(e), bistré(e)

swashbuckling [ˈswɔʃbʌklɪŋ] *adj* (*film*) de cape et d'épée

swastika [ˈswɔstɪkə] *n* croix gammée

SWAT *n abbr* (*US:* = *Special Weapons and Tactics*)

≈ CRS *f*

swat [swɔt] *vt* écraser ▷ *n* (*Brit: also:* **fly swat**) tapette *f*

swathe [sweɪð] *vt:* **to ~ in** (*bandages, blankets*) embobiner de

swatter ['swɔtə^r] *n* (*also:* **fly swatter**) tapette *f*

sway [sweɪ] *vi* se balancer, osciller; tanguer ▷ *vt* (*influence*) influencer ▷ *n* (*rule, power*): **~ (over)** emprise *f* (sur); **to hold ~ over sb** avoir de l'emprise sur qn

Swaziland ['swɑːzɪlænd] *n* Swaziland *m*

swear [swɛə^r] (*pt* **swore**, *pp* **sworn**) [swɔː^r, swɔːn] *vt, vi* jurer; **to ~ to sth** jurer de qch; **to ~ an oath** prêter serment

▸ **swear in** *vt* assermenter

swearword ['swɛəwəːd] *n* gros mot, juron *m*

sweat [swɛt] *n* sueur *f*, transpiration *f* ▷ *vi* suer; **in a ~** en sueur

sweatband ['swɛtbænd] *n* (*Sport*) bandeau *m*

sweater ['swɛtə^r] *n* tricot *m*, pull *m*

sweatshirt ['swɛtʃəːt] *n* sweat-shirt *m*

sweatshop ['swɛtʃɔp] *n* atelier *m* où les ouvriers sont exploités

sweaty ['swɛtɪ] *adj* en sueur, moite *or* mouillé(e) de sueur

Swede [swiːd] *n* Suédois(e)

swede [swiːd] *n* (*Brit*) rutabaga *m*

Sweden ['swiːdn] *n* Suède *f*

Swedish ['swiːdɪʃ] *adj* suédois(e) ▷ *n* (*Ling*) suédois *m*

sweep [swiːp] (*pt, pp* **swept**) [swɛpt] *n* coup *m* de balai; (*curve*) grande courbe; (*range*) champ *m*; (*also:* **chimney sweep**) ramoneur *m* ▷ *vt* balayer; (*subj: current*) emporter; (*subj: fashion, craze*) se répandre dans ▷ *vi* avancer majestueusement *or* rapidement; s'élancer; s'étendre

▸ **sweep away** *vt* balayer; entraîner; emporter

▸ **sweep past** *vi* passer majestueusement *or* rapidement

▸ **sweep up** *vt, vi* balayer

sweeper ['swiːpə^r] *n* (*person*) balayeur *m*; (*machine*) balayeuse *f*; (*Football*) libéro *m*

sweeping ['swiːpɪŋ] *adj* (*gesture*) large; circulaire; (*changes, reforms*) radical(e); **a ~ statement** une généralisation hâtive

sweepstake ['swiːpsteɪk] *n* sweepstake *m*

sweet [swiːt] *n* (*Brit: pudding*) dessert *m*; (*candy*) bonbon *m* ▷ *adj* doux (douce); (*not savoury*) sucré(e); (*fresh*) frais (fraîche), pur(e); (*kind*) gentil(le); (*baby*) mignon(ne) ▷ *adv:* **to smell ~** sentir bon; **to taste ~** avoir un goût sucré; **~ and sour** *adj* aigre-doux (douce)

sweetbread ['swiːtbrɛd] *n* ris *m* de veau

sweetcorn ['swiːtkɔːn] *n* maïs doux

sweeten ['swiːtn] *vt* sucrer; (*fig*) adoucir

sweetener ['swiːtnə^r] *n* (*Culin*) édulcorant *m*

sweetheart ['swiːthɑːt] *n* amoureux(-euse)

sweetly ['swiːtlɪ] *adv* (*smile*) gentiment; (*sing, play*) mélodieusement

sweetness ['swiːtnɪs] *n* douceur *f*; (*of taste*) goût sucré

sweet pea *n* pois *m* de senteur

sweet potato *n* patate douce

sweetshop ['swiːtʃɔp] *n* (*Brit*) confiserie *f*

sweet tooth *n:* **to have a ~** aimer les sucreries

swell [swɛl] (*pt* **-ed**, *pp* **swollen** *or* **-ed**) ['swəulən] *n* (*of sea*) houle *f* ▷ *adj* (*US: inf: excellent*) chouette ▷ *vt* (*increase*) grossir, augmenter ▷ *vi* (*increase*) grossir, augmenter; (*sound*) s'enfler; (*Med: also:* **swell up**) enfler

swelling ['swɛlɪŋ] *n* (*Med*) enflure *f*; (: *lump*) grosseur *f*

sweltering ['swɛltərɪŋ] *adj* étouffant(e), oppressant(e)

swept [swɛpt] *pt, pp of* **sweep**

swerve [swəːv] *vi* (*to avoid obstacle*) faire une embardée *or* un écart; (*off the road*) dévier

swift [swɪft] *n* (*bird*) martinet *m* ▷ *adj* rapide, prompt(e)

swiftly ['swɪftlɪ] *adv* rapidement, vite

swiftness ['swɪftnɪs] *n* rapidité *f*

swig [swɪg] *n* (*inf: drink*) lampée *f*

swill [swɪl] *n* pâtée *f* ▷ *vt* (*also:* **swill out, swill down**) laver à grande eau

swim [swɪm] (*pt* **swam**, *pp* **swum**) [swæm, swʌm] *n:* **to go for a ~** aller nager *or* se baigner ▷ *vi* nager; (*Sport*) faire de la natation; (*fig: head, room*) tourner ▷ *vt* traverser (à la nage); (*distance*) faire (à la nage); **to ~ a length** nager une longueur; **to go ~ming** aller nager

swimmer ['swɪmə^r] *n* nageur(-euse)

swimming ['swɪmɪŋ] *n* nage *f*, natation *f*

swimming baths *npl* (*Brit*) piscine *f*

swimming cap *n* bonnet *m* de bain

swimming costume *n* (*Brit*) maillot *m* (de bain)

swimmingly ['swɪmɪŋlɪ] *adv:* **to go ~** (*wonderfully*) se dérouler à merveille

swimming pool *n* piscine *f*

swimming trunks *npl* maillot *m* de bain

swimsuit ['swɪmsuːt] *n* maillot *m* (de bain)

swindle ['swɪndl] *n* escroquerie *f* ▷ *vt* escroquer

swindler ['swɪndlə^r] *n* escroc *m*

swine [swaɪn] *n* (*pl inv*) pourceau *m*, porc *m*; (*inf!*) salaud *m* (!)

swing [swɪŋ] (*pt, pp* **swung**) [swʌŋ] *n* (*in playground*) balançoire *f*; (*movement*) balancement *m*, oscillations *fpl*; (*change in opinion etc*) revirement *m*; (*Mus*) swing *m*; rythme *m* ▷ *vt* balancer, faire osciller; (*also:* **swing round**) tourner, faire virer ▷ *vi* se balancer, osciller; (*also:* **swing round**) virer, tourner; **a ~ to the left** (*Pol*) un revirement en faveur de la gauche; **to be in full ~** battre son plein; **to get into the ~ of things** se mettre dans le bain; **the road ~s south** la route prend la direction sud

swing bridge *n* pont tournant

swing door *n* (*Brit*) porte battante

swingeing ['swɪndʒɪŋ] *adj* (*Brit*) écrasant(e); considérable

swinging ['swɪŋɪŋ] *adj* rythmé(e); entraînant(e); (*fig*) dans le vent; **~ door** (*US*) porte battante

swipe [swaɪp] *n* grand coup; gifle *f* ▷ *vt* (*hit*) frapper à toute volée; gifler; (*inf: steal*) piquer;

(*credit card etc*) faire passer (dans la machine)

swipe card *n* carte *f* magnétique

swirl [swə:l] *n* tourbillon *m* ▷ *vi* tourbillonner, tournoyer

swish [swɪʃ] *adj* (*Brit inf: smart*) rupin(e) ▷ *vi* (*whip*) siffler; (*skirt, long grass*) bruire

Swiss [swɪs] *adj* suisse ▷ *n* (*pl inv*) Suisse(-esse)

Swiss French *adj* suisse romand(e)

Swiss German *adj* suisse-allemand(e)

Swiss roll *n* gâteau roulé

switch [swɪtʃ] *n* (*for light, radio etc*) bouton *m*; (*change*) changement *m*, revirement *m* ▷ *vt* (*change*) changer; (*exchange*) intervertir; (*invert*): **to ~ (round** *or* **over)** changer de place

▶ **switch off** *vt* éteindre; (*engine, machine*) arrêter; **could you ~ off the light?** pouvez-vous éteindre la lumière?

▶ **switch on** *vt* allumer; (*engine, machine*) mettre en marche; (*Brit: water supply*) ouvrir

switchback ['swɪtʃbæk] *n* (*Brit*) montagnes *fpl* russes

switchblade ['swɪtʃbleɪd] *n* (*also*: **switchblade knife**) couteau *m* à cran d'arrêt

switchboard ['swɪtʃbɔːd] *n* (*Tel*) standard *m*

switchboard operator *n* (*Tel*) standardiste *m/f*

Switzerland ['swɪtsələnd] *n* Suisse *f*

swivel ['swɪvl] *vi* (*also*: **swivel round**) pivoter, tourner

swollen ['swəulən] *pp of* **swell** ▷ *adj* (*ankle etc*) enflé(e)

swoon [swuːn] *vi* se pâmer

swoop [swuːp] *n* (*by police etc*) rafle *f*, descente *f*; (*of bird etc*) descente *f* en piqué ▷ *vi* (*bird: also*: **swoop down**) descendre en piqué, piquer

swop [swɔp] *n, vt* = **swap**

sword [sɔːd] *n* épée *f*

swordfish ['sɔːdfɪʃ] *n* espadon *m*

swore [swɔːʳ] *pt of* **swear**

sworn [swɔːn] *pp of* **swear** ▷ *adj* (*statement, evidence*) donné(e) sous serment; (*enemy*) juré(e)

swot [swɔt] *vt, vi* bûcher, potasser

swum [swʌm] *pp of* **swim**

swung [swʌŋ] *pt, pp of* **swing**

sycamore ['sɪkəmɔːʳ] *n* sycomore *m*

sycophant ['sɪkəfænt] *n* flagorneur(-euse)

sycophantic [sɪkə'fæntɪk] *adj* flagorneur(-euse)

Sydney ['sɪdnɪ] *n* Sydney

syllable ['sɪləbl] *n* syllabe *f*

syllabus ['sɪləbəs] *n* programme *m*; **on the ~** au programme

symbol ['sɪmbl] *n* symbole *m*

symbolic [sɪm'bɔlɪk], **symbolical** [sɪm'bɔlɪkl] *adj* symbolique

symbolism ['sɪmbəlɪzəm] *n* symbolisme *m*

symbolize ['sɪmbəlaɪz] *vt* symboliser

symmetrical [sɪ'mɛtrɪkl] *adj* symétrique

symmetry ['sɪmɪtrɪ] *n* symétrie *f*

sympathetic [sɪmpə'θɛtɪk] *adj* (*showing pity*) compatissant(e); (*understanding*) bienveillant(e), compréhensif(-ive); **~ towards** bien disposé(e) envers

sympathetically [sɪmpə'θɛtɪklɪ] *adv* avec compassion (*or* bienveillance)

sympathize ['sɪmpəθaɪz] *vi*: **to ~ with sb** plaindre qn; (*in grief*) s'associer à la douleur de qn; **to ~ with sth** comprendre qch

sympathizer ['sɪmpəθaɪzəʳ] *n* (*Pol*) sympathisant(e)

sympathy ['sɪmpəθɪ] *n* (*pity*) compassion *f*; **sympathies** *npl* (*support*) soutien *m*; **in ~ with** en accord avec; (*strike*) en *or* par solidarité avec; **with our deepest ~** en vous priant d'accepter nos sincères condoléances

symphonic [sɪm'fɔnɪk] *adj* symphonique

symphony ['sɪmfənɪ] *n* symphonie *f*

symphony orchestra *n* orchestre *m* symphonique

symposium [sɪm'pəuzɪəm] *n* symposium *m*

symptom ['sɪmptəm] *n* symptôme *m*; indice *m*

symptomatic [sɪmptə'mætɪk] *adj* symptomatique

synagogue ['sɪnəgɔg] *n* synagogue *f*

sync [sɪŋk] *n* (*inf*): **in/out of ~** bien/mal synchronisé(e); **they're in ~ with each other** (*fig*) le courant passe bien entre eux

synchromesh [sɪŋkrəu'mɛʃ] *n* (*Aut*) synchronisation *f*

synchronize ['sɪŋkrənaɪz] *vt* synchroniser ▷ *vi*: **to ~ with** se produire en même temps que

synchronized swimming ['sɪŋkrənaɪzd-] *n* natation synchronisée

syncopated ['sɪŋkəpeɪtɪd] *adj* syncopé(e)

syndicate ['sɪndɪkɪt] *n* syndicat *m*, coopérative *f*; (*Press*) agence *f* de presse

syndrome ['sɪndrəum] *n* syndrome *m*

synonym ['sɪnənɪm] *n* synonyme *m*

synonymous [sɪ'nɔnɪməs] *adj*: **~ (with)** synonyme (de)

synopsis (*pl* **synopses**) [sɪ'nɔpsɪs, -siːz] *n* résumé *m*, synopsis *m or f*

syntax ['sɪntæks] *n* syntaxe *f*

synthesis (*pl* **syntheses**) ['sɪnθəsɪs, -siːz] *n* synthèse *f*

synthesizer ['sɪnθəsaɪzəʳ] *n* (*Mus*) synthétiseur *m*

synthetic [sɪn'θɛtɪk] *adj* synthétique ▷ *n* matière *f* synthétique; **synthetics** *npl* textiles artificiels

syphilis ['sɪfɪlɪs] *n* syphilis *f*

syphon ['saɪfən] *n, vb* = **siphon**

Syria ['sɪrɪə] *n* Syrie *f*

Syrian ['sɪrɪən] *adj* syrien(ne) ▷ *n* Syrien(ne)

syringe [sɪ'rɪndʒ] *n* seringue *f*

syrup ['sɪrəp] *n* sirop *m*; (*Brit: also*: **golden syrup**) mélasse raffinée

syrupy ['sɪrəpɪ] *adj* sirupeux(-euse)

system ['sɪstəm] *n* système *m*; (*order*) méthode *f*; (*Anat*) organisme *m*

systematic [sɪstə'mætɪk] *adj* systématique; méthodique

system disk *n* (*Comput*) disque *m* système

systems analyst *n* analyste-programmeur *m/f*

Tt

T, t [tiː] n (letter) T, t m; **T for Tommy** T comme Thérèse

TA n abbr (Brit) = **Territorial Army**

ta [taː] excl (Brit inf) merci!

tab [tæb] n abbr = **tabulator** ▷ n (loop on coat etc) attache f; (label) étiquette f; (on drinks can etc) languette f; **to keep ~s on** (fig) surveiller

tabby ['tæbɪ] n (also: **tabby cat**) chat(te) tigré(e)

table ['teɪbl] n table f ▷ vt (Brit: motion etc) présenter; **to lay** or **set the ~** mettre le couvert or la table; **to clear the ~** débarrasser la table; **league ~** (Brit Football, Rugby) classement m (du championnat); **~ of contents** table des matières

tablecloth ['teɪblklɔθ] n nappe f

table d'hôte [taːbl'dəut] adj (meal) à prix fixe

table football n baby-foot m

table lamp n lampe décorative or de table

tablemat ['teɪblmæt] n (for plate) napperon m, set m; (for hot dish) dessous-de-plat m inv

table salt n sel fin or de table

tablespoon ['teɪblspuːn] n cuiller f de service; (also: **tablespoonful**: as measurement) cuillerée f à soupe

tablet ['tæblɪt] n (Med) comprimé m; (: for sucking) pastille f; (of stone) plaque f; **~ of soap** (Brit) savonnette f

table tennis n ping-pong m, tennis m de table

table wine n vin m de table

tabloid ['tæblɔɪd] n (newspaper) quotidien m populaire; voir article

- ● **TABLOID PRESS**
- ●
- ● Le terme tabloid press désigne les journaux
- ● populaires de demi-format où l'on trouve
- ● beaucoup de photos et qui adoptent un style
- ● très concis. Ce type de journaux vise des
- ● lecteurs s'intéressant aux faits divers ayant
- ● un parfum de scandale; voir "quality press".

taboo [tə'buː] adj, n tabou (m)

tabulate ['tæbjuleɪt] vt (data, figures) mettre sous forme de table(s)

tabulator ['tæbjuleɪtə'] n tabulateur m

tachograph ['tækəgrɑːf] n tachygraphe m

tachometer [tæ'kɔmɪtə'] n tachymètre m

tacit ['tæsɪt] adj tacite

taciturn ['tæsɪtəːn] adj taciturne

tack [tæk] n (nail) petit clou; (stitch) point m de bâti; (Naut) bord m, bordée f; (fig) direction f ▷ vt (nail) clouer; (sew) bâtir ▷ vi (Naut) tirer un or des bord(s); **to change ~** virer de bord; **on the wrong ~** (fig) sur la mauvaise voie; **to ~ sth on to (the end of) sth** (of letter, book) rajouter qch à la fin de qch

tackle ['tækl] n matériel m, équipement m; (for lifting) appareil m de levage; (Football, Rugby) plaquage m ▷ vt (difficulty, animal, burglar) s'attaquer à; (person: challenge) s'expliquer avec; (Football, Rugby) plaquer

tacky ['tækɪ] adj collant(e); (paint) pas sec (sèche); (inf: shabby) moche; (pej: poor-quality) minable; (: showing bad taste) ringard(e)

tact [tækt] n tact m

tactful ['tæktful] adj plein(e) de tact

tactfully ['tæktfəlɪ] adv avec tact

tactical ['tæktɪkl] adj tactique; **~ error** erreur f de tactique

tactician [tæk'tɪʃən] n tacticien(ne)

tactics ['tæktɪks] n, npl tactique f

tactless ['tæktlɪs] adj qui manque de tact

tactlessly ['tæktlɪslɪ] adv sans tact

tadpole ['tædpəul] n têtard m

Tadzhikistan [tædʒɪkɪ'staːn] n = **Tajikistan**

taffy ['tæfɪ] n (US) (bonbon m au) caramel m

tag [tæg] n étiquette f; **price/name ~** étiquette (portant le prix/le nom)
 ▶ **tag along** vi suivre

Tahiti [taː'hiːtɪ] n Tahiti m

tail [teɪl] n queue f; (of shirt) pan m ▷ vt (follow) suivre, filer; **tails** npl (suit) habit m; **to turn ~** se sauver à toutes jambes; see also **head**
 ▶ **tail away, tail off** vi (in size, quality etc) baisser peu à peu

tailback ['teɪlbæk] n (Brit) bouchon m

tail coat n habit m

tail end n bout m, fin f

tailgate ['teɪlgeɪt] n (Aut) hayon m arrière

tail light n (Aut) feu m arrière

tailor ['teɪlə'] n tailleur m (artisan) ▷ vt: **to ~ sth (to)** adapter qch exactement (à); **~'s (shop)**

(boutique f de) tailleur m

tailoring ['teɪlərɪŋ] n (cut) coupe f

tailor-made ['teɪlə'meɪd] adj fait(e) sur mesure; (fig) conçu(e) spécialement

tailwind ['teɪlwɪnd] n vent m arrière inv

taint [teɪnt] vt (meat, food) gâter; (fig: reputation) salir

tainted ['teɪntɪd] adj (food) gâté(e); (water, air) infecté(e); (fig) souillé(e)

Taiwan ['taɪ'wɑːn] n Taïwan (no article)

Taiwanese [taɪwə'niːz] adj taïwanais(e) ▷ n inv Taïwanais(e)

Tajikistan [tædʒɪkɪ'stɑːn] n Tadjikistan m/f

take [teɪk] (pt **took**, pp **-n**) [tuk, 'teɪkn] vt prendre; (gain: prize) remporter; (require: effort, courage) demander; (tolerate) accepter, supporter; (hold: passengers etc) contenir; (accompany) emmener, accompagner; (bring, carry) apporter, emporter; (exam) passer, se présenter à; (conduct: meeting) présider ▷ vi (dye, fire etc) prendre ▷ n (Cine) prise f de vues; **to ~ sth from** (drawer etc) prendre qch dans; (person) prendre qch à; **I ~ it that** je suppose que; **I took him for a doctor** je l'ai pris pour un docteur; **to ~ sb's hand** prendre qn par la main; **to ~ for a walk** (child, dog) emmener promener; **to be ~n ill** tomber malade; **to ~ it upon o.s. to do sth** prendre sur soi de faire qch; **~ the first (street) on the left** prenez la première à gauche; **it won't ~ long** ça ne prendra pas longtemps; **I was quite ~n with her/it** elle/cela m'a beaucoup plu

▶ **take after** vt fus ressembler à

▶ **take apart** vt démonter

▶ **take away** vt (carry off) emporter; (remove) enlever; (subtract) soustraire ▷ vi: **to ~ away from** diminuer

▶ **take back** vt (return) rendre, rapporter; (one's words) retirer

▶ **take down** vt (building) démolir; (dismantle: scaffolding) démonter; (letter etc) prendre, écrire

▶ **take in** vt (deceive) tromper, rouler; (understand) comprendre, saisir; (include) couvrir, inclure; (lodger) prendre; (orphan, stray dog) recueillir; (dress, waistband) reprendre

▶ **take off** vi (Aviat) décoller ▷ vt (remove) enlever; (imitate) imiter, pasticher

▶ **take on** vt (work) accepter, se charger de; (employee) prendre, embaucher; (opponent) accepter de se battre contre

▶ **take out** vt sortir; (remove) enlever; (invite) sortir avec; (licence) prendre, se procurer; **to ~ sth out of** enlever qch de; (out of drawer etc) prendre qch dans; **don't ~ it out on me!** ne t'en prends pas à moi!; **to ~ sb out to a restaurant** emmener qn au restaurant

▶ **take over** vt (business) reprendre ▷ vi: **to ~ over from sb** prendre la relève de qn

▶ **take to** vt fus (person) se prendre d'amitié pour; (activity) prendre goût à; **to ~ to doing sth** prendre l'habitude de faire qch

▶ **take up** vt (one's story) reprendre; (dress)

raccourcir; (occupy: time, space) prendre, occuper; (engage in: hobby etc) se mettre à; (accept: offer, challenge) accepter; (absorb: liquids) absorber ▷ vi: **to ~ up with sb** se lier d'amitié avec qn

takeaway ['teɪkəweɪ] (Brit) adj (food) à emporter ▷ n (shop, restaurant) ≈ magasin m qui vend des plats à emporter

take-home pay ['teɪkhəum-] n salaire net

taken ['teɪkən] pp of **take**

takeoff ['teɪkɔf] n (Aviat) décollage m

takeout ['teɪkaut] adj, n (US) = **takeaway**

takeover ['teɪkəuvəʳ] n (Comm) rachat m

takeover bid n offre publique d'achat, OPA f

takings ['teɪkɪŋz] npl (Comm) recette f

talc [tælk] n (also: **talcum powder**) talc m

tale [teɪl] n (story) conte m, histoire f; (account) récit m; (pej) histoire; **to tell ~s** (fig) rapporter

talent ['tælnt] n talent m, don m

talented ['tæləntɪd] adj doué(e), plein(e) de talent

talent scout n découvreur m de vedettes (or joueurs etc)

talisman ['tælɪzmən] n talisman m

talk [tɔːk] n (a speech) causerie f, exposé m; (conversation) discussion f; (interview) entretien m, propos mpl; (gossip) racontars mpl (pej) ▷ vi parler; (chatter) bavarder; **talks** npl (Pol etc) entretiens mpl; conférence f; **to give a ~** faire un exposé; **to ~ about** parler de; (converse) s'entretenir or parler de; **~ing of films, have you seen …?** à propos de films, as-tu vu …?; **to ~ sb out of/into doing** persuader qn de ne pas faire/de faire; **to ~ shop** parler métier or affaires

▶ **talk over** vt discuter (de)

talkative ['tɔːkətɪv] adj bavard(e)

talking point ['tɔːkɪŋ-] n sujet m de conversation

talking-to ['tɔːkɪŋtu] n: **to give sb a good ~** passer un savon à qn

talk show n (TV, Radio) émission-débat f

tall [tɔːl] adj (person) grand(e); (building, tree) haut(e); **to be 6 feet ~** ≈ mesurer 1 mètre 80; **how ~ are you?** combien mesurez-vous?

tallboy ['tɔːlbɔɪ] n (Brit) grande commode f

tallness ['tɔːlnɪs] n grande taille; hauteur f

tall story n histoire f invraisemblable

tally ['tælɪ] n compte m ▷ vi: **to ~ (with)** correspondre (à); **to keep a ~ of sth** tenir le compte de qch

talon ['tælən] n griffe f; (of eagle) serre f

tambourine [tæmbə'riːn] n tambourin m

tame [teɪm] adj apprivoisé(e); (fig: story, style) insipide

Tamil ['tæmɪl] adj tamoul(e) or tamil(e) ▷ n Tamoul(e) or Tamil(e); (Ling) tamoul m or tamil m

tamper ['tæmpəʳ] vi: **to ~ with** toucher à (en cachette ou sans permission)

tampon ['tæmpən] n tampon m hygiénique or périodique

tan [tæn] n (also: **suntan**) bronzage m ▷ vt, vi

bronzer, brunir ▷ *adj* (*colour*) marron clair *inv*; **to get a ~** bronzer

tandem ['tændəm] *n* tandem *m*

tandoori [tæn'duərɪ] *adj* tandouri

tang [tæŋ] *n* odeur (*or* saveur) piquante

tangent ['tændʒənt] *n* (*Math*) tangente *f*; **to go off at a ~** (*fig*) partir dans une digression

tangerine [tændʒə'riːn] *n* mandarine *f*

tangible ['tændʒəbl] *adj* tangible; **~ assets** biens réels

Tangier [tæn'dʒɪəᵣ] *n* Tanger

tangle ['tæŋgl] *n* enchevêtrement *m* ▷ *vt* enchevêtrer; **to get in(to) a ~** s'emmêler

tango ['tæŋgəu] *n* tango *m*

tank [tæŋk] *n* réservoir *m*; (*for processing*) cuve *f*; (*for fish*) aquarium *m*; (*Mil*) char *m* d'assaut, tank *m*

tankard ['tæŋkəd] *n* chope *f*

tanker ['tæŋkəᵣ] *n* (*ship*) pétrolier *m*, tanker *m*; (*truck*) camion-citerne *m*; (*Rail*) wagon-citerne *m*

tanned [tænd] *adj* bronzé(e)

tannin ['tænɪn] *n* tanin *m*

tanning ['tænɪŋ] *n* (*of leather*) tannage *m*

tannoy® ['tænɔɪ] *n* (*Brit*) haut-parleur *m*; **over the tannoy** par haut-parleur

tantalizing ['tæntəlaɪzɪŋ] *adj* (*smell*) extrêmement appétissant(e); (*offer*) terriblement tentant(e)

tantamount ['tæntəmaunt] *adj*: **~ to** qui équivaut à

tantrum ['tæntrəm] *n* accès *m* de colère; **to throw a ~** piquer une colère

Tanzania [tænzə'nɪə] *n* Tanzanie *f*

Tanzanian [tænzə'nɪən] *adj* tanzanien(ne) ▷ *n* Tanzanien(ne)

tap [tæp] *n* (*on sink etc*) robinet *m*; (*gentle blow*) petite tape ▷ *vt* frapper *or* taper légèrement; (*resources*) exploiter, utiliser; (*telephone*) mettre sur écoute; **on ~** (*beer*) en tonneau; (*fig: resources*) disponible

tap dancing ['tæpdɑːnsɪŋ] *n* claquettes *fpl*

tape [teɪp] *n* (*for tying*) ruban *m*; (*also:* **magnetic tape**) bande *f* (magnétique); (*cassette*) cassette *f*; (*sticky*) Scotch® *m* ▷ *vt* (*record*) enregistrer (au magnétoscope *or* sur cassette); (*stick*) coller avec du Scotch®; **on ~** (*song etc*) enregistré(e)

tape deck *n* platine *f* d'enregistrement

tape measure *n* mètre *m* à ruban

taper ['teɪpəᵣ] *n* cierge *m* ▷ *vi* s'effiler

tape recorder *n* magnétophone *m*

tapered ['teɪpəd], **tapering** ['teɪpərɪŋ] *adj* fuselé(e), effilé(e)

tapestry ['tæpɪstrɪ] *n* tapisserie *f*

tape-worm ['teɪpwəːm] *n* ver *m* solitaire, ténia *m*

tapioca [tæpɪ'əukə] *n* tapioca *m*

tappet ['tæpɪt] *n* (*Aut*) poussoir *m* (de soupape)

tar [tɑː] *n* goudron *m*; **low-/middle-~ cigarettes** cigarettes *fpl* à faible/moyenne teneur en goudron

tarantula [tə'ræntjulə] *n* tarentule *f*

tardy ['tɑːdɪ] *adj* tardif(-ive)

target ['tɑːgɪt] *n* cible *f*; (*fig: objective*) objectif *m*; **to be on ~** (*project*) progresser comme prévu

target practice *n* exercices *mpl* de tir (à la cible)

tariff ['tærɪf] *n* (*Comm*) tarif *m*; (*taxes*) tarif douanier

tarmac ['tɑːmæk] *n* (*Brit: on road*) macadam *m*; (*Aviat*) aire *f* d'envol ▷ *vt* (*Brit*) goudronner

tarnish ['tɑːnɪʃ] *vt* ternir

tarot ['tærəu] *n* tarot *m*

tarpaulin [tɑː'pɔːlɪn] *n* bâche goudronnée

tarragon ['tærəgən] *n* estragon *m*

tart [tɑːt] *n* (*Culin*) tarte *f*; (*Brit inf: pej: prostitute*) poule *f* ▷ *adj* (*flavour*) âpre, aigrelet(te)

  ▶ **tart up** *vt* (*inf*): **to ~ o.s. up** se faire beau (belle); (: *pej*) s'attifer

tartan ['tɑːtn] *n* tartan *m* ▷ *adj* écossais(e)

tartar ['tɑːtəᵣ] *n* (*on teeth*) tartre *m*

tartar sauce, tartare sauce *n* sauce *f* tartare

task [tɑːsk] *n* tâche *f*; **to take to ~** prendre à partie

task force *n* (*Mil, Police*) détachement spécial

taskmaster ['tɑːskmɑːstəᵣ] *n*: **he's a hard ~** il est très exigeant dans le travail

Tasmania [tæz'meɪnɪə] *n* Tasmanie *f*

tassel ['tæsl] *n* gland *m*; pompon *m*

taste [teɪst] *n* goût *m*; (*fig: glimpse, idea*) idée *f*, aperçu *m* ▷ *vt* goûter ▷ *vi*: **to ~ of** (*fish etc*) avoir le *or* un goût de; **it ~s like fish** ça a un *or* le goût de poisson, on dirait du poisson; **what does it ~ like?** quel goût ça a?; **you can ~ the garlic (in it)** on sent bien l'ail; **to have a ~ of sth** goûter (à) qch; **can I have a ~?** je peux goûter?; **to have a ~ for sth** aimer qch, avoir un penchant pour qch; **to be in good/bad** *or* **poor ~** être de bon/mauvais goût

taste bud *n* papille *f*

tasteful ['teɪstful] *adj* de bon goût

tastefully ['teɪstfəlɪ] *adv* avec goût

tasteless ['teɪstlɪs] *adj* (*food*) insipide; (*remark*) de mauvais goût

tasty ['teɪstɪ] *adj* savoureux(-euse), délicieux(-euse)

tattered ['tætəd] *adj see* **tatters**

tatters ['tætəz] *npl*: **in ~** (*also:* **tattered**) en lambeaux

tattoo [tə'tuː] *n* tatouage *m*; (*spectacle*) parade *f* militaire ▷ *vt* tatouer

tatty ['tætɪ] *adj* (*Brit inf*) défraîchi(e), en piteux état

taught [tɔːt] *pt, pp of* **teach**

taunt [tɔːnt] *n* raillerie *f* ▷ *vt* railler

Taurus ['tɔːrəs] *n* le Taureau; **to be ~** être du Taureau

taut [tɔːt] *adj* tendu(e)

tavern ['tævən] *n* taverne *f*

tawdry ['tɔːdrɪ] *adj* (d'un mauvais goût) criard

tawny ['tɔːnɪ] *adj* fauve (*couleur*)

tax [tæks] *n* (*on goods etc*) taxe *f*; (*on income*) impôts *mpl*, contributions *fpl* ▷ *vt* taxer; imposer; (*fig: patience etc*) mettre à l'épreuve; **before/after ~** avant/après l'impôt; **free of ~** exonéré(e) d'impôt

taxable ['tæksəbl] *adj* (*income*) imposable
tax allowance *n* part *f* du revenu non imposable, abattement *m* à la base
taxation [tæk'seɪʃən] *n* taxation *f*; impôts *mpl*, contributions *fpl*; **system of** ~ système fiscal
tax avoidance *n* évasion fiscale
tax collector *n* percepteur *m*
tax disc *n* (*Brit Aut*) vignette *f* (automobile)
tax evasion *n* fraude fiscale
tax exemption *n* exonération fiscale, exemption *f* d'impôts
tax exile *n* personne qui s'expatrie pour raisons fiscales
tax-free ['tæksfri:] *adj* exempt(e) d'impôts
tax haven *n* paradis fiscal
taxi ['tæksɪ] *n* taxi *m* ▷ *vi* (*Aviat*) rouler (lentement) au sol
taxidermist ['tæksɪdə:mɪst] *n* empailleur(-euse) (*d'animaux*)
taxi driver *n* chauffeur *m* de taxi
tax inspector *n* (*Brit*) percepteur *m*
taxi rank, (*Brit*) **taxi stand** *n* station *f* de taxis
tax payer [-peɪər] *n* contribuable *m/f*
tax rebate *n* ristourne *f* d'impôt
tax relief *n* dégrèvement *or* allègement fiscal, réduction *f* d'impôt
tax return *n* déclaration *f* d'impôts *or* de revenus
tax year *n* année fiscale
TB *n abbr* = **tuberculosis**
tbc *abbr* = **to be confirmed**
TD *n abbr* (*US*) = **Treasury Department**; (: *Football*) = **touchdown**
tea [ti:] *n* thé *m*; (*Brit: snack: for children*) goûter *m*; **high** ~ (*Brit*) collation combinant goûter et dîner
tea bag *n* sachet *m* de thé
tea break *n* (*Brit*) pause-thé *f*
teacake ['ti:keɪk] *n* (*Brit*) ≈ petit pain aux raisins
teach (*pt, pp* **taught**) [ti:tʃ, tɔ:t] *vt*: **to** ~ **sb sth, to** ~ **sth to sb** apprendre qch à qn; (*in school etc*) enseigner qch à qn ▷ *vi* enseigner; **it taught him a lesson** (*fig*) ça lui a servi de leçon
teacher ['ti:tʃər] *n* (*in secondary school*) professeur *m*; (*in primary school*) instituteur(-trice); **French** ~ professeur de français
teacher training college *n* (*for primary schools*) ≈ école normale d'instituteurs; (*for secondary schools*) collège *m* de formation pédagogique (*pour l'enseignement secondaire*)
teaching ['ti:tʃɪŋ] *n* enseignement *m*
teaching aids *npl* supports *mpl* pédagogiques
teaching hospital *n* (*Brit*) C.H.U. *m*, centre *m* hospitalo-universitaire
teaching staff *n* (*Brit*) enseignants *mpl*
tea cosy *n* couvre-théière *m*
teacup ['ti:kʌp] *n* tasse *f* à thé
teak [ti:k] *n* teck *m* ▷ *adj* en *or* de teck
tea leaves *npl* feuilles *fpl* de thé
team [ti:m] *n* équipe *f*; (*of animals*) attelage *m*
  ▶ **team up** *vi*: **to** ~ **up (with)** faire équipe (avec)
team games *npl* jeux *mpl* d'équipe
teamwork ['ti:mwə:k] *n* travail *m* d'équipe
tea party *n* thé *m* (*réception*)

teapot ['ti:pɔt] *n* théière *f*
tear[1] ['tɪər] *n* larme *f*; **in** ~**s** en larmes; **to burst into** ~**s** fondre en larmes
tear[2] [tɛər] (*pt* **tore**, *pp* **torn**) [tɔ:[r], tɔ:n] *n* déchirure *f* ▷ *vt* déchirer ▷ *vi* se déchirer; **to** ~ **to pieces** *or* **to bits** *or* **to shreds** mettre en pièces; (*fig*) démolir
  ▶ **tear along** *vi* (*rush*) aller à toute vitesse
  ▶ **tear apart** *vt* (*also fig*) déchirer
  ▶ **tear away** *vt*: **to** ~ **o.s. away (from sth)** (*fig*) s'arracher (de qch)
  ▶ **tear down** *vt* (*building, statue*) démolir; (*poster, flag*) arracher
  ▶ **tear off** *vt* (*sheet of paper etc*) arracher; (*one's clothes*) enlever à toute vitesse
  ▶ **tear out** *vt* (*sheet of paper, cheque*) arracher
  ▶ **tear up** *vt* (*sheet of paper etc*) déchirer, mettre en morceaux *or* pièces
tearaway ['tɛərəweɪ] *n* (*inf*) casse-cou *m inv*
teardrop ['tɪədrɔp] *n* larme *f*
tearful ['tɪəful] *adj* larmoyant(e)
tear gas ['tɪə-] *n* gaz *m* lacrymogène
tearoom ['ti:ru:m] *n* salon *m* de thé
tease [ti:z] *n* taquin(e) ▷ *vt* taquiner; (*unkindly*) tourmenter
tea set *n* service *m* à thé
teashop ['ti:ʃɔp] *n* (*Brit*) salon *m* de thé
teaspoon ['ti:spu:n] *n* petite cuiller; (*also:* **teaspoonful**: *as measurement*) ≈ cuillerée *f* à café
tea strainer *n* passoire *f* (à thé)
teat [ti:t] *n* tétine *f*
teatime ['ti:taɪm] *n* l'heure *f* du thé
tea towel *n* (*Brit*) torchon *m* (à vaisselle)
tea urn *n* fontaine *f* à thé
tech [tɛk] *n abbr* (*inf*) = **technology; technical college**
technical ['tɛknɪkl] *adj* technique
technical college *n* C.E.T. *m*, collège *m* d'enseignement technique
technicality [tɛknɪ'kælɪtɪ] *n* technicité *f*; (*detail*) détail *m* technique; **on a legal** ~ à cause de (*or* grâce à) l'application à la lettre d'une subtilité juridique; pour vice de forme
technically ['tɛknɪklɪ] *adv* techniquement; (*strictly speaking*) en théorie, en principe
technician [tɛk'nɪʃən] *n* technicien(ne)
technique [tɛk'ni:k] *n* technique *f*
techno ['tɛknəu] *n* (*Mus*) techno *f*
technocrat ['tɛknəkræt] *n* technocrate *m/f*
technological [tɛknə'lɔdʒɪkl] *adj* technologique
technologist [tɛk'nɔlədʒɪst] *n* technologue *m/f*
technology [tɛk'nɔlədʒɪ] *n* technologie *f*
teddy ['tɛdɪ], **teddy bear** *n* ours *m* (en peluche)
tedious ['ti:dɪəs] *adj* fastidieux(-euse)
tedium ['ti:dɪəm] *n* ennui *m*
tee [ti:] *n* (*Golf*) tee *m*
teem [ti:m] *vi*: **to** ~ **(with)** grouiller (de); **it is** ~**ing (with rain)** il pleut à torrents
teen [ti:n] *adj* = **teenage** ▷ *n* (*US*) = **teenager**
teenage ['ti:neɪdʒ] *adj* (*fashions etc*) pour jeunes, pour adolescents; (*child*) qui est adolescent(e)
teenager ['ti:neɪdʒər] *n* adolescent(e)

teens [ti:nz] *npl*: **to be in one's** ~ être adolescent(e)

tee-shirt ['ti:ʃəːt] *n* = **T-shirt**

teeter ['ti:təʳ] *vi* chanceler, vaciller

teeth [ti:θ] *npl of* **tooth**

teethe [ti:ð] *vi* percer ses dents

teething ring ['ti:ðɪŋ-] *n* anneau *m* (*pour bébé qui perce ses dents*)

teething troubles ['ti:ðɪŋ-] *npl* (*fig*) difficultés initiales

teetotal ['ti:'təutl] *adj* (*person*) qui ne boit jamais d'alcool

teetotaller, (US) **teetotaler** ['ti:'təutləʳ] *n* personne *f* qui ne boit jamais d'alcool

TEFL ['tɛfl] *n abbr* = **Teaching of English as a Foreign Language**

Teflon® ['tɛflɔn] *n* Téflon® *m*

Teheran [tɛə'rɑːn] *n* Téhéran

tel. *abbr* (= *telephone*) tél

Tel Aviv ['tɛlə'viːv] *n* Tel Aviv

telecast ['tɛlɪkɑːst] *vt* télédiffuser, téléviser

telecommunications ['tɛlɪkəmjuːnɪ'keɪʃənz] *n* télécommunications *fpl*

teleconferencing [tɛlɪ'kɔnfərənsɪŋ] *n* téléconférence(s) *f(pl)*

telegram ['tɛlɪɡræm] *n* télégramme *m*

telegraph ['tɛlɪɡrɑːf] *n* télégraphe *m*

telegraphic [tɛlɪ'ɡræfɪk] *adj* télégraphique

telegraph pole ['tɛlɪɡrɑːf-] *n* poteau *m* télégraphique

telegraph wire *n* fil *m* télégraphique

telepathic [tɛlɪ'pæθɪk] *adj* télépathique

telepathy [tə'lɛpəθɪ] *n* télépathie *f*

telephone ['tɛlɪfəun] *n* téléphone *m* ▷ *vt* (*person*) téléphoner à; (*message*) téléphoner; **to have a** ~ (*Brit*): **to be on the** ~ (*subscriber*) être abonné(e) au téléphone; **to be on the** ~ (*be speaking*) être au téléphone

telephone book *n* = **telephone directory**

telephone booth, (*Brit*) **telephone box** *n* cabine *f* téléphonique

telephone call *n* appel *m* téléphonique

telephone directory *n* annuaire *m* (du téléphone)

telephone exchange *n* central *m* (téléphonique)

telephone number *n* numéro *m* de téléphone

telephone operator *n* téléphoniste *m/f*, standardiste *m/f*

telephone tapping [-tæpɪŋ] *n* mise *f* sur écoute

telephonist [tə'lɛfənɪst] *n* (*Brit*) téléphoniste *m/f*

telephoto ['tɛlɪfəutəu] *adj*: ~ **lens** téléobjectif *m*

teleprinter ['tɛlɪprɪntəʳ] *n* téléscripteur *m*

telesales ['tɛlɪseɪlz] *npl* télévente *f*

telescope ['tɛlɪskəup] *n* télescope *m* ▷ *vi* se télescoper ▷ *vt* télescoper

telescopic [tɛlɪ'skɔpɪk] *adj* télescopique; (*umbrella*) à manche télescopique

Teletext® ['tɛlɪtɛkst] *n* télétexte *m*

telethon ['tɛlɪθɔn] *n* téléthon *m*

televise ['tɛlɪvaɪz] *vt* téléviser

television ['tɛlɪvɪʒən] *n* télévision *f*; **on** ~ à la télévision

television licence *n* (*Brit*) redevance *f* (de l'audio-visuel)

television programme *n* émission *f* de télévision

television set *n* poste *m* de télévision, téléviseur *m*

telex ['tɛlɛks] *n* télex *m* ▷ *vt* (*message*) envoyer par télex; (*person*) envoyer un télex à ▷ *vi* envoyer un télex

tell (*pt, pp* **told**) [tɛl, təuld] *vt* dire; (*relate: story*) raconter; (*distinguish*): **to** ~ **sth from** distinguer qch de ▷ *vi* (*talk*): **to** ~ **of** parler de; (*have effect*) se faire sentir, se voir; **to** ~ **sb to do** dire à qn de faire; **to** ~ **sb about sth** (*place, object etc*) parler de qch à qn; (*what happened etc*) raconter qch à qn; **to** ~ **the time** (*know how to*) savoir lire l'heure; **can you** ~ **me the time?** pourriez-vous me dire l'heure?; **(I)** ~ **you what, ...** écoute, ...; **I can't** ~ **them apart** je n'arrive pas à les distinguer

▶ **tell off** *vt* réprimander, gronder

▶ **tell on** *vt fus* (*inform against*) dénoncer, rapporter contre

teller ['tɛləʳ] *n* (*in bank*) caissier(-ière)

telling ['tɛlɪŋ] *adj* (*remark, detail*) révélateur(-trice)

telltale ['tɛlteɪl] *n* rapporteur(-euse) ▷ *adj* (*sign*) éloquent(e), révélateur(-trice)

telly ['tɛlɪ] *n abbr* (*Brit inf*: = *television*) télé *f*

temerity [tə'mɛrɪtɪ] *n* témérité *f*

temp [tɛmp] *n* (*Brit*: = *temporary worker*) intérimaire *m/f* ▷ *vi* travailler comme intérimaire

temper ['tɛmpəʳ] *n* (*nature*) caractère *m*; (*mood*) humeur *f*; (*fit of anger*) colère *f* ▷ *vt* (*moderate*) tempérer, adoucir; **to be in a** ~ être en colère; **to lose one's** ~ se mettre en colère; **to keep one's** ~ rester calme

temperament ['tɛmprəmənt] *n* (*nature*) tempérament *m*

temperamental [tɛmprə'mɛntl] *adj* capricieux(-euse)

temperance ['tɛmpərns] *n* modération *f*; (*in drinking*) tempérance *f*

temperate ['tɛmprət] *adj* modéré(e); (*climate*) tempéré(e)

temperature ['tɛmprətʃəʳ] *n* température *f*; **to have** *or* **run a** ~ avoir de la fièvre

temperature chart *n* (*Med*) feuille *f* de température

tempered ['tɛmpəd] *adj* (*steel*) trempé(e)

tempest ['tɛmpɪst] *n* tempête *f*

tempestuous [tɛm'pɛstjuəs] *adj* (*fig*) orageux(-euse); (: *person*) passionné(e)

tempi ['tɛmpiː] *npl of* **tempo**

template ['tɛmplɪt] *n* patron *m*

temple ['tɛmpl] *n* (*building*) temple *m*; (*Anat*) tempe *f*

templet ['tɛmplɪt] *n* = **template**

tempo (*pl* **-s** *or* **tempi**) ['tɛmpəu, 'tɛmpiː] *n* tempo *m*; (*fig: of life etc*) rythme *m*

temporal ['tɛmpərl] *adj* temporel(le)

temporarily ['tɛmpərərɪlɪ] *adv* temporairement; provisoirement

temporary ['tɛmpərərɪ] *adj* temporaire, provisoire; (*job, worker*) temporaire; **~ secretary** (secrétaire *f*) intérimaire *f*; **a ~ teacher** un professeur remplaçant *or* suppléant

temporize ['tɛmpəraɪz] *vi* atermoyer; transiger

tempt [tɛmpt] *vt* tenter; **to ~ sb into doing** induire qn à faire; **to be ~ed to do sth** être tenté(e) de faire qch

temptation [tɛmp'teɪʃən] *n* tentation *f*

tempting ['tɛmptɪŋ] *adj* tentant(e); (*food*) appétissant(e)

ten [tɛn] *num* dix ▷ *n*: **~s of thousands** des dizaines *fpl* de milliers

tenable ['tɛnəbl] *adj* défendable

tenacious [tə'neɪʃəs] *adj* tenace

tenacity [tə'næsɪtɪ] *n* ténacité *f*

tenancy ['tɛnənsɪ] *n* location *f*; état *m* de locataire

tenant ['tɛnənt] *n* locataire *m/f*

tend [tɛnd] *vt* s'occuper de; (*sick etc*) soigner ▷ *vi*: **to ~ to do** avoir tendance à faire; (*colour*): **to ~ to** tirer sur

tendency ['tɛndənsɪ] *n* tendance *f*

tender ['tɛndə^r] *adj* tendre; (*delicate*) délicat(e); (*sore*) sensible; (*affectionate*) tendre, doux (douce) ▷ *n* (*Comm: offer*) soumission *f*; (*money*): **legal ~** cours légal ▷ *vt* offrir; **to ~ one's resignation** donner sa démission; **to put in a ~ (for)** faire une soumission (pour); **to put work out to ~** (*Brit*) mettre un contrat en adjudication

tenderize ['tɛndəraɪz] *vt* (*Culin*) attendrir

tenderly ['tɛndəlɪ] *adv* tendrement

tenderness ['tɛndənɪs] *n* tendresse *f*; (*of meat*) tendreté *f*

tendon ['tɛndən] *n* tendon *m*

tenement ['tɛnəmənt] *n* immeuble *m* (de rapport)

Tenerife [tɛnə'riːf] *n* Ténérife *f*

tenet ['tɛnət] *n* principe *m*

Tenn. *abbr* (*US*) = **Tennessee**

tenner ['tɛnə^r] *n* (*Brit inf*) billet *m* de dix livres

tennis ['tɛnɪs] *n* tennis *m* ▷ *cpd* (*club, match, racket, player*) de tennis

tennis ball *n* balle *f* de tennis

tennis court *n* (court *m* de) tennis *m*

tennis elbow *n* (*Med*) synovite *f* du coude

tennis match *n* match *m* de tennis

tennis player *n* joueur(-euse) de tennis

tennis racket *n* raquette *f* de tennis

tennis shoes *npl* (chaussures *fpl* de) tennis *mpl*

tenor ['tɛnə^r] *n* (*Mus*) ténor *m*; (*of speech etc*) sens général

tenpin bowling ['tɛnpɪn-] *n* (*Brit*) bowling *m* (à 10 quilles)

tense [tɛns] *adj* tendu(e); (*person*) tendu, crispé(e) ▷ *n* (*Ling*) temps *m* ▷ *vt* (*tighten: muscles*) tendre

tenseness ['tɛnsnɪs] *n* tension *f*

tension ['tɛnʃən] *n* tension *f*

tent [tɛnt] *n* tente *f*

tentacle ['tɛntəkl] *n* tentacule *m*

tentative ['tɛntətɪv] *adj* timide, hésitant(e); (*conclusion*) provisoire

tenterhooks ['tɛntəhuks] *npl*: **on ~** sur des charbons ardents

tenth [tɛnθ] *num* dixième

tent peg *n* piquet *m* de tente

tent pole *n* montant *m* de tente

tenuous ['tɛnjuəs] *adj* ténu(e)

tenure ['tɛnjuə^r] *n* (*of property*) bail *m*; (*of job*) période *f* de jouissance; statut *m* de titulaire

tepid ['tɛpɪd] *adj* tiède

Ter. *abbr* = **terrace**

term [təːm] *n* (*limit*) terme *m*; (*word*) terme, mot *m*; (*Scol*) trimestre *m*; (*Law*) session *f* ▷ *vt* appeler; **terms** *npl* (*conditions*) conditions *fpl*; (*Comm*) tarif *m*; **~ of imprisonment** peine *f* de prison; **his ~ of office** la période où il était en fonction; **in the short/long ~** à court/long terme; **"easy ~s"** (*Comm*) "facilités de paiement"; **to come to ~s with** (*problem*) faire face à; **to be on good ~s with** bien s'entendre avec, être en bons termes avec

terminal ['təːmɪnl] *adj* terminal(e); (*disease*) dans sa phase terminale; (*patient*) incurable ▷ *n* (*Elec*) borne *f*; (*for oil, ore etc, also Comput*) terminal *m*; (*also*: **air terminal**) aérogare *f*; (*Brit: also*: **coach terminal**) gare routière

terminally ['təːmɪnlɪ] *adv*: **to be ~ ill** être condamné(e)

terminate ['təːmɪneɪt] *vt* mettre fin à; (*pregnancy*) interrompre ▷ *vi*: **to ~ in** finir en *or* par

termination [təːmɪ'neɪʃən] *n* fin *f*; cessation *f*; (*of contract*) résiliation *f*; **~ of pregnancy** (*Med*) interruption *f* de grossesse

termini ['təːmɪnaɪ] *npl of* **terminus**

terminology [təːmɪ'nɔlədʒɪ] *n* terminologie *f*

terminus (*pl* **termini**) ['təːmɪnəs, 'təːmɪnaɪ] *n* terminus *m inv*

termite ['təːmaɪt] *n* termite *m*

term paper *n* (*US University*) dissertation trimestrielle

terrace ['tɛrəs] *n* terrasse *f*; (*Brit: row of houses*) rangée *f* de maisons (*attenantes les unes aux autres*); **the ~s** (*Brit Sport*) les gradins *mpl*

terraced ['tɛrəst] *adj* (*garden*) en terrasses; (*in a row: house*) attenant(e) aux maisons voisines

terracotta ['tɛrə'kɔtə] *n* terre cuite

terrain [tɛ'reɪn] *n* terrain *m* (sol)

terrestrial [tɪ'rɛstrɪəl] *adj* terrestre

terrible ['tɛrɪbl] *adj* terrible, atroce; (*weather, work*) affreux(-euse), épouvantable

terribly ['tɛrɪblɪ] *adv* terriblement; (*very badly*) affreusement mal

terrier ['tɛrɪə^r] *n* terrier *m* (*chien*)

terrific [tə'rɪfɪk] *adj* (*very great*) fantastique, incroyable, terrible; (*wonderful*) formidable, sensationnel(le)

terrified ['tɛrɪfaɪd] *adj* terrifié(e); **to be ~ of sth**

avoir très peur de qch
terrify ['tɛrɪfaɪ] *vt* terrifier
terrifying ['tɛrɪfaɪɪŋ] *adj* terrifiant(e)
territorial [tɛrɪ'tɔːrɪəl] *adj* territorial(e)
territorial waters *npl* eaux territoriales
territory ['tɛrɪtərɪ] *n* territoire *m*
terror ['tɛrə^r] *n* terreur *f*
terrorism ['tɛrərɪzəm] *n* terrorisme *m*
terrorist ['tɛrərɪst] *n* terroriste *m/f*
terrorist attack *n* attentat *m* terroriste
terrorize ['tɛrəraɪz] *vt* terroriser
terse [təːs] *adj* (*style*) concis(e); (*reply*) laconique
tertiary ['təːʃərɪ] *adj* tertiaire; **~ education** (*Brit*) enseignement *m* postscolaire
TESL ['tɛsl] *n abbr* = **Teaching of English as a Second Language**
test [tɛst] *n* (*trial, check*) essai *m*; (: *of goods in factory*) contrôle *m*; (*of courage etc*) épreuve *f*; (*Med*) examen *m*; (*Chem*) analyse *f*; (*exam: of intelligence etc*) test *m* (d'aptitude); (*Scol*) interrogation *f* de contrôle; (*also:* **driving test**) (examen du) permis *m* de conduire ▷ *vt* essayer; contrôler; mettre à l'épreuve; examiner; analyser; tester; faire subir une interrogation à; **to put sth to the ~** mettre qch à l'épreuve
testament ['tɛstəmənt] *n* testament *m*; **the Old/New T~** l'Ancien/le Nouveau Testament
test ban *n* (*also:* **nuclear test ban**) interdiction *f* des essais nucléaires
test case *n* (*Law*) affaire *f* qui fait jurisprudence
testes ['tɛstiːz] *npl* testicules *mpl*
test flight *n* vol *m* d'essai
testicle ['tɛstɪkl] *n* testicule *m*
testify ['tɛstɪfaɪ] *vi* (*Law*) témoigner, déposer; **to ~ to sth** (*Law*) attester qch; (*gen*) témoigner de qch
testimonial [tɛstɪ'məunɪəl] *n* (*Brit: reference*) recommandation *f*; (*gift*) témoignage *m* d'estime
testimony ['tɛstɪmənɪ] *n* (*Law*) témoignage *m*, déposition *f*
testing ['tɛstɪŋ] *adj* (*situation, period*) difficile
test match *n* (*Cricket, Rugby*) match international
testosterone [tɛs'tɔstərəun] *n* testostérone *f*
test paper *n* (*Scol*) interrogation écrite
test pilot *n* pilote *m* d'essai
test tube *n* éprouvette *f*
test-tube baby ['tɛsttjuːb-] *n* bébé-éprouvette *m*
testy ['tɛstɪ] *adj* irritable
tetanus ['tɛtənəs] *n* tétanos *m*
tetchy ['tɛtʃɪ] *adj* hargneux(-euse)
tether ['tɛðə^r] *vt* attacher ▷ *n*: **at the end of one's ~** à bout (de patience)
Tex. *abbr* (*US*) = **Texas**
text [tɛkst] *n* texte *m*; (*on mobile phone*) texto *m*, SMS *m inv* ▷ *vt* (*inf*) envoyer un texto *or* SMS à
textbook ['tɛkstbuk] *n* manuel *m*
textile ['tɛkstaɪl] *n* textile *m*

text message *n* texto *m*, SMS *m inv*
text messaging [-'mɛsɪdʒɪŋ] *n* messagerie textuelle
textual ['tɛkstjuəl] *adj* textuel(le)
texture ['tɛkstʃə^r] *n* texture *f*; (*of skin, paper etc*) grain *m*
TGIF *abbr* (*inf*) = **thank God it's Friday**
TGWU *n abbr* (*Brit*: = *Transport and General Workers' Union*) *syndicat de transporteurs*
Thai [taɪ] *adj* thaïlandais(e) ▷ *n* Thaïlandais(e); (*Ling*) thaï *m*
Thailand ['taɪlænd] *n* Thaïlande *f*
Thames [tɛmz] *n*: **the (River) ~** la Tamise
than [ðæn, ðən] *conj* que; (*with numerals*): **more ~ 10/once** plus de 10/d'une fois; **I have more/less ~ you** j'en ai plus/moins que toi; **she has more apples ~ pears** elle a plus de pommes que de poires; **it is better to phone ~ to write** il vaut mieux téléphoner (plutôt) qu'écrire; **she is older ~ you think** elle est plus âgée que tu le crois; **no sooner did he leave ~ the phone rang** il venait de partir quand le téléphone a sonné
thank [θæŋk] *vt* remercier, dire merci à; **thanks** *npl* remerciements *mpl* ▷ *excl* merci!; **~ you (very much)** merci (beaucoup); **~ heavens, ~ God** Dieu merci; **~s to** (*prep*) grâce à
thankful ['θæŋkful] *adj*: **~ (for)** reconnaissant(e) (de); **~ for/that** (*relieved*) soulagé(e) de/que
thankfully ['θæŋkfəlɪ] *adv* avec reconnaissance; avec soulagement; (*fortunately*) heureusement; **~ there were few victims** il y eut fort heureusement peu de victimes
thankless ['θæŋklɪs] *adj* ingrat(e)
Thanksgiving ['θæŋksgɪvɪŋ], **Thanksgiving Day** *n* jour *m* d'action de grâce

⊙ KEYWORD

that [ðæt] *adj* (*demonstrative: pl* **those**) ce, cet + *vowel or h mute*, cette *f*; **that man/woman/book** cet homme/cette femme/ce livre; (*not this*) cet homme-là/cette femme-là/ce livre-là; **that one** celui-là (celle-là)
▷ *pron* **1** (*demonstrative: pl* **those**) ce; (*not this one*) cela, ça; (*that one*) celui (celle); **who's that?** qui est-ce?; **what's that?** qu'est-ce que c'est?; **is that you?** c'est toi?; **I prefer this to that** je préfère ceci à cela *or* ça; **that's what he said** c'est *or* voilà ce qu'il a dit; **will you eat all that?** tu vas manger tout ça?; **that is (to say)** c'est-à-dire, à savoir; **at** *or* **with that, he ...** là-dessus, il ...; **do it like that** fais-le comme ça
2 (*relative: subject*) qui; (: *object*) que; (: *after prep*) lequel (laquelle), lesquels (lesquelles) *pl*; **the book that I read** le livre que j'ai lu; **the books that are in the library** les livres qui sont dans la bibliothèque; **the box that I put it in** la boîte dans laquelle je l'ai mis; **the people that I spoke to** les gens auxquels *or* à qui j'ai parlé; **not that I know of** pas à ma connaissance

3 (relative: of time) où; **the day that he came** le jour où il est venu
▷ conj que; **he thought that I was ill** il pensait que j'étais malade
▷ adv (demonstrative): **I don't like it that much** ça ne me plaît pas tant que ça; **I didn't know it was that bad** je ne savais pas que c'était si or aussi mauvais; **that high** aussi haut; si haut; **it's about that high** c'est à peu près de cette hauteur

thatched [θætʃt] adj (roof) de chaume; **~ cottage** chaumière f
Thatcherism ['θætʃərɪzəm] n thatchérisme m
thaw [θɔ:] n dégel m ▷ vi (ice) fondre; (food) dégeler ▷ vt (food) (faire) dégeler; **it's ~ing** (weather) il dégèle

 KEYWORD

the [ði:, ðə] def art **1** (gen) le, la f, l' + vowel or h mute, les pl (NB: â + le(s) = **au(x)**; de + le = **du**; de + les = **des**); **the boy/girl/ink** le garçon/la fille/l'encre; **the children** les enfants; **the history of the world** l'histoire du monde; **give it to the postman** donne-le au facteur; **to play the piano/flute** jouer du piano/de la flûte
2 (+ adj to form n) le, la f, l' + vowel or h mute, les pl; **the rich and the poor** les riches et les pauvres; **to attempt the impossible** tenter l'impossible
3 (in titles): **Elizabeth the First** Elisabeth première; **Peter the Great** Pierre le Grand
4 (in comparisons): **the more he works, the more he earns** plus il travaille, plus il gagne de l'argent; **the sooner the better** le plus tôt sera le mieux

theatre, (US) **theater** ['θɪətəʳ] n théâtre m; (also: **lecture theatre**) amphithéâtre m, amphi m (inf); (Med: also: **operating theatre**) salle f d'opération
theatre-goer, (US) **theater-goer** ['θɪətəɡəuəʳ] n habitué(e) du théâtre
theatrical [θɪ'ætrɪkl] adj théâtral(e); **~ company** troupe f de théâtre
theft [θɛft] n vol m (larcin)
their [ðɛəʳ] adj leur, leurs pl; see also **my**
theirs [ðɛəz] pron le (la) leur, les leurs; **it is ~** c'est à eux; **a friend of ~** un de leurs amis; see also **mine**[1]
them [ðɛm, ðəm] pron (direct) les; (indirect) leur; (stressed, after prep) eux (elles); **I see ~** je les vois; **give ~ the book** donne-leur le livre; **give me a few of ~** donnez m'en quelques uns (or quelques unes); see also **me**
theme [θi:m] n thème m
theme park n parc m à thème
theme song n chanson principale
themselves [ðəm'sɛlvz] pl pron (reflexive) se; (emphatic, after prep) eux-mêmes (elles-mêmes); **between ~** entre eux (elles); see also **oneself**
then [ðɛn] adv (at that time) alors, à ce moment-

là; (next) puis, ensuite; (and also) et puis ▷ conj (therefore) alors, dans ce cas ▷ adj: **the ~ president** le président d'alors or de l'époque; **by ~** (past) à ce moment-là; (future) d'ici là; **from ~ on** dès lors; **before ~** avant; **until ~** jusqu'à ce moment-là, jusque-là; **and ~ what?** et puis après?; **what do you want me to do ~?** (afterwards) que veux-tu que je fasse ensuite?; (in that case) bon alors, qu'est-ce que je fais?
theologian [θɪə'ləudʒən] n théologien(ne)
theological [θɪə'lɔdʒɪkl] adj théologique
theology [θɪ'ɔlədʒɪ] n théologie f
theorem ['θɪərəm] n théorème m
theoretical [θɪə'rɛtɪkl] adj théorique
theorize ['θɪəraɪz] vi élaborer une théorie; (pej) faire des théories
theory ['θɪərɪ] n théorie f
therapeutic [θɛrə'pju:tɪk] adj thérapeutique
therapist ['θɛrəpɪst] n thérapeute m/f
therapy ['θɛrəpɪ] n thérapie f

 KEYWORD

there [ðɛəʳ] adv **1**: **there is**, **there are** il y a; **there are 3 of them** (people, things) il y en a 3; **there is no-one here/no bread left** il n'y a personne/il n'y a plus de pain; **there has been an accident** il y a eu un accident
2 (referring to place) là, là-bas; **it's there** c'est là(-bas); **in/on/up/down there** là-dedans/là-dessus/là-haut/en bas; **he went there on Friday** il y est allé vendredi; **to go there and back** faire l'aller-retour; **I want that book there** je veux ce livre-là; **there he is!** le voilà!
3: **there, there** (esp to child) allons, allons!

thereabouts ['ðɛərə'bauts] adv (place) par là, près de là; (amount) environ, à peu près
thereafter [ðɛər'ɑ:ftəʳ] adv par la suite
thereby ['ðɛəbaɪ] adv ainsi
therefore ['ðɛəfɔ:ʳ] adv donc, par conséquent
there's ['ðɛəz] = **there is**; **there has**
thereupon [ðɛərə'pɔn] adv (at that point) sur ce; (formal: on that subject) à ce sujet
thermal ['θə:ml] adj thermique; **~ paper/printer** papier m/imprimante f thermique; **~ underwear** sous-vêtements mpl en Thermolactyl®
thermodynamics ['θə:məudaɪ'næmɪks] n thermodynamique f
thermometer [θə'mɔmɪtəʳ] n thermomètre m
thermonuclear ['θə:məu'nju:klɪəʳ] adj thermonucléaire
Thermos® ['θə:məs] n (also: **Thermos flask**) thermos® m or f inv
thermostat ['θə:məustæt] n thermostat m
thesaurus [θɪ'sɔ:rəs] n dictionnaire m synonymique
these [ði:z] pl pron ceux-ci (celles-ci) ▷ pl adj ces; (not those): **~ books** ces livres-ci
thesis (pl **theses**) ['θi:sɪs, 'θi:si:z] n thèse f
they [ðeɪ] pl pron ils (elles); (stressed) eux (elles); **~**

say that ... (it is said that) on dit que ...

they'd [ðeɪd] = **they had**; **they would**

they'll [ðeɪl] = **they shall**; **they will**

they're [ðɛəʳ] = **they are**

they've [ðeɪv] = **they have**

thick [θɪk] adj épais(se); (crowd) dense; (stupid) bête, borné(e) ▷ n: **in the ~ of** au beau milieu de, en plein cœur de; **it's 20 cm ~** ça a 20 cm d'épaisseur

thicken [ˈθɪkn] vi s'épaissir ▷ vt (sauce etc) épaissir

thicket [ˈθɪkɪt] n fourré m, hallier m

thickly [ˈθɪklɪ] adv (spread) en couche épaisse; (cut) en tranches épaisses; **~ populated** à forte densité de population

thickness [ˈθɪknɪs] n épaisseur f

thickset [θɪkˈsɛt] adj trapu(e), costaud(e)

thick-skinned [θɪkˈskɪnd] adj (fig) peu sensible

thief (pl **thieves**) [θiːf, θiːvz] n voleur(-euse)

thieving [ˈθiːvɪŋ] n vol m (larcin)

thigh [θaɪ] n cuisse f

thighbone [ˈθaɪbəun] n fémur m

thimble [ˈθɪmbl] n dé m (à coudre)

thin [θɪn] adj mince; (skinny) maigre; (soup) peu épais(se); (hair, crowd) clairsemé(e); (fog) léger(-ère) ▷ vt (hair) éclaircir; (also: **thin down**: sauce, paint) délayer ▷ vi (fog) s'éclaircir; (also: **thin out**: crowd) se disperser; **his hair is ~ning** il se dégarnit

thing [θɪŋ] n chose f; (object) objet m; (contraption) truc m; **things** npl (belongings) affaires fpl; **first ~ (in the morning)** à la première heure, tout de suite (le matin); **last ~ (at night), he ...** juste avant de se coucher, il ...; **the ~ is ...** c'est que ...; **for one ~** d'abord; **the best ~ would be to** le mieux serait de; **how are ~s?** comment ça va?; **to have a ~ about** (be obsessed by) être obsédé(e) par; (hate) détester; **poor ~!** le (or la) pauvre!

think (pt, pp **thought**) [θɪŋk, θɔːt] vi penser, réfléchir ▷ vt penser, croire; (imagine) s'imaginer; **to ~ of** penser à; **what do you ~ of it?** qu'en pensez-vous?; **what did you ~ of them?** qu'avez-vous pensé d'eux?; **to ~ about sth/sb** penser à qch/qn; **I'll ~ about it** je vais y réfléchir; **to ~ of doing** avoir l'idée de faire; **I so/not** je crois or pense que oui/non; **to ~ well of** avoir une haute opinion de; **~ again!** attention, réfléchis bien!; **to ~ aloud** penser tout haut

▸ **think out** vt (plan) bien réfléchir à; (solution) trouver

▸ **think over** vt bien réfléchir à; **I'd like to ~ things over** (offer, suggestion) j'aimerais bien y réfléchir un peu

▸ **think through** vt étudier dans tous les détails

▸ **think up** vt inventer, trouver

thinking [ˈθɪŋkɪŋ] n: **to my (way of) ~** selon moi

think tank n groupe m de réflexion

thinly [ˈθɪnlɪ] adv (cut) en tranches fines; (spread) en couche mince

thinness [ˈθɪnnɪs] n minceur f; maigreur f

third [θəːd] num troisième ▷ n troisième m/f; (fraction) tiers m; (Aut) troisième (vitesse) f; (Brit Scol: degree) ≈ licence f avec mention passable; **a ~ of** le tiers de

third-degree burns [ˈθəːdɪgriː-] npl brûlures fpl au troisième degré

thirdly [ˈθəːdlɪ] adv troisièmement

third party insurance n (Brit) assurance f au tiers

third-rate [ˈθəːdˈreɪt] adj de qualité médiocre

Third World n: **the ~** le Tiers-Monde

thirst [θəːst] n soif f

thirsty [ˈθəːstɪ] adj qui a soif, assoiffé(e); (work) qui donne soif; **to be ~** avoir soif

thirteen [θəːˈtiːn] num treize

thirteenth [-ˈtiːnθ] num treizième

thirtieth [ˈθəːtɪɪθ] num trentième

thirty [ˈθəːtɪ] num trente

 KEYWORD

this [ðɪs] adj (demonstrative: pl **these**) ce, cet + vowel or h mute, cette f; **this man/woman/book** cet homme/cette femme/ce livre; (not that) cet homme-ci/cette femme-ci/ce livre-ci; **this one** celui-ci (celle-ci); **this time** cette fois-ci; **this time last year** l'année dernière à la même époque; **this way** (in this direction) par ici; (in this fashion) de cette façon, ainsi

▷ pron (demonstrative: pl **these**) ce; (not that one) celui-ci (celle-ci), ceci; **who's this?** qui est-ce?; **what's this?** qu'est-ce que c'est?; **I prefer this to that** je préfère ceci à cela; **they were talking of this and that** ils parlaient de choses et d'autres; **this is where I live** c'est ici que j'habite; **this is what he said** voici ce qu'il a dit; **this is Mr Brown** (in introductions) je vous présente Mr Brown; (in photo) c'est Mr Brown; (on telephone) ici Mr Brown

▷ adv (demonstrative): **it was about this big** c'était à peu près de cette grandeur or grand comme ça; **I didn't know it was this bad** je ne savais pas que c'était si or aussi mauvais

thistle [ˈθɪsl] n chardon m

thong [θɒŋ] n lanière f

thorn [θɔːn] n épine f

thorny [ˈθɔːnɪ] adj épineux(-euse)

thorough [ˈθʌrə] adj (search) minutieux(-euse); (knowledge, research) approfondi(e); (work, person) consciencieux(-euse); (cleaning) à fond

thoroughbred [ˈθʌrəbrɛd] n (horse) pur-sang m inv

thoroughfare [ˈθʌrəfɛəʳ] n rue f; **"no ~"** (Brit) "passage interdit"

thoroughgoing [ˈθʌrəgəuɪŋ] adj (analysis) approfondi(e); (reform) profond(e)

thoroughly [ˈθʌrəlɪ] adv (search) minutieusement; (study) en profondeur; (clean) à fond; (very) tout à fait; **he ~ agreed** il était tout à fait d'accord

thoroughness [ˈθʌrənɪs] n soin (méticuleux)

those [ðəuz] pl pron ceux-là (celles-là) ▷ pl adj

ces; (not these): ~ **books** ces livres-là

though [ðəu] conj bien que + sub, quoique + sub ▷ adv pourtant; **even** ~ quand bien même + conditional; **it's not easy,** ~ pourtant, ce n'est pas facile

thought [θɔ:t] pt, pp of **think** ▷ n pensée f; (idea) idée f; (opinion) avis m; (intention) intention f; **after much** ~ après mûre réflexion; **I've just had a** ~ je viens de penser à quelque chose; **to give sth some** ~ réfléchir à qch

thoughtful ['θɔ:tful] adj (deep in thought) pensif(-ive); (serious) réfléchi(e); (considerate) prévenant(e)

thoughtfully ['θɔ:tfəlɪ] adv pensivement; avec prévenance

thoughtless ['θɔ:tlɪs] adj qui manque de considération

thoughtlessly ['θɔ:tlɪslɪ] adv inconsidérément

thought-provoking ['θɔ:tprəvəukɪŋ] adj stimulant(e)

thousand ['θauzənd] num mille; **one** ~ mille; **two** ~ deux mille; **~s of** des milliers de

thousandth ['θauzəntθ] num millième

thrash [θræʃ] vt rouer de coups; (as punishment) donner une correction à; (inf: defeat) battre à plate(s) couture(s)

▶ **thrash about** vi se débattre
▶ **thrash out** vt débattre de

thrashing ['θræʃɪŋ] n: **to give sb a** ~; = **to thrash sb**

thread [θrɛd] n fil m; (of screw) pas m, filetage m ▷ vt (needle) enfiler; **to** ~ **one's way between** se faufiler entre

threadbare ['θrɛdbɛəʳ] adj râpé(e), élimé(e)

threat [θrɛt] n menace f; **to be under** ~ **of** être menacé(e) de

threaten ['θrɛtn] vi (storm) menacer ▷ vt: **to** ~ **sb with sth/to do** menacer qn de qch/de faire

threatening ['θrɛtnɪŋ] adj menaçant(e)

three [θri:] num trois

three-dimensional [θri:dɪ'mɛnʃənl] adj à trois dimensions; (film) en relief

threefold ['θri:fəuld] adv: **to increase** ~ tripler

three-piece suit ['θri:pi:s-] n complet m (avec gilet)

three-piece suite n salon m (canapé et deux fauteuils)

three-ply [θri:'plaɪ] adj (wood) à trois épaisseurs; (wool) trois fils inv

three-quarters [θri:'kwɔ:təz] npl trois-quarts mpl; ~ **full** aux trois-quarts plein

three-wheeler [θri:'wi:ləʳ] n (car) voiture f à trois roues

thresh [θrɛʃ] vt (Agr) battre

threshing machine ['θrɛʃɪŋ-] n batteuse f

threshold ['θrɛʃhəuld] n seuil m; **to be on the** ~ **of** (fig) être au seuil de

threshold agreement n (Econ) accord m d'indexation des salaires

threw [θru:] pt of **throw**

thrift [θrɪft] n économie f

thrifty ['θrɪftɪ] adj économe

thrill [θrɪl] n (excitement) émotion f, sensation forte; (shudder) frisson m ▷ vi tressaillir, frissonner ▷ vt (audience) électriser

thrilled [θrɪld] adj: ~ **(with)** ravi(e) de

thriller ['θrɪləʳ] n film m (or roman m or pièce f) à suspense

thrilling ['θrɪlɪŋ] adj (book, play etc) saisissant(e); (news, discovery) excitant(e)

thrive (pt **-d** or **throve**, pp **-d** or **thriven**) [θraɪv, θrəuv, 'θrɪvn] vi (grow) pousser or se développer bien; (business) prospérer; **he ~s on it** cela lui réussit

thriving ['θraɪvɪŋ] adj vigoureux(-euse); (business, community) prospère

throat [θrəut] n gorge f; **to have a sore** ~ avoir mal à la gorge

throb [θrɔb] n (of heart) pulsation f; (of engine) vibration f; (of pain) élancement m ▷ vi (heart) palpiter; (engine) vibrer; (pain) lanciner; (wound) causer des élancements; **my head is ~bing** j'ai des élancements dans la tête

throes [θrəuz] npl: **in the** ~ **of** au beau milieu de; en proie à; **in the** ~ **of death** à l'agonie

thrombosis [θrɔm'bəusɪs] n thrombose f

throne [θrəun] n trône m

throng ['θrɔŋ] n foule f ▷ vt se presser dans

throttle ['θrɔtl] n (Aut) accélérateur m ▷ vt étrangler

through [θru:] prep à travers; (time) pendant, durant; (by means of) par, par l'intermédiaire de; (owing to) à cause de ▷ adj (ticket, train, passage) direct(e) ▷ adv à travers; **(from) Monday** ~ **Friday** (US) de lundi à vendredi; **to let sb** ~ laisser passer qn; **to put sb** ~ **to sb** (Tel) passer qn à qn; **to be** ~ (Brit; Tel) avoir la communication; (esp US: have finished) avoir fini; **"no** ~ **traffic"** (US) "passage interdit"; **"no** ~ **road"** (Brit) "impasse"

throughout [θru:'aut] prep (place) partout dans; (time) durant tout(e) le (la) ▷ adv partout

throughput ['θru:put] n (of goods, materials) quantité de matières premières utilisée; (Comput) débit m

throve [θrəuv] pt of **thrive**

throw [θrəu] n jet m; (Sport) lancer m ▷ vt (pt **threw**, pp **-n**) [θru:, θrəun] lancer, jeter; (Sport) lancer; (rider) désarçonner; (fig) décontenancer; (pottery) tourner; **to** ~ **a party** donner une réception

▶ **throw about, throw around** vt (litter etc) éparpiller
▶ **throw away** vt jeter; (money) gaspiller
▶ **throw in** vt (Sport: ball) remettre en jeu; (include) ajouter
▶ **throw off** vt se débarrasser de
▶ **throw out** vt jeter; (reject) rejeter; (person) mettre à la porte
▶ **throw together** vt (clothes, meal etc) assembler à la hâte; (essay) bâcler
▶ **throw up** vi vomir

throwaway ['θrəuəweɪ] adj à jeter

throwback ['θrəubæk] n: **it's a** ~ **to** ça nous etc ramène à

throw-in ['θrəuɪn] *n* (*Sport*) remise *f* en jeu
thrown [θrəun] *pp of* **throw**
thru [θru:] (*US*) = **through**
thrush [θrʌʃ] *n* (*Zool*) grive *f*; (*Med: esp in children*) muguet *m*; (: *in women: Brit*) muguet vaginal
thrust [θrʌst] *n* (*Tech*) poussée *f* ▷ *vt* (*pt, pp* **thrust**) pousser brusquement; (*push in*) enfoncer
thrusting ['θrʌstɪŋ] *adj* dynamique; qui se met trop en avant
thud [θʌd] *n* bruit sourd
thug [θʌg] *n* voyou *m*
thumb [θʌm] *n* (*Anat*) pouce *m* ▷ *vt* (*book*) feuilleter; **to ~ a lift** faire de l'auto-stop, arrêter une voiture; **to give sb/sth the ~s up/~s down** donner/refuser de donner le feu vert à qn/qch
  ▶ **thumb through** *vt* (*book*) feuilleter
thumb index *n* répertoire *m* (à onglets)
thumbnail ['θʌmneɪl] *n* ongle *m* du pouce
thumbnail sketch *n* croquis *m*
thumbtack ['θʌmtæk] *n* (*US*) punaise *f* (*clou*)
thump [θʌmp] *n* grand coup; (*sound*) bruit sourd ▷ *vt* cogner sur ▷ *vi* cogner, frapper
thunder ['θʌndə*] *n* tonnerre *m* ▷ *vi* tonner; (*train etc*): **to ~ past** passer dans un grondement *or* un bruit de tonnerre
thunderbolt ['θʌndəbəult] *n* foudre *f*
thunderclap ['θʌndəklæp] *n* coup *m* de tonnerre
thunderous ['θʌndrəs] *adj* étourdissant(e)
thunderstorm ['θʌndəstɔ:m] *n* orage *m*
thunderstruck ['θʌndəstrʌk] *adj* (*fig*) abasourdi(e)
thundery ['θʌndərɪ] *adj* orageux(-euse)
Thursday ['θə:zdɪ] *n* jeudi *m*; *see also* **Tuesday**
thus [ðʌs] *adv* ainsi
thwart [θwɔ:t] *vt* contrecarrer
thyme [taɪm] *n* thym *m*
thyroid ['θaɪrɔɪd] *n* thyroïde *f*
tiara [tɪ'ɑ:rə] *n* (*woman's*) diadème *m*
Tibet [tɪ'bɛt] *n* Tibet *m*
Tibetan [tɪ'bɛtən] *adj* tibétain(e) ▷ *n* Tibétain(e); (*Ling*) tibétain *m*
tibia ['tɪbɪə] *n* tibia *m*
tic [tɪk] *n* tic (nerveux)
tick [tɪk] *n* (*sound: of clock*) tic-tac *m*; (*mark*) coche *f*; (*Zool*) tique *f*; (*Brit inf*): **in a ~** dans un instant; (*Brit inf: credit*): **to buy sth on ~** acheter qch à crédit ▷ *vi* faire tic-tac ▷ *vt* (*item on list*) cocher; **to put a ~ against sth** cocher qch
  ▶ **tick off** *vt* (*item on list*) cocher; (*person*) réprimander, attraper
  ▶ **tick over** *vi* (*Brit: engine*) tourner au ralenti; (: *fig*) aller *or* marcher doucettement
ticker tape ['tɪkə-] *n* bande *f* de téléscripteur; (*US: in celebrations*) ≈ serpentin *m*
ticket ['tɪkɪt] *n* billet *m*; (*for bus, tube*) ticket *m*; (*in shop: on goods*) étiquette *f*; (: *from cash register*) reçu *m*, ticket; (*for library*) carte *f*; (*also:* **parking ticket**) contravention *f*, p.-v. *m*; (*US Pol*) liste électorale (*soutenue par un parti*); **to get a (parking) ~** (*Aut*) attraper une contravention (pour stationnement illégal)
ticket agency *n* (*Theat*) agence *f* de spectacles

ticket barrier *n* (*Brit: Rail*) portillon *m* automatique
ticket collector *n* contrôleur(-euse)
ticket holder *n* personne munie d'un billet
ticket inspector *n* contrôleur(-euse)
ticket machine *n* billetterie *f* automatique
ticket office *n* guichet *m*, bureau *m* de vente des billets
tickle ['tɪkl] *n* chatouillement *m* ▷ *vi* chatouiller ▷ *vt* chatouiller; (*fig*) plaire à; faire rire
ticklish ['tɪklɪʃ] *adj* (*person*) chatouilleux(-euse); (*which tickles: blanket*) qui chatouille; (: *cough*) qui irrite; (*problem*) épineux(-euse)
tidal ['taɪdl] *adj* à marée
tidal wave *n* raz-de-marée *m inv*
tidbit ['tɪdbɪt] *n* (*esp US*) = **titbit**
tiddlywinks ['tɪdlɪwɪŋks] *n* jeu *m* de puce
tide [taɪd] *n* marée *f*; (*fig: of events*) cours *m* ▷ *vt*: **to ~ sb over** dépanner qn; **high/low ~** marée haute/basse
tidily ['taɪdɪlɪ] *adv* avec soin, soigneusement
tidiness ['taɪdɪnɪs] *n* bon ordre; goût *m* de l'ordre
tidy ['taɪdɪ] *adj* (*room*) bien rangé(e); (*dress, work*) net (nette), soigné(e); (*person*) ordonné(e), qui a de l'ordre; (: *in character*) soigneux(-euse); (*mind*) méthodique ▷ *vt* (*also:* **tidy up**) ranger; **to ~ o.s. up** s'arranger
tie [taɪ] *n* (*string etc*) cordon *m*; (*Brit: also:* **necktie**) cravate *f*; (*fig: link*) lien *m*; (*Sport: draw*) égalité *f* de points; match nul; (: *match*) rencontre *f*; (*US Rail*) traverse *f* ▷ *vt* (*parcel*) attacher; (*ribbon*) nouer ▷ *vi* (*Sport*) faire match nul; finir à égalité de points; **"black/white ~"** "smoking/habit de rigueur"; **family ~s** liens de famille; **to ~ sth in a bow** faire un nœud à *or* avec qch; **to ~ a knot in sth** faire un nœud à qch
  ▶ **tie down** *vt* attacher; (*fig*): **to ~ sb down to** contraindre qn à accepter; **to feel ~d down** (*by relationship*) se sentir coincé(e)
  ▶ **tie in** *vi*: **to ~ in (with)** (*correspond*) correspondre (à)
  ▶ **tie on** *vt* (*Brit: label etc*) attacher (avec une ficelle)
  ▶ **tie up** *vt* (*parcel*) ficeler; (*dog, boat*) attacher; (*prisoner*) ligoter; (*arrangements*) conclure; **to be ~d up** (*busy*) être pris(e) *or* occupé(e)
tie-break ['taɪbreɪk], **tie-breaker** ['taɪbreɪkə*] *n* (*Tennis*) tie-break *m*; (*in quiz*) question *f* subsidiaire
tie-on ['taɪɔn] *adj* (*Brit: label*) qui s'attache
tie-pin ['taɪpɪn] *n* (*Brit*) épingle *f* de cravate
tier [tɪə*] *n* gradin *m*; (*of cake*) étage *m*
Tierra del Fuego [tɪ'ɛrədɛl'fweɪgəu] *n* Terre *f* de Feu
tie tack *n* (*US*) épingle *f* de cravate
tiff [tɪf] *n* petite querelle
tiger ['taɪgə*] *n* tigre *m*
tight [taɪt] *adj* (*rope*) tendu(e), raide; (*clothes*) étroit(e), très juste; (*budget, programme, bend*) serré(e); (*control*) strict(e), sévère; (*inf: drunk*) ivre, rond(e) ▷ *adv* (*squeeze*) très fort; (*shut*) à bloc, hermétiquement; **to be packed ~** (*suitcase*)

être bourré(e); (*people*) être serré(e); **hold ~!** accrochez-vous bien!

tighten ['taɪtn] *vt* (*rope*) tendre; (*screw*) resserrer; (*control*) renforcer ▷ *vi* se tendre; se resserrer

tightfisted [taɪt'fɪstɪd] *adj* avare

tight-lipped ['taɪt'lɪpt] *adj*: **to be ~ (about sth)** (*silent*) ne pas desserrer les lèvres *or* les dents (au sujet de qch); **she was ~ with anger** elle pinçait les lèvres de colère

tightly ['taɪtlɪ] *adv* (*grasp*) bien, très fort

tightrope ['taɪtrəʊp] *n* corde *f* raide

tights [taɪts] *npl* (*Brit*) collant *m*

tigress ['taɪgrɪs] *n* tigresse *f*

tilde ['tɪldə] *n* tilde *m*

tile [taɪl] *n* (*on roof*) tuile *f*; (*on wall or floor*) carreau *m* ▷ *vt* (*floor, bathroom etc*) carreler

tiled [taɪld] *adj* en tuiles; carrelé(e)

till [tɪl] *n* caisse (enregistreuse) ▷ *vt* (*land*) cultiver ▷ *prep, conj* = **until**

tiller ['tɪlə'] *n* (*Naut*) barre *f* (du gouvernail)

tilt [tɪlt] *vt* pencher, incliner ▷ *vi* pencher, être incliné(e) ▷ *n* (*slope*) inclinaison *f*; **to wear one's hat at a ~** porter son chapeau incliné sur le côté; **(at) full ~** à toute vitesse

timber ['tɪmbə'] *n* (*material*) bois *m* de construction; (*trees*) arbres *mpl*

time [taɪm] *n* temps *m*; (*epoch: often pl*) époque *f*, temps; (*by clock*) heure *f*; (*moment*) moment *m*; (*occasion, also Math*) fois *f*; (*Mus*) mesure *f* ▷ *vt* (*race*) chronométrer; (*programme*) minuter; (*visit*) fixer; (*remark etc*) choisir le moment de; **a long ~** un long moment, longtemps; **four at a ~** quatre à la fois; **for the ~ being** pour le moment; **from ~ to ~** de temps en temps; **~ after ~, ~ and again** bien des fois; **at ~s** parfois; **in ~** (*soon enough*) à temps; (*after some time*) avec le temps, à la longue; (*Mus*) en mesure; **in a week's ~** dans une semaine; **in no ~** en un rien de temps; **any ~** n'importe quand; **on ~** à l'heure; **to be 30 minutes behind/ahead of ~** avoir 30 minutes de retard/d'avance; **by the ~ he arrived** quand il est arrivé, le temps qu'il arrive + *sub*; **5 ~s 5** 5 fois 5; **what ~ is it?** quelle heure est-il?; **what ~ do you make it?** quelle heure avez-vous?; **what ~ is the museum/ shop open?** à quelle heure ouvre le musée/ magasin?; **to have a good ~** bien s'amuser; **we** (*or* **they** *etc*) **had a hard ~** ça a été difficile *or* pénible; **~'s up!** c'est l'heure!; **I've no ~ for it** (*fig*) cela m'agace; **he'll do it in his own (good) ~** (*without being hurried*) il le fera quand il en aura le temps; **he'll do it in** *or* (*US*) **on his own ~** (*out of working hours*) il le fera à ses heures perdues; **to be behind the ~s** retarder (sur son temps)

time-and-motion study ['taɪmənd'məʊʃən-] *n* étude *f* des cadences

time bomb *n* bombe *f* à retardement

time clock *n* horloge pointeuse

time-consuming ['taɪmkənsju:mɪŋ] *adj* qui prend beaucoup de temps

time difference *n* décalage *m* horaire

time frame *n* délais *mpl*

time-honoured, (*US*) **time-honored** ['taɪmɔnəd] *adj* consacré(e)

timekeeper ['taɪmki:pə'] *n* (*Sport*) chronomètre *m*

time lag *n* (*Brit*) décalage *m*; (: *in travel*) décalage horaire

timeless ['taɪmlɪs] *adj* éternel(le)

time limit *n* limite *f* de temps, délai *m*

timely ['taɪmlɪ] *adj* opportun(e)

time off *n* temps *m* libre

timer ['taɪmə'] *n* (*in kitchen*) compte-minutes *m inv*; (*Tech*) minuteur *m*

time-saving ['taɪmseɪvɪŋ] *adj* qui fait gagner du temps

timescale ['taɪmskeɪl] *n* délais *mpl*

time-share ['taɪmʃɛə'] *n* maison *f*/ appartement *m* en multipropriété

time-sharing ['taɪmʃɛərɪŋ] *n* (*Comput*) temps partagé

time sheet *n* feuille *f* de présence

time signal *n* signal *m* horaire

time switch *n* (*Brit*) minuteur *m*; (: *for lighting*) minuterie *f*

timetable ['taɪmteɪbl] *n* (*Rail*) (indicateur *m*) horaire *m*; (*Scol*) emploi *m* du temps; (*programme of events etc*) programme *m*

time zone *n* fuseau *m* horaire

timid ['tɪmɪd] *adj* timide; (*easily scared*) peureux(-euse)

timidity [tɪ'mɪdɪtɪ] *n* timidité *f*

timing ['taɪmɪŋ] *n* minutage *m*; (*Sport*) chronométrage *m*; **the ~ of his resignation** le moment choisi pour sa démission

timing device *n* (*on bomb*) mécanisme *m* de retardement

timpani ['tɪmpənɪ] *npl* timbales *fpl*

tin [tɪn] *n* étain *m*; (*also:* **tin plate**) fer-blanc *m*; (*Brit: can*) boîte *f* (de conserve); (: *for baking*) moule *m* (à gâteau); (*for storage*) boîte *f*; **a ~ of paint** un pot de peinture

tinfoil ['tɪnfɔɪl] *n* papier *m* d'étain *or* d'aluminium

tinge [tɪndʒ] *n* nuance *f* ▷ *vt*: **~d with** teinté(e) de

tingle ['tɪŋgl] *n* picotement *m*; frisson *m* ▷ *vi* picoter; (*person*) avoir des picotements

tinker ['tɪŋkə'] *n* rétameur ambulant; (*gipsy*) romanichel *m*

> ► **tinker with** *vt fus* bricoler, rafistoler

tinkle ['tɪŋkl] *vi* tinter ▷ *n* (*inf*): **to give sb a ~** passer un coup de fil à qn

tin mine *n* mine *f* d'étain

tinned [tɪnd] *adj* (*Brit: food*) en boîte, en conserve

tinnitus ['tɪnɪtəs] *n* (*Med*) acouphène *m*

tinny ['tɪnɪ] *adj* métallique

tin opener [-'əupnə'] *n* (*Brit*) ouvre-boîte(s) *m*

tinsel ['tɪnsl] *n* guirlandes *fpl* de Noël (argentées)

tint [tɪnt] *n* teinte *f*; (*for hair*) shampooing colorant ▷ *vt* (*hair*) faire un shampooing colorant à

tinted ['tɪntɪd] *adj* (*hair*) teint(e); (*spectacles, glass*) teinté(e)

tiny ['taɪnɪ] *adj* minuscule

tip [tɪp] *n* (*end*) bout *m*; (*protective: on umbrella etc*) embout *m*; (*gratuity*) pourboire *m*; (*Brit: for coal*) terril *m*; (*Brit: for rubbish*) décharge *f*; (*advice*) tuyau *m* ▷ *vt* (*waiter*) donner un pourboire à; (*tilt*) incliner; (*overturn: also:* **tip over**) renverser; (*empty: also:* **tip out**) déverser; (*predict: winner etc*) pronostiquer; **he ~ped out the contents of the box** il a vidé le contenu de la boîte; **how much should I ~?** combien de pourboire est-ce qu'il faut laisser?

▶**tip off** *vt* prévenir, avertir

tip-off ['tɪpɔf] *n* (*hint*) tuyau *m*

tipped ['tɪpt] *adj* (*Brit: cigarette*) (à bout) filtre *inv*; **steel-~** à bout métallique, à embout de métal

Tipp-Ex® ['tɪpɛks] *n* (*Brit*) Tipp-Ex® *m*

tipple ['tɪpl] (*Brit*) *vi* picoler ▷ *n*: **to have a ~** boire un petit coup

tipster ['tɪpstəʳ] *n* (*Racing*) pronostiqueur *m*

tipsy ['tɪpsɪ] *adj* un peu ivre, éméché(e)

tiptoe ['tɪptəu] *n*: **on ~** sur la pointe des pieds

tiptop ['tɪptɔp] *adj*: **in ~ condition** en excellent état

tirade [taɪ'reɪd] *n* diatribe *f*

tire ['taɪəʳ] *n* (*US*) = **tyre** ▷ *vt* fatiguer ▷ *vi* se fatiguer

▶**tire out** *vt* épuiser

tired ['taɪəd] *adj* fatigué(e); **to be/feel/look ~** être/se sentir/avoir l'air fatigué; **to be ~ of** en avoir assez de, être las (lasse) de

tiredness ['taɪədnɪs] *n* fatigue *f*

tireless ['taɪəlɪs] *adj* infatigable, inlassable

tire pressure (*US*) = **tyre pressure**

tiresome ['taɪsəm] *adj* ennuyeux(-euse)

tiring ['taɪərɪŋ] *adj* fatigant(e)

tissue ['tɪʃuː] *n* tissu *m*; (*paper handkerchief*) mouchoir *m* en papier, kleenex® *m*

tissue paper *n* papier *m* de soie

tit [tɪt] *n* (*bird*) mésange *f*; (*inf: breast*) nichon *m*; **to give ~ for tat** rendre coup pour coup

titanium [tɪ'teɪnɪəm] *n* titane *m*

titbit ['tɪtbɪt] *n* (*food*) friandise *f*; (*before meal*) amuse-gueule *m inv*; (*news*) potin *m*

titillate ['tɪtɪleɪt] *vt* titiller, exciter

titivate ['tɪtɪveɪt] *vt* pomponner

title ['taɪtl] *n* titre *m*; (*Law: right*): **~ (to)** droit *m* (à)

title deed *n* (*Law*) titre (constitutif) de propriété

title page *n* page *f* de titre

title role *n* rôle principal

titter ['tɪtəʳ] *vi* rire (bêtement)

tittle-tattle ['tɪtltætl] *n* bavardages *mpl*

titular ['tɪtjuləʳ] *adj* (*in name only*) nominal(e)

tizzy ['tɪzɪ] *n*: **to be in a ~** être dans tous ses états

T-junction ['tiː'dʒʌŋkʃən] *n* croisement *m* en T

TM *n abbr* = **trademark; transcendental meditation**

TN *abbr* (*US*) = **Tennessee**

TNT *n abbr* (= *trinitrotoluene*) TNT *m*

KEYWORD

to [tuː, tə] *prep* (*with noun/pronoun*) **1** (*direction*) à; (*towards*) vers; envers; **to go to France/ Portugal/London/school** aller en France/au Portugal/à Londres/à l'école; **to go to Claude's/the doctor's** aller chez Claude/le docteur; **the road to Edinburgh** la route d'Édimbourg

2 (*as far as*) (jusqu')à; **to count to 10** compter jusqu'à 10; **from 40 to 50 people** de 40 à 50 personnes

3 (*with expressions of time*): **a quarter to 5** 5 heures moins le quart; **it's twenty to 3** il est 3 heures moins vingt

4 (*for, of*) de; **the key to the front door** la clé de la porte d'entrée; **a letter to his wife** une lettre (adressée) à sa femme

5 (*expressing indirect object*) à; **to give sth to sb** donner qch à qn; **to talk to sb** parler à qn; **it belongs to him** cela lui appartient, c'est à lui; **to be a danger to sb** être dangereux(-euse) pour qn

6 (*in relation to*) à; **3 goals to 2** 3 (buts) à 2; **30 miles to the gallon** ≈ 9,4 litres aux cent (km)

7 (*purpose, result*): **to come to sb's aid** venir au secours de qn, porter secours à qn; **to sentence sb to death** condamner qn à mort; **to my surprise** à ma grande surprise

▷ *prep* (*with vb*) **1** (*simple infinitive*): **to go/eat** aller/manger

2 (*following another vb*): **to want/try/start to do** vouloir/essayer de/commencer à faire

3 (*with vb omitted*): **I don't want to** je ne veux pas

4 (*purpose, result*) pour; **I did it to help you** je l'ai fait pour vous aider

5 (*equivalent to relative clause*): **I have things to do** j'ai des choses à faire; **the main thing is to try** l'important est d'essayer

6 (*after adjective etc*): **ready to go** prêt(e) à partir; **too old/young to ...** trop vieux/jeune pour ...

▷ *adv*: **push/pull the door to** tirez/poussez la porte; **to go to and fro** aller et venir

toad [təud] *n* crapaud *m*

toadstool ['təudstuːl] *n* champignon (vénéneux)

toady ['təudɪ] *vi* flatter bassement

toast [təust] *n* (*Culin*) pain grillé, toast *m*; (*drink, speech*) toast ▷ *vt* (*Culin*) faire griller; (*drink to*) porter un toast à; **a piece** *or* **slice of ~** un toast

toaster ['təustəʳ] *n* grille-pain *m inv*

toastmaster ['təustmɑːstəʳ] *n* animateur *m* pour réceptions

toast rack *n* porte-toast *m inv*

tobacco [tə'bækəu] *n* tabac *m*; **pipe ~** tabac à pipe

tobacconist [tə'bækənɪst] *n* marchand(e) de tabac; **~'s (shop)** (bureau *m* de) tabac *m*

Tobago [tə'beɪgəu] *n see* **Trinidad and Tobago**

toboggan [tə'bɔgən] *n* toboggan *m*; (*child's*) luge *f*

today [tə'deɪ] *adv, n* (*also fig*) aujourd'hui (*m*); **what day is it ~?** quel jour sommes-nous aujourd'hui?; **what date is it ~?** quelle est la date aujourd'hui?; **~ is the 4th of March**

aujourd'hui nous sommes le 4 mars; **a week ago** ~ il y a huit jours aujourd'hui

toddler ['tɒdlə^r] *n* enfant *m/f* qui commence à marcher, bambin *m*

toddy ['tɒdɪ] *n* grog *m*

to-do [tə'duː] *n* (*fuss*) histoire *f*, affaire *f*

toe [təʊ] *n* doigt *m* de pied, orteil *m*; (*of shoe*) bout *m* ▷ *vt*: **to ~ the line** (*fig*) obéir, se conformer; **big ~** gros orteil; **little ~** petit orteil

TOEFL *n abbr* = **Test(ing) of English as a Foreign Language**

toehold ['təʊhəʊld] *n* prise *f*

toenail ['təʊneɪl] *n* ongle *m* de l'orteil

toffee ['tɒfɪ] *n* caramel *m*

toffee apple *n* (*Brit*) pomme caramélisée

tofu ['təʊfuː] *n* fromage *m* de soja

toga ['təʊgə] *n* toge *f*

together [tə'gɛðə^r] *adv* ensemble; (*at same time*) en même temps; **~ with** (*prep*) avec

togetherness [tə'gɛðənɪs] *n* camaraderie *f*; intimité *f*

toggle switch ['tɒgl-] *n* (*Comput*) interrupteur *m* à bascule

Togo ['təʊgəʊ] *n* Togo *m*

togs [tɒgz] *npl* (*inf: clothes*) fringues *fpl*

toil [tɔɪl] *n* dur travail, labeur *m* ▷ *vi* travailler dur; peiner

toilet ['tɔɪlət] *n* (*Brit: lavatory*) toilettes *fpl*, cabinets *mpl* ▷ *cpd* (*bag, soap etc*) de toilette; **to go to the ~** aller aux toilettes; **where's the ~?** où sont les toilettes?

toilet bag *n* (*Brit*) nécessaire *m* de toilette

toilet bowl *n* cuvette *f* des W.-C.

toilet paper *n* papier *m* hygiénique

toiletries ['tɔɪlətrɪz] *npl* articles *mpl* de toilette

toilet roll *n* rouleau *m* de papier hygiénique

toilet water *n* eau *f* de toilette

to-ing and fro-ing ['tuːɪŋən'frəʊɪŋ] *n* (*Brit*) allées et venues *fpl*

token ['təʊkən] *n* (*sign*) marque *f*, témoignage *m*; (*metal disc*) jeton *m*; (*voucher*) bon *m*, coupon *m* ▷ *adj* (*fee, strike*) symbolique; **by the same ~** (*fig*) de même; **book/record ~** (*Brit*) chèque-livre/-disque *m*

tokenism ['təʊkənɪzəm] *n* (*Pol*): **it's just** ~ c'est une politique de pure forme

Tokyo ['təʊkjəʊ] *n* Tokyo

told [təʊld] *pt, pp of* **tell**

tolerable ['tɒlərəbl] *adj* (*bearable*) tolérable; (*fairly good*) passable

tolerably ['tɒlərəblɪ] *adv*: **~ good** tolérable

tolerance ['tɒlərns] *n* (*also Tech*) tolérance *f*

tolerant ['tɒlərnt] *adj*: **~ (of)** tolérant(e) (à l'égard de)

tolerate ['tɒləreɪt] *vt* supporter; (*Med, Tech*) tolérer

toleration [tɒlə'reɪʃən] *n* tolérance *f*

toll [təʊl] *n* (*tax, charge*) péage *m* ▷ *vi* (*bell*) sonner; **the accident ~ on the roads** le nombre des victimes de la route

tollbridge ['təʊlbrɪdʒ] *n* pont *m* à péage

toll call *n* (*US Tel*) appel *m* (à) longue distance

toll-free ['təʊl'friː] *adj* (*US*) gratuit(e) ▷ *adv* gratuitement

tomato [tə'mɑːtəʊ] (*pl* **-es**) *n* tomate *f*

tomato sauce *n* sauce *f* tomate

tomb [tuːm] *n* tombe *f*

tombola [tɒm'bəʊlə] *n* tombola *f*

tomboy ['tɒmbɔɪ] *n* garçon manqué

tombstone ['tuːmstəʊn] *n* pierre tombale

tomcat ['tɒmkæt] *n* matou *m*

tomorrow [tə'mɒrəʊ] *adv, n* (*also fig*) demain (*m*); **the day after ~** après-demain; **a week ~** demain en huit; **~ morning** demain matin

ton [tʌn] *n* tonne *f* (*Brit: = 1016 kg; US = 907 kg; metric = 1000 kg*); (*Naut: also:* **register ton**) tonneau *m* (= 2.83 cu.m*); **~s of** (*inf*) des tas de

tonal ['təʊnl] *adj* tonal(e)

tone [təʊn] *n* ton *m*; (*of radio, Brit Tel*) tonalité *f* ▷ *vi* (*also:* **tone in**) s'harmoniser
   ▸ **tone down** *vt* (*colour, criticism*) adoucir; (*sound*) baisser
   ▸ **tone up** *vt* (*muscles*) tonifier

tone-deaf [təʊn'dɛf] *adj* qui n'a pas d'oreille

toner ['təʊnə^r] *n* (*for photocopier*) encre *f*

Tonga [tɒŋə] *n* îles *fpl* Tonga

tongs [tɒŋz] *npl* pinces *fpl*; (*for coal*) pincettes *fpl*; (*for hair*) fer *m* à friser

tongue [tʌŋ] *n* langue *f*; **~ in cheek** (*adv*) ironiquement

tongue-tied ['tʌŋtaɪd] *adj* (*fig*) muet(te)

tonic ['tɒnɪk] *n* (*Med*) tonique *m*; (*Mus*) tonique *f*; (*also:* **tonic water**) Schweppes® *m*

tonight [tə'naɪt] *adv, n* cette nuit; (*this evening*) ce soir; **(I'll) see you ~!** à ce soir!

tonnage ['tʌnɪdʒ] *n* (*Naut*) tonnage *m*

tonne [tʌn] *n* (*Brit: metric ton*) tonne *f*

tonsil ['tɒnsl] *n* amygdale *f*; **to have one's ~s out** se faire opérer des amygdales

tonsillitis [tɒnsɪ'laɪtɪs] *n* amygdalite *f*; **to have ~** avoir une angine *or* une amygdalite

too [tuː] *adv* (*excessively*) trop; (*also*) aussi; **it's ~ sweet** c'est trop sucré; **I went ~** moi aussi, j'y suis allé; **~ much** (*as adv*) trop; (*as adj*) trop de; **~ many** (*adj*) trop de; **~ bad!** tant pis!

took [tʊk] *pt of* **take**

tool [tuːl] *n* outil *m*; (*fig*) instrument *m* ▷ *vt* travailler, ouvrager

tool box *n* boîte *f* à outils

tool kit *n* trousse *f* à outils

toot [tuːt] *n* coup *m* de sifflet (*or* de klaxon) ▷ *vi* siffler; (*with car-horn*) klaxonner

tooth (*pl* **teeth**) [tuːθ, tiːθ] *n* (*Anat, Tech*) dent *f*; **to have a ~ out** *or* (*US*) **pulled** se faire arracher une dent; **to brush one's teeth** se laver les dents; **by the skin of one's teeth** (*fig*) de justesse

toothache ['tuːθeɪk] *n* mal *m* de dents; **to have ~** avoir mal aux dents

toothbrush ['tuːθbrʌʃ] *n* brosse *f* à dents

toothpaste ['tuːθpeɪst] *n* (*pâte f*) dentifrice *m*

toothpick ['tuːθpɪk] *n* cure-dent *m*

tooth powder *n* poudre *f* dentifrice

top [tɒp] *n* (*of mountain, head*) sommet *m*; (*of page,*

ladder) haut *m*; (*of list, queue*) commencement *m*; (*of box, cupboard, table*) dessus *m*; (*lid: of box, jar*) couvercle *m*; (: *of bottle*) bouchon *m*; (*toy*) toupie *f*; (*Dress: blouse etc*) haut; (: *of pyjamas*) veste *f* ▷ *adj* du haut; (*in rank*) premier(-ière); (*best*) meilleur(e) ▷ *vt* (*exceed*) dépasser; (*be first in*) être en tête de; **the ~ of the milk** (*Brit*) la crème du lait; **at the ~ of the stairs/page/street** en haut de l'escalier/de la page/de la rue; **from ~ to bottom** de fond en comble; **on ~ of** sur; (*in addition to*) en plus de; **from ~ to toe** (*Brit*) de la tête aux pieds; **at the ~ of the list** en tête de liste; **at the ~ of one's voice** à tue-tête; **at ~ speed** à toute vitesse; **over the ~** (*inf: behaviour etc*) qui dépasse les limites
  ▸ **top up** (*Brit*), **top off** *vt* (*bottle*) remplir; (*salary*) compléter; **to ~ up one's mobile (phone)** recharger son compte
topaz ['təʊpæz] *n* topaze *f*
top-class ['tɔp'klɑːs] *adj* de première classe; (*Sport*) de haute compétition
topcoat ['tɔpkəʊt] *n* pardessus *m*
topflight ['tɔpflaɪt] *adj* excellent(e)
top floor *n* dernier étage
top hat *n* haut-de-forme *m*
top-heavy [tɔp'hɛvɪ] *adj* (*object*) trop lourd(e) du haut
topic ['tɔpɪk] *n* sujet *m*, thème *m*
topical ['tɔpɪkl] *adj* d'actualité
topless ['tɔplɪs] *adj* (*bather etc*) aux seins nus; ~ **swimsuit** monokini *m*
top-level ['tɔplɛvl] *adj* (*talks*) à l'échelon le plus élevé
topmost ['tɔpməʊst] *adj* le (la) plus haut(e)
top-notch ['tɔp'nɔtʃ] *adj* (*inf*) de premier ordre
topography [tə'pɔgrəfɪ] *n* topographie *f*
topping ['tɔpɪŋ] *n* (*Culin*) couche de crème, fromage *etc qui recouvre un plat*
topple ['tɔpl] *vt* renverser, faire tomber ▷ *vi* basculer; tomber
top-ranking ['tɔprænkɪŋ] *adj* très haut placé(e)
top-secret ['tɔp'siːkrɪt] *adj* ultra-secret(-ète)
top-security ['tɔpsə'kjʊərɪtɪ] *adj* (*Brit*) de haute sécurité
topsy-turvy ['tɔpsɪ'təːvɪ] *adj, adv* sens dessus-dessous
top-up ['tɔpʌp] *n* (*for mobile phone*) recharge *f*, minutes *fpl*; **would you like a ~?** je vous en remets *or* rajoute?
top-up card *n* (*for mobile phone*) recharge *f*
top-up loan *n* (*Brit*) prêt *m* complémentaire
torch [tɔːtʃ] *n* torche *f*; (*Brit: electric*) lampe *f* de poche
tore [tɔːʳ] *pt of* **tear²**
torment *n* ['tɔːmɛnt] tourment *m* ▷ *vt* [tɔː'mɛnt] tourmenter; (*fig: annoy*) agacer
torn [tɔːn] *pp of* **tear²** ▷ *adj*: ~ **between** (*fig*) tiraillé(e) entre
tornado [tɔː'neɪdəʊ] (*pl* -**es**) *n* tornade *f*
torpedo [tɔː'piːdəʊ] (*pl* -**es**) *n* torpille *f*
torpedo boat *n* torpilleur *m*
torpor ['tɔːpəʳ] *n* torpeur *f*

torrent ['tɔrnt] *n* torrent *m*
torrential [tɔ'rɛnʃl] *adj* torrentiel(le)
torrid ['tɔrɪd] *adj* torride; (*fig*) ardent(e)
torso ['tɔːsəʊ] *n* torse *m*
tortoise ['tɔːtəs] *n* tortue *f*
tortoiseshell ['tɔːtəʃɛl] *adj* en écaille
tortuous ['tɔːtjuəs] *adj* tortueux(-euse)
torture ['tɔːtʃəʳ] *n* torture *f* ▷ *vt* torturer
torturer ['tɔːtʃərəʳ] *n* tortionnaire *m*
Tory ['tɔːrɪ] *adj, n* (*Brit Pol*) tory *m/f*, conservateur(-trice)
toss [tɔs] *vt* lancer, jeter; (*Brit: pancake*) faire sauter; (*head*) rejeter en arrière ▷ *vi*: **to ~ up for sth** (*Brit*) jouer qch à pile ou face ▷ *n* (*movement: of head etc*) mouvement soudain; (*of coin*) tirage *m* à pile ou face; **to ~ a coin** jouer à pile ou face; **to ~ and turn** (*in bed*) se tourner et se retourner; **to win/lose the ~** gagner/perdre à pile ou face; (*Sport*) gagner/perdre le tirage au sort
tot [tɔt] *n* (*Brit: drink*) petit verre; (*child*) bambin *m*
  ▸ **tot up** *vt* (*Brit: figures*) additionner
total ['təʊtl] *adj* total(e) ▷ *n* total *m* ▷ *vt* (*add up*) faire le total de, additionner; (*amount to*) s'élever à; **in ~** au total
totalitarian [təʊtælɪ'tɛərɪən] *adj* totalitaire
totality [təʊ'tælɪtɪ] *n* totalité *f*
totally ['təʊtəlɪ] *adv* totalement
tote bag [təʊt-] *n* fourre-tout *m inv*
totem pole ['təʊtəm-] *n* mât *m* totémique
totter ['tɔtəʳ] *vi* chanceler; (*object, government*) être chancelant(e)
touch [tʌtʃ] *n* contact *m*, toucher *m*; (*sense, skill: of pianist etc*) toucher; (*fig: note, also Football*) touche *f* ▷ *vt* (*gen*) toucher; (*tamper with*) toucher à; **the personal ~** la petite note personnelle; **to put the finishing ~es to sth** mettre la dernière main à qch; **a ~ of** (*fig*) un petit peu de; une touche de; **in ~ with** en contact *or* rapport avec; **to get in ~ with** prendre contact avec; **I'll be in ~** je resterai en contact; **to lose ~** (*friends*) se perdre de vue; **to be out of ~ with events** ne pas être au courant de ce qui se passe
  ▸ **touch down** *vi* (*Aviat*) atterrir; (*on sea*) amerrir
  ▸ **touch on** *vt fus* (*topic*) effleurer, toucher
  ▸ **touch up** *vt* (*paint*) retoucher
touch-and-go ['tʌtʃən'gəʊ] *adj* incertain(e); **it was ~ whether we did it** nous avons failli ne pas le faire
touchdown ['tʌtʃdaun] *n* (*Aviat*) atterrissage *m*; (*on sea*) amerrissage *m*; (*US Football*) essai *m*
touched [tʌtʃt] *adj* (*moved*) touché(e); (*inf*) cinglé(e)
touching ['tʌtʃɪŋ] *adj* touchant(e), attendrissant(e)
touchline ['tʌtʃlaɪn] *n* (*Sport*) (ligne *f* de) touche *f*
touch-sensitive ['tʌtʃsɛnsɪtɪv] *adj* (*keypad*) à effleurement; (*screen*) tactile
touch-type ['tʌtʃtaɪp] *vi* taper au toucher
touchy ['tʌtʃɪ] *adj* (*person*) susceptible
tough [tʌf] *adj* dur(e); (*resistant*) résistant(e),

solide; (*meat*) dur, coriace; (*firm*) inflexible; (*journey*) pénible; (*task, problem, situation*) difficile; (*rough*) dur ▷ *n* (*gangster etc*) dur *m*; **~ luck!** pas de chance!; tant pis!

toughen ['tʌfn] *vt* rendre plus dur(e) (*or* plus résistant(e) *or* plus solide)

toughness ['tʌfnɪs] *n* dureté *f*; résistance *f*; solidité *f*

toupee ['tu:peɪ] *n* postiche *m*

tour ['tuəʳ] *n* voyage *m*; (*also:* **package tour**) voyage organisé; (*of town, museum*) tour *m*, visite *f*; (*by band*) tournée *f* ▷ *vt* visiter; **to go on a ~ of** (*museum, region*) visiter; **to go on ~** partir en tournée

tour guide *n* (*person*) guide *m/f*

touring ['tuərɪŋ] *n* voyages *mpl* touristiques, tourisme *m*

tourism ['tuərɪzm] *n* tourisme *m*

tourist ['tuərɪst] *n* touriste *m/f* ▷ *adv* (*travel*) en classe touriste ▷ *cpd* touristique; **the ~ trade** le tourisme

tourist class *n* (*Aviat*) classe *f* touriste

tourist office *n* syndicat *m* d'initiative

tournament ['tuənəmənt] *n* tournoi *m*

tourniquet ['tuənɪkeɪ] *n* (*Med*) garrot *m*

tour operator *n* (*Brit*) organisateur *m* de voyages, tour-opérateur *m*

tousled ['tauzld] *adj* (*hair*) ébouriffé(e)

tout [taut] *vi*: **to ~ for** essayer de raccrocher, racoler; **to ~ sth (around)** (*Brit*) essayer de placer *or* (re)vendre qch ▷ *n* (*Brit: ticket tout*) revendeur *m* de billets

tow [təu] *n*: **to give sb a ~** (*Aut*) remorquer qn ▷ *vt* remorquer; (*caravan, trailer*) tracter; **"on ~"**, (*US*) **"in ~"** (*Aut*) "véhicule en remorque"
▶ **tow away** *vt* (*subj: police*) emmener à la fourrière; (*: breakdown service*) remorquer

toward [tə'wɔ:d], **towards** [tə'wɔ:dz] *prep* vers; (*of attitude*) envers, à l'égard de; (*of purpose*) pour; **~(s) noon/the end of the year** vers midi/la fin de l'année; **to feel friendly ~(s) sb** être bien disposé envers qn

towel ['tauəl] *n* serviette *f* (de toilette); (*also:* **tea towel**) torchon *m*; **to throw in the ~** (*fig*) jeter l'éponge

towelling ['tauəlɪŋ] *n* (*fabric*) tissu-éponge *m*

towel rail, (*US*) **towel rack** *n* porte-serviettes *m* *inv*

tower ['tauəʳ] *n* tour *f* ▷ *vi* (*building, mountain*) se dresser (majestueusement); **to ~ above** *or* **over sb/sth** dominer qn/qch

tower block *n* (*Brit*) tour *f* (d'habitation)

towering ['tauərɪŋ] *adj* très haut(e), imposant(e)

towline ['təulaɪn] *n* (câble *m* de) remorque *f*

town [taun] *n* ville *f*; **to go to ~** aller en ville; (*fig*) y mettre le paquet; **in the ~** dans la ville, en ville; **to be out of ~** (*person*) être en déplacement

town centre *n* (*Brit*) centre *m* de la ville, centre-ville *m*

town clerk *n* ≈ secrétaire *m/f* de mairie

town council *n* conseil municipal

town crier [-'kraɪəʳ] *n* (*Brit*) crieur public

town hall *n* ≈ mairie *f*

townie ['taunɪ] *n* (*Brit inf*) citadin(e)

town plan *n* plan *m* de ville

town planner *n* urbaniste *m/f*

town planning *n* urbanisme *m*

township ['taunʃɪp] *n* banlieue noire (*établie sous le régime de l'apartheid*)

townspeople ['taunzpi:pl] *npl* citadins *mpl*

towpath ['təupɑ:θ] *n* (chemin *m* de) halage *m*

towrope ['təurəup] *n* (câble *m* de) remorque *f*

tow truck *n* (*US*) dépanneuse *f*

toxic ['tɔksɪk] *adj* toxique

toxin ['tɔksɪn] *n* toxine *f*

toy [tɔɪ] *n* jouet *m*
▶ **toy with** *vt fus* jouer avec; (*idea*) caresser

toyshop ['tɔɪʃɔp] *n* magasin *m* de jouets

trace [treɪs] *n* trace *f* ▷ *vt* (*draw*) tracer, dessiner; (*follow*) suivre la trace de; (*locate*) retrouver; **without ~** (*disappear*) sans laisser de traces; **there was no ~ of it** il n'y en avait pas trace

trace element *n* oligo-élément *m*

trachea [trə'kɪə] *n* (*Anat*) trachée *f*

tracing paper ['treɪsɪŋ-] *n* papier-calque *m*

track [træk] *n* (*mark*) trace *f*; (*path: gen*) chemin *m*, piste *f*; (*: of bullet etc*) trajectoire *f*; (*: of suspect, animal*) piste; (*Rail*) voie ferrée, rails *mpl*; (*on tape, Comput, Sport*) piste; (*on CD*) piste *f*; (*on record*) plage *f* ▷ *vt* suivre la trace *or* la piste de; **to keep ~ of** suivre; **to be on the right ~** (*fig*) être sur la bonne voie
▶ **track down** *vt* (*prey*) trouver et capturer; (*sth lost*) finir par retrouver

tracker dog ['trækə-] *n* (*Brit*) chien dressé pour suivre une piste

track events *npl* (*Sport*) épreuves *fpl* sur piste

tracking station ['trækɪŋ-] *n* (*Space*) centre *m* d'observation de satellites

track meet *n* (*US*) réunion sportive sur piste

track record *n*: **to have a good ~** (*fig*) avoir fait ses preuves

tracksuit ['træksu:t] *n* survêtement *m*

tract [trækt] *n* (*Geo*) étendue *f*, zone *f*; (*pamphlet*) tract *m*; **respiratory ~** (*Anat*) système *m* respiratoire

traction ['trækʃən] *n* traction *f*

tractor ['træktəʳ] *n* tracteur *m*

trade [treɪd] *n* commerce *m*; (*skill, job*) métier *m* ▷ *vi* faire du commerce ▷ *vt* (*exchange*): **to ~ sth (for sth)** échanger qch (contre qch); **to ~ with/ in** faire du commerce avec/le commerce de; **foreign ~** commerce extérieur; **Department of T~ and Industry (DTI)** (*Brit*) ministère *m* du Commerce et de l'Industrie
▶ **trade in** *vt* (*old car etc*) faire reprendre

trade barrier *n* barrière commerciale

trade deficit *n* déficit extérieur

Trade Descriptions Act *n* (*Brit*) loi contre les appellations et la publicité mensongères

trade discount *n* remise *f* au détaillant

trade fair *n* foire(-exposition) commerciale

trade-in ['treɪdɪn] *n* reprise *f*

trade-in price n prix m à la reprise
trademark ['treɪdmɑːk] n marque f de fabrique
trade mission n mission commerciale
trade name n marque déposée
trade-off ['treɪdɔf] n (exchange) échange f; (balancing) équilibre m
trader ['treɪdər] n commerçant(e), négociant(e)
trade secret n secret m de fabrication
tradesman ['treɪdzmən] (irreg) n (shopkeeper) commerçant m; (skilled worker) ouvrier qualifié
trade union n syndicat m
trade unionist [-'juːnjənɪst] n syndicaliste m/f
trade wind n alizé m
trading ['treɪdɪŋ] n affaires fpl, commerce m
trading estate n (Brit) zone industrielle
trading stamp n timbre-prime m
tradition [trə'dɪʃən] n tradition f; **traditions** npl coutumes fpl, traditions
traditional [trə'dɪʃənl] adj traditionnel(le)
traffic ['træfɪk] n trafic m; (cars) circulation f
▷ vi: **to ~ in** (pej: liquor, drugs) faire le trafic de
traffic calming [-'kɑːmɪŋ] n ralentissement m de la circulation
traffic circle n (US) rond-point m
traffic island n refuge m (pour piétons)
traffic jam n embouteillage m
trafficker ['træfɪkər] n trafiquant(e)
traffic lights npl feux mpl (de signalisation)
traffic offence n (Brit) infraction f au code de la route
traffic sign n panneau m de signalisation
traffic violation n (US) = **traffic offence**
traffic warden n contractuel(le)
tragedy ['trædʒədɪ] n tragédie f
tragic ['trædʒɪk] adj tragique
trail [treɪl] n (tracks) trace f, piste f; (path) chemin m, piste; (of smoke etc) traînée f ▷ vt (drag) traîner, tirer; (follow) suivre ▷ vi traîner; (in game, contest) être en retard; **to be on sb's ~** être sur la piste de qn
  ▶ **trail away, trail off** vi (sound, voice) s'évanouir; (interest) disparaître
  ▶ **trail behind** vi traîner, être à la traîne
trailer ['treɪlər] n (Aut) remorque f; (US) caravane f; (Cine) bande-annonce f
trailer truck n (US) (camion m) semi-remorque m
train [treɪn] n train m; (in underground) rame f; (of dress) traîne f; (Brit: series): **~ of events** série f d'événements ▷ vt (apprentice, doctor etc) former; (Sport) entraîner; (dog) dresser; (memory) exercer; (point: gun etc): **to ~ sth on** braquer qch sur ▷ vi recevoir sa formation; (Sport) s'entraîner; **one's ~ of thought** le fil de sa pensée; **to go by ~** voyager par le train or en train; **what time does the ~ from Paris get in?** à quelle heure arrive le train de Paris?; **is this the ~ for ...?** c'est bien le train pour ...?; **to ~ sb to do sth** apprendre à qn à faire qch; (employee) former qn à faire qch
train attendant n (US) employé(e) des

wagons-lits
trained [treɪnd] adj qualifié(e), qui a reçu une formation; dressé(e)
trainee [treɪ'niː] n stagiaire m/f; (in trade) apprenti(e)
trainer ['treɪnər] n (Sport) entraîneur(-euse); (of dogs etc) dresseur(-euse); **trainers** npl (shoes) chaussures fpl de sport
training ['treɪnɪŋ] n formation f; (Sport) entraînement m; (of dog etc) dressage m; **in ~** (Sport) à l'entraînement; (fit) en forme
training college n école professionnelle; (for teachers) ≈ école normale
training course n cours m de formation professionnelle
training shoes npl chaussures fpl de sport
traipse [treɪps] vi (se) traîner, déambuler
trait [treɪt] n trait m (de caractère)
traitor ['treɪtər] n traître m
trajectory [trə'dʒɛktərɪ] n trajectoire f
tram [træm] n (Brit: also: **tramcar**) tram(way) m
tramline ['træmlaɪn] n ligne f de tram(way)
tramp [træmp] n (person) vagabond(e), clochard(e); (inf: pej: woman): **to be a ~** être coureuse ▷ vi marcher d'un pas lourd ▷ vt (walk through: town, streets) parcourir à pied
trample ['træmpl] vt: **to ~ (underfoot)** piétiner; (fig) bafouer
trampoline ['træmpəliːn] n trampoline m
trance [trɑːns] n transe f; (Med) catalepsie f; **to go into a ~** entrer en transe
tranquil ['træŋkwɪl] adj tranquille
tranquillity [træŋ'kwɪlɪtɪ] n tranquillité f
tranquillizer, (US) **tranquilizer** ['træŋkwɪlaɪzər] n (Med) tranquillisant m
transact [træn'zækt] vt (business) traiter
transaction [træn'zækʃən] n transaction f; **transactions** npl (minutes) actes mpl; **cash ~** transaction au comptant
transatlantic ['trænzət'læntɪk] adj transatlantique
transcend [træn'sɛnd] vt transcender; (excel over) surpasser
transcendental [trænsɛn'dɛntl] adj: **~ meditation** méditation transcendantale
transcribe [træn'skraɪb] vt transcrire
transcript ['trænskrɪpt] n transcription f (texte)
transcription [træn'skrɪpʃən] n transcription f
transept ['trænsɛpt] n transept m
transfer n ['trænsfər] (gen, also Sport) transfert m; (Pol: of power) passation f; (of money) virement m; (picture, design) décalcomanie f; (: stick-on) autocollant m ▷ vt [træns'fəːr] transférer; passer; virer; décalquer; **to ~ the charges** (Brit Tel) téléphoner en P.C.V.; **by bank ~** par virement bancaire
transferable [træns'fəːrəbl] adj transmissible, transférable; **"not ~"** "personnel"
transfer desk n (Aviat) guichet m de transit
transfix [træns'fɪks] vt transpercer; (fig): **~ed with fear** paralysé(e) par la peur
transform [træns'fɔːm] vt transformer

transformation [trænsfə'meɪʃən] n
transformation f
transformer [træns'fɔ:mər] n (Elec)
transformateur m
transfusion [træns'fju:ʒən] n transfusion f
transgress [træns'grɛs] vt transgresser
transient ['trænzɪənt] adj transitoire,
éphémère
transistor [træn'zɪstər] n (Elec: also: **transistor
radio**) transistor m
transit ['trænzɪt] n: **in ~** en transit
transit camp n camp m de transit
transition [træn'zɪʃən] n transition f
transitional [træn'zɪʃənl] adj transitoire
transitive ['trænzɪtɪv] adj (Ling) transitif(-ive)
transit lounge n (Aviat) salle f de transit
transitory ['trænzɪtərɪ] adj transitoire
translate [trænz'leɪt] vt: **to ~ (from/into)**
traduire (du/en); **can you ~ this for me?**
pouvez-vous me traduire ceci?
translation [trænz'leɪʃən] n traduction f; (Scol:
as opposed to prose) version f
translator [trænz'leɪtər] n traducteur(-trice)
translucent [trænz'lu:snt] adj translucide
transmission [trænz'mɪʃən] n transmission f
transmit [trænz'mɪt] vt transmettre; (Radio, TV)
émettre
transmitter [trænz'mɪtər] n émetteur m
transparency [træns'pɛərnsɪ] n (Brit Phot)
diapositive f
transparent [træns'pærnt] adj transparent(e)
transpire [træns'paɪər] vi (become known): **it
finally ~d that ...** on a finalement appris que
...; (happen) arriver
transplant vt [træns'plɑ:nt] transplanter;
(seedlings) repiquer ▷ n ['trænsplɑ:nt] (Med)
transplantation f; **to have a heart ~** subir une
greffe du cœur
transport n ['trænspɔ:t] transport m ▷ vt
[træns'pɔ:t] transporter; **public ~** transports en
commun; **Department of T~** (Brit) ministère m
des Transports
transportation [trænspɔ:'teɪʃən] n (moyen m
de) transport m; (of prisoners) transportation f;
Department of T~ (US) ministère m des
Transports
transport café n (Brit) ≈ routier m
transpose [træns'pəuz] vt transposer
transsexual [trænz'sɛksjuəl] adj, n
transsexuel(le)
transverse ['trænzvə:s] adj transversal(e)
transvestite [trænz'vɛstaɪt] n travesti(e)
trap [træp] n (snare, trick) piège m; (carriage)
cabriolet m ▷ vt prendre au piège; (immobilize)
bloquer; (confine) coincer; **to set** or **lay a ~ (for
sb)** tendre un piège (à qn); **to shut one's ~** (inf)
la fermer
trap door n trappe f
trapeze [trə'pi:z] n trapèze m
trapper ['træpər] n trappeur m
trappings ['træpɪŋz] npl ornements mpl;
attributs mpl

trash [træʃ] n (pej: goods) camelote f; (: nonsense)
sottises fpl; (US: rubbish) ordures fpl
trash can n (US) poubelle f
trashy ['træʃɪ] adj (inf) de camelote, qui ne vaut
rien
trauma ['trɔ:mə] n traumatisme m
traumatic [trɔ:'mætɪk] adj traumatisant(e)
travel ['trævl] n voyage(s) m(pl) ▷ vi voyager;
(move) aller, se déplacer; (news, sound) se
propager ▷ vt (distance) parcourir; **this wine
doesn't ~ well** ce vin voyage mal
travel agency n agence f de voyages
travel agent n agent m de voyages
travel brochure n brochure f touristique
travel insurance n assurance-voyage f
traveller, (US) **traveler** ['trævlər] n
voyageur(-euse); (Comm) représentant m de
commerce
traveller's cheque, (US) **traveler's check** n
chèque m de voyage
travelling, (US) **traveling** ['trævlɪŋ] n voyage(s)
m(pl) ▷ adj (circus, exhibition) ambulant(e) ▷ cpd
(bag, clock) de voyage; (expenses) de déplacement
travelling salesman, (US) **traveling salesman**
(irreg) n voyageur m de commerce
travelogue ['trævələg] n (book, talk) récit m de
voyage; (film) documentaire m de voyage
travel-sick ['trævlsɪk] adj: **to get ~** avoir le mal
de la route (or de mer or de l'air)
travel sickness n mal m de la route (or de mer or
de l'air)
traverse ['trævəs] vt traverser
travesty ['trævəstɪ] n parodie f
trawler ['trɔ:lər] n chalutier m
tray [treɪ] n (for carrying) plateau m; (on desk)
corbeille f
treacherous ['trɛtʃərəs] adj traître(sse); (ground,
tide) dont il faut se méfier; **road conditions
are ~** l'état des routes est dangereux
treachery ['trɛtʃərɪ] n traîtrise f
treacle ['tri:kl] n mélasse f
tread [trɛd] n (step) pas m; (sound) bruit m de pas;
(of tyre) chape f, bande f de roulement ▷ vi (pt
trod, pp **trodden**) [trɔd, 'trɔdn] marcher
▶ **tread on** vt fus marcher sur
treadle ['trɛdl] n pédale f (de machine)
treas. abbr = **treasurer**
treason ['tri:zn] n trahison f
treasure ['trɛʒər] n trésor m ▷ vt (value) tenir
beaucoup à; (store) conserver précieusement
treasure hunt n chasse f au trésor
treasurer ['trɛʒərər] n trésorier(-ière)
treasury ['trɛʒərɪ] n trésorerie f; **the T~**, (US)
the T~ Department ≈ le ministère des
Finances
treasury bill n bon m du Trésor
treat [tri:t] n petit cadeau, petite surprise ▷ vt
traiter; **it was a ~** ça m'a (or nous a etc) vraiment
fait plaisir; **to ~ sb to sth** offrir qch à qn; **to ~
sth as a joke** prendre qch à la plaisanterie
treatise ['tri:tɪz] n traité m (ouvrage)
treatment ['tri:tmənt] n traitement m; **to have**

~ for sth (*Med*) suivre un traitement pour qch
treaty ['tri:tɪ] *n* traité *m*
treble ['trɛbl] *adj* triple ▷ *n* (*Mus*) soprano *m* ▷ *vt*, *vi* tripler
treble clef *n* clé *f* de sol
tree [tri:] *n* arbre *m*
tree-lined ['tri:laɪnd] *adj* bordé(e) d'arbres
treetop ['tri:tɔp] *n* cime *f* d'un arbre
tree trunk *n* tronc *m* d'arbre
trek [trɛk] *n* (*long walk*) randonnée *f*; (*tiring walk*) longue marche, trotte *f* ▷ *vi* (*as holiday*) faire de la randonnée
trellis ['trɛlɪs] *n* treillis *m*, treillage *m*
tremble ['trɛmbl] *vi* trembler
trembling ['trɛmblɪŋ] *n* tremblement *m* ▷ *adj* tremblant(e)
tremendous [trɪ'mɛndəs] *adj* (*enormous*) énorme; (*excellent*) formidable, fantastique
tremendously [trɪ'mɛndəslɪ] *adv* énormément, extrêmement + *adjective*; formidablement
tremor ['trɛməʳ] *n* tremblement *m*; (*also*: **earth tremor**) secousse *f* sismique
trench [trɛntʃ] *n* tranchée *f*
trench coat *n* trench-coat *m*
trench warfare *n* guerre *f* de tranchées
trend [trɛnd] *n* (*tendency*) tendance *f*; (*of events*) cours *m*; (*fashion*) mode *f*; **~ towards/away from doing** tendance à faire/à ne pas faire; **to set the ~** donner le ton; **to set a ~** lancer une mode
trendy ['trɛndɪ] *adj* (*idea, person*) dans le vent; (*clothes*) dernier cri *inv*
trepidation [trɛpɪ'deɪʃən] *n* vive agitation
trespass ['trɛspəs] *vi*: **to ~ on** s'introduire sans permission dans; (*fig*) empiéter sur; **"no ~ing"** "propriété privée", "défense d'entrer"
trespasser ['trɛspəsəʳ] *n* intrus(e); **"~s will be prosecuted"** "interdiction d'entrer sous peine de poursuites"
trestle ['trɛsl] *n* tréteau *m*
trestle table *n* table *f* à tréteaux
trial ['traɪəl] *n* (*Law*) procès *m*, jugement *m*; (*test: of machine etc*) essai *m*; (*worry*) souci *m*; **trials** *npl* (*unpleasant experiences*) épreuves *fpl*; (*Sport*) épreuves éliminatoires; **horse ~s** concours *m* hippique; **~ by jury** jugement par jury; **to be sent for ~** être traduit(e) en justice; **to be on ~** passer en jugement; **by ~ and error** par tâtonnements
trial balance *n* (*Comm*) balance *f* de vérification
trial basis *n*: **on a ~** pour une période d'essai
trial period *n* période *f* d'essai
trial run *n* essai *m*
triangle ['traɪæŋgl] *n* (*Math, Mus*) triangle *m*
triangular [traɪ'æŋgjuləʳ] *adj* triangulaire
triathlon [traɪ'æθlən] *n* triathlon *m*
tribal ['traɪbl] *adj* tribal(e)
tribe [traɪb] *n* tribu *f*
tribesman ['traɪbzmən] *n* membre *m* de la tribu
tribulation [trɪbju'leɪʃən] *n* tribulation *f*, malheur *m*
tribunal [traɪ'bju:nl] *n* tribunal *m*
tributary ['trɪbjutərɪ] *n* (*river*) affluent *m*

tribute ['trɪbju:t] *n* tribut *m*, hommage *m*; **to pay ~ to** rendre hommage à
trice [traɪs] *n*: **in a ~** en un clin d'œil
trick [trɪk] *n* (*magic*) tour *m*; (*joke, prank*) tour, farce *f*; (*skill, knack*) astuce *f*; (*Cards*) levée *f* ▷ *vt* attraper, rouler; **to play a ~ on sb** jouer un tour à qn; **to ~ sb into doing sth** persuader qn par la ruse de faire qch; **to ~ sb out of sth** obtenir qch de qn par la ruse; **it's a ~ of the light** c'est une illusion d'optique causée par la lumière; **that should do the ~** (*fam*) ça devrait faire l'affaire
trickery ['trɪkərɪ] *n* ruse *f*
trickle ['trɪkl] *n* (*of water etc*) filet *m* ▷ *vi* couler en un filet *or* goutte à goutte; **to ~ in/out** (*people*) entrer/sortir par petits groupes
trick question *n* question-piège *f*
trickster ['trɪkstəʳ] *n* arnaqueur(-euse), filou *m*
tricky ['trɪkɪ] *adj* difficile, délicat(e)
tricycle ['traɪsɪkl] *n* tricycle *m*
trifle ['traɪfl] *n* bagatelle *f*; (*Culin*) ≈ diplomate *m* ▷ *adv*: **a ~ long** un peu long ▷ *vi*: **to ~ with** traiter à la légère
trifling ['traɪflɪŋ] *adj* insignifiant(e)
trigger ['trɪgəʳ] *n* (*of gun*) gâchette *f*
  ▶ **trigger off** *vt* déclencher
trigonometry [trɪgə'nɔmətrɪ] *n* trigonométrie *f*
trilby ['trɪlbɪ] *n* (*Brit: also*: **trilby hat**) chapeau mou, feutre *m*
trill [trɪl] *n* (*of bird, Mus*) trille *m*
trilogy ['trɪlədʒɪ] *n* trilogie *f*
trim [trɪm] *adj* net(te); (*house, garden*) bien tenu(e); (*figure*) svelte ▷ *n* (*haircut etc*) légère coupe; (*embellishment*) finitions *fpl*; (*on car*) garnitures *fpl* ▷ *vt* (*cut*) couper légèrement; (*decorate*): **to ~ (with)** décorer (de); (*Naut: a sail*) gréer; **to keep in (good) ~** maintenir en (bon) état
trimmings ['trɪmɪŋz] *npl* décorations *fpl*; (*extras: gen Culin*) garniture *f*
Trinidad and Tobago ['trɪnɪdæd-] *n* Trinité et Tobago *f*
Trinity ['trɪnɪtɪ] *n*: **the ~** la Trinité
trinket ['trɪŋkɪt] *n* bibelot *m*; (*piece of jewellery*) colifichet *m*
trio ['tri:əu] *n* trio *m*
trip [trɪp] *n* voyage *m*; (*excursion*) excursion *f*; (*stumble*) faux pas ▷ *vi* faire un faux pas, trébucher; (*go lightly*) marcher d'un pas léger; **on a ~** en voyage
  ▶ **trip up** *vi* trébucher ▷ *vt* faire un croc-en-jambe à
tripartite [traɪ'pɑ:taɪt] *adj* triparti(e)
tripe [traɪp] *n* (*Culin*) tripes *fpl*; (*pej: rubbish*) idioties *fpl*
triple ['trɪpl] *adj* triple ▷ *adv*: **~ the distance/the speed** trois fois la distance/la vitesse
triple jump *n* triple saut *m*
triplets ['trɪplɪts] *npl* triplés(-ées)
triplicate ['trɪplɪkət] *n*: **in ~** en trois exemplaires
tripod ['traɪpɔd] *n* trépied *m*
Tripoli ['trɪpəlɪ] *n* Tripoli

tripper ['trɪpə^r] n (Brit) touriste m/f; excursionniste m/f

tripwire ['trɪpwaɪə^r] n fil m de déclenchement

trite [traɪt] adj banal(e)

triumph ['traɪʌmf] n triomphe m ▷ vi: **to ~ (over)** triompher (de)

triumphal [traɪ'ʌmfl] adj triomphal(e)

triumphant [traɪ'ʌmfənt] adj triomphant(e)

trivia ['trɪvɪə] npl futilités fpl

trivial ['trɪvɪəl] adj insignifiant(e); (commonplace) banal(e)

triviality [trɪvɪ'ælɪtɪ] n caractère insignifiant; banalité f

trivialize ['trɪvɪəlaɪz] vt rendre banal(e)

trod [trɒd] pt of **tread**

trodden ['trɒdn] pp of **tread**

trolley ['trɒlɪ] n chariot m

trolley bus n trolleybus m

trollop ['trɒləp] n prostituée f

trombone [trɒm'bəun] n trombone m

troop [tru:p] n bande f, groupe m ▷ vi: **to ~ in/ out** entrer/sortir en groupe; **troops** npl (Mil) troupes fpl; (: men) hommes mpl, soldats mpl; **~ing the colour** (Brit: ceremony) le salut au drapeau

troop carrier n (plane) avion m de transport de troupes; (Naut: also: **troopship**) transport m (navire)

trooper ['tru:pə^r] n (Mil) soldat m de cavalerie; (US: policeman) ≈ gendarme m

troopship ['tru:pʃɪp] n transport m (navire)

trophy ['trəufɪ] n trophée m

tropic ['trɒpɪk] n tropique m; **in the ~s** sous les tropiques; **T~ of Cancer/Capricorn** tropique du Cancer/Capricorne

tropical ['trɒpɪkl] adj tropical(e)

trot [trɒt] n trot m ▷ vi trotter; **on the ~** (Brit: fig) d'affilée

▶ **trot out** vt (excuse, reason) débiter; (names, facts) réciter les uns après les autres

trouble ['trʌbl] n difficulté(s) f(pl), problème(s) m(pl); (worry) ennuis mpl, soucis mpl; (bother, effort) peine f; (Pol) conflit(s) m(pl), troubles mpl; (Med): **stomach** etc ~ troubles gastriques etc ▷ vt (disturb) déranger, gêner; (worry) inquiéter ▷ vi: **to ~ to do** prendre la peine de faire; **troubles** npl (Pol etc) troubles; (personal) ennuis, soucis; **to be in ~** avoir des ennuis; (ship, climber etc) être en difficulté; **to have ~ doing sth** avoir du mal à faire qch; **to go to the ~ of doing** se donner le mal de faire; **it's no ~!** je vous en prie!; **please don't ~ yourself** je vous en prie, ne vous dérangez pas!; **the ~ is ...** le problème, c'est que ...; **what's the ~?** qu'est-ce qui ne va pas?

troubled ['trʌbld] adj (person) inquiet(-ète); (times, life) agité(e)

trouble-free ['trʌblfri:] adj sans problèmes or ennuis

troublemaker ['trʌblmeɪkə^r] n élément perturbateur, fauteur m de troubles

troubleshooter ['trʌblʃu:tə^r] n (in conflict) conciliateur m

troublesome ['trʌblsəm] adj (child) fatigant(e), difficile; (cough) gênant(e)

trouble spot n point chaud (fig)

troubling ['trʌblɪŋ] adj (times, thought) inquiétant(e)

trough [trɒf] n (also: **drinking trough**) abreuvoir m; (also: **feeding trough**) auge f; (depression) creux m; (channel) chenal m; **~ of low pressure** (Meteorology) dépression f

trounce [trauns] vt (defeat) battre à plates coutures

troupe [tru:p] n troupe f

trouser press n presse-pantalon m inv

trousers ['trauzəz] npl pantalon m; **short ~** (Brit) culottes courtes

trouser suit n (Brit) tailleur-pantalon m

trousseau (pl **-x** or **-s**) ['tru:səu, -z] n trousseau m

trout [traut] n (pl inv) truite f

trowel ['trauəl] n truelle f; (garden tool) déplantoir m

truant ['truənt] n: **to play ~** (Brit) faire l'école buissonnière

truce [tru:s] n trêve f

truck [trʌk] n camion m; (Rail) wagon m à plate-forme; (for luggage) chariot m (à bagages)

truck driver n camionneur m

trucker ['trʌkə^r] n (esp US) camionneur m

truck farm n (US) jardin maraîcher

trucking ['trʌkɪŋ] n (esp US) transport routier

trucking company n (US) entreprise f de transport (routier)

truck stop (US) n routier m, restaurant m de routiers

truculent ['trʌkjulənt] adj agressif(-ive)

trudge [trʌdʒ] vi marcher lourdement, se traîner

true [tru:] adj vrai(e); (accurate) exact(e); (genuine) vrai, véritable; (faithful) fidèle; (wall) d'aplomb; (beam) droit(e); (wheel) dans l'axe; **to come ~** se réaliser; **~ to life** réaliste

truffle ['trʌfl] n truffe f

truly ['tru:lɪ] adv vraiment, réellement; (truthfully) sans mentir; (faithfully) fidèlement; **yours ~** (in letter) je vous prie d'agréer, Monsieur (or Madame etc), l'expression de mes sentiments respectueux

trump [trʌmp] n atout m; **to turn up ~s** (fig) faire des miracles

trump card n atout m; (fig) carte maîtresse f

trumped-up [trʌmpt'ʌp] adj inventé(e) (de toutes pièces)

trumpet ['trʌmpɪt] n trompette f

truncated [trʌŋ'keɪtɪd] adj tronqué(e)

truncheon ['trʌntʃən] n bâton m (d'agent de police); matraque f

trundle ['trʌndl] vt, vi: **to ~ along** rouler bruyamment

trunk [trʌŋk] n (of tree, person) tronc m; (of elephant) trompe f; (case) malle f; (US Aut) coffre m; **trunks** npl (also: **swimming trunks**) maillot m or slip m de bain

trunk call n (Brit Tel) communication

interurbaine

trunk road *n* (*Brit*) ≈ (route *f*) nationale *f*

truss [trʌs] *n* (*Med*) bandage *m* herniaire ▷ *vt*: **to ~ (up)** (*Culin*) brider

trust [trʌst] *n* confiance *f*; (*responsibility*): **to place sth in sb's ~** confier la responsabilité de qch à qn; (*Law*) fidéicommis *m*; (*Comm*) trust *m* ▷ *vt* (*rely on*) avoir confiance en; (*entrust*): **to ~ sth to sb** confier qch à qn; (*hope*): **to ~ (that)** espérer (que); **to take sth on ~** accepter qch les yeux fermés; **in ~** (*Law*) par fidéicommis

trust company *n* société *f* fiduciaire

trusted ['trʌstɪd] *adj* en qui l'on a confiance

trustee [trʌs'tiː] *n* (*Law*) fidéicommissaire *m/f*; (*of school etc*) administrateur(-trice)

trustful ['trʌstful] *adj* confiant(e)

trust fund *n* fonds *m* en fidéicommis

trusting ['trʌstɪŋ] *adj* confiant(e)

trustworthy ['trʌstwəːðɪ] *adj* digne de confiance

trusty ['trʌstɪ] *adj* fidèle

truth [truːθ, *pl* truːðz] *n* vérité *f*

truthful ['truːθful] *adj* (*person*) qui dit la vérité; (*answer*) sincère; (*description*) exact(e), vrai(e)

truthfully ['truːθfəlɪ] *adv* sincèrement, sans mentir

truthfulness ['truːθfəlnɪs] *n* véracité *f*

try [traɪ] *n* essai *m*, tentative *f*; (*Rugby*) essai *m* ▷ *vt* (*attempt*) essayer, tenter; (*test: sth new: also*: **try out**) essayer, tester; (*Law: person*) juger; (*strain*) éprouver ▷ *vi* essayer; **to ~ to do** essayer de faire; (*seek*) chercher à faire; **to ~ one's (very) best** *or* **one's (very) hardest** faire de son mieux; **to give sth a ~** essayer qch

▸ **try on** *vt* (*clothes*) essayer; **to ~ it on** (*fig*) tenter le coup, bluffer

▸ **try out** *vt* essayer, mettre à l'essai

trying ['traɪɪŋ] *adj* pénible

tsar [zɑː'] *n* tsar *m*

T-shirt ['tiːʃəːt] *n* tee-shirt *m*

tsunami [tsʊ'nɑːmɪ] *n* tsunami *m*

T-square ['tiːskwɛə'] *n* équerre *f* en T

TT *adj abbr* (*Brit inf*) = **teetotal** ▷ *abbr* (*US*) = **Trust Territory**

tub [tʌb] *n* cuve *f*; (*for washing clothes*) baquet *m*; (*bath*) baignoire *f*

tuba ['tjuːbə] *n* tuba *m*

tubby ['tʌbɪ] *adj* rondelet(te)

tube [tjuːb] *n* tube *m*; (*Brit: underground*) métro *m*; (*for tyre*) chambre *f* à air; (*inf: television*): **the ~** la télé

tubeless ['tjuːblɪs] *adj* (*tyre*) sans chambre à air

tuber ['tjuːbə'] *n* (*Bot*) tubercule *m*

tuberculosis [tjubəːkju'ləʊsɪs] *n* tuberculose *f*

tube station *n* (*Brit*) station *f* de métro

tubing ['tjuːbɪŋ] *n* tubes *mpl*; **a piece of ~** un tube

tubular ['tjuːbjulə'] *adj* tubulaire

TUC *n abbr* (*Brit*: = *Trades Union Congress*) confédération *f* des syndicats britanniques

tuck [tʌk] *n* (*Sewing*) pli *m*, rempli *m* ▷ *vt* (*put*) mettre

▸ **tuck away** *vt* cacher, ranger; (*money*) mettre de côté; (*building*): **to be ~ed away** être caché(e)

▸ **tuck in** *vt* rentrer; (*child*) border ▷ *vi* (*eat*) manger de bon appétit; attaquer le repas

▸ **tuck up** *vt* (*child*) border

tuck shop *n* (*Brit Scol*) boutique *f* à provisions

Tuesday ['tjuːzdɪ] *n* mardi *m*; (**the date**) **today is ~ 23rd March** nous sommes aujourd'hui le mardi 23 mars; **on ~** mardi; **on ~s** le mardi; **every ~** tous les mardis, chaque mardi; **every other ~** un mardi sur deux; **last/next ~** mardi dernier/prochain; **~ next** mardi qui vient; **the following ~** le mardi suivant; **a week/fortnight on ~**, **~ week/fortnight** mardi en huit/quinze; **the ~ before last** l'autre mardi; **the ~ after next** mardi en huit; **~ morning/lunchtime/afternoon/evening** mardi matin/midi/après-midi/soir; **~ night** mardi soir; (*overnight*) la nuit de mardi (à mercredi); **~'s newspaper** le journal de mardi

tuft [tʌft] *n* touffe *f*

tug [tʌg] *n* (*ship*) remorqueur *m* ▷ *vt* tirer (sur)

tug-of-love [tʌgəv'lʌv] *n* lutte acharnée entre parents divorcés pour avoir la garde d'un enfant

tug-of-war [tʌgəv'wɔː'] *n* lutte *f* à la corde

tuition [tjuː'ɪʃən] *n* (*Brit: lessons*) leçons *fpl*; (: *private*) cours particuliers; (*US: fees*) frais *mpl* de scolarité

tulip ['tjuːlɪp] *n* tulipe *f*

tumble ['tʌmbl] *n* (*fall*) chute *f*, culbute *f* ▷ *vi* tomber, dégringoler; (*somersault*) faire une *or* des culbute(s) ▷ *vt* renverser, faire tomber; **to ~ to sth** (*inf*) réaliser qch

tumbledown ['tʌmbldaun] *adj* délabré(e)

tumble dryer *n* (*Brit*) séchoir *m* (à linge) à air chaud

tumbler ['tʌmblə'] *n* verre (droit), gobelet *m*

tummy ['tʌmɪ] *n* (*inf*) ventre *m*

tumour, (*US*) **tumor** ['tjuːmə'] *n* tumeur *f*

tumult ['tjuːmʌlt] *n* tumulte *m*

tumultuous [tjuː'mʌltjuəs] *adj* tumultueux(-euse)

tuna ['tjuːnə] *n* (*pl inv: also*: **tuna fish**) thon *m*

tune [tjuːn] *n* (*melody*) air *m* ▷ *vt* (*Mus*) accorder; (*Radio, TV, Aut*) régler, mettre au point; **to be in/out of ~** (*instrument*) être accordé/désaccordé; (*singer*) chanter juste/faux; **to be in/out of ~ with** (*fig*) être en accord/désaccord avec; **she was robbed to the ~ of £30,000** (*fig*) on lui a volé la jolie somme de 10 000 livres

▸ **tune in** *vi* (*Radio, TV*): **to ~ in (to)** se mettre à l'écoute (de)

▸ **tune up** *vi* (*musician*) accorder son instrument

tuneful ['tjuːnful] *adj* mélodieux(-euse)

tuner ['tjuːnə'] *n* (*radio set*) tuner *m*; **piano ~** accordeur *m* de pianos

tuner amplifier *n* ampli-tuner *m*

tungsten ['tʌŋstn] *n* tungstène *m*

tunic ['tjuːnɪk] *n* tunique *f*

tuning ['tjuːnɪŋ] *n* réglage *m*

tuning fork *n* diapason *m*

Tunis ['tjuːnɪs] *n* Tunis

Tunisia [tjuː'nɪzɪə] *n* Tunisie *f*

Tunisian [tjuː'nɪzɪən] *adj* tunisien(ne) ▷ *n* Tunisien(ne)

tunnel ['tʌnl] *n* tunnel *m*; (*in mine*) galerie *f* ▷ *vi* creuser un tunnel (*or* une galerie)

tunnel vision *n* (*Med*) rétrécissement *m* du champ visuel; (*fig*) vision étroite des choses

tunny ['tʌnɪ] *n* thon *m*

turban ['təːbən] *n* turban *m*

turbid ['təːbɪd] *adj* boueux(-euse)

turbine ['təːbaɪn] *n* turbine *f*

turbo ['təːbəu] *n* turbo *m*

turbojet [təːbəu'dʒɛt] *n* turboréacteur *m*

turboprop [təːbəu'prɔp] *n* (*engine*) turbopropulseur *m*

turbot ['təːbət] *n* (*pl inv*) turbot *m*

turbulence ['təːbjuləns] *n* (*Aviat*) turbulence *f*

turbulent ['təːbjulənt] *adj* turbulent(e); (*sea*) agité(e)

tureen [təˈriːn] *n* soupière *f*

turf [təːf] *n* gazon *m*; (*clod*) motte *f* (de gazon) ▷ *vt* gazonner; **the T~** le turf, les courses *fpl* ▶ **turf out** *vt* (*inf*) jeter; jeter dehors

turf accountant *n* (*Brit*) bookmaker *m*

turgid ['təːdʒɪd] *adj* (*speech*) pompeux(-euse)

Turin [tjuəˈrɪn] *n* Turin

Turk [təːk] *n* Turc (Turque)

Turkey ['təːkɪ] *n* Turquie *f*

turkey ['təːkɪ] *n* dindon *m*, dinde *f*

Turkish ['təːkɪʃ] *adj* turc (turque) ▷ *n* (*Ling*) turc *m*

Turkish bath *n* bain turc

Turkish delight *n* loukoum *m*

turmeric ['təːmərɪk] *n* curcuma *m*

turmoil ['təːmɔɪl] *n* trouble *m*, bouleversement *m*

turn [təːn] *n* tour *m*; (*in road*) tournant *m*; (*tendency: of mind, events*) tournure *f*; (*performance*) numéro *m*; (*Med*) crise *f*, attaque *f* ▷ *vt* tourner; (*collar, steak*) retourner; (*age*) atteindre; (*shape: wood, metal*) tourner; (*milk*) faire tourner; (*change*): **to ~ sth into** changer qch en ▷ *vi* (*object, wind, milk*) tourner; (*person: look back*) se (re)tourner; (*reverse direction*) faire demi-tour; (*change*) changer; (*become*) devenir; **to ~ into** se changer en, se transformer en; **a good ~** un service; **a bad ~** un mauvais tour; **it gave me quite a ~** ça m'a fait un coup; **"no left ~"** (*Aut*) "défense de tourner à gauche"; **~ left/right at the next junction** tournez à gauche/droite au prochain carrefour; **it's your ~** c'est (à) votre tour; **in ~** à son tour; à tour de rôle; **to take ~s** se relayer; **to take ~s at** faire à tour de rôle; **at the ~ of the year/century** à la fin de l'année/du siècle; **to take a ~ for the worse** (*situation, events*) empirer; **his health** *or* **he has taken a ~ for the worse** son état s'est aggravé
▶ **turn about** *vi* faire demi-tour; faire un demi-tour
▶ **turn around** *vi* (*person*) se retourner ▷ *vt* (*object*) tourner
▶ **turn away** *vi* se détourner, tourner la tête ▷ *vt*

(*reject: person*) renvoyer; (*: business*) refuser
▶ **turn back** *vi* revenir, faire demi-tour
▶ **turn down** *vt* (*refuse*) rejeter, refuser; (*reduce*) baisser; (*fold*) rabattre
▶ **turn in** *vi* (*inf: go to bed*) aller se coucher ▷ *vt* (*fold*) rentrer
▶ **turn off** *vi* (*from road*) tourner ▷ *vt* (*light, radio etc*) éteindre; (*tap*) fermer; (*engine*) arrêter; **I can't ~ the heating off** je n'arrive pas à éteindre le chauffage
▶ **turn on** *vt* (*light, radio etc*) allumer; (*tap*) ouvrir; (*engine*) mettre en marche; **I can't ~ the heating on** je n'arrive pas à allumer le chauffage
▶ **turn out** *vt* (*light, gas*) éteindre; (*produce: goods, novel, good pupils*) produire ▷ *vi* (*voters, troops*) se présenter; **to ~ out to be ...** s'avérer ..., se révéler ...
▶ **turn over** *vi* (*person*) se retourner ▷ *vt* (*object*) retourner; (*page*) tourner
▶ **turn round** *vi* faire demi-tour; (*rotate*) tourner
▶ **turn to** *vt fus*: **to ~ to sb** s'adresser à qn
▶ **turn up** *vi* (*person*) arriver, se pointer (*inf*); (*lost object*) être retrouvé(e) ▷ *vt* (*collar*) remonter; (*radio, heater*) mettre plus fort

turnabout ['təːnəbaut], **turnaround** ['təːnəraund] *n* volte-face *f inv*

turncoat ['təːnkəut] *n* renégat(e)

turned-up ['təːndʌp] *adj* (*nose*) retroussé(e)

turning ['təːnɪŋ] *n* (*in road*) tournant *m*; **the first ~ on the right** la première (rue *or* route) à droite

turning circle *n* (*Brit*) rayon *m* de braquage

turning point *n* (*fig*) tournant *m*, moment décisif

turning radius *n* (*US*) = **turning circle**

turnip ['təːnɪp] *n* navet *m*

turnout ['təːnaut] *n* (nombre *m* de personnes dans l')assistance *f*; (*of voters*) taux *m* de participation

turnover ['təːnəuvəʳ] *n* (*Comm: amount of money*) chiffre *m* d'affaires; (*: of goods*) roulement *m*; (*of staff*) renouvellement *m*, changement *m*; (*Culin*) sorte de chausson; **there is a rapid ~ in staff** le personnel change souvent

turnpike ['təːnpaɪk] *n* (*US*) autoroute *f* à péage

turnstile ['təːnstaɪl] *n* tourniquet *m* (d'entrée)

turntable ['təːnteɪbl] *n* (*on record player*) platine *f*

turn-up ['təːnʌp] *n* (*Brit: on trousers*) revers *m*

turpentine ['təːpəntaɪn] *n* (*also*: **turps**) (essence *f* de) térébenthine *f*

turquoise ['təːkwɔɪz] *n* (*stone*) turquoise *f* ▷ *adj* turquoise *inv*

turret ['tʌrɪt] *n* tourelle *f*

turtle ['təːtl] *n* tortue marine

turtleneck ['təːtlnɛk], **turtleneck sweater** *n* pullover *m* à col montant

Tuscany ['tʌskənɪ] *n* Toscane *f*

tusk [tʌsk] *n* défense *f* (d'éléphant)

tussle ['tʌsl] *n* bagarre *f*, mêlée *f*

tutor ['tjuːtəʳ] *n* (*Brit Scol: in college*) directeur(-trice) d'études; (*private teacher*) précepteur(-trice)

tutorial [tjuːˈtɔːrɪəl] *n* (*Scol*) (séance *f* de) travaux *mpl* pratiques

tuxedo [tʌkˈsiːdəu] *n* (*US*) smoking *m*

TV [tiːˈviː] *n abbr* (= *television*) télé *f*, TV *f*

TV dinner *n* plateau-repas surgelé

twaddle [ˈtwɔdl] *n* balivernes *fpl*

twang [twæŋ] *n* (*of instrument*) son vibrant; (*of voice*) ton nasillard ▷ *vi* vibrer ▷ *vt* (*guitar*) pincer les cordes de

tweak [twiːk] *vt* (*nose*) tordre; (*ear, hair*) tirer

tweed [twiːd] *n* tweed *m*

tweezers [ˈtwiːzəz] *npl* pince *f* à épiler

twelfth [twelfθ] *num* douzième

Twelfth Night *n* la fête des Rois

twelve [twelv] *num* douze; **at ~ (o'clock)** à midi; (*midnight*) à minuit

twentieth [ˈtwentɪɪθ] *num* vingtième

twenty [ˈtwentɪ] *num* vingt

twerp [twəːp] *n* (*inf*) imbécile *m/f*

twice [twaɪs] *adv* deux fois; **~ as much** deux fois plus; **~ a week** deux fois par semaine; **she is ~ your age** elle a deux fois ton âge

twiddle [ˈtwɪdl] *vt, vi*: **to ~ (with)** sth tripoter qch; **to ~ one's thumbs** (*fig*) se tourner les pouces

twig [twɪg] *n* brindille *f* ▷ *vt, vi* (*inf*) piger

twilight [ˈtwaɪlaɪt] *n* crépuscule *m*; (*morning*) aube *f*; **in the ~** dans la pénombre

twill [twɪl] *n* sergé *m*

twin [twɪn] *adj, n* jumeau(-elle) ▷ *vt* jumeler

twin-bedded room [ˈtwɪnˈbɛdɪd-] *n* = **twin room**

twin beds *npl* lits *mpl* jumeaux

twin-carburettor [ˈtwɪnkaːbjuˈrɛtər] *adj* à double carburateur

twine [twaɪn] *n* ficelle *f* ▷ *vi* (*plant*) s'enrouler

twin-engined [twɪnˈɛndʒɪnd] *adj* bimoteur; **~ aircraft** bimoteur *m*

twinge [twɪndʒ] *n* (*of pain*) élancement *m*; (*of conscience*) remords *m*

twinkle [ˈtwɪŋkl] *n* scintillement *m*; pétillement *m* ▷ *vi* scintiller; (*eyes*) pétiller

twin room *n* chambre *f* à deux lits

twin town *n* ville jumelée

twirl [twəːl] *n* tournoiement *m* ▷ *vt* faire tournoyer ▷ *vi* tournoyer

twist [twɪst] *n* torsion *f*, tour *m*; (*in wire, flex*) tortillon *m*; (*bend: in road*) tournant *m*; (*in story*) coup *m* de théâtre ▷ *vt* tordre; (*weave*) entortiller; (*roll around*) enrouler; (*fig*) déformer ▷ *vi* s'entortiller; s'enrouler; (*road, river*) serpenter; **to ~ one's ankle/wrist** (*Med*) se tordre la cheville/le poignet

twisted [ˈtwɪstɪd] *adj* (*wire, rope*) entortillé(e); (*ankle, wrist*) tordu(e), foulé(e); (*fig: logic, mind*) tordu

twit [twɪt] *n* (*inf*) crétin(e)

twitch [twɪtʃ] *n* (*pull*) coup sec, saccade *f*; (*nervous*) tic *m* ▷ *vi* se convulser; avoir un tic

two [tuː] *num* deux; **~ by ~**, **in ~s** par deux; **to put ~ and ~ together** (*fig*) faire le rapprochement

two-bit [tuːˈbɪt] *adj* (*esp US inf, pej*) de pacotille

two-door [tuːˈdɔːr] *adj* (*Aut*) à deux portes

two-faced [tuːˈfeɪst] *adj* (*pej: person*) faux (fausse)

twofold [ˈtuːfəuld] *adv*: **to increase ~** doubler ▷ *adj* (*increase*) de cent pour cent; (*reply*) en deux parties

two-piece [ˈtuːpiːs] *n* (*also*: **two-piece suit**) (costume *m*) deux-pièces *m inv*; (*also*: **two-piece swimsuit**) (maillot *m* de bain) deux-pièces

two-seater [tuːˈsiːtər] *n* (*plane*) (avion *m*) biplace *m*; (*car*) voiture *f* à deux places

twosome [ˈtuːsəm] *n* (*people*) couple *m*

two-stroke [ˈtuːstrəuk] *n* (*also*: **two-stroke engine**) moteur *m* à deux temps ▷ *adj* à deux temps

two-tone [ˈtuːtəun] *adj* (*in colour*) à deux tons

two-way [ˈtuːweɪ] *adj* (*traffic*) dans les deux sens; **~ radio** émetteur-récepteur *m*

TX *abbr* (*US*) = **Texas**

tycoon [taɪˈkuːn] *n*: **(business) ~** gros homme d'affaires

type [taɪp] *n* (*category*) genre *m*, espèce *f*; (*model*) modèle *m*; (*example*) type *m*; (*Typ*) type, caractère *m* ▷ *vt* (*letter etc*) taper (à la machine); **what ~ do you want?** quel genre voulez-vous?; **in bold/ italic ~** en caractères gras/en italiques

typecast [ˈtaɪpkaːst] *adj* condamné(e) à toujours jouer le même rôle

typeface [ˈtaɪpfeɪs] *n* police *f* (de caractères)

typescript [ˈtaɪpskrɪpt] *n* texte dactylographié

typeset [ˈtaɪpsɛt] *vt* composer (*en imprimerie*)

typesetter [ˈtaɪpsɛtər] *n* compositeur *m*

typewriter [ˈtaɪpraɪtər] *n* machine *f* à écrire

typewritten [ˈtaɪprɪtn] *adj* dactylographié(e)

typhoid [ˈtaɪfɔɪd] *n* typhoïde *f*

typhoon [taɪˈfuːn] *n* typhon *m*

typhus [ˈtaɪfəs] *n* typhus *m*

typical [ˈtɪpɪkl] *adj* typique, caractéristique

typically [ˈtɪpɪklɪ] *adv* (*as usual*) comme d'habitude; (*characteristically*) typiquement

typify [ˈtɪpɪfaɪ] *vt* être caractéristique de

typing [ˈtaɪpɪŋ] *n* dactylo(graphie) *f*

typing error *n* faute *f* de frappe

typing pool *n* pool *m* de dactylos

typist [ˈtaɪpɪst] *n* dactylo *m/f*

typo [ˈtaɪpəu] *n abbr* (*inf*: = *typographical error*) coquille *f*

typography [taɪˈpɔgrəfɪ] *n* typographie *f*

tyranny [ˈtɪrənɪ] *n* tyrannie *f*

tyrant [ˈtaɪrənt] *n* tyran *m*

tyre, (*US*) **tire** [ˈtaɪər] *n* pneu *m*

tyre pressure *n* (*Brit*) pression *f* (de gonflage)

Tyrol [tɪˈrəul] *n* Tyrol *m*

Tyrolean [tɪrəˈliːən], **Tyrolese** [tɪrəˈliːz] *adj* tyrolien(ne) ▷ *n* Tyrolien(ne)

Tyrrhenian Sea [tɪˈriːnɪən-] *n*: **the ~** la mer Tyrrhénienne

tzar [zaːr] *n* = **tsar**

Uu

U, u [juː] *n* (*letter*) U, u *m*; **U for Uncle** U comme Ursule

U *n abbr* (*Brit Cine*: = *universal*) ≈ tous publics

UAW *n abbr* (*US*: = *United Automobile Workers*) syndicat des ouvriers de l'automobile

UB40 *n abbr* (*Brit*: = *unemployment benefit form 40*) numéro de référence d'un formulaire d'inscription au chômage: par extension, le bénéficiaire

U-bend ['juːbɛnd] *n* (*Brit Aut*) coude *m*, virage *m* en épingle à cheveux; (*in pipe*) coude

ubiquitous [juːˈbɪkwɪtəs] *adj* doué(e) d'ubiquité, omniprésent(e)

UCAS ['juːkæs] *n abbr* (*Brit*) = **Universities and Colleges Admissions Service**

UDA *n abbr* (*Brit*) = **Ulster Defence Association**

UDC *n abbr* (*Brit*) = **Urban District Council**

udder ['ʌdəʳ] *n* pis *m*, mamelle *f*

UDI *n abbr* (*Brit Pol*) = **unilateral declaration of independence**

UDR *n abbr* (*Brit*) = **Ulster Defence Regiment**

UEFA [juːˈeɪfə] *n abbr* (= *Union of European Football Associations*) UEFA *f*

UFO ['juːfəu] *n abbr* (= *unidentified flying object*) ovni *m*

Uganda [juːˈgændə] *n* Ouganda *m*

Ugandan [juːˈgændən] *adj* ougandais(e) ⊳ *n* Ougandais(e)

UGC *n abbr* (*Brit*: = *University Grants Committee*) commission d'attribution des dotations aux universités

ugh [əːh] *excl* pouah!

ugliness ['ʌglɪnɪs] *n* laideur *f*

ugly ['ʌglɪ] *adj* laid(e), vilain(e); (*fig*) répugnant(e)

UHF *abbr* (= *ultra-high frequency*) UHF

UHT *adj abbr* = **ultra-heat treated**; **~ milk** lait *m* UHT *or* longue conservation

UK *n abbr* = **United Kingdom**

Ukraine [juːˈkreɪn] *n* Ukraine *f*

Ukrainian [juːˈkreɪnɪən] *adj* ukrainien(ne) ⊳ *n* Ukrainien(ne); (*Ling*) ukrainien *m*

ulcer ['ʌlsəʳ] *n* ulcère *m*; **mouth ~** aphte *f*

Ulster ['ʌlstəʳ] *n* Ulster *m*

ulterior [ʌlˈtɪərɪəʳ] *adj* ultérieur(e); **~ motive** arrière-pensée *f*

ultimate ['ʌltɪmət] *adj* ultime, final(e); (*authority*) suprême ⊳ *n*: **the ~ in luxury** le summum du luxe

ultimately ['ʌltɪmətlɪ] *adv* (*at last*) en fin de compte; (*fundamentally*) finalement; (*eventually*) par la suite

ultimatum (*pl* **-s** *or* **ultimata**) [ʌltɪˈmeɪtəm, -tə] *n* ultimatum *m*

ultrasonic [ʌltrəˈsɔnɪk] *adj* ultrasonique

ultrasound ['ʌltrəsaund] *n* (*Med*) ultrason *m*

ultraviolet ['ʌltrəˈvaɪəlɪt] *adj* ultraviolet(te)

umbilical [ʌmbɪˈlaɪkl] *adj*: **~ cord** cordon ombilical

umbrage ['ʌmbrɪdʒ] *n*: **to take ~** prendre ombrage, se froisser

umbrella [ʌmˈbrɛlə] *n* parapluie *m*; (*for sun*) parasol *m*; (*fig*): **under the ~ of** sous les auspices de; chapeauté(e) par

umlaut ['umlaut] *n* tréma *m*

umpire ['ʌmpaɪəʳ] *n* arbitre *m*; (*Tennis*) juge *m* de chaise ⊳ *vt* arbitrer

umpteen [ʌmpˈtiːn] *adj* je ne sais combien de; **for the ~th time** pour la nième fois

UMW *n abbr* (= *United Mineworkers of America*) syndicat des mineurs

UN *n abbr* = **United Nations**

unabashed [ʌnəˈbæʃt] *adj* nullement intimidé(e)

unabated [ʌnəˈbeɪtɪd] *adj* non diminué(e)

unable [ʌnˈeɪbl] *adj*: **to be ~ to** ne (pas) pouvoir, être dans l'impossibilité de; (*not capable*) être incapable de

unabridged [ʌnəˈbrɪdʒd] *adj* complet(-ète), intégral(e)

unacceptable [ʌnəkˈsɛptəbl] *adj* (*behaviour*) inadmissible; (*price, proposal*) inacceptable

unaccompanied [ʌnəˈkʌmpənɪd] *adj* (*child, lady*) non accompagné(e); (*singing, song*) sans accompagnement

unaccountably [ʌnəˈkauntəblɪ] *adv* inexplicablement

unaccounted [ʌnəˈkauntɪd] *adj*: **two passengers are ~ for** on est sans nouvelles de deux passagers

unaccustomed [ʌnəˈkʌstəmd] *adj* inaccoutumé(e), inhabituel(le); **to be ~ to sth** ne pas avoir l'habitude de qch

unacquainted [ʌnəˈkweɪntɪd] *adj*: **to be ~ with**

ne pas connaître

unadulterated [ʌnə'dʌltəreɪtɪd] *adj* pur(e), naturel(le)

unaffected [ʌnə'fɛktɪd] *adj* (*person, behaviour*) naturel(le); (*emotionally*): **to be ~ by** ne pas être touché(e) par

unafraid [ʌnə'freɪd] *adj*: **to be ~** ne pas avoir peur

unaided [ʌn'eɪdɪd] *adj* sans aide, tout(e) seul(e)

unanimity [juːnə'nɪmɪtɪ] *n* unanimité *f*

unanimous [juː'nænɪməs] *adj* unanime

unanimously [juː'nænɪməslɪ] *adv* à l'unanimité

unanswered [ʌn'ɑːnsəd] *adj* (*question, letter*) sans réponse

unappetizing [ʌn'æpɪtaɪzɪŋ] *adj* peu appétissant(e)

unappreciative [ʌnə'priːʃɪətɪv] *adj* indifférent(e)

unarmed [ʌn'ɑːmd] *adj* (*person*) non armé(e); (*combat*) sans armes

unashamed [ʌnə'ʃeɪmd] *adj* sans honte; impudent(e)

unassisted [ʌnə'sɪstɪd] *adj* non assisté(e) ▷ *adv* sans aide, tout(e) seul(e)

unassuming [ʌnə'sjuːmɪŋ] *adj* modeste, sans prétentions

unattached [ʌnə'tætʃt] *adj* libre, sans attaches

unattended [ʌnə'tɛndɪd] *adj* (*car, child, luggage*) sans surveillance

unattractive [ʌnə'træktɪv] *adj* peu attrayant(e); (*character*) peu sympathique

unauthorized [ʌn'ɔːθəraɪzd] *adj* non autorisé(e), sans autorisation

unavailable [ʌnə'veɪləbl] *adj* (*article, room, book*) (qui n'est) pas disponible; (*person*) (qui n'est) pas libre

unavoidable [ʌnə'vɔɪdəbl] *adj* inévitable

unavoidably [ʌnə'vɔɪdəblɪ] *adv* inévitablement

unaware [ʌnə'wɛəʳ] *adj*: **to be ~ of** ignorer, ne pas savoir, être inconscient(e) de

unawares [ʌnə'wɛəz] *adv* à l'improviste, au dépourvu

unbalanced [ʌn'bælənst] *adj* déséquilibré(e)

unbearable [ʌn'bɛərəbl] *adj* insupportable

unbeatable [ʌn'biːtəbl] *adj* imbattable

unbeaten [ʌn'biːtn] *adj* invaincu(e); (*record*) non battu(e)

unbecoming [ʌnbɪ'kʌmɪŋ] *adj* (*unseemly: language, behaviour*) malséant(e), inconvenant(e); (*unflattering: garment*) peu seyant(e)

unbeknown [ʌnbɪ'nəʊn], **unbeknownst** [ʌnbɪ'nəʊnst] *adv*: **~ to** à l'insu de

unbelief [ʌnbɪ'liːf] *n* incrédulité *f*

unbelievable [ʌnbɪ'liːvəbl] *adj* incroyable

unbelievingly [ʌnbɪ'liːvɪŋlɪ] *adv* avec incrédulité

unbend [ʌn'bɛnd] (*irreg: like* **bend**) *vi* se détendre ▷ *vt* (*wire*) redresser, détordre

unbending [ʌn'bɛndɪŋ] *adj* (*fig*) inflexible

unbiased, unbiassed [ʌn'baɪəst] *adj* impartial(e)

unblemished [ʌn'blɛmɪʃt] *adj* impeccable

unblock [ʌn'blɔk] *vt* (*pipe*) déboucher; (*road*) dégager

unborn [ʌn'bɔːn] *adj* à naître

unbounded [ʌn'baʊndɪd] *adj* sans bornes, illimité(e)

unbreakable [ʌn'breɪkəbl] *adj* incassable

unbridled [ʌn'braɪdld] *adj* débridé(e), déchaîné(e)

unbroken [ʌn'brəʊkn] *adj* intact(e); (*line*) continu(e); (*record*) non battu(e)

unbuckle [ʌn'bʌkl] *vt* déboucler

unburden [ʌn'bəːdn] *vt*: **to ~ o.s.** s'épancher, se livrer

unbutton [ʌn'bʌtn] *vt* déboutonner

uncalled-for [ʌn'kɔːldfɔːʳ] *adj* déplacé(e), injustifié(e)

uncanny [ʌn'kænɪ] *adj* étrange, troublant(e)

unceasing [ʌn'siːsɪŋ] *adj* incessant(e), continu(e)

unceremonious [ʌnsɛrɪ'məʊnɪəs] *adj* (*abrupt, rude*) brusque

uncertain [ʌn'səːtn] *adj* incertain(e); (*hesitant*) hésitant(e); **we were ~ whether ...** nous ne savions pas vraiment si ...; **in no ~ terms** sans équivoque possible

uncertainty [ʌn'səːtntɪ] *n* incertitude *f*, doutes *mpl*

unchallenged [ʌn'tʃælɪndʒd] *adj* (*gen*) incontesté(e); (*information*) non contesté(e); **to go ~** ne pas être contesté

unchanged [ʌn'tʃeɪndʒd] *adj* inchangé(e)

uncharitable [ʌn'tʃærɪtəbl] *adj* peu charitable

uncharted [ʌn'tʃɑːtɪd] *adj* inexploré(e)

unchecked [ʌn'tʃɛkt] *adj* non réprimé(e)

uncivilized [ʌn'sɪvɪlaɪzd] *adj* non civilisé(e); (*fig*) barbare

uncle ['ʌŋkl] *n* oncle *m*

unclear [ʌn'klɪəʳ] *adj* (qui n'est) pas clair(e) *or* évident(e); **I'm still ~ about what I'm supposed to do** je ne sais pas encore exactement ce que je dois faire

uncoil [ʌn'kɔɪl] *vt* dérouler ▷ *vi* se dérouler

uncomfortable [ʌn'kʌmfətəbl] *adj* inconfortable, peu confortable; (*uneasy*) mal à l'aise, gêné(e); (*situation*) désagréable

uncomfortably [ʌn'kʌmfətəblɪ] *adv* inconfortablement; d'un ton *etc* gêné *or* embarrassé; désagréablement

uncommitted [ʌnkə'mɪtɪd] *adj* (*attitude, country*) non engagé(e)

uncommon [ʌn'kɔmən] *adj* rare, singulier(-ière), peu commun(e)

uncommunicative [ʌnkə'mjuːnɪkətɪv] *adj* réservé(e)

uncomplicated [ʌn'kɔmplɪkeɪtɪd] *adj* simple, peu compliqué(e)

uncompromising [ʌn'kɔmprəmaɪzɪŋ] *adj* intransigeant(e), inflexible

unconcerned [ʌnkən'səːnd] *adj* (*unworried*): **to be ~ (about)** ne pas s'inquiéter (de)

unconditional [ʌnkən'dɪʃənl] *adj* sans

conditions

uncongenial [ʌnkən'dʒiːnɪəl] *adj* peu agréable

unconnected [ʌnkə'nɛktɪd] *adj* (*unrelated*): ~ **(with)** sans rapport (avec)

unconscious [ʌn'kɒnʃəs] *adj* sans connaissance, évanoui(e); (*unaware*): ~ **(of)** inconscient(e) (de) ▷ *n*: **the ~** l'inconscient *m*; **to knock sb ~** assommer qn

unconsciously [ʌn'kɒnʃəslɪ] *adv* inconsciemment

unconstitutional [ʌnkɒnstɪ'tjuːʃnl] *adj* anticonstitutionnel(le)

uncontested [ʌnkən'tɛstɪd] *adj* (*champion*) incontesté(e); (*Pol: seat*) non disputé(e)

uncontrollable [ʌnkən'trəuləbl] *adj* (*child, dog*) indiscipliné(e); (*temper, laughter*) irrépressible

uncontrolled [ʌnkən'trəuld] *adj* (*laughter, price rises*) incontrôlé(e)

unconventional [ʌnkən'vɛnʃənl] *adj* peu conventionnel(le)

unconvinced [ʌnkən'vɪnst] *adj*: **to be ~** ne pas être convaincu(e)

unconvincing [ʌnkən'vɪnsɪŋ] *adj* peu convaincant(e)

uncork [ʌn'kɔːk] *vt* déboucher

uncorroborated [ʌnkə'rɒbəreɪtɪd] *adj* non confirmé(e)

uncouth [ʌn'kuːθ] *adj* grossier(-ière), fruste

uncover [ʌn'kʌvəʳ] *vt* découvrir

unctuous ['ʌŋktjuəs] *adj* onctueux(-euse), mielleux(-euse)

undamaged [ʌn'dæmɪdʒd] *adj* (*goods*) intact(e), en bon état; (*fig: reputation*) intact

undaunted [ʌn'dɔːntɪd] *adj* non intimidé(e), inébranlable

undecided [ʌndɪ'saɪdɪd] *adj* indécis(e), irrésolu(e)

undelivered [ʌndɪ'lɪvəd] *adj* non remis(e), non livré(e)

undeniable [ʌndɪ'naɪəbl] *adj* indéniable, incontestable

under ['ʌndəʳ] *prep* sous; (*less than*) (de) moins de; au-dessous de; (*according to*) selon, en vertu de ▷ *adv* au-dessous; en dessous; **from ~ sth** de dessous *or* de sous qch; ~ **there** là-dessous; **in ~ 2 hours** en moins de 2 heures; ~ **anaesthetic** sous anesthésie; ~ **discussion** en discussion; ~ **the circumstances** étant donné les circonstances; ~ **repair** en (cours de) réparation

under... ['ʌndəʳ] *prefix* sous-

underage [ʌndər'eɪdʒ] *adj* qui n'a pas l'âge réglementaire

underarm ['ʌndərɑːm] *adv* par en-dessous ▷ *adj* (*throw*) par en-dessous; (*deodorant*) pour les aisselles

undercapitalized [ʌndə'kæpɪtəlaɪzd] *adj* sous-capitalisé(e)

undercarriage ['ʌndəkærɪdʒ] *n* (*Brit Aviat*) train *m* d'atterrissage

undercharge [ʌndə'tʃɑːdʒ] *vt* ne pas faire payer assez à

underclass ['ʌndəklɑːs] *n* ≈ quart-monde *m*

underclothes ['ʌndəkləuðz] *npl* sous-vêtements *mpl*; (*women's only*) dessous *mpl*

undercoat ['ʌndəkəut] *n* (*paint*) couche *f* de fond

undercover [ʌndə'kʌvəʳ] *adj* secret(-ète), clandestin(e)

undercurrent ['ʌndəkʌrnt] *n* courant sous-jacent

undercut [ʌndə'kʌt] *vt* (*irreg: like* **cut**) vendre moins cher que

underdeveloped ['ʌndədɪ'vɛləpt] *adj* sous-développé(e)

underdog ['ʌndədɒg] *n* opprimé *m*

underdone [ʌndə'dʌn] *adj* (*Culin*) saignant(e); (: *pej*) pas assez cuit(e)

underestimate [ʌndər'ɛstɪmeɪt] *vt* sous-estimer, mésestimer

underexposed ['ʌndərɪks'pəuzd] *adj* (*Phot*) sous-exposé(e)

underfed [ʌndə'fɛd] *adj* sous-alimenté(e)

underfoot [ʌndə'fut] *adv* sous les pieds

under-funded ['ʌndə'fʌndɪd] *adj*: **to be ~** (*organization*) ne pas être doté(e) de fonds suffisants

undergo [ʌndə'gəu] *vt* (*irreg: like* **go**) subir; (*treatment*) suivre; **the car is ~ing repairs** la voiture est en réparation

undergraduate [ʌndə'grædjuɪt] *n* étudiant(e) (qui prépare la licence) ▷ *cpd*: ~ **courses** cours *mpl* préparant à la licence

underground ['ʌndəgraund] *adj* souterrain(e); (*fig*) clandestin(e) ▷ *n* (*Brit: railway*) métro *m*; (*Pol*) clandestinité *f*

undergrowth ['ʌndəgrəuθ] *n* broussailles *fpl*, sous-bois *m*

underhand [ʌndə'hænd], **underhanded** [ʌndə'hændɪd] *adj* (*fig*) sournois(e), en dessous

underinsured [ʌndərɪn'ʃuəd] *adj* sous-assuré(e)

underlie [ʌndə'laɪ] *vt* (*irreg: like* **lie**) être à la base de; **the underlying cause** la cause sous-jacente

underline [ʌndə'laɪn] *vt* souligner

underling ['ʌndəlɪŋ] *n* (*pej*) sous-fifre *m*, subalterne *m*

undermanning [ʌndə'mænɪŋ] *n* pénurie *f* de main-d'œuvre

undermentioned [ʌndə'mɛnʃənd] *adj* mentionné(e) ci-dessous

undermine [ʌndə'maɪn] *vt* saper, miner

underneath [ʌndə'niːθ] *adv* (en) dessous ▷ *prep* sous, au-dessous de

undernourished [ʌndə'nʌrɪʃt] *adj* sous-alimenté(e)

underpaid [ʌndə'peɪd] *adj* sous-payé(e)

underpants ['ʌndəpænts] *npl* caleçon *m*, slip *m*

underpass ['ʌndəpɑːs] *n* (*Brit: for pedestrians*) passage souterrain; (: *for cars*) passage inférieur

underpin [ʌndə'pɪn] *vt* (*argument, case*) étayer

underplay [ʌndə'pleɪ] *vt* (*Brit*) minimiser

underpopulated [ʌndə'pɒpjuleɪtɪd] *adj* sous-peuplé(e)

underprice [ʌndə'praɪs] *vt* vendre à un prix trop bas

underprivileged [ˌʌndə'prɪvɪlɪdʒd] adj défavorisé(e)

underrate [ʌndə'reɪt] vt sous-estimer, mésestimer

underscore [ʌndə'skɔːʳ] vt souligner

underseal [ʌndə'siːl] vt (Brit) traiter contre la rouille

undersecretary ['ʌndə'sɛkrətrɪ] n sous-secrétaire m

undersell [ʌndə'sɛl] vt (irreg: like sell: competitors) vendre moins cher que

undershirt ['ʌndəʃəːt] n (US) tricot m de corps

undershorts ['ʌndəʃɔːts] npl (US) caleçon m, slip m

underside ['ʌndəsaɪd] n dessous m

undersigned ['ʌndə'saɪnd] adj, n soussigné(e) m/f

underskirt ['ʌndəskəːt] n (Brit) jupon m

understaffed [ʌndə'stɑːft] adj qui manque de personnel

understand [ʌndə'stænd] vt, vi (irreg: like stand) comprendre; **I don't ~** je ne comprends pas; **I ~ that ...** je me suis laissé dire que ..., je crois comprendre que ...; **to make o.s. understood** se faire comprendre

understandable [ʌndə'stændəbl] adj compréhensible

understanding [ʌndə'stændɪŋ] adj compréhensif(-ive) ▷ n compréhension f; (agreement) accord m; **to come to an ~ with sb** s'entendre avec qn; **on the ~ that ...** à condition que ...

understate [ʌndə'steɪt] vt minimiser

understatement ['ʌndəsteɪtmənt] n: **that's an ~** c'est (bien) peu dire, le terme est faible

understood [ʌndə'stud] pt, pp of **understand** ▷ adj entendu(e); (implied) sous-entendu(e)

understudy ['ʌndəstʌdɪ] n doublure f

undertake [ʌndə'teɪk] vt (irreg: like take: job, task) entreprendre; (duty) se charger de; **to ~ to do sth** s'engager à faire qch

undertaker ['ʌndəteɪkəʳ] n (Brit) entrepreneur m des pompes funèbres, croque-mort m

undertaking ['ʌndəteɪkɪŋ] n entreprise f; (promise) promesse f

undertone ['ʌndətəun] n (low voice): **in an ~** à mi-voix; (of criticism etc) nuance cachée

undervalue [ʌndə'væljuː] vt sous-estimer

underwater [ʌndə'wɔːtəʳ] adv sous l'eau ▷ adj sous-marin(e)

underway [ʌndə'weɪ] adj: **to be ~** (meeting, investigation) être en cours

underwear ['ʌndəwɛəʳ] n sous-vêtements mpl; (women's only) dessous mpl

underweight [ʌndə'weɪt] adj d'un poids insuffisant; (person) (trop) maigre

underwent [ʌndə'wɛnt] pt of **undergo**

underworld ['ʌndəwəːld] n (of crime) milieu m, pègre f

underwrite [ʌndə'raɪt] vt (Finance) garantir; (Insurance) souscrire

underwriter ['ʌndəraɪtəʳ] n (Insurance)

souscripteur m

undeserving [ʌndɪ'zəːvɪŋ] adj: **to be ~ of** ne pas mériter

undesirable [ʌndɪ'zaɪərəbl] adj peu souhaitable; (person, effect) indésirable

undeveloped [ʌndɪ'vɛləpt] adj (land, resources) non exploité(e)

undies ['ʌndɪz] npl (inf) dessous mpl, lingerie f

undiluted ['ʌndaɪ'luːtɪd] adj pur(e), non dilué(e)

undiplomatic ['ʌndɪplə'mætɪk] adj peu diplomatique, maladroit(e)

undischarged ['ʌndɪs'tʃɑːdʒd] adj: **~ bankrupt** failli(e) non réhabilité(e)

undisciplined [ʌn'dɪsɪplɪnd] adj indiscipliné(e)

undisguised ['ʌndɪs'gaɪzd] adj (dislike, amusement etc) franc (franche)

undisputed ['ʌndɪs'pjuːtɪd] adj incontesté(e)

undistinguished ['ʌndɪs'tɪŋgwɪʃt] adj médiocre, quelconque

undisturbed [ʌndɪs'təːbd] adj (sleep) tranquille, paisible; **to leave ~** ne pas déranger

undivided [ʌndɪ'vaɪdɪd] adj: **can I have your ~ attention?** puis-je avoir toute votre attention?

undo [ʌn'duː] vt (irreg: like do) défaire

undoing [ʌn'duːɪŋ] n ruine f, perte f

undone [ʌn'dʌn] pp of **undo** ▷ adj: **to come ~** se défaire

undoubted [ʌn'dautɪd] adj indubitable, certain(e)

undoubtedly [ʌn'dautɪdlɪ] adv sans aucun doute

undress [ʌn'drɛs] vi se déshabiller ▷ vt déshabiller

undrinkable [ʌn'drɪŋkəbl] adj (unpalatable) imbuvable; (poisonous) non potable

undue [ʌn'djuː] adj indu(e), excessif(-ive)

undulating ['ʌndjuleɪtɪŋ] adj ondoyant(e), onduleux(-euse)

unduly [ʌn'djuːlɪ] adv trop, excessivement

undying [ʌn'daɪɪŋ] adj éternel(le)

unearned [ʌn'əːnd] adj (praise, respect) immérité(e); **~ income** rentes fpl

unearth [ʌn'əːθ] vt déterrer; (fig) dénicher

unearthly [ʌn'əːθlɪ] adj surnaturel(le); (hour) indu(e), impossible

uneasy [ʌn'iːzɪ] adj mal à l'aise, gêné(e); (worried) inquiet(-ète); (feeling) désagréable; (peace, truce) fragile; **to feel ~ about doing sth** se sentir mal à l'aise à l'idée de faire qch

uneconomic ['ʌniːkə'nɔmɪk], **uneconomical** ['ʌniːkə'nɔmɪkl] adj peu économique; peu rentable

uneducated [ʌn'ɛdjukeɪtɪd] adj sans éducation

unemployed [ʌnɪm'plɔɪd] adj sans travail, au chômage ▷ n: **the ~** les chômeurs mpl

unemployment [ʌnɪm'plɔɪmənt] n chômage m

unemployment benefit, (US) **unemployment compensation** n allocation f de chômage

unending [ʌn'ɛndɪŋ] adj interminable

unenviable [ʌn'ɛnvɪəbl] adj peu enviable

unequal [ʌn'iːkwəl] adj inégal(e)

unequalled, (US) **unequaled** [ʌn'iːkwəld] adj

inégalé(e)

unequivocal [ʌnɪ'kwɪvəkl] *adj* (*answer*) sans équivoque; (*person*) catégorique

unerring [ʌn'ə:rɪŋ] *adj* infaillible, sûr(e)

UNESCO [ju:'nɛskəu] *n abbr* (= *United Nations Educational, Scientific and Cultural Organization*) UNESCO *f*

unethical [ʌn'εθɪkl] *adj* (*methods*) immoral(e); (*doctor's behaviour*) qui ne respecte pas l'éthique

uneven [ʌn'i:vn] *adj* inégal(e); (*quality, work*) irrégulier(-ière)

uneventful [ʌnɪ'vɛntful] *adj* tranquille, sans histoires

unexceptional [ʌnɪk'sɛpʃənl] *adj* banal(e), quelconque

unexciting [ʌnɪk'saɪtɪŋ] *adj* pas passionnant(e)

unexpected [ʌnɪk'spɛktɪd] *adj* inattendu(e), imprévu(e)

unexpectedly [ʌnɪk'spɛktɪdlɪ] *adv* (*succeed*) contre toute attente; (*arrive*) à l'improviste

unexplained [ʌnɪk'spleɪnd] *adj* inexpliqué(e)

unexploded [ʌnɪk'spləudɪd] *adj* non explosé(e) or éclaté(e)

unfailing [ʌn'feɪlɪŋ] *adj* inépuisable; infaillible

unfair [ʌn'fεəʳ] *adj*: **~ (to)** injuste (envers); **it's ~ that ...** il n'est pas juste que ...

unfair dismissal *n* licenciement abusif

unfairly [ʌn'fεəlɪ] *adv* injustement

unfaithful [ʌn'feɪθful] *adj* infidèle

unfamiliar [ʌnfə'mɪlɪəʳ] *adj* étrange, inconnu(e); **to be ~ with sth** mal connaître qch

unfashionable [ʌn'fæʃnəbl] *adj* (*clothes*) démodé(e); (*place*) peu chic *inv*; (*district*) déshérité(e), pas à la mode

unfasten [ʌn'fɑ:sn] *vt* défaire; (*belt, necklace*) détacher; (*open*) ouvrir

unfathomable [ʌn'fæðəməbl] *adj* insondable

unfavourable, (*US*) **unfavorable** [ʌn'feɪvrəbl] *adj* défavorable

unfavourably, (*US*) **unfavorably** [ʌn'feɪvrəblɪ] *adv*: **to look ~ upon** ne pas être favorable à

unfeeling [ʌn'fi:lɪŋ] *adj* insensible, dur(e)

unfinished [ʌn'fɪnɪʃt] *adj* inachevé(e)

unfit [ʌn'fɪt] *adj* (*physically: ill*) en mauvaise santé; (: *out of condition*) pas en forme; (*incompetent*): **~ (for)** impropre (à); (*work, service*) inapte (à)

unflagging [ʌn'flægɪŋ] *adj* infatigable, inlassable

unflappable [ʌn'flæpəbl] *adj* imperturbable

unflattering [ʌn'flætərɪŋ] *adj* (*dress, hairstyle*) qui n'avantage pas; (*remark*) peu flatteur(-euse)

unflinching [ʌn'flɪntʃɪŋ] *adj* stoïque

unfold [ʌn'fəuld] *vt* déplier; (*fig*) révéler, exposer ▷ *vi* se dérouler

unforeseeable [ʌnfɔ:'si:əbl] *adj* imprévisible

unforeseen ['ʌnfɔ:'si:n] *adj* imprévu(e)

unforgettable [ʌnfə'gɛtəbl] *adj* inoubliable

unforgivable [ʌnfə'gɪvəbl] *adj* impardonnable

unformatted [ʌn'fɔ:mætɪd] *adj* (*disk, text*) non formaté(e)

unfortunate [ʌn'fɔ:tʃnət] *adj* malheureux(-euse); (*event, remark*) malencontreux(-euse)

unfortunately [ʌn'fɔ:tʃnətlɪ] *adv* malheureusement

unfounded [ʌn'faundɪd] *adj* sans fondement

unfriendly [ʌn'frɛndlɪ] *adj* peu aimable, froid(e), inamical(e)

unfulfilled [ʌnful'fɪld] *adj* (*ambition, prophecy*) non réalisé(e); (*desire*) insatisfait(e); (*promise*) non tenu(e); (*terms of contract*) non rempli(e); (*person*) qui n'a pas su se réaliser

unfurl [ʌn'fə:l] *vt* déployer

unfurnished [ʌn'fə:nɪʃt] *adj* non meublé(e)

ungainly [ʌn'geɪnlɪ] *adj* gauche, dégingandé(e)

ungodly [ʌn'gɔdlɪ] *adj* impie; **at an ~ hour** à une heure indue

ungrateful [ʌn'greɪtful] *adj* qui manque de reconnaissance, ingrat(e)

unguarded [ʌn'gɑ:dɪd] *adj*: **~ moment** moment *m* d'inattention

unhappily [ʌn'hæpɪlɪ] *adv* tristement; (*unfortunately*) malheureusement

unhappiness [ʌn'hæpɪnɪs] *n* tristesse *f*, peine *f*

unhappy [ʌn'hæpɪ] *adj* triste, malheureux(-euse); (*unfortunate: remark etc*) malheureux(-euse); (*not pleased*): **~ with** mécontent(e) de, peu satisfait(e) de

unharmed [ʌn'hɑ:md] *adj* indemne, sain(e) et sauf (sauve)

UNHCR *n abbr* (= *United Nations High Commission for Refugees*) HCR *m*

unhealthy [ʌn'hɛlθɪ] *adj* (*gen*) malsain(e); (*person*) maladif(-ive)

unheard-of [ʌn'hə:dɔv] *adj* inouï(e), sans précédent

unhelpful [ʌn'hɛlpful] *adj* (*person*) peu serviable; (*advice*) peu utile

unhesitating [ʌn'hɛzɪteɪtɪŋ] *adj* (*loyalty*) spontané(e); (*reply, offer*) immédiat(e)

unholy [ʌn'həulɪ] *adj*: **an ~ alliance** une alliance contre nature; **he got home at an ~ hour** il est rentré à une heure impossible

unhook [ʌn'huk] *vt* décrocher; dégrafer

unhurt [ʌn'hə:t] *adj* indemne, sain(e) et sauf (sauve)

unhygienic ['ʌnhaɪ'dʒi:nɪk] *adj* antihygiénique

UNICEF ['ju:nɪsɛf] *n abbr* (= *United Nations International Children's Emergency Fund*) UNICEF *m*, FISE *m*

unicorn ['ju:nɪkɔ:n] *n* licorne *f*

unidentified [ʌnaɪ'dɛntɪfaɪd] *adj* non identifié(e); *see also* **UFO**

uniform ['ju:nɪfɔ:m] *n* uniforme *m* ▷ *adj* uniforme

uniformity [ju:nɪ'fɔ:mɪtɪ] *n* uniformité *f*

unify ['ju:nɪfaɪ] *vt* unifier

unilateral [ju:nɪ'lætərəl] *adj* unilatéral(e)

unimaginable [ʌnɪ'mædʒɪnəbl] *adj* inimaginable, inconcevable

unimaginative [ʌnɪ'mædʒɪnətɪv] *adj* sans imagination

unimpaired [ʌnɪm'pɛəd] *adj* intact(e)

unimportant [ʌnɪm'pɔ:tənt] *adj* sans importance

unimpressed [ʌnɪm'prɛst] *adj* pas impressionné(e)

uninhabited [ʌnɪn'hæbɪtɪd] *adj* inhabité(e)

uninhibited [ʌnɪn'hɪbɪtɪd] *adj* sans inhibitions; sans retenue

uninjured [ʌn'ɪndʒəd] *adj* indemne

uninspiring [ʌnɪn'spaɪərɪŋ] *adj* peu inspirant(e)

unintelligent [ʌnɪn'tɛlɪdʒənt] *adj* inintelligent(e)

unintentional [ʌnɪn'tɛnʃənəl] *adj* involontaire

unintentionally [ʌnɪn'tɛnʃnəlɪ] *adv* sans le vouloir

uninvited [ʌnɪn'vaɪtɪd] *adj* (*guest*) qui n'a pas été invité(e)

uninviting [ʌnɪn'vaɪtɪŋ] *adj* (*place*) peu attirant(e); (*food*) peu appétissant(e)

union ['ju:njən] *n* union *f*; (*also*: **trade union**) syndicat *m* ▷ *cpd* du syndicat, syndical(e)

unionize ['ju:njənaɪz] *vt* syndiquer

Union Jack *n* drapeau du Royaume-Uni

Union of Soviet Socialist Republics *n* (*formerly*) Union *f* des républiques socialistes soviétiques

union shop *n* entreprise où tous les travailleurs doivent être syndiqués

unique [ju:'ni:k] *adj* unique

unisex ['ju:nɪsɛks] *adj* unisexe

Unison ['ju:nɪsn] *n* (*trade union*) grand syndicat des services publics en Grande-Bretagne

unison ['ju:nɪsn] *n*: **in ~** à l'unisson, en chœur

unit ['ju:nɪt] *n* unité *f*; (*section: of furniture etc*) élément *m*, bloc *m*; (*team, squad*) groupe *m*, service *m*; **production ~** atelier *m* de fabrication; **kitchen ~** élément de cuisine; **sink ~** bloc-évier *m*

unit cost *n* coût *m* unitaire

unite [ju:'naɪt] *vt* unir ▷ *vi* s'unir

united [ju:'naɪtɪd] *adj* uni(e); (*country, party*) unifié(e); (*efforts*) conjugué(e)

United Arab Emirates *npl* Émirats Arabes Unis

United Kingdom *n* Royaume-Uni *m*

United Nations, United Nations Organization *n* (Organisation *f* des) Nations unies

United States, United States of America *n* États-Unis *mpl*

unit price *n* prix *m* unitaire

unit trust *n* (*Brit Comm*) fonds commun de placement, FCP *m*

unity ['ju:nɪtɪ] *n* unité *f*

Univ. *abbr* = **university**

universal [ju:nɪ'və:sl] *adj* universel(le)

universe ['ju:nɪvə:s] *n* univers *m*

university [ju:nɪ'və:sɪtɪ] *n* université *f* ▷ *cpd* (*student, professor*) d'université; (*education, year, degree*) universitaire

unjust [ʌn'dʒʌst] *adj* injuste

unjustifiable ['ʌndʒʌstɪ'faɪəbl] *adj* injustifiable

unjustified [ʌn'dʒʌstɪfaɪd] *adj* injustifié(e);

(*text*) non justifié(e)

unkempt [ʌn'kɛmpt] *adj* mal tenu(e), débraillé(e); mal peigné(e)

unkind [ʌn'kaɪnd] *adj* peu gentil(le), méchant(e)

unkindly [ʌn'kaɪndlɪ] *adv* (*treat, speak*) avec méchanceté

unknown [ʌn'nəun] *adj* inconnu(e); **~ to me** sans que je le sache; **~ quantity** (*Math, fig*) inconnue *f*

unladen [ʌn'leɪdn] *adj* (*ship, weight*) à vide

unlawful [ʌn'lɔ:ful] *adj* illégal(e)

unleaded [ʌn'lɛdɪd] *n* (*also*: **unleaded petrol**) essence *f* sans plomb

unleash [ʌn'li:ʃ] *vt* détacher; (*fig*) déchaîner, déclencher

unleavened [ʌn'lɛvnd] *adj* sans levain

unless [ʌn'lɛs] *conj*: **~ he leaves** à moins qu'il (ne) parte; **~ we leave** à moins de partir, à moins que nous (ne) partions; **~ otherwise stated** sauf indication contraire; **~ I am mistaken** si je ne me trompe

unlicensed [ʌn'laɪsnst] *adj* (*Brit*) non patenté(e) pour la vente des spiritueux

unlike [ʌn'laɪk] *adj* dissemblable, différent(e) ▷ *prep* à la différence de, contrairement à

unlikelihood [ʌn'laɪklɪhud] *n* improbabilité *f*

unlikely [ʌn'laɪklɪ] *adj* (*result, event*) improbable; (*explanation*) invraisemblable

unlimited [ʌn'lɪmɪtɪd] *adj* illimité(e)

unlisted ['ʌn'lɪstɪd] *adj* (*US Tel*) sur la liste rouge; (*Stock Exchange*) non coté(e) en Bourse

unlit [ʌn'lɪt] *adj* (*room*) non éclairé(e)

unload [ʌn'ləud] *vt* décharger

unlock [ʌn'lɔk] *vt* ouvrir

unlucky [ʌn'lʌkɪ] *adj* (*person*) malchanceux(-euse); (*object, number*) qui porte malheur; **to be ~** (*person*) ne pas avoir de chance

unmanageable [ʌn'mænɪdʒəbl] *adj* (*unwieldy: tool, vehicle*) peu maniable; (: *situation*) inextricable

unmanned [ʌn'mænd] *adj* sans équipage

unmannerly [ʌn'mænəlɪ] *adj* mal élevé(e), impoli(e)

unmarked [ʌn'ma:kt] *adj* (*unstained*) sans marque; **~ police car** voiture de police banalisée

unmarried [ʌn'mærɪd] *adj* célibataire

unmask [ʌn'ma:sk] *vt* démasquer

unmatched [ʌn'mætʃt] *adj* sans égal(e)

unmentionable [ʌn'mɛnʃnəbl] *adj* (*topic*) dont on ne parle pas; (*word*) qui ne se dit pas

unmerciful [ʌn'mə:sɪful] *adj* sans pitié

unmistakable, unmistakeable [ʌnmɪs'teɪkəbl] *adj* indubitable; qu'on ne peut pas ne pas reconnaître

unmitigated [ʌn'mɪtɪgeɪtɪd] *adj* non mitigé(e), absolu(e), pur(e)

unnamed [ʌn'neɪmd] *adj* (*nameless*) sans nom; (*anonymous*) anonyme

unnatural [ʌn'nætʃrəl] *adj* non naturel(le); (*perversion*) contre nature

unnecessary [ʌn'nɛsəsərɪ] *adj* inutile, superflu(e)

unnerve [ʌn'nə:v] *vt* faire perdre son sang-froid à

unnoticed [ʌn'nəutɪst] *adj* inaperçu(e); **to go ~** passer inaperçu

UNO ['ju:nəu] *n abbr* = **United Nations Organization**

unobservant [ʌnəb'zə:vnt] *adj* pas observateur(-trice)

unobtainable [ʌnəb'teɪnəbl] *adj* (*Tel*) impossible à obtenir

unobtrusive [ʌnəb'tru:sɪv] *adj* discret(-ète)

unoccupied [ʌn'ɔkjupaɪd] *adj* (*seat, table, Mil*) libre; (*house*) inoccupé(e)

unofficial [ʌnə'fɪʃl] *adj* (*news*) officieux(-euse), non officiel(le); (*strike*) ≈ sauvage

unopposed [ʌnə'pəuzd] *adj* sans opposition

unorthodox [ʌn'ɔ:θədɔks] *adj* peu orthodoxe

unpack [ʌn'pæk] *vi* défaire sa valise, déballer ses affaires ▷ *vt* (*suitcase*) défaire; (*belongings*) déballer

unpaid [ʌn'peɪd] *adj* (*bill*) impayé(e); (*holiday*) non-payé(e), sans salaire; (*work*) non rétribué(e); (*worker*) bénévole

unpalatable [ʌn'pælətəbl] *adj* (*truth*) désagréable (à entendre)

unparalleled [ʌn'pærəlɛld] *adj* incomparable, sans égal

unpatriotic ['ʌnpætrɪ'ɔtɪk] *adj* (*person*) manquant de patriotisme; (*speech, attitude*) antipatriotique

unplanned [ʌn'plænd] *adj* (*visit*) imprévu(e); (*baby*) non prévu(e)

unpleasant [ʌn'plɛznt] *adj* déplaisant(e), désagréable

unplug [ʌn'plʌg] *vt* débrancher

unpolluted [ʌnpə'lu:tɪd] *adj* non pollué(e)

unpopular [ʌn'pɔpjuləʳ] *adj* impopulaire; **to make o.s. ~ (with)** se rendre impopulaire (auprès de)

unprecedented [ʌn'prɛsɪdɛntɪd] *adj* sans précédent

unpredictable [ʌnprɪ'dɪktəbl] *adj* imprévisible

unprejudiced [ʌn'prɛdʒudɪst] *adj* (*not biased*) impartial(e); (*having no prejudices*) qui n'a pas de préjugés

unprepared [ʌnprɪ'pɛəd] *adj* (*person*) qui n'est pas suffisamment préparé(e); (*speech*) improvisé(e)

unprepossessing ['ʌnpri:pə'zɛsɪŋ] *adj* peu avenant(e)

unpretentious [ʌnprɪ'tɛnʃəs] *adj* sans prétention(s)

unprincipled [ʌn'prɪnsɪpld] *adj* sans principes

unproductive [ʌnprə'dʌktɪv] *adj* improductif(-ive); (*discussion*) stérile

unprofessional [ʌnprə'fɛʃənl] *adj* (*conduct*) contraire à la déontologie

unprofitable [ʌn'prɔfɪtəbl] *adj* non rentable

UNPROFOR [ʌn'prəufɔ:ʳ] *n abbr* (= *United Nations Protection Force*) FORPRONU *f*

unprotected ['ʌnprə'tɛktɪd] *adj* (*sex*) non protégé(e)

unprovoked [ʌnprə'vəukt] *adj* (*attack*) sans provocation

unpunished [ʌn'pʌnɪʃt] *adj* impuni(e); **to go ~** rester impuni

unqualified [ʌn'kwɔlɪfaɪd] *adj* (*teacher*) non diplômé(e), sans titres; (*success*) sans réserve, total(e); (*disaster*) total(e)

unquestionably [ʌn'kwɛstʃənəblɪ] *adv* incontestablement

unquestioning [ʌn'kwɛstʃənɪŋ] *adj* (*obedience, acceptance*) inconditionnel(le)

unravel [ʌn'rævl] *vt* démêler

unreal [ʌn'rɪəl] *adj* irréel(le); (*extraordinary*) incroyable

unrealistic ['ʌnrɪə'lɪstɪk] *adj* (*idea*) irréaliste; (*estimate*) peu réaliste

unreasonable [ʌn'ri:znəbl] *adj* qui n'est pas raisonnable; **to make ~ demands on sb** exiger trop de qn

unrecognizable [ʌn'rɛkəgnaɪzəbl] *adj* pas reconnaissable

unrecognized [ʌn'rɛkəgnaɪzd] *adj* (*talent, genius*) méconnu(e); (*Pol: régime*) non reconnu(e)

unrecorded [ʌnrɪ'kɔ:dɪd] *adj* non enregistré(e)

unrefined [ʌnrɪ'faɪnd] *adj* (*sugar, petroleum*) non raffiné(e)

unrehearsed [ʌnrɪ'hə:st] *adj* (*Theat etc*) qui n'a pas été répété(e); (*spontaneous*) spontané(e)

unrelated [ʌnrɪ'leɪtɪd] *adj* sans rapport; (*people*) sans lien de parenté

unrelenting [ʌnrɪ'lɛntɪŋ] *adj* implacable; acharné(e)

unreliable [ʌnrɪ'laɪəbl] *adj* sur qui (*or* quoi) on ne peut pas compter, peu fiable

unrelieved [ʌnrɪ'li:vd] *adj* (*monotony*) constant(e), uniforme

unremitting [ʌnrɪ'mɪtɪŋ] *adj* inlassable, infatigable, acharné(e)

unrepeatable [ʌnrɪ'pi:təbl] *adj* (*offer*) unique, exceptionnel(le)

unrepentant [ʌnrɪ'pɛntənt] *adj* impénitent(e)

unrepresentative ['ʌnrɛprɪ'zɛntətɪv] *adj*: **~ (of)** peu représentatif(-ive) (de)

unreserved [ʌnrɪ'zə:vd] *adj* (*seat*) non réservé(e); (*approval, admiration*) sans réserve

unreservedly [ʌnrɪ'zə:vɪdlɪ] *adv* sans réserve

unresponsive [ʌnrɪs'pɔnsɪv] *adj* insensible

unrest [ʌn'rɛst] *n* agitation *f*, troubles *mpl*

unrestricted [ʌnrɪ'strɪktɪd] *adj* illimité(e); **to have ~ access to** avoir librement accès *or* accès en tout temps à

unrewarded [ʌnrɪ'wɔ:dɪd] *adj* pas récompensé(e)

unripe [ʌn'raɪp] *adj* pas mûr(e)

unrivalled, (*US*) **unrivaled** [ʌn'raɪvəld] *adj* sans égal, incomparable

unroll [ʌn'rəul] *vt* dérouler

unruffled [ʌn'rʌfld] *adj* (*person*) imperturbable; (*hair*) qui n'est pas ébouriffé(e)

unruly [ʌn'ru:lɪ] *adj* indiscipliné(e)

unsafe [ʌn'seɪf] *adj* (*in danger*) en danger; (*journey, car*) dangereux(-euse); (*method*) hasardeux(-euse); ~ **to drink/eat** non potable/comestible

unsaid [ʌn'sɛd] *adj*: **to leave sth ~** passer qch sous silence

unsaleable, (*US*) **unsalable** [ʌn'seɪləbl] *adj* invendable

unsatisfactory ['ʌnsætɪs'fæktərɪ] *adj* peu satisfaisant(e), qui laisse à désirer

unsavoury, (*US*) **unsavory** [ʌn'seɪvərɪ] *adj* (*fig*) peu recommandable, répugnant(e)

unscathed [ʌn'skeɪðd] *adj* indemne

unscientific ['ʌnsaɪən'tɪfɪk] *adj* non scientifique

unscrew [ʌn'skru:] *vt* dévisser

unscrupulous [ʌn'skru:pjuləs] *adj* sans scrupules

unseat [ʌn'si:t] *vt* (*rider*) désarçonner; (*fig: official*) faire perdre son siège à

unsecured ['ʌnsɪ'kjuəd] *adj*: ~ **creditor** créancier(-ière) sans garantie

unseeded [ʌn'si:dɪd] *adj* (*Sport*) non classé(e)

unseemly [ʌn'si:mlɪ] *adj* inconvenant(e)

unseen [ʌn'si:n] *adj* (*person*) invisible; (*danger*) imprévu(e)

unselfish [ʌn'sɛlfɪʃ] *adj* désintéressé(e)

unsettled [ʌn'sɛtld] *adj* (*restless*) perturbé(e); (*unpredictable*) instable; incertain(e); (*not finalized*) non résolu(e)

unsettling [ʌn'sɛtlɪŋ] *adj* qui a un effet perturbateur

unshakable, unshakeable [ʌn'ʃeɪkəbl] *adj* inébranlable

unshaven [ʌn'ʃeɪvn] *adj* non or mal rasé(e)

unsightly [ʌn'saɪtlɪ] *adj* disgracieux(-euse), laid(e)

unskilled [ʌn'skɪld] *adj*: ~ **worker** manœuvre *m*

unsociable [ʌn'səuʃəbl] *adj* (*person*) peu sociable; (*behaviour*) qui manque de sociabilité

unsocial [ʌn'səuʃl] *adj* (*hours*) en dehors de l'horaire normal

unsold [ʌn'səuld] *adj* invendu(e), non vendu(e)

unsolicited [ʌnsə'lɪsɪtɪd] *adj* non sollicité(e)

unsophisticated [ʌnsə'fɪstɪkeɪtɪd] *adj* simple, naturel(le)

unsound [ʌn'saund] *adj* (*health*) chancelant(e); (*floor, foundations*) peu solide; (*policy, advice*) peu judicieux(-euse)

unspeakable [ʌn'spi:kəbl] *adj* indicible; (*awful*) innommable

unspoiled ['ʌn'spɔɪld], **unspoilt** ['ʌn'spɔɪlt] *adj* (*place*) non dégradé(e)

unspoken [ʌn'spəukn] *adj* (*word*) qui n'est pas prononcé(e); (*agreement, approval*) tacite

unstable [ʌn'steɪbl] *adj* instable

unsteady [ʌn'stɛdɪ] *adj* mal assuré(e), chancelant(e), instable

unstinting [ʌn'stɪntɪŋ] *adj* (*support*) total(e), sans réserve; (*generosity*) sans limites

unstuck [ʌn'stʌk] *adj*: **to come ~** se décoller; (*fig*) faire fiasco

unsubstantiated ['ʌnsəb'stænʃɪeɪtɪd] *adj* (*rumour*) qui n'est pas confirmé(e); (*accusation*) sans preuve

unsuccessful [ʌnsək'sɛsful] *adj* (*attempt*) infructueux(-euse); (*writer, proposal*) qui n'a pas de succès; (*marriage*) malheureux(-euse), qui ne réussit pas; **to be ~** (*in attempting sth*) ne pas réussir; ne pas avoir de succès; (*application*) ne pas être retenu(e)

unsuccessfully [ʌnsək'sɛsfəlɪ] *adv* en vain

unsuitable [ʌn'su:təbl] *adj* qui ne convient pas, peu approprié(e); (*time*) inopportun(e)

unsuited [ʌn'su:tɪd] *adj*: **to be ~ for** *or* **to** être inapte *or* impropre à

unsung ['ʌnsʌŋ] *adj*: **an ~ hero** un héros méconnu

unsupported [ʌnsə'pɔ:tɪd] *adj* (*claim*) non soutenu(e); (*theory*) qui n'est pas corroboré(e)

unsure [ʌn'ʃuə'] *adj* pas sûr(e); **to be ~ of o.s.** ne pas être sûr de soi, manquer de confiance en soi

unsuspecting [ʌnsə'spɛktɪŋ] *adj* qui ne se méfie pas

unsweetened [ʌn'swi:tnd] *adj* non sucré(e)

unswerving [ʌn'swə:vɪŋ] *adj* inébranlable

unsympathetic ['ʌnsɪmpə'θɛtɪk] *adj* hostile; (*unpleasant*) antipathique; ~ **to** indifférent(e) à

untangle [ʌn'tæŋgl] *vt* démêler, débrouiller

untapped [ʌn'tæpt] *adj* (*resources*) inexploité(e)

untaxed [ʌn'tækst] *adj* (*goods*) non taxé(e); (*income*) non imposé(e)

unthinkable [ʌn'θɪŋkəbl] *adj* impensable, inconcevable

unthinkingly [ʌn'θɪŋkɪŋlɪ] *adv* sans réfléchir

untidy [ʌn'taɪdɪ] *adj* (*room*) en désordre; (*appearance, person*) débraillé(e); (*person: in character*) sans ordre, désordonné; débraillé; (*work*) peu soigné(e)

untie [ʌn'taɪ] *vt* (*knot, parcel*) défaire; (*prisoner, dog*) détacher

until [ən'tɪl] *prep* jusqu'à; (*after negative*) avant ▷ *conj* jusqu'à ce que + *sub*, en attendant que + *sub*; (*in past, after negative*) avant que + *sub*; ~ **he comes** jusqu'à ce qu'il vienne, jusqu'à son arrivée; ~ **now** jusqu'à présent, jusqu'ici; ~ **then** jusque-là; **from morning ~ night** du matin au soir *or* jusqu'au soir

untimely [ʌn'taɪmlɪ] *adj* inopportun(e); (*death*) prématuré(e)

untold [ʌn'təuld] *adj* incalculable; indescriptible

untouched [ʌn'tʌtʃt] *adj* (*not used etc*) tel(le) quel(le), intact(e); (*safe: person*) indemne; (*unaffected*): ~ **by** indifférent(e) à

untoward [ʌntə'wɔ:d] *adj* fâcheux(-euse), malencontreux(-euse)

untrained ['ʌn'treɪnd] *adj* (*worker*) sans formation; (*troops*) sans entraînement; **to the ~ eye** à l'œil non exercé

untrammelled [ʌn'træmld] *adj* sans entraves

untranslatable [ʌntrænz'leɪtəbl] *adj* intraduisible

untrue [ʌn'tru:] *adj* (*statement*) faux (fausse)

untrustworthy [ʌn'trʌstwə:ðɪ] *adj* (*person*) pas digne de confiance, peu sûr(e)

unusable [ʌn'ju:zəbl] *adj* inutilisable

unused¹ [ʌn'ju:zd] *adj* (*new*) neuf (neuve)

unused² [ʌn'ju:st] *adj*: **to be ~ to sth/to doing sth** ne pas avoir l'habitude de qch/de faire qch

unusual [ʌn'ju:ʒuəl] *adj* insolite, exceptionnel(le), rare

unusually [ʌn'ju:ʒuəlɪ] *adv* exceptionnellement, particulièrement

unveil [ʌn'veɪl] *vt* dévoiler

unwanted [ʌn'wɔntɪd] *adj* (*child, pregnancy*) non désiré(e); (*clothes etc*) à donner

unwarranted [ʌn'wɔrəntɪd] *adj* injustifié(e)

unwary [ʌn'wɛərɪ] *adj* imprudent(e)

unwavering [ʌn'weɪvərɪŋ] *adj* inébranlable

unwelcome [ʌn'wɛlkəm] *adj* importun(e); **to feel ~** se sentir de trop

unwell [ʌn'wɛl] *adj* indisposé(e), souffrant(e); **to feel ~** ne pas se sentir bien

unwieldy [ʌn'wi:ldɪ] *adj* difficile à manier

unwilling [ʌn'wɪlɪŋ] *adj*: **to be ~ to do** ne pas vouloir faire

unwillingly [ʌn'wɪlɪŋlɪ] *adv* à contrecœur, contre son gré

unwind [ʌn'waɪnd] (*irreg: like* **wind**) *vt* dérouler ▷ *vi* (*relax*) se détendre

unwise [ʌn'waɪz] *adj* imprudent(e), peu judicieux(-euse)

unwitting [ʌn'wɪtɪŋ] *adj* involontaire

unwittingly [ʌn'wɪtɪŋlɪ] *adv* involontairement

unworkable [ʌn'wə:kəbl] *adj* (*plan etc*) inexploitable

unworthy [ʌn'wə:ðɪ] *adj* indigne

unwrap [ʌn'ræp] *vt* défaire; ouvrir

unwritten [ʌn'rɪtn] *adj* (*agreement*) tacite

unzip [ʌn'zɪp] *vt* ouvrir (la fermeture éclair de); (*Comput*) dézipper

 KEYWORD

up [ʌp] *prep*: **he went up the stairs/the hill** il a monté l'escalier/la colline; **the cat was up a tree** le chat était dans un arbre; **they live further up the street** ils habitent plus haut dans la rue; **go up that road and turn left** remontez la rue et tournez à gauche
▷ *vi* (*inf*): **she upped and left** elle a fichu le camp sans plus attendre
▷ *adv* **1** en haut; en l'air; (*upwards, higher*): **up in the sky/the mountains** (là-haut) dans le ciel/les montagnes; **put it a bit higher up** mettez-le un peu plus haut; **to stand up** (*get up*) se lever, se mettre debout; (*be standing*) être debout; **up there** là-haut; **up above** au-dessus; **"this side up"** "haut"
2: **to be up** (*out of bed*) être levé(e); (*prices*) avoir augmenté *or* monté; (*finished*): **when the year was up** à la fin de l'année; **time's up** c'est l'heure
3: **up to** (*as far as*) jusqu'à; **up to now** jusqu'à présent

4: **to be up to** (*depending on*): **it's up to you** c'est à vous de décider; (*equal to*): **he's not up to it** (*job, task etc*) il n'en est pas capable; (*inf: be doing*): **what is he up to?** qu'est-ce qu'il peut bien faire?
5 (*phrases*): **he's well up in** *or* **on ...** (*Brit: knowledgeable*) il s'y connaît en ...; **up with Leeds United!** vive Leeds United!; **what's up?** (*inf*) qu'est-ce qui ne va pas?; **what's up with him?** (*inf*) qu'est-ce qui lui arrive?
▷ *n*: **ups and downs** hauts et bas *mpl*

up-and-coming [ʌpənd'kʌmɪŋ] *adj* plein(e) d'avenir *or* de promesses

upbeat ['ʌpbi:t] *n* (*Mus*) levé *m*; (*in economy, prosperity*) amélioration *f* ▷ *adj* (*optimistic*) optimiste

upbraid [ʌp'breɪd] *vt* morigéner

upbringing ['ʌpbrɪŋɪŋ] *n* éducation *f*

upcoming ['ʌpkʌmɪŋ] *adj* tout(e) prochain(e)

update [ʌp'deɪt] *vt* mettre à jour

upend [ʌp'ɛnd] *vt* mettre debout

upfront [ʌp'frʌnt] *adj* (*open*) franc (franche) ▷ *adv* (*pay*) d'avance; **to be ~ about sth** ne rien cacher de qch

upgrade [ʌp'greɪd] *vt* (*person*) promouvoir; (*job*) revaloriser; (*property, equipment*) moderniser

upheaval [ʌp'hi:vl] *n* bouleversement *m*; (*in room*) branle-bas *m*; (*event*) crise *f*

uphill [ʌp'hɪl] *adj* qui monte; (*fig: task*) difficile, pénible ▷ *adv* (*face, look*) en amont, vers l'amont; (*go, move*) vers le haut, en haut; **to go ~** monter

uphold [ʌp'həʊld] *vt* (*irreg: like* **hold**) maintenir; soutenir

upholstery [ʌp'həʊlstərɪ] *n* rembourrage *m*; (*cover*) tissu *m* d'ameublement; (*of car*) garniture *f*

upkeep ['ʌpki:p] *n* entretien *m*

upmarket [ʌp'mɑ:kɪt] *adj* (*product*) haut de gamme *inv*; (*area*) chic *inv*

upon [ə'pɔn] *prep* sur

upper ['ʌpəʳ] *adj* supérieur(e); du dessus ▷ *n* (*of shoe*) empeigne *f*

upper class *n*: **the ~** ≈ la haute bourgeoisie

upper-class [ʌpə'klɑ:s] *adj* de la haute société, aristocratique; (*district*) élégant(e), huppé(e); (*accent, attitude*) caractéristique des classes supérieures

uppercut ['ʌpəkʌt] *n* uppercut *m*

upper hand *n*: **to have the ~** avoir le dessus

Upper House *n*: **the ~** (*in Britain*) la Chambre des Lords, la Chambre haute; (*in France, in the US etc*) le Sénat

uppermost ['ʌpəməʊst] *adj* le (la) plus haut(e), en dessus; **it was ~ in my mind** j'y pensais avant tout autre chose

upper sixth *n* terminale *f*

Upper Volta [-'vɔltə] *n* Haute Volta

upright ['ʌpraɪt] *adj* droit(e); (*fig*) droit, honnête ▷ *n* montant *m*

uprising ['ʌpraɪzɪŋ] *n* soulèvement *m*, insurrection *f*

uproar [ˈʌprɔːʳ] n tumulte m, vacarme m; (protests) protestations fpl

uproarious [ʌpˈrɔːrɪəs] adj (event etc) désopilant(e); ~ **laughter** un brouhaha de rires

uproot [ʌpˈruːt] vt déraciner

upset n [ˈʌpsɛt] dérangement m ▷ vt [ʌpˈsɛt] (irreg: like **set**: glass etc) renverser; (plan) déranger; (person: offend) contrarier; (: grieve) faire de la peine à; bouleverser ▷ adj [ʌpˈsɛt] contrarié(e); peiné(e); (stomach) détraqué(e), dérangé(e); **to get ~** (sad) devenir triste; (offended) se vexer; **to have a stomach ~** (Brit) avoir une indigestion

upset price n (US, Scottish) mise f à prix, prix m de départ

upsetting [ʌpˈsɛtɪŋ] adj (offending) vexant(e); (annoying) ennuyeux(-euse)

upshot [ˈʌpʃɒt] n résultat m; **the ~ of it all was that ...** il a résulté de tout cela que ...

upside down [ˈʌpsaɪd-] adv à l'envers; **to turn sth ~** (fig: place) mettre sens dessus dessous

upstage [ˈʌpˈsteɪdʒ] vt: **to ~ sb** souffler la vedette à qn

upstairs [ʌpˈstɛəz] adv en haut ▷ adj (room) du dessus, d'en haut ▷ n: **the ~** l'étage m; **there's no ~** il n'y a pas d'étage

upstart [ˈʌpstɑːt] n parvenu(e)

upstream [ʌpˈstriːm] adv en amont

upsurge [ˈʌpsəːdʒ] n (of enthusiasm etc) vague f

uptake [ˈʌpteɪk] n: **he is quick/slow on the ~** il comprend vite/est lent à comprendre

uptight [ʌpˈtaɪt] adj (inf) très tendu(e), crispé(e)

up-to-date [ˈʌptəˈdeɪt] adj moderne; (information) très récent(e)

upturn [ˈʌptəːn] n (in economy) reprise f

upturned [ˈʌptəːnd] adj (nose) retroussé(e)

upward [ˈʌpwəd] adj ascendant(e); vers le haut ▷ adv vers le haut; (more than): ~ **of** plus de; **and ~ et plus, et au-dessus**

upwardly-mobile [ˈʌpwədlɪˈməubaɪl] adj à mobilité sociale ascendante

upwards [ˈʌpwədz] adv vers le haut; (more than): ~ **of** plus de; **and ~** et plus, et au-dessus

URA n abbr (US) = **Urban Renewal Administration**

Ural Mountains [ˈjuərəl-] npl: **the ~** (also: **the Urals**) les monts mpl Oural, l'Oural m

uranium [juəˈreɪnɪəm] n uranium m

Uranus [juəˈreɪnəs] n Uranus f

urban [ˈəːbən] adj urbain(e)

urban clearway n rue f à stationnement interdit

urbane [əːˈbeɪn] adj urbain(e), courtois(e)

urbanization [əːbənaɪˈzeɪʃən] n urbanisation f

urchin [ˈəːtʃɪn] n gosse m, garnement m

Urdu [ˈuəduː] n ourdou m

urge [əːdʒ] n besoin (impératif), envie (pressante) ▷ vt (caution etc) recommander avec insistance; (person): **to ~ sb to do** exhorter qn à faire, pousser qn à faire, recommander vivement à qn de faire
  ▶ **urge on** vt pousser, presser

urgency [ˈəːdʒənsɪ] n urgence f; (of tone) insistance f

urgent [ˈəːdʒənt] adj urgent(e); (plea, tone) pressant(e)

urgently [ˈəːdʒəntlɪ] adv d'urgence, de toute urgence; (need) sans délai

urinal [ˈjuərɪnl] n (Brit: place) urinoir m

urinate [ˈjuərɪneɪt] vi uriner

urine [ˈjuərɪn] n urine f

URL abbr (= uniform resource locator) URL f

urn [əːn] n urne f; (also: **tea urn**) fontaine f à thé

Uruguay [ˈjuərəgwaɪ] n Uruguay m

Uruguayan [juərəˈgwaɪən] adj uruguayen(ne) ▷ n Uruguayen(ne)

US n abbr = **United States**

us [ʌs] pron nous; see also **me**

USA n abbr = **United States of America**; (Mil) = **United States Army**

usable [ˈjuːzəbl] adj utilisable

USAF n abbr = **United States Air Force**

usage [ˈjuːzɪdʒ] n usage m

USCG n abbr = **United States Coast Guard**

USDA n abbr = **United States Department of Agriculture**

USDAW [ˈʌzdɔː] n abbr (Brit: = Union of Shop, Distributive and Allied Workers) syndicat du commerce de détail et de la distribution

USDI n abbr = **United States Department of the Interior**

use n [juːs] emploi m, utilisation f; usage m; (usefulness) utilité f ▷ vt [juːz] se servir de, utiliser, employer; **in ~** en usage; **out of ~** hors d'usage; **to be of ~** servir, être utile; **to make ~ of sth** utiliser qch; **ready for ~** prêt à l'emploi; **it's no ~** ça ne sert à rien; **to have the ~ of** avoir l'usage de; **what's this ~d for?** à quoi est-ce que ça sert?; **she ~d to do it** elle le faisait (autrefois), elle avait coutume de le faire; **to be ~d to** avoir l'habitude de, être habitué(e) à; **to get ~d to** s'habituer à
  ▶ **use up** vt finir, épuiser; (food) consommer

used [juːzd] adj (car) d'occasion

useful [ˈjuːsful] adj utile; **to come in ~** être utile

usefulness [ˈjuːsfəlnɪs] n utilité f

useless [ˈjuːslɪs] adj inutile; (inf: person) nul(le)

user [ˈjuːzəʳ] n utilisateur(-trice), usager m

user-friendly [ˈjuːzəˈfrɛndlɪ] adj convivial(e), facile d'emploi

USES n abbr = **United States Employment Service**

usher [ˈʌʃəʳ] n placeur m ▷ vt: **to ~ sb in** faire entrer qn

usherette [ʌʃəˈrɛt] n (in cinema) ouvreuse f

USIA n abbr = **United States Information Agency**

USM n abbr = **United States Mail**; **United States Mint**

USN n abbr = **United States Navy**

USP n abbr = **unique selling proposition**

USPHS n abbr = **United States Public Health Service**

USPO n abbr = **United States Post Office**

USS *abbr* = **United States Ship (or Steamer)**
USSR *n abbr* = **Union of Soviet Socialist Republics**
usu. *abbr* = **usually**
usual ['juːʒuəl] *adj* habituel(le); **as** ~ comme d'habitude
usually ['juːʒuəlɪ] *adv* d'habitude, d'ordinaire
usurer ['juːʒərəʳ] *n* usurier(-ière)
usurp [juːˈzəːp] *vt* usurper
UT *abbr* (*US*) = **Utah**
utensil [juːˈtɛnsl] *n* ustensile *m*; **kitchen** ~**s** batterie *f* de cuisine
uterus ['juːtərəs] *n* utérus *m*
utilitarian [juːtɪlɪˈtɛərɪən] *adj* utilitaire
utility [juːˈtɪlɪtɪ] *n* utilité *f*; (*also*: **public utility**) service public

utility room *n* buanderie *f*
utilization [juːtɪlaɪˈzeɪʃən] *n* utilisation *f*
utilize ['juːtɪlaɪz] *vt* utiliser; (*make good use of*) exploiter
utmost ['ʌtməust] *adj* extrême, le (la) plus grand(e) ▷ *n*: **to do one's** ~ faire tout son possible; **of the** ~ **importance** d'une importance capitale, de la plus haute importance
utter ['ʌtəʳ] *adj* total(e), complet(-ète) ▷ *vt* prononcer, proférer; (*sounds*) émettre
utterance ['ʌtrns] *n* paroles *fpl*
utterly ['ʌtəlɪ] *adv* complètement, totalement
U-turn ['juːˈtəːn] *n* demi-tour *m*; (*fig*) volte-face *f inv*
Uzbekistan [ʌzbɛkɪˈstɑːn] *n* Ouzbékistan *m*

Vv

V, v [vi:] *n* (*letter*) V, v *m*; **V for Victor** V comme
Victor
v. *abbr* = **verse**; (= *vide*) v.; (= *versus*) vs; (= *volt*) V
VA, Va. *abbr* (*US*) = **Virginia**
vac [væk] *n abbr* (*Brit inf*) = **vacation**
vacancy ['veɪkənsɪ] *n* (*Brit: job*) poste vacant;
(*room*) chambre *f* disponible; **"no vacancies"**
"complet"
vacant ['veɪkənt] *adj* (*post*) vacant(e); (*seat etc*)
libre, disponible; (*expression*) distrait(e)
vacant lot *n* terrain inoccupé; (*for sale*) terrain à
vendre
vacate [və'keɪt] *vt* quitter
vacation [və'keɪʃən] *n* (*esp US*) vacances *fpl*; **to
take a ~** prendre des vacances; **on ~** en vacances
vacation course *n* cours *mpl* de vacances
vacationer [və'keɪʃənə'], (*US*) **vacationist**
[və'keɪʃənɪst] *n* vacancier(-ière)
vaccinate ['væksɪneɪt] *vt* vacciner
vaccination [væksɪ'neɪʃən] *n* vaccination *f*
vaccine ['væksi:n] *n* vaccin *m*
vacuum ['vækjum] *n* vide *m*
vacuum bottle *n* (*US*) = **vacuum flask**
vacuum cleaner *n* aspirateur *m*
vacuum flask *n* (*Brit*) bouteille *f* thermos®
vacuum-packed ['vækjumpækt] *adj* emballé(e)
sous vide
vagabond ['vægəbɔnd] *n* vagabond(e); (*tramp*)
chemineau *m*, clochard(e)
vagary ['veɪgərɪ] *n* caprice *m*
vagina [və'dʒaɪnə] *n* vagin *m*
vagrancy ['veɪgrənsɪ] *n* vagabondage *m*
vagrant ['veɪgrənt] *n* vagabond(e), mendiant(e)
vague [veɪg] *adj* vague, imprécis(e); (*blurred:
photo, memory*) flou(e); **I haven't the ~st idea** je
n'en ai pas la moindre idée
vaguely ['veɪglɪ] *adv* vaguement
vain [veɪn] *adj* (*useless*) vain(e); (*conceited*)
vaniteux(-euse); **in ~** en vain
valance ['væləns] *n* (*of bed*) tour *m* de lit
valedictory [vælɪ'dɪktərɪ] *adj* d'adieu
valentine ['væləntaɪn] *n* (*also*: **valentine card**)
carte *f* de la Saint-Valentin
Valentine's Day ['væləntaɪnz-] *n* Saint-
Valentin *f*
valet ['vælɪt] *n* valet *m* de chambre

valet parking *n* parcage *m* par les soins du
personnel (de l'hôtel *etc*)
valet service *n* (*for clothes*) pressing *m*; (*for car*)
nettoyage complet
valiant ['vælɪənt] *adj* vaillant(e),
courageux(-euse)
valid ['vælɪd] *adj* (*document*) valide, valable;
(*excuse*) valable
validate ['vælɪdeɪt] *vt* (*contract, document*) valider;
(*argument, claim*) prouver la justesse de,
confirmer
validity [və'lɪdɪtɪ] *n* validité *f*
valise [və'li:z] *n* sac *m* de voyage
valley ['vælɪ] *n* vallée *f*
valour, (*US*) **valor** ['vælə'] *n* courage *m*
valuable ['væljuəbl] *adj* (*jewel*) de grande valeur;
(*time, help*) précieux(-euse)
valuables ['væljuəblz] *npl* objets *mpl* de valeur
valuation [vælju'eɪʃən] *n* évaluation *f*,
expertise *f*
value ['vælju:] *n* valeur *f* ▷ *vt* (*fix price*) évaluer,
expertiser; (*appreciate*) apprécier; (*cherish*) tenir
à; **values** *npl* (*principles*) valeurs *fpl*; **you get
good ~ (for money) in that shop** vous en avez
pour votre argent dans ce magasin; **to lose (in)
~** (*currency*) baisser; (*property*) se déprécier; **to
gain (in) ~** (*currency*) monter; (*property*) prendre
de la valeur; **to be of great ~ to sb** (*fig*) être très
utile à qn
value added tax [-'ædɪd-] *n* (*Brit*) taxe *f* à la
valeur ajoutée
valued ['vælju:d] *adj* (*appreciated*) estimé(e)
valuer ['væljuə'] *n* expert *m* (en estimations)
valve [vælv] *n* (*in machine*) soupape *f*; (*on tyre*)
valve *f*; (*in radio*) lampe *f*; (*Med*) valve, valvule *f*
vampire ['væmpaɪə'] *n* vampire *m*
van [væn] *n* (*Aut*) camionnette *f*; (*Brit Rail*)
fourgon *m*
V and A *n abbr* (*Brit*) = **Victoria and Albert
Museum**
vandal ['vændl] *n* vandale *m/f*
vandalism ['vændəlɪzəm] *n* vandalisme *m*
vandalize ['vændəlaɪz] *vt* saccager
vanguard ['vængɑːd] *n* avant-garde *m*
vanilla [və'nɪlə] *n* vanille *f* ▷ *cpd* (*ice cream*) à la
vanille

vanish ['vænɪʃ] vi disparaître
vanity ['vænɪtɪ] n vanité f
vanity case n sac m de toilette
vantage ['vɑ:ntɪdʒ] n: ~ **point** bonne position
vaporize ['veɪpəraɪz] vt vaporiser ▷ vi se vaporiser
vapour, (US) **vapor** ['veɪpəʳ] n vapeur f; (on window) buée f
variable ['vɛərɪəbl] adj variable; (mood) changeant(e) ▷ n variable f
variance ['vɛərɪəns] n: **to be at ~ (with)** être en désaccord (avec); (facts) être en contradiction (avec)
variant ['vɛərɪənt] n variante f
variation [vɛərɪ'eɪʃən] n variation f; (in opinion) changement m
varicose ['værɪkəus] adj: ~ **veins** varices fpl
varied ['vɛərɪd] adj varié(e), divers(e)
variety [və'raɪətɪ] n variété f; (quantity) nombre m, quantité f; **a wide ~ of ...** une quantité or un grand nombre de ... (différent(e)s or divers(es)); **for a ~ of reasons** pour diverses raisons
variety show n (spectacle m de) variétés fpl
various ['vɛərɪəs] adj divers(e), différent(e); (several) divers, plusieurs; **at ~ times** (different) en diverses occasions; (several) à plusieurs reprises
varnish ['vɑ:nɪʃ] n vernis m; (for nails) vernis (à ongles) ▷ vt vernir; **to ~ one's nails** se vernir les ongles
vary ['vɛərɪ] vt, vi varier, changer; **to ~ with** or **according to** varier selon
varying ['vɛərɪɪŋ] adj variable
vase [vɑ:z] n vase m
vasectomy [væ'sɛktəmɪ] n vasectomie f
Vaseline® ['væsɪli:n] n vaseline f
vast [vɑ:st] adj vaste, immense; (amount, success) énorme
vastly ['vɑ:stlɪ] adv infiniment, extrêmement
vastness ['vɑ:stnɪs] n immensité f
VAT [væt] n abbr (Brit: = value added tax) TVA f
vat [væt] n cuve f
Vatican ['vætɪkən] n: **the ~** le Vatican
vatman ['vætmæn] (irreg) n (Brit inf) contrôleur m de la T.V.A.
vault [vɔ:lt] n (of roof) voûte f; (tomb) caveau m; (in bank) salle f des coffres; chambre forte; (jump) saut m ▷ vt (also: **vault over**) sauter (d'un bond)
vaunted ['vɔ:ntɪd] adj: **much-~** tant célébré(e)
VC n abbr = **vice-chairman**; (Brit: = Victoria Cross) distinction militaire
VCR n abbr = **video cassette recorder**
VD n abbr = **venereal disease**
VDU n abbr = **visual display unit**
veal [vi:l] n veau m
veer [vɪəʳ] vi tourner; (car, ship) virer
veg. [vɛdʒ] n abbr (Brit inf) = **vegetable**; **vegetables**
vegan ['vi:gən] n végétalien(ne)
vegeburger ['vɛdʒɪbə:gəʳ] n burger végétarien
vegetable ['vɛdʒtəbl] n légume m ▷ adj végétal(e)

vegetable garden n (jardin m) potager m
vegetarian [vɛdʒɪ'tɛərɪən] adj, n végétarien(ne); **do you have any ~ dishes?** avez-vous des plats végétariens?
vegetate ['vɛdʒɪteɪt] vi végéter
vegetation [vɛdʒɪ'teɪʃən] n végétation f
vegetative ['vɛdʒɪtətɪv] adj (lit) végétal(e); (fig) végétatif(-ive)
veggieburger ['vɛdʒɪbə:gəʳ] n = **vegeburger**
vehemence ['vi:ɪməns] n véhémence f, violence f
vehement ['vi:ɪmənt] adj violent(e), impétueux(-euse); (impassioned) ardent(e)
vehicle ['vi:ɪkl] n véhicule m
vehicular [vɪ'hɪkjuləʳ] adj: **"no ~ traffic"** "interdit à tout véhicule"
veil [veɪl] n voile m ▷ vt voiler; **under a ~ of secrecy** (fig) dans le plus grand secret
veiled [veɪld] adj voilé(e)
vein [veɪn] n veine f; (on leaf) nervure f; (fig: mood) esprit m
Velcro® ['vɛlkrəu] n velcro® m
vellum ['vɛləm] n (writing paper) vélin m
velocity [vɪ'lɔsɪtɪ] n vitesse f, vélocité f
velour, velours [və'luəʳ] n velours m
velvet ['vɛlvɪt] n velours m
vending machine ['vɛndɪŋ-] n distributeur m automatique
vendor ['vɛndəʳ] n vendeur(-euse); **street ~** marchand ambulant
veneer [və'nɪəʳ] n placage m de bois; (fig) vernis m
venerable ['vɛnərəbl] adj vénérable
venereal [vɪ'nɪərɪəl] adj: ~ **disease** maladie vénérienne
Venetian blind [vɪ'ni:ʃən-] n store vénitien
Venezuela [vɛnɛ'zweɪlə] n Venezuela m
Venezuelan [vɛnɛ'zweɪlən] adj vénézuélien(ne) ▷ n Vénézuélien(ne)
vengeance ['vɛndʒəns] n vengeance f; **with a ~** (fig) vraiment, pour de bon
vengeful ['vɛndʒful] adj vengeur(-geresse)
Venice ['vɛnɪs] n Venise f
venison ['vɛnɪsn] n venaison f
venom ['vɛnəm] n venin m
venomous ['vɛnəməs] adj venimeux(-euse)
vent [vɛnt] n conduit m d'aération; (in dress, jacket) fente f ▷ vt (fig: one's feelings) donner libre cours à
ventilate ['vɛntɪleɪt] vt (room) ventiler, aérer
ventilation [vɛntɪ'leɪʃən] n ventilation f, aération f
ventilation shaft n conduit m de ventilation or d'aération
ventilator ['vɛntɪleɪtəʳ] n ventilateur m
ventriloquist [vɛn'trɪləkwɪst] n ventriloque m/f
venture ['vɛntʃəʳ] n entreprise f ▷ vt risquer, hasarder ▷ vi s'aventurer, se risquer; **a business ~** une entreprise commerciale; **to ~ to do sth** se risquer à faire qch
venture capital n capital-risque m
venue ['vɛnju:] n lieu m; (of conference etc) lieu de

855

la réunion (or manifestation etc); (of match) lieu
de la rencontre
Venus ['vi:nəs] n (planet) Vénus f
veracity [və'ræsɪtɪ] n véracité f
veranda, verandah [və'rændə] n véranda f
verb [və:b] n verbe m
verbal ['və:bl] adj verbal(e); (translation)
littéral(e)
verbally ['və:bəlɪ] adv verbalement
verbatim [və:'beɪtɪm] adj, adv mot pour mot
verbose [və:'bəus] adj verbeux(-euse)
verdict ['və:dɪkt] n verdict m; ~ **of guilty/not
guilty** verdict de culpabilité/de non-culpabilité
verge [və:dʒ] n bord m; "**soft ~s**" (Brit)
"accotements non stabilisés"; **on the ~ of
doing** sur le point de faire
▸ **verge on** vt fus approcher de
verger ['və:dʒəʳ] n (Rel) bedeau m
verification [verɪfɪ'keɪʃən] n vérification f
verify ['verɪfaɪ] vt vérifier
veritable ['verɪtəbl] adj véritable
vermin ['və:mɪn] npl animaux mpl nuisibles;
(insects) vermine f
vermouth ['və:məθ] n vermouth m
vernacular [və'nækjuləʳ] n langue f
vernaculaire, dialecte m
versatile ['və:sətaɪl] adj polyvalent(e)
verse [və:s] n vers mpl; (stanza) strophe f; (in
Bible) verset m; **in ~** en vers
versed [və:st] adj: (**well-**)~ **in** versé(e) dans
version ['və:ʃən] n version f
versus ['və:səs] prep contre
vertebra (pl -e) ['və:tɪbrə, -bri:] n vertèbre f
vertebrate ['və:tɪbrɪt] n vertébré m
vertical ['və:tɪkl] adj vertical(e) ▸ n verticale f
vertically ['və:tɪklɪ] adv verticalement
vertigo ['və:tɪgəu] n vertige m; **to suffer from ~**
avoir des vertiges
verve [və:v] n brio m; enthousiasme m
very ['verɪ] adv très ▸ adj: **the ~ book which** le
livre même que; **the ~ thought (of it)** ... rien
que d'y penser ...; **at the ~ end** tout à la fin; **the
~ last** le tout dernier; **at the ~ least** au moins;
~ well très bien; **~ little** très peu; **~ much**
beaucoup
vespers ['vespəz] npl vêpres fpl
vessel ['vesl] n (Anat, Naut) vaisseau m; (container)
récipient m; see also **blood**
vest [vest] n (Brit: underwear) tricot m de corps;
(US: waistcoat) gilet m ▸ vt: **to ~ sb with sth, to ~
sth in sb** investir qn de qch
vested interest n: **to have a ~ in doing** avoir
tout intérêt à faire; **vested interests** npl
(Comm) droits acquis
vestibule ['vestɪbju:l] n vestibule m
vestige ['vestɪdʒ] n vestige m
vestry ['vestrɪ] n sacristie f
Vesuvius [vɪ'su:vɪəs] n Vésuve m
vet [vet] n abbr (Brit: = veterinary surgeon)
vétérinaire m/f; (US: = veteran) ancien(ne)
combattant(e) ▸ vt examiner minutieusement;
(text) revoir; (candidate) se renseigner

soigneusement sur; soumettre à une enquête
approfondie
veteran ['vetərn] n vétéran m; (also: **war
veteran**) ancien combattant ▸ adj: **she's a ~
campaigner for** ... cela fait très longtemps
qu'elle lutte pour ...
veteran car n voiture f d'époque
veterinarian [vetrɪ'neərɪən] n (US) = **veterinary
surgeon**
veterinary ['vetrɪnərɪ] adj vétérinaire
veterinary surgeon ['vetrɪnərɪ-] (Brit) n
vétérinaire m/f
veto ['vi:təu] n (pl -es) veto m ▸ vt opposer son
veto à; **to put a ~ on** mettre (or opposer) son
veto à
vetting ['vetɪŋ] n: **positive ~** enquête f de
sécurité
vex [veks] vt fâcher, contrarier
vexed [vekst] adj (question) controversé(e)
VFD n abbr (US) = **voluntary fire department**
VG n abbr (Brit: Scol etc: = very good) tb (= très bien)
VHF abbr (= very high frequency) VHF
VI abbr (US) = **Virgin Islands**
via ['vaɪə] prep par, via
viability [vaɪə'bɪlɪtɪ] n viabilité f
viable ['vaɪəbl] adj viable
viaduct ['vaɪədʌkt] n viaduc m
vial ['vaɪəl] n fiole f
vibes [vaɪbz] npl (inf): **I get good/bad ~ about it**
je le sens bien/ne le sens pas; **there are good/
bad ~ between us** entre nous le courant passe
bien/ne passe pas
vibrant ['vaɪbrnt] adj (sound, colour) vibrant(e)
vibraphone ['vaɪbrəfəun] n vibraphone m
vibrate [vaɪ'breɪt] vi: **to ~ (with)** vibrer (de);
(resound) retentir (de)
vibration [vaɪ'breɪʃən] n vibration f
vibrator [vaɪ'breɪtəʳ] n vibromasseur m
vicar ['vɪkəʳ] n pasteur m (de l'Église anglicane)
vicarage ['vɪkərɪdʒ] n presbytère m
vicarious [vɪ'keərɪəs] adj (pleasure, experience)
indirect(e)
vice [vaɪs] n (evil) vice m; (Tech) étau m
vice- [vaɪs] prefix vice-
vice-chairman [vaɪs'tʃeəmən] (irreg) n vice-
président(e)
vice-chancellor [vaɪs'tʃɑ:nsələʳ] n (Brit)
≈ président(e) d'université
vice-president [vaɪs'prezɪdənt] n vice-
président(e)
viceroy ['vaɪsrɔɪ] n vice-roi m
vice squad n ≈ brigade mondaine
vice versa ['vaɪsɪ'və:sə] adv vice versa
vicinity [vɪ'sɪnɪtɪ] n environs mpl, alentours mpl
vicious ['vɪʃəs] adj (remark) cruel(le), méchant(e);
(blow) brutal(e); (dog) méchant(e),
dangereux(-euse); **a ~ circle** un cercle vicieux
viciousness ['vɪʃəsnɪs] n méchanceté f, cruauté
f; brutalité f
vicissitudes [vɪ'sɪsɪtju:dz] npl vicissitudes fpl
victim ['vɪktɪm] n victime f; **to be the ~ of** être
victime de

victimization [vɪktɪmaɪ'zeɪʃən] n brimades fpl; représailles fpl
victimize ['vɪktɪmaɪz] vt brimer; exercer des représailles sur
victor ['vɪktər] n vainqueur m
Victorian [vɪk'tɔːrɪən] adj victorien(ne)
victorious [vɪk'tɔːrɪəs] adj victorieux(-euse)
victory ['vɪktərɪ] n victoire f; **to win a ~ over sb** remporter une victoire sur qn
video ['vɪdɪəʊ] n (video film) vidéo f; (also: **video cassette**) vidéocassette f; (also: **video cassette recorder**) magnétoscope m ▷ vt (with recorder) enregistrer; (with camera) filmer ▷ cpd vidéo inv
video camera n caméra f vidéo inv
video cassette n vidéocassette f
video cassette recorder n = **video recorder**
videodisc ['vɪdɪəʊdɪsk] n vidéodisque m
video game n jeu m vidéo inv
video nasty n vidéo à caractère violent ou pornographique
videophone ['vɪdɪəʊfəʊn] n visiophone m, vidéophone m
video recorder n magnétoscope m
video recording n enregistrement m (en) vidéo inv
video shop n vidéoclub m
video tape n bande f vidéo inv; (cassette) vidéocassette f
video wall n mur m d'images vidéo
vie [vaɪ] vi: **to ~ with** lutter avec, rivaliser avec
Vienna [vɪ'ɛnə] n Vienne
Vietnam, Viet Nam ['vjɛt'næm] n Viêt-nam or Vietnam m
Vietnamese [vjɛtnə'miːz] adj vietnamien(ne) ▷ n (pl inv) Vietnamien(ne); (Ling) vietnamien m
view [vjuː] n vue f; (opinion) avis m, vue ▷ vt voir, regarder; (situation) considérer; (house) visiter; **on ~** (in museum etc) exposé(e); **in full ~ of sb** sous les yeux de qn; **to be within ~ (of sth)** être à portée de vue (de qch); **an overall ~ of the situation** une vue d'ensemble de la situation; **in my ~** à mon avis; **in ~ of the fact that** étant donné que; **with a ~ to doing sth** dans l'intention de faire qch
viewdata ['vjuːdeɪtə] n (Brit) télétexte m (version téléphonique)
viewer ['vjuːər] n (viewfinder) viseur m; (small projector) visionneuse f; (TV) téléspectateur(-trice)
viewfinder ['vjuːfaɪndər] n viseur m
viewpoint ['vjuːpɔɪnt] n point m de vue
vigil ['vɪdʒɪl] n veille f; **to keep ~** veiller
vigilance ['vɪdʒɪləns] n vigilance f
vigilant ['vɪdʒɪlənt] adj vigilant(e)
vigilante [vɪdʒɪ'læntɪ] n justicier ou membre d'un groupe d'autodéfense
vigorous ['vɪgərəs] adj vigoureux(-euse)
vigour, (US) vigor ['vɪgər] n vigueur f
vile [vaɪl] adj (action) vil(e); (smell, food) abominable; (temper) massacrant(e)
vilify ['vɪlɪfaɪ] vt calomnier, vilipender
villa ['vɪlə] n villa f

village ['vɪlɪdʒ] n village m
villager ['vɪlɪdʒər] n villageois(e)
villain ['vɪlən] n (scoundrel) scélérat m; (Brit: criminal) bandit m; (in novel etc) traître m
VIN n abbr (US) = **vehicle identification number**
vinaigrette [vɪneɪ'grɛt] n vinaigrette f
vindicate ['vɪndɪkeɪt] vt défendre avec succès; justifier
vindication [vɪndɪ'keɪʃən] n: **in ~ of** pour justifier
vindictive [vɪn'dɪktɪv] adj vindicatif(-ive), rancunier(-ière)
vine [vaɪn] n vigne f; (climbing plant) plante grimpante
vinegar ['vɪnɪgər] n vinaigre m
vine grower n viticulteur m
vine-growing ['vaɪngrəʊɪŋ] adj viticole ▷ n viticulture f
vineyard ['vɪnjɑːd] n vignoble m
vintage ['vɪntɪdʒ] n (year) année f, millésime m ▷ cpd (car) d'époque; (wine) de grand cru; **the 1970 ~** le millésime 1970
vinyl ['vaɪnl] n vinyle m
viola [vɪ'əʊlə] n alto m
violate ['vaɪəleɪt] vt violer
violation [vaɪə'leɪʃən] n violation f; **in ~ of** (rule, law) en infraction à, en violation de
violence ['vaɪələns] n violence f; (Pol etc) incidents violents
violent ['vaɪələnt] adj violent(e); **a ~ dislike of sb/sth** une aversion profonde pour qn/qch
violently ['vaɪələntlɪ] adv violemment; (ill, angry) terriblement
violet ['vaɪələt] adj (colour) violet(te) ▷ n (plant) violette f
violin [vaɪə'lɪn] n violon m
violinist [vaɪə'lɪnɪst] n violoniste m/f
VIP n abbr (= very important person) VIP m
viper ['vaɪpər] n vipère f
viral ['vaɪərəl] adj viral(e)
virgin ['vəːdʒɪn] n vierge f ▷ adj vierge; **she is a ~** elle est vierge; **the Blessed V~** la Sainte Vierge
virginity [vəː'dʒɪnɪtɪ] n virginité f
Virgo ['vəːgəʊ] n la Vierge; **to be ~** être de la Vierge
virile ['vɪraɪl] adj viril(e)
virility [vɪ'rɪlɪtɪ] n virilité f
virtual ['vəːtjʊəl] adj (Comput, Physics) virtuel(le); (in effect): **it's a ~ impossibility** c'est quasiment impossible; **the ~ leader** le chef dans la pratique
virtually ['vəːtjʊəlɪ] adv (almost) pratiquement; **it is ~ impossible** c'est quasiment impossible
virtual reality n (Comput) réalité virtuelle
virtue ['vəːtjuː] n vertu f; (advantage) mérite m, avantage m; **by ~ of** en vertu or raison de
virtuosity [vəːtjʊ'ɔsɪtɪ] n virtuosité f
virtuoso [vəːtjʊ'əʊzəʊ] n virtuose m/f
virtuous ['vəːtjʊəs] adj vertueux(-euse)
virulent ['vɪrʊlənt] adj virulent(e)
virus ['vaɪərəs] n (Med, Comput) virus m
visa ['viːzə] n visa m

vis-à-vis [viːzəˈviː] *prep* vis-à-vis de

viscount [ˈvaɪkaunt] *n* vicomte *m*

viscous [ˈvɪskəs] *adj* visqueux(-euse), gluant(e)

vise [vaɪs] *n* (US Tech) = **vice**

visibility [vɪzɪˈbɪlɪtɪ] *n* visibilité *f*

visible [ˈvɪzəbl] *adj* visible; **~ exports/imports** exportations/importations *fpl* visibles

visibly [ˈvɪzəblɪ] *adv* visiblement

vision [ˈvɪʒən] *n* (sight) vue *f*, vision *f*; (foresight, in dream) vision

visionary [ˈvɪʒənrɪ] *n* visionnaire *m/f*

visit [ˈvɪzɪt] *n* visite *f*; (stay) séjour *m* ▷ *vt* (person: US: also: **visit with**) rendre visite à; (place) visiter; **on a private/official ~** en visite privée/officielle

visiting [ˈvɪzɪtɪŋ] *adj* (speaker, team) invité(e), de l'extérieur

visiting card *n* carte *f* de visite

visiting hours *npl* heures *fpl* de visite

visitor [ˈvɪzɪtəʳ] *n* visiteur(-euse); (to one's house) invité(e); (in hotel) client(e)

visitor centre, (US) **visitor center** *n* hall *m* or centre *m* d'accueil

visitors' book *n* livre *m* d'or; (in hotel) registre *m*

visor [ˈvaɪzəʳ] *n* visière *f*

VISTA [ˈvɪstə] *n abbr* (= Volunteers in Service to America) programme d'assistance bénévole aux régions pauvres

vista [ˈvɪstə] *n* vue *f*, perspective *f*

visual [ˈvɪzjuəl] *adj* visuel(le)

visual aid *n* support visuel (pour l'enseignement)

visual arts *npl* arts *mpl* plastiques

visual display unit *n* console *f* de visualisation, visuel *m*

visualize [ˈvɪzjuəlaɪz] *vt* se représenter; (foresee) prévoir

visually [ˈvɪzjuəlɪ] *adv* visuellement; **~ handicapped** handicapé(e) visuel(le)

visually-impaired [ˈvɪzjuəliɪmˈpɛəʳd] *adj* malvoyant(e)

vital [ˈvaɪtl] *adj* vital(e); **of ~ importance (to sb/sth)** d'une importance capitale (pour qn/qch)

vitality [vaɪˈtælɪtɪ] *n* vitalité *f*

vitally [ˈvaɪtəlɪ] *adv* extrêmement

vital statistics *npl* (of population) statistiques *fpl* démographiques; (inf: woman's) mensurations *fpl*

vitamin [ˈvɪtəmɪn] *n* vitamine *f*

vitiate [ˈvɪʃɪeɪt] *vt* vicier

vitreous [ˈvɪtrɪəs] *adj* (china) vitreux(-euse); (enamel) vitrifié(e)

vitriolic [vɪtrɪˈɔlɪk] *adj* (fig) venimeux(-euse)

viva [ˈvaɪvə] *n* (also: **viva voce**) (examen) oral

vivacious [vɪˈveɪʃəs] *adj* animé(e), qui a de la vivacité

vivacity [vɪˈvæsɪtɪ] *n* vivacité *f*

vivid [ˈvɪvɪd] *adj* (account) frappant(e), vivant(e); (light, imagination) vif (vive)

vividly [ˈvɪvɪdlɪ] *adv* (describe) d'une manière vivante; (remember) de façon précise

vivisection [vɪvɪˈsɛkʃən] *n* vivisection *f*

vixen [ˈvɪksn] *n* renarde *f*; (pej: woman) mégère *f*

viz [vɪz] *abbr* (= vide licet: namely) à savoir, c. à d.

VLF *abbr* = **very low frequency**

V-neck [ˈviːnɛk] *n* décolleté *m* en V

VOA *n abbr* (= Voice of America) voix *f* de l'Amérique (émissions de radio à destination de l'étranger)

vocabulary [vəuˈkæbjulərɪ] *n* vocabulaire *m*

vocal [ˈvəukl] *adj* vocal(e); (articulate) qui n'hésite pas à s'exprimer, qui sait faire entendre ses opinions; **vocals** *npl* voix *fpl*

vocal cords *npl* cordes vocales

vocalist [ˈvəukəlɪst] *n* chanteur(-euse)

vocation [vəuˈkeɪʃən] *n* vocation *f*

vocational [vəuˈkeɪʃənl] *adj* professionnel(le); **~ guidance/training** orientation/formation professionnelle

vociferous [vəˈsɪfərəs] *adj* bruyant(e)

vodka [ˈvɔdkə] *n* vodka *f*

vogue [vəug] *n* mode *f*; (popularity) vogue *f*; **to be in ~** être en vogue or à la mode

voice [vɔɪs] *n* voix *f*; (opinion) avis *m* ▷ *vt* (opinion) exprimer, formuler; **in a loud/soft ~** à voix haute/basse; **to give ~ to** exprimer

voice mail *n* (system) messagerie *f* vocale; (device) boîte *f* vocale

voice-over [ˈvɔɪsəuvəʳ] *n* voix off *f*

void [vɔɪd] *n* vide *m* ▷ *adj* (invalid) nul(le); (empty): **~ of** vide de, dépourvu(e) de

voile [vɔɪl] *n* voile *m* (tissu)

vol. *abbr* (= volume) vol

volatile [ˈvɔlətaɪl] *adj* volatil(e); (fig: person) versatile; (: situation) explosif(-ive)

volcanic [vɔlˈkænɪk] *adj* volcanique

volcano (pl **-es**) [vɔlˈkeɪnəu] *n* volcan *m*

volition [vəˈlɪʃən] *n*: **of one's own ~** de son propre gré

volley [ˈvɔlɪ] *n* (of gunfire) salve *f*; (of stones etc) pluie *f*, volée *f*; (Tennis etc) volée

volleyball [ˈvɔlɪbɔːl] *n* volley(-ball) *m*

volt [vəult] *n* volt *m*

voltage [ˈvəultɪdʒ] *n* tension *f*, voltage *m*; **high/low ~** haute/basse tension

voluble [ˈvɔljubl] *adj* volubile

volume [ˈvɔljuːm] *n* volume *m*; (of tank) capacité *f*; **~ one/two** (of book) tome un/deux; **his expression spoke ~s** son expression en disait long

volume control *n* (Radio, TV) bouton *m* de réglage du volume

volume discount *n* (Comm) remise *f* sur la quantité

voluminous [vəˈluːmɪnəs] *adj* volumineux(-euse)

voluntarily [ˈvɔləntrɪlɪ] *adv* volontairement; bénévolement

voluntary [ˈvɔləntərɪ] *adj* volontaire; (unpaid) bénévole

voluntary liquidation *n* (Comm) dépôt *m* de bilan

voluntary redundancy *n* (Brit) départ *m* volontaire (en cas de licenciements)

volunteer [vɔlən'tɪəʳ] *n* volontaire *m/f* ▷ *vt* (*information*) donner spontanément ▷ *vi* (*Mil*) s'engager comme volontaire; **to ~ to do** se proposer pour faire

voluptuous [və'lʌptjuəs] *adj* voluptueux(-euse)

vomit ['vɔmɪt] *n* vomissure *f* ▷ *vt, vi* vomir

voracious [və'reɪʃəs] *adj* vorace; (*reader*) avide

vote [vəut] *n* vote *m*, suffrage *m*; (*votes cast*) voix *f*, vote; (*franchise*) droit *m* de vote ▷ *vt* (*bill*) voter; (*chairman*) élire; (*propose*): **to ~ that** proposer que + *sub* ▷ *vi* voter; **to put sth to the ~, to take a ~ on sth** mettre qch aux voix, procéder à un vote sur qch; **~ for** *or* **in favour of/against** vote pour/contre; **to ~ to do sth** voter en faveur de faire qch; **~ of censure** motion *f* de censure; **~ of thanks** discours *m* de remerciement

voter ['vəutəʳ] *n* électeur(-trice)

voting ['vəutɪŋ] *n* scrutin *m*, vote *m*

voting paper *n* (*Brit*) bulletin *m* de vote

voting right *n* droit *m* de vote

vouch [vautʃ]: **to ~ for** *vt fus* se porter garant de

voucher ['vautʃəʳ] *n* (*for meal, petrol, gift*) bon *m*; (*receipt*) reçu *m*; **travel ~** bon *m* de transport

vow [vau] *n* vœu *m*, serment *m* ▷ *vi* jurer; **to take** *or* **make a ~ to do sth** faire le vœu de faire qch

vowel ['vauəl] *n* voyelle *f*

voyage ['vɔɪɪdʒ] *n* voyage *m* par mer, traversée *f*; (*by spacecraft*) voyage

voyeur [vwɑ:jə:ʳ] *n* voyeur *m*

VP *n abbr* = **vice-president**

vs *abbr* (= *versus*) vs

VSO *n abbr* (Brit: = *Voluntary Service Overseas*) ≈ coopération civile

VT, Vt. *abbr* (US) = **Vermont**

vulgar ['vʌlgəʳ] *adj* vulgaire

vulgarity [vʌl'gærɪtɪ] *n* vulgarité *f*

vulnerability [vʌlnərə'bɪlɪtɪ] *n* vulnérabilité *f*

vulnerable ['vʌlnərəbl] *adj* vulnérable

vulture ['vʌltʃəʳ] *n* vautour *m*

W, w ['dʌblju:] n (letter) W, w m; **W for William** W comme William

W abbr (= west) O; (Elec: = watt) W

WA abbr (US) = **Washington**

wad [wɔd] n (of cotton wool, paper) tampon m; (of banknotes etc) liasse f

wadding ['wɔdɪŋ] n rembourrage m

waddle ['wɔdl] vi se dandiner

wade [weɪd] vi: **to ~ through** marcher dans, patauger dans; (fig: book) venir à bout de ▷ vt passer à gué

wafer ['weɪfə'] n (Culin) gaufrette f; (Rel) pain m d'hostie; (Comput) tranche f (de silicium)

wafer-thin ['weɪfə'θɪn] adj ultra-mince, mince comme du papier à cigarette

waffle ['wɔfl] n (Culin) gaufre f; (inf) rabâchage m; remplissage m ▷ vi parler pour ne rien dire; faire du remplissage

waffle iron n gaufrier m

waft [wɔft] vt porter ▷ vi flotter

wag [wæg] vt agiter, remuer ▷ vi remuer; **the dog ~ged its tail** le chien a remué la queue

wage [weɪdʒ] n (also: **wages**) salaire m, paye f ▷ vt: **to ~ war** faire la guerre; **a day's ~s** un jour de salaire

wage claim n demande f d'augmentation de salaire

wage differential n éventail m des salaires

wage earner [-ə:nə'] n salarié(e); (breadwinner) soutien m de famille

wage freeze n blocage m des salaires

wage packet n (Brit) (enveloppe f de) paye f

wager ['weɪdʒə'] n pari m ▷ vt parier

waggle ['wægl] vt, vi remuer

wagon, waggon ['wægən] n (horse-drawn) chariot m; (Brit Rail) wagon m (de marchandises)

wail [weɪl] n gémissement m; (of siren) hurlement m ▷ vi gémir; (siren) hurler

waist [weɪst] n taille f, ceinture f

waistcoat ['weɪskəut] n (Brit) gilet m

waistline ['weɪstlaɪn] n (tour m de) taille f

wait [weɪt] n attente f ▷ vi attendre; **to ~ for sb/sth** attendre qn/qch; **to keep sb ~ing** faire attendre qn; **~ for me, please** attendez-moi, s'il vous plaît; **~ a minute!** un instant!;

"repairs while you ~" "réparations minute"; **I can't ~ to ...** (fig) je meurs d'envie de ...; **to lie in ~ for** guetter

▶ **wait behind** vi rester (à attendre)

▶ **wait on** vt fus servir

▶ **wait up** vi attendre, ne pas se coucher; **don't ~ up for me** ne m'attendez pas pour aller vous coucher

waiter ['weɪtə'] n garçon m (de café), serveur m

waiting ['weɪtɪŋ] n: **"no ~"** (Brit Aut) "stationnement interdit"

waiting list n liste f d'attente

waiting room n salle f d'attente

waitress ['weɪtrɪs] n serveuse f

waive [weɪv] vt renoncer à, abandonner

waiver ['weɪvə'] n dispense f

wake [weɪk] (pt woke or -d, pp woken or waked [wəuk, 'wəukn]) vt (also: **wake up**) réveiller ▷ vi (also: **wake up**) se réveiller ▷ n (for dead person) veillée f mortuaire; (Naut) sillage m; **to ~ up to sth** (fig) se rendre compte de qch; **in the ~ of** (fig) à la suite de; **to follow in sb's ~** (fig) marcher sur les traces de qn

waken ['weɪkn] vt, vi = **wake**

Wales [weɪlz] n pays m de Galles; **the Prince of ~** le prince de Galles

walk [wɔ:k] n promenade f; (short) petit tour; (gait) démarche f; (path) chemin m; (in park etc) allée f; (pace): **at a quick ~** d'un pas rapide ▷ vi marcher; (for pleasure, exercise) se promener ▷ vt (distance) faire à pied; (dog) promener; **10 minutes' ~ from** à 10 minutes de marche de; **to go for a ~** se promener; faire un tour; **from all ~s of life** de toutes conditions sociales; **I'll ~ you home** je vais vous raccompagner chez vous

▶ **walk out** vi (go out) sortir; (as protest) partir (en signe de protestation); (strike) se mettre en grève; **to ~ out on sb** quitter qn

walkabout ['wɔ:kəbaut] n: **to go (on a) ~** (VIP) prendre un bain de foule

walker ['wɔ:kə'] n (person) marcheur(-euse)

walkie-talkie ['wɔ:kɪ'tɔ:kɪ] n talkie-walkie m

walking ['wɔ:kɪŋ] n marche f à pied; **it's within ~ distance** on peut y aller à pied

walking holiday n vacances passées à faire de

guerre; **to make ~ (on)** faire la guerre (à)

walking shoes *npl* chaussures *fpl* de marche

walking stick *n* canne *f*

Walkman® ['wɔːkmən] *n* Walkman® *m*

walk-on ['wɔːkɔn] *adj* (*Theat: part*) de figurant(e)

walkout ['wɔːkaut] *n* (*of workers*) grève-surprise *f*

walkover ['wɔːkəuvə^r] *n* (*inf*) victoire *f* or examen *m etc* facile

walkway ['wɔːkweɪ] *n* promenade *f*, cheminement piéton

wall [wɔːl] *n* mur *m*; (*of tunnel, cave*) paroi *f*; **to go to the ~** (*fig: firm etc*) faire faillite
▸ **wall in** *vt* (*garden etc*) entourer d'un mur

wall cupboard *n* placard mural

walled [wɔːld] *adj* (*city*) fortifié(e)

wallet ['wɔlɪt] *n* portefeuille *m*; **I can't find my ~** je ne retrouve plus mon portefeuille

wallflower ['wɔːlflauə^r] *n* giroflée *f*; **to be a ~** (*fig*) faire tapisserie

wall hanging *n* tenture (murale), tapisserie *f*

wallop ['wɔləp] *vt* (*Brit inf*) taper sur, cogner

wallow ['wɔləu] *vi* se vautrer; **to ~ in one's grief** se complaire à sa douleur

wallpaper ['wɔːlpeɪpə^r] *n* papier peint ▷ *vt* tapisser

wall-to-wall ['wɔːltə'wɔːl] *adj*: **~ carpeting** moquette *f*

walnut ['wɔːlnʌt] *n* noix *f*; (*tree, wood*) noyer *m*

walrus (*pl* **walrus** *or* **-es**) ['wɔːlrəs] *n* morse *m*

waltz [wɔːls] *n* valse *f* ▷ *vi* valser

wan [wɔn] *adj* pâle; triste

wand [wɔnd] *n* (*also:* **magic wand**) baguette *f* (magique)

wander ['wɔndə^r] *vi* (*person*) errer, aller sans but; (*thoughts*) vagabonder; (*river*) serpenter ▷ *vt* errer dans

wanderer ['wɔndərə^r] *n* vagabond(e)

wandering ['wɔndrɪŋ] *adj* (*tribe*) nomade; (*minstrel, actor*) ambulant(e)

wane [weɪn] *vi* (*moon*) décroître; (*reputation*) décliner

wangle ['wæŋgl] (*Brit inf*) *vt* se débrouiller pour avoir; carotter ▷ *n* combine *f*, magouille *f*

wanker ['wæŋkə^r] *n* (*inf!*) branleur *m* (!)

want [wɔnt] *vt* vouloir; (*need*) avoir besoin de; (*lack*) manquer de ▷ *n* (*poverty*) pauvreté *f*, besoin *m*; **wants** *npl* (*needs*) besoins *mpl*; **to ~ to do** vouloir faire; **to ~ sb to do** vouloir que qn fasse; **you're ~ed on the phone** on vous demande au téléphone; **"cook ~ed"** "on demande un cuisinier"; **for ~ of** par manque de, faute de

want ads *npl* (*US*) petites annonces

wanted ['wɔntɪd] *adj* (*criminal*) recherché(e) par la police

wanting ['wɔntɪŋ] *adj*: **to be ~ (in)** manquer (de); **to be found ~** ne pas être à la hauteur

wanton ['wɔntn] *adj* capricieux(-euse), dévergondé(e)

war [wɔː^r] *n* guerre *f*; **to go to ~** se mettre en

warble ['wɔːbl] *n* (*of bird*) gazouillis *m* ▷ *vi* gazouiller

war cry *n* cri *m* de guerre

ward [wɔːd] *n* (*in hospital*) salle *f*; (*Pol*) section électorale; (*Law: child: also:* **ward of court**) pupille *m/f*
▸ **ward off** *vt* parer, éviter

warden ['wɔːdn] *n* (*Brit: of institution*) directeur(-trice); (*of park, game reserve*) gardien(ne); (*Brit: also:* **traffic warden**) contractuel(le); (*of youth hostel*) responsable *m/f*

warder ['wɔːdə^r] *n* (*Brit*) gardien *m* de prison

wardrobe ['wɔːdrəub] *n* (*cupboard*) armoire *f*; (*clothes*) garde-robe *f*; (*Theat*) costumes *mpl*

warehouse ['wɛəhaus] *n* entrepôt *m*

wares [wɛəz] *npl* marchandises *fpl*

warfare ['wɔːfɛə^r] *n* guerre *f*

war game *n* jeu *m* de stratégie militaire

warhead ['wɔːhɛd] *n* (*Mil*) ogive *f*

warily ['wɛərɪlɪ] *adv* avec prudence, avec précaution

warlike ['wɔːlaɪk] *adj* guerrier(-ière)

warm [wɔːm] *adj* chaud(e); (*person, thanks, welcome, applause*) chaleureux(-euse); (*supporter*) ardent(e), enthousiaste; **it's ~** il fait chaud; **I'm ~** j'ai chaud; **to keep sth ~** tenir qch au chaud; **with my ~est thanks/congratulations** avec mes remerciements/mes félicitations les plus sincères
▸ **warm up** *vi* (*person, room*) se réchauffer; (*water*) chauffer; (*athlete, discussion*) s'échauffer ▷ *vt* (*food*) (faire) réchauffer; (*water*) (faire) chauffer; (*engine*) faire chauffer

warm-blooded ['wɔːm'blʌdɪd] *adj* (*Zool*) à sang chaud

war memorial *n* monument *m* aux morts

warm-hearted [wɔːm'hɑːtɪd] *adj* affectueux(-euse)

warmly ['wɔːmlɪ] *adv* (*dress*) chaudement; (*thank, welcome*) chaleureusement

warmonger ['wɔːmʌŋgə^r] *n* belliciste *m/f*

warmongering ['wɔːmʌŋgrɪŋ] *n* propagande *f* belliciste, bellicisme *m*

warmth [wɔːmθ] *n* chaleur *f*

warm-up ['wɔːmʌp] *n* (*Sport*) période *f* d'échauffement

warn [wɔːn] *vt* avertir, prévenir; **to ~ sb (not) to do** conseiller à qn de (ne pas) faire

warning ['wɔːnɪŋ] *n* avertissement *m*; (*notice*) avis *m*; (*signal*) avertisseur *m*; **without (any) ~** (*suddenly*) inopinément; (*without notifying*) sans prévenir; **gale ~** (*Meteorology*) avis de grand vent

warning light *n* avertisseur lumineux

warning triangle *n* (*Aut*) triangle *m* de présignalisation

warp [wɔːp] *n* (*Textiles*) chaîne *f* ▷ *vi* (*wood*) travailler, se voiler *or* gauchir ▷ *vt* voiler; (*fig*) pervertir

warpath ['wɔːpɑːθ] *n*: **to be on the ~** (*fig*) être sur le sentier de la guerre

warped [wɔ:pt] *adj* (*wood*) gauchi(e); (*fig*) perverti(e)

warrant ['wɔrnt] *n* (*guarantee*) garantie *f*; (*Law:* *to arrest*) mandat *m* d'arrêt; (*: to search*) mandat de perquisition ▷ *vt* (*justify, merit*) justifier

warrant officer *n* (*Mil*) adjudant *m*; (*Naut*) premier-maître *m*

warranty ['wɔrəntɪ] *n* garantie *f*; **under ~** (*Comm*) sous garantie

warren ['wɔrən] *n* (*of rabbits*) terriers *mpl*, garenne *f*

warring ['wɔ:rɪŋ] *adj* (*nations*) en guerre; (*interests etc*) contradictoire, opposé(e)

warrior ['wɔrɪər] *n* guerrier(-ière)

Warsaw ['wɔ:sɔ:] *n* Varsovie

warship ['wɔ:ʃɪp] *n* navire *m* de guerre

wart [wɔ:t] *n* verrue *f*

wartime ['wɔ:taɪm] *n*: **in ~** en temps de guerre

wary ['wɛərɪ] *adj* prudent(e); **to be ~ about** *or* **of doing sth** hésiter beaucoup à faire qch

was [wɔz] *pt of* **be**

wash [wɔʃ] *vt* laver; (*sweep, carry: sea etc*) emporter, entraîner; (*: ashore*) rejeter ▷ *vi* se laver; (*sea*): **to ~ over/against sth** inonder/ baigner qch ▷ *n* (*paint*) badigeon *m*; (*clothes*) lessive *f*; (*washing programme*) lavage *m*; (*of ship*) sillage *m*; **to give sth a ~** laver qch; **to have a ~** se laver, faire sa toilette; **he was ~ed overboard** il a été emporté par une vague

  ▶ **wash away** *vt* (*stain*) enlever au lavage; (*subj: river etc*) emporter

  ▶ **wash down** *vt* laver; laver à grande eau

  ▶ **wash off** *vi* partir au lavage

  ▶ **wash up** *vi* (*Brit*) faire la vaisselle; (*US: have a wash*) se débarbouiller

Wash. *abbr* (*US*) = **Washington**

washable ['wɔʃəbl] *adj* lavable

washbasin ['wɔʃbeɪsn] *n* lavabo *m*

washer ['wɔʃər] *n* (*Tech*) rondelle *f*, joint *m*

washing ['wɔʃɪŋ] *n* (*Brit: linen etc: dirty*) linge *m*; (*: clean*) lessive *f*

washing line *n* (*Brit*) corde *f* à linge

washing machine *n* machine *f* à laver

washing powder *n* (*Brit*) lessive *f* (en poudre)

Washington ['wɔʃɪŋtən] *n* (*city, state*) Washington *m*

washing-up [wɔʃɪŋ'ʌp] *n* (*Brit*) vaisselle *f*

washing-up liquid *n* (*Brit*) produit *m* pour la vaisselle

wash-out ['wɔʃaut] *n* (*inf*) désastre *m*

washroom ['wɔʃrum] *n* (*US*) toilettes *fpl*

wasn't ['wɔznt] = **was not**

Wasp, WASP [wɔsp] *n abbr* (*US inf:* = *White Anglo-Saxon Protestant*) *surnom, souvent péjoratif, donné à l'américain de souche anglo-saxonne, aisé et de tendance conservatrice*

wasp [wɔsp] *n* guêpe *f*

waspish ['wɔspɪʃ] *adj* irritable

wastage ['weɪstɪdʒ] *n* gaspillage *m*; (*in manufacturing, transport etc*) déchet *m*

waste [weɪst] *n* gaspillage *m*; (*of time*) perte *f*; (*rubbish*) déchets *mpl*; (*also:* **household waste**)

ordures *fpl* ▷ *adj* (*energy, heat*) perdu(e); (*food*) inutilisé(e); (*land, ground: in city*) à l'abandon; (*: in country*) inculte, en friche; (*leftover*): **~ material** déchets ▷ *vt* gaspiller; (*time, opportunity*) perdre; **wastes** *npl* étendue *f* désertique; **it's a ~ of money** c'est de l'argent jeté en l'air; **to go to ~** être gaspillé(e); **to lay ~** (*destroy*) dévaster

  ▶ **waste away** *vi* dépérir

wastebasket ['weɪstbɑ:skɪt] *n* = **wastepaper basket**

waste disposal, waste disposal unit *n* (*Brit*) broyeur *m* d'ordures

wasteful ['weɪstful] *adj* gaspilleur(-euse); (*process*) peu économique

waste ground *n* (*Brit*) terrain *m* vague

wasteland ['weɪstlənd] *n* terres *fpl* à l'abandon; (*in town*) terrain(s) *m(pl)* vague(s)

wastepaper basket ['weɪstpeɪpə-] *n* corbeille *f* à papier

waste pipe *n* (tuyau *m* de) vidange *f*

waste products *npl* (*Industry*) déchets *mpl* (de fabrication)

waster ['weɪstər] *n* (*inf*) bon(ne) à rien

watch [wɔtʃ] *n* montre *f*; (*act of watching*) surveillance *f*; (*guard: Mil*) sentinelle *f*; (*: Naut*) homme *m* de quart; (*Naut: spell of duty*) quart *m* ▷ *vt* (*look at*) observer; (*: match, programme*) regarder; (*spy on, guard*) surveiller; (*be careful of*) faire attention à ▷ *vi* regarder; (*keep guard*) monter la garde; **to keep a close ~ on sb/sth** surveiller qn/qch de près; **to keep ~** faire le guet; **~ what you're doing** fais attention à ce que tu fais

  ▶ **watch out** *vi* faire attention

watchband ['wɔtʃbænd] *n* (*US*) bracelet *m* de montre

watchdog ['wɔtʃdɔg] *n* chien *m* de garde; (*fig*) gardien(ne)

watchful ['wɔtʃful] *adj* attentif(-ive), vigilant(e)

watchmaker ['wɔtʃmeɪkər] *n* horloger(-ère)

watchman ['wɔtʃmən] (*irreg*) *n* gardien *m*; (*also:* **night watchman**) veilleur *m* de nuit

watch stem *n* (*US*) remontoir *m*

watch strap ['wɔtʃstræp] *n* bracelet *m* de montre

watchword ['wɔtʃwə:d] *n* mot *m* de passe

water ['wɔ:tər] *n* eau *f* ▷ *vt* (*plant, garden*) arroser ▷ *vi* (*eyes*) larmoyer; **a drink of ~** un verre d'eau; **in British ~s** dans les eaux territoriales Britanniques; **to pass ~** uriner; **to make sb's mouth ~** mettre l'eau à la bouche de qn

  ▶ **water down** *vt* (*milk etc*) couper avec de l'eau; (*fig: story*) édulcorer

water closet *n* (*Brit*) w.-c. *mpl*, waters *mpl*

watercolour, (*US*) **watercolor** ['wɔ:təkʌlər] *n* aquarelle *f*; **watercolours** *npl* couleurs *fpl* pour aquarelle

water-cooled ['wɔ:təku:ld] *adj* à refroidissement par eau

watercress ['wɔ:təkrɛs] *n* cresson *m* (de

fontaine)

waterfall ['wɔ:təfɔ:l] n chute f d'eau

waterfront ['wɔ:təfrʌnt] n (seafront) front m de mer; (at docks) quais mpl

water heater n chauffe-eau m

water hole n mare f

water ice n (Brit) sorbet m

watering can ['wɔ:tərɪŋ-] n arrosoir m

water level n niveau m de l'eau; (of flood) niveau des eaux

water lily n nénuphar m

waterline ['wɔ:təlaɪn] n (Naut) ligne f de flottaison

waterlogged ['wɔ:təlɔgd] adj détrempé(e); imbibé(e) d'eau

water main n canalisation f d'eau

watermark ['wɔ:təmɑ:k] n (on paper) filigrane m

watermelon ['wɔ:təmɛlən] n pastèque f

water polo n water-polo m

waterproof ['wɔ:təpru:f] adj imperméable

water-repellent ['wɔ:tərɪpɛlnt] adj hydrofuge

watershed ['wɔ:təʃɛd] n (Geo) ligne f de partage des eaux; (fig) moment m critique, point décisif

water-skiing ['wɔ:təski:ɪŋ] n ski m nautique

water softener n adoucisseur m d'eau

water tank n réservoir m d'eau

watertight ['wɔ:tətaɪt] adj étanche

water vapour n vapeur f d'eau

waterway ['wɔ:təweɪ] n cours m d'eau navigable

waterworks ['wɔ:təwə:ks] npl station f hydraulique

watery ['wɔ:tərɪ] adj (colour) délavé(e); (coffee) trop faible

watt [wɔt] n watt m

wattage ['wɔtɪdʒ] n puissance f or consommation f en watts

wattle ['wɔtl] n clayonnage m

wave [weɪv] n vague f; (of hand) geste m, signe m; (Radio) onde f; (in hair) ondulation f; (fig: of enthusiasm, strikes etc) vague ▷ vi faire signe de la main; (flag) flotter au vent; (grass) ondoyer ▷ vt (handkerchief) agiter; (stick) brandir; (hair) onduler; **short/medium ~** (Radio) ondes courtes/moyennes; **long ~** (Radio) grandes ondes; **the new ~** (Cine, Mus) la nouvelle vague; **to ~ goodbye to sb** dire au revoir de la main à qn

▶ **wave aside**

▶ **wave away** vt (fig: suggestion, objection) rejeter, repousser; (: doubts) chasser; (person): **to ~ sb aside** faire signe à qn de s'écarter

waveband ['weɪvbænd] n bande f de fréquences

wavelength ['weɪvlɛŋθ] n longueur f d'ondes

waver ['weɪvəʳ] vi vaciller; (voice) trembler; (person) hésiter

wavy ['weɪvɪ] adj (hair, surface) ondulé(e); (line) onduleux(-euse)

wax [wæks] n cire f; (for skis) fart m ▷ vt cirer; (car) lustrer; (skis) farter ▷ vi (moon) croître

waxworks ['wækswə:ks] npl personnages mpl

de cire; musée m de cire

way [weɪ] n chemin m, voie f; (path, access) passage m; (distance) distance f; (direction) chemin, direction f; (manner) façon f, manière f; (habit) habitude f, façon; (condition) état m; **which ~?** — **this ~/that ~** par où or de quel côté? — par ici/par là; **to crawl one's ~ to ...** ramper jusqu'à ...; **to lie one's ~ out of it** s'en sortir par un mensonge; **to lose one's ~** perdre son chemin; **on the ~ (to)** en route (pour); **to be on one's ~** être en route; **to be in the ~** bloquer le passage; (fig) gêner; **to keep out of sb's ~** éviter qn; **it's a long ~ away** c'est loin d'ici; **the village is rather out of the ~** le village est plutôt à l'écart or isolé; **to go out of one's ~ to do** (fig) se donner beaucoup de mal pour faire; **to be under ~** (work, project) être en cours; **to make ~ (for sb/sth)** faire place (à qn/qch), s'écarter pour laisser passer (qn/qch); **to get one's own ~** arriver à ses fins; **put it the right ~ up** (Brit) mettez-le dans le bon sens; **to be the wrong ~ round** être à l'envers, ne pas être dans le bon sens; **he's in a bad ~** il va mal; **in a ~** dans un sens; **by the ~** à propos; **in some ~s** à certains égards; d'un côté; **in the ~ of** en fait de, comme; **by ~ of** (through) en passant par, via; (as a sort of) en guise de; **"~ in"** (Brit) "entrée"; **"~ out"** (Brit) "sortie"; **the ~ back** le chemin du retour; **this ~ and that** par-ci par-là; **"give ~"** (Brit Aut) "cédez la priorité"; **no ~!** (inf) pas question!

waybill ['weɪbɪl] n (Comm) récépissé m

waylay ['weɪleɪ] vt (irreg: like **lay**) attaquer; (fig): **I got waylaid** quelqu'un m'a accroché

wayside ['weɪsaɪd] n bord m de la route; **to fall by the ~** (fig) abandonner; (morally) quitter le droit chemin

way station n (US Rail) petite gare; (: fig) étape f

wayward ['weɪwəd] adj capricieux(-euse), entêté(e)

W.C. n abbr (Brit: = water closet) w.-c. mpl, waters mpl

WCC n abbr (= World Council of Churches) COE m (Conseil œcuménique des Églises)

we [wi:] pl pron nous

weak [wi:k] adj faible; (health) fragile; (beam etc) peu solide; (tea, coffee) léger(-ère); **to grow ~(er)** s'affaiblir, faiblir

weaken ['wi:kn] vi faiblir ▷ vt affaiblir

weak-kneed ['wi:k'ni:d] adj (fig) lâche, faible

weakling ['wi:klɪŋ] n gringalet m; faible m/f

weakly ['wi:klɪ] adj chétif(-ive) ▷ adv faiblement

weakness ['wi:knɪs] n faiblesse f; (fault) point m faible

wealth [wɛlθ] n (money, resources) richesse(s) f(pl); (of details) profusion f

wealth tax n impôt m sur la fortune

wealthy ['wɛlθɪ] adj riche

wean [wi:n] vt sevrer

weapon ['wɛpən] n arme f; **~s of mass destruction** armes fpl de destruction massive

wear [wɛə^r] (pt **wore**, pp **worn**) [wɔː^r, wɔːn] n (use) usage m; (deterioration through use) usure f ▷ vt (clothes) porter; (put on) mettre; (beard etc) avoir; (damage: through use) user ▷ vi (last) faire de l'usage; (rub etc through) s'user; **sports/baby~** vêtements mpl de sport/pour bébés; **evening ~** tenue f de soirée; **~ and tear** usure f; **to ~ a hole in sth** faire (à la longue) un trou dans qch
▸ **wear away** vt user, ronger ▷ vi s'user, être rongé(e)
▸ **wear down** vt user; (strength) épuiser
▸ **wear off** vi disparaître
▸ **wear on** vi se poursuivre; passer
▸ **wear out** vt user; (person, strength) épuiser
wearable ['wɛərəbl] adj mettable
wearily ['wɪərɪlɪ] adv avec lassitude
weariness ['wɪərɪnɪs] n épuisement m, lassitude f
wearisome ['wɪərɪsəm] adj (tiring) fatigant(e); (boring) ennuyeux(-euse)
weary ['wɪərɪ] adj (tired) épuisé(e); (dispirited) las (lasse); abattu(e) ▷ vt lasser ▷ vi: **to ~ of** se lasser de
weasel ['wiːzl] n (Zool) belette f
weather ['wɛðə^r] n temps m ▷ vt (wood) faire mûrir; (storm: lit, fig) essuyer; (crisis) survivre à; **what's the ~ like?** quel temps fait-il?; **under the ~** (fig: ill) mal fichu(e)
weather-beaten ['wɛðəbiːtn] adj (person) hâlé(e); (building) dégradé(e) par les intempéries
weather forecast n prévisions fpl météorologiques, météo f
weatherman ['wɛðəmæn] (irreg) n météorologue m
weatherproof ['wɛðəpruːf] adj (garment) imperméable; (building) étanche
weather report n bulletin m météo, météo f
weather vane [-veɪn] n = **weather cock**
weave (pt **wove**, pp **woven**) [wiːv, wəuv, 'wəuvn] vt (cloth) tisser; (basket) tresser ▷ vi (fig: pt, pp **weaved**) (move in and out) se faufiler
weaver ['wiːvə^r] n tisserand(e)
weaving ['wiːvɪŋ] n tissage m
web [wɛb] n (of spider) toile f; (on duck's foot) palmure f; (fig) tissu m; (Comput): **the (World-Wide) W~** le Web
web address n adresse f Web
webbed ['wɛbd] adj (foot) palmé(e)
webbing ['wɛbɪŋ] n (on chair) sangles fpl
webcam ['wɛbkæm] n webcam f
weblog ['wɛblɔg] n blog m, blogue m
web page n (Comput) page f Web
website ['wɛbsaɪt] n (Comput) site m web
wed [wɛd] (pt, pp **-ded**) vt épouser ▷ vi se marier ▷ n: **the newly-~s** les jeunes mariés
we'd [wiːd] = **we had; we would**
wedded ['wɛdɪd] pt, pp of **wed**
wedding ['wɛdɪŋ] n mariage m
wedding anniversary n anniversaire m de mariage; **silver/golden ~** noces fpl d'argent/d'or
wedding day n jour m du mariage

wedding dress n robe f de mariée
wedding present n cadeau m de mariage
wedding ring n alliance f
wedge [wɛdʒ] n (of wood etc) coin m; (under door etc) cale f; (of cake) part f ▷ vt (fix) caler; (push) enfoncer, coincer
wedge-heeled shoes ['wɛdʒhiːld-] npl chaussures fpl à semelles compensées
wedlock ['wɛdlɔk] n (union f du) mariage m
Wednesday ['wɛdnzdɪ] n mercredi m; for phrases see also **Tuesday**
wee [wiː] adj (Scottish) petit(e); tout(e) petit(e)
weed [wiːd] n mauvaise herbe f ▷ vt désherber
▸ **weed out** vt éliminer
weedkiller ['wiːdkɪlə^r] n désherbant m
weedy ['wiːdɪ] adj (man) gringalet
week [wiːk] n semaine f; **once/twice a ~** une fois/deux fois par semaine; **in two ~s' time** dans quinze jours; **a ~ today/on Tuesday** aujourd'hui/mardi en huit
weekday ['wiːkdeɪ] n jour m de semaine; (Comm) jour ouvrable; **on ~s** en semaine
weekend [wiːk'ɛnd] n week-end m
weekend case n sac m de voyage
weekly ['wiːklɪ] adv une fois par semaine, chaque semaine ▷ adj, n hebdomadaire (m)
weep [wiːp] (pt, pp **wept**) [wɛpt] vi (person) pleurer; (Med: wound etc) suinter
weeping willow ['wiːpɪŋ-] n saule pleureur
weepy ['wiːpɪ] n (inf: film) mélo m
weft [wɛft] n (Textiles) trame f
weigh [weɪ] vt, vi peser; **to ~ anchor** lever l'ancre; **to ~ the pros and cons** peser le pour et le contre
▸ **weigh down** vt (branch) faire plier; (fig: with worry) accabler
▸ **weigh out** vt (goods) peser
▸ **weigh up** vt examiner
weighbridge ['weɪbrɪdʒ] n pont-bascule m
weighing machine ['weɪɪŋ-] n balance f, bascule f
weight [weɪt] n poids m ▷ vt alourdir; (fig: factor) pondérer; **sold by ~** vendu au poids; **to put on/lose ~** grossir/maigrir; **~s and measures** poids et mesures
weighting ['weɪtɪŋ] n: **~ allowance** indemnité f de résidence
weightlessness ['weɪtlɪsnɪs] n apesanteur f
weightlifter ['weɪtlɪftə^r] n haltérophile m
weightlifting ['weɪtlɪftɪŋ] n haltérophilie f
weight training n musculation f
weighty ['weɪtɪ] adj lourd(e)
weir [wɪə^r] n barrage m
weird [wɪəd] adj bizarre; (eerie) surnaturel(le)
weirdo ['wɪədəu] n (inf) type m bizarre
welcome ['wɛlkəm] adj bienvenu(e) ▷ n accueil m ▷ vt accueillir; (also: **bid welcome**) souhaiter la bienvenue à; (be glad of) se réjouir de; **to be ~** être le (la) bienvenu(e); **to make sb ~** faire bon accueil à qn; **you're ~ to try** vous pouvez essayer si vous voulez; **you're ~!** (after thanks) de rien, il n'y a pas de quoi

welcoming ['wɛlkəmɪŋ] *adj* accueillant(e); (*speech*) d'accueil
weld [wɛld] *n* soudure *f* ▷ *vt* souder
welder ['wɛldə^r] *n* (*person*) soudeur *m*
welding ['wɛldɪŋ] *n* soudure *f* (autogène)
welfare ['wɛlfɛə^r] *n* (*wellbeing*) bien-être *m*; (*social aid*) assistance sociale
welfare state *n* État-providence *m*
welfare work *n* travail social
well [wɛl] *n* puits *m* ▷ *adv* bien ▷ *adj*: **to be ~** aller bien ▷ *excl* eh bien!; (*relief also*) bon!; (*resignation*) enfin!; **~ done!** bravo!; **I don't feel ~** je ne me sens pas bien; **get ~ soon!** remets-toi vite!; **to do ~** bien réussir; (*business*) prospérer; **to think ~ of sb** penser du bien de qn; **as ~** (*in addition*) aussi, également; **you might as ~ tell me** tu ferais aussi bien de me le dire; **as ~ as** aussi bien que *or* de; en plus de; **~, as I was saying** ... donc, comme je disais ...
 ▶ **well up** *vi* (*tears, emotions*) monter
we'll [wiːl] = **we will; we shall**
well-behaved ['wɛlbɪ'heɪvd] *adj* sage, obéissant(e)
well-being ['wɛl'biːɪŋ] *n* bien-être *m*
well-bred ['wɛl'brɛd] *adj* bien élevé(e)
well-built ['wɛl'bɪlt] *adj* (*house*) bien construit(e); (*person*) bien bâti(e)
well-chosen ['wɛl'tʃəuzn] *adj* (*remarks, words*) bien choisi(e), pertinent(e)
well-deserved ['wɛldɪ'zəːvd] *adj* (bien) mérité(e)
well-developed ['wɛldɪ'vɛləpt] *adj* (*girl*) bien fait(e)
well-disposed ['wɛldɪs'pəuzd] *adj*: **~ to(wards)** bien disposé(e) envers
well-dressed ['wɛl'drɛst] *adj* bien habillé(e), bien vêtu(e)
well-earned ['wɛl'əːnd] *adj* (*rest*) bien mérité(e)
well-groomed [-'gruːmd] *adj* très soigné(e)
well-heeled ['wɛl'hiːld] *adj* (*inf: wealthy*) fortuné(e), riche
wellies ['wɛlɪz] (*inf*) *npl* (*Brit*) = **wellingtons**
well-informed ['wɛlɪn'fɔːmd] *adj* (*having knowledge of sth*) bien renseigné(e); (*having general knowledge*) cultivé(e)
Wellington ['wɛlɪŋtən] *n* Wellington
wellingtons ['wɛlɪŋtənz] *npl* (*also*: **wellington boots**) bottes *fpl* en caoutchouc
well-kept ['wɛl'kɛpt] *adj* (*house, grounds*) bien tenu(e), bien entretenu(e); (*secret*) bien gardé(e); (*hair, hands*) soigné(e)
well-known ['wɛl'nəun] *adj* (*person*) bien connu(e)
well-mannered ['wɛl'mænəd] *adj* bien élevé(e)
well-meaning ['wɛl'miːnɪŋ] *adj* bien intentionné(e)
well-nigh ['wɛl'naɪ] *adv*: **~ impossible** pratiquement impossible
well-off ['wɛl'ɔf] *adj* aisé(e), assez riche
well-paid [wɛl'peɪd] *adj* bien payé(e)
well-read ['wɛl'rɛd] *adj* cultivé(e)
well-spoken ['wɛl'spəukn] *adj* (*person*) qui parle

bien; (*words*) bien choisi(e)
well-stocked ['wɛl'stɔkt] *adj* bien approvisionné(e)
well-timed ['wɛl'taɪmd] *adj* opportun(e)
well-to-do ['wɛltə'duː] *adj* aisé(e), assez riche
well-wisher ['wɛlwɪʃə^r] *n* ami(e), admirateur(-trice); **scores of ~s had gathered** de nombreux amis et admirateurs s'étaient rassemblés; **letters from ~s** des lettres d'encouragement
well-woman clinic ['wɛlwumən-] *n* centre prophylactique et thérapeutique pour femmes
Welsh [wɛlʃ] *adj* gallois(e) ▷ *n* (*Ling*) gallois *m*; **the Welsh** *npl* (*people*) les Gallois
Welsh Assembly *n* Parlement gallois
Welshman ['wɛlʃmən] (*irreg*) *n* Gallois *m*
Welsh rarebit *n* croûte *f* au fromage
Welshwoman ['wɛlʃwumən] (*irreg*) *n* Galloise *f*
welter ['wɛltə^r] *n* fatras *m*
went [wɛnt] *pt of* **go**
wept [wɛpt] *pt, pp of* **weep**
were [wəː^r] *pt of* **be**
we're [wɪə^r] = **we are**
weren't [wəːnt] = **were not**
werewolf (*pl* **-wolves**) ['wɪəwulf, -wulvz] *n* loup-garou *m*
west [wɛst] *n* ouest *m* ▷ *adj* (*wind*) d'ouest; (*side*) ouest *inv* ▷ *adv* à *or* vers l'ouest; **the W~** l'Occident *m*, l'Ouest
westbound ['wɛstbaund] *adj* en direction de l'ouest; (*carriageway*) ouest *inv*
West Country *n*: **the ~** le sud-ouest de l'Angleterre
westerly ['wɛstəlɪ] *adj* (*situation*) à l'ouest; (*wind*) d'ouest
western ['wɛstən] *adj* occidental(e), de *or* à l'ouest ▷ *n* (*Cine*) western *m*
westerner ['wɛstənə^r] *n* occidental(e)
westernized ['wɛstənaɪzd] *adj* occidentalisé(e)
West German (*formerly*) *adj* ouest-allemand(e) ▷ *n* Allemand(e) de l'Ouest
West Germany *n* (*formerly*) Allemagne *f* de l'Ouest
West Indian *adj* antillais(e) ▷ *n* Antillais(e)
West Indies [-'ɪndɪz] *npl* Antilles *fpl*
Westminster ['wɛstmɪnstə^r] *n* (*Brit Parliament*) Westminster *m*
westward ['wɛstwəd], **westwards** ['wɛstwədz] *adv* vers l'ouest
wet [wɛt] *adj* mouillé(e); (*damp*) humide; (*soaked: also*: **wet through**) trempé(e); (*rainy*) pluvieux(-euse) ▷ *vt*: **to ~ one's pants** *or* **o.s.** mouiller sa culotte, faire pipi dans sa culotte; **to get ~** se mouiller; **"~ paint"** "attention peinture fraîche"
wet blanket *n* (*fig*) rabat-joie *m inv*
wetness ['wɛtnɪs] *n* humidité *f*
wetsuit ['wɛtsuːt] *n* combinaison *f* de plongée
we've [wiːv] = **we have**
whack [wæk] *vt* donner un grand coup à
whacked [wækt] *adj* (*Brit inf: tired*) crevé(e)
whale [weɪl] *n* (*Zool*) baleine *f*

whaler ['weɪlə^r] *n* (*ship*) baleinier *m*
whaling ['weɪlɪŋ] *n* pêche *f* à la baleine
wharf (*pl* **wharves**) [wɔ:f, wɔ:vz] *n* quai *m*

 KEYWORD

what [wɔt] *adj* **1** (*in questions*) quel(le); **what size is he?** quelle taille fait-il?; **what colour is it?** de quelle couleur est-ce?; **what books do you need?** quels livres vous faut-il?
2 (*in exclamations*): **what a mess!** quel désordre!; **what a fool I am!** que je suis bête!
▷ *pron* **1** (*interrogative*) que; de/à/en *etc* quoi; **what are you doing?** que faites-vous?, qu'est-ce que vous faites?; **what is happening?** qu'est-ce qui se passe?, que se passe-t-il?; **what are you talking about?** de quoi parlez-vous?; **what are you thinking about?** à quoi pensez-vous?; **what is it called?** comment est-ce que ça s'appelle?; **what about me?** et moi?; **what about doing ...?** et si on faisait ...?
2 (*relative: subject*) ce qui; (*: direct object*) ce que; (*: indirect object*) ce à quoi, ce dont; **I saw what you did/was on the table** j'ai vu ce que vous avez fait/ce qui était sur la table; **tell me what you remember** dites-moi ce dont vous vous souvenez; **what I want is a cup of tea** ce que je veux, c'est une tasse de thé
▷ *excl* (*disbelieving*) quoi!, comment!

whatever [wɔt'ɛvə^r] *adj*: **take ~ book you prefer** prenez le livre que vous préférez, peu importe lequel; **~ book you take** quel que soit le livre que vous preniez ▷ *pron*: **do ~ is necessary** faites (tout) ce qui est nécessaire; **~ happens** quoi qu'il arrive; **no reason ~** *or* **whatsoever** pas la moindre raison; **nothing ~** *or* **whatsoever** rien du tout
whatsoever [wɔtsəu'ɛvə^r] *adj see* **whatever**
wheat [wi:t] *n* blé *m*, froment *m*
wheatgerm ['wi:tdʒə:m] *n* germe *m* de blé
wheatmeal ['wi:tmi:l] *n* farine bise
wheedle ['wi:dl] *vt*: **to ~ sb into doing sth** cajoler *or* enjôler qn pour qu'il fasse qch; **to ~ sth out of sb** obtenir qch de qn par des cajoleries
wheel [wi:l] *n* roue *f*; (*Aut: also:* **steering wheel**) volant *m*; (*Naut*) gouvernail *m* ▷ *vt* (*pram etc*) pousser, rouler ▷ *vi* (*birds*) tournoyer; (*also:* **wheel round**: *person*) se retourner, faire volte-face
wheelbarrow ['wi:lbærəu] *n* brouette *f*
wheelbase ['wi:lbeɪs] *n* empattement *m*
wheelchair ['wi:ltʃɛə^r] *n* fauteuil roulant
wheel clamp *n* (*Aut*) sabot *m* (de Denver)
wheeler-dealer ['wi:lə'di:lə^r] *n* (*pej*) combinard(e), affairiste *m/f*
wheelie-bin ['wi:lɪbɪn] *n* (*Brit*) poubelle *f* à roulettes
wheeling ['wi:lɪŋ] *n*: **~ and dealing** (*pej*) manigances *fpl*, magouilles *fpl*
wheeze [wi:z] *n* respiration bruyante

(*d'asthmatique*) ▷ *vi* respirer bruyamment
wheezy ['wi:zɪ] *adj* sifflant(e)

 KEYWORD

when [wen] *adv* quand; **when did he go?** quand est-ce qu'il est parti?
▷ *conj* **1** (*at, during, after the time that*) quand, lorsque; **she was reading when I came in** elle lisait quand *or* lorsque je suis entré
2 (*on, at which*): **on the day when I met him** le jour où je l'ai rencontré
3 (*whereas*) alors que; **I thought I was wrong when in fact I was right** j'ai cru que j'avais tort alors qu'en fait j'avais raison

whenever [wɛn'ɛvə^r] *adv* quand donc ▷ *conj* quand; (*every time that*) chaque fois que; **I go ~ I can** j'y vais quand *or* chaque fois que je le peux
where [wɛə^r] *adv, conj* où; **this is ~** c'est là que; **~ are you from?** d'où venez vous?
whereabouts ['wɛərəbauts] *adv* où donc ▷ *n*: **nobody knows his ~** personne ne sait où il se trouve
whereas [wɛər'æz] *conj* alors que
whereby [wɛə'baɪ] *adv* (*formal*) par lequel (*or* laquelle *etc*)
whereupon [wɛərə'pɔn] *adv* sur quoi, et sur ce
wherever [wɛər'ɛvə^r] *adv* où donc ▷ *conj* où que + *sub*; **sit ~ you like** asseyez-vous (là) où vous voulez
wherewithal ['wɛəwɪðə:l] *n*: **the ~ (to do sth)** les moyens *mpl* (de faire qch)
whet [wɛt] *vt* aiguiser
whether ['wɛðə^r] *conj* si; **I don't know ~ to accept or not** je ne sais pas si je dois accepter ou non; **it's doubtful ~** il est peu probable que + *sub*; **~ you go or not** que vous y alliez ou non
whey ['weɪ] *n* petit-lait *m*

 KEYWORD

which [wɪtʃ] *adj* **1** (*interrogative: direct, indirect*) quel(le); **which picture do you want?** quel tableau voulez-vous?; **which one?** lequel (laquelle)?
2: **in which case** auquel cas; **we got there at 8pm, by which time the cinema was full** quand nous sommes arrivés à 20h, le cinéma était complet
▷ *pron* **1** (*interrogative*) lequel (laquelle), lesquels (lesquelles) *pl*; **I don't mind which** peu importe lequel; **which (of these) are yours?** lesquels sont à vous?; **tell me which you want** dites-moi lesquels *or* ceux que vous voulez
2 (*relative: subject*) qui; (*: object*) que; sur/vers *etc* lequel (laquelle) (*NB: à + lequel = auquel; de + lequel = duquel*); **the apple which you ate/which is on the table** la pomme que vous avez mangée/qui est sur la table; **the chair on which you are sitting** la chaise sur laquelle vous êtes assis; **the book of which you spoke** le livre

dont vous avez parlé; **he said he knew, which is true/I was afraid of** il a dit qu'il le savait, ce qui est vrai/ce que je craignais; **after which** après quoi

whichever [wɪtʃˈɛvəʳ] *adj*: **take ~ book you prefer** prenez le livre que vous préférez, peu importe lequel; **~ book you take** quel que soit le livre que vous preniez; **~ way you** de quelque façon que vous + *sub*

whiff [wɪf] *n* bouffée *f*; **to catch a ~ of sth** sentir l'odeur de qch

while [waɪl] *n* moment *m* ▷ *conj* pendant que; (*as long as*) tant que; (*as, whereas*) alors que; (*though*) bien que + *sub*, quoique + *sub*; **for a ~** pendant quelque temps; **in a ~** dans un moment; **all the ~** pendant tout ce temps-là; **we'll make it worth your ~** nous vous récompenserons de votre peine
   ▶ **while away** *vt* (*time*) (faire) passer

whilst [waɪlst] *conj* = **while**

whim [wɪm] *n* caprice *m*

whimper [ˈwɪmpəʳ] *n* geignement *m* ▷ *vi* geindre

whimsical [ˈwɪmzɪkl] *adj* (*person*) capricieux(-euse); (*look*) étrange

whine [waɪn] *n* gémissement *m*; (*of engine, siren*) plainte stridente ▷ *vi* gémir, geindre, pleurnicher; (*dog, engine, siren*) gémir

whip [wɪp] *n* fouet *m*; (*for riding*) cravache *f*; (*Pol: person*) chef *m* de file (*assurant la discipline dans son groupe parlementaire*) ▷ *vt* fouetter; (*snatch*) enlever (*or* sortir) brusquement
   ▶ **whip up** *vt* (*cream*) fouetter; (*inf: meal*) préparer en vitesse; (*stir up: support*) stimuler; (*: feeling*) attiser, aviver; *voir article*

⬤ **WHIP**
⬤
⬤
⬤ Un *whip* est un député dont le rôle est, entre
⬤ autres, de s'assurer que les membres de son
⬤ parti sont régulièrement présents à la
⬤ "House of Commons", surtout lorsque les
⬤ votes ont lieu. Les convocations que les *whips*
⬤ envoient se distinguent, selon leur degré
⬤ d'importance, par le fait qu'elles sont
⬤ soulignées 1, 2 ou 3 fois (les "1-, 2-, ou 3-line
⬤ whips").

whiplash [ˈwɪplæʃ] *n* (*Med: also*: **whiplash injury**) coup *m* du lapin

whipped cream [wɪpt-] *n* crème fouettée

whipping boy [ˈwɪpɪŋ-] *n* (*fig*) bouc *m* émissaire

whip-round [ˈwɪpraund] *n* (*Brit*) collecte *f*

whirl [wəːl] *n* tourbillon *m* ▷ *vi* tourbillonner; (*dancers*) tournoyer ▷ *vt* faire tourbillonner; faire tournoyer

whirlpool [ˈwəːlpuːl] *n* tourbillon *m*

whirlwind [ˈwəːlwɪnd] *n* tornade *f*

whirr [wəːʳ] *vi* bruire; ronronner; vrombir

whisk [wɪsk] *n* (*Culin*) fouet *m* ▷ *vt* (*eggs*) fouetter, battre; **to ~ sb away** *or* **off** emmener

qn rapidement

whiskers [ˈwɪskəz] *npl* (*of animal*) moustaches *fpl*; (*of man*) favoris *mpl*

whisky, (*Irish, US*) **whiskey** [ˈwɪskɪ] *n* whisky *m*

whisper [ˈwɪspəʳ] *n* chuchotement *m*; (*fig: of leaves*) bruissement *m*; (*rumour*) rumeur *f* ▷ *vt*, *vi* chuchoter

whispering [ˈwɪspərɪŋ] *n* chuchotement(s) *m(pl)*

whist [wɪst] *n* (*Brit*) whist *m*

whistle [ˈwɪsl] *n* (*sound*) sifflement *m*; (*object*) sifflet *m* ▷ *vi* siffler ▷ *vt* siffler, siffloter

whistle-stop [ˈwɪslstɔp] *adj*: **to make a ~ tour of** (*Pol*) faire la tournée électorale des petits patelins de

Whit [wɪt] *n* la Pentecôte

white [waɪt] *adj* blanc (blanche); (*with fear*) blême ▷ *n* blanc *m*; (*person*) blanc (blanche); **to turn** *or* **go ~** (*person*) pâlir, blêmir; (*hair*) blanchir; **the ~s** (*washing*) le linge blanc; **tennis ~s** tenue *f* de tennis

whitebait [ˈwaɪtbeɪt] *n* blanchaille *f*

whiteboard [ˈwaɪtbɔːd] *n* tableau *m* blanc; **interactive ~** tableau *m* (blanc) interactif

white coffee *n* (*Brit*) café *m* au lait, (café) crème *m*

white-collar worker [ˈwaɪtkɔlə-] *n* employé(e) de bureau

white elephant *n* (*fig*) objet dispendieux et superflu

white goods *npl* (*appliances*) (gros) électroménager *m*; (*linen etc*) linge *m* de maison

white-hot [waɪtˈhɔt] *adj* (*metal*) incandescent(e)

White House *n* (*US*): **the ~** la Maison-Blanche; *voir article*

⬤ **WHITE HOUSE**
⬤
⬤ La *White House* est un grand bâtiment blanc
⬤ situé à Washington D.C. où réside le
⬤ Président des États-Unis. Par extension, ce
⬤ terme désigne l'exécutif américain.

white lie *n* pieux mensonge

whiteness [ˈwaɪtnɪs] *n* blancheur *f*

white noise *n* son *m* blanc

whiteout [ˈwaɪtaut] *n* jour blanc

white paper *n* (*Pol*) livre blanc

whitewash [ˈwaɪtwɔʃ] *n* (*paint*) lait *m* de chaux ▷ *vt* blanchir à la chaux; (*fig*) blanchir

whiting [ˈwaɪtɪŋ] *n* (*pl inv: fish*) merlan *m*

Whit Monday *n* le lundi de Pentecôte

Whitsun [ˈwɪtsn] *n* la Pentecôte

whittle [ˈwɪtl] *vt*: **to ~ away**, **to ~ down** (*costs*) réduire, rogner

whizz [wɪz] *vi* aller (*or* passer) à toute vitesse

whizz kid *n* (*inf*) petit prodige

WHO *n abbr* (= *World Health Organization*) OMS *f* (*Organisation mondiale de la Santé*)

who [huː] *pron* qui

whodunit [huːˈdʌnɪt] *n* (*inf*) roman policier

whoever [huː'ɛvəʳ] *pron*: ~ **finds it** celui (celle) qui le trouve (, qui que ce soit), quiconque le trouve; **ask ~ you like** demandez à qui vous voulez; ~ **he marries** qui que ce soit *or* quelle que soit la personne qu'il épouse; ~ **told you that?** qui a bien pu vous dire ça?, qui donc vous a dit ça?

whole [həul] *adj* (*complete*) entier(-ière), tout(e); (*not broken*) intact(e), complet(-ète) ▷ *n* (*entire unit*) tout *m*; (*all*): **the ~ of** la totalité de, tout(e) le (la); **the ~ lot (of it)** tout; **the ~ lot (of them)** tous (sans exception); **the ~ of the time** tout le temps; **the ~ of the town** la ville tout entière; **on the ~, as a ~** dans l'ensemble

wholefood ['həulfuːd] *n*, **wholefoods** ['həulfuːdz] *npl* aliments complets

wholehearted [həul'hɑːtɪd] *adj* sans réserve(s), sincère

wholeheartedly [həul'hɑːtɪdlɪ] *adv* sans réserve; **to agree ~** être entièrement d'accord

wholemeal ['həulmiːl] *adj* (*Brit: flour, bread*) complet(-ète)

whole note *n* (*US*) ronde *f*

wholesale ['həulseɪl] *n* (*vente f en*) gros *m* ▷ *adj* (*price*) de gros; (*destruction*) systématique

wholesaler ['həulseɪləʳ] *n* grossiste *m/f*

wholesome ['həulsəm] *adj* sain(e); (*advice*) salutaire

wholewheat ['həulwiːt] *adj* = **wholemeal**

wholly ['həulɪ] *adv* entièrement, tout à fait

 KEYWORD

whom [huːm] *pron* **1** (*interrogative*) qui; **whom did you see?** qui avez-vous vu?; **to whom did you give it?** à qui l'avez-vous donné?
2 (*relative*) que; à/de *etc* qui; **the man whom I saw/to whom I spoke** l'homme que j'ai vu/à qui j'ai parlé

whooping cough ['huːpɪŋ-] *n* coqueluche *f*

whoops [wuːps] *excl* (*also:* **whoops-a-daisy**) oups!, houp-là!

whoosh [wuʃ] *vi*: **the skiers ~ed past** les skieurs passèrent dans un glissement rapide

whopper ['wɔpəʳ] *n* (*inf: lie*) gros bobard; (: *large thing*) monstre *m*, phénomène *m*

whopping ['wɔpɪŋ] *adj* (*inf: big*) énorme

whore [hɔːʳ] *n* (*inf: pej*) putain *f*

 KEYWORD

whose [huːz] *adj* **1** (*possessive: interrogative*): **whose book is this?, whose is this book?** à qui est ce livre?; **whose pencil have you taken?** à qui est le crayon que vous avez pris?, c'est le crayon de qui que vous avez pris?; **whose daughter are you?** de qui êtes-vous la fille?
2 (*possessive: relative*): **the man whose son you rescued** l'homme dont *or* de qui vous avez sauvé le fils; **the girl whose sister you were speaking to** la fille à la sœur de qui *or* de laquelle vous parliez; **the woman whose car was stolen** la femme dont la voiture a été volée
▷ *pron* à qui; **whose is this?** à qui est ceci?; **I know whose it is** je sais à qui c'est

Who's Who ['huːz'huː] *n* ≈ Bottin Mondain

 KEYWORD

why [waɪ] *adv* pourquoi; **why is he late?** pourquoi est-il en retard?; **why not?** pourquoi pas?
▷ *conj*: **I wonder why he said that** je me demande pourquoi il a dit ça; **that's not why I'm here** ce n'est pas pour ça que je suis là; **the reason why** la raison pour laquelle
▷ *excl* eh bien!, tiens!; **why, it's you!** tiens, c'est vous!; **why, that's impossible!** voyons, c'est impossible!

whyever [waɪ'ɛvəʳ] *adv* pourquoi donc, mais pourquoi

WI *n abbr* (*Brit*: = *Women's Institute*) amicale de femmes au foyer ▷ *abbr* (*Geo*) = **West Indies**; (*US*) = **Wisconsin**

wick [wɪk] *n* mèche *f* (*de bougie*)

wicked ['wɪkɪd] *adj* méchant(e); (*mischievous: grin, look*) espiègle, malicieux(-euse); (*crime*) pervers(e); (*terrible: prices, weather*) épouvantable; (*inf: very good*) génial(e) (*inf*)

wicker ['wɪkəʳ] *n* osier *m*; (*also:* **wickerwork**) vannerie *f*

wicket ['wɪkɪt] *n* (*Cricket: stumps*) guichet *m*; (: *grass area*) espace compris entre les deux guichets

wicket keeper *n* (*Cricket*) gardien *m* de guichet

wide [waɪd] *adj* large; (*area, knowledge*) vaste, très étendu(e); (*choice*) grand(e) ▷ *adv*: **to open ~** ouvrir tout grand; **to shoot ~** tirer à côté; **it is 3 metres ~** cela fait 3 mètres de large

wide-angle lens ['waɪdæŋgl-] *n* objectif *m* grand-angulaire

wide-awake [waɪdə'weɪk] *adj* bien éveillé(e)

wide-eyed [waɪd'aɪd] *adj* aux yeux écarquillés; (*fig*) naïf(-ïve), crédule

widely ['waɪdlɪ] *adv* (*different*) radicalement; (*spaced*) sur une grande étendue; (*believed*) généralement; (*travel*) beaucoup; **to be ~ read** (*author*) être beaucoup lu(e); (*reader*) avoir beaucoup lu, être cultivé(e)

widen ['waɪdn] *vt* élargir ▷ *vi* s'élargir

wideness ['waɪdnɪs] *n* largeur *f*

wide open *adj* grand(e) ouvert(e)

wide-ranging [waɪd'reɪndʒɪŋ] *adj* (*survey, report*) vaste; (*interests*) divers(e)

widespread ['waɪdsprɛd] *adj* (*belief etc*) très répandu(e)

widow ['wɪdəu] *n* veuve *f*

widowed ['wɪdəud] *adj* (*qui est devenu(e)*) veuf (veuve)

widower ['wɪdəuəʳ] *n* veuf *m*

width [wɪdθ] *n* largeur *f*; **it's 7 metres in** ~ cela fait 7 mètres de large

widthways ['wɪdθweɪz] *adv* en largeur

wield [wiːld] *vt* (*sword*) manier; (*power*) exercer

wife (*pl* **wives**) [waɪf, waɪvz] *n* femme *f*, épouse *f*

WiFi ['waɪfaɪ] *n abbr* (= *wireless fidelity*) WiFi *m* ▷ *adj* (*hot spot, network*) WiFi *inv*

wig [wɪg] *n* perruque *f*

wigging ['wɪgɪŋ] *n* (*Brit inf*) savon *m*, engueulade *f*

wiggle ['wɪgl] *vt* agiter, remuer ▷ *vi* (*loose screw etc*) branler; (*worm*) se tortiller

wiggly ['wɪglɪ] *adj* (*line*) ondulé(e)

wild [waɪld] *adj* sauvage; (*sea*) déchaîné(e); (*idea, life*) fou (folle); (*behaviour*) déchaîné(e), extravagant(e); (*inf: angry*) hors de soi, furieux(-euse); (: *enthusiastic*): **to be ~ about** être fou (folle) *or* dingue de ▷ *n*: **the ~** la nature; **wilds** *npl* régions *fpl* sauvages

wild card *n* (*Comput*) caractère *m* de remplacement

wildcat ['waɪldkæt] *n* chat *m* sauvage

wildcat strike *n* grève *f* sauvage

wilderness ['wɪldənɪs] *n* désert *m*, région *f* sauvage

wildfire ['waɪldfaɪə'] *n*: **to spread like ~** se répandre comme une traînée de poudre

wild-goose chase [waɪld'guːs-] *n* (*fig*) fausse piste

wildlife ['waɪldlaɪf] *n* faune *f* (et flore *f*)

wildly ['waɪldlɪ] *adv* (*behave*) de manière déchaînée; (*applaud*) frénétiquement; (*hit, guess*) au hasard; (*happy*) follement

wiles [waɪlz] *npl* ruses *fpl*, artifices *mpl*

wilful, (US) **willful** ['wɪlful] *adj* (*person*) obstiné(e); (*action*) délibéré(e); (*crime*) prémédité(e)

 KEYWORD

will [wɪl] *aux vb* **1** (*forming future tense*): **I will finish it tomorrow** je le finirai demain; **I will have finished it by tomorrow** je l'aurai fini d'ici demain; **will you do it?** — **yes I will/no I won't** le ferez-vous? — oui/non; **you won't lose it, will you?** vous ne le perdrez pas, n'est-ce pas?

2 (*in conjectures, predictions*): **he will** *or* **he'll be there by now** il doit être arrivé à l'heure qu'il est; **that will be the postman** ça doit être le facteur

3 (*in commands, requests, offers*): **will you be quiet!** voulez-vous bien vous taire!; **will you help me?** est-ce que vous pouvez m'aider?; **will you have a cup of tea?** voulez-vous une tasse de thé?; **I won't put up with it!** je ne le tolérerai pas!

▷ *vt* (*pt, pp* **willed**): **to will sb to do** souhaiter ardemment que qn fasse; **he willed himself to go on** par un suprême effort de volonté, il continua

▷ *n* volonté *f*; (*document*) testament *m*; **to do sth of one's own free will** faire qch de son propre gré; **against one's will** à contre-cœur

willful ['wɪlful] *adj* (US) = **wilful**

willing ['wɪlɪŋ] *adj* de bonne volonté, serviable ▷ *n*: **to show ~** faire preuve de bonne volonté; **he's ~ to do it** il est disposé à le faire, il veut bien le faire

willingly ['wɪlɪŋlɪ] *adv* volontiers

willingness ['wɪlɪŋnɪs] *n* bonne volonté

will-o'-the-wisp ['wɪlədə'wɪsp] *n* (*also fig*) feu follet *m*

willow ['wɪləu] *n* saule *m*

willpower ['wɪlpauə'] *n* volonté *f*

willy-nilly ['wɪlɪ'nɪlɪ] *adv* bon gré mal gré

wilt [wɪlt] *vi* dépérir

Wilts [wɪlts] *abbr* (*Brit*) = **Wiltshire**

wily ['waɪlɪ] *adj* rusé(e)

wimp [wɪmp] *n* (*inf*) mauviette *f*

win [wɪn] (*pt, pp* **won**) [wʌn] *n* (*in sports etc*) victoire *f* ▷ *vt* (*battle, money*) gagner; (*prize, contract*) remporter; (*popularity*) acquérir ▷ *vi* gagner

▶ **win over** *vt* convaincre

▶ **win round** *vt* gagner, se concilier

wince [wɪns] *n* tressaillement *m* ▷ *vi* tressaillir

winch [wɪntʃ] *n* treuil *m*

Winchester disk ['wɪntʃɪstə-] *n* (*Comput*) disque *m* Winchester

wind¹ [wɪnd] *n* (*also Med*) vent *m*; (*breath*) souffle *m* ▷ *vt* (*take breath away*) couper le souffle à; **the ~(s)** (*Mus*) les instruments *mpl* à vent; **into** *or* **against the ~** contre le vent; **to get ~ of sth** (*fig*) avoir vent de qch; **to break ~** avoir des gaz

wind² [waɪnd] (*pt, pp* **wound**) [waɪnd, waund] *vt* enrouler; (*wrap*) envelopper; (*clock, toy*) remonter ▷ *vi* (*road, river*) serpenter

▶ **wind down** *vt* (*car window*) baisser; (*fig: production, business*) réduire progressivement

▶ **wind up** *vt* (*clock*) remonter; (*debate*) terminer, clôturer

windbreak ['wɪndbreɪk] *n* brise-vent *m inv*

windcheater ['wɪndtʃiːtə'], (US) **windbreaker** ['wɪndbreɪkə'] *n* anorak *m*

winder ['waɪndə'] *n* (*Brit: on watch*) remontoir *m*

windfall ['wɪndfɔːl] *n* coup *m* de chance

winding ['waɪndɪŋ] *adj* (*road*) sinueux(-euse); (*staircase*) tournant(e)

wind instrument *n* (*Mus*) instrument *m* à vent

windmill ['wɪndmɪl] *n* moulin *m* à vent

window ['wɪndəu] *n* fenêtre *f*; (*in car, train: also*: **windowpane**) vitre *f*; (*in shop etc*) vitrine *f*

window box *n* jardinière *f*

window cleaner *n* (*person*) laveur(-euse) de vitres

window dressing *n* arrangement *m* de la vitrine

window envelope *n* enveloppe *f* à fenêtre

window frame *n* châssis *m* de fenêtre

window ledge *n* rebord *m* de la fenêtre

window pane *n* vitre *f*, carreau *m*

window seat n (in vehicle) place f côté fenêtre
window-shopping ['wɪndəʊʃɔpɪŋ] n: **to go ~** faire du lèche-vitrines
windowsill ['wɪndəʊsɪl] n (inside) appui m de la fenêtre; (outside) rebord m de la fenêtre
windpipe ['wɪndpaɪp] n gosier m
wind power n énergie éolienne
windscreen ['wɪndskriːn] n pare-brise m inv
windscreen washer n lave-glace m inv
windscreen wiper, (US) **windshield wiper** [-waɪpəʳ] n essuie-glace m inv
windshield ['wɪndʃiːld] (US) n = **windscreen**
windsurfing ['wɪndsəːfɪŋ] n planche f à voile
windswept ['wɪndswɛpt] adj balayé(e) par le vent
wind tunnel n soufflerie f
windy ['wɪndɪ] adj (day) de vent, venteux(-euse); (place, weather) venteux; **it's ~** il y a du vent
wine [waɪn] n vin m ▷ vt: **to ~ and dine sb** offrir un dîner bien arrosé à qn
wine bar n bar m à vin
wine cellar n cave f à vins
wine glass n verre m à vin
wine list n carte f des vins
wine merchant n marchand(e) de vins
wine tasting [-teɪstɪŋ] n dégustation f (de vins)
wine waiter n sommelier m
wing [wɪŋ] n aile f; (in air force) groupe m d'escadrilles; **wings** npl (Theat) coulisses fpl
winger ['wɪŋəʳ] n (Sport) ailier m
wing mirror n (Brit) rétroviseur latéral
wing nut n papillon m, écrou m à ailettes
wingspan ['wɪŋspæn], **wingspread** ['wɪŋsprɛd] n envergure f
wink [wɪŋk] n clin m d'œil ▷ vi faire un clin d'œil; (blink) cligner des yeux
winkle [wɪŋkl] n bigorneau m
winner ['wɪnəʳ] n gagnant(e)
winning ['wɪnɪŋ] adj (team) gagnant(e); (goal) décisif(-ive); (charming) charmeur(-euse)
winning post n poteau m d'arrivée
winnings ['wɪnɪŋz] npl gains mpl
winsome ['wɪnsəm] adj avenant(e), engageant(e)
winter ['wɪntəʳ] n hiver m ▷ vi hiverner; **in ~** en hiver
winter sports npl sports mpl d'hiver
wintertime ['wɪntəʳtaɪm] n hiver m
wintry ['wɪntrɪ] adj hivernal(e)
wipe [waɪp] n coup m de torchon (or de chiffon or d'éponge); **to give sth a ~** donner un coup de torchon/de chiffon/d'éponge à qch ▷ vt essuyer; (erase: tape) effacer; **to ~ one's nose** se moucher
▶ **wipe off** vt essuyer
▶ **wipe out** vt (debt) éteindre, amortir; (memory) effacer; (destroy) anéantir
▶ **wipe up** vt essuyer
wire ['waɪəʳ] n fil m (de fer); (Elec) fil électrique; (Tel) télégramme m ▷ vt (fence) grillager; (house) faire l'installation électrique de; (also: **wire up**) brancher; (person: send telegram to) télégraphier à

wire brush n brosse f métallique
wire cutters [-kʌtəz] npl cisaille f
wireless ['waɪəlɪs] n (Brit) télégraphie f sans fil; (set) T.S.F. f
wire netting n treillis m métallique, grillage m
wire service n (US) revue f de presse (par téléscripteur)
wire-tapping ['waɪə'tæpɪŋ] n écoute f téléphonique
wiring ['waɪərɪŋ] n (Elec) installation f électrique
wiry ['waɪərɪ] adj noueux(-euse), nerveux(-euse)
Wis. abbr (US) = **Wisconsin**
wisdom ['wɪzdəm] n sagesse f; (of action) prudence f
wisdom tooth n dent f de sagesse
wise [waɪz] adj sage, prudent(e); (remark) judicieux(-euse); **I'm none the ~r** je ne suis pas plus avancé(e) pour autant
▶ **wise up** vi (inf): **to ~ up to** commencer à se rendre compte de
...wise [waɪz] suffix: **time~** en ce qui concerne le temps, question temps
wisecrack ['waɪzkræk] n sarcasme m
wish [wɪʃ] n (desire) désir m; (specific desire) souhait m, vœu m ▷ vt souhaiter, désirer, vouloir; **best ~es** (on birthday etc) meilleurs vœux; **with best ~es** (in letter) bien amicalement; **give her my best ~es** faites-lui mes amitiés; **to ~ sb goodbye** dire au revoir à qn; **he ~ed me well** il m'a souhaité bonne chance; **to ~ to do/sb to do** désirer or vouloir faire/que qn fasse; **to ~ for** souhaiter; **to ~ sth on sb** souhaiter qch à qn
wishbone ['wɪʃbəun] n fourchette f
wishful ['wɪʃful] adj: **it's ~ thinking** c'est prendre ses désirs pour des réalités
wishy-washy ['wɪʃɪ'wɔʃɪ] adj (inf: person) qui manque de caractère falot(e); (: ideas, thinking) faiblard(e)
wisp [wɪsp] n fine mèche (de cheveux); (of smoke) mince volute f; **a ~ of straw** un fétu de paille
wistful ['wɪstful] adj mélancolique
wit [wɪt] n (also: **wits**: intelligence) intelligence f, esprit m; (presence of mind) présence f d'esprit; (wittiness) esprit; (person) homme/femme d'esprit; **to be at one's ~s' end** (fig) ne plus savoir que faire; **to have one's ~s about one** avoir toute sa présence d'esprit, ne pas perdre la tête; **to ~** adv à savoir
witch [wɪtʃ] n sorcière f
witchcraft ['wɪtʃkrɑːft] n sorcellerie f
witch doctor n sorcier m
witch-hunt ['wɪtʃhʌnt] n chasse f aux sorcières

 KEYWORD

with [wɪð, wɪθ] prep **1** (in the company of) avec; (at the home of) chez; **we stayed with friends** nous avons logé chez des amis; **I'll be with you in a minute** je suis à vous dans un instant
2 (descriptive): **a room with a view** une chambre

avec vue; **the man with the grey hat/blue eyes** l'homme au chapeau gris/aux yeux bleus
3 (*indicating manner, means, cause*): **with tears in her eyes** les larmes aux yeux; **to walk with a stick** marcher avec une canne; **red with anger** rouge de colère; **to shake with fear** trembler de peur; **to fill sth with water** remplir qch d'eau
4 (*in phrases*): **I'm with you** (*I understand*) je vous suis; **to be with it** (*inf: up-to-date*) être dans le vent

withdraw [wɪθ'drɔ:] *vt* (*irreg: like* **draw**) retirer ▷ *vi* se retirer; (*go back on promise*) se rétracter; **to ~ into o.s.** se replier sur soi-même
withdrawal [wɪθ'drɔ:əl] *n* retrait *m*; (*Med*) état *m* de manque
withdrawal symptoms *npl*: **to have ~** être en état de manque, présenter les symptômes *mpl* de sevrage
withdrawn [wɪθ'drɔ:n] *pp of* **withdraw** ▷ *adj* (*person*) renfermé(e)
withdrew [wɪθ'dru:] *pt of* **withdraw**
wither ['wɪðər] *vi* se faner
withered ['wɪðəd] *adj* fané(e), flétri(e); (*limb*) atrophié(e)
withhold [wɪθ'həuld] *vt* (*irreg: like* **hold**: *money*) retenir; (*decision*) remettre; **to ~ (from)** (*permission*) refuser (à); (*information*) cacher (à)
within [wɪð'ɪn] *prep* à l'intérieur de ▷ *adv* à l'intérieur; **~ his reach** à sa portée; **~ sight of** en vue de; **~ a mile of** à moins d'un mille de; **~ the week** avant la fin de la semaine; **~ an hour from now** d'ici une heure; **to be ~ the law** être légal(e) *or* dans les limites de la légalité
without [wɪð'aut] *prep* sans; **~ a coat** sans manteau; **~ speaking** sans parler; **~ anybody knowing** sans que personne le sache; **to go or do ~ sth** se passer de qch
withstand [wɪθ'stænd] *vt* (*irreg: like* **stand**) résister à
witness ['wɪtnɪs] *n* (*person*) témoin *m*; (*evidence*) témoignage *m* ▷ *vt* (*event*) être témoin de; (*document*) attester l'authenticité de; **to bear ~ to sth** témoigner de qch; **~ for the prosecution/defence** témoin à charge/à décharge; **to ~ to sth/having seen sth** témoigner de qch/d'avoir vu qch
witness box, (*US*) **witness stand** *n* barre *f* des témoins
witticism ['wɪtɪsɪzəm] *n* mot *m* d'esprit
witty ['wɪtɪ] *adj* spirituel(le), plein(e) d'esprit
wives [waivz] *npl of* **wife**
wizard ['wɪzəd] *n* magicien *m*
wizened ['wɪznd] *adj* ratatiné(e)
wk *abbr* = **week**
Wm. *abbr* = **William**
WMD. *abbr* = **weapons of mass destruction**
WO *n abbr* = **warrant officer**
wobble ['wɔbl] *vi* trembler; (*chair*) branler
wobbly ['wɔblɪ] *adj* tremblant(e), branlant(e)
woe [wəu] *n* malheur *m*

woeful ['wəuful] *adj* (*sad*) malheureux(-euse); (*terrible*) affligeant(e)
wok [wɔk] *n* wok *m*
woke [wəuk] *pt of* **wake**
woken ['wəukn] *pp of* **wake**
wolf (*pl* **wolves**) [wulf, wulvz] *n* loup *m*
woman (*pl* **women**) ['wumən, 'wɪmɪn] *n* femme *f* ▷ *cpd*: **~ doctor** femme *f* médecin; **~ friend** amie *f*; **~ teacher** professeur *m* femme; **young ~** jeune femme; **women's page** (*Press*) page *f* des lectrices
womanize ['wumənaɪz] *vi* jouer les séducteurs
womanly ['wumənlɪ] *adj* féminin(e)
womb [wu:m] *n* (*Anat*) utérus *m*
women ['wɪmɪn] *npl of* **woman**
won [wʌn] *pt, pp of* **win**
wonder ['wʌndər] *n* merveille *f*, miracle *m*; (*feeling*) émerveillement *m* ▷ *vi*: **to ~ whether/why** se demander si/pourquoi; **to ~ at** (*surprise*) s'étonner de; (*admiration*) s'émerveiller de; **to ~ about** songer à; **it's no ~ that** il n'est pas étonnant que + *sub*
wonderful ['wʌndəful] *adj* merveilleux(-euse)
wonderfully ['wʌndəfəlɪ] *adv* (+ *adj*) merveilleusement; (+ *vb*) à merveille
wonky ['wɔŋkɪ] *adj* (*Brit inf*) qui ne va *or* ne marche pas très bien
wont [wəunt] *n*: **as is his/her ~** comme de coutume
won't [wəunt] = **will not**
woo [wu:] *vt* (*woman*) faire la cour à
wood [wud] *n* (*timber, forest*) bois *m* ▷ *cpd* de bois, en bois
wood carving *n* sculpture *f* en *or* sur bois
wooded ['wudɪd] *adj* boisé(e)
wooden ['wudn] *adj* en bois; (*fig: actor*) raide; (: *performance*) qui manque de naturel
woodland ['wudlənd] *n* forêt *f*, région boisée
woodpecker ['wudpɛkər] *n* pic *m* (*oiseau*)
wood pigeon *n* ramier *m*
woodwind ['wudwɪnd] *n* (*Mus*) bois *m*; **the ~** les bois *mpl*
woodwork ['wudwə:k] *n* menuiserie *f*
woodworm ['wudwə:m] *n* ver *m* du bois; **the table has got ~** la table est piquée des vers
woof [wuf] *n* (*of dog*) aboiement *m* ▷ *vi* aboyer; **~, ~!** oua, oua!
wool [wul] *n* laine *f*; **to pull the ~ over sb's eyes** (*fig*) en faire accroire à qn
woollen, (*US*) **woolen** ['wulən] *adj* de *or* en laine; (*industry*) lainier(-ière) ▷ *n*: **~s** lainages *mpl*
woolly, (*US*) **wooly** ['wulɪ] *adj* laineux(-euse); (*fig: ideas*) confus(e)
woozy ['wu:zɪ] *adj* (*inf*) dans les vapes
word [wə:d] *n* mot *m*; (*spoken*) mot, parole *f*; (*promise*) parole; (*news*) nouvelles *fpl* ▷ *vt* rédiger, formuler; **~ for ~** (*repeat*) mot pour mot; (*translate*) mot à mot; **what's the ~ for "pen" in French?** comment dit-on "pen" en français?; **to put sth into ~s** exprimer qch; **in other ~s** en d'autres termes; **to have a ~ with sb**

toucher un mot à qn; **to have ~s with sb** (*quarrel with*) avoir des mots avec qn; **to break/keep one's ~** manquer à sa parole/tenir (sa) parole; **I'll take your ~ for it** je vous crois sur parole; **to send ~ of** prévenir de; **to leave ~ (with sb/ for sb) that ...** laisser un mot (à qn/pour qn) disant que ...

wording ['wə:dɪŋ] *n* termes *mpl*, langage *m*; (*of document*) libellé *m*

word of mouth *n*: **by** *or* **through ~** de bouche à oreille

word-perfect ['wə:d'pə:fɪkt] *adj*: **he was ~ (in his speech** *etc*), **his speech** *etc* **was ~** il savait son discours *etc* sur le bout du doigt

word processing *n* traitement *m* de texte

word processor [-prəusɛsə^r] *n* machine *f* de traitement de texte

wordwrap ['wə:dræp] *n* (*Comput*) retour *m* (automatique) à la ligne

wordy ['wə:dɪ] *adj* verbeux(-euse)

wore [wɔː^r] *pt of* **wear**

work [wə:k] *n* travail *m*; (*Art, Literature*) œuvre *f* ▷ *vi* travailler; (*mechanism*) marcher, fonctionner; (*plan etc*) marcher; (*medicine*) agir ▷ *vt* (*clay, wood etc*) travailler; (*mine etc*) exploiter; (*machine*) faire marcher *or* fonctionner; (*miracles etc*) faire; **works** *n* (*Brit: factory*) usine *f* ▷ *npl* (*of clock, machine*) mécanisme *m*; **how does this ~?** comment est-ce que ça marche?; **the TV isn't ~ing** la télévision est en panne *or* ne marche pas; **to go to ~** aller travailler; **to set to ~**, **to start ~** se mettre à l'œuvre; **to be at ~ (on sth)** travailler (sur qch); **to be out of ~** être au chômage *or* sans emploi; **to ~ hard** travailler dur; **to ~ loose** se défaire, se desserrer; **road ~s** travaux *mpl* (d'entretien des routes)

▶ **work on** *vt fus* travailler à; (*principle*) se baser sur

▶ **work out** *vi* (*plans etc*) marcher; (*Sport*) s'entraîner ▷ *vt* (*problem*) résoudre; (*plan*) élaborer; **it ~s out at £100** ça fait 100 livres

▶ **work up** *vt*: **to get ~ed up** se mettre dans tous ses états

workable ['wə:kəbl] *adj* (*solution*) réalisable

workaholic [wə:kə'hɔlɪk] *n* bourreau *m* de travail

workbench ['wə:kbɛntʃ] *n* établi *m*

worked up [wə:kt-] *adj*: **to get ~** se mettre dans tous ses états

worker ['wə:kə^r] *n* travailleur(-euse), ouvrier(-ière); **office ~** employé(e) de bureau

work experience *n* stage *m*

workforce ['wə:kfɔ:s] *n* main-d'œuvre *f*

work-in ['wə:kɪn] *n* (*Brit*) occupation *f* d'usine *etc* (*sans arrêt de la production*)

working ['wə:kɪŋ] *adj* (*day, tools etc, conditions*) de travail; (*wife*) qui travaille; (*partner, population*) actif(-ive); **in ~ order** en état de marche; **a ~ knowledge of English** une connaissance toute pratique de l'anglais

working capital *n* (*Comm*) fonds *mpl* de roulement

working class *n* classe ouvrière ▷ *adj*: **working-class** ouvrier(-ière), de la classe ouvrière

working man (*irreg*) *n* travailleur *m*

working party *n* (*Brit*) groupe *m* de travail

working week *n* semaine *f* de travail

work-in-progress ['wə:kɪn'prəugrɛs] *n* (*Comm*) en-cours *m inv*; (: *value*) valeur *f* des en-cours

workload ['wə:kləud] *n* charge *f* de travail

workman ['wə:kmən] (*irreg*) *n* ouvrier *m*

workmanship ['wə:kmənʃɪp] *n* métier *m*, habileté *f*; facture *f*

workmate ['wə:kmeɪt] *n* collègue *m/f*

work of art *n* œuvre *f* d'art

workout ['wə:kaut] *n* (*Sport*) séance *f* d'entraînement

work permit *n* permis *m* de travail

workplace ['wə:kpleɪs] *n* lieu *m* de travail

works council *n* comité *m* d'entreprise

worksheet ['wə:kʃiːt] *n* (*Scol*) feuille *f* d'exercices; (*Comput*) feuille *f* de programmation

workshop ['wə:kʃɔp] *n* atelier *m*

work station *n* poste *m* de travail

work study *n* étude *f* du travail

work surface *n* plan *m* de travail

worktop ['wə:ktɔp] *n* plan *m* de travail

work-to-rule ['wə:ktə'ru:l] *n* (*Brit*) grève *f* du zèle

world [wə:ld] *n* monde *m* ▷ *cpd* (*champion*) du monde; (*power, war*) mondial(e); **all over the ~** dans le monde entier, partout dans le monde; **to think the ~ of sb** (*fig*) ne jurer que par qn; **what in the ~ is he doing?** qu'est-ce qu'il peut bien être en train de faire?; **to do sb a ~ of good** faire le plus grand bien à qn; **W~ War One/ Two**, **the First/Second W~ War** la Première/ Deuxième Guerre mondiale; **out of this ~** *adj* extraordinaire

World Cup *n*: **the ~** (*Football*) la Coupe du monde

world-famous [wə:ld'feɪməs] *adj* de renommée mondiale

worldly ['wə:ldlɪ] *adj* de ce monde

world music *n* world music *f*

World Series *n*: **the ~** (*US: Baseball*) le championnat national de baseball

world-wide ['wə:ld'waɪd] *adj* universel(le) ▷ *adv* dans le monde entier

World-Wide Web *n*: **the ~** le Web

worm [wə:m] *n* (*also*: **earthworm**) ver *m*

worn [wɔ:n] *pp of* **wear** ▷ *adj* usé(e)

worn-out ['wɔ:naut] *adj* (*object*) complètement usé(e); (*person*) épuisé(e)

worried ['wʌrɪd] *adj* inquiet(-ète); **to be ~ about sth** être inquiet au sujet de qch

worrier ['wʌrɪə^r] *n* inquiet(-ète)

worrisome ['wʌrɪsəm] *adj* inquiétant(e)

worry ['wʌrɪ] *n* souci *m* ▷ *vt* inquiéter ▷ *vi* s'inquiéter, se faire du souci; **to ~ about** *or* **over sth/sb** se faire du souci pour *or* à propos de qch/ qn

worrying ['wʌrɪɪŋ] *adj* inquiétant(e)

worse [wə:s] *adj* pire, plus mauvais(e) ▷ *adv*

plus mal ▷ *n* pire *m*; **to get ~** (*condition, situation*) empirer, se dégrader; **a change for the ~** une détérioration; **he is none the ~ for it** il ne s'en porte pas plus mal; **so much the ~ for you!** tant pis pour vous!

worsen ['wəːsn] *vt, vi* empirer

worse off *adj* moins à l'aise financièrement; (*fig*): **you'll be ~ this way** ça ira moins bien de cette façon; **he is now ~ than before** il se retrouve dans une situation pire qu'auparavant

worship ['wəːʃɪp] *n* culte *m* ▷ *vt* (*God*) rendre un culte à; (*person*) adorer; **Your W~** (*Brit: to mayor*) Monsieur le Maire; (: *to judge*) Monsieur le Juge

worshipper ['wəːʃɪpəʳ] *n* adorateur(-trice); (*in church*) fidèle *m/f*

worst [wəːst] *adj* le (la) pire, le (la) plus mauvais(e) ▷ *adv* le plus mal ▷ *n* pire *m*; **at ~** au pis aller; **if the ~ comes to the ~** si le pire doit arriver

worst-case ['wəːstkeɪs] *adj*: **the ~ scenario** le pire scénario *or* cas de figure

worsted ['wustɪd] *n*: **(wool) ~** laine peignée

worth [wəːθ] *n* valeur *f* ▷ *adj*: **to be ~** valoir; **how much is it ~?** ça vaut combien?; **it's ~ it** cela en vaut la peine, ça vaut la peine; **it is ~ one's while (to do)** ça vaut le coup (*inf*) (de faire); **50 pence ~ of apples** (pour) 50 pence de pommes

worthless ['wəːθlɪs] *adj* qui ne vaut rien

worthwhile ['wəːθ'waɪl] *adj* (*activity*) qui en vaut la peine; (*cause*) louable; **a ~ book** un livre qui vaut la peine d'être lu

worthy ['wəːðɪ] *adj* (*person*) digne; (*motive*) louable; **~ of** digne de

 KEYWORD

would [wud] *aux vb* **1** (*conditional tense*): **if you asked him he would do it** si vous le lui demandiez, il le ferait; **if you had asked him he would have done it** si vous le lui aviez demandé, il l'aurait fait

2 (*in offers, invitations, requests*): **would you like a biscuit?** voulez-vous un biscuit?; **would you close the door please?** voulez-vous fermer la porte, s'il vous plaît?

3 (*in indirect speech*): **I said I would do it** j'ai dit que je le ferais

4 (*emphatic*): **it WOULD have to snow today!** naturellement il neige aujourd'hui! *or* il fallait qu'il neige aujourd'hui!

5 (*insistence*): **she wouldn't do it** elle n'a pas voulu *or* elle a refusé de le faire

6 (*conjecture*): **it would have been midnight** il devait être minuit; **it would seem so** on dirait bien

7 (*indicating habit*): **he would go there on Mondays** il y allait le lundi

would-be ['wudbiː] *adj* (*pej*) soi-disant

wouldn't ['wudnt] = **would not**

wound¹ [wuːnd] *n* blessure *f* ▷ *vt* blesser; **~ed in**

the leg blessé à la jambe

wound² [waund] *pt, pp of* **wind²**

wove [wəuv] *pt of* **weave**

woven ['wəuvn] *pp of* **weave**

WP *n abbr* = **word processing**; **word processor** ▷ *abbr* (*Brit inf*) = **weather permitting**

WPC *n abbr* (*Brit*) = **woman police constable**

wpm *abbr* (= *words per minute*) mots/minute

WRAC *n abbr* (*Brit*: = *Women's Royal Army Corps*) auxiliaires féminines de l'armée de terre

WRAF *n abbr* (*Brit*: = *Women's Royal Air Force*) auxiliaires féminines de l'armée de l'air

wrangle ['ræŋgl] *n* dispute *f* ▷ *vi* se disputer

wrap [ræp] *n* (*stole*) écharpe *f*; (*cape*) pèlerine *f* ▷ *vt* (*also*: **wrap up**) envelopper; (*parcel*) emballer; (*wind*) enrouler; **under ~s** (*fig: plan, scheme*) secret(-ète)

wrapper ['ræpəʳ] *n* (*on chocolate etc*) papier *m*; (*Brit: of book*) couverture *f*

wrapping ['ræpɪŋ] *n* (*of sweet, chocolate*) papier *m*; (*of parcel*) emballage *m*

wrapping paper *n* papier *m* d'emballage; (*for gift*) papier cadeau

wrath [rɔθ] *n* courroux *m*

wreak [riːk] *vt* (*destruction*) entraîner; **to ~ havoc** faire des ravages; **to ~ vengeance on** se venger de, exercer sa vengeance sur

wreath [riːθ, *pl* riːðz] *n* couronne *f*

wreck [rɛk] *n* (*sea disaster*) naufrage *m*; (*ship*) épave *f*; (*vehicle*) véhicule accidentée; (*pej: person*) loque (humaine) ▷ *vt* démolir; (*ship*) provoquer le naufrage de; (*fig*) briser, ruiner

wreckage ['rɛkɪdʒ] *n* débris *mpl*; (*of building*) décombres *mpl*; (*of ship*) naufrage *m*

wrecker ['rɛkəʳ] *n* (*US: breakdown van*) dépanneuse *f*

WREN [rɛn] *n abbr* (*Brit*) *membre du* WRNS

wren [rɛn] *n* (*Zool*) troglodyte *m*

wrench [rɛntʃ] *n* (*Tech*) clé *f* (à écrous); (*tug*) violent mouvement de torsion; (*fig*) déchirement *m* ▷ *vt* tirer violemment sur, tordre; **to ~ sth from** arracher qch (violemment) à *or* de

wrest [rɛst] *vt*: **to ~ sth from sb** arracher *or* ravir qch à qn

wrestle ['rɛsl] *vi*: **to ~ (with sb)** lutter (avec qn); **to ~ with** (*fig*) se débattre avec, lutter contre

wrestler ['rɛsləʳ] *n* lutteur(-euse)

wrestling ['rɛslɪŋ] *n* lutte *f*; (*also*: **all-in wrestling**: *Brit*) catch *m*

wrestling match *n* rencontre *f* de lutte (*or* de catch)

wretch [rɛtʃ] *n* pauvre malheureux(-euse); **little ~!** (*often humorous*) petit(e) misérable!

wretched ['rɛtʃɪd] *adj* misérable; (*inf*) maudit(e)

wriggle ['rɪgl] *n* tortillement *m* ▷ *vi* (*also*: **wriggle about**) se tortiller

wring (*pt, pp* **wrung**) [rɪŋ, rʌŋ] *vt* tordre; (*wet clothes*) essorer; (*fig*): **to ~ sth out of** arracher qch à

wringer ['rɪŋəʳ] *n* essoreuse *f*

wringing ['rɪŋɪŋ] *adj* (*also*: **wringing wet**) tout

mouillé(e), trempé(e)

wrinkle ['rɪŋkl] n (on skin) ride f; (on paper etc) pli m ▷ vt rider, plisser ▷ vi se plisser

wrinkled ['rɪŋkld], **wrinkly** ['rɪŋklɪ] adj (fabric, paper) froissé(e), plissé(e); (surface) plissé; (skin) ridé(e), plissé

wrist [rɪst] n poignet m

wristband ['rɪstbænd] n (Brit: of shirt) poignet m; (: of watch) bracelet m

wrist watch ['rɪstwɔtʃ] n montre-bracelet f

writ [rɪt] n acte m judiciaire; **to issue a ~ against sb, to serve a ~ on sb** assigner qn en justice

writable ['raɪtəbl] adj (CD, DVD) inscriptible

write (pt **wrote**, pp **written**) [raɪt, rəut, 'rɪtn] vt, vi écrire; (prescription) rédiger; **to ~ sb a letter** écrire une lettre à qn

▶ **write away** vi: **to ~ away for** (information) (écrire pour) demander; (goods) (écrire pour) commander

▶ **write down** vt noter; (put in writing) mettre par écrit

▶ **write off** vt (debt) passer aux profits et pertes; (project) mettre une croix sur; (depreciate) amortir; (smash up: car etc) démolir complètement

▶ **write out** vt écrire; (copy) recopier

▶ **write up** vt rédiger

write-off ['raɪtɔf] n perte totale; **the car is a ~** la voiture est bonne pour la casse

write-protect ['raɪtprə'tɛkt] vt (Comput) protéger contre l'écriture

writer ['raɪtər] n auteur m, écrivain m

write-up ['raɪtʌp] n (review) critique f

writhe [raɪð] vi se tordre

writing ['raɪtɪŋ] n écriture f; (of author) œuvres fpl; **in ~** par écrit; **in my own ~** écrit(e) de ma main

writing case n nécessaire m de correspondance

writing desk n secrétaire m

writing paper n papier m à lettres

written ['rɪtn] pp of **write**

WRNS n abbr (Brit: = Women's Royal Naval Service) auxiliaires féminines de la marine

wrong [rɔŋ] adj (incorrect) faux (fausse); (incorrectly chosen: number, road etc) mauvais(e); (not suitable) qui ne convient pas; (wicked) mal; (unfair) injuste ▷ adv mal ▷ n tort m ▷ vt faire du tort à, léser; **to be ~** (answer) être faux (fausse); (in doing/saying) avoir tort (de dire/faire); **you are ~ to do it** tu as tort de le faire; **it's ~ to steal, stealing is ~** c'est mal de voler; **you are ~ about that, you've got it ~** tu te trompes; **to be in the ~** avoir tort; **what's ~?** qu'est-ce qui ne va pas?; **there's nothing ~** tout va bien; **what's ~ with the car?** qu'est-ce qu'elle a, la voiture?; **to go ~** (person) se tromper; (plan) mal tourner; (machine) se détraquer; **I took a ~ turning** je me suis trompé de route

wrongdoer ['rɔŋduːər] n malfaiteur m

wrong-foot [rɔŋ'fut] vt (Sport) prendre à contre-pied; (fig) prendre au dépourvu

wrongful ['rɔŋful] adj injustifié(e); **~ dismissal** (Industry) licenciement abusif

wrongly ['rɔŋlɪ] adv à tort; (answer, do, count) mal, incorrectement; (treat) injustement

wrong number n (Tel): **you have the ~** vous vous êtes trompé de numéro

wrong side n (of cloth) envers m

wrote [rəut] pt of **write**

wrought [rɔːt] adj: **~ iron** fer forgé

wrung [rʌŋ] pt, pp of **wring**

WRVS n abbr (Brit: = Women's Royal Voluntary Service) auxiliaires féminines bénévoles au service de la collectivité

wry [raɪ] adj désabusé(e)

wt. abbr (= weight) pds.

WV, W.Va. abbr (US) = **West Virginia**

WWW n abbr = **World-Wide Web**

WY, Wyo. abbr (US) = **Wyoming**

WYSIWYG ['wɪzɪwɪg] abbr (Comput: = what you see is what you get) ce que vous voyez est ce que vous aurez

X, x [ɛks] *n* (*letter*) X, x *m*; (*Brit Cine: formerly*) film interdit aux moins de 18 ans; **X for Xmas** X comme Xavier
Xerox® ['zɪərɔks] *n* (*also*: **Xerox machine**) photocopieuse *f*; (*photocopy*) photocopie *f* ▷ *vt* photocopier
XL *abbr* (= *extra large*) XL

Xmas ['ɛksməs] *n abbr* = **Christmas**
X-rated ['ɛks'reɪtɪd] *adj* (*US: film*) interdit(e) aux moins de 18 ans
X-ray ['ɛksreɪ] *n* (*ray*) rayon *m* X; (*photograph*) radio(graphie) *f* ▷ *vt* radiographier
xylophone ['zaɪləfəun] *n* xylophone *m*

Y, y [waɪ] *n* (*letter*) Y, y *m*; **Y for Yellow**, (*US*) **Y for Yoke** Y comme Yvonne

yacht [jɔt] *n* voilier *m*; (*motor, luxury yacht*) yacht *m*

yachting ['jɔtɪŋ] *n* yachting *m*, navigation *f* de plaisance

yachtsman ['jɔtsmən] (*irreg*) *n* yacht(s)man *m*

yam [jæm] *n* igname *f*

Yank [jæŋk], **Yankee** ['jæŋkɪ] *n* (*pej*) Amerloque *m/f*, Ricain(e)

yank [jæŋk] *vt* tirer d'un coup sec

yap [jæp] *vi* (*dog*) japper

yard [jɑːd] *n* (*of house etc*) cour *f*; (*US: garden*) jardin *m*; (*measure*) yard *m* (= 914 mm; 3 feet); **builder's ~** chantier *m*

yard sale *n* (*US*) brocante *f* (dans son propre jardin)

yardstick ['jɑːdstɪk] *n* (*fig*) mesure *f*, critère *m*

yarn [jɑːn] *n* fil *m*; (*tale*) longue histoire

yawn [jɔːn] *n* bâillement *m* ▷ *vi* bâiller

yawning ['jɔːnɪŋ] *adj* (*gap*) béant(e)

yd. *abbr* = **yard; yards**

yeah [jɛə] *adv* (*inf*) ouais

year [jɪəʳ] *n* an *m*, année *f*; (*Scol etc*) année; **every ~** tous les ans, chaque année; **this ~** cette année; **a** *or* **per ~** par an; **~ in, ~ out** année après année; **to be 8 ~s old** avoir 8 ans; **an eight-~-old child** un enfant de huit ans

yearbook ['jɪəbuk] *n* annuaire *m*

yearly ['jɪəlɪ] *adj* annuel(le) ▷ *adv* annuellement; **twice ~** deux fois par an

yearn [jəːn] *vi*: **to ~ for sth/to do** aspirer à qch/à faire

yearning ['jəːnɪŋ] *n* désir ardent, envie *f*

yeast [jiːst] *n* levure *f*

yell [jɛl] *n* hurlement *m*, cri *m* ▷ *vi* hurler

yellow ['jɛləu] *adj, n* jaune (*m*)

yellow fever *n* fièvre *f* jaune

yellowish ['jɛləuɪʃ] *adj* qui tire sur le jaune, jaunâtre (*pej*)

Yellow Pages® *npl* (*Tel*) pages *fpl* jaunes

Yellow Sea *n*: **the ~** la mer Jaune

yelp [jɛlp] *n* jappement *m*; glapissement *m* ▷ *vi* japper; glapir

Yemen ['jɛmən] *n* Yémen *m*

yen [jɛn] *n* (*currency*) yen *m*; (*craving*): **~ for/to do** grande envie de/de faire

yeoman ['jəumən] (*irreg*) *n*: **Y~ of the Guard** hallebardier *m* de la garde royale

yes [jɛs] *adv* oui; (*answering negative question*) si ▷ *n* oui *m*; **to say ~ (to)** dire oui (à)

yesterday ['jɛstədɪ] *adv, n* hier (*m*); **~ morning/evening** hier matin/soir; **the day before ~** avant-hier; **all day ~** toute la journée d'hier

yet [jɛt] *adv* encore; (*in questions*) déjà ▷ *conj* pourtant, néanmoins; **it is not finished ~** ce n'est pas encore fini *or* toujours pas fini; **must you go just ~?** dois-tu déjà partir?; **have you eaten ~?** vous avez déjà mangé?; **the best ~** le meilleur jusqu'ici *or* jusque-là; **as ~** jusqu'ici, encore; **a few days ~** encore quelques jours; **~ again** une fois de plus

yew [juː] *n* if *m*

Y-fronts® ['waɪfrʌnts] *npl* (*Brit*) slip *m* kangourou

YHA *n abbr* (*Brit*) = **Youth Hostels Association**

Yiddish ['jɪdɪʃ] *n* yiddish *m*

yield [jiːld] *n* production *f*, rendement *m*; (*Finance*) rapport *m* ▷ *vt* produire, rendre, rapporter; (*surrender*) céder ▷ *vi* céder; (*US Aut*) céder la priorité; **a ~ of 5%** un rendement de 5%

YMCA *n abbr* (= *Young Men's Christian Association*) ≈ union chrétienne de jeunes gens (UCJG)

yob ['jɔb], **yobbo** ['jɔbəu] *n* (*Brit inf*) loubar(d) *m*

yodel ['jəudl] *vi* faire des tyroliennes, jodler

yoga ['jəugə] *n* yoga *m*

yoghurt, yogurt ['jɔgət] *n* yaourt *m*

yoke [jəuk] *n* joug *m* ▷ *vt* (*also*: **yoke together**: *oxen*) accoupler

yolk [jəuk] *n* jaune *m* (d'œuf)

yonder ['jɔndəʳ] *adv* là(-bas)

yonks [jɔŋks] *npl* (*inf*): **for ~** très longtemps; **we've been here for ~** ça fait une éternité qu'on est ici; **we were there for ~** on est resté là pendant des lustres

Yorks [jɔːks] *abbr* (*Brit*) = **Yorkshire**

⬤ KEYWORD

you [juː] *pron* **1** (*subject*) tu; (*polite form*) vous; (*plural*) vous; **you are very kind** vous êtes très gentil; **you French enjoy your food** vous autres Français, vous aimez bien manger; **you and I will go** toi et moi *or* vous et moi, nous irons; **there you are!** vous voilà!

2 (*object: direct, indirect*) te, t' + *vowel*; vous; **I know you** je te *or* vous connais; **I gave it to you** je te l'ai donné, je vous l'ai donné

3 (*stressed*) toi; vous; **I told you to do it** c'est à toi *or* vous que j'ai dit de le faire

4 (*after prep, in comparisons*) toi; vous; **it's for you** c'est pour toi *or* vous; **she's younger than you** elle est plus jeune que toi *or* vous

5 (*impersonal: one*) on; **fresh air does you good** l'air frais fait du bien; **you never know** on ne sait jamais; **you can't do that!** ça ne se fait pas!

you'd [ju:d] = **you had**; **you would**
you'll [ju:l] = **you will**; **you shall**
young [jʌŋ] *adj* jeune ▷ *npl* (*of animal*) petits *mpl*; (*people*): **the ~** les jeunes, la jeunesse; **a ~ man** un jeune homme; **a ~ lady** (*unmarried*) une jeune fille, une demoiselle; (*married*) une jeune femme *or* dame; **my ~er brother** mon frère cadet; **the ~er generation** la jeune génération
younger [jʌŋɡəʳ] *adj* (*brother etc*) cadet(te)
youngish [jʌŋɪʃ] *adj* assez jeune
youngster [jʌŋstəʳ] *n* jeune *m/f*; (*child*) enfant *m/f*
your [jɔːʳ] *adj* ton (ta), tes *pl*; (*polite form, pl*) votre, vos *pl*; *see also* **my**
you're [juəʳ] = **you are**
yours [jɔːz] *pron* le (la) tien(ne), les tiens (tiennes); (*polite form, pl*) le (la) vôtre, les vôtres;

is it ~? c'est à toi (*or* à vous)?; **a friend of ~** un(e) de tes (*or* de vos) amis; *see also* **faithfully**; **sincerely**
yourself [jɔː'sɛlf] *pron* (*reflexive*) te; (: *polite form*) vous; (*after prep*) toi; vous; (*emphatic*) toi-même; vous-même; **you ~ told me** c'est vous qui me l'avez dit, vous me l'avez dit vous-même; *see also* **oneself**
yourselves [jɔː'sɛlvz] *pl pron* vous; (*emphatic*) vous-mêmes; *see also* **oneself**
youth [ju:θ] *n* jeunesse *f*; (*young man*) (*pl* **-s**) [ju:ðz] jeune homme *m*; **in my ~** dans ma jeunesse, quand j'étais jeune
youth club *n* centre *m* de jeunes
youthful [ju:θful] *adj* jeune; (*enthusiasm etc*) juvénile; (*misdemeanour*) de jeunesse
youthfulness [ju:θfəlnɪs] *n* jeunesse *f*
youth hostel *n* auberge *f* de jeunesse
youth movement *n* mouvement *m* de jeunes
you've [ju:v] = **you have**
yowl [jaul] *n* hurlement *m*; miaulement *m* ▷ *vi* hurler; miauler
YT *abbr* (*Canada*) = **Yukon Territory.**
Yugoslav [ju:ɡəuslɑːv] *adj* (*Hist*) yougoslave ▷ *n* Yougoslave *m/f*
Yugoslavia [ju:ɡəu'slɑːvɪə] *n* (*Hist*) Yougoslavie *f*
Yugoslavian [ju:ɡəu'slɑːvɪən] *adj* (*Hist*) yougoslave
yuppie [jʌpɪ] *n* yuppie *m/f*
YWCA *n abbr* (= *Young Women's Christian Association*) union chrétienne féminine

Zz

Z, z [zɛd, (US) zi:] n (letter) Z, z m; **Z for Zebra** Z comme Zoé
Zambia ['zæmbɪə] n Zambie f
Zambian ['zæmbɪən] adj zambien(ne) ▷ n Zambien(ne)
zany ['zeɪnɪ] adj farfelu(e), loufoque
zap [zæp] vt (Comput) effacer
zeal [zi:l] n (revolutionary etc) ferveur f; (keenness) ardeur f, zèle m
zealot ['zɛlət] n fanatique m/f
zealous ['zɛləs] adj fervent(e); ardent(e), zélé(e)
zebra ['zi:brə] n zèbre m
zebra crossing n (Brit) passage clouté or pour piétons
zenith ['zɛnɪθ] n (Astronomy) zénith m; (fig) zénith, apogée m
zero ['zɪərəu] n zéro m ▷ vi: **to ~ in on** (target) se diriger droit sur; **5° below ~** 5 degrés au-dessous de zéro
zero hour n l'heure f H
zero option n (Pol): **the ~** l'option f zéro
zero-rated ['zi:rəureɪtɪd] adj (Brit) exonéré(e) de TVA
zest [zɛst] n entrain m, élan m; (of lemon etc) zeste m
zigzag ['zɪgzæg] n zigzag m ▷ vi zigzaguer, faire des zigzags
Zimbabwe [zɪm'bɑːbwɪ] n Zimbabwe m
Zimbabwean [zɪm'bɑːbwɪən] adj
zimbabwéen(ne) ▷ n Zimbabwéen(ne)
Zimmer® ['zɪmər] n (also: **Zimmer frame**) déambulateur m
zinc [zɪŋk] n zinc m
Zionism ['zaɪənɪzəm] n sionisme m
Zionist ['zaɪənɪst] adj sioniste ▷ n Sioniste m/f
zip [zɪp] n (also: **zip fastener**) fermeture f éclair® or à glissière; (energy) entrain m ▷ vt (file) zipper; (also: **zip up**) fermer (avec une fermeture éclair®)
zip code n (US) code postal
zip file n (Comput) fichier m zip inv
zipper ['zɪpər] n (US) = **zip**
zit [zɪt] (inf) n bouton m
zither ['zɪðər] n cithare f
zodiac ['zəudɪæk] n zodiaque m
zombie ['zɔmbɪ] n (fig): **like a ~** avec l'air d'un zombie, comme un automate
zone [zəun] n zone f
zoo [zu:] n zoo m
zoological [zuə'lɔdʒɪkl] adj zoologique
zoologist [zu'ɔlədʒɪst] n zoologiste m/f
zoology [zu:'ɔlədʒɪ] n zoologie f
zoom [zu:m] vi: **to ~ past** passer en trombe; **to ~ in (on sb/sth)** (Phot, Cine) zoomer (sur qn/qch)
zoom lens n zoom m, objectif m à focale variable
zucchini [zu:'ki:nɪ] n (US) courgette f
Zulu ['zu:lu:] adj zoulou ▷ n Zoulou m/f
Zürich ['zjuərɪk] n Zurich